symptoms)/episodic with no in-terepisode residual symptoms
Continuous (specify if: with prominent negative symptoms)
Single episode in partial remission (specify if: with prominent negative symptoms)/single episode in full remission
Other or unspecified pattern

Paranoid type
Disorganized type
Catatonic type
Undifferentiated type
Residual type

Schizophreniform disorder
Specify if: without good prognostic features/with good prognostic features
Schizoaffective disorder
Specify type: bipolar type/depressive type
Delusional disorder
Specify type: erotomanic type/grandiose type/jealous type/persecutory type/somatic type/mixed type/unspecified type
Brief psychotic disorder
Specify if: with marked stressor(s)/without marked stressor(s)/with postpartum onset
Shared psychotic disorder
Psychotic disorder due to [indicate the general medical condition]
With delusions
With hallucinations
Substance-induced psychotic disorder
Specify if: with onset during intoxication/with onset during withdrawal
Psychotic disorder NOS

MOOD DISORDERS

Code current state of major depressive disorder or bipolar I disorder as mild, moderate, severe without psychotic features, severe with psychotic features (mood congruent or mood incongruent), in partial remission, in full remission, or unspecified.
Depressive disorders
Major depressive disorder
Single episode
Recurrent
Dysthymic disorder
[specify if: early onset/late onset; with atypical features]
Depressive disorder NOS
Bipolar disorders
Bipolar I disorder
Single manic episode [specify if: mixed]
Most recent episode hypomanic
Most recent episode manic
Most recent episode mixed
Most recent episode depressed
Most recent episode unspecified
Bipolar II disorder [specify (current or most recent episode): hypomanic/depressed]
Cyclothymic disorder
Bipolar disorder NOS
Mood disorder due to [indicate the general medical condition]
Substance-induced mood disorder [specify further]
Mood disorder NOS

ANXIETY DISORDERS

Panic disorder without agoraphobia
Panic disorder with agoraphobia
Agoraphobia without history of panic disorder
Specific phobia [specify type: animal type/natural environment type/blood-injection-injury type/situational type/other type]
Social phobia [specify if: generalized]

Obsessive-compulsive disorder [specify if: with poor insight]
Posttraumatic stress disorder [specify if: acute/chronic; with delayed onset]
Acute stress disorder
Generalized anxiety disorder
Anxiety disorder due to [indicate the general medical condition]
Substance-induced anxiety disorder [give more information]
Anxiety disorder NOS

SOMATOFORM DISORDERS

Somatization disorder
Undifferentiated somatoform disorder
Conversion disorder [specify type: with motor symptom or deficit/with sensory symptom or deficit/with seizures or convulsions/with mixed presentation]
Pain disorder
Associated with psychological factors
Associated with both psychological factors and a general medical condition [specify if: acute/chronic]
Hypochondriasis [specify if: with poor insight]
Body dysmorphic disorder
Somatoform disorder NOS

FACTITIOUS DISORDERS

[Four Disorders]

DISSOCIATIVE DISORDERS

Dissociative amnesia
Dissociative fugue
Dissociative identity disorder
Depersonalization disorder
Dissociative disorder NOS

SEXUAL AND GENDER IDENTITY DISORDERS

Sexual dysfunctions
The following specifiers apply to all primary sexual dysfunctions: lifelong type/acquired type; generalized type/situational type; due to psychological factors/due to combined factors
Sexual desire disorders
Hypoactive sexual desire disorder
Sexual aversion disorder
Sexual arousal disorders
Female sexual arousal disorder
Male erectile disorder
Orgasmic disorders
Female orgasmic disorder
Male orgasmic disorder
Premature ejaculation
Sexual pain disorders
Dyspareunia (not due to a general medical condition)
Vaginismus (not due to a general medical condition)
Sexual dysfunction due to a general medical condition [specify further]
Substance-induced sexual dysfunction
Sexual dysfunction NOS
Paraphilias
Exhibitionism
Fetishism
Frotteurism
Pedophilia [specify if: sexually attracted to males/females/both]
Sexual masochism
Sexual sadism
Transvestic fetishism [specify if: with gender dysphoria]
Voyeurism
Paraphilia NOS
Gender identity disorders
Gender identity disorder
In children
In adolescents or adults
[Specify if: sexually attracted to males/females/both/neither]

EATING DISORDERS

Anorexia nervosa [specify type: restricting type; binge-eating/purging type]
Bulimia nervosa [specify type: purging type/non-purging type]
Eating disorder NOS

SLEEP DISORDERS

Primary sleep disorders
Dyssomnias
Primary insomnia
Primary hypersomnia [specify if: recurrent]
Narcolepsy
Breathing-related sleep disorder
Circadian rhythm sleep disorder [specify type]
Dyssomnia NOS
Parasomnias
Nightmare disorder
Sleep terror disorder
Sleepwalking disorder
Parasomnia NOS [and eight other disorders]

IMPULSE-CONTROL DISORDERS NOT ELSEWHERE CLASSIFIED

Intermittent explosive disorder
Kleptomania
Pyromania
Pathological gambling
Trichotillomania
Impulse-control disorder NOS

ADJUSTMENT DISORDERS

Adjustment disorder with depressed mood/anxiety/with mixed anxiety and depressed mood/with disturbance of conduct/with mixed disturbance of emotions and conduct

PERSONALITY DISORDERS

Note: These are coded on Axis II
Paranoid personality disorder
Schizoid personality disorder
Schizotypal personality disorder
Antisocial personality disorder
Borderline personality disorder
Histrionic personality disorder
Narcissistic personality disorder
Avoidant personality disorder
Dependent personality disorder
Obsessive-compulsive personality disorder
Personality disorder NOS

OTHER CONDITIONS THAT MAY BE A FOCUS OF CLINICAL ATTENTION

Psychological factors affecting medical condition [six factors]

MEDICATION-INDUCED MOVEMENT DISORDERS

[Seven disorders]

RELATIONAL PROBLEMS

[Five problems]

PROBLEMS RELATED TO ABUSE AND NEGLECT

[Five problems]

ADDITIONAL CONDITIONS THAT MAY BE A FOCUS OF CLINICAL ATTENTION

[Thirteen conditions]

ADDITIONAL CODES

Unspecified mental disorder (nonpsychotic)
No diagnosis or condition on Axis I
Diagnosis or condition deferred on Axis I
No diagnosis on Axis II
Diagnosis deferred on Axis II

ABNORMAL PSYCHOLOGY AND MODERN LIFE

ELEVENTH EDITION

Robert C. Carson
Duke University

James N. Butcher
University of Minnesota

Susan Mineka
Northwestern University

Allyn and Bacon

Boston • London • Toronto • Sydney • Tokyo • Singapore

Executive Editor: Rebecca Pascal
Vice President, Director of Marketing: Joyce Nilsen
Full Service Production Manager: Joseph Vella
Project Coordination and Text Design: York Production Services
Electronic Page Makeup: York Production Services
Cover Administrator: Jenny Hart
Cover Designer: Studio Nine
Manufacturing Buyer: Megan Cochran

Copyright © 2000 by Allyn & Bacon
A Pearson Education Company
160 Gould Street
Needham Heights, MA 02194

Internet: www.abacon.com

Library of Congress Cataloging-in-Publication Data
Carson, Robert C., 1930–
    Abnormal psychology and modern life/Robert C. Carson, James N. Butcher,
Susan Mineka.—11th ed.
      p. cm.
    Includes bibliographical references and index.
    ISBN 0-321-03430-9
    1. Psychiatry.   2. Psychology, Pathological.   I. Butcher, James Neal, 1933– .
II. Mineka, Susan.   III. Title.
RC454.C275   1999
616.89—dc21   99–34830
                                          CIP

Printed in the United States of America.

10 9 8 7 6 5 4 3 2 1 VHP 03 02 01 00 99

Credits appear on pages A-1–A-2, which constitute a continuation of the copyright page.

BRIEF CONTENTS

DETAILED CONTENTS

PREFACE

Many of you may be familiar with *Abnormal Psychology and Modern Life* as the "Coleman" text that you used in your own undergraduate abnormal psychology class. This textbook has been providing an introduction to abnormal psychology since 1948 when James Coleman authored the first edition. Since the sixth edition in 1980, Bob Carson and Jim Butcher have focused diligently on updating this classic textbook, expanding its research focus to reflect the many changes in the field over the past two decades. Susan Mineka came onboard the author team in 1996, adding her own research expertise to help create the most comprehensive and accessible text for today's students. With each edition, we, as authors, feel the challenge and the "rush" of anticipation and eagerness that comes with the responsibility for an abnormal psychology treatise of uncommon historical distinction: a text that has thrived through eleven editions, educating more students about the field of abnormal psychology than any other textbook.

We believe the eleventh edition is even more thorough, timely, and dynamic, reflecting the state of the field, than the first edition of the book was in its time. As with each edition, we faced a dilemma common to many authors of abnormal psychology textbooks: how to examine at an appropriate depth and breadth the vast domain of abnormal behavior with an economy of words and timely illustrative material sufficient to maintain a reasonable length. That requirement, always a difficult challenge, has become more so over time as an ever-broadening range of research confronts us with important and exponentially increasing new knowledge that must be assimilated within the developing core of the discipline. Different authors and author teams manage this inherent conflict of aims in their own ways and with varying levels of successful compromise. Our resolution has been to sacrifice as little as possible in content coverage, while striving for crispness in prose and ever increasing clarity and accessibility.

The goal of this edition has been to produce the most accessible yet comprehensive text available, to provide students with an enjoyable learning experience and exposure to both the classic and contemporary research in the field. Several features of the revision support this aim.

RESEARCH HIGHLIGHTS IN THIS EDITION

Prior to beginning work on the eleventh edition, we engaged a large number of peers to review critically its immediate predecessor. This group included both notable experts in particular content areas and experienced teachers, in keeping with our aims to ensure both content accuracy as well as pedagogical efficacy. Their advice was invaluable in our formulation of a systematic revision plan for enhancing the appeal and educational impact of the new edition. The list below summarizes many of the types of changes we made in each chapter.

All topics covered in the text are informed by the most recent information available with over 1500 new references. In keeping with the rapidly developing knowledge of biological influences over the entire spectrum of abnormalities of behavior, we have given increased attention to such factors in numerous places throughout the text.

- *Chapter 1* features enhanced attention to the definition, assessment, and diagnosis of mental disorders and the impact of the DSM (Diagnostic and Statistical Manual) taxonomic format on the field at large.

- *Chapter 2* includes a new historic time line that addresses the contribution of major figures in abnormal psychology and provides new coverage of the theme of the treatment of women throughout the history of the field. A new "Highlight" feature on the history of medications has also been added.

- *Chapter 3* has been updated to include coverage of contemporary psychodynamic perspectives such as object relations, interpersonal, and attachment theories, with a focus on current research supporting these perspectives. This represents a significant enhancement of our treatment of general causal factors and viewpoints.

- *Chapter 4* contains a broadened interpretation of the biological changes that take place when a person experiences severe stress.

- *Chapter 5* discusses anxiety disorders with increased attention to the nature and function of worry in generalized anxiety disorder, and to the effects of attempted thought suppression in obsessive-compulsive disorder. Also, treatment approaches to the various anxiety disorders are addressed contiguously with each disorder to better highlight treatment rationales and how they are tailored to the primary features of each disorder. A new "Highlight" focuses on body dysmorphic disorder.

- *Chapter 6* includes discussion of mood disorders with expanded coverage of their relationship to creativity, using as examples famous persons in various fields of the arts including composers, artists, and poets. A new "Highlight" focuses on the interrelationships between depression and marital violence.

- *Chapter 7* draws out certain similarities and interrelations between somatoform and dissociative disorders. The continuing controversies revolving around the emergence of memories of abuse and the status of dissociative identity disorder are aired and updated.

- *Chapter 8* includes expanded coverage of the eating disorders to reflect the increasingly widespread occurrence of these dangerous disorders among young women.

- *Chapter 9* features expanded coverage of borderline and antisocial disorders, including new treatment approaches for the latter. A new "Highlight" discusses prevention of conduct disorder and antisocial personality disorder.

- *Chapter 10* offers a thorough updating of the use and abuse of alcohol and drugs in addition to a broadened interpretation of the biological impact of alcohol on the brain.

- *Chapter 11* focuses on sexual disorders and features new biological treatments for male sexual dysfunction. The controversy surrounding "Megan's Law"—including legal and ethical issues regarding what happens to convicted sex offenders who have been released—is discussed in a new "Highlight" feature.

- *Chapter 12* pays particular attention to updating the research evidence on the schizophrenias, which continues to be produced at an extraordinary rate. We have also examined more closely the competing neurodegenerative and neurodevelopmental perspectives.

- *Chapter 13* includes expanded discussion of traumatic brain injury and of learning disabilities, particularly dyslexia.

- *Chapter 14* discusses childhood disorders and features expanded coverage of the increasing problem of violent crime among youths in our society, drawing attention to the negative social impact of some types of psychopathology.

- *Chapter 15* includes broadened coverage of assessment to include the direct use of psychological test data in treatment planning and execution and the use of psychological testing data as a means of bringing about behavioral change.

- *Chapter 16* features an expanded discussion of the newest "atypical" antidepressant, antipsychotic, and antianxiety drugs, outlining their advantages as well as their drawbacks.

- *Chapter 17* introduces new material on the "efficacy" versus "effectiveness" distinction as applied to evaluating psychosocial treatments, and also on the increasingly important problems of racial/ethnic mismatches between therapist and client.

- *Chapter 18* introduces new conceptions and strategies in the area of prevention of mental disorders, using as a timely example the prevention of alcohol and drug abuse among adolescents.

INTEGRATED RESEARCH ON MULTICULTURAL AND CROSS-CULTURAL ISSUES

New coverage of multicultural and cross-cultural issues in abnormal psychology has been integrated into many chapters. For example, Chapter 1 provides a general overview of cultural influences in abnormality. Chapter 3 includes an entire section on the sociocultural viewpoint in abnormal psychology as well as sociocultural causal factors, including discussion of John Weisz's research on how cultural factors affect both how symptoms are expressed and how prevalent they are. Chapter 5 discusses general sociocultural causal factors for anxiety disorders, focusing on cultural differences in sources of worry and including discussion of Taijin Kyofusho. Chapter 6 discusses cross-cultural differences in depressive symptoms. Chapter 8 includes coverage of sociocultural factors in physical disease. Chapter 9 includes a section on sociocultural causal factors in personality disorders. Chapter 10 discusses sociocultural factors in alcohol abuse and dependence. Chapter 11 includes extensive discussion of cultural influences on sexual practices and standards. Chapter 12 includes discussion of sociocultural causal factors in schizophrenia. Chapter 13 discusses cultural-familial mental retardation and ends with a related section on unresolved issues in this area. Chapter 17 features discussion of psychotherapy and multiculturalism, highlighting the important issue of racial/ethnic mismatches between therapist and client.

ACCESSIBLE ORGANIZATION

The organization of *Abnormal Psychology and Modern Life* has to a large extent set the standard for the study of abnormal psychology. It provides a framework for understanding the field as a whole that will help enhance student comprehension and serves as a handy reference for future study or research.

Part 1, "Perspectives on Abnormal Behavior," sets forth a framework for understanding abnormal behavior, beginning with discussions of classification and scientific research in abnormal psychology (Chapter 1). A historical overview with a helpful new time line traces the changing views on mental disorder from ancient to modern times with a focus on the treatment of women and the difficulties of interpreting historical events over time (Chapter 2). This leads to a discussion of causal factors and viewpoints (Chapter 3). Throughout these chapters the reader is made aware of the diversity of the field and the interaction of biological, psychosocial, and sociocultural factors. The ideal of achieving a biopsychosocial integrative approach to understanding the causes of different disorders is emphasized.

Part 2, "Patterns of Abnormal (Maladaptive) Behavior" can be considered the core of the text. Here the clinical pictures, causal factors, and treatments and outcomes of maladaptive behavior patterns are examined for each category of disorders. This section begins with an examination of stress and adjustment disorders, followed by chapters on panic-based and anxiety-based disorders, mood disorders and suicide, somatoform and dissociative disorders, eating disorders and other compromises of physical health, personality disorders, substance-related and addictive disorders, sexual variants, abuse, and dysfunctions, schizophrenic and delusional disorders, brain disorders and other cognitive impairments, and disorders of childhood and adolescence.

Part 3 is a more comprehensive look at the clinical assessment, treatment, and prevention of disorders. It includes chapters on assessment, biological therapies, psychosocial therapies, and contemporary social issues pertaining to abnormalities of behavior.

HELPFUL FEATURES AND PEDAGOGY

The extensive research base and accessible organization of this book are supported by high-interest features and helpful pedagogy to further engage students and support learning.

- "Highlight" sections in each chapter expand on topics of particular interest. Two new types have been added to this edition. "Highlight: Modern Life" features applications of research to everyday life and current events. "Highlight: Cutting Edge" features the latest research methodologies/technologies and findings.

- "Unresolved Issues" sections at the end of each chapter demonstrate how far we have come and how far we have to go in our understanding of psychological

disorders. The topics included here provide insight into the future of the field.

- **Case Studies** of individuals with various disorders appear in color throughout the book. These cases have been expanded in this edition to provide even more real-life examples of many disorders covered in the text. Some are brief excerpts and others are detailed analyses. These cases bring disorders to life while reminding students of the human factor that is so intimately a part of the subject matter of this text.

- **Reproductions of paintings** by patients with various mental disorders are featured on the first page of each chapter with a brief biological sketch of each artist. These images also help illuminate the human side of psychological disorders. The placement of the artwork, however, is not keyed to particular disorders.

- **A chapter outline** introduces the content of each chapter and provides an overview of what is to come. This, and the extensive chapter summary found at the end of each chapter, are excellent tools for study and review.

- **Key Terms** appear in boldface type when first introduced and defined in the text. They are also listed at the end of each chapter and defined in the end of text glossary.

- **Expanded graphics.** Over several editions, we had imperceptibly (and inadvertently) altered the balance of text and graphical displays in favor of the former. Consequently, by the tenth edition the book had become quite somewhat dense in its visual aspect. We have remedied that situation by substantially increasing the proportion of graphical material included in each chapter.

HELPFUL ANCILLARY MATERIALS

The following items are available to support learning and teaching with the Eleventh Edition of *Abnormal Psychology and Modern Life.*

- **Student Study Guide (Beth Levy and Don Fowles):** Includes learning objectives, study questions, quizzes, and key terms for each chapter of the text, with an emphasis on stimulating critical thinking.

- **Telecourse Study Guide:** For those of you using this textbook with the Annenberg/CPB Telecourse, a special study guide is available to key the textbook content with the videos and provide helpful study aids.

- **Telecourse Faculty Guide:** For those of you using this textbook with the Annenberg/CPB Telecourse, a special faculty guide is available to help integrate the text with the telecourse videos.

- **Quick Guide to the Internet for Abnormal Psychology:** This helpful resource provides direct routes to research on particular mental disorders, contacts with support services, and Web locations of mental health/professional organizations. This guide makes searches on the Internet more efficient and provides helpful information about doing research on the Internet, such as how to cite Internet sources. It also directly links you and your students with the extensive Website that accompanies this textbook.

- **Instructor's Manual (Frank Prerost, Midwestern University):** Provides chapter overviews, learning objectives, lists of key terms, abstracts with discussion questions, suggested readings, discussion and lecture ideas, suggested films, and ideas for activities and projects to support and extend each chapter of the textbook.

- **Test Bank (Richard Leavy, Ohio Wesleyan University):** Containing over 100 multiple choice questions, 15 essay questions, and 20 short answer questions per chapter, this collection of test questions can also be edited using our state of the art computerized testing system.

- **Computerized Testing System:** Allyn and Bacon Test Manager is an integrated suite of testing and assessment tools for Windows and Macintosh. You can use Test Manager to create professional-looking exams in just minutes by building tests for the existing database of questions, editing questions, or adding you own. Course management features include a class roster, gradebook, and item analysis. Test Manager also has everything you need to create and administer online tests. For first-time users, there is a guided tour of the entire Test Manager system and screen wizards to walk you through each area.

- **Transparencies:** A collection of four-color transparencies is available upon adoption, to help extend visual learning beyond the textbook.

- **Powerpoint Presentations for Lecture:** A collection of preassembled Powerpoint slides highlighting key concepts in each chapter is available for easy use in your lectures.

- **Videotapes:** A collection of custom video segments highlighting issues related to diagnoses and treatment is available with adoption of this text. Videos from "The World of Abnormal Psychology" a telecourse produced by the Annenberg/CPB Project in conjunction with Toby Levine Communications, Alvin H.

Perlmutter, and Allyn and Bacon, are also available to qualified adopters. Please contact your local Allyn and Bacon representative or visit the Allyn and Bacon Website for more information.

- **Web Resources:** *Abnormal Psychology and Modern Life* is supported by an extensive Website with unique interactive case studies to allow students to immediately apply what they have learned in the textbook. This Website also includes practice tests, related Web links, and other helpful study aids for each chapter of the textbook. Visit www.abacon.com/carson for more information.

Acknowledgements

We want to single out for special praise and appreciation our development editor, Leslie Carr. A highly experienced editor of psychology textbooks, Leslie made numerous suggestions for places where cuts could be made to leave room for additions that are inevitable with progress in an area, as well as points that needed clarification, and suggestions for new headings, figures, and visual aids to improve readability. Such suggestions were especially helpful at the early stage of the revision, reflecting her great editorial wisdom. This editorial wisdom, combined with her enthusiasm for the project, are central to whatever success the current edition enjoys.

We are also greatly indebted to Dr. J. Michael Bailey of Northwestern University for his enormous help in revising and updating the coverage of sexual variants, abuse, and dysfunctions in Chapter 11. As a leading researcher in this important and controversial area, his advice on what to include in such a chapter and how to cover it in an interesting and sensitive fashion was invaluable.

Most of the revisions of the portion of this textbook written by Susan Mineka were completed while she was a Fellow at the Center for Advanced Study in the Behavioral Sciences in Stanford, California. She would like to acknowledge the John D. and Catherine T. MacArthur Foundation Grant #95-32005-0 for their generous financial support during that year (1997-1998). She would like to extend special thanks to the staff at the center for their role in making this such a special and stimulating year—indeed, a perfect place to work on such a project and related scholarly goals. She would also like to thank Dave Barlow, another Fellow in residence, who shared many ideas and much support as we pursued closely related tasks in revising our abnormal psychology textbooks and

Marta Fulop for her comments on the psychoanalytic and psychodynamic coverage.

Any project of this magnitude incurs author preoccupation that usurps "quality" time from deserving others. Robert Carson thanks his children, David, Carolyn, and Kelly, and his grandchildren, Hope, Lisa, and Steven, for their uncomplaining forbearance. James Butcher thanks his wife Carolyn L. Williams and his children, Holly Butcher, Sherry Butcher and Jay Butcher.

We would also like to thank the many reviewers who have contributed helpful comments on this and previous editions. These include Norman Anderson, National Institute of Mental Health and Duke University Medical Center; John Bates, Indiana University; Alfred Baumeister, Vanderbilt University; Mitchell Berman, University of Southern Mississippi; Ira Berstein, University of Texas at Arlington; Bruce Bongar, Pacific Graduate School of Psychology; Robert F. Bornstein, Fordham Univeristy-Lincoln Center; Linda Bosmajian, Hood College; Kenneth Bowers, University of Waterloo; Thomas G. Bowers, Penn State-Harrisburg; Wolfgang Bringmann, University of Southern Alabama; Alan Butler, University of Maine; James Calhoun, University of Georgia; Caryn Carlson, University of Texas at Austin; Dennis Carmody, St. Peter's College; Alan Carr, University College Dublin; Kathleen Carroll, Yale University School of Medicine; Lee Anna Clark, University of Iowa; David Cole, University of Notre Dame; Bruce Compas, University of Vermont; Eric Cooley, Western Oregon State; Robert Deluty, University of Maryland Baltimore County; Joan Doolittle, Anne Arundel Community College; John Exner, Rorschach Workshops; Kenneth L. Farr, University of Texas at Arlington; Anthony F. Fazio, University of Wisconsin, Milwaukee; Gary Ford, Stephen F. Austin State University; Don Fowles, University of Iowa; Sol Garfield, Washington University; Carlton Gass, Veterans Administration Medical Center-Miami; Paul Goldin, Metropolitan State of Denver, Ethan Gornstein, Columbia University; Lisa Green, Baldwin-Wallace College; Susan Hardin, University of Akron; March Henley, Delaware County Community College; Michael Hirt, Kent State University; Karen Horner, Ohio State University; William Iacono, University of Minnesota; Ira Iscoe, University of Texas at Austin; Fred Johnson, University of the District of Columbia; Gary Johnson, Normandale Community College; John Junginger, SUNY Binghamton; Stephen R. Kahoe, El Paso Community College; John Kihlstrom, Yale University; Marlyne Kilbey, Wayne State University; David Kosson, Chicago Medical School; Dennis Kreinbrook, Westmoreland County Community College; Michael J. Lambert, Brigham Young University; Connie Lanier, Central Piedmont Community College; Marvin W. Lee, Shenandoah University; Gerard Lenthall, Keene State College; Gloria Leon, University of Minnesota; Arnold LeUnes, Texas A & M University; Richard Lewine, Emory University; Patrick Logue, Duke University Medical Center; Steven R. Lopez, UCLA; Lester Luborsky, University of Pennsylvania; Donna K. McMillan, St. Olaf College; Edwin Megargee, Florida State University; Dorothy Mercer, Eastern Kentucky University; Linda Montgomery, University of Texas of the Permian Basin; Steve A. Nida, Franklin University; Eileen Palace, Tulane University Medical School; Dimitri Papageorgis, University of British Columbia; David L. Penn, Louisiana State University; John Poppleston, Akron University; Charles Prokop, Florida Institute of Technology; Paul Retzlaff, University of Northern Colorado; Clive Robins, Duke University Medical Center; William B. Scott, College of Wooster; Kenneth Sher, University of Missouri; Patricia J. Slocum, College of DuPage; Jerome Small, Youngstown State University; Gregory Smith, University of Kentucky; Cheryl L. Spinweber, University of California-San Diego; Kathleen Stafford, Court Diagnostic Clinic, Hudson, Ohio; Brian Stagner, Texas A & M University; Louis Stamps, University of Wisconsin-La Crosse; Veronica Stebbing, University College Dublin; Patricia Sutker, Veterans Medical Center-New Orleans; Alexander Troster, University of Kansas Medical Center; Samuel Turner, Medical University of South Carolina; Linda Van Egeren, Department of Veterans Affairs Medical Center-Minneapolis; Frank W. Weathers, UMASS Boston; Charles Wenar, Ohio State University; Fred Whitford, Montana State University; Jennifer Wilson, Duke University Medical Center; Richard Zinbarg, University of Oregon.

About the Authors

Robert Carson, a native New Englander, received his undergraduate degree in psychology at Brown University. His graduate training, culminating in the PhD in clinical psychology, occurred at Northwestern University. He has been a member of both the Medical and Arts and Sciences faculties at Duke University since 1960. In the course of that tenure he served as head of Duke Medical Center's Division of Medical Psychology and, in the Department of Psychology, as Director of its doctoral clinical program and as Chair. He has taught psychology to undergraduates virtually uninterruptedly since his senior year at Brown, and in 1993-94 was named a Distinguished Teacher in Duke University's Trinity College. Also, partly in recognition of his teaching contributions, he was appointed a G. Stanley Hall Lecturer by the American Psychological Association for 1989. Dr. Carson's scholarly interests are focused on the interpersonal dimensions of psychopathology, although he claims to work hard at remaining a generalist and avoiding excessive specialization.

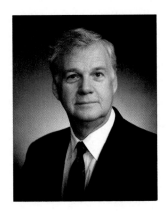

James N. Butcher was born in West Virginia. He enlisted in the Army at 17 years of age and served in the airborne infantry for three years, including a one-year tour in Korea during the Korean War. After military service, he attended Guilford College, graduating in 1960 with a BA in psychology. He received an MA in experimental psychology in 1962 and a PhD in clinical psychology from the University of North Carolina at Chapel Hill. He was awarded Doctor Honoris Causa from the Free University of Brussels, Belgium, in 1990.

He is currently Professor of Psychology in the Department of Psychology at the University of Minnesota and was Associate Director and Director of the Clinical Psychology Program at Minnesota for 19 years. He was a member of the University of Minnesota Press' MMPI Consultive Committee that undertook the revision of the MMPI in 1989. He was formerly the editor of Psychological Assessment, a journal of the American Psychological Association, and serves as consulting editor or reviewer for numerous other journals in psychology and psychiatry. Dr. Butcher has been actively involved in developing and organizing disaster response programs for dealing with human problems following airline disasters. He organized a model crisis intervention disaster response for the Minneapolis-St. Paul Airport, and organized and supervised the psychological services offered following two major airline disasters: Northwest Flight 255 in Detroit, Michigan, and Aloha Airlines on Maui.

He is a fellow of the American Psychological Association and the Society for Personality Assessment. He has published 40 books and more than 175 articles in the fields of abnormal psychology, cross-cultural psychology, and personality assessment.

Susan Mineka, born and raised in Ithaca, New York, received her undergraduate degree magna cum laude in psychology at Cornell University. She received a PhD in experimental psychology from the University of Pennsylvania in 1974, and later completed a formal clinical retraining program from 1981-1984. She taught at the University of Wisconsin-Madison and at the University of Texas at Austin before moving to Northwestern University in 1987. She has taught a wide range of undergraduate and graduate courses, including introductory psychology, learning, motivation, abnormal psychology, and cognitive-behavior therapy. Her current research interests include cognitive and behavioral approaches to understanding the etiology, maintenance, and treatment of anxiety and mood disorders. She is currently a Fellow of both the American Psychological Association and the American Psychological Society. She has served as Editor of the Journal of Abnormal Psychology (1990-1994) and is currently on the editorial boards of several of the leading journals in the field. She was also President of the Society for the Science of Clinical Psychology (1994-1995), and was President of the Midwestern Psychological Association (1997). She also served on the American Psychological Association's Board of Scientific Affairs (1992-1994, Chair 1994) and on the Executive Board of the Society for Research in Psychopathology (1992-1994). During 1997–1998 she was a fellow at the Center for Advanced Study in the Behavioral Sciences at Stanford.

Abnormal Psychology: An Overview

August Natterer (Neter), *Witch's Head*. Married and living in Germany, Neter (1868–1933) began to suffer from depression and hallucinations, and was institutionalized around 1907 with an acute phase of schizophrenia. Educated as an electrical engineer, he punctuated his images with precise details. This painting represents his recurring vision of a hostile Witch who created the world.

Virtually all of us have at least some interest in abnormalities of behavior, and probably a large majority of readers of this text will have had at least some direct experience with persons whose behavior they considered to be abnormal. Our awareness of abnormal behavior may be based, for example, on encounters with a person on the streets of our towns and cities who talks agitatedly to no obvious listener; with the parent of a friend who had to go into an alcohol or drug rehabilitation program; with the neighbor who was afraid to go outside; or the athlete who had to be hospitalized for an eating disorder. We hear about some multiple murder on the news and wonder how someone could do such a thing.

Abnormal behavior is thus a part of our common experience. It is the main purpose of this book to help you gain a better understanding of the variety of psychological problems that any of us may experience. It is easy to judge the loud and obnoxious drunk down the street or the youngster who seems constantly in conflict with authority, parental or otherwise. Understanding them, trying to figure out why they behave as they do, is quite another and usually far more challenging matter. As you will see, one of the themes reappearing throughout this book is that because people with and without psychological problems are all different and the influences on them complex and varied as well, there are few, if any, simple and straightforward explanations for abnormalities of behavior. Our hope is to increase your understanding so that when you encounter people exhibiting abnormal behavior or go through periods of psychological difficulty in your own life you'll be prepared to raise potentially productive questions as to what is going on, rather than merely to judge the behavior or feel overwhelmed by the problems you may be having.

This chapter sketches the outlines of the field of abnormal psychology and the varied training and activities of the people who work in it. It first covers the ways abnormal behavior can be defined and classified so as to enable mental health professionals to communicate with each other about the people they see. The issues here are probably more complex and controversial than you might expect. Having established this definitional framework, the chapter will then provide some basic information about the extent of behavioral abnormalities in the population at large. It also conveys how we study abnormal behavior—the methods psychologists and other mental health professionals use to uncover the information presented in subsequent chapters of the book.

Finally, the chapter is designed to give you a sense of this field as a fascinating work still very much in progress. This is not a field for those who want only cold, hard

These presumably "normal" persons crossing an intersection in New York City are a highly varied group despite the common situation they share. People with psychological problems are no less different one from the other in their reactions to the various influences impinging on them.

facts. As demonstrated throughout the text, simple facts by themselves—for example, that there are genetic contributions to a particular disorder—do not always yield very useful conclusions. Human behavior is fascinating because it is complexly organized, and this is no less true of those currently experiencing psychological difficulties. Often, what we are looking for are patterns among the various simple facts presented to us, but even that level of insight is sometimes still out of reach. For that reason, each chapter of this book ends with a section entitled Unresolved Issues to give you a sense of what those in the field—psychologists, social workers, psychiatrists, and other mental health professionals—are working on as they pursue their own clarity and understanding.

Let's open with three cases from our files, people we have dealt with as clinicians. These cases describe the problematic behavior they exhibit, with only modest alteration to preserve anonymity. During the course of this text, we hope to flesh out more of the questions and potential answers such behaviors raise.

Case Study, A Case of Suicide • Albert G., a 62-year-old professor at a small college in the Midwest, was immensely popular and well regarded by everyone who knew him. Students flocked to his classes; his professional colleagues sought his consultation and scholarly views; and he wrote, when his moods permitted, with penetrating insight and unusual candor. With such high praise and with obvious success, why did he kill himself—a victim of deep personal despair? He had lived a very organized and conscientious life, always concerned about how he was viewed by others. Although dwelling alone, he had had several close friends, yet no one knew of the personal plight he apparently had experienced. No one around him, not even his closest associates, had been aware of the depth of his despondent moods. The suicide left everyone in the community wondering about the psychological forces that could prompt someone as seemingly well-adjusted as Albert to end his life.

Case Study, Alcohol Shatters a Life • Sue D., a 38-year-old attorney, acknowledged to her treatment group that she did not know how long she had had a problem with alcohol and tranquilizer abuse. She had become painfully aware of her problems on an evening when she had gone to dinner with some friends and had lingered afterward in the restaurant bar to have a few drinks. She had drunk a great deal more than she had intended (as was often the case) and had gotten into a heated argument with other patrons and the manager of the bar. Sue explained how the situation had deteriorated. Objects had been thrown, the police had been called, and she had been arrested for public drunkenness and abuse of police officers. The police then had taken her to a detoxification center at the county hospital—the same hospital where she served as chief counsel for the law firm at which she worked. Sue told her group that the hospital administrator had been incensed, and the law firm partners had been embarrassed and outraged. Sue had been given the option of leaving the law firm or seeking treatment; she had chosen the latter and had begun a new phase of her life. She had entered a treatment program and was trying to understand how she had allowed her life to shatter as it had.

Case Study, Donald G.'s Insulting Voices • Donald G. was 33 years old when one of us became professionally involved with him. Although he was of relatively high measured intelligence, he had never been employed for more than a few days at a time and currently lives in a sheltered community setting—except for brief, but frequent, periods of rehospitalization because he has periods of marked agitation in which he hears voices heaping insulting and abusive comments upon him. Donald appeared awkward, moderately inappropriate in introducing extraneous content into his conversations, and painfully unsure of himself in most social situations. The voices had made their appearance quite suddenly and without obvious provocation at age 17 after a brief period of social withdrawal. At that time he was stubbornly insistent that the voices were coming, with malicious intent, from within a neighbor's house and were being transmitted electronically to the speakers of the family television set. More recently he had conceded that he somehow produces them within himself. During periods of deterioration he might be heard arguing vehemently with the voices, but for the most part was

now able to ignore them, though they are reportedly never entirely absent for sustained periods.

Prior to his breakdown, Donald had lived a relatively normal middle-class life, was reasonably popular among peers, had maintained passing grades in school, and had shown considerable athletic prowess, although his parents and teachers had often complained that he seemed inattentive and preoccupied. There was no evidence of his ever having abused drugs. Donald's prognosis (the likelihood that he would ever regain a full measure of functioning) was considered "guarded" by his professional caregivers.

Unfortunately, none of the seemingly senseless behavioral distortions depicted in these accounts, which represent recognized patterns of deviance, can be considered rare. As will be seen in this and subsequent chapters, there is no shortage of ideas purporting to explain them. Some of these ideas are promising, in the sense of having considerable scientific support, and some remain untested. Because so much about abnormal behavior and mental distress remains unexplained, another important goal of this book is to teach you how to discriminate among qualitative levels of supporting evidence. But first, we must deal with the elemental problem of trying to define our field of inquiry.

WHAT DO WE MEAN BY ABNORMAL BEHAVIOR?

To assess, treat, and prevent abnormal behavior, it is important to develop definitions of normal and abnormal and to specify criteria for distinguishing one from the other. Unfortunately, and often surprisingly to newcomers to the field, making such formal distinctions is far from easy and is fraught with numerous conceptual pitfalls. The word *abnormal* literally means "away from the normal," but note that we do not usually employ the term for those high-end behaviors that are better than, or superior to, normal performance. Genius is rarely if ever addressed in textbooks of abnormal psychology; mental retardation almost always is. We are already confronted, then, with a *valuational* consideration, one that necessarily will loom large in our discussion of these issues.

Even where we attempt to restrict consideration to the "subnormal" range, however, there remains the implication of deviation from some specified norm. But what is the norm? In the case of physical illness, the norm is the integrity of the body as a workable biological system; here, the boundary lines between normality and pathology are usually (but not always) clear: at any given point

The almost incredible skill professional athletes display is highly "abnormal" in a literal and statistical sense. Yet we do not consider it part of abnormal psychology because that field is concerned chiefly with undesirable behavioral deviations.

in time one is either healthy or one is not. For psychological disorder, however, we have no ideal, or even universally normal, model of human mental and behavioral functioning to use as a base of comparison. Thus we find considerable confusion and disagreement as to just what is or is not normal, a confusion aggravated by changing values and expectations in society at large. As recently as 25 years ago in our culture, the wearing of earrings by male persons regularly inspired questions about their mental health; now such adornments are quite routine.

Dilemmas of Definition

Nearly all of what we regard as "abnormal" in behavior we also regard as *undesirable.* From the standpoint of political democracy, society has no "right" to treat or otherwise seek to change abnormal behavior unless that behavior can be deemed undesirable—that is, contrary to the public interest. In any attempt to delineate the boundaries of the field, the problem of values and the associated problem of maintaining an *objective* point of view will never be far beneath the surface as you proceed through the pages of this text.

Despite the evident difficulties, the need for a consensus understanding about what is to be considered abnormality is, in certain contexts, quite compelling. These contexts include, for example, legal ones, matters concerning health insurance coverage, clinical decisions as to whether to undertake treatment, and the writing of abnormal psychology textbooks. We need, in other words, some sort of working definition of the subject matter that is to occupy our attention. The concepts of "behavioral abnormality," "mental disorder" and "mental illness" have tended to merge in recent decades, so that "abnormality" has become the functional equivalent of all of these notions. As a result it has tended to be seen as a subset of essentially *medical* problems. As we shall see, however, *mental disorders* are for the most part only loosely analogous to medical diseases as ordinarily conceived.

The DSM-IV Definition of Mental Disorder

The gold standard for defining mental disorder and its subclasses has become the American Psychiatric Association's *Diagnostic and Statistical Manual of Mental Disorders (DSM),* whose fourth edition (DSM-IV) was published in 1994. Here is how the DSM-IV defines mental disorder:

> [A mental disorder] is conceptualized as a clinically significant behavioral or psychological syndrome or pattern that occurs in an individual and that is associated with present distress (a painful symptom) or disability (impairment in one or more areas of functioning) or with a significantly increased risk of suffering death, pain, disability, or an important loss of freedom. In addition, this syndrome or pattern must not be merely an expectable and culturally sanctioned response to a particular event, for example, the death of a loved one. Whatever its original cause, it must currently be considered a manifestation of a behavioral, psychological, or biological dysfunction in the individual. Neither deviant behavior (e.g., political, religious, or sexual) nor conflicts that are primarily between the individual and society are mental disorders unless the deviance or conflict is a symptom of a dysfunction in the individual, as described above (American Psychiatric Association, 1994, pp. xxi–xxii).

The term *syndrome* refers to a group of clinical observations or symptoms that tend to co-occur. For example, feelings of despondency, lowered self-esteem, and preoccupation with negative thoughts constitute important parts of a depressive syndrome.

A noteworthy characteristic of this DSM definition of mental disorders is that it does not refer to the causes of mental disorder. It also carefully rules out, among other things, certain otherwise questionable behaviors that are culturally sanctioned, such as (depressive) grief following the death of a significant other, and it is careful also to assert that mental disorders are always the product of "dysfunctions," dysfunctions that in turn always reside in individuals. In other words, there are no mentally disordered groups per se, although such a concept might arguably apply where some significant proportion of a group's members *individually* qualify as mentally disordered.

While widely accepted, the DSM definition of mental disorder has by no means gone unchallenged. The value considerations involved in notions like *distress, disability,* and *enhanced risk* as well as the need to define the term *dysfunction* have all been raised as weaknesses of the definition, which is also regarded by many professionals as unduly tortuous and cumbersome. Psychologist Jerome Wakefield, for example, has proposed that the definition be reduced to its simplest terms:

> A mental disorder is a mental condition that (a) causes significant distress or disability, (b) is not merely an expectable response to a particular event, and (c) is a manifestation of a mental dysfunction (1992a, p. 235).

We shall examine these matters more closely in the Unresolved Issues section at the end of the chapter. In the final analysis, as you may already have suspected, any definition of abnormality or mental disorder must be somewhat arbitrary, and the DSM-IV definition is no exception. Nonetheless, attempted definitions have also had to consider that to some degree what is abnormal is culturally determined.

Cultural Influences in Abnormality

It is difficult to consider the concepts of normal and abnormal without reference to a given culture: abnormal behavior is behavior that deviates from the norms of the society in which it is enacted (e.g., see Gorenstein, 1992; Sarbin, 1997; Scheff, 1984; Ullmann & Krasner, 1975). While social and cultural contexts are obviously important, at its most extreme this position leads to the jarring conclusion that, for example, a Nazi concentration camp commandant of the early 1940s was acting "normally" in ordering and presiding over the cold-blooded murders of tens of thousands of men, women, and children of a group officially designated to be despised. In fact, from this point of view, actions in the victims' behalf, such as Oscar Schindler's famous "list" of Jews exempt from gassing and cremation, might be taken as pathologically self-endangering.

Certain actions, such as wild, dangerous, and seemingly out-of-control behaviors, are almost universally considered to be the product of mental disorder or its cultural equivalent (e.g., possession by spirits). But excluding this relatively rare phenomenon there is precious little agreement across the cultures of the world as to what is "abnormal." So, while it is important to acknowledge the critical significance of context, including prevailing social norms, in trying to understand behavior, it is also desirable to take

What is considered abnormal or deviant behavior in one society may be quite normal in another. We might consider this Arab woman's style of dress to be abnormal, but in her society it is the norm. What we consider normal may not be normal for everyone.

a firmer position regarding what is to be considered abnormal or disordered in behavior. Although it is likely that any definition of abnormality will involve value choices, it is probably better, everything considered, that these choices be explicitly stated rather than implicitly embedded in the widely varying norms of different cultures.

Mental Disorder as Maladaptive Behavior

Although some measure of social conformity is essential to group life, we suggest that the best criterion for determining the normality of behavior is not whether society accepts it, but whether the behavior fosters or threatens individual and group well-being. According to this perspective, **abnormal behavior** is *maladaptive behavior.* Even behavior that conforms strictly to contemporary societal values is abnormal, mentally disordered, if it seriously interferes with functioning and is self-defeating in its consequences.

In keeping with the above perspective as well as with the comprehensive aims of this text, *we define behavior as abnormal, a manifestation of mental disorder, if it is both persistent and in serious degree contrary to the continued well-being of the individual and/or that of the human community of which the individual is a member.* This "working definition" contains, of course, an explicit value judgment that ties the definition of mental disorder to the persistent enactment of behavior that produces harmful consequences for self and/or others.

Abnormal or disordered behavior defined in this manner includes the more traditional categories of mental disorders—such as alcoholism and schizophrenia—as well as, for example, self-destructive behaviors designed to establish a counterfeit "identity," promotion of intergroup hostility, destructive assaults on the environment in which all of us must live, irrational violence, and political corruption, regardless of whether such actions are condemned or condoned by a given society or subculture. All of these actions represent maladaptive behavior that impairs individual or group well-being. Typically they sooner or later lead to personal distress among those attracted to their temporary or illusory benefits, and often they bring about destructive group conflict as well.

CLASSIFYING ABNORMAL BEHAVIOR

Classification is important in any science, whether we are studying chemical elements, plants, planets, or people. With an agreed-upon classification system, we can be confident that we are communicating clearly. If someone says to you, I saw a dog running down the street, you can probably produce a mental image approximating in broad features the appearance of that dog—not from seeing it but rather from your knowledge of animal classifications. There are of course many breeds of dogs that vary widely in their configurations of size, color, muzzle length, etc., and yet we have little difficulty in recognizing the essential features of "dogness." "Dogness" is an example of what psychologists refer to as a cognitive prototype or pattern, about which we shall have more to say below.

In abnormal psychology, classification involves the attempt to delineate meaningful subvarieties of maladaptive behavior. Like defining abnormal behavior, classification of some kind is a necessary first step toward introducing order into our discussion of the nature, causes, and treatment of such behavior. It is intended to enable communication about particular clusters of abnormal behavior in agreed-upon and relatively precise ways. For example, we cannot conduct research on what might cause eating disorders unless we begin with a more or less clear definition of the behavior under examination; otherwise, we would be unable to select for intensive study persons whose behavior displays the aberrant eating patterns we hope to understand. There are other reasons for diagnostic classifications, too, such as gathering statistics on how common are the various types of disorder or meeting the needs of medical insurance companies (which insist on having formal diagnoses before they will authorize payment of claims).

Keep in mind that, just as with the process of defining abnormality itself, all classification is the product of human invention—it is, in essence, a matter of making generalizations based on what has been observed. Even when observations are precise and carefully made, the generalizations we arrive at go beyond those observations and hopefully enable us to make inferences about underlying similarities and differences. For example, it is common for people experiencing episodes of panic to feel they are about to die. When "panic" is carefully delineated, we find that it is not in fact associated with any enhanced risk of death but that the people experiencing such episodes tend to share certain other characteristics, such as recent exposure to highly stressful events.

It is not unusual for a classification system to be an ongoing work in progress as new knowledge demonstrates an earlier generalization to be incomplete or flawed. This has been the case on numerous occasions in the history of abnormal psychology, and we have no doubt that additional revisions will be necessary in the future. It is important to bear in mind, too, that formal classification is successfully accomplished only through precise techniques of psychological, or clinical, assessment—techniques that have been increasingly refined over the years. We offer an example of these techniques in a later section and discuss them in detail in Chapter 15, after we have looked thoroughly at the kinds of abnormal behavior classified thus far by judicious application of these observational methods.

Reliability and Validity

A classification system's usefulness depends largely on its reliability and validity. **Reliability** is the degree to which a measuring device produces the same result each time it is used to measure the same thing. If your scale showed a significantly different weight each time you stepped on it over some brief period, you would consider it a fairly unreliable measure of your body mass. In the context of classification, reliability is an index of the extent to which different observers can agree that a person's behavior fits a given diagnostic class. If observers cannot agree, it may mean that the classification criteria are not precise enough to determine whether the suspected disorder is present or absent.

The classification system must also be *valid*. **Validity** refers to the extent to which a measuring instrument actually measures what it is supposed to measure. In the case of mental disorder classification, validity is defined by the degree to which a diagnosis accurately conveys to us something clinically important about the person whose behavior fits the category, such as helping to predict the future course of the disorder. If, for example, a person is diagnosed as having schizophrenia, as was Donald G. (p. 3), we should be able to infer from that classification some fairly precise characteristics that differentiate the person from others considered normal, or from those suffering from other types of mental disorder. Thus, the diagnosis of schizophrenia implies a disorder of unusually stubborn persistence, with recurrent episodes being common.

Normally, validity presupposes reliability. If clinicians can't agree on the class to which a disordered person's behavior belongs, then the question of the validity of the diagnostic classifications that may be under consideration becomes an irrelevant issue. To put it another way, if we can't confidently pin down what the diagnosis is, then whatever useful information a given diagnosis might convey about the person being evaluated is lost. On the other hand, good reliability does not in itself guarantee validity. For example, handedness (left, right, ambidextrous) can be assessed with a high degree of reliability, but handedness accurately predicts neither mental health status nor countless other behavioral qualities on which people vary; that is, it is not a valid index of these qualities, although it may be for success in certain situations involving the game of baseball. In like manner, *reliable* assignment of a person's behavior to a given class of mental disorder will prove useful only to the extent that the validity of that class has been established through research. We will encounter the important concepts of reliability and validity again in the Unresolved Issues section and when we discuss specialized psychological assessment techniques in Chapter 15.

Differing Models of Classification

There appear to be three basic approaches currently possible for classifying abnormal behavior: the categorical, the dimensional, and the prototypal (Widiger & Frances, 1985). A *categorical* approach, similar to the diagnostic system of general medical diseases, assumes that (1) all human behavior can be divided into the categories of healthy and disordered, and (2) within the latter there exist discrete, nonoverlapping classes or types of disorder having a high degree of within-class homogeneity in both "symptoms" displayed and the underlying organization of the disorder identified.

The Dimensional Approach   The dimensional and prototypal approaches differ fundamentally in the assumptions they make, particularly in respect to the requirement of discrete and internally homogeneous classes of behavior. In a dimensional approach, it is assumed that a person's typical behavior is the product of differing strengths or intensities of behavior along several definable dimensions, such as

Even though a test may be reliable—produce the same results on repeat occasions—it may not predict the characteristics we are interested in. For example, this test of strength might be reliable over two occasions but not validly predict arm strength.

mood, emotional stability, aggressiveness, gender identity, anxiousness, interpersonal trust, clarity of thinking and communication, social introversion, and so on. The important dimensions, once established, would be the same for everyone. In this conception, people differ from one another in their configuration or profile of these dimensional traits (each ranging from very low to very high), not in terms of behavioral indications of a corresponding "dysfunctional" entity presumed to underlie and give rise to the disordered pattern of behavior. Normal could be discriminated from abnormal, then, by precise statistical criteria applied to dimensional intensities among unselected people in general, most of whom may be presumed to be close to average, or mentally "normal." We could decide, for example, that anything above the ninety-seventh normative percentile on *aggressiveness* and anything below the third normative percentile on *sociability* be considered "abnormal" findings.

Dimensionally based diagnosis would have the incidental benefit of directly addressing treatment options. Since the patient's profile of psychological characteristics will normally consist of deviantly high and low points, therapies can be designed to modulate those of excessive intensity (e.g., anxiety) and to enhance those that constitute deficit status (e.g., inhibited self-assertiveness).

Of course, in taking a dimensional approach it would be possible—perhaps even likely—to discover that such profiles tend to cluster together in types, and even that some of these types are correlated, though imperfectly, with recognizable sorts of gross behavioral malfunctions, such as anxiety disorders or depression. It is highly unlikely, however, that any individual's profile will exactly fit a narrowly defined type, or that the types identified will not have some overlapping features. This brings us to the matter of a prototypal approach.

The Prototypal Approach   A *prototype* (as the term is used here) is a conceptual entity depicting an idealized combination of characteristics that more or less regularly occur together in a less than perfect or standard way at the level of actual observation. Recall our earlier example of the "dogness" prototype. Prototypes, as that example demonstrates, are actually an aspect of our everyday thinking and experience. We can all readily generate in our mind's eye an image of a dog, while recognizing we have never seen nor ever will see two identical dogs. Thus, no member of a prototypally defined group may actually have all of the characteristics of the defined prototype, although it will have at least some of the more central of them. Also, some characteristics may be shared among differing prototypes—for example, many animals other than dogs have tails.

As we shall see, the official diagnostic criteria defining the various recognized classes of mental disorder, while explicitly intended to create categorical entities, more often than not result in prototypal ones. The central features of the various identified disorders are often somewhat vague, as are the boundaries purporting to separate one disorder from another. Much evidence suggests that a strict categorical approach to identifying differences among types of human behavior, whether normal or abnormal, may well be an unattainable goal (e.g., Carson, 1996; Lillienfeld & Marino, 1995). Bearing this in mind as we proceed may help you avoid some confusion. For example, we commonly find that two or more identified disorders regularly occur together in the same psychologically disordered individuals, a situation known as **comorbidity.** Does this really mean that such a person has two or more entirely separate and distinct disorders? In the typical instance, probably not.

DSM Classification of Mental Disorders

We have already introduced the *Diagnostic and Statistical Manual of Mental Disorders* (DSM). We return to it here because, in addition to attempting to define what is to be considered a mental disorder, this manual specifies what subtypes of mental disorder are currently officially recognized and provides for each a set of defining criteria. As already noted, the system purports to be a categorical one

having sharp boundaries separating the various disorders from one another, but it is in fact a prototypal one having much fuzziness of boundaries and interpenetration of the various "categories" of disorder it identifies.

The criteria that define the recognized categories of disorder consist for the most part of symptoms and signs. **Symptoms** generally refer to the patient's subjective description, the complaints she or he presents about what is wrong. **Signs,** on the other hand, refer to objective observations the diagnostician may make either directly (such as the patient's inability to look another person in the eye) or indirectly (such as the results of pertinent tests administered by a psychological examiner). For a given diagnosis to be made, the diagnostician must observe the particular criteria—the symptoms and signs asserted to define that diagnosis—to be met.

The Evolution of the DSM   As we have seen, the DSM is currently in its fourth edition (DSM-IV), this version having been published in May 1994. The classes of mental disorder recognized in the DSM-IV are reproduced on the endpapers of this book. The DSM-IV is the product of a four-decade evolution involving increasing refinement and precision in the identification and description of mental disorders. The first edition of the manual (DSM-I) appeared in 1952 and was largely an outgrowth of attempts to standardize diagnostic practices in coping with the widespread mental breakdowns occurring among military personnel in World War II. The 1968 DSM-II reflected the additional insights gleaned from a markedly expanded postwar research effort in mental health sponsored by the federal government. An only gradually recognized deficiency of both these early efforts was that the various types of disorder identified were described in narrative and jargon-laden terms that proved too vague for mental health professionals to agree on their meaning. The result was a serious limitation of diagnostic reliability; that is, two professionals examining the same patient might very well come up with completely different impressions of what disorder(s) the patient had.

To address this clinical and scientific impasse, the DSM-III of 1980 introduced a radically different approach, one intended to remove as far as possible the element of subjective judgment from the diagnostic process. It did so by adopting an "operational" method of defining the various disorders that would officially be recognized. This innovation meant that the DSM system would now specify the exact observations that must be made for a given diagnostic label to be applied. In a typical case, a specific number of signs or symptoms from a designated list must be present before a diagnosis can properly be assigned. The new approach, continued in DSM-III's revised version of 1987 (DSM-III-R) and in the 1994 DSM-IV, almost necessarily enhanced diagnostic reliability. Whether that enhancement has been of sufficient magnitude to fulfill the vital role a diagnostic system must play in both clinical and research domains remains somewhat controversial (e.g., see Kirk & Kutchins, 1992). As an example of the operational approach to diagnosis, the DSM-IV diagnostic criteria for *Somatization Disorder* are reproduced in Table 1.1.

The number of recognized mental disorders has increased enormously from DSM-I to DSM-IV, due both to the addition of new diagnoses and the elaborate subdivision of older ones. Since it is unlikely that the nature of the American psyche has changed all that much in the interim period, it seems more reasonable to assume that mental health professionals view their field in a different light than they did 40-odd years ago. It is now both more expanded and more finely differentiated into subsets of disorder.

The Limitations of DSM Classification As already noted, there are limits on the extent to which a conceptually strict categorical system may adequately represent the abnormalities of behavior to which human beings are subject. The real problems of real patients often do not fit into the precise lists of signs and symptoms that are the heart of the modern DSM effort. How should we deal, for example, with the patient who meets three of the criteria

for a particular diagnosis where four is the minimum threshold for rendering the diagnosis? In fact, as shown in Table 1.1 at least four different types of pain symptoms must be reported for a patient to be diagnosed with *Somatization Disorder;* what if he or she reports only three but meets all other criteria for that diagnosis? One result of the stricter criteria in DSM-IV is that some abnormal behavior may be assigned to wastebasket or residual categories, such as *Somatoform Disorder, Not Otherwise Specified* (NOS). When this occurs, validity suffers, since a category so broad can give only vague hints as to the nature of the disorders within it.

The clinical reality is that the disorders people actually suffer are often not as finely differentiated as is the DSM grid on which they must be mapped. Increasingly fine differentiation also produces, of course, more and more recognized types of disorder. Too often, we believe, the unintended effect is to sacrifice validity in an effort to maximize interdiagnostician agreement—reliability—which makes little sense. For example, blends of anxiety and depression are extremely common in a clinical population, and they typically show much overlap (correlation) in quantitative scientific investigations as well. Nevertheless, the DSM treats the two as generically distinct forms of disorder, with the consequence that a person

---

TABLE 1.1 DSM-IV DIAGNOSTIC CRITERIA FOR SOMATIZATION DISORDER

A. A history of many physical complaints beginning before age 30 years that occur over a period of several years and result in treatment being sought or significant impairment in social, occupational, or other important areas of functioning.

B. Each of the following criteria must have been met, with individual symptoms occurring at any time during the course of the disturbance:

   (1) *Four pain symptoms:* a history of pain related to at least four different sites or functions (e.g., head, abdomen, back, joints, extremities, chest, rectum, during menstruation, during sexual intercourse, or during urination)

   (2) *Two gastrointestinal symptoms:* a history of at least two gastrointestinal symptoms other than pain (e.g., nausea, bloating, vomiting other than during pregnancy, diarrhea, or intolerance of several different foods)

   (3) *One sexual symptom:* a history of at least one sexual or reproductive symptom other than pain (e.g., sexual indifference, erectile or ejaculatory dysfunction, irregular menses, excessive menstrual bleeding, vomiting throughout pregnancy)

   (4) *One pseudoneurological symptom:* a history of at least one symptom or deficit suggesting a neurological condition not limited to pain (conversion symptoms such as impaired coordination or balance, paralysis or localized weakness, difficulty swallowing or lump in throat, aphonia, urinary retention, hallucinations, loss of touch or pain sensation, double vision, blindness, deafness, seizures, dissociative symptoms such as amnesia; or loss of consciousness other than fainting

C. Either (1) or (2):

   (1) After appropriate investigation, each of the symptoms in Criterion B cannot be fully explained by a known general medical condition or the direct effects of a substance (e.g., a drug of abuse, a medication)

   (2) When there is a related general medical condition, the physical complaints or resulting social or occupational impairment are in excess of what would be expected from the history, physical examination, or laboratory findings

D. The symptoms are not intentionally produced or feigned (as in Factitious Disorder or Malingering).

Source: American Psychiatric Association, 1994, pp. 449–450.

who is clinically both anxious and depressed may receive two diagnoses, one for each of the supposedly separate conditions. There is no official category for mixed anxiety-depression, although the DSM-IV mentions such a syndrome in an appendix set aside for conditions proposed for further study. As we shall see in a later section, there is a more refined way of approaching this problem.

As already noted, instances of this kind where two or more supposedly separate disorders are found regularly to occur together in the same persons are known as *comorbidity*. Comorbidities occur very commonly within the DSM diagnostic system (e.g., see Kessler et al., 1994). If two or more designated disorders regularly co-occur, there is a high likelihood that they are related to one another in some fashion. Understanding such interrelations would doubtless be a significant help in understanding the nature and development of such mixed syndromes, but excepting the anxiety-depression overlap (see Mineka, Watson, & Clark, 1998) research in this area has to date been quite sparse.

In making these critical observations regarding contemporary DSM efforts, we do not intend to suggest we are unrespectful or unappreciative of either the difficulties of the task or the considerable advances in understanding those efforts have produced. Rather, our intent is to alert the thoughtful reader to the many perplexing problems of classification that remain to be solved. We would be uncomfortable with an approach that glossed

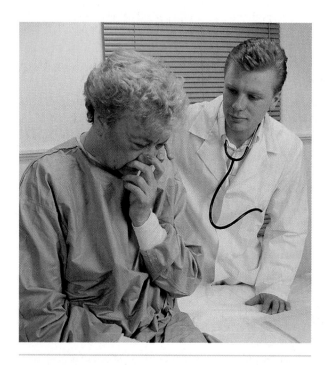

Many clinical situations require a rapid determination of the main characteristics of the presenting problem as well as assessment of any risk (e.g., suicide) involved. Diagnostic guidelines aid clinicians in making such judgments.

over difficulties and said, in effect, This is the way it is; learn it. Should you become puzzled and confused about particular issues of classification as we proceed, therefore, do not assume that the difficulty resides in you; it may instead reflect continuing problems in developing the basic taxonomy, or classification system, of the field.

The Five Axes of DSM-IV As has been the case since the advent of DSM-III in 1980, DSM-IV evaluates an individual according to five foci, or "axes." The first three axes assess an individual's present clinical status or condition:

Axis I. *The particular clinical syndromes or other conditions that may be a focus of clinical attention.* This would include schizophrenia, generalized anxiety disorder, major depression, and substance dependence. Axis I conditions are roughly analogous to the various illnesses and diseases recognized in general medicine.

Axis II. *Personality disorders.* A very broad group of disorders, discussed in Chapter 9, that encompasses a variety of problematic ways of relating to the world, such as histrionic personality disorder, paranoid personality disorder, or antisocial personality disorder. The last of these, for example, refers to an early-developing, persistent, and pervasive pattern of disregard for accepted standards of conduct, including legal ones. Axis II provides a means of coding for long-standing maladaptive personality traits that may or may not be involved in the development and expression of an Axis I disorder. Mental retardation is also diagnosed as an Axis II condition.

Axis III. *General medical conditions.* Listed here are any general medical conditions potentially relevant to understanding or management of the case. Axis III of DSM-IV may be used in conjunction with an Axis I diagnosis qualified by the phrase, "Due to [a specifically designated]" general medical condition—for example, where a major depressive disorder is conceived as resulting from unremitting pain associated with some chronic medical disease.

On any of these first three axes where the pertinent criteria are met more than one diagnosis is permissible, and in fact encouraged. That is, a person may be diagnosed as having multiple psychiatric syndromes, such as Panic Disorder and Major Depressive Disorder; disorders of personality, such as Dependent or Avoidant; or potentially relevant medical problems, such as Cirrhosis (liver disease often caused by excessive alcohol use) and Overdose, Cocaine. The last two DSM-IV axes are used to assess broader aspects of an individual's situation.

Axis IV. *Psychosocial and environmental problems.* This group deals with the stressors that may have contributed to the current disorder, particularly those that have been present during the prior year. The diagnostician is invited to use a checklist approach for various categories of *impinging life problems*—family, economic, occupational, legal, etc. For example, the phrase "Problems with Primary Support Group" may be included where a family disruption is judged to have contributed to the disorder.

Axis V. *Global assessment of functioning.* This is where clinicians note how well the individual is coping at the present time. A 100-point rating scale, the *Global Assessment of Functioning (GAF) Scale,* is provided for the examiner to assign a number summarizing a patient's overall functionability. The GAF Scale is reproduced in Table 1.2.

Axes IV and V, first introduced in DSM-III, are significant additions. Knowing the frustrations and demands a

---

TABLE 1.2   THE GLOBAL ASSESSMENT OF FUNCTIONING (GAF) SCALE

Consider psychological, social, and occupational functioning on a hypothetical continuum of mental health illness. Do not include impairment in functioning due to physical (or environmental) limitations. (*Note:* Use intermediate codes when appropriate, e.g., 45, 68, 72.)

Code	
100	Superior functioning in a wide range of activities, life's problems never seem to get out of hand,
91	is sought out by others because of his or her many positive qualities. No symptoms.
90	Absent or minimal symptoms (e.g., mild anxiety before an exam), good functioning in all areas, interested and involved in a wide range of activities, socially effective, generally satisfied with life, no more than every-
81	day problems or concerns (e.g., an occasional argument with family members).
80	If symptoms are present, they are transient and expectable reactions to psychosocial stressors (e.g., difficulty concentrating after family argument; no more than slight impairment in social, occupational, or school
71	functioning (e.g., temporarily falling behind in school work).
70	Some mild symptoms (e.g., depressed mood and mild insomnia) OR some difficulty in social, occupational, or school functioning (e.g., occasional truancy or theft within the household), but generally functioning
61	pretty well, has some meaningful interpersonal relationships.
60	Moderate symptoms (e.g., flat affect and circumstantial speech, occasional panic attacks) OR moderate difficulty in social, occupational, or school functioning (e.g., few friends, conflicts with peers or
51	coworkers).
50	Serious symptoms (e.g., suicidal ideation, severe obsessional rituals, frequent shoplifting) OR any serious impairment in social, occupational, or school functioning (e.g., no friends, unable to keep
41	a job).
40	Some impairment in reality testing or communication (e.g., speech is at times illogical, obscure, or irrelevant) OR major impairment in several areas, such as work or school, family relations, judgment, thinking or mood (e.g., depressed man avoids friends, neglects family, and is unable to work; child frequently beats up
31	younger children, is defiant at home, and is failing at school).
30	Behavior is considerably influenced by delusions or hallucinations OR serious impairment in communication or judgment (e.g., sometimes incoherent, acts grossly inappropriately, suicidal preoccupation) OR in-
21	ability to function in almost all areas (e.g., stays in bed all day; no job, home, or friends).
20	Some danger of hurting self or others (e.g., suicide attempts without clear expectation of death; frequently violent; manic excitement) OR occasionally fails to maintain minimal personal hygiene (e.g., smears feces)
11	OR gross impairment in communication (e.g., largely incoherent or mute).
10	Persistent danger of severely hurting self or others (e.g., recurrent violence) OR persistent inability to maintain minimal personal hygiene OR serious suicidal
1	act with expectation of death.
0	Inadequate information.

Source: American Psychiatric Association, 1994, p. 32.

person has been facing is important for understanding the context in which the problem behavior has developed. Knowing someone's general level of functioning conveys important information not necessarily contained in the entries for other axes and indicates how well the individual is coping with his or her problems. Some clinicians, however, object to the routine use of these axes for insurance forms and the like on the grounds that such use unnecessarily compromises a patient's right to privacy by revealing, for example, a recent divorce (Axis IV) or a suicide attempt (Axis V). Because of such concerns, Axes IV and V are now considered optional for diagnosis and in fact are rarely used in most clinical settings.

As an example of an extended DSM-IV diagnosis, let us consider the case of Albert G., the college professor described at the beginning of this chapter. Immediately before his suicide, his multiaxial diagnosis might have been depicted as shown in Table 1.3.

TABLE 1.3   DSM-IV FULL DIAGNOSIS OF ALBERT G.

- *Axis I*
  Major depressive disorder
- *Axis II*
  Obsessive-compulsive personality disorder
- *Axis III*
  None
- *Axis IV*
  No primary support group
  Social environment problem: living alone
- *Axis V*
  Global functioning: 20 (some danger of hurting self)

Main Categories of Axis I and Axis II Disorders   The different Axis I and II disorders are identified in the previously noted listing of DSM-IV mental disorder diagnoses appearing on the endpapers of this book. They also serve as the means by which the clinical material in this book is organized. These diagnoses may be regarded for purposes of clarity as fitting into several broad etiological (major causal) groupings, each containing several subgroupings:

- *Disorders secondary to gross destruction or malfunctioning of brain tissue,* as in Alzheimer's dementia and a wide range of other conditions based on permanent or reversible organic brain pathology. These disorders are described in Chapter 13.

- *Substance-use disorders,* involving problems such as habitual drug or alcohol abuse. These are discussed in Chapter 10.

- *Disorders of psychological or sociocultural origin having no known brain pathology* as a primary causal factor. This is

a very large group that includes a majority of the mental disorders discussed in this book, among them anxiety disorders (Chapter 5), somatoform and dissociative disorders (Chapter 7), psychophysiologic disorders (Chapter 8), psychosexual disorders (Chapter 11), and the Axis II personality disorders (Chapter 9). Traditionally, this group also includes severe mental disorders for which a specific organic brain pathology has not been demonstrated—such as major mood disorders (Chapter 6) and schizophrenia (Chapter 12), although it appears increasingly likely that they may be caused at least in part by certain types of aberrant brain functioning.

- *Disorders usually arising during childhood or adolescence,* including a broad group of disorders, featuring cognitive impairments such as mental retardation and specific learning disabilities (Chapter 13), and a large variety of behavioral problems, such as attention-deficit/hyperactivity disorder, which constitute deviations from the expected or normal path of development (Chapter 14).

In referring to mental disorders, several qualifying terms are commonly used. **Acute** is used to describe disorders of relatively short duration, usually under six months, such as transitory adjustment disorders (Chapter 4). In some contexts, it also connotes behavioral symptoms of high intensity. **Chronic** refers to long-standing and often permanent disorders, such as Alzheimer's dementia and some forms of schizophrenia. The term can also be applied generally to low-intensity disorders, since long-term difficulties are often of this sort. **Mild, moderate,** and **severe** are terms relating to varying points on a dimension of severity or seriousness. **Episodic** and **recurrent** are used to describe unstable disorder patterns that tend to come and go, as with some mood and schizophrenic conditions.

The Problem of Labeling   The psychiatric diagnoses of the sort typified by the DSM-IV system are not uniformly revered among mental health professionals (e.g., see Carson, 1997; Sarbin, 1997). Not even all psychiatrists (e.g., see Guze, 1995; Lidz, 1994; Tucker, 1998; Wilson, 1993) are content with them. One important and frequently voiced criticism is that a psychiatric diagnosis is little more than a label applied to a defined category of socially disapproved or otherwise problematic behavior. (Recall our discussion of the value considerations intrinsic to defining "mental disorder.")

The diagnostic label does not describe a person, nor necessarily any underlying pathological condition ("dysfunction") the person harbors, but rather some behavioral pattern associated with that person's current level of functioning. Yet once a label has been assigned, it may close off further inquiry. It is all too easy—even for professionals—to accept a label as an accurate and complete description of an individual rather than of that person's current behavior. When a person is labeled "depressed" or "schizophrenic," others will be more likely to make certain assumptions about that person that may or may not be accurate. In fact, a diagnostic label can make it hard to look at the person's behavior objectively, without preconceptions about how he or she will act. These expectations can influence even clinically important interactions and treatment choices. For example, arrival at the diagnosis Major Depressive Disorder may cut off any further inquiry about the patient's life situation and lead abruptly to a prescription for antidepressant medication (Tucker, 1998).

Once an individual is labeled, he or she may accept a redefined identity and play out the expectations of that role. ("I'm nothing but a substance abuser, I might as well do drugs—everyone expects me to anyway. Furthermore, since this is a condition deemed to be not in my control, it is pointless for me to be an active participant in my treatment.") This acquisition of a new social identity can be harmful for a variety of reasons. The pejorative and stigmatizing implications of many psychiatric labels can mark people as second-class citizens with severe limitations, often presumed to be permanent (Jones et al., 1984; Link et al., 1987). They can also have devastating effects on a person's morale, self-esteem, and relationships with others. The person so labeled may decide he or she "is" their diagnosis and adopt the latter, so to speak, as a life "career."

Clearly, it is important and in the disordered person's best interests for mental health professionals to be circumspect in the diagnostic process, in their use of labels, and in ensuring confidentiality with respect to both. A related change has developed over the past 50 years regarding the person who goes to see a mental health professional. For years the traditional term for such a person has been *patient*, which is closely associated with a medically sick person and a passive stance, waiting (patiently) for the doctor's cure. Today many such professionals, especially those trained in nonmedical settings, prefer the term *client* because it implies more responsibility and participation on the part of an individual for bringing about his or her own recovery. We shall be using these terms interchangeably in this text.

Assessment and Diagnosis

When a client first meets with a clinician, he or she usually presents a complaint—"I have headaches almost every day"; or "My marriage is falling apart." This presenting complaint initiates a process of assessment, through which the clinician attempts to understand the nature and extent of the problem. At times this process of inquiry is convoluted and challenging, with the clinician in a role reminis-

Gladys Burr (shown here with her attorney) is a tragic example of the dangers of labeling. Involuntarily committed by her mother (apparently because of some personality problems) in 1936 at the age of 29, Ms. Burr was diagnosed as psychotic and was later declared to be mentally retarded. Though a number of IQ tests administered from 1946 to 1961 showed her to be of normal intelligence, and though a number of doctors stated that she was of normal intelligence and should be released, she was confined in a residential center for the mentally retarded or in a state boarding home until 1978. Though a court did give her a financial reward in compensation, surely nothing can compensate for 42 years of unnecessary and involuntary commitment.

cent of Sherlock Holmes. On other occasions assessment is a relatively straightforward matter in which the clinician may, with a high probability of being correct, come to a rapid conclusion about the basis for the complaint and the proper disposition of the case. Pediatricians whose practices tend to be confined to a local clientele, for example, know what childhood infections are "going around" at a given time. A child who has complaints that mimic the characteristic symptom profile for a common infection will likely be found to have that disease. The conscientious pediatrician will usually want to confirm an initial diagnostic impression with lab studies that identify the infectious organism involved before initiating specifically targeted treatment, even when the diagnosis is pretty clear.

Using assessment to confirm diagnostic impressions is thus a matter of good practice even in the most routine clinical situations. For the mental health practitioner, few clinical situations are as routine as our pediatric example, and adequate techniques for confirming initial impressions may prove far more elusive. With rare exceptions, the lab work essential to much medical assessment is irrelevant in this domain. Psychological disorders usually lack identifying biological characteristics. Furthermore, they are always interlaced with the personalities of the individuals suffering them and usually with their entire social circumstances. Every instance of abnormal behavior is likely to be the product of a number of contributing factors, many of which may not be immediately apparent or even evident after many months of intense scrutiny in the course of psychotherapy. As this last statement implies, psychological assessment or diagnosis can be an ongoing process that proceeds along with treatment efforts rather than only preceding them.

Considered in this context, a DSM diagnosis per se may be of limited usefulness. The DSM-IV acknowledges this in its Introduction:

> Making a DSM-IV diagnosis is only the first step in a comprehensive evaluation. To formulate an adequate treatment plan, the clinician will invariably require considerable additional information about the person being evaluated beyond that required to make a DSM-IV diagnosis (American Psychiatric Association, 1994, p. xxv).

Nevertheless, arriving at such a diagnosis is usually required, at least in the form of a "diagnostic impression," before the commencement of clinical services to the person seeking them. This is necessitated, perhaps unwisely, by medical insurance requirements and long-standing clinical administrative tradition.

The invariably required additional information for adequate clinical assessment may be extensive and extremely difficult to unearth. A host of specialized techniques, such as various psychological tests, have been developed to aid in the assessment. We examine these techniques in some detail in Chapter 15. For now, we concentrate on the process of arriving at a DSM-IV diagnosis. For the most part, in keeping with psychiatric tradition, that process is interview-based. That is, the examiner engages the patient (or perhaps a family member of the patient) in a conversation designed to elicit the information necessary to place the patient in one or more DSM diagnostic categories. The interviewer introduces various questions and probes, typically becoming increasingly specific as he or she develops diagnostic hypotheses and checks these out with additional probes relating to the criteria for particular DSM diagnoses. Physicians in general medical practice do something similar in the course of an examination.

Unstructured Interviews Diagnostic interviews are of two general types, unstructured and structured. In the *unstructured interview*, the examiner follows no preexisting plan with respect to content and sequence of the probes introduced. Unstructured interviews, as their name implies, are somewhat freewheeling. The therapist/clinician asks questions as they occur to him or her, in part based on the responses to previous questions. For example, if the pa-

tient/client mentioned a father who traveled a lot when he or she was a child, the clinician might ask, "Did you miss your father?" or (pursuing a different tack), "How did your mother handle that?" rather than being required to ask the next question in a predetermined list of questions. Many clinical examiners prefer this unfettered approach because it permits maximum freedom to formulate probes and to follow perhaps idiosyncratic "leads." In the above example, the clinician might have chosen to ask about the mother's reaction on the basis of a developing suspicion that mother may have been depressed during the client's childhood years. There is one serious drawback to the freewheeling style: the information gained in the unstructured interview may to a greater or lesser extent be particular to the content of that interview. Should another clinician interview the same patient, he or she might come up with a different clinical picture, or in extreme cases quite literally with a "different" interviewee.

Structured Interviews The *structured interview* probes the client in a manner that is highly controlled. Guided by a sort of master plan (sometimes to the extent of specifying the examiner's exact wording), the clinician using a structured interview is typically seeking to discover if the person's symptoms and signs "fit" diagnostic criteria that are more precise and "operational" than in the past. The use of more precise criteria and highly structured diagnostic interviewing has substantially improved diagnostic reliability (Wiens, 1991), but the structured interview format is still used only sporadically in routine clinical work. Nevertheless, the precision of clinical research, including epidemiologic research to be discussed below, has profited enormously with these developments.

There are a number of structured diagnostic interviews that may be used in various contexts. In clinical and research situations, a popular instrument has been the Structured Clinical Interview for DSM Diagnosis (SCID), which yields, almost automatically so to speak, diagnoses carefully attuned to the DSM diagnostic criteria. A portion of the SCID focused on Somatization Disorder is presented in Highlight 1.1. Another structured diagnostic instrument, the "mental status examination," has actually been around in various forms a very long time and is still taught to medical students; by posing various mental tasks to the patient, it quickly assesses mental efficiency and (especially cognitive) functioning.

The Mental Health "Team"

In many clinical settings diagnosis and assessment may involve a number of participants who take differing roles in the process and who gather data helpful to a comprehensive evaluation of the client's situation from several perspectives and many different sources. The latter may include family

Sample Items from the Somatization Disorder Section of the Structured Clinical Interview for DSM Diagnosis (SCID)

IF: CURRENT PSYCHOTIC DISORDER OR IN RESIDUAL PHASE OF SCHIZOPHRENIA, CHECK HERE _____ AND SKIP TO NEXT MODULE.

Screening Questions

Over the last several years what has your physical health been like?

How often have you had to go to a doctor because you weren't feeling well? (What for?)

IF YES: Was the doctor always able to find out what was wrong, or were there times when the doctor said there was nothing wrong but you were still convinced something was wrong?

(Do you worry much about your physical health? Does your doctor think you worry too much?)

IF NOTHING SUGGESTS THE POSSIBILITY OF A SOMATOFORM DISORDER, CHECK HERE _____ AND GO TO THE NEXT MODULE.

Somatization Disorder

How old were you when you first started to have a lot of physical problems or illnesses?

FOR EACH SYMPTOM REPORTED DETERMINE THAT CRITERIA ARE MET BY SUCH QUESTIONS AS:

Did you tell a doctor about (symptom)?

What was the diagnosis? (What did the doctor say was causing it?)

Was anything abnormal found on tests or X rays?

Were you taking any medications, drugs, or alcohol around the time you were having (symptom)?

Did you take any medicine for it?

Did it interfere with your life a lot?

Now I am going to ask about specific physical symptoms you may have had in the past few years.

Have you had a lot of trouble with . . .

vomiting (when not pregnant)?

abdominal or belly pain (when not menstruating)?

nausea—feeling sick to your stomach?

excessive gas or bloating?

loose bowels or diarrhea?

Have there been any foods you couldn't eat because they made you sick? What are they?

Have you ever had pain . . .

in your arms or legs?

in your back?

in your joints?

when you urinate?

anywhere else?

Have you ever . . .

had a period of amnesia—that is, a period of several hours or days when you couldn't remember anything afterward about what happened during that time?

had trouble swallowing?

lost your voice for more than a few minutes?

been completely deaf for a period of time?

been completely blind for more than a few seconds?

had a seizure or convulsion?

been paralyzed or had periods of weakness in your limbs?

been completely unable to urinate?

Now I'm going to ask you some questions about sex.

Would you say that your sex life has been important to you or could you have gotten along as well without it?

Have you often had any other sexual problem, like not being able to get an erection?

Have you experienced problems with menstruation? What?

Did you vomit throughout any pregnancy? ■

Source: Adapted from Spitzer et al., 1988.

MODERN LIFE

Personnel in Mental Health

Professional

Clinical Psychologist

Ph.D. in psychology, with both research and clinical skill specialization. One-year internship in a psychiatric hospital or mental health center. Or, Psy.D. in psychology (a professional degree with more clinical than research specialization) plus one-year internship in a psychiatric hospital or mental health center.

Counseling Psychologist

Ph.D. in psychology plus internship in a marital- or student-counseling setting; normally, a counseling psychologist deals with adjustment problems not involving severe mental disorder.

School Psychologist

Ideally, a person having doctoral training in child-clinical psychology, with additional training and experience in academic and learning problems. At present, many school systems lack the resources to maintain an adequate school psychology program.

Psychiatrist

M.D. with residency training (usually three years) in a psychiatric hospital or mental health facility.

Psychoanalyst

M.D. or Ph.D. plus intensive training in the theory and practice of psychoanalysis.

Psychiatric Social Worker

M.S.W., or Ph.D. with specialized clinical training in mental health settings.

Psychiatric Nurse

R.N. certification plus specialized training in the care and treatment of psychiatric clients. Nurses can attain M.A. and Ph.D. in psychiatric nursing.

Occupational Therapist

B.S. in occupational therapy plus internship training with physically or psychologically handicapped individuals, helping them make the most of their resources.

Pastoral Counselor

Ministerial background plus training in psychology. Internship in mental health facility as a chaplain.

Paraprofessional

Community Mental Health Worker

Person with limited professional training who works under professional direction; usually involved in crisis intervention.

Alcohol- or Drug-Abuse Counselor

Limited professional training but trained in the evaluation and management of alcohol- and drug-abuse problems.

In both mental health clinics and hospitals, personnel from several fields may function as an interdisciplinary team—for example, a psychiatrist, a clinical psychologist, a psychiatric social worker, a psychiatric nurse, and an occupational therapist may work together. ■

members, friends, school officials (if the client is a child or adolescent), and mental health professionals and social agencies with which the client may have had prior contact. The client is then "staffed" in a meeting attended by all these contributors in an attempt to process and integrate all the available information, arrive at a consensus diagnosis, and plan the initial phase of treatment intervention. The Modern Life box (Highlight 1.2) briefly summarizes the training and professional identities of the mental health personnel likely to be found on such assessment teams.

Diagnostic classification is a useful, although sometimes overestimated, tool. One of its main uses has been that of estimating the magnitude and types of mental disorders found in differing populations. We now turn to that problem.

THE EXTENT OF ABNORMAL BEHAVIOR

How many people actually have diagnosable psychological disorders today? The frequency or infrequency of particular disorders is an important consideration for a number of reasons. For one, researchers in the mental health field need to have a clear understanding of the nature and extent of abnormal behaviors in various groups of people because this may provide clues about their causes. For example, if only men and women who play ice hockey end up with a given disorder, then something about the sport—its tolerance of hostile aggression, its training, or its equipment—is a likely source of the problem. Additionally, mental health planners need to have a clear picture of the nature and extent of psychological problems within the citizenry in order to determine how resources, such as funding of research projects or services provided by community mental health centers, can be most effectively allocated.

Before we can discuss the extent of mental disorders in society we must clarify how psychological problems are counted. **Epidemiology** is the study of the distribution of diseases, disorders, or health-related behaviors in a given population. Mental health epidemiology refers to the study of the distribution of mental disorders. A key component of an epidemiological survey is determining the magnitude of the problem being studied—how frequently a particular disorder becomes a problem. There are several ways of doing this. The term **prevalence** refers to the proportion of active cases in a population that can be identified at a given point in, or during a given period of, time. For example, *point prevalence* refers (as the term implies) to the estimated proportion of actual, active cases of the disorder in a given population at any instant in time. Prevalence is to be distinguished from **incidence,** which refers to the *occurrence (onset) rate* of a given disorder in a given population, often expressed as a cumulative ratio of onsets per unit population over some time period—say one year. For example, schizophrenia is estimated to have an *incidence* in the U.S. as high as 2 per 1000 persons per year (Tien & Eaton, 1992). Incidence rates include recovered cases as well as people who may have died in the past year. Increasingly employed in the contemporary literature is a measure termed **lifetime prevalence,** which is the proportion of living persons in a population ever having had the disorder up to the time of epidemiologic assess-

Appearances are sometimes deceiving. Much real mental disorder is not obvious, and the frankly bizarre does not always signify abnormality. Modern epidemiologic researchers employ trained interviewers and refined assessment techniques to determine the presence or absence of various mental disorders in the population of interest.

ment; it, too, includes recovered cases. For example, the *lifetime prevalence* for schizophrenia (and schizophrenia-like) disorders is estimated at 0.7 percent of the noninstitutionalized U.S. population (Kessler et al., 1994). Its *point prevalence* is thought to be in the range of 0.2 to 2.0 percent (American Psychiatric Association, 1994).

Two major national mental health epidemiology studies, with direct and formal diagnostic assessment of participants, have been carried out in the United States in recent years. One, the Epidemiologic Catchment Area (ECA) study, concentrated on sampling the citizens of five communities: Baltimore, New Haven, St. Louis, Durham (NC), and Los Angeles (Myers et al., 1984; Regier et al., 1988; Regier et al., 1993). The other, the Na-

TABLE 1.4 LIFETIME AND 12-MONTH PREVALENCE OF MAJOR TYPES OF DISORDER AS REPORTED IN THE NATIONAL COMOR-BIDITY STUDY

	Male		Female		Total	
	Lifetime	12-month	Lifetime	12-month	Lifetime	12-month
	%	%	%			
Any mood disorder	14.7	8.5	23.9	14.1	19.3	11.3
Any anxiety disorder	19.2	11.8	30.5	22.6	24.9	17.2
Any substance abuse disorder	35.4	16.1	17.9	6.6	26.6	11.3
Nonaffective psychosis[*]	0.6	0.5	0.8	0.6	0.7	0.5
Any NCS-assessed disorder	48.7	27.7	47.3	31.2	48.0	29.5

[*]Includes schizophrenia, schizophreniform disorder, schizoaffective disorder, delusional disorder, and atypical psychosis.

Source: Kessler et al., 1994, p. 12.

tional Comorbidity Survey (NCS), was more extensive in sampling the entire U.S. population and had a number of sophisticated methodological improvements as well (Kessler et al., 1994). Since the main results of the two studies are fairly similar, we focus here on the NCS.

Table 1.4 summarizes the NCS findings with respect to 12-month and lifetime prevalence estimates (percentage of persons affected) among noninstitutionalized American male and female adolescents and adults (ages 15–54) for the various broad categories of Axis I disorders considered. It is important to note that the NCS study largely excluded Axis II (personality) disorders.

By any reasonable measure, these are sobering statistics. They tell us that at some time in their lives roughly half of the U.S. population between 15 and 54 will have had a diagnosable Axis I mental disorder, a quarter to a third of them within any one year. An astounding 35 percent of males will at some time in their lives have abused substances to the point of qualifying for a mental disorder diagnosis, and nearly one-quarter of women will have qualified for a serious mood disorder (mostly major depression). These NCS figures confirmed much other epidemiologic data in showing declining rates for most disorders with age progression and higher socioeconomic status.

The percentages of the NCS study also show a familiar pattern of gender differences. Women tend to be diagnosed as having more mood and anxiety disorders than do men. The opposite pattern holds for substance use disorders and for antisocial personality disorder. These trends may reflect assessment bias or actual gender differences. Both possibilities will be examined more fully as we address the separate disorders in later chapters of the book.

A final finding of note from the NCS study was the widespread occurrence of comorbidity among diagnosed disorders. Specifically, 56 percent of the respondents with a history of at least one disorder also had two or more additional disorders (for example, a person who drinks excessively may also be depressed and have an anxiety disorder). These persons with a history of three or more comorbid disorders, estimated to be one-sixth of the U.S. population or some 43 million people, tended to have disorders in the more severe ranges and would appear to represent a special group of unusually high psychological vulnerability.

As was true of NCS respondents, most people with significant psychological problems are not now hospitalized in large state or county psychiatric institutions. Of those who are hospitalized, most receive these services in other types of inpatient settings, such as the psychiatric units of general hospitals (Narrow et al., 1993). Various surveys indicate that admission to mental hospitals has decreased substantially over the past 45 years. The development of medications that control the more socially disruptive symptoms of some severe disorders is one reason for this change. The dramatic declines in the use of public mental hospitals have been accompanied by a steady rise in admissions to private psychiatric hospitals and to psychiatric facilities in general hospitals, most of them also privately sponsored (Kiesler & Simpkins, 1993; Lee & Goodwin, 1987). Because of their high costs, stays in private inpatient facilities tend to be much shorter than those in large public institutions. This trend away from use of the latter, often referred to as *deinstitutionalization,* will be discussed more extensively in Chapter 18.

People with psychological problems are now more likely to receive treatment in outpatient facilities such as community mental health centers (Narrow et al., 1993). However, evidence suggests that only about 25 percent of those with psychological problems actually receive any professional treatment at all (Regier et al., 1993; Robins et al., 1984). Of persons receiving any kind of help for their problems, about 40 percent rely on voluntary support networks, such as family, friends, and organized clubs that provide supportive information on coping problems as well as social interaction with other ex-patients (Narrow et al., 1993). The overall trends in the management of mental health problems are thus toward increased privatization, decreased duration of inpatient stays, and increased use of both professional and nonprofessional resources within the community.

RESEARCH IN ABNORMAL PSYCHOLOGY

Like the data derived from the ECA and NCS studies described above, the facts and ideas you will learn from this book are the products of scientific studies of maladaptive behavior. For those epidemiological studies, people were assessed and counted, and the results of this quantification of their problems were tabulated. You are probably already familiar with scientific methods in general and their uses in various areas of psychology. Certain issues and problems arise in applying these methods to understanding the nature, causes, and treatment of abnormal behavior; thus some review is appropriate before we move on. Our review will be organized around the major approaches used in studying abnormal behavior: (1) direct observation of behavior, (2) hypotheses about behavior, (3) sampling and generalization, (4) correlation and causation, (5) experimental strategies, (6) case studies, and (7) retrospective and prospective strategies.

Observation of Behavior

As in virtually all other sciences, the bedrock of psychological knowledge is observation. The focus of such observations is variable and includes the overt actions of an organism, certain of its measurable internal states and behaviors (e.g., its physiological processes), and at the human level verbal reports about inner processes or events. It is the last of these sources of information that is by far the most troublesome and yet often the most interesting and potentially useful. For example, mental events are fundamentally *private* events, forever inaccessible to anyone else, and so impossible to confirm objectively. Science normally demands such confirmation by others as a means of ensuring accuracy in the observations made. This constraint on public accessibility to important, pri-

mary "data" has been a source of considerable difficulty for the discipline of psychology throughout its history. For example, in its earliest years as a science psychology was focused on the relations between physical "stimuli" (e.g., a tone of a certain cycles-per-second frequency) and the subjective experience of the person hearing the tone. It was quickly learned that these "naive" reports of personal sensory experience left much to be desired in terms of the scientific aims of the experimenter. The solution was to train experimental subjects in how to give accurate accounts of their own sensory experience, an ability that had erroneously been taken for granted.

In the field of abnormal psychology, researchers must inevitably be concerned with inner processes such as thoughts, feelings, and interpretations of external events, for much of the theoretical bedrock of the field relates precisely to these private happenings. It follows that these researchers are to a remarkable extent dependent on subjects' reporting of this otherwise inaccessible inner experience. As a result, much research effort has gone into the development of specialized techniques, such as precisely calibrated rating scales, for maximizing accurate/consistent reporting of this experience.

Similar, although somewhat less problematic, considerations apply to observations of the overt behavior of research subjects, many of whom in this field would be members of particular diagnostic groupings. As we saw in the case of diagnostic interviewing, these observations must be reliable if they are to serve as a useful basis for deriving inferences about the organization and underpinnings of the behavior being investigated. Hence, it has become routine in such investigations to employ observers who are trained to watch and record behavior systematically, using scientifically developed techniques. Elaine Walker and her colleagues (1993), for example, used family home movies to study the childhood behavior of individuals who did and did not qualify for a diagnosis of schizophrenia as adults. The training of assistants to observe and record the often subtle behavioral differences between these groups of children must have been as arduous as it was critical to producing an important set of findings (discussed in Chapter 12). And even here more than one observer is typically employed until the reliability of each of their recordings is established beyond doubt.

Forming Hypotheses About Behavior

To make sense of observed behavior, all of us, including researchers, generate *hypotheses,* more or less plausible ideas to explain something—in this case, behavior. All empirical sciences use hypotheses, although these hypotheses appear to be more closely tied to observable phenomena in the more established physical sciences.

For example, the concept of electricity is actually hypothetical. Scientists have only observed the effects of this presumed entity, but these effects are extremely reliable and predictable; hence we believe in the real existence of electricity. Most people have less confidence in a construct such as repressed memories, as we shall see in later chapters.

These considerations are particularly important in the study of abnormal behavior. For the most part, we understand the behavior of the people we meet, at least to the extent necessary to carry on ordinary social interactions. Even when we observe something unexpected in a person's behavior, we can usually empathize enough to have a sense of "where they're coming from," of the factors that may have contributed to the behavior, for example. Almost by definition, abnormal behavior is far more difficult to fathom. It is extraordinary, and our minds are therefore attracted to extraordinary explanations of it—to extraordinary hypotheses. Whether these hypotheses can account satisfactorily for abnormal behavior is open to question, but it is clear that we need them in order to begin to understand. Behavior never explains itself, whether it is normal or abnormal.

Several competing hypotheses typically exist to explain the complex patterns we find in abnormal behavior.

The deranged man shown here in the custody of a police officer had made a bloody and murderous attack on numerous passengers of a Long Island Railroad train. Many differing hypotheses purport to explain such behavior, but none is at present sufficient in itself to do so. Our best guess is that an interaction of genetic, biological, psychosocial, developmental, and environmental factors operate together in some probably unique and still obscure fashion.

In fact, these hypotheses tend to cluster together in distinctive approaches or viewpoints. For example, we might try to explain a person's fearfulness by reference to an inherited biological anomaly, to traumatic childhood experiences, to having been "taught" by parents that the world is a fearsome place, or to all of these influences operating together. These general viewpoints are addressed in Chapter 3. For now, we merely wish to emphasize that all forms of psychological inquiry begin with observations of behavior, and that much of the subject matter of abnormal psychology is built on hypotheses that account more or less adequately for observed behavior declared to be disordered.

These viewpoints and the hypotheses they lead us toward are important because they frequently determine the therapeutic approaches used to treat an abnormality. For example, suppose we are confronted with someone who washes his or her hands 60 to 100 times a day, causing serious injury to the skin and underlying tissues. If we conclude that this behavior is a result of subtle neurological damage, we would try to discover the nature of the individual's disease in the hope of administering a cure. If we view the behavior as the symbolic cleansing of sinful thoughts, we would try to unearth and address the sources of the person's excessive scrupulousness. If we regard the hand-washing symptom as merely the product of unfortunate conditioning or learning, we would devise a means of counterconditioning to eliminate the problematic behavior. These different approaches reflect different concepts of the causes of the abnormal behavior and are discussed in detail in Chapter 3. Without such concepts—if we are limited merely to observing behavior itself—we would be left with no means of grasping abnormal behavior, and few clues as to what should be done to change it.

Sampling and Generalization

Research in abnormal psychology is concerned with gaining enhanced understanding and, where possible, control of (that is, the ability to alter in predictable ways) abnormal behavior. Although we can occasionally get important leads from the intensive observation of a single case of a given disorder, such a strategy rarely yields enough information to allow us to reach firm conclusions. The basic difficulty with this strategy is that we cannot know whether our observations pertain to the disorder, to unrelated characteristics of the person with the disorder, to some combination of these factors, or even to characteristics of the observer. One person's sexual disorder may have little in common with that of another. We need to study a larger group in order to know which of our observations are generalizable.

Using Groups to Identify Common Factors

For these reasons, we generally place greater reliance on research studies using groups of individuals who show roughly equivalent abnormalities of behavior. Typically, several people in such studies share one characteristic (the problematic behavior) while varying widely on others. We can then infer that anything else they have in common, such as having a chronically depressed parent, may be related to the behavioral abnormality—provided, of course, that the characteristic is not widely shared by people who do not have the abnormality. If the abnormality arises from different sources in different people (which might in itself be an important finding), we would probably have considerable difficulty identifying with precision the patterns underlying the abnormality. In fact, difficulties of this sort appear to be impeding our progress in respect to several of the disorders we will consider in later chapters.

If we wanted to research the problem of major psychological depression, for example, a first step would be to determine criteria for identifying persons believed to be affected with the condition. DSM-IV provides a set of such criteria, among them unrelievable sadness, diminished or absent pleasure response, fatigue, and sleep disturbances. We would then need to find people who fit our criteria. Obviously, we could never hope to study all of the people in the world who meet our criteria; we would use instead a technique called **sampling,** in which we would select as subjects a limited number of depressed persons who appear to be representative of the much larger group of individuals having major depressive disorders. That is, our sample should mirror the larger group in terms of disorder severity and duration as well as any potentially important demographics such as average age, gender, and marital status. Ideally, the sample would be randomly selected from the larger depressed population, which is tantamount to ensuring that every person in that population has an equal chance of being included in our study sample. Such a procedure would automatically adjust for potential biases in sample selection. Normally, however, that degree of rigor in sample selection is for practical reasons unachievable, so researchers settle for approximations to random sample selection. The requirement of representativeness is imposed because we would hope to generalize our sample findings to the larger group. We could legitimately do so only to the extent that our sample is truly reflective in all relevant respects of the population to which we hope to generalize.

As we have learned from the results of poorly designed public opinion polls, nonrepresentative sampling can produce erroneous conclusions about the larger group we wish to study. For example, if our research group of depressed people consisted only of college-educated members of the middle to upper-middle class, we might be tempted to attribute some characteristic—say a tendency to drink wine with dinner—to depression sufferers that is in fact not true of depressed people in general, such as those less educated or from a different socioeconomic group.

Criterion and Control Groups

Suppose we had a hypothesis that stress led to depression. We would need to be certain that the levels of prior stress experienced by our depressed subjects were not similar to findings about other mental disorder groups, or the general population. If everyone experienced the same amount of stress, then prior stress would not be useful in telling us anything about depression per se. Researchers use a **control group,** a sample of people who do *not* exhibit the disorder being studied but who are comparable in all other respects to the **criterion group,** members of which do exhibit the disorder. Typically, the control group is psychologically "normal" according to specified criteria. We can then compare the two groups in certain areas—such as reported prior stress experienced—to determine if they differ. They would in fact almost certainly differ if only because of chance factors, but we have powerful statistical techniques to determine whether or not such observed differences are truly significant. If we found, for example, that major depressives had significantly more prior stress than the normals, we might be tempted to pursue our hypothesis further and consider that the experience of unusual stress is causally related to the onset of major depression. Entertaining this hypothesis assumes, of course, that the people in our study have reported their stressful experiences accurately, a sometimes dubious assumption. Depression, for example, might cause people to review past innocuous (factually unstressful) events in a negative light. At most, in fact, we would have found an association, or correlation, between *reported* prior stress and the experience of major depression. (See Chapters 3 and 6 for further discussion of this issue.)

The Difference Between Correlation and Causation

In the above example (which happens to depict an actual circumstance in the scientific literature on depression), we could not legitimately conclude from our findings alone that the experience of severe prior stress *causes* the onset of major depression. There are simply too many alternative ways to account for such an association, including the possibility that depressed persons are more prone than others to remember stressful events in their immediate pasts. Correlation, in this case between higher levels of reported stress and depression, does not imply causation.

The mere correlation, or association, of two or more variables can never by itself be taken as evidence of causation—that is, a relationship in which one of the associated variables (i.e., stress) *causes* the outcome of the other (i.e., depression). This is an important caveat to bear in mind, especially so in the field of abnormal psychology. Many studies in abnormal psychology show that two (or more) things regularly occur together, such as poverty and retarded intellectual development or depression and reported prior stressors. For example, at one time it was thought that marijuana *caused* juvenile delinquency because so many young offenders smoked it. Yet most of these juveniles also grew up in high crime neighborhoods with abundant models of adult criminal behavior. When marijuana smoking among youths moved into the well-to-do suburbs, the correlation between it and juvenile delinquency dropped precipitously. In other words, any causal relationship was probably one involving the quality of neighborhoods, not the smoking of pot. Correlated variables may well be related to one another in some kind of causal context, but the relationship could take a variety of forms:

> Variable *a* causes variable *b* (or vice versa).
>
> Variable *a* and variable *b* are both caused by variable *c.*
>
> Variables *a* and *b* are both involved in a complex pattern of variables influencing *a* and *b* in similar ways. For example, there is a strong correlation between (1) the number of churches or synagogues and (2) the number of bars to be found in cities across the U.S. Does one cause the other? No, both are "caused" by (3), the size of the cities' populations.

To take another instance, coming from a broken home has been established as a significant correlate of many forms of abnormal behavior. Yet we cannot conclude that marital rupture in itself causes abnormality because many other potential causes of abnormality have been found to be associated with parental separation or divorce—socioeconomic distress, family disharmony, alcoholism in one or both parents, a move to a new neighborhood or school, the difficulties of adjusting to a single

Though a dysfunctional family relationship may be a correlate of some forms of abnormal behavior, this is not necessarily a causal factor because there may be many other ways of accounting for a particular mental disorder.

parent's new love relationships, and so forth. Unfortunately, such complexity is the rule rather than the exception when attempting to understand how abnormal behavior becomes established.

Statistical techniques of relatively recent development (such as path analysis) that take into account how variables predict and are related to one another through time are frequently helpful in disentangling correlated factors. These techniques give us much greater confidence in our causal inferences, but they still cannot prove a cause and effect relationship.

Even though correlational studies may not be able to pin down causal relationships, they can be a powerful and rich source of inference. They often suggest causal hypotheses and occasionally provide crucial data that confirm or refute these hypotheses. As a measure of their usefulness, we need only reflect on what the science of astronomy would be without correlational studies, since astronomers cannot manipulate the variables they study, such as the relative positions and movements of stars and planets.

Correlational studies have been useful in many areas of abnormal psychology but especially so in epidemiological research. **Epidemiological studies** attempt to establish the pattern of occurrence of certain disorders (in our case, mental disorders) in different times, places, and groups of people. Where we find significant variations in the incidence or prevalence of a disorder, we ask why. For example, why is it (as noted earlier) that women experience a much higher rate of depression than men in the United States? This question has prompted a great deal of research, as well as speculation, regarding the plight of women in our society, as will be seen in Chapter 6.

Experimental Strategies in Abnormal Psychology

Correlational research has the character of taking things as they are and determining covariations among observed phenomena. Do things vary together in a direct, corresponding manner, as in female gender and increased risk of depression; in an inverse manner such as high socioeconomic status and generally less risk of mental disorder; or are the variables in question perhaps entirely independent of one another, such that a given state or level of one variable fails to predict reliably anything about that of another, as in our earlier example of handedness and mental disorder? And as just noted, the documentation of covariations (associations) between variables may still leave us perplexed as to the causal pattern producing them.

Scientific research is most rigorous, and its findings most reliable, when it employs the full power of the experimental method. In such cases, scientists control all factors, except one, that could have an effect on a variable or outcome of interest; then they actively manipulate that one factor, often referred to as the **independent variable.** If the outcome of interest, often called the **dependent variable,** is observed to change as the manipulated factor is changed, that factor can be regarded as a cause of the outcome. For example, if a proposed treatment is provided to a given group of patients but withheld from an otherwise completely comparable one, and if the former group experiences positive changes significantly in excess of the latter group, then a powerful causal inference can be made regarding the treatment's efficacy.

Unfortunately, the experimental method cannot be applied to many problems of abnormal psychology. There are both practical and ethical reasons for this. Suppose, for example, we wanted to do an experiment to evaluate the hypothesis that stressful events can cause major depression. Our ideal experimental approach would be to choose at random two groups of normal adults for a longitudinal study—a study in which the same subjects are followed over a prolonged period of time. The individuals in one group would be subjected in systematic fashion to a rigorous program of contrived (but believable) stressful harassment, such as repeated breakdown of their computers' hard drives, resulting in loss of data already entered. Subjects in the other (control) group would spend the same amount of time in some comparable but smooth-running activity. Naturally occurring stressors in both groups would be monitored as well to ensure that the experimental (stressed) group

was in fact more stressed. Some weeks or months later the subjects of both groups would be assessed as to symptoms meeting DSM-IV criteria for Major Depressive Episode—for example, persistently depressed mood, diminished interest or pleasure in usual activities, significant weight loss, sleep disturbance, etc.). If the group of stressed subjects had significantly more occurrences of major depressive episodes than controls, our causal hypothesis would be confirmed: prior stress causes depression. But it would of course be ethically unacceptable to treat people in a manner that is deliberately callous, destructive, and potentially dangerous (e.g., depressive episodes enhance the risk of suicide), even though the experiment itself would be methodologically sound.

Many variables of potential importance in abnormal behavior cannot be manipulated in the active way the experimental method demands, quite apart from the constraints ethical considerations may impose. Fortunately, we have made great progress in the statistical control of variables that do not yield to the classic form of experimental control. Statistical controls allow us in effect to "adjust" for otherwise uncontrolled (or uncontrollable) variables. For example, the prevalence of a number of mental disorders appears to vary inversely with socioeconomic status. Using statistical controls, we can correct for any differences in socioeconomic status existing between our experimental and control groups to the extent that these differences are shown to affect the results we get. Alternatively, we can make sure that socioeconomic statuses of members of our control group exist in exactly the same proportions as those in the pathological group we wish to study, but such a proportional distribution might be difficult to achieve. This might also inadvertently create an additional problem: If we insist that socioeconomic statuses in our control group exactly mirror those in the experimental group rather than those in the general population, then our control group may no longer be representative of the general population. As this example shows, the proper design of research studies in abnormal psychology must take a variety of factors into account.

Animal Research   The experimental method is sometimes used in causal research with animals, though here, too, ethical considerations apply. Such animal studies are conceptual simulations, so to speak, of the processes thought to be involved in the development of abnormal human behavior. Experiments of this kind are generally known as **analogue studies**—studies in which a researcher attempts to emulate the conditions hypothesized as leading to abnormality. These experiments attempt to establish the causes of maladaptive behavior by inducing a model of the behavior in subhuman species. The major scientific problem is, of course, to establish commonality between the contrived behavior and the real thing as it occurs naturally in the course of human development.

A case in point is Martin Seligman's research on the hypothesis that *learned helplessness* is a cause of depression in humans (Seligman, 1975). Laboratory experiments with dogs had demonstrated that, when subjected to repeated experiences of painful, unpredictable, inescapable electric shock, these dogs lost their ability to learn a simple escape routine to avoid further shock. They just sat and endured the pain. This observation led Seligman to argue that human depression (which he equated with the reaction of the helpless dogs) is a reaction to the experience of one's behavior having no effect on one's environment. As a result, the animal or person "learns" they are helpless to do anything. Experiments attempting to induce learned helplessness in humans and to determine if that state would produce mild and reversible depressions were sometimes disappointing. Human subjects did not always respond with helplessness to noncontingency situations, many of them actually showing enhanced effort following the frustrating experiences (see the February 1978 issue of *Journal of Abnormal Psychology,* Volume 87).

Reacting to these disappointing results, Seligman and his colleagues (Abramson, Seligman, & Teasdale, 1978) modified the learned helplessness theory of depression. They suggested that a noncontingency experience should have a depression-inducing effect only on those persons prone to interpret failure-to-cope experiences in a negative way—specifically by attributing them to personal (internal) characteristics that are pervasive (global) and relatively permanent (stable). ("I'm such a clod; I never get anything right and I never will.") This idea has fared considerably better in subsequent research, which will be reviewed in Chapter 6. Curiously, the original concept of learned helplessness may be a better model of human anxiety disorders than of depression, as will be seen in Chapter 5.

In this case, despite the earlier disappointment, which illustrates the hazards involved in generalizing too readily from laboratory models to the real world, the learned helplessness analogue generated much research and thereby clarified certain aspects of an important psychopathological problem relating to depression. In addition, its range of application has turned out to be probably considerably broader than was originally anticipated. We count that as a successful outcome.

Research on the Efficacy of Therapy The necessarily limited role of the experimental method in research on causes of abnormal behavior does not extend to treatment research, where it has proved indispensable. It is a relatively simple and straightforward matter to set up a study in which a proposed treatment is given to a designated group of patients and withheld from a similar group of patients. Should the treated group show significantly more improvement than the latter, we can have confidence in the treatment's efficacy. It is nonetheless true that we may still not know why the treatment works, although investigators are becoming increasingly sophisticated about teasing out the mechanisms whereby therapeutic change is induced (e.g., see Hollon, DeRubeis, & Evans, 1987; Kazdin, 1994)

Special techniques must usually be employed in treatment research to ensure that the two groups are in fact comparable in every respect except the presence or absence of the proposed active treatment agent. Once a treatment has proved effective, it can subsequently be employed for members of the original control group, leading to improved functioning for everyone.

Sometimes this "waiting list" control group strategy is deemed inadvisable for ethical or other reasons. For example, withholding a treatment of already demonstrated efficacy just to evaluate some newly proposed treatment may needlessly prolong mental anguish among control subjects and should require stringent safeguards regarding the potential costs versus benefits of conducting the particular research project (Imber et al., 1986). In this case an alternative research design may call for a compar-

Analogue studies in which generalizations are made from laboratory models to the real world may fail to make convincing connections. Results of testing—using rats, mice, dogs, or monkeys, for example, in a laboratory setting—may not hold up when extended to humans.

ison of two (or more) treatments in different equivalent groups. Typically in this type of study the efficacy of one of the treatments, the control condition, has already been proved. Such comparative outcome research has much to recommend it and is being increasingly employed (Barlow & Hofman, 1997; VandenBos, 1986).

Clinical Case Studies

Most disorders are still studied individually, using the traditional clinical case study method. A **case study** is an in-depth examination of an individual or family that draws from a number of data sources, including interviews and psychological testing. The clinical investigator, who is usually also a patient's therapist, intensively observes an individual's behavior and searches background facts that may be influencing the case. A case study includes a set of hypotheses about what is causing the problem and a guide to treatment planning. For example, the therapist may develop a hunch that the patient was taught inordinate levels of fearfulness by overconcerned parents, the effects of which are now contributing to the patient's clinical condition. The therapist must then decide on how to confirm or disconfirm this hypothesis of disruptive parental influence, which if confirmed at some reasonable level of probability will necessitate therapeutic attention to overcoming the damaging effects of parental depiction of the world in excessively dangerous terms. These hypotheses and therapeutic strategies may be revised as necessary, based on a patient's response to treatment interventions. This strategy is sometimes called an *N equals 1 experiment* (with *N* referring to the number of subjects in the experiment), especially when the precise relationships between successive treatment interventions (or their withdrawal) and patient responses are systematically monitored.

Much can be learned when skilled clinicians use the case study method, but the information acquired is often relevant only to the individual being studied and may be flawed, especially if we seek to apply it to other cases involving an apparently similar abnormality. When there is only one observer and one subject, and when the observations are made in a relatively uncontrolled context, the conclusions we can draw are very narrow and may be mistaken.

Retrospective Versus Prospective Strategies

The classic method of trying to uncover the probable causes of abnormal behavior has involved a retrospective (i.e., looking backward) approach. We start with present disordered behavior and work back from there to try to reconstruct the client's developmental history in the hope of determining what went wrong during its course. Our source material is limited to the patient's recollections and such other data as we may be able to unearth in diaries, records, memories of other family members, etc. The **retrospective strategy** involves many pitfalls. Memories are faulty and selective, tending to emphasize items that confirm the client's already-adopted view of his or her situation. As we saw in our example of major depressives, there are certain difficulties in attempting to reconstruct the pasts of people already experiencing a disorder. Apart from the fact that a disordered person may not be the most accurate or objective source of information, such a strategy invites investigators to discover what they expect to discover about the background factors theoretically linked to a disorder. For example, it is now clear that many false memories of ritual satanic abuse during childhood were implanted by therapists overzealously believing this to be a source of certain types of disorder (Spanos, 1996). Even outside observers of the client are likely to engage in 20/20 hindsight, reinterpreting the person's past behavior in light of his or her present problems.

One way around these difficulties is to utilize documents and records, such as school reports, dated before the emergence of the disorder. While this *archival strategy* has on occasion been productively employed, it obviously depends on the accidental availability of the precise information needed. Few investigators are attracted to research that is so "chancy" in its payoff.

Prospective strategies focus on individuals who have a higher-than-average likelihood of becoming psychologically disordered *before* abnormal behavior shows up. We can have much more confidence in our hypotheses about the causes of a disorder if we have been tracking various influences and measuring them ahead of time. When our hypotheses correctly predict the behavior a group of individuals will develop, we are much closer to establishing a causal relationship. In a typical instance, children sharing a risk factor known to be associated with relatively high rates of subsequent breakdown (such as having been born to a schizophrenic mother) are studied over the course of years. Those who do break down are compared with those who do not in the hope that crucial differentiating factors will be discovered.

As a group, researchers in abnormal behavior have learned there are few easy answers. In fact, the study of behavioral abnormalities has enriched the discipline of psychology by enhancing our understanding of how enormously complex the origins of human behavior really are.

THE ORIENTATION OF THIS BOOK

One of our main purposes in this book is to educate you in an approach to abnormal behavior that is scientific and humanistic in the best senses of both terms. Our more specific intent is to introduce you to the thoughtful examination of abnormal behavior and its place in contemporary society. We will focus on all the major types of mental disorder, particularly those patterns that seem most relevant to a broad, basic understanding of maladaptive behavior. We want to emphasize the unity of human behavior, the idea that abnormality is merely an exaggeration of human qualities all of us possess.

Throughout this text we assume that a sound and comprehensive study of abnormal behavior should be based on the following principles:

1. *A scientific approach to abnormal behavior.* Any comprehensive view of human behavior must draw upon concepts and research findings from a variety of scientific fields. Of particular relevance are genetics, biochemistry, neurophysiology, sociology, anthropology, and of course psychology. Common scientific concepts, such as causal processes, developmental influences, control groups, dependent variables, placebos, and various theoretical positions, will figure in our discussion.

   In this general context, you are encouraged to take a critical and evaluative attitude toward the research findings presented in this text and in other sources. When properly conducted, scientific research provides us with information that has a high probability of being accurate, but many research findings are subject to various sorts of errors and unintended biases and are thus open to serious questions. We intend to show you some of the recurrent sources of these errors and to some extent teach you how to evaluate and interpret research outcomes in this field. We think the benefits of acquiring such skills will persist long after your course in abnormal psychology will have ended, and will make it possible for you to understand and appreciate at perhaps a somewhat advanced level the research the field produces on into the future.

2. *An awareness of our common human concerns.* Insights into hope, faith, courage, love, grief, despair, death, and the quest for values and meaning are not readily obtainable in a laboratory. We must supplement what science with its present methods can teach by turning to literature, drama, autobiographical accounts, and even art, history, and religion to seek a greater understanding of these aspects of human psychological functioning. Science, while limited, is apt to be quite precise; the arts and humanities, while limitless, are normally less so.

3. *Respect for the dignity, integrity, and growth potential of all persons, particularly those individuals whose current functioning may be compromised by psychological problems mild or severe in magnitude.* In attempting to provide a perspective on abnormal behavior, we will focus not only on how maladaptive patterns are perceived by clinical psychologists and other mental health personnel, but also on how such disorders feel to and are perceived by those experiencing them and their friends and families. Historically, many of the disorders we'll look at have been conceptualized in extremely pessimistic terms and their victims as "hopeless cases." We reject that attitude as both unproved in most instances and as containing the seeds of its own fulfillment.

We will focus on four significant aspects of each abnormal pattern of behavior: (1) the clinical picture, in which we will describe what is going on with the disorder; (2) the possible causal factors; (3) treatments; and (4) outcomes. In each case, we will examine the evidence for biological, psychosocial (psychological and interpersonal), and sociocultural (the broader social environment of culture and subculture) influences. In short, we will try consistently to give you a sense of the total context in which abnormalities of behavior occur.

Because this is a psychology book, much of our focus will be on the psychosocial factors involved in abnormal behavior. The most challenging adaptational problems we face in a future of rapid change and ever-increasing demand on adaptational resources tend to be psychosocial in nature. Even in respect to our physical health, there are increasing signs that ultimate solutions will depend on a far greater sophistication about ourselves as psychosocial, as well as biological, entities—an idea we examine in detail in Chapter 8. The impressive advances in medicine and biomedical treatment of certain disorders are still limited in their ability to manage or overcome ineffective, self-defeating, or dangerous behavior patterns. For example, it is not presently even conceivable that a prescription medication or a brain operation might be fashioned that will convert a person lacking essential skills of sociability or perseverance into one capable of effectively negotiating the complexities of modern life. Accomplishing this requires both an enhanced understanding of the psychosocial underpinnings of social competence and the development of remedial techniques of unprecedented power. The challenge is very great, but also we think very exciting.

UNRESOLVED ISSUES

The DSM

As we have seen, the DSM is the current standard for defining what a mental disorder is and for differentiating among its supposed subtypes. It is a far from perfect system, as even its principal authors acknowledge (Frances et al., 1991). It is clear that the increasingly "operational" DSM approach has helped us achieve respectable levels of reliability in the diagnostic process, particularly where structured diagnostic interviews are employed. However, the validity of the diagnoses in the current DSM remains the subject of controversy. As noted earlier, recent editions of the DSM have tended to sacrifice validity to improve interdiagnostician agreement, or reliability. They have done this mostly by pinpointing more readily observable surface characteristics. But having diagnosticians agree on assignment of patients to a diagnosis of questionable validity or meaning does not in and of itself constitute an exceptional level of progress.

It is difficult to satisfy simultaneously the dual requirements of reliability and validity in diagnosing mental disorders. This is due to the enormous complexity of the factors underlying and determining human behavior. It is also due, according to many observers, to our having chosen an inadequate model for organizing our observations of behavioral abnormalities. As you will see in the next two chapters, a medical or disease metaphor has tended to dominate the history of the field of psychopathology and the way we view abnormal behavior. That is, the various types of abnormal behavior have tended to be seen as the "symptomatic" outward manifestation of an underlying illness ("dysfunction").

The Definitional Problem

The problems begin right at the beginning—in the DSM-IV definition of "mental disorder." As you will recall, this definition requires that problematic behavior must be "a symptom of a dysfunction in the individual" if it is to qualify as an instance of mental disorder. What does this expression mean? The problematic behavior cannot itself be the "dysfunction" for that would be like saying mental disorders are due to mental disorders.

Identifying this flaw in the definition, Jerome Wakefield (1992a, 1992b, 1997) has proposed that "dysfunction" be interpreted as referring to some underlying mechanism that fails to perform according to "design." There are various logical and philosophical problems with this proposed solution (e.g., see Bergner, 1997; Carson, 1997; Lillienthal & Marino, 1995), whose detailed discussion here would take us too far afield. Probably its most glaring deficiency is an obvious one: namely that, with rare exception, no such defectively operating mechanisms have ever been precisely identified. Moreover, to imagine that we might some day be able to pinpoint a distinctive underlying dysfunction for each of the nearly 300 DSM diagnoses seems extremely farfetched. The *symptom/underlying disease model* is thus at once both conjectural and potentially deceiving, inviting us to look for causes in places where none may exist. Maladaptive behavior that is consistent with an individual's biological propensities (e.g., temperamental aggressiveness) and developmental experience (e.g., childhood neglect or abuse) need not, after all, be forced into the metaphor of broken machinery in order for us to be able to make sense of it.

The Overlap/Comorbidity Problem

We have already had occasion to comment on another difficulty with the DSM diagnostic system—that is, the widespread overlap of the diagnoses identified. Consistent with the adopted medical disease metaphor, the DSM-IV attempts to treat mental disorder as consisting

Most of this book will be devoted to a presentation of well-established patterns of mental disorder and to special problem behaviors of our time that are more controversial but directly relevant. Initially, however, to give you a sense of where the field is coming from, we will trace the development of contemporary views of abnormal behavior from early beliefs and practices to the major views now underlying attempts to explain what makes human beings behave as they do.

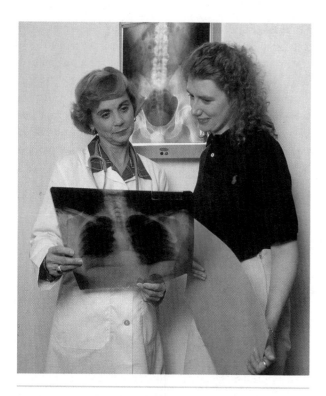

Though the symptom/underlying disease model is useful for strictly physical illness, when applied to mental disorder it tends to invite us to look for causes in places where none may exist.

of a large number of discrete (nonoverlapping) categories, much the way medical/physical diseases are categorized and diagnosed. This insistence on a categorical format for mental disorder diagnoses that (as we have argued) are primarily prototypal in nature is a source of much confusion and misdirected effort in the field at large. The DSM categories establish groupings that are neither internally homogeneous nor cleanly separated at the boundaries.

There is undoubtedly a certain economy of communication, especially among experienced professionals, in adopting the categorical approach, provided one consistently bears in mind that this organizational schema is largely in the nature of a convenient fiction, that the domain is in reality not nearly so exquisitely differentiated. The DSM-IV makes clear in its Introduction (American Psychiatric Association, 1994, pp. xv–xxv) that its primary purpose is to facilitate in a pragmatic manner clinical and research objectives. Unfortunately, it has proved difficult to limit the DSM's influence to this pragmatic aim. In many contexts, including legal ones (see Chapter 18), DSM categories become reified (i.e., assumed to constitute concrete, real phenomena, as ordained by nature) to unintended levels, thereby encouraging unwarranted inferences about the origins of mentally disordered be-

havior—for example, that these must always be exotic and wholly different from the origins of normal behavior.

One epidemiological study found that over 43 million U.S. citizens between the ages of 15 and 54 could by current DSM standards be declared to have had three or more *separate* and almost exclusively Axis I mental disorders in their lifetimes (Kessler et al., 1994). The inclusion of the full gamut of Axis II disorders in this important NCS study would without question have resulted in a marked increase in the numbers of persons sharing multiple mental disorder diagnoses. There is growing evidence in fact that even the distinction between Axis I (symptomatic disorders) and Axis II (personality disorders) of the DSM may be rationally and empirically unjustified (Benjamin, 1994; Greenberg, 1997; Lillienfeld, Waldman, & Israel, 1994; Livesly et al., 1994). The upshot seems to be that the modern DSM effort has resulted in a confusing array of interrelated psychological difficulties that are conceived to be separate and independent entities of disorder, even though there is massive evidence against such a view. Some (e.g., Carson, 1997; Greenberg, 1997; Westen & Shedler, 1999a, 1999b) think it will be needlessly difficult to make fundamental progress in psychopathological research in the face of this pervasive inaccuracy in ordering the phenomena constituting the field of inquiry.

A good example of the problems posed by the DSM model and of a potential solution to them is provided in recent research concerning the substantial comorbidity of anxiety disorders (Chapter 5) and depression (Chapter 6), as previously noted. Mineka, Watson, and Clark (1998) describe what is in effect a component, dimensionalized analysis of both anxiety and depressive disorders, concluding that each has some shared and some distinctive features, and that the various recognized types of anxiety disorder probably also have their own distinctive component features that vary in overlap with the depression experience. According to their analysis of the available evidence, for example, a general distress factor indexed by measures of "Negative Affect" (feeling distressed, stymied, and self-doubting) is common to both the anxiety disorders and depression and is chiefly responsible for the observed anxiety-depression diagnostic comorbidity.

The Expanding Horizons of "Mental Disorder"

Because the concept of mental disorder, as we have seen, lacks a truly objective means of settling on its limits, and because it is in the economic and other interests of mental health professionals to designate larger and larger segments of human behavior as within the purview of "mentally disordered," there is constant pressure to include in the DSM more and more kinds of socially undesirable behavior. For example, one recent proposal was to include "Road Rage" (anger at other drivers) as a newly discovered mental disorder in the next edition of the DSM (Sharkey, 1997). There is considerable informal evidence that the steering committee responsible for the production of DSM-IV worked hard to fend off a large number of such frivolous proposals, and in fact they largely succeeded in curtailing additional diagnoses beyond those appearing in the previous edition (DSM-III-R) by adopting stringent criteria for inclusion. Nevertheless, this promises to be an uphill battle. Mental health professionals, like the members of other professions, tend to view the world through a lens that enhances the importance of phenomena relating to their own expertise. In addition, inclusion of a disorder in the DSM is a prerequisite for health insurers' reimbursement of services rendered.

It is thus in the interests of the public at large to keep a wary eye on proposed expansions of the "mentally disordered" domain. It is conceivable that failure to do so would eventually lead to a situation wherein almost anything but the most bland, conformist, and conventional of behaviors may be declared a manifestation of mental disorder. By that point the concept will have become so indiscriminate as to lose most of its scientifically productive meaning.

Though some mental health professionals have serious reservations about the prevailing classificatory and diagnostic procedures, most do not recommend that these procedures be summarily abandoned or ignored. While far from ideal, they constitute the standard language of the field for both formal (especially research-based) and informal communication. Familiarity with the system in use is thus vital for the serious student. We hope, however, that this discussion has given you a more sophisticated perspective on the classificatory issues facing the field.

SUMMARY

Encountering instances of seemingly abnormal behavior is a common experience for nearly all of us, which is not surprising in light of prevalence rates indicating that about half of all Americans will at some time in their lives have a diagnosable Axis I mental disorder. Having some understanding of mental disorder, which this book attempts to provide, is therefore highly desirable.

Difficulties in understanding, however, are probably more abundant than is necessary or justified, even with respect to so primary an issue as defining the scope of the field. The formal definition of mental disorder, as offered in the fourth edition of the *Diagnostic and Statistical Manual of Mental Disorders* (DSM-IV), has certain problems that limit its clarity (what are these imputed "dysfunctions"?) and objectivity (who shall decide what is "harmful"?). There is probably no perfect or value-free solution to the definitional problem, but the authors opt for one emphasizing behavioral maladaptiveness. Importantly, the latter position does not locate all mental disorder within individuals.

There are also problems with the category type of classification system adopted in DSM-IV. Notably, the categories result in neither convincing within-class homogeneity nor between-class discrimination, in turn leading, among other difficulties, to very high levels of comorbidity among disorders. One potential solution to this problem would be that of dimensionalizing the phenomena of mental disorder. Another would be the ex-

plicit adoption of a prototypal approach to the organization of the field, which is what the DSM-IV in fact provides without acknowledging that it does so. For all of its problems, however, knowledge of the DSM is essential to serious study in the field.

The most certain way to avoid misconception and error is to adopt a scientific attitude and approach to the study of abnormal behavior. This involves, among other things, a focus on research and research methods, including an appreciation of the distinction between what is observable and what is hypothetical or inferred. Much of the content of abnormal psychology falls into the latter category. Research on abnormal conditions, if it is to produce valid results, must be done on people who are truly representative of the diagnostic groups to which they purportedly belong—a requirement that is often difficult to satisfy. We must also remain alert to the fact that mere correlation does not establish a causal relationship between the variables in question. Researchers use experimental methods and prospective research designs to resolve questions of causality, but these approaches are not always appropriate and may not always be effective. The individual case study method, despite its weaknesses, remains a frequently used investigative technique.

A primary aim of the authors of this book is to combine the best of both science and humanism in introducing the reader to the study of abnormal psychology.

KEY TERMS

abnormal behavior (p. 5)

reliability (p. 6)

validity (p. 6)

comorbidity (p. 8)

symptoms (p. 8)

signs (p. 8)

axes (of DSM) (p. 10)

acute (p. 12)

chronic (p. 12)

mild (p. 12)

moderate (p. 12)

severe (p. 12)

episodic (p. 12)

recurrent (p. 12)

epidemiology (p. 17)

prevalence (p. 17)

incidence (p. 17)

lifetime prevalence (p. 17)

sampling (p. 21)

control group (p. 21)

criterion group (p. 21)

epidemiological studies (p. 22)

independent variable (p. 23)

dependent variable (p. 23)

analogue studies (p. 23)

case study (p. 25)

retrospective strategy (p. 25)

prospective strategy (p. 25)

Historical Views of Abnormal Behavior

Frank Karl Bühler (Pohl), *Untitled*. Born in Offenburg in 1864, Bühler worked as an art metalworker and lecturer but was dismissed from his position at a vocational school for his "bizarre behavior." Diagnosed with schizophrenia and institutionalized, he suffered hallucinations and withdrew into his autistic world. He was later killed by the Nazis. His artwork is rather sophisticated, and shows evidence of his academic schooling.

There is humor as well as tragedy to some of the missteps and misconceptions that are part of the history of our efforts to understand abnormal behavior. But it is equally true that many modern scientific concepts and treatments have their counterparts in approaches tried long ago. For example, free association—a technique used in twentieth-century psychoanalytic therapy—is described by the Greek playwright Aristophanes in his play *The Clouds* (423 B.C.). The scene in which Socrates tries to calm and bring self-knowledge to Strepsiades even contains a couch.

In this chapter, we will trace the evolution of views and treatments of psychopathology from ancient times to the twentieth century. In a broad sense, we will see an evolution from beliefs we consider today as superstition to those based on scientific awareness—from a focus on supernatural causes to a knowledge of natural causes. The course of this evolution has often been marked by periods of advancement or unique individual contributions followed by long years of inactivity or unproductive backward steps.

As we will see, current views of abnormal behavior have been shaped by the prevailing attitudes of past times and the advances of science. Each has contributed to the growth—and often the stagnation—of the other. For example, during certain periods in ancient Greece, the human body was considered sacred. Since autopsies on human beings were not performed, the understanding of human anatomy or biological processes was impeded. Much later, during the nineteenth and early twentieth centuries, the belief that a biological (medical) solution was needed to cure mental disorders frustrated investigation into psychological causes. Even today, with renewed emphasis on biological causes and treatments, the focus on psychological causes and treatment is sometimes undervalued.

If we think that we have today arrived at a knowledgeable and humane approach to treating the mentally ill, we should think again. We are still bound by culturally conditioned constraints and beliefs. For many, attitudes toward people who are different are still formed, at least in part, by superstition and fear. Even today one can find superstition and nonscientific thinking influencing the way people behave. As news accounts periodically unveil, animal sacrifice and satanic rituals are still with us and even some of our leaders have succumbed to using astrological charts in making important decisions!

ABNORMAL BEHAVIOR IN ANCIENT TIMES

Although human life presumably appeared on earth some 3 million or more years ago, written records extend back only a few thousand years. Thus our knowledge of our early ancestors is limited.

Two Egyptian papyri dating from the sixteenth century B.C. have provided some clues into the earliest interest in the treatment of diseases and behavior disorders. The Edwin Smith papyrus (named after its nineteenth-century discoverer) contains detailed descriptions of the treatment of wounds and other surgical operations. In it, the brain is described—possibly for the first time in history—and the writing clearly shows that the brain was recognized as the site of mental functions. We may think this remarkable for the sixteenth century B.C.; it becomes even more remarkable once we realize that this papyrus is believed to be a copy of an earlier work from about 3000 B.C. The Ebers papyrus provides another perspective on treatment. It covers internal medicine and the circulatory system but relies more on incantations and magic for explaining and curing diseases that had unknown causes. Although surgical techniques may have been used, they were probably coupled with prayers and the like that reflected the prevailing view of the origin of behavior disorders, to which we now turn.

Demonology, Gods, and Magic

References to abnormal behavior in early writings show that the Chinese, Egyptians, Hebrews, and Greeks often attributed such behavior to a demon or god who had taken possession of a person. This belief is not surprising if we remember that "good" and "bad" spirits were widely used to explain lightning, thunder, earthquakes, storms, fires, sickness, and many other events that otherwise seemed incomprehensible. It was a simple and logical step to extend this theory to peculiar and incomprehensible behavior as well.

The decision as to whether the "possession" involved good spirits or evil spirits usually depended on an individual's symptoms. If a person's speech or behavior appeared to have a religious or mystical significance, it was usually thought that he or she was possessed by a good spirit or god. Such people were often treated with considerable awe and respect, for it was thought that they had supernatural powers.

Most possessions, however, were considered to be the work of an angry god or an evil spirit, particularly when a person became excited or overactive and engaged in behavior contrary to religious teachings. Among the ancient Hebrews, for example, such possessions were thought to represent the wrath and punishment of God. Moses is quoted in the Bible as saying, "The Lord shall smite thee with madness." Apparently this punishment was thought to involve the withdrawal of God's protection and the abandonment of the person to the forces of evil. In such cases, every effort was made to rid the person of the evil spirit. Jesus reportedly cured a man with an "unclean spirit" by transferring the devils that plagued him to a herd of swine who, in turn, became possessed and "ran violently down a steep place into the sea" (Mark 5:1–13).

The primary type of treatment for demonic possession was exorcism, which included various techniques for casting an evil spirit out of an afflicted person. These techniques varied considerably but typically included magic, prayer, incantation, noisemaking, and the use of various horrible-tasting concoctions, such as purgatives made from sheep's dung and wine. More severe measures, such as starving or flogging, were sometimes used in extreme cases to make the body of a possessed person such an unpleasant place that an evil spirit would be driven out. We will look more closely at exorcism as a treatment in the Middle Ages later in this chapter. The continuing popularity of movies and books on possession and exorcism suggests, and recent newspaper accounts of animal sacrifices and witchcraft preoccupation (ostensibly going on today) confirm, that these primitive ideas still have appeal.

Exorcism was originally the task of shamans or persons regarded as having healing powers, but it was eventually taken over in Egypt and Greece by priests, who apparently served as holy people, physicians, psychologists, and magicians. Many of their cures remained based in magical rites. Although these priests typically believed in demonology and used established exorcistic practices, many of them were thought to treat people with mental disturbances in a more humane way. For example, in ancient Greece, the priests had patients sleep in the temples of the god Asclepius. Supposedly, the dreams they had there would reveal what they needed to do to get better. The priests supplemented prayer and incantation with kindness, suggestion, and recreational measures, such as plays, riding, walking, and harmonious music.

Hippocrates' Early Medical Concepts

The Greek temples of healing ushered in the Golden Age of Greece under the Athenian leader Pericles (461–429 B.C.). During this time, considerable progress was made in the understanding and treatment of mental disorders. Interestingly, this progress was made in spite of the fact that Greeks of this time considered the human body sacred and thus little could be learned of human anatomy or physiology. During this period the Greek physician Hippocrates (460–377 B.C.), often referred to as the father

Hippocrates' (460–377 B.C.) belief that mental disease was the result of natural causes and brain pathology was revolutionary for its time.

of modern medicine, received his training and made substantial contributions to the field.

Hippocrates denied that deities and demons intervened in the development of illnesses and insisted that mental disorders had natural causes and required treatments like other diseases. He believed that the brain was the central organ of intellectual activity and that mental disorders were due to brain pathology. He also emphasized the importance of heredity and predisposition and pointed out that injuries to the head could cause sensory and motor disorders.

Hippocrates classified all mental disorders into three general categories—mania, melancholia, and phrenitis (brain fever)—and gave detailed clinical descriptions of the specific disorders included in each category. He relied heavily on clinical observation, and his descriptions, which were based on daily clinical records of his patients, were surprisingly thorough. Hippocrates considered dreams to be important in understanding a patient's personality. On this point, he not only elaborated on the thinking set forth by the priests in the temples of Asclepius but also was a harbinger of a basic concept of modern psychodynamic psychotherapy.

The treatments advocated by Hippocrates were far in advance of the exorcistic practices then prevalent. For the treatment of melancholia, for example, he prescribed a regular and tranquil life, sobriety and abstinence from all excesses, a vegetable diet, celibacy, exercise short of fatigue, and bleeding if indicated. He also believed in the importance of the environment and often removed his patients from their families.

Hippocrates' emphasis on the natural causes of diseases, clinical observation, and brain pathology as the root of mental disorders was truly revolutionary. Like his contemporaries, however, Hippocrates had little knowledge of physiology. He believed that hysteria (the appearance of physical illness in the absence of organic pathology) was restricted to women and was caused by the uterus wandering to various parts of the body, pining for children. (See Highlight 2.1.) For this "disease," Hippocrates recommended marriage as the best remedy. He also believed in the existence of four bodily fluids or humors—blood, black bile, yellow bile, and phlegm. Although the concept of humors went far beyond demonology, it was too crude physiologically to be of much therapeutic value. Yet in its emphasis on the importance of bodily balances to mental health, it may be seen as a precursor of today's focus on the need for biochemical balances to maintain normal brain functioning and good health.

Early Philosophical Conceptions of Consciousness and Mental Discovery

The problem of dealing with mentally disturbed individuals who have committed criminal acts was studied by the Greek philosopher Plato (429–347 B.C.). He wrote that such persons were in some "obvious" sense not responsible for their acts and should not receive punishment in the same way as normal persons: ". . . someone may commit an act when mad or afflicted with disease. . . . [If so,] let him pay simply for the damage; and let him be exempt from other punishment." Plato also made provision for mental cases to be cared for in the community. In making these humane suggestions, Plato was addressing issues with which we are still grappling today—for example, the issue of insanity as a legal defense. **Insanity** is a legal term for mental disorder that implies a lack of understanding of what is right or wrong as required by law and therefore a lack of responsibility for one's acts and an inability to manage one's affairs. Even today the question of whether a person's mental condition at the time of a crime is relevant to a legal defense is widely debated. (We will return to this issue in Chapter 18.)

Plato viewed psychological phenomena as responses of the whole organism, reflecting its internal state and

natural appetites. He also seems to have anticipated Freud's insight into the functions of fantasies and dreams as substitute satisfactions. In *The Republic,* Plato emphasized the importance of individual differences in intellectual and other abilities, pointing to the role of sociocultural influences in shaping thinking and behavior. His ideas regarding treatment included a provision for "hospital" care for individuals who developed beliefs that were contrary to the broader social order. There they would have periodic conversations analogous to psychotherapy to promote the health of their souls (Milns, 1986). Despite these modern ideas, however, Plato shared the belief of his time that mental disorders were in part divinely caused.

The celebrated Greek philosopher Aristotle (384–322 B.C.), who was a pupil of Plato, wrote extensively on mental disorders. Among his most lasting contributions to psychology are his descriptions of consciousness. He too anticipated Freud in his view of "thinking" as directed striving toward the elimination of pain and the attainment of pleasure. On the question of whether mental disorders could be caused by psychological factors such as frustration and conflict, Aristotle discussed the possibility and rejected it; his lead on this issue was widely followed. Aristotle generally believed the Hippocratic theory of disturbances in the bile. For example, he thought that very hot bile generated amorous desires, verbal fluency, and suicidal impulses.

Later Greek and Roman Thought

Hippocrates' work was continued by some of the later Greek and Roman physicians. Particularly in Alexandria, Egypt (which became a center of Greek culture after its founding in 332 B.C. by Alexander the Great), medical practices developed to a high level, and the temples dedicated to Saturn were first-rate sanatoriums. Pleasant surroundings were considered of great therapeutic value for mental patients, who were provided with constant activities, including parties, dances, walks in the temple gardens, rowing along the Nile, and musical concerts. Physicians of this time also used a wide range of therapeutic measures, including dieting, massage, hydrotherapy, gymnastics, and education, as well as some less desirable practices, such as bleeding, purging, and mechanical restraints.

One of the most influential Greek physicians was Galen (A.D. 130–200), who practiced in Rome. Although he elaborated on the Hippocratic tradition, he did not contribute much that was new to the treatment or clinical descriptions of mental disorders. Rather, he made a num-

Highlight 2.1

Misperceptions About Women in the History of Abnormal Behavior

Woman have often been unfairly cast in the history of abnormal behavior perhaps because most of those writing the history of the field have been men who may not have sufficiently understood women's experiences. The reproductive role of women, for example, has been associated with various psychological "disorders" in past efforts to understand or explain mental disorders. The off-target interpretations of women in the history of abnormal psychology also came about in some part because women in our society have often been victimized by broader social attitudes centering on issues of gender and on procreation. The role expectations that have often been placed on women with respect to procreation at different periods in history have often produced enormous adaptive challenges and considerable malaise. With more women entering higher education, another perspective of history, particularly with respect to social influences on mental disorders in women, has begun to bring more balance in the ways women have been viewed over time (Tomes, 1994). One can still find today, however, social role attitudes and expectations that result in a great deal of uncertainty and anxiety in women.

An exploration of women's experiences over the issue of childlessness reveals considerable unhappiness and unpleasantness. Having the ability or the potential to reproduce our species is a marvelous power that women possess. However, this gift has also brought its share of difficult life circumstances, troubling role expectations, and a modicum of tragedy along with it. In an informative book, *Barren in the Promised Land,* historian Elaine May (1995) has traced the history of America's social expectations about reproduction and the impact that both reproduction and infertility have on women. May examined the consequences of childlessness in America and detailed many ways in which society's expectations of women and the obsession with fertility has created great anguish among women in our society. At various times throughout history social expectations have dictated very different attitudes toward childbearing, and women have been subjected to extremely different social expectations surrounding procreation. A few of the diverse social climates will be noted as an example:

- In the early periods of American history when fertility and procreation were associated with survival of the species, women were thought to have a manifest destiny to bear many children. Failure to have children produced the social stigma of "barrenness," was considered by some to represent a moral failing on the part of the woman.
- During the widespread slave trade of the seventeenth and eighteenth centuries, many African-American women were forced to bear children as a trade commodity.
- In the early twentieth century, during the throes of the eugenics movement, many women, usually lower class or ethnic minority women, were sterilized because they were considered "unfit" for motherhood.
- At present some social attitudes appear to encourage women who chose career over family to defer or forgo having children. This decision, however, sometimes results in later regret and soul searching.

We can see that the varying—often extremely difficult—roles in which women have been placed in the past can lead to considerable unhappiness and possibly psychological disorders. Historical analyses such as May's can hopefully begin to offset to some extent the biases that have been put forth in past historical accounts as a result of social expectations. ■

ber of original contributions concerning the anatomy of the nervous system. (These findings were based on dissections of animals because human autopsies were still not allowed.) Galen also maintained a scientific approach to the field, dividing the causes of psychological disorders into physical and mental categories. Among the causes he named were injuries to the head, alcoholic excess, shock, fear, adolescence, menstrual changes, economic reverses, and disappointment in love.

Roman medicine reflected the characteristic pragmatism of the Roman people. Roman physicians wanted to make their patients comfortable and thus used pleasant physical therapies, such as warm baths and massage. They also followed the principle of *contrariis contrarius* (opposite by opposite)—for example, having their patients drink chilled wine while they were in a warm tub.

Although historians generally consider the fall of Rome at the end of the fifth century to be the dividing line between ancient and medieval times, the "Dark Ages" in the history of abnormal psychology began much earlier, with Galen's death in A.D. 200. The contributions of Hippocrates and the later Greek and Roman physicians were soon lost in the welter of popular superstition, and though some exceptions can be found, most of the physicians of Rome returned to some sort of belief in demonology as an underlying factor in abnormal behavior.

Galen (A.D. 130–200) believed that psychological disorders could have either physical causes, such as injuries to the head, or mental causes, such as disappointment in love.

VIEWS OF ABNORMALITY DURING THE MIDDLE AGES

During the Middle Ages, the more scientific aspects of Greek medicine survived in the Islamic countries of the Middle East. The first mental hospital was established in Baghdad in A.D. 792; it was soon followed by others in Damascus and Aleppo (Polvan, 1969). In these hospitals, the mentally disturbed individuals received humane treatment. The outstanding figure in Islamic medicine was Avicenna from Arabia (c. 980–1037), called the "prince of physicians" (Campbell, 1926) and author of *The Canon of Medicine,* perhaps the most widely studied medical work ever written. In his writings, Avicenna frequently referred to hysteria, epilepsy, manic reactions, and melancholia. The following story shows his unique approach to the treatment of a young prince suffering from a mental disorder:

> A certain prince was afflicted with melancholia, and suffered from the delusion that he was a cow . . . he would low like a cow, causing annoyance to everyone, . . . crying "Kill me so that a good stew may be made of my flesh," finally . . .

he would eat nothing. . . . Avicenna was persuaded to take the case. . . . First of all he sent a message to the patient bidding him be of good cheer because the butcher was coming to slaughter him, whereat . . . the sick man rejoiced. Some time afterwards Avicenna, holding a knife in his hand, entered the sickroom saying, "Where is this cow that I may kill it?" The patient lowed like a cow to indicate where he was. By Avicenna's orders he was laid on the ground bound hand and foot. Avicenna then felt him all over and said, "He is too lean, and not ready to be killed; he must be fattened." Then they offered him suitable food of which he now partook eagerly, and gradually he gained strength, got rid of his delusion, and was completely cured. (Browne, 1921, pp. 88–89)

Unfortunately, most Western medical practitioners of Avicenna's time dealt with mental patients in a far different way. The advances made by the thinkers of antiquity had little impact on the ways most people approached abnormal behavior.

During the Middle Ages in Europe (c. 500–1500), scientific inquiry into abnormal behavior was limited, and the treatment of psychologically disturbed individuals was more often characterized by ritual or superstition than by attempts to understand an individual's condition. In contrast to Avicenna's era in the Islamic countries

Islamic physician Avicenna (c. 980–1037) approached the treatment of mental disorder with humane practices unknown to Western medical practitioners of the time.

of the Middle East or to the period of enlightenment during the seventeenth and eighteenth centuries, the Middle Ages in Europe can largely be characterized as void with respect to scientific thinking and the humane treatment of the mentally disturbed. A similar sequence of events occurred in other parts of the world, as can be seen in Highlight 2.2.

Mental disorders were quite prevalent throughout the Middle Ages in Europe, especially so toward the end of the period, when medieval institutions, social structures, and beliefs began to change drastically. During this time, supernatural explanations of the causes of mental illness grew in popularity. Within this environment, it obviously was difficult to make great strides in the understanding and treatment of abnormal behavior. Although the influence of theology was growing rapidly, "sin" was not always cited as a causal factor in mental illness. For example, Kroll and Bachrach (1984) examined 57 episodes of mental illness, ranging from madness and possession to alcohol and epilepsy. They found sin implicated in only nine cases (16 percent). To understand better this elusive period of history, let us look at two events of the times— mass madness and exorcism—to see how they relate to views of abnormal behavior.

Mass Madness   During the last half of the Middle Ages in Europe, a peculiar trend emerged in efforts to understand abnormal behavior. It involved **mass madness**—the widespread occurrence of group behavior disorders that were apparently cases of hysteria. Whole groups of people were affected simultaneously. Dancing manias (epidemics of raving, jumping, dancing, and convulsions) were reported as early as the tenth century. One such episode, occurring in Italy early in the thirteenth century was known as **tarantism.** This dancing mania later spread to Germany and the rest of Europe, where it was known as **Saint Vitus's dance.** The behavior was similar to the ancient orgiastic rites by which people had worshiped the Greek god Dionysus. These rites had been banned with the advent of Christianity, but they were deeply embedded in the culture and were apparently kept alive in secret gatherings (which probably led to considerable guilt and conflict). Then, with time, the meaning of the dances changed. The old rites reappeared, but they were attributed to symptoms of the tarantula's bite. The participants were no longer sinners but the unwilling victims of the tarantula's spirit. The dancing became the "cure" and is the source of the dance we know today as the tarantella.

Isolated rural areas were also afflicted with outbreaks of **lycanthropy**—a condition in which people believed themselves to be possessed by wolves and imitated their behavior. In 1541 a case was reported in which a lycanthrope told his captors, in confidence, that he was really a wolf but that his skin was smooth on the surface because all the hairs were on the inside (Stone, 1937). To cure him of his delusions, his extremities were amputated, following which he died, still uncured.

Mass madness occurred periodically into the seventeenth century but apparently reached its peak during the fourteenth and fifteenth centuries—a period noted for social oppression, famine, and epidemic diseases. During this period, Europe was ravaged by a plague known as the Black Death, which killed millions (some estimates say 50 percent of the population of Europe died) and severely disrupted social organization. Undoubtedly, many of the peculiar cases of mass madness were related to the depression, fear, and wild mysticism engendered by the terrible events of this period. People simply could not believe that frightening catastrophes such as the Black Death could have natural causes and thus could be within our power to control, prevent, or even create.

Today so-called mass hysteria occurs occasionally; the affliction usually mimics some type of physical disorder,

Early Views of Mental Disorders in China

The following passage is taken from an ancient Chinese medical text supposedly written by Huang Ti (c. 2674 B.C.), the third legendary emperor. Historians now believe that the text was written at a later date, possibly during the seventh century B.C.:

> The person suffering from excited insanity initially feels sad, eating and sleeping less; he then becomes grandiose, feeling that he is very smart and noble, talking and scolding day and night, singing, behaving strangely, seeing strange things, hearing strange voices, believing that he can see the devil or gods. (Tseng, 1973, p. 570)

Even at this early date, Chinese medicine was based on a belief in natural rather than supernatural causes for illnesses. For example, in the concept of Yin and Yang, the human body, like the cosmos, is divided into positive and negative forces that both complement and contradict each other. If the two forces are balanced, the result is physical and mental health; if they are not, illness will result. Thus treatments focused on restoring balance: "As treatment for such an excited condition withholding food was suggested, since food was considered to be the source of positive force and the patient was thought to be in need of a decrease in such force" (p. 570).

Chinese medicine reached a relatively sophisticated level during the second century, and Chung Ching, who has been called the Hippocrates of China, wrote two well-known medical works around A.D. 200. Like Hippocrates, he based his views of physical and mental disorders on clinical observations, and he implicated organ pathologies as primary causes. However, he also believed that stressful psychological conditions could cause organ pathologies, and his treatments, like those of Hippocrates, utilized both drugs and the regaining of emotional balance through appropriate activities.

As in the West, Chinese views of mental disorders regressed to a belief in supernatural forces as causal agents. From the later part of the second century through the early part of the ninth century, ghosts and devils were implicated in "ghost-evil" insanity, which presumably resulted from possession by evil spirits. The "Dark Ages" in China, however, were not as severe—in terms of the treatment of mental patients—nor as long lasting as in the West. A return to biological, somatic (bodily) views and an emphasis on psychosocial factors occurred in the centuries that followed. ■

such as fainting spells or convulsive movements. In 1982, after a nationwide story about some Chicago-area residents poisoned by Tylenol capsules, California health officials reported a sudden wave of illness among some 200 people who drank soda at a high school football game. No objective cause for the illness could be found, and officials speculated that most sufferers had been experiencing a kind of mass hysteria related to the Tylenol incident (United Press International, 1982). Another case of apparent mass hysteria occurred among hundreds of West Bank Palestinian girls in April 1983. This episode threatened to have serious political repercussions because some Arab and Israeli leaders initially thought that the girls

had been poisoned by Israelis; health officials later concluded that psychological factors had played a key role in most of the cases (Hefez, 1985).

Exorcism and Witchcraft   In the Middle Ages in Europe, management of the mentally disturbed was left largely to the clergy. Monasteries served as refuges and places of confinement. During the early part of the medieval period, the mentally disturbed were, for the most part, treated with considerable kindness. "Treatment" consisted of prayer, holy water, sanctified ointments, the breath or spittle of the priests, the touching of relics, visits to holy places, and mild forms of **exorcism.** In some

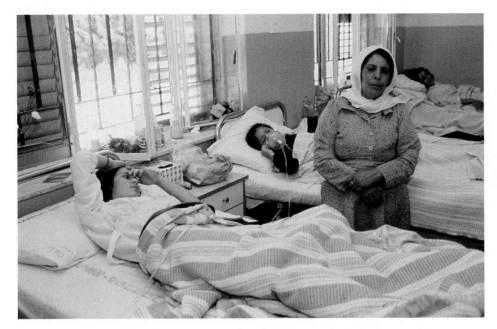

Mass disorders seem to occur during periods of widespread public fear and stress, such as that felt by these West Bank Palestinian schoolgirls, who developed the same mysterious physical symptoms in April 1983. Although Arab leaders at first suspected the girls had been the victims of an Israeli poison plot, it was later thought that psychological factors had played an important role in the appearance of their symptoms.

monasteries and shrines, exorcisms were performed by the gentle "laying on of hands." Such methods were often joined with vaguely understood medical treatments derived mainly from Galen, which gave rise to prescriptions such as the following: "For a fiend-sick man: When a devil possesses a man, or controls him from within with disease, a spewdrink of lupin, bishopswort, henbane, garlic. Pound these together, add ale and holy water" (Cockayne, 1864–1866). Interestingly, there has been a recent resurgence of superstition, for example, one can find those who believe that supernatural forces cause psychological problems and that "cures" should involve exorcism to rid people of unwanted characteristics or "spells." Occasionally exorcism is still practiced.

It had long been thought that during the Middle Ages, many mentally disturbed people were accused of being witches and thus were punished and often killed (e.g., Zilboorg & Henry, 1941). But some more recent interpretations have questioned the extent to which this was so. Schoeneman (1984), for example, in a review of the literature, found that "the typical accused witch was not a mentally ill person but an impoverished woman with a sharp tongue and a bad temper" (p. 301). He goes on to say that "witchcraft was, in fact, never considered a variety of possession either by witch hunters, the general populace, or modern historians" (p. 306). To say "never" may be overstating the case; clearly, some mentally ill people were punished as witches. Otherwise, as you will see in the next section, why did some physicians and thinkers go to great lengths to expose the fallacies of the connection? In the case of witchcraft and mental illness,

the confusion may be due, in part, to a confusion about demonic possession. Even Robert Burton (1576–1640) an enlightened physican-scholar, in his classic work *Anatomy of Melancholia* (1621) (the older term for depression), considered demonic possession as a potential cause of the disorder. There were two types of demonically possessed people—those physically possessed were considered mad; those spiritually possessed were likely considered witches. With time, the distinctions between these two categories may have blurred in the eyes of historians, thus resulting in a less-than-accurate perception that witchcraft and mental illness were connected more frequently than was the case.

The changing view of the relationship between witchcraft and mental illness points to an even broader issue—the difficulties of interpreting historical events accurately. We will discuss this concept in more depth in the Unresolved Issues section at the end of this chapter.

Toward Humanitarian Approaches

During the latter part of the Middle Ages and the early Renaissance, scientific questioning reemerged and a movement emphasizing the importance of specifically human interests and concerns began—a movement (still with us today) that can be loosely referred to as humanism. Consequently, the superstitious beliefs that had retarded the understanding and therapeutic treatment of mental disorders began to be challenged.

As the notion spread in the Middle Ages that madness was caused by satanic possession, exorcism became a treatment of choice.

The Resurgence of Scientific Questioning in Europe

Paracelsus, a Swiss physician (1490–1541), was an early critic of superstitious beliefs about possession. He insisted that the dancing mania was not a possession but a form of disease, and that it should be treated as such. He also postulated a conflict between the instinctual and spiritual nature of human beings, formulated the idea of psychic causes for mental illness, and advocated treatment by "bodily magnetism," later called hypnosis (Mora, 1967). Although Paracelsus rejected demonology, his view of abnormal behavior was colored by his belief in astral influences (lunatic is derived from the Latin word *luna* or "moon"). He was convinced that the moon exercised a supernatural influence over the brain—an idea, incidentally, that persists among some people today. Paracelsus defied the medical and theological traditions of his time; he often burned the works of Galen and others of whom he disapproved. Had he been more restrained and diplomatic in his efforts, he might have exerted more influence over the scientific thinking of his day. Instead, he became known more for his arrogance than for his scientific advances.

During the sixteenth century, Teresa of Avila (1515–1582) a Spanish nun who was later canonized, made an extraordinary conceptual leap that has influenced thinking to the present day. Teresa, in charge of a group of cloistered nuns who had become hysterical and were therefore in danger from the Spanish Inquisition, argued convincingly that her nuns were not possessed but rather were "as if sick" (*comas enfermas*). Apparently, she did not mean that they were sick of body. Rather, in the expression "as if," we have what is perhaps the first suggestion that a mind can be ill just as a body can be ill. It was a momentous suggestion, which apparently began as a kind of metaphor but was, with time, accepted as fact: People came to see mental illness as an entity, and the "as if" dropped out of use (Sarbin & Juhasz, 1967).

Johann Weyer (1515–1588), a German physician and writer who wrote under the Latin name of Joannus Wierus, was so deeply disturbed by the imprisonment, torture, and burning of people accused of witchcraft that he made a careful study of the entire problem. About 1563 he published a book, *The Deception of Demons*, which contains a step-by-step rebuttal of the *Malleus Maleficarum*, a witch-hunting handbook published in 1486 for use in recognizing and dealing with those suspected of being witches. In his book, Weyer argued that a considerable number, if not all, of those imprisoned, tortured, and burned for witchcraft were really sick in mind or body, and consequently that great wrongs were being committed against innocent people. Weyer's work received the approval of a few outstanding physicians and theologians of his time. Mostly, however, it met with vehement protest and condemnation.

Weyer was one of the first physicians to specialize in mental disorders, and his wide experience and progressive views justify his reputation as the founder of modern psychopathology. Unfortunately, however, he was too far ahead of his time. He was scorned by his peers, many of whom called him "Weirus Hereticus" and "Weirus Insanus." His works were banned by the Church and remained so until the twentieth century.

Perhaps there is no better illustration of the developing spirit of scientific skepticism in the sixteenth century than the works of the Oxford-educated Reginald Scot (1538–1599). Scot devoted his life to exposing the fallacies of witchcraft and demonology. In his book, *Discovery of Witchcraft*, published in 1584, he convincingly and daringly denied the existence of demons, devils, and evil spirits as the cause of mental disorders:

> These women are but diseased wretches suffering from melancholy, and their words, actions, reasoning, and gestures show that sickness has affected their brains and impaired their powers of judgment (In Castiglioni, 1946, p. 253).

King James I of England (1566–1625), however, came to the rescue of demonology, personally refuted Scot's thesis, and ordered his book seized and burned.

The clergy, however, were beginning to question the practices of the time. For example, St. Vincent de Paul (1576–1660), at the risk of his life, declared: "Mental disease is no different to bodily disease and Christianity demands of the humane and powerful to protect, and the skillful to relieve the one as well as the other."

In the face of such persistent advocates of science, who continued their testimonies throughout the next two centuries, demonology and superstition gave ground. These advocates gradually paved the way for the return of observation and reason, which culminated in the development of modern experimental and clinical approaches.

The Establishment of Early Asylums and Shrines

From the sixteenth century on, special institutions called **asylums,** meant solely for the care of the mentally ill, grew in number. The early asylums were begun as a way of removing from society troublesome individuals who could not care for themselves. Although scientific inquiry into understanding abnormal behavior was on the increase, most early asylums, often referred to as madhouses, were not pleasant places or "hospitals" but primarily residences or storage places for the insane. The unfortunate residents lived and died amid conditions of incredible filth and cruelty.

Cultural Variation in Early Asylums In 1547 the monastery of St. Mary of Bethlehem at London was officially made into an asylum by Henry VIII. Its name soon was contracted to Bedlam, and it became widely known for its deplorable conditions and practices. The more violent patients were exhibited to the public for one penny a look, and the more harmless inmates were forced to seek charity on the streets of London in the manner described by Shakespeare: "Bedlam beggars, who, with roaring voices . . . Sometime with lunatic bans, sometime with prayers, enforce their charity" (*King Lear*, II. iii).

Such asylums for the mentally ill were gradually established in other countries. The San Hipolito, established in Mexico in 1566 by philanthropist Bernardino Alvares, was the first asylum established in the Americas. The first such hospital in France, La Maison de Charenton, was founded in 1641 in a suburb of Paris. An asylum was established in Moscow in 1764, and the notorious Lunatics' Tower in Vienna was constructed in 1784. This structure was a showplace in Old Vienna, an ornately decorated round tower within which were square rooms. The doctors and "keepers" lived in the square rooms, while the patients were confined in the spaces between the walls of the rooms and the outside of the tower. The patients were put on exhibit to the public for a small fee.

These early asylums were primarily modifications of penal institutions, and the inmates were treated more like beasts than like human beings. The following passage describes the treatment of the chronically insane in La Bicêtre, a hospital in Paris. This treatment was typical of the asylums of the period and continued through most of the eighteenth century.

> The patients were ordinarily shackled to the walls of their dark, unlighted cells by iron collars which held them flat against the wall and permitted little movement. Ofttimes there were also iron hoops around the waists of the patients and both their hands and feet were chained. Although these chains usually permitted enough movement that the patients could feed themselves out of bowls, they often kept them from being able to lie down at night. Since little was known about nutrition, and the patients were presumed to be animals anyway, little attention was paid to whether they were adequately fed or to whether the food was good or bad. The cells were furnished only with straw and were never swept or cleaned; the patient remained in the midst of all the accumulated odor. No one visited the cells except at feeding time, no provision was made for warmth, and even the most elementary gestures of humanity were lacking. (Modified from Selling, 1943, pp. 54–55)

In the United States, the Pennsylvania Hospital at Philadelphia, completed under the guidance of Benjamin Franklin in 1756, provided some cells or wards for mental patients. The Public Hospital in Williamsburg, Virginia, constructed in 1773, was the first hospital in the United States devoted exclusively to mental patients. The treatment of mental patients in the United States was no better than that offered by European institutions. Zwelling's (1985) review of Public Hospital's treatment methods shows that, initially, the philosophy of treatment involved the view that patients needed to choose rationality over insanity. Thus the treatment techniques were aggressive, aimed at restoring a "physical balance in the body and brain." These techniques, though based on the scientific views of the day, were designed to intimidate patients. They included powerful drugs, water treatments, bleeding and blistering, electrical shocks, and physical restraints. For example, a violent patient might be plunged into ice water or a listless patient into hot water; frenzied patients might be administered drugs to exhaust them; or patients might be bled in order to drain their system of "harmful" fluids. Early estimates of the cure rate for patients at the hospital were only about 20 percent.

Even as late as 1830, new patients had their heads shaved, were dressed in straitjackets, put on sparse diets, compelled to swallow some active purgative, and placed in dark cells. If these procedures did not quiet unruly or excited patients, more severe measures, such as starvation, solitary confinement, cold baths, and other torture-like methods, were used (Bennett, 1947).

The Geel Shrine   There were a few bright spots in this otherwise bleak situation. Out of the more humane Christian tradition of prayer, laying on of hands (or holy touch), and visits to shrines, there arose several great shrines where treatment by kindness and love stood out in marked contrast to prevailing conditions. The shrine at Geel in Belgium, visited since the thirteenth century, is probably the most famous. Legend has it that hidden in the forest of Geel is the body of a young princess who, upon the death of her mother, had dedicated her life to the poor and mentally disturbed. She was later slain by her incestuous father. Years later, five lunatics who spent the night in the forest recovered their mental health. Villagers believed that the princess, reincarnated as St. Dymphna, was responsible for the cures. Pilgrimages to Geel were organized for the mentally sick; many of the patients stayed on to live with the local inhabitants (Karnesh & Zucker, 1945). The colony of Geel has continued its work into modern times (Aring, 1974, 1975a; Belgian Consulate, 1994). Today, a new psychiatric hospital has been built in Geel, and nearly 1000 mental patients live in private homes with "foster families," work in community-based centers, and suffer few restrictions other than not drinking alcohol. Many types of mental disorders are represented, including schizophrenia, mood disorder, antisocial personality, and mental retardation. Ordinarily, patients remain in Geel until they are considered recovered by a supervising therapist. It is unfortunate that the great humanitarian work of this colony—and the opportunity it affords to study the treatment of patients in a family and community setting—has received so little recognition.

Humanitarian Reform

Clearly, by the late eighteenth century, most mental hospitals in Europe and America were in great need of reform. The humanitarian treatment of patients received great impetus from the work of Philippe Pinel (1745–1826) in France.

Pinel's Experiment   In 1792, shortly after the first phase of the French Revolution, Pinel was placed in charge of La Bicêtre in Paris. In this capacity, he received the grudging permission of the Revolutionary Commune to remove the chains from some of the inmates as an experiment to test his views that mental patients should be treated with kindness and consideration—as sick people, not as vicious beasts or criminals. Had his experiment proved a failure, Pinel might have lost his head, but fortunately it was a great success. Chains were removed; sunny rooms were provided; patients were permitted to exercise on the hospital grounds; and kindness was extended to these poor beings, some of whom had been chained in dungeons for 30 years or more. The effect was almost miraculous. The previous noise, filth, and abuse were replaced by order and peace. As Pinel said: "The whole discipline was marked with regularity and kindness which had the most favorable effect on the insane themselves, rendering even the most furious more tractable" (Selling, 1943, p. 65).

Interestingly, a historical document, subsequently found in the French Archives, raises some question about the beginning of humanitarian reforms in France. The document provided by Jean-Baptiste Pussin (Pinel's predecessor at the Bicêtre) indicated that he had been the head of the hospital beginning in 1784 and had removed some of the chains from patients and employed more humane straitjackets instead. He also pointed out in the document that he had issued orders forbidding the staff from beating patients (Weiner, 1979).

Regardless of whether Pussin or Pinel began the reform at the Bicêtre, Pinel is nevertheless given the credit for carrying out the extensive humanitarian effort (Reisman, 1991). The reactions of these patients when all their chains were removed for the first time was telling. One patient, an English officer who had years before killed a guard in an attack of fury, tottered outside on legs weak from lack of use, and for the first time in some 40 years saw the sun and sky. With tears in his eyes he exclaimed, "Oh, how beautiful!" (Zilboorg & Henry, 1941, p. 323). When night came, he voluntarily returned to his cell, which had been cleaned during his absence, to fall peacefully asleep on his new bed. After two years of orderly behavior, including helping to handle other patients, he was pronounced recovered and permitted to leave the hospital. Pinel himself was once saved from a mob that accused him of antirevolutionary activities by a soldier whom he had freed from asylum chains.

Pinel was later given charge of La Salpêtrière hospital, where the same reorganization was instituted with similar results. La Bicêtre and La Salpêtrière hospitals thus became the first modern hospitals for the care of the insane. Pinel's successor, Jean Esquirol (1772–1840), continued Pinel's good work at La Salpêtrière and, in addi-

This painting shows Philippe Pinel supervising the unchaining of inmates at La Bicêtre hospital. Pinel's experiment represented both a great reform and a major step in devising humanitarian methods of treating mental disorders.

tion, helped establish ten new mental hospitals. Incidentally, in his classic textbook *Mental Maladies,* Esquirol attributes the origin of the humane treatment at La Bicêtre to Pinel and makes no mention of Pussin as having initiated reforms:

> . . . but Pinel made himself master of it, and changed the lot of the insane. The chains were broken, the insane were treated with humanity, hope gained hearts, and a more rational system of therapeutics, directed to the treatment. (1845, p. 10)

These hospitals put France in the forefront of humane treatment for the mentally disturbed and "signalled

Viewed from a contemporary perspective the scene depicted in this nineteenth-century drawing appears inhumane and degrading. However, hydrotherapy treatment, as shown here at St. Anne's Hospital in Paris in 1868, was considered a standard treatment method.

the end of the indiscriminate mixture of paupers and criminals, the physically sick, and the mentally deranged" (Rosenblatt, 1984, p. 246).

Tuke's Work in England   At about the same time that Pinel was reforming La Bicêtre, an English Quaker named William Tuke (1732–1822) established the York Retreat, a pleasant country house where mental patients lived, worked, and rested in a kindly religious atmosphere (Narby, 1982). This retreat represented the culmination of a noble battle against the brutality, ignorance, and indifference of his time.

As word of Pinel's amazing results spread to England, Tuke's small force of Quakers gradually gained support from John Connolly, Samuel Hitch, and other great English medical practitioners. In 1841 Hitch introduced trained nurses into the wards at the Gloucester Asylum and put trained supervisors at the head of the nursing staffs. These innovations, quite revolutionary at the time, were of great importance not only in improving the care of mental patients but also in changing public attitudes toward the mentally disturbed by showing that they deserved better treatment.

Rush and Moral Management in America   The success of Pinel's and Tuke's humanitarian experiments revolutionized the treatment of mental patients throughout the Western world. In the United States, this revolution was reflected in the work of Benjamin Rush

(1745–1813), the founder of American psychiatry, who incidentally had earlier been one of the signers of the Declaration of Independence. While associated with the Pennsylvania Hospital in 1783, Rush encouraged more humane treatment of the mentally ill; wrote the first systematic treatise on psychiatry in America, *Medical Inquiries and Observations upon the Diseases of the Mind* (1812); and was the first American to organize a course in psychiatry. But even he did not escape entirely from established beliefs of his time. His medical theory was tainted with astrology, and his principal remedies were bloodletting and purgatives. In addition, he invented and used a device called "the tranquilizing chair," which was probably more torturous than tranquil for patients. The chair was thought to lessen the force of the blood on the head while the muscles are relaxed. Despite these limitations, we can consider Rush an important transitional figure between the old era and the new.

During the early part of this period of humanitarian reform, the use of **moral management**—a wide-ranging

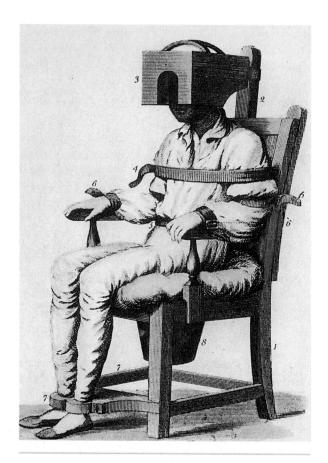

Early engraving depicting a chair similar to the "tranquilizing chair" developed by Benjamin Rush around 1800. An agitated patient was strapped in and then whirled around rapidly until he or she became more docile.

method of treatment that focused on a patient's social, individual, and occupational needs—became relatively widespread. This approach, which stemmed largely from the work of Pinel and Tuke, began in Europe during the late eighteenth century and in America during the early nineteenth century. Rees (1957) described the approach this way:

> The insane came to be regarded as normal people who had lost their reason as a result of having been exposed to severe psychological and social stresses. These stresses were called the moral causes of insanity, and moral treatment aimed at relieving the patient by friendly association, discussion of his difficulties, and the daily pursuit of purposeful activity; in other words, social therapy, individual therapy, and occupational therapy. (pp. 306–307)

Changes at Williamsburg's Public Hospital reflected this change in attitude. First, the hospital was renamed the Williamsburg Lunatic Asylum to reflect "the view that the mentally ill were innocent victims who required protection from society" (Zwelling, 1985, p. 30). Treatment regimens were also changed. There were fewer physical restraints, more open wards, and opportunities to practice positive activities such as farming and carpentry. Social activities, some involving members of the opposite sex, were incorporated into the daily activities of the patients.

Moral treatment in asylums was actually part of a broader movement in which more humane treatment of physical illness in hospitals was being provided for patients, usually people from the poorer classes (Luchins, 1990). A great deal more emphasis was placed in both the general hospitals and asylums on the patients' moral and spiritual development and on rehabilitation of their "character" than on their physical or mental disorders, perhaps because very little effective treatment was available for these conditions at the time. The treatment or rehabilitation of the physical or mental disorders was usually through manual labor and spiritual discussion along with humane treatment.

Moral management achieved a high degree of effectiveness—all the more amazing because it was done without the benefit of the antipsychotic drugs used today and because many of the patients were probably suffering from syphilis, the then-incurable disease of the central nervous system. In the 20-year period between 1833 and 1853, Worcester State Hospital's discharge rate for patients who had been ill less than one year before admission was 71 percent. Even for patients with a longer preadmission disorder, the discharge rate was 59 percent (Bockhoven, 1972).

Despite its reported effectiveness in many cases, moral management was nearly abandoned by the latter part of the nineteenth century. The reasons were many and varied. Among the more obvious ones were the ethnic prejudice that came with the rising immigrant population, leading to tension between staff and patients; the failure of the movement's leaders to train their own replacements; and the overextension of hospital facilities, reflecting the misguided belief that bigger hospitals would differ from smaller ones only in size.

Two other reasons for the demise of moral management are, in retrospect, truly ironic. One was the rise of the **mental hygiene movement,** which advocated a method of treatment that focused almost exclusively on the physical well-being of hospitalized mental patients. Although the creature comforts of patients may have improved under the mental hygienists, the patients received no help for their mental problems and thus were subtly condemned to helplessness and dependency.

Advances in biomedical science also contributed to the demise of moral management and the rise of the mental hygiene movement. These advances fostered the notion that all mental disorders would eventually yield to biological explanations and biologically based treatments (Luchins, 1990). Thus the psychological and social environment of a patient was considered largely irrelevant; the best one could do was keep the patient comfortable until a biological cure was discovered. Needless to say, the anticipated biological cure-all did not arrive, and by the late 1940s and early 1950s discharge rates were down to about 30 percent. We do better today, with discharge rates above 90 percent, but these improved rates are a recent development due to many factors, including advances in drug therapy and a trend to release many patients for continued care in their communities. Controversy over inpatient psychiatric care is still with us today. As you will see in Chapter 18, where the issue of deinstitutionalization is discussed, there is great concern that patients might be released from hospital care before they are ready. Part of this problem comes from the fact that the care that is available in the community often does not meet acceptable standards. (See Highlight 2.3 Modern Life, which discusses psychiatric hospitalization.)

Notwithstanding its negative effects on the use of moral management, the mental hygiene movement has accounted for many humanitarian accomplishments.

Dix and the Mental Hygiene Movement Dorothea Dix (1802–1887) was an energetic New England schoolteacher who became a champion of poor and "forgotten" people in prisons and mental institutions for decades during the nineteenth century. Dix, herself a child of very difficult and impoverished circumstances (Viney, 1996), later became an important driving force in humane treatment for psychiatric patients. As a young adult she worked as a schoolteacher but was later forced into early retirement because of recurring attacks of tuberculosis. In 1841 she began to teach in a women's prison. Through this contact she became acquainted with the deplorable conditions in jails, almshouses, and asylums. In a "Memorial" submitted to the U.S. Congress in 1848, she stated that she had seen

> more than 9000 idiots, epileptics and insane in the United States, destitute of appropriate care and protection . . . bound with galling chains, bowed beneath fetters and heavy iron bails attached to drag-chains, lacerated with ropes, scouraged with rods and terrified beneath storms of execration and cruel blows; now subject to jibes and scorn and torturing tricks; now abandoned to the most outrageous violations. (Zilboorg & Henry, 1941, pp. 583–584)

As a result of her findings, Dix carried on a zealous campaign between 1841 and 1881 that aroused people and legislatures to do something about the inhuman treatment accorded the mentally ill. Through her efforts, the mental hygiene movement grew in America: millions of dollars were raised to build suitable hospitals, and 20 states responded directly to her appeals. Not only was she instrumental in improving conditions in American hospitals, but she directed the opening of two large institutions in Canada and completely reformed the asylum system in Scotland and several other countries. She is credited with establishing 32 mental hospitals, an astonishing record considering the ignorance and superstition that still prevailed in the field of mental health. She rounded out her career by organizing the nursing forces of the northern armies during the Civil War. A resolution presented by the U.S. Congress in 1901 characterized her as "among the noblest examples of humanity in all history" (Karnesh, with Zucker, 1945, p. 18).

Later critics have claimed that establishing hospitals for the mentally ill and increasing the number of people in them created overcrowded facilities and custodial care (Bockhoven, 1972; Dain, 1964). These critics have claimed further that housing patients in institutions away from society, interfered with the treatment of the day (moral therapy) and deferred the search for more appropriate and effective treatments for mental disorders (Bockhoven, 1972). These criticisms, however, do not consider the context in which Dix's contributions wer' made (see the Unresolved Issues section at the end of ' chapter). Her advocacy of the humane treatment

MODERN LIFE

Psychiatric Hospitalization

During the last decades of the twentieth century, our society has seemingly come full circle with respect to providing humane care for the mentally ill in the hospital environment. Recent years have seen great efforts to close down mental hospitals and to return psychiatrically disturbed people to the community, ostensibly as a means of providing more integrated and humane treatment than was available in the "isolated" environment of the psychiatric hospital. Large numbers of psychiatric hospitals have now closed and there has been a significant reduction in state and county mental hospital populations, from over a half million in 1950 (Lerman, 1981) to about 100,000 in recent years (Narrow et al., 1993). These reductions are all the more impressive given that the U.S. population increased substantially over those years. This movement, referred to as **deinstitutionalization,** although motivated by benevolent goals, appears to have created great difficulties for many psychologically disturbed persons and for many communities as well (see Chapter 18 for a full discussion).

The original impetus for the deinstitutionalization policy of recent years was that it was considered more humane (and cost effective) to treat disturbed people outside of the large mental hospitals because it would prevent people from acquiring negative adaptations to hospital confinement. Many professionals were concerned that the mental hospitals were becoming permanent refuges for disturbed people who were "escaping" from the demands of everyday living and were settling into a chronic sick role with a permanent excuse for letting other people take care of them. There was great hope that new medications (see Chapter 16) would promote a healthy readjustment and enable former patients to live more productive lives outside the hospital. The overall philosophy of deinstitutionalization also included the idea that patients would be treated outside of inpatient facilities except for possibly brief periods of hospitalization necessitated by occasional periods of intense crisis. There has been the be-

lief that society wanted and could financially afford to provide better community-based care for chronic patients outside of large mental hospitals. The various approaches that have been implemented to circumvent patient failures to readjust to the community have not been particularly successful at reducing hospital readmissions. For example, after-care treatment in the community—that is, a routine of careful follow-up by trained professional staff who assist disturbed people in establishing close ties with their families and communities and provide them with positive expectations about their recovery—has not been sufficient. Many former patients have not fared well at community living.

The deinstitutionalization movement has generated a great deal of controversy—many authorities now speak of the "abandonment" of chronic patients to a cruel and harsh existence. Evidence of this failure to successfully treat psychiatric patients in the community can be readily seen in our cities: Many of the people living on the streets in large cities today are homeless mentally ill who wander the streets of their neighborhoods. The problems caused by deinstitutalization appear to be due, in no small part, to the failure of society to develop the planned community efforts to fill the gaps in mental health services in the community (Grob, 1994).

The mental institution, once thought to be the most humane way to manage problems of the severely mentally ill, has now come to be seen as obsolete or as an evil alternative and is viewed as more of a problem than a solution to mental health problems. Yet, it is clear that closing mental hospitals and providing treatment for severely disturbed people in the community has not proved to be the panacea it was touted to be only a few years ago. The role of the psychiatric hospital in helping those with severe psychiatric problems is likely to undergo further evolution as society again finds itself unable to deal effectively with the problems that severe mental illness can create if ignored or left unattended. ■

Dorothea Dix (1802–1887) was a tireless reformer who made great strides in changing public attitudes toward the mentally ill.

mentally ill stood in stark contrast to the cruel treatment common at the time (Viney & Bartsch, 1984).

Nineteenth-Century Views of the Causes and Treatment of Mental Disorders

Most of us hold certain views or attitudes not because we have thought them through carefully or molded them out of our experiences but because they were imparted to us through family, school, or social influences—the broad cultural and societal pressures that remain hidden until long after they have ceased to exert their influence. It often takes decades or longer for well-ingrained cultural viewpoints to be amenable to objective interpretation from a different perspective.

Viewed from our contemporary vantage point, for example, well-meaning professionals during the nineteenth century were often quite naive and inaccurate in the ways they conceptualized mental health problems

and generally ineffective in their attempts to treat them. Our understanding of the impact of broader cultural influences in understanding nineteenth-century concepts of mental disorder has recently been illuminated by a historical analysis of the Victorian period by Janet Oppenheim (1991). In an interesting and informative discussion, Oppenheim provides a view of how that era's notions of morality influenced doctors' attempts to understand and treat depression during this "socially repressive" period in England's history.

In the early part of the nineteenth century, mental hospitals were controlled essentially by lay persons because of the prominence of moral management in the treatment of "lunatics." Medical professionals—or *alienists,* as psychiatrists were called at this time in reference to treating the "alienated," or insane—had a relatively inconsequential role in the care of the insane and management of the asylums of the day. Moreover, effective treatments for mental disorders were unavailable, with the only measures being such procedures as drugging, bleeding, or purging, which produced few objective results. However, during the latter part of the century, alienists gained control of the insane asylums and incorporated the traditional moral management therapy into their other rudimentary physical-medical procedures. Over time, the alienists came to have more status and influence in society and during the latter part of the century were influential as purveyors of morality, touting the benefits of Victorian morality as important to good mental health. In this era mental disorders were only vaguely understood, and conditions such as depression were considered to be the result of nervous exhaustion—that is, psychiatrists of the time thought that emotional problems were caused by the expenditure of energy or depletion of bodily energies as a result of excesses in living (see Highlight 2.4). The mental deterioration or "shattered nerves" that supposedly resulted from a person's using up precious nerve force came to be referred to as *neurasthenia,* a condition that involved pervasive feelings of low mood, lack of energy, and physical symptoms that were considered to be related in part to "life style" problems brought on by the demands of civilization. These vague symptoms, viewed by the alienists/psychiatrists as a definable medical condition, were then considered treatable by medical men of the times.

Changing Attitudes Toward Mental Health in the Early Twentieth Century

It is difficult to partition modern views of abnormal behavior into discrete, uniform attitudes or to trace their

Victorian Views of Depression

The Victorians looked upon the notion of depression as a result of energy-depleting activities. In men, for example, the nerve force was thought to be easily depleted through such activities as work, sexual intercourse (see Chapter 11), or even excessive study. Many famous historical figures, such as John Stuart Mill, Charles Dickens, William James, and Herbert Spencer, to mention only a few, were considered to be affected by "nerves" or neurasthenia at some point. Victorian physicians attempted to restore their depleted nerve forces through such means as long vacations, rest, and hydrotherapy, and tonics such as laudanum (an opiate), mercury, and barbiturates.

The Victorian view of women was even more negative—they were seen as extremely fragile, cursed by their biological nature, and especially vulnerable to emotional illness. Nineteenth-century doctors believed that women's nervous problems were tied to their uterus, and signs of anxiety or depression were routinely attributed to uterine disturbances. Interestingly, Victorian men (especially doctors and husbands) "expected women to experience neither sexual desire nor pleasure, and

that, owing in part to utter ignorance about their own bodies, women did, in fact, go through life in a state of sexual anaesthesia" (Oppenheim, 1991 p. 200). Oppenheim points out that Victorian society, with its view that women were inferior to men (biologically, intellectually, and morally) served to keep women out of academic and occupational roles. She points out: "There is no doubt that, generally speaking, the nineteenth-century medical profession considered women's bodies to be defective—suitable companions for their inadequate minds" (p. 190).

The perspective on the powerful and pervasive influence of Victorian thinking provided by Oppenheim gives us more than an interesting picture of the workings of the nineteenth-century mind. It causes us to wonder about the resiliency and veracity of our present-day views. How will our current explanatory views and treatments stand up against viewpoints that will emerge over the coming generations? In a hundred years, will our contemporary views appear as biased and narrow as do those of the medical practitioners of the nineteenth century when viewed from our present perspective? ■

historical precedents without appearing arbitrary and overly simplistic. However, a brief, selective overview here will bring us into the twentieth century and set the scene for our discussion of the major viewpoints and causal considerations in Chapter 3. By the end of the nineteenth century, the mental hospital or asylum—"the big house on the hill"—with its fortresslike appearance, had become a familiar landmark in America. In it, mental patients lived under relatively harsh conditions despite the inroads made by moral management. To the general public, however, the asylum was an eerie place, and its occupants a strange and frightening lot. Little was done by the resident psychiatrists to educate the public to reduce the general fear and horror of insanity. A principal reason for this silence, of course, was that early psychiatrists had little actual information to impart.

Gradually, however, important strides were made toward changing the general public's attitude toward mental patients. In America, the pioneering work of Dix was followed by that of Clifford Beers (1876–1943), whose book *A Mind That Found Itself* was published in 1908. Beers, a Yale graduate, described his own mental collapse and told of the bad treatment he received in three typical institutions of the day. He also explained his eventual recovery in the home of a friendly attendant. Although chains and other torture devices had long since been given up, the straitjacket was still widely used as a means of "quieting" excited patients. Beers experienced this treatment and supplied a vivid description of what such painful immobilization of the arms means to an overwrought mental patient:

Clifford Beers (1876–1943) used his own experiences of incarceration in mental institutions to wage a campaign of public awareness about the need for changes in attitudes toward and treatment of mental patients.

No one incident of my whole life has ever impressed itself more indelibly on my memory. Within one hour's time I was suffering pain as intense as any I ever endured, and before the night had passed that pain had become almost unbearable. My right hand was so held that the tip of one of my fingers was all but cut by the nail of another, and soon knife-like pains began to shoot through my right arm as far as the shoulder. If there be any so curious as to wish to get a slight idea of my agony, let him bite a finger tip as hard as he can without drawing blood. Let him continue the operation for two or three minutes. Then let him multiply that effect, if he can, by two or three hundred. In my case, after four or five hours the excess of pain rendered me partially insensible to it. But for nine hundred minutes—fifteen consecutive hours—I remained in that strait-jacket; and not until the twelfth hour, about breakfast time the next morning, did an attendant so much as loosen a cord. (Beers, 1970, pp. 127–128)

After Beers recovered, he began a campaign to make people realize that such treatment was no way to handle the sick. He soon won the interest and support of many public-spirited individuals, including the eminent psychologist William James and the "dean of American psychiatry," Adolf Meyer.

THE BEGINNING OF THE MODERN ERA

While the mental hygiene movement was gaining ground in the United States during the latter years of the nineteenth century, great technological discoveries were occurring both at home and abroad. These advances helped begin what we know today as the scientific, or experimentally oriented, view of abnormal behavior and the application of scientific knowledge to the treatment of disturbed individuals. We will describe four major themes in abnormal psychology that spanned the nineteenth and twentieth centuries, generating powerful influences on our contemporary perspectives in abnormal behavior. These will be divided into four lines of development (1) biological discoveries, (2) development of a classification system for the mental disorders, (3) the emergence of psychological causation views, and (4) experimental psychological research developments.

Establishing the Link Between the Brain and Mental Disorder

The most immediately apparent advances were in the study of the biological and anatomical factors underlying both physical and mental disorders. A major biomedical breakthrough, for example, came with the discovery of the organic factors underlying *general paresis*—syphilis of the brain. One of the most serious mental illnesses of the day, general paresis produced paralysis and insanity and typically caused death within two to five years. This scientific discovery, however, did not occur overnight; it required the combined efforts of many scientists and researchers for nearly a century.

General Paresis and Syphilis   The discovery of a cure for general paresis began in 1825, when the French physician A. L. J. Bayle differentiated general paresis as a specific type of mental disorder. Bayle gave a complete and accurate description of the symptom pattern of paresis and convincingly presented his reasons for believing paresis to be a distinct disorder. Many years later, in 1897, the Viennese psychiatrist Richard von Krafft-Ebing conducted experiments involving the inoculation of paretic patients with matter from syphilitic sores. None of the patients developed secondary symptoms of syphilis, which led to the conclusion that they must previously have been infected. This crucial experiment established the relationship of general paresis to syphilis. It was almost a decade later, in 1906, when von Wassermann developed a blood test for syphilis. This development made it possible to check for the presence of the deadly spirochetes in the bloodstream of an individual before the more serious consequences of infection appeared. Finally, in 1917 Julius von Wagner-Jauregg, chief of the psychiatric clinic of the University of Vienna, introduced the malarial fever treatment of syphilis and paresis because the high fever associated with malaria killed off the spirochete. He infected nine paretic patients with the blood of a soldier who was ill with malaria and found marked improvement paretic symptoms in three patients and apparent recovery in three others.

Though today we have penicillin as an effective, simpler treatment of syphilis, the early malarial treatment represented, for the first time in history, a clear-cut conquest of a mental disorder by medical science. The field of abnormal psychology had come a long way—from superstitious beliefs to scientific proof of how brain pathology can cause a specific disorder. This breakthrough raised great hopes in the medical community that organic bases would be found for many other mental disorders—perhaps for all of them.

Brain Pathology as a Causal Factor   With the emergence of modern experimental science in the early part of the eighteenth century, knowledge of anatomy, physiology, neurology, chemistry, and general medicine increased rapidly. These advances led to the gradual identification of the biological, or organic, pathology underlying many physical ailments. Scientists began to focus on diseased body organs as the cause of physical ailments. It was only another step for these researchers to assume that mental disorder was an illness based on the pathology of an organ—in this case, the brain. In 1757 Albrecht von Haller (1708–1777), in his *Elements of Physiology,* emphasized the importance of the brain in psychic functions and advocated postmortem dissection to study the brains of the insane. The first systematic presentation of this viewpoint, however, was made by the German psychiatrist Wilhelm Griesinger (1817–1868). In his textbook *The Pathology and Therapy of Psychic Disorders,* published in 1845, Griesinger insisted that all mental disorders could be explained in terms of brain pathology. Following the discovery that brain pathology resulted in general paresis, other successes followed. The brain pathology in cerebral arteriosclerosis and in the senile mental disorders was established by Alois Alzheimer and

other investigators. Eventually in the twentieth century, the organic pathologies underlying the toxic mental disorders (disorders caused by toxic substances such as lead), certain types of mental retardation, and other mental illnesses were discovered.

It is important to note here that although the discovery of the organic bases of mental disorders may have addressed the *how* behind causation, it did not, in most cases, address the question of *why*. This situation is sometimes true to this day. For example, although we know what causes certain "presenile" mental disorders—brain pathology—we do not yet know why some individuals are afflicted and others are not. Nonetheless, we can predict quite accurately the courses of these disorders. This ability is due not only to a greater understanding of the organic factors involved but also, in large part, to the work of a follower of Griesinger, Emil Kraepelin.

The Beginnings of a Classification System   Emil Kraepelin (1856–1926) played a dominant role in the early development of the biological viewpoint. His textbook *Lehrbuch der Psychiatrie,* published in 1883, not only emphasized the importance of brain pathology in mental disorders but also made several related contributions that helped establish this viewpoint. The most important of these contributions was his system of classification of mental disorders, which became the forerunner of today's DSM-IV (discussed in Chapter 1). Kraepelin noted that certain symptom patterns occurred together regularly enough to be regarded as specific types of mental disease. He then proceeded to describe and clarify these types of mental disorders, working out a scheme of classification that is the basis of our present system. The integration of the clinical material underlying this classification was a herculean task and represented a major contribution to the field of psychopathology.

Kraepelin saw each type of mental disorder as distinct from the others and thought that the course of each was as predetermined and predictable as the course of measles. Thus the outcome of a given type of disorder could presumably be predicted even if it could not yet be controlled. Such conclusions led to widespread interest in the accurate description and classification of mental disorders.

Advances Achieved as a Result of Early Biological Views   Although early biologically based thinking was perhaps too widely adopted before its limitations were recognized, it represented the first great advance of modern science toward the understanding and treatment of mental disorder. (See Highlight 2.5 for more recent historic advances in biological therapy-medications.) In turn, there was an enormous research effort to discover specific causes of disorders that would yield to specific medical treatments; researchers looked for damage or disease in particular sections of the brain to find the causes underlying different disorders. Such efforts necessarily involved differentiating various forms of abnormality, leading to a promising system for classifying separate disorders. These were substantial accomplishments. Not all of the consequences of this early thinking were positive, however. Because the disorders best understood in terms of the then-available knowledge were those in which brain damage or deterioration was a central feature (as in general paresis), there naturally developed an expectation that all abnormal behavior would eventually be explained by reference to gross brain pathology. To be sure, organic mental disorders do occur (and we will describe them in Chapter 13), but the vast majority of abnormal behavior is not clearly associated with physical damage to brain tissue. Nonetheless, the medical model—a conceptual model that is inappropriate for much abnormal behavior—became stubbornly entrenched by these early but limited successes. It is important to note that a *medical-model* orientation is not limited to biological viewpoints on the nature of mental disorder. It has also extended into psychosocial theorizing by adopting a symptom/underlying-cause point of view. This point of view assumes that abnormal behavior, even though it may be psychological (rather than biological) in nature, is a symptom of some sort of underlying, internal pathology or "illness"—just as a fever is a symptom of an underlying infection. As we will see shortly, Freud, who was a physician, took this approach in developing his psychoanalytic theory of abnormal behavior.

Establishing the Psychological Basis of Mental Disorder

Despite the emphasis on biological research, understanding of the psychological factors in mental disorders was progressing, too, with the first major steps being taken by Sigmund Freud (1856–1939), generally acknowledged as the most frequently cited psychological theorist of the twentieth century (Street, 1994). During five decades of observation, treatment, and writing, Freud developed a comprehensive theory of psychopathology that emphasized the inner dynamics of unconscious motives (often referred to as *psychodynam-*

ics) that are at the heart of the **psychoanalytic perspective.** The methods he used to study and treat patients came to be called **psychoanalysis.** We can trace the ancestral roots of psychoanalysis in a somewhat unexpected place—the study of hypnosis, especially in its relation to hysteria. Hypnosis, an induced state of relaxation in which a person is highly open to suggestion, first came into widespread use in late eighteenth- and early nineteenth-century France.

Mesmerism   Our efforts to understand psychological causation of mental disorder start with Franz Anton Mesmer (1734–1815), an Austrian physician who further developed Paracelsus' ideas about the influence of the planets on the human body. Mesmer believed that the planets affected a universal magnetic fluid in the body, the distribution of which determined health or disease. In attempting to find cures for mental disorders, Mesmer concluded that all people possessed magnetic forces that could be used to influence the distribution of the magnetic fluid in other people, thus effecting cures.

Mesmer attempted to put his views into practice in Vienna and various other cities, but it was in Paris in 1778 that he gained a broad following. There he opened a clinic in which he treated all kinds of diseases by "animal magnetism." In a dark room, patients were seated around a tub containing various chemicals, and iron rods protruding from the tub were applied to the affected areas of the patients' bodies. Accompanied by music, Mesmer appeared in a lilac robe, passing from one patient to another and touching each one with his hands or his wand. By this means, Mesmer was reportedly able to remove hysterical anesthesias and paralyses. He also demonstrated most of the phenomena later connected with the use of hypnosis.

Eventually branded a charlatan by his medical colleagues, Mesmer was forced to leave Paris and he quickly faded into obscurity. His methods and results, however, were at the center of scientific controversy for many years—in fact, **mesmerism,** as his technique came to be known, was as much a source of heated discussion in the early nineteenth century as psychoanalysis became in the early twentieth century. This discussion led to a renewed interest in hypnosis itself as an explanation of the "cures" that took place.

The Nancy School   Ambrose August Liébeault (1823–1904), a French physician who practiced in the town of Nancy, used hypnosis successfully in his practice. Also in Nancy at the time was a professor of medicine, Hippolyte

Highlight 2.5

Historic Search for Medications to Cure Mental Disorders

Although there were early efforts to use drugs to treat mental disorders, the effective use of medications has a very recent history. For centuries physicians have sought a medicinal cure for mental disorder. One of the earliest extant treatises on the use of drugs to treat mental disorders is the work of the Roman physician Galen (A.D. 130–200). Galen coined the term *apotherapy* for the use of medications to treat human disorders and his writing detail both the concoction of various medications and clinical use of drug therapy with patients experiencing mental disorders. Most of his medications were laxatives and emetics (purgatives) that were used to cleanse the individuals body of non-human materials believed to be causing the person's ills. During the Middle Ages, another notable but highly controversial physician-chemist named Paracelsus (1490–1541) experimented with various chemicals as medications to treat human disorders. Although he used many of the same substances that were widely used by Galen and others—including laxatives and even a substance referred to as "mummy powder" (ground up particles of mummies)—he also experimented with various other seemingly more potent substances such as mercury (also thought to be the key ingredient for synthesizing gold) to treat human disorders.

Despite the many physicians of antiquity who sought cures through medicine, the highly successful use of medication for severe mental disorder has a much briefer history—about 50 years. Nevertheless, this rapidly developing field has made a great impact in a relatively short time on both the treatment and understanding of mental disorders. We will describe here recent historic developments in the area of psychotropic medication—two drugs that emerged in the 1950s with remarkable success. (The use of medication to treat mental disorders will be described more fully in Chapter 16.)

The first of the medications, *reserpine,* was used for centuries as an herbal folk medicine in India. The root, Rauwolfia serpentina was prescribed for a wide array of afflictions, including serpent bites, epilepsy, cataracts, and insanity. The Indian name for the root, *pagla-ka-dawa,* means insanity herb. In 1931, Sen and Bose (Bose, 1932) published an article in an Indian medical journal about the usefulness of Rauwolfia in treating high blood pressure and insanity and in 1943 an article in the *Indian Medical Gazette* reported on the possible beneficial

---

Bernheim (1840–1919), who became interested in the relationship between hysteria and hypnosis. His interest was the result of Liébeault's success in curing by hypnosis a patient who Bernheim had been treating unsuccessfully by more conventional methods for four years (Selling, 1943). Bernheim and Liébeault worked together to develop the hypothesis that hypnotism and hysteria were related and that both were due to suggestion (Brown & Menninger, 1940). Their hypothesis was based on two lines of evidence: (1) the phenomena observed in hysteria, such as paralysis of an arm, inability to hear, or anesthetic areas in which an individual could be stuck with a pin without feeling pain (all of which occurred when there was apparently nothing organically wrong), could be produced in normal subjects by means of hypnosis; and (2) the same symptoms also could be removed by means of hypnosis. Thus it seemed likely that hysteria was a sort of self-hypnosis. The physicians who accepted this view ultimately came to be known as the **Nancy School.**

Meanwhile, Jean Charcot (1825–1893), who was head of the Salpêtrière Hospital in Paris and the leading neurologist of his time, had been experimenting with some of the phenomena described by the mesmerists. As a re-

effects of the root for treating manic depression and schizophrenia. However, further progress in the development of this drug was sidetracked during World War II. In the early 1950s the active ingredient in Rauwolfia, reserpine, was isolated by Ciba, a Swiss drug company, and in 1953 the psychiatrist R. A. Hakim wrote a prize winning paper in India on using Rauwolfia in treating psychosis (cited in Gupta, Deb, & Kahali, 1943). Today reserpine has been surpassed as a treatment for psychoses because of the development of other drugs and because of the side effect symptoms of reserpine (tremor referred to as Parkinsonian symptoms). Today reserpine is mostly used in the treatment of hypertension.

The second psychoactive drug to emerge in the 1950s as a treatment for severe mental disorder was *chlorpromazine*. A German chemist named Bernthesen, searching for compounds that would operate as dyes, first developed the drug in the latter part of the nineteenth century. He synthesized a compound that is referred to as the *phenothiazines*. Paul Erlich, a medical researcher and father of the field of chemotherapy, thought that this compound might be effective in treating human diseases by killing nonhuman cells while preserving human tissue. The drug was first tried as a means of treating malaria, and by the 1930s, was being employed as an anaesthetic because of its sedating qualities. In 1951, the French surgeon, Henri Labroit,

employed the drug as an "artificial hibernator" to prevent shock among surgical patients. It was not until 1952 that two French psychiatrists, Jean Delay and Pierre Deniker, finding that the drug reduced psychotic symptoms, began to use chlorpromazine to treat psychiatric patients.

The almost magic impact of antipsychotic medication was immediately felt in the psychiatric community in the United States. By 1956, the first year of widespread use of reserpine and chlorpromazine, the impact on psychiatric hospitalization had begun to show a remarkable effect. The previously increasing admission rate to psychiatric hospitals leveled off at 560,000 psychiatric inpatients in the United States. This number dropped to 490,000 by 1964 and to 300,000 by 1971!

The effectiveness of drugs at reducing psychotic symptoms has also led researchers to develop more specific causal hypotheses for mental disorders like schizophrenia. Researchers have noted that antipsychotic drugs like the phenothiazines modify the levels of dopamine, a neurotransmitter that is associated with schizophrenia. These observations have led theoreticians to the "dopamine hypothesis"—that the metabolism of dopamine is a associated with the cause of schizophrenia. This development will be discussed further in Chapter 12. ■

Sources: Frankenberg, 1994; Green, 1951; Moriarty, Alagna, & Lake, 1984; Pachter, 1951.

---

sult of his research, Charcot disagreed with the findings of the Nancy School and insisted that degenerative brain changes led to hysteria. In this, Charcot was eventually proved wrong, but work on the problem by so outstanding a scientist did a great deal to awaken medical and scientific interest in hysteria.

The dispute between Charcot and the Nancy School was one of the major debates of medical history, during which many harsh words were spoken on both sides. The adherents of the Nancy School finally triumphed, representing the first recognition of a psychologically caused mental disorder. This recognition spurred more research

on the behavior underlying hysteria and other disorders. Soon it was suggested that psychological factors were also involved in anxiety states, phobias, and other psychopathologies. Eventually, Charcot himself was won over to the new point of view and did much to promote the study of psychological factors in various mental disorders.

The debate over whether mental disorders are caused by biological or psychological factors continues to this day. The Nancy School/Charcot debate represented a major step forward for psychology, however. Toward the end of the nineteenth century, it was clear that mental disorders could have either psychological bases or biological

Mesmer believed that the distribution of magnetic fluid in the body was responsible for determining health or disease. He further thought that all people possessed magnetic forces that could be used to influence the distribution of fluid in others, thus effecting cures. In this painting of his therapy, Mesmer, standing on the far right, holding a wand, was eventually branded a fraud by his colleagues. His theories did, however, demonstrate most of the phenomena later connected with the use of hypnosis.

bases, or both. With this recognition, a major question remained to be answered: How do the psychologically based mental disorders actually develop?

The Beginnings of Psychoanalysis   The first systematic attempt to answer this question was made by Sigmund Freud (1856–1939). Freud was a brilliant young Viennese neurologist who received an appointment as lecturer on nervous diseases at the University of Vienna. In 1885 he went to study under Charcot and later became acquainted with the work of Liébeault and Bernheim at Nancy. He was impressed by their use of hypnosis with hysterical patients and came away convinced that powerful mental processes could remain hidden from consciousness.

On his return to Vienna, Freud worked in collaboration with another physician, Josef Breuer (1842–1925), who had introduced an interesting innovation in the use

of hypnosis with his patients. Unlike hypnotists before him, Freud directed his patients to talk freely about their problems while under hypnosis. The patients usually displayed considerable emotion, and on awakening from their hypnotic states felt a significant emotional release, which was called a **catharsis.** This simple innovation in the use of hypnosis proved to be of great significance: It not only helped patients discharge their emotional tensions by discussing their problems, but it also revealed to the therapist the nature of the difficulties that had brought about certain symptoms. The patients, on awakening, saw no relationship between their problems and their hysterical symptoms.

It was this approach that thus led to the discovery of the **unconscious**—that portion of the mind that contains experiences of which a person is unaware—and with it the belief that processes outside of a person's awareness can play an important role in the determination of behavior. In 1893 Freud and Breuer published their joint paper *On the Psychical Mechanisms of Hysterical Phenomena,* which was one of the great milestones in the study of the dynamics of the conscious and unconscious. Freud soon discovered, moreover, that he could dispense with hypnosis entirely. By encouraging patients to say whatever came into their minds without regard to logic or propriety, Freud found that patients would eventually overcome inner obstacles to remembering and would discuss their problems freely. Two related methods allowed him to understand patients' conscious and unconscious thought processes. One method, **free association,** involved having patients talk freely about themselves, thereby providing information about their feelings, motives, and so forth. A second method, **dream analysis,** involved having patients record and describe their dreams. These techniques helped analysts and patients gain insights and achieve a more adequate understanding of emotional problems. Freud devoted the rest of his long and energetic life to the development and elaboration of psychoanalytic principles. His views were formally introduced to American scientists in 1909, when he was invited to deliver a series of lectures at Clark University by the eminent psychologist G. Stanley Hall, who was then president of the university. These lectures created a great deal of controversy and helped popularize psychoanalytic concepts to scientists as well as the general public.

We will return to a more complete discussion of the psychoanalytic viewpoint in Chapter 3. Next, we will discuss the early developments of psychological research and the evolution of the behavioral perspective in viewing abnormal behavior. Freud's lively and seminal views earned a substantial following over his long career that continues even today— more than a hundred years after he began writing. Numerous other clinician theorists such as Carl Jung, Alfred Adler, and Harry Stack Sullivan launched "spin-off" theories that have contributed a great deal to the elaboration of the psychoanalytic viewpoint. More will be said of these views in Chapter 3.

The Evolution of the Psychological Research Tradition

We consider the origins to much of the scientific thinking in contemporary psychology to lie in early rigorous efforts to objectively study psychological processes as demonstrated by Wilhelm Wundt (1832–1920) and William James (1842–1910). Although the early work of these experimental psychologists did not bear directly on clinical practice or our understanding of abnormal behavior, this tradition was clearly influential a few decades later in molding the thinking of the psychologists who brought these rigorous attitudes into the clinic.

The Early Psychological Laboratories   In 1879 Wilhelm Wundt established the first experimental psychology laboratory at the University of Leipzig. While studying the psychological factors involved in memory and sensation, Wundt and his colleagues devised many basic experimental methods and strategies. Early contributors to the empirical study of abnormal behavior were directly influenced by Wundt; they followed his experimental

Psychoanalysis was introduced to North America at a famous meeting at Clark University in Worcester, Massachusetts, in 1909. Among those present were (back row) A. A. Brill, Ernest Jones, and Sandor Ferenczi; (front row) Sigmund Freud, G. Stanley Hall, and Carl Jung.

methodology and also used some of his research strategies to study clinical problems. For example, a student of Wundt's, J. McKeen Cattell (1860–1944), brought Wundt's experimental methods to the United States and used them to assess individual differences in mental processing. He and other students of Wundt's work established research laboratories throughout the United States.

It was not until 1896, however, that another of Wundt's students, Lightner Witmer (1867–1956), combined research with application and established the first American psychological clinic at the University of Pennsylvania. Witmer's clinic focused on the problems of mentally deficient children, in terms of both research and therapy. Witmer, considered to be the founder of clinical psychology (McReynolds, 1996, 1997), was influential in encouraging others to become involved in the new profession. Other clinics were soon established. One clinic of great importance was the Chicago Juvenile Psychopathic Institute (later called the Institute of Juvenile Research), established in 1909 by William Healy (1869–1963). Healy was the first to view juvenile delinquency as a symptom of urbanization, not as a result of inner psychological problems. In so doing, he was among the first to seize upon a new area of causation—environmental, or sociocultural, factors.

By the first decade of the twentieth century, psychological laboratories and clinics were burgeoning, and a great deal of research was being generated (Reisman, 1991). The rapid and objective communication of scientific findings was perhaps as important in the development of modern psychology (or any science) as the collection and interpretation of research findings. This period saw the origin of many scientific journals for the dissemination of research and theoretical discoveries. Two notable publications in the field of abnormal psychology were the *Journal of Abnormal Psychology,* founded by Morton Prince in 1906, and *The Psychological Clinic,* founded by Lightner Witmer in 1907. (Interestingly, Prince was a psychiatrist who created an outlet for papers on abnormal psychology that were not biological in nature.) As the years have passed, the number of journals has grown. The American Psychological Association now publishes 29 scientific journals, many of which focus on research into abnormal behavior and personality functioning.

The Behavioral Perspective   While psychoanalysis dominated thought about abnormal behavior at the end of the nineteenth and in the early twentieth century, another school—behaviorism—was emerging out of experimental psychology to challenge its supremacy as theories of learning began to be employed to understand abnormal behavior. Behavioral psychologists believed that the study of

subjective experience—through the techniques of free association and dream analysis—did not provide acceptable scientific data, because such observations were not open to verification by other investigators. In their view, only the study of directly observable behavior and the stimuli and reinforcing conditions that "control" it could serve as a basis for formulating scientific principles of human behavior.

The **behavioral perspective** is organized around a central theme: the role of learning in human behavior. Although this perspective was initially developed through research in the laboratory rather than through clinical practice with disturbed individuals, its implications for explaining and treating maladaptive behavior soon became evident.

Classical Conditioning   The origins of the behavioral view of abnormal behavior and its treatment are tied to experimental work on the form of learning known as **classical conditioning.** This work began with the discovery of the conditioned reflex by Russian physiologist Ivan Pavlov (1849–1936). Around the turn of the century, Pavlov demonstrated that dogs would gradually begin to salivate to a nonfood stimulus, such as a bell, after the stimulus had been regularly accompanied by food.

Pavlov's discoveries in classical conditioning excited a young American psychologist, John B. Watson (1878–1958), who was searching for objective ways to study human behavior. Watson reasoned that if psychology was to become a true science, it must abandon the subjectivity of inner sensations and other "mental" events and limit itself to what could be objectively observed. What better way to do this than to observe systematic changes in behavior brought about simply by rearranging stimulus conditions? Watson thus changed the focus of psychology to the study of overt behavior, an approach he called **behaviorism.**

Watson, a man of impressive energy and demeanor, saw great possibilities in behaviorism, and he was quick to point them out to his fellow scientists and a curious public. He boasted that, through conditioning, he could train any healthy child to become whatever sort of adult one wished. He also challenged the psychoanalysts and the more biologically oriented psychologists of his day by suggesting that abnormal behavior was the product of unfortunate, inadvertent earlier conditioning and could be modified through reconditioning.

By the 1930s Watson had made an enormous impact on American psychology. Watson's approach placed heavy emphasis on the role of the social environment in conditioning personality development and behavior, both normal and abnormal. Today's behaviorally oriented psychologists still accept many of the basic tenets of Watson's doctrine, although they are more cautious in their claims.

Ivan Pavlov (1849–1936), a pioneer in demonstrating the part conditioning plays in behavior, is shown here with his staff and some of the apparatus used to condition reflexes in dogs.

Operant Conditioning While Pavlov and Watson were studying antecedent stimulus conditions and their relation to behavioral responses, E. L. Thorndike (1874–1949) and subsequently B. F. Skinner (1904–1990) were exploring a different kind of conditioning—one in which the consequences of behavior influence behavior. Behavior that operates on the environment may be instrumental in producing certain outcomes, and those outcomes, in turn, determine the likelihood that the behavior will be repeated on similar occasions. For example, Thorndike studied how cats could learn a particular response such as pulling a chain if that response was followed by food reinforcement. This type of learning came to be called *instrumental conditioning* and was later renamed **operant conditioning** by Skinner.

In this chapter we have touched upon several important trends in the evolution of the field of abnormal psychology and have recounted the contributions of numerous individuals from history that brought us to our current prevailing views. The vast amount of information available can cause confusion and controversy when it comes to obtaining an integrated view of behavior and causation. We may have left supernatural beliefs behind, but we have moved into something far more complex in trying to determine the role of natural factors—be they biological, psychological, or sociocultural—in abnormal

B. F. Skinner (1904–1990) formulated the concept of operant conditioning, in which reinforcers could be used to make a response more or less probable and frequent.

behavior. For a recap of some of the key contributors to the field of abnormal psychology, see the timeline summary on pages 58–59.

Major Figures in the Early History of Abnormal Psychology

Hippocrates

THE ANCIENT WORLD

Hippocrates (460–377 B.C.) A Greek physician who believed that mental disease was the result of natural causes and brain pathology rather than demonology.

Plato (429–347 B.C.) A Greek philosopher who believed that mental patients should be treated humanely and should not be held responsible for their actions.

Aristotle (384–322 B.C.) A Greek philosopher and a pupil of Plato who believed in the Hippocratic theory that various agents, or humors, within the body, when imbalanced, were responsible for mental disorders. Aristotle rejected the notion of psychological factors as causes of mental disorders.

Galen

Galen (A.D. 130–200) A Greek physician and advocate of the Hippocratic tradition who contributed much to our understanding of the nervous system. Galen divided the causes of mental disorders into physical and mental categories.

Avicenna

THE MIDDLE AGES

Avicenna (980–1037) An Islamic Arabian-born physician who adopted principles of humane treatment for the mentally disturbed at a time when Western approaches to mental illness were the opposite.

Martin Luther (1483–1546) A German theologian and leader of the Reformation who held the belief, common to his time, that the mentally disturbed were possessed by the devil.

Paracelsus (1490–1541) A Swiss physician who rejected demonology as a cause of abnormal behavior. Paracelsus believed in psychic causes of mental illness.

THE SIXTEENTH THROUGH THE EIGHTEENTH CENTURIES

Teresa of Avila (1515–1582) A Canonized Spanish nun who argued that mental disorder was an illness of the mind.

Johann Weyer (1515–1588) A German physician who argued against demonology and was ostracized by his peers and the Church for his progressive views.

Reginald Scot (1538–1599) An Englishman who refuted the notion of demons as the cause of mental disorders and was castigated by King James I.

Teresa of Avila

UNRESOLVED ISSUES

Interpreting Historical Events

One would think that trying to look back in history to get a picture of events that occurred long ago would not be a difficult task—that it would be a simple matter of reviewing some history books and some publications from the time in question. However, our views of history and our understanding of events are constantly open to reinterpretation. As Schudson (1995) recently pointed out: "Collective memory, more than individual memory, at least in liberal pluralistic societies, is provisional. It is always open to contestation" (p. 16). Any number of obstacles can stand in the way of our gaining an accurate picture of the attitudes and behaviors of people who lived hundreds of years ago. This has certainly been the case with our views of the Middle Ages (Kroll & Bachrach, 1984).

The foremost problem in retrospective psychological analysis is that we cannot rely on direct observation, a hallmark of psychological research. Instead, we must turn to written documents or historical surveys of the times. Though these sources are often full of fascinating information, they may not reveal directly the information we seek; we must therefore extrapolate "facts" from the information we have, which is not always an easy task. We are restricted in our conclusions by the documents or sources available to us. Attempting to learn about people's attitudes and subtle social perceptions hundreds of years ago by examining surviving church documents or biographical accounts is less than ideal. First, we inevitably view these documents out of the context in which they were written. Second, we do not know

Benjamin Rush

Robert Burton (1576–1640) An Oxford scholar who wrote a classic, influential treatise on depression, *Anatomy of Melancholia*, in 1621.

William Tuke (1732–1822) An English Quaker who established the York Retreat, where mental patients lived in humane surroundings.

Philippe Pinel (1745–1826) A French physician who pioneered the use of moral management in La Bicêtre and La Salpêtrière hospitals in France, where mental patients were treated in a humane way.

Benjamin Rush (1745–1813) An American physician and the founder of American psychiatry who used moral management, based on Pinel's humanitarian methods, to treat the mentally disturbed.

THE NINETEENTH AND EARLY TWENTIETH CENTURIES

Dorothea Dix (1802–1887) An American teacher who founded the mental hygiene movement in the United States, which focused on the physical well-being of mental patients in hospitals.

Clifford Beers (1876–1943) An American who campaigned to change public attitudes toward mental patients after his own experiences in mental institutions.

Franz Anton Mesmer (1734–1815) An Austrian physician who conducted early investigations into hypnosis as a medical treatment.

Emil Kraepelin (1856–1926), A German psychiatrist who developed the first diagnostic system.

Dorothea Dix

Sigmund Freud

Sigmund Freud (1856–1938) The founder of the school of psychological therapy known as psychoanalysis.

Wilhelm Wundt (1832–1920) A German scientist who established the first experimental psychology laboratory in 1879 and subsequently influenced the empirical study of abnormal behavior.

J. McKeen Cattell (1860–1944) An American psychologist who adopted Wundt's methods and studied individual differences in mental processing.

Lightner Witmer (1867–1956) An American psychologist who established the first psychological clinic in the United States, focusing on problems of mentally deficient children. He also founded the journal *The Psychological Clinic* in 1896.

Ivan Pavlov (1849–1936) A Russian physiologist who published classical studies in the psychology of learning.

William Healy (1869–1963) An American psychologist who established the Chicago Juvenile Psychopathic Institute and advanced the idea that mental illness was due to environmental or sociocultural factors.

John B. Watson (1878–1958) Conducted early research into learning principles and came to be known as the father of behaviorism.

John B. Watson

whether the authors had ulterior motives—or what the real purposes were behind the documents. For example, some historians have concluded erroneously that people of the Middle Ages considered sin to be a major causal factor in mental illness. This misconception may have been due in part to zealous authors invoking "God's punishment" against the victims of mental illnesses who happened to be their enemies. Apparently, if the victims happened to be friends, sin was typically not mentioned as a causal factor (Kroll & Bachrach, 1984). Such writings, of course, are biased, but we may have no way of knowing this. The fewer the sources surveyed, the more likely that any existing bias will go undetected.

In other cases, concepts important to historical interpretation may have quite a different meaning to us today than they did in the past. Or the meaning may simply be unclear. Kroll and Bachrach (1984) pointed out that the concept of "possession"—so critical to our views of the Middle Ages—is

> a very vague and complex concept for which we have no helpful natural models. Our language fails us, except for colourful analogies and metaphors. Just as the term "nervous breakdown" means different things to different people, so too "possession" means and meant many different things, and undoubtedly had a different range of meanings to medieval persons from what it has to us. (p. 510)

This kind of uncertainty can make definitive assessments of the happenings during the Middle Ages difficult—if not impossible.

Bias can come into play during interpretation, also. Our interpretations of historical events or previously held beliefs can be colored by our own views of normal and abnormal. In fact, it is difficult to conduct a retrospective analysis without taking current perspectives and values as a starting point. For example, our modern beliefs about the Middle Ages have led, says Schoeneman (1984), to our contemporary misinterpretation that, during the fifteenth and sixteenth centuries, the mentally ill were typically accused of being witches. For most of us, this interpretation—albeit a wrong one—makes sense simply because we do not understand the medieval perspective on witchcraft.

Although reevaluations of the Middle Ages have minimized the views that demonology, sin, and witchcraft played a key role in the medieval understanding of mental illness, it is also clear that in some cases, these concepts were associated with mental illness. Wherein lies the truth? It appears that the last word has not been written on the Middle Ages, nor on any period of our history, for that matter. At best, historical views—and, therefore, retrospective psychological studies—must be held as working hypotheses that are open to change as new perspectives are applied to history or "new" historical documents are discovered.

On a related topic, some authorities interested in the area of applying psychological thought to the interpretation of historical events have proposed the field of *psychohistory* (DeMause, 1981), which according to Lawton (1990) involves "the interdisciplinary study of why man has acted as he has in history, prominently utilizing psychoanalytic principles" (p. 353). This approach to history (which is not without its critics; see Shephard, 1979) has attempted to provide penetrating analyses of historical figures or historical events using psychological theory, particularly psychoanalysis, to explain events. Such an approach to studying or reinterpreting historical events is fraught with validational problems and may be viewed as providing "plausible" applications of the particular theory in question rather than as revelations of fact about the event itself. Historical events, of course, are often ambiguous and open to considerable interpretation and reinterpretation before they become "written history." The final version of a particular event is often debated long after the ink has dried on the historical tomes reporting and interpreting it.

Even when historical events are relatively recent it may not be an easy task for well-meaning individuals to accurately reconstruct what actually happened. A recent example of the difficulties of conducting a psychological reconstruction of historical events, or "psychological autopsy," can be found in the highly publicized case of the explosion aboard the *USS Iowa*. In 1989, an explosion in a gun emplacement on this U.S. Navy ship killed 47 people on board and led to the retirement of the famous battleship. Investigation of the incident by the Navy and the FBI initially ruled out the possibility of accident or sabotage and placed the blame for the accident on a sailor who was alleged to be a psychologically disturbed homosexual who was thought to have intentionally caused the accident in an effort to commit suicide. A controversy followed, prompting a congressional investigation into the accident and the Navy's attribution of blame to the sailor. As part of the congressional panel to evaluate the potential cause of the accident and evaluate whether the sailor being accused of creating the accident had done so, 14 noted psychologists were asked to review the existing information about the sailor in question and develop a psychological autopsy concerning the sailor's psychological state at the time of the incident. Eleven of the 14 panelists were critical of the Navy's conclusions and raised doubts about the FBI's report on the sailor's mental health status at the time of the accident. Considerable disagreement was found in the expert opinion reports, especially for detailed judgments, and agreement was obtained for only the broad categories. Recent studies (Otto, Poythress, Starr, & Darkes, 1993) have suggested caution in the use of psychological autopsies for such cases because the expert reviewers were notably inconsistent in their judgments.

SUMMARY

Understanding of abnormal behavior over the centuries has not proceeded smoothly or uniformly; the steps have been uneven with great gaps between, and unusual, even bizarre views or beliefs have often sidetracked researchers and theorists. The dominant social, economic, and religious views of the times have had a profound influence over how people view abnormal behavior, as have advances in the physical and biological sciences. Great strides have been made in our understanding of abnormal behavior in the twentieth century, and we can trace a general movement away from superstitions and "magic" toward reasoned, scientific studies.

In the ancient world superstitions were followed by the emergence of medical concepts in many places, such as Egypt and Greece; many of these concepts were developed and refined by Roman physicians. With the fall of Rome near the end of the fifth century A.D., most Europeans returned to superstitious views, which dominated popular thinking about mental disorders for over 1000 years. In the fifteenth and sixteenth centuries, it was still widely believed, even by scholars, that mentally disturbed people were possessed by a devil.

During the latter stages of the Middle Ages and early Renaissance, a spirit of scientific questioning reappeared in

Europe, and several noted physicians spoke out against inhumane treatments, arguing that "possessed" individuals were actually "sick of mind" and should be treated as such. With this recognition of a need for the special treatment of disturbed people came the founding of various "asylums" toward the end of the sixteenth century. However, with institutionalization came the isolation and maltreatment of mental patients; slowly, this situation was recognized, and in the eighteenth century, further efforts were made to help afflicted individuals by providing them with better living conditions and humane treatment, though these were likely the exception rather than the rule.

The nineteenth and early twentieth centuries witnessed a number of scientific and humanitarian advances. The work of Philippe Pinel in France, William Tuke in England, and Benjamin Rush and Dorothea Dix in the United States prepared the way for several important developments in contemporary abnormal psychology. Among these were the gradual acceptance of mental patients as afflicted individuals who needed and deserved professional attention; the success of biomedical methods as applied to disorders; and the growth of scientific research into the biological, psychological, and sociocultural roots of abnormal behavior.

In the nineteenth century great technological discoveries and scientific advancements were made in the biological sciences that aided in the understanding and treatment of disturbed individuals. A major biomedical breakthrough, for example, came with the discovery of the organic factors underlying general paresis—syphilis of the brain—one of the most serious mental illnesses of the day.

Our modern scientific views of abnormal behavior have several historical branches. Three main themes were highlighted in this chapter: (1) the biological, (2) the psychodynamic, and (3) the psychological research viewpoints. These viewpoints will be further addressed in Chapter 3.

In the early part of the eighteenth century, knowledge of anatomy, physiology, neurology, chemistry, and general medicine increased rapidly. These advances led to the identification of the biological, or organic, pathology underlying many physical ailments. The development of a psychiatric classification system by Kraepelin played a dominant role in the early development of the biological viewpoint. Kraepelin's work (a forerunner to the DSM system) helped to establish the importance of brain pathology in mental disorders and made several related contributions that helped establish this viewpoint.

The first major steps toward understanding psychological factors in mental disorders were taken by Sigmund Freud. During five decades of observation, treatment, and writing, he developed a theory of psychopathology, known as psychoanalysis, that emphasized the inner dynamics of unconscious motives. Over the last half century, other clinicians have modified and revised Freud's theory, evolving into new psychodynamic perspectives.

Finally, the scientific investigation into psychological factors and human behavior began to make progress in the latter part of the nineteenth century also. The end of the nineteenth and the early twentieth centuries saw experimental psychology evolve into clinical psychology with the development of clinics to study as well as intervene in abnormal behavior. Two major schools of learning paralleled this development and behaviorism emerged as an explanatory model in abnormal psychology. The behavioral perspective is organized around a central theme—that learning plays an important role in human behavior. Although this perspective was initially developed through research in the laboratory, unlike psychoanalysis, which emerged out of clinical practice with disturbed individuals, it has been shown to have important implications for explaining and treating maladaptive behavior.

Understanding the history of viewpoints on psychopathology, with its forward steps and its reverses, helps us understand the emergence of modern concepts of abnormal behavior. This knowledge also provides us with a perspective for understanding current and future advances.

KEY TERMS

insanity (p. 34)

mass madness (p. 37)

tarantism (p. 37)

Saint Vitus's dance (p. 37)

lycanthropy (p. 37)

exorcism (p. 38)

asylums (p. 41)

moral management (p. 44)

mental hygiene movement (p. 45)

deinstitutionalization (p. 46)

psychoanalytic perspective (p. 51)

psychoanalysis (p. 51)

mesmerism (p. 51)

Nancy School (p. 52)

catharsis (p. 54)

unconscious (p. 54)

free association (p. 55)

dream analysis (p. 55)

behavioral perspective (p. 56)

classical conditioning (p. 56)

behaviorism (p. 56)

operant conditioning (p. 57)

CHAPTER THREE

Causal Factors and Viewpoints in Abnormal Psychology

Elsie Blankenhorn, *Banknote*. Born in 1873, Blankenhorn grew up in a privileged family. Her father suffered with manic depression, and died in 1906. After his death, she was hospitalized in a private psychiatric clinic, where she remained until 1921. Diagnosed with catatonia and dementia praecox, she recorded her private, inner thoughts in diaries and albums. She often drew bank notes with imaginary numbers and "guardian angels."

We saw in the last chapter that speculation about the causes of abnormal behavior goes back very far in human history. From early times those who observed disordered behavior grappled with the question of its cause. Hippocrates, for example, suggested that an imbalance in bodily humors produced abnormal behavior. To other observers the cause was possession by demons or evil spirits. Later, bodily dysfunction was suggested as a cause.

Each attempt at identifying a cause brought with it a theory, or model, of abnormal behavior. Hippocrates' theory, a type of disease model, posited the existence of four bodily humors that were connected with certain kinds of behavior. Other theories similarly grew out of attempts to identify causes.

Today we are still puzzling over the causes of abnormal behavior, and speculation about causes continues to give rise to new models of abnormality. Since the beginning of this century, several important schools of thought developed elaborate models to explain the origins of abnormal behavior and to suggest how it might be treated. We will discuss each of these theoretical perspectives in this chapter, giving attention to the causal factors each has identified.

We will first consider biological viewpoints. These emphasize genetic and organic conditions that impair brain and bodily functioning and lead to psychopathology. From there we will move on to psychosocial approaches. Of the psychosocial viewpoints, the psychodynamic focuses on intrapsychic conflicts that lead to anxiety; the behavioral, on faulty learning; and the cognitive-behavioral, on types of information processing that lead to distorted thinking. We will look briefly, too, at the sociocultural viewpoint, which focuses on pathological social conditions and the importance of differing cultural backgrounds in shaping both vulnerability to psychopathology and the form psychopathology may take. In recent years, many theorists working in this area have come to recognize the need for a more integrative viewpoint called the *biopsychosocial viewpoint* that acknowledges the idea that biological, psychosocial, and sociocultural factors all interact and play a role. First, however, we need to address the nature of causation of abnormal behavior.

Causes and Risk Factors for Abnormal Behavior

Central to the field of abnormal psychology are questions about what causes people to behave maladaptively. If we knew the causes for given disorders, we might be able to prevent conditions that lead to them and perhaps reverse those that maintain them. We could also classify and diagnose disorders better if we clearly understood their causes rather than relying on clusters of symptoms, as we usually do now.

Although understanding the causes of abnormal behavior is clearly a desirable goal, it is enormously difficult to achieve because human behavior is so complex. Even the simplest human behavior, such as speaking or writing a single word, is the product of thousands of prior events—the connections among which are not always clear. Attempting to understand a person's life in causal terms, even an "adaptive" life, is a task of enormous magnitude; when the life is a maladaptive one, it is even more difficult. As a result, many investigators now prefer to speak of risk factors (variables correlated with an abnormal outcome) rather than of causes. Nevertheless, understanding causes remains the ultimate goal.

In analyzing causal factors of abnormal behavior, it is helpful to consider (1) the distinctions between necessary, sufficient, and contributory causes; (2) the problem of feedback and circularity in abnormal behavior; and (3) the concept of diathesis-stress as a broad causal model of abnormal behavior.

Necessary, Sufficient, and Contributory Causes

Regardless of one's theoretical perspective, several terms can be used to specify the role a factor plays in the **etiology,** or causal pattern, of abnormal behavior. A **necessary cause** is a condition that must exist for a disorder to occur. For example, general paresis—a degenerative brain disorder—cannot develop unless a person has previously contracted syphilis. A necessary cause, however, is not always sufficient by itself to cause a disorder—other factors may also be required. Many mental disorders do not seem to have necessary causes, although there continues to be a search for such causes.

A **sufficient cause** of a disorder is a condition that guarantees the occurrence of a disorder. For example, one current theory hypothesizes that hopelessness is a sufficient cause of depression (Abramson, Metalsky, & Alloy, 1989; Abramson, Alloy, & Metalsky 1995). According to this theory, if you are hopeless enough about your future, then you will become depressed. However, a sufficient cause may not be a necessary cause. Continuing with the depression example, Abramson and colleagues (1989) acknowledge that hopelessness is not a necessary cause of depression—there are other causes of depression as well.

Finally, what we study most often in psychopathology research are contributory causes. A **contributory cause** is one that increases the probability of developing a disorder but that is neither necessary nor sufficient for the disorder to occur. For example, parental rejection could increase the probability that a child may have difficulty in handling close personal relationships later or may increase the probability that being rejected in a relationship in adulthood might precipitate depression. We say here that parental rejection is a contributory cause for the person's later difficulties, but it is neither necessary nor sufficient (Abramson et al., 1989; Abramson, Alloy, & Metalsky, 1995).

In addition to distinguishing between necessary, sufficient, and contributory causes of abnormal behavior, we must also consider the time frame under which the different causes operate. Some causal factors occurring relatively early in life may not show their effects for many years; these would be considered *distal* causal factors that may contribute to a predisposition to develop a disorder. For example, loss of a parent early in life may serve as a distal contributory cause predisposing the person to depression in adulthood. By contrast, other causal factors operate shortly before the occurrence of the symptoms of a disorder; these would be considered *proximal* causal factors. A proximal causal factor may be a condition that proves too much for a person and triggers a disorder. Examples are a crushing disappointment at work or school, or loss of a loved one. Sometimes proximal or precipitating causes may seem insignificant and related only slightly, if at all, to the more distal causes. In short, it is the straw that breaks the camel's back. For example, leaving dirty clothes lying on the bathroom floor may be a minor annoyance in a basically well-adjusted family, but the same act can cause a heated argument in a family already experiencing major difficulties.

A *reinforcing* cause is a condition that tends to maintain maladaptive behavior that is already occurring. An example is the extra attention, sympathy, and removal from unwanted responsibility that may come when a person is ill; these pleasant experiences may unintentionally discourage recovery. Another example occurs in cases of severe depression where the depressed person's behavior may alienate friends and family, leading to a greater sense of rejection that reinforces the existing depression (Joiner, 1995; Joiner & Metalsky, 1995; Monroe & Simons, 1991).

For many forms of psychopathology we do not yet have a clear understanding of whether there are necessary or sufficient causes, although this remains the goal of much current research. However, we do have a good understanding of many of the contributory causes for most forms of psychopathology. Some of the distal contributory causes, to be discussed later in this chapter, set up vulnerability during childhood for disorder later in life. Other more proximal contributory causes may bring on a disorder directly, and yet others may contribute to the maintenance of a disorder. This complex causal picture is further complicated by the fact that what may be a proximal cause for a problem at one stage in life may also serve as a distal contributory cause, setting up a predisposition for another disorder later in life. For example, the death of a parent can be a proximal cause of a child's subsequent grief reaction that might last a few months or a year; however, the parent's death may also serve as a distal contributory factor that increases the probability that when the child grows up he or she may become depressed in response to certain stressors.

Feedback and Circularity in Abnormal Behavior

Traditionally in the sciences, the task of determining cause-and-effect relationships has focused on isolating the condition X (cause) that could be demonstrated to lead to condition Y (effect). For example, when the alcohol content of the blood reaches a certain level, alcoholic intoxication occurs. Where more than one causal factor is involved, the term *causal pattern* has been used. Here conditions A, B, C, etc., lead to condition Y. In either case, this concept of cause follows a simple linear model in which a given variable or set of variables leads to a result either immediately after or later in time.

In the behavioral sciences, and particularly in abnormal psychology, such simple cause-and-effect sequences are very rare. This happens not only because we usually deal with a multitude of interacting causes, but also because we often have difficulty distinguishing between what is cause and what is effect. In abnormal behavior, the effects of feedback and the existence of mutual, two-way influences must be taken into account. Consider the following situation:

Case Study, Drinking and Distancing • A husband and wife are undergoing counseling for difficulties in their marriage. The husband accuses his wife of drinking excessively, while the wife accuses her husband of rejecting her and showing no affection. In explaining her frustrations to the therapist, the wife views the situation as "I drink because my husband rejects me." The husband sees the problem differently: "I reject my wife because she drinks too much."

Over time, a vicious circle has developed in which the husband has increasingly withdrawn as his wife has increasingly lost control of her drinking. It is extremely difficult, if not impossible, to differentiate cause from effect. Rather, the problem has become a vicious circle: each person influences and maintains the behavior of the other.

Even more subtle intermixing of cause and effect occur regularly in the lives of disturbed people. Consider the following scenario:

Case Study, Perceived Hostility Leads to Rejection • A boy with a history of disturbed interactions with his parents routinely misinterprets the intentions of his peers as being hostile. He develops defensive strategies to counteract the supposed hostility of those around him, such as the rejection of others' efforts to be friendly, which he misinterprets as patronizing. His behavior is difficult for others to deal with, even when their intentions are benign. Confronted by the boy's prickly behavior they become defensive, hostile, and rejecting, thus confirming and strengthening the boy's distorted expectations. In this manner, each opportunity for new experience and new learning is in fact subverted and becomes another encounter with a social environment that seems perversely and persistently hostile—exactly in line with the boy's expectations.

These examples illustrate that our concepts of causal relationships must take into account the complex factors of feedback, patterns of interaction, and circularity.

Diathesis-Stress Models

One feature that many of the viewpoints or models of abnormal behavior that we will be discussing in this chapter have in common is that they can be considered to be diathesis-stress models. A predisposition toward developing a disorder is termed a *diathesis*. It can derive from biological, psychosocial, and/or sociocultural causal factors, and the different viewpoints that we will be discussing tend to emphasize the importance of different kinds of diatheses. Many mental disorders are believed to develop as the result of some kind of stressor operating on a person who has a diathesis for the type of disorder that emerges. Hence we will discuss what are commonly known as **diathesis-stress models** of abnormal behavior (e.g., Meehl, 1962; Metalsky et al., 1982; Rosenthal, 1963). To translate these terms into the types of causal factors described earlier, the diathesis is a relatively distal necessary or contributory cause, but it is not sufficient to cause the disorder. Instead, there must be a more proximal

cause (the stressor), which may also be contributory or necessary but is generally not sufficient by itself to cause the disorder. In the past these models often had limited use because it was impossible to identify diatheses or stressors independently of one another or of an occurrence of maladaptive behavior. However, increasingly sophisticated methods of measuring both diatheses and stressors have developed that have made many of these models more useful (e.g., Kessler, 1997; Monroe & Simons, 1991).

Stress, the response of an individual to demands that he or she perceives as taxing or exceeding his or her personal resources (Lazarus & Folkman, 1984) will be the focus of Chapter 4. The presence of a diathesis is often only inferred after stressful circumstances have led to maladaptive behavior. To further complicate matters, factors contributing to the development of a diathesis are themselves sometimes highly potent stressors, as when a child experiences the death of a parent and may thereby acquire a predisposition or diathesis for becoming depressed later in life.

In recent years, attention has been focused on the concept of **protective factors,** which are influences that modify a person's response to an environmental stressor, making it less likely that the person will experience the adverse consequences of the stressor (Masten & Coatsworth, 1995, 1998; Rolf et al., 1990; Rutter, 1985). One important protective factor in childhood is having a family environment in which at least one parent is warm and supportive, allowing the development of a good attachment relationship between the child and parent (Hetherington & Parke, 1993; Masten & Coatsworth, 1998). However, protective factors are not necessarily positive experiences. Indeed, sometimes exposure to stressful experiences that are dealt with successfully can promote a sense of self-confidence or self-esteem and thereby serve as a protective factor; thus, some stressors paradoxically promote coping. This has sometimes been referred to as a "steeling" or "inoculation" effect, and is most likely to occur with moderate rather than with mild or extreme stressors (Hetherington, 1991; Rutter, 1987a). And some protective factors have nothing to do with experiences at all, but are simply some quality or attribute of a person. For example, girls are less vulnerable than boys to many psychosocial stressors such as parental conflict and to physical hazards for reasons that are not yet well understood (Rutter, 1982). In addition, other protective attributes include having an easy temperament, high self-esteem, high intelligence, school achievement (Hetherington, 1991; Hetherington &

A child growing up under conditions of adversity may be protected from problems later in life if he or she has a warm and supportive relationship with some adult—in this case a grandmother. Encouraging children to ask questions, taking the time to listen to their problems and concerns, and trying to understand the conflicts and pressures they face are the important elements of such a supportive and protective relationship.

Parke, 1993; Masten & Coatsworth, 1995, 1998; Rutter, 1987a).

Protective factors most often, but not always, lead to **resilience**—the ability to adapt successfully to even very difficult circumstances. An example would be the child who perseveres in school despite his parent's drug addiction or physical abuse (Masten, Best, & Garmezy, 1990, p. 426; Masten & Coatsworth, 1995, 1998). The term resilience has been used to describe three distinct phenomena: "(1) good outcomes despite high-risk status, (2) sustained competence under threat, and (3) recovery from trauma" (Masten et al., 1990, p. 426). A more everyday way of thinking of resilience is in terms of "overcoming the odds" against you. There is increasing evidence that if a child's fundamental systems of adaptation (such as intelligence and cognitive development, ability to self-regulate, good mastery motivation) are operating normally, that most threatening circumstances will have minimal impact. Problems tend to arise either when one or more of these systems of adaptation are weak to begin with (e.g., low intelligence), or when a stressor damages one or more of these systems (e.g., when a parent dies), or when the level of challenge far exceeds human capacity to adapt (e.g., exposure to chronic trauma as in war or chronic maltreatment) (Masten & Coatsworth, 1995, 1998). We should also note, however, that resilience should not be thought of as an all-or-none capacity, and some research has shown that resilient children (that is,

those showing high social competence despite high stress) may nonetheless also experience considerable self-reported emotional distress. Moreover, children who show resilience in one domain may show significant difficulties in other domains (Luther, Doernberger, & Zigler, 1993).

In sum, we can distinguish between causes of abnormal behavior that lie within and are part of the biological makeup or prior experience of a person—diatheses, vulnerabilities, or predispositions—and those that pertain to current challenges in a person's life—stressors. The diathesis (or diatheses) can involve either necessary or contributory causal factors, but it is not by itself sufficient to cause the disorder. The stressors may also be necessary or contributory but generally not sufficient by themselves to cause the disorder. In addition, we can also examine protective factors, which may derive either from particular types of experiences or from certain qualities of the person, that can promote resilience in the face of vulnerability and stress. Most protective factors are probably contributory rather than necessary or sufficient to produce resilience. Different models of abnormal behavior, as we shall see in the sections that follow, identify different diatheses and different stressors as the route to abnormality, and different protective factors as the route to resilience in the face of adversity.

This discussion should make it very clear that diathesis-stress models need to be considered in a broad framework of multicausal developmental models. Specifically, in the course of development a child may acquire a variety of cumulative risk factors that may interact with each other in determining risk for psychopathology. These risk factors also interact, however, with a variety of protective processes, and sometimes with stressors, to determine whether the child develops in a normal and adaptive way as opposed to showing signs of maladaptive behavior and psychopathology, either in childhood, adolesence, or adulthood. It is also important to note, however, that to understand what is abnormal one must always have a good understanding of normal human development. This has been the focus of the rapidly growing field of **developmental psychopathology,** which focuses on determining what is abnormal at any point in development by comparing and contrasting it with normal and expected changes that occur in the course of development. For example, an intense fear of the dark in 3-to-5-year-old child may not be considered abnormal given that most children have at least one specific fear into early adolescence (Barlow, 1988). However, an intense fear of the dark in a high school or college-aged student would be considered abnormal.

MODELS OR VIEWPOINTS FOR UNDERSTANDING ABNORMAL BEHAVIOR

As already noted, in attempting to uncover the causes of abnormal behavior, we rarely find clear-cut answers as we sometimes do in the case of physical disease. In the preceding chapter, for example, we examined many interpretations developed over the centuries to explain deviant behavior, from theories of supernatural possession to naturally occurring biological causes. Alternative viewpoints of the causes of abnormal behavior have emerged because no single approach satisfactorily explains all abnormal behavior. Each different viewpoint focuses on important facets of behavior, although each falls short of providing a complete explanation. We now look at several models or viewpoints that dominate today's approaches to understanding the causes of abnormal behavior. They also form the basis for the types of therapy we will discuss, both with the discussion of the disorders themselves and in more depth in Chapters 16 and 17. All these viewpoints derive from the events described in Chapter 2, and, because they continue to evolve to meet new ideas and discoveries, some of them may well represent tomorrow's "history."

Students are often perplexed by the fact that, in the behavioral sciences, there are several competing explanations for the same thing. In general, the more complex the phenomenon being investigated, the greater the number of viewpoints that develop in an attempt to explain it.

Inevitably, not all these viewpoints are equally valid. As you will see, the applicability of a viewpoint is often determined by the extent to which it helps an observer understand a given phenomenon, and its validity is usually determined by whether it can be supported through empirical research.

The Value of Viewpoints

The viewpoints to be discussed here help mental health professionals explain abnormal behavior. They help us understand disorders on three broad fronts: their clinical pictures (the symptoms of the disorders), their causal factors, and their treatments. In each case, these viewpoints help professionals organize the observations they have made, provide a system of thought in which to place the observed data, and suggest areas of focus for treatment.

Unfortunately, theoretical orientations in science often retain a strong hold over their adherents, even in the face of contradictory evidence and valid alternative explanations of the same phenomena. They may remain blind to these "hints" that their point of view is limited until some new insight is achieved that resolves the problems left unsolved. These new insights constitute *paradigm shifts*, fundamental reorganizations of how people think about an entire field of science (Kuhn, 1962). For example, the sun was thought to revolve around the earth until Copernicus proposed the radical idea that the earth revolved around the sun, causing a major paradigm shift in astronomy and physics.

Sigmund Freud, as we saw in Chapter 2, helped shift the focus of abnormal psychology from biological illness or moral infirmity to unconscious mental processes within the person. In recent years there seem to have been two paradigm shifts occurring in parallel in the study of abnormal behavior. First, a slightly different newer biological viewpoint is having a significant impact and is the dominant force in psychiatry. Second, the behavioral and cognitive-behavioral viewpoints have become the dominant paradigms among most research-oriented clinical psychologists. In the long run, however, we also know from biological, psychosocial, and sociocultural research that only an integrated approach is likely to provide anything close to a full understanding of the origins of various forms of psychopathology, or a long-lasting cure for many serious forms of psychopathology.

Multidimensional, Eclectic, and Integrative Approaches

Many researchers and practitioners do not subscribe to a single theoretical perspective. Rather, they take an eclectic approach, drawing on what they see as the best principles or techniques from several viewpoints. Some integrate these different techniques into their own somewhat unique approach, and others use different viewpoints and techniques for different types of psychopathology. Either of these approaches often seem to work at a practical level and their use reflects a growing trend by some practitioners not to be bound to any one viewpoint. We will return to this issue in the Unresolved Issues section of this chapter, where we further discuss eclectic and integrative approaches.

However, we must first understand the major different viewpoints of abnormal behavior and their perspectives on the causes of such behavior. Our survey will be descriptive. We do not intend to advocate one viewpoint over another. Rather, we will present information about the key ideas of each perspective, along with information about attempts to evaluate their validity. We will also describe the kinds of causal factors that each model tends to emphasize. As we will see, different models often have different perspectives on how and why a particular causal factor is involved in a given disorder.

THE BIOLOGICAL VIEWPOINTS

As we saw in the discussion of general paresis and its link to syphillis in Chapter 2, the biological viewpoint focuses on mental disorders as *diseases,* many of the primary symptoms of which are cognitive or behavioral rather than physiological or anatomical. Mental disorders are thus viewed as disorders of the central nervous system, the autonomic nervous system, or the endocrine system, that are either inherited or caused by some pathological process. Neither psychological factors nor a person's psychosocial environment is believed to play a causal role in the mental disorder. Although at one time people taking this viewpoint hoped to find simple biological explanations, today most people recognize that such explanations are usually unlikely to be quite so simple. Therefore, a less extreme version of the biological viewpoint has emerged—the biopsychological viewpoint—which allows for other causal factors but focuses primarily on the genetic, biochemical, and other biological processes that have become imbalanced (for whatever reason) and are disrupting normal behavior.

As discussed in Chapter 2, the disorders first recognized as having biological or organic components were those associated with gross destruction of brain tissue. These disorders were neurological diseases—that is, they resulted from the disruption of brain functioning by physical or chemical means and often involved psychological or behavioral aberrations. However, neurological damage does not necessarily result in abnormal behavior.

Likewise, the bizarre thought content of delusions and other abnormal mental states is probably never, in itself, the direct result of brain damage. Clearly, a person's behavioral impairment (such as memory loss) may be readily accounted for by structural damage to the brain, but it is not so apparent how such damage produces the sometimes bizarre content of the person's thoughts or behavior. For example, we can understand how the loss of neurons in general paresis can lead to difficulties in executing certain tasks, but the fact that a person claims to be Napoleon is not likely to be the result simply of a loss of neurons. Such behavior must be the product of some sort of functional integration of different neural structures, some of which have been "programmed" by personality and learning based on past experience.

Today we know that many conditions (for example, brain inflammation or high fever) temporarily disrupt the information-processing capabilities of the brain without inflicting permanent damage or death to the neural cells involved. In these cases, normal functioning is altered by the context (especially the chemical context) in which the neural cells operate. The most familiar example occurs during alcohol intoxication when disruptive or otherwise inappropriate behavior is sometimes indulged in that would normally be inhibited. In sum, many processes short of brain damage can affect the functional capacity of the brain and thus change behavior.

BIOLOGICAL CAUSAL FACTORS

In this section we will focus on five categories of biological factors that seem particularly relevant to the development of maladaptive behavior: (1) neurotransmitter and hormonal imbalances in the brain, (2) genetic vulnerabilities, (3) constitutional liabilities, (4) brain dysfunction and neural plasticity, and (5) physical deprivation or disruption. Each of these categories encompasses a number of conditions that influence the quality and functioning of our bodies and our behavior. They are not necessarily independent of each other, and they often occur in varying combinations in different people.

Neurotransmitter and Hormonal Imbalances

In order for the brain to function adequately neurons, or excited nerve cells, need to be able to communicate

People's behavior during alcohol intoxication is one good example of how a temporary biological condition can dramatically affect their functioning—in this case engaging in behavior that normally would be inhibited.

effectively with one another. The site of communication from the axon of one neuron to the dendrites or cell body of another neuron is the **synapse** (or *synaptic cleft*)—a tiny filled space between neurons. These interneuronal (or transsynaptic) transmissions are accomplished by chemicals called **neurotransmitters** that are released into the synaptic cleft by the presynaptic neuron when a nerve impulse occurs (for details see Highlight 3.1). There are many different kinds of neurotransmitters; some increase the likelihood that the postsynaptic neuron will "fire" (produce an impulse), while others inhibit the impulse. Whether the neural message is successfully transmitted to the postsynaptic neuron depends, among other things, on the concentration of certain neurotransmitters within the synaptic cleft.

Imbalances of Neurotransmitters The belief that *neurotransmitter imbalances* in the brain can result in abnormal behavior is one of the basic tenets of the biological perspective today. Sometimes psychological stress can bring on neurotransmitter imbalances. These imbalances can be created in a variety of ways (see figure in Highlight 3.1). For example, there may be excessive production and release of the neurotransmitter substance into the synapses, causing a functional excess in levels of that neurotransmitter. Alternatively, there may be dysfunctions in the normal processes by which neurotransmitters, once released into the synapse, are

deactivated. Ordinarily this deactivation occurs in one of two ways. After being released into the synaptic cleft, the neurotransmitter substance either is deactivated by enzymes present in the synapse or, more commonly, it is reabsorbed or sucked back into the presynaptic axon button, a process called *re-uptake.* Dysfunctions can create neurotransmitter imbalances either when the deactivation enzymes present in the synapse are deficient, or when there is a slowing of the ordinary process of re-uptake. Finally, there may also be problems with the receptors in the postsynaptic neuron, which may be either abnormally sensitive or abnormally insensitive. As we will see, different disorders are thought to stem from different patterns of neurotransmitter imbalances. Moreover, different drugs used to treat various disorders are often believed to operate through correcting these imbalances. For example, the widely prescribed antidepressant Prozac appears to slow down the re-uptake process of the neurotransmitter serotonin (see Chapters 6 and 16).

Although there are dozens of different kinds of neurotransmitters, there are four that have been most extensively studied in relationship to psychopathology: (1) norepinephrine, (2) dopamine, (3) serotonin, and (4) GABA. The first three are all part of a class of neurotransmitters called *monoamines* because they are each synthesized from a single amino acid (monoamine means one amine). Dopamine and norepinephrine are most closely related to one another

Neurotransmission and Abnormal Behavior

A nerve impulse, which is electrical in nature, travels from the cell body of a neuron (nerve cell) down the axon. Although there is only one axon for each neuron, axons have branches at their end, called *axonal endings* or *terminal buttons.* These are the sites where neurotransmitter substances get released into a synapse—a tiny fluid-filled gap between the axon endings of one neuron (the presynaptic neuron) and the dendrites or cell body of another neuron (the postsynaptic neuron). The synapse is the site of neural transmission—that is, of communication—between neurons. The neurotransmitter substances are contained within synaptic vesicles near the axon endings. When a nerve impulse reaches the axon endings, the synaptic vesicles travel to the presynaptic membrane of the axon and release the neurotransmitter substance into the synapse. The neurotransmitter substances released into the synapse then act on the postsynaptic membrane of the dendrite of the receiving neuron, which has specialized places called *receptor sites* where the neurotransmitter substances pass on their message. The receptor sites then initiate the receiving cell's response. The neurotransmitters can either stimulate that postsynaptic neuron to initiate an impulse or can inhibit impulse transmission. The message transmitted is thus a chemical one, and it may be either excitatory or inhibitory in nature—that is, it may either cause the postsynaptic neuron to fire or it may inhibit its firing. Some important neurotransmitters deliver inhibitory messages and others deliver excitatory messages. Both kinds of messages are important. Once the neurotransmitter substance is released into the synapse, it does not stay around indefinitely (so that the second neuron does not continue firing in the absence of a real impulse). Sometimes the neurotransmitters are quickly destroyed by an enzyme, such as monoamine oxidase, or sometimes they are returned to storage vesicles in the axonal button by a "re-uptake" mechanism—a process by which they are effectively sucked back up into the axon ending.

Given that many forms of psychopathology have been associated with various imbalances in neurotransmitter substances, and with altered sensitivities of receptor sites, it is not surprising that many of the medications used to treat various disorders have as their site of action the synapse. For example, certain medications act to increase or decrease the concentrations of pertinent neurotransmitters in the synaptic gap. They may do so by affecting the actions of the enzymes that ordinarily break down the neurotransmitter substances in the synapse, or by blocking the re-uptake process, or by altering the sensitivity of the receptor sites. ∎

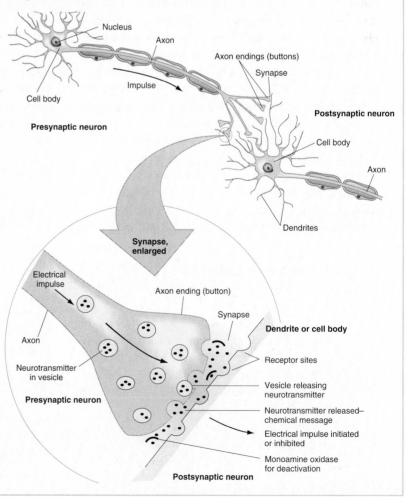

(both are called *catecholamines*) because they are both synthesized from a common amino acid. Norepinephrine has been implicated as playing an important role in the emergency reactions our bodies show when we are exposed to an acutely stressful or dangerous situation, as will be discussed more extensively in Chapters 4 and 5. Dopamine has been implicated in schizophrenia, although as we will see in Chapter 12 the early simple hypothesis that schizophrenia is caused by excessively high levels of dopamine is not entirely correct. Moreover, altered dopamine functioning is also implicated in other disorders as well. Serotonin is synthesized from a different amino acid than are the catecholamines and is called an *indolamine*. It has been found to have important effects in the way we process information from our environment (e.g., Spoont, 1992) and seems to play a role in emotional disorders such as anxiety and depression as well as suicide, as we will see in Chapters 5 and 6. Finally, GABA (short for *gamma aminobutryic acid*) was the most recently discovered of the neurotransmitters and it is strongly implicated in anxiety, as will be discussed in Chapter 5.

Hormonal Imbalances   Some forms of psychopathology have also been linked *to hormonal imbalances*. **Hormones** are chemical messengers secreted by a set of endocrine glands in our bodies. Each of the endocrine glands produce and release its own set of hormones, which travel through our bloodstream and affect various parts of our brain and body. Our central nervous system is linked to the endocrine system (in what is known as the *neuroendocrine system*) by the effects of the hypothalamus on the pituitary gland (see Figure 3.1), which is the master gland of the body that produces a variety of hormones that regulate or control the other endocrine glands. One particularly important set of interactions occurs in the *hypothalamic-pituitary-adrenal- cortical axis*. Activation of this axis involves messages from the hypothalamus to the pituitary, which then stimulates the cortical part of the adrenal gland (located on top of the kidney) to produce epinephrine (adrenaline) and the stress hormone cortisol. As we will see, malfunction of this system has been implicated in various forms of psychopathology. Sex hormones are produced by the gonadal glands, and imbalance in these (such as the male hormones—the *androgens*) can also contribute to maladaptive behavior.

Hormonal influences on the developing nervous system also seem to contribute to some of the differences between behavior in men and women. Although we know that social views of gender and other social learning experiences can sometimes override such influences, some biological influence still shows up in gender-related differences in behavior (Collaer & Hines, 1995; Ehrhardt & Meyer-Bahlburg, 1981; Money & Ehrhardt, 1972). For example, girls who were ex-

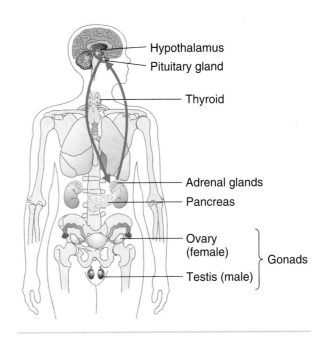

FIGURE 3.1
This figure illustrates some of the major glands of the endocrine system, which produce and release hormones into the bloodstream. The hypothalamic-pituitary-adrenal-cortical axis is also shown. The hypothalamus and pituitary are closely connected, and messages from the hypothalamus periodically send signals to the pituitary (the master gland), which in turn sends messages to the cortical part of adrenal glands (above the kidneys) to release epinephrine and the stress hormone cortisol.

posed prenatally to high levels of male hormones are likely to show higher levels of tomboyism and a preference for toys usually preferred by boys (trucks versus dolls) (Berenbaum & Hines, 1992; Collaer & Hines, 1995; Money & Ehrhardt, 1972). In adulthood, men clearly show more aggressive behavior than women based on evidence from evolutionary, cross-cultural, developmental, and biological-hormonal sources (e.g., Archer, 1994, 1995; Eagly & Steffen, 1986).

Genetic Vulnerabilities

The biochemical processes described above are themselves affected by genes. Although behavior is never determined exclusively by genes, substantial evidence shows that some mental disorders have a hereditary component. The genetic transmission of traits or vulnerabilities from one generation to the next is, by definition, a biological process. Thus, the many recent studies suggesting that heredity is an important predisposing causal factor for a number of different disorders—such as depression, schizophrenia, and alcoholism—support the biological viewpoint (e.g., Plomin, DeFries, McClearn, & Rutter, 1997). In these cases it is important to note that the genetic source of vulnerability does not manifest itself until later in life—adolescence or adulthood. It also seems to be the case that many broad temperamental features of newborns and children are genetically influenced. For example, some children are just naturally more shy or anxious, while others are more outgoing (e.g., Carey & DiLalla, 1994; Kagan, 1993).

In the field of abnormal psychology, genetic influences rarely express themselves in a simple and straightforward manner. This is because behavior, unlike some physical characteristics such as eye color, is not determined exclusively by genetic endowment: It is a product of the organism's interaction with the environment. In other words, genes can affect behavior only indirectly. Gene "expression" is normally not a simple outcome of the information encoded in DNA, but is rather the end product of an intricate process that may be influenced by the internal (e.g., intrauterine) and external environment.

The essential characteristics of human inheritance are basically the same for all people. Inheritance begins at conception, when a female's egg cell is fertilized by a male sperm cell. The resulting embryo receives a genetic code that provides potentialities for development and behavior throughout a lifetime. The specific features of genetic endowment vary widely. Except for identical twins, no two humans ever begin life with the same endowment. Thus heredity not only provides the potentialities for development and behavior typical of the species but it is also an important source of individual differences. Heredity determines not the specifics of human behavior but rather the ranges within which characteristic behavior can be modified by environmental or experiential influences. For example, a child born with an introverted disposition may become more or less introverted depending on various experiences growing up, but it is unlikely that he or she will ever be truly extraverted.

Some inherited defects interfere directly with the normal development of the brain. Other more subtle defects can leave a person susceptible to severe mental disorders. These subtle influences are usually transmitted in the genetic code itself, showing up as metabolic or biochemical variations from an ideally functional norm. The form of mental retardation known as phenylketonuria (PKU), for example, is produced by a genetically determined deficiency that makes the body unable to adequately metabolize a chemical compound present in many foods (phenylalanine) (see Chapter 13). (But see also Highlight 3.2.) Other genetic defects are believed to affect adversely the delicate regulation of brain biochemistry.

Chromosomal Abnormalities The chainlike structures within a cell nucleus that contain the genes are called chromosomes, as illustrated in Figure 3.2. Advances in research have enabled us to readily detect *chromosomal abnormalities*—irregularities in the chromosomal structure—even before birth, thus making it possible to study

their effects on future development and behavior. Normal human cells have 46 chromosomes containing the genetic materials in which the hereditary plan is encoded. When fertilization takes place, the normal inheritance consists of 23 pairs of chromosomes, one of each pair from the mother and one from the father. Twenty-two of these chromosome pairs are called *autosomes;* they determine by their biochemical action general anatomical and physiological characteristics. The remaining pair, the *sex chromosomes,* determine an individual's sex. In a female both of these sex chromosomes—one from each parent—are designated as X chromosomes. In a male, the sex chromosome from the mother is an X, but that from the father is a Y chromosome.

Research in developmental genetics has shown that abnormalities in the structure or number of the chromosomes are associated with a wide range of malformations and disorders. For example, Down syndrome is a type of mental retardation (also associated with certain recognizable facial features) in which there is a trisomy (a set of three chromosomes instead of two) in chromosome 21 (see Chapter 13). Here the extra chromosome is the primary cause of the disorder. Anomalies may also occur in the sex chromosomes, producing a variety of complications that may predispose a person to develop abnormal behavior.

The Relationship of Genotypes to Phenotypes

Genes are the long molecules of DNA (deoxyribonucleic acid) that are present at various locations on a chromosome. Genes could be likened to beads on a necklace (the chromosome). Individual genes may contain information that causes bodily processes to malfunction, although we cannot yet predict with any great certainty the occurrence of most such malfunctions.

A person's total genetic endowment is referred to as his or her **genotype.** The observed structural and functional characteristics that result from an interaction of the genotype and the environment are referred to as a person's **phenotype.** In some cases the genotypic vulnerability present at birth will not manifest its effect on the phenotype until much later in life. In many cases, the genotype may shape the environmental experiences a child has, thus affecting the phenotype in yet another very important way. For example, a child who may be genetically predisposed to aggressive behavior may be rejected by his or her peers in early grades because of aggressive behavior. Such rejection may lead the child to go on to associate with similarly aggressive and delinquent peers in later grades, leading to an increased likelihood of developing a full-blown pattern of delinquency in adolescence. When the genotype shapes the environmental ex-

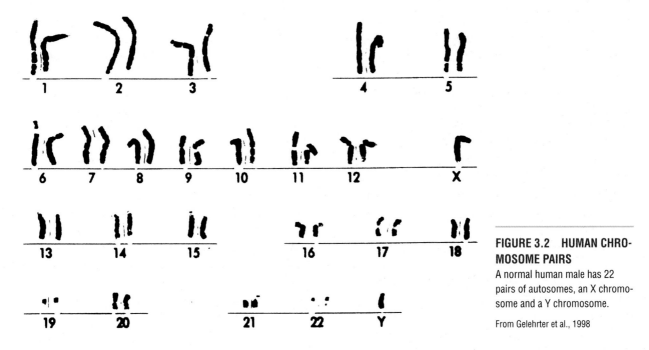

FIGURE 3.2 HUMAN CHRO-MOSOME PAIRS

A normal human male has 22 pairs of autosomes, an X chromosome and a Y chromosome.

From Gelehrter et al., 1998

periences a child has in this way, we refer to this phenomenon as a **genotype-environment correlation.**

Genotype-Environment Correlations Researchers have found three ways in which an individual's genotype may shape his or her environment (Plomin et al., 1997; Scarr, 1992).

- *The genotype may have what has been termed a passive effect on the environment resulting from the genetic similarity of parents and children.* Such genetic similarity is likely to result in the parents automatically creating an environment compatible with the child's predisposition. For example, highly intelligent parents may provide a highly stimulating environment for their child, thus creating an environment that will interact in a positive way with the child's genetic endowment for high intelligence.

- *The child's genotype may evoke particular kinds of reactions from the social and physical environment—a so-called evocative effect.* For example, active, happy babies evoke more positive responses from others than do passive, unresponsive infants (Lytton, 1980). Similarly, musically talented children may be picked out at school and given special opportunities (Plomin et al., 1997).

- *The child's genotype may play a more active role in shaping the environment—a so-called active effect.* In this case the child seeks out or builds an environment that is congenial. Extraverted children may seek the company of others, for example, thereby enhancing their own tendencies to be sociable

(Baumrind, 1991; Plomin et al., 1997). Active and evocative genotype-environment correlations become more important as the child grows up and experiences more environments outside the family (Plomin et al., 1997).

Genotype-Environment Interactions With the type of genotype-environment correlations just discussed we see the effects that genes have on a child's exposure to the environment. But an additional fascinating complication is that people with different genotypes may be differentially sensitive or susceptible to their environments; this is known as a **genotype-environment interaction.** One important example is illustrated by the disorder mentioned earlier—PKU-induced mental retardation. Children with the genetic vulnerability to PKU react very differently to foods with phenylalanine than do normal children because they cannot metabolize the phenylalanine, and as its metabolic products build up they damage the brain (Plomin et al., 1997). Another example occurs in people who are at genetic risk for depression who have been shown to be more likely to respond to stressful life events by becoming depressed than are people without the genetic risk factors (Kendler et al., 1995; Plomin et al., 1997).

The Nature of Genetic Effects on Mental Disorders
It appears likely that many of the most interesting (if still largely obscure) genetic influences in normal and abnor-

mal behavior typically operate *polygenically*—that is, through the action of many genes together in some sort of additive or interactive fashion (e.g., Plomin, 1990; Plomin et al., 1997; Torgersen, 1993). A genetically vulnerable person has inherited a large number of these genes that collectively represent faulty heredity. These faulty genes may in turn lead to structural abnormalities in the central nervous system, to errors in the regulation of brain chemistry, or to excesses or deficiencies in the reactivity of the autonomic nervous system, which is involved in mediating many of our emotional responses. These various processes serve to predispose the person to later difficulties.

The few instances in which relatively straightforward predictions of mental disorders can be made on the basis of known laws of inheritance invariably involve gross neurological impairment. In such cases, abnormal behavior arises in part as a consequence of a central nervous system malfunction, such as occurs in Huntington's disease; such conditions will be discussed in Chapter 13.

Methods for Studying Genetic Influences Although advances have been made in identifying faulty genetic endowment (including locating genes responsible for certain physical anomalies), we are not yet able to isolate specific defects for mental disorders on the genes themselves. Therefore most of the information we have on the role of genetic factors in mental disorders is based not on studies of genes but on studies of people who are related to one another. There are three primary methods that are used in *behavior genetics,* the field that focuses on studying the heritability of mental disorders (as well as other aspects of psychological functioning): (1) the pedigree, or family history method, (2) the twin method, and (3) the adoption method

The **pedigree,** or **family history, method** requires that an investigator observe samples of relatives of each *proband* or *index case* (the subject, or carrier, of the trait or disorder in question) in order to see whether the incidence increases in proportion to the degree of hereditary relationship. In addition, the incidence of the trait in a normal population is compared (as a control) with its incidence among the relatives of the index cases. The central limitation of this method is that people who are more closely related genetically also usually tend to share more similar environments, making it difficult to disentangle genetic and environmental effects.

The **twin method** is the second approach used to study genetic influences on abnormal behavior. *Identical or monozygotic twins* share the same genetic endowment because they develop from a single zygote, or fertilized egg. Thus if a given disorder or trait were completely heritable, one would expect the **concordance rate**—the percentage of twins sharing the disorder or trait—to be 100 percent. That is, if one identical twin had a particular disorder, the other twin would as well. There are virtually no forms of psychopathology where the concordance rates for identical twins are this high, and so we can safely conclude that virtually no disorders are completely heritable. However, as we will see, there are relatively high concordance rates for identical twins in some common and severe forms of psychopathology. These concordance rates are particularly meaningful when they differ from those found for nonidentical twins. *Nonidentical* or *dizygotic twins* do not share any more genes than do siblings from the same parents because they develop from two different fertilized eggs. One would therefore expect concordance rates for a disorder to be much lower for dizygotic (DZ) than for monozygotic (MZ) twins if the disorder had a strong genetic component because DZs have much less genetic similarity. So evidence for genetic transmission of a trait or a disorder can be obtained by comparing the concordance rates between identical and nonidentical twins. For most of the disorders we will discuss, concordance rates are much lower for nonidentical twins than for identical twins.

Some researchers have argued that higher concordance rates for a disorder in monozygotic twins than in dizygotic twins do not provide conclusive evidence for a genetic contribution because the possibility always remains that identical twins are treated more similarly by their parents than are nonidentical twins (Baker & Daniels, 1990; Torgersen, 1993). However, recent studies that have examined this possibility have provided reasonably strong evidence that the genetic similarity is more important than the similarity of the parents' behavior (e.g., Hettema, Neale, & Kendler, 1995; Plomin et al., 1997).

The ideal study of genetic factors involves identical twins who have been reared apart in significantly different environments. Obviously, finding such twins is extremely difficult (there are probably only a few hundred pairs in the United States), and only a few such studies with small numbers have been conducted. For example, Gottesman (1991) noted that only 14 pairs of identical twins reared apart where one has a diagnosis of schizophrenia had ever been studied. Although this sample is too small to be definitive, it is of interest to note that the concordance rates for schizophrenia for these identical twins reared apart was very similar to that reported for

This set of identical twins from Bouchard's University of Minnesota study of the relative roles of genetics and environment provides some striking support for the prominence of genetic influences on personality traits and attitudes (Bouchard et al., 1990). Jim Springer (left) and Jim Lewis (right) were separated four weeks after their birth in 1940. They grew up 45 miles apart in Ohio. After they were reunited in 1979, they discovered they had some eerie similarities: Both chain-smoked Salems, both drove the same model blue Chevrolet, both chewed their fingernails, and both had dogs named Toy. Further, they had both vacationed in the same neighborhood in Florida. When tested for such personality traits as sociability and self-control, they responded almost identically.

identical twins reared together, suggesting that genes, rather than the family environment play a considerable role in that disorder.

The third method used to study genetic influences is the **adoption method.** In one variation on this method, the biological parents of individuals who have a given disorder (and who had been given up for adoption shortly after birth) are compared with the biological parents of individuals without the disorder (who were also adopted shortly after birth) to determine their rates of disorder. If there is a genetic influence, one expects to find higher rates of the disorder in the biological relatives of those with the disorder than in those without the disorder. In another variation, one compares the rates of disorder in the adopted-away offspring of biological parents with a disorder with that seen in the adopted-away offspring of normal biological parents. If there is a genetic influence, then there should be higher rates of disorder in the adopted-away offspring of the biological parents with the disorder.

Although each of these methods alone has its pitfalls of interpretation, if the results from studies using all three strategies converge, one can draw reasonably strong conclusions about the genetic influence on a disorder (Plomin et al., 1997; Rutter, 1991a). Highlight 3.2 considers various misconceptions about studies of genetics and psychopathology.

Because the three types of heritability studies separate heredity from environment to some extent, they also allow for testing the influence of environmental factors and even for differentiating "shared" and "nonshared" environmental influences (Plomin & Daniels, 1987; Plomin et al., 1997). *Shared environmental influences* are those that would affect all children in a family similarly, such as overcrowding or poverty, and sometimes family discord. *Nonshared environmental influences* are those in which different children in a family differ. These would include experiences at school, but also some features of upbringing in the home that may not be the same for all children, as when a parent treats one child in a qualitatively different way from another. An example of the latter would be when parents who are quarreling and showing hostility to one another draw some children into the conflict but others are able to remain outside it (Rutter et al., 1993). For many important psychological characteristics and forms of psychopathology, nonshared influences appear to be more important—that is, experiences that are specific to a child may do more to influence his or her behavior and adjustment than experiences shared by all children in the family (Plomin et al., 1997; Rutter, 1991a).

Constitutional Liabilities

The term *constitutional liability* is used to describe any detrimental characteristic that is either innate or acquired so early—often prenatally—and in such strength that it is functionally similar to a genetic characteristic. Physical handicaps and temperament are among the

"Nature, Nurture, and Psychopathology: A New Look at an Old Topic"

People have abundant misconceptions and stereotypes about studies of genetic influences on behavior and psychopathology. Several of the more important ones are presented here: (Plomin et al., 1997; Rutter, 1991a; Rutter et al., 1993)

1. *Strong genetic effects mean that environmental influences must be unimportant.* Even if we are discussing a trait or disorder that has a strong genetic influence, environmental factors can have a major impact on the level of that trait. Height, for example, is strongly genetically determined and yet nutritional factors have a very large effect on the actual height a person attains. Between 1960 and 1990 the average height of boys reared in London increased about 10 cm due to improvements in diet, in spite of the fact that there were not genetic changes in the same time period (Tizard, 1975).

2. *Genes provide a limit to potential.* One's potential can change if one's environment changes, as the above example illustrates. Another example comes from children born to socially disadvantaged parents who are adopted and reared with socially advantaged parents. These children have a mean IQ about 12 points higher than those reared in the socially disadvantaged environment (Capron & Duyme, 1989; Plomin et al., 1997).

3. *Genetic strategies are of no value for studying environmental influences.* The opposite is true because genetic research strategies provide critical tests of the influence of environmental factors. For example, because monozygotic twins have identical genes, concordance rates of less than 100 percent clearly illustrate the importance of environmental influences, particularly those of the nonshared environment (Plomin et al., 1997).

4. *Nature and nurture are separate.* Genetic effects "operate mainly through their effect on susceptibility to environmental influences" (Rutter, 1991a, p. 129). For example, babies born with the genetic defect causing phenylketonuria (PKU), a metabolic disease, only develop the disease if they are environmentally exposed to diets with phenylalanine. In addition, genes affect the kinds of experiences people have, as is immediately evident if one thinks about the effects that gender, IQ, and temperament have on one's life experiences (Plomin et al., 1997).

5. *Genetic effects diminish with age.* Although many people assume that genetic effects should be maximal at birth, with environmental influences getting stronger with increasing age, it is now evident that this is not true (Plomin, 1986). For height, weight, and IQ, dizygotic twins are more alike than are monozygotic twins at birth, but over time dizygotic twins show greater differences than monozygotic twins. For whatever the reasons, many genetic effects on psychological characteristics increase with age up to at least middle childhood. Moreover, other genetic effects do not appear until much later in life, as in cases like Huntington's disease, to be discussed in Chapter 13.

6. *Disorders that run in families must be genetic and those that do not run in families must not be genetic.* Many examples contradict these misconceptions. For example, juvenile delinquency and conduct disorder tend to run in families, and yet this seems to be due primarily not to genetic but rather to environmental influences (McGuffin & Gottesman, 1985). Conversely, autism is such a rare disorder that it doesn't appear to run in families (only about 3 percent of siblings have the disorder), and yet there seems to be a very powerful genetic effect (Plomin et al., 1997; Rutter, 1991b). ■

many traits included in this category. We will briefly explore the role of these constitutional factors in the etiology of maladaptive behavior.

Physical Handicaps Embryologic abnormalities or environmental conditions operating before or after birth may result in physical defects. The most common birth difficulty associated with later mental disorders (including learning disabilities, and emotional and behavioral disturbances) is low birth weight (5 pounds or less); approximately 6 to 7 percent of all babies born in the United States in 1985 were of low birth weight (Kopp & Kaler, 1989) and current projections are that this will still be true in the year 2000 (Barnard, Morisett, & Spieker, 1993). Low birth weight is most often a factor in premature births but can also occur in full-term births. Prenatal conditions that can lead to premature birth and to low birth weight include nutritional deficiencies, disease, exposure to radiation, drugs, severe emotional stress, or the mother's excessive use of alcohol or tobacco. As might be expected, socioeconomic status is related to fetal and birth difficulties, the incidence of which is several times greater among mothers of lower socioeconomic levels (Kopp & Kaler, 1989). Because low birth weight is often associated with so many other environmental adversities, if is often difficult to disentangle which actually play a causal role in the negative outcomes that may ensue.

Fortunately, early intervention programs for the mothers of low birth weight infants, as well as for the infants, can be quite effective, at least in the short term, in preventing some of the problems often associated with low birth weight (e.g., Hetherington & Parke, 1993). However, one recent study that followed the low birth weight children for five years after their three year intervention program found that at 8 years of age some of the gains had been lost; at best only modest beneficial effects remained, and then only for the moderately low birth weight children (the severely low birth weight children had lost all the earlier advantages of having been in the intervention program) (McCarton et al., 1997). Thus more long-term interventions may be necessary to prevent the many difficulties often associated with very low birth weight.

Temperament Newborns differ in how they react to particular kinds of stimuli. Some are startled by slight sounds or cry if sunlight hits their faces; others are seemingly insensitive to such stimulation. These reactions differ from baby to baby and are examples of characteristic behaviors that appear to have been established before any extensive interaction with the environment. These behaviors are regarded as constitutional rather than genetic because they are probably due to more than genetic influences alone; prenatal and postnatal environmental factors may also play a role in their development (Kagan, 1993). Behaviors like these are one component of **temperament,** which involves not only reactivity but also characteristic ways of self-regulation. When we say that babies differ in temperament, we mean that they differ in systematic ways in their emotional and arousal responses to various stimuli, and in their tendency to approach, withdraw, or attend to various situations (Rothbart & Ahadi, 1994).

Our early temperament is thought to be the substrate from which our personality develops. Starting at about 2 to 3 months of age, approximately five dimensions of temperament can be identified, although some of these emerge later than others: (1) fearfulness, (2) irritability and frustration, (3) positive affect, (4) activity level, and (5) attentional persistence. These seem to be related to the three important dimensions of adult personality: (1) neuroticism or negative emotionality, (2) extraversion or positive emotionality, and (3) constraint (conscientiousness and agreeableness) (Rothbart & Ahadi, 1994; Watson, Clark, & Harkness, 1994). The infant dimensions of fearfulness and irritability correspond to the adult dimension of neuroticism—the disposition to experience negative affect. The infant dimensions of positive affect and possibly activity level seem related to the adult dimension of extraversion, and the infant dimension of attentional persistence seems related to the adult dimension of constraint or control. At least some aspects of temperament show a moderate degree of stability from late in the first year of life through at least middle childhood (e.g., Kagan, 1993, 1997).

Just as we saw in the discussion of gene-environment correlations, the temperament of an infant or young child has profound effects on a variety of important developmental processes (Rothbart & Ahadi, 1994). For example, a child with a fearful temperament has many opportunities for the classical conditioning of fear to situations in which fear is provoked; later the child may learn to avoid entering those feared situations and recent evidence suggests they may be especially likely to learn to fear social situations (Kagan, 1997). A child with a low threshold for distress may also learn to regulate distress by keeping the level of stimulation low, whereas a child with a high need for stimulation may do things to increase excitement (Rothbart & Ahadi, 1994).

Given these profound effects on various basic developmental processes, it is not surprising that temperament may also set the stage for the development of various forms of psychopathology later in life. For example, children who are fearful in many situations have been labeled *behaviorally inhibited* by Kagan and his colleagues. This trait has a significant heritable component (Kagan, 1993; Matheny, 1989), and when it is stable, it is a risk factor for the development of anxiety disorders later in childhood and probably in adulthood (Biederman et al., 1990; Hirshfeld et al., 1992; Kagan, 1993, 1997). Conversely, 2-year-old children who are highly *uninhibited,* showing little fear of anything, may have difficulty learning moral standards for their behavior from parents or society (Rothbart & Ahadi, 1994), and they have been shown at age 13 to exhibit more aggressive and delinquent behavior (Schwartz, Snidman, & Kagan, 1996). If these personality ingredients were combined with high levels of hostility, the stage could be set for the development of conduct disorder and antisocial personality disorder (Harpur, Hart, & Hare, 1993).

Brain Dysfunction and Neural Plasticity

Significant damage of brain tissue places a person at risk for psychopathology, but specific brain lesions are rarely a primary cause of psychiatric disorder (Eisenberg, 1990). The incidence of such damage increases notably among the elderly, mostly because of the aging process itself (often resulting in Alzheimer's disease) or associated cardiovascular insufficiency, both of which will be discussed in Chapter 13. Brain damage in the elderly sometimes leads to abnormal behavior. In addition, it also increases vulnerability by making a person less able to cope.

Clearly then, gross brain pathology, in which there are observable defects in brain tissue, occurs in only a small percentage of people with abnormal behavior. However, more subtle deficiencies of brain function are now implicated in many of the disorders that we will discuss throughout this book. Advances in our understanding of how these abnormalities in brain structure and function contribute to psychopathology have been increasing at a rapid pace in the past decade with the increased availability of sophisticated new neuroimaging techniques to study the function and structure of the brain (see Chapter 15 for detailed discussion). These and other kinds of techniques to study brain structure and function have been showing that genetic programs for brain development are not as rigid and deterministic as was once believed (e.g., Nelson & Blum, 1997). For example, pregnant monkeys who are exposed to unpredictable loud sounds have infants who are jittery and show neurochemical abnormalities (specifically elevated levels of circulating catecholamines) (Schneider, 1992). Moreover,

many environmental events that occur postnatally also affect the brain development of the infant and child (Nelson & Blum, 1997). For example, the formation of new neural connections (or synapses) after birth is dramatically affected by the experience a young organism has (e.g., Greenough & Black, 1992). Rats reared in enriched environments (as opposed to isolation) show heavier and thicker cell development in certain portions of the cortex (as well as more synapses per neuron). In addition, monkeys reared from birth in social isolation show neuroanatomical abnormalities in brain regions that contribute to emotional and cognitive functioning and not surprisingly show a variety of behavioral and emotional abnormalities (Ginsberg, Hof, McKinney, & Morrison, 1993 a, b).

This work on neural and behavioral plasticity, in combination with the work described earlier on genotype-environment correlations, make it clear why developmental psychopathologists have been devoting increasing attention to a **developmental systems approach,** which acknowledges not only that genetic activity influences neural activity, which in turn influences behavior, which in turn influences the environment, but also that these influences are bidirectional. As illustrated in Figure 3.3, various aspects of our environment (physical, social, and cultural) also influence our behavior, which in turn affects our neural activity and this in turn can even influence genetic activity (Gottlieb, 1992; Gottlieb, Wahlsten, & Lickliter, 1998).

Physical Deprivation or Disruption

Through a remarkable set of complex processes, our digestive, circulatory, and other bodily functions work to maintain our body's physiological equilibrium and integration. However, injuries and diseases strike all of us from time to time and upset our normal equilibrium. The psychological repercussions from such events can be profound. Depressions, for example, frequently accompany significant physical illnesses, in part because illnesses painfully remind us of the limits of our control over our lives. Even without serious illness or disability people may experience challenges to their equilibriums. In the following sections, we deal with two such situations: deprivation of basic physiological needs and nonoptimal levels of stimulation.

Deprivation of Basic Physiological Needs The most basic human requirements are those for food, oxygen, water, sleep, and the elimination of wastes. Insufficient rest, inadequate diet, or working too hard when ill,

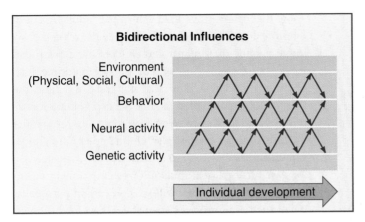

FIGURE 3.3   BIDIRECTIONAL INFLUENCES
A systems view of psychobiological development.

Source: Gilbert Gottlieb, from *Individual Development and Evolution: The Genesis of Novel Behavior.* New York: Oxford University Press, 1992. Copyright © 1992 by Oxford University Press. Reprinted with permission.

can all interfere with a person's ability to cope and predispose him or her to a variety of problems. Prisoners have sometimes been broken by nothing more persuasive than the systematic prevention of sleep or deprivation of food over a period of several days. Experimental studies of volunteers who have gone without sleep for periods of 72 to 98 hours show increasing psychological problems as the sleep loss progresses—including disorientation for time and place and feelings of depersonalization.

It is also now recognized that chronic but even relatively mild sleep deprivation can have adverse emotional consequences in children and adolescents. For example, in an extensive review of the empirical literature Carskadon (1990) demonstrated that over the course of adolescence there is a pattern of decreasing total sleep time. This pattern was associated with a good deal of daytime sleepiness. She argued that the performance lapses that are associated with excessive sleepiness can in turn lead to an increased vulnerability to accidents and to the use of caffeine and alcohol, and to mood and behavior problems.

Prolonged food deprivation also affects psychological functioning. Some of these effects were demonstrated in a pioneering study of semistarvation carried out by Keys and his associates (1950) during World War II. Thirty-two conscientious objectors served as volunteer subjects and were put on low-calorie diets characteristic of European famine areas for a period of six months, followed by a three-month period of nutritional rehabilitation. The men had an average weight loss of 24 percent and showed dramatic personality and behavioral changes. They became irritable, unsociable, and increasingly unable to concentrate on or daydream about anything but food, sometimes lying and stealing food to obtain additional food. Near the end of the six months, the men's predominant mood was one of gloom and depression, accompanied by apathy, feelings of inadequacy, and loss of interest in sex.

There may also be some very long-term consequences of such severe weight loss. For example, when a group of former World War II and Korean War POWs who had lost 35 percent or more of their original body weight while in captivity were tested more than 30 years later, they performed more poorly on a variety of tests of cognitive functioning than did other former POWs who had not lost this much weight (Sutker et al., 1990, 1995). In addition, Polivy and colleagues (1994) found that former POWs who had lost a great deal of weight as POWs reported higher than expected levels of binge eating in the interim years.

Perhaps the most tragic deprivation is seen in young children who are malnourished, with estimates by the World Health Organization being that 40 to 60 percent of the world's children suffer from mild to moderate malnutrition (Lozoff, 1989). In some parts of the world 3 to 7 percent may suffer from severe malnutrition, which is associated with a host of other potentially damaging variables such as parental neglect and limited access to health care (Brozek & Schurch, 1984; Lozoff, 1989) impairs physical development and lowers resistance to disease. But it also stunts brain growth, results in markedly lowered intelligence, and enhances risk for disorders such as attention-deficit disorder (which leads to attentional problems, increased distractibility, and interference with school performance) (Amcoff, 1980; Galler, 1984; Lozoff, 1989). In a postmortem study of infants who had died of malnutrition during their first year of life, Winick (1976) found the total brain cell content to be 60 percent below that of normal infants.

At least in Western countries such as the United States, recent evidence has been accumulating that malnutrition is more common in families where the mother is traditionally passive in childcare. If the mothers are taught to give their infants nutritional supplements (assuming they are available), many of the adverse effects of

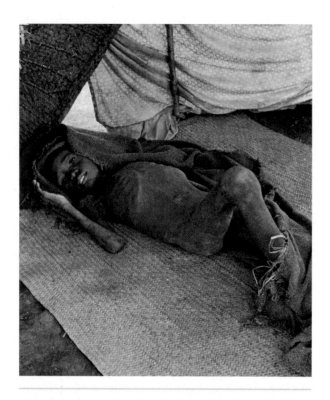

Children who are severely malnourished show stunted growth and lowered intelligence. This makes them vulnerable to attentional problems and hence, impaired school performance. An unstimulating environment has also been shown to stunt brain development.

early malnutrition can be reversed as the babies gain more energy and are more open to the socialization process which is so important for normal intellectual growth (Sameroff, 1995).

Stimulation and Activity We have known for some time that healthy mental development depends on a child's receiving adequate amounts of stimulation from the environment. In addition to psychological vulnerabilities that can be induced by too little stimulation, and which will be discussed later, the *physical* development of the brain is adversely affected by an unstimulating environment. Conversely, many animal studies demonstrate enhanced biological development produced by conditions of special stimulation, such as enriched and complex environments in which many different activities can be engaged in. These include positive changes in brain chemistry and structural changes in many parts of the brain, such as increases in numbers of synapses and dendrites (Diamond, 1988; Nelson & Blum, 1997; Swain et al., 1995).

On the other hand, there are limits to how much stimulation is beneficial to a developing organism. We know that sensory overload can impair adult functioning, and although we do not yet have evidence on this, we might assume that infants and children are similarly affected. In general, we each seem to have an optimal level of stimulation and activity that may vary over time, but that must be maintained for normal psychological functioning. Under excessive pressure, we may strive to reduce the level of input and activity. On the other hand, under some conditions—such as boredom—we may strive to increase the level of stimulation by doing something engaging. In Chapter 9, we will see that certain personality types, such as antisocial personalities, have higher-than-average needs for excitement.

The Impact of the Biological Viewpoint

Biological discoveries have profoundly affected the way we think about human behavior. We now recognize the important role of biochemical factors and innate characteristics, many of which are genetically determined, in both normal and abnormal behavior. In addition, since the 1950s we have witnessed many new developments in the use of drugs that can dramatically alter the severity and course of certain mental disorders—particularly the more severe ones like schizophrenia. We know to some extent what biochemical changes are caused by taking these drugs, and we can evaluate their effects by noting whether changes in behavioral, cognitive, and emotional symptoms occur in a patient. The host of new drugs has brought a great deal of attention to the biological viewpoint, not only in scientific circles but also in the popular media. Biological treatments seem to have more immediate results than other available therapies, and the hope is that they may in most cases lead to a "cure-all"—immediate results with seemingly little effort.

However, as Gorenstein (1992) has argued, there are several common errors in the way many people interpret the meaning of recent biological advances. For example, some prominent biological psychiatrists have suggested that if we can show that a particular biological attribute is causally related to a particular abnormal mental condition, then that mental condition can objectively be considered an illness (e.g., Andreason, 1984; Kety, 1974; Gorenstein, 1992, p. 119). But as Gorenstein points out, it is illusory to think that establishing biological differences between, for example, schizophrenics and nonschizophrenics in and of itself substantiates that schizophrenia is an illness. All behavioral traits such as introversion and extraversion, or high and low sensation seeking, are characterized by distinctive biological characteristics and yet we do not label these traits as illnesses. Thus the decision about what constitutes a mental illness or disorder ultimately still rests on subjective opinion regarding the functional effects of the disordered behavior. Establishing the biological substrate does not bear on this issue because all behavior—normal and abnormal—has a biological substrate. The second important misconception discussed by Gorenstein (1992) concerns the idea that most, if not all, mental disorders are biological conditions with biological causes (Andreason, 1984; Kety, 1974). Given that all of our cognitions and behavior are ultimately reducible to a set of biological events occurring in the brain, it is a mistake to distinguish between psychological and biological causes in this way. As Gorenstein argues, psychological causes can be distinguished from biological causes "only prior to their entry into the central nervous system" (p. 123). This is because once a psychological cause has had its effect on a person, the effect of that psychological event is also mediated through the activities of the central nervous system. In actuality then, if we find some dysfunction of the nervous system, this dysfunction could as well have arisen from psychosocial as from biological causes.

At a more general level we must remind ourselves again that few, if any, mental disorders are independent of people's personalities or of the problems they face in trying to live their lives. We will examine viewpoints that emphasize these psychosocial and sociocultural considerations in the pages that follow, keeping in mind that the ultimate challenge will be to integrate these varying perspectives into a theoretically consistent biopsychosocial perspective on psychopathology.

THE PSYCHOSOCIAL VIEWPOINTS

There are many more psychosocial interpretations of abnormal behavior than biological ones, reflecting a wider range of opinions regarding how to best understand humans not just as biological organisms but also as people with motives, desires, perceptions, etc. We will examine in some depth three perspectives on human nature and behavior: psychodynamic, behavioral, and cognitive-behavioral. There are also two other perspectives. One is the humanistic perspective, which focuses on freeing people from disabling assumptions and attitudes so that they can live fuller lives. Its emphasis is thus on growth and self-actualization rather than on curing diseases or alleviating disorders. The other is the existential perspective, which is less optimistic and emphasizes the difficulties inherent in self-fulfillment. Highlight 3.3 presents a few of the major themes of humanistic and existential

perspectives and Chapter 17 will later consider their approach to psychotherapy—one that focuses on fostering growth toward a socially constructive and personally fulfilling way of life.

The three viewpoints we will discuss represent distinct and sometimes conflicting orientations, but they are in many ways complementary. All of them emphasize the importance of early experience and an awareness of social influences and psychological processes within an individual, hence the term psychosocial viewpoints as a descriptive label. After describing these different psychosocial models we will consider a variety of psychosocial causal factors known to be associated with abnormal behavior and discuss how some of the psychosocial models would explain their effects.

The Psychodynamic Perspectives

As discussed in Chapter 2, Sigmund Freud founded the psychoanalytic school, which emphasized the role of unconscious processes in the determination of both normal and abnormal behavior. A key concept here is the *unconscious.* Freud thought that the conscious part of the mind represents a relatively small area, while the unconscious part, like the submerged part of an iceberg, is the much larger portion. In the depths of the unconscious are the hurtful memories, forbidden desires, and other experiences that have been repressed—that is, pushed out of consciousness. However, unconscious material continues to seek expression and comes out in fantasies, dreams, slips of the tongue, and so forth, as well as when under hypnosis. Until such unconscious material is brought to awareness and integrated into the conscious part of the mind—for example, through psychoanalysis—it may lead to irrational and maladaptive behavior.

The actual techniques of psychoanalysis as a form of treatment for mental disorders are based on the general principles underlying Freud's theory of personality. They are very complex and will not be dealt with in detail here (although Chapter 17 presents further discussion). For our purposes, a general overview of the principles of classical psychoanalytic theory will suffice. For those wishing more information, good resources include Alexander's (1948) *Fundamentals of Psychoanalysis* and any of Freud's original works.

The Structure of Personality: Id, Ego, and Superego
Freud theorized that a person's behavior results from the interaction of three key components of the personality or psyche: the id, ego, and superego. The **id** is the

The Humanistic and Existential Perspectives

The Humanistic Perspective

The *humanistic perspective* views human nature as basically "good." It emphasizes present conscious processes—paying less attention to unconscious processes and past causes—and places strong emphasis on each person's inherent capacity for responsible self-direction. Humanistic psychologists think that much of the empirical research designed to investigate causal factors is too simplistic to uncover the complexities of human behavior. Thus the humanistic perspective tends to be as much a statement of values—how we ought to view the human condition—as it is an attempt to account for human behavior, at least among persons beset by personal problems. Psychotherapists who adhere to the humanistic perspective focus on freeing people from disabling assumptions and attitudes so that they can live fuller lives. Its emphasis is thus on growth and self-actualization rather than on curing diseases or alleviating disorders.

The humanistic approach emerged as a major perspective in psychology during the 1950s and 1960s when many middle-class Americans began to feel materially affluent and spiritually empty. It is optimistically concerned with an individual's future rather than his or her past. This perspective is also concerned with processes about which we have as yet little scientific information—love, hope, creativity, values, meaning, personal growth, and self-fulfillment. Although not readily subject to empirical investigation, certain underlying themes and principles of humanistic psychology can be identified. Two of these are described here.

The Self as a Unifying Theme

Humanists of the 1950s and 1960s focused their perspective on the concept of *self*. Among humanistic psychologists, Carl Rogers (1902–1987) developed the most systematic formulation of the *self-concept*, based largely on his pioneering research into the nature of the psychotherapeutic process.

Rogers (1951, 1959) stated his views in a series of propositions that may be summarized as follows:

- Each individual exists in a private world of experience of which the *I, me,* or *myself* is the center.
- The most basic striving of an individual is toward the maintenance, enhancement, and actualization of the self.
- An individual reacts to situations in terms of the way he or she perceives them, in ways consistent with his or her self-concept and view of the world.
- A perceived threat to the self is followed by a defense—including a tightening of perception and behavior and the introduction of self-defense mechanisms.
- An individual's inner tendencies are toward health and wholeness; under normal conditions, a person behaves in rational and constructive ways and chooses pathways toward personal growth and self-actualization.

In using the concept of self as a unifying theme, humanistic psychologists emphasize the importance of individuality. In studying human nature, psychologists are thus faced with the dual task of describing the uniqueness of each person and identifying the characteristics that all people share.

A Focus on Values and Personal Growth

Humanistic psychologists emphasize values and the process of choice in guiding behavior and achieving meaningful and fulfilling lives. They consider it crucial that each of us develop values based on our own experiences and evaluations rather than blindly accepting the values of others; otherwise, we deny our own experiences and lose touch with our feelings. To evaluate and choose for ourselves requires a clear sense of our own identity—the discovery of who we are, what sort of person we want to become, and why. Only in this way can we become *self-actualizing,* meaning that we are achieving our full potential. According to the humanistic view, psychopathology is essentially the blocking or distortion of personal growth and the natural tendency toward physical and mental health. Such blocking or distortion is generally the result of one or more of these causal factors: (1) the exaggerated use of ego-defense mechanisms that leave an individual increasingly out of touch with reality; (2) unfavorable social conditions and faulty learning; and (3) excessive stress.

The Existential Perspective

During the middle part of the twentieth century, as the humanistic perspective was becoming an influential force in the field of psychology, a related intellectual movement centered in Europe was also beginning to have a notable impact. This movement was *existentialism,* a philosophical outlook with roots in the work of such existential thinkers as Martin Heidegger and Søren Kierkegaard.

The existential perspective resembles humanism in its emphasis on the uniqueness of each individual, the quest for values and meanings, and the existence of freedom for self-direction and self-fulfillment. However, it represents a less optimistic view of human beings and places more emphasis on the irrational tendencies and the difficulties inherent in self-fulfillment—particularly in a modern, bureaucratic, and dehumanizing mass society. In short, living is much more of a "confrontation" for the existentialists than for the humanists. Existential thinkers are especially concerned with the inner experiences of an individual in his or her attempts to understand and deal with the deepest human problems. There are several basic tenets of existentialism:

- *Existence and essence:* A basic theme of existentialism is that our existence is a given, but what we make of it—our essence—is up to us. An adolescent boy who defiantly blurts out, "Well, I didn't ask to be born," is stating a profound truth, but in existential terms it is completely irrelevant. Whether he asked to be born or not, he is in the world and answerable for himself—for one human life. It is his responsibility to shape the kind of person he is to become and to live a meaningful and constructive life.

- *Choice, freedom, and courage:* Our essence is created by our choices, because our choices reflect the values on which we base and order our lives. As Sartre said, "I am my choices." In choosing what sort of people to become, we have absolute freedom; even refusing to choose represents a choice. Thus the locus of value is within each individual. We are inescapably the architects of our own lives.

- *Meaning, value, and obligation:* A central theme in the existential perspective is the will-to-meaning. This trait is considered a basic human characteristic and is primarily a matter of finding satisfying values and guiding one's life by them. Existentialism also places strong emphasis on our obligations to each other. The most important consideration is not what we can get out of life but what we can contribute to it by having socially constructive values and making socially constructive choices.

- *Existential anxiety and the encounter with nothingness.* A final existential theme, nonbeing, or nothingness, adds an urgent and painful note to the human situation. In its ultimate form, nothingness is death, which is the inescapable fate of all human beings. The awareness of our inevitable death and its implications for our living can lead to existential anxiety—a deep concern over whether we are living meaningful and fulfilling lives. We can overcome our existential anxiety and deny victory to nothingness by living a life that counts for something.

Thus, existential psychologists focus on the importance of establishing values and acquiring a level of spiritual maturity worthy of the freedom and dignity bestowed by one's humanness. It is the avoidance of such central issues that creates corrupted, meaningless, and wasted lives. Much abnormal behavior, therefore, is seen as the product of a failure to deal constructively with existential despair and frustration. ■

source of instinctual drives and the first structure to appear in infancy. These drives are inherited and considered to be of two opposing types: (1) *life instincts,* which are constructive drives primarily of a sexual nature and which constitute the **libido,** the basic energy of life; and (2) *death instincts,* which are destructive drives and tend toward aggression, destruction, and eventual death. Freud used the term *sexual* in a broad sense to refer to almost anything pleasurable, from eating to painting. The id operates on the **pleasure principle,** engaging in completely selfish and pleasure-oriented behavior, concerned only with the immediate gratification of instinctual needs without reference to reality or moral considerations. Although the id can generate mental images and wish-fulfilling fantasies, referred to as **primary process thinking,** it cannot undertake the realistic actions needed to meet instinctual demands.

Consequently, after the first few months of life a second part of the personality, as viewed by Freud, develops— the ego. The **ego** mediates between the demands of the id and the realities of the external world. For example, during toilet training the child learns to control a bodily function to meet parental-societal expectations, and it is the developing ego that takes the role of mediating between the physical needs of the body/id and the need to find an appropriate place and time. The basic purpose of the ego is to meet id demands, but in such a way as to ensure the well-being and survival of the individual. This role requires the use of reason and other intellectual resources in dealing with the external world, as well as the exercise of control over id demands. The ego's adaptive measures are referred to as **secondary process thinking,** and the ego operates on the **reality principle.** Freud viewed id demands, especially sexual and aggressive strivings, as inherently in conflict with the rules and prohibitions imposed by society.

As a child grows and gradually learns the rules of parents and society regarding right and wrong, Freud postulated that a third part of the personality gradually emerges from the ego—the **superego.** The superego is the outgrowth of internalizing the taboos and moral values of society. It is essentially what we refer to as the *conscience;* it is concerned with right and wrong. As the superego develops, it becomes an inner control system that deals with the uninhibited desires of the id. The superego operates through the ego system and strives to compel the ego to inhibit desires that are considered wrong or immoral. Because the ego mediates between fulfilling the desires of the id, the demands of reality, and the moral constraints of the superego, it is often called the *executive branch of the personality.*

Freud believed that the interplay of id, ego, and superego is of crucial significance in determining behavior. Often inner mental conflicts arise because the three subsystems are striving for different goals. These conflicts are called **intrapsychic conflicts** and, if unresolved, lead to mental disorder.

Anxiety, Defense Mechanisms, and the Unconscious

The concept of *anxiety*—generalized feelings of fear and apprehension—is prominent in the psychoanalytic viewpoint because it is an almost universal symptom of neurotic disorders. Indeed, Freud believed that anxiety played a key causal role in most of the forms of psychopathology that will be discussed in this book. Sometimes the anxiety is overtly experienced and sometimes it is repressed, and then transformed into, and manifested in other overt symptoms. Freud distinguished three types of anxiety, or "psychic pain," that people can suffer: (1) *reality anxiety,* arising from actual dangers or threats in the external world; (2) *neurotic anxiety,* caused by the id's impulses threatening to break through ego controls into behavior that will be punished in some way; and (3) *moral anxiety,* arising from a real or contemplated action that is in conflict with an individual's superego and arouses feelings of guilt.

Anxiety is a warning of impending real or imagined dangers as well as a painful experience, and forces an individual to take corrective action. Often, the ego can cope with objective anxiety through rational measures. However, neurotic and moral anxiety, because they are unconscious, usually cannot be dealt with through rational measures. In these cases the ego resorts to irrational protective measures that are referred to as **ego-defense mechanisms** and are described in Table 3.1. These defense mechanisms discharge or soothe anxiety, but they do so by helping a person push painful ideas out of consciousness (such as when we "forget" a dental appointment rather than by dealing directly with the problem). These mechanisms result in a distorted view of reality, although some are clearly more adaptive than others.

Psychosexual Stages of Development   In addition to his concept of the structure of personality, Freud also conceptualized five **psychosexual stages of development** that we all pass through from infancy through puberty. Each stage is characterized by a dominant mode of achieving libidinal (sexual) pleasure:

> **Oral stage:** During the first two years of life, the mouth is the principal erogenous zone; an infant's greatest source of gratification is sucking, a process that is necessary for feeding.

TABLE 3.1 EGO-DEFENSE MECHANISMS

Mechanism	Example
Acting out. Engaging in antisocial or excesssive behavior without regard to negative consequences as a way of dealing with emotional stress.	An unhappy, frustrated man has several indiscriminate affairs without regard to the negative effects of the behavior.
Denial of reality. Protecting the self from an unpleasant reality by the refusal to perceive or face it.	A smoker concludes that the evidence linking cigarette use to health problems is scientifically worthless.
Displacement. Discharging pent-up feelings, often of hostility, on objects less dangerous than those arousing the feelings.	A woman harassed by her boss at work initiates an argument with her husband.
Fixation. Attaching oneself in an unreasonable or exaggerated way to some person, or arresting emotional development on a childhood or adolescent level.	An unmarried, middle-aged man still depends on his mother to provide his basic needs.
Projection. Attributing one's unacceptable motives or characteristics to others.	An expansionist-minded dictator of a totalitarian state is convinced that neighboring countries are planning to invade.
Rationalization. Using contrived "explanations" to conceal or disguise unworthy motives for one's behavior.	A fanatical racist uses ambiguous passages from Scripture to justify his hostile actions toward minorities.
Reaction formation. Preventing the awareness of expression of unacceptable desires by an exaggerated adoption of seemingly opposite behavior.	A man troubled by homosexual urges initiates a zealous community campaign to stamp out gay bars.
Regression. Retreating to an earlier developmental level involving less mature behavior and responsibility.	A man whose self-esteem has been shattered reverts to childlike "show-off" behavior and exhibits his genitals to young girls.
Repression. Preventing painful or dangerous thoughts from entering consciousness.	A mother's occasional murderous impulses toward her hyperactive 2-year-old are denied access to awareness.
Sublimation. Channeling frustrated sexual energy into substitutive activities.	A sexually frustrated artist paints wildly erotic pictures.
Undoing. Atoning for or magically trying to dispel unacceptable desires or acts.	A teenager who feels guilty about masturbation ritually touches a doorknob a prescribed number of times following each occurrence of the act.

Source: Based on A. Freud (1946); American Psychiatric Association (1994), pp. 751–753.

Anal stage: From ages 2 to 3, the anus provides the major source of pleasurable stimulation during the time when toilet training is often going on and there are urges both for retention and elimination.

Phallic stage: From ages 3 to 5 or 6, self-manipulation of the genitals provides the major source of pleasurable sensation.

Latency stage: From ages 6 to 12, sexual motivations recede in importance as a child becomes preoccupied with developing skills and other activities.

Genital stage: After puberty, the deepest feelings of pleasure come from sexual relations.

Freud believed that appropriate gratification during each stage is important if a person is not to be stuck or *fixated* at that level. For example, he maintained that an infant who does not receive adequate oral gratification may be prone to excessive eating or drinking in adult life.

The Oedipus Complex and the Electra Complex

In general, each stage of development places demands on an individual and arouses conflicts that Freud believed must be resolved. One of the most important conflicts occurs during the phallic stage, when the pleasures of self-stimulation and accompanying fantasies pave the way for the **Oedipus complex.** Oedipus, according to Greek mythology, unknowingly killed his father and married his mother. Each young boy, Freud thought, symbolically relives the Oedipus drama. He longs for his mother

The demands of the id are evident in early childhood. According to Freud, babies pass through an oral stage, in which sucking is a dominant pleasure.

sexually and views his father as a hated rival; however, each young boy also fears that his father will take revenge on his son's lust by cutting off his penis. This **castration anxiety** forces the boy to repress his sexual desire for his mother and his hostility toward his father. Eventually, if all goes well, the boy identifies with his father and comes to have only harmless affection for his mother.

The **Electra complex** is the female counterpart of the Oedipus complex and is also drawn from a Greek tragedy. It is based on the view that each girl desires to possess her father and to replace her mother. Freud also believed that each girl at this stage experiences penis envy so that she can be more like her father and brothers. While the boy renounces his lust for his mother out of fear of castration, no such threat can realistically be posed for the girl. Her emergence from the complex is milder and less complete than the boy's. She essentially settles for a promissory note: One day she will have a man of her own who can give her a baby—which unconsciously serves as a type of penis substitute.

For either sex, resolution of this conflict is considered essential if a young adult is to develop satisfactory heterosexual relationships. The psychoanalytic perspective holds that the best we can hope for is a compromise among our warring inclinations, and to realize as much instinctual gratification as possible with minimal punishment and guilt. This perspective thus presents a deterministic view of human behavior that minimizes ratio-

nality and freedom of self-determination. On a group level, it interprets violence, war, and related phenomena as the inevitable products of the aggressive and destructive instincts present in human nature.

Newer Psychodynamic Perspectives   In seeking to understand his patients and develop his theories, Freud was chiefly concerned with the workings of the id, its nature as a source of energy, and the manner in which this id energy could be channeled or transformed. He also focused on the superego but paid relatively little attention to the importance of the ego. Later theorists developed some of Freud's basic ideas in three somewhat different directions. One new direction was started by his daughter Anna Freud (1895–1982), who was much more concerned with how the ego performed its central functions as the "executive" of personality. She and some of the more influential second generation of psychodynamic theorists refined and elaborated on the ego-defense reactions, and put the ego in the foreground, giving it an important organizing role in personality development. This school became known as *ego psychology*. A second new direction was started by theorists who focused on very early aspects of the mother-infant relationship, and the third influential second generation psychodynamic theorists focused on social determinants of behavior and on the importance of people's interpersonal relationships. In all three of these new directions, the original emphasis of traditional (Freudian) psychoanalytic theory on the primacy of libidinal energies and intrapsychic conflicts is gone. The term psychodynamic generally refers to any of these second generation theories that stemmed out of Freud's original psychoanalytic theory in some important way, and yet also departs from it in significant ways.

Object-Relations Theory   The object-relations approach had its origins in the so-called Budapest School of Psychoanalysis whose most prominent figure was Sandor Ferenczi—a colleague and friend of Freud. The representatives of this school focused more on the importance of the pre-Oedipal phase to personality development and psychopathology. Freud had believed that events happening during the Oedipal stage were key to the development of neurotic symptoms but Ferenczi believed that pre-Oedipal relationships were even more important. This approach focuses neither on the nature of the id nor the ego, but rather on the objects toward which the infant and young child has directed these impulses and which the infant and young child has introjected (incorporated)

Anna Freud (1895–1982) elaborated the theory of ego-defense mechanisms and pioneered the psychoanalytic treatment of children.

Margaret Mahler (1897–1985) elaborated the object-relations approach, which many see as the main focus of contemporary psychoanalysis.

D.W. Winnicott (1896–1971), a British object-relations theorist, emphasized that the infant psyche develops through relationships, especially with the mother, who helps create a good "holding environment" as the infant begins to develop a small degree of independence.

into his or her own personality. *Object* in this context refers to the symbolic representation of another person in the infant or child's environment, most often a parent. The concept of **introjection** refers to an internal process in which the infant or child incorporates symbolically, through images and memories, important people in his or her life. For example, the child might internalize the image of a parent's scowling face. Later, this symbol, or representation of the outer object (also known as the *inner object*), can influence how a person experiences events and behaves.

Some of the earliest developments of this object-relations emphasis in psychodynamic thought took place in the 1930s in England under the leadership of Melanie Klein (a student of Ferenczi's), W. R. D. Fairbairn, and D. W. Winnicott. Although there are many variations on **object-relations theory,** what they share is a focus on "individuals' interactions with external and internal (real and imagined) other people, and to the relationship between their internal and external object worlds" (Greenberg & Mitchell, 1983, pp. 13–14). These theorists developed the general notion that internalized objects could have various conflicting properties—such as exciting or attractive versus hostile, frustrating, or rejecting—and moreover that these objects could split off from the central ego and maintain independent existences, thus giving rise to inner conflicts. For example, a child might internalize images of a punishing father; that image becomes a harsh self-critic. An individual experiencing such splitting among internalized objects is, so to speak, "the servant of

many masters" and cannot therefore lead an integrated, orderly life.

The work of Margaret Mahler (1897–1985), who also used to belong to Ferenczi's circle, in the United States complemented and added additional insights to this approach (see, for example, Mahler, 1976). Mahler pointed out that a very young child does not differentiate between self and object. Only gradually does a child gain an internal representation of self as distinct from representations of other objects. Only gradually is object constancy achieved (in which, for instance, the mother of yesterday is seen as the same object as the mother of today). This process involves a developmental phase of separation-individuation which starts at 4 to 5 months of age and is not completed until sometime later at about age 3 (Greenberg & Mitchell, 1983). Thus, the first three years of life involves the birth of the individual from the symbiotic relationship with the mother to the separated individual. Successful completion of separation-individuation is essential for the achievement of personal maturity.

In recent years many other American analysts have become advocates of the object-relations point of view. Among them is Otto Kernberg, noted especially for his studies of both borderline and narcissistic personalities (see Chapter 9). Kernberg's view is that the borderline personality, whose chief characteristic is instability (especially in personal relationships), is an individual who is unable to achieve a full and stable personal identity (self) because of an inability to integrate and reconcile pathological internalized objects. These newer developments in

According to object relations theorists, children incorporate or *introject* symbolic aspect of important people in their lives (such as their parents) and then carry this representation with them as part of their developing personalities.

psychodynamic theory emphasize interpersonal relationships and how the quality of early pre-Oedipal relationships affects a person's subsequent ability to achieve fulfilling adult interactions.

The Interpersonal Perspective We are social beings, and much of what we are is a product of our relationships with others. It is logical to expect that much of psychopathology reflects this fact—that psychopathology is rooted in the unfortunate tendencies we have developed while dealing with our interpersonal environments. Abnormal behavior has a great deal of impact on our relationships with other people. Hence it should not be surprising that many theorists conclude that abnormal behavior is best understood by analyzing our relationships, past and present, with other people. This is the focus of the **interpersonal perspective.**

The roots of the interpersonal perspective lie in earlier developments in the psychodynamic movement. The defection in 1911 of Alfred Adler (1870–1937) from the psychoanalytic viewpoint of his teacher, Freud, grew out of Adler's emphasis on social rather than inner determinants of behavior. Adler objected to the prominence Freud gave to instincts as the basic driving forces of personality. In Adler's view, people were inherently social beings motivated primarily by the desire to belong to and participate in a group.

Over time, a number of other psychodynamic theorists also took issue with psychoanalytic theory for its neglect of crucial social factors. Among the best known of these theorists were Erich Fromm (1900–1980) and Karen Horney (1885–1952). Fromm focused on the orientations, or dispositions (exploitive, for example), that people adopted in their interactions with others. He believed that these orientations to the social environment were the bases of much psychopathology. Horney independently developed a similar view and, in particular, vigorously rejected Freud's demeaning psychoanalytic view of women (for instance, the idea that women experience penis envy). According to Horney, "femininity" was a product of the culturally determined social learning that most women experienced.

Erik Erikson (1902–1994) also extended the interpersonal aspects of psychoanalytic theory. He elaborated and broadened Freud's psychosexual stages into more socially oriented concepts, describing crises or conflicts that occurred at eight stages, each of which could be resolved in a healthy or unhealthy way. For example, during what Freud called the oral stage, when a child is preoccupied with oral gratification, Erikson believed that a child's real development centered on learning either "basic trust" of his or her social world or "basic mistrust." Although these crises are never fully resolved, failure to develop toward the appropriate pole of each crisis handicaps an individual during later stages. Trust, for instance, is needed for later competence in many areas of life. A clear sense of identity is necessary for a satisfying intimacy with another person; such intimacy, in turn, is important for becoming a nurturing parent.

Sullivan's Interpersonal Theory Another well-known interpersonal theorist was Harry Stack Sullivan (1892–1949), an American psychiatrist. Sullivan offered a comprehensive and systematic theory of personality that was explicit interpersonal. Sullivan (1953) maintained that the concept of personality had meaning only when defined in terms of a person's characteristic ways of relating to others. He argued that personality development proceeded through various stages involving different pat-

Erich Fromm (1900–1980) focused on the orientations that people adopt in their interactions with others. He believed that these basic orientations to the social environment were the bases of much psychopathology.

Erik Erikson (1902–1994) elaborated and broadened Freud's psychosexual stages into more socially oriented concepts. Erikson described conflicts that occurred at eight stages, each of which could be resolved in a healthy or unhealthy way.

Karen Horney (1885–1952) was trained in Freudian theory, but she rejected Freud's demeaning psychoanalytic view of women. She believed that "femininity" was a product of the culturally determined social learning that most women experience.

terns of interpersonal relationships. Early in life, for example, a child becomes socialized mainly through interactions with parents, and somewhat later peer relationships become increasingly important. In young adulthood, intimate relationships are established, culminating typically in marriage. Failure to progress satisfactorily through these various stages paves the way for maladaptive behavior.

Sullivan was concerned with the anxiety-arousing aspects of interpersonal relationships during early childhood (rather than Freud's emphasis on anxiety as being a signal of unconscious conflict). Because an infant is completely dependent on parents and siblings for meeting all needs, a lack of love and care leads to insecurity and what can be an overwhelming sense of anxiety. He defined security as the freedom from anxiety. He also believed that anxiety about anxiety is fundamental to much psychopathology. His emphasis on anxiety to psychopathology was even greater than Freud's (Greenberg & Mitchell, 1983). Sullivan also emphasized the role of early childhood relationships in shaping the self-concept. For example, if a little girl perceives that others are rejecting her, she may view herself in a similar light and develop a negative self-image that almost inevitably leads to maladjustment.

Interpersonal Accommodation and Attachment Other contributions to the interpersonal perspective come from the study of **interpersonal accommodation,** which is the process through which two people develop patterns of communication and interaction that enable them to attain common goals, meet mutual needs, and build a satisfying relationship. People use many cues, both verbal and nonverbal, to interpret what is really being said to them. When communication and interpersonal accommodation fail and a relationship does not meet the needs of one or both partners, it is likely to be characterized by conflict, dissension, and eventually dissolution. The principles of interpersonal behavioral accommodation have been analyzed at length by Benjamin (1982, 1993), Carson (1979), and Wiggins (1982).

Finally, Bowlby's *attachment theory,* which can in many ways be seen as having its roots in the interpersonal and object-relations' perspectives, has become an enormously influential theory in child psychology and child psychiatry, as well as adult psychopathology. Drawing on Freud and others from these perspectives, Bowlby's theory (1969, 1973, 1980) emphasizes the importance of early experience, especially early experience with attachment relationships, as laying the foundation for later functioning throughout childhood, adolescent, and adulthood. He emphasized the importance of the quality of parental care

The interpersonal model is based largely on the work of Harry Stack Sullivan (1892–1949), who believed that personality had meaning only in relation to interaction with others.

to the development of secure attachments, but also saw the infants as playing a more active role in shaping the course of their own development than had most of the earlier theorists (Carlson & Sroufe, 1995).

Impact of the Psychodynamic Perspectives In historical perspective, Freudian psychoanalysis can be seen as the first systematic approach to show how human psychological processes can result in mental disorders. Much as the biological perspective had replaced superstition with organic pathology as the suspected cause of mental disorders, the psychoanalytic perspective replaced brain pathology with intrapsychic conflict and exaggerated ego defenses as the suspected cause of at least some mental disorders.

Freud greatly advanced our understanding of both normal and abnormal behavior. Many of his original concepts have become fundamental to our thinking about human nature and behavior. Two of Freud's contributions stand out as particularly noteworthy:

1. He developed therapeutic techniques such as free association and dream analysis for becoming acquainted with both the conscious and unconscious aspects of mental life. The results thus obtained led Freud to emphasize (a) the extent to which unconscious motives and defense mechanisms affect behavior, (b) the importance of early childhood experiences in later personality adjustment and maladjustment, and (c) the importance of sexual fac-

tors in human behavior and mental disorders. Although, as we have said, Freud used the term sexual in a much broader sense than usual, the idea struck a common chord, and the role of sexual factors in human behavior was finally brought out into the open as an appropriate topic for scientific investigation.

2. He demonstrated that certain abnormal mental phenomena occur in the attempt to cope with difficult problems and are simply exaggerations of normal ego-defense mechanisms. This realization that the same psychological principles apply to both normal and abnormal behavior dissipated much of the mystery and fear surrounding mental disorders.

The psychoanalytic perspective has come under attack, however, from many directions—from other perspectives as well as from theorists within the psychodynamic tradition. Two important criticisms of traditional psychoanalytic theory center on its failure as a scientific theory to explain abnormal behavior. First, many believe that it fails to recognize sufficiently the scientific limits of personal reports of experience as the primary mode of obtaining information, although its defenders claim they are nonetheless useful. Second, there is a lack of scientific evidence to support many of its explanatory assumptions or the effectiveness of traditional psychoanalysis. In addition, Freudian theory in particular has been criticized for an overemphasis on the sex drive, for its demeaning view of women, for pessimism about basic human nature, for exaggerating the role of unconscious processes, and for failing to consider motives toward personal growth and fulfillment.

Impact of Newer Psychodynamic Perspectives The second generation of psychodynamic theorists has done much to overcome some of these objections. There are a number of psychotherapy researchers who have begun to document the utility of various psychodynamic therapeutic techniques, as well as the effectiveness of psychodynamic psychotherapy for certain problems (e.g., Crits-Christoph, 1992; Henry, Strupp, Schacht, & Gaston, 1994). In addition, these psychodynamic researchers have begun to make significant progress in developing reasonably reliable ways of measuring key concepts in psychodynamic theory such as a person's core (yet unconscious) conflictual relationships (e.g., Henry et al., 1994; Horowitz et al., 1991; Luborsky & Crits-Cristoph, 1990). Progress has also been made in understanding how the process of psychodynamic therapy works (e.g., Henry et al., 1994; Weiss & Sampson, 1986). Moreover, Bowlby's attachment theory has begun to generate an enormous amount of research supporting many of its basic tenets about normal and abnormal child development and adult psychopathology (e.g., Carlson & Sroufe, 1995).

The interpersonal perspective which views unsatisfactory relationships in the past or present as the primary causes of many forms of maladaptive behavior has also done a good deal to begin to establish its scientific validity. In the area of diagnosis, many supporters of the interpersonal perspective believe that the reliability and validity of psychological diagnoses could be improved if a new system based on interpersonal functioning were developed, and some progress has been made toward developing such a system (e.g., Benjamin, 1982, 1993). The focus of interpersonal therapy is on alleviating problem-causing relationships and on helping people achieve more satisfactory relationships. Such therapy is concerned with verbal and nonverbal communication, social roles, processes of accommodation, causal attributions (including those supposedly motivating the behavior of others), and the general interpersonal context of behavior. The therapy situation itself can be used as a vehicle for learning new interpersonal skills. Considerable research has been conducted to determine what are the most important aspects of the therapeutic process for successful outcomes (e.g., Koss & Shiang, 1994). Moreover, in recent years, major progress has been made in documenting the effectiveness of interpersonal psychotherapy in the treatment of disorders such as depression and bulimia, an eating disorder discussed in Chapter 8 (Fairburn et al., 1993; Klerman et al., 1994).

Although the interpersonal approach still lacks a fully adequate scientific grounding, it has generated considerable enthusiasm among researchers in recent years. The major impact of the interpersonal perspective has been its focus on the key role a person's close relationships play in determining whether behavior will be effective or maladaptive.

The Behavioral Perspective

The behavioral perspective arose in the early twentieth century in part as a reaction against the unscientific methods of psychoanalysis. Behavioral psychologists believed that the study of subjective experience—through the techniques of free association and dream analysis—did not provide acceptable scientific data, because such observations were not open to verification by other investigators. In their view, only the study of directly observable behavior and the stimuli and reinforcing conditions that control it could serve as a basis for understanding human behavior, normal or abnormal.

The behavioral perspective is organized around a central theme: the role of learning in human behavior. This emphasis on learning fit well within the context of the modern industrial age in a country with democratic ideals, claiming that "all men are created equal." Although this perspective was initially developed through research in the laboratory rather than through clinical practice with disturbed patients, its implications for explaining and treating maladaptive behavior soon became evident. As discussed in Chapter 2, the roots of the behavioral perspective came from the study of classical conditioning by Ivan Pavlov and from the study of instrumental conditioning by Edward Thorndike (later renamed operant conditioning by B. F. Skinner). In the United States, John Watson did much to promote the behavioral approach to psychology with his book *Behaviorism* (1924).

As we have noted, *learning*—the modification of behavior as a consequence of experience—provides the central theme of the behavioral approach. Because most human behavior is learned, the behaviorists addressed themselves to the question of how learning occurs. They focused on the effects of environmental conditions (stimuli) on the acquisition, modification, and possible elimination of various types of response patterns—both adaptive and maladaptive.

Classical Conditioning A specific stimulus may come to elicit a specific response through the process of **classical conditioning.** For example, although food naturally elicits salivation, a stimulus that reliably precedes the presentation of food will also come to elicit salivation. In this case, food is the *unconditioned stimulus* (UCS), and salivation is the *unconditioned response* (UCR). A stimulus that precedes food delivery and eventually elicits salivation is called a *conditioned stimulus* (CS). Conditioning has occurred when presentation of the conditioned stimulus alone elicits salivation—the *conditioned response* (CR). Pavlov, for instance, sounded a tone (the soon-to-be conditioned stimulus) just before he presented food (the unconditioned stimulus) to his dogs (Pavlov, 1927). After a number of tone-food pairings, the dogs salivated (the conditioned response) to the tone (the conditioned stimulus) alone. The dogs learned that the tone was a reliable predictor of food delivery and came to respond to it in a similar fashion.

The hallmark of classical conditioning is that a formerly neutral stimulus—the CS—acquires the capacity to elicit biologically adaptive responses through repeated pairings with the UCS. However, we also now know that this process of classical conditioning is not as blind or automatic as once thought. Rather, it seems that animals (and people) actively acquire information about what CSs allow them to predict, expect, or prepare for a biologically significant event (the UCS). Indeed, only CSs that provide reliable and nonredundant information about the occurrence of a UCS will acquire the capacity to elicit CRs (Hall, 1994; Rescorla, 1988). For example, if UCSs occur as often without being preceded by a CS as they do with the CS, conditioning will not occur because the CS in this case does not provide reliable information about the occurrence of the UCS. Figure 3.4 illustrates how this process occurs.

Classically conditioned responses are well maintained over time; that is, they are not simply forgotten. However, if a CS is repeatedly presented without the UCS, the conditioned response will gradually extinguish. This gradual process, known as **extinction,** should not be confused with the idea of unlearning because we know that the response may return at some future point in time (a phenomenon Pavlov called **spontaneous recovery**). Moreover, a somewhat weaker CR may also still be elicited in different environmental contexts than that in which the extinction process took place (Bouton, 1994, 1997). Thus, any extinction of fear that has taken place in a therapist's office may not necessarily generalize completely and automatically to other contexts outside the therapist's office. As we will see, these principles of extinction and spontaneous recovery have important implications for many forms of behavioral treatment.

The chief importance of classical conditioning in abnormal psychology is the fact that many physiological and emotional responses can be conditioned, including those relating to fear, anxiety, sexual arousal, and those stimulated by drugs of abuse. Thus, for example, one can learn a fear of the dark if fear-producing stimuli (such as frightening dreams or fantasies) occur regularly during conditions of darkness, or one can acquire a fear of snakes if bitten by a snake.

Instrumental Conditioning In **instrumental** (or **operant**) **conditioning** an individual learns how to achieve a desired goal. The goal in question may be to obtain something that is rewarding or to escape from something that is unpleasant. Essential here is the concept of **reinforcement,** which refers to the delivery of a reward or a pleasant stimulus, or to escape from an aversive stimulus. New responses are learned and tend to recur if they are reinforced. Although it was originally thought that instrumental conditioning, like classical conditioning, consisted of simple strengthening of a stimulus-response connection, it is now believed that the person learns a *response-outcome expectancy* (Mackintosh, 1983), and if sufficiently motivated for that outcome (e.g., being hungry) the person will make the response that it has learned produces the outcome (e.g., opening the refrigerator).

Initially a high rate of reinforcement may be necessary to establish an instrumental response, but lesser rates are usually sufficient to maintain it. In fact, an instrumental response appears to be especially persistent when reinforcement is intermittent—when the reinforcing stimulus does not invariably follow the response—as demonstrated in gambling when occasional wins seem to maintain high rates of response. However, when reinforcement is consistently withheld over time, the conditioned response—whether classical or instrumental—gradually extinguishes. In short, the subject eventually stops making the response.

A special problem arises in extinguishing a response in situations in which a subject has been conditioned to

FIGURE 3.4
CLASSICAL CONDITIONING
Before conditioning, the CS has no capacity to elicit fear, but after being repeatedly followed by a painful UCS that elicits pain and fear, the CS gradually acquires the capacity to elicit a fear CR. If there are also interpersed trials in which the UCS occurs not preceded by the CS, conditioning does not occur because in this case the CS does not have good predictive power about the occurrence of the UCS.

Classical Conditioning

Prior to conditioning:
Conditioned stimulus (neutral) (CS) ....Orientation response to light
　　　(Light)
Unconditioned stimulus (UCS)......................Unconditioned response (UCR)
　　　(Painful stimulus)　　　　　　　　　　　　　　　(Pain and fear)

During conditioning:
Conditioned stimulus (light) (CS)
　　　　　　　+　　　　　　　.........................Conditioned response (fear) (CR)
Unconditioned stimulus (UCS)
　　　(painful stimulus)

Following conditioning:
Conditioned stimulus (alone) (CS) ....Conditioned response (fear) (CR)

anticipate an aversive event and to make an instrumental response to avoid it. For example, a boy who has nearly drowned in a swimming pool may develop a fear of water and a *conditioned avoidance response* in which he consistently avoids all large bodies of water. When he sees a pond, lake, or swimming pool, he feels anxious; running away and avoiding contact lessens his anxiety and is thus reinforcing. As a result, his avoidance response is highly resistant to extinction. It also prevents him from having experiences with water that could bring about extinction of his fear. In later discussions, we will see that conditioned avoidance responses play a role in many patterns of abnormal behavior.

As we grow up, instrumental learning becomes an important mechanism for discriminating between what will prove rewarding and what will prove unrewarding—and thus for acquiring the behaviors essential for coping with our world. Unfortunately, there is no guarantee that what we learn will always be useful. We may learn to value things that seem attractive in the short run, such as cigarettes or alcohol, but that can actually hurt us in the long run, or we may learn coping patterns such as helplessness, bullying, or other irresponsible behaviors that are maladaptive rather than adaptive in the long run.

Generalization and Discrimination In both classical and instrumental conditioning, when a response is conditioned to one stimulus or set of stimulus conditions, it can be evoked by other, similar stimuli; this process is called **generalization.** A person who fears bees, for example, may generalize that fear to all flying insects.

A process complementary to generalization is **discrimination,** which occurs when a person learns to distinguish between similar stimuli and to respond differently to them. The ability to discriminate may be brought about through differential reinforcement. For example, because red strawberries taste good and green ones do not, a conditioned discrimination will occur if a person has experience with both. According to the behavioral perspective, complex processes like perceiving, forming concepts, and solving problems are all based on this basic discriminative learning process.

The concepts of generalization and discrimination have many implications for the development of maladaptive behavior. Although generalization enables us to use past experiences in sizing up new situations, the possibility always exists of making inappropriate generalizations—as when a troubled adolescent fails to discriminate between friendly and hostile "joshing" from peers. In some instances, a vital discrimination seems to be beyond an individual's capability—as when a bigoted person deals with others as stereotypes rather than as individuals—and may lead to inappropriate and maladaptive behavior.

Observational Learning Human and nonhuman primates are also capable of learning through observation alone—that is, without directly experiencing an unconditioned stimulus (for classical conditioning) or a reinforcement (for operant conditioning). For example, as we will see in Chapter 5, children can acquire fears simply through observing a parent or peer behaving fearfully with some object or situation that the child was not initially afraid of. In this case, the fear of the parent or peer is experienced vicariously and becomes attached to the formerly neutral object (Mineka & Cook, 1993). For observational operant learning, in the 1960s Bandura did a classic series of experiments on how children will observationally learn various novel aggressive responses toward a large Bobo doll after they had observed models being reinforced for these responses (cf. Bandura, 1969). Although the children themselves were never directly reinforced for showing these novel aggressive responses, they nonetheless showed them when given the opportunity to interact with the Bobo doll themselves. The possibilities for observational conditioning of both classical and operant responses greatly expand our opportunities for learning both adaptive and maladaptive behavior.

Impact of the Behavioral Perspective The principles of conditioning had been fairly well worked out by 1950 when John Dollard and Neal Miller published their classic work *Personality and Psychotherapy,* which reinterpreted psychoanalytic theory in the terminology of learning principles. They asserted that the ungoverned pleasure-seeking impulses of Freud's id were merely an aspect of the principle of reinforcement (the behavior of organisms being generally determined by the maximization of pleasure, which occurs when obtaining a reinforcement, and the minimization of pain, which occurs when escaping an aversive stimulus); that anxiety was merely a conditioned fear response; that repression was merely conditioned thought-stoppage reinforced by anxiety reduction; and so on. The groundwork was thus laid for a behavioral assault on the prevailingly psychodynamic doctrines of the time. Early efforts to apply learning principles in the treatment of abnormal behavior, such as those by Salter (1949) and Wolpe (1958), were met with much resistance by the well-entrenched supporters of psychoanalysis; it was not until the 1960s and 1970s that behavior therapy became established as a powerful way of viewing and treating abnormal behavior.

By means of relatively few basic concepts, behaviorism attempts to explain the acquisition, modification,

Neal Miller (b. 1909), along with John Dollard, reinterpreted psychoanalytic theory into the language of learning principles in their classic work *Personality and Psychotherapy.*

and extinction of nearly all types of behavior. Maladaptive behavior is viewed as essentially the result of (1) a failure to learn necessary adaptive behaviors or competencies, such as how to establish satisfying personal relationships; or (2) the learning of ineffective or maladaptive responses. Maladaptive behavior is thus the result of learning that has gone awry and is defined in terms of specific, observable, undesirable responses.

For the behaviorist, the focus of therapy is on changing specific behaviors and emotional responses—eliminating undesirable reactions (such as phobic fears or frequent temper tantrums) and learning desirable ones for certain mentally retarded or chronically mentally ill individuals (such as better social skills or learning to clothe and feed oneself). Many different behavioral techniques have been developed, based on the systematic application of learning principles. For example, fears and phobias can be successfully treated by prolonged exposure to feared objects or situations—a kind of extinction procedure derived from principles of extinction of classically conditioned responses. Using principles of operant conditioning, chronically mentally ill people can be retaught basic living skills like clothing and feeding themselves through the use of tokens that are earned for appropriate behavior and that can be turned in for desirable rewards (candy,

cigarettes, passes to go outside, etc.) Many other examples of these techniques will be given in later chapters.

The behavioral approach has been heralded for its precision and objectivity, for its wealth of research, and for its demonstrated effectiveness in changing specific behaviors. A behavior therapist specifies what behavior is to be changed and how it is to be changed. Later, the effectiveness of the therapy can be evaluated objectively by the degree to which the stated goals have been achieved. On the other hand, the behavioral perspective has been criticized for being concerned only with symptoms. However, this criticism is considered unfair by many contemporary behavior therapists given that successful symptom-focused treatment often ends up having very positive effects on other aspects of a person's life (e.g., Borkovec, Abel, & Newman, 1995; Telch et al., 1995). It has also been criticized for ignoring other issues that may be important for those seeking help, such as searching for a sense of self-direction or meaning in life. Yet others have argued that it oversimplifies human behavior and cannot explain all of its complexities. This latter criticism, however, stems at least in part from misunderstandings about the complexities of current developments in behavioral approaches such as will be discussed in Chapter 5 (e.g., Mineka & Zinbarg, 1996). Whatever its limitations, the behavioral perspective has had and continues to have a tremendous impact on contemporary views of human nature, behavior, and psychopathology.

The Cognitive-Behavioral Perspective

The behavioral perspective was a reaction to the subjectivism of an earlier era in psychology and in its radical form sought to banish private mental events from psychological study because they were unobservable and therefore deemed unsuitable for scientific research. Some proponents of radical behaviorism even refused to use such terms as mind and thought. Ironically, it, too, has been challenged for its shortcomings by members of its own ranks, as well as by psychologists and psychiatrists originally trained in the psychodynamic tradition. The challenge centered on the claim of the radical behaviorists that covert mental or cognitive processes could not be studied scientifically simply because they were not observable.

Since the 1950s psychologists, including some learning theorists, have focused on cognitive processes and their impact on behavior. Cognitive psychology involves the study of basic information-processing mechanisms, such as attention and memory, as well as higher mental processes such as thinking, planning, and decision making. In many respects, the current emphasis within psychology as a whole on understanding all of these facets of normal human cognition was originally a reaction against the relatively mechanistic nature of the traditional radical behavioral viewpoint, including its failure to attend to the importance of mental processes—both in their own right and because of their influence on emotions and behavior.

Developments in clinical psychology have paralleled this reorientation in psychology as a whole. In many instances, the developments in this area were led by individuals who were formerly identified with the behavioral tradition in clinical psychology. The **cognitive** or **cognitive-behavioral perspective** on abnormal behavior focuses on how thoughts and information processing can become distorted and lead to maladaptive emotions and behavior. Unlike behaviorism's focus on overt behavior, the cognitive view treats thoughts as "behaviors" that can be studied empirically and that can become the focus of attention in therapy. For example, a woman who is depressed and is asked to express the thoughts running through her head might respond with "I can never do anything right" or "No one will ever love me."

In addition, by studying the patterns of distorted information processing exhibited by people with various forms of psychopathology, the mechanisms that may be involved in the maintenance of certain disorders have been illuminated. For example, depressed individuals show memory biases favoring memory for negative information relative to positive or neutral information. Such biases are likely to help reinforce or maintain one's current depressed state (e.g., Mathews & MacLeod, 1994; Mineka, Watson, & Clark, 1998; Mineka & Zinbarg, 1998). Today the cognitive-behavioral perspective is highly influential, both because of the successes it has had in developing effective treatments for many disorders and because of the insights it has provided into the importance of distorted cognitions in understanding abnormal behavior.

Albert Bandura (b. 1925), a learning theorist who developed a cognitive-behavioral perspective, placed considerable emphasis on the cognitive aspects of learning. Bandura stressed that human beings regulate their behavior by internal symbolic processes—thoughts. That is, they learn *by internal reinforcement*. We prepare ourselves for difficult tasks, for example, by visualizing what the consequences would be if we did not perform them. Thus we take our automobiles to the garage in the fall and have the antifreeze checked because we can "see" ourselves stranded on a road in winter. We do not always require external reinforcement to alter our behavior patterns; with our cognitive abilities we can solve many problems internally. Bandura (1974) went so far as to say that hu-

man beings have "a capacity for self-direction" (p. 861). Bandura later developed a theory of *self-efficacy*—the belief that you can achieve a desired goal (1977a; 1986). His belief was that cognitive-behavioral treatments work in large part by improving self-efficacy.

Attributions, Attributional Style, and Psychopathology *Attribution theory* has also contributed significantly to the cognitive-behavioral approach (Anderson, Krull, & Weiner, 1996; Fiske & Taylor, 1991; Heider, 1958). **Attributions** simply refer to the process of assigning causes to things that happen. We may attribute causes to external events, such as rewards or punishments ("He did it for the money"); or we may assume that the causes are internal—that they derive from traits within ourselves or others. Causal attributions help us explain our own or other people's behaviors and make it possible to predict what we or others are likely to do in the future. A student who fails a test may attribute the failure to lack of intelligence (a personal trait) or to ambiguous test questions or unclear directions (environmental causes).

Attribution theorists have been interested in whether different forms of psychopathology are associated with characteristic attributional styles. *Attributional style* refers to a characteristic way that an individual may tend to make attributions for bad events or for good events. For example, depressed people tend to attribute bad events to internal, stable, and global causes ("I failed the test because I'm stupid" as opposed to "I failed the test because the teacher was in a bad mood and graded it unfairly"). However inaccurate our attributions may be, they become important parts of our view of the world and can have significant effects on our emotional well-being. They can also make us see other people and ourselves as unchanging and unchangeable, leading us to be inflexible in our relationships (Abramson, Seligman, & Teasdale, 1978; Buchanan & Seligman, 1995).

Cognitive Therapy Another pioneering cognitive theorist, Aaron Beck (b. 1921), adapted the concept of schemas from cognitive psychology (e.g., Neisser, 1967, 1982). A **schema** is an underlying representation of knowledge that guides the current processing of information and often leads to distortions in attention, memory, and comprehension. According to Beck (1967, 1976; Beck & Freeman, 1990), different forms of psychopathology are characterized by different maladaptive schemas that have developed as a function of adverse early learning experiences and that lead to the distortions in thinking characteristic of certain disorders such as anxiety, depression, and personality disorders.

Albert Bandura (b. 1925) stressed that people learn more by internal than external reinforcement. They can visualize the consequences of their actions rather than rely exclusively on environmental reinforcements.

Aaron Beck (b. 1921) pioneered the development of cognitive theories of depression, anxiety, and personality disorders. He also developed highly effective cognitive-behavioral treatments for these disorders.

Fundamental to his perspective is the idea that the way we interpret events and experiences determines our emotional reactions to them. Suppose, for example, that you are sitting in your living room and hear a crash in the adjacent dining room. You remember that you had left the window open in the dining room, and conclude that a gust of wind must have knocked over your favorite new vase that was sitting on the table. What would your emotional reaction be? Probably you would be annoyed or angry with yourself for either having left the window open or for having left the vase out (or both!). But suppose, on the other hand, that you conclude that a burglar must have climbed in the open window. What would your emotional reaction be then? In all likelihood, you would feel frightened. Thus your interpretation of the same event (hearing a crash in the next room) fundamentally determines your emotional reaction to it.

Beck's work has had the greatest impact on the development of cognitive-behavioral treatment approaches to various forms of psychopathology and he is generally considered the founding father of cognitive therapy. Following Beck's lead, cognitive-behavioral theoreticians and clinicians have simply shifted their focus from overt behavior itself to the underlying cognitions assumed to be producing that behavior. The issue then becomes one of altering the maladaptive cognitions, including the underlying maladaptive schemas. For example, cognitive-behavioral clinicians are concerned with their clients' self-statements—with what they say to themselves by way of interpreting their experiences. For example, people who interpret what happens in their lives as a negative reflection of their self-worth are likely to feel depressed; people who interpret a sensation that their heart is racing as meaning they may have a heart attack and may die are likely to have a panic attack. Cognitive-behavioral clinicians use a variety of techniques designed to alter whatever negative cognitive bias the client harbors (for example, see Beck, Hollon et al., 1985; Hollon & Beck, 1994). This is in contrast to, for example, psychodynamic practice, which assumes that diverse problems are due to a limited array of intrapsychic conflicts (such as an unresolved Oedipus complex) and tends not to focus treatment techniques directly on a person's particular problems or complaints. The most widely used cognitive-behavioral therapies, Albert Ellis's rational-emotive therapy and Beck's cognitive-behavioral treatment, will be described in greater detail in Chapters 5, 6, 9, and 17.

The Impact of the Cognitive-Behavioral Perspective   The cognitive-behavioral viewpoint has had a powerful impact on contemporary clinical psychology. Many researchers and clinicians have found support for the principle of altering human behavior through changing the way people think about themselves and

Some interpret terrifying scenes in a horror movie and the sensations of their heart pounding as a sign of excitement and having a good time; others intepret the same scenes and sensations as if something danger-ous and scary is *really* happening. Cognitive-behavioral psychologists emphasize that the way we interpret an event can dramatically color our emotional reactions to it.

others. Many traditional behaviorists, however, are skeptical of the cognitive-behavioral viewpoint. B. F. Skinner (1990), in his last major address, remained true to behaviorism. He questioned the move away from principles of operant conditioning and toward cognitive behaviorism. He reminded his audience that cognitions are not observable phenomena and, as such, cannot be relied on as solid empirical data. Although Skinner is gone, this debate will surely continue. Indeed, Wolpe

(1988, 1993), who was another founder of behavior therapy, remained highly critical of the cognitive per-spective until his death in 1997.

What the Adoption of a Perspective Does and Does Not Do

Each of the psychosocial perspectives on human behavior—psychodynamic, behavioral, and cognitive-behavioral—contributes to our understanding of psychopathology, but none alone can account for the complex variety of human maladaptive behaviors. Each perspective depends on generalizations from limited observations and research. In attempting to explain a complex disorder such as alcoholism, for example, the more traditional psychodynamic viewpoint focuses on intrapsychic conflict and anxiety that the person attempts to reduce through the intake of alcohol; the more recent interpersonal variant on the psychodynamic perspective focuses on difficulties in a person's past and present relationships that contribute to drinking; the behavioral viewpoint focuses on faulty learning of habits to reduce stress (drinking alcohol) and environmental conditions that may be exacerbating or maintaining the condition; and the cognitive-behavioral viewpoint focuses on maladaptive thinking, including deficits in problem solving and information processing such as irrational beliefs about the need for alcohol to reduce stress.

Thus adopting one perspective or another has important consequences: It influences our *perception* of maladaptive behavior, the *types of evidence* we look for, and *the way in which we are likely to interpret data*. In the following section we will discuss a range of psychosocial causal factors that have been implicated in the origins of maladaptive behavior. We will also illustrate how some of these different viewpoints would provide contrasting (or sometimes complementary) explanations for how they exert their effects. In later chapters, we will discuss relevant concepts from all these viewpoints as they relate to different forms of psychopathology, and in many instances, we will contrast different ways of explaining and treating the same disorder.

PSYCHOSOCIAL CAUSAL FACTORS

We begin life with few built-in patterns and a great capacity to learn from experience. What we do learn from our experiences may help us face challenges resourcefully and lead to resilience in the face of future stressors. Unfortunately, some of our experiences may be much less helpful in our later lives, and we may be deeply influenced by factors in early childhood over which we have no control. In this section we will examine the psychosocial factors that make people vulnerable to disorder or that may precipitate disorder. Psychosocial factors are those developmental influences that may handicap a person psychologically, making him or her less resourceful in coping with events.

After briefly examining the central role played by our perceptions of ourselves and our world which derive from our schemas and self-schemas, we will review specific influences that may distort the cognitive structures on which good psychological functioning depends. We will focus on four categories of psychosocial causal factors that exemplify the range of factors that have been studied: (1) early deprivation or trauma, (2) inadequate parenting styles, (3) marital discord and divorce structures, and (4) maladaptive peer relationships. Such factors typically do not operate alone. They interact with each other and with other psychosocial factors, with particular genetic and constitutional factors, and with particular settings or environments.

Our Views of the World and of Ourselves: Schemas and Self-Schemas

Fundamental to determining what we know, want, and do are some basic assumptions that we make about ourselves, our world, and the relationship between the two. Each of the different viewpoints we have described uses somewhat different terminology to describe the nature of these basic assumptions about ourselves and our worlds. However, both for the sake of simplicity and because it is perhaps the dominant research-oriented approach today, we will use terminology from the cognitive perspective to describe these assumptions that make up our frames of reference—our *schemas* about other people and the world around us, and our *self-schemas* or ideas that we have about our own attributes. Because what we can learn or perceive directly through our senses can provide only an approximate representation of "reality," we need cognitive frameworks to fill in the gaps and make sense out of what we can observe and experience.

As already noted, a *schema* is an organized representation of prior knowledge about a concept or about some stimulus that helps guide our processing of current information (Alloy & Tabachnik, 1984; Fiske & Taylor, 1991). Our schemas about the world around us and about ourselves are our guides, one might say, through the complexities of living in the world as we understand it. We all have schemas about other people (for example, expectations that they are lazy or ambitious, or that they are very career-oriented or very marriage-minded), as well as

Our self-schemas—our frames of reference for what we are, what we might become, and what is important to us—influence our choice of goals and our confidence in being able to attain them. A key element of this older woman's self-schema was that she could accomplish her lifelong goal of obtaining a college education once her children were grown in spite of the fact that she was nearly 40 years older than the average college student.

schemas about social roles (for example, expectations about what appropriate behaviors for a widow are) and about events (for example, what appropriate sequences of events are for a particular situation such as someone coping with a loss) (Fiske & Taylor, 1991).

Our **self-schemas** include our views on what we are, what we might become, and what is important to us. Other aspects of our self-schema concern our notions of the various roles we occupy or might occupy in our social environment, such as woman, man, student, parent, physician, American, older person, and so on. The various aspects of a person's self-schema also can be construed as his or her *self-identity*. Most people have clear ideas about at least some of their own personal attributes, and less clear ideas about other attributes (Fiske & Taylor, 1991).

Schemas about the world and self-schemas are vital to our ability to engage in effective and organized behavior because they guide and streamline our processing of information, allowing us to focus on what are the most relevant and important bits of information from the amazingly complex array of possible information that is available to our senses. However, schemas are also sources of psychological vulnerabilities because some of our schemas or certain aspects of our self-schema may be distorted and inaccurate. In addition, some schemas—even distorted ones—may be held with conviction, making them resistant to change. This is in part because we are usually not completely conscious of our schemas. In other words, although our daily decisions and behavior are largely shaped by these frames of reference, we may be unaware of the assumptions on which they are based—or even of having made assumptions at all. We think that we are simply seeing things the way they are and often do not often consider the fact that other pictures of the "real" world might be possible or that other rules for "right" might exist.

New experiences tend to be worked into our existing cognitive frameworks, even if the new information has to be reinterpreted or distorted to make it fit—a process known as **assimilation.** We tend to cling to existing assumptions and reject or change new information that contradicts them. **Accommodation**—changing our existing frameworks to make it possible to incorporate discrepant information—is more difficult and threatening, especially when important assumptions are challenged. Accommodation is, of course, a basic goal of psychosocial therapies—explicitly in the case of the cognitive and cognitive-behavioral variants, but deeply embedded in virtually all other approaches as well. This process makes major therapeutic change a difficult task.

Variations in Schemas and Personal Growth A person's failure to acquire appropriate principles or rules in cognitive organization can make him or her vulnerable to psychological problems later in life. Because of differences in temperament, abilities, and experiences, children differ enormously in what kinds of competencies they develop, in what kinds of ways they learn to categorize their experiences, in what kinds of values and goals they have, and in how they learn to deal with their impulses and regulate their behavior (e.g., Mischel, 1990, 1993). These learned variations make some children far better prepared than others for further learning and personal growth. The ability to make effective use of new experience depends very much on the degree to which past learning has created cognitive structures that facilitate the integration of the novel or unexpected. A well-prepared child will be able to assimilate or when necessary accommodate new experience in ways that will enhance growth; a child with less adequate cognitive foundations may be confused, unreceptive to new information, and psychologically vulnerable. It is mainly

for this reason that most theories of personality development, and all of the psychosocial viewpoints of abnormal behavior just described, emphasize the importance of early experience in shaping the main directions that a person's coping style will take.

Predictability and Controllability A good example of ways in which the events making up one child's experiences may be vastly different from those of another is whether they are predictable or controllable. At one extreme are children who grow up in stable and lovingly indulgent environments, buffered to a large extent from the harsher realities of the world; at the other extreme are children whose experiences consist of constant exposure to unpredictable and uncontrollable frightening events or unspeakable cruelties. Such different experiences have corresponding effects on the adult's schemas about the world and about the self: Some suggest a world that is uniformly loving, unthreatening and benign, which of course it is not; others a jungle in which safety and perhaps even life itself is constantly in the balance. Given a preference in terms of likely outcomes, most of us would opt for the former of these sets of experiences. However, these actually may not be the best blueprint for engaging the real world, because it may be important to encounter some stresses and learn ways to deal with them in order to gain a sense of control (Seligman, 1975) or self-efficacy (Bandura, 1977a, 1986).

Exposure to multiple uncontrollable and unpredictable frightening events is likely to leave a person vulnerable to *anxiety,* a central problem in a number of the mental disorders to be discussed in this book. For example, Barlow's (1988) and Mineka's (1985a) models acknowledge some biological vulnerability to stressful circumstances in creating anxiety, but they also emphasize the importance of experience with negative outcomes perceived to be unpredictable and uncontrollable, based on a review of pertinent research (see also Mineka & Zinbarg, 1996, 1998). A clinically anxious person is someone whose schemas include strong possibilities that terrible things over which he or she has no control may happen unpredictably, and that the world is a dangerous place. It is not difficult to imagine developmental scenarios that would lead a person to have schemas with these elements as prominent characteristics.

Finally, it appears that some uncontrollable experiences to which children are subjected are so overwhelming that they do not develop a coherent self-schema. This situation is perhaps seen most clearly in cases of dissociative identity disorder, where separate personalities have developed separate self-schemas that may be completely walled off from one another. We have learned in recent years that dissociative identity disorder (formerly called "multiple personality disorder"; see Chapter 7) may be associated with repeated, traumatic sexual and physical abuse in childhood. The main point here is that a fragmented sense of identity, whatever its origin—and it is frequently traumatic—invites the development of abnormal behaviors. On this the psychosocial viewpoints all concur; they differ primarily in the mechanisms through which they hypothesize these abnormal behaviors develop.

Early Deprivation or Trauma

Fortunately, experiences of the intensity and persistence just noted as occurring in dissociative identity disorder, although more common than was thought only a decade ago, are nevertheless relatively rare. There are, however, other kinds of experiences that, while less dramatic and chilling, may leave children with deep and sometimes irreversible psychic scars. The deprivation of needed resources normally supplied by parents or parental surrogates is one such circumstance. The needed resources range from food and shelter, to love and attention.

Parental deprivation of such resources can occur in several forms. For example, it can occur even in intact families where, for one reason or another, parents are unable (for instance, because of mental disorder) or unwilling to provide for a child's needs for close and frequent human contact. But the most severe manifestations of deprivation are usually seen among abandoned or orphaned children who may either be institutionalized or placed in a succession of unwholesome foster homes.

We can interpret the consequences of parental deprivation from several psychosocial viewpoints. Such deprivation might result in fixation at the oral stage of psychosexual development (Freud); it might interfere with the development of basic trust (Erikson); it might stunt the development of the child's capacity for relatively anxiety-free exchanges of tenderness and intimacy with others (Sullivan); it might retard the attainment of needed skills because of a lack of available reinforcements (Skinner); or it might result in the child acquiring dysfunctional schemas and self-schemas in which relationships are represented as unstable, untrustworthy, and without affection (Beck). Any of these viewpoints might be the best way of conceptualizing the problems that arise in a particular case, or some combination of them might be superior to any one.

Institutionalization As noted, in some cases children are raised in an institution where, compared with an ordinary home, there is likely to be less warmth and physical contact; less intellectual, emotional, and social stimulation; and a lack of encouragement and help in positive learning. As we are witnessing today in some countries, where institutionalization of young children is all too common, the long-range prognosis for children suffering early and prolonged parental deprivation through institutionalization is considered unfavorable (Quinton & Rutter, 1988; Quinton, Rutter, & Liddle, 1984; Rutter, 1990; Rutter & Quinton, 1984a). It is clear that many children deprived of normal parenting in infancy and early childhood show maladaptive personality development and are at risk for psychopathology. Institutionalization later in childhood in a child who has already had good attachment experiences is not so damaging (Rutter, 1987a, 1987b). However, even among those institutionalized at an early age, some show resilience and do well in adulthood. One important protective factor found to influence this was whether the child went from the institution into a harmonious family or a discordant one, with better outcomes among those who entered harmonious homes (Rutter, 1990). Other influential protective factors were having some good experiences at school, whether in the form of social relationships, or athletic or academic success, or having a supportive marital partner in adulthood; these successes probably contributed to a better sense of self-esteem or self-efficacy (Quinton & Rutter, 1988; Rutter, 1985, 1990).

Deprivation and Abuse in the Home Most infants subjected to parental deprivation are not separated from their parents, but rather suffer from inadequate care at home. In these situations parents typically neglect or devote little attention to their children and are generally rejecting. In the United States approximately two million reports of abuse and neglect are made annually, and over half are found to be accurate (Cicchetti & Toth, 1995a). Parental rejection of a child may be demonstrated in various ways—by physical neglect, denial of love and affection, lack of interest in the child's activities and achievements, failure to spend time with the child, and lack of respect for the child's rights and feelings. In a minority of cases, it also involves cruel and abusive treatment. Parental rejection may be partial or complete, passive or active, or subtly or overtly cruel.

In February 1994 during a drug raid, Chicago police discovered 19 children in this freezing, squalid cockroach-infested apartment. The stove in the kitchen did not work, and children were found sharing food with dogs off the floor. The six adults in the apartment were charged with child neglect, and child abuse charges were also considered. Growing up in such a setting may predispose children to later psychological problems.

The effects of such deprivation and rejection may be very serious. For example, Bullard and his colleagues (1967) delineated a "failure to thrive" syndrome that "is a serious disorder of growth and development frequently requiring admission to the hospital. In its acute phase it significantly compromises the health and sometimes endangers the life of the child" (p. 689). The problem is fairly common in low-income families, with estimates at about 6 percent of children born at medical centers serving low-income families (Lozoff, 1989). Such children are thought to be at risk for behavior problems and delays in development (Sameroff, 1995). The syndrome may sometimes occur in a child who has become severely depressed (Attie & Brooks-Gunn, 1995), and it may sometimes occur in children whose parents find them oppositional or "bad" and have difficulty feeding them (Sameroff, 1995). However, it is also now clear that this syndrome often has prenatal origins, with a disproportionate number having had low birth weights (Lozoff, 1989).

Outright parental abuse (physical or sexual or both) of children has also been associated with many other negative effects on the development of its victims, although some studies have suggested that, at least among infants, gross neglect may be worse than having an abusive relationship. Abused children often have a tendency to be overly aggressive (both verbally and physically) and some even respond with anger and aggression to friendly overtures from peers (e.g., Cicchetti & Toth, 1995a; Emery & Laumann-Billings, 1998). Researchers have also found that maltreated children have difficulties in linguistic de-

velopment and significant problems in emotional and social functioning, including depression and anxiety and impaired relationships with peers, who tend to avoid or reject them (Cicchetti & Toth, 1995a, b; Emery & Laumann-Billings, 1998; Rogosch, Cicchetti, & Aber, 1995; Toth & Cicchetti, 1996).

Abused and maltreated infants and toddlers are also quite likely to develop atypical patterns of attachment—most often a disorganized and disoriented style of attachment (Cicchetti & Toth, 1995a; Crittenden & Ainsworth, 1989), characterized by bizarre, disorganized, and inconsistent behavior with the caregiver. A significant portion of these children will continue to show these "confused" patterns of relating to their mother up to at least age 13. A review of research in this area concluded that "The findings on the prevalence and stability of insecure and atypical attachments in maltreated children point to the extreme risk these children face in achieving adaptive outcomes in others domains of interpersonal relationships. Internal representational models of these insecure and often atypical attachments, with their complementary models of self and others, may generalize to new relationships, leading to negative expectations of how others will behave and how successful the self will be in relation to others" (Cicchetti & Toth, 1995a, p. 549). Study of these maladaptive attachment styles is one small example of the major contributions Bowlby's attachment theory (1969, 1973, 1980) has made to our understanding of abnormal developmental patterns.

These negative expectations mean that the detrimental effects of such early traumas may never be completely overcome, partly because experiences that would provide the necessary relearning may be selectively avoided. A child whose schemas do not include the possibility that others can be trusted may not venture out toward others far enough to learn that some people in the world are in fact trustworthy, which is consistent with findings that they tend to be socially withdrawn from peers (Cicchetti & Toth, 1995a). This idea is also supported by the findings of Dodge and colleagues (1990, 1995) who found that abused children tend to attribute hostile intent to negative interactions with peers and to be more likely to think an aggressive response will have a positive outcome. Moreover, this tendency to attribute hostile intent seemed to at least partially mediate the development of aggressive behavior. That these effects may be enduring is supported by recent reviews of the long-term consequences of physical abuse (into adolescence and adulthood) which concluded that childhood physical abuse predicts both familial and nonfamilial violence in adolescence and adulthood, especially in abused men (Cicchetti

& Toth, 1995a; Emery & Laumann-Billings, 1998; Mali-nosky-Rummell & Hansen, 1993). Physical abuse was also found to be associated with self-injurious and suicidal behaviors, as well as anxiety, depression, and personality disorders. Another study found previously abused and neglected individuals continued to have lower IQs and reading ability compared to well-matched controls into adulthood (Perez & Widom, 1994). There is also increasing evidence that maltreated children, not surprisingly, show a variety of physiological disturbances (Cicchetti & Toth, 1995a).

A significant proportion of parents who reject or abuse their children have themselves been the victims of parental rejection. Their early history of rejection or abuse would clearly have had damaging effects on their schemas and self-schemas, and probably resulted in a failure to internalize good models of parenting. Kaufman and Zigler (1989) estimated that there is about a 30 percent chance of this pattern of intergenerational transmission of abuse (see also Cicchetti & Toth, 1995a).

Nevertheless maltreated children—whether the maltreatment comes from abuse or from deprivation—can improve to at least some extent when the caregiving environment improves (Cicchetti & Toth, 1995a; Emery & Laumnann-Billings, 1998; Masten & O'Connor, 1989). Moreover, there are always a range of effects, and those who were least likely to show these negative outcomes tended to have one or more protective factors, such as a good relationship with some adult during childhood, a higher IQ, positive school experiences, or physical attractiveness, among others.

Success at school—such as winning a spelling bee—may be a protective factor that helps a child overcome disadvantages such as parental deprivation or institutionalization.

Other Childhood Traumas   Most of us have had one-time traumatic experiences that temporarily shattered our feelings of security, adequacy, and worth and influenced our perceptions of ourselves and our environment. The term *psychic trauma* is used to describe any aversive (unpleasant) experience that has harmful psychological effects on an individual. The following illustrates such an incident:

> **Case Study, An Adopted Child** • I believe the most traumatic experience of my entire life happened one April evening when I was 11. I was not too sure of how I had become a member of the family, although my parents had thought it wise to tell me that I was adopted. That much I knew, but what the term adopted meant was something else entirely. One evening after my step-brother and I had retired, he proceeded to explain it to me—with a vehemence I shall never forget. He made it clear that I wasn't a "real" member of the family, that my parents didn't "really" love me, and that I wasn't even wanted around the place. That was one night I vividly recall crying myself to sleep. That experience undoubtedly played a major role in making me feel insecure and inferior.

Traumas of this sort are apt to leave psychological wounds that may never completely heal. As a result, later stress that reactivates these wounds may be particularly difficult for an individual to handle; this often explains why one person has difficulty with a problem that is not especially stressful to another. Conditioned responses, which in cognitive terms are acquired expectancies that a particular event will follow from another, are also readily established in situations that evoke strong emotions; such responses are often highly resistant to extinction. Thus one traumatic experience of almost drowning in a deep lake may be sufficient to establish a fear of water that endures for years or a lifetime. Conditioned responses stemming from traumatic experiences may also generalize to other situations. For example, the child who has learned to fear water may also come to fear riding in boats and other situations associated with even the remotest possibility of drowning. Young children are thus especially prone to acquiring intense anxieties that remain resistant to modification even as their coping resources develop over time.

Separation   Bowlby (1960, 1973) summarized the traumatic effects for children from 2 to 5 years old of being separated from their parents during prolonged periods of hospitalization. First, there are the short-term or acute effects of the separation, which can include significant despair during the separation and detachment from the parents upon reunion; Bowlby considered this to be a normal response to prolonged separation, even in securely attached infants. Children who undergo such separations may develop an insecure attachment. In addition, there can be longer-term effects of early separation from one or both parents. For example, such separations can cause an increased vulnerability to stressors in adulthood, making it more likely that the person will become depressed (Bowlby, 1980). As with other early traumatic experiences, the long-term effects of separation depend heavily on the support and reassurance given a child by parents or other significant people, which is most likely if the child has a secure relationship with at least one parent (Carlson & Sroufe, 1995; Lease & Ollendick, 1993; Main & Weston, 1981). Thus, not all children who experience even a parent's death exhibit discernible long-term effects (Brown, Harris, & Bifulco, 1985; Rutter, 1985).

Inadequate Parenting Styles

Even in the absence of severe deprivation, neglect, or trauma, many kinds of deviations in parenting can have profound effects on a child's subsequent ability to cope with life's challenges, and thus create vulnerability to various forms of psychopathology. Therefore, although their explanations vary considerably, the psychosocial viewpoints on abnormal behavior all focus attention on the behavioral tendencies a child acquires in the course of early social interaction with others—chiefly parents or parental surrogates.

You should keep in mind that a parent-child relationship is always bidirectional: As with any continuing relationship, the behavior of each person affects the behavior of the other. Some children are easier to love than others; some parents are more sensitive than others to an infant's needs. In occasional cases, we are able to identify characteristics in an infant that have been largely responsible for an unsatisfactory relationship between parent and child. A common example occurs in parents who have babies with high levels of negative emotionality (that is, they are very prone to negative moods). For example, Rutter and Quinton (1984b) found that parents tended to react with irritability, hostility, and criticism to children who were high in negative mood and low on adaptability. This in turn may set such children at risk for psychopathology because they become "a focus for discord" in the family (Rutter, 1990, p. 191). Because parents find it difficult and stressful to deal with babies who are high on negative emotionality, many of these infants may be more prone to developing avoidant styles of attachment than are infants who are not high on negative emotionality (Rothbart, Posner, & Hershey, 1995). Although these examples illustrate that characteristics of an infant can contribute to unsatisfactory attachment relationships, in most cases the influence of a parent on his or her child is likely to be more important in shaping a child's behavior, as we will see in the following sections.

Parental Psychopathology In general, it has been found that parents who have various forms of psychopathology, including schizophrenia, depression, antisocial personality disorder, and alcoholism, tend to have children who are at heightened risk for a wide range of developmental difficulties. Although some of these effects undoubtedly have a genetic component, many researchers believe that genetic effects cannot account for all of the adverse effects that parental psychopathology has on children. For example, the children of seriously depressed parents are at enhanced risk for disorder themselves (Cicchetti & Toth, 1995b, 1998; Gotlib & Avison, 1993), at least partly because depression makes for unskillful parenting—notably including inattentiveness to a child's many needs (Gelfand & Teti, 1990) and being ineffective in managing and disciplining the child (Cicchetti & Toth, 1995b, 1998). Not only do depressed mothers rate their children as having more psychological and physical problems than do nondepressed mothers, but independent observers also rate infants of depressed mothers as more unhappy and tenser than infants of nondepressed mothers. They are also more likely to have insecure attachment relationships than are children of nondepressed mothers (Cicchetti & Toth, 1995b).

In addition, children of alcoholics have elevated rates of truancy and substance abuse and a greater likelihood of dropping out of school, as well as higher levels of anxiety and depression and lower levels of self-esteem (Chassin, Rogosch, & Barrera, 1991; Gotlib & Avison, 1993), although many children of alcoholics do not have difficulties. Although most research on this topic has focused on the effects of disordered mothers on their children, attention has also been drawn to the fact that disordered fathers also make significant contributions to child and adolescent psychopathology, especially to problems such as conduct disorder, delinquency, and attention deficit disorder (Phares & Compas, 1992).

In spite of the profound effects that parental psychopathology can have on children, it should also be noted that many children raised in such families do just fine because of a variety of protective factors that may be present. For example, a child living with a parent with a serious disorder who also has a warm and nurturing relationship with the other parent, or with another adult outside the family, has a significant protective factor. Other important protective factors that promote resilience include having good intellectual skills, social and academic competence, and being appealing to adults (Masten et al., 1990; Masten & Coatsworth, 1995, 1998).

Parenting Styles: Warmth and Control There are also less extreme differences in parenting styles than may occur with various forms of parental psychopathology that nonetheless can have a significant impact on a child's development and increase their risk for psychopathology. In the past, discipline was conceived of as a method for both punishing undesirable behavior and preventing or deterring such behavior in the future. Discipline is now thought of more positively as providing needed structure and guidance for promoting a child's healthy growth. Such guidance provides a child with schemas similar to outcomes actually meted out by the world, contingent on a person's behavior. The person thus informed has a sense of control over these outcomes and is free to make deliberate choices. When punishment is deemed necessary, it is important that a parent make clear exactly what behavior is considered inappropriate. It is also important that the child know what behavior is expected, and that positive and consistent methods of discipline be worked out for dealing with infractions. In general, a child should be allowed independence in keeping with his or her level of maturity. Unfortunately, these judgments are not always easy to make.

Researchers have been interested in the degree to which parenting styles—including their disciplinary

This father, who is helping his child with homework, has an authoritative parenting style. He has a warm and supportive relationship with his son, but also sets clear limits and restrictions—for example, about how much homework must be done before his son is allowed to watch TV.

styles—affect children's behavior over the course of development. Four types of parenting styles have been identified that seem to be related to different developmental outcomes for the children: (1) authoritative, (2) authoritarian, (3) permissive/indulgent, and (4) neglectful/uninvolved. These styles vary in the degree of *parental warmth* (amount of support, encouragement, and affection versus shame, rejection, and hostility) and in the degree of *parental control* (extent of discipline and monitoring versus being largely unsupervised) (Emery & Kitzman, 1995; Maccoby & Martin, 1983).

Authoritative Parenting The *authoritative style* is one in which the parents are both very warm and very careful to set clear limits and restrictions regarding certain kinds of behaviors, but also allow considerable freedom within certain limits. This style of parenting is associated with the most positive early social development, with the children tending to be energetic and friendly and showing development of general competencies for dealing with others and with their environments (Baumrind, 1975, 1993; Emery & Kitzman, 1995). When followed into adolescence in a longitudinal study, children of authoritative parents continued to show positive outcomes.

Authoritarian Parenting Parents with an *authoritarian style* are high on control but low on warmth, and their children tend to be conflicted, irritable, and moody (Baumrind, 1975, 1993). When followed into adolescence, these children had more negative outcomes, with the boys doing particularly poorly in social and cognitive skills. If such authoritarian parents also use overly *severe discipline* in the form of physical punishment—as opposed to the withdrawal of approval and privileges—the result tends to be increased aggressive behavior on the part of the child (Emery & Kitzman, 1995; Eron et al., 1974; Patterson, 1979). Apparently, physical punishment provides a model of aggressive behavior that the child emulates and incorporates into his or her own self-schema (Millon & Davis, 1995).

Permissive-Indulgent Parenting A third parenting style is the *permissive-indulgent style*, in which parents are high on warmth but low on discipline and control. This style of parenting is associated with impulsive and aggressive behavior in children (Baumrind, 1967; Hetherington & Parke, 1993). Overly indulged children are characteristically spoiled, selfish, inconsiderate, and demanding. In a classic study Sears (1961) found that much permissiveness and little discipline in a home were correlated positively with antisocial, aggressive behavior, particularly during middle and later childhood. Unlike rejected and emotionally deprived children, indulged children enter readily into interpersonal relationships, but they exploit people for their own purposes in the same way that they have learned to exploit their parents (Millon & Davis, 1995). Overly indulged children also tend to be impatient, and to approach problems in an aggressive and demanding manner (Baumrind, 1971, 1975). In short, they have self-schemas with significant "entitlement" features. Confusion and difficulties in adjustment may occur when "reality" forces them to reassess their assumptions about themselves and the world.

Neglectful-Uninvolved Parenting Finally, parents who are low both on warmth and on control represent the *neglectful-uninvolved style*. This style of parental uninvolvement is associated with disruptions in attachment during childhood (Egeland & Sroufe, 1981), and with moodiness, low self-esteem, and conduct problems later in childhood (Baumrind, 1991; Hetherington & Parke, 1993). These children of uninvolved parents also have problems with peer relations and with academic performance (Hetherington & Parke, 1993).

When examining only the effects of restrictiveness (ignoring the warmth variable), research has shown that restrictiveness can serve as a protective factor for children growing up in high-risk environments, as defined by a combination of family occupation and education level, minority status, and absence of a father (Baldwin, Baldwin, & Cole, 1990). Among high-risk children, those who did well in terms of cognitive outcome (IQ and school achievement) tended to have more restrictive and less democratic parents. Indeed, restrictiveness was positively related to cognitive outcome only among high-risk children and not among low-risk children. Restrictiveness was also particularly helpful for families living in areas with high crime rates.

Inadequate, Irrational, and Angry Communication Parents sometimes discourage a child from asking questions and in other ways fail to foster the information exchange essential for helping the child develop essential competencies. Inadequate communication may take a number of forms. Some parents are too busy or preoccupied with their own concerns to listen to their children and to try to understand the conflicts and pressures they are facing. As a consequence, these parents often fail to give needed support and assistance, particularly when there is a crisis. Other parents have forgotten that the world often looks different to a child or adolescent—rapid social change can lead to a communication gap between generations. In other instances, faulty communica-

tion may take more deviant forms in which messages become completely garbled because a listener distorts, disconfirms, or ignores a speaker's intended meaning.

Children are often exposed to high levels of anger and conflict. The anger can occur in the context of marital discord, abuse, or parental psychopathology, and it is often associated with psychological problems in children (Emery & Kitzman, 1995; Schneider-Rosen & Cicchetti, 1984). This is not surprising given that children often become distressed and emotionally aroused by such background anger, just as they do when abused (Cummings, 1987; Emery, 1989; Emery & Kitzman, 1995). Not surprisingly, abused children are even more frightened by parental anger—especially unresolved anger—than are nonabused children (Hennessy, Rabideau, Cicchetti, & Cummings, 1994).

Marital Discord and Divorce

The disturbed parent-child patterns so far described, such as parental rejection, are rarely found in severe form unless the total familial context is also abnormal. Thus disturbed family structure is an overarching risk factor that increases an individual's vulnerability to particular stressors. We will distinguish between intact families where there is significant marital discord and families that have been disrupted by divorce or separation.

Marital Discord In some cases of marital discord or conflict, one or both of the parents is not gaining satisfaction from the relationship. One spouse may express feelings of frustration and disillusionment in hostile ways such as nagging, criticizing, and doing things purposely to annoy the other person. Whatever the reasons for the difficulties, seriously discordant relationships of long standing are likely to be frustrating, hurtful, and generally damaging in their effects on the adults and their children (Emery & Kitzman, 1995). One recent study found that children could be buffered against many of the damaging effects of marital conflict if one or both parents had the following characteristics: warmth, proneness to giving praise and approval, and ability to inhibit rejecting behavior toward their children (Katz & Gottman, 1997). Another recent study found that children who had high levels of support from their peers were also buffered against the negative effects of marital discord in their parents (Wasserstein & La Greca, 1996).

More severe cases of marital discord may expose children to one or more of the stressors we have already discussed: child abuse or neglect, the effects of living with a parent with a serious mental disorder, authoritarian or neglectful/uninvolved parenting, and spouse abuse. In all these cases, the children are caught up in an unwholesome and irrational psychological environment and as they grow up they may find it difficult to establish and maintain marital and other intimate relationships.

Divorced Families In many cases a family is incomplete as a result of death, divorce, separation, or some other circumstance. Due partly to a growing cultural acceptance of divorce, more than a million divorces now occur yearly in the United States (U.S. Bureau of the Census, 1992). Estimates are that about 20 percent of children under the age of 18 are living in a single-parent household—some with unwed parents and some with divorced parents. Nearly one half of marriages end in divorce and it is estimated that 50 to 60 percent of children born in the 1990s will live at some point in single parent families (Hetherington, Bridges, & Insabella, 1998).

Effects of Divorce on Parents Unhappy marriages are difficult, but ending a marital relationship can also be enormously stressful for the adults, both mentally and physically. Divorced and separated persons are overrepresented among psychiatric patients, although the direction of the causal relationship is not always clear. In their comprehensive review of the effects of divorce on adults, Amato and Keith (1991a) concluded that it is a major source of psychopathology, as well as physical illness, death, suicide, and homicide.

Effects of Divorce on Children Divorce can have traumatic effects on children, too. Feelings of insecurity and rejection may be aggravated by conflicting loyalties and, sometimes, by the spoiling the children receive while staying with one of the parents. Not surprisingly, some children do develop serious maladaptive responses. Temperamentally difficult children are likely to have a more difficult time adjusting than are temperamentally easy children (Hetherington, Stanley-Hagan, & Anderson, 1989). Somewhat ironically, these also may be the children whose parents are more likely to divorce, perhaps because having difficult children is likely to exacerbate marital problems (Block, Block, & Gjerde, 1986). Delinquency and a wide range of other psychological problems are much more frequent among children and adolescents from divorced families than among those from intact families, although it is likely that a contributing factor here is prior or continuing parental strife (Chase-Lansdale, Cherlin, & Kiernan, 1995; Rutter, 1971, 1979). Finally, a number of studies have demonstrated that there may well be long-term effects of divorce on adaptive

functioning into adulthood in as much as many studies have found lower educational attainment, lower incomes, lower life-satisfaction, and an increased probability of being on welfare and having children out of wedlock in young adults from divorced families (Amato & Keith, 1991b; Chase-Lansdale et al., 1995; Hetherington et al., 1998). Children from divorced families are also more likely to have their own marriages end in divorce. One 70-year longitudinal study of gifted children born around 1910 found that those whose parents had divorced before the children were 21 died an average of four years sooner than those whose parents did not divorce before they were 21 (Tucker et al., 1997).

Nevertheless, many children adjust quite well to the divorce of their parents. Indeed, a quantitative review of 92 studies on parental divorce and the well-being of children conducted on 13,000 children since the 1950s concluded that the average negative effects of divorce on children are actually quite modest in size (Amato & Keith, 1991a; see also Chase-Lansdale et al., 1995; Emery & Kitzman, 1995; Hetherington et al., 1998), as are the negative effects persisting into adulthood (Amato & Keith, 1991b). They also found that the effects seem to be decreasing over the past four decades (particularly since 1970), perhaps because the stigma of divorce is decreasing (Amato & Keith, 1991a, b). The domains of well-being that were examined in childhood included school achievement, conduct problems, psychological and social adjustment, self-concept, and parent-child relations. Children in the middle-age range (grade school to high school) had slightly worse outcomes than preschool-age and college-age children (Amato & Keith, 1991a). The domains in adulthood that were examined included psychological well-being, family well-being, socioeconomic well-being, and physical health (Amato & Keith, 1991b; Emery & Kitzman, 1995).

The effects of divorce on children are often more favorable than the effects of remaining in a home torn by marital conflict and dissension (Emery & Kitzman, 1995; Hetherington et al., 1998; Amato & Keith, 1991a). At one time it was thought that the detrimental effects of divorce might be minimized if a successful remarriage provided an adequate environment for child rearing. Unfortunately, however, the Amato and Keith (1991a) review revealed that such children living with a stepparent were no better off than children living with a single parent, although this was more true for girls than for boys. Indeed, some studies have found that the period of adjustment to remarriage may be longer than that for divorce (Hetherington et al., 1989). Other studies have shown that children—especially very young children—living with a stepparent are at increased risk for physical abuse and even death by the stepparent, relative to children living with two biological parents (Daly & Wilson, 1988, 1996).

Maladaptive Peer Relationships

Another important set of relationships outside the family usually begins in the preschool years—those involving age-mates, or peers. Normally, these neighborhood or school relationships involve a much broader range of possible experiences than do the more constrained and established relationships within families. When a child ventures into the world independently, he or she is faced with a number of complicated and unpredictable challenges. The potential for problems and failure is considerable.

Children at this stage are hardly masters of the fine points of human relationships or diplomacy. Empathy—the appreciation of another's situation, perspective, and feelings—is at best only primitively developed, as can be seen in a child who turns on and rejects a current playmate when a more favored candidate arrives. The child's own immediate satisfaction tends to be the primary goal of any interaction, and there is only an uncertain recognition that cooperation and collaboration may bring even greater benefits. A substantial minority of children seems somehow ill-equipped for the rigors and competition of the school years, most likely by virtue of temperamental factors and deficits in the psychosocial climate of their families. A significant number of them withdraw from their peers; a large number of others (especially among males) adopt physically intimidating and aggressive lifestyles. The neighborhood bully and the menacing school yard loner are examples. Neither of these routes bode well for good mental health outcomes (e.g., Coie et al., 1992; Coie & Cillessen, 1993; Dodge et al., 1997).

Fortunately, there is another side to this coin. If peer relations have their developmental hazards, they can also be sources of key learning experiences that stand an individual in good stead for years, perhaps for a lifetime. For a resourceful youngster, the give-and-take, the winning and losing, the successes and failures of the school years provide superb training in coming to grips with the real world and with his or her developing self—its capabilities and limitations, its attractive and unattractive qualities. The experience of intimacy with another, with a friend, has its beginning in this period of intense social involvement. If all has gone well in the early juvenile years, a child emerges into adolescence with a considerable reper-

Juvenile socializing is a risky business in which a child's hard-won prestige in a group is probably perceived as being constantly in jeopardy. Actually, reputation and status in a group tend to be stable, and a child who has been rejected by peers is likely to continue to have problems in peer relationships.

toire of social knowledge and skills—often known as social competence. Such an adolescent can effectively adapt his or her behavior to the requirements of a situation and communicate, as appropriate, his or her thoughts and feelings to others. Practice and experience in intimate communication with others makes possible a transition from attraction, infatuation, and mere sexual curiosity to genuine love and commitment. Such resources can be strong protective factors against frustration, demoralization, despair, and mental disorder (Masten & Coatsworth, 1998).

Although the scenario just outlined seems reasonable, it lacked until recently a strong empirical research foundation. In fact, the developmental period it addresses had been largely ignored by the major personality theorists, Erikson and Sullivan being notable exceptions. In the last 25 years, however, research into risk factors associated with children's peer relations has been accelerating. Some of the more important of these findings are briefly summarized in the following section.

Sources of Popularity Versus Rejection What determines which children will be popular and which will be rejected? By far the most consistent correlate of popularity among juveniles is being seen as friendly and outgoing (Hartup, 1983). The causal relationship between popularity and friendliness is indeterminate and probably involved in complex ways with other variables, such as intelligence and physical attractiveness.

Far more attention has been devoted to identifying why some children are persistently rejected by their peers.

One large factor is an excessively demanding or aggressive approach to ongoing peer activities, but this factor by no means characterizes the behavior of all children rejected by their peers. A smaller group of children is apparently rejected because of their own social withdrawal or submissiveness. Others are rejected for unknown reasons; evidently some reasons are quite subtle (Coie, 1990).

Many rejected children have poor entry skills in seeking to join ongoing group activities: They draw attention to themselves in disruptive ways and may make unjustified aversive comments to others. Consequently they frequently become the focal point of verbal and physical aggression (Coie & Kupersmidt, 1983; Coie & Dodge, 1988). Indeed, approximately half of rejected boys are highly aggressive (Coie & Cillessen, 1993); another large subset who may become chronic victims of rejection are not aggressive but are highly unassertive and quite submissive toward their peers (Schwartz, Dodge, & Coie, 1993). More generally, Dodge and colleagues (1980; see Crick & Dodge, 1994, for a review) have described the aggressive children as taking offense too readily and as attributing hostile intent to the teasing of their peers, escalating confrontations to unintended levels. They also tend to take a more punitive and less forgiving attitude toward such situations (Coie et al., 1991). Aggression toward peers in the fifth grade was the best predictor of juvenile delinquency and school dropout seven years later (see also Coie et al., 1992; Coie & Cillessen, 1993). One causal pathway for this association has been supported by Patterson, Capaldi, and Bank (1991; see also Dishion, 1994). Building on the finding that aggression is the best predictor of peer rejection (Coie et al., 1990), they found that peer rejection often leads a child to associate with deviant peers several years later, which in turn is associated with a tendency toward juvenile delinquency.

In the end, rejection leads to social isolation, often self-imposed (Dodge, Coie, & Brakke, 1982; Hymel & Rubin, 1985). Coie (1990) pointed out that such isolation is likely to have serious consequences because it deprives a child of further opportunities to learn the rules of social behavior and interchange, rules that become more sophisticated and subtle with increasing age. Repeated social failure is the usual result, with further damaging effects on self-confidence and self-esteem, as well as sometimes leading to loneliness and depression (Burks, Dodge, & Price, 1995). Kupersmidt, Burchinal, and Patterson (1995) reported that 9- to 13-year-old children who were rejected by their peers were more likely to show aggression and delinquency over the next four years than were nonrejected children.

A child's position in a group tends, in the absence of intervention, to remain stable, especially by the fifth grade and beyond. On average, "stars" tend to remain stars and "rejects," rejects. For example, in one study almost half of the fifth graders who were rejected by their peers continued to be rejected over the next five years (Coie & Dodge, 1983). Some of this happens because other children tend to explain the behavior of the rejected child in terms of stable characteristics of the child. Because they have negative expectations of the rejected child, they act more negatively toward the child, thus setting up a kind of self-fulfilling prophecy for the interaction between the rejected child and his peers.

In summary, both logic and research findings lead to a similar conclusion: A child who fails to establish a satisfactory relationship with peers during the developmental years is deprived of a crucial set of background experiences and is at higher-than-average risk for a variety of negative outcomes in adolescence and adulthood (Burks et al., 1995; Kupersmidt et al., 1990). Peer social problems in childhood have been linked to a variety of breakdowns in later adaptive functioning, including depression, school dropout, and delinquency. Although these correlational data do not in themselves permit strong causal inferences, they constitute important links in a highly plausible causal chain. However, one should also remember that the peer social problems may also be early markers of disorders that have a heritable component but that do not become full-blown until later in adolescence or adulthood. In actuality, what is often going on is that the peer social problems are indeed in part reflecting some heritable diathesis, but in turn are also serving as stressors that make it more likely that the underlying vulnerability will lead to full-blown disorder later on (Parker et al., 1995).

THE SOCIOCULTURAL VIEWPOINT

By the beginning of the twentieth century, sociology and anthropology had emerged as independent scientific disciplines and were making rapid strides toward understanding the role of sociocultural factors in human development and behavior. Early sociocultural theorists included such notables as Ruth Benedict, Ralph Linton, Abram Kardiner, Margaret Mead, and Franz Boas. Their investigations and writings showed that individual personality development reflected the larger society—its institutions, norms, values, ideas, and—as well as the immediate family and other groups. Studies also made clear the relationship between sociocultural conditions and mental disorders—between the particular stressors in a society and the types of mental disorders that typically occur in it. Further studies showed that the patterns of both physical and mental disorders in a given society could change over time as sociocultural conditions changed. These discoveries have added new dimensions to modern perspectives on abnormal behavior (Westermeyer & Janca, 1997).

Uncovering Sociocultural Factors Through Cross-Cultural Studies

The sociocultural viewpoint is concerned with the impact of the social environment on mental disorder, but the relationships between maladaptive behavior and sociocultural factors such as poverty, discrimination, or illiteracy are complex. It is one thing to observe that a person with a psychological disorder has come from a harsh environment. It is quite another thing, however, to show empirically that these circumstances were either necessary or sufficient conditions for producing the disorder. Part of the problem relates to the impossibility of conducting controlled experiments. Investigators cannot ethically rear children with similar genetic or biological traits in diverse social or economic environments in order to find out which variables affect development and adjustment.

Nevertheless, natural occurrences have provided laboratories for researchers. Groups of human beings have been exposed to very different environments, from the Arctic to the tropics to the desert. These societies have developed different means of economic subsistence and different types of family structures. Accordingly, highly diverse social and political systems have developed. Nature has indeed done social scientists a great favor by providing such a wide array of human groups for study. Several researchers have suggested that cross-cultural research can enhance our knowledge about the range of variation that is possible in human behavioral and emotional development, as well as being a way of generating ideas about what causes normal and abnormal behavior, which can later be tested more rigorously in the laboratory (e.g., Weisz et al., 1996).

Research supports the view that many psychological disturbances—in both adults and children—are universal, appearing in most cultures studied (Al-Issa, 1982; Butcher, 1996; Kleinman, 1988; Verhulst & Achenbach, 1995). For example, although the incidences and symptoms vary, the pattern of behaviors we call schizophrenia (Chapter 12) can be found among almost all peoples, from the most primitive to the most technologically advanced. Recent

studies have also shown that certain psychological symptoms, as measured by the Minnesota Multiphasic Personality Inventory (MMPI-2; see Chapter 15), were consistently found among similarly diagnosed clinical groups in many other countries (e.g., Butcher, 1996).

Nevertheless, although some universal symptoms appear, cultural factors do influence abnormal behavior. Human biology does not operate in a vacuum; cultural demands serve as causal factors and modifying influences in psychopathology. For example, sociocultural factors often create stress for an individual (Al-Issa, 1982; Cohler, Stott, & Musick, 1995). For example, children growing up in an oppressive society that offers few rewards and many hassles are likely to experience more stress and thus be more vulnerable to disorder than children growing up in a society that offers ample rewards and considerable social support. In addition, growing up during a period of great fear, such as during a war, a famine, or a period of persecution, can make a child vulnerable to psychological problems.

Cultural Differences in Which Disorders Develop and How They Are Experienced Sociocultural factors also appear to influence which disorders develop, the forms that they take, and their courses. A good example of this point is a comparison study by Butcher (1996) of psychiatric patients from Italy, Switzerland, Chile, India, Greece, and the United States who were all diagnosed with paranoid schizophrenia. Patients with this diagnosis produced similar general personality patterns on the MMPI in spite of coming from widely differing cultures. However, such cross-cultural comparisons can also reveal differences. For example, in one study the Italian patients also showed an exaggerated pattern of physical complaints significantly greater than that of the Swiss and the American patients, regardless of clinical diagnosis (Butcher & Pancheri, 1976).

In another example, Kleinman (1986, 1988) traced the different ways that Chinese people (in Taiwan and in the People's Republic of China) deal with stress compared with Westerners. He found that in Western societies depression was a frequent reaction to individual stress. In China, on the other hand, he noted a relatively low rate of reported depression. Instead, the effects of stress were more typically manifested in physical problems, such as fatigue, weakness, and other complaints. Moreover, Kleinman and Good (1985) surveyed the experience of depression across cultures. Their data show that important elements of depression in Western societies—for example, the acute sense of guilt typically experienced—do not appear in other cultures. They also point out that the symptoms of depression (or dysphoria), such as sadness, hopelessness, unhappiness, lack of pleasure in the things of the world and in social relationships, have dramatically different meanings in different societies. For Buddhists, seeking pleasure from things of the world and social relationships is the basis of all suffering; a willful disengagement is thus the first step on the road to salvation. For Shi'ite Muslims in Iran, grief is a religious experience, associated with recognition of the tragic consequences of living justly in an unjust world; the ability to experience dysphoria fully is thus a marker of depth of personality and understanding. Several examples of abnormal behavior that appear only in certain cultures are given in Highlight 3.4 on culture-bound syndromes.

Culture and Over- and Under-controlled Behavior Fascinating issues are also raised by recent studies

Culture can influence not only what mental disorders develop, if any, but also *how* they are experienced. Stress is often a precipitant of depression in Western cultures. However, in Taiwan and the People's Republic of China, people who are under stress tend to experience physical problems such as fatigue or weakness.

of childhood psychopathology in different cultures. In cultures such as that of Thailand, adults are said to be highly intolerant of *undercontrolled behavior* such as aggression, disobedience, and disrespectful acts in their children. Children are explicitly taught to be polite and deferential and to inhibit any expression of anger. This raises interesting questions about whether childhood problems of undercontrolled behavior would be lower in Thailand than in the United States where such behavior seems to be tolerated to a greater extent. Conversely it also raises the question of whether *overcontrolled behavior* problems such as shyness, anxiety, and depression would be overrepresented in Thailand relative to the United States.

Two cross-national studies (Weisz, Sywanlert et al., 1987, 1993) have confirmed that Thai children and adolescents do indeed have a greater prevalence of overcontrolled problems than do American children. Although there were no differences in the rate of undercontrolled problems between the two countries, there were differences in the kind of undercontrolled behavior problems reported. For example, Thai adolescents had higher scores than American adolescents on indirect and subtle forms of undercontrol not involving interpersonal aggression, such as having difficulty concentrating or being cruel to animals; American adolescents on the other hand had higher scores than Thai adolescents on behaviors like fighting, bullying, and disobeying at school (Weisz et al., 1993). However, these findings are further complicated by the fact that Thai and American parents differ a good deal in which problems they will bring for treatment. In general, Thai parents seem less likely to refer their children for psychological treatment than are American parents (Weisz & Weiss, 1991; Weisz et al., 1996). This may be in part because of their Buddhist belief in the transience of problems and their optimism that their child's behavior will improve. Alternatively, Thai parents may not refer their children with undercontrolled problems for treatment simply because these problems are so unacceptable that they are embarrassed to go public with them (Weisz et al., 1996).

Related findings have also emerged from studies comparing Jamaican and American children. Jamaicans come from an Afro-British tradition that is also intolerant of acting out behavior and that promotes politeness and respectfulness. Accordingly, it is not surprising that Jamaican children were more likely to be referred to a clinic for overcontrolled behavior than were American children, whereas American children were more likely to be referred for undercontrolled behavior than were Ja-

Culture-Bound Syndromes

Name of Disorder	Culture	Description
Amok	Malaysia (also observed in Laos, the Philippines, Polynesia, Papua New Guinea, Puerto Rico)	A disorder characterized by sudden, wild outbursts of violent aggression or homicidal behavior in which an afflicted person may kill or injure others. This rage disorder is usually found in males who are rather withdrawn, quiet, brooding and inoffensive prior to the onset of the disorder. Episodes are often precipitated by a perceived slight or insult. Several stages have been observed: Typically in the first stage the person becomes more withdrawn; then a period of brooding follows in which a loss of reality contact is evident. Ideas of persecution and anger predominate. Finally, a phase of automatism or *Amok* occurs, in which the person jumps up, yells, grabs a knife, and stabs people or objects within reach. Exhaustion and depression usually follow, with amnesia for the rage period.
Latah	Malaysia and Indonesia (also Japan, Siberia, and the Philippines)	Hypersensitivity to sudden fright often occurring in middle-aged women of low intelligence who are subservient and self-effacing. The disorder is precipitated by the word snake or by tickling. It is characterized by *echolalia* (repetition of the words and sentences of others) and *echopraxia* (repetition of the acts of others). A disturbed individual may also show dissociative or trancelike behavior.
Koro	Southeast Asia and China (particularly Malaysia)	A fear reaction or anxiety state in which a man fears that his penis will withdraw into his abdomen and he may die. This reaction may appear after sexual overindulgence or excessive masturbation. The anxiety is typically very intense and of sudden onset. The condition is "treated" by having the penis held firmly by the patient or by family members or friends. Often the penis is clamped to a wooden box.
Windigo	Algonquin Indian hunters	A fear reaction in which a hunter becomes anxious and agitated, convinced that he is bewitched. Fears center on his being turned into a cannibal by the power of a monster with an insatiable craving for human flesh.
Kitsunetsuki	Japan	A disorder in which victims believe that they are possessed by foxes and are said to change their facial expressions to resemble foxes. Entire families are often possessed and banned by the community. This reaction occurs in rural areas of Japan where people are superstitious and relatively uneducated.
Taijin kyofusho (TKS)	Japan	A relatively common psychiatric disorder in Japan in which an individual develops a fear of offending or hurting other people through being awkward in social situations or because of an imagined physical defect or problem. The excessive concern over how a person presents himself or herself in social situations is the salient problem.
Zar	North Africa and Middle East	A person who believes he or she is possessed by a spirit and may experience a dissociative episode during which shouting, laughing, singing, or weeping may occur. The person may also show apathy and withdrawal, not eating or working.

Source: Based on Bartholomew (1997); Chowdhury (1996); Hatta (1996); Kiev (1972); Kirmayer (1991, 1995); Lebra (1976); Lewis & Ednie (1997); Sheung-Tak (1996); Simons and Hughes (1985); American Psychiatric Association (1994).

maican children (Lambert, Weisz, & Knight, 1989). These findings may reflect either differences in prevalence rates of over- and under-controlled behavior in each nation or they may reflect differences between Jamaican and American parents' judgments about what problems need treatment (Lambert et al., 1992).

The Need for More Cross-cultural Study All of these findings illustrate an important point—the need for greater study of cultural influences on psychopathology. This neglected area of research may yet answer many questions about the origins and courses of behavior problems (Cohler et al., 1995; Marsella et al., 1985). Yet even with strong evidence of cultural influences on psychopathology, many professionals may fail to adopt an appropriate cultural perspective when dealing with mental illness. Many cross-cultural researchers have noted a reluctance of "mainstream" psychologists and psychiatrists to incorporate the cross-cultural perspective in their research and clinical practices even when their patients or subjects are from diverse cultures (e.g., Clark, 1987; Cohler et al., 1995; Kleinman, 1988). This occurs despite increasing research showing that patients may do better when treated by therapists from their own ethnic group (or at least by someone familiar with the patient's culture) (Sue et al., 1991; Tharp, 1991; Yeh et al., 1994). In a shrinking world, with instant communication and easy transportation, it is crucial for our sciences and professions to take a world view. In fact, Kleinman and Good (1985) consider cultural factors so important to our understanding of depressive disorders that they have urged the psychiatric community to incorporate another axis in the DSM diagnostic system to reflect cultural factors in psychopathology. Although this has not yet happened, authors of DSM-IV (1994) did include an appendix in which they lay out the ways in which cultural factors should be considered when making psychiatric diagnoses. They also provided a glossary of culture-bound syndromes that usually occur only in specific societies or cultural areas and are described as "localized, folk, diagnostic categories" (p. 844). Some of these are described in the And Modern Life box.

Sociocultural Influences in Our Own Society

As was noted in Chapter 1, the study of the incidence and distribution of physical and mental disorders in a population (as in the research just cited) is called *epidemiology.* The epidemiological approach implicates not only the social conditions and high-risk areas that are correlated with a high incidence of given disorders, but also the groups for whom the risk of pathology is especially high—for example, refugees from other countries (Cohler et al., 1995; Vega & Rumbaut, 1991). Throughout this text we will point out many high-risk groups with respect to suicide, drug dependence, and other maladaptive behavior patterns. This information provides a basis for formulating prevention and treatment programs; in turn, the effectiveness of these programs can be evaluated.

With the gradual recognition of sociocultural influences, what was previously an almost exclusive concern with individual patients has broadened to include a concern with societal, communal, familial, and other group settings as factors in mental disorders. Sociocultural research has led to programs designed to improve the social conditions that foster maladaptive behavior and mental disorder, and to community facilities for the early detection, treatment, and long-range prevention of mental disorder. In Chapter 18 we will examine some clinical facilities and other programs—both governmental and private—that have been established as a result of community efforts.

Sociocultural Causal Factors

We will begin our discussion of the sociocultural factors that increase our vulnerability to the development of abnormal behavior by considering the role of culture in affecting an individual's behavior patterns. For reasons of temperament, conditioning, and other individual factors, not all people adopt the prevailing cultural patterns. This situation is especially common in Western society, where we are exposed to many competing values and patterns. We will also examine several factors in the social environment that may increase vulnerability: low socioeconomic class, disorder-engendering social roles, prejudice and discrimination, economic and employment problems, and social change and uncertainty. However, as already noted, it is important to remember that with sociocultural research it is perhaps even more difficult than with biological or psychosocial research to identify true causal factors. Nevertheless, documenting the association between various sociocultural factors and abnormal behavior provides an important first step for developing hypotheses about causal processes.

The Sociocultural Environment

In much the same way that we receive a genetic inheritance that is the end product of millions of years of biological evolution, we also receive a sociocultural inheritance that is the end product of thousands of years of social evolution. The significance of this inheritance was well pointed out by Aldous Huxley (1965):

> The native or genetic capacities of today's bright city child are no better than the native capacities of a bright child born into a family of Upper Paleolithic cave-dwellers. But whereas the contemporary bright baby may grow up to become almost anything—a Presbyterian engineer, for example, a piano-playing Marxist, a professor of biochemistry who is a mystical agnostic and likes to paint in water colours—the Paleolithic baby could not possibly have grown into anything except a hunter or food-gatherer, using the crudest of stone tools and thinking about his narrow world of trees and swamps in terms of some hazy system of magic. Ancient and modern, the two babies are indistinguishable. . . . But the adults into whom the babies will grow are profoundly dissimilar; and they are dissimilar because in one of them very few, and in the other a good many, of the baby's inborn potentialities have been actualized. (p. 69)

Because each group fosters its own cultural patterns by systematically teaching its offspring, all its members tend to be somewhat alike—to conform to certain basic personality types. Children reared among headhunters become headhunters; children reared in societies that do not sanction violence learn to settle their differences in nonviolent ways. The more uniform and thorough the education of the younger members of a group, the more alike they will become. Thus in a society characterized by a limited and consistent point of view, there are not the wide individual differences typical in a society like ours, where children have contact with diverse, often conflicting, beliefs. Even in our society, however, there are certain core values that most of us consider essential.

Subgroups within a general sociocultural environment—such as family, sex, age, class, occupational, ethnic, and religious groups—foster beliefs and norms of their own, largely by means of social roles that their members learn to adopt. Expected role behaviors exist for a student, a teacher, an army officer, a priest, a nurse, and so on. Because most people are members of various subgroups, they are subject to various role demands, which also change over time. In fact, an individual's life can be viewed as a succession of roles—child, student, worker, spouse, parent, and senior citizen. When social roles are conflicting, unclear, or uncomfortable, or when an individual is unable to achieve a satisfactory role in a group, healthy personality development may be impaired—just as it is when a child is rejected by juvenile peer groups.

The extent to which role expectations can influence development is well illustrated by masculine and feminine roles in our own society and their effects on person-

ality development and on behavior. In recent years, a combination of masculine and feminine traits (androgyny) has often been claimed to be psychologically ideal for both men and women. Many people, however, continue to show evidence of having been strongly affected by traditional assigned masculine and feminine roles. Moreover, there is accumulating evidence that the acceptance of gender-role assignments has substantial implications for mental health. In general, studies show that low "masculinity" is associated with maladaptive behavior and vulnerability to disorder for either biological sex, possibly because this condition tends to be strongly associated with deficient self-esteem (Carson, 1989). Baucom (1983), for example, has shown that high-feminine-sex-typed (low masculinity) women tend to reject opportunities to lead group problem-solving situations. He likens this effect to learned helplessness, which, as we have seen, has in turn been suggested as a causal factor in anxiety (Barlow, 1988; Mineka, 1985a; Mineka & Zinbarg, 1996) and depression (Abramson et al., 1978; Seligman, 1975). Given findings like these, it should not be too surprising that women show much higher rates of anxiety and depressive disorders (see Chapters 5 and 6).

Pathogenic Societal Influences

There are many sources of pathogenic social influences, some of which stem from socioeconomic factors and others from sociocultural factors regarding role expectations and the destructive forces of prejudice and discrimination. Some of the more important ones will be examined in the following sections.

Low Socioeconomic Status and Unemployment

In our society, an inverse correlation exists between socioeconomic status (SES) and the prevalence of abnormal behavior—the lower the socioeconomic class, the higher the incidence of abnormal behavior (e.g., Kessler et al., 1994). The strength of the correlation seems to vary with different types of disorder, however. For example, antisocial personality disorder is strongly related to social class, occurring at three times the rate in the lowest income category as in the highest income category, whereas depressive disorders occur only about 50 percent more often in the lowest income category as in the highest income category (Kessler et al., 1994).

We do not understand all the reasons for the more general inverse relationship. There is evidence that some people with mental disorders slide down to the lower rungs of the economic ladder and remain there because they do not have the economic or personal resources to climb back up

(Gottesman, 1991). These people will often have children who also show abnormal behavior for a whole host of reasons, including biological reasons such as increased risk for prenatal complications leading to low birth weight. At the same time, more affluent people are better able to get prompt help or to conceal their problems. In addition, it is almost certainly true that people living in poverty encounter more, and more severe, stressors in their lives than do people in the middle and upper classes, and they usually have fewer resources for dealing with them. Thus the tendency for some forms of abnormal behavior to appear more frequently in lower socioeconomic groups may be at least partly due to increased stress in the people at risk (Gottesman, 1991; Hobfoll et al., 1995).

Children from lower SES families also tend to have more problems. A number of studies have documented a strong relationship between the poverty status of parents and lower IQs in children at least up to 5 years of age, with persistent poverty having the most adverse effects (Duncan et al., 1994; McLoyd, 1998). These adverse effects of poverty on cognitive functioning seem to occur as a function of a variety of factors associated with poverty, including poor physical health or low birth weight at birth, higher risk of prenatal exposure to drugs, higher risk of lead poisoning, and less cognitive stimulation in the home environment (McLoyd, 1998). Moreover, Dodge and colleagues (1994) found that low socioeconomic status of parents as assessed when children were in preschool significantly predicted teacher- and peer-rated acting out and aggressive behaviors over the next four years. Nevertheless, findings from a longitudinal study of inner-city children in Boston showed that in spite of coming from high-risk socioeconomic background, many of the boys did very well and showed upward mobility. Resilience here was best indicated by childhood IQ and having adequate functioning as a child in school, family, and peer relationships (Felsman & Valliant, 1987; Long & Valliant, 1984; Masten & Coatsworth, 1995).

In addition to studies of the effects of poverty on children, other studies have examined the effects of unemployment per se on adults and children. Such studies have repeatedly found unemployment to be associated with enhanced vulnerability and thus to elevated rates of abnormal behavior (Dew, Penkower, & Bromet, 1991; Dooley & Catalano, 1980). Recession and inflation coupled with high unemployment are sources of chronic anxiety for many people. Unemployment has placed a burden on a sizable segment of our population, bringing with it both financial hardships, self-devaluation, demor-

In our society the lower the socioeconomic class, the higher the incidence of abnormal behavior. The conditions under which lower-class youngsters are reared tend to inhibit the development of coping skills. Many individuals, however, emerge from low socioeconomic environments with strong, highly adaptive personalities and skills.

alization, and emotional distress. In fact, unemployment can be as damaging psychologically as it is financially.

Research on the effects of unemployment was intense in the Great Depression of the 1930s (Eisenberg & Lazarsfeld, 1938), but during the period of economic prosperity following World War II interest in the topic waned. However, interest was rekindled in the 1970s and 1980s when severe economic recessions were experienced worldwide and moderately high rates of employment became a seemingly permanent part of modern society. More recent crises in the 1990s have centered around the effects that corporate restructuring and downsizing has had on upper middle class people who find themselves having to look for work at much lower incomes than in the past. We certainly have not come close to solving the human problems such major economic shifts entail.

Periods of extensive unemployment are typically accompanied by adverse effects on mental and physical health. In particular, rates of depression, marital problems, and somatic complaints increase during periods of unemployment, but usually normalize following reemployment (Dew et al., 1991; Jones, 1992). It is not simply that those who are mentally unstable tend to lose their jobs. These effects occur even when mental health status before unemployment is taken into account. The psychological and physical health problems are more severe in lower socioeconomic groups (Jones, 1992). It also seems that physical violence among couples is associated with unemployment, although the causal direction is unclear (Dew et al., 1991). Not surprisingly, the wives of unemployed men also are adversely affected, with higher levels of anxiety, depression, and hostility, which seems to be at least partially caused by the distress of the unemployed husband (Dew, Bromet, & Schulberg, 1987). In addition, children can be seriously affected. In the worst cases, the unemployed fathers engage in child abuse, with many studies documenting an association between child abuse and father's unemployment (Cicchetti & Lynch, 1995; Dew et al., 1991). In one prospective study, all the children born on Kauai, Hawaii, in 1955 were followed until age 18 (Werner & Smith, 1982). One of the best predictors distinguishing children (especially boys) who experienced significant problems with mental health or delinquency from those who did not was whether the father had lost his job when his children were small.

Maternal unemployment can also have adverse effects—especially if the mother is single. For example, McLoyd and colleagues (1994; McLoyd, 1998) found that single African-American mothers who were unemployed (relative to those who were employed) showed more frequent punishment of their adolescent children, which in turn led to cognitive distress and depressive symptoms in the adolescents.

Disorder-Engendering Social Roles

An organized society, even an "advanced" one, sometimes asks its members to perform roles in which the prescribed behaviors either are deviant themselves or may produce maladaptive reactions. Soldier's who are called upon by their superiors (and ultimately by his society) to deliberately kill and maim other human beings may subsequently develop serious feelings of guilt. They may also have latent emotional problems resulting from the horrors commonly experienced in combat and hence be vulnerable to disorder. As a nation, we are still struggling with the many problems of this type that have emerged among veterans of the Vietnam War (Kulka et al., 1990), as discussed in Chapter 4. The feeling of guilt over atrocities committed were especially pronounced in Vietnam veterans.

Prejudice and Discrimination in Race, Gender, and Culture

Vast numbers of people in our society have been subjected to demoralizing stereotypes and overt discrimination in areas such as employment, education, and housing. We have made progress in race relations since the 1960s, but the lingering effects of mistrust and discomfort among various ethnic and racial groups can be clearly observed on almost any college campus. For the most part, students socialize informally only with members of their own subcultures, despite the attempts of many well-meaning college administrators to break down the barriers. The tendency of students to avoid crossing these barriers needlessly limits their educational experiences and probably contributes to continued misinformation about, and prejudice toward, others. Prejudice against minority groups may play a role in explaining why these groups sometimes show increased prevalence of certain mental disorders (Cohler et al., 1995; Kessler et al., 1994).

We have made progress in recognizing the demeaning and often disabling social roles our society has historically assigned to women. Again though, much remains to be done. As already noted, many more women than men suffer from various emotional disorders, notably depression and many anxiety disorders. Mental health professionals believe this is a consequence both of the vulnerabilities (such as passivity and dependence) intrinsic to the traditional roles assigned to women, and possibly of the special stressors with which many modern women must cope (being full-time mothers, full-time homemakers, and full-time employees) as their traditional roles rapidly change. However, it should also be noted that working outside the home has also been shown to be a protective factor against depression under at least some circumstances (e.g., Brown & Harris, 1978).

Social Change and Uncertainty

The rate and pervasiveness of change today are different from anything our ancestors ever experienced. All aspects of our lives are affected—our education, our jobs, our families, our leisure pursuits, our finances, and our beliefs and values. Constantly trying to keep up with the numerous adjustments demanded by these changes is a source of constant and considerable stress. Simultaneously, we confront inevitable crises as the earth's consumable natural resources dwindle and as our environment becomes increasingly noxious with pollutants. Certain neighborhoods have increasing problems with drugs and crime. No longer are Americans confident that the future will be better than the past or that technology will solve all our problems. On the contrary, our attempts to cope with existing problems increasingly seem to create new problems that are as bad or worse. The resulting despair, demoralization, and sense of helplessness are well-established predisposing conditions for abnormal reactions to stressful events (Dohrenwend et al., 1980; Seligman 1990, 1998).

UNRESOLVED ISSUES

Theoretical Viewpoints and the Causes of Abnormal Behavior

The viewpoints described in this chapter are theoretical constructions devised to orient psychologists in the study of abnormal behavior. As a set of hypothetical guidelines, each viewpoint speaks to the importance and integrity of its own position to the exclusion of other explanations. Most psychodynamically oriented clinicians, for example, value those traditional writings and beliefs consistent with Freudian or later psychodynamic theories, and they minimize or ignore the teachings of opposing viewpoints. They usually adhere to prescribed practices of psychodynamic therapy and do not use other methods, such as desensitization therapy.

Advantages of Having a Theoretical Viewpoint

Theoretical integrity and adherence to a systematic viewpoint has a key advantage: It provides a consistent approach to orient one's practice or research efforts. Once mastered, the methodology can guide a practitioner or researcher through the complex web of human problems. Theoretical adherence has its disadvantages, however. By excluding other possible explanations, it can blind researchers to other factors that may be equally important.

However, the fact is that none of the theories to date addresses the whole spectrum of abnormality—each is limited in its focus. Two general trends have occurred as a result. First, the original model or theory may be revised by expanding or modifying some elements of the system. There are many examples of such corrective interpretations, such as Adler's or Jung's modification of Freudian theory or the more recent cognitive-behavioral approach as a modification of behavior therapy. But many of the early Freudian theorists did not accept the neo-Freudian additions, and many classical behavior therapists today do not accept the revisions proposed by cognitive behaviorists. Therefore, theoretical viewpoints tend to multiply and coexist—each with its own proponents—rather than being assimilated into previous views.

The Eclectic Approach

Alternatively, aspects of two or more diverse approaches may be combined in a more general, eclectic approach.

As already noted, explanations based on single viewpoints are likely to be incomplete. In practice, many psychologists have responded to the existence of many perspectives by adopting an eclectic stance—that is, they accept working ideas from several existing viewpoints and use whichever they find to be useful. For example, a psychologist using an eclectic approach might accept causal explanations from psychodynamic theory while applying techniques of anxiety reduction derived from behavior therapy. Another psychologist might combine techniques from the cognitive-behavioral approach with those from the interpersonal approach. Purists in the field—those advocating a single viewpoint—are skeptical about eclecticism, claiming that the eclectic approach tends to lack integrity and produces a "crazy quilt" of activity with little rationale and inconsistent practice. This criticism may be true, but the approach certainly works for many psychologists.

Typically, those using an eclectic approach make no attempt to synthesize the theoretical perspectives. Although the approach can work in practical settings, it is not successful at a theoretical level because the underlying principles of many of the theoretical perspectives are incompatible as they now stand. Thus the eclectic approach still falls short of the final goal, which is to tackle the theoretical clutter and develop a single, comprehensive, internally consistent viewpoint that accurately reflects what we know empirically about abnormal behavior. It may be unrealistic to expect a single theoretical viewpoint to be broad enough to explain abnormal behavior in general and specific enough to accurately predict the symptoms and causes of specific disorders. Nevertheless, such a unified viewpoint is the challenge for the next generation of theorists in the field of abnormal psychology.

The Biopsychosocial, Unified Approach

At present the one attempt at such a unified perspective is called the *biopsychosocial viewpoint*, and it acknowledges the interaction of biological, psychosocial, and sociocultural causal factors in the development of abnormal behavior. The biopsychosocial model was first articulated in order to account for the effects of psychological and sociocultural factors in physical health and has now become the dominant viewpoint in the fields of health psychology and behavioral medicine (see Chapter 8). However, it has also now been extended to the study of many other disorders as well.

The biopsychosocial viewpoint fits well with the conclusion that most disorders, especially those occurring beyond childhood, are the result of many causal factors—biological, psychosocial, and sociocultural. Moreover, for any person the particular combination of causal factors may be relatively unique, or at least not widely shared by large numbers of people with the same disorder. For example, some children may become delinquents because of having a heavy genetic loading for antisocial behavior, while others may become delinquent because of environmental influences such as living in an area with a large number of gangs. Nevertheless, we can still have a scientific understanding of many of the causes of abnormal behavior even if we cannot predict such behavior with exact certainty in each individual case and are often left with a rather large array of "unexplained" influences.

SUMMARY

In most instances the occurrence of abnormal or maladaptive behavior is the joint product of a person's vulnerability (diathesis) to disorder and of certain stressors that challenge his or her coping resources. Such vulnerabilities may be necessary or contributory causal factors, but they are not generally sufficient to cause disorder. Some of the major contributory causal influences are reviewed in this chapter. We also distinguished between relatively distal causal factors and those that are more proximal. There are also a variety of protective factors that can promote more positive developmental outcomes even in persons who have the diathesis for a disorder.

Both the distal (long-term) and the proximal (immediate) causes of mental disorder may involve biological, psychosocial, and sociocultural factors. These three classes of factors can interact with each other in complicated ways. At present there are many different points of view on the interpretation and treatment of abnormal behavior. We discussed biological, psychosocial, and sociocultural viewpoints, each of which tends to emphasize the importance of causal factors of the same type.

The early biological viewpoint focused on brain damage as a model for the understanding of abnormality. Modern biological thinking about mental disorders has focused more on the biochemistry of brain functioning, as well as other more subtle forms of brain dysfunction. In examining biologically based vulnerabilities, we must consider genetic endowment (including chromosomal irregularities), brain dysfunction and neural plasticity, physical deprivation, and temperament. Investigations in this area show much promise for advancing our knowledge of how the mind and the body interact to produce maladaptive behavior.

The psychosocial viewpoints on abnormal behavior, which deal with human psychology rather than biology, necessarily are more varied than the biological perspective. The oldest of these perspectives is Freudian psychoanalytic theory. For many years this view was preoccupied with questions about libidinal energies and their containment, but more recently it has shown a distinctly social or interpersonal thrust under the influence of object-relations theory. Object-relations theorists also emphasize the importance of the quality of very early (pre-Oedipal) mother-infant relationships for normal development. The originators of the interpersonal perspective were defectors from the psychoanalytic ranks who took exception to the Freudian emphasis on the internal determinants of motivation and behavior. As a group, interpersonal theorists have emphasized that important aspects of human personality have social or interpersonal origins. This viewpoint sees unsatisfactory relationships in the past or present as the primary causes of maladaptive behaviors. Psychoanalysis and closely related approaches are termed psychodynamic in recognition of their attention to inner, often unconscious forces.

The behavioral perspective on abnormal behavior, which was rooted in the desire to make psychology an objective science, was slow in overcoming a dominant psychodynamic bias, but in the last 30 years it has established itself as a significant force. Behaviorism focuses on the role of learning in human behavior. It views maladaptive behavior either as a failure of learning appropriate behaviors, or learning maladaptive behaviors.

Initially a spin-off from (and in part a reaction against) the behavioral perspective, the cognitive-behavioral viewpoint attempts to incorporate the complexities of human cognition in a rigorous, information-processing framework. This viewpoint attempts to alter maladaptive thinking and improve a person's abilities to solve problems and to plan.

For psychosocially determined causes or sources of vulnerability, the situation is somewhat more complicated than it is for biological causes. It is clear, however, that people's schemas and self-schemas play a central role in the way that they process information and in the kinds of attributions and values concerning the world that they have. The efficiency, accuracy, and coherence of a person's schemas and self-schemas appear to provide an important protection against breakdown. Sources of psychosocially determined vulnerability include early social deprivation or severe emotional trauma, inadequate parenting styles, marital discord and divorce, and maladaptive peer relationships.

The sociocultural viewpoint is concerned with the social environment as a contributor to mental disorder because sociocultural variables are also important sources of vulnerability, or, conversely, of resistance to it. The incidence of particular disorders varies widely among different cultures. Unfortunately, we know little of the specific factors involved in these variations. In our own culture, certain prescribed roles, such as those relating to gender, appear to be more predisposing to disorder than others. Low socioeconomic status is also associated with greater risk for various disorders, possibly because it is often difficult for economically distressed families to provide their offspring with sufficient coping resources. Ad-

ditionally, certain roles evolved by given cultures may in themselves be maladaptive, and certain large-scale cultural trends, such as rapid technological advance, may increase stress while lessening the effectiveness of traditional coping resources.

Such findings reveal that we are still a long way from the goal of a complete understanding of abnormal behavior. The many theoretical perspectives that exist have given us a start, and a good one at that—but they fall short. To obtain a more comprehensive understanding of mental disorder, we must draw on a variety of sources, including the findings of genetics, biochemistry, psychology, sociology, and so forth. The biopsychosocial approach comes closest, but in many ways it is merely a descriptive acknowledgment of these complex interactions rather than a clearly articulated theory of how they interact. It is the task of future generations of theorists to devise a general theory of psychopathology, if indeed one is possible.

KEY TERMS

etiology (p. 63)

necessary cause (p. 63)

sufficient cause (p. 63)

contributory cause (p. 64)

diathesis-stress models (p. 65)

protective factors (p. 65)

resilience (p. 66)

developmental psychopathology (p. 67)

synapse (p. 69)

neurotransmitters (p. 69)

hormones (p. 71)

genotype (p. 72)

phenotype (p. 72)

genotype-environment correlation (p. 73)

genotype-environment interaction (p. 73)

pedigree (family history) method (p. 74)

twin method (p. 74)

concordance rates (p. 74)

adoption method (p. 75)

temperament (p. 77)

developmental systems approach (p. 78)

id (p. 81)

libido (p. 84)

pleasure principle (p. 84)

primary process thinking (p. 84)

ego (p. 84)

secondary process thinking (p. 84)

reality principle (p. 84)

superego (p. 84)

intrapsychic conflicts (p. 84)

ego-defense mechanisms (p. 84)

psychosexual stages of development (p. 84)

Oedipus complex (p. 85)

castration anxiety (p. 86)

Electra complex (p. 86)

introjection (p. 87)

object-relations theory (p. 87)

interpersonal perspective (p. 88)

interpersonal accommodation (p. 89)

classical conditioning (p. 91)

extinction (p. 92)

spontaneous recovery (p. 92)

instrumental (or operant) conditioning (p. 92)

reinforcement (p. 92)

generalization (p. 93)

discrimination (p. 93)

cognitive-behavioral perspective (p. 95)

attributions (p. 95)

schema (p. 95)

self-schema (p. 98)

assimilation (p. 99)

accommodation (p. 99)

Stress and Adjustment Disorders

Paul Goesch, *Horus Remembered*. Born in 1885, Goesch was a German artist and highly successful architect. He was hospitalized at the age of 36 after suffering mental problems for some years. He lived in an institution near Berlin until 1940, when he was removed by the Nazis to Austria and murdered there with other mental patients.

It is probably not necessary to point out that life can be stressful. Everyone faces a different mix of adjustive demands in life, and any one of us may break down if the going gets tough enough. Under conditions of overwhelming stress, even a previously stable person may develop temporary (transient) psychological problems and lose the capacity to gain pleasure from life (Berenbaum & Connelly, 1993). This breakdown may be sudden, as in the case of a person who has gone through a severe accident or fire, or it may be gradual, as in the case of a person, in a deteriorating marriage or other intimate relationship, who has been subjected to prolonged periods of tension and challenges to his or her self-esteem. Most often a person recovers once a stressful situation is over, although in some cases there may be long-lasting damage to self-concept and an increased vulnerability to certain types of stressors. Today's stress can be tomorrow's vulnerability. In the case of a person who is quite vulnerable to begin with, of course, a stressful situation may precipitate more serious and lasting psychopathology.

In Chapter 3 we focused on the diathesis, or vulnerability, half of the diathesis-stress model of abnormal behavior. We saw that our vulnerabilities, whether biological or psychological, can predispose us to develop abnormal behavior. In this chapter we will focus on the role of stress as a precipitating causal factor in abnormal behavior. We will see that, at times, the impact of stress depends not only on its severity, but on a person's preexisting vulnerabilities as well. It is important to remember here that many of the factors that contribute to diatheses are also sources of stress. This is especially true of psychosocial factors, such as emotional deprivation, inadequate parenting, and the like. In this chapter our focus will be on the precipitating nature of stress; in Chapter 3 we focused on its predisposing nature. As you read the chapter, however, keep in mind that people are different in the way they perceive, interpret, and cope with stress and traumatic events.

Research findings and clinical observations on the relationship between stress and psychopathology are so substantial that the role of stressors in symptom development is now formally emphasized in diagnostic formulations. In DSM-IV (American Psychiatric Association, 1994), for example, a diagnostician can specify on Axis IV the specific psychosocial stressors facing a person. The Axis IV scale is particularly useful in relation to three Axis I categories: adjustment disorder, acute stress disorder, and post-traumatic stress disorder (acute, chronic, or delayed). These disorders involve patterns of psychological and behavioral disturbances that occur in response to identifiable stressors. The key differences between them lie not only in the severity of the disturbances but also in the natures of the stressors and the time frames during which the disorders occur. In these disorders, the stressors supposedly can be identified as causal factors and specified on Axis IV.

In this chapter, we will first look at what stress is, the factors that affect it, and how we react to it, focusing on some specific situations that result in severe stress and their effects on physical health and adjustment. We will then examine severe, catastrophic stress situations that precipitate the development of post-traumatic stress disorders. In the last part of the chapter, we will look at attempts made by mental health workers to intervene in the stress process either to prevent stress reactions or to limit their intensity and duration once they have developed.

WHAT IS STRESS?

Life would be simple indeed if all of our needs were automatically satisfied. In reality, however, many obstacles, both personal and environmental, prevent this ideal situation. We may be too short for professional basketball or have less money than we need. Such obstacles place adjustive demands on us and can lead to stress. The term *stress* has typically been used to refer both to the adjustive demands placed on an organism and to the organism's internal biological and psychological responses to such demands. To avoid confusion, we will refer to adjustive demands as **stressors,** to the effects they create within an organism as **stress,** and to efforts to deal with stress as **coping strategies.** Note that separating these constructs is somewhat arbitrary, as Neufeld (1990) has pointed out: stress is a by-product of poor or inadequate coping. For the purpose of study, however, making the distinction between stress and stressors can be of help. What is important to remember in the long run is that the two concepts—stress and coping—are interrelated and dependent on each other.

All situations, positive and negative, that require adjustment can be stressful. Thus, according to Canadian physiologist Hans Selye (1956, 1976a), the notion of stress can be broken down further into **eustress** (positive stress) and **distress** (negative stress). (In most cases, the stress experienced during a wedding would be eustress; during a funeral, distress.) Both types of stress tax a person's resources and coping skills, though distress typically has the potential to do more damage. In the following sections, we will look at (1) categories of stressors, (2) factors predisposing a person to stress, and (3) the unique and changing stressor patterns that characterize each person's life.

Categories of Stressors

Adjustive demands, or stressors, stem from sources that fall into three basic categories: (1) frustrations, (2) conflicts, and (3) pressures. Though we will consider these categories separately, they are closely interrelated.

Frustrations   When a person's strivings are thwarted, either by obstacles that block progress toward a desired goal or by the absence of an appropriate goal, frustration occurs. Frustrations can be particularly difficult for a person to cope with because they often lead to self-devaluation, making the person feel that he or she has failed in some way or is incompetent. One young man with whom one of the authors is acquainted became so frustrated over his financial problems, working two jobs, and school pressures that he simply left the university, telling a friend "I can't take this anymore!"

A wide range of obstacles, both external and internal, can lead to frustration. Prejudice and discrimination, unfulfillment in a job, and the death of a loved one are common frustrations stemming from the environment; physical handicaps, limited ability to perform certain tasks, loneliness, guilt, and inadequate self-control are sources of frustration based on personal limitations.

Conflicts   In many instances stress results from the simultaneous occurrence of two or more incompatible needs or motives: The requirements of one preclude satisfaction of the others—for example, the woman who loves her job but must decide whether to uproot her family for a promotion. In essence she has a choice to make, and she will experience conflict while trying to make it. Conflicts with which everyone has to cope may be classified as *approach-avoidance*, *double-approach*, and *double-avoidance types* (see Table 4.1). Classifying conflicts in this manner is somewhat arbitrary, and various combinations among the different types are perhaps the rule rather than the exception. Thus a double-approach conflict between alternative careers may also have its approach-avoidance aspects because of the responsibilities that either will impose. Regardless of how we categorize conflicts, they represent a major source of stress that can often become overwhelming in intensity.

Pressures   Stress may stem not only from frustrations and conflicts but also from pressures to achieve specific goals or to behave in particular ways. In general, pressures force us to speed up, intensify effort, or change the direction of goal-oriented behavior. All of us encounter many everyday pressures, and we often handle them without undue difficulty. In some instances, however, pressures seriously tax our coping resources, and if they become excessive, they may lead to maladaptive behavior.

Living in extreme proverty with insufficient life resources can be a powerful stressor in a person's life at any age, but especially for children.

TABLE 4.1 CLASSIFICATION OF CONFLICT SITUATIONS

1. *Approach-avoidance conflicts* involve strong tendencies to approach and to avoid the same goal. Mary has been offered an appealing new job in another department of the company in which she is employed. The job is one that she has had her eye on for several years and includes a substantial pay raise and better benefits. Unfortunately, her ex-husband with whom she has been having great difficulty, also works in that department. She becomes very upset when she has to deal with him and is concerned that the work atmosphere would be unbearable.

2. *Double-approach conflicts* involve choosing between two or more desirable goals. Though the experience may cause more eustress than distress, the stress is still real and the choice difficult. In either case, the person gives up something. Charles G. is faced with a decision that many would envy but is giving him a lot of sleepless nights. He has been admitted into two graduate programs that have almost equal appeal. One is a program at a highly prestigious university whose graduates tend to get the best positions. The other school is also highly respected (not as much as the first school) and has exactly the type of specialization he has wanted with an outstanding faculty. Choosing one, of course, means turning down the other. He has been vacillating between the choices, sometimes changing his decision every five minutes.

3. *Double-avoidance conflicts* are those in which the choices are between undesirable alternatives. Neither choice will bring satisfaction, so the task is to decide which course of action will be least disagreeable—that is, the least stressful. Jenny's mother sent her an airline ticket to enable her to attend an "important" family outing the likes of which Jenny has grown to despise. She is considering a course of action that she finds very distasteful—lying to her mother about being so busy that she cannot attend. She knows that if she fails to go her mother will be very punitive but the family gatherings have become very stressful.

Pressures can originate from external or internal sources. Students may feel under severe pressure to make good grades because their parents demand it, or they may submit themselves to such pressure because they want to get into graduate school. The long hours of study, the tension of examinations, and the sustained concentration of effort over many years result in considerable stress for many students. Many students preparing for important, career-determining examinations, such as the Graduate Record Exam (GRE) or the Medical College Admissions Test (MCAT), experience considerable anxiety as the examination date approaches. Fifty premedical students reported their anxiety levels for 17 days before and 17 days after the MCAT. The experience of anxiety was greater in the days preceding the examination with peak anxiety occurring as the examination day approached (Bolger, 1990). People who were prone to dealing with stress by overusing defense mechanisms, such as wishful thinking or self-blame, tended to show increased maladaptive behavior and increased anxiety under high stress. Performance on the examination, however, did not appear to be related to the use of various coping strategies to deal with the stress; that is, those students who used maladaptive behaviors did not appear to do worse on the exam.

Occupational demands can also be highly stressful, and many jobs make severe demands in terms of responsibility, time, and performance (Snow & Kline, 1995). Although we have arbitrarily separated stress into three categories, it appears that a given situation may involve elements of all three categories. The following case illustrates this point:

Case Study, Dejected Premed Student • A premed student whose lifelong ambition was to become a doctor received rejection letters from all the medical schools to which he had applied. This unexpected blow left him feeling depressed and empty. He felt extreme frustration over his failure and conflict over what his next steps should be. He was experiencing pressure from his family and peers to try again, but he was also overwhelmed by a sense of failure. He felt so bitter that he wanted to drop everything and become a beach bum or a blackjack dealer in Las Vegas. The loss of self-esteem he was experiencing left him with no realistic backup plans and little interest in pursuing alternative careers.

Although a particular stressor may predominate in any situation, we rarely deal with an isolated demand. Instead, we usually confront a continuously changing pattern of interrelated and sometimes contradictory demands.

Factors Predisposing a Person to Stress

The severity of stress is gauged by the degree to which it disrupts functioning. The actual degree of disruption that occurs or is threatened depends partly on a stressor's characteristics and partly on a person's resources, both personal and situational, for meeting the demands resulting from the stress and the relationship between the two. Everyone faces a unique pattern of adjustive demands. This fact is partly due to differences in the way people perceive and interpret similar situations, but also, objectively, no two people are faced with exactly the same pattern of stressors. In the following sections, we examine the factors that predispose individuals to react poorly to external demands. We will then explore the ways people cope with stressful situations.

The Nature of the Stressor   The impact of a stressor depends on a wide range of factors—among them the importance of the stressor to the person, the duration of the stress, the cumulative effect of stressors in the person's life, whether the stressor appears along with other stressors, whether the stressor is "natural" or artificial and whether it has prominence in the person's life, and whether or not that stressor is seen by the victim as being within his or her control. Although most minor stressors, such as misplacing one's keys, may be dealt with as a matter of course, stressors that involve important aspects of a person's life—such as the death of a loved one, a divorce, a job loss, or a serious illness—tend to be highly stressful for most people. Furthermore, the longer a stressor operates, the more severe its effects. Prolonged exhaustion, for example, imposes a more intense stress than does temporary fatigue. Also, stressors often appear to have a cumulative effect (Singer, 1980). A married couple may maintain amicable relations through a long series of minor irritations or frustrations only to dissolve the relationship in the face of one last straw of a precipitating stressor. Sometimes, key stressors in a person's life center on a continuing, difficult life situation. These stressors are considered chronic, or long-lasting. A person may be frustrated in a boring and unrewarding job from which there is seemingly no escape, suffer for years in an unhappy and conflictful marriage, or be severely frustrated by a physical handicap or a long-term health problem.

Encountering a number of stressors at the same time also makes a difference. If a man has a heart attack, loses his job, and receives news that his son has been arrested for selling drugs all at the same time, the resulting stress will be more severe than if these events occurred separately.

Finally, the symptoms of stress intensify when a person is more closely involved in an immediately traumatic situation. Pynoos and colleagues (1987) conducted an extensive investigation of children's symptoms and behavior one month after a shooting incident in a schoolyard (one child was killed and several others wounded when a sniper randomly fired into the playground). A total of 159 children from the school were interviewed. Depending on where they were—on the playground, in the school, in the neighborhood, on the way home, absent from school, or out of the vicinity—the children experienced different stress levels. Children on the playground, closest to the shooting, had the most severe symptoms, whereas children on vacation or who were not at school during the shooting experienced no symptoms.

The Experience of Crisis   From time to time, most of us experience periods of especially acute (sudden and intense) stress. The term **crisis** is used to refer to times when a stressful situation approaches or exceeds the adaptive capacities of a person or group. Crises are often especially stressful because the stressors are so potent that the coping techniques we typically use do not work. Some authorities distinguish stress from trauma in this way: a traumatic situation overwhelms a person's ability to cope whereas stress does not necessarily overwhelm the person.

A crisis may occur as a result of a traumatic divorce, a natural disaster such as a flood, or the aftermath of an injury or disease that forces difficult readjustments in a person's self-concept and way of life. Estimates of how often such crises occur in the life of the average person range from about once every ten years to about once every two years. In view of our complex and rapidly changing society, the latter estimate may be more realistic. A recent survey by Elliott (1997) found that 72 percent of a large random sample of adults in the United States reported some form of trauma that had occurred in their lives. In another study, trauma symptoms were commonly (23.1 percent) found to accompany motor vehicle accidents (Ehlers, Mayou, & Bryant, 1998).

The outcome of such crises has a profound influence on a person's subsequent adjustment. If a crisis leads a person to develop an effective new method of coping, perhaps joining a gym or a social group, he or she may emerge from the crisis even better adjusted than before. If the crisis impairs the person's ability to cope with similar stressors in the future because of the expectation of failure, then his or her overall adjustment will suffer. For this reason, **crisis intervention**—providing psychological help in times of severe and special stress—has become an important element in contemporary treatment and prevention approaches. We will discuss such intervention in more detail in Chapter 18.

Long-Term Follow-up of Nuclear Disaster Victims

In April 1986, an accident at the Chernobyl nuclear power plant in the Ukraine produced a radiation leak that was 65,000 times greater than the accident at the Three Mile Island nuclear plant in the United States. In greatest jeopardy were the power plant employees and the disaster response team that worked to seal off the damaged reactor building and to secure the other reactors to prevent further damage. The power plant operators, several of whom were among the over 200 lives claimed by the accident, were especially vulnerable to radioactivity exposure. Negative health consequences of the nuclear disaster have been extensive—for example, increases in thyroid cancer, leukemia, and congenital malformations have been noted (Bard, Verger, & Hubert, 1997). In a major study of the long-term psychological consequences of radioactivity exposure, physicians and psychologists from the Specialized Center for Disaster Medicine Protection of the Russian Ministry of Health have conducted follow-up studies of the survivors of the accident. Operators who were working at Chernobyl during the accident were evaluated four times over a 20-month period. The evaluations involved about 100 employees at each testing time. The research team also tested a control group of nuclear plant operators from plants that were some distance from the Chernobyl site. In addition to the physical examinations, each employee was also given a battery of psychological tests, including the Russian language version of the Minnesota Multiphasic Personality Inventory (MMPI). (See Chapter 15 for discussion of the MMPI.)

The postdisaster evaluation demonstrated significant increases in symptoms of stress such as physical problems, depression, interpersonal conflict, social alienation, and lack of concern for others. Those tested also showed an increase in mistrust of information being provided by the government (Koscheyev et al., 1993). ■

are also reduced. This study found that men who had lost a spouse were more often depressed than women who had done so. The reasons for this finding remain unclear, though others have found similar results as well (e.g., Stroebe & Stroebe, 1983). It could be that the women had a closer network of friends from the outset, which may have reduced their vulnerability to depression (Kershner, Cohen, & Coyne, 1998).

In other situations, a person may be adversely affected by other family members who are experiencing problems. The level of tension for all family members can be increased if one member experiences extreme difficulty, such as a chronic or life-threatening illness or a psychiatric disability. A person whose spouse is experiencing psychological disturbance is likely to experience more stress than one whose spouse is psychologically in better shape (Yager, Grant, & Bolus, 1984). The stress of the illness is compounded by the loss of support.

Often a culture offers specific rituals or courses of action that support people as they attempt to deal with certain types of stress. For example, most religions provide rituals that help the bereaved, and in some faiths, confession and atonement help people deal with stresses related to guilt and self-recrimination.

In sum, the interaction between the nature of a stressor and a person's resources for dealing with it largely determines the severity of stress. However great a challenge, it creates little stress if a person feels they can easily handle it. Having looked at some of the factors influencing the ways in which people react to stress, we will now examine some of the ways people cope with stressful events.

Coping with Stress

In general, increased levels of stress threaten a person's well-being and produce automatic, persistent attempts to relieve the tension. In short, stress forces a person to do something. What is done depends on many influences. Sometimes inner factors such as a person's frame of reference, motives, competencies, or stress tolerance play the dominant role in determining his or her coping strategies. For example, a person who has successfully handled adversity in the past may be better equipped to deal with similar problems in the future (Major, Richards, Cooper, Cozzarelli, & Zubek, 1997; Masten & Coatsworth, 1998). (See the discussion on resilience in Chapter 3.) At other times, environmental conditions such as social demands and expectations are of primary importance. Any stress reaction, of course, reflects the interplay of inner strategies and outer conditions, some more influential than others but all working together to make the person react in a certain way. Ironically, some people *create* stress for themselves rather than coping. Recent studies have shown that stressful situations might be in part related to or produced by the person's cognitions. For example, if you're feeling depressed or anxious already, you may perceive a friend's canceling a movie date as more stressful than if you are not depressed or anxious. That is, a vicious cycle occurs, causing some people to generate the life events that in turn produce their psychological adjustment problems (Simons et al., 1993).

Next we will consider some general principles dealing with personal adjustment and coping; we will then examine some characteristic stages that occur when an individual's adaptive functioning is threatened.

In reviewing certain general principles of coping with stress, it is helpful to conceptualize three interactional levels: (1) on a biological level, there are immunological defenses and damage-repair mechanisms; (2) on a psychological and interpersonal level, there are learned coping patterns, self-defenses, and support from family and friends; and (3) on a sociocultural level, there are group resources, such as labor unions, religious organizations, and law-enforcement agencies.

The failure of coping efforts on any of these levels may seriously increase a person's vulnerability on other levels. For example, a breakdown of immunological defenses may impair not only bodily functioning, but psychological functioning as well; chronically poor psychological coping patterns may lead to other diseases; or the failure of a group on which a person depends may seriously interfere with his or her ability to satisfy basic needs. The impact of stress on bodily functioning and physical disorder will be discussed more fully in Chapter 8.

In coping with stress, a person is confronted with two challenges: (1) to meet the requirements of the stressor, and (2) to protect oneself from psychological damage and disorganization. When a person feels competent to handle a stressful situation, a task-oriented response is typical—that is, behavior is directed primarily at dealing with the requirements of the stressor. Typically, this response means the person objectively appraises the situation, works out alternative solutions, decides on an appropriate strategy, takes action, and evaluates feedback. The steps in a task-oriented response—whether the actions turn out to be effective or ineffective—are generally flexible enough to enable a person to change course.

Task-Oriented Coping A **task-oriented response** may involve making changes in one's self, one's surroundings, or both, depending on the situation. The action may be overt, as in showing one's spouse more affection, or it may be covert, as in lowering one's level of aspiration. The action may involve retreating from the problem, attacking it directly, or trying to find a workable compromise. Any of these actions are appropriate under certain circumstances. For instance, if one is faced with a situation of overwhelming physical danger, such as a forest fire, the logical task-oriented response might well be to run.

Defense-Oriented Coping When a person's feelings of adequacy are seriously threatened by a stressor, a

one's job and being unable to find suitable employment has been common in the United States since the Great Depression of the 1930s. The frequent restructuring of businesses has resulted in the laying off of many people, transforming many thriving communities into depressed areas and many industrious employees into unemployed or underemployed people. In almost any community one can find workers who have been laid off from jobs they had held for many years and who are facing the end of their unemployment compensation. The following case is typical of the problems that unemployment can bring.

Case Study, An Unemployed Construction Foreman •

David C., a 49-year-old construction foreman who was married and had two children attending college, had worked for a large building construction firm since he graduated from high school. One afternoon his company, without warning, filed for bankruptcy, closed down its remaining job sites, and began to liquidate its resources. David was stunned. The unexpected changes in his life were not easy for him to face. Early efforts to find other employment were met only with frustration because other construction companies were experiencing similar economic problems and layoffs.

After a few weeks his savings were depleted, and he took a step he never dreamed possible: He applied for unemployment compensation. This action was a tremendous blow to his self-esteem. He had always been self-sufficient and had taken great pride in being a hard worker and a good provider for his family. He was particularly upset at not being able to pay the tuition and living costs for his two sons in college and he felt a great sense of failure when they remained on their summer jobs rather than returning to school. His wife, who had never worked outside the home since their marriage, took a job in a local department store to meet some of the family's living expenses.

After some searching David seemingly gave up on finding a job and began to spend more time in bars. His drinking problem intensified. When he returned home in the evenings, he sulked around the house and rebuffed most attempts by other family members to socialize or communicate. During this period family arguments were so frequent that Joel, his eldest son, felt that he couldn't tolerate the tension any more and enlisted in the army. In February, eight months after he lost his job, David saw a notice in the newspaper indicating that a local company was taking applications for 25 construction jobs the following Monday. He arrived at the company's employment office early on Monday morning only to find that there were about 3000 other applicants ahead of him some who had arrived the day before and had stood in line all night in the bitter cold. He left the lot dejected. That same week the bank initiated foreclosure proceedings on his house because he had not made a mortgage payment in seven months. He was forced to sell his house and move into an apartment.

For the next year David still could not find work in his community. Finally, after he had exhausted his unemployment benefits, he and a fellow employee left their families and moved to another city in the Southeast to find work. David planned to have his wife follow him when he got settled. She, however, had by that time been enjoying some success on her job and refused to move away. After several months of living apart, David's wife filed for a divorce. No further information is available on David.

Managing the stress associated with unemployment requires great coping strength. Some people can deal with setbacks and can adapt without suffering long-range adjustment difficulties once the initial stressful situation has ended. The impact of chronic unemployment, however, can be shattering and can have serious long-term effects. People shown here are waiting in line to file for unemployment at the New York State Department of Labor at a time when the unemployment rate rose to a three-year high of 5.9 percent in November 1990.

Unemployment is a problem in some population subgroups. For example, many young minority males live in a permanent economic depression that is more pervasive and just as debilitating as the Great Depression was for the white majority (Department of Labor, 1999). Indeed, for young black men, rates of unemployment are over twice those for whites. The long-range psychological consequences of unemployment can be great. Some people can deal with setbacks such as David experienced and can adapt without long-range adjustment difficulties once the initial stressful situation has ended. For others, however, unemployment can have serious long-term effects. The impact of chronic unemployment on a person's self-concept, sense of worth, and feeling of belongingness is shattering, especially in an affluent society.

Stress from Bereavement

The sudden unexpected death of a loved one accounts for about one-third of all PTSD cases seen in a community (Breslau, Kessler, Chilcoat et al., 1998). When someone close to us dies, we are psychologically capsized. Often the first reaction is disbelief. Then, as we begin to realize the significance of the death, our feelings of sadness, grief, and despair (even, perhaps, anger at the departed person) frequently overwhelm us.

Grief over the loss of a loved one is a natural process that allows the survivors to mourn their loss and then free themselves for life without the departed person. Some people do not go through the typical process of grieving, perhaps because of their personality makeups (defensive coping styles) or as a consequence of their particular situations. A person may, for instance, be expected to be stoical about his or her feelings or may have to manage the family's affairs. Another person may develop exaggerated or prolonged depressions after the grieving process should have ended. A normal grieving process typically lasts up to about a year and may involve negative health effects such as high blood pressure, changes in eating habits, and even thoughts of suicide (Prigerson, Bierhals, Kasl, Reynolds et al., 1997).

Complicated or prolonged bereavement is often found in situations where there has been an untimely or unexpected death (Kim & Jacobs, 1995). Pathological reactions to death are also more likely to occur in people who have a history of emotional problems or who harbor a great deal of resentment and hostility toward the deceased, thus experiencing intense guilt. They are usually profoundly depressed and may, in some instances, be suffering from major depression (see Chapter 6). The following case illustrates an extreme pattern of withdrawal or pathological grief reaction (and, in this instance, a positive outcome) following a tragic death.

Case Study, Nadine's Grief • Nadine, a 66-year-old former high school teacher, lived with Charles, age 67, her husband of 40 years (also a retired teacher). The couple had been nearly inseparable since they met—they even taught at the same schools during most of their teaching careers. They lived in a semirural community where they had worked and had raised their three children, all of whom had married and moved to a large metropolitan area about 100 miles away. For years they had planned their retirement and had hoped to travel around the country visiting friends. A week before their fortieth anniversary, Charles had a heart attack and, after five days in the intensive care unit, had a second heart attack and died.

Nadine took Charles's death quite hard. Even though she had a great deal of emotional support from her many friends and her children, she had great difficulty adjusting. Elaine, one of her daughters, came and stayed a few days and encouraged her to come to the city for a while. Nadine declined the persistent invitation even though she had little to do at home. Friends called on her frequently, but she seemed almost to resent their presence. In the months following the funeral, Nadine's reclusive behavior persisted. Several well wishers reported to Elaine

Loss of a loved one is one of the most intense stressors experienced by people. These Bosnians grieving at a new grave site show the powerful emotions experienced during grief.

that her mother was not doing well and was not even leaving the house to go shopping. They reported that Nadine sat alone in the darkened house not answering the phone and showing reluctance to come to the door. She had lost interest in activities she had once enjoyed.

Greatly worried about her mother's welfare, Elaine organized a campaign to get her mother out of the house and back to doing the things she had formerly enjoyed. Each of Nadine's children and their families took turns visiting and taking her places until she finally began to show interest in living again. In time, Nadine agreed to come to each of their homes for visits. This proved a therapeutic step—Nadine had always been fond of children and took pleasure in the time spent with her eight grandchildren—and she actually extended the visits longer than she had planned.

Stress from Divorce or Separation

The deterioration or ending of an intimate relationship is a potent stressor and a frequent reason why people seek psychological treatment. Divorce, though more generally accepted today, is still a tragic and usually stressful outcome to a once close and trusting relationship. We noted in Chapter 3 that marital disruption is a major source of vulnerability to psychopathology: People who are recently divorced or separated are markedly overrepresented among people with psychological problems.

Many factors make a divorce or separation unpleasant and stressful for everyone concerned: the acknowledgment of failure in a relationship important both personally and culturally; the necessity of explaining the failure to family and friends; the loss of valuable friendships that often accompanies the rupture; the economic uncertainties and hardships that both partners frequently experience; and, when children are involved, the problem of custody, including court battles, living arrangements, and so on.

After the divorce or separation, new problems typically emerge. The readjustment to a single life, perhaps after many years of marriage, can be a difficult experience. Since in many cases it seems that friends as well as assets have to be divided, new friendships need to be made. New romantic relationships may require a great deal of personal change. Even when the separation has been relatively amicable, new strength to adapt and cope is needed. Thus it is not surprising that divorce may motivate the task-oriented coping response of seeking counseling after the breakup of a significant relationship.

We will look now at some characteristics of catastrophic events and our differing reactions to them. Then we will turn to some specific stressor events that can cause post-traumatic stress disorder.

POST-TRAUMATIC STRESS DISORDER: REACTIONS TO CATASTROPHIC EVENTS

Many potential sources of trauma exist in contemporary society, and post-traumatic stress disorder symptoms are by no means rare in the general population. Accidents, for example, are quite common. One study in Israel found that 10 percent of survivors of serious traffic accidents suffered symptoms of PTSD one to six months after the accident (Brom, Kleber, & Hofman, 1993). Another source of trauma in contemporary society is violence, which often results in long-term adjustment problems for victims (Norris & Kaniasty, 1994; Falsetti et al., 1995). General population surveys have recently shown that we live in a violent and dangerous world. Four out of ten Americans have been exposed to significant traumatic events before the age of 30 and 9 percent of young adults met the diagnostic criteria for PTSD (Breslau et al., 1991).

Many people, if not most, who are exposed to plane crashes, automobile accidents, explosions, fires, earthquakes, tornadoes, sexual assaults, or other terrifying experiences show psychological shock reactions such as confusion and disorganization. The symptoms may vary greatly, depending on the nature and severity of the terrifying experience, the degree of surprise, and the personality makeup of the person. Consider the following examples: over half of the survivors of the disastrous Coconut Grove nightclub fire which took the lives of 492 people in Boston in 1942 required treatment for severe psychological shock (Adler, 1943). Psychological evaluations of 8 of the 64 survivors of the collision of two jet planes on Santa Cruz de Tenerife Island in 1977, in which 580 people died, indicated that all eight suffered from serious emotional problems stemming directly from the accident (Perlberg, 1979).

Post-traumatic stress disorder includes the following symptoms:

- *The traumatic event is persistently reexperienced by the person.* He or she may have intrusive, recurring thoughts or repetitive nightmares about the event (Joseph, Williams, & Yule, 1995). A study of college students who experienced the Loma Prieta earthquake in 1989 in the San Francisco area confirmed this long-held belief about traumatic events influencing the experience of nightmares. Wood and colleagues (1992) found that students who experienced the earthquake had substantially more nightmares and more nightmares about earthquakes than students who did not experience the earthquake.

- *The person persistently avoids stimuli associated with the trauma.* For example, he or she tries to avoid activities related to the incident or blocks out the memory of certain aspects of the experience. Situations that recall the traumatic experience provoke anxiety.

- *The person may experience persistent symptoms of increased arousal.* These may include chronic tension and irritability, often accompanied by insomnia, the inability to tolerate noise, and the complaint that "I just can't seem to relax."

- *The individual may experience impaired concentration and memory.*

- *The person may experience feelings of depression.* In some cases he or she may withdraw from social contact and avoid experiences that might increase excitation—commonly manifested in the avoidance of interpersonal involvement, loss of sexual interest, and an attitude of "peace and quiet at any price."

Clearly, PTSD includes elements of anxiety—generalized feelings of fear and apprehension—but since it bears such a close relationship to the experience of major stress, we cover it here and follow in Chapter 5 with coverage of the other anxiety disorders.

Distinguishing Between Acute Stress Disorder and Post-Traumatic Stress Disorder The DSM-IV provides two major classifications for PTSD that differ largely in terms of severity of the symptom pattern shown: Acute Stress Disorder and Post-Traumatic Stress Disorder. These two disorders are described in Table 4.2 and Table 4.3. Acute stress disorder occurs within four weeks of the traumatic event and lasts for a minimum of two days and a maximum of four weeks. If the symptoms last longer, the appropriate diagnosis is post-traumatic stress disorder. The diagnosis, which is not given unless the symptoms last for at least one month, can be further specified in terms of when the symptoms begin. If the symptoms be-

---

TABLE 4.2 ACUTE STRESS DISORDER

In order to receive an Acute Stress Disorder diagnosis, the individual needs to meet the following criteria as adapted from the DSM-IV:

- The person has been exposed to a traumatic situation in which both of the following conditions were present: He or she experienced, witnessed, or were confronted with an event that involved actual or threatened death or serious injury, or a serious threat to the physical integrity of self or others. The person's response also involved the feeling of intense fear, helplessness, or horror.
- During or following the distressing event, the person has three (or more) of the following dissociative symptoms:
  1. A subjective sense of numbing, detachment, or absence of emotional responsiveness
  2. A reduction in awareness of his or her surroundings (e.g., "being in a daze")
  3. Derealization
  4. Depersonalization
  5. Dissociative amnesia (i.e., inability to recall an important aspect of the trauma)
- The person persistently reexperiences the trauma by at least one of the following symptoms: recurrent images of the trauma, thoughts, dreams, illusions, flashback episodes, or a sense of reliving the experience, or persistent distress on exposure to reminders of the traumatic event.
- The person shows a marked avoidance of stimuli that arouse recollections of the trauma (e.g., thoughts, feelings, conversations, activities, places, or people).
- The person has marked symptoms of anxiety or increased arousal (e.g., difficulty sleeping, irritability, poor concentration, hypervigilance, exaggerated startle response, motor restlessness).
- The disturbance following the trauma causes clinically significant distress or impairment in social, occupational, or other important areas of functioning or impairs the individual's ability to pursue some necessary task, such as obtaining necessary assistance or mobilizing personal resources by telling family members about the traumatic experience.
- The disturbance lasts for a minimum of 2 days and a maximum of 4 weeks and occurs within 14 weeks of the traumatic event.
- The disturbance is not due to the direct physiological effects of a substance (e.g., a drug of abuse, a medication) or a general medical condition, is not better accounted for by Brief Psychotic Disorder, and is not merely an exacerbation of a preexisting Axis I or Axis II disorder.

Source: American Psychiatric Association, 1994.

TABLE 4.3 POST-TRAUMATIC STRESS DISORDER

The Post-Traumatic Stress Disorder diagnosis in DSM-IV takes into consideration many of the same elements of the Acute Stress Disorder and differs largely in terms of degree and duration of symptoms:

- The person has been exposed to a traumatic situation in which both of the following were present: he or she experienced, witnessed, or were confronted with an event or events that involved actual or threatened death or serious injury, or a threat to the physical integrity of self or others. And their response to the situation involved intense fear, helplessness, or horror.
- The person persistently reexperiences the trauma in one or more of the following ways:
    1. Recurrent and intrusive distressing recollections of the event, including images, thoughts, or perceptions.
    2. Recurrent distressing dreams of the event.
    3. Acting or feeling as if the traumatic event were recurring includes a sense of reliving the experience, illusions, hallucinations, and dissociative flashback episodes, including those that occur on awakening or when intoxicated.
    4. Intense psychological distress at exposure to internal or external cues that symbolize or resemble an aspect of the traumatic event.
    5. Physiological reactive or exposure to internal of external cues that symbolize or resemble an aspect of the traumatic event.
- Persistent avoidance of stimuli associated with the trauma and numbing of general responsiveness (not present before the trauma), as indicated by three (or more) of the following:
    1. Efforts to avoid thoughts, feelings, or conversations associated with the trauma
    2. Efforts to avoid activities, places, or people that arouse recollections of the trauma
    3. Inability to recall an important aspect of the trauma
    4. Markedly diminished interest or participation in significant activities
    5. Feeling of detachment or estrangement from others
    6. Restricted range of affect (e.g., unable to have loving feelings)
    7. Sense of a foreshortened future (e.g., does not expect to have a career, marriage, children, or a normal life span)
- Persistent symptoms of increased arousal (not present before the trauma) as indicated by two or more of the following: difficulty falling or staying asleep; irritability or outbursts of anger; difficulty concentrating; hypervigilance; or showing an exaggerated startle response.
- The duration of the disturbance is more than 1 month.
- The person's disturbance causes him or her clinically significant distress or impairment in social, occupational, or other important areas of functioning.

The clinician making the PTSD diagnosis needs also to specify whether the condition is:

Acute: if duration of symptoms is less than 3 months

Chronic: if duration of symptoms is 3 months or more

The clinician must further indicate if the condition occurs with Delayed Onset: if onset of symptoms is at least 6 months after the stressor.

Source: American Psychiatric Association, 1994.

gin within six months of the traumatic event, then the reaction is considered to be acute. If symptoms begin more than six months after the traumatic situation, the reaction is considered to be delayed. The delayed version of PTSD is less well defined and more difficult to diagnose than disorders that emerge shortly after the precipitating incident. Some authorities have questioned whether a delayed reaction should be diagnosed as a PTSD at all; instead, some would categorize such a reaction as some other anxiety-based disorder. It is important to keep in mind that

the criteria for post-traumatic stress disorders specify that the reactions last for at least one month.

A **disaster syndrome** appears to characterize the reactions of many victims of major catastrophes in which great loss or public suffering has been identified (see Highlight 4.2). This syndrome may be described in terms of the reactions during the traumatic experience, the initial reactions after it (the acute post-traumatic stress), and the long-lasting or late-arising complications (the chronic or delayed post-traumatic stress).

Highlight 4.2

Problems of Recovery in the Aftermath of a Killer Hurricane

In September 1989 one of the most powerful and destructive hurricanes of all times, Hurricane Hugo, came ashore in the vicinity of Charleston, South Carolina, bringing with it winds that were estimated at 175 miles per hour and a tidal wave ranging from 12 to 23 feet high. More than 35 people were killed and hundreds of houses and buildings were destroyed, leaving tens of thousands of people homeless. Hundreds of thousands of people were without services such as electricity, and nearly 300,000 people were left without work.

Among the most seriously affected victims of Hugo were young children. Belter and Shannon (1993) found that children showed a significant increase in the number and severity of problem behaviors after the hurricane, including dependent and demanding behavior, frustration, irritability, temper tantrums, and sleep difficulties (p. 97). Symptoms of post-traumatic stress disorder in children continued to persist even months after the hurricane. Swenson and colleagues (1991) reported that 28 percent of the children they examined had displayed emotional and behavioral problems immediately after the hurricane, 29 percent continued to have problems three months after the hurricane; 16 percent showed problems at seven to nine months following the hurricane; and 6 percent still had problems one year later.

In another study, Garrison and colleagues (1993) followed up 1264 adolescents between the ages of 11 and 17 who lived in three South Carolina communities hit by Hurricane Hugo and administered a 174-item questionnaire. The extent of the stress from the hurricane is reflected in the fact that 12 percent of the youngsters reported that they had to move out of their homes, 4 percent reported that someone close to them was injured in the hurricane, 10 percent were actually injured themselves, and 71 percent reported experiencing fear of being injured. The most frequent PTSD symptoms reported by the adolescents were detachment (36 percent), avoidance of feelings or thoughts related to the hurricane (36 percent), irritability and anger (25 percent), and physiological arousal (20 percent). The total number of reported PTSD symptoms was associated with severity of exposure to the hurricane. Overall, 5 percent of the adolescents in the study reported severe and extensive enough symptoms to receive a PTSD diagnosis. The recovery process following the disaster was sped up considerably by several community-based programs aimed at helping victim's deal with the immediate crisis and to readjust to a difficult set of environmental circumstances following the disaster. Crisis intervention services were made available immediately following the disaster to provide brief counseling and outreach programs to needy victims (Joyner & Swenson, 1993). In addition, school-based social support programs were provided to assist the children in their reentry to school (Stewart et al., 1992). ■

A victim's initial responses following a disaster typically involve three stages: (1) the shock stage, in which the victim is stunned, dazed, and apathetic; (2) the suggestible stage, in which the victim tends to be passive, suggestible, and willing to take directions from rescue workers or others; and (3) the recovery stage, in which the victim may be tense and apprehensive and show generalized anxiety, but gradually regains psychological equilibrium often showing a need to repeatedly tell about the catastrophic event. It is in the third stage that post-traumatic stress disorder may develop. Recurrent nightmares and the typical need to tell the same story about the disaster again and again appear to be mechanisms for reducing anxiety and desensitizing the self to the traumatic experience. Tension, apprehensiveness, and hypersensitivity appear to be residual effects of the shock reaction and to reflect the person's realization that the world can become overwhelmingly dangerous and threatening.

In some cases, the clinical picture may be complicated by intense grief and depression. When a person feels that his or her own personal inadequacy contributed to the loss of loved ones in a disaster, the picture may be further complicated by strong feelings of guilt, and the post-traumatic stress may last for months. This pattern is well illustrated in the following case of a husband who failed to save his wife in the jet crash at Tenerife in 1977.

Case Study, A Survivor's Guilt and Depression • Martin's story is quite tragic. He lost his beloved wife of 37 years and blames himself for her death, because he sat stunned and motionless for some 25 seconds after the [other plane] hit. He saw nothing but fire and smoke in the aisles, but he roused himself and led his wife to a jagged hole above and behind his seat. Martin climbed out onto the wing and reached down and took hold of his wife's hand, but an explosion from within literally blew her out of his hands and pushed him back and down onto the wing. He reached the runway, turned to go back after her, but the plane blew up seconds later.

[Five months later] Martin was depressed and bored, had wild dreams, a short temper and became easily confused and irritated. "What I saw there will terrify me forever," he says. He told [the psychologist who interviewed him] that he avoided television and movies, because he couldn't know when a frightening scene would appear (Perlberg, 1979, pp. 49–50).

In some instances the guilt of the survivors seems to center on the belief that they deserved to survive no more or perhaps even less than those who died. As one flight attendant explained after the crash of a Miami-bound jet in the Florida Everglades that took many lives, "I kept thinking, I'm alive. Thank God. But I wondered why I was spared. I felt, It's not fair" (*Time,* Jan. 15, 1973, p. 53).

Extreme post-traumatic symptoms following serious accidents are not uncommon. Blanchard, Hickling, Barton, and Taylor (1996) followed up a group of motor vehicle accident victims, who had sought medical attention as a result of their accidents. They found that one-third of those who initially met PTSD diagnostic criteria had not experienced a reduction in symptoms at a 12-month follow-up. In another incident, one month after a mass-murder spree by a gunman in Texas, psychologists interviewed 136 terrorized survivors and diagnosed 20 percent of the men and 36 percent of the women as having

PTSD. In a recent review and comparison of all published disaster research in which estimates of post-disaster psychopathology were included, on average 17 percent of victims showed psychological adjustment problems in the aftermath of the disaster (Rubonis & Bickman, 1991), which is similar to the findings of La Greca, Silverman, Vernberg, and Prinstein (1996) that 18 percent of the children studied after Hurricane Andrew had symptoms of PTSD. Green and colleagues (1992) and Green and Lindy (1994) followed up 193 victims of the tragic Buffalo Creek flood 14 years later, finding that symptoms of past and present PTSD were diagnosable in a significant portion of the sample. As we have seen, feelings of guilt about having failed to protect loved ones that perished may be quite intense, especially in situations where some responsibility can be directly assigned.

A person's traumatic reaction state may be more complicated in cases of severe loss. For example, following the Oakland/Berkeley firestorm in which 24 people died and 3125 others lost their homes, Koopman, Clasesen, and Spiegel (1997) reported that those who experienced major loss (like their home) were likely to experience a series of stressful changes. Similarly, those who become disabled find that their lives have markedly changed. An individual who becomes paralyzed in an automobile accident in which his wife is killed not only has to deal with the grief over losing a close relationship but must do so during a long period of rehabilitation and severely changed life. The psychological effects of disability compensation may also complicate the recovery. Personal damage lawsuits tend to prolong post-traumatic symptoms because of the difficulties of litigation (Egendorf, 1986; Okura, 1975).

Dealing with the consequences of natural disasters can require great efforts at adaptation as shown by the people in this flood. Some studies have shown that as many as 20 percent of children exposed to disaster trauma may suffer adjustment disorders in the aftermath of a disaster.

Causal Factors in Post-Traumatic Stress

Most people function relatively well in catastrophes, and, in fact, many behave with heroism (Rachman, 1990). Whether or not someone develops post-traumatic stress disorder depends on a number of factors. Some research suggests that personality seems to play a role in reducing vulnerability to stress when the stressors are severe (Clark, Watson, & Mineka, 1994). At high levels of traumatic exposure, the nature of the traumatic stressor itself appears to account for most of the stress-response variance (e.g., Ursano, Boydstun, & Wheatley, 1981); however, there appears to be greater likelihood of post-traumatic disorder among women than among men (Breslau, Davis et al., 1997). In other words, everyone has a breaking point, and at sufficiently high levels of stress the average person can be expected to develop some psychological difficulties (which may be either short-lived or long-term) following a traumatic event.

Even a well-seasoned police officer can experience a disabling level of stress, as shown in the following case.

Case Study, A Police Officer's Post-Traumatic Stress •
Don had been a model police officer during his 14 years on the force. He was highly evaluated by his superiors, had a master's degree in social work, and had attained the rank of sergeant. While patrolling in a squad car, he heard that there had been an aircraft accident, and he quickly drove to the scene to give aid to any survivors. When he arrived he wandered around in a daze looking for someone to help but there was only destruction. He later remembered the next few days as a bad dream.

He was quite depressed for several days after the cleanup, had no appetite, couldn't sleep, and was impotent. Images and recollections of the accident would come to him out of nowhere. He reported having a recurring dream in which he would come upon an airplane crash while driving a car or flying a plane. In his dream, he would rush to the wreckage and help some passengers to safety.

Don decided that he needed help and sought counseling. Because of his deteriorating mood and physical condition, he was placed on medical leave from the police force. Eight months after the accident he was still in therapy and had not returned to work. During therapy it became apparent that Don had been experiencing a great deal of personal dissatisfaction and anger prior to the crash. His prolonged psychological disorder was not only a result of his anguish over the air crash but also a vehicle for expressing other problems. (Based on Davidson, 1979a, 1979b; O'Brien, 1979.)

In all cases of post-traumatic stress, conditioned fear—the fear associated with the traumatic experi-

ence—appears to be a key causal factor. Thus prompt psychotherapy following a traumatic experience is considered important in preventing conditioned fear from establishing itself and becoming resistant to change.

We will now explore several instances of post-traumatic stress disorder, examining both the immediate and long-range effects of several debilitating situations: rape, military combat, imprisonment as a POW or in a concentration camp, and severe threats to safety and security.

The Trauma of Rape

Rape involves the act of forcing someone to engage in sexual intercourse against his or her will—a situation that can inflict severe trauma on a victim. In our society rape occurs with an alarming frequency (see Chapter 11 for further discussion). In most cases, the victim is a woman. Rape is the most frequent cause of PTSD in women (Kessler, Sonnega, Bromet, Hughes, & Nelson, 1995). In Chapter 11 we consider the pathology of rapists; our concern in this chapter is with a victim's response to rape, which can vary depending on a number of factors. In *stranger rape*—a rape in which the victim does not know the offender—the victim is likely to experience strong fear of physical harm and death. In *acquaintance rape* the reaction is apt to be slightly different (Ellison, 1977; Frazier & Burnett, 1994). In such a situation the victim may feel not only fear but also betrayal by someone she had trusted. She may feel more responsible for what happened and experience greater guilt. She may also be more hesitant to seek help or report the rape to the police out of fear that she will be held partially responsible for it.

The age and life circumstances of a victim may also influence her reaction (Adam, Everett, & O'Neal, 1992). For a young child who knows nothing about sexual behavior, rape can lead to sexual scars and confusion, particularly if the child is encouraged to forget about the experience without thoroughly talking it over first (Browne & Finkelhor, 1986). For young adult women, rape can increase the conflicts over independence and separation that are normal in this age group. In an effort to be helpful, parents of these victims may encourage various forms of regression, such as moving back to the family home, which may prevent mastery of this developmental phase. Married rape victims with children face the task of explaining their experience to their children. Sometimes the sense of vulnerability that results from rape leaves a woman feeling temporarily unable to care for her children.

Husbands and boyfriends, if unsympathetic to what a woman is undergoing after being raped, can negatively influence a rape victim's adjustment by their attitudes and behavior. Rejection, blaming, uncontrolled anger at the offender, or insistence on a quick resumption of sexual activity can serve to increase a victim's negative feelings.

McCann et al. (1988) found that the experience of rape affected women in five areas of a life functioning. First, physical disturbances, including hyperarousal or anxiousness (typical symptoms of PTSD), were common. One recent study found that women who had a history of sexual assault tended to see themselves as in poorer health (Golding, Cooper, & George, 1997). Second, women who had been sexually assaulted tended to experience emotional problems, such as anxiety, depressed mood, and low self-esteem. Fierman and colleagues (1993) found that prior trauma, particularly sexual abuse, physical abuse, and rape were prominent in the life histories of patients seeking treatment at an anxiety clinic. Falsetti and colleagues (1995) reported that 94 percent of their sample of women with panic disorders had histories of criminal victimization. Third, following rape, women tended to report cognitive dysfunction, including disturbed concentration and the experience of intrusive thoughts (Valentiner, Foa, Riggs, & Gershuny, 1996). Fourth, many women reported having atypical behavioral acts, such as aggressive, antisocial actions, and substance abuse after being raped. Finally, many women who experience rape tend to report having interference in their social relationships, including sexual problems, intimacy problems, and further victimization in sexual relationship. All these symptoms reflect those of PTSD.

Coping with Rape Research with rape victims soon after the trauma has provided clear insights into the emotional turmoil and psychological processes they go through in coping with their experiences (Burgess & Holmstrom, 1974, 1976; Frazier & Schauben, 1994; Frazier & Burnett, 1994). Coping actually begins even before the rape occurs and ends many months after the attack. The following categories summarize these findings and integrate the feelings and problems women experience at different points of their traumas.

Anticipatory phase: This period occurs before an actual rape, when an offender "sets up" a victim and the victim begins to perceive that a dangerous situation exists. In the early minutes of this phase, the victim often uses defense mechanisms such as denial to preserve an illusion of invulnerability. Common thoughts are "This isn't really happening to me" or "He doesn't really mean that."

Impact phase: This phase begins with a victim's recognition that she is actually going to be raped and ends when the rape is over. The victim's first reaction is usually intense fear for her life, a fear much stronger than her fear of the sexual act itself. Symonds (1976) has described the paralytic effect of intense fear on victims of crime, showing that this fear usually leads to varying degrees of disintegration in the victim's functioning and possibly to complete inability to act. Roth and Lebowitz (1988) found that the sexual trauma "confronts the individual" with emotions and images that are difficult to manage and may have long-term adjustment consequences. When the victim later recalls her behavior during the assault, she may feel guilty about not reacting more efficiently, and she needs to be reassured that her actions were normal.

Post-traumatic recoil phase: This phase begins immediately after a rape. Burgess and Holmstrom (1974, 1976) observed two emotional styles among the rape victims they interviewed in hospital emergency rooms: (1) an expressed style, in which feelings of fear and anxiety were shown through crying, sobbing, and restlessness, and (2) a controlled style, in which feelings appeared to be masked by a calm, controlled, subdued facade. Regardless of style, most victims felt guilty about the way they had reacted to the offender and wished that they had reacted faster or fought harder. (Excessive self-blame has been associated with poor long-term adjustment [Meyer & Taylor, 1986].) Feelings of dependency were increased, and victims often had to be encouraged and helped to call friends or parents and make other arrangements.

Reconstitution phase: This phase begins as a victim starts to make plans for leaving the emergency room or crisis center. It ends, often many months later, when the stress of the rape has been assimilated, the experience shared with significant others, and the victim's self-concept restored. Certain behaviors and symptoms are typical during this phase:

1. Self-protective activities, such as changing one's telephone number and moving to a new residence, are common. The victim's fear is often well justified at this point because, even in the unlikely event that the offender has been arrested and charged with rape, he is often out on bail.

2. Frightening nightmares in which the rape is relived are common. As the victim moves closer to-

ward assimilating the experience, the content of the dreams may gradually shift until the victim successfully fights off the assailant.

3. Phobias often develop immediately following rape, including fear of the indoors or outdoors (depending on where the rape took place), fear of being alone, fear of crowds, fear of being followed, and sexual fears.

Long-Term Effects Whether a rape victim will experience serious psychological problems depends to a large extent on her past coping skills and level of psychological functioning. A previously well-adjusted woman usually will regain her prior equilibrium, but rape can precipitate severe pathology in a woman with psychological difficulties (Meyer & Taylor, 1986). Victims' perceptions as to whether they were able to control future circumstances influenced the recovery process. Women who tended to blame themselves or thought more about *why* the rape occurred were slower to recover from the trauma than those who believed that future assaults were less likely (Frazier & Schauben, 1994). When problems do continue, or when they become manifest later in a delayed post-traumatic stress disorder, they are likely to involve anxiety, depression, withdrawal, and heterosexual relationship difficulties (Gold, 1986; Koss, 1983; Meyer & Taylor, 1986).

Counseling Rape Victims The women's movement has played a crucial role in establishing specialized rape counseling services, such as hotlines and rape crisis centers often staffed by trained paraprofessionals who provide general support for victims, both individually and in groups. Many crisis centers also have victim advocacy services in which a trained volunteer accompanies a woman to a hospital or police station, helps her understand the procedures, and assists her with red tape. The advocate may also accompany the person to meetings with legal representatives and to the trial, experiences that tend to temporarily reactivate the trauma of the rape.

The Trauma of Military Combat

Many people who have been involved in the turmoil of war experience devastating psychological problems for months or even years afterward (Barrett, Resnick et al., 1996). During World War I, traumatic reactions to combat conditions were called *shell shock,* a term coined by a British pathologist, Col. Frederick Mott (1919), who regarded these reactions as organic conditions produced by

minute brain hemorrhages. It was gradually realized, however, that only a small percentage of such cases represented physical injury. Most victims were suffering instead from the general combat situation, with its physical fatigue, ever-present threat of death or mutilation, and severe psychological shocks. During World War II, traumatic reactions to combat passed through a number of classifications, such as operational fatigue and war neuroses, before finally being termed combat fatigue or combat exhaustion in the Korean and Vietnam wars. Even the latter terms were none too aptly chosen, because they implied that physical exhaustion played a more important role than was usually the case. They did, however, serve to distinguish such disorders from other psychological disorders such as drug use that happened to occur under war conditions but might well have occurred in civilian life.

It has been estimated that in World War II, 10 percent of Americans in combat developed combat exhaustion (the term used for post-traumatic disorders during World War II). However, the actual incidence is not known because many soldiers received supportive therapy at their battalion aid stations and were returned to combat within a few hours. In fact, combat exhaustion caused the single greatest loss of personnel during that war (Bloch, 1969). During the Korean War the incidence of combat exhaustion dropped from an initial high of over 6 percent to 3.7 percent; 27 percent of medical discharges were for psychiatric reasons (Bell, 1958). In the Vietnam War the figure dropped to less than 1.5 percent for combat exhaustion, with a negligible number of discharges for psychiatric disorders (Allerton, 1970; Bourne, 1970).

However, research has shown a high prevalence of post-traumatic stress disorder for Vietnam veterans. Though combat exhaustion, or acute stress disorder as it is known today, was not as great a factor as in previous wars, combat-related stress apparently manifested itself later and was clearly related to combat *experience* not fatigue (Goldberg et al, 1990).

A further analysis was conducted to assess the relationship between the degree of combat exposure and the later development of post-traumatic stress disorder. The researchers found that men who had experienced high levels of combat had a greater prevalence of post-traumatic stress symptoms than those who had had lower levels of combat exposure (Bremner, Southwick, & Charney, 1995).

Clinical Picture in Combat-Related Stress The specific symptoms of combat-related stress vary considerably, depending on the type of duty, the severity and nature of the traumatic experience, and the personality of

| Highlight 4.3 | *MODERN LIFE* |

The High Emotional Cost of Peacekeeping

Peacekeeping missions to strife-torn countries have been launched as humanitarian efforts designed to serve only peaceful purposes—to protect the civilian population by placing neutral forces between warring factions and in providing security for relief efforts to the civilian population. However, the duties and responsibilities of the personnel involved in these deployments can be very ambiguous and "mission creep" can actually embroil the peacekeepers in intense conflict for which they were unprepared. Indeed, some "non-combat" military assignments such as in Somalia and Bosnia can be as stressful as wartime experience and can result in tragedies that can be highly traumatic for those involved.

A tragic example came about as a result of young men and women in the military who were sent on a humanitarian mission to feed thousands of starving civilians in Somalia. Some armed Somali militants did not accept the outside help and aggressively resisted the peacekeeping efforts. On June 5, 1993, 24 Pakastani peacekeepers were killed when their mission was "expanded" to include closing down a radio station being used by one of the factions for anti-UN propaganda. Then in October 1993, 18 American soldiers were killed in an expedition to capture one of the Somali warlords. Television broadcasts provided vivid accounts of the action and horrible pictures of some of the American soldier's bodies being dragged

Even peace keeping missions can prove as stressful or as tragic as wartime duty as shown in this horrible scene of an American soldier's body being dragged through the streets of Mogadishu.

through the streets in defiance of the UN presence. The mission was altered substantially after these incidents.

Many of those deployed in this humanitarian mission experienced significant stress as a result of their assignment. Some also experienced post-traumatic symptoms in the months following their deployment. Recent studies by Litz and colleagues (Litz, Orsillo, Friedman, Ehlich et al., 1997; Litz, King, King et al., 1997) reported the prevalence of post-traumatic stress symptoms among military personnel who were deployed on the peacekeeping mission to Somalia. They surveyed 3461 active duty personnel, finding that 8 percent of the soldiers showed PTSD symptoms at a 5-month follow-up. ∎

---

the person. Just being in a war zone with the ever-present possibility that a shell can explode and kill or injure anyone in the area is a frightening experience (Zeidner, 1993). (See Highlight 4.3 Modern Life for a discussion of the stresses of some non-combat duty among soldiers). In fact, civilians living in war zones are also at risk for PTSD. Studies of 492 Israeli elementary school children who were exposed to SCUD missile attacks during the war with Iraq found that higher stress responses occurred in areas that were hit by missiles (Schwarzwald et al., 1993). In another study, the anxiety levels of the civilians

exposed to the threat of attack were significantly higher during the war than when retested when the war was over (Weizman et al., 1994). Moreover, anxiety was higher during the evenings (when the SCUD attacks usually occurred) than during the day.

One study evaluated the self-reports of 251 Vietnam veterans grouping them according to three levels of experienced stress: (1) exposed to combat; (2) exposed to abusive violence in combat; and (3) participated in abusive violence in combat (Laufer, Brett, & Gallops, 1985). They found that post-traumatic symptoms, including intrusive imagery, hyperarousal, numbing, and cognitive disruption, were associated with exposure to combat violence. Participation in abusive violence was most highly associated with more severe pathologies marked by cognitive disruptions, such as depression. The authors concluded that the clinical picture of post-traumatic stress disorder varies according to the stressors experienced. Combat involvement is also not the only stressor in a war zone. Soldiers involved in graves registration duties (i.e., handling corpses) had high rates of PTSD symptoms such as anger, anxiety, and somatic complaints compared with soldiers not assigned to such duties (McCarroll, Ursano, & Fullerton, 1995). Moreover, some people entering the military are more vulnerable to developing stress-related symptoms than others.

Despite these variations, however, the general clinical picture was surprisingly uniform for soldiers who developed combat stress in different wars. The first symptoms were increasing irritability and sensitivity, sleep disturbances, and often-recurrent nightmares. A recent empirical study of the emotional components of PTSD in combat veterans found anger and anger-control problems to be a strong component in post-traumatic stress among combat veterans (Chemtob et al., 1994).

The recorded cases of combat-related stress among soldiers in various wars show that the common symptom usually has been the feeling of overwhelming anxiety. In comparison, it is interesting to note that most physically wounded soldiers have shown less anxiety or less combat exhaustion symptoms than non-physically wounded soldiers except in cases of permanent mutilation. Apparently a wound, in providing an acceptable escape from a stressful combat situation, removes the source of anxiety. A similar finding was reported among Israeli soldiers hospitalized during the five-to-six-week Yom Kippur War in 1973 when Egyptian and Syrian forces attacked Israel (Merbaum & Hefez, 1976). In fact, it is not unusual for soldiers to admit that they have prayed to be hit or to have something honorable happen to them to remove them from battle. When approaching full recovery and the necessity of returning to combat, injured soldiers sometimes show prolonged symptoms or delayed traumatic reactions of nervousness, insomnia, and other symptoms that were nonexistent when they were first hospitalized.

Prisoners of War and Holocaust Survivors

Among the most stressful and persistently troubling wartime experiences is that of being a prisoner of war (Beal, 1995; Page Engdahl et al., 1997). Although some people have been able to adjust to the stress (especially if part of a supportive group), the past shows us that the toll on most prisoners is great. About 40 percent of the American prisoners in Japanese POW camps during World War II died during their imprisonment; an even higher number of prisoners of Nazi concentration camps died. Survivors of Nazi concentration camps often sustained residual organic and psychological damage along

It has been estimated that in World War II, 10 percent of Americans in combat developed combat exhaustion. The stress of combat clearly took its toll on this Marine who had just finished two days of heavy fighting in the Pacific.

with a lowered tolerance to stress of any kind. Symptoms were often extensive and commonly included anxiety, insomnia, headaches, irritability, depression, nightmares, impaired sexual potency, and functional diarrhea (which occurs in any situation of stress, even relatively mild stress). Such symptoms were attributed not only to the psychological stressors but also to biological stressors, such as head injuries, prolonged malnutrition, and serious infectious diseases (Sigal et al., 1973; Warnes, 1973).

Among returning POWs, the effects of the psychological trauma they had suffered were often masked by the feelings of relief and jubilation that accompanied release from confinement. Even when there was little evidence of residual physical pathology, however, survivors of prisoner-of-war camps commonly showed impaired resistance to physical illness, low frustration tolerance, frequent dependence on alcohol and drugs, irritability, and other indications of emotional instability (Chambers, 1952; Goldsmith & Cretekos, 1969; Hunter, 1978; Strange & Brown, 1970; Wilbur, 1973). Many veterans experience, at times, overwhelming anger over minor events that for some is difficult to control. Such maladaptive behaviors may require intervention even years after the stress of military combat has faded (Chemtob, Novaco, Hamada, & Gross, 1997). There is also evidence to suggest that combat exposure could result in severe adjustment problems, including antisocial behavior (Barrett, Resnick, Foy, & Dansky, 1996).

In a retrospective study of psychological maladjustment symptoms following repatriation, Engdahl and colleagues (1993) interviewed a large sample of former POWs and found that half of them reported symptoms that met standard criteria for PTSD in the year following their releases from captivity; nearly a third met PTSD criteria 40 to 50 years after their wartime experiences, indicating the marked persistence of the effects of war trauma.

Another measure of the toll taken by the prolonged stress of being in a POW or concentration camp is the higher death rate after return to civilian life. Among returning World War II POWs from the Pacific area, Wolff (1960) found that within the first six years, nine times as many died from tuberculosis as would have been expected in civilian life, four times as many from gastrointestinal disorders, over twice as many from cancer, heart disease, and suicide, and three times as many from accidents. Many problems of adjustment and post-traumatic symptoms can be found in POWs many years after their release (Sutker & Allain, 1995). Bullman and Kang (1997) found an increased risk of death due to external causes (for example, from overdose and accidents) associated with PTSD in Vietnam veterans.

Some of the lingering problems experienced by former POWs might be a direct result of harsh treatment and starvation during captivity. Sutker and colleagues (1992) conducted a study of memory and cognitive performance of POW survivors and found that those who experienced the greatest trauma-induced weight loss, defined as greater than 35 percent of their pre-captive weight, performed significantly worse on memory tasks than POWs who experienced less malnutrition.

Causal Factors in Combat Stress Problems In a combat situation, with the continual threat of injury or death and repeated narrow escapes, a person's ordinary coping methods are relatively useless. The adequacy and security the person has known in the relatively safe and dependable civilian world are completely undermined. At the same time, we must not overlook the fact that most soldiers subjected to combat have not become psychiatric casualties, although most of them have evidenced severe fear reactions and other symptoms of personality disorganization that were not serious enough to be incapacitating. In addition, many soldiers have tolerated almost unbelievable stress before they have broken, while others have become casualties under conditions of relatively slight combat stress or even as noncombatants—for example, during basic training.

In order to understand traumatic reactions to combat, we need to look at factors such as constitutional predisposition, personal maturity, loyalty to one's unit, and confidence in one's officers as well as at the actual stress experienced.

Temperament Do constitutional differences in sensitivity, vigor, and temperament affect a soldier's resistance to combat stress? They probably do, but little actual evidence supports this assumption. We have more information about the conditions of battle that tax a soldier's emotional and physical stamina. Add other factors that often occur in combat situations such as severe climatic conditions, malnutrition, and disease to the strain of continual emotional mobilization, and the result is a general lowering of a person's physical and psychological resistance to all stressors.

Psychosocial Factors A number of psychological and interpersonal factors may contribute to the overall stress experienced by soldiers and predispose them to break down under combat. Such factors include reductions in personal freedom, frustrations of all sorts, and separation from home and loved ones. Central, of course, are the many stresses arising from combat, including constant fear, unpredictable and largely uncontrollable circumstances, the necessity of killing, and prolonged harsh conditions.

Personality (which is shaped by temperamental differences beginning in infancy) is an important determinant of adjustment to military experiences. Personality characteristics that lower a person's resistance to stress or to particular stressors may be important in determining his or her reactions to combat. Personal immaturity sometimes stemming from parental overprotection is commonly cited as making a soldier more vulnerable to combat stress. Worthington (1978) found that American soldiers who experienced problems readjusting after they returned home from the Vietnam War also tended to have had greater difficulties before and during their military service than soldiers who adjusted readily. In their study of the personality characteristics of Israeli soldiers who had broken down in combat during the Yom Kippur War, Merbaum and Hefez (1976) found that over 25 percent reported having had psychological treatment prior to the war. Another 12 percent had experienced difficulties previously in the six-day Israeli-Arab war of 1967. Thus about 37 percent of these soldiers had clear histories of some personality instability that may have predisposed them to break down under combat stress. On the other hand, of the other soldiers who broke down, over 60 percent had not shown earlier difficulties and would not have been considered to be at risk for such breakdown.

A background of personal maladjustment does not always make a person a poor risk for withstanding combat stress. Some people are so accustomed to anxiety that they cope with it more or less automatically, whereas soldiers who are feeling severe anxiety for the first time may be terrified by the experience, lose their self-confidence, and go to pieces.

Sociocultural Factors Several sociocultural factors play an important part in determining a person's adjustment to combat. These general factors include clarity and acceptability of war goals, identification with the combat unit, esprit de corps, and quality of leadership.

An important consideration is how clear and acceptable the war's goals are to a person. If the goals can be concretely integrated into the soldier's values in terms of his or her "stake" in the war and the worth and importance of what he or she is doing, this will help support the soldier psychologically. Another important factor is a person's identification with the combat unit. In fact the stronger the sense of group identification, the less chance that a soldier will break down in combat. Feelings of *esprit de corps* influence a person's morale and adjustment to extreme circumstances. Finally, the quality of leadership and confidence in one's unit are of vital importance in a soldier's adjustment to combat. If a soldier respects his or her leaders, has confidence in their judgment and ability, and can accept them as relatively strong parental

or sibling figures, the soldier's morale and resistance to stress are bolstered. On the other hand, lack of confidence or dislike of leaders is detrimental to morale and to combat stress tolerance.

It also appears that returning to an unaccepting social environment can increase a soldier's vulnerability to post-traumatic stress. For example, in a one-year follow-up of Israeli men who had been psychiatric war casualties during the Yom Kippur War, Merbaum (1977) found that they not only continued to show extreme anxiety, depression, and extensive physical complaints, but in many instances they appeared to have become more disturbed over time. Merbaum hypothesized that their psychological deterioration had probably been due to the unaccepting attitudes of the community; in a country so reliant on the strength of its army for survival, considerable stigma is attached to psychological breakdown in combat. Because of the stigma, many of the men were experiencing not only isolation within their communities, but also self-recrimination about what they perceived as failure on their own parts. These feelings exacerbated the soldiers' already stressful situations. In a more recent follow-up study of Yom Kippur War veterans, Solomon, and Kleinhauz (1996) reported residual PTSD symptoms (intrusive thinking and avoidance) were present in war veterans compared with controls 18 years after the war ended.

Long-Term Effects of Post-Traumatic Stress In some cases, soldiers who have experienced combat exhaustion may show symptoms of post-traumatic stress for sustained periods of time. In cases of delayed post-traumatic stress, some soldiers who have stood up exceptionally well under intensive combat situations have experienced post-traumatic stress only upon their return home, often in response to relatively minor stresses that they had handled easily before. Evidently, these soldiers have suffered long-term damage to their adaptive capabilities, in some cases complicated by memories of killing enemy soldiers or civilians as well as feelings that are tinged with guilt and anxiety (Haley, 1978; Horowitz & Solomon, 1978).

In a study of Vietnam returnees, Strange and Brown (1970) compared combat and noncombat veterans who were experiencing emotional difficulties. The combat group showed a higher incidence of depression and of difficulties in close interpersonal relationships. They also showed a higher incidence of aggressive and suicidal threats but did not actually carry them out. In a later study of Vietnam veterans who were making a satisfactory readjustment to civilian life, DeFazio, Rustin, and Diamond (1975) found that the combat veterans still

Many factors may contribute to traumatic reactions to combat—constitutional predisposition, personal immaturity, compromised loyalty to one's unit, diminished confidence in one's officers, as well as the actual stress experienced. Thus, although combat situations completely undermine a person's ordinary coping methods, some soldiers can tolerate great stress without becoming psychiatric casualties, while others may break down under only slight combat stress.

reported certain symptoms twice as often as the noncombat veterans. The nature and extent of delayed post-traumatic stress disorder are somewhat controversial (Burstein, 1985). Reported cases of delayed stress syndrome among Vietnam combat veterans are often difficult to relate explicitly to combat stress because these people may also have other significant adjustment problems. People with adjustment difficulties may erroneously attribute their present problems to specific incidents from their past, such as experiences in combat. The wide publicity recently given to delayed post-traumatic stress disorder has made it easy for clinicians to find a

precipitating cause in their patients' backgrounds. Indeed, the frequency with which this disorder has recently been diagnosed in some settings suggests that its increased use is as much a result of its plausibility and popularity as of its true incidence.

Severe Threats to Personal Safety and Security

Some of the most traumatic and psychologically disabling circumstances a person can experience involve those in which they face drastic threat to their personal security. Even living in a modern, civilized world is no guarantee of having uninterrupted peaceful pursuit of our dreams and ambitions. All too often in the modern world we hear about tragic sociopolitical circumstances that require large populations to leave their homeland and join a scattered trail of refugees to some unknown place with horribly lawless and inhumane treatment.

In this section we will briefly describe some extreme situations that are among the most stressful circumstances for anyone to cope with, and which often result in long-range psychological adjustment problems for the victims. We will examine three traumatic circumstances: (1) forced migration to a strange land; (2) being held hostage; and (3) torture. Although such circumstances are extreme and unlikely for most of us to encounter, they are all too frequent in our oftentimes turbulent world. The suffering shown by the Vietnamese refugee described in Highlight 4.4 is not unique. It is estimated that more than 16 million refugees exist in today's world, mostly from developing countries, with only about 11 percent of them relocating in developed nations like the United States and Canada (Brandel, 1980). Most refugees move between third-world countries. For example, more than 1.5 million Kurdish refugees from Iraq have either fled to Iran or live near the Iraq-Turkey border in makeshift living quarters, and there are countless numbers of Rwandan refugees living in Zaire.

In the United States, recent refugees have come from many countries—Ethiopia, the former Soviet Union, Iran, Cuba, Haiti, Laos, Vietnam, Cambodia, and Somalia. The Southeast Asians who began arriving in America after 1975 perhaps had the most difficult adjustment. Although many of these people were functioning well in their homeland and in time became successful and happy American citizens, others have had difficulty adjusting (Carlson & Rosser-Hogan, 1993; Clarke, Sack, & Goff, 1993; Westermeyer, Williams, & Nguyen, 1991). Refugees who have low self-esteem tend to be the ones who have

Highlight 4.4

The Trauma of Forced Relocation

Being uprooted from home is a disturbing event that violates a person's sense of security. News broadcasts report on such traumas regularly: a hazardous substance fire in Canada forced 1663 families to evacuate their homes for 18 days (Breton, Valla, & Lambert, 1993) and 24,000 people were killed and hundreds left homeless in a volcano/mudslide in South America. It is not surprising that in such circumstances the accompanying stress can be severe. Imagine, then, the trauma of refugees who are forced not only to leave their homes but also their homelands and to face the stress of adapting to a new and unfamiliar culture. For those who come to the United States, the land of opportunity may seem a nightmare rather than a haven. Such was the case for Pham, a 34-year-old Vietnamese refugee who killed his sons and himself. Because Pham had no past history of mental disorder and seemed to function reasonably well, it is likely that he was experiencing symptoms of poor adaptation to his new environment: Pham's ordeal began with a comfortable life in a wealthy Vietnamese family and a good job as a Saigon pharmacist. It ended after six months in the United States in a small two-bedroom apartment in Washington, D.C. The county police called it a murder-suicide. Police believe that the refugee, a lab technician in a local community college's work-study program, administered the poison to his own family and then took his own life. Only Pham's wife survived the administration of the poison. Two seven-page suicide notes, one in Vietnamese and one in English, began, "To whom it may concern. We committed suicide by cyanide. The reason is that I lost my mind. I cannot live here like a normal person . . . ."

Pham, according to relatives, had been depressed over what he considered his financial and social failures in America. He was despondent over having to study five years to become a pharmacist here and about his difficulties communicating in English. Pham was a dutiful son who had never been away from home before leaving for the United States. He was homesick for his native country and for the parents who remained behind. "He had a lot of expectations about America," said one relative, "He just could not cope." ■

Source: Adapted from the *Washington Star,* December 8, 1980.

the most difficulty adjusting to new cultures (Nesdale, Rooney, & Smith, 1997). For example, a ten-year longitudinal study of Hmong refugees from Laos found that many refugees had made considerable progress in their acculturation (Westermeyer, Neider, & Callies, 1989). Many had improved economically—about 55 percent were employed, with incomes approaching those of the general population. The percentage of people initially living on welfare had dropped from 53 to 29 percent after ten years. As a group, psychological adjustment had also improved, with symptoms of phobia, somatization, and low self-esteem showing the most positive changes. Considerable problems remain, however. Many refugees still have not learned the language, some seemingly have settled permanently onto the welfare rolls, and some show symptoms such as anxiety, hostility, and paranoia that have changed little over the period studied. Although many refugees have adapted to their new culture, many are still experiencing considerable adjustment problems even after ten years in the United States (Hinton, Tiet et al., 1997; Westermeyer, 1989) or in other refugee countries such as Norway (Hauff & Vaglum, 1994).

Many adults who emigrate—especially those forced to leave their homes—experience a high degree of stress and psychological adjustment problems. However, even greater degrees of stress can occur with their children (Rousseau, Drapeau, & Corin, 1996). In a study of Chinese migrants to Canada, Short and Johnston (1997) found that the degree of stress in children was often buffered by greater adjustment in the parents. Their study highlighted the importance of measuring stress levels of adults and implementing strategies to alleviate their "settlement concerns" in order to lower the level of stress for children.

The Trauma of Being Held Hostage Hostage taking seems to increase each year. Not only are politically driven hostage-taking situations becoming more frequent, but kidnappings in the United States for economic or other motives also seem on the rise. Clearly such situations can produce disabling psychological symptoms in victims (Allodi, 1994). The following case reported by Sonnenberg (1988) describes a man who experienced a horrifying ordeal that left him with intense symptoms of anxiety and distress for months following the incident:

Case Study, Abduction and Its Aftermath • Mr. A. was a married accountant, the father of two, in his early thirties. One night, while out performing an errand, he was attacked by a group of youths. These youngsters made him get into their car, and took him to a deserted country road.

There they pulled him from the car and began beating and kicking him. They took his wallet, began taunting him about its contents (they had learned his name, his occupation, and the names of his wife and children), and threatened to go to his home and harm these family members. Finally, after brutalizing him for several hours, they tied him to a tree, one youth held a gun to his head, and after he begged and pleaded for his life, the armed assailant pulled the trigger. The gun was empty, but at the moment the trigger was pulled the victim defecated and urinated in his pants. Then the youths untied him and left him on the road.

This man slowly made his way to a gas station he had seen during his abduction, and called the police. [One of the authors] was called to examine him, and did so at intervals for the next 2 years. The diagnosis was PTSD. He had clearly experienced an event outside the range of normal human experience, and was at first reexperiencing the event in various ways: intrusive recollections, nightmares, flashbacks, and extreme fear upon seeing groups of unsavory looking youths. He was initially remarkably numb in other respects: he withdrew from the members of his family and lost interest in his job. He felt generally estranged and detached. He expected to die in the near future. There were also symptoms of increased psychophysiologic arousal: poor sleeping, difficulty concentrating, exaggerated startle response, and when we first spoke about his abduction in detail, he actually soiled himself at the moment he described doing so during the original traumatic experience.

This man received treatment during the next 2 years from another psychiatrist, consisting of twice-weekly intensive individual psychotherapy sessions and the concurrent administration of a tricyclic antidepressant. The individual psychotherapy consisted of discussions that focused on the sense of shame

and guilt this man felt over his behavior during his abduction. He wished he had been more stoic and had not pleaded for his life. With the understanding help of his psychotherapist, he came to see that he could accept responsibility for his behavior during his captivity, that his murderous rage at his abductors was understandable, as was his desire for revenge and that his response to his experience was not remarkable compared with what others might have done and felt. Eventually he began to discuss his experience with his wife and friends, and by the end of the 2 years over which [the author] followed him, he was essentially without symptoms, although he still became somewhat anxious when he saw groups of tough-looking youths. Most importantly, his relationship with his wife and children was warm and close, and he was again interested in his work. (p. 585)

Psychological Trauma among Victims of Torture Among the most highly stressful experiences human beings have reported have been those inhuman acts perpetrated upon them by other human beings in the form of systematic torture. From the beginning of human history to the present, some people have been subjecting other people to pain, humiliation, and degradation for political or inexplicable personal reasons (Jaranson & Popkin, 1998). For example, Allden and colleagues (1996) reported that 38 percent of Burmese political dissidents who escaped to Thailand had been tortured before their escape. History and literature are full of personal accounts of intense suffering and lifelong dread resulting from maltreatment by ruthless captors. Psychological symptoms experienced after torture have been well documented and involve a range of problems, including physical symptoms (such as pain, nervousness, insomnia, tremors, weakness, fainting, sweating, and diarrhea); psychological symptoms (such as night terrors and nightmares, depression, suspiciousness, social withdrawal and alienation, irritability, and aggressiveness); cognitive impairments (such as concentration problems, disorientation, confusion, and memory deficits); and unacceptable behaviors (such as aggressiveness, impulsivity, and suicidal attempts) (see Başoğlu & Mineka, 1992; Mollica et al., 1990).

Most of what we know about the psychological consequences of torture comes from anecdotal reports by victims. More recently, the experiences of torture victims have been empirically evaluated in a well-controlled study of victims by Metin Başoğlu and his colleagues in an effort to understand the psychological factors involved, the long-term consequences of torture, and possible rehabilitation strategies. Başoğlu and colleagues (1994) report the results of a unique empirical study in which 55 former Turkish prisoners who were political activists were com-

Many Burmese political dissidents who later escaped to Thailand experienced torture before their escape.

pared with 55 political activists who were not tortured. The torture victims and control subjects were identified through articles and ads in newspapers and political journals. The investigators were able to closely match the victims and controls on a number of variables, including age, gender, education level, ethnic status, and occupation. They used a number of standard assessment techniques to obtain an objective picture of each person's adjustment and psychological symptoms—a psychiatric interview and a number of standardized psychological tests including the Turkish language MMPI, the Beck Depression Scale, and the State-Trait Anxiety Inventory.

Although the victims of torture were for the most part not found to be extremely psychiatrically disturbed compared with the controls, the victims of imprisonment and torture were found to experience significant symptoms of post-traumatic stress disorder related to being uprooted, being a refugee, living in a repressive political environment, and living through related traumatic events. Moreover Başoğlu and his colleagues also found evidence sufficient to conclude that torture induces psychological effects independent of other stressors (Başoğlu et al., 1994). Interestingly, the authors found that traumatic experience from torture had a differential impact depending on the manner in which torture was applied—that is, whether the torture was perceived by the victim as uncontrollable and unpredictable (Başoğlu & Mineka, 1992). Victims who were able to assert some ele-

ment of cognitive control over the circumstances (for example, who were able to predict and ready themselves for the pain they were about to experience) tended to be less affected over the long term (see Highlight 4.5). They came to this conclusion:

> Prior knowledge of and preparedness for torture, strong commitment to a cause, immunization against traumatic stress as a result of repeated exposure, and strong social supports appear to have protective value against PTSD in survivors of torture. (p. 76)

In a further follow-up study of torture victims, Başoğlu, Mineka and colleagues (1997) found additional support for the idea that psychological preparedness for trauma is an extremely important protective factor for lessening the psychological effects of torture.

TREATMENT AND PREVENTION OF STRESS DISORDERS

In general, the more stable and better-integrated a personality and the more favorable a person's life situation, the more quickly he or she will recover from a severe stress reaction. Many people who experience a disaster benefit from at least some psychological counseling, no matter how brief, to begin coping with their experiences (Shelby & Tredinnick, 1995). Brom, Kleber, and Defares (1989) conducted a controlled study of the effectiveness

Unpredictable and Uncontrollable Stressors

For the past 30 years, extensive research in animals has shown that two of the most important determinants of how an organism responds to stress are whether the stressors are unpredictable or uncontrollable or both. An unpredictable stressor occurs without warning and its nature may be unforeseen. With an uncontrollable stressor, there is no way to respond to reduce its impact, such as by escape or avoidance. In general, both people and animals are more stressed by unpredictable and uncontrollable stressors than by stressors that are of equal physical magnitude but that are either predictable or controllable or both (e.g., Mineka & Zinbarg, 1996).

There are many parallels in the symptoms of PTSD and the behavioral and physiological consequences of unpredictable and uncontrollable stressors in animals (e.g., Başoğlu & Mineka, 1992; Foa, Zinbarg, & Olasov-Rothbaum, 1992; Friedman & Yehuda 1997; Mineka & Zinbarg, 1996). It is known, for example, that uncontrollable stressors stimulate some brain systems and increase levels of central and peripheral norepinephrine (Friedman & Yehuda, 1997; Southwick, Yehuda, & Morgan, 1995). This led PTSD researchers to hypothesize that administration of a drug called yohimbine to persons with PTSD might increase their symptoms, because yohimbine (a naturally occurring substance) is known to activate noradrenergic neurons. Consistent with this hypothesis, Southwick and colleagues (1995) found that 40 percent of a group of 20 Vietnam veterans with PTSD experienced flashbacks. In addition, the veterans with PTSD showed increases in other symptoms, such as intrusive traumatic thoughts, emotional numbing, and grief.

Uncontrollable stressors in animals are also known to cause stress-induced analgesia (SIA), or diminished sensitivity to pain. Formerly neutral conditioned stimuli that are paired with uncontrollable stressors can also become conditioned to elicit this analgesia. This SIA is known to work through the production of endogenous, or internally produced, opiate-like substances in the brain (Southwick et al., 1995; van der Kolk & Saporta, 1993). PTSD researchers now believe that many of the symptoms of emotional numbing seen in people with PTSD may be caused by this same kind of SIA, rather than being a psychological defensive reaction against remembering the trauma. Consistent with this are results from a study by Pitman and his colleagues (1990) in which veterans with and without PTSD who watched a film depicting combat in Vietnam (certainly a conditioned stimulus for trauma) were later given a pain sensitivity test. Those with PTSD showed reduced pain sensitivity relative to those without PTSD. Those with PTSD also showed a relative blunting of emotional responses to the film. This and other studies support the idea that the symptoms of emotional numbing in PTSD stem from the opioid-mediated SIA that has developed because of the experience with uncontrollable stressors.

If unpredictable and uncontrollable stressors are most likely to produce PTSD, what factors might influence which of the people who experience those stressors will be most likely to develop PTSD? Again, researchers have turned to the animal literature for answers (e.g., Mineka & Zinbarg, 1996). For example, it is known that prior experience with uncontrollable stressors can sensitize the organism—that is, make it more susceptible to the negative consequences of later experiences with uncontrollable trauma. Several studies of PTSD have confirmed that this is indeed the case, with victims of childhood abuse being more susceptible to PTSD in response to both sexual and nonsexual assault in adulthood (see Foa et al., 1992; Mineka & Zinbarg, 1996). In addition, soldiers who had been physically abused in childhood were more likely to develop PTSD during the Vietnam war (Post, Weiss, & Smith, 1995).

Considerable research now supports the hypotheses that perceptions of uncontrollability and unpredictability play an important role in the development and maintenance of PTSD symptoms. Moreover, the animal literature showing that prior experiences with uncontrollable stressors may sensitize an organism to the negative effects of subsequent experience with other uncontrollable stressors has led to important new findings regarding which individuals may be most susceptible to PTSD. ■

of brief therapy with people experiencing PTSD and found that treatment immediately following the traumatic event significantly reduced the PTSD symptoms. Sixty percent of the treated persons showed improvement while only 26 percent of the untreated group improved. They also found, however, that treatment did not benefit everyone and that some people maintained their PTSD symptoms even after therapy was terminated.

Treatment is often required, too, for disaster area workers. Many people called to the scene of a disaster to assist victims later experience post-traumatic stress disorder themselves. Epstein, Fullerton, and Ursano (1998) found that workers who provide support to bereaved families of disaster victims are at risk for increased illness, psychiatric symptoms, and negative psychological well-being for up to a 18 months following the disaster. They also reported that individuals with lower levels of education, those who had exposure to grotesque burns, and had strong feelings of numbness following exposure, were more likely to experience later psychological symptoms following an air disaster.

Supportive therapy and proper rest (induced by sedatives if necessary) usually can alleviate symptoms that lead to post-traumatic stress disorder (Morgan, 1995; Everly, 1995). Repetitive talking about the experience and constantly reliving it in fantasies or nightmares may serve as built-in repair mechanisms to help a person adjust to the traumatic event.

As mentioned earlier in the section on coping, the treatment of stress-related psychological problems is most effective when intervention is applied early or as soon as possible following the traumatic events. We will describe some medications that have been considered useful in providing relief from the symptoms of post-traumatic stress disorder; however, psychopharmacotherapy works best in the context of psychological treatment. We will also describe effective approaches to reduction of symptoms related to stress.

Stress Prevention or Reduction

If we know that extreme or prolonged stress can produce maladaptive psychological reactions that have predictable courses, is it possible to intervene early in the process to prevent the development of emotional disorder? In some situations it may be possible to prevent maladaptive responses to stress by preparing a person in advance to deal with the stress. This approach to stress management has been shown to be effective in cases where the person is facing a known traumatic event, such as major surgery or the breakup of a relationship. In these cases a professional attempts to prepare the person in advance to cope better with the stressful event through developing more realistic and adaptive attitudes about the problem.

When a predictable and unusually stressful situation is about to occur, is it possible to inoculate a person by providing information about likely stressors ahead of time and suggesting ways of coping with them? If preparation for battle stressors can help soldiers avoid breakdowns, why not prepare other people to effectively meet anticipated stressors? The use of cognitive-behavioral techniques to help people manage potentially stressful situations or difficult events has been widely explored (Beech, Burns, & Sheffield, 1982; MacDonald & Kuiper, 1983; Meichenbaum & Cameron, 1983). This preventive strategy, often referred to as **stress-inoculation training,** prepares people to tolerate an anticipated threat by changing the things they say to themselves before the crisis. A three-stage process is employed. The first stage provides information about the stressful situation and about ways people can deal with such dangers. In the second stage, self-statements that promote effective adaptation—for example, "Don't worry, this little pain is just part of the treatment"—are rehearsed. In the third stage, the person practices making such self-statements while being exposed to a variety of ego-threatening or pain-threatening stressors, such as unpredictable electric shocks, stress-inducing films, or sudden cold. This last phase allows the person to apply the new coping skills learned earlier. We shall discuss stress-inoculation training and the use of self-statements in greater detail in Chapter 17. Now we will examine ways in which post-traumatic symptoms are treated.

Treatment of Post-Traumatic Stress Symptoms

Medications Several medications are used to provide relief for intense PTSD symptoms. Antidepressants are sometimes helpful in improving PTSD symptoms of depression, intrusion, and avoidance (Marshall & Klein, 1995; Shaley, Bonne, & Eth, 1996). However, since the symptoms can fluctuate over a brief period of time, careful monitoring of medications or dosage is required. The use of medication tends to be focused on specific symptoms; for example, intrusive distressing symptoms or nightmares, images of horrible events, startle reaction, and so forth (see Chapter 16). Vargas and Davidson (1993) concluded that psychotherapy along with medications were more effective in improving PTSD symptoms than medications taken alone.

Crisis Intervention Therapy A brief problem-focused counseling approach referred to as *crisis intervention* (see Chapter 18) may aid a victim of a traumatic event in readjusting to life after the stressful situation has

Loss of a loved one is one of the most intense stressors that people experience. The family shown here is grieving the loss of a loved one in the Swissair air disaster at sea off the coast of Nova Scotia.

ended. In brief crisis-oriented therapy with people in a crisis situation, the disaster victim is provided emotional support and is encouraged to talk about their experiences during the crisis (Cigrang, Pace, & Yasuhara, 1995). People who are able to deal with their emotional reactions during the crisis are better able to adjust to life circumstances following the disaster (Chemtob, Tomas, Law, & Cremniter, 1997).

Direct Therapeutic Exposure

One behaviorally oriented treatment strategy that has been used effectively with PTSD clients is *direct therapeutic exposure* (Fairbank et al., 1993). In this approach, the client is exposed or reintroduced to stimuli that have come to be feared or associated with the traumatic event (McIvor & Turner, 1995). This procedure involves repeated or extended exposure, either *in vivo* or in the imagination, to objectively harmless but feared stimuli for the purpose of reducing anxiety (Fairbank et al., 1993).

Exposure to stimuli that have come to be associated with fear-producing situations might also be supplemented by other behavioral techniques in an effort to re-

duce the symptoms of PTSD. For example, the use of traditional behavioral therapy methods such as relaxation training and assertiveness training might also be found to be effective in helping a client deal with the anxiety following a traumatic event.

The following case shows the effectiveness of this approach:

Case Study, Therapy for an Angry Vet with PTSD • A male veteran diagnosed with PTSD and substance abuse was enrolled in a treatment program and received anger management treatment. He began attending the anger management groups in May 1992 and continues to attend a drop-in anger management support group regularly.

John is a 45-year-old, divorced, Hispanic, Vietnam veteran, with a 25-year history of alcohol and heroin dependence. He grew up in Texas, graduated from high school, and served in the Navy from July 1969 to April 1971. During his tour in Vietnam, John saw significant combat, including friendly and hostile incoming fire. He took part in amphibious invasions and engaged the enemy in fire fights. John saw many of his comrades killed, including his best friend who was killed only a few feet away from him by an exploding land mine. He also witnessed many atrocities, including the killing of Vietnamese civilians.

John began using alcohol and heroin while in Vietnam. Following his discharge, he experienced symptoms of depression, fearfulness, hypervigilance, and isolation. John began to increase his alcohol and heroin use in an attempt to decrease these feelings. Although trained as a welder, John was unable to hold steady employment. Prior to his entry into treatment for PTSD, he was hospitalized on several occasions for depression and two suicide attempts. John was arrested more than 30 times for assault and disorderly conduct.

In 1990, John began outpatient treatment in the Post-Traumatic Stress Disorder Clinic at the San Francisco Veterans Affairs Medical Center. He engaged in group psychotherpy and received pharmacotherapy; however, he continued to abuse alcohol and heroin and displayed significant behavioral difficulties, including occasional assaults. In December 1991, John was hospitalized in the inpatient PTSD program following an escalation of angry outbursts, including an incident in which, apparently without provocation, he swung a stick at a man he encountered on a walk.

At the time of his admission to both the treatment program and the anger management group in May 1992, John reported that he had not used alcohol or other drugs for one month. He complained, however, of intrusive thoughts and memories, nightmares, flashbacks, sleep disturbance, poor concentration, and frequent outbursts of anger.

During his initial sessions in the anger management group, John reported high levels of irritability and anger, and very low frustration tolerance. On one occasion, he destroyed personal property during an episode of rage. Over the course of several weeks in the group, John became skilled at monitoring his anger by using the anger meter and identifying the physical, emotional, and situational cues that led to his escalation of anger. He also became aware of his hostile self-talk, and began to use anger management strategies, such as time-out and an exercise program, to control his anger effectively. By the eighth week of treatment, John was regularly practicing assertiveness techniques, such as conflict resolution. His improvement is exemplified by an incident that occurred during his tenth week of treatment. John reported that he had become angered when he learned that his landlord had let his ex-wife into his apartment without his permission. Rather than acting out aggressively against the landlord or destroying property, John spoke directly to his landlord, resolving the incident assertively.

John has continued to make significant progress. He completed the 12-week group and continues to attend an anger management support group for clients in the program. He has maintained his abstinence throughout his treatment in the program. He has become significantly less isolated, having formed friendships with group members, and has enrolled in a work training program. He has progressed from angry outbursts and violently acting out to taking brief time-outs and assertively resolving conflicts. John is now more confident in his ability to negotiate difficult situations, can identify anger-provoking situations, and can manage his anger effectively with specific cognitive and behavioral techniques (Reilley, Clark, Shopshire, Lewis, & Sorensen, 1994, p. 406).

UNRESOLVED ISSUES

The Abuse of PTSD and Other Stress Diagnoses

This chapter has addressed the role of stress in producing psychological disorders. A considerable amount of research has substantiated the link between severe stress or trauma and subsequent psychological problems. People may react to stressful situations in ways that are quite disabling. Many symptoms of post-traumatic stress disorder can interfere with psychological functioning, at least for a time, and can require considerable adaptive effort to overcome.

In recent years, alleged psychological disability as a result of post-traumatic stress disorder has been used in both civil and criminal cases (Slovenko, 1994). PTSD has been used as a defense in court cases to justify criminal acts according to the not guilty by reason of insanity plea (see Chapter 18). A recent case illustrates the sometimes loose connection between PTSD and deviant behavior.

Case Study • In January 1987 an employee of an air cargo company, who had been fired from his job the day before, returned to the office dressed in army fatigues and carrying a sawed-off shotgun. He chased several employees away from the office and took his former supervisor hostage. He held his supervisor at gunpoint for about 1 1/2 hours, making him beg for his life. During this time he fired about 21 shots at desks, computers, and windows, destroying a great deal of property. Once the hostage-taking situation ended, the former employee was arrested on charges of property destruction and assault with a deadly weapon. He reportedly claimed that he was extremely distraught and was suffering a post-traumatic stress disorder. He explained that he had just seen the movie *Platoon,* which brought back horrible memories of Vietnam and had resulted in his becoming enraged. However, a check of his background and military records showed that he had never been in Vietnam and had actually spent his service time in a low stress noncombat environment.

There have been a number of similar incidences in which alleged post-traumatic symptoms have been incorporated into the legal defense strategy of individuals facing felony convictions. For example, one recent dramatic case is of a World War II POW veteran who killed his daughter's estranged husband. He later claimed that he committed this act because of the "ghosts of the past." He claimed that he was afraid for his life when his son-in-law approached him, and he shot him because he thought he was going to be "beaten to death" (*Los Angeles Times,* Sept. 8, 1997).

The frequent sensational nature and resulting publicity of some cases may give the impression that the use of the PTSD defense is on the increase. A recent study of insanity plea defendants showed that concerns over widespread abuse of the PTSD insanity defense are unfounded because the defense is not used as frequently as is often supposed. Appelbaum and colleagues (1993) found that in 8163 defendants pleading insanity between 1980 and 1986 only 28 (0.3 percent) had been given PTSD diagnoses. People with a PTSD diagnosis employing the insanity defense were, however, more likely to be able to avoid pretrial detention than those in the control group of non-PTSD defendants (Appelbaum et al., 1993).

The PTSD syndrome is more frequently being used in civil court cases, such as those involving compensation and personal injury. For example, in one case (*Albertson's*

Panic, Anxiety, and Their Disorders

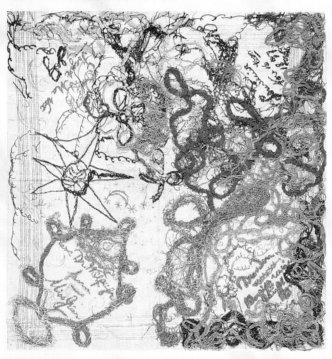

G. (Miss G.), *Untitled.* Miss G. was diagnosed with depression, and in 1897 chose to express herself—like most Victorian women of her time—by embroidering on a linen handkerchief. Like any woman proud of her sewing accomplishments, she signed and dated her tangled handiwork.

Overwhelming stress, as we noted in the last chapter, can produce psychological problems in anyone. Even stable, well-adjusted people may break down if forced to face extensive combat stress, torture, or devastating natural disaster, for example. But for some people, everyday problems can be disturbing. Faced with the normal demands of life—socializing with friends, waiting in line for a bus, being on an airplane, touching a doorknob—they experience the arousal of serious fear or anxiety. In the most severe cases, people with anxiety problems may be unable even to leave their homes or may spend much of their time in maladaptive behavior, such as constant hand washing.

Anxiety—a general feeling of apprehension about possible danger—was in Freud's formulation a sign of an inner battle or conflict between some primitive desire (from the id) and prohibitions against its expression (from the ego and superego). Sometimes this anxiety seemed evident to him in clients who were obviously fearful and nervous. Today the DSM has identified such cases within a group of disorders that share obvious symptoms and features of anxiety known as the *anxiety disorders,* which will be the focus of this chapter.

Historically, anxiety disorders were considered to be examples of **neurotic behavior,** which involved the exaggerated use of avoidance behaviors (such as not leaving home) or defense mechanisms (such as rationalizing that making a trip by car is "more convenient" than confronting the feared airplane ride). Although neurotic behavior is maladaptive and self-defeating, a neurotic person is not out of touch with reality, incoherent, or dangerous. Nevertheless, such a person's social relations and work performance are likely to be impaired by their efforts to cope with their fear—whether by avoiding it or taking extreme precautions to guard against it.

The idea of **neurosis** has a long history and is still used in psychodynamic professional circles, and in casual conversation by the general public. Freud challenged earlier long-held beliefs that neurosis was due to neurological malfunction and argued instead that it was caused by intrapsychic conflict. To Freud, neurosis was a *psychological disorder* that resulted when there was anxiety that was a sign of intrapsychic conflict. As already noted, sometimes this anxiety was very evident, as it was in clients who were obviously fearful or anxious. To complicate matters, however, he also believed that the anxiety might *not* be obvious, either to the person involved or to others, if psychological defense mechanisms were able to deflect or mask it. Yet, in his view, it still was causing the neurotic behavior in such cases as well. For example, Freud believed that many of his patient's physical complaints (such as temporary blindness or paralysis) were caused by anxiety—chiefly

about sexual or aggressive feelings they were uncomfortable with. Freud's ideas required inferring that anxiety somehow existed in the mind and caused neurotic behavior even though it could not be observed or measured.

Since 1980, the approach of each edition of the DSM has been to avoid such inferences about the causes of disorders. Therefore, although we still hear and use the term *neurosis,* the DSM has separated what used to be officially called neuroses into different categories based on their symptoms, which *can* be observed and measured. People with anxiety disorders, which we shall be considering in this chapter, show prominent symptoms of anxiety. One of the anxiety disorders—post-traumatic stress disorder—was already discussed in Chapter 4. Most of the other disorders that Freud considered neuroses, but that did not involve obvious anxiety symptoms, have been reclassified and will be discussed in Chapter 7 (the dissociative and somatoform disorders). One final category of neurotic disorders (depressive neurosis) is now included with the other mood disorders which will be discussed in Chapter 6.

In recent years, Freud's views on the nature of neurosis have been criticized as too theoretical and not sufficiently tied to the real world. This is because Freud believed anxiety to be key not only to disorders where anxiety symptoms are obvious but also to many disorders in which there are few, if any, actual symptoms of anxiety. The DSM's grouping of disorders that share obvious symptoms and features has allowed major advances to be made in understanding their causes and treatment. One reason for this is that the diagnostic criteria for the different disorders are now much more clearly defined. The diagnostician or therapist need not make inferences about underlying unobservable inner states, such as anxiety that is thought to be present but not observable because it is "defended against." As a consequence, the reliability of diagnoses is higher than it was previously, allowing investigators to study much more homogeneous groups of people who share a common diagnosis. This greatly facilitates our ability to learn what causes the disorders and how best to treat them.

We now begin by discussing the nature of fear and anxiety as emotional states, both of which have an extremely important adaptive value but to which humans at times seem all too vulnerable. We will then move to a discussion of the anxiety disorders as described in DSM-IV and of causal factors and optimal modes of treatment for each disorder.

THE FEAR AND ANXIETY RESPONSE PATTERNS

The task of defining *fear* and *anxiety* is difficult; there has never been complete agreement whether the two emotions are indeed distinct from each other. Historically, the most common way of distinguishing between fear and anxiety has been whether there is a clear and obvious source of danger that would be regarded as real by most people. When the source of danger is obvious, the experienced emotion has been called fear. With anxiety, however, we frequently cannot specify clearly what the danger is. Intuitively, anxiety seems to be experienced as an unpleasant inner state in which we are anticipating some dreadful thing happening that is not entirely predictable from our actual circumstances. For example, the term *anxious apprehension* is often used to describe this state (Barlow, 1991a; Barlow, Chorpita, & Turovsky, 1996).

In recent years, many prominent researchers have proposed a more fundamental distinction between fear or panic, and anxiety (e.g., Barlow et al., 1996; Gray, 1991; Gray & McNaughton, 1996). According to these theorists, **fear** or **panic** is a basic emotion that involves the activation of the "fight-or-flight" response of the sympathetic nervous system, allowing us to respond quickly when faced with any imminent threat.

Fear or panic is a basic emotion that occurs in many higher animals and humans. It is usually associated with a distinctive facial expression such as expressed here, and involves activation of the "fight or flight" response of the sympathetic nervous system. This allows us to respond rapidly when faced with a dangerous situation, such as being threatened by a predator. In humans who are having a panic attack there is no external threat; panic occurs because of some misfiring of this response system.

Such threats range from dangerous predators who preyed on our early ancestors, and which may still be encountered (for example, by hikers in wilderness areas), to threats that derive from more modern sources of danger, such as facing someone with a loaded gun, or being in an airplane that has started to plunge earthward. Fear has three components: (1) cognitive/subjective components ("I feel afraid"), (2) physiological components (such as increased heart rate and heavy breathing), and (3) behavioral components (a strong urge to escape) (Lang, 1968, 1971). These components are only "loosely coupled" (Lang, 1985), which means that someone might show, for example, physiological and behavioral indications of fear without much of the subjective component, or vice versa. For the fear response to serve its adaptive purpose of enabling us to escape or avoid danger, it must be activated with great speed. Indeed, subjectively we often seem to go from a normal state to a state of intense fear almost instantaneously. Not surprisingly, given its adaptive value for helping us escape from sources of danger, this is not a uniquely human emotion but one that is shared by many animals.

For our purposes here, we will follow the conceptualization of David Barlow, who argues that anxiety, in contrast to fear, is best thought of as a complex blend of emotions and cognitions that is much more diffuse than fear. At the cognitive/subjective level, anxiety involves negative mood, worry about possible future threat or danger, self-preoccupation, and a sense of being unable to predict the future threat or to control it if it occurs (Barlow, 1988; Barlow et al., 1996). Rather than involving the activation of the fight-or-flight response itself, as we see with fear, anxiety involves preparing for that response should it become necessary ("Something awful may happen and I had better be ready for it if it does"). As with fear, anxiety involves not only cognitive/subjective components but also physiological and behavioral components. At a physiological level, anxiety involves a state of chronic overarousal which may reflect the state of readiness for dealing with danger should it occur (preparation for, or priming of, the fight-or-flight response). At a behavioral level, anxiety may involve a strong tendency to avoid situations where the danger or threat might be encountered, but there is no immediate urge to flee associated with anxiety as there is with fear (Barlow, 1988; Barlow et al., 1996). The adaptive value of anxiety may derive from the fact that it helps us plan for and prepare for possible threat, and in mild to moderate degrees, anxiety actually enhances learning and performance. But although anxiety is often adaptive in mild or moderate degrees, it is maladaptive when it becomes chronic and severe, as we generally see in people diagnosed with anxiety disorders, including post-traumatic stress disorder as discussed in Chapter 4.

Although there are many threatening situations that provoke fear or anxiety unconditionally, many of our sources of fear and anxiety are learned. Human and non-human animal experimentation going back many decades has established that the basic fear and anxiety response patterns are highly conditionable. That is, previously neutral and novel stimuli that are repeatedly paired with, and reliably predict, aversive events (such as mild electric shocks) can acquire the capacity to elicit fear or anxiety themselves. Of course, few human infants or children are subjected to electric shocks, but many have experiences that are inherently aversive or painful. And, as we have increasingly discovered in recent years, some have unspeakably cruel and terrifying experiences visited upon them by disturbed parents or other adults. For example, a girl who sees and hears her father physically abuse her mother in the evening may become anxious as soon as she hears her father's car arrive in the driveway at the end of the day. In such situations a wide variety of initially neutral stimuli may accidentally come to serve as cues that something threatening and unpleasant is about to happen. These neutral stimuli may consist not only of external cues, but also of internal bodily sensations such as stomach or intestinal contractions or heart palpitations. As a result of such pairings, these conditioned stimuli can themselves become fear- or anxiety-provoking. In addition, the richly elaborate mental life that we humans enjoy means that our thoughts and images become capable of eliciting the fear or anxiety response pattern. In this scenario virtually any type of novel stimulus (external, mental, or internal bodily sensations) that reliably precedes and predicts an aversive event would be expected to acquire the tendency to elicit fear or anxiety. For example, the girl described above whose father beats her mother might well come to feel anxious even when thinking about her father.

OVERVIEW OF THE ANXIETY DISORDERS

An **anxiety disorder,** as the term suggests, has an unrealistic, irrational fear or anxiety of disabling intensity at its core and also as its principal and most obvious manifestation. DSM-IV recognizes seven primary types of anxiety disorder: phobic disorders of the "specific" or of the "social" type, panic disorder with or without agoraphobia, generalized anxiety disorder, obsessive-compulsive disorder, and post-traumatic stress disorder. The last of these, basically a prolonged reaction to traumatic stressors, was discussed in Chapter 4 and will not be considered here.

Anxiety disorders are relatively common, affecting more than 23 million Americans each year and costing the United States $46.6 billion in 1990 in direct and indirect costs (nearly one-third of the nation's total mental health bill of $148 billion) (National Institute of Mental Health, 1998). In

the National Comorbidity Survey, the most recent large epidemiological study, anxiety disorders as a group were the most common kind of disorder for women, affecting approximately 30 percent of the female population at some point in their lives, and the second most common kind of disorder for men, affecting approximately 19 percent of the male population at some point (Kessler et al., 1994). Twelve-month prevalence rates for women were 23 percent and for men were 12 percent. In terms of specific anxiety disorders, phobias were the second most common psychiatric disorder reported for women (with major depression being the most common) and the fourth most common for men (behind alcohol abuse, alcohol dependence, and major depression).

It is also very common for a person diagnosed with one anxiety disorder to be diagnosed with one or more additional anxiety disorders, as well as with a mood disorder (discussed in Chapter 6; see Highlight 6.3 for a discussion of anxiety/depression comorbidity). For example, in the National Comorbidity Survey about 40 to 50 percent of those who ever had a phobic disorder (specific, social, or agoraphobia) in their lifetime also had a depressive disorder at some point in their lifetime and 57 to 75 percent also had another anxiety disorder at some point in their lifetime (Magee et al., 1996; see also Mineka, Watson, & Clark, 1998).

PHOBIC DISORDERS

A **phobia** is a persistent and disproportionate fear of some specific object or situation that presents little or no actual danger to a person. When a person with a phobia encounters a feared object, he or she will often experience the fight-or-flight response discussed earlier, which prepares the person to escape from the situation. Thus, physiologically and behaviorally the phobic response is often identical to that which would occur in an encounter with an objectively terrifying situation, such as being chased down a hiking trail by a grizzly bear. In the phobic's case, however, the situation eliciting this response is not especially dangerous—it could be a bridge or a bus, for example. Phobics go to great lengths to avoid such encounters with their phobic stimulus, or sometimes even a seemingly innocent representation of it, such as a photograph. In DSM-IV there are three main categories of phobias: (1) specific phobia, (2) social phobia, and (3) agoraphobia. **Specific phobias** (formerly known as *simple phobias*) may involve fears of other species (snake and spider phobias being the most common) or fears of various aspects of the environment, such as water, heights, tunnels, or bridges. **Social phobias** involve fears of social situations in which a person is exposed to the scrutiny of others and is afraid of acting in a humiliating or embarrassing way. Social phobias may be circumscribed (as in fear of public speaking) or generalized (as in fear of many different sorts of social interactions). Traditionally, *agoraphobia* was thought to involve, somewhat paradoxically, a fear of both open and enclosed spaces. However, as discussed later, it is now understood that agoraphobia most often stems from anxiety about having a panic attack (discussed below and the basic activation of the fight-or-flight response discussed above) in situations where escape might prove difficult or embarrassing. The apparent paradox is resolved in this view because escape is difficult from both open and enclosed spaces. Because it is no longer considered to be closely related to the specific phobias, we will discuss agoraphobia in the context of panic disorder, as is done in DSM-IV.

Specific Phobias

A person is diagnosed as having a specific phobia if he or she shows strong and persistent fear triggered by the presence of (or anticipation of an encounter with) a specific object or situation. The level of fear must also be excessive or unreasonable relative to the actual danger posed by the object or situation. When individuals with specific phobias encounter a phobic stimulus, they almost always show an immediate fear response that often resembles a panic attack except for the existence of a clear external trigger (American Psychiatric Association, 1994, p. 410). The avoidance of the feared situation, or the distress experienced in the feared situation, must also interfere significantly with normal functioning or produce marked distress. Table 5.1 lists some common specific phobias and their objects, clearly illustrating the wide variety of situations around which specific phobias may be centered. In DSM-IV there are now five subtypes of specific phobias listed: (1) animal subtype (e.g., snakes or spiders); (2) natural environment subtype (e.g., heights or water); (3) blood-injection-injury subtype (see below); (4) situational subtype (e.g., airplanes or elevators); (5) atypical subtype (e.g., choking or vomiting).

Some of these specific phobias involve exaggerated fears of things that many of us fear to some extent, such as darkness, fire, disease, spiders, and snakes. Others, such as phobias of water or crowds, involve situations that do not elicit fear in most people. Many of us have at least a few minor irrational fears, but in phobic disorders such fears are intense and often interfere significantly with everyday activities. For example, claustrophobic persons may go to great lengths to avoid entering a small room or an elevator, even if this means climbing many flights of stairs or turning down jobs that might require them to take an elevator. This avoidance is a cardinal characteristic of phobias; it occurs both because the phobic response itself is so unpleasant and because of phobic person's irrational appraisal of the likelihood that something terrible will happen.

People with claustrophobia may find elevators so frightening that they go to great lengths to avoid them. If for some reason they have to take an elevator, they will be very frightened and may have thoughts about the elevator falling, the doors never opening, or there not being enough air to breathe.

The following case is typical of specific phobia.

Case Study, A Pilot's Wife's Fear of Heights and Enclosed Spaces • Mary, a married mother of three, was 47 at the time she first sought treatment for both claustrophobia and acrophobia. She reported having been intensely afraid of enclosed spaces and of heights since her teens. She remembered having been locked in closets by her older siblings when she was a child; the siblings also confined her under blankets to scare her, and added to her fright by showing her pictures of spiders after releasing her from under the blankets. She traced the onset of her claustrophobia to those traumatic incidents, but she had no idea why she was afraid of heights. While her children had been growing up, she had been a housewife and had managed to live a fairly normal life in spite of her two specific phobias. However, her children were now

TABLE 5.1   COMMON SPECIFIC PHOBIAS

Acrophobia	Heights
Algophobia	Pain
Astraphobia	Thunderstorms, lightning
Claustrophobia	Enclosed places
Hydrophobia	Water
Monophobia	Being alone
Mysophobia	Contamination or germs
Nyctophobia	Darkness
Ochlophobia	Crowds
Pathophobia	Disease
Pyrophobia	Fire
Zoophobia	Animals or some particular animal

grown and she wanted to find a job outside her home. This was proving to be very difficult, however, because she could not take elevators and was not comfortable being on anything other than the first floor of an office building because of her fear of heights. Moreover, her husband had for some years been working for an airline, which entitled him to free airline tickets for himself and his wife. The fact that she could not fly (primarily because of her claustrophobia but to some extent because of her acrophobia as well) had become a sore point in her marriage because they both wanted to be able to take advantage of these free tickets to see far-away parts of the United States and Europe. Thus, although she had had these phobias for many years, they had only become truly disabling in recent years as her life circumstances had changed and she could no longer easily avoid heights or enclosed spaces.

People who suffer from phobias usually know that their fears are somewhat irrational, but they say that they cannot help themselves. If they attempt to approach the phobic situation, they are overcome with fear or anxiety, which may vary from mild feelings of apprehension and distress (usually while still at some distance) to a full-fledged activation of the fight-or-flight response very similar to a panic attack. Regardless of how it begins, phobic behavior tends to be reinforced by the reduction in anxiety that occurs each time a feared situation is avoided. In addition, phobias may sometimes be maintained in part by secondary gains (benefits derived from being disabled), such as increased attention, sympathy, and some control over the behavior of others. For example, a phobia for driving may result in a homemaker being able to escape from responsibilities outside the home, such as grocery shopping or transporting children to and from school. Phobias, then, in addition to being primary manifestations of irrational, acquired fears, may sometimes serve the interests of seemingly remote objectives, although usually without the sufferer's awareness.

Blood-Injection-Injury Phobia   One category of specific phobias that probably occurs in about 3 to 4 percent of the population has a number of interesting and unique characteristics (Öst & Hellström, 1997; Page, 1994). In **blood-injection-injury phobia** the afflicted person shows a unique physiological response when confronted with the sight of blood or injury. Rather than showing the simple increase in heart rate and blood pressure that is seen when most phobics encounter their phobic object, these people show an initial acceleration, followed by a dramatic drop in both heart rate and blood pressure. This is often accompanied by nausea, dizziness, and fainting. Indeed, it has been estimated that about 75 percent of people with blood-injury phobia have a history of fainting in these situations (Öst & Hellström, 1997).

Interestingly, blood-injury phobics only show this unique physiological response pattern in the presence of blood and injury stimuli; in the presence of other feared objects they show the more typical physiological response pattern characteristic of the fight-or-flight response (see Öst & Hugdahl, 1985). This category of phobia also has a strong familial component, with as many as two-thirds of blood-injury phobics having at least one first-degree relative who is also blood phobic. Whether this reflects a genetic effect of common environmental experiences shared by members of the same family is still unclear (Neale et al., 1994; Page & Martin, 1998). From an evolutionary and functional standpoint, this unique physiological response pattern may have evolved for a specific purpose: by fainting, the person being attacked might inhibit further attack (Marks & Nesse, 1991).

Age of Onset and Gender Differences in Specific Phobias   Specific phobias are quite common, especially in women. Results of the National Comorbidity Survey revealed a lifetime prevalence rate of over 16 percent for women and nearly 7 percent for men (Kessler et al., 1994; Magee et al., 1996). The relative sex ratios vary considerably according to the type of specific phobia. For example, about 90 to 95 percent of people with animal phobias are women, but the sex ratio is less than two to one for blood-injury phobia. The average age of onset for different types of specific phobias also varies widely. Animal phobias usually begin in childhood (where they are actually equally common in boys and girls, but boys tend to "outgrow" them), as do blood-injury phobias, dental phobias, and natural environment phobias such as heights and water. However, other phobias, such as claustrophobia and agoraphobia, tend to begin in adolescence and early adulthood (American Psychiatric Association, 1994; Öst, 1987).

Psychosocial Causal Factors   There are a variety of psychosocial causal factors that have been implicated in the origins of specific phobias, ranging from deep-seated

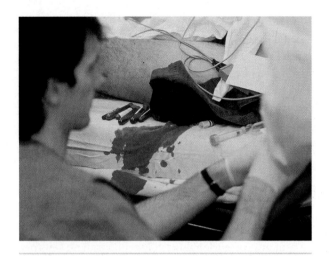

People with blood-injury phobia are terrified of being confronted with scenes involving blood or injury and often faint if they do encounter such a scene. Such people go to great lengths to avoid doctors and hospitals, sometimes to the extent of avoiding necessary medical treatments.

psychodynamic conflicts to relatively straightforward traumatic conditioning of fear.

Psychodynamic Viewpoint According to the *psychodynamic* view of the origins of phobias, phobias represent a defense against anxiety that stems from repressed impulses from the id. Because it is too dangerous to "know" the repressed id impulse, the anxiety is displaced onto some external object or situation that has some symbolic relationship to the real object of the anxiety. For example, in his classic case of Little Hans, Freud (1909) postulated that 5-year-old Hans had developed a phobia for horses as a result of anxiety stemming from a repressed Oedipal conflict. Specifically, Freud believed that Hans unconsciously desired his mother based on a conversation she reported occurred with her when he was in the bathtub and wanted her to touch his penis or "widdler" and so was so jealous of his father (whose penis was larger) that he wanted to kill him to get him out of the way so he could have his mother all to himself. This led him to assume (by projection) that his father wanted to "kill'" him or at least castrate him. The intense internal conflict created by all these unconscious feelings was not acceptable to Hans's conscious mind, according to Freud, and so the anxiety was displaced onto horses, which supposedly bore some symbolic relationship to his father.

Although widely accepted among psychoanalytic theorists as a prototypical case for how phobias are acquired, this account has been criticized as being far too speculative (e.g., Wolpe & Rachman, 1960). Moreover, an alternative and much simpler account of the origins of Hans's phobia for horses derives from learning theory. In particular, when Hans was 4 years old he had witnessed an accident with a horse in which the horse was badly hurt; Hans

had become very upset at witnessing this incident and had later begun to avoid leaving the house so as to not encounter horses in the street. So according to Wolpe and Rachman, Hans's phobia can be seen as having originated from an instance of traumatic classical conditioning.

Phobias as Learned Behavior More generally, there are many instances in which the principles of classical conditioning appear to account for the acquisition of irrational fears and phobias. As noted earlier, the fear response has been shown in countless experiments to be readily conditioned to previously neutral stimuli when they are paired with traumatic or painful events. Moreover, from the principles of classical conditioning we would also expect that, once acquired, phobic fears would *generalize* to other similar objects or situations. Recall, for example, that in Mary's case her generalized claustrophobia had probably been caused by multiple incidents as a child when her siblings locked her in closets and confined her under blankets to scare her. The powerful role of classical conditioning in the development of phobias was supported in a survey by Öst and Hugdahl (1981). These investigators administered questionnaires to 106 adult phobic clients concerning, among other things, the purported origins of their fears. In describing the situations they considered as sources of their phobias, 58 percent cited traumatic conditioning experiences. Direct traumatic conditioning may be especially common in the onset of dental phobia (Kent, 1997), claustrophobia (Rachman, 1997), and accident phobia (Kuch, 1997).

Direct traumatic conditioning is not the only way in which people can learn irrational fears. Indeed, much human learning, including the learning of fears, is observational. Simply watching a frightening event can be distressing, and this includes watching a phobic person behaving fearfully with his or her phobic object. In this case, fears can be transmitted from one person to another through a process of *vicarious* or *observational* classical conditioning. Merely observing the fear of another in a given situation may cause the observer to acquire a fear of that situation. Indeed, the Öst and Hugdahl study mentioned earlier found that 17 percent of their phobic clients described their phobias as having originated from instances of vicarious conditioning.

Just as much of our knowledge about classical conditioning of fear comes from research with animals, vicarious conditioning of intense fears has also been demonstrated in animal research, using rhesus monkey subjects. In these experiments, Mineka and Cook and their colleagues (e.g., 1984, 1991, 1993) showed that laboratory-reared monkeys who were not initially afraid of snakes rapidly developed a phobic-like fear of snakes simply through observing a wild-reared monkey behaving fearfully with snakes. Significant fear was acquired after only 4 to 8 minutes of exposure to the wild-reared monkey with snakes, and there were no signs that the fear had diminished three months later. Moreover, the monkeys could also learn to be afraid simply through watching a videotape of the wild-reared model monkey behaving fearfully with snakes—suggesting that the mass media may play a role in vicariously conditioning fears and phobias in people (Cook & Mineka, 1990).

Conditioning models of phobia acquisition have often been criticized because at first glance they do not appear to account for why so many people who undergo traumatic experiences do *not* develop intense or persistent fears or phobias. In other words, given all the traumas some people undergo, why don't more people develop phobias (Rachman, 1990)? Much of the answer to this question seems to stem from differences in life experiences that affect the outcome of a given conditioning experience. The traditional view was that phobias originate from simple instances of traumatic conditioning or avoidance learning occurring more or less in a vacuum in a person's life. Instead, we now know that many experiences that occur before, during, and after a given traumatic or observational conditioning experience affect how much fear is experienced, conditioned, or maintained over time. For example, years of positive experiences with friendly dogs before experiencing a dog bite will probably keep the bite victim from developing a dog phobia. So to understand individual differences in the development and maintenance of phobias, it is important to understand the role of different life experiences, or experiential variables, in which persons undergoing the same trauma may differ (Mineka, 1985a, 1985b; Mineka & Zinbarg, 1996, 1998).

The example of good "dog experience" immunizing one from developing a dog phobia after a dog bite shows the importance of one's familiarity with an object or situation in determining the likelihood that a phobia develops following a fear-conditioning experience. Indeed, there are several studies showing that children who have had more previous nontraumatic encounters with a dentist are less likely to develop dental anxiety if subsequently traumatized than are those with fewer previous nontraumatic encounters when they are traumatized (de Jongh et al., 1995; Kent, 1997). Moreover, Mineka and Cook (1986) showed that monkeys who simply *watched* nonfearful monkeys behaving nonfearfully with snakes were immunized against acquiring a fear of snakes when subsequently exposed to fearful monkeys behaving fearfully with snakes. Thus direct experience with an object may not even be necessary for immunization to occur. By analogy, if a child has extensive exposure to a nonfearful parent or peer behaving nonfearfully with the phobic object or situation of his or her other parent, this may immunize the child against the effects of later seeing the phobic parent behaving fearfully with that object.

Monkeys who watch a model monkey (such as the one illustrated here) behaving fearfully with a live boa constrictor will rapidly acquire an intense fear of snakes themselves. Fears can thus be learned vicariously, without any direct traumatic experience.

Events that occur *during* a conditioning experience, as well as before it, are also important in determining the level of fear that is conditioned. For example, experiencing an inescapable and uncontrollable event such as having a traumatic encounter with a dog that one cannot escape (such as, for example, being bitten by a dog in a rageful attack) seems to condition fear much more powerfully than experiencing the same intensity of trauma that one can escape from or to some extent control (Mineka, 1985a, 1985b; Mineka & Zinbarg, 1996). In addition, the experiences that a person has *after* a conditioning experience may affect whether the conditioned fear is maintained or strengthened. A person who is exposed to a more intense traumatic experience (not paired with the conditioned stimulus) after the first may be likely to become more fearful of the conditioned stimulus (Rescorla, 1974; White & Davey, 1989). This so-called *inflation effect* suggests that a person who acquired, for example, a mild fear of automobiles following a minor crash might be expected to develop a full-blown phobia if he or she later were physically assaulted even though no automobile was present during the assault (Davey, 1997; Mineka, 1985a, 1985b; Mineka & Zinbarg, 1996). Even verbal information that later alters one's interpretation of the dangerousness of a previous trauma (for example, being told "You're lucky to be alive because the man who held you up at the bank last week is a known killer") can be sufficient to cause the level of fear to be inflated (Davey, 1997). These examples show that the factors involved in the origins and

A person who has good experiences with a potentially phobic stimulus, such as the young woman romping here with her dog, is likely to be immunized from later acquiring a fear of dogs even if she has a traumatic encounter with one.

maintenance of fears and phobias are more complex than suggested by the traditional conditioning view.

Recently it has been suggested that *cognitive* variables may help maintain phobias once they have been acquired. It is now well known that our cognitions or thoughts have a powerful influence on our emotional state, as well as vice versa. Recent research suggests that people with phobias are constantly on the alert for their phobic objects or situations or other stimuli relevant to their phobia. Nonphobic persons, on the other hand, tend to direct their attention away from threatening stimuli (see Mineka, 1992, for a review). In addition, phobics also markedly overestimate the probability that feared objects have been or will be followed by aversive events. This bias may help maintain or strengthen phobic fears with the passage of time

(Davey, 1997; Mineka, 1992; Öhman & Mineka, 1999; Tomarken, Sutton, & Mineka, 1995).

Genetic and Temperamental Causal Factors Two very different types of biological variables may affect the acquisition of phobias. First, genetic and temperamental or personality variables are known to affect the speed and strength of conditioning of fear (Eysenck, 1965; Gray, 1987; Pavlov, 1927). That is, people are more or less likely to acquire phobias depending on their temperament or personality. Indeed, Kagan and his colleagues have found that children defined as *behaviorally inhibited* (excessively timid, shy, etc.) at 21 months of age were at higher risk for the development of multiple specific phobias at 7 to 8 years of age than were uninhibited children (32 versus 5 percent). The average number of reported fears in the inhibited group was three to four per child (Biederman et al., 1990).

In addition, there are several studies suggesting a modest genetic contribution to the development of specific phobias. For example, one study found that there was an elevated risk of specific phobias (but not social phobia or panic disorder) in first degree relatives of those who had been diagnosed with specific phobia (Fyer et al., 1995). A large female twin study found a somewhat higher concordance rate for specific phobias in monozygotic twins than in dizygotic twins for animal phobias but not for situational phobias (like heights or water) (Kendler et al., 1992b). The same study found evidence that there may be two different types of genetic factors involved, the first being a modest inherited tendency to develop any specific phobia, and the second being a modest inherited tendency to develop a particular type of specific phobia (e.g., snakes versus heights), although much more information is needed before this conclusion can be drawn with any degree of certainty.

Preparedness and the Nonrandom Distribution of Fears and Phobias Our evolutionary history has affected which stimuli we are most likely to come to fear. For example, people are much more likely to have phobias of snakes, water, heights, and enclosed spaces than of bicycles, knives, or cars, even though the latter objects may be at least as likely to be associated with trauma. These observations are contrary to what would be expected from traditional conditioning theory, which held that all objects associated with trauma would be equally likely to become objects of fear. Accordingly, some theorists have argued that primates and humans may be prepared biologically to rapidly associate certain kinds of objects—such as snakes, spiders water, and enclosed spaces—with aversive events (e.g., Öhman, 1996; Öhman & Mineka, 1999; Seligman, 1971). They have argued that this *preparedness* occurs because there may have been a selective advantage in the course of evolution for primates and humans who rapidly acquired fears of certain objects or situations that posed threats to our early ancestors. Thus prepared fears are not inborn or innate but rather easily acquired or especially resistant to extinction.

Two lines of evidence now support the preparedness theory of phobias. In one important series of experiments using human subjects, Arne Öhman and his colleagues (e.g., Öhman, Dimberg, & Öst, 1985; Öhman, 1996) found that fear was conditioned more effectively to fear-relevant stimuli (slides of snakes and spiders) than to fear-irrelevant stimuli (slides of flowers and mushrooms). The experimenters also found that once the subjects acquired the conditioned responses, these could be elicited even when the subjects' exposure to the fear-relevant stimulus (but not to fear-irrelevant stimuli) was subliminal (that is, presentation was so brief that it was not consciously perceived). This subliminal activation of responses to phobic stimuli may help to account for certain aspects of the irrationality of phobias. That is, phobics may not be able to control their fear because the fear may arise from cognitive structures that are not under conscious control (Öhman & Soares, 1993; Öhman & Mineka, 1999).

Moreover, monkeys can easily acquire fears of fear-relevant stimuli such as toy snakes and toy crocodiles, but not of fear-irrelevant stimuli such as flowers or a toy rabbit (Cook & Mineka, 1989, 1990). Thus, both monkeys and humans seem to selectively associate certain fear-relevant stimuli such as snakes or crocodiles with threat or danger. It is also noteworthy that unlike the human subjects in the studies from Öhman's laboratory described above, these laboratory-reared monkeys had no prior exposure to or experience with any of the fear-relevant or fear-irrelevant stimuli before participating in these experiments. Thus these results more clearly support the preparedness hypothesis, which implicates evolutionary factors as being responsible for these biased associations. It remains possible that human subjects showed superior conditioning to snakes or spiders because they had preexisting negative associations based on prior experiences with snakes or spiders, rather than because of evolutionary factors (Öhman & Mineka, 1999).

Treating Specific Phobias The behavior therapy most commonly used in the treatment of specific phobias involves controlled *exposure* to the stimuli or situations that elicit phobic fear. Here clients are gradually placed—symbolically or increasingly under "real life" conditions—in those situations they find most frightening. In the original variant known as *systematic desensitization,* clients are first trained in the techniques of deep muscle

relaxation and asked to develop a hierarchy of situations they fear, ranging at the bottom from only mildly anxiety-provoking to the top at maximally fear-provoking. Then, while remaining in a state of relaxation, they are asked to imagine their fear-producing situations, starting with those lowest in a hierarchy and gradually moving up the hierarchy as the fear of the scenes lower in the hierarchy extinguishes (Wolpe, 1958, 1988). Other more efficient forms of treatment (requiring less time in therapy) involve graded exposure to fear-producing stimuli and do not rely on the use of relaxation or imaginal exposure. Instead, clients are encouraged to expose themselves (either with the aid of a therapist or friend, or alone) to their actual feared situations for long enough periods of time that their fear begins to subside. It is often found that a variant on this procedure known as *participant modeling* is even more effective than exposure alone. With participant modeling, developed by Bandura in the

People are more likely to acquire fears of objects or situations that once posed a threat to our evolutionary ancestors than of objects that did not exist in our early evolutionary history (such as cars and knives). Such prepared fears include a fear of heights.

One variation on exposure therapy is called participant modeling. Here the therapist models how to touch and pick up a live tarantula and encourages the spider-phobic client to imitate her behavior: This treatment is graduated, with the client's first task being simply to touch the tarantula from the outside of the cage, then to touch the tarantula with a stick, then with a gloved hand, then with a bare hand, and finally to let the tarantula crawl over his hand. This is a highly effective treatment, with the most spider-phobic clients being able to reach the top of the hierarchy within 60 to 90 minutes.

1960s, the therapist models ways of interacting with the phobic stimulus or situation in calm and nonfearful ways (Bandura, 1969, 1977a, 1997b). All of these techniques enable clients to learn that these situations are not as frightening as they had thought and that their anxiety, albeit unpleasant, is not harmful and will gradually dissipate (Craske & Rowe, 1997; Foa & Kozak, 1986; Mineka & Thomas, 1999). Exposure-based treatments are widely considered to be the treatment of choice for specific phobias (Craske & Rowe, 1997) and recent research has shown that for certain phobias, such as small animal phobias, flying phobia, and blood-injury phobia, it can often be highly effective when conducted in a single long session (up to 3 hours) (Öst, 1997).

An example of the use of exposure therapy comes from the treatment of Mary, the housewife whose acrophobia and claustrophobia was described earlier.

Case Study, Mary's Treatment • Treatment consisted of 13 sessions of graduated exposure exercises in which the therapist first accompanied Mary into mildly fear-provoking situations, and then gradually into more and more fear-provoking situations. She also engaged in homework doing these exposure exercises by herself. The prolonged in vivo ("real life") exposure sessions lasted as long as necessary for her anxiety to subside. Initial sessions focused on her claustrophobia and getting her to be able to ride for a few floors in an elevator, first with the therapist and then alone. Later she took longer elevator rides in taller buildings. Exposure for the acrophobia consisted of walking around the periphery of the inner atrium on the top floor of a tall hotel, and later spending time at a mountain vista overlook spot. The top of the claustrophobia hierarchy consisted of taking a tour of an underground cave. After 13 sessions Mary successfully took a flight with her husband to Europe and climbed to the top of many tall tourist sites there.

In recent years a number of researchers have sought to determine whether the addition of cognitive techniques to these exposure-based techniques can produce additional gains. In general, the results of studies using cognitive techniques alone have not produced as good results as those using exposure-based techniques, and addition of cognitive techniques has not generally added much (Craske & Rowe, 1997). There are no known effective pharmacotherapies for specific phobias.

Social Phobia

Social phobia was only identified as a distinct form of phobia in the late 1960s (Marks, 1969). Fear of negative evaluation by others may be the hallmark of social phobia (Hope & Heimberg, 1993). As currently conceptualized in DSM-IV, there are two subtypes of social phobia—specific and generalized. People with *specific social phobias* have disabling fears of one or more discrete social situations in which they fear they may be exposed to the scrutiny of others and may act in an embarrassing or humiliating manner (e.g., public speaking, urinating in a public bathroom, or eating or writing in public). Because of their fears, they either avoid these situations or endure them with great distress. Intense fear of public speaking is the single most common specific social phobia. Individuals with *generalized social phobia* have significant fears of most social situations (including both public performance situations *and* situations requiring social interactions), and often also share a diagnosis of avoidant personality disorder (see Chapter 9) (e.g., Skodol et al., 1995; Turner, Beidel, & Townsley, 1992). That these are truly *social* phobias becomes clear when one observes that these people have no difficulty performing the same acts (e.g., speaking, urinating, or eating) when alone.

The diagnosis of social phobia is very common, with estimates from the recent National Comorbidity Survey that about 11 percent of men and 15 percent of women qualify for a diagnosis of social phobia at some point in their lives (Kessler et al., 1994). These estimates are much higher than previous estimates because in the past the diagnostic criteria specified that a social phobic had to avoid certain social situations to qualify for the diagnosis. However, presently one can qualify for the diagnosis if the social situations are not necessarily *avoided* but are *endured with great distress,* which is the case with many people who now qualify for the diagnosis (Magee et al., 1996). Moreover, there is also some evidence that the prevalence of social phobia is increasing in younger generations (Magee et al., 1996). Unlike specific phobias, which most often originate in childhood, social phobias typically begin during adolescence or early adulthood (Hope & Heimberg, 1993; Wells & Clark, 1997). Over half of persons with social phobia suffer from one or more additional anxiety disorders at some point in their lives (e.g., panic disorder, generalized anxiety disorder, or specific phobia, or PTSD). Approximately 40 percent also suffer from a depressive disorder at some point (Magee et al., 1996). Moreover, approximately one-third also abuse alcohol in order to reduce their anxi-

ety and help them face their feared situations (for example, drinking *before* going to a party) (Magee et al., 1996).

The case of Paul is typical of social phobia (except that not all social phobics have full-blown panic attacks, as Paul did, in their social phobic situations).

> **Case Study, A Surgeon's Social Phobia** • Paul was a single white male in his mid-30s when he first presented for treatment at an anxiety clinic. He was a surgeon who practiced at a large local hospital. He reported a 13-year history of social phobia. He had very few social outlets because of his persistent concerns that people would notice how nervous he was in social situations, and he had not dated in many years for the same reasons. He was convinced that people would perceive him as foolish or crazy, and particularly worried that people would notice how his jaw tensed up when around other people. He frequently chewed gum in public situations because he thought that this kept his face from looking distorted. Importantly, he had no particular problems talking with people in professional situations. He was, for example, quite calm talking with patients before and after surgery. During surgery when his face was covered with a mask, he also had no trouble carrying out surgical tasks and no trouble interacting with the other surgeons and nurses in the room. The trouble began when he left the operating room and had to make small talk with the other doctors and nurses, or with the patient's family. He frequently had panic attacks in these social situations where he had to make eye contact and social chit-chat. During the panic attacks he experienced heart palpitations, fears of going crazy, and a sense of his mind "shutting down." The most specific trigger for these fears and panic attacks was making eye contact in social situations. Because the panic attacks occurred only in social situations he was diagnosed as having social phobia rather than panic disorder.
>
> Paul reported that his social phobia and panic had begun about 13 years earlier at a time when he was under a great deal of stress. His family's business had failed, his parents had divorced, and his mother had had a heart attack. It was in this context of multiple stressors that a personally traumatic incident probably triggered the onset of his social phobia. One day he had come home from medical school to find his best friend in bed with his fiancée. It was about one month later that he had his first panic attack and started avoiding social situations.

Interaction of Psychosocial and Biological Causal Factors Social phobias involve learned behavior that have been shaped by evolutionary factors. Such learning is most likely to occur in people who are genetically or temperamentally at risk.

Social Phobias as Learned Behavior Like specific phobias, social phobias seem to often originate out of simple instances of direct or vicarious classical conditioning, such as experiencing or witnessing a perceived social defeat or humiliation, or being or witnessing the target of anger or criticism. In one study, 58 percent of social phobics recalled direct traumatic conditioning experiences as having been involved in the origin of their social phobia (Öst & Hugdahl, 1981); another study found that this was true for 56 percent of specific social phobics and 44 percent of generalized social phobics (Townsley et al., 1995). Öst and Hugdahl also reported that another 13 percent of their subjects recalled vicarious conditioning experiences of some sort as having been involved in the origin of their social phobia. Other research suggests that generalized social phobics may be especially likely to have grown up with parents who were socially isolated and who devalued sociability, thus providing ample opportunity for vicarious learning of social fears (Bruch, 1989; Rosenbaum et al., 1994).

Social Fears and Phobias in an Evolutionary Context Social fears and phobias by definition involve fear of members of one's own species; this is in contrast, for example, to animal fears and phobias, which involve fear of potential predators. The latter probably evolved to help activation of the fight-or-flight response as a reaction to threat from potential predators and may be most likely to originate early in development because the young are most vulnerable to predation. Öhman and his colleagues have theorized that social fears and phobias, by contrast, evolved as a by-product of dominance hierarchies that are a common social arrangement among animals like primates (Öhman et al., 1985). Dominance hierarchies are established through aggressive encounters between members of a social group, and a defeated individual typically displays fear and submissive behavior but only rarely attempts to escape the situation completely. Thus, they argue, it is not surprising that social phobics are more likely to endure being in their feared situation than to run away and escape it as animal phobics are likely to do. They further note that it is probably not coincidental that social phobias most often originate in adolescence and early adulthood, which is also when dominance conflicts are most prominent.

Preparedness and Social Phobia Given this way of thinking about social phobia in an evolutionary context, Öhman and his colleagues have extended the preparedness theory of specific phobias discussed above to the understanding of social phobia. Earlier we presented the theory that humans may have an evolutionarily based preparedness to acquire fears of certain objects or situations that may once have posed a threat to our early ancestors. But it seems that we also have an evolutionarily based predisposition to acquire fears of social stimuli signaling dominance and aggression from other humans.

These social stimuli include facial expressions of anger or contempt. In a series of experiments paralleling those described for specific phobias, Öhman and his colleagues have demonstrated that subjects develop stronger conditioned responses when slides of angry faces are paired with mild electric shocks than when happy or neutral faces are paired with the same shocks. Moreover, they also demonstrated that this superior conditioning only occurs when the angry facial expression is directed at the subject (Dimberg & Öhman, 1983). Finally, they have also demonstrated that even very brief presentations of the angry face that are not consciously perceived are sufficient to activate the conditioned responses (Öhman, Dimberg, & Esteves, 1989; Öhman, 1996). Such results may help to account for the seemingly irrational quality of social phobia, in that the emotional reaction can be activated without a person's awareness of any threat.

Genetic and Temperamental Factors As with specific phobias, not all persons who undergo or witness traumatic social humiliation or defeat go on to develop full-blown social phobia. Recent results from a very large study of female twins suggests that there is a modest genetic contribution to social phobia; estimates were that the proportion of variance due to genetic factors was about 30 percent (Kendler et al., 1992b). Such results are also consistent with the results of two family studies which found that the first-degree relatives of social phobics were more than two to three times as likely to also share a diagnosis of social phobia (but not specific phobias or agoraphobia) as were the relatives of normal controls (Fyer et al., 1993, 1995). Nevertheless, more research is needed before the exact contribution of genetic and environmental variables can be disentangled.

The temperamental variable that appears to be of greatest importance is behavioral inhibition. Infants who are easily distressed by unfamiliar stimuli are at increased risk for becoming fearful during childhood, and by adolescence show increased risk of developing social phobia (Kagan, 1997). Another longitudinal study found that children who were high on behavioral inhibition between ages 8 and 12, defined as wariness of strangers, were much more likely to have a less positive and less active social life in young adulthood, and the men were also more likely to be emotionally distressed (Gest, 1997).

Perceptions of Uncontrollability It also seems that a similar range of individual differences in experience that make an individual vulnerable to developing specific phobias are also likely to affect a person's vulnerability for developing social phobia (see Barlow, 1988; Mineka & Zinbarg, 1995). For example, exposure to uncontrollable

Infants and young children who are easily distressed are sometimes high on the temperamental variable called behavioral inhibition. Such infants show an increased risk of developing social phobia in adolescence.

stressful events (such as Paul finding his fiancée in bed with his best friend) may play an important role. Perceptions of uncontrollability often lead to submissive and unassertive behavior such as that characteristic of socially anxious or phobic persons. This may be especially likely if the perceptions of uncontrollability stem from an actual social defeat, which is known in animals to lead to both increased submissive behavior and increased fear (Mineka & Zinbarg, 1995). Consistent with this, it has also been found that social phobics have a diminished sense of personal control over events in their lives; they are particularly prone to beliefs that control over events is primarily determined by "powerful others" (Cloitre et al., 1992).

Cognitive Variables In recent years increased attention has also been paid to the role that cognitive factors play in the onset and maintenance of social phobia. Beck and colleagues (1985) suggested that social phobics tend to expect that other people will reject or negatively evaluate them, leading to a sense of vulnerability in the presence of other persons who might potentially pose a threat. These *danger schemas* (see Chapter 3) of social phobics lead them to be hypervigilant to cues that people around them are negative or critical, leading them to spend a great deal of their time paying attention to and evaluating possible negative evaluations by others (Clark, 1997). In a recent elaboration of this theory, Clark and Wells (1995; Wells & Clark, 1997) have argued that the schemas of social phobics also include expectations that they will behave "in an inept and unacceptable fashion and that such behavior will have disastrous consequences in terms of loss of status, loss of worth, and rejection" (pp. 69–70). Such expectations lead social phobics to be preoccupied with their bodily responses in social situations and to overestimate how easily others will detect their anxiety. Such intense self-preoccupation during social situations interferes with their actual ability to interact in as skillful a fashion as they might if they were not so preoccupied. This in turn may lead to a vicious circle in which their somewhat awkward behavior may indeed lead others to react to them in a less friendly fashion, thus confirming their expectations (Clark, 1997; Clark & Wells, 1995; Wells & Clark, 1997). Although still quite new, this recent cognitive model of social phobia has received impressive empirical support from a number of studies (Clark, 1997).

Treating Social Phobia In contrast to specific phobias, there are effective medications for social phobia which have received increasing attention in the past decade. There have been some promising results with the use of beta-blockers (drugs often used to treat high blood pressure) such as Inderal on an occasional basis—especially for performance anxiety such as shown by actors or musicians (Gitlin, 1996). These medications seem to work because they help control peripheral autonomic arousal symptoms such as trembling hands or voice. However, it appears that for full-blown social phobia other categories of drugs are more effective (den Boer et al., 1996). These include several categories of antidepressants (including the monoamine oxidase inhibitors and the selective-serotonin-reuptake inhibitors discussed in Chapter 6) and some antianxiety or *anxiolytic* drugs. One negative factor associated with the use of medication for treating what tends to be a chronic condition like social phobia, is that relapse rates upon discontinuation of the drug tend to be quite high (Hayward & Wardle, 1997; Potts & Davidson, 1995).

There are also very effective forms of behavior therapy, and of cognitive-behavior therapy, for social phobia. Behavioral treatments were developed first and generally involve prolonged exposure to social situations that evoke fear, often in a graduated manner—in a fashion parallel to that done with specific phobias. More recently, as research has revealed the underlying distorted cognitions that characterize social phobia, cognitive techniques have been added to these behavioral techniques, generating a form of cognitive-behavior therapy. Here a therapist attempts to help clients with social phobia identify their underlying negative automatic thoughts ("I've got nothing interesting to say" or "no one is interested in me"), which are often irrational and generally involve discrete predictions about what will happen to them in various social situations. After helping clients understand that these automatic thoughts often involve cognitive distortions, the therapist then helps the clients change these inner thoughts and beliefs through logical reanalysis. Although these techniques were first developed by Aaron Beck for the treatment of depression, they have now been successfully applied to the treatment of social phobia (Clark, 1997; Heimberg & Juster, 1995). Whether adding a cognitive therapy component to the already established behavioral treatments of these three disorders enhances treatment efficacy is still a matter of some debate in the literature (e.g, Clark, 1997; Feske & Chambless, 1995; Taylor, 1996). Moreover, there is also reason to believe that more recently developed and refined versions of cognitive-behavior therapy may ultimately prove superior (Clark, 1997). A distinct advantage that behavioral and cognitive-behavior therapy techniques have over medication is that they produce much more long-lasting improvement, with very low relapse rates; indeed clients often continue to improve after treatment is over.

An example of successful combined treatment can be seen in the case of Paul, the surgeon described earlier who had social phobia.

Case Study, Paul's Treatment • Since the onset of his social phobia 13 years earlier, Paul had taken a tricyclic antidepressant at one point, which had helped stop his panic attacks, although he continued to fear them intensely and still avoided social situations and thus had little effect on his social phobia. He had also been in supportive psychotherapy, which helped his depression at the time but not his social phobia or his panic. At the time he came for treatment at an anxiety clinic he was not on any medication or in any other form of treatment. Treatment consisted of 14 weeks of cognitive-behavior therapy. By the end of treatment he was not panicking at all and was quite comfortable in most social situations he had previously avoided. He was seeing old friends that he had avoided for years because of his anxiety, and was beginning to date. Indeed, he even asked his female therapist for a date during the last treatment session!

PANIC DISORDER WITH AND WITHOUT AGORAPHOBIA

Diagnostically, **panic disorder** is defined and characterized by the occurrence of "unexpected" panic attacks that often seem to come "out of the blue." According to the DSM-IV definition, the person must have experienced recurrent unexpected attacks and must have been persistently concerned about having another attack or worried about the consequences of having an attack (e.g., of "losing control" or "going crazy") for at least a month. To qualify as a full-blown panic attack, there must be abrupt onset of at least 4 of 13 symptoms (such as shortness of breath, heart palpitations, sweating, dizziness, depersonalization (a feeling of being detached from one's body) or derealization (a feeling that the external world is strange or unreal), fear of dying, of "going crazy," or of "losing control". Such attacks are often "unexpected" or "uncued" in the sense that they do not appear to be provoked by identifiable aspects of the immediate situation. Indeed, they sometimes occur in situations in which they might be least expected, such as during relaxation or during sleep (known as *nocturnal panic*). In other cases, however, the panic attacks are said to be "situationally predisposed" in that they only occur sometimes while in a particular situation, such as while driving a car or being in a crowd. The stark terror of a panic attack typically subsides within a matter of minutes.

Given that 10 out of the 13 symptoms of a panic attack are somatic, it may not be too surprising that many people experiencing such an attack do not identify it as a panic attack, and instead think that they are, for example, having a heart attack. As many as 90 percent of these people may show up repeatedly at emergency rooms or at their physicians' offices for what they are convinced is a medical problem—usually cardiac, respiratory, or neurological (Hirshfeld, 1996). Unfortunately, a correct diagnosis of the problem is often not made for years in spite of numerous costly medical tests that produce normal results. Such delays in correct diagnosis, and wasted time and money on unnecessary medical costs, are avoided if the person sees a physician who is familiar with the condition or one who refers the person to a mental health professional (Hirshfeld, 1996; Katon, 1994). This is also important because panic disorder causes considerable impairment in social and physical functioning (approximately equal to that caused by major depression, Hirshfeld, 1996), and because panic disorder can contribute to the development of, or exacerbation of, a variety of medical problems (Schmidt & Telch, 1997). Finally, recently evidence has been accumulating that 30 to 60 percent of persons who experience a chest pain syndrome, but who have normal coronary arteries (no evidence of heart disease), actually have a previously undiagnosed panic disorder. Thus physicians who have patients complaining of chest pain, but who show no evidence of coronary artery disease should be given a psychiatric interview to determine whether they have panic disorder (Carter et al., 1997).

Distinguishing Features Between Panic and Anxiety

The two features of panic attacks that distinguish them from other types of anxiety are their characteristic brevity and their intensity. In a panic attack the symptoms develop abruptly and usually reach a peak intensity within 10 minutes; the attacks usually subside in 20 to 30 minutes and rarely last more than an hour. Periods of anxiety, by contrast, do not usually have such an abrupt onset, are more long-lasting, and the symptoms are not as intense. If we go back to the distinction drawn at the beginning of the chapter between fear and anxiety, it is important to note that a number of influential contemporary researchers of panic believe that a panic attack is simply the activation of the fight-or-flight response of the sympathetic nervous system (Gray, 1987; Gray & McNaughton, 1996), which is identified with the emotion of fear for some theorists (e.g., Antony & Barlow, 1996; Barlow, 1988; Barlow et al., 1996). Barlow refers to a panic attack as a "false alarm" where there is no obvious trigger, as opposed to the "true alarm" that occurs when one confronts a grizzly bear, or a "learned alarm" that occurs when one encounters a phobic object. Thus for Barlow the primary feature that distinguishes the panic attacks occurring in panic disorder from the phobic responses seen when specific and social phobics encounter their phobic object or situation is simply whether there is an identifiable external trigger. As discussed earlier, anxiety, in contrast to phobic fear and panic, is a more complex and diffuse blend of emotions and cognitions, including high levels of negative affect, worry about future threat, and a sense of preparation for dealing with danger should it occur.

The case of Mindy Markowitz is typical of someone who has panic disorder without agoraphobia.

Case Study, An Art Director's Panic Attacks • Mindy Markowitz is an attractive, stylishly dressed 25-year-old art director for a trade magazine who comes to an anxiety clinic after reading about the clinic program in the newspaper. She is seeking treatment for "panic attacks" that have occurred with increasing frequency over the past year, often two or three times a day. These attacks begin with a sudden intense wave of "horrible fear" that seems to come out of nowhere, sometimes during the day, sometimes waking her from sleep. She begins to tremble, is nauseated, sweats profusely, feels as though she is choking, and fears that she will lose control and do something crazy, like run screaming into the street.

Mindy remembers first having attacks like this when she was in high school. She was dating a boy her parents disapproved of, and had to do a lot of "sneaking around" to avoid confrontations with them. At the same time, she was under a lot of pressure as the principal designer of her high school yearbook, and was applying to Ivy League colleges. She remembers that her first panic attack occurred just after the yearbook went to press and she was accepted by Harvard, Yale, and Brown. The attacks lasted only a few minutes, and she would just "sit through them." She was worried enough to mention them to her mother; but because she was otherwise perfectly healthy, she did not seek treatment. ◄

Mindy has had panic attacks intermittently over the 8 years since her first attack, sometimes not for many months, but sometimes, as now, several times a day. There have been extreme variations in the intensity of the attacks, some being so severe and debilitating that she has had to take a day off from work.

Mindy has always functioned extremely well in school, at work, and in her social life, apart from her panic attacks and a brief period of depression at age 19 when she broke up with a boyfriend. She is a lively, friendly person who is respected by her friends and colleagues both for her intelligence and creativity and for her ability to mediate disputes.

Mindy has never limited her activities, even during the times that she was having frequent, severe attacks, although she might stay home from work for a day because she was exhausted from multiple attacks. She has never associated the attacks with particular places. She says, for example, that she is as likely to have an attack at home in her own bed as on the subway, so there is no point in avoiding the subway. Whether she has an attack on the subway, in a supermarket, or at home by herself, she says, "I just tough it out" (Spitzer et al., 1994).

Agoraphobia

Historically, agoraphobia was thought to involve a fear of the "agora"—the Greek word for public places of assembly (Marks, 1987). And indeed the most commonly feared and avoided situations for agoraphobics include streets and crowded places such as shopping malls, movie theaters, and sports arenas. Standing in line can be particularly difficult. However, agoraphobics also usually fear one or more forms of travel, and commonly avoid cars, buses, airplanes, and subway trains. What is the common theme that underlies this seemingly diverse cluster of fears? Today it is thought that **agoraphobia** usually develops as a complication of having panic attacks (which can be quite terrifying) in one or more of such situations. Agoraphobics, concerned they may have a panic attack or get sick, are anxious about being in places or situations from which escape would be physically difficult or psychologically embarrassing, or in which immediate help would be unavailable in the event that something bad happened (American Psychiatric Association, 1994). In cases of moderate severity these people may even be uncomfortable venturing outside their homes alone, doing so only with significant anxiety. In very severe cases agoraphobia is a terribly disabling disorder in which a person cannot go beyond the narrow confines of home, or even particular parts of the home.

Agoraphobia Without Panic   Although agoraphobia is a frequent complication of panic disorder, it can also occur in the absence of prior full-blown panic attacks. In the latter instance a common pattern is that of a gradually spreading fearfulness in which more and more aspects of the environment outside the home acquire threatening properties. Cases of agoraphobia without panic are extremely rare in clinical settings, and when they are seen there is often a history of what are called limited symptom attacks (with fewer than four symptoms) or of some other unpredictable somatic ailment such as epilepsy or colitis where the person may fear sudden physical incapacitation (Barlow, 1988; McNally, 1994). However, cases of agoraphobia without panic are not uncommon in epidemiological studies (e.g., Eaton & Keyl, 1990; Kessler et al., 1994). The reasons for this are unclear at the present time and little research attention has yet been directed toward understanding agoraphobia without panic. Some believe that in many cases where this disorder has been diagnosed, it would more appropriately be characterized as a kind of specific phobia if correct diagnostic procedures were used (McNally, 1994).

The case of Anne Watson is in many respects typical of panic disorder with agoraphobia:

Case Study, A Mother with Panic Disorder with Agoraphobia • Ms. Watson, married mother of two and age 45 at her first clinic contact, experienced her first panic attack some

Severe agoraphobics are often fearful of venturing out of their homes into public places, in part because of fear of having a panic attack in a place in which escape might prove physically difficult or psychologically embarrassing. They may even become housebound unless accompanied by a spouse or trusted companion.

two years earlier, several months after the sudden death of an uncle to whom she had been extremely close while growing up. While returning home from work one evening she had the feeling that she couldn't catch her breath. Immediately thereafter her heart began to pound, she broke out in a cold sweat, and she had a sense of unreality. Feeling immobilized by a leaden quality in her legs, she became certain she would pass out or die before she could reach home. Soliciting help from a passerby, she was able to engage a cab, directing the driver to take her to the nearest hospital emergency room. Her ensuing physical examination revealed no abnormalities apart from a slightly elevated heart rate, which subsided to normal limits before the examination was completed. She regained composure rapidly and was able to return home on her own.

Four weeks later, after the incident had been all but forgotten, Ms. Watson had a second similar attack while at home preparing a meal. Four more occurred in the next several weeks, all of them surprises, and she began to despair about discovering their source. She also noticed that she was becoming anxious about the probability of additional attacks. Consultation with the family physician yielded a diagnosis of "nervous strain" and a prescription for antianxiety medication. The medication made Ms. Watson calmer, but seemed to have no effect on the continuing panics. She discovered alcohol was even more effective than the medication in relieving her tension and began to drink excessively, which only increased the worry and concern of her husband.

As the attacks continued, Ms. Watson began to dread going out of the house alone. She feared that while out she would have an attack and would be stranded and helpless. She stopped riding the subway to work out of fear she might be trapped in a car between stops when an attack struck, preferring instead to walk the 20 blocks between her home and work. She also severely curtailed her social and recreational activities—previously frequent and enjoyed—because an attack might occur, necessitating an abrupt and embarrassing flight from the scene. When household duties and the like required brief driving excursions, she surreptitiously put these off until she could be accompanied by one of the children or a neighbor. Despite these drastic alterations of lifestyle and her growing unhappiness and desperation, however, she remained her normal self when at home or when her husband accompanied her away from home (Adapted from Spitzer et al., 1983).

We consider panic disorder and agoraphobia together because accumulating research evidence suggests that they share some basic properties, including a possible genetic linkage (e.g., Noyes et al., 1986, 1987). As already noted, many people with an agoraphobic pattern report a history of repeated panic attacks, and it appears that in most cases agoraphobia develops as a secondary reaction to the experience of panic. That is, after having experienced a few panic attacks, the person begins to develop a fear of the situations in which the attacks have occurred, which gradually spreads to involve fear of other situations where attacks *might* occur. The person experiences this anticipatory anxiety much of the time when he or she thinks about having to leave home for any reason.

Prevalence and Age of Onset of Panic Disorder with and without Agoraphobia

Panic disorder with and without agoraphobia affects many people. For example, the National Comorbidity Survey found approximately 3.5 percent of the adult population had panic disorder at some time in their life; 1.5 percent also had agoraphobia. Approximately another 5 percent qualified for a diagnosis of agoraphobia without panic (Kessler et al., 1994). The same study found that, as for social phobia, the prevalence of panic disorder seems to be increasing in younger generations (Magee et al., 1996).

The age of onset for panic disorder with or without agoraphobia is most common between 15 and 24, especially for men, but it can also begin when people, especially women, are in their 30s and 40s (Eaton et al., 1994; Hirshfeld, 1996). Once it begins, it tends to have a chronic course, although the intensity of symptoms often waxes and wanes over time (Ehlers, 1995; Wolfe & Maser, 1994). In the past many studies found panic disorder without agoraphobia to be almost as common in men as in women, but the latest epidemiological results suggest this is not so, with the prevalence being about twice as common in women as in men (Eaton et al., 1994). Findings regarding gender differences have been much more consistent for agoraphobia, which occurs much more frequently in women than in men. Indeed, the percentage of women increases as the extent of agoraphobic avoidance increases, and among severe agoraphobics approximately 80 percent are female (Bekker, 1996; Reich, Noyes, & Troughton, 1987). The most common explanation of this finding is a sociocultural one. That is, in our culture (and many others as well), it is more acceptable for women experiencing panic to avoid the situations they fear, or to depend on having a trusted companion accompany them when they enter their feared situations. Men who experience panic are more prone to "tough it out" because of societal expectations. Supporting this idea, Chambless and Mason (1986) administered a sex-role scale to both male and female agoraphobics and found that the less "masculine" one scores on the scale, the more extensive the agoraphobic avoidance, for both males and females. A recent review noted several studies supporting the idea that the lack of masculine traits such as having an assertive and instrumental approach to life may play a role in accounting for the large sex difference in agoraphobia (Bekker, 1996); that is, women experiencing panic attacks who do not have an assertive approach to life may be more prone to develop the passive-dependent behavior characteristic of agoraphobia. However, there is a relatively small amount of good research on this topic and much more is needed before we really understand why so many more women than men become severely agoraphobic.

Comorbidity with Other Disorders

Persons with panic disorder with or without agoraphobia often have one or more additional diagnoses, including generalized anxiety, social phobia, simple phobia, depression, and alcohol abuse (Brown, 1996; Craske & Barlow, 1993; Magee et al., 1996). Current estimates are that 30 to 50 percent of persons with panic disorder will experience a serious depression at some point in their lives (Gorman & Coplan, 1996). Not uncommonly, they may also meet criteria for dependent or avoidant personality disorder (a personality disorder is diagnosed when a person has personality traits that are inflexible and maladaptive and that cause significant impairment or distress; see Chapter 9) (Craske & Barlow, 1993). There is also considerable recent controversy over whether clients with panic disorder show an increased risk of suicidal ideation and suicide attempts. Recent reviews concluded that there is little evidence that panic disorder, by itself, increases the risk for suicide, although it may do so indirectly by increasing risk for depression and substance use, both of which are risk factors for suicide (Hornig & McNally, 1995; McNally, 1994; see also Warshaw et al., 1995).

The Timing of a First Panic Attack

Although panic attacks themselves appear to come "out of the blue," their initial appearance frequently follows feelings of distress (Lelliott et al., 1989) or some highly stressful life circumstance, such as the loss of a loved one, loss of an important relationship, loss of a job, or criminal victimization (see Falsetti et al., 1995, for a review; Manfro et al., 1996). Indeed, according to averages across many studies, approximately 80 to 90 percent of clients report their first panic attack as having occurred after one or more negative life events. Thus, the timing of the initial attacks is usually not random but rather associated with generally stressful life circumstances, as was evident in both of the case histories of Mindy Markowitz and Ms. Watson described above.

Nevertheless, not all people who have a panic attack following a stressful event go on to develop full-blown panic disorder. In fact, occasional panic attacks occur in many people who do not have panic disorder or agoraphobia. Indeed, current estimates are that 7 to 30 percent of adults have experienced at least one panic attack in their lifetime, but most have not gone on to develop full-blown panic disorder. Occasional panic attacks also commonly occur in persons who have other anxiety disorders and/or major depression (Barlow, Brown, & Craske, 1994; Brown, 1996). Given that panic attacks occur much more commonly than does panic disorder, this leads us to the important question: What causes full-blown panic disorder to develop in only a subset of these people? Several very different prominent theories about the causes of panic disorder have addressed this question.

Biological Causal Factors

A variety of research findings have led biological psychiatrists to hypothesize that panic disorder results from a biochemical abnormality in the brains of clients with the dis-

order. The initial argument was that panic must be qualitatively different from generalized anxiety (discussed below)—not just a more severe form of anxiety, as was previously thought (Klein, 1981). Support for this idea came from an apparent finding that imipramine (a tricyclic antidepressant drug) appeared to block panic attacks in agoraphobics without affecting their anticipatory anxiety. If imipramine affected panic but not anxiety, then panic must not simply be a more severe form of anxiety.

Klein (1981) and others (Sheehan, 1982, 1983) argued that panic attacks are alarm reactions that are caused by biochemical dysfunctions. In a more recent elaboration on this idea Klein (1993) has argued that this alarm mechanism may stem from persons with panic disorder being overly sensitive to rising levels of carbon dioxide (one of the two components of air we breathe) in the brain. Through the course of evolution humans have evolved a "suffocation alarm mechanism," in order to deal with the very real dangerous possibility of suffocation. According to this hypothesis, people with panic disorder have an overly sensitive suffocation monitor, which erroneously detects signals of lack of useful air when they experience breathing difficulties (as are common in panic disorder). Research directed at testing this theory has yielded mixed results (e.g., Coplan & Klein, 1996; McNally, 1994; McNally & Eke, 1996).

The Role of Norepinephrine and Serotonin The biochemical dysfunction hypothesis appears to be supported by numerous studies over the past 30 years that have shown that panic clients are much more likely to experience panic attacks in studies in which they are exposed to a variety of *biological challenge procedures* than are normal people or other psychiatric controls. These biological challenge procedures (ranging from taking various drugs to inhaling air with altered amounts of carbon dioxide) put stress on certain neurobiological systems, which in turn produce intense physical symptoms (such as increased heart rate and blood pressure) often culminating in a panic attack for clients with panic disorder. For example, infusions of sodium lactate, a substance that resembles the lactate produced by our bodies during exercise (e.g., Gorman et al., 1989; Hollander et al., 1989), or the inhalation of carbon dioxide (e.g., Woods et al., 1987), or the ingestion of caffeine or a chemical compound called yohimbine (e.g., Uhde, 1990) can produce panic attacks in panic disorder clients at a much higher rate than in normal subjects (see Coplan & Klein, 1996, for a review). Unfortunately, there is such a broad range of pharmacological agents that provoke panic (hence the term *panic provocation agents*), some of which are associated with quite different and even mutually exclusive neurobiological processes, that no single neurobiological mechanism could possibly be implicated (Antony & Barlow, 1996; van den Hout, 1988). This has led biologically oriented theorists to speculate that there are multiple hetergeneous biological causes of panic (Krystal, Deutsch, & Charney, 1996). However, as discussed below in the section on cognitive and behavioral causal factors, there does seem to be simpler psychological accounts of this pattern of results.

Panic and the Brain   One prominent theory about the neurobiology of panic implicates a particular area of the brain—the locus coeruleus in the brain stem (see Figure 5.1)—and a particular neurotransmitter—norepinephrine—which is centrally involved in brain activity in this area. For example, Redmond (1985) showed that electrical stimulation of the locus coeruleus in monkeys leads to a response that strongly resembles a panic attack; moreover, destruction of this area leaves the monkey seemingly unable to experience fear even in the presence of real danger. In addition, some of the drugs most commonly used in the treatment of panic disorder—the tricyclic antidepressants such as imipramine and the monamine oxidase inhibitors—are also known to decrease

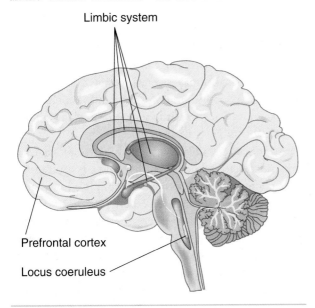

Limbic system

Prefrontal cortex

Locus coeruleus

FIGURE 5.1   A BIOLOGICAL THEORY OF PANIC, ANXIETY, AND AGORAPHOBIA
According to one theory, panic attacks may arise from abnormal activity in the locus coeruleus, a small area in the brain stem. The anticipatory anxiety that people develop about having another panic attack is thought to arise from activity in the limbic system. Phobic avoidance, a learned response, may involve activity of the prefrontal cortex (Gorman et al., 1989).

norepinephrine function (Goodard, Woods, & Charney, 1996; Redmond, 1985). Thus, it is possible that abnormal norepinephrine activity in the locus coeruleus may play a causal role in panic attacks (e.g., Goodard et al., 1996). More research is certainly needed before we have a complete understanding of the neurobiology of panic, however. At present the evidence for this theory is mixed, and it is not likely to explain all cases of panic disorder (Goodard et al., 1996; McNally, 1994).

Indeed, more recently another brain structure in the midbrain—the central periaqueductal gray—has also been implicated as playing a central role in the generation of panic attacks (Gray & McNaughton, 1996). Moreover, because of recent evidence that drugs that selectively affect another neurotransmitter—serotonin—are very useful in the treatment of panic disorder, attention has been drawn to the likelihood of alterations in serotonin transmission in panic disorder as well as alterations in norepinephrine transmission. Current theory suggests that serotonin may have an inhibitory effect on norepinephrine function in the central gray area and/or the locus coeruleus, acting to inhibit surges of norepinephrine activity that are thought to occur during a panic attack (Goddard et al., 1996; Gray & McNaughton, 1996).

But panic attacks are only one component of panic disorder. As we have seen, persons with panic disorder also experience anticipatory anxiety about the possible occurrence of another attack, and those with agoraphobia also engage in phobic avoidance behavior. It seems likely that different brain areas are involved in these different aspects of panic disorder. The panic attacks themselves arise from activity in the locus coeruleus in the brain stem (and/or the central gray in the midbrain) and involve "storms of autonomic nervous system activity" (Gorman et al., 1989, p. 150). For people who have one or more panic attacks and who go on to develop significant anticipatory anxiety about having another, the limbic system (a part of the brain below the cortex that is very involved in emotional behavior) generates this anxiety, which often involves a vague sense that future attacks may occur and be dangerous. Because there are well-defined pathways between the locus coeruleus and the limbic system, Gorman and colleagues (1989) propose that panic attacks may produce generalized or anticipatory anxiety through a kind of *kindling* phenomenon: Repeated stimulation of the limbic system by discharges from the locus coeruleus (panic attacks) might lower the threshold for stimulation of anxiety from the limbic system. Finally, they argue that the phobic avoidance seen with agoraphobia is truly a learned phenomenon that is controlled by the prefrontal cortex, which is the part of the brain involved in learning (see Figure 5.1). Gray and McNaughton (1996) have also summarized more recent evidence for the role of the limbic system in anticipatory anxiety (see also Charney, Grillon, & Bremner, 1998).

Genetic Factors   There is also evidence that panic disorder tends to run in families. Many studies have shown that first-degree relatives of panic clients are more likely to experience panic disorder than are relatives of controls (Mackinnon & Foley, 1996; McNally, 1994), and monozygotic twins are somewhat more likely to be concordant for the diagnosis than are dizygotic twins (Torgersen, 1983; Kendler et al., 1992b, 1993a, 1995). However, it should also be emphasized that what heritability does exist is modest. For example, Kendler and colleagues (1992b, 1995), in a large female twin study, estimated that 35 to 39 percent of the variance in liability to agoraphobia and panic disorder was due to genetic factors. Some studies have suggested that this heritability is specific for panic disorder (e.g., Crowe et al., 1983; Noyes et al., 1986, 1987), but a recent large female twin study suggests there is overlap in the genetic vulnerability factors for panic disorder and phobias (Kendler et al., 1995).

Cognitive and Behavioral Causal Factors

One early hypothesis about the origins of panic and agoraphobia was the "fear of fear" hypothesis (Goldstein & Chambless, 1978). According to this theory, agoraphobics come to fear the experience of a panic attack because it is so terrifying. They become hyperalert to their bodily sensations and begin to interpret mild signs of anxiety as a signal that a panic attack may occur; they then react with anxiety to their anxiety. If they gradually also come to fear a range of places in which panic might occur, they develop agoraphobic avoidance. In a more recent elaboration of this model, they have argued that agoraphobia also involves a fear of other emotions such as anger and depression (Williams, Chambless, & Ahrens, 1997). Relatedly, several theorists have argued that panic disorder involves **interoceptive fears**—that is, fear of various internal bodily sensations. These fears may have come about through a process of interoceptive conditioning in which various internal bodily sensations that have been associated with panic attacks acquire the capacity to provoke panic themselves. For example, heart palpitations may occur at the beginning of a full-blown attack and because they become predictors of the rest of the attack, they may acquire the capacity to provoke panic (Antony & Barlow, 1996; Mineka & Zinbarg, 1996; van den Hout, 1988).

The Cognitive Theory of Panic   Building on these behavioral hypotheses, Beck and Emery (1985) and Clark (1986, 1988, 1997) proposed a cognitive model of panic. According to this model, panic clients are hypersensitive to their bodily sensations and are very prone to giving them the direst possible interpretation. Clark refers to this as a tendency to catastrophize about the meaning of their bodily sensations. For example, a panic patient might notice that his heart is racing and conclude that he is having a heart attack. That very frightening thought causes many more physical symptoms of fear or anxiety, which provides further fuel for the catastrophic thoughts, leading to a vicious cycle culminating in a panic attack. Or if someone feels dizzy and interprets this as meaning that she is going to faint or that she may have a brain tumor, this could culminate in a panic attack through the same kind of vicious cycle (see Figure 5.2). It should be noted that the person is often not aware of making these catastrophic interpretations; rather the thoughts are often just barely out of the realm of their awareness (Rapee, 1996). These "automatic thoughts," as Beck calls them are in a sense, however, the triggers of panic. Taken literally, then, this model suggests that panic attacks don't really "come out of the blue" but rather are triggered by these automatic thoughts, which may or may not be conscious (although they can be brought into awareness through cognitive therapy).

The key difference between the cognitive model and the interoceptive "fear of fear" models is the importance for the cognitive model of the *meaning* the person places on bodily sensations, which causes panic attacks to occur when the person makes catastrophic interpretations about certain bodily sensations. Such catastrophic cognitions are not necessary with the interoceptive conditioning model (Antony & Barlow, 1996).

At present cognitive theorists are not sure what factors lead a person to develop this tendency to catastrophize about his or her bodily sensations. One possibility is that it comes from learning experiences prior to a first attack, such as observing parents model illness-related behavior or having panic attacks (Ehlers, 1993). Another possibility is that the tendency to catastrophize could develop after the first attack because of the way doctors and significant others respond to that attack (Clark, 1997). But however this tendency develops, cognitive theory hypothesizes that among the people who have had at least one panic attack (estimates range from 7 to 30 percent of the population), it is those who have this tendency to catastrophize who will be the ones likely to go on to develop panic disorder (Clark, 1997). Thus, the cognitive model may not always adequately explain why an initial panic

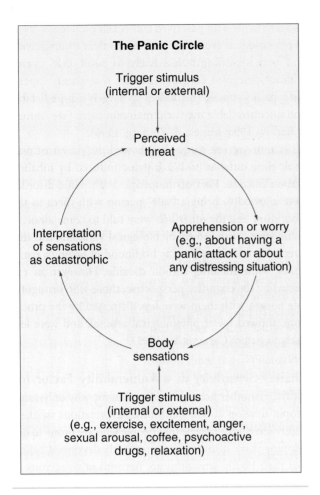

The Panic Circle

Trigger stimulus
(internal or external)

↓

Perceived
threat

Apprehension or worry
(e.g., about having a
panic attack or about
any distressing situation)

Interpretation
of sensations
as catastrophic

Body
sensations

Trigger stimulus
(internal or external)
(e.g., exercise, excitement, anger,
sexual arousal, coffee, psychoactive
drugs, relaxation)

FIGURE 5.2   THE PANIC CIRCLE
Any kind of perceived threat may lead to apprehension or worry, which is accompanied by various bodily sensations. According to the cognitive model of panic, if a person then catastrophizes about the meaning of his or her bodily sensations, this will raise the level of perceived threat, thus creating more apprehension and worry, as well as more physical symptoms, which fuel further catastrophic thoughts. This vicious cycle can culminate in a panic attack. The initial physical sensations need not arise from the perceived threat (as in the top of the circle), but may come from other sources (such as exercise, anger, or psychoactive drugs). (Adapted from Clark, 1986.)

The tendency to catastrophize about bodily sensations, such as having difficulty catching one's breath, may play a casual role in the spiraling of anxiety or worry into a panic attack. But how this tendency develops is not yet well understood.

attack occurs, but it does provide a plausible account of why only a small subset of people who have experienced one or more panic attacks go on to develop panic disorder. Obviously, however, longitudinal prospective studies will be needed to provide definitive tests of this aspect of the theory.

In spite of the fact that we still lack such prospective studies, several lines of evidence are consistent with the cognitive model of panic. For example, many studies have demonstrated that panic clients are more likely to interpret their bodily sensations in a catastrophic manner (e.g., Hibbert, 1984; see Clark, 1997, for a review).

Moreover, one study showed that activation of catastrophic misinterpretations through simply having panic clients read aloud pairs of words such as "palpitations-dying," "breathless-suffocate," or "numbness-stroke" was sufficient to induce panic in over 80 percent of the panic clients tested (Clark, 1997). That is, simply thinking about panic-related sensations and their feared consequences was sufficient to induce panic. The model also predicts that changing clients' cognitions about their bodily symptoms should reduce or prevent panic. Evidence from cognitive therapy for panic is consistent with this prediction (D. M. Clark et al., 1994; see below). In addition, however, a brief explanation of what to expect in a panic provocation study can prevent panic (Clark, 1997). Clients with panic disorder were either given a brief but detailed explanation of what physical symptoms to expect from their infusion of sodium

never do. After having had several hundred, let alone several thousand, panic attacks without a heart attack, one would think that this catastrophic thought would have been adequately disconfirmed to go away. Recent evidence suggests that panic clients frequently engage in "safety behaviors" before or during an attack and they tend to attribute the lack of catastrophe to their having engaged in this safety behavior. For example, panic clients who think they are having a heart attack during panic may rest and slow down their breathing during the attack; they later attribute not having had a heart attack to these behaviors. Other clients who think they may faint will tend to lean against solid objects, and clients who fear they are going crazy may try hard to control their thinking (Clark, 1997; Salkovskis et al., 1996). This research suggests that it is important during treatment to identify these safety behaviors so that the clients can try giving them up and finally see that their feared catastrophe still does not occur.

Cognitive Biases and the Maintenance of Panic

Finally, there are also many studies that underscore the fact that people with panic disorder are biased in the way they process threatening information. Such people are more prone to interpreting ambiguous bodily sensations as threatening (Clark, 1997), and they seem to show a bias to remember threatening information (McNally, 1994, 1996; see also Becker, Rinck, & Margraf, 1994). There is also evidence that their attention is particularly drawn to threatening information, especially information about physical threat, and that they are especially good at detecting their own heartbeats (Ehlers & Breuer, 1996). Whether these information-processing biases play a causal role in panic disorder is unclear, but they are certainly likely to help maintain the disorder once it has begun.

In summary, research into both biological and psychological factors involved in panic disorder has provided important insights into this disorder in the 15 years since it was first identified as a distinct disorder. It seems unlikely that research from either tradition alone will ever be able to provide a complete account of this disorder, and we eagerly await more attempts at synthesizing and integrating findings from these different traditions (McNally, 1994).

Treating Panic Disorder and Agoraphobia

Medications Many clients with panic disorder (with or without agoraphobia) are prescribed drugs from the benzodiazepine category such as Xanax. They frequently show some symptom relief with these minor tranquilizers or (anxiolytics or antianxiety drugs), and some are able to function more effectively. However, the effects are generally much smaller (when compared with the effects of placebo) than is generally recognized by the public. These drugs also tend to lose their effectiveness after a number of weeks (Barlow, 1988). The anxiolytic drugs can also have quite undesirable side effects such as drowsiness and sedation, which lead to impaired cognitive and motor performance. Furthermore, it is not uncommon for a patient to develop an increasing tolerance for and persistent dependence on a drug—these drugs have considerable addictive potential. Withdrawal from these drugs can be slow and difficult, and very often precipitates relapse. With panic disorder, if the withdrawal is not done very gradually (for example over a period of 2 to 4 months) the client is likely to experience what has been called "rebound panic," which may be worse than the original panic (Ballenger, 1996). In addition, many people expect too much of a treatment that merely reduces symptoms without affecting the underlying problem, and the masking of their symptoms may discourage them from seeking needed psychotherapy that may have more long-lasting effects. Moreover, some studies have shown that taking medications simultaneously with behavior therapy can interfere with the long-term effects of effective behavioral or cognitive-behavior treatments described below (Barlow et al., submitted; Marks et al., 1993; Hayward & Wardle, 1997).

The other category of medication that is useful in the treatment of panic disorder and agoraphobia is the antidepressants (including the monamine oxidase inhibitors, the tricyclics, and the selective-serotonin reuptake inhibitors). These drugs have both advantages and disadvantages when compared with anxiolytics. One major advantage is that they are not addictive. However, one disadvantage is that they take several weeks before they have any beneficial effects and so are not useful in the acute situation that a person having a panic attack or extreme anxiety may come to a doctor with. Troublesome side effects (such as dry mouth and blurred vision, or interference with sexual arousal) can also be a serious problem with the antidepressants. Thus, a large number of these clients refuse to take the drug or stop taking the drug because of the side effects (Wolfe & Maser, 1994), or simply because many have an almost phobic-like response to the idea of taking any medication (Ballenger, 1996). Moreover, relapse rates are quite high once the drugs are discontinued.

Behavioral and Cognitive-Behavior Treatments
The original behavioral treatment for agoraphobia that was developed in the early 1970s involved prolonged exposure, often with the help of a therapist or family member, to feared situations. Such exposure-based treatments proved quite effective, generally helping about 60 percent of agoraphobic clients show clinically significant improvement. Such results, which left approximately 40 percent not improved to a clinically significant degree, led to further research designed to improve success rates (McNally, 1994).

One possible limitation of exposure-based treatments was that they had not targeted panic attacks per se. In the mid-1980s, two new techniques were developed as the recognition of the centrality of panic attacks to most people with this condition was increasing. One of these new techniques involves a new variant on exposure known as *interoceptive exposure*. Given the prominent fears that people with panic disorder have of their bodily sensations, the idea is that fear of these internal sensations should be treated in the same way that fear of external agoraphobic situations is treated—namely, through prolonged exposure to those internal sensations so that the fear may extinguish. Thus, panic clients are asked to do a variety of exercises (such as hyperventilating, shaking their head from side to side, running in place, holding their breath, ingesting caffeine, etc.) that bring on physical sensations they may fear. Whichever exercises bring on the symptoms that most resemble the symptoms they experience during panic are then targeted for practice so that extinction of the anxiety that accompanies these physical sensations may occur.

The second kind of techniques that have been added are cognitive techniques, in recognition of the importance of catastrophic automatic thoughts to at least the maintenance of this condition. Highlight 5.2 illustrates one kind of integrative cognitive-behavior treatment approach for panic disorder. These newer cognitive-behavior treatments that target not only agoraphobic avoidance but also panic attacks per se, generally seem to produce better results than were obtained with the original exposure therapy techniques that focused exclusively on exposure to external (exteroceptive) situations (Clark, 1996, 1997; McNally, 1994), although at least two studies showed that combining interoceptive and exteroceptive exposure may produce as good results as a treatment package that adds cognitive techniques (Margraf & Schneider, 1991; Telch, 1995). Indeed, in most of the studies conducted using one of the variants on these treatments 75 to 95 percent of people with panic disorder were panic free at the end of 8 to 14 weeks of treatment,

and gains are well maintained at one year follow-up (Clark, 1996).

What about the combination of medication and cognitive-behavior therapy? As alluded to earlier, in the short term this may produce a superior result to either type of treatment alone (as has been found in some but not all studies), but in the long term after medication has been tapered, clients who have been on medication, even when they also received behavioral or cognitive-behavior treatment, seem to show a greater likelihood of relapse (Barlow et al., submitted; Marks et al., 1993), perhaps because they have attributed their gains to the medication rather than their personal efforts (Başoğlu et al., 1994).

GENERALIZED ANXIETY DISORDER

People with generalized anxiety disorder, unlike those with other anxiety disorders, do not have any very effective anxiety-avoidance mechanisms. Thus, although victims of other anxiety disorders can to some extent allay their anxieties through avoidance behavior, seemingly unavoidable feelings of threat and anxiety are the central feature of this disorder.

Generalized anxiety disorder (GAD) is characterized by chronic excessive worry about a number of events or activities. This state was originally described as *free-floating anxiety* because it was not anchored to a specific object or situation as with specific or social phobias. DSM-IV criteria specify that the worry must occur more days than not for at least six months and that it must be experienced as difficult to control. Its content may not be exclusively related to the worry associated with another concurrent Axis I disorder, such as the possibility of having a panic attack. The subjective experience of excessive worry must also be accompanied by at least three of the following six symptoms: (1) restlessness or feelings of being keyed up or on edge, (2) a sense of being easily fatigued, (3) difficulty concentrating or mind going blank, (4) irritability, (5) muscle tension, and (6) sleep disturbance. In previous DSMs, symptoms of autonomic hyperactivity were also included (such as shortness of breath, rapid pulse, sweating, dizziness, and nausea), but these were dropped from DSM-IV when it was found in a multisite study that none of these symptoms were endorsed with much frequency in clients diagnosed with GAD (Brown, O'Leary, or Barlow, 1993). Indeed, GAD clients respond to laboratory stressors with less autonomic responding than do nonanxious controls. Instead, they respond to

Cognitive-Behavior Therapy for Panic Disorder

The cognitive model of panic disorder has been responsible for the formulation of a new treatment that has been shown to be highly effective in over a dozen different studies in at least four countries (Wolfe & Maser, 1994). Although the treatments used in the different research studies vary somewhat, there are many common threads that identify each as a form of cognitive-behavior therapy. In one version of the treatment used at a panic disorder treatment clinic codirected by one of the authors, a 14-session treatment format is used (modified from Barlow & Cerny, 1988).

There are three aspects to the treatment. First, clients are taught about the cognitive model of panic through the use of numerous examples from their own experiences with panic, as well as the experiences of other people with the disorder. Through learning about the panic circle (Figure 5.2, p. 179), they come to see how their tendency to catastrophize about the meaning of their bodily sensations is likely to spiral initially low levels of anxiety into full-blown panic. Over the first three or four sessions clients are taught to identify their own automatic thoughts during panic attacks, as well as during anxiety-provoking situations. They are then taught about the logical er-

rors that people who have panic are prone to making and to subject their own automatic thoughts to a logical reanalysis. For example, a person who fears having a heart attack is asked at the first sign of heart palpitations to examine the evidence that this might be true (e.g., when did the doctor last tell him that his heart was perfectly healthy?), and what the likelihood is of having a heart attack at age 30, etc. Alternatively, someone afraid of making a fool of herself in a restaurant if she has a panic attack and has to leave, is asked not only to evaluate the evidence that her friends would think this made her look foolish, but also to examine her standards for her own behavior and whether they are higher than the standards she has for other people (e.g., would she think other people were foolish if they had to leave a restaurant during a panic attack?), as well as whether she is engaging in all-or-none thinking (e.g., her friends might be concerned about her without thinking she was a fool).

In later sessions the cognitive part of the treatment is focused on teaching people how to decatastrophize—that is, to learn how to think through what the worst possible outcome might be if they did have a panic attack (e.g., if they had a panic attack while

such stressors with high levels of psychic and muscle tension (Brown et al., 1993).

General Characteristics

The general picture of people suffering from generalized anxiety disorder is that they live in a relatively constant state of tension, worry, and diffuse uneasiness. The fundamental process is one of *anxious apprehension,* which is defined as a future-oriented mood state in which a person attempts to be constantly ready to deal with upcoming negative events (Barlow et al., 1996; Brown et al., 1993). This mood state is characterized by high levels of

negative affect, chronic overarousal, and a sense of uncontrollability (Barlow et al., 1996). Although anxious apprehension is also part of other anxiety disorders (e.g., the agoraphobic is anxious about future panic attacks and about dying; the social phobic is anxious about possible negative social evaluation), it is the essence of GAD, leading Barlow and others to refer to GAD as the "basic" anxiety disorder (Wells & Butler, 1997).

In addition to their excessive levels of worry and anxious apprehension, people with generalized anxiety disorder often have difficulty concentrating and making decisions, dreading to make a mistake. They may engage in certain subtle avoidance activities such as procrastination

driving they might have to pull their car over to the side of the road until the attack subsided). Usually once they learn to decatastrophize, the entire experience of panic becomes less terrifying, although still quite unpleasant (and no attempts are made to decatastrophize death!).

The second part of the treatment involves teaching people with panic disorder two techniques that lower their overall level of physical arousal and tension. This includes training in deep muscle relaxation, followed by training in how to breathe from the diaphragm. By learning how to relax they reduce the number of physical symptoms of anxiety from which panic attacks tend to spiral. The breathing retraining is important not only as a relaxation tool, but also because many people with panic disorder have a chronic tendency to hyperventilate (to overbreathe, which is adaptive during exercise but not at other times). Hyperventilation is known to create a variety of unpleasant physical sensations such as lightheadedness, dizziness, and tightness of the chest, which often occur during panic attacks. (You can see this for yourself by breathing very fast and deeply for 1 to 2 minutes.) By learning how to counteract this tendency to hyperventilate, these clients have a new coping tool to use that will reduce the likelihood that they are themselves creating some of the symptoms they are so frightened of.

The third part of the treatment involves exposure to feared situations and feared bodily sensations. Because of the importance of interoceptive fears (fears of bodily sensations), clients are asked to do a variety of exercises with the therapist that bring on different bodily sensations. These include hyperventilating, breathing through a straw, shaking one's head from side to side, jogging in place, holding one's breath for a minute, etc. After each exercise, clients describe the sensations produced, how similar these sensations are to those that they experience during panic, and how scary those sensations are. Whichever exercises produce symptoms most similar to their own during panic attacks are targeted for practice. The idea is that if clients practice these exercises, their anxiety about these sensations will gradually extinguish. Moreover, they will also learn a sense of control over producing the sensations, which may help reduce the anxiety the sensations create when they appear to come out of the blue. By about the ninth session, clients who also have extensive agoraphobic avoidance begin to expose themselves to their feared situations for long enough so that their anxiety comes down. This part of the treatment is delayed until this point so that clients have a variety of coping skills (cognitive techniques, as well as relaxation and breathing skills) that should help them deal with these feared situations better than they have been able to do so in the past. ■

or checking, but these are generally not very effective in reducing anxiety. They also tend to show a marked vigilance for possible signs of threat in their environment. Commonly, they complain of muscle tension, especially in the neck and upper shoulder region, and sleep disturbances including insomnia and nightmares. (See Table 5.2 for the frequency of different symptoms in GAD.)

No matter how well things seem to be going, people with generalized anxiety disorder are apprehensive and anxious. Their nearly constant worries leave them continually upset, uneasy, and discouraged. In one study their most common spheres of worry were found to be family, work, finances, and personal illness (Roemer, Molina, & Borkovec, 1997). Not only do they have difficulty making decisions, after they have managed to make a decision they worry endlessly over possible errors and unforeseen circumstances that may prove the decision wrong and lead to disaster. Even after going to bed, people suffering from GAD are not likely to find relief from their worries. Often, they review each mistake, real or imagined, recent or remotely past. When they are not reviewing and regretting the events of the past, they are anticipating all the difficulties that may arise in the future. They have no appreciation of the logic most of us use in concluding that it is pointless to torment ourselves about possible outcomes over which we have no control. Al-

Muscle tension, chronic overarousal, restlessness, and difficulty concentrating are all symptoms that people with generalized anxiety disorder may have. Such individuals also worry excessively and are hypervigilant for possible signs of threat in their environment.

though it may seem at times that they are actually looking for things to worry about, it is their feeling that they cannot control their tendency to worry.

Prevalence and Age of Onset

Generalized anxiety disorder is a relatively common condition, with current estimates that it is experienced by approximately 3 percent of the population in any one-year period and 5 percent at some point in their lives (Kessler et al., 1994). This makes it slightly more common than panic disorder with or without agoraphobia. GAD is approximately twice as common in women than men (a somewhat less dramatic difference than is seen with many specific phobias or severe agoraphobia). (See Table 5.3 for summaries of gender differences in the different anxiety disorders.) Although GAD is quite common, most people with this disorder do manage to function in spite of their high levels of worry and anxiety; perhaps because of this, they are less likely to come to clinics for psychological treatment than are people with panic disorder or major depression, which are frequently more debilitating conditions. Although they may not present for psychological treatment as often as do clients with certain other conditions, they do show up in physician's offices with medical complaints (such as muscle tension or fatigue) at very high rates; indeed, like people with panic disorder they are generally considered to be over-users of health care resources (Roy-Byrne & Katon, 1997; Schweizer & Rickels, 1997).

Age of onset is often difficult to determine, with 60 to 80 percent of clients reporting that they remember having been anxious nearly all their lives; many others report a slow and insidious onset (Rapee & Barlow, 1993; Wells & Butler, 1997). In recent years this has led many to sug-

---

TABLE 5.2 FREQUENCY OF SYMPTOMS IN 100 CASES OF GENERALIZED ANXIETY DISORDER

Affective/Somatic	%	Cognitive/Behavioral	%
Unable to relax	97	Difficulty concentrating	86
Tense	86	Fear losing control	76
Frightened	79	Fear being rejected	72
Jumpy	72	Unable to control thoughts	72
Unsteady	62	Confusion	69
Weakness all over	59	Mind blurred	66
Hands (only) sweating	52	Inability to recall	55
Terrified	52	Sentences disconnected	45
Heart racing	48	Blocking in speech	45
Face flushed	48	Fear of being attacked	35
Wobbly	45	Fear of dying	35
Sweating all over	38	Hands trembling	31
Difficult breathing	35	Body swaying	31
Urgent need to urinate	35	Stuttering	24
Nausea	31		
Diarrhea	31		
Faint/dizzy feeling	28		
Face is pale	24		
Feeling of choking	14		
Actual fainting	3		

Source: Adapted from Beck and Emery (1985), pp. 87–88.

TABLE 5.3   GENDER DIFFERENCES IN THE ANXIETY DISORDERS: LIFETIME PREVALENCE ESTIMATES

Disorder	Prevalence in Men (%)	Prevalence in Women (%)	Ratio
Specific phobias	6.7	15.7	2.34
Social phobia	11.1	15.5	1.4
Panic disorder	0.8	2.0	2.5
Generalized anxiety disorder	3.6	6.6	1.8
Obsessive-compulsive disorder	2.0	2.9	1.45
Post-traumatic stress disorder	5	10.4	2.08

Sources: Barlow, 1988; Eaton et al., 1994; Karno et al., 1988; Kessler et al., 1994; Magee et al., 1996).

Note: Because these figures are from different studies and may not be strictly comparable, they should be taken as approximations of current estimates of gender differences.

gest that GAD might be reconceptualized as a personality disorder (see Chapter 9) given its lifelong presentation, unlike that of most of the other anxiety disorders, which usually have a more acute onset (Rapee & Barlow, 1993; Sanderson & Wetzler, 1991). Clients themselves also tend to think of their anxiety and worry as a personality characteristic (Wells & Butler, 1997).

Comorbidity with Other Disorders

Generalized anxiety disorder often co-occurs with other Axis I disorders, especially other anxiety and mood disorders. The most common additional anxiety disorders are panic disorder with agoraphobia, social phobia, and specific phobia (Wittchen et al., 1994). In addition, many people with GAD experience occasional panic attacks without qualifying for a full-blown diagnosis of panic disorder (Barlow, 1988). Many of these people show mild to moderate depression as well as chronic anxiety (Brown et al., 1993; Schweizer & Rickels, 1996; Wells & Butler, 1997). This finding is not unexpected in view of their generally gloomy outlook on the world. Nor is it surprising that excessive use of tranquilizing drugs, sleeping pills, and alcohol often complicates the clinical picture in generalized anxiety disorder.

The following case is fairly typical of generalized anxiety disorder.

Case Study, A Graduate Student with GAD • John was a 26-year-old single graduate student in the social sciences at a prestigious university. Although he reported that he had had problems with anxiety nearly all his life, including as a child, the past 7 to 8 years since he had left home and gone to college had been worse. During the past year his anxiety had seriously interfered with his functioning. He reported worries about several dif-

ferent spheres of his life. He was very concerned about his own health and that of his parents. During one incident a few months earlier, he had thought that his heart was beating slower than usual and he had experienced some tingling sensations; this led him to worry that he might die. In another incident he had heard his name being paged over a loudspeaker in an airport and worried that someone at home must be dying. He was also very worried about his future because he had had trouble completing his master's thesis on time given his high level of anxiety. He also worried excessively about getting a bad grade even though he had never had one during four years at a prestigious Ivy League university or at his equally prestigious graduate institution. In classes he worried excessively about what the professor and other students thought of him and tended not to talk unless the class was small and he was quite confident about the topic. Although he had a number of friends, he had never had a girlfriend because of his shyness about dating. He had no problem talking or socializing with women as long as it was not defined as a dating situation. He worried that he should only date a woman if he was quite sure it could be a serious relationship from the outset. He also worried excessively that if a woman did not want to date him that it meant that he was boring.

In addition to his worries, John reported muscle tension and easy fatiguability. He also reported great difficulty concentrating and a considerable amount of restlessness and pacing. When he couldn't work he spent a great deal of time daydreaming, which worried him because he didn't seem able to control it. At times he had difficulty falling asleep if he was particularly anxious, but at other times he slept excessively, in part to escape from his worries. He frequently experienced dizziness and palpitations, and in the past had had full-blown panic attacks. Overall, he reported frequently feeling paralyzed and unable to do things.

Both of John's parents were professionals; his mother was also quite anxious and had been treated for panic disorder. He

volves more extended and involved rumination and appraisal about possible future threats. Nevertheless, it may be the occurrence of negative automatic thoughts that initiates a bout of worrying on a particular topic (Wells & Butler, 1997). Borkovec (1994) and colleagues have investigated both what people with GAD think the benefits are of worrying as well as what actual functions the process of worry serve. The five most common benefits people with GAD think derive from worrying are: (1) superstitious avoidance of catastrophe ("worrying makes it less likely that the feared event will occur"); (2) actual avoidance of catastrophe ("worrying helps to generate ways of avoiding or preventing catastrophe"); (3) avoidance of deeper emotional topics ("worrying about most of the things I worry about is a way to distract myself from worrying about even more emotional things, things that I don't want to think about"); (4) coping and preparation ("worrying about a predicted negative event helps me to prepare for its occurrence"); (5) motivating device ("worrying helps to motivate me to accomplish the work that needs to be done") (Borkovec, 1994, pp. 16–17).

Exciting new developments in the understanding of what functions worry actually serves have given new understanding to why the worry process is so self-sustaining and why it is perceived as so uncontrollable. When people with GAD worry, their emotional and physiological response to aversive imagery is actually suppressed. This suppression of emotional and aversive physiological responding serves to reinforce (that is, increase the probability of) the process of worry. Because worry suppresses physiological responding, it also serves to keep the person from fully experiencing or processing the topic that is being worried about and it is known that such full processing is necessary if extinction of that anxiety is to occur (Borkovec, 1994). Thus the threatening meaning of the topic being worried about is maintained.

Moreover, although worry serves an immediate dampening function for physiological arousal, it is also associated with a more long-term maintenance of emotional disturbance. For example, Wells and Papageorgiou (1995) had people watch a gruesome film. Following the film some were told to relax and settle down, some were told to imagine the events in the film, and some were told to worry in verbal form about the film. Over the next several days people in the worry condition showed the most intrusive images from the film. Wells and Butler (1997, p. 167) concluded "Individuals who are prone to worry . . . perhaps to avoid images, are likely to engage in an activity that pollutes the stream of consciousness with an increasing frequency of intrusive thoughts." Finally, there is now some evidence that attempts to control thoughts and

worry may paradoxically lead to increased experience of intrusive thoughts and enhanced perception of being unable to control them (Wells & Butler, 1997).

Cognitive Biases for Threatening Information In addition to having frequent thoughts with threatening content, people with GAD process threatening information in a biased way. Many studies have shown that generally anxious people tend to have their attention drawn toward threat cues when there is a mixture of threat and nonthreat cues in the environment. Nonanxious people show, if anything, the opposite bias, tending to have their attention drawn away from threat cues (see Mathews & MacLeod, 1994; Mineka & Nugent, 1995; Mineka et al., 1998, for reviews). Moreover, this different perception of threat cues occurs at a very early stage of information processing, even before the information has entered the person's conscious awareness. This automatic, unconscious attentional bias would seem to have the effect of reinforcing or even enhancing the person's current emotional state. That is, if when one is already anxious, one's attention is automatically drawn toward threat cues in the environment, this would only seem to make the anxiety worse. Generally anxious people also have a much stronger tendency to interpret ambiguous information in a threatening way than do nonanxious individuals. For example, when clinically anxious subjects read a series of ambiguous sentences (e.g., "The doctor examined little Emma's growth," or "They discussed the priest's convictions"), they are more likely to remember the threatening meaning of the sentences than are nonanxious controls (Eysenck et al., 1991; see also MacLeod & Cohen, 1993; Williams, Watts, MacLeod & Mathews, 1997).

Given these strong attentional and interpretive biases for threat cues, one might well expect that anxious persons would also be especially likely to remember the threat cues they have encountered. However, the weight of the evidence at present suggests that this is not the case (Mathews & MacLeod, 1994; Mineka & Nugent, 1995; Mineka et al., 1998; Williams et al., 1997). It seems that the vigilance for threat cues that underlies the attentional bias is also somewhat paradoxically associated with *avoidance* of further elaboration of those threat cues; such elaboration would be necessary to show a memory bias.

In summary, several cognitive variables seem to promote the onset of generalized anxiety as well as its maintenance. Experience with unpredictable and/or uncontrollable life events may promote both current anxiety as well as a vulnerability to anxiety in the presence of future stressors (Barlow, 1988; Barlow et al., 1996; Mineka,

1985a; Mineka & Zinbarg, 1996). In addition, schemas that one develops early in life about how to cope with strange and dangerous situations and about how to survive may leave one prone to developing automatic thoughts focused on possible threats. The content of such thoughts surely helps to maintain anxiety, as does the process of worry itself. Finally, for anxiety-prone people, anxiety affects the processing of threatening information in such a way that they automatically pay attention to threatening cues in their environment. Moreover, they are prone to interpret ambiguous information in a threatening manner. Yet they do not seem to have especially good memory for the threatening cues they encounter.

Biological Causal Factors

Genetic Factors Although evidence regarding genetic factors in GAD is mixed, it does seem likely that there is a modest heritability, as for the other anxiety disorders (Kendler et al., 1992a; MacKinnon & Foley, 1996; Plomin et al., 1997). Part of the problem for research in this area has been the evolving nature of our understanding of GAD and what its diagnostic criteria are. GAD was only introduced as a diagnostic category in 1980. Thus many of the people participating in studies before then who had been diagnosed with "anxiety states" may have included a mixture of GAD and panic disorder clients. Moreover, even since 1980 the diagnostic criteria for GAD have changed significantly with each revision of the DSM, making it difficult to compare the results of studies done at different times (MacKinnon & Foley, 1996). One large twin study reveals exactly how heritability estimates vary as a function of one's definition of GAD (Kendler et al., 1992a).

There are also many questions as to the degree of specificity of transmission of GAD and the other anxiety disorders. For example, some studies support the idea that GAD and panic disorder have separate genetic diatheses, while other studies suggest they may have a common diathesis (MacKinnon & Foley, 1996). The evidence is increasingly strong, however, that GAD and major depressive disorder (to be discussed in Chapter 6) do share a common underlying genetic diathesis (Kendler et al., 1992d, 1996).

Recently scientists reported having identified a specific gene related to anxiety and neuroticism. This gene affects the brain's ability to use the neurotransmitter serotonin. This is one of the first times that a specific gene has been identified that affects an important human personality trait—specifically, who is prone to anxiety and other negative moods and who is prone to a more stable, laid-back attitude. The gene affects what is called the *serotonin transporter*—molecules that are separate from serotonin itself but allow surrounding nerve cells to respond to serotonin (Lesch et al., 1996).

The scientists emphasized that the size of the relationship between this transporter gene and neuroticism is quite small, accounting for only about 4 percent of the variance in people's neuroticism levels. Thus many other as yet unidentified genes as well as experiential factors combine with this gene to determine a person's level of neuroticism (Goldman, 1996). Nevertheless, these findings are considered very important because neuroticism is one of the three or four most basic human personality dimensions (Watson, Clark, & Harkness, 1994) and because people with high levels of neuroticism are known to be at increased risk for both anxiety and depressive disorders (Clark, Watson, & Mineka, 1994).

A Functional Deficiency of GABA In the 1950s certain drugs were found to reduce anxiety. This category of drugs, the benzodiazepines, includes some of today's most prescribed psychoactive drugs (e.g., Valium, Librium, and most recently Xanax). Discovery of the marked effects that these drugs have on generalized anxiety was followed in the 1970s by the finding that the drugs probably exert their effects through stimulating the action of gamma aminobutyric acid (GABA), a neurotransmitter now strongly implicated in generalized anxiety (Redmond, 1985). It appears that highly anxious people have a kind of functional deficiency in GABA, which ordinarily plays an important role in the way our brain inhibits anxiety in stressful situations. The benzodiazepine drugs appear to reduce anxiety by increasing GABA activity in certain parts of the brain known to be implicated in anxiety, such as the limbic system. Whether the functional deficiency in GABA in anxious people causes their anxiety or occurs as a consequence of it is not yet known, but it does appear that this functional deficiency would promote the maintenance of anxiety.

More recently, a new class of drugs that reduce anxiety has been discovered—the azaspirones (with buspirone being the one most commonly used). As researchers have sought to determine how this class of drugs work, they have discovered that another neurotransmitter—serotonin—is also involved in modulating anxiety. However, the exact mechanisms remain unknown and are likely to be very complicated (Glitz & Balon, 1996). At present, it seems that GABA, serotonin, and perhaps norepinephrine all play a role in anxiety but the ways in which they interact remain unknown.

Neurobiological Differences Between Anxiety and Panic It is also important to reemphasize here that the neurobiological factors implicated in panic attacks and generalized anxiety are *not* the same (Charney et al., 1998; Gray & McNaughton, 1996). As we noted at the outset of this chapter, contemporary theorists are drawing a distinction between fear, or panic, and anxiety that is far more fundamental than the old one that anxiety is simply fear without a known source. Fear and panic involve the activation of the fight-or-flight response, and the brain area and neurotransmitters that seem most strongly implicated in these emotional responses are the locus coeruleus in the brain stem, and/or the central gray in the midbrain, and the neurotransmitter norepinephrine. Generalized anxiety or anxious apprehension is a more diffuse emotional state involving arousal and a preparation for possible impending threat, and the brain area and neurotransmitters that seem most strongly implicated are the limbic system and GABA (Gorman et al., 1989; Redmond, 1985). More recently, some involvement of serotonin has been suggested for both conditions but quite probably in somewhat different ways.

Treating Generalized Anxiety Disorder

As already noted, many clients with generalized anxiety disorder are seen by family physicians rather than by mental health professionals; they are seeking relief from their "nerves" or anxieties and/or their various functional (psychogenic) physical problems. Most often in such cases drugs from the benzodiazepine (anxiolytic) category such as Valium are used—and misused—for tension relief and for relaxation; they also reduce subjective anxiety and may reduce emotional reactivity to new stressors. As noted earlier for panic disorder, these drugs are generally not as effective as believed by the general public, and their effectiveness often wears off after a few weeks of continuous medication. Moreover, they are quite habit forming and difficult to taper. As mentioned above, busipirone (from the azaspirone category) also seems effective. It has an advantage over the benzodiazepines in that it is not addictive but it has the disadvantage that a therapeutic response may take several weeks (Glitz & Balon, 1996). Several categories of antidepressant medications have also been shown to be useful in the treatment of GAD (Gitlin, 1996).

Cognitive-behavior therapy for generalized anxiety disorder has also become increasingly effective in recent years as refinements in the techniques are made. It usually involves a combination of behavioral techniques such as training in deep muscle relaxation and cognitive restructuring techniques aimed at reducing worry and its negative content. Although GAD initially appeared to be

among the most difficult of the anxiety disorders to treat, recent advances have been made, and a number of studies have now shown very effective treatment outcomes for 60 to 70 percent of persons with the condition (Wells & Butler, 1997).

Case Study, Cognitive-Behavior Therapy for John's GAD

● The case of John, the graduate student with GAD discussed earlier, serves as an example of the success of cognitive-behavior therapy with this condition. Before seeking treatment with a cognitive-behavior therapist, he had seen someone at a student counseling center for several months the previous year but hadn't found the "talk therapy" very useful. He had heard from his mother that cognitive-behavior therapy might be useful and had sought a referral for such treatment. He was in treatment for about six months, during which time he found training in deep muscle relaxation helpful in reducing his overall level of tension. In addition, cognitive restructuring (see Chapters 3 and 17) helped reduce his worry levels considerably; indeed, he reported that he was worrying much less about all spheres of his life. He still had problems with procrastinating when he had deadlines, but this too was improving. He also began socializing more frequently and had tentatively begun dating when treatment ended for financial reasons. He was better able to see that if a woman didn't wish to go out with him again, this did not mean that he was boring but simply that they might not be a good match.

OBSESSIVE-COMPULSIVE DISORDER

Diagnostically **obsessive-compulsive disorder (OCD)** is defined by the occurrence of unwanted and intrusive obsessive thoughts or distressing images; these are usually accompanied by compulsive behaviors designed to neutralize the obsessive thoughts or images or to prevent some dreaded event or situation. More specifically, according to DSM-IV, **obsessions** involve persistent and recurrent intrusive thoughts, images, or impulses that are experienced as disturbing and inappropriate. People who have such obsessions try to ignore or suppress them, or to neutralize them with some other thought or action. **Compulsions** can involve either overt repetitive behaviors (such as hand washing, checking, or ordering) or more covert mental acts (such as counting, praying, or saying certain words silently). A person with this disorder usually feels driven to perform this compulsive behavior in response to an obsession, and there are often very rigid rules regarding how the compulsive behavior should be performed. The compulsive behaviors are performed with the goal of preventing or reducing distress or preventing some dreaded event or situation, even though

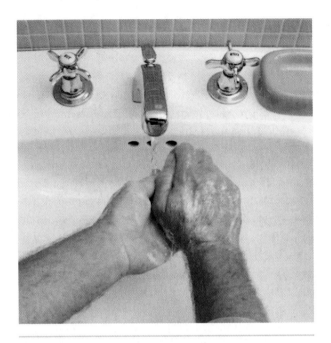

Many of us show some compulsive behavior, but people with obsessive-compulsive disorder feel compelled to repeatedly perform some act in response to an obsession in order to reduce the anxiety or discomfort created by the obsession. Although the person may realize that the behavior is excessive or unreasonable, be or she does not feel able to control the urge. Obsessive-compulsive washers may spend hours a day washing, and may even use abrasive cleansers to the point that their bands bleed.

they are not usually very realistically connected with what they are designed to neutralize or prevent, or are clearly excessive (American Psychiatric Association, 1994). In addition, the person must recognize that the obsession is the product of his own mind rather than being imposed from without (as might occur in schizophrenia). It is also now recognized that there is a continuum of "insight" among obsessive-compulsives about exactly how senseless and excessive their obsessions and compulsions are (Riggs & Foa, 1993). In most cases these people do have some recognition that their obsessions or compulsions are excessive or unreasonable, but they cannot seem to control them; in a minority of cases this insight is absent most of the time. Finally, the DSM-IV diagnosis requires that this seemingly involuntary behavior cause a person marked distress, consume excessive time (over an hour a day), or interfere with occupational or social functioning.

The following is a fairly typical case of severe obsessive-compulsive disorder.

Case Study, An Artist's Obsessions with Confessing •
Mark was a 28-year-old single male with severe obsessions about causing harm to others, including committing crimes. The obsessions were accompanied by lengthy and excessive checking rituals. At the time he came to an anxiety disorder clinic, he was no longer able to live by himself, and had been forced to move back home with his parents after having lived for several years on his own since college. His obsessions about harming others or confessing to crimes were so severe that he was virtually confined to his room and could only leave it if he had a tape recorder with him so that he would have a record of any crimes he confessed to. The clinic was several hours' drive from his home; his mother usually had to drive. One day when he drove he began obsessing that he had caused an accident at an intersection and felt compelled to spend several hours driving and walking around all parts of that intersection to find evidence of the accident. He could not speak on the phone for fear of confessing some crime that he had not committed, and he could not mail a letter for the same reason. He also could not go into a store alone or into public bathrooms, where he feared he might write a confession on the wall.

Mark was a very bright young man with considerable artistic talent. He had finished college at a prestigious school for people interested in the arts and had begun a successful career as a young artist when the obsessions began in his early 20s. At first they were focused on the possibility that he would be implicated in some crime that he had not committed; only later did they evolve to the point that he was actually afraid that he might commit a crime and confess to it. The checking rituals and avoidance of all places where such confessions might occur eventually led to his having to give up his career and his own apartment and move back in with his family.

Prevalence and Age of Onset

Although once thought to be an extremely rare disorder (e.g., Black, 1974, reviewed studies estimating the prevalence at 0.05 percent), estimates from the Epidemiologic Catchment Area study indicate that obsessive-compulsive disorder is much more prevalent than was once thought (see Antony, Downie, & Swinson, 1998). Specifically, the average one-year prevalence rate of OCD in this composite sample was 1.6 percent, and the average lifetime prevalence was 2.5 percent (Robins & Regier, 1991), and these figures appear to be similar in other cultures that have been studied (Gibbs, 1996). Divorced (or separated) and unemployed people were somewhat overrepresented (Karno et al., 1988), which is not surprising given the difficulties this disorder creates for interpersonal and occupational functioning. Contrary to earlier reports suggesting a preponderance of OCD among females, these newer figures show little or no gender difference, making OCD very different from most of the rest of the anxiety disorders in this regard. Although the disorder generally begins in late adolescence or early adulthood, it is not uncommon in children, where its symptoms are strikingly similar to those of adult cases (March & Leonard, 1998; Valeni et al., 1994). Childhood onset is often associated with greater severity. In most cases the disorder has a gradual onset, but once it becomes a serious condition it tends to be chronic, although the severity of symptoms usually waxes and wanes in intensity over time (e.g., Rasmussen & Eisen, 1991).

Characteristics of OCD

Most people with obsessive-compulsive disorder who present for treatment experience both obsessions and compulsions. Although earlier estimates were that as many as 25 percent experienced pure obsessional disorder without any compulsive rituals (Rachman & Hodgson, 1980), recent estimates from research conducted in the development of the DSM-IV are that over 90 percent of those who come for treatment experience both obsessions and compulsions. When mental rituals or compulsions such as counting are also included as compulsive behaviors, this figure jumps to 98 percent. In 90 percent of cases the compulsions are seen as functionally related to the obsessions (Riggs & Foa, 1993). For example, it can be predicted that someone with an obsession about dirt and contamination will have washing rituals. However, in epidemiological samples where people in the community are being diagnosed, but who are often not presenting for treatment, the picture that emerges is rather different. In one such study, 40 percent experienced obsessions only, and 30 percent experienced compulsions only (Weissman et al., 1994; see Gibbs, 1996, for a review).

Most of us have experienced minor obsessive thoughts, such as whether we remembered to lock the door or turn the stove off. In addition, most of us occasionally engage in repetitive or stereotyped behavior, such as checking the stove or the lock on the door, or stepping over cracks on a sidewalk. In the case of obsessive-compulsive disorder, however, the thoughts are much more persistent and distressing, they generally appear irrational or excessive to the individual, and along with the associated compulsive acts they interfere considerably with everyday behavior. Nevertheless, research indicates that normal and abnormal obsessions and compulsive behaviors exist on a continuum, with the primary difference being in the frequency and intensity of the obsessions and in the degree to which the obsessions and compulsions are troubling and to which they are resisted

(Gibbs, 1996; Rachman & Hodgson, 1980; Salkovskis & Kirk, 1997).

Types of Obsessive Thoughts Obsessive thoughts may center on a variety of topics. A recent review concluded that in patient and nonpatient (epidemiological community) samples, the content of obsessions consist most often of contamination fears, fears of harming self or others, and pathological doubt. Other fairly common themes are concerns about or need for symmetry, sexual obsessions, and obsessions concerning religion or aggressions. These themes are quite consistent cross-culturally and across the lifespan (Gibbs, 1996).

Obsessive thoughts involving themes of violence or aggression might include a wife being obsessed with the idea that she might poison her husband, or a daughter constantly imagining pushing her mother down a flight of stairs. Even though such obsessive thoughts are only very rarely carried out in action, they remain a source of often excruciating torment to a person plagued with them. This pattern is well illustrated in a classic case described by Kraines (1948) of a woman who

> . . . complained of having "terrible thoughts." When she thought of her boyfriend she wished he were dead; when her mother went down the stairs, she "wished she'd fall and break her neck"; when her sister spoke of going to the beach with her infant daughter, the patient "hoped that they would both drown." These thoughts "make me hysterical. I love them; why should I wish such terrible things to happen? It drives me wild, makes me feel I'm crazy and don't belong to society; maybe it's best for me to end it all than to go on thinking such terrible things about those I love." (p. 183)

Types of Compulsions People with OCD feel compelled to perform repeatedly acts that often seem pointless and absurd even to them and that they in some sense do not want to perform. These compulsive acts in patient samples are of five primary types: cleaning, checking, repeating, ordering/arranging, and counting (Antony et al., 1998), with many people showing multiple kinds of rituals. For a smaller number the compulsions are to perform various everyday acts such as eating or dressing extremely slowly (primary obsessional slowness), and for others the compulsions are to have things exactly symmetrical or "evened up" (Rasmussen & Eisen, 1991). Washing rituals vary from relatively mild ritual-like behavior, such as spending 15 to 20 minutes washing one's hands after going to the bathroom, to more extreme behavior, such as washing one's hands with disinfectants for hours every day to the point that the hands bleed. Washing rituals appear to be far less common in nonpatient samples than in patient samples. Checking rituals also vary from relatively mild, such as checking all the lights, appliances, and locks two or three times before leaving the house, to very extreme, such as going back to an intersection where one thinks one may have run over a pedestrian and spending hours checking for any sign of the imagined accident, much as Mark did. Both cleaning and checking rituals are often performed a specific number of times and thus also involve counting. Compulsive rituals are sometimes covert or cognitive in nature, involving feelings and thoughts (see Table 5.4). The performance of the compulsive act or the ritualized series of acts usually brings a feeling of reduced tension and satisfaction (Rachman & Hodgson, 1980; Salkovskis & Kirk, 1997).

Consistent Themes Given the range of content of both obsessions and compulsive rituals, considerable attention has been devoted to the issue of whether OCD is a homogeneous disorder, or rather several different disorders. For example, a distinction is often made between "cleaners" and "checkers," with the former having obsessions about contamination accompanied by cleaning rituals, and the latter having obsessions about causing harm to others, leading to checking rituals. However, problems with this distinction arise when one notes that many people with OCD have both cleaning and checking rituals, and the primary type of ritual may change over time (Gibbs, 1996; Rapoport, 1989). Moreover, some studies comparing different possible subgroups on a host of demographic variables and clinical features have found very few differences. Thus, the disorder seems more homogeneous than one might guess given the many different ways in which it presents itself (Rasmussen & Eisen, 1991). Certain factors seem consistent across nearly all the different clinical presentations: (1) anxiety is the affective symptom (except with primary obsessional slowness); (2) nearly all people afflicted with OCD fear that something terrible will happen to themselves or others for which they will be responsible; and (3) compulsions usually reduce the anxiety, at least in the short term.

Another consistent theme across different cases of obsessive-compulsive disorder lies in its characterization as a "what if" illness (Rasmussen & Eisen, 1991). Most clients with obsessive-compulsive disorder are continually worried about the possibility that something terrible will happen. "If there is a one in a million chance that something terrible will happen, they somehow convince themselves that it will happen to them ... [e.g.] 'The very fact that it is within the realm of possibility, however unlikely, that I will stab my baby, or poison my child, is enough to terrify me so that I can think of nothing else no matter how hard I try.'" (Rasmussen & Eisen, 1991, p. 37). This tendency to judge risks unrealistically seems to be a very important feature of OCD.

TABLE 5.4 COGNITIVE AND MOTOR BEHAVIOR PATTERNS IN OBSESSIVE-COMPULSIVE DISORDER

	Symptoms	Examples
Cognitive	**Obsessions.** Recurrent, persistent ideas, thoughts, images, or impulses involuntarily coming to awareness.	A person has ideas of contamination, dread, guilt; urges to kill, attack, injure, confess, or steal.
	Ruminations. Forced preoccupation with thoughts about a particular topic, associated with brooding, doubting, and inconclusive speculation.	A person spends several hours per day in worried anticipation that a former lover may attempt to reestablish contact.
	Cognitive rituals. Elaborate series of mental acts the client feels compelled to complete. Termination depends on proper performance.	Before retiring for the evening, a client feels required to recite mentally a long series of prayers learned in childhood.
Motor	**Compulsive motor rituals.** Elaborate, often time-consuming activities frequently associated with everyday functions such as eating, toileting, grooming, dressing, and sexual activity.	A patient evidences hand washing (sometimes reaching 400 or more washes per day), compulsive counting (e.g, of passersby), or "checking" of objects.
	Compulsive avoidances. Substitute actions performed instead of appropriate behavior that induces anxiety.	A student becomes involved in several distracting activities before exams, leaving no time to study.

MODERN LIFE

Body Dysmorphic Disorder

The Clinical Picture Body dysmorphic disorder (BDD) is officially classified in DSM-IV as a somatoform disorder, but most researchers and clinicians consider it to be more closely related to OCD, indeed often calling it an OCD-spectrum disorder. Katharine Phillips (1996) has carefully described the condition in *The Broken Mirror: Understanding and Treating Body Dysmorphic Disorder,* a book written for people who suffer from this disorder as well as for their families and clinicians. People with BDD are obsessed with some perceived flaw or flaws in their appearance. They may focus on almost any body part: their skin has blemishes, their breasts are too small, their face is too thin (or too fat) or disfigured by blood vessels that others find repulsive, etc. Some of the more common locations for perceived defects include skin (65%), hair (50%), nose (38%), eyes (20%), legs/knees (18%), chin/jaw (13%), breasts/chest/nipples (12%), stomach/waist (11%), lips (11%), body build (11%), face size/shape (10%) (Phillips, 1996). These are not the ordinary concerns that most of us have about our appearance; they are far more extreme, leading in many cases to complete preoccupation and significant emotional pain. For example, many BDD sufferers are afraid to date or go to parties because they do not want people to see them with their perceived defect. In severe cases, they may become so isolated that they lock themselves up in their house and never go out. In most cases others do not see the defects that the person with BDD has, or if they do, they see only a very minor defect within the normal range.

Sufferers of BDD commonly make their way into the office of a dermatologist or plastic surgeon. An astute doctor will not do the requested procedures and may instead make a referral to a psychologist or psychiatrist. All too often though the patient does get what he or she requests—and unfortunately is almost never satisfied with the outcome. Some patients have repeated surgeries or unnecessary dermatological procedures.

Another common feature of BDD is that people with this condition frequently seek reassurance from friends and family about their defects but the reassurances almost never provide more than very temporary relief. And if 20 people tell them that they look fine, but one person acknowledges some minor problem, it is the latter comment that they will tend to focus on. They also frequently seek reassurance for themselves by checking their appearance in the mirror countless times in a day. Sometimes they may think their perceived defect may not look as bad at other times, which means that by looking in the mirror they are in effect often putting themselves on an emotional roller coaster. They also commonly compare their body parts with others and scrutinize others very carefully. They frequently try to camouflage their perceived defect through clothing or makeup, or by maintaining unusual postures. It is also quite common that they engage in excessive grooming behavior (for example, spending hours fixing their hair or applying makeup).

Relationship to OCD At this point the similarities to OCD should be fairly obvious. Like people with OCD, those with BDD have prominent obsessions and they engage in a variety of ritualistic-like behaviors such as reassurance seek-

Comorbidity with Other Disorders   As with all of the anxiety disorders, obsessive-compulsive disorder frequently co-occurs with other mood and anxiety disorders. Depression is especially common, with estimates suggesting that as many as 67 percent of those with OCD may experience major depression at some time in their life (Gibbs, 1996). Given the chronic and debilitating nature of this disorder, it may not be surprising that many develop depression at least partly in response to having OCD.

The anxiety disorders with which OCD most often co-occurs include social phobia, panic disorder, and specific phobia (e.g., Antony et al., 1998). The most common personality disorders (see Chapter 9) in people with

People with body dysmorphic disorder often seek plastic surgery for what they perceive to be serious flaws in their appearance. Here the actress Goldie Hawn in *First Wives Club* plays a woman who is unhappy with her lips, wishing them to be fuller in shape. She has plastic surgery to make them fuller, and yet is still quite unhappy with the outcome, as is typical of individuals with body dysmorphic disorder who undergo such surgery.

ing, mirror checking, comparing themselves to others, camouflage, etc. But in addition to these symptoms similarities, increasingly research is suggesting an overlapping set of causes. For example, the same kinds of treatment that work for OCD are also the treatments of choice for BDD. In the case of medications, it is clearly the drugs that work on serotonin (clomipramine and the selective serotonin reuptake inhibitors) that are most effective. In the case of behavior therapy it is a variant on exposure and response prevention treatment (see Highlight 5.4) which is most effective (Phillips, 1996).

Why Now? BDD has clearly existed for centuries if not for all time. Why has it only been studied in the literature fairly recently? It seems likely that it has been understudied because most people with this condition never seek psychological or psychiatric treatment. Rather they suffer silently or they go to dermatologists or plastic surgeons (Phillips, 1996). Reasons for this secrecy and shame include worries that others will think they are superficial, silly or vain, and that if they mention their perceived defect others will notice it and focus more on it.

Part of the reason more are now seeking treatment is because the disorder has received a good deal of media attention in the past decade, including being discussed on some daily talk shows where it is sometimes called "imaginary defect disorder." Phillips and others estimate that it is not a rare disorder, perhaps affecting 1 to 2 percent of the general population, up to 8 percent of people with depression, and up to 12 percent of people seeking psychological help in outpatient treatment settings. It occurs only slightly more often in women than men. It commonly co-occurs with either a mood disorder, social phobia, or obsessive-compulsive disorder (Veale et al., 1996). As increasing attention is focused on this disorder, hopefully the secrecy and shame often surrounding it will decrease and more people will seek treatment. ∎

OCD are dependent and avoidant. Indeed Baer and colleagues (1992), found that about 25 percent of 55 OCD clients met criteria for either avoidant and dependent personality disorders, with a subset having both (Summerfeldt, Huta, & Swinson, 1998).

Another disorder that has only been studied extensively in the past decade—**body dysmorphic disorder** **(BDD)**—also co-occurs rather commonly with OCD (indeed 12 percent of patients with OCD also had body dysmorphic disorder in one large study) and is thought by most researchers in this area to be a closely related disorder (e.g., Phillips, 1996; Simeon et al., 1995). See Highlight 5.3 for a discussion of body dysmorphic disorder.

Psychosocial Causal Factors

Psychoanalytic Viewpoint   Until recently the dominant theories of the origins of obsessive-compulsive disorder were the psychoanalytic and behavioral views. According to Freud's psychoanalytic view, a person with OCD has been unable to cope with the instinctual conflicts of the Oedipal stage and has either never advanced beyond this stage or has regressed back to an earlier stage of psychosexual development. Specifically, such a person is thought to be fixated in the anal stage of development (about 2 years of age) when children are thought to derive sensual pleasure from defecating, both as physical release and as a creative act ("Mommy, see what I made!"). This is also the time at which parents are often attempting to toilet train their children, which involves learning to control and delay these urges. If parents are too harsh and make the child feel bad and dirty about soiling himself or herself, they may instill rage in the child, as well as guilt and shame about these drives. According to this theory, the intense conflict that may develop between impulses from the id to let go, and the ego to control and withhold, leads to the development of defense mechanisms that may ultimately produce obsessive-compulsive symptoms.

The four primary defense mechanisms thought to be used are (1) isolation, (2) displacement, (3) reaction formation, and (4) undoing (Nemiah, 1975; Sturgis, 1993). With *isolation,* the associations between a blasphemous thought and the feeling that would ordinarily be associated with it are disconnected. Thus, the person might think about violence without experiencing anger, isolating himself from the affect associated with the distressing situation. With *displacement,* the person substitutes one thought or activity for another that is more frightening or threatening. With *reaction formation,* the person thinks and acts in a fashion that is opposite to his or her true impulses. For example, someone who was obsessed with thoughts of harming her children might become a "supermom." Finally, with *undoing* the person tries to obtain forgiveness for some imagined transgression through some magical compulsive behavior. For example, someone with blasphemous thoughts might engage in extensive praying and cleaning rituals (see Sturgis, 1993). Unfortunately, there has been virtually no empirical research documenting any of the major tenets of this theory, and the treatment that stems from it has not proved to be useful in treating OCD.

The Behavioral Viewpoint   The dominant behavioral view of obsessive-compulsive disorder derives from O. H.

Mowrer's two-process theory of avoidance learning (1947). According to this theory, neutral stimuli become associated with aversive stimuli through a process of classical conditioning and come to elicit anxiety. For example, touching a doorknob or shaking hands might become associated with the "scary" idea of contamination. Once having made this association, the person may discover that the anxiety produced by shaking hands or touching a doorknob may be reduced by an activity like hand washing. By washing his or her hands extensively, the anxiety would be reduced and the washing response would be reinforced, making it more likely to occur again in the future when anxiety about contamination was evoked in other situations (Rachman & Shafran, 1998). Once learned, such avoidance responses are extremely resistant to extinction (Mineka & Zinbarg, 1996; Salkovskis & Kirk, 1997).

Several classic experiments conducted by Rachman and Hodgson (1980) supported these ideas. They found that for most clients with OCD, exposure to a situation that provoked their obsession (e.g., a doorknob or toilet seat for someone with obsessions about contamination) did indeed produce distress, which would continue for a moderate amount of time and then gradually dissipate. If the patient was allowed to engage in the compulsive ritual immediately after the provocation, however, his or her anxiety would generally decrease rapidly. This model predicts then that exposure to feared objects or situations should be useful in treating OCD if the exposure is followed by prevention of the ritual, allowing the patient to see that the anxiety will subside naturally in time without the ritual (see also Rachman & Shafran, 1998). And this is indeed the core of the most effective form of behavior therapy for OCD (see below and Highlight 5.4). Thus, the behavioral model has been very useful in helping us understand what factors may help to maintain obsessive-compulsive behavior, and it has also been useful in generating an effective form of treatment. However, it has not been helpful in explaining why people with OCD develop obsessions in the first place, and why they have such abnormal assessments of risk.

OCD and Preparedness   Just as the conditioning view of phobias has been revitalized through the addition of the preparedness concept, which puts phobias in the evolutionary context of what fears may have been adaptive for our early ancestors, so too has our understanding of obsessive-compulsive disorder increased through looking at it in an evolutionary context. For example, one group of researchers found that the preparedness concept as applied to phobias was also relevant to understanding the nonrandom distribution of obsessive thoughts and compulsive rituals (De Silva, Rachman, & Seligman, 1977). For example, thoughts about dirt and contamination associated with compulsive washing are so common as to make their occurrence seem nonrandom. The researchers developed a rating system for the "preparedness" of different kinds of objects or situations based on estimates of the level of probable danger that they posed to pretechnological humans. Ratings of preparedness of compulsive behaviors were based on estimates that those behaviors almost certainly defended pretechnological people against danger. These ratings were applied to the content of the obsessions, compulsions, and phobias for 82 cases of OCD and 69 cases of phobia. The contents of the great majority of both obsessions and phobias were rated as highly prepared, as were the ratings of most compulsive behaviors (such as washing off animal feces or checking fire hazards). The overall consensus seems to be that humans' obsessions with dirt and contamination and certain other potentially dangerous situations did not arise out of a vacuum but rather have deep evolutionary roots (Mineka & Zinbarg, 1996).

In addition, some theorists have argued that the displacement activities that many species of animals engage in under situations of conflict or high arousal bear a significant resemblance to the compulsive rituals seen in obsessive-compulsive disorder (Holland, 1974; Mineka, 1985a; Mineka & Zinbarg, 1996; Winslow & Insel, 1991). Displacement activities often involve grooming (such as a bird preening his feathers) or nesting under conditions of high conflict or frustration, and may therefore be related to the grooming (such as washing) or tidying rituals seen in obsessive-compulsives, which are often provoked by anxiety, discomfort, or distress brought about by obsessive thoughts or images.

The Role of Memory Cognitive factors have also been implicated in obsessive-compulsive disorder. Sher, Frost, and Otis (1983; see also Sher et al., 1989), for example, have shown that people with checking compulsions show poor memory for their behavioral acts, such as "Did I check to see if the stove was off?" Having a poor memory for one's actions could easily be seen as contributing to the repetitive nature of checking rituals. More recently, there is increasing evidence that people with OCD do indeed have impairments in their nonverbal memory but not their verbal memory (Trivedi, 1996). They also have low confidence in their memory ability (Gibbs, 1996; Trivedi, 1996).

The Effects of Attempting to Suppress Obsessive Thoughts It has now been shown that when normal people attempt to suppress unwanted thoughts (for example, "Don't think about white bears") they may find a paradoxical increase in those thoughts later (Wegner, 1994). Moreover, two other studies with normal subjects showed that thought suppression during a negative mood produced a connection between the thought and the negative mood. When the negative mood occurred again later the thought was more easily experienced, or when the thought was later experienced the mood returned (Wenzlaff, Wegner, & Klein, 1991). They concluded that if people try not to think of something, "unintentionally they bond that thought to their mood such that each will later make the other return" (p. 507).

Given the findings of Rachman that people with normal and abnormal obsessions differ primarily in the degree to which their thoughts are resisted and found unacceptable, it may be that a major factor contributing to the frequency of obsessive thoughts and negative moods may be these attempts to suppress them, leading to paradoxical increases. For example, in one study normal people were asked to describe some negative intrusive thought they had had recently. When they were then asked to suppress that thought over the next 4-day period, they experienced more than twice as many of these thoughts as did people who were simply instructed to record the thought if they experienced it (Trinder & Salkovskis, 1994). Moreover, those instructed to suppress the thought also rated the thoughts as causing more discomfort. In addition, when OCD clients were asked to record intrusive thoughts in a diary, both on days when they were told to try to suppress those thoughts and on days without instructions to suppress, the OCD clients reported approximately twice as many intrusive thoughts on the days they were attempting to suppress them (Salkovskis & Kirk, 1997). This is similar to the idea discussed earlier regarding the paradoxical effects that attempts of people with generalized anxiety disorder to control worry may lead to an increase in intrusive thoughts.

Biological Causal Factors

In the past 20 years there has been an explosion of research investigating the possible biological basis for obsessive-compulsive disorder. Some studies have sought to discover whether there is a genetic contribution to this disorder. Others have explored whether there are

Exposure and Response Prevention

Steketee and Foa (1985) presented the following case as an illustration of their recommended approach to the treatment of obsessive-compulsive disorders. The patient, June, was a 26-year-old recently married nursing graduate who complained of washing and cleaning problems so severe that she was unable to seek work in her profession. On initial evaluation she was agitated and distressed, feeling helpless to control her need to take at least two 45-minute showers daily and, in addition, to wash her hands some 20 times a day for 5 minutes. She also spent a great deal of time wiping various objects with alcohol. Inquiry soon determined that she was terrified of becoming "contaminated," particularly by bird, animal, or human feces, which she took great pains to avoid. She also had problems with garbage and with dead animals on the road. Previous treatment by systematic desensitization, tranquilizing drugs, and "cognitive restructuring" had been ineffective. Her marriage was now threatened owing to her husband's frustration with her excessive cleanliness.

Exposure Treatment

The therapist and patient worked together to create a hierarchy of upsetting stimuli, rating them on a scale of 1 through 100 according to their capacities to evoke disgust and the impulse to wash. For example, the patient gave ratings of 100 to touching dog feces (if unable to wash immediately), 90 to automobile tires (which may have contacted a dead animal), and 40 to the outside doorknob of a public bathroom (the inside doorknob rated 80). Subsequently, in treatment sessions three times weekly, June was instructed to expose herself deliberately to these stimuli either in guided fantasy (in vitro) or directly (in vivo), beginning with those rated relatively low in the hierarchy and moving gradually to the more severely threatening ones.

In addition to the exposures conducted during therapy sessions, "homework" was liberally assigned. Subjective ratings of discomfort were carefully monitored during these encounters. On one occasion well into treatment, the therapist drove with the patient to a place where she had observed a dead cat on the roadside and insisted that the patient approach the "smelly" corpse and touch it with a stick. The stick and a pebble lying close by were presented to the patient with the instruction that she keep

structural brain abnormalities associated with OCD, and yet others whether there are abnormalities in specific neurotransmitter systems associated with OCD. The accumulating evidence from all three kinds of studies is that biological causal factors are probably more clearly implicated in the causes of OCD than in any of the other anxiety disorders.

Genetic Influences Genetic studies have included both twin studies and family studies. Evidence from twin studies reveals a moderately high concordance rate for monozygotic twins and a lower rate for dizygotic twins. A recent review of 14 published studies included 80 monozygotic twins, of whom 54 were concordant for the diagnosis of OCD, and 29 dizygotic twins, of whom 9 were concordant. This is consistent with a moderate genetic heritability (Billett, Richter, & Kennedy, 1998). Most family studies have also found substantially higher rates of OCD in first-degree relatives of OCD clients than would be expected based on current estimates of the prevalence of OCD, with estimates that about 10 percent of first-degree relatives have diagnosable OCD (Pauls et al., 1995). With both twin and family studies, estimates of a genetic contribution go up if twins or family members who have some obsessive-compulsive symptoms (but not full-blown OCD) are included (Pauls et al., 1995). Finally, there is also quite convincing evidence of a genetic contribution to some forms of OCD given that OCD is linked

them in her pocket and touch them frequently throughout the day. The patient was also told to drive her car past the spot on subsequent days.

The therapist made "home visits" to assist the patient in facing her problems in that setting, touching contaminated objects and places (such as a porch railing soiled with pigeon droppings) and contaminating (by unwashed touch) clean ones. Systematic exposure continued until the patient appeared at ease with a particular confrontation and her discomfort rating concerning it dropped to the 40 to 50 range.

Response Prevention

After obtaining June's commitment to the full treatment procedure (which had previously been explained) in the fourth session, the therapist instituted a no-washing rule. Specifically, the patient was to remain unwashed for a period of five days, after which she could take a 10-minute shower to be followed by another wash-free five days. As anticipated, June was notably upset by this proposed regimen and strongly doubted she could carry it off. The therapist was encouraging but insistent, promising support through the hard times, and the patient was successful in

curbing her frequent impulses to wash. A transition to "normal washing and cleaning behavior" was instituted shortly before the end of the planned 15 therapy sessions. This plan consisted of one 10-minute shower per day and hand washings not to exceed six per day at mealtimes, after bathroom use, and after touching clearly soiled or greasy objects.

Because June's discomfort ratings remained somewhat high (maximum 70, but only briefly) following the planned 15 sessions, a few additional follow-up sessions were given. In an evaluation nine months following the initiation of treatment, June described herself as "definitely a lot better . . . maybe 80 percent." She acknowledged that she still had obsessions "once every week or two" (such as "driving over someone"), but she was now employed and her relationship with her husband was much improved. She felt she was living a "normal life."

As Steketee and Foa pointed out, obsessive-compulsive disorders rarely remit completely; even a successfully treated patient will usually have some residual obsessive problems or rituals, as in June's case. The treatment undertaken here was of course direct and rigorous and was based on a behavioral formulation. It appears to have been the treatment of choice. ∎

---

to Tourette's syndrome—a disorder characterized by chronic motor and vocal tics, which is suspected to have a genetic basis (see Chapter 13). For example, one study found that 23 percent of first-degree relatives of clients with Tourette's syndrome had diagnosable OCD (Pauls et al., 1986, 1991). Moreover, nearly 5 percent of the first degree relatives of persons with OCD were found to have Tourette's syndrome or other chronic tics whereas only one percent of the relatives of normal controls received a diagnosis of Tourette's or chronic tics (Pauls et al., 1995). In general, it seems that there is probably a moderate genetic contribution to OCD, although it may be a rather nonspecific "neurotic" predisposition (Black et al., 1992; MacKinnon & Foley, 1996). However, more research is

needed with new genetic methodologies before the exact nature of this contribution will be completely understood.

Abnormalities in Brain Function The search for structural abnormalities in the brains of OCD clients has also been intense in the past 15 years but the results of seven major studies have not revealed a consistent pattern of structural abnormalities (Brody & Baxter, 1996; Cottraux & Gérard, 1998; Trivedi, 1996). In addition, as major advances have been made in techniques used to study the *functioning* of brain structures, attempts have been made to determine whether some brain structures may show abnormalities in how they function, even if they do not show abnormalities of structure per se. Findings from at least a half dozen studies using positron emission tomography (PET) scans have shown that clients with OCD have abnormally active metabolic levels in the orbital prefrontal cortex, the caudate nucleus, and the cingulate cortex (see Brody & Baxter, 1996; Cottraux & Gérard, 1998; Trivedi, 1996, for reviews). Some of these studies have also shown some normalization of at least some of these abnormalities with successful treatment either through the use of medication or behavior therapy (Brody & Baxter, 1996; Cottraux & Gérard, 1998; Trivedi, 1996). There are also findings that implicate abnormalities in the functioning of the basal ganglia (Cottraux & Gérard, 1998; Insel, 1992; Trivedi, 1996), although it is possible that this may be true for only a subset of clients with OCD (Piggot et al., 1996).

Exactly how these areas are implicated is unclear as yet, although several different theories are currently being tested. For example, Baxter et al. (1991) have speculated that the primary dysfunction in OCD may be in an area of the brain called the *striatum,* which is involved in the preparation of appropriate behavioral responses. They cite evidence that when this area is not functioning properly inappropriate behavioral responses may occur, including repeated behaviors such as occur in OCD. They further hypothesize that in OCD there is a dysfunctional interaction of this area with certain areas of the cortex, leading those higher brain areas to become abnormally active. This causes sensations, thoughts, and behaviors that would normally be inhibited (if the striatum were functioning properly) to not be inhibited in clients with OCD. In this case impulses toward aggression, sex, hygiene, and danger ("the stuff of obsessions," p. 116) that most people keep under control with relative ease "leak through" as obsessions in the patient with OCD and lead to distractions from ordinary goal-directed behavior. This would in turn cause the cortex to "cope" through the use of mechanisms such as compulsive rituals in order to dampen the concerns raised by the obsessive thoughts (Baxter et al., 1991, 1992; Brody & Baxter, 1996; Trivedi, 1996).

The Role of Serotonin Pharmacological studies of obsessive-compulsive disorder intensified with the discovery that a drug called Anafranil (clomipramine) is often effective in the treatment of obsessive-compulsive disorder. Although the drug was first discovered to be useful in the treatment of OCD in the late 1960s, double-blind placebo-controlled studies clearly documenting its effectiveness in the treatment of OCD did not

begin to appear until the 1980s (see DeVeaugh-Geiss, 1991). Clomipramine is closely related to other tricyclic antidepressants (see Chapter 6) but is more effective than they are in the treatment of OCD (Murphy et al., 1996). It seems very likely that clomipramine is more effective with OCD than the other tricyclics because it has greater effects on the neurotransmitter serotonin, which is now strongly implicated in OCD. This is also in keeping with the fact that several other antidepressant drugs such as fluoxetine (Prozac) that also have relatively selective effects on serotonin have also been shown to be about equally useful in the treatment of OCD (Dolberg et al., 1996; Koran et al., 1996; Murphy et al., 1996). Indeed, OCD is quite different from the other anxiety and mood disorders in that it most clearly shows a preferential response to drugs that affect serotonin. The other anxiety and mood disorders respond to a wider range of drugs (Dolberg et al., 1996a, 1996b, Murphy et al., 1996).

The exact nature of the dysfunction in serotonergic systems in OCD is as yet unclear (see Gross, Sasson, Chopra, & Zohar, 1998; Murphy et al., 1996). Clomipramine, like Prozac, is known to inhibit the reuptake of serotonin after it has been released into the synapse. This would seem to suggest that it operates through increasing the availability of serotonin, which in turn would seem to suggest that OCD may be characterized by deficiencies in serotonin levels. Unfortunately, however, the story is much more complicated because it is also known from several studies that administration of a drug that is a serotonin-agonist (causing release of serotonin) results in increases in obsessive-compulsive symptoms (Dolberg et al., 1996a, 1996b; Murphy et al., 1996), suggesting that OCD may be characterized by excessively high levels of serotonin. The complex picture that seems to be emerging is that increased serotonin activity and increased sensitivity of some brain structures to serotonin may be involved in OCD symptoms. In this view, long-term administration of clomipramine or Prozac causes a down-regulation of certain serotonin receptors (Dolberg et al., 1996a, 1996b). That is, although the immediate effect of clomipramine or Prozac may be to increase serotonin levels, the long-term effects are quite different. This is consistent with the finding that these drugs must be taken for at least 6 to 12 weeks before significant improvement in OCD symptoms occurs (Dolberg et al., 1996a, 1996b; Liebowitz & Hollander, 1991). However, it is also becoming clear that dysfunction in serotonergic systems cannot by itself fully explain this complex disorder. Other neurotransmitter systems and functional brain abnormalities in certain structures also seem to be involved (Hollander et al., 1992).

In summary, there is now a substantial body of evidence implicating biological causal factors in OCD. This evidence comes from genetic studies, from studies of structural brain functioning, and from psychopharmacological studies. Although the exact nature of these factors and how they are interrelated is not yet understood, major research efforts are currently underway and are sure to enhance our understanding of this very serious and disabling disorder in the next decade.

Treating Obsessive-Compulsive Behavior

As mentioned in the biological causal factors section, research in the early 1980s began to show that medications that affect the neurotransmitter serotonin seem to be the only class of medication studied to date that has reasonably good effects in treating persons with OCD. These selective serotonin-reuptake inhibitors (such as clomipramine or Anafranil, and fluoxetine or Prozac) appear to reduce the intensity of the symptoms of this disorder, with approximately 50 to 70 percent of OCD clients showing at least a 25 percent reduction in symptoms (relative to 4 to 5 percent on placebo) (Dolberg et al., 1996a, 1996b; Koran et al., 1996). Some clients may show greater improvement than this, but approximately 30 to 50 percent do not show what is considered to be clinically significant improvement.

A major disadvantage of drug treatment for OCD, as for other anxiety disorders, is that relapse rates are very high following discontinuation of the drug (approximately 90 percent, Dolberg et al., 1996). Thus many clients who do not seek alternative forms of behavior therapy that have more long-lasting benefits may have to stay on these drugs indefinitely given that OCD, like other anxiety disorders, tends to be a chronic condition if left untreated.

With OCD, a behavioral treatment involving a combination of exposure and (compulsive) response prevention may be in the long run the most effective approach to the difficult problem of obsessive-compulsive disorders (e.g., Foa, Franklin, & Kozak, 1998; Steketee, 1993). This treatment involves having the OCD client repeatedly expose himself or herself to stimuli that will provoke their obsession (such as touching the bottom of their shoe or a toilet seat in a public bathroom for someone with compulsive washing), and then prevent

them from engaging in their compulsive rituals, which they ordinarily would engage in to reduce the anxiety/distress provoked by their obsession. Preventing the rituals is essential so that they can see that the anxiety created by the obsession will dissipate naturally if they allow enough time to pass. This treatment tends to help clients who stick with the treatment, with most showing a 50 to 70 percent reduction in symptoms (Steketee, 1993). On average about 50 percent are much improved or very much improved, and another 25 percent are moderately improved. These results are generally considered superior to those obtained with medication (Foa et al., 1998).

The successful use of this treatment in the case of Mark, the young artist with severe OCD, is described here briefly.

> **Case Study, Mark's Treatment** • Mark was initially treated with medication and with exposure and response prevention. He found the side effects of the medication (clomipramine) intolerable and gave it up within a few weeks. For the behavioral treatment, he was directed to get rid of the tape recorder and was given a series of exercises in which he exposed himself to feared situations where he might confess to a crime or cause harm to others, including making phone calls, mailing letters, and entering stores and public bathrooms (all things he had been unable to do). Checking rituals (including the tape recorder) were prevented. Although the initial round of treatment was not especially helpful, in part because of the distance and difficulty of getting to treatment, he did eventually commit to more intensive treatment by moving to a small apartment closer to the clinic and did quite well.

More detailed examination of this treatment is provided in Highlight 5.4.

Finally, because OCD in its most severe form is such a crippling and disabling disorder, in recent years psychiatrists have begun to reexamine the usefulness of certain neurosurgical techniques for the treatment of severe intractable OCD (which may be the case for as many as 10 percent of people diagnosed with OCD) (Mindus, Rasmussen, & Lindquist, 1994). Before such surgery is even contemplated, the person must have had severe OCD for at least 5 years and not responded to all of the known treatments discussed so far (both behavior therapy and several medications). Several studies have now shown that a significant number of intractable cases with all other known treatments do respond quite well to neurosurgery designed to destroy brain tissue in one of the areas implicated in this condition (Pigott & Seay, 1998). These techniques will be discussed in greater detail in Chapter 16.

GENERAL SOCIOCULTURAL CAUSAL FACTORS FOR ALL ANXIETY DISORDERS

Cross-cultural research suggests that although anxiety is a universal emotion and anxiety disorders probably exist in all human societies, there are many differences in prevalence and in the form of expression of the different disorders in different cultures (Good & Kleinman, 1985; Kirmayer, Young, & Hayton, 1995).

Cultural Differences in Sources of Worry

In the Yoruba culture of Nigeria, there are three primary clusters of symptoms associated with generalized anxiety: (1) worry, (2) dreams, and (3) bodily complaints. The sources of worry are very different than in Western society, however, and they focus on creating and maintaining a large family, and on fertility. Dreams are a major source of anxiety because they are thought to indicate that one may be bewitched. Somatic complaints are also unusual from a Western standpoint. Common ones include "Occasionally I experience heat sensation in my head," I have the feeling of something like water in my brain," "Things like ants keep on creeping in various parts of my brain," and "I am convinced some types of worms are in my head" (Ebigbo, 1982; Good & Kleinman, 1985). Nigerians with this syndrome also often have paranoid fears of malevolent attack by witchcraft (Kirmayer et al., 1995). In India as well there are many more worries about being possessed by spirits and about sexual inadequacy than are seen in generalized anxiety in Western cultures (Carstairs & Kapur, 1976; Good & Kleinman, 1985).

Another culture-related syndrome that occurs in places like China is *Koro*, which for men involves intense acute fear that their penis is shrinking into the body and when this process is complete the sufferer will die. For women, the fear is that their nipples are retracting and their breasts shrinking. Koro tends to occur in epidemics—especially in cultural minority groups when their survival is threatened. It occurs in a cultural context where there are concerns about male sexual potency (Kirmayer et al., 1995).

Taijin Kyofusho

There is also some evidence that the form that certain anxiety disorders take has actually evolved so as to fit within certain cultural patterns. A good example is the Japanese disorder *taijin kyofusho* (TKS), which is related to the Western diagnosis of social phobia. Like social phobia, it refers to a fear of interpersonal relations or a fear of social situations (Kirmayer, 1991; Kleinknecht, et al., 1997; Tseng et al., 1992). However, Westerners with social phobia are afraid of social situations where they may be the object of scrutiny or criticism. By contrast, most people with TKS have a single dominant symptom, which in the past was a fear of blushing but currently seems to be most often a phobia about eye contact—symptoms not mentioned in the DSM-IV description of social phobia (Kirmayer, 1991). Body dysmorphic disorder—the fear that some part of the body is defective or malformed (see Highlight 5.3 Modern Life, p. 196)—is also commonly associated with TKS sufferers, who have a morbid fear of embarrassing or offending others through their inappropriate behavior or their perceived physical defects. That is, they may think that their blushing or eye contact, or their emitting an offensive odor, or their imagined deformity, is causing others significant discomfort. This fear of bringing shame on others or offending them is what leads to social avoidance (Kleinknecht et al., 1997).

Kirmayer (1991; Kirmayer et al., 1995) has argued that the pattern of symptoms that occurs in *taijin kyofusho* has clearly been shaped by cultural factors. Japanese children are raised to be highly dependent on their mothers and to have a fear of the outside world, especially strangers. As babies and young children, they are praised for being obedient and docile. There is also a great deal of emphasis on implicit communication—being able to guess another's thoughts and feelings and being sensitive to them. People who make too much eye contact are likely to be considered to be aggressive and insensitive, and children are taught to look at the throat of people with whom they are conversing rather than into their eyes. The society is also very hierarchical and structured, and many subtleties in language and facial communication are used to communicate one's response to social status.

Kirmayer compares the effects of such Japanese cultural patterns on the symptoms seen in *taijin kyofusho* with the effects of Western cultural patterns on the symptoms seen in social phobia:

> The delusional fear of harming others through one's tense or inappropriate social behavior is rooted in Japanese concerns about the social presentation of self. Other-centered group conformity puts the individual on stage at all times and transforms ordinary awkwardness into a more serious social or moral failing. In Western society, where individu-

ality is emphasized, concern with the feelings of the other does not reach a comparable intensity and so does not promote the formation of rigid preoccupations with injuring or offending others. (Kirmayer, 1991, p. 24)

At a more general level, cross-cultural researchers have noted that recognition of the cognitive component of most anxiety disorders leads one to expect many cross-cultural variations in the form that different anxiety disorders take. Anxiety disorders can be considered to be, at least in part, disorders of the interpretive process. Because cultures influence the categories and schemas that we use to interpret our symptoms of distress, there are bound to be significant differences in the form that anxiety disorders take in different cultures (e.g., Good & Kleinman, 1985; Kirmayer et al., 1995).

GENERAL ISSUES REGARDING TREATMENTS AND OUTCOMES

As seen above in the discussion of each anxiety disorder, treatment may involve a wide range of goals and procedures: alleviating distressing symptoms such as generalized anxiety or panic, changing a person's basically defensive and avoidant lifestyle as in specific and social phobias, or both. Treatment may include medications or psychotherapy, or some combination of these approaches. Most people with anxiety disorders respond quite well to at least certain forms of treatment, although the prognosis may be less favorable when the person has comorbid depression or personality disorders, or severe intractible OCD.

Probably a majority of the misprescribed and abused drugs referred to here are the anxiolytic drugs (minor tranquilizers) used in the treatment of several of anxiety disorders—most notably GAD and panic disorder. A major disadvantage of all drug treatments for anxiety disorders is that relapse rates range from moderate to very high following discontinuation of the drug, and this is especially true of the anxiolytics from the benzodiazepine category, which are also highly addictive, setting up the potential for serious withdrawal symptoms. Thus many clients who do not seek alternative forms of psychotherapy that have more long-lasting benefits may have to stay on these drugs indefinitely given that most of the anxiety disorders tend to be chronic conditions if left untreated. This problem can sometimes be overcome through combining drug and psychosocial treatments, with the goal being to withdraw clients from the drug after they have gained the skills from psychotherapy necessary to deal with their panic or anxiety symptoms directly. However, the results of several recent studies have also shown that such combined treatment may not always have such beneficial effects in the long-term, especially if the patient attributes their gains to the drugs rather than their personal efforts (Barlow et al., submitted; Başoğlu et al., 1994; Marks et al., 1993).

As for traditional psychotherapies that will be discussed more in Chapter 17, most of these are oriented toward helping clients achieve greater understanding of themselves, their problems, and their relationships, and toward helping clients develop healthier attitudes and better coping skills. The various types of therapy included in this general category differ somewhat in their specific goals and procedures—each reflecting the particular psychosocial perspective on which it is based. The psychodynamic approach is specifically directed at helping the patient uncover the repressed conflict that is thought to underlie the symptoms of the anxiety disorder; there is little if any focus on the symptoms themselves. Although traditional psychodynamic psychotherapy may be useful in treating many of the general life problems that a person with an anxiety disorder may have, it does not have an impressive record for helping reduce the prominent symptoms of the anxiety disorder itself. For example, psychodynamic psychotherapy for the treatment of panic attacks or agoraphobia (Wolfe & Maser, 1994), or for obsessive-compulsive disorder (Foa et al., 1998), or specific or social phobias has not proved effective.

Instead, as we have seen, the psychotherapeutic treatments of choice for anxiety disorders all clearly involve behavior therapy techniques or cognitive-behavioral therapy techniques. Behavior and cognitive-behavioral therapy are usually directed toward changing specific "target behaviors"—such as removing phobias—or toward changing specific negative patterns of thinking that maintain anxiety (such as the catastrophic thinking involved in panic disorder), but they often seem to have more far-reaching positive results (Barlow, 1993; Borkovec et al., 1995; Telch et al., 1995). For example, a client who overcomes a specific phobia or panic disorder or generalized anxiety disorder may gain confidence in his or her ability to overcome other problems. Ultimately, the person learns that coping effectively with life's demands and stressors is more rewarding than trying to avoid them. Although outcomes vary considerably, it appears that from 70 to 90 percent of the people who receive appropriate kinds of help for their anxiety disorder obtain substantial benefit from it (Barlow, 1993).

UNRESOLVED ISSUES

Interdisciplinary Research on the Anxiety Disorders

Many of the advances in our understanding of anxiety disorders have been made by biological psychiatrists and psychologists who search for the genetic vulnerabilities, as well as for the biochemical abnormalities and abnormalities of function, that underlie them. Progress in understanding the neurobiology of the anxiety disorders has occurred in tandem with increased understanding of which drug therapies are most effective in treating them. This is because insights derived from neurobiology often lead to new ideas for drugs that may work, and new findings about drugs that are effective often provide new insights about what the neurobiology of a disorder may be.

At the same time many other advances have been made by cognitive and behaviorally oriented psychologists and psychiatrists who search for the psychological vulnerabilities and causes of anxiety disorders. Progress in understanding the cognitive and behavioral factors involved has also occurred in parallel with increased understanding of how best to treat anxiety disorders with cognitive and behavioral therapies. Again, research in this area is a two-way street, with findings about the psychopathology of the disorders giving new insights into possible new effective treatments and vice versa.

What is unfortunate is that these two different lines of research have so often proceeded along relatively independent and unrelated paths. All too often these approaches are pitted against each another as if a disorder has either biological or psychological causes, or as if drugs or psychotherapeutic treatments always constitute the best approach. Clearly this is not generally the case with most forms of psychopathology.

As discussed in Chapter 3, all of our cognitions and behaviors are ultimately reducible to a set of biological events occurring in the brain. What we need to understand is how the events occurring at one level of analysis (cognitive or behavioral) affect events occurring at another level of analysis (physiological) and vice versa.

Adding another layer of complexity, we also need to examine the sociocultural context in which disorders arise and how this can affect the way in which the disorder manifests itself. This is important because there certainly seem to be more cultural variations in the manifestations of disorders such as the anxiety disorders than exist for most medical disorders such as pneumonia, colds, or cancer. This leads us to the importance of developing a coherent biopsychosocial approach to understanding these disorders. Yet progress in this regard for anxiety disorders has been slow.

What are the impediments to this kind of progress? Some seem to stem simply from difficulties mental health professionals with the different orientations have in communicating with one another because of lack of knowledge and understanding of other approaches. For most psychologists, reading and understanding the research reports regarding the neurobiology of these disorders is a difficult task because of their relative lack of knowledge of neuroscience—a field that is advancing at a rapid rate. And for many neuroscientists and biological psychiatrists, reading and understanding the research reports regarding cognitive and behavioral factors associated with these disorders may also be difficult because of their lack of training in these areas.

But lack of knowledge is not the only, or necessarily even the major impediment to progress in developing a biopsychosocial approach to understanding these disorders. Many of the problems stem from the fact that many of these mental health professionals are simply entrenched in their beliefs about the superiority of one approach relative to another. Yet there is hope that this situation may change. Today there are more interdisciplinary research teams consisting of professionals trained in all of these perspectives than there ever have been in the past. They are working on both the psychopathology and the treatment of anxiety disorders. The work of such interdisciplinary teams will be critical to the advancement of a biopsychosocial integrative perspective on these disorders.

SUMMARY

This chapter has been concerned with maladaptive behavior patterns that appear to have anxiety or panic or both at their core. The anxiety disorders were initially considered a subset of the neuroses, but recent versions of the DSM-III and DSM-IV have largely abandoned this term. Fear or panic is a basic emotion that involves activation of the fight-or-flight response of the autonomic nervous system. Anxiety is a more diffuse blend of emotions that includes high levels of negative affect, worry about possible threat or danger, and the sense of being unable to predict threat or to control it if it occurs. Although we all have identifiable, rational, realistic sources of anxieties at times, people with anxiety disorders, by definition, have irrational sources of, and unrealistic levels of, anxiety.

As we have seen, anxiety and panic are each associated with a number of distinct anxiety disorder syndromes. With specific phobias, there is an intense and irrational fear of specific objects or situations; when confronted with a feared object, the phobic person often shows activation of the fight-or-flight response, which is also associated with panic. In social phobia, a person has disabling fears of one or more social situations usually because of fears of negative evaluation by others or of acting in an embarrassing or humiliating manner; in some cases a social phobic may actually experience panic attacks in social situations.

In panic disorder, a person experiences unexpected panic attacks that often create a sense of stark terror, which usually subsides in a matter of minutes. Many people who experience panic attacks develop anxious apprehension about experiencing another one because the attacks can be so terrifying. Many also develop agoraphobic avoidance of situations in which they fear that they might have an attack and would find it difficult to escape or would be especially embarrassed. In cases of severe agoraphobia, the person may become housebound except perhaps when accompanied by a spouse or trusted companion.

In generalized anxiety disorder a person has chronic and excessively high levels of worry about a number of events or activities, and responds to stress with high levels of psychic and muscle tension. In obsessive-compulsive disorder a person experiences unwanted and intrusive distressing thoughts or images that are usually accompanied by compulsive behaviors designed to neutralize those thoughts or images. Checking and cleaning rituals are most common.

Many sources of fear and anxiety are believed to be acquired through conditioning or other learning mechanisms, although some people are more constitutionally predisposed than are others to acquire such responses. Specific phobias do not tend to involve a random or arbitrary group of objects or situations associated with trauma. Instead, we seem to have a biologically based preparedness to acquire fears of objects or situations that posed a threat to our early ancestors.

We also seem to have an evolutionarily based predisposition to acquire fears of social stimuli signaling dominance and aggression from other humans, including facial expressions of anger or contempt. Social phobics are also preoccupied with negative self-evaluative thoughts that tend to interfere with their ability to interact in a socially skillful fashion.

One prominent theory of panic disorder is that this condition may develop in people who are prone to making catastrophic misinterpretations of their bodily sensations, a tendency that may be related to preexisting high levels of anxiety sensitivity. Other biological theories of panic disorder emphasize that the disorder may result from biochemical abnormalities in the brain as well as abnormal activity of the neurotransmitter norepinephrine and probably also serotonin. Panic attacks may arise from the brain areas called the locus coeruleus and the central periacqueductal gray.

Generalized anxiety disorder may occur in people who have had extensive experience with unpredictable and/or uncontrollable life events. In addition, people with generalized anxiety seem to have schemas about how to cope with strange and dangerous situations that promote automatic thoughts focused on possible threats. The neurobiological factors implicated in generalized anxiety are a functional deficiency in the neurotransmitter GABA, which is involved in inhibiting anxiety in stressful situations; the limbic system is the brain area most involved. Thus different neurotransmitters and brain areas are involved in panic attacks and generalized anxiety.

Biological causal factors also seem to be involved in obsessive-compulsive disorder, with evidence coming from genetic studies, studies of structural brain functioning, and psychopharmacological studies. Once this disorder begins, the anxiety-reducing qualities of the compulsive behaviors may help to maintain the disorder. For all the anxiety disorders, once a person has the disorder, mood-congruent information processing, such as attentional and interpretive biases, seems to help maintain them.

Many people with anxiety disorders are treated by physicians, often with drugs designed to allay anxiety. Such treatment focuses on suppressing the symptoms, and it is not without dangers. A number of alternative means of achieving anxiety reduction are available. In general, the cognitive and behavioral therapies have a very good track record with the anxiety disorders. Behavior therapies focus on prolonged exposure to feared situations to allow fear or anxiety to habituate; with obsessive-compulsive disorder the rituals also must be prevented following exposure to the feared situations. Cognitive therapies focus on getting clients to understand their underlying automatic thoughts, which often involve cognitive distortions such as unrealistic predictions of catastrophes that in reality are very unlikely to occur. Once clients can identify these automatic thoughts, therapy focuses on helping them change these inner thoughts and beliefs through a process of logical reanalysis known as cognitive restructuring.

KEY TERMS

anxiety (p. 159)

neurotic behavior (p. 159)

neurosis (p. 159)

fear (p. 160)

panic (p. 160)

anxiety disorder (p. 161)

phobia (p. 161)

specific phobia (p. 161)

social phobia (p. 161)

blood-injection-injury phobia (p. 163)

panic disorder (p. 172)

agoraphobia (p. 174)

interoceptive fears (p. 178)

generalized anxiety disorder (GAD) (p. 183)

obsessive-compulsive disorder (OCD) (p. 192)

obsessions (p. 192)

compulsions (p. 192)

body dysmorphic disorder (BDD) (p. 197)

Mood Disorders and Suicide

Franz Bühler (Pohl),
Untitled (1909-1916).
Bühler was born in
Offenburg in 1864, and
worked as an art
metalworker and lecturer,
but was dismissed from
his position at a vocational
school for his "bizarre
behavior." Diagnosed with
schizophrenia and
institutionalized, he
suffered hallucinations
and withdrew into his
autistic world. He was
later killed by the Nazis.
His artwork is rather
sophisticated, and shows
evidence of his academic
schooling.

Most of us get depressed from time to time. Failing an exam, not getting into one's first choice college or graduate school, breaking up with a romantic partner are all examples of events that can precipitate a depressed mood in many people. However, **mood disorders** involve much more severe alterations in mood, and for much more prolonged periods of time. In such cases the disturbances of mood are intense and persistent enough to be clearly maladaptive, often leading to serious problems in relationships and work performance. In fact, recent estimates are that depression ranked fourth among 150 health conditions in terms of "disease-burden" to society in 1990— that is, total direct costs (such as for treatment) and indirect costs (such as days missed at work, disability, premature deaths, etc.). Moreover, the forecast was that by 2020, depression would be the single leading cause of death (Murray & Lopez, 1996). Consider the following case.

Case Study, A Very Successful "Total Failure" • A prominent businesswoman, Margaret, in her middle years, noted for her energy and productivity, was unexpectedly deserted by her husband for a younger woman. Following her initial shock and rage, she began to have uncontrollable weeping spells and doubts about her business acumen. Decision making became an ordeal. Her spirits rapidly worsened, and she began to spend more and more time in bed, refusing to deal with anyone. Her alcohol consumption increased to the point that she was seldom entirely sober. Within a period of weeks, serious financial losses were incurred owing to her inability, or refusal, to keep her affairs in order. She felt she was a "total failure," a self-attribution that was entirely resistant to alteration by a review of her considerable achievements; indeed, her self-criticism gradually spread to all aspects of her life and her personal history. Finally, members of her family, having become alarmed, essentially forced her to accept an appointment with a clinical psychologist.

Was something "wrong" with Margaret, or was she merely experiencing normal human emotions due to her husband's departure? The psychologist concluded that she was suffering from a mood disorder and initiated treatment. The diagnosis, based on the severity of the symptoms and the degree of impairment, was major depressive disorder.

When significant mood change brings about behavior that seriously endangers a person's welfare, psychologists and other mental health professionals conclude that the person has a mood disorder. Mood disorders are diverse in nature, as is illustrated by the many types of de-

pression recognized in the DSM-IV, listed in Table 6.1. Nevertheless, in all mood disorders (formerly called affective disorders), extremes of emotion or *affect*—soaring elation or deep depression—dominate the clinical picture. Other symptoms are also present, but the abnormal mood is the defining feature.

WHAT ARE MOOD DISORDERS?

The two key moods involved in mood disorders are **mania,** characterized by intense and unrealistic feelings of excitement and euphoria, and **depression,** which involves feelings of extraordinary sadness and dejection. Some people experience both of these kinds of moods at one time or another, but other people only experience the depression. These mood states are often conceived to be at opposite ends of a mood continuum, with normal mood in the middle. Although this concept is accurate to a degree, it cannot explain every instance of mood disorder, because in some cases a patient may have symptoms of mania and depression at the same time. In these cases, the person experiences rapidly alternating moods such as sadness, euphoria, and irritability, all within the same episode of illness.

Our discussion will be organized around the distinction between unipolar and bipolar forms of the mood disorders. In **unipolar disorders,** which are much more frequent, the person experiences only depressive episodes. In **bipolar disorders,** the person experiences both manic and depressive episodes. This distinction is prominent in DSM-IV, and although the unipolar and bipolar forms of mood disorder may not be wholly separate and distinct, there are sufficient differences in symptoms, causal factors, and treatments that it is useful to make this distinction. It is also customary to differentiate the mood disorders by (1) *severity*—the number of dysfunctions experienced in various areas of living and the relative degree of impairment evidenced in those areas; and (2) *duration*—whether the disorder is acute, chronic, or intermittent (with periods of relatively normal functioning between the episodes of disorder). The following discussion reflects these customary divisions as well.

Within each of these general categories of unipolar and bipolar disorders, we begin with the milder mood disturbances. From there, we will move to disorders in which a person's functioning is moderately to severely impaired, as in the case of Margaret described at the outset. Research suggests that we can conceive of mild mood disturbances as being largely on the same continuum as the more severe disorders on which this chapter will fo-

TABLE 6.1   VARIETIES OF DEPRESSION ACCORDING TO DSM-IV

	Diagnosis	Main Features
Unipolar Disorders	**Dysthymia**	For at least the past two years, the person has been bothered for most of the day, for more days than not, by a depressed mood, and at least two other depressive symptoms, but not of sufficient persistence or severity to meet the criteria for major depression. The person cannot have had any manic or hypomanic episodes.
	Adjustment disorder with depressed mood	The person reacts with a maladaptively depressed mood to some identifiable stressor occurring within the past three months. Symptoms stemming from bereavement do not qualify. Once the stressor has terminated, the symptoms must remit within 6 months.
	Major depressive disorder	The person has one or more major depressive episodes in the absence of any manic or hypomanic episodes. Symptoms of a major depressive episode include prominent and persistent depressed mood or loss of pleasure for at least two weeks, accompanied by four or more symptoms such as poor appetite, insomnia, psychomotor retardation, fatigue, feelings of worthlessness or guilt, inability to concentrate, and thoughts of death or suicide.
Bipolar Disorders	**Cyclothymia, depressed**	At present or during the past two years, the person has experienced episodes resembling dysthymia, but also has had one or more periods of hypomania—characterized by elevated, expansive, or irritable mood not of psychotic proportions.
	Bipolar I disorder, depressed	The person experiences a major depressive episode (as in major depressive disorder) and has had one or more manic episodes.
	Bipolar II disorder, depressed	The person experiences a major depressive episode and has had one or more hypomanic episodes.
Other Mood Disorders	**Mood disorder due to a general medical condition**	The person has notably depressed mood, including symptoms associated with major depression, whose primary cause is considered to be due to the direct physiological effects of a general medical condition. The medical conditions include degenerative neurological conditions such as Parkinson's disease, stroke, various metabolic and endocrine conditions, viral infections (including HIV), and certain cancers.
	Substance-induced mood disorder	The person has a prominent and persistent depression that is judged to be due to the direct physiological effects of some drug. The drug may be a drug of abuse, or a medication. The depression may occur in association with intoxication by the drug, or in association with withdrawal from the drug.

cus. Many think that the differences are chiefly of degree, not of kind, a conclusion supported in several recent reviews of the evidence (e.g., Vredenbrug, Flett, & Krames, 1993; Watson et al., 1995b). Others advocate the idea that

there are qualitative differences between mild and moderate depression and severe depression (e.g., Coyne, 1994). Moreover, as we will see even within the categories of unipolar and bipolar disorder, in addition to differences of severity there is considerable heterogeneity of the *ways* in which the mood disorders manifest themselves. Thus there are multiple different subtypes of both unipolar and bipolar disorders. This adds greatly to the complexity of understanding the causal factors of mood disorders because of the likelihood that at least somewhat different causal pathways are important for different subtypes.

The Prevalence of Mood Disorders

Major mood disorders occur with alarming frequency—at least 10 to 20 times more frequently than schizophrenia, for example, and at about the same rate as all the anxiety disorders taken together. Of the two types of serious mood disorders, *unipolar major depression* is much more common, and its occurrence has apparently increased in recent years (Kaelber, Moul, & Farmer 1995; Lewinsohn et al., 1993). The most recent results from the National Comorbidity Survey (Kessler et al., 1994) found lifetime prevalence rates of major depression for males at nearly 13 percent, and lifetime prevalence rates for females at 21 percent (12-month prevalence rates were nearly 8 percent for men and nearly 13 percent for women). These figures illustrate the nearly universal observation that unipolar depression is much more common in women than in men; this difference is similar to the sex differences for many anxiety disorders (see Chapter 5). The issue of sex differences in unipolar depression will be discussed in detail later in the chapter (Highlight 6.1 on page 238). The other type of mood disorder, *bipolar disorder* (in which both manic and depressive episodes occur), is much less common. Estimates of lifetime risk range from 0.4 to 1.6 percent, and there is no discernible difference in the prevalence rates between sexes. Similar rates were found in the recent National Comorbidity Survey (Kessler et al., 1994).

Depression Throughout the Life Cycle

Although most mood disorder cases occur during early and middle adulthood, such reactions may occur anytime from early childhood to old age. For example, one study found that about one-quarter of adults reported the first onset of unipolar depression in childhood or adolescence (Sorenson, Rutter, & Aneshensel, 1991). Depression was once thought not to occur in childhood, but we now know that this is not the case. Although relatively rare, major depressions have been observed in preadolescent youngsters, with estimates that about 2 percent of school age children meet criteria for some form of unipolar disorder, with perhaps another 2 percent exhibiting

chronic mild depression (see Speier et al., 1995, for a review). Even infants may experience a form of depression (commonly known as anaclitic depression or despair) if they are separated for a prolonged period from their attachment figure (usually their mother) (Bowlby, 1973, 1980; Speier et al., 1995). Although there is not universal agreement about whether this is simply a "normal" depressive response to loss, Bowlby (1980) has made a persuasive case that this form of depression observed in infants is at least a "prototype" for depression seen in adulthood.

Although significant depressions do occur in infancy and childhood, the incidence of depression rises sharply during adolescence—a period of great turmoil for many people. Recent figures also suggest that the average age of onset for adolescent depression has been decreasing over the past decade (Lewinsohn, et al., 1993; Speier et al., 1995). It is also during this time period that sex differences in rates of depression first emerge (Nolen-Hoeksema & Girgus, 1994). (See Chapter 14 for further discussion of childhood and adolescent depression.)

Suicide is a distressingly frequent outcome (and always a potential outcome) of significant depressions, both unipolar and bipolar. In fact, depressive episodes are undoubtedly the most common of the predisposing causes leading to suicide. The latter part of this chapter includes a discussion of the causes and prevention of suicide.

UNIPOLAR MOOD DISORDERS

Sadness, discouragement, pessimism, and hopelessness about being able to improve matters are familiar feelings to most people. Depression is unpleasant when we are in it, but it usually does not last long. Sometimes it seems almost to be self-limiting, turning off after a period of days or weeks, or after it has reached a certain intensity level. Sometimes we may experience it as having been in some sense useful: We were stuck, and now we can move on; what bothered us was easier to get out of than we thought it could be, and our new perspective may offer new possibilities.

This scenario contains hints that may be significant to our understanding of depression generally. For example, that mild depression may actually be adaptive in the long run; that much of the "work" of depression seems to involve facing images, thoughts, and feelings that one would normally avoid; and that depression may sometimes be self-limiting. These considerations suggest that the capacity to experience depression may be "normal"—even desirable—if the depression is brief and mild. They also suggest the idea of normal depressions—depressions we would expect to occur in anyone undergoing painful but common life events, such as significant personal, interpersonal, or economic losses.

Depressions That Are Not Mood Disorders

Normal depressions are almost always the result of recent stress. In fact, as discussed in Chapter 4, some depressions are considered adjustment disorders (those that develop in response to stressors) rather than mood disorders. However, such sharp distinctions may not be accurate. Indeed, many depressions meeting criteria as "major" are also clearly related to the prior occurrence of stress (Brown & Harris, 1978; Kessler, 1997; Monroe & Simons, 1991). We will consider some of the milder forms of normal depression in the following sections.

Loss and the Grieving Process   We usually think of grief as the psychological process one goes through following the death of a loved one—a process that appears to be more damaging for men than women (Stroebe & Stroebe, 1983). Although this may be the most common and intense cause of grieving, many other types of loss will give rise to a similar state. Loss of a favored status or position, separation or divorce, financial loss, the breakup of a romantic relationship, retirement, separation from a friend, absence from home for the first time, or even the loss of a cherished pet may all give rise to symptoms of acute grief.

Whatever its source, grief has certain characteristic qualities. Indeed, Bowlby (1980) has observed that there are usually four phases of response to the loss of a spouse or close family member:

1. Numbing and disbelief that may last from a few hours to a week and which may be interrupted by outbursts of intense distress, panic, or anger

2. Yearning and searching for the dead person, which may last for months or occasionally for years

3. Disorganization and despair

4. Some level of reorganization

In the second phase (which resembles anxiety more than depression), the grieving person may show great restlessness, insomnia, and preoccupation with the dead person; anger is also very common in this phase and is entirely normal. The intensity of the yearning and search gradually diminishes. The third phase of despair sets in when the person finally accepts the loss as permanent and finds it is necessary to discard old patterns of think-

ing, feeling, and acting, including establishing a new identity (e.g., as a widow or widower). During this phase, the person may meet the criteria for a major depression. Gradually, however, most people pass into the fourth phase and begin to rebuild their lives. The ability to respond to the external world is gradually regained, sadness abates, zest returns, and a person emerges into a more productive engagement with the challenges of life. This has generally been considered to be the *normal* pattern. The process of grieving following bereavement is normally completed within one year (Clayton, 1982). Some people, however, become stuck somewhere in the middle of the sequence, and if depressive symptoms persist beyond the first year after loss, therapeutic intervention may be called for. This is often called chronic grief and may occur in 10 to 20 percent of bereaved individuals (Jacobs, 1993; Middleton et al., 1996).

Ignoring for the moment such potential complications, it is easy to see grief as having an adaptive function

We usually think of grief as the psychological process a person goes through following the death of a loved one. We see here a man grieving at his wife's grave. Grief may accompany other types of loss as well, including separation or divorce, or loss of a pet.

Major Depressive Disorder

The diagnostic criteria for **major depressive disorder** require that the person exhibit more symptoms than are required for dysthymia and the symptoms be more persistent (not interwoven with periods of normal mood). An affected person must experience either markedly depressed mood or marked loss of interest in pleasurable activities most of every day for at least two weeks. In addition, the person must experience at least four more of the following symptoms during the same period: (1) fatigue or loss of energy; (2) insomnia or hypersomnia (that is, too little or too much sleep); (3) decreased appetite and significant weight loss without dieting (or, much more rarely, their opposites); (4) psychomotor agitation or retardation (a slowdown of mental and physical activity); (5) diminished ability to think or concentrate; (6) self-denunciation to the point of claiming worthlessness or guilt out of proportion to any past indiscretions; and (7) recurrent thoughts of death or thoughts of suicide.

Most of these symptoms (at least five, including either sad mood, or loss of interest or pleasure) must be present all day and nearly every day for two consecutive weeks before the diagnosis is applicable. The diagnosis of major depression is not made if a patient has ever experi-

enced a manic or hypomanic episode; in such a case, the current depression is viewed as a depressive episode of bipolar disorder, which is discussed in the next section.

It should be noted that few, if any, depressions—including milder ones—occur in the absence of significant anxiety (Akiskal, 1997; Mineka et al., 1998). As discussed later in this chapter, the issues surrounding the co-occurrence of depression and anxiety, which have received an enormous amount of attention in recent years, are very complex (see Highlight 6.2 on page 240).

The following conversation between a therapist and a 34-year-old woman illustrates a major depression of moderate severity.

than I had and when something bad happened to them I was glad. . . . All my flaws stand out and I am repugnant to everyone. [Sighs] I am a miserable failure. . . . There is no hope for me.

Cognitive and Motivational Symptoms As this conversation between a woman and her therapist illustrates, a person with major depression shows not only mood symptoms of sadness but also a variety of cognitive and motivational symptoms that are more severe than in milder forms of depression. In this case the person shows various cognitive distortions, including being firmly convinced that she is a failure and that her family also thinks so. She vacillates between anger at her friends and family for not being trustworthy, and self-hatred and self-blame. Because of her sense of hopelessness about her future, she shows no motivation to try to improve her situation. Her problems with friends who appear to no longer be close to her occur commonly with depression because, as we will see, most people find it aversive to be around depressed persons.

Subtypes of Major Depression Several subcategories of major depression have been defined according to the particular symptom patterns displayed. Such efforts are driven mostly by the hope of distinguishing causes and effective treatments for the different subtypes. One such subcategory in DSM-IV is major depression of the **melancholic type.** This designation is applied when, in addition to meeting the criteria for major depression, a patient has either loss of interest or pleasure in almost all activities, or does not react to usually pleasurable stimuli or desired events. In addition, the patient must also experience at least three of the following: (1) early morning awakenings, (2) depression being worse in the morning, (3) marked psychomotor retardation or agitation, (4) significant loss of appetite and weight, (5) inappropriate or excessive guilt, or (6) the depressed mood has a qualitative difference from the sadness experienced following a loss or during a nonmelancholic depression. This severe subtype of depression is associated with a higher genetic loading than other forms of depression (Kendler, 1997). It has also been found that patients with this subtype of depression may be more likely to respond to electroconvulsive treatment or to tricyclic antidepressant medications than to selective serotonin reuptake inhibitors (Gitlin, 1996; Roose et al., 1994). The chief theoretical importance of the melancholia con-

Someone who has major depression is not only sad, but also shows a host of other symptoms such as feelings of worthlessnss or guilt, diminished ability to think or concentrate, loss of energy, loss of appetite, and sometimes recurrent thoughts of death or suicide.

cept is that it is strongly linked in the psychiatric literature to the idea of *endogenous* causation—that is, to the notion that certain depressions are caused "from within," so to speak, and are unrelated to any stressful events in a patient's life. We will have more to say about this in a later section.

Psychotic symptoms, characterized by loss of contact with reality, and including delusions (false beliefs) or hallucinations (false sensory perceptions), may sometimes accompany the other symptoms of major depression. In such cases a diagnosis of **severe major depressive episode with psychotic features** is made. Ordinarily, any delusions or hallucinations present are **mood-congruent**— that is, they seem in some sense "appropriate" to serious depression because the content is negative in tone. Additional examples of mood-congruent delusions might involve themes of personal inadequacy, guilt, deserved punishment, death, disease, and so forth. For example, the delusional idea that one's internal organs have totally deteriorated—an idea sometimes held by severely depressed people—ties in with the mood of a despondent person. In contrast, the idea that one has been chosen by the Deity for a special mission to save humankind is inconsistent with the self-abnegation normally seen in depression. The latter type of disordered thinking is termed **mood-incongruent**—that is, delusional thinking that is inconsistent with the predominant mood. Mood-incongruent thinking is usually associated with a poorer prognosis. Psychotically depressed individuals are more likely to show some of the symptoms of melancholia and to have a poorer long-term prognosis than are nonpsychotic depressives (Coryell, 1997).

Distinguishing Major Depression Discriminating major depression from other forms of depressive disorder is not always easy. Major depression may coexist with dysthymia in some people, a condition given the designation "double depression" (Keller & Shapiro, 1982; Hirschfeld & Hanks, 1997). Double depressives are people who are moderately depressed on a chronic basis and who undergo increased problems from time to time, during which they manifest "major" depressive symptoms. Among clinical samples of dysthymics, the experience of double depression appears to be common, although it may be much less common in dysthymics who never seek treatment (Akiskal, 1997). For example, in one clinical sample of dysthymics studied by Klein, 54 percent were in a major depressive episode at the time they sought treatment, and 75 percent reported a lifetime history of one or major depressive episodes; other studies have found comparable or even higher rates of double depression in dysthymics (Keller et al., 1997; Klein et al., 1993). Although nearly all double depressives appear to recover from their major depressive episode (at least for awhile), less than half are likely to recover from the dysthymia as well (Keller et al., 1997).

Depression as a Recurrent Disorder When a diagnosis of major depression is made, it is usually also specified whether this is a *single* (initial) episode or a *recurrent* episode (one or more previous episodes have already occurred). This reflects the fact that depressive episodes are usually time-limited (with the average duration of an untreated episode being about six months according to DSM-IV). In a large untreated sample of depressed women, certain predictors pointed to a longer time to spontaneous remission of symptoms: having financial difficulties, obsessive-compulsive symptoms, severe stressful life events, and high genetic risk (Kendler, Walters, & Kessler, 1997). However, depressions often recur following a period of remission of symptoms for at least two months. In recent years **recurrence** has been distinguished from **relapse,** where the latter term refers to the return of symptoms within a fairly short period of time and probably reflects the fact that the underlying episode of depression has not yet run its course (Frank et al., 1991; Keller et al., 1982). Relapse may commonly occur, for example, when pharmacotherapy is terminated prematurely after symptoms have remitted but before the underlying episode is really over (Hollon et al., 1996; Shelton et al., 1991).

The proportion of patients who will exhibit a recurrence of major depression is difficult to estimate reliably; studies have found wide variations. Based on an extensive review of nearly all studies done between 1970 and 1993, Piccinelli and Wilkinson (1994) estimated that 26 percent of patients experienced a recurrence within one year of recovery and 76 percent experienced a recurrence within ten years of recovery. The same review estimated that approximately 10 to 12 percent show persistent depression over five- and ten-year follow-up (see also Keller et al., 1997). There is also evidence that the probability of recurrence increases with the number of prior episodes. Conversely, the probability of recurrence seems to decrease the longer the person remains symptom free. People with psychotic depression are somewhat more likely to relapse than those without psychotic features, and later episodes are also more likely to be characterized by psychotic features than is true for patients whose first episode is not characterized by psychotic features (Coryell, 1997).

Persons who experience recurrent depressions can be distinguished from those who experience only a single episode in a number of ways. Those with some form of recurrent depression show not only greater severity in terms of number and frequency of symptoms, but also many more suicide attempts, a much higher proportion with a family history of depression, more work and social impairment, and higher divorce rates (Merikangas, Wicki, & Angst, 1994). They also have more impaired social functioning between episodes (Keller et al., 1997).

Most of these estimates of recurrence rates come from samples of treated patients, and it is also important to determine whether comparable rates of recurrence occur in untreated samples. Using a large community sample, Lewinsohn, Zeiss, and Duncan (1989) found the probability of relapse or recurrence was 46 percent over the lifetime, somewhat lower than those reported in most other studies for treated patients. Younger subjects were more prone to have a recurrence. The occurrence of stressful life events also made recurrence more likely (see Gotlib & Hammen, 1992).

The traditional view has been that between episodes, a person suffering from a recurrent major mood disorder is essentially normal. This view has been increasingly called into question as more research data have become available (Coryell & Winokur, 1982, 1992), and some have raised the possibility that major depressive episodes may leave "scars" that may leave a person at risk for future recurrences. Such scars might include fears about having another depression, continuing low-grade symptoms, including resignation, pessimism, or insecurity. Evidence of the scar hypothesis at this point is mixed (Klein et al., 1993; Rohde, Lewinsohn, & Seeley, 1990). The probability of depression leaving scars may be especially likely in younger persons and in those who have experienced multiple episodes (Gotlib & Hammen, 1992), and in those with the melancholic subtype of depression who appear to continue to show residual cognitive and neuropsychological deficits between episodes (Marcos et al., 1994).

Seasonal Affective Disorder   Some people who experience recurrent depressive episodes show a seasonal pattern, commonly known as **seasonal affective disorder.** To meet DSM-IV criteria for recurrent major depression with a seasonal pattern, the person must have had at least two episodes of depression in the past two years occurring at the same time of the year (most commonly the fall or winter), and full remission must also have occurred at the same time of the year (most commonly the spring). In addition, the person cannot have had other nonseasonal depressive episodes in the same two-year period, and most of their lifetime depressive episodes must have been of the seasonal variety. Prevalence rates suggest that winter seasonal affective disorder is more common in people living at higher latitudes (northern climates) and in younger people. As will be discussed later, there has been a great deal of interesting research on this relatively recently identified subtype of depression.

BIPOLAR DISORDERS

As we have seen, despite their seeming opposition, depression and mania are sometimes closely related; and some people even experience both states simultaneously. As with the unipolar disorders, the severity of disturbance in bipolar disorder ranges from mild to moderate

People who live in higher latitudes (northern climates for those in the northern hemisphere) are more likely to exhibit seasonal affective disorder in which depression occurs primarily in the fall and winter months and tends to remit in the spring or summer months.

to severe. In the mild to moderate range the disorder is known as *cyclothymia,* and in the moderate to severe range the disorder is known as *bipolar disorder.*

Cyclothymia

As we have noted, mania is in some ways the opposite of depression. It is a state involving excessive levels of excitement, elation, or euphoria, often liberally mixed with inflated self-esteem or grandiosity and the assumption of great powers. Periods of intense irritability are also often intermixed (Whybrow, 1997). In its milder forms it is known as **hypomania.** It has long been recognized that some people are subject to cyclical mood changes with relative excesses of hypomania and depression that, though substantial, are not disabling. These, in essence, are the symptoms of the disorder known as **cyclothymia** (see Table 6.1).

Changes in the DSM classification reflect current thinking about cyclothymia. In DSM-I and DSM-II, this pattern was included under the category of personality disorders (see Chapter 9). By contrast, the DSM-III-R and DSM-IV definitions of cyclothymia make the pattern sound like a less serious version of major bipolar disorder, minus certain extreme symptoms and psychotic features, such as delusions, and minus the marked impairment caused by full-blown manic or major depressive episodes. In the depressed phase of cyclothymia, a person's mood is dejected, and he or she experiences a distinct loss of interest or pleasure in usual activities and pasttimes. In addition, the person may exhibit sleep irregularity (too much or too little); low energy levels; feelings of inadequacy; decreased efficiency, productivity, talkativeness, and cognitive sharpness; social withdrawal; restriction of pleasurable activities, including a relative lack of interest in sex; a pessimistic and brooding attitude; and tearfulness. A cyclothymic does not, however, experience enough of the symptoms, or experience them persistently enough, to qualify for a diagnosis of major depression (similar to someone with dysthymia except without the duration criterion).

Symptoms of the hypomanic phase of cyclothymia are essentially the opposite of the symptoms of dysthymia, except that the sleep disturbance is invariably one of an apparent decreased need for sleep. As in the case of bipolar disorder, no obvious precipitating circumstance may be evident for the abrupt change in mood and an affected person may have significant periods between episodes in which he or she functions in a relatively adaptive manner. To qualify for a diagnosis of cyclothymia, however, there must be at least a two-year span during which there are numerous periods with hypomanic and depressed symptoms (only one year is required for adolescents and children).

As already noted, many clinicians feel that cyclothymia is but a milder variant of bipolar disorder, and evidence for this view has in recent years become quite compelling (Whybrow, 1997). For example, there are people with cyclothymic personality organization who have some symptoms of cyclothymia, although not enough to qualify for the diagnosis. These people are at higher-than-average risk for serious mood disorder episodes (e.g., Goplerud & Depue, 1985; Klein & Depue, 1984; Klein, Depue, & Slater, 1985, 1986). Using a group of college students, researchers developed a hypomanic personality inventory scale that postdicted (that is, identified those individuals who had had) not only hypomanic episodes but other maladaptive patterns, including depression. This study is significant because it suggests that people who experience cyclothymia have a distinctive personality style which includes some symptoms of cyclothymia even when they are not in a hypomanic or a depressive episode (see also Akiskal, Khani, & Scott-Strauss, 1979; Akiskal, 1989; Whybrow, 1997).

The following case illustrates cyclothymia.

Case Study, A Cyclothymic Car Salesman • A 29-year-old car salesman was referred by his current girlfriend, a psychiatric nurse, who suspected he had a mood disorder, even though the patient was reluctant to admit that he might be a "moody" person. According to him, since the age of 14 he has experienced repeated alternating cycles that he terms "good times and bad times." During a "bad" period, usually lasting four to seven days, he oversleeps 10 to 14 hours daily, lacks energy, confidence, and motivation—"just vegetating," as he puts it. Often he abruptly shifts, characteristically upon waking up in the morning, to a three-to-four-day stretch of overconfidence, heightened social awareness, promiscuity, and sharpened thinking—"things would flash in my mind." At such times he indulges in alcohol to enhance the experience, but also to help him sleep. Occasionally the "good" periods last seven to ten days, but culminate in irritable and hostile outbursts, which often herald the transition back to another period of "bad" days. He admits to frequent use of marijuana, which he claims helps him "adjust" to daily routines.

In school, A's and B's alternated with C's and D's, with the result that the patient was considered a bright student whose performance was mediocre overall because of "unstable motivation." As a car salesman his performance has also been uneven, with "good days" canceling out the "bad days"; yet even during his "good days" he is sometimes perilously argumentative with customers and loses sales that appeared sure. Although considered a charming man in many social circles, he alienates friends when he is hostile and irritable. He typically accumulates social obligations during the "bad" days and takes care of them all at once on the first day of a "good" period. (Spitzer et al., 1994, pp. 155–156)

In short, cyclothymia consists of mood swings that, at either extreme, are clearly maladaptive but of insufficient intensity to merit the major disorder designation.

Bipolar Disorders

Although recurrent cycles of mania and melancholia were recognized as early as the sixth century, it remained for Kraepelin, in 1899, to introduce the term *manic-depressive insanity* and to clarify the clinical picture. Kraepelin described the disorder as a series of attacks of elation and depression, with periods of relative normality in between, and a generally favorable prognosis. Today DSM-IV calls this illness **bipolar disorder.**

Bipolar disorder is distinguished from major depression by at least one episode of mania. Any given episode is classified as depressive, manic, or mixed, according to its predominant features. The depressed or manic classification is self-explanatory. A mixed episode is characterized by symptoms of both manic and major depressive episodes, whether the symptoms are either intermixed or alternate rapidly every few days. Such cases were once thought to be relatively rare but are increasingly recognized as relatively common (Cassidy et al., 1998).

Even though a patient may be exhibiting only manic symptoms, it is assumed that a bipolar disorder exists and that a depressive episode will eventually occur. Thus, there are no officially recognized "unipolar" manic or hypomanic counterparts to dysthymia or major depression. The implicit assumption is that all mania-like behaviors must be part of a cyclothymic or bipolar disorder, or perhaps exist along a continuum on which these two conditions fall. Although some researchers have noted the probable existence of a unipolar type of manic disorder (Andreasen, 1982; Nurnberger et al., 1979), critics of this diagnosis argue that such patients usually have bipolar relatives and may well have had mild depressions that went unrecognized (Winokur & Tsuang, 1996).

Bipolar disorder, even more than major depression, is typically a recurrent disorder; single episodes are extremely rare (Winokur & Tsuang, 1996). As with unipolar major depression, the recurrences can be seasonal in nature, in which case **bipolar disorder with a seasonal pattern** is diagnosed. Although most patients with bipolar disorder experience periods of remission when they are relatively symptom free, as many as 20 to 30 percent continue to experience significant impairment (occupational and/or interpersonal) and mood lability. Moreover, a few chronic patients continue to meet diagnostic criteria over long periods of time, even years, sometimes despite the successive application of all standard treatments. It is not known whether these "refractory" cases represent fundamentally different psychopathological entities (Akiskal & Simmons, 1985).

Features of Bipolar Disorder The features of the depressive form of bipolar disorder are usually clinically indistinguishable from those of major depression (Perris, 1992; American Psychiatric Association, 1994), although some studies do report higher rates of psychomotor retardation, oversleeping, and overeating in the depressed phase of bipolar disorder (Cassano et al., 1992; Whybrow, 1997). Nevertheless, the essential difference is that these depressive episodes alternate with manic ones. In about two-thirds of cases, the manic episodes either immediately precede or immediately follow a depressive episode; in other cases the manic and depressive episodes are separated by intervals of relatively normal functioning. Before modern treatments were available, the periods of disorder often gradually lengthened over a person's lifetime, leaving the person in one phase of the illness or the other nearly all the time (Whybrow, 1997).

DSM-IV also identified a form of bipolar disorder called *Bipolar II disorder,* in which the person may not experience full-blown manic episodes, but has experienced clear-cut hypomanic episodes (as in cyclothymia). That this is indeed a distinct disorder is suggested by findings that Bipolar II disorder evolves into Bipolar I disorder (the type already described with full-blown manic episodes—usually simply called "bipolar disorder") in less than 5 percent of cases (Coryell, Endicott, & Keller, 1987). If Bipolar II disorder were simply a milder early version of Bipolar I disorder, one would expect that a much higher percentage of cases of Bipolar II would evolve into Bipolar I disorder. Figure 6.1 illustrates the different kinds of patterns of manic and depressive episodes that can be seen in bipolar disorder.

Manic symptoms in bipolar disorder tend to be extreme, and there is significant impairment of occupational and social functioning. A person who experiences a manic episode has a markedly elevated, euphoric, and expansive mood, often interrupted by occasional outbursts of irritability or even violence—particularly when others refuse to go along with the manic person's antics and schemes. This mood must persist for at least a week to qualify for a diagnosis. In addition, three or more of the following symptoms must also occur in the same time period: A notable increase in goal-directed activity may occur, which sometimes may appear as an unrelievable restlessness, and mental activity may also speed up, so that the person may evidence a "flight of ideas" or thoughts that "race" through the brain. Distractibility, high levels of verbal output in speech or in writing, and a severely decreased need for sleep may also occur. In addition, inflated self-esteem is common and when severe becomes frankly delusional, so that the person harbors feelings of enormous grandeur and power. Finally, personal and cultural inhibitions loosen, and the person may indulge in foolish ventures with a high potential for painful consequences, such as foolish business ventures, major spending sprees, and sexual indiscretions.

A recent large study of 237 manic patients also revealed that during manic episodes some patients also report intermixed symptoms of depressed mood, anxiety, guilt, and suicidal thoughts (Cassidy et al., 1998). Although no prior research had revealed such findings so clearly (except for the symptoms of irritability), it is very much in keeping with clinical observations of manic patients. One possible explanation is that the dysphoria comes from feelings of being out of control with their manic behaviors and feelings (Barlow et al., 1996). Mixed episodes seem to be more common in women than in men (Leibenluft, 1996).

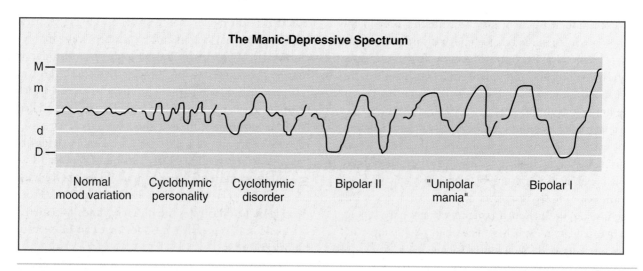

FIGURE 6.1   THE MANIC-DEPRESSIVE SPECTRUM
There is spectrum of bipolarity in moods. All of us have our ups and downs, which we refer to as normal mood variation. People with a cyclothymic person-ality have more marked and regular mood swings, and people with cyclothymic disorder go through periods during which they meet the criteria for dys-thymia (except for the two-year duration), and other periods when they meet criteria for hypomania. People with Bipolar II disorder have periods of major depression as well as periods of hypomania. Unipolar mania is an extremely rare condition. Finally, people with Bipolar I disorder have periods of major de-pression and periods of mania. (Adapted from Goodwin & Jamison, 1990.)

Source: From Frederick K. Goodwin and Kay J. Jamison, *Manic Depressive Illness.* Copyright © 1990 Oxford University Press, Inc. Used by permission of Oxford University Press.

The following conversation illustrates a manic episode of moderate severity. The patient is a 46-year-old woman.

Case Study, Therapy Session with a Moderately Manic Patient

DOCTOR: Hello, how are you today?

PATIENT: Fine, fine, and how are you, Doc? You're looking pretty good. I never felt better in my life. Could I go for a schnapps now. Say, you're new around here, I never saw you before—and not bad! How's about you and me stepping out tonight if I can get that sour old bat-tleship of a nurse to give me back my dress. It's low cut and it'll wow 'em. Even in this old rag, all the doc-tors give me the eye. You know I'm a model. Yep, I was number one—used to dazzle them in New York, London, and Paris. Hollywood has been angling with me for a contract.

DOCTOR: Is that what you did before you came here?

PATIENT: I was a society queen . . . entertainer of kings and presidents. I've got five grown sons and I wore out three husbands getting them . . . about ready for a couple of more now. There's no woman like me, smart, brainy, beautiful, and sexy. You can see I don't believe in playing myself down. If you are good and

know you're good you have to speak out, and I know what I've got.

DOCTOR: Why are you in this hospital?

PATIENT: That's just the trouble. My husbands never could un-derstand me. I was too far above them. I need some-one like me with savoir faire you know, somebody that can get around, intelligent, lots on the ball. Say, where can I get a schnapps around here—always like one before dinner. Someday I'll cook you a meal. I've got special recipes like you never ate before . . . sauces, wines, desserts. Boy, it's making me hungry. Say, have you got anything for me to do around here? I've been showing these slowpokes how to make up beds but I want something more in line with my talents.

DOCTOR: What would you like to do?

PATIENT: Well, I'm thinking of organizing a show, singing, danc-ing, jokes. I can do it all myself but I want to know what you think about it. I'll bet there's some schnapps in the kitchen. I'll look around later. You know what we need here . . . a dance at night. I could play the piano, and teach them the latest steps. Wherever I go I'm the life of the party.

This case is particularly illustrative of the inflated self-esteem characteristic of a manic person. The erotic suggestiveness and impatience with routine seen here are also common features of manic episodes.

Because a person who is depressed cannot be diagnosed as bipolar unless he or she has exhibited at least one manic episode in the past, many people with bipolar disorder whose initial episode or episodes are depressive will be misdiagnosed at first, and possibly throughout their lives (if no manic episodes are observed or reported, or if they die before a manic episode is experienced). Estimates vary widely across studies (0 to 37.5 percent), but averaging across studies a recent review estimated that about 10 to 13 percent of people who have an initial major depressive episode will later have a manic or hypomanic episode and at that time will be diagnosed as having Bipolar I or II disorder (Akiskal et al., 1995).

Such misdiagnoses are unfortunate and important because there are different treatments of choice for unipolar and bipolar depression. Moreover, there is even evidence suggesting that some antidepressant drugs used to treat what is thought to be unipolar depression may actually precipitate manic episodes in patients who actually have as yet undetected bipolar disorder, thus worsening the course of the illness (Goodwin & Ghaemi, 1998; Whybrow, 1997). On the other hand, misdiagnosis is automatically prevented if a person first has manic symptoms: By DSM-IV definition, this would be a bipolar disorder even though, as already noted, some researchers believe that a very rare unipolar form of manic disorder may actually exist.

People with bipolar disorder seem in some ways to be even more unfortunate than those who suffer from recurrent major depression. On average they suffer from more episodes during their lifetimes than do persons with unipolar disorder (although these episodes tend to be somewhat shorter). Indeed, according to DSM-IV more than 90 percent of those who have one manic episode will go on to have further episodes (see also Coryell et al., 1995). As many as 5 to 10 percent of persons with bipolar disorder experience at least four or more episodes (either manic or depressive) every year, a pattern known as **rapid cycling.** In fact, those who go through periods of rapid cycling usually experience many more than four episodes a year; in one treatment clinic for this condition, the average was 16 episodes a year (Whybrow, 1997). Rapid cycling is more common in women than men and is sometimes precipitated by taking certain kinds of antidepressants (Leibenluft, 1996; Whybrow, 1997). Fortunately, for many, rapid cycling is a temporary phenomenon and gradually disappears (Coryell et al., 1995).

Overall, the probabilities of "full recovery" from bipolar disorder (that is, being symptom-free for a period of four to seven years) are discouraging. One 10-year prospective study of over 200 patients found that 24 percent had re-

Many highly creative people are believed to have had bipolar disorder, going through periods of intense productivity in their creative medium during manic phases, and often through unproductive periods when clinically depressed. Two such individuals are the German composer Robert Schumann (1810–1856) and the English novelist Virginia Woolf (1882–1941). Schumann was committed to a mental asylum in 1854 and died there two years later. Woolf committed suicide by drowning herself.

lapsed within six months of recovery; 77 percent had had at least one new episode within four years of recovery, and 82 percent by seven years (Coryell et al., 1995). Many of theses recurrences occurred in spite of maintenance lithium therapy discussed later in this chapter.

Schizoaffective Disorder

Occasionally, clinicians are confronted with a patient whose mood disorder is as severe as those seen in the major depressive or bipolar disorders but whose mental and cognitive processes are so out of touch with reality as to suggest the presence of a schizophrenic psychosis (see Chapter 12). Such cases are likely to be diagnosed as **schizoaffective disorder** in the DSM-IV category. To receive this diagnosis, a person must have a period of illness during which he or she meets criteria for both a major mood disorder (unipolar or bipolar) and at least two major symptoms of schizophrenia (such as hallucinations and delusions). However, during at least two weeks of the illness they must experience the schizophrenic symptoms in the absence of prominent mood symptoms; and they must meet criteria for a mood disorder for a substantial portion of the period of illness. In spite of its inclusion in the DSM, the diagnosis of schizoaffective disorder is a controversial one. Some clinicians believe these persons are basically schizophrenic; others believe they have primarily psychotic mood disorders; and still others consider this disorder a distinct entity with some recent good evidence supporting its validity as a separate category (Kendler et al., 1995).

The often severe disturbances of psychological functioning seen in these cases, such as mood-incongruent delusions and hallucinations, are indeed reminiscent of schizophrenic phenomena. Unlike schizophrenia, however, the schizoaffective pattern tends to be highly episodic, with a relatively good prognosis for individual attacks and often with relatively lucid periods between episodes. Although it was once thought that schizoaffective patients had a relatively good prognosis for full recovery, recently published follow-up data on these patients cast considerable doubt on such a benign outlook (Kendler et al., 1995; Winokur & Tsuang, 1996). According to DSM-IV, the prognosis is probably better than that for schizophrenia but considerably worse than that for mood disorders (see also Kendler et al., 1995; Winokur & Tsuang, 1996).

CAUSAL FACTORS IN UNIPOLAR DISORDERS

In considering the development of major mood disorders, we again find it useful to examine the possible roles of biological, psychosocial, and sociocultural factors. We will first examine what is known about the causes of unipolar disorders, followed by a discussion of the causes of bipolar disorders.

Biological Causal Factors

It has long been known that a variety of diseases and drugs can affect mood, sometimes leading to depression, and sometimes to elation or even hypomania. Indeed, this idea goes back to Hippocrates, who hypothesized that depression was caused by an excess of "black bile" in the system (c. 400 B.C.). Thus, it is not surprising that researchers have sought to determine whether there is a biological basis for at least some of the depressive disorders. Investigators attempting to establish a biological basis for unipolar disorders have considered genetic and constitutional factors as well as neurophysiological, neuroendocrinological, and biochemical alterations. A good deal of attention has also been focused on disturbances in many of our biological rhythms, including the effects of seasonal variations in light and darkness.

Hereditary Factors The prevalence of mood disorders is higher among blood relatives of persons with clinically diagnosed mood disorders than in the population at large (e.g., Plomin et al., 1997). Some studies have suggested that this higher prevalence of mood disorders in first-degree relatives is especially true for endogenous or melancholic depression (relative to other types of unipolar depression), but other studies have not found such a difference (see Katz & McGuffin, 1993; Plomin et al., 1997). Because of the difficulties of disentangling hereditary and environmental influences, however, a higher rate of disorder among family members can never in itself be taken as conclusive proof of genetic causation.

Twin studies have also suggested that there may be a moderate genetic contribution to unipolar depression. Plomin et al. (1997) reviewed evidence from five studies showing that monozygotic co-twins of a twin with unipolar major depression are about two to four times as likely to develop major depression as are dizygotic co-twins of a depressed twin. However, the actual rates of concordance differ quite a bit, at least in part because of differences in diagnostic criteria used across studies—a problem that is almost inevitable since diagnostic criteria change over time as our understanding of diagnostic subtypes changes. For example, one large twin study used a variety of different definitions of "major depression" that have been used over the years and found that heritability estimates ranged from 33 to 45 percent—simply resulting from the use of different definitions of depression. The evidence for a genetic contribution is much less consistent for milder forms of unipolar depression such as dysthymia (Katz & McGuffin, 1993; Plomin et al., 1997; Roth & Mountjoy, 1997), and indeed some twin studies have not found any evidence of a genetic contribution to these milder but more chronic forms of unipolar depression.

A number of years ago the adoption method of genetic research was applied to the study of mood disorders. If a predisposition to develop a given disorder is heritable, it should show up (so the logic goes) more often among biological relatives of the affected adoptees than among biological relatives of control adoptees. Of the limited number of adoption studies on mood disorders published thus far, the most adequate is one that found that unipolar depression occurred in 2.1 percent of the biological relatives of the severely depressed subjects and in 0.3 percent of the biological relatives of control cases (a seven-fold increase); completed suicide was 13 times more likely among biological relatives of depressed patients (3.9 percent) than in biological relatives of control cases (0.3 percent) (Wender et al., 1986). Although these are substantial differences, the actual numbers are probably underestimates because the study relied exclusively on medical records without direct interviews and family history information.

In spite of the weak results from adoption studies, based on the rest of the family and twin evidence presented so far, the case for some hereditary contribution in the causal patterns of unipolar major depression is quite strong, although not as strong as for bipolar disorder (Katz & McGuffin, 1993; Plomin et al., 1997). For example, several good studies estimate that genes contribute between 33 to 50 percent of the variance in the tendency to develop (that is, the liability for) unipolar depression. However, any genetic contribution to more minor depressive disorders is likely to be very modest at best (Roth & Mountjoy, 1997).

Biochemical Factors   Starting in the 1960s, the view that depression may arise from disruptions in the delicate balance of neurotransmitter substances that regulate and mediate the activity of the brain's nerve cells, or neurons, has received a great deal of attention. Neurotransmitters, released by the activated presynaptic neuron, mediate the transfer of nerve impulses across the synaptic cleft from one neuron to the next in a neuronal pathway; they may either stimulate or inhibit the firing of the next neuron in the chain (see Highlight 3.1 on p. 70).

A large body of evidence suggests that various biological therapies (discussed later in the chapter) often used to treat severe mood disorders—such as electroconvulsive therapy and antidepressant drugs—may affect the concentrations or the activity of neurotransmitters at the synapse and thus determine the extent to which particular brain pathways are relatively volatile or sluggish in conducting messages. In fact, the largely accidental discovery of these treatments (particularly the antidepressant drugs), and initial explanations of how they work, are what encouraged the development of biochemical theories of the etiology of major depression.

Early attention in the 1960s and 1970s focused primarily on three neurotransmitter substances of the monoamine class—norepinephrine, dopamine, and serotonin—because researchers observed that antidepressant medications seemed to have the effect of increasing their availability at synaptic junctions. This observation led to the monoamine hypothesis—that depression was at least sometimes due to an absolute or relative depletion of one or all of these neurotransmitters at important receptor sites in the brain (Schildkraut, 1965). This depletion could come about either through impaired synthesis of these neurotransmitters in the presynaptic neuron, or through increased degradation of the neurotransmitters once released into the synapse, or through altered function of postsynaptic receptors (Thase & Howland, 1995).

However, it is now clear, some 35 years later, that no such straightforward mechanism is likely to provide the answers we need (e.g., Shelton et al., 1991; Thase & Howland, 1995; Whybrow, 1997). For example, some studies have found exactly the opposite of what is predicted by the monoamine hypothesis—that is, net increases in norepinephrine activity in depressed patients (see Thase & Howland, 1995, for a review). In addition, it is also now known that even though the immediate short-term effects of antidepressant drugs are to increase the availability of norepinephrine and serotonin, the long-term effects of these drugs (when they actually begin to have their clinical effects two to four weeks later) are to produce functional *decreases* in available norepinephrine and serotonin by reducing the number of several different norepinephrine and serotonin receptors in the postsynaptic neurons, thereby reducing the number of sites where messages can be transferred.

Unfortunately, the early monoamine theory has not been replaced by a compelling alternative. Initially, research attention shifted to a concern that depression may be associated with abnormal receptor systems (see Highlight 3.1)—that is, the large molecules on a postsynaptic neuron to which neurotransmitters bearing the appropriate chemical codes selectively bond—much like a lock and key that must fit together or match to work (Sedvall et al., 1986; Thase & Howland, 1995). This shift of attention occurred because of findings that antidepressant drugs, when administered for at least several weeks (long enough to have a therapeutic antidepressant effect), decrease the number and sensitivity of certain types of receptors and increase the responsiveness of others (Shelton et al., 1991; Thase & Howland, 1995). Unfortunately, the yield from such studies has not yet provided any firm etiological conclusions; as we will see, attention has shifted in the past 15 years toward more integrative theories that do not focus exclusively on biochemical systems and to the extent that they do focus on biochemical systems, it is more on their interactions than on single neurotransmitters.

Neuroendocrine and Neurophysiological Factors

There has also been a good deal of research on the possible neurophysiological and neuroendocrine (hormonal) correlates of some distinguishable forms of mood disorder (Checkley, 1992; Shelton et al., 1991; Thase & Howland, 1995). Ideas about hormonal influences on mood have a long history. One contemporary theory (e.g., Holsboer, 1992; Stokes & Sikes, 1987; Thase & Howland, 1995) has focused on the hypothalamic-pituitary-adrenal axis, and in particular on the hormone *cortisol,* which is excreted by the outermost portion of the adrenal glands and is regulated through a complex feedback loop (see Figure 3.1). Blood plasma levels of this substance are known to be elevated in from 50 to 60 percent of seriously depressed patients (Holsboer, 1992), suggesting a possible clue of etiological significance. Even more intriguing, however, is the finding that a potent suppressor of plasma cortisol in normal individuals, *dexamethasone,* either fails entirely to suppress or fails to sustain suppression of cortisol in about 45 percent of seriously depressed patients (Shelton et al., 1991; Thase & Howland, 1995). This means that the complex feedback loop involved in regulation of the entire hypothalamic-pituitary-adrenal-cortical axis is not operating properly in these "dexamethasone non-suppressors."

These findings, in themselves essentially undisputed, gave rise some years ago to widespread use of the *dexamethasone suppression test (DST)* in assessing depressed individuals. At first it was suggested that DST nonsuppressor patients constitute a distinct subgroup among depressed people—namely, the group sometimes referred to as having an "endogenous" or melancholic form of depression (Holsboer, 1992). Consistent with this idea was evidence showing that nonsuppression is in fact correlated with clinical severity (and occurs in 60 to 90 percent of the most severe melancholic and psychotic depressives). It is also correlated with positive response to drug treatment—another feature of melancholic depression (e.g., Shelton et al., 1991; Thase & Howland, 1995). However, over time it has become apparent that several other groups of psychiatric patients exhibit high rates of nonsuppression, calling into question the specificity and hence the diagnostic utility of the DST for depression (Goodwin & Jamison, 1990; Thase & Howland, 1995). This suggests that nonsuppression may merely be a nonspecific indicator of generalized mental distress.

The other endocrine system that has relevance to depression is the hypothalamic-pituitary-thyroid axis, because it is known that disturbances to this axis are also linked to mood disorders (Checkley, 1992; Marangell et al., 1997; Thase & Howland, 1995). For example, people with low thyroid levels (a condition known as *hypothyroidism*) often become depressed. In addition, about 25 to 40 percent of depressed patients who have normal thyroid levels show dysregulation of this axis as evidenced through abnormal responses to thyrotropin-releasing hormone (which through a complex sequence of steps leads to increased levels of thyroid hormone). In addition, administration of the same thyrotropin-releasing hormone improves the mood and sense of motivation and coping for both normal and psychiatric subjects (Loosen, 1986; Shelton et al., 1991). As with the dexamethasone suppression test, however, abnormal response to thyrotropin-releasing hormone also occurs in a number of other psychiatric and medical illnesses, and so it is not useful as a diagnostic tool (Thase & Howland, 1995).

Other exciting neurophysiological research in recent years has followed up on earlier neurological findings showing that lesions of the left (but not the right) anterior or prefrontal cortex (as, for example, from having a stroke in that region) often lead to depression (e.g., Robinson & Downhill, 1995). This led to the idea that perhaps depression in people without brain lesions is nonetheless linked to lowered levels of brain activity in this same region. Several recent studies have supported this idea. When one measures the electroencephalographic (EEG) activity of both cerebral hemispheres in depressed patients, one finds that there is an asymmetry or imbalance in the EEG activity of the two sides of the anterior (prefrontal) regions of the brain. In particular, depressed persons show relatively low activity in the left hemisphere in these regions (Henriques & Davidson, 1991; Davidson, 1998). It also seems that this may be a risk marker for depression, since patients in remission show the same pattern (Henriques &

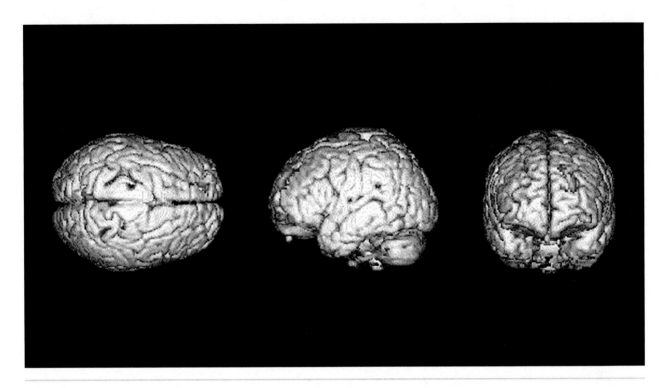

A PET scan from the Thase and Howland 1995 study showing decreased metabolism in the interior regions of the cerebral hemispheres.

Davidson, 1990), as do children at risk for depression (Tomarken, Siemien, & Garber, 1994). Studies using brain imaging techniques such as positron emission tomography (PET) also suggest that severely depressed patients show decreased metabolism in the anterior (prefrontal) regions of the cerebral hemispheres and especially on the left side (see Thase & Howland, 1995, for a review). Although this is a relatively new area of research, it seems to hold promise as a way of identifying persons at risk, both for an initial episode and for recurrent episodes.

Sleep and Other Biological Rhythms Although findings of sleep disturbances in depressed patients have existed as long as depression has been studied, only recently have some of these findings been linked to more general disturbances in biological rhythms. As we will see, these links provide some of today's most interesting biologically based etiological hypotheses.

Sleep is characterized by five stages that occur in a relatively invariant sequence throughout the night (Stages 1 to 4 of non-REM sleep, and REM sleep). REM sleep (rapid eye movement sleep) is characterized by rapid eye movements and dreaming, as well as other bodily changes; the first REM period does not usually begin until near the end of the first sleep cycle, about 75 to 80 min-

utes into sleep. Depressed patients, especially those with melancholic features, show a variety of sleep problems, ranging from early morning awakening, periodic awakening during the night (poor sleep maintenance), and, for some, difficulty falling asleep. Such changes occur in about 80 percent of hospitalized depressed patients and about 50 percent of depressed outpatients. Moreover, research using EEG recordings has found that many depressed patients enter the first period of REM sleep after only 60 minutes or less of sleep (i.e., less than the typical 75 to 80 minutes), as well as show greater amounts of REM sleep early in the night, than are seen in nondepressed persons. One recent study found this to be the most common in endogenous depression (65 percent), and least common in nonendogenous major depression (35 percent) (Rush et al., 1997). Because this is the period of the night when most deep sleep (Stages 3 and 4) usually occurs, the depressed person also receives a lower than normal *amount* of deep sleep. These findings suggest disturbances in both the overall sleep-wake cycle rhythms and the REM sleep rhythm (Shelton et al., 1991; Thase & Howland, 1995). Some of these sleep disturbances remain even when the depression remits, and one recent study found that some of them are present in people who are at high genetic risk for depression (Lauer et al., 1995).

Circadian Rhythms Humans have many other circadian (24-hour or daily) cycles other than sleep, including body temperature, propensity to REM sleep, and secretion of cortisol, thyroid-stimulating hormone, and melatonin (a hormone secreted by the pineal gland at the base of the brain during the dark). These circadian rhythms are controlled by two related central "oscillators," which act like internal biological clocks. The strong oscillator (so named because it is relatively impervious to environmental influence) controls the regulation of body temperature, hormones such as cortisol, and REM sleep rhythms. The weak oscillator (so named because it does readily respond to environmental influence) controls the rest-activity and sleep-wake cycles (Goodwin & Jamison, 1990). Research has found some abnormalities in all of these rhythms in depressed patients, though not all patients show abnormalities in all rhythms (Shelton et al., 1991; Thase & Howland, 1995). Although there is no agreement yet about the exact nature of the dysfunctions, there seems to be increasing agreement that some kind of circadian rhythm dysfunction is not just a symptom of depression but may actually play a causal role in many of the clinical features of depression. Two current theories that need further research are (1) that the size or magnitude of the circadian rhythms are blunted, or (2) that the various circadian rhythms that are normally well synchronized become desynchronized (Thase & Howland, 1995).

Several theorists have even gone so far as to propose that the primary biological disturbance in depression is in the regulation of the circadian system, with alterations in neurotransmitters occurring as a secondary consequence to the disturbed rhythms (Goodwin & Jamison, 1990; Healy & Williams, 1988). An alternative comprehensive theory is one hypothesizing that there is a dysregulation in one or more neurotransmitter systems in depression (Siever & Davis, 1985). These irregularities in neurotransmitter activity are thought in turn to be responsible for the changes in the neuroendocrine system and in the circadian rhythms. These theories can account for many of the seeming discrepancies of prior findings in the literature, but considerably more research is required to determine how valid they are (see Shelton et al., 1991; Thase & Howland, 1995).

Sunlight and Seasons Another rather different kind of rhythm abnormality or disturbance may be seen in subtype of unipolar depression known as *seasonal affective disorder* discussed earlier. In this subtype of mood disorder, most patients seem to be responsive to the total quantity of available light in the environment (Oren & Rosenthal, 1992), with a majority (but not all) becoming depressed in the fall and winter and normalizing in the spring and summer (Wehr et al., 1986; Whybrow, 1997). Research in animals has also documented that many seasonal variations in basic functions such as sleep, activity, and appetite are related to the amount of light in a day (which except near the equator is much greater in summer than in winter). For depressed patients who fit the seasonal pattern, they usually showed increased appetite and hypersomnia rather than decreased appetite and insomnia (Dalgleish Rosen, & Marks, 1996). They also have clear disturbances in their circadian cycles, showing weaker 24-hour patterns than normal individuals (Teicher et al., 1997). There is now a good deal of research on patients with seasonal affective disorder demonstrating the therapeutic use of controlled exposure to light, even artificial light (Oren & Rosenthal., 1992; Dalgleish et al., 1996). The mechanisms through which light therapy works for seasonal affective disorder are still not well understood, but research in this area is giving many clues to the underlying biological dysfunctions, and it still remains possible that light therapy works by reestablishing normal biological rhythms (Fava & Rosenbaum, 1995).

Summary of Biological Causal Factors A comprehensive review of the biological factors implicated in major depression (Thase & Howland, 1995) summarized the primary findings as follows:

- Any simple theory such as the early monoamine theory of depression is clearly not supported. Depression is not caused simply by isolated deficits in one or more neurotransmitter systems. Moreover, given the heterogeneity of unipolar depression (e.g., dysthymia, unipolar depression with or without melancholic and psychotic features), it is highly unlikely that any single abnormality would be found in all patients.

- Severe depressions (especially those with melancholic and/or psychotic features) are clearly associated with multiple interacting disturbances in neurobiological regulation, including neurochemical, neuroendocrine, and neurophysiological systems.

- There is far greater evidence for biological abnormalities in severe depressive syndromes; those with dysthymia or uncomplicated major depression (which make up about 75 percent of those seen in community surveys) may show few if any biological abnormalities.

- Some biological disturbances occur only when the person is actively depressed (e.g., high levels of cortisol, poor sleep efficiency, increased norepinephrine activity), but others are more like traits and remain present between episodes (e.g., reduced REM latency and reduced deep sleep).

- Biological disturbances occur in several different functional neurobiological systems. For example, the behavioral facilitation system (e.g., Depue & Spoont, 1986) which underlies appetite behaviors such as eating, sexual behavior, and goal-directed behaviors more generally, is clearly impaired in those people who experience reduced appetite and libido, loss of interest and pleasure. In addition, the stress response system is chronically overactivated during severe depression as indicated, for example, by high levels of cortisol. Regulation of biological rhythms is also clearly disturbed. Finally, executive functions of the cortex, which include problem solving and the ability to concentrate, are also clearly impaired and may be related to the findings of reduced activity in the left prefrontal cortex. (See Thase & Howland, 1995, for more details.)

Psychosocial Causal Factors

Growing awareness of biological factors in the etiology of unipolar depressive disorders does not, of course, imply that psychosocial factors are irrelevant. Indeed, evidence for important psychological causal factors in most mood disorders is at least as strong as evidence for biological factors. However, biochemical and psychosocial approaches to understanding the mood disorders can be made compatible because in many ways they are simply working at different levels of analysis. As discussed in Chapter 3, psychological and behavioral factors implicated in causing depression ultimately are reducible to a set of biological events occurring in the brain and central nervous system, even if how this occurs is not yet completely understood.

Stressful Life Events as Causal Factors   Psychosocial stressors are known to be involved in the onset of a variety of disorders, ranging from some of the anxiety disorders to schizophrenia, but nowhere has their role been more carefully studied than in the case of unipolar depression (e.g., Kessler, 1997). Indeed, many investigators have been impressed with the high incidence of stressful life events that apparently serve as precipitating factors for unipolar depression (Kessler, 1997). The most frequently encountered precipitating circumstances in depression include the following:

- Situations that tend to lower self-esteem, like being fired or failing an important exam.

- The thwarting of an important goal or the posing of an insoluble dilemma, such as being told the fellowship you were counting on to support you in graduate school is no longer available.

- Developing a physical disease or abnormality that activates ideas of deterioration or death, such as being diagnosed with cancer.

- Single stressors of overwhelming magnitude, such as the death of a child for a parent.

- Several stressors occurring in a series, such as the breakup of an important romantic relationship, followed by doing poorly at school or work.

- Insidious stressors unrecognized as such by an affected person, such as living with a depressed or physically disabled person who needs a lot of care.

Perhaps not surprisingly, separations from people important in one's life (through death, for example) are strongly associated with depression, although such losses tend to precede other disorders as well (Kessler, 1997). Another serious stressor that has been the focus of study only fairly recently is caregiving to a spouse with a debilitating disease such as Alzheimer's (formerly known as senility), which is known to be associated with the onset of both major depression and generalized anxiety disorder for the caregiver (e.g., Russo et al., 1995). Finally, in recent years there has been attention paid to the fact that depressed people sometimes generate stressful life events in part as a byproduct of their depressed state (e.g., Davila et al., 1995; Hammen, 1991). For example, depression is associated with poor interpersonal problem solving (such as resolving conflicts with a spouse or child), which in turn leads to higher levels of interpersonal stress, which in turn leads to further symptoms of depression. This may also involve failure to keep up with routine tasks such as paying bills, which may result in getting in trouble with the telephone or electric company or the Internal Revenue Service.

Research on stress and the onset of depression is complicated by the fact that depressed people have a distinctly negative view of themselves and the world around them (Beck, 1967), and so at least to some extent their perceptions of stress may *result* from the cognitive symptoms of their disorder rather than causing their disorder (Kessler, 1997; Monroe & Simons, 1991). That is, because of their pessimistic outlook, they may evaluate events as stressful that an independent evaluator (or a nondepressed friend) would not. Therefore researchers have developed more complex and sophisticated measures of life stress that do not rely on the depressed person's self-report of how stressful an event is (e.g., Brown & Harris, 1978; Dohrenwend et al., 1995; Kessler, 1997). But because relatively few studies have used these more sophisticated strategies, much of the research literature on the association of depression and life stress as assessed by self-report is difficult to evaluate.

In several studies using these sophisticated measurements of life stress, Brown and Harris (1978, 1989) have concluded that depression often follows from one or more severely stressful events, usually involving some loss or exit from one's social sphere. (Interestingly, events signifying danger or threat were found more likely to precede the onset of anxiety disorders [Finlay-Jones & Brown, 1981; Paykel, 1982b]). Indeed, when comparing the incidence of such stressful events in depressed subjects with that in nondepressed controls, Brown and Harris (1978) estimated that stressful life events played a causal role in the depression of about 50 percent of their subjects. In another sophisticated study, Dohrenwend and colleagues (1986) found that depressed patients had more negative life events of three types in the year before the onset of their depression than did nondepressed controls: physical illness and injury, fateful loss events such as death or divorce, and events that disrupted their social network such as having to move to a new state because of one's job. Kessler's recent review (1997) of this literature also suggests that the relationship between stressful life events and depression is much stronger in people who have had one or more previous episodes than in those who are having their first onset.

Endogenous Depression For one subtype of major mood disorder that is not officially recognized in DSM-IV but is still widely discussed in the literature—*endogenous depression*—there is a strong implication that it occurs *de novo*—out of the blue, so to speak. If endogenous depression occurs in the absence of significant psychosocial antecedents, it must be caused entirely from within. This idea of endogenous causation is most compatible with a strong version of the biomedical model. However, there is at least some evidence that the onset of so-called endogenous depressions does not differ substantially from other forms of depression in terms of the frequency with which major life events are associated with their onset (e.g., Bebbington et al., 1988). Indeed, the problems in defining exactly what is meant by endogenous depression, as well as findings that it is often associated with precipitating life events, may be part of the reason why it is not officially recognized in DSM-IV (although major depression with melancholia is a similar construct).

Chronic Strains Whether mildly stressful events and chronic strains are also associated with the onset of de-

pression is more controversial. Using their sophisticated strategies for assessing life stress, Brown and his colleagues, and Dohrenwend and his colleagues, have not found minor stressful events, and only occasionally chronic strains, to be associated with the onset of clinical depression (e.g., Dohrenwend et al., 1995). However, other studies have found minor events and chronic strains to be associated with the onset of depression (e.g., Bebbington et al., 1988; Billings, Cronkite, & Moos, 1983; Lewinsohn, Hoberman, & Rosenbaum, 1988). Although these are well-conducted studies, their results should be interpreted with some caution given that subjects rated stressful events at the follow-up period when they were depressed, and this may have colored their perceptions of what constituted minor life events and chronic strains. Given the dozens of studies in this area, it is perhaps best to rely on findings from a review of the literature that concluded that chronic stressors (such as poverty) and minor events may be associated with an increase in depressive symptoms but probably not major depression (Monroe & Simons, 1991).

Individual Differences in Responses to Stressors If we take the position—and the available research data seem

If a woman living in poverty is already genetically at risk for depression, the stresses associated with living in poverty may be especially likely to precipitate a major depression.

to justify doing so—that some people are constitutionally more prone than others to develop mood disorders, then it would seem reasonable to suppose that such high-risk persons would be more susceptible to the effects of severely stressful events. Recent evidence has shown that, at least for women, those at genetic risk for depression not only experienced more stressful life events (Kendler & Karkowski-Shuman, 1997), but they are also more sensitive to them (Kendler et al., 1995). That is, they are three times more likely than those not at genetic risk to respond to severely stressful life events with depression. However, there is also evidence for the idea that a large percentage of the population (perhaps half) is at risk for depression if they are exposed to one or more severe life events (Monroe & Simons, 1991). For example, Brown and Harris (1978) found that among depressed women, more than 60 percent (compared with about 20 percent of nondepressed women) had had one or more severe life events in the past two to six months. Looked at from a different perspective, with one severe life event the odds were about 50/50 of becoming depressed, but with two severe events the odds were about 75/25 of becoming depressed, and with three or more severe events 100 percent of the women became depressed (although there was a very small sample in this category). This suggests that nearly any person who experiences a series of misfortunes can become clinically depressed.

Vulnerability and Invulnerabilty Factors It is obvious from these findings, however, that not everyone with one or two severe life events becomes depressed. What makes one vulnerable or invulnerable? Brown and Harris (1978) found some interesting answers in their classic study of women living in a poor area of inner London. Of women experiencing a severe event, there were four factors associated with not becoming depressed: (1) having an intimate relationship with a spouse or lover, (2) having no more than three children still at home, (3) having a part-time or full-time job outside the home, and (4) having a serious religious commitment. Conversely, not having a close relationship with a spouse or lover, having three children under five at home, not having a job, and having lost a parent by death before the age of 11 were strongly associated with the onset of depression following a major negative life event. Finally, the genetic evidence discussed above suggests that those at low genetic risk for depression will be more invulnerable to the effects of major stressors and those at high genetic risk more vulnerable (Kendler et al., 1995).

How Stressors Act One way in which stressors may act is through their effects on biochemical and hormonal bal-

ances, and on biological rhythms (see Chapter 4). Whybrow (1997), in a summary of research in this area, suggest that psychosocial stressors may cause long-term changes in brain functioning and that these changes may play a role in the development of mood disorders. Essentially the same point has been made by other leading researchers in the field (Akiskal, 1979; Thase et al., 1985; Thase & Howland, 1995).

Types of Diathesis-Stress Models for Unipolar Depression We can now turn to the more general question of how stress interacts with various types of vulnerability factors to produce depression. As noted in Chapter 3, psychopathology researchers have long advocated the use of the **diathesis-stress model** for understanding the development of certain kinds of psychopathology such as schizophrenia and they have more recently begun to do so for depression as well. The idea is that people who eventually develop a disorder differ in some underlying way from those who do not, and this underlying difference is known as their diathesis (or predisposition). However, among those with the diathesis, only those who experience stress will actually develop the disorder. Originally it was assumed that the diathesis was constitutional or biological in origin (e.g., Meehl, 1962; Rosenthal, 1963), but more recently depression researchers have also begun to propose diatheses for depression that are cognitive and social rather than constitutional (e.g., Abramson et al., 1989, 1995; Metalsky et al., 1982).

One kind of diathesis-stress model for depression has already been discussed in the context of biological causal factors. As we saw, there is substantial evidence for some heritability for unipolar depression. Yet even among monozygotic twins there is only about 50 percent concordance, suggesting that a large role is left for environmental factors such as stressful life events in determining which of those who inherit the predisposition will develop the disorder. Moreover, at present we do not know what the nature of this genetic predisposition is. It may be some kind of constitutional weakness, for example, or it may be a personality trait.

Personality and Cognitive Diatheses Another general kind of diathesis-stress model for depression proposes that personality variables play a role in predisposition to depression. In two reviews of many studies of this type, researchers concluded that there was good evidence that neuroticism is the primary personality variable that serves as a vulnerability factor for depression (and anxiety as well) (Clark et al., 1994; Parker & Hadzi-Pavlovic, 1997).

Neuroticism Personality psychologists currently use the term *neuroticism* or negative affectivity to refer to a stable and heritable personality trait that involves a temperamental sensitivity to negative stimuli (Tellegen, 1985). That is, people who are high on this trait are prone to experiencing a broad range of negative moods, including not only sadness, but also anxiety, guilt, and hostility. In addition to serving as a vulnerability factor, neuroticism is also associated with a worse prognosis for complete recovery from depression. L.A. Clark and colleagues (1994) also concluded that there is some evidence (but more limited than that for neuroticism) that low levels of extraversion or positive affectivity may also serve as a vulnerability factor for depression. Positive affectivity involves a disposition to feel joyful, energetic, bold, proud, enthusiastic, and confident; people low on this disposition tend to feel unenthusiastic, unenergetic, dull, flat, and bored. It is therefore not surprising that this might make them more prone to depression.

There are several other personality dimensions and cognitive diatheses that have also been associated with a vulnerability to depression that will be discussed in more detail later in the context of cognitive theories of depression. The cognitive diatheses focus on particular negative patterns of thinking that people prone to depression may have, which make them more prone to become depressed when faced with one or more stressful life events. For example, people who attribute negative events to internal, stable, and global causes may be more prone to becoming depressed than do people who attribute the same events to unstable and specific causes (e.g., Abramson et al., 1978, 1989, 1995). A pessimistic or depressive attribution for receiving a low grade on an exam, for example, would be "I'm stupid" (i.e., the cause is internal—"I," stable because intelligence is not likely to change much, and global because stupidity is likely to affect a wide range of issues in one's life). A more optimistic attribution for the same event would be "The teacher made up the test in a bad mood and made it especially difficult" (i.e., the cause is external—the teacher, unstable because the teacher hopefully isn't always in a bad mood, and specific because it was only this one teacher for this one course).

Early Parental Loss as a Diathesis Another diathesis-stress model is based on evidence that early parental loss through death or permanent separation can create a vulnerability for depression. Beck (1967) provided some early clinical observations on this point in the context of his cognitive model of depression, although such a diathesis can be formulated in psychodynamic terms as well. Considerable research since that time has documented such observations. For example, in the classic Brown and Harris (1978) study, the incidence of depression was three times higher in women who had lost their mother before the age of 11 (see also Bowlby, 1980). Moreover, Brown and Harris also found that the type of loss (by death versus by divorce or separation) also affected the severity of the depression experienced in adulthood. Women who had experienced loss by death were more likely to develop severe psychotic depression, whereas women who had experienced loss by divorce or separation were more likely to develop less severe neurotic depression (see also Barnes & Prosen, 1985; Roy, 1985, for similar results). If parental loss occurs through suicide, it doubtless adds an additional layer of problems for child survivors and potentially into adulthood as well.

However, a number of studies have not found any evidence that early parental loss produces a vulnerability to depression in adulthood. In a comprehensive review, Gotlib and Hammen (1992) concluded that it seems that the contradictory findings can be resolved if one considers the quality of parental care following the loss. In cases where the child continues to receive good parental care, a vulnerability to depression may not be created. However, if parental loss is followed by poor parental care, a vulnerability to depression is likely to be created (Bifulco, Brown, & Harris, 1987; Harris, Brown, & Bifulco, 1986). More generally, Kessler (1997) has reviewed evidence that the early lives of depressed adults were often marked by a variety of childhood adversities (ranging from family turmoil to parental psychopathology and physical or sexual abuse), independent of parental loss. On average, depressed adults tend to remember more strained and unhappy relationships with their parents than do nondepressed adults, and mothers and siblings have tended to corroborate the depressed patients' memories (Brewin, Andrews, & Gotlib, 1993). Thus, poor early parenting, whether or not it occurs in the context of parental loss, seems to create a vulnerability to depression in adolescence and adulthood; this may be especially true for people with dysthymia beginning in adolescence, compared to people with major depression (Lizardi et al., 1995).

Summary of Diathesis-Stress Models Several different diathesis-stress models have been proposed for depression. Some propose a genetic or constitutional diathesis, which in conjunction with stressful life events can lead to depression. Other models suggest that personality variables, such as neuroticism, or cognitive variables such as pessimism or dysfunctional beliefs provide the diathesis, which in interaction with negative life events can produce depression. Finally, models proposing the importance of parental loss or poor parental care, especially in early childhood, have also received a good deal of attention. It should be understood that none of these models is mutually exclusive, and some may simply be describing the same diathesis in different terms or at different levels of analysis. For example, there is probably a genetic basis for neuroticism (Carey & DiLalla, 1994), and neuroticism seems to be correlated with pessimism (L. A. Clark et al., 1994; Luten, Ralph, & Mineka, 1997), and so these two proposed diatheses may be closely interrelated. Moreover, poor early parenting and parental loss have been strongly implicated in the formation of some of the other cognitive diatheses (Beck, 1967; Bowlby, 1980). Thus, these two proposed diatheses may simply differ in whether they operate distally (poor early parenting) or proximally (negative thinking patterns) in contributing to vulnerability for depression.

We now turn to five major psychological theories of depression that have received much attention in recent years.

Psychodynamic Theories   In his classic paper "Mourning and Melancholia" (1917), Freud noted the important similarity that we discussed earlier between the symptoms of clinical depression and the symptoms seen in someone mourning a lost loved one. Freud and a colleague, Karl Abraham (1911/1960a, 1916/1960b), both hypothesized that when a loved one dies, the mourner regresses to the oral stage of development (when the infant cannot distinguish self from others) and introjects or incorporates the lost person, feeling all the same feelings toward the self as toward the lost person. These feelings were thought to include anger and hostility because Freud believed that we unconsciously hold negative feelings toward those we love, in part because of their power over us. Freud hypothesized that depression could also occur in response to imagined or symbolic losses. For example, a student who fails in school or who fails at a romantic relationship may experience this symbolically as a loss of her parents' love.

The primary difference that Freud observed between mourning and depression was that depressed people show lower self-esteem and are more self-critical. He further hypothesized that these self-accusations are really unconsciously directed at the lost love object (real or symbolic), and do not occur in normal grief, if the person has had a childhood characterized by good attachment relationships. By contrast, the person who is predisposed to becoming depressed is someone who has either experienced the loss of a mother or whose parents did not fulfill the infant's needs for nurturance and love. In both cases, the infant will grow up feeling unworthy of love, have low self-esteem, and be prone to depression when faced with real or symbolic losses (Bemporad, 1995).

Later psychodynamic theorists such as Klein (1934) and Jacobson (1971) emphasized even more than did Freud the importance of the quality of the early mother-infant relationship in establishing a vulnerability (or invulnerability) to depression. Bowlby (1973, 1980), who started as a psychoanalyst and later developed the integrative approach known as attachment theory discussed in Chapter 3, also extensively documented a child's need for a secure attachment to parental figures in order to be resistant to depression (and anxiety) in later life. As we saw earlier, much research supports this position. Bowlby also described two personality types—the anxiously attached and the compulsively self-reliant—which predispose one to depression. People who are anxiously attached are overly dependent on significant others and fear abandonment, and they are hypothesized to become this way because of perceived or real parental neglect in childhood. People who are compulsively self-reliant have little desire for interpersonal relations, and they are hypothesized to become this way because their parents were critical or rejecting (Ouimette & Klein, 1993). At the same time these later theorists emphasized a decrease in or threat to self-esteem as a critical issue (Bibring, 1953) and de-emphasized the idea of regression to an oral stage of development (Jacobson, 1971).

Perhaps the most important contribution of the psychodynamic approaches to depression has been to note the importance of loss (both real and symbolic or imagined) to the onset of depression and to note the striking similarities between the symptoms of mourning and the symptoms of depression (Bowlby, 1980). Even theorists who disagree with many of the specific details of these theories have found it imperative that their own theories also be able to account for these basic observations.

Behavioral Theories   Over the past 25 years several variations on behavioral theories of depression have been proposed. For example, Ferster (1973, 1974) argued that depression could be equated with a state of extinction from positive reinforcement—that is, a state in which the person's responses no longer produce positive reinforcement. He noted that this was consistent with the idea that major losses in one's life—which we know can precipitate depression—can be associated with loss of significant sources of reinforcement such as when an important relationship ends, and there is a subsequent loss of friendship, a sexual partner, etc. Lewinsohn (1974; Lewinsohn et al., 1985; Lewinsohn & Gotlib, 1995) elaborated on this model and proposed that depression can be elicited when a person's behavior no longer brings the accustomed reinforcement or gratification—for example, when someone loses a job. The failure to receive positive reinforcement contingent on one's responses, or an increase in the rate of negative reinforcements, leads in turn to a reduction in effort and activity, thus resulting in even less chance of coping with aversive conditions and achieving need gratification. One problem that can lead to a low rate of positive reinforcement is a deficit in social skills, which makes it difficult for a person to obtain rewards that stem from social interactions. For example, a person with poor social skills such as making conversation will likely have difficulty making and maintaining friends, and therefore have a relative lack of the rewards stemming from friendships. Another problem may be the lack of reinforcers due to environmental circumstances (e.g., being sick and confined to home). Finally, some people simply find more activities reinforcing than do others, and people's sensitivity to reinforcers can change as they become depressed because loss of pleasure in normal activities is a common symptom of depression; moreover, people also differ in sensitivity to negative reinforcers—for example, some people are highly sensitive to mild criticism whereas others are not.

Research shows that depressed persons do indeed receive fewer positive verbal reinforcements from their families than do nondepressed persons and fewer social reinforcements in their lives in general. As we have already seen, they also tend to experience more negative events. Moreover, their moods seem to vary with both their positive and their negative reinforcement rates. They also have lower levels of activity and report less pleasure from seemingly positive events (see Lewinsohn & Gotlib, 1995; Rehm & Tyndall, 1993).

Although much of this research is consistent with the behavioral theory, the findings only show that depressed persons may have a low rate of response-contingent positive reinforcement (such as the rewards stemming from having close friends), or a high rate of negative reinforcement (such as major life stressors or chronic strains). However, they cannot demonstrate that depression is *caused* by these factors. Instead it may be that some of the primary symptoms of depression, such as low levels of energy and pessimism, instead cause the depressed person to experience these lower rates of reinforcement (Carson & Carson, 1984). More recently behavioral theories have evolved to include an emphasis on personality and cognitive variables that may interact with behavioral variables to produce depression (Lewinsohn & Gotlib, 1995).

Beck's Cognitive Theory   One of the most prominent theories of depression for over 30 years has been that of Aaron Beck—a psychiatrist who became disenchanted with psychodynamic theories of depression early in his career and developed his own cognitive theory of depression (Beck, 1967). Whereas the most prominent

symptoms of depression have generally been considered to be the affective or mood symptoms, Beck hypothesized that the cognitive symptoms of depression may often precede and cause the affective or mood symptoms rather than vice versa. That is, if you think that you're a failure or that you're ugly, it would not be surprising if those thoughts led to a depressed mood. According to Beck, it is these negative cognitions that are central to depression, rather than, for example, the low rates of reinforcement postulated by the behavioral view.

There are several important features of Beck's theory (e.g., Beck 1967, 1983; Sacco & Beck, 1995). First, there are the underlying **depressogenic schemas** or **dysfunctional beliefs,** which are rigid, extreme, and counterproductive. An example of a dysfunctional belief (that the person may well not be consciously aware of) is "If everyone doesn't love me, then my life is worthless." According to Beck and others, such a belief would predispose the person holding it to develop depression if he or she perceived social rejection. Alternatively, if the dysfunctional belief was "If I'm not perfectly successful, then I'm a nobody," then the person would be likely to develop negative thoughts and depressed affect if he or she felt a failure.

These depression-producing beliefs are thought to develop during childhood and adolescence as a function of one's experiences with one's parents and with significant others (teachers, peers, etc.). Children who lose a parent or who have poor parenting are prone to develop

If a movie or rock star comes to expect the constant attention of adoring fans that he gets used to receiving wherever he goes, he might begin to develop a dysfunctional belief (that he is not consciously aware of) such as "If everybody doesn't love me, my life is worthless." At a later point in time when under stress (particularly under the effect of a stressor such as losing attention or affection of someone close), he might become prone to developing depression according to Beck's theory.

such depressogenic schemas. The schemas or beliefs are thought to serve as the underlying diathesis or vulnerability to develop depression, although they may lie dormant for years in the absence of significant stressors. However, when dysfunctional beliefs are activated by current stressors, they tend to fuel the current thinking pattern, creating a pattern of **negative automatic thoughts**—thoughts that often occur just below the surface of awareness and involve unpleasant pessimistic predictions. These pessimistic predictions tend to center on the three themes of what Beck calls the **negative cognitive triad:** (1) negative thoughts about the *self* ("I'm ugly"; "I'm worthless"; "I'm a failure"), (2) negative thoughts about one's experiences and the surrounding *world* ("No one loves me"; "People treat me badly"); and (3) negative thoughts about one's *future* ("It's hopeless because things will always be this way").

Along with the dysfunctional beliefs that fuel the negative cognitive triad once they are activated, Beck also postulates that the negative cognitive triad tends to be maintained by a variety of cognitive biases or distortions, among them:

- *Dichotomous or all-or-none reasoning,* which involves a tendency to think in extremes. For example, someone might discount a less-than-perfect performance by saying "If I can't get it 100 percent right, there's no point in doing it at all."

- *Selective abstraction,* which involves a tendency to focus on one negative detail of a situation while ignoring the other elements of the situation. Someone might say "I didn't have a moment of pleasure or fun today" not because this is true but because he or she selectively remembered the negative things and not the positive things that happened.

- *Arbitrary inference,* which involves jumping to a conclusion based on minimal or no evidence. A depressed person might say after an initial homework assignment from a cognitive therapist did not work: "This therapy will never work for me."

- *Overgeneralization,* which involves a tendency to draw a sweeping conclusion from a single, perhaps rather unimportant, event. For example, someone who makes one mistake may conclude "Everything I do goes wrong." (Examples taken from Fennell, 1989, p. 193.)

It is easy to see how each of these cognitive distortions tends to maintain the negative cognitive triad. That is, if the content of your thoughts regarding your views of your self, your world, and your future is already negative, and you tend to minimize the good things that happen to you

or to draw negative conclusions based on minimal evidence, those negative thoughts are not likely to disappear. In addition, just as the underlying dysfunctional beliefs (such as "If everybody doesn't love me then my life is worthless") elicit the negative cognitive triad when activated, so too does the negative thinking produced by the negative triad serve to reinforce those underlying beliefs. Thus, each of these components of Beck's cognitive theory serves to reinforce the others, as shown in Figure 6.2. Moreover, as already noted, these negative thoughts can be expected to produce some of the other symptoms of depression, such as sadness, dejection, and lack of motivation.

Personality Variables as Additional Vulnerability Factors Beck (1983) identified two different types of people who may be prone to depression when negative life events occur to which their personality makes them particularly sensitive

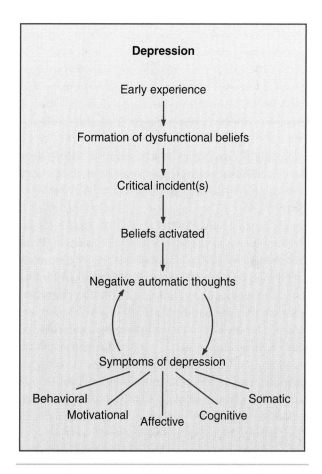

FIGURE 6.2 BECK'S COGNITIVE MODEL OF DEPRESSION
According to Beck's cognitive model of depression, certain kinds of early experiences can lead to the formation of dysfunctional assumptions that leave a person vulnerable to depression later in life if certain critical incidents (stressors) serve to activate those assumptions. Once activated, these dysfunctional assumptions trigger automatic thoughts that in turn produce depressive symptoms, which further fuel the depressive automatic thoughts. (Adapted from Fennel, 1989.)

(termed *congruent events*). First, there are people high on *sociotropy*, who are excessively concerned with interpersonal dependency and who are overly sensitive to interpersonal losses or rejections. Second, there are people high on *autonomy*, who are excessively concerned with achievement issues and who tend to be highly self-critical; these people are especially sensitive to achievement failures. It is of great interest that these two personality types resemble those identified by contemporary psychodynamic researchers in the object-relations and ego psychology traditions (e.g. Blatt, 1974; Bowlby, 1980; see Ouimette & Klein, 1993, for a review).

Research on these ideas has provided reasonably good support for the hypothesis that highly sociotropic people are especially vulnerable to negative interpersonal events (relative to their sensitivity to achievement failures) and are likely to become depressed when faced with them. Evidence supporting the idea that highly autonomous or self-critical subjects are especially vulnerable to becoming depressed in response to achievement failures is less consistent, but there are some supportive findings (Blatt & Zuroff, 1992; L. A. Clark et al., 1994; Coyne & Whiffen, 1995). In both cases, evidence appears to be strongest that these personality variables may predict *relapse* (more strongly than first onset) in response to congruent events (Coyne & Whiffen, 1995).

Evaluating Beck's Theory as a Descriptive Theory Over the past 30 years an enormous amount of research has been conducted testing various other aspects of Beck's theory. As we will see in a later section on treatment, it has generated a very effective form of treatment for depression known as cognitive therapy. In addition, it has been well supported as a descriptive theory. Depressed patients are considerably more negative in their thinking than are nondepressed persons, and than they themselves are when they are not depressed. Moreover, there is also evidence for the negative cognitive triad—depressed persons do think more negatively about themselves and the world around them than do nondepressed persons and are quite negative about the future—especially their own future. The negative thinking that Beck describes seems to occur in all subtypes of depression studied to date (see Clark & Steer, 1996; Haaga, Dyck, & Ernst, 1991).

In addition to evidence showing that depressed people have negative automatic thoughts revolving around the themes of the negative cognitive triad, there is also some evidence supporting the existence of cognitive biases in depression. For example, depressed people show better or biased recall of negative information, whereas nondepressed people tend to show a bias for positive information. The bias occurs whether or not the information involves autobiographical material (about their own lives) or emotionally meaningful words (lonely, blue, dejected versus confident,

exuberant, outgoing) presented by an experimenter (Mathews & MacLeod, 1994; Mineka & Nugent, 1995; Mineka et al., 1998). In addition, depressed people are more likely to draw negative conclusions that go beyond the information presented in a scenario than are nondepressed people, and to underestimate the positive feedback they have received (Haaga et al., 1991). It is easy to see how these biases can play an important role in maintaining depression. For example, if you're already depressed and your memory is biased so that you primarily remember the bad things that have happened to you, it is easy to see how this is likely to maintain or exacerbate the depression. Teasdale (1988) has called this the vicious cycle of depression (see also Teasdale, 1996).

Evaluating the Causal Aspects of Beck's Theory Although research supports most features of the descriptive aspects of Beck's theory, research directed toward confirming the *causal* hypotheses of Beck's theory has had more mixed findings. For example, it has been difficult to find convincing support for the hypothesis that the depressogenic schemas or dysfunctional beliefs thought to reflect the underlying vulnerability to depression are actually present when the person is not depressed (either before an episode of depression or following recovery). In addition, tests of the causal hypothesis of Beck's theory regarding the onset of depression have also provided mixed results. That is, most studies that have measured vulnerability at Time 1 and followed subjects for one or more months, have not found that a measure of vulnerability, in interaction with stressful life events, predicts depression at Time 2. However, several recent reviews (Haaga et al., 1991; Kwon & Oei, 1994; Sacco & Beck, 1995) concluded that there has not yet been an adequate test of the causal aspects of the theory and that it would be premature to dismiss it at this point in time.

The Helplessness and Hopelessness Theories of Depression A second set of interrelated cognitive theories of depression has also generated an enormous amount of research over the past 25 years. Whereas Beck's theory originated out of his clinical observations of the pervasive patterns of negative thinking seen in depressed patients, the learned helplessness theory of depression originated out of observations in an animal research laboratory. Martin Seligman (1974, 1975) first proposed that the laboratory phenomenon known as **learned helplessness** might provide a useful animal model of depression. In the late 1960s Seligman and his colleagues (Maier, Seligman, & Solomon, 1969; Overmier and Seligman, 1967) noted that laboratory dogs who were first exposed to uncontrollable shocks later showed major deficits in learning in a different situation that they could control shocks. Animals first exposed to equal amounts of controllable shocks showed no such deficits. Indeed, when the uncontrollably shocked animals were put in the new situation with potentially controllable shocks, they didn't even seem to try to learn whether there was some way to control the shocks; instead they seemed to simply passively accept the shocks.

Seligman and his colleagues proposed the learned helplessness hypothesis to explain these effects. This hypothesis states that when an organism learns that it has no control over aversive events such as shock, this "learned helplessness" will produce three kinds of deficits: (1) *motivational deficits:* if you have already learned that you have no control, why bother trying? This was consistent with observations that the helpless animals did not initiate many responses on their own—that is, they didn't even try to escape the shocks in the new situation; (2) *cognitive deficits:* if you've learned that you have no control, this interferes with your future ability to learn that you can have control. This was consistent with observations that even when a dog made an occasional response to escape the shock, it did not seem to notice that its response had brought relief and returned to passively accepting the shock on future trials; (3) *emotional deficits:* learning that you have no control produces passivity and perhaps depression. It was this observation (that the animals looked depressed) that captured Seligman's attention and led ultimately to his proposing a learned helplessness model of depression.

Subsequent research demonstrated that helpless animals also show lower levels of aggression, loss of appetite and weight, and a variety of physiological changes in neurotransmitter levels. After demonstrating that the learned helplessness phenomenon occurred across species, including humans (Hiroto & Seligman, 1975), Seligman went on to propose that learned helplessness may underlie some types of human depression. That is, people undergoing stressful life events over which they have little or no control develop a syndrome like the helplessness syndrome seen in animals.

Similarities Between Depression and Helplessness Seligman noted that there were many symptom similarities between helplessness and depression. For example, both helpless animals and depressed humans show lowered initiation of voluntary responses, or what is known in the depression literature as "paralysis of will." In addition, both show a negative cognitive set, and here he noted the similarities between the cognitive deficits seen in helpless animals and the pervasive negative thinking seen in depressives noted by Beck. Moreover, the lack of aggression and loss of appetite, as well as the physiological changes observed, seemed to be parallel in helplessness and depression.

The idea of helplessness being central to depression was not entirely new, as investigators of widely differing theoretical orientations had emphasized that feelings of helplessness and hopelessness are basic to depressive reactions (e.g., Bibring, 1953). However, none of the earlier proposals about the role of helplessness in depression were stated in a testable form as was Seligman's model. Thus it is not surprising that the learned helplessness model of depression quickly attracted a great deal of attention and much research was devoted to testing it. Highlight 6.1 discusses the helplessness approach, as well as other approaches to understanding sex differences in unipolar depression.

The Role of Attributional Style By 1978, there was a substantial amount of evidence supporting the helplessness theory as well as some that was critical. This was the point at which Abramson, Seligman, and Teasdale (1978) published a major reformulation of the theory that took into account some of the critiques and better acknowledged some of the complexities of what humans do when faced with uncontrollable events (complexities that are not necessarily shared by animals). In particular, they proposed that when people (probably unlike animals) are exposed to uncontrollable negative events, they ask themselves, why? The kinds of **attributions** that people make about uncontrollable events are, in turn, central to whether they become depressed. They proposed three critical dimensions on which attributions are made: (1) internal/external, (2) global/specific, and (3) stable/unstable. As noted earlier, a depressogenic or pessimistic attribution for a negative event would be an internal, stable, and global one. For example, if your boyfriend treats you badly and you conclude that "It's because I'm ugly and boring" you are much more likely to become depressed than if you conclude that "it's because he's in a bad mood today after failing his exam and he is taking it out on me." Moreover, as noted in the diathesis-stress section earlier, Abramson and colleagues also hypothesized that people have a relatively stable and consistent style for making attributions and that people who have a pessimistic or depressogenic style are at risk for depression when faced with uncontrollable negative life events. That is, the pessimistic attributional style is a vulnerability or diathesis for depression.

Since it was proposed in 1978, the *reformulated helplessness theory* has generated an enormous amount of research. Many studies have shown that depressed people do indeed have this kind of pessimistic attributional style (e.g., Abramson et al., 1995; Buchanan & Seligman, 1995). However, the evidence in support of the vulnerability hypothesis is much more mixed. As with Beck's vulnerability construct (dysfunctional attitudes), evidence seems to suggest that the pessimistic attributional style seems to go away when the person has recovered from depression, raising questions about whether it is more an effect of depression than a vulnerability factor. In addition, studies that have examined the ability of this diathesis to predict the onset of depression in interac-

Sex Differences in Unipolar Depression

It has long been observed that women are about twice as likely to become clinically depressed (to have dysthymia or unipolar depression) as are men. These differences occur in most countries around the world, with the few exceptions coming from developing and rural countries such as people in Nigeria and Iran. In the United States, this sex difference starts in adolescence and continues until about age 65, when it seems to disappear. Yet among school age children, boys are more likely to be diagnosed with depression than girls (Nolen-Hoeksema & Girgus, 1994).

Questions have been raised about whether these differences stem from some kind of artifact, such as young women in adolescence becoming more willing to report their feelings, but the data do not support this idea (Brems, 1995; Nolen-Hoeksema, 1990). What kinds of theories have been proposed that can explain this interesting collection of observations?

One set of theories is biological—for example, suggestions have been made that hormonal factors account for the differences. Studies examining this hypothesis have not been very supportive, however (Brems, 1995; Nolen-Hoeksema, 1990; Nolen-Hoeksema & Girgus, 1994). Other biological theories have proposed that among women and men sharing a common genetic diathesis, women are more likely to become depressed and men are more likely to become alcoholic. Research has also addressed the possibility that women are simply more predisposed to depression because of some kind of mutant gene on the X chromosome (of which women have two and men only one). However, research does not support any of these biological hypotheses,

leading us to look at social and psychological factors (Brems, 1995; Nolen-Hoeksema, 1990).

One psychological theory has proposed that by virtue of their roles in society women are more prone to experiencing a sense of lack of control over negative life events. These feelings of helplessness might stem from any or all of the following: poverty, discrimination in the workplace leading to unemployment or underemployment, the relative imbalance of power in many heterosexual relationships, high rates of sexual and physical abuse against women (either currently or previously in childhood), role overload (e.g., being a working wife and mother), and less perceived control for women over traits valued by men when choosing a long-term mate (e.g., beauty, thinness, and youth) (Ben Hamida, Mineka, & Bailey, 1998). There is at least some evidence that each of these conditions is associated with higher-than-expected rates of depression, but whether the effects involve a sense of helplessness has not been established (Brems, 1995; Nolen-Hoeksema, 1990; Whiffen & Clark, 1997). Nevertheless, this remains a plausible hypothesis in need of further research designed directly to test it.

Another intriguing hypothesis is that women have different responses to being in a depressed mood than do men, and it may be these different responses that lead to differences in the severity and duration of depression for women and men. In particular, it seems that women are more likely to ruminate when they become depressed. *Rumination* includes responses such as trying to figure out why you are depressed, crying to relieve tension, or talking to your friends

tion with negative life events have produced mixed results (Abramson et al., 1989; Barnett & Gotlib, 1988b; Peterson, Maier, & Seligman, 1993). However, this theory, like Beck's, is sufficiently complex that it is difficult to provide a critical test of it, and probably no one study has yet done so.

The Hopelessness Theory of Depression In 1989, a further revision of reformulated helplessness theory was presented—known as the *hopelessness theory* (Abramson et al., 1989). Although many elements of the earlier theory were similar, these investigators proposed that having a

about your depression. It is known that rumination is likely to maintain or exacerbate depression, in part by interfering with instrumental behavior (i.e., taking action), and engaging in effective interpersonal problem solving (Lyubomirsky & Nolen-Hoeksema, 1995; Nolen-Hoeksema, Morrow, & Fredrickson, 1993). Moreover, self-focused rumination leads people to increased recall of more negative autobiographical memories, thereby enhancing the vicious cycle of depression (Lyubomirsky, Caldwell, & Nolen-Hoeksema, in press; Teasdale, 1988)

Men, by contrast, are more likely to engage in a distracting activity when they get in a depressed mood, and distraction seems to reduce depression (Nolen-Hoeksema, 1990). Distraction might include going to a movie, playing a sport, or avoiding thinking about why you are depressed. The origin of these sex differences in response to depression is unclear, but if further research supports this hypothesis, it would certainly suggest that a prevention strategy for girls would be to teach them distraction rather than rumination as a response to depression.

Finally, we must consider why the sex differences only start in adolescence (Nolen-Hoeksema & Girgus, 1994), beginning to emerge between ages 13 and 15 and reaching its most dramatic peak between ages 15 and 18 (Hankin, Abramson et al., 1998). This is a time of rapid physiological, environmental, and psychological changes known to create turmoil for many adolescents, but why are adolescent females more likely to become depressed? There is evidence that the development of secondary sexual characteristics is harder psychologically for girls than for boys. Body dissatisfaction goes up for females at this time, and down for males; moreover, body dissatisfaction is more closely related to self-esteem for girls than for boys. Much of girls' dissatisfaction with their bodies comes from their realization of the discrepancy between our society's ideal of a thin, prepubescent body shape for females and the fact that they are gaining fat as they mature sexually.

In addition, this is a time of an increase in sex role socialization. Girls tend to have increased pressure to assume a feminine sex role, and if they accept this somewhat nonassertive, dependent role they may be predisposed to anxiety and depression. But if they reject this role, they may in turn be rejected by the opposite sex. One piece of evidence consistent with this hypothesis is that adolescent girls do perceive competence as a liability and tend to conceal their intelligence. Indeed, one study showed a significant positive correlation between IQ and depression in adolescent girls. For boys, by contrast, there was a small negative correlation between IQ and depression (Block, Gjerde, & Block, 1991). Again, much research remains to be done to fully reveal how sex differences in depression emerge in adolescence, but these are intriguing ideas that will be pursued in the future (Nolen-Hoeksema & Girgus, 1994). At present the evidence is most consistent with the overall idea that a variety of gender differences in personality and behavioral style that are already present in childhood (e.g., girls being less assertive and aggressive, and more ruminative in response to distress) then interact with the increased challenges occurring in adolescence to produce increased risk for depression in adolescent girls. For example, if a girl enters adolescence with a less assertive and more ruminative style of coping and she is then confronted with threats of abuse or harassment, or has restricted choices or is devalued because of her gender, she may be less able to cope with these adolescent challenges and more likely to become depressed (Nolen-Hoeksema & Girgus, 1994, pp. 438–439). ∎

pessimistic attributional style in conjunction with one or more negative life events was not sufficient to produce depression unless one first experienced a state of hopelessness. A *hopelessness expectancy* was defined by the perception that one had no control over what was going to happen and by absolute certainty that an important bad outcome was going to occur or that a highly desired good outcome was not going to occur. Such expectations may themselves be a sufficient condition for depression, although this may be true for only a subset of depressives.

Highlight 6.2 *CUTTING EDGE*

Comorbidity of Anxiety and Mood Disorders

Questions regarding whether depression and anxiety can be differentiated in a reliable and valid way have received a good deal of attention over the years. Only recently, however, have researchers begun to make significant advances in understanding the real scope of the problem. The overlap between measures of depression and anxiety occurs at all levels of analysis—patient self-report, clinician ratings, diagnosis, and family/genetic factors (Clark & Watson, 1991a, 1991b; Mineka et al., 1998). That is, persons who rate themselves high on a scale for symptoms of anxiety also tend to rate themselves high on a scale for symptoms of depression, and clinicians rating these same individuals do the same thing. Moreover, the overlap also occurs at the diagnostic level. One recent review of the literature estimated that just over half of the patients who receive a diagnosis of a mood disorder also receive a diagnosis of an anxiety disorder at some point in their lives, and vice versa (Mineka et al., 1998).

Finally, there is also considerable evidence from genetic and family studies of the close relationship between anxiety and depressive disorders (Clark & Watson, 1991a, 1991b; Kendler et al., 1995; Kendler, 1996; Mineka et al., 1998). Several very large twin studies and a recent review have shown that the liability for depression and generalized anxiety disorder comes from the same genetic factors, and which disorder develops is a result of what environmental experiences occur (Kendler et al., 1992d, 1995; Kendler 1996). By contrast, the genetic relationship between panic disorder and depression, and between the other anxiety disorders and de-pression is more modest (Kendler et al., 1995; Mineka et al., 1998).

At present the dominant theoretical approach to understanding the overlap between depressive and anxiety symptoms is that most of the measures used to measure both sets of symptoms tap the broad mood and personality dimension of *negative affect,* which includes affective states such as distress, anger, fear, guilt, and worry (Clark & Watson, 1991a, 1991b; Clark et al., 1994; Tellegen, 1985; Watson et al., 1995a, 1995b). Both depressed and anxious individuals cannot be distinguished on the basis of their high level of negative affect. But these researchers have also shown that anxiety and depression can be distinguished on the basis of a second dimension of mood and personality known as *positive affect,* which includes affective states such as excitement, delight, interest, and pride. Depressed persons tend to be characterized by low levels of positive affect, but anxious individuals are not. That is, only depressed individuals show the signs of fatigue and lack of energy and enthusiasm characteristic of low positive affect. Clark and Watson have also shown that some anxious (especially panic patients), but not depressed people tend to be characterized by high levels of yet another mood dimension known as *anxious hyperarousal,* symptoms of which include racing heart, trembling, dizziness, and shortness of breath. This tripartite model of anxiety and depression thus explains what features for anxiety and depression are common to both (high negative affect) and what features are distinct (low positive affect for depression, and anxious hyperarousal for panic)

Research is currently testing this theory. A major longitudinal prospective study of college students who are hypothesized to be at high risk for unipolar depression because they have a pessimistic attibutional style and have dysfunctional beliefs is beginning to yield evidence quite supportive of some of the major tenets of the theory (Alloy & Abramson, 1997). For example, students in the high-risk group were seven times more likely to develop an episode of major depression in a two year follow-up period than were those in the low-risk group. Moreover, the high-risk students who also had a tendency to ruminate about their negative thoughts and moods were even more likely to become depressed than did the nonruminators. (See also Lynd-Stevenson [1996] for related results.)

(Mineka et al., 1998). Each of the other anxiety disorders has its own separate and relatively unique component as well (Brown et al., 1998; Mineka et al., 1998; Zinbarg & Barlow, 1996).

Beck and D. A. Clark have presented evidence that there is also some discriminability of anxiety and depression based on the kinds of cognitions the patients show (e.g., D. A. Clark, Beck, & Beck, 1994a; D. A. Clark, Steer, & Beck, 1994b; Steer et al., 1995). For example, cognitions about loss, failure, and hopelessness are more common in major depression and dysthymia than in panic disorder and generalized anxiety disorder (although they are elevated in all of these disorders). Threat-related cognitions were significantly elevated in panic disorder (but not generalized anxiety disorder) relative to major depression and dysthymia.

There are also several features of comorbidity between anxiety and mood disorders at the diagnostic level that raise interesting questions about what the common and distinct causal factors may be. For example, there is usually a sequential relationship between the symptoms of anxiety and depression, both within an episode and between episodes. For example, Bowlby (1973, 1980) described a biphasic response to separation and loss in which the first phase appears to be one of agitation and anxiety, followed by despair and depression. And across a lifetime, individuals are more likely to experience an anxiety disorder first and a depressive disorder later, rather than vice versa (Alloy et al., 1990; Kessler, 1997; Mineka et al., 1998). There is also differential comorbidity between depression and the different anxiety disorders, with panic disorder and obsessive-compulsive disorder being more likely to be accompanied by depression

than, for example, simple or social phobia (Kessler et al., 1996; Mineka et al., 1998).

Alloy and colleagues (1990; see also Mineka et al. 1998) proposed an expansion of the hopelessness model of depression to account for these and other features of comorbidity. In their helplessness/hopelessness model they propose that anxiety and anxiety disorders are characterized by prominent feelings of helplessness. People with these disorders expect that they may be helpless in controlling important outcomes, but they also believe that future control might be possible and so are likely to experience increased arousal and anxiety and an intense scanning of the environment in efforts to gain control. If the person becomes convinced of his or her helplessness to control important outcomes but is still uncertain about whether the bad outcome will actually occur, a mixed anxiety/depression syndrome is likely to emerge. And finally, if the person is convinced not only of his or her helplessness but also becomes certain that bad outcomes will occur, helplessness becomes hopelessness and depression sets in. Alloy and colleagues show how this perspective can explain certain features of comorbidity between anxiety and depressive disorders. For example, the sequential relationship is explained by the fact that one is likely to go through a stage of feeling helpless for some time before one becomes totally hopeless. And some anxiety disorders may be more associated with depression precisely because the symptoms of the disorder themselves (for example, obsessive thoughts and compulsions, and panic attacks) are so distressing and seemingly uncontrollable as to create a more certain form of helplessness, leading to the mixed anxiety/depressive diagnostic picture. ■

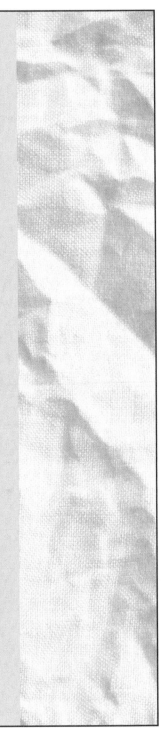

However, these results are still somewhat preliminary in that they have not yet presented findings regarding whether stress interacts with negative cognitive styles in the way postulated by the theory. The theory has also been criticized for proposing hopelessness as a *cause* of depression (as well as a symptom) when most investigators have considered it to be only a *symptom* of depres-

sion. This is similar to the points made earlier regarding Beck's negative cognitive triad and Seligman's pessimistic attributional style, which may only be concomitants or correlates of depression rather than causes. Nevertheless, the hopelessness theory, like the other cognitive theories, is likely to remain a significant area of research for the foreseeable future. Highlight 6.2 discusses how the helplessness and hopelessness theories help explain why anxiety and depression are so often comorbid.

Interpersonal Effects of Mood Disorders Although there is no interpersonal theory of depression that is as clearly articulated as are the cognitive theories, there has nevertheless been a considerable amount of research in the past two decades on interpersonal factors in depression. As we will see, interpersonal problems and social skills deficits may well play a causal role in at least some cases of depression. In addition, depression creates many interpersonal difficulties—with strangers and friends as well as with family members (Hammen, 1991, 1995). We will start by discussing the way in which interpersonal problems can play a causal role in depression.

Lack of Social Support and Social Skills Deficits We noted earlier that Brown and Harris (1978) had found that women without a close confiding relationship were more vulnerable to depression. Since that time, many more studies have supported the idea that people who lack social support are more vulnerable to becoming depressed and that depressed individuals have smaller and less supportive social networks (e.g., Gotlib & Hammen, 1992; Holohan and Moos, 1991). These findings are not just due to a negative reporting bias, because the findings were confirmed by nondepressed family members (Billings et al., 1983). These restricted social networks seem to precede the onset of depression, and although depressed persons may have more social contact when their symptoms remit, their social networks are still more restricted than those of never-depressed persons. In addition, depressives have social skills deficits. For example, they seem to speak more slowly and monotonously and to maintain less eye contact; they are also poorer than nondepressed people at solving interpersonal problems (e.g., Gotlib & Hammen, 1992).

The Effects of Depression on Others Depressed people not only have interpersonal problems, but their own behavior also seems to make these problems worse. For example, the behavior of a depressed individual often places others in the position of providing sympathy, support, and care. Such positive reinforcement does not necessarily follow, however. Depressive behavior can, and over time frequently does, elicit negative feelings and rejection in other people, including strangers, roommates, and spouses (Coyne, 1976; Hokanson et al., 1989; see Gotlib & Hammen, 1992; Nolan, Mineka, & Gotlib, submitted, for reviews). In fact, merely being around a depressed person may induce depressed feelings or negative affect in others (Howes, Hokanson, & Loewenstein, 1985;

People without social support networks are more prone to depression when faced with major stressors. Depressed people also have smaller and less supportive social support networks while they are depressed and to some extent even after their depression has remitted.

Joiner & Metalsky, 1995) and may make a nondepressed person less willing to interact again with the depressed person. If the other people with whom a depressed person interacts are prone to guilt feelings, a depressed person may elicit considerable sympathy and support, at least over the short term. More commonly, the ultimate result is probably a downwardly spiraling relationship from which others finally withdraw, making the depressed person feel worse (e.g., Coyne, 1976; Joiner & Metalsky, 1995).

Marriage and Family Life In recent years interpersonal aspects of depression have also been carefully studied in the context of marital and family relationships. Gotlib and Hammen (1992) reviewed evidence that between one-third and one-half of all couples experiencing marital distress have at least one partner with clinical depression. In addition, it is known that marital distress predicts a poor prognosis for a depressed spouse whose symptoms have remitted. That is, a person whose depression clears up is likely to relapse if he or she has an unsatisfying marriage (Butzlaff & Hooley, 1998; Hooley & Teasdale, 1989).

(

As already noted, the high co-occurrence of marital distress and depression may occur because the depressed partner's behavior triggers negative affect in their spouses along the lines discussed above with strangers and roommates. In reviewing the literature on this topic, Gotlib and Hammen (1992) concluded that depressed people and their spouses tend to perceive their interactions as marked by tension and hostility, which often persist even after the depressed spouse recovers. But there is also evidence that marital distress can lead to depression as well, because marital distress often precedes a depressive episode and is frequently identified as a precipitant of depression and as a reason for seeking treatment (see Gotlib & Hammen, 1992). Thus the evidence suggests both that marital distress can lead to depression and that depression can lead to marital distress. Highlight 6.3, Depression and Marital Violence, discusses how depression also all too often sets the occasion for marital violence.

The effects of depression in one family member extend to infants, children, and adolescents, as well. Parental depression puts children at high risk for many problems, but especially for depression (Murray et al., 1996; Puig-Antich et al., 1989). For adolescent girls, it also increases risk for conduct problems (Davies & Windle, 1997). A skeptic may argue that such studies merely prove that these disorders are genetically transmitted. However, genetic transmission as a sole explanation becomes less likely when we consider that there are many studies documenting the damaging effects of negative interactional patterns between depressed mothers and their children. For example, depressed mothers show more friction and have less playful, mutually rewarding interactions with their children (see Gotlib & Hammen, 1992; Murray & Cooper, 1997). They are also less sensitively attuned to their infants and less affirming of their infant's experiences (Murray et al., 1996). So although genetically determined vulnerability may be involved, psychosocial influences probably play a more decisive role, and most evidence points to the maternal interactional style rather than the depressive symptoms per se as playing the most decisive role in the negative outcomes on infants and children (Murray & Cooper, 1997).

Summary of Psychosocial Causal Factors There are many different psychological theories regarding what causes unipolar depression, ranging from the psychodynamic to the cognitive and interpersonal. Some, such as Beck's cognitive theory and the reformulated helplessness and hopelessness theories, are clearly formulated as

In a large proportion of couples experiencing marital distress, at least one of the partners is clinically depressed. Marital distress also predicts a relativly poor prognosis for the depressed partner.

diathesis-stress models, where the diathesis is seen as cognitive in nature. The psychodynamic and interpersonal approaches both emphasize the importance of early experiential variables (such as the quality of the parent-child relationship) in determining vulnerability to depression. Each of these theories captures interesting aspects of the causal pathways to depression, and given the probable heterogeneity of unipolar depression it is unlikely that any one theory will ever successfully explain all of the variance regarding who does and who does not become depressed when faced with comparable stressful life circumstances.

CAUSAL FACTORS IN BIPOLAR DISORDER

As for unipolar disorder, there are a host of causal factors involved in bipolar disorder that have been posited over the past century. However, biological causal factors are clearly dominant and the role of psychosocial causal factors has received significantly less attention in the literature.

Biological Causal Factors

Hereditary Factors As we have already noted, there is a significant genetic component to bipolar disorder, one that is stronger than that for unipolar disorder. A recent summary of studies using refined diagnostic procedures suggests that about 9 percent of the first-degree relatives of a person with bipolar illness can also be expected to have bipolar disorder (nine times the rate of the disorder in the general population) (Katz & McGuffin, 1993;

MODERN LIFE

Depression and Marital Violence

A strong concordance exists between distressed adult relationships and the presence of a mood disorder in one or both partners (Fruzzetti, 1996; Gotlib & Hammen, 1992; O'Leary, Christian, & Mendell, 1994). These forms of relationship distress may include the occurrence of violent abuse.

It has long been known that mood-disordered persons have an enhanced risk for engaging in violence, including family violence. Until fairly recently, however, virtually all of that enhanced risk was thought to be related to the lack of control and disinhibition associated with manic or hypomanic episodes. Continuing research developments, beginning in the 1980s (e.g., Maiuro et al., 1988), increasingly call that view into question and implicate depressive disorders in the occurrence of much violence, specifically domestic violence.

Men who attack their partners violently—some women also attack men, but usually less violently (Jacobson et al., 1994; O'Leary, 1995)—commonly do so as a means of attempting, by inspiring fear in the partner, to control a situation they perceive as threatening their "proprietary" assumptions about the partnership (e.g., Maiuro et al., 1988; Murphy, Meyer, & O'Leary, 1994; Wilson & Daly, 1996). Such men tend to be highly emotionally dependent on their partners, despite appearances to the contrary, and they tolerate poorly signs of a partner's autonomy. Their underlying sense of inadequacy fuels their desperate attempts to maintain control over the partnership. Too often, the result is a violent attack (Murphy, Meyer, & O'Leary, 1994).

Many partnered men who experience marital distress and become depressed tend to be "unsuccessful," either chronically or in response to recent reversals of fortune. Self-perceived "failure," in terms of conventional male values such as providing for the economic needs of the family, is thus often a complicating factor (Pan, Neidig, & O'Leary, 1994; Vinokur, Price, & Caplan, 1996). Although these men frequently show evidence of high levels of "rejection sensitivity," their behavior in fact invites rejection, which increases the likelihood of heightened relationship friction (Downey & Feldman, 1996) and thus the further development of depressive symptoms (Fruzzetti, 1996). In this process of escalating dysphoria, many men turn to alcohol or other disinhibiting drugs as a type of "self-medication" to reduce stress and relieve depression, thus making it even more likely that they will impulsively attempt a violent solution to end their acute despair (Leonard & Senchak, 1996; Pan, Neidig, & O'Leary, 1994). Like other dysfunctional reactions to a deteriorating relationship, this one, too, almost always makes matters worse.

The causal relationships among depression, marital distress, and familial violence thus appear to be mutually reinforcing and multidirec-

---

Plomin et al., 1997). The first-degree relatives of a person with bipolar disorder are also at elevated risk for unipolar major depression, although the reverse is not true.

Although family studies cannot by themselves establish a genetic basis for the disorder, results from twin studies also point to a genetic basis. The concordance rates for these disorders are much higher for identical than for fraternal twins (Kallman, 1958; Mendlewicz, 1985; Perris, 1979), and one particularly good study by Bertelsen, Harvald, and Hauge (1977) estimated that monozygotic twins were over three times more likely to be concordant (67

percent) for a diagnosis of bipolar disorder than were dizygotic twins (20 percent). About three-quarters of the affected cotwins had the same form of the disorder (bipolar), but nearly one-quarter had unipolar disorder. This study suggests that genes account for over 80 percent of the variance in the tendency to develop (that is, the liability for) bipolar depression. This is higher than heritability estimates for unipolar disorder or any of the other major adult psychiatric disorders, including schizophrenia (Torrey et al., 1994). It is of interest that Kraepelin (1922), who first identified manic-depressive illness, also estimated

tional in nature. In fact, the victims of physical abuse are themselves likely to become clinically depressed (O'Leary, 1995), thus diminishing their abilities to take effective action. Once these behaviors are established as a pattern, it becomes extremely difficult, even with professional help, to disentangle cause from effect and to restore mutual understanding, respect, trust, and effective nonviolent functioning. Unfortunately, as pointed out by Fruzzetti (1996), the DSM, which recognizes disorders as exclusively "within" individuals, provides no adequate diagnostic recognition of this common scenario.

Despite the difficulties of establishing primacy within the entangled causal pattern in abusive relationships, contemporary research suggests that there is often evidence of problematic early attachment processes among the people involved. Deriving from the work of Bowlby (1980) in England, psychologists have in recent years developed apparently reliable and valid means of measuring adults' attachment propensities (Griffin & Bartholomew, 1994), usually differentiating among three "levels" having significant implications for adult relationships. A person with a *secure* attachment pattern comfortably "connects with" and engages others at optimal levels of intimacy and mutual autonomy. *Insecure* attachment patterns include the *anxious-ambivalent*, involving high intimacy needs mixed with anxiety and conflictful, unstable attachments, and the *avoidant*, which involves an active distancing of the self from others. The general hypothesis advanced here is that partners with insecure attachment patterns, particularly the anxious-ambivalent variety, are at significantly increased risk for marital distress, depression, and domestic violence.

In support of this hypothesis, Woike, Osier, and Candela (1996) recently demonstrated a significantly high level of violent relationship imagery (male perpetrators, female victims) among anxious-attachment male college students. Anxious-attachment women in this study had more violent imagery specifically involving female victims than did secure or avoidant-attachment women. The import of such findings, however, may go beyond mere violent imagery. Maiuro and colleagues (1988) found evidence of disturbed attachment patterns in their sample of domestically violent men. Moreover, relationship difficulties associated with insecure attachment patterns may surface early in romantic pairing, as demonstrated by Simpson, Rholes, and Phillips (1996) in a study of college-age dating couples. In addition, Roberts, Gotlib, and Kassell (1996) have recently demonstrated what appears to be a causal relationship between attachment insecurity and the emergence of depressive symptoms, as mediated by self-esteem deficits. As already noted, depressive symptoms in the marital context are associated with a substantially enhanced risk of domestic violence, which sometimes proves deadly. ∎

that about 80 percent of his cases were predisposed to the disorder by a "hereditary taint" (Katz & McGuffin, 1993).

The finding of elevated rates of both bipolar and unipolar forms of the disorder in the relatives of bipolars can be taken in one of two ways. One possibility is that bipolar disorder does not "breed true"—that is, that bipolar genes do not specifically predispose for bipolar disorder, but also for unipolar disorder. This possibility would be of considerable theoretical interest given the current trend to treat unipolar and bipolar disorders as separate conditions. Alternatively, others have noted that these elevations in rates of unipolar depression in the relatives of bipolars may not actually be much greater than would be expected by chance given that unipolar disorder is so much more prevalent in the general population than is bipolar disorder. In the latter case, the conclusion that bipolar disorder does not "breed true" would be unwarranted.

Efforts to locate the chromosomal site of the implicated gene or genes in this genetic transmission of bipolar disorder suggest that they are likely polygenic. Overall, no consistent support yet exists for any specific mode of genetic transmission of the bipolar disorders according to several comprehensive reviews (e.g., Goodwin & Ghaemi, 1998; Plomin et al., 1997).

Biochemical Factors   Much research effort in the past few decades has been directed toward finding the biological substrate of bipolar disorder. The early monoamine hypothesis for unipolar disorder discussed earlier was extended to bipolar disorder with the hypothesis being that if depression was caused by deficiencies of norepinephrine and/or serotonin, then perhaps mania is caused by excesses of these neurotransmitters. Although there is some evidence for increased norepinephrine activity during manic episodes, serotonin activity appears to be low in both depressive and manic phases. More recently it has been suggested that norepinephrine, serotonin, and dopamine are all involved in regulating our mood states (Whybrow, 1997). Disturbances in the balance of these neurotransmitters seem to be the key to understanding this debilitating illness that can send its victims on an emotional roller-coaster, although exactly how is not yet clear (Goodwin & Jamison, 1990; Whybrow, 1997). Evidence for the role of dopamine stems in part from observations that addictive drugs often stimulate dopamine and the reward centers in the brain and produce manic-like behavior. Thus, in mania both dopamine and norepinephrine appear to be elevated. This may be related to why antipsychotic drugs (which lower dopamine levels) can be helpful in reducing the psychotic symptoms of mania (Whybrow, 1997).

One of the thorniest issues that must be addressed by any theory is how lithium, the most effective and widely used drug in the treatment of bipolar disorder, can stabilize individuals from both depressive and manic episodes. We know that lithium is closely related chemically to sodium and that sodium plays a key role in the passage of the neural impulse down an axon. Therefore, questions have been raised regarding whether bipolar patients have abnormalities in the way ions (such as sodium) are transported across the neural membranes. Although the abnormality has not yet been identified, research suggests that there is indeed some such kind of abnormality in bipolar disorder (Goodwin & Jamison, 1990; Whybrow, 1997). One possible account of the effectiveness of lithium is that it may substitute for sodium ions.

Other Biological Causal Factors   Some hormonal research on bipolar depression has focused on the hypothalamic-pituitary-adrenal axis. Bipolar patients, when depressed, show evidence of abnormalities on the dexa-

methasone suppression test (DST), described earlier, at about the same rate as do unipolar depressed patients. When manic, however, their rate of abnormalities has generally (but not always) been found to be much lower (Goodwin & Jamison, 1990). Research has also focused on abnormalities of the hypothalamic-pituitary-thyroid axis because abnormalities of thyroid function are frequently accompanied by changes in mood. Many bipolar patients have subtle but significant abnormalities in the functioning of this axis, and administration of thyroid hormone is known at times to make antidepressant drugs work better (Goodwin & Jamison, 1990; Whybrow, 1997). However, thyroid hormone can also precipitate manic episodes in bipolar patients (Wehr & Goodwin, 1987). Finally, some investigators have suggested that the most effective drugs for the treatment of bipolar disorder—lithium and carbamazepine—may alter the functioning of this axis (Goodwin & Jamison, 1990).

There is also considerable evidence regarding disturbances in biological rhythms in bipolar disorder. During manic episodes, bipolar patients tend to sleep very little (seemingly by choice, not because of insomnia). During depressive episodes, they tend toward hypersomnia (too much sleep), but they do not appear to show the reduced latency to REM sleep seen in unipolar patients (Goodwin & Jamison, 1990; Whybrow, 1997). Bipolar disorder also sometimes shows a seasonal pattern as does unipolar disorder, suggesting disturbances of different biological rhythms that may nonetheless derive from circadian abnormalities. Given the cyclic nature of the disorder itself, this focus on disturbances in biological rhythms holds promise for future integrative theories of the biological underpinnings of bipolar disorder. This is particularly true because bipolar patients seem especially sensitive to any changes in their daily cycles, requiring a resetting of their biological clocks (Whybrow, 1997). Indeed, Goodwin and Jamison (1990) formulated a bold hypothesis worthy of further investigation: "The genetic defect in manic-depressive illness involves the circadian pacemaker or systems that modulate it" (p. 589).

With the modern technology of positron emission tomography (PET) scans, it has even proved possible to visualize variation in brain glucose metabolic rates in depressed and manic states. Whybrow (1997) summarized evidence from studies using PET and other neuroimaging techniques that, whereas blood flow to the left prefrontal cortex is reduced during depression, during mania it is reduced in the right frontal and temporal regions. During normal mood, blood flow across the two brain

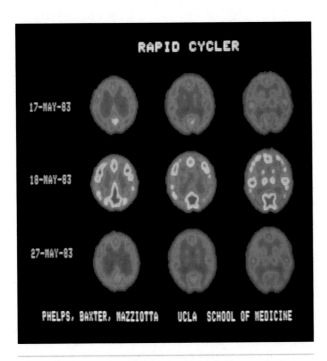

RAPID CYCLER

17-MAY-83

18-MAY-83

27-MAY-83

PHELPS, BAXTER, MAZZIOTTA   UCLA SCHOOL OF MEDICINE

Shown here are positron emission tomography (PET) scans of identical planes of the brain of a rapid-cycling bipolar patient. The top and bottom sets of planes were obtained on days in which the patient was depressed; the middle set was obtained on a hypomanic day. Colors of scans correspond to glucose (sugar) metabolic rates in the respective brain areas, the reds and yellows representing high rates and the blues and greens low rates.

hemispheres is approximately equal. Thus there are shifting patterns of brain activity during mania and during depressed and normal moods. The photograph above illustrates PET scans of a person with bipolar disorder, showing additional aspects of the differences in patterns of brain glucose metabolic rates during both manic and depressed phases.

Psychosocial Causal Factors in Bipolar Disorder

Stressful Life Events Early in the course of bipolar disorder, stressful life events preceding manic or depressive episodes may be precipitants, just as Kraepelin had noted in his clinical observations (Goodwin & Jamison, 1990). It has long been argued that as the illness unfolds, the manic and depressive episodes become more autonomous and do not usually seem to be precipitated by stressful events (e.g., Post, 1992). Some of these conclusions may be premature, however, given that most studies addressing this issue have relied on patients' memories of events before episodes, which may be unreliable (John-

son & Roberts, 1995). In several good prospective studies using the most sophisticated stress measurement techniques, Ellicott and Hammen and colleagues (1990; Hammen, 1995) followed patients with established bipolar disorder for one to two years. They found a significant association between the occurrence of high levels of stress and the experience of manic, hypomanic, or depressive episodes. Moreover, they did not find that stress played any less important a role in precipitating episodes for people who had had more episodes of illness (Hammen, 1995; Swendsen et al., 1995). Indeed, one study even found that patients with more prior episodes were *more* likely to have episodes following major stressors than patients with fewer prior episodes (Hammen & Gitlin, 1997). Finally, a recent study found that patients who experienced severe negative events took on average three times longer to recover from an episode than those without a severe negative event (395 versus 112 days) (Johnson & Miller, 1997). Even minor negative events were found to increase time to recovery (Johnson et al., 1997).

How might stressful life events operate to increase chance of relapse? One hypothesized mechanism is through the destabilizing effects that stressful life events may have on critical biological rhythms, which as already discussed are strongly implicated in biological views on bipolar disorder. Although evidence in support of this idea is still preliminary, it appears to be a promising hypothesis (Johnson & Roberts, 1995).

One interesting example of the apparent role of aversive life events as precipitating causes in bipolar attacks has been described by Ellicott and colleagues (1990, p. 1997).

Case Study, Life Changes and Bipolar Disorder • Mr. A., a 30-year-old man, had been given a diagnosis of bipolar I disorder at age 21. He had had two manic episodes and multiple minor depressions and hypomanic episodes before treatment at the affective disorders clinic. After entering the study, he remained asymptomatic on a regimen of lithium carbonate and had no severely threatening life events (those rated four or five on the objective threat scale) during the first six months of observations. Then the patient reported a severely threatening event that involved a month-long financial investigation at his workplace. Directly afterward he experienced a mild subsyndromal depression, which spontaneously resolved after 18 days. Several weeks later, however, Mr. A reported three severely threatening events over the course of a month, two of which were employment-related changes that jeopardized his job, and one of which involved a major estrangement from his live-in girlfriend. One week after these events, he had a two-week manic episode, which was controlled on an outpatient basis with an increased dose of lithium and which subsided into hypomania that persisted over three months.

There is also some recent evidence that personality and cognitive variables may interact with stress in determining the likelihood of relapse. For example, one study found that bipolar individuals who were highly introverted or obsessional were especially responsive to stress (Swendsen et al., 1995). Another found that students with a pessimistic attributional style who also had negative life events showed an increase in depressive symptoms whether they were bipolar or unipolar depressives (Alloy et al., 1997).

Psychodynamic Views   According to psychodynamic theorists, manic and depressive disorders may be viewed as two different but related defense-oriented strategies for dealing with severe stress. Manic persons try to escape their difficulties by a "flight into reality"—that is, they try to avoid the pain of their inner lives through outer-world distractions. In hypomania, the less severe form, this type of reaction to stress is shown by a person who goes on a round of parties to try to forget a broken love affair or tries to escape from a threatening life situation by restless action, occupying every moment with work, athletics, sexual affairs, and countless other activities—all performed with professed gusto but not necessarily with true enjoyment. In full-blown mania, this pattern is exaggerated. With a tremendous expenditure of energy, a manic person tries to deny feelings of helplessness and hopelessness and to play a role of domineering competence. Once this mode of coping with difficulties is adopted, it is maintained until it has spent itself in emotional exhaustion, for the only other alternative is an admission of defeat and inevitable depression. Thus as a manic episode proceeds, any defensive value it might originally have had is negated, for thought processes are speeded up to a point where an individual can no longer process incoming information with any degree of efficiency. This results in behavior that is highly erratic at best and incomprehensible at the extreme.

Although a manic person may appear to have high self-esteem (and even be quite grandiose), there is one study supporting the idea that this may be a defensive posture. Winters and Neale (1985) used two measures of self-esteem in a study of normals and patients with

unipolar disorder and manic disorder in remission (i.e., between episodes). In the direct measure of self-esteem, the normals and remitted manics reported higher self-esteem than did the unipolar depressives. But on another indirect task that all subjects thought was a measure of their memory, the remitted manics scored more like the unipolar depressives, revealing that they indeed had lower self-esteem than that seen in normals.

According to psychodynamic views about bipolar disorder, the shift from mania to depression may tend to occur when the defensive function of the manic reaction breaks down. Similarly, the shift from depression to mania may tend to occur when an individual, devalued and guilt-ridden by inactivity and an inability to cope, finally feels compelled to attempt some countermeasure, however desperate. Although the view of manic and depressive reactions as extreme defenses may seem plausible up to a point, it is difficult to account satisfactorily for the more extreme versions of these states without acknowledging the importance of biological causal factors. The effectiveness of biological treatment in alleviating severe episodes lends support to the importance of biological causal factors.

SOCIOCULTURAL FACTORS AFFECTING UNIPOLAR AND BIPOLAR DISORDERS

Research on the association of sociocultural factors with both bipolar and unipolar mood disorders is discussed together because much of the research conducted in this area has not made clear-cut diagnostic distinctions between the two types of disorder. The prevalence of mood disorders seems to vary considerably among different societies: In some, mania is more frequent, while in others, depression is more common. However, it has been difficult to provide conclusive evidence on this because of various methodological problems, including widely differing diagnostic practices in different cultures, and because the symptoms of depression also appear to vary considerably across cultures (Kaelber et al., 1995).

Cross-Cultural Differences in Depressive Symptoms

Even in those nonindustrialized countries where depressive disorders are relatively common, Marsella's (1980) comprehensive review of the cross-cultural literature on depression left little doubt that it generally

In some cultures the concept of depression as we know it simply does not exist. For example, Australian aborigines who are "depressed" show none of the guilt and self-abnegation commonly seen in more "developed" countries. They also do not show suicidal tendencies, but instead are more likely to vent their hostilities onto others rather than onto themselves.

takes a different form from that customarily seen in our society. For example, in some non-Western cultures like China where rates of depression are low, the psychological symptoms of depression are often not present. Instead people exhibit so-called somatic and vegetative manifestations, such as sleep disturbance, loss of appetite, weight loss, and loss of sexual interest (Kleinman, 1986; see also Goodwin & Jamison, 1990). Interestingly, in some such cultures there is not even a concept of depression that would be reasonably comparable to our own. The psychological components that seem to be missing are the feelings of guilt and self-recrimination that are so commonly seen in the "developed" countries (Kidson & Jones, 1968; Lorr & Klett, 1968; Zung, 1969). In fact, among several groups of Australian aborigines, Kidson and Jones (1968) found not only an absence of guilt and self-recrimination in depressive reactions but also no incidence of attempted or actual suicide. In connection with the latter finding, they stated, "The absence of suicide can perhaps be explained as a consequence of strong fears of death and also because of the tendency to act out and project hostile impulses" (p. 415). That is, these groups of aborigines are more likely to vent their hostility onto others than onto themselves through suicide.

A Belief in Self-Sufficiency

In spite of the difficulties in drawing definitive conclusions about cross-cultural differences, a number of interesting cross-cultural findings raise provocative questions about the kinds of factors that promote high versus low rates of mood disorders. For example, in early studies, Carothers (1947, 1951, 1959) found manic disorders to be fairly common among the East Africans he studied, but depressive disorders relatively rare—the opposite of their incidence in the United States. He attributed the low incidence of depressive disorders to the fact that in traditional African cultures individuals have not usually been held personally responsible for failures and misfortunes. The culture of the Kenya Africans Carothers observed may be taken as fairly typical in this respect (1947, 1951, 1953). Their behavior was largely group-determined, and therefore they were not confronted with problems of self-sufficiency, choice, and responsibility, which are so prominent in Western cultures. Setting high achievement goals was discouraged (so there was little room for disappointment or failure in this regard). They were humble toward the harsh environment they lived in and always expected the worst from it. Responsibility and blame for misfortunes were attributed to outside forces; because they weren't personally responsible there were few opportunities for self-devaluation. Needless to say, much has changed in Africa since Carothers made these observations, and more recent data suggest a quite different picture. In general, it appears that as societies take on the ways of Western culture, their members become more prone to developing Western-style mood disorders (Marsella, 1980).

Relieving Losses

Yet there are still societies relatively untouched by Western culture, such as the Kaluli—a primitive tribe in New Guinea studied by Scheiffelin (1984), where it is still very difficult to detect any sign of depression. A summary of Scheiffelin's work by Seligman (1990) provides interesting suggestions regarding why this might be the case:

> Briefly, the Kaluli do not seem to have despair, hopelessness, depression, or suicide in the way we know it. What they do have is quite interesting. If you lose something valuable, such as your pig, you have a right to recompense. There are rituals (such as dancing and screaming at the neighbor who you think killed the pig) that are recognized by the society. When you demand recompense for loss, either the neighbor or the whole tribe takes note of your condition and usually recompenses you one way or another. The point I want to make here is that reciprocity between the culture and the in-

ders. For most moderately to seriously depressed patients, including those with dysthymia (Kocsis et al., 1997), the drug treatment of choice since the 1960s until the past decade had been one of the standard antidepressants (called *tricyclics* because of their chemical structure), such as Tofranil (imipramine) (Gitlin, 1996; Nemeroff & Schatzberg, 1998). The efficacy of the tricyclics has been demonstrated in hundreds of studies where the response of depressed patients given these drugs has been compared with the response of patients given a placebo. Unfortunately, the tricyclics have unpleasant side effects such as dry mouth, constipation, sexual dysfunction, and weight gain, and many patients do not continue long enough with the drug for it to have its antidepressant effect. In addition, because these drugs are highly toxic when taken in large doses, there is some risk in prescribing them for suicidal patients who might use them for an overdose. (See also Chapter 16.) Finally, if a patient has bipolar disorder (either known or not yet diagnosed because of no prior manic episode), treatment with an antidepressant can sometimes precipitate a manic episode or precipitate rapid-cycling form of bipolar disorder (Nemeroff & Schatzberg, 1998).

Selective Serotonin Re-uptake Inhibitors

For all these reasons, physicians are increasingly choosing to prescribe one of the antidepressants from the *selective serotonin re-uptake inhibitors* (SSRIs), a new category of drugs that tend to have many fewer side effects and are better tolerated by patients, as well as being less toxic in large doses. One of these, Prozac (fluoxetine), is now extremely popular among physicians in various specialties, not only to treat significant depression but also for people with mild depressive symptoms (Gitlin, 1996; Nemeroff & Schatzberg, 1998). The primary negative side effects about the SSRIs about which patients complain are that many these drugs cause orgasmic problems or lowered interest in sexual activity.

Prescriptions for Prozac are being written at a rate that seems excessive; modest distress or unhappiness should not, we think, be an occasion for taking drugs but rather for seriously examining one's life and perhaps seeking psychotherapy. There are many interesting and controversial questions about the ethics of prescribing drugs to essentially healthy people because the drugs make them feel more energetic, outgoing, and productive than they have ever been. Recently these have been discussed widely in the popular media because of the the controversial best-selling book *Listening to Prozac*

(Kramer, 1993), written by a psychiatrist who describes his own dilemmas in deciding when and how long to continue his patients (many of whom are not depressed) on this drug. This question is considered further in Chapter 16 (Highlight 16.2 Modern Life).

The Course of Treatment with Antidepressant Drugs

Unfortunately, antidepressant drugs usually require at least several weeks to take effect. Also, discontinuing the drugs when symptoms have remitted may result in relapse. Recall that the natural course of a depressive episode if left untreated is typically six to nine months. Thus if depressed patients take drugs for three to four months and then stop because they are feeling better, they are likely to relapse because the underlying depressive episodes were actually still present and only their symptomatic expression had been suppressed (Gitlin, 1996; Nemeroff & Schatzberg, 1998). Because depression tends to be a recurrent disorder, there are also increasing trends to continue patients for very long periods of time on the drugs in order to prevent recurrence. For example, Frank and colleagues (1990) continued patients on moderate doses of imipramine for three years and found that only about 20 percent showed a recurrence, compared with about 90 percent of those maintained on placebo for the same time period. Thus, when properly prescribed, these drugs are often effective in prevention as well as treatment for patients subject to recurrent episodes (Gitlin, 1996; Nemeroff & Schatzberg, 1998) (see also Chapter 16).

Lithium and Other Mood-Stabilizing Drugs

Lithium therapy has now become widely used as a *mood stabilizer* in the treatment of both depressive and manic episodes of bipolar disorder. The term *mood stabilizer* is often used to describe these drugs because they have both anti-manic and anti-depressant effects—i.e., mood-stabilizing effects in either direction. It is often effective in preventing cycling between manic and depressive episodes (although not necessarily for patients with rapid cycling), and bipolar patients are frequently maintained on lithium therapy over long time periods. Early studies indicated that lithium was considered an effective preventive for approximately 65 percent of patients suffering repeated bipolar attacks (Prien, 1992), but other studies present a more pessimistic picture, with several large studies finding only slightly over one-third of patients remaining free of an episode over a five-year follow-up period. Nevertheless, maintenance on lithium clearly leads to having *fewer* episodes than are experienced by patients who discontinue their medication. In a quantitative study of patients discontinuing medication, the risk of having a new episode was 28 times higher per month when not on medication as when on medication (Nemeroff & Schatzberg, 1998).

Lithium therapy has some unpleasant side effects, such as lethargy, decreased motor coordination, and gastrointestinal difficulties in some patients. Long-term use of lithium has also been associated with kidney malfunction and sometimes permanent kidney damage (Gitlin, 1996; Goodwin & Jamison, 1990). Not surprisingly these side effects, combined with the fact that many bipolar patients seem to miss the highs and the abundance of energy associated with their hypomanic and manic episodes, sometimes create problems with compliance to taking the drug (see Highlight 16.4).

More recently there has also been emerging evidence for the usefulness of another category of drugs known as the *anticonvulsants* (such as carbamazepine and valproate) in the treatment of bipolar disorder (Nemeroff & Schatzberg, 1998). These drugs may often be effective in patients who do not respond well to lithium or who have unacceptable side effects from it (Nemeroff & Schatzberg, 1998) (see also Chapter 16). Both bipolar and unipolar patients who show signs of psychosis (hallucinations and delusions) may also receive treatments with *antipsychotic* medications (see Chapters 12 and 16) in conjunction with their antidepressant or mood-stabilizing drugs (Nemeroff & Schatzberg, 1998).

Electroconvulsive Therapy   Because antidepressants often take three to four weeks to produce significant improvement, *electroconvulsive therapy* (ECT) is often used with severely depressed patients who may present an immediate and serious suicidal risk including those with psychotic or melancholic features (Gitlin, 1996; Weiner & Krystal, 1994). ECT is also used with patients who have not responded to other forms of pharmacological treatment; it is frequently considered the treatment of choice for the elderly who often either cannot take antidepressant medications or who do not respond well to them (Niederehe & Schneider, 1998). When selection criteria for this form of treatment are carefully observed, a complete remission of symptoms occurs after about 6 to 12 treatments (with two or three per week being typical), meaning that a majority of severely depressed patients can be vastly better in two to four weeks (Gitlin, 1996). Maintenance dosages of antidepressant and antianxiety

drugs are then ordinarily used to maintain the treatment gains achieved, until the depression has run its course. ECT is also very useful in the treatment of manic episodes, with recent reviews of the evidence suggesting that it is associated with remission or marked improvement in 80 percent of manic patients (Gitlin, 1996; Mukherjee, Sackeim, & Schnur, 1994). However, maintenance on mood-stabilizing drugs following ECT is still usually required to prevent relapse (Gitlin, 1996) (see also Chapter 16).

Psychotherapy

In the best of circumstances, the drugs or drugs plus electroconvulsive therapy that are used in the treatment of depression are combined with individual or group psychotherapy directed at helping a patient develop a more stable long-range adjustment. Considerable evidence also suggests that certain forms of psychotherapy for depression, alone or in combination with drugs, significantly decrease the likelihood of relapse within a two-year follow-up period (Hollon & Beck, 1994; Hollon, DeRubeis, & Evans, 1996). Although these results are encouraging, no study has as yet followed patients for long enough to know whether these treatments are also effective in preventing recurrence—that is, a new depressive episode. Studies on the efficacy of combining drugs and psychotherapy have been reviewed by Klerman and colleagues (1994), who concluded that whether combined treatment is really superior to either kind of treatment alone is as yet unclear.

As our discussion of the factors influencing the occurrence of depression may have suggested, proposed psychosocial treatments for unipolar depression have proliferated at an extraordinary rate over the years. In addition to depression-focused modifications of traditional therapies, a number of specialized systems of psychotherapy have been developed that specifically address the problem of unipolar depression, and yet others that specifically address the problems of people with bipolar disorder. By and large, these psychosocial therapies are intended for outpatient (nonpsychotic) treatment, but they are increasingly applied in inpatient settings as well (e.g., Craighead, Craighead, & Iladi, 1998; Thase et al., 1991).

Cognitive-Behavioral Therapy   Two of the best-known of these depression-specific psychotherapies for unipolar depression are the cognitive-behavioral approach of Beck and colleagues (Beck et al., 1979) and the interpersonal therapy (IPT) program developed by Klerman, Weissman, and colleagues (Klerman et al., 1984). Both are relatively brief approaches (10 to 20 sessions) that focus on here-and-now problems rather than on the more remote causal issues that are often focused on in psychodynamic psychotherapy. For example, cognitive-behavioral techniques consist of highly structured, systematic attempts to teach people with unipolar depression to evaluate their beliefs and negative automatic thoughts systematically. They are also taught to identify and correct their biases or distortions of information processing, and to uncover and challenge their underlying depressogenic assumptions. Cognitive therapy relies heavily on an empirical approach, in that patients are taught to treat their beliefs as hypotheses that can be tested through the use of behavioral experiments.

An example of challenging a negative automatic thought through a behavioral experiment can be seen in the following interchange between a cognitive therapist and a depressed patient.

Case Study, Therapy Session: "My Husband Doesn't Love Me Any More"

PATIENT: My husband doesn't love me any more.

THERAPIST: That must be a very distressing thought. What makes you think that he doesn't love you?

PATIENT: Well, when he comes in in the evening, he never wants to talk to me. He just wants to sit and watch TV. Then he goes straight off to bed.

THERAPIST: OK. Now, is there any evidence, anything he does, that goes against the idea that he doesn't love you?

PATIENT: I can't think of any. Well, no, wait a minute. Actually it was my birthday a couple of weeks ago, and he gave me a watch which is really lovely. I'd seen them advertised and mentioned I liked it, and he took notice and went and got me one.

THERAPIST: Right. Now how does that fit with the idea that he doesn't love you?

PATIENT: Well, I suppose it doesn't really, does it? But then why is he like that in the evening?

THERAPIST: I suppose him not loving you any more is one possible reason. Are there any other possible reasons?

PATIENT: Well, he has been working very hard lately. I mean, he's late home most nights, and he had to go in to the office at the weekend. So I suppose it could be that.

THERAPIST: It could, couldn't it? How could you find out if that's it?

PATIENT: Well, I could say I've noticed how tired he looks and ask him how he's feeling and how the work's going. I haven't done that, I've just been getting annoyed because he doesn't pay any attention to me.

THERAPIST: That sounds like an excellent idea. How would you like to make that a homework task for this week? (From Fennell, 1989.)

Another example of trying to challenge an underlying depressogenic assumption of having to be loved (once this has been discovered in the course of treatment) occurs in the following interchange.

Case Study, Therapy Session: "I Must Be Loved"

PATIENT: Not being loved leads automatically to unhappiness.

THERAPIST: Not being loved is a "nonevent." How can a nonevent lead automatically to something?

PATIENT: I just don't believe anyone could be happy without being loved.

THERAPIST: This is your belief. If you believe something, this belief will dictate your emotional reactions.

PATIENT: I don't understand that.

THERAPIST: If you believe something, you're going to act and feel as if it were true, whether it is or not.

PATIENT: You mean if I believe I'll be unhappy without love, it's only my belief causing my unhappiness?

THERAPIST: And when you feel unhappy, you probably say to yourself, "See, I was right. If I don't have love, I am bound to be unhappy."

PATIENT: How can I get out of this trap?

THERAPIST: You could experiment with your belief about having to be loved. Force yourself to suspend this belief and see what happens. Pay attention to the natural consequences created by your belief. For example, can you picture yourself on a tropical island with all the delicious fruits and other food available?

PATIENT: Yes, it looks pretty good.

THERAPIST: Now, imagine that there are primitive people on the island. They are friendly and helpful, but they do not love you. None of them loves you.

PATIENT: I can picture that.

THERAPIST: How do you feel in your fantasy?

PATIENT: Relaxed and comfortable.

THERAPIST: So you can see that it does not necessarily follow that if you aren't loved, you will be unhappy. (From Beck et al., 1979, p. 260.)

The usefulness of cognitive therapy has been amply documented in dozens of studies, including several studies with unipolar depressed inpatients and with patients diagnosed with depression with melancholic features (Craighead et al., 1998; Hollon & Beck, 1994). It may have a special advantage in preventing relapse, although evidence of whether it can also prevent recurrence is not yet available (Hollon et al., 1996; Simons et al., 1986). When compared with pharmacotherapy, it seems to be at least as effective (DeRubeis, 1997). Nevertheless, some have questioned whether adequate tests of the comparative efficacy of cognitive therapy versus pharmacotherapy have yet been adequately conducted (Hollon et al., 1996; Hollon & Beck, 1994). (See also Chapter 17.)

Interpersonal Therapy The interpersonal therapy (IPT) approach has not yet been subjected to as extensive an evaluation as has cognitive-behavior therapy. The findings of a carefully designed multisite study sponsored by the National Institute of Mental Health, however, strongly supported its effectiveness and as well as that of cognitive therapy. When immediate posttherapy outcomes were compared, both these psychosocial treatment approaches proved as effective as antidepressant drugs for milder cases of major depression, and in some instances even severe ones (Elkin et al., 1989; this important study is further described in Chapter 17). The question has also been addressed whether IPT can be useful in long-term follow-up for individuals with severe recurrent unipolar depression (Craighead et al., 1998; Frank et al., 1990). Patients who received continued treatment with IPT once a month or who received continued medication were much less likely to have a recurrence than those maintained on placebo over a three year follow-up period.

Family and Marital Therapy Of course, in any treatment program, it is important to deal with unusual stressors in a patient's life, because an unfavorable life situation may lead to a recurrence of the depression and may necessitate longer treatment. This point has been well established in studies that extended to the mood disorders, the well-established finding that relapse in schizophrenia, as well as unipolar and bipolar disorders, is correlated with certain noxious elements in family life (Butzlaff & Hooley, 1998; Hooley, in press). Behavior by a spouse that can be interpreted by a former patient as criticism seems especially likely to produce depression relapse. For example, some types of couples or family interventions directed at reducing the level of expressed emotion or hostility, described in Chapter 17, have been found to be very useful in preventing relapse in these situations (e.g., Miklowitz, 1996). For bipolar disorder, such family therapy in conjunction with medication significantly reduces the chance of relapse. In addition, for married people who are depressed and having marital discord, it has been shown that marital therapy (focusing on the marital discord rather than the depressed spouse alone) is as effective as cognitive therapy in reducing unipolar depression for the depressed spouse. The marital therapy had the further advantage of also producing greater increases in marital satisfaction than did the cognitive therapy (Beach & O'Leary, 1992; Craighead et al., 1998; Jacobsen et al., 1991).

Even without formal therapy, as we have noted, the great majority of manic and depressed patients recover from a given episode within less than a year. With the modern methods of treatment discussed here, the general outlook has become increasingly favorable. Although relapses may occur in some instances, these can now often be prevented by maintenance therapy—either through continuation of medication and/or through follow-up therapy sessions at regular intervals.

At the same time, the mortality rate for depressed patients appears to be significantly higher than that for the general population, partly because of the higher incidence of suicide, but some studies also indicate an excess of deaths due to natural causes as well (see Coryell & Winokur, 1992; Futterman et al., 1995), including coronary heart disease (Frasure-Smith et al., 1993, 1995) (see Chapter 8). Manic patients also have a high risk of death, due to such circumstances as accidents (with or without alcohol as a contributing factor), neglect of proper health precautions, or physical exhaustion (Coryell & Winokur, 1992). Thus, although the development of effective drugs and other new approaches to therapy have brought greatly improved outcomes for patients with mood disorders, the need clearly remains for still more effective treatment methods, both immediate and long-term. Also, a great need remains to study the factors that put people at risk for depressive disorders and to apply relevant findings to early intervention and prevention.

Suicide

The risk of **suicide**—taking one's own life—is a significant factor in all depressive states. Although it is obvious that people also commit suicide for reasons other

Known Risk Factors for Adolescent Suicide Studies attempting to distinguish who is at risk for a completed suicide, as opposed to a nonfatal attempted suicide, find that conduct disorder and substance abuse (especially alcohol) are relatively more common in the completers, and mood disorders are relatively more common among the nonfatal attempters (Berman & Jobes, 1992). However, these differences are only relative, and each of these forms of psychopathology puts an adolescent at risk for both a nonfatal attempt and a completed suicide. Among those with two or more of these disorders, risk for completion increases. Availability of firearms in the home is also more common in those who complete suicide than in those who attempt it (King, 1997).

Why is there such a surge in suicide attempts and completed suicides in adolescence? Two rather obvious reasons are that this is also a period during which depression, alcohol and drug use, and conduct disorder problems also show increasing prevalence, and as already noted these are all associated with risk for suicide. In addition, adolescents may be more sensitive than younger children to feelings of lack of control they may have in maladaptive family settings. Moreover, they may have limited problem-solving ability and a limited ability to project positive ways in which their lives might improve in the future (King, 1997). That is, they have difficulty in "seeing beyond" their immediate situation.

In addition, exposure to suicide through the media has led to reports of aggregate increases in adolescent suicide, perhaps because adolescents are highly susceptible to suggestion and imitative behavior (Berman & Jobes, 1992). However, research in the past decade on this idea that suicide can be contagious has shown that although it is a real effect, it is a relatively small contributor to the magnitude of the problem. Estimates are that between 1 and 13 percent of adolescent suicides occur as a result of contagion factors (Velting & Gould, 1997).

Many college students seem peculiarly vulnerable to the development of suicidal motivations. The combined stressors of academic demands, social interaction problems, and career choices—perhaps interacting with challenges to their basic values—evidently make it impossible for some students to continue making the adjustments their life situations demand. Some 10,000 college students in the United States attempt suicide each year, and over 1,000 of them succeed. Reflecting the general trend, approximately three times as many female as male students attempt suicide, but more males than females succeed. For an overview of warning signs for student suicide, see Highlight 6.4.

Other Psychosocial Factors Associated with Suicide The specific factors leading a person to suicide may take many forms. For example, one middle-aged man developed profound feelings of guilt after being promoted to the presidency of the bank for which he worked; shortly after his promotion, he fatally slit his throat. Such "success suicides" are undoubtedly related to those occasional depressive episodes that seem to be precipitated by positive life events. Much more often, suicide is associated with negative events, such as severe financial reverses, imprisonment, or interpersonal crises of various sorts. The common denominator may be either that these events lead to the loss of a sense of meaning to life and/or to hopelessness about the future (Beck et al., 1985; Eyman & Eyman, 1992), which can both produce, independently or in combination, a mental state that looks to suicide as a possible way out. Nevertheless, some research suggests that hopelessness about the future may be a better long-term predictor of suicide (say one or two years later) than it is for the short term (weeks or months) (D.C. Clark, 1995).

Historically, researchers have proposed several theoretical rationales for suicidal behavior. As a group, these theories tend to be abstract, even impersonal, and therefore to miss something in depicting the emotional charge of the suicidal act. A leading suicidologist for over 30 years, Shneidman has written extensively about "the suicidal mind." Recently he wrote

> In almost every case suicide is caused by pain, a certain kind of pain—psychological pain, or "Psychache". . . . Suicidal death, in other words, is an escape from pain. . . . Pain is nature's great signal. Pain warns us; pain both mobilizes us and saps our strength; pain, by its very nature, makes us want to stop it or escape from it. . . . Psychache is the hurt, anguish, or ache that takes hold in the mind. It is intrinsically psychological, the pain of excessively felt shame, guilt, fear, anxiety, loneliness, angst, and dread of growing old or of dying badly. When psychache occurs, its introspective reality is undeniable. Suicide happens when the psychache is deemed unbearable and death is actively sought to stop the unceasing flow of painful consciousness. Suicide is a tragic drama in the mind. (Shneidman, 1997, pp. 23, 24, 29).

Another theoretical analysis of suicide offered by Baumeister (1990) also captures this notion of escape from intolerable experience. Baumeister conceives of suicide as basically an escape from self, or at least self-awareness. In this effort a person achieves a "cognitive deconstruction," which entails both irrationality and disinhibition, such that drastic action becomes acceptable.

But what psychological factors lead one to this state? A recent review of the literature on the etiology of suici-

Warning Signs for Student Suicide

A change in a student's mood and behavior is a significant warning of possible suicide. Characteristically, the student becomes depressed and withdrawn, undergoes a marked decline in self-esteem, and shows deterioration in personal hygiene. These signs are accompanied by a profound loss of interest in studies. Often he or she stops attending classes and stays at home most of the day. Usually, the student's distress is communicated to at least one other person, often in the form of a veiled suicide warning.

When college students attempt suicide, one of the first explanations to occur to those around them is that they may have been doing poorly in school. As a group, however, they are superior students, and though they tend to expect a great deal of themselves in terms of academic achievement, their grades and academic competition are not regarded as significant precipitating stressors. Also, although many lose interest in their studies before becoming suicidal and thus receive worse grades, the loss of interest appears to be associated with depression and withdrawal caused by other problems. Moreover, when academic failure does appear to trigger suicidal behavior—in a minority of cases—the actual cause of the behavior is generally considered to be loss of self-esteem and failure to live up to parental expectations, rather than academic failure itself.

For most suicidal students, both male and female, the major precipitating stressor appears to be either the failure to establish, or the loss of, a close interpersonal relationship. Often the breakup of a romance is the key precipitating factor. It has also been noted that significantly more suicide attempts and suicides are made by students from families that have experienced separation, divorce, or the death of a parent.

Although most colleges and universities have mental health facilities to assist distressed students, few suicidal students seek professional help. Thus it is of vital importance for those around a suicidal student to notice the warning signs and try to obtain assistance. ■

dal behavior concluded that it is the end product of a long sequence of events that begins in childhood. There is evidence that people who become suicidal often came from backgrounds in which there was some combination of a good deal of family psychopathology (alcoholism, depression, suicidal behavior), child maltreatment (physical or sexual abuse), and/or or family instability. These early experiences are in turn associated with the child and later the adult having low self-esteem, hopelessness, poor problem-solving skills. Thus early negative experiences of these sorts affect the person's cognitive functioning in a very negative way, and these cognitive deficits may in turn mediate the link with suicidal behavior (Yang & Clum, 1996). Much research remains to be conducted to determine the validity of this model, but it is an intriguing one, linking early childhood events (distal causal factors) with adult cognitive functioning that in turn provides the proximal vulnerability to suicidal thinking and behavior when a person faces some apparent crisis that precipitates the suicide attempt.

Biological Causal Factors There is a fair amount of evidence that suicide sometimes runs in families and that genetic factors may play a role in risk for suicide (Arango & Underwood, 1997). For example, several studies have shown that the biological relatives of adoptees who commit suicide have higher rates of suicide than do the adoptive relatives (e.g., Wender et al., 1986). Moreover, the concordance rates for suicide in monozygotic twins is about five times higher than that in fraternal twins. Moreover, this genetic vulnerability may also be linked to the biochemical correlates of suicide that have now been found in numerous studies. Accumulating evidence shows that suicide victims often have alterations in serotonin functioning, with reduced serotonergic activity being associated with increased suicide risk—especially for violent suicide. Such studies have been conducted not only in postmortem studies of suicide victims but also in people who have made suicide attempts but survived, and this association appears to be independent of psychiatric diagnosis of the suicide attempter or victim (Arango

& Underwood, 1997). People hospitalized for a suicide attempt who have low serotonin levels are ten times more likely to kill themselves in the next year than are those without low serotonin levels. In addition, even in nonsuicidal individuals, low serotonin levels are associated with a tendency toward impulsive violent behavior (Harvard Mental Health Newsletter, 1996). Unfortunately, research in this area has not tended to focus on the extent to which the same genetic and other biological factors implicated in suicide overlap with those implicated in unipolar and bipolar depression.

Sociocultural Factors Suicide rates appear to vary considerably from one society to another. Hungary, with an annual incidence of more than 40 per 100,000, has the world's highest rate (about four times the rate in the United States), although this may be declining slightly since the recent democratization of the government (Velting & Gould, 1997). Other Western countries with high rates—20 per 100,000 or higher—include Switzerland, Finland, Austria, Sweden, Denmark, and Germany. Rates in Japan are also high. The United States has a rate of approximately 11 or 12 per 100,000, which is roughly comparable to that of Canada. Countries with low rates (less than 9 per 100,000) include Egypt, Greece, Italy, Israel, Spain, Mexico, and Ireland (World Health Organization, 1987). As mentioned earlier, among certain groups, such as the aborigines of the western Australian desert, the suicide rate drops to zero—possibly as a result of a strong, culturally determined fear of death (Kidson & Jones, 1968). These estimates should, however, be considered in light of the fact that there are wide differences across countries in the criteria used for determining whether a death was due to suicide (Hawton, 1992), and such differences may well contribute to the apparent differences in suicide rates.

Religious taboos concerning suicide and the attitudes of a society toward death are apparently important determinants of suicide rates. Both Catholicism and Islam strongly condemn suicide, and suicide rates in Catholic and Islamic countries are correspondingly low. In fact, most societies have developed strong sanctions against suicide, and many still regard it as a crime as well as a sin.

Japan is one of the few societies in which suicide has been socially approved under certain circumstances—for example, in response to conditions that bring disgrace to an individual or group. During World War II, many Japanese villagers were reported to have committed mass suicide when faced with imminent capture by

Allied forces. There were also reports of group suicide by Japanese military personnel under threat of defeat. In the case of the *kamikaze,* Japanese pilots who deliberately crashed their explosives-laden planes into American warships during the war's final stages, self-destruction was a way of demonstrating complete personal commitment to the national purpose. It is estimated that 1000 young Japanese pilots destroyed themselves in this exercise of patriotic zeal. Despite the effectiveness of such an attack, one can hardly imagine its being ordered by an American commander, or such an order being obeyed by American pilots. Nevertheless, comparable acts of self-destruction do still occur today in the Middle East where Muslim extremists may commit suicide in order to ensure that a car-bomb explodes in a designated target.

There are also interesting cross-cultural gender differences in whether men or women are more likely to attempt and complete suicide. Although women are more likely to attempt and men to complete suicide in the United States, the same is not true in many other countries. For example, in India, Poland, and Finland, men are more likely than women to engage in nonfatal suicide attempts, and in other countries such as Canada and Sri Lanka rates are similar for men and women. Moreover, in China, India, and Papua New Guinea, women are more likely to complete suicide than men (Canetto, 1997).

In a pioneering study of sociocultural factors in suicide, the French sociologist Emile Durkheim (1897/1951) attempted to relate differences in suicide rates to differences in group cohesiveness. Analyzing records of suicides in different countries and for different historical periods, Durkheim concluded that the greatest deterrent to committing suicide in times of personal stress is a sense of involvement and identity with other people. More contemporary studies tend to confirm this idea, showing, for example, that being married and having kids tends to protect one from suicide (Maris, 1997).

Durkheim's views also appear relevant to understanding the higher incidence of suicide among subgroups in our society who are subjected to conditions of uncertainty and social disorganization in the absence of strong group ties. For example, there is a well-known association between unemployment and suicide (especially for men), which may primarily be related to the effects that unemployment has on mental health (Hawton, 1992; Maris, 1997). Similarly, suicide rates have been found to be higher than average among people who are "downwardly mobile" (or who fear they may become so) and among groups undergoing severe social pressures. For example, in 1932 at the height of the Great Depression in the United States, the suicide rate increased from less than 10 to 17.4 per 100,000; during the early years of the severe recession of the mid- and late 1970s, the suicide rate also increased (National Institute of Mental Health, 1976; Wekstein, 1979). Following the same pattern, we could point to the environmental pressures such as unemployment and alienation that appear to contribute to the high rate of suicide among black youth in our society.

Suicidal Ambivalence

There is often ambivalence that accompanies thoughts of suicide. Some people do not really wish to die, but instead want to communicate a dramatic message to others concerning their distress. Their suicide attempts involve nonlethal methods such as minimal drug ingestion or minor wrist-slashing. They usually arrange matters so that intervention by others is almost inevitable. This group is disproportionately female in the United States, perhaps because women have been socialized to feel helpless and to fantasize being rescued (Canetto, 1997). In contrast, some people are seemingly intent on dying. They give little or no warning of their intent, and they generally rely on the more violent and certain means of suicide, such as shooting themselves or jumping from high places. Investigators have estimated that this group makes up only a small minority of the suicidal population. Successful preventive intervention with this group is extremely difficult.

There is another subset of people who are ambivalent about dying and tend to leave the question of death to fate. Although loss of a love relationship, financial problems, or feelings of meaninglessness may be present, a person in this group still entertains some hope of working things out. The methods used for the suicide attempt are often dangerous but moderately slow acting, such as drug ingestion. The feeling during such attempts can be summed up as, "If I die the conflict is settled, but if I am rescued that is what is meant to be." Often the people in this group lead stormy, stress-filled lives and make repeated suicide attempts.

After an unsuccessful attempt, a marked reduction in emotional turmoil usually occurs. This is especially true if the attempt was expected to be lethal, such as jumping in front of a train. Such people, may explain their survival in terms of supernatural intervention—that is, "they had been chosen to continue living" (O'-Donnell, Farmer, & Catalan, 1996). This reduction in turmoil is usually not stable, however, and subsequent suicidal behavior may follow. In the year following a suicide attempt, repetition of the behavior is common, with 12 to 25 percent of attempters being referred to the same hospital within a year. There is an increased risk that the second attempt will be fatal, especially if the first attempt was a serious one (Hawton, 1992). Long-term follow-up of those who have made a suicide attempt show that about 7 to 10 percent will eventually die by suicide (D.C. Clark, 1995). Moreover, of people who do kill themselves, about 20 to 40 percent have a history of one or more previous attempts; however, nearly half of those who commit suicide have no previous attempts (D.C. Clark, 1995).

Communication of Suicidal Intent Research has clearly disproved the tragic belief that those who threaten to take their lives seldom do so. A recent review of many studies conducted around the world that involved interviewing friends and relatives of people who had committed suicide revealed that more than 40 percent had communicated their suicidal intent in very clear and specific terms, and another 30 percent had talked about death or dying in the months preceding suicide. These communications were usually made to several people and occurred within a few weeks or months before the suicide (D.C. Clark, 1995). Nevertheless, it should also be remembered that such information is always gathered after the fact and most of those interviewed say the suicide came as a surprise.

It is also interesting that most of these communications of intent are to friends and family members and not to mental health professionals. Indeed, nearly 50 percent of people who die by suicide have never seen a mental health professional in their lifetime, and only 25 to 30 percent are under the care of one at the time of their death (Clark & Fawcett, 1992). This is generally even true of those with major depression. One study in Finland showed that only 45 percent of individuals with a diagnosis of major depression who had committed suicide were receiving any kind of psychiatric treatment at the time of death, and it was generally minimal and inadequate (Isometsä et al., 1994).

Indirect threats to friends and family members typically include references to being better off dead, discussions of suicide methods and burial, statements such as "If I see you again . . . ," and dire predictions about the future. Whether direct or indirect, communication of suicidal intent usually represents a warning and a cry for help. The person is trying to express distress and ambivalence about suicide. As several investigators have pointed out, many people who are contemplating suicide feel that living may be preferable if they can obtain the understanding and support of their family and friends. Failing to receive it after a suicidal threat, they go on to actual suicide.

Suicide Notes Several investigators have analyzed suicide notes in an effort to understand better the motives and feelings of people who take their own lives. In several large studies of completed suicides, it has been found that only about 15 to 25 percent left notes, usually addressed to relatives or friends (Maris, 1997). The notes, usually coherent and legible, were either mailed, found on the person's body, or located near the suicide scene. In terms of emotional content, the suicide notes were categorized in one classic study into those showing positive, negative, neutral, and mixed affect (Tuckman, Kleiner, & Lavell, 1959). The emotional content of the notes was rated, in decreasing order of frequency, positive, neutral, mixed, and negative in content.

An understanding of the reasons for or motives underlying note writing (or its absence) could possibly help make the bases of these variations clearer. For example, the motivation for writing a note with positive content may stem from the desire to be remembered positively. More specifically, statements of love and concern may be motivated by the desire to reassure the survivor of the worth of their relationship.

Suicide Prevention and Intervention

Preventing suicide is extremely difficult. One complicating factor is that most people who are depressed and contemplating suicide do not realize that their thinking is restricted and irrational and that they are in need of assistance. As we have seen, less than one-third voluntarily seek psychological help, and most of those who do probably do not receive adequate care. More are likely to visit a doctor's office with multiple vague complaints of physical symptoms that go undetected by the doctor as symptoms of depression or alcoholism. Others are brought to the attention of mental health personnel by family members or friends who are concerned because the person appears depressed or has made suicide threats. The vast majority, however, do not receive the assistance they desperately need. As we have seen, most people who attempt suicide do not really want to die and give prior warning of their intentions; if a person's cry for

help can be heard in time, it is often possible to intervene successfully.

Currently, the main thrust of preventive efforts is on crisis intervention. Efforts are gradually being extended, however, to the broader tasks of alleviating long-term stressful conditions known to be associated with suicidal behavior and trying to better understand and cope with the suicide problem in high-risk groups (Hawton, 1992).

Crisis Intervention The primary objective of crisis intervention is to help a person cope with an immediate life crisis. If a serious suicide attempt has been made, the first step involves emergency medical treatment, usually in the emergency room of a general hospital or clinic. It appears, however, that only about 10 percent of suicide attempts are considered of sufficient severity to warrant intensive medical care. Most people who attempt suicide, after initial treatment, are referred to inpatient or outpatient mental health facilities (D.C. Clark, 1995; Comstock, 1992). This is important because, as already noted, the suicide rate for previous attempters is much higher than that for the population in general, and so it is apparent that those who have attempted suicide remain a relatively high-risk group.

When people contemplating suicide are willing to discuss their problems with someone at a suicide prevention center, it is often possible to avert an actual suicide attempt. Here the primary objective is to help these people regain their ability to cope with their immediate problems—and to do so as quickly as possible. Emphasis is usually placed on (1) maintaining contact with a person over a short period of time—usually one to six contacts; (2) helping the person realize that acute distress is impairing his or her ability to assess the situation accurately and to choose among possible alternatives; (3) helping the person see that other ways of dealing with the problem are available and preferable to suicide; (4) taking a highly directive and supportive role; and (5) helping the person see that the present distress and emotional turmoil will not be endless. When feasible, counselors may elicit the understanding and emotional support of family members or friends; and, of course, they may make frequent use of relevant community agencies. Admittedly, however, these are stopgap measures and do not constitute complete therapy.

It is important to distinguish between (1) individuals who have demonstrated relatively stable adjustment but have been overwhelmed by some acute stress—about 35 to 40 percent of people coming to the attention

In recent years, the availability of competent assistance at times of suicidal crisis has been expanded through the establishment of suicide prevention centers. These centers are geared toward crisis intervention—usually via 24-hour telephone hotlines.

thousand such hotlines in the United States, but less than 200 are members of the American Association of Suicidology, raising questions about the quality of care offered by the majority (Seeley, 1997). These centers are geared primarily toward crisis intervention, usually via the 24-hour-a-day availability of telephone contact. Some centers, however, offer long-term therapy programs, and they can refer suicidal people to other community agencies and organizations for special types of assistance. Suicide prevention centers are staffed by a variety of personnel: psychologists, psychiatrists, social workers, clergy, and trained volunteers. Although initially there was some doubt about the wisdom of using nonprofessionals in the important first-contact role, experience has shown that the empathic concern and peer-type relationship provided by a caring volunteer can be highly effective in helping a person through a suicidal crisis. Unfortunately, good information on the assessment of the effects of these centers has not revealed much impact on suicide rates, except perhaps in young women who are the primary users (Hawton, 1992; Seeley, 1997).

One difficult problem with which suicide prevention centers must deal is that most people who use them do not follow up their initial contact by seeking additional help from the center or other treatment agencies. Therefore, some suicide prevention centers have made more systematic attempts to expand their services to better meet the needs of clients, including the introduction of long-range after-care or maintenance-therapy programs. Unfortunately, one recent prospective study of nearly 300 suicide attempters randomly assigned to an intensive psychosocial treatment program aimed at prevention of further attempts versus a "care as usual" condition revealed no differences in further suicide attempts at a one-year follow-up (van der Sande et al., 1997).

Focus on High-Risk Groups and Other Measures

Many investigators have emphasized the need for broadly based preventive programs aimed at alleviating the life problems of people who are in high-risk groups for suicide. Few such programs have actually been initiated, but one approach has been to involve older men—a high-risk group—in social and interpersonal roles that help others. These roles may lessen their frequent feelings of isolation and meaninglessness. Among this group, such feelings often stem from forced retirement, financial problems, the death of loved ones, impaired physical health, and feeling unwanted.

of hospitals and suicide prevention centers; and (2) individuals who have been tenuously adjusted for some time and in whom the current suicidal crisis represents an intensification of ongoing problems—about 60 to 65 percent of suicidal cases. For people in the first group, crisis intervention is usually sufficient to help them cope with the immediate stress and regain their equilibrium. For people in the second group, crisis intervention may also be sufficient to help them deal with the present problem, but with their lifestyle of "staggering from one crisis to another," they are likely to require more comprehensive therapy.

Since the 1960s, the availability of competent assistance at times of suicidal crisis has been expanded through the establishment of hotlines for suicide prevention centers. At present, there are more than several

Other measures to broaden the scope of suicide prevention programs include focusing efforts on the training of clergy, nurses, police, teachers, and other professional personnel who come in contact with many people in their communities. An important aspect of such training is to increase their alertness for, and sensitivity to, suicidal threats. For ex- ample, a parishioner might intensely clasp the hand of a minister after church services and say, "Pray for me." Because such a request is quite normal, a minister who is not alert to suicidal cries for help might reply with a simple, "Yes, I will" and turn to the next person in line—only to receive the news a few days later that the parishioner has committed suicide.

UNRESOLVED ISSUES

Mood Disorders and Suicide

Most of us respect the preservation of human life as a worthwhile value. Thus in our society suicide is generally considered not only tragic but "wrong." Efforts to prevent suicide, however, also involve ethical problems. If people wish to take their own lives, what obligation— or right—do others have to interfere? Not all societies have taken the position that others should interfere when someone wishes to commit suicide. For example, the classical Greeks believed in dignity in death, and people who were extremely ill could get permission from the state to commit suicide. Officials of the state gave out hemlock (a poison) to those who received such permission (Humphry & Wickett, 1986). In certain Western European countries such as the Netherlands today, the law also allows terminally ill people to be given access to drugs that they can use to commit suicide (Silverman, 1997).

By contrast, in the United States there is heated debate even today about the right of people who are terminally ill or who suffer chronic and debilitating pain to shorten their agony. One group, the Hemlock Society, supports the rights of terminally ill people to get help in terminating their own life when they wish (called *assisted suicide* or *voluntary euthanasia*); the society also provides support groups for people making this decision. Several other groups press related issues at a legislative level. One physician in Michigan, Dr. Jack Kevorkian, has helped over 130 gravely ill people commit suicide, and in so doing has tried to get Michigan to pass laws permitting such acts. The state, however, tried to block Kevorkian from assisting in any further suicides, and at several points he was even imprisoned and his medical license was revoked because he refused to obey injunctions that instructed him to not assist with any further suicides. In 1998 Kevorkian invited further attention and prosecution by releasing a videotape showing him assisting in a suicide. This was aired on the CBS program *60 Minutes* for millions to watch. He was later charged, and convicted in April 1999, of second de- gree murder. He intends to appeal the verdict. In spite of the failure to pass laws supporting assisted suicide for such gravely ill individuals (indeed, Michigan passed a law prohibiting assisted suicide!), there has been increasing sympathy on the part of substantial numbers of people for this position (Silverman, 1997). Arguments against this position have included fears that the right to suicide might be abused. For example, people who are terminally ill and severely incapacitated might feel pressured to end their own lives rather than burden their families with their care, or the cost of their care in a medical facility or hospice. However, the Netherlands, where assisted suicide is legal, has not seen this happen, as advocates for this position in this country are pointing out.

But what about the rights of suicidal people who are not terminally ill and who have dependent children, parents, a spouse, or other loved ones who will be adversely affected, perhaps permanently (Lukas & Seiden, 1990), by their death? Here a person's "right to suicide," reduced to such nonabstract terms, is not immediately obvious. The right to suicide is even less clear in the case of those who are ambivalent about taking their lives and who might, through intervention, regain their perspective and see alternative ways of dealing with their distress. Still, who has the right to prevent another's self-destruction?

Possibly the early suicidologists erred in focusing on suicide "prevention." Others have suggested suicide "intervention" as both a more appropriate term and as descriptive of a more ethically defensible professional approach to suicidal behavior. Suicide intervention, according to this perspective, embodies a more neutral moral stance to suicide than does prevention—it means interceding without the implication of preventing the act—and, in certain circumstances, such as when people are terminally ill, may even hold out the possibility of facilitating the suicidal person's objective (e.g., Nelson, 1984; Silverman, 1997).

Here, however, we should reemphasize that the great majority of people who attempt suicide either do not really want to die or are ambivalent about taking their lives; and even for the minority who do wish to die, the desire is often a transient one. With improvement in a person's life situation and a lifting of depression, the suicidal crisis is likely to pass and not recur.

The dilemma becomes even more intense when prevention requires that a person be hospitalized involuntarily; when personal items, such as belts and sharp objects, are taken away; and when calming medication is more or less forcibly administered. Sometimes considerable restriction is needed to calm the individual. Not uncommonly, particularly in these litigious times, the responsible clinician feels trapped between threats of legal action on either side of the issue. Undue restriction might lead to a civil rights suit, whereas failure to employ all available safeguards could, in the case of the patient's injury or death, lead to a potentially ruinous malpractice claim initiated by the patient's family (Fremouw et al., 1990). Currently, it appears that most practitioners resolve this dilemma by taking the most cautious and conservative course. Thus many patients are hospitalized with insufficient clinical justification. Even where the decision to hospitalize is made on good grounds, however, preventive efforts may be fruitless, as truly determined

persons may find a way to commit suicide even on a "suicide watch."

Thus, the vexing ethical problems of whether and to what extent one should intervene in cases of threatened suicide have now been complicated by no less vexing legal ones. As in other areas of professional practice, clinical judgment is no longer the exclusive consideration in intervention decisions. The ramifications of clinical decisions spread widely to matters that were formerly remote or irrelevant, such as the cost of malpractice insurance or the estimated likelihood that a patient or his or her family will sue. Because this is a societal problem, the solutions—if any—will have to be societal ones.

Admittedly, the preceding considerations do not resolve the issue of a person's basic right to suicide. As in the case of most complex ethical issues, no simple answer is apparent. Unless and until sufficient evidence confirms this alleged right—and society agrees on the conditions under which it may appropriately be exercised—it thus seems the wiser course to encourage existing suicide prevention (intervention) programs and to foster research into suicidal behavior with the hope of reducing the toll in human life and misery taken each year by suicide.

SUMMARY

Mood disorders (formerly called affective disorders) are those in which extreme variations in mood—either low or high—are the predominant feature. We all experience such variations at mild to moderate levels in the natural course of life. For some people, however, the extremity of a mood in either direction is causally related to behavior that most would consider maladaptive. This chapter described the official categories of disorder associated with such maladaptive mood variations.

The large majority of people with these disorders have some form of unipolar depression—dysthymia or major depression. In these disorders the person experiences a range of affective, cognitive, and motivational symptoms including persistent sadness, negative thoughts about the self and the future, and lack of energy or initiative to engage in formerly pleasurable activities. Basic biological functioning is often also altered—for example, the sleep pattern may be dramatically altered or the person may become uninterested in food or eating.

In the bipolar disorders (cyclothymia, and Bipolar I and II disorders), the person experiences episodes of both depression and hypomania or mania. During manic or hypomanic episodes, the symptoms are essentially the oppo-

site of those during a depressive episode. Unipolar disorders are much more common than bipolar disorders.

For unipolar disorders, there are both biological and psychosocial causal factors. Among biological causal factors, there is evidence of a modest genetic contribution to the vulnerability for major depression, but probably not for dysthymia. Although we do not yet understand how biological factors are involved in causing major depression, there are many reasons to think that biological factors do indeed play an important causal role. For example, severe depressions are clearly associated with multiple interacting disturbances in neurobiological regulation, including neurochemical, neurooendocrine, and neurophysiological systems. Disruptions in circadian and seasonal rhythms in depression also support the role of biological factors; much of the most exciting biological research on depression in recent years has focused on circadian rhythm dysfunction and how it may account for many of the clinical features of depression.

There are also many important theories regarding psychosocial causes of unipolar depression. Beck's cognitive theory and the reformulated helplessness and hopelessness theories are formulated as diathesis-stress models, where the diathesis is cognitive in nature (e.g., dysfunctional beliefs and pessimistic attributional style, respectively). Personality variables such as neuroticism, sociotropy, and autonomy may also serve as diatheses for depression. Psychodynamic and interpersonal theories emphasize the importance of early experiences (especially early losses and the quality of the parent-child relationship) as setting up a predisposition for depression. Although no single theory can successfully explain all of the causes of depression, it is unlikely that any one theory will ever explain all of the causal pathways to unipolar depression, which is undoubtedly multiply determined.

For bipolar disorders, biological causal factors play an even stronger role than for unipolar disorders. The genetic contribution to bipolar disorder is probably stronger than for any other major psychiatric disorder. Biochemical imbalances and abnormalities of the hypothalamic-pituitary-adrenal axis are also clearly implicated, although the exact nature of the abnormalities remains to be determined. There is also clear evidence regarding disturbances in biological rhythms in bipolar disorder. One major challenge is to determine how one drug—lithium—can play a role in reducing both manic symptoms and depressive symptoms. Stressful life events may be involved in precipitating manic or depressive episodes, but it is unlikely that they cause the disorder, as opposed to affecting the timing and frequency of episodes of illness.

Biologically based treatments, such as drugs or electroconvulsive therapy, are often used in the treatment of the more severe or major disorders. Increasingly, however, psychosocial treatments are also being used with good effectiveness in many cases of these more severe disorders, as well as the milder forms of mood disorder. Considerable evidence suggests that recurrent depression is best treated by specialized forms of psychosocial treatment or by maintenance for prolonged periods on drugs.

Suicide is a constant danger with depressive syndromes of any type or severity. Accordingly, an assessment of suicide risk is essential in the proper management of depressive disorders. A small minority of suicides appears unavoidable—chiefly those of the deliberate type where the person really wants to die and uses a highly lethal method. A substantial amount of suicidal behavior (for example, taking nonlethal or slow-acting drugs where the likelihood of discovery is high) is motivated more by a desire for indirect interpersonal communication than by a wish to die. Somewhere between these extremes is a large group of people who are ambivalent about killing themselves and who initiate dangerous actions that they may or may not carry to completion, depending on momentary events and impulses. Suicide prevention programs generally consist of crisis intervention in the form of suicide hotlines and although these are undoubtedly effective in some cases in averting fatal suicide attempt, the long-term success of treatment aimed at preventing suicide in those at high risk is much less clear at the present time.

KEY TERMS

mood disorders (p. 210)

mania (p. 210)

depression (p. 210)

unipolar disorder (p. 210)

bipolar disorder (p. 210)

dysthymia (p. 214)

adjustment disorder with depressed mood (p. 215)

major depressive disorder (p. 216)

melancholic type (p. 217)

severe major depressive episode with psychotic features (p. 217)

mood-congruent (p. 217)

mood-incongruent (p. 218)

recurrence (p. 218)

relapse (p. 218)

seasonal affective disorder (p. 219)

hypomania (p. 219)

cyclothymia (p. 219)

bipolar disorder (p. 220)

bipolar disorder with a seasonal pattern (p. 221)

rapid cycling (p. 223)

schizoaffective disorder (p. 224)

diathesis-stress model (p. 231)

pessimistic attributional style (p. 232)

depressogenic schemas (p. 234)

dysfunctional beliefs (p. 234)

negative automatic thoughts (p. 235)

negative cognitive triad (p. 235)

learned helplessness (p. 236)

attributions (p. 237)

suicide (p. 255)

Somatoform and Dissociative Disorders

Josef Forster, *Untitled* (after 1916). Born in 1878, Forster worked as a paperhanger and a decorator. Little is known about him, other than the fact that he was diagnosed with schizophrenia, and remained single until his death, sometime after 1941. In this painterly illusion, the figure seems to float silently between two worlds.

Think about a period in your own life in which you were having serious problems. Perhaps you can also recall the disorganizing effects of these stressful events. Perhaps you began to feel physical pains or just felt like you were walking around in a daze. Certainly the disorders to be examined in this chapter will seem to most readers much less familiar and less readily grasped as merely exaggerated forms of everyday psychological phenomena such as feelings of depression or anxiety. However, reflecting on the subtler effects of stress, such as feelings of just not being all there, may make the disorders we are about to discuss a little more concrete. Somatoform and dissociative processes appear to involve more complex and convoluted mental operations than those we have so far encountered. As a result, they confront the field of psychopathology with some of its most fascinating and difficult challenges.

The **somatoform disorders** are a group of conditions involving physical complaints or disabilities that occur without any evidence of physical pathology to account for them. Despite the range of clinical manifestations—from blindness to paralysis—they share one key feature: all are expressions of psychological difficulties in the "body language" of medical problems that on careful examination cannot be documented to exist. Equally key to these disorders is the fact that the affected patients are *not* merely faking symptoms and attempting to deceive others; for the most part they genuinely and sometimes passionately believe something is terribly wrong with their bodies. They therefore show up in large numbers in the practices of primary care physicians, who then have the often difficult task of deciding how to manage their complaints.

The **dissociative disorders,** on the other hand, are conditions involving a disruption in a person's sense of personal identity. Included here are some of the more dramatic phenomena to be observed in the entire domain of psychopathology: people who cannot recall who they are or where they may have come from, or who split themselves into two or more individuals having independent "personalities" and autobiographical memories. The term *dissociation* refers to this type of splitting process wherein some part of the person's experience of self and the world becomes autonomous from and normally inaccessible to conscious appraisal and executive direction of the main or "host" personality.

As we have seen (Chapter 5), both somatoform and dissociative disorders were once included with the anxiety disorders under the general rubric *neuroses* or *psychoneuroses.* Our reason for including them together here in a single chapter goes beyond historical precedence. There is growing empirical evidence (e.g., Nijenhuis et al., 1998; Pribor et al., 1993; Ross, 1997; Saxe et al., 1994; van der Kolk et al., 1996) of a significant link between dissociative tendencies on the one hand and the likelihood of experiencing somatoform symptoms on the other. We begin our discussion with the somatoform disorders.

SOMATOFORM DISORDERS

Soma means "body," and somatoform disorders involve patterns in which individuals complain of bodily symptoms that suggest the presence of medical problems, but for which no organic basis can be found that satisfactorily explains the symptoms. Such individuals are typically preoccupied with their state of health and with various presumed disorders or diseases of bodily organs.

In our discussion, we will focus on four more or less distinct somatoform patterns: (1) somatization disorder, (2) hypochondriasis, (3) pain disorder, and (4) conversion disorder. Although all four involve the "neurotic" development or elaboration of physical disabilities, the patterns of causation and the most effective treatment approaches may differ somewhat. The diagnosis of undifferentiated somatoform disorder is reserved for those persistent (i.e., a duration of at least six months) unfounded complaints of insufficient clarity or intensity to meet criteria for a more specific somatoform disorder. DSM-IV also includes a sixth syndrome under the somatoform rubric, body dysmorphic disorder, in which there is a preoccupation with some imagined defect in one's physical appearance. As noted in Chapter 5, our view is that this type of problem is best considered a variant of obsessive-compulsive disorder.

Somatization Disorder

Somatization disorder is characterized by multiple complaints of physical ailments over a long period, beginning before age 30, that are inadequately explained by independent findings of physical illness or injury and that lead to medical treatment or to significant life impairment. Not surprisingly, therefore, somatization disorder is relatively common among patients in primary medical care settings around the world (Gureje et al., 1997).

A diagnostician need not be convinced that these claimed illnesses actually existed in a patient's background history; the mere reporting of them is sufficient. As noted in Chapter 1, the DSM-IV provides a list of four types and levels of symptoms that, where each is present to at least a minimal degree, qualify as justifying a diagnosis of somatization disorder. We review them here:

1. *Four pain symptoms:* The patient must report a history of pain experienced with respect to at least four different sites or functions—for example, head, abdomen, back, joints, or rectum, or during menstruation, sexual intercourse, or urination.

2. *Two gastrointestinal symptoms:* The patient must report a history of at least two symptoms, other than pain, pertaining to the gastrointestinal system—such as nausea, bloating, diarrhea, multiple food intolerances, or vomiting when not pregnant.

3. *One sexual symptom:* The patient must report at least one reproductive system symptom other than pain—as for example sexual indifference or dysfunction, menstrual irregularity, vomiting throughout pregnancy.

4. *One pseudoneurological symptom:* The patient must report a history of at least one symptom, not limited to pain, suggestive of a neurological condition—for example, various symptoms that mimic sensory or motor impairments such as loss of sensation or involuntary muscle contraction in a hand; or symptoms involving anomalies of consciousness or memory—for example, an episode of dissociative amnesia, to be described later.

The main features of somatization disorder are illustrated in the following case summary, which also involves a secondary diagnosis of depression:

Case Study, A Woman and Her As-Yet-Undiscovered Illness • This 38-year-old married woman, the mother of five children, reports to a mental health clinic with the chief complaint of depression, meeting diagnostic criteria for major depressive disorder, the latest of several such episodes. Her marriage, which began at age 17, has been a chronically unhappy one; her husband is described as an alcoholic with an unstable work history, and there have been frequent arguments revolving around finances, her sexual indifference, and her complaints of pain during intercourse.

The history reveals that the patient had herself abused alcohol between ages 19 and 29, but has been abstinent since. She describes herself as nervous since childhood and as having been continuously sickly beginning in her youth; she believes she has a not-yet-discovered physical illness. She experiences chest pain and reportedly has been told by doctors that she has a "nervous heart." She sees physicians frequently for abdominal pain, having been diagnosed on one occasion as having a "spastic colon."

In addition to M.D. physicians she has consulted chiropractors and osteopaths for backaches, pains in her extremities, and a feeling of anesthesia in her fingertips. She was recently admitted to a hospital following complaints of abdominal and chest pain and of vomiting, during which admission she received a hysterectomy. Following the surgery she has been troubled by spells of anxiety, fainting, vomiting, food intolerance, and weakness and fatigue. Physical examinations reveal completely negative findings.

The patient attributes her depression to hormonal irregularities, and she continues to seek a medical explanation of her other problems as well. (Adapted from Spitzer et al., 1994, pp. 404–405)

Somatization disorder, formerly called Briquet's syndrome after the French physician who first described it, has not been as extensively researched as the other somatoform disorders. It is believed to be about ten times more common among women than among men, with a lifetime prevalence of up to 2 percent (American Psychiatric Association, 1994). Despite its significant prevalence in medical settings, therefore, we remain quite uncertain about its developmental course and specific etiology.

There is evidence of a familial linkage with antisocial personality disorder (see Chapter 9), one that could have some genetic basis. There is also some speculation, based on opposite prevalence discrepancies for these disorders in men and women, that a common underlying predisposition tends to lead to antisocial behavior in men and to somatization in women (Guze et al, 1986; Lilienfeld, 1992; Sigvardson et al., 1984). Both disorders also appear disproportionally prevalent among those of lower socioeconomic status (Lilienfeld, 1992), which somewhat clouds the meaning of their familial association. Even accepting the dubious assumption of an entirely genetic basis for family linkage, however, it is far from clear (1) how any such genetic influence might encourage such outcomes, (2) why they should vary with gender, and (3) what is the role, if any, of low socioeconomic status in contributing to either disorder. Conceivably, the associations observed here may have the common theme of gross family disorganization, which is also known to be associated with various forms of child abuse.

Hypochondriasis

The differences between somatization disorder and **hypochondriasis** remain conceptually unclear, although the DSM-IV diagnostic criteria for the two do achieve a practical separation between them. Evidently, the two disorders (if they are in fact distinct) are closely related (see Noyes et al., 1993). The main differences seem to be that hypochondriasis may have its onset after age 30, and that the abnormal health concerns characteristic of hypochondriasis need not focus on any particular set of symptoms nor on a profusion of them. A hypochondriacal person mostly focuses on the idea that he or she has a serious disease, such as tuberculosis or lung cancer, rather than claiming various symptoms or physical disabilities.

Hypochondriasis is one of the most frequently seen somatoform patterns, with a prevalence in general medical practice of between 4 and 9 percent. The disorder is characterized by multiple and stubbornly held complaints about possible physical illness even though no evidence of such illness can be found. Hypochondriacal complaints are usually not restricted to any physiologically coherent symptom pattern; rather, they express a preoccupation with health matters and unrealistic fears of disease. Although hypochondriacal people repeatedly seek medical advice, their concerns are not in the least lessened by their doctors' reassurances—in fact they are frequently disappointed when no physical problem is found.

Major Characteristics Individuals with hypochondriasis may complain of uncomfortable and peculiar sensations in the general area of the stomach, chest, head, genitals, or anywhere else in the body. They usually have trouble giving a precise description of their symptoms, however. They may begin by mentioning pain in the stomach, which on further questioning is not really a pain but a gnawing sensation, or perhaps a feeling of heat, or of pressure, whose locus may now on more careful observation migrate to a neighboring portion of the abdomen, and so on. The mental orientation of these individuals keeps them constantly on the alert for new symptoms, the description of which may challenge the capacity of mere language to communicate.

Hypochondriacal patients are likely to be avid readers of popular magazines on medical topics and are apt to feel certain that they are suffering from every new disease they read or hear about. They are major consumers of over-the-counter (and often virtually worthless) remedies touted in ads as being able to alleviate vaguely described problems such as "tired blood" or "irregularity." Tuberculosis, cancer, exotic infections, and numerous other diseases are readily self-diagnosed by these individuals. Their morbid preoccupation with bodily processes, coupled with their often limited knowledge of medical pathology (but see the case below), leads to some interesting diagnoses. One patient diagnosed his condition as

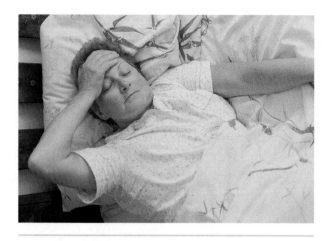

Hypochondriacal individuals are preoccupied with health matters and unrealistic fears of disease. They are convinced that they have symptoms of physical illness, but their complaints typically do not conform to any coherent symptom pattern, and they usually have trouble giving a precise description of their symptoms.

"ptosis of the transvex colon," and added, "If I am just half as bad off as I think, I am a dead pigeon."

This attitude appears to be typical: Such individuals are sure they are seriously ill and cannot recover. Yet—and this is revealing—despite their exaggerated concerns over their health, they do not usually show the intense fear or anxiety that might be expected of those suffering from such horrible ills. In fact they are usually in good physical condition. Nevertheless, they are sincere in their conviction that the symptoms they detect represent real illness. They are not **malingering**—consciously faking symptoms to achieve specific goals external to the medical context—although an attentive listener may get the impression that something more is being communicated in these complaints.

The following case captures a typical clinical picture in hypochondriasis and incidentally demonstrates that a high level of medical sophistication does not necessarily rule out a person's developing this disorder.

Case Study, A Radiologist's Abdominal Mass • This 38-year-old physician radiologist initiated his first psychiatric consultation following his 9-year-old son's accidentally discovering his father palpating (examining by touch) his own abdomen and saying to him, "What do you think it is this time, Dad?" The radiologist describes the incident and his accompanying anger and shame with tears in his eyes. He also describes his recent return from a ten-day stay at a famous out-of-state medical diagnostic center to which he had been referred by an exasperated gastroenterologist colleague who'd reportedly "reached the end of the line" with his radiologist patient. The extensive physical and laboratory examinations performed at the center had revealed no significant physical disease, a conclusion the patient reports with resentment and disappointment rather than relief.

The patient's history reveals a long-standing pattern of over-concern about personal health matters, beginning at age 13 and exacerbated by his medical school experience. Until fairly recently, however, he had maintained reasonable control over these concerns, in part because he was embarrassed to reveal them to other physicians. He is conscientious and successful in his profession and active in community life. However, he spends much of his leisure time at home alone in bed. His wife, like his son, has become increasingly impatient with his morbid preoccupation about life-threatening but undetectable diseases.

In describing his current symptoms the patient refers to his becoming increasingly aware over the past several months of various sounds and sensations emanating from his abdomen and of his sometimes being able to feel a "firm mass" in its left lower quadrant. His tentative diagnosis is carcinoma (cancer) of the colon. He tests his stool for blood weekly and palpates his abdomen for 15 to 20 minutes every 2 to 3 days. He has performed several X-ray studies of himself in secrecy after hours at his office. Generally discouraged in demeanor, the patient brightens notably in describing a clinically insignificant finding of a urethral anomaly, the result of a laboratory test he had had performed on himself. (Adapted from Spitzer et al., 1994, pp. 88–90.)

As in this case, hypochondriacal persons often show a notable preoccupation with digestive and excretory functions. Some keep charts of their bowel movements, and most are able to give detailed information concerning diet, constipation, and related matters. Many, as suggested earlier, use a wide range of self-medications of the type frequently advertised on television. However, they do not show the losses or distortions of sensory, motor, and visceral functioning that occur in conversion disorder (to be discussed in a later section); nor do their complaints have the bizarre delusional quality—such as "insides rotting away" or "lungs drying up"—that occurs in some psychotic disorders.

More Than Meets the Eye? Most of us as children learn well the lesson that, when we are sick, special comforts and attention are provided and, furthermore, that we are excused from a number of responsibilities or at least are not expected to perform certain chores up to par. This lesson has been learned all too well by the hypochondriacal adult. Such an adult is in effect saying (1) I deserve more of your attention and concern, and (2)

You may not legitimately expect me to perform as a well person would. Typically these messages are conveyed with more than a touch of angry rebuke or whining, inconsolable demand.

It is a reasonable assumption that these patients have, as a group, more deep-seated problems than merely a fear of disease, and most hypochondriacs also meet criteria for other Axis I psychiatric diagnoses (Barsky, Wyshak, & Klerman, 1992). Moreover, Barsky and colleagues (1994) have indicated reports of significantly elevated psychological trauma, including violence and sexual abuse, in the childhood histories of hypochondriacal patients, compared with controls. These authors also found their hypochondriacal patients to report much childhood sickness and missing of school, suggesting that the pattern of communicating psychic distress by reference to physical malfunction was learned quite early.

In short, hypochondriasis may be viewed as a certain type of needful interpersonal communication as well as a disorder involving abnormal preoccupation with disease. Treatment of the latter in the absence of an appreciation of the former frequently produces clinical frustration, if not exasperation. In fact, it may be that the (understandable) impatience with which many physicians react to these patients has the unintended effect of maintaining or increasing their fears of abandonment and an early demise from some terrible condition that remains undetected by an insufficiently caring physician (Kirmayer, Robbins, & Paris, 1994; Noyes et al., 1993). Highlight 7.1 presents an interesting research finding on this point.

Pain Disorder

Pain disorder is characterized by the report of pain of sufficient duration and severity to cause significant life disruption in the absence of objective findings of medical pathology that would explain pain experience and behavior of the magnitude observed. DSM-IV specifies two coded subdiagnoses of (1) pain disorder associated with psychological factors, and (2) pain disorder associated with both psychological factors and a general medical condition. The first subdiagnosis applies where any coexisting general medical condition is considered of minimal causal significance in the pain complaint; the second applies where the experienced pain is considered to be out of proportion to an established medical condition that might cause some pain. When general medical conditions are implicated in pain, they are coded on Axis III. Medically unexplained pain associated with sexual inter-

Hypochondriasis and "Real" Illness

What happens if a hypochondriacal patient should become sick with a genuinely serious medical condition? A preliminary answer to this question is provided in a controlled longitudinal study of hypochondriacal individuals recently published by Barsky and colleagues (1998).

In this study, patients meeting diagnostic criteria for hypochondriasis were intensively studied at clinic intake and then again four to five years later, and compared with a similar group of clinic patients who were not hypochondriacal. The main findings confirm that hypochondriasis is often a stubbornly persistent disorder, with 63.5 percent of these patients still meeting criteria for hypochondriasis at follow-up. In general, these more persistently hypochondriacal patients ("nonremitters") were more severely disordered (e.g., having higher "disease conviction" and more somatic complaints) at intake than those who no longer met hypochondriacal diagnostic criteria at follow-up ("remitters").

There was an interesting twist to these findings, however: during the follow-up interval hypochondriasis remitters had acquired significantly more (real) major medical problems than had their nonremitting counterparts. In other words, it appears that hypochondriacal tendencies were reduced by the occurrence of serious medical conditions. The authors comment on this as follows:

> The qualitative interviews support the quantitative findings in suggesting that serious medical illness sometimes ameliorated hypochondriacal symptoms because it served to legitimize the patients' complaints, sanction their assumption of the sick role, and lessen the skepticism with which they had previously been regarded . . . . As one noted, "Now that I know Dr. X is paying attention to me, I can believe him if he says nothing serious is wrong." (p. 744) ■

---

course is diagnosed as dyspareunia, a sexual disorder (see Chapter 11).

The Subjectivity of Pain In approaching the phenomenon of pain it is important to bear in mind that it is *always* a subjective experience. Pain perceived or experienced does not exist in a perfect correlation with observable tissue damage or irritation. This partial independence of physical dysfunction and psychological experience also means that it is possible to treat pain associated with real physical causes psychologically (see Gatchel & Turk, 1996; Keefe & Williams, 1989; Keefe & Lefebvre, 1997).

Pain is also always private. We have no way of gauging with certainty the actual extent of a patient's pain. We are reduced to rough estimates based on "pain behavior," which includes the patient's verbal report of feeling it as well as observations of grimacing, restricted mobility, "protective" movements, favoring the alternate limb, etc. However, simply because it is fundamentally impossible to assess pain with pinpoint accuracy, this does not justify the conclusion that a patient is faking or exaggerating his or her pain, although such judgments are regrettably frequent in clinical situations.

Pain disorder is fairly common among psychiatric patients (Katon, Egan, & Miller, 1985) and is more often diagnosed among women. There is considerable evidence that, even where some physical basis for pain is present, its experienced intensity is a function of the level of stress the patient is currently undergoing. For example, Schwartz, Slater, and Birchler (1994) have reported a study in which chronic back pain patients subjected to a prior contrived stressful circumstance reported more pain and engaged in more nonverbal pain behavior than a comparable group exposed to an emotionally neutral prior circumstance.

The reported pain may be vaguely located in the area of the heart or other vital organs, or it may center in the lower back or limbs. (Tension headaches and migraines are not included here, since they involve demonstrable physiological changes, such as muscle contractions.) People with predominantly *psychogenic* (that is, psychologi-

Despite the thoroughly believable quality of this man's suffering, the experience of pain is always subjective and private. Pain does not exist in perfect correlation with observable tissue damage or irritation.

cally caused) pain disorders may adopt an invalid lifestyle. They tend to "doctor-shop" in the hope of finding both a physical confirmation of their pain and some medication to relieve their suffering. This behavior continues even if several visits to doctors fail to indicate any underlying physical problem. Sadly enough, in many cases somatoform pain patients actually wind up being disabled—either through addiction to pain medication or through the crippling effects of surgery they have been able to obtain as treatment for their condition. The following case is illustrative.

Case Study, Pain Disorder and Lost Youth • An attractive, socially prominent, middle-aged woman developed a severe pain, increasing over time, in her right breast. Over a period of several years she consulted numerous physicians in various specialties, none of whom was able to establish any objective medical reason for the pain despite the employment of every known diagnostic procedure that might yield an answer; the painful breast was, so far as could be determined using the most advanced methods available, anatomically and physiologically normal. Increasingly desperate, she so pressured one of her physicians that he recommended she consider mastectomy (surgical removal of the breast), and she did in fact travel to a tertiary-care, university medical center to request this operation.

Fortunately, the surgeon to whom she was assigned was a compassionate and psychologically sophisticated man. He sensed that this pain was somehow associated with the woman's concerns about growing older and losing her sexual attractiveness, which had been central to her self-esteem and feelings of worth since adolescence. He skillfully diverted her to an experienced psychotherapist. In somewhat less than a year of work with this therapist the patient was free of pain and in general far more comfortable with herself and her life.

Unnecessary, mutilating surgery was in this case averted; sometimes, in pain disorder, it is not.

Conversion Disorder

Conversion disorder, known originally as *hysteria,* involves a pattern in which symptoms of some physical malfunction or loss of control appear without any underlying organic pathology. These symptoms often mimic neurological disorders of one kind or another and are thus described as "pseudoneurological" in nature. Conversion disorder is one of the most intriguing and baffling patterns in psychopathology, and we still have much to learn about it. Nevertheless, contemporary research relating to the problem has been notably sparse.

As we mentioned in Chapter 2, the term *hysteria* was derived from the Greek word meaning uterus. It was thought by Hippocrates and other ancient Greeks that this disorder was restricted to women, and that it was caused by sexual difficulties, particularly by the wandering of a frustrated womb to various parts of the body because of sexual desires and a yearning for children. Thus the uterus might lodge in the throat and cause choking sensations, or in the spleen, resulting in temper tantrums. Hippocrates considered marriage the best remedy for the affliction. Freud used the term *conversion hysteria* for these disorders because he believed that the symptoms were an expression of repressed sexual energy—that is, the unconscious conflict a person felt about his or her sexual desires was converted into a bodily disturbance. For example, a person's guilty feelings about masturbation might be solved by developing a paralyzed hand. This was not done consciously, of course, and the person was not aware of the origin or meaning of the physical symptom.

Escape and Secondary Gain In contemporary psychopathology, reactions of this type are no longer interpreted in Freudian terms as the conversion of sexual conflicts or other psychological problems into physical symptoms. Though still called a *conversion disorder,* the physical symptoms are now usually seen as serving the rather obvious function of providing a plausible excuse, enabling an individual to escape or avoid an intolerably stressful situation without having to take responsibility for doing so. Relatedly, the term **secondary gain,** which originally referred to advantages of the symptom(s) beyond the "primary gain" of neutralizing intrapsychic conflict, has also been retained. Generally, it is used to refer to any "external" circumstance, such as attention from loved ones or financial compensation, that would tend to reinforce the maintenance of disability. With the diminished importance accorded to intrapsychic "gain," the distinction between primary and secondary gain has become rather blurred over the course of time. "Secondary gain" does retain a more pejorative connotation of active management of outcomes by the display of symptoms.

Decreasing Incidence Conversion disorders were once relatively common in civilian and especially in military life. In World War I, conversion disorder was the most frequently diagnosed psychiatric syndrome among soldiers; it was also relatively common during World War II. Conversion disorder typically occurred under highly stressful combat conditions and involved men who would ordinarily be considered stable. Here, conversion symptoms—such as paralysis of the legs—enabled a soldier to avoid an anxiety-arousing combat situation without being labeled a coward or being subjected to court-martial.

Today conversion disorders constitute only some 1 to 3 percent of all disorders referred for mental health treatment. Interestingly enough, their decreasing incidence seems to be closely related to our growing sophistication about medical and psychological disorders: A conversion disorder apparently loses its defensive function if it can be readily shown to lack an organic basis. In an age that no longer believes in such phenomena as being "struck blind" or suddenly afflicted with an unusual and dramatic paraplegia, the cases that do occur increasingly simulate more exotic physical diseases that are harder to diagnose, such as convulsive seizures or seeming malfunction of internal organs. As noted above, more common in contemporary conversion disorders are symptoms not so obviously and directly related to the nature of the problem with which the patient, without awareness, is attempting to cope. The following case is illustrative:

Case Study, A Desperate Wife's Vertigo • A 46-year-old housewife, mother of four children, was referred for psychiatric evaluation of her frequent and incapacitating attacks of dizziness accompanied by nausea, in the course of which the environment would take on a "shimmering" appearance and she would have the experience of "floating" and inability to maintain her balance. Consultation with an internist, a neurologist, and an otolaryngologist had resulted in no satisfactory medical explanation for these experiences; she was, in fact, pronounced physically fit.

The patient readily admitted to some marital difficulties, chiefly revolving around her spouse's verbal abuse and excessive criticism of her and their children. Nevertheless, she declared that she very much loved and needed her husband, and she saw no connection between her dizziness "attacks" and his occasionally unpleasant behavior.

Careful evaluation, however, revealed that her attacks almost always occurred in late afternoon, at about the time her husband returned from work, and when he was usually most grumpy and critical; she admitted that she dreaded his arrival because he would usually complain about the messiness of the house and the dinner she had planned. With the onset of her attacks, she normally would have to lie on a couch and would not feel "up" for doing anything until 7:00 or 8:00 P.M., with the result that her husband and the children would eat at local fast-food establishments. The patient would spend the rest of the evening watching TV, usually falling asleep and not returning to the couple's bedroom until 2:00 or 3:00 A.M. Meanwhile, the husband watched TV in the bedroom until *he* fell asleep. Communication between the couple was thus kept to a minimum. (Adapted from Spitzer et al., 1994, pp. 244–245.)

Here we see with particular clarity how "functional" a conversion disorder may be in the overall psychic economy of the patient, despite its imposing a certain cost in illness or disability.

The range of symptoms in conversion disorder is practically as diverse as for physically based ailments. In describing the clinical picture in conversion disorder, it is useful to think in terms of three categories of symptoms: (1) sensory, (2) motor, and (3) visceral.

Sensory Symptoms Any of the senses may be involved in sensory conversion reactions. The most common forms are as follows:

Anesthesia—loss of sensitivity

Hypesthesia—partial loss of sensitivity

Hyperesthesia—excessive sensitivity

Analgesia—loss of sensitivity to pain

Paresthesia—exceptional sensations, such as tingling or heat

You may be wondering why somatoform pain disorder, given its essential similarity to the symptoms just listed, is not included here as merely another form of sensory conversion disorder. Why is it a separate category? The DSM-IV offers no satisfactory answer to this question. It may be that it was given separate status because it appears to occur far more frequently than other conversion phenomena.

Some idea of the range of sensory symptoms that may occur in conversion disorders can be gleaned from Ironside and Batchelor's (1945) classic study of hysterical visual symptoms among airmen in World War II. They found blurred vision, photophobia (extreme sensitivity to light), double vision, night blindness, a combination of intermittent visual failure and amnesia, deficient stereopsis (the tendency to look past an object during attempts to focus on it), restriction in the visual field, intermittent loss of vision in one eye, color blindness, jumbling of print during attempts to read, and failing day vision. They also found that the symptoms of each airman were closely related to his performance duties. Night fliers, for example, were more subject to night blindness, while day fliers more often developed failing day vision.

The other senses may also be subject to a wide range of problems. A puzzling and unsolved question in conversion blindness and deafness is whether affected persons actually cannot see or hear, or whether the sensory information is received but screened from consciousness. In general, the evidence supports the idea that the sensory input is registered but is somehow screened from explicit conscious recognition. Numerous demonstrations of this type of phenomenon occur in the literature on hypnosis, which has, for good reason, been closely associated historically with conversion phenomena (see Hilgard, 1994). Virtually all of the symptoms seen in conversion disorder can be reproduced on a temporary basis by hypnotic suggestion, particularly among highly hypnotizable subjects. Hypnotized subjects and conversion patients also share certain anomalies that suggest their sensory losses are not absolute. For example, hysterically blind persons rarely endanger themselves by walking into hazardous situations, and a normal subject hypnotically induced to be unable to see an object in his or her path will nevertheless avoid walking into it.

Motor Symptoms Motor conversion reactions also cover a wide range of symptoms, but only the most common need be mentioned here.

Paralysis conversion reactions are usually confined to a single limb, such as an arm or a leg, and the loss of function is usually selective. For example, in writer's cramp, a person cannot write but may be able to use the same muscles in shuffling a deck of cards or playing the piano. *Tremors* (muscular shaking or trembling) and *tics* (localized muscular twitches) are common. Occasionally, symptoms include contractures, which usually involve flexing of the fingers and toes, or rigidity of the larger joints, such as the elbows and knees. Paralyses and contractures frequently lead to walking disturbances. A person with a rigid knee joint may be forced to throw his or her leg out in a sort of arc as he or she walks. Another walking disturbance is *astasia-abasia,* in which an individual can usually control leg movements when sitting or lying down, but can hardly stand and has a grotesque, disorganized walk, with both legs wobbling about in every direction.

The most common speech-related conversion disturbances are *aphonia,* in which an individual is able to talk only in a whisper, and *mutism,* in which he or she cannot speak at all. Interestingly enough, a person who can talk only in a whisper can usually cough in a normal manner. In true, organic laryngeal paralysis both the cough and the voice are affected. Aphonia is a relatively common conversion reaction and usually occurs after some emotional shock, whereas mutism is relatively rare. Occasionally, symptoms may involve convulsions, similar to those in epilepsy. People with such symptoms, however, show few of the usual characteristics of true epilepsy—they rarely, if ever, injure themselves in falls; their pupillary reflex to light remains unaffected; they are able to control excretory functions; and they rarely have attacks when others are not present.

Visceral Symptoms The DSM-IV recognizes four subtypes of Conversion Disorder according to the kinds of symptoms displayed: (1) sensory, (2) motor, (3) seizure or convulsion, and (4) "mixed." Traditionally, however, a number of other fairly common symptom patterns seemingly referring to alterations in the functioning of internal organs have also been considered to be basically conversion phenomena. A wide range of medically unexplained visceral symptom patterns is involved, such as "lump in the throat" and choking sensations, coughing spells, difficulty in breathing, cold and clammy extremities, belching, nausea, vomiting, and so on. Occasionally, persistent hiccoughing or sneezing occurs.

Actual organic symptoms may be simulated to an almost unbelievable degree. In a pseudoattack of acute

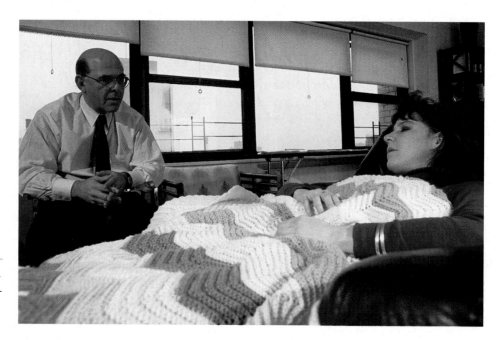

Virtually all the symptoms of conversion disorder can be temporarily reproduced by hypnotic suggestions.

appendicitis, a person not only may evidence lower-abdominal pain and other typical symptoms, but also may have a temperature far above normal. Conversion-reaction cases of malaria and tuberculosis have also been cited in the literature. In the latter, for example, an individual may show all the usual symptoms—coughing, loss of weight, recurrent fever, and night sweats—without actual organic disease. Numerous cases of pseudopregnancy (formerly called pseudocyesis) have been reported, in which menstruation may cease, the abdominal area and breasts may enlarge, and the woman may experience morning sickness.

Diagnosis in Conversion Disorder   Because the symptoms in conversion disorder can simulate almost every known disease, accurate diagnosis can be a serious problem. However, in addition to specialized medical techniques, several criteria are commonly used for distinguishing between conversion disorders and true organic disturbances:

- *A certain unconcern ("la belle indifférence"), in which the patient describes what is wrong in a rather matter-of-fact way, with little of the anxiety and fear that would be expected in a person with a paralyzed arm or loss of sight.* Mucha and Reinhardt (1970) reported that all of the 56 conversion disordered military student fliers in their study showed this pattern, seeming to be unconcerned about long-range effects of their disabilities. In itself, however, unconcernedness cannot be taken as a reliable sign of conversion; some stoic persons with genuine organic pathology show a

similar disregard, and some conversion patients exhibit a level of concern "appropriate" to the disabilities they display.

- *The frequent failure of the dysfunction to conform clearly to the symptoms of the particular disease or disorder simulated.* For example, little or no wasting away or atrophy of a "paralyzed" limb occurs in paralyses that are conversion reactions, except in rare and long-standing cases.

- *The selective nature of the dysfunction.* As already noted, in conversion blindness the affected individual does not usually bump into people or objects; "paralyzed" muscles can be used for some activities but not others; and uncontrolled contractures (muscular rigidities) usually disappear during sleep.

- *Under hypnosis or narcosis (a sleeplike state induced by drugs) the symptoms can usually be removed, shifted, or reinduced at the suggestion of the therapist.* Similarly, if the person is suddenly awakened from a sound sleep, he or she may be tricked into using a "paralyzed" limb.

Distinguishing Conversion from Malingering/Factitious Disorder

Sometimes, of course, persons do deliberately and consciously feign disability or illness. For these instances, the DSM distinguishes between *malingering* and *factitious disorder* on the basis of the feigning person's apparent goals. As noted earlier, the malingering person is seen as seeking a specific outcome, such as an award of money or

Highlight 7.2

Factitious Disorder by Proxy

In a somewhat bizarre variant of factitious disorder, the person invalidly seeking medical or mental health professional attention intentionally feigns or induces medical or psychological symptoms in another person who is under his or her care. In a typical instance, a mother presents her own child for treatment of a medical condition she has deliberately caused, disclaiming any knowledge of its origin. The majority of such cases involve the gastrointestinal, genitourinary, or central nervous systems, apparently because diseases or dysfunctions in these systems are most readily simulated by excessive administration of widely available drugs (e.g., emetics, laxatives, diuretics, CNS stimulants or depressants) or other illness-inducing chemicals (such as cleaning products). Of course, the health of such victims is often genuinely endangered in being repeatedly abused by these measures, sometimes necessitating social service or law enforcement intervention. Reports of presumably accidental victim death are not rare in these "proxy" cases.

Such cases tend to come to be viewed suspiciously when the victim's clinical presentation is atypical, when lab results are inconsistent with each other or with recognized diseases, or when there are unduly frequent returns or increasingly urgent visits to the same hospital or clinic. If the perpetrator becomes aware of suspicions (s)he may abruptly terminate contact with the medical facility, only to show up at another one to recycle the entire procedure. Those practicing factitious disorder by proxy tend to have extensive medical knowledge, not uncommonly having been employed in medical settings. They often seem to have a fascination, or preoccupation, with things medical, and may themselves have a history of factitious disorder—now perhaps held in check by the proxy strategy.

Not surprisingly, factitious disorder by proxy perpetrators often have other problems, especially somatoform or personality disorders. As a group, they are given to exaggeration if not frank lying about themselves and their life experiences. The disorder is commonly precipitated by life stressors, particularly marital conflict or disruption.

---

avoidance of an unwanted duty or obligation. In **factitious disorder,** the person's goal is the more general one of maintaining such personal benefits as the "sick role" may provide, including the attention and concern of medical personnel. Frequently these patients surreptitiously alter their own physiology—for example by taking drugs—in order to simulate various real illnesses (see Highlight 7.2 for an interesting variation). In the past, factitious disorder has variously been called Munchausen syndrome, hospital addiction, polysurgical addiction, and professional patient syndrome.

It is usually possible to distinguish between a conversion (or other somatoform) disorder and frank malingering or factitiously "sick" role-playing with a fair degree of confidence. Persons engaged in the latter strategies are consciously perpetrating frauds by faking the symptoms of diseases or disabilities, and this fact is reflected in their demeanor. Individuals with conversion disorders are usually dramatic and apparently naive; they are concerned mainly with the symptoms and willingly discuss them, often in excruciating detail. If inconsistencies in their behaviors are pointed out, they are usually unperturbed. Persons who are feigning symptoms, on the other hand, are inclined to be defensive, evasive, and suspicious; they are usually reluctant to be examined and slow to talk about their symptoms, lest the pretense be discovered. Should inconsistencies in their behaviors be pointed out, deliberate deceivers as a rule immediately become more defensive. Thus conversion disorder and deliberate faking of illness are considered distinct patterns.

The phenomenon of *mass hysteria,* as typified by outbreaks of Saint Vitus' dance and biting manias during the Middle Ages, is a form of conversion disorder that has become relatively rare in modern times. As we saw in Chapter 2, however, some outbreaks do still occur (for recent examples, see page 38). In all cases, suggestibility clearly plays a major role—a conversion reaction in one person rapidly spreads to others for whom, one suspects, the appearance of having the imputed "condition" has some sort of psychic payoff.

Precipitating Circumstances

In the development of a conversion disorder, the following chain of events typically occurs: the patient experiences (1) a desire to escape from some unpleasant situation; (2) and then a fleeting wish to be sick in order to avoid the situation (this wish, however, is suppressed as unfeasible or unworthy); and, finally, under additional or continued stress, (3) begins to show the appearance of the symptoms of some physical ailment. The individual typically sees no relation between the symptoms and the stress situation. The particular symptoms that occur are usually those of a previous illness or are copied from other sources, such as symptoms observed among relatives, seen on television, or read about in magazines. The symptoms may also be superimposed on an existing organic ailment, associated with anticipated secondary gains, or symbolically related to major conflict situations in the individual's life, as in the previously mentioned case of the wife with vertigo.

Sometimes, conversion disorders seem to stem from feelings of guilt and the necessity for self-punishment. In one case, for example, a female patient developed a marked tremor and partial paralysis of the right arm and hand after she had physically attacked her father. During this incident, she had clutched at and torn open his shirt with her right hand, and apparently the subsequent paralysis represented a sort of symbolic punishment of the "guilty party," while simultaneously preventing a recurrence of her hostile and forbidden behavior.

Whatever specific factors may be involved in a given instance, the basic motivational pattern underlying most conversion disorders seems to be to avoid or reduce anxiety-arousing stress by getting sick—thus converting an unresolvable emotional problem into a face-saving physical one. Once this response is learned, it is maintained because it is repeatedly reinforced—both by anxiety reduction and by whatever gains (in terms of sympathy and support or more material compensation) that result from being disabled.

Causal Factors in Somatoform Disorders

We have a relatively limited knowledge of causal and risk factors in the somatoform disorders. For unknown reasons, they have not been the subject of a great deal of systematic research effort in recent years. We summarize in what follows findings that have been reasonably well established.

Biological Factors The precise role of genetic and constitutional factors in somatoform disorder has not been clearly defined. Limited evidence suggests a modest genetic contribution to somatoform disorders generally (Cloninger et al., 1984; Guze et al., 1986; Noyes et al., 1997; Sigvardsson et al., 1984), but observed familial concordance for somatoform behaviors might also be the result of learning from exposure to somatizing parents or siblings (see, Kreitman et al., 1965; Kriechman, 1987)

Bishop, Mobley, and Farr (1978) reported the curious observation from a large series of cases that somatoform disorders involving nervous system and musculoskeletal symptoms showed a pronounced tendency to be located on the left side of the body, a finding supported by other research as well (Galin, Diamond, & Braff, 1977; Stern, 1977). Since the right side of the brain generally controls the left side of the body, and vice versa, this would suggest that the right cerebral hemisphere (which is known to be involved chiefly with nonverbal mental processes) may have some special importance in mediating these types of disorders. We might speculate, for example, that the right brain is chiefly involved because much somatoform behavior is readily conceived as a form of nonverbal communication with the environment, a sort of pantomime of involuntary incapacity to perform obligations. Beyond that, however, the meaning of the finding remains obscure.

Psychosocial Factors Given the heterogeneous nature of the somatoform disorders, emphasized in a review of pertinent research by Iezzi and Adams (1993), it should perhaps come as no surprise that these problems are often accompanied by other psychiatric disorders as well, notably depression and anxiety disorders (e.g., Boyd et al., 1984; Ebert & Martus, 1994). As a group, then, somatizing patients exhibit widespread difficulties in their emotional lives, exhibiting a pattern of negative affect and emotional vulnerability frequently referred to as *neuroticism* (Lipowski, 1988; see also Chapter 5). Neuroticism as a personality trait has been shown to include facets of anxiety, angry hostility, depression, self-consciousness, impulsiveness, and vulnerability (Costa & Widiger, 1994), a combination of characteristics often associated with medical complaints that prove on careful examination to be spurious (Costa & McCrae, 1987). However, the range of disorders for which neuroticism is a risk factor appears very broad. It is far from specific to disorders of the somatoform type.

Possibly somewhat more specific is a reported history of childhood abuse. There is increasing evidence (e.g., Barsky et al., 1994; Ross, 1997; Salmon & Calderbank, 1996; van der Kolk, 1997) of a significant association between the development of somatizing symptom patterns and memories of having been seriously abused as a child. If confirmed, such an association would be one of several convergences with dissociative disorders, to be discussed below.

Another group of patients showing frequent somatoform patterns are those who seem unwilling or unable to communicate their personal distress in other than somatic language (Bach & Bach, 1995; Joucamaa et al., 1996). They tend to focus on and amplify body sensations almost to the exclusion of attending to their own subjective attitudes and feelings, which if negative in character (as is often the case) are referred to some supposedly malfunctioning body part. The term *alexithymia*, literally absence of speech about feelings, has been coined to denote this personality pattern (Sifneos, 1973, 1996). Contrary to common belief, the so-called hysterical (now histrionic) personality disorder pattern (see Chapter 9) is not strongly associated with risk for conversion disorder (Iezzi & Adams, 1993).

Sociocultural Factors The prevalence of somatoform disorders appears to vary considerably among differing cultures (Isaac et al., 1995; Janca et al., 1995). There are several non-Western cultures (e.g., the Chinese) in which, unlike our own, frank expression of emotional distress is considered unacceptable. We would thus expect somatizing patterns to be relatively more common in these areas, and this expectation appears to be borne out (see, Katon, Kleinman, & Rosen, 1982; Kirmayer, 1984).

The old diagnostic term *"neurasthenia"* (literally weakened nerves), referring to medically unexplained chronic complaints of physical weakness and fatigue, is still applied frequently by mental health practitioners in many other parts of the world, including China. It does not appear as an independent diagnosis in DSM-IV, although the inherently vague diagnosis *Undifferentiated Somatoform Disorder* may be employed for patients presenting with this clinical picture. Possibly the DSM authors wished to avoid confusion with the increasingly diagnosed *chronic fatigue syndrome*, the attributed causal roots of which remain in dispute. In part for that reason, the diagnosis remains a somewhat controversial one. In any event, it appears that the idea of psychologically caused fatigue is less accepted here than in other parts of the world, probably with a consequent constraining effect on prevalence rates—some of it artifactual (if it's not in the DSM it's not likely to be counted).

Treatment and Outcomes in Somatoform Disorders

Most authorities recommend caution in using medical (e.g., drug) interventions in the treatment of somatoform disorders. Where there is no alternative (many of these patients, convinced of the realness of their symptoms, adamantly refuse psychosocial therapies), antianxiety and antidepressant medication are sometimes useful in making the patient more comfortable. Drugs are rarely effective in achieving sustained relief of primary symptoms, and the antianxiety drugs in particular entail a substantial risk of inducing dependency. In many instances the best treatment turns out to be no treatment at all, but rather the provision of support, reassurance, and nonthreatening explanations as to causal factors; frequent office visits and contrived medical reexaminations may be helpful in this general approach. With the exception of conversion disorder and pain syndromes, however, the prognosis for full recovery from somatoform disorders is not encouraging (Barsky et al., 1998; Iezzi & Adams, 1993).

The development of behavior and cognitive-behavior therapies for both conversion and pain disorders (and as noted we have doubts about the validity of this distinction), and their evaluation in controlled clinical trials, shows some real promise (e.g., see Blanchard,

In many instances the best treatment for somatoform disorders turns out to be no treatment at all. Providing support and reassurance, even with office visits and contrived examinations may be the best treatment of all. The prognosis for full recovery from somatoform disorders is not encouraging.

1994; Gatchel & Turk, 1996; Iezzi & Adams, 1993). We suspect that the direct approach of behaviorally oriented therapies in, for example, eliminating sources of secondary gain would in itself hasten a positive therapeutic outcome in conversion disorders, but there exist as yet no entirely convincing data on the ultimate confirmation of this hypothesis.

DISSOCIATIVE DISORDERS

The concept of dissociation, which is at least a century old (Kihlstrom, 1994), refers to the human mind's capacity to mediate complex mental activity in channels split off from or independent of conscious awareness.

We all dissociate all of the time: when we start the car while thinking about all we have to do that day, or wash the dishes while talking on the phone, with little or no conscious attention to the task in which we're engaged. As these everyday examples of *automatisms* suggest, there is nothing inherently pathological about dissociation itself, and in fact a strong argument can be made that it is an extremely adaptive mechanism that allows us to carry out many of the functions of living with maximum efficiency (Epstein, 1994). Similarly, the achievement of *multitasking* in the design of desktop computers (thus allowing the machine to work on several problems simultaneously in the "background") has been hailed as a major advance. We humans have been doing it for millennia, or, as Hilgard (1977) has put it:

> The unity of consciousness is illusory. Man does more than one thing at a time—all the time—and the conscious representation of these actions is never complete. (p. 1)

In short, much of an individual's mental life involves nonconscious processes that are to a large extent autonomous with respect to deliberate, self-aware monitoring and direction. Such unaware processing extends to the areas of memory and perception, where it can be demonstrated that persons routinely remember things they do not consciously remember and perceive things they cannot report they have perceived, called **implicit memory** and **implicit perception,** respectively (Kihlstrom, Tataryn, & Hoyt, 1993). As we have seen, the general idea of unconscious mental processes has been embraced by psychodynamically oriented clinicians for many years. In the past quarter-century it has become a mainstay in the rapidly developing field of cognitive psychology.

In certain clinical conditions, however, this multichannel quality of human cognition appears to lose some sort of overall, integrative control. When this happens, the affected person may be unable to access information that is normally in the forefront of consciousness, such as his or her own personal identity. In addition, the person may become subject to the influence of cognitive subsystems not normally accessible to awareness, as when psychologically healthy individuals initiate motor activity in response to the content of a dream. Or, to put it another way, the normally useful capacity to maintain ongoing mental activity outside of awareness appears to be subverted and misused for the purpose of managing severe psychological threat. When that happens we observe the behavioral outcomes known as **dissociative disorders.**

Like somatoform disorders, dissociative disorders appear mainly to be ways of avoiding anxiety and stress and of managing life problems that threaten to overwhelm the person's usual coping resources. Both types of disorder also permit a person to deny personal responsibility for his or her "unacceptable" wishes or behavior. Kihlstrom (1994) in fact makes a strong argument that conversion disorders *are* dissociative disorders in every important sense of the term, an idea first put forward in the nineteenth century. In the case of DSM-defined dissociative disorders, however, the person avoids the stress by *pathologically dissociating*—in essence by escaping from his or her own autobiographical memory, or personal identity. The DSM-IV recognizes several types of pathological dissociation, as detailed below.

Dissociative Amnesia and Fugue

Amnesia is partial or total inability to recall or identify past experience. Persistent amnesia may occur in neurotic and psychotic disorders and in organic brain pathology, including traumatic brain injury and diseases of the central nervous system. If the amnesia is caused by brain pathology, it usually involves an actual retention failure. That is, either the information contained in experience is not registered and does not enter memory storage, or, if stored, it cannot be retrieved; it is truly and almost always permanently lost (Hirst, 1982).

Types of Dissociative Amnesia **Psychogenic** or **dissociative amnesia,** on the other hand, is usually limited to a failure to recall. In this disorder, forgotten personal information is still there beneath the level of consciousness, as sometimes becomes apparent under hypnosis or narcosis (sodium amytal, or so-called truth serum) interviews, and in cases where the amnesia spontaneously clears up. Four types of psychogenic amnesia are recognized: *localized* (a person remembers nothing that happened during a specific period—usually the first few

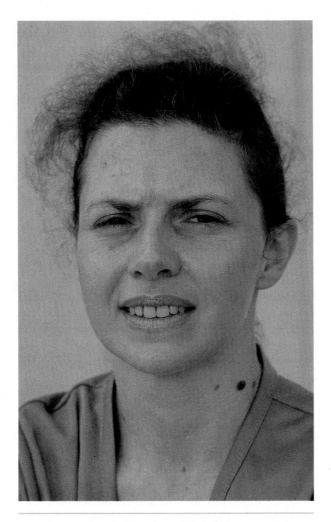

This woman, dubbed "Jane Doe," was emaciated, incoherent, partially clothed, covered by insect and animal bites, and near death when discovered by a Florida park ranger in September 1980. Her recovery was further complicated by a rare form of psychogenic amnesia, generalized amnesia, in which she had lost the memory of her name, her past, and her ability to read and write. Judging from her accent, linguistic experts said the woman was probably from Illinois. Although interviews conducted under the effect of drugs revealed that the woman had apparently had a Catholic education, her few childhood memories were so common that they were meaningless. In a dramatic attempt to recover her past, Jane Doe and her doctor appeared on Good Morning America and appealed to her relatives to step forward. The response was overwhelming, and authorities came to believe that Jane Doe was the daughter of a couple from Roselle, Illinois, whose daughter had gone to the Fort Lauderdale area to open a boutique. Their last contact with their daughter had been a phone call in 1976. Despite the couple's certainty, Jane Doe was never able to remember her past.

As already noted, psychogenic (or dissociative) amnesia is fairly common in initial reactions to intolerably traumatic experiences, such as those occurring during wartime combat conditions or immediately after catastrophic events. Some troubled persons, however, develop such amnesias in the face of stressful life situations with which most people deal more effectively.

Typical Symptoms   In typical dissociative amnesic reactions, individuals cannot remember their names, do not know how old they are or where they live, and do not recognize their parents, spouses, relatives, or friends. Yet their basic habit patterns—such as their abilities to read, talk, perform skilled work, and so on—remain intact, and they seem normal aside from the memory deficit (Coons & Millstein, 1992). Another way of putting this is that only a particular type of memory is affected, the type of memory psychologists refer to as episodic (pertaining to events experienced), or autobiographical. The other recognized forms of memory—semantic (pertaining to language and concepts), procedural (how to do things), perceptual representation (imaging), and short-term storage—almost always remain intact (Tulving, 1993).

Fugue States   A person may retreat still further from real-life problems by going into an amnesic state called a **fugue**, which as the term implies (*fugue* means "flight" in French) is a defense by actual flight—a person is not only amnesic but also departs from home surroundings, often assuming a partially or completely new identity. Days, weeks, or sometimes even years later, such persons may suddenly find themselves in strange places, not knowing how they got there and with apparently complete amnesia for their fugue periods. Their activities during their fugues may vary from merely going on a round of motion pictures to traveling across the country, entering a new occupation, and starting a whole new way of life. Virtually all of what we know about fugues is based on clinical observation; there has been little if any systematic study of the phenomenon.

The pattern in dissociative amnesia, it should be noted, is essentially similar to that in conversion symptoms, except that instead of avoiding some unpleasant situation by becoming physically dysfunctional, a person avoids thoughts about the situation or in the extreme leaves the scene. Apparently, the urgent wish for one's personal situation to be other than what it is serves as the basis of an amnesic reaction and its elaboration into fugue. Threatening information becomes inaccessible, apparently owing to some sort of "automatic" cognitive blockage (often described as *repression*). This is the "pure

hours following some traumatic event); *selective* (a person forgets some but not all of what happened during a given period); *generalized* (a person forgets his or her entire life history); and *continuous* (a person remembers nothing beyond a certain point in the past). The latter two types occur only rarely.

case" scenario. In other instances there is evidence that the individual consciously suppresses the threatening information by avoiding (via distraction, etc.) thoughts and associative threads that may lead to its exposure in awareness; physically leaving the scene where threatening cues abound is one way of maintaining freedom from troublesome facts that might otherwise present themselves.

People experiencing dissociative amnesia are typically faced with extremely unpleasant situations from which they see no escape. Often, they previously had experienced conscious impulses to forget and run away but were too inhibited to accept that solution. Eventually, however, the stress becomes so intolerable that they suppress large segments of their personalities and all memory for the stressful situations. As already noted, this type of amnesia is highly selective and normally involves only material that is basically intolerable or threatening to the self. During a dissociative fugue, an individual appears normal and is able to engage in complex activities. Normally the activities chosen reflect a rather different lifestyle from the previous one, the rejection of which is usually obvious. Such behavior is well illustrated in the following case.

Case Study, A Middle Manager's Dissociative Fugue • Burt Tate, a 42-year-old short-order cook in a small-town diner, was brought to the attention of local police following a heated altercation with another man at the diner. Questioned by the police, he gave his name as Burt Tate and indicated that he had arrived in town several weeks earlier. However, he could produce no official identification and could not tell the officers where he had previously lived and worked. No charges were proffered and no arrest made, but Burt was asked to accompany the officers to the emergency room of a local hospital so that he might be examined, to which he agreed.

Burt's physical examination was negative for evidence of recent head trauma or any other medical abnormality, and there was no indication of drug or alcohol abuse. He was oriented as to current time and place, but manifested no recall of his personal history prior to his arrival in town. He did not seem especially concerned about his total lack of a remembered past. He was kept in the hospital overnight for observation and discharged the following day.

Meanwhile, the police instituted missing-person search procedures and discovered that Burt matched the description of one Gene Saunders, a resident of a city some 200 miles away who had disappeared a month earlier. The wife of Mr. Saunders was brought to the town and confirmed the real identity of Burt, who, now noticeably anxious, stated that he did not recognize Mrs. Saunders.

Prior to his disappearance, Gene Saunders, a middle-level manager in a large manufacturing firm, had been experiencing considerable difficulties at work and at home. A number of stressful work problems, including failure to get an expected promotion, the loss through resignation of some of his key staff, failure of his section to meet production goals, and increased criticism from his superior—all occurring within a brief time frame—had upset his normal equanimity. He had become morose and withdrawn at home, and had been critical of his wife and children. Two days before he had left, he had had a violent argument with his 18-year-old son, who'd declared his father a failure and had stormed out of the house to go live with friends. (Adapted from Spitzer et al., 1989, pp. 215–16.)

Dissociative Identity Disorder

Dissociative identity disorder (DID), formerly multiple personality disorder (MPD), is a dramatic dissociative pattern, usually having identifiable stressor precipitants, in which a patient manifests at least two more or less complete *systems of identity.* When well-developed (many "alter" identities are quite fragmentary), each such system has distinctive emotional and thought processes and represents a separate entity having relatively stable characteristics. The individual may change from one identity to another at periods varying from a few minutes to several years, though shorter time frames are more common. One, the original personality, is normally the **host personality;** other identities are usually strikingly different from the host personality and often from one another; one may be carefree and fun-loving, and another quiet, studious, and serious. Needs and behaviors inhibited in the main or host personality are usually liberally displayed by the others. The case of Mary Kendall is illustrative.

Case Study, Mary, Marian and Other Alters • Mary, a 35-year-old divorced social worker, had a somewhat rare condition in her right forearm and hand, one of several general medical problems, that caused her chronic pain. Medical management of this pain had proven problematic, and it was decided to teach her self-hypnosis as a means whereby she might control it. She proved an excellent hypnotic subject and quickly learned effective pain-control technique.

Her hypnotist-trainer, a psychiatrist, describes Mary's life in rather unappealing terms. She is said to be competent professionally but has an "arid" personal and social life. Although her brief marriage ended some ten years ago, she evidences little interest in men and doesn't seem to have any close friends. She spends most of her free time doing volunteer work in a hospice, a type of supportive alternative care facility where terminally ill patients go to die.

In the course of the hypnotic training Mary's psychiatrist discovered that she seemed to have substantial gaps in her memory. One phenomenon in particular was very puzzling: she reported that she could not account for what seemed an extraordinary depletion of the gasoline in her car's tank. She would arrive home from work with a nearly full tank, and by the following morning as she began her trip to work would notice that the tank was now only half-full. When it was advised that she keep track of her odometer readings she discovered that on many nights on which she insisted she'd remained at home the odometer showed significant accumulations of up to 100 miles. The psychiatrist, by now strongly suspecting that Mary had a dissociative disorder, also established that there were large gaps in her memories of childhood. He shifted his focus to exploring the apparently widespread dissociative difficulties.

In the course of one of the continuing hypnotic sessions the psychiatrist again asked about "lost time," and was greeted with a response in a wholly different voice tone that said, "It's about time you knew about me." Marian, an apparently well-established alter identity, went on to describe the trips she was fond of taking at night, during which she traveled to various scenic resort areas to "work out problems." It soon became apparent that Marian was an extraordinarily abrupt and hostile "person," the epitome in these respects of everything the compliant and self-sacrificing Mary was not. Marian regarded Mary with unmitigated contempt, and asserted that "worrying about anyone but yourself is a waste of time."

In due course some six other alter identities emerged, all rather saliently arranged in characteristic behavior along a dimension anchored at one end by traits of marked compliance/dependency and at the other of equally marked aggressiveness/autonomy. There was notable competition among the alters for time spent "out," and Marian was often so provocative as to frighten some of the more timid others, which included a six-year-old child. When one of the hostile adult alters seriously threatened suicide, the alarmed therapist insisted on consulting the other identities, to which the intended suicidal alter responded with charges of violation of doctor-patient confidentiality!

Mary's history, as gradually pieced together, included memories of physical and sexual abuse by her father as well as others during her childhood. She also reported considerable feelings of guilt for not having protected her siblings from similar abuse. Her mother was described as not especially physically abusive but as having abdicated to a large extent the maternal role, forcing Mary from a young age to assume these duties in the family.

Four years of subsequent psychotherapy resulted in only modest success in achieving a true "integration" of these diverse trends in Mary Kendall's selfhood. (Adapted from Spitzer et al., 1994, pp. 56–57)

The number of **alter identities** in DID varies, but in two substantial series of cases evaluated by questionnaire

it averaged an amazing 15 (Ross, 1989). The historical trend, in fact, seems to be one of increasing multiplicity, suggesting the operation of social factors, perhaps even some "competition" among these patients and/or their therapists in numbers of alters identified (Spanos, 1996; Spanos & Burgess, 1994). As already noted, the quality of alters' existence varies considerably from being robust, persistent, and complexly organized to being merely fragmentary, amorphous, and fleeting; for example, a given alter may never come "out," and is only referred to by other alters. Hence it is not entirely clear what these accounts may tell us. The fact that alters are usually strikingly different from the host or primary personality leads to the inference that the alters express rejected parts of the original self. Alter physical characteristics are also highly varied and have been known to include nonhuman species.

The Nature of Alters Much of the reason for abandoning the older diagnostic term "multiple personality disorder" in cases involving DID was the growing recognition that it conveyed misleading information in suggesting multiple occupancy of space, time, and victims' bodies by differing, but fully organized and coherent, "personalities." But alters are not in fact in any meaningful sense of the word *personalities*. They are pretended, fragmented parts of a single person and serve as devices to manage otherwise unmanageable psychological distress. Colin Ross (1997), a major contributor to the DID literature, explains it as follows:

> The most important thing to understand is that alter personalities are not people. They are not even personalities. . . . It is probably impossible to construct a satisfactory definition of an alter personality. . . . Alter personalities are highly stylized enactments of inner conflicts, drives, memories, and feelings. At the same time, they are dissociated packets of behavior developed for transaction with the outside world. They are fragmented parts of one person. There is only one person. The patient's conviction that there is more than one person in her is a dissociative delusion. . . . DID is an elaborate pretending. The patient *pretends* that she is more than one person, in a very convincing manner. She actually believes it herself. (p. 144)

Common Alter "Roles" Certain roles are extremely common in the alter repertoires of DID patients. These include the roles of Child, Protector, and Persecutor; an Opposite Sex alter, who may share one of these other roles, is also present in most cases (Ross,

1989, 1997). Normally, alters know of the existence of the host personality and of each other, but the host or primary personality is not "permitted" explicit knowledge of these others occupying his or her space, time, and body. Mutual and unidirectional amnesias among the alters also sometimes occur. Interestingly, very often one alter personality knows everything and, if cooperative, may be a valuable consultant for the therapist.

Incidence and Prevalence—Why Are They Increasing?

Owing to their dramatic nature, dual and multiple identities have received a great deal of attention and publicity in fiction, television, and motion pictures. Actually, however, they were rare—or at least rarely diagnosed—in clinical practice until relatively recently. Prior to approximately the last three decades, in fact, only slightly more than 100 cases could be found in the psychological and psychiatric literature worldwide. Their diagnosed occurrence has increased enormously in recent years. No wholly complete or satisfactory explanation exists for such a drastic change in the occurrence base rate.

Some of the increase, however, is almost certainly artifactual, the product of increased acceptance of the diagnosis by clinicians, who traditionally have been somewhat skeptical of the astonishing behavior these patients often display—such as undergoing sudden and dramatic shifts in personal identity before their eyes. More females than males are diagnosed as having the disorder, with the ratio being about nine to one; most patients are in their 20s or 30s at the point of diagnosis (Ross, 1997). The pronounced gender discrepancy is believed by some to be due to the much greater proportion of childhood sexual abuse victimization among females than males (Tricket & Putnam, 1993).

Beginning in about 1980, prior scattered reports of instances of childhood abuse in the histories of adult DID patients began building into what would become a crescendo. That a strong association exists between a diagnosis of DID and a *reported* history that includes significant abuse—sexual, generalized, or both—is now beyond question. What remains to be settled, as we shall see in later sections of the chapter, is the trustworthiness of such memories of abusive childhoods in these patients.

The DID Diagnosis: Continuing Controversy

However, questions about the substantive status of sepa-

rate identities or about the role of childhood abuse in contributing to the development of DID do not exhaust the controversial issues surrounding this concept and may in some sense put the cart before the horse. As already suggested, the issue of possible factitious or malingering origins has dogged the diagnosis of DID for at least a century, and many contemporary mental health professionals doubt the validity of the diagnosis or the existence of any such syndrome as other than the deliberate enactment of a drama-rich role. These doubts are reinforced by the suspicion that overzealous clinicians, by virtue of undue fascination with the clinical phenomena and unwise use of techniques like hypnosis, are themselves responsible for eliciting this "disorder" in highly suggestible patients (e.g., see McHugh, 1995; Spanos, 1996). The latter criticism has a ring of truth, but it fails to account convincingly for all of the observations reported—such as the occasional independent corroboration of apparently dissociative pretreatment events. Cynicism about the concept of DID has also been encouraged by the frequency with which it has been used by defendants and their attorneys to escape punishment for crimes ("My other personality did it."). This defense was used, unsuccessfully, in the famous case of the Hillside Strangler, Kenneth Bianchi (Orne, Dinges, & Orne, 1984).

It is also true, as Spanos, Weekes, and Bertrand (1985) have demonstrated, that normal college students can be induced by suggestion to exhibit some of the phenomena seen in DID, including the adoption of a second personality. Such role-playing demonstrations are interesting, but they do not answer, nor even convincingly address, the question of the reality of DID. That subjects might be able to give a convincing portrayal of a person with a broken leg would not, after all, establish the nonexistence of broken legs.

Our own view of the controversy surrounding DID is that it is too often formulated in terms of an absolute dichotomy: It is viewed either as a completely genuine disorder affecting a helpless and passive victim, or as a completely dissembled fabrication orchestrated by an unscrupulous person seeking unfair advantages. There is of course a wide range of possibilities between these two extreme positions. Our increasing knowledge concerning widespread evidence of separate (dissociated) memory subsystems and nonconscious active mental processing, indicates that much highly organized mental activity is normally carried on in the background, outside of awareness. We should also note the possible existence of a numerically significant group of persons who may be especially prone to a pathological variant of this process (Waller, Putnam, & Carlson, 1996; Waller & Ross, 1997). Numerous studies indicate that the separate identities harbored by DID patients may be physiologically and cognitively distinct. For example, brain scans of various alters may be quite different. Since such differences cannot in any obvious way be intentionally simulated (Armstrong, 1995; Eich et al, 1997; Miller, 1989; Miller et al., 1991; Osgood & Luria, 1954; Putnam, Zahn, & Post, 1995; Silberman et al., 1985), these studies suggest that, whatever DID may be, it is in many cases more than mere feigning or role-playing.

Accordingly, questions about whether a given behavior is consciously or unconsciously motivated, genuine or feigned, intended or unintended, deliberate or spontaneous, and so on, are as a general rule oversimplified. So far as we can tell, the human mind does not operate in these dichotomous ways, and undue preoccupation with unanswerable questions can distract us from the task of understanding the adaptational processes in which the patient is engaged.

We can reframe the question and ask if we believe that many cases of DID are characterized by apparently severe disruptions in memory, identity, and behavioral state modulation. Then the answer, based on available evidence, will almost necessarily be "yes." The vagaries involved in declaring certain types of behavior to be manifestations of "mental disorder" go all the way back to issues first addressed in Chapter 1. One thing is clear: Many of the persons qualifying for the DID diagnosis are miserable, severely stressed human beings. If a mental disorder diagnosis must be a prerequisite for them to receive help, then we are loath to declare that judgment uniformly mistaken.

Depersonalization Disorder

A more common dissociative disorder that occurs mostly in adolescents and young adults is **depersonalization disorder,** in which there is a loss of the sense of self. Individuals with this disorder feel that they are, all of a sudden, different—for example, that they are other people or that their bodies have drastically changed—have become quite grotesque, for example. A related, and commonly accompanying, experience is that of **derealization,** in which the external world is perceived as distorted in various ways; it may be experienced as lacking a stable and palpable existence, for example.

Frequently, the altered states are reported as out-of-body experiences in which individuals feel that they are, for a time, floating above their physical bodies and observing what is going on below. Mild forms of the experience are extremely common and are no cause for alarm. Reports of out-of-body experiences have included perceptions of visiting other planets or relatives who are in other cities. The disorder is often precipitated by acute stress resulting from an infectious illness, an accident, or some other traumatic event, as in the following case.

> **Case Study, A Young Woman's "Traveling"** • Charlotte D., a recently separated 19-year-old woman, was referred to an outpatient mental health service by her physician because she had experienced several "spells" in which her mind left her body and went to a strange place in another state. The first instance had occurred two months earlier, a few days after her husband had left her without explanation. Since then, she had had four episodes of "traveling" that had occurred during her waking state and had lasted for about 15 to 20 minutes. She described her experiences as a dreamy feeling in which her arms and legs were not attached to her body and other people around her were perceived as zombielike. Typically she felt dizzy and had pains in her stomach for hours after each spell.

In a recent clinical study of 30 cases of depersonalization disorder, Simeon et al. (1997) noted a widespread occurrence of comorbid personality disorders (Chapter 9), especially avoidant, borderline, and obsessive-compulsive. They also noted that the disorder appeared to be highly treatment resistant. Taken together, these findings suggest that clinically significant levels of depersonalization tend to occur in unstable, vulnerable individuals having numerous other problems. These patients also reported more childhood trauma than a nondissociative control group, but the traumatic experiences described tended to be milder than those reported by, for example, DID patients.

The lifetime prevalence of depersonalization disorder is unknown. Individuals who experience depersonalized states, and they are many, are usually able to function normally between episodes. With more severe manifestations, as in the preceding case, the experience can be quite frightening and may cause a victim to become concerned about imminent mental collapse. Such fears are usually unfounded. Sometimes, however, feel-

In depersonalization/derealization disorders the world is often experienced as hazy and indistinct.

ings of depersonalization are early manifestations of impending decompensation and the development of psychotic states of a schizophreniform type, discussed in Chapter 12. In either case professional help in dealing with the precipitating stressors and reducing anxiety may be helpful.

Causal Factors in Dissociative Disorders

Because of a dearth of pertinent research, relatively little is known (beyond what has already been reported) about causal patterns involved in dissociative amnesia, fugue, and depersonalization disorder. For that reason,

we shall concentrate here on suspected causal factors in DID.

Modifying to a considerable extent his previously expressed (1989) views emphasizing the almost unique importance of childhood traumatic abuse in the etiology of DID, Ross (1997) has more recently suggested four separate "pathways" that may lead to the emergence of the DID syndrome. The pathways are not mutually exclusive, and a given case may incorporate a mixture of two or more of them. He describes them as follows.

1. *The childhood abuse pathway:* This is the original and still widely held conception that DID arises from the child's attempts to cope with an overwhelming sense of hopelessness and powerlessness in the face of repeated traumatic abuse. Lacking other resources or routes of escape, the child creates "stable internal persons who are always available for attachment, safety, security, and nurturing" (Ross, 1997, p. 65).

2. *The childhood neglect pathway:* This is a variant form of childhood trauma in which the child is not physically or sexually abused so much as left to his or her own devices, perhaps being locked in closets or basements or left unattended over long periods of time. Here, mothers of such children are usually described as psychiatrically impaired themselves—with problems such as depression, schizophrenia, chronic alcohol abuse, or even DID.

3. *The factitious pathway:* Here the symptoms of DID are displayed as typically one of several "scams" the person employs in engaging the health care system. There is usually an elaborate medical-surgical history and often multiple prior psychiatric diagnoses. Ross (1997) regards the factitious pathway (when uncontaminated with others) as representing a more severe psychiatric problem than pure abuse pathway DID.

4. *The iatrogenic pathway.* The term *iatrogenic* as used in general medicine means treatment-induced. In including this pathway Ross acknowledges the widespread evidence that some cases of DID arise as a consequence of incompetent and misguided treatment for misdiagnosed other types of disorder—most notably bipolar (Chapter 6), post-traumatic stress (Chapter 4), or mixed syndromes involving some dissociative elements. We shall have more to say about the iatrogenic pathway in the Unresolved Issues section at the end of this chapter.

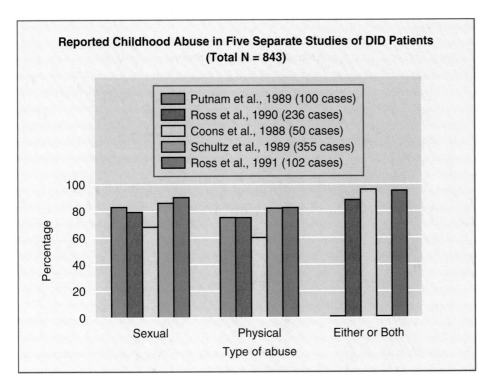

**Reported Childhood Abuse in Five Separate Studies of DID Patients
(Total N = 843)**

Putnam et al., 1989 (100 cases)
Ross et al., 1990 (236 cases)
Coons et al., 1988 (50 cases)
Schultz et al., 1989 (355 cases)
Ross et al., 1991 (102 cases)

Percentage

Type of abuse

Sexual   Physical   Either or Both

FIGURE 7.1
Reported childhood abuse in five separate studies of DID patients (Total N=843)

Most of the available research purporting to shed light on the potential causes of DID has been oriented to more "pure form" cases, which in the above scheme would include the first two trauma-based pathways. We review that research below, but the reader should be forewarned that it is unevenly distributed and in certain areas quite sparse.

Biological Factors   We have found no convincing evidence of a genetic contribution to pathological dissociation. The same conclusion is echoed in a recent twin study reported by Waller and Ross (1997). Nevertheless, we would not be surprised if future research should uncover a modest risk from this source. Certainly it would be premature to rule out the possibility of a heightened innate dissociative capacity in patients experiencing these disorders (Braun & Sachs, 1985).

Psychosocial Factors   A study of 71 sexually abused children likened their reactions to post-traumatic stress disorder (see Chapter 4) (Wolfe, Gentile, & Wolfe, 1989). Evidence is building impressively in support of the notion that DID is largely a type of post-traumatic dissociative disorder (see Brown, 1994; Zelikovsky & Lynn, 1994). It must be emphasized, however, that sexual abuse rarely occurs in the absence of serious overall family pathology, many aspects of which (e.g., continuously threatened dis-

solution of the child's primary support system) could themselves be traumatizing (Briere & Elliott, 1993; Nash et al., 1993; Tillman, Nash, & Lerner, 1994). In any event, it is not difficult to imagine how the development of partially independent (dissociated) subsystems that constitute alter identities could serve important adaptive and coping functions for individuals who were severely and repeatedly traumatized as children, perhaps particularly (although doubtless not exclusively) by incestuous sexual abuse. As Ross (1997) has put it, "What is DID? DID is a little girl imagining that the abuse is happening to someone else" (p. 59).

Figure 7.1 depicts the percentages of abuse reported by the victims in five separate studies involving a total of 843 DID patients. The reported specifically sexual abuse in such studies, moreover, often goes well beyond inappropriate touching or fondling and includes attempted intercourse and oral/anal penetration (e.g., Ross et al., 1991).

The message of these data is amplified in a recently reported and uniquely documented study of 12 convicted murderers diagnosed as having DID, 11 men and one woman. In this study, Lewis and colleagues (1997) searched medical, psychiatric, social service, school, military, and prison records, and records of interviews with family members and others, to determine the actual occurrence of prior abuse. In addition, they examined scars on the bodies of their subjects; 11 of the 12

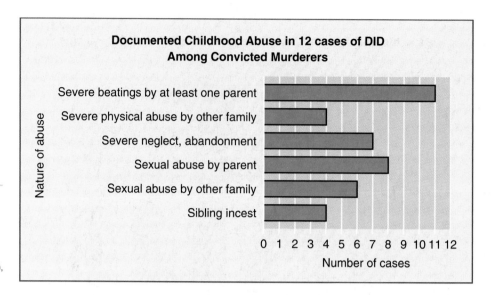

FIGURE 7.2
Documented childhood abuse in
12 cases of DID among convicted
murderers

Source: Adapted from Lewis et al., (1997),
Table 2, pp. 1708–1709.

had them, and they were mostly consistent with abuse reports. As determined by these methods, all 12 had been abused as children, and this abuse—both general and sexual—was notably severe. Interestingly, these victims are reported as not for the most part remembering their childhood abuse, or remembering it only partially when queried. Figure 7.2 summarizes these results. Unfortunately, this study did not include a control group of otherwise comparable murderers not evidencing DID symptomatology. Hence we cannot be certain that the childhood abuse of these subjects is not as much (or more) associated with conviction for murder as it is with the development of DID; nor is it unreasonable to assume that dissociative experiences would be encouraged by lengthy incarceration. Still, it seems unwise to ignore entirely the information provided by this flawed but otherwise impressive and logistically demanding investigation.

Case reports, notably including the rather famous one of Sybil, who is reported to have been repeatedly tortured and nearly killed by her psychotic mother (Schreiber, 1973), describe the cruelty that some DID patients suffered as children as gut-wrenching in its severity. However, reports of widespread sexual and other forms of childhood abuse as causal factors in DID, as well as in certain other disorders, have become a matter of controversy in recent years. In some cases, these reports are the result of false memories, which are in turn a product of highly leading and suggestive techniques by convinced but inadequately skilled psychotherapists (e.g., see Yapko, 1994). While we have no doubt this sort of thing has happened, and with tragic consequences to innocent

families, it is also true that brutal abuse of children occurs too often and that it can have devastating effects on normal development, among other things probably encouraging pathological dissociation (see Nash et al., 1993; Trickett & Putnam, 1993). The issue of false memory is more extensively considered in the Unresolved Issues section at the end of this chapter.

Does DID occur in the absence of a history of severe childhood trauma? If we accept the seemingly reasonable notion of differing but often intersecting "pathways" leading to the clinical manifestations of DID, as described earlier, then the appropriate answer would be "probably

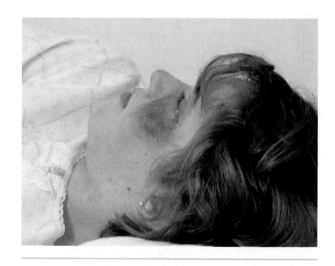

Though recovered memories are controversial, there is evidence that physical and sexual abuse is correlated with dissociative disorders. As one researcher put it, "What is DID? DID is a little girl imagining that abuse is happening to someone else."

yes." We would expect in such cases, however, to see in these people evidence of other factors encouraging the development of dissociative tendencies, such as ease of hypnotizability (Butler et al., 1996) and a high capacity for personal absorption (inward focus of attention) and fantasy (Kihlstrom, Glisky, & Angiulo, 1994). The Dissociative Experiences Scale (Bernstein & Putnam, 1986), a self-administered questionnaire that taps into the absorption trait as well as episodes of dissociative experiences, has been widely used to measure dissociative tendencies and has garnered considerable support as a valid predictor of dissociative symptoms (Carlson & Armstrong, 1994). In fact, a subset of the items of the scale can be validly used to identify individuals who are members of a class of *pathological dissociators* (Waller, Putnam, & Carlson, 1996). Of course, it is possible that most high scorers have a history of childhood trauma.

Sociocultural Factors   There seems little doubt that the incidence and prevalence of dissociative disorders, especially their more dramatic forms such as DID, are strongly influenced by the degree to which such phenomena are accepted or tolerated as either normal or as legitimate mental disorders by the surrounding cultural context. And, as seen in our own society, acceptance and tolerance as legitimate disorders are likely to vary over time.

Many seemingly related phenomena, such as spirit possession, occur in abundance in many different parts of the world where the local culture sanctions them (Krippner, 1994). Instances of what our dominant culture might regard as pathological dissociation are not always maladaptive and need not be construed in these negative, mental disorder terms. As Stanley Krippner puts it, "People can create personalities as required to defend themselves against trauma, to conform to cultural pressures, or to meet the expectations of a psychotherapist, medium, or exorcist. This malleability has both adaptive and maladaptive aspects" (1994, p. 358). Considered from this perspective, we are again confronted with the stubborn problem of trying to disentangle issues of widely varying values from what we define as mental disorder, discussed in Chapter 1. Is it really so bad to fragment one's identity to cope with traumatic events? Or is some of our concern based on Western values of self and rationality?

Treatment and Outcomes in Dissociative Disorders

As in the case of trying to discern causal factors, little is known about treatment and outcomes in dissociative amnesias, fugues, and depersonalization disorder. In depersonalization disorder, we have the already mentioned research showing that the disorder is resistant to treatment, but that judgment was based on only 30 cases and was mainly impressionistic rather than deriving from a rigorous and controlled quantitative analysis (Simeon et al., 1997). In dissociative amnesia and fugue, where a limited number of individual case reports are essentially all we have, the yield is even less. We therefore again concentrate on the treatment of DID.

Most therapists of DID patients set "integration" (that is, some level of amalgamation of the previously separate alters, together with their collective merging into the host personality) as the primary goal of treatment. However, given the diverse, frequently destructive, and often amorphous or fragmentary qualities of alters, we are not sure we understand the meaning of the term as used in this context. A reasonable criterion of therapeutic success would be that the alters no longer emerge, or that they have markedly diminished power to assume executive control of the host's behavior or otherwise interfere with his or her adjustment efforts. Perhaps one or the other of these outcomes is what is meant by "integration," but at present the specific meaning of the term as it pertains to DID patients is not clear.

Rigorously designed and controlled studies on the treatment of DID are, so far as we know, nonexistent. Most reports in the literature are treatment summaries of single cases, with widely varying treatment approaches employed, and widely varying outcomes reported. Where therapy for larger groups of DID patients has been studied, as in a report by Coons (1986), the outcomes have been mixed. Ellason and Ross (1997) have recently reported on a two-year post-discharge follow-up of DID patients originally treated in a specialized inpatient unit. Fifty-four of an original 135 such patients were located and systematically assessed. These patients, especially those achieving "integration," generally showed marked improvements in various aspects of their lives. These results may suggest some reason for treatment optimism, but we must wonder about the clinical status of the other 81 "lost" patients, a substantial majority of those originally treated. Our guess would be that, on average, they have done less well; that is, we think it likely that the 54 ex-patients located is a sample biased in favor of good outcomes.

Given an apparent diversity of treatment approaches, it would be helpful from at least a research standpoint if some agreement could be reached on what characteristics a maximally promising treatment approach would have.

Along this line, Kluft (1993) has offered a three-stage model for the treatment of DID, one endorsed in a more recent work on the same subject by Horevitz and Loewenstein (1994). The following stages are identified:

1. *Stabilization:* The therapist and client establish ground rules for the nature of the therapeutic relationship, share their understandings of the problem, explore issues of trust between them, and develop ways to help prevent further fragmenting in the face of stress. These ground rules include a statement of circumstances— for example, threats of bodily harm to the therapist or his or her family members made by any alter—that would prompt the immediate termination of therapy.

2. *Working through the trauma and resolution of dissociative defenses:* This phase, obviously the critical therapeutic one, is said to involve three essential tasks: (a) the client must begin to deal effectively with amnesia and the propensity to "switch" among differing identity states; (b) he or she must face and deal with dissociative memories, reconnecting them to real-life events; and (c) he or she must reestablish connections between distinct, seemingly separate, identity states. Clearly, successful negotiation of this critical phase of treatment requires therapeutic skills of the highest order, as well as attitudes of patience and forbearance not abundantly available in the human community. In short, the therapist *must* be strongly committed as well as professionally competent; regrettably, not all are (see Chapter 17).

3. *Postintegration therapy:* This is basically a stage of repair and compensation for the multiple deficiencies left in the wake of (often) years of pseudo-adjustment accomplished by means of dissociative strategies. Huge gaps may appear in the patient's skills, knowledge, and general functioning, and there is often a sense of profound loneliness and detachment owing to the requirement to resume living in a world that is in many respects wholly unfamiliar. Also, patients are now feeling/acknowledging intensely painful memories they had before avoided. Grief concerning the "loss" of a comforting if very costly adjustment is frequently a complicating feature. This last phase of therapy is said to be often long (one to two years) and arduous for both patient and therapist.

The general outline of this treatment plan makes a good deal of sense and deserves careful empirical evaluation. Unfortunately, it is by no means certain that the considerable funding needed to launch such a project will become available at any time in the foreseeable future. The phenomena of DID are at the center of raging controversies about their nature and about related issues such as the sexual abuse of children and the validity of recovered memories of abuse. We will deal with these considerations in the Unresolved Issues below. Meanwhile, we note that prospective research funding agencies are normally reluctant to involve themselves in such high-profile controversial issues.

UNRESOLVED ISSUES

DID and Childhood Trauma

In the 1990s a chasm developed in the ranks of mental health professionals over the validity of the Dissociative Identity Disorder concept and the related issues of "recovered" memories of childhood abuse, particularly sexual abuse, which were asserted to be a major causal factor in the production of severe adult dissociative pathology. In what is undoubtedly an oversimplification, we may generalize that the major players in this conflict have been, on the one hand, the "believers," mostly the private practitioners who have undertaken to treat people with these conditions and, on the other, the "disbelievers," mostly the more academic and science-oriented mental health professionals who, while sympathetic to people suffering such symptoms, as a group have doubted the validity of both the diagnosis and its alleged source in childhood abuse.

As is well known, the controversy has moved beyond professional debate and has become a major public issue, leading to countless legal proceedings. DID patients have sued their parents for having inflicted abuse; they have also

sued therapists and institutions for implanting memories of abuse they now believe did not occur. Parents, asserting they have been falsely accused, have formed an international support organization—the False Memory Syndrome Foundation—and have sometimes sued therapists for damages secondary to the latters' alleged induction of false memories of parental abuse. Many families have been torn apart in the fallout from this remarkable climate of suspicion, accusation, litigation, and unrelenting hostility.

Although the validity of the DID diagnosis and the purported origins of it in childhood abuse are basically separate questions, they have tended to become fused in the course of the debate. Hence those who doubt the validity of memories of abuse are also likely to regard the phenomena of DID as dramatic role-playing, encouraged or induced—like the abusive memories—by misguided therapy (e.g., see Spanos, 1996). Believers, on the other hand, usually take both DID and the idea of abuse as its cause to be established beyond doubt (e.g., see Lewis et al., 1997).

To a large extent, therefore, the controversy is rooted in disagreements about the nature, reliability, and malleability of human autobiographical memory. With rare exception, evidence for childhood abuse as a cause of DID is restricted to "recovered memories" (i.e., memories not originally accessible) of adult persons being treated for dissociative experiences, the idea being that such memories had—prior to treatment—been "repressed" owing to their traumatic nature. Treatment, according to the view of believers, dismantles the repressive defense and thus makes available to awareness an essentially accurate memory recording of the past abuse.

Disbelievers counter with the scientifically well-supported argument that human memory of past events does not operate in this computer-like manner, retrieving with perfect accuracy an unadulterated record of information previously "input." Rather, human memory is *constructive,* and very much subject to modification or revision based on the experience of events happening after any original memory trace is established (Schacter, Norman, & Koustaal, 1998). Directly addressing the abuse issue, Kirsch, Lynn, and Rhue (1993) put it this way:

> A traumatic history . . . consists not only of past childhood events but also of the person's interpretations, embellishments, and distortions of those events from the perspective of recent events, accomplishments, behaviors, and relationships that constitute life in the present. . . . In short, memory is not immutable or preserved like a fly in amber, nor is the mind like a vast storehouse of indelible impressions, facts, and information. Indeed, the memory literature indicates that ordinary memory is fallible and that certain subjects place an inordinate degree of confidence in their remembrances. . . . (p. 18)

There can be little doubt that, by the outset of the 1990s, many poorly trained therapists uninformed with respect to how the human memory system works bought into the notion that a suitably vigorous therapeutic approach could uncover a true and accurate record of the traumatic childhood experiences of their clients. In addition, many were convinced that certain adult symptoms and complaints, rather common ones at that (e.g., headaches, poor self-esteem, unexplained anxiety), were themselves indicative of a history of childhood trauma (e.g., see Bass & Davis, 1988; Bloom, 1990), hence justifying a relentless demand that the client remember the traumatic abuse. Persuaded by the therapist's certainty and persistence, accompanied by liberal use of confusion-inducing procedures such as hypnotic trance states, many clients did eventually "remember" such incidents, confirming the therapist's "expert" opinion.

Attempting to mediate the conflict and provide guidance to its members and the public on the issues involved, the American Psychological Association (APA) convened a bipartisan panel of experts, the Working Group on the Investigation of Memories of Childhood Abuse in the mid-1990s. As one further measure of the amount of dissent and controversy raging in this field, the APA's chief executive officer, Raymond Fowler reports that (electronic mail, February 27, 1997), "the working group agreed on almost nothing." The upshot is that the public and many less directly involved professionals remain entirely divided and confused, as of this writing, on what to believe about dissociative phenomena and their connection (if any) with actual childhood abuse.

Until there is clear, unimpeachable evidence to compel a consensus among responsible members of both the clinical and the scientific communities, the most reasonable thing to do is to insist that clinicians treating persons suspected of having these conditions be held to the highest of standards of professional practice, as described below. As already noted, it was evidence of deviance from those standards, that has been an important source of the impatience, irritation, and anger emanating from the more scientifically inclined in the mental health professions. Since this poor practice has resulted from ignorance and confusion rather than any deliberate attempt to be harmful to patients, there is hope that the present situation may be alleviated by a more informed and cautious approach to the clinical situation.

A notable step forward in this regard has been the welcome appearance of a thoughtful book addressing this extremely complex clinical problem—*Recovered Memories of Abuse: Assessment, Therapy, Forensics* by Kenneth Pope and Laura Brown (1996). This book acknowledges the possibly "real" occurrence of DID and related clinical syndromes, as well as the possibility of a genuine causal link between the disorder and prior childhood abuse. Completely frank in confronting the contentious issues pervading the field, it recommends procedures that would lessen the likelihood of error on the part of perhaps overzealous practitioners.

Pope and Brown emphasize the importance of professional competence in three areas: intellectual, emotional, and procedural. The last of these refers to skill in actually carrying out the elements of a carefully formulated assessment and treatment plan.

Intellectual competence, as the term implies, refers to the adequacy of the practitioner's knowledge of the basic psychological processes likely to be involved where possible abuse becomes an issue—such as memory functioning, developmental theory, and the nature and consequences of psychic trauma. Included here would be a sophisticated understanding of the common pitfalls involved in developing inferences from observations, thus encouraging practitioners to be self-critical as they form their ideas about a case. Emotional competence refers to the practitioner's resilience and resourcefulness in coping with the frequently dramatic clinical material that may come to light in working with patients who have recovered memories of abuse. The therapist who "loses it" in this regard—by, for example, prematurely becoming the client's champion in seeking punishment of her "evil" parents—is likely to make serious mistakes in case management. Pope and Brown recommend frequent consultation with professional colleagues, or in more serious instances perhaps even personal therapy, for practitioners who may find themselves becoming swept up by their work with this challenging clinical population.

SUMMARY

Originally considered subvarieties of the general class known as neurotic disorders, somatoform and dissociative disorders came to be recognized as separate and distinct general types of disorder in their own right in contemporary versions of the DSM. They continue to share certain similarities, both being covert ways of avoiding psychological stress while denying personal responsibility for doing so. There are suggestions, as well, that both are associated with traumatic childhood experiences, and they are frequently comorbid.

Somatoform disorders are those in which psychological problems are manifested in physical disorders (or complaints of physical disorders) that mimic medical conditions but for which there can be found no evidence of corresponding organic pathology. They include somatization disorder (chronic absence of a sense of physical wellness), hypochondriasis (anxious preoccupation with self-attributed disease), pain disorder (experienced pain disproportional to objective findings of disease), and conversion disorder (relatively specific malfunction in the sensory, motor, or visceral apparatus). Secondary gain, or external benefits that accrue to the person by virtue of being disabled, may complicate the picture in somatoform disorders and interfere with treatment progress. While there are certain known risk factors for the development of these disorders, such as neuroticism, etiologic hypotheses remain for the most part nonspecific. With the exception of pain and con-

version disorder, treatment prospects generally are not encouraging.

In dissociative disorders the normal processes regulating awareness and the multichannel capacities of the mind apparently become disorganized, leading to various anomalies of consciousness and personal identity. These include functional amnesic states with or without fugue, the dramatic phenomena of dissociative identity disorder (DID) in which the individual may harbor a multitude of seemingly autonomous personalities or fragments thereof, and the far more common depersonalization disorder in which the person has a sense of lost connection with the self. The incidence/prevalence of diagnosed DID has increased markedly over the last three decades, suggesting it is a disorder whose occurrence is strongly affected by trends in the sociocultural milieu. Certain traits of personality such as capacity for absorption appear to facilitate dissociative experiences, and there is growing evidence that traumatic abuse in childhood is a specific risk factor, especially for the development of DID. Treatment of dissociative disorders, especially DID, is regarded as difficult, and in well-established cases the prospects for complete recovery may be quite limited.

Dissociative identity disorder remains highly controversial as a concept, as does its purported specific association with traumatic childhood abuse, among professional experts in the field. Much public confusion and conflict is thus a continuing problem.

KEY TERMS

somatoform disorders (p. 268)

dissociative disorders (p. 268)

somatization disorder (p. 268)

hypochondriasis (p. 269)

malingering (p. 270)

pain disorder (p. 271)

conversion disorder (p. 273)

secondary gain (p. 274)

factitious disorder (p. 277)

implicit memory (p. 280)

implicit perception (p. 280)

dissociative disorders (p. 280)

psychogenic or dissociative amnesia (p. 280)

fugue (p. 281)

dissociative identity disorder (p. 282)

host personality (p. 282)

alter identities (p. 283)

depersonalization disorder (p. 285)

derealization (p. 285)

CHAPTER EIGHT

Eating Disorders and Other Psychological Compromises of Physical Health

Elsie Blankenhorn, *Untitled*. Born in 1873, Blankenhorn grew up in a privileged family. Her father suffered with manic depression, and died in 1906. After his death, she was hospitalized in a private psychiatric clinic, where she remained until 1921. Diagnosed with catatonia and dementia praecox, she recorded her private, inner thoughts in diaries and albums. She often drew bank notes with imaginary numbers and "guardian angels."

Traditionally, the medical profession has concentrated its efforts on understanding and influencing anatomical and physiological factors in disease. In psychopathology, on the other hand, interest centered primarily on the discovery and remedy of psychological factors associated with mental disorders. Today we realize that both these approaches are limited: Although a disorder may be primarily physical or primarily psychological, it is always a disorder of the whole person—not just of the body or the psyche.

Today, the mind and body are seen more as a two-way street. Fatigue or a bad cold may lower tolerance for psychological stress; an emotional upset may lower resistance to physical disease; a woman's attempts to meet contemporary standards of beauty may plunge her into a dangerous confrontation with starvation; other maladaptive behaviors, such as excessive alcohol use, may contribute to the impairment of various organs, like the brain and liver. Furthermore, a person's overall life situation has much to do with the onset of a disorder, its nature, duration, and prognosis.

Recovery from a physical or mental disorder is apt to be more rapid for a patient eager to get back to work and to family and friends than for the one who will be returning to a frustrating job or an unpleasant home life. As we have seen in previous chapters, sociocultural influences affect the types and incidence of disorders found in members of different cultures and gender and age groups. The ailments to which people are most vulnerable—whether physical, psychological, or both—are determined in no small part by when, where, and how they live. In short, an individual is a biopsychosocial unit.

Behavioral medicine is the broad interdisciplinary approach to the treatment of physical disorders thought to have psychosocial factors as major aspects in their causation and/or maintenance. The field thus includes professionals from many disciplines—including medicine, psychology, and sociology—who take into account biological, psychological, and sociocultural influences when considering a person's health. Its emphasis, however, is essentially on the role psychological factors play in the occurrence, maintenance, and prevention of physical illness.

In this chapter we address largely **psychogenic illnesses**—psychologically induced or maintained diseases. Some psychologists have adopted this as an area of major professional interest. **Health psychology** is a psychological subspecialty within the behavioral medicine approach that deals with psychology's contributions to the diagnosis, treatment, and prevention of psychological components of physical dysfunction. Since the 1970s, the field has developed rapidly and has had a notable impact over

virtually the entire range of clinical medicine (Belar, 1997; Hafen et al., 1996).

A behavioral medicine approach to physical illness examines the broad biopsychosocial context of the following problem areas (adapted from Gentry, 1984):

- The psychological factors such as critical life events, characteristic behavior, and personality organization, which may predispose an individual to physical illness.

- The ways in which the negative effects of stress can be reduced by personal resources, such as coping styles, social supports, and certain personality traits.

- The biological mechanisms by which human physiology is altered by stressors, particularly those arising from maladaptive behavior, and the effects of stress on the immune, endocrine, gastrointestinal, and cardiovascular systems, among others.

- The psychological processes involved in the health choices individuals make with respect to such matters as hazardous lifestyles, health care decisions, and adherence to preventive regimens.

- The factors—biomedical, behavioral, self-regulative, cultural, social, and interpersonal (for example, aspects of the practitioner-patient relationship)—that determine compliance with sound medical advice.

- The effectiveness of psychological measures, such as health education and behavior modification, in altering unhealthy lifestyles and in directly reducing illness and illness behavior at both individual and community levels.

Behavioral medicine, and the subspecialty health psychology within it, are concerned with the psychological processes involved in the health choices people make as well as the psychological and biological factors predisposing them to physical illness.

From this perspective, for example, a patient's current psychological depression may both contribute to the advancement of cardiovascular disease (Glassman & Shapiro, 1998; see also Highlight 8.3) and hinder its effective treatment by making the patient less likely to adhere to a prescribed exercise regimen. Behavioral medicine thus gives health practitioners extra tools for conceptualizing and treating problems. It encourages them to consider job or family circumstances, for example, which, if addressed, may make treatment of the primary medical problem more successful. Far from being of merely supplementary significance—icing on the cake, so to speak—the behavioral medicine viewpoint may be critical in determining clinical outcomes, including survival versus death.

Before DSM-III, most psychogenic medical illnesses were categorized as *psychophysiologic disorders* (and before that as *psychosomatic disorders*). The focus in these earlier times was on specific body system diseases, such as peptic ulcer, traditionally (though in this case erroneously) thought to have primarily psychological origins. In 1980, with the adoption of DSM-III, the category of psychophysiologic disorders was dropped, largely because of the newer perspective that emphasizes the psychological component of all physical illnesses. That is, the attempt to specify particular diseases as having psychological components in their etiology or maintenance came to be seen as both limiting and misleading, because it was increasingly understood that the absence of such components in any disease would in fact be quite rare. As we have seen, in DSM-IV patients are now rated separately on different axes for psychiatric symptom disorders (Axis I), personality disorders (Axis II), and accompanying physical disorders or General Medical Conditions (Axis III). Thus there is no place on the first two axes for the classic psychosomatic disorders.

To permit some sort of psychiatric coding for the many medical conditions that we now recognize may involve psychological contributions, Axis I provides a major category called *Psychological Factors Affecting Medical Condition.* The suspected contributing factors are specified under six subcategories: (1) mental disorder, (2) psychological symptoms, (3) personality traits or coping style, (4) maladaptive health behaviors, (6) stress-related physiological response, or (7) other/unspecified. This diagnosis is to be used when a general medical condition such as high blood pressure, coded on Axis III, involves psychological factors that have either definitely or probably played a significant role in initiating or exacerbating the illness. Obviously, this decision is intended to be left to the diagnostician's judgment, because no sharp line of demarcation exists between a significant and a less significant role for psychological factors.

The diseases for which there is at least some clinical or research evidence of psychogenic involvement have been identified in Hafen and colleagues (1996) recent comprehensive review of mind-body relationships in the medical arena. For convenient access, they are listed in Table 8.1.

In this chapter, we will first take up the unfortunately common and sometimes life-threatening eating disorders, focusing on anorexia nervosa and bulimia nervosa. In the DSM-IV, these disorders are included within the separate, main category of **Eating Disorders.** Because of their contemporary importance and relatively circumscribed nature, we discuss these disorders as a self-contained unit and include suspected causal factors and treatment options. From there we will move to a general consideration of the role of psychological factors in physical health and illness, including influences on the immune system. To provide concrete illustrations of applications in specific disease processes, we will examine in some detail the psychology of cardiovascular diseases, one of which—coronary heart disease—remains the leading cause of death among Americans, and in briefer fashion the extremely common problem of psychogenic headache. Then we will examine major causal pathways, and, finally, highlight several treatment approaches in this rapidly developing area.

EATING DISORDERS

In February 1983, fans of the Carpenters, a musical group that had dominated the pop/soft rock recording market throughout the 1970s, were shocked to learn of the death of lead singer and sometime drummer Karen Carpenter, age 32. The cause of death was listed as cardiac arrest, secondary to chronic starvation. Karen, whose hits like "Close to You" and "We've Only Just Begun" may still occasionally be heard on the radio, was the victim of the eating disorder known as *anorexia nervosa.* She had struggled with the problem, mostly in secrecy, before its effects became obvious in her appearance, for nearly a decade prior to her demise.

Princess Diana of the United Kingdom had also developed an eating disorder. It began at age 20, virtually from the outset of her difficult and unhappy marriage to Prince Charles, who had made critical remarks about her weight during their engagement, and over time increasingly distanced himself from her. Diana's binging and purging (mostly self-induced vomiting) continued, with variations in intensity, at least until the couple formally separated. Like many persons adopting an eating-disordered

TABLE 8.1 MEDICAL CONDITIONS THOUGHT TO BE INFLUENCED BY PSYCHOLOGICAL FACTORS IN TERMS OF ETIOLOGY, AGGRAVATION, OR MAINTENANCE

Accidental injuries	Diabetic blood sugar dysregulation
Alcohol and drug toxicity	Eating disorders
Allergies	Headaches
Arthritis	High medical usage
Asthma	Hypertension
Back pain	Insomnia
Cancer	Irritable bowel syndrome
Colds and other infections	Menstrual difficulties
Coronary heart disease	Pregnancy complications
Delayed surgical recovery	Sexual dysfunctions
Dental cavities, gingivitis	Stomach ulcers

Source: From Hafen et al., 1996.

lifestyle, the Princess was able to contain or ignore speculation about her problems in this area until she decided herself to make them public, some years before her death in a car accident in 1997. Diana's type of eating disorder is called *bulimia nervosa* (for more detail about these two cases, see Meyer & Osborne, 1996, ch. 10).

Although vastly different in background, these two women shared more than untimely and tragic deaths. The most obvious similarity is their celebrity status and their consequent high level of exposure to public scrutiny. Each woman in her own way made perfectionistic demands on herself. Incomprehensibly to many observers, both of these famous women felt lonely and unloved much of the time. Significant women in each of their lives, including their mothers, were less than devoted and affectionate toward them and tended to be highly controlling. The fathers of both women appear to have been largely disengaged from the process of rearing their daughters. As we shall see, there are some hints here that coincide with what we have begun to learn about the origins of eating disorders.

As observed in the case of Karen Carpenter, anorexia nervosa, in particular, is often a stubbornly persistent and life-threatening disorder. Its associated mortality rate, the highest for any psychiatric disorder (Sullivan, 1995), may be as high as 20 percent over an extended period, with death usually the result of either the physiologic consequences of starvation or more intentionally suicidal behavior. This is one of few very sharp contrasts to bulimia nervosa, where death as a direct outcome of the disorder is rare (Keel & Mitchell, 1997; Mitchell, Pomeroy, & Adson, 1997). There is growing evidence that the severe anorexic, even should she survive, may suffer from irreversible brain atrophy (Garner, 1997; Lambe et al., 1997).

Definitions and Gender Differences

Anorexia nervosa and bulimia nervosa, which are considered separate syndromes, are coded as *adult* eating disorders in DSM-IV. In fact, neither syndrome, especially bulimia nervosa, occurs in appreciable numbers before adolescence, and onset after age 25 appears rare, although good epidemiologic data on this point are lacking. Also, the overwhelming number of persons with these disorders are female—on the order of 90 to 95 percent. This marked gender imbalance suggests that, for reasons not yet fully understood, variables associated with gender may be centrally involved in the nature and genesis of these disorders.

Little is reliably known about these eating disorder syndromes in men because of their relative rarity. The limited research information we have about males with anorexic or bulimic eating patterns indicates, interestingly, that a very substantial proportion (up to about half) of them are homosexual, bisexual, or asexual in their sexual preferences (Carlat, Camargo, & Herzog, 1997; Licavoli & Orland, 1997). Unfortunately, this finding has not yet received follow-up attention. Because the overwhelming proportion of research studies on these conditions has been carried out on females, we will confine ourselves here to the typical instances involving adolescent girls or young women.

Clinical Picture and Diagnostic Criteria in Anorexia

Anorexia nervosa has been officially recognized as a distinct disorder for more than a century. The central features of the syndrome, as defined in DSM-IV, are an intense fear of gaining weight coupled with refusal to maintain adequate nutrition, usually associated with an obviously erroneous complaint of being "fat"; loss of original body weight at least to a level (approximately) 85 percent of that expected on the basis of height/weight norms (or, in those still in a period of growth, a discrepancy from average projected weight gain that constitutes about a 15 percent shortfall); disturbance of body image (i.e., the patient has a distorted perception of her own body) or undue influence of the latter in determining self-evaluation; and, in postmenarchial females, absence of at least three consecutive menstrual periods. Associated features that are typically present include marked overactivity and a pattern that emphasizes either severe dietary restriction or binge-eating (with or without compulsive purging). This distinction is coded diagnostically with *Restricting* or *Binge-eating/Purging* subtype designations, respectively. The latter subtype represents one of several links with bulimia nervosa, as discussed below. Methods of purging, besides self-induced vomiting, include the misuse of laxatives, diuretics, and enemas, which as a group are largely ineffective means of curtailing the absorption of calories.

Anorexia nervosa patients having a predominantly restricting pattern tend generally to be obsessional and tightly self-controlled in their everyday style; they may in fact exhibit obsessive-compulsive symptoms (see Chapter 5). They are often socially awkward and may maintain considerable distance and isolation from peers. In contrast, patients exhibiting the binge/purge or bulimia-like pattern normally show considerably less restraint and inhibition, and many of them have problems of impulse control in areas other than eating—such as substance abuse (Gleaves & Eberenz, 1993; Walsh & Garner, 1997). The binge/purge pattern is thought to be associated with a longer duration of disorder and a poorer prognosis for recovery (Herzog, Schellberg, & Deter, 1997).

Clinical Picture and Diagnostic Criteria in Bulimia

Unlike anorexia nervosa, the specific recognition of bulimia nervosa as a psychiatric syndrome is relatively recent; it is not mentioned in the DSM-II of 1968. Russell (1997), in fact, has concluded on the basis of historical review that bulimia nervosa, as presently defined, is a new disorder, "virtually unknown until the latter half of the twentieth century" (p. 20). The apparent hesitancy about recognizing bulimic behavior as psychopathological may be due to its lacking a completely clear differentiation from the concerns and practices of many "normal" young women (Stice et al., 1998). In the DSM-IV, criteria for the

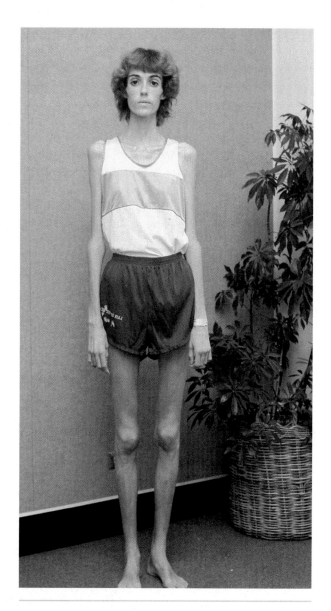

Though this anorexic woman's appearance is shocking to us, she is likely convinced that she is "fat." This distorted view of the true nature of one's body weight is a central feature of anorexia nervosa, along with a refusal to maintain weight within the normal limits for age and height. Anorexia often begins as an extension of normal dieting, but what distinguishes a normal dieter from one who converts dieting into a dangerous activity remains not fully understood.

diagnosis of **bulimia nervosa** emphasize (1) the frequent occurrence of binge-eating episodes accompanied by a sense of loss of control of the overeating process, and (2) recurrent inappropriate behavior intended to prevent weight gain. The latter includes, in addition to the use of purgatives, such measures as dietary fasting, excessive exercise, and the taking of thyroid medication to enhance metabolic rate. Additional criteria refer to frequency and duration—both (1) and (2) at least twice a week, on average, for three months—and, as with anorexia nervosa, undue influence on behavior of the person's body image. Finally, bulimia nervosa may not be diagnosed if these episodes occur only when the person also meets criteria for anorexia nervosa; that is, the anorexia nervosa diagnosis of binge/purge subtype "trumps" the bulimia nervosa one, primarily because of the much greater mortality associated with the former type of disorder, as noted above. In any event, a central issue that is easily obscured in making these fine distinctions is that these girls and young women typically share a common overwhelming fear—that of being, or of becoming, "fat."

The DSM-IV recognizes *Purging* and *Nonpurging* subtypes of bulimia nervosa based on whether or not, in the current episode, the person has employed purgative methods of preventing weight gain (as opposed to excessive exercise, for example). The distinction is not as trivial as it may seem because purging types are often more psychologically disturbed and are more likely to experience physical problems associated with purging, such as electrolyte imbalances, mineral deficiencies, and tooth erosion from frequent regurgitation of stomach acids. Whereas the typical anorexia nervosa patient engages in much denial regarding the seriousness of her disorder and may remain seemingly unaware of the shock and concern with which others view her emaciated condition, the mind-set of the average bulimia nervosa patient is anything but complacent. Preoccupied with shame, guilt, self-deprecation, and efforts at concealment, she struggles painfully and often unsuccessfully on a daily basis to master the impulse to binge. The case described in Highlight 8.1 depicts a typical pattern.

In addition to anorexia and bulimia nervosa, the DSM-IV allows the diagnosis *Eating Disorder Not Otherwise Specified* (EDNOS), which encompasses approximately one-third of all eating disorder patients seeking treatment and is therefore also quite a heterogeneous category. The majority of conditions described under this rubric are sub-threshold varieties of phenomena common to either anorexia nervosa or bulimia nervosa (or both)—for example, a woman who meets all criteria for anorexia nervosa except for disrupted menstrual periods. An exception is the not uncommon **Binge-Eating Disorder (BED),** which is proposed as a separate disorder distinct from bulimia nervosa, Nonpurging type. Here the individual binges at a level comparable to bulimia nervosa patients but does not regularly engage in any form of inappropriate "compensatory" behavior to limit weight gain (even exercise). Not surprisingly, most such persons are overweight, but that is apparently not a factor distinguishing them from the group of Nonpurging bulimia nervosa patients (Walsh &

The public's understanding of the eating disorder, bulimia nervosa was undoubtedly furthered by Princess Diana's courage in discussing her own successful treatment for the disorder and the feelings that contributed to it.

Garner, 1997). Being overweight per se, by the way, does not necessarily indicate an eating disorder, although some markedly overweight persons have a variety of psychological problems, as discussed in Chapter 10.

Distinguishing Among Diagnoses

As is perhaps implied in the large proportion of eating disordered patients falling within the EDNOS category, the diagnosis of an eating disorder can be difficult. The distinction between normal and disordered eating, particularly in a time when very large numbers of young women perceive themselves to be overweight and therefore indulge in one or another form of "dieting," is at best a fuzzy and blurred one. And, as also indicated in the well-populated EDNOS category, failure to meet diagnostic criteria for either anorexia nervosa or bulimia nervosa does not imply that the individual is free of disorder. As is also seen from the foregoing, the distinction between anorexia nervosa and bulimia nervosa is often less than clear. In fact, many persons presently meeting criteria for bulimia nervosa have been diagnosed with anorexia nervosa in the past and, to a lesser extent, vice versa (Garner & Garfinkel, 1997).

Eating disorder diagnoses are commonly associated with other diagnosable psychiatric conditions—that is, the occurrence of "comorbidity" with other recognized disorders is frequent. Anorexia nervosa patients often also meet criteria for clinical depression (Kaye, Weltzin, & Hsu, 1993), and, those with the restricting type, for obsessive-compulsive disorder (Halmi et al., 1991). The frequent co-occurrence of substance abuse disorders in the binge/purge subtype of anorexia nervosa and in bulimia nervosa has already been mentioned. Comorbid Personality Disorder (Axis II) diagnoses, especially those in the anxious-fearful range (Cluster C; see Chapter 9), are also common in anorexia nervosa, particularly the restricting subtype (Skodol et al., 1993). Roughly comparable comorbidities, including much depression, have also been found for the bulimia nervosa disorder. Some patients with bulimia nervosa, with its more impulsive trends, also show signs of anxiety disorders, either of the generalized or social phobia types. Borderline or other Cluster B (dramatic, emotional, erratic) problems are the most commonly diagnosed Axis II comorbid personality disorders (American Psychiatric Association, 1994). Less is known about comorbidity in BED. Some evidence (Wilson, 1993) suggests that alcohol abuse is less common in this group than in binge/purge anorexia nervosa or in bulimia nervosa patients, and also that there is less comorbidity with other psychiatric disorders (Telch & Stice, 1998).

Table 8.2 summarizes the diagnostic criteria differentiating anorexic and bulimic subtypes and binge-eating disorders.

Prevalence of Eating Disorders

It is generally agreed that the prevalence of eating disorders, particularly bulimia nervosa, has increased markedly over the past four decades. Moreover, this increase appears to be "real," and not significantly the product of heightened sensitivity and subsequently, diagnosis, among clinicians, as is suspected for Dissociative Identity Disorder (Chapter 7). The reasons for the increase are not fully understood, but most authorities point to changing norms regarding the "ideal" size and shape of women as one decisive factor. The female "curves" once almost uniformly admired by both men and women are now considered unattractive and undesirable, particularly by many women. Added to this external motivation is the fact that the personal security and solid self-esteem that would doubtless be powerful bulwarks against such influences are apparently not easy to acquire or maintain among adolescent girls and young women in our post-modern society—about which we shall have more to say below.

The point prevalences of the full syndromes among adolescent and young adult women in the United States

TABLE 8.2 DIFFERENTIAL DIAGNOSTIC CRITERIA IN ANOREXIA NERVOSA, BULIMIA NERVOSA, AND BINGE-EATING DISORDER

Criterion	*Anorexia*		*Bulimia*		*Binge Eating*
	Restricting	**Binge/ Purge**	**Purging**	**Non- purging**	
Maintain extremely low weight	yes	yes	no	no	no
Fear of weight gain, becoming fat	yes	yes	yes	yes	no
Denial of seriously low weight	?	?	no	no	no
Body image distortion	?	?	no	no	no
Amenorrhea	yes	yes	no	no	no
Frequent binge eating	no	?	yes	yes	yes
Frequent purging	no	?	yes	no	no
Frequent use of nonpurging methods to avoid weight gain	yes	no	yes	yes	no
Sensed lack of control over eating	no	no	yes	yes	yes
Self-evaluation unduly influenced by shape/weight	?	?	yes	yes	no

Notes: Based on criteria sets provided in the DSM-IV. ? = the feature may or may not be present, as in the form of an either-or criterion alternative.

A Bulimic's Morning

Nicole awakens in her cold dark room and already wishes it was time to go back to bed. She dreads the thought of going through this day, which will be like so many others in her recent past. She asks herself the same question every morning: "Will I be able to make it through the day without being totally obsessed by thoughts of food, or will I blow it again and spend the day bingeing?" She tells herself that today she will begin a new life, today she will start to live like a normal human being. However, she is not at all convinced that the choice is hers.

She feels fat and wants to lose weight, so she decides to start a new diet: "This time it'll be for real! I know I'll feel good about myself if I'm thinner. I want to start my exercises again because I want to make my body more attractive." Nicole plans her breakfast, but decides not to eat until she has worked out for a half hour or so. She tries not to think about food since she is not really hungry. She feels anxiety about the day ahead of her. "It's this tension," she rationalizes. That is what is making her want to eat.

Nicole showers and dresses and plans her schedule for the day—classes, studying, and meals. She plans this schedule in great detail, listing where she will be at every minute and what she will eat at every meal. She does not want to leave blocks of time when she might feel tempted to binge. "It's time to exercise, but I don't really want to; I feel lazy. Why do I always feel so lazy? What happened to the will power I used to have?" Gradually, Nicole feels the bingeing signal coming on. Halfheartedly she tries to fight it, remembering the promises she made to herself about changing. She also knows how she is going to feel at the end of the day if she spends it bingeing. Ultimately, Nicole decides to give into her urges because, for the moment, she would rather eat.

Since Nicole is not going to exercise, because she wants to eat, she decides that she might as well eat some "good" food. She makes a poached egg and toast and brews a cup of coffee, all of which goes down in about thirty seconds. She knows this is the beginning of several hours of craziness!

After rummaging through the cupboards, Nicole realizes that she does not have any binge food. It is cold and snowy outside and she has to be at school fairly soon, but she bundles up and runs down the street. First she stops at the bakery for a bagful of sweets—

are estimated to be between 0.5 and 1.0 percent for anorexia nervosa, and between 1.0 and 3.0 for bulimia nervosa (American Psychiatric Association, 1994). As we have seen, however, such specifically identifiable cases account for only some two-thirds of persons seeking help for eating disorders. We may thus conservatively estimate the point prevalence of all diagnosable eating disorders among postpubertal American females to be minimally 4.0 percent—i.e., at least 4 in 100 such persons may be expected to have an eating disorder of sufficient severity to warrant clinical intervention.

The overall prevalence estimate undoubtedly masks significant variations among demographic groups. Historically, these disorders have been largely confined to the white majority of middle to upper socioeconomic status.

A variety of observations suggest that these disorders are now becoming prevalent among the less privileged of our population. Nor is this phenomenon limited to the United States. Le Grange, Telch, and Tibbs (1998) recently reported widespread eating disorder difficulties among both Caucasian and non-Caucasian South African college students. Among American women of college age, 10 percent or more of them acknowledge some symptoms of eating disorder, which may or may not be severe enough to meet diagnostic criteria (G. Leon, personal communication, November 12, 1997; Heatherton et al., 1995). For some, this will prove a temporary condition, according to a recently published ten-year follow-up of persons who were in college at initial assessment (Heatherton et al., 1997). At follow-up, the

cookies and doughnuts. While munching on these, she stops and buys a few bagels. Then a quick run to the grocery store for granola and milk. At the last minute, Nicole adds several candy bars. By the time she is finished, she has spent over fifteen dollars.

Nicole can hardly believe that she is going to put all of this food, this junk, into her body; even so, her adrenaline is flowing and all she wants to do is eat, think about eating, and anticipate getting it over with. She winces at the thought of how many pounds all of this food represents, but knows she will throw it up afterward. There is no need to worry.

At home Nicole makes herself a few bowls of cereal and milk, which she gobbles down with some of the bagels smothered with butter, cream cheese, and jelly (not to mention the goodies from the bakery and the candy bars which she is still working on). She drowns all of this with huge cups of coffee and milk, which help speed up the process even more. All this has taken no longer than forty-five minutes, and Nicole feels as though she has been moving at ninety miles an hour.

Nicole dreads reaching this stage, where she is so full that she absolutely has to stop eating. She will throw up, which she feels she has to do but which repels her. At this point, she has to acknowledge that she's been bingeing. She wishes she were dreaming, but knows all too well that this is real. The thought of actually digesting all of those calories, all of that junk, terrifies her.

In her bathroom, Nicole ties her hair back, turns on the shower (so none of the neighbors can hear her), drinks a big glass of water, and proceeds to force herself to vomit. She feels sick, ashamed, and incredulous that she is really doing this. Yet she feels trapped—she does not know how to break out of this pattern. As her stomach empties, she steps on and off the scale to make sure she has not gained any weight.

Nicole knows she needs help, but she wants someone else to make it all go away. As she crashes on her bed to recuperate, her head is spinning. "I'll never do this again," she vows. "Starting tomorrow, I'm going to change. I'll go on a fast for a week and then I'll feel better." Unfortunately, deep inside, Nicole does not believe any of this. She knows this will not be the last time. Reluctantly, she leaves for school, late and unwilling to face the work and responsibilities that lie ahead. She almost feels as though she could eat again to avoid going to school. She wonders how many hours it will be until she starts her next binge, and she wishes she had never gotten out of bed this morning. ■

Source: Boskind-White and White (1983) pp. 29–32.

women in this study had experienced significant declines in disordered eating and increased satisfaction with their bodies, despite continuing preoccupation with losing weight. In contrast, many men in the study reported increased concern about their eating habits.

Generalized Risk and Causal Factors in Eating Disorders

In discussing the origins of eating disorders it is useful to distinguish general vulnerabilities, those characteristics that seem implicated in a variety of disordered outcomes, from those influences that appear to be relatively specific to the development of eating problems. In this section we will first review those factors that appear to contribute to the prevalence of a range of problems, including eating disorders, among young women in our society. There appear to be a number of these risk factors that raise the overall likelihood of developing an eating disorder of some kind but are not specific to either eating (as opposed to other types of) disorders or to the particular form in which an eating disorder may be manifested, such as anorexia nervosa, bulimia nervosa, or BED. Following that, we will take up and review what is known or suspected about anorexia nervosa and bulimia nervosa in terms of specific elements of developmental history that may contribute to the disordered outcome. (To date, little of a reliable nature is known about the origins of BED.) It should be understood from the outset, however, that eating disorders (like most other disorders) are undoubtedly multidetermined, and therefore it is unlikely that compelling single factors as causes will be discovered.

Self-Ideal Body Image Discordance That there is now a general sociocultural factor idealizing extremes of thinness in women in "advanced" Western cultures (and, by cultural diffusion, elsewhere) is beyond question. Nearly all instances of eating disorder in general begin with the "normal" dieting that is extremely common among young women in our culture. As several converging lines of evidence indicate (e.g., Fallon & Rozin, 1985; Rodin, 1993; Wiseman et al., 1992; Zellner, Harner, & Adler, 1989), one important product of these thinness pressures is that girls and women often develop highly intrusive and pervasive perceptual biases regarding how "fat" they are. Probably the most important of these are the perceptual discrepancies between the image the girl or young woman has of her own body and the "ideal" female form as represented in contemporary media. Such perceptual biases lead girls and women to believe that men prefer more slender shapes than they in fact do. Figure 8.1 illustrates this set of findings.

Most studies indicate that this phenomenon is quite specific to females, perhaps adding to (or being a significant cause of) the decreases in self-esteem mid-adolescent girls regularly experience. Young males—as a group—remain unaffected by any special slenderness value (perhaps because they are not the subjects of such concerted image-making). Somewhat curiously, and in marked contrast to anorexia nervosa and bulimia nervosa patients, most binge-eating disorder patients do not appear to overvalue thinness, although they do disparage their own bodies (Marcus, 1997).

Such widespread self-ideal discrepancies might be less disconcerting if most of the young women thus affected had a reasonable chance of attaining their body ideal by simply not exceeding an average caloric intake or maintaining a healthy weight. In fact, as pointed out by Garner (1997), the average body weight of American young women has been *increasing* over at least the past four decades, probably as a consequence of general improvements in pediatric health care and other factors such as widespread availability of high-calorie foods. As women's average weight has been increasing over the period 1959 to 1988, the weight of such cultural icons of attractiveness as *Playboy* centerfolds and Miss America contestants *decreased* at a roughly comparable rate. Figure 8.2 depicts these trends.

It is nevertheless worth noting that recent representatives in both the entertainment media mentioned seem physically robust in comparison with contemporary fash-

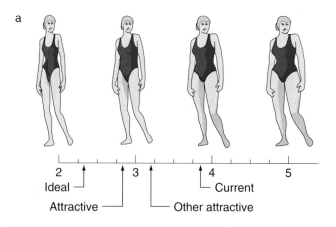

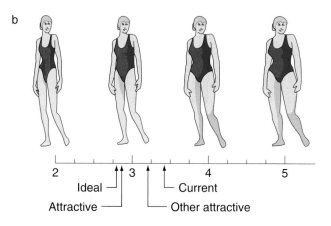

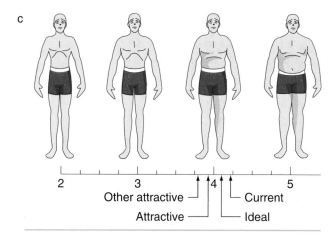

FIGURE 8.1 EATING DISORDER STATUS AND GENDER AS DETERMINANTS OF DESIRABLE BODY SHAPE
Indicated are mean ratings of women identified as having abnormal eating patterns (a), of women having normal eating patterns (b), and of a demographically comparable group of men (c). All subjects rated their "current figure," their "ideal figure," and the figure thought most attractive by the opposite sex (labeled attractive). Also included are the actual mean ratings of "most attractive" provided by oppostie-sex subjects (labeled other "attractive"). *Source:* Zellner, Harner, & Adler (1989).

ion models, many of whom appear—and are encouraged to appear—clearly undernourished. The unreality of the ideal is also seen in the size and shape of the Barbie doll,

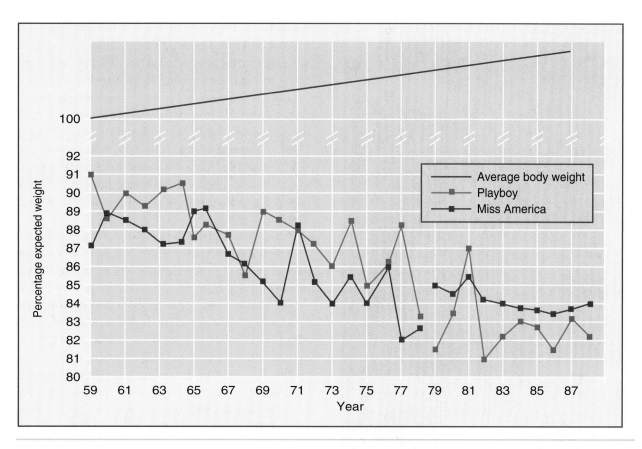

FIGURE 8.2   PRORATED TREND OF WOMEN'S ACTUAL BODY WEIGHTS COMPARED WITH THE TREND FOR PLAYBOY CENTERFOLDS AND MISS AMERICA CONTESTANTS

Changes in the average percentage of expected weight of *Playboy* centerfolds and Miss America contestants. 1959–1978 (data from Garner, Garfinkel, Schwartz, & Thompson, 1980) and 1979–1988 (data from Wiseman, Gray, Masimann, & Ahrens, 1992). The function above the broken verticals represents prorated changes in the average weights for women over the first 20 year period based on the 1959 and revised 1979 Society of Actuaries norms—a trend that has continued according to later population studies. Adapted from Garner (1997), p. 148.

to which most American girls receive much exposure. It has been calculated that, for an average woman to achieve Barbie-like proportions, she would have to be 7 feet 2 inches tall, lose 10 inches from her waist circumference, and gain 12 inches to that of her bust (Moser, 1989).

Biological Considerations   As with many other disorders, the tendency to develop an eating problem runs in families and may therefore indicate some hereditary contribution (Strober, 1995; Walters et al., 1992). Garner (1997) also points out the implications of set-point theory, which refers to the well-established tendency for persons' bodies to "resist" marked variation from some sort of biologically determined individual norm (the "set point"), at least over limited time periods. Thus any individual intent on achieving and maintaining a significant decrease in body mass below his or her individual set-point may face the opposition of innate compensatory

homeostatic mechanisms shared by all of us. Garner (1997) states the idea as follows:

> Generally speaking, body weight resists change. Weight appears to be physiologically regulated around a "set point," or a weight that one's body tries to "defend." Significant deviations from this weight result in a myriad of physiological compensations aimed at returning the organism to this set point (p. 149).

One important consequence of these "physiological compensations" for persons intent on losing weight would most likely be that of enhancing their hunger drive—in severe instances to perhaps extreme peaks of demand, thus motivating pathologic psychological vigilance in the case of anorexia and a significant cause, possibly the main cause, of "uncontrollable" binge eating in bulimia. Chronic dieting would thus enhance the likelihood of the person's encountering periods of seemingly irresistible impulses to gorge on large amounts of high-caloric food.

As the female ideal represented by models grows thinner, a young girl's sense of the discrepancy between her own real weight and her fantasized ideal grows, creating a loss of self-esteem as well as a desire to attain an ever-more impossible weight that can only be reached by compulsive dieting.

Psychopathologic Vulnerability   As has been noted in earlier chapters, some people are more susceptible than others to the development of self-defeating reactions to the inevitable challenges of life. The sources of this fragility are undoubtedly partly inherited, but they are also the outcome of experiences of stressors, the methods employed by the individual to address them, and the relative success of those methods in reestablishing a forward developmental course.

The extensive pattern of comorbid diagnoses in cases of eating disorder, noted above, suggests that many of the

people having them may be generally ill-equipped to deal with life problems in a resourceful manner. Psychologists often refer to this generalized vulnerability pattern as one involving high "neuroticism" in the person's personality makeup, as discussed in Chapter 5. Such people may be anxious, angry, hostile, depressed, self-conscious, impulsive, and highly vulnerable to stressors (Costa & Widiger, 1994). A longitudinal study involving youngsters at high risk for eating disorders, confirmed that general "negative affect" predicts a high risk for eating disorder, but its effects are associated with other psychopathology as well (Leon et al., 1997).

Childhood sexual abuse provides another example of a single risk factor having very diffuse associations across a broad range of dissimilar disorders, including bulimia nervosa (Fairburn et al., 1997; Fallon & Wonderlich, 1997). That is, such abuse (assuming report accuracy) appears significantly associated with some sort of generalized vulnerability to psychological disorder. However, recalling earlier text discussions (see Chapter 7, for example), we cannot be certain that such abuse is, in itself, a contributory *cause* in the disorders with which it has been associated, partly because it occurs for the most part in the context of gross family disorganization, which alone could be an equal or even more potent factor in enhancing vulnerability. This hypothesized relationship among childhood sexual abuse, family disorganization, and bulimia nervosa has been supported in a well-designed community-based study of British young women (Fairburn et al., 1997). The findings indicated that bulimics, as compared with other psychiatric subjects, were more likely to come from families with parental alcoholism and low parental contact. On the other hand, reports of childhood sexual (or physical) abuse for the most part did not differentiate bulimics from general psychiatric subjects, although both disordered groups reported significantly more such abuse than normal controls.

Dysfunctional Cognitive Styles   People with eating disorders, like those with depression (which is often comorbid with these disorders as we have seen), tend to exhibit distorted ways of thinking and of processing information received from the environment. They routinely engage in dichotomous, all-or-nothing thinking and fail to appreciate the fine gradations in which most of life experience actually presents itself. Thus objects of attention are either good or bad, beautiful or ugly, sinful or sublime, stoical or indulgent, fat or thin, etc., with no intervening levels. This type of thinking reflects inadequacies in representing reality on the part of the eating disordered person/perceiver, and hence leads to behavior that does not match the actual requirements of situations confronting the person (e.g., see Butow, Beumont, & Touyz, 1993; Garner, Vitousek, & Pike, 1997). For example, a preanorexic in one of her typically frequent mirror assessments is likely to see any slight deviation from the prescribed ideal body size and shape as totally disgusting and as indicating the grossest of deficiencies in self-restraint and general character.

Specific Risk and Causal Factors in Anorexia and Bulimia Nervosa

In addition to sharing the generalized risk factors reviewed above, adolescents and young women who develop anorexia or bulimia also tend to share many personality characteristics and background features that may be more specific to these types of disorder. There may also be some subtle differences encouraging either an anorexic or a bulimic solution to the particular problems encountered by these unfortunate persons, but as a general rule our research efforts are not sufficiently advanced to detect them reliably. In trying to pinpoint these more specific causal factors, it is also important, of course, to distinguish between qualities of eating disorder patients and their families that may be the *result* of the eating disorders rather than contributory in a causal sense. Garner et al. (1997) for example, point to a number of "starvation symptoms," such as irritability and anger, that may falsely be presumed to be a prominent aspect of the patient's premorbid personality, rather than a product of self-starvation.

Personality Characteristics

The girls and young women who go on to develop anorexia nervosa often show the following characteristics (Strober, 1997):

- Tend to be highly emotionally reserved and cognitively inhibited.
- Prefer routine, orderly, and predictable environments; and adapt poorly to change.
- Show heightened conformity and deference to others.
- Avoid risk and react to appetitive or affectively stressful events with strong feelings of distress.
- Focus excessively on perfectionism.

  In short, the anorexic carries with her a disposition to avoid whatever is novel, intense, or unfamiliar; to have nagging self-doubt and to ruminate; to shun intimate ties with others, especially those outside her immediate family; and to persevere, even in the absence of tangible reward (Strober, 1997, p. 233).

These qualities are almost the antitheses of what is required by the new demands placed on a girl with the advent of puberty or upon confronting numerous other developmentally normal life changes, such as going off to college, where being able to adapt easily to new situations is highly advantageous.

Consistent with its relatively recent "discovery," the personality antecedents of bulimia appear not to be as well articulated as in anorexia and more heterogeneous. Within this constraint of less reliable knowledge, however, the premorbid characteristics of many bulimia nervosa patients are seen as similar to those noted above (e.g., Gleaves & Eberenz, 1993). Research on bulimics has found one subgroup sharing characteristics of emotional instability and impulsivity (Vitousek & Manke, 1994).

Nearly all authorities agree that, like persons with anorexia nervosa, a large proportion of bulimia nervosa patients show a long-standing pattern of excessive perfectionism (Garner & Garfinkel, 1997), which appears to manifest itself in widespread negative self-evaluation (e.g., see Fairburn et al., 1997), particularly if the person perceives herself to be overweight (Joiner et al., 1997a). Maturity fears (fears of becoming adult) may be another shared characteristic of both anorexia- and bulimia-disposed persons (Garner, Vitousek, & Pike, 1997; Joiner et al., 1997b).

Family Patterns

Clinicians dealing with the anorexia nervosa disorder have for decades been impressed with certain problems that seem regularly to characterize the families out of which these distressed young women emerge, so much so that many advocate a family therapy approach to treatment intervention. In fact, an important root of family therapy as it is practiced today (see Chapter 17) derives from early work on therapy with anorexics and their families (Dare & Eisler, 1997). This connection with family problems is amply supported in the comments of anorexia nervosa patients themselves. They usually describe their mothers in unflattering terms: excessively dominant, intrusive, overbearing, and markedly ambivalent in dispensing affection. By contrast, their fathers are usually described as emotional absentees. However, in attempting to depict family characteristics associated with eating disorders, we must register again the general caution that these observations may sometimes be contaminated by the impact the eating disorder has on family functioning. That is, the causal connection, if any, might be in the other direction.

The portrait of families of anorexic patients painted by the research and clinical literature is generally consistent with the portrayal rendered by the girls and young

Research has shown that the families of anorexic girls tend to be intolerant of disagreements and subtly undermining of daughters' efforts at autonomy, perhaps by being overly critical or through an abundance of advice. As a result, their daughters may be tempted to please their parents' perfectionism and exert their own will in the one area where they are clearly in control: their bodies.

women themselves. Families of anorexics are described as showing the following characteristics:

- Limited tolerance of disharmonious affect or psychological tension
- An emphasis on propriety and rule-mindedness
- Parental overdirection of the child or subtle discouragement of autonomous strivings
- Poor skills in conflict resolution (Adapted from Strober, 1997, p. 234.)

To this list may be added the frequent finding that many of these families evidence long-standing preoccupations regarding the desirability of thinness, dieting, and a good physical appearance (Garner & Garfinkel, 1997).

We can thus conceive of a typical developmental course in which the compliance and perfectionism of the preanorexic girl is an adaptation to the rigid rules and control of a family system intolerant of deviation or disharmony. In such a situation and without supportive parents daughters are left with little personal foundation, external support, or instrumental means to express the normal strivings for individuality and autonomy that are enhanced with the onset of adolescence. In this situation the daughter "rebels" in one of the few ways available in this family system—by becoming a super-perfect exemplar of the values of thinness and of propriety and restraint with respect to the indulgence of needs, even the very basic one of hunger. In effect, she "turns the tables"

on the oppressive influences dominating her life. She retains this "autonomous" position with a stubborn fierceness and relentlessness that is routinely impressive even to clinicians with long experience in the field.

The essentials of this admittedly somewhat speculative scenario of how anorexia nervosa may develop were advanced a number of years ago by psychiatrist Hilde Bruch (1986, posthumously published), who until her death in 1984 was generally considered the world's leading authority on the psychotherapy of anorexic disorders. Bruch saw the anorexic person as attempting to camouflage an undeveloped and amorphous selfhood by being different, even unique, in a special and fiercely independent way.

Findings about family patterns in bulimia suggest, again, a number of similarities with anorexia nervosa. For example, in the previously noted study of British bulimic subjects by Fairburn and colleagues (1997), bulimic women were statistically differentiated from the general psychiatric control group (and from the normal one) on such risk factor items as high parental expectations; other family members dieting; and degree of critical comment from other family members about shape, weight, or eating.

In a more quantitatively oriented examination of similarities and differences in the family patterns of anorexic and bulimic subjects, Humphrey (1989) has analyzed the actual interactions of families with either an anorexic or a bulimic daughter using the Structural Analysis of Social Behavior (SASB; Benjamin, 1974, 1996). SASB is a highly systematic technique for measuring the nature of interpersonal relationships. The parents of anorexic young women were found to communicate with their daughters in abnormally complicated ways, providing double messages that at once communicated both nurturant affection and disregard of the daughters' attempts to express themselves. For example, parents might suggest an alternative birthday gift more expensive than one their daughter had specifically requested, thus undercutting her desires and interests. In turn, the anorexic daughters displayed behaviors that wavered between self-expression and submission to the conformity demands issued by parents. Disturbed family dynamics involving this sort of undercutting of the daughters' autonomy were also observed for bulimic young women.

This controlling quality of parents' interactions with their bulimic daughters—despite the parents' overt intentions to be helpful or generous—was more recently confirmed in a new study by Ratti, Humphrey, and Lyons (1996). Such parental behaviors appear to encourage daughters to attack themselves and shows up as disparaged self-image (see, e.g., Benjamin, 1996)—a propensity

Wonderlich, Klein, and Council (1996) found abnormally present in their sample of bulimic women. They may also make daughters susceptible to "internalizing" dysfunctional thinness values (Mason & Cheney, 1996). In short, our available knowledge suggests that both anorexic and bulimic individuals have a common problem of being deeply but ambivalently involved with their parents in power struggles concerning their autonomy and identity. Such problems are, of course, a notable adolescent developmental hurdle in our culture and so are far from exclusive to persons with eating disorders. The evidence suggests that there may be something special about the families of eating disordered women, in that they appear to fail in providing the measured support for autonomous functioning that would enable these young women to negotiate successfully the challenge of becoming, unambivalently, fully functioning independent persons.

Treatment of Eating Disorders

The therapeutic management of eating disorders is multifaceted, complicated in no small part by the fact that, in the case of anorexia, failure can result in the patient's death. Fortunately, there are a large number of procedures available, including hospitalization if the situation is desperate. These can be brought to bear to (1) stabilize the patient and (2) maximize chances for full and lasting recovery. Hospitalization permits control of the patient's environment, and of her food intake (if necessary by measures such as tube feeding), to an extent not possible in more natural settings. Ultimate success, however, depends on whether the patient becomes committed to change—which is not always to be assumed. Karen Carpenter, with whose tragic example we opened this section, found numerous opportunities, including hospitalization, that might have put her on a different and life-saving path. Unfortunately, she appears to have been highly dependent on family support, and so was unable to find within herself the motivation to eat (Meyer & Osborne, 1996).

Treatment of Anorexia Nervosa Efforts to treat the psychological aspects of anorexia must frequently wait until the patient is renourished and her weight reestablished to a level that will ensure both survival and the ability to profit from an emotionally demanding psychological intervention. Not uncommonly, this involves hospitalization under conditions of rigorous dietary control and monitoring of progress toward a targeted range of weight gain (Andersen, Bowers, & Evans, 1997). Normally, this short-term effort is successful. What is less re-

liable is the anorexic person's ability to maintain these gains. This is in fact extremely doubtful without treatment that is also designed to modify or eradicate the psychological conditions fueling anorexic behavior.

There are many varieties of psychosocial interventions available and potentially useful in reversing the problems underlying anorexia. These broad approaches and their central features are described more fully in Chapter 17. Most of what we know about their successful use in the treatment of anorexia comes from published case reports. Unfortunately, and unlike the situation with bulimia, there have been surprisingly few controlled studies to allow for a truly informed choice among these psychosocial treatments. This is probably due in large measure to the fact that successful treatment of anorexia, by whatever means, takes a long time. As we shall see, cognitive behavioral therapy (CBT) has proved very effective in bulimia, and because anorexia shares many similarities with it, CBT is often attempted in cases of anorexia.

A highly detailed model for the application of CBT techniques in anorexia emphasizes the *differences* between the average bulimic and anorexic patient (such as the frequently uncertain motivation and the pronounced social deficits of the anorexic), and builds into the treatment plan techniques for managing the special problems of the anorexic, such as her predictable distancing and distrust of the therapist (Garner, Vitousek, & Pike, 1997).

Treatment of Bulimia Nervosa One of the more dramatic successes of research in psychopathology and its treatment in recent decades has been related to the unmatched success of CBT in the treatment of bulimia nervosa. Multiple controlled studies of immediate posttreatment and long-term follow-up outcomes of CBT treatment of bulimia nervosa have established CBT as the clear treatment of choice for this disorder (e.g., Agras et al., 1992; Fairburn et al., 1993, 1995; Fichter et al., 1991; Leitenberg et al., 1994; Walsh et al., 1997; Wilson & Fairburn, 1993, 1998). Such studies have included competitive comparisons with medication therapy (chiefly antidepressants) and generally show CBT to be clearly superior. In fact, combining these two approaches produces only a modest increment in effectiveness over that achievable with CBT alone (Wilson & Fairburn, 1998). For a more comprehensive review of the overall evidence the reader may consult Wilson, Fairburn, and Agras (1997).

The "behavioral" component of CBT for bulimia is focused on normalizing eating patterns—ending bingeing and purging and teaching the person instead to eat small amounts more regularly. For example, the patient is put on a prescribed schedule for eating, one emphasizing temporal regularity rather than amounts eaten. The "cognitive" elements of the treatment address the dysfunctional thought patterns usually present in bulimia, such as the "all or nothing" thinking described above. For example, the tendency to divide all foods into "good" and "bad" categories is disputed by providing factual information and by arranging for the patient to demonstrate to herself that ingesting "bad" food does not inevitably lead to a total loss of control over eating.

Treatment of Binge-Eating Disorder Little of a systematic nature is known about effective treatment for binge-eating disorder (BED), probably because this is a heterogeneous and relatively neglected category of disorder. Undoubtedly most instances have some overlap with both anorexia and bulimia. Hence clinicians have tended to try to adapt relevant aspects of the treatment of these disorders to the particular clinical picture presented by the BED patient. This is well illustrated in the approach advocated by Marcus (1997), who emphasizes the adaptation of already established CBT techniques in anorexia nervosa and bulimia nervosa to the special circumstances of the BED patient. Such patients are typically overweight and subject to chaotic eating patterns. They also typically have a variety of illogical and contradictory "rules" about food ingestion—for example, sharing with bulimics a rigid distinction between "good" and "bad" foods. They may also have stereotypic attitudes about the character flaws of overweight people and so lack the self-esteem that might motivate them to stop their bingeing.

Many BED patients are failed veterans of various diet plans based on unproven and sometimes nonsensical principles, adding to their burden of misinformation, confusion, and sense of failure. Significant depression is a common comorbid condition for binge eaters. Thus a judiciously planned program of CBT, together with the provision of corrective and factual information on nutrition and weight loss, could be helpful to many of these people. Fairburn and Carter (1997) suggest the addition of selected self-help reading materials to such a therapeutic program.

While eating disorders are clearly psychological disorders affecting physical health, it is also reasonable to conceive of eating disorders as disorders of impulse control, with anorexics having too much and bulimics and BED patients having too little, resulting in serious threats to physical health. In the remainder of this chapter we will be looking at additional ways in which psychological issues are involved in physical health maintenance or its compromise.

GENERAL PSYCHOLOGICAL FACTORS IN HEALTH AND DISEASE

Research has repeatedly shown that mental and emotional processes are somehow implicated both in good health and in most physical diseases. In this section we will outline the main phenomena relating to psychosocial influences on biological health in general, specifying, where possible, the mechanisms involved. We will begin our survey with observations on health, attitudes, and coping resources. We move from there to an examination of the autonomic nervous system and its potential effects on health. We then consider what may eventually be recognized as the most basic and general topic in this area—the immune system and the compromise of its functioning by psychological states and stressful events. The section ends with a brief discussion of lifestyle and its implications for physical health maintenance.

Health, Attitudes, and Coping Resources

The negative health effects of stressful life events were outlined in Chapter 4. Here we shall examine this relationship in greater detail, discussing the psychological aspects of immune functioning and of cardiovascular reactivity. We begin by examining attitudes and personality factors that appear to be implicated in health maintenance or deterioration.

Hopeless and helpless attitudes can have devastating effects on organic functioning. For example, a sense of hopelessness accelerates progression of atherosclerosis, the underlying process leading to heart attacks and strokes (Everson et al., 1997). Today, many surgeons will delay a major operation until they are convinced that a patient is reasonably optimistic about the outcome. Optimism in a more positive, everyday sense seems to serve as a buffer against disease (Scheier & Carver, 1987, 1992), though one can be too optimistic about one's health status, perhaps leading to dangerous neglect of health care (e.g., Davison & Prkachin, 1997; Fisher & Fisher, 1992; Friedman, Hawley, & Tucker, 1994; Kalichman, Hunter, & Kelly, 1993; Tennen & Affleck, 1987).

The Two Faces of Optimism Optimism, then, has two faces—at least as it pertains to health matters. Its more positive aspect appears related to a person's sense of *efficacy,* of being able to cope with any adversity that may arise. Optimism's more problematic form is seen in defensive denial, an unwillingness or inability to acknowledge illness, symptoms, or potential threats to well-being.

Persistent negative affect has been shown to be associated with health endangerment.

The defensive type of optimism is not only unhelpful in the health context, but actually constitutes a significantly enhanced risk for health problems (e.g., see Davidson & Prkachin, 1997; Shedler, Mayman, & Manis, 1993).

People with too little optimism of the more positive kind experience a psychological sense of helplessness, and as we also saw in Chapter 4 this can be associated with poor health outcomes (e.g., Fawzy et al., 1993). In an interesting study of hall-of-fame baseball players, Peterson and Seligman (1987) found that in this group of athletes negative attitudes were significantly associated with health problems following their active playing years. Recently, Peterson and colleagues (1998) reported a significantly elevated mortality rate among a group of intellectually gifted individuals who had, a half-century earlier, a tendency to treat negative events as catastrophes. Similarly, a follow-up study of Harvard graduates having pessimistic attitudes at age 25 demonstrated them to have an elevated incidence of physical disease at ages 45 to 60 (Peterson, Seligman, & Vaillant, 1988).

Negative Emotions and Physical Illness In other instances, it is the particular nature of a person's coping

resources rather than their attitude that is suspect. The most familiar example here is the Type A behavior pattern, discussed below. When certain ordinary hassles or problems of life (such as having to wait in line) habitually provoke extremes of behavior (such as rage or explosive frustration), a person is designated "Type A." A large body of evidence has implicated a component of this coping style as a significant risk factor for coronary heart disease. More generally, any type of chronic negative affect seems to enhance the risk of disease (Friedman & Booth-Kewley, 1987b; Hafen et al., 1996), although it must also be noted that, through its association with the personality trait of *neuroticism*, mentioned earlier, negative emotion increases complaints about health problems that cannot be medically documented (Costa & McCrae, 1987; Thoreson & Powell, 1992; Watson & Pennebaker, 1989). Neuroticism, incidentally, is associated with increased occurrence of negative life events such as divorce (Magnus et al., 1993), which themselves are linked with disease onset. As these examples illustrate, the relationships between personality and health often prove to be very complex (Friedman, Hawley, & Tucker, 1994).

Often it appears that any severe stress serves to facilitate, precipitate, or aggravate a physical disorder in a person already predisposed to it. This assumption is in keeping with the diathesis-stress model we discussed in Chapter 3. A person with allergies may find his or her resistance further lowered by emotional tension; similarly, as we will see, when an invading virus has already entered a person's body—as is thought to be the case in multiple sclerosis, for example—emotional stress may interfere with the body's normal defensive forces or immunological system. In like manner, any stress may tend to aggravate and maintain certain disorders, such as migraine headaches (Levor et al., 1986) or rheumatoid arthritis (Affleck et al., 1994).

Psychological Factors in Health and Healing The relationship between psychological factors and good health has also been well documented (e.g., Jones, 1977; Hafen et al., 1996). Positive emotions often seem to protect against physical disease or to be associated with speedy and uncomplicated recoveries when disease does strike (O'Leary, 1985), a fact that complicates efforts to determine the true effectiveness of new treatment techniques, such as new drugs. A patient who believes a treatment is going to be effective has a much better chance of showing improvement than does one who is neutral or pessimistic—even when the treatment is subsequently shown to have no direct or relevant physiological effects.

This reaction is known generally as the **placebo effect,** and it accounts in part for the controversies that arise periodically between the scientific community and the general public regarding the efficacy of certain drugs or other treatments.

It has even been suggested that, had it not been for the placebo effect, the medical profession as we know it would not have survived to the twentieth century, because until the early 1900s medical practitioners had little else to offer disease sufferers; indeed, many widely employed specific treatments (e.g., bleeding) were plainly harmful. The profession's survival and prosperity from ancient times is to a large extent a demonstration of the power of faith in healing (Shapiro & Morris, 1978). Thus the fundamental intimacy of the mind and body is perhaps nowhere better documented than in the history of the medical profession itself.

Fight or Flight and Nowhere to Go Our cave-dwelling ancestors needed organ systems that could rapidly prepare their bodies for the intense life-or-death struggles that were part of their daily existence. Nature provided these in the form of a rather elaborate apparatus for dramatically enhancing energy mobilization on a short-term basis. The events making this emergency reaction possible involve chiefly the sympathetic division of the autonomic nervous system. It was termed the "fight-or-flight response" in 1929 by the distinguished physiologist Walter B. Cannon (1871–1945), thus underscoring its apparent function either in fleeing danger or subduing an aggressor. In describing the fight-or-flight pattern, Cannon noted that, with the advance of civilization, to a degree these reactions have become obsolete. Today, because we are rarely able to flee or physically attack a threat (such as a noisy neighbor or traffic congestion), no effective avenue exists for the prompt discharge of the high states of physiologic readiness that may be triggered in these situations. In Cannon's view (and the views of many contemporary investigators), this state of affairs, when unduly repetitive or long-continued, produces tissue breakdown—that is, disease, such as high blood pressure (hypertension).

The arousal of the autonomic nervous system involves many component processes, some of them subtle or even silent in terms of being readily observed. With increasing levels of arousal, we can directly observe the more dramatic manifestations: increased breathing and heart rate, increased sweating, increased muscle tone, and flushing; a keen observer will note pupillary dilation, enhancing vision. With adequate instrumentation, we could

The physiological arousal behind this cat's response, while useful for fleeing danger or defending against an aggressor, is not so useful to humans today and takes its toll on tissues and systems if it is not promptly discharged.

also observe increased blood pressure, the dumping of sugar reserves into the blood, redistribution of blood pooled in the viscera to the peripheral or voluntary musculature, and enhanced secretion of powerful neurotransmitters. All of these changes are sometimes referred to collectively as the alarm reaction (Selye, 1976b), the first phase of a general adaptation syndrome described in Chapter 4. These changes are the body's response to a "battle stations" signal from the brain. Such a system was not evolved for dealing with trifling circumstances, and it is hardly surprising that such widespread and potent effects, if not permitted to subside, might over time lead to organic pathology.

Coming to a similar conclusion, the early psychosomatic theorists, notably including Flanders Dunbar (1943) and Franz Alexander (1950), reasoned that chronic *internal* sources of threat could place physical health in serious jeopardy. In other words, unremitting psychological stress of the type found in, for example, chronic anxiety disorders (Chapter 5) might actually cause physical damage to vital organs. These early theorists appear to have been largely on the right track, although—as so often happens in psychology and in science generally—many of their conceptions have proved inaccurate or oversimplified.

The link between prior stress and the occurrence of physical illness includes various types of disease not thought to involve excessive autonomic nervous system activity in their causal pattern. It includes certain forms of cancer, for example. These correlational observations suggest the involvement of a very generalized type of vulnerability that stress may also induce. Specifically, it suggests that stress may compromise immune functioning. Put another way, the harmful physical effects of stress may involve not only the "alarm" stage of the general adaptation syndrome, but the "resistance" one as well. We turn now to the evidence addressing this question.

Psychosocial Factors and the Immune System

The immune system's responsiveness to invasion by a foreign substance can be readily seen through laboratory examination of samples of blood or certain body fluids such as saliva. Early studies examining the association between stress and immune functioning rapidly established an association between the occurrence of presumably stressful circumstances (e.g., medical school exams) and diminished immune reactivity. Such immune system compromise would make a person more susceptible to infections, among other negative effects. Although observations linking disease onset to prior stress have been robust and reliable, they have been for the most part correlational in nature. In addition, there is some evidence of substantial individual differences in this type of reactivity to stress (Manuck et al., 1991). Before moving into the substantive issues, however, we need to describe the basics of immune functioning.

Elements of the Human Immune System   While much remains to be learned about the details of immunologic functioning, particularly in regard to psychosocial influences, certain broad outlines are now fairly well understood.

The immune system is traditionally divided into two branches, humoral and cellular. The humoral branch refers to the activity of B-cells and the antibodies they produce. Cellular immune function, on the other hand, is mediated by T-cells, whose effects, while widespread, do not include antibody production. When an organism is invaded by an antigen—that is, a substance recognized as "foreign"—B- and T-cells become activated and multiply rapidly, deploying the various forms of counterattack mediated by each type of cell.

B-cells, which are formed in the bone marrow, perform their defensive function by producing antibodies that circulate in the blood serum. B-cell (or humoral immune) functioning is involved chiefly with detection of and protection against the more common varieties of bacterial infection. Several descendant forms of the progenitor stem cell develop to maturity as T-cells in the thymus. T-cells mediate immune reactions that, while slower, are both more extensive and more direct in character. These include: (1) destruction of certain types of antigens, especially nonbacterial ones such as viruses and neoplasms (tumor cells); (2) regulation and in certain instances activation of the other, antibody-based division of the defense system; and (3) termination of the immune response when danger subsides. T-cells mainly generate an attack that is highly specific to a given invading antigen.

The protective activity of the B- and T-cells is supported and reinforced by other specialized components of the system—most notably natural killer cells, macrophages (literally, big eaters), and granulocytes. The front line of immune defense is thus contained within this highly differentiated system of white cells that circulate freely in the blood or remain as resident reinforcements in the lymph nodes. The immune system's response to antigen invasion is thus generalized and intricately orchestrated, requiring the intact functioning of numerous components. As will be seen, it is by now a virtual certainty that the brain is centrally involved in this control of immune system events.

Psychosocial Compromise of the Immune Response   As a disease of the immune system, AIDS provides a good illustration of the interrelationship between stress and the immune response. Though stress may not *cause* AIDS to be expressed in the HIV-positive person, it apparently weakens further the body's already compromised immune response (Kiecolt-Glaser & Glaser, 1988, 1992). For example, Antoni and colleagues (1990) reported preliminary results indicating that behavioral interventions, such as aerobic exercise, had positive psychological and immunocompetence effects among groups of uninfected high-risk and early-stage infected gay men. More recently, Kemeny and colleagues (1994) presented evidence suggesting that a depressed mood was associated with enhanced HIV-1 activity among infected gay men, confirming in this group the more general point that psychological depression compromises immune function (Herbert & Cohen, 1993). It also enhances the likelihood of continued high risk behavior in as yet uninfected men (Kalichman et al., 1997a). Inasmuch as we now have effective treatments for depression, notably in-

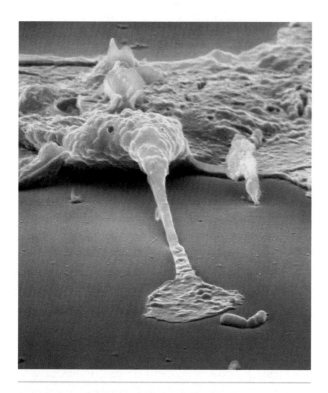

A macrophage reaches out to eat bacteria. Macrophages are important components of the immune system because they initiate the action of B-cells and T-cells against bacterial, or antigen, invasion.

cluding psychosocial ones such as cognitive-behavior therapy (e.g., DeRubeis, 1997; Hollon et al., 1992), the current almost exclusive focus on pharmacological approaches in treating AIDS may be neglecting an important alternative.

The original correlational evidence of a stress-illness relationship has now been fortified by studies permitting a stronger causal inference concerning the role of stress in reducing immunocompetence. Strauman, Lemieux, and Coe (1993) designed an experiment that (temporarily) manipulated the self-evaluations of their subjects. They found that natural killer cell cytotoxicity (i.e., its power to eradicate an antigen) was significantly diminished with induced negative self-evaluations, an effect that was especially strong for persons who were determined to be anxious and/or dysphoric in mood before the experiment. Another experimental demonstration deliberately exposed quarantined, healthy volunteer subjects to a common cold virus and assessed the outcome in terms of actual contraction of an upper respiratory infection. Stressful life events, self-perceived stress, and negative emotion, all assessed before exposure, each significantly predicted which subjects would become ill with colds (Cohen, Tyrrell, & Smith, 1993).

As already suggested, depression or negative affect may turn out to have special significance with respect to the suppression of immune protection. A review of the evidence by Weisse (1992) indicates a strong association between dysphoric mood and compromised immune function, one that appears to be at least partially independent of specific situations or events that may have provoked depressed feelings; that is, the state of being depressed *in itself* adds something beyond any negative effects of the stressors precipitating this mood. Another review of the relevant research found that depressive affect was reliably associated with lowered numbers of white cells following foreign protein challenge, lowered natural killer cell activity, and lowered quantities of several varieties of circulating white cells (Herbert & Cohen, 1993). A possibly related finding: health care use diminished with recovery from depressive disorders among members of a health maintenance organization (Von Korff et al., 1992).

The list of conditions demonstrated to be associated with diminished immune function is in fact a long one. Besides psychological depression it includes sleep deprivation, marathon running, space flight, and death of a spouse (Schleifer, Keller, & Stein, 1985; Schleifer et al., 1989; Vasiljeva et al., 1989). Cacioppo and colleagues (1998) have recently added caregiving to a demented person such as an Alzheimer patient (see Chapter 13) to the list. Immune responsiveness has been shown to vary with even normal, diurnal mood variations (Stone et al., 1987). A group of researchers at Ohio State University has repeatedly demonstrated the compromise of white blood cell proliferation, including diminished natural killer cell activity, among medical students undergoing the stress of academic examinations (Glaser et al., 1985, 1987). Natural killer cells are believed to play a key role in tumor surveillance and the control of viral infections.

Psychoneuroimmunology Indications of strong relationships between certain negative psychological states and diminished immune system functioning suggest some sort of central mediating mechanism that presides over the interaction. The obvious candidate for such a role is the central nervous system, specifically the brain. Such considerations have led to the development of the field of **psychoneuroimmunology,** which explores psychological interactions in the brain's control of immune responsiveness by way of its control over neural, neurochemical, and endocrinological (hormonal) processes. Although still relatively new, the field has developed in a rapid and impressive manner (see Maier & Watkins,

1998, and Maier, Watkins, & Fleshner, 1994, for an overview).

The Hypothalamic-Pituitary-Adrenocortical Axis If stressors, in particular psychosocial or mental ones, can impair the immune response through some type of brain mediation, a conclusion supported by the weight of evidence (Antoni et al., 1990; Jemmott & Locke, 1984; Kiecolt-Glaser & Glaser, 1992; Maier et al., 1994, 1998), how do they do it? What pathway or pathways of influence are involved?

Until fairly recently, most researchers were convinced that the primary pathway was the hypothalamic-pituitary-adrenocortical (HPA) axis. According to this hypothesis, the processing of stressful events in the brain causes hypothalamic activation of the pituitary, which in turn stimulates the adrenal cortex to secrete excessive levels of adrenocortical hormones, substances known to have powerfully negative (as well as some positive) effects on immune functioning. In fact, corticosteroids such as cortisone are used to treat diseases where suppression of the immune system is desired, as in rheumatoid arthritis, an "autoimmune" disease in which the immune system makes a mistake and attacks healthy tissue.

Other Neurochemicals and Immune Function More recent research findings and conceptual refinements have turned up a host of strong competitors to the HPA interpretation. For example, we now know that a number of other hormones, including growth hormone, testosterone, and estrogen, respond to stress and also affect immune competence. The same is true of a variety of more exotic neurochemicals, including the endorphins (endogenous peptide substances that mimic the action of opium).

The link between psychosocial stressors and the immune system may be even more direct, however. The discovery of nerve endings in thymus, spleen, and lymph nodes, tissues literally teeming with white blood cells, suggests the possibility of direct neural control of the secretion of immunologic agents. It is now known, too, that white blood cell surfaces contain receptors for circulating neurochemicals (Rogers, 1989). We must assume that the presence of these receptors on these cells is not accidental and that the cells respond in some way to messages conveyed by brain-regulated substances in the bloodstream, such as various peptides.

Conditioned Immunosuppression Perhaps most unexpectedly, immunosuppression can be classically conditioned (Ader & Cohen, 1984; Maier et al., 1994)—that is, it can come to be elicited as an ac-

quired response to previously neutral stimuli, just as Pavlov's dogs learned to salivate to a tone. Conceivably, even mental stimuli such as thoughts or images could thus come to activate immunosuppression if they were regularly paired with immunosuppressive events (operating as unconditioned stimuli). For example, the one to three years of immunosuppression believed to follow the death of a spouse (Hafen et al., 1996, p. 25) might be due to repeatedly evoked images of a lost and more pleasant past, images that became conditioned stimuli for immunosuppression through association with the latter during an earlier period of intense grieving.

Immune Feedback Complicating the picture of the effects of psychosocial stressors on the immune system is the fact that the influences are bidirectional. Maier and colleagues (Maier et al., 1994; Maier & Watkins, 1998) present strong evidence that a person's behavior and psychological states do indeed affect immune functioning, but the status of immunologic defenses also feeds back to affect current mental states and behavioral dispositions by affecting the blood levels of circulating neurochemicals, which in turn modify brain states. Such a feedback loop might, for example, account for the frequently observed effect of stress in inducing psychological depression. That is, stressors may evoke immunosuppression that could in turn result in chemical signals to the brain having the effect of inducing depressive thoughts and behavior.

Stressor Toxicity While efforts to relate specific stressors to specific physical diseases have not generally been successful, stress is becoming a key underlying theme in our understanding of the development and course of virtually all organic illness. Stress may serve as a predisposing, precipitating, or reinforcing factor in the causal pattern, or it may merely aggravate a condition that might have occurred anyway. Even stress that is treatment-related, as in aggressive therapy for certain cancers, may carry its own measure of risk for compromising defensive resources by seriously diminishing the patient's quality of life, as pointed out by Anderson, Kiecolt-Glaser, and Glaser (1994). Post-traumatic stress may continue to have destructive health effects long after the traumatic event, as suggested in the long-term problematic health histories of women (and men) who have been victims of sexual assault (Golding, 1994; Golding, Cooper, & George, 1997). Often stress appears to speed up the onset or increase the severity of a disorder, and to interfere with the body's immunological defenses and other homeostatic repair

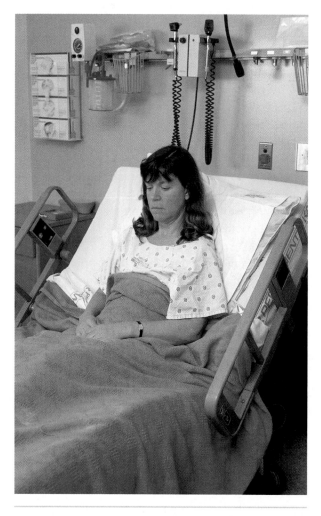

Just as stress can disrupt the immune system and make a person vulnerable to disease, so can being sick and the taxing of the immune system make a person vulnerable psychologically—to anxiety and depression, for example.

functions. Presuming that we all have one organ system in our bodies that is relatively vulnerable, a high, chronic level of stress puts us at risk for a breakdown of that organ system, and perhaps others, sooner or later.

Lifestyle as a Factor in Health Endangerment

Our increasing understanding of the biological mechanisms involved in our psychological and physiological states has meant that a great deal of attention is today being paid to the role of lifestyle in the development or maintenance of many health problems. Numerous aspects of the way we live are now considered influential in the development of some severe physical problems: diet—particularly overeating and consuming too many high-fat, low-fiber foods; lack of exercise; smoking cigarettes; family estrangement and divorce; excessive alcohol

and drug use; constantly facing high-stress situations; and even ineffective ways of dealing with day-to-day problems are but a few of the many lifestyle patterns that are viewed as contributing causes.

Lifestyle factors—habits or behavior patterns presumably under our own control—play a major role in three of the leading causes of death in this country: coronary heart disease, automobile accidents, and alcohol-related deaths. Meanwhile, we continue to struggle with the AIDS epidemic. Despite widespread knowledge that use of the latex condom is an effective measure for preventing transmission of the HIV-1 retrovirus, very large numbers of sexually active persons (both homosexual and heterosexual) continue their high-risk behavior (Bryan, Aiken, & West, 1997; Carey et al., 1997; Fisher & Fisher, 1992; Kalichman, Kelly, & Rompa, 1997b; Kalichman et al., 1997a; Kelly & Murphy, 1992).

Even in cases where virtual proof of causation exists, such as cigarette smoking, it is difficult for many people to change their lifestyles to reduce their risk of disease—an incentive that may seem very remote for currently healthy people. Significant and lasting change is generally hard to accomplish, and this is especially true where available rewards are immediate and powerful, as in the case of addictions (Chapter 10). After having two heart attacks and surgery to remove a cancerous lung, one man continued to smoke two and a half packs of cigarettes a day even though he frequently said, "I know these things are killing me a little at a time . . . but they have become so much a part of my life I can't live without them!"

PSYCHOLOGICAL FACTORS AND CARDIOVASCULAR DISEASE

Diseases of the cardiovascular system (the heart and its connected tree of vessels through which its pumping action distributes and retrieves blood) remain the most serious health problem confronting Americans and their health care professionals in terms of deaths accounted for and disabilities experienced. The bulk of the difficulty consists of three interrelated clinical conditions: (1) hypertension (high blood pressure), (2) coronary heart disease (CHD), where arteries supplying blood to the heart muscle itself become clogged, and (3) stroke, where the same types of clogging affect arterial supply to the brain. Of these, we deal here with hypertension and CHD; stroke, which is in many ways similar to CHD in its etiology, is covered in Chapter 13.

Essential Hypertension

When a physiologically normal person is calm, his or her heartbeat is regular, pulse is even, blood pressure is relatively low, and visceral organs are well supplied with blood. With stress, however, the vessels of the visceral organs constrict, and blood flows in greater quantity to the muscles of the trunk and limbs—part of the flight-or-fight pattern described earlier. With the tightening of the tiny vessels supplying the visceral organs, the heart must work harder. As it beats faster and with greater force, the pulse quickens and blood pressure mounts. Usually, when the crisis passes, the body resumes normal functioning and the blood pressure returns to normal. Under continuing emotional strain, however, high blood pressure may become chronic.

Blood pressure below 140/90 is considered "normotensive;" blood pressure above 160/100 is considered unambiguously "high." (By convention, the first number given is the *systolic* pressure, that occurring when the heart contracts; the second is the *diastolic* or between-beat pressure). Consistent readings between these extremes are designated "borderline," as is a pattern in which a person fluctuates between normotensive and high pressures (Turner, 1994). Much evidence indicates that borderline readings are a risk factor for the development of definite, sustained hypertension, a disease estimated to afflict over 40 million Americans. For reasons that are not entirely clear, the incidence of hypertension is about twice as high among blacks as among whites (Anderson & Jackson, 1987; Edwards, 1973; Fray & Douglas, 1993; Mays, 1974; Myers & McClure, 1993), making it a more serious health problem in this population than even sickle-cell anemia (a serious and periodically very painful malformation of red blood cells that mainly affects blacks). Many clinicians and investigators hold the view that hypertension begins with a biological predisposition to high cardiovascular reactivity to stress (see, e.g., Tuomisto 1997; Turner, 1994) and then, given untoward life circumstances, progresses through borderline to frank hypertension in the adult years.

Other organic malfunctions known to induce hypertension account for only a small percentage of hypertension cases; the large remainder are given the designation **essential hypertension,** meaning no specific physical cause is known. Essential hypertension is often symptomless until its effects become manifest in medical complications. In addition to enhancing significantly the likelihood of CHD and stroke, it is often a causal factor in occlusive disease of the peripheral arteries, congestive heart failure (due to the heart's inability to overcome the resistance of constricted arteries), kidney failure, blindness, and a number of other serious physical ailments.

High blood pressure is thus an insidious and dangerous disorder. Ironically, it is both simple and painless to detect by means of the familiar inflated arm cuff, automated versions of which are now widely available for self-testing at shopping centers and the like. The normal regulation of blood pressure, however, is so complex that when it goes awry in a particular case, identifying the causal factors can be extremely difficult (Herd, 1984). Kidney dysfunction, for example, may be a cause, an effect, or both, of dangerously elevated pressures. Hypertension can also result from excessive sodium (e.g., salt) in the diet, or from excessive metabolic retention of sodium.

Hypertension and African-Americans The stresses of inner-city life, poverty, and explicit racial prejudice have been identified as probably playing a key role in the high incidence of hypertension among African-Americans (Anderson & Jackson, 1987; Anderson & McNeilly, 1993; Mays, 1974). "John Henryism," named for a mythical black folk hero who toiled relentlessly in the face of limited resources and overwhelming odds against him, provides an accurate description of many blacks who succumb to hypertension (see, e.g., Anderson & McNeilly, 1993; Myers & McClure, 1993). Heavy salt use is common in the dietary preferences of blacks, and in addition there is some evidence that the black population, as a group, excessively retains ingested sodium, a condition resulting in fluid retention and endocrine changes that in turn elevate blood pressure. (Anderson & McNeilly, 1993). Too, some people carry their stress around with them, as in the Type A behavior pattern (described below), which is associated with elevated systolic and diastolic blood pressure (Lyness, 1993).

The classical psychoanalytic interpretation of hypertension is that affected people suffer from suppressed rage, and scattered and somewhat dated evidence supports this hypothesis (Gentry et al., 1982; Spielberger et al., 1985; Stone & Hokanson, 1969). Although suppressed hostility might be expected to run high among inner-city residents, including African-Americans (Anderson & McNeilly, 1993; Harburgh et al., 1973; Myers & McClure, 1993), the suppressed-rage hypothesis cannot be said to be firmly established with respect to all, or even necessarily a majority, of affected persons. Findings by Esler and colleagues (1977) suggest that, in the subgroup of hypertensive people who do show suppressed hostility, it is often accompanied by high levels of submissiveness, overcontrol, and guilt.

Anger and Hypertension A variant of the suppressed-rage hypothesis was proposed by McClelland (1979). According to this view, an affected individual is driven not so much by rage and the need to suppress it as by power motives and the need to inhibit their expression. Unexpressed anger is then a frequent accompaniment. In a well-conceived study designed to test these ideas, McClelland found that personality measures of need for power and activity inhibition were indeed jointly associated with elevated blood pressures. Moreover, he demonstrated that this inhibited power motive syndrome in men in their 30s significantly predicted elevated blood pressure and signs of hypertensive disease in these same men 20 years later.

It may be, however, that it is the inhibition or suppression of strong urges to perform acts that are poorly tolerated by society that underlies psychogenic hypertension. (In the case of African-Americans, simply aspiring to a certain job, profession, or neighborhood may qualify as an act poorly tolerated by society.) Conflictual states of this sort are by no means rare and, as noted in earlier chapters, are at the conceptual center of certain psychodynamic notions pertaining to neurotic processes. Some evidence supporting this more general notion was obtained by Jorgensen et al. (1996) in a quantitative review of studies concerned with personality variables and elevated blood pressure.

Coronary Heart Disease and the Type A Behavior Pattern

Coronary heart disease (CHD) is a potentially lethal blockage of the arteries supplying blood to the heart muscle, or myocardium. Its chief clinical manifestations are (1) angina pectoris, severe chest pain signaling that the delivery of oxygenated blood to the affected area of the heart is insufficient for its current workload; (2) myocardial infarction, functionally complete blockage of a section of the coronary arterial system, resulting in death of the myocardial tissue supplied by that arterial branch; and (3) disturbance of the heart's electrical conduction consequent to arterial blockage, resulting in disruption or interruption of the hearts pumping action, often leading to death. Many instances of sudden cardiac death, in which victims have no prior history of CHD symptoms, are attributed to silent CHD. This often occurs when a piece of the atherosclerotic material adhering to the arterial walls (a "plaque") breaks loose and lodges in a smaller vessel, blocking it (see Highlight 8.2).

While CHD-related deaths in the United States have declined dramatically in recent years, this decline has oc-

curred at the end of a long period, comprising most of the twentieth century, of rising CHD-related mortality. CHD retains today the dubious distinction of being the nation's number one killer, despite impressive advances in treatment (such as various types of coronary artery surgery) and markedly enhanced appreciation of risk factors, some of which (elevated low density serum cholesterol, smoking, lack of exercise, obesity, and hypertension, for example) are potentially reversible.

The known biological risk factors for CHD, which include heredity in addition to those just mentioned, explain less than half of the CHD-related outcomes people actually experience. In other words, much of the causal pattern for CHD development (or, for that matter, for its failure to develop) remains a mystery. Noting this circumstance, cardiovascular researchers have increasingly turned their attention to psychosocial and personality factors contributing to the disease's development. Attempts to refine and precisely specify the psychological contribution to the development of the disease for the most part have involved identification of the crucial components of what M. Friedman and Rosenman (1959) first labeled the **Type A behavior pattern.**

Characteristics of Type A Personalities Excessive competitive drive even when it is unnecessary, impatience or time urgency, and hostility are the hallmarks of Type A behavior as Friedman and Rosenman (1959) originally conceived it. It manifests itself in accelerated speech and motor activity. The contrasting Type B pattern, to which little descriptive attention has been paid, is negatively defined in terms of the absence of Type A characteristics.

The relationship between Type A behavior and CHD, while intuitively appealing, has been hard to assess. Various approaches to the assessment of Type A behavior have been developed, but unfortunately, the various assessment measures for the A/B typology do not produce consistent results (i.e., do not produce the same orderings of people on extent of Type A-ness). This situation suggests continuing problems in the construct's definition and the likelihood that differing measurement approaches emphasize different components of the Type A pattern. This measurement problem may be the main reason why a few studies have failed to find a Type A–CHD relationship (Fischman, 1987; Thoreson & Powell, 1992). Moreover, some evidence shows that not all components of the Type A pattern are equally predictive of CHD, or even of differing pathological manifestations within the CHD syndrome, such as angina versus infarction (Krantz & Glass, 1984).

Heart Attack

We have all heard the old story about the faint-hearted guard dog who, on being told "Attack," had one. Attack is now a common word in our vocabulary, as well it should be since heart attacks kill over half a million Americans each year. The incidence of heart disease among Americans is one of the highest in the world; about 30 million people are affected. (Some countries have a higher rate, including France, or a lower one, such as Japan.) But what is a heart attack? Technically, it is the result of a *myocardial infarction*—that is, a blockage of the arteries that feed the heart. When such an artery is blocked, the oxygen-starved muscles of the heart begin to die. Depending on how much of the heart is damaged and how badly, the results can vary from almost complete recovery to death.

Blockage of the coronary vessels that feed the heart is usually caused by one of three things: a clot lodged in the vessel, a prolonged contraction of the vessel walls, or atherosclerosis. Atherosclerosis is the result of the buildup of a number of substances, such as fat, fibrin (formed in clots), parts of dead cells, and calcium. These substances reduce the elasticity of the vessel, and by decreasing its diameter, they raise blood pressure, just as you raise the pressure in a garden hose by holding your thumb over the end. No one knows what causes atherosclerosis, but a number of things can speed its development, such as smoking cigarettes and, probably, eating animal fat and cholesterol. Other factors include age, hypertension, diabetes, stress, heredity, gender (males have more heart attacks), and a Type A behavior pattern.

The warnings of heart attack are often (but not always) (1) a pain that spreads along the shoulders, arm, neck, or jaw; (2) sudden sweating; (3) a heavy pressure and pain in the center of the chest; and (4) nausea, vomiting, and shortness of breath. The symptoms may come and go. People who have not developed a strong and efficient cardiovascular system through exercise are particularly susceptible to *angina pectoris* (chest pain), which occurs when the heart fails to receive enough blood, particularly during times of stress or exercise. It should not be confused with a true heart attack, although it may forecast one in the future. The pain may be relieved by stopping the unusual exercise or by reducing the stress levels. Blood flow to the heart can be increased by an exercise program or by surgically inserting vessels from other parts of the body (a coronary bypass). Certain chemicals, such as nitroglycerin, also dilate the heart's vessels and increase the circulation of blood there.

Another form of heart attack results in a phenomenon called *sudden death*. The death may be due to chaotic and uncoordinated contractions of the ventricles, often brought on by an unanticipated myocardial infarction. The contractions do not move blood along and, after a few spasms, the heart may stop entirely. Many people afflicted in such a way mysteriously fall dead in their tracks. Some, however, can be saved if they are helped in time. In fact, victims of any form of heart attack stand a much greater chance of surviving if they are treated immediately. In many metropolitan areas, citizens are being trained in cardiopulmonary resuscitation (CPR) to help restore a victim's circulation in such emergencies. CPR continues the flow of blood to the brain, where sensitive tissues die quickly without oxygen. In Seattle, Washington, with an extensive citizen-training program, passersby have performed about one-third of the city's resuscitations. Their success rate is higher than that of professionals because they usually reach victims sooner. ■

Source: Adapted from Wallace (1987).

CUTTING EDGE

Depression and Coronary Heart Disease

Until the past few years the primary psychological variable recognized as affecting coronary heart disease (CHD) was Type A behavior—particularly the hostility component (see pages 316–321). Now, however, we are learning that depression also dramatically affects risk for CHD and has a negative effect on the progression of CHD once it has been diagnosed (Shapiro, 1996; Glassman & Shapiro, 1998). At first, it was noticed that people with heart disease were more likely to be depressed than were healthy people. Several studies have shown that 15 to 20 percent of people who have a heart attack are clinically depressed—a much higher figure than would be expected in the general population (Chesney, 1996; Shapiro, 1996). Such findings led investigators to examine the effects of depression on the course of CHD, and several studies now indicate that heart attack patients who are depressed at the time of their heart attack or shortly afterward show a greatly increased risk for future coronary events and cardiac death (Chesney, 1996; Shapiro, 1996). For example, Frasure-Smith and colleagues (1993) initially followed 222 patients for six months after they had had a heart attack. These investigators found that the clinically depressed patients were five times more likely to die in the next six months than were their nondepressed counterparts. Moreover, depression was as good a predictor of death from heart disease as were medical variables such as prior heart attacks or poor heart functioning. After adjusting for these other variables, it was estimated that the relative risk of death associated with depression was still four times greater. Frasure-Smith and colleagues (1995) assessed these patients again eighteen months after their initial heart attack and found that depression as assessed within ten days of the initial heart attack was associated with a nearly eightfold increase in mortality (Shapiro, 1996). Ladwig and colleagues (1994) reached similar conclusions.

Other studies have shown that clinical depression is a risk factor for later developing CHD. For example, Pratt and her colleagues (1996) followed over 1,500 men and women with no prior history of heart disease for fourteen years. They found that 8 percent of those who had suffered major depression at one time and 6 percent of those who had suffered mild depression at some point, had a heart attack during the fourteen-year follow-up interval. By contrast, only 3 percent of those without a history of depression suffered heart attacks. When medical history and other variables were taken into account, those who had suffered major depression were found to be four times more likely to have had a heart attack. Similar findings had also been reported in several earlier studies (Chesney, 1996; Scheier & Bridges, 1995; Shapiro, 1996).

Two mechanisms have been proposed to explain the association between depression and CHD. The first possiblity is that depressed people may engage in more behaviors known to put people at risk for CHD. For example, depressed people are less likely to eat well or exercise, are more likely to smoke, and are perhaps less likely to take medications for conditions such as high blood pressure (Chesney, 1996; Kolata, 1997). Depressed people are also known to lack social support, another factor linked to CHD (Eriksen, 1994).

Second, it may be that depression is linked to CHD through biochemical mechanisms. As discussed in Chapter 6, many depressed people have elevated levels of the stress hormone cortisol. They also have elevated rates of norepinephrine in their blood, which can increase blood pressure and heart rate (Kolata, 1997). So, although depressed people may appear lethargic, their elevated stress hormones may damage their hearts. It has also been shown that depressed persons show lower heart rate variability in response to behavioral changes (such as walking versus sitting down when heart rate should change). High heart rate levels and low heart rate variability are also known to be associated with changes in sympathetic-parasympathetic balance, which may increase cardiac arrhythmias that often precede sudden death (Chesney, 1996; Frasure-Smith et al., 1993).

Given the high levels of comorbidity between anxiety and mood disorders discussed in Chapter 6, it is not surprising that a similar link might also be found between anxiety and CHD. Several studies suggest such a relationship. For example, De Silva and colleagues (1993) found that patients with established CHD (such as coronary artery disease, angina, or prior heart attack) were at increased risk for sudden death when exposed to anxiety-provoking stressors. A recent study by Leor and colleagues (1996) found a transient fivefold increase in sudden cardiac death in the days immediately following a 1994 California earthquake. The deaths were associated primarily with the emotional stress caused by the earthquake (Shapiro, 1996). Another study has documented a relationship between phobic anxiety and increased risk for sudden cardiac death. Kawachi and colleagues (1994a) followed nearly 34,000 male professionals who had been assessed for panic disorder, agoraphobia, and generalized anxiety for two years. Men with the highest levels of phobic anxiety were three times more likely to have a fatal heart attack than were men with the lowest levels of phobic anxiety. Sudden cardiac death was six times higher in the men with the highest levels of anxiety. However, there was *no* association found between anxiety and *nonfatal* attacks. The findings were replicated in a second study of nearly 2,300 men who were participating in a Normative Aging study (Kawachi et al., 1994b, 1995).

Given these strong associations between depression (and anxiety) and risk for CHD, increasing attention is being paid to the need for treatment interventions. Most people with clinical depression are untreated, creating unnecessary added risk for CHD. Of those with major depression at the time of a heart attack, approximately one-half remain depressed or have relapsed one year later without treatment (Hance et al., 1996). Yet there is promising evidence that various treatments can help post-heart-attack patients who are depressed. Linden and colleagues (1996) did a review of the literature on psychosocial interventions for depression in CHD patients. They found good evidence that psychosocial interventions can decrease depression, systolic blood pressure, heart rate, and cholesterol levels. Moreover, patients who did not receive psychosocial treatment were 1.7 times more likely to die from their CHD, and 1.8 times more likely to have another heart attack in a two-year follow-up period than were patients who were treated for their depression and anxiety. Drug treaments are also considered more promising than in the past because the new class of antidepressants, the SSRIs (see Chapters 6 and 16), are not contraindicated for patients with CHD as older tricylic antidepressants often were (Chesney, 1996; Shapiro, 1996). Finally, a recent study has shown that cardiac rehabilitation and exercise programs that are frequently suggested to patients who have had a heart attack to improve their physical condition also have significant effects on improving depression (Milani et al., 1996).

Fortunately, the findings reviewed above have not gone unnoticed by researchers at the National Heart, Lung, and Blood Institute of the National Institutes of Health. A large study is now being conducted of 3,000 heart attack patients at eight clinical sites across the United States to investigate whether interventions directed at decreasing depression immediately after a heart attack actually reduce the risk of future heart attacks and cardiac death. This is one more indication of the influence that behavioral medicine is having on drawing attention to the importance of psychological rather than purely medical variables in prevention of the leading cause of death in the United States today. ■

The Type A behavior pattern may be observed in certain individuals under stressful or challenging circumstances. The pattern involves excessive competitiveness, impatience, hostility, and accelerated speech and motor activity.

Overall, a strong consensus has developed that the pattern's "free floating" (i.e., nonspecific, cynically distrustful) hostility component, perhaps in association with status insecurity ("Am I good enough?") and frequent, intense anger arousal, is the aspect most closely correlated with demonstrable coronary artery deterioration. The more "workaholic" aspects of Type A as originally conceived appear not to be part of what has come to be called its "toxic core" (M. Friedman & Ulmer, 1984; Hafen et al., 1996; Krantz & Glass, 1984; Williams et al., 1980; Williams, Barefoot, & Shekelle, 1985; Wood, 1986). As Hafen and colleagues (1996) put it, "The real difference between workaholics and Type A personalities seems to lie with hostility. The workaholic seldom is hostile. The Type A is almost always hostile" (p. 149).

However, there remains some inconsistency and uncertainty regarding the measurement of the A/B-Type variable and identification of its most significant components (Hearn, Murray, & Luepker, 1989; Thoreson & Powell, 1992). Anxiety and depression may be as important as anger and hostility in the correlational network that includes CHD development (Booth-Kewley & H. Friedman, 1987). There is now in fact a large body of evidence linking depression and the occurrence of CHD (see Highlight 8.3).

Research on Type A and CHD In spite of some continuing conceptual and measurement uncertainties, it remains difficult to dispute the original evidence that the general cluster of reactions identified as the Type A pattern is a significant predictor of CHD, independent of other risk factors. While several studies support such a conclusion, including one involving Chinese subjects (Boyuan, 1988), two in particular stand out because their prospective designs circumvent many of the interpretation problems attending less powerful investigative strategies. (For example, evaluating personality factors *after* a diagnosis of CHD could lead subjects to distort their levels of hostility or anxiety based on preconceived notions of a coronary-prone personality type.) These studies are described below.

The Western Collaborative Group Study (WCGS) project involved some 3150 healthy men between the ages of 35 and 59 who on entry were typed as to A or B status. They were then carefully followed for a period of eight and a half years. Type As were found to be approximately twice as likely as Type Bs to have developed CHD (angina or myocardial infarctions) during the follow-up period. This greater risk remained even when other risk factors were statistically eliminated from consideration. When the data for a younger group of men (ages 39 to 49 on entry into the project) were considered separately, CHD was proportionately *six* times more prevalent among Type As than Type Bs (Rosenman et al., 1975). The findings also linked the Type A pattern to recurrent myocardial infarctions (Jenkins, Zyzanski, & Rosenman, 1976) and to sudden cardiac death (M. Friedman et al., 1973).

One aspect of the well-known Framingham Heart Study (the second major study of Type A behavior and CHD), begun in 1948 and involving long-term follow-up of a large sample of men and women from Framingham, Massachusetts, also provides evidence supporting Type A behavior as a coronary risk factor. Some 1700 CHD-free subjects were typed as to A or B status in the mid-1960s. Analysis of the data for CHD occurrence during an eight-year follow-up period not only confirmed the major findings of the WCGS project but extended them to women as well. In fact, the twofold increase in CHD risk reported for Type A men was almost exactly replicated for Type A women. Somewhat curiously, the CHD–Type A association among males in this study was limited to those of white-collar socioeconomic status (Haynes, Feinleib, & Kannel, 1980). Also, some question has been raised about the validity of the results for female subjects (Thoreson &

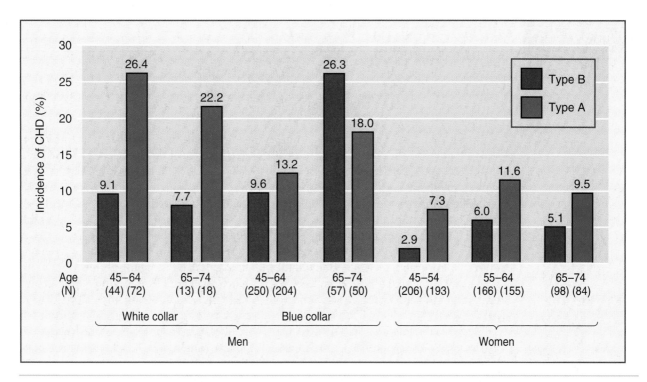

FIGURE 8.3   THE TYPE A BEHAVIOR PATTERN AND CORONARY HEART DISEASE
The graph depicts the percent incidence of coronary heart disease (CHD) over an eight-year period among subjects of the Framingham Heart Study. Subjects are distinguished according to age, sex, occupation (men only), and Type A versus Type B behavior pattern. Note the substantial rise in CHD among Type A women and men of white-collar occupations over their Type B counterparts. The failure to confirm this finding among blue-collar males remains unexplained.

Powell, 1992), and as Hafen and colleagues (1996) point out, most other studies have pointed to depression as having a stronger association with CHD among women. Figure 8.3 summarizes the Framingham results.

Taken together, these and other studies meet most of the stringent criteria established by epidemiologists to justify the assumption of a cause-effect relationship in disease genesis. That is, the evidence overall suggests that some aspect of the Type A behavior pattern—possibly one involving general negative affect that remains unexpressed (Endicott, 1989; H. Friedman & Booth-Kewley, 1987a)—is implicated in the development of a potentially lethal organic malfunction (CHD) among some people. Also, a quantitative review by Lyness (1993) has confirmed that Type A individuals do show elevated cardiovascular reactivity to a variety of stressful situations. It is important to note, however, that precise definition of the psychosocial antecedents of CHD has remained somewhat elusive and controversial. Clearly, the factors leading to CHD are extremely complicated at the level of the individual case.

Nevertheless, the theoretical importance of these psychosocial influences in advancing our understanding of basic processes underlying CHD is considerable. Beyond that, they raise the possibility of saving lives by devising preventive therapeutic interventions to alter the Type A reaction pattern (or more precisely its negative affect component) in persons at risk, such as those having genetic liability or hypertension. Work in this area has yielded encouraging results (Nunes, Frank, & Kornfield, 1987). In general, the best-designed studies have generated the most optimistic conclusions (Thoreson & Powell, 1992), suggesting that not only does hostile, negative emotional style cause CHD, but that changing one's emotional style can reduce the risk of it.

Highlight 8.4 Modern Life, Psychological Factors in Headaches, describes a less dangerous but far more common problem having significant psychogenic roots—that of recurrent headache.

GENERAL CAUSAL FACTORS IN PHYSICAL DISEASE

We have been exploring at a general level the manner in which negative thinking and attitudes, autonomic excess, stressor-induced immunosuppression, and health-endangering lifestyles can compromise a person's biological

MODERN LIFE

Psychological Factors in Headaches

Although headaches can result from a wide range of organic conditions, most of them seem to be related to emotional tension, as many sufferers confirm. More than 50 million Americans suffer from frequent tension or migraine headaches, with the overall incidence apparently being higher among women than men. In one survey, Andrasik, Holroyd, and Abell (1979) found that 52 percent of a large group of college students reported headaches at least once or twice a week.

Research in this area has focused primarily on migraine headache, an intense pain that recurs periodically. Although typically involving only one side of the head, migraine is sometimes more generalized; it may also shift from side to side. Migraine was described extensively by medical writers of antiquity, but the cause of the pain remained a mystery until the 1940s, when interest was focused on pain-sensitive structures of the head. The *"classic" migraine* occurs in two phases. The first is the *aura*, a variably experienced but painless disturbance having odd sensory (particularly visual), motor, and/or mood components. Once thought to be primarily the subjective effects of sudden changes in vascular diameter and hence blood flow to the brain, the aura is now believed to stem from alterations in the brain's electrical activity. The two conceptions are not, of course, mutually exclusive. In any event, when the involved pathophysiology reaches pain-sensitive tissues, it is thought, the second phase of intense pain (often experienced as throbbing) begins. Frequently excruciating in severity, it may last for hours, days, or in rare cases weeks. Nausea and vomiting sometimes accompany a migraine attack.

The *"common" migraine*, whose prevalence is actually higher than the classic variety (about 70 versus 30 percent of migraine headaches), is distinguished chiefly by the absence of an aura. Onset is often experienced, therefore, as abrupt and unpredictable. As in the classic type, the pain is likely to be localized to a particular region of the head, and it is also commonly of excruciating intensity. Fortunately for the sufferer, common migraines tend to resolve themselves within one to several hours. They may, however, recur within relatively brief intervals.

Sometimes confused with common migraine (and sometimes called *migrainous neuralgia*) are *cluster headaches*, short periods of severe, stabbing pain usually centered over one eye. Cluster headaches are most often observed in men.

It seems increasingly likely that the tendencies to be subject to migraine and cluster headaches are related to variants of normal physiology, some of them probably inherited. Cluster headaches, for example, are now thought to be due to a disorder of histamine metabolism. In some individuals, therefore, the role of stress in provoking migraine or cluster headaches may be minimal to nonexistent.

The vast majority of headaches—almost 90 percent of those treated by physicians—

integrity, going on to discuss apparently specific psychogenic contributions, insofar as these are known, to the etiology of three extremely common and sometimes life-threatening physical conditions: essential hypertension, coronary heart disease, and recurrent headaches. However, this is by no means an exhaustive cataloging of the physical ills that may have psychogenic roots.

In this section we return to a more general level of analysis to complete our picture of psychological contri-

butions in physical illness. We will be particularly concerned with the problem of specificity—of why, under stress, one person develops anorexia, another hypertension, and still another tension headaches.

Biological Factors

Obviously, biological factors are involved in all disease. We focus here on those factors likely to have a role in de-are so-called **simple tension headaches.** They appear to be particularly common as accompaniments of depressed mood, but generally the role of emotional upset in contributing to their onset is fairly obvious. With these headaches, emotional stress seems to lead to contraction of the muscles surrounding the skull; these contractions may be painful in themselves, but in addition may result in vascular constrictions that also cause headache pain. Though further studies are needed, it may be that the physiological processes are similar for the two types of headaches—tension and migraine—and that the difference is rather one of degree, with migraine involving greater vascular (or other central physiologic) disruption. Certainly it is true that many people suffer headaches that appear to have both vascular and muscular origins.

Both tension and migraine headaches usually appear during adolescence and recur periodically during stressful times. The pain can often be relieved with analgesics, with muscle-relaxant or more specifically targeted drugs, or with certain relaxation-inducing psychological procedures (Blanchard, 1994; Blanchard et al., 1990a; Carlson & Hoyle, 1993). These latter procedures include **biofeedback,** a technique in which a person is taught to influence his or her own physiological processes (Blanchard, 1992; Blanchard et al., 1990b). Of the two types, migraine headaches are usually more painful and slower to respond to treatment than simple tension headaches. Overall,

however, these psychological techniques for headache control have amassed an impressive record, and done so with "side effects" (e.g., decreased anxiety and depression) that are generally positive in nature (Blanchard, 1992).

The presumed psychological predispositions for psychogenic headaches are less clear than in the case of other disorders considered in this chapter. Also, the interaction of personality factors with particular types of stressors appears to be especially important for headache sufferers (Levor et al., 1986). For example, highly organized people may be especially affected by events that disrupt their schedules. In fact, clinicians historically have held the view that it is important to the typical headache-prone person to feel "on top of things" and in control of events impinging on him or her (e.g., Hafen et al., 1996; Williams, 1977).

Traditional beliefs about headache-proneness and personality factors may not apply in the case of migraine. Psychological tests of migraine sufferers revealed relatively normal profiles. Tension headache sufferers showed the greatest psychopathology (Andrasik et al., 1982). There is also some independent evidence (Lehrer & Murphy, 1991) that tension headache sufferers are unusually reactive to stress and to the experience of pain. These findings support the suggestion already made that tension headaches might be more indicative of psychological problems per se than migraine headaches. ■

termining the adequacy of a person's response to psychological stressors.

Genetic Factors   In general, our understanding of genetic contributions to disease, including those believed to have strong psychogenic origins, remains fairly limited. In addition to a dearth of adequate research in many areas, the field involves many complexities. Genetic contributions may involve (1) an underlying physical vulnera-

bility for acquiring the disease in question, such as excessive cardiovascular reactivity in hypertension; (2) the psychological makeup of the individual and his or her stress tolerance, such as an aggressive or inhibited temperament; and (3) the nature of any interaction between (1) and (2). If biological and psychological contributions to enhanced risk are both partly inherited, then disentangling their separate influences is bound to be difficult— all the more so if the expression of one influence is somehow modified by the presence of the other (i.e., they "interact").

Despite these difficulties of interpretation, nearly all diseases of multifactor origin can be shown to run in families to at least some extent. However, social learning (for example, children modeling the inadequate coping skills of their parents) could be a factor in such family resemblances. As in other areas of psychopathology, in assessing the psychogenic aspects of physical illness we struggle with the problem of differentiating the effects of shared genes from those of shared environments.

Presumably, discoveries will be forthcoming over time with continuing progress of the Human Genome Project, a vast, federally sponsored effort to identify the complete genetic mapping of human life. There is good reason to believe that additional inherited disease vulnerabilities, as well as health-relevant behavioral tendencies, will be included in these discoveries. Plomin (1998), for example, has recently discussed the identification of differing alleles of a gene on chromosome 11 that codes for the dopamine-4 (D4) receptor on neuronal dendrites. Dopamine is an important catecholamine neurotransmitter, and its D4 receptor is believed to be involved in the functioning of the brain's limbic system, which in turn is known to mediate many emotional and motivational processes that could be implicated in the development of psychogenic disease.

Psychosocial Interaction As such research progresses, we may reasonably expect that the pathological expression of any inherited vulnerability to disease will usually be modified by the person's psychosocial life circumstances. For example, the role of heredity in CHD has been much studied and is known to be substantial. The subjects in one classic study consisted of 32 pairs of identical male twins between 42 and 67 years of age, in which only one twin in each pair suffered from CHD. The genetic contribution in such twinships is of course constant for each pair, thus controlling for this factor. Since one of the twins of each pair had CHD, we may assume that the other was at comparable *genetic* risk. The investigators found that the twins suffering from heart disease were more work-oriented, took less leisure time, had more home problems, and in general experienced greater dissatisfactions in their lives than their healthier twin brothers (Liljefors & Rahe, 1970). In this case, the shared genetic liability for CHD was expressed only in those twins whose lives had an excess of psychosocial disorganization. That is, the actual effects of a probably substantial (especially in light of the relatively young age range of the subjects) genetic risk appear to have been

moderated by the factor of lifestyle. Interpretive complexities of this sort will probably remain even after we have a complete mapping of human DNA.

Differences in Autonomic Reactivity and Somatic Weakness In our earlier discussion (Chapter 3) of vulnerability and causal factors, we noted that individuals vary significantly temperament. Even very young infants reveal marked differences in their sensitivities to aversive stimuli; some infants react to such stressors by developing fevers, others by digestive upsets, and still others by sleep disturbances. Such differences in reactivity continue into adult life and presumably help account for individual differences in susceptibility to psychogenic diseases and for the types of diseases a given person is most likely to develop. As suggested earlier, for example, a person who has an inherited tendency to respond to stressors with increased cardiac output and vasoconstriction may be at special risk for chronic hypertension (Friedman & Iwai, 1976; Turner, 1994). In like manner, a person who reacts with increased intestinal motility will be more likely to develop what is termed the "irritable bowel syndrome."

Sometimes a particular organ is especially vulnerable because of heredity, illness, or prior trauma. A person who has inherited or developed a weak stomach will be prone to gastrointestinal upsets during anger or anxiety. Presumably, the weakest link in the chain of visceral organs will be the organ affected. Caution must be exercised, however, to avoid *ex post facto* reasoning, because it would not be safe to conclude that when a particular organ system is affected it must have been weak to begin with. Also, as we will see, conditioning may play a key role in determining which organ system is involved.

Disruption of Physiological Equilibrium The human organism is an extremely complex biological system whose adequate functioning and survival depend on an elaborate network of monitors and feedback mechanisms to maintain vital processes within certain quantitative limits. The site of most of this homeostatic regulation is the brain itself, although many of the details of how it performs these functions remain quite speculative. According to one hypothesis, these control mechanisms may fail in their regulation of autonomic nervous system arousal, so that an individual's emotional response is exaggerated in intensity and his or her physiological equilibrium is not regained within normal time limits following the occurrence of stressful events (Anderson & McNeilly, 1993; Halberstam, 1972; Lebedev, 1967; Schwartz, 1989; Turner, 1994). Such control failures might then lead to chronically excessive autonomic activation, as appears to be the case in essential hypertension, for example. In addition, excessive hypothalamic activation may be associated with attendant dysregulation of circulating adrenocortical hormones, which are involved in the body's immunity to disease. More generally, we have seen that breakdowns in a number of different pathways can compromise immune competence during the brain's processing of stressor events.

In assessing the role of biological factors in psychogenic diseases, most investigators would take into consideration each of the factors we have described. Perhaps the greatest emphasis at present would be placed on a person's characteristic autonomic activity, the vulnerability of affected organ systems, and possible constitutionally based or acquired alterations in the control mechanisms of the brain that normally regulate the autonomic nervous system and hormonal functioning.

Psychosocial Factors

Though evidence suggests that psychological factors play a prominent role in causing many diseases, it is still not entirely clear what particular factors are involved or how they exert their effects. Also, research has been inconsistent and sometimes contradictory. Investigators have examined personality characteristics (including failure to learn adequate coping patterns), interpersonal relationships, and the learning of biological dysfunctions.

Personality Characteristics   If we could delineate with clarity a "disease-prone" or "hypertensive" personality linked to particular diseases, it would be of great value in understanding, assessing, and treating illnesses, and perhaps even in preventing them. Just as useful would be a clear picture of the so-called "disease-resistant" personality—characterized in the literature as one possessing a high degree of "hardiness"—or the ability to withstand stress and bounce back from it (e.g., see Hafen et al., 1996). Research justifies the generalization that negative attitudes about oneself, the world (including its people), and the future are associated with higher levels of physical and mental illness (especially depression). But, as we've seen in the case of attempts to define the "coronary-prone" (Type A) personality, our efforts to identify more specific types of association between personality characteristics and particular diseases tend to founder in the face of the variability of people and of the diseases they contract.

For example, although Kidson (1973) found hypertensive patients as a group to be significantly more inse-

cure, anxious, sensitive, and angry than a nonhypertensive control group, a sizable number of the control-group members also showed these characteristics. Similarly, the association of Type A behavior (or some limited component of it) with CHD and heart attacks must be tempered with the observation that most Type As do not have coronary problems, and some Type Bs do (see again Figure 8.3 on page 321). As we have emphasized, the relationships between particular personality variables and disease processes, while often clearly important, tend to be complex and difficult to pin down (see Friedman et al., 1994).

So even though personality makeup seems to play an important role, we still do not know why some people with predisposing personality characteristics do not develop a particular disease, nor can we account adequately for the wide range of personality types among people who suffer from the same medical condition. Usually, we

Even though many Type As don't have coronary problems while some Type Bs do, personality makeup seems to play an important role in predisposing a person to illness—or to health, as suggested here.

can only conclude that particular personality factors are weakly but significantly correlated with the occurrence of certain illnesses.

Interpersonal Relationships as Sources of Protection In our previous discussions we have repeatedly noted the destructive effects that stressful interpersonal patterns—including marital unhappiness and divorce—may have on personality adjustment. Such patterns may also influence physiological functioning. In fact, death rates from varied causes, including physical disease, are markedly higher in people who have recently undergone marital problems or divorce than in the general population (Bloom et al., 1978; Burman & Margolin, 1989; Siegel, 1986). Loss of a spouse through death also puts the survivor at elevated risk, but men are more adversely affected by the death of their wives than women are by the death of their husbands (Hafen et al., 1996; Stroebe & Stroebe, 1983).

Findings such as the above suggest that being "connected" with others in mutually supportive ways—as in well-functioning families—is a significant protective factor in maintaining physical health. Available research strongly supports that conclusion and extends it beyond the confines of the family. Having a good social support system is a significant predictor of good health maintenance; by contrast, being alone and lonely predicts to multiple illnesses and death from multiple causes (Hafen et al., 1996). Lynch (1977), in a book entitled *The Broken Heart*, argues convincingly that the relatively high incidence of heart disease in industrialized communities stems in part from the absence of positive human relationships. Well-known Stanford University psychiatrist David Spiegel (1991) reported himself as "stunned" by finding that a group of seriously ill breast cancer patients who had been assigned to group therapy (and thus developed strong, mutually supportive ties) survived on average twice as long as a comparable group of women given only standard medical treatment.

The Learning of Illnesses Although Pavlov and many subsequent investigators have demonstrated that autonomic responses can be conditioned—as in the case of salivation—it was long assumed that people could not learn to control such responses "voluntarily." We now know that this assumption was wrong. Not only can autonomic reactivity be conditioned involuntarily via the classical Pavlovian model, but operant conditioning of the autonomic nervous system can also take place.

Thus the hypothesis has developed that certain physical disorders may arise through accidental rein-

forcement of symptom and behavioral patterns. "A child who is repeatedly allowed to stay home from school when he has an upset stomach may be learning the visceral responses of chronic indigestion" (Lang, 1970, p. 86). Similarly, an adolescent girl may get little or no attention from being "good," but if she starves herself to the point of severe weight loss she may become the center of attention. If this pattern is continued, she might learn to avoid weight gain at all costs and correspondingly learn a profound aversion to food. The increasing alarm of her parents and others would presumably serve as a potent reinforcement for her to continue avoiding food.

Although causal factors other than conditioning are now thought to play a role in most cases of psychogenic illness, it seems clear that regardless of how a physical symptom may have developed, it may be elicited by suggestion and maintained by the reinforcement provided by **secondary gains,** indirect benefits derived from the illness behavior. The role of suggestion was demonstrated by a classic study in which 19 of 40 volunteer asthmatic subjects developed asthma symptoms after breathing the mist of a salt solution that they were falsely told contained allergens, such as dust or pollen. In fact, 12 of the subjects had full-fledged asthma attacks. When the subjects then took what they thought was a drug to combat asthma (actually the same salt mist), their symptoms disappeared immediately (Bleeker, 1968). This study clearly shows the effect of suggestion on an autonomically mediated response. Why the other 21 subjects remained unaffected is not clear.

In short, it appears that some physical disorders may be acquired, maintained, or both in much the same way as other behavior patterns. Indeed, this finding is a basic tenet of behavioral medicine and health psychology, one aspect of which examines how various behavior modification and psychotherapeutic techniques can alter overt and covert reactions to physical disease processes (Blanchard, 1994; Bradley & Prokop, 1982; Gentry, 1984; Hafen et al., 1996; Stone et al., 1987; Williams & Gentry, 1977; see also the August 1992 [vol. 60, no. 4] special issue of the *Journal of Consulting and Clinical Psychology*). Behavior modification has also been used in the management of pain (Keefe, Dunsmore, & Burnett, 1992), a serious complication of many medical diseases. Severe or chronic pain diminishes the patient's quality of life beyond any impediments caused by the disease itself, and may therefore impair immune function and the body's own resources for healing. Successful teaching of pain management techniques may thus have a retarding effect on the primary disease that is causing the pain.

Sociocultural Factors

As we have seen, the incidence of specific disorders, both physical and mental, varies in different societies, in different strata of the same society, and over time. In general, what Cannon (1929) called diseases of civilization do not occur among nonindustrialized societies like the aborigines of the Australian Western Desert (Kidson & Jones, 1968), the Navajo Indians of Arizona, or certain isolated groups in South America (Stein, 1970). As these societies are exposed to social change, however, gastrointestinal, cardiovascular, and other psychogenic diseases begin to make their appearances. There is evidence of change in the nature and incidence of such disorders in Japan, paralleling the tremendous social changes that have taken place there since World War II (Ikemi et al., 1974). For example, the incidence of hypertension and coronary heart disease have increased markedly with the postwar westernization of Japanese culture.

As we have seen, nearly all authorities are in agreement that the current epidemic of eating disorders among young American women is largely a product of sociocultural influences, in particular a media-promoted obsession with extreme thinness as the ideal female form. As noted earlier, there is growing evidence that this once very middle-class white American dilemma is now spreading through other populations. In addition to unrealistic thinness standards, we should also note in this connection the extremely difficult and contradictory role expectations our culture now imposes on young women about to assume "adult" age status. They are to be sexually attractive, competitive and economically successful, and flawless homemakers and mothers. Small wonder that some adolescent girls develop "maturity fears" and elect to remain children, at least physically.

In general, it appears that any sociocultural conditions that markedly increase life stress tend to play havoc with the biological human organism and lead to an increase in disease as well as other physical and mental problems.

Treatments and Outcomes

Though a particular environmental stressor may have been a key causal factor in the development of a physical illness, removal of this stressor, even combined with learning more effective coping techniques, may not be enough to bring about recovery if organic changes have taken place; such changes may have become chronic and irreversible.

As in the case of treatment for the severe starvation seen in anorexia nervosa, treatment of psychogenic physical illnesses must begin with a thorough assessment of the nature and seriousness of the organic pathology involved. Since the latter may prove progressive and/or life-threatening, immediate medical intervention may prove necessary to curtail or reverse the pathological condition. Once the patient is sufficiently stabilized medically, wisdom would dictate the need for a comprehensive intervention plan based on behavioral medicine principles. The latter would be designed to alter or ameliorate on a permanent basis those psychosocial and sociocultural factors that appear to have been implicated in the development or maintenance of the patient's illness.

Except for conditions involving serious organic pathology, treatment methods are similar to those for mental disorders in general. The outcomes are likewise reasonably favorable. Instead of going into detail concerning the methods of treatment and the outcomes for each type of disorder, we shall briefly summarize the general treatment measures currently used. More detailed discussion of these therapies can be found in Chapters 16 and 17.

Biological Measures

Aside from immediate and long-range medical measures, such as emergency care for a hypertensive crisis or bypass surgery for coronary heart disease, biological treatment often involves the use of tranquilizer medications of the benzodiazepine family (e.g., Valium, Xanax) aimed at reducing emotional tension. Obviously, such drugs do not address the stressful situation or the coping reactions involved. By alleviating emotional tension and distress symptoms, however, they may provide a person with an opportunity to regroup his or her resources and develop more effective means of coping with life problems. Of course, health professionals must guard against too readily prescribing tranquilizers to insulate patients against everyday stress that they might be better off facing and resolving in some manner. Some patients may also come to rely too much on their prescriptions for easy cures, and such palliative, symptomatic treatment may divert needed attention from a persistently destructive lifestyle. The development of physiologic dependence on these tension-relieving medications is also a very real danger to be considered.

Where a chronically depressed mood is judged to be a significant etiologic factor, a trial of antidepressant medication may be indicated. Modern antidepressants, such as the serotonin-specific re-uptake inhibitors (SSRIs, such as Prozac and Zoloft), have far fewer unpleasant side effects than their earlier counterparts and are thus more readily tolerated by patients who may already be distressed by a multitude of physical symptoms. As with the use of tranquilizers, however, there may be disadvantages to moving too quickly to this palliative form of intervention for depression. Other methods, such as cognitive-behavioral therapy in which the patient becomes more aware of and actively begins to question his or her negative assumptions, may provide a more lasting means of altering those factors responsible for the depressive mood state.

Other drugs, such as those used to control high blood pressure, are prescribed on a more specific basis. The development of the nicotine-delivering skin patch and nicotine-containing chewing gum have been a boon to many persons seeking to overcome the smoking habit.

Psychosocial Measures

One-on-one, nonspecifically directed, verbally oriented psychotherapies—aimed at helping patients understand their personality problems—have been, with certain exceptions, relatively ineffective in the treatment of psychophysiological problems. The most effective therapies

Lifestyle, particularly one in which physical exercise is a central companion, is a significant factor in health maintenance.

are cognitive-behavior therapy (CBT) variant, considered earlier in our discussion of treatment for bulimia nervosa. (See Chapter 17 for further discussion of the therapies mentioned in this section.)

Traditional Psychotherapy It is interesting to note here that, although psychoanalytic theory has emphasized associations between emotions and pathological visceral states, it has had little impact on the treatment of psychogenic physical disorders (Agras, 1982). That is, the treatment literature does not reveal psychoanalytic approaches to have contributed much in the way of producing reliable and predictable therapeutic results. On the other hand, "opening up," as by writing expressively about life problems under a systematic regimen, does seem to be an effective therapy for many persons having psychogenic illnesses (Pennebaker, 1997; Smyth, 1998). For example, Kelley, Lumley, and Leisen (1997), using this method, recently demonstrated positive changes in the functioning of affected joints among a group of rheumatoid arthritis patients. As in this study, patients undergoing the therapy often experience *increases* in emotional distress during the active phase of treatment (writing), but then show improvement in their medical status over follow-up. There are at least two potential sources of these treatment benefits: (1) the opportunity afforded for emotional catharsis or "blowing off steam," and (2) the encouragement such writing gives to rethinking and recasting life problems—a type of self-administered cognitive therapy. So far, the "active ingredients" of this prescribed writing therapy have not been precisely identified.

Biofeedback Somewhat ironically in light of its focus on altering physiological states, biofeedback treatment for psychogenic diseases (see Chapter 17), though showing modest success (for example, in treating headache [Blanchard, 1992, 1994; Blanchard et al., 1990b]), had until recently generally failed to live up to the enthusiasm it generated when first introduced some 30 years ago. Overall, its effects proved so small and transient as to lack substantial clinical significance, and they rarely exceeded those that could be obtained in simpler (and less expensive) ways, as by providing systematic relaxation training without biofeedback equipment (Carlson & Hoyle, 1993; Reed, Katkin, & Goldband, 1986) or teaching patients how to meditate (Hafen et al., 1996).

That situation may now be changing, although it is still not entirely clear that biofeedback is anything more than an elaborate means to teach patients how to relax. In any event, biofeedback practitioners and their equipment have become much more sophisticated in the interim, and there have been increasingly favorable reports in recent years regarding efficacy in the behavioral medicine area. For example, Flor and Birbaumer (1993) have reported impressive effectiveness, especially in long-term follow-up, for electromyographic (muscle tonus) biofeedback in the control of musculoskeletal pain.

Behavior Therapy   Behavior modification techniques are based on the assumption that because autonomic responses can be learned, they can be unlearned. In one now classic case, the patient, June C., was a 17-year-old girl who had been sneezing every few seconds of her waking hours for a period of five months. Medical experts had been unable to help her. Eventually a psychologist volunteered to attempt treatment by behavior therapy.

A Case of Nonstop Sneezing • The therapist used a relatively simple, low power electric-shock device, activated by sound—the sound of June's sneezes. Electrodes were attached to her forearm for 30 minutes, and every time she sneezed she got a mild electric shock. After a ten-minute break, the electrodes were put on the other arm. In little more than four hours, June's sneezes, which had been reverberating every 40 seconds, stopped. Since then, she had had only a few ordinary sneezes, none of the dry, racking kind that had been draining her strength for so long. "We hope the absence of sneezes will last," said the therapist cautiously. "So do I," snapped June. "I never want to see that machine again." (*Time*, June 17, 1966, p. 72)

A follow-up report of the case indicated that, with the addition of modest "maintenance therapy," the intractable sneezing had not recurred over a period of 16 months (Kushner, 1968).

Many studies have examined the effects of various behavioral relaxation techniques on selected stress-related illnesses (Carlson & Hoyle, 1993; Hafen et al., 1996). Results obtained have been variable, though generally encouraging. For example, simple tension headaches have proved quite amenable to general relaxation treatment procedures (Blanchard, 1992; Blanchard et al., 1990a; Cox, Freundlich, & Meyer, 1975; Tasto & Hinkle, 1973). The same kinds of procedures have not been as effective when used to treat essential hypertension (Blanchard et al., 1979; Johnson, 1987; Schwartz, 1978; Surwit, Shapiro, & Good, 1978), especially as compared with hypertensive medication (Wadden et al., 1985).

In general, the effectiveness of an exclusively behavioral approach in treating psychogenic physical disorders

remains to be established. It may turn out that the greatest contribution of behavioral approaches will be in the area of altering self-injurious habits, such as smoking and excessive alcohol use, in systematic programs that teach self-control and lifestyle alteration (Blanchard & Andrasik, 1982; Goldfried & Merbaum, 1973; Weisenberg, 1977). Such programs may have particular importance in recovery from heart attack (Ketterer, 1993; Oldenburg et al., 1985). Relatedly, some success has been reported in modifying Type A lifestyles (Nunes et al., 1987; Thoreson & Powell, 1992).

Cognitive-Behavior Therapy   As we have seen, cognitive-behavior therapy (CBT) has shown striking success in the treatment of bulimia nervosa. Similarly, CBT has proven an effective intervention for headache (Blanchard, 1992; Blanchard et al., 1990a, 1990b) as well as other types of pain (Keefe et al., 1992). CBT-oriented family therapy was markedly more successful than routine pediatric care in alleviating childrens' complaints of recurrent abdominal pain, as reported in a study by Sanders and colleagues (1994). More recently Deale and colleagues (1997) showed CBT to be an effective treatment for "chronic fatigue syndrome," whose etiologic status continues to be a matter of controversy (e.g., Jason et al., 1997).

Some CBT techniques have also been used for the general purpose of stress management (Hafen et al., 1996). In one study, these techniques were shown to be effective at reducing maladaptive behaviors—such as rushing, impatience, and hostility—characteristic of Type A personalities (Jenni & Wollersheim, 1979). In two studies designed to teach patients how to cope better with life stresses that precipitated headaches, researchers showed that stress-management techniques could decrease the frequency of headaches (Holroyd & Andrasik, 1978; Holroyd, Andrasik, & Westbrook, 1977). More generally, Kobasa (1985) and other researchers have experimented with cognitive-behavior methods to increase hardiness, the ability to withstand stressful circumstances and remain healthy. Though we will look at these techniques in more detail in Chapter 17, they basically involve teaching people to use more effective coping skills to lower their experiences of stress and thus reduce the occurrence of physical symptoms and illness.

Sociocultural Measures

Sociocultural treatment measures are targeted more toward preventive efforts and are typically applied to selected populations or subcultural groups thought to be at risk for developing disorders as will be discussed more in Chapter 18. Within these groups, efforts are made to alter certain lifestyle behaviors to reduce the overall level of susceptibility to a disorder. For example, cigarette smoking is associated with increased risk for lung cancer and heart disease; to reduce the general risk of these scourges, persistent efforts have been made to reduce or prevent smoking. Similarly, some association exists between high-cholesterol diets and coronary heart disease; and efforts are made to convince people to alter their diets to reduce the rate of coronary heart disease in the total population. Obviously, such intervention efforts involve substantial amounts of persuasion—often employing the media and, in the case of smoking, even restrictive

changes in federal and local laws (such as airline, restaurant, and workplace smoking policies).

As we learn more about the role of biological, psychosocial, and sociocultural factors in the etiology of disease, it becomes increasingly possible to identify high-risk persons and groups—such as excessively diet-conscious adolescent girls, heart attack–prone personalities with chronic negative affect, sexually active young singles, and groups living in precarious and rapidly changing life situations. This ability in turn enables treatment efforts to focus on early intervention and prevention. In this context, programs aimed at fostering changes in maladaptive lifestyles and at remedying pathological social conditions seem eminently worthwhile, indeed life-saving.

UNRESOLVED ISSUES

Medical Education and Practice

In orienting remarks offered in the closing sections of Chapter 1, we noted that a full understanding of mental and behavioral abnormalities requires that a strictly objective and scientific approach to the field be supplemented by insights into human qualities not easily addressed by scientific methods. We mentioned, for example, hope, faith, courage, and despair. That caveat is particularly relevant in the present context—the interface of abnormal psychology and physical medicine. As is evident in this chapter, that interface is an extremely broad one, cutting across virtually the whole spectrum of medical disease.

Over most of its history, as we have suggested in the present chapter, the medical profession survived and prospered not so much because it had available effective remedies for illnesses, but because physicians were able unwittingly to rely on the considerable power of the placebo response in their patients. As medicine moved into the modern era, it became increasingly an applied aspect of a rapidly advancing and technologically sophisticated biological science. Enormous progress has been made in the control and actual conquering of many diseases that were once scourges of humankind, essentially all of it due to medicine's adoption of a relentlessly scientific approach.

There are increasing signs, however, that something valuable may have been lost in this enthusiastic embrace of science and the "objectivity" it both bestows on and

demands of its practitioners. The inherent temptation is for the physician to become a mere technician who administers to objectified patients (or in a worse scenario to objectified parts of patients) the marvels of modern medical science. That temptation is exacerbated by economic trends and the related development of "managed care" medicine, wherein physician options are bureaucratically curtailed and patients are often "processed" in assembly-line fashion. There is obvious and growing public restlessness about this model of "service delivery," as seen, for example, in increasing interest in "alternative" varieties of medicine, an explosion of medical self-help publications, and a heightened interest among members of the U.S. Congress in the details of medical practice.

Considering the advances of behavioral medicine in shedding light on the intricate connections of mind, body, and society in disease processes, as surveyed in this chapter, these trends in medical practice would appear in many ways to be the antithesis of what is needed for a truly comprehensive understanding of the complex nature of an individual illness and modes of approach to preventing or treating it. Put another way, the ongoing reorganization of the medical care delivery system seems thus far to have ignored what behavioral medicine has taught us, and to that extent has assumed a model of disease management that is no longer entirely valid, if it ever was.

SUMMARY

This chapter began with an analysis of adolescent and young adult eating disorders, which have reached epidemic proportions in the United States and elsewhere.

These disorders occur chiefly in females and are thought to be due in large part to a media-supported and unrealistic standard of thinness in defining feminine attractiveness and beauty. Although there is considerable heterogeneity in eating-disorder patterns, we focused on three main types: (1) anorexia nervosa—severe food restriction with or without binge eating and purging; (2) bulimia nervosa—frequent binge eating with compensatory behaviors involving either purging or nonpurging methods; and (3) binge-eating disorder (BED), frequent binge eating with little or no accompanying compensatory behavior. Of these, by far the most dangerous is the anorexia nervosa pattern because of the sometimes lethal consequences of starvation as well as more directly suicidal behavior. Certain personality characteristics and family patterns, such as perfectionism, tend to be shared among eating-disorder patients. The treatment of anorexia nervosa is especially difficult and often prolonged.

Research has clearly established that emotional factors influence the development of many other physical disorders and play an important role in the course of disease processes. The official Axis I diagnostic classification, Psychological Factors Affecting Medical Condition, is an acknowledgment of our enhanced appreciation of the widespread nature of such effects. Likewise, the relatively new field of behavioral medicine has its origins in the general recognition of these influences and seeks to extend our conception of disease beyond the traditional medical preoccupation with the physical breakdown of organs and organ systems.

At the most general level, the influence of psychological variables on health is seen in excessive autonomic nervous system responses to stressor conditions, sometimes resulting directly in organ damage. It is also seen in the increasing evidence that psychosocial challenges, including negative emotional states, can impair the immune system's ability to respond, leaving a person more vulnerable to disease-producing agents. Damaging habits and lifestyles also enhance risk for physical disease, as in the notable instances of cigarette smoking and high-risk sexual behavior.

Psychogenic vulnerability to particular diseases may be somewhat specific in nature, although not so specific as early doctrines implied. The distressingly common diseases of hypertension and coronary heart disease seem to be linked to chronic negative emotions. The Type A behavior pattern, or rather its generalized hostility component, is now well established as an independent risk factor for the frequently fatal CHD. Evidence relating to general and specific psychosocial factors, including the extent and quality of relationships with others, in the etiology of multiple other physical diseases continues to show promise.

Biological factors, including genetic vulnerabilities, excessive autonomic reactivity, and possible organ weaknesses, must of course continue to be given prominent attention in the search for etiological patterns. They must also be a part of treatment considerations whenever physical disease occurs, regardless of strong evidence of psychological contributions to its development.

A common factor in much psychosocially mediated physical disease is inadequacy in an individual's coping resources for managing stressful life circumstances. Cognitive-behavior therapy, in particular, shows much promise in alleviating this type of health-endangering problem.

KEY TERMS

behavioral medicine (p. 294)

psychogenic illness (p. 294)

health psychology (p. 294)

eating disorders (p. 295)

anorexia nervosa (p. 296)

bulimia nervosa (p. 297)

binge-eating disorder (BED) (p. 298)

placebo effect (p. 310)

psychoneuroimmunology (p. 312)

essential hypertension (p. 315)

Type A behavior pattern (p. 316)

simple tension headaches (p. 323)

biofeedback (p. 323)

secondary gains (p. 326)

Personality Disorders

Oskar Herzberg, *Untitled.* Herzberg, who worked as a servant and a typesetter in Frankfurt, spent time in several German mental institutions before undergoing psychiatric treatment from 1912-1914 for senile-mania. Fascinated by astronomical events, his narrative images have a naïve, child-like quality.

Ideally, people continue to grow and change throughout their lives. Successful adjustment through the life cycle is, after all, mostly a matter of flexibly adapting to the changing demands, opportunities, and limitations associated with different stages of life. Nevertheless, a person's broadly characteristic traits, coping styles, and ways of interacting in the social environment emerge during childhood and normally crystalize into established patterns by the end of adolescence or early adulthood. These patterns constitute the individual's *personality*—the unique pattern of traits and behaviors that characterize the individual.

For most of us, our adult personality is attuned to the demands of society. In other words, we readily comply with societal expectations. In contrast, there are certain people who, although not necessarily displaying obvious symptoms of an Axis I disorder, nevertheless seem somehow ill-equipped to become fully functioning members of society. For these individuals, personality formation has led to some traits that are so inflexible and maladaptive that they are unable to perform adequately at least some of the varied roles expected of them by their societies.

These people might be diagnosed as having **personality disorders,** which were formerly known as *character disorders.* Personality disorders typically do not stem from debilitating reactions to stress, as in post-traumatic stress disorder or many cases of major depression. Rather, the disorders to be examined here stem largely from the gradual development of inflexible and distorted personality and behavioral patterns, which result in persistently maladaptive ways of perceiving, thinking about, and relating to the world. These maladaptive approaches usually significantly impair at least some aspects of functioning and in some cases cause a good deal of subjective distress. For example, people with avoidant personality disorder are so shy and hypersensitive to rejection that they actively avoid most social interactions.

The category of personality disorders is broad, encompassing behavioral problems that differ greatly in form and severity. In the milder cases we find people who generally function adequately but who would be described by their relatives, friends, or associates as troublesome, eccentric, or difficult to get to know. They have characteristic ways of approaching situations and people that make them either have difficulties developing close relationships with others, or have difficulties getting along with those with whom they have close relationships. However, they are often quite capable or even gifted in some ways. In more severe cases, we find people whose extreme and often unethical "acting out" against society makes them less able to function in a normal setting; many are incarcerated in prisons or maximum security hospitals, although some are able to manipulate others and keep from getting caught.

There is not a great deal of evidence on the prevalence of personality disorders, in part because many people with such disorders never come in contact with mental health or legal agencies. Many individuals with a subset of the personality disorders are identified through the correctional system or through court-ordered psychological evaluations stemming from family problems such as physical abuse. Others eventually show up in alcohol treatment programs or in psychiatric emergency rooms after a suicide attempt. Nevertheless, estimates of the prevalence of one serious personality disorder, antisocial personality, were reported in a very large epidemiological study to be between 2.1 and 3.3 percent in the three study sites (Robins et al., 1984). More recent estimates concur that about 2 to 3 percent of individuals in the United States and Canada have antisocial personality disorder (Weissman, 1993). Weissman's (1993) comprehensive summary of epidemiological studies of all the personality disorders concluded that about 10 to 13 percent of the population meet the criteria for a personality disorder at some point in their lifetime. There are some suggestions that personality disorders have a tendency to decrease after age 50, but more research is needed (Abrams & Horowitz, 1996; Cohen et al., 1994). Not surprisingly, personality disorders are more common among psychiatric patients.

In the DSM-IV, as in DSM-III and DSM-III-R, the personality disorders are coded on a separate axis, Axis II (along with mental retardation, see Chapter 13), because they are regarded as being different enough from the standard psychiatric syndromes (which are coded on Axis I) to warrant separate classification. As already noted, the personality disorder section of Axis II represents long-standing personality traits that are thought to be inflexible and maladaptive and that cause social or occupational adjustment problems or personal distress. These reaction patterns are so deeply embedded in the personality structure (for whatever reason) that they are extremely resistant to modification. Although a person might be diagnosed on Axis II only, he or she could instead be diagnosed on both Axes I and II, which would reflect the existence of both a currently active mental disorder and a more chronic, underlying personality disorder. For example, someone with avoidant personality disorder might also develop major depression.

In the 20 years since DSM-III first identified personality disorders on a separate axis of disorders, there has been a great deal of research directed at understanding their nature and increasingly more research about how they develop. In this chapter, we will consider each of the types of disordered personalities that have been identified and then examine one of them—antisocial personality—in greater detail to give you an idea of the extensive research in this area.

Personality disorders are often associated with a number of the Axis I disorders that have been and will be considered in other chapters, such as anxiety disorders (Chapters 4 and 5), mood disorders (Chapter 6), alcoholism (Chapter 10), sexual deviations (Chapter 11), and delinquency (Chapter 14) (e.g., Ruegg & Frances, 1995). The behavioral patterns associated with personality disorders are in some cases also similar to those related to head injuries or other brain pathologies. In such cases, these behaviors might be evidence of organic brain disorders, which we consider in Chapter 13. These qualifications aside, let us move on to an examination of personality disorders.

CLINICAL FEATURES OF PERSONALITY DISORDERS

People with personality disorders often cause at least as much difficulty in the lives of others as in their own lives. Other people tend to find the behavior of individuals with personality disorders confusing, exasperating, unpredictable, and, in varying degrees, unacceptable—although rarely as bizarre or out of contact with reality as that of people with psychotic disorders. Some people with personality disorders experience a good deal of emotional suffering, although others do not, at least not obviously. Their behavioral deviations are persistent and seem to be intrinsic to their personalities. They have difficulty taking part in mutually respectful and satisfying social relationships. Whatever the particular trait patterns affected individuals have developed (obstinacy, covert hostility, suspiciousness, or fear of rejection, for example), these patterns color their reactions to each new situation and lead to a repetition of the same maladaptive behaviors. For example, a dependent person may wear out a relationship with someone, such as a spouse, by incessant and extraordinary demands such as never leaving them alone; after that partner leaves, the person may immediately into another dependent relationship and repeat the behavior. Thus personality disorders are marked by considerable consistency over time, with no apparent learning from previous troubles.

In the past, these persistent disorders were thought to center on and evolve from personality characteristics referred to as *temperament* or *character traits,* suggesting the possibility of hereditary or constitutional influences.

As discussed in Chapter 3, temperamental differences emerge early in infancy and involve differences in one's inborn disposition to react affectively to environmental stimuli, such as being very shy and frightened by novel stimuli versus being more outgoing and not easily frightened. One way of thinking about temperament is that it lays the early foundation for the development of the adult personality, but it is not the sole determinant of adult personality. The possibility of genetic transmission of a liability for some of these disorders, particularly antisocial and schizotypal personality, has been receiving strong support in the research literature (Nigg & Goldsmith, 1994).

More recently, however, environmental and social factors, particularly learning-based habit patterns and maladaptive cognitive styles, have also been receiving more attention as possible causal factors (Millon & Davis, 1996). Many of these maladaptive habits and cognitive styles may originate in disturbed parent-child attachment relationships, rather than deriving simply from temperamental differences. Early attachment relationships are thought by developmental psychologists to create models for children of what adult relationships should be like. If early models are not healthy, this may predispose the child to a pattern of personality development that can lead to the diagnosis of personality disorder later in life.

DSM-IV's Five Criteria

The essential feature of a Personality Disorder is an enduring pattern of inner experience and behavior that deviates markedly from the expectations of the individual's culture. The definition of personality disorders in the DSM-IV is based on five criteria:

- *Criterion A:* This pattern must be manifested in at least two of the following areas: cognition, affectivity, interpersonal functioning, or impulse control.

- *Criterion B:* This enduring pattern must be inflexible and pervasive across a broad range of personal and social situations.

- *Criterion C:* This pattern leads to clinically significant distress.

- *Criterion D:* The pattern is stable and of long duration, and its onset can be traced back at least to adolescence or early adulthood.

- *Criterion E:* The pattern is not better accounted for as a manifestation or consequence of another mental disorder

Specific diagnostic criteria are also provided for each of the Personality Disorders (American Psychiatric Association, 1994, p. 630); these will be discussed later in the chapter.

Difficulties in Diagnosing Personality Disorders

A special caution is in order regarding the personality disorders. Perhaps more misdiagnoses occur here than in any other categories. There are a number of reasons for this problem. One is that personality disorders are not as sharply defined as most Axis I diagnostic categories. Although DSM-IV includes criteria that must be met for a particular personality disorder diagnosis, these criteria are often not very precise or easy to follow in practice. For example, it may be difficult to diagnose reliably whether someone meets a criterion for dependent personality disorder such as "goes to excessive lengths to obtain nurturance and support from others," or "has difficulty making everyday decisions without an excessive amount of advice and reassurance from others" (e.g., Tryer, 1995). Because the criteria for personality disorders are defined by inferred traits or consistent patterns of behavior rather than by objective behavioral standards, more judgment is required from the clinician making the diagnosis than is the case for many Axis I disorders. Nevertheless, with the recent development of semistructured interviews for the diagnosis of personality disorders, diagnostic reliability has increased substantially. However, because the different structured interviews often result in different diagnoses (e.g., Oldham et al., 1992), there are still substantial problems with the reliability and validity of these diagnoses (Widiger & Sanderson, 1995). Moreover, British researchers often argue that diagnosing based on information provided by people who know the patient may be more reliable and valid than diagnosing based solely on interviews of the patients himself or herself (Tryer, 1995).

A second problem is that the diagnostic categories are not mutually exclusive: People often show characteristics of more than one personality disorder (Tryer, 1995; Widiger & Sanderson, 1995). For example, someone might show the suspiciousness, mistrust, avoidance of blame, and guardedness of paranoid personality disorder, along with the withdrawal, absence of friends, and aloofness that characterize schizoid personality disorder. It should be noted, however, that this problem also occurs with Axis I disorders, where many individuals also qualify for more than one diagnosis.

One of the problems with the diagnostic categories of personality disorders is that the exact same observable behaviors may be associated with different personality disorders and yet have different meanings with each disorder. For example, this woman's behavior and expression looking out this closed window could suggest the suspiciousness and avoidance of blame seen in paranoid personality disorder, or it could indicate social withdrawal and absence of friends that characterize schizoid personality disorder, or it could indicate social anxiety about interacting with others becuase of fear of being rejected or negatively evaluated as seen in avoidant personality disorder.

A third reason for diagnostic problems is that the personality characteristics that define personality disorders are dimensional in nature—that is, they range from normal expressions to pathological exaggerations and can be found, on a smaller scale and less intensely expressed, in many normal people (Carson, 1996; Clark & Livesley, 1994; Livesley et al., 1994; Widiger & Sanderson, 1995). For example, liking one's work and being conscientious about the details of one's job does not make one an obsessive-compulsive personality, nor does being economically dependent automatically make a spouse a dependent personality. Applying diagnostic labels to people who are in some cases functioning reasonably well is always risky; it is especially so where the diagnosis involves judgment about characteristics that are also common in normal people.

These problems can lead to unreliability of diagnoses and in fact they often do (Widiger & Sanderson, 1995). Someday a more accurate way of diagnosing the personality disorders may be devised. In the meantime, however, the categorical system of symptoms and traits will continue to be used with the recognition that it is more dependent on the observer's judgment than one might wish. Several theorists have attempted to deal with the problems inherent in categorizing personality disorders (e.g., Clark & Livesley, 1994; Costa & Widiger, 1994; Livesley et al., 1994; Tyrer, 1995; Widiger & Frances, 1994; Widiger & Sanderson, 1995); however, no clearly consistent theoretical view on the classification of personality disorders currently exists. With these cautions, we will look now at the elusive and often exasperating clinical features of the personality disorders. It is important to bear in mind, however, that we will be describing the prototype for each personality disorder. In reality, it is rare for any individual to fit these "ideal" descriptions. (See also Chapter 1.)

CATEGORIES OF PERSONALITY DISORDERS

The DSM-IV personality disorders are grouped into three clusters on the basis of similarities among the disorders. As already noted, many people meet the criteria for more than one personality disorder, including those from different clusters.

- *Cluster A:* Includes paranoid, schizoid, and schizotypal personality disorders. People with these disorders often seem odd or eccentric, with unusual behavior ranging from distrust and suspiciousness to social detachment.

- *Cluster B:* Includes histrionic, narcissistic, antisocial, and borderline personality disorders. Individuals with these disorders have in common a tendency to be dramatic, emotional, and erratic. Their impulsive behavior, often involving antisocial activities, is more colorful, more forceful, and more likely to bring them into contact with mental health or legal authorities than the behaviors characterizing disorders in the first cluster.

- *Cluster C:* Includes avoidant, dependent, and obsessive-compulsive personality disorders. In contrast to the other clusters, anxiety and fearfulness are often part of these disorders, making it difficult in some cases to distinguish them from anxiety-based disorders. People with these disorders, because of their anxieties, are more likely to seek help.

Two additional personality disorders—depressive and passive-aggressive personality disorders—are listed in DSM-IV in a provisional category in the appendix. (See Table 9.1 for a summary of personality disorder diagnoses.)

Paranoid Personality Disorder

Individuals with **paranoid personality disorder** have a pervasive suspiciousness and distrust of others. They tend to see themselves as blameless, instead finding fault for their own mistakes and failures in others—even to the point of ascribing evil motives to others. Such people are constantly expecting trickery and looking for clues to validate their expectations, while disregarding all evidence to the contrary. They are often preoccupied with doubts about the loyalty of friends, leading to a reluctance to confide in others. They also may be hypersensitive, as indicated by a tendency to read threatening meanings into benign remarks. They also commonly bear grudges, are unwilling to forgive perceived insults and slights, and are quick to react with anger (Bernstein, Useda, & Siever, 1995; Widiger & Frances, 1994). It is important to keep in mind that paranoid personalities are not usually psychotic; that is, most of the time they are in clear contact with reality, although they may experience transient psychotic symptoms (Thompson-Pope & Turkat, 1993). Another disorder, paranoid schizophrenia, to be discussed in Chapter 12, shares some symptoms found in paranoid personality. Paranoid schizophrenics have additional problems, however, including more persistent loss of reality contact and extreme cognitive and behavioral disorganization, such as delusions and hallucinations. Moreover, studies examining the genetic relationship between paranoid personality disorder and schizophrenia have produced mixed results and there are some suggestions that paranoid personality disorder may be more closely related to Axis I delusional disorder (see Chapter 12) than to schizophrenia (Bernstein et al., 1995).

The following case demonstrates well the behaviors characteristic of paranoid personality disorder.

Case Study, A Paranoid Construction Worker • A 40-year-old construction worker believes that his coworkers do not like him and fears that someone might let his scaffolding slip in order to cause him injury on the job. This concern followed a recent disagreement on the lunch line when the patient felt that a coworker was sneaking ahead and complained to him. He began noticing his new "enemy" laughing with the other men and often wondered if he were the butt of their mockery. He thought of confronting them, but decided that the whole issue might just be

TABLE 9.1 SUMMARY OF PERSONALITY DISORDERS

Personality Disorder	Characteristics
Cluster A	
Paranoid	Suspiciousness and mistrust of others; tendency to see self as blameless; on guard for perceived attacks by others
Schizoid	Impaired social relationships; inability and lack of desire to form attachments to others
Schizotypal	Peculiar thought patterns; oddities of perception and speech that interfere with communication and social interaction
Cluster B	
Histrionic	Self-dramatization; overconcern with attractiveness; tendency to irritability and temper outbursts if attention seeking is frustrated
Narcissistic	Grandiosity; preoccupation with receiving attention; self-promoting; lack of empathy
Antisocial	Lack of moral or ethical development; inability to follow approved models of behavior; deceitfulness; shameless manipulation of others; history of conduct problems as a child
Borderline	Impulsiveness, inappropriate anger; drastic mood shifts; chronic feelings of boredom; attempts at self-mutilation or suicide
Cluster C	
Avoidant	Hypersensitivity to rejection or social derogation; shyness; insecurity in social interaction and initiating relationships
Dependent	Difficulty in separating in relationships; discomfort at being alone; subordination of needs in order to keep others involved in a relationship; indecisiveness
Obsessive-compulsive	Excessive concern with order, rules, and trivial details; perfectionistic; lack of expressiveness and warmth; difficulty in relaxing and having fun
Provisional Categories	
Passive-aggressive	Negativistic attitudes and passive resistance to adequate performance expressed through indirect means, such as complaining, being sullen and argumentative, expressing envy and resentment toward those who are more fortunate
Depressive	Pervasive depressive cognitions. Persistent unhappiness or dejection. Feeling of inadequacy, guilt, and self-criticism

in his own mind, and that he might get himself into more trouble by taking any action.

The patient offers little spontaneous information, sits tensely in the chair, is wide-eyed and carefully tracks all movements in the room. He reads between the lines of the interviewer's questions, feels criticized, and imagines that the interviewer is siding with his coworkers. He makes it clear that he would not have come to the personnel clinic at all except for his need for sleep medication.

He was a loner as a boy and felt that other children would form cliques and be mean to him. He did poorly in school, but blamed his teachers—he claimed that they preferred girls or boys who were "sissies." He dropped out of school and has since been a hard and effective worker; but he feels he never gets the breaks. He believes that he has been discriminated against because of his Catholicism, but can offer little convincing evidence. He gets on poorly with bosses and coworkers, is unable to appreciate joking around, and does best in situations where he can work and have lunch alone. He has switched jobs many times because he felt he was being mistreated.

The patient is distant and demanding with his family. His children call him "Sir" and know that it is wise to be "seen but not heard" when he is around. At home he can never comfortably sit still and is always busy at some chore or another. He prefers not to have people visit his house and becomes restless when his wife is away visiting others. (Spitzer et al., 1981, p. 37)

This pervasive suspiciousness and mistrust of other people leave a paranoid personality prone to numerous difficulties and hurts in interpersonal relationships. These difficulties typically lead the person to be continually "on guard" for perceived attacks by others.

Schizoid Personality Disorder

Individuals with **schizoid personality disorder** usually show an inability to form social relationships and a lack of interest in doing so. Consequently they typically do not have good friends, with the possible exception of close relatives. Such people are unable to express their feelings and are seen by others as cold and distant; they often lack social skills and can be classified as loners or introverts, with solitary interests and occupations (Widiger & Frances, 1994). They tend not to take pleasure in many activities, including sexual activity. Commonly they may even appear indifferent to praise or criticism from others. More generally, they are not very emotionally reactive, rarely experiencing strong positive or negative emotions, which contributes to their appearing cold and aloof (Widiger et al., 1994).

Early theorists considered a schizoid personality to be a likely precursor to the development of schizophrenia. This viewpoint has been challenged in recent times, however (Kalus, Bernstein, & Siever, 1995). Research on the possible genetic transmission of schizoid personality has failed to establish either a link between the two disorders or the hereditary basis of schizoid personality. Siever and Davis (1991), in their theoretical comparison of schizoid and schizotypal personality disorders (to be considered in the next section), considered the schizotypal personality to be more closely linked genetically to the positive symptoms of schizophrenia, in which people are often out of touch with reality, showing hallucinations and delusions. However, they also recognized that schizoid personality disorder may show some links with the so-called negative symptoms of schizophrenia (see Chapter 12) which include anhedonia and social withdrawal (see also Kalus et al., 1995). Nevertheless, two more recent reviews of the literature also suggest that evidence for a genetic link between schizotypal personality disorder and schizophrenia is much stronger (Kendler & Gardner, 1997; Nigg & Goldsmith, 1994).

The following case of a schizoid personality illustrates a fairly severe personality problem in a man who had been functioning adequately as judged both by occupational criteria and by his own standards of "happiness." When he sought help, it was at the encouragement of his supervisor and his physician.

Case Study, A Schizoid Computer Analyst • Bill D., a highly intelligent but quite introverted and withdrawn 33-year-old computer analyst, was referred for psychological evaluation by his physician, who was concerned that Bill might be depressed and unhappy. At the suggestion of his supervisor, Bill had recently gone to the physician for rather vague physical complaints and because of his gloomy outlook on life. Bill had virtually no contact with other people. He lived alone in his apartment, worked in a small office by himself, and usually saw no one at work except for the occasional visits of his supervisor to give him new work and pick up completed projects. He ate lunch by himself and about once a week, on nice days, went to the zoo for his lunch break.

Bill was a lifelong loner; as a child he had had few friends and always had preferred solitary activities over family outings (he was the oldest of five children). In high school he had never dated and in college had gone out with a woman only once—and that was with a group of students after a game. He had been active in sports, however, and had played varsity football in both high school and college. In college he had spent a lot of time with one relatively close friend—mostly drinking. However, this friend now lived in another city.

Bill reported rather matter-of-factly that he had a hard time making friends; he never knew what to say in a conversation. On a number of occasions he had thought of becoming friends with other people but simply couldn't think of the right words, so "the conversation just died." He reported that he had given some

People with schizoid personality disorder are often loners interested in solitary pursuits, such as assembling odd collections of objects.

thought lately to changing his life in an attempt to be more "positive," but it never had seemed worth the trouble. It was easier for him not to make the effort because he became embarrassed when someone tried to talk with him. He was happiest when he was alone.

In short, the central problem of the person with a schizoid personality is that they neither desire nor enjoy close relationships with other people. It is as though the needs for love, belonging, and approval fail to develop in these people—or if they had been there earlier in development they had somehow disappeared at an early stage. The result is a profound barrenness of interpersonal experience.

Schizotypal Personality Disorder

Individuals with **schizotypal personality disorder** are not only excessively introverted and have pervasive social and interpersonal deficits; they also have cognitive and perceptual distortions and eccentricities in their communication and behavior (Widiger & Frances, 1994). Although schizotypal and schizoid personalities are both characterized by social isolation and withdrawal, the two can be distinguished in that schizotypal personality—but not schizoid personality—also involves oddities of thought, perception, or speech. Although reality contact is usually maintained, highly personalized and superstitious thinking are characteristic of people with schizotypal personality, and under extreme stress they may experience *transient* psychotic symptoms (Thompson-Pope & Turkat, 1993; Widiger & Frances, 1994). Indeed, they often believe that they have magical powers and may engage in magical rituals. Their oddities in thinking, talking, and other behaviors are similar to those often seen in more severe forms in schizophrenic patients; in fact, they are sometimes first diagnosed as exhibiting simple or latent schizophrenia. Several studies have found that the symptoms of cognitive malfunctioning included in schizotypal personality disorder were more useful in making a clinical diagnosis than were symptoms of social isolation, inadequate rapport, and social anxiety (Siever, Bernstein, & Silverman, 1995; Widiger & Frances, 1994). The cognitive symptoms that were useful in making the diagnosis included cognitive perceptual problems, magical thinking (for example, belief in telepathy and superstitions), ideas of reference (the belief that conversations or gestures of others have special meaning or personal significance), odd speech, and suspicious beliefs (see also Thompson-Pope & Turkat, 1993).

The prevalence of this disorder in the general population is estimated at about 3 percent (American Psychiatric Association, 1994). A genetic and biological association with schizophrenia has been clearly documented (Kendler & Gardner, 1997; Meehl, 1990a; Nigg & Goldsmith, 1994). Indeed, several studies have documented that patients with schizotypal personality disorder (Siever et al., 1995), as well as college students with schizotypal personality disorder (Lencz et al., 1993), have the same deficit in their ability to track a moving target visually that is common in schizophrenia (see Chapter 12). They also show attentional deficits (Lees-Roitman et al., 1997) and working memory deficits (e.g., being able to remember a span of digits) common in schizophrenia (Squires-Wheeler et al., 1997). In fact the term schizotypal is an abbreviation for "schizophrenic genotype" (Rado, 1956), and many consider it to be part of a spectrum of schizophrenia that often occurs in the first-degree relatives of schizophrenics (Kendler & Gardner, 1997; Nigg & Goldsmith, 1994). Moreover, teenagers who have a schizotypal personality type have been shown to be at increased risk for developing schizophrenia and schizophrenia-spectrum disorders in adulthood (Siever et al., 1995; Tykra, Cannon et al., 1995). The following case is fairly typical.

Case Study, The Disconnectedness of a Schizotypal Woman • The patient is a 32-year-old unmarried, unemployed woman on welfare who complains that she feels "spacey." Her feelings of detachment have gradually become stronger and more uncomfortable. For many hours each day she feels as if she were watching herself move through life, and the world around her seems unreal. She feels especially strange when she looks into a mirror. For many years she has felt able to read people's minds by a "kind of clairvoyance I don't understand." According to her, several people in her family apparently also have this ability. She is preoccupied by the thought that she has some special mission in life, but is not sure what it is; she is not particularly religious. She is very self-conscious in public, often feels that people are paying special attention to her, and sometimes thinks that strangers cross the street to avoid her. She has no friends, feels lonely and isolated, and spends much of each day lost in fantasies or watching TV soap operas.

The patient speaks in a vague, abstract, digressive manner, generally just missing the point, but she is never incoherent. She seems shy, suspicious, and afraid she will be criticized. She has no gross loss of reality testing, such as hallucinations or delusions. She has never had treatment for emotional problems. She has had occasional jobs, but drifts away from them because of lack of interest (Spitzer et al., 1989, pp. 173–174).

The distinguishing feature of a schizotypal person is peculiar thought patterns, which are in turn associated with a loosening—although not a complete rupture—of ties to reality. The individual appears to lack some key integrative competence of the sort that enables most of us to "keep it all together" and move our lives toward some personal goals. As a result, many basic abilities, such as being able to communicate clearly, are never fully mastered, and the person tends to drift aimlessly and unproductively through the adult years.

Histrionic Personality Disorder

Excessive attention-seeking behavior and emotionality are the key characteristics of individuals with **histrionic personality disorder.** They tend to feel unappreciated if not the center of attention, and their lively, dramatic, and often excessively extraverted styles often ensure that they can charm others into attending to them. But these qualities do not lead to stable and satisfying relationships because others tire of providing this level of attention. In seeking attention, their appearance and behavior are often quite theatrical and emotional, as well as sexually provocative and seductive. Their style of speech may be dramatic but is also quite impressionistic and lacking in detail. People with histrionic personality disorder are often highly suggestible and consider relationships to be closer than they are. Their sexual adjustment is usually poor (Apt & Hurlbert, 1994) and their interpersonal relationships are stormy because they may attempt to control their partner through seductive behavior and emotional manipulation, but they also show a good deal of dependence. Usually they are considered to be self-centered, vain, and overconcerned about the approval of others, who see them as overly reactive, shallow, and insincere. The prevalence in the general population is estimated at 2 to 3 percent and it seems to occur somewhat more often in women than men, although whether this is because of interviewer bias or a criterion bias is as yet unclear (American Psychiatric Association, 1994; Pfohl, 1995; Widiger, 1998). For example, the idea that an interviewer bias may play a role here comes from a study done where clinicians read fictitious case histories of men and women with histrionic personality disorder and antisocial personality disorder; the gender of the cases was manipulated by the investigators (Ford & Widiger, 1989). Clinicians were much more likely to diagnose the women as having histrionic personality disorder and the men as having antisocial personality disorder even though the rest of the information about the cases was identical. The idea that a criterion bias may also be playing a role stems

from observations that many of the criteria for histrionic personality disorder (overdramatization, vanity, seductiveness, and overconcern with physical appearance) are more likely to occur in Western society in women than in men. This automatically increases the chances that women might be diagnosed as having the disorder that includes so many of these features as criteria. The following case illustrates the histrionic personality pattern.

> **Case Study, A Secretary with Histrionic Disorder** • Pam, a 22-year-old secretary, was causing numerous problems for her supervisor and coworkers. According to her supervisor, Pam was unable to carry out her duties without constant guidance. Seemingly helpless and dependent, she would overreact to minor events and job pressures with irritability and occasional temper tantrums. If others placed unwanted demands on her, she would complain of physical problems, such as nausea or headaches; furthermore, she frequently missed work altogether. To top it off, Pam was flirtatious and often demandingly seductive toward the men in the office.
>
> As a result of her frequent absenteeism and her disruptive behavior in the office, Pam's supervisor and the personnel manager recommended that she be given a psychological evaluation and counseling in the Employee Assistance Program. She went to the first appointment with the psychologist but failed to return for follow-up visits. She was finally given a discharge notice after several incidents of temper outbursts at work.

Both Pam's physical complaints and her seductive behavior are examples of attention-seeking tactics commonly found in the histrionic personality pattern. When these tactics fail to bring about the desired result, irritability and temper outbursts typically follow.

Narcissistic Personality Disorder

Individuals with **narcissistic personality disorder** show an exaggerated sense of self-importance, a preoccupation with being admired, and a lack of empathy for the feelings of others (Blais, Hilsenroth, & Castlebury, 1997). Ronningstam and Gunderson (1989) reported that grandiosity was the most generalizable criterion for diagnosing narcissistic patients and was used most often in making a diagnosis, although they later found in a prospective study that grandiosity was the symptom most likely to diminish with time (Ronningstam et al., 1995). The grandiosity of narcissistic patients is manifested by a strong tendency to overestimate their abilities and accomplishments, while often concurrently underestimating the abilities and accomplishments of others.

People with histrionic personality disorder often engage in seductive and attention-seeking behavior—appearing in public in scanty clothing, for example.

Their sense of entitlement is frequently a source of astonishment to others, although they themselves seem to regard their lavish expectations as merely what they deserve. They behave in stereotypical ways (for example, with constant self-references and bragging) to gain the acclaim and recognition that feeds their grandiose expectations and their fantasies of unlimited success, power, beauty, or brilliance. Because they believe they are so special, they often think they can only be understood by other high-status people, or should only associate with such people. These tactics, to those around them, appear to be excessive efforts to make themselves look good.

Narcissistic personalities share another central element—they are unwilling to take the perspective of others, to see things other than "through their own eyes." In more general terms, they lack the capacity for empathy, which is an essential ingredient for mature relationships. In this sense all children begin life as narcissists and only gradually acquire a perspective-taking ability. For reasons that are far from entirely understood, some children do not show normal progress in this respect, and indeed, in extreme cases, show little or none. The latter may grow up to become adult narcissistic personalities. Along with the lack of empathy, narcissistic persons not uncommonly take advantage of others to achieve their own ends and often show arrogant, snobbish, or haughty behaviors and attitudes. Finally, they are often very envious of other

people, or believe that other people are envious of them (Gunderson, Ronningstam, & Smith, 1995).

Most researchers and clinicians believe that people with narcissistic personality disorder have a very fragile sense of self-esteem underneath all their grandiosity. This may be why they are often preoccupied with what others think, why they show such a great need for admiration, and why they are so preoccupied with fantasies of outstanding achievement. Not surprisingly, they are also very sensitive to criticism, which may leave them feeling humiliated, empty, or full of rage (Widiger & Frances, 1994). The following case is illustrative.

Case Study, A Narcissistic Graduate Student • A 25-year-old, single graduate student complains to his psychoanalyst of difficulty completing his Ph.D. in English literature and expresses concerns about his relationships with women. He believes that his thesis topic may profoundly increase the level of understanding in his discipline and make him famous, but so far he has not been able to get past the third chapter. His mentor does not seem sufficiently impressed with his ideas, and the patient is furious at him, but also self-doubting and ashamed. He blames his mentor for his lack of progress, and thinks that he deserves more help with his grand idea, that his mentor should help with some of the research. The patient brags about his creativity and complains that other people are "jealous" of his insight. He is very envious of students who are moving along faster than he and regards them as "dull drones and ass-kissers." He prides himself on the brilliance of his class participation and imagines someday becoming a great professor.

He becomes rapidly infatuated with women and has powerful and persistent fantasies about each new woman he meets, but after several experiences of sexual intercourse feels disappointed and finds them dumb, clinging, and physically repugnant. He has many "friends," but they turn over quickly, and no one relationship lasts very long. People get tired of his continual self-promotion and lack of consideration of them. For example, he was lonely at Christmas and insisted that his best friend stay in town rather than visit his family. The friend refused, criticizing the patient's self-centeredness; and the patient, enraged, decided never to see this friend again. (Spitzer et al., 1981, pp. 52–53)

Narcissistic personality disorder may be more frequently observed in men than in women (American Psychiatric Association, 1994; Golomb et al., 1995), although not all studies show this. Compared with some of the other personality disorders, it is thought to be relatively rare, with estimates that it occurs in about 1 percent of the population. Given the overlapping features between histrionic and narcissistic personality disorders, Widiger and Trull (1993) attempted to summarize the major differences in this way: "The histrionic tends to be more emotional and dramatic than the narcissistic, and whereas both may be promiscuous, the narcissistic is more dispassionately exploitative, while the histrionic is more overtly needy. Both will be exhibitionistic, but the histrionic seeks attention, whereas the narcissistic seeks admiration" (p. 388).

Individuals with narcissistic personality patterns may not seek psychological treatment because they view themselves as nearly perfect and in no need of change. Those who do enter treatment often do so at the insistence of another person, such as a husband or wife, and may terminate therapy prematurely—particularly if their therapist is confrontational and questions their self-serving behavior. Most of what is known about narcissistic personality disorder has emerged from psychoanalytic therapy and later ego-analytic and self-psychology writings (Kernberg, 1984, 1985, 1996; Kohut & Wolff, 1978). The psychodynamic treatment approach may be the most viable therapy, because a long-term treatment relationship seems needed to bring about changes in these patients' persistent self-oriented patterns (Kernberg, 1985, 1996). However, there are unfortunately no controlled studies to date documenting the effectiveness of this (or any other) form of treatment for narcissistic personality disorder.

Antisocial Personality Disorder

Individuals with **antisocial personality disorder (ASPD)** continually violate and show disregard for the rights of others through deceitful, aggressive, or antisocial behavior, typically without remorse or loyalty to anyone. They tend to be impulsive, irritable, and aggressive, and show a pattern of generally irresponsible behavior. Moreover, according to the DSM, this pattern of behavior must have been occurring since the age of 15, and before age 15, the person must have had symptoms of conduct disorder, a similar disorder occurring in children and young adolescents who show persistent patterns of aggression toward people or animals, destruction of property, deceitfulness or theft, and serious violation of rules at home or in school (see Chapter 14.) Some people with antisocial personalities have enough intelligence and social charm to devise and carry out elaborate schemes for conning large numbers of people. Impostors frequently fit into this category. This disorder is much more common in men than in women, with a lifetime prevalence of about 3 percent in men and about 1 percent in women (e.g., Golomb et al., 1995; Robins et al., 1984). Because this pattern has been studied more fully than the others, it will be examined in some detail later in this chapter. A brief clinical description should suffice here.

Case Study, A Thief with ASPD • Mark, a 22-year-old, came to a psychology clinic on court order. He was awaiting trial for car theft and armed robbery. His case records revealed that he had a long history of arrests beginning at age 9, when he had been picked up for vandalism. He had been expelled from high school for truancy and disruptive behavior. On a number of occasions he had run away from home for days or weeks at a time—always returning in a disheveled and "rundown" condition. To date he had not held a job for more than a few days at a time, even though his generally charming manner enabled him to obtain work readily. He was described as a loner, with few friends. Though initially charming, Mark usually soon antagonized those he met with his aggressive, self-oriented behavior.

Mark was generally affable and complimentary during the therapy session. At the end of it, he enthusiastically told the therapist how much he'd benefited from the counseling and looked forward to future sessions. Mark's first session was his last. Shortly after it, he skipped bail and presumably left town to avoid his trial.

Given that there is some overlap in the criteria for narcissistic and antisocial personality disorders Widiger and Trull (1993) noted that the most basic distinction is that "The narcissist's exploitation would be more for the purpose of demonstrating domination, prestige, and superiority rather than for the personal, material gain of the antisocial personality" (p. 388).

Borderline Personality Disorder

Individuals with **borderline personality disorder (BPD)** show a pattern of behavior characterized by impulsivity and instability in interpersonal relationships, self-image, and moods. The term *borderline personality* has a long and rather confusing history (Widiger & Trull, 1993). Originally it was most often used to refer to a condition that was thought to occupy the "border" between neurotic and psychotic disorders (as in the term *borderline schizophrenia*). However, this sense of the term *borderline* later became identified with schizotypal personality disorder, which as we have discussed is biologically related to schizophrenia. Since DSM-III, the term *borderline personality disorder* has been used for people who have "enduring personality features of instability and vulnerability" (Widiger & Trull, 1993, p. 372) and it is no longer considered to be biologically related to schizophrenia.

People with borderline personalities show serious disturbances in basic identity. Their sense of self is highly unstable. Given this extremely unstable self-image, it is not surprising that they also have highly unstable interpersonal relationships. For example, they may make desperate efforts to avoid real or imagined abandonment, perhaps because their fears of abandonment are so intense. Feeling slighted, they might, for example, become verbally abusive toward loved ones or might threaten suicide over minor setbacks. Given such behaviors, it is not surprising that they commonly have a history of intense but stormy relationships, typically involving overidealizations of friends or lovers that later end in bitter disillusionment and disappointment (Gunderson, Zanarini, & Kisiel, 1995). Their mood is also highly unstable. For example, they may display intense outbursts with little provocation and have difficulty controlling their anger. They tend to have a low tolerance for frustration, as well as chronic feelings of emptiness. Associated with the sense of emptiness is a common intolerance for being alone. Their extreme affective instability is reflected in drastic mood shifts and impulsive or erratic self-destructive behaviors, such as binges of gambling, sex, substance abuse, binge-eating, or reckless driving. Suicide attempts, often flagrantly manipulative, are frequently part of the clinical picture (Soloff et al., 1994), and self-mutilation is one of the most discriminating signs for borderline personality (Widiger et al., 1986). In some cases the self-injurious

behavior is associated with relief from anxiety or dysphoria and research has documented that it may even be associated with analgesia (absence of the experience of pain in the presence of a theoretically painful stimulus) (Figueroa & Silk, 1997; Russ et al., 1994). Suicide attempts among those with borderline personality disorder are not always simply manipulative, with prospective studies suggesting that 3 to 9 percent may ultimately complete suicide (Soloff et al., 1994). The following prototypic case illustrates the frequent risk of suicide and self-mutilation among borderline personalities.

> **Case Study, Self-Mutilation in a Woman with Borderline Personality Disorder** • A 26-year-old unemployed woman was referred for admission to a hospital by her therapist because of intense suicidal preoccupation and urges to mutilate herself with a razor.
>
> The patient was apparently well until her junior year in high school, when she became preoccupied with religion and philosophy, avoided friends, and was filled with doubt about who she was. Academically she did well, but later, during college, her performance declined. In college she began to use a variety of drugs, abandoned the religion of her family, and seemed to be searching for a charismatic religious figure with whom to identify. At times massive anxiety swept over her and she found it would suddenly vanish if she cut her forearm with a razor blade.
>
> Three years ago she began psychotherapy, and initially rapidly idealized her therapist as being incredibly intuitive and empathic. Later she became hostile and demanding of him, requiring more and more sessions, sometimes two in one day. Her life centered on her therapist, by this time to the exclusion of everyone else. Although her hostility toward her therapist was obvious, she could neither see it nor control it. Her difficulties with her therapist culminated in many episodes of her forearm cutting and suicidal threats, which led to the referral for admission. (Spitzer et al., 1994, p. 233)

Clinical observation of people with borderline personality disorder points strongly to a problem of achieving a coherent sense of self as a key predisposing causal factor. These people somehow fail to complete the process of achieving a coherent and stable self-identity, and this failure leads to complications in interpersonal relationships.

Although people with borderline personality disorder are usually aware of their circumstances and surroundings, they may have relatively short or transient episodes in which they appear to be out of contact with reality and experience delusions or other psychotic-like symptoms, such as hallucinations, paranoid beliefs, body image distortions, or dissociative symptoms. Among inpatients with severe borderline personality disorder the frequency and duration of psychotic symptoms may be greater. Estimates are that 20 to 40 percent of people with borderline personality disorder experience transient, circumscribed delusions (false beliefs) and hallucinations (false sensory perceptions) (Gunderson et al., 1995). Among patients with dissociative symptoms, the risk for self-mutilation seems especially high (Brodsky, Cloitre, & Dulit, 1995).

Estimates are that about 2 percent of the population may qualify for the diagnosis of borderline personality disorder, although they represent a disproportionate number of patients in both inpatient and outpatient clinical settings (Widiger & Trull, 1993). There are estimates that about 8 percent of outpatients and about 15 percent of inpatients seeking treatment have borderline personality disorder. Approximately 75 percent of individuals receiving this diagnosis are women.

Comorbidity with Other Axis I Disorders   Given their many and varied symptoms and problems with their sense of personal identity, it is not surprising that this personality disorder commonly co-occurs with a variety of Axis I disorders, ranging from mood and anxiety disorders (especially panic and PTSD), to substance use and eating disorders (Widiger & Trull, 1993). The relationship with mood disorders is especially strong, with about 50 percent of those with BPD also qualifying for a mood disorder diagnosis at some time (Widiger & Trull, 1993). Indeed, in the past this has led some to suggest that borderline disorders are closer to "the border of affective [psychoses]" rather than schizophrenic psychoses (Akiskal et al., 1985, p. 45) or that borderline personality disorder may represent "a literally borderline condition of both personality and mood pathology" (Widiger & Trull, 1993, p. 377). That is, borderline personalities have both a disturbance in the ability to regulate their moods, and a pathological organization of the personality (Soloff, Cornelius, & George, 1991).

Some of the overlap between borderline personality and depression occurs because of the overlap in the symptoms that are required for a diagnosis of borderline personality and for mood disorders. In spite of this seemingly special relationship between BPD and mood disorders, the consensus today is that the relationship between these disorders is actually not a special or unique one (Gunderson & Philips, 1991). For example, other Axis II disorders are actually more commonly associated with depression than is borderline personality disorder. More-

over, depression as experienced by the borderline personality is apparently somewhat different from that of other depressives in that it is more often characterized by chronic feelings of loneliness (Soloff et al., 1991; Westen et al., as cited in Gunderson & Philips, 1991). Borderline patients are also much more likely to view their relationships with family and friends as hostile and noncohesive and to show more pervasive dysfunction in social relationships than do depressives (Benjamin & Wonderlich, 1994; Sack et al., 1996). In addition, borderline patients with depression do not show as good a response to the most common classes of antidepressant medication as do other depressed patients (Gitlin, 1996; Gunderson & Philips, 1991).

Comorbidity with Other Personality Disorders
There is also substantial co-ocurrence of borderline personality disorder with other personality disorders—especially histrionic, dependent, antisocial, and schizotypal personality disorders. Nevertheless, Widiger and Trull (1993) noted that a prototypical borderline personality can be distinguished from these other personality disorders in the following way: "The prototypic borderline's exploitative use of others is usually an angry and impulsive response to disappointment, whereas the antisocial's is a guiltless and calculated effort for personal gain. Sexuality may play a more central role in the relationships of histrionics than in borderlines, evident in the histrionic's tendency to eroticize situations, to compete with members of the same sex, and to be inappropriately seductive. The prototypic schizotypal lacks the emotionality of the borderline, and tends to be more isolated, odd and peculiar" (p. 377).

Avoidant Personality Disorder

Individuals with **avoidant personality disorder** have a pattern of extreme social inhibition and introversion leading to lifelong patterns of limited social relationships and reluctance to enter into social interactions. Because of their hypersensitivity to, and their fear of, criticism and rebuff, they do not seek out other people; yet they desire affection and are often lonely and bored. Unlike schizoid personalities, they do not enjoy their aloneness; their inability to relate comfortably to other people causes acute anxiety and is accompanied by low self-esteem and excessive self-consciousness. Because of their hypersensitivity to any sign of rejection or social derogation, they may readily see ridicule or disparagement where none was intended, as shown by the following case.

Case Study, A Librarian with Avoidant Personality Disorder • Sally, a 35-year-old librarian, lived a relatively isolated life and had few acquaintances and no close personal friends. From childhood on, she had been very shy and had withdrawn from close ties with others to keep from being hurt or criticized. Two years before she entered therapy, she had had a date to go to a party with an acquaintance she had met at the library. The moment they had arrived at the party, Sally had felt extremely uncomfortable because she had not been "dressed properly." She left in a hurry and refused to see her acquaintance again. It was because of her continuing concern over this incident that—two years later—Sally decided to go into therapy, even though she dreaded the possibility that the psychologist would be critical of her.

In the early treatment sessions, she sat silently much of the time, finding it too difficult to talk about herself. After several sessions, she grew to trust the therapist, and she related numerous incidents in her early years in which she had been "devastated" by her alcoholic father's obnoxious behavior in public. Though she had tried to keep her school friends from knowing about her family problems, when this had become impossible she instead had limited her friendships, thus protecting herself from possible embarrassment or criticism.

When Sally first began therapy, she avoided meeting people unless she could be assured that they would "like her." With therapy that focused on enhancing her assertiveness and social skills, she made some progress in her ability to approach and talk with people.

Sally's extreme need to avoid situations in which she might be embarrassed is the keynote of the avoidant personality. Life is full of risks; yet such people cannot face even the slightest risk of embarrassment or criticism. They want guarantees of success before they will participate—and if they cannot have them, they just will not play the game.

Some research suggests that avoidant personality may be a biologically based disorder often starting in infancy or childhood that is reinforced by environmental factors to become a highly stable and chronic behavioral pattern (Alden & Kapp, 1988; Kagan, 1997; Kagan, Reznick, & Snidman, 1988). The key difference between the loner with schizoid personality disorder and the loner who is avoidant is that the one with an avoidant personality is hypersensitive to criticism, shy, and insecure, while the one with a schizoid personality is aloof, cold, and indifferent to criticism (Millon & Martinez, 1995). Another difficult distinction is between dependent and avoidant personalities. In this case, dependent personalities have great difficulty separating in relationships because of

feelings of incompetence on their own, while avoidant personalities have problems initiating them because of fearing criticism or rejection (Millon & Martinez, 1995). In addition, the primary focus of the dependent personality is on being taken care of, whereas the primary focus of the avoidant personality is on avoidance of humiliation and rejection (American Psychiatric Association, 1994). It should also be noted, however, these two disorders co-occur rather frequently.

Another major problem is in distinguishing avoidant personality disorder and generalized social phobia (Chapter 5). For example, numerous studies found substantial overlap between these two disorders, with a general conclusion that avoidant personality disorder may simply be a somewhat more severe manifestation of generalized social phobia (Alpert et al., 1997; Holt, Heimberg, & Hope, 1992; Noyes et al., 1995; Turner et al., 1992). This is consistent with the finding in these studies

The key difference between the loner with schizoid personality disorder and the loner who is avoidant is that the avoidant personality is hypersensitive to criticism, shy, and insecure. The schizoid personality is cold, aloof, and indifferent to criticism.

that there are cases of generalized social phobia without avoidant personality disorder, but very few cases of avoidant personality disorder without generalized social phobia, as well as with findings of somewhat higher levels of dysfunction and distress in the individuals with avoidant personality disorder, including more consistent feelings of low self-esteem (Millon & Martinez, 1995). Moreover, these conditions may both respond to similar psychopharmacological treatments (Gitlin, 1996; Liebowitz et al., 1992). These findings led Widiger (1992) to suggest that these two disorders "may represent boundary conditions of the anxiety and personality disorders that involve essentially the same psychopathology" (p. 341). DSM-IV has recently come to the same conclusion, noting that they overlap so extensively "that they may be alternative conceptualizations of the same or similar conditions" (pp. 663–664).

Dependent Personality Disorder

Individuals with **dependent personality disorder** show extreme dependence on other people, particularly the need to be taken care of, which leads to clinging and submissive behavior. They also show acute discomfort—even panic—at the possibility of separation or sometimes of simply having to be alone, often leading to excessive reliance on emergency medical services (Bornstein, 1992, 1997). These individuals usually build their lives around other people and subordinate their own needs or views to keep these people involved with them, often leading to indiscriminate selection of mates. They often fail to get appropriately angry with others because of a fear of losing their support, which means that they may remain in psychologically or physically abusive relationships. They have great difficulty making even simple everyday decisions without a great deal of advice and reassurance. This may be because they lack self-confidence and feel helpless even when they have actually developed good work skills or other competencies. They may function well as long as they are not required to be on their own. In the following case, a woman with a dependent personality experienced such distress following desertion by her husband that she sought help.

Case Study, A Mother with Dependent Personality Disorder • Sarah D., a 32-year-old mother of two and a part-time tax accountant, came to a crisis center late one evening after Michael, her husband of a year and a half, abused her physically and then left home. Although he never physically harmed the children, he frequently threatened to do so when he was drunk.

Sarah appeared acutely anxious and worried about the future and "needed to be told what to do." She wanted her husband to come back and seemed rather unconcerned about his regular pattern of physical abuse. At the time, Michael was an unemployed resident in a day treatment program at a halfway house for paroled drug abusers that taught abstinence from all addictive substances through harassment and group cohesiveness. He was almost always in a surly mood and "ready to explode."

Although Sarah had a well-paying job, she voiced great concern about being able to make it on her own. She realized that it was foolish to be "dependent" on her husband, whom she referred to as a "real loser." (She had had a similar relationship with her first husband, who had left her and her oldest child when she was 18.) Several times in the past few months, Sarah had made up her mind to get out of the marriage but couldn't bring herself to break away. She would threaten to leave, but when the time came to do so, she would "freeze in the door" with a numbness in her body and a sinking feeling in her stomach at the thought of "not being with Michael."

As a result of their lack of confidence, dependent personalities passively allow other people to take over the major decisions in their lives—such as where they will live and work, what friends they will have, and even how they will spend their time. These individuals typically appear "selfless" and bland, since they usually feel they have no right to express even mild individuality. They are often preoccupied with a fear of being left to take care of themselves, and if one relationship ends they often will seek out a new one with great urgency. It is quite common that people with dependent personality disorder have a comorbid diagnosis of anxiety disorders (especially social phobia, panic disorder, or generalized anxiety disorder) (Bornstein, 1995). Among patients with eating disorders, dependent personality disorder is also quite common.

Some features of dependent personality disorder overlap with those of borderline, histrionic, and avoidant personality disorders, but there are differences as well. For example, both borderline personalities and dependent personalities fear abandonment. However, the borderline reacts with feelings of emptiness or rage if abandonment occurs, whereas the dependent personality reacts initially with submissiveness and appeasement, and if abandonment occurs with an urgent seeking of a new relationship. Moreover, the dependent personality does not have the pattern of intense and stormy relationships that the borderline does. Histrionic and dependent personalities both have strong needs for reassurance and approval. However, the style of the histrionic personality is much more gregarious, flamboyant, and actively demanding of attention, whereas the dependent is more docile and self-effacing. Finally, as already noted, the avoidant and dependent personalities share feelings of inadequacy and hypersensitivity, but the avoidant personality is more socially timid and avoids relationships rather than be rejected, whereas the dependent seeks out relationships with others in spite of the fear of being rejected (Hirschfeld, Shea, & Weise, 1995).

Obsessive-Compulsive Personality Disorder

Perfectionism and an excessive concern with maintaining order characterize those individuals with **obsessive-compulsive personality disorder (OCPD)**. They are also preoccupied with maintaining mental and interpersonal control through careful attention to rules and schedules. They are very careful in what they do so as not to make mistakes, and they will often repeatedly check for possible mistakes. Because the details they are preoccupied with are often trivial, they therefore use their time poorly. This perfectionism is also often quite dysfunctional in that it can result in their never finishing projects. They also tend to be devoted to work to the exclusion of leisure activities and may have difficulty relaxing or doing anything just for fun (Widiger & Frances, 1994).

According to current views, the central feature of people with obsessive-compulsive personality disorder is that they are excessively conscientious, which includes the disposition to be deliberate, disciplined, competent, achievement-striving, and organized as well as quite inflexible about moral or ethical issues (Widiger & Frances, 1994). They may also have difficulty getting rid of old and worn out household items and may be quite stingy or miserly as well. At an interpersonal level, they have difficulty delegating tasks to others and are quite rigid and stubborn. Not surprisingly, other people tend to view obsessive-compulsive personalities as rigid, stiff, and cold.

It was once thought that obsessive-compulsive personality disorder served as a diathesis for full-blown obsessive-compulsive disorder (discussed in Chapter 5). However, this is generally not considered to be the case today (Pfohl & Blum, 1995), although some consider the evidence still to be inconclusive. For example, two studies by Baer and colleagues (1990, 1992) found that only 6 to 16 percent of patients with obsessive-compulsive disorder met the criteria for obsessive-compulsive personality disorder; another more recent study found 30 percent met the criteria for OCPD (Diaferia et al., 1997). These figures would surely be higher if this personality disorder served as a diathesis for obsessive-compulsive disorder (Pollak, 1995). Moreover, reviews of the literature suggest

that about 35 percent of people with obsessive-compulsive disorder have no obsessive-compulsive personality traits whatsoever (Barlow, 1988), and that two other personality disorders—dependent and avoidant—are actually more commonly associated with obsessive-compulsive disorder (Pfohl & Blum, 1995).

To underscore the distinction between these two disorders, recall that with full-blown obsessive-compulsive disorder a person suffers from the persistent intrusion of particular undesired thoughts or images (obsessions) that are a source of extreme anxiety or distress. The anxiety or distress can only be reduced through the performance of compulsive rituals (such as cleaning or checking) and much of the person's life may be absorbed by the time taken to perform these rituals over and over again. By contrast, people with obsessive-compulsive personality disorder have lifestyles characterized by overconscientiousness, inflexibility, and perfectionism, but without the presence of true obsessions or compulsive rituals. Although they may be anxious about getting all their work done in keeping with their exacting standards, they are not anxious about their compulsiveness itself, as individuals with obsessive-compulsive disorder usually are. An example of obsessive-compulsive personality is reflected in the following case.

> **Case Study, Alan, An Obsessive-Compulsive Personality** • Alan appeared to be well suited to his work as a train dispatcher. He was conscientious, perfectionistic, and attended to minute details. However, he was not close to his coworkers and, reportedly, they thought him "off." He would get quite upset if even minor variations to his daily routine occurred. For example, he would become tense and irritable if coworkers did not follow exactly his elaborately constructed schedules and plans. If he became tied up in traffic, he would beat the steering wheel and swear at other drivers for holding him up.
>
> In short, Alan got little pleasure out of life and worried constantly about minor problems. His rigid routines were impossible to maintain, and he often developed tension headaches or stomachaches when he couldn't keep his complicated plans in order. His physician, noting the frequency of his physical complaints and his generally perfectionistic approach to life, referred him for a psychological evaluation. Psychotherapy was recommended to him, although the prognosis for significant behavioral change was considered questionable. He did not follow up on the treatment recommendations because he felt that he could not afford the time away from work.

Some features of obsessive-compulsive personality disorder overlap with some features of narcissistic, anti-

A person with obsessive-compulsive personality disorder is highly perfectionistic, leading to serious problems finishing various projects. They are also excessively devoted to work. In addition, they are quite inflexible about moral and ethical issues and have difficulty delegating tasks to others. They are also inclined to be ungenerous with themselves and others.

social, and schizoid personality disorder, although there are also distinguishing features. For example, individuals with both obsessive-compulsive and narcissistic personality disorder may be highly perfectionistic, but the narcissistic individual is more grandiose and likely to believe he or she has achieved perfection, whereas the obsessive-compulsive personality is often quite self-critical. Individuals with narcissistic and antisocial personality disorder may also share the lack of generosity toward others that characterizes obsessive-compulsive personality, but the former tend to indulge themselves, whereas obsessive-compulsives are equally unwilling to be generous with themselves and others. Finally, both the schizoid and the obsessive-compulsive personality may have a certain amount of formality and social detachment, but only the schizoid personality lacks the capacity for close relationships. The obsessive-compulsive personality has difficulty in interpersonal relationships because of excessive devotion to work and because of difficulty expressing emotions.

Provisional Categories of Personality Disorder in DSM-IV

Passive-Aggressive Personality Disorder One of the most controversial personality disorders is **passive-aggressive personality disorder.** One reason for the controversy over this diagnosis is that empirical support for the reliability and validity of this diagnosis is limited. This is in part because it may be more of a situational reaction than a personality trait, occuring particularly in situations where the person resents being confined and

having to follow various rules and regulations (Widiger & Chat, 1994). Thus, although this disorder was previously included in DSM-III and DSM-III-R, it has been placed in an appendix in DSM-IV, with somewhat new criteria that still need further study before the new conceptualization can be validated (Millon & Radovanov, 1995).

As currently conceptualized, people with passive-aggressive personality disorder show a pervasive pattern of passive resistance to demands in social or work situations. They also show a strong pattern of negativistic attitudes unrelated to any concurrent diagnosis of major depressive disorder or dysthymia. Their passive resistance to demands is shown in many ways, ranging from simple resistance to fulfilling routine tasks, to being sullen or argumentative, or alternating between defiance and submission. They commonly complain of being misunderstood and unappreciated, and at the same time may be highly critical or scornful of authority. They also complain about their personal misfortunes and are envious of others who appear more fortunate.

The passive-aggressive personality pattern is shown in the following case.

> **Case Study, A Passive-Aggressive Psychiatrist •** A 34-year-old psychiatrist is 15 minutes late for his first appointment. He had recently been asked to resign from his job in a mental health center because, according to his boss, he had frequently been late for work and meetings, missed appointments, forgot about assignments, was late with his statistics, refused to follow instructions, and seemed unmotivated. The patient was surprised and resentful—he thought he had been doing a particularly good job under trying circumstances and experienced his boss as excessively obsessive and demanding. Nonetheless, he reported a long-standing pattern of difficulties with authority. . . .
>
> The patient is unhappily married. He complains that his wife does not understand him and is a "nitpicker." She complains that he is unreliable and stubborn. He refuses to do anything around the house and often fails to complete the few tasks he has accepted as within his responsibility. Tax forms are submitted several months late; bills are not paid. The patient is sociable and has considerable charm, but friends generally become annoyed at his unwillingness to go along with the wishes of the group (for example, if a restaurant is not his choice, he may sulk all night or "forget" to bring his wallet. (From Spitzer et al., 1989, pp. 107–108)

In sum, we can see in a passive-aggressive personality a pattern of never confronting a problem situation directly, but rather showing passive resistance through procrastination, forgetfulness, or sulking. These characteristic ways of reacting to problems are frustrating for others, who must deal with the inefficient behavior, and frustrating for the individual because such behavior typically does not productively resolve problems.

Depressive Personality Disorder   A second provisional category in the DSM-IV Appendix is **depressive personality disorder.** People with this disorder show a pattern of depressive cognitions and behaviors that begins by early adulthood and is pervasive in nature. Their usual mood state is one of unhappiness or dejection and they tend to feel inadequate, worthless, or guilty. They tend to be highly self-critical and may be judgmental toward others as well. They also tend to be pessimistic and prone to worry. Although the emphasis here is more on distorted cognitions and interpersonal traits than is true for dysthymic disorder (see Chapter 6), many questions remain about the validity of the distinction between these two diagnoses (Hirshfeld, 1994). In particular, it may not be possible to distinguish early-onset dysthymia from depressive personality disorder. Nevertheless, Klein and colleagues (Klein et al., 1993; Klein & Shih, 1998) have provided preliminary evidence that the depressive personality diagnosis is somewhat distinct and that most patients who receive the diagnosis do not meet the criteria for dysthymia; it appears to be associated with fewer depressive symptoms than dysthymia (see also Hirshfeld, 1994). Thus, it remains possible that the pervasive cognitive traits of pessimism, guilt, and self-criticism seen in depressive personality disorder may not be best characterized as a disorder in mood regulation, which is the way dysthymia is characterized (Hirshfeld, 1994; Widiger & Chat, 1994). However, other questions remain about the overlap between this provisional diagnostic category and other related personality disorders—especially dependent, avoidant, and obsessive-compulsive (Philips et al., 1995).

Overview of Personality Disorders

Aaron Beck and his colleagues have proposed a useful integrative scheme that may highlight some of the commonalties and differences among the personality disorders (Beck & Freeman, 1990; Pretzer & Beck, 1996). In their view people with personality disorders can be characterized on several different dimensions, including the kinds of interpersonal strategies they use. Differing interpersonal strategies include different uses of interpersonal space. For example:

Individuals may move or place themselves against, toward, away from, above, or under others. The dependent moves <u>toward</u> and often <u>below</u> (submissive, subservient). Another "type" <u>stays still</u> and may obstruct others: the passive-aggressive. The narcissists position themselves <u>above</u> others. The compulsive may move <u>above</u> in the interest of control. The schizoid moves <u>away</u>, and the avoidant moves closer and then <u>backs off</u>. The histrionic personalities use the space to <u>draw others</u> toward them. . . . These vectors may be regarded as the visible manifestations of specific interpersonal strategies associated with specific personality disorders. (Beck & Freeman, 1990, p. 40)

Each personality disorder is also characterized by a different set of behavior patterns that are overdeveloped, and another set of behavior patterns that are underdeveloped. In many cases the deficient behaviors are somehow counterparts to the overdeveloped features (Beck & Freeman, 1990; Pretzer & Beck, 1996). These over- and under-developed patterns are illustrated in Table 9.2.

Finally, Beck and colleagues also propose that each personality disorder is characterized by different core dysfunctional beliefs that people with personality disorders have about themselves and the world around them. For example, a woman with avoidant personality disorder is likely to see herself as inept or incompetent, and to view others as potentially critical or demeaning. Her core belief is likely to be "It's terrible to be rejected, put down . . . If people know the real me they will reject me" (Pretzer & Beck, 1996, p. 60). A man with the related dependent personality disorder is also likely to see himself as incompetent, but also as needy and weak, and to view strong others as all-supportive and competent. His core belief is likely to be "[I] need people to survive and be happy" and/or "need a steady flow of support" (Pretzer & Beck, 1996, p. 60). For the dramatic, emotional Cluster B personality disorders, Beck and colleagues propose that people with narcissistic personality disorder see themselves as special and unique; they view others as inferior and seek admiration from them "primarily to document their own grandiosity and preserve their own superior status" (Beck & Freeman, 1990, p. 49). Their core beliefs might include "Because I'm special, I deserve special rules," "I'm above the rules," and "I'm better than others" (Pretzer & Beck, 1996, p. 60). Of the odd or eccentric Cluster A personality disorders, Beck and colleagues propose that people with schizoid personality disorder would tend to view themselves as self-sufficient loners and to view others as intrusive. Their core beliefs might be "I am basically alone" (Beck & Freeman, 1990, p. 51) or "Relationships are messy [and] undesirable" (Pretzer & Beck, 1996, p. 60).

TABLE 9.2 TYPICAL OVERDEVELOPED AND UNDERDEVELOPED STRATEGIES

Personality Disorder	Overdeveloped	Underdeveloped
Obsessive-compulsive	Control	Spontaneity
	Responsibility	Playfulness
Dependent	Help seeking	Self-sufficiency
	Clinging	Mobility
Passive-aggressive	Autonomy	Intimacy
	Resistance	Assertiveness
	Passivity	Activity
	Sabotage	Cooperativeness
Paranoid	Vigilance	Serenity
	Mistrust	Trust
Narcissistic	Self-aggrandizement	Sharing
	Competitiveness	Group identification
Antisocial	Combativeness	Empathy
	Exploitativeness	Reciprocity
	Predation	Social sensitivity
Schizoid	Autonomy	Intimacy
	Isolation	Reciprocity
Avoidant	Social vulnerability	Self-assertion
	Avoidance	Gregariousness
	Inhibition	
Histrionic	Exhibitionism	Reflectiveness
	Expressiveness	Control
	Impressionism	Systematization

Source: From Beck and Freeman (1990), p. 42.

CAUSAL FACTORS IN PERSONALITY DISORDERS

Little is yet known about the causal factors in personality disorders, partly because such disorders have only received consistent attention since DSM-III was published in 1980 and partly because they are less amenable to thorough study. One major problem in studying the causes of personality disorders stems from the high level of comorbidity among them. For example, in a review of four studies, Widiger and colleagues found that 85 percent of patients who qualified for one personality disorder diagnosis also qualified for at least one more, and many qualified for several more (Widiger & Rogers, 1989; Widiger et al., 1991). Even in a nonpatient sample, Zimmerman and Coryell (1989) found that of those with one personality disorder, almost 25 percent had at least one more. This substantial comorbidity adds to the difficulties in studying the causes of these disorders because of the difficulty untangling which causal factors are associated with which personality disorder.

An additional problem is that many people with these disorders are never seen by clinical personnel. Typically, those who do come to the attention of clinicians or legal authorities have already developed a full-blown disorder, so that only *retrospective* study is possible—that is, going back through what records may exist in an effort to reconstruct the chain of events that may have led to the disorder. As we have seen, researchers have more confidence in *prospective* studies, in which groups of people are observed before a disorder appears and followed over a period of time to see which ones develop problems and what causal factors have been present.

Biological Causal Factors

Of possible biological factors, it has been suggested that infants' constitutional reaction tendencies (high or low vitality, behavioral inhibition, and so on) may predispose them to the development of particular personality disorders. Given that most personality traits have been found to be moderately heritable (e.g., Carey & DiLalla, 1994), it is not surprising that there is increasing evidence for genetic contributions to certain personality disorders (Livesley et al., 1994; Nigg & Goldsmith, 1994; Plomin et al., 1997; Siever & Davis, 1991). For example, some research suggests that genetic factors may be important for the development of paranoid personality disorder (Nigg & Goldsmith, 1994), schizotypal personality disorder (Kendler et al., 1991; Nigg & Goldsmith, 1994), borderline personality (Widiger & Trull, 1993), and antisocial personality disorder (Carey, 1997; Gottesman & Goldsmith, 1994).

In addition, some progress is being made in understanding the psychobiological substrate of at least some of the personality disorders (Depue, 1996; Hollander et al., 1994; Siever & Davis, 1991). For example, people with borderline personality disorder appear to be characterized by lowered functioning of the neurotransmitter *serotonin,* which may be why they show impulsive-aggressive behavior as in parasuicidal acts such as cutting their arms with a knife (Figueroa & Silk, 1997; Hollander et al., 1994). Patients with borderline personality disorder may also show disturbances in the regulation of noradrenergic neurotransmitters (the deficits may be in function, receptors, or concentration) that are similar to those seen in chronic stress conditions such as PTSD (see Chapter 4). In particular, their hyperresponsive noradrenergic system may be related to their hypersensitivity to environmental changes (Figueroa & Silk, 1997). In addition, deficits in the dopamine systems may be related to a disposition toward transient psychotic symptoms (Kernberg, 1996). Nevertheless, as with the Axis I disorders, none of the personality disorders is entirely heritable and none can be understood solely from a biological perspective. Thus psychosocial and sociocultural causal factors must also play crucial roles in their origins, and our understanding of these disorders at a psychological level must supplement any understanding of their biological underpinnings. The ultimate goal would be to achieve a biopsychosocial perspective on the origins of each personality disorder, but we are far from that goal today.

Psychological Causal Factors

Early Learning Experiences Among psychological factors, early learning is usually assumed to contribute the most in predisposing a person to develop a personality disorder, yet there is little research to support this belief. A significant number of studies have suggested that abuse and neglect in childhood may be related to the development of certain personality disorders. For example, in what is perhaps the largest and best designed study to date, Zanarini and colleagues (1997) reported on the re-

sults of detailed interviews of over 350 patients with borderline personality disorder and over 100 with other personality disorders (interviewers were blind as to diagnostic status). Patients with borderline personality disorder reported significantly higher rates of abuse than patients with other personality disorders: emotional abuse (73 versus 51 percent), verbal abuse (76 versus 52 percent), physical abuse (59 versus 34 percent), and sexual abuse (61 versus 32 percent), as well as higher rates of emotional withdrawal (55 versus 32 percent). Repeated sexual abuse was usually by someone other than a parent and almost always occurred in conjunction with at least one other type of abuse and neglect. Overall about 90 percent of patients with borderline personality disorder reported some type of childhood abuse and neglect. Although this and many other related studies (e.g., Norden et al., 1995) are suggestive that borderline personality disorder (and perhaps other personality disorders as well) is often associated with early childhood trauma, the studies are not without their shortcomings inasmuch as they rely on retrospective self-reports of individuals who are known for their exaggerated and distorted views of other people (Ruegg & Frances, 1995; Rutter & Maughan, 1997). Moreover, the nature of the stressors involved seems to be somewhat nonspecific (Widiger & Trull, 1993), and although the rates of abuse and neglect may seem rather alarming it must still be remembered that the majority of children who experience early abuse and neglect do not end up with serious personality disorders or psychopathology (Rutter & Maughan, 1997).

The Psychodynamic View Psychodynamic theorists such as Otto Kernberg (1984; 1996) and Heinz Kohut (1977) have also written a great deal in recent years about the origins of several of the personality disorders—most notably borderline, antisocial, histrionic, and narcissistic personality disorders. For example, with regard to narcissistic personality disorder Kohut argues that all children go through a phase of primitive grandiosity during which they think that all events and needs revolve around them. For normal development beyond this phase to occur, according to this view, parents must do some mirroring of the infant's grandiosity. This helps the child develop normal levels of self-confidence. So for example, Kohut argued "However grave the blows may be to which the child's grandiosity is exposed by the realities of life, the proud smile of the parents will keep alive a bit of the original omnipotence, to be retained as the nucleus of the self-confidence and inner security about one's worth that sustain the healthy person throughout his life" (Kohut &

Otto Kernberg (b. 1928) is an influential contemporary psychoanalytic theorist who has written a great deal about borderline and narcissistic personality disorders.

Heinz Kohut (1913-1981), another contemporary psychoanalytic thinker, theorized that poor parenting can cause narcissistic personality disorder by failing to build a child's normal self-confidence.

Wolff, 1978, p. 182; from Widiger & Trull, 1993). Kohut further proposed that narcissistic personality disorder is likely to develop if parents are neglectful, devaluing, or unempathetic to the child; this individual will be perpetually searching for affirmation of this idealized and grandiose sense of self. Although this theory has been very influential among psychodynamic clinicians, it unfortunately has no real empirical support. And indeed it is interesting to note that Theodore Millon—a personality disorder researcher from the social learning tradition of Bandura—has argued quite the opposite. He believes that narcissistic personality disorder comes from parental overvaluation (Millon & Davis, 1996). For example, he has proposed that "these parents pamper and indulge their youngsters in ways that teach them that their every wish is a command, that they can receive without getting in return, and that they deserve prominence without even minimal effort" (Millon, 1981, p. 175; from Widiger & Trull, 1993). That theorists from these two quite different traditions (psychoanalytic and social learning) can come to such opposite conclusions illustrates the current poverty of knowledge regarding particular antecedents for these disorders. The only disorder for which there is a good deal of research on causal factors is antisocial personality disorder, which is discussed at length below.

Another current variant on psychodynamic thinking about the origins of personality disorders stems from the interpersonal approach to psychopathology and psychotherapy (see Chapter 3). Benjamin's (1996a, 1996b)

sophisticated approach to understanding the psychopathology of both Axis I and Axis II personality disorders provides the most empirically sound approach to understanding how different interpersonal and intrapsychic factors are involved in the origins of different disorders. This approach quantifies a patient's interpersonal and intrapsychic aspects of relationships and is beginning to yield important insights not only about the probable origins of personality disorders but also about how best to treat them.

Sociocultural Causal Factors

Sociocultural factors contributing to personality disorders are even less well defined. We do know that the incidence and form of psychopathology in general vary somewhat with time and place and the same may be true for personality disorders, although evidence on this point is sketchy at best. Moreover, some clinicians believe that personality disorders have increased in American society in recent years. If this claim is true, we can expect to find the increase related to changes in our culture's general priorities and activities. Is our emphasis on impulse gratification, instant solutions, and pain-free benefits leading more people to develop the self-centered lifestyles that we see in more extreme forms in the personality disorders? Only further research can clarify this issue, which will be discussed further at the end of the antisocial personality disorder section.

TREATMENTS AND OUTCOMES

Personality disorders seem especially resistant to therapy. Valliant (1987) made this observation:

> Certainly, treating personality disorder is not easy. Indeed, we often identify personality disorders precisely because they do not respond to treatment. Due to defects in genes, socialization, or maturation, personality-disordered individuals have difficulty learning what society wishes to teach them. . . . Individuals with personality disorder need care that is very similar to the care required by adolescents. Indeed, adolescents do not need therapy at all: they need time and space to internalize the valuable facets of their parents and their society. . . . Like adolescents, individuals with personality disorders need opportunities to internalize fresh role models and to make peace with the imperfect familial figures who are already within. (p. 154)

In addition, it is well known that people who have both an Axis I disorder and a personality disorder do not, on average, do as well in treatment for their Axis I disorders as do patients without comorbid personality disorders, especially if the treatment approach is not modified to account for the personality disorder (Pretzer & Beck, 1996). That is, having one or more personality disorders often makes it harder to treat disorders such as anxiety and depressive disorders, in part because people with personality disorders, almost by definition, have rigid ingrained personality traits that often make them resist doing the things that would help improve their Axis I condition. Other reasons that personality disorders may complicate treatment of Axis I conditions is that people with personality disorders often have difficulties establishing good therapeutic relationships with their therapist (see Chapter 17 for the importance of this) and that people with personality disorders are more likely to terminate treatment prematurely (van Velzen & Emmelkamp, 1996).

In many cases, people with personality disorders who are seen clinically are there as part of another person's treatment—as, for example, in couples counseling, where a partner identified as the "patient" has a spouse with a personality disorder. Or a child referred to a child guidance center may have a parent with a personality disorder. In these cases, of course, the problems of the so-called patient may be due in no small measure to the great strain caused by the family member with a personality disorder. A narcissistic father, who is so self-centered and demanding of attention from others that family relationships are constantly strained, leaves little room for small children to grow into self-respecting adults. Likewise, a mother with dependent personality disorder, whose typical manner of responding to others is to be highly submissive and clinging and fearful of separation, may create an unhealthy family atmosphere that distorts a child's development.

A child subjected to such extreme, inescapable, and often irrational behavior on the part of one or both parents may become the weak link that breaks, bringing the family into therapy. Many a child or family therapist has quickly concluded after seeing a child in a family context that psychological attention, if it is to be effective at all, must be focused on the parental relationships. The following case clearly illustrates this problem.

> **Case Study, The Child of a Father with Paranoid Personality Disorder** • Mrs. A. brought her 7-year-old son, Christopher, to a mental health center for treatment because he was fearful of going out and recently had been having bad nightmares. Mrs. A. sought help at the recommendation of the school social worker after Chris refused to return to school. She voiced a great deal of concern for Chris and agreed to cooperate in the treatment by attending parent effectiveness training sessions. However, she seemed quite reluctant to talk about getting her husband involved in the treatment. After much encouragement, she agreed to try to bring him to the next session, but he adamantly refused to participate. Mrs. A described him as a "very proud and strong-willed man" who was quite suspicious of other people. She felt that he might be afraid people would blame him for Chris's problems. She reported that he had been having a lot of problems lately—he had seemed quite bitter and resentful over some local political issues and tended to blame others (particularly minorities) for his problems. He refused to come to the clinic because he "doesn't like social workers."
>
> After several sessions of therapy, Mrs. A. confessed to her therapist that her husband's rigid and suspicious behavior was disrupting the family. He would often come home from work and accuse her of, for example, "talking with Jewish men." He was a domineering person who set strict house rules and enforced them with loud threats and intimidation. Both Mrs. A. and Chris were fearful of his tyrannical demands, but his suspicious nature made it difficult for them to explain anything to him. Mrs. A. also felt a great deal of sympathy for her husband because she felt that deep down inside he was frightened; she reported that he kept numerous guns around the house and several locks on the doors for protection against outsiders, whom he feared. Thus it became clear that her husband had at least certain features of paranoid personality disorder and that this was creating a great deal of difficulty for the family.

Because many people with personality disorders—especially those from the odd/eccentric Cluster A and the erratic/dramatic Cluster B—enter treatment only at someone else's insistence, they often do not believe that they need to change. Consequently people with such personality disorders typically put the responsibility for treatment on others and are adept at avoiding the focus of therapy themselves. In addition, the difficulties they have in forming and maintaining good relationships generally tend to make a therapeutic relationship fragile or stormy. For those from the erratic/dramatic Cluster B, the pattern of acting out, typical in their other relationships, is carried into the therapy situation, and instead of dealing with their problems at the verbal level, they may become angry at their therapist and loudly disrupt the sessions. These patients may also behave in socially inappropriate ways outside the sessions to show their therapist that the therapy is not working.

When questioned about such behavior, these people often drop out of treatment or become even more entrenched defending their inappropriate behavior. In some cases, however, confrontation can be quite effective. Individuals who become very involved in group therapy, or who are sufficiently "hooked" into couples therapy may not flee the sessions when their behavior comes under scrutiny, because the intense feedback from peers or spouse often is more acceptable than confrontation by a therapist in individual treatment (Gurman & Kniskern, 1978; Lubin, 1976).

Adapting Therapeutic Techniques to Specific Personality Disorders

In some situations, therapeutic techniques must be modified. For example, recognizing that traditional individual psychotherapy tends to encourage dependency in people already too dependent (such as in dependent, histrionic, and borderline personality disorders), it is often useful to develop treatment strategies specifically aimed at altering a dependent person's basic lifestyle instead of fostering it. Patients from the anxious/fearful Cluster C, such as dependent and avoidant personalities, may be hypersensitive to any perceived criticism from the therapist and may quit prematurely for such reasons. In such cases the therapist has to be extremely careful to make sure that this does not happen. One approach is to ask the patient for feedback about the therapist's behavior and attitude at the end of each session day (e.g, patients can be asked to rate their therapists on qualities such as listening well, explaining homework clearly, etc.) (Beck & Freeman, 1990). By letting the patient give feedback and discussing possible changes for future sessions, the therapist appears nondefensive and yet also encourages and reinforces assertive criticism on the part of the patient.

Such specific therapeutic techniques are a central part of the relatively new cognitive approach to personality disorders (see again Table 9.2) (Beck & Freeman, 1990; Pretzer & Beck, 1996). The cognitive approach assumes that the dysfunctional feelings and behavior associated with the personality disorders are largely the result of schemas that tend to produce consistently biased judgments, as well as tendencies to make cognitive errors in many types of situations. Schemas, as we saw in Chapter 3, involve specific rules that govern information processing and behavior. They are of many types—for example, we have personal, familial, cultural, religious, gender, and occupational schemas. Changing the underlying dysfunctional schemas is at the heart of cognitive therapy for personality disorders, and doing so is particularly difficult because these schemas are held in place by behavioral, cognitive, and emotional elements. Nevertheless, through the usual cognitive techniques of monitoring automatic thoughts, challenging faulty logic, and assigning behavioral tasks that hopefully help to challenge the patient's dysfunctional assumptions and beliefs, cognitive therapists may have made a significant step in advancing treatment for personality disorders. At this point, for most disorders there are only case studies or uncontrolled clinical studies, rather than controlled treatment studies, but the results do seem promising (Crits-Christoph, 1998; Pretzer & Beck, 1996).

In general, therapy for people with severe personality disorders may be more effective in situations where acting-out behavior can be constrained. Outpatient treatment is often not promising because severe acting out can disrupt the course of treatment. In addition, many patients with borderline personality disorder are hospitalized for safety reasons because of their frequent suicidal behavior (Silk et al., 1994; Norton & Hinshelwood, 1996).

Treating Borderline Personality Disorder

Of all the personality disorders there has probably been more attention paid to the treatment of borderline personality disorder, in part because treatment prognosis (probable outcome) for borderline personality disorder patients is typically considered to be guarded because of their long-standing problems and extreme instability. Because borderline patients are usually difficult to manage due to their behavioral problems and acting out tendencies, treatment often involves a judicious use of both psychological and biological treatment methods (Gitlin, 1996). The use of drugs is especially controversial with this disorder because it is so frequently associated with suicidal behavior. Nevertheless, several reviews of the evidence for psychopharmacological treatment of borderline personality disorder have concluded that low doses of antipsychotic medication (see Chapter 16) have modest but significant effects that are broad-based; that is, patients show some improvement in depression, anxiety, suicidality, rejection sensitivity, and psychotic symptoms (Gitlin, 1996; Woo-Ming & Siever, 1998). These reviews also concluded that benzodiazepines (anxiolytics) and tricylic antidepressants are generally ineffective in the treatment of borderline personality disorder, but that antidepressant drugs from the same class as Prozac (SSRIs) are promising, as are MAO inhibitors (see Chapters 6 and 16). Lithium may also be useful in reducing irritability, suicidality and angry behavior (Woo-Ming & Siever, 1998). In general, the drugs are used as an adjunct to psychological treatment.

Psychosocial Treatments Traditional psychosocial treatments for borderline personality disorder involve variants of psychodynamic psychotherapy, which is adapted for the particular problems of persons with this disorder. For example, Kernberg (1985, 1996) has developed a form of psychodynamic psychotherapy for borderline personality disorder that is much more directive than is typical psychodynamic treatment. The primary goal of treatment is seen as strengthening the weak egos of these individuals, with a particular focus on their primary defense mechanism of *splitting,* which leads them to black-and-white, all-or-none thinking, as well as to rapid shifts in their reactions to other people (including the therapist) as "all good" or "all bad." Although this treatment can be effective in some cases, it is expensive and time-consuming (often lasting a good number of years) and is only beginning to be subjected to controlled research.

Probably the most promising treatment for borderline personality disorder is Marsha Linehan's (1987, 1993) recently developed *dialectical behavior therapy,* which is a kind of cognitive behavior therapy specifically designed for treating borderline personality disorder. Linehan believes that it is the inability to tolerate strong states of negative affect that is central to this disorder, and one of the primary goals of treatment is to encourage patients to accept this negative affect without engaging in self-destructive or other maladaptive behaviors. Accordingly, she has developed a problem-focused treatment based on a clear hierarchy of goals: (1) decreasing suicidal behavior; (2) decreasing behaviors that interfere with therapy, such as missing sessions, lying, and getting hospitalized; (3) decreasing escapist behaviors that interfere with a stable lifestyle, such as substance abuse; (4) increasing behavioral skills in order to regulate emotions,

to increase interpersonal skills, and to increase tolerance for distress; and (5) other goals the patient chooses. Suicidal behaviors are the first target "simply because psychotherapy is not effective with dead patients" (Linehan, 1987, p. 329) and because this indicates these behaviors are taken very seriously.

Dialectical behavior therapy combines individual and group components, with the group setting focusing more on the skills training for interpersonal skills, emotion regulation, and stress tolerance. This all occurs in the presence of a therapist who is taught to accept the patient for who he or she is (almost a client-centered focus), in spite of the very behaviors on the part of the patients that make it so difficult to do so (such as bursts of rage, suicidal behaviors, missing appointments, etc.). Linehan, like Carl Rogers, makes a clear distinction between *accepting* the patient for who he or she is, and *approving* of the patient's behavior. For example, a therapist cannot approve of self-mutilation, but he or she should indicate acceptance of that as part of a patient's problem.

Efficacy Studies Results from one important controlled study using this form of treatment have been very encouraging (Linehan et al., 1991; Linehan, Heard, & Armstrong, 1993; Linehan et al., 1994). The researchers compared borderline patients who received dialectical behavior therapy with patients receiving treatment as usual in the community over a one-year treatment period, followed by a one-year follow-up period. Patients who received dialectical behavior therapy showed greater reduction in self-destructive and suicidal behaviors, as well as in levels of anger, than did those in the treatment-as-usual group. The patients who received dialectical behavior therapy were also more likely to stay in treatment and to require fewer days of hospitalization. At follow-up they were also doing better occupationally and were rated as better adjusted in terms of interpersonal and emotional regulation skills than the control group. Although these results may seem modest in some ways, they are considered extraordinary by most therapists who work with this population. Many psychodynamic therapists are incorporating important components of this treatment into their own treatment of persons with borderline personality.

Treating Other Personality Disorders

Treating Other Cluster A and B Disorders Treatment of schizotypal personality disorder is not, so far, as promising as some of the recent advances that have been made in the treatment of borderline personality disorder. For example, Gitlin (1996) summarized evidence showing that low doses of antipsychotic drugs may result in modest improvements, but no treatment has yet produced anything approaching a cure for most people with this disorder (see also Woo-Ming & Siever, 1998). Other than uncontrolled studies or single cases, no systematic studies of treating people with either paranoid or schizoid disorder exist (Gitlin, 1996; Pretzer & Beck, 1996). There is also little other than uncontrolled studies or singles cases documenting the effectiveness of either cognitive therapy or medication for the treatment of narcissistic, antisocial, or histrionic personality disorders (Gitlin 1996; Pretzer & Beck, 1996).

Treating Cluster C Disorders Treatment of some of the personality disorders from Cluster C, such as dependent and avoidant personality disorder, has not been extensively studied but appears more promising than for many of those from Clusters A and B. For example, Mehlum and colleagues (1991) compared the outcome of inpatient treatment two to five years later for patients with borderline, schizotypal, dependent, and avoidant personality disorders. Those with Cluster C personality disorders showed marked symptom reduction and good overall outcome; patients with borderline personality disorder showed only moderate symptom reduction and fair overall outcome; and those with schizotypal personality disorder also showed moderate symptom reduction but poor overall outcome. In addition, Winston and colleagues (1994) found significant improvement in patients with Cluster C disorders using a form of short-term psychotherapy that is active and confrontational (see also Pretzer & Beck, 1996). Finally, there is also some evidence that antidepressants that are MAO inhibitors may sometimes help in the treatment of avoidant personality disorder given that it is almost always comorbid with generalized social phobia, which can also be treated with MAO inhibitors (Gitlin, 1996; Woo-Ming & Siever, 1998). Finally, there is suggestive evidence from case studies that several other classes of antidepressants may be useful in treating avoidant personality disorder (Woo-Ming & Siever, 1998).

ANTISOCIAL PERSONALITY AND PSYCHOPATHY

As we have seen, the outstanding characteristics of people with antisocial personality disorder (ASPD) is their tendency to persistently disregard and violate the rights of others. They do this through a combination of deceitful, aggressive, or antisocial behavior, with little or no sign of remorse. Basically, these people have a lifelong pattern of unsocialized and irresponsible behavior, with little regard for safety—either their own or that of others. These characteristics bring them into repeated conflict with society.

Only individuals 18 or over are diagnosed as antisocial personalities. According to DSM-IV, this diagnosis is made if the following criteria are met:

- *At least three behavioral problems occurring after age 15,* such as repeatedly performing acts that are grounds for arrest, repeated deceitfulness, impulsivity or failure to plan for the future, irritability and aggressiveness, disregard for safety, consistent irresponsibility in work or financial matters, and lack of remorse.

- *At least three instances of deviant behavior before age 15,* such as aggression toward people or animals, destruction of property, deceitfulness or theft, and serious violation of rules (symptoms of conduct disorder—see Chapter 14).

- *The antisocial behavior is not a symptom of another mental disorder such as schizophrenia or a manic episode.*

Psychopathy and ASPD

The use of the term *antisocial personality disorder* dates back only to DSM-III in 1980, but many of the central features of this disorder have long been labeled **psychopathy** or *sociopathy.* Although several investigators identified the syndrome in the nineteenth century under such labels as "moral insanity" (Prichard, 1835), psychopathy was first carefully described by Cleckley (1941, 1982) in the 1940s. In addition to the defining features of antisocial personality in DSM-III and DSM-IV, psychopathy also includes such traits as lack of empathy, inflated and arrogant self-appraisal, and glib and superficial charm. With its strong emphasis on behavioral criteria that can be measured reasonably objectively, DSM-III and IV have broken from the tradition of psychopathy researchers, in an attempt to increase the reliability of the diagnosis (the level of agreement of clinicians on the diagnosis). However, much less attention has been paid to its validity—that is, whether it measures a meaningful construct and whether that construct is the same as psychopathy.

Two Dimensions of Psychopathy Research over the past 20 years by Robert Hare and his colleagues suggests that ASPD and psychopathy are related but differ in significant ways. Hare (1980, 1991; Hart & Hare, 1997) developed a 20-item Psychopathy Checklist as a way for clinicians and researchers to diagnose psychopathy based on the Cleckley criteria. Extensive research with this checklist has shown that there are two related but separable dimensions of psychopathy, with each predicting different types of behavior. The first dimension involves the affective and interpersonal core of the disorder and reflects traits such as lack of remorse, callousness, selfishness, and an exploitative use of others. The second dimension reflects behavior—the aspects of psychopathy involving an antisocial, impulsive, and socially deviant lifestyle. The second dimension is much more closely related to the DSM-III and DSM-IV diagnosis of antisocial personality disorder than is the first dimension (Hare, Hart, & Harpur, 1991; Hart & Hare 1997). Not surprisingly, therefore, when comparisons have been made in prison settings of what percentage of prison inmates qualify for a diagnosis of psychopathy versus antisocial personality disorder, it is typically found that a higher percentage qualify for ASPD than for psychopathy. That is, a significant number of the inmates show the antisocial, deviant, and aggressive behaviors that result in their meeting the criteria for a diagnosis of antisocial personality disorder, but not enough of the selfish, callous, and exploitative behaviors to qualify for a diagnosis of psychopathy. The prevalence of antisocial personality disorder in the general population is estimated to be about 3 percent for males and about 1 percent for females based on several large epidemiological studies (American Psychiatric Association, 1994). There are no epidemiological studies estimating the prevalence of psychopathy as diagnosed by Hare's Psychopathy Checklist.

An additional concern among researchers is that the current conceptualization of antisocial personality disorder may not include what may be a substantial segment of society who show many of the features of the first affective and interpersonal dimension of psychopathy but not as many features of the second antisocial dimension, or at least few enough that they do not get into trouble with the law.

These issues remain highly controversial. Although there was considerable discussion about expanding the DSM-IV criteria for antisocial personality disorder to include more of the traditional affective and interpersonal features of psychopathy, a conservative approach was taken and such changes were not made (Widiger & Corbit, 1995). DSM-IV does note that in prison and forensic settings, where by definition we are dealing with criminals (or alleged criminals) who have engaged in antisocial behavior, psychopathic traits of lack of empathy or remorse, and glib and superficial charm, may be useful

in making more valid diagnoses than relying on antisocial behavioral criteria alone. In addition, many researchers are likely to continue studying the Cleckley/Hare psychopathy diagnosis rather than the DSM-IV diagnosis of antisocial personality disorder. This is both because of the long and rich research tradition on psychopathy and because the psychopathy diagnosis has been shown to be a better predictor of a variety of important facets of criminal behavior than is the antisocial personality disorder diagnosis. Overall, a diagnosis of psychopathy appears to be the single best predictor we have of violence (Hart, 1998; Hart & Hare, 1997). Moreover, there is also some evidence that violent psychopaths may be more likely than violent nonpsychopaths to show instrumental preplanned, goal-oriented violent offenses, relative to reactive aggression that occurs out of hostility in response to some provocation of perceived threat (Cornell et al., 1996).

The controversy over the use of a psychopathy diagnosis or a diagnosis of antisocial personality disorder is not likely to be solved soon, and unfortunately different researchers in this area make different choices, leading to some confusion when trying to interpret the research on causal factors. In the sections that follow we will attempt to be clear which diagnostic category was being used in different studies, because the causal factors may well not be identical.

Whichever diagnosis is used, individuals with antisocial personality disorder or with psychopathy include a mixed group of individuals: unprincipled business professionals, high-pressure evangelists, crooked politicians, impostors, drug pushers, and assorted criminals. Few of these people find their way into community clinics or mental hospitals. A larger number are confined in jail, but as already noted, a history of repeated legal or social offenses is certainly not sufficient justification for assuming that an individual is psychopathic or has antisocial personality disorder. It is believed that a large number of psychopathic individuals manage to stay out of correctional institutions, although they tend to be in constant conflict with authority (see Highlight 9.1).

The Clinical Picture in Antisocial Personality and Psychopathy

Often charming, spontaneous, and likable on first acquaintance, psychopaths and antisocial personalities are deceitful and manipulative, callously using others to achieve their own ends. Often they seem to live in a series of present moments, without consideration for the past or future. The following example is illustrative.

Wanted: Everyday Psychopaths

Most of antisocial personalities have been conducted on institutionalized persons, leaving us ignorant about the large number who never get caught. Widom (1977) tried an ingenious approach for reaching this large group. She ran advertisements in the local newspapers which read:

> Are you adventurous? Psychologist studying adventurous, carefree people who've led exciting, impulsive lives. If you're the kind of person who'd do almost anything for a dare and want to participate in a paid experiment, send name, address, phone, and short biography proving how interesting you are to. . . . (p. 675)

Widom had hoped to attract psychopathic individuals and apparently did just that. When given a battery of tests, those who responded turned out to be similar in personality makeup to institutionalized psychopathic individuals. Although she did not go further than a personality assessment of these individuals, her method suggests a way of making contact with samples of uninstitutionalized psychopaths.

Since Widom's study, little has been done to improve our understanding of noninstitutionalized psychopaths (other than some studies in analogue populations that differ in many ways). A major stumbling block has been the need for a test to assess psychopathy in such populations given that the PCL was designed for institutionalized populations. Fortunately, a self-report instrument has been developed recently specifically to help assess and study psychopathy in noncriminal populations (Lilienfeld & Andrews, 1996). It appears to have good psychometric properties and should be useful in further research on this understudied group of individuals. ■

Case Study, Two Psychopaths' Idea of a Practical Joke
• Two 18-year-old youths went to visit a teenager at her home. Finding no one there, they broke into the house, damaged a number of valuable paintings and other furnishings, and stole a quantity of liquor and a television set. They sold the TV to a mutual friend for a small sum of money. On their apprehension by the police, they at first denied the entire venture and then later insisted that it was all a "practical joke." They did not consider their behavior particularly inappropriate, nor did they think any sort of restitution for damage was called for.

Also included in the general category of antisocial and psychopathic individuals are hostile people who are prone to acting out impulses in remorseless and often senseless violence. In other cases, antisocial or psychopathic persons show periods of reliability and are capable of assuming responsibility and pursuing long-range goals, but they do so in unethical ways with a complete lack of consideration for the rights and well-being of others.

To fill in the clinical picture, let us begin by summarizing characteristics that psychopaths and antisocial personalities tend to share. We will then describe a case that illustrates the wide range of behavioral patterns that may be involved. Although all the characteristics examined in the following sections are not usually found in a particular case, they are typical of psychopaths as described by Cleckley (1941, 1982). Many people with antisocial personality disorder also share at least a subset of these characteristics, although they are not all criteria for the diagnosis in DSM-IV.

Inadequate Conscience Development   Psychopaths appear unable to understand and accept ethical values except on a verbal level. They glibly claim to adhere to high moral standards that have no apparent connection with their behavior. In short, their conscience development is severely retarded or nonexistent, although their intellectual development is typically normal. Nevertheless, intelligence is one trait that has different relationships with the two dimensions of psychopathy. The first dimension, having to do with selfish, callous, exploitative personality features, is generally unrelated to intelligence; but the second dimension, associated with chronic antisocial behavior, is negatively related to intelligence at least among criminal psychopaths and children with conduct disorder (Carey & Goldman, 1997; Moffitt, 1993b; Frick, 1998). Indeed, there is some evidence that intelligence seems to serve as a protective factor for adolescents who are at risk for psychopathy or antisocial personality in adulthood (Hawkins, Arthur, & Olson, 1997). For example, several studies found that many adolescents with conduct disorder who are known to be predisposed to antisocial personality or psychopathy never get involved in criminal behavior because they are positively influenced by schooling. Thus they presumably focus their energies on more socially accepted behaviors (e.g., White, Moffitt, & Silva, 1989).

Psychopaths tend to "act out" tensions and problems rather than worry them out. Their apparent lack of anxiety and guilt, combined with the appearance of sincerity and candor, may enable them to avoid suspicion and detection for stealing and other illegal activities. They often show contempt for those they are able to take advantage of—their "marks."

Irresponsible and Impulsive Behavior Psychopaths generally have a callous disregard for the rights, needs, and well-being of others. They have learned to take rather than earn what they want. Prone to thrill seeking and deviant and unconventional behavior, they often break the law impulsively and without regard for the consequences. They seldom forgo immediate pleasure for future gains and long-range goals. They live in the present, without realistically considering either past or future. External reality is used for immediate personal gratification. Unable to endure routine or to shoulder responsibility, they are often unable to hold a steady job.

Many studies have shown that antisocial personalities and perhaps psychopaths have high rates of alcoholism and other substance abuse-dependence disorders (e.g., Cloninger, Bayon, & Przybeck, 1997; Sher & Trull, 1994). In examining the relationship of substance abuse to the two different dimensions of psychopathy assessed by Hare's Psychopathy Checklist, Smith and Newman (1990) found that substance abuse was related only to the dimension reflecting antisocial deviant behavior, not to the dimension reflecting egocentric, callous, and exploitative personality traits. A more recent quantitative review also confirms that alcohol abuse is related to the antisocial deviant behavior dimension of psychopathy, not to the interpersonal and affective dimension (Hemphill, Hart, & Hare, 1994).

The relationship between antisocial behavior and substance abuse is sufficiently strong that some have questioned whether there may be a common factor lead-ing to both alcoholism and antisocial personality. Studies of genetic factors involved in the predisposition to antisocial personality and to alcoholism are inconsistent, with some supporting the idea that the two disorders are genetically independent and others suggesting that there is at least some genetic involvement in their high level of comorbidity (Carey & Goldman, 1997; Sher & Trull, 1994; Sutker, Bugg, & West, 1993).

Rejection of Authority Psychopaths behave as if social regulations do not apply to them: They do not play by the rules of the game. Frequently they have a history of difficulties with educational and law enforcement authorities. Yet although they often drift into criminal activities, they are not typically calculating, professional criminals. Despite the difficulties they get into and the punishments they may receive, they go on behaving as if they are immune from the consequences of their actions.

Ability to Impress and Exploit Others Often psychopaths are charming and likable, with a disarming manner that easily wins friends. Typically, they have a good sense of humor and an optimistic outlook. Although frequent liars, they usually will seem sincerely sorry if caught in a lie and promise to make amends—but will not do so. They seem to have good insight into other people's needs and weaknesses and are adept at exploiting them. For example, many psychopaths engage in unethical sales schemes in which they use their charm and the confidence they inspire in others to make "easy money." They readily find excuses and rationalizations for their antisocial conduct, typically projecting the blame onto someone else. Thus they are often able to convince other people—as well as themselves—that they are free of fault.

Inability to Maintain Good Relationships Although initially able to win the liking and friendship of other people, psychopaths are seldom able to keep close friends. Irresponsible and egocentric, they are usually cynical, unsympathetic, ungrateful, and remorseless in their dealings. They seemingly cannot understand love in others or give it in return. Psychopaths pose a menace not only to chance acquaintances but also to their family and friends. Violence toward family members is common. Manipulative and exploitative in sexual relationships, psychopaths are irresponsible and unfaithful mates. Although they often promise to change, they rarely do so for long.

Serial killer Ted Bundy exhibited antisocial behavior at its most extreme and dangerous. He showed the classic psychopathic traits of good looks, charm, and intelligence. But he was also highly manipulative and showed a total lack of remorse for his victims. Bundy's clean-cut image, which he used to get close to his victims—all young women whom he sexually abused and then murdered—was so convincing as to be chilling when the magnitude of his acts became apparent. Bundy was executed in Florida in 1989.

Hare, who has conducted more research on psychopathy than any other individual, recently summarized the prototypic psychopath in the following manner:

Conceptualizing psychopaths as remorseless predators helped me to make sense of what often appears to be senseless behavior. These are individuals who, lacking in conscience and feelings for others, find it easy to use charm, manipulation, intimidation, and violence to control others and to satisfy their own social needs. They cold-bloodedly take what they want and do as they please, violating social norms and expectations without the slightest sense of guilt or regret. Their depredations affect virtually everyone at one time or another, because they form a significant proportion of persistent criminals, drug dealers, spouse and child abusers, swindlers and con men. . . . They are well represented in the business and corporate world, particu-

larly during chaotic restructuring, where the rules and their enforcement are lax and accountability is difficult to determine (Babiak, 1995). Many psychopaths emerge as "patriots" and "saviors" in societies experiencing social, economic, and political upheaval (e.g., Rawanda, the former Yugoslavia, and the former Soviet Union). They wrap themselves in the flag, and enrich themselves by callously exploiting ethnic, cultural, or racial tensions and grievances. (1998b, pp. 128–129)

Patterns of Behavior Psychopathy is illustrated in the following classic case study published by Hare (1970).

Case Study, A Psychopath in Action • Donald S., 30 years old, has just completed a three-year prison term for fraud, bigamy, false pretenses, and escaping lawful custody. The circumstances leading up to these offenses are interesting and consistent with his past behavior. With less than a month left to serve on an earlier 18-month term for fraud, he faked illness and escaped from the prison hospital. During the ten months of freedom that followed, he engaged in a variety of illegal enterprises; the activity that resulted in his recapture was typical of his method of operation. By passing himself off as the "field executive" of an international philanthropic foundation, he was able to enlist the aid of several religious organizations in a fund-raising campaign. The campaign moved slowly at first, and in an attempt to speed things up, he arranged an interview with the local TV station. His performance during the interview was so impressive that funds started to pour in. However, unfortunately for Donald, the interview was also carried on a national news network. He was recognized and quickly arrested. During the ensuing trial it became evident that he experienced no sense of wrongdoing for his activities. He maintained, for example, that his passionate plea for funds "primed the pump"—that is, induced people to give to other charities as well as to the one he professed to represent. At the same time, he stated that most donations to charity are made by those who feel guilty about something and who therefore deserve to be bilked. This ability to rationalize his behavior and his lack of self-criticism were also evident in his attempts to solicit aid from the very people he had misled. Perhaps it is a tribute to his persuasiveness that a number of individuals actually did come to his support. During his three-year prison term, Donald spent much time searching for legal loopholes and writing to outside authorities, including local lawyers, the Prime Minister of Canada, and a Canadian representative to the United Nations. In each case he verbally attacked them for representing the authority and injustice responsible for his predicament. At the same time he requested them to intercede on his behalf and in the name of the justice they professed to represent.

While in prison he was used as a subject in some of the author's research. On his release he applied for admission to a university and, by way of reference, told the registrar that he had been one of the author's research colleagues! Several months later the author received a letter from him requesting a letter of recommendation on behalf of Donald's application for a job.

Background. Donald was the youngest of three boys born to middle-class parents. Both of his brothers led normal, productive lives. His father spent a great deal of time with his business; when he was home he tended to be moody and to drink heavily when things were not going right. Donald's mother was a gentle, timid woman who tried to please her husband and to maintain a semblance of family harmony. When she discovered her children engaged in some mischief, she would threaten to tell their father. However, she seldom carried out these threats because she did not want to disturb her husband and because his reactions were likely to be dependent on his mood at the time; on some occasions he would fly into a rage and beat the children and on others he would administer a verbal reprimand, sometimes mild and sometimes severe.

By all accounts Donald was considered a willful and difficult child. When his desire for candy or toys was frustrated he would begin with a show of affection, and if this failed he would throw a temper tantrum; the latter was seldom necessary because his angelic appearance and artful ways usually got him what he wanted. Similar tactics were used to avoid punishment for his numerous misdeeds. At first he would attempt to cover up with an elaborate facade of lies, often shifting the blame to his brothers. If this did not work, he would give a convincing display of remorse and contrition. When punishment was unavoidable he would become sullenly defiant, regarding it as an unjustifiable tax on his pleasures.

Although he was obviously very intelligent, his school years were academically undistinguished. He was restless, easily bored, and frequently truant. His behavior in the presence of the teacher or some other authority was usually quite good, but when he was on his own he generally got himself or others into trouble. Although he was often suspected of being the culprit, he was adept at talking his way out of difficulty.

Donald's misbehavior as a child took many forms including lying, cheating, petty theft, and the bullying of smaller children. As he grew older he became more and more interested in sex, gambling, and alcohol. When he was 14 he made crude sexual advances toward a younger girl, and when she threatened to tell her parents he locked her in a shed. It was about 16 hours before she was found. Donald at first denied knowledge of the incident, later stating that she had seduced him and that the door must have locked itself. He expressed no concern for the anguish experienced by the girl and her parents . . . His parents were able to prevent charges being brought against him. Nevertheless, incidents of this sort were becoming more frequent and, in an attempt to prevent further embarrassment to the family, he was sent away to a private boarding school. . . .

A Ladies' Man. When he was 17, Donald left the boarding school, forged his father's name to a large check, and spent about a year traveling around the world. He apparently lived well, using a combination of charm, physical attractiveness, and false pretenses to finance his way. During subsequent years he held a succession of jobs, never . . . for more than a few months. Throughout this period he was charged with a variety of crimes, including theft, drunkenness in a public place, assault, and many traffic violations. In most cases he was either fined or given a light sentence.

His sexual experiences were frequent, casual, and callous. When he was 22 he married a 41-year-old woman whom he had met in a bar. Several other marriages followed, all bigamous. In each case the pattern was the same: he would marry someone on impulse, let her support him for several months, and then leave. One marriage was particularly interesting. After being charged with fraud Donald was sent to a psychiatric institution for a period of observation. While there he came to the attention of a female member of the professional staff. His charm, physical attractiveness, and convincing promises to reform led her to intervene on his behalf. He was given a suspended sentence and they were married a week later. At first things went reasonably well, but when she refused to pay some of his gambling debts he forged her name to a check and left. He was soon caught and given an 18-month prison term. . . . He escaped with less than a month left to serve.

It is interesting to note that Donald sees nothing particularly wrong with his behavior, nor does he express remorse or guilt for using others and causing them grief. Although his behavior is self-defeating in the long run, he considers it to be practical and possessed of good sense. Periodic punishments do nothing to decrease his egotism and confidence in his own abilities. . . . His behavior is entirely egocentric, and his needs are satisfied without any concern for the feelings and welfare of others. (Hare, 1970, pp. 1–4)

The repetitive behavior pattern shown by Donald is common among people diagnosed as psychopathic. Interestingly, many psychopaths and antisocial personalities do eventually settle down to responsible positions in their community. Evidence shows that there seems to be a strong drop with age in the antisocial behavior associated with the second dimension of psychopathy, although the first dimension of egocentric, callous and remorseless traits appears to be fairly stable across the lifespan of the psychopath (Cloninger et al., 1997; Harpur & Hare, 1997).

Causal Factors in Psychopathy and Antisocial Personality

As is the case with all the personality disorders discussed here, the causal factors in psychopathy and antisocial personality are still not fully understood. As always in the study of psychopathology, our perspective is complicated by the fact that the causal factors involved appear to differ from case to case, as well as from one socioeconomic level to another. However, far more research has been conducted on the causes of psychopathy and antisocial personality than on any of the other personality disorders, so we are beginning to have a clearer picture of what some of the more important causal factors are. Contemporary research has variously stressed the causal roles of genetic factors, constitutional deficiencies, deficiencies in aversive emotional arousal, more general emotional deficits, the early learning of antisocial behavior as a coping style, and the influence of particular family and environmental patterns.

Because an antisocial person's impulsiveness, acting out, and intolerance of discipline tend to appear early in life, several investigators have focused on the role of biological factors as causative agents in psychopathic behaviors. The following sections focus on some of these biological factors.

Genetic Influences Most behavior genetic research has focused on genetic influences on criminality rather than on psychopathy per se. There have been many studies using the twin method of comparing concordance rates between monozygotic and dizygotic twins, as well as a number of studies using the adoption method where rates of criminal behavior in the adopted-away children of criminals are compared with the rates of criminal behavior in adopted-away children of normals. The results of both kinds of studies show a modest heritability for antisocial or criminal behavior (Carey & Goldman, 1997; Gottesman & Goldsmith, 1994; Lykken, 1995; Nigg & Goldsmith, 1994) and at least one study reached similar conclusions for psychopathy (Schulsinger, 1972). These effects are stronger for adult criminality than for adolescent criminality (Rutter, 1996). However, researchers also note that strong environmental influences (to be discussed later) interact with genetic predispositions to determine which individuals become criminals or antisocial personalities (Carey & Goldman, 1997; Lykken, 1995). Moreover, it is certainly clear that genetic factors cannot account for the dramatic rises in crime that have occurred in the United States and the United Kingdom since 1960, nor for the tenfold higher murder rate in the United States than in the United Kingdom (Rutter, 1996).

Deficient Aversive Emotional Arousal and Conditioning Research evidence indicates that psychopaths show deficient aversive emotional arousal; this condition presumably renders them less prone to fear and anxiety in stressful situations and less prone to normal conscience development and socialization. This lack of anxiety is more associated with the egocentric, callous, exploitative dimension of psychopathy rather than with the antisocial behavior dimension (which may have a slight positive association with anxiety) (Frick, 1998; Harpur et al., 1989; Lykken, 1995).

In an early classic study, for example, Lykken (1957) found that psychopaths showed deficient conditioning of anxiety when anticipating punishment and were slow at learning to stop responding in order to avoid punishment (see Eysenck, 1960, for a related early study). As a result, psychopaths presumably fail to acquire many of the conditioned reactions essential to normal passive avoidance of punishment, conscience development, and socialization (Trasler, 1978). Hare has recently summarized work on this issue by stating that "It is the emotionally charged thought, images, and internal dialogue that give the 'bite' to conscience, account for its powerful control over behavior, and generate guilt and remorse for transgressions. This is something that psychopaths cannot understand. For them conscience is little more than an intellectual awareness of rules others make up—empty words (1998, p. 112)."

An impressive array of studies that support these early ideas of Lykken and Eysenck showing that psychopaths are deficient in the conditioning of anxiety (e.g., Fowles, 1993; Fowles & Missel, 1994; Hare, 1978a, 1998; Lykken, 1995). Because such conditioning may underlie successful avoidance of punishment, this may also explain why their impulsive behavior goes unchecked. According to Fowles, the deficient anxiety conditioning seems to stem from psychopaths' having a deficient *behavioral inhibition system* (Fowles, 1980, 1993; Fowles & Missel, 1994; see also Newman, 1997). The behavioral inhibition system has been proposed by Gray (1987; Gray & McNaughton, 1996) to be the neural system underlying anxiety. It is also the neural system responsible for learning to inhibit responses to cues signalling punishment; this kind of so-called *passive avoidance learning* depends on conditioning of anxiety to the cue and the response when they will be followed by punishment. It is called *passive* avoidance learning because one learns to avoid punishment by *not* making a response (for example, by not commiting robbery one avoids punishment). Thus, deficiencies in this neural system are associated both with deficits in anxiety conditioning and with deficits in learning to avoid punishment through passive avoidance.

The second important neural system in Gray's model is the *behavioral activation system*: This system activates behavior in response to cues for reward (positive reinforcement), as well as to cues for *active* avoidance of threatened punishment (such as in lying or running away to avoid punishment that one has been threatened with). Activation of this system is associated with positive emotions such as hope and relief. According to Fowles' theory, the behavioral activation system is thought to be normal or possibly overactive in psychopaths, which may explain why they are quite focused on obtaining reward. Moreover, if they are caught in a misdeed, they are also very focused on actively avoiding threatened punishment (e.g., through deceit and lies, or running away). This hypothesis of Fowles that psychopaths have a deficient behavioral inhibition system and a normal or possibly overactive behavioral activation system seems to be able to account for three features of psychopathy: (1) psychopaths' deficient conditioning of anxiety to signals for punishment, (2) their difficulty learning to inhibit responses that may result in punishment (such as illegal and antisocial acts), and (3) their normal or hypernormal active avoidance of punishment (by deceit, lies, and escape behavior) when actively threatened with punishment (Fowles, 1993, p. 9; see also Hare, 1998).

This last element prompted a modification. Fowles and Missel (1994) noted that although psychopaths do seem to be deficient in the kind of anxiety seen in *anticipation* of punishment, they may not be deficient in the kind of fear or panic response discussed in Chapter 5 in the face of a threatening stimulus, which is driven by different neural systems—namely, those responsible for the fight-or-flight response. In support of this idea, Fowles cites evidence from Schalling (1978) who distinguished between psychic anxiety (anticipatory worry and concern) and somatic anxiety (panic, cardiovascular symptoms, and muscle tenseness). Schalling found that psychopaths were low only in psychic anxiety, but not in somatic anxiety.

More General Emotional Deficits   Researchers have also been interested in whether there are more general emotional deficits in psychopaths than simply in the conditioning of anxiety (Fowles & Missel, 1994; Hare, 1998). Psychopaths show less significant physiological reactivity to distress cues (slides of people crying, obviously quite distressed) than did nonpsychopaths, confirming the idea that they are low on empathy (Blair et al, 1997). However, they were not underresponsive to unconditioned threat cues such as slides of sharks, pointed guns, or angry faces.

Both humans and animals show a larger startle response if a startle probe stimulus (such as a loud noise) is presented when the person is already in an anxious state (like Schalling's psychic anxiety) (e.g., Patrick, Bradley, & Lang, 1993). When comparing psychopathic and nonpsychopathic prisoners, Patrick and colleagues found that the psychopaths did not show this effect, although the nonpsychopathic prisoners did. Indeed, the psychopaths showed smaller startle responses when viewing unpleasant and pleasant slides than when watching neutral slides, suggesting the emotional valence of the stimuli meant little to them (Hare, 1998). Patrick, Cuthbert, and Lang (1994) further showed that when asked to imagine frightening and neutral situations, psychopathic prisoners showed reduced physiological reactivity to the fearful imagery relative to that seen in the nonpsychopathic prisoners, suggesting that the imaginal process of psychopaths are "emotionally flat" (Hare, 1998, p. 112).

In a recent summary of research on emotional deficits in psychopathy, Hare stated "Psychopaths . . . seem to have difficulty in fully understanding and using words that for normal people refer to ordinary emotional events and feelings. . . . It is as if emotion is a second language for psychopaths, a language that requires a considerable amount of . . . cognitive effort on their part" (1998, p. 115).

Early Parental Loss, Parental Rejection, and Inconsistency   Perhaps the most popular generalization about the development of psychopathy and antisocial personality is the assumption of some form of early disturbance in family relationships. Some of the earliest ideas about the origins of these disorders stemmed from early observations that an unusually high number of antisocial individuals have experienced the trauma of losing a parent at an early age—usually through the separation or divorce of their parents. For example, Greer (1964) found that 60 percent of one group of antisocial persons he studied had lost a parent during childhood, compared with 28 percent for a control group of other psychologically maladjusted persons and 27 percent for a control group of normal subjects. However, 30 years ago Hare (1970) had already suggested that the factor of key significance was not the parental loss per se, but rather the emotional disturbances in family relationships created before the departure of a parent; as discussed below, recent research has clearly confirmed this suggestion.

In Chapter 3, we noted that slow conscience development and aggression are among the damaging effects of parental rejection, abuse, and neglect, accompanied by inconsistent discipline. It has now been documented that children who had experienced substantiated child abuse and neglect were more likely to show symptoms of ASPD in adulthood than were children matched on age, race, sex, and social class (Luntz & Widom, 1994). Moreover, children whose mothers had experienced birth complications and who had been rejected by their mothers were especially likely to be predisposed to violent crime in adulthood (Raine, Brennan, & Mednick, 1994).

However, parental rejection and inconsistency alone are not sufficient explanations for the origins of psychopathy or antisocial personality. These same conditions have been implicated in a wide range of later maladaptive behaviors, and many children coming from such family backgrounds do not become psychopathic or antisocial or show any other serious psychopathology. Thus further explanation is needed. In the following section we present an integrated developmental perspective with multiple interacting causal pathways.

A Developmental Perspective on Psychopathy and Antisocial Personality

It has long been known that these disorders generally begin early in childhood, especially for boys, and that the number of antisocial behaviors exhibited in childhood is the single best predictor of who develops an adult diagnosis of psychopathy or antisocial personality (Robins, 1978). These early antisocial symptoms included "theft, incorrigibility, running away from home, truancy, associating with other delinquent children, staying out past the hour allowed, discipline problems in school and school retardation" (Robins, 1978, p. 260), and today are associated with a diagnosis of conduct disorder.

In addition, the age of onset of such antisocial symptoms was another predictor of adult antisocial personality, even when the number of childhood symptoms was controlled (Robins, 1991; Robins & Price, 1991); earlier onset was associated with greater likelihood of developing adult antisocial personality. Our understanding of the factors associated with the development of such behavior patterns in childhood, often leading to a diagnosis of conduct disorder (discussed more extensively in Chapter 14), has increased tremendously in the past 20 years. Because of its importance for understanding the causes of psychopathy and antisocial personality, it will briefly be reviewed here.

The initial problems that children who go on to develop adult antisocial personality disorder usually exhibit

Antisocial personality disorder in adulthood is always preceded by conduct disorder in adolescence (usually early-onset conduct disorder). However, not all adolescents with conduct disorder (especially late-onset conduct disorder) go on to become adult antisocial personalities.

often lead to one of two diagnoses. The first is *oppositional defiant disorder,* which is characterized by a pattern of hostile and defiant behavior toward authority figures that usually begins by the age of six years. Prospective studies have indicated a common developmental sequence from oppositional defiant disorder to conduct disorder, which does not usually begin until age nine. As will be discussed more extensively in Chapter 14, it is children with this early history of oppositional defiant disorder, followed by early-onset conduct disorder, who are most likely to develop antisocial personality disorder, psychopathy, or other serious problems as adults. By contrast, those who develop conduct disorder in adolescence do not usually become psychopaths or antisocial personalities but instead have problems limited to the adolescent years (Hinshaw, 1994; Moffitt, 1993a). As summarized by Hinshaw (1994), the typical pattern in the prepsychopath is as follows:

> For the prototypic "early onset" child, irritable, difficult temperamental style in infancy yields to harshly defiant, argumentative behavior during preschool; early indexes of fighting, lying, and petty theft by the beginning of grade school; assault and sexual precocity in preadolescence; robbery and substance abuse by midadolescence; and repetitive criminal activities, callous relationships, and spousal and

child abuse in adulthood (Caspi & Moffitt, 1995; Moffitt, 1993a). Thus antisocial activities persist, but they change in form markedly with development. (Hinshaw, 1994, p. 21)

The second early diagnosis that is often a precursor to adult psychopathy or ASPD is attention deficit hyperactivity disorder (ADHD). ADHD is characterized by restless, inattentive, and impulsive behavior, a short attention span, and high distractibility. When ADHD occurs with conduct disorder (which happens in 30 to 50 percent of cases), this leads to a high likelihood that the person will develop adult psychopathy (Lyman, 1996; McBurnett & Pfiffner, 1998). Indeed, Lyman (1996, 1997) has recently referred to children with ADHD and conduct disorder as "fledgling psychopaths" and has recently developed a childhood version of the PCL to assess these individuals who may be specifically predisposed to adult psychopathy rather than ASPD.

There is increasing evidence that genetic propensities leading to mild neuropsychological problems such as those leading to hyperactivity or attentional difficulties, along with a difficult temperament may be important predisposing factors for early-onset conduct disorder. The behavioral problems that these predisposing factors create have a cascade of pervasive effects over time. For example, Moffitt and Lynam (1994) presented this hypothesis:

> How might neuropsychological risk initiate a chain of events that culminates in antisocial disorders? One possibility is that such behavioral deficits evoke a chain of failed parent-child encounters. . . . Children with difficult temperaments and early behavior problems pose a challenge to even the most resourceful, loving, and patient families. . . . Even more disturbing, an infant's neurological health status has been shown to be related to risk for maltreatment and neglect. . . . A toddler's problem behaviors may affect his parents' disciplinary strategies. . . . Children characterized by a "difficult temperament" in infancy are more likely to resist their mothers' efforts to control them. . . . Children's oppositional behaviors often provoke and force adult family members to counter with highly punitive and angry responses. . . . Children who coerce parents into providing short-term payoffs in the immediate situation may thereby learn an interactional style that continues to "work" in similar ways in later social encounters and with different interaction partners. . . . The child with neuropsychological problems and difficult behavior may learn early to rely on offensive interpersonal tactics. If he generalized antisocial tactics to other settings, his style may consolidate into a syndrome of conduct disorder. (pp. 245–247)

In addition, many other psychosocial and sociocultural contextual variables contribute to the probability that a child with the genetic or constitutional liabilities discussed above will develop conduct disorder, and later adult psy-

chopathy or antisocial personality disorder. As summarized by Patterson and colleagues (Capaldi & Patterson, 1994; Dishion & Patterson, 1997), these include parents' own antisocial behavior, divorce and other parental transitions, low socioeconomic status, poor neighborhoods, and parental stress and depression. All of these contribute to poor and ineffective parenting skills—especially ineffective discipline, monitoring, and supervision. "These children are trained by the family directly in antisocial behavior by coercive interchanges and indirectly by lack of monitoring and consistent discipline" (Capaldi & Patterson, 1994, p. 169; see also Dishion & Patterson, 1997). This in turn all too often leads to association with deviant peers and the opportunity for further learning of antisocial behavior. Their mediational model of how all this occurs is illustrated in Figure 9.1.

In summary, individuals with psychopathy and antisocial personality show patterns of deviant behavior from early on in childhood, at first often in the form of oppositional defiant disorder, and then in the form of early onset conduct disorder. Increasingly our understanding of the causal factors suggests that varying combinations of biological, psychosocial, and sociocultural factors appear to be involved. In other words, this is one disorder for which a biopsychosocial approach is absolutely critical.

Sociocultural Causal Factors and Psychopathy
Cross-cultural research on psychopathy reveals that it is a disorder that occurs in a wide range of cultures, including nonindustrialized ones as diverse as the Inuit of northwest Alaska and the Yorubas of Nigeria. The Yorubas concept of a psychopath is of "a person who always goes his own way regardless of others, who is uncooperative, full of malice, and bullheaded" and the Inuit's concept is of someone whose "mind knows what to do but he does not do it. . . . This is an abstract term for the breaking of the many rules when awareness of the rules is not in question" (Murphy, 1976, p. 1026, cited in Cooke, 1996, p. 23). Nevertheless, the exact manifestations of the disorder based on cultural factors, and the prevalence of the disorder also seems to vary due to sociocultural influences that encourage or discourage its development.

Regarding different cross-cultural manifestations of the disorder, one of the primary symptoms where cultural variations occur is in the frequency of aggressive and violent behavior. Socialization forces have an enormous impact on the expression of aggressive impulses and thus it is not surprising that in some cultures people we would call psychopaths may be much less likely to engage in aggressive, especially violent behavior (Cooke, 1996). Thus, it is not surprising that cultures like the Chinese show much lower rates of aggressive behavior than seen in most Western cultures.

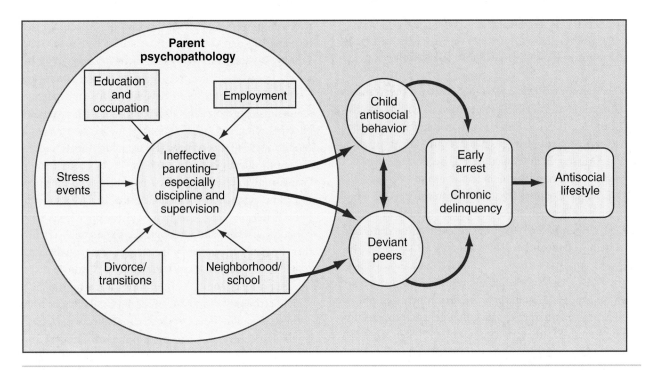

FIGURE 9.1

A model for the association of family context and antisocial behavior. Each of the contextual variables in this model has been shown to be related to antisocial behavior in adults. Antisocial behavior in girls is far less common and has also been found to be less stable over time, making it more difficult to predict (Capaldi & Patterson, 1994).

Moreover, cultures can be classified along a dimension distinguishing between individualistic and collectivist societies. Competitiveness, self-confidence, and independence from others is emphasized in relatively individualistic societies, whereas contributions to the group, acceptance of authority, and stability of relationships are encouraged in relatively collectivist societies (Cooke, 1996). Not surprisingly, we would expect that individualistic societies (such as our own) would be more likely to promote some of the behavioral characteristics which, carried to the extreme, result in psychopathy. These characteristics include "glibness and superficiality, grandiosity, promiscuity . . . together with a lack of responsibility within relationships" and "the competitiveness . . . associated not only with higher crime rates but also with increases in . . . deceptive, manipulative, and parasitic behavior" (Cooke, 1996, p. 27). Although the evidence bearing on this is minimal, it is interesting to note that estimates of the prevalence of antisocial personality in Taiwan, a relatively collectivist society, are much lower than in the United States (approximately 0.1 to 0.2 percent versus 1.5 to 5 percent). This intriguing preliminary work on sociocultural factors contributing to both the symptomatology of psychopathy as well as its prevalence is in its infancy, but it is likely to provide important new insights into the origins of this disorder in the years to come.

Treatments and Outcomes in Psychopathic and Antisocial Personality

Because most people with psychopathic and antisocial personalities do not exhibit obvious psychopathology and can function effectively in many respects, they seldom come to the attention of mental hospitals or clinics. Those who run afoul of the law may participate in rehabilitation programs in penal institutions, but they are rarely changed by them. Even if more and better therapeutic facilities were available, effective treatment would still be a challenging task.

In general, traditional psychotherapeutic approaches have not proved effective in altering psychopathic and antisocial personalities. Factors inherent in the psychopath's personality—the inability to trust, to feel as others do, to learn from experience, and to accept responsibility for one's actions—apparently make the prognosis for psychodynamic psychotherapy very poor (Lösel, 1998). In addition, therapists must be vigilant for the possibility that the psychopathic patient may attempt to manipulate them, and that the information provided about the patient's life is likely to contain distortions and fabrications (Lösel, 1998). Nor have biological treatment measures for psychopathic personalities—including electroconvulsive therapy or drugs—fared much better. There is some evidence that antipsychotic drugs that might be expected to reduce aggressive behavioral disturbances in psychopaths who also show schizotypal symptoms may have beneficial effects on certain symptoms (Lösel, 1998). Antianxiety drugs seem to be contraindicated, however, given that they would be expected to further diminish functioning of the behavioral inhibition system, which is already hypoactive in psychopathy (Lösel, 1998). Drugs such as lithium and carbazemine used to treat bipolar disorder have had some success in treating the aggressive impulsive behavior of violent aggressive criminals (Gitlin, 1996; Lösel, 1998). Finally, there have recently been some tentative but promising results using antidepressants from the SSRI category, which can sometimes reduce aggressive impulsive behavior and increase interpersonal skills (Lösel, 1998). However, none of these biological treatments have substantial impact on the disorder as a whole and much work remains to be done to determine more clearly which medications are most promising and for which symptoms.

Cognitive-Behavior Treatments Cognitive-behavior therapists have developed multifaceted techniques that appear to offer some promise of more effective treatment (Lösel, 1998; Rice & Harris, 1997). These treatments need to be targeted to the risk level that a particular offender poses, with higher levels of service and treatment perhaps reserved for higher risk cases (unless further research shows that such treatments are simply not effective for such offenders), as well as to the specific needs of each offender. Common targets of cognitive-behavior interventions with psychopathy or ASPD include the following (Lösel, 1998):

- Improving social skills
- Increasing self-control
- Increasing self-critical thinking
- Increasing social perspective-taking
- Victim awareness
- Anger management
- Improving vocational competencies
- Interpersonal problem-solving
- Changing antisocial attitudes
- Curing drug addiction
- Reducing contacts with antisocial peers
- Improving positive interactions with nonantisocial peers

Such programs require a controlled situation in which the therapist can administer or withhold reinforcement and the individual cannot leave treatment (such as an inpatient or prison setting). The controlled situation seems necessary for treatment to succeed.

When treating antisocial behavior, we are dealing with a total lifestyle rather than with a specific maladaptive behavior, like a phobia, that can be targeted for treatment. Without a controlled situation, the intermittent reinforcement of short-term gains and successful avoidance of punishments, combined with a lack of anxiety and guilt, leave an antisocial individual with little motivation to change. Punishment by itself is ineffective for changing antisocial behavior.

Beck and Freeman's (1990) cognitive treatment for personality disorders also offers an interesting approach that can be incorporated into the treatment of antisocial personality disorder by focusing on improving social and moral behavior by examining self-serving dysfunctional beliefs that psychopaths tend to have. These include "Wanting something or wanting to avoid something justifies my actions"; "I always make good choices"; "The views of others are irrelevant to my decisions, unless they directly control my immediate consequences"; and "Undesirable consequences will not occur or will not matter to me" (Beck & Freeman, 1990, p. 154). In cognitive therapy, the therapist tries to guide the patient toward higher and more abstract kinds of thinking using principles that are based on theories of moral and cognitive development. This is done through guided discussions, structured cognitive exercises, and behavioral experiments. The following case illustrates how a cognitive therapy session with an antisocial personality is conducted.

Case Study, Cognitive Therapy with a Psychopath

THERAPIST: How well has the "beat-the-system" approach actually worked out for you over time?

BRETT: It works great . . . until someone catches on or starts to catch on. Then you have to scrap that plan and come up with a new one.

THERAPIST: How difficult was it, you know, to cover up one scheme and come up with a new one?

BRETT: Sometimes it was really easy. There are some real pigeons out there.

THERAPIST: Was it always easy?

BRETT: Well, no. Sometimes it was a real bitch. . . . Seems like I'm always needing a good plan to beat the system.

THERAPIST: Do you think it's ever easier to go with the system instead of trying to beat it in some way?

BRETT: Well, after all that I have been through, I would have to say yes, there have been times that going with the system would have been easier in the long run . . . But . . . it's such a challenge to beat the system. It feels exciting when I come up with a new plan and think I can make it work. Going with the system might not even occur to me.

THERAPIST: So what you choose to do is dictated by how excited you feel about your idea, your plan?

BRETT: Yeah.

THERAPIST: Yet several of your plans have actually ended up costing you and creating hassles in the long run.

BRETT: Yeah.

THERAPIST: How does that fit with your goal of having an easy, carefree life where you don't have to work too hard?

BRETT: It doesn't. [pause] So how do I get the easy life, Doc? . . .

THERAPIST: Do you ever think about what all your choices are and weigh them out, according to what consequences each one would have?

BRETT: Not usually. Usually, I just go for beating the system.

THERAPIST: What do you think would happen if you thought about other options. . . .

BRETT: I don't know.

THERAPIST: Is there some situation that you are dealing with right now in your life that you have to come up with money for, and you have to figure out how you are going to do it?

BRETT: Yeah . . . how I'm going to afford to rent my apartment, the lease on the nightclub property, getting the place ready to open for business, and still pay my lawyer. . . .

[Later in the session after discussing options]

THERAPIST: So it sounds like you have several options for dealing with your current financial situation. Most of the time in the past, you have dealt with financial demands by getting involved in some beat-the-system scheme. . . . This time, you have discussed several possibilities. Which do you think will be the easiest and best in the long run?

BRETT: Fix up the space at the club and move in.

(From Beck & Freeman, 1990, pp. 171–172.)

Although cognitive therapy along such lines seems quite promising, at present there are only case studies documenting its effectiveness (Davidson & Tryer, 1996). It seems unlikely that cognitive therapy by itself will be highly effective but when combined with some of the behavioral treatments described above, it may be quite useful.

How effective are the best of these multifaceted cognitive-behaviorally oriented treatment programs? In general the effects to date are significant but only modest in size, although they are somewhat more effective in

treating young offenders (teenagers) than older offenders, perhaps because the former group includes a higher proportion of adolescent-limited conduct disorder described above, and the latter group includes a higher proportion of hard-core lifelong psychopaths. Indeed, the available evidence suggests that psychopathy is probably more difficult to treat than antisocial personality disorder (Lösel, 1998; Rice & Harris, 1997). These modest results have tended to have an effect on public policy of simply pushing for harsher penalties and executions, policies that leading researchers in this area suggest "will fail as effective social policies" and rest on the false conclusion that such treatments have clearly been shown to be ineffective (Rice & Harris, 1997, p. 432). Rather it is better to acknowledge that research on developing effective treatments for psychopathy and antisocial personality is still in its very early stages and much work remains to be done.

Fortunately, many psychopathic and antisocial personalities improve after the age of 40 even without treatment, possibly because of weaker biological drives, better insight into self-defeating behaviors, and the cumulative effects of social conditioning. Such individuals are often referred to as "burned-out psychopaths." Hare, McPherson, and Forth (1988) confirmed the hypothesis that psychopaths tend to burn out over time. They followed up a group of male psychopaths and tracked their criminal careers beyond age 40. They found a clear and dramatic reduction in criminal behavior after age 40. They were quick to note, however, that even with this reduction in criminal behavior, over 50 percent of these people continued being arrested after age 40. Even with the prospect that they might eventually engage in less destructive behavior, psychopaths can create a great deal of havoc before they reach 40—as well as afterward if they do not change. Moreover, Harpur and Hare (1994) have also shown that it is only the antisocial behavioral dimension of psychopathy that diminishes with age; the egocentric, callous, and exploitative affective and interpersonal dimension does not.

In view of the distress and unhappiness that psychopaths inflict on others and the social damage they cause, it seems desirable—and more economical in the long run—to put increased effort into the development of effective prevention programs. At present there is considerable ongoing longitudinal prevention research on children at risk for conduct disorder. See Highlight 9.2 Modern Life, Prevention of Psychopathy and Antisocial Personality Disorder, for a review of the highlights of such prevention programs.

MODERN LIFE

Prevention of Psychopathy and Antisocial Personality Disorder

Given that conduct disorder seems to always be a precursor of antisocial personality disorder and psychopathy, and that it is difficult to treat (Southam-Geron & Kendall, 1997; see Chapter 14), the best approach seems to be a preventive one oriented both toward minimizing some of the developmental and environmental risk factors described earlier and in breaking some of the vicious cycles that these at-risk children seem to get themselves into. The early results of many of these prevention efforts seem promising, but it will be many years before we understand their true potential for preventing adult psychopathy and antisocial personality disorder.

Given the life-course developmental model for the etiology of ASPD described above, the idea of prevention becomes very complex because there are a host of different stages at which preventive interventions can and probably should be implemented. Some interventions with mothers estimated to be at high risk (namely poor, first time, and often single mothers) for producing children that could be at risk include prenatal care aimed at improving maternal nutrition, decreasing smoking and other substance use, as well as improving parenting skills (Olds et al., 1986, 1994; Reid & Eddy, 1997). One such intensive intervention study starting at 30 weeks into pregnancy and lasting for the first two years of the child's life produced very impressive results (Olds et al., 1994).

During the transition to school years, Patterson and colleagues have developed programs targeting the family environment which teach effective parental discipline and supervision. At-risk children whose families receive such interventions do better academically, are less likely to associate with delinquent peers, and are less likely to get involved in drug use. Such family or parent training can even be effective in reducing

and preventing further antisocial behavior in children and adolescents already engaged in antisocial behavior, although conducting the intervention with pre-elementary school aged children was more effective and less labor intensive (see Reid & Eddy, 1997, for a review). Nevertheless, at any stage such interventions have been shown to be effective in reducing offending rate and amount of time spent incarcerated.

Other prevention efforts have targetted the school environment, or school and family environments concurrently. Although such programs are generally more difficult to implement for a variety of reasons, some significant advances have been made in developing such programs. One especially promising ongoing multisite intervention study of this sort is called the FAST Track (Families and Schools Together) intervention. Kindergarten students who attend high risk schools (generally inner city and poor) and who already show poor peer relations and high levels of disruptive behavior are recruited for this intensive program which includes parent training and school interventions. There is a focus on targeting interpersonal problem-solving skills, emotional awareness abilities, and self-control skills. Teachers are taught how to manage disruptive behavior and parents are informed of information their children are taught. Early results are very promising in terms of reducing later conduct problems. Children in FAST Track are also less likely to be nominated by peers as aggressive, and to be better liked and to show better reading skills (Coie, 1996; Reid & Eddy, 1997). Although such interventions are costly, if they can prevent (or at least dramatically reduce) the extremely costly effects on society of these children developing full-blown adult ASPD or psychopathy, the long-term benefits will outweigh the initial costs. ■

UNRESOLVED ISSUES

Axis II of DSM-IV

While reading this chapter, you may have had some difficulty in capturing a clear, distinctive picture of each of the personality disorders. It is quite likely that as you studied the descriptions of the different disorders, the characteristics and attributes of some of them, say the schizoid personality disorder, seemed to blend with other conditions, such as the schizotypal or avoidant personality disorders. Although we attempted to highlight the apparent differences between prototypic cases of the different personality disorders with the greatest potential for overlap, in most cases people do not neatly fit these prototypes and instead qualify for more than one personality disorder. Indeed, as already noted, Widiger and Rogers (1989; Widiger et al., 1991) reported that an average of 85 percent of patients with one personality disorder also qualified for at least one other personality disorder, and some studies have found that patients were given an average of four or more personality disorder diagnoses (Shea, 1995; Skodol et al., 1991). In addition, one of the *most common* diagnoses is a grab-bag category of "Personality disorder not otherwise specified" (e.g., Tryer, 1995; Widiger & Corbit, 1995); this category is reserved for persons who do not cleanly fit within any of the ten categories, but rather share features from several different categories.

Further complicating matters is the fact that the different semistructured interviews and self-report inventories that have been developed to make personality disorder diagnosis more reliable tend to show only modest agreement on what personality disorder(s) a person has (Oldham et al., 1992; Widiger & Sanderson, 1995). In other words, Axis II diagnoses are considerably less reliable than are diagnoses made for Axis I disorders. Finally, Clark (1992) has also reviewed evidence showing poor stability of personality disorder diagnoses over time, which should not be given the DSM definition of personality disorder as an "enduring pattern" of inflexible and maladaptive behavior.

Axis II diagnoses are unreliable (that is, there is a good deal of interrater disagreement about who qualifies for a diagnosis) for several reasons. One major difficulty stems from the assumption in DSM-IV that we can make a clear distinction between the presence and absence of a personality disorder (Livesley, 1995; Widiger & Sanderson, 1995). The personality processes classified on Axis II are *dimensional* in nature; that is, the data on which Axis II classifications are made are underlying personality traits that people vary on in terms of degree. For example, everyone is suspicious at times, but the degree to which this trait exists in someone with paranoid person-

ality disorder is extreme. Suspiciousness can be viewed as a personality dimension on which essentially all people can be rated or given scores. The scores might range, on an illustrative "scale of suspiciousness," as follows:

Extremely Low		Low		Average		High		Extremely High	
0	10	20	30	40	50	60	70	80	90 100

Many studies have been conducted attempting to find discrete breaks in such personality dimensions—that is, points at which normal behavior becomes clearly distinct from pathological behavior—and none have been found (Widiger & Sanderson, 1995). Indeed, Zimmerman and Coryell (1990) concluded that personality disorder "scores are continuously distributed without points of rarity to indicate where to make the distinction between normality and pathology" (p. 690). Moreover, when changes are made in the cut-points or threshold for diagnosis of a personality disorder, as was done for several personality disorders when DSM-III was revised to DSM-III-R, this can have drastic effects in the apparent prevalence rates of a particular personality disorder diagnosis. For example, the revisions resulted in "an 800 percent increase in the rate of schizoid personality disorder and a 350 percent increase in narcissistic personality disorder" (Morey, 1988a, p. 575).

A second problem inherent in Axis II classifications involves the fact that there are enormous differences in the kinds of symptoms that people can have who nevertheless obtain the same diagnosis (Clark, 1992; Widiger & Sanderson, 1995). For example, to obtain a diagnosis of DSM-III-R borderline personality disorder, a person had to meet five out of eight possible symptom criteria (in DSM-IV, it is five out of nine). Widiger and colleagues calculated that this meant that there were 93 different ways (through different combinations of symptoms) to meet the DSM-III-R criteria for borderline personality disorder (Widiger, 1993; Widiger & Sanderson, 1995). Moreover, this also meant that two people with the same diagnosis might share only two symptoms. For example, one person might meet criteria 1–5, and a second person might meet criteria 4–8. By contrast, a third individual who met only criteria 1–4 would obtain no borderline personality diagnosis at all and yet surely would be more similar to the first person than would the first two people be to each other (Clark, 1992; Widiger & Sanderson, 1995). Even more amazing were the comparable figures for the number of different ways to meet DSM-III-R criteria for antisocial personality disorder, which were calculated to be nearly 150 million different ways (Widiger & Sanderson, 1995).

Both researchers and clinicians are somewhat dissatisfied with Axis II. This situation is due in part to the difficulties in applying the system and to its relative unreliability. Moreover, in actual clinical practice, the multiaxial system is seldom applied to its fullest. Although information about Axis I diagnoses is usually recorded on patients' charts (because it is required for insurance and administrative purposes), information about other axes, including Axis II, is frequently omitted because their concepts are not easy to diagnose reliably. Moreover, the presence of an Axis II diagnosis is often used as a source of pessimism about the prognosis for a good response to treatment (Livesley et al., 1994).

Nevertheless, the developers of DSM-III made an important theoretical leap when they recognized the importance of weighing premorbid personality factors in the clinical picture and thus developed the second axis. Use of the Axis II concepts can lead to a better understanding of a case, particularly with regard to treatment outcomes. Strong, ingrained personality characteristics can work against treatment interventions. The use of Axis II forces a clinician to attend to these long-standing and difficult-to-change personality factors in planning treatment.

What can be done to resolve the difficulties with Axis II? Most researchers feel that the psychiatric community should give up on the typological approach to classification in favor of a dimensional approach and rating methods that would take into account the relative "amounts" of the primary traits shown by patients. We will have more to say on this issue as it applies to children in Chapter 14. Some of the resistance to the dimensional approach to classification stems from the fact that medically oriented practitioners have a pronounced preference for categorical diagnosis. Moreover, there are fears that the dimensional approach to personality measurement might not be accepted because sound quantitative ratings might involve far too much time for most busy clinicians

both to learn and to apply. Nevertheless, reviews of the evidence show that many clinicians are unhappy with the current categorical system, which is cumbersome when used properly because of the need to assess nearly 80 diagnostic criteria for DSM-IV personality disorders (Widiger, 1993; Widiger & Sanderson, 1995). Indeed, Widiger has argued persuasively that the use of a dimensional model might require less time because it would reduce the redundancy and overlap that currently exists across the categories.

If the present categorical classification system continues to be used, a clearer set of classification rules is needed to make the categories more accurate and more mutually exclusive. The classification rules would need to be made more exhaustive and to incorporate behaviors and traits that do not overlap with other categories. However, there is little reason for optimism here because such attempts have already been made in revising DSM-III to DSM-III-R and DSM-IV. So although such an undertaking might be desirable, it may in the final analysis be scientifically impossible. There appear to be few if any "pure" clusters for grouping people's maladaptive personality traits into the type of neat pigeonholes ideally required by a categorical approach.

In sum, the ultimate status of Axis II in future editions of the DSM is uncertain. Many problems inherent in using typological classes for essentially dimensional behavior (traits) have yet to be resolved, although they are now almost universally recognized. One of the primary reasons that dimensional models have not yet replaced categorical models is that a number of different dimensional systems have been proposed, and there is as yet no clear evidence as to which one is best (Clark & Livesley, 1994; Livesley, 1995; Widiger & Sanderson, 1995). Moreover, some have argued that personality disorders should be included on Axis I along with the other Axis I disorders, saving Axis II for a description of each person's personality profile—normal or abnormal (Livesley et al., 1994; Livesley, 1995).

SUMMARY

Personality disorders, in general, appear to be extreme or exaggerated patterns of personality traits that predispose an individual to maladaptive behavior. A number of personality disorders have been delineated in which there are persistent maladaptive patterns of perceiving, thinking, and relating to the environment. Three general clusters of personality disorders have been described. (1) Cluster A, which includes individuals with paranoid, schizoid, and schizotypal personality disorders, who seem odd or ec-

centric; (2) Cluster B, which includes individuals with histrionic, narcissistic, antisocial, and borderline personality disorders, who share a common tendency to be dramatic, emotional, and erratic; and (3) Cluster C, which includes individuals with avoidant, dependent, and obsessive-compulsive personality disorders who show fearfulness or tension as in anxiety-based disorders. Two provisional personality disorders are also listed for further study in the appendix of DSM-IV: the passive-aggressive and depressive personality disorders. The acceptability and utility of these disorders by researchers and practicing clinicians has not yet been determined.

There is as yet little research into what causes many of the personality disorders. According to some evidence, constitutional and genetic causal factors play a role in borderline, paranoid, schizotypal, and antisocial personality disorders. However, none of the disorders is entirely heritable, and current work is being directed at understanding which psychological factors also play a causal role. Some evidence suggests that early childhood abuse may play a role in causing borderline personality disorder, but prospective studies are needed to draw definitive conclusions about this. In addition to the relative lack of research on causal factors for personality disorders, there is also relatively little good research about how best to treat these difficult disorders. Treatment of the Cluster C disorders, which includes dependent and avoidant personality disorder, seems most promising, although a new form of cognitive-behavior therapy for borderline personality disorder (dialectical behavior therapy) also shows considerable promise in treating this very serious condition. Cluster A disorders such as schizotypal and paranoid are most difficult to treat.

One of the most notable of the personality disorders is the antisocial, or psychopathic, personality disorder. In this disorder, a person is callous and unethical, without loyalty or close relationships, but often with superficial charm and intelligence. Constitutional, learning, and adverse environmental factors seem to be important in causing the disorder. Some evidence suggests that genetic factors may also predispose an individual to develop this disorder. Psychopaths also show deficiencies in aversive emotional arousal and show poor conditioning of anxiety and passive avoidance, which seems to reflect an underactive behavioral inhibition system—the neural substrate for anxiety. They also seem to show more general emotional deficits. The disorder often begins and is recognized in childhood or early adolescence, but only persons who are 18 or over are given the diagnosis of antisocial personality.

Treatment of psychopaths is difficult, because they rarely see any need for change and tend to blame other people for their problems. Traditional psychotherapy is typically ineffective, but where control is possible, as in institutional settings, multifaceted cognitive-behavior approaches have had some modest success.

Finally, there are many theoretical and practical problems with the personality disorders as currently described in the DSM-IV. One problem is that even with the use of structured interviews the reliability of diagnosing personality disorders is less than ideal. In addition, the high number of people who are diagnosed with more than one personality disorder, or with personality disorder not otherwise specified, suggests that the categories as currently described do not really describe most people's personality problems adequately. Finally, most researchers and clinicians agree that a dimensional approach to understanding personality disorders is preferable, but as yet there has been no agreement regarding which of the possible dimensional approaches that has been studied is best.

KEY TERMS

personality disorders (p. 333)
paranoid personality disorder (p. 336)
schizoid personality disorder (p. 338)
schizotypal personality disorder (p. 339)
histrionic personality disorder (p. 340)
narcissistic personality disorder (p. 340)
antisocial personality disorder (ASPD) (p. 342)

borderline personality disorder (BPD) (p. 343)
avoidant personality disorder (p. 344)
dependent personality disorder (p. 346)
obsessive-compulsive personality disorder (OCPD) (p. 347)
passive-aggressive personality disorder (p. 348)
depressive personality disorder (p. 349)
psychopathy (p. 356)

CHAPTER TEN

Substance-Related and Other Addictive Disorders

August Natterer (Neter), *The Miraculous Shepherd (II)*. Neter was married and living in Germany when he began to suffer from depression and hallucinations, and was institutionalized around 1907 with an acute phase of schizophrenia. Educated as an electrical engineer, he chose to punctuate his images with precise details. This painting represents his recurring vision of a hostile Witch who created the world.

The increasing problem of substance abuse and dependence in our society has drawn both public and scientific attention. Although our present knowledge is far from complete, investigating these problems as maladaptive patterns of adjustment to life's demands, with no social stigma involved, has led to clear progress in understanding and treatment. Such an approach, of course, does not mean that an individual bears no personal responsibility in the development of a problem; the widespread notion that drug dependence and abuse can be viewed as forms of "disease" should not imply that the individual is a passive participant in the addiction process. Individual lifestyles and personality features are thought by many to play important roles in the development of addictive disorders and are central themes in some types of treatment.

Addictive behavior, behavior based on the pathological need for a substance or activity, may involve the abuse of substances, such as nicotine, alcohol, or cocaine, or the excessive ingestion of high-caloric food, resulting in extreme obesity. Addictive behavior is one of the most pervasive and intransigent mental health problems facing our society today. Addictive disorders can be seen all around us: in extremely high rates of alcoholism, in tragic exposés of cocaine abuse among star athletes and entertainers, and in reports of pathological gambling, which has increased with the widening opportunity for legalized gambling today.

The most commonly used problem substances are the **psychoactive drugs,** those drugs that affect mental functioning: alcohol, nicotine, barbiturates, minor tranquilizers, amphetamines, heroin, and marijuana. Some of these drugs, such as alcohol and nicotine, can be purchased legally by adults; others, such as the barbiturates, can be used legally under medical supervision; still others, such as heroin, are illegal.

The diagnostic classification of addictive or psychoactive substance-related disorders is divided into two major categories. First, psychoactive substance-induced organic mental disorders and syndromes (the latter of which are included within the organic mental disorders) are those conditions that involve *organic impairment* resulting from the ingestion of psychoactive substances—for example, an alcohol abuse dementia disorder involving amnesia, formerly known as Korsakoff's syndrome. These conditions stem from **toxicity,** the poisonous nature of the substance (leading to, for example, amphetamine delusional disorder, alcoholic intoxication, or cannabis delirium), or physiological changes in the brain due to vitamin deficiency.

A number of addictive disorders are covered in the second category, which focuses on the maladaptive behaviors resulting from regular and consistent use of a substance and includes psychoactive substance-abuse and substance-dependence disorders. The system of classification for substance abuse disorders that is followed by both DSM-IV and by ICD-10 (*International Classification of Disease,* published by the World Health Organization) provides two major categories: (1) substance dependence disorders and (2) substance abuse disorders (see Highlight 10.1) Although some researchers and clinicians disagree with the dichotomous grouping, others consider this classification approach to have both research and clinical utility (Maisto & McKay, 1995).

Psychoactive substance abuse generally involves a pathological use of a substance resulting in potentially hazardous behavior, such as driving while intoxicated, or in continued use despite a persistent social, psychological, occupational, or health problem. **Psychoactive substance dependence** includes more severe forms of substance-use disorders and usually involves a marked physiological need for increasing amounts of a substance to achieve the desired effects. Dependence in these disorders means that an individual will show a tolerance for a drug or withdrawal symptoms when the drug is unavailable. **Tolerance**—the need for increased amounts of a substance to achieve the desired effects—results from biochemical changes in the body that affect the rate of metabolism and elimination of alcohol from the body. When alcohol is ingested, it is absorbed into the bloodstream and distributed to other parts of the body. **Withdrawal symptoms** are physical symptoms, such as sweating, tremors, and tension, that accompany abstinence from the drug.

In addition to the abuse and dependence disorders that involve particular substances such as alcohol, there are disorders that have all the features of an addictive condition, such as excessive eating, but do not involve substances with chemically addicting properties. Two of these disorders, excessive overeating and pathological gambling, are discussed in this chapter because the maladaptive behaviors involved and the treatment approaches shown to be effective suggest that they are quite similar to the various drug-use and drug-induced disorders. Because alcohol is one of the most common and most researched of abused substances, we will begin our discussion there. Much of our knowledge of long-term effects, causes, and addictive mechanisms apply to some degree to other substances as well.

ALCOHOL ABUSE AND DEPENDENCE

The terms *alcoholic* and *alcoholism* have been subject to some controversy and have been used differently by various groups in the past. There is a trend today to use a

Highlight 10.1

Criteria for Substance Dependence and Substance Use Disorders According to DSM-IV

Substance Dependence Disorder

This is a maladaptive pattern of substance use that leads to clinically significant impairment or distress when at least three of the following have occurred any time in the last 12 months:

- Tolerance, as defined by either of the following:
  a. There is a need for markedly increased amounts of the substance to achieve intoxication or desired effect.
  b. There is a substantially diminished effect with continued use of the same amount of the substance. (It takes more of the substance to produce the effects it first had.)
- Withdrawal, as shown by either of the following problems:
  a. The individual shows the characteristic withdrawal syndrome for the substance.
  b. The same or closely related substance is taken to relieve or avoid withdrawal symptoms.
- The substance is often taken in larger amounts or over a longer period than was initially intended.
- There is a persistent desire or unsuccessful effort to cut down or control substance use.
- The person spends a great deal of time engaging in activities necessary to obtain the substance, use the substance, or recover from its effects.

- The person has given up or reduced the amount of important social, occupational, or recreational activities they have been involved in.
- The substance use is continued despite knowledge of having a persistent or recurrent physical or psychological problem that is likely to have been caused or exacerbated by the substance.

Substance Abuse Disorder

- This is a maladaptive pattern of substance use that leads to clinically significant impairment or distress, as shown by at least one of the following problems that occurred within a 12-month period.
  a. Recurrent substance use that resulted in a failure to fulfill some major role obligations at work, school, or home.
  b. Recurrent substance use in situations in which it is physically hazardous.
  c. Recurrent substance-related legal problems.
  d. Continued substance use despite having persistent or recurrent social or interpersonal problems caused or exacerbated by the effects of the substance.
- The person does not have symptoms or problems that have met the criteria for Substance Dependence for this class of substance. ■

Source: Adapted from American Psychiatric Association (1994).

more restrictive definition. For example, the World Health Organization no longer recommends the term *alcoholism* but prefers the term *alcohol dependence syndrome*—"a state, psychic and usually also physical, resulting from taking alcohol, characterized by behavioral and other responses that always include a compulsion to take alcohol on a continuous or periodic basis in order to ex-

perience its psychic effects, and sometimes to avoid the discomfort of its absence; tolerance may or may not be present" (1992, p. 4). However, because alcoholic and alcoholism are still widely used in practice, we will continue to use these terms in this book.

People of many ancient cultures, including the Egyptian, Greek, and Roman, made extensive and often excessive use of alcohol. Beer was first made in Egypt around 3000 B.C. The oldest surviving wine-making formulas were recorded by Marcus Cato in Italy almost a century and a half before the birth of Christ. About A.D. 800, the process of distillation was developed by an Arabian alchemist, thus making possible an increase in both the range and the potency of alcoholic beverages. Problems with excessive use of alcohol were observed almost as early as its use began. Cambyses, King of Persia in the sixth century B.C., has the dubious distinction of being one of the first alcoholics on record.

The term **alcoholic** is often used to refer to a person with a serious drinking problem, whose drinking impairs his or her life adjustment in terms of health, personal relationships, and occupational functioning. Likewise, the term **alcoholism** refers to a dependence on alcohol that seriously interferes with life adjustment.

The Prevalence, Comorbidity, and Demographics of Alcoholism

However defined, alcoholism is a major problem in the United States. A large NIMH epidemiological study found the lifetime prevalence for alcoholism in the United States to be 13.4 percent. One in seven people meet the criteria for alcohol abuse (Grant, 1997).

The potentially detrimental effects of excessive alcohol use—for an individual, his or her loved ones, and society—are legion. Heavy drinking is associated with vulnerability to injury (Shepherd & Brickley, 1996). The life span of the average alcoholic is about 12 years shorter than that of the average citizen, and alcohol now ranks as the third major cause of death in the United States, behind coronary heart disease and cancer. Alcohol significantly lowers performance on cognitive ability tasks such as problem solving—and the more complex the task the more impairment (Pickworth, Rohrer, & Fant, 1997). Organic impairment, including brain shrinkage, occurs in a high proportion of alcoholics (Errico, Parsons, & King, 1991; Lishman, Jacobson, & Acker, 1987), especially among *binge drinkers,* people who abuse alcohol following periods of sobriety (Hunt, 1993).

Over 37 percent of alcohol abusers suffer from at least one coexisting mental disorder (Rovner, 1990). Depression ranks high among the mental disorders often comorbid with alcoholism, not surprisingly since alcohol is a depressant (Kranzler, Del Boca, & Rounsaville, 1997). About 10 percent of alcoholics commit suicide (Miles, 1977), and over 18 percent are found to have a history of suicide attempts (Black et al., 1986).

In addition to the serious problems excessive drinkers create for themselves, they also pose serious difficulties for others (Gortner et al., 1997). Alcohol abuse is associated with over half the deaths and major injuries suffered in automobile accidents each year (Brewer, Morris, et al. 1994), and with about 50 percent of all murders (Bennett & Lehman, 1996), 40 percent of all assaults, over 50 percent of all rapes (Seto & Barbaree, 1995), and 30 percent of all suicides. About one out of every three arrests in the United States is related to alcohol abuse. Violent offenders have higher rates of alcohol problems than the general population (Martin, 1992). In a survey of alcohol-related violence in Norway, Rossow (1996) reported that 3 percent of adults in the general population sample reported having taken part in a fight when they were intoxicated. These individuals were most often young people who drank frequently and visited public places to drink. Interestingly, in a study of substance abuse and violent crime in the United States, Dawkins (1997) found that alcohol was more frequently associated with both violent and nonviolent crime than other drugs such as marijuana.

Alcoholism in the United States cuts across all age, educational, occupational, and socioeconomic boundaries. It is considered a serious problem in industry, in the professions, and in the military; it is found among such seemingly unlikely candidates as priests, airline pilots, politicians, surgeons, law enforcement officers, and teenagers. For example, in a survey of over 70,000 pilots, those with prior DWI convictions were found to be at greater risk for a pilot-error accident (McFadden, 1997). The once popular image of the alcoholic as an unkempt resident of skid row is clearly inaccurate. Further myths about alcoholism are noted in Table 10.1.

Most problem drinkers are men, with about five times the frequency of women (Helzer et al., 1990). There do not appear to be important differences in rates of alcohol abuse between black and white Americans. It appears, too, that problem drinking may develop during any life period from early childhood through old age. One study reported that 64.9 percent of their sample of high school students indicated a moderate use of alcohol and 18.8 percent of these reported a misuse of alcohol (Mann, Chassin, & Sher, 1987). Marriage, having higher levels of education, and being older are associated with a lower incidence of alcoholism (Helzer et al., 1991). Survey's of alcoholism rates across different cultural groups in North America and Asia have found varying rates of disorder across diverse cultural samples (Caetano et al., 1998).

The course of alcoholism can be both "erratic and fluctuating." A recent survey found that some alcoholics go through long periods of abstinence. Of 600 respon-

Alcohol is associated with over half of the deaths and serious injuries suffered in automobile accidents in the United States each year.

dents in the study (most of whom were alcohol dependent) over half (56 percent) had periods of abstinence for three months and 16 percent reported a period of five years of abstinence (Schuckit, Tipp, Smith, & Buckholz, 1997). It is therefore important to keep in mind that the course of alcoholism can vary, even including periods of remission.

The Clinical Picture of Alcohol Abuse and Dependence

The Roman poet Horace, in the first century B.C., wrote lyrically about the effects of wine: "It discloses secrets; ratifies and confirms our hopes; thrusts the coward forth to battle; eases the anxious mind of its burden; instructs in arts. Whom has not a cheerful glass made eloquent! Whom not quite free and easy from pinching poverty!" Unfortunately, the effects of alcohol are not always so benign or beneficial. According to a Japanese proverb, "First the man takes a drink, then the drink takes a drink, and then the drink takes the man."

Alcohol's Effects on the Brain Alcohol has complex and seemingly contradictory effects on the brain. At lower levels, alcohol stimulates certain brain cells and activates the brain's "pleasure areas," which release opium-like endogenous opioids that are stored in the body (Braun, 1996; Van Ree, 1996). At higher levels alcohol depresses brain functioning, inhibiting one of the brain's excitatory neurotransmitters, glutamate, which in turn slows down activity in parts of the brain. Inhibition of

glutamate in the brain impairs the organism's ability to learn and affects the higher brain centers, impairing judgment and other rational processes and lowering self-control. As behavioral restraints decline, a drinker may indulge in the satisfaction of impulses ordinarily held in check. Some degree of motor uncoordination soon becomes apparent, and the drinker's discrimination and perception of cold, pain, and other discomforts are dulled. Typically the drinker experiences a sense of warmth, expansiveness, and well-being. In such a mood, unpleasant realities are screened out and the drinker's feelings of self-esteem and adequacy rise. Casual acquaintances become the best and most understanding of friends, and the drinker enters a generally pleasant world of unreality in which worries are temporarily left behind. Interestingly, a recent investigation by Sayette (1994) showed that when intoxicated people describe themselves they are more likely to downplay their negative characteristics more than do sober subjects. That is, they tend to disclose fewer negative items in their speech in a self-protective effort.

When the alcohol content of the bloodstream reaches 0.10 percent (0.08 in some states), the individual is considered to be intoxicated, at least with respect to driving a vehicle. Muscular coordination, speech, and vision are impaired, and thought processes are confused. Even before this level of intoxication is reached, however, judgment becomes impaired to such an extent that the person misjudges his or her condition. For example, drinkers tend to express confidence in their ability to drive safely

TABLE 10.1 SOME COMMON MISCONCEPTIONS ABOUT ALCOHOL AND ALCOHOLISM

Fiction	Fact
Alcohol is a stimulant.	Alcohol is actually both a nervous system stimulant and a depressant.
You can always detect alcohol on the breath of a person who has been drinking.	It is not always possible to detect the presence of alcohol. Some individuals successfully cover up their alcohol use for years.
One ounce of 86-proof liquor contains more alcohol than two 12-ounce cans of beer.	Actually two 12-ounce cans of beer contain more than an ounce of alcohol.
Alcohol can help a person sleep more soundly.	Alcohol may actually interfere with sound sleep.
Impaired judgment does not occur before there are obvious signs of intoxication.	In fact, impaired judgment can occur long before motor signs of intoxication are apparent.
An individual will get more intoxicated by mixing liquors than by taking comparable amounts of one kind—e.g., bourbon, Scotch, or vodka.	It is the actual amount of alcohol in the bloodstream rather than the mix that determines intoxication.
Drinking several cups of coffee can counteract the effects of alcohol and enable a drinker to "sober up."	Drinking coffee does not affect the level of intoxication.
Exercise or a cold shower helps speed up the metabolism of alcohol.	Exercise and cold showers are futile attempts to increase alcohol metabolism.
People with "strong wills" need not be concerned about becoming alcoholics.	Alcohol is seductive and can lower the resistance of even the "strongest will."
Alcohol cannot produce a true addiction in the same sense that heroin can.	Alcohol has strong addictive properties.
One cannot become an alcoholic by drinking just beer.	One can consume a considerable amount of alcohol by drinking beer. It is, of course, the amount of alcohol that determines whether one becomes an alcoholic.
Alcohol is far less dangerous than marijuana.	There are considerably more individuals in treatment programs for alcohol problems than for marijuana abuse.
In a heavy drinker, damage to the liver shows up long before brain damage appears.	Heavy alcohol use can be manifested in organic brain damage before liver damage is detected.
The physiological withdrawal reaction from heroin is considered more dangerous than is withdrawal from alcohol.	The physiological symptoms accompanying withdrawal from heroin are no more frightening or traumatic to an individual than alcohol withdrawal. Actually, alcohol withdrawal is potentially more lethal than opiate withdrawal.
Everybody drinks.	Actually, 28 percent of men and 50 percent of women in the United States are abstainers.

long after such actions are in fact quite unsafe. When the blood-alcohol level reaches approximately 0.5 percent (although the level differs somewhat between individuals) the entire neural balance is upset and the individual passes out. Unconsciousness apparently acts as a safety device, because concentrations above 0.55 percent are usually lethal (see Table 10.2).

In general, it is the amount of alcohol actually concentrated in the bodily fluids, not the amount consumed, that determines intoxication. The effects of alcohol, however, vary for different drinkers, depending on their physical condition, the amount of food in their stomach, and

the duration of their drinking. In addition, alcohol users may gradually build up a tolerance for the drug so that ever-increasing amounts may be needed to produce the desired effects. Women metabolize alcohol less effectively than men and thus become intoxicated on lesser amounts of alcohol (Gordis et al., 1995). Drinkers' attitudes are important, too: Although actual motor and intellectual abilities decline in direct ratio to the blood concentration of alcohol, many people who consciously try to do so can maintain apparent control over their behavior, showing few outward signs of being intoxicated even after drinking relatively large amounts of alcohol.

TABLE 10.2   ALCOHOL LEVELS IN THE BLOOD AFTER DRINKS TAKEN ON AN EMPTY STOMACH BY A 150-POUND MALE DRINKING FOR ONE HOUR

Effects	Time for Alcohol to Leave the Body (Hours)	Alcohol Concentration in Blood (Percentage)	Amount of Beverage
Slight changes in feeling	1	0.025	1 cocktail (1 1/2 oz. whiskey) *or* 5 1/2 oz. ordinary wine *or* 1 bottle beer (12 oz.)
Feelings of warmth, mental relaxation	2	0.05	2 cocktails 11 oz. ordinary wine *or* 2 bottles beer
Exaggerated emotion and behavior—talkative, noisy, or morose	4	0.07	3 cocktails 16 1/2 oz. ordinary wine *or* 4 bottles beer
Clumsiness—unsteadiness in standing or walking	6	0.1	4 cocktails 22 oz. ordinary wine *or* 6 bottles beer
Gross intoxication	10	0.15	6 cocktails 27 1/2 oz ordinary wine *or* 1/2 pint whiskey
Calories			
4 oz. wine	100		
12 oz. beer	150		
1 oz. whisky	70		

Note: Blood-alcohol level following given intake differs according to a person's weight, the length of the drinking time, and the person's sex.

Source: Bellerson, 1997; Ray & Ksir, 1995.

Exactly how alcohol works on the brain is only beginning to be understood, but several physiological effects are common. The first is a tendency toward decreased sexual inhibition but, simultaneously, lowered sexual performance. As Shakespeare wrote in *Macbeth,* alcohol "provokes the desire, but it takes away the performance." An appreciable number of alcohol abusers also experience blackouts—lapses of memory. At first these occur at high blood-alcohol levels, and a drinker may carry on a rational conversation or engage in other relatively complex activities but have no trace of recall the next day. For heavy drinkers, even moderate drinking can elicit memory lapses. Another phenomenon associated with alcoholic intoxication is the hangover, which many drinkers experience at one time or another. As yet, no one has come up with a satisfactory explanation or remedy for the symptoms of headache, nausea, and fatigue characteristic of the hangover.

Development of Alcohol Dependence   Excessive drinking can be viewed as progressing insidiously from early- to middle- to late-stage alcoholism, although some alcoholics do not follow this progressively developing pattern. Table 10.3 presents some of the common early warning signs of excessive drinking.

Although many investigators have maintained that alcohol is a dangerous systemic poison even in small amounts, others believe that in moderate amounts it is not harmful to most people. Some studies have shown that small amounts of red wine can even serve as a protective factor in coronary disease (Brody, 1996). For pregnant women, however, even moderate amounts are believed to be dangerous; in fact, no safe level has been established, as is discussed in Highlight 10.2. The photo on page 380 shows the differences in the brain of a normal teenager and those born with fetal alcohol syndrome (FAS), a condition caused by excessive alcohol consumption during pregnancy and which results in birth defects such as mental retardation.

The Physical Effects of Chronic Alcohol Use   For individuals who drink to excess, the clinical picture is

TABLE 10.3 EARLY WARNING SIGNS OF DRINKING PROBLEMS

1. *Frequent desire*—increase in desire, often evidenced by eager anticipation of drinking after work and careful attention to maintaining supply.

2. *Increased consumption*—increase that seems gradual but is marked from month to month. An individual may begin to worry at this point and lie about the amount consumed.

3. *Extreme behavior*—commission of various acts that leave an individual feeling guilty and embarrassed the next day.

4. *"Pulling blanks"*—inability to remember what happened during an alcoholic bout.

5. *Morning drinking*—either as a means of reducing a hangover or as a "bracer" to help start the day.

   A person who exhibits this pattern is well on the road to abusive drinking. The progression is likely to be facilitated if there is environmental support for heavy or excessive drinking from the person's spouse, job situation, or sociocultural setting.

highly unfavorable (Maher, 1997). For one, the alcohol that is taken in must be assimilated by the body, except for about 5 to 10 percent that is eliminated through breath, urine, and perspiration. The work of assimilation is done by the liver, but when large amounts of alcohol are ingested, the liver may be seriously overworked and eventually suffer irreversible damage. In fact, from 15 to 30 percent of heavy drinkers develop cirrhosis of the liver, a disorder involving extensive stiffening of the blood vessels. About 40 to 90 percent of the 26,000 annual cirrhosis deaths every year are alcohol related (Du-Four, Stinson, & Cases, 1993). Alcohol-related cirrhosis is a problem in other countries as well. The Medical Council on Alcoholism in England (1997) recently reported an increase in liver disease in England and Wales, particularly in women.

Alcohol is also a high-calorie drug. A pint of whiskey—enough to make about eight to ten ordinary cocktails—provides about 1200 calories, which is approximately half the ordinary caloric requirement for a day (Flier, Underhill, & Lieber, 1995). Thus consumption of alcohol reduces a drinker's appetite for other food. Because alcohol has no nutritional value, the excessive drinker often suffers from malnutrition (Derr & Gutman, 1994). Furthermore, heavy drinking impairs the

body's ability to utilize nutrients, so the nutritional deficiency cannot be made up by popping vitamins. Alcoholics also experience increased gastrointestinal symptoms such as stomach pains (Fields et al., 1994).

Psychosocial Affects of Alcohol Abuse and Dependence   In addition to various physical problems, an excessive drinker usually suffers from chronic fatigue, oversensitivity, and depression. Initially, alcohol may seem to provide a useful crutch for dealing with the stresses of life, especially during periods of acute stress, by helping screen out intolerable realities and enhancing the drinker's feelings of adequacy and worth. The excessive use of alcohol becomes counterproductive, however, resulting in lowered feelings of adequacy and worth, impaired reasoning and judgment, and gradual personality deterioration. Behavior typically becomes coarse and inappropriate, and the drinker assumes increasingly less responsibility, loses pride in personal appearance, neglects spouse and family, and becomes generally touchy, irritable, and unwilling to discuss the problem.

As judgment becomes impaired, an excessive drinker may be unable to hold a job and generally becomes unqualified to cope with new demands that arise. General personality disorganization and deterioration may be re-

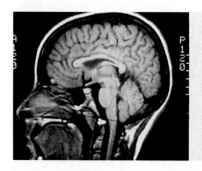 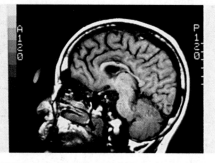 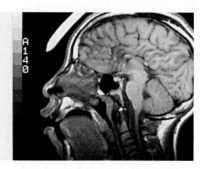

MRIs of three children: (left) Normal control, 13 year old female; (center) FAS, 13 year old male with focal thinning of the corpus callosum; (right) FAS, 14 year old male with complete agenesis of the corpus callosum.

Source: Mattson, S.N., Jernigan, T.L., and Riley, E.P. (1994). MRI and prenatal alcohol exposure. *Alcohol Health & Research World, 18* (1), 49–52.

Highlight 10.2

Fetal Alcohol Syndrome: How Much Drinking Is Too Much?

Research indicates that heavy drinking by expectant mothers can affect the health of unborn babies. Newborn infants whose mothers drank heavily during pregnancy have been found to have frequent physical and behavioral abnormalities (Alison, 1994; see the photo on page 380 of brain damage in a child with fetal alcohol syndrome) and may experience symptoms of withdrawal (Thomas & Riley, 1998). For example, such infants have shown growth deficiencies, facial and limb irregularities, and central nervous system dysfunction (Mattson, Riley et al., 1998; Mattson & Riley, 1998; Short & Hess, 1995). As noted in *The Third Report on Alcohol and Health* (HEW, 1978), alcohol abuse in pregnant women is the third-leading cause of birth defects (the first two being Down syndrome and spina bifida, the latter referring to the incomplete formation and fusion of the spinal canal and one of the leading causes of mental retardation (Abel, 1988; Niccols, 1994) and ADHD (Nanson & Hiscock, 1990)). Fetal alcohol syndrome is also associated with the development of mental disorder in adults (Famy, Streissguth, & Unis, 1998). Although data on fetal alcohol syndrome are often difficult to obtain, estimates range from 1 to 3 per 1000 births (Abel, 1990) in the general population to 25 per 1000 in women who are chronic alcoholics (Abel, 1988). Research in laboratory animals has confirmed the devastating neurological effects of alcohol exposure in utero (Hannigan, 1996). Interestingly, nearly all cases of fetal alcohol syndrome occur in the United States and not in other countries, some of which have higher rates of alcohol use than the United States. The phenomenon of fetal alcohol syndrome has been referred to as an "American Paradox" (Abel, 1998), with researchers noting that fetal alcohol syndrome is strongly related to socioeconomic class.

How much drinking endangers a newborn's health? The HEW report warns against drinking more than 1 ounce of alcohol per day or the equivalent (one 12-ounce can of beer or one 5-ounce glass of wine, for example). The actual amount of alcohol that can safely be ingested during pregnancy is not known, but it is clear that existing evidence for fetal alcohol syndrome is strongest when applied to heavy alcohol users rather than light to moderate users (Kolata, 1981b). Nonetheless, the Surgeon General and many medical experts have concurred that pregnant women should abstain from using alcohol as the "safest course" until safe amounts of alcohol consumption can be determined (Raskin, 1993).

Unfortunately, treatment resources have traditionally been focused on and developed for men, in part because substance-abuse problems have been more common among men. However, with more women, including pregnant women, developing alcohol-abuse problems, an important new need has developed for providing treatment services to future mothers and their babies. Treatment programs need to be developed that aid pregnant women and protect their children (Finkelstein, 1993). ■

flected in loss of employment and marital breakup. By this time, the drinker's general health is likely to have deteriorated, and brain and liver damage may have occurred. For example, there is some evidence that an alcoholic's brain could be accumulating diffuse organic damage even when no extreme organic symptoms are present (Lishman, 1990). As discussed in Chapter 13, other researchers have found extensive alcohol consumption to be associated with an increased amount of neurological deficit in later life (Parsons, 1998).

Psychoses Associated with Alcoholism Several acute psychotic reactions fit the diagnostic classification of substance-induced disorders. These reactions may develop

The effects of fetal alcohol syndrome can be both dramatic and long-lasting. This child shows some of the permanent physical abnormalities characteristic of the syndrome: widely spaced eyes, short broad nose, underdeveloped upper lip, and receding chin.

in people who have been drinking excessively over long periods of time or who have a reduced tolerance for alcohol for other reasons—for example, because of brain lesions. Such acute reactions usually last only a short time and generally consist of confusion, excitement, and delirium. There is some evidence to suggest that delirium might be associated with lower levels of thiamine in alcoholics (Holzbeck, 1996). These disorders are often called alcoholic psychoses because they are marked by a temporary loss of contact with reality. Two commonly recognized psychotic reactions will be briefly described.

Among those who drink excessively for a long time, a reaction known as *alcohol withdrawal delirium* (formerly known as *delirium tremens*) may occur. This reaction usually happens following a prolonged drinking spree when the person is in a state of withdrawal. Slight noises or sudden moving objects may cause considerable excitement and agitation. The full-blown symptoms include (1) disorientation for time and place in which, for example, a person may mistake the hospital for a church or jail, no longer recognize friends, or identify hospital attendants as old acquaintances; (2) vivid hallucinations, particularly of small, fast-moving animals like snakes, rats, and roaches, which are clearly localized in space; (3) acute fear, in which these animals may change in form, size, or color in terrifying ways; (4) extreme suggestibility, in which a person can be made to see almost any animal if its presence is merely suggested; (5) marked tremors of

the hands, tongue, and lips; and (6) other symptoms, including perspiration, fever, a rapid and weak heartbeat, a coated tongue, and foul breath.

The delirium typically lasts from three to six days and is generally followed by a deep sleep. When a person awakens, few symptoms—aside from possible slight remorse—remain, but frequently the individual is badly scared and may not resume drinking for several weeks or months. Usually, however, drinking is eventually resumed, followed by a return to the hospital with a new attack. The death rate from withdrawal delirium as a result of convulsions, heart failure, and other complications once approximated 10 percent (Tavel, 1962). With drugs such as chlordiazepoxide, however, the current death rate during withdrawal delirium and acute alcoholic withdrawal has been markedly reduced.

A second alcohol-related psychosis is the disorder referred to as *alcohol amnestic disorder* (formerly known as *Korsakoff's syndrome*). This condition was first described by the Russian psychiatrist Korsakoff in 1887 and is one of the most severe alcohol-related disorders (Oscar-Berman, Shagrin, Evert, & Epstein, 1997). The outstanding symptom is a memory defect (particularly with regard to recent events), which is sometimes accompanied by falsification of events (confabulation). Persons with this disorder may not recognize pictures, faces, rooms, and other objects that they have just seen, although they may feel that these people or objects are familiar. Such people increasingly tend to fill in their memory gaps with reminiscences and fanciful tales that lead to unconnected and distorted associations. These individuals may appear to be delirious, delusional, and disoriented for time and place, but ordinarily their confusion and disordered actions are closely related to their attempts to fill in memory gaps. The memory disturbance itself seems related to an inability to form new associations in a manner that renders them readily retrievable. Such a reaction usually occurs in older alcoholics, after many years of excessive drinking. These patients have also been observed to show other cognitive impairments such as planning deficits (Joyce & Robbins, 1991) and intellectual decline. Research with sophisticated brain-imaging techniques has found that patients with alcohol amnestic disorders show cortical lesions (Jernigan et al., 1991; Kopelman, 1991).

Case Study, A 48-Year-Old Homeless Veteran with Alcohol Amnestic Disorder • Averill B. was brought into the detoxification unit of a local county hospital by the police following an incident at a crowded city park. He was arrested because of his assaultive behavior toward others (he was walking through the crowded groups of sunbathers muttering to himself, kicking at people). At admission to the hospital, Averill was disoriented (did not know where he was), incoherent, and confused. When asked his name he paused a moment, scratched his head and said "George Washington." When asked about what he was doing at the park he indicated that he was "marching in a parade in his honor."

The symptoms of alcohol amnesic disorder are now thought to be due to vitamin B (thiamine) deficiency and other dietary inadequacies. Although it had been believed that a diet rich in vitamins and minerals generally restores a patient to more normal physical and mental health, recent evidence suggests otherwise. Lishman (1990) reported that alcohol amnestic disorder did not respond well to thiamine replacement. Some memory functioning appears to be restored with prolonged abstinence. However, some personality deterioration usually remains in the form of memory impairment, blunted intellectual capacity, and lowered moral and ethical standards.

Biological Factors in the Abuse of and Dependence on Alcohol and Other Substances

In trying to identify the causes of problem drinking, some researchers have stressed the role of genetic and biochemical factors; others have pointed to psychosocial factors, viewing problem drinking as a maladaptive pattern of adjustment to the stress of life; and still others have emphasized sociocultural factors, such as the availability of alcohol and social approval of excessive drinking. As with most other forms of maladaptive behavior, it appears that there may be several types of alcohol dependence, each with somewhat different patterns of biological, psychosocial, and sociocultural causal factors.

How do substances such as alcohol, cocaine, or opium (discussed below) come to have such powerful effects—an overpowering hold that occurs in some people after only a few uses of a drug? Although the exact mechanisms are not fully agreed on by experts in the field, two important factors are apparently involved. The first is the ability of some drugs to activate areas of the brain that produce intrinsic pleasure and immediate, powerful reward. The second factor involves the person's biological makeup or constitution, which includes both his or her genetic inheritance as well as the environmental influences (learning factors) that enter into the need to seek mind-altering substances to an increasing degree. The development of an alcohol addiction is a complex process involving many elements—constitutional vulnerability and environmental encouragement as well as the unique biochemical properties of certain psychoactive substances. The exact role that each of these ingredients plays in the addiction process has not been fully determined (and indeed may differ somewhat for each individual); however, each appears to contribute substantially to the process (Kalint 1989; Liebman & Cooper, 1989; Office of Technological Assessment, 1993; Sandbak, Murison et al., 1998). Let's examine each of these elements in more detail.

The Neurobiology of Addiction Let's first examine the role that drugs like alcohol play in the process of addiction. Drugs differ in terms of their biochemical properties as well as how rapidly they enter the brain. There are several routes of administration—oral, nasal, and intravenous. Alcohol is usually drunk, the slowest route, while cocaine is often self-administered by injection or taken nasally. Central to the neurochemical process underlying addiction is the role the drug plays in activating the "pleasure pathway." The **mesocorticolimbic dopamine pathway (MCLP)** is the center of psychoactive drug activation in the brain. The MCLP is made up of axons or neuronal cells in the middle portion of the brain known as the ventral tegmental area (see Figure 10.1) and connects to other brain centers such the nucleus accumbens and then to the frontal cortex. This neuronal system is involved in such functions as control of emotions, memory, and gratification. Alcohol is rewarding in that it produces euphoria by stimulating this area in the brain. Research has shown that direct electrical stimulation of the MCLP produces great pleasure and has strong reinforcing properties (Liebman & Cooper, 1989). Psychoactive drugs operate to change the brain's normal functioning and to activate the pleasure pathway. Drugs that activate the brain reward system obtain reinforcing action and, thereby, promote further use. The exposure of the brain to drug changes its neurochemical structure and results in a number of behavioral effects. With continued use of the drug, neuroadaptation or tolerance and dependence develop (see Figure 10.1).

Craving and Genetic Vulnerability The possibility of a genetic predisposition to developing alcohol-abuse problems has been widely researched. Alcoholism clearly tends to run in families (Dawson, Harford, & Grant, 1992). A review of 39 studies of families of 6251 alcoholics and 4083 nonalcoholics who had been followed over 40 years reported that almost one–third of alcoholics had at least one parent with an alcohol problem (Cotton, 1979). Likewise, a study of children of alcoholics by Cloninger and colleagues (1986) reported

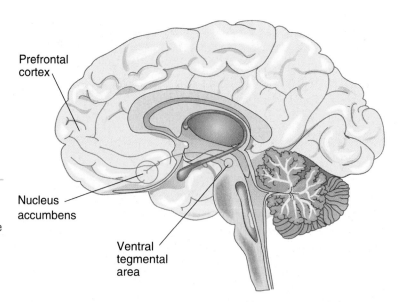

FIGURE 10.1 THE MESOCORTICOLIMBIC PATHWAY

The mesocorticolimbic pathway (MCLP), running from the ventral tegmental area to the nucleus accumbens to the frontal cortex is central to the release of the neurotransmitter dopamine and in mediating the rewarding properties of drugs (Office of Technology Assessment, 1993).

strong evidence for the inheritance of alcoholism. They found that, for males, having one alcoholic parent increased the rate of alcoholism from 11.4 percent to 29.5 percent, and having two alcoholic parents increased the rate to 41.2 percent. For females with no alcoholic parents, the rate was 5.0 percent; for those with one alcoholic parent, the rate was 9.5 percent; and for those with two alcoholic parents, it was 25.0 percent.

Much of the research on alcoholism has been conducted with persons who have been hospitalized for alcohol-related problems. Thus it is often difficult to know which symptoms or behaviors being investigated existed before the individual became "alcoholic" and which are the result of many years of abuse. An interesting problem for researchers in the search for causal factors in alcoholism and substance abuse in general is how to determine if the behavior being investigated is antecedent to the substance abuse caused by the abuse itself. One approach to understanding the precursors to alcoholism is to study prealcoholic personalities—individuals who are at high risk for substance abuse but who are not yet affected by alcohol.

An alcohol-risk personality has been described as an individual (usually an alcoholic's child) who has an inherited predisposition toward alcohol abuse and who is impulsive, prefers taking high risks, is emotionally unstable, has difficulty planning and organizing behavior, has problems in predicting the consequences of his or her actions, has many psychological problems, finds that alcohol is helpful in coping with stress, does not experience hangovers, and finds alcohol rewarding (Finn, 1990).

Research has shown that prealcoholic men (at present, most of this research has been done on men, in part because of the greater frequency of this problem for men) show different physiological patterns than nonalcoholic men in several respects. Prealcoholic men tend to feel a greater lessening of feelings of stress with alcohol ingestion than do nonalcoholic men (Finn & Pihl, 1987; Finn, Sharkansky et al., 1997). They also show different alpha wave patterns on EEG (Stewart, Finn, & Pihl, 1990). Prealcoholic men were found to show larger conditioned physiological responses to alcohol cues than were individuals who were considered at a low risk for alcoholism, according to Earlywine and Finn (1990). These results suggest that prealcoholic men may be more prone to develop tolerance for alcohol than low-risk men.

In support of possible genetic factors in alcoholism, a Japanese team has shown that rats that were bred to lack a particular gene (FYN) stayed drunk longer than normal mice (Miyakawa, Yagi et al., 1997). These rats were hypersensitive to the hypnotic effect of alcohol. In addition, some research has suggested that certain ethnic groups, particularly Asians and Native Americans have abnormal physiological reactions to alcohol—a phenomenon referred to as "alcohol flush reaction." Fenna and colleagues (1971) and Wolff (1972) found that Asian and Eskimo subjects showed a hypersensitive reaction, including flushing of the skin, a drop in blood pressure, heart palpitations, and nausea following the ingestion of alcohol. The physiological reaction is found in roughly half of all Asians (Chen & Yeh, 1997) and results from a mutant enzyme that fails to break down alcohol molecules in the liver during the metabolic process (Takeshita et al., 1993). Although cultural factors cannot be ruled out (Schaefer, 1978), the relatively lower rates of alcoholism among Asian groups might be related to the extreme discomfort associated with the alcohol flush reaction (Higuci, Matsushita et al., 1994).

Research has begun to accumulate that genetic factors contribute substantially to the development of alcohol preference. Research with animals, for example, has shown that strains of animals can be bred to have very high preference for alcohol (McBride et al., 1992). Moreover, genetic factors are likely to be involved in increased susceptibility or sensitivity to the effects of drugs. For example, low doses of alcohol or other addictive substances might be more stimulating to some people as a result of inherited differences in the mesocorticolimbic dopamine pathway described earlier (Liebman & Cooper, 1989). It seems increasingly likely that inherited factors affect an individual's response to psychoactive substances like alcohol.

Nevertheless, genetics alone are not the whole story and the role they play in the development of alcoholism remains unclear. We will return to this topic in the "Unresolved Issues" section at the end of this chapter. The genetic mechanism or model for the generally agreed upon observation that alcoholism is familial is insufficient to explain the behavior fully. That is, genetic transmission in the case of alcoholism does not follow the hereditary pattern found in other strictly genetic disorders.

Genetic Influences and Learning When we talk about familial or constitutional differences, we are not strictly limiting our explanation to genetic inheritance. Rather, learning factors appear to play an important part in the development of constitutional reaction tendencies. Having a genetic predisposition or biological vulnerability to alcoholism, of course, is not a sufficient cause of the disorder. The person must be exposed to the substance to a sufficient degree for the addictive behavior to appear. In the case of alcohol, almost everyone in America is exposed to the drug to some extent—in most cases through peer pressure, parental example, and advertising. The development of alcoholism involves living in an environment that promotes initial as well as continuing use of the substance. People become conditioned to stimuli and tend to respond in particular ways as a result of learning. Learning appears to play an important part in the development of substance abuse and antisocial personality disorders (see Chapter 9). There clearly are numerous reinforcements for using alcohol in our social environments and everyday lives. Furthermore, the use of alcohol

in a social context is often a sufficient reason for many people to continue using the drug. However, research has also shown that psychoactive drugs such as alcohol contain *intrinsic* rewarding properties that provide pleasure in and of itself—apart from the social context or its operation to diminish worry or frustration. As we saw earlier, the drug stimulates pleasure centers in the brain, and once use begins the substance develops a reward system of its own.

Psychosocial Causal Factors in Alcohol Abuse and Dependence

Not only do alcoholics become physiologically dependent on alcohol, they develop a powerful psychological dependence as well—they become socially dependent upon the drug to help them enjoy social situations. Because excessive drinking is ultimately so destructive to a person's total life adjustment, the question arises as to how psychological dependence is learned. A number of psychosocial factors have been advanced as possible answers.

Failures in Parental Guidance Stable family relationships and parental guidance are extremely important molding influences for children, and this stability is often lacking in families of alcoholics. Children who have parents who are extensive alcohol or drug abusers are vulnerable to developing substance abuse and related problems themselves. The experiences and lessons we learn from important figures in our early years have a significant impact, one way or another, on us as adults. Parent substance use is associated with early adolescent drug use (Hops et al., 1996). Children who are exposed to negative role models early in their lives or experience other negative circumstances because the adults around them provide limited guidance often falter on the difficult steps they must take in life (Vega et al., 1993). These formative experiences can have a direct influence on whether a youngster becomes involved in maladaptive behavior such as alcohol or drug abuse. These negative parental models can have longer range negative consequences once children leave the family situation. For example, in a study of college student health behavior, college freshmen from families with alcoholic parents viewed their families as less healthy and had more problematic family relationships than those with nonalcoholic parents (Deming, Chase, & Karesh, 1996).

In one program of research aimed at evaluating the possibility that negative socialization factors might influence alcohol use, Chassin and colleagues (1993) replicated findings that alcohol abuse in parents was associated with substance use in adolescents. They then evaluated several possible mediating factors that can influence adolescents in initiating alcohol use. They found that parenting skills or parental behavior was associated with substance use in adolescents. Alcoholic parents are less likely to keep track of what their children are doing, and this lack of monitoring often leads to the adolescent's affiliation with drug-using peers. In addition, Chassin and colleagues found that stress and negative affect (more prevalent in families with an alcoholic parent) were associated with alcohol use in adolescents. They reported that "parental alcoholism was associated with increases in negative uncontrollable life events which, in turn, were linked to negative affect, to associations with drug-using peers, and to substance use" (p. 16). More recently, in a follow-up study Chassin et al. (1996) reported that although fathers' monitoring, stress, and negative affect were mediators in adolescent alcohol abuse, there are likely to be other factors involved because the direct effect of fathers' alcoholism was strong, even after controlling for stress and negative affect.

Psychological Vulnerability

Is there an "alcoholic personality"—a type of character organization that predisposes a person to use alcohol rather than some other defensive pattern of coping with stress? Do some individuals self-medicate or reduce their discomfort by excessive use of alcohol? In efforts to answer this question, investigators have found that many potential alcoholics tend to be emotionally immature, expect a great deal of the world, require an inordinate amount of praise and appreciation, react to failure with marked feelings of hurt and inferiority, have low frustration tolerance, and feel inadequate and unsure of their abilities to fulfill expected male or female roles. Persons at high risk for developing alcoholism are significantly more impulsive and aggressive than those at low risk for abusing alcohol (Morey, Skinner, & Blashfield, 1984).

In recent years substantial research has focused on the link between alcohol-abuse disorders and other disorders such as antisocial personality, depression, and schizophrenia. About half of the persons with schizophrenia have either alcohol or drug-abuse dependency as well (Kosten, 1997). With respect to antisocial personality and alcohol abuse, the relationship is strong (Harford & Parker, 1994; Kwapil, 1996) though by no means completely overlapping or clear in terms of which (if either) disorder causes which (Carroll, Ball, & Rounsaville, 1993). High rates of substance abuse are found among antisocial personalities

The excessive use of alcohol may lead to depression or a depressed person may turn to the excessive use of alcohol.

(Clark, Watson, & Reynolds, 1995), and in a survey of eight alcohol treatment programs Morganstern, Langenbucher and colleagues (1997) found that 57.9 percent had a personality disorder, with 22.7 percent meeting criteria for antisocial personality disorder.

While such findings provide promising leads for understanding the causes of alcoholism, it is difficult to assess the role of specific personality characteristics in the development of the disorder. Certainly many people with similar personality characteristics do not become alcoholics, and others with dissimilar ones do. The only characteristic that appears common to the backgrounds of most problem drinkers is personal maladjustment, yet most maladjusted people do not become alcoholics. An alcoholic's personality may be as much a result as a cause of his or her dependence on alcohol—for example, the excessive use of alcohol may lead to depression, or a depressed person may turn to the excessive use of alcohol, or both.

The two psychopathological conditions that have been most frequently linked to addictive disorders are depression (Kranzler et al., 1997) and antisocial personality (Cadoret et al., 1985; Rounsaville, Kranzler et al., 1998). By far, most of the research has related antisocial personality (discussed in Chapter 9) and addictive disorders, with about 75 to 80 percent of the studies showing a strong association (Alterman, 1988) and conduct disorder (Slutsky, Heath et al., 1998). However, other diagnostic groups have also been found to co-occur—for example, schizophrenia (Buckley et al., 1994); borderline personality (Miller et al., 1993b); anxiety disorders (Deas-Nesmith, Brady, & Campbell, 1998); and bipolar disorder (Mason, & Ownby, 1998).

Some research has suggested that there is a relationship between depressive disorders and alcohol abuse, and there may be gender differences in the association between these disorders. One group of researchers (Moscato, Russell et al., 1997) found the degree of association between depression and alcohol abuse problems stronger among women. In addition, some authorities have suggested that patients who are comorbid alcoholic-depressives may be exhibiting both diseases distinctly (Coryell et al., 1992).

For whatever reason they co-occur, the presence of other mental disorders in alcohol or drug-abusing patients is a very important consideration when it comes to treatment. In order to ensure more effective treatment with these complicated problems, Brems and Johnson (1997) recommended that treatment of co-occurring mental health problems involve the following: more cross-disciplinary collaboration, greater integration of substance abuse and mental health treatments, and modification of training of caregivers to sensitize them to the difficulties of treating patients with comorbid disorders.

Stress, Tension Reduction, and Reinforcement

A number of investigators have pointed out that the typical alcoholic is discontented with his or her life and is unable or unwilling to tolerate tension and stress. For example, in a large sample of Norwegians, Watten (1995) found that there was a high degree of association between alcohol consumption and negative affectivity such as anxiety and somatic complaints. In other words, the subjects drank to relax. In this view, anyone who finds alcohol to be tension-reducing is in danger of becoming an alcoholic, even without an especially stressful life situation. However, as a sole explanatory hypothesis, the tension-reduction causal model is difficult to accept. For example, if this process were a main cause, we would expect alcoholism to be far more common than it is, since alcohol tends to reduce tension for most people who use it. In addition, this model does not explain why some excessive drinkers are able to maintain control over their drinking and continue to function in society while others are not.

Cox and Klinger (1988; Cooper, 1994) describe a motivational model of alcohol use that places a great deal of responsibility on the individual. According to this view, the final common pathway of alcohol use is motivation; that is, a person decides, consciously or unconsciously, whether to consume a particular drink of alcohol. Alcohol is consumed to bring about affective changes, such as the mood-altering effects, and even indirect effects, such as peer approval. In short, alcohol is consumed because it is reinforcing to the individual.

Expectatations of Social Success

In recent years a number of investigators have been exploring the idea that cognitive expectation might play an important role both in the initiation of drinking and in the maintenance of drinking behavior once the person has begun to use alcohol (Connors, Maisto, & Derman, 1994; Marlatt, Baer et al., 1998). Many people, especially young adolescents, expect that alcohol use will lower tension and anxiety and increase sexual desire and pleasure in life (Seto & Barbaree, 1995). In this view, often referred to as the *reciprocal influence model*, adolescents begin drinking as a result of expectations that alcohol will increase their popularity and acceptance by their peers. Research has shown that expectancies of social benefit can influence adolescents' decisions to start drinking and predicts their consumption of alcohol (Christiansen et al., 1989).

This view—that adolescents' expectations that drinking will ease their feelings of social awkwardness might influence their drinking behavior—provides professionals with an important and potentially powerful means of deterring, or at least delaying, the onset of, drinking among young people. From this perspective, alcohol use in teenagers can be countered by providing young people with more effective social tools and ways of altering these expectancies before drinking begins. Smith and colleagues (1995) have suggested that prevention efforts should be targeted at children before they begin to drink to avoid the positive feedback cycle of reciprocal reinforcement between expectancy and drinking (see the discussion on alcohol use prevention in Chapter 18).

Time and experience does have a moderating influence over these alcohol expectancies. There is clear evidence to suggest that these expectancies become less influential over time or age. In a longitudinal study of college drinking, Sher, Wood, and colleagues (1996) found that there was a significant decrease in outcome expectancy over time. Older students showed less expectation of the benefits of alcohol than beginning students (see Highlight 10.3 on binge drinking in college).

Marital and Other Intimate Relationships

Excessive drinking often begins during crisis periods in marital or other intimate personal relationships, particularly crises that lead to hurt and self-devaluation. The marital relationship may actually serve to maintain the pattern of excessive drinking. In one case, Evelyn C., a 36-year-old homemaker, began to drink to excess during times of extreme marital distress, particularly when her husband of three years began staying out all night and physically abusing her when he came back home. Marital partners may

Binge Drinking in College

Scott K., an 18-year-old college freshman from a prestigious university in Boston, went to a party at an off-campus fraternity house he was pledging. During an evening that was filled with heavy drinking, Scott lapsed into unconsciousness and his heart stopped. Although he was rushed to the emergency room where medics attempted to revive him, it was too late—he died without regaining consciousness. His blood-alcohol level at the time was .41—an amount that is four times the legal limit for driving in the state (Goldberg, 1997). This tragic incident occurred just a few weeks after another college student in Louisiana had died and 12 classmates had to be hospitalized for alcohol poisoning after an evening of drinking. Deaths due to alcohol poisoning, though seemingly more tragic when they occur among the young, are not uncommon. In fact, about 4000 people a year die of alcohol poisoning (Goldberg, 1997). However, the greatest number of alcohol-related deaths among college-age people (National Institute of Drug Abuse, 1981) involves driving while intoxicated.

These alcohol-related problems are not isolated incidents on college campuses nor are they only of recent vintage. Such problems as fighting, property damage, drunk driving, sexual assaults, falling deaths, to mention only the more serious, are relatively common around colleges and universities and have been more or less a part of the university environment for centuries. Moreover, binge drinking among college students is an international problem. College students in the United Kingdom, for example, have been shown to have an even higher rate of alcohol consumption, hangovers, blackouts, and missed classes than American college students (Delk & Meilman, 1996) and in Australia 34 percent of respondents reported mixing alcohol and driving and have greater concerns about drinking to excess than students in Israel, the United States, and Singapore (Isralowitz, Borowski et al., 1992). Whether they occur following off-campus parties or on one of the annual "break aways" to Panama City or Atlanta, binge drinking episodes are commonly associated with negative consequences. (Cities such as Fort Lauderdale, Florida, have discouraged these gatherings because of their adverse consequences.)

These incidents serve to highlight the serious problem of binge drinking in a population that is at an exceptionally high risk for substance abuse disorder. Although explicit criteria for what is a problem drinker can be debated (DeCourville & Sadova, 1997) most would concede that the outcome of college binge drinking such as these instances can be highly problematic.

How extensive is college binge drinking? In spite of the fact that alcohol use is illegal for most undergraduates, binge drinking on campus is widespread (Rabow & Duncan-Schill, 1995). In fact, 44 percent of college students in the United States are binge drinkers according to a survey by Wechsler, Davenport, Dowdall, Moeykens, and Castillo

behave toward each other in ways that promote or enable the spouse's excessive drinking. For example, a husband who lives with an alcoholic wife is often unaware of the fact that, gradually and inevitably, many of the decisions he makes every day are based on the expectation that his wife will be drinking. These expectations, in turn, may make the drinking behavior more likely. Thus one important concern in many treatment programs today involves identifying relationship patterns that tend to foster the drinking in the alcohol-abusing person. That is, such programs try to identify the personality or lifestyle factors in a relationship that serve to promote, maintain, or justify the drinking behavior of an alcoholic. Eventually an entire marriage may center on the drinking of an alcoholic spouse. In some instances, the husband or wife may also begin to drink excessively, possibly through the reinforcement of such behavior by the drinking mate or to blank out the disillusionment, frustration, and resentment that are often elicited by an

(1994), and Goodwin (1992) reports that 98 percent of fraternity and sorority members drink some amount every week. Wechsler and colleagues (1994) conducted a nation-wide survey of 140 college campuses in 40 states and obtained survey information per-taining to the drinking behavior and health consequences of drinking on 17,592 students (with approximately a 69 percent response rate.) Students completed a 20-page survey of their drinking practices including such in-formation as recency of last drink, how many times they had five drinks or more in a row, and how many times they had four drinks in a row. In addition they were asked to provide information as to whether they experienced any of the following consequences after drinking: had a hangover, missed a class, got behind in schoolwork, did something they later regretted, forgot where they were or what they did, argued with friends, engaged in unplanned sexual activities, failed to use protection when having sex, damaged prop-erty, got into trouble with the campus police, got hurt or required medical treatment for an alcohol overdose.

The colleges surveyed in the study varied widely as to the extent of binge drinking in their student body. As one might expect—some colleges earn reputations as being "party schools"—some institutions had a large num-ber of students (70 percent) that are heavily involved in alcohol and binge drinking, but the problem occurred across most college campuses to a degree. Binge drinking tended to vary with age, with those between 17 to 23 years of age having much higher rates than older students. There is some tendency for students to moderate their drinking over time. Alcohol is not as central in the lives of older students as with younger students who, along with older individuals in general, ap-pear to have lowered expectancies of benefit from using alcohol (Sher et al., 1996).

The consequences of college binge drink-ing can indeed be great. In their survey, Wechsler and colleagues (1994) reported that there was a strong positive relationship be-tween the frequency of binge drinking and al-cohol-related health and life problems. In fact, binge drinkers were nearly 10 times more likely than nonbinge drinkers to engage in unplanned sexual activity, not use protec-tion when having sex, get into trouble with campus police, damage property, or get hurt after drinking. Men and women tended to re-port similar problems except that men tended to engage in more property damage than women. Over 16 percent of the men and 9 percent of the women reported having got-ten in trouble with the campus police. About 47 percent of the frequent binge drinkers in-dicated that they had experienced five or more of the problems surveyed compared with 14 percent of the nonbinge drinkers.

Interestingly, in a recent follow-up sur-vey of college drinking in 1997. Wechsler and colleagues (1998) reported strikingly similar results—2 out of 5 students (about 42.7 per-cent) were considered binge drinkers in the more recent study as compared with 44.1 percent in the earlier study. ■

alcoholic spouse. Of course, such relationships are not re-stricted to marital partners but may also occur in those in-volved in love affairs or close friendships.

Excessive use of alcohol is one of the most frequent causes of divorce in the United States (Fillmore et al., 1994), and often a hidden factor in the two most com-mon causes—financial and sexual problems. The deterio-ration in alcoholics' interpersonal relationships, of course, further augments the stress and disorganization in their lives. The break-up of marital relationships can be a highly stressful situation for many people. The stress of divorce and the often erratic adjustment period that follows can lead to increased substance-abuse problems.

Family relationship problems have also been found to be central to the development of alcoholism. In a longitu-dinal study of possible etiological factors in alcohol abuse, Vaillant and Milofsky (1982) described six family relationship factors that were significantly associated with the development of alcoholism in the individuals they studied. The most important family variables that were considered to predispose the individual to substance use problems were the presence of an alcoholic father, the existence of acute marital conflict, lax maternal supervision and inconsistent discipline, having many family moves during their early years, having a lack of "attachment" to the father, and having no family cohesiveness.

Sociocultural Factors

In a general sense, our culture has become dependent on alcohol as a social lubricant and a means of reducing tension. Thus numerous investigators have pointed to the role of sociocultural as well as physiological and psychological factors in the high rate of alcohol abuse and dependence among Americans (Vega et al., 1993).

The effect of cultural attitudes toward drinking is well illustrated by Muslims and Mormons, whose religious values prohibit the use of alcohol, and by orthodox Jews, who have traditionally limited its use largely to religious rituals. The incidence of alcoholism among these groups is minimal. In comparison, the incidence of alcoholism is high among Europeans, who comprise less than 15 percent of the world's population yet consume about half the alcohol (Sulkunen, 1976). Interestingly, Europe and six countries that have been influenced by European culture—Argentina, Canada, Chile, Japan, the United States, and New Zealand—make up less than 20 percent of the world's population yet consume 80 percent of the alcohol (Barry, 1982). Alcohol abuse continues to be a problem in Europe and these problems have been noted to have great consequence in terms of accidents (Lehto, 1995), crime (Rittson, 1995), increased liver disease (Medical Council on Alcoholism, 1997), and the extent to which young people are becoming involved in substance use problems (Anderson & Lehto, 1995). The French appear to have the highest rate of alcoholism in the world, approximately 15 percent of the population. France has both the highest per capita alcohol consumption and the highest death rate from cirrhosis of the liver (Noble, 1979). In addition, France shows the highest prevalence rates: In a broad survey of hospital patients 18 percent (25 percent for men and 7 percent for women) were reported to have alcohol use disorders though only 6 percent of admissions were for alcohol problems (Reynaud, Leleu et al., 1997). In Sweden, another country with high rates of alcoholism, the proportion of hospital admissions attributed to alcohol was 13.2 percent for men and 1.1 percent for women (Andreason & Brandt, 1997). Thus it appears that religious sanctions and social customs can determine

The cultural influences on alcoholism are clear when one looks at the extremely low incidence of alcoholism among Muslims, Mormons and orthodox Jews, whose religious values prohibit drinking except in religious services.

whether alcohol is one of the coping methods commonly used in a given group or society.

The behavior that is manifested under the influence of alcohol appears to be influenced by cultural factors. Lindman and Lang (1994), in a study of alcohol-related behavior in eight countries, found that most subjects expressed the view that aggressive behavior frequently followed after drinking "many" drinks; however, the expectation that alcohol leads to aggression is related to cultural traditions and early exposure to violent or aggressive behavior.

In sum, we can identify many reasons why people drink—as well as many conditions that can predispose them to do so and reinforce drinking behavior—but the combination of factors that result in a person's becoming an alcoholic are still unknown.

Treatment of Alcoholism

Alcohol abuse and dependence are difficult to treat because many alcoholics refuse to admit that they have a problem or seek assistance before they "hit bottom," and many that do go into treatment leave before therapy is completed. Di Clemente (1993) refers to the addictions as "diseases of denial." In a survey that included more than 60,000 treated alcoholics, Booth, Cook, and Blow (1992) reported that 11 percent left treatment against medical advice. When alcoholics are confronted with their drinking problem, they may react with denial or become angry at the "messenger" and withdraw from this person (Miller & Rollnick, 1991).

A multidisciplinary approach to the treatment of drinking problems appears to be most effective because the problems are often complex, requiring flexibility and individualization of treatment procedures (Margolis & Zweben, 1998). Also, an alcoholic's needs change as treatment progresses. Treatment program objectives usually include detoxification, physical rehabilitation, control over alcohol-abuse behavior, and development of an individual's realization that he or she can cope with the problems of living and lead a much more rewarding life without alcohol. Traditional treatment programs usually have as their goal abstinence from alcohol. However, some programs attempt to promote controlled drinking as a treatment goal for problem drinkers. No matter what the treatment method, however, relapse is common and is seen as part of the treatment and recovery process by many in the field.

Use of Medications in Treating Alcoholics Biological approaches include a variety of treatment measures such as medications to reduce cravings, to ease the detoxification process, and to treat co-occurring mental health problems that are thought to potentially underlie the drinking behavior (Romach & Sellers, 1998).

Medications to Block the Desire to Drink Disulfiram (Antabuse), a drug that causes violent vomiting when followed by ingestion of alcohol, may be administered to prevent an immediate return to drinking (Chic et al., 1992). Adelman and Weiss (1989), studying the efficacy of different treatment strategies with alcoholics, reported that alcohol treatment programs that use Antabuse may have clear advantages over programs that do not in that they usually suppress drinking when the drug is taken regularly. However, such deterrent therapy is seldom advocated as the sole approach, because pharmacological methods alone have not proved effective in treating alcoholism (Gorlick, 1993). For example, since the drug is usually self-administered, an alcoholic may simply discontinue the use of Antabuse when he or she is released from a hospital or clinic and begins to drink again. In fact, the primary value of drugs of this type seems to be their ability to interrupt the alcoholic cycle for a period of time, during which therapy may be undertaken. Uncomfortable side effects may accompany the use of Antabuse; for example, alcohol-based after-shave lotion can be absorbed through the skin, resulting in illness. Moreover, the cost of Antabuse treatment, since it requires careful medical maintenance, is higher than for many other, more effective treatments (Holder et al., 1991).

Another type of medication that has been used in a promising line of research (Anton, 1996; Columbus, et al., 1995) is *Naltrexone,* an opiate antagonist that helps reduce the "craving" for alcohol that alcoholics experience by blocking the pleasure producing effects of alcohol. O'Malley, Jaffe, Rode, and Rounsaville (1996) have shown that Naltrexone reduced the alcohol intake and lowered the incentive to drink for alcoholics compared with a control sample who were given a placebo.

Medications to Lower the Side Effects of Acute Withdrawal In acute intoxication, the initial focus is on detoxification (the elimination of alcoholic substances from an individual's body), the treatment of withdrawal symptoms described earlier, and a medical regimen for physical rehabilitation. One of the primary goals in treatment of withdrawal symptoms is to reduce the physical symptoms characteristic of the syndrome, such as insomnia, headache, gastrointestinal distress, and tremulousness. Central to the treatment are the prevention of heart arrhythmias, seizures, delirium, and death (Bohn, 1993). These steps can usually best be handled in a hospital or clinic, where drugs such as Valium have largely revolutionized the treatment of withdrawal symptoms. Such drugs overcome motor excitement, nausea, and vomiting; prevent withdrawal delirium and convulsions; and help alleviate the tension and anxiety associated with withdrawal. Concern is growing, however, that the use of tranquilizers at this stage does not promote long-term recovery and may foster addiction to another substance. Accordingly, some detoxification clinics are exploring alternative approaches, including a gradual weaning from alcohol instead of a sudden cutoff. Maintenance doses of mild tranquilizers are sometimes given to patients withdrawing from alcohol to reduce anxiety and help them sleep. Such use of tranquilizers may be less effective than no treatment at all, however. Usually patients must learn to abstain from tranquilizers as well as from alcohol, because they tend to misuse both. Further, under the influence of tranquilizers, patients may even return to alcohol use.

Medications to Treat Co-occurring Disorders Tranquilizing medications are also used in the treatment of alcoholism in ways other than easing withdrawal symptoms. For example, medications such as *desimpramine* are used to treat comorbid depression symptoms and alcohol consumption (Anton, 1996).

Psychological Treatment Approaches Detoxification is optimally followed by psychological treatment, including family counseling and the use of community resources relating to employment and other aspects of a person's social readjustment. Although individual psychotherapy is sometimes effective, the focus of psychosocial measures in the alcoholism treatment more often involves group therapy, environmental intervention, behavior therapy, and the approach used by Alcoholics Anonymous and family groups such as Al-Anon and Al-Ateen.

Group Therapy In the confrontational give-and-take of group therapy (see Chapter 17), alcoholics are often forced to face their problems (perhaps for the first time) and their tendencies to deny or to minimize their involvement in their troubles when they describe them to a knowing audience of "peers." It may be difficult for them to hide or deny drinking problems when they are confronted by persons who have had similar problems and similar guises but have come to recognize them. These treatment group situations can be extremely difficult for alcoholics who have been engrossed in denial of their own responsibilities; but they also provide the opportunity for them to see new possibilities for coping with circumstances that have led to their difficulties. Often, but by no means always, this problem recognition paves the way for learning more effective methods of coping and other positive steps toward dealing with their drinking problem.

In some instances, the spouses of alcoholics and even their children may be invited to join in group therapy meetings. In other situations, family treatment is itself the central focus of therapeutic efforts. In this case, the alcoholic is seen as a member of a disturbed family in which all the members have a responsibility for cooperating in treatment. Because family members are frequently the people most victimized by the alcoholic's addiction, they often tend to be judgmental and punitive, and the alcoholic, who has already passed harsh judgment on himself or herself, tolerates this further source of devaluation poorly. In other instances, family members may unwittingly encourage an alcoholic to remain addicted—for example, a man with a need to dominate his wife may find that a continually drunken and remorseful spouse best meets his needs.

Environmental Intervention As with other serious maladaptive behaviors, a total treatment program for alcoholism usually requires measures to alleviate a patient's aversive life situation. Environmental support has been shown to be an important ingredient to an alcoholic's recovery (Booth et al., 1992a; 1992b). As a result of their drinking, alcoholics often become estranged from family and friends and either lose or jeopardize their jobs. As a result they are often lonely and live in impoverished neighborhoods. Typically the reaction of those around them is not as understanding or supportive as it would be if the alcoholic had a physical illness of comparable magnitude. Simply helping alcoholics learn more effec-

tive coping techniques may not be enough if their social environment remains hostile and threatening. For alcoholics who have been hospitalized, halfway houses—designed to assist them in their return to family and community—are often important adjuncts to their total treatment program.

The relapses and continued deterioration that alcoholics often experience are associated with their lack of close relationships with family or friends, as well as living in a stressful environment. In general, it appears unlikely that an alcoholic will remain abstinent after treatment unless the negative psychosocial factors that operated in the past also change for the better.

Behavior Therapy One interesting and often effective form of treatment for alcohol-abuse disorders is behavior therapy, of which several types exist. One is *aversive conditioning,* involving the presentation of a wide range of noxious stimuli with alcohol consumption in order to suppress drinking behavior. For example, the ingestion of alcohol might be paired with an electric shock or a drug that produces nausea.

A variety of pharmacological and other deterrent measures can be used in behavior therapy after detoxification. One approach involves an intramuscular injection of emetine hydrochloride, an emetic. Before experiencing the nausea that results from the injection, a patient is given alcohol, so that the sight, smell, and taste of the beverage become associated with severe retching and vomiting. That is, a conditioned aversion to taste and smell of alcohol develops. With repetition, this classical conditioning procedure acts as a strong deterrent to further drinking—probably in part because it adds an immediate and unpleasant physiological consequence to the more general socially aversive consequences of excessive drinking.

Behavioral and cognitive behavioral approaches often target behaviors that are thought to contribute to use of alcohol—for example, depression. Research has shown that cognitive-behavioral interventions can both improve the person's mood state and lower substance abuse (Brown, Evans, Miller et al. 1997). Another behavioral approach that has shown substantial benefit has been behavioral couples therapy. More benefit at lower cost was found for behavioral couples therapy than for individual behavior therapy (Fals-Stewart, O'Farrell, & Birchler, 1997).

One of the most effective contemporary procedures for treating alcoholics has been the cognitive-behavioral approach recommended by Alan Marlatt (1985) and Marlatt, Baer, and colleagues (1998). This approach combines cognitive-behavioral strategies of intervention with social-learning theory and modeling of behavior. The approach, often referred to as a skills-training procedure, is usually aimed at younger problem drinkers who are considered to be at risk for developing more severe drinking problems because of alcoholism in their family history or their heavy current consumption level. This approach relies on such techniques as imparting specific knowledge about alcohol, developing coping skills in situations associated with increased risk of alcohol use, modifying cognitions and expectancies, and acquiring stress-management skills. This cognitive-behavioral approach clearly has intuitive appeal; however, its relative effectiveness has yet to be demonstrated. Holder and colleagues (1991) reported that this approach tends to be less effective than other behavioral methods such as skills-training procedures.

Self-control training techniques (Miller, Brown et al. 1995), in which the goal of therapy is to get alcoholics to reduce alcohol intake without necessarily abstaining altogether, have a great deal of appeal for some drinkers. There is now even a computer-based self-control training program available that has been shown to reduce problem drinking in a controlled study (Hester & Delaney, 1997). It is difficult, of course, for individuals who are extremely dependent on the effects of alcohol to abstain totally from drinking. Thus many alcoholics fail to complete traditional treatment programs. The idea that they might be able to learn to control their drinking and at the same time enjoy the continued use of alcohol might serve as a motivating element (Lang & Kidorf, 1990).

Controlled Drinking Versus Abstinence   Other psychological techniques have also received attention in recent years, partly because they are based on the hypothesis that some problem drinkers need not give up drinking altogether but can learn to drink moderately (Lang & Kidorf, 1990; Miller, 1978; Sobell & Sobell, 1995). Several approaches to learning controlled drinking have been attempted (McMurran & Hollin, 1993), and research has suggested that some alcoholics can learn to control their alcohol intake (Miller, 1978; Senft, Polen et al., 1997). Miller and colleagues (1986) evaluated the results of four long-term follow-up studies of controlled-drinking treatment programs. Although they found a clear trend of increased numbers of abstainers and relapsed cases at long-term follow-up, they also found that a consistent percentage (15 percent) of subjects across the four studies controlled their drinking. The researchers concluded that controlled drinking was more likely to be successful in persons with less severe alcohol problems. The finding that some individuals are able to maintain some control over their drinking after treatment (and not remain totally abstinent) was also reported by Polich, Armor, and

Braiker (1981). These researchers found that 18 percent of the alcoholics they studied had reportedly been able to drink socially without problems during the six-month follow-up of treatment.

There are clear differences among treatment agencies and professionals with respect to their willingness to apply controlled-drinking strategies versus abstinence in alcohol treatment (Heather, 1995; Hsieh & Srebalus, 1997). Controlled-drinking programs (often referred to as *harm minimization*) have been reportedly successful in Australia. Dawe and Richmond (1997) reported a study in which the emphasis was shifted from total abstinence to one of "reducing hazardous" alcohol consumption." Of the 179 agencies surveyed, 66 percent reported that giving advice about controlled drinking as a treatment goal was met with reported success.

Many people in the field have rejected the idea that alcoholics can learn to control their drinking and insist on a total abstinence approach. The debate over whether alcoholics can learn moderate drinking continues after 25 years. Some researchers (Heather, 1995; Kahler, 1995; and Sobell & Sobell, 1995) maintain the efficacy of controlled drinking while others such as Glatt (1995) point to difficulties with alcoholics being able to maintain control. The debate as to the efficacy of controlled drinking has waned somewhat (Sobell & Sobell, 1995), and there has been acceptance of the notion that some individuals with alcohol-abuse problems can gain control over their drinking. However, this view of alcohol treatment is still in the minority. Most workers in the field still assume that total abstinence should be the goal for all problem drinkers. Some groups, such as Alcoholics Anonymous, are adamant in their opposition to programs aimed at controlled drinking for alcohol-dependent individuals.

Alcoholics Anonymous   A practical approach to alcoholism that has reportedly met with considerable success is that of Alcoholics Anonymous (AA). This organization was started in 1935 by two men, Dr. Bob and Bill W. in Akron, Ohio. Bill W. recovered from alcoholism through a "fundamental spiritual change," and immediately sought out Dr. Bob, who, with Bill's assistance, achieved recovery. They in turn began to help other alcoholics. Since that time, AA has grown to over 56,000 groups in the United States and Canada with an annual growth rate of about 6 to 7 percent (Alcoholics Anonymous, 1997). In addition, AA groups have been established in many other countries.

Alcoholics Anonymous operates primarily as a self-help counseling program in which both person-to-person

The people shown in this group meeting are following the widely adopted "Twelve-step program" for remaining abstinent from alcohol. Though the effectiveness of such programs is not exactly known, AA is one of the most popular alcohol treatment programs. It promotes total abstinence rather than controlled drinking.

and group relationships are emphasized. AA accepts both teenagers and adults with drinking problems, has no dues or fees, does not keep records or case histories, does not participate in political causes, and is not affiliated with any religious sect, although spiritual development is a key aspect of its treatment approach. To ensure anonymity, only first names are used. Meetings are devoted partly to social activities, but they consist mainly of discussions of the participants' problems with alcohol, often with testimonials from those who have recovered from alcoholism. Recovered members usually contrast their lives before they broke their alcohol dependence with the lives they now live without alcohol. We should point out here that the term *alcoholic* is used by AA and its affiliates to refer either to persons who currently are drinking excessively or to people who have recovered from such problems but must, according to AA philosophy, continue to abstain from alcohol consumption in the future. That is, in the AA view, one is an alcoholic for life, whether or not one is drinking; one is never "cured" of alcoholism but is instead "in recovery."

An important aspect of AA's rehabilitation program is that it lifts the burden of personal responsibility by helping alcoholics accept that alcoholism, like many other problems, is bigger than they are. Henceforth, they can see themselves not as weak-willed or lacking in moral strength, but rather simply as having an affliction—they cannot drink—just as other people may not be able to tolerate certain types of medication. By mutual help and reassurance from group members who have shared similar experiences, many alcoholics acquire insight into their problems, a new sense of purpose, greater ego strength, and more effective coping techniques. Continued participation in the group, of course, helps prevent the crisis of a relapse.

Affiliated movements, such as Al-Anon family groups and Al-Ateen (with over 35,000 groups in the United States and Canada), are designed to bring family members together to share common experiences and problems, to gain understanding of the nature of alcoholism, and to learn techniques for dealing with their own problems in the situation. There have also been some "spin-off" alcohol rehabilitation programs that follow this social-modelling approach using peer-oriented treatment that evolved from the AA approach (Borkman, Kaskutas, Room et al. 1998). These approaches may follow the AA model but include other treatment methods as well (Wallace, 1996).

The reported success of Alcoholics Anonymous is based primarily on anecdotal information rather than objective study of treatment outcomes since AA does not participate in external comparative research efforts. Brandsma, Maultsby, and Welsh (1980), however, included an AA program in their extensive comparative study of alcoholism treatments. The success of this treatment method with severe alcoholics was quite limited. One important finding was that the AA method had high dropout rates compared with other therapies. About half of the people who come to AA drop out of the program within three months. Chappel (1993) attributes the very high dropout rate to alcoholics' denial that they have problems, resistance to external pressure, and resistance to AA itself. Apparently many alcoholics are unable to accept the quasi-religious quality of the sessions and the group testimonial format that is so much a part of the AA program. In the Brandsma study, the participants who were assigned to the AA group subsequently encountered more life difficulties and drank more than people in other treatment groups. On the positive side, however, a recent study by Morganstern, Labouvie and colleagues (1997) reported that affiliation with AA after alcohol treatment was associated with better outcomes than non–AA involvement and a study by Tonigan, Toscova, and Miller (1995) found that AA involvement was strongly associated with success in outpatient samples.

Outcome Studies and Issues in Treatment The outcome of alcoholism treatment varies considerably, depending on the population studied and on the treatment facilities and procedures employed. They range from low rates of success for hard-core alcoholics to recoveries of 70 to 90 percent where modern treatment and aftercare procedures are used. Rounsaville and colleagues (1987) reported that psychopathology was influential in treatment outcomes for alcoholics. Alcoholics who were also diagnosed as having a personality disorder or affective disorder tended to have poorer outcomes in alcohol treatment than those for whom the diagnosis was simply alcoholism.

In their extensive four-year follow-up of a large group of treated alcoholics, Polich and colleagues (1981) found that alcoholics were difficult to treat regardless of the method used. Only 7 percent of the total sample (922 males) abstained from alcohol use throughout the four-year period, and 54 percent continued to show alcohol-related problems. (In addition, 36 percent of the sample demonstrated alcohol-dependence symptoms, and another 18 percent showed adverse consequences—such as arrests—from drinking.) On the positive side, however, this study can be viewed as demonstrating a clear beneficial effect of treatment for some people. Although 54 percent of the subjects showed drinking problems at follow-up, over 90 percent had had serious drinking problems at the beginning of treatment—a significant reduction. Interestingly, although only 7 percent of the alcoholics had been able to abstain from drinking for the full four-year period, others had abstained for shorter periods. For example, 21 percent had abstained for one year or more, and an additional 7 percent had abstained for six months. One interesting finding supports the view that some alcoholics may be able to learn to control their alcohol use without having to totally abstain from drinking—18 percent of the alcoholics had been able to drink without problems during the six-month period before follow-up.

Treatment is most likely to be effective when an individual realizes that he or she needs help, when adequate treatment facilities are available, and when the individual attends treatment regularly. Having a positive relationship with the therapist was associated with better treatment outcome and better outcome (Connors et al., 1997). One important new treatment strategy is aimed at reinforcing treatment motivation and abstinence early in the treatment process by providing "check-up" follow-ups on drinking behavior. Miller, Benefield, and Tonigan (1993) reported that "Drinking Check-Up" sessions during the early stages of therapy resulted in a reduction of drinking in the first six weeks of therapy as compared with clients who did not have check-up sessions.

Some researchers have maintained that treatment for alcohol use and abuse disorders would be more effective if important patient characteristics were taken into account in providing therapy (Mattson, Allen, Longabaugh et al., 1994). That is, patients with certain personality characteristics or with differing degrees of severity might do better in a specific therapeutic approach rather than a different one. This view was evaluated in an extensive study of patient-treatment matching (referred to as Project MATCH) that was sponsored by the National Institute on Alcohol Abuse and Alcoholism (NIAAA). This extensive recently completed study, initiated in 1989, involved 1,726 patients who were treated in 26 alcohol treatment programs in the United States by 80 different therapists from three treatment approaches. The research design included two separate and equal study branches in order to incorporate both an inpatient and an outpatient treatment component.

Project MATCH compared the treatment effectiveness of three different approaches to alcohol treatment: (1) a twelve-step program along the lines of Alcoholics Anonymous (but not sponsored by AA) was referred to as Twelve-Step Facilitation Therapy (TSF); (2) a cognitive-behavior therapy program (CBT); and (3) a treatment technique referred to as Motivational Enhancement Therapy (MET), which attempts to get clients to assume responsibility for helping themselves. These approaches were chosen because they had been reported to have potential for clear matching as well as being considered to be effective in treating alcoholics (Gordis, 1997). The researchers in Project MATCH evaluated patients on ten characteristics that had been shown in the literature to be related to treatment outcome (Babor, 1996; Project MATCH Group, 1997): diagnosis as alcoholics, cognitive impairment, conceptual ability level, gender, desire to seek meaning in life, motivation, psychiatric severity, severity of alcohol involvement, social support for drinking versus abstinence, and presence of sociopathy (personality disorder).

The results of this study were unexpected—matching the patients to particular treatments did not appear to be important to having an effective outcome. The treatments studied all had equal outcomes. Gordis (1997) concluded that "it is likely that patients in competently run alcoholism treatment programs will do as well with one of the three treatments studied as with the others."

Programs in the Workplace Alcohol and violence in the workplace has increasingly been a problem in the United States (Bennett & Lehman, 1996). Many organizations have implemented measures to provide more internal and external security in order to reduce the amount of substance abuse and violence-related abuse in the workplace (Bush & O'Shea, 1996). One of the most effective means of reducing and lowering the impact of alcohol-abuse problems in the workplace has involved the introduction of Employee Assistance Programs (EAPs). Such programs, which are aimed at providing mental health services to employees, have proven highly effective in detecting drinking problems early, in referring drinkers for treatment, and in ensuring the effectiveness of after-care procedures. When we realize that an estimated 5 percent of the nation's workforce are severe alcoholics, and an additional 5 percent are considered alcohol abusers, it is apparent that such programs can have a major impact on coping with the alcohol problem in our society (Alander & Campbell, 1975).

Inpatient or Outpatient Treatment As described earlier, there is some controversy over whether inpatient treatment for alcohol problems is required or whether alcoholics can be treated successfully as outpatients. Clearly, if outpatient therapy were as effective as inpatient treatment, several distinct advantages could be found. For example, patients could remain in the community with their families and jobs where, many would say, their ultimate adjustment needs to be made. Moreover, outpatient treatment is more cost-effective, an important factor that is a prominent issue in health care today. Unfortunately, some studies have reported a clear advantage of inpatient treatment (75 percent completion rate) over outpatient programs (18 percent completion rate) (Wickizer et al., 1994). At the present stage of research on treatment effectiveness, neither inpatient nor outpatient therapy has won the majority of followers. The relative effectiveness of inpatient versus outpatient therapy for alcoholics remains controversial, and research supports both sides of the issue (Adelman & Weiss, 1993; Cocores, 1991; Collins, 1993).

The Value of Professional Treatment In their study of various treatments of chronic, severe alcohol problems, Brandsma and colleagues (1980) found that direct treatment—whether professional or paraprofessional, insight-oriented or cognitive-behavior therapy—was more effective than an untreated control condition. The investigators randomly assigned chronic alcoholics to treatment groups—insight-oriented therapy, rational-behavior therapy, Alcoholics Anonymous, self-help (paraprofessional) therapy—or to a nontreatment control group. One important finding was that professional treatment was more effective than nonprofessional treatment, although either of the two major therapeutic orientations (insight-oriented versus rational-behavior therapy) was equally effective. As noted above, Alcoholics Anonymous was the least effective, partly due to a high dropout rate.

Relapse Prevention One of the greatest problems in the treatment of addictive disorders, such as alcoholism or any of the conditions described in this chapter, is maintaining abstinence or self-control once the behavioral excesses have been checked. Most alcohol treatment programs show high success rates in "curing" the addictive problems, but many programs show lessening rates of abstinence or controlled drinking at various periods of follow-up. Many treatment programs do not pay sufficient attention to the important element of maintaining effective behavior and preventing relapse into previous maladaptive patterns.

Given the fact that alcoholics are highly vulnerable to relapse, some researchers have focused on the important need to help them remain abstinent In one cognitive-behavior approach, relapse behavior is a key factor in alcohol treatment (Marlatt, 1985; Marlatt & Vandenbos, 1997). The behaviors underlying relapse are seen as "indulgent behaviors" that are based on an individual's learning his-

It is difficult for many people to remain abstinent from alcohol because of the luring appeal of advertisements and displays as shown in this picture. Given the fact that alcoholics are highly vulnerable to relapse, many experts believe that treatment should also include teaching the alcoholic to expect slips and not see them as huge failures, which can then provide the rationale for such thinking as "Well, I've blown my abstinence. I might as well go get drunk."

tory. When an individual is abstinent or has an addiction under control, he or she gains a sense of personal control over the indulgent behavior. The longer the person is able to maintain this control, the greater the sense of achievement—the self-efficacy or confidence—and the greater the chance that he or she will be able to cope with the addiction and maintain control. However, a person may violate this rule of abstinence through a gradual, perhaps unconscious, process rather than through the sudden "falling off the wagon" that constitutes the traditional view of craving and relapse. In the cognitive-behavior view, a person may inadvertently make a series of mini-decisions, even while maintaining abstinence, that begin a chain of behaviors making relapse inevitable. For example, an abstinent alcoholic who buys a quart of bourbon just in case his friends drop by or a dieting obese woman who changes her route to work to include a pass by the bakery are both unconsciously preparing the way for relapse.

Another type of relapse behavior involves the "abstinence violation effect," in which even minor transgressions are seen by the abstainer to have drastic significance. The effect works this way: An abstinent person may hold that he or she should not, under any circumstance, transgress or give in to the old habit. Abstinence-oriented treatment programs are particularly guided by this prohibitive rule. What happens, then, when an abstinent man becomes somewhat self-indulgent and takes a drink offered by an old friend? He may lose some of the sense of self-efficacy, the confidence needed to control his drinking. Since the vow of abstinence has been violated, he may feel guilty about giving in to the temptation and rationalize that he "has blown it and become a drunk again, so why not go all the way?"

In relapse prevention treatment, clients are taught to recognize the apparently irrelevant decisions that serve as early warning signals of the possibility of relapse. High-risk situations such as parties or sports events are targeted, and the individuals learn to assess their own vulnerability to relapse. Clients are also trained not to become so discouraged that they lose their confidence if they do relapse. Some cognitive-behavior therapists have employed a "planned relapse" phase in the treatment to supervise an individual's cognitive-behavior strategies to help the client through this important problem area. In other words, if patients are taught to expect a relapse, they are better able to handle it.

DRUG ABUSE AND DEPENDENCE

Aside from alcohol, the psychoactive drugs most commonly associated with abuse and dependence in our society appear to be (1) narcotics, such as opium and its derivatives; (2) sedatives, such as barbiturates; (3) stimulants, such as cocaine and amphetamines; (4) antianxiety drugs, such as benzodiazepines; and (5) hallucinogens, such as LSD and PCP. (These and other drugs are summarized in Table 10.4.) Caffeine and nicotine are also drugs of dependence, and disorders associated with tobacco withdrawal and caffeine intoxication are in-

TABLE 10.4 PSYCHOACTIVE DRUGS COMMONLY INVOLVED IN DRUG ABUSE

Classification	Drug	Effect
Sedatives	Alcohol (ethanol)	Reduce tension Facilitate social interaction "Blot out" feelings or events

	Barbiturates
	  Nembutal (pentobarbital)
	  Seconal (secobarbital)
	  Veronal (barbital)
	  Tuinal (secobarbital and amobarbital)
		Reduce tension

Stimulants	Amphetamines
	  Benzedrine (amphetamine)
	  Dexedrine (dextroamphetamine)
	  Methedrine (methamphetamine)
	  Cocaine (coca)
		Increase feelings of alertness and confidence
		Decrease feelings of fatigue
		Stay awake for long periods
		Decrease feelings of fatigue
		Increase endurance
		Stimulate sex drive

Narcotics	Opium and its derivatives
	  Opium
	  Morphine
	  Codeine
	  Heroin
		Alleviate physical pain
		Induce relaxation and pleasant reverie
		Alleviate anxiety and tension

	Methadone (synthetic narcotic)	Treatment of heroin dependence

Psychedelics and hallucinogens	Cannabis
	  Marijuana
	  Hashish
		Induce changes in mood, thought, and behavior

	Mescaline (peyote)
	  Psilocybin (psychotogenic mushrooms)
	  LSD (lysergic acid diethylamide-25)
	  PCP (phencyclidine)
		"Expand" one's mind
		Induce stupor

Antianxiety drugs (minor tranquilizers)	Librium (chlordiazepoxide) Miltown (meprobamate) Valium (diazepam) Xanax	Alleviate tension and anxiety Induce relaxation and sleep

Note: This list is by no means complete; for example, it does not include newer drugs, such as Ritalin, which are designed to produce multiple effects; it does not include the less commonly used volatile hydrocarbons, such as glue, paint thinner, gasoline, cleaning fluid, and nail-polish remover, which are highly dangerous when sniffed for their psychoactive effects; and it does not include the antipsychotic and antidepressant drugs, which are abused, but relatively rarely. We shall deal with these and the antianxiety drugs in our discussion of drug therapy in Chapter 16.

Causal Factors in Opiate Abuse and Dependence

No single causal pattern fits all addictions to narcotic drugs. A study by Fulmer and Lapidus (1980) concluded that the three most frequently cited reasons for beginning to use heroin were pleasure, curiosity, and peer pressure. Pleasure was the single most widespread reason—given by 81 percent of addicts. Other reasons, such as a desire to escape life stress, personal maladjustment, and sociocultural conditions, also play a part (Bry, McKeon, & Pandina, 1982).

Although the following categorization of causal factors is somewhat artificial, it does provide a convenient means of ordering our discussion.

Neural Bases for Physiological Addiction Research teams have isolated and studied receptor sites for narcotic drugs in the brain (Goldstein et al., 1974; Pert & Snyder, 1973; Office of Technology Assessment, 1993). Such receptor sites are specific nerve cells into which given psychoactive drugs fit like keys into the proper locks. This interaction of drug and brain cells apparently results in a drug's action, and in the case of narcotic drugs, may lead to addiction.

The human body produces its own opiumlike substances, called **endorphins,** in the brain and pituitary gland. These substances are produced in response to stimulation and are believed to play a role in an organism's reaction to pain (Bolles & Fanselow, 1982). Some investigators have suspected that endorphins may play a role in drug addiction, speculating that chronic underproduction of endorphins may lead to a craving for narcotic drugs. Research on the role of endorphins in drug addiction has generally been inconclusive and disappointing and no effective treatment has resulted from this line of research.

Addiction Associated with Psychopathology A high incidence of antisocial personality has been found among heroin addicts (Alterman, McDermott et al., 1998). In a comparison between a group of 45 young institutionalized male addicts and a control group of nonaddicts, Gilbert and Lombardi (1967) found that distinguishing features were "the addict's antisocial traits, his depression, tension, insecurity, and feelings of inadequacy, and his difficulty in forming warm and lasting interpersonal relationships" (p. 536). Meyer and Mirin (1979) found that opiate addicts were highly impulsive and showed an inability to delay gratification. Kosten and Rounsaville (1986) reported that about 68 percent of heroin abusers were also diagnosed as having a personality disorder. As in the case of alcoholism, however, it is essential to exercise caution in distinguishing between personality traits before and after addiction; the

high incidence of psychopathology among narcotics addicts may in part result from, rather than precede, the long-term effects of addiction.

Addiction Associated with Sociocultural Factors In our society a so-called narcotics subculture exists in which addicts can obtain drugs and protect themselves against society's sanctions. Apparently the majority of narcotics addicts participate in this drug culture. The decision to join this culture has important future implications, for from that point on addicts will center their activities on their drug-user role. In short, addiction becomes a way of life. In a recent survey in three large cities in Texas, Maddux and colleagues (1994) found that the majority of illicit drug injectors were predominantly undereducated and unemployed individuals from minority groups.

With time, most young addicts who join the drug culture become increasingly withdrawn, indifferent to their friends (except those in the drug group), and apathetic about sexual activity (Tremble et al., 1994). They are likely to abandon scholastic and athletic endeavors and to show a marked reduction in competitive and achievement strivings. Most of these addicts appear to lack good sex-role identification and to experience feelings of inadequacy when confronted with the demands of adulthood. While feeling progressively isolated from the broader culture, their feelings of group belongingness are bolstered by continued association with the addict milieu; at the same time, they come to view drugs both as a means of revolt against authority and conventional values and as a device for alleviating personal anxieties and tensions.

Treatments and Outcomes Treatment for narcotic addiction is initially similar to that for alcoholism in that it involves building up an addict both physically and psychologically and providing help through the withdrawal period. Addicts often dread the discomfort of withdrawal, but in a hospital setting it is less abrupt and usually involves the administration of a medication that eases the distress.

After physical withdrawal has been completed, treatment focuses on helping a former addict make an adequate adjustment to his or her community and abstain from the further use of narcotics. Traditionally, however, the prognosis has been unfavorable. Withdrawal from heroin does not remove the craving for the drug. A key target in treatment of heroin addiction must be the alleviation of this craving. One approach to dealing with the physiological craving for heroin was pioneered by a research team at Rockefeller University in New York. Their approach involved the use of the drug **methadone** in conjunction with a rehabilitation program (counseling, group therapy, and other procedures) directed toward the "total resocialization" of addicts. Methadone hydrochloride is a synthetic narcotic that is related to heroin and possesses qualities that are equally addictive physiologically. Its usefulness in treatment lies in the fact that it satisfies an addict's craving for heroin without producing serious psychological impairment, if only because it is administered as a "treatment" in a formal clinical context.

Research has shown the effectiveness of methadone at reducing the dependence upon heroin (Moolchan & Hoffman, 1994; Silverman, Higgins, Brooner, & Montoya, 1996); however, methadone alone may only be effective for a small minority of heroin abusers. Psychotherapy along with methadone increases the effectiveness of treatment (Woody et al., 1987). Moreover, more recent research has underscored the importance of providing psychosocial support in addition to methadone (McLellan, Arndt et al., 1993). Some addicts on methadone get involved with other drugs such as cocaine; therefore procedures need to be developed for reducing use of other substances while being treated for heroin addiction (Silverman et al., 1996).

The practice of weaning addicts from heroin only to addict them to another narcotic drug that may be required for life is also questionable. Methadone advocates, however, point out that addicts on methadone can function normally and hold jobs, which is not possible for most heroin addicts. In addition, methadone is available legally, and its quality is controlled by government standards. Nor is it necessary to increase the dosage over time. In fact, some patients can eventually stop taking methadone without danger of relapse to heroin addiction. Many heroin addicts can undergo methadone treatment without initial hospitalization, and during treatment they are able to hold jobs and function in their family and community settings (Newman & Cates, 1977).

Improvements in methadone maintenance treatment over the past few years have increased its attractiveness for treating heroin abusers and have improved its overall success rates. The increased success rates for methadone treatment have been attributed to the use of additional drugs like clonidine (an antihypertensive drug used to treat essential hypertension and prevent headache), which aid in the detoxification process and reduce the discomfort of withdrawal symptoms.

Even though it is a clearly better alternative to continued heroin use, being in a methadone maintenance program is no picnic. Methadone patients often must resort to great secrecy about their program participation in an effort to accommodate to society, hold a job, and even to

relate to friends and family. One crucial element in beating the drug abuse problem seems to be for the addict to develop a drug-free social network—a task that is often difficult in methadone programs.

A new medication, buprenorphine, has been used to treat heroin addiction. It promises an equally effective substitute for heroin but has fewer side effects than methadone (Blaine, 1992). Buprenorphine operates as a partial antagonist to heroin (Lewis & Walter, 1992) and produces the "feelings of contentment" associated with heroin use (Mendelson & Mello, 1992). Yet the drug does not produce the physical dependency that is characteristic of heroin (Grant & Sonti, 1994) and can be discontinued without severe withdrawal symptoms. As with methadone therapy, buprenorphine appears to work best at maintaining abstinence if it is provided along with behavior therapy (Bickel, Amass, Higgins, Badger, & Esch, 1997).

Cocaine and Amphetamines (Stimulants)

In contrast to narcotics, which depress or slow down the action of the central nervous system, cocaine and amphetamines stimulate or speed it up.

Cocaine Like opium, **cocaine** is a plant product discovered and used since ancient times. It was widely used in the pre-Columbian world of Mexico and Peru (Guerra, 1971). Because of its typically high price for many years in the United States, cocaine was considered as the "high" for the affluent. However, with increased availability and lowering of prices, the drug's use increased significantly in the United States during the 1980s and 1990s—to the point that it was considered epidemic, especially among middle- and upper-income groups.

Cocaine-related emergency room visits increased substantially between 1978 and 1995. In 1995 cocaine involved 27 percent of all drug-related emergency room visits (DAWN Survey, 1996) with most of these being persons seeking detoxification. In Memphis, Tennessee, 59 percent of people arrested for reckless driving tested positive for cocaine abuse (Brookoff et al., 1994).

Like the opiates, cocaine may be ingested by sniffing, swallowing, or injecting. Also like the opiates, it precipitates a euphoric state of four to six hours' duration, during which a user experiences feelings of confidence and contentment. However, this blissful state may be preceded by headache, dizziness, and restlessness. When cocaine is chronically abused, acute toxic psychotic symptoms may occur—including frightening visual, auditory, and tactual hallucination similar to those in acute schizophrenia.

Unlike the opiates, cocaine stimulates the cortex of the brain, inducing sleeplessness and excitement as well as stimulating and accentuating sexual feelings. Dependence on cocaine also differs somewhat from dependence on opiates. It was believed that tolerance was not increased appreciably with cocaine use. However, acute tolerance has now been demonstrated, and some chronic tolerance, a more persistent habituation, may occur as well (Jones, 1984). The previous view that cocaine abusers did not develop physiological dependence on the drug also has changed. Gawin and Kleber (1986) demonstrated that chronic abusers who become abstinent develop uniform, depression-like symptoms, but the symptoms are transient.

Our broadened knowledge about cocaine abuse, particularly with respect to the many health and social problems resulting from dependence on the drug, has resulted in considerable modification of professional views of cocaine over the past 20 years. For example, the modifications in DSM-IV diagnostic classification reflect a significant increase in our knowledge of cocaine's addictive properties. A new disorder is described, cocaine withdrawal, which involves symptoms of depression, fatigue, disturbed sleep, and increased dreaming (Foltin & Fischman, 1997). The psychological and life problems experienced by cocaine users are often great. Employment, family, psychological, and legal problems are all more likely to occur among cocaine and crack users than nonusers. Tardiff and colleagues (1994) reported that 31 percent of murder victims in New York City tested positive for cocaine. Many life problems experienced by cocaine abusers result in part from the considerable amounts of money that are required to support their habits.

Increased sexual activity, often trading sex for drugs, is associated with crack cocaine use (Weatherby et al., 1992), as has engaging in sexual activity with anonymous partners (Balshem et al., 1992). Problems in sexual functioning have been reported to be associated with crack cocaine use. Kim and colleagues (1992) reported that most users develop a disinterest and sexual dysfunction with prolonged usage.

Women who use cocaine when they are pregnant place their babies at risk for both health and psychological problems. Although recent research has suggested that there is no "fetal crack syndrome" as has been shown with alcohol-abusing mothers (Azar, 1997), children of crack-using mothers are at risk of being maltreated as infants as well of losing their mother during infancy. Wasserman and Leventhal (1993) studied a group of cocaine-exposed children and a controlled sample of nonexposed children for a 24-month period following their birth. They found that children who were regularly exposed to cocaine in utero were more likely to be mistreated (23 percent) versus only 4 percent of controls. The courts today are be-

ginning to take a stern stance with respect to mothers who take cocaine during pregnancy to the detriment of their fetus. In one recent case a woman who lost her fetus as a result of crack use faced a murder charge for killing her unborn child (Associated Press, December 3, 1997). She pleaded guilty to involuntary manslaughter and received a three-year suspended sentence.

Treatment for psychological dependence on cocaine does not differ appreciably from that for other drugs that involve physiological dependence. Kosten (1989) reported that effective cocaine-abuse treatment includes the use of medications, such as desipramine and naltrexone (Kosten et al., 1992) to reduce cravings and the use of psychological therapy to ensure treatment compliance. The feelings of tension and depression that accompany absence of the drug have to be dealt with during the immediate withdrawal period.

Some success in the treatment of cocaine abusers has been reported. Carroll, Power, and colleagues (1993; 1993b) have shown that many cocaine abusers did well in

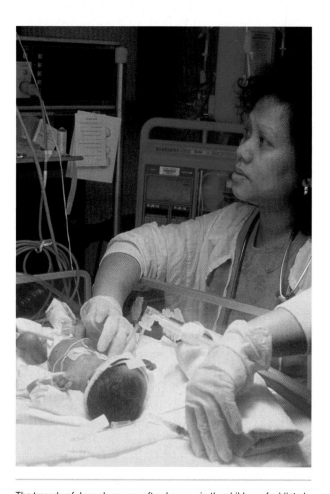

The tragedy of drug abuse can often be seen in the children of addicted mothers. This infant displays many of the characteristic features of the "crack baby," such as low birth weight.

maintaining treatment goals and one-third were abstinent at a 12-month follow-up. Several factors were associated with poorer outcomes—severity of abuse, poorer psychiatric functioning, and presence of concurrent alcoholism. One of the problems clinicians face in working with cocaine abusers is that only 42 percent of those in one study were retained in treatment for six or more sessions (Kleinman et al., 1992). Another problem encountered in drug treatment is that many of the cocaine-dependent patients have severe antisocial personality disorders—a situation resulting in treatment resistance (Leal, Ziedonis, & Kosten, 1994) or are "psychosis-prone" personalities (Kwapil, 1996). Arndt and colleagues (1994) found that cocaine-dependent patients with antisocial personality characteristics made few therapeutic gains while those without antisocial features made significant progress.

Amphetamines The earliest **amphetamine** to be introduced—Benzedrine, or amphetamine sulfate—was first synthesized in 1927 and became available in drugstores in the early 1930s as an inhalant to relieve stuffy noses. However, the manufacturers soon learned that some customers were chewing the wicks in the inhalers for "kicks." Thus the stimulating effects of amphetamine sulfate were discovered by the public before the drug was formally prescribed as a stimulant by physicians. In the late 1930s two newer amphetamines were introduced—Dexedrine (dextroamphetamine) and Methedrine (methamphetamine hydrochloride, also known as *speed*). The latter preparation is a far more potent stimulant of the central nervous system than either Benzedrine or Dexedrine and hence is considered more dangerous. In fact its abuse can be lethal.

Initially these preparations were considered to be "wonder pills" that helped people stay alert and awake and function temporarily at a level beyond normal. During World War II, military interest was aroused in the stimulating effects of these drugs, and they were used by both Allied and German soldiers to ward off fatigue (Jarvik, 1967). Similarly, among civilians, amphetamines came to be widely used by night workers, long-distance truck drivers, students cramming for exams, and athletes striving to improve their performances. It was also discovered that amphetamines tended to suppress appetite, and they became popular with people trying to lose weight. In addition, they were often used to counteract the effects of barbiturates or other sleeping pills that had been taken the night before. As a result of their many uses, amphetamines were widely prescribed by doctors.

Today amphetamines are occasionally used medically for curbing the appetite when weight reduction is desirable; for treating individuals suffering from narcolepsy, a disorder in which people cannot prevent themselves from continually falling asleep during the day; and for treating hyperactive children. Curiously enough, amphetamines have a calming rather than a stimulating effect on many of these youngsters (see Chapter 14). Amphetamines are also sometimes prescribed for alleviating mild feelings of depression, relieving fatigue, and maintaining alertness for sustained periods of time. By far, the most frequent use of amphetamines is for recreational purposes—with the most typical user being a young person interested in the high that the drug induces (Klee, 1998).

Since the passage of the Controlled Substance Act of 1970 (Drug Enforcement Administration, 1979), amphetamines have been classified as Schedule II controlled substances—that is, drugs with high abuse potential that require a prescription for each purchase. As a result, medical use of amphetamines has declined in the United States in recent years, and they are more difficult to obtain legally. However, it is often easy to find illegal sources of amphetamines, which thus remain among the most widely abused drugs. Amphetamines are among the most widely used illicit drugs in other countries as well—for example, Australia (Lintzeris, Holgate, & Dunlop, 1996). In the past few years, there has been a slight decrease in metamphetamine-related visits to emergency rooms during the mid-1990s because there has been a "shortage" of the illegal drug (DAWN Survey, 1996), in part, because of more effective policing efforts that have curtailed the supply.

Causes and Effects of Amphetamine Abuse Despite their legitimate medical uses, amphetamines are not a magical source of extra mental or physical energy and instead serve to push users toward greater expenditures of their own resources—often to a point of hazardous fatigue. Amphetamines are psychologically and physically addictive and the body does build up tolerance to them rapidly (Wise, 1996). Thus habituated users may use the drugs in amounts that would be lethal to nonusers. In some instances, users inject the drug to get faster and more intense results.

For a person who exceeds prescribed dosages, amphetamine consumption results in heightened blood pressure, enlarged pupils, unclear or rapid speech, profuse sweating, tremors, excitability, loss of appetite, confusion, and sleeplessness. Injected in large quantities, Methedrine can raise blood pressure enough to cause immediate death. In addition, chronic abuse of amphetamines can result in brain damage and a wide range of psychopathology, including a disorder known as amphetamine psychosis, which appears similar to paranoid schizophrenia. Suicide, homicide, assault, and various other acts of violence are associated with amphetamine abuse.

Treatments and Outcomes Withdrawal from amphetamines is usually safe, but recent evidence suggests that physiological addiction can be a factor to consider in the treatment (Wise & Munn, 1995). In some instances abrupt withdrawal from the chronic, excessive use of amphetamines can result in cramping, nausea, diarrhea, and even convulsions. Moreover, abrupt abstinence commonly results in feelings of weariness and depression. The depression usually reaches its peak in 48 to 72 hours, often remains intense for a day or two, and then tends to lessen gradually over a period of several days. Mild feelings of depression and lassitude may persist for weeks or even months. If brain damage has occurred, residual effects may also include impaired ability to concentrate, learn, and remember, with resulting social, economic, and personality deterioration.

Barbiturates (Sedatives)

In the 1930s, powerful sedatives called **barbiturates** were developed. Although barbiturates have legitimate medical uses, they are extremely dangerous drugs commonly associated with both physiological and psychological dependence and with lethal overdoses.

Effects of Barbiturates Barbiturates were once widely used by physicians to calm patients and induce sleep. They act as depressants—somewhat like alcohol—to slow down the action of the central nervous system and significantly reduce performance on cognitive tasks (Pickworth et al., 1997). Shortly after taking a barbiturate, an individual experiences a feeling of relaxation in which tensions seem to disappear, followed by a physical and intellectual lassitude and a tendency toward drowsiness and sleep—the intensity of such feelings depending on the type and amount of the barbiturate taken. Strong doses produce sleep almost immediately; excessive doses are lethal because they result in paralysis of the brain's respiratory centers. Pentobarbital, a common barbiturate, appears to actually have more sedating characteristics than alcohol (Mintzer, Guarino et al., 1997). Impaired decision making and problem solving, sluggishness, slow speech and sudden mood shifts are also common effects of barbiturates.

Excessive use of barbiturates leads to increased tolerance as well as to physiological and psychological dependence. It can also lead to brain damage and personality

deterioration. Unlike opiates, tolerance of barbiturates does not increase the amount needed to cause death. This fact means that users can easily ingest fatal overdoses, either intentionally or accidentally.

Causal Factors in Barbiturate Abuse and Dependence Though many young people experiment with barbiturates, or downers, most do not become dependent. In fact, the people who do become dependent on barbiturates tend to be middle-aged and older people who often rely on them as "sleeping pills" and who do not commonly use other classes of drugs (except, possibly, alcohol and minor tranquilizers). Often these people are referred to as silent abusers because they take the drugs in the privacy of their homes and ordinarily do not become public nuisances.

Barbiturates are commonly used with alcohol. Some users claim they can achieve an intense high by combining barbiturates, amphetamines, and alcohol. However, one possible effect of combining barbiturates and alcohol is death, because each drug potentiates (increases the action of) the other.

Treatments and Outcomes As with many other drugs, it is often essential in treatment to distinguish between barbiturate intoxication, which results from the toxic effects of overdose, and the symptoms associated with drug withdrawal because different procedures are required. With barbiturates, withdrawal symptoms are more dangerous, severe, and long-lasting than in opiate withdrawal. A patient going through barbiturate withdrawal becomes anxious and apprehensive and manifests coarse tremors of the hands and face; additional symptoms commonly include insomnia, weakness, nausea, vomiting, abdominal cramps, rapid heart rate, elevated blood pressure, and loss of weight. An acute delirious psychosis may develop.

For persons used to taking large dosages, withdrawal symptoms may last for as long as a month, but usually they tend to abate by the end of the first week. Fortunately, the withdrawal symptoms in barbiturate addiction can be minimized by administering increasingly smaller doses of the barbiturate itself or another drug producing similar effects. The withdrawal program is still a dangerous one, however, especially if barbiturate addiction is complicated by alcoholism or dependence on other drugs.

LSD and Related Drugs (Hallucinogens)

The **hallucinogens** are drugs whose properties are thought to induce hallucinations. However, these preparations usually do not in fact "create" sensory images but distort them, so that an individual sees or hears things in different and unusual ways. These drugs are often referred to as *psychedelics*. The major drugs in this category are LSD (lysergic acid diethylamide), mescaline, and psilocybin. Not long ago, Phencyclidine (PCP, or "angel dust") became popular as well. Our present discussion will be restricted largely to LSD because of its unusual hallucinogenic properties.

LSD The most potent of the hallucinogens, the odorless, colorless, and tasteless drug **LSD** can produce intoxication with an amount smaller than a grain of salt. It is a chemically synthesized substance first discovered by the Swiss chemist Albert Hoffman in 1938. Hoffman was not aware of the potent hallucinatory qualities of LSD until he swallowed a small amount. This is his report of the experience:

> Last Friday, April 16, 1943, I was forced to stop my work in the laboratory in the middle of the afternoon and to go home, as I was seized by a peculiar restlessness associated with a sensation of mild dizziness. On arriving home, I lay down and sank into a kind of drunkenness which was not unpleasant and which was characterized by extreme activity of imagination. As I lay in a dazed condition with my eyes closed (I experienced daylight as disagreeably bright) there surged upon me an uninterrupted stream of fantastic images of extraordinary plasticity and vividness and accompanied by an intense kaleidoscope-like play of colors. This condition gradually passed off after about two hours. (Hoffman, 1971, p. 23)

Hoffman followed up this experience with a series of planned self-observations with LSD, some of which he described as "harrowing." Researchers thought LSD might be useful for the induction and study of hallucinogenic states or "model psychoses," which were thought to be related to schizophrenia. About 1950, LSD was introduced into the United States for purposes of such research and to ascertain whether it might have medical or therapeutic uses. Despite considerable research, however, LSD has not proven therapeutically useful.

After taking LSD, a person typically goes through about eight hours of changes in sensory perception, mood swings, and feelings of depersonalization and detachment. The LSD experience is not always pleasant. It can be extremely traumatic, and the distorted objects and sounds, the illusory colors, and the new thoughts can be menacing and terrifying. For example, a British law student tried to "continue time" by using a dental drill to bore a hole in his head while under the influence of LSD (Rorvik, 1970). In other instances, people undergoing "bad trips" have set themselves aflame, jumped from high places, and taken other drugs that proved lethal in combination with LSD.

An interesting and unusual phenomenon that may occur following the use of LSD is a **flashback,** an involuntary recurrence of perceptual distortions or hallucinations weeks or even months after taking the drug. Flashbacks appear to be relatively rare among people who have taken LSD only once—although they do sometimes occur. One study found that continued effects on visual function were apparent at least two years following LSD use. In this study, Abraham and Wolf (1988) reported that individuals who had used LSD for a week were shown to have reduced visual sensitivity to light during dark adaptation and showed other visual problems compared with controls.

Despite the possibility of adverse reactions, LSD was widely publicized during the 1960s, and a number of relatively well-known people experimented with it and gave glowing accounts of their "trips." During this period, use of LSD was advocated by some, based on the conviction that the drug could "expand the mind" and enable one to use talents and realize potentials previously undetected. However, no evidence exists that LSD enhances creative activity: No recognized works of art have been produced under the influence of the drug or as a consequence of a psychedelic experience. Although several artists have claimed improved creativity stemming from their LSD experiences, objective observers recognize few, if any, improvements in the work of these artists. It should also be pointed out that although users of LSD do not develop physiological dependence, some frequent users have been known to develop psychological dependence in the sense that they focus their life around LSD experiences.

For acute psychoses induced by LSD intoxication, treatment requires hospitalization and is primarily a medical matter. Often the outcome in such cases depends on a person's stability before taking the drug. Fortunately, brief psychotherapy is usually effective in treating psychological reliance on LSD and in preventing the recurrence of flashbacks. Therapy is aimed at helping the individual work through the painful experience induced by the drug and integrate it into his or her self-schema.

Mescaline and Psilocybin Two other hallucinogens are **mescaline,** which is derived from the small, disclike growths (mescal buttons) at the top of the peyote cactus, and **psilocybin,** which is obtained from a variety of "sacred" Mexican mushrooms known as *Psilocybe mexicana.* These drugs have been used for centuries in the ceremonial rites of native peoples living in Mexico, the American

Southwest, and Central and South America. In fact, they were used by the Aztecs for such purposes long before the Spanish invasion. Both drugs have mind-altering and hallucinogenic properties, but their principal effect appears to be enabling an individual to see, hear, and otherwise experience events in unaccustomed ways—transporting him or her into a realm of "nonordinary reality." As with LSD, no definite evidence shows that mescaline and psilocybin actually "expand consciousness" or create new ideas; rather, they mainly alter or distort experience.

Marijuana

Although **marijuana** may be classified as a mild hallucinogen, there are significant differences in the nature, intensity, and duration of its effects as compared with those induced by LSD, mescaline, and other major hallucinogens. Marijuana comes from the leaves and flowering tops of the hemp plant, *Cannabis sativa.* The plant grows in mild climates throughout the world, including parts of India, Africa, Mexico, South America, and the United States. In its prepared state, marijuana consists chiefly of the dried green leaves—hence the colloquial name *grass.* It is ordinarily smoked in the form of cigarettes (called *reefers* or *joints*) or in pipes. In some cultures the leaves are steeped in hot water and the liquid is drunk, much as one might drink tea. Marijuana is related to a stronger drug, **hashish,** which is derived from the resin exuded by the cannabis plant and made into a gummy powder. Hashish, like marijuana, is usually smoked.

Both marijuana and hashish use can be traced far back into history. Cannabis was apparently known in ancient China (Blum, 1969; Culliton, 1970) and was listed in the herbal compendiums of the Chinese emperor Shen Nung, written about 2737 B.C. Until the late 1960s, marijuana use in the United States was confined largely to members of lower socioeconomic minority groups and to people in entertainment and related fields.

Marijuana-related problems requiring emergency room admissions are on the increase. Since the 1960s, the use of marijuana among youth dramatically increased, and during the early 1970s it was estimated that over half the teenagers and young adults in America had experimented with marijuana, with about 10 percent presumably going from occasional to habitual use. Kandel and colleagues (1986) reported that among 24- and 25-year-old subjects, about 78 percent of males and 69 percent of females had tried marijuana. A recent epidemiological survey reported that over one-third of persons in the National Household Survey on Drug Abuse (N = 17,747 in 1995) reported that they had used marijuana in the past

(Bobashev & Anthony, 1998). In a survey of drug-related visits to the emergency room (DAWN Survey, 1996) the number of visits related to marijuana use increased over 17 percent in both 1994 and 1995. There has been a 200 percent increase in admissions since 1990. Many of these emergency room visits, as one might suspect, involved the use of other substances along with marijuana.

Effects of Marijuana The specific effects of marijuana vary greatly, depending on the quality and dosage of the drug, the personality and mood of the user, the user's past experiences with the drug, the social setting, and the user's expectations. However, considerable consensus exists among regular users that when marijuana is smoked and inhaled, a state of slight intoxication results. This state is one of mild euphoria distinguished by increased feelings of well-being, heightened perceptual acuity, and pleasant relaxation, often accompanied by a sensation of drifting or floating away. Sensory inputs are intensified. Often a person's sense of time is stretched or distorted, so that an event lasting but a few seconds may seem to cover a much longer span. Short-term memory may also be affected, as when one notices a bite taken out of a sandwich but does not remember having taken it. For most users, pleasurable experiences, including sexual intercourse, are reportedly enhanced. When smoked, marijuana is rapidly absorbed and its effects appear within seconds to minutes but seldom last more than two to three hours.

Marijuana may lead to unpleasant as well as pleasant experiences. For example, if a person uses the drug while in an unhappy, angry, suspicious, or frightened mood, these feelings may be magnified. With higher dosages and with certain unstable or susceptible individuals, marijuana can produce extreme euphoria, hilarity, and overtalkativeness but it can also produce intense anxiety and depression as well as delusions, hallucinations, and other psychotic-like behavior. Evidence (Tien & Anthony, 1990) suggests a strong relationship between daily marijuana use and the occurrence of self-reported psychotic symptoms.

Marijuana's short-range physiological effects include a moderate increase in heart rate, a slowing of reaction time, a slight contraction of pupil size, bloodshot and itchy eyes, a dry mouth, and an increased appetite. Furthermore, marijuana induces memory dysfunction and a slowing of information processing (Mathew, Wilson, & Melges, 1992). Continued use of high dosages over time tends to produce lethargy and passivity. In such cases marijuana appears to have a depressant and a hallucinogenic effect. The effects of long-term and habitual marijuana use are still under investigation, although a number of possible adverse side effects have been related to the prolonged, heavy use of marijuana. For example, marijuana use tends to diminish self-control. One recent study exploring past substance-use history in incarcerated murderers reported that among men who committed murder, marijuana was the most commonly used drug. One-third indicated that they used the drug before the homicide, and two-thirds were experiencing some effects of the drug at the time of the murder (Spunt et al., 1994).

Marijuana has often been compared to heroin, but the two drugs have little in common with respect either to tolerance or to physiological dependence. Marijuana does not lead to physiological dependence, as heroin does, so discontinued use is not accompanied by withdrawal symptoms. Marijuana can, however, lead to psychological dependence, in which a person experiences a strong need for the drug whenever he or she feels anxious and tense. In fact, one recent study reported that 16 percent of their sample of marijuana users reported having withdrawal-like symptoms such as nervousness, tensions, sleep problems, and appetite change (Weisbeck, Schuckit et al., 1996).

Psychological treatment methods have been shown to be effective in reducing marijuana use in adults who are dependent on the drug (Zweben & O'Connell, 1992). As with other addictive drugs, there may be among the users many individuals with serious antisocial or "psychosis-prone" personalities (Kwapil, 1996). Treatment of marijuana use is hampered by the fact that there might be an underlying personality disorder. One study compared the

Group counseling is a common treatment for psychological dependence on drugs. In the give-and-take of group therapy, drug abusers may be able to face the consequences of their addiction and to see new possibilities for coping with it.

effectiveness of two treatments, Relapse Prevention (RP) and Support Group (SSP), with marijuana-dependent adults (Stephens, Roffman, & Simpson, 1994). Both treatment conditions resulted in substantial reduction in marijuana use in the 12 months following treatment. Relapse prevention and support discussion sessions were equally effective in bringing about changes in marijuana use.

OTHER ADDICTIVE DISORDERS: HYPEROBESITY AND PATHOLOGICAL GAMBLING

Not all addictive disorders involve the use of substances with chemical properties that induce dependency. People can develop "addictions" to certain activities that can be just as life-threatening as severe alcoholism and just as damaging, psychologically and socially, as drug abuse. We include two such disorders in this chapter—hyperobesity and pathological gambling. They are similar to other addictions in their behavioral manifestations, their etiologies, and their resistance to treatments.

Extreme Obesity

To get an idea of how extensive the problem of obesity is, just look around and count the number of people who are seriously overweight. If one defines obesity as 20 percent in excess of desirable weight, then 24 percent of men and 27 percent of women are obese (Kuczmarski, 1992). Moreover, obesity appears to be a problem that persists over time. DiPietro, Mossberg, and Stunkard (1994) reported on a 40-year follow-up of 504 overweight children, the majority of whom remained overweight as adults.

In this discussion, we are particularly concerned with **hyperobesity**—often called morbid obesity—which we define as being 100 pounds or more above ideal body weight. Such hyperobesity can be a dangerous, life-threatening disorder, resulting in such conditions as diabetes, musculoskeletal problems, high blood pressure, and other cardiovascular diseases that may place a person at high risk for a heart attack. Although some cases of extreme obesity result from metabolic or hormonal disorders, most obese persons simply take in more calories than they burn.

Hyperobesity, as a disorder, may be placed in several diagnostic categories, depending on which characteristics are emphasized. If we focus on the physical changes, for example, we may view obesity as having both psychological and physical components. Many clinicians, however, view the central problem not as the excessive weight itself, but as the long-standing habit of overeating. Thus obesity resulting from gross, habitual overeating is considered to be more like the problems found in the personality disorders—especially those ingrained personality problems that involve loss of control over an appetite of some kind (Leon et al., 1978; Orford, 1985).

Causes of Persistent Overeating

What prompts a person to overeat to the point of hyperobesity, despite an awareness of the detrimental health effects, the negative body image that results (Sarwer et al., 1998), and a consciousness of the strong social prejudice in favor of the "body beautiful"? Several potential causal factors have been explored (Drewnowski, 1996); although results are not conclusive, biological and learning factors seem to be of great importance.

Biological Factors Some people seem able to eat high-calorie foods without significant weight gain, while others become overweight easily and engage in a constant struggle to maintain their weight. Most people gain weight with advancing age, but this gain could be related to reduced activity and to the fact that older people are likely to continue their earlier eating habits even though they need fewer calories. As already indicated, some people have metabolic or endocrine anomalies that can produce obesity at any age, though these cases seem to be relatively rare.

Genetic inheritance contributes substantially to the tendency for some people to become obese, or alternatively to remain thin. Findings in a study of twins reared apart have shown that genetics plays an important part in body weight (Stunkard et al., 1990). Adult obesity is related to the number and size of the adipose cells (fat cells) in the body (Heymsfield, Allison et al., 1995). People who are obese and hyperobese have markedly more adipose cells than do people of normal weight (Peeke & Chrousos, 1995). When weight is lost, the size of the cells is reduced, but not their number. Some evidence suggests that the total number of adipose cells stays the same from childhood on (Crisp et al., 1970). It is possible that overfeeding infants and young children may cause them to develop more adipose cells and may thus predispose them to weight problems in adulthood.

Psychosocial Factors Factors other than biological endowment play an important role in obesity (Jeffrey & French, 1996; Fairburn, Doll et al., 1998). In many cases the key determinants of excessive eating and obesity appear to be family behavior patterns. In some families, a high fat, high calorie diet or an overemphasis on food may produce obesity in many or all family members. In such families, a fat baby may be seen as a healthy baby, and there may be great pressure on infants and children to eat more than they want. In other families, eating (or overeating) becomes a habitual means of alleviating emotional distress (Musante, Costanzo, & Friedman, 1998).

Several psychological views address the causes of gross habitual overeating. According to the psychoanalytic view, obese individuals are fixated at the oral stage of psychosexual development (Bychowski, 1950). They are believed to orient their lives around oral gratification (through excessive eating) because their libidinal energies and psychological growth have not advanced to a more mature level. This view has been elaborated by Bruch (1973) and by Schneider (1995), who distinguishes between developmental obesity and reactive obesity. Bruch saw developmental obesity as a childhood response to parental rejection or other severe disturbances in the parent-child relationship. Supposedly, the parents compensate for their emotional rejection by overfeeding and overprotecting the child. Such children never learn to distinguish different internal signals because their parents respond to all signs of distress by giving them food. Bruch saw this pattern as leading to a distorted perception of internal states—that is, not knowing when enough food has been ingested.

Bruch defined reactive obesity as obesity that occurs in adults as a reaction to trauma or stress. Here, overeating is thought to function as a defense mechanism to lessen feelings of distress or depression. There is evidence to support the idea that many obese people experience other psychological problems such as depression. For example, one study reported that 26 percent of patients seeking weight-loss treatment were diagnosed as having a mood disorder and 55 percent had at least one diagnosis of mood disorder in their lifetime (Goldsmith et al., 1992). Other research has found that a striking percentage of eating-disorder subjects binge eat in response to aversive emotional states such as feeling depressed or anxious (Kenardy, Arnow, & Agras, 1996).

According to the cognitive-behavior viewpoint, a person's weight gain and his or her tendency to maintain excessive weight can be explained quite simply in terms of learning principles (Fairburn, Doll et al., 1998). For all of us, eating behavior is determined in part by conditioned responses to a wide range of environmental stimuli. For example, people are encouraged to eat at parties and movies, while watching TV, and even at work. Eating is

Though biological endowment may play an important role in obesity and hyperobesity, in many cases, the key determinant of obesity is family behavior patterns such as an overemphasis on food and the consumption of a high-fat, high-calorie diet.

reinforced in all these situations, and it is difficult to avoid the many inducements to eat. Thus a wide assortment of seemingly avoidable reinforcers and conditioned stimuli enter the lives of most Americans.

Obese people, however, have been shown to be conditioned to more cues—both internal and external—than people of normal weight. Anxiety, anger, boredom, and social inducements all may lead to overeating. Eating in response to such cues is then reinforced because the taste of good food is pleasurable and the individual's emotional tension is reduced. This reinforcement increases the probability that overeating will continue and worsen. Binge-eating, ingesting large amounts of food over short periods of time, is a prominent factor in obesity in some individuals. Many people entering into weight-control programs report engaging in binge-eating (Wilson & Fairburn, 1993).

With such frequent overfeeding, obese people may then learn not to respond to feeling "full" as most people do, no longer feeling full when they have had enough. Meanwhile, physical activity, because its short-term effects are often aversive rather than pleasant, tends not to be reinforced, especially as pounds accumulate. Thus obese individuals may become less and less active.

Sociocultural Factors Different cultures have different concepts of human beauty. Some value slimness; others,

a rounded contour. In some cultures, obesity is valued as a sign of social influence and power. However, within our own society, obesity seems to be related to social class, occurring six times as often in lower-class adults and nine times more often in lower-class youngsters (Ernst & Harlan, 1991). Obesity may be related to high-carbohydrate diets in lower-class families, however. Adolescents are at high risk for developing eating disorders (Sanders, Kapphahn, & Steiner, 1998). For example, Lissau and Sorenson (1994) found that children who were seriously neglected as children had a greater risk of obesity in young adulthood than well-cared for children.

Treatment of Extreme Obesity Losing weight is a preoccupation of many Americans; diet books, dietary aids, and weight-loss programs are big business. Diet plans abound, with new programs emerging as often as clothing fads. The success rates of most of these devices and programs are quite low (Brownell & Wadden, 1992).

A number of weight-loss group programs are conducted by organizations like Overeaters Anonymous and Weight Watchers (Weiner, 1998). These programs provide strong group pressures to reduce weight by public praise of weight losses and public disapproval and "punishments" for failures. Thus they provide community support and encouragement to maintain better eating habits.

Fasting or starvation diets under medically controlled conditions generally produce weight losses in extremely obese patients, with some studies reporting losses of over 100 pounds. This method of rapid weight loss, however, may involve several dangerous potential complications, such as hypertension, gout, and kidney failure (Munro & Duncan, 1972). Recently, two brands of diet pills (Phen-Fen and Redux) were removed from the market by the U.S. Food and Drug Administration because their use, even over a short time, resulted in heart disease.

Another questionable medical treatment of extremely obese patients has centered on the use of drugs to reduce appetite. Diet pills, such as amphetamines, suppress the desire for food and, as a result, have been used extensively. Again, however, maintenance of weight loss once the diet pills are gone often becomes a problem. Moreover, diet pills often present an additional problem of their own. As we have seen, amphetamines are addicting substances and are particularly dangerous when used in combination with other substances, such as alcohol. The general ineffectiveness of amphetamines for long-term weight control plus their high abuse potential has made these drugs of doubtful value in weight-reduction programs.

Given that severe obesity presents a major health risk for hypertension, heart disease, pulmonary insufficiency, and arthritis, it is no wonder that extreme treatment measures are often considered necessary to help severely obese patients who cannot lose weight by other means. One very extreme method for treating obesity involves the bariatric or gastric bypass surgery (Benotti & Forse, 1995). This surgical procedure involves surgically placing lines of staples in the intestines to develop a holding pouch for food that is ingested. This procedure limits the amount of food in the stomach since the food in the pouch is excreted as waste and not absorbed into the system. Although this surgical procedure does result in substantial immediate weight loss (40 to 60 percent of body weight) there are a number of negative side effects including gallstones, metabolic changes, and lifestyle problems. Moreover, it appears that many patients continue their binge-eating after surgery (Kalarchian, Wilson et al., 1998) and tend to regain their weight over an 18-month period (Hsu, Benotti et al., 1998).

The most effective psychological treatment procedures for extremely obese patients are behavioral management methods. A number of methods using positive reinforcement, self-monitoring, and self-reward can produce moderate weight loss over time (Agras, Telch et al., 1997). In general these procedures, based on positive reinforcement, are more effective than classical conditioning procedures, such as aversive conditioning in which shock or unpleasant thoughts may be paired with eating behavior. Considerable support for treatment of binge-eating using cognitive-behavior methods has been found (Carter & Fairburn, 1998; Wilson & Fairburn, 1993). Two recent studies have shown that highly motivated people can lose weight and keep it off (Klem, Wing et al., 1997; Tinker & Tucker, 1997). In these studies clients identified strong reasons for losing weight such as medical problems aggravated by obesity (for example, varicose veins) or concerns over their appearance. These individuals were able to reduce their weight through diet and exercise in a long-term weight-loss program.

However, not every obese person has the strong motivation to lose weight under a behavior management regimen. The evidence is overwhelming that most approaches are ineffective at producing weight loss (Garner & Wooley, 1991). Obese people undergoing very low calorie diets that produce dramatic weight loss during the program tend to gain back the weight and are higher at follow-up than those on a gradual (balanced diet) weight-loss program (Wadden, Foster, & Letizia, 1994). High but stable weight maintenance is preferable to the weight fluctuation that commonly results from most treatment and dietary programs (Garner & Wooley, 1991).

The treatment of extremely obese patients is often a difficult and frustrating task for all concerned. Even with the most effective treatment procedures, failures abound, partly due to the necessity of self-motivation in treatment.

Impact of Failed Weight-Loss Treatment Programs Most obese patients who seek professional help have failed on many diets in the past and tend to experience a "roller-coaster" effect rather than stabilizing at a lower, more desired weight. The weight-fluctuation effect, so much a part of most weight-loss programs, has prompted some authorities to rethink the weight-loss program goals in order to avoid both the roller-coaster effect and to prevent the negative self-views so prominent among individuals who start out with great intentions and high expectations only to fail and then appear to themselves and others as a "failure." Obese people may feel a great sense of shame and failure because they have tried many times and many diets but fail to lose weight or else regain the weight soon afterward. Brownell and Wadden (1992) found that their patients had undertaken an average of five major diets on which they lost (and eventually regained) a total of 56 kg or 123.2 pounds. They have proposed a somewhat different model for losing weight, which includes establishing a "reasonable weight," a weight that can be practically obtainable, which may differ somewhat from what the person might consider desirable but which is more realistic and more readily maintained through such means as low-fat diets and exercise.

Pathological Gambling

Judging from written history and the studies of anthropologists, gambling has occurred and continues to occur almost universally and among all social strata. In the United States today, with the legalized and widely promoted government gambling enterprises, the problems of pathological gambling are increasing (Politzer, Yesalis, & Hudak, 1992; Volberg, 1994). **Pathological gambling,** also known as *compulsive gambling,* is a progressive disorder characterized by continuous or periodic loss of control over gambling; a preoccupation with gambling and obtaining money for gambling; irrational behavior; and continuation of the gambling behavior in spite of adverse consequences (Rosenthal, 1992). Estimates place the number of pathological gamblers in the United States at between 1.2 and 2.3 percent of the adult population (Volberg, 1990; Volberg & Steadman, 1989). Miller and Westermeyer (1996) found that gambling was ten times the estimated rate among the general population of Veterans Administration patients. Both men and women appear to be vulnerable to pathological gambling. One recent study of slot machine addicts reported that there were no gender differences associated with people who become hooked on slot machines (Ohtsuka, Bruton et al., 1997).

Although pathological gambling does not involve a chemically addictive substance, it can be considered an addictive disorder because of the personality factors that tend to characterize compulsive gamblers, the difficulties attributable to compulsive gambling, and the treatment problems involved. Like other addictions, pathological gambling involves behavior maintained by short-term gains despite long-term disruption of an individual's life.

Clinical Picture in Pathological Gambling Gambling in our society takes many forms, including casino gambling, betting on horse races (legally or otherwise), numbers games, lotteries, dice, bingo, and cards. The exact sums that change hands in legal and illegal gambling are unknown, but it has been estimated that habitual gamblers in the United States lose more than $20 billion each year.

If one were to define gambling in its broadest sense, even investing in the stock market might be considered a game of chance. In any event, gambling appears to be one of our major national pastimes, with some 50 percent of the population gambling at one time or another on anything from Saturday night poker games to the outcome of sporting events. Usually, such gambling is a harmless form of social entertainment; an individual places a bet and waits for the result. Win or lose, the game is over. But while most people can gamble and then get on with their life, an estimated 6 to 10 million Americans get "hooked" on gambling. The following case is illustrative.

Case Study, A Compulsive Gambler • John was a handsome 40-year-old man with slightly graying hair who managed an automobile dealership for his father. For the previous two years, he had increasingly neglected his job and was deep in debt as a result of gambling. He had gambled heavily since his twenties. Gambling had caused quarrels in his first marriage and finally a divorce. He had married his second wife without telling her of his problem, but it eventually created such difficulty that she had left him.

John joined an encounter group in the stated hope that he might be helped with his problem. In early group sessions, he proved to be an intelligent, well-educated man who seemed to understand his gambling problem and its self-defeating nature. He stated that he had started gambling after winning some money at the horse races. This experience convinced him that he could supplement his income by gambling judiciously. However, his subsequent gambling—which frequently involved all-night poker games, trips to Las Vegas, and betting on the races—almost always resulted in heavy losses.

In the group, John talked about his gambling freely and coherently—candidly admitting that he enjoyed the excitement of gambling more than sexual relations with his wife. He was actually glad his family had left because it relieved him of responsibility toward them and alleviated his guilt for neglecting them. He acknowledged that his feelings and behavior were inappropriate and self-defeating, but he stated that he was "sick" and that he desperately needed help.

It soon became apparent that although John was willing to talk about his problem, he was not prepared to take constructive steps to deal with it. He wanted the group to accept him in the role of a pathological gambler who could not be expected to "cure" himself. At the group's suggestion, he attended a few meetings of Gamblers Anonymous but found them "irrelevant." It was also suggested that he try aversive therapy, but he felt this would not help him.

While attending the group sessions, John apparently continued to gamble and to lose. After the eighth encounter group session, he did not return. Through inquiry by one of the members, it was learned that he had been arrested for embezzling funds from his father's business, but that his father had somehow managed to have the charges dropped. John reportedly then left for another state. His subsequent history is unknown.

Whatever an individual gambler's situation, compulsive gambling significantly affects the social, psychological, and economic well-being of the gambler's family (Lorenz & Shuttlesworth, 1983). In fact, one study found that a high proportion of pathological gamblers commit crimes that are related to gambling (Blaszczynski, McConaghy, & Frankova, 1989).

Causal Factors in Pathological Gambling   Little systematic research on pathological gambling has been done, and the causal factors behind it are not yet well understood. Pathological gambling seems to be a learned pattern that is highly resistant to extinction. As the case of John illustrates, many people who become pathological gamblers have won a substantial sum of money the first time they gambled; chance alone would dictate that a certain percentage of people would have such "beginner's luck." The reinforcement a person receives during this introductory phase may be a significant factor in later pathological gambling. Because anyone is likely to win from time to time, the principles of intermittent reinforcement—the most potent reinforcement schedule for operant conditioning (see Chapter 3)—could explain an addict's continued gambling despite excessive losses.

Despite their awareness that the odds are against them, and despite the fact that they rarely or never repeat their early success, compulsive gamblers continue to gamble avidly. To "stake" their gambling, they often dissipate their savings, neglect their families, default on bills, and borrow money from friends and loan companies. Eventually, they may resort to embezzlement, writing bad checks, or other illegal means of obtaining money, feeling sure that their luck will change and that they will be able to repay what they have taken. Whereas others view their gambling as unethical and disruptive, they are likely to see themselves as taking "calculated risks" to build a lucrative business. Often they feel alone and resentful that others do not understand their activities.

In a pioneering and well-controlled study of former pathological gamblers, Rosten (1961) found that as a group they tended to be rebellious, unconventional individuals who did not seem to fully understand the ethical norms of society. Half of the group described themselves as "hating regulations." Of 30 men studied, 12 had served time in jail for embezzlement and other crimes directly

The lure of legalized casino gambling has increased the extent of pathological gambling in the United States in recent years.

connected with their gambling. Rosten also found that these men were unrealistic in their thinking and prone to seeking highly stimulating situations. In the subjects' own words, they "loved excitement" and "needed action." Although the men admitted that they had known objectively the all-but-impossible odds they faced while gambling, they had felt that these odds did not apply to them. Often they had the unshakable feeling that "tonight is my night"; typically, they had also followed the so-called Monte Carlo fallacy—that after so many losses, their turn was coming up and they would hit it big. Many of the men discussed the extent to which they had "fooled" themselves by elaborate rationalizations. For example, one gambler described his previous rationalizations as covering all contingencies: "When I was ahead, I could gamble because I was playing with others' money. When I was behind, I had to get even. When I was even, I hadn't lost any money" (Rosten, 1961, p. 67). It is of interest to note that within a few months after the study, 13 of Rosten's 30 subjects either had returned to heavy gambling, had started to drink excessively, or had not been heard from and were presumed to be gambling again.

Later studies strongly support Rosten's findings. They describe pathological gamblers as typically immature, rebellious, thrill-seeking, superstitious, and basically psychopathic (Bolen & Boyd, 1968; Custer, 1982; Graham, 1978a). The most comprehensive study is that of Livingston (1974), who observed, interviewed, and tested 55 mostly working-class men who had joined Gamblers Anonymous to try to stop gambling. Livingston found that these men often referred to their "past immaturity" in explaining their habitual gambling. They also described themselves as having a "big ego" and acknowledged a strong need for recognition and adulation from others. Although these men had usually been able to cover their losses early in their gambling careers, the course was downhill, leading to financial, marital, job, and often legal problems. Eventually, things got so bad that it seemed the only way out of their difficulties was the way they got into them—by gambling.

Cultural factors also appear to be important in developing gambling problems. Research with Southeast Asian refugee populations highlights the role of cultural influences in gambling. Pathological gambling is a particular problem among Southeast Asian refugees, especially those from Laos. Surveys of mental health problems have reported almost epidemic problems with gambling among such groups (Aronoff, 1987; Ganju & Quan, 1987). For example, Aronoff (1987) reported that 54 percent of informants in the Laos group reported gambling as a significant problem. This causes serious adaptation difficulties for refugees because family members who gamble away the limited resources available to them (for example, food stamps) can place additional stress on those facing the challenge of adapting to a new culture.

Pathological gambling problems are not new to Southeast Asians because gambling is reportedly common within their own cultures. However, these problems have apparently become more serious and more widespread in the United States. Several reasons can be cited for these increased gambling problems: (1) the social sanctions that worked to control excessive gambling in Southeast Asia are absent; (2) refugees experience considerable stress, and gambling serves temporarily to relieve cares (reportedly, when they are in their "casinos," many refugees feel, at least temporarily, as though they are still in their native lands); (3) many refugees are unable to find employment, and gambling helps pass the time; and (4) gambling lures refugees with the possibility of great rewards and the opportunity to regain all they lost during migration (Ganju & Quan, 1987).

Treatments and Outcomes Treatment of pathological gamblers has tended to follow along the lines of other addictive disorders. The most extensive treatment approach used with pathological gamblers is cognitive-behavior therapy (Viets, Lopez, & Miller, 1997). For example, one recent controlled study of pathological gamblers using cognitive and behavioral treatment for impulse control problems have been reported. Sylvain, Ladouceur, and Boisvert (1997) provided cognitive-behavior therapy for 58 pathological gamblers who were recruited through the media. Although, 18 participants dropped out at the outset and 11 quit during therapy, the persons remaining in treatment showed significant improvement. Of those actually completing therapy, 86 percent were considered to be "no longer" pathological gamblers at the end of a one-year follow-up.

Some pathological gamblers who want to change find help through membership in Gamblers Anonymous. This organization was founded in 1957 in Los Angeles by two pathological gamblers who found that they could help each other control their gambling by talking about their experiences. Since then, groups have been formed in most major American cities. The groups are modeled after Alcoholics Anonymous, and they view those who gamble as personally responsible for their own actions. The only requirement for membership is an expressed desire to stop gambling. In group discussions, members share experiences and try to gain insights into the irrationality of their gambling and to realize its inevitable consequences. As with Alcoholics Anonymous, members try to help each other maintain control and prevent relapses. Unfortunately, only a small fraction of pathological gamblers find their way into Gamblers Anonymous. Of those who do, only about one in ten manages to overcome the addiction to gambling (Strine, 1971).

A novel, pioneering inpatient treatment program for pathological gamblers was developed at the Brecksville, Ohio, Veterans' Administration Medical Center (1981). The Brecksville treatment program, which lasts for a minimum of 28 days, is integrated into the alcohol treatment program. Five inpatient beds in the 55-bed unit are set aside for pathological gamblers. Alcoholics and gamblers are housed together and share many common program elements because their problems are viewed as similar. The treatment goals for gamblers include abstinence from gambling, major lifestyle changes, participation in Gamblers Anonymous programs, and the acquisition of more adaptive forms of recreation.

Pathological gambling is on the increase in the United States (Custer, 1982). Liberalized gambling legislation has permitted state-operated lotteries, horse racing, and gambling casinos in an effort to increase state tax revenues. In the context of this apparent environ-mental support and "official" sanction for gambling, it is likely that pathological gambling will increase substantially as more and more people "try their luck." Given that pathological gamblers are resistant to treatment, it is likely, too, that our future efforts toward developing more effective preventive and treatment approaches will need to be increased as this problem continues to grow.

UNRESOLVED ISSUES

Genetics of Alcoholism

The origin of alcohol-abuse problems has puzzled researchers for some time. At different periods in our history, various views have dominated. At times, authorities have tended toward the view that sociocultural factors (including sin and personal degradation) are the primary sources of alcohol abuse. One theme that has persisted, however, is the idea that some individuals are more prone to developing alcoholism than are others. Are some people more genetically predisposed to alcohol abuse? Several avenues of research have shown the relevance of genetic factors in the development of alcoholism (Plomin et al., 1997).

Many experts today agree that genetics are likely to play an important role in developing sensitivity to the addictive power of drugs like alcohol (Gardner, 1997; Koob & Nestler, 1997; Hyman, 1994). Research has shown that mice can be bred to have a sensitivity or preference for alcohol (Hyman, 1994). People, like mice, vary considerably in their preference for alcohol—some have an inherent like for the drug, others a dislike for it. Research has shown that some people, such as the sons of alcoholics, have a high risk for developing problems with alcohol because of the inherent motivation or sensitivity to the drug (Conrod, Pihl, & Vassileva, 1998).

Research on the children of alcoholics who were adopted to other (nonalcoholic) families has also provided useful information bearing on the genetics of alcoholism. Studies have been conducted of alcoholics' children who were placed for adoption early in life and so did not come under the environmental influences of their biological parents. For example, Goodwin and colleagues (1973) found that children of alcoholic parents who had been adopted by nonalcoholic foster parents had nearly twice the number of alcohol problems by their late 20s as did a control group of adopted children whose real parents were not alcoholics. In another study, Goodwin and colleagues (1974) compared the sons of alcoholic parents who were adopted in infancy by nonalcoholic parents with those raised by their alcoholic parents. Both adopted and nonadopted sons later evidenced high rates of alcoholism—25 percent and 17 percent, respectively. These investigators concluded that being born to an alcoholic parent, rather than being raised by one, increased the risk of a son's becoming an alcoholic.

Other researchers have attempted to determine if individuals who have a genetic "risk" for alcoholism—such as children of alcoholics—show signs of a predisposition toward alcoholism (McGue, Pickens, & Svikis, 1992). Evidence for increased alcoholism risk includes such factors as a decreased intensity of subjective feelings of intoxication, a smaller decrease in motor performance, and less body sway after alcohol ingestion. Along with these behavioral indices, increases in prolactin (a pituitary hormone) levels after low doses of alcohol have been thought to occur in individuals with a predisposition to alcohol-abuse disorders. Research into these risk factors in alcohol predisposition typically involves obtaining a sample of highly susceptible individuals, such as children of alcoholics, and a sample of controls, and then determining if certain variables (one or more of the risk factors) distinguish the groups. Research by Schuckit and Gould (1988) has shown that alcohol susceptibility indicators significantly separate sons of alcoholics from matched controls. Further evidence for a genetic basis in alcoholism has come from the search for underlying mechanisms for the transmission of alcohol abuse or susceptibility to alcoholism. Hoffman and Tabakoff (1996) have hypothesized that alcohol-induced changes in neuroreceptors might play a role in tolerance to alcohol and in alcohol dependency. They suggest that decreased dopamine, which occurs during withdrawal, might be involved in the individual's compulsion to initiate or to maintain drinking behavior, however, studies have not consistently found such a link for daughters of alcoholics (McGue, 1998).

The evidence on the genetic basis of alcoholism continues to be debated, however, and other experts are not convinced of the primary role of genetics in alcoholism.

Some have employed the evidence that genetics appear to play a stronger role in men than in women (Merikangas & Swendsen, 1997) to question the relative power of genetics as an explanatory factor in substance abuse. Searles (1991) points to the ambiguous evidence for the genetics of alcoholism and cautions against interpreting genetics as a causal factor in the development of alcoholism. Negative results have been found in both adoptive studies and in studies designed to follow up the behavior of high-risk individuals. It is clear that the great majority of children who have alcoholic parents do not themselves become alcoholics—whether or not they are raised by their real parents. The successful outcomes—that is, children of alcoholics who make successful life adjustments—have not been sufficiently studied. In one study of high-risk children of alcoholics, a group of young men 19 to 20 years of age who were presumably at high risk for developing alcoholism were carefully studied for symptoms of psychopathology. Schulsinger and colleagues (1986) found no differences in psychopathology or alcohol-abuse behavior from a control sample similar to the general population. In another study of high-risk individuals, Alterman, Searles, and Hall (1989) failed to find differences in drinking behavior or alcohol-related symptoms between a group of high-risk subjects (those who had alcoholic fathers) and a group of non–high-risk subjects.

Although much evidence implicates genetic factors in alcoholism, we do not know the precise role genetic factors play in the etiology of alcoholism. Available evidence suggests that they might be important as predisposing causes, or that they might contribute in combination with constitutional variables (such as susceptibility to the effects of alcohol) in the development of alcoholism. (So a constitutional predispostion to alcoholism could be acquired as well as inherited.) It is not known whether acquired biological conditions, such as endocrine or enzyme imbalances, increase an individual's vulnerability to alcoholism.

At present, it appears that the genetic interpretation of alcoholism remains an attractive hypothesis; however, additional research is needed for us to hold this view with confidence. It is not likely that genetics alone will account for the full range of alcohol and drug problems. Social circumstances are still considered to be powerful forces in providing both the availability and motivation to use alcohol and other drugs. McGue (1998) has noted that the mechanisms of genetic influence should be viewed as compatible, rather than competitive, with psychological and social determinants of this disorder.

SUMMARY

Addictive disorders—such as alcohol or drug abuse, extreme overeating, and pathological gambling—are among the most widespread and intransigent mental health problems facing us today. Alcohol- and drug-abuse problems can be viewed as psychoactive substance-induced organic mental disorders or as psychoactive substance-abuse and substance-dependence disorders. Many problems of alcohol or drug use involve difficulties that stem solely from the intoxicating effects of the substances. Dependence occurs when an individual develops a tolerance for the substance or exhibits withdrawal symptoms when the substance is not available. Several psychoses related to alcoholism have been identified: idiosyncratic intoxication, withdrawal delirium, chronic alcoholic hallucinosis, and dementia associated with alcoholism.

Drug-abuse disorders may involve physiological dependence on substances, such as opiates—particularly heroin—or barbiturates; however, psychological dependence may also occur with any of the drugs that are commonly used today—for example, marijuana or cocaine.

A number of factors are considered important in the etiology of alcoholism. Some substances such as alcohol or opium stimulate brain centers that produce euphoria—which then becomes a desired goal to attain. It is widely believed that genetic factors may play some role in causing susceptibility through such biological avenues as metabolic rates and sensitivity to alcohol. Psychological factors—such as psychological vulnerability, stress, and the desire for tension reduction—and marital and other relationships are also seen as important etiologic elements in alcohol-use disorders. Although the existence of an "alcoholic personality type" has been disavowed by most theorists, a variety of personality factors apparently play an important role in the development and expression of addictive disorders. Finally, sociocultural factors, such as different attitudes toward alcohol seen in different cultures, may predispose individuals to alcoholism.

Possible causal factors in drug abuse include the influence of peer groups, the existence of a so-called drug culture, and the availability of drugs as tension reducers or as pain relievers. Some recent research has explored a possible physiological basis for drug abuse. The discovery of endorphins, morphine-like substances produced by the body, has raised speculation that a biochemical basis to drug addiction may exist. The so-called "pleasure pathway"—the mesocorticolimbic dopamine pathway (MCLP)—has come under a great deal of study in recent years as the possible potential anatomic site underlying the addictions.

The treatment of individuals who abuse alcohol or drugs is generally difficult and often fails. Many reasons can be found for this poor prognosis: The abuse may reflect a long history of psychological difficulties; interpersonal and marital distress may be involved; and financial and legal problems may be present. In addition, all such problems must be dealt with by an individual who denies that problems exist and is not motivated to work on them.

Several approaches to the treatment of chronic alcoholism or drug abuse have been developed. Frequently, the situation requires biological or medical measures—for example, medication to deal with withdrawal symptoms and withdrawal delirium, or dietary evaluation and treatment for malnutrition. Psychological therapies, such as group therapy and behavioral interventions, may be effective with some alcoholic or drug-abusing individuals. Another source of help for alcoholics is Alcoholics Anonymous; however, the extent of successful outcomes with this program has not been sufficiently studied.

Most treatment programs show reasonably high success rates in the initial "curing" of addictive problems but lowered success rates at follow-up. Recent research on relapse prevention has contributed new insights into the problems of self-control once addictive behaviors have been checked. Part of this approach involves making individuals aware of factors that can lead to relapse and preparing them to deal with such setbacks. Most treatment programs require abstinence; however, over the past 20 years, research has suggested that some alcoholics can learn to control their drinking while continuing to drink socially. The controversy surrounding controlled drinking continues.

Not all addictive disorders involve the use of substances such as alcohol or drugs. Some people eat to excess, endangering their health. Others gamble to such an extent that they wreck their lives and damage or destroy their family relationships. These disorders—extreme obesity and pathological gambling—involve many of the same psychological mechanisms that seem to underlie chronic alcoholism or drug addiction. Treatment approaches found to be effective for alcoholism and drug abuse appear to work about as well with obese clients and pathological gamblers. Many of the same difficulties, especially concerning response to treatment and relapse, also plague the treatment of extremely obese persons and compulsive gamblers.

KEY TERMS

addictive behavior (p. 374)

psychoactive drugs (p. 374)

toxicity (p. 374)

psychoactive substance abuse (p. 374)

psychoactive substance dependence (p. 374)

tolerance (p. 374)

withdrawal symptoms (p. 374)

alcoholic (p. 376)

alcoholism (p. 376)

mesocorticolimbic dopamine pathway (MCLP) (p. 383)

caffeine (p. 398)

nicotine (p. 398)

opium (p. 400)

morphine (p. 400)

heroin (p. 400)

endorphins (p. 402)

methadone (p. 402)

cocaine (p. 403)

amphetamine (p. 405)

barbiturates (p. 406)

hallucinogens (p. 406)

LSD (p. 407)

flashback (p. 407)

mescaline (p. 407)

psilocybin (p. 407)

marijuana (p. 408)

hashish (p. 408)

hyperobesity (p. 409)

pathological gambling (p. 413)

Sexual Variants, Abuse, and Dysfunctions

Dwight Mackintosh, *My Mother Baking Bread, 1988*. Mackintosh, born in 1906 in California, was admitted to a mental institution at age 16 after having become "unmanageable at home." He remained in state mental hospitals until the deinstitutionalization movement inspired his release in 1978. His brother took him to the Creative Growth Art Center in Oakland, where he began to draw and paint earnestly. People are the primary subject of his art, and drawing his only way of expressing his interest in them; otherwise, he is deeply withdrawn.

Loving, sexually satisfying relationships contribute a great deal to our happiness, and if we are not in such relationships, we are apt to spend a great deal of time, effort, and emotional energy looking for them. Sexuality is a central concern of our lives, influencing with whom we fall in love and mate, and how happy we are with them and with ourselves.

In this chapter we shall first look at the psychological problems that make sexual fulfillment especially difficult for some people—the vast majority of them men—who develop unusual sexual interests that are difficult to satisfy in a socially acceptable manner. For example, exhibitionists are sexually aroused by showing their genitals to strangers, who are likely to be disgusted and frightened. Thus exhibitionists' sexual expression often requires the discomfort of others, a situation that is not only socially unacceptable, but potentially traumatic to the unwilling viewer. Other sexual variants may be problematic primarily to the individual: Transsexualism, for example, is a disorder involving discomfort with one's biological sex and a strong desire to be of the opposite sex. Still other variants, such as fetishism, in which sexual interest centers on some inanimate object or body part, involve behaviors that, although bizarre and unusual, do not clearly harm anyone. Perhaps no other area covered in this book exposes the difficulties in defining boundaries between normality and psychopathology as clearly as variant sexuality does. Later, we address this issue explicitly and in greater detail, focusing especially on homosexuality, which illustrates the influence of cultural norms on what is classified as psychopathological.

The second category of problems we shall consider is **sexual abuse,** a pattern of pressured or forced sexual contact. It has especially devastating social effects, and we will therefore focus special attention on this topic. During the past decade or so, there has been a tremendous increase in attention to the problem of sexual abuse of both children and adults (most adult victims being women). Research has addressed both the causes and consequences of sexual abuse. As we shall see, some related issues, such as the reality of repressed memories of sexual abuse are extremely controversial.

The third category of sexual difficulties examined in this chapter is sexual dysfunctions, which include problems that impede satisfactory performance of sexual acts. Premature ejaculation, for example, causes men to reach orgasm much earlier than they and their partners find satisfying. The question of what is normal and what is not, which often appears in discussions of variant sexuality, is much less of an issue with sexual dysfunctions because people who have sexual dysfunctions (or their part-

ners) typically view them as problems. Nevertheless, questions do arise concerning realistic expectations. Few people function ideally all the time, and many less-than-ideal conditions are common. For example, many young men ejaculate more rapidly than they would like but slow down as they age. Many women do not have orgasms during sexual intercourse, yet find intercourse enjoyable and satisfying.

Much less is known about sexual deviations, abuse, and dysfunctions than is known about many of the other disorders we have considered thus far in this book, such as anxiety and depression. The major clinical psychology and psychiatry journals have relatively few articles related to sexual dysfunctions and deviations, and there are also many fewer sex researchers than depression and anxiety researchers. One major reason is the sex taboo. Although sex is an important concern for most people, many have difficulty talking about it openly. This makes it difficult to obtain knowledge about even the most basic facts, such as the frequency of various sexual practices, feelings, and attitudes. This is especially true when the relevant behaviors are socially ostracized, such as homosexuality. It is difficult both to ask people about such behaviors and to trust their answers.

A second reason why sex research has progressed less rapidly is that many issues related to sexuality—including homosexuality, teenage sexuality, abortion, and childhood sexual abuse—are among our most divisive and controversial. In fact, sex research is itself controversial. Two large-scale sex surveys were halted because of political opposition even after being officially approved and deemed scientifically meritorious (Udry, 1993). Fortunately, one of these was funded privately, although on a much smaller scale, and it is now considered the definitive study for the 1990s (Laumann et al., 1994). Senator Jesse Helms and others had argued that sex researchers tended to approve of premarital sex and homosexuality, and that this would likely bias the results of the surveys. Perhaps in part because of the controversial nature of sex research, it is not well funded. For example, although sex offenders are widely feared and millions of dollars are spent keeping convicted sex offenders behind bars every year, the National Institute of Mental Health spent only $1.2 million on sex offender research in 1993, compared with $125.3 million on depression (Goode, 1994).

Despite these significant barriers, we do know some things about sexual variants and dysfunctions. Clinical investigations have provided rich descriptions of many sexual variants. Etiological research on sexual dysfunctions and deviations, although in its infancy, has shown promise for some disorders, and we discuss these developments.

Loving, sexually satisfying relationships contribute a great deal to our happiness, but our understanding of them has advanced slowly, largely because they are so difficult for people to talk about openly and because funding for research is often hard to come by.

Before we turn to specific disorders, we examine sociocultural influences on sexual behavior and attitudes in general. We take this excursion first in order to provide some perspective about cross-cultural variability in standards of sexual conduct, and to encourage special caution in classifying sexual practices as "abnormal" or "deviant."

Sociocultural Influences on Sexual Practices and Standards

Although some aspects of sexuality and mating, such as men's greater emphasis on their partner's attractiveness, are cross-culturally universal (Buss, 1989), others are quite variable. For example, all known cultures have taboos against sex between close relatives, but attitudes toward premarital sex vary considerably (Frayser, 1985). Ideas about acceptable sexual behavior also change over time. Less than 100 years ago, for example, sexual modesty was such that women's arms and legs were always

hidden in public. Nowadays, actors are shown nude in movies and sometimes even on television.

Despite the substantial variability in sexual attitudes and behavior in different times and places, people typically behave as if the sexual standards of their time and place were obviously correct, and they are intolerant of sexual nonconformity. Sexual nonconformists are often considered evil or sick. We do not mean to suggest that such judgments are always arbitrary. There has probably never existed a society in which Jeffrey Dahmer, who was sexually aroused by killing men, having sex with them, storing their corpses, and sometimes eating them, would be considered psychologically normal. Nevertheless, it is useful to be aware of historical and cultural influences on sexuality. When the expression or the acceptance of a certain behavior varies considerably across eras and cultures, we should at least pause to consider whether our own stance is the most appropriate one.

Because the influence of time and place are so important in shaping sexual behavior and attitudes, we begin by exploring three cases that illustrate how opinions about "acceptable" and "normal" sexual behavior may change dramatically over time, and may differ dramatically from one culture to another. In the first case, America during the mid-1800s, a set of beliefs about sexuality, "degeneracy theory," led to highly conservative sexual practices and dire warnings about most kinds of sexual "indulgence." In the second case, we look briefly at the Sambia tribe in New Guinea, in which a set of beliefs about sexuality has led to sexual practices unknown in Western culture. In Sambian society, all normal adolescent males go through a stage of homosexuality before switching rather abruptly to heterosexuality in adulthood. Finally, in the third case, we consider the status of homosexuality in Western culture. We focus here on the mental health profession's decision in the 1970s to change its view of homosexual behavior.

Case 1: Degeneracy and Abstinence Theory

During the 1750s, the Swiss physician Simon Tissot developed *degeneracy theory,* the central belief of which was that semen is necessary for physical and sexual vigor in men and for masculine characteristics such as beard growth (Money, 1985, 1986). He based this theory on observations about human eunuchs and castrated animals. Of course, we now know that the loss of the male hormone testosterone, and not of semen, is responsible for relevant characteristics of eunuchs and castrated animals. Based on his theory, however, Tissot asserted that two practices were especially harmful: masturbation and patronizing prostitutes. Both of these practices wasted the vital fluid, semen, as well as (in his view) overstimulating and exhausting the nervous system. Tissot also recommended that married people engage solely in procreative sex to avoid the waste of semen. (See again Highlight 2.4 for further discussion of nineteenth-century views on abnormal behavior.)

A descendant of degeneracy theory, *abstinence theory*, was advocated in America during the 1830s by the Reverend Sylvester Graham (Money, 1985, 1986). The three cornerstones of his crusade for public health were healthy food (Graham crackers were named for him), physical fitness, and sexual abstinence. Graham's most famous successor, Dr. John Harvey Kellogg, began practicing medicine in the 1870s. He ardently disapproved of masturbation and urged parents to be wary of signs that their children were indulging in it. He published a paper on the 39 signs of "the secret vice," which included, among others, weakness, early symptoms of consumption (TB), sudden change in disposition, lassitude, dullness of the eyes, premature and defective development, sleeplessness, fickleness, untrustworthiness, bashfulness, love of solitude, unnatural boldness, mock piety, and round shoulders.

As a physician, Kellogg was professionally admired and publicly influential, earning a fortune publishing books discouraging masturbation. His recommended treatments for "the secret vice" were quite extreme. For example, he advocated that especially persistent masturbation in boys be treated by sewing the foreskin with silver wire, or as a last resort, circumcision without anesthesia. Female masturbation was to be treated by burning the clitoris with carbolic acid. Besides deploring masturbation, Kellogg, like Graham, was especially concerned with dietary health. He urged people to eat more cereals and nuts and less meat, because he believed that eating meat increased sexual desire. Thus, Kellogg's cornflakes were invented "almost literally, as anti-masturbation food" (Money, 1986, p. 186). Although Kellogg married, it appears that he slept alone and never consummated his marriage.

Given the influence of physicians like Kellogg, it should perhaps come as no surprise that many people believed that masturbation caused insanity (Hare, 1962). This hypothesis had started with the anonymous publication in the early eighteenth century in London of a book entitled *Onania, or the Heinous Sin of Self-Pollution*. It asserted that masturbation was a common cause of insanity. This idea probably arose from observations that many patients in mental asylums masturbated openly (unlike sane people, who are more likely to do it in private) and

that the age at which masturbation tends to begin (at puberty in adolescence) precedes by several years the age when the first signs of insanity often begin (late adolescence and young adulthood) (Abramson & Seligman, 1977). The idea that masturbation may cause insanity appeared in some psychiatry textbooks as late as the 1940s.

The most influential American political opponent of sexual expression was Anthony Comstock. A contemporary of Kellogg, he formed the Society for the Suppression of Vice and in 1873 successfully lobbied Congress to pass laws against "obscenity," which he construed quite broadly. As an inspector with the post office, he became, in effect, the national censor. His targets included female nudity in art classes and medical books pertaining to sexuality. He believed that lust led to psychological degeneracy (Money, 1985, 1986).

Although abstinence theory and associated attitudes seem highly puritanical by today's standards, they have had a long-lasting influence on attitudes toward sex in American and other Western cultures. It was not until 1972 that the American Medical Association declared: "Masturbation is a normal part of adolescent sexual development and requires no medical management" (American Medical Association Committee on Human Sexuality, 1972, p. 40). Around the same time, the Boy Scout Manual dropped its antimasturbation warnings. Nonetheless, in 1994 Jocelyn Elders was fired as U.S. Surgeon General for suggesting publicly that sex education courses should include discussion of masturbation.

Case 2: Ritualized Homosexuality in Melanesia

Melanesia is a group of islands in the South Pacific that has been intensively studied by anthropologists, who have uncovered cultural influences on sexuality unlike any known in the West. Between 10 and 20 percent of Melanesian societies practice a form of homosexuality within the context of male initiation rituals that all male members of society must experience.

The best studied society has been the Sambia of Papua New Guinea (Herdt & Stoller, 1990). Two beliefs are related to Sambian sexual practices: *semen conservation* and *female pollution*. Like Tissot, the Sambians believe that semen is important for many things, including physical growth, strength, and spirituality. Furthermore, they believe that it takes many inseminations (and much semen) to impregnate a woman. Finally, they believe that semen cannot easily be replenished by the body and so must be conserved or obtained elsewhere. The female pollution doctrine refers to the belief that the female body is unhealthy to males, primarily due to menstrual fluids. At menarche, Sambian women are secretly initiated in the menstrual hut forbidden to all males.

In order to obtain or maintain adequate amounts of semen, young Sambian males practice semen exchange with each other. Beginning as boys, they learn to practice fellatio (oral sex) in order to ingest sperm. At first, they take only the oral role, but after puberty they can take the penetrative role, inseminating younger boys. Ritualized homosexuality among the Sambian men is seen as an exchange of sexual pleasure for vital semen. (It is ironic that although both the Sambian and Victorian-era Americans believed in semen conservation, their solutions to the problem were radically different.) When Sambian males are well past puberty, they begin the transition to heterosexuality. At this time the female body is thought to be less dangerous because the males have ingested protective semen over the previous years. For a time, they may begin having sex with women and still participate in fellatio with younger boys, but homosexual behavior stops after the birth of a man's first child. Most of the Sambian men make the transition to exclusive adult heterosexuality without problems. Those few who do not are somewhat ironically considered misfits.

An interesting evolutionary hypothesis notes that the Melanesian societies practicing ritualized homosexuality have highly male-biased sex ratios, probably due to what is suspected to be a high incidence of female infanticide (Oles, 1994). According to this hypothesis, requisite homosexuality is a tactic used by older males to limit the arena of mate competition by channeling potential rivals' (i.e., young men's) sexuality into homoerotic behavior, making adolescent and young women exclusively available to older males. By this hypothesis, the female pollution ideology is a scare tactic used for the same end.

Whatever its explanation, ritualized homosexuality among the Melanesians is a striking example of the influence of culture on sexual attitudes and behavior. A Melanesian adolescent who refused to practice homosexuality would be viewed as abnormal, and such adolescents are apparently absent or rare. Homosexuality among the Sambia is not the same as homosexuality in contemporary America, with the possible exception of those Sambian men who have difficulty making the heterosexual transition.

Case 3: Homosexuality and American Psychiatry

During the past half century, the status of homosexuality has changed enormously both within psychiatry and psy-

chology and for society in general. In the not-too-distant past, homosexuality was a taboo topic. Now, movies, talk shows, and television sitcoms and dramas address the topic explicitly by including gay men and lesbians in leading roles. As we shall see, developments in psychiatry and psychology have played an important role in these changes. Homosexuality was officially removed from the DSM (where it had previously been classed as a sexual deviation) in 1973 and today is no longer regarded as a psychological disorder. A brief survey of attitudes toward homosexuality within the mental health profession itself again illustrates how attitudes toward various expressions of human sexuality may change over time.

Homosexuality as Sickness Reading the medical and psychological literature on homosexuality written before 1970 can be a jarring experience, especially if one subscribes to views prevalent today. Relevant articles included "Effeminate homosexuality: A disease of childhood" and "On the cure of homosexuality." It is only fair to note, however, that the view that homosexual people are mentally ill was relatively tolerant compared with some earlier views. During the first half of this century, those who did not believe that homosexual people were mentally ill and in need of treatment tended to believe that they were criminals in need of incarceration (Bayer, 1981). British and American cultures had long taken punitive approaches to homosexual behavior. In the sixteenth century King Henry VIII of England declared "the detestable and abominable vice of buggery [anal sex]" a felony punishable by death, and it was not until 1861 that the maximum penalty was reduced to ten years' imprisonment. Similarly, in the United States laws were very repressive until recently, and even now homosexual behavior continues to be a criminal offense in some states. Thus the belief that homosexuality is an illness seems somewhat less intolerant in historical context.

During the late nineteenth and early twentieth centuries, several prominent theorists suggested that homosexuality was consistent with psychological normality. The famous sexologists Havelock Ellis and Magnus Hirshfeld believed that homosexuality is natural and nonpathological. Although, as we shall see, psychoanalysts became the most vigorous proponents of the disease position, Freud's own attitude toward homosexual people was remarkably progressive for the time and is well expressed in his touching "Letter to an American Mother" (1935):

Dear Mrs. . . .

I gather from your letter that your son is a homosexual. I am most impressed by the fact that you do not mention this term yourself in your information about him. May I question you, why you avoid it? Homosexuality is assuredly no advantage, but it is nothing to be ashamed of, no vice, no degradation, it cannot be classified as an illness; we consider it to be a variation of the sexual function produced by a certain arrest of sexual development. Many highly respectable individuals of ancient and modern times have been homosexuals, several of the greatest men among them (Plato, Michelangelo, Leonardo da Vinci, etc.). It is a great injustice to persecute homosexuality as a crime, and cruelty too. . . .

By asking me if I can help, you mean, I suppose, if I can abolish homosexuality and make normal heterosexuality take its place. The answer is, in a general way, we cannot promise to achieve it. . . .

Sincerely yours with kind wishes,
Freud

Beginning in the 1940s, psychoanalysts, led by Sandor Rado, began to take a more pessimistic view of the mental health of homosexual people, and a more optimistic view of the likely success of therapy to induce heterosexuality. In contrast to Freud's view that homosexual impulses were universal, Rado (1962) believed that homosexuality was found only in people whose heterosexual desires were too psychologically threatening. He viewed homosexuality as an escape from heterosexuality and therefore incompatible with mental health. This general view was adopted and articulated further by Irving Bieber and Charles Socarides, who stressed the role of "highly pathologic parent-child relationships" (Bieber et al., 1962). They believed that in the case of male homosexuality, domineering, emotionally smothering mothers, and detached, hostile fathers prevented boys from identifying closely with the fathers, a step they hypothesized was necessary to normal psychological development. It may have been important that these psychoanalysts based their opinions primarily on their experiences seeing gay men in therapy, who are likely to be more psychologically troubled than other gay men.

Homosexuality as Nonpathological Variation

Around 1950, the view of homosexuality as sickness began to be challenged by both scientists and homosexual people themselves. Scientific blows to the pathology position included Alfred Kinsey's finding that homosexual behavior was much more common than had been previously believed, although as we shall see, we now know that his estimates were too high (Kinsey, Pomeroy, & Martin, 1948; Kinsey et al., 1953). Perhaps the most influential studies were performed by Evelyn Hooker (1957). She demonstrated that trained psychologists could not distinguish the psychological tests of homosexual and heterosexual subjects.

Gay men and lesbians also began to challenge psychiatric orthodoxy. Beginning in the 1950s, homophile organizations encouraged frank discussion of the status of homosexuality and spawned committed opponents of the homosexuality-as-illness position. The 1960s saw the birth of the radical gay liberation movement, which took the more uncompromising stance that "gay is good." The decade closed with the famous Stonewall riot in New York City, sparked by police mistreatment of gay men, which provided a clear signal that homosexual people would no longer passively accept their status as second-class citizens. By the 1970s, openly gay psychiatrists and psychologists were working from within the mental health profession to change the orthodox position. Specifically, they wished to have homosexuality removed from the *Diagnostic and Statistical Manual of Psychiatric Disorders* (DSM-II).

In 1973, after acrimonious debate, the Board of Trustees of the American Psychiatric Association (APA) voted to remove homosexuality from DSM-II. This move was opposed by some APA members, who argued that the board abandoned scientific principles because of political pressure. They prevailed on the APA to put the matter before its membership in a referendum, and in 1974 the membership voted 5,854 to 3,810, to remove homosexuality from DSM-II. This episode was both a milestone for gay rights and an embarrassment for psychiatry, and more generally, for advocates of psychodiagnosis. The spectacle of the psychiatric nomenclature being modified on the basis of a vote rather than the scientific consensus of experts appeared to confirm what psychodiagnosis' harshest critics, such as Thomas Szasz (1974), had been saying, that the label "mental illness" merely reflects the values of mental health professionals.

We believe the APA made a correct decision in removing homosexuality from DSM-II because the vast majority of evidence shows that homosexuality is compatible with psychological normality. Furthermore, we do not find the resolution of this issue by vote to be especially problematic. The classification of any behavior as psychopathology necessitates a value judgment that the behavior is undesirable (see also Chapter 1). This value judgment is usually implicit and unchallenged—for example, few people deny the impairment and pain caused by schizophrenia, even among schizophrenic patients themselves. Challenges by gay and lesbian people forced mental health professionals to confront the values question explicitly, and they made the correct determination that homosexuality is not a psychological disorder. See Highlight 11.1 for further discussion of homosexuality as a normal sexual variation.

Despite the fact that homosexuality is considered a normal sexual variation and compatible with psychological normality, discrimination and violence against homosexuals remains a very significant problem today.

SEXUAL AND GENDER VARIANTS

We now turn to the problematic sexual variants included in DSM-IV. There are two general categories: paraphilias and gender identity disorders.

The Paraphilias

The **paraphilias** are a group of persistent sexual behavior patterns in which unusual objects, rituals, or situations are required for full sexual satisfaction. Although mild forms of these conditions probably have occurred in the lives of many normal people, a paraphilic person is distinguished by the insistence and relative exclusivity with which his or her sexuality focuses on the acts or objects in question—without which orgasm is often impossible. Paraphilias also frequently have a compulsive quality, with some paraphilic individuals requiring orgasmic release as often as four to ten times per day (Money, 1986, p. 133). Paraphilic individuals may or may not have persistent desires to change their sexual preferences. Some paraphilias require a partner, and a fortunate paraphilic individual may discover another person with a reciprocal paraphilia—as in sexual sadomasochism discussed below—which may then lead to a lasting although by conventional standards somewhat bizarre love affair. Fairly common is a situation in which a sexually normal person becomes unwittingly involved in a paraphilic person's ritualized sexual program, only gradually discovering that he or she is a mere accessory, a sort of stage prop, in the latter's sexual drama. Because nearly all paraphilic persons are male (a fact whose etiological implications we consider later), we use masculine pronouns to refer to them.

The DSM-IV recognizes eight specific paraphilias: (1) fetishism, (2) transvestic fetishism, (3) voyeurism, (4) exhibitionism, (5) sexual sadism, (6) sexual masochism, (7) pedophilia, and (8) frotteurism (rubbing against a nonconsenting person). An additional category, Paraphilias Not Otherwise Specified, includes several rarer disorders such as telephone scatologia (obscene phone calls), necrophilia (sexual desire for corpses), and coprophilia (sexual arousal to feces). Of the specified paraphilias, we will discuss all but frotteurism, a category that is relatively new and not yet satisfactorily researched. Our discussion of pedophilia is postponed, however, until a later section concerning sexual abuse.

Fetishism   In **fetishism,** sexual interest typically centers on some inanimate object, such as an article of clothing, or some body part. (DSM-IV states that a fetish is diagnosed only when the object is inanimate, but most sex researchers have not traditionally made this distinction.) As is generally true for the paraphilias, males are most commonly involved in cases of fetishism; reported cases of female fetishists are extremely rare (Mason, 1997). The range of fetishistic objects includes hair, ears, hands, underclothing, shoes, perfume, and similar objects associated with the opposite sex. The mode of using these objects to achieve sexual excitation and gratification varies considerably, but it commonly involves kissing, fondling, tasting, or smelling the objects. Fetishism does not normally interfere with the rights of others, except in an incidental way such as asking the partner to wear the object during sexual encounters. Many men have a strong sexual fascination for paraphernalia such as brassieres, garter belts, hose, and high heels. Although such men do not typically meet diagnostic criteria for fetishism, because the paraphernalia are not necessary or strongly preferred for sexual arousal (as is required to be diagnosed as having a fetish), they do illustrate the high frequency of fetish-like preferences among men.

To obtain the required object, a fetishistic person may commit burglary, theft, or even assault. Probably the articles most commonly stolen by fetishistic individuals are women's undergarments. One young boy was found to have accumulated over 100 pairs of underpants from a lingerie shop when he was apprehended. In such cases the excitement and suspense of the criminal act itself typically reinforce the sexual stimulation and sometimes actually constitute the fetish—the stolen article being of little importance. For example, one adolescent admitted entering many homes in which the entering itself usually sufficed to induce an orgasm. When it did not, he was able to achieve sexual satisfaction by taking some "token," such as money or jewelry.

Frequently, fetishistic behavior consists of masturbation in association with a fetishistic object. Here, of course, it is difficult to draw a line between fetishistic activity and the effort to increase the sexual excitation and satisfaction of masturbation through the use of pictures and other articles associated with a desired sexual object. Using such articles in masturbation is a common practice and not usually considered pathological. Where antisocial behavior, such as breaking and entering, is involved, however, everyone can agree that the practice is fetishistic. For example, Marshall (1974) reported a rather unusual case of a young university student who had a "trouser fetish"; he would steal the trousers of teenagers and then use them in physical contact during masturbation. A somewhat different, but not atypical, pattern of fetishism is illustrated by the case of a man whose fetish was women's shoes and legs:

> The fetishist in this case was arrested several times for loitering in public places, such as railroad stations and libraries, watching women's legs. Finally he chanced on a novel solution to his problem. Posing as an agent for a hosiery firm, he rented a large room, advertised for models, and took motion pictures of a number of women walking and seated with their legs displayed to best advantage. He then used these pictures to achieve sexual satisfaction and found that they continued to be adequate for the purpose. (Adapted from Grant, 1953)

Most theories of the etiology fetishism emphasize the importance of classical conditioning. It is not difficult to imagine how women's underwear might become eroticized by its close association with sex and the female body. Rubber fetishism may depend on the fact that training pants are made of rubber. If so, then as plastic replaces rubber, plastic fetishes may become more com-

mon (Money, 1986, p. 65; see also Mason, 1997). It is important to emphasize that differential experiences do not seem sufficient to explain why some men develop fetishes. Although perhaps most rubber fetishists wore rubber training pants, most men who wore such pants do not develop fetishes. It seems likely that this is because there are individual differences in conditionability of sexual responses. Men high in sexual conditionability would be prone to developing one or more fetishes. We will later return to the role of conditioning in the development of paraphilias, in general.

Transvestic Fetishism   The achievement of sexual arousal and satisfaction by "cross-dressing"—that is, dressing as a member of the opposite sex—is called **transvestic fetishism.** Typically, the onset of transvestism is during adolescence and involves masturbation while wearing female clothing or undergarments. Blanchard (1989, 1992) has termed the psychological motivation of transvestites autogynephilia: paraphilic sexual arousal by the thought or fantasy of being women (Blanchard, 1991, 1993). The great sexologist Magnus Hirschfeld first identified a class of cross-dressing men who are sexually aroused by the image of themselves as women: "They feel attracted not by the women outside them, but by the woman inside them" (Hirschfeld, 1948, p. 167). Although some gay men dress "in drag" on occasion, they do not typically do this for sexual pleasure and hence are not transvestic fetishists. The vast majority of transvestites are heterosexual (Talamini, 1982). Transvestites may fuse the idea of being a woman with their sexual attractions toward real women in fantasies in which they are engaging in lesbian interactions (Blanchard, 1991). Buckner (1970) formulated a description of the "ordinary" male transvestite from a survey of 262 transvestites conducted by the magazine *Transvestia*:

> He is probably married (about two–thirds are); if he is married he probably has children (about two-thirds do). Almost all of these transvestites said they were exclusively heterosexual—in fact, the rate of "homosexuality" was less than the average for the entire population. The transvestic behavior generally consists of privately dressing in the clothes of a woman, at home, in secret . . . The transvestite generally does not run into trouble with the law. His cross-dressing causes difficulties for very few people besides himself and his wife. (p. 381)

This clinical picture has not changed since Buckner's report; nor, unfortunately, has the state of knowledge about etiology, about which very little is known (Zucker & Blanchard, 1997). The following is a fairly typical case of transvestic fetishism and illustrates both the typical early onset of transvestic fetishism and the difficulties the condition may raise in a marriage:

Case Study, A Transvestite's Dilemma • Mr. A., a 65-year-old security guard, formerly a fishing-boat captain, is distressed about his wife's objections to his wearing a nightgown at home in the evening, now that his youngest child has left home. His appearance and demeanor, except when he is dressing in women's clothes, are always appropriately masculine, and he is exclusively heterosexual. Occasionally, over the past five years, he has worn an inconspicuous item of female clothing even when dressed as a man, sometimes a pair of panties, sometimes an ambiguous pinkie ring. He always carries a photograph of himself dressed as a woman.

His first recollection of an interest in female clothing was putting on his sister's bloomers at age 12, an act accompanied by sexual excitement. He continued periodically to put on women's underpants—an activity that invariably resulted in an erection, sometimes a spontaneous emission, sometimes masturbation, but never accompanied by fantasy. Although he occasionally wished to be a girl, he never fantasized himself as one. He was competitive and aggressive with other boys and always acted "masculine." During his single years he was always attracted to girls, but was shy about sex. Following his marriage at age 22, he had his first heterosexual intercourse.

His involvement with female clothes was of the same intensity even after his marriage. Beginning at age 45, after a chance exposure to a magazine called *Transvestia,* he began to increase his cross-dressing activity. He learned there were other men like himself, and he became more and more preoccupied with female clothing in fantasy and progressed to periodically dressing completely as a woman. More recently he has become involved in a transvestite network, writing to other transvestites contacted through the magazine and occasionally attending transvestite parties. Cross-dressing at these parties has been the only time that he has cross-dressed outside his home.

Although still committed to his marriage, sex with his wife has dwindled over the past 20 years as his waking thoughts and activities have become increasingly centered on cross-dressing. Over time this activity has become less eroticized and more an end in itself, but it still is a source of some sexual excitement. He always has an increased urge to dress as a woman when under stress; it has a tranquilizing effect. If particular circumstances prevent him from cross-dressing, he feels extremely frustrated . . .

Because of disruptions in his early life, the patient has always treasured the steadfastness of his wife and the order of his home. He told his wife about his cross-dressing practice when they were married, and she was accepting so long as he kept it to himself. Nevertheless, he felt guilty, particularly after he began complete cross-dressing, and periodically he attempted to renounce the practice, throwing out all his female clothes and makeup. His children served as a barrier to his giving free rein to his impulses. Following his retirement from fishing, and in the absence of his children, he finds himself more drawn to cross-dressing, more in conflict with his wife, and more depressed. (Spitzer et al., 1994)

As we have indicated, transvestic fetishism may complicate a relationship. However, like other kinds of

Studies have shown that men who cross-dress may actually feel less anxiety and shyness when in their female roles. Although a transvestic man may therefore enjoy excursions into the social roles of the other sex, he may also be markedly distressed by urges to do so, and, if married, his transvestism may also cause difficulties for his wife. Cross-dressers are seeking out others of their kind to deal with their special problems in support groups like the one shown.

fetishism, it causes overt harm to others only when accompanied by such illegal acts as theft or destruction of property. This is not always the case with the other paraphilias, many of which do contain a definite element of injury or significant risk of injury—physical or psychological—to one or more of the parties involved in a sexual encounter. Typically these practices have strong legal sanctions against them. We shall consider only the most common forms of these paraphilias: voyeurism, exhibitionism, sadism, and masochism.

Voyeurism The synonymous terms **voyeurism,** *scotophilia,* and *inspectionalism* refer to the achievement of sexual pleasure through clandestine peeping. It occurs as a sexual offense primarily among young men. These Peeping Toms, as they are commonly called, usually observe females who are undressing or couples engaging in sexual relations. Frequently they masturbate during their peeping activity.

How do young men develop this pattern? First, viewing the body of an attractive female seems to be quite stimulating sexually for many, if not most, men. In addition, the privacy and mystery that have traditionally surrounded sexual activities tend to increase curiosity about them. Second, if a young man with such curiosity feels shy and inadequate in his relations with the other sex, it is not too surprising for him to accept the substitute of voyeurism. In this way he satisfies his curiosity and to some extent meets his sexual needs without the trauma of actually approaching a female, and thus without the rejection and lowered self-status that such an approach might bring. In fact voyeuristic activities often provide important compensatory feelings of power and secret domination over an unsuspecting victim, which may contribute to the maintenance of this pattern. Also, of course, the suspense and danger associated with voyeurism may lead to emotional excitement and a reinforcement of the sexual stimulation. A voyeur does not normally seek sexual activity with those he observes. If a voyeur manages to find a wife in spite of his interpersonal difficulties, as many do, he is rarely well-adjusted sexually in his relationship with his wife, as the following case illustrates:

Case Study, A Peeping Tom • A young married college student had an attic apartment that was extremely hot during the summer months. To enable him to attend school, his wife worked; she came home at night tired and irritable and not in the mood for sexual relations. In addition, "the damned springs in the bed squeaked." In order "to obtain some sexual gratification"

the youth would peer through his binoculars at the room next door and occasionally saw the young couple there engaged in erotic activities. This stimulated him greatly, and he thus decided to extend his peeping to a sorority house. During his second venture, however, he was reported and apprehended by the police. This offender was quite immature for his age, rather puritanical in his attitude toward masturbation, and prone to indulge in rich but immature sexual fantasies.

Although more permissive laws concerning "adult" movies, videos, and magazines have probably removed much of the secrecy from sexual behavior and also have provided an alternative source of gratification for would-be voyeurs, their actual effects on the prevalence of voyeurism is a matter of speculation because there never have been any good epidemiological data on the prevalence of voyeurism (Kaplan & Krueger, 1997). For many voyeurs, these movies and magazines probably do not provide an adequate substitute for secretly watching the sexual behavior of an unsuspecting couple or the "real-life" nudity of a woman who mistakenly believes she enjoys privacy.

Although a voyeur may become reckless in his behavior and thus may be detected and assaulted by his victims, voyeurism does not ordinarily have any serious criminal or antisocial aspects. In fact many people probably have some voyeuristic inclinations, which are checked by practical considerations, such as the possibility of being caught, and ethical attitudes concerning the right to privacy. On the other hand, strong voyeuristic tendencies are sometimes accompanied by other, more bizarre elements in a peeper's sexual arousal pattern that might signal far more serious problems. For example, their sex lives may be confined to voyeuristic activities to the exclusion of interactions with a real partner.

Exhibitionism The word **exhibitionism** (*indecent exposure* in legal terms) describes the intentional exposure of the genitals to others (generally strangers) in inappropriate circumstances and without their consent. The exposure may take place in some secluded location, such as a park, or in a more public place, such as a department store, church, theater, or bus. In cities an exhibitionist often drives by schools or bus stops, exhibits himself while in the car, and then drives rapidly away. In many instances the exposure is repeated under fairly constant conditions, such as only in churches or buses, or in the same general vicinity and at the same time of day. In one case, a youth exhibited himself only at the top of an escalator in a large department store. The type of victim too is usually fairly consistent for an individual exhibitionist. For a male offender, this ordinarily involves a young or middle-aged female who is not known to the offender, though children and adolescents may also be targeted disproportionately (Murphy, 1997). Exhibitionism is the most common sexual offense reported to the police in the United States, Canada, and Europe, accounting for about one-third of all sexual offenses (Murphy, 1997). According to some estimates as many as 20 percent of women may have been the target of either exhibitionism or voyeurism (Kaplan & Kruger, 1997; Meyer, 1995).

Exhibitionism is most common during the warm spring and summer months, and most offenders are young adult males. Practically all occupational groups are represented. Often exhibitionism by males in public or semipublic places is reported to the police, although some women simply ignore such incidents. In some instances, exposure of the genitals is accompanied by suggestive gestures or masturbation, but more often there is only exposure. Although it is considered relatively rare, a hostile exposer may accompany exhibitionism with aggressive acts and may assault a victim. Some research indicates a subclass of exhibitionists who may best be considered as having antisocial personality disorder, as described in Chapter 9 (Forgac & Michaels, 1982; Kaplan & Krueger, 1997). A significant minority of exhibitionists have also committed coercive sex crimes against adults or children (Murphy, 1997).

Despite the rarity of assaultive behavior in these cases, and the fact that most exhibitionists are not aggressive and dangerous criminals, an exhibitionistic act nevertheless takes place without the viewer's consent and may be emotionally upsetting, as is indeed the perpetrator's intent. This intrusive quality of the act, together with its explicit violation of propriety norms respecting "private parts," assures condemnation. Thus society considers exhibitionism a criminal offense.

Sadism The term **sadism** is derived from the name of the Marquis de Sade (1740–1814), who for sexual purposes inflicted such cruelty on his victims that he was eventually committed as insane. Although the term's meaning has broadened to denote cruelty in general, we will use it in its restricted sense to mean the achievement of sexual stimulation and gratification by inflicting physical or psychic pain or humiliation on a sexual partner. A closely related pattern is the practice of "bondage and discipline" (B & D), which may include tying a person up, hitting or spanking, and so on, to enhance sexual excitement. These elements of a sadist's erotic interest suggest a

psychological association with rape (Marshall & Barbaree, 1990a), discussed in a later section. The arousal of sadistic individuals thus heavily depends on the infliction of suffering, or the appearance of it, on their partners.

The pain may be inflicted by such means as whipping, biting, or pinching; the act may vary in intensity, from fantasy to severe mutilation and even murder. Mild degrees of sadism (and masochism, discussed below) are involved in the sexual foreplay customs of many cultures, and some couples in our own society—both heterosexual and homosexual—regularly engage in such practices. It is important to distinguish transient or occasional interest in sadomasochistic practices from sadism as a paraphilia. Surveys have found that perhaps 5 to 10 percent of men and women enjoy sadistic or masochistic activities occasionally (Baumeister & Butler, 1997). Paraphilic sadism and masochism, in which sadomasochistic activities are the preferred or exclusive means to sexual gratification, appear to be rare, and like all paraphilias, occur almost exclusively in men.

In some cases, sadistic activities lead up to or terminate in actual sexual relations; in others, full sexual gratification is obtained from the sadistic practice alone. A sadist, for example, may slash a woman with a razor or stick her with a needle, experiencing an orgasm in the process. The peculiar and extreme associations that may occur are shown by the case of a young man who entered a strange woman's apartment, held a chloroformed rag to her face until she lost consciousness, and branded her on the thigh with a hot iron. She was not molested in any other way.

Sometimes sadistic activities are associated with animals or with fetishistic objects instead of other human beings. East (1946) cited the case of a man who stole women's shoes, which he then slashed savagely with a knife. When he was in prison, he was found mutilating photographs that other prisoners kept in their cells by cutting the throats of the women in them. He admitted that he derived full sexual gratification from this procedure.

In other instances, gratification is achieved only if mutilation is performed directly on a victim. Many serial killers are sexual sadists. One study characterized 20 sexually sadistic serial killers, responsible for 149 murders throughout the United States and Canada, (Warren, Dietz, & Hazelwood, 1996). Most were white males in their late twenties or early thirties. Their murders were remarkably consistent over time, reflecting sexual arousal to the pain, fear, and panic of their victims. Choreographed assaults allowed them to carefully control their victims' deaths. Some of the men reported that the God-like sense of being in control of the life and death of another human being was especially exhilarating. The sample exhibited a number of other paraphilias, including fetishism and exhibitionism. Eighty-five percent of the sample reported consistent violent sexual fantasies, and 75 percent collected materials of a violent theme, including audiotapes, videotapes, pictures, or sketches of the subject's sadistic acts or sexually sadistic pornography. The majority of the men also exhibited extensive antisocial behavior, suggesting that a lack of conscience contributed to their homicidal acts.

Notorious serial killers include Ted Bundy who was executed in 1989. Bundy confessed to the murder of over 30 young women, almost all of whom fit a target type: women with long hair parted in the middle. Bundy admitted that he used his victims to re-create for him the covers of detective magazines or scenes from "slasher movies." Jeffrey Dahmer, who was also a serious alcoholic, was convicted in 1992 of having mutilated and murdered 15 boys and young men, generally having sex with them after death. (He was subsequently murdered in prison.) Although many sadists have had chaotic childhoods, both Bundy and Dahmer came from middle-class families and loving parents. Unfortunately, we do not have a good understanding of the causal factors involved in these extreme cases of sadism.

Masochism The term **masochism** is derived from the name of the Austrian novelist Leopold V. Sacher-Masoch (1836–1895), whose fictional characters dwelt lovingly on the sexual pleasure of pain. As in the case of the term *sadism,* the meaning of masochism has been broadened beyond sexual connotations, so that it includes deriving pleasure from self-denial, from expiatory physical suffering, such as that of the religious flagellants, and from hardship and suffering in general. Here we restrict our discussion to the sexual aspects of masochistic behavior.

In masochism, a person experiences sexual stimulation and gratification from the experience of pain and degradation in relating to a lover. Interpersonal masochistic activities require the participation of at least two people—one superior "disciplinarian" and one obedient "slave." Such arrangements are not uncommon in either heterosexual or homosexual relationships. Masochists do not usually want, or cooperate with, true sexual sadists, but with individuals willing to hurt or humiliate them within limits they set. Masochism appears to be much more common than sadism (Baumeister & Butler, 1997). Sadomasochistic activities, including bondage-and-discipline, are often performed commu-

nally, within "dungeons" popular in major cities. Such activities might involve men being bound and whipped by women called dominatrixes wearing tight leather or rubber outfits. These activities are playful rather than frightening, at least to the participants.

One particularly dangerous form of masochism, called *autoerotic asphyxia,* involves self-strangulation to the point of oxygen deprivation. Coroners in most major U.S. cities are familiar with cases in which the deceased is found hanged next to masochistic pornographic literature or other sexual paraphernalia. Accidental deaths attributable from this practice have been estimated to range between 250 and 1000 per year in the United States (Uva, 1995). The following is a case of autoerotic asphyxia with a tragic ending.

Case Study, Autoerotic Asphyxia • A woman heard a man shouting for help and went to his apartment door. Calling through the door, she asked the man inside if he needed help.

"Yes," he said. "Break the door down."

"Is this a joke?"

"No."

The woman returned with her two sons, who broke into the apartment. They found the man lying on the floor, his hands tied behind him, his legs bent back, and his ankles secured to his hands. A mop handle had been placed behind his knees. He was visibly distraught, sweating, and short of breath, and his hands were turning blue. He had defecated and urinated in his trousers. In his kitchen the woman found a knife and freed him.

When police officers arrived and questioned the man, he stated that he had returned home that afternoon, fallen asleep on his couch, and awakened an hour later only to find himself hopelessly bound. The officers noted that the apartment door had been locked when the neighbors broke in. The man continued his story. As far as he knew, he had no enemies, and certainly no friends capable of this kind of practical joke. The officers questioned him about the rope. The man explained that, because he had considered moving in the near future, he kept a bag of rope in his bedroom. Near the couch lay a torn bag, numerous short lengths of thin rope, and a steak knife.

When the officers filed their report, they noted that "this could possibly be a sexual deviation act." Interviewed the next day, the man confessed to binding himself in the position in which he was found.

A month later, the police were called back to the same man's apartment. A building manager had discovered him face down on the floor in his apartment. A paper bag covered his head like a hood. When the police arrived, the man was breathing rapidly with a satin cloth stuffed in his mouth. Rope was stretched around his head and mouth and wrapped his chest and waist.

Several lengths ran from his back to his crotch, and ropes at his ankles had left deep marks. A broom handle locked his elbows behind his back. Once freed, the man explained, "While doing isometric exercises, I got tangled up in the rope." . . .

Two years passed and the man moved on to another job. He failed to appear for work one Monday morning. A fellow employee found him dead in his apartment. During their investigation, police were able to reconstruct the man's final minutes. On the preceding Friday, he had bound himself in the following manner: sitting on his bed and crossing his ankles, left over right, he had bound them together with twine. Fastening a tie around his neck, he then secured the tie to an 86-inch pole behind his back. Aligning the pole with his left side, the upper end crossing the front of his left shoulder, he placed his hands behind his bent legs and there, leaving his wrists 4 inches apart, secured them with a length of rope. He then tied the rope that secured his wrists to the pole and to an electric cord girdling his waist. Thus bound, he lay on his bed on his back and stretched his legs. By thus applying pressure to the pole, still secured to the tie around his neck, he strangled himself. In order to save himself, he might have rolled over onto his side and drawn up his legs; but the upper end of the pole pressed against the wall. He was locked into place. (Spitzer et al., 1994)

Causal Factors and Treatments for Paraphilias

Many paraphilic individuals have explanations for their unusual sexual preferences. For example, an amputee paraphilic (whose preference is a partner with a missing limb) recalled that his fascination with female amputees originated during adolescence. He was neglected emotionally by his cold family but heard a family member express sympathetic feelings for an amputee. He developed the wish that he would become an amputee and thus earn their sympathy. This story raises many questions. Emotionally cold families are not uncommon, and sympathy for amputees is nearly universal. Surely, not every male in a cold family who detects sympathy for amputees develops an amputee paraphilia. Such stories do not necessarily have any validity. We are often unaware of the forces that shape us (Nisbett & Wilson, 1977).

At least two facts about paraphilia are likely to be etiologically important. First, as we have already noted, almost all paraphiliacs are male. Indeed, females with paraphilias are so rare that they are found in the literature only as case reports. Second, people with paraphilias often have more than one (American Psychiatric Association, 1994; Maletzky, 1998). For example, the corpses of men who died accidentally in the course of autoerotic asphyxia are partially or fully cross-dressed in 25 to 33 percent of cases (Blanchard & Hucker, 1991). There is no ob-

vious reason for the association between masochism and transvestism. Why should it be so?

Money (1986) has suggested that male vulnerability to paraphilias is closely linked to their greater dependency on visual sexual imagery. Perhaps sexual arousal in men depends on physical stimulus features to a greater degree than in women, whose arousal may depend more on emotional context, such as being in love with a partner. If so, men may be more vulnerable to forming sexual associations to nonsexual stimuli.

The fact that men with one paraphilia often have others suggests that such men are especially vulnerable. Freund and Blanchard (1993) have suggested that the vulnerability is to errors in what they call *erotic target location*. According to this theory, although most men become heterosexual, they are not born with that orientation but instead must learn through a process of classical conditioning which stimuli together constitute a female sex partner, who is their target stimulus. This is the process of erotic target location. Perhaps certain men have nervous systems prone to errors in targeting, possibly because they acquire these associations especially easily, which might also help to explain the incidence of multiple paraphilias. (An analogous process may be hypothesized to cause the development of paraphilias in homosexual persons.) This theory is somewhat more

Men's vulnerability to paraphilias such as fetishism may be a result of their greater dependency on physical stimuli. This in turn makes them more likely to form sexual associations to nonsexual stimuli, such as women's legs or high-heeled shoes, quite possibly through a process of classical conditioning.

useful in explaining paraphilias such as transvestism and certain fetishes (e.g., for women's underwear), in which the sexual stimuli are related to feminine characteristics, than it is for explaining others, such as masochism, in which the paraphilic target has no obvious association with normal sexual activities.

Treatments for Paraphilias Over the past 30 years significant progress has been made in developing moderately effective treatments for the paraphilias, although treatment research on these populations generally lags behind that for most other disorders discussed in this book. One problem is that most people with paraphilias do not seek treatment for these conditions, but rather receive it only after they have been caught and detained in jail or prison. Thus, their motivations for change may often stem more from a desire to get released than from a genuine desire to change. Moreover, many do not readily admit all of their deviant behavior and do not consider their therapist an ally if, as is often the case, the therapist must report on the offender's progress to prison authorities or parole boards (Maletzky, 1998).

Nevertheless, treatments that combine cognitive and behavioral elements have been shown to be moderately successful in effecting changes in deviant arousal and behavioral patterns in a significant number of cases. Moreover, there is increasing evidence suggesting that these treatments can result in significantly reduced rates of recidivism than seen in untreated offenders, although the most compelling evidence would stem from research with untreated control groups, which is generally not conducted because of ethical reasons (Maletzky, 1998). In other words, if a potentially effective treatment exists, how can one defend on ethical grounds withholding that treatment from the standpoint of the potential victims who could be saved?

One key component of treatment involves techniques commonly known as *aversion therapy*—aversive conditioning to deviant sexual fantasies. Although early treatments tended to use electric shock as the unconditioned stimulus, in the past 15 years greater success has been found using what is called *assisted covert sensitization*, which involves having the patient imagine a deviant sexual arousal scene. At the point where arousal is high, the patient imagines aversive consequences (simple *covert sensitization*) and a foul odor is introduced via an open vial or an automated odor pump to help condition a real aversion to these deviant scenes (hence the term *assisted covert sensitization*). Variations on this technique are employed in most cognitive-behavioral treatment programs in recent years (Maletzky, 1998).

Other important components of cognitive-behavioral treatment programs for paraphiliacs include social skills training (McFall, 1990; Maletzky, 1998) and restructuring cognitive distortions that may be helping to maintain the deviant sexual arousal and behavior patterns. For example, men with exhibitionism often misattribute blame ("She kept looking at me like she was expecting it"), debase their victims ("She was just a slut anyway"), and minimize the consequences ("I never touched her so I couldn't have hurt her"). Other paraphilias have similar patterns of cognitive distortions, although the content may differ. Through work with a therapist, the patients can begin to identify these cognitive distortions and to learn self-corrective messages that, with work, can become more automatic and reflexive and contribute to their overall improvement (Maletzky, 1998).

Using treatment programs that combine these and other elements, a recently completed study of approximately 1500 offenders who had been followed for at least one year with very stringent criteria for success (i.e., they completed all treatment sessions, they reported no covert or overt deviant sexual behavior at the end of treatment or one year follow-up, they showed no deviant sexual arousal as measured with a penile plethysmograph (which measures erectile responses directly) at the end of treatment or follow-up, and they had no repeat legal charges), success rates were rather impressive (Maletzky, 1998). Rates of success for transvestic fetishism were the lowest (nearly 79 percent) and rates for exhibitionism, voyeurism and fetishism were the highest (approximately 95 percent). Nevertheless much work remains to be done in this area, especially in light of the fact that these treatments which have shown very promising results are not yet widely available.

Gender Identity Disorders

Gender identity refers to one's sense of maleness or femaleness and may be distinguished from *gender role*, which refers to the masculinity and femininity of one's overt behavior (Money, 1988, p. 77). Of all behavioral traits, gender identity may have the strongest correlation with biological sex, but the correlation is imperfect. Some rare individuals feel extreme discomfort with their biological sex and strongly desire to change to the opposite sex. Indeed, some adults with gender identity disorders, often called transsexuals, do opt for expensive and complicated surgery to accomplish just that. In DSM-IV **gender identity disorder** is characterized by two components: (1) a strong and persistent **cross-gender identification**—that is the desire to be, or the insistence that one is, of the opposite sex—and (2) **gender dysphoria**—persistent discomfort about one's biological sex or the sense that the gender role of that sex is inappropriate (American Psychiatric Association, 1994). The disorder may occur in children or adults, and in males or females.

Gender Identity Disorder of Childhood   Boys with gender identity disorder show a marked preoccupation with traditionally feminine activities (Zucker & Bradley, 1995). They may prefer to dress in female clothing. They enjoy stereotypical games of girls, such as playing dolls, house (in which they usually play the mother), drawing pictures of beautiful girls, and watching television programs with favorite female characters. They usually avoid rough-and-tumble play. They may express the desire to be a girl. Girls with gender identity disorder typically balk at parents' attempts to dress them in traditional feminine clothes such as dresses. They prefer boys' clothing and short hair, and they may be misidentified by strangers as boys. Fantasy heroes typically include powerful male figures like Batman and Superman. They show little interest in doll playing or dressing up, and increased interest in sports. Although mere tomboys frequently have many or most of those traits, girls with gender identity disorder are distinguished by their desire to be a boy, or to grow up as a man. Boys with gender identity disorder are often ostracized as "sissies" by their peers. Young girls with gender identity disorder are treated better by their peers, as cross-gender behavior in girls is better tolerated (Zucker, Sanikhani, & Bradley, 1997). In clinic-referred gender identity disorder, boys outnumber girls five to one. An appreciable percentage of that imbalance may reflect greater parental concern about femininity in boys than masculinity in girls.

The most common adult outcome of boys with gender identity disorder appears to be homosexuality rather than transsexualism (Bradley & Zucker, 1997). In Richard Green's (1987) study of 44 very feminine boys, only one sought sex change surgery as an adult. About three-quarters became gay or bisexual men who were evidently satisfied with their biological sex. There have been no prospective studies of girls with gender identity disorder. A recent analysis of retrospective reports of lesbians' sex-atypical behavior suggests that very masculine girls are more likely than other girls to become homosexual, but that most of them probably grow up as heterosexual women (Bailey & Zucker, 1995). Thus the vast majority of children with gender identity disorder probably become homosexual or heterosexual adults, with only a small minority becoming transsexuals. If such children typically adjust well in adulthood, should they be considered to have a mental disorder?

One argument for considering children with atypical childhood gender identity to be disordered is that such children are often greatly distressed and thus should receive treatment. They suffer for two general reasons. First, by definition (i.e., current diagnostic criteria) they are unhappy with their biological sex. Second, as we have noted, they are likely to be mistreated by their peers and to have strained relations with their parents. An argument against considering such children "disordered" is that the primary obstacle to their happiness is a society that is intolerant of cross-gender behavior. Moreover, unlike some other behaviors that society stigmatizes, such as criminality and cruelty, cross-gender behavior harms no one. Thus, labeling children with atypical gender identity as "sick" shifts the blame from society, where it belongs. The diagnostic status of gender identity disorder of childhood therefore deserves serious debate.

Children with gender identity disorder are often brought by their parents for psychotherapy. Specialists attempt both to treat the child's unhappiness with his or her biological sex and to ease strained relations with parents and peers. Therapists try to improve peer and parental relations by teaching such children how to reduce their cross-gender behavior, especially in situations where it might cause interpersonal problems. Gender dysphoria is typically treated psychodynamically—that is, by examining inner conflicts. Controlled studies evaluating such treatment remain to be conducted.

Transsexualism   Transsexuals are adults with gender identity disorder. Many, perhaps most, transsexuals desire to change their sex, and surgical advances have made this goal partially feasible, although expensive. **Transsexualism** is apparently a very rare disorder. European studies suggest that approximately 1 per 30,000 adult males and 1 per 100,000 adult females seek sex reassignment surgery. Until recently, most researchers assumed that transsexualism was the adult version of childhood gender identity disorder, and indeed this is often the case. That is, many transsexuals had gender identity disorder as children (despite the fact that most children with gender identity disorder do not become transsexual), and their adult behavior is analogous. This appears to be the case for all female-to-male transsexuals (i.e., individuals born female who become male). Virtually all such individuals recall being extremely

Dr. Richard Raskin, a physician and professional tennis player, became Renee Richards through transsexual surgery.

tomboyish, with masculinity persisting unabated until adulthood. Most, but not all, female-to-male transsexuals are sexually attracted to women. One female-to-male transsexual had these recollections:

> [I have felt different] as far as I can remember. Three years old. I remember wanting to be a boy. Wearing boy's clothes and wanting to do all the things boys do. I remember my mother as I was growing up saying, "Are you ever going to be a lady? Are you ever going to wear women's clothing?" These kind of things as far back as I can remember. I can remember as I got a little older always looking at women, always wanting a woman . . . I feel like a man, and I feel like my loving a woman is perfectly normal. (Green, 1992, p. 102)

In contrast to female-to-male transsexuals, there are two kinds of male-to-female transsexuals, with very different causes and developmental courses: homosexual and autogynephilic transsexuals (Blanchard, 1989). Homosexual transsexuals might be conceptualized as extremely feminine gay men who also wish to change their sex. In contrast, autogynephilic transsexuals appear to have a paraphilia in which their attraction is to the image of themselves as a woman. This distinction is not currently made in the DSM. Although it may not be relevant for treatment purposes (both types of transsexuals are appropriate for sex reassignment surgery), it is fundamental for understanding the diverse psychology

of male-to-female transsexualism. A homosexual male-to-female transsexual is a genetic male who describes himself as a woman trapped in a man's body and who is sexually attracted to men. Such men seek a sex change operation in part so that as women they will have the ability to attract heterosexual male partners (Freund et al., 1974). Although homosexual transsexuals are attracted to members of their own genetic sex, they resent being labeled gay because they do not feel that they belong to their genetic sex (Adams & McAnulty, 1993). Nevertheless, from an etiological standpoint homosexual transsexualism probably overlaps with ordinary homosexuality. What in rare cases causes gay men who are extremely feminine to want to change their sex is not yet well understood.

Homosexual transsexuals generally have gender identity disorder from childhood. One adult homosexual male-to-female transsexual recalled the following:

> I used to like to play with girls. I never did like to play with boys. I wanted to play jacks. I wanted to jump rope and all those things. The lady in the schoolyard used to always tell me to go play with the boys. I found it distasteful. I wanted to play with the girls. I wanted to play the girl games. I remember one day the teacher said, "If you play with the girls one more day, I am going to bring a dress to school and make you wear it all day long. How would you like that?" Well, I would have liked it. (Green, 1992, p. 101)

Because most children with gender identity disorder do not become transsexual adults (but instead become gay men), there must be other important determinants of transsexualism. One study of men found that being raised in a religious Catholic family where homosexuality was condemned, coupled with cross-gender behavior in boyhood, was related to transsexual rather than homosexual outcomes (Hellman et al., 1981). These investigators suggested that for these men, transsexualism was a way of being sexually involved with males while still avoiding homosexuality per se. If this is true, then homosexual transsexualism should become rarer as homosexuality becomes less stigmatized. The difference between homosexual transsexualism and cross-gendered homosexuality (that is, homosexuality accompanied by behavior more typical of the opposite sex) is probably more in degree than in kind. The 1990 documentary film *Paris Is Burning* depicts gay African-American men who devote a considerable amount of time, money, and energy trying to look like beautiful women. One of the men in that film describes how he had considered but decided against a sex-change operation. Another man intends to obtain the operation when he can afford it. Although probably only the second of these two men would merit the diagnosis of transsexualism, they are clearly very similar.

Autogynephilic transsexualism (Blanchard, 1989, 1992) appears to occur only in genetic males, and its primary clinical feature is **autogynephilia**—a paraphilia characterized by sexual arousal at the thought or fantasy of being a woman (Blanchard, 1991; 1993). Indeed, autogynephilic transsexuals usually report a history of transvestic fetishism, although it is not uncommon for them to deny such a history. Reasons for such denial include shame at the idea of having a "perversion," and the fact that in the past, men with transvestism could not obtain sex reassignment surgery. Some autogynephilic transsexuals may genuinely never have engaged in transvestism per se, but in most of these cases, there is other evidence for autogynephilia. For example, unlike other transvestites, autogynephilic transsexuals fantasize that they have female genitalia. Perhaps because of this fantasy, their gender dysphoria is especially acute, motivating their desire for sex reassignment surgery. Autogynephilic transsexuals may report sexual attraction either to women, both men and women, or to neither. Research has shown that these subtypes of autogynephilic transsexuals are very similar to each other and differ from homosexual transsexuals in important respects beyond their sexual orientations (R. Blanchard, 1985, 1989, 1991). Unlike homosexual transsexuals, autogynephilic transsexuals do not appear to have been especially feminine in childhood or adulthood. Autogynephilic transsexuals typically seek sex-reassignment surgery much later than homosexual transsexuals (R. Blanchard, 1994). The causes of autogynephilic transsexualism probably overlap etiologically with the causes of other paraphilias but as of yet are not well understood.

Treatment Psychotherapy is usually not helpful in aiding transsexuals resolve their gender dysphoria (Tollison & Adams, 1979). The only treatment that has been shown to be effective is surgical sex reassignment. Initially, transsexuals awaiting surgery are given hormone treatment. Biological men are given estrogens to facilitate breast growth, skin softening, and shrinking of muscles. Biological women are given testosterone, which suppresses menstruation, increases facial and body hair, and deepens the voice. Typically, transsexuals must live for a lengthy period of many months with hormonal therapy, and they generally must live for at least a year as the gender they wish to become. If they successfully complete the trial period, they undergo surgery and continue to take hormones indefinitely. In male-to-female transsexuals, this entails removal of the penis and testes and the creation of an artificial vagina. Moreover, they must undergo extensive electrolysis to remove their beards and body hair. They also have to learn to raise the pitch of their voice. Female-to-male transsexuals typically are given mastectomies and hysterectomies and often other plastic surgery to alter various facial features (such as the Adam's apple).

Because relevant surgical techniques are still rather primitive and very expensive, only a subset of female-to-male transsexuals seek an artificial penis (which is not capable of normal erection and so they must rely on artificial supports to have intercourse anyway); the rest function sexually without a penis. As surgical techniques advance, this will very likely change. A review of the outcome literature found that 87 percent of 220 male-to-female transsexuals had satisfactory outcomes (meaning that they did not regret their decisions), and that 97 percent of 130 female-to-male transsexuals had successful outcomes (Green & Fleming, 1990). Blanchard (1985) also reported that the majority of transsexuals are satisfied with the outcome of sex reassignment surgery, although there is variability in the degree of satisfaction. In general, those who were reasonably well adjusted before surgery do better following surgery, and those with preexisting psychopathology are less likely to do well. In spite of the reasonably good success record for transsexual patients who are carefully chosen, such surgery remains controversial because some professionals continue to maintain that it is inappropriate to treat psychological disorders through drastic anatomical changes (e.g., McHugh, 1992).

Sexual abuse

Sexual abuse is sexual contact that involves physical or psychological coercion, or at least one individual who cannot reasonably consent to the contact (e.g., a child). Such abuse includes pedophilia, rape, and incest, and concerns society more than any other sexual problem. It is somewhat ironic, then, that of these, only pedophilia is included in DSM-IV. (Furthermore, the restrictive definition of pedophilia employed there probably excludes most cases of childhood sexual abuse, because many of the victims have gone through puberty and pedophilia applies only to abuse of prepubertal children.) This partly reflects the seriousness with which society views these offenses and its preference for treating coercive sex offenders as criminals rather than as having a mental disorder. However, the fact that rape, for example, is not included as a DSM-IV category need not deter us. The research literature of abnormal psychology is increasingly addressing topics related to sexual abuse of both children and adults and how it may be implicated in the causal pathways to a variety of disorders (see Chapters 3, 4, 7 and 9). Because of this and because sexual abuse is an extremely important social problem, we have included a thorough treatment here.

Childhood Sexual Abuse

The past decade has seen intense concern about childhood sexual abuse, with an accompanying increase in relevant research. A search of the electronic database *Medline* found only 72 articles about childhood sexual abuse from 1975 to 1984. The number of relevant articles published during the next decade grew nearly tenfold, to 693. (In contrast, the number of articles about schizophrenia only doubled during that same time period.) One of the most frequently cited articles in psychology during the past 15 years concerned the varied nature of the impact of childhood sexual abuse on psychological functioning (Browne & Finkelhor, 1986), ranging from depression to self-destructive behavior, anxiety, low self-esteem, substance abuse and sexual maladjustment.

There are at least three reasons for the marked increase in interest in childhood sexual abuse. First, much evidence suggests that, broadly defined, childhood sexual abuse is common, much more so than was once assumed. Second, several mental disorders have been linked to childhood sexual abuse; thus, such abuse may be important in the etiology of some disorders. Third, some dramatic and well-publicized cases involving allegations of childhood sexual abuse have raised very controversial issues, such as the validity of children's testimony and recovered memories of sexual abuse. We shall consider all three of these issues in turn.

Prevalence of Childhood Sexual Abuse   The prevalence of childhood sexual abuse depends on its definition, which has varied substantially across studies (Salter, 1991). For example, different studies use different definitions of "childhood," with the upper age limit ranging from age 12 to as high as 19. Some studies have counted any kind of sexual interaction, even that which does not include physical contact (e.g., exhibitionism), others have counted only physical contact, and other have counted only genital contact. Other important factors that have varied across studies include the age difference between offenders and victims and whether or not force was used. Depending on these factors, prevalence figures have ranged from less than 5 percent to more than 30 percent. Even the lowest plausible figures are sufficiently high to concern us.

Consequences of Childhood Sexual Abuse   Childhood sexual abuse may have both short-term and long-term consequences. The most common short-term consequences include fears, post-traumatic stress disorder, sexual inappropriateness (e.g., touching others' genitals or talking about sexual acts), and poor self-esteem (Kendall-Tackett, Williams, & Finkelhor, 1993). Approximately one-third of sexually abused children show no symptoms. Thus, there is no single "sexual abuse" syndrome.

A number of studies have found associations between reports of childhood sexual abuse and adult psychopathology, including borderline personality disorder (Herman et al., 1989; Ogata et al., 1990), somatization disorder (Morris, 1989), dissociative symptoms (Chu & Dill, 1990), chronic pelvic pain (Walker et al., 1988), and dissociative identity disorder (Coons, 1986b). A wide variety of sexual symptoms have been alleged to result from early sexual abuse (Bass & Davis, 1986; Browne & Finkelhor, 1986), ranging, for example, from aversion to sex to sexual promiscuity. Our knowledge about the long-term consequences of childhood sexual abuse is more uncertain than about the short-term consequences, primarily due to the difficulties of establishing causal links between early experiences and adult behavior (discussed more fully in the Unresolved Issues section at the end of this chapter).

Controversies Concerning Childhood Sexual Abuse

Several high-profile criminal trials have highlighted the limitations of our knowledge concerning questions of great scientific and practical importance. Two general types of cases have been prosecuted. In the first, children have accused adults working in daycare settings of extensive, often bizarre, sexual abuse. The most controversial aspect of these cases has been the degree to which children's accusations could be trusted. The second type of case concerns adults who claim to have repressed and completely forgotten memories of early sexual abuse and who then "recovered" the memories during adulthood, typically while seeing a therapist who believes that repressed memories of childhood sexual abuse are a very common cause of adult psychopathology. The most controversial aspect of these cases is the validity of the "recovered" memories.

Children's Testimony

Several cases involving alleged sexual abuse in daycare settings shocked the country during the past decade. The most notorious was the McMartin Preschool case in California. In 1983 Judy Johnson complained to police in Manhattan Beach, California, that her son had been molested by Raymond Buckey, who helped run the McMartin Preschool, which her son attended. Johnson's complaints grew increasingly bizarre. For example, she accused Buckey of sodomizing her son while he stuck the boy's head in a toilet and of making him ride naked on a horse. Johnson was diagnosed with acute paranoid schizophrenia, and she died of alcohol-related liver disease in 1986. By the time she died, prosecutors no longer needed her. Children at the preschool who were interviewed began to tell fantastically lurid stories—for example, that children were forced to dig up dead bodies at cemeteries, jump out of airplanes, and kill animals with bats. Nevertheless, prosecutors and many McMartin parents believed the children (Carlson, 1990). Buckey and his mother (who owned the day care) were tried in a trial that took two and a half years and cost $15 million. The jury acquitted Ms. Buckey on all counts, and failed to convict Raymond Buckey on any; however, he was freed only after a retrial, having spent five years in jail. The jurors' principal reason for not finding the defendants guilty was their concern that interviewers had coaxed the children into telling stories of abuse using leading or coercive methods of questioning as described in Chapter 7.

Because children are susceptible to the influence of others and cannot always distinguish fact from fantasy,

the accuracy of their testimony is a crucial issue. Anatomically correct dolls have often been used during interviews to explore allegations of sexual abuse in young children. As discussed in Highlight 11.2, the few empirical studies investigating their use have shown that young children questioned with an anatomically correct doll may allege that they have been touched in places that they were not touched, and more generally that the use of such dolls does not improve the accuracy of the reports of where (or even if) they were touched (Ceci, 1995).

Recovered Memories of Sexual Abuse

In 1990 a young woman named Eileen Franklin testified in court that she had seen her father rape and murder an eight-year-old playmate 20 years earlier. Remarkably, despite her claim to have witnessed the murder, she had no memory of the event until she "recovered" the memory by accident in adulthood. (Franklin's father was convicted and given a life sentence, although in 1995 the conviction was overturned because of two serious constitutional errors made during the original trial that might have affected the jury's verdict.) In 1993, Steven Cook accused Chicago Roman Catholic Cardinal Joseph Bernardin and another priest of sexually abusing Cook 17 years earlier, when Cook was 17 years old. Cook also claimed he had forgotten the abuse for many years, recovering the memory only during therapy. Cook later withdrew his charges against Bernardin because of concern that his own "recovered memory" may have been invalid, and even later he made a personal apology to Cardinal Bernadin for having made the accusation.

Recent evidence has suggested that the use of anatomically correct dolls to question young children about where they may have been touched in alleged incidents of sexual abuse does not improve the accuracy of their testimony relative to verbal interviews alone.

CUTTING EDGE

The Reliability of Children's Reports of Past Events

In recent years, as more and more children are being brought forward to testify in court about alleged physical and sexual abuse by parents or other adults, researchers have become increasingly concerned about determining how reliable we can expect the testimony of children—especially that of *young* children—to be. Because abuse of children is distressingly common, children's reports of such abuse must always be taken seriously. Increasingly, however, doubt is being cast on the accuracy of young children's testimony, especially when they have been subjected to repeated interviews over many months with highly leading questions, sometimes in a coercive atmosphere. Unfortunately, this appears to be the way in which such children are sometimes treated before the trials in which they testify.

Stephen Ceci, a leading developmental psychologist studying this problem, has recently summarized a series of experiments that casts grave doubt on young children's testimony if they have been exposed repeatedly to suggestive interviews over long intervals of time (Ceci, 1995). For example, Ceci has summarized evidence that preschoolers have greater difficulty distinguishing between real and imagined acts (such as deciding whether they really touched their nose or only imagined touching it) than do older children or adults (Foley et al., 1989). In one of his own experiments, Ceci and his colleagues had an adult interview young children weekly for ten weeks about whether certain actual events (such as getting in an accident that required stitches) and certain fictitious events (such as getting their hand caught in a mousetrap and having to go to the hospital to get it removed) had occurred. In one version of this experiment, each week interviewers asked the children to think hard about whether the event had happened and prompted the children to visualize the scene. After ten such weekly interviews, children were given a forensic interview by a new adult (in a forensic interview, the interviewer first tries to make the child comfort-able, then elicits a free narrative about what the child remembers happening, and then asks probing questions). All interviews were videotaped. The results were very striking. Over half the preschool children (58 percent) claimed that at least one of the fictitious events had actually happened to them, and 27 percent of the children claimed that nearly all of the fictitious events had happened to them. Their narratives describing these fictitious events were often elaborate, embellished, and coherent, and the children generally showed emotion appropriate to the event. Moreover, it appeared that the children actually believed these events had happened to them, because Ceci and the children's parents were sometimes unable to talk them out of their false reports, with the children often protesting "but it really did happen. I remember it" (Ceci, 1995, p. 103). When Ceci showed these videotapes to many psychologists who specialize in interviewing children, the psychologists' accuracy at detecting real events from fictitious events was no better than chance. Similar results have been obtained for judges, social workers, and psychiatrists. Ceci concluded: "Repeatedly thinking about a fictitious event can lead some preschool children to produce vivid, detailed reports that professionals are unable to discern from their reports of actual events" (1995, p. 103).

In another important study called the "Sam Stone Study," Leichtman and Ceci (1995) interviewed preschool children four times over ten weeks for details about a previously staged two-minute visit by a stranger named Sam Stone to their daycare center. Some of the children were given no prior information about Sam Stone before his visit and were never asked suggestive questions during the four interviews; other children were given a stereotype about Sam Stone before his visit (such as that he was clumsy: "That Sam Stone is always getting into accidents and breaking things") and were also given leading questions during the four interviews (for example, "Remember that time Sam Stone . . .

spilled chocolate on that white teddy bear? Did he do it on purpose or by accident?"). One month later, after the four subsequent interviews were completed (about 14 weeks after Sam Stone's visit), all children were interviewed with forensic procedures by a new interviewer, who asked about two events that had not happened during Sam Stone's visit—whether he had soiled a teddy bear and/or ripped a book. For the children given no prior stereotype about Sam Stone and no leading questions during the initial four interviews, only 10 percent of the youngest preschoolers claimed that Sam Stone had done either of these two nonevents, and when gently challenged about this, only 2.5 percent stuck to the story that Sam had done these things. (Older preschoolers seldom committed such errors.) By contrast, for the younger preschoolers who were given a prior stereotype that Sam Stone was clumsy and who had been asked leading questions during the four interviews, a startling 72 percent of the youngest children claimed that Sam Stone had either soiled the teddy bear or ripped the book, or both. When gently challenged, 44 percent continued to claim that they had seen him do these things. Leichtman and Ceci tested the believability of these reports by showing the videotapes of some of the forensic interviews to over 1000 researchers and clinicians who work with children. When asked about which events actually occurred during Sam Stone's visit and to rate the children for the accuracy of their testimony, the majority of the professionals were highly inaccurate. Indeed, the videotape of the child who was least accurate was rated as being most credible, and the videotape of the child who was most accurate was rated as least credible. Leichtman and Ceci (1995) concluded: "It is not that the members of these audiences were worse than anyone else at assessing which children gave accurate accounts, but that the accuracy of children's reports is extremely difficult to discern when children have been subjected to repeated erroneous suggestions over long retention intervals, especially when coupled with the induction of stereotypes" (p. 20).

Finally, Ceci's work also challenges the use of anatomically correct dolls (dolls with bodies showing the sex organs) to symboli-

cally represent actions, at least for very young children. Bruck and colleagues (1995) studied 70 three-year-old boys and girls who were visiting their pediatrician, 35 of whom were given a genital exam (which involved touching of the genital area but no genital insertions) and 35 of whom were not given a genital exam. Mothers were present during these exams. Five minutes later, with the mother still present, the children were asked to describe where the doctor had touched them. They were then presented anatomical dolls and asked to point on the dolls where the doctor had touched them. When interviewed verbally, most of the children who had not received a genital exam correctly refrained from stating that their genitals had been touched. However, when given the anatomical doll, nearly 60 percent of those who had not received a genital exam claimed that the doctor had made genital and/or anal insertions and done other acts to be concerned about. On the other hand, just over half of the children who had been given a genital exam claimed that their genitals had not been touched, even though they had. Thus it seemed that the use of anatomical dolls failed to improve the accuracy of the three-year-olds' reports of what did or did not happen. A previous study by Goodman and Aman (1990) of five-year-olds also did not find that the use of anatomical dolls was useful in eliciting information, although their subjects rarely reported genital contact that had not actually been made. This and other studies have led Ceci and his colleagues to conclude that "although older children do make fewer errors, there is still no convincing evidence that dolls improve their reporting" (Bruck et al., 1995).

In summary, although young children are capable of correct recall of what happened to them, they are also susceptible to a greater variety of sources of postevent distortion than are older children and adults. Nevertheless, even adults are also susceptible to a variety of sources of postevent distortion to a lesser degree (Loftus, Feldman, & Dashiell, 1995; see again Highlight 7.3), and so the differences should be seen as a matter of degree rather than of kind (Ceci, 1995). ■

The possibility that traumatic experiences can be utterly forgotten due to repression and then somehow recovered intact years later has been heatedly debated during the past few years. Some have argued that repressed memories are common (Herman, 1993) and are responsible for a great deal of psychopathology. In a controversial but very popular book, *The Courage to Heal,* journalists Ellen Bass and Laura Davis asserted: "If you are unable to remember any specific instances [of sexual abuse] . . . but still have the feeling that something abusive happened to you, it probably did" (1988, p. 21). Some therapists routinely give this book to their clients, and those clients often do report "recovering" such memories. Those skeptical about recovery of repressed memories point out that even normal unrepressed memories can be highly inaccurate and that false memories can be induced experimentally (Loftus, 1993; Loftus et al., 1995, in press). For example, in one study an adolescent was told (falsely) that as a young boy, he had gotten lost in a shopping mall, had become quite frightened, then was rescued by a kind man. Although at first the young man had no memory of the event; within a couple of weeks, he had vivid memories of the event, including what the man looked like and what he was wearing.

At the time of this writing, the validity of memories of childhood sexual abuse that arise during therapy remains extremely controversial. False memories can be induced, and some writers believe that the concept of repressed memory is invalid. In their view, virtually all "recovered memories" are false (Crews, 1995; Loftus & Ketcham, 1994). Others believe that false memories rarely occur, and that recovered memories are typically valid (e.g., Pope, 1996). As evidence, they offer cases like that of Ross Cheit. In 1992, Cheit, a Brown University professor, was talking to his sister about her son participating in after-school activities, when he began to feel depressed and disturbed. Shortly afterward, he thought about a man, William Farmer, who had managed a summer camp that Cheit attended when he was the age of his nephew, and recalled repeated sexual abuse by Farmer. Farmer has subsequently acknowledged sexually abusing Cheit. Williams (1994) found that 38 percent of women with a documented history of childhood sexual abuse failed to report that they had been abused when interviewed in adulthood. Those who are skeptical of recovered memory argue that those data are not directly analogous to recovered memory during psychotherapy. If, prior to remembering, Ross Cheit had been asked directly whether Farmer had sexually abused him, would he have said "no," or would such inquiry have rapidly led to

memory? Was it a case of repressed memory, or a case of not thinking about an unpleasant experience? Regarding the fact that many women did not report their childhood sexual abuse experiences, alternative explanations to repressed memory include the possibility that the women did not want to tell the interviewers, or that they had simply forgotten, rather than repressed, their experiences (Loftus, Feldman, & Garry, 1994). Psychologists equally familiar with the evidence have bitterly opposed each other on this issue, and as discussed in Chapter 7, a task force assembled by the American Psychological Association to study the issue failed to reach a consensus.

The issue of recovered memories has divided not only academics and clinicians but families as well. Many parents have been accused by their children of early sexual abuse due to recovered memories. Some children have sued their parents for damages, and some courts have ruled that the statute of limitations applies from the date at which an offense is remembered, not from the date it occurred (Green, 1992). Recently, a father successfully sued his daughter's therapist for inducing what he claimed were false memories that he had abused her (Johnston, 1997). A large group of parents who say that they were falsely accused by their children of sexual abuse has organized as the False Memory Syndrome Foundation (Gardner, 1993). (Actually, the founder of the organization is a woman who accused her parents of sexual abuse and then recanted because she came to the realization that the abuse had never happened.) The foundation has been accused by others as a front for shielding pedophiles (Herman, 1994). The debate concerning recovered memories of sexual abuse is one of the most important and interesting contemporary controversies in the domains of psychopathology and mental health (see Unresolved Issues in Chapter 7).

Pedophilia

Pedophilia is a paraphilia in which an adult's preferred or exclusive sexual partner is a prepubertal child. It is important to emphasize that pedophilia is defined by the bodily maturity, not the age, of the preferred partner. Thus studies of childhood sexual abuse, which typically define childhood based on an age range that may extend well into adolescence, do not necessarily concern pedophilia. Nearly all pedophiles are male, and about two-thirds of their victims are girls, typically between the ages of 8 and 11 (Marshall, 1997). The proportion of pedophilic interactions that are technically homosexual is much higher than the rate of homosexuality in the general population. This does not, however, mean that homosexual men have a greater propensity to become sexually involved with children than do heterosexual men (Freund, Watson, & Rienzo, 1989). Rather, it reflects the fact that many pedophiles are relatively indifferent to the sex of their victim, provided that he or she is a certain age (Freund & Kuban, 1993).

Pedophilia frequently involves manipulation of the child's genitals. It used to be thought that sexual penetration was rare; however, one study found that such penetration occurred in more than half of cases and that use of physical force or violence occurred in 89 percent (Stermac, Hall, & Henskens, 1989). Although penetration and associated violence are often injurious to the child, injuries are usually a by-product rather than a goal, as would be true with a sadist.

Studies investigating the sexual responses of pedophiles have achieved quite consistent results (Barbaree, 1990). Such studies tend to use a *penile phlethysmograph* in order to directly measure erectile responses to sexual stimuli rather than relying on self-report. (A plethysmograph consists of an expandable band placed around the penis, connected to a recording device.) In general, men who have molested nonfamilial female children have shown greater sexual arousal to pictures of nude or partially clad girls than have matched nonoffenders. Interestingly, however, as a group the offenders also responded strongly to adult women. Men who have molested nonfamilial male children have tended to respond sexually to both adult men and women. Although pedophiles thus show deviant sexual arousal patterns, they also appear capable, under some circumstances, of arousal to adults. Consequently, deviant sexual preference alone may not explain why some men become pedophiles. Other factors include cognitive and nonsexual motivational factors. For example, child molesters are more likely than nonoffenders to believe that children will benefit from sexual contacts with adults and that children often initiate such contact (Segal & Stermac, 1990). Motivationally, many pedophiles appear to desire mastery or dominance over another individual, and some idealize aspects of childhood such as innocence, unconditional love, or simplicity. Indeed, perhaps the most common type of pedophile is someone who is an interpersonally unskilled man drawn to children because he feels in control in relationships with them.

There has been a rash of pedophilia among a group long considered to be highly trustworthy: the Catholic clergy. Although the majority of priests are innocent of sexual wrongdoing, the Catholic Church has admitted that a significant minority have committed sexual abuse, including pedophilia. At least 400 priests were charged with sexual abuse during the 1980s, and $400 million has been paid in damages since 1985 (Samborn, 1994). The most serious scandal to date involved James R. Porter, a 57-year-old father of four who is alleged to have sexually abused as many as 100 children when he was a priest in Massachusetts during the 1960s. The case was complicated by the fact that his initial accuser claimed to have recovered memories of sexual abuse. Porter has since admitted to his offenses and was convicted of molesting his children's baby-sitter in 1987. The Church settled a multimillion-dollar suit with 25 men whom Porter had abused while a priest. Because of the scandals, there have been calls for the Church to take more aggressive steps to find, isolate, and treat abusive priests (Greeley, 1993).

Incest

Culturally prohibited sexual relations (up to and including coitus) between family members, such as a brother and sister or a parent and child, are known as **incest.** Although a few societies have approved of incestuous relationships—at one time it was the established practice for Egyptian pharaohs to marry their sisters to prevent the royal blood from being "contaminated"—the incest taboo is virtually universal among human societies. Incest often produces children with mental and physical problems. For example, in one study, 15 of 38 offspring of incestuous unions had been admitted to hospitals for treatment of mental retardation (Jancar & Johnston, 1990). These consequences of matings between close relatives reflect the action of rare recessive genes with negative effects. Close genetic relatives are much more likely than nonrelatives to share the same bad genes, and hence to have children with two of them. Presumably for this reason, many nonhuman animal species, and all known primates, avoid matings between close relatives. The mechanism for human incest avoidance appears to be lack of sexual interest in people to whom one is continuously exposed from an early age. For example, biologically unrelated children who were raised together in Israeli kibbutzim rarely marry or have affairs with others from their rearing group when they become adults (Shepher, 1971). Evolutionarily, this makes sense. In most cultures, children reared together will be biologically related siblings.

Incest is traditionally defined as sex between biological relatives. Recent trends toward nontraditional family

James R. Porter, a former Roman Catholic priest, was convicted of pedophilia that had been committed many years earlier. His conviction occurred after a number of persons came forward with reports of his earlier abuse when they were members of his church as children.

compositions such as stepparents and stepchildren have led some researchers to expand the definition of incest to legal relatives. There are no adverse genetic consequences of matings between relatives-in-law, and thus the incest taboo might be expected to operate less effectively between them. On the other hand, it is conceivable that a young woman who is sexually molested by her stepfather could suffer every bit as much, psychologically, as one who is molested by her biological father. At present there are no relevant studies examining this question.

In our own society, the actual incidence of incest is difficult to estimate because it usually comes to light only when reported to law enforcement or other agencies. It is almost certainly more common than is generally believed, in part because many victims are reluctant to report the incest or do not consider themselves victimized (De Young, 1982; Maisch, 1972). The incidence of "intrafamilial sexual abuse" coming to the attention of professionals approached 100,000 in 1985 (Williams & Finkelhor, 1990). Brother-sister incest is clearly the most common form of incest, even though it is rarely reported (Masters et al., 1992). Indeed in two studies, brother-sister incest was reported as being five times more common than the next most common pattern—father-daughter incest (Gebhard et al., 1965; Kinsey et al., 1948, 1953). Mother-son incest is thought to be relatively rare. In a study of 78 cases of incest, which excluded the brother-sister variety, Maisch (1972) found that the father-daughter and stepfather-stepdaughter varieties accounted for fully 85 percent of the sample; mother-son incest accounted for only 4 percent. It seems that girls living with stepfathers are at especially high risk for incest, perhaps because there is less of an incest taboo among nonblood relatives (Finkelhor, 1984; Masters et al., 1992; Russell, 1986). In occasional cases, multiple patterns of incest may exist within the same family, and some incestuous fathers involve all of their daughters serially as they become pubescent.

Incestuous fathers tend to be of lower intelligence than other fathers, but they do not typically evidence serious psychopathology (Williams & Finkelhor, 1990). Indeed, they are often shy and conventional and claim devotion to their families (Masters et al., 1992). Most incestuous offenders are not pedophiles; only one-fifth to one-third have pedophilic arousal patterns (Langevin et al., 1985; Marshall, Barbaree, & Christophe, 1986). Most incestuous fathers have experienced substantial sexual dysfunction with their wives or adult partners. They have also tended to avoid child-care or nurturing activities that may otherwise have led them to treat their children as children, rather than sexual objects. Although not especially nurturing, incestuous fathers tend to be overprotective of their victims, which might represent an attempt to isolate and monopolize them. Incestuous families tend to be low in community involvement and high in conflict avoidance. The wives of men who commit incest were often sexually abused themselves as children, and in more than two-thirds of such cases the wife often did not help or protect her child even if she knew about the incest (Masters et al., 1992). Despite these associations, no one pattern adequately describes all incestuous fathers and families.

Rape

The term **rape** describes sexual activity that occurs under actual or threatened forcible coercion of one person by another. In most states, legal definitions restrict forcible rape to forced intercourse or penetration of a bodily orifice by a penis or other object. Statutory rape is sexual activity with a person who is legally defined (by *statute* or law) to be under the age of consent (18 in most states). Statutory rape is considered to have occurred regardless of the apparent willingness of an underage partner. In the vast majority of cases, rape is a crime of men against women, although in prison settings it is often men against men. As with childhood sexual abuse, several issues related to rape are scientifically and politically controversial. Two especially controversial questions are how frequently rape occurs and whether rape is primarily motivated by sex or aggression.

Prevalence   It might seem to be fairly straightforward to estimate the prevalence of rape, but different studies have varied wildly in their estimates (Lynch, 1996). Figures may vary according to both the precise definition of rape used and the way that the information is gathered (direct or indirect questions, for example). The FBI routinely gathers statistics on most major crimes reported to local law enforcement agencies throughout the country. The incidence of unreported rapes can be estimated from the National Crime Survey of the Bureau of Justice Statistics (BJS), which drew on a probability sample of 59,000 households. In this survey, respondents were asked whether they had experienced "forced or coerced sexual intercourse." The incidence of reported rapes between 1979 and 1990 was fairly stable, at between 70 and 80 rapes per 100,000 women, per year (Federal Bureau of Investigation, 1991). The incidence of total (reported and unreported) rapes was approximately double these. Projecting to lifetime risk, most reasonable assumptions lead to the estimate that approximately 5 to 7 percent of women will be victims of rape or attempted rape (Gilbert, 1992) during the course of their lives.

The National Women's Study (Resnick, Kilpatrick, Dansky, Saunders, & Best, 1993) asked approximately 2,000 women whether "a man or boy ever made you have sex by using force or threatening to harm [you] or someone close to [you]." When sex was defined as completed vaginal or anal penetration, or forced oral sex, 13 percent of women said that this had occurred sometime during their lives, a much higher rate than the BJS statistics. The two surveys differed in a number of respects that may have contributed to the difference, but it is not clear

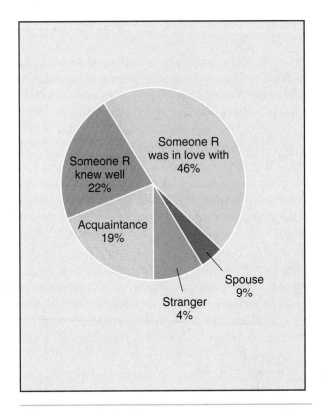

FIGURE 11.1   RELATIONSHIP OF WOMEN RESPONDENTS TO A MAN WHO FORCED THEM TO DO SOMETHING SEXUAL.
Note: Sample size = 204. This includes female respondents who reported that they had ever been "forced to do something sexual that they did not want to do by a man." Eighty-six women (or about 30 percent of all women) reported that they had been forced sexually by more than one person; they are not represented in the figure but in the distribution of relationships to persons forcing is similar.

which figures provide a more accurate lifetime estimate (Lynch, 1996). Even the lower figure is much higher than desirable.

Is Rape Motivated by Sex or Aggression?   Traditionally, rape has been classified as a sex crime, and society has assumed that the rapist was motivated by lust. However, some feminist scholars have challenged this view, arguing instead that rape is motivated by the need to dominate, to assert power, and to humiliate a victim rather than by sexual desire for her (Brownmiller, 1975). Before evaluating the argument that rape is about aggression and not about sex, it is important to emphasize one undeniable fact. Whatever motivates the rapist, rape victims do not find rape to be sexually pleasurable. The myth that they sometimes do is dangerous and probably has encouraged some men to rape and some juries to excuse rapists. Rape is among women's worst fears (Gordon, 1992). Even in the context of a romantic relationship, women rate forced sex as the most destructive act a partner can perform (Buss, 1994). Moreover, from the perspective of the victim, rape is always an act of violence, whatever the rapist's motivation.

Some writers have evaluated some of the reasons offered by those who believe rape is not sexually motivated, and found them unconvincing (Ellis, 1989; Palmer, 1988). For example, although many rapists have stable sexual partners, it is not uncommon for men to desire multiple sexual outlets. Brownmiller (1975) noted that rape victims include females of all ages and degrees of physical attractiveness. Although this is true, the age distribution of rape victims is not random but includes a very high proportion of women in their teens and early twenties. This age distribution is quite different from the distribution of other violent crimes, in which the elderly are overrepresented because of their vulnerability. In contrast, less than 5 percent of rape victims are over the age of 50 (Groth, 1979). The fact that older women are raped very rarely despite their increased vulnerability to violent crime in general supports the interpretation that rapists prefer younger (and more attractive) victims. Rapists themselves have described their preferred victims as the "'American dream ideal'—a nice, friendly, young, pretty, middle-class, white female" (Geis, 1977, p. 27). Furthermore, rapists usually cite sexual motivation as a very important cause of their actions (Smithyman, 1978, p. iv). Finally, as we shall see, at least some rapists share features of paraphiliacs, such as a characteristic arousal pattern to abnormal (in their case, rape) stimuli, and multiple paraphilias (Abel & Rouleau, 1990). Paraphiliacs are typically highly sexually motivated. Thus, in our view, sexual desire is a factor in motivating many rapists. At the same time we agree with David Finkelhor, who states that "The debate about the sexual motivation of sexual abuse is something of an unfortunate red herring . . . the goal should be to explain how the sexual component fits in" (1984, pp. 34–35).

Recently some progress has been made toward Finkelhor's goal. Two prominent researchers studying sex offenders, Raymond Knight and Robert Prentky, have developed a classification system for rapists that shows all rapists have both aggressive and sexual motives, but to varying degrees. Two of the subtypes they have identified are motivated primarily by aggression, and two of the subtypes are motivated primarily by distorted sexual motives (1990; Knight, Prentky, & Cerce, 1994). In a study validating this classification system, Barbaree and colleagues (1994) found that the rapists of the sexual subtypes showed greater sexual arousal to taped scenes of rape than did rapists of the aggressive subtypes. Further research validating this classification system should be useful in helping to design better treatments for the different subtypes of rapists.

Rape and Its Aftermath Rape tends to be a repetitive activity rather than an isolated act, and most rapes are planned events. About 80 percent of rapists commit the act in the neighborhoods in which they reside; most rapes take place in an urban setting at night. The specific scene of the rape varies greatly, however. The act may occur on a lonely street after dark, in an automobile in a large shopping center's parking lot, in the elevator or hallway of a building, and in other situations where a victim has little chance of assistance. Rapists have also entered apartments or homes by pretending to be making deliveries or repairs. In fact, rapes occur most often in the victim's home.

About a third or more of all rapes involve more than one offender, and often they are accompanied by beatings. The remainder are single-offender rapes in which the victim and the offender may know each other; the closer the relationship, the more brutally the victim may be beaten. When a victim struggles against her attacker, she is likely to receive more severe injuries or in rare cases to be killed. On the other hand, one study found that when the victim was able to cry out and run away, she was more likely to be successful in avoiding the rape (Selkin, 1975).

As discussed in Chapter 4, in addition to the physical trauma inflicted on a victim, the psychological trauma may be severe, leading to what has been called a rape trauma syndrome (Burgess & Holmstrom, 1974) or PTSD (Becker & Kaplan, 1991). One especially unfortunate factor in rape is the possibility of pregnancy; another is the chance of contracting a sexually transmitted disease. A rape may also have a negative impact on a victim's marriage or other intimate relationships. The situation is likely to be particularly upsetting to a husband or boyfriend if he has been forced to watch the rape, as is occasionally the case when a victim is raped by the members of a juvenile gang.

The concept of "victim-precipitated" rape, a favorite of defense attorneys and of some police and court jurisdictions, turns out on close examination to be a myth. According to this view, a victim, although often bruised both psychologically and physically—if not worse—is regarded as the cause of the crime, often on such grounds as the alleged provocativeness of her clothing, her past sexual behavior, or her presence in a location considered risky (Stermac, Segal, & Gillis, 1990). The attacker, on the other hand, is treated as unable to quell his lust in the face of such irresistible provocation—and therefore not legally responsible for the act. A society as troubled as ours is by sexual assault can ill-afford this type of nonsensical and myth-based jurisprudence; in nearly a century of combined clinical practice none of the authors has ever encountered a woman who desired to be raped, nor have we ever heard a convincing account of any such case. Despite evidence to the contrary, however, the harmful and dangerous concept that women want to be forced into sex is persistent and widespread (Segal & Stermac, 1990).

Women who are repeated victims of rape are especially likely to be suspected of provoking the attacks. In fact such women tend to be significantly dysfunctional in many areas of their lives, and they also tend to be victims in situations other than rape, perhaps including other forms of sexual traumatization such as being the victim of a voyeur or exhibitionist, or being sexually assaulted in less extreme ways than full-blown rape (Koss & Dinero, 1989). Far from being the seductresses of popular folklore, they are often quite ineffectual and inadequate (sometimes because of the effects of a prior history of abuse) with insufficient personal resources to fend off those who would exploit them (Ellis, Atkeson, & Calhoun, 1982; Myers et al., 1985).

Rape, even at its least violent, is a bullying, intrusive violation of another person's integrity, selfhood, and personal boundaries that deserves to be viewed with more gravity—and its victims with more compassion and sensitivity—than is usually the case. Much still remains to be done in providing services to these victims (Koss, 1983), many of whom suffer from moderately severe posttraumatic stress disorder (see Chapter 4).

Rapists Based on information gathered by the FBI about arrested and convicted rapists, rape is usually a young man's crime. According to FBI Uniform Crime Reports, about 60 percent of all rapists arrested are under 25 years of age, with the greatest concentration in the 18-to-24 age group. Of the rapists who get into police records, about 30 to 50 percent are married and living with their wives at the time of the crime. As a group, they come from the low end of the socioeconomic ladder and commonly have a prior criminal record (Masters et al., 1992). Typically they are unskilled workers with low intelligence, low education, and low income. The large majority have prior criminal records. About half were drinking heavily or drunk when they committed the rape. Seventy percent were strangers to the victims.

How similar are incarcerated rapists and other rapists? Data suggest both important similarities and differences. In one study, 71 college date rapists (that is, an acquaintance who rapes a woman typically in a context of a date or other social interaction) described themselves as more sexually active and successful compared with other men (Kanin, 1985). Because they were more sexually driven, however, they felt more sexually deprived. Date rapists also tend to have a "hostile masculine personality" (Malamuth, Linz, Heavey, & Barnes, 1995), involving hostility toward women and femininity (including positive feminine traits such as nurturance), and an exaggerated mas-

Alex Kelly, a young man from a wealthy family who certainly does not fit our stereotype of a rapist, was convicted in 1997 of raping a 16 year old girl in 1986, and was sentenced to sixteen years in prison. While awaiting his trial in 1987, Kelly fled the United States and spent eight years as an international fugitive before being caught and returned to the United States for trial.

culinity emphasizing power, control and machismo. Knight (1997) has found that both date rapists and incarcerated rapists are characterized by promiscuity, hostile masculinity, and an emotionally detached, predatory personality (i.e., the personality style of a psychopath). What distinguishes them, primarily, is that incarcerated rapists show much higher levels of impulsive, antisocial behavior. Impulsive, antisocial men are more likely to commit multiple, serious offenses leading to incarceration.

The case can be made that some rapists have a paraphilia—not different in its essentials from the paraphilias already discussed (Abel & Rouleau, 1990). Many rapists have many features of paraphiliacs. For example, they often report having recurrent, repetitive, and compulsive urges to rape. They typically try to control the urges, but the urges eventually become so strong that they act on them. Many rapists have other paraphilias. In one study of 126 rapists, for example, 28 percent had interest in exhibitionism and 18 percent in voyeurism (Abel & Rouleau, 1990). Most important, rapists have a characteristic pattern of sexual arousal (Abel & Rouleau, 1990; Lohr, Adams, & Davis, 1997). Most rapists are similar to normal nonoffending men in being sexually aroused to depictions of mutually satisfying, consensual intercourse. However, in contrast to normal men, many rapists are also sexually aroused to depictions of sexual assaults. Evidently, they are less sensitive to the inhibitory mechanisms that prevent most men from seeking sexual gratification coercively. A small minority of rapists, characterized by very violent assaults, are aroused more to assault than to sexual stimuli. They appear to be sexual sadists.

Rapists also show some deficits in their cognitive appraisals of women's feelings and intentions (Segal & Stermac, 1990). For example, they have difficulty decoding women's negative cues during social interactions. This could lead to inappropriate behaviors that women would experience as sexually intrusive. In one study, for example, rapists and nonrapist offenders were shown a series of vignettes of heterosexual couples interacting, and subjects were asked to guess which emotional cues were being portrayed. Rapists were significantly less accurate than the control groups (violent nonrapists and nonviolent nonrapists) in interpreting cues. Moreover, rapists were especially bad at reading women's cues, and errors associated with negative cues were most common (Lipton, McDonel, & McFall, 1987).

Conviction rates for rape are low, and most men who have raped are free in the community. In fact, one study (reported in Abel & Rouleau, 1990) found that 907 separate acts of rape were reported by only 126 nonincarcerated offenders, an average of 7 per offender.

In recent years, new rape laws have been adopted by a majority of states, many of them based on the "Michigan model," which describes four degrees of criminal sexual conduct, with different punishment levels for different degrees of seriousness. In calling the offense criminal sexual conduct rather than rape, the Michigan law also appropriately places the emphasis on the offender rather than the victim. Unfortunately, most sexual assaults are not reported, and of those that are, less than 10 percent result in conviction (Darke, 1990). Convictions often bring light sentences, and a jail term does not dissuade a substantial number of offenders from repeating their crimes. The upshot, we reiterate, is that the large majority of rapists are not in prison but out among us.

Treatment and Recidivism of Sex Offenders

Soon after his release from prison, convicted sex offender Earl Shriner forced a seven-year-old boy off his bike in the woods near Tacoma, Washington, then raped and stabbed him before cutting off the boy's penis. Just before his release from prison, Shriner had confided to a cellmate that he still had fantasies of molesting and murdering children (Popkin, 1994). In a similar case, seven-year-old Megan Kanka was sexually molested and murdered by a convicted pedophile living in her neighborhood. Cases such as these have inspired a number of measures to protect society from sexual predators. (See Highlight 11.3 Modern Life, "Megan's Law.") There is growing intolerance about sex offenders who repeat their crimes. The case of Willie Horton, who sexually assaulted a woman while out on parole, figured prominently in the defeat of Michael Dukakis in the 1988 presidential election (Dukakis, then Governor of Massachusetts, was accused of permitting the parole). But are such stories representative? Are sex offenders typically incurable? Should they receive life sentences on the presumption that they are bound to offend again? Or have they been unfairly singled out due to media sensationalism when they really are responsive to treatment (Berlin & Malin, 1991)? The efficacy of treatment for sex offenders is controversial—as, it seems, are so many issues related to sexual abuse (Furby, Weinrott, & Blackshaw, 1989; Marshall, 1993; Marshall & Pithers, 1994; Quinsey et al., 1993; Rice, Quinsey, & Harris, 1991).

Goals of Treatment Therapies for sex offenders are very similar to those described above for the paraphilias, typically having at least one of the following three goals: to modify patterns of sexual arousal, to modify cognitions and social skills to allow more appropriate sexual interactions with adult partners, or to reduce sexual drive. Attempts to modify sexual arousal patterns usually involve aversion therapy. In aversion therapy a paraphilic stimulus, such as a slide of a nude pre-pubescent girl for a pedophile, is paired with an aversive event, such as forced inhalation of noxious odors or a shock to the arm. Alternatively, inhalation of the noxious odors or delivery of the shock may be conditional on penile response; if penile erection exceeds some minimum criterion, shock occurs; otherwise, no shock occurs. An alternative to electric aversion therapy is covert sensitization, in which the patient imagines a highly aversive event while viewing or imagining a paraphilic stimulus, or assisted covert sensitization in which a foul odor is introduced to induce nausea at the point of peak arousal. Another method for reducing deviant arousal is satiation, in which the patient first masturbates to orgasm while fantasizing about sexually appropriate scenes, then continues masturbating after switching to his paraphilic fantasies. The deviant fantasy is continued for an hour each session, the goal being to produce boredom (Maletzky, 1998).

Reduction of deviant sexual arousal is probably insufficient. Deviant arousal patterns need to be replaced by arousal to acceptable stimuli (Maletzky, 1998; Quinsey & Earls, 1990). Most often investigators have attempted to pair the pleasurable stimuli of orgasm with sexual fantasies involving sex between consenting adults. Patients are asked to masturbate while thinking of deviant fantasies. At the moment of ejaculatory inevitability, the patient switches his fantasy to a more appropriate theme. The moment of switching themes is gradually moved backward in time until, ideally, the patient can rely entirely on appropriate themes. Both therapies are intended to reduce inappropriate sexual arousal, and those intended to increase nondeviant sexual arousal have been shown to be somewhat effective in the laboratory (Maletzky, 1998; Quinsey & Earls, 1990). However, there are at least two concerns about their practical effectiveness. First, some sex offenders can fake phallometric measurements of sexual preference by inhibiting their attention to the deviant stimuli (Maletzky, 1998; Quinsey & Earls, 1990). Thus their actual sexual preferences may not change despite apparent progress. Second, the laboratory is an artificial setting, and it is important to demonstrate that therapeutic change generalizes to the patient's outside world, which may be especially problematic if his motivation wanes following treatment.

Cognitive restructuring attempts to eliminate sex offenders' cognitive distortions, because these may play a role in sexual abuse (Maletzky, 1998). For example, an incest offender who stated "If my ten-year-old daughter had said no I would have stopped," might be challenged about a number of implied distortions. For example, he has implied that a child can consent to have sex with an adult, that if a child does not say no she has consented, and that it is the child's responsibility to stop sexual contact. Another approach is to have offenders who have been sexually abused themselves recount their experience, and then link these experiences with those of the offenders' victims. Social-skills training aims to help sex offenders (especially rapists) learn to process social information from women more effectively (Maletzky, 1998; McFall, 1990). For example, some men read positive sexual connotations into women's neutral or negative messages, or believe that women's refusals of sexual advances reflect "playing hard to get." Training typically involves interaction of patients and female partners, who can give the patients feedback on their response to their interaction. Cognitive treatment of sex offenders has shown some promise (Maletzky, 1998; Marshall & Barabaree, 1990b), although relevant studies have some important limitations, which we shall consider later. Social-skills training by itself has not yet received solid empirical support (McFall, 1990).

Effectiveness of Psychosocial Treatments Although some reviews of the treatment literature have reached positive conclusions (e.g., Marshall et al., 1991), some studies have also provided rather disturbing results about the long-term effectiveness of such treatments (Emmelkamp, 1994; Rice et al., 1991). For example, in one important study Quinsey and colleagues (1991) followed 136 child molesters for an average of six years following their release from imprisonment. Nearly half had committed another violent or sexual offense, and this rate of recidivism did not differ among the 50 men who had received aversion therapy and the 86 men who had not. Moreover, the degree of aversion that was conditioned during treatment was not a significant predictor of recidivism. Some studies have had somewhat more promising results, including Maletzky's (1998) important study of over 4000 rapists and pedophiles. Although the study unfortunately does not have an untreated control group like the Quinsey et al. study did, and to date only one-year follow-up results exist for all the offenders, the success rates were very promising—75 percent for rapists, and 80 to 95 percent for different types of pedophiles. And this was using very stringent criteria for success (i.e., they completed all treatment sessions, they reported no covert or overt deviant sexual behavior at the end of treatment or at the one-year follow-up, they showed no deviant sexual arousal as measured with a penile plethsymograph at the end of treatment or follow-up, and they had no repeat legal charges). Nevertheless, much work remains to be done and it is probably most accurate to say that at the present time we simply do not know how likely it is that various treatments will significantly reduce sex offenders' likelihood of recidivism (Maletzky, 1998; Quinsey et al., 1993) and the treatments that show promise are not yet widely in use.

Biological and Surgical Treatments The most controversial treatment for sex offenders involves castration, either surgical removal of the testes or the hormonal treatment sometimes called "chemical castration" (Besharov, 1992; Bradford, 1990; Money, 1986, pp. 135–45). Both surgical and chemical castration lower the testosterone level, which in turn lowers the sex drive, allowing the offender to resist any inappropriate impulses. Chemical castration has most often involved the administration of antiandrogen steroid hormones such as Depo-Provera (technically, medroxyprogesterone acetate or MPA). Recently, an uncontrolled study of the drug lupron (technically, triptorelin) yielded dramatic results: 30 men with paraphilias reported an average of 48 deviant fantasies per week prior to therapy, and no such fantasies during treatment (Rosler & Witztum, 1998). Lupron is especially effective at reducing testosterone and has fewer bad side effects than drugs such as Depo-Provera. Studies of surgical castration of sex offenders conducted in Europe suggest similar results. These studies have typically included diverse categories of offenders, from pedophiles to rapists of adult women. Follow-up has sometimes exceeded 10 years. Recidivism rates of castrated offenders are typically less than 3 percent, compared with greater than 50 percent of uncastrated of-

MODERN LIFE

Megan's Law

On July 29, 1994, seven-year-old Megan Kanka, from Hamilton Township, N.J., was walking home from her friend's house. Just before she reached her front door, a neighbor invited her to his house to see his new puppy. The neighbor, Jesse Timmendequas, 33, was a landscaper who had lived across the street for about a year. Unknown to Megan, Megan's parents, or anyone else in the neighborhood, he was also a twice-convicted child molester (and lived with two other convicted sex offenders). When Megan followed him inside, he led her to an upstairs bedroom, strangled her unconscious with his belt, raped her, and asphyxiated her with a plastic bag. Timmendequas then placed Megan's body in a toolbox, drove to a soccer field and dumped it near a portable toilet. Subsequently, Timmendequas was apprehended, convicted, and sentenced to death.

Megan's murder sparked outrage that dangerous sex offenders could move into a neighborhood without notifying the community of their presence. In response, the New Jersey state legislature passed Megan's Law, which mandated that upon release, convicted sex offenders register with police, and that authorities notify neighbors of convicted sex offenders by distributing flyers, alerting local organizations, and canvassing door-to-door. Similar laws have been passed in many other states, and it is now possible in California to examine a CD-ROM containing the name, picture, and legal history of convicted sex offenders subject to that state's Megan's Law. Some states post sex offenders' identities on Internet websites.

Delaware will soon require sex offense convictions to be indicated on driver's licenses.

Although Megan's Laws have been enormously popular with state legislators and citizens, they have not been uncontroversial. Civil libertarians have objected to community notification requirements, which, they argue, endanger released offenders (who have arguably paid their debts to society) and also prevent them from integrating successfully back into society. Although the various Megan's Laws are intended to protect potential victims rather than encourage harassment of sex offenders, the latter has occurred. For example, in July 1993 the home of convicted child rapist Joseph Gallardo was burned to the ground after citizens in Snohomish County, Washington, learned he was about to be paroled. John Becerra, a convicted sex offender, moved into a two-story home in the New York City area in December 1995, hoping to begin a new life with his wife and their nine-year-old son. But he and his family found themselves the target of a persistent campaign of protests by their neighbors. Signs around the neighborhood warned, "Beware of Sex Offender," their car was vandalized, and rallies were held outside their home. A second problem is that "sex offender" status applies to some cases that seem clearly inappropriate for Megan's Law notification. For example, an 18-year-old Wisconsin man, convicted of sexual assault after impregnating his 15-year-old girlfriend (whom he intended to marry) discovered that under Wisconsin's Megan's Law, he must provide a DNA sample and register as a convicted sex offender

fenders (Berlin, 1994; Bradford, 1990; Green, 1992; Wille & Beier, 1989). However, many feel that the treatment is brutal and dehumanizing (Gunn, 1993). Interestingly, most recent cases have involved a request by the sex offender himself to be castrated in exchange for a lighter sentence.

Increasingly many treatment programs use a combination of hormone therapy and cognitive behavioral treatments, with the hope being that eventually the hormone treatment can be tapered after the offender has learned techniques for impulse control (Maletzky, 1998). However, the single most important defect of nearly all available studies is the lack of randomly assigned controls who were equally motivated for treatment. Some have argued that denying treatment to sex offenders is

for the next 15 years. Finally, the limited relevant data have brought the effectiveness of Megan's Laws into question. A 1995 Washington state study found that in the period before that state's Megan's Law, 22% of sex offenders who had been arrested committed another sex crime. After the law went into effect, the rate was quite similar, 19% (Schenk, 1998).

Recognition that some sex offenses have high recidivism rates, and uncertainty whether treatment helps, have led some states to pass laws that require involuntary commitment of dangerous offenders to psychiatric facilities even after their sentence has been served. Leroy Hendricks was convicted five times of molesting children and admitted that only his death could guarantee that he would commit no further offenses. In 1994, Kansas prosecutors invoked state law to prevent his release after he served 10 years in prison, but this action was challenged as unconstitutional. The primary objection was that holding Hendricks after his sentence amounted to giving him a second punishment for the same offense. In 1997 the U.S. Supreme Court ruled narrowly (5–4) that people such as Hendricks can be held if they are considered mentally abnormal and are likely to commit new crimes. Early signs are that once committed, few sex offenders will be released.

In order to ensure that released sex offenders will not reoffend, some states have passed legislation requiring chemical or surgical castration for certain types of sex offenders. For example, California now requires that repeat child molesters undergo chemical castration as a condition of parole. Michigan has passed a similar law applying to repeat rapists. Civil libertarians, exemplified by the ACLU, have argued that such requirements violate the Constitution's ban on cruel and unusual punishment, because of potentially severe side effects. Furthermore, because the treatment may affect both sex drive and spermatogenesis, civil libertarians argue, required chemical castration violates "reproductive privacy rights."

Finally, some highly publicized cases in which children or adolescents were lured by sexual predators over the Internet (e.g., in "chat rooms") sparked federal legislation, the Child Pornography Prevention Act of 1996, which expanded the definition of illegal child pornography to include images not necessarily based on a real child, such as cartoon images. Legislators were motivated, in part, by the belief that pedophiles used cartoons to demonstrate desired sexual activities to children. Specifically, the law forbids "visual depiction [that] is, or appears to be, of a minor engaging in sexually explicit conduct." Civil libertarians have been concerned that the law is too broad, worrying for example, that it could be used to ban underwear advertisements featuring children, as well as serious art. Under a similar state law, Oklahoma removed from public circulation copies of the acclaimed film, *The Tin Drum*, because it included scenes in which the child star crawls into bed with an actress and, beneath a heavy, woolen blanket which entirely obscures both actors, mimics intercourse with her. ∎

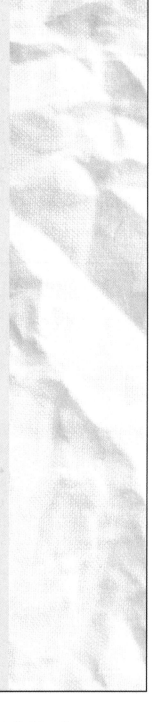

unethical (e.g., Marshall et al., 1991). However, this could only be true if the treatment were effective, and it is unclear at this point if it is. Research in this area is further complicated by the fact that the outcome variable in most studies is whether the man is reconvicted for another sex offense during the follow-up period. Because most sex offenses go unpunished (the offender is often never even caught, let alone convicted), this will exaggerate the apparent effectiveness of treatment, and underestimate the dangerousness of sex offenders. Given the social importance of the questions of whether sex offenders can be helped and how likely they are to reoffend, we hope that society will devote the resources necessary to answer them.

It is possible both to acknowledge that sex offenders cause immense human suffering and to feel sympathy for their plight. Many sex offenders have been burdened with a deviant sexual arousal pattern that has caused them great personal and legal trouble. Consider the case of Scott Murphy, a convicted pedophile:

> He lives alone with a friend, works odd hours and doesn't go out of his way to meet neighbors. Ironically, Murphy has never been prouder of his behavior. He admits he'll never be cured and will always be attracted to young boys. But he says he is now making every attempt to steer clear of them: "I went from constantly living my whole life to molest kids to now living my whole life to not molest kids." It's a 24-hour-a-day job. On the highway, Murphy keeps at a distance to guarantee he makes no eye contact with the young passengers in school buses. When the Sunday paper arrives at home, he immediately throws out the coupon section because the glossy ads often depict attractive boy models. He refuses to leave the office when kids might be walking to or from school and got rid of his television so the sit-com images of young boys wouldn't distract him. (Popkin, 1994, p. 67)

Society cannot allow Murphy to act on his sexual preference; nor can his past crimes be forgotten. Nevertheless, in deciding how to treat people like Scott Murphy, it is humane to remember that many of them have a tormented inner life.

Sexual Dysfunctions

The term **sexual dysfunction** refers to impairment either in the desire for sexual gratification or in the ability to achieve it. They vary markedly in degree, and regardless of which partner is alleged to be dysfunctional, the enjoyment of sex by both parties in a relationship is typically adversely affected. They occur in both heterosexual and homosexual couples. In some cases, sexual dysfunctions are caused by dysfunctional psychosexual adjustment and learning. In others, organic factors are most important. In recent years, both explanations and treatment of sexual dysfunction have become increasingly physiological (Rosen & Leiblum, 1995).

Today we understand that there are four relatively distinct phases of the human sexual response (Masters and Johnson, 1966; 1970; 1975). Disorders can occur in any of the first three phases (American Psychiatric Association, 1994). The first phase is the **desire phase,** which consists of fantasies about sexual activity or a sense of desire to have sexual activity. The second phase is the **excitement phase,** during which there is generally both a subjective sense of sexual pleasure and physiological changes that accompany this subjective pleasure, including penile erection in the male and vaginal lubrication and enlargement in the female. The third phase is **orgasm,** during which there is a release of sexual tension and a peaking of sexual pleasure. The final phase is **resolution,** during which the person has a sense of relaxation and well-being. We will first describe the most common dysfunctions that accompany the first three phases and then discuss issues of causation and treatment. Table 11.2 summarizes the dysfunctions we will be covering here.

TABLE 11.2 SEXUAL DYSFUNCTIONS

Dysfunctions	Characteristics
Dysfunctions of Sexual Desire	
Hypoactive sexual desire disorder	Little or no sexual drive or interest
Sexual aversion disorder	Total lack of interest in sex and avoidance of sexual contact
Dysfunctions of Sexual Arousal	
Male erectile disorder	Inability to achieve or maintain an erection (formerly known as impotence)
Female sexual arousal disorder	Nonresponsiveness to erotic stimulation both physically and emotionally (formerly known as frigidity)
Dysfunctions of Orgasm	
Premature ejaculation	Unsatisfactorily brief period between the beginning of sexual stimulation and the occurrence of ejaculation
Male orgasmic disorder	Inability to ejaculate during intercourse (also known as retarded ejaculation)
Female orgasmic disorder	Difficulty in achieving orgasm, either manually or during sexual intercourse
Sexual Pain Disorders	
Vaginismus	Involuntary muscle spasm at the entrance to the vagina that prevents penetration and sexual intercourse
Dyspareunia	Painful coitus; may have either an organic or psychological basis

Sexual dysfunctions can occur at the desire, excitement, or orgasm phases of the sexual response cycle. Many people, if not most, will experience some sexual dysfunction sometime during their lives. If it becomes chronic or highly disturbing to one or both partners, it warrants treatment.

How common are sexual dysfunctions? It is obviously difficult to do large-scale research on such a sensitive topic. Nevertheless, the National Health and Social Life Survey (Laumann et al., 1994) assessed sexual problems during the previous year in 3,432 randomly ascertained Americans. Although they did not use DSM diagnostic criteria, the researchers inquired about similar problems. For women, the most common complaints were lack of sexual interest (33%) and inability to experience orgasm (24%). For men, climaxing too early (29%), anxiety about sexual performance (17%), and lack of sexual interest (16%) were reported most frequently. Altogether 45% of men and 55% of women reported some dysfunction during the past year. Clearly, a high percentage of people will experience sexual dysfunction sometime during their lives.

Dysfunctions of Sexual Desire

Sexual Desire Disorders Researchers have delineated two types of sexual desire disorders. The first is **hypoactive sexual desire disorder.** It is a dysfunction in which either a man or a woman shows little or no sexual drive or interest. It is assumed in most cases that the biological basis of the sex drive remains unimpaired (see Schreiner-Engel et al., 1989), but that for some reason sexual motivation is blocked. These people usually come to the attention of clinicians only at the request of their partners, who typically complain of insufficient sexual interaction. This fact exposes one problem with the diagnosis, because it is known that preferences for frequency of sexual contact vary widely among otherwise normal individuals. Who is to decide what is "not enough"? DSM-IV explicitly indicates that this judgment is left to the clinician, taking into account the person's age and the context of his or her life. Nevertheless, there do appear to be some people who are almost totally lacking in sexual desire. In extreme cases, sex actually becomes psychologically aversive, and warrants a diagnosis of **sexual aversion disorder,** the second type of sexual desire disorder. With this disorder the person shows extreme aversion to, and avoidance of, all genital sexual contact with a partner.

Depression may contribute to some cases of sexual desire disorders (Rosen & Leiblum, 1987). Although sexual desire disorders typically occur in the absence of obvious organic pathology, there is evidence that organic factors may sometimes play a role. Sexual arousal in both men and women depends on testosterone (Sherwin, 1988; Alexander and Sherwin, 1993). The increase in sexual desire problems with age may be in part attributable to declining levels of testosterone, but evidence regarding the utility of testosterone replacement therapy suggests it is usually not beneficial except possibly in women whose ovaries have been removed (Segraves & Althof, 1998). Although there has been interest in the possibility that a drug might be found to increase sexual desire since antiquity, no effective aphrodisiacs yet exist.

Sexual desire disorder appears to be the most common female sexual dysfunction (Laumann et al., 1994). Despite this fact, it has inspired far less etiological and treatment research than have male dysfunctions, especially erectile disorder and premature ejaculation. One main reason for this disparity is doubtless the centrality that many men place on their ability to perform sexually. There has also been, until recently, a general neglect of female sexuality and an implicit societal attitude that women simply do not care much about sex. It also appears that female sexuality may be in some senses more complicated than male sexuality, and this complexity may slow progress toward etiological theories and interventions. For example, it appears that the correlation between subjective sexual arousal and physiological sexual arousal (i.e., genital response) is much lower for women than for men (Heiman, 1980; Laan & Everaerd, 1995). That is, it is not uncommon for women to feel unaroused sexually, but to have some genital response; the reverse also occurs frequently. The significance of this desychrony between female genital and subjective arousal to female sexual dysfunction remains to be determined (Andersen & Cyranowski, 1995). There is an indication that sexual arousal disorder in women is increasing rapidly (Beck, 1995). We hope that such research increases commensurate with the importance and prevalence of the problem.

Dysfunctions of Sexual Arousal

Male Erectile Disorder Inability to achieve or maintain an erection sufficient for successful sexual intercourse was formerly called *impotence*. It is now known as **male erectile disorder** or *erectile insufficiency*. In lifelong erectile disorder a man has never been able to sustain an erection long enough to accomplish a satisfactory duration of penetration. In acquired or situational erectile disorder, a man has had at least one successful experience of coitus but is presently unable to produce or maintain the required level of penile rigidity. Lifelong insufficiency is a relatively rare disorder, but it has been estimated that half or more of the male population has had some experiences of erectile insufficiency on at least a temporary basis.

Masters and Johnson (1975; Masters et al., 1992) and Kaplan (1975, 1987) believed that erectile dysfunction is primarily a function of anxiety about sexual performance. In other reviews of the accumulated evidence, however, Barlow and colleagues (Beck & Barlow, 1984; Sbrocco & Barlow, 1996) have played down the role of anxiety per se—which under some circumstances can actually enhance sexual performance in normally function-

ing men and women (Barlow, Sakheim, & Beck, 1983; Hoon, Wincze, & Hoon, 1977; Palace & Gorzalka, 1990; see Sbrocco & Barlow, 1996, for a review). For example, in one study sexually functional male subjects in a laboratory experiment were made anxious by being told that there was a 60 percent chance of receiving electric shock while watching an erotic film unless they had an average-sized erection; these men actually showed more sexual arousal to the film than did men who were not threatened with shock (Barlow et al., 1983).

Instead of anxiety per se, Barlow and colleagues emphasized that it is the cognitive distractions frequently associated with anxiety in dysfunctional people that seem to interfere with their sexual arousal. For example, one study found that nondysfunctional men who were distracted by material they were listening to on earphones while watching an erotic film showed less sexual arousal than did men who were not distracted (Abrahamson et al., 1985). The distraction in this study had nothing to do with anxiety but it nonetheless interfered with sexual arousal in normal men. Barlow and colleagues believe that sexually dysfunctional men and women get distracted by negative thoughts about their performance during a sexual encounter (such as "I'll never get aroused" or "She will think I'm inadequate"). It seems to be this preoccupation with negative thoughts, rather than anxiety per se, that is responsible for inhibiting sexual arousal. Thus cognitive factors such as negative thoughts about performance have powerful effects on the physiology of sexual arousal. Another study consistent with this theory confirmed that dysfunctional men with erectile problems differ from functional men in being more easily distracted by cues about their performance, resulting in smaller erections during erotic stimulation (Abrahamson et al., 1989). Such self-defeating thoughts not only decrease pleasure but can also increase anxiety if the erection does not happen (Malatesta & Adams, 1993), and this in turn can fuel further negative self-defeating thoughts (Sbrocco & Barlow, 1996).

Erectile problems are a common consequence of aging. Prolonged or permanent erectile disorder before the age of 60 is relatively rare. One study found that more than half of married men over 70 had some erectile difficulties (Diokno, Brown, & Herzog, 1990). Studies have indicated that men and women in their 80s and 90s are often quite capable of enjoying intercourse (Kaplan, 1974; Malatesta & Adams, 1993; Masters et al., 1992). For example, in one study of 202 healthy men and women between ages 80 and 102, it was found that nearly two-thirds of the men and one-third of the women were still having sexual intercourse, although this was not generally their most common form of sexual activity (Bretschneider & McCoy, 1988).

Increased erectile dysfunction with age, and erectile disorder in general, are increasingly viewed as medical rather than psychological problems (Rosen, 1996). The most frequent cause of erectile disorder in older men is vascular disease, resulting in decreased blood flow to the penis or in diminished ability of the penis to hold blood to maintain an erection. Thus, hardening of the arteries, high blood pressure, and other diseases causing vascular problems are often causes of erectile disorder. Smoking, obesity, and alcohol abuse are associated lifestyle factors. Diseases that affect the nervous system, such as multiple sclerosis, can also cause erectile problems. Increased erectile problems with age are mainly due to cumulative vascular damage. For young men, one cause of erectile problems is having had priapism, or an erection that will not diminish, even after a couple of hours, typically unaccompanied by sexual excitement. Priapism can occur as a result of prolonged sexual activity, disease, or the side effect of certain medications. Untreated cases result in erectile dysfunction approximately 50 percent of the time (Starck, Branna, & Tallen, 1994), and thus should be treated as a medical emergency.

Distinguishing between psychogenic and organically caused erectile disorder for diagnostic purposes is at best a complicated process. The normal man has several erections per night, associated with periods of REM (rapid eye movement) sleep. Some researchers have suggested that organically based erectile disorder can be distinguished from psychogenically based erectile disorder by noting an absence of these nocturnal erections. However, it now appears that many other factors must also be evaluated in order to establish a proper diagnosis (Malatesta & Adams, 1993), because the nocturnal penile erection procedure has been found, by itself, to produce unreliable results (Mohr & Beutler, 1990). An important implication of these assessment difficulties is that we have probably again made the common error of assuming a mutually exclusive dichotomy (organic versus psychogenic), where such pure cases may in fact be the exception rather than the rule (Tiefer & Melman, 1989).

A variety of treatments—primarily medical—have been employed in recent years, often when cognitive-behavioral treatments have failed. These include drugs such as yohimbine, injections of smooth muscle relaxing drugs into the penile erection chambers (corpora cavernosa), and even a vacuum pump (Rosen, 1996). In extreme cases, penile implants may be used. These devices can be inflated to provide erection on demand. They are made of silicone rubber or polyurethane rubber. Most consist of two inflatable cylinders implanted in the penis. These are connected to a reservoir filled with fluid implanted in the abdomen and a manual pump implanted in scrotum. Some models combine parts. In order to get an erection, the pump must be squeezed.

These treatments have generally shown success in clinical trials, although they are rather extreme interventions that often evoke bothersome side effects (Rosen & Leiblum, 1995). Perhaps for these reasons, there has been immense interest in the revolutionary new drug Viagra (Sildenalfil). Viagra works by facilitating nitric oxide (that is making it more available), the primary neurotransmitter involved in penile erection. Viagra is taken orally, at least one hour before sexual activity. Unlike some other biological treatments for erectile dysfunction, Viagra promotes erection only if sexual desire is present.

Clinical trials of Viagra have been impressive. In a double-blind study, over 70 percent of men receiving at least 50 mg of Viagra reported that their erections had improved, compared with fewer than 30 percent of men receiving a placebo (Carlson, 1997, see also Goldstein et al., 1998). Side effects were relatively uncommon and not serious (e.g., the most common side effect, headache, was reported by 11 percent of patients), provided the person does not have serious preexisting heart problems in which case it can be very dangerous (even life-threatening). Based on these results, there has been immense public interest in the drug, and some analysts have predicted that Viagra may be the most commercially successful drug ever marketed. During the first two weeks after it was released in April 1998, approximately 150,000 prescriptions were written for it. This is an indication of both the high prevalence of sexual dysfunction and the importance that people attach to sexual performance.

Female Sexual Arousal Disorder Formerly and somewhat pejoratively referred to as *frigidity*, **female sexual arousal disorder**—the absence of sexual arousal feelings and an unresponsiveness to most or all forms of erotic stimulation—is in many ways the female counterpart of erectile disorder. Its chief physical manifestation is a failure to produce the characteristic swelling and lubrication of the vulva and vaginal tissues during sexual stimulation, a condition that may make intercourse quite uncomfortable. To be diagnosed, the disturbance must cause the woman marked distress or interpersonal difficulty. The diagnosis of female sexual arousal disorder by itself is rare (Segraves & Segraves, 1991). Although the causes of this disorder are not well understood, possible reasons for this inhibition of sexual feeling range from early sexual traumatization, to excessive and distorted so-

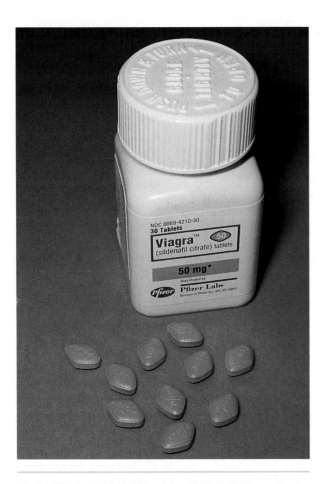

The drug Viagra works by making nitric oxide, the primary neurotransmitter in penile erection, more available. It is taken orally, about an hour before sexual activity. Unlike some other biological treatments for sexual dysfunction, Viagra only works if sexual desire is present.

cialization about the evils of sex, to dislike of, or disgust with a current partner's sexuality.

Given its rarity, it is not surprising that no treatment studies have been conducted. The widespread use of vaginal lubricants may effectively mask and treat the disorder in many women (Rosen & Leiblum, 1995). Some recent research suggests that under certain conditions, women's genital arousal can be increased by increasing their autonomic arousal—for example, via exercise or anxiety (Meston & Gorzalka, 1996; Palace, 1995). However, this work is preliminary and the findings complicated (e.g., the effects of exercise may not become manifest until half an hour after activity and may depend on beliefs about a woman's own level of sexual excitement). Finally, there has been great interest in the possibility that Viagra will have positive effects for women analogous to those for men (Kolata, 1998). Female genital response probably depends in large part on the same neurotransmitter systems as does male genital response, and thus it is plausible that

Viagra will be effective in women as well. Although therapeutic trials in women have begun in Europe, results of those trials are unavailable at this time.

Orgasmic Disorders

Premature Ejaculation   **Premature ejaculation** refers to persistent and recurrent onset of orgasm and ejaculation with minimal sexual stimulation. It may occur before, on, or shortly after penetration and before the man wants it to. The consequences include failure of the partner to achieve satisfaction and, often, acute embarrassment for the prematurely ejaculating man, with disruptive anxiety about recurrence on future occasions. Men who have had this problem from their first sexual encounter often try to diminish sexual excitement, by avoidance of stimulation, self-distraction, and "spectatoring," or psychologically taking the role of an observer rather than a participant (Metz, Pryor, Nesvacil, Abuzzahab, & Koznar, 1997).

An exact definition of prematurity is necessarily somewhat arbitrary. Some time ago LoPiccolo (1978) suggested that an inability to tolerate as much as 4 minutes of stimulation without ejaculation is a reasonable indicator that a man may be in need of sex therapy. Such guidelines are not included in DSM-IV and have generally been discarded because they are subject to numerous qualifications (Masters et al., 1992). For example, the age of a client must be considered—the alleged "quick trigger" of the younger man being more than a mere myth (McCarthy, 1989). Approximately half of young men complain of early ejaculation (Frank, Anderson, & Rubenstein, 1978). Not surprisingly, premature ejaculation is most likely after a lengthy abstinence (Malatesta & Adams, 1993; Spiess, Geer, & O'Donohue, 1984). DSM-IV acknowledges these many factors that may affect time to ejaculation by noting that the diagnosis is made only if ejaculation occurs before, on, or shortly after penetration and before the man wants it to. Premature ejaculation is the most prevalent male sexual dysfunction (Laumann et al., 1994; Segraves & Althof, 1998). Indeed some estimate that 15 to 20 percent of American men have at least a moderate degree of difficulty in controlling rapid ejaculation (Masters et al., 1992).

In sexually normal men the ejaculatory reflex is to a considerable extent under voluntary control. They monitor their sensations during sexual stimulation and are somehow able, perhaps by judicious use of distraction, to forestall the point of ejaculatory inevitability until they decide to "let go" (Kaplan, 1987). Premature ejaculators are for some reason unable to use this technique effectively. Explanations have ranged from psychological factors such as increased anxiety (Kaplan, 1987) to physiological factors such as increased penile sensitivity (Gospodinoff, 1989). Presently, however, no explanation has much empirical support.

For many years, sex therapists have primarily considered premature ejaculation to be psychogenically caused and highly treatable via behavioral therapy, such as the pause-and-squeeze technique (Masters & Johnson, 1970). This technique requires the man to monitor his sexual arousal during sexual activity. When arousal is intense enough that the man feels that ejaculation might occur soon, he pauses, and he or his partner squeezes the head of the penis for a few moments, until the feeling of pending ejaculation passes. Initial reports suggested that this technique was approximately 90 percent effective; more recent studies have reported a much lower overall success rate (Rosen & Leiblum, 1995; Segraves & Althof, 1998). In recent years, for men with whom behavioral treatments have not worked, there has been increasing interest in possible use of pharmacological interventions. Antidepressants such as fluoxetine (Prozac) and clomipramine that block serotonin re-uptake have been found to prolong ejaculatory latency in men with premature ejaculation (Rowland & Slob, 1997; Segraves & Althof, 1998); some can be taken about 6 hours before anticipated intercourse, and others must be taken every day. Although available research suggests that these drugs are quite effective, the precise physiological mechanism by which they work remains unclear. Moreover, to date evidence suggests that the drugs work only as long as they are being taken (Segraves & Althof, 1998).

Male Orgasmic Disorder   Sometimes called *retarded ejaculation* or *inhibited male orgasm,* **male orgasmic disorder** refers to the inability to ejaculate during intercourse. Men who are completely unable to ejaculate are rare. About 85 percent of men who have difficulty ejaculating during intercourse can nevertheless achieve orgasm by other means of stimulation, notably through solitary masturbation (Masters et al., 1992). In milder cases a man can ejaculate in the presence of a partner, but only by means of manual or oral stimulation (Kaplan, 1987). On rare occasions retarded ejaculation may be partner-specific; that is, it occurs only with a particular partner but not with others (Apfelbaum, 1989). The problem in these cases is therefore largely one of psychological inhibition or overcontrol, and it thus seems that substantial "symbolic" and interpersonal elements may exist in this dysfunction. Psychological treatments emphasize the reduction of performance anxiety, in addition

to increasing genital stimulation (Rosen & Leiblum, 1995; Segraves & Althof, 1998). In other cases, retarded ejaculation can be related to specific physiological problems such as multiple sclerosis, or the use of certain medications. We noted that antidepressants blocking serotonin re-uptake appear to be an effective treatment for premature ejaculation. In other men, they sometimes delay or prevent orgasm to an unpleasant extent (Ashton, Hamer, & Rosen; 1997; Rosen & Leiblum, 1995). These side effects are common (Gitlin, 1996), but can often be treated pharmacologically (Ahston et al., 1997).

Female Orgasmic Disorder   Many women who are readily sexually excitable and who otherwise enjoy sexual activity nevertheless experience **female orgasmic disorder** (formerly *inhibited female orgasm*)—persistent or recurrent delay in or absence of orgasm following a normal sexual excitement phase. Of these women, many do not routinely experience orgasm during sexual intercourse without direct supplemental stimulation of the clitoris; indeed this pattern is so common that it is not generally considered dysfunctional. A small percentage of women are able to achieve orgasm only through direct mechanical stimulation of the clitoris, as in vigorous digital manipulation, oral stimulation, or the use of an electric vibrator. Even fewer are unable to have the experience under any known conditions of stimulation; this condition is called lifelong orgasmic dysfunction, analogous to lifelong erectile insufficiency in males.

What causes female orgasmic disorder is not well understood but a multitude of contributory factors have been hypothesized. For example, some women feel fearful and inadequate in sexual relations. A woman may be uncertain whether her partner finds her sexually attractive, and this may lead to anxiety and tension that interfere with her sexual enjoyment. Or she may feel inadequate because she is unable to have an orgasm or does so infrequently. Sometimes a nonorgasmic woman will pretend to have orgasms to make her sexual partner feel fully adequate. The longer a woman maintains such a pretense, however, the more likely she is to become confused and frustrated; in addition, she is likely to resent her partner for being insensitive to her real feelings and needs. This in turn only adds to her sexual difficulties.

The diagnosis of orgasmic dysfunction is complicated by the fact that the subjective quality of orgasm varies widely among women, within the same woman from time to time, and depending on mode of stimulation. Thus precise evaluations of occurrence and quality are difficult (Malatesta & Adams, 1993; Segraves & Althof, 1998). The criteria to be applied are also unclear in the vast middle range of orgasmic responsiveness. Most clinicians agree that a woman with lifelong orgasmic disorder needs treatment if she is to become orgasmic, and that a woman at the other extreme who routinely climaxes with relatively brief intercourse, or perhaps even with only breast stimulation or fantasy, does not. Differences of opinion become notable, however, as we move away from these extremes into the range in which most women's experiences actually fall (Masters et al., 1992; Segraves & Althof, 1998). Our own view is that this question is best left to a woman herself to answer; if she is dissatisfied about her responsiveness, and if there is a reasonable likelihood that treatment will help, then she should seek it.

Regarding treatment, it is important to distinguish between lifelong and situational female orgasmic dysfunction. Treatment of the former, typically beginning with instruction and guided practice in masturbating to orgasm, has a high likelihood of success (Andersen, 1983; Segraves & Althof, 1998), while "situational" anorgasmia (where a woman may experience orgasm in some situations, with certain kinds of stimulation, or with certain partners, but not under the precise conditions she desires) often proves more difficult to treat, perhaps in part because it is often associated with relationship difficulties that may also be difficult to treat (Beck, 1992).

Dysfunctions Involving Sexual Pain

Vaginismus   An involuntary spasm of the muscles at the entrance to the vagina (not due to a physical disorder) that prevents penetration and sexual intercourse is called **vaginismus.** Evidently these muscles are readily conditionable to respond with intense contraction to stimuli associated with impending penetration. In some cases, women who suffer from vaginismus also have sexual arousal disorder, possibly as a result of conditioned

fears associated with earlier traumatic sexual experiences. In most cases, however, they show normal sexual arousal but are still afflicted with this disorder (Masters et al., 1992). It is not always possible to identify the "unconditioned stimuli" presumed to have been involved in the acquisition of vaginismus (Kaplan, 1987), probably because the disorder is sometimes "overdetermined" in the sense of having multiple causal links (Segraves & Althof, 1998). This form of sexual dysfunction is relatively rare, but, when it occurs, it is likely to be extremely distressing for both an affected woman and her partner, sometimes leading to erectile or ejaculatory dysfunction in the partner (Leiblum et al., 1989; Segraves & Althof, 1998). Treatment of vaginismus typically involves a combination of banning intercourse, training of the vaginal muscles, and graduated self-insertion of vaginal dilators of increasing size. It generally appears to be effective (Rosen & Leiblum, 1995; Segraves & Althof, 1998).

Dyspareunia   Painful coitus, or **dyspareunia,** can occur in men but is far more common in women (Lazarus, 1989). This is the form of sexual dysfunction most likely to have an obvious organic basis—for example, in association with infections or structural pathology of the sex organs. It may sometimes have a psychological basis, however, as in the case of a woman who has an aversion to sexual intercourse and experiences her displeasure as intense physical discomfort; in such cases the designation "functional" is used. Understandably, dyspareunia is often associated with vaginismus. Treatment of this problem usually requires addressing the specific organic or psychological problems that contribute to it, but often there may also be a conditioned psychological response that needs psychological intervention as well (Segraves & Althof, 1998).

UNRESOLVED ISSUES

Long-Term Consequences of Childhood Sexual Abuse

Does sexual abuse *cause* mental disorders? Many studies during the past decade have linked recollections of childhood sexual abuse with adult psychopathology. Typically, the studies have compared the prevalence of abuse memories in patients (usually women) with and without a certain diagnosis. For example, a study might compare the prevalence of memories of childhood sexual abuse in women with borderline personality disorder to that in women with other personality disorders. The best-established associa-

tions between childhood sexual abuse and adult disorders are with borderline personality disorder (Chapter 9) and dissociative identity disorder (Chapter 7). Relevant studies are often interpreted as showing that childhood sexual abuse is a causal factor in these disorders (Anderson et al., 1993; Paris, Zweig-Frank, & Guzder, 1994; Sanders & Giolas, 1991; Waller, 1994; Glod, 1993; Whitman & Munkel, 1991); however, the available evidence is insufficient to establish a causal link. This is because establishing causation on the basis of retrospective studies is fraught with methodological perils, and furthermore, a number of other plausible interpretations of the findings have not been excluded (Rutter & Maughn, 1997). A recent, highly controversial quantitative review of 59 studies examining the relationship between childhood sexual abuse and more general psychopathology in college students that sexual abuse has on later adjustment (Rind et al., 1998).

First, consider the association between childhood sexual abuse and borderline personality disorder (discussed in Chapter 9). Although early sexual abuse may well cause the personality disorder, a number of other explanations of the association are also conceivable (Bailey & Shriver, in press). For example, it may be family pathology generally, and not sexual abuse per se, that causes borderline personality disorder. In this case sexual abuse would merely be a noncausal correlate of the true causal factors, which might include, for example, hostility between parents or the lack of appropriate expressions of parental love.

Alternatively, relatives of individuals with borderline personality disorder may be genetically or environmentally predisposed to commit impulsive acts such as sexual abuse. There is evidence that borderline personality traits run in families, though it is currently unclear if this is due to genetic factors (Nigg & Goldsmith, 1994). Regardless, this suggests that the association between childhood sexual abuse and adult borderline personality disorder could reflect the familiality of borderline personality traits rather than a causal association.

Another possibility is that this association is with *reports* of childhood sexual abuse rather than its actual occurrence. Persons with borderline personality disorder are known to be highly manipulative. If they believe they could receive extra sympathy by claiming abuse, they may be inclined to do so whether or not it actually occurred. Finally, borderline personality disorder is often characterized by sexual impulsivity. It is conceivable that even during childhood, individuals who will later be diagnosed with borderline personality disorder behaved in ways that made them more vulnerable to sexual advances of exploitative adults.

The association between childhood sexual abuse and dissociative identity disorder (discussed in Chapter 7) raises an additional alternative hypothesis about causation. This is the possibility that both dissociative identity disorder and (false) memories of childhood sexual abuse can be iatrogenic (literally, doctor-produced) phenomena, unintentional by-products of therapy (McHugh, 1992; Spanos, 1994). Highly hypnotizable people are especially likely to produce, under suggestion, a number of responses that resemble symptoms of dissociative identity disorder, including amnesia and the enactment of multiple selves (Spanos, 1994). Indeed,

Nicholas Spanos (1994) has argued that both dissociative identity disorder and hypnotic responding are intentional behaviors aimed at meeting the expectations of experimenters, therapists, or hypnotists. Highly suggestible and hypnotizable people may also be especially likely to produce memories of childhood sexual abuse for therapists who suggest to patients that such abuse is a likely cause of dissociative identity disorder or other problems (McHugh, 1993; Spanos, 1994). Thus, the combination of suggestible patients and overly zealous therapists who "find what they are looking for" may account for the association between memories of sexual abuse and dissociative identity disorder.

We are not asserting that any of these alternatives is more likely than the possibility that sexual abuse causes borderline personality disorder or dissociative identity disorder. Moreover, we do not wish to minimize the pain that true victims of childhood sexual abuse often feel. However, scientific hypotheses succeed by the elimination of plausible rivals. If we wish to understand the consequences of childhood sexual abuse, we shall have to ask, and answer, methodologically and emotionally challenging questions.

Several lines of research may be helpful. For example, prospective studies of sexually abused children could eliminate the possibility that either intentional or unconscious retrospective distortion produced the associations. Similarly, studies following young children could conceivably discern whether certain behavioral tendencies related to adult diagnoses sometimes preceded sexual abuse. Studies of borderline personality disorder patients who were adopted could falsify a genetic hypothesis. If sexual abuse was found to be as common among such patients as among those reared with their biological relatives, this would show that the association was not due to genes causing both borderline personality disorder and sexual abuse. It would also be desirable for theorists to specify more precisely the hypothesized causal mechanisms linking childhood sexual abuse to specific disorders. For example, through what mechanism would childhood sexual abuse so often lead to borderline personality disorder? If theories become more explicit, they will be easier to test.

Researchers of other disorders have faced similar challenges. For example, depression researchers have had to consider several alternative explanations for the association between depression and memories of recent stress, and they have found that the association is not entirely a causal one (Monroe & Simons, 1991). Research on childhood sexual abuse is still in its infancy, and so it is not surprising that available studies are not yet definitive. Progress will require more sophisticated designs and more attention to alternative hypotheses.

SUMMARY

Defining boundaries between normality and psychopathology in the area of variant sexuality may be more difficult than for any other topic covered in this book. Sociocultural influences on what have been viewed as normal or aberrant sexual practices abound, giving us reason to pause when we reflect on our own views of what is aberrant. Degeneracy theory and abstinence theory were very influential for long periods of time in the United States and many other Western cultures and led to very conservative views on heterosexual sexuality. The hypothesis that masturbation can cause insanity was also influential for several centuries and appeared in some psychiatry textbooks until the 1940s. In contrast to Western culture, in Melanesia homosexuality is practiced by all adolescent males in the context of male sexual initiation rites. In young adulthood, they make a rather abrupt transition to heterosexuality, in most cases without apparent difficulty. Until rather recently, in many Western cultures homosexuality was viewed as either criminal behavior or as a form of mental illness. However, since 1972 homosexuality is no longer considered by mental health professionals to be abnormal and is considered a normal sexual variant. Currently much research attention is being directed toward understanding the causal factors that determine sexual orientation. The causal factors being explored include a probable genetic component as well as various environmental variables.

Sexual deviations in the form of paraphilias involve persistent patterns of sexual behavior and arousal in which unusual objects, rituals, or situations are required for full sexual satisfaction. They almost always occur in males. The paraphilias include (1) fetishes (in which sexual interest centers on some inanimate object or anatomical part), (2) transvestic fetishism (which involves sexual arousal occurring through cross-dressing behavior), (3) voyeurism (in which sexual pleasure occurs through clandestine peeping), (4) exhibitionism (in which sexual pleasure occurs when the man exposes his genitals to others without their consent), (5) sadism (in which sexual arousal occurs through inflicting cruelty on one's sexual partner), (6) masochism (in which sexual arousal occurs when pain is inflicted on oneself), and (7) pedophilia (in which sexual attraction occurs to prepubescent children). What causes paraphilias is not well understood. One theory is that males are vulnerable to problems in erotic target location. In this view men are not born with an automatic attraction to either women or men but instead must learn which stimuli constitute a female or male sexual partner. Perhaps some men have nervous systems more prone to errors in targeting; this might explain why so many men with paraphilias have more than one.

Gender identity disorders occur in children and adults. Childhood gender identity disorder occurs in children who have cross-gender identification and gender dysphoria. Most boys who have this disorder grow up to have a homosexual orientation; a few become transsexuals. Prospective studies of girls who have this disorder have not yet been reported. Transsexualism is a very rare disorder in which the person believes that he or she is trapped in the body of the wrong sex. It is now recognized that there are two distinct types of transsexuals: homosexual transsexuals (who are attracted to the people of their same biological sex) and autogynephilic transsexuals (who may be attracted to people of either sex and whose gender dysphoria is related to a paraphilia). The only known effective treatment for transsexuals is a sex-change operation. Although its use remains highly controversial, it does appear to have fairly high success rates when the people are carefully diagnosed as being true transsexuals.

There are three overlapping categories of sexual abuse: pedophilia (another form of paraphilia), incest, and rape. All three kinds of abuse occur at alarming rates today, although it is difficult to estimate their true prevalence. There are also many controversies surrounding how perpetrators of any of these categories of sexual abuse are discovered. These include controversies about the accuracy of children's testimony and about the accuracy of recovered memories of sexual abuse that may often occur in psychotherapy. Pedophiles engage in sexual activity with prepubescent children, and quite commonly they are indifferent to the sex of the child. Incest involves sexual molestation of family members; it overlaps with pedophilia when the sexual molestation is of young children. Rape can occur among strangers or among people who know each other, and involves force or threat of force. All sexual abuse can have serious short-term and long-term consequences for its victims. What leads people to engage in sexual abuse is poorly understood at this time. Treatment of sex offenders has not as yet proved highly effective in most cases, although promising research in this area is being conducted.

Sexual dysfunction involves impairment either in the desire for sexual gratification or in the ability to achieve it. There are generally considered to be four phases of the human sexual response: the desire phase, the excitement phase, the orgasm phase, and the resolution phase. Dysfunctions can occur around any of the first three phases. Both men and women can experience hypoactive sexual desire disorder, in which they have little or no interest in sex. In more extreme cases, they may develop sexual aversion disorder, which involves a strong disinclination to sexual activity. Dysfunctions of the arousal phase include male erectile disorder and female arousal disorder. Male erectile disorder can occur for psychological or physiological reasons, or a combination of the two. Dysfunc-

tions of orgasm for men include premature ejaculation and male orgasmic disorder (retarded ejaculation), and for women include female orgasmic disorder. There are also two sexual pain disorders: vaginismus, which occurs in women, and dyspareunia (painful coitus), which can occur in women and occasionally in men. In the past 25 years remarkable progress has been made in the treatment of sexual dysfunctions, and for some of these dysfunctions the success rates for treatment are quite high.

KEY TERMS

sexual abuse (p. 420)

paraphilias (p. 425)

fetishism (p. 425)

transvestic fetishism (p. 428)

voyeurism (p. 430)

exhibitionism (p. 430)

sadism (p. 431)

masochism (p. 432)

gender identity disorder (p. 434)

cross-gender identification (p. 434)

gender dysphoria (p. 435)

transsexualism (p. 435)

autogynephilia (p. 437)

pedophilia (p. 442)

incest (p. 443)

rape (p. 445)

sexual dysfunction (p. 452)

desire phase (p. 452)

excitement phase (p. 452)

orgasm (p. 452)

resolution (p. 452)

hypoactive sexual desire disorder (p. 453)

sexual aversion disorder (p. 453)

male erectile disorder (p. 454)

female sexual arousal disorder (p. 455)

premature ejaculation (p. 456)

male orgasmic disorder (p. 457)

female orgasmic disorder (p. 457)

vaginismus (p. 458)

dyspareunia (p. 458)

The Schizophrenias and Delusional Disorder

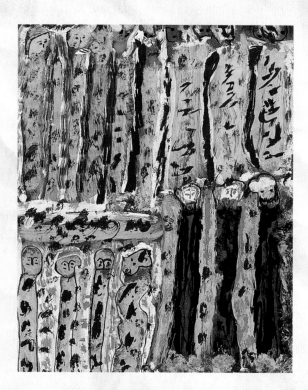

John (*J.B.*) Murry, *Untitled* (1986). After continually seeing visions, J. B. Murry (1908-1988) was first jailed, then hospitalized for his behavior. He later began to draw colorful, ghost-like depictions of his visions, with a script that he said was dictated directly by God. Hundreds of drawings adorned his house in Georgia, where he settled with his family. Murry ceremoniously read his "spirit drawings" to his church congregation, and gave away many of his artworks to church members.

You probably already have some familiarity with the term *schizophrenia*. We use its plural form, **the schizophrenias,** for this chapter title in recognition of the growing consensus that what is meant by "schizophrenia" encompasses several differing types of relatively severe mental disorder. As the American Psychiatric Association (1997) has recently put it, "It is likely that schizophrenia is the final common pathway for a group of disorders with a variety of etiologies, courses, and outcomes" (p. 49).

Nevertheless, the DSM-IV provides diagnostic criteria for only "Schizophrenia," thus treating it as though it were a singular entity. To avoid confusion, therefore, and also for the sake of convenience, we frequently employ the singular form of the term in what follows. It should be understood, however, that the diagnostic criteria for the diagnosis of schizophrenia are probably a manifestation of an unknown number of differing pathological conditions sharing a "final common pathway"—a striking and essential feature: a significant loss of contact with reality, often referred to as **psychosis.**

The hallmark of the schizophrenias is thus a more or less sharp break with the world in which most less disturbed people live, a world that is rooted in a basic consensus about what is true and real in our shared experience. The typical schizophrenic person is someone who has lost or become detached from a set of anchoring points fundamental to adequate mental integration and communication with the surrounding human environment. These individuals may, for example, claim to be God or assert that their brains are hooked up to the CIA via satellite, or they may appear to have "disconnected" themselves from all psychological commerce with other human beings. To those around the schizophrenic person during an active phase of the disorder, he or she appears alien, incomprehensible, unpredictable, and often frightening.

If we look more closely, trying to identify the component processes underlying this detachment from reality, we observe many differing psychological abnormalities in persons whose behavior meets criteria for the schizophrenia diagnosis. These include extreme oddities in action, thinking, perception, feeling, sense of self, and manner of relating to others, with the features displayed varying from one patient to another. This heterogeneity extends well beyond differences in clinically significant behavior and includes marked variations in background features—such as genetic and environmental risk factors, course and duration of the disorder(s) in different people (notably including males versus females), responses to treatment efforts, and the exceptionally wide range of outcomes these patients experience.

This chapter, then, will describe the pieces of the schizophrenia puzzle as we now know them. It is impor-

To those around the schizophrenic person during an active phase of the disorder, he or she appears alien, incomprehensible, unpredictable, and often frightening.

tant that you bear in mind from the outset that not all of the pieces or their presumed interconnections have been found, so our puzzle remains fragmented and incomplete—more so here than perhaps in any other area of psychopathology.

We will in addition consider in this chapter the condition the DSM-IV calls **delusional disorder,** whose main features were formerly included under the classic rubric *paranoia,* or *"true" paranoia* (to distinguish it from the paranoid subtype of schizophrenia, described below). Patients with delusional disorder, like many schizophrenic persons, nurture, give voice to, and sometimes take actions based on, beliefs that are considered completely false and absurd by those around them. Unlike schizophrenic individuals, however, persons with delusional disorder may otherwise behave quite normally. Their behavior does not show the gross disorganization and performance deficiencies characteristic of schizophrenia, and general behavioral deterioration is rarely observed in this disorder, even when it proves chronic.

THE SCHIZOPHRENIAS

The disorders now called schizophrenia were at one time attributed to a type of mental deterioration beginning early in life. In 1860 the Belgian psychiatrist Benedict Morel described the case of a 13-year-old boy who had formerly been the most brilliant pupil in his school but who gradually lost interest in his studies, became increasingly withdrawn, lethargic, seclusive, and quiet, and appeared to have forgotten everything he had learned. He talked frequently of killing his father. Morel thought the boy's intellectual, moral, and physical functions had deteriorated as a result of brain degeneration of hereditary origin, and hence were irrecoverable. He used the term *démence précoce* (mental deterioration at an early age) to describe the condition and to distinguish it from the dementing disorders associated with old age.

Origins of the Schizophrenia Concept

The Latin form of this term—*dementia praecox*—was subsequently adopted in the late nineteenth century by the German psychiatrist Emil Kraepelin to refer to a group of conditions that all seemed to have the feature of mental deterioration beginning early in life. Actually, however, the term is somewhat misleading. There is no compelling evidence of progressive (i.e., worsening over time) brain degeneration in the natural course of the disorder (Cannon, 1998; Russell et al., 1997). Also, where progressive degeneration has been observed, it sometimes appears to have been treatment-induced by virtue of excessive dosing with antipsychotic medication (Cohen, 1997; Gur et al., 1998). We will address this issue further in the section on neuroanatomical factors. Finally, schizophrenic symptoms sometimes make their first appearance well into middle age or beyond, although onset in adolescence or early adulthood is far more typical.

It remained for a Swiss psychiatrist, Eugen Bleuler, to introduce in 1911 a more acceptable descriptive term for this general class of disorders. He used *"schizophrenia"* (split mind) because he thought the condition was characterized primarily by disorganization of thought processes, a lack of coherence between thought and emotion, and an inward orientation away (split off) from reality. The splitting thus does not refer to multiple personalities, an entirely different form of disorder discussed in Chapter 7 (and now called dissociative identity disorder). Instead, in schizophrenia there is a split within the intellect, between the intellect and emotion, and between the intellect and external reality. The subtitle of Bleuler's monograph on the subject (Bleuler, 1911/1950) was *The Group of Schizophrenias,* indicating his own belief in multiple forms in which this basic psychic splitting might be manifested.

Prevalence and Onset

Global prevalence rates for the schizophrenias are difficult to pin down because of substantial variations over time and place in the criteria for defining cases. In addition, cross-cultural research in psychopathology generally is fraught with many pitfalls for the unwary investigator. Among other problems, such research is subject to distorting biases arising where investigators apply the unexamined assumptions of their own culture to observations made about the behavior of members of cultures that may be very different (Tsai et al., in press; Lewis-Fernández & Kleinman, 1994). For example, in some cultures the belief that one is in direct contact with a god who resides in a particular animal or tree is not divorced from reality as it is in our culture. Problems of this sort are likely to be amplified where, as in the case of the schizophrenias, the essential nature of the disordered entity remains conceptually unclear.

Some believe that schizophrenia occurs at an approximately constant rate in most if not all societies of the world. However, the pertinent epidemiological data (e.g., Eaton, 1985; Jablensky et al., 1992; Stevens & Hallick, 1992; Torrey, 1987) do not as a general rule support this uniformity assumption. One exception, recently discussed by Allen (1997), is that schizophrenia appears to be both rarer and of less severe quality in traditional, small-scale societies than it is in modern, well-developed ones. Accordingly, we are hesitant to attempt any sort of global assessment of prevalence rates for the schizophrenias.

We can be more certain of our ground if we concentrate on DSM-defined schizophrenia in the United States, where, as was discussed in Chapter 1, psychiatric epidemiology is relatively advanced. As was reported in that chapter, the *point prevalence* of schizophrenia in the United States is believed to be in the range of 0.2 to 2.0 percent of the population (American Psychiatric Association, 1994). *Lifetime prevalence* is estimated at 0.7 percent among persons not currently institutionalized (Kessler et al., 1994). During any given year approximately 1 percent of adult U.S. citizens, over 2 million persons, meet diagnostic criteria for schizophrenia (Regier et al., 1993). The *incidence* or cumulative occurrence rate of new cases of schizophrenia in the United States could be as high as 0.2 percent per year (Tien & Eaton, 1992).

In recent years schizophrenia has been the primary diagnosis for nearly 40 percent of all admissions to state and county mental hospitals, far outstripping all other diagnostic categories; it has been the second most frequent primary diagnosis (the first being either mood or alcohol-related disorders) for every other type of inpatient psychiatric admission, including private hospitals (Manderscheid et al., 1985). Forty-five percent of schizophrenic persons receiving hospital care during a given year receive that care in state and county mental hospitals, a proportion exceeded only by patients with severe cognitive impairments such as Alzheimer's dementia. During any given year, more than 1 million people in the United States receive outpatient care for a primary diagnosis of schizophrenia (Narrow et al., 1993). Because schizophrenic persons often require prolonged or repeated hospitalization, they have historically occupied about half of all available mental hospital beds in this country.

Although schizophrenic disorders sometimes first occur during childhood or old age, about three-fourths of all initial onsets occur between the ages of 15 and 45, with a median age in the mid-20s. The prevalence rate, overall, appears to be about the same for males and females, but males tend to have earlier onsets (early to mid-20s versus late 20s for females), and many investigators believe males develop more severe forms of these disorders (Iacono & Beiser, 1992; Marcus et al., 1993; Tien & Eaton, 1992). That belief is consistent with a recent brain imaging study by Nopoulos, Flaum, and Andreasen (1997) showing schizophrenia-related anomalies of brain structure (discussed below) to be more severe in male than in female patients. Interestingly, the male-female difference in age of onset reverses with increasing age range, and late-onset (35 and older) schizophrenia is significantly more common among women than men (Jeste & Heaton, 1994). Figure 12.1 depicts this reversal. There is also some evidence that this late-onset pattern in women is associated with a severe clinical presentation (Hafner et al., 1998). The schizophrenias, because of their complexity, their high rate of incidence (especially at the beginning of adult life), and their tendency to recur or become chronic, are considered the most serious of all mental disorders, as well as among the most baffling.

THE CLINICAL PICTURE IN SCHIZOPHRENIA

Since the days of Bleuler, two general symptom patterns or syndromes of schizophrenia have been differentiated. Today they are called **positive-** and **negative-syndrome schizophrenia** (e.g., Andreasen, 1985; Andreasen et al., 1995). Positive signs and symptoms are those in which something has been added to a normal repertoire of behavior and experience, such as marked emotional turmoil, motor agitation, delusional interpretation of events, or hallucinations. Negative signs and symptoms, by contrast, refer to an absence or deficit of behaviors

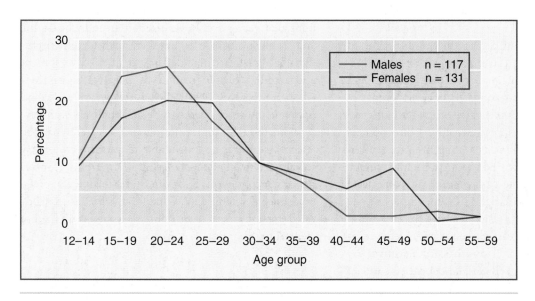

FIGURE 12.1
Age distribution of onset of schizophrenia (first sign of mental disorder) for men and women.
Source: Haffner et al. (1998).

TABLE 12.1 DIAGNOSTIC SIGNS DISTINGUISHING THE POSITIVE-NEGATIVE AND TYPE I–TYPE II SUBSYNDROMES IN SCHIZOPHRENIA

Positive Subsyndrome	Negative Subsyndrome
Hallucinations	Emotional flattening
Delusions	Poverty of speech
Derailment of associations	Asociality
Bizarre behavior	Apathy
Minimal cognitive impairment	Significant cognitive impairment
Sudden onset	Insidious onset
Variable course	Chronic course
Type I	**Type II**
The above plus:	*The above plus:*
Good response to drugs	Uncertain response to drugs
Limbic system abnormalities	Frontal lobe abnormalities
Normal brain ventricles	Enlarged brain ventricles

normally present in a person's repertoire, such as emotional expressiveness, communicative speech, or reactivity to environmental events. A related differentiation, with more emphasis on biological variables and speed of onset, refers to essentially these same patterns as **Type I** and **Type II schizophrenia,** respectively (Crow, 1985). The two systems are compared in Table 12.1. Although most patients exhibit both positive and negative signs during the course of their disorders (Breier et al., 1994; Guelfi, Faustman, & Csernansky, 1989), a preponderance of negative symptoms in the clinical picture has increasingly been shown to have relatively grave prognostic significance (e.g., Fenton & McGlashan, 1994; McGlashan & Fenton, 1993).

In recent years a third pattern, that of disorganized schizophrenia has been recognized as yet another cluster of schizophrenic signs that is partially independent of the other two (e.g., Ratakonda et al., 1998; Toomey et al., 1997). As the term implies, this is a pattern characterized chiefly by chaotic and seemingly directionless speech and behavior, and in fact it has been recognized as one of the classic subtypes of schizophrenia ("hebephrenia") over the past century. To complicate matters, Dolphus and colleagues (1996), employing the statistical technique of cluster analysis, recently suggested that there are at least *four* discriminable patterns of schizophrenia signs: (1) positive, (2) negative, (3) disorganized, and (4) mixed. Since most patients in fact display a "mixed" picture, especially over time, it is not clear that this proposal adds much to our understanding. It may also be noted that "disorganized" behavior

was considered a *negative* sign in earlier formulations of the positive-negative distinction.

It is important to keep in mind that the positivity/negativity distinction is *not* dichotomous. In fact, it is not even necessarily a single dimension. Research evidence indicates that these polar terms would better be conceived as the end points of an uninterrupted continuum, or possibly two separate and largely independent continua, both of which are for some reason involved in manifest schizophrenic behavior.

Whatever the combination or relative proportion of positive and negative signs in particular instances, schizophrenia encompasses many specific manifestations that vary greatly over time in an individual's life and from one person to another. Such largely unpredictable variations include the extent of development and rapidity of progression of negative signs (McGlashan & Fenton, 1993). The basic experience in schizophrenia, however, seems to be disorganization in perception, thought, and emotion to the extent that the affected person is no longer able to perform customary social roles in an adequate fashion. The DSM-IV specifies in concrete terms a list of criteria for the diagnosis, reproduced in Table 12.2. What follows is a more elaborated version of the schizophrenia construct as it has evolved to this point.

Disturbance of Associative Linking

Often referred to as *formal thought disorder,* associative disturbance is usually considered a prime indicator of a

Positive signs and symptoms are those in which something has been added to normal behavior or experience–emotional turmoil, hallucinations, or motor agitation, for example. Negative symptoms, such as depicted here, refer to behavioral and emotional deficits and generally indicate a poorer prognosis.

schizophrenic disorder. Basically, an affected person fails to make sense, despite seeming to conform to the semantic and syntactic rules governing verbal communication. The failure is not attributable to low intelligence, poor education, or cultural deprivation. Meehl (1962) aptly referred to the process as one of "cognitive slippage"; others have referred to it as "derailment" or "loosening" of associations, or "incoherence." However labeled, the phenomenon is readily recognized by experienced clinicians: The patient seems to be using words in combinations that sound communicative, but the listener can understand little or nothing of what point he or she is trying to make. As an example from the files of one of the authors, consider the following excerpt from a letter addressed to Queen Beatrix of the Netherlands by a highly intelligent schizophrenic man:

Case Study, An Example of Cognitive Slippage • I have also "killed" my ex-wife, [name], in a 2.5 to 3.0 hours sex bout in Devon Pennsylvania in 1976, while two Pitcairns were residing in my next room closet, hearing the event. Enclosed, please find my urology report, indicating that my male genitals, specifically my penis, are within normal size and that I'm capable of normal intercourse with any woman, signed by Dr. [name], a urologist and surgeon who performed a circumcision on me in 1982. *Conclusion:* I cannot be a nincompoop in a physical sense (unless Society would feed me chemicals for my picture in the nincompoop book).

This example has a relatively intact structure. In more extreme instances, communication becomes little more than gibberish, a "word salad."

Disturbance of Thought Content

Disturbances in the content of thought typically involve certain standard types of **delusions** or false beliefs (Oltmanns & Maher, 1988). Prominent among these are beliefs that one's thoughts, feelings, or actions are being controlled by external agents; that one's private thoughts are being broadcast indiscriminately to others; that thoughts are being inserted into one's brain by alien forces; that some mysterious agency has robbed one of one's thoughts; or that some neutral environmental event (such as a television program or a billboard) has an intended personal meaning, often termed an "idea of reference." Other absurd propositions, including delusions of grotesque bodily changes, are regularly observed.

Disruption of Perception

Major perceptual disruption often accompanies the criteria already indicated. The patient seems unable to sort out and process the great mass of sensory information to which all of us are constantly exposed. As a result, stimuli overwhelm the meager resources the person has for information processing. This point is illustrated in the following statements of schizophrenic people: "I feel like I'm too alert . . . everything seems to come pouring in at once . . . I can't seem to keep anything out . . . ." "My nerves seem supersensitive . . . objects seem brighter . . . noises are louder . . . my feelings are so intense . . . things seem so vivid and they come at me like a flood from a broken dam." "It

TABLE 12.2   DSM-IV CRITERIA FOR THE DIAGNOSIS OF SCHIZOPHRENIA

A. *Characteristic symptoms:* Two (or more) of the following, each present for a significant portion of time during a 1-month period (or less if successfully treated):

1. delusions
2. hallucinations
3. disorganized speech (e.g., frequent derailment or incoherence)
4. grossly disorganized or catatonic behavior
5. negative symptoms, i.e., affective flattening, alogia [little speech, or little substance of ideas contained in speech], or avolition [deficient or absence of "will"]

Note: Only one Criterion A symptom is required if delusions are bizarre or hallucinations consist of a voice keeping up a running commentary on the person's behavior or thoughts, or two or more voices conversing with each other.

B. *Social/occupational dysfunction:* For a significant portion of the time since the onset of the disturbance, one or more major areas of functioning such as work, interpersonal relations, or self-care are markedly below the level achieved prior to the onset (or when the onset is in childhood or adolescence, failure to achieve expected level of interpersonal, academic, or occupational achievement).

C. *Duration:* Continuous signs of the disturbance persist for at least 6 months. This 6-month period must include at least 1 month of symptoms (or less if successfully treated) that meet Criterion A (i.e., active phase symptoms) and may include periods of prodomal or residual symptoms. During these prodomal or residual periods, the signs of the disturbance may be manifested by only negative symptoms or two or more symptoms listed in Criterion A present in an attenuated form (e.g., odd beliefs, unusual perceptual experiences).

D. *Schizoaffective and Mood Disorder exclusion:* Schizoaffective Disorder and Mood Disorder With Psychotic Features have been ruled out because either (1) no Major Depressive, Manic, or Mixed Episodes have occurred concurrently with active-phase symptoms; or (2) if mood episodes have occurred during active-phase symptoms, their total duration has been brief relative to the duration of the active and residual periods.

E. *Substance/general medical condition exclusion:* The disturbance is not due to the direct physiologic effects of a substance (e.g., a drug of abuse, a medication) or a general medical condition.

F. *Relationship to a Pervasive Developmental Disorder:* If there is a history of Autistic Disorder or another Pervasive Developmental Disorder, the additional diagnosis of Schizophrenia is made only if prominent delusions or hallucinations are also present for at least a month (or less if successfully treated).

Source: American Psychiatric Association, 1994, pp. 285–286.

seems like nothing ever stops. Thoughts just keep coming in and racing round in my head . . . and getting broken up . . . sort of into pieces of thoughts and images . . . like tearing up a picture. And everything is out of control . . . I can't seem to stop it." It is estimated that approximately 50 percent of patients diagnosed as schizophrenic experience this breakdown of perceptual selectivity during the onset of their disorders. Other even more dramatic perceptual phenomena include **hallucinations**—false perceptions, such as voices that only the schizophrenic person can hear. Hallucinations in the schizophrenias are most often auditory, although they can also be visual and even olfactory. The typical hallucination is one in which a voice (or voices) keeps up a running commentary on the person's behaviors or thoughts. Some investigators (e.g., Stern & Silbersweig, 1998) hypothesize that hal-

lucinations in schizophrenia are the result of malfunctioning neural feedback connections between differing brain regions.

Emotional Dysfunction

The schizophrenic syndromes are often said to include an element of clearly inappropriate emotion, or affect. In the more severe or chronic cases, the picture is usually one of apparent anhedonia (inability to experience joy or pleasure) and emotional shallowness or "blunting" (lack of intensity or clear definition). The person may appear virtually emotionless, so that even the most compelling and dramatic events produce at most an intellectual recognition of what is happening. We must be cautious in interpreting this sign, however, because evidence suggests that the deficit is only one of expressiveness, not of feeling per se (Berenbaum & Oltmanns, 1992; Dworkin et al., 1998; Kring, 1998; Kring et al., 1993). In other instances, particularly in the acute phases, the person may show strong affect, but the emotion clashes with the situation or with the content of his or her thoughts. For example, the person may respond to news of a parent's death with gleeful hilarity.

Confused Sense of Self

Schizophrenic persons may feel confused about their identity to the point of loss of a subjective sense of self or of personal agency. Delusional assumption of a new identity, including a unique one such as Jesus Christ or the Virgin Mary, is not uncommon. In other instances the person may be perplexed about aspects of his or her own body, including its gender, or may be uncertain about the boundaries separating the self from the rest of the world. The latter confusion is often associated with frightening "cosmic" or "oceanic" feelings of being somehow intimately tied up with universal powers, including God or the Devil. These feelings appear to be related to ideas of external control and similar delusions.

Disrupted Volition

Goal-directed activity is almost universally disrupted in schizophrenic individuals. The impairment always occurs in areas of routine daily functioning, such as work, social relations, and self-care, such that observers note that the person is not himself or herself any more. The picture is thus one of deterioration from a previously mastered standard of performance in everyday affairs. For example, the person may no longer maintain minimal standards of personal hygiene, or may evidence a profound disregard of personal safety and health. Many researchers attribute these disruptions of "executive" behavior to some sort of impairment in the functioning of the prefrontal region of the cerebral cortex (Lenzeweger & Dworkin, 1998).

Retreat to an Inner World

Ties to the external world are almost by definition loosened in the schizophrenic disorders. In extreme instances the withdrawal from reality seems deliberate and involves active disengagement from the environment. This rejection of the external world may be accompanied by the elaboration of an inner world in which the person develops illogical and fantastic ideas, including the creation of strange beings who interact with the person in various self-directed dramas.

Disturbed Motor Behavior

Various peculiarities of movement are sometimes observed in the schizophrenias; indeed, this is the chief and defining characteristic of catatonic schizophrenia, of which more will be said later. These motor disturbances range from an excited sort of hyperactivity to a marked decrease in all movement or an apparent clumsiness. Also included here are various forms of rigid posturing, mutism, ritualistic mannerisms, and bizarre grimacing.

Continuing Problems in Defining Schizophrenia

As we have seen, what we call "schizophrenia" in all probability encompasses a variety of disordered processes of varied etiology, developmental pattern, and outcome—perhaps more so here than in the case of any other psychiatric diagnosis. This leads to much heterogeneity at the clinical, observational level, which is the level at which DSM diagnoses are with rare exception designed to operate. Pinning down the essential features of "schizophrenic" behavior is therefore more than usually dependent on the judgments of acknowledged experts in the field, rather than on established and reliable scientific data. In fact, criteria for the diagnosis of schizophrenia have varied considerably over the past century (Hegarty et al., 1994). While no reasonable person doubts the reality of the behavioral phenomena described above, it has proved difficult to identify or to formulate in exact terms a common core for this presumed psychopathological entity.

Despite the dramatic quality of the associated clinical phenomena, therefore, it must be kept in mind that schizophrenia remains a *provisional construct* (Andreasen & Carpenter, 1993), one whose definition has evolved and changed over time—with substantial effects on incidence/prevalence rates relative to other disorders (Carson & Sanislow, 1993), and even—as we shall see—on observed clinical outcomes for persons assigned the diagnosis. Criteria for applying the diagnosis will almost certainly change in more than trivial ways with future changes in conceptualization.

TABLE 12.3 TYPES OF SCHIZOPHRENIA

Type	Characteristics
Undifferentiated type	A pattern of symptoms in which there is a rapidly changing mixture of all or most of the primary indicators of schizophrenia. Commonly observed are indications of perplexity, confusion, emotional turmoil, delusions of reference, excitement, dream-like autism, depression, and fear. Most often this picture is seen in patients who are in the process of breaking down and becoming schizophrenic. It is also seen, however, when major changes are occurring in the adjustive demands impinging on a person with an already-established schizophrenic psychosis. In such cases, it frequently foreshadows an impending change to another primary schizophrenic subtype.
Paranoid type	A symptom picture dominated by absurd, illogical, and changeable delusions, frequently accompanied by vivid hallucinations, with a resulting impairment of critical judgment and erratic, unpredictable, and occasionally dangerous behavior. In chronic cases, there is usually less disorganization of behavior than in other types of schizophrenia, and less extreme withdrawal from social interaction.
Catatonic type	Often characterized by alternating periods of extreme withdrawal and extreme excitement, although in some cases one or the other reaction predominates. In the withdrawal reaction there is a sudden loss of all animation and a tendency to remain motionless for hours or even days in a single position. The clinical picture may undergo an abrupt change, with excitement coming on suddenly, wherein an individual may talk or shout incoherently, pace rapidly, and engage in uninhibited, impulsive, and frenzied behavior. In this state, an individual may be dangerous.
Disorganized type	Usually occurs at an earlier age than most other types of schizophrenia, and represents a more severe disintegration of the personality. Emotional distortion and blunting typically are manifested in inappropriate laughter and silliness, peculiar mannerisms, and bizarre, often obscene, behavior.
Residual type	Mild indications of schizophrenia shown by individuals in remission following a schizophrenic episode.

THE CLASSIC SUBTYPES OF SCHIZOPHRENIA

Recent editions of the DSM have listed five subtypes of schizophrenia, based on the differing clinical pictures long thought to be variants of a common theme of disorder; they are summarized in Table 12.3. We will focus on four of these here: undifferentiated, catatonic, disorganized, and paranoid. Of these, the undifferentiated and paranoid types are the most common today.

Undifferentiated Type

As the term implies, the diagnosis of **schizophrenia, undifferentiated type,** is something of a wastebasket category. A person so diagnosed meets the usual criteria for schizophrenia—including (in varying combinations) delusions, hallucinations, disordered thoughts, and bizarre behaviors—but does not clearly fit into one of the other types because of a mixed symptom picture. People in the acute, early phases of a schizophrenic breakdown

frequently exhibit undifferentiated symptoms, as do those who are in transitional phases from one to another of the standard subtypes.

Probably most instances of acute, rapid-onset schizophrenic breakdown occurring for the first time appear undifferentiated in type. However, current diagnostic criteria (that is, DSM-IV) preclude the diagnosis of schizophrenia unless there have been signs of the disorder for at least six months, by which time a stable pattern may develop, consistent with a more definite indication of type. Some schizophrenic patients, on the other hand, remain undifferentiated over long time periods. The case of Rick Wheeler is illustrative of the latter course.

Case Study, He Thought He Could Move Mountains • Rick Wheeler, 26 years old, neatly groomed, and friendly and cheerful in disposition, was removed from an airplane by airport police because he was creating a disturbance—from his own account probably because he was "on another dimension." On arrest, he was oriented to the extent of knowing where he was, his name, and the current date, but his report of these facts was em-

This painting was made by a male patient diagnosed as suffering from undifferentiated schizophrenia. Over a period of about nine years, he did hundreds of paintings in which the tops of the heads of males were always missing, though the females were complete. Although the therapist tried several maneuvers to get him to paint a man's head, the patient never did.

bedded in a peculiar and circumstantial context involving science fiction themes. Investigation revealed he had been discharged from a nearby state mental hospital three days earlier. He was brought to another hospital by police.

On admission, physical examination and laboratory studies were normal, but Rick claimed he was Jesus Christ and that he could move mountains. His speech was extremely difficult to follow because of incoherence and derailment. For example, he explained his wish to leave the city, "because things happen here I don't approve of. I approve of other things but I don't approve of the other things. And believe me it's worse for them in the end." He complained that the Devil wanted to kill him and that his food contained "ground-up corpses." He was born, he claimed, from his father's sexual organs.

Background investigation revealed that Rick's difficulties began, after a successful academic start, in elementary school: "I could comprehend but I couldn't store . . . it's like looking at something but being unable to take it in." He thereafter maintained a D average until he dropped out halfway through his junior year of high school. He had never held a full-time job, and his social adjustment had always been poor. He showed no interest in women until he married, at age 19, a patient he'd met during one of the earliest of some 20 of his hospitalizations, beginning at age 16. A daughter was born from this match, but Rick had lost track of both her and his wife; he had shown no further interest in women. Rick himself was the eldest of five children; there was no known mental disorder in any of his first-degree (that is, siblings and parents) relatives.

Unable to maintain employment, Rick had been supported mainly on federal disability welfare and by virtue of patienthood in public hospitals. His hospital admissions and discharges showed a substantial correlation with his varying financial status; that is, he tended to be released from the hospital around the first of the month, when his welfare check was due, and to be readmitted (or alternatively sent to jail) following some public altercation after his money had run out. Numerous attempts to commit Rick to the hospital indefinitely on an involuntary basis had failed because he was able to appear competent at court appearances. He had, however, been declared incompetent to receive his own checks, and various relatives had stepped forward to handle his finances. Now they are afraid to do so because Rick set his grandmother's house afire, having concluded (erroneously, as it turned out) that she was withholding some of his money. He had also threatened others and had been arrested several times for carrying concealed weapons.

In the latest hospitalization, two different antipsychotic medications were tried over a period of five weeks with no discernible improvement. Rick still claimed supernatural powers and special connections with several national governments; was still refusing food because of its contamination with ground corpses; and was still threatening bodily harm to people he found uncooperative. A further attempt was made to commit him and to place his affairs under legal guardianship. As Rick had rather boastfully predicted, this attempt failed because of his lucid defense of himself, and the court dismissed the action. He was discharged to a protected boarding house but disappeared four days later. (Adapted from Spitzer et al., 1983, pp. 153–155)

Most patients who show this type of chaotic, undifferentiated pattern do not have the early and slowly developing, insidious onset—one associated with poor prognosis—that we see in Rick's case. On the contrary, the breakdown erupts suddenly out of the context of a seemingly unremarkable life history, usually following a period of notable stress. The episode usually clears up in a matter of weeks or, at most, months. Recurrent episodes, however, are not uncommon, especially in the absence of vigorous follow-up treatment. Should this "schizophreniform" (see below) disturbance exceed six months duration, it may qualify for the diagnosis of schizophrenia. In some few instances, treatment efforts are unsuccessful, and the mixed symptoms of the early undifferentiated disorder slide into a more chronic phase, typically developing both the more specific symptoms of other subtypes as well as increasingly severe negative symptoms.

Catatonic Type

The central feature of **schizophrenia, catatonic type,** is pronounced motor signs, either of an excited or a stuporous type, which sometimes make for difficulty in differentiating this condition from a psychotic mood disorder. The clinical picture is often an early manifestation of a disorder that will become chronic and intractable unless the underlying process is somehow arrested. Though at one time common in Europe and North America, catatonic reactions have become less frequent in recent years.

Some of these patients are highly suggestible and will automatically obey commands or imitate the actions of others (echopraxia) or mimic their phrases (echolalia). If a patient's arm is raised to an awkward and uncomfortable position, he or she may keep it there for minutes or even hours. Ordinarily, patients in a catatonic stupor stubbornly resist any effort to change their position and may become mute, resist all attempts at feeding, and refuse to comply with even the slightest request. They pay no attention to bowel or bladder control and may drool. Their facial expression is typically vacant, and their skin appears waxy. Threats and painful stimuli have no effect, and they may have to be dressed and washed by nursing personnel.

Catatonic patients may pass suddenly from states of extreme stupor to great excitement, during which they seem to be under great "pressure of activity" and may become violent, being in these respects indistinguishable from some bipolar manic patients. They may talk or shout excitedly and incoherently, pace rapidly back and forth, openly indulge in sexual activities, attempt self-mutilation or even suicide, or impulsively attack and try to kill others. The suddenness and extreme frenzy of these attacks make such patients dangerous to both themselves and others. The following case illustrates some of the symptoms typical of catatonic reactions.

Case Study, Catatonia in a 16-Year-Old • Todd Phillips, a 16-year-old high school student, was referred to a psychiatric hospital by his family physician. His family had been very upset by his increasingly strange behavior over the preceding eight months. They had consulted their family physician, who treated him with small doses of antipsychotic medication, without any improvement.

Although Todd has had many problems since he was a small child, there was a distinct change about eight months ago. He began spending more and more time in his room and seemed uninterested in doing many of his usual activities. His grades dropped. He started stuttering. He used to weigh about 215 pounds, but began to eat less, and lost 35 pounds. For no apparent reason, he started drinking large quantities of water.

More recently, there was a change for the worse. A few months ago he began taking Tai Chi lessons and often stood for long periods in karatelike positions, oblivious to what was going on around him. He stopped doing his homework. He took an inordinately long time to get dressed, eat his meals, or bathe. Before getting dressed in the morning he would go through an elaborate ritual of arranging his clothes on the bed before putting them on. When his parents asked him a question, he repeated the question over and over and did not seem to hear or understand what was said.

At school he received demerits for the first time for being late to class. His family began to lose patience with him when he eventually refused to go to school. When his father tried to get him out of bed in the morning, he lay motionless, sometimes having wet the bed during the night. It was at this point that his parents, in desperation, consulted their family physician.

When first seen in the hospital, Todd was a disheveled looking, somewhat obese adolescent, standing motionless in the center of the room with his head flexed forward and his hands at his sides. He appeared perplexed, but was correctly oriented to time and place. He was able to do simple calculations, and his recent and remote memory were intact. He answered questions slowly and in a peculiar manner. An example of his speech follows:

Q: Why did you come to the hospital?

A: Why did I come? Why did I come to the hospital? I came to the hospital because of crazy things with my hands. Sometimes my hands jump up like that . . . wait a minute . . . I guess its happening. . . . Well, yes, see it's been happening [Makes robotlike gestures with his hands.]

Q: What thoughts go through your head?

A: What thoughts go through my head? What thoughts go through my head? Well, I think about things . . . like . . . yes, well . . . I think thoughts . . . I have thoughts. I think thoughts.

Q: What thoughts?

A: What thoughts? What kinds of thoughts? I think thoughts.

Q: Do you hear voices?

A: Do I hear voices? I hear voices. People talk. Do I hear voices? No. . . . People talk. I hear voices. I hear voices when people talk.

Q: Are you sick?

A: Am I sick? No I'm not sick . . . these fidgeting habits, these fidgeting habits. I have habits. I have fidgeting habits.

Throughout the examination he made repetitive chewing and biting motions. Occasionally, when questioned, he would smile enigmatically. He seemed unresponsive to much of what was going on around him. His infrequent movements were slow and jerky, and he often assumed the karatelike postures that his parents described, in which he would remain frozen. If the examiner placed the patient's hands in an awkward position the patient remained frozen in that position for several minutes. (Spitzer et al., 1983, pp. 139–140)

Although the matter is far from settled, some clinicians interpret a catatonic patient's immobility as a way of coping with his or her reduced filtering ability and increased vulnerability to stimulation: It seems to provide a feeling of some control over external sources of stimulation, though not necessarily over inner ones. Freeman (1960) has cited the explanation advanced by one patient: "I did not want to move, because if I did everything changed around me and upset me horribly so I remained still to hold onto a sense of permanence" (p. 932).

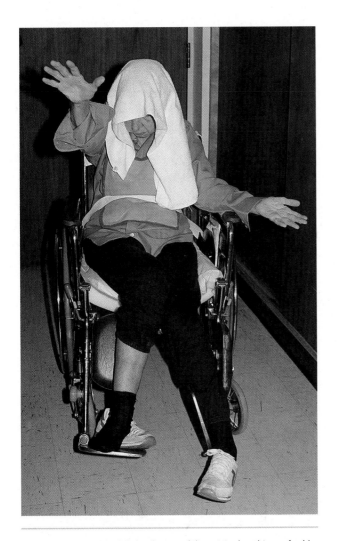

Peculiar posturing is a defining feature of the catatonic subtype of schizophrenia.

Disorganized Type

Compared with the other subtypes of schizophrenia, **schizophrenia, disorganized type,** usually occurs at an earlier age and represents a more severe disintegration of the personality. Fortunately, like catatonia, it is relatively uncommon. In pre-DSM-III classifications, this type was called *hebephrenic* schizophrenia.

Typically, an affected person has a history of oddness, overscrupulousness about trivial things, and preoccupation with obscure religious and philosophical issues. Frequently, he or she broods over the dire results of masturbation or minor infractions of social conventions. While schoolmates are enjoying normal play and social activities, this person gradually becomes more seclusive and more preoccupied with fantasies.

As the disorder progresses, the person becomes emotionally indifferent and infantile. A silly smile and inappropriate, shallow laughter after little or no provocation are common symptoms. If asked the reason for his or her laughter, the patient may state that he or she does not know or may volunteer some wholly irrelevant and unsatisfactory explanation. Speech becomes incoherent and may include considerable baby talk, childish giggling, a repetitious use of similar-sounding words, and a derailing of associated thoughts that may give a punlike quality to speech. The patient may invent new words (neologisms). In some instances, speech becomes wholly incomprehensible.

Hallucinations, particularly auditory ones, are common. The voices heard by these patients may accuse them of immoral practices, "pour filth" into their minds, and call them vile names. Delusions are usually of a sexual, religious, hypochondriacal, or persecutory nature, and they are typically changeable, unsystematized, and fantastic. For example, one woman insisted not only that she was being followed by enemies but that she had already been killed a number of times. Another claimed that a long tube extended from the Kremlin directly to her uterus, through which she was being invaded by Russians.

In occasional cases, individuals become hostile and aggressive. They may exhibit peculiar mannerisms and other bizarre forms of behavior. These behaviors may take the form of odd facial grimaces; talking and gesturing to themselves; sudden, inexplicable laughter and weeping; and in some cases an abnormal interest in urine and feces, which they may smear on walls and even on themselves. Obscene behavior and the absence of any modesty or sense of shame are characteristic. Although they may exhibit outbursts of anger and temper tantrums in connection with fantasies, they are indifferent to real-life situations, no matter how horrifying or gruesome the latter may be. The clinical picture in disorganized schizophrenia is exemplified in the following interview.

Case Study, "I am a 'looner' . . . a bachelor" • The patient was a divorcee, 32 years of age, who had come to the hospital with bizarre delusions, hallucinations, and severe personality disintegration. She had a record of alcoholism, promiscuity, and possible incestuous relations with a brother. The following conversation shows typical hebephrenic responses to questioning.

DOCTOR: How do you feel today?

PATIENT: Fine.

DOCTOR: When did you come here?

PATIENT: 1416, you remember, doctor [silly giggle].

DOCTOR: Do you know why you are here?

PATIENT: Well, in 1951 I changed into two men. President Truman was judge at my trial. I was convicted and hung [silly giggle]. My brother and I were given back our normal bodies 5 years ago. I am a policewoman. I keep a dictaphone concealed on my person.

DOCTOR: Can you tell me the name of this place?

PATIENT: I have not been a drinker for 16 years. I am taking a mental rest after a "carter" assignment or "quill." You know, a "penwrap." I had contracts with Warner Brothers Studios and Eugene broke phonograph records but Mike protested. I have been with the police department for 35 years. I am made of flesh and blood—see doctor [pulling up her dress].

DOCTOR: Are you married?

PATIENT: No. I am not attracted to men [silly giggle]. I have a companionship arrangement with my brother. I am a "looner" . . . a bachelor.

The prognosis is generally poor if a person develops disorganized schizophrenia. At this stage of deterioration no form of treatment intervention yet discovered has a high likelihood of effecting more than a modest recovery.

Paranoid Type

Formerly about one-half of all schizophrenic first admissions to hospitals were diagnosed as **schizophrenia, paranoid type.** In recent years, however, the prevalence of the paranoid type has shown a substantial decrease, while the undifferentiated type has shown a marked increase. The reasons for these changes are uncertain but may relate to the promptness with which newly diagnosed schizophrenic (or schizophreniform) patients are now put on antipsychotic medication, which has an especially powerful effect in suppressing "positive" symptoms such as paranoid delusions.

Frequently, paranoid-type schizophrenic persons show histories of increasing suspiciousness and of severe difficulties in interpersonal relationships. The eventual clinical picture is dominated by absurd, illogical, and often changing delusions. Persecutory delusions are the most frequent and may involve a wide range of bizarre ideas and plots. An individual may become highly suspicious of relatives or associates and may complain of being watched, followed, poisoned, talked about, or influenced by various tormenting devices rigged up by "enemies."

In addition to persecutory themes, themes of grandeur are also common in paranoid-type delusions. Persons with such delusions may, for example, claim to be the world's greatest economist or philosopher, or some prominent person of the past, such as Franklin Roosevelt, Joan of Arc, or even God. These delusions are frequently accompanied by vivid auditory, visual, and other hallucinations. Patients may hear singing, or God speaking, or the voices of their enemies, or they may see angels or feel damaging rays piercing their bodies at various points.

An individual's thinking and behavior become centered on the themes of persecution, grandeur, or both in a pathological "paranoid construction" that—for all its distortion of reality—provides a sense of identity and importance perhaps not otherwise attainable for the person. There thus tends to be a higher level of adaptive coping and of cognitive integrative skills in a paranoid-type schizophrenic person than in other schizophrenic individuals, although these differences are not large and are not consistent across all cognitive domains (Zalewski et al., 1998).

Despite this modest relative "advantage" that paranoid-type schizophrenic individuals enjoy, such people are far from easy to deal with. The weaving of delusions and hallucinations into a paranoid construction results in a loss of critical judgment and in erratic, unpredictable behavior. In response to a command from a "voice," such a person may commit violent acts. Thus, paranoid schizophrenic patients can sometimes be dangerous, as when they attack people they are convinced have been persecuting them. Somewhat paradoxically, such problems are exacerbated by the fact that such people show less bizarre behavior and less extreme withdrawal from the outside world than individuals with other types of schizophrenia; as a consequence, they are less likely to be confined in protective environments.

The following conversation between a clinician and a man diagnosed as having chronic paranoid schizophrenia illustrates well the illogical, delusional symptom picture, together with continued attention to misinterpreted sensory data, that these individuals experience:

A patient diagnosed as a paranoid schizophrenic was unable to respond at all when asked by a therapist to make an original drawing. Therefore, with the therapist's help, a picture (top left) was selected from a magazine for the patient to copy. One of his first attempts (top right) was a pencil drawing on manila paper showing great visual distortion, as well as an inability to use colors and difficulty in using letters of the alphabet. The evident visual distortion was a diagnostic aid for the therapist, who was able to learn from it that the patient, who was extremely fearful, saw things in this distorted way, aggravating his fear. In the picture at bottom left, the patient has shown obvious improvement, although it was not until a year after therapy began that he was able to execute a painting with the realism of the picture at bottom right.

Case Study, A Case of Paranoid Schizophrenia

DOCTOR: What's your name?

PATIENT: Who are you?

DOCTOR: I'm a doctor. Who are you?

PATIENT: I can't tell you who I am.

DOCTOR: Why can't you tell me?

PATIENT: You wouldn't believe me.

DOCTOR: What are you doing here?

PATIENT: Well, I've been sent here to thwart the Russians. I'm the only one in the world who knows how to deal with them. They got their spies all around here though to get me, but I'm smarter than any of them.

DOCTOR: What are you going to do to thwart the Russians?

PATIENT: I'm organizing.

DOCTOR: Whom are you going to organize?

PATIENT: Everybody. I'm the only man in the world who can do that, but they're trying to get me. But I'm going to use my atomic bomb media to blow them up.

DOCTOR: You must be a terribly important person then.

PATIENT: Well, of course.

DOCTOR: What do you call yourself?

PATIENT: You used to know me as Franklin D. Roosevelt.

DOCTOR: Isn't he dead?

PATIENT: Sure he's dead, but I'm alive.

DOCTOR: But you're Franklin D. Roosevelt?

PATIENT: His spirit. He, God, and I figured this out. And now I'm going to make a race of healthy people. My agents are lining them up. Say, who are you?

DOCTOR: I'm a doctor here.

PATIENT: You don't look like a doctor. You look like a Russian to me.

DOCTOR: How can you tell a Russian from one of your agents?

PATIENT: I read eyes. I get all my signs from eyes. I look into your eyes and get all my signs from them.

DOCTOR: Do you sometimes hear voices telling you someone is a Russian?

PATIENT: No, I just look into eyes. I got a mirror here to look into my own eyes. I know everything that's going on. I can tell by the color, by the way it's shaped.

DOCTOR: Did you have any trouble with people before you came here?

PATIENT: Well, only the Russians. They were trying to surround me in my neighborhood. One day they tried to drop a bomb on me from the fire escape.

DOCTOR: How could you tell it was a bomb?

PATIENT: I just knew.

Despite a considerable longevity, the formal subtyping scheme described above has never proved very productive either clinically (e.g., patients frequently and apparently spontaneously change in subtype over time) or in shedding light on more basic issues such as the nature of a "common core," if any, of the schizophrenia experience.

Other Schizophrenic Patterns

The remaining subcategories of schizophrenia contained in DSM-IV deserve brief mention. **Schizophrenia, residual type,** which is the fifth officially recognized type of schizophrenia, is a category used for people who have experienced an episode of schizophrenia from which they have recovered sufficiently so as not to show prominent psychotic symptoms. They nevertheless still manifest some mild signs of their past disorder, such as odd beliefs, flat affect, or eccentric behavior.

As was noted in Chapter 6, the term **schizoaffective disorder** (bipolar or depressive subtype) is applied to individuals who show features of both schizophrenia and severe affective disorder. In the DSM-IV classification, this disorder is not considered to be a formal subtype of schizophrenic disorder, although it is listed in the same section of the manual and shares the numerical code of the schizophrenias. Thus, although treated as a separate disorder, its status within the DSM system is left somewhat unclear—reflecting some continuing controversy in the field as to where it really belongs.

Schizophreniform disorder is a category reserved for schizophrenia-like psychoses of less than six months duration. It may include any of the symptoms described in the preceding sections but is probably most often seen in an undifferentiated form. Brief psychotic states of this sort may or may not be related to subsequent psychiatric disorder (Strakowski, 1994). At present, however, all recent-onset cases of true schizophrenia presumably must first receive a diagnosis of schizophreniform disorder. Because of the possibility of an early and lasting remission in a first episode of schizophrenic breakdown, prognosis for schizophreniform

disorder (where it is a manifestation of recent-onset schizophrenic symptoms) is better than for established forms of schizophrenia, and it appears likely that by keeping it out of the formal category of schizophrenic disorder the potentially harmful effects of labeling may be reduced.

Causal Factors in Schizophrenia

Despite an enormous research effort going back many years and continuing to the present day, the causal factors underlying the schizophrenias remain unclear, particularly in their details. Primary responsibility has been attributed variously to (1) biological factors; (2) psychosocial factors, including pathogenic interpersonal and family patterns, and decompensation under excessive stress; and (3) sociocultural factors, especially as influences on the types and local prevalence of schizophrenic disorders. These three sets of factors are not mutually exclusive, of course, and it seems likely that each is involved in at least some cases. We will discuss biological factors first and in relatively greater detail because of the prominence they have attained in contemporary thinking about schizophrenia.

Biological Factors in Schizophrenia

Research relating to biological factors implicated in the causal pattern leading to schizophrenia has been concentrated on genetics and on various biochemical, neurophysiological, and neuroanatomical processes. Each of these research foci will be discussed in what follows.

Genetic Influences It has been known for many decades that disorders of the schizophrenic type tend to "run in families," giving rise to the notion of "tainted" genes as an important causal factor. In fact, the evidence for higher-than-expected rates of schizophrenia among biological relatives of "index" cases (that is, the diagnosed group of people who provide the starting point for inquiry, also called "probands") is overwhelming. Moreover, that evidence includes a strong correlation between closeness of the blood relationship (i.e., level of gene-sharing or consanguinity) and degree of concordance for the diagnosis, as depicted in Figure 12.2.

Of course, and as we have repeatedly emphasized, the interpretation of such familial concordance patterns is never completely straightforward, in part because of the strong relationship between the sharing of genes and the sharing of the environments in which those genes express themselves. As the genetic research itself teaches us, individual environments (including prenatal ones) have a powerful effect in determining outcomes with respect to schizophrenia (Moldin & Gottesman, 1997). Thus evidence of a shared family trait, while persuasive, remains incomplete because of the difficulty of figuring out where genetic influences end and environmental ones begin.

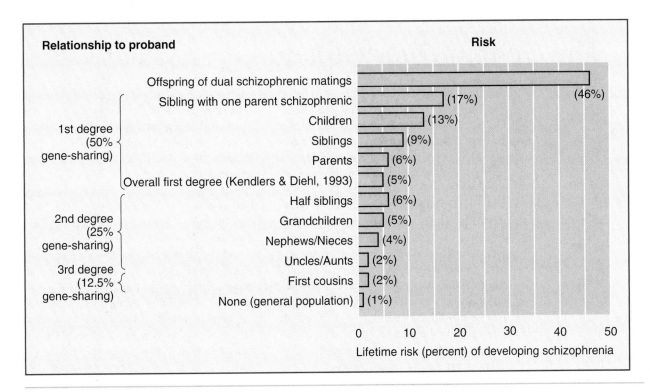

FIGURE 12.2

Lifetime risk of developing schizophrenia as a function of closeness of blood relationship (consanguinity). Adapted from Gottesman (1991). Included is a somewhat discrepant risk estimate derived from a thorough analysis of worldwide data on first-degree relatives of schizophrenic probands by Kendler and Diehl (1993). Discrepancies of this sort are not unusual in such "pedigree" research, reflecting differences in approach as well as biased observations. Twin concordance data are omitted here, but are presented in Figure 12.3.

Indeed, it is entirely possible—if not likely—that implicated genes may sometimes most importantly express themselves through their control of the environments to which individuals are exposed (Kraemer, 1997; Phelps, Davis, & Schwartz, 1997; Rutter, 1997; Saudino, 1997). For example, an inherited temperament such as *introversion* will almost certainly determine in some measure the reactions of the social environment to the person who has it. A shy person may tend to go unnoticed or be socially inept from lack of experience and social anxiety. If environmental reactions materially contribute to the occurrence of disorder, say depression or paranoid suspiciousness, it would be misleading at best to assign causal prominence to the person's genes, when in fact the more direct and immediate cause may be a noxious environmental response.

The still-open question of the direct heritability of schizophrenia-proneness would be easier to answer if we could (1) identify the exact mechanism whereby gene biochemical products (and those are the only immediate products genes have) alter the probability of becoming schizophrenic and/or (2) isolate and identify the particular gene or genes involved. Unfortunately, and despite the dramatic progress of genetics research in recent years, neither of these seems at present an attainable goal. While some investigators continue to hold the view that the genetic influence in schizophrenia is confined to one or at most a very few genes, the evidence points strongly toward *polygenic* involvement. That is, current expert thinking emphasizes the notion of a multiplicity of genes that must somehow operate in concert to enhance the genetic schizophrenia risk (Gottesman, 1991; Kendler & Diehl, 1993; Moldin & Gottesman, 1997). If that proves to be the case, pinning down the genes involved will be a very difficult undertaking, as confirmed in a recent study attempting to identify genes common to schizophrenia by Levinson and colleagues (1998).

It will be helpful for the student to bear in mind these continuing uncertainties as we review below the available data on twin and adoption studies of schizophrenia.

Twin Studies   The general strategy of twin studies was discussed in Chapter 3 and more specifically in relation to anxiety and mood disorders in Chapters 5 and 6. As with the mood disorders, schizophrenia concordance rates for identical twins are routinely, and over very many studies, found to be significantly higher than those for fraternal twins or ordinary siblings. The most famous case of concordance for schizophrenia among identical siblings is the Genain quadruplets, summarized in Highlight 12.1.

The Genain Quadruplets

Sometime in the early 1930s, quadruplet girls were born to Mr. and Mrs. Henry Genain, the product of a marriage occasioned by Mr. Genain's threatening to kill the reluctant Mrs. Genain unless she consented to it. Except for their low birth weights, ranging from Nora's 4 1b, 8 oz., to Hester's 3 1b (Iris and Myra being in-between), the girls appeared to be reasonably normal babies, albeit premature. Hester had to be fitted with a truss (an abdominal compression device) because of a hernia but was nevertheless discharged from the hospital with her sisters as basically healthy some six weeks after the birth. Each of these genetically identical girls was to become schizophrenic before the age of 25, an outcome that would be expected to occur by chance only once in approximately 1.5 billion births. What we know of this family is the product of an intensive and lengthy on-site study carried out by staff of the National Institute of Mental Health (Rosenthal, 1963) and provides a window on the interacting influences operating in the schizophrenias.

Notwithstanding their genetic identity and physical similarity, the girls were treated as though they were two sets of twins—a superior and talented set consisting of Nora and Myra, and an inferior, problematic set consisting of Iris and Hester. Hester—the "runt of the litter"—was regarded from an early age as oversexed. (Possibly because of irritation from her truss, Hester began to masturbate regularly by the age of three, a habit she continued for many years to the dismay of her parents.) Complying with parental attributions, the girls did in fact pair up for purposes of mutual support and intimacy; when threatened from the outside, however, they became a true foursome. Such threats were frequent because of the girls' celebrity status, causing them to become socially isolated. This isolation was encouraged by their parents, both of whom had anxieties of their own about "the outside world."

Mr. Genain's job was not very demanding, and he spent most of his time drinking and expressing his various fears and obsessions to his family. Prominent among these were fears that break-ins would occur at the home unless he patrolled the premises constantly with a loaded gun, and, especially as the girls developed into adolescence, that they would get into sexual trouble or be raped unless he watched over them with total dedication. He imposed extreme restrictions and surveillance on the girls until the time of their breakdowns. Beginning at an early age and persisting through early adulthood, Mr. Genain insisted on being present when his daughters dressed and undressed. He even insisted on watching them change their sanitary pads during menstruation. He was himself sexually promiscuous and was reported to have sexually molested at least two of his daughters.

Mr. Genain's preoccupation with sexuality, while extreme, was matched by that of his wife. Mrs. Genain managed to see sexuality and sexual threats in the most innocuous circumstances and yet seemingly ignored real sexual

activity occurring in the home. When the girls complained to her about Mr. Genain's sexual approaches, she rationalized that Mr. Genain was merely testing their virtue; if they objected to his advances, then clearly all was well. Hester, the chronic masturbator, was a particular thorn in her side—all the more so when she discovered that, at about age 12, Hester had introduced Iris to the practice of mutual masturbation, which Iris found pleasing. Apparently unable to think of any more appropriate response to this dilemma, the parents—on the questionable advice of a physician—forced the two girls to submit to clitoral circumcisions, a drastic measure but one that nevertheless failed to alter the offending behavior.

Hester had her first breakdown while still in high school, at age 18. Nora's breakdown followed, at age 20. Iris "just went to pieces" at age 22. Myra, who had maintained the most independence from her disturbed parents, did not show signs of schizophrenia until age 24. It may be significant that in the cases of Nora, Iris, and Myra, deterioration began shortly after an incident in which a man had made rather insistent "improper advances." The initial clinical pictures displayed by the young women were in most respects quite similar, with undifferentiated and changing features and an abundance of "positive" signs.

Despite these early clinical similarities, the courses and outcomes of their disorders differed markedly and, to some extent, in ways that might have been predicted from manifestations that appeared quite early. The quads' outcomes show a corresponding pattern. At the time of Rosenthal's 1963 report, Myra was working steadily, married, and doing well. Nora was making a marginal adjustment outside the hospital. Iris was still fluctuating between periods of severe disturbance and relative lucidity in which she could manage brief stays outside of the hospital. Hester remained continuously hospitalized in a condition of severe psychosis and was considered essentially a "hopeless case."

It is a tribute to the scientific diligence of the NIMH staff and to David Rosenthal, who maintained both a human and a scientific interest in this unfortunate family, that we had a follow-up report some 20 years after the original one (DeLisi et al., 1984; Mirsky et al., 1984; Sargent, 1982a). In general, the relative adjustment of the sisters, then in their 50s, remained in 1982 as it had been in the 1960s. Myra continued to do well and had had two children in the interim. The other three women were living at home with their mother, with Nora continuing to show a higher level of functioning than Iris or Hester. All of the quads were on continuous medication, and even the beleaguered Hester appeared to have overcome to an extent her originally dismal prognosis.

It is of considerable interest that newly developed techniques of neurological assessment showed that Nora had impairments of the central nervous system similar to those of Hester, and yet her outcome seemed far better than that of Hester or even Iris. It is possible that the original pairing of Iris with Hester was inappropriate (at least in the limited sense implied here) and destructive of Iris's development. In any event, we see that the quads, despite their identical heredity, array themselves along a considerable range of the possible outcomes associated with schizophrenic breakdown.

We have here, then, four genetically identical women, all of whom experienced schizophrenic disorders. The disorders, however, have been different in severity, chronicity, and eventual outcome. Obviously these differences must be ascribed to differences in the environments the quads experienced, including their intrauterine environments, which presumably contributed to their modest variations detectable at birth. Clearly Hester, possibly most compromised biologically and in relative parental disfavor from the beginning, faced the harshest environmental conditions, followed closely by her "twin," Iris. The outcome for these women has been grim. Myra was the most favored youngster and the one who experienced the least objectionable parental attention, partly owing to a greater independence and assertiveness than her sisters displayed. Nora was a close second in this respect but had the misfortune of being her incestuous father's "favorite." In the more recent assessments, Nora was also shown to have a compromised central nervous system (specifically, an imbalance of metabolic rates in different brain areas) comparable to that of Hester. Though Nora has not done as well as Myra, she has emerged as clearly superior in functioning to the other two sisters. We see here the considerable power of environmental forces in determining personal destiny, even in schizophrenia. ■

Although the incidence of schizophrenia among twins is no greater than for the general population, study after study has shown a higher concordance for schizophrenia among identical (monozygotic—MZ) twins over people related in any other way, including fraternal (dizygotic—DZ) twinship. Depending on a variety of factors, the degree of this difference varies substantially from one study to another.

Torrey and colleagues (1994) have published a review of the major literature worldwide on twin studies in schizophrenia. Their findings are summarized in Figure 12.3. Noting in particular overall pairwise concordance rates of 28 and 6 percent in MZ versus DZ twinships, respectively, we may conclude that a reduction in shared genes from 100 percent to 50 percent reduces the risk of schizophrenia nearly 80 percent. Also, 50 percent gene-sharing with a schizophrenic proband is associated with a lifetime risk (6 percent) that, while low in absolute terms, is markedly higher than that of the general population.

If schizophrenia were exclusively a genetic disorder, the concordance rate for identical twins would, of course, be 100 percent. In fact, however, there are more discordant than concordant pairs. On the other hand, concordance of significant magnitude clearly exists, and twin studies show us that predisposition for the disorder is associated with genetic variables. As already noted, the correct interpretation of this finding is not as straightforward as one might wish.

A good example of these interpretive hazards is provided in studies of identical twins who are discordant for the diagnosis of schizophrenia. These are sets of twins in which one member of the pair meets diagnostic criteria for schizophrenia but the other does not. Such cases, because they render the genetic variable constant, have the potential of revealing postnatal environmental factors critical in the development of schizophrenia. Unfortunately, this ideal turns out to be difficult, perhaps impossible, to realize. As pointed out by Torrey and colleagues (1994), we can be certain that identical twins are in fact biologically identical only at the moment of the original splitting of the zygote. From that point on, recent studies show, a host of influences may intervene that could differentially affect the development of the two embryos. These include chromosomal changes and gene mutations, differences in circulation and oxygenation, differential response on exposure to infectious agents and to drugs and chemicals, and congenital brain anomalies.

These potentially disruptive conditions, when they occur, are more likely to be shared by MZ than by DZ twins. As recently pointed out by Phelps, Davis, and Schwartz (1997), for example, some two-thirds of MZ embryos are "monochorionic," meaning they share their blood supply; so far as has been determined DZ twins never do. The higher concordance rate for schizophrenia in MZ than in DZ twins might be a consequence, at least in part, of a higher rate of shared pathogenic factors

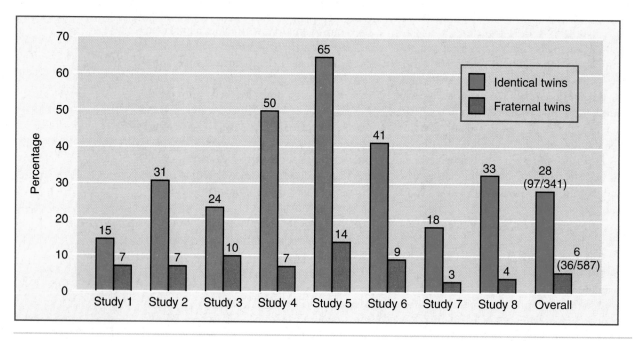

FIGURE 12.3

Pairwise twin concordance rates for schizophrenia found in eight methodologically adequate studies (adapted from Torrey et al., 1994, p. 11).

other than tainted genes—for example, an inadequate maternal blood supply, which would affect MZ embryos more similarly than DZ ones. Another possibility is that shared genes produce a shared anomalous condition, such as retarded motor coordination, which then may adversely affect the twins' development in similar or dissimilar ways.

The most thorough and searching of available investigations of discordant schizophrenia outcomes among MZ twins was reported by Torrey and colleagues (1994). The study involved 27 pairs of MZ twins who were discordant for the schizophrenia diagnosis. The main statistically significant differences separating the schizophrenic from their nonschizophrenic co-twins were as follows:

- Approximately 30 percent of the discordant *affected* twins were described as having been different during early childhood (e.g., shy and withdrawn, aggressive, or odd). Many of these differences were suggestive of early central nervous system dysfunction.

- Discordant affected twins showed widespread changes in brain structure, in particular bilateral decrements in size of the hippocampus-amygdala. However, changes in brain structure were uncorrelated with clinical aspects of the disorder, indicating that the behavioral manifestations of schizophrenia were apparently determined by something other than aberrant brain structure per se.

- Discordant affected twins showed prominent alterations in brain function as assessed by cerebral blood flow, neuropsychological tests, neurological examination, and smooth pursuit eye movement (see p. 484). Reduced blood flow to the frontal lobes ("hypofrontality") was especially prominent and was associated with reduced size of the anterior hippocampus. Moderate or severe cognitive impairment in neuropsychological tests was observed in 14 of the 27 affected twins. The nonschizophrenic co-twins of discordant pairs, while less neurologically impaired than their disordered siblings, were more impaired than a set of control MZ twins where both members of the twinship were considered psychiatrically normal.

- When schizophrenic persons from discordant and concordant pairs were compared, no significant differences in clinical or potential etiologic variables were found.

These results would seem to establish beyond reasonable doubt that genetically identical individuals can manifest widespread biological differences, particularly in neurological integrity, that are associated with relative risk for the development of schizophrenia. It should be noted, however, that none of the findings is of sufficient magnitude to predict outcomes for individual cases. Also, there were a few striking inconsistencies in the data, such that in these few cases the well twin appeared more biologically compromised than his or her schizophrenic co-twin. As the authors acknowledge, the results of this study, while intriguing, in themselves provide no clear resolution of basic questions concerning the ultimate source or sources of vulnerability to the development of schizophrenia. They do, of course, strongly implicate neurological anomalies as often playing a role in the causal pattern.

Returning to the specific issue of genetic influences, a seemingly cleaner investigative strategy employing discordant twins was pioneered by Fischer (1971, 1973). Reasoning that genetic influence, if present, would show up in the *offspring* of the *nonschizophrenic* twins of discordant pairs, she found exactly that outcome in a search of official records in Denmark. Gottesman and Bertelson (1989), in a follow-up of Fischer's subjects, have reported an age-corrected schizophrenia incidence rate (that is, a rate taking into account predicted breakdowns for subjects not yet beyond the age of risk) of 17.4 percent for the offspring of the nonschizophrenic monozygotic twins. This rate, which far exceeds normal expectancy, was not significantly different from that for offspring of the schizophrenic members of discordant pairs, or from that for offspring of schizophrenic dizygotic twins. Assuming that exposure to schizophrenic aunts and uncles would have, at most, limited etiologic significance, these results give impressive support to the genetic hypothesis. They also, as the authors note, indicate that the implicated predisposition may remain "unexpressed" (as in the nonschizophrenic twins of discordant pairs) unless "released" by unknown environmental factors.

Adoption Studies   Several studies have attempted to overcome the shortcomings of the twin method in achieving a true separation of hereditary from environmental influences by using what is called the adoption strategy. Here concordance rates for schizophrenia are compared for the biological and the adoptive relatives of persons who have been adopted out of their biological families at an early age (preferably at birth) and have subsequently become schizophrenic. If concordance is greater among the patients' biological than adoptive relatives, a hereditary influence is strongly suggested; the reverse pattern would of course argue for environmental causation. There are several procedural variants to this basic method, as indicated in what follows.

A follow-up study of 47 people who had been born to schizophrenic mothers in a state mental hospital and placed with relatives or in foster homes shortly after birth found that 16.6 percent of these subjects were later diagnosed as schizophrenic. In contrast, none of the 50 control subjects selected from among residents of the same foster homes—whose biological mothers were not schizophrenic—later became schizophrenic. In addition to the greater probability of being diagnosed schizophrenic, the offspring of schizophrenic mothers were more likely to be diagnosed as mentally retarded, neurotic, and psychopathic (that is, antisocial). They also had been involved more frequently in criminal activities and had spent more time in penal institutions (Heston, 1966). These findings suggest that any genetic liability conveyed by the mothers is not specific to schizophrenia but also includes a liability for other forms of psychopathology.

A large-scale and multifaceted adoption study was undertaken in Denmark with American investigators working in collaboration with Danish professionals (Kendler & Gruenberg, 1984; Kendler, Gruenberg, & Kinney, 1994a; Kety, 1987; Kety et al., 1968, 1978, 1994; Rosenthal et al., 1968; Wender et al., 1974). Using a national sample of schizophrenic adoptees and their biological and adoptive relatives (together with suitable control cases), the data show a preponderance of schizophrenia and "schizophrenia spectrum" (which includes schizotypal and paranoid personality disorder) problems in the biological relatives of schizophrenic adoptees. By contrast, adoptive relatives of schizophrenic adoptees had an unremarkable incidence rate for schizophrenia.

The Danish adoption studies did not include independent assessments of the child-rearing adequacy of the adoptive families into which index (those who became schizophrenic) and control (those who did not) youngsters had been placed. It remained for Tienari and colleagues (Tienari et al., 1985, 1987, 1994; Tienari, 1991) to add this feature to their research plan. This study, still in progress, involves a follow-up of the adopted-away children of all women in Finland hospitalized for schizophrenia, beginning in 1960. These index children as they grow into adulthood are compared with a comparable group of control adoptees whose biological mothers were normal. The trend of the results is already clear, reaching high levels of statistical significance. There is the familiar finding that the index adoptees have developed more, and more serious (including schizophrenia), psychopathology than the controls. Most of this psychopathology, however, is concentrated in the index group reared by poorly functioning adoptive parents—for example, parents showing high levels of communication deviance (see below). Index adoptees reared by well-functioning adoptive parents had substantially less psychopathology, and control cases reared in disorganized adoptive families experienced more serious psychopathology as adults than did their counterparts raised in "healthy" families.

Supporting earlier work, these results show a moderate genetic effect—the differential "healthy" and disorder rates of index versus control adoptees irrespective of adoptive family context. However, parental inadequacy and disturbed communication has a substantial impact on outcome for both index and control cases. Further, the findings indicate a strong interaction between genetic vulnerability and an unfavorable family environment in the causal pathway leading to schizophrenia. Unfortunately, we cannot be certain that the emergence of odd or psychotic behavior in adoptees did not precede and cause, in whole or in part, the disorganization of their adoptive families. Analyses to examine this possibility are in progress (e.g., Wahlberg et al., 1997), but so far provide no definitive support for this alternative interpretation. Some independent work reported by Kinney and colleagues (1997) also fails to show diminished mental health in adoptive parents raising children who became schizophrenic. Everything considered, the Finnish Adoption Study (as it is called) has provided strong confirmation of the diathesis-stress model as it applies to the origins of schizophrenia.

Studies of High-Risk Children The prospective research strategy of long-term monitoring of children known to be at high risk for schizophrenia (by virtue of having been born to a schizophrenic parent) is basically intended to identify the environmental factors that cause breakdown (or resistance to it) in predisposed people. As we have seen in Chapter 1, this strategy, pioneered by Mednick and Schulsinger (1968) and followed up by numerous additional research projects (for reviews see Cornblatt et al., 1992; Erlenmeyer-Kimling & Cornblatt, 1992; Garmezy, 1978a, 1978b; Neale & Oltmanns, 1980; Rieder, 1979; Watt et al., 1984), has thus far not paid off very well in terms of isolating specific environmental factors. In saying this, however, we must acknowledge both the enormous difficulties that attend long-term and complicated projects of this sort and our own admiration for those who undertake them.

Although the available results of high-risk studies have generally proved difficult to interpret, they have supported the observation that having a schizophrenic parent is a good predictor of psychological disorder, including schizophrenia (e.g., Erlenmeyer-Kimling et al.,

1997). It seems likely that some of this predictability comes about as a result of the genetic transmission of vulnerability to schizophrenia. However, as in the case of the Torrey and colleagues (1994) discordant twin study described above, many of these studies point to evidence of subtle neurological impairment in those children who later become schizophrenic. It is conceivable that schizophrenia in a mother somehow interferes with the maintenance of a healthy gestational environment for her child, producing the effect noted (see, e.g., Jones et al., 1998).

Summing up, the question of genetic transmissibility of a predisposition to schizophrenia is not as easily answered as it may appear to be when first posed. We are convinced that some genetic influence does make certain individuals abnormally vulnerable to schizophrenia. The data suggest that no such genetic contribution to etiology is sufficient in itself to produce schizophrenia, and they provide no basis for concluding that such a contribution is a necessary condition for a schizophrenic outcome. Indeed, most people who develop schizophrenia have no close relatives who are also known to have had the disorder—although, as we shall see, some of these normal relatives may share biological anomalies statistically associated with a schizophrenia diagnosis. Based on the best available studies, the aggregate average risk of schizophrenia for first-degree (sharing 50 percent genes) relatives of index cases is 4.8 percent, approximately nine times the rate for normal control cases (Kendler & Diehl, 1993).

Biochemical Factors The idea that serious mental disorders are due to "chemical imbalances" in the brain is now commonplace. To be useful to clinicians and researchers, however, such an idea must be reformulated into hypotheses that are as explicit and specific as possible. We cannot effectively address the general question of possible biochemically based contributions to the onset or maintenance of schizophrenic behaviors in the absence of clues that tell us where to look and what to look for. At present, as in the case of the severe mood disorders, the search is governed largely by attempts to discover the site and nature of central nervous system effects induced by drugs that diminish the behavioral expression of the disorder. In general, drugs that do so are ones found to alter (by up- or down-regulation) the likelihood that a nerve impulse arriving at a synapse will cross the synapse and fire the next neuron in the chain.

In schizophrenia research, the most attractive of these specific ideas has been the dopamine hypothesis (Meltzer & Stahl, 1976), based on the observation that all of the early antischizophrenic drugs (called *neuroleptics*) had the common property of blocking dopamine-mediated neural transmission. Dopamine is a catecholamine neurotransmitter like norepinephrine, of which it is a chemical precursor. It appears to be the main neurotransmitter for perhaps a half-dozen identified brain pathways. According to the dopamine hypothesis, then, schizophrenia is the product of an excess of dopamine activity at certain synaptic sites. Variants of this view include hypotheses that a schizophrenic person has too many postsynaptic dopamine receptors or that these receptors have for some reason become supersensitive. In recent years, however, the dopamine hypothesis has proved oversimplistic and inadequate as a general formulation of etiology (Carlsson, 1988; Csernansky & Grace, 1998; Grace & Moore, 1998; Koreen et al., 1994; Lieberman & Koreen, 1993).

Dopamine-blocking drugs, for example, are therapeutically nonspecific for schizophrenia (that is, they are also used effectively to treat psychotic symptoms associated with various other disordered states, such as neuropsychological disorders, some manias, and even drug-induced bad trips). Additionally, the receptor-blocking effect is accomplished too quickly (within hours) to be consistent with the clinical picture of a gradual improvement (often over several weeks) following initiation of neuroleptic drug therapy in schizophrenia. In other words, if only excess dopamine activity were the cause of schizophrenia, these drugs should have ameliorative effects almost immediately; they usually do not. Moreover, their therapeutic activity depends not so much on curtailing excessive dopaminergic activity as on reducing it to *abnormally* low levels, which creates additional problems of an often serious nature (e.g., tardive dyskinesia; see Chapter 16).

Recent research has shown the dopaminergic systems within the brain to be far more complicated than was originally thought. For example, we now know that several types of dopamine receptor sites exist on the dendrites of postsynaptic neurons (labeled D_2, D_4, etc.), that these are involved in differing biochemical processes, and that differing antipsychotic drugs act upon them in varying ways. The "second-generation" or "atypical" antipsychotic drugs such as Clozaril (clozapine), Zyprexa (olanzapine), and Risperdal (risperidone) have a side-effect profile that is very different (and generally more benign) from that of the original neuroleptics, one of several indications that their antipsychotic modes of action differ significantly from that of the "typical" drugs such as Thorazine (chlorpromazine) and Haldol (haloperidol) (see Chapter 16). That is not to suggest that their principal effects necessarily involve something other than dopamine brain pathways, which continue to be seen as somehow generally implicated in the schizophrenias (O'Donnell & Grace, 1998). We just don't, as yet, know how.

Other biochemical theories of schizophrenia have been, and doubtless will continue to be, advanced, but to date no other such theory appears anywhere near as promising as has the dopamine theory through much of the past 30 years (Lieberman & Koreen, 1993). The fact is that the brain chemistry of schizophrenia remains very imperfectly understood. Ultimately, it seems likely that a complete understanding of the biochemistry of these disorders will have to include a sense of how other influences, such as aberrations of neural circuitry, may interact with whatever biochemical abnormalities are discovered to accompany schizophrenic behavior (Csernansky & Grace, 1998).

Neurophysiological Factors Much recent research has focused on the role of neurophysiological disturbances in schizophrenia, such as an imbalance in various neurophysiologic processes (e.g., those involved in eye movement control—see below) and inappropriate autonomic arousal. Such disordered physiology would disrupt normal attentional and information-processing capabilities, and there seems to be a growing consensus that disturbances of this type underlie the cognitive and perceptual distortions characteristic of schizophrenia. Andreasen, Paradiso, and O'Leary (1998) refer to this process as one of "cognitive dysmetria," a type of "poor mental coordination" that results in "difficulty in prioritizing, processing, coordinating, and responding to information" (p. 203).

One aspect of this "dysmetria" is a highly reliable finding of a specific attentional difficulty in schizophrenia. A substantial proportion of schizophrenic persons are found to be deficient in their ability to track a moving target visually, a skill referred to as *smooth pursuit eye movement* (*SPEM*) (Holzman et al., 1988, 1998; Levy et al., 1983, 1993; Lieberman et al., 1993a). The deficiency is sometimes attributed to a disorder of nonvoluntary attention, one likely related to an impaired ability to detect the velocity of moving visual stimuli. Unfortunately, the potential significance of this clue is obscured by the fact that this type of speed discrimination is highly complex in organization and involves the participation of numerous widely disseminated brain processes (Holzman et al., 1998).

An impressive amount of evidence also indicates that many close relatives of schizophrenics share this SPEM deficit (e.g., Clementz et al., 1992; Iacono et al., 1992; Kuechenmeister et al., 1977; Levy et al., 1994), far more in fact than share the diagnosis (Levy et al., 1993). This would suggest an inherited source for the difficulty while simultaneously ruling it out as a specific indicator for the disorder, a conclusion confirmed in a recent study by Keefe and colleagues (1997). As shown below, much other evidence suggests the presence of widespread neurophysiologic risk factors for schizophrenia, ones that do not necessarily eventuate in the development of the disorder itself.

Numerous related findings indicate that persons who are merely at increased risk for schizophrenia for one or another reason, such as heredity, often experience difficulties in maintaining attention, in processing information, and in certain other indicators of deficit cognitive functioning prior to any schizophrenic breakdown (Cornblatt & Keilp, 1994; Dworkin et al., 1993; Finkelstein et al., 1997; Fish et al., 1992; Green, Nuechterlein, & Breitmeyer, 1997; Kinney et al., 1997; Kwapil et al., 1997; Marcus et al., 1985, 1993; Roitman et al., 1997).

Also possibly related to attentional deficits in schizophrenia are certain anomalies shown by many schizophrenic persons in electroencephalographic (brain wave) reactions to momentary sensory stimulation (Friedman & Squires-Wheeler, 1994; Pritchard, 1986). This abnormal brain reaction to stimulation may also be characteristic of subjects merely at enhanced risk for the disorder (Stelmack, Houlihan, & McGarry-Roberts, 1993). Neurologic abnormalities, such as reflex hyperactivity and deficit performance in neuropsychological testing (see Chapter 15), have also been found to be shared by the nonpsychotic close relatives of schizophrenic individuals (Ismail, Cantor-Graae, & McNeil, 1998; Kinney, Woods, & Yurgelun-Todd, 1986; Kremen et al., 1994; Torrey et al., 1994).

We should also note the evidence that many persons diagnosed as having a schizotypal personality pattern (see Chapter 9) show behavioral deficits, such as poor perceptual-motor coordination or distinctive anomalies in reaction-time performance, suggestive of subtle neurological impairment (Lenzenweger, 1994, 1998; Lenzenweger & Korfine, 1994; Rosenbaum, Shore, & Chapin, 1988; Siever, 1985). This schizotypal pattern is conceived as one manifestation of a general schizophrenia spectrum of disorder and to render the person at risk for the full syndrome (Kwapil et al., 1997; Lenzenweger, 1994, 1998; Meehl, 1990a).

Additional research literature, going back many decades, documents an enormous variety of other ways in which attentional and cognitive processes seemingly dependent on intact neurophysiologic functioning are disrupted among schizophrenic persons. The disjointed array of findings reported remains baffling; as yet, there is no wholly satisfactory conceptual framework within which the pieces of the schizophrenia puzzle can be put together. Indeed, a recent issue of the authoritative *Schizophrenia Bulletin* (vol.

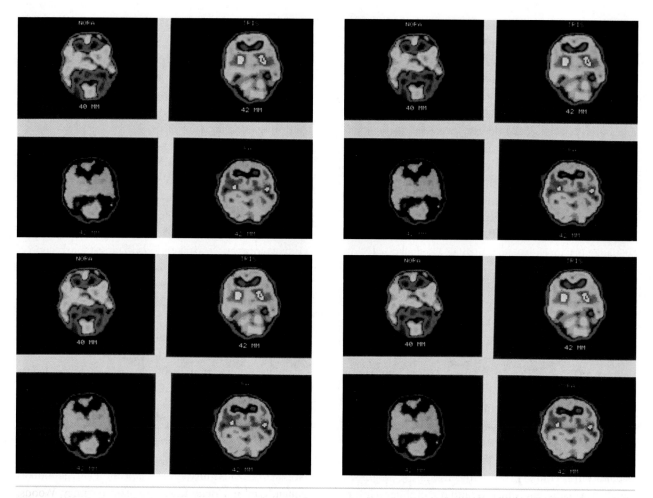

PET scans of the Genian quadruplets suggest a possible psychosocial impact resulting from the early matching of two pairs of co-twins. The scans indicate comparatively more severe brain impairment for Hester and Nora. The large areas of blue and yellow show that their brains consume lower levels of glucose, one indicator of lessened brain activity. The orange spots on the scan of Iris and Myra suggest more normal energy usage. Yet it is Iris, originally "matched" with Hester, who has had the poorer clinical outcome than either Nora or Myra. (Delisi et al., 1984)

24, no. 2, 1998) is devoted to the presentation of an array of "pathophysiologic models" purporting to integrate and explain many of the research findings reviewed in this section. While there are many instances of agreement on the facts, there is substantial divergence on how to interpret them.

Neuroanatomical Factors Abnormal neurophysiological processes in schizophrenia could be genetic in origin, but some at least could also be the product of biological deviations caused by other factors, as suggested in the discordant MZ twin data reviewed earlier. Problems of this sort could as likely arise from unknown intrauterine conditions or mechanical difficulties in the birth process as from faulty genes. Obstetrical complications, such as an unduly short gestational period (premature birth), in the histories of people who later become schizophrenic appear to be well above normative expectations (Cannon et al., 1993; Gureje, Bamidele, & Raji, 1994; Jones et al.,

1998; Torrey et al., 1994), although it is possible that resultant early brain injury contributes to schizophrenic outcomes only among genetically predisposed persons (see Mednick et al., 1998; Marcus et al., 1993). Such observations have led to a resurgence of interest in an old question—that of the anatomical intactness of the schizophrenic brain—to which we now turn.

Research on the structural properties of the brain in living subjects was largely unproductive until the development of modern computer-dependent technologies, such as computerized axial tomography (CAT), positron emission tomography (PET), and magnetic resonance imaging (MRI). The use of these techniques in the study of schizophrenic people's brains has developed at an accelerating pace in recent years, with important results.

Brain Mass Anomalies Much evidence now indicates that in a minority of cases of schizophrenia, particularly among those of chronic, negative-symptom course, there is an abnormal enlargement of the brain's ventricles—the hollow areas filled with cerebrospinal fluid lying deep within the core (Andreasen et al., 1986; Carpenter et al., 1993; Gur & Pearlson, 1993; Gur et al., 1994; Marsh et al., 1997; Pearlson et al., 1989; Raz, 1993; Stevens, 1997). Several other associated anatomical anomalies, such as enlarged sulci (the fissures in the surface of the cerebral cortex), are often reported as well. In fact, the same anomalies are sometimes found in the normal family members of schizophrenic patients (Cannon & Marco, 1994; DeLisi et al., 1986b) and in the high-risk offspring of schizophrenic mothers (Cannon et al., 1993, 1994). In the latter instance, they appear to be associated with low birth weight and the possibility of fetal damage from some unknown agent, possibly infectious (Lyon et al., 1989; Silverton et al., 1985).

Because the brain normally occupies fully the rigid enclosure of the skull, enlarged ventricles imply a loss of brain tissue mass—possibly some type of atrophy or degeneration. Enlarged sulci have a similar significance. Some findings (e.g., Nestor et al., 1993) indicate deficient size of temporal lobe structures as well, but the evidence here is contradictory (Dwork, 1997). Bogerts (1993), in reviewing some 50 postmortem studies of schizophrenics' brains, concluded that the findings are generally not consistent with the notion of *progressive degeneration* and favor the hypothesis of some type of anomaly in prenatal brain development that becomes manifest as schizophrenia (and as reduced brain volume) in young adulthood. Arnold and colleagues (1998)

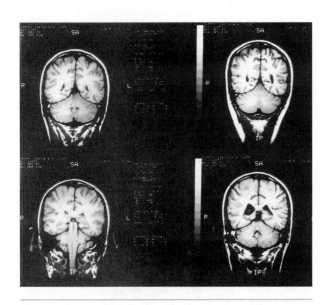

MRI scans of discordant monozygotic twins. In the schizophrenic twin (right), the brain's ventricles are larger than in the normal twin's brain (left).

present data in support of this conclusion from a sample of the brains of elderly schizophrenic patients. Additionally, data on neuropsychological test performance (Heaton et al., 1994) and an extensive review by Cannon and colleagues (1998) of the pertinent literature come to essentially the same conclusion of a static rather than a worsening anomaly.

These rather consistent findings relate to an ongoing controversy as to whether the supposed anatomical substrates of schizophrenia are best considered due to a *neurodegenerative* or to a *neurodevelopmental* process (Buchanan, Stevens, & Carpenter, 1997; Csernansky & Bardgett, 1998). It should be noted that these are not mutually incompatible conceptions. The establishment of some type of static lesion would not rule out the possibility of later progressive changes in brain anatomy. In given instances, either or both might be true. However, little progress has been made in differentiating any such subgroups at the level of clinical observation (Buchanan & Carpenter, 1997; Stevens, 1997). The increasingly important neurodevelopmental *conception* is discussed below.

The findings of a particular brain anomaly associated with some cases is of enormous potential significance for at least the types of schizophrenia primarily implicated. As already noted, it has been suggested that at least some of these brain abnormalities could be due to long-term or excessive use of antipsychotic medication (Breggin, 1990; Cohen, 1997), a hypothesis receiving partial confirmation in a recently reported MRI study by Gur and colleagues (1998). However, examinations of the brains of schizophrenic people who have never taken neuroleptic drugs show that this type of brain anomaly is not limited to patients having histories of excessive or long exposure to these compounds (e.g., Lieberman et al., 1993b; Saykin et al., 1994; Weinberger et al., 1982; Zipursky et al., 1998). The observation of similar abnormalities among normal family members who have not taken these drugs also supports the conclusion that, whatever may be the role of drugs in contributing to brain mass decrement, they are not necessary causes for its occurrence.

Deficit Localization   Much research effort in recent years has focused on the question of what particular brain structures may be especially involved in contributing to the development of the symptoms common to schizophrenia. In an overall review of neuroimaging studies in schizophrenia, Gur and Pearlson (1993) concluded that the evidence implicates primarily three brain regions: the frontal, the temporolimbic (i.e., the temporal lobes and the adjacent, interior limbic system structures such as the hippocampus), and the basal ganglia (subcortical neural centers chiefly involved in integrative functions). More recent reviews by Cannon and colleagues (1998) and Weinberger (1997) implicate the first two of these. Virtually all authorities agree, however, that few of the findings are specific for schizophrenia, being also observed (usually in lesser degree) in other conditions, such as the severe mood disorders.

Concerning the frontal and prefrontal regions, many studies have demonstrated abnormally low frontal lobe activation—called *hypofrontality*—among schizophrenic persons when they engage in tasks supposedly requiring substantial frontal lobe involvement, such as the Wisconsin Card Sorting Test (WCST). Evidence of such hypofrontality has been reported for only the schizophrenic co-twins of discordant monozygotic twin pairs (Berman et al., 1992), for never-medicated patients (Buchsbaum et al., 1992), and especially for patients having high levels of negative versus positive symptoms (Andreasen et al., 1992; Wolkin et al., 1992). It should be cautioned, however, that the levels of hypofrontality observed among schizophrenic persons are often only marginally, albeit statistically significantly, different from levels observed in normal control subjects, with much overlap between the groups (e.g., Buchsbaum et al., 1992). Dysfunctional frontal lobes are believed to be especially important in accounting for *negative* signs and symptoms, and perhaps also attentional-cognitive deficits (Cannon et al., 1998; Goldman-Rakic & Selemon, 1997).

There is also considerable evidence relating to the special involvement of temporolimbic structures in schizophrenia (Cannon, 1998; Bogerts, 1997; Haber & Fudge, 1997). It is somewhat less consistent and more controversial than that relating to the frontal area, having many unresolved or unreconciled findings (Crow, 1997; Weinberger, 1997). The consensus appears to be that these centers, perhaps especially the left-sided (i.e., for most people, dominant-side) ones, are somehow implicated, and that they have a particular role in the production of *positive* signs and symptoms (Bogerts, 1997; Cannon et al., 1998; Woodruff et al., 1997). The conclusion of temporolimbic involvement is consistent with the types of abnormal functioning observed in an extensive neuropsychological investigation of unmedicated, first-episode schizophrenic patients reported by Saykin and colleagues (1994).

Neurodevelopmental Issues Given all these findings, noted schizophrenia researcher Timothy Crow (1997) has recently voiced a persistent question that has quietly frustrated many of his colleagues around the world: "Where is the primary lesion in schizophrenia and what is its nature?" He goes on to note this:

The problem is that many changes in many different anatomical structures are reported. Which of these is reliably associated with the disease process? If, as seems likely, there is more than one such change, which is primary and which secondary?. . . . We need to find changes characteristic at least of a subtype of psychopathology. . . . But there is an embarrassment of riches. (p. 521)

There are indeed very many reports of neuroanatomical differences between schizophrenic (or those at enhanced risk for it) and normal individuals, only the major of them reviewed here. And it is also true that they point to no obvious candidate uniformly present in all cases of schizophrenia, or even in all cases of recognized subtypes of schizophrenia. Could it be the case that there is *no "primary lesion"* in schizophrenia or any of its subtypes? Increasing numbers of contemporary investigators are approaching an affirmative answer to that question.

The nature of this new thinking is by no means completely developed or uniformly expressed, but its essential kernel involves the idea that what we call schizophrenia is due to a probably variable aberration in the basic circuitry, the basic wiring, of the brain itself. Most forms of the idea include the notion of an early, even prenatal, insult to the brain, one that may have detectable neurological effects in early childhood but will not necessarily result in the later development of schizophrenia. The latter arises where the initial injury somehow interferes with normal brain synapse development during a period of intensive synaptic reorganization, for most people occurring during adolescence or early adulthood. Conceivable candidates here include neuronal cell "pruning," cell migration, and programmed cell death, all processes known to occur normally during postnatal phases of brain development (see Weickert & Weinberger, 1998, for a useful overview).

Fetuses or newborns sustaining the earlier insult, according to the developmental view, are at elevated risk for missing or misconnected circuitry arising during cell reorganization. They are thus more "vulnerable" (have an enhanced *diathesis*) to developing schizophrenia (e.g., see Walker & Diforio, 1997). The hypothesized relationship between such neurological involvement and clinical outcomes is depicted in Figure 12.4. Such deficiencies in "wiring," would not, of course, be directly observable by available methods of brain scanning. Certain research findings of recent years, some already described and more described below, appear consistent with this type of etiologic scenario.

For a number of years researchers have noted that people who become schizophrenic are more likely than people in general to have been born in the winter and early spring months—about an 8 percent deviation

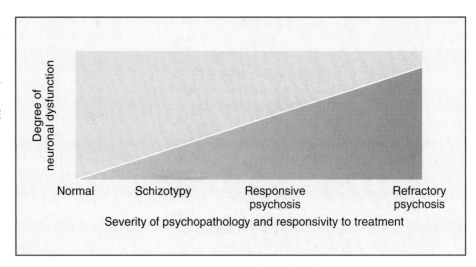

FIGURE 12.4 RELATIONSHIP BETWEEN INCREASING DAMAGE TO NEURONAL CIRCUITS AND CLINICAL PHENOMENOLOGY. Clinical psychopathology and the capacity to respond to typical antipsychotic drugs may occur on a physiological continuum in relationships to degree of neuropathology.

Source: From Csernansky & Bardgett, (1998).

from norms (DeLisi, Crow, & Hirsch, 1986a). This peculiar observation, which itself is now beyond dispute, has given rise to a variety of hypotheses involving what has come to be called the "season of birth effect" in the development of schizophrenia. Some of these relate directly to the question of compromised brain integrity in schizophrenia, as was suggested early on by Bradbury and Miller (1985). Their best guess as to origin was some type of infectious process or obstetrical complications, or both.

Accumulating evidence suggests that Bradbury and Miller were on the right track. For example, Wright and colleagues (1995) found that maternal influenza in the second trimester of pregnancy is associated with impaired fetal growth, enhanced obstetrical complications, and later-developing schizophrenia. Several studies have suggested that, historically, influenza epidemics are associated at a higher-than-chance level with the gestation periods of fetuses who later became schizophrenic. The latest of these studies as of this writing, reported by Takei and colleagues (1997), identifies the supposedly critical peak infectious period as the fifth gestational month. Here, risk of influenza exposure in the critical period was associated with enlarged ventricles and sulci among a group of 83 schizophrenic patients, relative to controls. Seemingly important and possibly related findings, reported by Torrey and colleagues (1993), establish a strong correlation between the occurrence of stillbirths and the live births of persons who become schizophrenic, both being elevated in winter months. The investigators suggest that there appears to be a common factor for both stillbirths and schizophrenia risk, presumably some infectious agent; in the one case, according to this hypothesis, it leads to death of the fetus, while in the other to brain changes that enhance vulnerability to schizophrenia.

An ingenious series of studies reported by Elaine Walker and her colleagues (Grimes & Walker, 1994; Walker et al., 1993, 1994) illustrates in compelling fashion the association between early neurodevelopmental deviation and schizophrenia risk. These investigators gathered family home movies made during the childhoods of 32 persons who eventually developed schizophrenia. Trained observers made "blind" (i.e., they were uninformed as to outcomes) ratings of certain dimensions of the emotional (Grimes & Walker, 1994) and facial expressions (Walker et al., 1993), motor skills, and neuromotor abnormalities (Walker et al., 1994) of these children and of their healthy-outcome siblings from the same movie clips.

The facial and emotional expressions, and the motor competence, of the preschizophrenic and the healthy-outcome children were found by the raters to differ significantly and in ways apparently disadvantageous to the former group. The preschizophrenic children showed less—and less positive than negative—emotionality, had poorer motor skills, and showed a higher rate of peculiar movements, such as tic-like muscle contractions, suggestive of neuromotor abnormalities. In other words, these children, in some instances before age two, were already showing behavioral abnormalities not unlike those already suggested. It is a reasonable hypothesis, therefore, that these preschizophrenic children as a group suffered from subtle neurological impairment of unknown origin. We again remind you, however, that (1) these early-appearing subtle impairments are probably not progressive, (2) they do not inevitably eventuate in a diagnosis of schizophrenia, and (3) they will almost inevitably impact the child's social environment, probably often in negative ways—so, once again, an interaction with one's environment is likely also to be a factor.

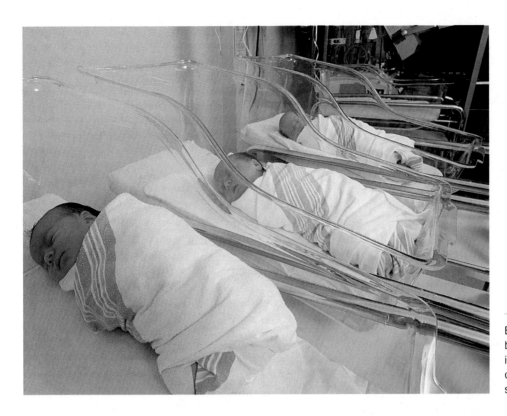

Early, even prenatal damage to the brain, whether through a mother's illness or other insult, is another of the diatheses associated with schizophrenia.

Interpreting the Biological Evidence: Diathesis/ Stress The role of biological factors in the etiology of schizophrenia has been established. Impressive as the evidence is, however, we remain uncertain about precisely how biological factors, operating either singly or in combination, are implicated in inducing schizophrenic outcomes. Nor do we know which factors are most important—either in the aggregate or in individual cases.

In summary, then, biologically oriented research, particularly in recent years, has given us a wealth of new insights regarding the nature of schizophrenia and some of the sources of vulnerability to it. Our best bet at present is that it will prove not to provide a complete answer to the riddle of schizophrenia—that is, biological findings will have to be supplemented by pertinent psychosocial and sociocultural research in order to provide a comprehensive understanding, and eventually control, of the problem. This is hardly an extraordinary conclusion; the general diathesis-stress model, whose origins largely derive from schizophrenia research, envisages exactly that sort of scenario (e.g., Walker & Diforio, 1997; Zubin & Spring, 1977). We turn now to an examination of the evidence relating to psychosocial influences in schizophrenia.

Psychosocial Factors in Schizophrenia

Some behavioral scientists (e.g., Whitaker, 1992) dispute the idea that schizophrenia is caused primarily by biological factors. It is unfortunate and counterproductive that biological and psychosocial research are often conceived as mutually antagonistic and that they rarely make contact with one another (Carson & Sanislow, 1993). Although much lip service is paid to the evidence of interaction between biological and psychosocial variables in schizophrenia, studies that actually examine the interaction are rare. Hopefully, they will become better funded and so more common in coming years.

A good illustration of the potential of such interactionally oriented research is afforded by the home movie studies of Walker and colleagues as reported above. As was noted, it is extremely likely that the (presumably) neurologically based behavioral deficits of the preschizophrenic children would be noticed and responded to in negative ways by others coming in contact with them. The child who rarely manifests joy (even on celebratory family occasions such as birthdays), whose emotional expressiveness is prevailingly in the bland to negative range, who is motorically clumsy or awkward, and who may evidence peculiar involuntary movements, is likely to have a far less stress-free early life than the child endowed with the opposite characteristics. Minimally, such a scenario suggests that the occurrence of challenging life events ("stress") that may affect social and personality development is not independent of a potentially pathogenic biological "diathesis." In fact, this idea has been a central element in the important contributions of psychologist Paul Meehl (1962, 1989, 1990a) in tracing the developmental course of schizophrenic outcomes. Berenbaum and Fujita (1994) have offered a similar conceptualization.

Notwithstanding its potential importance, research on psychosocial factors in the development of schizophrenia has been exceedingly sparse in recent years, especially as compared with the research investment in biological correlates. As a result, much of the available psychosocially oriented research in schizophrenia is seriously dated. Much of it is also of questionable quality, in part because it was planned and carried out in an era of less rigorous standards, and one in which less was in fact known about the proper design of research studies. It could also be argued that as a general rule research on psychosocial variables is inherently more complex and difficult than biologically oriented research. For these reasons, our discussion of psychosocial causal factors in schizophrenia will be relatively brief.

Damaging Parent-Child and Family Interactions

Studies of interactions in families having schizophrenic offspring have focused on such factors as (1) schizophrenogenic (schizophrenia-causing) parents; (2) destructive parental interactions; and (3) faulty communication. The focus of research has shifted in recent years from parent-child to total family interactions. We will therefore deal here with the latter two of these foci. Before we proceed, however, let us take a moment to gain some perspective on this sensitive topic.

In the early years of attention to family variables in schizophrenia, beginning in the 1950s, parents were routinely assumed to have caused their children's disorders through hostility, deliberate rejection, or gross parental ineptitude. Many professionals blamed parents, and their feedback to them was often angry and insensitive, if not brutal. We hope that nothing in the following discussion appears to condone such attitudes. Most of the parents we have known, whether or not they experienced the "bad luck" (Meehl, 1978, 1989) of schizophrenia in a child, have done the best that could reasonably be expected, within the limits of their own situations, to foster their children's happiness and success. Some parents are cruel and abusive, but there is no evidence that such a pattern is especially associated with schizophrenic outcomes. Apart from the fact that blaming parents does not help and may indeed worsen matters, blame could only be based on an oversimplified and erroneous notion of how people come to be schizophrenic.

One further caveat: Studies have shown a high incidence of emotional disturbances and conflict in the families from which schizophrenic persons emerge (e.g., Hirsch & Leff, 1975). As we've repeatedly emphasized, however, we cannot reasonably assume that disturbance always passes from parent to offspring; it can work in the other direction as well. Whatever the original source of the difficulty, it appears that once it begins the members of a family may stimulate each other to increasingly pathological behavior. For example, studies by Mishler and Waxler (1968) and Liem (1974) both found that parents' attempts to deal with the disturbed behavior of schizophrenic sons and daughters had pathological effects on their own behavior and communication patterns. In fact, the bidirectionality of effects may be the single most robust finding we have gleaned from studying the families of schizophrenic people.

Destructive Parental Interactions Of particular interest here is the work of Theodore Lidz and his associates, which continued over some two decades. In an initial intensive clinical study of 14 families with schizophrenic offspring, Lidz, Fleck, and Cornelison (1965) failed to find a single parental couple that functioned in a reasonably effective and well-integrated manner. Eight of the 14 couples lived in a state of severe chronic discord in which continuation of the marriage was constantly threatened. The other six couples in this study had achieved a state of equilibrium in which the relationship was maintained at the expense of a basic distortion in family relationships; in these cases, family members entered into a "collusion" in which the seriously disturbed behavior (e.g., a frankly delusional construction of some aspect of reality) of one or the other parent was redefined as normal and justified by consensual rationalization.

Schizophrenic people often have psychologically healthy siblings who were raised with them in the same families. How have these siblings escaped the presumed pathology of the family context? A possible answer is that they were not biologically predisposed. But it is also probably true, as emphasized by the Lidz group, that the subculture of a family is not constant—that every child raised within a family experiences a unique family pattern. Thus, a given child may experience a greater degree of exposure to family pathology, as through parental overinvolvement, than his or her more fortunate siblings.

Faulty Communication Gregory Bateson (1959, 1960) was one of the first investigators to emphasize the conflicting and confusing nature of communications among members of families experiencing a schizophrenic outcome. He used the term *double-bind communication* to describe one such pattern. In this pattern the parent presents to the child ideas, feelings, and demands that are mutually incompatible. For example, a mother may be verbally loving and accepting but emotionally anxious and rejecting; or she may complain about her son's lack of affection but freeze up or punish him when he approaches her affectionately. The mother subtly but effectively prohibits comment on such paradoxes, and the father is too ineffectual or distanced to intervene. In essence, according to Bateson's etiologic hypothesis, such a son is continually placed in situations where he cannot win, and he becomes increasingly anxious; presumably, such disorganized and contradictory communications in the family come to be reflected in his own thinking. However, no solid confirmation of the pathogenicity of double-bind communications has ever been reported.

Singer and Wynne (1963, 1965a, 1965b) linked the thought disorders in schizophrenia to two styles of thinking and communication in the family—amorphous and fragmented. The amorphous pattern is characterized by a failure in differentiation; here, attention toward feelings, objects, or people is loosely organized, vague, and drifting. Fragmented thinking involves greater differentiation but lowered integration, with erratic and disruptive shifts in communication. In their later research, Singer and Wynne (Singer, Wynne, & Toohey, 1978; Wynne, Toohey, & Doane, 1979) used the term *communication deviance* (or "transactional style deviance") to refer to these deficiencies of precision and coherence they regarded as being at the heart of the purported negative effects parents have on their preschizophrenic children.

In a longitudinal study (Doane et al., 1981; Goldstein, 1985; Goldstein et al., 1978; Goldstein & Strachan, 1987;

Destructive interaction patterns between parents toward children have been shown to be correlated with the development of schizophrenia in those at risk, and the relapse of discharged patients diagnosed with the disorder. Yet not all children in such families become schizophrenic. A possible reason for this discrepancy is that every child in a family experiences that family in their own way.

Lewis, Rodnick, & Goldstein, 1981), subjects who had been psychological clinic patients, but not schizophrenic, as adolescents were followed into adulthood. The findings confirmed such an effect. High parental communication deviance (as defined above), measured during their children's adolescence, did indeed predict the occurrence of adult schizophrenic spectrum disorders among these offspring. A family atmosphere of negative affect appeared to increase the likelihood of such outcomes. However, the study's design cannot rule out the possibility of a common genetic influence affecting both parents and offspring, one leading to odd communication in parents and (independently) to schizophrenia in offspring. That possibility is rendered unlikely by findings from the previously described Finnish Adoption Study, where (adoptive) parent communication deviance was associated with the development of serious psychopathology in adoptees (Tienari et al., 1994).

The Role of Excessive Life Stress and Expressed Emotion A marked increase in the severity of life stress has been found during the ten-week period prior to a person's schizophrenic breakdown (Brown, 1972). Problems typically centered on difficulties in intimate personal relationships, such as a breakup. Another study found interpersonal stressors to be significantly more common among schizophrenic people than among members of a matched control group (Schwartz & Myers, 1977). We also note that life stressors, like schizophrenia itself, have a higher co-occurrence rate in twins than in ordinary siblings (Kendler et al., 1993b), thus suggesting that some part of the elevated concordance for schizophrenia in twins may be due as much to shared stress as shared genes.

Whether or not poor relations with parents and family members is a cause of schizophrenia, we do know that *relapse* into schizophrenia following remission is associated with a certain type of negative communication, called **expressed emotion (EE),** directed at the patient by family members (Butzlaff & Hooley, 1998; Hooley & Hiller, 1998; Linszen et al., 1997; Miklowitz, Goldstein, & Falloon, 1983; Vaughn et al., 1984). Two components appear critical in the pathogenic effects of EE: emotional overinvolvement (intrusiveness) with the ex-patient, and excessive criticism of him or her. Interestingly, the recent quantitative review of pertinent research by Butzlaff and Hooley (1998) shows that the EE-relapse association is generally robust but strongest among patients having a chronic course. Expressed emotion may be especially intense where family members harbor the view that the disorder and its symptoms are under the voluntary control of the patient (Weisman et al., 1993). But here, too, the communication problems are likely to be two-way (Hooley & Hiller, 1998).

Some research shows EE to *predict* schizophrenia before its initial onset (Goldstein, 1985), and strongly suggests that its role in relapse is a directly causal one (Nuechterlein, Snyder, & Mintz, 1992). Also, attempts to reduce EE and associated behaviors in family members have been very impressive in terms of relapse prevention (Falloon et al., 1985; Hogarty et al., 1986; Leff et al., 1982; McFarlane et al., 1995). Familial Expressed Emotion has thus turned out to be a quite potent variable in the precipitation of schizophrenic episodes. As Hooley and Hiller (1998) suggest, it is now time to turn our attention to gaining a fuller understanding of how it does this.

As noted earlier, the course of decompensation (deterioration, disorganization of thought and personality) in primarily positive-syndrome, Type I schizophrenia tends to be sudden, while that in primarily negative-syndrome, Type II schizophrenia tends to be gradual, though often finally more profound: The actual degree of decompensation may vary markedly, depending on the severity of stress and the makeup of the individual. The course of recovery or recompensation may also be relatively rapid or slow. Similarly, the degree of recovery may be complete, even leading to a better-adjusted person than before; it may be partial but sufficient for adequate independent living ("social recovery"); or it may be nonexistent, with some individuals eventually developing an intractable, chronic, prevailingly negative-syndrome schizophrenia (see Fenton & McGlashan, 1994).

Sociocultural Factors in Schizophrenia

As was noted earlier, prevalence rates for schizophrenia appear to vary substantially around the world. Granting the already acknowledged hazards of such cross-cultural comparisons, there is at least a twofold to threefold—and possibly considerably greater—variation in occurrence of the disorder in the various social groupings and geographic regions for which epidemiologic data are available (Gottesman, 1991; Stevens & Hallick, 1992). No satisfactory biological explanation for this variation has been identified (Kirch, 1993), and the possibility that the differences reflect intercultural social factors (e.g., religious beliefs and practices, family organization and values) that modify the schizophrenia risk cannot be ruled out (Torrey, 1987). If there are cultural factors that both enhance and diminish the risk for schizophrenia, it would obviously be of great value to understand how these operate. Surprisingly little attention has been directed to this question, so we remain largely ignorant of any such influences.

We also noted earlier that schizophrenia seems to occur less often and with diminished severity in traditional, less "well-developed" cultures (Allen, 1997). Systematic differences in the content and form of schizophrenia between cultures and even subcultures have been documented by various investigators over many years. Often, cases within a particular subculture tend to have a distinctive form. For example, among the aborigines of West Malaysia, Kinzie and Bolton (1973) found the positive syndrome type to be by far the most common manifestation; they also noted that symptom content often had an obvious cultural overlay, such as "seeing a river ghost" or "men-like spirits or talking to one's soul" (p. 773).

Focusing on sociocultural factors within the United States, there is now a huge body of evidence going back to the 1930s indicating that the lower the socioeconomic status, the higher the prevalence of schizophrenia. Although it has quite reasonably been suggested (e.g., by Kohn, 1973) that the conditions of lower-class existence are themselves stressful and in addition impair an individual's ability to deal resourcefully with stress, there is also compelling evidence that lower-class membership can be a *result* of schizophrenia or its socially debilitating behavioral antecedents. Affected individuals often drift downward on the socioeconomic ladder because the early signs of impending disorder prevent them from finding jobs or developing human relationships that might otherwise provide economic stability (Gottesman, 1991). As we discuss in Chapter 18, many such cases may be found among the homeless mentally disordered.

Schizophrenia seems to occur less often and with less severity among undeveloped cultures. One study of the aborigines of West Malaysia found that the positive symptoms of schizophrenia were more common there than in other parts of the world and centered on cultural beliefs, such as hallucinations of a river ghost or male spirits who spoke to the person's soul.

Proportionally far more blacks than whites in the United States receive a diagnosis of schizophrenia. However, this imbalance appears to be primarily if not exclusively artifactual. Differences between African-American and Caucasian prevalence rates and clinical pictures for schizophrenia diminish markedly when social class, education, and related socioeconomic conditions are equated (Lindsey & Paul, 1989; Snowden & Cheung, 1990). Indeed, Brekke and Barrio (1997) report a diminished intensity of schizophrenic symptoms, relative to those of whites, among both black and Latino patients when socioeconomic class is controlled.

In general, then, there appears to be no one clinical entity or causal sequence in schizophrenia. Rather we seem to be dealing with several types of psychologically maladaptive processes resulting from an interaction of biological, psychosocial, and sociocultural factors; the role of these factors undoubtedly varies according to the given case and clinical picture. Often the interaction appears to involve a vicious spiral that, once initiated, propels the person into a process of decreasing availability of coping resources in the face of increasing demands for performance adequacy. Some people panic and undergo a sort of psychobiological collapse; others appear to become gradually apathetic and demoralized, retreating from the unmanageable and perhaps (to them) unintelligible real world both physically and psychologically. Whatever the initial picture, outcomes are not at first notably predictable (Endicott et al., 1986; Strakowski, 1994; Vaillant, 1978) and typically become more so only after weeks, months, or, in some cases of rapidly altering clinical pictures, even years.

TREATMENTS AND OUTCOMES

Before the 1950s the prognosis for schizophrenia was generally considered extremely unfavorable, even hopeless. Patients receiving the diagnosis, unless their families were wealthy and could afford the expense of private psychiatric hospitalization, were routinely shuttled to remote, forbidding, overcrowded, and environmentally bleak public hospitals. Once "safely" incarcerated they were treated—if at all—by poorly trained, overworked, demoralized staff with largely ineffective techniques that were often, in addition, objectively cruel (e.g., straitjackets) or predictably terrifying (e.g., electroconvulsive "shock" therapy, as it was originally called). As often as not, perhaps after a brief trial at one or more of the inad-

equate "therapies" offered, the patient was simply left to adjust to an institution he or she was never expected to leave (Deutsch, 1948). Such an adjustment in most instances ensured the erosion of capacities and skills essential to self-maintenance outside of the institution. Thus, complying with the self-fulfilling prophecies of their dismal prognoses, most admitted patients, in fact, did not ever leave.

The Effects of Antipsychotic Medication

For most schizophrenic persons, the outlook today is not nearly so bleak. Improvement came with dramatic suddenness when the phenothiazine class of drugs—then referred to as "major tranquilizers"—were introduced in the mid-1950s. Pharmacotherapy (treatment by drugs) with these potent compounds transformed the environment of mental hospitals practically "overnight" by virtually eliminating the ever-present threat of wild, dangerous, or otherwise anxiety-producing patient behaviors. Patients did indeed become "tranquil." These changes were so abrupt and compelling that it is difficult now to convey the extent of their effects, particularly on the morale and optimism of hospital staffs. The latter now seemingly had the means to reliably normalize patient behavior, even to the extent of releasing many patients, who could be maintained on the drugs in outpatient facilities. With further advances in psychopharmacology, one might even contemplate *curing* schizophrenia. A new and far more hopeful era had finally arrived.

Newer and better (mostly in the sense of reduced problematic side effects) antipsychotic drugs did in fact make their appearance in the interim, and they continue today to be introduced at a high rate (see Chapter 16). A schizophrenic person who enters a mental hospital or other facility as a first-time inpatient today has an 80 to 90 percent chance of being discharged within a matter of weeks or, at most, months. A minority of these early discharge patients recover permanently and without notable residual problems. Unfortunately, the rate of readmission remains extremely high, and many schizophrenic patients experience repeated discharges and readmissions in what is commonly referred to as the "revolving door" pattern. Also, some persons who become schizophrenic—estimated to be about 10 percent—continue to be resistant to drug (or any other) treatment and undergo an irreversible negative syndrome and/or disorganized deterioration.

In some relatively few instances the progression of the disorder cannot be interrupted by any known intervention techniques. This deteriorating course can occur remarkably rapidly, reaching a stable state of profound dilapidation in a year or less. More typically, it develops over several years, normally stabilizing at a low functioning level within five years (Fenton & McGlashan, 1994; McGlashan & Fenton, 1993). The hope of a reliable "cure" for schizophrenia has not materialized, nor can it be discerned anywhere on the horizon. Antipsychotic medications are not a cure. Consider in this regard the remarks of the recently deceased Harvard social psychologist Roger Brown, who once attended a meeting of Schizophrenics Anonymous in order to familiarize himself with the problems of these people:

> [The group leader] began with an optimistic testimony about how things were going with him, designed in part to buck up the others. Some of them also spoke hopefully; others were silent and stared at the floor throughout. I gradually felt hope draining out of the group as they began to talk of their inability to hold jobs, of living on welfare, of finding themselves overwhelmed by simple demands. Nothing bizarre was said or done; there was rather a pervasive sense of inadequacy, of lives in which each day was a dreadful trial. Doughnuts and coffee were served, and then each one, still alone, trailed off into the Cambridge night.
>
> What I saw a little of at that meeting of Schizophrenics Anonymous is simply that there is something about schizophrenia that the antipsychotic drugs do not cure or even always remit on a long-term basis (Brown & Herrnstein, 1975, p. 641).

What Brown saw as lacking in the club membership is what mental health professionals call **social recovery**—the ability to manage independently as an economically effective and interpersonally connected member of one's society. These members were not "psychotic," and most probably would not currently meet criteria for the schizophrenia diagnosis—excepting possibly the *residual* subtype. Antipsychotic drugs can usually resolve psychotic symptoms, and in their newer, "atypical" versions often without distressing side effects (Sheitman et al., 1998). Can they, by themselves, reverse that substantial part of the schizophrenia experience that so often leaves victims unable either to work or to love in satisfying and productive ways?

In a landmark study Hegarty and colleagues (1994) did a quantitative analysis of worldwide clinical outcomes in treated schizophrenia on a decade-by-decade basis from 1895 through 1991. Criteria employed for declaring a patient to be "improved" following treatment were essentially those defining the concept of social recovery. The results of the study, which involved 51,800 schizophrenic patients and 311, 400 person-years of pa-

tient follow-up, are depicted in Figure 12.5. Note that there was in fact an increase in social recoveries following the introduction of antipsychotic medication (decades 1956–1975). That increase, however, was a quite modest one—going roughly from 40 to 50 percent socially recovered. It then evaporated, which the authors argue was due to increased stringency in diagnostic criteria for schizophrenia—i.e., on average more seriously disturbed patients were included in these later years. A smaller-scale but similar study by Warner (1994) confirms the main findings reported here. Overall, we find these results sobering and disappointing.

On a more optimistic note, the disappointing performance of the antipsychotic drugs in the above study relate only to the older "typical" compounds such as chlorpromazine and haloperidol, and may conceivably be overcome with further advances in pharmacologic therapy. Sheitman and colleagues (1998) identify a number of newer "atypical" antipsychotics in various stages of development and use, any of which might produce a better record in social recovery terms. Unfortunately, none has as yet been adequately evaluated with respect to this relatively demanding criterion (see Chapter 16 for further discussion).

In light of the limited success of the older antipsychotic drugs, it is somewhat disconcerting to realize that for several recent decades they were virtually the only treatment offered to many schizophrenic patients. That may now be changing, as described in what follows.

Psychosocial Approaches in Treating Schizophrenia

As a group, mental health professionals of the present era have only gradually come to realize the serious limitations of an exclusively pharmacological approach to the treatment of schizophrenia. In fact, so dominant was this viewpoint that some extremely promising alternative approaches appearing in the decades prior to the 1990s were quite simply ignored by the majority of the professional mental health community. Included here, for example, were a therapeutic community–based program of "self-help" for patients moved from the hospital to a commercially failed motel and given minimal professional oversight (Fairweather et al., 1969; Fairweather, 1980), and a rigorous token economy "social learning" program (see Chapter 17) for chronic state hospital patients (Paul & Lentz, 1977). Neither of these involved extensive use of medication and both produced exciting results in terms of patient progress. Also largely ignored was a report of a well-designed study demonstrating the superiority of

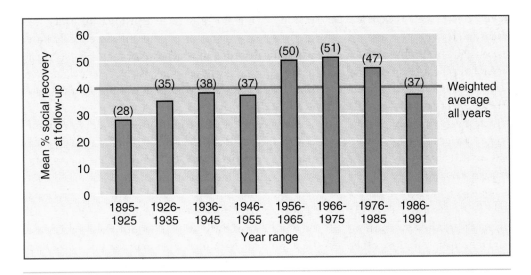

FIGURE 12.5

Percentage of followed-up schizophrenic patients attaining social recovery over the past century. Adapted from Hegarty et al., 1994; percentages have been rounded off to the nearest whole number.

specialized individual psychotherapy (by highly experienced therapists) to antipsychotic medication in treating schizophrenia (Karon & Vandenbos, 1981).

Perhaps the most notable indication of a changing perspective on the treatment of schizophrenia is the content of the recently published American Psychiatric Association's (1997) *Practice Guideline for the Treatment of Patients with Schizophrenia.* This document contains the expected comprehensive recommendations on managing the medication of patients in various phases and at differing severities of disorder, but it also makes a host of recommendations relating to the desirability of vigorous psychosocial intervention as well. In making these recommendations, the *Practice Guideline* takes notice of the development in recent years of a number of relatively new and demonstrably effective psychosocial initiatives in ameliorating the problems of schizophrenic patients, particularly those problems that seem largely unresponsive to antipsychotic drugs (Kopelowicz & Liberman, 1998). Some of these initiatives, normally used in conjunction with medication, are briefly described below.

Family Therapy Although family therapy-type approaches are by no means new in the treatment of schizophrenia, there is a renewed emphasis on their importance—due in no small measure to research findings on the relapse hazards of familial expressed emotion (EE) as reviewed above. Family therapy would appear to be an excellent medium for identifying instances of EE and for teaching family members how to control or avoid it (Tarrier & Barrowclough, 1990).

Individual Psychotherapy One-on-one individual psychotherapy of schizophrenia has a rich history but had largely fallen by the wayside under the onslaught of the antipsychotics and by virtue of some reports that it (particularly in its more psychodynamic forms) made schizophrenic patients worse. However, Hogarty and colleagues (1997a, 1997b) report on a controlled three-year trial of what they call "personal therapy." This treatment was very effective in enhancing social adjustment and social role performance of discharged patients. Personal therapy is described as involving a staged, nonpsychodynamic approach oriented to the learning of coping skills for managing emotion and stressful events. We do not know in what manner, if any, it differs from cognitive-behavior therapy. In favorably commenting on this program, Fenton and McGlashan (1997) assert the need for a flexible individual psychotherapy component in virtually all treatment packages for schizophrenia.

Social-Skills Training and Community Treatment Training in social skills (e.g., see Bellack et al., 1997; Dilk & Bond, 1996; Halford & Haynes, 1991) is also a useful procedure for overcoming the embarrassment, ineptitude, awkwardness, and attentional "cluelessness" displayed in social situations by many persons who've undergone episodes of schizophrenia.

Somewhat belatedly, we now understand that many schizophrenic patients discharged into the community have great difficulty in marshaling resources and getting their lives organized (see Chapter 18). Included here is some propensity to become involved in substance abuse, often as self-medication for unpleasant antipsychotic drug side effects (Kosten & Ziedonis, 1997). There is therefore considerable need for persistent and vigorous community-based follow-up and aid in managing life problems. Such programs, reviewed by Mueser and colleagues (1998), are often referred to as **assertive community treatment (ACT)** or **intensive case management (ICM).** Typically, they involve multidisciplinary teams having limited caseloads to ensure that discharged patients don't get overlooked and "lost," a frequent occurrence where the local mental health system is poorly organized. In general, the more intensive the services, the larger the effect in clinical improvement and social functioning (Brekke et al., 1997).

Finally, there is the question of coordinating continuing antipsychotic medication, if needed, with these other, nonmedical services. When done well, the patient benefits substantially (Klerman et al., 1994; Kopelowicz, 1997).

A Problem: System Inertia These psychosocially based efforts to compensate for the shortcomings of antipsychotic medication in treating schizophrenia are not at present generally "in place" and functioning as intended. An intensive effort to assess the degree of conformity of actual practice to a set of previously issued treatment guidelines similar to those described above in the mental health systems of two states found that conformity was generally less than 50 percent, especially in regard to the psychosocial enhancements recommended (Lehman et al., 1998). We suspect that a national compliance assessment effort covering all 50 states would not produce a more encouraging picture at this time. Actual mental health practice, at least within most state systems, fails to keep pace with what is known to be maximally effective in restoring schizophrenic patients to active and productive citizenship. In this sense we seem to have continued a very long-standing pattern of limited horizons for and neglect of this portion of the population.

DELUSIONAL DISORDER (PARANOIA)

The term **paranoia** has been in use a long time. The ancient Greeks and Romans used it to refer more or less indiscriminately to any mental disorder. Our present, more limited use of the term stems from the nineteenth century and the work of Emil Kraepelin, who reserved it for cases showing delusions and impaired contact with reality but without the bizarreness, fragmentation, and severe personality disorganization characteristic of schizophrenia.

Currently two main types of psychoses are included under the DSM-IV headings relating to (nonschizo-

phrenic) paranoid disorders: **delusional disorder,** formerly called paranoia or paranoid disorder, and **shared psychotic disorder,** in which two or more people usually of the same family develop persistent, interlocking delusional ideas. The latter condition was historically known as *folie à deux.*

Brief episodes (i.e., lasting one month or less) of otherwise uncomplicated delusional thinking are included in the category **brief psychotic disorder.** Our focus in this section will be on delusional disorder. As there is little recent literature on this disorder—it is not currently a "hot" research topic—we will be forced to rely primarily on a number of early studies. Because these studies used the traditional terminology *paranoia* and *paranoid disorder,* we will use those terms and the newer *delusional disorder* classification interchangeably.

Diagnosis of Delusional Disorder

The diagnosis of delusional disorder may be rendered difficult at times because of the imprecision of the term *delusion.* It is not always possible to determine the truth or falsity of an idea, and some ideas that are either patently false or empirically unconfirmable are held with sincerity and conviction by very many people. For example, a significant number of people believe the Nazi Holocaust against European Jewry never happened, despite overwhelming evidence to the contrary (e.g., Weinberg & Elieli, 1995). For this reason, formal definitions of delusion (as in DSM-IV) usually specify that an idea must be held as preposterous by the majority of a person's own community. As the example of Columbus's much ridiculed fifteenth-century belief that the earth is round shows, however, this criterion does not always solve the problem of differentiating truth from falsehood.

Paranoid thinking is not necessarily so different from normal thinking as we would perhaps like to think (see, e.g., Oltmanns & Maher, 1988). Newman, Duff, and Baumeister (1997) have recently demonstrated the creation of "defensive projection" (attributing one's own undesirable characteristics to others) among normal subjects by simply having them try actively to suppress thoughts of their own shortcomings. Paradoxically, such attempts at thought suppression often produce involuntary intrusions of the targeted thoughts, in this case involving threats to self-esteem, into conscious awareness. The threat is apparently diminished by attributing the same shortcomings to others.

The problem also remains of differentiating delusional disorder from paranoid personality disorder

(Chapter 9), which also involves a judgment call as to whether or not clearly eccentric and convoluted thinking merits the designation "delusional"—that is, "psychotic."

DSM-IV requires that diagnoses of delusional disorder be specified by type, based on the predominant theme of the delusions present. These types are as follows:

- *Persecutory type:* The predominant delusional theme is that one (or someone to whom one is closely related) is being subjected to some kind of malevolent treatment, such as spying, stalking, or the spreading of false rumors of illegal or immoral behavior. Legal actions of one sort or another are often instituted to redress the alleged injustice, and in extreme cases more direct and dangerous modes of counteraction are employed, such as attempted (and sometimes completed) murder.

- *Jealous type:* The predominant theme is that one's sexual partner is being unfaithful.

- *Erotomanic type:* The predominant theme is that some person of higher status, frequently someone of considerable prominence, is in love with or wants to start a sexual liaison with the delusional person.

- *Somatic type:* The predominant theme is an unshakable belief about having some physical illness or disorder whose nature is delusionally absurd.

- *Grandiose type:* The predominant theme is that one is a person of extraordinary status, power, ability, talent, beauty, etc., or that one has a special relationship with someone having such attributes, usually someone of celebrity status.

- *Mixed:* This diagnosis is used where there are combinations of the above but when no single theme predominates.

Of these types, the persecutory is by far the most common, and our discussion will deal primarily with this form of the disorder.

Although the formal diagnosis of delusional disorder is rare in clinic and mental hospital populations, this observation provides a somewhat misleading picture of its actual occurrence. Many exploited inventors, fanatical reformers, self-styled prophets, morbidly jealous spouses, persecuted teachers, business executives, or other employees fall into this category. Unless they become a serious nuisance, these people are usually able to maintain themselves in the community and do not recognize their paranoid condition nor seek help to alleviate it. In some instances, however, they are potentially dangerous, and in virtually all instances they are inveterate "injustice-detectors," inclined to undertake retributive actions of one sort or another against their supposed tormenters.

The Clinical Picture in Delusional Disorder

A paranoid, or delusionally disordered, individual feels singled out and taken advantage of, mistreated, plotted against, stolen from, spied on, ignored, or otherwise mistreated by enemies. The delusional system usually centers on one major theme, such as financial matters, a job, an invention, a conspiracy, or an unfaithful spouse. For example, a woman who is failing on the job may insist that her fellow workers and superiors have it in for her because they are envious of her great ability and efficiency. As a result, she may quit her job and go to work elsewhere, only to find friction developing again and her new job in jeopardy. Now she may become convinced that the first company has written to her present employer and has turned everyone against her so that she has not been given a fair chance. With time, more and more of the environment is integrated into her delusional system as each additional experience is misconstrued and interpreted in the light of her delusional ideas. Highlight 12.2 lists the characteristics typical of the development of paranoid thinking.

Although ideas of persecution predominate, many paranoid individuals develop delusions of grandeur in which they endow themselves with superior or unique abilities. Such exalted ideas usually center on messianic missions, political or social reforms, or remarkable inventions. Paranoid people who are religious may consider themselves appointed by God to save the world and may spend most of their time preaching and crusading. Threats of fire and brimstone, burning in hell, and similar persuasive devices are liberally employed. Many paranoid people become attached to extremist political movements and are tireless and fanatical crusaders, although they often do their cause more harm than good by their self-righteousness and their scornful intolerance of contrary views.

Aside from the delusional system, such an individual may appear perfectly normal in conversation, emotionality, and conduct. Hallucinations and the other obvious signs of psychopathology are rarely found. This normal appearance, together with the logical and coherent way in which the delusional ideas are presented, may make the individual most convincing. Persons awash in their own uncertainties, such as many joiners of religious cults established by delusionally inspired leaders, are especially vulnerable to these often charismatic inducements to believe. Indeed, as several tragic events of recent years remind us, the "message" may prove so powerful as to undergird voluntary mass suicide.

Highlight 12.2

Sequence of Events in a Paranoid Mode of Thinking

A number of investigators have concluded that the most useful perspective from which to view paranoia is in terms of a *mode of thinking*. The sequence of events that appears to characterize this mode of thinking may be summarized as follows:

1. *Suspiciousness:* The individual mistrusts the motives of others, fears he or she will be taken advantage of, and is constantly on the alert.
2. *Projective thinking:* The individual selectively perceives the actions of others to confirm suspicions and blames others for his or her failures.
3. *Hostility:* The individual responds to alleged injustices and mistreatment with anger and hostility and becomes increasingly suspicious.
4. *Paranoid illumination:* The moment when everything "falls into place"; the in-

dividual finally understands the strange feelings and events being experienced.
5. *Delusions:* The individual has delusions of influence and persecution that may be based on "some grain of truth," presented in a logical and convincing way; often, the later development of delusions of grandeur.

Over time, a paranoid individual may incorporate additional life areas, people, and events into the delusional system, creating a "pseudo-community" whose purpose is to carry out some action against him or her. Paranoid individuals who respond in this manner may come to feel that all the attention they are receiving from others is indicative of their unique abilities and importance, thus paving the way for delusions of grandeur. ■

Source: Based in part on Meissner (1978) and Swanson, Bohnert, and Smith (1970).

The following more mundane case is typical.

Case Study, A Foggy Delusion • An engineer developed detailed plans for eliminating the fog in San Francisco and other large cities by means of a system of reflectors that would heat the air by solar radiation and cause the fog to lift. The company for which he worked examined the plans and found them unsound. This rejection upset him greatly and he resigned his position, stating that the other engineers in the company were not qualified to pass judgment on any complex and advanced engineering projects like his. Instead of attempting to obtain other employment, he then devoted full time trying to find some other engineering firm that would have the vision and technical proficiency to see the great potential of his idea. He would present his plans convincingly but become highly suspicious and hostile when questions concerning their feasibility were raised. Eventually, he became convinced that there was a conspiracy among a large number of engineering firms to steal his plans and use them for their own profit. He reported his suspicions to the po-

lice, threatening to do something about the situation himself unless they took action. As a consequence, he was hospitalized for observation and diagnosed as suffering from paranoia.

Causal Factors in Delusional Disorder

Most of us on various occasions may wonder if we are not jinxed, when it seems as if everything we do goes wrong and the cards seem to be stacked against us. Many people go through life feeling underrated and frustrated, brooding over fancied or real failures to achieve their goals. What distinguishes the pre-paranoid individual is that he or she develops an unerring tendency to locate the blame for untoward life events in injustices committed by other people (Kinderman & Bentall, 1997).

We have already noted that individuals with paranoid schizophrenia tend to show less of the extensive cognitive disorganization seen in other forms of schizophrenia. Also, while the maintenance of a severely paranoid fix on the world does indeed require drastic contortions of a

The insistent way the owner of this car has chosen to broadcast his or her ideas which are hostile, suspicious, and a distortion of factual evidence, indicate delusional thinking.

person's basic cognitive resources, it also requires that the person be relatively deft in dealing with the information the environment provides. If an individual were so impaired cognitively as to be unable to function on a day-by-day basis, the alertness and selectively efficient information processing essential to the effective maintenance of an organized delusional system would, of course, be unavailable. Implied in these observations is the idea that severe disruption of cognitive processes per se may not be implicated in the causal pattern leading to delusional, or paranoid, forms of psychosis, and might indeed be a factor that, if present, would discourage their development.

Some studies have shown that pre-paranoid individuals do not generally show a history of normal play with other children or good socialization in terms of warm, affectionate relationships (Sarvis, 1962; Schwartz, 1963; Swanson et al., 1970). Their standoffish and relatively unfriendly interpersonal style may make them understandably unpopular with peers—in effect, an aversive stimulus. Thus an unduly suspicious or coldly rejecting person frequently becomes a target of actual discrimination and mistreatment. He or she may develop feelings of being singled out as "different" and vaguely unacceptable, enhancing self-consciousness and undue wariness in dealing with others (Lemert, 1962).

Where delusional disorder develops, it usually does so gradually, as perceived failures and seeming betrayals force these individuals to rely on their tendency to blame others. To avoid self-devaluation, they ruminate about "logical" reasons for their lack of success and become hypervigilant for clues that may provide a self-esteem–preserving answer. Why were they denied a much-deserved recognition or promotion? Why was it given to someone obviously far less qualified? They scrutinize the environment, search for hidden meanings, and ask leading questions. They overly personalize innocent events and ponder like a detective over the "evidence" they are able to unearth, trying to fit it into some sort of meaningful picture. And as the picture is elaborated, their resultant behavior enhances the likelihood their suspicions will be confirmed. This development of "paranoid social cognition" is well described in a recent analysis by Roderick Kramer (1998), whose summary graphic appears in Figure 12.6.

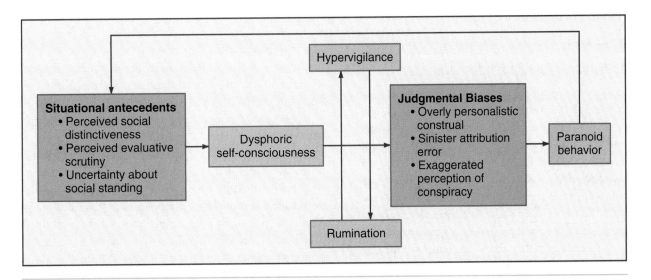

FIGURE 12.6   PARANOID SOCIAL COGNITION

Source: From R.M. Kramer (1998).

Gradually the picture begins to crystallize—a process commonly referred to as "paranoid illumination." Formerly only a suspicion, it now becomes obvious that such individuals are being singled out for some reason, that other people are working against them, that their rights are being trampled, that they are being interfered with in unscrupulous ways. In essence, these individuals protect themselves against the intolerable assumption, "There is something wrong with me," with the defensive transformation, "They are doing something unjust to me." They have failed not because of any inferiority or lack on their part, but because others are working against them. They are on the side of good and the progress of humankind, while their enemies are allied with the forces of evil. With this as their fundamental defensive premise, they proceed to distort and falsify the facts to fit it and gradually develop a logical, fixed, delusional system. This process has been referred to as the building up of a paranoid "pseudo-community" in which an individual organizes surrounding people (both real and sometimes imaginary) into a structured group whose purpose it is to carry out some despicable or violent action against him or her (Cameron, 1959).

Treatments and Outcomes in Delusional Disorder

We do not have established, empirically validated approaches for the treatment of delusional disorders. It is generally conceded that, once a delusional system is well established, it is extremely difficult to dismantle. It is usually impossible to communicate with such individuals in a rational way concerning their problems. In addition, they are not prone to seek treatment, which many would interpret as an unacceptable admission of weakness, but are more likely to seek justice for all the wrong done to them.

An offer of medication—even if any genuinely promising ones were available—is very likely to be refused, and it may indeed be woven into a delusional system involving conspiracy and intended harm. Nor is hospitalization likely to help, for delusionally disordered persons are likely to see it as a form of unjust incarceration and persecution. If forcibly hospitalized, they are apt to regard themselves as superior to hospital staff as well as other patients and will usually complain that their families and the staff have conspired to have them "put away" illegally and for no valid reason. Not uncommonly, they seek legal redress, and sometimes they are successful in gaining a court-ordered release, particularly if they have not as yet been charged with any crime. Seeing nothing wrong with themselves, they refuse to cooperate or participate in anything resembling "treatment."

Eventually, however, many hospitalized delusional persons realize that their failure to curb their actions or expression of their delusional ideas will result in prolonged hospitalization. As a result, they may make a pretext of renouncing their delusions, admitting that they did hold such ideas but claiming that they now realize the ideas are absurd and are giving them up. After their release, they are often more reserved in expressing their ideas and in annoying other people, but they are usually far from recovered. Thus the prognosis for complete recovery from paranoia has traditionally been unfavorable.

UNRESOLVED ISSUES

The Overlooked Value of Psychosocial Intervention in the Schizophrenias

The disorders we call the schizophrenias confront society with the massive problem of how to take care of people who seem unable, or unmotivated, to take care of themselves. Neither institutionalization nor deinstitutionalization has worked (see Chapter 18). And the traditional antipsychotic drugs have proved, as we have seen, insufficiently effective in promoting social recovery—though the newer ones show some greater promise. In overestimating their real properties, we have largely failed to take advantage of the access the antipsychotic drugs have given us to rebuilding patient resources in such a manner as to ensure successful reentry into society's mainstream. A dispassionate analysis of the problem, as well as much pertinent research evidence, indicates that an enormously expanded effort at the psychosocial level of intervention is needed if we are to ease the massive personal, familial, and societal tragedies that the schizophrenias inflict.

As recent research reviewed in this chapter has also shown, however, merely identifying what is needed in a more comprehensive approach to the problem by no means ensures that these measures will be carried out. The main difficulty appears twofold: (1) professional inertia and (2) monetary expense. A potential third problem, that of patient noncompliance in taking prescribed medication, may be significantly eased with the development of new compounds having minimal noxious side effects.

We have already noted the failure of the professional community to pick up on promising treatment leads that deviated from standard practice. We need to find ways of overcoming the often ideologically based prejudices of professionals and institute in their stead a renewed respect for what the research evidence is actually telling us. The challenge of inertia is not trivial, but neither is it insurmountable.

The economic investment involved in approaching the treatment of schizophrenia in the manner suggested by the best of currently available research knowledge is very high. Indications are that it is going to be enormously personnel-intensive, and those personnel will need to have resources and skills that are expensive. However, the other side of this coin, the societal economic losses sustained by large numbers of economically dependent, unemployable adults who have high rates of utilization of expensive facilities are also expensive—estimated in the United States to be in excess of $70 billion annually (Wyatt et al., 1995). A recent literature review by Gabbard and colleagues (1997) emphasizes the economic *savings* realized where individual psychotherapy is employed in the treatment of severe mental disorders, including schizophrenia. It is a virtual certainty that "society"—that is, taxpayers—will pay one way or another. The advantage of restoring lives in the process makes the choice, it seems to the authors, a "no-brainer."

SUMMARY

The schizophrenic disorders, involving largely psychotic phenomena, include some of the most extreme deviations to be found in the domain of psychopathology. Markedly heterogeneous in their organization, they manifest a profile of disordered functioning in the areas of cognitive incoherence, content of thought, perception, emotional expression, identity confusion, disrupted volition, retreat into a personal world, and peculiarities of motor behavior.

Classical subtypes of schizophrenia include undifferentiated (mixed symptoms not fitting into other categories or moving rapidly among them), catatonic (involving chiefly motor symptoms), disorganized (incoherent, silly, or inappropriate affect and behavior), and paranoid (persistent ideas or hallucinations regarding persecution or grandiosity, or other themes). Modern research has tended to focus on positive-syndrome (e.g., hallucinations and delusions) versus negative-syndrome (e.g., emotional blunting, poverty of speech) schizophrenia. Given these variations as well as other anomalies, some have questioned the validity of the schizophrenia diagnosis. Schizophrenia is best seen as a "provisional construct" that probably encompasses several different disorders.

Hardly anybody questions the existence of a cluster of behaviors, called the schizophrenias, that are baffling in their departure from the realities of common experience. Such behaviors have been correlated with biological, psychosocial, and sociocultural variables. There appears to be a hereditary component in the causal pattern, one that may or may not interact with other biological variables, such as early neurological compromise, in enhancing risk for developing the disorder. Current biological thinking emphasizes a developmental view in which an early (including prenatal) brain anomaly results in a failure of the brain's circuitry to align itself properly during a later phase of synaptic reorganization.

The weight of evidence indicates that biological factors alone will not account for most instances of schizophrenia. It indicates powerful, but as yet poorly understood, contributions from psychosocial and sociocultural sources. Research findings at all levels of observation suggest that complex interactions involving numerous influences, probably different in different patients, are involved.

The delusional (paranoid) disorders, in which schizophrenic disorganization seems not to be a significant factor, form a subgroup of psychoses that have not received much study in recent years. A paranoid individual harbors ideas of persecution, grandiosity, both, or more rarely of other consensually false content. The person, however, is usually otherwise functional—including, often, highly organized cognitive functioning—in areas that do not impinge on the delusional thought structure (the paranoid illumination) in which the person is centrally involved. These people can often function at a marginal level in society. Some of them, however, become dangerous. Treatment of chronically paranoid persons is currently difficult, at best.

The treatment of schizophrenia in recent decades has probably relied too heavily on antipsychotic medication, which often does little to promote social recovery. A variety of psychosocial treatment initiatives have promising records in this area. By and large, they have not been deployed at the levels required. The latter remains an unresolved issue.

KEY TERMS

the schizophrenias (p. 463)

psychosis (p. 463)

delusional disorder (p. 463)

positive-syndrome schizophrenia (p. 465)

negative-syndrome schizophrenia (p. 465)

Type I schizophrenia (p. 465)

Type II schizophrenia (p. 465)

delusion (p. 467)

hallucination (p. 468)

undifferentiated schizophrenia (p. 470)

catatonic schizophrenia (p. 471)

disorganized schizophrenia (p. 473)

paranoid schizophrenia (p. 474)

residual schizophrenia (p. 476)

schizoaffective disorder (p. 476)

schizophreniform disorder (p. 476)

expressed emotion (EE) (p. 491)

social recovery (p. 494)

assertive community treatment (ACT) (p. 496)

intensive case management (ICM) (p. 496)

paranoia (p. 496)

delusional disorder (p. 496)

shared psychotic disorder (p. 496)

brief psychotic disorder (p. 496)

CHAPTER **THIRTEEN**

Brain Disorders and Other Cognitive Impairments

Arthur F. Becker (Buhr),
The Kiss. Diagnosed as a
degenerative imbecile,
Becker recorded soft pencil
impressions on paper,
surrounded by narratives.
His strange figures, only
half-human in form, have
barely discernible features.

Some psychological problems arise as a result of damage or defects in the brain tissue. The brain is the organ of behavior: it processes relevant available information from external and internal environments (including itself) and selects and executes action patterns stored in its memory banks. Damage to the brain may therefore disrupt effective thought, feeling, and behavior. The relationship between mental deficits associated with organic brain defects and abnormal behavior is complicated and often unclear, largely because the brain and its functions are so intertwined.

When structural defects in the brain are present before birth or occur at an early age, mental retardation may result, its severity depending to a large extent on the magnitude of the defect. Some people who sustain prenatal or perinatal (that is, during birth) brain damage may experience normal mental development in most aspects of behavior but suffer from specific cognitive or motor deficits, such as learning disorders or spasticity (excessive muscle contraction that impairs motor performance).

Sometimes the intact brain sustains damage after it has completed normal biological development. A wide variety of injuries, diseases, and toxic substances may cause the functional impairment or death of neurons or their connections, which may lead to obvious deficits in psychological functioning. In some cases such damage is associated with behavior that is not only impaired but also highly maladaptive—even psychotic. People who sustain serious brain damage after they have mastered the basic tasks of life are in a very different situation from those who start life with a deficit of this kind. When brain injury occurs in an older child or adult, there is a loss in established functioning. This loss—this deprivation of already acquired and customary skills—can be painfully obvious to the victim, adding an often pronounced psychological burden to the organic one. In other cases the impairment may extend to the capacity for realistic self-appraisal, leaving these patients relatively unaware of their losses and thus poorly motivated for rehabilitation.

In this chapter we will first discuss those disorders that occur when the normal adolescent or adult brain has suffered significant organic impairment or damage, following which we will move to a consideration of compromised brain functioning that is either congenital or arises in the earliest phases of psychological development.

BRAIN IMPAIRMENT AND ADULT DISORDER

Prior to the DSM-IV of 1994, most of the disorders to be considered in this section were called **organic mental disorders,** an outmoded term that failed to distinguish

between the direct *neurological* consequences of brain injury, including various cognitive deficits, and the *psychopathological* problems sometimes accompanying such injury, such as depression or paranoid delusions. Since the latter types of abnormal "mental" phenomena are common in people with no demonstrable brain anomalies, the implication that they were in some other cases caused by brain damage was at best unproved and at worst possibly seriously misleading.

The destruction of brain tissue may involve only limited behavioral deficits or a wide range of psychological impairments, depending on (1) the nature, location, and extent of neural damage; (2) the premorbid (predisorder) competence and personality of the individual; (3) the individual's total life situation; and (4) the amount of time since the first appearance of the condition. Although the degree of mental impairment is usually directly related to the extent of damage, in some cases involving relatively severe brain damage, mental change is astonishingly slight; in other cases of apparently mild and limited damage there may be profoundly altered functioning.

Neuropsychological Disorders and Brain Damage

The fundamental disorders we shall be dealing with in this section are always in the strictest sense *neuropsychological* ones, although psychopathological problems may be associated with them. Some "mental" symptoms are therefore the more or less direct product of the physical interruption of established neural pathways in the brain. The bases of these symptoms are relatively well understood, and the symptoms themselves have relatively constant features in people with comparable types of brain injury in terms of location and extent. For example, attention is often impaired with mild to moderate diffuse (widespread) damage, such as might occur with moderate oxygen deprivation or the ingestion of toxic substances such as mercury. Such a person, for example, may complain of memory problems due to an inability to sustain focused retrieval efforts, while showing an intact ability to store new information. Severe diffuse damage results in dementia, described later.

In contrast to diffuse damage, *focal brain lesions* are circumscribed areas of abnormal change in brain structure, such as might occur with a sharply defined traumatic injury or an interruption of blood supply (commonly called *stroke*) to a part of the brain. With progressive brain disease, such as Alzheimer's disease or expanding brain tumors, one may see a gradual spreading over more and more focal sites, leading to permanent damage that is both diffuse and severe. Some consequences of organic brain disorders that have mainly focal origins but commonly appear in the context of progressively diffuse damage are as follows:

1. *Impairment of memory:* The individual has notable trouble remembering recent events and less trouble remembering events of the remote past, with a tendency in some patients to confabulate—that is, to invent memories to fill in gaps. In severe instances no new experience can be retained for more than a few minutes. It either fails entirely to be stored in long-term memory or is stored in a way that provides no means for it to be readily retrieved at a later time.

2. *Impairment of orientation:* The individual is unable to locate himself or herself accurately, especially in time but also in space or in relation to the personal identities of self or others.

3. *Impairment of learning, comprehension, and judgment:* The individual's thinking becomes clouded, sluggish, and/or inaccurate. The person may lose the ability to plan with foresight or to understand abstract concepts and hence to process anything but the simplest of information, often described as thought impoverishment.

4. *Impairment of emotional control or modulation:* The individual manifests emotional overreactivity and easy arousal to laughter, tears, rage, and other extreme emotions.

5. *Apathy or emotional blunting:* The individual shows little emotion, especially where deterioration is advanced.

6. *Impairment in the initiation of behavior:* The individual lacks self-starting capability and may have to be repeatedly reminded about what to do next, even where the behavior involved remains well within the person's range of competence. This is sometimes referred to as loss of "executive" function.

7. *Impairment of controls over matters of propriety and ethical conduct:* The individual may manifest a marked lowering of personal standards in appearance, personal hygiene, sexuality, language, and so on.

8. *Impairment of receptive and expressive communication:* The individual may be unable to comprehend written or spoken language, or may be unable to express his or her own thoughts orally or in writing.

9. *Impaired visuospatial ability:* The individual has difficulty in coordinating motor activity with the characteristics of the visual environment, affecting performance in graphomotor (handwriting and drawing), constructional (e.g., assembling things), and other tasks dependent on such skills.

The Neuropsychology/Psychopathology Interaction Most people who have a neuropsychological disorder do not develop psychopathological symptoms, such as panic attacks, dissociative episodes, or delusions, although many will show at least mild deficits in cognitive processing and self-regulation. The psychopathological symptoms that do sometimes accompany brain impairment are less predictable than those just listed and more likely to show individual nuances consistent with the prior personality and the total psychological situation confronting the patient. It is erroneous to assume that a psychological disorder—for example, a serious depression accompanying deficits produced by brain injury—is necessarily and completely explained by reference to the patient's brain damage; it might better be explained in terms of the psychological challenge presented by the patient's awareness of dramatically lessened competence.

Significant impairment may have variable effects on individuals. A person is a functional unit and reacts as such to all stressors, whether they are organic or psychological. A well-functioning and resourceful personality can usually withstand brain damage (or any other stress) better than a rigid, immature, or otherwise psychologically handicapped one—except where brain damage is so severe or its location so critical as to destroy the integrity of the personality. Similarly, an individual who has a favorable life situation is likely to have a better prognosis than one who does not, a conclusion that extends to children suffering traumatic brain injuries (Yeates et al., 1997). In recent years, the concept of *brain reserve capacity* has been employed increasingly to account for the fact that intelligent, well-educated, mentally active people have enhanced resistance to mental and behavioral deterioration following significant brain injury (e.g., see Mori et al., 1997a; Schmand et al., 1997a). Because the brain is the center for the integration of behavior, however, there are limits to the amount of brain damage that anyone can tolerate or compensate for without exhibiting behavior that is decidedly abnormal.

Hardware and Software (A Useful, Though Crude, Analogy) We believe that it is somewhat hazardous to employ computer analogies in discussions of the brain and mental processes. However, such an analogy seems to be useful in the context of the present discussion of the relationship of brain impairment to behavioral abnormalities.

When computers fail to do what we want and expect them to do for us, our troubleshooting speculations normally begin with two possibilities: (1) a hardware problem—perhaps a "sticky" chip, a deficient power supply, or a defective resistor or capacitor; or (2) a software problem, such as having a "bug" in our program of procedural instructions or an error in the data we load into a machine that is in perfect working order.

We may thus consider the intact human brain to be a highly programmable system of hardware, and psychosocial experience in both its developmental and current aspects to be functionally equivalent to software. Using our analogy, neuropsychological disorders by definition have hardware defects as their primary cause. In other words, in such situations the brain cannot perform the physical operations called for by virtue of a breakdown in one or another (or several) of its components. The direct "symptoms" of such a breakdown, such as those listed above, should be predictable from a knowledge of how these components work. In general, our knowledge in this area of the direct effects of various types of brain damage is relatively advanced.

A breakdown in the brain's hardware will necessarily have pervasive effects on the processing of software, or past and present experience. Indeed, in the case of extensive hardware damage, much or perhaps most previously loaded information may be lost because the structural components in which it had been encoded are no longer operative; new information for the same reason fails to be adequately loaded. Such a condition is known clinically as *dementia*. With less extensive hardware damage, we see effects that depend to a considerable extent on the particular characteristics of the software that constitutes the record of an individual's life experience, which is unique. The delusion that one is Napoleon, rather common in the nineteenth century, would not have been seen in a patient who lived before Napoleon became famous. Such symptoms are at most only indirect manifestations of organic hardware breakdown; their content is obviously a product of life experience, and they sometimes occur in the absence of any demonstrable hardware breakdown at all. In this case, we must consider the possibility that they are due entirely to serious flaws in the individual's personality, or (in our analogy) software.

General Clinical Features of Neuropsychological Disorders With possibly minor exceptions, cell bodies and neural pathways in the brain do not have the power of regeneration, which means that their destruction is permanent. Some functions lost as a result of actual brain damage may be relearned, typically at a compromised and less efficient level, or the injured person may develop techniques to compensate for what is missing. When recovery of function following brain injury is rapid, which

often happens, much of this is due to the resolution of temporary conditions, such as edema (swelling), produced in tissue spared from actual damage. Recovery from disabilities following an irreversible brain lesion may be relatively complete or limited, and it may proceed rapidly or slowly. Because there are limits to compensatory capacities of the brain, however, brain damage leads to more or less extensive permanent diminishment or loss of function over a wide range of physical and psychological abilities. In general, as already noted, the greater the amount of tissue damage, the greater the impairment of function.

The location of the damage may also play a significant role in determining a patient's ultimate neuropsychological status. The brain is highly specialized, each part—each cell in fact—making a unique contribution to the functional whole of an organism's activity (see Figure 13.1). Thus the two hemispheres, while interacting intimately at many levels, are involved in somewhat different types of mental processing. For example, functions that are dependent on serial (i.e., ordered) processing of familiar information, such as language or solving mathematical equations, take place mostly in the left hemisphere for nearly everyone. The right hemisphere is generally specialized for configurational or *gestalt* (i.e., appreciation of patterns) processing, which is best suited for grasping overall meanings in novel situations, reasoning on a nonverbal, intuitive level, and appreciation of spatial relations. Even within hemispheres, the various lobes and areas within lobes mediate somewhat specialized functions.

Although none of these relationships between brain location and behavior can be considered constant or uni-

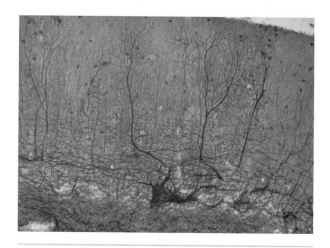

With possibly minor exceptions, cell bodies and neural pathways in the brain do not have the power of regeneration, which means that their destruction is permanent. In general, the greater the tissue damage, the greater the impairment.

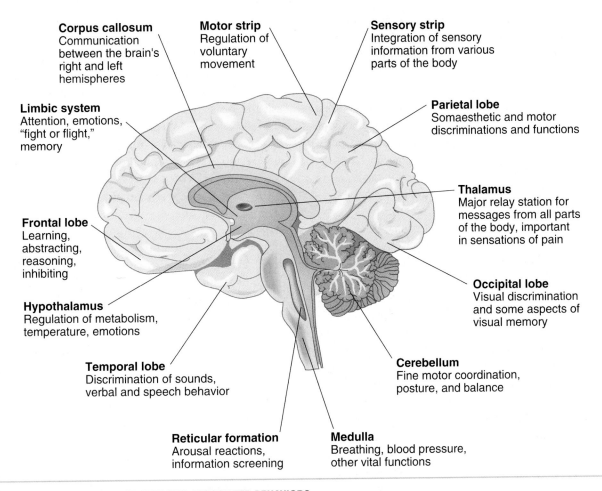

Corpus callosum
Communication
between the brain's
right and left
hemispheres

Motor strip
Regulation of
voluntary
movement

Sensory strip
Integration of sensory
information from various
parts of the body

Limbic system
Attention, emotions,
"fight or flight,"
memory

Parietal lobe
Somaesthetic and motor
discriminations and functions

Frontal lobe
Learning,
abstracting,
reasoning,
inhibiting

Thalamus
Major relay station for
messages from all parts
of the body, important
in sensations of pain

Hypothalamus
Regulation of metabolism,
temperature, emotions

Occipital lobe
Visual discrimination
and some aspects of
visual memory

Temporal lobe
Discrimination of sounds,
verbal and speech behavior

Cerebellum
Fine motor coordination,
posture, and balance

Reticular formation
Arousal reactions,
information screening

Medulla
Breathing, blood pressure,
other vital functions

FIGURE 13.1 BRAIN STRUCTURES AND ASSOCIATED BEHAVIORS

versal, it is possible to make broad generalizations about the likely effects of damage to particular parts of the brain. Damage to the frontal areas, for example, is associated with either of two contrasting clinical pictures: (1) behavioral inertia, passivity, apathy, and an inability to give up a given stream of associations or initiate a new one (perseverative thought); or (2) impulsiveness, distractibility, and insufficient ethical restraint. Damage to specific areas of the right parietal lobe may produce impairment of visual-motor coordination or distortions of body image, while damage to the left parietal area may impair certain aspects of language function, including reading and writing, as well as arithmetical abilities.

Damage to certain structures within the temporal lobes disrupts an early stage of memory storage. Extensive bilateral temporal damage can produce a syndrome in which remote memory remains relatively intact but nothing new can be stored for later retrieval. Damage to other structures within the temporal lobes is associated with disturbances of eating, sexuality, and the emotions, probably by way of disrupting the functioning of the ad-

jacent limbic system, a center deep in the brain regulating these "primitive" functions, apparently by way of extensive communication with controlling frontal-lobe structures.

Occipital damage produces a variety of visual impairments and visual association deficits, the nature of the deficit depending on the particular site of the lesion. For example, a person may be unable to recognize familiar faces or to visualize and understand symbolic stimuli correctly. Unfortunately, many types of brain disease are general and therefore diffuse in their destructive effects, causing multiple and widespread interruptions of the brain's circuitry.

Diagnostic Issues in Neuropsychological Disorders The DSM-IV presents the diagnostic coding of various neuropsychological disorders in different and somewhat inconsistent ways. Traditionally, these disorders have been classified by disease entity or recognizable medical disorder, such as Huntington's disease, general paresis, and so on. That is, the principal etiologic factor, the underlying neurological disease process, was specified in the diagnostic term applied. As we have seen, however, such basically medical disorders that may have various kinds of associated mental symptoms are normally coded not on Axis I but on Axis III of the DSM-IV. The associated mental conditions are then typically coded on Axis I, normally with the qualifying phrase, "Due to [a specified General Medical Condition]" (i.e., the disease process indicated on Axis III). Many of the common neuropsychological disorders are handled in this manner, but there are important exceptions, as noted below.

Some pathologic brain changes that may produce significant mental symptoms are related to the pathogenic effects of abusing certain substances, such as long-term, excessive alcohol consumption (see Chapter 10). In these cases a specific etiologic notation is included in the Axis I diagnosis, as in Substance-Induced Persisting Amnestic Disorder (referring to a circumscribed and characteristic type of memory impairment). DSM-IV also deals in a special way with certain conditions, often progressive, that result in pronounced and generalized cognitive deterioration, or dementia. Here the presumed underlying neurological disease process is sometimes included in the Axis I designation, and also on Axis III as well. Thus, notable cognitive impairment associated with cerebrovascular disease might have a DSM-IV diagnostic code as follows:

Axis I: Vascular Dementia

Axis III: Occlusion, cerebral artery

There is a degree of redundancy here inasmuch as the Axis I term already implies the existence of cerebral artery blockage, or "occlusion." The important *Dementia of the Alzheimer's Type* Axis I diagnosis is managed in a similar way, with *Alzheimer's disease* being designated on Axis III.

Bearing in mind these basic and potentially confusing issues concerning relationships between the brain, mental contents and processes, behavior, and formal diagnosis, we move now to a consideration of several of the more common and important neuropsychological clinical syndromes.

Neuropsychological Symptom Syndromes

As we have seen, a *syndrome* is a group of signs and symptoms that tend to cluster together. The neuropsychological syndromes include many such indicators similar to those that occur in the schizophrenias, the mood disorders, and certain Axis II personality disorders, but

in these syndromes they are assumed to reflect underlying brain pathology. The specific brain pathology may vary; it may be the result of brain disease or of the withdrawal of a chemical substance on which a person has become physiologically dependent. For our purposes, we will group these syndromes into six categories: (1) delirium, (2) dementia, (3) amnestic syndrome, (4) neuropsychological delusional syndrome, (5) neuropsychological mood syndrome, and (6) neuropsychological personality syndrome.

We should note that more than one syndrome may be present at a time in a given patient and that syndromes and patterns of syndromes may change over a particular disorder's course of development. As already noted, the behavior associated with some syndromes involving brain damage mimics the types of disorders we have described in previous chapters. Clinicians always need to be alert to the possibility that brain impairment itself may be directly responsible for the clinical phenomena observed. Failure to do so could result in serious diagnostic errors, as when a clinician falsely attributes a mood change to psychological causes and fails to consider what may actually be a neuropsychological origin, such as a brain tumor (Geschwind, 1975; Malamud, 1975; Purisch & Sbordone, 1997; Weinberger, 1984).

Delirium The syndrome called **delirium** is characterized by the relatively rapid onset of widespread disorganization of the higher mental processes; it is caused by a generalized disturbance in brain metabolism. Delirium may result from several conditions, including head injury, toxic or metabolic disturbances, oxygen deprivation, insufficient delivery of blood to brain tissues, or precipitous withdrawal from alcohol or other drugs in an addicted person. Information-processing capacities are impaired, affecting such basic functions as attention, perception, memory, and thinking; and the patient may have frightening hallucinations. The syndrome often includes abnormal psychomotor activity, such as wild thrashing about, and disturbance of the sleep cycle. Delirium reflects a breakdown in the functional integrity of the brain. In this respect, it may be seen as only one step above coma and, in fact, it may lead to coma. A delirious person is essentially unable to carry out purposeful mental activity of any kind; current experience appears to make no contact with the person's previously acquired store of knowledge. Delirious states tend to be acute conditions that rarely last more than a week, terminating in recovery or, less often, in death due to the underlying injury or disease.

Dementia The essential feature of **dementia** is the normally progressive deterioration of brain functioning occurring after the completion of brain maturation (that is, after about 15 years of age). Early in the course of the disease, an individual is alert and fairly well attuned to events in the environment. Episodic (memory for events), but not necessarily semantic (language and concept), memory functioning is typically affected in the early stages, especially memory for recent events. Patients with dementia also show increasingly marked deficits in abstract thinking, the acquisition of new knowledge or skills, visuospatial comprehension, motor control, problem solving, and judgment. Personality deterioration and loss of motivation accompany these other deficits. Normally, dementia is also accompanied by an impairment in emotional control and in moral and ethical sensibilities; for example, the person may engage in crude solicitations for sex. Dementia may be progressive or static, more often the former; occasionally it is even reversible. Its course depends to a large extent on its underlying causes.

The factors causing dementia are many and varied. They include degenerative processes that usually, but not always, affect older individuals. Other causes may be repeated cerebrovascular accidents (strokes); certain infectious diseases, such as syphilis, meningitis, and AIDS; intracranial tumors and abscesses; certain dietary deficiencies; severe or repeated head injury; anoxia (lack of oxygen); and the ingestion or inhalation of toxic substances. As Table 13.1 indicates, the most common cause of dementia is degenerative brain disease, particularly Alzheimer's disease.

The Amnestic Syndrome The essential feature of the **amnestic syndrome** is a striking deficit in the ability to recall ongoing events more than a few minutes after they have taken place. Immediate memory and, to a lesser extent, memory for events that occurred before the disorder's development may remain largely intact, as does memory for words and concepts. An amnestic individual, then, is typically constrained to live for the most part only in the present or the remote past; the recent past is for most practical purposes unavailable. We should add here that the question of whether the recent past is unavailable in some absolute sense is subject to differing interpretations. Some evidence suggests that these individuals may recognize or even recollect events of the recent past if given sufficient cues, which would indicate that the information has been acquired. Thus, some part of the memory difficulty may involve a defective retrieval mechanism rather than a failure of memory storage per se.

In contrast to the dementia syndrome, overall cognitive functioning in the amnestic syndrome may remain relatively intact. The affected person may thus be able to execute complex tasks if the nature of the task provides its own distinctive cues as to the stages of the task already completed; if it does not, then the individual may become hopelessly enmeshed in recycling through the same procedure. Theoretically, the disorder involves chiefly the relationship between the short-term and long-term memory systems; the contents of the former, always limited in scope and ephemeral in duration, are not stored in a way that permits ready accessibility or retrieval (Hirst, 1982).

TABLE 13.1 DEMENTIA IN 417 PATIENTS FULLY EVALUATED FOR DEMENTIA

Diagnosis	Number	Percent
Alzheimer's disease or dementia of unknown cause	199	47.7
Alcoholic dementia	42	10.0
Multi-infarct dementia [Vascular dementia]	39	9.4
Normal pressure hydrocephalus	25	6.0
Intracranial masses [tumors]	20	4.8
Huntington's disease	12	2.9
Drug toxicity	10	2.4
Post-traumatic	7	1.7
Other identified dementing diseases[a]	28	6.7
Pseudodementias[b]	28	6.7
Dementia uncertain	7	1.7

[a]Including epilepsy, subarachnoid hemorrhage, encephalitis, amyotropic lateral sclerosis, Parkinson's disease, hyperthyroidism, syphilis, liver disease, and cerebral anoxia episode, all less than 1 percent incidence.

[b]Including depression (16), schizophrenia (5), mania (2), "hysteria" (1), and not demented (4).

Source: Based on Wells (1979).

In the most common forms of amnestic syndrome—those associated with alcohol or barbiturate addiction—the disorder may be irreversible; the person never regains the ability to acquire new information in a way that ensures its availability when needed. A wide range of other pathogenic factors, such as a correctable medical condition, may produce the amnestic syndrome. In these cases, depending on the nature and extent of damage to the affected neural structures and on the treatment undertaken, the syndrome may in time abate wholly, in part, or hardly at all. A wide range of techniques has been developed to assist the good-prognosis amnestic patient in remembering recent events (e.g., Gouvier et al., 1997).

The Neuropsychological Delusional Syndrome

In **neuropsychological delusional syndrome,** false beliefs or belief systems arise in a setting of known or suspected brain impairment and are considered to be due primarily to the accompanying organic brain pathology. These delusions vary in content depending to some extent on the particular etiology involved. For example, a distinctly paranoid, suspicious, and persecutory delusional system is commonly seen with long-standing abuse of amphetamine drugs, whereas grandiose and expansive delusions are more characteristic of the now fortunately rare advanced neurosyphilis (general paresis). Many early Alzheimer patients develop jealousy delusions, accusing their often elderly spouses of sexual infidelity. Other etiological factors in the neuropsychological delusional syndrome include head injury and intracranial tumors.

Neuropsychological Mood Syndrome

Some cases of serious mood disturbance appear to be caused by disruptions in the normal physiology of cerebral function. Such conditions may closely resemble the symptoms seen in either depressive or manic mood disorders. Severe depressive syndromes, whether or not associated with organic pathology, may on superficial examination appear as dementias, in which case the term *pseudodementia* is often applied. On the other hand, subjective complaints among the elderly of, for example, memory loss may be an accurate harbinger of developing dementia (Schmand et al., 1997b). The neuropsychological mood reaction may be minimal or severe, and the course of the disorder varies widely, depending on the nature of the organic pathology. **Neuropsychological mood syndromes** may be caused by cerebrovascular accidents (strokes), Parkinson's disease, head injury, withdrawal of certain drugs, intracranial tumors or tumors of the hormone-secreting organs, and excessive use of steroid (adrenocortical hormone) drugs or certain other medications. Of course, an

This man has Parkinson's disease, which may be associated with a neuropsychological mood syndrome, a cluster of symptoms that closely resembles those seen in either depressive or manic mood disorders

awareness of lost function or a hopeless outlook might itself make a person depressed, so special care needs to be taken in the diagnostic process when there is reason to believe the patient harbors pessimistic thoughts about his or her clinical outcome (see Teri & Wagner, 1992; Teri et al., 1997).

Neuropsychological Personality Syndromes

A change in an individual's general personality style or traits following brain injury of one or another origin is the essential feature of **neuropsychological personality syndromes.** Normally the change is in a socially negative direction; it may include impaired social judgment, lessened control of emotions and impulses, diminished concern about the consequences of one's behavior, and an inability to sustain goal-directed activity. Many different causes are associated with the neuropsychological personality syndromes, and the course of the disorder depends on its etiology. Occasionally, as when it is induced by medication, the personality change may be transitory. Often, however, it is the first sign of impending deterioration, as when a kindly and gentle old man makes sexual advances toward a child or when a conservative executive suddenly begins to engage in unwise financial dealings. Much evidence indicates that a common feature in the organic personality syndrome may be damage to the frontal lobes (Bennett, Dittmar, & Ho, 1997; Sherwin & Geschwind, 1978; Stuss, Gow, & Heatherington, 1992), perhaps especially the right frontal (Borod, 1992).

The DSM-IV classification lists several different mental disorders in which brain impairment or other general medical conditions are believed to be contributory; many of these are related to substance abuse and involve only temporary physiological disruption (see Chapter 10).

The disorders we will discuss in the following sections are longer-term disorders in which major, usually permanent, brain pathology occurs but in which an individual's emotional, motivational, and behavioral reactions to the loss of function also play an important role. Indeed, as was earlier suggested, it is often impossible to distinguish between maladaptive behavior that is directly caused by neuropsychological dysfunction from that which is basically part of an individual's psychological reaction to the deficits and disabilities experienced (Bennett et al., 1997; Fabrega, 1981; Geschwind, 1975; Teri & Wagner, 1992).

The three types of neuropsychological mental disorder we will discuss in greater detail are (1) HIV-1 infection of the brain, (2) dementia of the Alzheimer's type, (3) and disorders involving traumatic head injury. Vascular (formerly multi-infarct) dementia will be briefly addressed following the section on Alzheimer's, chiefly as a contrast to that disease.

Neuropsychological Disorder with HIV-1 Infection

As we saw in Chapter 8, the devastating effects on the immune system produced by infection with the HIV Type 1 virus renders its victims susceptible to a wide variety of other infectious agents. When neuropsychological syndromes were first observed among AIDS patients early in the 1980s, it was assumed that they were due to secondary infections of this sort or to the brain tumors also associated with immune system incompetence. Then, in 1983, Snider and colleagues published the first systematic evidence that the presence of the HIV-1 virus (or a mutant form of it) could itself result in the destruction of brain cells. Since then, several different forms of such HIV-induced central nervous system pathology have been identified, some of which appear to be associated with the emergence of psychotic (e.g., delusional) phenomena (Sewell et al., 1994). To date, however, most attention has focused on the **AIDS dementia complex (ADC),** a generalized loss of cognitive functioning affecting a substantial proportion of AIDS patients.

The neuropathology of ADC involves various changes in the brain, among them generalized atrophy, edema, inflammation, and patches of demyelination (loss of the myelin sheath surrounding nerve fibers), as described by various investigators (Adams & Ferraro, 1997; Gabuzda & Hirsch, 1987; Gray, Gherardi, & Scaravilli, 1988; Price et al., 1988a; Sewell et al., 1994). No brain area may be spared, but the damage appears concentrated in subcortical regions, notably the central white matter, the tissue surrounding the ventricles, and deeper gray matter structures such as the basal ganglia and thalamus. Fully 90 percent of AIDS patients show evidence of such changes on autopsy (Adams & Ferraro, 1997).

Prominent Features The neuropsychological features of AIDS, which tend to appear as a late phase of HIV infection (although often before the full development of AIDS itself), usually begin with psychomotor slowing, diminished concentration, mild memory difficulties, and perhaps slight motor clumsiness. Progression is typically rapid after this point, with clear-cut dementia appearing in many cases within one year, although considerably longer periods have been reported. In general, and consistent with autopsy findings, the neuropsychological evidence points primarily to a disruption of brain function at the subcortical level; the most reliably reported finding is that of notably delayed reaction time (Law & Mapou, 1997). The later phases of ADC can be quite grim and include behavioral regression, confusion, psychotic thinking, apathy, and marked withdrawal, leading before death to an incontinent, bedridden state (Navia, Jordan, & Price, 1986; Price et al., 1988a, 1988b).

Prevalence Studies Thirty-eight percent of 121 living AIDS patients studied by Navia and colleagues (1986) met DSM criteria for dementia. Patients with **AIDS-related complex (ARC),** a pre-AIDS manifestation of HIV infection involving minor infections, various nonspecific symptoms (such as unexplained fever), and blood cell count abnormalities, may also experience cognitive difficulty, although it may be too subtle to be readily detected on clinical observation or the more standard neuropsychological test batteries (Law & Mapou, 1997). In one study (Grant et al., 1987), 54 percent of ARC patients demonstrated definite impairment on a neuropsychological test battery. Other studies, reviewed by Grant and Heaton (1990) and by Law and Mapou (1997), have shown inconsistent evidence of neuropsychological compromise in asymptomatic pre-ARC people who are merely infected with the HIV-1 virus. Significant numbers of infected persons were found to be neuropsychologically compromised in a cross-national study reported by Maj and colleagues (1994), although these investigators emphasize the subtlety of the deficits detected and their lack of substantial impact on social functioning in otherwise asymptomatic persons. Depression, a frequent accompaniment of HIV infection, does not appear to account for the compromised neuropsychological test performance observed in these patients (Beason-Hazen, Nasrallah, & Bornstein, 1994; Law & Mapou, 1997).

Infection with the HIV-1 virus poses a substantial threat to the anatomical integrity of the brain, in addition to its immune system effects. As of this writing, it is not known what protects the minority of AIDS patients who show no central nervous system involvement during the entire course of their illnesses.

The question of treatment for ADC is of course intimately tied to that involving control or eradication of the HIV-1 infection itself. Until fairly recently, it was impossible to feel confident about our prospects because of the enormous and unprecedented challenges presented by the complex structure and life cycle of this retrovirus (McCutchan, 1990). This picture is now improving with advances in antiviral therapy, and there is considerable evidence that these agents can improve cognitive and neurological functioning—although complete restoration is not a likely outcome (Adams & Ferraro, 1997; Law & Mapou, 1997). Unfortunately, experience with zidovudine (AZT) therapy indicates that this encouraging effect may prove temporary because the virus adapts over time to the presence of antiviral agents.

It remains true therefore that prevention of infection is the only certain defensive strategy, a circumstance not unlike the problem posed by neurosyphilis, another sexually transmitted and potentially dementing disease, in an earlier era. In general, humankind has not done well in controlling the spread of sexually transmitted diseases through cautious sexual behavior, and, as was noted in Chapter 8, that pattern seems to be repeating itself with respect to the HIV-1 virus.

Dementia of the Alzheimer's Type

While the dementia complicating many cases of HIV-1 infection is a very serious concern, especially for the family and friends of victims, it is dwarfed in magnitude by the problems our society faces in coping with the dementias that are the most salient aspect of Alzheimer's disease, officially (as on Axis I of DSM-IV) termed **Dementia of the Alzheimer's Type (DAT).** DAT takes its name from Alois Alzheimer, a German neuropsychiatrist, who first described it in 1907.

It is a commonplace observation that the organs of the body deteriorate with aging. The cause or causes of this deterioration, however, remain largely obscure; science has not yet solved the riddle of aging. Of course, the brain—truly the master organ—is not spared in the aging process. Over time it too wears out, or degenerates. Mental disorders that sometimes accompany this brain degeneration and occur in old age have traditionally been called **senile dementias.** Unfortunately, a number of rare conditions result in degenerative changes in brain tissue earlier in life. Disorders associated with such earlier degeneration of the brain are known as **presenile dementias.**

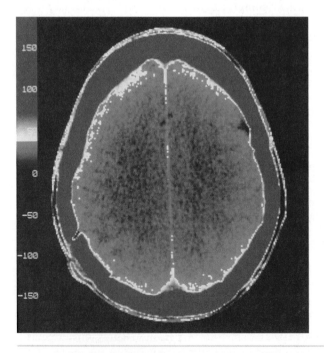
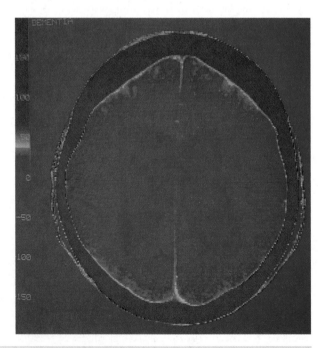

Dramatic differences show up in these CAT scans of a normal brain (left) and the brain of a person afflicted with probable Alzheimer's dementia (right). The dark blue areas in both hemispheres of the diseased brain indicate an enlargement of the ventricles (the large, hollow spaces deep within the brain) due to the degeneration of the brain tissue.

Highlight 13.1

Presenile Dementias

In addition to early-onset Alzheimer's disease, two other forms of presenile dementia occur with sufficient frequency to deserve mention: Pick's disease and Huntington's disease.

Pick's Disease

Even rarer than early-onset Alzheimer's disease, Pick's disease (first described by Arnold Pick of Prague in 1892) is a degenerative disorder of the brain, usually having its onset in people between the ages of 45 and 50. Its cause is unknown. Women are apparently more subject to Pick's disease than men, at a ratio of about three to two. Onset is slow and insidious, involving difficulty in thinking, slight memory defects, easy fatigability, and, often, character changes with a lowering of many social inhibitions. At first there is a circumscribed atrophy of the frontal and temporal lobes; as the atrophy becomes more severe, the mental deterioration becomes progressively greater and includes apathy and disorientation as well as the impairment of judgment and other intellectual functions. The disease usually runs a fatal course within two to seven years.

Huntington's Disease

Huntington's disease is a genetically determined (autosomal dominant) degenerative disorder of the central nervous system. It was first described by the American neurologist George Huntington in 1872. With an incidence rate of about 5 cases per 100,000 people, the disease usually occurs in individuals between 30 and 50 years of age. Behavior deterioration often becomes apparent several years before there are any detectable neurological manifestations. The disease itself is characterized by a chronic, progressive chorea (involuntary and irregular twitching, jerking movements) with mental deterioration leading to dementia and death within 10 to 20 years. Although Huntington's disease cannot be cured or even arrested at the present time, it can be prevented, at least in theory, by genetic counseling, because its occurrence is a function of known genetic laws. ■

Not only is the age of onset different in the presenile dementias, but they are also distinguished from the senile dementias by their different behavioral manifestations and brain tissue alterations (see Highlight 13.1). One important exception is Alzheimer's disease, which is a typical and common senile disorder but which can, in some people, occur well before old age. Alzheimer's disease is associated with a characteristic dementia syndrome having an imperceptible onset and a usually slow but progressively deteriorating course, terminating in delirium and death.

The Clinical Picture in DAT The diagnosis of DAT is often difficult and uncertain (Debettignies et al., 1997), a major reason being that it is not possible to establish definitely the presence of the distinctive Alzheimer neuropathology (described below) in living patients. The diagnosis is normally rendered only after all other potential causes of dementia are ruled out by case and family history, physical examination, and laboratory tests. Brain imaging techniques, such as that of magnetic resonance imaging (MRI), may provide supportive evidence in showing enlarged ventricles or widening in the folds (sulci) of the cerebral cortex, indicating brain atrophy. Unfortunately, several other disease conditions, as well as normal aging, result in a similar type of atrophy—making it impossible at present to definitively diagnose Alzheimer's without an autopsy. Much contemporary research is therefore devoted to the discovery of valid antemortem (before death) criteria for the diagnosis of DAT.

The onset of Alzheimer's disease in older people is usually gradual, involving slow mental deterioration. In some cases a physical ailment or some other stressful event is a dividing point, but usually an individual passes into a demented state almost imperceptibly, so that it is impossible to date the onset of the disorder precisely. The clinical picture may vary markedly from one person to another, depending on the nature and extent of brain degeneration, the premorbid personality of the individual, the particular stressors present, and the degree of environmental support.

Signs often begin with the person's gradual withdrawal from active engagement with life. There is a narrowing of social activities and interests, a lessening of mental alertness and adaptability, and a lowering of tolerance to new ideas and changes in routine. Often thoughts and activities become self-centered and childlike, including a preoccupation with the bodily functions of eating, digestion, and excretion. As these changes—typical in a lesser degree of many older people—become more severe, additional symptoms, such as impaired memory for recent events, "empty" speech (in which grammar and syntax remain intact but vague and seemingly pointless expressions replace meaningful conversational exchange—e.g., "It's a nice day, but it might rain."), messiness, impaired judgment, agitation, and periods of confusion, make their appearance. Specific symptoms may vary considerably from patient to patient and from day to day for the same patient; thus the clinical picture is by no means uniform until the terminal stages, when the patient is reduced to a vegetative level. There is also, of course, individual variation in the rapidity of the disorder's progression. In rare instances the symptoms may reverse and partial function may return, but in true DAT this reversal will invariably prove temporary.

The end stages of Alzheimer's disease involve a depressingly similar pattern of reduction to a vegetative existence and ultimate death from some disease that overwhelms an affected person's limited defensive resources. Before this point, there is, as noted, some distinctiveness in patient behavior. Allowing for individual differences, a given victim is likely to show one of the several dominant behavioral manifestations described in the following paragraphs.

Approximately half of all DAT patients display a course of simple deterioration. That is, they gradually lose various mental capacities, typically beginning with memory for recent events and progressing to disorientation, poor judgment, neglect of personal hygiene, and loss of contact with reality to an extent precluding independent functioning as adults. Distinctly psychopathological symptoms (such as delusions), if they occur at all, are likely to be transitory and inconsistent over time. The following case—involving a man who had retired some seven years prior to his hospitalization—is typical of simple deterioration resulting from DAT:

Case Study, An Engineer with DAT • During the past five years, he had shown a progressive loss of interest in his surroundings and during the last year had become increasingly "childish." His wife and eldest son had brought him to the hospital because they felt they could no longer care for him in their home, particularly because of the grandchildren. They stated that he had become careless in his eating and other personal habits and was restless and prone to wandering about at night. He could not seem to remember anything that had happened during the day but was garrulous concerning events of his childhood and middle years.

After admission to the hospital, the patient seemed to deteriorate rapidly. He could rarely remember what had happened a few minutes before, although his memory for remote events of his childhood remained good. When he was visited by his wife and children, he mistook them for old friends, nor could he recall anything about the visit a few minutes after they had departed. The following brief conversation with the patient, which took place after he had been in the hospital for nine months and about three months before his death, shows his disorientation for time and person:

DOCTOR: How are you today, Mr. ____

PATIENT: Oh . . . hello [looks at doctor in rather puzzled way as if trying to make out who he is].

DOCTOR: Do you know where you are now?

PATIENT: Why yes . . . I am at home. I must paint the house this summer. It has needed painting for a long time but it seems like I just keep putting it off.

DOCTOR: Can you tell me the day today?

PATIENT: Isn't today Sunday . . . why, yes, the children are coming over for dinner today. We always have dinner for the whole family on Sunday. My wife was here just a minute ago but I guess she has gone back into the kitchen.

In a less frequent manifestation of Alzheimer's disease, the patient develops a decidedly paranoid orientation to the environment, becoming markedly suspicious and often convinced that others are engaged in various injurious plots and schemes. Uncooperativeness and verbal abuse are common accompaniments, making the task of caregiving significantly more stressful. In the early phases of this reaction pattern, the cognitive deficits characteristic of Alzheimer's disease (memory loss, disorientation) may not be prominent, perhaps enabling the person to be quite observant and even logical in building the case for others' threatening activities. Though themes of victimization predominate in this form of the disorder, also common is the so-called jealousy delusion in which the person persistently accuses his or her partner or spouse—who is often of advanced age and physically debilitated—of being sexually unfaithful. Family members may be accused of various foul deeds, such as poisoning the patient's food or plotting to steal the patient's funds. Fortunately, punitive retribution in the form of physical attacks on the "evildoers" is not especially common, but a combative pattern does occasionally occur, complicating the patient's management. In a recent study of physically aggressive DAT patients, Gilley and associates (1997) found that 80 percent of them were delusional.

Paranoid orientations tend to develop in people who have been sensitive and suspicious. Existing personality tendencies are apparently intensified by degenerative brain changes and the stress accompanying advancing age. As a general rule, advanced-stage Alzheimer's patients are unlikely to be aware of their own cognitive deficits (Vasterling, Seltzer, & Watrous, 1997; Wagner et al., 1997), and hence do not attribute negative events to this source.

Other patterns seen in Alzheimer's patients are comparatively infrequent. Some patients are confused but amiable, usually showing marked memory impairment and a tendency to engage in seemingly pointless activities, such as hoarding useless objects or repetitively performing household tasks in a ritualized manner. Other patients become severely agitated, with or without an accompanying hand-wringing depression. Depressed Alzheimer's patients tend to develop extremely morbid preoccupations and delusions, such as hypochondriacal ideas about having various horrible diseases, often seen as punishment for past sins. Suicide is a possibility in such cases should a patient be physically capable of carrying out the act.

When we picture a typical Alzheimer patient, we imagine a person of advanced age. Although most patients are older, for some, DAT is a presenile dementia that begins in their 40s or 50s; in such cases the progress of the disease and its associated dementia is often rapid (Heyman et al., 1987). Considerable evidence suggests an especially substantial genetic contribution in early-onset DAT (Davies, 1986), although different genes may well be involved in different families (Breitner et al., 1993). These early-onset cases, occurring in comparatively young and vigorous patients, portray the tragedy of Alzheimer's disease in an especially stark light.

With appropriate treatment, which may include medication and the maintenance of a calm, reassuring, and unprovocative social milieu, many people with Alzheimer's disease show some symptom alleviation. In general, however, deterioration continues its downward course over a period of months or years. Eventually, patients become

oblivious of their surroundings, bedridden, and reduced to a vegetative existence. Resistance to disease is lowered, and death usually results from pneumonia or some other respiratory or cardiac problem.

Prevalence of DAT The magnitude of the problem of DAT—often seriously underestimated—is already straining societal and family resources, both economic (Ernst et al., 1997; Max, 1993) and emotional (see below). As shown in Table 13.1 (see page 509), the disorder is believed to account for a large proportion of all cases of dementia of whatever cause. The ratio is doubtless considerably higher for older people. It is estimated that one of every six people in the United States over age 65 is clinically demented, and that one of every ten people in this age range suffers from DAT (Evans et al., 1989). The prevalence rate of DAT may approach 50 percent by age 85 (Fisher & Carstensen, 1990), and a United Kingdom study indicates that, in each five-year interval from ages 75 to 89, there is an approximate doubling of the rate of new cases of DAT (Paykel et al., 1994). There are thus over 4 million living victims in the United States alone, and the number is increasing rapidly with the advancing age of the population. It is estimated that about 30 to 40 percent of nursing home residents are DAT patients. Some of these patients reside in mental hospitals or other types of institutional settings. Most, however, live in the community, typically with family members (Gurland & Cross, 1982), a circumstance that is often extremely stressful for caregivers (Brane, 1986; Fisher & Carstensen, 1990; Intrieri & Rapp, 1994; Shaw et al., 1997).

The future prospects regarding DAT prevalence are somewhat alarming. Survival to at least age 65 is becoming increasingly routine, and after the first decade of the twenty-first century, the first members of the enormous post–World War II baby boom generation will enter the age range of maximum risk. If we have not solved the problem of preventing (or halting in its early stages) DAT by that time or shortly thereafter, society will be faced with the overwhelming problem of caring for millions of demented but otherwise reasonably healthy senior citizens. These citizens may be expected to be subject to marked agitation, disappearances owing to wandering, inappropriate sexual behavior, uncontrolled eating habits, sleep disturbances, senselessly repetitive behaviors, hoarding of useless items, and unpredictable aggressive outbursts, among other problems. The adverse family, social, and economic consequences, already considerable in magnitude, could become devastating (Fisher & Carstensen, 1990).

Some brain diseases, Alzheimer's among them, can be diagnosed with certainty only at autopsy. Clinicians must be conscientious in their diagnostic efforts with live patients because of the potentially serious consequences of error.

Causal Factors in DAT The quickening pace of research on Alzheimer's has already yielded many intriguing leads, as we shall see. It has also shown, however, that the etiology of the disease is complex and varying—not simply a matter of having been born with the wrong genes and getting on in years. We will focus our discussion on the known neuropathology of DAT and on the still puzzling genetic-environmental interaction that seems implicated in its causation.

Neuropathology The structural neuropathology of the Alzheimer's brain has been known for some time. Readily determined by microscopic examination of tissue specimens, it has three elements: (1) the widespread appearance of *senile plaques,* small areas of dark-colored matter that are in part the debris of damaged nerve terminals; (2) the tangling of the normally regular patterning of

neurofibrils (strandlike protein filaments) within neuronal cell bodies; and (3) the abnormal appearance of small holes in neuronal tissue, called *granulovacuoles,* which derive from cell degeneration. Absolute confirmation of the diagnosis of DAT at present rests on observation of these changes in tissue samples, which is why it can normally be accomplished only after a patient has died. When sufficiently numerous, these microscopic alterations of the brain's substance lead to generalized brain atrophy, which as already noted may be visualized in live patients by imaging techniques.

Another notable alteration in DAT concerns the neurotransmitter acetylcholine (ACh), which is known to be important in the mediation of memory. While there is widespread destruction of neurons in DAT, particularly in the area of the hippocampus (Adler, 1994; Mori et al., 1997b), evidence suggests that among the earliest and most severely affected are a cluster of cell bodies located in the basal forebrain and involved in the release of ACh (Whitehouse et al., 1982). This observation and related ones (e.g., Wester et al., 1988) have given rise to the ACh depletion theory of DAT etiology, hypothesizing that a primary cause of the disease is insufficient availability of ACh in the brain. Although the evidence is not conclusive, the theory does integrate an impressive array of research data. For example, a temporary DAT-like syndrome may be produced in normal subjects who are given ACh-blocking drugs (Kopelman, 1986). The relatively new drug tacrine (Cognex), which increases available brain ACh, is temporarily helpful in improving cognitive function in some DAT patients (Whitehouse, 1993). Also, the reduction in brain ACh activity in DAT patients is correlated with the extent of neuronal damage (i.e., plaques, tangles) they have sustained (Debettignles et al., 1997).

If we make the reasonable assumption that ACh depletion plays at least some role in the production of DAT symptoms, there is still the question of what place it occupies in the presumed causal chain. What, for example, causes the degeneration of ACh-releasing cells? Several hypotheses purport to answer such questions, but none has so far gained a consensus acceptance.

Some investigators have taken the more direct approach of trying to discover the sources of the primary DAT lesions such as neurofibrillary tangles and senile plaques. An important observation concerning the plaques is that at the core of the cell debris is a sticky protein substance called *beta amyloid.* This substance (and a chemical precursor to it) also occurs in abnormal abundance in other parts of DAT patients' brains (see Gaj-

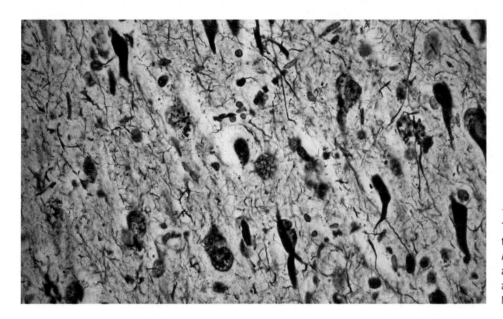

This photomicrograph of a brain tissue specimen from an Alzheimer's patient shows the characteristic plaques (dark patches) and neurofibrillary tangles (irregular pattern of strand-like fibers).

dusek, 1986; Hardy et al., 1986; Kang et al., 1987), and it is therefore believed to be somehow involved in the etiology of the disease. In fact, beta amyloid has recently been shown to be in itself neurotoxic, causing cell death (Seppa, 1998). As yet, however, the source and the specific role of the abnormal accumulation of this protein in the DAT brain remain unclear.

Gene-Environment Interaction in DAT A general vulnerability to the development of DAT, even in very late-onset cases, may be inherited (Breitner, 1986; Breitner et al., 1993; Davies, 1986; Martin et al., 1997; Mohs et al., 1987; Sturt, 1986). Much of this evidence points to a genetic connection with Down syndrome (to be discussed later in the chapter), which is usually due to a trisomy (tripling) involving chromosome 21. Most people with Down syndrome who survive beyond about age 40 develop a DAT-like dementia (Bauer & Shea, 1986; Janicki & Dalton, 1993), with similar neuropathological changes (Schapiro & Rapoport, 1987). Anomalies of chromosome 21 have also been implicated in DAT (e.g., Van Broeckhoven et al., 1987), although it is clear that this chromosome cannot be the only site of origin for genetic influences in enhancing disease vulnerability (Breitner et al., 1993; Clark & Goate, 1993).

As in other varieties of psychopathology, it remains a puzzle as to how genetic influences manifest themselves in increasing risk of disorder. A partial answer to that puzzle in the case of DAT has become available over the past decade by virtue of the discovery that differing forms (genetic alleles) of a blood protein called *apolipoprotein-E (ApoE)* differentially predict risk for

late-onset DAT. Three such alleles have been identified, and everyone inherits two of them, one from each parent. One of these alleles, called ε4 (and fortunately relatively infrequent), significantly enhances risk for late-onset DAT. Thus, a person may inherit zero, one, or two of the ε4 forms, and his or her risk correspondingly increases in that order. Another such allele, ε2, (also relatively infrequent) seems to convey protection against late-onset DAT, and thus the fairly rare ε2/2 person is an unusually lucky one from this perspective. The remaining and most common allele form, ε3, is of "neutral" significance in predicting to DAT (e.g., see Katzman et al., 1997; Lopez et al., 1997; Martin et al., 1997; Plassman & Breitner, 1997).

Exciting as they are, however, these recent discoveries still do not account for all cases of DAT, not even all cases of late-onset DAT (e.g., see Bergem, Engedal, & Kringlen, 1997). Many people inheriting the most risky ApoE pattern do not succumb to DAT, and some who do succumb to the disease have no such risk factor. Substantial numbers of monozygotic twins are discordant for the disease (Bergem et al., 1997; Breitner et al., 1993). That important observation is most readily understood by positing some sort of critical environmental influence—such as significant prior head trauma—that may operate in concert with a genetic vulnerability to produce the pathologic outcome. On this point, Gatz and associates, (1994) note that many eventually fatal organ system failures, Alzheimer's disease among them, seem to be the product not of a single or even a limited array of specific causal factors. Rather, they are the result of an accumulation of risk factors, both genetic and environmental, that ultimately exceed some clinical threshold and produce disease. Advancing age, of course, increases exposure to risks. This view leaves open the possibility of reducing or delaying the occurrence of DAT through deliberately limiting exposure to risks—such as environmental toxins or excessive alcohol consumption—some of which are potentially controllable.

Treatments and Outcomes in DAT   There is as yet no known treatment for DAT—medical, psychosocial, re-training-based, or rehabilitative, including attempts at preserving or replenishing brain ACh—that produces a sustained reversal or interruption of the deteriorating course. Until some means of accomplishing such an effect appears, we will have to content ourselves with palliative measures that diminish patient and caregiver distress and relieve as far as possible those complications of the disorder, such as combativeness, that increase the difficulties of management.

Several of the common problematic behaviors that are associated with DAT (and with other dementing disorders as well), include wandering off, incontinence, inappropriate sexual behavior, and inadequate self-care skills. These can be somewhat controlled using behavioral approaches, such as systematic contingent reinforcement (see Chapter 17). Such therapies need not be dependent on complex cognitive and communicational abilities, which are apt to be lacking in these patients. They may therefore be particularly appropriate for therapeutic intervention with this group. In general, reports of results are moderately encouraging in terms of reducing unnecessary frustration and embarrassment for the patient and difficulty for the caregiver (Fisher & Carstensen, 1990; Mintzer et al., 1997; Teri et al., 1997).

There has also been active treatment research focused on the consistent findings of ACh depletion in DAT. The reasoning here is that it might be possible to improve functioning by administering drugs that enhance the availability of brain ACh. Currently, the most effective way of doing so is by inhibiting the production of acetylcholinesterase, the principal enzyme involved in the metabolic breakdown of ACh. This is the rationale for the drug tacrine (Cognex). The findings so far available, however, indicate effects that are mostly quite limited and inconsistent (Rainer, 1997; Whitehouse, 1993). Rainer (1997) has recently suggested that a natural acetylcholinesterase inhibitor, galanthamine, derived from certain plant species, has more promise, but research on its use is presently very limited.

Other medications may be of some help for patients who experience difficulty in modulating their emotions and impulses. Some depressed DAT patients respond reasonably well to antidepressant or stimulant medication. Where medications are used, however, dosages must be carefully monitored because unanticipated effects are common and because the frequently debilitated state of these patients makes them susceptible to an exaggerated response.

As we have seen, neuronal cells that have died with the advance of Alzheimer's neuropathology are permanently lost; hence, even if some treatment were found to terminate a patient's progressive loss of brain tissue, he or she would still be left seriously impaired. The real key to effective intervention must therefore be seen as preventive, or at least as deployable at the first sign of Alzheimer's onset, sparing the bulk of the brain's neurons. Eventually, for example, we might be able to identify and reduce or eliminate the environmental hazards that play a role in stimulating the development of Alzheimer's (Gatz et al., 1994). Clearly, however, the most promising development in regard to prevention possibilities relates to the apolipoprotein (ApoE) research described above. Conceivably, it will prove possible to fashion interventions—for example, by administering targeted drugs—that counteract pathogenic processes associated with inheritance of the highest-risk ApoE allele patterns (e.g., ε3/4, ε4/4). That would truly be a momentous achievement.

Treating Caregivers   In the meantime, any comprehensive approach to therapeutic intervention must consider the extremely difficult situation of caregivers. With advancing DAT, they are confronted not only with many challenging management problems but also with the "social death" of the patient as a person and their own "anticipatory grief" (Gilhooly et al., 1994). They are, as a group, at extraordinarily high risk for depression (Cohen & Eisdorfer, 1988), perhaps especially if they are husbands caring for impaired wives (Robinson-Whelen & Kiecolt-Glaser, 1997; Tower, Kasl, & Moritz, 1997). They tend to consume high quantities of psychotropic medication themselves and to report many stress symptoms (George, 1984; Hinrichsen & Niederehe, 1994). Because the basic problem usually seems to be one of high and sustained stress, any measures found successful in the reduction and management of stress and the enhancement of coping resources could be helpful in easing caregivers' burdens (Costa, Whitfield, & Stewart, 1989). Group support programs, for example, may produce measurable reductions in experienced stress and depression (e.g., Glosser & Wexler, 1985; Hebert et al., 1994; Kahan et al., 1985).

The stress on children or spouses of taking care of DAT patients is enormous. Group support programs can help reduce this stress and the depressive symptoms that may accompany it.

Whether or not, or at what point, to institutionalize a DAT patient whose requirements for care threaten to overwhelm his or her spouse or other family members can be a vexing and emotional decision (Cohen et al., 1993). It can also be one with significant financial implications because, on average, nursing home care is about twice as costly as home care (Hu, Huang, & Cartwright, 1986). As we have seen, most DAT patients are cared for at home, mostly for emotional reasons, such as continuing love, loyalty, and a sense of obligation to the stricken parent or partner. In one sense at least, the home care decision is a justifiable one; the move to an institution, particularly one lacking in social stimulation and support, may result in an abrupt worsening of symptoms and sometimes a markedly enhanced rate of deterioration—demonstrating once again the power of psychosocial influences even in the case of widespread brain destruction. On the other hand, the emergence of marked confusion, gross and argumentative demeanor, stuporous depression, inappropriate sexual behavior, and disorientation for time, place, and person, not to mention possible sudden eruption of combative violence, can put an intolerable strain on caregivers. Because in all likelihood such conditions will worsen over time, wisdom dictates an early rather than a late removal to an institution, which

in any event is where most DAT patients will have to spend their final weeks, months, or years.

Vascular Dementia

Vascular dementia (VAD), formerly *multi-infarct dementia,* is frequently confused with DAT because of its similar clinical picture of progressive dementia and its increasing incidence and prevalence rates with advancing age. It is actually an entirely different disease in terms of its underlying neuropathology. In this disorder, a series of circumscribed cerebral infarcts—interruptions of the blood supply to minute areas of the brain because of arterial disease, commonly known as "small strokes"—cumulatively destroy neurons over expanding brain regions. The affected regions become soft and may degenerate over time, leaving only cavities. Although this disorder tends to have a more heterogeneous early clinical picture than DAT (Wallin & Blennow, 1993), the progressive loss of cells leads to brain atrophy and behavioral impairments that ultimately mimic those of DAT (Bowler et al, 1997). The decline, however, is less smooth because of (1) the discrete character of each infarct event; (2) variations over time in the volume of blood delivered by a seriously clogged artery, producing variations in the functional adequacy of cells that have not yet succumbed to oxygen deprivation; and (3) a tendency for vascular dementia to be associated with more severe behavioral complications, such as violence (Sultzer et al., 1993). VAD is far less common than DAT, accounting for only some 10 percent of dementia cases. One reason for this is that VAD has a much shorter average course because of a patient's vulnerability to sudden death from a large infarct or one that affects vital centers. Occasionally, an unfortunate patient will be discovered to have both DAT and VAD, commonly referred to as "mixed" dementia (Cohen et al., 1997).

The medical treatment of VAD, while hazardous and complicated, offers slightly more hope at this time than that of DAT. Unlike DAT, the basic problem of cerebral arteriosclerosis can be medically managed to some extent, perhaps decreasing the likelihood of further strokes.

The psychological and behavioral aspects of the dementia caused by DAT and VAD are similar in many respects, and any management measure found useful in one is likely to be applicable in the other. Likewise, the maintenance of any gains achieved cannot be taken for granted because of the generally progressive nature of the underlying brain pathology. The daunting problems facing caregivers are also much the same in the two conditions, indicating the appropriateness of support groups, stress reduction techniques, and the like.

Disorders Involving Head Injury

Traumatic brain injuries (TBI) occur frequently, on the order of 7 to 8 million per year in the United States. Most of these are the result of motor vehicle crashes. A sizable number of cases are the result of bullets or other objects actually penetrating the cranium. Significant brain damage is sustained in some 500,000 of these instances of TBI, and in some 70,000 to 90,000 of those it is of sufficient severity to preclude return to normal functioning (Bennet, Ditmar, & Ho, 1997). Nevertheless, relatively few people with TBIs find their way into mental hospitals because many head injuries do not involve appreciable damage to the brain, and even where they do, psychopathological complications are often not observed. In DSM-IV, brain injuries having notable, long-standing effects on adaptive functioning are coded on Axis I using the appropriate syndromal descriptive phrase, with the qualifier "due to head trauma."

The Clinical Picture in Head Injury Disorders

Clinicians distinguish three general types of TBI because the clinical pictures and residual problems vary somewhat among them: (1) closed head injury (CHI), in which the cranium remains intact; (2) penetrating head injury (PHI), in which the cranium, as well as the underlying brain, are penetrated by some object, such as a bullet; and (3) skull fracture, with or without compression of the brain by fragmented bone concavity. Post-trauma epilepsy, for example, is unusual in CHI but a rather common outcome of the other two forms of head injury. The damage to the brain in CHI is indirect, so to speak, produced by inertial forces that cause it to come into violent contact with the interior skull wall, or rotational forces that twist the brain mass relative to the brain stem. Not uncommonly, CHI also causes diffuse neuron damage because the inertial force (e.g., violent movement of the rigid cranium is arrested by contact with an unyielding object, but the softer brain tissue within keeps moving) has a shearing effect on nerve fibers and their synaptic interconnections.

Neuropsychologically significant head injuries usually give rise to immediate acute reactions, such as unconsciousness and disruption of circulatory, metabolic, and neurotransmitter regulation. Normally, if a head injury is sufficiently severe to result in unconsciousness, the person experiences *retrograde amnesia,* or inability to recall events immediately preceding the injury. Apparently, such trauma interferes with the brain's capacity to consolidate into long-term storage the events that were still being processed at the time of the trauma. *Anterograde amnesia* (also called post-traumatic amnesia) refers to an inability to effectively store in memory events happening during variable periods of time *after* the trauma. It is also frequently observed and is regarded by many as a negative prognostic sign.

A person rendered unconscious by a head injury usually passes through stages of stupor and confusion on the way to recovering clear consciousness. This recovery of consciousness may be complete in the course of minutes, or it may take hours or days. In rare cases an individual may live for extended periods of time without regaining consciousness, a condition known as coma. In such cases the prognosis for substantial improvement is poor. In some instances, significant cognitive or personality alterations following injury are observed even where a person experiences no loss of consciousness.

Following a severe cerebral injury and loss of consciousness, a person's pulse, temperature, blood pressure, and important aspects of brain metabolism are all affected, and survival may be uncertain. The duration of the resultant coma is generally related to the severity of the injury. If the patient survives, coma may be followed by delirium, in which acute excitement is manifested, with disorientation, hallucinations, and generally agitated, restless, and confused activity. Often the patient talks incessantly in a disconnected fashion, with no insight into the disturbed condition. Gradually the confusion clears up and the individual regains contact with reality.

The persistence and severity of post-trauma disruptions of brain function depend on the degree and type of injury. They may lead to early death or may clear up entirely. Quite often, as already noted, they develop into chronic disorders in which the individual's future cognitive and behavioral functioning is seriously compromised. In relatively severe but nonfatal brain injury, most of the recovery that will be experienced tends to occur in the earliest post-trauma phase, although sometimes return of function may still occur after several years. Individual courses of recovery are highly variable (Crepeau & Scherzer, 1993; Powell & Wilson, 1994).

Fortunately, the brain, encased in the hard shell of the skull, is an extraordinarily well-protected organ. But even so, a hard blow on the head may result in a skull fracture in which portions of bone press on or are driven into the brain tissue. Even without a fracture, the force of the blow may result in small, pinpoint hemorrhages throughout the brain or in the rupturing of larger blood vessels in the brain. Some degree of bleeding, or *intracranial hemor-*

rhage, can occur with even relatively low-impact head injuries; while potentially serious, minute levels of bleeding may require no intervention. In severe injuries, there may be gross bleeding or hemorrhaging at the site of the damage. Enough blood may accumulate within the rigid confines of the skull that disruptive pressure is exerted on neighboring regions of the brain; a common form of this problem is the *subdural hematoma,* which, if not relieved by aspiration (drawing out) of the excess blood, may endanger vital brain functions or produce permanent neuronal damage. When the hemorrhaging involves small spots of bleeding—often microscopic sleeves of red cells encircling tiny blood vessels—the condition is referred to as *petechial hemorrhages.* Some evidence shows tiny, scattered petechial hemorrhages in most brain injuries, but in fatal cases they are usually multiple or generalized throughout the brain. Serious levels of brain swelling, or *cerebral edema,* occur in many cases of severe damage, increasing the risk of significant mental impairment or death unless promptly treated.

Professional boxers are likely to suffer such petechial hemorrhaging from repeated blows to the head; they may develop a form of encephalopathy (characterized by an area or areas of permanently damaged brain tissue) from the accumulated damage of such injuries. Consequently, some former boxers suffer from impaired memory, slurred speech, inability to concentrate, involuntary movements, and other symptoms—a condition popularly referred to as being "punch-drunk."

Even where a TBI seems relatively mild with good return of function, careful neuropsychological assessment may reveal subtle residual impairment. Large numbers of relatively mild closed-head brain *concussions* (violent shock to tissues) and *contusions* (bruises) occur every year as a result of auto collisions, athletic injuries, falls, and other mishaps. Temporary loss of consciousness and postimpact confusion are the most common and salient immediate symptoms. There is considerable controversy about whether these mild brain injuries produce significant long-standing symptoms or impairments of various abilities (Dikmen & Levin, 1993; Zasler, 1993). Brown, Fann, and Grant (1994), for example, have made a strong argument that "postconcussional disorder" should be included in the DSM as a separate diagnosis based on evidence of diffuse postinjury changes in cognitive ability (e.g., memory deficiencies), personality (e.g., increased impulsivity), brain anatomy (e.g., enlarged ventricles), brain electrophysiology (e.g., electroencephalographic abnormalities—see Chapter 15), and general life functioning (e.g., employment difficulties). So far, at least, that argument has not prevailed, although the recom-

Though Phineas Gage survived when a tamping iron entered his face and shot through his head, his personality was so altered that his friends found that he was "no longer Gage."

mended diagnosis is included as one of a large number of provisional candidates said to need "further study" in a DSM-IV appendix.

Perhaps the most famous historical example of traumatic brain injury is the celebrated American crowbar case reported by Dr. J. M. Harlow in 1868. (Dr. Harlow's original report was reprinted in *History of Psychiatry,* 1993. Vol. 4, pp. 271–281.) Because it is of both historical and descriptive significance, it merits our attention:

Case Study, The Change in Phineas Gage • The accident occurred in Cavendish, Vermont, on the line of the Rutland and Burlington Railroad, at that time being built, on the 13th of September, 1848, and was occasioned by the premature explosion of a blast, when this iron, known to blasters as a tamping iron, and which I now show you, was shot through the face and head.

The subject of it was Phineas P. Gage, a perfectly healthy, strong and active young man, twenty-five years of age . . . Gage was foreman of a gang of men employed in excavating rock, for the road way . . . .

The missile entered by its pointed end, the left side of the face, immediately anterior to the angle of the lower jaw, and passing obliquely upwards, and obliquely backwards, emerged in the median line, at the back part of the frontal bone, near the coronal suture. . . .

The iron which thus traversed the head, is round and rendered comparatively smooth by use, and is three feet seven inches in length, one and one fourth inches in its largest diameter, and weighs thirteen and one fourth pounds. . . .

> The patient was thrown upon his back by the explosion, and gave a few convulsive motions of the extremities, but spoke in a few minutes. His men (with whom he was a great favorite) took him in their arms and carried him to the road, only a few rods distant, and put him into an ox cart, in which he rode, supported in a sitting posture, fully three quarters of a mile to his hotel. He got out of the cart himself, with a little assistance from his men, and an hour afterwards (with what I could aid him by taking hold of his left arm) walked up a long flight of stairs, and got upon the bed in the room where he was dressed. He seemed perfectly conscious, but was becoming exhausted from the hemorrhage, which by this time, was quite profuse, the blood pouring from the lacerated sinus in the top of his head, and also finding its way into the stomach, which ejected it as often as every fifteen or twenty minutes. He bore his sufferings with firmness, and directed my attention to the hole in his cheek, saying, "the iron entered there and passed through my head."

Some time later Dr. Harlow made the following report:

> His physical health is good, and I am inclined to say that he has recovered. Has no pain in head, but says it has a queer feeling which he is not able to describe. Applied for his situation as foreman, but is undecided whether to work or travel. His contractors, who regarded him as the most efficient and capable foreman in their employ previous to his injury considered the change in his mind so marked that they could not give him his place again. The equilibrium or balance, so to speak, between his intellectual faculties and animal propensities, seems to have been destroyed. He is fitful, irreverent, indulging at times in the grossest profanity (which was not previously his custom), manifesting but little deference for his fellows, impatient of restraint or advice when it conflicts with his desires, at times pertinaciously obstinate, yet capricious and vacillating, devising many plans of future operations, which are no sooner arranged than they are abandoned in turn for others . . . his mind is radically changed, so decidedly that his friends and acquaintances said he was "no longer Gage."

It is evident from the above account that Gage acquired a severe frontal brain wound as well as a neuropsychological personality syndrome from his encounter with the tamping iron. As Stuss and colleagues (1992) have noted, Gage's persistent post-trauma difficulties are fairly characteristic for severe frontal-lobe damage; emotional dyscontrol and personality alterations, including impairment of self-reflective awareness, are often prominent features of behavior change due to this type of injury. In general, however, personality disturbances secondary to traumatic brain injury are somewhat unpredictable owing to the varied structural pathology apt to be involved in such injuries (Prigatano, 1992).

Treatments and Outcomes Immediate treatment for brain damage due to head injury is primarily a medical matter. Prompt treatment may prevent further injury or damage—for example, when pooled blood under pressure must be removed from the skull. In many instances, including some that may initially be considered "mild," immediate medical treatment may have to be supplemented by a long-range program of reeducation and rehabilitation.

Although many TBI patients show few residual effects from their injury, particularly if they have experienced only a brief loss of consciousness, other patients sustain definite and long-lasting impairment. Common aftereffects of moderate brain injury are chronic headaches, anxiety, irritability, dizziness, easy fatigability, and impaired memory and concentration. Where the brain damage is extensive, a patient's general intellectual level may be markedly reduced, especially if he or she has suffered severe temporal- or parietal-lobe lesions. Most victims have significant delays in returning to their occupations, and many are unable to return at all (Bennett, Dittmar, & Ho, 1997; Dikmen et al., 1994; Goran, Fabiano, & Crewe, 1997); other losses of adult social role functioning are also common (Hallett et al., 1994). In addition, various specific neurological and psychological defects may follow localized brain damage, as we have seen. Some 24 percent of TBI cases, overall, develop posttraumatic epilepsy, presumably owing to the growth of scar tissue in the brain. Seizures usually develop within two years of the head injury, but sometimes much later.

In a minority of brain injury cases, notable personality changes occur, such as those described in the historic case of Phineas Gage. Other kinds of personality changes include passivity, loss of drive and spontaneity, agitation, anxiety, depression, and paranoid suspiciousness. Like cognitive changes, the kinds of personality changes that emerge in severely damaged people will depend, in large measure, on the site and extent of their injury (Prigatano, 1992).

The great majority of people suffering from mild concussions improve to a near normal status within a short time. With moderate brain injuries, it takes longer for patients to reach their maximum level of improvement, and many suffer from headaches and other symptoms for prolonged periods. A few develop chronic, incapacitating symptoms. In severe brain injury cases, the prognosis is less favorable (Jennett et al., 1976; Powell & Wilson, 1994). Many of these patients have to adjust to lower levels of occupational and social functioning (Bennett, Dittmar, & Ho, 1997; Dikmen et al., 1994), while others are so impaired intellectually that they require continuing supervision and, sometimes, institutionalization. Even in cases where considerable amounts of brain tissue have been destroyed, however, some patients are able to become socially independent. In many cases there is improvement with time, due largely to reeducation and to intact brain areas taking over new functions (Powell & Wilson, 1994).

Children who undergo significant traumatic brain injury are more likely to be adversely affected the younger they are at the time of injury and the less language, fine motor and other competencies they have. The severity of their injury, the degree to which their environment (such as parents) are accommodating or difficult will also affect the child's recovery (Anderson et al., 1997; Taylor & Alden, 1997; Yeates et al., 1997). When the injury is mild, most children emerge without lasting negative effects (Satz et al., 1997).

Treatment of traumatic brain injury beyond the purely medical phase is often difficult, protracted, and expensive. Its core is a careful and continuing assessment of neuropsychological functioning and the design of interventions intended to overcome remaining deficits. Many disciplines may become involved in the latter, such as neurology, psychology, neuropsychology, occupational therapy, physical therapy, speech/language therapy, cognitive rehabilitation, prevocational and vocational services, and recreational therapy. As often as not, treatment consists of providing patients with new techniques to compensate for losses that may well be permanent (Bennett, Dittmar, & Ho, 1997).

In general, outcomes in cases of TBI are most favorable when there is (1) a short period of unconsciousness or post-traumatic anterograde amnesia; (2) no or minimal cognitive impairment; (3) a well-functioning pre-injury personality; (4) higher educational attainment; (5) a stable pre-injury work history; (6) motivation to recover or make the most of residual capacities; (7) a favorable life situation to which to return; (8) early intervention; and (9) an appropriate program of rehabilitation and retraining (Bennett, Dittmar, & Ho, 1997; Brooks, 1974; Dikmen et al., 1994; Diller & Gordon, 1981; Mackay, 1994).

The outlook for individuals who are also victims of alcoholism, drug dependence, or other medical problems may be unfavorable. Alcoholics, in particular, are prone to head injuries and other accidents and do not have good improvement records, possibly because many of them also have brain deficits related to excessive drinking (Mearns & Lees-Haley, 1993). Severe emotional prob-

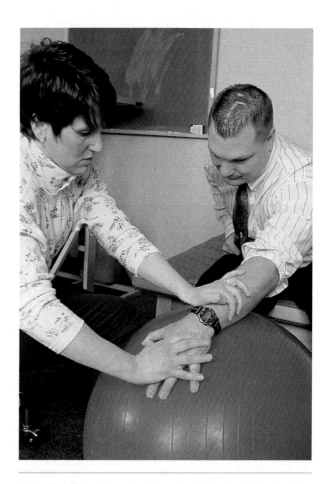

This police officer, who received a gunshot head wound in the line of duty, is receiving therapy to improve muscle tone and function in his left arm.

lems sometimes appear to predispose an individual to car crashes and other violent events and also may delay recovery.

MENTAL RETARDATION

The American Psychiatric Association (1994) in DSM-IV defines mental retardation as "significantly subaverage general intellectual functioning . . . that is accompanied by significant limitations in adaptive functioning" (p. 39) in certain skill areas such as self-care, work, health, and safety. To qualify for the diagnosis, these problems must have begun before the age of 18. Mental retardation is thus defined in terms of level of performance as well as intelligence. The definition says nothing about causal factors, which may be primarily biological, psychosocial, sociocultural, or a combination of these. By definition, any functional equivalent of mental retardation that has its onset after age 17 must be considered a dementia rather than mental retardation. The distinction is an important one, because, as was pointed out early in the chapter, the psychological situation of a person who acquires a pronounced impairment of intellectual functioning after attaining maturity is vastly different from that of a person whose intellectual resources were subnormal throughout all or most of his or her development.

In contrast to other developmental disorders (see Chapter 14 and the specific learning disorders discussed below), mental retardation is coded on Axis II of DSM-IV, along with the personality disorders. Mental retardation, like other DSM diagnostic categories, is treated as a specific type of disorder, although it may occur in combination with other disorders appearing on either Axis I or Axis II. In fact other psychiatric disorders, especially psychoses (Jacobson, 1990), occur at a markedly higher rate among retarded people than in the general population (Borthwick-Duffy, 1994; Sturmey & Sevin, 1993).

Mental retardation occurs among children throughout the world. In its most severe forms, it is a source of great hardship to parents as well as an economic and social burden on a community. The point prevalence rate of diagnosed mental retardation in the United States is estimated to be about 1 percent, which would indicate a population estimate of some 2.6 million people. In fact, however, prevalence is extremely difficult to pin down precisely because definitions of mental retardation vary considerably (Roeleveld, Zielhuis, & Gabreels, 1997). Most states have laws providing that persons with IQs below 70 who show socially incompetent or persistently problematic behavior can be classified as mentally retarded, and if judged otherwise unmanageable may be placed in an institution. Informally, IQ scores between about 70 and 90 are often referred to as "borderline" or (in the upper part of the range) "dull-normal."

Initial diagnoses of mental retardation seem to increase markedly at ages 5 to 6, to peak at age 15, and to drop off sharply after that. For the most part, these age-related changes in time of first diagnosis reflect changes in life demands. During early childhood, individuals with only a mild degree of intellectual impairment, who constitute the vast majority of the mentally retarded, often appear to be normal. Their subaverage intellectual functioning becomes apparent only when difficulties with schoolwork lead to a diagnostic evaluation. When adequate facilities are available for their education, children in this group can usually master essential school skills and achieve a satisfactory level of socially adaptive behavior. Following the school years, they usually make a more or less acceptable adjustment in the community and thus lose the identity of being mentally retarded.

Levels of Mental Retardation

The DSM-IV recognizes four degrees of severity of mental retardation. These are indicated in Table 13.2, together with their corresponding IQ ranges.

It is important to remind ourselves once again that any classification system in the behavioral field will have strong features of both arbitrariness and pragmatism. In mental retardation, attempts to define varying levels of impairment have tended to rely increasingly on measurement—largely by means of standardized intelligence (IQ) tests (Maclean, 1997). In the previously quoted DSM-IV definition, for example, the phrase "significantly subaverage general intellectual functioning" translates directly and officially into an IQ test score that is more than two standard deviations below the population mean. That mean, which represents the average test performance for children of a given age, is 100. The standard deviation of most IQ tests is about 15 points, and approximately two-thirds of the population score between plus and minus one standard deviation unit from the mean—that is, between 85 and 115. Thus a score of two standard deviations below the mean would be an IQ of approximately 70. Under the assumption that IQ scores are normally distributed in the familiar bell-shaped curve, about 2.5 percent of the population would score in the range below 70.

It is not necessarily improper to define mental retardation in this way, provided we keep in mind the implications of the definition. IQ tests are not infallible, and performance on them is affected by numerous factors such as motivation, fatigue, and current state of health. Also, the original IQ tests were devised for the explicit purpose of predicting academic achievement among schoolchildren. Thus when we speak of varying levels of mental retardation, we are to a great extent speaking of levels of ability to succeed at schoolwork.

Of course, this reliance on IQ scores is tempered somewhat by the other main part of the definition—the presence of concurrent "significant limitations in adaptive functioning." The same dual criteria are involved in the officially recognized "levels" of retardation, although

TABLE 13.2   RETARDATION SEVERITY AND IQ RANGES

Diagnosed Level of Mental Retardation	Corresponding IQ Range
Mild retardation	50–55 to approximately 70
Moderate retardation	35–40 to 50–55
Severe retardation	20–25 to 35–40
Profound retardation	below 20–25

the IQ score often tends in practice to be the dominant consideration. This emphasis on the IQ score is reasonable at the lower end of the scale, because a person with an IQ of 50 or below will inevitably exhibit gross deficiencies in overall adaptive behavior as well. At the higher ranges of "retarded" IQ scores, however, behavioral adaptiveness and IQ score seem to be at least partially independent of one another. Some individuals with lower IQs function better than those with higher ones. It should also be noted that differing social environments, such as rural versus urban, are differentially demanding both intellectually and behaviorally. Growing up in a small, highly integrated farming community, for example, poses less challenge than does, say, growing up in Manhattan.

The various levels of mental retardation, as defined in DSM-IV, are described in greater detail in the following sections.

Mild Mental Retardation   Mildly retarded individuals constitute by far the largest number of those diagnosed as mentally retarded. Within the educational context, people in this group are considered "educable," and their intellectual levels as adults are comparable with those of average 8- to 11-year-old children. Statements such as the latter, however, should not be taken too literally. A mildly retarded adult with a mental age of, say, 10 (that is, intelligence test performance is at the level of the average 10-year-old) may not in fact be comparable to the normal 10-year-old in information-processing ability or speed (Weiss, Weisz, & Bromfield, 1986). On the other hand, he or she will normally have had far more experience in living, which would tend to raise the IQ score.

The social adjustment of mildly retarded people often approximates that of adolescents, although they tend to lack normal adolescents' imagination, inventiveness, and judgment. Ordinarily, they do not show signs of brain pathology or other physical anomalies, but often they require some measure of supervision because of their limited abilities to foresee the consequences of their actions. Individuals at a somewhat higher, "borderline" IQ level (about 71–84) may also need special services to maximize their potentials (Zetlin & Murtaugh, 1990). With early diagnosis, parental assistance, and special educational programs, the great majority of borderline and mildly retarded individuals can adjust socially, master simple academic and occupational skills, and become self-supporting citizens (Maclean, 1997; Schalock, Harper, & Carver, 1981).

Moderate Mental Retardation   Moderately retarded individuals are likely to fall in the educational category of

Mildly retarded individuals constitute the largest number of those labeled mentally retarded. With help, a great majority of these individuals can adjust socially, master simple academic and occupational skills, and become self-supporting citizens.

"trainable," which means that they are presumed able to master certain routine skills, such as cooking or minor janitorial work, if provided specialized instruction in these activities. In adult life, individuals classified as moderately retarded attain intellectual levels similar to those of average four- to seven-year-old children. Although some can be taught to read and write a little and may manage to achieve a fair command of spoken language, their rate of learning is slow, and their level of conceptualizing extremely limited. Physically, they usually appear clumsy and ungainly, and they suffer from bodily deformities and poor motor coordination. Some of these moderately retarded people are hostile and aggressive; more typically they present an affable, unthreatening personality picture. Very rarely, extraordinary specialized skills, such as outstanding musical ability (see Hill, 1975), are found in moderately retarded individuals; well documented empirically, these phenomena have never been adequately explained. In general, with early diagnosis, parental help, and adequate opportunities for training, most moderately retarded individuals can achieve partial independence in daily self-care, acceptable behavior, and economic sustenance in a family or other sheltered environment.

Severe Mental Retardation   Severely retarded individuals are sometimes referred to as dependent retarded.

In these individuals, motor and speech development are severely retarded, and sensory defects and motor handicaps are common. They can develop limited levels of personal hygiene and self-help skills, which somewhat lessen their dependence, but they are always dependent on others for care. However, many profit to some extent from training and can perform simple occupational tasks under supervision.

Profound Mental Retardation The term *life-support retarded* is sometimes used to refer to profoundly retarded individuals. Most of these people are severely deficient in adaptive behavior and unable to master any but the simplest tasks. Useful speech, if it develops at all, is rudimentary. Severe physical deformities, central nervous system pathology, and retarded growth are typical; convulsive seizures, mutism, deafness, and other physical anomalies are also common. These individuals must remain in custodial care all their lives. They tend, however, to have poor health and low resistance to disease and thus a short life expectancy.

Severe and profound cases of mental retardation can usually be readily diagnosed in infancy because of the presence of obvious physical malformations, grossly delayed development (e.g., taking solid food), and other obvious symptoms of abnormality. Although these individuals show a marked impairment of overall intellectual functioning, they may have considerably more ability in some areas than in others. It should also be noted that, despite their limitations, they can be rewarding, loyal, and affectionate social partners to understanding others.

Until relatively recently, the American Psychiatric Association (sponsor of DSM-IV) and the American Association on Mental Retardation (AAMR) generally agreed on definitions of mental retardation and specifications of levels or degrees of it. In 1992 the AAMR broke away from this tradition (Luckasson et al., 1992), adopting IQ 75 as the cutoff point for the diagnosis of mental retardation (thus expanding the pool of eligibles). In addition, the AAMR proposal substitutes the patterns and intensity of supports needed—intermittent, limited, extensive, and pervasive—for the levels of severity indicated above; the steps of the two systems for characterizing severity are not directly comparable. Several more technical revisions of standard diagnostic procedure are also called for in the AAMR approach. Many professionals have voiced criticism of the new AAMR-proposed guidelines and view this divergence of approaches as unfortunate and as increasing the potential for disagreement and confusion in rendering the mental retardation diagnosis (e.g., Greenspan, 1997;

MacMillan, Gresham, & Siperstein, 1993). It seems clear, however, that the AAMR intent was to advance its agenda to provide increased services for retarded persons.

Brain Defects in Mental Retardation

Some cases of mental retardation—something on the order of 25 percent—occur in association with known organic brain pathology. In these cases, retardation is virtually always at least moderate, and it is often severe. Profound retardation, fortunately rare, always includes obvious organic impairment. Organically caused retardation is in essential respects similar to dementia as earlier described, except for a different history of prior functioning. In this section we will consider five biological conditions that may lead to mental retardation, noting some of the possible interrelations between them. Then we will review some of the major clinical types of mental retardation associated with these organic causes.

Genetic-Chromosomal Factors Mental retardation tends to run in families. This tendency is particularly true of mild retardation. Poverty and sociocultural deprivation, however, also tend to run in families, and with early and continued exposure to such conditions, even the inheritance of average intellectual potential may not prevent subaverage intellectual functioning.

Genetic and chromosomal factors play a much clearer role in the etiology of relatively infrequent but more severe types of mental retardation, such as Down syndrome (discussed below) or an inheritable condition known as *fragile X,* a constriction or breaking off of the end portion of the long arm of the X sex chromosome that appears determined by a specific gene defect (de Vries et al., 1994). In such conditions genetic aberrations are responsible for metabolic alterations that adversely affect the brain's development. Genetic defects leading to metabolic alterations may, of course, involve many other developmental anomalies besides mental retardation. In general, mental retardation associated with known genetic-chromosomal defects is moderate to severe in degree.

Infections and Toxic Agents Mental retardation may be associated with a wide range of conditions due to infection. If a pregnant woman is infected with syphilis or HIV-1, or if she gets German measles, her child may suffer brain damage. Brain damage may also result from infections occurring after birth, such as viral encephalitis.

A number of toxic agents, such as carbon monoxide and lead, may cause brain damage during fetal development or after birth. In rare instances, immunological agents, such as antitetanus serum or typhoid vaccine, may lead to brain damage. Similarly, certain drugs, including an excess of alcohol (see Chapter 10), taken by a pregnant woman may lead to congenital malformations; an overdose of drugs administered to an infant may result in toxicity and brain damage. In rare cases, brain damage results from incompatibility in blood types between mother and fetus. Fortunately, early diagnosis and blood transfusions can now minimize the effects of such incompatibility.

Prematurity and Trauma (Physical Injury) Follow-up studies of children born prematurely and weighing less than about 5.5 pounds at birth have revealed a high incidence of neurological disorders and often mental retardation. In fact, very small premature babies are many times more likely to be mentally retarded than normal-sized infants.

Physical injury at birth can also result in retardation. Isaacson (1970) has estimated that in 1 birth out of 1000 brain damage occurs that will prevent the child from reaching the intelligence level of an average 12-year-old. Although the fetus is normally well protected by its fluid-filled bag during gestation, and its skull appears designed to resist delivery stressors, accidents do happen during delivery and after birth. Difficulties in labor due to malposition of the fetus or other complications may irreparably damage the infant's brain. Bleeding within the brain is probably the most common result of such birth trauma. *Hypoxia*—lack of sufficient oxygen to the brain stemming from delayed breathing or other causes—is another type of birth trauma that may damage the brain.

Ionizing Radiation In recent decades a good deal of scientific attention has been focused on the damaging effects of ionizing radiation on sex cells and other bodily cells and tissues. Radiation may act directly on the fertilized ovum or may produce gene mutations in the sex cells of either or both parents, which, in turn, may lead to defective offspring. Sources of harmful radiation were once limited primarily to high-energy X rays used in medicine for diagnosis and therapy, but the list has grown to include nuclear weapons testing and leakages at nuclear power plants, among others.

Malnutrition and Other Biological Factors It has long been believed that dietary deficiencies in protein and other essential nutrients during early development can result in irreversible physical and mental damage.

However, current thinking on the association between malnutrition and mental retardation outcomes suggests that the direct causal link originally posited may be oversimplified or incomplete. In a review of the problem, Ricciuti (1993) cites growing evidence that the negative impact of malnutrition on mental development may be more indirect by altering a child's responsiveness, curiosity, and motivation to learn. These losses would then lead, according to this hypothesis, to a relative retardation of intellectual facility. The implication here is that at least some malnutrition-associated intellectual deficit is a special case of psychosocial deprivation, also involved in retardation outcomes, as described below.

A limited number of cases of mental retardation are clearly associated with organic brain pathology. In some instances—particularly of the severe and profound types—the specific causes are uncertain or unknown, al-

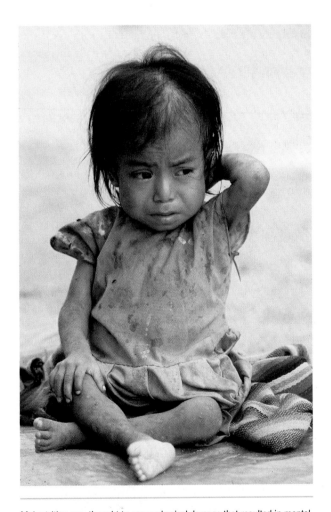

Malnutrition was thought to cause physical damage that resulted in mental retardation, but today the impact of malnutrition on mental development is viewed as more complicated. Listlessness and lack of responsiveness, curiosity and motivation associated with malnutrition may result in a type of environmental deprivation that also limits intellectual development.

though extensive brain pathology is evident. In the following sections we will deal with three relatively well-understood types of organically caused mental retardation.

Organic Retardation Syndromes

Mental retardation stemming primarily from biological causes can be classified into several recognizable clinical types, of which Down syndrome, phenylketonuria, and cranial anomalies will be discussed here. Table 13.3 presents information on several other well-known forms.

Down Syndrome   First described by Langdon Down in 1866, **Down syndrome** is the best known of the clinical conditions associated with moderate and severe mental retardation. About 1 in every 600 babies born in the United States is diagnosed as having Down syndrome, a condition that creates irreversible limitations on survivability, intellectual achievement, and competence in managing life tasks. In fact, among adults with this disorder, adaptive abilities seem to *decrease* with increasing age, especially after 40 (Collacott & Cooper, 1997). The

availability of amniocentesis and of chorionic villus sampling has made it possible to detect in utero the extra genetic material involved in Down syndrome, most often a trisomy of chromosome 21, yielding 47 rather than the normal 46 chromosomes. The possibility of elective abortion should the fetus prove chromosomally defective, while helpful for individual families, appears not to have affected substantially the overall incidence of the disorder. Because of a high rate of testing of older pregnant women and of demographic shifts involving high pregnancy rates among still-pubescent girls, most Down syndrome infants in recent decades have been born to mothers under 35 years of age, not a group for whom chromosomal assessment is routinely recommended (Evans & Hamerton, 1985).

A number of physical features are often found among children with Down syndrome, but few of these children have all of the characteristics commonly thought of as typifying this group. In such children, the eyes appear almond-shaped, and the skin of the eyelids tends to be abnormally thick. The face and nose are often flat and broad, as is the back of the head. The tongue, which

TABLE 13.3   OTHER DISORDERS SOMETIMES ASSOCIATED WITH MENTAL RETARDATION

Clinical Type	Symptoms	Causes
No. 18 trisomy syndrome	Peculiar pattern of multiple congenital anomalies, the most common being low-set malformed ears, flexion of fingers, small jaw, and heart defects	Autosomal anomaly of chromosome 18
Tay-Sachs disease	Hypertonicity, listlessness, blindness, progressive spastic paralysis, and convulsions (death by the third year)	Disorder of lipoid metabolism, carried by a single recessive gene
Turner's syndrome	In females only; webbing of neck, increased carrying angle of forearm, and sexual infantilism	Sex chromosome anomaly (XO); mental retardation may occur but is infrequent
Klinefelter's syndrome	In males only; features vary from case to case, the only constant finding being the presence of small testes after puberty	Sex chromosome anomaly (XXY)
Niemann-Pick's disease	Onset usually in infancy, with loss of weight, dehydration, and progressive paralysis	Disorder of lipoid metabolism
Bilirubin encephalopathy	Abnormal levels of bilirubin (a toxic substance released by red cell destruction) in the blood; motor incoordination frequent	Often, Rh (ABO) blood group incompatibility between mother and fetus
Rubella, congenital	Visual difficulties most common, with cataracts and retinal problems often occurring together and with deafness and anomalies in the valves and septa of the heart	The mother's contraction of rubella (German measles) during the first few months of her pregnancy

Source: Based on American Psychiatric Association (1968, 1972); Clarke, Clarke, and Berg (1985); Holvey and Talbott (1972); Robinson and Robinson (1976).

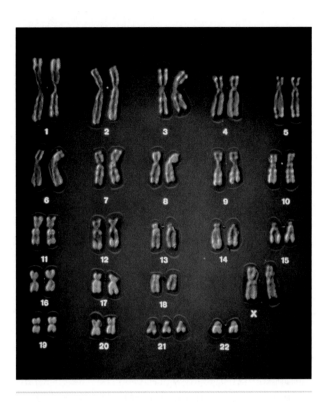

This is a reproduction (karyotype) of the chromosomes of a female patient with Down syndrome. Note the triple (rather than the normal paired) representation at chromosome 21.

seems too large for the mouth, may show deep fissures. The iris of the eye is frequently speckled. The neck is often short and broad, as are the hands. The fingers are stubby, and the little finger is often more noticeably curved than the other fingers. Although facial surgery is sometimes tried to correct the more stigmatizing features, its success is often limited (Dodd & Leahy, 1989; Katz & Kravetz, 1989). Also, parental acceptance of the Down syndrome child is inversely related to their support of such surgery (Katz, Kravetz & Marks, 1997).

Interestingly, there appears to be little, if any, correlation between the extent of physical anomalies and the degree of mental retardation in individuals with Down syndrome. Death rates for children with Down syndrome have decreased dramatically in the past century. In 1919, the life expectancy at birth for such children was about nine years; most of the deaths were due to gross physical problems, and a large proportion occurred in the first year. Thanks to antibiotics, surgical correction of lethal anatomical defects such as holes in the walls separating the heart's chambers, and better general medical care, many more of these children now live to adulthood (Hijji et al., 1997; Jancar & Jancar, 1996). Nevertheless, they appear as a group to experience an accelerated aging process (Hasegawa et al., 1997).

Despite their problems, children with Down syndrome are usually able to learn self-help skills, acceptable social behavior, and routine manual skills that enable them to be of assistance in a family or institutional setting. The traditional view has been that Down syndrome youngsters are unusually placid and affectionate. Research has questioned the validity of this generalization. These children may indeed be very docile, but probably in no greater proportion than normal youngsters; they may also be equally (or more) difficult in various areas (Bridges & Cicchetti, 1982). In general, the quality of a child's social relationships depends on both IQ level and a supportive home environment (Sloper et al., 1990). Down syndrome adults may manifest less maladaptive behavior than comparable persons with other types of learning disability (Collacott et al., 1998).

Research has also suggested that the intellectual defect in Down syndrome may not be consistent across various abilities. Down syndrome children tend to remain relatively unimpaired in their appreciation of spatial relationships and in visual-motor coordination, although some evidence disputes this conclusion (Uecker et al., 1993); research data are quite consistent in showing that they have their greatest deficits in verbal and language-related skills (Azari et al., 1994; Mahoney, Glover, & Finger, 1981; Silverstein et al., 1982). Since spatial functions are known to be partially localized in the right cerebral hemisphere, and language-related functions in the left cerebral hemisphere, some investigators speculate that the syndrome is especially crippling to the left hemisphere.

Today many more Down syndrome children are living to adulthood than in the past and are able to learn self-help, social and manual skills. It is not unusual for Down syndrome children to be mainstreamed to some extent with unimpaired children, such as this girl in a ballet class. Down syndrome children tend to remain relatively unimpaired in their appreciation of spatial relationships and visual-motor coordination: they show their greatest deficits in verbal and language-related skills.

Chromosomal abnormalities other than the 21 trisomy may occasionally be involved in the etiology of Down syndrome. However, the extra version of chromosome 21 is present in at least 94 percent of cases meeting strict Down syndrome diagnostic criteria. As was noted earlier, it may be significant that this is the same chromosome that has been implicated in recent research on Alzheimer's disease, especially since persons with Down syndrome are at extremely high risk for Alzheimer's as they get into and beyond their late 30s (Bauer & Shea, 1986; Cole et al., 1994; Prasher & Kirshnan, 1993; Reid, 1985; Schapiro, Haxby, & Grady, 1992). Interestingly, the apoE risk factor now so prominent in research on Alzheimer's appears not to be a significant element in the dementia experienced by Down syndrome adults (Prasher et al., 1997).

The reason for the trisomy of chromosome 21 is not clear, but the defect seems definitely related to parental age at conception. It has been known for many years that the incidence of Down syndrome increases on an accelerating slope (from the 20s on) with increasing age of the mother. A woman in her 20s has about 1 chance in 2000 of conceiving a Down syndrome baby, whereas the risk for a woman in her 40s is 1 in 50 (Holvey & Talbott, 1972). As in the case of all birth defects, the risk of having a Down syndrome baby is also high for very young mothers whose reproductive systems have not yet fully matured. The advanced maternal age correlation led naturally to the inference that an older woman's capacity to produce a chromosomally normal fetus was somehow impaired by the aging process. This observed effect obscured for many years a potential male contribution, since older men tend to have older women partners.

Subsequent research has indicated that the father's age at conception is also implicated in Down syndrome, particularly at higher ages (Hook, 1980; Stene et al., 1981). In one study involving 1279 cases of Down syndrome in Japan, Matsunaga and associates (1978) demonstrated an overall increase in incidence with advancing paternal age when maternal age was controlled. The risk for fathers aged 55 years and over was more than twice that for fathers in their early 20s. Curiously, these investigators noted that, in their sample, fathers in their early 40s had a lower risk factor than slightly younger as well as older men.

Thus it seems that advancing age in either parent increases the risk of the trisomy 21 anomaly, although the maternal age effect is the larger one. As yet we do not understand how aging produces this effect. A reasonable guess is that aging is related to cumulative exposure to varied environmental hazards, such as radiation, that might have adverse effects on the processes involved in zygote formation or development.

Phenylketonuria   In **phenylketonuria** (**PKU**), a baby appears normal at birth but lacks a liver enzyme needed to break down phenylalanine, an amino acid found in many foods. The genetic error results in retardation only when significant quantities of phenylalanine are ingested, something that is virtually certain to occur if the child's condition remains undiagnosed. If the condition is undetected, the amount of phenylalanine in the blood increases and eventually produces brain damage.

The disorder usually becomes apparent between 6 and 12 months after birth, although such symptoms as vomiting, a peculiar odor, infantile eczema, and seizures may occur during the early weeks of life. Often the first symptoms noticed are signs of mental retardation, which may be moderate to severe depending on the degree to which the disease has progressed. Lack of motor coordination and other neurological problems caused by the brain damage are also common, and often the eyes, skin, and hair of untreated PKU patients are very pale. PKU was unidentified until 1934, when a Norwegian mother sought to learn the reason for her child's mental retardation and peculiar musty odor. She consulted with many physicians to no avail until Dr. Asbjorn Folling found phenylpyruvic acid in the child's urine and concluded that the child had a disorder of phenylalanine metabolism (Centerwall & Centerwall, 1961).

The early detection of PKU by examining urine for the presence of phenylpyruvic acid is now routine in developed countries, and dietary treatment (such as the elimination of phenylalanine-containing foods) and related procedures can be used to prevent the disorder. With early detection and treatment—preferably before an infant is six months old—the deterioration process can usually be arrested so that levels of intellectual functioning may range from borderline to normal. A few children suffer mental retardation despite restricted phenylalanine intake and other measures, however. Dietary restriction in late-diagnosed PKU may improve the clinical picture somewhat, but there is no real substitute for early detection and prompt intervention (Pavone et al., 1993).

For a baby to inherit PKU, it appears that both parents must carry the recessive genes. Thus when one child in a family is discovered to have PKU, it is especially critical that other children in the family be screened as well. Also, a pregnant PKU mother whose risk status has been successfully addressed by early dietary intervention may damage her at-risk fetus unless she maintains rigorous control of phenylalanine intake.

Cranial Anomalies Mental retardation is associated with a number of conditions that involve alterations in head size and shape and for which the causal factors have not been definitely established (Maclean, 1997; Robinson & Robinson, 1976). In the rare condition known as **macrocephaly** (large-headedness), for example, there is an increase in the size and weight of the brain, an enlargement of the skull, visual impairment, convulsions, and other neurological symptoms, resulting from the abnormal growth of glia cells that form the supporting structure for brain tissue. Other more common cranial anomalies include *microcephaly* and *hydrocephalus*, which we will discuss in more detail.

Microcephaly The term **microcephaly** means "small-headedness." It refers to a type of mental retardation resulting from impaired development of the brain and a consequent failure of the cranium to attain normal size. In an early study of postmortem examinations of microcephalic individuals' brains, Greenfield and Wolfson (1935) reported that practically all cases examined showed development to have been arrested at the fourth or fifth month of fetal life.

The most obvious characteristic of microcephaly is the small head, the circumference of which rarely exceeds 17 inches, as compared with the normal size of approximately 22 inches. Penrose (1963) also described microcephalic youngsters as being invariably short in stature but having relatively normal musculature and sex organs. Beyond these characteristics, they differ considerably from one another in appearance, although there is a tendency for the skull to be cone-shaped, with a receding chin and forehead. Microcephalic children fall within the moderate, severe, and profound categories of mental retardation, but most show little language development and are extremely limited in mental capacity.

Microcephaly may result from a wide range of factors that impair brain development, including intrauterine infections and pelvic irradiation during the mother's early months of pregnancy. Miller (1970) noted a number of cases of microcephaly in Hiroshima and Nagasaki that apparently resulted from the atomic bomb explosions during World War II. The role of genetic factors is not clear, although there is speculation that a single recessive gene is involved in a primary, inherited form of the disorder (Robinson & Robinson, 1976). Treatment is ineffective once faulty development has occurred; at present, preventive measures focus on the avoidance of infection and radiation during pregnancy.

Hydrocephalus **Hydrocephalus** is a relatively rare condition in which the accumulation of an abnormal amount of cerebrospinal fluid within the cranium causes damage to the brain tissues and enlargement of the skull. In congenital cases, the head is either already enlarged at birth or begins to enlarge soon thereafter, presumably as a result of a disturbance in the formation, absorption, or circulation of the cerebrospinal fluid. The disorder can also develop in infancy or early childhood, following the development of a brain tumor, subdural hematoma, meningitis, or other conditions. In these cases the condition appears to result from a blockage of the cerebrospinal pathways and an accumulation of fluid in certain brain areas.

The clinical picture in hydrocephalus depends on the extent of neural damage, which, in turn, depends on the age at onset and the duration and severity of the disorder. In chronic cases, the chief symptom is the gradual enlargement of the upper part of the head out of proportion to the face and the rest of the body. While the expansion of the skull helps minimize destructive pressure on the brain, serious brain damage occurs nonetheless. This damage leads to intellectual impairment and such other effects as convulsions and impairment or loss of sight and hearing. The degree of intellectual impairment varies, being severe or profound in advanced cases.

A good deal of attention has been directed to the surgical treatment of hydrocephalus, in which shunting devices are inserted to drain cerebrospinal fluid. With early diagnosis and treatment, this condition can usually be arrested before severe brain damage has occurred (Geisz & Steinhausen, 1974). Even with significant brain damage, carefully planned and early interventions that take into account both strengths and weaknesses in intellectual functioning may minimize disability (Baron & Goldberger, 1993).

Cultural-Familial Mental Retardation

Investigators used to believe that all mental retardation was the result of faulty genes or of other causes of brain impairment. In recent decades, however, it has become apparent that adverse sociocultural conditions, particularly those involving a deprivation of normal environmental stimulation, may play a primary role in the etiology of mental retardation. Two subtypes of mental retardation fall in this general category: (1) mental retardation associated with extreme sensory and social deprivation, such as prolonged isolation during the developmental years, as is occasionally inflicted on children by disturbed parents; and (2) **cultural-familial retardation,** in which a child is not subjected to extreme isolation but rather suffers from an inferior quality of interaction with the cultural environment and with other people. Because such sociocultural impoverishment may be associated with genetic deficiency in some cases, a child born to a family in such circumstances may be doubly jeopardized. In any event, it has proved all but impossible to assess the differential influences of nature and nurture in these cases.

Because most mental retardation is of the cultural-familial type, our discussion will focus on it. Table 13.4 depicts the average IQs of 586 Milwaukee children in differing age ranges. The children were separated according to whether or not the IQs of their mothers, all of whom dwelt in slum areas under deprived circumstances, fell below 80. Note that the two groups of children did not differ in IQ at ages 1 through 2 and that both groups scored within the normal range. The children whose mothers had IQs of 80 or above continued to manifest average IQs in the normal range through age 14. However, children of mothers of IQ less than 80 showed, on average, a progressive (and, after age 6, nonreversing) decline in IQ with advancing age, approaching the upper limits of the mental retardation range by age 14. Such a progressive loss is not easy to reconcile with a hereditary interpretation; it suggests, rather, the cumulative effects of a deficient environment, one that is associated with the mothers' IQ levels.

The effect may be due to the inadequacy of low IQ mothers in stimulating intellectual growth. Although this conclusion is consistent with most more recently acquired evidence (e.g., Camp et al., 1998), it would be tragic to convert such evidence to an assignment of blame against disadvantaged women. They need help, not blame, and when they get this help, the IQs of their children may be substantially elevated (Garber, 1988; Ramey & Haskins, 1981; Turkheimer, 1991; Zigler & Muenchow, 1992; Zigler & Styfco, 1994).

Whatever the specific etiology, children whose retardation is cultural-familial in origin are usually only

The causal pattern in cultural-familial mental retardation is believed to include an impoverished and intellectually deprived developmental history.

mildly retarded. They show no identifiable brain pathology and are usually not diagnosed as mentally retarded until they enter school and have difficulties with their studies. As many investigators have pointed out, most of these children come from economically deprived, unstable, and often disrupted family backgrounds characterized by a lack of intellectual stimulation, an inferior quality of interaction with others, and general environmental deprivation (e.g., Birns & Bridger, 1977; Braginsky & Braginsky, 1974; Feuerstein, 1977):

> They are raised in homes with absent fathers and with physically or emotionally unavailable mothers. During in-

TABLE 13.4   AVERAGE IQS OF 586 MILWAUKEE CHILDREN

Maternal IQ	*Age of Children in Years*						
	1–3	**3–5**	**5–7**	**7–9**	**9–11**	**11–14**	**14+**
80+ (*n* = 48)	95	93	90	94	87.5	94	90
< 80 (*n* = 40)	95	76	84	80	75	70	67.5

Source: Adapted from Garber (1988, p. 23).

fancy they are not exposed to the same quality and quantity of tactile and kinesthetic stimulations as other children. Often they are left unattended in a crib or on the floor of the dwelling. Although there are noises, odors, and colors in the environment, the stimuli are not as organized as those found in middle-class and upper-class environments. For example, the number of words they hear is limited, with sentences brief and most commands carrying a negative connotation. (Tarjan & Eisenberg, 1972, p. 16)

Since a child's current level of intellectual functioning is based largely on previous learning—and since school-work requires complex skills, such as being able to control one's attention, follow instructions, and recognize the meaning of a considerable range of words—these children are at a disadvantage from the beginning because they have not had an opportunity to learn requisite background skills or to be motivated toward learning. Thus with each succeeding year, unless remedial measures are undertaken, they tend to fall further behind in school performance.

The Problem of Assessment

Because mental retardation is defined in terms of both intellectual (academic) and social competence, it is essential to assess both of these characteristics before labeling a person mentally retarded. Unfortunately, neither of these tasks is easy. Errors in IQ assessment can stem from a variety of sources, including (1) errors in administering and scoring tests; (2) the personal characteristics of a child, such as a language problem or lack of motivation to do well on tests; (3) temporary disrupting circumstances in the child's life, such as illness or family stress; and (4) limitations in the tests themselves.

Although the assessment of social competence may seem less complicated, especially if it is based on clinical observations and ratings, it is subject to many of the same errors as the measurement of IQ. In the elaborated version of adaptive skills assessment proposed by the AAMR (Luckasson et al., 1992), noted above, many of the skills included, such as responsivity to subtle social cues, cannot be reliably measured with existing techniques (MacMillan et al., 1993). Also, the criteria used by the person or persons doing the assessing are of particular importance. For example, if children are well adapted socially to life in an urban ghetto but not to the demands of a formal school setting, should they be evaluated as having a high, intermediate, or low level of social competence? Competence for what? It is doubtful that judgments of this kind can be made objectively—that is, without reference to particular value orientations.

To label a child mentally retarded is likely to have profound effects on both the child's self-concept and the reactions of others, and thus on his or her entire future life. Most immediately, it may lead to a disadvantaged upbringing by discouraged, demoralized parents (Richardson, Koller, & Katz, 1985), to say nothing of the likely effects on overburdened schoolteachers. Over the long term, such a label may become a self-fulfilling prophecy fueled by the tendency to behave in ways consistent with one's self-concept and others' expectations. Obviously it is a label that has profound ethical and social implications. On the other hand, making the formal diagnosis in many jurisdictions admits the child and his or her family to a host of special services, including specialized education, that may well not otherwise be available. Clearly, the decision is one needing careful thought and a highly individualized approach.

Treatments, Outcomes, and Prevention

A number of programs have demonstrated that significant changes in adaptive capacity are possible through special education and other rehabilitative measures. The degree of change that can be expected is related, of course, to an individual's particular situation and level of mental retardation.

Treatment Facilities and Methods One problem that causes anxiety for the parents of a mentally retarded child is whether to put the child in an institution. Most authorities agree that this should be considered a "last resort," in light of the unfavorable outcomes normally experienced—particularly in regard to the erosion of self-care skills (Lynch, Kellow, & Willson, 1997). In general, children who are institutionalized fall into two groups: (1) those who, in infancy and childhood, manifest severe mental retardation and associated physical impairment, and who enter an institution at an early age; and (2) those who have no physical impairments but show relatively mild mental retardation and a failure to adjust socially in adolescence, eventually being institutionalized chiefly because of delinquency or other problem behavior (see Stattin & Klackenberg-Larsson, 1993). In these cases, social incompetence is the main factor in the decision. The families of those in the first group come from all socioeconomic levels, whereas a significantly higher percentage of the families of those in the second group come from lower educational and occupational strata.

The effect of being institutionalized in adolescence depends heavily, of course, on an institution's facilities as well as on individual factors. For the many retarded teenagers who do not have families in a position to help them achieve a satisfactory adjustment, community-oriented residential care seems a particularly effective alternative (Alexander, Huganir, & Zigler, 1985; Landesman-Dwyer, 1981; Seidl, 1974; Thacher, 1978), although for maximum effectiveness great care must be taken in adequately assessing needs and in the recruitment of staff personnel (Petronko, Harris, & Kormann, 1994). Unfortunately, many neighborhoods resist the location of such facilities within their confines and reject integration of residents into the local society (Short, 1997).

For the mentally retarded who do not require institutionalization, educational and training facilities have historically been woefully inadequate. It still appears that a very substantial proportion of mentally retarded people in the United States are never reached by services appropriate to their specific needs (Luckasson et al., 1992; Tyor & Bell, 1984).

This neglect is especially tragic in view of what we now know about helping these people. For example, classes for the mildly retarded, which usually emphasize reading and other basic school subjects, budgeting and money matters, and the development of occupational skills, have succeeded in helping many people become independent, productive community members. Classes for the moderately and severely retarded usually have more limited objectives, but they emphasize the development of self-care and other skills—e.g., toilet habits (Wilder et al., 1997)—that enable individuals to function adequately and to be of assistance in either a family (see, e.g., Heller, Miller, & Factor, 1997) or institutional setting. Just mastering toilet training and learning to eat and dress properly may mean the difference between remaining at home or in a community residence and being institutionalized.

Today there are probably under 80,000 individuals still in institutions for the retarded, less than half the number that were residents a mere 30 years ago. Even many of these more seriously affected persons are being helped to be partly self-supporting in community programs (Brown, 1977; Landesman-Dwyer, 1981; Maclean, 1997; McDonnell et al., 1993; Robinson & Robinson, 1976; Thacher, 1978). These developments reflect both the new optimism that has come to prevail and also, in many instances, new laws and judicial decisions favorable to the rights of retarded people and their families. A notable example is Public Law 94–142, passed by Congress in 1975 and since modified several times (see Hayden, 1998, for an update). This statute, termed the Education for All Handicapped Children Act, asserts the right of mentally retarded people to be educated at public expense in the least restrictive environment possible.

During the 1970s, there was a rapid increase in alternate forms of care for the mentally retarded (Tyor & Bell, 1984). These included, but were not limited to, the use of decentralized regional facilities for short-term evaluation and training; small private hospitals specializing in rehabilitative techniques; group homes or halfway houses integrated into the local community; nursing homes for the elderly retarded; the placement of severely retarded children in more enriched foster-home environments; and varied forms of support to the family for own-home care. The last three decades, in short, have seen a marked enhancement of alternative modes of dealing with retarded citizens, rendering obsolete (and often leading to the closure of) many public institutions formerly devoted exclusively to this type of care.

Education and Mainstreaming Typically, educational and training procedures involve mapping out target areas of improvement, such as personal grooming, social behavior, basic academic skills, and (for retarded adults) simple occupational skills (see Forness & Kavale, 1993). Within each area, specific skills are divided into simple components that can be learned and reinforced before more complex behaviors are required. Training that builds on step-by-step progression can bring retarded individuals repeated experiences of success and lead to substantial progress even by those previously regarded as uneducable (see McDonnell et al., 1993).

For mildly retarded youngsters, the question of what schooling is best is likely to challenge both parents and school officials. Parents have fought for and largely gained access to special education classes *within* public schools, having learned that isolation from peers tends to compound the problem. Too often, however, success in getting a retarded child into a public school has meant that the child is treated as very special indeed and—along with other retarded students—becomes isolated within the school. We have now learned that this type of special education may have serious limitations in terms of a child's social and educational development, and that many such children fare better by attending regular classes for at least much of the day. Of course, this type of approach—called **mainstreaming**—does require careful planning, a high level of teacher skill, and facilitative teacher attitudes (Birns & Bridger, 1977; Borg & Ascione, 1982; Budoff, 1977; Hanrahan, Goodman, & Rapagna, 1990; Kozleski & Jackson, 1993; Stafford & Green, 1993).

Substantial research has led to the conclusion that mainstreaming is not the hoped-for panacea for retarded children (Gottlieb, 1981). Such programs are difficult to launch and to maintain (Lieberman, 1982); their success (or lack of it) seems to depend largely on such change-resistant influences as teacher attitudes and overall classroom climate (Haywood, Meyers, & Switsky, 1982; Miller, 1989; Schumm & Vaughn, 1992). Moreover, any educational gains may come at the expense of deficits in self-esteem suffered by handicapped children as they interact intensively with more cognitively advantaged peers (Haywood et al., 1982; Santich & Kavanaugh, 1997). Gresham (1982) argues that such dangers may be decreased or eliminated if retarded children are given social skills training before they enter a mainstream classroom. Also, when the situation is sensitively managed, the normal classmates of mainstreamed children may themselves derive benefits from the experience (Lincoln et al., 1992). A variant of mainstreaming called the Parallel Alternate Curriculum program, which emphasizes specialized instruction in a regular classroom setting, has shown much promise. Even here, however, much attention must be given to teaching-staff development (Chandler, 1985; Smith & Smith, 1985).

A reasonable conclusion at this time is that school systems should not attempt mainstreaming without a great deal of advance planning and preparation. In other words, mere window dressing to achieve an appearance of progressive educational practice is not enough; the system's leadership must be thoroughly committed to overcoming deeply entrenched attitudes and procedures within the education bureaucracy to ensure the success of the effort.

Frontiers in Prevention Since the 1960s, programs geared toward preventing mental retardation have focused on reaching high-risk children early with the intensive cognitive stimulation believed to underlie the sound development of mental ability. Project Head Start is a well-known example operating at the local community level, one whose effectiveness is difficult to measure and therefore subject to controversy (Gamble & Zigler, 1989). In fact, however, local Head Start programs have varied widely in their organizational and management expertise and in their commitment to making a difference in the lives of their child clientele. Perhaps inevitably, too, politics and bureaucratic bumbling have often served to dull the cutting edge Head Start was fashioned to provide (Zigler & Muenchow, 1992). In the end, no program of early intervention can guarantee a successful outcome. Nevertheless, the available outcome data are clear in showing that well-managed Head Start programs have amassed a very creditable record in launching children on the path to educational and occupational accomplishment; considering the stakes in failed and socially costly

lives, they appear to be an excellent community investment (Zigler & Styfco, 1994).

Somewhat sobering is the possibility that the educational performance of many Head Start children increases primarily because of temporarily enhanced motivation rather than higher rates of cognitive development (Zigler et al., 1982). Where the environment continues to be harmful over time, the gain for many youngsters exposed to short-term enrichment programs may be lost (Garber, 1988; Gray & Ramsey, 1982; Switsky, 1997). Obviously, much remains to be learned and done in the area of maintaining early gains. Where notable and sustainable gains have not been unequivocally demonstrated, the necessary financial investment may attract the kind of short-sighted political opposition commonly directed at expensive social programs (see Chafel, 1992). The irony is that the money is spent anyway, usually at compounded rates of increase, on such things as ADC (welfare-based aid to dependent children), chronic institutionalization, correctional facilities, and the "war on drugs."

The federal initiatives begun in the 1960s during the Kennedy administration have eroded over the years. Demands on the federal budget for programs seen as having greater national priority have increased, and the funds committed for helping the retarded have suffered devaluation through inflation. Beginning with the Nixon administration of the early 1970s, serious cutbacks were made in training and research in all of the mental health disciplines. The trend became steadily worse after that time as the national debt increased to unprecedented levels and as many states likewise experienced severe fiscal problems. As a result, we were not able to capitalize fully on our increased understanding of how to reverse or prevent the deficits experienced by mentally retarded youngsters and adults. With the ending of the Cold War and increasing signs of a prosperous economy developing on a worldwide basis, it is perhaps time to renew our commitment to the prevention of mental retardation.

LEARNING DISORDERS

In contrast to generalized developmental disorders such as mental retardation and autism (addressed in Chapter 14), **specific learning disorders** have a circumscribed character and may occur in children who are otherwise normal or even gifted in their overall functioning (Ferri, Gregg, & Heggoy, 1997). The inadequate development may be manifested in language, speech, mathematical, or motor-skills areas, and it is not due to any reliably demonstrable physical or neurological defect. Of these types of problems, the best known and most researched is a variety of reading/writing difficulties known collectively as *dyslexia*. In dyslexia, the individual manifests problems in word recognition and reading comprehension; often he or she is found markedly deficient in spelling as well. On assessment of reading skill, these persons routinely omit, add, and distort words, and their reading is typically painfully slow and halting.

The diagnosis of learning disorder is restricted to those cases in which there is clear impairment in school performance or (if the person is not a student) in daily living activities, not due to mental retardation or a pervasive developmental disorder, such as autism. Skill deficits due to attention-deficit hyperactivity disorder, described in Chapter 14, are coded under that diagnosis. This coding presents another diagnostic dilemma because some investigators hold that an attentional deficit is basic to many learning disorders; evidence for the latter view is equivocal (see Faraone et al., 1993b). We will focus in this section on specific developmental disorders involving academic skills, also known as specific learning disabilities, or—in DSM-IV terms—simply *learning disorders*. Children (and adults) with these disorders are more generally said to be *learning disabled* (LD). Significantly more boys than girls are diagnosed as learning disabled, but proportional estimates of this gender discrepancy have varied widely from study to study. Also, some investigators believe the observation is itself biased, owing to the greater likelihood of LD boys to come to the attention of authorities because of conduct problems.

The Clinical Picture in Learning Disorders

Learning disabled children are initially identified as such because of an apparent disparity between their expected academic achievement level and their actual academic performance in one or more school subjects, such as math, spelling, writing, or reading. Typically, these children have overall IQs, family backgrounds, and exposure to cultural norms and symbols that are consistent with at least average achievement in school. They do not have obvious crippling emotional problems, nor do they seem to be lacking in motivation, cooperativeness, or eagerness to please their teachers and parents—at least not at the outset of their formal education. Nevertheless, they fail, often abysmally and usually with a stubborn, puzzling persistence. Why? As we will see, satisfactory answers are hard to come by.

Frustration for teachers, school officials, parents, professional helpers, and perhaps most notably for the victims themselves (although the last may go unnoticed in the general turmoil) is virtually guaranteed in this scenario, and it is likely to complicate efforts to find a solution. Charles Wenar (1990) poignantly depicts the problem:

> You are a child clinical psychologist. It has been a rough day. The climax was a phone call to the principal of Wykwyre Junior High School. It is the kind of suburban school in which children from two-swimming-pool families do not speak to children from one-swimming-pool families. The call had been about Jon Hastings, a 16-year-old with a long history of school failures. The intelligence test showed him to be bright enough to do college work, and yet he is only in the eighth grade. He is articulate, has a talent for making miniature rockets and speedboats, and a real flair for drawing cartoons. Yet the written word is Jon's nemesis. He reads laboriously one word at a time, while his writing is even more painfully slow. Because of repeated failures and because he is now a social misfit with peers, he has begun cutting up in class and talking back to the teacher.
>
> You had phoned the principal to suggest ways of bypassing Jon's reading disability. Since he is sufficiently bright to absorb most of the lecture material, could he be given oral examinations every now and then? If he were taught to type, could he type instead of writing his examinations? Would the principal consider introducing special classes for all the learning-disabled children?
>
> The principal was suave and ingratiating and a compendium of the resistances you have run up against in the past. He "understood your concern" but asked that you "look at the situation from my point of view." The school had "tried everything possible to no avail," "the boy is incorrigible," "you can't help a child unless the child wants help," and finally—you could feel this one coming, since you had heard it so often—"I can't give one student a favor without giving a favor to all of them. I'd have half the mothers in my office next day demanding something extra to pull their child's grades up." (p. 197)

It is unfortunately the case that LD, despite its having been recognized as a distinct and rather common type of disorder for more than 40 years, and despite its having generated a voluminous research literature, still fails to be given the status it deserves in many school jurisdictions. Instead, as in the preceding example, the familiar diversion of blaming the victim and of attributing the affected child's problems to various character deficiencies is still routinely employed by many classroom teachers and school administrators, whether in public or private settings (see Bearn & Smith, 1998; Fischer, 1993; Moats & Lyon, 1993). Where lockstep uniformity is the rule, as it is in most public and many alternative educational systems, a youngster who learns academic skills slowly or in a different way is treated as a troublemaker, as a threat to the prevailing theory of education.

The consequences of these encounters between LD children and rigidly doctrinaire or regimented school systems can be disastrous to a child's self-esteem and general psychological well-being, and research indicates that these effects do not necessarily dissipate after secondary schooling ends (Aspis, 1997; Brinckerhoff, 1993; Bruck, 1987; Cooper, 1997; Ferri, Gregg, & Heggoy, 1997; Khan, Cowan, & Roy, 1997; Michaels, Lazar, & Risucci, 1997; Saracoglu, Minden, & Wilchesky, 1989; Walters & Croen, 1993; Wilczenski, 1993). Thus even where LD difficulties are no longer a significant impediment, an individual may bear the scars of many painful school-related episodes of failure into maturity and beyond.

But there is also a brighter side to this picture. High levels of general talent and of motivation to overcome the obstacle of a learning disorder sometimes produces a life of extraordinary achievement. Sir Winston Churchill, British statesman, author, and inspiring WWII wartime leader, is said to have been dyslexic as a child. The same attribution is made to Woodrow Wilson, former university professor and president of the United States, and to Nelson Rockefeller, former governor of New York and vice president of the United States. Such examples remind us that the "bad luck" and personal adversity of having a learning disorder need not be uniformly limiting; quite the contrary.

Causal Factors in Learning Disorders

Probably the most generally held view of the cause of specific learning disabilities is that they are the products of subtle central nervous system impairments. In particular, these disabilities are thought to result from some sort of immaturity, deficiency, or dysregulation limited to those brain functions supposedly mediating, for normal children, the cognitive skills that LD children cannot efficiently acquire. For example, many researchers believe that language-related LDs such as dyslexia are associated with a failure of the brain to develop in a normally asymmetrical manner with respect to the right and left hemispheres. Specifically, portions of the left hemisphere, where language function is normally mediated, for unknown reasons appear to remain relatively underdeveloped in many dyslexic individuals (Beaton, 1997; Obrzut, Paquette, & Flores, 1997).

A few years back the term *minimal brain dysfunction (MBD)* was in popular use to refer to such presumed organic malfunction—until it was generally recognized that nobody had the slightest idea what the term really meant. While some LD children show definite or highly suggestive evidence of brain disease, such as cerebral palsy,

epilepsy, or a history of severe head trauma (e.g., Yule & Rutter, 1985), the large majority do not. In others, there may be subtle indications, "soft signs," of neurological compromise, but again such findings are by no means routine. Overall, there is little evidence of a specific central nervous system dysfunction among LD children generally (Durrant, 1994; Schwartz & Johnson, 1985), although some recent work with functional magnetic resonance imaging (see Chapter 15) has suggested that dyslexic individuals may have a deficiency of physiologic activation in a brain center believed to be involved with rapid visual processing (Travis, 1996).

There is also growing evidence that many dyslexic persons suffer from a potentially treatable (through training, drill, etc.) deficiency of phonological processing (e.g, Brown, 1997; Busink, 1997; Faust, Dimitrovsky, & Davidi, 1997). That is, they have difficulty understanding correctly words and parts of words (phonemes) as units of sound, and therefore cannot make efficient use of implicit "hearing" of what they are attempting to read. Stein and Walsh (1997), however, dispute this emphasis on the purely phonological, arguing that the research evidence indicates lessened ability to manage the temporal processing of fast incoming sensory information in the visual and motor, as well as the phonological, "systems." This notion of multiple deficits in skills related to reading was supported in a well-designed study recently reported by Badian (1997).

Some investigators believe that the various forms of LD, or vulnerability to develop them, may be genetically transmitted. This issue seems not to have been studied with the same intensity or methodologic rigor as in other disorders. Two family pedigree studies, those of Hallgren (1950) and Finucci and colleagues (1976), showed evidence of familial concordance for reading disorders (dyslexia), and Owen (1978) cites a twin study in which monozygocity was associated with 100 percent concordance for reading disorders. Identification of a gene region for dyslexia on chromosome 6 has been reported (*Science News,* October 22, 1994, p. 271). Although it would be somewhat surprising if a single gene were to be identified as the causal factor in all cases of reading disorder, the hypothesis of a genetic contribution to at least the dyslexic form of LD appears increasingly promising. A recent twin study of mathematics disability has also turned up evidence of some genetic contribution to this form of LD (Alarcon et al., 1997).

Summing up, biological or organic hypotheses concerning the etiology of LD, though widely held, tend to be vague on mechanisms and—excepting dyslexia—do not have an exceptionally strong record of evidence supporting them. They continue to have a sort of intuitive appeal that is at least as great as alternative psychosocial theories of causation.

The apparent complexity of the psychological processes involved in LD (see Ceci & Baker, 1987) evidently makes it difficult to do definitive studies on potential causal factors. Thus the research that is available, most of it again directed to the problem of dyslexia, tends to be riddled with problems of subject selection, inappropriate controls, and other serious methodological flaws (Durrant, 1994; Lyon & Moats, 1997; Vellutino, 1987).

Despite what appears to be a multitude of seemingly differing factors involved in LD, there may yet be some common elements. This is the position taken by Worden (1986), who argues that we should study what characterizes the approaches taken by good learners to be able to identify the areas of significant weakness from which LD children suffer. Specialized training can then be employed to remedy the specific deficiencies involved. He offers the following list as an example of defining intervention aims:

1. What memory strategies are used by normal or good learners, and in what manner do these differ from those employed by LD children?

2. How do normal or good learners monitor their ongoing performances? For example, how do good learners use performance information to gauge where they are being successful and where not, and to introduce corrective action as needed?

3. What metastrategy information is used by good learners and not by LD children? For example, do LD children understand the advantage of having a strategy at all, as in dealing with the time constraints of many school tasks?

4. What motivates good learners, and how does this differ from the motivation of poor learners? Is a learner's orientation one of seeking success or of avoiding failure? To what is success or failure attributed: individual ability, task difficulty, chance, or some other factor?

Worden's approach to analyzing the complex issues involved in academic skill acquisition strikes us as a potentially useful means of disentangling the complex array of educational challenges the LD child presents in the school setting. However, even precise information on the manner in which LD children's learning approaches differ from those of normal children would still leave us with unanswered questions about the sources of these differences. Nevertheless, pursuit of this idea might produce a set of rational, fine-tuned strategies for intervening to correct LD children's inefficient modes of learning.

Treatments and Outcomes

Because we do not yet have a confident grasp on what is "wrong" with the average LD child, we have had limited success in treating these children. While many informal and single-case reports claim success for various treatment approaches, there are few well-designed and well-executed outcome studies on specific treatments for LD problems. Focusing on reading disorders, where most of the effort has been concentrated, Gittelman's (1983) review contains little evidence of impressive results. Moreover, any short-term gains that are made tend in many cases to diminish or even disappear over time (Yule & Rutter, 1985).

Ellis (1993) has offered a comprehensive intervention model to facilitate learning in LD—called Integrative Strategy Instruction (ISI)—which has inspired considerable interest among professionals in the field (see Houck, 1993; Hutchinson, 1993; Parker, 1993; Walsh, 1993). Organized according to particular content areas, it envisions a variety of teacher-directed instructional strategies directed at key aspects of the learning process: orienting, framing, applying, and extending. Although the model appears not to have been rigorously tested for efficacy, its knowledge-based and systematic character is a welcome addition to the analysis of the educational problems presented by LD children. Its application would seem to demand, however, high levels of administrative flexibility, teacher skill, and teacher motivation, none of which can be taken for granted in the average school environment (see Bearn & Smith, 1998; Hutchinson, 1993; Male & May, 1997; Parker, 1993).

It is encouraging that increasing efforts are being made to identify and provide services for LD students in higher education settings. Many of these students are sufficiently bright and resourceful to circumvent lower-level educational barriers to find themselves confronted with challenges requiring skills they simply do not have (Ferri, Gregg, & Heggoy, 1997). Walters and Croen (1993), for example, describe such efforts in a medical school environment; they stress the need for early identification, provision of appropriate support, and arranging minimal accommodations for medical students having LD problems. Yanok (1993) describes an apparently successful developmental education program for LD college students, thus providing for these individuals an "equal educational opportunity."

We have only limited data on the long-term, adult adjustments of people who grew up with the personal, academic, and social problems LD generally entails. Two studies of college students with LD (Gregg & Hoy, 1989; Saracoglu et al., 1989) suggested that as a group they continue to have problems—academic, personal, and social—into the postsecondary education years. In a community survey of LD adults, Khan and Roy (1997) found that some 50 percent of them had "personality abnormalities." Cato and Rice (1982) extracted from the available literature a lengthy list of somewhat discouraging problems experienced by the typical LD adult. These include—in addition to expected difficulties with self-confidence—continuing problems with deficits in the ordinary skills, such as math, that these people originally encountered as children. The authors did note, however, that there are considerable individual differences in these outcomes, thus reminding us that some adults with LD are able to manage very well.

UNRESOLVED ISSUES

Cultural-Familial Retardation

The problem of cultural-familial mental retardation, which has no biological markers, continues to be a frustrating and all-too-common one—complicated in no small measure by sensitive issues of race relations and imputed ethnic differences in native abilities. No scientifically respectable evidence suggests that the quality of brain tissue is in any degree correlated with race or ethnicity. A great deal of evidence, on the other hand, shows that different ethnic groups, on average, vary considerably in performance on standardized tests designed to predict academic achievement. The very controversial book *The Bell Curve* (Herrnstein & Murray, 1994) contains the most recent comprehensive discussion of such intergroup differences in average IQ test scores. Do such tests more or less directly measure "intelligence" as we have long been encouraged to believe? In fact, IQ tests are and have always been validated primarily on their ability to predict school performance.

Schools may reasonably be viewed as having the principal function of transmitting a culture's approved products from earlier to later generations; approved products are those deemed valuable by a cultural elite. So-called intelligence tests, then, are designed to measure the facility with which a child may be expected to acquire and adequately process what the school offers. It does not seem farfetched to suggest that a child's performance in school will be determined to a considerable extent by the amount of prior and continuing extracurricular exposure he or she has to the products of the dominant culture that the school represents. Indeed, we have a fair amount of empirical evidence showing that this is so. We also have a fair amount of empirical evidence suggesting that a person's IQ ("intelligence" quotient) rises significantly with enhanced exposure to these cultural products. It is therefore more than a mere possibility that what IQ tests mostly measure is prior exposure to approved cultural products. Considered from this perspective, the notion of a "culture-free" IQ test that would also do well at predicting school grades is a practical impossibility.

The fact that African Americans are disproportionately represented among those labeled "retarded" is clearly related to the prominence of the IQ measure in the definition of retardation. African Americans have a persistent 15-point deficit, on average, relative to whites on this type of test. However interpreted—whether in terms of "test bias" or in terms of a "real" difference (and from the preceding argument we suggest that these are the same things)—one implication seems clear. Namely, African Americans as a group are seriously disadvantaged in engagements with the standard educational system. Relative success in such engagements, as already noted, is mostly what IQ tests are designed to predict, and for the most part they do so effectively. If, as is often said (we have our own small doubts), conventional academic success leads to such happiness and riches as are attainable in our larger culture, then enormously disproportionate numbers of African Americans will continue to be excluded from the good life unless some remedy for this problem can be found.

As we have seen, serious and broad-based efforts to find a remedy were begun in the 1960s, Project Head Start being a notable example. Much was learned in the programs that were launched during that era, one of the most important lessons being that genuine and sustained advance was costly and difficult. For example, we learned that the gains in academic skill acquired in an enriched preschool experience, as in Head Start, were not lasting without a more general environmental enrichment. However, subsequent changes in national priorities and in the political atmosphere, particularly at the federal level, precluded a vigorous follow-up of these initiatives. We have not regained momentum in this area, nor does it appear likely, as of this writing, that we soon will. If progress in laying to rest the Cold War and in the achievement of "the new world order" were happily to continue, however, sufficient funds and energies might be liberated to contemplate seriously a new national order, one in which all of our children might truly be granted equal opportunity. It is a cruel deception, in our judgment, to suggest that they have it now.

SUMMARY

The neuropsychological mental disorders are those in which mental symptoms of a neurologic or psychopathologic sort (such as cognitive deterioration and delusions, respectively) are presumed to appear as a result of malfunction of the brain's hardware, typically involving the destruction of brain tissue. Generally, these disorders are in some primary sense physical diseases and are accordingly coded on Axis III of DSM-IV, in addition to a descriptive Axis I coding that pertains to the nature of the mental symptoms manifested. The current DSM recognizes certain characteristic neuropsychological syndromes that form a basis for an Axis I psychiatric diagnosis where the precise organic etiology is unknown or is implied in an accompanying Axis III disease; those discussed here are delirium, dementia, amnestic syndrome, and neuropsychological delusional, mood, and personality syndromes. These syndromes are conceived as the primary behavioral indicators for organic brain disease. Some of them mimic disorders in which no gross brain pathology can be demonstrated, which may present problems in diagnosis.

Neuropsychological disorders may be acute and transitory; in this case, brain functioning is only temporarily compromised. Chronic neuropsychological disorders, on which we have focused, involve the permanent loss of neural cells. Psychosocial interventions are often helpful in minimizing psychopathologic reactions in the chronically disordered, although these people will remain neurologically disabled.

The primary causes of brain tissue destruction are many and varied; common ones include certain infectious diseases (such as the HIV-1 virus), brain tumors, physical trauma, degenerative processes (as in Alzheimer's disease), and cerebrovascular arteriosclerosis, often manifested as vascular dementia. The correlation between neurologic brain impairment and psychiatric disorder, however, is not an especially strong one: Some people who have severe damage develop no severe mental symptoms, while others with slight damage have extreme reactions. Although such inconsistencies are not completely understood, it appears that an individual's premorbid personality and life situation are also important in determining his or her reactions to brain damage.

Elderly people are at particular risk for the development of chronic organic mental disorders, especially those related to brain degeneration caused by Alzheimer's disease. As at younger ages, the reaction to brain damage is determined by many nonbiological factors. With disproportionate increases in the numbers of elderly people in the population, and the upcoming wave of baby boomers who will become at risk beginning early in the twenty-first century, we face staggering social, emotional, and economic problems unless some way can be found to prevent or effectively treat Alzheimer's disease.

When serious organic brain impairment occurs before the age of 18, and especially where it is congenital or is acquired shortly after birth, the cognitive and behavioral deficits experienced are referred to as mental retardation. Relatively common forms of such mental retardation, which in these cases is normally at least moderate in severity, include Down syndrome, phenylketonuria (PKU), and certain cranial anomalies. This organic type of mental deficit accounts for only some 25 percent of all cases of mental retardation. Mental retardation diagnoses, regardless of the underlying origins of the deficit condition, are always coded on Axis II of DSM-IV.

The large majority—some 75 percent—of mental retardation cases are unrelated to obvious physical defects and are considered cultural-familial in origin, a term that acknowledges our inability to disentangle genetic and environmental influences in the disorder. Caution is warranted in applying the label mentally retarded, in part because of the heavy reliance on IQ test scores in its definition. The IQ test is—and always has been—a measure of academic skill, not of ability to survive and perhaps even prosper in other areas of life. A variety of evidence points to the conclusion that cultural-familial retardation may be treatable and even preventable, provided we can find the means of providing the necessary cognitive stimulation to socially and economically deprived children.

Specific learning disorders are those in which failure of mastery is limited to circumscribed areas, chiefly involving academic skills such as reading; general cognitive ability may be normal or superior. Affected children are commonly described as learning disabled (LD). Here again some localized defect in brain development is usually considered the primary cause, although independent corroboration of an organic cause is the exception rather than the rule. These disorders create great turmoil and frustration in victims, their families, schools, and professional helpers. Various remedies, most involving training regimens of one sort or another, are tried and apparently are sometimes successful. However, solid outcome research in the area of intervention techniques is seriously lacking. The long-term prognosis for LD is in general not particularly encouraging.

KEY TERMS

organic mental disorders (p. 504)

delerium (p. 508)

dementia (p. 509)

amnestic syndrome (p. 509)

neuropsychological delusional sybdrome (p. 510)

neuropsychological mood syndrome (p. 510)

neuropsychological personality syndrome (p. 510)

AIDS dementia complex (ADC) (p. 511)

AIDS-related complex (ARC) (p. 511)

Dementia of the Alzheimer's Type (DAT) (p. 512)

senile dementia (p. 512)

presenile dementia (p. 512)

vascular dementia (VAD) (p. 519)

traumatic brain injury (TBI) (p. 520)

Down syndrome (p. 528)

phenylketonuria (PKU) (p. 530)

macrocephaly (p. 531)

microcephaly (p. 531)

hydrocephalus (p. 531)

cultural-familial retardation (p. 532)

mainstreaming (p. 534)

specific learning disorders (p. 535)

Disorders of Childhood and Adolescence

Henry J. Darger, *At Sunbeam Creak Captured by Foe-West-Side B, 1950.* Although institutionalized at a young age for behavioral problems, Darger later worked as a janitor until he retired at the age of 81. It was then that his landlord discovered the artist's enormous collection of delicate paintings depicting an imaginary saga of seven young tortured and victimized slave girls.

Until the twentieth century, little account was taken of the special characteristics of psychopathology in children; maladaptive patterns considered relatively specific to childhood, such as autism, received virtually no attention at all. Only with the advent of the mental health movement and the availability of child guidance facilities, have marked strides been made in assessing, treating, and understanding the maladaptive behavior patterns of children and adolescents. Still progress in child psychopathology has lagged behind adult psychopathology. In fact, as we will see, initially, the problems of childhood were seen simply as downward extensions of adult-oriented diagnostic systems.

The prevailing view was one of children as "miniature adults." But this view failed to take into account special problems, such as those associated with the developmental changes that normally take place in a child or adolescent. Only recently have we come to realize that we cannot fully understand childhood disorders without taking into account these developmental processes. Today, even though great progress has been made in providing treatment for disturbed children, our facilities are still woefully inadequate in relation to the magnitude of the task, and most problem children do not receive psychological attention. The numbers of children affected by psychological problems are considerable.

Multisite studies in several countries have provided estimates of childhood disorder that range from 17 to 22 percent (Costello, 1989; Institute of Medicine, 1989; Verhulst & Koot, 1992; and Zill & Schoenborn, 1990). In New Zealand a group of 1600 birth cohort children (children born near in the same time period, 1975–1976, at Queen Mary Hospital in Dunedin, N.Z.) have been followed for over 21 years. The follow-up study has been designed to obtain longitudinal data on such outcomes as health and behavioral problems and possible correlates of psychopathology. During the course of this longitudinal study, about one in four children have developed a psychological disorder (McGee, Feehan, & Williams, 1995).

In most studies, maladjustment is found more commonly among boys than girls. In one survey of psychological disorder in children, Anderson and colleagues (1987) found that 17.6 percent of 11-year-old children studied had one or more disorders with boys and girls diagnosed at a ratio of 1.7 boys to 1 girl. The most prevalent disorders were attention-deficit hyperactivity disorder and separation anxiety disorders. Zill and Schoenborn (1990) reported that rates of childhood disorders varied by gender with boys having higher rates of emotional problems over the childhood and adolescent years. However, for some diagnostic problems, such as eating disorders, rates for girls are higher than for boys.

In the first section of this chapter we will note some general characteristics of maladaptive behavior in children compared with adult disorders. Next we will examine the issues surrounding the diagnostic classification of children's disorders. Then we will look at a number of important disorders of childhood and adolescence. In the final section we will give detailed consideration to some of the special factors involved in both the treatment and prevention of children's problems.

MALADAPTIVE BEHAVIOR IN DIFFERENT LIFE PERIODS

Because of the manner in which personality develops, the various steps in growth and development, and the differing stressors people face in childhood, adolescence, and adulthood, we would expect to find some differences in maladaptive behavior in these periods. Childhood disorders have special characteristics that require careful consideration. Disorders in young people need to be understood along with developmental changes they are undergoing in the normal process of growing up. Psychological maturity is related to growth of the brain which matures in stages with growth occurring even in late adolescence (ages 17 to 21) (Hudspeth & Pribram, 1992). Many problematic behaviors and threats to adjustment emerge over the course of normal development (Kazdin, 1992). Indeed, several behaviors that characterize maladjustment or emotional disturbance are relatively common in childhood. *Developmental science* (Hetherington, 1998) and more specifically, **developmental psychopathology** (Cicchetti & Rogosch, 1999)—are two fields devoted to studying the origins and course of individual maladaptation in the context of normal growth processes.

It is important to view a child's behavior in reference to normal childhood development. We cannot understand or consider a child's behavior as abnormal without determining whether the behavior in question is appropriate for the child's age. Behavior such as temper tantrums or eating inedible objects might be viewed as symptoms of abnormal behavior at age ten but not at age two. Despite the somewhat distinctive characteristics of childhood disturbances at different ages, there is no sharp

childhood problems and among researchers attempting to broaden our understanding of childhood psychopathology, that the then-current ways of viewing psychological disorders in children and adolescents were inappropriate and inaccurate for several reasons.

The greatest problem stemmed from the fact that the same classification system that had been developed for adults was used for childhood problems—yet many disorders such as autism, learning disabilities, and school phobias have no counterpart in adult psychopathology. The early systems also ignored the fact that in childhood disorders, environmental factors play an important part in the expression of symptoms—that is, symptoms are highly influenced by a family's acceptance or rejection of the behavior. For example, either extreme tolerance of deviant behavior such as accepting a child's frequent school refusal as "normal" or total rejection and neglect could lead a child's extreme behavior to be viewed as normal. In addition, symptoms were not considered with respect to a child's developmental level. Some of the problem behaviors might be considered age-appropriate, and troubling behaviors might simply be ones the child will eventually outgrow.

The Categorical Strategy

Over the years, discontent with the classification system for childhood behavior problems has led to considerable rethinking, discussion, and empirical investigation of the issues related to diagnosis. You may recall that in Chapters 1 and 9 we discussed various methods of classification. In the classification of childhood disorders, two of these methods—the categorical and the dimensional—have both been prominent. The first approach, a *categorical strategy,* is typically used by clinicians and has evolved from previous diagnostic classification systems. DSM-IV is an example of a categorical strategy: A clinician or, in the case of DSM-IV, a panel of clinicians arrives at a descriptive class or category by reviewing the diagnostic literature on the behaviors that appear to define that class of children. For example, the similar behaviors that appear in children who are judged to fit the diagnostic class *attention-deficit hyperactivity disorder* are used as the defining criteria of that class.

The Dimensional Strategy

The second approach—which is rarely used by clinicians but which is favored by many empirical researchers in psychopathology—is a *dimensional strategy.* This approach involves the application of sophisticated statistical methods to provide clear behavior clusters or dimensions for the widely observed symptoms manifested by children. A researcher gathers his or her symptomatic information through teachers', parents', or clinicians' observations or through a child's presenting symptoms—that is, the behaviors characteristic of the clinical picture at the time the child is first seen by professional personnel. The researcher then allows the statistical method—for example, factor analysis—to determine the various behavior dimensions evidenced by an individual child. The Child Behavior Checklist (CBCL) is the most widely researched and used dimensional strategy for assessing childhood behavior problems. Achenbach (1985) and colleagues (Achenbach, Howell et al., 1995; Achenbach, Howell, & McConaughy, 1995) used parent and teacher ratings of the symptoms of problem children and followed up these children after six years. They found that this dimensional approach to childhood psychopathology detected developmental variations that "may be masked" by the use of categorical diagnostic cutoffs.

Contrasting Categorical and Dimensional Strategies

Both categorical and dimensional strategies are based on observation of a child's behavior, and both result in classifying the child according to the presence or absence of symptoms or problem behaviors. There are marked differences between the systems, however. The categorical strategy can require the presence of relatively few symptoms to arrive at a diagnosis while the dimensional strategy usually requires the presence of a number of related symptoms before an individual is considered to have a problem—that is, it usually takes a number of related symptoms on a particular dimension to be considered extreme. As a result, a categorical system will tend to have many categories defined by few, sometimes quite rare, behaviors, while dimensional approaches typically involve a small number of general classes covering numerous related behaviors.

Broadly, the categorical approach follows the disease model of psychopathology and attempts to classify problem behavior in children into meaningful classes of mental disorders to provide useful prognoses and treatments. The dimensional approach is based on the idea that these behaviors are continuous and are found even among many normal children; it attempts to provide an objective classification scheme for assessing the relative frequency of these behavioral problems in an individual or group. It is possible to see benefits and problems in both these approaches to classification. Because this textbook focuses on the clinical manifestation of disorders, including infrequent symptoms that would be minimized in a dimensional approach, we will, for practical purposes, follow the DSM-IV classification system of childhood and adolescent disorders. Keep in mind, however, that the approach taken here is only one possible way of viewing disorders.

DISORDERS OF CHILDHOOD

We discuss here several disorders of childhood with a focus on describing the clinical picture of each syndrome, while also surveying the possible causal factors and outlining treatment approaches that have proved effective. A broader discussion of treatment methods can be found in Chapters 16 and 17.

The disorders that will be covered are attention-deficit hyperactivity disorder, conduct disorder, anxiety disorders of childhood, depressive disorders, several special symptom disorders, and autism. Some of these disorders are more transient than many of the abnormal behavior patterns of adulthood discussed in earlier chapters and are also perhaps more amenable to treatment. As we will see, if treatment is not received, childhood developmental problems sometimes merge almost imperceptibly into more serious and chronic disorders as the child passes into adulthood, or they manifest themselves later as different disorders (Gelfand, Jenson, & Drew, 1988).

Attention-Deficit Hyperactivity Disorder

Attention-deficit hyperactivity disorder (ADHD), often referred to as hyperactivity, is characterized by difficulties that interfere with effective task-oriented behavior in children—particularly impulsivity, excessive motor activity, and difficulties in sustaining attention. The symptoms of ADHD are relatively common among children seen at child guidance centers. In fact, hyperactive children are the most frequent psychological referrals to mental health and pediatric facilities, and the disorder is usually thought to occur in about 3 to 5 percent of school-age children (Goldman et al., 1998). However, one recent study reported a much higher prevalence rate of 16.1 percent for all types of ADHD (Wolrich, Hannah et al., 1998). The disorder occurs most frequently among preadolescent boys—it is six to nine times more prevalent among boys than girls (DSM-IV). ADHD occurs with the greatest frequency before age eight and tends to become less frequent and with briefer episodes thereafter. Some residual effects, such as attention difficulties, may persist into adolescence or adulthood (Odell, Warren et al.,

1997) although, as we will see, some authorities doubt the authenticity of this syndrome in adults (Bhandary, 1997).

The Clinical Picture in Attention-Deficit Hyperactivity Disorder As the term implies, ADHD hyperactive children show excessive or exaggerated muscular activity such as aimless or haphazard running or fidgeting. This disorder exists in other cultures—for example, among Chinese schoolboys (Leung, Luk et al., 1996), who show an essentially similar pattern as youngsters in the United States with ADHD. Difficulty in sustaining attention is another central feature of the disorder. Hyperactive children are highly distractible and often fail to follow instructions or respond to demands placed on them (Leung & Connolly, 1996). Impulsive behavior and a low frustration tolerance are also characteristic. Perhaps as a result of their behavioral problems, hyperactive children are often lower in intelligence, usually about 7 to 15 IQ points below average. Hyperactive children tend to talk incessantly and to be socially intrusive and immature. In a recent study of 916 youths in New Zealand, adolescents with ADHD and conduct disorder had higher rates of driving offenses than other adolescents (Nada-Raja, Langley, McGee, Williams, Begg, & Reeder, 1997).

Children with ADHD generally affect the people around them negatively. Hyperactive children usually have great difficulties in getting along with their parents because they do not obey rules. Their behavior problems also result in their being viewed negatively by their peers. In general, however, hyperactive children do not appear to be anxious, although their overactivity, restlessness, and distractibility are often interpreted as indications of anxiety. Usually they do poorly in school, commonly showing specific learning disabilities, such as difficulties in reading or in learning other basic school subjects. Hyperactive children also pose behavior problems in the elementary grades. The following case reveals a typical clinical picture.

Case Study, A Hyperactive 8-Year-Old Girl • Gina was referred to a community clinic because of overactive, inattentive, and disruptive behavior. She was a problem to her teacher and to other students because of her hyperactivity and her uninhibited behavior. She would impulsively hit other children, knock things off their desks, and erase material on the blackboard, and damage books and other school property. She seemed to be in perpetual motion talking, moving about, and darting from one area of the classroom to another. She demanded an inordinate amount of attention from her parents and her teacher, and she was intensely jealous of other children, including her own

Children with ADHD are described as overactive, impulsive, and having a low tolerance for frustration and an inability to delay gratification. Incessant talkers, they tend not to obey rules and often run the risk of a multitude of problems with schoolwork, teachers, and other students.

brother and sister. Despite her hyperactive behavior, inferior school performance, and other problems, she was considerably above average in intelligence. Nevertheless, she felt stupid and had a seriously devaluated self-image. Neurological tests revealed no significant organic brain disorder.

Causal Factors in Attention-Deficit Hyperactivity Disorder The cause or causes of ADHD in children is debated (Breggin & Breggin, 1995). The extent to which the problem occurring in ADHD children results from environmental or biological factors remains unclear although recent research points to both genetic (Nadder, Silberg et al., 1998) and social environmental precursors (Hechtman, 1996). Many researchers consider potential biological factors, such as genetic inheritance, to be likely important precursors in developing ADHD (Levy, Barr, & Sunohara, 1998). The potential genetic basis for ADHD has not, however, been firmly established, although there is some support for the idea that ADHD is a familial disorder (Faraone, Biederman, & Milberger, 1994a). For example, one study reported that siblings of ADHD children were more likely to have had academic tutoring and to have been placed in special classes than controls (Faraone et al., 1993b). Moreover, brothers of identified ADHD children were more likely to have lower scores on reading tests than controls.

One early viewpoint that received a great deal of public attention suggested that hyperactivity in children may be produced by dietary factors, particularly food coloring (Feingold, 1977). However, the food-additive theory of hyperactivity has generally been discredited (Mattes & Gittelman, 1981; Stare, Whelan, & Sheridan, 1980). Firm conclusions as to the potential biological basis for ADHD must await further research.

The search for psychological causes of hyperactivity has had similarly inconclusive results. Investigators have not clearly established any psychological causes for the disorder, although they have emphasized both temperament and learning factors. Some evidence shows that the home environment is influential in the development of the disorder (Paternite & Loney, 1980). One study suggested that family pathology, particularly parental personality problems, leads to hyperactivity in children. Morrison (1980) found that many parents of hyperactive children had psychological problems; for example, a large number were found to have clinical diagnoses of personality disorder or hysteria. Currently, ADHD is considered to have multiple causes and effects (Hinshaw, Zupan et al., 1997).

Treatments and Outcomes Although the hyperactive syndrome was first described more than 100 years ago, disagreement remains over the most effective methods of treatment, especially regarding the use of drugs to calm a hyperactive child. Yet, this approach to treating hyperactive children has great appeal in the medical community; a recent survey (Runnheim, Frankenberger, & Hazelkorn 1996) found that 40 percent of junior high school children and 15 percent of high school children with emotional and behavioral problems and ADHD were prescribed medication, mostly **Ritalin** (methylphenidate), an amphetamine.

Interestingly, research has shown that cerebral stimulants, such as amphetamines, have a quieting effect on children—just the opposite of what we would expect from their effects on adults (Pelham et al., 1992). Such medication decreases hyperactive children's overactivity and distractibility and at the same time increases their attention and ability to concentrate. As a result they are often able to function much better at school (Arnett, Fischer, & Newby, 1996). Some authorities (Pliszka, 1991) consider stimulants the first drug of choice for treating ADHD. Fava (1997) concluded that Ritalin can often lower the amount of aggressiveness in hyperactive children. In fact, many hyperactive children whose behavior has not been acceptable in regular classes can function and progress in a relatively normal manner when they use such drugs. The medication does not appear to affect their intelligence but instead seems to help them use their basic capacities more effectively (Klorman et al. 1994). Although the drugs do not *cure* hyperactivity, they have reduced the behavioral symptoms in about one-half to two-thirds of the cases in which medication appears warranted. For example, it has been found that medication reduced the problems of inattention but not the impulsivity in hyperactive children (Matier et al., 1992).

Another medication, **Pemoline,** which is being used in the treatment of ADHD, is chemically very different from Ritalin (Faigel & Heligensten, 1996) with less adverse side effects. Pemoline has been found to have beneficial effects on improved classroom behavior by enhancing cognitive processing without side effects (Pelham, Swanson, et al., 1997). Other research has suggested that those who do not respond to Pemoline might be at too low a dosage level (Heiligenstein & Anders, 1996). In general, Pemoline is considered to be a safe medication for adolescents and young adults with attentional deficits to take on a long-term basis to enhance their performance.

While the short-term pharmacologic effect of stimulants on the symptoms of hyperactive children is well established, their long-term effects are not well known (Safer, 1997). Carlson and Bunner (1993) reported that studies of achievement over long periods of time failed to show that medication has beneficial effects. Some concern has been expressed about the effects of the drugs, particularly when used in heavy dosages over time. Some questions that have been raised concerning the use of these drugs are discussed in Highlight 14.2. The pharmacologic similarity of methylphenidate and cocaine have

caused some investigators concern over its use in treatment of ADHD (Volkow et al., 1995). However, there has not been any reported abuse of methylphenidate. The use of drug therapy with children will be taken up again in Chapter 16.

Another effective approach to treating hyperactive children involves the use of behavior therapy techniques featuring positive reinforcement and the structuring of learning materials and tasks in a way that minimizes error and maximizes immediate feedback and success (Frazier & Merrill, 1998; Goldstein & Goldstein, 1998)—for example, providing immediate praise to a hyperactive boy for stopping to think through a task he has been assigned before he starts to do it. The use of behavioral treatment methods (see Chapter 17) for hyperactivity has reportedly been quite successful, at least for short-term gains.

The use of behavior therapy with medication in a total treatment program has reportedly shown good success. Pelham and colleagues (1993) found that both behavior modification and medication therapy significantly reduced ADHD. Medication, however, appeared to be the more effective element in the treatment.

ADHD Beyond Adolescence Even though behavioral interventions and medication have reportedly enjoyed short-term successes, there has been insufficient critical evaluation of the long-term effects of either treatment method. Even without treatment, hyperactive behavior tends to diminish by the time some of the children reach their middle teens. One follow-up study of the drug treatment of 75 children over a 10- to 12-year period reported that young adults who had been hyperactive children had less education than control subjects and had a history of more auto accidents and more geographical moves. Research has suggested that only a minority of the formerly hyperactive subjects continued their antisocial behavior into adulthood or developed psychopathologies One study found major depressive disorder to be relatively rare among ADHD patients (Alpert, Maddocks et al., 1996).

Some researchers, however, have reported that a percentage of hyperactive children retain ADHD into early adulthood or go on to have other psychological problems such as overly aggressive behavior or substance abuse in their late teens and early adulthood. For example, Carroll and Rounsaville (1993) found that 34.6 percent of treatment-seeking cocaine abusers in their study met the criteria for ADHD when they were children. In a 16-year follow-up study of ADHD children, about 25 percent never completed high school, compared with 2 percent for controls (Mannuzza et al., 1993). This finding is simi-

Drug Therapy with Children Diagnosed as ADHD

One of the most widely used treatments for attention-deficit hyperactivity disorder (ADHD) is psychostimulant medication (Horn et al., 1991). It is estimated that as many as 750,000 children receive medication, such as Ritalin, for overactive behavior every day (Safer & Krager, 1988). These medications are found to be effective in about 75 percent of hyperactive children (DuPaul & Barkley, 1990).

The use of psychostimulant drugs with hyperactive children frequently meets with enthusiasm on the part of parents, school administrators, and clinicians because of their demonstrated effectiveness in controlling disruptive behavior, at least over short periods (Gittelman-Klein, 1987). The reduction in negative behavior, it is assumed, promotes more effective learning and enables the child to adapt better to the school environment and to get along better with peers. However, a number of questions have been raised concerning the increasing use of drugs in the treatment of hyperactive children. The principal questions include the following:

1. *Who is being selected for treatment?* It is important that an accurate diagnosis be obtained before drug treatment is initiated. However, many question the adequacy of the assessment procedures used in identifying children who actually need medication. For example, a clearcut distinction is not always made between children who appear to need drug therapy because of hyperactivity and children whose inattention and restlessness may be the result of hunger, crowded classrooms, irrelevant curriculum content, or anxiety and depression stemming from problems at home.

2. *Are drugs sometimes being used simply to control the child's behavior for the convenience of adults—for example, to keep peace in the classroom?* Those who raise this question point to the possibility that children who manifest bewilderment, anger, restlessness, or lethargy at school may only be showing a normal reaction to educational procedures that fail to spark their interest or meet their needs. These investigators maintain that to label such children as

"sick"—as evidencing hyperactivity or some other behavior disorder—and to treat them through medication is to sidestep the difficult and expensive alternative of providing better educational programs.

3. *Are the effects of medication worth the side effects that accompany its use?* Drugs like Ritalin sometimes have undesirable side effects, such as severe insomnia, decreased appetite, dysphoria, dizziness, and headaches. Recently these drugs have also been suspected as a cause of growth retardation. Appropriate therapeutic dosages are often difficult to ensure and higher-than-therapeutic dosages are not uncommon. Excessive dosages have been found to produce brief paranoid psychoses in some individuals (Greenhill, 1992). Even with drugs that seem to produce minimal side effects, the possibility of adverse long-range effects resulting from sustained use during early growth and development is still being assessed.

4. *Are the drugs suitable for children?* In some cases, practitioners have used triclycic medications (see Chapter 6), such as desipramine, to treat children with ADHD who also are considered to have problems of comorbid depression. Extreme caution needs to be exercised in the use of tricyclics because a number of deaths have been reported with this medication (Campbell & Cueva, 1995).

In general, drug therapy for children should be used with extreme caution, and only with those children for whom other alternatives simply do not work. It is also important that drug therapy be undertaken only with the informed consent of the parent, as well as that of the child if he or she is old enough, and that the child not be given the sole responsibility for taking the medication—a procedure that can lead to misuse of the drug (Vitiello & Jensen, 1997). At the same time, it is important to recognize that the drugs do help some children. Finally, children who do benefit from drug therapy also need other therapeutic measures for dealing with coexisting problems, such as learning deficiencies and psychological, interpersonal, and family difficulties (DuPaul & Barkley, 1990; Greenhill, 1992) ∎

lar to an earlier study by Gittelman and colleagues (1985) that evaluated and followed up a group of 101 boys aged 6 through 12 who showed hyperactivity, contrasting their later adjustment, at 16 to 23 years of age, with a control sample of 100 nonhyperactive boys. Although most boys who had been diagnosed as hyperactive showed diminished symptom patterns in later adolescence and early adulthood, the full attention-deficit disorder persisted in 31 percent of the hyperactive boys, while only 3 percent of the control sample showed hyperactive symptoms at follow-up.

More longitudinal research is clearly needed to conclude that children with ADHD go on to develop similar or other problems in adulthood. However, some of the research cited suggests that a significant percentage of adolescents do retain their problems into later life.

Conduct Disorder and Oppositional Defiant Disorder

The next group of disorders centers on a child's or an adolescent's relationship to social norms and rules of conduct. In both **conduct disorder** and **oppositional defiant disorder,** aggressive or antisocial behavior is the focus. As we will see, oppositional defiant disorders are usually apparent by about age 6 while conduct disorders tend to be seen by age 9. Both disorders are closely linked. However, with these disorders, it is important to distinguish between persistent antisocial acts, such as setting fires, in which the rights of others are violated, and the less serious pranks often carried out by normal children and adolescents. We should point out, too, that conduct disorders and oppositional defiant disorders involve misdeeds that may or may not be against the law; **juvenile delinquency** (discussed in the Unresolved Issues section at the end of this chapter) is the legal term used to refer to violations of the law committed by minors.

The behavior described in the following sections may appear to be similar to the early stages in the development of antisocial personality disorder, discussed in Chapter 9. Indeed, the personality characteristics and causal considerations are much the same. It is difficult, if not impossible, to distinguish among a conduct disorder, a predelinquent pattern of behavior, and the early stages in the development of an antisocial personality. Highlight 14.3 Modern Life, which focuses on youth violence, provides a closer look at juvenile delinquency, one aspect of this problem.) Behaviorally, the patterns are alike and may simply represent three ways of describing or accounting for the same uncontrollable behavior. As described in Chapter 9, adult antisocial personalities, as children, showed the aggressive behavior and rule viola-

tions that often are labeled conduct disorders, and many came into contact with the authorities as a result of this delinquent behavior. There is substantial evidence that in some children disruptive behavior problems develop gradually from childhood onward in an orderly fashion (Loeber et al., 1992), and there is also considerable evidence for a substantial continuity of early onset conduct disorder problems from childhood to adulthood (Offord & Bennett, 1996). Fortunately, however, not all children who are described as having conduct disorders or who engage in delinquent behavior grow up to become antisocial personalities or commit themselves to lives of crime. As we will see, although the conduct disorders are quite serious and complex to treat, there are effective ways of working with these disordered children.

Clinical Picture in Oppositional Defiant Disorders An important precursor of the antisocial behavior seen in children who develop conduct disorder is often what is now called *oppositional defiant disorder* (Biederman, Faraone et al., 1996). The essential feature is a recurrent pattern of negativistic, defiant, disobedient, and hostile behavior toward authority figures that persists for at least six months (American Psychiatric Association, 1994, p. 91). This disorder usually begins by the age of six, whereas full-blown conduct disorder does not typically begin until the age of nine or later. Prospective studies have found a developmental sequence from oppositional defiant disorder to conduct disorder, with common risk factors for both conditions (Hinshaw, 1994). That is, virtually all cases of conduct disorder were preceded developmentally by oppositional defiant disorder, although only about 25 percent of children with oppositional defiant disorder go on to develop conduct disorder within a three-year period (Lahey et al., 1992). The risk factors for both include family discord, socioeconomic disadvantage, and antisocial behavior in the parents (Hinshaw, 1994).

The Clinical Picture in Conduct Disorders The essential symptomatic behavior in the conduct disorders involves a persistent, repetitive violation of rules and a disregard for the rights of others. The following case is typical of children with conduct disorder and illustrates many of the features commonly found.

Case Study, An Eight-Year-Old Boy with Conduct Disorder • Craig had already established himself as a social outcast by the time he entered first grade. Previously, he had been ex-

Highlight 14.3 MODERN LIFE

Youth Violence: A Problem Too Big for America?

Terrie A., a seventh-grade African-American student who lives in a run-down urban community, is too terrified to fall asleep in her own bed. Instead, she now sleeps on the floor of a small room that is shared by her two younger brothers. Two nights earlier, as she was falling asleep, a bullet crashed through her window just inches above her head. This drive-by-shooting has not been her only exposure to violence in her life. Her father, whom she never really knew, had been murdered when she was less than one year old. More recently two of her classmates had been gunned down in separate shooting incidents. One of these children was actually shot by another boy who had brought a handgun to school.

Violent crime among the young has increased substantially over the past decade. Homicide is now the eleventh leading cause of death in the United States and occurs around 26,000 times a year (Center for Disease Control, 1994). Although homicide committed by young people makes up only 16 percent of the total (people over age 18 commit the majority of violent crimes), the rate has increased substantially in recent years among juveniles (Stanton, Baldwin, & Rachuba, 1997). Violent behavior is the most frequent reason for referral for mental health services among youth (Achenbach & Howell, 1993). Violent crimes and the possibility of being victimized are not uniform across all segments of society. Rates of violence are five times higher for boys than for girls. Moreover, rates among African-American males are ten times higher than for whites. O'Donnell (1995) reported that almost half of all deaths of African-American teenagers involved firearms. Violent crime is more common in urban areas than in rural or suburban communities. Marans and Cohen (1993) surveyed sixth-, eighth-, and tenth-grade children and found that 40 percent of inner-city children had witnessed at least one violent crime. Both the home (Finkelhor, 1984; Rivera, Mueller et al., 1997) and the school (Kachur, Stennies, Powell et al., 1996)—places that one might consider as

usually safe environments—are increasingly found to be settings for violence. For example, Kachur and colleagues (1996) reported that over a recent two-year period (1992–1994) 105 school-associated violent deaths occurred in the United States.

Although there is a high rate of diagnosable mental disorders found among violent youth, particularly conduct disorder and oppositional defiant disorder, the antisocial patterns are more heterogeneous, reflecting a broad range of diagnostic categories. Similarly, no single cause has been pinpointed for the crimes of violence committed by young people in our society. Numerous potential causes have been suggested, ranging from biological influences, family disruption, and parent-child interactions to sociocultural factors (Hinshaw & Anderson, 1996).

Behavior genetic studies (Cadoret, Leve, & Devor, 1997 and Goldsmith & Gottesman, 1996) have generally concluded that violent behavior is strongly influenced by genetics. Although not viewed as the primary causal element, genetic influence appears to increase the risk of antisocial and violent behavior and that hostility needs to be taken into account in any causal search. Another variable that has received recent attention in understanding youth violence is referred to as neuropsychological dysfunction. Cortical dysfunctioning as reflected in lowered verbal reasoning and low emotional control are contributory factors in adolescent violent behavior. Most researchers working in the biological causation areas do not consider these factors as the only or even the primary causal influence. Rather, researchers such as Moffitt and Lynam (1994) view these as biological vulnerabilities that serve to increase the individual's susceptibility to negative environmental influences.

Among the seemingly powerful psychosocial factors leading up to youth violence is a negative home environment—a situation that appears to be one of the strongest influences in producing violence-prone children. For example, when parental role models provide frustrating and unstructured environments and when parents themselves are antisocial, conduct problems and aggressive behavior patterns are more likely to emerge as early-onset problems (Patterson, 1996). The broader social context in which children become socialized can also be instrumental in producing children who commit violent crimes. Extreme poverty and family disruption are considered powerful breeding grounds for violence. Emotional upheaval and frustration emerge from disruptive family situations producing a state of malaise and hopelessness. The environmental "pull" for negative behavior in the form of negative models for aggression that are prominent in the social context serve to reinforce aggression as a behavior to emulate (Osofsky, 1995). For example, the television programs and movies from which our young people often obtain their adult role models show a plethora of violent episodes. One television news documentary recently reported that the average child in America is estimated to be exposed to thousands of murders on television and in movies during the course of a single year. Such exposure to violence as a means of solving frustrating situations is an all too common message sent to our youth who tune into TV or attend movies. Richters and Martinez (1993) studied the impact of children's exposure to violence in the community and found that exposure was related to aggressive symptoms but that the effect was lessened when the family was considered stable. That is, family stability tended to serve as a protective factor in the context of violence exposure.

The solutions to violent crime among our youth are even more elusive and complex than its causes. There are no surefire curative procedures available to practitioners who are faced with the challenge of helping violent clients. In our medication-oriented society, treatment for many conditions will often focus upon the use of drugs—especially in the case of violent behavior. There are, at present, however, no FDA approved medications for treatment of patho-

logic aggression and no drug companies have applied for approval of such medications (Fava, 1997). Likewise, psychotherapy has proved to have limited usefulness in treating violence-prone people (Blackburn, 1993; Tate, Repucci, & Mulvey, 1995). The most effective psychological treatment intervention for violent and aggressive behavior has been the use of behavioral modification techniques in an institutional treatment milieu (Alpert & Spillman, 1997). However, treatment interventions such as these usually come only after children or adolescents have already engaged in extremely violent behavior and caused themselves and others possibly irreparable harm.

Prevention of violent crimes, though potentially the most desirable solution, is perhaps the most difficult strategy to implement. Poverty, a commonly viewed source of disenfranchisement, underlying aggression is not easy to cure. Other more limited context factors that are aimed at potential sources of aggressive behavior—television violence—do not seem easy to combat either. The connection between TV violence and juvenile violence has become the focus of broad attention, and great efforts are being placed on reducing the amount of TV violence to which children are exposed—such as a TV rating system. However, the ultimate impact of these efforts may be difficult to evaluate for many years.

Our society has yet to face up to the enormous problem of violent behavior among youth. Although recognized as a problem by our political-social leaders, a workable solution to this problem continues to evade us. Incarceration of violent criminals and segregating them from society appears to be the most trusted solution to violent crime in America. More prison facilities are being built, and laws affecting violent juvenile crimes are being made tougher. Yet incarceration of young violent offenders is not an effective solution to the problem of violence in our society—and may in fact be a training ground for adult offenders—and new cases seem to flow endlessly into the courts. ■

Hostility and aggressive behavior have been found to play a role in the development of conduct disorder. Children who develop this disorder early in childhood are at special risk for problems later in life.

pelled from kindergarten two times in two years for being un- manageable. His mother brought him to a mental health center at the insistence of the school when she attempted to enroll him in the first grade. Within the first week of school, Craig's quarrel- some and defiant behavior had tried the special education teacher, who was reputedly "excellent" with problem children like him, to the point where she recommended his suspension from school. His classmates likewise were completely unsympa- thetic to Craig, whom they viewed as a bully. At even the slight- est sign of movement on his part, the other children would tell the teacher that Craig was being bad again.

At home, Craig was uncontrollable. His mother and six other children lived with his domineering grandmother. Craig's mother was ineffective at disciplining or managing her children. She worked long hours as a domestic maid and did not feel like has- sling with the children when she got home. Her present hus- band, the father of the three youngest children (including Craig), had deserted the family.

Conduct-disordered children, as Craig's behavior il- lustrates, show a deficit in social behavior (Happe & Frith, 1996). In general, they manifest such characteris- tics as overt or covert hostility, disobedience, physical and verbal aggressiveness, quarrelsomeness, vengefulness, and destructiveness. Lying, solitary stealing, and temper tantrums are common. Such children tend to be sexually uninhibited and inclined toward sexual aggressiveness. Some may engage in firesetting (Forehand et al., 1991; Puri, Baxter, & Cordess, 1996), vandalism, robbery, and even homicidal acts. Conduct-disordered children and adolescents also frequently are comorbid for substance abuse disorder (Grilo, Becker et al., 1996) or depressive symptoms (O'Connor et al., 1998). Zoccolillo, Meyers,

and Assiter (1997) found that conduct disorder was a risk factor for unwed pregnancy and substance abuse in teenage girls; other researchers have found that conduct disorder has been associated with obesity in adulthood (Pine, Cohen et al. 1997).

Causal Factors in Conduct Disorders   Our under- standing of what factors are associated with the develop- ment of conduct problems in childhood has increased tremendously in the past 15 years. Several factors will be covered in the sections that follow.

A Self-Perpetuating Cycle   Evidence has accumulated that a genetic predisposition leading to low verbal intelligence, mild neuropsychological problems, and difficult tempera- ment can set the stage for early-onset conduct disorder through a set of self-perpetuating mechanisms (Slutsky, Heath et al., 1997; Moffitt & Lynam, 1994). The child's dif- ficult temperament may lead to an insecure attachment because parents find it hard to engage in the good parent- ing that would lead to a secure attachment. In addition, low verbal intelligence and/or mild neuropsychological deficits that have been documented in many of these chil- dren—some of which may involve deficiencies in self- control functions such as sustaining attention, planning, self-monitoring, inhibiting unsuccessful or impulsive be- haviors—may help set the stage for a lifelong course of difficulties. In attempting to explain why the relatively mild neuropsychological deficits typically seen can have such pervasive effects, Moffitt and Lynam (1994) hypoth- esize that the effects of early neuropsychological vulnera- bilities are amplified over time as children interact with their environment. This fosters the development of later conduct disorder. They provide the following scenario as an illustration of how conduct problems develop. A preschooler has problems understanding language and tends to resist his mother's efforts to read to him. This deficit then delays the child's readiness for school. When he does enter school, the typical busy curriculum does not allow teachers to focus their attention on students at his low readiness level. Over time, and after a few years of school failure, the child will be chronologically older than his classmates—setting the stage for social rejection. At some point the child might be placed into remedial pro- grams that contain other pupils who have similar behav- ioral disorders as well as learning disabilities. Their in- volvement with conduct-disordered peers exposes them to delinquent behaviors that the child adopts in order to gain acceptance by his peers. (1994, pp. 243–244.)

Age of Onset and Links to Antisocial Personality Disor- der   Children who develop conduct disorder at an earlier age are much more likely to develop psychopathy or antisocial personality disorder as adults than are adolescents who develop conduct disorder suddenly in adolescence (Hinshaw, 1994; Moffitt, 1993b). Thus it is the pervasiveness of the problems first associated with oppositional defiant disorder, and then with conduct disorder, which is the pattern associated with an adult diagnosis of psychopathy or antisocial personality. Although only about 25 to 40 percent of cases of early-onset conduct disorder go on to develop adult antisocial personality disorder, over 80 percent of boys with early-onset conduct disorder do continue to have multiple problems of social dysfunction (in friendships, intimate relationships, and vocational activities) even if they do not meet full criteria for antisocial personality disorder (Hinshaw, 1994; Zoccolillo et al., 1992). By contrast, most adolescents who develop conduct disorder in adolescence do not go on to become adult psychopaths or antisocial personalities but instead have problems limited to the adolescent years. These adolescent-onset cases also do not share the same set of risk factors that the child-onset cases have, including low verbal intelligence, neuropsychological deficits, and impulsive and attentional problems (Hinshaw, 1994; Moffitt & Lynam, 1994).

Environmental Factors In addition to these genetic or constitutional liabilities that may predispose to conduct disorder and adult psychopathy and antisocial personality, Kazdin (1995) underscored the importance of family and social context factors as causal variables in conduct disorder. For example, having a confused "idea" or relationship with the primary caregiver can result in disorganized early attachment and can signal later aggression in the child (Lyons-Ruth, 1996). In addition, environmental factors may interact as well, as noted in the case of Craig, who was rejected by his peers because they did not like his overly aggressive behavior. This situation has been found in the research literature as well: Children who are aggressive and socially unskilled are often rejected by their peers and such rejection can lead to "a spiraling sequence" of social interactions with peers that exacerbates the tendency toward antisocial behavior (Dodge, 1980; Coie & Lenox, 1994). This socially rejected subgroup of aggressive children are also at the highest risk for adolescent delinquency and probably for adult antisocial personality. In addition, parents and teachers may react with strong negative affect, such as anger, to aggressive children (Capaldi & Patterson, 1994), and they may in turn reject these aggressive children. The combination of rejection by parents, peers, and teachers leads these children to become isolated and alienated. Not surprisingly,

they often turn to deviant peer groups for companionship (Coie & Lenox, 1994), at which point a good deal of imitation of the antisocial behavior of their deviant peer models may occur (see Chapter 3).

Investigators generally seem to agree that the family setting of a conduct-disordered child is typically characterized by ineffective parenting, rejection, harsh and inconsistent discipline, and often parental neglect (Frick, 1998; Patterson, 1996). Frequently, the parents have an unstable marital relationship (Osborn, 1992), are emotionally disturbed or sociopathic, and do not provide the child with consistent guidance, acceptance, or affection. Recently Patterson (1996) concluded that parents who are themselves appraised as having antisocial characteristics are very likely to be ineffective in their parental skills.

Family discord, such as the conflict and disharmony accompanying divorce, can be instrumental in the development of conduct disorders (Chess & Thomas, 1984; Robins, 1991). In a disproportionate number of cases, the child may have a single parent, a stepparent, or a series of stepparents. Regardless of whether the family is intact, a child in a conflict-charged home feels overtly rejected. For example, Rutter and Quinton (1984b) concluded that family discord and hostility were the primary factors defining the relationship between disturbed parents and disturbed children; this is particularly true with respect to the development of conduct disorders in children and adolescents. Such discord and hostility are conceptualized as contributing to poor and ineffective parenting skills—especially ineffective discipline and supervision. These children are trained by the family directly in antisocial behavior by coercive interchanges and indirectly by lack of monitoring and consistent discipline (Capaldi & Patterson, 1994, p. 169). This in turn all too often leads to association with deviant peers and the opportunity for further learning of antisocial behavior.

In addition to these familial factors, a number of broader psychosocial and sociocultural variables increase the probability that a child will develop conduct disorder, and later adult psychopathy or antisocial personality disorder. Low socioeconomic status, poor neighborhoods, parental stress, and depression all appear to increase the likelihood that a child will become enmeshed in this cycle (Capaldi & Patterson, 1994).

Treatments and Outcomes Treatment for oppositional defiant disorder and conduct disorder tends to focus on the dysfunctional family patterns described above and on finding ways to alter the child's aggressive or otherwise maladaptive behaviors.

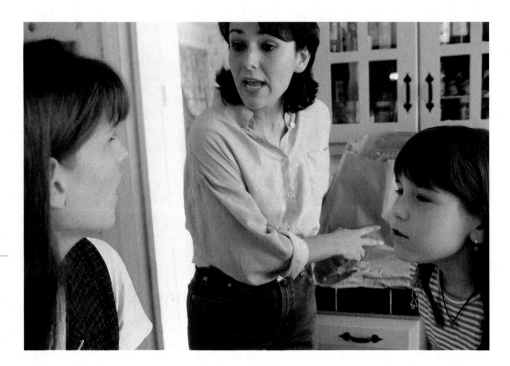

Ineffective parenting, harsh and inconsistent discipline, parental neglect and marital discord all contribute to ODD and conduct disorders. So do poverty, parental stress and depression.

The Cohesive Family Model Therapy for a conduct-disordered child is likely to be ineffective unless some means can be found for modifying the child's environment. One interesting and often effective treatment strategy with conduct disorder in children is the *cohesive family model* (Patterson et al., 1991; Webster-Stratton, 1991). In this family–group-oriented approach parents of conduct-disordered children are viewed as lacking in parenting skills and as having failed to socialize the children by behaving in inconsistent ways, thereby reinforcing inappropriate behavior. Children learn to escape or avoid parental criticism by escalating their negative behavior. This tactic in turn increases their parents aversive interactions and criticism. The child observes the increased anger in his or her parents and models this aggressive pattern. The parental attention to the child's negative behaviors actually serves to reinforce the negative, aggressive behavior instead of suppressing it. Viewing the genesis of conduct problems as emerging from such interactions places the treatment focus on the interaction between the child and the parents (Patterson et al., 1991).

Obtaining treatment cooperation from parents who are themselves in conflict with each other is a difficult process. Often an overburdened parent who is separated or divorced and working simply does not have the time or inclination to learn and practice a more adequate parental role. In some cases, the circumstances may call for a child to be removed from the home and placed in a foster home or institution, with the expectation of a later return to the home if intervening therapy with the parent or parents appears to justify it.

Unfortunately, children who are removed to new environments often interpret this removal as further rejection, not only by their parents but by society as well. Unless the changed environment offers a warm, kindly, and accepting yet consistent and firm setting, such children are likely to make little progress. Even then, treatment may have only a temporary effect. Faretra (1981) followed up 66 aggressive and disturbed adolescents who had been admitted to an inpatient unit. She found that antisocial and criminal behavior persisted into adulthood though with a lessening of psychiatric involvement. Many conduct-disordered children go on to have personality disorders as adults (Rutter, 1988; Zeitlin, 1986).

By and large, our society tends to take a punitive, rather than rehabilitative, attitude toward an antisocial, aggressive youth. Thus the emphasis is on punishment and on "teaching the child a lesson." Such treatment, however, appears to intensify rather than correct the behavior. Where treatment is unsuccessful, the end product is likely to be an antisocial personality with aggressive behavior.

Behavioral Techniques The advent of behavior therapy techniques has, however, made the outlook brighter for children who manifest conduct disorders (Kazdin, 1998). Teaching control techniques to the parents of such children is particularly important, so that they function as therapists in reinforcing desirable behavior and modifying the environmental conditions that have been reinforcing maladaptive behavior. The changes brought about when they consistently accept and reward their child's positive behavior and stop focusing attention on the negative behavior may finally change their perception of and feelings toward the child, leading to the basic acceptance that the child has so badly needed.

Though effective techniques for behavioral management can be taught to parents, they often have difficulty carrying out treatment plans. If this is the case, other techniques, such as family therapy or parental counseling, are used to ensure that the parent or person responsible for the child's discipline is sufficiently assertive to follow through on the program.

Anxiety Disorders of Childhood and Adolescence

In modern society, no one is totally insulated from anxiety-producing events or situations. Most children are vulnerable to fears and uncertainties as a normal part of growing up. Children with anxiety disorders however, are more extreme in their behavior than those experiencing "normal" anxiety. These children appear to share many of the following characteristics: oversensitivity, unrealistic fears, shyness and timidity, pervasive feelings of inadequacy, sleep disturbances, and fear of school. Children diagnosed as suffering from an anxiety disorder typically attempt to cope with their fears by becoming overly dependent on others for support and help. In DSM-IV, anxiety disorders of childhood and adolescence are similar to anxiety disorders in adults (Albano, Chorpita, & Barlow, 1996).

Anxiety disorders are apparently quite common in the general population. In fact, 9.7 percent of one community-based school sample clearly met diagnostic criteria for an anxiety-based disorder (Dadds, Spence et al., 1997) with a greater preponderance of anxiety-based disorder found in girls (Lewinsohn et al., 1998). Obsessive-compulsive disorders (OCD) are apparently not as rare in children as they were once thought to be but occur with a frequency of between 0.5 and 2 percent (Thomsen, 1998). Two additional anxiety disorders of children and adolescence, *separation anxiety disorder* and *selective mutism,* will be described in more detail.

Separation Anxiety Disorder **Separation anxiety disorder** is the most common of the childhood anxiety disorders (Bernstein & Borchardt, 1991), reportedly occurring with a prevalence of 2.4 percent of children in a population health study (Bowen, Offord, & Boyle, 1990). Children with separation anxiety disorder are characterized by unrealistic fears, oversensitivity, self-consciousness, nightmares, and chronic anxiety. They lack self-confidence, are apprehensive in new situations, and tend to be immature for their age. Such children are described by their parents as shy, sensitive, nervous, submissive, easily discouraged, worried, and frequently moved to tears. Typically, they are overly dependent, particularly on their parents. The essential feature in the clinical picture of this disorder is excessive anxiety about separation from major attachment figures, such as mother, and from familiar home surroundings. In many cases a clear psychosocial stressor can be identified, such as the death of a relative or a pet. The following case illustrates the clinical picture in this disorder.

> **Case Study, Separation Anxiety in a Six-Year-Old Boy •**
> Johnny was a highly sensitive six-year-old who suffered from numerous fears, nightmares, and chronic anxiety. He was terrified of being separated from his mother, even for a brief period. When his mother tried to enroll him in kindergarten, he became so upset when she left the room that the principal arranged for her to remain in the classroom. After two weeks, however, this arrangement had to be discontinued, and Johnny had to be withdrawn from kindergarten because his mother could not leave him even for a few minutes. Later, when his mother attempted to enroll him in the first grade, Johnny manifested the same intense anxiety and unwillingness to be separated from her. At the suggestion of the school counselor, Johnny's mother brought him to a community clinic for assistance with the problem. The therapist, who initially saw Johnny and his mother, was wearing a white clinic jacket, which led to a severe panic reaction on Johnny's part. His mother had to hold him to keep him from running away, and he did not settle down until the therapist removed his jacket. Johnny's mother explained that he is terrified of doctors, and it is almost impossible to get him to a physician even when he is sick.

When children with separation anxiety disorder are actually separated from their attachment figures, they typically become preoccupied with morbid fears, such as the worry that their parents are going to become ill or die. They cling helplessly to adults, have difficulty sleeping, and they become intensely demanding. Separation anxiety is more common in girls (Majcher & Pollack, 1996), and the disorder is not very stable in children—44 percent of youngsters showed recovery at a four-year follow-up (Cantwell & Baker, 1989). However, some children go on to exhibit *school refusal problems* (a fear of leaving home and parents to attend school) and continue to have adjustment difficulty over time and make difficult work and life adjustments later.

Selective Mutism   Another anxiety-based disorder sometimes found in childhood is **selective mutism,** a condition that involves the persistent failure to speak in specific social situations—for example, in school or in social groups—and is considered to interfere with educational or social adjustment. This disorder should be diagnosed only if the child actually has the ability to speak and knows the language. Moreover, in order for this disorder to be diagnosed the condition must have lasted for a month and not be limited to the first month of school when many children are shy or inhibited.

Selective, formerly referred to as elective, mutism is apparently quite rare in clinical populations and most typically seen at preschool age. The disorder occurs in all social strata, and in about one-third of the cases studied the child showed early signs of the problem such as shyness and internalizing behavior (Steinhausen & Juzi, 1996).

Both genetic and learning factors have been cited as possible causal factors underlying the disorder. Simmons, Goode, and Fombonne (1997) reported a case in which the mute child experienced a chromosomal abnormality. Steinhausen and Adamek (1997) reported some evidence that genetic factors played a part in selective mutism because these cases tended to occur more frequently in families in which taciturn behavior was prominent. Evidence for cultural or learning factors has also been presented. Black and Uhde (1995) found that the severity of mutism varied markedly in different environmental settings and reported that social anxiety was most commonly associated with mutism.

Selective mutism is treated much like other anxiety-based disorders. One study reported that the symptoms were reduced substantially with fluoxetine (Motavalli, 1995); however, family-based psychological treatment is the most common therapeutic approach used (Tatem & DelCampo, 1995).

Causal Factors in Anxiety Disorders   A number of causal factors have been emphasized in explanations of the childhood anxiety disorders. The more important appear to be the following:

1. Anxious children often manifest an unusual constitutional sensitivity that makes them easily conditionable by aversive stimuli. For example, they may be

readily upset by even small disappointments—a lost toy or encounter with an overeager dog. They then have a harder time calming down, a fact that can result in a buildup and generalization of surplus fear reactions.

2. The child can become anxious because of early illnesses, accidents, or losses that involved pain and discomfort. The traumatic effect of experiences such as hospitalization make such children feel insecure and inadequate. The traumatic nature of certain life changes, such as moving away from friends and into a new situation, can also have an intensely negative effect on a child's adjustment. Kashani and colleagues (1981a) found that the most common recent life event for children receiving psychiatric care was moving to a new school district.

3. Overanxious children often have the modeling effect of an overanxious and protective parent who sensitizes a child to the dangers and threats of the outside world. Often the parent's overprotectiveness communicates a lack of confidence in the child's ability to cope, thus reinforcing the child's feelings of inadequacy (Dadds, Heard, & Rapee, 1991).

4. Indifferent or detached parents also foster anxiety in their children. Although the child is not necessarily rejected, neither is he or she adequately supported in mastering essential competencies and in gaining a positive self-concept. Repeated experiences of failure, stemming from poor learning skills, may lead to subsequent patterns of anxiety or withdrawal in the face of "threatening" situations. Other children may perform adequately but are overcritical of themselves and feel intensely anxious and devalued when they perceive themselves as failing to do well enough to earn their parents' love and respect.

5. The role that social-environmental factors might play in the development of anxiety-based disorders, though important, is not clearly understood. A recent cross-cultural study of fears (Ollendick et al., 1996) reported that significant differences were found between American, Australian, Nigerian, and Chinese children and adolescents. These authors suggested that cultures which favor inhibition, compliance, and obedience appear to increase the levels of fear reported. In another study in the United States, Last and Perrin (1993) reported that there were some differences between African-American and white children with respect to types of anxiety disorders. White children were more likely to present with school refusal than African-American children, who showed

more PTSD symptoms. This difference might result from differing patterns of referral in African-American or white families or it might reflect differing environmental stressors placed on the children.

6. A recent study found a strong association between exposure to violence and a reduced sense of security and psychological well-being (Kliewer et al., 1998). The child's vulnerability to anxiety and depression may be set in place by his or her early experiences of feeling a lack of "control" over reinforcing environmental events (Chorpita & Barlow, 1998). Children who experience a sense of diminished control over negative environmental factors may become more vulnerable to the development of anxiety than those children who gain a sense of efficacy in managing stressful circumstances.

Treatments and Outcomes The anxiety disorders of childhood may continue into adolescence and young adulthood, first leading to maladaptive avoidance behavior and later to increasingly idiosyncratic thinking and behavior or an inability to "fit in" with a peer group. Typically, however, this is not the case. As affected children grow and have wider interactions in school and in peer-group activities, they often benefit from experiences such as making friends and succeeding at given tasks. Teachers who are aware of the needs of both overanxious and shy, withdrawn children are often able to ensure successful experiences for them that help alleviate anxiety.

Psychopharmacological treatment of anxiety disorders in children and adolescents is becoming more common today, although the effectiveness of drugs such as imipramine with these problems have questionable efficacy. Moreover, one factor contributing to caution in using medications in these disorders is the diagnostic uncertainty involved. Anxiety is often found to coexist with other conditions, particularly depression (Gittelman, 1988) and ADHD (Pliszka, 1989). Often there is not the diagnostic clarity required for cautious use of antianxiety medication.

Behavior therapy procedures, sometimes used in school settings, often help anxious children. Such procedures include assertiveness training, to provide help with mastering essential competencies, and desensitization to reduce anxious behavior. Recently, a group of researchers reported the successful use of cognitive-behavioral treatment with 94 nine- to 13-year-old children with anxiety disorders (Kendall, Flannery-Schroeder et al. 1997). Behavioral treatment approaches such as desensitization must be explicitly tailored to a child's particular problem, and in vivo methods (using real-life situations graded in terms of anxiety arousing) tend to be more effective than having the child "imagine" situations.

An interesting and effective cognitive-behavioral anxiety prevention and treatment study was recently implemented in Australia. In an effort to identify and reduce anxiousness in young adolescents, Dadds, Spence, and colleagues (1997) identified 314 children out of a sample of 1786 seven- to 14-year-olds in a school system in Brisbane, Australia, who met the criteria for an anxiety disorder. They contacted parents of these anxious children to engage them in the treatment intervention and 128 of the parents agreed to participate. The treatment intervention involved holding group sessions with the children in which they were taught to recognize their anxious feelings and deal with them more effectively than they otherwise would have. In addition, the parents were taught behavioral management procedures to deal more effectively with the child's behavior. Six months after therapy was completed, significant anxiety reduction was shown for the treatment group compared with an untreated control sample.

Childhood Depression

Although the field of childhood psychopathology was somewhat slow to accept the notion that children suffer from depressive disorders (Hammen & Rudolph, 1996), clinicians working with children in mental health settings have long noted a pattern of symptoms that seemed indicative of depression. Spitz (1946) first described the problem, which he called *anaclitic depression,* as a behavior pattern, similar to adult depression, that occurred in infants and children experiencing prolonged separation from their mothers. This specific childhood depression syndrome included slowed development and such symptomatic behavior as weepiness, sadness, immobility, and apathy.

More recent research has confirmed that depression in children and adolescents occurs with high frequency. The point prevalence (the rate at the time of the assessment) of major depressive disorder in children has been estimated to be between 0.4 and 2.5 percent and for adolescents between 4.0 and 8.3 percent (Birmaher, Ryan et al., 1996). The lifetime prevalence for major depressive disorders in adolescence is between 15 and 20 percent (Harrington, Rutter, & Fombonne, 1996). A survey of 1710 high school students found that point revalence was 2.9 percent, that lifetime prevalence was 20.4 percent, and that suicidal ideation at some time in their lives in this sample was high—19 percent (Lewinsohn et al., 1996). Before adolescence, rates of depression are somewhat higher in boys, but depression occurs at about twice the rate for adolescent girls as for adolescent boys (Hankin et al., 1998). Lewinsohn and colleagues (1993) also reported that 7.1 percent of the adolescents surveyed reported having attempted suicide in the past and, in a more recent epidemiological study, Lewinsohn, Rohde, and Seeley (1994) pointed out that 1.7 percent of adolescents between 14 and 18 had made a suicide attempt.

The Clinical Picture in Childhood Depression

Childhood depression includes behaviors such as withdrawal, crying, avoidance of eye contact, physical complaints, poor appetite, and even aggressive behavior and in some cases suicide (Pfeffer, 1996). One recent epidemiological study (Cohen et al., 1998) reported an association between somatic illness and childhood depressive illness, suggesting that there may be some common etiological factors.

Currently, childhood depression is classified according to the same DSM-IV diagnostic criteria used in the adult system (Kovacs, 1996). The only modification for children is that irritability is often found as a major symptom and can be substituted for depressed mood as seen in the following case reported by Hammen and Rudolph (1996).

Case Study, A Case of Irritability as a Primary Symptom of Depression • Joey is a 10-year-old boy whose mother and teacher have shared their concerns about his irritability and temper tantrums displayed both at home and at school. With little provocation, he bursts into tears and yells and throws objects. In class he seems to have difficulty concentrating and seems easily distracted. Increasingly shunned by his peers, he plays by himself at recess, and at home he spends most of his time in his room watching TV. His mother notes that he has been sleeping poorly and has gained 10 pounds over the past couple of months from constant snacking. A consultation with the school psychologists has ruled out learning disabilities or attention-deficit disorder; instead, she says, he is a deeply unhappy child who expresses feelings of worthlessness and hopelessness—and even a wish that he would die. These experiences probably began about six months ago when his father, divorced from Joey's mother for several years, remarried and moved to another town where he spends far less time with Joey (pp. 153–154).

The use of adult diagnostic depressive categories with children is considered to be appropriate by many. Lobovits and Handel (1985), for example, found that adult diagnostic categories such as dysthymia or major depression could be reliably used with children. They conclude that the use of such criteria with children offers a useful starting point for untangling the confusion surrounding the diagnosis and prevalence rate of childhood disorder (p. 52).

Causal Factors in Childhood Depression The causal factors described in the childhood anxiety disorders are pertinent to the depressive disorders as well.

Biological Factors There appears to be an association between parental depression and behavioral and mood problems in children (Thapar & McGuffin, 1996). Children of parents with major depression were more impaired, received more psychological treatment, and had more psychological diagnoses than children of parents with no psychological disorders (Kramer, Warner et al., 1998; Mufson, Weissman, & Warner, 1992). A controlled study of family history and onset of depression found that children from mood disordered families had significantly higher rates of depression than those from nondisordered families (Kovacs, Devlin et al., 1997). The suicide attempt rate has also been shown to be higher for children of depressed parents (7.8 percent) than for the offspring of control parents (Weissman et al., 1992). Children who have experienced past stressful events are susceptible to states of depression that make them vulnerable to suicidal thinking under stress (Brent, Moritz, & Liotus, 1996). All these correlations suggest a potential genetic component to childhood depression, but in each case learning could also be the causal factor.

Learning Factors Learning maladaptive behaviors appears to be important in childhood depressive disorders (Kaslow, Deering, & Racusin, 1994). Children who are exposed to negative parental behavior or negative emotional states may develop depressed affect themselves. For example, depression has been found to be more common in divorced families (Palosaari & Laippala, 1996).

Can children learn depressed mood from their depressed parent? One important area of research is focusing on the mother-child interaction in the transmission of depressed affect. Specifically, investigators have been evaluating the possibility that mothers who are depressed, through their interactions with their infants, transfer their low mood to them. Depression among mothers is not uncommon and can result from several sources. Of course, many women who are clinically depressed have children. Some women, however, become depressed during pregnancy or following the delivery of their child, in part because of exhaustion and hormonal changes that can affect mood. Several investigators have reported that marital distress, delivery complications, and difficulties with the infant are also associated with depression in mothers (Campbell et al., 1990; Sameroff, Seifer, & Zax, 1982).

Extensive research supports the view that the patterns of mother-infant behavior are critical to the development of attachment in a child and that depression in the mother can adversely affect the infant (Martinez, Malphurs et al., 1996). Dysphoric mothers do not respond effectively to their children (Goldsmith and Rogoff, 1997). Depressed mothers tend to be less sensitively attuned to their infants and more negative to the child than nondepressed mothers (Murray, Fiori-Cowley et al., 1996). Other research has shown that negative (depressed) affect and constricted mood on the part of a mother, which shows up as unresponsive facial expressions and irritable behavior, can produce similar responses in her infant (Cohn & Tronick, 1983; Tronick & Cohn, 1989). Interestingly, the negative impact of depressed mothers' interaction style has also been studied at the physiological level. Infants have been reported to exhibit greater frontal brain electrical activity during the expression of negative emotionality by their mothers (Dawson, Panagiotides et al., 1997).

The extent to which an infant's negative response to a caregiver's depressed, constricted mood results in later childhood depression has not been fully determined. This research is highly suggestive, however, and it may eventually lead to a fuller understanding of the possible link between a caregiver's mood and a child's behavior.

Another important line of research in childhood depression involves the cognitive-behavioral perspective. Considerable evidence has accumulated that depressive symptoms are positively correlated with the tendency to attribute positive events to external, specific, and unstable causes and negative events to internal, global, and stable causes (Hinshaw, 1992). For example, the child may learn to attribute peer rejection or teasing to a mistaken belief that he or she has some internal flaw. Hinshaw (1994) considers the tendency to develop distorted mental representations an important cause of disorders such as depression and conduct disorder. In addition, children who tend to show symptoms of depression tend to underestimate their self-competence over time (Cole et al., 1998).

Treatments and Outcomes The view that childhood and adolescent depression is like adult depression (Ryan et al., 1987) has prompted researchers to treat children

Mothers who are depressed may transmit their depression to their children by their lack of responsiveness to the child as a result of their own depression. Unfortunately, depression among mothers is all-too common. Exhaustion, marital distress as a result of the arrival of children in a couple's lives, delivery complications and the difficulties of particular babies may all play a part.

displaying mood disorders, particularly adolescents who are viewed as suicidal (Greenhill & Waslick, 1997), with medications that have worked with adults. Research on the effectiveness of antidepressant medication with children is contradictory at best. Some recent studies using fluoxetine (Prozac) with depressed adolescents have shown the drug to be more effective than a placebo (Emslie, Rush et al., 1997; DeVane & Floyd, 1996), although complete remission of symptoms was seldom obtained. However, another study by Sommers-Flannagan and Sommers-Flannagan (1996), an extensive evaluation of antidepressant medication treatment for children and adolescents, concluded that currently available antidepressant medications do not show improvement greater than a placebo. Antidepressant medication with children and adolescents may have some undesirable side effects (i.e., nausea, headaches, nervousness, insomnia, and even seizures). Four accidental deaths with desipramine have been reported (Campbell & Cueva, 1995).

An important facet of psychological therapy with children, whether for depression or anxiety or other disorders, is providing a supportive emotional environment for them to learn more adaptive coping strategies and effective emotional expression. Older children and adolescents can often benefit from a positive therapeutic relationship in which they can discuss their feelings openly. Younger children or those with less developed verbal skills may benefit from play therapy. Controlled studies of psychological treatment with depressed adolescents have shown significantly reduced symptoms with cognitive-behavior therapy (Brent, Holder et al., 1997) with ideas derived from Beck's cognitive-behavioral approach as discussed in Chapter 6 (Ackerson et al., 1998). Rawson and Tabb (1993) showed that short-term residential treatment was effective with depressed children ages 8 to 14.

An important aspect in the treatment of depression in young people is the necessity of a suicide appraisal (Berman & Jobes, 1991), as illustrated by the following case.

Case Study, A Depressed Boy and His Family. • Jack, a ten-year-old boy, was admitted to a child psychiatric hospital unit after he attempted to stab himself in the stomach with a medium-sized kitchen knife. The suicide attempt was foiled by his mother, who pulled the knife away from her son. This suicide attempt occurred immediately after Jack had an argument with his father. Jack felt that his "father hates me" and that "I would be better off dead." A variety of factors made Jack vulnerable to suicidal tendencies. Jack grew up in an atmosphere in which there was intense disagreement between his parents. His father drank heavily and when drunk would physically assault his mother. Jack's mother was chronically depressed and often said that "life is not worth living." However, she loved her son and felt that because he needed her, she must continue to work and manage the home. Jack has a serious learning disability, and he struggled to maintain his school grades. He had a private tutor who helped him overcome some of his sad feelings and shame. Often, however, when teased by his classmates, he thought about ending his life. (Pfeffer, 1981, pp. 218–219)

Depressed mood has come to be viewed as an important risk factor in suicide among children and adolescents (Ivarsson, Larsson, & Gillberg, 1998; Pfeffer, 1996). About 7 to 10 percent of adolescents report having made at least one suicide attempt (Safer, 1997). Children who attempt suicide are at greater risk for subsequent suicidal episodes than nonattempters, particularly within the first two years after their initial attempt (Pfeffer et al., 1994). Among the childhood disorders, then, depression especially merits aggressive treatment.

Symptom Disorders: Enuresis, Encopresis, Sleepwalking, and Tics

The childhood disorders we will deal with in this section—elimination disorders (enuresis and encopresis), sleepwalking, and tics—typically involve a single outstanding symptom rather than a pervasive maladaptive pattern.

Functional Enuresis The term **enuresis** refers to the habitual involuntary discharge of urine, usually at night, after the age of expected continence (age five). In DSM-IV, functional enuresis refers to bedwetting that is not organically caused. Children who have primary functional enuresis have never been continent; children who have secondary functional enuresis have been continent for at least a year but have regressed.

Enuresis may vary in frequency, from nightly occurrence to occasional instances when a child is under considerable stress or is unduly tired. It has been estimated that some 4 to 5 million children and adolescents in the United States suffer from the inconvenience and embarrassment of this disorder. Estimates of the prevalence of enuresis reported in DSM-IV are 7 percent for boys and 3 percent for girls at age five; 3 percent for boys and 2 percent for girls at age ten; and 1 percent for boys and almost nonexistent for girls at age eighteen. Research has shown that there are clear sex differences in enuresis as well as age differences. In one extensive epidemiological study of enuresis in Holland, Verhulst and colleagues (1985) determined that between the ages of five and eight, enuresis is about two to three times more common among boys than among girls. The percentages for boys also diminish at a slower rate; the decline for girls between ages four and six is about 71 percent, while the decline for boys is only 16 percent. The authors recommend that the age criteria for boys' enuresis be extended to age eight because it is at about age nine that approximately the same percentage of boys as girls reach "dryness"—that is, wetting the bed less than once a month.

Enuresis may result from a variety of organic conditions, such as disturbed cerebral control of the bladder (Kaada & Retvedt, 1981), neurological dysfunction (Lunsing et al., 1991), or other medical factors such as medication side effects (Took & Buck, 1996) or having a small functional bladder capacity and weak urethral spinchter

(Dahl, 1992). One group of researchers reported that 11 percent of their enuretic patients had disorders of the urinary tract (Watanabe et al., 1994). However, most investigators have pointed to a number of other possible causal factors: (1) faulty learning, resulting in the failure to acquire inhibition of reflexive bladder emptying; (2) personal immaturity, associated with or stemming from emotional problems; (3) disturbed family interactions, particularly those that lead to sustained anxiety, hostility, or both; and (4) stressful events (Haug Schnabel, 1992). For example, a child may regress to bedwetting when a new baby enters the family and becomes the center of attention.

Medical treatment of enuresis typically centers on using medications, such as imipramine, in which the mechanism underlying the action of the drug is unclear but it may simply decrease the deepest stages of sleep to light sleep enabling the child to recognize bodily needs more effectively (Dahl, 1992). More recently, an intranasal desmopressin (DDAVP) has been used to help children manage urine more effectively. This medication, a hormone replacement, apparently increases urine concentration, decreases urine volume, and therefore reduces the need to urinate (Dahl, 1992). The use of this medication to treat enuretic children is no panacea. One disadvantage to using this drug is that it is effective only with a small subset of enuretic children and then only temporarily. Another disadvantage is that desmopressin is an expensive treatment. Bath, Morton, Uing, and Williams (1995) recently reported that treatment with desmopressin was disappointing but concluded that this treatment had some utility as a method to enable children to stay dry for brief periods of time—for example, at a camp or on a holiday. Recently Moffatt (1997) suggested that DDAVP had an important place in treating nocturnal enuresis particularly for youngsters who have not responded well to behavioral treatment methods. It is well to remember that medications by themselves do not cure enuresis and that there is frequent relapse when the drug is discontinued or the child habituates to the medication (Dahl, 1992).

Conditioning procedures have proved to be the most effective treatment of enuresis (Friman & Warzak, 1990). Mowrer and Mowrer (1938) introduced a procedure in which a child may sleep on a pad that is wired to a battery-operated bell. At the first few drops of urine, the bell is set off, thus awakening the child. Through conditioning, the child comes to associate bladder tension with awakening.

With or without treatment, the incidence of enuresis tends to decrease significantly with age, but many experts still believe that enuresis should be treated in childhood

because no way currently exists to identify which children will remain enuretic into adulthood. In a recent comparison and evaluation of research on the treatment of bedwetting, Houts, Berman, and Abramson (1994) concluded that treated children were more improved at follow-up than nontreated children. They also found that the use of learning-based procedures was more effective in reducing bedwetting than were medications.

Functional Encopresis The term **encopresis** describes children who have not learned appropriate toileting for bowel movements after age four. This condition is less common than enuresis; however, DSM IV estimates that about 1 percent of five-year-olds have encopresis. A study of 102 cases of encopretic children provided the following list of characteristics: The average age of children with encopresis was seven, with a range from ages four to thirteen. About one-third of encopretic children were also enuretic; and a large sex difference was found, with about six times more boys than girls in the sample. Many of the children soiled their clothing when they were under stress. A common time was in the late afternoon after school; few children actually had this problem at school. Most of the children reported that they did not know when they needed to have a bowel movement or were too shy to use the bathrooms at school.

Many encopretic children suffer from constipation; thus an important element in the diagnosis of the disorder involves a physical examination to determine whether physiological factors are contributing to the disorder. The treatment of encopresis usually involves both medical and psychological aspects (Dawson, Griffith, & Boeke, 1990). One study found that of the encopretic children treated by medical and behavioral procedures in that sample, more than half were cured—that is, no additional incidents occurred within six months following treatment. An additional 25 percent were improved (Levine & Bakow, 1975).

Sleepwalking (Somnambulism) Though the onset of sleepwalking disorder is usually between the ages of 6 and 12, the disorder is classified broadly under sleep disorders in DSM-IV rather than under disorders of infancy, childhood, and adolescence. The symptoms of **sleepwalking disorder** involve repeated episodes in which a person leaves his or her bed and walks around without being conscious of the experience or remembering it later.

Statistics are meager but the incidence of one episode of sleepwalking reported for children in DSM-IV is high—between 10 and 30 percent. However, the incidence for repeated episodes is low, from 1 to 5 percent. Children subject to this problem usually go to sleep in a normal manner but arise during the second or third hour of sleep. They may walk to another room of the house or even outside, and they may engage in complex activities. Finally they return to bed and in the morning remember nothing that has taken place. While moving about, sleepwalkers' eyes are partially or fully open; they avoid obstacles, listen when spoken to, and ordinarily respond to commands, such as to return to bed. Shaking them will usually awaken sleepwalkers, and they will be surprised and perplexed at finding themselves in an unexpected place. Sleepwalking episodes usually last from 15 to 30 minutes. The causes of sleepwalking are not fully understood. Sleepwalking takes place during NREM (non–rapid eye movement) sleep. It appears to be related to some anxiety-arousing situation that has just occurred or is expected to occur in the near future (Klackenberg, 1987).

Little attention has been given to the treatment of sleepwalking. Clement (1970), however, reported on the treatment of a seven-year-old boy through behavior therapy. During treatment, the therapist learned that just before each sleepwalking episode the boy usually had a nightmare about being chased by "a big black bug." After his nightmare began, he perspired freely, moaned and talked in his sleep, tossed and turned, and finally got up and walked through the house. He did not remember the sleepwalking episode when he awoke the next morning. Assessment data revealed no neurological or other medical problems and indicated that he was of normal intelligence. He was, however, found to be a very anxious, guilt-ridden little boy who avoided performing assertive and aggressive behaviors appropriate to his age and sex (p. 23). The therapist focused treatment on having his mother awaken the boy each time he showed signs of an impending episode. After washing his face with cold water and making sure he was fully awake, the mother would return him to bed, where he was to hit and tear up a picture of the big black bug. (At the start of the treatment program, he had made up several of these drawings.)

Eventually, the nightmare was associated with awakening, and he learned to wake up on most occasions when he was having a bad dream. Clement considered the basic behavior therapy model in this case to follow that used in the conditioning treatment for enuresis, where a waking response is elicited by an intense stimulus just as urination is beginning and be-

comes associated with, and eventually prevents, nocturnal bedwetting.

Tics A **tic** is a persistent, intermittent muscle twitch or spasm, usually limited to a localized muscle group. The term is used broadly to include blinking the eye, twitching the mouth, licking the lips, shrugging the shoulders, twisting the neck, clearing the throat, blowing the nose, and grimacing, among other actions. Tics occur most frequently between the ages of 2 and 14 (Evans, King, & Leckman, 1996). In some instances, as in clearing the throat, an individual may be aware of the tic when it occurs, but usually he or she performs the act habitually and does not notice it. In fact, many individuals do not even realize they have a tic unless someone brings it to their attention. A recent cross-cultural examination of tics found a similar pattern in research and clinical case reports from other countries (Staley, Ward, & Shady, 1997). Moreover, the age of onset (average 7 to 8 years of age) and predominant gender (male) of cases was reported to be similar across cultures.

The psychological impact tics can have on an adolescent is exemplified in the following case.

Case Study, An Adolescent's Facial Tic • An adolescent who had wanted very much to be a teacher told the school counselor that he was thinking of giving up his plans. When asked the reason, he explained that several friends had told him that he had a persistent twitching of the mouth muscles when he answered questions in class. He had been unaware of this muscle twitch and even after being told about it could not tell when it took place. However, he became acutely self-conscious and was reluctant to answer questions or enter into class discussions. As a result, his general level of tension increased, and so did the frequency of the tic, which now became apparent even when he was talking to his friends. Thus a vicious circle had been established. Fortunately, it proved amenable to treatment by conditioning and assertiveness training.

Tourette's syndrome is an extreme tic disorder involving multiple motor and vocal patterns. This disorder typically involves uncontrollable head movements with accompanying sounds, such as grunts, clicks, yelps, sniffs, or words. Some, and possibly most tics are preceded by an urge or sensation that seems to be relieved by the execution of the tic. Tics are thus often difficult to differentiate from compulsions—thus they are sometimes referred to as "compulsive tics" (Jankovic, 1997). About one-third of individuals with Tourette's syndrome manifest *coprolalia,* which is a complex vocal tic involving the uttering of obscenities. The average age of onset for Tourette's syndrome is 7, and most cases have an onset before age 14 and it frequently persists into adulthood. The disorder is about three times more frequent among males. Although the exact cause of Tourette's syndrome is undetermined, evidence suggests an organic basis for the syndrome. Because children with Tourette's syndrome can have substantial adjustment problems at school (Nolan & Gadow, 1997), interventions designed to aid their adjustment and to modify the reactions of peers to them need to be made. School psychologists can play an effective part through behavioral intervention strategies in the social adjustment of the child affected with Tourette's syndrome (Walter & Carter, 1997) by helping to arrange the child's environment to be more accepting of such unusual behaviors.

There are many types of tics and many of these appear to be associated with the presence of other psychological disorders (Cardona et al., 1997), particularly obsessive-compulsive disorder (OCD). Most tics, however, do not have an organic basis but usually stem from psychological causes, such as self-consciousness or tension in social situations and they are usually associated with severity of behavioral problems (Rosenberg, Brown, & Singer, 1995). As in the case of the adolescent boy previously described, an individual's awareness of the tic often increases tension and the occurrence of the tic.

Tics have been successfully treated by means of medications. Neuroleptic drugs are the most predictably effective tic-suppressing drugs (Kurlan, 1997). Clonazepam, clonidine, and tiapride have all shown effectiveness in reducing motor tics; however, tiapride has shown the greatest decrease in the intensity and frequency of tics (Drtikova et al., 1997) Campbell and Cueva (1995) reported that both haloperidol and pimozide reduced the severity of tics by about 65 percent but thought that haloperidol was the more effective of the two medications.

Behavioral intervention techniques have also been used successfully in treating tics. One successful program involved several sequential elements, beginning with awareness training, relaxation training, and the development of incompatible responses and then progressing to cognitive therapy and the modification of overall style of action. Finally, perfectionist expectations about self-image (often found in children and adolescents with tics) are addressed through cognitive restructuring (O'Connor et al., 1998).

PERVASIVE DEVELOPMENTAL DISORDER: AUTISM

The **pervasive developmental disorders (PDD)** are a group of severely disabling conditions considered to be among the most difficult to understand and treat. They make up about 3.2 percent of cases seen in inpatient settings (Sverd, Sheth, Fuss, & Levine, 1995). They are considered to be the result of some structural differences in the brain that are usually evident at birth or become apparent as the child begins to develop (Siegel, 1996). There is fairly good diagnostic agreement in the determination of pervasive developmental disorder in children whether one follows the DSM-IV or ICD-10 (the International Classification of Disease Published by the World Health Organization), which have slightly different criteria for some disorders (Sponheim, 1996). There are several pervasive developmental disorders covered in DSM-IV—for example, **Asberger's disorder,** which is a "severe and sustained impairment in social interaction" that involves marked stereotypic (repetitive) behavior and inflexible adherence to routines (Gillberg, 1998). This pattern of behavior usually appears later than other pervasive developmental disorders such as autism but nevertheless involves substantial long-term psychological disability.

One of the most frequent and most puzzling and disabling of the pervasive developmental disorders and the one that we will address in more detail is autistic disorder, often referred to as **autism** or childhood autism. It is a developmental disorder that involves a wide range of problematic behaviors, including deficits in language, perceptual, and motor development; defective reality testing; and an inability to function in social situations. The following case illustrates some of the behaviors that may be seen in an autistic child.

> **Case Study, A Case of Autism** • The boy is five years old. When spoken to, he turns his head away. Sometimes he mumbles unintelligibly. He is neither toilet trained nor able to feed himself. He actively resists being touched. He dislikes sounds and is uncommunicative. He cannot relate to others and avoids looking anyone in the eye. He often engages in routine manipulative activities, such as dropping an object, picking it up, and dropping it again. He shows a pathological need for sameness. While seated, he often rocks back and forth in a rhythmic motion for hours. Any change in routine is highly upsetting to him.

Autism in infancy and childhood was first described by Kanner (1943). It afflicts some 80,000 American children—about 6.5 children in 10,000—and occurs about four or five times more frequently among boys than girls (Gillberg, 1995). A large epidemiological study of four regions of France reported similar rates, 4.9 per 10,000, with boys about two to one (Fombonne & du Mazaubrun, 1992). Autism is usually identified before a child is 30 months of age and may be suspected in the early weeks of life. A recent study found that autistic behavior such as lack of empathy, attention to others, and ability to imitate is shown as early as at 20 months (Charman, Swettenham, Baron-Cohen et al. 1997). Autistic children come from all socioeconomic levels.

The Clinical Picture in Autism Disorder

Autistic children show varying degrees of impairments and capabilities. In this section we will discuss some of the behaviors that may be evident in autism. A cardinal and typical sign is that a child seems apart or aloof from others, even in the earliest stages of life (Adrien et al., 1992). Mothers often remember such babies as never being cuddly, never reaching out when being picked up, never smiling or looking at them while being fed, and never appearing to notice the comings and goings of other people.

A Social Deficit Typically, autistic children do not show any need for affection or contact with anyone, usually not even seeming to know or care who their parents are. Several recent studies, however, have questioned this view that autistic children are emotionally flat. These studies (Capps et al., 1993) have shown that autistic children do express emotions and should not be considered as having an apparent lack of emotional reaction as noted in traditional descriptions of the disorder. Sigman (1996) has characterized the seeming inability of autistic children to respond to others as a lack of social understanding—a deficit in the ability to attend to social cues from others. The autistic child is thought to have a "mind blindness," an inability to take the attitude of or to "see" things as others do. For example, an autistic child appears limited in the ability to understand where another person is pointing. Additionally, autistic children show deficits in attention and in locating and orienting to sounds in their environment (Townsend, Harris, & Courchesne, 1996).

The lack of social interaction among autistic children has been well described by numerous studies in the past. In a recent behavioral observation study by Lord and Magill-Evans (1995) the authors noted that autistic youngsters engaged in fewer social interactions than other children; however, they also made the important

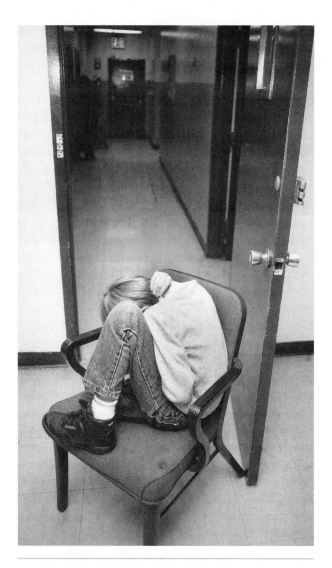

Extreme withdrawal from others is typical of autistic children.

observation that autistic children did not play—particularly did not show spontaneous play. In fact, much of the time nothing was going on.

An Absence of Speech The absence of or severely restricted use of speech is characteristic of autistic children, who have been considered to have an imitative deficit and do not effectively learn by imitation (Smith & Bryson, 1994). This dysfunction might explain the characteristic absence or limited use of speech by autistic children. If speech is present, it is almost never used to communicate except in the most rudimentary fashion, as by saying yes in answer to a question or by the use of **echolalia**—the parrotlike repetition of a few words. Although the echoing of parents' verbal behavior is found to a small degree in normal children as they experiment with their ability to produce articulate speech, persistent echolalia is found in about 75 percent of autistic children (Prizant, 1983). Some research has focused on trying to understand if echolalia in autistic children is functional. Prizant and Duchan (1981) analyzed echolalic verbalizations previously believed to be meaningless according to tone, latency, and other speech characteristics. They concluded that, far from being meaningless, these verbalizations could help clinicians or researchers understand the communicative and cognitive functioning of autistic children. Nevertheless, these utterances remain highly cryptic and are, of course, an inadequate substitute for true language functioning.

The usual picture of an autistic child as lacking in language ability and being wholly withdrawn is probably oversimplified. Researchers have found that autistic children vary considerably in language skill and at least some autistic children do comprehend language, even though they may not use it to express themselves as other children do (Wetherby & Prizant, 1992).

Autistic children seem to actively arrange the environment on their own terms in an effort to exclude or limit variety and intervention from other people, preferring instead a limited and solitary routine. Autistic children often show an active aversion to auditory stimuli, crying even at the sound of a parent's voice. The pattern is not always consistent, however; autistic children may at one moment be severely agitated or panicked by a very soft sound and at another time be totally oblivious to loud noise.

Self-Stimulation Self-stimulation is often characteristic of autistic children, usually taking the form of such repetitive movements as head banging, spinning, and rocking, which may continue by the hour. Other bizarre as well as repetitive behaviors are typical. Such behavior is well described by Schreibman and Charlop-Christie (1998) and illustrated in in the case of a young autistic boy.

Case Study, Repetitive Behavior in an Autistic Boy • A. was described as a screaming, severely disturbed child who ran around in circles making high-pitched sounds for hours. He also liked to sit in boxes, under mats, and [under] blankets. He habitually piled up all furniture and bedding in the center of the room. At times he was thought deaf though he also showed extreme fear of loud noises. He refused all food except in a bottle, refused to wear clothes, chewed stones and paper, whirled himself, and spun objects. . . . He played repetitively with the same toys for months, lining things in rows, collected objects such as bottle tops, and insisted on having two of everything, one in

each hand. He became extremely upset if interrupted and if the order or arrangement of things were altered. (Gajzago & Prior, 1974, p. 264)

Intellectual Ability In contrast to the behavior just described, some autistic children are skilled at fitting objects together. Thus their performance on puzzles or form boards may be average or above. Even in the manipulation of objects, however, difficulty with meaning is apparent. For example, when pictures are to be arranged in an order that tells a story, autistic children show a marked deficiency in performance. Moreover, autistic adolescents, even those who are well functioning, have difficulty with symbolic tasks such as pantomime, in which they are asked to recall motor actions such as imitation of tasks with imagined objects (e.g., ironing) yet they might perform well with real objects (Rogers, Benetto et al., 1996).

Although some have regarded autistic children as potentially of normal intelligence, this view has been challenged by a number of investigators who consider most of these children to be mentally retarded. Prior and Wherry (1986) reported that about three-fourths of autistic children were mentally retarded. Some autistic children, however, show markedly discrepant and relatively isolated abilities, such as astounding memory capabilities, as Dustin Hoffman depicted in the movie, *Rain Man*. In this context, Goodman (1989) described the case of an "autistic-savant" who showed unusual ability at an early age in calendar calculating (rapidly determining the day of any calendar date in history) as well as in other areas, such as naming the capitals of most states and countries and rapid calculation that allowed him to win a lot of money in Las Vegas. Nevertheless, his language development was severely retarded, and he showed the indifference to others and related symptoms characteristic of autistic children.

Much has been learned recently about the cognitive deficits of autistic children (Bennetto, Pennington et al., 1996). Compared with other groups of children on cognitive or intellectual tasks, autistic children often show marked impairment. For example, autistic children are significantly impaired on memory tasks when compared with both normal and retarded children. Autistic children particularly show a deficit in representing mental states—that is, they appear to have deficits in social reasoning but can manipulate objects (Scott & Baron-Cohen, 1996). Carpentieri and Morgan (1996) found that the cognitive impairment in autistic children is reflected in greater impairment in adaptive behaviors than in mentally retarded children without autism. Whether the frequently observed cognitive impairment in autism is the result of actual organic brain damage or of motivational deficits has not been clearly established. Koegel and Mentis (1985) have raised the possibility that the deficits result at least partly from motivational differences; they found that autistic children can learn and perform tasks at a higher level if motivation for a task is found and appropriate reinforcement is provided.

Maintaining Sameness   Many autistic children become preoccupied with and form strong attachments to unusual objects, such as rocks, light switches, film negatives, or keys. In some instances the object is so large or bizarre that merely carrying it around interferes with other activities. When their preoccupation with the object is disturbed—for example, by its removal or by attempts to substitute something in its place—or when anything familiar in their environment is altered even slightly, they may have a violent temper tantrum or a crying spell that continues until the familiar situation is restored. Thus autistic children are often said to be "obsessed with the maintenance of sameness." Furthermore, autistic children have been referred to as "negativistic" because they seemingly do not comply with requests. However, this observation has been questioned in a study by Volkmar, Hoder, and Cohen (1985). They found that, under the carefully structured and reinforcing conditions in a clinic setting, autistic children generally complied with requests made by staff.

In summary, autistic children typically show difficulties in relationships to other people, in perceptual-cognitive functioning, in language development, and in the development of a sense of identity (L. K. Wing, 1976). They also engage in bizarre and repetitive activities, demonstrate a fascination with unusual objects, and show an obsessive need to maintain environmental sameness. This is indeed a heavy set of handicaps. Almost two-thirds of autistic patients will be dependent on others as adults (Gilbert, 1991).

Causal Factors in Autism

The precise cause or causes of autism are unknown. However, evidence has accumulated that defective genes or damage from radiation or other conditions during prenatal development may play a significant role in the etiologic picture (Abramson et al., 1992; Rutter, 1991b; Waterhouse & Fein, 1997). Evidence for a genetic contribution to autism comes from examining the risk for autism in the siblings of autistic children. The best estimates are that families with one autistic child show a 3 to 5 percent risk of a sibling being autistic as well. Although this figure may seem low in an absolute sense, it is in fact extremely high given the population frequency of autism in the population.

Twin studies have also consistently shown higher concordance rates among monozygotic than among dizygotic twins (Bailey, Le Couteur et al., 1995). The conclusion from family and twin studies is that 80 to 90 percent of the variance in risk for autism is based on genetic factors, making it probably the most heritable of the various forms of psychopathology discussed in this text (Rutter, 1991b; LeCouteur, Bailey, Goode, Pickles, Robertson, Gottesman, & Rutter, 1996). Nevertheless, the exact mode of genetic transmission is not yet understood, and it seems likely that relatives may also show an increased risk for other cognitive and social deficits that are milder in form than true autism (Smalley, 1991). In other words, there may be a spectrum of disorders related to autism.

It seems likely at this point that the disorder we call autism involves both multiple kinds of deficits (Howlin, 1998; Mesibov et al, 1997) and multiple etiologic pathways (Gillberg, 1990). Thus we should perhaps not expect to find large risk factors accounting for all autistic outcomes, or even exceptional levels of consistency from one study to another where differing samples of autistic youngsters have been evaluated. Some investigators have pointed to the existence of a possible genetic defect, a fragile site on the X chromosome, referred to as the fragile X syndrome (Brown et al., 1986; Tsai & Ghaziuddin, 1992) that may occur in about 8 percent of autistic males (Smalley, 1991). In addition, 15 to 20 percent of males with the fragile X syndrome are also diagnosed with autism, further suggesting a link between the two syndromes. Nevertheless, there also appear to be differences between autism and the fragile X syndrome, suggesting that there are some qualitative differences between the two syndromes (Smalley, 1991). Even subtler constitutional defects may also exist in autism. One recent case report noted an association of autism with pituitary deficiency (Gingell, Parmar, & Sungum-Paliwal, 1996). Most recent investigators believe that autism begins with some type of inborn defect that impairs an infant's perceptual-cognitive functioning—the ability to process incoming stimuli and to relate to the world.

Sociocultural factors have also been postulated as causal elements in autism. In his early studies of childhood autism, Kanner (1943) concluded that an innate disorder in a child is exacerbated by a cold and unresponsive mother, the first factor resulting in social withdrawal and the second tending to maintain this isolation. Most investigators, however, have failed to find the parents of autistic children to be "emotional refrigerators" (Schreibman et al., 1998; Wolff & Morris, 1971) and Kanner's views have been generally discredited.

Clearly, much remains to be learned about the etiology of childhood autism. It appears most reasonable to suppose, however, that this disorder normally begins with an inborn defect or defects in brain functioning, regardless of what other causal factors may subsequently become involved.

Treatments and Outcomes

Treatment prognosis for autistic disorder is poor, and those diagnosed with autism, because of the severity of the problems, are often insufficiently treated (Wherry, 1996). Moreover, because of the typically poor response to treatment, autistic children are often subjected to a range of fads and "novel" approaches which turn out to be equally ineffective.

Medical Treatment   In the past, the use of medications to treat autistic children has not proven effective (Rutter, 1985). The drug most often used in the treatment of autism is haloperidol (Haldol), an antipsychotic medication (Campbell, 1987), but the data on its effectiveness do not warrant use unless a child's behavior is unmanageable by other means (Sloman, 1991). More recently, the drug clonidine, an antihypertensive medication, has been used with reportedly moderate effects at reducing the severity of the symptoms (Fankhauser et al., 1992). If irritability and aggressiveness are present, the medical management of such cases might involve use of medications to lower the level of aggression (Fava, 1997; Leventhal, Cook, & Lord, 1998). Although there are no surefire medications approved for this purpose, the drug clomipramine has had some observed beneficial effect. However, no currently available medication reduces the symptoms of autism enough to encourage general use. We will thus direct our attention to a variety of psychological procedures that have been more successful in treating autistic children.

Behavioral Treatment   Behavior therapy in an institutional setting has been used successfully in the elimination of self-injurious behavior, the mastery of the fundamentals of social behavior, and the development of some language skills (Charlop-Christie et al., 1998). Ivar Lovaas (1987), a pioneer in behavioral treatment of autistic

children, reported highly positive results from a long-term experimental treatment program of autistic children. Of the treated children, 47 percent achieved normal intellectual functioning and another 40 percent attained the mildly retarded level. In comparison, only 2 percent of the untreated, control children achieved normal functioning and 45 percent attained mildly retarded functioning. These remarkable results did, however, require a considerable staffing effort, with well-qualified therapists working with each child at least 40 hours per week for two years. Interestingly, studies on the effectiveness of behavior therapy with institutionalized children have found that children who were discharged to their parents continued to improve, whereas those who remained in an institution tended to lose much of what they had gained (Lovaas, 1977).

Some of the other most impressive results with autistic children have been obtained in projects that involve parents, with treatment in the home preferable to hospital-based therapy (Mesibov et al., 1997). Treatment contracts with parents specify the desired behavior changes in their child and spell out the explicit techniques for bringing about these changes. Such contracting acknowledges the value of the parents as potential agents of change (Huynen, Lutzker et al., 1996). Perhaps the most favorable results are those of Schreibman and Koegel (1975), who reported successful outcomes in the treatment of 10 out of 16 autistic children. These investigators relied heavily on the use of parents as therapists to reinforce normal behavior in their children. They concluded that autism is potentially a "defeatable horror."

Some studies show that intensive behavioral treatment of autistic children, requiring a significant investment of time and energy on the part of therapist and parents, can bring improvement, particularly if this treatment continues at home rather than in an institution.

The Effectiveness of Treatment It is too early to evaluate the long-term effectiveness of these newer treatment methods or the degree of improvement they actually bring about. The prognosis for autistic children, particularly for children showing symptoms before the age of two, is poor. Commonly, the long-term results of autism treatments have been unfavorable. A great deal of attention has been given to high-functioning autistic children (children who meet the criteria for autism yet develop functional speech). Ritvo and colleagues (1988) studied 11 parents whom they believed met diagnostic criteria for autism (they were identified through having had children who were autistic). These individuals had been able to make modest adjustments to life, hold down jobs, and get married. The outcome in autism is often problematic, however.

One important factor limiting treatment success is the problems autistic children experience in generalizing behavior outside the treatment context (Handleman, Gill, & Alessandri, 1988). Children with severe developmental disabilities do not transfer skills across situations very well. Consequently, learned behavior in one situation does not appear to help them meet challenges in others. This important component needs to be addressed if training or treatment programs are to be successful. Changes in the law in 1990 with respect to providing services for disabled children (Public Law 101–476) ensure equal access to an appropriate education in the least restrictive environment for all children. It is likely that more focus will be placed on integrating school-age children with autism into traditional learning environments.

At our present state of knowledge, the long-term prognosis for many autistic children is still guarded. Even with intensive long-term care in a clinical facility, where gratifying improvements may be brought about in specific behaviors, autistic children are a long way from becoming normal. Some make substantial improvement during childhood, only to deteriorate, showing symptom aggravation, at the onset of puberty (Gillberg & Schaumann, 1981). In spite of a few remarkable cases of dramatic success, the overall prognosis for autistic children remains guarded. Less than one-fourth of the autistic children who receive treatment appear to attain even marginal adjustment in later life.

Providing parental care to autistic children is more trying and stressful than for normal or mentally retarded children (Kasari & Sigman, 1997). Parents of autistic children often find themselves in the extremely frustrating situation of trying to understand their autistic child, providing day-to-day care, and searching for possible educational resources for their child in the present health and educational environment. There are many more questions than answers, and parents of autistic children often find themselves in the dark about the best way to proceed to gain an understanding of their child's potential and the best means of helping him or her realize that potential. In an unusually informative book on the topic of autism, *The World of the Austitic Child,* Siegel (1996) provides a very valuable guide for understanding and dealing with the problems of educating and treating autistic children. She discusses the impact that having an autistic child can have on the family—both parents and siblings—and describes ways of dealing with the problems, including the possible need of psychological treatment for parents or siblings of autistic children. The book is particularly valuable in providing clues as to how parents can obtain available resources for educating and treating autistic children in the confusing educational environment. The issue of residential placement, clearly a necessity in some situations and families, is also an important decision to which parents of autistic children must come to terms. Recently, efforts are being made to promote the development and growth of autistic people over their life spans in what has been referred to as the Eden Model (Holmes, 1998). In this approach, professionals and families recognize that the autistic individuals may need to have different therapeutic regimes at different periods of their lives, and the available resources need to be structured to provide for changing needs as they grow older.

PLANNING BETTER PROGRAMS TO HELP CHILDREN AND ADOLESCENTS

In our discussion of several problems of childhood and adolescence, we have noted the wide range of treatment procedures available, as well as the marked differences in outcomes. In concluding the chapter, we will discuss certain special factors associated with the treatment of children, the problem of child abuse, and the need for child advocacy and the rights of children, to prevent the occurrence of negative conditions that inhibit their optimal development.

Special Factors Associated with Treatment for Children and Adolescents

Mental health treatment, psychotherapy, and behavior therapy have been found to be as effective with children and adolescents as with adults (Kazdin, 1998; Weisz, Weiss, & Donenberg, 1992), but treatment conducted in laboratory-controlled studies are more effective than "real world" treatment situations (Weisz & Donenberg, 1995). There are a number of special factors to consider in relation to treatment for children and adolescents.

Child's Inability to Seek Assistance

Most emotionally disturbed children who need assistance are not in a position to ask for it themselves or to transport themselves to and from child treatment clinics. Thus, unlike an adult, who can usually seek help, a child is dependent, primarily on his or her parents. Adults should realize when a child needs professional help and take the initiative in obtaining it. Sometimes, however, adults neglect this responsibility. Plotkin (1981) has pointed out: "Parents have traditionally had the right to consent to health services for their children. In situations where the interest of the parents and children differ, the rule has had unfortunate consequences and has left treatment professionals in a quandary" (p. 121).

The law identifies four areas in which treatment without parental consent is permitted: (1) in the case of mature minors (those considered to be capable of making decisions about themselves); (2) in the case of emancipated minors (those living independently away from their parents); (3) in emergency situations; and (4) in situations in which a court orders treatment. Many children, of course, come to the attention of treatment agencies as a consequence of school referrals, delinquent acts, or parental abuse.

Vulnerabilities Placing Children at Risk for Developing Emotional Problems

Many families provide an undesirable environment for their growing children (Ammerman et al., 1998). Studies have shown that up to a fourth of American children may be living in inadequate homes and 7.6 percent of American youth have reported spending at least one night in a shelter, public place, or abandoned building (Ringwalt, Greene et al., 1998). Disruptive childhood experiences have been found to be a risk factor for adult problems. For example, a recent epidemiological study (Susser, Moore, & Link, 1993) reported that 23 percent of newly homeless men in New York city reported a history of out-of-home care as children, and another study by Caudill and colleagues (1994) reported that clients with a parental history of substance abuse were at over twice the risk for antisocial personality disorders.

Children growing up in troubled homes are at a double disadvantage. Not only are they deprived from the standpoint of environmental influence on their personality development (Crouch & Milner, 1993), but they also lack parents who will perceive their need for help and actively seek and participate in treatment programs. Inadequate or inattentive parenting can result in a failure to recognize serious signs of developing emotional problems.

High-risk behaviors or conditions need to be recognized and taken into consideration (Harrington & Clark, 1998). For example, there are a number of behaviors such as engaging in sexual acts, using alcohol or drugs, or delinquent behavior, that young people might engage in that place them at great risk for developing later emotional problems. Moreover, there are situations that can "happen" to young people—physical or sexual abuse, parental divorce, family turbulence, and homelessness—that place young people at great risk for emotional distress and subsequent maladaptive behavior. Dodge, Lochman, and colleagues (1997) found that children from homes with harsh discipline and physical abuse, for example, were more likely to be aggressive and conduct-disordered than those from homes with less harsh discipline and from nonabusing families.

Parents as Well as Child Needing Treatment

Because many of the behavior disorders specific to childhood appear to grow out of pathogenic family interactions, it is often essential for the parents, as well as their child, to receive treatment. In some instances, in fact, the treatment program may focus on the parents entirely, as in the case of child abuse.

Increasingly, then, the treatment of children has come to mean family therapy, in which one or both parents, along with the child and siblings, may participate in all phases of the program. (See Highlight 14.4 and Highlight 14.5 for a discussion of treatment approaches with children and adolescents.) Many therapists have discovered that fathers are particularly difficult to engage in the treatment process. For working parents and for parents who basically reject the affected child, such treatment may be difficult to arrange (Gaudin, 1993), especially in the case of poorer families who lack transportation and money. Thus both parental and economic factors help determine which emotionally disturbed children will receive assistance.

Family Therapy as a Means of Helping Children

For a number of reasons, therapeutic intervention with children experiencing psychological problems is often a more complicated process than providing psychotherapy for adults. The source of a child's problem and the means for changing behavior are often not within the child's power but instead are imbedded in the context of complex family interaction patterns. To remedy the child's problems, it is often necessary to alter those pathological family interaction patterns that produce or maintain the child's behavior, such as treating an entire family in a group context (Sandberg, Johnson et al., 1997).

Several family therapy approaches have been developed (Minuchin, 1974; Patterson et al., 1991). These differ in some important ways—for example, in terms of how the family is defined (whether to include extended family members); what the treatment process will focus on (whether communications between the family members or the aberrant behavior of the problem family members is the focus); what procedures are used in treatment (analyzing and interpreting hidden messages in the family communications or altering the reward

and punishment contingencies through behavioral assessment and reinforcement). Regardless of their differences, all family therapies view a child's problems, at least in part, as an outgrowth of pathological interaction patterns within the family, and they attempt to bring about positive change in family members through analysis and modification of the deviant family patterns (Carr, 1997).

How effective is family therapy at improving disruptive family relationships and promoting a more positive atmosphere for children? Hazelrigg, Cooper, and Borduin (1987), after comparing the research to date on family therapy, concluded that family therapy had positive effects when contrasted with no-treatment control samples or with alternative treatment approaches, such as individual therapy. In a recent meta-analytic study that included the results of 163 treatment trials, Shadish and colleagues (1993) found that the average therapy client was better off at termination than 70 percent of the clients in nontreatment conditions. They concluded that treatment outcome research strongly supported the effectiveness of family therapy. ■

Possibility of Using Parents as Change Agents
In essence, the parents are trained in techniques that enable them to help their child. Typically, such training focuses on helping the parents to understand the child's behavior disorder and to learn to reinforce adaptive behavior while withholding reinforcement for undesirable behavior. Encouraging results have been obtained with parents who care about their children and want to help (Forehand, 1993; Webster-Stratton, 1991). Kazdin, Holland, and Crowley (1997) described a number of barriers to parental involvement in treatment that resulted in dropout from therapy. Factors such as coming from a disadvantaged background, hav-

ing parents who were antisocial, or having parents who were under great stress tended to result in premature treatment termination.

Problem of Placing Child Outside the Family
Most communities have juvenile facilities that, day or night, will provide protective care and custody for young victims of unfit homes, abandonment, abuse, neglect, and related conditions. Depending on the home situation and the special needs of the child, he or she will later either be returned to his or her parents or placed elsewhere. In the latter instance, four types of facilities are commonly relied on: (1) foster homes, (2)

Using Play Therapy to Resolve Psychological Problems

Even if a child's problems are viewed as primary and in need of specific therapeutic intervention, he or she may not be motivated for therapy or sufficiently verbal to gain understanding through psychotherapeutic methods that work with adults. Consequently, effective psychological treatment with children may involve using more indirect methods of therapy or providing individual psychological therapy for children in a less intrusive and more familiar way through play therapy (Sperling, 1997).

As a treatment technique, play therapy emerged out of efforts to apply psychodynamic therapy to children. Because children are not able to talk about their problems in the way adults are, having not yet developed the self-awareness necessary, this limits the application of traditional psychodynamic therapy methods to children. Children tend to be oriented to the present and lack the capability for insight and self-scrutiny that therapy requires. Their perceptions of their therapist differ from those of adult patients, and they may have an unrealistic view that the therapist can magically change their environment (Wenar, 1990).

Through their play, children often express their feelings, fears, and emotions in a direct and uncensored fashion, providing a clinician with a clearer picture of problems and feelings. The activity of play has become a valuable source of obtaining personality and problem information about children, particularly when the sessions are consistent with their developmental level (Lewis, 1997).

In a play therapy session, the therapist usually needs to provide some structure or to guide play activities so that the child can express pertinent feelings. This might mean that the therapist asks direct questions of the child during the play session, such as: "Is the doll happy now?" or "What makes the doll cry?" In addition to using play activity as a means of understanding a troubled child's problems, it also provides a medium for bringing about change in the child's behavior. A central process in play therapy is that the therapist, through interpretation, providing emotional support, and clarification of feelings (often by labeling them for the child), provides the child with a corrective emotional experience. That is, the therapist provides the child with an accepting and trusting relationship that promotes healthier personality and relationship development. The play therapy situation enables the child to reexperience conflict or problems in the safety of the therapy setting, thereby providing a chance to conquer fears, to acclimate to necessary life changes, or to gain a feeling of security to replace the anxiety and uncertainty.

How effective is play therapy in reducing a child's problems and promoting better adjustment? When compared with adult treatment studies, play therapy compares quite favorably. Casey and Berman (1985) conducted a careful study of treatment research with children and concluded that such treatment "appears to match the efficacy of psychotherapy with adults" (p. 395). Play therapy was found to be as effective as other types of treatment, such as behavior therapy. In another recent study in which play therapy was integrated into an eight-week intervention program to treat conduct-disordered children, the subjects showed significant gain at a two-year follow-up (McDonald, Bellingham et al., 1997). ■

Children can often express their feelings more directly through play than in words, as shown in this play therapy session.

private institutions for the care of children, (3) county or state institutions, or (4) the homes of relatives. At any one time, more than half a million children are living in foster-care facilities.

The quality of a child's new home is of course a crucial determinant of whether the child's problems will be alleviated or made worse. Although efforts are made to screen the placement facilities and maintain contact with the situation through follow-up visits, there have been too many reported cases of mistreatment in the new home. In cases of child abuse, child abandonment, or a serious childhood behavior problem that parents cannot control, it has often been assumed that the only feasible action was to take the child out of the home and find a temporary substitute. With such a child's own home so obviously inadequate, the hope has been that a more stable outside placement would be better. But when children are taken from their homes and placed in an institution (which promptly tries to change them) or in a series of foster homes (where they obviously do not really belong), they are likely to feel rejected by their own parents, unwanted by their new caretakers, rootless, constantly insecure, lonely, and bitter.

Accordingly, the trend today is toward permanent planning. First, every effort is made to hold a family together and to give the parents the support and guidance they need for adequate childrearing. If this is impossible, then efforts are made to free the child legally for adoption and to find an adoptive home as soon as possible. This, of course, means that the public agencies need specially trained staffs with reasonable caseloads and access to resources that they and their clients may need.

Value of Intervening Before Problems Become Acute

Over the last 20 years, a primary concern of many researchers and clinicians has been to identify and provide early help for children who are at special risk (Athey, O'Malley et al., 1997). Rather than wait until these children develop acute psychological problems that may require therapy or major changes in living arrangements, psychologists are attempting to identify conditions in such children's lives that seem likely to bring about or maintain behavior problems and, where such conditions exist, to intervene before a child's development has been seriously distorted (Cicchetti & Toth, 1998). An example of this approach is provided in the work of Steele and Forehand (1997). These investigators found that children of parents who have a chronic medical condition (fathers were diagnosed as hav-

ing hemophilia, many were HIV positive) were vulnerable to developing internalizing problems and avoidant behavior, particularly when the parent-child relationship was weak. These symptoms in the child were associated with depression in the parent. The authors concluded that clinicians may be able to reduce the impact of parental chronic illness by strengthening the parent-child relationship and decreasing the child's use of avoidant strategies.

As described in Chapter 4, another type of early intervention has been developed in response to the special vulnerability children experience in the wake of disaster such as a hurricane, accident, or trauma such as a hostage-taking or shooting. Children and adolescents often require considerable support and attention to deal with traumatic events, a circumstance that is all too frequent in today's world. Individual and small-group psychological therapy might be implemented for victims of trauma (Gillis, 1993), support programs might operate through school-based interventions (Klingman, 1993), or community-based programs might be implemented to reduce the post-traumatic symptoms and prevent the occurrence of long-term maladjustment problems (see the discussion on crisis intervention techniques in Chapter 18).

Such early intervention has the double goal of reducing the stressors in a child's life and strengthening the child's coping mechanisms. If successful, it can effectively reduce the number and intensity of later problems, thus averting problems for both the individuals concerned and the broader society. It is apparent that children's needs can be met only if adequate preventive and treatment facilities for children exist and are available to the children who need assistance. In the next section, we will look at the specific issue of child abuse, which is of growing concern to researchers and practitioners who want to know what causes it and how it can be prevented.

Child Abuse

In contemporary society, we deplore the idea that children were commonly mistreated in the past. Society's goals today encompass the ideals of kind and gentle treatment of our children and we collectively believe that the future of our society depends upon the proper care of our young. However, this lofty ideal is clearly not realized, as a growing and troublesome number of cases of child maltreatment makes clear. Child abuse is an increasing concern in the United States (Lung & Daro, 1996). A recent survey of reported child abuse incidents in the United States found that child abuse reports increased 1.7 percent in 1995, with a total number of incidents exceeding 3.1 million. An estimated 1215 children were killed in 1995 in child abuse incidents (National Committee to Prevent Child Abuse, 1996). The excessive use of alcohol or drugs in the family appears to increase the risk of violent death in the home (Rivera, Mueller et al., 1997). Some evidence suggests that boys are more often physically abused than girls. It is usually clear that many children brought to the attention of legal agencies for abuse have been abused before. Moreover, the significantly higher rates of having been abused as a child among psychiatric inpatients suggest a likely causal role such maltreatment has in the development of severe psychopathology in the child (Read, 1997).

The seriousness of the child abuse problem in our society was not realized until the 1960s, when researchers began to report case after case like the following two.

Case Study, Two Cases of Child Abuse • The mother of a 29-month-old boy claimed he was a behavior problem, beat him with a stick and screwdriver handle, dropped him on the floor, beat his head on the wall or threw him against it, choked him to force his mouth open to eat, and burned him on the face and hands. After she had severely beaten him, the mother found the child dead.

Because her 2½-year-old daughter did not respond readily enough to toilet training, the mother became indignant and in a fit of temper over the child's inability to control a bowel movement gave her an enema with near scalding water. To save the child's life, a doctor was forced to perform a colostomy (Earl, 1965).

Many abused children show impaired cognitive ability and memory when compared with control children (Friedrich, Einbender, & Luecke, 1983). In addition, abused children are likely to show problems in social adjustment and are particularly likely to feel that the outcomes of events are determined by external factors beyond their own control (Kinzl & Biebl, 1992; Toth, Manly, & Cicchetti, 1992). They are also more likely to experience depressive symptoms (Bushnell, Wells, & Oakley-Browne, 1992; Emery & Laumann-Billings, 1998). As a result, abused children are dramatically less likely to assume personal responsibility for themselves, and they generally demonstrate less interpersonal sensitivity than control children. Child abuse and neglect may initiate a chain of violence. Child abuse is also associated with delinquent and criminal behavior when the victim grows up. Maxfield and Widom (1996), in a follow-up study of 908 people who were abused as children, found that their arrest rate for nontraffic offenses was significantly higher than a control sample of nonabused children.

Abused children also tend to show other more self-destructive behavior than nonabused children and physically abused children may be more likely to abuse their own children when they become parents (Malinosky-Rummel & Hansen, 1993). Childhood victimization was also found to be significantly related to the number of lifetime symptoms of antisocial personality disorder and predictive of a diagnosis of antisocial disorder in a recent study by Luntz and Widom (1994) and psychosis (Read, 1997).

Sexual Abuse   When the abuse involves a sexual component, such as incest or rape, the long-range consequences can be profound (Kendall-Tackett et al., 1993). Although recent analyses have questioned the impact of sexual abuse on child development (Rind et al., 1998) some research has suggested that people who have been sexually abused are more likely to develop substance abuse problems (Hernandez, 1992). Watkins and Bentovim (1992) reported that approximately 2 to 5 percent of men in the adult population have been sexually abused, often resulting in lifelong negative consequences such as sexual problems (e.g., exhibitionism, homophobic behavior, depression, anxiety) and even a tendency to recapitulate this experience as an adult. Jackson and colleagues (1990) found that women who had experienced intrafamily sexual abuse had significantly poorer social adjustment, especially in dating relationships. The women also reported significantly lower sexual satisfaction, more sexual dysfunctions, and lower self-esteem than control women. Adults who have been sexually abused as children often show serious psychological symptoms such as a tendency to use dissociative defense mechanisms to excess, excessive preoccupation with bodily functions, and lowered self-esteem (Nash et al., 1993) or to disengage as a means of handling stress as an adult (Coffey, Leitenberg et al., 1996).

The role of sexual abuse in causing psychological problems has recently been the subject of several longitudinal studies. A number of investigators have followed up sexually abused children to study the long-term effects of abuse on a victim's behavior. A large percentage of sexually abused children experience intense psychological symptoms following the incident (for example, 74 percent reported by Bentovim, Boston, & Van Elburg, 1987). At follow-up, however, the improvement often seems dramatic. Similarly, several other studies have reported substantial improvement of sexually abused victims at follow-up (Bentovim et al., 1987; Conte, Berliner, & Schuerman, 1986). One study found that 55 percent of victims had substantially improved at follow-up 18 months later, particularly in terms of sleeping problems, fears of the offender, and anxiety. However, 28 percent of the victims showed worsening behavior (Gomes-Schwartz, Horowitz, & Cardarelli, 1990).

Several investigators have conceptualized the residual symptoms of sexual abuse as a type of post-traumatic stress disorder (PTSD) because the symptoms experienced are similar; for example, nightmares, flashbacks, sleep problems, and feelings of estrangement (Donaldson & Gardner, 1985) and PTSD symptoms are strongly associated with abuse (Koltek, Wilkes, & Atkinson, 1998). However, other investigators (e.g., Finkelhor, 1990) object to this explanation on grounds that viewing these symptoms as an example of PTSD will "lead us to miss some of [the] most serious effects" of the sexual abuse experience, such as prolonged depression or anxiety (p. 329).

Causal Factors in Child Abuse Since the 1960s, a great deal of research has been aimed at finding out which parents abuse their children and why, in the hope that ultimately these parents can be stopped, or better yet, prevented, from abusing their children. It is important to realize that in most cases it is not possible to find a single cause of child abuse. As Jay Belsky (1993) has pointed out, "There is no one pathway to these disturbances in parenting; rather, maltreatment seems to arise when stressors outweigh supports and risks are greater than protective factors" (p. 427). We now know that there are multiple pathways to abuse (Emery & Laumann-Billings, 1998). Parents who physically abuse their children tend to be young, with most under 30. In the majority of reported cases, they come from the lower-socioeconomic levels (Peterson & Brown, 1994). An important common factor among families with abusing parents is a higher-than-average degree of frustration; many stressors are present in their lives, including marital discord, high unemployment, and alcohol abuse (Cicchetti & Toth, 1998). Recent evidence suggests that these high levels of caregiver stress play an important part in child abuse and neglect (Hillson & Kuiper, 1994). Many incidents of physical abuse occur as parental reactions to a child's misbehavior in areas such as fighting, sexual behavior, aggression, and so on (Herrenkohl, Herrenkohl, & Egolf, 1983). Although no clear and consistent personality pattern emerges as typical of child-abusing parents, they seem to show a

higher-than-average rate of psychological disturbance (Serrano et al., 1979). Some evidence from personality testing shows that they tend to be aggressive, nonconforming, selfish, and lacking in appropriate impulse control (Lund, 1975).

The Prevention of Child Abuse Because of complexities involved in the area of child abuse and neglect, interventions need to be implemented on multiple levels including individual, familial, and community (Becker, Alpert et al., 1995). Practitioners and child protection agencies have attempted to reduce the amount and impact of child abuse. Their efforts include the following:

1. Community education programs have been developed to increase public awareness of the problem. Television advertisements have been especially effective at sensitizing parents and children to potential abuse.

2. Child protection teams have been organized by many state and county welfare departments to investigate and intervene in reported cases of child abuse.

3. Teams of mental health specialists in many community mental health centers are working to evaluate and provide psychological treatment for both abused children and their parents.

4. Parent support groups, often made up of former child abusers, are forming that can offer abusing parents or those at risk for child abuse alternative ways of behaving toward their children. All states require physicians and other professionals to report cases of child abuse that come to their attention.

One of the most effective treatment strategies for eliminating or reducing child abuse involves parent-focused interventions that include teaching parents clearly defined child training strategies aimed at improving childrearing skills (Wolfe & Wekerle, 1993). Research aimed at enabling early intervention with parents identified as likely to abuse their children has been promising. Wolfe and colleagues (1988) identified women who were at high risk for maltreatment of their children. They randomly assigned mothers to either a treatment or a control group. The treatment consisted of behaviorally oriented parent training that provided child management skills, instruction in child care, modeling, rehearsal instructions to give clear, concise demands, and the use of "time out" as a punishment. The study showed that this early intervention reduced the risk for child abuse among the mothers provided the treatment. Through such efforts on many levels, it is hoped that children will be spared abuse and that abusive or potentially abusive parents will be helped to be more effective and nurturant.

Unfortunately, child abuse all too frequently produces maladaptive social behavior in its victims. The treatment of abused children needs to address the problems of social adjustment, depression, and poor interpersonal skills that these children exhibit. An interesting treatment approach to reducing the negative consequences of child abuse is the use of peers to help modify abused children's tendency to withdraw and improve their poor social skills. Fantuzzo and colleagues (1988) trained peer confederates to make play overtures to abused children. They found that peer-initiated efforts were more effective at increasing the social interaction of withdrawn children than adult-initiated treatment efforts. Further work on rehabilitative efforts is needed to assist these unfortunate children in overcoming the psychologically disabling effects of being abused.

Child Advocacy Programs

Today there are over 63 million people under age 18 in the United States (Bureau of the Census, 1995). Unfortunately both treatment and preventive programs for our society's children have been and remain inadequate to deal with the extent of psychological problems among children and adolescents. In 1989, the United Nations General Assembly adopted the UN Convention on the Rights of the Child, which provides a detailed definition of the rights of children in political, economic, social and cultural areas. This international recognition of the rights of children can potentially have a great impact on promoting humane treatment of children (Wilcox & Naimark, 1991).

In the United States one approach that has been designed to meet mental health needs, mental health child advocacy, has been prominent in recent years. Advocacy programs attempt to help children or others receive services that they need but often are unable to obtain for themselves. In some cases, advocacy seeks to better conditions for underserved populations by changing the system (McLoyd, 1998; Ramey & Ramey, 1998).

Twice in recent years the federal government has established a National Center for Child Advocacy to coordinate the many kinds of work for children's welfare performed by different government agencies. Both times the new agency proved ineffective and was given up after a year or so. Currently, the fragmentation in children's services means that different agencies serve different needs; no government agency is charged with considering the whole child and planning comprehensively for children who need help.

Outside the federal government, until recently, advocacy efforts for children have been supported largely by legal and special-interest citizen's groups, such as the Children's Defense Fund, a public-interest organization based in Washington, D.C. Mental health professionals have typically not been involved. Today, however, there is greater interdisciplinary involvement in attempts to provide effective advocacy programs for children (Gentry & Eron, 1993; Hermalin & Morell, 1986).

Although such programs have made important local gains toward bettering conditions for mentally disabled children, a great deal of confusion, inconsistency, and uncertainty still persist in the advocacy movement as a whole

The agencies designed to protect children are often so overburdened and fragmented that children referred to them for ongoing monitoring and protection may be abused anyway. Such was the case of Eliza Izquierdo, a little girl abused by her mother over many years.

(Levine & Perkins, 1987), and the need for improving the accountability of mental health services for children still exists (Burchard & Schafer, 1992). In addition, the mood at both federal and state levels has for some time been to cut back on funds for social services. Some important beginning steps have been taken in the work toward child advocacy, and new efforts to identify and help high-risk children have been made (National Advisory Mental Health Council, 1990). If the direction and momentum of these efforts can be maintained and if sufficient financial support for them can be procured, the psychological environment for children could substantially improve.

UNRESOLVED ISSUES

Can Society Deal with Delinquent Behavior?

One of the most troublesome and extensive problems in childhood and adolescence is delinquent behavior. This behavior includes such acts as destruction of property, violence against other people, and various behaviors contrary to the needs and rights of others and in violation of society's laws. The term *juvenile delinquency* is a legal one; it refers to illegal acts committed by individuals under the age of 16, 17, or 18 (depending on state law). It is not recognized in DSM-IV as a disorder. Children under eight who commit crimes are not considered delinquents, because it is assumed that they are too immature to understand the significance and consequences of their actions. As a legal issue, delinquency is generally regarded as calling for some punishment or corrective action.

The actual incidence of juvenile delinquency is difficult to determine because many delinquent acts are not reported. However, the data that are available are alarming:

- Of the 2 million young people who go through the juvenile courts each year in the United States, about a million and a half were for delinquent acts and the remainder for status offenses, such as running away, that are not considered crimes for adults. About one teenager out of every 15 in the nation was arrested. Well over half of the juveniles who are arrested each year have prior police records (Federal Bureau of Investigation, 1995).

- In 1995 there were 68,910 juvenile delinquents being held in correctional facilities in the United States. There were 1785 status offenders being held.

- Although most juvenile crime is committed by males, the rate has also risen for females. Female delinquents are commonly apprehended for drug use, sexual offenses, running away from home, and incorrigibility, but crimes against property, such as stealing, have also markedly increased among this group.

- Male delinquents are commonly arrested for drug usage and crimes against property; to a lesser extent, they are arrested for armed robbery, aggravated assault, and other crimes against people.

- Both the incidence and the severity of delinquent behavior are disproportionately high for lower-class adolescents. It may also be noted that the delinquency rate for socially disadvantaged youths appears about equal for whites and nonwhites (Federal Bureau of Investigation, 1995).

Only a small group of "continuous" delinquents actually evolve from oppositional defiant behavior to conduct disorder then to adult antisocial personality while most people who engage in delinquent acts as adolescents do not follow this trend Moffitt (1993a). The individuals who show adolescence-limited delinquency are thought to do so as a result of social mimicry—they mimic their more antisocial peers but discontinue this behavior when they begin to respond to other factors in their environment. As they mature, they thus lose their motivation for delinquency and gain rewards for more socially acceptable events in their environment. Aggressive or violent behaviors resulting in delinquency are not always "continuous" from early aggressiveness. Some violent behavior actually occurs in later adolescents without precursors (Loeber & Stouthamer-Loeber, 1998). Several key variables seem to play a part in the genesis of delinquency: personal pathology, pathogenic family patterns, and undesirable peer relationships.

Personal Pathology as a Cause of Delinquency

A number of investigators have attempted to understand delinquents in terms of pervasive patterns and sources of personal pathology.

Genetic Determinants Although the research on genetic determinants of antisocial behavior is far from conclusive, some evidence suggests possible hereditary contributions to criminality. Schulsinger (1980) identified 57 sociopathic adoptees from psychiatric and police files in Denmark and matched them with 57 nonsociopathic control adoptees on the basis of age, sex, social class, geographic region, and age at adoption. He found that natural parents of the adopted sociopaths, particularly fathers, were more likely to have sociopathic characteristics than the natural parents of the controls. Because these natural parents had little contact with their offspring, thus reducing the possibility of environmental influence, the results are interpreted as reflecting the possibility of some genetic transmission of a predisposition to antisocial behavior.

Brain Damage and Learning Disability   In a distinct minority of delinquency cases (an estimated 1 percent or less), brain pathology results in lowered inhibitory controls and a tendency toward episodes of violent behavior. Such adolescents are often hyperactive, impulsive, emotionally unstable, and unable to inhibit themselves when strongly stimulated. Fortunately, their inner controls appear to improve during later adolescence and young adulthood. The actual role intellectual factors, particularly learning disabilities, play in causing juvenile delinquency is still being debated (Lombardo & Lombardo, 1991; Lynam, Moffitt, & Stouthamer-Loeber, 1993).

Psychological Disorders   A small percentage of delinquent acts appear to be directly associated with behavior disorders such as hyperactivity (Loeber & Farrington, 1998). Delinquent acts associated with psychotic behavior often involve a pattern of prolonged emotional hurt and turmoil, culminating, after long frustration, in an outburst of violent behavior. In the case of psychologically disturbed delinquents, the delinquent act is a by-product of severe personality maladjustment rather than a reflection of antisocial attitudes.

Antisocial Traits   Many habitual delinquents appear to share the traits typical of antisocial personalities. They are impulsive, defiant, resentful, devoid of feelings of remorse or guilt, incapable of establishing and maintaining close interpersonal ties, and seemingly unable to profit from experience. Because they lack needed reality and ethical controls, they often engage in seemingly senseless acts that are not planned but occur on the spur of the moment. They may steal a small sum of money they do not need, or they may steal a car, drive it a few blocks, and abandon it. In some instances, they engage in impulsive acts of violence that are not committed for personal gain but rather reflect underlying resentment and hostility toward the world. In essence, these individuals are unsocialized.

Drug Abuse   Many delinquent acts—particularly theft, prostitution, and assault—are directly associated with alcohol or drug use (Leukefeld et al., 1998). Most adolescents who abuse hard drugs, such as heroin, are forced to steal to maintain their habit, which can be very expensive. In the case of female addicts, theft may be combined with or replaced by prostitution as a means of obtaining money.

Pathogenic Family Patterns as a Cause of Delinquency

In evaluating the role of pathogenic family patterns in delinquency, it should be emphasized that a given pattern is only one of many interacting factors. Of the various patterns that have been emphasized in the research on juvenile delinquency, the following appear to be the most important.

Parental Absence or Family Conflict   Delinquency appears to be much more common among youths coming from homes in which parents have separated or divorced than from homes in which a parent has died, suggesting that parental conflict may be a key element in causing delinquency. The effects of parental absence vary—for example, parental separation or divorce may be less troubling for children than parental conflict and dissension. It is parental disharmony and conflict in lieu of a stable home life that appears to be an important causal variable.

Parental Rejection and Faulty Discipline   In many cases, one or both parents reject a child. When the father is the rejecting parent, it is difficult for a boy to identify with him and use him as a model for his own development. In a classic early study of 26 aggressively delinquent boys, Bandura and Walters (1963) reported a pattern in which rejection by the father was combined with inconsistent handling of the boy by both parents. To complicate the pathogenic picture, the father typically used physically punitive methods of discipline, thus modeling aggressive behavior and augmenting the hostility that the boy already felt toward him. The end result of such a pattern was a hostile, defiant, inadequately socialized youth who lacked normal inner controls and tended to act out his aggressive impulses in antisocial behavior. The detrimental effects of parental rejection and inconsistent discipline are by no means attributable only to fathers. Researchers have found that such behavior by either parent can be associated with aggression, lying, stealing, running away from home, and a wide range of other difficulties (Lefkowitz et al., 1977). Antisocial parental models—alcoholism, brutality, antisocial attitudes, failure to provide, frequent unnecessary absences from home, and other characteristics that made the father or mother an inadequate and unacceptable model—are often found in the parents of delinquents (Bandura, 1973).

Relationships Outside the Family Some research suggests that the parents' interpersonal relationships outside the family may contribute to their children's delinquency (Griest & Wells, 1983). Wahler (1980) found that the children's acting-out behavior was inversely related to the amount of friendly contacts that parents had outside the home. Wahler, Hughey, and Gordon (1981) reported that mothers who are isolated or who have negative community interactions are less likely to track or control their children's behavior in the community than parents who have friendly relationships outside the family.

Undesirable Peer Relationships

Delinquency tends to be a shared experience. In their study of delinquents in the Flint, Michigan, area, Haney and Gold (1973) found that about two-thirds of delinquent acts were committed in association with one or two other people, and most of the remainder involved three or four other people. Usually the offender and the companion or companions were of the same sex. Interestingly, girls were more likely than boys to have a constant friend or companion in delinquency.

Broad social conditions may also tend to produce or support delinquency. Interrelated factors that appear to be of key importance include alienation and rebellion, social rejection, and the psychological support afforded by membership in a delinquent gang. A recent report of the Office of Juvenile Justice and Delinquency Prevention estimated that there are 23,388 youth gangs with 664,906 members in the United States. Every state and every large city has a gang problem. Apparently, gangs are cropping up in small rural towns across the United States as well. The gang experience is male oriented; only about 3 percent of gang members are female. In 1995 there were 46,359 gang related crimes and 1072 gang-related murders reported (Office of Juvenile Justice and Delinquency Prevention, 1995).

The problem of gang membership is most prevalent in lower-socioeconomic areas and more common among ethnic minority adolescents (48 percent African Americans; 43 percent Hispanic Americans) than among Caucasians. Though there are many reasons for joining gangs, most members appear to feel inadequate in and rejected by the larger society. Gang membership gives

Youth gangs offer acceptance and affection that are often absent in the adolescent's home and school environment.

members a sense of belonging and a means of gaining some measure of status and approval. It may also represent a means of committing robberies and other illegal activities for financial gain, acts that an individual could not successfully perform alone.

Dealing with Delinquency

If juvenile institutions and training schools have adequate facilities and personnel, they can be of great help to youths who need to be removed from aversive environments. These institutions can give adolescents a chance to learn about themselves and their world, to further their education and develop needed skills, and to find purpose and meaning in their lives. In such settings, young people may have the opportunity to receive psychological counseling and group therapy. It is of key importance here that peer group pressures be channeled in the direction of resocialization, rather than toward repetitive delinquent behavior. Behavior therapy techniques based on the assumption that delinquent behavior is learned, maintained, and changed according to the same principles as other learned behavior have shown promise in the rehabilitation of juvenile offenders who require institutionalization (Ammerman & Hersen, 1997). Counseling with parents and related environmental changes are generally of vital importance in a total rehabilitation program.

Probation is widely used with juvenile offenders and may be granted either in lieu of or after a period of institutionalization. Many delinquents can be guided into constructive behavior without being removed from their family or community. The recidivism rate for delinquents, the most commonly used measure for assessing rehabilitation programs, depends heavily on the type of offenders being dealt with and on the particular facility or procedures used. The overall recidivism rate for delinquents sent to training schools has been estimated to be high (Federal Bureau of Investigation, 1995). Because many crimes are committed by juveniles who have been recently released from custody or who were not incarcerated after being arrested, a number of state officials have become advocates of stiffer penalties for some types of juvenile crime.

SUMMARY

Children used to be viewed as "miniature" adults. It was not until the second half of the twentieth century that a diagnostic classification system focused clearly on the special problems of children.

Two broad approaches to the classification of childhood and adolescent behavior problems have been undertaken: a categorical strategy, reflected most extensively in the DSM-IV, and a dimensional strategy. Both classification approaches involve organized classes of observed behaviors. In the categorical strategy, symptoms of behavior problems are grouped together as syndromes based on clinical observations. In the dimensional strategy, a broad range of observed behaviors are submitted to multivariate statistical techniques; the symptoms that group together make up the diagnostic classes referred to as "dimensions."

In this chapter, the DSM-IV classification system is followed in order to provide clinical descriptions of a wide range of childhood behavior problems. Attention-deficit hyperactivity disorder is one of the more frequent behavior problems of childhood. In this disorder, the child shows impulsive, overactive behavior that interferes with his or her ability to accomplish tasks. There is some controversy over the explicit criteria used to distinguish hyperactive children from "normal" children or from children who exhibit other behavior disorders, such as conduct disorders. This lack of clarity in defining hyperactivity increases the difficulty of determining causal factors for the disorder. The major approaches to treating hyperactive children have been medication and behavior therapy. Using medications, such as amphetamines, with children is somewhat controversial. Behavior therapy, particularly cognitive-behavioral methods, has shown a great deal of promise in modifying the behavior of hyperactive children.

Another common behavior problem among children is that of conduct disorder. In this disorder, a child engages in persistent aggressive or antisocial acts. In cases where the child's misdeeds involve illegal activities, the terms *delinquent* or *juvenile delinquent* may be applied. A number of potential causes of conduct disorder or delinquent behavior have been determined, ranging from biological factors to personal pathology to social conditions. Treatment of conduct disorders and delinquent behavior is often frustrating and difficult; treatment is likely to be ineffective unless some means can be found for modifying a child's environment.

Other disorders, such as the childhood anxiety or depressive disorders, are quite different from the conduct disorders. Children who suffer from these disorders typically do not cause difficulty for others through their aggressive conduct. Rather they are fearful, shy, withdrawn, insecure, and have difficulty adapting to outside demands. The anxiety disorders may be characterized by extreme anxiety, withdrawal, or avoidance behavior. A likely cause for these disorders is early family relationships that generate anxiety and prevent the child from developing more adaptive coping skills. Behavior therapy approaches such as assertiveness training and desensitization may be helpful in treating this kind of disorder.

Several other disorders of childhood involve behavior problems centering on a single outstanding symptom rather than pervasive maladaptive patterns. The symptoms may involve enuresis, encopresis, sleepwalking, or tics. Treatment of these disorders is generally more successful than in the other disorders just described.

The chapter then addresses one of the most severe and inexplicable childhood disorders, autism. In this disorder, extreme maladaptive behavior occurs during the early years and prevents affected children from developing psychologically. Autistic children, for example, seem to remain aloof from others, never responding to or seemingly not caring about what goes on around them. Many never learn to speak. It is likely that the disorder has a genetic and biological basis. Neither medical nor psychological treatment has been able to normalize the behavior of autistic children, but newer instructional and behavior-modification techniques have sometimes scored significant gains in improving their ability to function. In general, the present long-term prognosis in autism appears guarded at best.

A number of potential causal factors were considered for the disorders of childhood and adolescence. Although genetic predisposition appears to be important in several disorders, parental psychopathology, family disruption, and stressful circumstances, such as parental death or desertion and child abuse, can have an important causal in-

fluence. Recent research has underscored the importance of multiple risk factors in the development of psychopathology.

There are special problems, and special opportunities, involved in treating childhood disorders. The need for preventive and treatment programs for children is always growing, and in recent years the concept of child advocacy has become a reality in some states. Child abuse is a serious problem that has and continues to foster both research and clinical efforts into finding causes and devising preventive measures and treatment. Another problem that takes a great toll on both the individual and community is juvenile crime or delinquency. Unfortunately, the financing and resources necessary for such services are not always readily available, and the future of programs for improving psychological environments for children remains uncertain.

KEY TERMS

developmental psychopathology (p. 543)

attention-deficit hyperactivity disorder (ADHD) (p. 547)

Ritalin (p. 549)

Pemoline (p. 549)

conduct disorder (p. 551)

oppositional defiant disorder (p. 551)

juvenile delinquency (p. 551)

separation anxiety disorder (p. 557)

selective mutism (p. 558)

enuresis (p. 562)

encopresis (p. 563)

sleepwalking disorder (p. 563)

tic (p. 564)

Tourette's syndrome (p. 564)

pervasive developmental disorders (PDD) (p. 565)

Asberger's Disorder (p. 565)

autism (p. 565)

echolalia (p. 566)

Clinical Assessment

Carlo Zinelli, *Untitled.* Zinelli (1916-1974) developed anxiety while in the Italian military, and became increasingly disoriented until 1947, when he was committed to a psychiatric hospital in Verona. He began his artistic career by drawing grafitti on the hospital walls, but when a studio was set up, he painted every day. In this painting above, the silhouetted form appears surrounded by the hallucinations that confronted the schizophrenic artist.

Most often, a patient's "presenting complaint" to a clinician—the behavioral, emotional, or physical discomfort that has prompted him or her to seek help—initiates a process of assessment. The clinician attempts to understand the nature and extent of the problem for which help is being sought. At times this process of inquiry is convoluted and challenging, reminiscent of a Sherlock Holmes exercise in inductive and deductive logic. On other occasions assessment is a relatively straightforward matter in which the clinician may, with a high probability of being correct, come to a rapid conclusion about the basis for the complaint and the proper disposition of the case. Pediatricians whose practices tend to be confined to a local clientele, for example, know what childhood infections are "going around" at a given time. A child who has complaints that mimic the characteristic symptom profile for a common infection will likely be found to have that disease. Even so, the conscientious pediatrician will usually want to confirm an initial diagnostic impression with lab studies that identify the infectious organism involved before initiating specifically targeted treatment.

For the mental health practitioner, few clinical situations are as routine as our pediatric example, and adequate techniques for confirming initial impressions may prove far more elusive. With rare exceptions, the "lab work" essential to much medical assessment is irrelevant. Psychological disorders usually lack identifying biological characteristics. Furthermore, they are always interlaced with the personalities of the individuals suffering them and usually with the entire surrounding social fabric.

As we have seen, mental disturbances are likely to be the product of a complex organization of contributing factors, many of which may not be apparent either immediately or after many months of intense scrutiny in the course of psychotherapy. As this last statement implies, psychological assessment or diagnosis can be an ongoing process that proceeds along with, rather than only preceding, treatment efforts.

As we have seen in earlier chapters, even where a specific diagnosis may be confidently determined, it will normally be of little direct clinical significance beyond a descriptive summary of the behavioral observations the clinician has been able to make. It will not reveal, as do most medical diagnoses, the underlying pathologic processes producing the condition (for example, fever) that is observed. For these reasons the assessment of mental disorders is usually more difficult, more uncertain, and more protracted than it is for physical diseases. It is no less critically important, however. No rational, specific treatment plan can be instituted without at least some general notion of what problems need to be addressed. As treatment proceeds, it is guided by the clinician's continuing assessment of the client's problems.

We will focus in this chapter on the initial *clinical assessment*—a procedure by which clinicians, using psychological tests, observation, and interviews, develop a summary of the client's symptoms and problems. Assessment is an ongoing process and may be important at other points during treatment—for example to assess outcome. In the initial clinical assessment an attempt is made to identify the main dimensions of a client's problem and to predict the likely course of events under various conditions. It is at this initial stage that crucial decisions have to be made—such as what if any treatment approach is to be offered, whether the problem will require hospitalization, to what extent family members will need to be included as co-clients, and so on. Sometimes these decisions must be made quickly, as in emergency conditions, and without recourse to critical information that would probably (but not necessarily) become available with extended client contact. As will be seen, various psychological measurement instruments are employed to maximize assessment efficiency in this type of pretreatment examination process (Gaw & Beutler, 1995).

A less obvious but equally important function of pretreatment assessment is that of establishing baselines for various psychological functions so that the effects produced by treatment can be measured. Criteria based on these measurements may be established as part of the treatment plan, such that the therapy is considered successful and is terminated only when the client's behavior meets these predetermined criteria. Also, as will be seen in Chapters 16 and 17, comparison of posttreatment with pretreatment assessment results is an essential feature of many research projects designed to evaluate the effectiveness of various therapies.

There are two other relatively common applications of psychological assessments described in this chapter. The first involves using assessments to determine whether an individual is experiencing psychological adjustment problems for use in court testimony. The second is the use of psychological assessment instruments in screening candidates for various roles and occupations. Here the effort is basically one of identifying persons who appear to be psychologically unfit for the type of assignment or work sought. For example, a police recruit who appears to have uncertain control of anger and aggressive impulses may need to be counseled about possibly adopting another occupational goal, or about seeking therapy to remedy a lack of control that could be dangerous in an occupation involving both great stress and constant access to lethal weapons.

In this chapter, we will review some of the more commonly used assessment procedures and show how the data obtained can be integrated into a coherent clinical picture for use in making decisions about referral and treatment. Our survey will include a discussion of neurological and neuropsychological assessment, the clinical interview, behavioral observation, and personality assessment through the use of projective and objective psychological tests.

Let us look first at what, exactly, a clinician is trying to learn during the psychological assessment of a client.

THE BASIC ELEMENTS IN ASSESSMENT

What does a clinician need to know? First, of course, the presenting problem must be identified. Is it a situational problem precipitated by some environmental stressor such as divorce or unemployment, a manifestation of a more pervasive and long-term disorder, or is it perhaps some combination of the two? Is there any evidence of recent deterioration in cognitive functioning? What is the duration of the current complaint and how is the person dealing with the problem? What, if any, prior help has been sought? Are there indications of self-defeating behavior and personality deterioration, or is the individual using available personal and environmental resources in a good effort to cope? How pervasively has the problem affected the person's performance of important social roles? Does the individual's symptomatic behavior fit any of the diagnostic patterns in the DSM-IV?

The Relationship Between Diagnosis and Assessment

It is often important to have an adequate classification of the presenting problem for a number of reasons. In many cases, a formal diagnosis is necessary before insurance claims can be filed. Clinically, knowledge of a person's type of disorder can help in planning and managing the appropriate treatment. Administratively, it is essential to know the range of diagnostic problems that are represented among the patient or client population and for which treatment facilities need to be available. If most patients at a facility have been diagnosed as having personality disorders, for example, then the staffing, physical environment, and treatment facilities should be arranged accordingly. Thus, the nature of the difficulty needs to be understood as clearly as possible, including a categorization if appropriate.

Taking a Social History

For most clinical purposes, a formal diagnostic classification per se is much less important than having a basic understanding of the individual's history, intellectual func-

tioning, personality characteristics, and environmental pressures and resources. That is, an adequate assessment includes much more than the diagnostic label. For example, it should include an objective description of the person's behavior. How does the person characteristically respond to other people? Are there excesses in behavior present, such as eating or drinking too much? Are there notable deficits, as, for example, in social skills? How appropriate is the person's behavior? Is the person manifesting behavior that would be acceptable in some contexts but is often displayed where it is plainly unresponsive to the situation or to reasonable social expectations? Excesses, deficits, and appropriateness are key dimensions to be noted if the clinician is to understand the particular disorder that has brought the individual to the clinic or hospital.

Personality Factors In addition, assessment needs to include a description of any relevant long-term personality characteristics. Has the person typically responded in deviant ways to particular kinds of situations—for example, those requiring submission to legitimate authority? Do there seem to be personality traits or behavior patterns that predispose the individual to behave in maladaptive ways across a broad range of circumstances? Does the person tend to become enmeshed with others to the point of losing his or her identity, or is he or she so self-contained that intimate exchange is routinely aborted? Is the person able to accept help from others? Is the person capable of genuine affection, or of accepting appropriate responsibility for the welfare of others? Such questions are necessarily at the heart of many assessment efforts.

The Social Context It is also important to assess the social context in which the individual operates. What kinds of environmental demands are typically placed on the person, and what supports or special stressors exist in his or her life situation? For example, being the primary caretaker for a spouse suffering from Alzheimer's disease is sufficiently challenging that relatively few can manage the task without significant psychological impairment, especially where outside supports are lacking. As we have seen, the DSM-IV classification includes guidelines for rating both the severity of the stressors in a person's current environment and the level of a person's overall adjustment in meeting the demands of a complex social environment.

The diverse and often conflicting bits of information about the individual's personality traits, behavior patterns, environmental demands, and so on must then be integrated into a consistent and meaningful picture. Some clinicians refer to this picture as a **dynamic formulation,** because it not only describes the current situation but includes

An adequate assessment requires more than a clinical diagnosis. It needs to encompass a basic understanding of the person's intellectual functioning, personality characteristics, and environmental pressures and resources. It is important to assess the social context in which the person finds himself or herself in order for a psychological assessment to be complete.

hypotheses about what is driving the person to behave in maladaptive ways. At this point in the assessment, the clinician should have a plausible explanation—for example, for why a normally passive and mild-mannered man suddenly flew into a rage and started breaking up furniture.

The formulation should allow the clinician to develop hypotheses about the client's future behavior as well. What is the likelihood of improvement or deterioration if the person's problems are left untreated? Which behaviors should be the initial focus of change, and what treatment methods are likely to be most efficient in producing this change? How much change might reasonably be expected from a particular type of treatment?

Where feasible, decisions about treatment are made collaboratively with the consent and approval of the individual. In cases of severe disorder, however, they may have to be made without the patient's participation or in rare instances even without consulting responsible family members. As has already been indicated, a knowledge of the patient's strengths and resources is important; in short, what qualities does the patient bring to treatment that can enhance the chances of improvement?

Because a wide range of factors can play important roles in causing and maintaining maladaptive behavior, assessment may involve the coordinated use of physical, psychological, and environmental assessment procedures. As we have indicated, however, the nature and comprehensiveness of clinical assessments vary according to the problem and the treatment agency's facilities. Assessment by phone in a suicide prevention center (Stelmachers, 1995), for example, is quite different from assessment aimed at determining whether a hospitalized patient is sufficiently intelligent, verbal, and psychologically minded to be likely to profit significantly from individual psychotherapy.

The Influence of Professional Orientation

How clinicians go about the assessment process often depends on their basic treatment orientations. For example, a biologically oriented clinician—typically a psychiatrist or other medical practitioner—will likely focus on biological assessment methods aimed at determining any underlying organic malfunctioning that may be causing the maladaptive behavior. A psychodynamic or psychoanalytically oriented clinician may choose unstructured personality assessment techniques, such as the Rorschach inkblots or the Thematic Apperception Test (TAT), to identify latent intrapsychic conflicts or they may simply proceed with therapy, expecting these conflicts to naturally emerge as part of the treatment process (see the Unresolved Issues Section at the end of this chapter). A behaviorally oriented clinician, in an effort to determine the functional relationships between environmental events or reinforcements and the abnormal behavior, will rely on such techniques as behavioral observation and systematic self-monitoring to identify maladaptive learned patterns; for a cognitively oriented behaviorist, the focus would shift to the dysfunctional thoughts supposedly mediating those patterns. A humanistically oriented clinician might use interview techniques to uncover blocked or distorted personal growth, and an interpersonally oriented clinician might use such techniques as personal confrontations and behavioral observations to pinpoint difficulties in interpersonal relationships.

The preceding examples represent general trends and are in no way meant to imply that clinicians of a particular orientation limit themselves to a particular assessment method or that each assessment technique is limited to a particular theoretical orientation. Such trends are instead a matter of emphasis and point to the fact that certain types of assessments are more conducive than others to uncovering particular causal factors, or for eliciting information about symptomatic behavior central to understanding and treating the disorder within a given conceptual framework.

As you will see in what follows, both physical and psychosocial data can be extremely important to understanding the patient in a clinical assessment evaluation. In the sections below we will examine in some detail an actual psychological study that has drawn on a variety of assessment data.

Trust and Rapport Between the Clinician and the Client

In order for psychological assessment to proceed effectively and provide a clear understanding of behavior and symptoms, the client being evaluated must feel comfortable with the clinician. In a clinical assessment situation this means that a client needs to feel that the testing will help the practitioner gain a clear understanding of his or her problems and to understand how the tests will be used and how the psychologist will incorporate them in the clinical evaluation. The clinician should explain what will happen during assessment and how the information gathered will help provide a clearer picture of the problems the client is facing.

It is important for the clinician to be aware of the fact that people being assessed in mental health settings are asked to provide a great deal of personal information about their feelings and behaviors. Clients need to be assured that the feelings, beliefs, attitudes, and personal history that they are disclosing will be used appropriately, kept in strict confidence, and made available only to therapists or others involved in the case. An important aspect of confidentiality is that the test results are only released to a third party if the client signs an appropriate release form. In cases in which the person is being tested for a third party, such as the court system, the client in effect becomes the referring source—the judge ordering the evaluation—not the individual being tested. In these cases the testing relationship is likely to be strained and rapport is likely to be difficult. Of course, in a court-ordered evaluation the person's test-taking behavior is likely to be very different from what it would be otherwise, and the test interpretation needs to reflect this different motivational set.

Clients being tested in a clinical situation are usually highly motivated to be evaluated and usually like to know the results of the testing. They usually are eager for some definition to their discomfort. Moreover, providing test feedback in a clinical setting can be an important element in the treatment process (Beutler, 1995). Interestingly, when patients are given appropriate feedback on test results, they tend to improve—just from gaining a perspective on their problems from the testing. The test feedback

process itself can be a powerful clinical intervention (Finn & Tonsager, 1997). When persons who were not provided psychological test feedback were compared with patients who were provided with feedback, the latter group showed a significant decline in reported symptoms and an increase in measured self-esteem as a result of having a clearer understanding of their own resources.

Assessment of the Physical Organism

In some situations or with certain psychological problems, a medical evaluation is necessary to rule out physical abnormalities that may be causing or contributing to the problem. The medical evaluation may include both a general physical and special examinations aimed at assessing the structural (anatomical) and functional (physiological) integrity of the brain as a behaviorally significant physical system (Rozensky, Sweet, & Tovian, 1997).

The General Physical Examination

A physical examination consists of the kinds of procedures most of us have experienced in getting a "medical checkup." Typically, a medical history is obtained and the major systems of the body are checked (DeGowin, 1994). This part of the assessment procedure is of obvious import for disorders that entail physical problems, such as somatoform, addictive, and organic brain syndromes. In addition, a variety of organic conditions, including various hormonal irregularities, can produce in some people behavioral symptoms that closely mimic those of mental disorders usually considered to have predominantly psychosocial origins. A case in point is the problem of chronic back pain in which psychological factors might play an important part. A diagnostic error in this type of situation resulting in surgery that proves ineffective could prove costly; hence, in equivocal cases most clinicians insist on a medical clearance before initiating psychosocially based interventions.

The Neurological Examination

Because brain pathology is sometimes involved or suspected to underlie some mental disorders, a specialized neurological examination can be given in addition to the general medical examination. This may involve getting an **electroencephalogram (EEG)** to assess brain-wave patterns in awake and sleeping states. An EEG is a graphic record of the brain's electrical activity. It is obtained by placing electrodes on the scalp and amplifying the minute brain-wave impulses from various brain areas; these amplified impulses drive oscillating pens whose deviations are traced on a strip of paper moving at a constant speed. Much is known about the normal pattern of brain impulses in waking and sleeping states and under various conditions of sensory stimulation. Significant divergences from the normal pattern can thus reflect abnormalities of brain function, such as might be caused by a brain tumor or other lesion. When an EEG reveals a **dysrhythmia** in the brain's electrical activity, other specialized techniques may be used in an attempt to arrive at a more precise diagnosis of the problem.

Anatomical Brain Scans Radiological technology, such as **computerized axial tomography,** known in brief as the **CAT scan,** is one of these specialized techniques. Through the use of X rays, a CAT scan reveals images of parts of the brain that might be diseased. This procedure has revolutionized neurological study in recent years by providing rapid access, without surgery, to accurate information about the localization and extent of anomalies in the brain's structural characteristics. The procedure involves the use of computer analysis applied to X-ray beams across sections of a patient's brain to produce images that a neurologist can then interpret.

CAT scans have been increasingly replaced by **magnetic resonance imaging (MRI)** as the technique of choice in detecting structural (anatomical) anomalies in the central nervous system, particularly the brain. The images of the interior of the brain are frequently sharper with MRI than with CAT because of the former's superior ability to differentiate subtle variations in soft tissue. In addition, the MRI procedure is normally far less complicated to administer, and it does not (like CAT) subject the patient to ionizing radiation or protracted X-ray of the site of interest and yet the images obtained are often decidedly clearer. Essentially, MRI involves the precise measurement of variations in magnetic fields that are caused by the varying amounts of water content of various organs and parts of organs. In this manner the anatomical structure of a cross section at any given plane through an organ such as the brain can be computed and graphically depicted with astonishing structural differentiation and clarity. MRI thus makes possible, by noninvasive means, visualization of all but the most minute abnormalities of brain structure. It has been particularly useful in confirming degenerative brain processes, as manifested, for example, in enlarged cerebrospinal fluid spaces within the brain. Therefore, MRI studies have considerable potential to illuminate the contribution of brain anomalies to "nonorganic" psychoses, such as schizophrenia, and some progress in this area has in fact been made, as noted in Chapter 12. The major problem encountered with MRI is that some patients have a claustrophobic reaction to being placed into the narrow cylin-

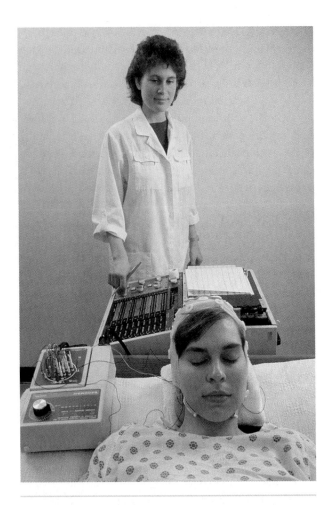

An electroencephalogram (EEG), a graphic record of the brain's electrical activity, is obtained by placing electrodes on the scalp that pick up brain impulses.

der of the MRI machine, necessitated for containing the magnetic field and blocking out external radio signals.

PET Scans: A Metabolic Portrait Another scanning technique is **positron emission tomography,** the **PET scan.** Though a CAT scan is limited to distinguishing anatomical features, such as the shape of a particular internal structure, a PET scan allows for an appraisal of how an organ is functioning by measuring metabolic processes (Mazziotta, 1996). The PET scan provides metabolic portraits by tracking natural compounds, like glucose, as they are metabolized by the brain or other organs. By revealing areas of differential metabolic activity, the PET scan enables a medical specialist to obtain more clear-cut diagnoses of brain pathology by, for example, pinpointing sites responsible for epileptic seizures, trauma from head injury or stroke, and brain tumors. Thus the PET scan may be able to reveal problems that are not immediately apparent anatomically. Moreover, the use of PET scans in research on brain pathology occurring in abnormal conditions such as schizophrenia, depression, and alcoholism has the potential of leading to important discoveries about the organic processes underlying these disorders, thus providing clues to more effective treatment (Zametkin & Liotta, 1997). Unfortunately, PET scans have been of limited value thus far because of the low fidelity pictures obtained. To date this procedure has been more valuable as a research technique than a clinical diagnostic procedure.

The Functional MRI   The technique known as **functional MRI (fMRI)** has only recently been developed and has not yet been extensively applied in the study of psychopathology. As originally developed and employed, MRI could reveal brain *structure* but not brain *activity*. For the latter, clinicians and investigators remained dependent on positron emission tomography (PET) scans, whose principal shortcoming is the very expensive requirement of having a cyclotron nearby to produce the short-lived radioactive atoms needed to carry out the procedure. The required introduction of radioactive substances, albeit short-lived ones, into the patient's body was also worrisome to many clinicians. It was apparent by the mid-1980s that adapting the MRI technique would be of tremendous advantage in revealing the workings of the brain as well as its anatomy, hence functional MRI (Bigler, 1996). This breakthrough, considered by many to be the most revolutionary of all the imaging techniques, was accomplished in the early 1990s, as reported in the *Harvard Health Letter* in January 1997.

The specific mechanisms underlying fMRI assessment (not to mention those involved in MRI itself) are too technical to be reviewed in detail here. Simply put, in its most common form fMRI measures changes in local oxygenation (i.e., blood flow) of specific areas of brain tissue that in turn depend on neuronal activity in those specific regions. Ongoing psychological activity, such as sensations, images, and thoughts can thus be "mapped," at least in principle, revealing the specific areas of the brain that appear to be involved in their neurophysiological mediation. Because the measurement of change in this context is critically time-dependent, the emergence of fMRI required the development of high-speed devices for enhancing the recording process as well as the computerized analysis of incoming data. These improvements are now widely available and will doubtless lead to a marked increase in studies of disordered persons using functional imaging.

To date, however, little has been published yet in the area of mental disorder, most of the work thus far having concentrated on mapping the visual area of the cerebral cortex (Kosslyn et al., 1993). This region is in fact believed to be involved in the processing of rapidly moving visual stimuli (as reading entails), thus providing a potentially important clue concerning the origins of reading disorders.

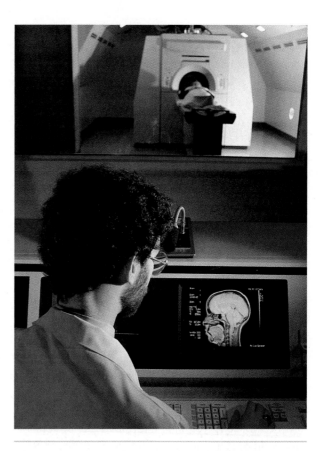

Until relatively recently our knowledge of human brain functioning has been acquired only through anatomical studies and inferences from behavior. Over the past decade rapidly evolving brain imagery technology, as shown in this picture, has been providing more detailed information about both the structure and the functioning of the human brain.

In another recently published study, also involving small samples, Breiter and colleagues (1996) reported abnormally high activation in several brain regions among obsessive-compulsive subjects when they were challenged with simulated "provocative" stimuli such as holding a "contaminated" towel. Unfortunately, even minimal head movement during critical phases of the examination precludes obtaining an adequate fMRI (or MRI) recording. Many mentally disordered patients are highly tense and agitated, particularly when challenged with stressors. In addition, many of the tasks mental health researchers might wish to employ in such assessments (e.g., approach to or avoidance of phobic stimuli) are not physically possible if the patient cannot move his or her head.

Several investigators have recently become involved in the use of fMRI to try to pinpoint areas of aberrant brain functioning in schizophrenia (McCarley et al., 1996). For example, Cohen and Green (1995) have reported an association between the occurrence of auditory hallucinations among persons diagnosed as schizophrenic and activation of brain centers believed to be involved in the reception of speech.

Given the unique advantages of fMRI brain imaging, mental health researchers will continue to find ways to cope with the relatively minor problems it poses for often distraught psychiatric patients. The scientific future of the approach thus appears ensured.

The Neuropsychological Examination

The techniques described so far are fairly accurate in identifying abnormalities in the brain's physical properties. Such abnormalities are very often accompanied by gross impairments in behavior and varied psychological deficits, although the nature of the latter may not be accurately predicted even after precisely localizing these physical abnormalities. Also, behavioral and psychological impairments due to organic brain abnormalities may become manifest before any organic brain lesion is detectable by scanning or other means. In these instances reliable techniques are needed to measure any alteration in behavioral or psychological functioning that has occurred because of the organic brain pathology. This need is met by a growing cadre of psychologists specializing in **neuropsychological assessment,** which involves the use of an expanding array of testing devices to measure a person's cognitive, perceptual, and motor performance as clues to the extent and location of brain damage (Grant & Adams, 1996; Spreen & Strauss, 1998).

In many instances of known or suspected organic brain involvement, a clinical neuropsychologist will administer a test battery to a patient. The person's performance on standardized tasks, particularly perceptual-motor ones, can give valuable clues about any cognitive and intellectual impairment following brain damage (LaRue & Swanda, 1997; Lezak, 1995; Reitan & Wolfson, 1985). Such testing can even provide clues as to the probable location of the brain damage, though PET scans, MRIs, and other physical tests are more effective in determining the exact location of the injury.

Many neuropsychologists prefer to select a highly individualized array of tests to administer, depending on a patient's case history and other available information. Others opt for a battery consisting of a standard set of tests that have been preselected so as to sample in a systematic and comprehensive manner a broad range of psychological competencies known to be adversely affected by various types of brain injury. The use of a constant set of tests has many research and clinical advantages, although it may compromise flexibility. One such standard procedure, widely used, is the Halstead-Reitan battery, whose components are described in Highlight 15.1.

Typically taking about six hours to administer, the Halstead-Reitan can be a problem in some clinical settings where time and funding are limited (Heaton, Grant,

& Matthews, 1991). Understandably, examinee fatigue may also be a limiting factor, particularly where a patient is not well. In some cases, other neuropsychological assessment measures that address more specific abilities or tasks such as memory (Psychological Corporation, 1997) or symptoms of dementia (Storandt & Vanden Bos, 1994) might be employed in lieu of the extensive battery. These instruments, as well as others of similar purpose and construction, provide their information without the risks attendant to more invasive neurological examination procedures. Despite these factors, the Halstead-Reitan battery continues to grow in use because it yields a great deal of useful information about a patient's cognitive and motor processes (LaRue & Swanda, 1997) that is not available through other means.

In summary, the medical and neuropsychological sciences are developing many new procedures to assess brain functioning and behavioral manifestations of organic disorder (Snyder & Nussbaum, 1998). Medical procedures to assess organic brain damage include EEGs and CAT, PET, and MRI scans. The new technology holds a great deal of promise for detecting and evaluating organic brain dysfunction and for providing increased understanding of brain functioning through graphic mapping of the brain. Neuropsychological testing provides a clinician with important behavioral information on how organic brain damage is affecting a person's present functioning. In cases where the psychological difficulty is thought to be the result of nonorganic causes psychosocial assessment is used.

Psychosocial Assessment

Psychosocial assessment attempts to provide a realistic picture of an individual in interaction with his or her social environment. This picture includes relevant information concerning the individual's personality makeup and present level of functioning, as well as information about the stressors and resources in his or her life situation. For example, early in the process, clinicians may act like puzzle solvers, absorbing as much information about the client as possible—present feelings, attitudes, memories, demographic facts, and so on—and trying to fit the pieces together into a meaningful pattern. They typically formulate hypotheses and discard or confirm them as they proceed. Starting with a global technique, such as a clinical interview described below, clinicians may later select more specific assessment tasks or tests. The following are some of the psychosocial procedures that may be used.

Assessment Interviews

An assessment interview, often considered the central element of the assessment process, usually involves a face-

Highlight 15.1

Neuropsychological Examinations: Determining Brain-Behavior Relationships

The Halstead-Reitan battery is a neuropsychological examination composed of several tests and variables from which an "index of impairment" can be computed (Reitan & Wolfson, 1985). In addition, it provides specific information about a subject's functioning in several skill areas. Though it typically takes 4 to 6 hours to complete and requires substantial administrative time, it is being used increasingly in neurological evaluations because it yields a great deal of useful information about an individual's cognitive and motor processes (LaRue & Swanda, 1997; Reitan & Wolfson, 1985). The Halstead-Reitan battery for adults is made up of the following tests:

1. *Halstead Category Test:* Measures a subject's ability to learn and remember material and can provide clues as to his or her judgment and impulsivity. The subject is presented with a stimulus (on a screen) that suggests a number between 1 and 4. The subject presses a button indicating the number they believe was suggested. A correct choice is followed by the sound of a pleasant doorbell and an incorrect choice by a loud buzzer. The person is required to determine from the pattern of buzzers and bells what the underlying principle of the correct choice is.
2. *Tactual Performance Test:* Measures a subject's motor speed, response to the unfamiliar, and ability to learn and use tactile and kinesthetic cues. The test consists of a board that has spaces for ten blocks of varied shapes. The subject

is blindfolded (never actually seeing the board) and asked to place the blocks into the correct grooves in the board. Later, the subject is asked to draw the blocks and the board from tactile memory.
3. *Rhythm Test:* Measures attention and sustained concentration through an auditory perception task. It is a subtest of Seashore's Test of musical talent and includes 30 pairs of rhythmic beats that are presented on a tape recorder. On this test, a subject is required to determine if the pairs are the same or different.
4. *Speech Sounds Perception Test:* Determines if an individual can identify spoken words. Nonsense words are presented on a tape recorder, and the subject is asked to identify the presented word from a list of four printed words. This task measures the subject's concentration, attention, and comprehension.
5. *The Finger Oscillation Task:* Measures the speed at which an individual can depress a lever with the index finger. Several trials are given with each hand.

In addition to the Halstead-Reitan battery, other tests, referred to as allied procedures, may be used in a neuropsychology laboratory. For example, Boll (1980) recommends the use of the modified Halstead-Wepman Aphasia Screening Test for obtaining information about a subject's language ability and about his or her abilities to identify numbers and body parts, to follow directions, to spell, and to pantomime simple actions. ■

to-face interaction in which a clinician obtains information about various aspects of a patient's situation, behavior, and personality makeup. The interview may vary from a simple set of questions or prompts, to a more extended and detailed format. It may be relatively open in character, with an interviewer making moment-to-

moment decisions about his or her next question based on responses to prior ones, or it may be more tightly controlled and structured so as to ensure that a particular set of questions is covered. In the latter case, the interviewer may choose from a number of highly structured, standardized interview formats whose reliability has been established in prior research. As used here, *reliability* means simply that two or more interviewers assessing the same client will generate highly similar conclusions about the client, a type of consensus that research shows can by no means be taken for granted.

Structured and Unstructured Interviews Although we know of few clinicians who express enthusiasm for the more controlled and structured type of assessment interview (preferring the freedom to explore as they feel responses merit), the research data show it to yield far more reliable results, in general, than the more flexible format. There appears to be widespread overconfidence among clinicians in the accuracy of their own methods and judgments (Garb, 1989; Taylor & Meux, 1997). On the other hand, every rule has its exceptions, and we have seen brilliantly conducted assessment interviews where each question was fashioned on the spur of the moment. In most instances, however, an assessor would be wise to conduct an interview that is carefully structured in terms of goals, comprehensive symptom review, other content to be explored, and the type of relationship the interviewer attempts to establish with the person. Such an approach is likely to minimize error over the long term, although we acknowledge that a more creative and spontaneous interview format may be more productive in particular clinical situations.

The reliability of the assessment interview may also be enhanced by the use of rating scales that help focus inquiry and quantify the interview data. For example, the

Whether one uses a structured or unstructured interview, it is important for those using this form of psychological assessment to have their goals clearly in mind and to attempt to establish a comprehensive list of symptoms and problems the person wishes to explore, and to pay attention to the kind of relationship that is being established in the interview.

person may be rated on a three-, five-, or seven-point scale with respect to self-esteem, anxiety, and various other characteristics. Such a structured and preselected format is particularly effective in giving a comprehensive impression or "profile" of the subject and his or her life situation, and in revealing specific problems or crises—such as marital difficulties, drug dependence, or suicidal fantasies—that may require immediate therapeutic intervention.

As already suggested, clinical interviews can be subject to error because they rely upon human judgment to choose the questions and process the information. Evidence of this unreliability includes the fact that different clinicians have often arrived at different formal diagnoses based on interview data they elicit for a particular patient. It is chiefly for this reason that recent versions of the DSM (that is, III, III-R, and IV) have emphasized an "operational" assessment approach, one that specifies observable criteria for diagnosis and provides specific guidelines for making diagnostic judgments. A clinician who is seeking to render a formal diagnosis thus must incorporate at least minimal structure into the interview or risk missing data essential to such a diagnosis. "Winging it" has limited use in this type of assessment process. Although the available data on the improved reliability of psychiatric diagnoses have shown the operational approach to have decided advantages, there has also doubtless been some cost in reducing interviewer flexibility and in encouraging undue preoccupation with observable "signs" at the expense of overall understanding of patient functioning.

Computerized Interviewing As was suggested in Chapter 1, the developments just described can be characterized as favoring the removal of the diagnostician, as a subjective judge, from the diagnostic process; to the degree possible, diagnosis is rendered "automatic." But if a human judge is unnecessary—perhaps even a troublesome source of error—then why not take the further step of computerizing the diagnostic process? Computers, after all, are superb at remembering and following explicitly stated rules for decision making. Where clinically feasible, they can even be used on-line to ask the same sorts of questions, and elicit the same sorts of answers, as would a human interviewer; that is, a patient can be "interviewed" by a computer terminal or console (Kobak, Taylor et al., 1997).

Substantial efforts of this sort have already been developed. Computer programs with highly sophisticated branching subroutines are available to "tailor-make" a diagnostic interview for a patient. Stein (1987), for example, described a program called the Computerized Diagnostic Interview for Children that can conduct a standard psychiatric interview. Several more specific clinical assessment tasks have been adapted for computer administration. For example, Fowler and colleagues (1987) have designed a Clinical Problem Checklist that can provide a therapist with an overview of a client's presenting symptoms. Allen and Skinner (1987) have designed a computer program that takes down a client's alcohol- and drug-abuse history, and Giannetti (1987) has a computer program that records a client's social history. All these programs are fairly easy to administer and can provide a clinician with a wealth of reliable and useful data. A computer-based diagnostic interview program for DSM-IV that can be quite valuable to the clinician conducting a diagnostic evaluation has also been published (First et al., 1997) (see Highlight 15.2).

Despite the progress made in reducing subjective factors by computerizing or otherwise making various aspects of the assessment process relatively automatic, it is important to understand that excessive reliance on such techniques can introduce error. The complexity of human behavior is bound to produce many exceptions to any rule. In the final analysis, therefore, there is probably no adequate substitute for expert clinical judgment. Where such judgment is available when needed, these techniques can substantially improve assessment efficiency.

The Clinical Observation of Behavior

One of the traditional and most useful assessment tools that a clinician has available is direct observation of a patient's characteristic behavior (Cone, 1998). The main purpose of direct observation is to learn more about the person's psychological functioning through the objective description of appearance and behavior in various contexts. Clinical observation refers to the clinician's objective description of the person's appearance and behavior—his or her personal hygiene, emotional responses, any depression, anxiety, aggression, hallucinations or delusions he or she may manifest. Ideally, clinical observation takes place in the natural environment (such as classroom or home) but it is more likely to take place upon admission to a clinic or hospital (Leichtman, 1995). For example, a brief description is usually made of a subject's behavior on hospital admission, and more detailed observations are made periodically on the ward.

In addition to making their own observations, many clinicians enlist their patients' help by providing instruction in **self-monitoring**—self-observation and objective reporting of behavior, thoughts, and feelings as they occur in various natural settings. Such a method can be a

valuable aid in determining the kinds of situations, possibly previously unrecognized, in which maladaptive behavior is likely to be evoked, and numerous studies also show it to have therapeutic benefits in its own right. Alternatively, a patient may be asked to fill out a more or less formal self-report or a checklist concerning problematic reactions experienced in various situations. Many instruments have been published in the professional literature and are commercially available to clinicians. These approaches recognize that people are excellent sources of information about themselves. Assuming that the right questions are asked and that people are willing to disclose information about themselves, the results can have a crucial bearing on treatment planning—for example, by providing essential information for structuring a behavioral or cognitive-behavioral treatment intervention.

Rating Scales   As in the case of interviews, the use of **rating scales** in clinical observation and in self-reports helps not only to organize information but also to encourage reliability and objectivity (Aiken, 1996). That is, the formal structure of a scale is likely to keep the observer inferences to a minimum. The most useful rating scales commonly used are those that enable a rater to indicate not only the presence or absence of a trait or behavior but also its prominence (Streiner & Norman, 1996). The following is an example of such a rating-scale item; the observer would check the most appropriate alternative.
Sexual behavior

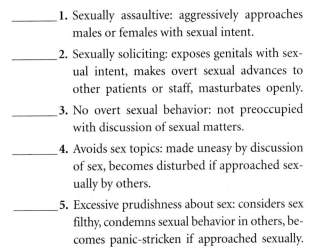

_____ 1. Sexually assaultive: aggressively approaches males or females with sexual intent.

_____ 2. Sexually soliciting: exposes genitals with sexual intent, makes overt sexual advances to other patients or staff, masturbates openly.

_____ 3. No overt sexual behavior: not preoccupied with discussion of sexual matters.

_____ 4. Avoids sex topics: made uneasy by discussion of sex, becomes disturbed if approached sexually by others.

_____ 5. Excessive prudishness about sex: considers sex filthy, condemns sexual behavior in others, becomes panic-stricken if approached sexually.

Ratings like these may be made not only as part of an initial evaluation but also to check on the course or outcome of treatment.

One of the rating scales most widely used for recording observations in clinical practice and in psychiatric research is the *Brief Psychiatric Rating Scale (BPRS).* The BPRS provides a structured and quantifiable format for

Clinical Diagnosis by Computer: The D-Tree

The process of clinical diagnosis can be a complicated and difficult one at times. The current clinical diagnosis system, DSM-IV, contains a number of explicit rules for each diagnostic category that define the symptoms and behavior that the patient must show to meet the particular diagnosis. The diagnostic system was developed in such a way that if the diagnostic criteria are explicitly followed the appropriate diagnostic "match" will be reliably made. One difficulty, of course, is that there are many different diagnostic categories with similar exclusion and inclusion rules. Therefore, the clinician needs to approach the classification task in a highly systematic manner—for example, following a branching strategy until the appropriate diagnostic classification is reached. The recommended diagnostic process follows a "decision tree" approach. Such an approach allows the practitioner to follow the hierarchial structure of DSM-IV and ask the appropriate questions for each diagnostic question until the most appropriate category is reached.

A decision tree begins with a set of particular clinical features. "When one of these features is a prominent part of the presenting clinical picture, the clinician can follow the series of questions to rule in or out various disorders" (American Psychiatric Association, 1994). Several standard decision trees are provided in DSM-IV—for example, a decision tree to develop a differential diagnosis of mental disorders due to a general medical condition and a decision tree to differentially diagnose psychotic disorders. The decision tree approach to classification is illustrated in Figure 15.1. The clinician follows the logical flowchart and determines the presence or absence of the criteria for the patient in question.

The branching strategy for the decision tree presents the clinician with a sequence of specific diagnostic questions such as "are hallucinations present," to which "yes"

or "no" responses determine the appropriate next question until a particular diagnosis is confirmed. Given the fact that a clinician can be presented with all of the appropriate questions in a systematic manner, this decision sequence could be asked and recorded in a very automatic, systematic way by a computer. The diagnostic process, in terms of the appropriate sequence of questions to address, has been demonstrated to be effectively accomplished by computer. Michael First, a noted psychiatrist who has a substantial background and education in computer programming, wrote a diagnostic program for DSM-III-R that came to be widely used by psychiatrists for both clinical assessment and training. He has recently revised this computer program, the D-Tree (First, Williams, & Spitzer, 1997) to provide DSM-IV diagnoses.

The D-Tree computer software is designed to guide the practitioner through the diagnostic process by presenting appropriate questions to the clinician. When all relevant information is provided, the computer gives the most likely DSM-IV diagnosis. If the clinician fails to provide the needed information in response to a question, the program halts and an instruction urges the clinician to seek the needed information. For example, if the D-Tree program requests information about whether the patient has had auditory hallucinations and the practitioner has failed to assess this area, then he or she might reinterview the patient to obtain the needed data. The D-Tree program has been a highly successful means of providing reliable clinical diagnoses as well as serving as a training guide for DSM-IV. Practitioners who use this computer aid soon become aware of the explicit rules to follow in developing DSM-IV diagnoses and the need to obtain clear verification of all the elements of a diagnosis before conclusions are reached about the patient. ■

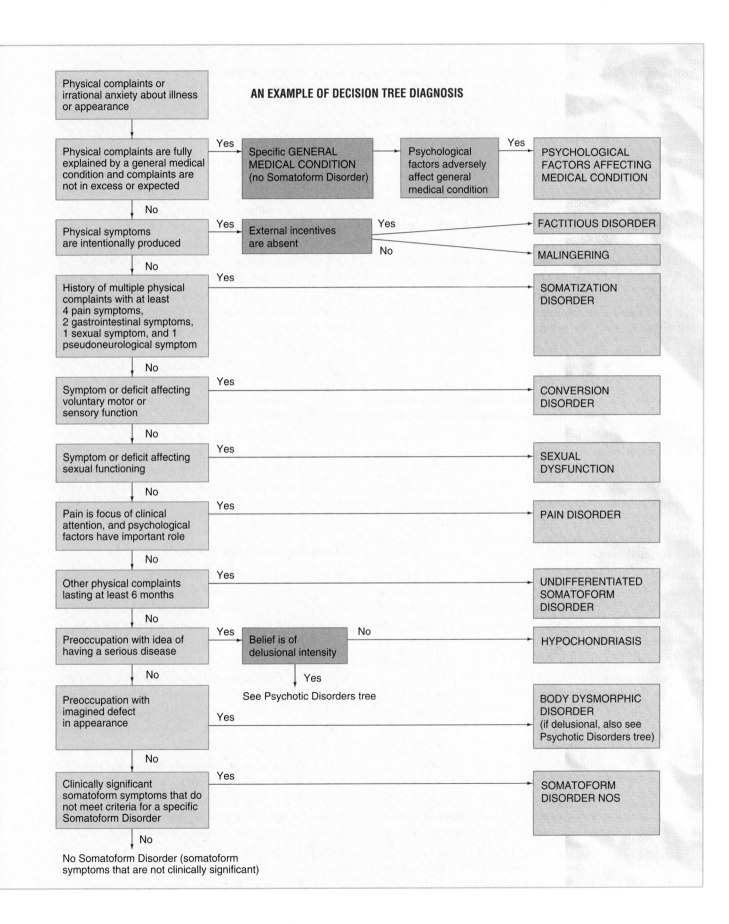

AN EXAMPLE OF DECISION TREE DIAGNOSIS

rating clinical symptoms, such as somatic concern, anxiety, emotional withdrawal, guilt feelings, hostility, suspiciousness, and unusual thought patterns. It contains 18 scales that are scored from ratings made by a clinician following an interview with a patient. The distinct patterns of behavior reflected in the BPRS ratings enable clinicians to make a standardized comparison of their patients' symptoms with the behavior of other psychiatric patients (Overall & Hollister, 1982). The BPRS has been found to be an extremely useful instrument in clinical research (for example, see Beauford, McNiel, & Binder, 1997; Inch, Crossley et al., 1997), especially for the purpose of assigning patients to treatment groups on the basis of similarity in symptoms, but it is not widely used for making treatment or diagnostic decisions in clinical practice. A similar but more specifically targeted instrument, the *Hamilton Rating Scale for Depression (HRSD)*, has become almost the standard in this respect for selecting clinically depressed research subjects, and also for assessing the response of such subjects to various treatments (see Otto, Fava et al., 1997).

Kinds of Clinical Observations Observations made in clinical settings by trained observers can provide behavioral data useful in ongoing clinical management (Gaynor, Baird, & Nelson-Gray, 1998). Paul and colleagues (Mariotto, Paul, & Licht, 1995; Paul & Lentz, 1977; Rich, Paul, & Mariotto, 1988), for example, have developed a comprehensive behavioral assessment program that they have implemented experimentally in a number of hospitals. The program includes evaluating the behavior of chronic patients and monitoring the activities of staff members working with them. Through the use of observational rating systems, they have been able to measure staff behavior in the daily management of patients and ongoing patient behavior on the ward. The behavioral ratings can be used to pinpoint specific behaviors to be changed on the part of members of either group.

The procedures described above focus on a subject's overt behavior, omitting the often equally important consideration of concurrent mental events—that is, the individual's ongoing thoughts. In an attempt to sample naturally occurring thoughts, psychologists are experimenting with having individuals carry small electronic beepers that produce a signal, such as a soft tone, at unexpected intervals. At each signal, the person is to write down or electronically record whatever thoughts the signal interrupted. These "thought reports" can then be analyzed in various ways, and they can be used for some kinds of personality assessment and diagnosis as well as

for monitoring progress in psychological therapy (Klinger & Kroll-Mensing, 1995).

In situations where it is not feasible to observe behavior in everyday settings—as when a subject is institutionalized—an entire family may be asked to meet together in the clinic or hospital where their interactions and difficulties can be observed and studied. In other cases, a social worker may obtain relevant data by visiting a subject's home, talking with family members and others, and observing the stressors and resources in the subject's life situation. In addition to providing important assessment data, this procedure incorporates the "observers" into the therapy program, thereby enhancing the therapy.

In still other situations where observation in a natural setting is not possible, a clinician may construct or contrive observational opportunities that can provide information about a person's response to particular circumstances. For example, a person who has a phobia for snakes might be placed in a situation where snake-like objects and pictures are presented to assess the severity of the fear and the extent of the avoidance behavior.

An often-used procedure that enables a clinician to observe a client's behavior directly is **role playing.** The client is instructed to play a part—for example, someone standing up for his or her rights. Role playing a situation like this not only can provide assessment information for the clinician but also can serve as a vehicle for new learning for the client.

Psychological Tests

Interviews and behavioral observation are relatively direct attempts to determine a person's beliefs, attitudes, and problems. Psychological tests, on the other hand, are a more indirect means of assessing psychological characteristics. Scientifically developed psychological tests (as opposed to the recreational ones sometimes appearing in newspapers and magazines) are standardized sets of procedures or tasks for obtaining samples of behavior; a subject's responses to the standardized stimuli are compared with those of other people having comparable demographic characteristics, usually through established test norms or test score distributions. From these comparisons, a clinician can then draw inferences about how much the person's psychological qualities differ from those of a reference group, typically a psychologically normal one. Among the characteristics these tests can measure are coping patterns, motive patterns, personality characteristics, role behaviors, values, levels of depression or anxiety, and intellectual functioning. Impressive ad-

A psychologist administering the WISC-III, an intelligence test that provides information about how well a child performs on a variety of cognitive challenges. An individually administered test such as this can require considerable time—often 2 to 3 hours—to give, score, and interpret; as such, it is appropriate to use these types of tests primarily when intelligence testing is considered critical to the diagnosis.

vances in the technology of test development have in fact made it possible to develop instruments of acceptable reliability and validity to measure almost any conceivable psychological characteristic on which people may vary.

Although psychological tests are more precise and often more reliable than interviews or some observational techniques, they are far from perfect tools. Their value often depends on the competence of the clinician who interprets them (see Highlight 15.3). In general, they are useful diagnostic tools for psychologists in much the same way that blood tests, X-ray films, or MRI scans are useful to physicians. In all these cases, pathology may be revealed in people who appear to be normal, or a general impression of "something wrong" can be checked against more precise information.

Two general categories of psychological tests for use in clinical practice are *intelligence tests* and *personality tests.* We discuss each in the following sections.

Intelligence Tests A clinician can choose from a wide range of intelligence tests. The Wechsler Intelligence Scale for Children–Revised (WISC–III) and the current edition of the Stanford-Binet Intelligence Scale are widely used in clinical settings for measuring the intellectual abilities of children. Probably the most commonly used test for measuring adult intelligence is the Wechsler Adult Intelligence Scale–Revised (WAIS–III) (Psychological Corporation, 1997). It includes both verbal and performance material and consists of 11 subtests. A brief description of two of the subtests will serve to illustrate the type of functions the WAIS–III measures:

- *Vocabulary (verbal):* This subtest consists of a list of words to define that are presented orally to the individual. This task is designed to evaluate the individual's vocabulary, which has been shown to be highly related to general intelligence.

- *Digit Span (performance):* This subtest, a test of short-term memory, consists of having a sequence of numbers administered orally. The individual is asked to repeat the digits in the order administered. Another task in this subtest involves remembering the numbers, holding them in memory, and reversing the order sequence—the individual is instructed to say them backwards (Psychological Corporation, 1997).

Individually administered intelligence tests—such as the WISC–III, WAIS–III, and the Stanford-Binet— typically require two to three hours to administer, score, and interpret. In many clinical situations, there is not sufficient time or funding to use these tests. In cases where intellectual impairment or organic brain damage is thought to be central to a patient's problem, intelligence testing may be the most crucial diagnostic procedure in the test battery. Moreover, information about cognitive functioning can provide valuable clues as to a person's intellectual resources in dealing with problems (Zetzer & Beutler, 1995). Yet in many clinical settings and for many clinical cases, gaining a thorough understanding of a client's problems and initiating a treatment program do not require knowing the kind of detailed information about intellectual functioning these instruments provide. In these cases, intelligence testing would not be recommended.

Projective Personality Tests There are a great many tests designed to measure personal characteristics other

The Automated Practice: Use of the Computer in Psychological Testing

Perhaps the most dramatic innovation in clinical assessment during the last 40 years has been the increasing sophistication and use of computers in individual assessment. As we have seen, computers are effectively used in assessment both to gather information directly from an individual and to put together and evaluate all the information that has been gathered previously through interviews, tests, and other assessment procedures (Bloom, 1992). By comparing the incoming information with data previously stored in its memory banks, a computer can perform a wide range of assessment tasks (Garb, 1995). It can supply a probable diagnosis, indicate the likelihood of certain kinds of behavior, suggest the most appropriate form of treatment, predict the outcome, and print out a summary report concerning the subject. In many of these functions, a computer is actually superior to a clinician because it is more efficient and accurate in recalling stored material.

With the increased efficiency and reliability accompanying the use of computers in clinical practice, one might expect a near unanimous welcoming of computers into the clinic. This is not completely the case, however, and some practitioners we know even resist the use of "modern" techniques such as E-mail, fax machines, and computerized billing in their practice. We will discuss these general issues in turn. (McMinn, Buchanan et al., 1999.)

Some clinicians are reluctant to use computer-based test interpretations in spite of their demonstrated utility and low cost. Even though many clinics and independent practitioners use microcomputers for record keeping and billing purposes, a smaller number incorporate computer-based clinical assessment procedures into their practice. Possible reasons for the underutilization of computer-based assessment procedures include the following:

- Practitioners trained before the computer age may feel uncomfortable with computers or may not have time to become acquainted with them.

- Many practitioners limit their practice to psychological treatment and do not do extensive pretreatment assessments of their cases. Many also have little interest in, or time for, the systematic evaluation of treatment efficacy that periodic formal assessments would facilitate.

- To some clinicians the impersonal and mechanized look of the booklets and answer sheets common to much computerized assessment is contrary to the image and style of warm and personal engagement they hope to convey to clients.

- Some clinicians view computer-based assessment as a threat to their own functioning. Some are concerned that computer-assessment specialists seek to replace human diagnostic functioning with automated reports (Matarazzo, 1986). Others are concerned that less well-qualified practitioners may use such reports and "set up shop" as competitors.

Some of these concerns are not unlike those expressed by many craftspersons or production personnel in industry when computers and robots come to the workplace. Are human mental health practitioners in danger of being replaced by computers? Not at all. Computers in psychological assessment have intrinsic limitations consigning them to an accessory role in the process; they would not be useful, in fact quite the contrary, if employed as the sole means of evaluation. It is the clinician who must assume the major organizing role and accept the responsibility for an assessment. An unqualified person wholly dependent on computerized reports for carrying on a practice would quickly be identified as incompetent by discerning referral sources, and probably by most self-referred clients; a thriving practice would not be a likely outcome. On the other hand, judicious use of computerized assessment can free up much time for doing those things that can only be accomplished by the personal application of high levels of clinical skill and wisdom (Carson, 1990b). ■

than intellectual facility. It is customary to group these personality tests into projective and objective tests. **Projective tests** are unstructured in that they rely on various ambiguous stimuli, such as inkblots or pictures, rather than explicit verbal questions, and the person's responses are not limited to the "true," "false," or "cannot say" variety. Through their interpretations of these ambiguous materials, people reveal a good deal about their personal preoccupations, conflicts, motives, coping techniques, and other personality characteristics. An assumption underlying the use of projective techniques is that in trying to make sense out of vague, unstructured stimuli, individuals "project" their own problems, motives, and wishes into the situation, inasmuch as they have little else on which to rely in formulating their responses to these materials (Lerner, 1995). Such responses are akin to the childhood pastime of detecting familiar scenes in cloud formations, with the important exception that the stimuli are in this case fixed and largely the same for all subjects. It is the latter circumstance that permits determination of the normative range of responses to the test materials, which in turn can be used to identify objectively deviant responding. Thus projective tests are aimed at discovering the ways in which an individual's past learning and personality structure may lead him or her to organize and perceive ambiguous information from the environment. Prominent among the several projective tests in common use are the Rorschach Test, the Thematic Apperception Test, and sentence-completion tests.

The Rorschach The **Rorschach Test** is named after the Swiss psychiatrist Hermann Rorschach, who initiated experimental use of inkblots in personality assessment in 1911. The test uses ten inkblot pictures to which a subject responds in succession after being instructed as follows (Exner, 1993):

> People may see many different things in these inkblot pictures; now tell me what you see, what it makes you think of, what it means to you.

The following excerpts are taken from the responses of a subject to one of the actual blots:

> This looks like two men with genital organs exposed. They have had a terrible fight and blood has splashed up against the wall. They have knives or sharp instruments in their hands and have just cut up a body. They have already taken out the lungs and other organs. The body is dismembered . . . nothing remains but a shell . . . the pelvic region. They were fighting as to who will complete the final dismemberment . . . like two vultures swooping down . . . .

The Rorschach Test, which uses inkblots similar to those illustrated here, is a well-known projective test.

The extremely gory, violent content of this response was not common for the particular blot, nor for any other blot in the series. While no responsible examiner would base conclusions on a single instance, such content was consistent with other data from this subject, who was diagnosed as an antisocial personality with strong hostility.

Use of the Rorschach in clinical assessment is complicated and requires considerable training (Exner & Weiner, 1995; Weiner, 1998). Methods of administering the test vary, and some approaches can take several hours and hence must compete for time with other essential clinical services. Furthermore, the results of the Rorschach can be unreliable because of the subjective nature of test interpretations. For example, interpreters might disagree on the symbolic significance to a particular response "a house in flames." One person might interpret this particular response as suggesting great feelings of anxiety whereas another interpreter might see the response as suggesting a desire on the part of the patient to set fires. Another reason for the diminished use in projective testing today comes from the fact that many clinical treatments used in today's mental health facilities

FIGURE 15.1

```
SUBJECT NAME:ESTEBAN.MMPI                AGE:21  SEX:M  RACE:W  MS:Sin  ED:14


              SEMANTIC INTERPRETATION OF THE RORSCHACH
              PROTOCOL UTILIZING THE COMPREHENSIVE SYSTEM
              (COPYRIGHT 1976, 1985 BY JOHN E. EXNER, JR.)


     THE FOLLOWING COMPUTER-BASED INTERPRETATION IS DERIVED ** EXCLUSIVELY **
FROM THE STRUCTURAL DATA OF THE RECORD AND DOES NOT INCLUDE CONSIDERATION OF
THE SEQUENCE OF SCORES OR THE VERBAL MATERIAL. IT IS INTENDED AS A GUIDE FROM
WHICH THE INTERPRETER OF THE TOTAL PROTOCOL CAN PROCEED TO STUDY AND REFINE
THE HYPOTHESES GENERATED FROM THESE ACTUARIAL FINDINGS.


                             * * * * *

 1.  THE RECORD APPEARS TO BE VALID AND INTERPRETIVELY USEFUL.

 2.  THIS IS THE TYPE OF PERSON WHO IS PRONE TO TRY TO OVERSIMPLIFY STIMULI
     IN ORDER TO MAKE THE WORLD LESS THREATENING AND/OR DEMANDING.  THIS
     BASIC COPING STYLE TENDS TO BE PERVASIVE WHEN NEW SITUATIONS AND/OR
     STRESSES OCCUR. WHEN DONE TO EXCESS, AS APPEARS TO BE THE CASE HERE,
     THE SUBJECT IS LIKELY TO EXPERIENCE FREQUENT SOCIAL DIFFICULTIES
     BECAUSE THE STYLE PROMOTES A NEGLECT OF THE DEMANDS AND/OR
     EXPECTATIONS OF THE ENVIRONMENT.

 3.  THIS SUBJECT USUALLY HAS ENOUGH RESOURCE ACCESSABLE TO PARTICIPATE
     MEANINGFULLY IN THE FORMULATION AND DIRECTION OF RESPONSES.  TOLERANCE
     FOR STRESS IS LIKE THAT OF MOST PEOPLE, THAT IS, CONTROLS USUALLY WILL
     NOT FALTER UNLESS THE STRESS IS UNEXPECTED AND INTENSE OR PROLONGED
     UNREASONABLY.

 4.  THERE IS EVIDENCE INDICATING THE PRESENCE OF CONSIDERABLE SUBJECTIVELY
     FELT DISTRESS.

 5.  THIS SUBJECT TENDS TO INTERNALIZE FEELINGS MUCH MORE THAN IS CUSTOMARY
     AND THIS OFTEN RESULTS IN SUBSTANTIAL DISCOMFORT THAT CAN TAKE THE
     FORM OF TENSION AND/OR ANXIETY.

 6.  THIS IS THE TYPE OF PERSON WHO PREFERS TO DELAY MAKING RESPONSES IN
     COPING SITUATIONS UNTIL TIME HAS BEEN ALLOWED TO CONSIDER RESPONSE
     POSSIBILITIES AND THEIR POTENTIAL CONSEQUENCES.  SUCH PEOPLE LIKE TO
     KEEP THEIR EMOTIONS ASIDE UNDER THESE CONDITIONS.

 7.  THIS PERSON TENDS TO USE DELIBERATE THINKING MORE FOR THE PURPOSE OF
     CREATING FANTASY THROUGH WHICH TO IGNORE THE WORLD THAN TO CONFRONT
     PROBLEMS DIRECTLY. THIS IS A SERIOUS PROBLEM BECAUSE THE BASIC COPING
     STYLE IS BEING USED MORE FOR FLIGHT THAN TO ADAPT TO THE EXTERNAL
     WORLD.

 8.  THIS TYPE OF PERSON IS NOT VERY FLEXIBLE IN THINKING, VALUES, OR
     ATTITUDES.   IN EFFECT, PEOPLE SUCH AS THIS HAVE SOME DIFFICULTY IN
     SHIFTING PERSPECTIVES OR VIEWPOINTS.
=============================================================================
(c)1976, 1985 by John E. Exner, Jr.
```

```
SUBJECT NAME:ESTEBAN.MMPI                AGE:21  SEX:M  RACE:W  MS:Sin  ED:14
     PAGE -3-

=============================================================================
     IMPULSIVENESS ALTHOUGH SOME DECISIONS AND BEHAVIORS THAT RESULT MAY
     HAVE THAT FEATURE.  IT IS A CONSEQUENCE OF NEGLECT IN SCANNING AND
     ORGANIZING TACTICS WHICH MAY BE THE PRODUCT OF A PERCEPTUAL DEFICIT,
     PSYCHOLOGICAL HABITS DEVELOPED EARLY IN LIFE, OR CAN BE A FUNCTION OF
     COGNITIVE DISARRAY PROVOKED BY NEUROLOGICALLY RELATED OR
     PSYCHOPATHOLOGICAL PROBLEMS. IT SHOULD ALSO BE NOTED FOR THIS SUBJECT
     THAT THE COMPOSITE OF HASTY SCANNING OF STIMULUS FIELDS PLUS LIMITED
     EMOTIONAL CONTROLS IS ONE IMPORTANT FACTOR THAT LEADS TO IMPULSIVE
     LIKE BEHAVIORS.

20.  THIS PERSON USUALLY SEEKS AN ECONOMICAL APPROACH TO PROBLEM SOLVING OR
     COPING BY FOCUSING MORE ON THE EASILY MANAGED ASPECTS OF A SITUATION
     AND TENDING TO NEGLECT BROADER ISSUES THAT MAY BE PRESENT.  THIS IS
     TYPICAL OF MANY PEOPLE AND CAN BE AN ASSET.  HOWEVER, IT CAN ALSO
     BECOME A LIABILITY IN MORE COMPLEX AND DEMANDING SITUATIONS THAT
     REQUIRE HIGHER LEVELS OF MOTIVATION AND EFFORT TO ACHIEVE EFFECTIVE
     RESULTS.

21.  THIS PERSON IS SOMEWHAT CONSERVATIVE IN SETTING GOALS.  USUALLY PEOPLE
     LIKE THIS WANT TO COMMIT THEMSELVES ONLY TO OBJECTIVES WHICH OFFER A
     SIGNIFICANT PROBABILITY OF SUCCESS.

22.  THIS PERSON TENDS TO USE INTELLECTUALIZATION AS A BASIC TACTIC TO
     CONTEND WITH EMOTIONAL THREATS AND STRESSES. PEOPLE LIKE THIS ARE
     OFTEN VERY RESISTIVE DURING EARLY PHASES OF INTERVENTION AS THIS
     TENDENCY TOWARD DENIAL CAUSES THEM TO AVOID ANY AFFECTIVE
     CONFRONTATIONS.

                    * * *  END OF REPORT  * * *




=============================================================================
(c)1976, 1985 by John E. Exner, Jr.
```

FIGURE 15.1

Semantic interpretation of the Rorschach protocol utilizing the comprehensive system.

```
SUBJECT NAME:ESTEBAN.MMPI                AGE:21  SEX:M  RACE:W  MS:Sin  ED:14
     PAGE -2-

=============================================================================
 9.  THERE IS A STRONG POSSIBILITY THAT THIS IS A PERSON WHO PREFERS TO
     AVOID INITIATING BEHAVIORS, AND INSTEAD, TENDS TOWARDS A MORE PASSIVE
     ROLE IN PROBLEM SOLVING AND INTERPERSONAL RELATIONSHIPS.

10.  THIS SUBJECT DOES NOT MODULATE EMOTIONAL DISPLAYS AS MUCH AS MOST
     ADULTS AND, BECAUSE OF THIS, IS PRONE TO BECOME VERY INFLUENCED BY
     FEELINGS IN MOST THINKING, DECISIONS, AND BEHAVIORS.

11.  THIS IS A PERSON WHO IS VERY ATTRACTED TO BEING AROUND EMOTIONAL
     STIMULI. THIS MAY POSE A SIGNIFICANT PROBLEM IN ADAPTATION BECAUSE OF
     PROBLEMS IN CONTROL. THAT IS, THE MORE EMOTIONAL STIMULI BEING
     PROCESSED, THE GREATER THE DEMAND FOR EMOTIONAL EXCHANGE. IF THAT
     EXCHANGE IS NOT WELL CONTROLLED, PROBLEMS CAN EASILY OCCUR.

12.  THIS IS AN INDIVIDUAL WHO DOES NOT EXPERIENCE NEEDS FOR CLOSENESS IN
     WAYS THAT ARE COMMON TO MOST PEOPLE.  AS A RESULT, THEY ARE TYPICALLY
     LESS COMFORTABLE IN INTERPERSONAL SITUATIONS, HAVE SOME DIFFICULTIES
     IN CREATING AND SUSTAINING DEEP RELATIONSHIPS, ARE MORE CONCERNED WITH
     ISSUES OF PERSONAL SPACE, AND MAY APPEAR MUCH MORE GUARDED AND/OR
     DISTANT TO OTHERS.

13.  THIS SUBJECT HAS AS MUCH INTEREST IN OTHERS AS DO MOST ADULTS AND
     CHILDREN. HOWEVER, THE SUBJECT DOES NOT APPEAR TO HAVE A VERY
     REALISTIC UNDERSTANDING OF PEOPLE.  INSTEAD, CONCEPTIONS OF OTHERS
     TEND TO BE DERIVED MORE FROM IMAGINATION THAN FROM REAL EXPERIENCE.

14.  THIS SUBJECT APPEARS TO HAVE AN UNUSUAL BODY PREOCCUPATION.

15.  THIS SUBJECT APPEARS TO HAVE A MARKED SEXUAL PREOCCUPATION.

16.  THIS SUBJECT IS VERY PRONE TO INTERPRET STIMULUS CUES IN A UNIQUE AND
     OVERPERSONALIZED MANNER.  PEOPLE SUCH AS THIS OFTEN VIEW THEIR WORLD
     WITH THEIR OWN SPECIAL SET OF BIASES AND ARE LESS CONCERNED WITH BEING
     CONVENTIONAL AND/OR ACCEPTABLE TO OTHERS.

17.  IN SPITE OF THE ABOVE MENTIONED TENDENCY TO MISINTERPRET OR OVERPERSON-
     ALIZE THE INTERPRETATION OF STIMULUS CUES, THE SUBJECT DOES TEND TO
     RESPOND IN CONVENTIONAL WAYS TO SITUATIONS IN WHICH CONVENTIONAL OR
     EXPECTED RESPONSES ARE OBVIOUS AND EASILY IDENTIFIED.

18.  MUCH OF THE COGNITIVE ACTIVITY OF THIS SUBJECT IS LESS SOPHISTICATED
     OR LESS MATURE THAN IS EXPECTED. THIS MAY BE A FUNCTION OF A
     DEVELOPMENTAL LAG, DISORGANIZATION, OR MAY SIMPLY REFLECT A RELUCTANCE
     TO COMMIT RESOURCES TO A TASK.

19.  THIS SUBJECT TENDS TO SCAN A STIMULUS FIELD HASTILY AND NOT
     METHODICALLY.  THESE KINDS OF PEOPLE OFTEN COME TO DECISIONS
     PREMATURELY AND ERRONEOUSLY SIMPLY BECAUSE THEY HAVE NOT PROCESSED ALL
     AVAILABLE INFORMATION ADEQUATELY.  THIS SHOULD NOT BE CONFUSED WITH
=============================================================================
(c)1976, 1985 by John E. Exner, Jr.
```

generally require specific behavioral descriptions rather than descriptions of deep-seated personality dynamics, such as those that typically result from Rorschach Test interpretation.

The Rorschach has been criticized, to some extent unfairly, as an instrument with low or negligible validity. In the hands of a skilled interpreter, the Rorschach has been shown to be useful in uncovering certain psychodynamic issues, such as the impact of unconscious motivations on current perceptions of others. Furthermore, there have been attempts to move beyond the original discursive and free-wheeling interpretive approaches and to objectify Rorschach interpretations by clearly specifying test variables and empirically exploring their relationship to external criteria, such as clinical diagnosis (Exner, 1995). However, the extent to which the Rorschach provides valid information beyond what is available from other, more economical instruments, has not been demonstrated.

The Rorschach, although generally considered an open-ended, subjective instrument aimed at studying a person's personality as a uniquely organized system ("idiographically"), has recently been adapted for computer interpretation. Exner (1987) has developed a computer-based interpretation system for the

Rorschach that, after scored responses are input, provides scoring summaries and a listing of likely personality descriptions and references about a person's adjustment (see Figure 15.1). The Exner Comprehensive Rorschach System may answer the criticism that Rorschach interpretation is unreliable, because the computer output provides a reliable and invariant set of descriptors for any given set of Rorschach scores. Assuming that clinicians agree on the scoring of particular responses, the computer outputs—that is, the interpretations—will be the same. Butcher and Rouse (1996) recently reviewed the clinical assessment research literature over the past 20 years including the major clinical assessment methods and found that the Rorschach was the second most frequently researched clinical instrument, the MMPI/MMPI-2 (discussed below) being first.

The Thematic Apperception Test The **Thematic Apperception Test (TAT)** was introduced in 1935 by its coauthors, C.D. Morgan and Henry Murray of the Harvard Psychological Clinic. It still is widely used in clinical practice today (Rossini & Moretti, 1997). The TAT uses a series of simple pictures, some highly representational and others quite abstract, about which a subject is instructed to make up stories. The content of the pictures, much of it depicting people in various contexts, is highly ambiguous as to actions and motives, so that subjects tend to project their own conflicts and worries into it.

Several scoring and interpretation systems have been developed to focus on different aspects of a subject's stories, such as expressions of needs (Atkinson, 1992), the person's perception of reality (Arnold, 1962), and the person's fantasies (Klinger, 1979). Generally these systems are time-consuming, and little evidence shows that they make a clinically significant contribution. Hence, most often a clinician simply makes a qualitative and subjective determination of how the story content reflects the person's underlying traits, motives, and preoccupations. Such interpretations often depend as much on "art" as on "science," and there is much room for error in such an informal procedure.

An example of the way a subject's problems may be reflected in TAT stories is shown in the following case, which is based on Card 1 (a picture of a boy staring at a violin on a table in front of him). The client, David, was a 15-year-old boy who had been referred to the clinic by his parents because of their concern about his withdrawal and poor work at school:

The Thematic Apperception Test (TAT) asks a subject to develop stories about the people depicted in a series of drawings. The patient's stories about the people shown in the cards are thought to reflect personality characteristics, motives, beliefs, attitudes, problems, and symptoms of the person taking the test.

Case Study, David's TAT Response • David was generally cooperative during the testing although he remained rather unemotional and unenthusiastic throughout. When he was given Card 1 of the TAT, he paused for over a minute, carefully scrutinizing the card.

"I think this is a . . . uh . . . machine gun . . . yeah, it's a machine gun. The guy is staring at it. Maybe he got it for his birthday or stole it or something." [Pause. The examiner reminded him that he was to make up a story about the picture.]

"OK. This boy, I'll call him Karl, found this machine gun . . . a Browning automatic rifle . . . in his garage. He kept it in his room for protection. One day he decided to take it to school to quiet down the jocks that lord it over everyone. When he walked into the locker hall, he cut loose on the top jock, Amos, and wasted him. Nobody bothered him after that because they knew he kept the BAR in his locker."

It was inferred from this story that David was experiencing a high level of frustration and anger in his life. The extent of this anger was reflected in his perception of the violin in the picture as a machine gun—a potential instrument of violence. The clinician concluded that David was feeling threatened not only by people at school but even in his own home where he needed "protection." This example shows how stories based on TAT cards may provide a clinician with information about a person's conflicts and worries as well as clues as to how the person is handling these problems.

The TAT has been criticized on several grounds in recent years. There is a "dated" quality to the test stimuli: the pictures, developed in the 1930s, appear quaint to many contemporary subjects who have difficulty identifying with the characters in the pictures. Subjects will often preface their stories with, "This is something from a movie I saw on the Late Show." Additionally, the TAT can require a great deal of time to administer and interpret. Interpretation of responses to the TAT is generally subjective and limits the reliability and validity of the test. Again, however, we must note that some examiners, notably those who have long experience in the instrument's use, are capable of astonishingly accurate interpretations with TAT stories. Typically, they have difficulty in teaching these skills to others. On reflection, such an observation should not be unduly surprising, but it does point to the essentially "artistic" element involved at this skill level.

Sentence Completion Test Another projective procedure that has proved useful in personality assessment is the **sentence-completion test.** There are a number of such tests designed for children, adolescents, and adults (for example, see Novy, Blumentritt et al., 1997). Such tests consist of the beginnings of sentences that a subject is asked to complete, as in these examples:

1. I wish _____
2. My mother _____
3. Sex _____
4. I hate_____
5. People_____

Sentence-completion tests, linked somewhat to the free-association method, are somewhat more structured than the Rorschach and most other projective tests. They help examiners pinpoint important clues to an individual's problems, attitudes, and symptoms through the content of his or her responses. Interpretation of the item responses, however, is generally subjective and unreliable. Despite the fact that the test stimuli (the sentence stems) are standard, interpretation is usually done in an ad hoc manner and without benefit of norms.

In sum, projective tests have an important place in many clinical settings, particularly those that attempt to obtain a comprehensive picture of a person's psychodynamic functioning and have the necessary trained staff to conduct extensive individual psychological evaluations. The great strengths of projective techniques—their unstructured nature and their focus on the unique aspects of personality—are at the same time their weaknesses because they make interpretation subjective, unreliable, and difficult to validate. Moreover, projective tests typically require a great deal of time to administer and advanced skill to interpret—both scarce quantities in many clinical settings.

Objective Personality Tests **Objective tests** are structured—that is, they typically use questionnaires, self-inventories, or rating scales in which questions or items are carefully phrased and alternative responses are specified as choices. They therefore involve a far more controlled format than projective devices and thus are more amenable to objectively based quantification. One virtue of such quantification is that of precision, which in turn enhances the reliability of test outcomes.

The MMPI One of the major structured inventories for personality assessment is the **Minnesota Multiphasic Personality Inventory (MMPI),** now called the **MMPI-2** after a revision in 1989. We focus on it here because in many ways it is the prototype and the standard of this class of instruments.

Several years in development, the MMPI was introduced for general use in 1943 by Starke Hathaway and J. C. McKinley; it is today the most widely used personality test for both clinical assessment and psychopathology research in the United States (Lees-Haley, Smith et al., 1996; Piotrowski & Keller, 1992) and is the assessment instrument most frequently taught in graduate clinical psychology programs (Piotrowski & Zalewski, 1993). Moreover, translated versions of the inventory are widely used internationally (the original MMPI was translated into more than 115 languages and used in over 46 countries, Butcher, 1984). International use of the revised inventory is increasing at a fast rate with over 25 translations since it was published in 1989 (Butcher, 1996).

The original MMPI, a kind of self-report technique, consisted of 550 items covering topics ranging from physical condition and psychological states to moral and social attitudes. Normally, subjects are encouraged to answer all of the items either *true* or *false.* Some sample items follow:

I sometimes keep on at a thing until others lose their patience with me.   T F

Bad words, often terrible words, come into my mind and I cannot get rid of them.   T F

I often feel as if things were not real.   T F

Someone has it in for me.   T F

(Hathaway & McKinley, 1951, p. 28)

The Clinical Scales of the MMPI The pool of items for the MMPI was originally administered to a large group of normal individuals (affectionately called the "Minnesota normals") and several quite homogeneous groups of patients having particular psychiatric diagnoses. Answers to all the items were then item-analyzed to see which ones differentiated the various groups. On the basis of the findings, ten clinical scales were constructed each consisting of the items that were answered by one of the patient groups in the direction opposite to the predominant response of the normal group. This rather ingenious method of scorable item selection, known as *empirical keying,* was original to the MMPI and doubtless accounts for much of the instrument's power. Note that it involves no subjective prejudgment about the "meaning" of a true or false answer to any item; that meaning resides entirely in whether or not the answer is the same as that deviantly given by patients of varying diagnoses. Should an examinee's pattern of true/false responses closely approximate that of a particular pathological group, it is a reasonable inference that he or she shares other psychiatrically significant characteristics with that group—and may in fact "psychologically" be a member of that group. (See the MMPI-2 profile of Esteban in Highlight 15.4.)

Each of these ten "clinical" scales thus measures tendencies to respond in psychologically deviant ways. Raw scores on these scales are compared with the corresponding scores of the normal population, many of whom did (and do) answer a few items in the critical direction, and the results are plotted on the standard MMPI profile form. By drawing a line connecting the scores for the different scales, a clinician can construct a profile that shows how far from normal a patient's performance is on each of the scales. The *Schizophrenia scale,* for example (and to reiterate the basic strategy), is made up of the items that schizophrenic patients consistently answered in a way that differentiated them from normal individuals. People who score high (relative to norms) on this scale, though not necessarily schizophrenic, often show

propensities typical of the schizophrenic population. For instance, high scorers on this scale may be socially inept, withdrawn, and have peculiar thought processes; they may have diminished contact with reality and in severe cases may have delusions and hallucinations.

The MMPI also includes a number of validity scales to detect whether a patient has answered the questions in a straightforward, honest manner. For example, there is one scale that detects lying or claiming extreme virtue as well as several scales to detect faking or malingering. Extreme endorsement of the items on any of these scales may invalidate the test, while lesser endorsements frequently contribute important interpretive insights. In addition to the validity scales and the ten clinical scales, a number of "special" problem scales have been devised—for example to detect problems of substance abuse, marital distress, and posttraumatic stress disorder.

Clinically, the MMPI is used in several ways to evaluate a patient's personality characteristics and clinical problems. Perhaps the most typical use of the MMPI is as a *diagnostic standard.* As we have seen, the individual's profile pattern is compared with profiles of known patient groups. If the profile matches a group, information about patients in this group can suggest a broad *descriptive diagnosis* for the patient under study. Another approach to MMPI interpretation, *content interpretation,* is used to supplement the empirical correlates provided in the described approach. Here, a clinician focuses on the content themes in a person's response to the inventory. For example, if an individual endorses an unusually large number of items about fears, a clinician might well conclude that the subject is preoccupied with fear.

Criticisms of the MMPI The original MMPI, in spite of being the most widely used personality measure, has not been without its critics. Some psychodynamically oriented clinicians felt that the MMPI (like other structured, objective tests) was superficial and did not adequately reflect the complexities of an individual taking the test. Some behaviorally oriented critics, on the other hand, criticized the MMPI, and in fact the entire genre of personality tests, as being too oriented toward measuring unobservable "mentalistic" constructs, such as traits.

A more specific criticism was leveled at the datedness of the MMPI. (The original MMPI dated from the early 1940s.) In response to these criticisms, the publisher of

Esteban's MMPI-2 Profile and Computer-Based Report

Esteban was first tested with the original MMPI. His responses from that testing were converted to the MMPI-2 format by J. N. Butcher (1993). The computer-based report for the MMPI-2 norms is provided. The validity scales are shown in Figure 15.2 in the left column in which the word "MALE" appears). The clinical scales are to the right. The special scales are not included in this version of the profile. (Table 15.1 on page 606 describes each of these scales.) Based on the scores originally obtained and those you see displayed in the chart, a computer produced the narrative descriptions given here. Hypotheses about the psychological functioning of Esteban from a computer-generated report of his Rorschach protocol performed by the Exner Comprehensive Rorschach System are presented on page 600–601.

Computer-Based Report: The MMPI-2

Profile Validity

This MMPI-2 profile should be interpreted with caution. There is some possibility that the clinical report is an exaggerated picture of Esteban's present situation. He presented an unusual number of psychological problems and symptoms. His test-taking attitudes should be evaluated to determine if his response pattern is a valid approach to the testing. This extreme response set could result from poor reading ability, confusion, disorientation, stress, or a need to seek attention for his problems. Clinical patients with this profile are often confused and distractible, and they show memory problems. Evidence of delusions and thought disorder may be present.

Symptomatic Pattern

Esteban's MMPI-2 profile reflects a high degree of psychological distress at this time. The client is presenting with a mixed pattern of psychological symptoms. He appears to be tense, apathetic, and withdrawn, and is experiencing some personality deterioration. He seems to be quite confused and disorganized, and probably secretly broods about unusual beliefs and suspicions. Autistic behavior and inappropriate affect are characteristic features of individuals with this profile. Some evidence of an active psychotic process is apparent. He may have delusions and occult preoccupations, and may feel that others are against him because of his beliefs. In interviews, he is likely to be vague, circumstantial, and tangential, and may be quite preoccupied with abstract ideas.

He is having problems concentrating, feels agitated, and is functioning at a very low level of psychological efficiency. He feels apathetic and indifferent, and that he is a passive participant in life. He also feels that he has little energy left over from mere survival to expend on any pleasure in life. He may be showing signs of serious psychopathology such as delusions, problems in thinking, and inappropriate affect. His long-standing lack of achievement and his work behavior have caused him many problems.

Many individuals with this profile consider committing suicide and Esteban may actually have serious plans for self-destruction.

He experiences some conflicts concerning his sex-role identity, appearing somewhat passive and effeminate in his orientation toward life. He may appear somewhat insecure in the masculine role and may be uncomfortable in his relationships with women.

Esteban's response content indicates that he is preoccupied with feeling guilty and unworthy, and feels that he deserves to be punished for wrongs he has committed. He feels regretful and unhappy about life, complains about having no zest for life, and seems plagued by anxiety and worry about the future. According to his response content, there is a strong possibility that he has contemplated suicide. A careful evaluation of this possibility is suggested. He views his physical health as failing and reports numerous somatic complaints. He feels that life is no longer worthwhile and that he is losing control of his thought processes. He reports in his response content that he feels things more, or more intensely, than others do.

Interpersonal Relations

Disturbed interpersonal relationships are characteristic of individuals with this profile type. Esteban feels vulnerable to interpersonal hurt, lacks trust, and may never form close, satisfying interpersonal ties. He feels very insecure in relationships and may be preoccupied with guilt and self-defeating behavior. Many individuals with this profile are so self-preoccupied and unskilled in sex-role behavior that they never develop rewarding heterosexual relationships. Some never marry.

Behavioral Stability

Individuals with this profile type often lead chronically stormy, chaotic lives.

Diagnostic Considerations

The most likely diagnosis for individuals with this MMPI-2 profile type is Schizophrenia, possibly Paranoid type, or Paranoid Disorder. Similar clients tend to also have features of an affective disorder. In addition, there seems to be a long-standing pattern of maladjustment that is characteristic of people with severe personality disorders.

Because this behavioral pattern may also be associated with Organic Brain Syndrome or Substance-Induced Organic Mental Disorder, these possibilities should be evaluated.

Treatment Considerations

Individuals with this profile may be experiencing considerable personality deterioration, which may require hospitalization if they are considered dangerous to themselves or others.

Psychotropic medication may reduce their thinking disturbance and mood disorder. Outpatient treatment may be complicated by their regressed or disorganized behavior. Multiple-problem life situations and difficulties forming interpersonal relationships make patients with this profile poor candidates for relationship-based psychotherapy. Day treatment programs or other such structured settings may be helpful in providing a stabilizing treatment environment. Long-term adjustment is a problem. Frequent, brief "management" therapy contacts may be helpful in structuring his activities. Insight-oriented or relationship therapies tend not to be helpful for individuals with these severe problems and may actually exacerbate the symptoms. Esteban probably would have difficulty establishing a trusting working relationship with a therapist. ∎

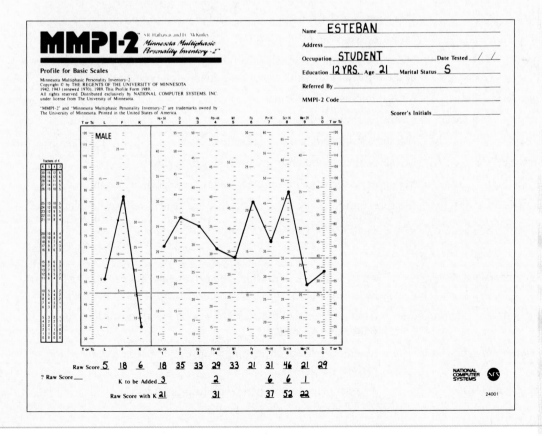

the MMPI sponsored a revision of the instrument. This revised MMPI, designated MMPI-2 for adults, became available for general professional use in mid-1989 (Butcher et al., 1989) and the MMPI-A, for adolescents (Butcher et al., 1992) was published in 1992. Perhaps inevitably, in light of the distinction of its forebear and the strong loyalties to it, some early reservations were expressed. However, the MMPI-2 has now effectively replaced the original instrument which is no longer available from the publisher. The revised versions of the MMPI have been validated in several clinical studies to date (Archer, Griffin, & Aiduk, 1995; Butcher, Rouse, & Perry, 1999).

The MMPI-2 The MMPI-2 was developed to rectify the problems that had been noted about the original MMPI. We will provide a brief discussion of the use of the MMPI-2 in clinical assessment. The scales listed on the standard original MMPI-2 profile form are described in Table 15.1.

TABLE 15.1   THE SCALES OF THE MMPI-2

Validity Scales

Cannot say score (?)	Measures the total number of unanswered items
Lie scale (L)	Measures the tendency to claim excessive virtue or to try to present an overall favorable image
Infrequency scale (F)	Measures the tendency to falsely claim or exaggerate psychological problems in the first part of the booklet; alternatively, detects random responding
Infrequency scale (FB)	Measures the tendency to falsely claim or exaggerate psychological problems on items toward the end of the booklet
Defensiveness scale (K)	Measures the tendency to see oneself in an unrealistically positive way
Response Inconsistency	Measures the tendency to endorse items in an inconsistent or random manner scale (VRIN)
Response Inconsistency	Measures the tendency to endorse items in an inconsistent true or false manner scale (TRIN)

Clinical Scales

Scale 1	*Hypochondriasis* (Hs)	Measures excessive somatic concern and physical complaints
Scale 2	*Depression* (D)	Measures symptomatic depression
Scale 3	*Hysteria* (Hy)	Measures hysteroid personality features such as a "rose-colored glasses" view of the world and the tendency to develop physical problems under stress
Scale 4	*Psychopathic deviate* (Pd)	Measures antisocial tendencies
Scale 5	*Masculinity-femininity* (Mf)	Measures gender-role reversal
Scale 6	*Paranoia* (Pa)	Measures suspicious, paranoid ideation
Scale 7	*Psychasthenia* (Pt)	Measures anxiety and obsessive, worrying behavior
Scale 8	*Schizophrenia* (Sc)	Measures peculiarities in thinking, feeling, and social behavior
Scale 9	*Hypomania* (Ma)	Measures unrealistically elated mood state and tendencies to yield to impulses
Scale 0	*Social introversion* (Si)	Measures social anxiety, withdrawal, and overcontrol

Special Scales

Scale APS	*Addiction Proneness Scale*	Assesses the extent to which the person matches personality features of people in substance use treatment
Scale AAS	*Addiction Acknowledgment Scale*	Assesses the extent to which the person has acknowledged substance abuse problems
Scale MAC-R	*Mac Andrew Addiction Scale*	An empirical scale measuring proneness to become addicted to various substances
MDS	*Marital Distress Scale*	Assesses perceived marital relationship problems

The original item pool was edited and modernized to eliminate expressions that were out of date and to delete objectionable items (about 14 percent of the items required alteration). Additional items were written to address additional problem areas, such as treatment compliance, Type A behavior, suicide, and personality problems. Two separate item pools were established: an adult form and an adolescent form, designated MMPI-A. The new adult normative sample for MMPI-2—2600 subjects randomly sampled from seven communities across the United States—is considerably more representative of the American population than was that for the original MMPI. Efforts were made to include representative groups from different racial and ethnic backgrounds, age groups, and social classes.

The adolescent form of the MMPI (MMPI-A) was standardized on 815 girls and 805 boys who were students in public and private schools in seven regions of the United States. Designed for use with youngsters aged 14 through 18, it contains a number of new scales. Its basic clinical scales, as in the case of MMPI-2, are the same as for the original MMPI.

Experience with the revised versions to date indicates that practitioners are able, with little change in their interpretive approaches, to use it in the same way they did the original instrument. Recent research (Brems & Lloyd, 1995; Clark, 1996) has provided strong support for the use of the revised versions of the MMPI. The clinical scales, which have been retained in their original form apart from minimal item deletion or rewording, seem, as expected, to measure the same properties of personality organization and functioning as they always have. A comparable stability of meaning is observed for the standard validity scales (also essentially unchanged), which have been reinforced with three additional scales to detect tendencies to respond untruthfully to some items. The essential psychometric comparability of the main scales of the two adult versions has been empirically demonstrated by BenPorath and Butcher (1989).

Overall, then, the authors of MMPI-2 have retained the central elements of the original instrument but have added a number of features and refinements to it, including provision for systematic "content" profile analysis. As was the authors' intent, the scales of MMPI-2 correlate highly with those of the original MMPI.

Advantages of Objective Personality Tests Another kind of objective self-report personality inventory uses the statistical procedure of **factor analysis,** a method for reducing a large array of intercorrelated measures to the minimum number of "factors" necessary to account for the observed overlap or associations among them. Because their scales are a product of such a refinement process, tests of this type are considered to measure purportedly basic and relatively independent personality traits. The goal is to measure one trait at a time with maximum precision and selectivity; a personality profile can then be drawn showing the degree to which several such methodologically rarefied traits are characteristic of an individual, as well as the overall pattern of the traits.

Self-report inventories, such as the MMPI, have a number of advantages over other types of personality tests. They are cost-effective, highly reliable, and objective; they also can be scored and interpreted, or if desired even administered, by computer. A number of general criticisms, however, have been leveled against the use of self-report inventories. As we have seen, some clinicians consider them to be too mechanistic to accurately portray the complexity of human beings and their problems. Also, because these tests require a subject to read, comprehend, and answer verbal material, patients who are illiterate or confused cannot take the test. Furthermore, the individual's cooperation is required in self-report inventories, and it is possible that the subject may distort his or her answers to create a particular impression. The validity scales of the MMPI-2 are a direct attempt to deal with this last criticism.

Scientifically constructed objective personality inventories, because of their scoring formats and emphasis on test validation, lend themselves particularly well to automated interpretation. The earliest practical applications of computer technology to test scoring and interpretation involved the MMPI. Over 40 years ago, psychologists at the Mayo Clinic programmed a computer to score and interpret clinical profiles. A number of other highly sophisticated MMPI and MMPI-2 interpretation systems have subsequently been developed (Butcher, 1995; Fowler, 1987). Computer-based MMPI interpretation systems typically employ powerful **actuarial procedures** (Grove & Meehl, 1996). In such systems, descriptions of the actual behavior or other established characteristics of many subjects with particular patterns of test scores have been stored in the computer. Whenever a person turns up with one of these test score patterns, the appropriate description is printed out in the computer's evaluation. Such descriptions have been written and stored for a number of different test score patterns, most of them based on MMPI-2 scores.

The accumulation of precise actuarial data for an instrument like the MMPI-2 is difficult, time-consuming, and expensive. This is in part because of the complexity of the instrument itself, since the potential number of significantly different MMPI-2 profile patterns is legion. The profiles of many subjects therefore do not "fit" the profile types for which actuarial data are available. Problems of actuarial data acquisition also arise at the other end, the behaviors or problems that are to be detected or predicted by the instrument. Many conditions that are of vital clinical importance are relatively rare (for example, suicide) or are psychologically complex (for example, possible psychogenic components in a patient's physical illness), thus making it difficult to accumulate a sufficient number of cases to serve as an adequate actuarial data base. In these situations, the interpretive program writer is forced to fall back on general clinical lore and wisdom to formulate clinical descriptions appropriate to the types of profiles actually obtained. Hence, the best programs are written by expert clinicians who have long experience with the instrument and keep up with its continuously developing research base (Carson, 1990b).

Examples of computer-generated descriptions for the case of Esteban appear in the evaluations reprinted in Highlight 15.4. Sometimes the different paragraphs generated by the computer will have inconsistencies resulting from the fact that different parts of a subject's test pattern call up different paragraphs from the computer. The computer simply prints out blindly what has been found to be typical for people making similar scores on the various clinical scales. The computer cannot integrate the descriptions it picks up, however. At this point the human element comes in: In the clinical use of computers, it is always essential that a trained professional further interpret and monitor the assessment data (American Psychological Association, 1986).

Computerized personality assessment is no longer a novelty, but an important, dependable adjunct to clinical assessment. Computerized psychological evaluations are a quick and efficient means of providing a clinician with needed information early in the decision-making process.

Psychological Assessment in Forensic or Legal Cases

One of the most extensive and fastest-growing applications of psychological tests involves their use in court

cases. As with the clinical settings, the MMPI-2 is the most frequently administered test in forensic settings (Lees-Haley et al., 1996) and is widely used in personnel selection for positions of public trust such as airline pilots and police officers (see Highlight 15.5 on the use of psychological tests in personnel screening).

Many different psychological tests have been employed to evaluate defendants or litigants. If there is a question of cognitive impairment, the WAIS-III or a Halstead-Reitan Neuropsychological Battery might be used. When an individual's psychological adjustment is an issue, the MMPI-2 is the most frequently employed psychological test (Pope, Butcher, & Seelen, 1993) because of its objectivity (less reliant upon interpreter's judgment) and extensive validity base. Due in large part to their scientific acceptability, well-known psychological tests, such as the WAIS-III and MMPI-2, are widely accepted by courts as appropriate assessment instruments. In order for a test to be allowed into testimony, it must be deemed to be an accepted standard. The primary means of ensuring that tests are appropriate for court testimony is that they are standardized and are not experimental procedures (Ogloff, 1995; Pope et al., 1993). Applications range from assessments to provide information about the mental state of felons on trial (Megargee, 1995, 1997), to assess the psychological adjustment of litigants in civil court cases (Butcher & Miller, 1998), and to aid in the determination of child custody in divorce cases (Bathurst, Gottfried, & Gottfried, 1997).

The three situations in which psychological tests are most often used in court settings are illustrated in the following cases.

Cast Study, Assessing Sanity • Mr. A., a 34-year-old man, on trial for serial rapes, alleged that he was not guilty of the crimes for which he was charged due to insanity. His counsel pleaded that he suffered from multiple personality disorder and that the alleged crimes were committed under the influence of "another personality"; the man was not aware that he was committing a crime. The prosecution employed a team of experts (a psychiatrist and two psychologists) to evaluate the defendant for multiple personality disorder or Dissociative Identity Disorder. The evaluation included a psychiatric interview, personal history, and a battery of psychological tests, including the MMPI, TAT, and Rorschach. The results of the evaluation were not consistent with a diagnosis of multiple personality disorder or Dissociative Identity Disorder but instead suggested malingering.

Assessing Trauma • In a civil law suit, Ms. B., age 29, sought damages from her employer following an incident in which she complained that she had been sexually harassed by the manager of her department. She alleged that on a number of occasions his blatant sexual advances had caused her great anguish and difficulty in her marriage. She claimed that her psychological adjustment during and after the harassment incidents had been extremely difficult and had prevented her from effectively pursuing her work. Her therapist supported a diagnosis of post-traumatic stress disorder in her case. (The manager involved in the incident was fired from the company.) Defense attorneys sought a psychological evaluation of Ms. B.

A psychiatric interview and psychological tests were administered, including the Beck Depression Inventory, MMPI-2, TAT, and Rorschach. The conclusions were that she was probably experiencing some post-traumatic symptoms at the time of the evaluation, but that there was evidence that she was exaggerating her symptoms and her disability. Before the trial, the case was settled out of court for a small portion of the original amount claimed.

Custody Battles • In a family court case, Mr. & Ms. T. were both seeking custody of their three-year-old daughter following an acrimonious divorce. During the proceedings, Mr. T., a successful contractor, accused (wrongly as it turned out) Ms. T. of sexually abusing their daughter and sought the termination of her parental rights. A court-appointed psychological evaluation was conducted to assess the emotional stability of Ms. T. and to appraise her suitability as a parent. The court-appointed psychologist did not find that Ms. T. suffered from emotional problems that would make her an unfit mother. Following the trial, the court ruled in favor of full custody for Ms. T. with supervised visits for Mr. T. In addition, the court awarded her $1,000,000 in damages as a result of the false accusation of abuse.

Psychological tests, though for the most part developed for other than court applications, have been found to provide valuable information for court cases—particularly if they contain a means of assessing the person's test-taking attitudes. The MMPI-2, for example, contains several measures that provide an appraisal of the person's cooperativeness or frankness in responding to the test items (Berry, 1995). Because many litigants or defendants in criminal cases, when tested, attempt to present themselves in a particular way (for example, to appear disturbed in the case of an insanity plea or impecca-

One of the fastest-growing applications of psychological tests involves their use in court cases.

bly virtuous when trying to present a false or exaggerated physical injury), their motivations to "fake good" or "fake bad" tend to result in noncredible test patterns.

Although psychological tests may be considered very useful in some forensic circumstances, their use has clear limitations (Faust, Ziskin, & Hiers, 1991; Faust, 1994; Heilbrun, 1992). The use of psychological assessment in court is nevertheless widespread and likely to become more common in the future, given the increasing number of situations in which mental health adjustment is becoming an issue for courts to evaluate.

A Psychological Case Study: Esteban

In this section, we will illustrate psychological assessment through a diagnostic case study of a young man who presented a complicated clinical picture that was substantially clarified through psychological and neuropsychological assessment. This is an unusual case in several respects: The young man's problems were quite severe and involved both psychological and organic elements; the case involved cross-cultural considerations—the young man was from South America and assessment was done in both English and Spanish (the latter only as necessary); and a number of psychological specialists participated in the assessment study, including a neuropsychologist, a behaviorally oriented clinical psychologist, a Hispanic clinical psychologist, and a psychiatrist.

MODERN LIFE

The Use of Psychological Tests in Personnel Screening

Some occupations—including those of airline flight crews, police officers, firefighters, air-traffic controllers, nuclear power plant workers, and certain military specialties—require a consistently high level of psychological performance and greater emotional stability than others; these jobs allow for less personal variation in performance. Disabling personality traits or behavior problems in such employees can be extremely dangerous to other employees and to the public. For example, someone who behaves in an irresponsible manner in a nuclear power plant control room may significantly endanger the operation of the facility, which may result in a failure to recognize problems requiring prompt and decisive action. Personality problems that may lead a police officer to using excessive force in an arrest are not simply an internal police matter; they are also a significant issue of concern for all of us. The potential for job failure or for psychological maladjustment can be so great in some high-stress occupations that measures need to be taken in the hiring process to evaluate applicants for emotional adjustment.

The use of personality tests in personnel screening has a long tradition. In fact, the first formal use of a standardized personality scale in the United States, the Woodworth Personal Data Sheet, was implemented to screen out World War I draftees who were psychologically unfit for military service (Woodworth, 1920). Today, psychological tests are widely used for personnel screening in occupations that require a high degree of emotional stability or great public trust.

An important distinction needs to be made between personnel selection and per-

sonnel screening or, phrased differently, between "screening in" versus "screening out" job candidates. In the first instance, one is looking for certain traits; in the second, one is testing to make sure certain vulnerabilities are *not* there. In situations where certain psychological characteristics are desired for a particular job, a psychologist would choose instruments that directly assess those qualities, such as the 16 Personality Factor Inventory (Cattell et al., 1988), which measures "normal" personality characteristics, such as dominance or sociability.

Personnel screening for emotional stability and potentially irresponsible behavior, on the other hand, requires a somewhat different set of assumptions. One assumption is that personality or emotional problems, such as poor reality contact, impulsivity, or pathological indecisiveness, would adversely affect the way in which a person would function in a critical job. In this situation, a psychologist could choose an instrument to assess the presence of personality problems, such as the MMPI-2. To extend an earlier example, in police officer selection, an applicant with an MMPI-2 profile pattern reflecting tendencies toward extreme aggressiveness, making hasty generalizations about others, and impulsivity would be eliminated from consideration or would undergo further evaluation to determine if these personality factors had resulted in negative job behaviors in the past.

Issues in Personality Test Job Screening

Before implementing psychological assessment for preemployment screening, an ethically responsible psychologist needs to consider a number of issues to determine both the relevance and appropriateness of the

Social History Esteban, a 21-year-old student from Colombia, had been enrolled in an English-language program at a small college in the United States. He had

become disruptive in school, evidencing loud, obnoxious behavior in class and quarreling with his roommates (whom he accused of stealing his wallet). After a

procedures to be used. The following questions need to be addressed:

1. *How should the preemployment test be used, or how much weight should be given to a particular test in preemployment decisions?* Psychological tests should not be the sole means of determining whether a person is hired. Instruments like the MMPI-2 should be used in conjunction with an employment interview, a background check, an evaluation of previous work record, and so on.

2. *Is the use of a psychological test an unwarranted invasion of privacy?* Undeniably, many (and perhaps in a certain sense all) psychological tests—especially personality tests like the MMPI-2 that ask personal questions—can be considered to invade an individual's privacy by asking many personal questions concerning symptoms, attitudes, and lifestyles. An important consideration, however, involves determining whether a particular test used is a warranted invasion of privacy—that is, determining whether the particular placement decisions being made are consistent with the greater interests of society. For some occupations, such decisions are deemed justifiable; it is considered within the criterion of "public good" that people being placed in positions of high responsibility are emotionally stable according to the best information available. For most occupations, however, psychological screening is unnecessary and unwarranted.

3. *Are the procedures fair to all candidates, including members of ethnic minorities?* The question of the fairness of psychological tests in personnel screening is an important one. In order for a psychological test

to be considered appropriate (both ethically and legally) for use in personnel selection situations, it must be demonstrated that the test does not unfairly portray or discriminate against ethnic minorities. This question needs to be addressed for each psychological test or personnel procedure used. The tests used must also have a demonstrated validity for the particular test application. In the case of the MMPI, which is the most widely used clinical test in personnel screening, minority group performance has been widely studied—for example, African-American (Ben-Porath, Shondrick, & Stafford, 1994), Hispanics (Velasquez et al., 1997), Chinese American (Keefe, Sue et al., 1996) and American Indian (Tinius & Ben-Porath, 1993). If a person can read the items (a foreign language version can be administered, if necessary), the MMPI-2 does not portray or discriminate against various ethnic minority subjects in an unfair manner. Given the more representative normative sample for MMPI-2, it is even less likely than its predecessor to present a problem in this respect.

4. *Tests need to be used in the light of the American with Disabilities Act (1991).* It is important that the assessment program be in compliance with federal guidelines and that individuals are not discriminated against because of a disability, including a mental disability. A recent court decision, *Miller* v. *City of Springfield (1998)*, found that the use of the MMPI-2 in selection of police officers does not constitute discrimination based on the ADA and that appropriate psychological screening is job-related and consistent with business necessity where the selection of police officers is concerned. ■

period of time during which his behavior did not improve, he was expelled from the program. The director of the program indicated that he felt Esteban needed

psychological help for his problems, which included not only the behavioral problems but also, reportedly, severe headaches and confused thinking. The director added that Esteban would be considered for readmission only if he showed significant improvement in therapy.

On hearing of his expulsion, Esteban's parents, who were well-to-do international banking entrepreneurs, flew in from Colombia and arranged for a complete physical examination for him at a well-known medical center in New York. After an extensive medical and neurological examination to determine the source of his headaches and confusion, Esteban was diagnosed as having some "diffuse" brain impairment, but he was found to be otherwise in good health. His parents then sought a further, more definitive neurological examination. The neurologist at the second hospital recommended a psychological and neuropsychological examination because he suspected that Esteban's mild neurological condition would not account for his extreme psychological and behavioral symptoms. He referred the family to a psychologist for assessment and treatment. Esteban was experiencing a number of pressing situational problems—for example, his behavior problems continued, he appeared anxious to find a new English program, and, as we will see, he had some hard issues to face about his career aspirations to become a physician. Therefore, the psychologist decided to begin with therapy immediately, concurrent with the additional assessment evaluation.

Interviews and Behavior Observations Esteban was seen in the initial session with his parents. The interview was conducted in English with some translation into Spanish (mostly by Esteban) because the parents knew little English. Throughout the session, Esteban was disorganized and distractible. He had difficulty keeping to the topic being discussed and periodically interrupted his own conversation with seemingly random impulses to show the interviewer papers, books, pamphlets, and the like from his knapsack. He talked incessantly, often loudly. He was not at all defensive about his problems but talked freely about his symptoms and attitudes. His behavior resembled that of a hyperactive child—he was excitable, impulsive, and immature. He did not appear to be psychotic; he reported no hallucinations or delusions and was in contact with reality. He related well with the interviewer, seemed to enjoy the session, and expressed an interest in having additional sessions.

During subsequent interviews, Esteban expressed frequent physical complaints, such as headaches, tension, and sleeping problems. He reported that he had a great deal of difficulty concentrating on his studies. He could not study because he always found other things to do—particularly talking about religion. He was seemingly outgoing and sociable and had no difficulty initiating conversations with other people. He tended, however, to say socially inappropriate things or become frustrated and lose his temper easily. For example, during one family interview, he became enraged and kicked his mother.

Family History Esteban's father was a Spanish-Colombian banker in his mid-sixties. He was well-dressed, somewhat passive, though visibly quite warm toward his son. He had his share of difficulties in recent years; severe business problems coupled with two heart attacks had brought on a depressive episode that had left him ineffective in dealing with his business. His wife and her brother, an attorney from Madrid, had to straighten out the business problems. She reported that her husband had had several depressive episodes in the past and that Esteban's moods resembled her husband's in his earlier years.

Esteban's mother was a tense, worried, and somewhat hypochondriacal woman who appeared to be rather domineering. Before the first and second interviews, she handed the therapist, in secret, written "explanations" of her son's problems. Her own history revealed that she was unhappy in her marriage and that she lived only for her children, on whom she doted.

Esteban's brother, Juan, was an engineering student at an American university and apparently was doing well academically and socially. He was one year older than Esteban.

Esteban's childhood had been marked with problems. His mother reported that although he had been a good baby—noting that he had been pretty happy as a small child—he had changed after age two and a half. At about that time, he had fallen on his head and was unconscious for a while; he was not hospitalized. Beginning in the preschool years, he exhibited behavioral problems, including temper tantrums, negativism, and an inability to get along with peers. These problems continued when he began school. He frequently refused to go to school, had periods of aggressive behavior, and appeared in general to be "hyperactive." It appeared that he was probably overprotected and "infantilized" by his mother.

Esteban was quite close to his brother Juan, with whom he reported having had extensive homosexual relations when they were growing up. The "darkest day" in Esteban's life was reportedly when Juan broke off the homosexual relationship with him at age 16 and told him to "go and find men." Although he later carried on a platonic relationship with a woman in Colombia, it was never a serious one. Esteban had strong homosexual urges of which he was consciously aware and attempted to control through a growing preoccupation with religion.

Esteban had been in psychotherapy on several occasions since he was 11 years old. After he graduated from high school, he attended law school in Colombia for a quarter, but dropped out because he "wanted to become a doctor instead." (In Colombia, professional schools are combined with college.) He left school, according to his parents' report, because he could not adapt. He worked for a time in the family business but had difficulty getting along with other employees and was encouraged to try other work. When that failed, his parents sent him to the United States to study English, rationalizing that Colombia was not as good an environment for him as the United States.

Intelligence Testing Esteban underwent psychological testing to evaluate further the possibility of neurological deficits and to determine if he had the intellectual capabilities to proceed with a demanding academic career. He scored in the borderline to average range of intelligence on the WAIS-R (English version) and on the WAIS (Spanish version). He was particularly deficient in tasks involving practical judgment, common sense, concentration, visual-motor coordination, and concept formation. In addition, on memory tests, he showed a below average memory ability, such as a poor immediate recall of ideas from paragraphs read aloud (in both English and Spanish). Under most circumstances, people with similar deficits are able to live comfortable, fulfilling lives in careers whose formal intellectual demands are relatively modest. It was clear from the test data and Esteban's behavior during testing that his stated career aspirations—seemingly nurtured by his parents—exceeded his abilities and might well be a factor in much of his frustration.

Personality Testing Esteban was given both the Rorschach Test and the MMPI. Both tests have been used extensively with Hispanic subjects. The Rorschach is believed by some to be particularly well-suited for cases like Esteban's because the test stimuli are relatively unstructured and not culture-bound. Esteban's performance on the Rorschach revealed tension, anxiety, and a preoccupation with morbid topics. He appeared to be overly concerned about his health, prone to depression,

indecisive and yet at other times impulsive and careless. His responses were often immature and he showed a strong and persistent ambivalence toward females. In some responses, he viewed females in highly aggressive ways—often a fusion of sexual and aggressive images was evident. In general, he demonstrated aloofness and an inability to relate well to other people. Although his Rorschach responses suggested that he could view the world in conventional ways and was probably not psychotic, at times he had difficulty controlling his impulses. Esteban's Rorschach protocol was computer analyzed using the Exner Comprehensive Rorschach System (see Figure 15.1).

Esteban took the original version of the MMPI in both English and Spanish. His MMPI profile was virtually identical in both languages. It has been converted to MMPI-2 format and is reproduced in Highlight 15.4 (page 604) along with the MMPI-2-based computer interpretation of his test scores.

Summary of the Psychological Assessment of Esteban Esteban showed mild neurological deficits on neuropsychological testing and borderline intellectual ability. He clearly did not have the academic ability to pursue a medical career. Demanding intellectual tasks placed a great deal of stress on him and resulted in frustration. Furthermore, his poor memory made learning complex material very difficult.

The MMPI-2 interpretation indicated that Esteban's disorganized behavior and symptomatic patterns reflected a serious psychological disorder. Although he was not currently psychotic, both his past behavior and his test performance suggested that he was functioning marginally and that he showed the potential for personality deterioration in some situations.

Esteban's most salient psychological problems concerned his tendency to become frustrated and his ready loss of impulse control. He was volatile and became upset easily. Additionally, it appeared that Esteban's relative isolation during his early years (due in part to his overprotective mother) did not prepare him to function adequately in many social situations. Another important problem area for Esteban was in psychosexual adjustment. The psychological test results and his personal history clearly indicated a gender-identity confusion.

Within the parameters of DSM-IV, Esteban would receive an Axis I diagnosis of organic personality syndrome and an Axis II diagnosis of borderline personality disorder. Furthermore, it was recommended that he undertake social-skills training and that—rather than a career in medicine—he be encouraged to pursue occupational goals more in keeping with his abilities. Psychotropic medication (Lithium and Mellaril) were prescribed for his emotional control problems.

A Follow-up Note Esteban was seen in psychological therapy twice a week and was kept on medication. He was also seen in a social-skills training program for ten sessions. Through the help of his therapist, he was admitted to a less-demanding English program, which seemed more appropriate for his abilities.

For the first six months, Esteban made considerable progress, especially after his behavior became somewhat stabilized, largely, it appeared, as a result of the medications. He became less impulsive and more in control of his anger. He successfully completed the English classes in which he was enrolled. During this period, he lived with his mother, who had taken up a temporary residence near the college. She then returned to Colombia, and Esteban moved into an apartment with a roommate, with whom, however, he had increasing difficulty.

Several weeks after his mother left, Esteban quit going to therapy and quit taking his medication. He began to frequent local gay bars, at first out of curiosity but later to seek male lovers. At the same time, his preoccupation with religion increased and he moved into a house near campus that was operated by a fundamentalist religious cult. His parents, quite concerned by his overt homosexual behavior (which he described in detail over the phone, adding the suggestion that they visit the gay bar with him), returned to the United States. Realizing that they could not stay permanently to supervise Esteban, they then sought a residential treatment program that would provide him with a more structured living arrangement. All assessment and therapy records were forwarded to those in charge of the residential program.

THE INTEGRATION OF ASSESSMENT DATA

As assessment data are collected, their significance must be interpreted so that they can be integrated into a coherent working model for use in planning or changing treatment. Clinicians in individual private practice normally assume this often arduous task on their own.

In a clinic or hospital setting, assessment data are usually evaluated in a staff conference attended by members of an interdisciplinary team (perhaps a clinical psychologist, a psychiatrist, a social worker, and other mental health personnel) who are concerned with the decisions to be made regarding treatment. By putting together all the information they have gathered, they can see whether the findings complement each other and form a definitive clinical picture or whether gaps or discrepancies exist that necessitate further investigation.

This integration of all the data gathered at the time of an original assessment may lead to agreement on a tentative diagnostic classification for a patient. In any case, the findings of each member of the team, as well as the recommendations for treatment, are entered in the case record, so that it will always be possible to check back and see why a certain course of therapy was undertaken, how accurate the clinical assessment was, and how valid the treatment decision turned out to be.

New assessment data collected during the course of therapy provide feedback on its effectiveness and serve as a basis for making needed modifications in an ongoing treatment program. As we have noted, clinical assessment data are also commonly used in evaluating the final outcome of therapy and in comparing the effectiveness of different therapeutic and preventive approaches.

Ethical Issues in Assessment

The decisions made on the basis of assessment data may have far-reaching implications for the people involved. A staff decision may determine whether a depressed person will be hospitalized or remain with his or her family or whether an accused person will be declared competent to stand trial. Thus a valid decision, based on accurate assessment data, is of far more than theoretical importance. Because of the impact that assessment can have on the lives of others, it is important that those involved keep several possible factors in mind in evaluating test results:

1. *Potential cultural bias of the instrument or the clinician:* There is the possibility that psychological tests may not elicit valid information from a patient from a minority group (Gray-Little, 1995). A clinician from one sociocultural background may have trouble assessing objectively the behavior of someone from another background, such as a Southeast Asian refugee. It is important to ensure, as Timbrook and Graham (1994) have done with the MMPI-2, that the instrument can be confidently used with persons from minority groups.

In a clinic or hospital setting, assessment data are usually evaluated in a staff conference attended by members of an interdisciplinary team—including, for example, a clinical psychologist, a psychiatrist, a social worker, and a psychiatric nurse. Sharing findings may lead to a diagnostic classification for a patient and a course of treatment. Staff decisions can have far-reaching consequences for patients: as such, it is important that clinicians be aware of the limitations of assessment.

2. *Theoretical orientation of the clinician:* Assessment is inevitably influenced by a clinician's assumptions, perceptions, and theoretical orientation. For example, a psychoanalyst and a behaviorist might assess the same behaviors quite differently. The psychoanalytically oriented professional would likely view behaviors as reflecting underlying motives whereas the behavioral clinician would likely view the behavior in the context of the immediate or preceding stimulus situation. If the differing assessments should lead to treatment recommendations of significantly differing efficacy for a client's problems, these biases could have serious repercussions.

3. *Underemphasis on the external situation:* Many clinicians overemphasize personality traits as the cause of patients' problems without due attention to the possible role of stressors or other circumstances in their life situations. An undue focus on a patient's personality, which may be encouraged by some assessment techniques, can divert attention from potentially critical environmental factors.

4. *Insufficient validation:* Many psychological assessment procedures have not been sufficiently vali-

dated. For example, unlike many of the personality scales, widely used procedures for behavioral observation and behavioral self-report have not been subjected to strict psychometric validation. The tendency on the part of clinicians to accept the results of these procedures at face value has recently been giving way to a broader recognition of the need for more explicit validation.

5. *Inaccurate data or premature evaluation:* There is always the possibility that some assessment data—and any diagnostic label or treatment based on them—may be inaccurate. Some risk is always involved in making predictions for an individual on the basis of group data or averages; although "schizophrenic" symptoms actually imply a difficult treatment course—for example, some people who have them recover quickly even without treatment and never experience another episode. Inaccurate data or premature conclusions not only may lead to a misunderstanding of a patient's problem, but may close off attempts to get further information, with possibly grave consequences for the patient.

UNRESOLVED ISSUES

Incorporating Psychological Test Data into Therapy—An Unfulfilled Relationship

In spite of the fact that assessment-oriented psychologists have made a strong case for the utility of incorporating conclusions from psychological tests into treatment planning, many psychotherapists and psychotherapy researchers do not routinely make use of this information (Ben-Porath, 1997; Nelson & Adams, 1997).

The practice of psychotherapy has seemingly been very little influenced by the extensive assessment literature. For example, in a recent issue of the *Journal of Consulting and Clinical Psychology* (1998, vol. 66), which was devoted to surveying empirically based treatments, none of the contributors included any discussion of the power of incorporating empirically based psychological assessment results into the treatment process (see Kendall, 1998). Yet an assessment-oriented journal published by the American Psychological Association (*Psychological Assessment*, 1997, vol. 9), offered an extensive series on the topic. Research has provided clear evidence of the likely beneficial effects of psychological assessment in the treatment process (Ben-Porath, 1997; Finn & Tonsager, 1997; Haynes, Lesen, & Blaine, 1997; Harkness & Lilienfield, 1997; Nelson & Adams, 1997). A great deal of research on the use of psychological tests in treatment planning and evaluation has been published. For example, with respect to one psychological test, the MMPI, over 1,000 articles have been published about the use of the instrument in pre-treatment planning or in evaluating the results of therapy (Rouse, Sullivan, & Taylor, 1997). This extensive research appears to have had little impact on the way therapy is conducted.

Interestingly, there is growing evidence to indicate that the results of psychological tests can, when sensitively shared with clients, bring about remarkable personality change and insight in clients (Miller & Rollnick, 1991; Finn & Tonsager, 1997; Newman & Greenway, 1997) have shown that personality information from tests given to clients early in the intervention can bring about improved self-esteem and a lowering of psychological symptoms. Test feedback alone produced therapeutic results that were comparable or better than therapy without psychological test feedback.

Why do many trained psychotherapists begin and continue their treatment without incorporating objective psychological information into the process? Several possible explanations come to mind:

- *Training:* One factor that accounts for this low utilization of tests in therapy is that some therapists are trained in programs that do not provide coursework in clinical assessment techniques. Some graduate training programs have de-emphasized training in psychological assessment in recent years. Many therapists have not received training in interpreting psychological tests and therefore have not been apprised of the dramatic results that can be obtained with the sensitive use of test results in therapy.

- *Theoretical bias:* Some schools of psychotherapy in the past (particularly client-centered therapy and some narrow behavioral viewpoints) have specifically argued against using testing information in therapy because test results are not considered pertinent to the intervention or are thought to "bias" the therapist in a detrimental way. For example, a therapist who is informed through testing that a male client probably has a severe problem with alcohol might allow this circumstance to "interfere" with the task of developing an understanding of the client's relationship problems as he is presenting them.

- *Cost:* Some professionals have cited cost of assessment as a reason for not including assessment information in the treatment process. (See the discussion on managed care in Chapter 18.) Ironically, although assessment has been shown to positively impact outcome when properly integrated into the treatment process, it appears to be the easiest aspect of the clinical process to dispense with under the fiscal reality of managed care. Even though assessment information early in the therapy can guide the treatment process effectively (Ben-Porath, 1997), some managed care organizations place limits (in terms of time or dollars) that can be utilized in assessment. Some have eliminated assessment altogether in the treatment planning process. Thus the information that can help ensure successful treatment outcome is often not available to the practitioner who then enters into a short-term, limited treatment arrangement with the client and must arrive at a sound assessment of the problems while at the same time treating them through therapy. Therapy is often conducted and indeed completed, or at least terminated, without the therapist ever arriving at a clear picture of the patient's problems and personality.

SUMMARY

Clinical assessment is one of the most important and complex activities facing mental health professionals. The extent to which a person's problems are understood and appropriately treated depend largely on the adequacy of the psychological assessment. The goals of psychological assessment include identifying and describing the individual's symptoms; determining the chronicity and severity of the problem; evaluating the potential causal factors in the person's background; and exploring the individual's personal resources, which might be assets in his or her treatment program.

Interdisciplinary sources of assessment data include both physical evaluation methods and psychosocial assessment techniques. Because many psychological problems have physical components, either as underlying causal factors or as symptom patterns, it is often important to include a medical examination in the psychological assessment. In cases where organic brain damage is suspected, it is important to have neurological tests—such as an EEG or a CAT, PET, or MRI scan—to aid in determining the site and extent of organic brain disorder. In addition, it may be important to have the person take a battery of neuropsychological tests to determine if or in what manner the underlying brain disorder is affecting his or her mental and behavioral capabilities.

Psychosocial assessment methods are techniques for gathering relevant psychological information for clinical decisions about patients. The most widely used and most flexible psychosocial assessment methods are the clinical interview and behavior observation. These methods provide a wealth of clinical information. They may be subject, however, to extraneous influences that make them somewhat unreliable, and structured interview formats and objective behavior rating scales have been developed to improve their reliability.

Whereas interviews and behavior observations attempt to assess an individual's beliefs, attitudes, and symptoms directly, psychological tests attempt to measure these aspects of personality indirectly. Psychological tests include standardized stimuli for collecting behavior samples that can be compared with other individuals through test norms. Two different personality testing approaches have been developed: (1) projective tests, such as the Rorschach, in which unstructured stimuli are presented to a subject, who then "projects" meaning or structure on to the stimulus, thereby revealing "hidden" motives, feelings, and so on; and (2) objective tests, or personality inventories, in which a subject is required to read and respond to itemized statements or questions. Objective personality tests provide a cost-effective means of collecting a great deal of personality information rapidly. The MMPI, the most widely used and validated objective personality inventory, as well as the MMPI-2 and MMPI-A, its recently revised offspring, provide a number of clinically relevant scales for describing abnormal behavior.

Psychological tests are widely used in settings other than clinical assessment situations. For example, tests like the MMPI-2, because of their objectivity in describing personality, are widely used in courts for assessing questions such as whether an individual is competent to stand trial or whether a personal injury claimant is suffering from stress following an alleged injury. Another nonclinical setting in which personality assessment is widely used is for personnel screening for positions that require emotionally stable people such as airline pilots, police officers, and nuclear power plant workers.

Possibly the most dramatic recent innovation in clinical assessment involves the widespread use of computers in the administration, scoring, and interpretation of psychological tests. It is now possible to obtain immediate interpretation of psychological test results, either through a direct computer interactive approach or through a modem to a computer network that interprets tests. In the past few years, rapid developments have been taking place in the computer assessment area. It is conceivable that within the next few years most clinical assessments will involve computers in some capacity, either for administration, scoring, and interpretation or for completing an entire test battery. Of course, mental health professionals will still play a major role in determining the appropriateness and adequacy of the computer's diagnostic output.

KEY TERMS

dynamic formulation (p. 586)
electroencephalogram (EEG) (p. 588)
dysrhythmia (p. 588)
computerized axial tomography (CAT scan) (p. 588)
magnetic resonance imaging (MRI) (p. 588)
positron emission tomography (PET scan) (p. 589)
functional MRI (fMRI) (p. 589)
neuropsychological assessment (p. 590)
self-monitoring (p. 593)
rating scales (p. 593)

role playing (p. 596)
projective tests (p. 599)
Rorschach Test (p. 599)
Thematic Apperception Test (TAT) (p. 600)
sentence-completion test (p. 602)
objective tests (p. 602)
Minnesota Multiphasic Personality Inventory (MMPI) (p. 602)
factor analysis (p. 607)
actuarial procedures (p. 608)

Biologically Based Therapies

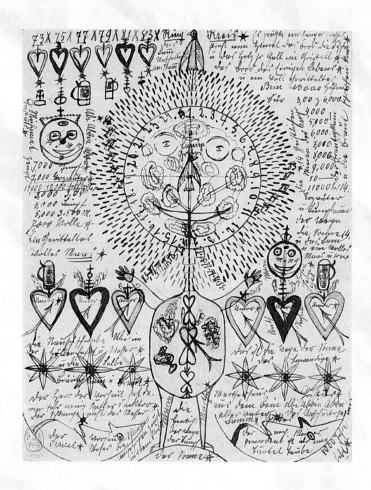

Johann Knopf (Knüpfer), Lamb of God. Knüpfer (1866-1910) lived at home and worked at a variety of manual jobs until he was nearly 30 years old. He married, unhappily, and left his wife, eventually becoming a vagrant. He attempted suicide in 1902 and was committed to a mental hospital near Heidelberg. Once there, Knüpfer began to draw. His art is detailed and orderly, and often illustrates religious preoccupations.

The concept of therapy is not new. Throughout recorded history, human beings have tried to help each other with life's problems—including mental disorders—in both informal and formal ways. In Chapter 2 we noted the wide range of procedures that have historically been advocated for helping the mentally disturbed—from exorcism to incarceration and torture, from understanding and kindness to the most extreme cruelty.

Today both biological and psychological procedures are used in attempts to help individuals overcome psychopathology. In this chapter we will focus on biological methods that have evolved for the treatment of mental disorders, such as the schizophrenias, mood disorders, and disorders in which severe anxiety is central. In Chapter 17 we will focus on psychological approaches.

EARLY ATTEMPTS AT BIOLOGICAL INTERVENTION

The idea that a disordered mind might be set straight by treatment directed at the body goes back, as we have seen, to ancient times. From Hippocrates in ancient Greece, to Paracelsus in medieval Europe, to Kraepelin in Europe at the turn of this century, and on to modern psychiatrists, there have always been those who believed that, ultimately, the cure for mental problems rested in the alteration of an organism's biological state. Today we still have no reliable knowledge of point-to-point correspondence between certain behaviors and particular events in the brain at cellular or subcellular levels. Nonetheless, the dictum "no twisted thought without a twisted molecule," while philosophically and scientifically naive in certain respects, has been deeply internalized by many workers in the mental health field. For them, it is but a small step to conclude that the search for treatment methods should concentrate on finding effective means of rearranging or reconstituting aberrant molecules—of changing the presumed physical substrate of abnormal behavior.

The history of psychiatry reflects interesting, though by today's standards often extreme and primitive, methods of treating mental illness by altering bodily processes. Some have been widely used in several periods of history. For example, ridding the body of unwanted substances by purging (with laxatives and emetics) was a typical treatment in ancient Rome, during the medieval period, and during the eighteenth century (Agnew, 1985). In fact, purging was so widespread during some periods, particularly the eighteenth century, that it was a common practice in medicine and among people in general. Other seemingly more barbaric techniques, such as bleeding,

have been widely used as treatments of the mentally disordered just as they have been used for a broad range of physical diseases. The use of bleeding was apparently consistent and acceptable to the views of medical science in the eighteenth century. Interestingly, many medical procedures were derived from or paralleled research and development in other sciences. For example, after the discovery of electricity, many efforts to use electrical stimulation to alter mental states ensued. Early electrical devices were used to stimulate patients' nerves, muscles, and organs as a treatment for a variety of illnesses. The rationale behind early somatic efforts to "treat" mental patients was often unclear, although frightening patients out of their madness or punishing the demons within may have been as much a reason as was any belief that an individual's bodily processes were being restored.

In general, as more has been learned in the various subfields of medicine, treatment measures have become more benign and less risky. As researchers come to understand scientifically the nature of a disorder, they typically have then been able to develop biological treatments that are more precisely designed to meet a given problem. The specificity of these new treatments usually means that they have fewer potentially damaging side effects.

By 1917, with the discovery of Wagner-Jauregg that general paresis, or neurosyphilis, could be curbed by intentionally infecting a patient with malaria (the consequent fevers were lethal to the spirochete), the stage was set for the development of extraordinarily bold but often hazardous new treatments (see Chapter 2). We will look now at two treatments that emerged during this period: the convulsive therapies and psychosurgery.

Coma and Convulsive Therapies

The first acknowledged medical use of inducing convulsions to treat individuals with mental disorders has been attributed to the Swiss physician-alchemist Paracelsus (1493–1591). He reported a case in which he induced a patient to drink camphor until he experienced convulsions (Mowbray, 1959; Abrams, 1997) in order to cure him of his "lunacy." During the eighteenth century, camphor-induced convulsions were used by several physicians to treat mania—in 1764 by von Aurenbrugger, in 1785 by Oliver, and in 1798 by Weickhardt (see Abrams, 1997). The cure seems to have been forgotten or was not widely adopted, and no use of it was reported during the nineteenth century.

The modern originator of convulsion therapy was Von Meduna, a Hungarian physician, who was apparently unaware of these early efforts to use camphor in the induction of convulsions to treat mania when he published his own observations on inducing epileptic seizures to treat schizophrenia in 1934. Von Meduna speculated—erroneously, as it turned out—that schizophrenia rarely occurred in people with epilepsy. This observation led to the inference that schizophrenia and epilepsy were somehow incompatible, and that one might be able to cure schizophrenia by inducing convulsions. Von Meduna conducted his first experiments on rats and then used camphor to induce convulsions in a schizophrenic patient who relatively quickly regained lucidity after the convulsive therapy. Shortly afterward, Von Meduna began to use a drug called Metrazol rather than camphor to induce convulsions because it operated more rapidly. Von Meduna's work, though not without its critics, provided a great deal of hope that some mental disorders that were previously unresponsive to treatment might now be treatable (Abrams, 1997).

Insulin Coma Therapy Rarely used today, **insulin coma therapy** was introduced by Sakel in 1932 as a physiological treatment for schizophrenia and was also used as a treatment for morphine withdrawal. The technique involved administration of increasing amounts of insulin (a hormone that regulates sugar metabolism in the body) daily until a patient went into "shock"—actually a hypoglycemic coma caused by an acute deficiency of glucose (sugar) in the blood. Coma-inducing doses of insulin were administered daily thereafter until the patient had experienced approximately 50 comas, each an hour or more in duration. The comas were terminated by administering glucose. This treatment caused profound biological and physiological stress, especially to the cardiovascular and nervous systems. The patient had to be closely monitored both during and after the comatose state because of a variety of medical complications that might ensue, including some that could have been fatal.

The results of insulin coma therapy were generally disappointing. Where patients showed improvement, it had been difficult to determine whether it was due to the experience of the comas or to some other aspect of the treatment, such as the markedly increased attention of the medical staff. Moreover, patients who did improve tended to be those who would improve readily under other treatment regimens as well; severe, chronic schizophrenic patients remained for the most part unimproved. Finally, the relapse rate for those who improved was high. With such a record—and in the face of marked medical risks—it is hardly surprising that the use of this therapeutic method has largely disappeared (Abrams, 1997).

Electroconvulsive Shock Therapy Shortly after the discovery of electricity, mild electrical stimulation was used in the treatment of mental disorders as a way of stimulating convulsions without drugs. As early as 1849 the physician John Charles Bucknill, working with asylum patients, used electrical stimulation of the skin and potassium oxide to successfully treat patients with melancholic depression (Beveridge & Renvoize, 1988). During the latter part of the nineteenth century, the therapeutic use of electrical stimulation was fairly widespread. Toward the end of the century, however, concern over its safe use resulted in a diminished use of electricity for treatment.

The potential value of electrostimulation therapy was reconsidered after Von Meduna's encouraging work on Metrazol-induced seizures in the treatment of mental disorders. In 1938 two Italian physicians, U. Cerletti and L. Bini, after visiting a slaughterhouse and seeing animals rendered unconscious by electric shock, tried the simplest method of all—that of passing an electric current through a patient's head. The method, which became known as **electroconvulsive therapy (ECT),** is much more widely used today than insulin therapy, mostly because of its effectiveness in alleviating depressive and manic episodes. Although ECT is known to be effective, the mechanism by which it works has never been adequately explained. Some researchers believe that the therapeutic effect is brought about by changes in the levels of certain neurotransmitters or by changes in receptor sensitivity but the mechanism of action remains a mystery (Abrams, 1997; Gitlin, 1996). However, at least one important study has shown that the location in the brain that was stimulated and the degree of current density within different pathways determined how effective the ECT was in relieving depression. So even though all patients had generalized seizures, of those receiving stimulation of certain pathways only 17 percent were responders, but of those receiving stimulation of other pathways 70 percent were responders. Thus, engagement of particular neural systems seemed critical to making the treatment effective. Such information should thus begin to help unravel the mystery surrounding the mechanism of action of ECT (Sackheim et al., 1993).

There are two types of ECT—bilateral and unilateral. The latter is a more recent introduction and is considered less intrusive. We will review both here. The technique of administering ECT has changed considerably since it was developed by Cerletti and Bini, although the basic procedure remains similar: Constant current brief electrical pulses of either high or low intensity are passed from one side of a patient's head to the other for up to about 1.5

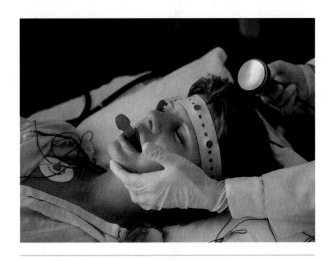

A patient administered electroconvulsive therapy (ECT) today is given sedative and muscle-relaxant premedication to prevent violent contractions. In the days before such medication was available, the initial seizure was sometimes so violent as to fracture vertebrae.

seconds. The patient immediately loses consciousness and undergoes marked muscle contractions (Abrams, 1997; Gitlin, 1996). Today, anesthetics and muscle-relaxant premedications are used to prevent violent contractions and careful, continuous monitoring during the procedure lowers side effects and risk. In the days before such medication was available, the initial seizure was sometimes so violent as to fracture vertebrae, one of several potential complications of this therapy.

After awakening several minutes later, the patient has amnesia for the period immediately preceding the therapy and is usually somewhat confused for the next hour or so. Normally, a treatment series consists of less than a dozen sessions, although occasionally more are needed (Gitlin, 1996). With repeated treatments, usually administered three times weekly, the patient gradually becomes disoriented, a state that usually clears after termination of the treatments.

Some years ago, a modification in the standard method of administering ECT was introduced. Instead of placing the electrodes on each side of the head in the temple region, thereby causing a transverse flow of current through both cerebral hemispheres, the new procedure involves limiting current flow through only one side of the brain, typically the nondominant (right side, for most people). This procedure is called unilateral ECT, and strong evidence shows that it lessens distressing side effects (such as memory impairment) without decreasing therapeutic effectiveness if higher dose electrical currents are used. However, other studies suggest that it may not be as effective as bilateral ECT, and so many suggest starting with unilateral ECT and switching to bilateral after

five or six treatments if no improvement is seen (Abrams, 1997; Gitlin, 1996).

The results of ECT in alleviating some cases of depression are generally acknowledged. A dramatic early example of successful ECT treatments is provided in the autobiographical account of Lenore McCall (1947/1961), who suffered a severe depressive disorder in her middle years.

Case Study, An Early Account of Treatment with ECT • Ms. McCall, a well-educated woman of affluent circumstances and the mother of three children, noticed a feeling of persistent fatigue as the first sign of her impending descent into depression. Too fearful to seek help, she at first attempted to fight off her increasingly profound apathy by engaging in excessive activity, a defensive strategy that accomplished little but the depletion of her remaining strength and emotional reserves.

In due course, she noticed that her mental processes seemed to be deteriorating—her memory appeared impaired and she could concentrate only with great difficulty. Emotionally, she felt an enormous loneliness, bleakness of experience, and increasingly intense fear about what was happening to her mind. She came to view her past small errors of commission and omission as the most heinous of crimes and increasingly withdrew from contact with her husband and children. Eventually, at her husband's and her physician's insistence, she was hospitalized despite her own vigorous resistance. She felt betrayed, and shortly thereafter attempted suicide by shattering a drinking glass and ingesting its fragments; to her great disappointment, she survived.

Ms. McCall thereafter spent nearly four years continuously in two separate mental hospitals, during which time she deteriorated further. She was silent and withdrawn, behaved in a mechanical fashion, lost an alarming amount of weight, and underwent a seemingly premature aging process. She felt that she emitted an offensive odor. At this time, ECT was introduced into the therapeutic procedures in use at her hospital.

A series of ECT treatments was given to Ms. McCall over about a three-month period. Then, one day, she woke up in the morning with a totally changed outlook: "I sat up suddenly, my heart pounding. I looked around the room and a sweep of wonder surged over me. God in heaven, I'm well. I'm myself . . . ." After a brief period of convalescence, she went home to her husband and children to try to pick up the threads of their painfully severed lives. She did so, and then wrote the engrossing and informative book from which this history is taken.

At present, the use of ECT is still considered somewhat controversial. There have been a number of malpractice lawsuits brought against psychiatrists who use

ECT, primarily over the failure to obtain appropriate patient consent, which can be very difficult when patients may not be legally competent to give such consent because of their illness (Abrams, 1997; Leong & Eth, 1991). However, many authorities support the use of ECT as the only effective way of dealing with some severely depressed and suicidal patients—especially if they have not responded to several different antidepressant medications. If is often the treatment of choice for severely depressed women who are pregnant (who should not take antidepressants) and for the elderly who may have medical conditions which may make antidepressant drugs contraindicated because of dangerous or intolerable side effects (Gitlin, 1996). Moreover, numerous reviews evaluating the research on ECT over the past 50 years, concluded that ECT is also an effective treatment for patients with manic disorders who have not responded to pharmacotherapy (80 percent effective overall with difficult to treat patients) (e.g., Abrams, 1997; Mukherjee, Sackeim, & Schnur, 1994). For example, Husain and colleagues (1993) reported on the use of a long-term (two-year) treatment of an elderly woman with recurring mania. The authors pointed out that the ECT (81 sessions in all) was the only effective means of controlling her manic episodes and proved to be both safe and cost-effective.

The use of ECT is somewhat more controversial than it was in, say the 1940s, because little else of proven efficacy was then available. Today there are effective alternative approaches—such as antidepressant medication—in abundance. Moreover, memory impairment resulting from the ECT can remain for some months (Gitlin, 1996). However, earlier concerns that it might produce structural damage to the brain have been laid to rest and it is now clear that at least properly administered ECT does not produce any structural damage to the brain (Devanand et al., 1994; Gitlin, 1996).

In 1985 the National Institute of Mental Health sponsored a Consensus Development Conference on electroconvulsive therapy to evaluate the issues surrounding the use of ECT (National Institute of Mental Health, 1985a). A panel of experts in psychiatry, psychology, neurology, psychopharmacology, epidemiology, and law, along with several laypersons, considered evidence as to (1) the effectiveness of ECT for patients with various disorders; (2) the risks of ECT; (3) the indications for administration of ECT; and (4) the best ways to implement ECT with patients.

The panel recognized a number of potential risks associated with the use of ECT and concluded that these risks have been virtually eliminated. Mortality following ECT, a significant problem in the early days of the treat-

ment, has also been significantly reduced to about 2.9 deaths per 10,000 patients. The injury and mortality rates are considered comparable to other somatic treatments. The panel reached a number of conclusions as to which disorders responded best to ECT. They agreed that the effect of ECT was well established for some types of depression, particularly psychotic depression (see Chapter 6). They also concluded that ECT can be effectively used with some types of manic disorders, particularly acute mania. On the other hand, they found that ECT was not particularly effective with some forms of depression, such as dysthymic disorder. Although ECT is sometimes used with certain types of schizophrenia, the evidence for effectiveness is not convincing. The NIMH consensus panel concluded that relapse rates for depression or mania following ECT were high unless the treatment was followed by maintenance doses of medication for unipolar or bipolar disorder; sometimes maintenance ECT treatments are given at increasingly long intervals for up to six months (Abrams, 1997). More recently, the American Psychiatric Association (1992) and the Canadian Psychiatric Association (Enns & Reiss, 1992) established clearer guidelines and standards for using ECT, training staff who conduct ECT, and policies for obtaining informed consent from patients.

Despite all the questions and controversy, the therapeutic efficacy of ECT, at least for some depressions and acute mania, is well established in the research literature (Abrams, 1997; Gitlin, 1996) and in personal testimonials from those who have been helped by it (Endler, 1990).

Neurosurgery

Brain surgery used in the treatment of functional or central nervous system disorders has sometimes been called **psychosurgery.** Mindus and colleagues (1993), however, object to this term because the "psyche" is not being operated upon. They prefer to use the term **neurosurgery** instead. We will use both terms in this text to refer to brain surgery for emotional disorders.

Although brain surgery was used occasionally in the nineteenth century to treat mental disorders by relieving pressure in the brain (Berrios, 1990), it was not considered a treatment for psychological problems until this century. In 1935 in Portugal, Antonio Moniz introduced a neurosurgical procedure in which the frontal lobes of the brain were severed from the deeper centers underlying them. This technique eventually evolved into an operation known as **prefrontal lobotomy.** This operation stands as a dubious tribute to the extremes to which professionals have sometimes been driven in their search for

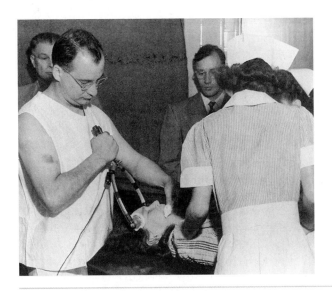
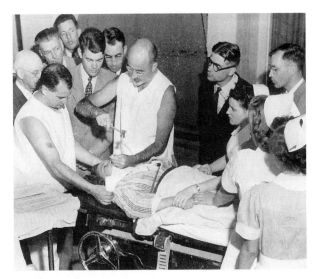

Shown here is a demonstration of a transorbital lobotomy, which was used extensively in this country from the 1940s until the late 1950s. First, a doctor administers ECT to anesthetize the patient (left). Immediately following ECT, another doctor performs the actual lobotomy (right). It is estimated that tens of thousands of patients were subjected to such procedures, resulting in permanent brain damage (which was, after all, the actual intent of the procedure) and sometimes death.

effective treatments for the psychoses. In retrospect, it is ironic that this procedure—which results in permanent structural changes in the brain of the patient and has been highly criticized by many within the profession—won Moniz the 1949 Nobel Prize in Medicine.

In the two decades between 1935 and 1955 (after which the new antipsychotic drugs became widely available), tens of thousands of mental patients in this country and abroad were subjected to prefrontal lobotomy and related neurosurgical procedures. In fact, in some settings, as many as 50 patients were treated in a single day (Freeman, 1959). As is often the case with newly developed therapeutic techniques, initial reports of results tended to be enthusiastic, downplaying complications (including a 1 to 4 percent death rate) and undesirable side effects. It was eventually recognized, however, that the "side effects" of psychosurgery could be very undesirable indeed. In some instances they included a permanent inability to inhibit impulses; in others, an unnatural "tranquility," with undesirable shallowness or absence of feeling. By 1951 the Soviet Union had banned all such operations; though rarely performed today, they are still permitted by law in the United States and in many other countries and, as we will see, have been making a comeback in modified form as a psychiatric treatment today for some difficult-to-treat disorders. See Highlight 16.1 for an illustration of the sometimes tragic outcome of lobotomy.

The advent of the major antipsychotic drugs caused an immediate decrease in the widespread use of psy-

chosurgery, especially prefrontal lobotomy. Such operations are rare today and are used only as a last resort for the intractable psychoses, severely and chronically debilitating obsessive-compulsive disorders, and occasionally for the control of severe pain in cases of terminal illness.

In his 1986 book *Great and Desperate Cures,* Elliot Valenstein examined the historical basis of psychosurgery and explained how an unproven and potentially life-threatening treatment could have emerged in a field devoted to scientific explanation and become an accepted treatment method with little empirical justification. He concluded that factors underlying this premature and "desperate" acceptance of psychosurgery included psychiatry's need to "gain respectability" as a medical science by having an organic-surgical treatment method; the professional rivalry between psychiatry, neurology, and neurosurgery; and the need to provide a cost-effective treatment and maintain control over mental hospitals.

When neurosurgery is employed today for psychiatric disorders, it is a far more circumspect procedure than in the heyday of lobotomies. Patients are more carefully screened and given more careful postoperative monitoring. Moreover, today the permanent damage to the brain has been substantially minimized and fewer detrimental side effects follow. Modern surgical techniques involve the selective destruction of minute areas of the brain; for example, in the "cingulotomy" procedure—which seems to relieve the subjective experience of pain, including "psychic" pain—a small bundle of

The Accomplishments and Subsequent Tragedy of Rosemary Kennedy

One of the tragic victims of the zeal to perform prefrontal lobotomies to alleviate behavior problems was Rosemary Kennedy, the sister of President John F. Kennedy and Senators Robert and Edward Kennedy. Rosemary was the third child of Joseph and Rose Kennedy, born during the height of the flu epidemic of 1918. She was a beautiful baby, with a sweet temperament, but as she grew, her mother became more and more concerned about her developmental delays compared to her brothers and sisters. When the family finally concluded that Rosemary was retarded, probably since birth from unknown causes, the best experts in the country at the time could offer no guidance: "We went from doctor to doctor. From all, we heard the same answer: 'I'm sorry, but we can do nothing.' For my husband and me it was nerve-racking and incomprehensible" (Goodwin, 1988, p. 416).

Rose Kennedy and the family rebelled against the suggestion that Rosemary be institutionalized. Instead, she was kept at home with the benefit of a special governess and many private tutors. She participated fully in the Kennedy's family activities, and she made considerable progress. Doris Kearns Goodwin (1988), a biographer of the Fitzgerald and Kennedy families, described an arithmetic paper that the 9-year-old Rosemary completed on February 21, 1927. She correctly answered several multiplication (428 times 32) and division (3924 divided by 6) problems. By the age of 18 years, Rosemary had obtained a fifth-grade level in English and remained at the fourth-grade level in math that she had obtained by age 9.

Because of the considerable stigma associated with mental retardation at the time, Rosemary's parents kept her condition hidden from those outside the family, a major task given the scrutiny of the family by the press. Although her parents and siblings were always nearby to protect her, Rosemary developed the social skills needed to be presented successfully as a debutante and later to the King and Queen of England at Buckingham Palace. The British press complimented Rose Kennedy for her beautiful daughters, never even noticing Rosemary's mental retardation.

Unfortunately, Rosemary's behavior deteriorated around the beginning of World War II when the family returned to the United States from England, where Joseph Kennedy had been ambassador. There are several possible explanations for this deterioration, including her increasing frustration about not being able to do all the things her siblings were able to do and having to leave the school in England where she had felt successful. The 21-year-old Rosemary became quite violent and frequently ran away from home or her convent school. There was considerable concern for her safety, and Joseph Kennedy—without Rose's knowledge—turned to the medical experts of the time, searching for a solution.

These experts convinced Joe that the miracle treatment lay in prefrontal lobotomy. Rosemary Kennedy became one of the thousands submitted to that "desperate" cure. In Rosemary's case, the surgery was a tragic failure—all her previous accomplishments were wiped out, leaving little of her former personality and adaptive ability intact: "They knew right away that it wasn't successful. You could see by looking at her that something was wrong, for her head was tilted and her capacity to speak was almost entirely gone. There was no question now that she could no longer take care of herself and that the only answer was an institution." (Ann Gargan King, a cousin, as reported by Goodwin, 1988, p. 744) ■

nerve fibers connecting the frontal lobes with a deeper structure known as the limbic system is interrupted with virtually pinpoint precision (Jenike et al., 1991). Another type of neurosurgery—the "capsulotomy" procedure, originally developed in Sweden—is a surgical operation that involves drilling very small holes in the patient's skull (employing careful measurement) and inserting tiny thermal electrodes in the brain. The electrodes are heated up, which destroys the adjacent cellular structures. Reportedly, patients do not experience subjective distress from the procedures (Meyerson & Mindus, 1988; Sweet & Meyerson, 1990). More recent innovative variations on these techniques allow functional neurosurgery without any need to drill through the skull by using a gamma knife or proton beam (Rauch & Jenike, 1998). Contemporary use of neurosurgery in the treatment of severe mental disorders is recommended only for patients who have not responded to all other forms of treatment considered standard for the disorder for a period of five years, and who are experiencing extreme and disabling symptoms. Patients are accepted for neurosurgical treatment only if they are rationally capable of understanding the procedure and provide informed consent (Rauch & Jenike, 1998).

Although there have not yet been enough controlled studies of these new psychosurgery techniques published at this time to warrant firm conclusions, research has been encouraging for at least one disorder. For example, Mindus and colleagues (1993, 1994) described an overall satisfactory result of psychosurgery in 253 severe obsessive-compulsive patients. About one half of these patients were found to show at least a 35 percent reduction in intensity of symptoms after surgery. Also important to the acceptability of an experimental procedure is the relative absence of negative side effects (occasionally patients may experience some seizures or transient headaches); effects on cognition or personality are rare (Rauch & Jenike, 1998). In this respect, Mindus and colleagues (1993) reported that no deaths occurred as a result of the psychosurgery and that the risk of suicide (often reported as a frequent outcome of psychosurgery in the past) was not found to be increased in patients who had undergone the procedure.

PSYCHOPHARMACOLOGICAL METHODS OF TREATMENT

A long-term goal of medicine has been to discover drugs that can effectively combat the ravages of mental disorder. This goal, one of the pursuits of **psychophar-**

macology, the science of determining which drugs work to alleviate which disorders and why they do so, has until the last few decades remained elusive. Early efforts in this direction were limited largely to a search for drugs that would have soothing, calming, or sleep-inducing effects—drugs that would make it easier to manage distraught, excited, and sometimes violent patients. Little thought was given to the possibility that the status and course of the disorder itself might actually be brought under control by appropriate medication; the focus was on rendering a patient's overt behavior more manageable and thereby making restraints, such as straitjackets, unnecessary.

As the field of psychopharmacology developed, many such compounds were introduced and tried in the mental hospital setting. Almost without exception, however, those that produced the desired calming effects proved to have serious shortcomings. At effective dosage levels, they often produced severe drowsiness if not outright sleep, and many of them were dangerously addicting. On the whole, little real progress was made in this field until the mid-1950s, at which point, as we will see, a genuine revolution in the treatment of the more severe disorders occurred. This breakthrough was followed shortly by the discovery of drugs helpful in the treatment of the less severe anxiety-based disorders, and also by recognition of the therapeutic benefits of antidepressants and lithium salts for the mood disorders.

In the next section we will trace the discovery of the four types of chemical agents now commonly used in therapy for mental disorders: (1) antipsychotic drugs, (2) antidepressant drugs, (3) antianxiety drugs (minor tranquilizers), and (4) lithium (as well as other mood-stabilizing drugs). These drugs are sometimes referred to as *psychotropic* (literally, mind-turning or mind-altering) *drugs,* in that their main effect is on an individual's mental life. As we examine drugs used in therapy, it is important to remember that people differ in how rapidly they metabolize drugs—that is, in how quickly their bodies break down the drugs once ingested. What this means is that people differ, too, in what dosage of a drug they may need to experience the desired therapeutic effect. Determining correct dosage is a critical factor of drug therapy because too much or too little of a drug can be ineffective and (in the case of too much) even life-threatening, depending on the individual.

Antipsychotic Drugs

The traditional **antipsychotic drugs** as a group are called *neuroleptics* and are also sometimes called *major* *tranquilizers,* but this latter term is somewhat misleading for they do more than tranquilize. They are used with the major disorders, such as the schizophrenias and psychotic mood disorders. Although they do indeed produce a calming effect on many patients, their unique quality is that of somehow alleviating or reducing the intensity of psychotic symptoms, such as delusions and hallucinations. In some cases, in fact, a patient who is already excessively "tranquil" (for example, withdrawn or immobile) becomes active and responsive to the environment under treatment by these drugs. In contrast, the *antianxiety drugs* (often referred to as the *minor tranquilizers*), to be described shortly, are effective in reducing tension without in any way affecting psychotic symptoms.

Although the benefits of the antipsychotic drugs or neuroleptics have often been exaggerated, it is difficult to convey the truly enormous influence they have had in altering the environment of the typical mental hospital. One of the authors, as part of his training, worked several months in the maximum security ward of one such hospital just before the introduction of this type of medication in 1955. The ward patients fulfilled the common stereotypes of individuals "gone mad." Bizarreness, nudity, wild screaming, and an ever-present threat of violence pervaded the atmosphere. Fearfulness and a nearly total preoccupation with the maintenance of control characterized the staff's attitude. Such an attitude was not unrealistic in terms of the frequency of serious physical assaults by patients, but it was hardly conducive to the development or maintenance of an effective therapeutic program.

Then, quite suddenly—within a period of perhaps a month—all of this dramatically changed. The patients began receiving the new antipsychotic medication (chlorpromazine). The ward became a place in which one could get to know one's patients on a personal level and perhaps even initiate programs of "milieu therapy," a form of psychosocial therapy in which the entire facility is regarded as a therapeutic community, and the emphasis is on developing a meaningful and constructive environment in which the patients participate in the regulation of their own activities. Promising reports of changes in hospital environments began to appear in the professional literature. A new era in hospital treatment had arrived, aided enormously and in many instances actually made possible by the development of these extraordinary drugs.

This new era was brought about because the first of the phenothiazine family of drugs, *chlorpromazine*

(Thorazine), was being synthesized in the early 1950s by one of the major pharmaceutical houses. Chlorpromazine soon became the treatment of choice for schizophrenia. The remarkable early successes reported with chlorpromazine led quickly to a bandwagon effect among other pharmaceutical companies, who began to manufacture and market their own variants of the basic phenothiazine compound. Some of the best-known variants are trifluoperazine (Stelazine), promazine (Sparine), prochlorperazine (Compazine), thioridazine (Mellaril), perphenazine (Trilafon), and fluphenazine (Prolixin). Currently, too, there are a number of other classes of nonphenothiazine antipsychotic drugs available in the United States, of which the best known are probably haloperidol (Haldol) and clozapine (Clozaril). This diversity becomes less bewildering when it is remembered that virtually all of the antipsychotics accomplish a common biochemical effect— namely, the blocking of dopamine receptors, as was noted in Chapter 12. However, they vary significantly in the potency of the dopamine blockade they produce. See Table 16.1 for some of the more commonly used neuroleptic drugs.

Most studies have found that approximately 60 percent of schizophrenic patients treated with some traditional antipsychotic medication show a near complete remission of positive symptoms within six weeks (compared to only about 20 percent of those treated with a placebo). Nevertheless, 20 to 30 percent seem resistant to these medications—especially those patients with prominent negative symptoms or chronic schizophrenia (Sheitman et al., 1998). Moreover, these drugs are also useful in treating other disorders with psychotic symptoms such as mania, psychotic depression, schizoaffective disorder, and they are occasionally used to treat transient psychotic symptoms when they occur in people with borderline personality disorder and schizotypal personality disorder (Gitlin, 1996). Finally, they are also useful in treating Tourette's syndrome and in relieving some of the symptoms of some dementias like Alzheimer's disease— especially the delusions, hallucinations, and paranoia that can occur with this condition, as well as the agitated behavior these patients often exhibit (see Chapter 13) (Gitlin, 1996).

Side Effects with Traditional Antipsychotics With persistent use or at high dosages, however, all of these preparations have varying degrees of troublesome side effects, such as dryness of the mouth and throat, seda-

TABLE 16.1 FREQUENTLY USED ANTIPSYCHOTIC DRUGS

Class	Generic Name	Trade Name	Used to Treat	Effects and Side Effects
Antipsychotic				
(a) Low potency dopamine blockade	chlorpromazine thioridazine mesoridazine	Thorazine Mellaril Serentil	Psychotic (especially schizophrenia) symptoms, such as extreme agitation, delusions, and hallucinations; aggressive or violent behavior	Somewhat variable in achieving intended purpose of suppression of psychotic symptoms. Side effects, such as dry mouth, are often uncomfortable. In long-term use may produce motor disturbances, such as Parkinsonism and tardive dyskinesia
(b) Middle potency dopamine blockade	perphenazine kixaoube molindone thiothixene trifluoperazine	Trilafon Loxitane Moban Navane Stelazane		
(c) High potency dopamine blockade	haloperidol fluphenazine	Haldol Prolixin		
(d) Atypical	clozapine	Clozaril	Schizophrenia	Suppresses psychotic thinking. Side effects include sedation, seizure, hypotension, fever, vomiting.
	risperidone	Risperdal	Schizophrenia	Like clozapine, it suppresses psychotic thinking, but appears to produce fewer negative side effects.

Source: Based on data from Bohn (1993); Dunner (1993); Gitlin (1996); Goodman et al. (1985); Nathan & Gorman (1998); Preskorn & Burke (1992); Tacke (1989).

tion, and weight gain. In addition they produce what are known as *extrapyramidal symptoms,* which mimic the classic symptoms of Parkinson's disease: tremor of extremities, muscle tightening, akinesia (characterized by a decrease in spontaneous movements), and akathisia (motor restlessness characterized by fidgety, purposeless movements) (Gitlin, 1996). Which side effects develop appears to depend on the particular compound used in relation to the particular vulnerabilities of the treated patient. Many of these side effects are temporary and may be relieved by substituting another drug of the same class, by switching to a different class of drug, or by reducing the dosage.

For certain patients, a particularly troublesome side effect of long-term antipsychotic drug treatment is the development of **tardive dyskinesia**—a disfiguring disturbance of motor control, particularly of the facial muscles. In a minority of cases tardive dyskinesia can be progressive and irreversible and this is why it is considered so serious. Symptoms of tardive dyskinesia, which often seem to disappear when a patient is asleep, are both dramatic to an observer and disabling to the

patient. The symptoms involve involuntary thrusting movements of the tongue, chewing movements, lip smacking, eyeblinking, and dancing-like movements in the extremeties. These movements are all involuntary and patients are often not even aware of them (Gitlin, 1996). The disturbance is believed to be due to the chronic blockade of dopamine in the brain, creating supersensitive dopamine receptors. Side effects of tardive dyskinesia can start to occur in a subset of people taking these medications months to years after the antipsychotic drug treatment is initiated and even after the treatment has been stopped or the drug reduced in dosage.

If people continue to take these traditional antipsychotic medications (as is usually recommended to reduce the chance of relapse), estimates are that 4 to 5 percent of new cases of tardive dyskinesia will develop per year for the first five years of treatment. It may occur in an even higher percentage of alcohol-abusing schizophrenics (Dixon et al., 1992; Olivera, Kiefer, & Manley, 1990) and is especially likely in people over 55. It is also more common in women and in people with a nonschizophrenic diagnosis (e.g., a psychotic mood disorder). The manifestation of the disturbance appears to fluctuate in patients over time (Gitlin, 1996). The use of antipsychotic medications in treatment is sometimes discontinued if a patient shows symptoms of tardive dyskinesia. Although there are medications that control the symptoms of tardive dyskinesia, they produce unpleasant side effects of their own (Gitlin, 1996). In some cases where the patient continues to display psychotic symptoms, the use of antipsychotic medication treatment may be resumed. Basically, the costs and benefits of staying on the antipsychotic medication must be balanced on an individual case basis with symptoms of tardive dyskinesia. To reduce the chances of this disturbance during the drug treatment of chronic schizophrenics, clinicians are sometimes using what is called "target dosing," which entails administering a drug when symptoms appear or are likely to appear rather than giving continuous dosages, as commonly practiced in the past, although this practice is usually associated with more relapses (Sheitman et al., 1998). Yet another trend in the treatment of schizophrenia involves the application of lower doses of standard drugs to reduce negative side effects, although there are greater risks of relapse with this approach as well (Sheitman et al., 1998).

The range of effects achieved by the antipsychotic drugs may be illustrated by two brief case histories of patients who served as subjects in a clinical research project designed to evaluate differing treatment approaches to the schizophrenias (Grinspoon, Ewalt, & Shader, 1972):

Case Study, Two Cases of Treatment with Antipsychotics

• Ms. W. was a 19-year-old, white, married woman who was admitted to the treatment unit as a result of gradually increasing agitation and hallucinations over a three-month period. At the outset of her hospitalization, Ms. W. continued to have auditory and visual hallucinations and appeared frightened, angry, and confused. She believed that she had a unique relationship with God or the devil. Her thought content displayed loosening of associations, and her affect was inappropriate to this content. Her condition continued to deteriorate for more than two weeks, at which point medication was begun.

Ms. W. was assigned to a treatment group in which the patients were receiving thioridazine (Mellaril). She responded dramatically during the first week of treatment. Her behavior became, for the most part, quiet and appropriate, and she made some attempts at socialization. She continued to improve, but by the fourth week of treatment began to show signs of mild depression. Her medication was increased, and she resumed her favorable course. By the sixth week she was dealing with various reality issues in her life in a reasonably effective manner, and by the ninth week she was spending considerable time at home, returning to the hospital in a pleasant and cheerful mood. She was discharged exactly 100 days after her admission, being then completely free of symptoms.

Mr. S., the eldest of three sons in a fairly religious Jewish family, was admitted to the hospital after developing marked paranoid ideation and hallucinations during his first weeks of college. He had looked forward to going to college, an elite New England school, but his insecurity once on campus caused him to become unduly boastful about his drinking prowess and women. He stayed up late at night to engage in "bull sessions" and neglected his studies and other responsibilities. Within ten days he panicked about his ability to keep up and tried frantically to rearrange his course schedule and his life, to no avail.

His sense of incompetence was transformed over time into the idea that others—including all the students in his dormitory—were against him, and that fellow male students were perhaps flirting homosexually with him. By the time of his referral to the college infirmary, he was convinced that the college was a fraud he would have to expose, that the CIA was plotting against him, and that someone was going to kill him. He heard voices and smelled strange odors. He also showed a marked loosening of associations and flat, inappropriate affect. At the time of his transfer to the hospital, he was diagnosed as an acute paranoid schizophrenic.

Mr. S. was assigned to a treatment group receiving haloperidol (Haldol). His initial response to treatment was rapid and favorable, but observers noted that his behavior remained immature. Then suddenly during the fifth week of treatment, he became tense, negativistic, and hostile. Thereafter, he gradually became less defiant and angry, and he responded well to a day-care program prescribed by his therapist, although he was nervous and apprehensive about being outside the hospital. He was discharged as improved ten weeks after the initiation of his drug therapy.

Three months later Mr. S. was readmitted to the hospital. Although he had done well at first, he had begun to deteriorate concurrently with his doctor-monitored withdrawal from haloperidol. His behavior showed increasing signs of a lack of effective control. He began to set random fires and was described by the investigators as "sociopathic." Two days after his readmission, he signed himself out of the hospital "against medical advice." His parents immediately arranged for his confinement in another hospital, and the investigators subsequently lost contact with him.

Recent Alternative Atypical Antipsychotic Drugs

Recent research with treatment-resistant schizophrenics has focused on possible alternative drugs—now generally known as the atypical antipsychotics. The first such compound to be developed that differs from the other conventional neuroleptics, clozapine (Clozaril), has produced very promising results (Gitlin, 1996; Kinon & Lieberman, 1996; Sheitman et al., 1998). Research has suggested that approximately 30 percent of patients who have failed to respond to at least three traditional neuroleptics may benefit from clozapine if it is continued for several months (Sheitman et al., 1998). Moreover, there is evidence that clozapine and related drugs may effectively treat both the positive and the negative symptoms of schizophrenia whereas the older traditional neuroleptics worked mainly on the positive symptoms such as hallunications and delusions. This represents a major advance in that traditional medication treatment often left the schizophrenic person with a great deal of amotivational and asocial behavior (for a discussion of negative symptoms, see Chapter 12).

Further research on the side effects of this drug is indicated, however, because some studies have found that about 1 percent of the patients taking the drug develop an immune deficiency that is life-threatening and that has resulted in the death of several patients. Even though clozapine has been heralded as the most effective treatment for schizophrenia, its use requires considerable caution and careful monitoring. The potentially lethal characteristic of the drug requires a highly structured blood-monitoring system along with the medication to guard against its misuse. Unfortunately, the cost of the drug in combination with this monitoring system makes the treatment expensive and has threatened to drastically limit its availability for many patients needing the drug (Gitlin, 1996; Sheitman et al., 1998). Such economic considerations may be shortsighted. Meltzer and colleagues (1993) have shown that clozapine can be very cost-effective by reducing the need for rehospitalization.

Four newer atypical antipsychotic drugs which have been less well studied than clozapine are risperidone, sertindole, quetiapine, and olanzapine. These drugs, similar to clozapine, suppress psychotic thinking also without as many of the negative side effects associated with antipsychotic medications such as the phenothiazines, particularly tardive dyskinesia (Gitlin, 1996; Sheitman et al., 1998). Moreover, like clozapine they also treat the negative as well as the positive symptoms of schizophrenia and yet they do not seem to have the same risk of pro-

ducing the life-threatening immune condition that clozapine has. Because of all these benefits to these newer atypical antipsychotic medications, contemporary research is addressing the issue of whether these medications should be used as a first course of treatment in order to prevent the deterioration that is often seen with schizophrenia if and when multiple active psychotic breakdowns occur. It is currently hypothesized, and some considerable research supports the idea, that these atypical antipsychotics operate on different dopamine receptors (and probably other neurotransmitter systems as well) than do the traditional antipsychotic medications (Kinon & Lieberman, 1996).

Antidepressant Drugs

The initial **antidepressant drugs** made their appearance shortly after the introduction of chlorpromazine in the late 1950s and their initial discoveries were quite serendipitous. Although many of these drugs were initially introduced as antidepressants they have also been found to be effective with other disorders. There are several basic classes of antidepressant compounds (see Table 16.2) and we will discuss them in the order in which they were discovered historically, although it should be noted from the outset that the newer classes are much more widely used today.

Monoamine Oxidase (MAO) Inhibitors The first group, the *monoamine oxidase (MAO) inhibitors,* include isocarboxazid (Marplan), phenelzine (Nardil), tranylcypromine (Parnate) and selegiline (Eldepryl) (see Chapter 6). These drugs were initially being studied for the treatment of tuberculosis and were found to elevate the mood of tuberculosis patients (Gitlin, 1996). They were later shown to be effective in treating depressed patients. They inhibit the activity of monoamine oxidase, an enzyme present in the synaptic cleft that helps break down the monoamine neurotransmitters (such as serotonin and norepinephrine) that have been released into the cleft. As discussed in Chapter 6, the early monoamine hypothesis of depression proposed that these drugs work through increasing the availability of the monoamines by working against their breakdown. Today we know that their effects are much more complex than this, but we still don't know exactly how they operate to reduce depression. They are not widely used today largely because of the dietary restrictions that need to be imposed on patients taking them and because of a number of unpleasant side effects. Nevertheless, they are used in certain

TABLE 16.2 FREQUENTLY USED ANTIDEPRESSANT DRUGS AND MOOD-STABILIZING DRUGS

Class	Generic Name	Trade Name	Used to Treat	Effects and Side Effects
(a) Tricyclics and related drugs	imipramine amitriptyline desipramine nortriptyline protriptyline doxepin trimipramine clomipramine	Tofranil Elavil Norpramin Aventyl Vivactil Sinequan Surmontil Anafranil	Relatively severe depressive symptoms, especially of psychotic severity and unipolar in type; some also used in treatment of panic disorder, OCD and bulimia.	Somewhat variable in alleviating symptoms, and noticeable effects may be delayed up to 3–5 weeks. Side effects may cause discomfort. Not safe in overdose.
(b) Monoamine oxidase (MAO) inhibitors currently available	phenelzine tranylcypromine selegiline	Nardil Parnate Eldepryl	Depression, panic disorder, and social phobia.	Multiple side effects—some of them dangerous. Use of MAO inhibitors requires dietary restrictions.
(c) Selective serotonin re-uptake inhibitors (SSRIs)	fluoxetine fluvoxamine sertraline paroxetine	Prozac Luvox Zoloft Paxil	Depressive symptoms, OCD, panic disorder, bulimia.	Effects take about 3 weeks. Side-effect profile is favorable, though some nausea, insomnia, and sexual dysfunction have been reported.
(d) Atypical antidepressants	trazodone	Desyrel	Depression	Less likelihood of response than TCAs. Not much used today. Minimal risk of overdose. Side effects include cognitive slowing.
	bupropion venlafaxine nefazodone	Wellbutrin Effexor Serzone	Depression	Used with patients who have not responded to TCAs or SSRIs. Relatively few side effects and relatively safe in overdose.
(e) Antimanic (bipolar) or mood stabilizers	lithium carbonate	Eskalith Lithane Lithonate	Manic episodes and some severe depressions, particularly recurrent ones or those alternating with mania	Usually effective in resolving manic episodes, but highly variable in effects on depression, probably because the latter is a less homogeneous grouping. Multiple side effects unless carefully monitored; high toxicity potential.
	carbamazepine	Tegretol	Bipolar disorder—especially manic episodes	Effective in treating bipolar disorders. Neurotoxic side effects have been noted, including unsteady gait, tremor, ataxia, and increased restlessness.
	valproate	Depakote	Bipolar disorder—especially manic episodes	Fewer side effects than lithium. Often used with bipolar patients who cannot take lithium.

Source: Based on data from Bohn (1993); Dunner (1993); Gitlin (1996); Goodman et al. (1985); Keck & McElroy (1998); Nathan & Gorman (1998); Preskorn & Burke (1992); Tacke (1989).

cases of atypical depression characterized by hypersomnia and overeating that do not respond well to other classes of antidepressant medication (Nemeroff & Schatzberg, 1998).

Tricyclic Antidepressants (TCAs) Another group of antidepressants, the tricyclics or TCAs, operate to inhibit the re-uptake of norepinephrine and serotonin (to a lesser extent) once they have been released into the synapse. Their discovery was also serendipitous in that the first one—imipramine—was being studied as a possible treatment for schizophrenia and was found to elevate the mood of depressed schizophrenics. As discussed in Chapter 6, the theory that these drugs work by increasing norepinephrine activity is now known to be oversimplified. In particular, although the immediate short-term effects of tricyclics are to increase the availability of norepinephrine and serotonin in the synapses, the long-term effects of these drugs (when they begin to have their clinical effects after three to five weeks) are to produce functional decreases in available norepinephrine and serotonin (Gitlin, 1996; Thase et al., 1995). It is also known that when the tricyclics are taken for several weeks they alter a number of other aspects of cellular functioning, including how receptors function and how cells respond to activation of receptors and the synthesis of neurotransmitters. Because these alterations in cellular functioning parallel the time course for these drugs to exert their antidepressant effects, one or more of these changes are likely to be involved in mediating their antidepressant effects (see Figure 16.1).

Mike Wallace, from CBS's hugely successful program *60 Minutes,* is one of many public figures who has been open with the public about his experience with depression.

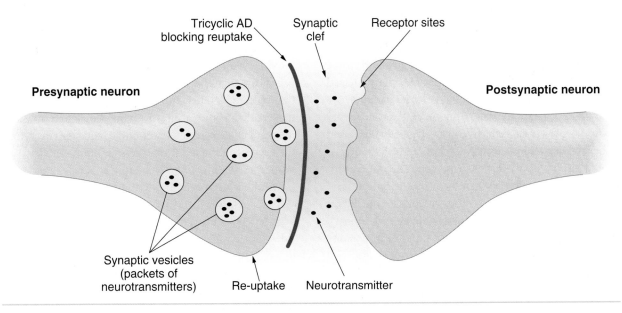

FIGURE 16.1 TRICYCLIC ANTIDEPRESSANTS AS REUPTAKE BLOCKERS

Adapted from Gitlin, 1996, p. 287.

Until the past decade, of the main classes of antidepressants, the tricyclics and their variants have been most often used. This is largely because other available medications such as the MAO inhibitors are more toxic and require troublesome dietary restrictions; in addition, they are widely believed to have less potent therapeutic effects. Nevertheless, some patients who do not respond favorably to tricyclics will subsequently do well on an MAO inhibitor—especially as already noted those with atypical depression. Although the MAO inhibitors are more toxic than the tricyclics, the tricyclics also have unpleasant side effects such as dry mouth, fatigue, dizziness, blurred vision, constipation, and occasional erectile dysfunction in men. Therefore, some patients do not continue taking the drug long enough for it to have its antidepressant effect. In addition, because these drugs are highly toxic when taken in large doses, there is some risk in prescribing them for suicidal patients who might use them for an overdose. Commonly used tricyclics are imipramine (Tofranil), amitriptyline (Elavil), desipramine (Norpramin), and nortriptyline (Aventyl).

Selective Serotonin Re-uptake Inhibitors (SSRIs)

A "second generation" of antidepressants began to be released in 1988 and has since come to dominate the market. These are the selective serotonin re-uptake inhibitors (SSRIs), such as fluoxetine (Prozac), sertraline (Zoloft), and paroxeteine (Paxil), and they are chemically unrelated to other antidepressant medications. As their name implies, the SSRIs serve to inhibit the re-uptake of serotonin following its release into the synapse. Unlike the tricyclics, they selectively inhibit the re-uptake of serotonin rather than inhibiting the re-uptake of both serotonin and norepinephrine. This class of antidepressant drugs was the first designed from the outset based on knowledge about the biochemical imbalances known to be involved in the mood disorders. The SSRIs have become the preferred class of antidepressant drugs in the 1990s because they are thought to be relatively "safe" drugs in that they are easier to use, have fewer side effects, and are generally not found to be fatal in overdose as the tricyclics can be. However, it should also be noted that they are generally not considered to be more effective than the classic tricyclic antidepressants—they are simply more acceptable and better tolerated by many patients. (See Highlight 16.2 Modern Life "Has Pharmacology Opened the Door to Personality Change?" for a discussion of some of the more controversial aspects of the use of SSRIs.)

Clinical trials with the SSRIs have reported that patients tend to improve after about three to five weeks of treatment with the drug. Several adverse side effects of the SSRIs are not uncommonly reported, particularly nausea, diarrhea, nervousness, insomnia, and sexual dysfunction (ranging from decreased arousal, to erectile dysfunction and/or delayed time to orgasm) (Gitlin, 1996; Nemeroff & Schatzberg, 1998). Although there were some early reports that Prozac was associated with suicidal urges (e.g., Cole & Bodkin, 1990; Papp & Gorman, 1990), more recent studies have found Prozac and the other SSRIs to be no more associated with suicide than other antidepressants (Gitlin, 1996). Because they have fewer side effects and are safer and easier to use, prescriptions for antidepressant medication have increased substantially in the United States since 1988. Prozac alone had been prescribed to well over 25 million Americans by 1997 (Nemeroff & Schatzberg, 1998).

Atypical Antidepressants

There is currently a heterogeneous new group of antidepressants that are not only quite different from each other but also from the other antidepressants. For example, trazodone (Desyrel) was the first antidepressant to be introduced in the United States that was not lethal when taken in overdose. It is thought to have weak serotonin re-uptake blocking effects and it acts as an antagonist to serotonin receptors. Trazodone appeared on introduction to be a very promising drug but it has heavy sedating properties that limit its usefulness; some use it in combination with SSRIs to be taken at night, helping to counter the adverse effects the SSRIs often have on sleep. It can in rare cases, however, produce permanent erectile dysfunction in men (Gitlin, 1996; Nemeroff & Schatzberg, 1998).

A more promising antidepressant introduced in 1989 is bupropion (Wellbutrin). It does not block re-uptake of either serotonin or norepinephrine but it does seem to increase noradrenegic function through other mechanisms (Gitlin, 1996). It appears to be comparably effective to the tricylic antidepressants and the SSRIs but it does not have the undesirable effects of producing sexual dysfunction that are the major reason why many people find the SSRIs unacceptable. It also has fewer unpleasant side effects than the tricyclics although it can cause insomnia, anxiety, and headaches (Gitlin, 1996; Nemeroff & Schatzberg, 1998).

Another promising new antidepressant is venlafaxine (Effexor) released in 1994. Although it blocks re-uptake of both norepinephrine and serotonin, as do the tricyclics, its side-effect profile resembles that of the SSRIs rather than that of the tricyclics, and it is relatively safe in overdose. One advantage of this drug is that it appears to help a significant number of patients who have not responded well to other antidepressants and it appears more effective than the SSRIs in the treatment of severe major depression. It

Has Pharmacology Opened the Door to Personality Change?

The drug Prozac (fluoxetine) and others pharmacologically similar to it in primarily inhibiting the re-uptake mechanism for the neurotransmitter serotonin, such as Paxil (paroxetine) and Zoloft (sertraline), are now among the drugs most prescribed by physicians. Originally considered antidepressants for use in the specific psychiatric treatment of relatively severe mood disorders, they are now also widely employed by many physicians, even nonpsychiatrists, to ease patients' often vague complaints of feeling unhappy. In this respect they have come to occupy a role in general medical practice not unlike that of the benzodiazepines (antianxiety agents such as Valium) during the 1970s and 1980s. The pharmacologic message appears to be that many people feel "better" when they have lots of serotonin available in the neuronal synapses of their brains.

What is the nature of this "feeling better"? Can we account for it in terms of more specific psychoactive properties of these drugs? These questions have been addressed in a thoughtful and scholarly manner by psychiatrist Peter Kramer (1993) in his popular and in certain respects startling book *Listening to Prozac*. Kramer's thesis is that Prozac does more than merely ameliorate depressive states—it actually in many instances transforms personality, usually in a very positive, self-esteem–enhancing way. He reports cases in which people claim to be functioning far better than they were before becoming depressed—literally "better than well"—or to have discovered, while on the drug, a "true" self different from and more satisfying than their previous self. In light of such remarkable effects on subjective well-being, patients are often understandably reluctant to give up the drug. That aspect, too, is reminiscent of the serious problems the overuse of benzodiazepines eventually produced.

Kramer examines several hypotheses concerning the basic psychological processes affected by Prozac, but he essentially suggests that the person on the drug experiences a diminished sensitivity to disapproval, criticism, or rejection by others. Obviously, such an effect would be of considerable benefit to those inhibited persons, not rare in the human species, who are overly dependent on maintaining uninterrupted signs of affection and approval from others, and who are miserable when they receive negative feedback. But just as obviously, there is a limit to the adaptiveness of any such increased insensitivity to one's environment, such as can be observed in situations where the person may appear almost entirely oblivious of others' opinions of his or her behavior. It is a bit disconcerting to contemplate living in a world in which that level of subjective social invulnerability and insensitivity toward others would be shared by everyone.

To his considerable credit, Kramer addresses forthrightly the disturbing questions raised by the availability of a prescription drug that seems not only to ameliorate disorder but in addition, for many persons, to alter their personalities, albeit mostly in ways they find pleasing. Recovery from disorder may in this context be superseded by other and quite different goals, ones with which psychiatrists or other professionals may be unprepared to deal. And Kramer is undoubtedly correct in his prediction that Prozac will prove to be only among the first of a large number of "legitimate" drugs having comparable personality-altering properties that will eventually become available. To put it another way, it seems likely that we might enter an era of "cosmetic psychopharmacology," conceivably one in which persons may even get to choose major aspects of their personalities, just as some now do the shapes of their noses. Such considerations give rise to the bizarre and somewhat ghastly conjecture that one day many social groups may be composed of pharmacologically synthetic personalities. Kramer, in the authors' judgment, has performed a valuable service in alerting us to the profound problems as well as to the promise of anticipated developments in the field of psychopharmacology. ■

also appears to act more quickly—approximately two weeks rather than three to five weeks as is more typical for the SSRIs (Gitlin, 1996; Nemeroff & Schatzberg, 1998).

Finally, nefazadone (Serzone), which was only released in 1995, acts in some ways like the SSRIs to block serotonin re-uptake but it also has other more complex effects on serotonin as well. One of the major advantages it has over the SSRIs is that it does not reduce sexual responsiveness and does not produce insomnia. Like venlafaxine, it appears to operate somewhat more quickly than the SSRIs in producing its initial antidepressant effect. However, it cannot be used in combination with certain antihistamines commonly used to treat colds and allergies, and it also cannot be used in combination with antianxiety drugs from the benzodiazepine category (Nemeroff & Schatzberg, 1998).

Pharmacological treatment for depression often produces dramatic results. Improvement in response to antidepressant medication is in sharp contrast to the effects of antipsychotic medications, which apparently only suppress schizophrenic symptoms. This statement, however, must be tempered with the observation that persons suffering from severe depression, unlike people with severe schizophrenia, often respond to any treatment (such as a placebo drug) or even no treatment at all (Nermeroff & Schatzberg, 1998). However, depression is often a recurrent disorder, and so drugs have to be administered over long periods. If the drugs are discontinued when symptoms have just remitted, there is a high probability of relapse, probably because the underlying depressive episode is still present and only its symptomatic expression has been suppressed (Frank et al., 1990). Long-term administration of these drugs is often effective in preventing relaspe as well as in preventing recurrent episodes in patients who are susceptible to recurrence (Gitlin, 1996; Nemeroff & Schatzberg, 1998).

Over the past 15 years, a great deal of research has been undertaken to determine how drugs operate to alleviate depression and which treatment or combination of treatments is appropriate for patients who are depressed (Gitlin, 1996; Nemeroff & Schatzberg, 1998). Overall, the use of antidepressant medications in the treatment of depressive episodes has shown considerable short-term effectiveness in spite of our lack of specific understanding of how they work and with what type of patient particular treatments are best suited. Nevertheless, a small minority of severely depressed patients respond to none of the currently available antidepressant compounds, in which case alternative modes of intervention, such as ECT, may be tried.

Using Antidepressants to Treat Anxiety Disorders, Bulimia, and Personality Disorders In addition to their usefulness in treating depression, the antidepressant drugs are also widely used in the treatment of various other disorders. For example, as discussed in Chapter 5, some of the tricyclic antidepressants (especially imipramine and clomipramine) are useful in the treatment of panic disorder (Roy-Byrne & Cowley, 1998; Wolfe & Maser, 1994); moreover there is preliminary evidence that the SSRIs may be useful as well (Gitlin, 1996; Roy-Byrne & Cowley, 1998). However, some people with panic disorder are greatly bothered by the side effects of the tricyclic drugs (which create some of the symptoms to which panic patients are hypersensitive) and so they quickly discontinue the medication. In the past decade a number of studies have suggested fluvoxamine, a SSRI rather than tricyclic antidepressant, is also a promising in the treatment of panic disorder (Roy-Byrne & Cowley, 1998).

In addition, several antidepressant drugs are used in the treatment of obsessive-compulsive disorder (see Chapter 5). Clomipramine (a tricyclic antidepressant that has greater effects on serotonin activity than do other tricyclics) has generally been considered to be the drug treatment of choice for obsessive-compulsive disorder. However, drugs from the SSRI category (such as Prozac) also show considerable promise and have fewer troublesome side effects than does clomipramine (Gitlin, 1996; Rauch & Jenike, 1998). Antidepressants have also been used effectively in the treatment of generalized anxiety disorder (Gitlin, 1996; Roy-Byrne & Cowley, 1998). Moreover, the monoamine oxidase inhibitors have been shown to be effective in the treatment of social phobia and there is some promising evidence that SSRIs may also be effective (Gitlin, 1996; Roy-Byrne & Cowley, 1998).

Both tricyclic antidepressant drugs and the SSRIs are also widely used in the treatment of bulimia. Many, but not all, studies have shown that these antidepressants are useful in reducing binge-eating and purging, relative to placebo (Gitlin, 1996; Wilson & Fairburn, 1998). Finally, patients with Cluster B personality disorders such as borderline personality may show a decrease in certain symptoms if they take SSRIs, most notably a decrease in mood lability, impulsiveness, and irritability, although good controlled research on this topic is in its early stages.

Antianxiety Drugs

If it is true, as some have observed, that ours is the age of anxiety, it is certainly no less true that ours is also the age of the search for anxiety reducers. Millions of prescription medications alleged to contain anxiety- and tension-relieving substances are consumed daily by the American public. In addition, Americans use other methods to reduce their anxiety—ranging from biofeedback to the practice of ancient Eastern religious rituals—that promise to relieve "uptight" feelings. The nonprescription drug market, which includes alcoholic beverages, marijuana, and decidedly more problematic substances, has had an unprecedented growth rate since the 1960s, much of it presumably due to the same widespread wish for anxiety relief.

Besides the barbiturates (see Chapter 10), which are seldom used in treatment today because they have high addictive potential and a low margin of dosage safety, two additional classes of prescription **antianxiety drugs** (also known as *anxiolytics* or *minor tranquilizers*) have been used over the past 40 years. Table 16.3 lists antianxiety drugs in both classes. The first of these were released around 1960 and are called the *propanediols* (mostly meprobamate compounds). They seem to operate mainly through the reduction of muscular tension, which in turn is experienced by a patient as calming and emotionally soothing. Although they were initially thought to be nonaddictive and safe in overdose, both of these supposed advantages to the barbiturates were later found to be false. Consequently, they are rarely used today.

The other class of antianxiety drugs is the *benzodiazepines* and the first of these were also first released in the early 1960s. Until recently, their use in this country was increasing at an alarming rate; however, thanks to effective public warnings about the addictive potential of these drugs, this trend is now leveling off (see Highlight 16.3). Under this rubric are included chlordiazepoxide (Librium), diazepam (Valium), oxazepam (Serax), clonazepam (Klonopin), flurazepam (Dalmane), and alprazolam (Xanax). In experimental studies on animals, the most striking effect of these drugs has been the recurrence of behavior previously inhibited by conditioned anxiety, without serious impairment in overall behavioral efficiency. Benzodiazepines, in other words, somehow selectively diminish generalized anxiety yet leave adaptive behaviors largely intact. They are thus far superior to many other types of anxiety-reducing drugs, which tend to produce widespread negative effects on adaptive functioning.

Side Effects of Antianxiety Drugs Nevertheless, all of the benzodiazepine antianxiety drugs have a basically sedative effect on an organism, and many patients treated with them complain of drowsiness and lethargy—not too surprising given that these drugs are also among those most commonly used to treat insomnia. We must also emphasize that all of these drugs have the serious potential of inducing

TABLE 16.3 FREQUENTLY USED ANTIANXIETY DRUGS (MINOR TRANQUILLIZERS)

Class	Generic Name	Trade Name	Used to Treat	Effects and Side Effects
(a) Propanediols (rarely used today)	meprobamate	Equanil Miltown	Nonpsychotic personality problems in which anxiety, tension, or panic attacks are prominent features; also used as anticonvulsants and as sleep-inducers (especially flurazepam, triazolan, and temazepan)	Somewhat variable in achieving intended purpose of tension reduction. Used often to treat alcohol withdrawal symptoms. Side effects include drowsiness and lethargy.
(b) benzodiazepines	diazepam chlordiazepoxide flurazepam oxazepam clorazepate alprazolam clonazepan triazolan temazepan lorazepan	Valium Librium Dalmane Serax Tranxene Xanax Klonopin Halcion Restoril Ativan		
(c) new anxiolytics	buspirone	Buspar	Generalized anxiety disorder	Effects take 1–4 weeks to occur. Not useful in treating acute anxiety. Not addictive or sedating. No addiction potential.

Source: Based on data from Bohn (1993); Dunner (1993); Gitlin (1996); Goodman et al. (1985); Nathan & Gorman (1998); Preskorn & Burke (1992); Tacke (1989).

dependence when used unwisely or in excess (Gitlin, 1996; Roy-Byrne & Cowley, 1998). Because of their potential for producing dependence, withdrawal from these drugs can be extremely difficult and must generally be accomplished slowly over a matter of weeks or months. This is especially true of the high-potency benzodiazapine Xanax, which is widely used in the treatment of panic disorder (see Chapter 5). Moreover, relapse rates following discontinuation of these drugs is extremely high (Roy-Byrne & Cowley, 1998). For example, as many as 60 to 80 percent of panic patients relapse following discontinuation of Xanax (McNally, 1994). This is probably mostly because the drugs treat the symptoms of these disorders which tend to be chronic conditions (although they do wax and wane in intensity).

The range of application of antianxiety drugs is quite broad. They are used in all manner of conditions in which tension and anxiety may be significant components, including anxiety-based and psychophysiologic disorders. They are also used as supplementary treatment in certain neurological disorders to control such symptoms as convulsive seizures, but they have little place in the treatment of the psychoses. They are among the most widely prescribed drugs available to physicians, a fact that has caused concern among some leaders in the medical and psychiatric fields because of their addictive potential and sedating effects.

Effects on GABA Continuing research on benzodiazepines and related compounds is turning up promising leads that will almost certainly result in important future advances in the treatment of anxiety and other conditions. It is now known that the benzodiazapines probably exert their effects through stimulating the action of *gamma aminobutyric acid (GABA)*, a neurotransmitter now thought to be functionally deficient in people with generalized anxiety (Gitlin, 1996; Roy-Byrne & Cowley, 1998). GABA—an inhibitory neurotransmitter—ordinarily plays an important role in the way our brain inhibits anxiety in stressful situations. The benzodiazepines appear to enhance GABA activity in certain parts of the brain known to be implicated in anxiety, such as the limbic system, and therefore inhibit anxiety in a way that is not necessary in a nonanxious person with normal levels of GABA activity. Additionally, because these compounds also have sedative, muscle-relaxant, and anticonvulsive properties, it might be possible to differentiate specific receptors for each and to discover variant compounds that will selectively bind to them. Research in this area has important implications for our basic understanding of brain processes, in addition to its obvious clinical import.

Buspirone The only new class of antianxiety medication that has been released since the early 1960s is buspirone (Buspar), which is completely unrelated to the benzodiazepines and is thought to act in complex ways on serotonergic functioning rather than on GABA. It has been shown to be equally effective as the benzodiazpines in treating generalized anxiety disorder (Gitlin, 1996; Roy-Byrne & Cowley, 1998), although patients who have previously taken benzodiazepines tend not respond as well as do ones who have never taken them. This is probably because buspirone does not have as many relaxing properties as do the benzodiazepines and hence is less reinforcing. In fact, the primary drawback to its use is that it takes two to four weeks for it to exert its anxiolytic effects and therefore is not useful in acute situations or in treating insomnia. Its primary advantage is that it has no addiction potential and is not sedating—the primary drawbacks of the benzodiazepines.

Lithium and Other Mood-Stablizing Drugs for the Bipolar Mood Disorders

In the late 1940s John Cade in Australia discovered that lithium salts, such as lithium carbonate, were effective in treating manic disorders. One of Cade's (1949) own cases serves well as an illustration of the effects of lithium treatment.

Case Study, An Early Case of Lithium Treatment • Mr. W. B. was a 51-year-old man who had been in a state of chronic manic excitement for five years. So obnoxious and destructive was his behavior that he had long been regarded as the most difficult patient on his ward in the hospital.

He was started on treatment with a lithium compound, and within three weeks his behavior had improved to the point that transfer to the convalescent ward was deemed appropriate. He remained in the hospital for another two months, during which his behavior continued to be essentially normal. Prior to discharge, he was switched to another form of lithium salts because the one he had been taking had caused stomach upset.

He was soon back at his job and living a happy and productive life. In fact, he felt so well that, contrary to instructions, he stopped taking his lithium. Thereafter he steadily became more irritable and erratic; some six months following his discharge, he had to cease work. In another five weeks he was back at the hospital in an acute manic state.

Lithium therapy was immediately reestablished, with prompt positive results. In another month Mr. W. B. was pronounced ready to return to home and work, provided he would continue taking a prescribed dosage of lithium.

It was about 20 years before lithium treatment was introduced in the United States around 1970. There were at least two reasons for this delay. First, it had been used as a

Chemically Induced Sleep: Is It Worth the Risks?

Estimates are that about one-third of the population has at least occasional insomnia and this is clearly higher among those with many of the disorders discussed in this book. Although most do not seek treatment, many do. Each year about 4 percent of the U.S. population obtain a prescription for medication to help them sleep (Gitlin, 1996). Prescriptions for the benzodiazepine class of antianxiety drugs, some of which are also called *hypnotics,* are the most widely used sleep medications. The most common hypnotics prescribed specifically for this purpose are flurazepam (Dalmane), triazolam (Halcion), and temazepan (Restoril), although other benzodiazepines not officially categorized as hypnotics are also often prescribed (such as Valium and Xanax). These drugs are prescribed for many patients hospitalized for physical disease.

Reacting to this overuse of anxiety medication, the Institute of Medicine (IOM) of the National Academy of Sciences issued a report outlining the hazards of this remedy for sleeping difficulties. Noting that the barbiturates justly deserve their reputation as dangerous drugs, the IOM report indicated that the benzodiazepines may be just as risky, and in some cases more so. For example, flurazepam, while not quite as addicting as the barbiturates, remains in the body in the form of metabolites far longer than do the barbiturates, resulting in a buildup of toxic substances that may reach a critical level within a week of regular ingestion. Although flurazepam overdose is usually not in itself lethal, it may interact with other drugs, such as alcohol, to produce lethal effects. Because of these readily misunderstood characteristics, the IOM concluded that, overall, flu-

razepam does not diminish the number of deaths attributable to sleeping pill medication, relative to earlier types of "hypnotic" drugs, such as the barbiturates. However, many of the other hypnotics do not have as long-lasting effects as flurazepam. Although they may be less toxic, they are actually associated with a great risk of causing dependence and precipitating withdrawal.

One relatively new sleeping medication— zoepidem (Ambien)—released in 1993 shows some similarities to the benzodiazepines but it also has some unique effects and is not considered to be a benzodiazepine. Many experts think it is safer than the benzodiazepines in being less likely to be associated with withdrawal reactions (Gitlin, 1996).

Recognizing the possible dangers in overuse of hypnotics (and other benzodiazepines) there has been a decline in prescriptions over the past 15 to 20 years. However, many people still believe they are overprescribed. A particularly worrisome aspect of this problem is the fact that a certain amount of benign "insomnia" naturally accompanies advancing age. Nevertheless, elderly people receive some 39 percent of all sleeping pill prescriptions. For these individuals there is a possible danger that the occasional side effects of these drugs, which can sometimes include daytime lethargy and clouding of consciousness, may be considered indicators of senile deterioration by family members and even by professional caretakers. Considering the risks involved in taking these drugs, it seems appropriate to keep in mind that losing some sleep now and then is usually not a life-threatening problem. ■

salt substitute for patients with hypertension in the 1940s and 1950s when its toxic side effects were not appreciated. Some tragic deaths resulted, making the medical community very wary of using it for any reason. Second, because it is a naturally occuring compound, it is unpatentable. This

meant that drug companies did not find it profitable to investigate its effects. Nevertheless, by the mid-1970s it was regarded as a wonder drug in psychiatry (Gitlin, 1996).

Wonder drug or not, there are significant limitations in its use. First, if not used at the proper dosage, lithium

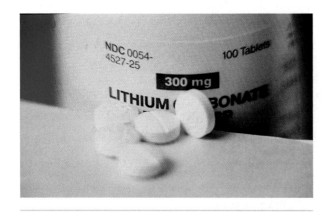

Lithium treatment requires careful monitoring of the dosage—too much can be lethal and too little is ineffective. There is no doubt, however, that the drug has been a boon to those people who have experienced repeated bouts with mania, depression, or both throughout their adult lives.

can be toxic, causing numerous side effects, such as delirium, convulsions, and even death. At the same time, if lithium is to have any notable therapeutic effect, it must be used in quantities within the range of potential dangerousness, which varies among different individuals. Thus, at the outset of lithium treatment, a patient's blood levels of lithium must be monitored carefully in relation to observable behavioral effects so that the minimum effective dosage can be established. For each individual, there is a relatively narrow range of effectiveness for the drug. Too little of the drug and the therapeutic effect will be negligible; too much of the drug and the effect could be lethal. In addition to these potentially dangerous side effects, lithium has some other unpleasant side effects in some patients, such as lethargy, decreased motor coordination, gastrointestinal difficulties, increased thirst and urination, and weight gain. Moreover, many bipolar patients seem to miss the highs and the abundance of energy associated with their hypomanic episodes, so when faced with unpleasant side effects and the loss of these highs, they may stop taking the drug. Highlight 16.4 describes the reasons that a prominent clinical psychologist who is an expert on bipolar disorder and suffers from it herself had difficulty for many years getting herself to take the medication consistently.

Even though we still do not know how it works, there can be no doubt at this point concerning lithium's remarkable effectiveness in at least partially resolving about 70 percent of clearly defined manic states—usually within seven to ten days, although it is sometimes more effective when used in conjunction with an antipsychotic drug or a benzodiazepine (Keck & McElroy, 1998). In addition, as we saw in Chapter 6, lithium is sometimes successful in relieving depression, although probably primarily in those patients with bipolar depression. Nevertheless, there may be a subclass of unipolar depressive patients who benefit from lithium treatment (Abou-Saleh, 1992; Gitlin, 1996).

The drug has been a boon, especially to those people who had experienced repeated bouts with mania, depression, or both throughout their adult lives. For many, these cycles can now be modulated or even prevented by regular maintenance doses of lithium—for example, by taking a single tablet each morning and evening. Psychiatry may thus have achieved its first essentially preventive treatment method—although, for some patients maintained on the drug for lengthy periods, there may be serious complications, including thyroid dysfunction and occasional kidney damage, as well as memory and motor-speed problems (Gitlin, 1996). There is also increasing evidence that the prevention of further attacks of mania by lithium maintenance treatment may be less reliable than was once thought. For example, several studies maintaining bipolar patients on lithium for five years or more found only just over one-third remained in remission. Nevertheless, discontinuation of lithium is also very risky, with estimates that the probability of relapse after withdrawal are 28 times higher than when on it, with about 50 percent relapsing within six months (Keck & McElroy, 1998).

The biochemical basis of lithium's therapeutic effect is unknown. One hypothesis is that lithium, being a mineral salt, may have an effect on electrolyte balances, which may alter the activities of many neurotransmitter systems in the brain, which is consistent with its diverse clinical effects (Gitlin, 1996). So far, however, this connection remains largely speculative. Clearly, the riddle of exactly what occurs will be solved only by more and better research.

Other Mood-Stabilizing Drugs Recently two other drugs have also been used with considerable success to treat bipolar disorders: carbamazepine (Tegretol) and valproate (Depakote). Initially used extensively as anticonvulsant agents to control epileptic seizures, these drugs have been found effective in the treatment of acute mania, in prevention of future bipolar episodes, and in reducing aggressivity in bipolar disorders (Gitlin, 1996; Keck & McElroy, 1996). However, they are probably less effective than lithium in the treatment of bipolar depressive episodes. Carbamazepine has been associated with significant side effects, especially neurological problems, such as an dizziness, unsteady balance, sedation, lethargy, and nausea (Keck & McElroy, 1998). As such, careful

The Many Sides of a Lithium Regimen

A prominent clinical psychologist, Kay Jamison (1995), has recently written *An Unquiet Mind,* a very moving autobiography in which she describes her own battle with bipolar disorder—a disorder on which she is one of the world's leading authorities. On the issue of her reluctance to take medication regularly, she wrote:

Even though I was a clinician and a scientist, and even though I could read the research literature and see the inevitable, bleak consequences of not taking lithium, I for many years after my initial diagnosis was reluctant to take my medications as prescribed. Why was I so unwilling? Why did it take having to go through more episodes of mania, followed by long suicidal depressions, before I would take lithium in a medically sensible way?

Some of my reluctance, no doubt, stemmed from a fundamental denial that what I had was a real disease. This is a common reaction that follows, rather counterintuitively, in the wake of early episodes of manic-depressive illness. Moods are such an essential part of the substance of life, of one's notion of oneself, that even psychotic extremes in mood and behavior somehow can be seen as temporary, even understandable reactions to what life has dealt. . . . It was difficult to give up the high flights of mind and mood, even though the depressions that inevitably followed nearly cost me my life.

My family and friends expected that I would welcome being "normal," be appreciative of lithium, and take in stride having normal energy and sleep. But if you have had stars at your feet and rings of planets through your hands, are used to sleeping only four or five hours a night and now sleep eight, are used to staying up all night for days and weeks in a row and now cannot, it is a very real adjustment to blend into a three piece suit schedule, which, while comfortable to many, is new, restrictive, seemingly less productive, and maddeningly less intoxicating. People say, when I complain of being less lively, less energetic, less high-spirited, "Well, now you're just like the rest of us," meaning among other things, to be reassuring. But I compare myself with my former self, not with others. Not only that, I tend to compare my current self with the best I have been, which is when I have been mildly manic. . . .

There has never been any question that lithium worked very well for me . . . but the drug strongly affected my mental life. I found myself beholden to a medication that also caused severe nausea and vomiting many times a month. . . .

[Years later] Lowering my lithium level had allowed not only a clarity of thinking, but also a vividness and intensity of experience, back into my life; these elements had once formed the core of my normal temperament and their absence had left gaping hollows in the way I could respond to the world. The too rigid structuring of my moods and temperament which had resulted from a higher dose of lithium, made me less resilient to stress than a lower dose, which . . . allowed my mind and emotions to sway a bit. Therefore, and rather oddly, there was a new solidness to both my thinking and emotions. (Jamison, 1995, pp. 91–93, 167). ■

monitoring of treatment, as with lithium use, is required. This is especially true because in a few patients carbamazepine has been known to cause a bone marrow reaction that can be fatal. Valproate probably has the fewest and mildest side effects, which can include nausea, diarrhea, sedation, tremor, and weight gain.

Drug Therapy for Children

Our discussion of the use of drugs in treating maladaptive behavior would be incomplete without some reiteration of their role in the management of childhood disturbances and disorders. We have already addressed this matter to some extent in Chapter 14. Although our society has often been too quick to label as deviant (and thus to "treat") various annoy-ing or inconvenient behaviors in which children sometimes indulge, it is nevertheless true that some children have seri-ous psychological disorders. It is also true that some of them may be helped by the judicious use of medication.

Antianxiety, antipsychotic, and antidepressant medica-tions, as well as lithium, have all been used effectively with children who are excessively anxious or "nervous," psychotic, depressed, or manic, respectively (Gitlin, 1996). However, to date for most of these disorders we still lack the research base needed to have high confidence in the efficacy of these drugs in children (i.e., double-blind placebo controlled studies). Moreover, considerable caution must be exercised in the use of these powerful drugs with children to be certain that dosage levels are within tolerable limits for a small and as yet biologically immature organism. Excessive blood lev-els of these drugs can be physically dangerous.

A majority of children and adolescents with attention deficit hyperactivity disorder benefit dramatically, and paradoxically, from drugs that stimulate the central ner-vous system (Gitlin, 1996; Greenhill, 1998). As we saw in Chapter 14, three stimulant drugs from the amphetamine category are used, with methylphenidate (Ritalin) being the most widely used. The primary effects on the child or adolescent with ADHD are increased attention span, de-creased distractibility and hyperactivity, and increased stability of mood. Numerous studies have also shown that hyperactive children treated with Ritalin show im-proved peer and family relationships and improved school performance. Normally, a child thus helped is kept on the drug through adolescence and sometimes into adulthood, although sometimes attempts to taper from the drug result in showing that it is no longer needed (Gitlin, 1996; Greenhill, 1998).

UNRESOLVED ISSUES

Medication and/or Psychotherapy?

Modern psychopharmacology has brought a reduction in the severity and chronicity of many types of psy-chopathology, particularly the psychoses. It has helped many individuals who would otherwise require hospital-ization to function in their family and community set-tings; it has led to the earlier discharge of those who do require hospitalization and to the greater effectiveness of after-care programs; and it has made restraints and locked wards largely obsolete. All in all, pharmacological therapy not only has largely outmoded more drastic forms of treatment but has led to a much more favorable hospital climate for patients and staff alike.

Nevertheless, a number of complications and limita-tions arise in the use of psychotropic drugs. Aside from possible undesirable side effects, the problem of match-ing drug and dosage to the needs of a given individual is often a difficult one, and it is sometimes necessary to change medication in the course of treatment. In addi-tion, the use of medications in isolation from other treat-ment methods for some disorders may not be ideal be-cause drugs themselves do not generally cure disorders. As many investigators have pointed out, drugs tend to al-leviate symptoms by inducing biochemical changes—not by bringing an individual to grips with personal or situa-tional factors that may be reinforcing maladaptive behav-iors. Although the reduction in anxiety, depression, dis-turbed thinking, and other symptoms may tempt therapists to regard a patient as "recovered," the observa-tions of relatively high relapse rates when drugs are dis-continued for a variety of disorders suggest otherwise. For many disorders a variety of empirically validated forms of psychotherapy may produce more long-lasting benefits than medications alone unless the medications are continued indefinitely.

On the other hand, for some disorders for which there are known effective medications, the failure to in-corporate medication into a psychotherapeutic treatment program can also lead to very serious problems. A court case, *Osherhoff* v. *Chestnut Lodge,* raised a number of is-sues concerning the importance of making an accurate clinical diagnosis, the effectiveness of medication, and the choice of appropriate treatment interventions (Kler-man, 1990). Osherhoff, a physician, was severely de-pressed and functioning so ineffectively that his family hospitalized him at Chestnut Lodge, an exclusively psy-choanalytic treatment facility. He was treated with inten-sive psychoanalytic treatment, without medication, four times a week. After several months, his family became concerned over his lack of progress; he had lost 40 pounds, was experiencing severe sleep disturbance, had marked psychomotor agitation to the point that his pac-ing caused his feet to become swollen and blistered. The family sought a reevaluation of his case. The staff, in a case conference, decided to continue the treatment pro-gram that had been initiated. Dr. Osherhoff's condition worsened and his family had him discharged and admit-ted into another facility where he was treated with a com-bination of phenothiazines and tricyclic antidepressants. He improved markedly and was discharged in three months. Later he filed a suit claiming that Chestnut Lodge had not administered the proper treatment—drug therapy—which had caused him to lose a year of employment in his medical practice. Preliminary court arbitration indicated an initial award of damages to Dr. Osherhoff; however, the case was settled out of court before a final judgment was rendered. A number of complicated issues were involved in the case, but the finding that therapists may be liable for failing to provide medication to patients with certain disorders for which there are known effective medications is an important and potentially disruptive new development in the field.

For severe psychopathology that tends to be resistant to treatment—such as that seen with schizophrenia, bipolar disorder, unipolar major depression, and some of the personality disorders—the combination of chemical and psychological forms of therapy is fast becoming the major thrust of current research and treatment. This integrative approach involves the combined use of psychotropic medication and psychosocial approaches, such as cognitive or behavior therapy or psychodynamic psychotherapy. The use of drugs can facilitate the patient's accessibility to psychotherapy and can serve to reduce noncompliant behavior in therapy. In many cases, the psychotherapy may be directed at the family of the patient in order to educate them about the nature of the patient's illness and to reduce high levels of expressed emotion in the family because it is widely known that patients with many severe disorders who return to families (say, after being hospitalized) with high levels of expressed emotion are much more prone to relapse (Butzlaff & Hooley, 1998). Overall, there is some reason to be optimistic about the combined use of drugs and psychosocial approaches, especially in the more severe disorders, such as schizophrenia and bipolar disorder, although in these cases the psychotherapy often cannot start until a psychotic episode has at least begun to subside. Here is the description by one bipolar patient, who also happens to be a prominent clinical scientist, of the need for both medication and psychotherapy:

> At this point in my existence, I cannot imagine leading a normal life without both taking lithium and having had the benefits of psychotherapy. Lithium prevents my seductive but disastrous highs, diminishes my depressions, clears out the wool and webbing from my disordered thinking, slows me down, gentles me out, keeps me from ruining my career and relationships, keeps me out of a hospital, alive, and makes psychotherapy possible. But ineffably, psychotherapy heals. It makes some sense of the confusion, reins in the terrifying thoughts and feelings, returns some control and hope and possibility of learning from it all. Pills cannot, do not, ease one back into reality; they only bring one back

> headlong, careening, and faster than can be endured at times. Psychotherapy is a sanctuary; it is a battleground; it is a place I have been psychotic, neurotic, elated, confused, and despairing beyond belief. But, always, it is where I have believed—or learned to believe—that I might someday be able to contend with all of this.

> No pill can help me deal with the problem of not wanting to take pills; likewise, no amount of psychotherapy alone can prevent my manias and depressions. I need both. It is an odd thing, owing life to pills, one's own quirks and tenacities, and this unique, strange, and ultimately profound relationship called psychotherapy. (From the autobiography of Kay Jamison, *An Unquiet Mind,* 1995, pp. 88–89.)

The issue of combined treatment for other disorders such as unipolar depression or anxiety disorders is somewhat less clear-cut, however. A review by Hollon and Beck (1994) concluded that at present evidence suggests only a modest superiority of combined treatment over cognitive or drug treatment alone for many such disorders. Moreover, little progress has been made in identifying patient characteristics or other clinical factors that relate to success by a given treatment method. There are still no clear indications that patients with particular characteristics respond better to medication as opposed to cognitive therapy (Hollon & Beck, 1994). There has been some belief that medication is superior to psychotherapy in the treatment of *severe* depression. As discussed more extensively in Chapter 17, one very large NIMH collaborative study (Elkin et al., 1989) for the treatment of depression concluded that medications were superior to cognitive therapy in the treatment of severe depression, and recent medical guidelines have been based on the results of that one study. DeRubeis (1997), however, has challenged this conclusion in a quantitative review of the literature. Collapsing the results of four very similar studies. DeRubeis found that cognitive therapy is as effective as medication in the treatment of severe depression. He noted that only one study (the NIMH collaborative study), which accounts for only a third of the relevant results, found medications to be superior to cognitive therapy. And even in the NIMH study cognitive therapy did more poorly only at two of the three study sites. Finally, the other three studies actually showed a slight advantage to cognitive therapy over medication (DeRubeis, 1997). Persons, Thase, and Crits-Cristoph (1996) reached a very similar conclusion in a more descriptive review of the research literature on cognitive therapy versus medication. This is just one example of the complications inherent in trying to make recommendations to patients as to which form of treatment they are most likely to respond to.

SUMMARY

Except for the development of electroconvulsive therapy (ECT) beginning in 1938, the biological approach to the treatment of mental disorders, at least on this continent and in Europe, had made little headway until about 1955. Indeed, some of the early biological treatments, such as insulin coma therapy and lobotomy, may have done more harm than good, as did many early medical treatments for purely physical diseases.

The mode of therapeutic action of ECT, which continues to be fairly widely used, is not yet understood. There is little doubt, however, of its efficacy for certain patients, especially those suffering from severe depression. Appropriate premedication together with other modifications in technique have made this treatment relatively safe and, for the most part, have checked the serious or long-term side effects. Nevertheless, some controversy about this method of treatment persists. Obviously, ECT should be used with caution and circumspection, and preferably only after less dramatic methods have been tried and have failed.

The antipsychotic compound chlorpromazine (Thorazine) became widely available in the mid-1950s. It was followed shortly by numerous other related antipsychotic drugs (neuroleptics) and more recently by nonrelated atypical antipsychotic drugs, of proven effectiveness in diminishing psychotic (especially schizophrenic) symptoms. Thus was initiated a true revolution in the treatment of severe mental disorders—one that, among other things, permanently altered the environment and the function of mental hospitals. Within a short period, too, the antidepressant medications became available to help patients with severe depression. They are also widely used in the treatment of several anxiety disorders and show significant promise in the treatment of bulimia. Finally, in 1970 (after a long delay in its introduction in this country), the antimanic drug lithium was recognized as having major therapeutic significance. With the availability of these three types of drugs, the major psychoses—for the first time in history—now came to be seen as generally quite effectively treatable.

Meanwhile, antianxiety drugs (mild tranquilizers) had been developed that circumvented many of the problems of the barbiturates used earlier in combating excessive tension and anxiety. This development extended the benefit of effective drug treatment to many people who were struggling with neurotic problems or with high-stress life circumstances. The meprobamates (for example, Equanil) were the first of these new antianxiety drugs but were largely superseded by the more potent and safer benzodiazepines (such as Valium and Xanax) for general use. A recent welcome addition to the list of antianxiety drugs is buspirone (Buspar) which does not produce sedation or dependence but is not useful in the acute situation.

Finally, the admittedly impressive gains in biological treatment methods may cause us to lose sight of important psychological processes that may be intrinsic to any mental disorder. In fact, some evidence shows that combinations of biologically and psychologically based approaches may be more successful than either alone, at least with some of the more severe disorders.

KEY TERMS

insulin coma therapy (p. 620)
electroconvulsive therapy (ECT) (p. 620)
psychosurgery (p. 622)
neurosurgery (p. 622)
prefrontal lobotomy (p. 622)

psychopharmacology (p. 625)
antipsychotic drugs (p. 625)
tardive dyskinesia (p. 627)
antidepressant drugs (p. 629)
antianxiety drugs (p. 635)

Psychologically Based Therapies

Paul Goesch, *Dream Fantasy.* A German artist and highly successful architect, Goesch (born in 1885) was hospitalized at the age of 36 after suffering mental problems for some years. He lived in an institution near Berlin until 1940, when he was removed by the Nazis to Austria and murdered there with other mental patients.

Most of us have experienced a time or situation when we were dramatically helped by talking things over with a relative or friend. As a noted psychoanalyst, Franz Alexander (1946) pointed out long ago, formal psychotherapy as practiced by a mental health professional has much in common with this familiar experience. Most therapists, like all good listeners, rely on a repertoire of receptiveness, warmth, empathy, and take a nonjudgmental approach to the problems their client's present. Most, however, also introduce into the relationship psychological interventions that are designed to promote new understandings, behaviors, or both on the client's part. The fact that these interventions are deliberately planned and systematically guided by certain theoretical preconceptions (of the kind discussed in Chapter 3) is what distinguishes professional **psychotherapy**—the treatment of mental disorders by psychological methods—from more informal helping relationships. As we will see, it is these theoretical differences that largely distinguish a given type of psychotherapy from the others available.

The belief that people with psychological problems can change—can learn more adaptive ways of perceiving, evaluating, and behaving—is the conviction underlying all psychotherapy. Achieving these changes is by no means easy. Sometimes a person's view of the world and self-concept are distorted as a result of a faulty parent-child relationship reinforced by many years of life experiences. In other instances, unsatisfying or inadequate occupational, marital, or social functioning requires major changes in a person's life situation, in addition to psychotherapy. It often seems easier to hold to one's present problematic but familiar course than to risk change and the unpredictability it entails. Therapy often takes time. Even a highly skilled and experienced therapist cannot undo an individual's entire past history and prepare him or her to cope with difficult life situations in a fully adequate manner in a short time. Psychotherapists offer no magical transformations of either selfhood or the realities in which people live their lives. Nevertheless, psychotherapy holds promise in even the most severe mental disorders, and indeed for certain of them, such as the Axis II personality disorders, may provide the only realistic hope for significant and lasting change. Contrary to common opinion, psychotherapy often proves to be less expensive in the long run than alternative modes of intervention (Gabbard et al., 1997).

To help a person achieve constructive change, a psychotherapist may attempt to (1) change maladaptive behavior patterns; (2) minimize or eliminate environmental conditions that may be causing or maintaining such behavior; (3) improve the person's interpersonal and other competencies; (4) resolve disabling conflicts among motives; (5) modify individuals' dysfunctional beliefs about themselves and their world; (6) reduce or remove distressing or disabling emotional reactions; and (7) foster a clear-cut sense of identity. All these strategies can open pathways to a more meaningful and fulfilling existence. Depending on a therapist's theoretical background and training, he or she will be likely to focus on some of these strategies more than others.

It has been estimated that several hundred therapeutic approaches exist, ranging from psychoanalysis to Zen meditation. Although the advent of managed care has had a constraining influence on the practice of psychotherapy, as it has on the delivery of other health care services, many varieties of approach compete for the shrinking financial resources available. We suspect that a significant proportion of the less well-established of these will not survive the increasingly stringent demands for empirically demonstrated efficacy that come with the managed care philosophy.

Nevertheless, the last few decades have witnessed a stream of "new therapies"—each winning avid proponents and followers for a time. The faddism in the popular literature on self-change might give the casual reader the idea that the entire field of psychotherapy is in constant flux. In reality, professional psychotherapy has shown both considerable stability over time and coherence around a few basic orientations, even though these vary appreciably in the "visions" they embody of the world and of human nature (Andrews, 1989a). This chapter will explore the most widely used and accepted of these formal psychological treatment approaches.

An Overview of Psychological Treatment

Before we turn our attention to specific psychological intervention techniques, we will attempt to gain perspective by considering more closely the individuals involved in therapy and their relationship.

Why Do People Seek Therapy?

People who receive psychotherapy vary widely in their problems and their motivations to solve them. Perhaps the most obvious candidates for psychological treatment are individuals experiencing sudden and highly stressful situations such as a divorce or unemployment, people who feel so overwhelmed by the crisis conditions in which they find themselves that they cannot manage on their own. These people typically feel quite vulnerable and tend to be open to psychological treatment because they are motivated to alter their present intolerable mental states. They often respond well to short-term, directive, crisis-oriented treatment (to be discussed in Chapter 18). In such situations, clients may gain considerably, in a brief time, from the outside perspective provided by their therapist.

Some people enter psychological therapy somewhat as a surprise to themselves. Perhaps they had consulted a physician for their headache or stomach pain, only to be told that there was nothing physically wrong with them. Such individuals, referred to a therapist, may at first resist the idea that their physical symptoms are emotionally based, especially if the referring physician has been brusque or unclear as to the rationale for his or her judgment. Motivation to enter treatment differs widely among psychotherapy clients. Reluctant clients may come from many sources—for example, an alcoholic whose spouse threatens "either therapy or divorce," or a suspected felon whose attorney advises that things will go better at trial if it can be announced that the suspect has "entered therapy." In general, males are far more reluctant to enter therapy than are females, probably for the same reasons that they resist asking for directions when lost (Real, 1997; Shay, 1996). A substantial number of angry parents bring their children to therapists with demands that their child's "uncontrollable behavior," viewed as independent of the family context, be "fixed." These parents may be surprised and reluctant to recognize their role in their child's behavior patterns.

Many people entering therapy have experienced long-term psychological distress and have had lengthy histories of maladjustment. They may have had interpersonal problems, such as an inability to be comfortable with intimacy, or may have felt susceptible to low moods that are difficult for them to dispel. Chronic unhappiness and inability to feel confident and secure may finally prompt them to seek outside help. These people seek psychological assistance out of dissatisfaction and despair. They may enter treatment with a high degree of motivation, but, as therapy proceeds, their persistent patterns of maladaptive behavior may become resistant forces with which a therapist must contend. For example, a narcissistic client who anticipates therapist praise and admiration may become disenchanted and hostile when these are not forthcoming.

Some people who enter therapy have problems that would be considered relatively normal. That is, they appear to have achieved success, have financial stability, have generally accepting and loving families, and have ac-

People have many different reasons for entering psychological therapy. It may be that they have been referred by their physician, or perhaps their spouse demands it; others seek help because of long-standing problems that affect their ability to function as happily as they would like; still others seek a deeper understanding of themselves and a greater sense of fulfillment in their lives.

complished many of their life goals. They enter therapy not out of personal despair or impossible interpersonal involvements, but out of a sense that they have not lived up to their own expectations and realized their own potential. These people, partly because their problems are more manageable than the problems of others, may make substantial gains in personal growth. Much of these therapeutic gains can be attributed to their high degree of motivation and personal resources. Individuals who seem to have the best prognosis for personality change, according to repeated research outcomes, have been described in terms of the so-called YAVIS pattern (Schofield, 1964)—they are Young, Attractive, Verbal, Intelligent, and Successful. Ironically, those who tend to do best in psychotherapy are those who seem objectively to need it least (Garfield, 1994; Luborsky et al., 1988).

Psychotherapy, however, is not just for people who have clearly defined problems, high levels of motivation, and an ability to gain ready insight into their behavior. Psychotherapeutic interventions have been applied to a wide variety of chronic problems. Even a severely disturbed psychotic client may profit from a therapeutic relationship that takes into account his or her level of functioning and maintains therapeutic subgoals that are within the client's present capabilities (e.g, see Hogarty et al., 1997a, 1997b).

It should be clear from this brief description of individuals in psychological therapy that there is indeed no "typical" client, nor, as we will see, is there a "model" therapy. No currently used form of therapy is applicable to all types of clients, and all of the standard therapies can document some successes. Most authorities agree that client variables, such as motivation and the seriousness of the problem, are exceedingly important to the outcome of therapy (Garfield, 1994; Lambert & Bergin, 1994; Rounsaville, Weissman, & Prusoff, 1981). As we will see, the various therapies have relatively greater success when a therapist takes the characteristics of a particular client into account in determining treatment approaches.

Who Provides Psychotherapeutic Services?

Members of many different professions have traditionally provided advice and counsel to individuals in emotional distress. Physicians, in addition to caring for their clients' physical problems, often become trusted advisers in emotional matters as well. In past eras, before the advent of health maintenance organizations and highly differentiated medical specialties, the family physician was called on for virtually all health questions. Even today, the medical practitioner—although he or she may have little psychological background and limited time to spend with individual clients—may be asked to give consultation in psychological matters. Many physicians are trained to recognize psychological problems that are beyond their expertise and to refer patients to psychological specialists.

Another professional group that deals extensively with emotional problems is the clergy. Members of the clergy are usually in intimate contact with the emotional needs and problems of their congregations. A minister, priest, or rabbi is frequently the first professional to encounter a person experiencing an emotional crisis. Although some clergy are trained mental health counselors, most limit their counseling to religious matters and spiritual support and do not attempt to provide psychotherapy. Rather, like general-practice physicians, they are trained to recognize problems that require professional management and refer seriously disturbed people to mental health specialists.

The three types of mental health professionals who most often administer psychological treatment in mental health settings are clinical psychologists, psychiatrists, and psychiatric social workers. These professions were briefly described in Chapter 1 (see Highlight 1.2 Modern Life, page 16). The medical training and licensure qualifications of psychiatrists permit them in addition to administer somatic therapies, such as electroconvulsive therapy, and to prescribe the psychoactive medications described in Chapter 16.

In a clinic or hospital, as opposed to an individual practice setting, a wide range of medical, psychological, and social work procedures may be used. These range from the use of drugs to individual or group psychotherapy and to home, school, or job visits aimed at modifying adverse conditions in a client's life—for example, helping a teacher become more understanding and supportive of a child client's needs. Often the latter is as important as treatment directed toward modifying the client's personality makeup, behavior, or both.

This willingness to use a variety of procedures is reflected in the frequent use of a team approach to assessment and treatment, particularly in group practice and institutional settings. This approach ideally involves the coordinated efforts of medical, psychological, social work, and other mental health personnel working together as the needs of each case warrant. Also of key importance is the current practice of providing treatment facilities in the community. Instead of considering maladjustment as an individual's private misery, which in the past often required confinement in a distant mental hospital, this approach integrates family and community resources in the total treatment approach.

The Therapeutic Relationship

The therapeutic relationship is formed out of what both a client and a therapist bring to the therapeutic situation. The outcome of psychotherapy will normally be dependent on whether the client and therapist are successful in achieving a productive *working alliance* (Horvath & Greenberg, 1994; Krupnick et al., 1996). The client's major contribution is his or her motivation. Just as physical medicine, properly used, essentially frees and cooperates with the body's own healing mechanisms, an important ally for a psychotherapist is the client's own drive toward wholeness and toward the development of unrealized potentialities. Although this inner drive is often obscured in severely disturbed clients, most anxious and confused people are sufficiently discouraged with their situation to be eager to cooperate in any program that holds hope for improvement.

The Therapeutic Alliance The establishment of an effective psychotherapeutic "working alliance" between client and therapist is seen by most investigators and practitioners as the bedrock of psychotherapeutic gain. Our own joint experience as therapists, in the aggregate comprising close to a century, affirms that basic observation. Provided there is this firm footing to the client-therapist relationship, it can withstand painful self-disclosure and the almost inevitable trials and tribulations associated with the induction of a new worldview, a more functional emotional reactivity, and a refined and expanded repertoire of new behaviors in clients.

Effective psychotherapy requires a good "working alliance," another term for a good therapeutic relationship.

Obviously, a primary and essential element in building such an alliance is that of accurate and broad-band *communication,* a mutuality of understanding that goes beyond the mere dictionary meaning of words to include cultural nuances, "body language," variations of inflection, argot or slang meanings, some mutual acquaintance with and appreciation for each other's subcultural developmental heritage, etc. In general, ease of attaining the requisite level of mutuality will be proportional to the degree of shared experience in the backgrounds of client and therapist. In an increasingly multicultural and socioeconomically disparate society, therefore, the requirement of some minimally shared frame of reference for client and therapist communication and empathic understanding would seem less and less readily achieved. This issue will be further addressed in a later section.

Other Qualities Enhancing Therapy As already noted, the client's motivation to change is a crucial element in determining the quality of the therapeutic alliance and hence the level of success likely to be achieved in the therapeutic effort. A wise therapist is appropriately cautious about accepting an unmotivated client. Not all prospective clients, regardless of their need for treatment, are ready for the temporary discomfort that effective therapy may entail. As already noted, many men, in particular, have difficulty in bringing themselves to accept the conditions good therapy may impose, such as the requirement of reporting their innermost feelings (Real, 1997; Shay, 1996). Even the motivation of self-referred clients may dissipate in the face of the painful confrontations with self and past experiences that good therapy may require.

Almost as important as motivation is a client's expectation of receiving help. This expectancy is often suffi-

cient in itself to bring about substantial improvement (Fisher & Greenberg, 1997a; Frank, 1978; Lambert, Shapiro, & Bergin, 1986). Just as a placebo often lessens pain for someone who believes it will do so, a person who expects to be helped by psychotherapy is likely to be helped, almost regardless of the particular methods used by a therapist. The downside of this fact is that if a therapy or a therapist fails for whatever reason to inspire client confidence, that treatment effort is likely to be compromised in effectiveness.

To the art of therapy, a therapist brings a variety of professional skills and methods intended to help individuals see themselves and their situations more objectively—that is, to gain a different perspective. Besides helping provide a new perspective, most therapy situations also offer a client a protected setting in which he or she is helped to practice new ways of feeling and acting, gradually developing both the courage and the ability to take responsibility for acting in more effective and satisfying ways.

To bring about such changes, an effective psychotherapist must interact with a client in such a manner as to discourage old and dysfunctional behavior patterns and to induce new and more functional ones in their place. Because clients will present varying challenges in this regard, the therapist must be flexible enough to use a variety of interactive styles. Effective therapy depends, at least to some extent, on a good match between client and therapist (Talley, Strupp, & Morey, 1990). Hence, a therapist's own personality is necessarily a factor of some importance in determining therapeutic outcomes, quite aside from his or her background and training or the particular formal treatment plan adopted (Beutler, Machado, & Neufeldt, 1994; Blatt et al., 1996a; Lambert, 1989). For example, a therapist who inadvertently but unfailingly takes charge in finding solutions for clients' problems will have considerable difficulty in working with people presenting serious difficulties in the area of inhibited autonomy, as in dependent personality disorder.

Despite general agreement among psychotherapists on these aspects of the client-therapist relationship, professionals can and do differ in their assessments and treatments of psychological disorders. This statement should not be surprising, of course. Even in the treatment of physical disorders, we sometimes find that physicians disagree. In psychopathology, such disagreements are even more common. The differing viewpoints on human motivation and behavior outlined in Chapter 3 lead to quite different appraisals of exactly what "the problem" is and how a person should be helped to overcome it. The next sections provide a perspective on the historical evolution of the several main types of therapy available and on how they are able to coexist and complement one another, despite their evident different emphases.

PSYCHODYNAMIC THERAPIES

Psychodynamic therapy is a psychological treatment approach that focuses on individual personality dynamics, usually from a psychoanalytic or some psychoanalytically derived perspective (see Chapter 3). In keeping with Freud's fascination with the principles of thermodynamics, the underlying model relates to the channeling and transformations that occur in the "energy" contained in human drives and motives. The therapy is mainly practiced in two basic forms: *classical psychoanalysis,* and *psychoanalytically oriented psychotherapy.* As developed by Freud and his immediate followers, classical psychoanalysis is an intensive (at least three sessions per week), long-term procedure for uncovering repressed memories, thoughts, fears, and conflicts presumably stemming from problems in early psychosexual development—and helping individuals come to terms with them in light of the realities of adult life. For example, excessive orderliness and a grim and humorless focus on rigorous self-control would likely be viewed as deriving from difficulties in early toilet training.

It is thought that gaining insight into such repressed material frees individuals from the need to keep wasting their energies on repressing the urge to "let go" and other defense mechanisms. Instead, they can bring their personality resources to bear on consciously resolving the anxieties that prompted the repression in the first place. Freed from the effort of keeping threatening thoughts out of consciousness (so the theory states), they can turn their energies to better personality integration and more effective living.

In psychoanalytically oriented psychotherapy the treatment and the ideas guiding it may depart substantially from the principles and procedures laid out by orthodox Freudian theory, yet the therapy is usually still loosely based on psychoanalytic concepts. For example, many psychoanalytically oriented therapists schedule less frequent sessions, such as once per week, and sit face-to-face with the client instead of having the latter recline on a couch with the analyst out of sight behind them. Likewise, the relatively passive stance of the analyst (primarily listening to the client's "free associations," and rarely offering "interpretations") is replaced with an active conversational style in which the therapist attempts to clarify distortions and gaps in the client's construction of the

origins and consequences of his or her problems, thus challenging client "defenses" as they present themselves. It is widely believed that this more direct approach significantly shortens total treatment time. We will examine first Freud's original treatment methods, in part because of their historical significance and enormous influence; we will then look briefly at some of the contemporary modifications of psychodynamic therapy, which for the most part focus on interpersonal processes.

Freudian Psychoanalysis

Psychoanalysis is a system of therapy that evolved over a period of years during Freud's long career. It is not an easy system of therapy to describe, and the problem is complicated by the fact that many people have inaccurate conceptions of it based on cartoons and other forms of caricature. The best way to begin our discussion is to describe the four basic techniques of this form of therapy: (1) free association, (2) analysis of dreams, (3) analysis of resistance, and (4) analysis of transference. Then we will note some of the most important changes that have taken place in psychodynamic therapy since Freud's time.

Free Association As we saw in Chapter 2, Freud for a time used hypnosis in his early work to free repressed thoughts from his clients' unconscious. Later, he stopped using hypnosis in favor of **free association**—a more direct method of gaining access to a person's hidden thoughts and fears

The basic rule of free association is that an individual must say whatever comes into his or her mind, regardless of how personal, painful, or seemingly irrelevant it may be. Usually a client lies in a relaxed position on a couch and gives a running account of all the thoughts, feelings, and desires that come to mind as one idea leads to another. The therapist normally takes a position behind the client so as not to in any way distract or disrupt the free flow of associations.

Although such a running account of whatever comes into one's mind may seem random, Freud did not view it as such; rather, he believed that associations are determined like other events. As we have seen, he also thought that the conscious represents a relatively small part of the mind, while the preconscious and unconscious are the much larger portions. The purpose of free association is to explore thoroughly the contents of the preconscious, that part of mind considered subject to conscious attention but largely ignored. The preconscious contents, it is thought, contain derivatives of repressed unconscious material, which if properly "interpreted" can lead to an uncovering of the latter. Analytic interpretation involves a therapist's tying together a client's often disconnected ideas, beliefs, actions, and so forth into a meaningful explanation to help the client gain insight into the relationship between his or her maladaptive behavior and the repressed (unconscious) events and fantasies that drive it.

Analysis of Dreams   Another important, related procedure for uncovering unconscious material is the analysis of dreams. When a person is asleep, repressive defenses are said to be lowered and forbidden desires and feelings may find an outlet in dreams. For this reason, dreams have been referred to as the "royal road to the unconscious." Some motives, however, are so unacceptable to an individual that even in dreams they are not revealed openly but are expressed in disguised or symbolic form. Thus a dream has two kinds of content: (1) **manifest content,** which is the dream as it appears to the dreamer, and (2) **latent content,** which is composed of the actual motives that are seeking expression but are so painful or unacceptable that they are disguised.

It is a therapist's task to uncover these disguised meanings by studying the images that appear in the manifest content of a client's dream and his or her preconscious associations to them. For example, a client's dream of being engulfed in a tidal wave may be interpreted by a therapist as indicating that the client feels in danger of

being overwhelmed by inadequately repressed fears and/or hostilities.

Analysis of Resistance   During the process of free association or of associating to dreams, an individual may evidence **resistance**—an unwillingness or inability to talk about certain thoughts, motives, or experiences (Strean, 1985). For example, a client may be talking about an important childhood experience and then suddenly switch topics, perhaps stating, "It really isn't that important," or "It is too absurd to discuss." Resistance may also be evidenced by the client's giving a too-glib interpretation of some association, or coming late to an appointment, or even "forgetting" an appointment altogether. Because resistance prevents painful and threatening material from entering awareness, its sources must be sought if an individual is to face the problem and learn to deal with it in a realistic manner.

Analysis of Transference   As client and therapist interact, the relationship between them may become complex and emotionally involved. Often people carry over and unconsciously apply to their therapist attitudes and feelings that they had in their relations with a parent or other person close to them in the past, a process known as **transference.** Thus clients may react to their analyst as they did to that earlier person and feel the same love, hostility, or

In classic psychoanalysis the patient lies in a relaxed position, facing away from the psychoanalyst. The idea behind this is that in this position he or she is better able to let thoughts go and say whatever comes to mind without trying to gauge the therapist's reactions. The therapist, too, is able to listen more freely for themes and patterns in the material when relieved of the conventions of face-to-face contact.

rejection that they felt long ago. If the analyst is operating according to the prescribed role of maintaining an impersonal stance of detached attention, the often affect-laden reactions of the client can be interpreted, it is held, as a type of projection—inappropriate to the present situation, yet highly revealing of central issues in the client's life. For example, should the client vehemently (but factually incorrectly) condemn the therapist for a lack of caring and attention to the client's needs, this would be seen as a "transference" to the therapist of attitudes acquired (possibly on valid grounds) in childhood interactions with parents or other key relationships.

In helping the client to understand and acknowledge the transference relationship, a therapist may provide the client with insight as to the meaning of his or her reactions to others. In doing so he or she may also introduce a corrective emotional experience by refusing as it were to engage the person on the basis of his or her unwarranted assumptions about the nature of the therapeutic relationship. If the client expects rejection and criticism, for example, the therapist is careful to maintain a neutral manner. In this way it may be possible for the individual to recognize these assumptions and to "work through" the conflict in feelings about the real parent or perhaps to overcome feelings of hostility and self-devaluation that stemmed from the earlier parental rejection. In essence, the negative effects of an undesirable early relationship are counteracted by working through a similar emotional conflict with the therapist in a therapeutic setting. A person's reliving of a pathogenic past relationship in a sense re-creates the neurosis in real life, and therefore this experience is often referred to as a *transference neurosis*.

It is not possible here to consider at length the complexities of transference relationships, but we can stress that a client's attitudes toward his or her therapist usually do not follow such simple patterns as our examples suggest. Often the client is ambivalent—distrusting the therapist and feeling hostile toward him or her as a symbol of authority, but at the same time seeking acceptance and love. In addition, the problems of transference are not confined to the client, for the therapist may also have a mixture of feelings toward the client. This phenomenon is known as **counter-transference** (the therapist reacts in accord with the client's transferred attributions rather than objectively) and must be recognized and handled properly by the therapist. For this reason, it is considered important that therapists have a thorough understanding of their own motives, conflicts, and "weak spots"; in fact, all psychoanalysts themselves undergo psychoanalysis before they begin independent practice.

The resolution of the transference neurosis is said to be the key element in effecting a psychoanalytic "cure." Such resolution can occur only if an analyst successfully avoids the pitfalls of counter-transference. That is, the analyst needs to keep track of his or her own transference or reaction to a client's behavior. Failure to do so risks merely repeating in the therapy relationship the typical relationship difficulties characterizing the client's adult life. Analysis of transference and counter-transference are also part of most psychodynamic derivatives of classical psychoanalysis, to which we now turn.

Psychodynamic Therapy Since Freud

The original version of psychoanalysis is practiced only rarely today. Arduous and expensive in time, money, and emotional commitment, it may take several years until both analyst and client are satisfied that all major issues in the client's life have been satisfactorily resolved. In light of these heavy demands, most psychoanalytic/psychodynamic therapists have worked out modifications in procedure designed to shorten the time and expense required. Mann (1973), for example, described an approach that follows psychoanalytic concepts but is confined to a 12-session treatment course aimed at symptom relief. Other brief psychodynamically oriented approaches have been reviewed by Anderson and Lambert (1995), Henry and colleagues (1994), and Messer and Warren (1995). In general, these therapies seem not to lose anything in effectiveness relative to full psychoanalysis.

Interpersonal Therapy Contemporary psychodynamic approaches to therapy tend to have a strongly *interpersonal* focus. They emphasize, in other words, what traditional Freudians would consider transferential and counter-transferential phenomena, with the important extension of this concept to virtually all of a disturbed person's relationships, rather than considering such distortions of interpersonal processes a unique product of the classical psychoanalytic treatment situation. First articulated in this country by Harry Stack Sullivan (see Chapter 3), the central idea is that all of us at all times involuntarily invoke schemas acquired from our earliest interactions with others, such as parents, in interpreting what is going on in our current relationships. Where those earlier relationships have had problematic features, such as rejection or abuse, the "introjected" characteristics of those earlier interaction partners may distort in various ways the ability to process accurately and objectively the information contained in current interpersonal transactions. Thus, the formerly abused or rejected person may come to operate under the implicit (unconscious) assumption that the world is generally rejecting and/or abusive. The mistrust stemming from this belief is bound to negatively affect current relationship possibilities—in the worst instances possibly even leading (because of the reactions of others to the client's wariness, reticence, or counteraggression) to a further confirmation for that client of the world's being a nasty if not dangerous place, an instance of self-fulfilling prophecy (e.g., see Carson, 1982; Wachtel, 1993).

Object Relations, Self Psychology, and Other Interpersonal Variations
The most extensive revisions of classical psychoanalytic theory undertaken within recent decades have been those relating to the *object relations* ("objects" in psychoanalytic jargon are other people) and to a lesser extent the *attachment* and *self psychology* perspectives (see Chapter 3; also Cashdan [1988]; Freedheim, [1992]). Whether or not psychotherapy investigators and clinicians use the term "object relations" (or the alternatives) to denote their approach to the work of psychotherapy, increasing numbers of them describe procedures that focus on interpersonal relationship issues, particularly as they play themselves out in the client-therapist relationship (e.g., Benjamin, 1996; Crits-Christoff & Connoly, in press; Frank & Spanier, 1995; Horowitz, 1996; Kiesler, 1996; Klerman et al., 1984; Strupp & Binder, 1984). Highlight 17.1 present an example of this general type of psychotherapy.

The greatest contribution of the interpersonal approach may be its role in the developing movement toward "integration" of the various forms of therapy, about which more is said below. Numerous contemporary investigators and clinicians (e.g., Beutler, 1992; Blatt et al., 1996b; Lazarus, 1997a, 1997b; Linehan, 1993; Safran, 1990a, 1990b; Wachtel, 1997) have pointed to the multiple ways in which interpersonal issues play a central role in psychodynamic, behavioral, cognitive, and even psychopharmacological therapies.

Psychodynamic interpersonally oriented therapists vary considerably in their time focus: whether they concentrate on remote events of the past or current ("the here and now") interpersonal situations and impasses—including those of the therapy itself—or some balance of the two. Probably, as already suggested, most seek to expose, bring to awareness, and modify the effects of the remote developmental sources of the difficulties the client is currently experiencing. These therapies generally retain, then, the classical psychoanalytic goal of under-

standing the present in terms of the past. What they ignore are the psychoanalytic notions of staged libidinal energy transformations and of entirely internal (and impersonal) drives that are channeled into psychopathological symptom formation.

Evaluating Psychodynamic Therapy

Classical psychoanalysis is routinely criticized by outsiders for being relatively time-consuming and expensive; for being based on a questionable, stultified, and sometimes cultlike approach to human nature; for neglecting a client's immediate problems in the search for unconscious conflicts in the remote past; and for inadequate proof of general effectiveness. Concerning the last of these, we note that, with a few exceptions, analysts have been less than eager to subject their treatment outcomes to rigorous scrutiny. When they have done so (see Smith et al., 1980; Wallerstein, 1989) the results have generally not been impressive, especially when considered in relation to the usually optimistic goals and considerable investments involved.

Nevertheless, many people do feel that they have profited from psychoanalysis—particularly in terms of greater self-understanding, relief from inner conflict and anxiety, and improved interpersonal relationships. Psychodynamic psychotherapy remains the treatment of choice for many individuals who are seeking extensive insight into themselves and broad-based personality change. In trying to reconcile these observations we may be confronting two different standards of evaluating therapeutic outcomes—that of *efficacy* (involving maximally rigorous controlled research designs) on the one hand and *effectiveness* (a looser but probably overall more realistic standard) on the other, a distinction that has become prominent in the literature only in the last few years (Seligman, 1995). We address that issue in a later section.

Turning our attention to the usually far briefer versions of psychodynamic-interpersonal therapies, the situation appears brighter—even under an efficacy standard—although much work with outcomes on specific groups of clients remains to be accomplished. Anderson and Lambert (1995) have published a useful summary, involving quantitative analysis, of 26 efficacy studies of brief psychodynamic psychotherapy. In general, the demonstrated results of this type of therapy are quite impressive. We would single out in particular the interpersonal therapy model developed by Klerman and associates (1984), originally targeted for the problem of

Highlight 17.1

An Example of Psychodynamic-Interpersonal Psychotherapy

The case presented here is that of a 43-year-old, never-married, college-educated woman with a diagnosis of Borderline Personality Disorder (BPD-see Chapter 9). Her history included two suicide attempts, one of them quite serious, and earlier bouts with alcohol dependence and eating disorder. As is not uncommon in instances of BPD, her former therapist had essentially given up on attempts to help this notably self-destructive woman and had referred her to the current therapist, who was working under the auspices of a free-service, but time-limited, psychotherapy research project. At the outset, the therapist was extremely careful to lay out the terms of the therapeutic contract, which specifically excluded the therapist's "materializing" on demand should the patient need help during other than scheduled sessions. In this segment, the therapist engages the prominent abandonment theme in the client's life (a characteristic theme in BPD) and relates it to their own relationship.

CLIENT: Uhh, last spring, a year ago, I can't remember, a year ago, yeah. I started seeing him just about this time. And I went out with him, you know, a couple of months, till May, maybe, or something, I don't know. And he was really very good to me. He made me feel important. He used to come, I was working the late shift then, and he used to work his schedule around. . . mine, which was really very nice. We ate breakfast or something, and then he just, you know, then all of a sudden he just changed his feelings, and decided he wanted nothing to do with me ever again.

THERAPIST: Hmm.

CLIENT: And never did.

THERAPIST: Out of the blue?

CLIENT: Out of the blue. Completely out of the blue. I mean there's only one thing. It wasn't completely out of the blue because, the week before this happened, I got very depressed, and I don't know what it was. It had nothing to do with him, it was just, I didn't go to work. I think it was just from lack of sleep, and I just was very, I went to bed for like six days. I was just in bed, and I said I was sick and I wasn't sick, I just didn't want anybody to know what was really, you know that I was so depressed. And I didn't really get out of bed for six days and he, came over one day, he just, maybe he knew, I don't know. I think he just couldn't stand seeing me like that. I mean I was pretending to feel good. I wasn't. You know, he didn't see me lying in my bed. Like I got up, I took a shower, and I, you know, I pretended like everything was okay.

THERAPIST: Hmm.

CLIENT: He didn't like the fact that I took off work for a couple of days.

THERAPIST: Oh. Sounds like exactly the kind of guy you'd expect, if you're not functioning perfectly, he runs the other way.

CLIENT: And he did.

THERAPIST: How did you happen to meet that particular guy?

CLIENT: He was my friend Sally's cousin. . . . And I met him at another friend's wedding, which was a year ago. And I thought he was completely different from who he was.

THERAPIST: Well, when I said to you how did you happen to meet that kind of guy, I was just curious that you happened to meet somebody who exactly fulfilled your fear, at least in your mind. A few days of not feeling terrific, and he was out the door.

CLIENT: I don't know how, but I did. And I didn't think he was anything like that, I thought he was understanding and, you know, sweet. And I didn't really think that at all. But it happened anyway. In fact, I let my guard down, I think, you know, I was like—

THERAPIST: Hmmm. Just what you were afraid would happen, happened.

CLIENT: And I'm afraid it will happen with Doug [the new boyfriend].

THERAPIST: Is your guard up or down here?

CLIENT: Hmm, I don't really feel like it's anywhere, you know. I don't feel like my guard is up, and I don't feel like, I mean I guess you do because you keep asking me.

THERAPIST: Well, you certainly don't let too much distress come through. You know you tell me your concerns, but you always seem together and matter-of-fact so there's kind of a mix. Your message is "I have these problems," but your manner is "I know how to take care of myself, I'll just not get too involved, I'll make sure I look okay to the world and Doug." So it's an interesting mix. You say the problems, but you look more or less in control, just that you're not happy with what you think is gonna come out of this . . .

CLIENT: No.

THERAPIST: . . . which you think will be negative. You look like you're on top of the situation, almost precisely because you can predict and plan for your disappointment.

CLIENT: Yeah, but I'm not really in control because I feel that if I look in control, I just will be.

THERAPIST: Hmm, you're sort of in control by expecting the worst.

CLIENT: Yeah, I guess it's so I don't look stupid to me or anybody else if I knew it was coming anyway, you know. I mean I would like to tell Doug that I feel this way and I'd like him to know, but for what reason, I don't know.

THERAPIST: For what reason to tell him?

CLIENT: Yeah.

THERAPIST: Other than for that's the way you feel.

CLIENT: I mean it's not always good to let everybody know all your feelings, you know.

THERAPIST: You see, it sounds like you're sort of assuming he could be two kinds of people. Either he's somebody you could tell how you feel and he'd be understanding or he could be somebody you tell how you feel and he'd drop you because you have a weakness. Sounds like you could imagine both people, but you're betting on the second one.

CLIENT: Right, I am. But I don't know, I don't think my guard is up here. I know what you're saying, but, I don't even know how I would let anybody know my feelings anyway.

THERAPIST: You don't know how?

CLIENT: Not really. You know.

THERAPIST: Are you afraid that if your feelings came through, that if they really broke through. . . .

CLIENT: Yes.

THERAPIST: If they really broke through . . . you were afraid that I wouldn't want to hear it either. I wouldn't want any part of your weakness or your sadness.

CLIENT: Maybe. And I'm also afraid sometimes when I, when things get to be too much that I'd just break down, and that's not what I want to happen.

THERAPIST: [interrupts] And if you broke down, I'd walk away.

CLIENT: Yeah, and then, also for me, I can't do that anymore, I can't go get into bed for days, you know.

THERAPIST: The only way to break down is to be in bed for days.

CLIENT: Sometimes.

THERAPIST: You see that's an action, that's not putting into words.

CLIENT: I know. Cause I just don't think about it, I sleep and I lay there.

THERAPIST: So it's kinda avoiding the thinking and feeling by acting.

CLIENT: Yeah, yeah it's true. ∎

Source: From Foelsch and Kernberg (1998), pp. 86–88.

depression, where it has demonstrated value (Frank & Spanier, 1995). It has since been shown to be a promising treatment for bulimia nervosa (Fairburn et al., 1993), and it is doubtless being investigated at the present time in other clinical contexts as well.

BEHAVIOR THERAPY

Although the use of conditioning techniques in therapy has a long history, it was not until the 1960s that **behavior therapy**—the use of therapeutic procedures based (as originally formulated) on the principles of classical and operant conditioning—really came into its own.

In the behavioral perspective, as we saw in Chapter 3, a maladjusted person (unless suffering from brain pathology) is seen as differing from other people only in (1) having failed to acquire competencies needed for coping with the problems of living, (2) having learned faulty reactions or coping patterns that are being maintained by some kind of reinforcement, or (3) both. Thus a behavior therapist specifies in advance the precise maladaptive behaviors to be modified and the adaptive behaviors to be achieved, as well as the specific learning principles or procedures to be used in producing the desired results.

Instead of exploring past traumatic events or inner conflicts, behavior therapists attempt to modify problem behaviors directly by extinguishing or counter-conditioning maladaptive reactions, such as anxiety, or by manipulating environmental contingencies—that is, by the use of reward, suspension of reward, or, occasionally, punishment to shape overt actions. Indeed, for the strict behaviorist, "personality" does not exist except in the form of a collection of modifiable habits. Behavior therapy techniques seem especially effective in altering maladaptive behavior when a reinforcement is administered contingent on a desired response, and when a person knows what is expected and why the reinforcement is given. The ultimate goal, of course, is not only to achieve the desired responses but to bring them under the control and self-monitoring of the individual.

We have cited many examples of the application of behavior therapy in earlier chapters. In this section, we will elaborate briefly on the key techniques of behavior therapy.

Guided Exposure

As we saw in Chapter 5, and as conceived by behavioral theory, most people with anxiety disorders are reacting to factually benign internal or external stimuli with the acquired (learned, classically conditioned) response of anxiety. Since the days of Pavlov (see Chapter 2), it has been

known that one can remove ("extinguish") such a classically conditioned response by repeated presentations of the pertinent stimuli in the absence of "reinforcement," which in this case would be some dreadful event (e.g., death) whose imminence is signaled by the occurrence of the evoking stimuli. One might logically wonder, if this is the case, why anxiety disorders don't cure themselves, since such dreadful events as a phobic's fear of a bridge collapsing are highly unlikely to happen should these evoking stimuli (the bridge) present themselves? The problem is that anxiety-disordered clients also learn artful and often complicated ways of avoiding confrontation with these disturbing stimuli, being reinforced in that effort by a relatively prompt reduction in anticipatory distress. But in so doing they deprive themselves of the opportunity to unlearn (extinguish) the anxiety response. Guided exposure (to these anxiety-provoking stimuli) is the technique behavior therapists have developed to ensure the unlearning of the anxiety reaction. It has two basic variations: systematic desensitization and in vivo exposure.

Systematic Desensitization   The process of extinguishing maladaptive reactions can be applied to behavior that is positively or negatively reinforced. Of the two, behavior that is negatively reinforced—reinforced by the successful avoidance of a painful situation—is harder to deal with because, as just noted, the avoidant client never gets a chance to find out that the expected aversive consequences do not in fact come about.

One technique that has proved useful in extinguishing negatively reinforced behavior involves eliciting an antagonistic or competing response. Because it is difficult if not impossible to feel both pleasant and anxious at the same time, the method of **systematic desensitization** is aimed at teaching a person to relax or behave in some other way that is inconsistent with anxiety while in the presence (real or imagined) of the anxiety-producing stimulus. It may therefore be considered a type of counter-conditioning procedure. The term *systematic* refers to the carefully graduated manner in which the person is exposed to the feared stimulus, the procedural opposite of some forms of in vivo exposure, a behavioral technique described below.

The prototype of systematic desensitization is the classic experiment of Mary Cover Jones (1924), in which she successfully eliminated a small boy's fears of a white rabbit and other furry animals. She began by bringing the rabbit just inside the door at the far end of the room while the boy, Peter, was eating. On successive days, the rabbit was gradually brought closer until Peter could pat it with one hand while eating with the other. Joseph Wolpe (1958; Rachman & Hodgson, 1980) elaborated on the procedure developed by Jones and devised the term *systematic desensitization* to refer to it. On the assumption that most anxiety-based patterns are, fundamentally, conditioned responses, Wolpe worked out a way to train a client to remain calm and relaxed in situations that formerly produced anxiety. Wolpe's approach is elegant in its simplicity, and his method is equally straightforward.

A client is first taught to enter a state of relaxation, typically by progressive concentration on relaxing various muscle groups. Meanwhile, in collaboration with the therapist, an anxiety hierarchy is constructed consisting of imagined scenes graded as to their capacity to elicit anxiety. For example, were the problem one of disabling sexual anxiety, a low-anxiety scene might be a candlelight dinner with the prospective partner, while a high-anxiety scene might be imagining the penis actually entering the vagina. Active therapy sessions consist of repeatedly imagining the scenes in the hierarchy under conditions of deep relaxation, beginning with the minimum anxiety items and gradually working toward those rated in the more extreme ranges. A session is terminated at any point where the client reports experiencing significant anxiety, the next session resuming at a lower point in the hierarchy.

Treatment continues until all items in the hierarchy can be imagined without notable discomfort, at which point the client's real-life difficulties will typically have shown substantial improvement. The usual duration of a desensitization session is about 30 minutes, and the ses-

sions are often given two to three times per week. The overall therapy program may, of course, take a number of weeks or even months. Typically, however, clients begin to make significant real-life therapeutic gains early in treatment (Kennedy & Kimura, 1974). As in the case of psychodynamic therapy, the original model has now been largely supplanted by briefer and more direct techniques, as described below.

Several variants of systematic desensitization have been devised. One variation involves the use of a tape recorder to enable a client to carry out the desensitization process at home. Another utilizes group desensitization procedures—as in marathon desensitization groups, in which the entire program is compressed into a few days of intensive treatment. One of the present authors routinely employs hypnosis to induce relaxation (the standard relaxation training can be quite tedious) and to achieve vividness in the imagining of hierarchy scenes. Highlight 17.2 focuses on a more recently developed therapy whose principle effective ingredient appears to be imaginal exposure. Perhaps the most important contemporary variation is "in vivo" desensitization, which typically involves graduated exposure to actual (unrealistically) feared situations.

In vivo exposure Following the introduction and rapidly established success of Wolpe's systematic desensitization procedure, behavior therapy researchers turned their attention to discovering the differential contribution to therapeutic success of the several components of this technique (i.e., relaxation training, graduated introduction of anxiety-inducing stimuli, imaginal exposure to the latter). By the mid-1980s it had become apparent that the central ingredient was in fact *exposure* to the here-to-fore avoided anxiety-provoking stimuli, the remaining components being seen largely as facilitating that exposure. (Relaxation training, by itself, can be a useful procedure for many stress-related disorders, as we have seen.)

With the recognition that exposure is the key element in treating many forms of anxiety disorder, therapists were freed to explore a variety of quite direct approaches to having clients repeatedly experience the actual—not merely imaginal—internal (e.g., heartbeat irregularities) or external (e.g., high places) stimuli that had been identified as producing anxiety reactions. Such approaches are often referred to as **in vivo** (as opposed to **in vitro**, or imaginal) **exposure.**

Imaginal procedures have some limitations, an obvious one being that not all persons are capable of vividly

Joseph Wolpe is shown here conducting systematic desensitization therapy to reduce a client's anxiety. The client, in a relaxed state. is told to imagine the weakest anxiety on her list of anxiety-producing stimuli. If she feels anxious, she is instructed to stop imagining and relax again.

Highlight 17.2

EMDR: Only Another Exposure Treatment?

The emergence of Eye Movement Desensitization and Reprocessing (EMDR) therapy was announced by its originator Francine Shapiro over a decade ago (Shapiro, 1989). It has been strongly promoted as an unusually effective and "breakthrough" treatment for various (chiefly anxiety-based) disorders in various publications (Shapiro, 1995, 1996; Shapiro & Forest, 1997) and through the formation of an EMDR Institute in Pacific Grove, California. It has proven highly attractive to some clinicians, mostly private practitioners, over 22, 000 of whom at this writing have been certified—after obtaining institute-sponsored training—as competent to carry out the procedure (EMDR Institute, 1997).

The commercial, promotional, and proprietary tenor of EMDR's development, together with its emphasis on the unlikely technique of inducing lateral eye movements in the client, by the therapist's wagging of a finger, was almost certain to raise eyebrows in the professional mental health community, and it did (e.g., see Acierno et al., 1994). Some of that reaction has taken the form of vigorous critiques of the theoretical and evidential basis of the extraordinary claims of success (e.g., curing posttraumatic stress disorder in one session) made by EMDR proponents. We focus on the latter controversy here.

Among a host of other critics (e.g., Foa & Meadows, 1997), Jeffrey Lohr and colleagues (Lohr et al., 1995; Lohr, Tolin, & Lilienfeld, 1998) have provided what are the most searching and comprehensive examinations of the now substantial EMDR research literature in two successive reviews. Their conclusions may be summarized as follows:

• The entire EMDR treatment package contains several elements already known to have powerful therapeutic effects, such as imaginal exposure and cognitive restructuring.
• The induction of lateral eye movement (or other lateralized movement, such as finger tapping) is superfluous in accounting for results.
• Much of the positive effect of EMDR is attributable to nonspecific treatment variables, such as placebo reactions.
• EMDR-supportive results tend to be limited to client verbal report indices.
• The theoretical underpinnings of EMDR, chiefly the notion that lateralized movement accelerates processing of affective-cognitive information, has little or no basis in scientific fact.

It would seem, therefore, that EMDR proponents have been overly enthusiastic in selling their wares. In so doing, they have attracted the kind of critical attention reviewed above. Some of them now say they have been held to a higher standard than proponents of other therapies. That may well be true, but who is responsible?

Further research will doubtless clarify the nature and efficacy of EMDR. Meanwhile, we are inclined to consider it a variant of exposure therapy. ■

imagining the required scenes. In a study of clients with agoraphobia, Emmelkamp and Wessels (1975) concluded that prolonged exposure in vivo plainly proved superior to simple reliance on the imagination, and in recent years the in vivo exposure procedure seems to have gained a definite ascendancy over that of in vitro imagining wherever it is possible to identify in concrete terms those situations evoking anxiety, and to induce the client to confront them directly (Barlow, 1988, 1993). However, some anxiety-inducing situations are not readily or judiciously reproducible in real life, as when they refer to memories of unique past events such as natural disasters, or when in

In vivo exposure is a technique that involves placing an individual in a real-life anxiety-arousing situation with the goal of extinguishing the conditioned avoidance of an anxiety-provoking stimulus, as well as anxiety itself. For example, a client with a fear of heights may be taken to the top of a tall building to demonstrate that the feared consequences do not occur.

logically oriented therapists have begun to experiment with computerized *virtual reality* means of exposing clients to scenes that would be unwise, inconvenient, or impossible to recreate in real life (e.g., Rothbaum et al., 1995a, 1995b, 1996). The technique appears to have considerable promise.

A modification of in vivo experience that involves repeated exposure to the somatic cues usually preceding panic (for example, heart palpitations experienced at the beginning of a false alarm; see Chapter 5), rather than to traumatizing situations themselves, may be one way to avoid undesirable reactions to exposure treatment. Accumulating evidence shows that it is these sorts of bodily cues that trigger full-blown anxiety attacks. Barlow and associates (e.g., Barlow et al., 1989; Craske & Barlow, 1993) have developed effective procedures for extinguishing this type of chain reaction—for example, by teaching clients to self-induce some of their false alarm symptoms repeatedly so that habituation can occur (*interoceptive exposure*). In an important study in which the exposure to anticipatory cues procedure was a centerpiece in a treatment package for panic disorder, this treatment was demonstrated to be far superior to drug treatment with alprazolam (Xanax), a benzodiazepine compound touted as having strong antipanic properties, but one also noted for its addictive potential (Klosko et al., 1990).

Where a therapist has a choice—that is, depending on the nature of the problem and on client cooperation and tolerance—in vivo procedures seem to have an edge in efficiency and possibly in ultimate efficacy over those employing imagery as the mode of confrontation (Emmelkamp, 1994). Overall, the outcome record for exposure treatments is impressive (Emmelkamp, 1994; Nathan & Gorman, 1998; Roth & Fonagy, 1996).

Aversion Therapy

Aversion therapy involves modifying undesirable behavior by the old-fashioned method of punishment. Punishment may involve either the removal of highly desired reinforcers or the use of aversive stimuli, but the basic idea is to reduce the "temptation value" of stimuli that elicit undesirable behavior. Probably the most commonly used aversive stimuli today are drugs having noxious effects, such as Antabuse, which induces nausea and vomiting when the person ingests alcohol (see Chapter 10). In another variant, the offending client is instructed to wear a substantial elastic band on the wrist and to "snap" it when temptation arises, thus administering self-punishment. In the past, painful electric shock was commonly employed in programs that paired it with the occurrence of

vivo exposure to them might be objectively dangerous. For example, it is desirable for the traumatized rape victim to confront the circumstances surrounding the attack (Calhoun & Resick, 1993), but it would obviously be foolhardy to recommend that she walk around crime-infested neighborhoods at night. In addition, an occasional client is so fearful that he or she cannot be induced to confront directly the anxiety-arousing situation (Emmelkamp & Wessels, 1975). Imaginal procedures remain, therefore, a vital part of the therapeutic exposure armamentarium.

On the other hand, the exposure procedure can be made relatively bearable without diminished effectiveness for even a severely fearful client by increasing therapist support and active guidance during exposure, as was demonstrated by Williams and Zane (1989) in a study involving the treatment of agoraphobia. Also, some techno-

the undesirable behavior, contributing to aversion therapy's "negative image" among some segments of the public. Aversion therapy has been used in the treatment of a wide range of maladaptive behaviors, including smoking, drinking, overeating, drug dependence, gambling, sexual deviance, and bizarre psychotic behavior.

Another variant of aversion therapy is called *covert* or *vicarious sensitization,* in which an attempt is made to induce unpleasant feelings such as disgust or fear in association with tempting stimuli through a process of classical conditioning (Maletsky, 1998). For example, Weinrot and Riggan (1996) describe a procedure in which adolescent sexual offenders view specially prepared videotapes that graphically depict plausible consequences of engaging in deviant behavior, such as being raped during prison confinement or being shamed and rejected by opposite-sex peers who know of the offense. Many offenders are described as complaining of nausea while viewing these videos.

Aversion therapy is primarily a way—sometimes quite an effective one—of stopping maladaptive responses for a brief period of time. With this interruption, an opportunity exists for substituting new behavior or for changing a lifestyle by encouraging more adaptive alternative patterns that will prove reinforcing in themselves. This point is particularly important because otherwise a client may simply refrain from maladaptive responses in unsafe therapy situations, where such behavior leads to immediate aversive results, but keep making them in safe real-life situations, where there is no fear of immediate discomfort. Also, there is little likelihood that a previously gratifying but maladaptive behavior pattern will be permanently relinquished unless alternative forms of gratification are learned during the aversion therapy. A therapist who believes it possible to take away something without giving something back is likely to be disappointed. This is an important point in regard to the treatment of addictions and paraphilias, one often not appreciated in otherwise well-designed treatment programs.

Modeling

As the name implies, **modeling** involves the learning of skills through imitating another person, such as a parent or therapist, who performs the behavior to be acquired. A younger client may be exposed to behaviors or roles in peers who act as assistants to the therapist and then be encouraged to imitate and practice the desired new responses. For example, modeling may be used to promote the learning of simple skills, such as self-feeding in a profoundly mentally retarded child, or more complex ones, such as being more effective in social situations for a shy, withdrawn adolescent. In work with children, especially,

Positive reinforcement is an effective technique for managing behavior problems, with food or other treats or privileges often used as reinforcers. This autistic child is being reinforced for some positive behavior by being stroked with a feather tickler.

effective decision making and problem solving may be modeled where the therapist "thinks out loud" about everyday choices that present themselves in the course of therapy (Kendall, 1990; Kendall & Braswell, 1985).

Modeling and imitation are adjunctive aspects of various forms of behavior as well as other types of therapy. For example, in an early classic work Bandura (1964) found that live modeling of fearlessness combined with instruction and guided exposure was the most effective treatment for snake phobia, resulting in the elimination of phobic reactions in over 90 percent of the cases treated. The photographs involving the treatment of spider phobia on page 168 of this text provide a graphic example of a similar combined approach.

Systematic Use of Reinforcement

Often referred to as *contingency management,* systematic programs involving the management of reinforcement to suppress (extinguish) unwanted behavior or to elicit and maintain effective behavior have achieved notable success, particularly but by no means exclusively in institutional settings.

The suppression of problematic behavior may be as simple as removing the reinforcements supporting it, provided of course the latter can be identified. Sometimes the identification is relatively easy, as in the following case. In other instances, it may require extremely careful and detailed observation and analysis for the therapist to learn what is maintaining the maladaptive behavior.

Case Study, Behavior Therapy for a Show-Off • Billy, a 6-year-old first grader, was brought to a psychological clinic by his parents because he hated school and his teacher had told them that his showing-off behavior was disrupting the class and making him unpopular. It became apparent in observing Billy and his parents during the initial interview that both his mother and father were noncritical and approving of everything he did. After further assessment, a three-phase program of therapy was undertaken: (1) the parents were helped to discriminate between showing-off behavior and appropriate behavior on Billy's part; (2) the parents were instructed to show a loss of interest and attention when Billy engaged in showing-off behavior while continuing to show their approval of appropriate behavior; and (3) Billy's teacher was instructed to ignore Billy, insofar as it was feasible, when he engaged in showing-off behavior, and to devote her attention at those times to children who were behaving more appropriately.

Although Billy's showing-off behavior in class increased during the first few days of this behavior therapy program, it diminished markedly thereafter when it was no longer reinforced by his parents and teacher. As his maladaptive behavior diminished, he was better accepted by his classmates, which, in turn, helped reinforce more appropriate behavior patterns and changed his negative attitude toward school.

Billy's was a case in which unwanted behavior was eliminated by eliminating its reinforcers. On other occasions therapy is required to establish desired behaviors that are missing. Response shaping, token economies, and behavioral contracting are among the most widely used of such techniques.

Response Shaping Positive reinforcement is often used in **response shaping**—that is, in establishing by gradual approximation a response that is actively resisted or is not initially in an individual's behavior repertoire. This technique has been used extensively in working with children's behavior problems. The following classic case reported by Wolf, Risley, and Mees (1964) is illustrative:

Case Study, Shaping the Behavior of an Autistic Boy • A 3-year-old autistic boy lacked normal verbal and social behavior. He did not eat properly, engaged in self-destructive behavior, such as banging his head and scratching his face, and manifested ungovernable tantrums. He had recently had a cataract operation, and required glasses for the development of normal vision. He refused to wear his glasses, however, and broke pair after pair.

The technique of shaping was decided on to counteract the problem with his glasses. Initially, the boy was trained to expect a bit of candy or fruit at the sound of a toy noisemaker. Then training was begun with empty eyeglass frames. First the boy was reinforced with the candy or fruit for picking them up, then for holding them, then for carrying them around, then for bringing the frames closer to the eyes, and then for putting the empty frames on his head at any angle. Through successive approximations, the boy finally learned to wear his glasses, with their corrective lenses, up to twelve hours a day.

Token Economies Approval and other intangible reinforcers may be ineffective in behavior modification programs, especially those dealing with severely maladaptive behavior. In such instances, appropriate behaviors may be rewarded with tangible reinforcers in the form of tokens that can later be exchanged for desired objects or privileges (Kazdin, 1980). In ground-breaking work with hospitalized schizophrenic clients, for example, Ayllon and Azrin (1968) found that using the commissary, listening to records, and going to movies were considered highly desirable activities by most clients. Consequently, these activities were chosen as reinforcers for socially appropriate behavior. To participate in any of them, a client had to earn a number of tokens by demonstrating appropriate ward behavior. In Chapter 18, we will describe another token economy program, an extraordinarily successful one, with chronic hospitalized clients who had been considered resistant to treatment (Paul, 1982; Paul & Lentz, 1977).

Token economies have been used to establish adaptive behaviors ranging from elementary responses, such as eating and making one's bed, to the daily performance of responsible hospital jobs. In the latter instance, the token economy resembles the outside world where an individual is paid for his or her work in tokens (money) that can later be exchanged for desired objects and activities. The use of tokens as reinforcers for appropriate behavior has a number of distinct advantages: (1) the number of tokens earned depends directly on the amount of desirable behavior shown; (2) tokens, like money in the outside world, may be made a general medium of currency in terms of what they will "purchase;" hence they are not readily subject to satiation and tend to maintain their incentive value; (3) tokens can reduce the delay that often occurs between appropriate performance and reinforcement; (4) the number of tokens earned and the way in which they are "spent" are largely up to the client; and (5) tokens tend to bridge the gap between the institutional environment and the demands and system of payment that will be encountered in the outside world.

The ultimate goal in token economies, as in other programs involving initially extrinsic reinforcement, is not only to achieve desired responses but to bring such responses to a level where their adaptive consequences will be reinforcing in their own right—intrinsically reinforcing—thus enabling natural rather than artificial rewards to maintain the desired behavior. For example, extrinsic reinforcers may be used initially to help children overcome reading difficulties, but once a child becomes proficient in reading, this skill will presumably provide intrinsic reinforcement as the child comes to enjoy reading for its own sake.

Although their effectiveness has been clearly demonstrated with chronic schizophrenic clients, mentally retarded residents in institutional settings, and children, the use of token economies has not been extensive in recent years (Paul & Menditto, 1992). In part, this neglect is a result of budget-inspired reductions in trained hospital treatment staffs, which are required for the effective management of such programs (Paul, Stuve, & Cross, 1997). Token economies are also poorly understood by laypersons, many of whom see them as inhumane or crassly manipulative. If these people are "sick," so the thought goes, they should have medicine and not be expected to "perform" for simple amenities. Unfortunately, such thinking makes for chronic social disability.

Behavioral Contracting A technique called **behavioral contracting** is used in some types of psychotherapy and behavior therapy to identify the behaviors that are to be changed and to maximize the probability that these changes will occur and be maintained (Nelson & Mowry, 1976). By definition, a contract is an agreement between two or more parties—such as a therapist and a client, a parent and a teenager, or a husband and a wife—that governs the nature of an exchange. The agreement, often in writing, specifies a client's obligations to change as well as the responsibilities of the other party to provide something the client wants in return, such as tangible rewards, privileges, or therapeutic attention. Behavior therapists frequently make behavioral contracting an explicit focus of treatment, thus helping establish the treatment as a joint enterprise for which both parties have responsibility. A common application of contracting is in behavioral couples therapy, where the principles governing the exchange of "reinforcements" between the distressed parties

is formally negotiated and sometimes even committed to writing (e.g., Cordova & Jacobson, 1993). For example, a husband may agree to try a new restaurant once a month in exchange for his wife's commitment to talk about the children's school work no more than three times weekly. These techniques have a good record in outcome studies (Shadish et al., 1993).

Behavioral contracting can facilitate therapy in several ways: (1) the structuring of the treatment relationship can be explicitly stated, giving the client a clear idea of each person's role in the treatment; (2) the actual responsibilities of the client are outlined and a system of rewards is built in for changed behavior; (3) the limitations of the treatment, in terms of the length and focus of the sessions, are specified; (4) by agreement, some behaviors (for example, the client's sexual orientation) may be eliminated from the treatment focus, thereby establishing the appropriate content of the treatment sessions; (5) clear treatment goals can be defined; and (6) criteria for determining success or failure in achieving these goals can be built into the program.

Sometimes a contract is negotiated between a disruptive child and a teacher, according to which the child will maintain or receive certain privileges as long as he or she behaves in accordance with the contract. Usually the school principal is also a party to such a contract to ensure the enforcement of certain conditions that the teacher may not be in a position to enforce, such as removing the child from the classroom for engaging in certain types of misbehavior.

We know of no therapist who seriously believes in the long-term feasibility of such formal therapeutic contracts as a means of regulating interpersonal behavior. Rather, as in the case of aversion therapy, contracts provide an opportunity to interrupt for a time self-sustaining dysfunctional behavior, thus permitting the emergence of new responses that may prove more adaptive and satisfying.

Biofeedback Treatment Historically, it was generally believed that voluntary control over physiological processes, such as heart rate, galvanic skin response, and blood pressure, was not possible. In the early 1960s, however, this view began to change. A number of investigators, aided by the development of sensitive electronic instruments that could accurately measure physiological responses, demonstrated that many of the processes formerly thought to be involuntary were modifiable by operant learning procedures. Kimmel (1974) demonstrated, for example, that the galvanic skin response, reflecting

The importance of the autonomic nervous system in abnormal behavior has long been recognized. Autonomic arousal is an important factor in anxiety states. Biofeedback is a behavioral technique meant to reduce this arousal and its anxiety component.

the activity of sweat glands, could be conditioned by operant learning techniques.

The importance of the autonomic nervous system in the development of abnormal behavior has long been recognized. For example, autonomic arousal is an important factor in anxiety states. Thus many researchers have applied techniques developed in the autonomic conditioning studies in an attempt to modify the internal environment of troubled persons to bring about more adaptive behavior—for instance, to modify heart rates in clients with irregular heartbeats (Weiss & Engel, 1971), to treat stuttering by feeding back information on the electric potential of muscles in the speech apparatus (Lanyon, Barrington, & Newman, 1976), and to reduce lower-back pain (Wolf, Nacht, & Kelly, 1982) and chronic headaches (Blanchard et al., 1983).

This treatment approach—in which a person is taught to influence his or her own physiological processes—is referred to as **biofeedback.** Several steps are typical in the process of biofeedback treatment: (1) monitoring the physiological response that is to be modified (perhaps blood pressure or skin temperature); (2) converting the information to a visual or auditory signal; and (3) providing a means of prompt feedback—indicating to a subject as rapidly as possible when the desired change is taking place (Blanchard & Epstein, 1978). Given this feedback, the subject may then seek to reduce his or her emotionality, as by lowering the skin temperature. For the most part, biofeedback is oriented to reducing the reactivity of some organ system innervated by the autonomic nervous system—very often a physiological component of the anxiety response.

Although there is general agreement that many physiological processes can be regulated to some extent by learning, the application of biofeedback procedures to alter abnormal behavior has produced equivocal results. Demonstrations of clinical biofeedback applications abound, but carefully controlled research has often not supported earlier impressions of widespread clinically significant improvement. The effects of biofeedback procedures are generally small and often do not generalize to situations outside the laboratory, where the biofeedback devices are not present (Blanchard & Young 1973, 1974). There is good evidence nevertheless that tension headache victims may respond quite favorably to biofeedback (Blanchard, 1994). Also, Flor and Birbaumer (1993) demonstrated in a well-controlled study a rather impressive effect of electromyographic (muscle tension) biofeedback in the control of musculoskeletal pain of the back and jaw, one that survived a 24-month follow-up.

Unfortunately, the latter study did not include a relaxation training comparison group. Where that comparison has been made, biofeedback usually has not been shown to be any more effective than relaxation training, leading to the suggestion that biofeedback may simply be a more elaborate (and usually more costly) means of teaching clients relaxation (Blanchard & Epstein, 1978; Blanchard et al., 1980; Tarler-Beniolo, 1978). Relaxation training, in itself, continues to amass a very creditable record in the treatment of various medical conditions, as shown in a quantitative review by Carlson and Hoyle (1993), as well as various mental disorders where anxiety is a substantial component (Nathan & Gorman, 1998; Roth & Fonagy, 1996). Although no final judgment can as yet be made, we would note that—as with almost any treatment procedure—a small percentage of clients may be expected to show an unusually good response to biofeedback treatment.

Evaluating Behavior Therapy

Compared with psychodynamic and other psychotherapies, behavior therapy appears to have three distinct advantages. First, the treatment approach is precise. The target behaviors to be modified are specified, the methods to be used are clearly delineated, and the results can be readily evaluated (Marks, 1982). Second, the use of explicit learning principles is a sound basis for effective interventions as a result of their demonstrated scientific validity (Borkovec, 1997; Kazdin & Wilson, 1978). Third, the economy of time and costs is quite good. Not surprisingly, then, the overall outcomes achieved with behavior therapy compare very favorably with those of other approaches (Nathan & Gorman, 1998; Roth & Fonagy, 1996; Smith et al., 1980). Behavior therapy usually achieves results in a short period of time because it is generally directed to specific symptoms, leading to faster relief of a client's distress and to lower costs.

As with other approaches, the range of effectiveness of behavior therapy is not unlimited, and it works better with certain kinds of problems than with others. Generally, the more pervasive and vaguely defined the client's problem, the less likely that behavior therapy will be useful. For example, it appears to be only rarely employed to treat Axis II personality disorders, where specific symptoms are rare. On the other hand, behavioral techniques are the backbone of modern approaches to treating sexual dysfunctions, as discussed in Chapter 11. Quantitative reviews of therapeutic outcomes confirm the expectation that behavior therapy has a particular place in the treatment of anxiety disorders, where the powerful exposure techniques of behavior therapy can be brought to bear (Andrews & Harvey, 1981; Chambless et al., 1998; Clum et al., 1993; Nathan & Gorman, 1998). The massive quantitative review conducted by Smith and colleagues (1980) in fact reveals the less expected finding of a relatively good outcome record with the psychoses. Thus, although behavior therapy is not a cure-all, it has earned in a relatively brief period a highly respected place among the available psychosocial treatment approaches.

COGNITIVE AND COGNITIVE-BEHAVIORAL THERAPY

As we have seen, early behavior therapists focused on observable behavior. They regarded the inner thoughts of their clients as not really part of the causal chain, and in their zeal to be objective they focused on the relationship between observable behaviors and observable reinforcing conditions. Thus they were often viewed as mechanistic technicians who simply manipulated their clients without considering them as people. Eventually, however, some behavior therapists such as Joseph Wolpe began to pay attention to covert behavior as in the use of imagined frightening scenes as a therapeutic technique. While Wolpe's focus was not on the role or manipulation of cognitive processes per se, starting in the 1970s a number of behavior therapists began to reappraise the importance of "private events"—thoughts, perceptions, evaluations, and self-statements—seeing them as processes that mediate the effects of objective stimulus conditions and thus help determine behavior and emotions (Borkovec, 1985; Mahoney & Arnkoff, 1978).

Cognitive and **cognitive-behavioral therapy** (terms for the most part used interchangeably) stem from both cognitive psychology, with its emphasis on the effects of thoughts on behavior and on the study of the nature of our cognitive processes, and behaviorism, with its rigorous methodology and performance-oriented focus. At the present time, there is no single set of techniques that define cognitively oriented psychotherapy. Rather, numerous methods are being developed with varying emphases. Two main themes seem to characterize them all, however: (1) the conviction that cognitive processes influence emotion, motivation, and behavior; and (2) the use of cognitive and behavior-change techniques in a pragmatic (hypothesis-testing) manner.

That is, much of the content of the therapy sessions and homework assignments is analogous to experiments in which a therapist and a client apply learning principles to alter the client's biased and dysfunctional cognitions, continuously evaluating the effects that these changes have on subsequent thoughts, feelings, and overt behavior. For example, a young man believing that his interest will be rebuffed by any woman he approaches would be led into a searching analysis of the reasons why he holds this belief. The client might then be assigned the task of "testing" this dysfunctional "hypothesis" by actually approaching seemingly appropriate women he admires. The results of the "test" would then be thoroughly analyzed with the cognitive therapist, and, if necessary, any cognitive "errors" that may have interfered with a skillful performance are discussed and corrected.

The exact nature of the relationship between emotion, cognition, and behavior is a venerable philosophical problem that remains far from clear even today. Can it be, for example, that thoughts cause emotions and behavior? Any serious discussion of such an issue would take us far afield, but it is important to understand that the intellectual status of cognitive therapy is not without controversy. Aaron Beck (Beck & Weishaar, 1989), an important leader in the field, acknowledges that disordered cognitions are not a cause of abnormal behavior or emotions, but rather are an intrinsic (yet alterable) element of such behavior and emotions. If the critical cognitive components can be changed, according to this view, then the behavior and maladaptive emotions will change. In our discussion, we will focus on three approaches to cognitive-behavior therapy: (1) the rational emotive behavior therapy of Albert Ellis, (2) the stress-inoculation training of Donald Meichenbaum, and (3) the cognitive therapies of Aaron Beck.

Rational Emotive Behavior Therapy

One of the earliest developed of the behaviorally oriented cognitive therapies is the rational-emotive therapy (now called **rational emotive behavior therapy—REBT**) of Albert Ellis (1958, 1973, 1975, 1989; Ellis & Dryden, 1997). REBT attempts to change a client's maladaptive thought processes, on which maladaptive emotional responses and thus behavior are presumed to depend. In its infancy, REBT was viewed skeptically by many professionals who doubted its effectiveness, but it has now become one of the most widely used therapeutic approaches (Ellis, 1989).

Ellis posited that a well-functioning individual behaves rationally and in tune with empirical reality. For Ellis, thoughts do have causal primacy in behavior, notably emotional behavior. Unfortunately, many of us have learned unrealistic beliefs and perfectionistic values that cause us to expect too much of ourselves, leading us to behave irrationally and then to feel unnecessarily that we are worthless failures. For example, a person may continually think, "I should be able to win everyone's love and approval" or "I should be thoroughly adequate and competent in everything I do." Such unrealistic assumptions and self-demands inevitably lead to ineffective and self-defeating behavior in the real world, which reacts accordingly, and then to the recognition of failure and the emotional response of self-devaluation. This emotional response is thus the necessary consequence not of reality, but of an individual's faulty expectations, interpretations, and self-demands.

As a more specific example, consider a man who has an intense depressive reaction of despair with deep feelings of worthlessness, unlovability, and self-devaluation when he fails to get an expected promotion at work. With a stronger self-concept and a more realistic picture of both himself and his employment situation, his emotional reaction might have been less severe and one more in keeping with an objective appraisal of his goals and

Cognitive-behavior therapy is geared toward uncovering and changing the faulty beliefs and unrealistic assumptions that can warp our perceptions of ourselves and events and contribute to depression and other disorders.

how to meet them. It is his interpretation of the situation and of himself, rather than the objective facts, that has led to his intense and crippling emotional reaction.

Ellis (1970) believes that one or more core irrational beliefs, reproduced in Table 17.1, are specific to and at the root of most psychological maladjustment.

The task of rational emotive behavior therapy is to restructure an individual's belief system and self-evaluation, especially with respect to the irrational "shoulds," "oughts," and "musts" that are preventing a more positive sense of self-worth and a creative, emotionally satisfying, and fulfilling life. Several methods are used. One method is to dispute a person's false beliefs through rational confrontation. For example, an REBT therapist dealing with the disappointed worker noted above might ask, "Why should your failure to get the promotion mean that you

TABLE 17.1   ELLIS'S CORE IRRATIONAL BELIEFS

One should be loved by everyone for everything one does.

Certain acts are awful or wicked, and people who perform them should be severely punished.

It is horrible when things are not the way we would like them to be.

If something may be dangerous or fearsome, one should be terribly upset about it.

It is better to avoid life problems, if possible, than to face them.

One needs something stronger or more powerful than oneself to rely on.

One should be thoroughly competent, intelligent, and achieving in all respects.

Because something once affected one's life, it will indefinitely affect it.

One must have perfect and certain self-control.

Happiness can be achieved by inertia and inaction.

We have virtually no control over our emotions and cannot help having certain feelings.

---

are worthless?" Here the therapist would teach the client to identify and dispute the beliefs that were producing the negative emotional consequences.

An REBT therapist also uses behaviorally oriented techniques, usually to help clients practice living in accord with their new beliefs and philosophy. Sometimes, for example, homework assignments are given to encourage clients to have new experiences and break negative chains of behavior. Clients might be instructed to reward themselves by an external reinforcer, such as a food treat, after working 15 minutes at disputing their beliefs. Another method of self-reinforcement might be through private self-statements such as "You are doing a really good job." Embracing such a belief, incidentally, will probably have positive effects whether or not it is factually true. There is abundant evidence that people in general maintain their self-esteem in part by deceiving themselves that things are better than they are (Bandura, 1986; Taylor & Brown, 1988). A modest level of "irrationality" is thus not, per se, a risk factor for mental disorder.

Although the techniques differ dramatically, in some ways the philosophy underlying rational emotive behavior therapy can be viewed as somewhat similar to that underlying humanistic therapy (to be discussed in a later section) because both take a clear stand on personal worth and human values. Rational emotive behavior therapy aims at increasing an individual's feelings of self-worth and clearing the way for self-actualization by removing the false beliefs that have been stumbling blocks to personal growth.

Stress-Inoculation Therapy

A second cognitive-behavioral approach to treatment is **stress-inoculation therapy** (**SIT**)—a type of self-instructional training focused on altering self-statements an individual routinely makes in stress-producing situations. Here the approach is to restructure these statements so as to improve functioning under stressful conditions (Meichenbaum, 1985, 1993). Like other cognitive-behavioral therapies, stress-inoculation therapy assumes that a person's problems result from maladaptive beliefs that are leading to negative emotional states and maladaptive behavior, familiar elements in the causal chain cognitive theorists have posited.

SIT usually involves three stages. In the initial phase, cognitive preparation, client and therapist together explore the client's beliefs and attitudes about problem situations and the self-statements to which they are leading. The focus is on how the person's self-talk can influence later performance and behavior. Together, the therapist and the client agree on new self-statements that would be more adaptive. In the second phase of stress inoculation—skill acquisition and rehearsal—more adaptive self-statements are learned and practiced. For example, a person attempting to cope with the "feeling of being overwhelmed" would rehearse self-statements such as the following:

- When fear comes, just pause.
- Keep the focus on the present; what is it you have to do?
- Label your fear from 0 to 10 and watch it change.
- You should expect your fear to rise.
- Don't try to eliminate fear totally; just keep it manageable.
- You can convince yourself to do it. You can reason fear away.
- It will be over shortly.

- It's not the worst thing that can happen.
- Just think about something else.
- Do something that will prevent you from thinking about fear.
- Describe what is around you. That way you won't think about worrying. (Meichenbaum, 1974, p. 16)

The third phase of SIT, application and practice, involves applying the new coping strategies in actual situations. This practice is scheduled in such a way that the client attempts easier situations first and only gradually enters more stressful situations as he or she feels confident of mastering them.

As its title implies, SIT was originally designed to help people cope with situations that cause them significant stress or anxiety, such as public speaking. Its range of application has broadened considerably in recent years. For example, Ross and Berger (1996) describe a controlled study in which a SIT intervention was notably successful (diminished pain and anxiety, lessened recuperative time) for male athletes undergoing arthroscopic knee surgery.

Beck's Cognitive Therapies

Aaron Beck's cognitive therapy approach was originally developed for the treatment of depression (Beck et al., 1979; Hollon & Beck, 1978) and was later extended to anxiety disorders, eating disorders and obesity, conduct disorder in children, personality disorders, and substance abuse (Beck, 1985; Beck & Emery, 1985; Beck et al., 1990, 1993; Hollon & Beck, 1994). Recently its use has been extended by Deale and associates (1997) to the controversial *chronic fatigue syndrome* diagnosis (see Chapters 7 and 8). One basic assumption underlying this approach is that problems like depression result from clients' illogical thinking about themselves, the world they live in, and the future.

In the initial phases clients are made aware of the connection between their patterns of thinking and their emotional responses. They are taught at first simply to identify their own automatic thoughts—e.g., "This event is a total disaster."—and to keep records of their thought content and their emotional reactions (e.g., see Clark, 1997). With the therapist's help, they then learn about the logical errors in their thinking, and to challenge the validity of these automatic thoughts. The errors in the logic behind their thinking lead them to (1) selectively perceive the world as harmful while ignoring evidence to the contrary; (2) overgeneralize on the basis of limited exam-

ples—for example, seeing themselves as totally worthless because they were laid off at work; (3) magnify the significance of undesirable events—for example, seeing the job loss as the end of the world for them; and (4) engage in absolutistic thinking—for example, exaggerating the importance of someone's mildly critical comment and perceiving it as proof of their instant descent from goodness to worthlessness.

In Beck's cognitive therapy, clients do not change their beliefs by debate and persuasion as is common in rational emotive behavior therapy; rather, as we have seen, they are encouraged to gather information about themselves. Together, a therapist and a client identify the client's beliefs and expectations and formulate them as hypotheses to be tested, as described earlier. They then design ways in which the client can check out these hypotheses in the real world. These disconfirmation experiments are planned to give the individual successful experiences, thereby interrupting the destructive sequence previously described. They are arranged according to difficulty, so that the least difficult (or risky) tasks will be accomplished successfully before the more difficult ones are attempted (see Highlight 17.3).

In the treatment of depression, sometimes a client and a therapist schedule the client's daily activities on an hour-by-hour basis. Such activity scheduling is an important part of therapy with depressed individuals because reducing such clients' inactivity interrupts their tendencies to ruminate about themselves. An important part of the arrangement is the scheduling of pleasurable events, because many depressed clients have lost the capacity for gaining pleasure from their own activities. Both the scheduled pleasurable activities and the rewarding experiences that derive from carrying out the behavioral experiments tend to increase an individual's satisfaction and positive mood—for example, resuming sex with a partner, previously avoided because of an erroneous but untested expectation of rejection.

Besides planning the behavioral assignments, evaluating the results in subsequent sessions, and planning further disconfirmation experiments, such therapy sessions for depression include several other cognitive emphases. For example, the client is encouraged to discover underlying dysfunctional assumptions or depression-inducing schemas that may be leading to self-defeating tendencies. These generally become evident over the course of therapy as the client and the therapist examine the themes of the client's automatic thoughts. Because these dysfunctional schemas are seen as creating the person's vulnerability to depression, this phase of treatment is considered

Cognitive-Behavioral Therapy for a Case of Depression

Rush, Khatami, and Beck (1975) have reported several cases of successful treatment using cognitive clarification and behavioral assignments for clients with recurring chronic depression. The following case illustrates their approach:

A 53-year-old white male engineer's initial depressive episode 15 years ago necessitated several months absence from work. Following medication and psychotherapy, he was asymptomatic up to four years ago. At that time, sadness, pessimism, loss of appetite and weight, and heavy use of alcohol returned.

Two years later, he was hospitalized for six weeks and treated with lithium and imipramine. He had three subsequent hospitalizations with adequate trials of several different tricyclics [antidepressant drugs]. During his last hospitalization, two weeks prior to initiating cognitive-behavioral therapy, he was treated with 10 sessions of ECT [electroconvulsive therapy]. His symptoms were only partially relieved with these various treatments.

When the client started cognitive-behavioral therapy, he showed moderate psychomotor retardation. He was anxious, sad, tearful, and pessimistic. He was self-depreciating and self-reproachful without any interest in life. He reported decreased appetite, early morning awakening, lack of sexual interest, and worries about his physical health. Initially he was treated with weekly sessions for 3 months, then bi-weekly for 2 months. Treatment, terminated after 5 months, consisted of 20 sessions. He was evaluated 12 months after the conclusion of therapy.

Therapist and client set an initial goal of his becoming physically active (i.e., doing more things no matter how small or trivial). The client and his wife kept a separate list of his activities. The list included raking leaves, having dinner, and assisting his wife in apartment sales, etc. His cognitive distortions were identified by comparing his assessment of each activity with that of his wife. Alternative ways of interpreting his experiences were then considered.

In comparing his wife's resumé of his past experiences, he became aware that he had (1) undervalued his past by failing to mention many previous accomplishments, (2) regarded himself as far more responsible for his failures than she did, and (3) concluded that he was worthless since he had not succeeded in attaining certain goals in the past. When the two accounts were contrasted he could discern many of his cognitive distortions. In subsequent sessions, his wife continued to serve as an objectifier. In midtherapy, the client compiled a list of new attitudes that he had acquired since initiating therapy. These included:

1. I am starting at a lower level of functioning at my job, but it will improve if I persist.
2. I know that once I get going in the morning, everything will run all right for the rest of the day.
3. I can't achieve everything at once.
4. I have my periods of ups and downs, but in the long run I feel better.
5. My expectations from my job and life should be scaled down to a realistic level.
6. Giving in to avoidance never helps and only leads to further avoidance.

He was instructed to re-read this list daily for several weeks even though he already knew the content. The log was continued, and subsequent assumptions reflected in the log were compared to the assumptions listed above.

As the client became gradually less depressed, he returned to his job for the first time in two years. He undertook new activities (e.g., camping, going out of town) as he continued his log. (pp. 400–401)

The focus of the therapy was on encouraging the client to restructure his thought content to reduce the negative self-judgments and to evaluate his actual achievements more realistically. Making and reviewing the list of new attitudes gave the client more perspective on his life situation, which resulted in an improved mood, less self-blame, and more willingness to risk alternative behavior. ∎

The negative emotional impact of situations and events such as rejection and isolation can lead to "catastrophizing," which may increase performance deficits. Cognitive therapy is "decatastrophizing."

essential in ensuring resistance to relapse when the client faces stressful life events in the future. That is, without changing the underlying cognitive vulnerability factors, the client may show short-term improvement but will still be subject to recurrent depression.

The general approach is similar for disorders other than depression, although the exact focus of the treatment, of course, differs if one is treating a client with panic disorder, generalized anxiety, bulimia, or substance abuse. For example, as was seen in Chapter 5, in panic disorder the focus is on identifying the automatic thoughts about feared bodily sensations and on teaching the client to correct logical errors in those automatic thoughts—basically to decatastrophize the experience of panic (Clark, 1986; Clark et al., 1994). For generalized anxiety disorder, the client is taught to correct the tendencies to overestimate the presence and likelihood of danger and to underestimate his or her ability to cope in a variety of situations (Beck & Emery, 1985; Wells & Butler, 1977). In bulimia, the cognitive approach proposes that the person has overvalued ideas about body weight and shape, which are often fueled by low self-esteem and fears of being unattractive. These beliefs are thought to lead to a tendency to diet excessively, which in turn increases the probability of losing control by bingeing and purging. The cognitive part of the treatment involves getting these clients to identify and change their maladaptive beliefs regarding weight and body image, as well as about what foods are "safe" or "dangerous" (Agras, 1993; Fairburn et al., 1993; Wilson, Fairburn, & Agras, 1997).

Evaluating Cognitive-Behavioral Therapies

In spite of the widespread attention and popularity that Ellis's rational emotive behavior therapy has enjoyed,

surprisingly little research has been conducted to document its efficacy—especially for carefully diagnosed clinical populations (Hollon & Beck, 1994). It has been shown to be useful in reducing test anxiety and speech anxiety, but it is inferior to exposure-based therapies in the treatment of more severe anxiety disorders such as agoraphobia, social phobia (Haaga & Davison, 1989, 1992), and probably obsessive-compulsive disorder (Franklin & Foa, 1998). It has not yet been compared with cognitive or interpersonal therapy for the treatment of depression (discussed in Chapter 6), so we don't know whether it is as effective as these two proven treatments. In general, it may be most useful in helping generally healthy people to cope better with everyday stress and perhaps prevent them from developing full-blown anxiety or depressive disorders (Haaga & Davison, 1989, 1992).

Stress-inoculation therapy has been successfully used with a number of clinical problems, including anger (Novaco, 1977, 1979), pain (Turk, Meichenbaum, & Genest, 1983; Masters et al., 1987), Type A behavior (Jenni & Wollersheim, 1979), mild forms of anxiety (Meichenbaum, 1975), and, as already noted, the consequences of knee surgery (Ross & Berger, 1996). (See also Denicola & Sandler, 1980; Holcomb, 1979; Klepac et al., 1981.) This approach is particularly suited to increasing the adaptive capabilities of individuals who have shown a vulnerability to developing problems in certain stressful situations. In addition to its value as a therapeutic technique for identified problems, stress-inoculation therapy may be a useful method for preventing behavior disorders. Although the preventive value of SIT has not been demonstrated by rigorous empirical study, many believe that the prevalence of maladaptive behavior might be reduced if more individuals' general coping skills were improved (e.g., Meichenbaum & Jaremko, 1983).

A review of research evaluating Beck's type of cognitive treatment methods suggests that these approaches to intervention are extremely effective in alleviating many different types of disorders (see Hollon & Beck, 1994, for a comprehensive review). In the case of depression, considerable evidence, reviewed in Chapters 6 and 16, suggests that cognitive-behavioral therapy is arguably at least comparable to drug treatment in all but the most severe cases (e.g., psychotic depression). Moreover, it has superior long-term advantages: several studies have shown that relapse in the one to two years of posttreatment was less likely if a client had been treated with cognitive therapy, whether or not there was also treatment with antidepressant drugs (Craighead, Craighead, & Ilardi, 1998). Additionally, Antonuccio, Thomas, and Danton (1997) have recently demonstrated this therapy to be more economical than treatment with the drug fluoxetine (Prozac), including for severe cases.

Although clinical depression was the first disorder for which there was good documented efficacy, many empirical studies in the past decade have compared cognitive-behavioral methods with other treatment approaches for a variety of other clinical disorders. The most dramatic recent results have been in the treatment of panic disorder and generalized anxiety disorder (Chapter 5), but cognitive-behavioral therapy is also now seen as the treatment of choice for bulimia (see Chapter 8; Garner & Garfinkel, 1997) and conduct disorder in children (Chapter 14; Hollon & Beck, 1994). There are also promising results in the treatment of substance abuse (Chapter 10; Beck et al., 1993) and of certain personality disorders (Chapter 9; Beck et al., 1990; Linehan, 1993).

The combined use of cognitive and behavior therapy approaches is now quite routine. There remains disagreement about whether the effects of cognitive treatments are actually the result of cognitive changes, as the cognitive theorists propose (Hollon & Beck, 1994; Hollon, DeRubeis, & Evans, 1987). But at least for depression and panic disorder it does appear that cognitive change is the best predictor of long-term outcome, as would be predicted by cognitive theory (Hollon, Evans, & DeRubeis, 1990). We anticipate that in the next few years more attention will be devoted to these important questions about how cognitive-behavioral therapy works. (See the Fall 1997 issue of *Behavior Therapy* [vol. 28, no. 4] for related interesting discussions by experts in the field.) Indeed, these questions have assumed increased importance in light of the striking and widely documented success of this mode of therapy.

Humanistic-Experiential Therapies

The humanistic-experiential therapies emerged as significant treatment approaches during the post–World War II era. To a large extent, they developed in reaction to the psychodynamic perspective, which many feel does not accurately take into account either the existential problems or the full potentialities of human beings. In a society dominated by self-interest, mechanization, computerization, mass deception, and mindless bureaucracy, proponents of the humanistic-experiential therapies see psychopathology as stemming in many cases from problems of alienation, depersonalization, loneliness, and a failure to find meaning and genuine fulfillment. Problems of this sort, it is held, are not likely to be solved either by delving into forgotten memories or by correcting specific maladaptive behaviors.

The humanistic-experiential therapies follow some variant of the general humanistic and existential perspective outlined in Chapter 3. They are based on the assumption that we have both the freedom and the responsibility to control our own behavior—that we can reflect on our problems, make choices, and take positive action. Whereas some behavior therapists see themselves as "behavior engineers," responsible only for changing specific behaviors they deem problematic by appropriate modifications in a person's environment, humanistic-experiential therapists feel that a client must take most of the responsibility for the direction and success of therapy, with a therapist merely serving as counselor, guide, and facilitator. These therapies may be carried out with individual clients or with groups of clients (see Highlight 17.4). Although humanistic-experiential therapies differ among themselves in details, their central focus is always that of expanding a client's "awareness."

Client-Centered Therapy

The **Client-Centered (person-centered) therapy** of Carl Rogers (1902–1987) focuses on the natural power of the organism to heal itself (Rogers, 1951, 1961, 1966). Rogers rejected both Freud's view of the primacy of irrational instinct and of the therapist's role as prober, interpreter, and director of the therapeutic process. He saw psychotherapy as a process of removing the constraints and hobbling restrictions that often prevent this process from operating. These constraints, he believed, grow out of unrealistic demands that people tend to place on themselves when they believe, as a condition of self-worth, that they should not have certain kinds of feelings, such as hostility. By denying that they do in fact have such feelings, they become unaware of their actual "gut" reactions. As they lose touch with their own genuine experience, the result is lowered integration, impaired personal relationships, and various forms of maladjustment.

The primary objective of Rogerian therapy is to resolve this incongruence—to help clients become able to accept and be themselves. To this end, client-centered therapists establish a psychological climate in which clients can feel unconditionally accepted, understood, and valued as people. Within this context, the therapist employs *nondirective* techniques such as empathic reflecting or restatement of the client's descriptions of life difficulties. If all goes well, clients begin to feel free for perhaps the first time to explore their real feelings and thoughts and to accept hates and angers and ugly feelings

Highlight 17.4

Group Therapy

The treatment of clients in groups first received impetus in the military during World War II, when psychotherapists were in short supply. Group therapy was found to be effective in dealing with a variety of problems, and it rapidly became an important therapeutic approach in civilian life. In fact, all the major systematic approaches to psychotherapy that we have discussed—psychoanalysis, behavior therapy, and so on—have been applied in group as well as individual settings.

Group therapy has traditionally involved a relatively small group of clients in a clinic or hospital setting, using a variety of procedures depending on the age, needs, and potentialities of the clients and the orientation of the therapists. The degree of structure and of client participation in the group process varies in different types of groups. Most often, groups are informal, and many follow the format of encounter groups. Occasionally, however, more or less formal lectures and visual materials are presented to clients as a group. For example, a group of alcoholic clients may be shown a film depicting the detrimental effects of excessive drinking on the human body, with a group discussion afterward. Although this approach by itself has not proved effective in combating alcoholism, it is often a useful adjunct to other forms of group therapy.

An interesting form of group therapy is psychodrama, based on role-playing techniques. A client, assisted by staff members or other clients, is encouraged to act out problem situations in a theater-like setting. This technique frees the individual to express anxieties and hostilities or relive traumatic experiences in a situation that simulates real life but is more sheltered. The goal is to help the client achieve emotional catharsis, increased understanding, and improved interpersonal competencies. This form of therapy, developed initially by Moreno (1959), has proved beneficial for the clients who make up the audience as well as for those who participate on the stage (Sundberg & Tyler, 1962; Yablonsky, 1975).

Group therapy may also be almost completely unstructured, as in activity groups where children with emotional problems are allowed to act out their aggressions in the safety and control of the group setting.

In a review of contemporary group therapy research, Bednar and Kaul (1994) concluded that the field is in need of more penetrating observations regarding the processes central to group treatment, which might in turn lead to more productive conceptualizations about what, uniquely, group therapies might offer in the domain of mental health treatment. ■

as parts of themselves. As their self-concept becomes more congruent with their actual experiencing, they become more self-accepting and more open to new experience and new perspectives; in short, they become better-integrated people.

In contrast to most other forms of therapy, the client-centered therapist does not give answers or interpret what a client says or probe for unconscious conflicts or even steer the client onto certain topics. Rather he or she simply listens attentively and acceptingly to what the client wants to talk about, interrupting only to restate in different words what the client is saying. Such restatements, without any judgment or interpretation

by the therapist, help the client clarify further the feelings and ideas that he or she is exploring—really to look at them and acknowledge them. The following excerpt from a therapist's second interview with a young woman will serve to illustrate these techniques of reflection and clarification:

Case Study, An Example of Client-Centered Therapy

ALICE: I was thinking about this business of standards. I somehow developed a sort of a knack, I guess, of—well—habit—of trying to make people feel at

Carl Rogers (1902–1987) contributed significantly to the humanistic perspective with his systematic formulation of the concept of self, which emphasizes the importance of individuality and a striving toward what Rogers called self-actualization.

ease around me, or to make things go along smoothly. . . .

COUNSELOR: In other words, what you did was always in the direction of trying to keep things smooth and to make other people feel better and to smooth the situation.

ALICE: Yes. I think that's what it was. Now the reason why I did it probably was—I mean, not that I was a good little Samaritan going around making other people happy, but that was probably the role that felt easiest for me to play. I'd been doing it around home so much. I just didn't stand up for my own convictions, until I don't know whether I have any convictions to stand up for.

COUNSELOR: You feel that for a long time you've been playing the role of kind of smoothing out the frictions or differences or what not.

ALICE: M-hm.

COUNSELOR: Rather than having any opinion or reaction of your own in the situation. Is that it?

ALICE: That's it. Or that I haven't been really honestly being myself, or actually knowing what my real self is, and that I've been just playing a sort of a false role. Whatever role no one else was playing, and that needed to be played at the time, I'd try to fill it in. (Rogers, 1951, pp. 152–153)

In a now somewhat dated survey of trends in psychotherapy and counseling, Rogers was rated one of the most influential psychotherapists among clinical practi-

tioners (Smith, 1982). In addition to his influence in clinical settings, Rogers was a pioneer in attempting to carry out empirical research on psychotherapy. Introducing the practice of systematic recording of therapy sessions, he was later able to make objective analyses of what was said, of the client-counselor relationship, and of the ongoing processes in these therapy sessions. He was also able to compare a client's behavior and attitudes at different stages of therapy. These comparisons revealed a typical sequence: Early sessions were dominated by negative feelings and discouragement. Then, after a time, tentative statements of hope and greater self-acceptance began to appear. Eventually, positive feelings, a reaching out toward others, greater self-confidence, and interest in future plans appeared. This characteristic sequence gave support to Rogers's hypothesis that, once freed to do so, individuals have the capacity to lead themselves to psychological health.

Pure client-centered psychotherapy, as originally practiced, is rarely used today in North America; it has continued to be a relatively popular approach in European centers (Greenberg, Elliott, & Lietaer, 1994). In its heyday here (roughly from the 1940s through the 1970s) it opened the way for a variety of humanistically oriented therapies in which the focus is a client's present conscious problems and in which it is assumed that the client is the primary actor in the curative process, with the therapist essentially being a facilitator. The newer humanistic therapies thus accept Rogers's concept of an active self, capable of sound value choices; they also emphasize the importance of a high degree of empathy, warmth, and unconditional positive regard from the therapist. They differ from original client-centered therapy in having found various shortcuts by which the therapist, going beyond simple reflection and clarification, can hasten and help focus the client's search for wholeness. Such a therapist might, for example, directly confront a client's deceitful mode of self-presentation. It is still the client's search and the client's insights that are seen as central in therapy, however.

Existential Therapy

Several important concepts underlie existential psychotherapy. The existentialist perspective, like the client-centered, emphasizes the importance of the human situation *as perceived by an individual.* The focus is thus on the person's own phenomenologic experience rather than on any notion of objective reality, being in this respect a forerunner of so-called postmodern thought. Existentialists are deeply concerned about the predicament of humankind, the breakdown of traditional faith, the alienation and depersonalization of individuals in contemporary society, and the lack of meaning in peoples' lives. They see people, however, as having a high degree of freedom and thus as capable both of doing something about their predicament and of being responsible for doing the best they can. The unique ability of human beings to be aware of their mortality and to reflect on and question their existence confronts them with the responsibility for *being*—for deciding what kind of person to become within the constraint of a single lifetime, for establishing their own values, and for actualizing their potentialities.

Existential therapists do not follow any rigidly prescribed procedures, but emphasize the uniqueness of each individual and his or her "way of being in the world." They stress the importance of being aware of one's own existence—challenging an individual directly with questions concerning the meaning and purpose of existence—and of the therapeutic encounter, the complex relationship established between two interacting human beings in the therapeutic situation as they both try to be open and "authentic." In contrast to both psychoanalysis and behavior therapy, existential therapy calls for therapists to share themselves—their feelings, their values, and their own existence.

Besides being authentic themselves, it is the task of existential therapists to keep a client responding authentically to the inescapable intersubjectivity of relations with others (Havens, 1974; May, 1969). For example, if a client says, "I hate you just like I hated my father," a therapist might respond by saying, "I am not your father, I am me, and you have to deal with me as Dr. S., not as your father." The focus is on the here and now—on what a person is choosing to do, and therefore to be, at this moment. This sense of immediacy, of the urgency of experience, is the touchstone of existential therapy and sets the stage for the individual to clarify and choose between alternative ways of being.

Gestalt Therapy

In German, the term *gestalt* means "whole," and gestalt therapy emphasizes the unity of mind and body—placing strong emphasis on the need to integrate thought, feeling, and action. Gestalt therapy was developed by Frederick (Fritz) Perls (1967, 1969) as a means of teaching clients to recognize the bodily processes and emotions they had been blocking off from awareness. As with the client-centered and existential approaches, the main goal of gestalt therapy is to increase an individual's self-awareness and self-acceptance.

Although gestalt therapy is commonly used in a group setting, the emphasis is on one person at a time with whom a therapist works intensively, attempting to help identify aspects of the individual's self or world that are not being acknowledged in awareness. The individual may be asked to act out fantasies concerning feelings and conflicts, or to be one part of a conflict while sitting in one chair and then switch chairs to take the part of the adversary. Often the therapist or other group members will ask questions like, "What are you aware of in your body now?" or "What does it feel like in your gut when you think of that?"

In Perls's approach to therapy, a good deal of emphasis is also placed on dreams, but with an emphasis very different from that of classical psychoanalysis. In gestalt theory, every element of a dream, including seemingly inconsequential, impersonal objects, are considered to be representations of unacknowledged aspects of the dreamer's self. The therapist urges the client to suspend normal critical judgment and to "be" the object in the dream, reporting then on the experience. For example, Perls asked a middle-aged woman who had dreamed of a lake to "be" the lake, with the following result:

> **Case Study, An Excerpt from a Gestalt Therapy Session**
> • I'm a lake . . . I'm drying up, and disappearing, soaking into the earth . . . [with a touch of surprise] dying. . . . But when I soak into the earth, I become a part of the earth—so maybe I water the surrounding area, so . . . even in the lake, even in my bed, flowers can grow [sighs]. . . . New life can grow . . . from me [cries]. . . . [sadly, but with conviction] I can paint—I can create—I can create beauty. I can no longer reproduce. . . . but I . . . I'm . . . I . . . keep wanting to say I'm food . . . I . . . as water becomes . . . I water the earth, and give life-growing things, the water—they need both the earth and water, and the . . . and the air and the sun, but as the water from the lake, I can play a part in something, and producing—feeding. (Perls, 1969, pp. 81–82)

In gestalt therapy sessions, the focus is on the more obvious elements of a person's behavior. Such sessions are often called "gestalt awareness training" because the therapeutic results of the experience stem from the process of becoming more aware of one's total self and environment. The technique of working through unresolved conflicts is called "taking care of unfinished business." We all go through life, according to gestalt theory, with unfinished or unresolved traumas and conflicts. We carry the excess baggage of these unfinished situations into new relationships and tend to reenact them in our relations with other people. If we are able to complete our past unfinished business, we then have less psychological tension to cope with and can be more realistically aware of ourselves and our world.

Expressing themselves in front of the group, perhaps taking the part of first one and then another fragment of a scene, and denied the use of their usual techniques for avoiding self-awareness, gestalt therapy clients are said to be brought to an "impasse," at which point they must confront their feelings and conflicts. According to Perls, "In the safe emergency of the therapeutic situation, the neurotic discovers that the world does not fall to pieces if he or she gets angry, sexy, joyous, mournful" (1967, p. 331). Thus clients find that they can, after all, get beyond "impasses" on their own.

Evaluating the Humanistic-Experiential Therapies

The humanistic-experiential therapies have been criticized for their lack of highly systematized models of human behavior and its specific aberrations, their lack of agreed-upon therapeutic procedures, and their vagueness about what is supposed to happen between client and therapist. These very features, however, are seen by many proponents of this general approach as contributing to its strength and vitality. Systematized theories can reduce individuals to abstractions, which can diminish their perceived worth and deny their uniqueness. Because people are so different, we should expect that different techniques are appropriate for different cases. Modern-era, controlled research on the outcomes produced by the humanistic-existential therapies is relatively sparse; when such outcomes are compared with those of behavioral and cognitive-behavioral therapies, they tend to be inferior (Greenberg, Elliott, & Lietaer, 1994). Earlier outcome research on client-centered therapy, chiefly involving clients with mild problems, was encouraging (e.g., Rogers & Dymond, 1954), but a later trial of this therapy with schizophrenic clients proved disappointing (Rogers et al., 1967). Early research on the effects of gestalt therapy showed it to have a respectable, though unspectacular, record (Smith et al., 1980).

On the other hand, many of the humanistic-experiential concepts—the uniqueness of each individual, the importance of therapist genuineness, the satisfaction that comes from developing and using one's potentials, the importance of the search for meaning and fulfillment, and the human power for choice and self-direction—have had a major impact on our contemporary views of both human nature and the nature of good psychotherapy.

Therapy for Interpersonal Relationships

Many problems brought to practitioners are explicitly relationship problems. That is, the presenting complaint is not so much one of dissatisfaction with self or one's own behavior as one of the inability to achieve satisfactory accords with significant others. A common example is couples' or marital distress. The maladaptive behavior is in these instances shared between the members of the relationship; it is, to use the contemporary term, "systemic" (Gurman, Kniskern, & Pinsof, 1986). A **family system approach** makes the assumption that the within-family behavior of a particular family member is to a large extent under the influence of the behaviors and communication patterns of other family members; it is, in other words, the product of a "system," one that may be amenable to both understanding and change. Problems deriving from the in-place *system* require therapeutic techniques that focus on relationships as much as or more than on individuals.

As was seen in Chapter 11, for example, many problems presenting as individual sexual dysfunctions turn out to be systemic in character. In this section, we will explore the growing fields of couples and family therapy as examples of this type of multiple-client intervention. In general, these therapies, when placed in the context of helping individuals to change, focus on altering the reactions of the interpersonal environment to the behavior of each involved person. It is important to note that couples and family therapies can be and are conducted from any of the perspectives discussed in this chapter and in Chapter 3 (see Alexander, Holtzworth-Munroe, & Jameson's review, 1994, for examples). Thus *behavioral marital therapy*, often utilizing a contracting approach, is one of several widely available variations on the theme.

Couples Counseling (Marital Therapy)

The large numbers of couples seeking help with relationship problems, doubtless in part a product of the conflicts that arise because of changing gender role expectations, have made couples counseling a growing field of therapy. Typically the couple is seen together, and therapy focuses on clarifying and improving their interactions and relationships. Although it is quite routine at the start of couples therapy for each partner to secretly harbor the idea that only the other will have to do the changing (e.g., Cordova & Jacobson, 1993), it is almost always necessary that both partners alter their reactions to the other. For this reason, seeing both members of a couple is generally more effective than working with only one (Gurman & Kniskern, 1978).

Couples counseling, or **marital therapy,** includes a wide range of concepts and procedures. Most therapists emphasize mutual need gratification, social role expectations, communication patterns, and similar interpersonal factors. Not surprisingly, happily married couples tend to differ from unhappily married couples in remaining best friends, talking more to each other, keeping channels of communication open, making more use of nonverbal communication, and showing more sensitivity to each other's feelings and needs. For example, in a study comparing distressed versus nondistressed couples, Margolin and Wampold (1981) found that nondistressed couples showed much more problem-solving behavior than distressed couples, a result found often in studies of this sort. The extremely common scenario, "He never talks to me, he withdraws" versus "All she ever does is bitch and complain, so who needs to talk?" is one whose resolution obviously calls for considerable problem-solving skill, not to mention a degree of maturity and patience in employing it.

Faulty role expectations often play havoc with marital adjustment. For example, Paul (1971) cited the case of a couple who came for marital therapy when the 39-year-old husband was about to divorce his wife to marry a much younger woman. During therapy, he broke into sobs of grief as he recalled the death of his Aunt Anna, who had always accepted him as he was and created an atmosphere of peace and contentment. In reviewing this incident, the husband realized that his girlfriend represented his lifelong search for another Aunt Anna. This led to a reconciliation with his wife, who was now more understanding of his needs, feelings, and role expectations and thus altered her behavior toward her husband accordingly. Of course, not all partners would be so accommodating.

One of the difficulties in couples therapy is the intense emotional involvement of the partners, which makes it difficult for them to perceive and accept the realities of their relationship. Often wives can see clearly what is "wrong" with their husbands but not what attitudes and behaviors of their own are contributing to the relationship impasse, while husbands tend to have remarkable "insight" into their wives' flaws but not their own. To help correct this problem, videotape recordings have been used increasingly to recapture crucial moments of intense interaction between the partners. By watching playbacks of these tapes after immediate tensions have diminished, the partners can gain a fuller awareness of the nature of their interactions. Thus a husband may realize for the first time that he tries to dominate rather than listen to his wife and consider her needs and expectations, or a wife may realize that she is continually undermining her husband's feelings of worth and self-esteem. The following statement was made by a young wife after viewing a videotape playback of the couple's first therapy session.

Case Study, A Couple's First Therapy Session • See! There it is—loud and clear! As usual you didn't let me express my feelings or opinions, you just interrupted me with your own. You're always telling me what I think without asking me what I think. And I can see what I have been doing in response—withdrawing into silence. I feel like, what's the use of talking.

In achieving this shared insight about a dominant pattern in their interactions, the couple was able to work out a much more satisfactory marital relationship within a few months.

Other relatively new and innovative approaches to couples therapy include training the partners to use Rogerian nondirective techniques in listening to each other and helping each other clarify and verbalize their feelings and reactions. A mutual readiness to really listen and try to understand what the other is experiencing—and an acceptance of whatever comes out in this process—can be therapeutic for both individuals, thus producing a more open and honest relationship in the future.

Behavioral therapy has also been used to bring about desired changes in marital relationships. The partners, for example, may be taught to reinforce instances of desired behavior while withdrawing reinforcement for undesired behavior. In a study comparing behavioral with insight-oriented psychodynamic marital therapy, neither proved superior to the other, but both significantly outperformed a waiting-list control condition (Snyder & Wills, 1989).

How generally effective are couples therapies at resolving relationship crises and promoting more effective marriages or intimate partnerships? One study involved a five-year follow-up of 320 former therapy clients and compared their divorce rates with those of the general population (Cookerly, 1980). In cases in which both partners underwent therapy together, 56.4 percent had remained married for the five-year period; in cases in which individual types of therapy were used, 29 percent had remained married. All forms of therapy were associated with significantly better results in keeping marriages together than was characteristic of general population norms. This positive result is also generally supported in Christensen and Heavey's (1999) more recent review of numerous outcome studies. Finally, couples therapy has been successfully used as an adjunct in the treatment of individual problems, such as depression, phobias, alcohol abuse, and sexual dysfunction (Alexander et al., 1994; Jacobson, Holtzworth-Munroe, & Schmaling, 1989; Roth & Fonagy, 1996; Shadish et al., 1993). Behavioral marital therapy, in particular, has been found a valuable adjunctive approach in the treatment of major depression among clients who are also experiencing marital discord

(Craighead, Craighead, & Ilardi, 1998), a numerically substantial subgroup. Despite this generally positive picture, however, Goffman's (1998) recent overall review of the marital therapy field suggests it is currently in a state of stagnation, especially in regard to advances in theory.

Of course, a motivational factor in outcome assessments of couples therapy makes their interpretation somewhat difficult. People strongly motivated to stay in their relationships are more likely to give couples therapy a serious try than their less motivated counterparts. Such motivation may itself, irrespective of therapy, make for partnership longevity or, perhaps, tolerance of partner abnormality. On the other hand, as we have seen, strong motivation is a key element in the likely success of any psychological therapy, so the research on outcomes of couples therapy has a certain face validity even acknowledging some lack of clarity about the role of motivational variations.

Family Systems Therapy

Therapy for a family obviously overlaps with couples and marital therapy but has somewhat different roots. Whereas marital therapy developed in response to the large number of clients who came for assistance with couples' problems, family therapy began with the finding that many people who had shown marked improvement in individual therapy—often in institutional settings—had a relapse on their return home. It soon became ap-

parent that many of these people came from disturbed family settings that required modification if they were to maintain their gains.

Considered from a *family system viewpoint*, the problem or disorder shown by an "identified client" is often only a symptom of a larger family problem. A careful study of the family of a disturbed child, for example, may reveal that the child is merely reflecting the pathology of the family unit. As a result, most family therapists share the view that the family—not simply the designated "client"—must be directly involved in therapy if lasting improvement is to be achieved. This conclusion is increasingly supported in attempts to understand relapse after recovery from even severe disorders, as in the work on expressed emotion (EE) in mood disorders and schizophrenia (see Chapters 6 and 12).

One influential approach to family therapy is the **conjoint family therapy** of Virginia Satir (1967); unfortunately, its popularity is not matched by a notable research record demonstrating its efficacy. Satir's emphasis is on improving faulty communications, interactions, and relationships among family members and on fostering a family system that better meets the needs of each member. Another seminal approach to resolving family disturbances is called **structural family therapy** (Minuchin, 1974). This approach, explicitly based on systems theory, holds that, if the family context can be changed, then the individual members will have altered experi-

Treatment of the entire family may be desirable where abnormal behavior patterns in individuals are maintained by family dynamics.

ences in the family and will behave differently in accordance with the changed requirements of the new family context. Thus an important goal of structural family therapy is to change the organization of the family in such a way that the family members will behave more supportively and less pathogenically toward each other.

Structural family therapy is focused on present interactions and requires an active but not directive approach on the part of a therapist. Initially, the therapist gathers information about the family—a structural map of the typical family interaction patterns—by acting like one of the family and participating in the family interactions as an insider. In this way, the therapist discovers whether the family system has rigid or flexible boundaries, who dominates the power structure, who gets blamed when things go wrong, and so on.

Armed with this understanding, the therapist operates as an agent for altering the interaction among the members, which often has transactional characteristics of enmeshment (overinvolvement), overprotectiveness, rigidity, and poor conflict resolution skills. The "identified client" is often found to play an important role in the family's mode of conflict avoidance. For example, Aponte and Hoffman (1973) reported the successful use of structural family therapy in treating an anorexic 14-year-old girl:

Case Study, Family Therapy for a Daughter's Anorexia •

Analyzing the communications in the family, the therapists saw a competitive struggle for the father's attention and observed that the girl, Laura, was able (covertly, so to speak) to succeed in this competition and get cuddly attention from her father by not eating. To bring the hidden dynamics out into the open, they worked at getting the family members to express their desires more directly—in words instead of through cryptic behavioral messages such as self-starvation. In time, Laura became much more able to verbalize her wishes for affection and gave up the unacceptable and dangerous method of not eating.

As discussed in Chapter 8, structural family therapy has a quite good record of success in the treatment of anorexia nervosa (Dare & Eisler, 1997). It has also been used successfully in the treatment of bulimia nervosa (Schwartz, Barrett, & Saba, 1983), childhood psychosomatic disorders (Minuchin et al., 1975), and narcotic addiction (Stanton & Todd, 1976).

As with couples problems, maladaptive family relationships associated with various types of clinical problems in identified clients have also been successfully overcome by behaviorally oriented therapies (Nathan &

Gorman, 1998; Roth & Fonagy, 1996). With this type of therapy, the therapist's primary task may be seen as reducing the negative effect of the family on the identified client as well as that of the client for other family members. "The therapist does this by actively manipulating the relationship (by instruction, role-playing, etc.) between members so that the relationship changes to a more positively reinforcing and reciprocal one" (Huff, 1969, p. 26).

In an early review of family therapy approaches, Gurman and Kniskern (1978) concluded that structural family therapy had had more impressive results than most other experientially and psychodynamically oriented approaches they had considered. By the time of their subsequent review eight years later (Gurman et al., 1986), the conclusion had shifted somewhat to favor behavioral interventions—one measure of the tremendous momentum generated by behavioral approaches and now shared by the cognitive-behavioral. A more recent quantitative review of outcomes by Shadish and colleagues (1993) supports the high standing accorded behavioral procedures in therapeutic work with families.

ECLECTICISM AND THE INTEGRATION OF THE PSYCHOTHERAPIES

The various "schools" of psychotherapy described in this and all the other chapters in this book used to be more in opposition to one another than they are today. For example, early behaviorists were adamant in their criticism of psychoanalysis as inefficient and mystical. The analysts reacted vehemently with counterarguments, usually to the effect that behavioral therapies were superficial and treated only symptoms, while psychoanalytic treatments sought deeper and more permanent cures. And both the behaviorists and the analysts were contemptuous of humanistic-existential approaches as involving unwise personalization of the therapy process, as being too "touchy-feely." The early behaviorists were also in fact notably suspicious and sometimes frankly hostile when the general "cognitive revolution" in psychology began to make inroads into what they considered their turf. Today *cognitive-behavioral therapy* is widely practiced—an amalgamation that would have been unthinkable to psychologists in the early 1960s.

The evolution just mentioned is actually part of a larger movement toward a relaxation of boundaries and a willingness of therapists to explore differing ways of approaching clinical problems, a process sometimes called *multimodal therapy* (Lazarus, 1981; 1985; 1997b). Most

Psychologically based treatment approaches became commonplace during the 20th century.

psychotherapists when asked today what is their orientation will reply "eclectic," which usually means that they try to borrow and combine concepts and techniques from various schools depending on what seems best for the individual case. This inclusiveness even extends to efforts to combine individual and family systems therapies (e.g., Feldman, 1992; E. Wachtel, 1994), and combined biological and psychosocial approaches (e.g., Feldman & Feldman, 1997; Klerman et al., 1994; Pinsof, 1995; see also Chapter 16). The integration of the psychotherapies has been the topic of numerous recent books and articles (e.g., Gold & Striker, 1993; Goldfried, Greenberg, & Marmar, 1990; Norcross & Goldfried, 1992; Wachtel, 1997). It appears to be a movement whose time has come.

Since no single therapy has proved to be effective at all times in all clinical situations, it seems reasonable to many to attempt to use the best components among them, often in combination. This has been done a number of ways. One such approach might be to try to identify the common threads shared by all or most varieties of therapy, such as empathic listening and nonjudgmental acceptance, and work from there to try to achieve clarity as to how these presumably powerful common factors produce the therapeutic effects they do. Little productive advance has emerged from this idea, and the integrationists seem to be after a more far-reaching goal.

Another integration strategy would be that of borrowing divergent techniques of therapy and recombining them in maximally effective ways. For example, a psychodynamicist might employ the gestalt two-chair technique to have the client explore the interplay between the two sides of a supposedly unconscious intrapsychic conflict. Probably most therapists of whatever stripe use contingent reinforcement (by their relative activity and atten-

tion versus their silence or inattention), whether deliberate or not, to guide clients into areas deemed to have special import. It is already apparent, then, that therapy "integration" can have different meanings. It is one thing, for example, to advocate a liberal borrowing of tactics and strategies from the various standard brands of therapy—using whatever "works," sometimes called *technical eclecticism*—but it is quite another and far more ambitious goal to seek the integration of their theoretical underpinnings. The latter are for the most part unique to each brand, and it is not obvious how they can be intermeshed. Paul Wachtel (1977, 1987, 1993, 1997) is one theorist conversant with several of these languages—the psychodynamic, the behavioral, the cognitive, the interpersonal, and family systems. He moves among these differing traditions with seeming comfort and ease while generating insightful ideas in the process. However, such flexible talent appears to be fairly rare in the field at large.

Meanwhile, not all mental health professionals agree that attempts at *theoretical* integration are worthwhile—even assuming modest success is possible, and some deny that possibility. Whatever their individual failings, and in the absence to date of a grand, overriding theory of therapy, the major schools of psychotherapy provide their respective practitioners with a coherent, internally consistent framework for conceptualizing what "the problem" is and for formulating what needs to be set in motion to eradicate it.

There is a "middle ground" here—namely, for the therapist to retain a loose allegiance to whatever theoretical orientation seems right for him or her but to remain alert to and, where justified, to experiment with specific techniques developed within other frameworks if they have promise of furthering the designated theory-specific therapeutic aims (i.e., uncovering the unconscious, changing dysfunctional cognitions, liberating constraints on awareness, etc.).

If a grand, overriding theory of psychotherapy does emerge from the efforts of the psychotherapy integrationists or from other sources, our guess is that it will be accompanied by dramatic new insights about the nature of mental disorders. At present, we still know too little that is ironclad about the "inner workings" of both disorder and its treatment, which is what permits radically differing conceptions to thrive side-by-side.

How DOES ONE MEASURE SUCCESS IN PSYCHOTHERAPY?

Evaluating the success of psychological treatment is a difficult enterprise for several reasons. At best, it is an inexact process, dependent on imperfect measurement and outcome data. Attempts at estimating clients' gains in therapy generally depend on one or more of the following sources of information: (1) a therapist's impression of changes that have occurred, (2) a client's reports of change, (3) reports from the client's family or friends, (4) comparison of pretreatment and posttreatment scores on personality test scores or on other test instruments designed to measure relevant facets of psychological functioning, and (5) measures of change in selected overt behaviors.

Unfortunately, each of these sources has its own limitations. A therapist may not be the best judge of a client's progress, since any therapist is likely to be biased in favor of seeing himself or herself as competent and successful. In addition, the therapist typically has only a limited observational sample, the client's in-session behavior, from which to make judgments of overall change. Furthermore, therapists can inflate improvement averages by deliberately or subtly encouraging difficult clients to discontinue therapy. And incidentally, the problem of how to deal with early dropouts complicates many therapy-outcome studies. For example, are these former clients to be counted as successes or as failures when in fact they have received little or none of the therapy being evaluated? From a certain point of view they probably shouldn't be counted at all, but this decision raises additional problems, such as the possible unrepresentativeness of the clients *not* dropping out—making it difficult to arrive at an unequivocal conclusion about the effectiveness of *this* kind of therapy for *that* type of client.

A client, also, is not necessarily a reliable source of information on therapeutic outcomes. Clients may not only want to think they are getting better for various personal reasons, but they may report that they are being helped in an attempt to please the therapist. In addition, because therapy often requires a considerable investment of time, money, and sometimes emotional distress, the idea that it has been useless is a dissonant one. Family and relatives may also be inclined to "see" the improvement they had hoped for, although they often seem to be more realistic than either the therapist or the client in their evaluations of outcome.

Clinical ratings by an outside independent observer are sometimes used in psychotherapy-outcome research to evaluate the progress of a client; these may be more objective than ratings by those directly involved in the therapy. Another widely used objective measure of client change is performance on various psychological tests. A client evaluated in this way takes a battery of tests before and after therapy and the differences in scores are assumed to reflect progress or its lack, or occasionally even deterioration. Although such tests may indeed show changes, these may sometimes be artifactual, as with *regression to the mean* phenomena (Speer, 1992), where very high (or low) scores tend on repeated measurement to drift toward the average of their own distributions—yielding a false impression that some real change has been documented. Also, the particular tests selected are likely to focus on the theoretical predictions of the therapist or researcher. They are not necessarily valid predictors of changes, if any, the therapy actually induces, nor of how the client will behave in real life. Without follow-up assessment they can also provide little information on how enduring any change is likely to be.

Objectifying and Quantifying Change

Generalized terms such as *recovery, marked improvement,* and *moderate improvement,* often used in outcome research in the past, are open to considerable differences in interpretation. Today there is a strong trend to use more quantitatively precise modes of measuring change. For example, the Beck Depression Inventory (a self-report measure of depression intensity) and the Hamilton Rating Scale for Depression (a set of rating scales used by clinicians to measure the same thing) both yield summary scores and have become almost standard in the pre- and post-therapy assessment of depression. Changes in preselected and specifically denoted behaviors that are systematically monitored, such as hand-washing counts for a client obsessed with contamination, appear to be the safest measures of outcome. Such techniques, including client self-monitoring, have been widely and effectively used, mainly by behavior and cognitive-behavioral therapists. Even under the best of measurement circumstances, however, there is always the possibility that improvement will be attributed to the particular form of treatment used, when it is in fact a product of placebo effects, other events in a client's life, or even of spontaneous change. This relates to the matter of experimental control, of which we shall have more to say in the Unresolved Issues section at the end of this chapter.

Would Change Occur Anyway?

In this context, it is pertinent to ask what happens to disturbed people who do not obtain formal treatment. In view of the many ways that people can help each other, it is not surprising that often considerable improvement occurs without professional therapeutic intervention. Relevant here is the observation that treatment offered by professional therapists has not, in general, been clearly demonstrated to be superior in outcome to nonprofessionally administered therapies (Christensen & Jacobson, 1994). Also, some forms of psychopathology, such as manic and depressive episodes and some instances of schizophreniform disorder, appear to run a fairly brief course with or without treatment, and there are many other instances in which disturbed people improve over time for reasons that are not apparent.

Even if many emotionally disturbed persons tend to improve over time without psychotherapy, it seems clear that psychotherapy can often accelerate improvement or ensure desired behavior change that might not otherwise occur (Lambert & Bergin, 1994; Telch, 1981). Most researchers today would agree that psychotherapy is more effective than no treatment, and indeed the pertinent evidence, widely cited throughout this chapter and the entire text, confirms this strongly. The chances of an average client benefiting significantly from psychological treatment are, overall, impressive (Lambert & Bergin, 1994).

Furthermore, improvement seems a function of the number of therapy sessions undertaken—with the largest gains achieved early (that is, within six months) in the therapeutic relationship (Howard et al., 1986). In one large-scale survey undertaken by *Consumers Union* (see Seligman, 1995, 1998) longer-term therapy was associated with a superior improvement record as judged by the clients themselves.

Can Therapy be Harmful?

The outcomes of psychotherapy do not range from neutral (no effect) to positive, but rather seem to encompass a significant negative or deteriorative effect. Some clients are *harmed* in their encounters with psychotherapists (Lambert & Bergin, 1994; Mays & Franks, 1985; Strupp, Hadley, & Gomes-Schwartz, 1977). The extreme is client suicide, although we certainly do not suggest that all such outcomes could be avoided with more skillful psychotherapy. In any event, some client-psychotherapist relationships, approaching perhaps 10 percent (Lambert & Bergin, 1994), apparently result in the client's being worse off than if psychotherapy had never been undertaken.

Obvious ruptures of the therapeutic alliance—what Binder and Strupp (1997) refer to as "negative process," in which client and therapist become embroiled in a mutually antagonistic and downwardly spiraling course—account for only a portion of the failures. In other instances a bewildering network of interactive factors operate together and idiosyncratically in an individual case (for example, the match of therapist and client personality characteristics) to produce deteriorating outcomes. Our

impression, supported by some evidence reviewed by Lambert (1989) and Lambert and Bergin (1994), is that certain therapists, probably for reasons of personality, just do not do well with certain types of client problems. In light of these intangible factors, we take it as the responsibility of all therapists to monitor their work with various types of clients to discover any such deficiencies, and to refer promptly to other therapists those clients with whom they may be ill-equipped to work.

A special case of therapeutic harm is the problem of sex between therapist and client, typically seduction of a client (or former client) by a therapist, which is considered unethical conduct. Given the frequently intense and intimate quality of therapeutic relationships, it is not surprising that sexual attraction arises. What is distressing is the apparent frequency with which it is manifested in exploitive and unprofessional behavior on the part of therapists—all the more so in light of the fact that virtually all authorities agree that such liaisons are nearly always destructive of good client functioning in the long run (Pope, Sonne, & Holroyd, 1993).

Even allowing for the likelihood of occasional fraudulent or frivolous client complaints in this area—estimated at 4 percent (Pope & Vetter, 1991)—the well-established occurrence of this type of event indicates an unacceptable level of misconduct, and probable client injury, among people holding themselves out to be psychotherapists (in most jurisdictions not a legally regulated self-description). A prospective client seeking therapy needs to be sufficiently wary to determine that the therapist chosen is one of the large majority committed to high ethical and professional standards.

PSYCHOTHERAPY AND SOCIETY

Psychosocial interventions to modify the behavior of individuals intersect with important social issues on many levels. Two of the more significant of these points of contact concern (1) the question of societal values and (2) the rapidly evolving multiculturalism of the society in which we live. We address each of these concerns here.

Social Values and Psychotherapy

The criticism has been raised—from both inside and outside the mental health professions—that psychotherapy can be viewed as an attempt to get people adjusted to a "sick" society rather than to encourage them to work toward its improvement. As a consequence, psychotherapy has often been considered the guardian of the status quo. This issue is perhaps easier for us to place in perspective by looking at other cultures. For example, there had been frequent allegations that psychiatry was used as a means of political control in the former Soviet Union, an abuse that was eventually officially acknowledged (see *Schizophrenia Bulletin,* 1990, vol. 16, no. 4). It is encouraging to note that these practices had been all but universally condemned by the international mental health community. Although few people make the claim that psychiatry in the Western world is used to gain control over social critics, there is nevertheless the possibility that therapists are, in some ways, placed in the roles of "gatekeepers" of social values. Such charges, of course, bring us back to the question we raised in Chapter 1: What do we mean by abnormal? Our answer to that question can only be made in the light of our values.

In a broader perspective, there is the complex and controversial issue of the role of values in science. Psychotherapy is not, or at least should not be, a system of ethics; it is a set of tools to be used at the discretion of a therapist in pursuit of a client's welfare. Thus mental health professionals are confronted with the same kinds of questions that confront scientists in general. Should a physical scientist who helps develop thermonuclear weapons be morally concerned about how they are used? Similarly, should a psychologist or behavioral scientist who develops powerful techniques to influence or control behavior be concerned about how they are used?

Many psychologists and other scientists try to sidestep this issue by insisting that science is value-free—that it is concerned only with gathering facts, not with how they are applied. Each time therapists decide that one behavior should be eliminated or substituted for another, however, they are making a value judgment. For example, is a therapist to assume the depression of a young homemaker-mother who is abused by a drunken husband to be an internally based disorder requiring "treatment," as once would have been routine? Or does the therapist perhaps have a larger responsibility to look beyond individual pathology and confront the abnormality of the marital relationship? Therapy takes place in a context that involves the values of the therapist, the client, and the society in which they live. There are strong pressures on a therapist—from parents, schools, courts, and other social institutions—to help people adjust to the world as it is. At the same time, there are many counterpressures, particularly from young people who are seeking support in their attempts (granted, sometimes overdone) to become authentic people rather than blind conformists.

The dilemma in which contemporary therapists may find themselves is illustrated by the following case.

Case Study, Who Needs Therapy? • A 15-year-old high school sophomore is sent to a therapist because her parents have discovered that she has been having sexual intercourse with her boyfriend. The girl tells the therapist that she thoroughly enjoys such relations and feels no guilt or remorse over her behavior, even though her parents strongly disapprove. In addition, she reports that she is quite aware of the danger of becoming pregnant and is careful to take contraceptive measures.

What is the role of the therapist in such a case? Should the girl be encouraged to conform to her parents' mores and postpone sexual activity until she is older and more mature? Or should the parents be helped to adjust to the pattern of sexual behavior she has chosen? What should be the therapist's goal? As was noted earlier, it is not unusual to find some individuals being referred for psychological treatment because their behavior, not particularly destructive or disturbing, has caused concern among family members who wish the therapist to "fix" them.

It is apparent that there are diametrically opposed ways of dealing with problems in therapy. It is often left to individual therapists to decide what path to take, and this requires value decisions on their part concerning what is best for an individual and for the larger society.

Psychotherapy and Cultural Diversity

As was noted earlier, the establishment and maintenance of an effective psychotherapeutic "working alliance" between client and therapist is generally regarded as a crucial and indispensable element in determining the relative success of the outcome. What does this mean then for a client whose background is considerably different from that of the therapist?

There is a quite large but somewhat unwieldy literature, reviewed by Sue, Zane, and Young (1994), on this subject. Generalizable conclusions are hard to formulate because of the complexity of the issues encountered, such as the marked heterogeneity on various dimensions *within* particular ethnic groups in the United States. For example, the significance of client-therapist ethnic match for Mexican-American clients in the Los Angeles area appears to depend on whether or not English is the client's primary language—if it is not, then such clients have better outcomes when the therapist is also of Mexican-American heritage (Sue et al., 1991).

Overall, however, there is as yet no solid evidence that psychotherapeutic outcomes are diminished when client and therapist are of different race or ethnicity (Beutler et al., 1994; Sue, Zane, & Young, 1994). However, Atkinson

(1983) and Atkinson and associates (1986) found that African-American clients experience greater rapport and satisfaction with African-American than with white therapists, and other evidence suggests they may be more amenable to self-disclosure when the therapist is also African American (Jackson & Kirschner, 1973). Similarly, Mexican Americans state a strong preference for therapists sharing this ethnic background and express the view that such therapists are more "credible" than Anglo therapists would be (Lopez, Lopez, & Fong, 1991; Ponce & Atkinson, 1989). Little is reliably known about such attitudinal dispositions among other minority groups.

Because of the history of slavery and continued overt and subtle racism, oppression, and discrimination in the United States, the psychotherapy of African-Americans by white mental health professionals may pose special problems around the issue of rage. Rage is said to be a common, everyday experience among many African Americans, yet the larger society has a very low tolerance

for its expression. Unexpressed rage leads to despair and the mental health consequences thereof. The white therapist, who may have little personal acquaintance with rage and who may share the larger culture's proscriptions regarding it, may have a hard time recognizing its signs or dealing effectively with it in his or her African-American clients, thus failing to engage what may be a central issue in these clients' lives (see Hardy & Laszloffy, 1995, for a focused discussion of the problem).

One way of coping with the general problem of mismatched ethnicity in client-therapist pairings would be to increase proportions of minority persons in the mental health professions. While these professions have been fairly aggressive in recruiting qualified minority persons into their ranks over roughly the past 25 years, the yield has been less impressive than the effort, in large part because minority status is often associated with disadvantaged economic and educational resources, and with the erosion of confidence in one's abilities to overcome challenges and obstacles.

UNRESOLVED ISSUES

Efficacy Versus Effectiveness

When a pharmaceutical company develops a new drug, it must obtain approval of the drug from the federal Food and Drug Administration (FDA) before that drug can be marketed. This involves, among other things, demonstrating through research on human subjects that the drug has efficacy—that is, that it does what it is supposed to do in curing or relieving some target medical condition. These tests, using voluntary and informed patients as subjects, are called *randomized clinical trials* (RCTs) or more simply *efficacy trials*. Although these trials may become quite elaborate, the basic design is one of randomly assigning (e.g., by the flip of a coin) half the patients to the supposedly "active" drug and the other half to a visually identical but physiologically inactive placebo. Usually, neither the patient nor the prescriber is informed which is to be administered, that information being retained in coded fashion by a third party; this procedure is called *double-blinding* and attempts to ensure that expectations on the part of the patient and prescriber play no role in the study. After a predetermined treatment interval, the code is broken and the active or placebo status of all subjects is revealed. If subjects on the active drug have improved in health significantly more than placebo subjects, the investigator is entitled to claim this to be evidence of the drug's efficacy. Obviously, the same design could be

modified to competitively compare the efficacy of two or more active drugs, with the option of adding a placebo condition. Thousands of such studies are in progress daily across the country, usually in academic medical settings and financially supported by the pharmaceutical industry.

Would-be investigators of psychosocial therapy outcomes have often attempted to apply this research design to their own field of inquiry, though with some necessary modifications. A significant and persistent frustration has been the difficulty of concocting a credible psychosocial analogue to a placebo pill. Most such research has thus adopted the strategy of either competitively comparing two or more purportedly "active" therapies or of using a no treatment ("wait list") control of the same duration as the active treatment. Also, therapists, even those acknowledging allegiance to the same school are, left to their own devices, quite different in the manner in which they deliver "their" therapy. Pills of the same chemical compound and dosage will have, at most, minuscule variations. Hence, in order to test the agreed-upon ingredients of, let us say, therapy X it becomes necessary to develop a *manual* specifying these, and then to train (and monitor) the research therapists to make sure their therapy sessions do not deviate significantly from the procedures outlined in the manual (e.g., see Sanderson & Woody, 1995).

The result is a **"manualized" therapy** in which any personal characteristics of the therapist that may subtly modify the style or delivery of the manualized therapy, such as a charismatic "presence," are typically considered a null factor and ignored, probably erroneously. There is in fact much evidence that therapist personal characteristics are important determinants of therapeutic outcome (e.g., see Beutler, Machado, & Neufeldt, 1994; Blatt et al., 1996a; Lambert, 1989). Although manualized therapies originated principally to standardize psychosocial treatments to fit the randomized clinical trial paradigm, some would extend their use to routine clinical practice after efficacy for particular disorders has been established (e.g., see Wilson, 1998).

Efficacy or RCT studies of psychosocial treatments are increasingly common, in part a response to demands for quality control in health service delivery. These time-limited studies typically focus on patients having a single DSM-IV diagnosis (those with comorbid psychiatric diagnoses being excluded) and involve two or more treatment or control (e.g., wait list) conditions where at least one of the treatment conditions is a psychosocial one (another could be some biological therapy, such as a particular drug). Client-subjects are randomly assigned to these conditions, whose effects, if any, are evaluated systematically with a common battery of assessment instruments, usually administered both before and after treatment.

Efficacy studies of the outcomes of specific psychosocial treatment procedures are considered to be the most rigorous type of evaluation we have for establishing that a given therapy "works" for clients with a given DSM-IV diagnosis. Treatments meeting this standard are often described as "empirically validated" or "empirically supported," and various lists of such treatments are now routinely published and updated (e.g., Chambless et al., 1998; Nathan & Gorman, 1998; Roth & Fonagy, 1996).

But note again that the focus here is on a specifically defined therapy applied to a specific (and noncomorbid) DSM-defined disorder, in keeping with the adopted analogy of specific drugs for specific medical illnesses. Other variables, such as patient characteristics other than designated diagnosis (e.g., see Barber & Muenz, 1996) and therapist characteristics other than the manualized script to be implemented (e.g., see Blatt et al., 1996a) are left out of the evaluation. As already noted, there is much evidence that, for psychosocial therapies, these may be crucial omissions (Bergin & Garfield, 1994; see also Garfield, 1998).

Mental health professionals are divided on both the value and the wisdom of lists of RCT-supported therapies, the opposition basing its arguments chiefly on the undoubtedly large discrepancy between the tightly controlled conditions of RCTs and what practicing clinicians actually deal with (see the November 1995 issue of *Consumer Reports;* also Seligman, 1995, 1998). They argue that therapeutic *effectiveness* is not the same thing as *efficacy,* with its connotations of tightly controlled experiments, and that less rigorous but more realistic and equally "empirical" effectiveness studies can tell us as much or even more about improving psychotherapeutic practice.

In one sense, at least, they have a point. Psychotherapy as practiced out in the field differs of necessity in numerous and obviously important ways from the psychotherapy of an efficacy trial (see Table 17.2). Some practitioners are so impressed with the differences that they declare efficacy trials to be irrelevant to their work. The latter is probably too extreme a judgment, but it is true that the relative "purity" of the RCT is seldom approached in the real world of clinical practice. We are inclined to agree with Seligman (1998) that, for the present, efficacy and effectiveness studies complement each other and that we will profit best by combining the strengths of both.

TABLE 17.2 COMMON IMPORTANT DIFFERENCES BETWEEN "EFFICACY" AND "EFFECTIVENESS" PSYCHOTHERAPY OUTCOME STUDIES

Efficacy Studies	Effectiveness Studies
Specified time (sessions) limit.	No specified time (session) limit.
Client often may not have comorbid mental disorders.	Client may have comorbid mental disorders.
Random assignment to predetermined treatment conditions.	Individually selected treatment approach.
Manualized delivery of treatment condition.	Flexible delivery of treatment approach.
No switching to another therapy type.	Switching to another therapy type permitted.
Predetermined outcome measures, not selected by client.	Treatment goals collaboratively decided.

SUMMARY

Psychological treatment is aimed at the reduction of abnormal behavior in individuals through psychological means. The goals of psychotherapy include changing maladaptive behavior, minimizing or eliminating stressful environmental conditions, reducing negative affect, improving interpersonal competencies, resolving personal conflicts, modifying a person's inaccurate assumptions about himself or herself, and fostering a more positive self-image. Although these goals are by no means easy to achieve, psychological treatment methods have been shown to be generally effective in promoting adaptive psychological functioning in many troubled people.

Many approaches to psychological treatment (schools of psychotherapy) have been developed to treat individuals with psychological disorders. One of the oldest approaches to psychological treatment, classical psychoanalysis, was originated a century ago by Sigmund Freud. It is rarely practiced today. Several psychodynamic variants of therapy have developed out of the psychoanalytic tradition. These approaches accept some elements of Freudian theory but diverge on key points, such as the length of time to be devoted to therapy or the role of primitive psychosexual drives in personality dynamics. For the most part, they emphasize interpersonal processes as affected by early interactions with significant others.

A second major approach to psychological intervention is behavior therapy. Originating over 50 years ago, behavior therapy has come to be used extensively in treating clinical problems. Behavior therapy approaches make use of a number of techniques, such as guided exposure and biofeedback as well as aversion therapy, modeling, and reinforcement approaches. Recently, behavior therapy methods have been applied to private events—that is, thoughts or cognitions—with a great deal of success. Known as cognitive or cognitive-behavioral therapy, this approach attempts to modify a person's self-statements and construal of events to change his or her behavior. Cognitive-behavioral methods have been used for a wide variety of clinical problems—from depression to anger control—and with a range of clinical populations.

Several other psychological treatment methods have been referred to as humanistic-experiential therapies. One of the earliest of these approaches is the client-centered, or person-centered, therapy of Carl Rogers. This treatment approach, originating in the 1940s, has received broad acceptance and has provided a valuable conceptualization of the client-therapist interaction as well as specific techniques for generating personal change or personal growth in motivated clients.

In addition to individual treatment approaches, some psychological treatment methods are applied to problematic relationships through marital or family therapy. These approaches typically assume that a person's problems lie partly in his or her interactions with others. Consequently, the focus of treatment is to change ways of interacting among individuals in the social or family context.

In recent years a concerted attempt has been made to integrate the various available conceptions and techniques of inducing behavioral change. This effort is a result of the recognition that elements from differing approaches can be used to increase our understanding of troubled clients and to bring about desired alterations of functioning. A key element in all therapies is the development of an effective "working alliance." A principal social issue in psychotherapy is the problem of ensuring the development of a good therapeutic working alliance between persons of widely differing cultural, ethnic, and socioeconomic backgrounds.

Evaluation of the success of psychotherapy in producing desired changes in clients is difficult. Two levels of standards for doing so have evolved, those of efficacy and of effectiveness. Research in psychotherapy, however, has shown that most treatment approaches are more effective than no treatment at all. However, therapy can also go awry, causing psychological deterioration. Beyond the question of evaluating the success of psychotherapy lie other, larger questions involving the ethical dilemmas posed by therapy. Does psychotherapy encourage conformity to the status quo? Should it do this? These constitute some of the difficult moral and social issues that daily confront mental health professionals.

KEY TERMS

psychotherapy (p. 644)

psychodynamic therapy (p. 648)

free association (p. 648)

manifest content (p. 649)

latent content (p. 649)

resistance (p. 649)

transference (p. 649)

counter-transference (p. 650)

behavior therapy (p. 654)

systematic desensitization (p. 654)

Contemporary Issues in Abnormal Psychology

Martin Ramirez, *Untitled*, 1950. Ramirez moved from Mexico to California around 1905, where he entered a mental institution and spent the rest of his life. Having lost his speech, he began to make crayon and graphite drawings, and collages on scraps of paper. His work often depicted a figure suspended in illusionistic, deep space by enclosures such as doorways or tunnels.

We have covered a great number of topics and issues pertinent to understanding abnormal behavior from a contemporary perspective on these pages. The final chapter of this book has traditionally been somewhat of a forum for several important topics in abnormal psychology that have only briefly been noted in earlier chapters. These issues are very important to understanding the field of abnormal psychology and will give the reader a broader perspective on ways our society deals with, or in some cases fails to deal with, abnormal behavior.

We begin with the topic of prevention of mental disorders. Over the years, most mental health efforts have been largely restorative, geared toward helping people only after they have already developed serious problems. Seemingly, a more effective strategy would be to try to catch problems before they become severe, or better yet, to establish conditions in which psychological disorders will not occur. Unfortunately, the causes of many mental disorders are either not sufficiently understood or specific enough to enable practitioners to initiate targeted preventive programs. As a result, prevention in the mental health field is still based largely on hypotheses about what works rather than on substantial empirical research. Nonetheless, many professionals believe that preventive mental health efforts are worthwhile. We will begin with a review of preventive strategies and then examine the kinds of measures that are being taken to prevent maladaptive behavior or limit its seriousness.

Next, we will explore several legal issues pertinent to psychiatric care and hospitalization of people with severe psychological problems: commitment, deinstitutionalization, and assessment of dangerousness. Closely related to these factors are the matters of (1) a therapist's duty to warn others if a client threatens violence and (2) the use—and some think abuse—of the insanity defense as a plea in capital crimes. We will then briefly survey the scope of organized efforts for mental health both in the United States and throughout the world. Finally, we will conclude the chapter by considering what each of us can do to foster mental health.

PERSPECTIVES ON PREVENTION

In the past the concepts of primary, secondary, and tertiary prevention were widely used in public health efforts to describe general strategies of disease prevention. These terms were derived from public health strategies employed for understanding and controlling infectious physical diseases, and were thought to provide a useful perspective in the mental health field as well.

However, for years there was a relative lack of progress in prevention (Albee, 1996). Heller (1996), for example, noted that "Until the last decade anything approaching a true prevention science did not exist" (p. 1124). In the early 1990s the U.S. Congress directed the National Institute of Mental Health (NIMH) to work with the Institute of Medicine (IOM) to develop a report detailing a long-term prevention research program. Among other things, the IOM report provided a new conceptualization of prevention that clarified the definitions of prevention to focus attention on the distinction between prevention and treatment efforts (Munoz, Mrazek, & Haggerty, 1996). Prevention efforts are now classified into three subcategories:

1. *Universal interventions:* Efforts that are aimed at influencing the general population.

2. *Selective interventions:* Efforts that are aimed at a specific subgroup of the population that would be considered at risk for developing mental health problems—for example, adolescents or ethnic minorities.

3. *Indicated interventions:* Efforts that are directed to high-risk individuals who are identified as having minimal but detectable symptoms of mental disorder but who do not meet criteria for clinical diagnosis—for example, individuals forced from their homes due to a flood or some other disaster.

As shown in Figure 18.1, preventive efforts are clearly differentiated from treatment and maintenance interventions.

Universal Interventions

Universal interventions are concerned with two key tasks: (1) altering conditions that can cause or contribute to mental disorders (risk factors) and (2) establishing conditions that foster positive mental health (protective factors). Epidemiological studies (as discussed in Chapter 1) are particularly important in this area because they help investigators obtain information about the incidence and distribution of various maladaptive behaviors needing prevention efforts (Dohrenwend, 1997). These findings can then be used to suggest what preventive efforts might be most appropriate. For example, various epidemiological studies and reviews have shown that certain groups are at high risk for mental disorders: recently divorced people (Bloom et al., 1978); the physically disabled (Freeman, Malkin, & Hastings, 1975); elderly people living alone (Neugarten, 1977); physically abused children (Malinosky-Rummel & Hansen, 1993); and peo-

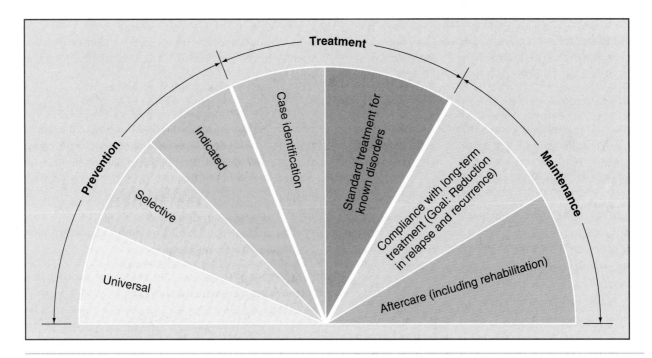

FIGURE 18.1   CLASSIFICATION OF PREVENTION STRATEGIES, TREATMENT, AND MAINTENANCE
The traditional terminology for describing general strategies of disease prevention in the field of public health has been revised to provide a more useful perspective on prevention efforts. The new classification system for prevention (universal, selective, and indicated strategies) is shown in this context as distinct from treatment, and maintenance approaches mental health problems.
Source: Mrazek and Haggerty (1994).

ple who have been uprooted from their homes (Westermeyer et al., 1991). Although findings such as these may be the basis for immediate selective or indicated prevention, they may also aid in universal prevention by telling us what to look for and where to look—in essence by focusing our efforts in the right direction. Universal prevention is very broad. It includes biological, psychosocial, and sociocultural efforts. Virtually any effort that is aimed at improving the human condition, at making life more fulfilling and meaningful, would be considered to be part of universal prevention of mental disorder.

Biological Measures   Biologically based universal strategies for prevention begin with developing adaptive lifestyles. Many of the goals of health psychology (see Chapter 8) can be viewed as universal prevention strategies. Such efforts geared toward improving diet, establishing a routine of physical exercise, and developing overall good health habits can do much to improve physical well-being. To the extent that physical illness always produces some sort of psychological stress that can result in such problems as depression, good health is prevention with respect to good mental health.

Psychosocial Measures   In viewing normality as optimal development and high functioning as the goal

rather than the mere absence of pathology, we imply that people need opportunities to learn physical, intellectual, emotional, and social competencies. The first requirement for psychosocial "health" is that a person develop the skills needed for effective problem solving, for expressing emotions constructively, and for satisfying relationships with others; failure to develop these "protective" skills places the individual at a serious disadvantage in coping with stresses and often unavoidable mental disorder risk factors.

The second requirement for psychosocial health is that a person acquire an accurate frame of reference on which to build his or her identity. We have seen repeatedly that when people's assumptions about themselves or their world are inaccurate, their behavior is likely to be maladaptive. Likewise, an inability to find satisfying values that foster a meaningful and fulfilling life constitutes a fertile source of maladjustment and mental disorders. Consider for example, the young woman who believes that being thin can bring happiness and so becomes anorexic.

The third requirement for psychosocial health is that a person be prepared for the types of problems likely to be encountered during given life stages. For example, pregnancy and childbirth usually have a great deal of emotional significance for both parents; in addition, the

This billboard is an example of a universal prevention effort which is concerned with risk factors, altering conditions that can cause or contribute to disorder, and protective factors, establishing conditions that foster health.

arrival of a new infant in the home places an enormously increased demand on the resources of caregivers and may disturb family equilibrium or exacerbate an already disturbed marital situation. Young people who want to marry and have children must be prepared for the tasks of building a mutually satisfying relationship and helping children develop their abilities. The latter is a particularly formidable responsibility for teenage parents, who are themselves still struggling to become independent adults. Similarly, a person needs to be prepared adequately for other developmental tasks characteristic of given life periods, including retirement and old age.

In recent years, psychosocial measures aimed at prevention have received a great deal of attention. The field of behavioral medicine has had substantial influence here. As we saw in Chapter 8, efforts are being made to change the psychological factors underlying unhealthful habits, such as smoking, excessive drinking, and poor eating habits, that may be contributing to the development of both physical and psychological problems.

Sociocultural Measures The relationship between an individual and his or her community is a reciprocal one, a fact Americans sometimes forget in a culture that has historically placed an unusually high value on individualism. We need autonomy and freedom to be ourselves, but we also need to belong and contribute to a community. As has been demonstrated many times throughout this book, without a supportive community, individual development is stifled.

At the same time, without responsible, psychologically healthy individuals, the community will not thrive and, in turn, cannot be supportive. When a community begins to fail (as noted by such circumstances as the flight of the more economically successful people to the suburbs, leaving a largely impoverished inner city), there is considerable danger that the failure will become self-sustaining; the psychosocially impaired victims of disorganized communities lack the wherewithal to create better communities to protect and sustain the psychological health of those who come after them, thus resulting in a persistently unprotective environment. Sociocultural efforts toward universal prevention are focused on making the community as safe and attractive as possible for the individuals within it.

With our growing realization of the role pathological social conditions play in producing maladaptive behavior (in socially impoverished communities), increased attention must be devoted to creating social conditions that will foster healthy development and functioning in individuals. Efforts to create these conditions are seen in a broad spectrum of social measures—ranging from public education and Social Security to economic planning and social legislation directed at ensuring adequate health care for all citizens.

Selective Interventions

Preventing mental health problems through social change in the community is difficult. Although the whole psychological climate can ultimately be changed by a social movement, such as the civil rights movement of the 1960s, the payoff of such efforts is generally far in the future and may be difficult or impossible to predict or measure. Efforts at psychologically desirable social change are also likely to involve ideological and political issues that may inspire powerful opposition, including opposition from government itself. According to an analysis by Humphreys and Rappaport (1993), for example, the Reagan and Bush administrations during the 1980s severely undercut Community Mental Health Center social programs in favor of agencies involved in the "war on drugs." This effort, in redirecting attention and funds to purported defects of individual character, was said to be more in keeping with a conservative political philosophy that viewed the basic problem as one of personal moral weakness ("How should kids deal with a drug-saturated environment? Just say no."), *not* social disorganization. Although drug abuse *is* a matter of individual behavior, it does not follow that countermeasures must be individually directed. Some examples of more selective and effective programs will be discussed in what follows.

An Illustration of Selective Prevention Strategies
Though difficult to formulate and even more difficult to mobilize and carry out, **selective intervention** can bring about major improvements if successful. In this section we will look at the mobilization of prevention resources aimed at curtailing or reducing the problem of teenage alcohol and drug abuse.

Drug use among most adolescent groups has declined in recent times (National Institute of Drug Abuse, 1996b), but teenage drug and alcohol use is still viewed as one of today's most significant psychological and community problems. Prominent social forces such as attractive television advertising, the influence of peer groups, negative parental role models, and the ready availability of many drugs are instrumental in promoting the early use of alcohol in young people.

Recent years have witnessed an alarming rate of marijuana and alcohol use, particularly binge drinking, among adolescents (National Institute of Drugs Abuse, 1996a). A recent survey found that 55 percent of eighth graders, 71 percent of tenth graders, 81 percent of twelfth graders, and 90 percent of college students have tried alcohol. Heavy drinking, defined as five or more drinks in a row, has shown an alarming rate of incidence (15 percent for eighth graders, 24 percent for tenth graders, 30 percent for twelfth graders, and 40 percent for college students). Heavy alcohol use among young people can lead to tragic consequences such as motor vehicle accidents involving emergency room admissions (National Insti-

tute of Drug Abuse, 1996a) or those in which several young people die as a result of drinking and driving (National Highway Safety Administration, 1990).

Because the factors that entice adolescents to begin using alcohol and drugs are seemingly under social control, it might appear reasonable to think that if these forces could be counterbalanced with equally powerful alternative influences, the rate of substance abuse might be delayed or even blocked altogether. This is easier said than done. Our government has approached the drug abuse problem with three broad strategies, all of which have proved insufficient:

1. *Interdicting and reducing the supply of drugs available:* The reduction of supply by policing our borders has had little impact on the availability of drugs. Drug interdiction programs do little to affect the supply of the two drugs most abused by adolescents—alcohol and tobacco—which are, of course, available in corner stores and even in the adolescent's home. The reduction of the supply of these drugs to adolescents seems virtually impossible.

2. *Providing treatment services for those who develop drug problems:* Although much money is spent each year on treatment, treating substance abuse is perhaps the least effective avenue to reducing the problem. Addictive disorders are very difficult to overcome, and treatment failure-relapse is the rule rather than the exception. Therapeutic programs for those addicted to drugs or alcohol, though necessary, are not the answer to eliminating or even significantly reducing the problems in our society.

3. *Encouraging prevention:* By far the most desirable and potentially most powerful means of reducing the drug problem in our country is through prevention methods aimed at alerting citizens to the problems of drugs and teaching young people ways to avoid using them (Botvin & Botvin, 1992; Botvin, Baker, Dusenbury, Botvin, & Diaz, 1995). Though past efforts have had limited success in easing adolescent drug use, initially promising prevention efforts have often failed to show the desired reduction in substance use for a number of reasons. The intervention typically has not been conducted for long enough to show the desired effect; the intervention efforts have not been powerful enough to make a sufficient impact on the participants; or the strategy may not have been well implemented.

It is clear that traditional health or psychological intervention models, aimed at individual remediation only after a youngster has become addicted to narcotics or alcohol, have not significantly reduced the problem of drug and alcohol abuse among teenagers. Moreover, these treatment approaches are typically implemented only after the child has seriously compromised his or her life opportunities through drug or alcohol use. Recent epidemiological research has confirmed that early alcohol use is a "powerful predictor of lifetime alcohol abuse and dependence" (Grant & Dawson, 1997). In recent years prevention specialists have taken a more proactive position. They have attempted to establish programs that prevent the development of abuse disorders before young people become so involved with drugs or alcohol that their lives are altered to the point that future adjustment becomes difficult, if not impossible. These recent prevention strategies have taken several diverse and hopeful directions, addressing somewhat different aspects of teenagers' lives. We will examine several efforts that show promise and then discuss the limitations of these prevention approaches.

Education Programs Drug and alcohol education programs represent a prevention strategy aimed at providing information about the damaging effects of these substances. Many are school-based and are usually premised on the idea that if children are made aware of the dangers of drugs and alcohol, they will choose not to begin using them. Englander-Golden and colleagues (1986), for example, provided "Say it straight" training to sixth through eighth graders in which they taught them both the dangers of drug and alcohol abuse and how to be assertive enough to resist drugs and alcohol in spite of peer pressure. In a follow-up evaluation, these investigators reported that youngsters who were trained in the program had a lower rate of drug- and alcohol-related suspensions from school than did children who received no training.

Intervention Programs for High-Risk Teens Intervention programs involve identifying high-risk teenagers and providing special approaches to circumvent their further use of alcohol or potentially dangerous drugs (Petraitis, Flay, Miller et al., 1998). Programs such as these are often school-based efforts and are not strictly prevention programs; rather, they are treatment programs that provide early intervention for high-risk teens who are vulnerable to drug or alcohol use, in order to reduce the likelihood of their becoming further involved with these substances. One such program involved the early identification of young people who were having difficulties in school because of drug and alcohol use. Teachers and administrators were trained to identify and counter alcohol- and drug-use

Efforts to teach schoolchildren about the dangers of drugs before they reach the age of maximum risk are based on the premise that if children are made aware of the dangers of drugs and alcohol they will chose not to use them.

problems through a fair and consistently enforced drug and alcohol policy in the schools (Newman et al., 1989).

Parent Education and Family-Based Intervention Programs Because parents typically underestimate their own children's drug and alcohol use (Silverman & Silverman, 1987), several programs have been aimed at increasing parents' awareness of the extent of the problem and at teaching them ways to deal with drug and alcohol use in the family context. These programs teach parents how to recognize drug- or alcohol-abuse problems so that youngsters can be diverted away from negative and self-destructive behaviors. One such program worked with parents whose children were about to become teenagers (Grady, Gersick, & Boratynski, 1985). It first assessed parents' skill in dealing with drug-related issues, then trained parents to understand and respond empathically to youngsters who might be exposed to drugs during their adolescent years. Parents were then taught how to respond effectively to their children's questions and concerns and to help them consider alternative, more adaptive behavior.

Other family-oriented programs have aimed at strengthening family bonds and providing more positive family relationships to insulate a child from external negative influences. For example, one program focused on involving parents or a family in the positive socialization of a child by increasing communications within the family and by teaching the parents how to deal with the child's problem behavior (DeMarsh & Kumpfer, 1985).

When there is a parental drug or alcohol problem, it can be difficult to gain family cooperation in the treatment program, and many programs have reported low rates of participation. In an effort to increase the participation rate, Szapocznik and colleagues (1988) used family-systems therapeutic techniques (both communication skills and behavior management techniques) to reduce the resistance of families to drug treatment. They reported that 77 percent of the families completed the treatment program, compared with only 25 percent in a control condition.

Peer Group Influence Programs Peers exert a powerful influence on teenagers in every aspect of their lives, including drug and alcohol abuse. Programs designed to help youngsters overcome negative pressures from peers focus on teaching social skills and assertiveness. Of course, peer pressure can also positively influence a teen not to use drugs or alcohol—and many programs focus on the positive aspects of peer pressure (Swadi & Zeitlin, 1988). Peer influence seems much more powerful than the influence of others, including teachers and parents.

Programs to Increase Self-Esteem Programs designed to increase a sense of self-worth attempt to ensure that young people will be able to fend for themselves more assuredly and not fall into dependent, negative relationships with stronger and more dominant peers. One such program provided teenagers with social-skills training and the modeling of appropriate behaviors to reduce drug use and other related negative behaviors, such as truancy (Pentz, 1983). In another program, Botvin (1983) relied on cognitive-behavioral intervention techniques (for example, self-talk) to enhance teenagers' feelings of competency in basic life skills and improve their problem-solving skills. This approach has been thought to be effective in reducing the impact of tobacco, alcohol, and marijuana use (Botvin et al., 1990).

Mass Media and Modeling Programs Recognizing the huge "market" potential of teenagers, advertisers have been adept in exploiting the tremendous value that the appearance of sophistication has for this age group. Most youngsters are bombarded with drug- or alcohol-related stimuli in movies and other visual blitzes and in TV commercials, which are aired at those times that children may be most likely to view them. Several recent efforts have been aimed at deglamorizing or counteracting these messages by showing commercials that graphically depict the negative aspects of alcohol and drug use (Coombs, Paulson, & Palley, 1988; Schilling & McAlister, 1990).

Combined Prevention Programs The various prevention strategies discussed here are by no means mutually exclusive. Most newer programs do not rely on a single intervention strategy but incorporate two or more (Wagenaar & Perry, 1995). Project Northland—an exemplary program of research geared to the prevention of alcohol abuse—targets junior high school students in northeastern Minnesota but also involves a much broader community-wide intervention effort (Perry et al., 1993; Perry, Williams et al., 1996). This program is discussed in Highlight 18.1.

These projects have clearly shown an effective path toward reducing the extent of substance abuse in young people. Carefully implemented educational programs along with teaching young people the skills needed to resist the onslaught of demands to begin using alcohol and drugs that appear to inundate them at around the sixth or seventh grade are powerful interventions. Armed with appropriate information and having practice at resisting others around them, adolescents can make the decision *not* to use alcohol or drugs stick. The visible success of these programs has come to the attention of educators in other school districts, and a number of efforts are under way to "export" these laboratory programs for broader use in America's schools. Recently, the Northland approach has been adapted for a prevention project in Russia as a means of fighting alcohol abuse—one of the most serious health problems in that country (Grechanaia, Romanova et al., 1997).

Indicated Intervention

Indicated intervention emphasizes the early detection and prompt treatment of maladaptive behavior in a person's family and community setting. In some cases—for example, in a crisis or after a disaster—indicated prevention involves immediate and relatively brief intervention to prevent any long-term behavioral consequences. We will later examine in some depth an indicated prevention effort after an airplane crash.

Crisis Intervention Often, people in crisis are in a state of acute turmoil and feel overwhelmed and incapable of dealing with the stress by themselves. They do not have time to wait for the customary initial therapy appointment, nor are they usually in a position to continue therapy over a sustained period of time. They need immediate assistance. Crisis intervention has emerged in

CUTTING EDGE

Preventing Alcohol Abuse

Project Northland is a research study designed to prevent or reduce alcohol use among adolescents by using a multilevel community-based approach (Williams & Perry, 1998). The investigators have conducted their program in 24 school districts in northern Minnesota, an area that had been notorious for high rates of substance abuse. It uses a number of forms of intervention: a social-behavioral curriculum in the schools to make students aware of the issues, parent education programs, peer leadership, and developing community-wide activities to alter the messages that young people typically receive about alcohol. Assessments were made annually to measure the use of alcohol among the identified target population and the control samples. The program is based on a set of four activity booklets students complete as homework assignments with their parents over a period of four weeks. Each booklet has activities that contain explicit behavioral objectives (for example, how to establish family rules about drinking). Elected peer leaders give students activity tasks each week, with the assistance of their teachers. These sessions are conducted in small groups.

Before the intervention program begins, teachers receive a four-hour teacher training session. Elected peer group leaders attend a two-hour training session. During the intervention phase of the program each child is asked to return score cards (signed by parents to record participation) on a prominently displayed scoreboard. Students receive prizes for completion of the first two booklets (e.g., a pen) and a T-shirt at the end of the program. The program ends with an event at each school that brings fifth-graders and their parents together for an evening program. During the week before the evening event, students work together in pairs on poster projects with alcohol-related messages that are presented to parents during the evening event.

Project Northland staff has been able to maintain broad participation in the program over three years and have shown that multilevel, targeted prevention programs for young adolescents are effective in reducing alcohol use among adolescents. Adolescents in the experimental condition show clearly lower levels of alcohol use than in the control schools. Alcohol use, cigarette smoking, and marijuana use was reduced by 21 percent by adolescents in the intervention schools as compared to those in the control schools.

Another extensive and comprehensive substance abuse prevention program was recently completed by Botvin and his colleagues (Botvin et al., 1995). This five-year program involved 3597 adolescents in 56 public schools, who were followed for five years beginning in the seventh grade. The initial intervention consisted of 15 classes, ten booster sessions in the eighth grade, and five booster sessions in the ninth grade. The adolescents were taught specific drug-resistance skills and general life skills in a classroom-based program. Like the Northland Project, this study found that drug abuse prevention programs conducted during junior high school "can produce meaningful and durable reductions" in tobacco, alcohol, and marijuana use if they teach social resistance skills. Significant reductions in substance use were reported for the experimental schools compared with the control schools. There were 44 percent fewer drug users and 66 percent fewer polydrug users (tobacco, marijuana, and alcohol) in the prevention group. It was, however, found necessary to provide booster sessions in order for the effect to be maintained. ∎

response to a widespread need for immediate help for individuals and families confronted with especially stressful situations—be they disasters or family situations that have become intolerable (Butcher & Dunn, 1989; Everly, 1995; Greenfield, Hechtman, & Tremblay, 1995; Morgan, 1995). As discussed in Chapter 4, two approaches are

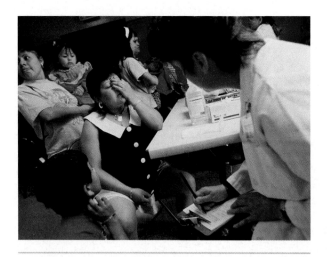

The provision of crisis counseling during the aftermath of a disaster—in this case, the Los Angeles earthquake—has been shown to reduce long-term maladaptive reactions.

widely used: (1) short-term crisis therapy, involving face-to-face discussion, and (2) telephone hot lines, which are usually handled either by professional mental health personnel or by paraprofessionals—lay people who have been trained for this work.

Short-Term Crisis Intervention Short-term crisis therapy, as the name implies, is of brief duration and focuses on the immediate problem with which an individual or family is having difficulty. Although medical problems may also require emergency treatment, we are concerned here with personal or family problems of an emotional nature. In such crisis situations, a therapist is usually very active, helping to clarify the problem, suggesting plans of action, providing reassurance, and otherwise giving needed information and support. In essence, the therapist tries to provide as much help as the individual or family will accept.

If the problem involves psychological disturbance in one of the family members, emphasis is usually placed on mobilizing the support of other family members. Often this enables the person to avoid hospitalization and a disruption of family life. Crisis intervention may also involve bringing other mental health or medical personnel into the treatment picture. Most individuals and families who come for short-term crisis therapy do not continue in treatment for more than one to six sessions. An example of crisis intervention as an indicated preventive effort is given in Highlight 18.2.

Telephone Hot Line As we noted in Chapter 4, the telephone hot line has become a common approach to dealing with people undergoing crises. Today all major cities in the United States and most smaller ones have developed some form of telephone hot line to help people undergoing periods of severe stress. Although the threat of suicide is the most dramatic example, the range of problems that people call about is virtually unlimited—from breaking up with someone to being on a bad drug trip. In addition, there are specific hot lines in many communities for rape victims and for runaways who need assistance.

As with other crisis intervention, a person handling hot-line calls is confronted with the problem of rapidly assessing what is wrong and how bad it is. Even if an accurate assessment is possible and the hot-line worker does everything within his or her power to help the caller, a distraught person may hang up without leaving any name, telephone number, or address. This can be a deeply disturbing experience for the hot-line counselor—particularly if, for example, the caller has announced that he or she has just swallowed a lethal dose of sleeping pills. Even in less severe cases, of course, the hot-line worker may never learn whether the caller's problem has been solved. In other instances, however, the caller may be induced to come in for counseling, making more personal contact possible.

For a therapist or volunteer counselor, crisis therapy can be the most discouraging of any intervention approach that we have discussed in this book. The urgency of the intervention and the frequent inability to provide any therapeutic closure or follow-up are probably key factors in this discouragement. Free clinics and crisis centers have reported that their counselors—many of whom are volunteers—tend to burn out after a short period of time. Despite the high frustration level of this work, however, crisis intervention counselors fill a crucial need in the mental health field, particularly for the young people who make up most of their clients. This need is recognized by the many community mental health centers and general hospitals that provide emergency psychological services, either through hot lines or walk-in services. For thousands of people in desperate trouble, an invaluable social support is provided by the fact that there is somewhere they can go for immediate help or someone they can call who will listen to their problems and try to help them. Thus the continuing need for crisis intervention services and telephone hot lines is evident.

An Illustration of Indicated Prevention The immediate consequences of an air crash are devastating. Survivors typically have traumatic responses to the accident that impair their immediate functioning and place great demands on their psychological adjustment for

Crisis Intervention in Troubled Families

Family crises can result from many sources; for example, a family may lose its home through economic emergency, or a family member may die or become severely ill, or one of the family members may become psychotic, or, as in the following case, one of the family members may attempt suicide:

A 17-year-old girl, Leah, was brought into the emergency department of a general hospital by her mother, father, and maternal grandmother. She had walked into her parents' bedroom earlier in the morning and announced that she had swallowed all her mother's pills. The parents had brought their daughter for emergency medical treatment and were enraged when a psychiatrist was called. The history was obtained from mother, since Leah said little, and mother answered every question. During the interview, father paced in and out of the room, repeatedly declaring that he was taking his daughter home. He aggressively asked each person who entered the room "What do you want?" but each time left before a response was possible. Grandmother sat in the room, announcing from time to time, "That girl always makes trouble." Leah was the oldest of three children. None of them attended school. According to mother, she tutored them at home. Mother also worked outside of the home and complained about how much she had to do. Leah "won't even go to the store alone, so I must accompany her everywhere." Mother said that her husband had told her not to bother with Leah, who would only get married and leave them anyway. But she (mother) had to "bother" because Leah could not go out alone in their neighborhood.

When asked about the suicide attempt, Leah said she would "do it again" if she went home. She wanted to talk to someone about the fights with mother that made her so angry she wanted to die. Mother said it was father's fault. He worked erratically, drank heavily, and made them live in a bad house in a poor neighborhood. They had terrible neighbors who were "nosey" and bothered them.

Since Leah had indicated she still had suicidal intentions and the family conflict continued unabated, hospitalization was recommended. In response, Leah immediately announced she was better and would go home. She said she would not stay in the hospital. Her mother said she could never persuade her to stay and the family gathered itself up to leave (Kress, 1984, p. 419–420).

The family crisis in this case brought to light several difficult problems that threatened the integrity of the family organization. While Leah appeared to be the most disturbed, other family members seemed to have significant psychological problems that directly affected the family strife as well. The suicide attempt required outside intervention. Not only was an immediate solution needed for the present emergency, but psychological intervention for the longer-term problem of the family's inability to resolve conflict was recommended. However, the closed, almost reclusive, nature of the family suggested that treatment for the individuals involved and for the disturbed family relationships, though needed, was not likely to be accepted at that point. Neither Leah nor her father appeared open to examining their problems or to changing their behavior. Unfortunately, we have no follow-up on the case of Leah. This is often the situation in crisis therapy, where the intervention efforts are limited to what can be accomplished only during the immediate crisis; that is, many such clients never return for more therapy, no matter how adamant the crisis worker's recommendation that they do so.

As is by now obvious, crisis intervention therapy with families is usually different and more limited in scope than family therapy as described in Chapter 17. The goals of family crisis intervention do not involve changing the basic family functioning, as in family therapy, but are usually limited to returning a disrupted family to precrisis functioning (Umana, Gross, & McConville, 1980). For example, the mental health practitioner's task in the case of Leah involved resolving the immediate emergency and helping ease her life-threatening state of mind while, hopefully, engaging her family in future family or individual treatment to resolve the pressing problems that appeared to have caused the immediate crisis. Unfortunately, this did not happen. ■

weeks after the disaster. Family members of victims often experience extensive psychological trauma after the accident; they may need to make extensive changes during their loved one's lengthy recovery period or, they may need to make major life changes to adjust to their loved one's death. Even rescue personnel caught up in dealing with the aftermath of an airline disaster may suffer from post-traumatic stress disorder.

In many respects the emotional responses of and adjustive demands placed on air crash victims are similar to those of victims of natural disasters, such as hurricanes, floods, earthquakes, and volcanic eruptions (McFarlane, Clayer, & Bookless, 1997). A number of special considerations, however, influence the intensity of the problems that are seen following airplane crashes: Typically airplane crashes are sudden and unexpected; they are usually quite chaotic in terms of their destruction; and they usually occur away from one's familiar settings and with people who are strangers. Consequently, the sense of community that characterizes response to many disasters is lacking. In addition, the impact of an air disaster affects a larger number of people than those immediately involved in the accident itself.

Air disasters differ from natural disasters in another important respect—they usually involve considerable blame and anger that can aggravate or intensify the emotional reactions of survivors even months after the crash. Most airports are required to have a disaster plan that includes rescue and evacuation procedures to deal with an airplane crash. Some airport disaster plans have incorporated a psychological support program to provide emergency mental health services to survivors and the family members of crash victims as well as to rescue workers (Butcher & Dunn, 1989; Carlier, Lambert, & Gersons, 1997).

These programs are viewed as indicated prevention efforts in that they are aimed at providing emergency psychological services in order to prevent the development of psychological disorders or to reduce the severity of such problems if they occur. Three types of indicated prevention services have been shown to be effective in dealing with the psychological problems related to air disasters: (1) immediate crisis intervention services to crash survivors and surviving family members; (2) crisis telephone hot-line services to provide information and referrals to victims who lack crisis intervention services; and (3) postdisaster debriefing sessions for secondary victims, such as rescue personnel, affected by the disaster. We will look at each of these services briefly.

Immediate Crisis Intervention Services Timing is critical to crisis intervention, which, when supplied in the im-

mediate aftermath of a disaster, can reduce the emotional distress experienced and can result in a more effective future psychological adjustment (Butcher & Hatcher, 1988). Crisis intervention treatment involves providing a victim with a supportive, understanding crisis-intervention specialist to enable the victim to express his or her intense feelings about the incident.

First of all, a crisis counselor provides objective emotional support and tries to provide a long-term perspective—to allow victims to see that there is hope of surviving psychologically. A crisis counselor also serves as a source of information and a buffer against misinformation coming from rumor. Disasters are always followed by periods of confusion, misinformation, and negative emotional states. One important role of the mental health professional in disaster response efforts is to obtain, decipher, and clearly communicate to victims the most accurate picture of the situation obtainable at the moment.

Finally, a crisis counselor provides practical suggestions to promote adaptation. In an extreme crisis people often lose perspective and "forget" that they are usually quite effective in dealing with life problems. An important facet of the mental health professional's role in dealing with disaster victims is to guide them through the difficult times by providing a perspective on the problems being faced and by offering valuable guidance for alleviating those problems.

Crisis Telephone Hot-Line Counseling Services After an air disaster, confusion prevails, as does considerable psychological turmoil among passengers and crew members. Inaccurate information and anxiety-producing doubts can create a state of tension that results in demoralization and negative behavior, such as absenteeism from work, excessive drinking, and morale problems.

An effective way to deal with this psychological uncertainty and reduce the negative atmosphere following an air disaster is to provide telephone counseling services—an informational hot line of sorts—for all those who feel the need to discuss their concerns, be they airline employees or the families of passengers. For example, a 24-hour crisis telephone hot-line counseling service was established shortly after the crash of an airliner in Detroit, Michigan, in 1987 in which 156 people died; it continued in operation for four weeks. This service was staffed by qualified psychologists in crisis management who provided counseling, information, and referral services.

Postdisaster Debriefing Sessions Those who appear to function well at the disaster site may experience difficulties after the immediate crisis has subsided, and they have returned to family and normal duties. Even experienced disaster workers who are well trained and effective at the site can be affected later by the pressures and problems experienced during the disaster.

The desire to "unwind" in a psychologically safe environment and to share one's experience of the disaster are universal needs of people following a traumatic situation. Debriefing sessions are designed to provide those who might be directly affected by the accident an opportunity to relate their experiences and to express their feelings and concerns about the disaster. Chemtob and colleagues (1997), for example, have explored the use of debriefing sessions—sessions designed to allow victims to describe their experiences and learn about the reactions of others—and found this approach to be effective in reducing the emotional reactions to traumatic events.

Immediate crisis intervention, telephone hot-line counseling, and debriefing programs have become standard efforts following major disasters to help victims and emergency workers return more quickly and effectively to normal functioning. By reducing the impact of a tragedy, these programs attempt to prevent the development of more severe psychological disorders. Prevention efforts have not been sufficient to eliminate the need for psychiatric treatment in both outpatient and inpatient mental health facilities. Mental health rehabilitative efforts are important aspects of the contemporary mental health system and will be discussed in the following sections.

The Mental Hospital as a Therapeutic Community

In cases where individuals might be considered dangerous to themselves or others (Richards, Smith et al., 1997) or where their symptoms are so severe that they are unable to care for themselves in the community, psychiatric hospitalization may be required. Most of the traditional forms of therapy that we discussed in Chapters 16 and 17 may, of course, be used in a hospital setting to help restore the patient to functioning. In addition, in many mental hospitals these techniques are being supplemented by efforts to make the hospital environment itself a "therapeutic community" (Jones, 1953; Paul & Lentz, 1977; Whiteley, 1991). That is, all the ongoing activities of the hospital are brought into the total treatment program, and the environment, or milieu, is a crucial aspect of the therapy. This approach is thus often referred to as **milieu therapy** (Coombe, 1996). Three general therapeutic principles guide this approach to treatment:

1. Staff expectations are clearly communicated to patients. Both positive and negative feedback are used to encourage appropriate verbalizations and actions by patients.

2. Patients are encouraged to become involved in all decisions made and all actions taken concerning them. A self-care, do-it-yourself attitude prevails.

3. All patients belong to social groups on the ward. The experience of group cohesiveness gives the patients support and encouragement, and the related process of group pressure helps exert control over their behavior.

In a therapeutic community, as few restraints as possible are placed on patients' freedom, and the orientation is toward encouraging patients to take responsibility for their behavior and to participate actively in their treatment programs. Open wards permit patients to use the grounds and premises. Self-government programs give patients responsibility for managing their own affairs and those of the ward. All hospital personnel are expected to treat the patients as human beings who merit consideration and courtesy. The interaction among patients— whether in group therapy sessions, social events, or other activities—is planned in such a way as to be of therapeutic benefit. In fact, it is becoming apparent that often the most beneficial aspect of a therapeutic community is the interaction among the patients themselves. Differences in social roles and backgrounds may make empathy between staff and patients difficult, but fellow patients have been there—they have had similar problems and breakdowns and have experienced the anxiety and humiliation of being labeled mentally ill and hospitalized. Thus, constructive relationships frequently develop among patients in a supportive, encouraging milieu.

Another successful method for helping patients take increased responsibility for their own behavior is the use of **social-learning programs.** Such programs normally make use of learning principles and techniques, such as token economies (see Chapter 17), to shape more socially acceptable behavior (Corrigan, 1995, 1997; Paul & Menditto, 1992; Paul, Stuve, & Cross, 1997).

A persistent concern with hospitalization is that the mental hospital may become a permanent refuge from the world, either because it offers total escape from the demands of everyday living or because it encourages patients to settle into a chronic sick role with a permanent excuse for letting other people take care of them. Over the past three decades there has been considerable effort aimed at reducing the population of inpatients by closing hospitals and treating patients with mental disorders on an outpatient basis. This effort, often referred to as *deinstitutionalization,* was initiated to prevent the often negative experiences many psychiatric patients have had when confined to a mental hospital for long periods of time. To keep the focus on returning patients to the community and on preventing a return to the institution, contemporary hospital staffs try to establish close ties with patients' families and communities and to provide them with positive expectations about the patient's recovery.

The rise of the biological therapies described in Chapter 16 has meant that between 70 and 90 percent of patients labeled as psychotic and admitted to mental hospitals can now be discharged within a few weeks, or at most a few months. Recent estimates suggest that there are about 2 to 3 million chronically mentally ill individuals in America, of whom about half reside in mental hospitals and the other half live in nursing homes or in the community (Narrow et al., 1993; Regier et al., 1993).

Even where disorders have become chronic, effective treatment methods have been developed. In one of the most extensive and well-controlled studies of chronic hospitalized patients, Paul and Lentz (1977) compared the relative effectiveness of three treatment approaches:

1. *Milieu therapy,* focused on structuring a patient's environment to provide clear communications of expectations, and to get the patient involved in the treatment and participating in the therapeutic community through the group process.

2. *A social-learning treatment program,* organized around learning principles and using a rigorously programmed token economy system, with ward staff as reinforcing agents. Undesirable behavior was not reinforced, whereas the accumulation of many tokens through effective functioning could result in attractive lifestyle amenities not normally available in public mental hospitals.

3. *Traditional mental hospital treatments,* including pharmacotherapy, occupational therapy, recreational therapy, activity therapy, and individual or group therapy. No systematic application of milieu therapy or the social-learning program was given to this group.

The treatment project covered a period of six years, with an initial phase of staff training, patient assessment, and baseline recording; a treatment phase; an aftercare phase; and a long (year and a half) follow-up. The changes targeted included resocialization, the learning of new roles, and the reduction or elimination of bizarre behavior. There were 28 chronic schizophrenic patients in each treatment group, matched for age, sex, socioeconomic level, symptoms, and duration of hospitalization. The results of the study were impressive. Both milieu therapy and the social-learning program produced sig-

nificant improvement in overall functioning and resulted in more successful hospital releases than the traditional hospital care. The behaviorally based social-learning program, however, was clearly superior to the more diffuse program of milieu therapy, as evidenced by the fact that over 90 percent of the released patients from the social-learning program remained continuously in the community, compared with 70 percent of the released patients who had had milieu therapy. The figure for the traditional treatment program was less than 50 percent.

Despite the promise of the token economy approach, emulating as it does certain "real world" principles of exchange the patient will face outside the institution, it has not fared particularly well in terms of public acceptance (Paul & Menditto, 1992). Many feel that it is cruel and inhumane to expect mental patients to govern their behavior in accordance with a prescribed schedule of reinforcements. One might ask in this connection, however, whether it is more humane to consign the patient to the status of a passive and helpless recipient of whatever the environment may somewhat unpredictably have to offer, which in many institutional settings is not very much. Is that truly the message we would wish to convey about the patient's relationship to his or her environment? Probably not, especially in light of the considerable evidence that chronic mental patients are as a group surprisingly adept at making successful adaptations that are within their range of control.

Aftercare Programs Even where hospitalization has successfully modified maladaptive behavior and a patient has learned needed occupational and interpersonal skills, readjustment in the community following release may still be difficult. Many studies have shown that in the past up to 45 percent of schizophrenic patients have been readmitted within the first year after their discharge. Aftercare programs can help smooth the transition from institutional to community life and reduce the number of relapses. However, some individuals do not function well in aftercare programs. Owen, Jones, and colleagues (1997) found that clients who were likely to hold unskilled employment, to be nonpsychotic, to have committed a crime, or to be more transient tended to be noncompliant in aftercare programs. The investigators concluded that many of the post-discharge patients did not "fit" the services typically offered to released psychiatric inpatients. Those with less severe symptoms may fail because they appear to aftercare staff as *not* needing much service while most services are geared to those patients exhibiting more extreme symptoms—thus indicating that the mental health system responds most to the "squeaky wheel."

Aftercare, such as that offered by this halfway house, can ease the transition from hospital to community life.

Aftercare is the responsibility of community mental health facilities and personnel, the community as a whole, and, of course, the person's family. Its goal is to ensure that released patients will be helped to make an adequate readjustment and return to full participation in their home and community with a minimum of delay and difficulty. Sometimes aftercare includes a "halfway" period in which a released patient has a gradual return to the outside world in what were formerly termed halfway houses. Community-based treatment programs, now referred to as aftercare programs, are live-in facilities that serve as a home base for former patients as they make the transition back to adequate functioning in the community. Typically, community-based facilities are run not by professional mental health personnel but by the residents themselves.

There is even some evidence that community-based living is preferable to hospital confinement for some patients who are still actively psychotic. In a noteworthy program with a group of seriously disturbed mental patients, Fairweather (1980), Fairweather and colleagues (1969),

and Fairweather and Fergus (1993) demonstrated that these patients could function in the community, living in a patient-run facility, even to the extent of responsibly (and profitably) operating a service business. Initially, a member of the research staff coordinated the daily operations of the "Lodge," but he was shortly replaced by a layperson. The patients were given full responsibility for operating the Lodge, for regulating each other's behavior, for earning money, and for purchasing and preparing food. Forty months after their discharge, a comparison was made of these former patients and a comparable group of 75 patients who had been discharged at the same time but had not had the Lodge experience. Whereas most members of the Lodge facility were able to hold income-producing jobs, to manage their daily lives, and to adjust in the outside world, the majority of those who had not had the community group-living experience were unable to adjust to life on the outside and required rehospitalization.

Similar community-based treatment facilities have been established for alcoholics, drug addicts, and other people attempting to make an adjustment into the community after institutionalization. Such facilities may be said to be specialized in the sense that all residents share similar backgrounds and problems, and this seems to contribute to the facilities' effectiveness.

Although some patients continue to have mental health problems including suicide attempts (Fenton, McGlashan et al., 1997) and many encounter problems of gaining the acceptance and support of the community (Fairweather, 1994) efforts to treat severely disturbed patients in the community are often very successful. However, as Dennes (1974) pointed out in the early years of the growth of community-based treatment, this requires educational and other social measures directed toward increasing community understanding, acceptance, and tolerance of troubled people who may differ somewhat from community norms. The viability of such an approach, however, is demonstrated in the example of Geel, Belgium—"the town that cares"—which we discussed in Chapter 2.

Recently there has been a great deal of criticism of the mental health system's inadequate provision of aftercare for the mentally ill patients who are released into the community (Torrey, 1997). This problem will be discussed later in this chapter.

CONTROVERSIAL LEGAL ISSUES AND THE MENTALLY DISORDERED

A number of important issues are related to the legal status of the mentally ill—the subject matter of **forensic psychology** or **forensic psychiatry**—and they center on the rights of mental patients and the rights of members of society to be protected from disturbed individuals and vice versa. For a survey of some of the legal rights that have been gained for the mentally ill over the years, see Highlight 18.3.

The issues we will cover in this section are those that have been the center of controversy for many years. We will first review the procedures involved in involuntarily committing disturbed and dangerous individuals to psychiatric institutions. Next, we will turn to the assessment of "dangerousness" in disturbed persons; we will also discuss a related issue, which has become of key concern to psychotherapists—the fairly recent court decision that psychotherapists have a duty to protect potential victims of any threatened violence by their patients even if this means ignoring their ethical and legal obligations to client confidentiality. In addition, we will examine the controversial insanity defense for capital crimes as well as the issue of deinstitutionalization, or what some have called the premature "dumping" of mental patients into the community. As you will see, homeless shelters in metropolitan communities have become a "makeshift alternative" to inpatient mental health care (Haugland, Sigel et al., 1997). In the Unresolved Issues section at the end of this chapter, we will discuss the impact that managed care is having on mental health services.

The Commitment Process

Persons with psychological problems or behaviors that are so extreme and severe as to pose a threat to themselves or others may require protective confinement. Those who commit crimes, whether or not they have a psychological disorder, are dealt with primarily through the judicial system—arrest, court trial, and, if convicted, possible confinement in a penal institution. Persons who are judged to be potentially dangerous because of their psychological state may, after civil commitment procedures, be confined in a mental institution. The steps in the commitment process vary slightly depending on state law (we will here use Minnesota as our model), the locally available community mental health resources, and the nature of the problem. For example, commitment procedures for a mentally retarded person will be different from those for a person with an alcohol-abuse problem.

A distinction should be made here between voluntary hospitalization and involuntary commitment. In most cases, people enter mental institutions without a court order; that is, they accept voluntary commitment or hospitalization. In these cases, they can, with sufficient notice, leave the hospital if they wish. In cases in which a person is believed to be dangerous or unable to provide for his or her own care, the need for involuntary commitment may arise.

Being mentally ill is not sufficient grounds for placing a person in a mental institution against his or her will. Although procedures vary somewhat from state to state, several conditions beyond mental illness usually must be met before formal commitment can occur (Simon & Aaronson, 1988). In brief, such individuals must be judged to be as follows:

- Dangerous to themselves, or to others
- Incapable of providing for their basic physical needs
- Unable to make responsible decisions about hospitalization
- And/or in need of treatment or care in a hospital

The use of the "dangerousness" complaint as grounds for civil commitment has apparently increased (McNeil & Binder, 1986). Typically, filing a petition for a commitment hearing is the first step in the process of committing a person involuntarily. This petition is usually filed by a concerned person, such as a relative, physician, or mental health professional. When a petition is filed, a judge appoints two examiners to evaluate the "proposed patient." In Minnesota, for example, one examiner must be a physician (not necessarily a psychiatrist); the other can be a psychiatrist or a psychologist. The patient is asked to appear voluntarily for psychiatric examination before the commitment hearing. The hearing must be held within 14 days, which can be extended for 30 more days if good cause for the extension can be shown. The law requires that the court-appointed examiners interview the patient before the hearing.

If a person is committed to a mental hospital for treatment, the hospital must report to the court within 60 days as to whether the person needs to be confined even longer. If no report is given by the hospital, the patient must be released. If the hospital indicates that the person needs further treatment, then the commitment period becomes indeterminate, subject to periodic reevaluations.

Because the decision to commit a person is based on the conclusions of others about the person's capabilities and his or her potential for dangerous behavior, the civil commitment process leaves open the possibility of the unwarranted violation of a person's civil rights. As a consequence, most states have stringent safeguards in the procedures to ensure that any person who is the subject of a petition for commitment is granted due process, including rights to formal hearings with representation by

Patient Advocacy: Important Court Decisions Regarding Patient Rights

Several important court decisions have helped establish certain basic rights for individuals suffering from mental disorders, but they have also curtailed these rights with continuing controversy:

- *Right to treatment:* In 1972, a U.S. District Court in Alabama made a landmark decision in the case of *Wyatt* v. *Stickney.* The ruling held that a mentally ill or mentally retarded person had a right to receive treatment. Since the decision, the state of Alabama has increased its budget for the treatment of mental health and mental retardation by 300 percent (see Winick, 1997).

- *Freedom from custodial confinement:* In 1975, the U.S. Supreme Court upheld the principle that patients have a right to freedom from custodial confinement if they are not dangerous to themselves or others and if they can safely survive outside of custody. In the *Donaldson* v. *O'Connor* decision, the defendants were required to pay Donaldson $10,000 for having kept him in custody without providing treatment.

- *Right to compensation for work:* In 1973, a U.S. District Court ruled in the case of *Souder* v. *Brennan* (the secretary of labor) that a patient in a nonfederal mental institution who performed work must be paid according to the Fair Labor Standards Act. Although a 1978 Supreme Court ruling nullified the part of the lower court's decision dealing with state hospitals, the ruling still applied to mentally ill and mentally retarded patients in private facilities.

- *Right to live in a community:* In 1974, the U.S. District Court decided, in the case of *Staff* v. *Miller,* that released state mental hospital patients had a right to live in "adult homes" in the community.

- *Right to less restrictive treatment:* In 1975, a U.S. District Court issued a landmark decision in the case of *Dixon* v. *Weinberger.* The ruling established the right of individuals to receive treatment in less restrictive facilities than mental institutions.

- *Right to legal counsel at commitment hearings:* The State Supreme Court of Wisconsin decided in 1976, in the case of *Memmel* v. *Mundy,* that an individual had the right to legal counsel during the commitment process.

- *Right to refuse treatment:* Several court decisions have provided rulings and some states have enacted legislation permitting patients to refuse certain treatments, such as electroconvulsive therapy and psychosurgery.

- *The need for confinement must be shown by clear, convincing evidence:* In 1979, the U.S. Supreme Court ruled, in the case of *Addington* v. *Texas,* that a person's need to be kept in an institution must be based on demonstrable evidence.

- *Limitation on patients' rights to refuse psychotropic medication:* In 1990 the U.S. Supreme Court ruled, in *Washington* v. *Harper,* that a Washington state prison could override a disturbed prisoner's refusal of psychotropic medications, based on a finding that the prison's review process adequately protected the patient's rights. We see in this instance that changes in the national political climate can reverse prior trends appearing to favor patients' rights.

Source: Hermann (1990); National Association for Mental Health (1979); and Mental Health Law Project (1987). ∎

legal counsel. If there is not time to get a court order for commitment or if there is imminent danger, however, the law allows emergency hospitalization without a formal commitment hearing. In such cases, a physician must sign a statement saying that an imminent danger exists. The patient can then be picked up (usually by the police) and detained under a "hold order," usually not to exceed 72 hours, unless a petition for commitment is filed within that period.

Involuntary commitment in a psychiatric facility is, in large part, contingent on a determination that a person is dangerous and needs to be confined out of a need to protect himself or herself or society. Once committed, a patient may not consent to treatment—a situation that faces mental health professionals working in psychiatric facilities (Grisso & Appelbaum, 1998). We will now turn to the important question of evaluating patients in terms of their potential dangerousness.

The Assessment of "Dangerousness"

As we have seen, though most psychiatric patients are not considered dangerous and need no special safety precautions, some are violent and require close supervision— perhaps confinement until they are no longer dangerous. Few psychiatric patients are assaultive at or prior to their admission to psychiatric facilities. Rates of assaultiveness vary from setting to setting, though in all reported studies the overall number of assaultive patients is relatively low. Nevertheless, the issue, involving as it does life and death considerations, deserves careful scrutiny as to *any* enhanced risk of violence. A history of violent behavior (Bonta et al., 1998) as well as a some classes of mental disorder appear to be a significant factor for the occurrence of violence, as an increasing number of clinical researchers in recent years have discovered. Although most currently disordered persons show no tendency toward violence (Lamberg, 1998), an increased risk of violence appears more likely among some who are *currently experiencing* psychotic symptoms (Tardiff, 1998). Several disorders that have an increased risk for violent behavior are schizophrenia, mania, personality disorder, substance abuse and more rare conditions of organic brain injury and Huntington's disease. One recent study from Finland (Eronen, Hakola, & Tiihonen, 1996) reported that homicidal behavior among former patients was increased eightfold with the diagnosis of schizophrenia and tenfold with diagnoses of antisocial personality or alcoholism. Violence among psychiatric patients is especially prominent for patients who abuse alcohol (Steadman, Mulvey et al., 1998).

The determination that a patient is potentially dangerous is a difficult one to make (Heilbrun, 1997). A 43-year-old homeless Cuban refugee, for example, who had only a few days earlier undergone a psychiatric evaluation and been released, stabbed two tourists to death on the Staten Island Ferry because "God told him to kill" (Triplett, 1986). Obviously, determining potential dangerousness is a crucial judgment for mental health professionals to make—not only from a therapeutic standpoint, to ensure that the most appropriate treatment is conducted, but also from the legal point of view of responsibility to the larger society.

The assessment of dangerousness is one of the most important decisions faced by professionals working in the field of law and psychology and one in which mental health professionals are likely to be asked to make in criminal case proceedings (Sigel & Kane, 1997). A clinician has a clear responsibility to attempt to protect the public from potential violence or other uncontrolled behavior of dangerous patients. A dramatic incident of a failure to assess the extent of a patient's dangerousness was reported by Gorin (1980, 1982) on the television news program *60 Minutes*:

> In December, 1979, Mrs. Eva B. was brutally stabbed to death by her former husband while a police dispatcher listened to her terrified screams over the telephone. Only hours before the stabbing incident occurred, Mr. B., who had attacked Mrs. B. eight times in the past, had been judged by two staff psychiatrists not to be dangerous. He had then been released, as part of his treatment, on a temporary pass from the Pilgrim State Hospital in New York. The hospital staff had released Mr. B. from confinement at this time despite the fact that both the judge and the prosecuting attorney who had been involved in his trial (for attempting to kill his wife) had independently written the New York State Department of Mental Health recommending that Mr. B. be held in the strictest confinement because of his persistent threats against Mrs. B. (Indeed, on two previous occasions, Mr. B. had escaped from the hospital and attempted to kill her.) The judge and attorney had also recommended that Mrs. B. should be warned if Mr. B. was released. Ironically, six hours after she had been murdered, a telegram from the hospital was delivered to Mrs. B.'s home warning her that her husband had not returned from his pass.

Looking beyond what appears to be some failure to follow through on the court's recommendations, this case illustrates a number of difficult yet critical dilemmas involved in trying to identify or predict dangerousness in psychiatric patients. First, it emphasizes the fact that some people are capable of uncontrolled violent behavior and hence are potentially dangerous if left unsupervised in the community. It also reflects the dilemma faced by mental health professionals who, attempting to rehabilitate disturbed patients by gradually easing them back into society, must exhibit some degree of trust in these individuals. Finally, and critically, it illustrates the fact that it is very difficult—for professionals and laypersons alike—to accurately appraise "dangerousness" in some individuals.

Attempts to Predict Dangerousness It is usually an easy matter to determine, after the fact, that a person has committed a violent act or acts and has demonstrated "dangerous behavior." The difficulty comes when one attempts to determine in advance if the person is going to commit some particular violent act—a process referred to as conducting a risk assessment (Borum, 1996). Assessing a general state of "dangerousness" or appraising whether groups of offenders might be at risk for dangerous behavior is not the same thing as the far more formidable task of predicting whether a designated violent act will occur. How well do mental health professionals do in predicting the occurrence of dangerous acts? A general answer to this question would have to be "not as well as we would like." There are several problems to be considered in coming to an adequate appreciation of the difficulties of the task. Perhaps the foremost is that the definition of what is "dangerous" is itself unclear—depending as it turns out to a large extent, on who is asked. Some people have a limited or restrictive definition of what behaviors are dangerous and are willing to tolerate more aggressive behavior than others, who in turn view a broader range of behaviors as potentially dangerous.

Violent acts are particularly difficult to predict because they are apparently determined as much by situational circumstances (for example, whether a person was under the influence of alcohol) as they are by an individual's personality traits or violent predispositions. It is, of course, impossible to predict with any great certainty what environmental circumstances are going to occur or what particular circumstances will provoke or instigate aggression for any given violently disposed person. One obvious and significantly predictive risk factor is a past history of violence (Megargee, 1993), but clinicians are not always able to unearth this type of background information.

As already noted, some types of patients, particularly actively schizophrenic and manic individuals (Binder & McNiel, 1988) or patients with well-entrenched delusions (de Pauw & Szulecka, 1988), are far more likely to commit violent acts than the average for the mental patient group as a whole. Martell and Dietz (1992) reported a

Predicting who will become violent is very difficult. Mental health professionals typically err on the conservative side, considering some patients as more violent prone than they actually are. At the same time, they have an obligation to integrate disordered individuals back into society, a move that has occasionally met with tragic results.

study of persons convicted of pushing or attempting to push unsuspecting victims, about half of whom were killed or seriously injured, into the paths of trains approaching subway stations in New York City. Most of the perpetrators of this gruesome crime, whose incidence has risen in recent years, were both psychotic and homeless at the time of the act.

Mental health professionals typically err on the conservative side when assessing "violence proneness" in a patient; that is, they overpredict violence. They consider some individuals more dangerous than they actually are and, in general, predict a greater percentage of clients to be dangerous, requiring protective confinement, than actually become involved in violent acts (Megargee, 1995). Such a trend is of course quite understandable from the standpoint of the practitioner, considering the potentially serious consequences of a "false negative" judgment. It is likely, however, that many innocent patients thereby sustain a violation of their civil rights. Given a certain irreducible level of uncertainty in the prediction of violence, it is not obvious how this dilemma can be completely resolved.

Methods for Assessing Potential for Dangerousness Evaluating a person's potential for committing violent acts is difficult because only part of the equation is available for study:

Predisposing personality + Environmental instigation
= Aggressive act

As we have noted, psychologists and psychiatrists usually do not know enough about the environmental circumstances the person will encounter to evaluate what the instigation to aggression will be. Predictions of dangerousness focus, then, primarily on aspects of the individual's personality.

The two major sources of personality information are data from personality tests and the individual's previous history. Personality testing can reveal whether the individual shows personality traits of hostility, aggressiveness, impulsiveness, poor judgment, and so on. Notwithstanding the already noted readiness of practitioners to predict the likelihood of violence based on such factors, many individuals having these characteristics never do act on them. The use of previous history—such as having committed prior aggression, having verbalized threats of aggression, having an available means of committing violence (such as possession of a gun), and so on—are useful predictors (Monahan, 1981). Like personality testing, however, these data focus only on the individual factors and do not account for the situational forces that impinge on the person, which may include notably provocative behavior on the part of the victim (Megargee, 1995).

The prediction of violence is even more difficult in the case of an overcontrolled offender, one of whose more salient characteristics is a subaverage level of manifestly aggressive behavior prior to the commission of an aggressive act, very often an extremely violent one. Megargee (1970) studied extensively the "overcontrolled hostile" person who is the epitome of well-controlled behavior but who, typically on only one occasion, loses control and murderously attacks another person. Examples of this type of killer are dramatic: the high school honor student, reportedly civic-minded and fond of helping sick and old people, who is arrested for torturing and killing a three-year-old girl in his neighborhood; or the mild, passive father of four who loses his temper over being cheated by a car dealer and beats the man to death with a tire iron. These examples illustrate the most difficult type of aggressive behavior to predict—the sudden, violent, impulsive act of a seemingly well-controlled and "normal" individual. However difficult, there is often the requirement for the mental health professional to conduct a risk assessment on individuals in forensic settings (Grisso & Tomkins, 1996).

The complex problem of risk assessment or prediction of dangerousness can be likened to the task of predicting the weather. "Ultimately, the goal of a warning system in mental health law is the same as the goal of a warning system in meteorology: to maximize the number of people who take appropriate and timely actions for the safety of life and property" (Monahan & Steadman, 1997, p. 937). In other words, both warning systems start with a detection of the dangerous event and culminate in taking actions to avoid the predicted problem.

The Duty to Protect: Implications of the Tarasoff Decision   What should a therapist do on learning that a patient is planning to harm another person? Can the therapist violate the legally sanctioned confidence of the therapy contract and take action to prevent the patient from committing the act? Today in most states the therapist not only can violate confidentiality with impunity but may be required by law to do so—that is, to take action to protect persons from the threat of imminent violence against them. In its original form, this requirement was conceived as a duty to warn the prospective victim. The duty-to-warn legal doctrine was given a great deal of impetus in a California court ruling in 1976 in the case of *Tarasoff* v. *the Regents of the University of California et al.* (Mills, Sullivan, & Eth, 1987).

In this case, Prosenjit Poddar was being seen in outpatient psychotherapy by a psychologist at the university mental health facility. During his treatment, Mr. Poddar indicated that he intended to kill his former girlfriend, Tatiana Tarasoff, when she returned from vacation. The psychologist, concerned about the threat, discussed the case with his supervisors, and they agreed that Poddar was dangerous and should be committed for further observation and treatment. They informed the campus police, who picked up Poddar for questioning and subsequently judged him to be rational and released him after he promised to leave Ms. Tarasoff alone. Poddar then terminated treatment with the psychologist. About two months later, he stabbed Ms. Tarasoff to death. Her parents later sued the University of California and its staff involved in the case for their failure to hospitalize Poddar and their failure to warn Tarasoff about the threat to her life. In due course the California Supreme Court in 1974 ruled that the defendants were not liable for failing to hospitalize Poddar; it did, however, find them liable for their failure to warn the victim. Ironically, Prosenjit Poddar, the criminal, was released on a trial technicality and returned home to India. In a later analysis of the case, Knapp (1980) said that the court ruled that difficulty in determining dangerousness does not exempt a psychotherapist from attempting to protect others when a determination of dangerousness exists. The court acknowledged that confidentiality was important to the psychotherapeutic relationship but stated that the protection privilege ends where the public peril begins (p. 610).

The duty-to-warn ruling—which has come to be known as the **Tarasoff decision**—while spelling out a therapist's responsibility in situations where there has been an explicit threat on a specific person's life, left other areas of application unclear. For example, does this ruling apply in cases where a patient threatens to commit suicide, and how might the therapist's responsibility be met in such a case? What if anything should a therapist do when the object of violence is not clearly named—for example, when global threats are made? Would the duty-to-warn ruling hold up in other states? Or might deleterious effects on patient-therapist relationships outweigh any public benefit to be derived from the duty to warn? Responding to mounting pressures for clarification, chiefly from mental health professional organizations, the California Supreme Court issued a revised opinion in 1976, called *Tarasoff* or the "duty to warn doctrine." In this decision the Court ruled that the duty was to *protect,* rather than specifically to warn, the prospective victim, but it left vague the question of how this duty might be discharged—presumably in order to provide practitioners with enhanced latitude in dealing with danger to third parties. However, the granting of such latitude would seem to carry with it the possibility of being held liable for providing inadequate protection based on rules not yet formulated at the time intervention is contemplated, as was the problem for the original *Tarasoff* defendants. Meanwhile, numerous other lawsuits in other jurisdictions have been filed and adjudicated in inconsistent and confusing ways (Mills et al., 1987).

The many perplexing issues for practitioners left in the wake of *Tarasoff* were partly resolved, at least in California, by the legislature's adoption in 1985 of a new state law essentially establishing that the duty to protect is discharged if the therapist makes "reasonable efforts" to inform potential victims *and* an appropriate law enforcement agency of the pending threat. In other jurisdictions, however, the inconsistent judicial fallout from *Tarasoff* has continued and has been a source of much anxiety and confusion among mental health professionals, many of whom continue to believe on ethical and clinical grounds that strict confidentiality is an absolute and inviolable trust. A small minority of states—for example, Maryland and Pennsylvania—has explicitly affirmed the latter position, abandoning *Tarasoff* altogether (Mills et al., 1987). Official professional ethics codes, such as that of the American Psychological Association (1992), normally compel compliance with relevant law regardless of personal predilections to the contrary. Where the law is itself vague or equivocal, however, as it often is in this area, there is of course much room for idiosyncratic and biased interpretation.

The Insanity Defense

The picture in the February 13, 1992, issue of *Time* said it all. The largest section offered Jeffrey Dahmer, on trial for the murder, dismemberment, and cannibalization of 15 men in Milwaukee. The top right-hand section pictured David Berkowitz, the "Son of Sam," who terrorized New York City for 13 months in 1976–1977 while killing six people and wounding seven others. The bottom right-hand frame showed John Hinckley, the would-be assassin of President Ronald Reagan in 1981 (Steadman et al., 1993, p. 1)

What linked the three infamous persons named here, apart from their murderous exploits, was their shared claim that they were in fact not legally responsible for their criminal acts. That is, each attempted to use the so-called **insanity defense**—also known as the **NGRI plea** ("not guilty by reason of insanity")—as a means of avoiding the legally prescribed consequences of their crimes. In technical legal terms, these men were invoking the ancient doctrine that their acts, while guilty ones (*actus rea*), lacked moral blameworthiness because they were unaccompanied by the corresponding (and, for a guilty judgment, legally mandated) intentional state of mind (*mens rea*)—the underlying assumption being that "insanity" somehow precludes or absolves the harboring of a guilty intent. (See Highlight 18.4 on controversial insanity defense pleas involving "poisoned" states of mind or altered personality states.) Whatever the legal issues involved in this doctrine—and these on the face of it would appear to be legion—they were rendered moot in the Dahmer and Berkowitz cases because the planned insanity defenses proved unsuccessful, as is the usual outcome (Steadman et al., 1993).

The outcome of the Hinckley case was different in a number of important respects because the jury in this instance considered the defendant to be acting "outside of reason" and "not guilty by reason of insanity." At trial, in June 1982, Hinckley was acquitted on those grounds, a verdict that immediately unleashed a storm of public protest and of widespread, often unduly hasty attempts to reform the law pertaining to the NGRI defense so as to make it a less-attractive option to capital case defendants and their attorneys. Hinckley himself was committed to the care of a federally operated high-security mental hospital, ostensibly to be involuntarily retained there until such time as his

in capital crimes might reflect negative social attitudes toward the insane and that there is a "culture of punishment" that contributes to the reaction against the insanity plea (Perlin, 1996). There has been some concern, especially in cases of high visibility, that guilty (in the *actus rea* sense) defendants may feign mental disorder and fraudulently profit from this plea in avoiding criminal responsibility. Good defense attorneys are of course aware of this public cynicism, which is likely to be shared by juries, and attempt to counteract it in various ways, often by portraying their purportedly "insane at the time of the act" clients to have been themselves victims of extraordinarily heinous and traumatic acts at an earlier time. Some of them undoubtedly were, but the strategy of creating sympathy while offering a plausible reason for the "insane" act would have a compelling attraction in any case. The insanity defense is often *not* employed where it is appropriate, as it would have been for example, in two high-visibility cases—one involving John Salvi (the abortion clinic assassin) and the other Theodore Kaczynski (the Unabomber). Apparently neither defendant wanted his mental state to be a part of the proceedings. In both cases severe delusional disorder (see Chapter 12) was likely to have played a significant role in their crimes.

Despite some features that make it an appealing option to consider, especially where the undisputed facts are strongly aligned against the defendant, the NGRI defense has actually been employed quite rarely—in less than 2 percent of capital cases in the United States over time (Steadman et al., 1993). Studies have confirmed the fact,

however, that persons acquitted of crimes by reason of insanity spend less time, on the whole, in a psychiatric hospital than persons who are convicted of crimes spend in prison (Kahn & Raifman, 1981; Pasewark, Pantle, & Steadman, 1982). In addition, states differ widely in the amount of time that persons found not guilty by reason of insanity are actually confined. For example, one recent study by Callahan and Silver (1998) reported that in the states of Ohio and Maryland nearly all persons acquitted by NGRI have been released within five years whereas in Connecticut and New York conditional release has been much more difficult to obtain.

Up to this point in the discussion, we have used the term "insanity defense" loosely, which is anathema to actual legal practice; we must now become more attentive to the many more precise legal nuances involved. Established precedents defining the insanity defense are as follows:

1. *The M'Naughten Rule (1843):* Under this ruling, often referred to as the "knowing right from wrong" rule, people are believed to be sane unless it can be proved that, at the time of committing the act, they were laboring under such a defect of reason (from a disease of the mind) that they did not know the nature and quality of the act they were doing—or, if they did know they were committing the act, they did not know that what they were doing was wrong.

2. *The irresistible impulse rule (1887):* A second precedent in the insanity defense is the doctrine of the "irresistible impulse." This view holds that accused persons might not be responsible for their acts, even if

Even where evidence of mental disorder exists, as in the case of Ted Kaczynski, the Unabomber, defendants may refuse the use of the insanity defense, preferring to keep their mental states out of the proceedings.

they knew that what they were doing was wrong (according to the M'Naughten Rule), if they had lost the power to choose between right and wrong. That is, they could not avoid doing the act in question because they were compelled beyond their will to commit the act (Fersch, 1980).

3. *The Durham Rule:* In 1954, Judge David Bazelon, in a decision of the U.S. Court of Appeals, broadened the insanity defense further. Bazelon did not believe that the previous precedents allowed for a sufficient application of established scientific knowledge of mental illness and proposed a test that would be based on this knowledge. Under this rule, often referred to as the "product test," the accused is "not criminally responsible if his or her unlawful act was the product of mental disease or mental defect."

4. *The American Law Institute (ALI) standard (1962):* Often referred to as the "substantial capacity test" for insanity, this test combines the cognitive aspect of M'Naughten with the volitional focus of irresistible impulse in holding that the perpetrator is not legally responsible if at the time of the act he or she, owing to mental disease or defect, lacked "substantial capacity" either to appreciate its criminal character or to conform his or her behavior to the law's requirements.

5. *The Federal Insanity Defense Reform Act (IDRA):* Adopted by Congress in 1984 as the standard regarding the insanity defense to be applied in all federal jurisdictions, this act abolished the volitional element of the ALI standard and modified the cognitive one to read "unable to appreciate," thus bringing the definition quite close to M'Naughten. IDRA also specified that the mental disorder involved must be a severe one, and shifted the burden of proof from the prosecution to the defense; that is, the defense must clearly and convincingly establish the defendant's insanity, as opposed to the prior requirement that the prosecution clearly and convincingly demonstrate the defendant to have been sane when the prohibited act was committed.

This shifting of the burden of proof for the insanity defense, by the way, was an extremely common reform instituted by the states in the wake of protests of excessive laxity provoked by the Hinckley acquittal. Like the many other types of reform proposed at that time, the intent was to discourage use of the insanity defense and to make its success improbable if it *were* used. Unlike the average reform instituted, this one proved quite effective in altering litigation practices in the intended direction, according to the extensive data gathered by Steadman and colleagues (1993).

At the present time, most states and the District of Columbia subscribe to a version of either the ALI or the more restrictive M'Naughten standard. New York is a special case. While it uses a version of M'Naughten to define insanity, with the burden of proof on the defense, an elaborate procedural code has been enacted whose effect is to promote fairness in outcomes while ensuring lengthy and restrictive hospital commitment for defendants judged to be dangerous; it appears to have worked well (Steadman et al., 1993). In some jurisdictions, when an insanity plea is filed, the case is submitted for pretrial screening, which includes a psychiatric evaluation, review of records, and appraisal of criminal responsibility. In one recent study of 190 defendants who entered a plea of not criminally responsible, the following outcomes were obtained: 105 were judged to be criminally responsible; charges on 34 were dropped; 8 cases were agreed by both the prosecution and defense to be insane and not responsible. A total of 134 withdrew their insanity pleas (Janofsky, Dunn et al., 1996). The insanity defense was thought in their study to be somewhat of a "rich man's defense" in that such cases involved private attorneys rather than public defenders.

In a recent study Silver (1995) found that the successful use of the NGRI defense varied widely between states. In addition, Silver reported that the length of confinement was more related to the judged seriousness of the crime than to whether the person was employing a NGRI defense. In one recent study (Cirinclone, Steadman, & McGreeve, 1995) an NGRI plea was most likely to be successful if one or more of the following factors were present:

- A diagnosed mental disorder, particularly major mental disorders
- A female defendant
- The violent crime was other than murder
- There had been prior mental hospitalizations

Three states—Idaho, Montana, and Utah—have entirely abolished the attribution of insanity as an acceptable defense for wrongdoing, a somewhat draconian solution that compensates in clarity for what some feel it lacks in compassion. As expected, the insanity acquittals did in fact decline. However, in Montana there was a corresponding rise in the use of "incompetent to stand trial" in which the charges were actually dismissed, in large part, negating the "desired result" of doing away with the insanity defense (Callahan, Robbins et al., 1995).

As we have seen, with the expansion of the diagnostic classification of mental disorder, a broad range of behaviors can be defined as mental disease or defect. Which mental diseases serve to excuse a defendant from criminal responsibility? Generally, under the M'Naughten ruling, psychotic disorders were the basis of the insanity defense, although that would appear an arguable proposition; but under the Durham or ALI Rules other conditions (such as personality disorder or dissociative disorder) might also apply.

How, then, is guilt or innocence determined? Many authorities believe that the insanity defense requires of the courts an impossible task—to determine guilt or innocence by reason of insanity on the basis of psychiatric testimony. Perlin (1996) recently reported that there is actually high agreement between experts as to the defendant's sanity; in a number of cases, conflicting testimony has resulted because both the prosecution and the defense have "their" panel of expert psychiatric witnesses, who are in complete disagreement (Fersch, 1980; Marvit, 1981).

It may well be that the notion of not guilty by reason of insanity, while defensible and humane in some abstract sense, is so flawed conceptually and procedurally that we are in need of a serious rethinking of the entire matter. Meanwhile, it would seem wise to employ stringent standards for the insanity defense, such as the federal IDRA rules or the relevant and carefully considered statutory procedures enacted in New York State (see Steadman et al., 1993, for details).

Finally, it should be noted that several states have adopted the optional plea/verdict of **guilty but mentally ill (GBMI).** In these cases, a defendant may be sentenced but placed in a treatment facility rather than in a prison. This two-part judgment serves to prevent the type of situation in which a person commits a murder, is found not guilty by reason of insanity, is turned over to a mental health facility, is found to be rational and in no further need of treatment by the hospital staff, and is unconditionally released to the community after only a minimal period of confinement. Under the two-part decision, such a person would remain in the custody of the correctional department until the full sentence is served. Marvit (1981) has suggested that this approach might "realistically balance the interest of the mentally ill offender's rights and the community's need to control criminal behavior" (p. 23). However, in Georgia, one of the states adopting this option, GBMI defendants received longer sentences and longer periods of confinement than those pleading NGRI and losing. Overall, outcomes from use of the GBMI standard, often employed in a plea-bargaining strategy, have been disappointing (Steadman et al., 1993).

Deinstitutionalization

The population of psychiatric patients in the United States has shrunk considerably over the past 25 years. Between 1970 and 1992 the number of state mental hospitals dropped from 310 to 273 and the patient population has been reduced by 73 percent (Witkin, Atay, & Manderscheid, 1998). **Deinstitutionalization**—the movement to close down mental hospitals and to treat persons with severe mental disorder in the community—has been the source of considerable controversy. Some authorities consider the emptying of the mental hospitals to be a positive expression of society's desire to free previously confined persons, while others speak of the "abandonment" of chronic patients to a cruel and harsh existence, which for many includes homelessness. Many citizens, too, complain of being harassed, intimidated, and frightened by obviously disturbed persons wandering the streets of their neighborhoods. The problems are real enough, but they have come about to a large extent because the planned community efforts to fill the gaps in service never really materialized at effective levels (Grob, 1994).

There has indeed been a significant reduction in state and county mental hospital populations, from over a half million in 1950 (Lerman, 1981) to about 100,000 in the 1990s (Narrow et al., 1993); these figures are even more staggering when we consider that at the same time the U.S. population grew by nearly 100 million. A number of factors have interacted to alter the pattern of mental hospital admissions and discharges over the past 40 years. As has been noted in previous chapters, the introduction of the antipsychotic drugs made it possible for many patients who would formerly have required confinement to be released into the community. The availability of these drugs led many to believe (falsely) that all mental health problems could be managed with medication. In addition, the changing treatment philosophy and the desire to eliminate mental institutions was accompanied by the belief that society wanted and could financially afford to provide better community-based care for chronic patients outside of large mental hospitals.

In theory, the movement to close the public mental hospitals seemed workable. According to plan, many community-based mental health centers would be opened and would provide continuing care to the residents of hospitals after discharge. Residents would be given welfare funds (supposedly costing the government less than it takes to maintain large mental hospitals) and would be administered medication to keep them stabilized until they could obtain continuing care. Many patients would be discharged to home and family, while others would be placed in smaller, homelike board-and-care facilities or nursing homes.

Many unforeseen problems arose, however. Many residents of mental institutions had no families or homes to go to; board-and-care facilities were often substandard; the community mental health centers were ill-prepared and insufficiently funded to provide needed services for chronic patients, particularly as national funding priorities shifted during the 1980s (Humphreys & Rappaport, 1993); many patients had not been carefully selected for discharge and were not ready for community living; and many of those who were discharged were not followed up sufficiently or with enough regularity to ensure their successful adaptation outside the hospital. One recent court case (*Albright* v. *Abington Memorial Hospital,* 1997) involved charges that the hospital failed to provide sufficient care for a seriously disturbed woman who later killed herself in a fire. Countless patients have been discharged to fates that were even more harsh than the conditions in any of the hospitals (Westermeyer, 1987). The following case illustrates the situation.

Some homeless people, casualties of indiscriminate deinstitutionalization, are seriously mentally disordered.

Case Study, From Deinstitutionalization to Homelessness and Back • Dave B., 49 years old, had been hospitalized for 25 years in a state mental hospital. When the hospital was scheduled for phaseout, many of the patients, particularly those who were regressed or aggressive, were transferred to another state hospital. Dave was a borderline mentally retarded man who had periodic episodes of psychosis. At the time of hospital closing, however, he was not hallucinating and was "reasonably intact." Dave was considered to be one of the "less disturbed" residents because his psychotic behavior was less pronounced and he presented no dangerous problems.

He was discharged to a board-and-care facility (actually an old hotel whose clientele consisted mostly of former inpatients). At first, Dave seemed to fit in well at the facility; mostly he sat in his room or in the outside hallway, and he caused no trouble for the caretakers. Two weeks after he arrived, he wandered off the hotel grounds and was missing for several days. The police eventually found him living in the city dump. He had apparently quit taking his medication and when he was discovered he was regressed and catatonic. He was readmitted to a state hospital.

Homelessness   By the early 1980s cases like Dave's had become commonplace in large cities throughout the nation. Vagrants and "bag ladies" appeared in abundance on city streets and in transport terminals, and the virtually always overwhelmed shelters for homeless persons hastily expanded in futile efforts to contain the tide of recently discharged patients. Street crime soared, as did the death rate among these hapless persons who were for the most part wholly lacking in survival resources for the harsh urban environment. As Westermeyer (1982a) noted:

> Patients are returned to the community, armed with drugs to control their illness. The worst aspects of their illnesses may be under control. But many of the patients are not ready to function in society. They need a gradual reintroduction—facilities where someone else can see that they take their drugs, see their psychiatrists, get food, clothing, and shelter. Such care is too often more than families can provide and such services are not generally available in a community. As a result, the numbers of bag ladies and men, vagrants and mentally disabled people, living in lonely hotels and dangerous streets, have burgeoned. (p. 2)

The full extent of problems created by deinstitutionalization is not precisely known. The ambiguity comes, in part, from the scarcity of rigorous follow-up data on patients who have been discharged from mental hospitals. There have not been a sufficient number of adequate research studies in this area. Moreover, such research investigations have tended to be difficult to conduct because the patients are transient and are hard to keep track of over time. Certainly not all homeless people are former mental patients, but evidence suggests that deinstitutionalization has contributed substantially to the number of homeless people (Lamb, 1984) and to the number of mentally ill people in prison (Butterfield, 1998; Powell et al., 1997). Researchers have also demonstrated that a greater percentage of homeless people have significant psychopathology, as reflected in higher rates of hospitalization and felony convictions, than people who have homes (see Fischer et al., 1986). More recently, Rossi (1990) estimated that 33 percent of homeless individuals suffer from chronic mental disorder. Goldfinger, Schutt, and colleagues (1996) reported that 84 percent of the homeless people in the study abused various substances.

In spite of the problems just described, some data on patient discharge and outcome status support the deinstitutionalization process (Braun et al., 1981) These same researchers, however, also concluded that deinstitutionalization is likely to be unsuccessful if continuing care in the community is not available or if it is inadequate.

The various approaches that have been implemented to circumvent patient failures to readjust to the community have not been particularly successful at reducing hospital readmissions and therefore at further reducing the average daily census in state hospitals. Nevertheless, advocates for deinstitutionalization continue to maintain that this is the most desirable approach to treating the chronically mental ill. The controversy over deinstitutionalization is likely to continue over some time, with advocates on both sides of the issue, until more definitive research is conducted.

Who Is Hospitalized? Meanwhile, the extent to which private (as opposed to publicly supported) mental health care, particularly private hospitalization, has expanded to fill at least part of the gap left by deinstitutionalization and inadequate funding for community mental health centers is not generally recognized. Deinstitutionalization notwithstanding, some 70 percent of all the dollars spent on mental health care are spent for hospitalization, much of it of the acute, short-term variety. These data, gathered by Kiesler and Simpkins (1993; Kiesler, 1993), indicate that the national investment in this rela-

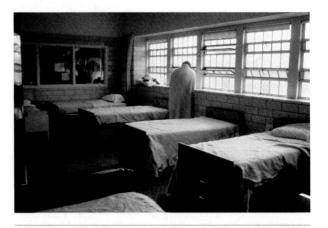

The extent of problems created by deinstitutionalization is not fully known, but some evidence suggests that the emptying of mental hospitals has contributed to the number of homeless people. Deinstitutionalization is not likely to be successful unless continuing care is available and adequate in the community, and unless it allows for readmission to the hospital for short periods if necessary.

tively very costly type of approach is a huge one—in fact constituting an "unnoticed majority" of the total mental health intervention effort of the nation. Many of these inpatient stays, moreover, occur in nonspecialized (i.e., nonpsychiatric) units of general hospitals, a setting whose overall effectiveness in dealing with mental patients is questionable.

Care in specialized, private mental hospitals or in specialized psychiatric units of private medical centers has long been an option for those families able to afford it. However, the mental health system appears to be undergoing considerable change at this time, due in large part to changes in funding for mental health care, with the result already noted. There has been some "privatization" of the mental health system (Dorwart et al., 1989), in cases where private insurance companies have agreed to cover the cost of inpatient mental health services. Several large private hospital corporations have, to some extent, filled the treatment void left by the public mental hospital cutbacks and are providing inpatient psychiatric care for a large number of patients currently receiving any type of formal treatment. **Health maintenance organizations** (HMOs) tend to place limits on inpatient care as with outpatient treatment. (See the Unresolved Issues section at the end of this chapter.) The demographics of the inpatient population has shifted in favor of a more socioeconomically advantaged group—that is, those who have medical insurance that contains provisions for psychiatric hospitalization. Because mental disorders are often chronic, this type of insurance tends to be very expensive (and hence aversive to employers), excluding many persons and families in less than affluent circumstances and with limited inpatient stays. With the continuing downsizing of public facilities, where do people with mental disorders go? Some of them, as we have seen, go into the streets.

Another related development in the care of chronic mental patients is the growth and expansion of private nursing home facilities, particularly for the elderly mentally disordered. Since the deinstitutionalization movement spurred the discharge of psychiatric patients into the community, alternative care facilities have expanded to fill the need for continued care (Morlock, 1989). This expansion of facilities for the elderly has been made possible through financial incentives provided by Medicare to fund treatment. Nursing homes have become the largest single setting to care for the chronic mentally ill. Mentally ill persons make up over 51 percent of the nursing home population at present (Goldman, Feder, & Scanlon, 1986).

The federal government is struggling with the problem of how to cope with the enormous costs involved in attempting to provide adequate and universal medical insurance coverage for all citizens. A huge part of the problem of needed health care reform is related to the escalating costs of hospitalization, felt by many to be out of control. It remains to be seen at this point whether the mental health sector will receive due consideration in whatever arrangements are finally enacted by the Congress. A factor of considerable importance here is the possibility that private hospitalization has come to be overutilized, relative to other less expensive but at least equally effective forms of intervention (e.g., outpatient care), in the mental health and substance abuse arenas (Kiesler, 1993; Kiesler & Simpkins, 1993; VandenBos, 1993). Plausible alternatives that do not involve inpatient care include enhanced preventive intervention and rehabilitative psychotherapy (VandenBos, 1993).

ORGANIZED EFFORTS FOR MENTAL HEALTH

Public awareness of the magnitude and severity of our contemporary mental health problem and the interest of government, professional, and lay organizations have prompted programs directed at better understanding, more effective treatment, and long-range prevention. Efforts to improve mental health are apparent not only in our society but also in many other countries they involve,

and international as well as national and local organizations and approaches.

U.S. Efforts for Mental Health

In the United States, the primary responsibility for dealing with mental disorders fell initially to state and local agencies. During World War II, however, the extent of mental disorders in the United States was brought to public attention when a large number of young men—two out of every seven recruits—were rejected for military service for psychiatric reasons. This discovery led to a variety of organized measures for coping with the nation's mental health problem.

The Federal Government and Mental Health   In 1946, aware of the need for more research, training, and services in the field of mental health, Congress passed its first comprehensive mental health bill, the National Mental Health Act, which laid the basis for the federal government's programs in the 1950s and 1960s.

The bill provided for the establishment in 1946 of the National Institute of Mental Health (NIMH) in Washington, D.C. The agency was to serve as a central research and training center and as headquarters for the administration of a grant-in-aid program designed to foster research and training elsewhere in the nation and to help state and local communities expand and improve their own mental health services. New powers were conferred on the NIMH in 1956, when Congress, under Title V of the Health Amendments Act, authorized the institute to provide "mental health project grants" for experimental studies, pilot projects, surveys, and general research having to do with the understanding, assessment, treatment, and aftercare of mental disorders. Today the status of NIMH is that of a separate institute under the National Institutes of Health, within the Department of Health and Human Services.

The NIMH (1) conducts and supports research on the biological, psychosocial, and sociocultural aspects of mental disorders; (2) supports the training of professional and paraprofessional personnel in the mental health field; (3) assists communities in planning, establishing, and maintaining more effective mental health programs; and (4) provides information on mental health to the public and to the scientific community. Two companion institutes—the National Institute on Alcohol Abuse and Alcoholism (NIAAA) and the National Institute on Drug Abuse (NIDA)—perform comparable functions in these more specialized fields.

Although the federal government provides leadership and financial aid, the states and local organizations actually plan and run most NIMH programs. In addition, the states establish, maintain, and supervise their own mental hospitals and clinics, leading to considerable variation in the adequacy with which these responsibilities are met. A number of states have also pioneered, through their legislation, a variety of mental health services: the development of community mental health centers; rehabilitation services in the community for former patients; and facilities for dealing with alcoholism, drug abuse, and other special mental health problems. The Northland Project described earlier is one of these programs. In the 1980s, federal support for mental health programs diminished considerably. Most state and local governments, which were expected to assume much of the support of mental health activities, have not been able to fund programs and facilities at 1960s and 1970s levels. As a result, many programs devoted to mental health training, research, and service have been greatly reduced or even abandoned, even as the need for them has increased. As to the future, there is, as already noted, considerable uncertainty about the extent to which problems of mental health will be included in forthcoming revisions of national health care policy, and about what forms any such inclusion might take.

Professional Organizations and Mental Health A number of national professional organizations exist in the mental health field. These include the American Psychological Association (APA), the American Psychological Society (APS), the American Psychiatric Association (APA), the American Medical Association (AMA), the Association for the Advancement of Behavior Therapy (AABT), and the American Association for Social Work.

One of the most important functions of these organizations is to set and maintain high professional and ethical standards within their special areas. This function may include (1) establishing and reviewing training qualifications for professional and paraprofessional personnel; (2) setting standards and procedures for the accreditation of undergraduate and graduate training programs; (3) setting standards for the accreditation of clinics, hospitals, or other service operations and carrying out inspections to see that the standards are followed; and (4) investigating reported cases of unethical or unprofessional conduct and taking disciplinary action when necessary.

A second key function of these professional organizations involves communication and information exchange within their areas via meetings, symposia, workshops, re-

fresher courses, the publication of professional and scientific journals, and related activities. In addition, all such organizations sponsor programs of public education as a means of advancing the interests of their professions, drawing attention to mental health needs, and attracting students to careers in their areas.

A third key function of professional organizations, one that is receiving increasing attention, is the application of insights and methods to contemporary social problems—for example, in lobbying national and local government agencies to provide more services for homeless people. Professional mental health organizations are in a unique position to serve as consultants on mental health problems and programs.

The Role of Voluntary Mental Health Organizations and Agencies Although professional mental health personnel and organizations can give expert technical advice with regard to mental health needs and programs, real progress in helping plan and implement these programs must come from informed and concerned citizens. In fact, it has been repeatedly, and quite rightly, stated that it is primarily concerned nonprofessionals who have blazed the trails in the mental health field.

Prominent among the many voluntary mental health agencies is the National Association for Mental Health (NAMH). This organization was founded in 1909 by Clifford Beers and expanded by the merger of the National Committee for Mental Hygiene, the National Mental Health Foundation, and the Psychiatric Foundation; it was further expanded in 1962 by merging with the National Organization for Mentally Ill Children. Through its national governing body and some 330 local affiliates, the NAMH works for the improvement of services in community clinics and mental hospitals; it helps recruit, train, and place volunteers for service in treatment and aftercare programs; and it works for enlightened mental health legislation and for the provision of needed facilities and personnel. It also carries on special educational programs aimed at fostering positive mental health and helping people understand mental disorders. In addition, the National Association for Mental Health has been actively involved in many court decisions affecting patient rights (NAMH, 1997). In several cases the NAMH has sponsored litigation or served as *amicus curiae* (friend of the court) in efforts to establish the rights of mental patients to treatment, to freedom from custodial confinement, to freedom to live in the community, and to protection of their confidentiality.

With a program and organization similar to that of the NAMH, the National Association for Retarded Citizens

(NARC) works to reduce the incidence of mental retardation, to seek community and residential treatment centers and services for the retarded, and to carry on a program of education aimed at better public understanding of retarded individuals and greater support for legislation on their behalf. The NARC also fosters scientific research into mental retardation, the recruitment and training of volunteer workers, and programs of community action.

These and other voluntary health organizations, such as Alcoholics Anonymous and the National Alliance for the Mentally Ill (NAMI), need the backing of a wide constituency of knowledgeable and involved citizens in order to succeed.

Mental Health Resources in Private Industry Personal problems—such as marital distress or other family problems, alcohol or drug abuse, financial difficulties, or job-related stress—can adversely affect employee morale and performance. Psychological difficulties among employees may result in numerous problems, such as absenteeism, accident proneness, poor productivity, and high job turnover. The National Institute for Occupational Safety and Health (NIOSH) recognizes psychological disorders as one of the ten leading work-related health problems (Millar, 1990), and work-related mental health risk factors may be increasing with changes in the economy, in technology, and in demographic factors in the workforce (Sauter, Murphy, & Hurrell, 1990). Today, with the passage of the Americans with Disabilities Act, people with psychiatric problems cannot be discriminated against in the workplace. Employers are encouraged to alter the workplace, as needed, to accommodate the needs of persons with mental illness. Although this is often resisted by employers on grounds that it is too costly to hire psychiatrically impaired persons, great benefits for society can result from integrating people with disabilities but who have appropriate skills into productive jobs (Kramer, 1998).

While a great deal more research is needed in the identification of specific mental health risk factors in work situations, available knowledge (e.g., Sauter et al., 1990) suggests that serious unrecognized problems may exist in the following areas of job design and conditions of work.

1. *Work load and pace:* The critical factor here appears to be the degree of *control* the worker may have over the pace of work rather than output demand per se. Machine-paced assembly work may be particularly hazardous to mental health.

2. *Work schedule:* Rotating "shifts" and night work have been associated with elevated risk for psychological difficulties.

3. *Role stressors:* Role ambiguity (e.g., who has responsibility for what?), said to be common in many work situations, has a negative impact on mental and physical health, as does role conflict (incompatible role demands).

4. *Career security factors:* Feelings of insecurity relating to issues such as job future or obsolescence, career development, and encouragement of early retirement adversely affect mental and physical health.

5. *Interpersonal relations:* Poor or unsupportive relationships among work colleagues significantly increase the risk for untoward psychological reactions.

6. *Job content:* Job dissatisfaction and poor mental health have been associated with work assignments involving fragmented, narrow, invariant tasks that allow for little creativity or sense of meaning with respect to contribution to the ultimate product.

Many corporations have long recognized the importance of worker mental health and of enhancing mental health-promoting factors in the workplace, and yet it has been a relatively recent phenomenon to see them act on this knowledge. Today many companies have expanded their "obligations" to employees to include numerous psychological services. Often referred to as employee-assistance programs (EAPs), these are the means through which larger corporations can actively provide mental health services to employees and their family members. In general, employers have been slower to deal with issues of job design and work environment as additional means of maximizing worker mental health.

International Efforts for Mental Health

Mental health of course is a major problem not only in the United States but in the rest of the world. Indeed, many of the unfavorable conditions in this country with regard to the causes and treatment of mental disorders are greatly magnified in poorer countries and countries with repressive governments. The severity of the world mental health problem is shown in the World Health Organization's estimates that mental disorders affect more than 200 million people worldwide. The recognition of this great problem served to bring about the formation of several international organizations at the end of World War II. We will briefly discuss here the World Health Organization and the World Federation for Mental Health.

The World Health Organization The World Health Organization (WHO) has always been keenly aware of the close interrelationships between physical, psychosocial, and sociocultural factors—such as the influence of rapid change and social disruption on both physical and mental health; the impossibility of major progress toward mental health in societies where a large proportion of the population suffer from malnutrition, parasites, and disease; and the frequent psychological and cultural barriers to successful programs in family planning and public health.

Formed after World War II as part of the United Nations system, WHO's earliest focus was on physical diseases; through its efforts dramatic progress has been made toward the conquest of ancient scourges like smallpox and malaria. Over the years, mental health, too, became an increasing concern among the member countries. In response, WHO's present program now integrates mental health concerns with the broad problems of overall health and socioeconomic development that must be faced by member countries (World Health Organization, 1997).

WHO has headquarters in Geneva and regional offices in Africa, the Americas, Southeast Asia, Europe, the Eastern Mediterranean, and the Western Pacific. Hence its activities extend into areas with diverse physical environments, types of social organization, and mental health facilities. It enters a country only on invitation, helping identify the basic health needs of each country and working with the local authorities to plan and carry out the most useful and appropriate programs. Where possible, it strives to make its services available over a period of several years to ensure continuity and success for the programs that are undertaken.

Another important contribution of WHO has been its International Classification of Diseases (ICD), which enables clinicians and researchers in different countries to use a uniform set of diagnostic categories. As we saw in Chapter 1 the American Psychiatric Association's DSM-IV classification has been coordinated with the WHO ICD-10 classification (Sartorius et al., 1993).

The World Federation for Mental Health   The World Federation for Mental Health was established in 1948 as an international congress of nongovernmental organizations and individuals concerned with mental health. Its purpose is to promote international cooperation between governmental and nongovernmental mental health agencies, and its membership now extends to more than 50 countries. The federation has been granted consultative status by WHO and it assists the UN agencies by collecting information on mental health conditions all over the world (World Health Organization, 1997).

We have now seen something of the maze of local, national, and international measures that are being undertaken in the mental health field. We can expect these efforts to continue. Furthermore, we can expect to see more and more mental health problems unraveled to reveal discoverable causes and to respond to treatment and prevention by scientific means. The 1990s have already witnessed an amazing openness and a diminishing of previously impassable borders. Along with this increased interchange of ideas and cooperation, we expect to see a broader interchange of mental health collaboration. Reductions in international tension and a greater international cooperation in the sciences and health planning will likely promote more sharing of information and views on mental health.

CHALLENGES FOR THE FUTURE

The media confront us daily with the stark truth that we have a long way to go before our dreams of a better world are realized. Many question whether the United States or any other technologically advanced nation can achieve mental health for the majority of its citizens in our time. Racism, poverty, youth violence, terrorism, the uprooting of developing world populations, and other social problems that contribute to mental disorder sometimes seem insurmountable.

Events in the rest of the world affect us also, both directly and indirectly. Worldwide economic instability and shortages and the possibility of the destruction of our planet's life support system breed widespread anxiety about the future. The vast resources we have spent on military programs over the past half-century to protect against perceived threats have absorbed funds and energy that otherwise might have been turned to meeting human and social needs here and elsewhere in the world. The limited resources we are now willing to apply to solving mental health problems prevent the solution of major problems resulting from drug and alcohol abuse, homelessness, broken families, and squalid living conditions for many.

The Need for Planning

It seems imperative that more effective planning be done at community, national, and international levels if mental health problems are going to be reduced or eliminated. Many challenges must be met if we are to create a better world for ourselves and future generations. Without slackening our efforts to meet needs at home, we will probably find it increasingly essential to participate more broadly in international measures toward reducing group tensions and promoting mental health and a better world for people everywhere. At the same time, we can expect that measures undertaken to reduce international conflict and improve the general condition of humankind will make their contribution to our own nation's social progress and mental health. Both kinds of measures will require understanding and moral commitment from concerned citizens.

Within our own country, as well as the rest of the industrialized world, progress in prolonging life has brought with it burgeoning problems in the prevalence of disorders associated with advanced age, particularly in the area of dementing conditions such as Alzheimer's disease. As was noted in Chapter 13, there can be no assurance at this time that we will find the means of eradicating or arresting this threat before it has overwhelmed us in terms of the numbers of already living people affected. Planning and preparation would seem our only rational hope of forestalling a potential disaster of unprecedented yet predictable magnitude; we need to make a beginning.

The Individual's Contribution

Each man can make a difference, and each man should try.
—JOHN F. KENNEDY

The history of abnormal psychology provides clear examples of individuals whose efforts were instrumental in changing thinking about problems. Recall that Pinel took off the chains, Dorothea Dix initiated a movement to improve the conditions of asylums, and Clifford Beers inspired the modern mental health movement with his autobiographical account of his own experience with mental illness. Who may lead the next revolution in mental health is anyone's guess. What is clear is that a great deal can be accomplished by individual effort.

When students become aware of the tremendous scope of the mental health problem both nationally and internationally and the woefully inadequate facilities for coping with it, they often ask, "What can I do?" Thus it seems appropriate to suggest a few of the lines of action interested students can profitably take.

Many opportunities in mental health work are open to trained personnel, both professional and paraprofessional. Social work, clinical psychology, psychiatry, and other mental health occupations are rewarding in terms of personal fulfillment. In addition, many occupations, ranging from law enforcement to teaching and the ministry, can and do play key roles in the mental health and well-being of many people. Training in all these fields usually offers individuals opportunities to work in community clinics and related facilities, to gain experience in understanding the needs and problems of people in distress, and to become familiar with community resources.

Citizens can find many ways to be of direct service if they are familiar with national and international resources and programs, and if they invest the effort necessary to learn about their community's special needs and problems. Whatever their roles in life—student, teacher, police officer, lawyer, homemaker, business executive, or trade unionist—their interests are directly at stake. For although the mental health of a nation may be manifested in many ways—in its purposes, courage, moral responsibility, scientific and cultural achievements, and quality of daily life—its health and resources derive ultimately from the individuals within it. In a participatory democracy, it is they who plan and implement the nation's goals.

Besides accepting some measure of responsibility for the mental health of others through the quality of one's own interpersonal relationships, there are several other constructive courses of action open to each citizen, including (1) serving as a volunteer in a mental hospital, community mental health center, or service organization; (2) supporting realistic measures for ensuring comprehensive health services for all age groups; and (3) working toward improved public education, responsible government, the alleviation of group prejudice, and the establishment of a more sane and harmonious world.

All of us are concerned with mental health for personal as well as altruistic reasons, for we want to overcome the harassing problems of contemporary living and find our share of happiness in a meaningful and fulfilling life. To do so, we may sometimes need the courage to admit that our problems are too much for us. When existence seems futile or the going becomes too difficult, it may help to remind ourselves of the following basic facts, which have been emphasized throughout this text: From time to time, each of us has serious difficulties in coping with the problems of living. During such crisis periods, we may need psychological and related assistance. Such difficulties are not a disgrace; they can happen to anyone if the stress is sufficiently severe. The early detection and correction of maladaptive behavior is of great importance in preventing the development of more severe or chronic conditions. Preventive measures—primary, secondary, and tertiary—are the most effective long-range approach to the solution of both individual and group mental health problems.

Recognizing these facts is essential because statistics show that almost all of us will at some time in our lives have to deal with severely maladaptive behavior or mental disorder either in ourselves or in someone close to us. Our interdependence and the loss to us all, individually and collectively, when any one of us fails to achieve his or her potential are eloquently expressed in the famous lines of John Donne (1624):

No man is an island, entire of itself; every man is a piece of the continent, a part of the main. If a clod be washed away by the sea, Europe is the less, as well as if a promontory were, as well as if a manor of thy friends or of thine own were: any man's death diminishes me, because I am involved in mankind, and therefore never send to know for whom the bell tolls; it tolls for thee.

UNRESOLVED ISSUES

The Crisis in Mental Health Care

About one out of every three Americans experiences psychological problems that could qualify him or her for a psychiatric diagnosis (Regier et al., 1988) and about one in five with a disorder receives mental health treatment (Castro, 1993). It has been estimated that psychiatric treatment accounts for about one-quarter of all hospital days in America (Kiesler & Sibulkin, 1987). Health care costs in general are reportedly rising more rapidly than any other aspect of the American economy (Resnick & DeLeon, 1995). Some businesses have spent as much on health care for employees as they earned (O'Conner, 1996). Over the past decade, health care costs have skyrocketed as the number of people receiving services has increased over 30 percent per year (Giles, 1993). As we have seen in this chapter, mental health treatment is valuable for preventing as well as easing mental disorders. Yet, the current crisis in health care has meant that mental health treatment is less readily available and less often reimbursed.

In response to these needs, health care administrators have created a diverse array of programs in an attempt to provide services at a cost that society can afford. **Managed health care** refers to a system of corporations that secure services from hospitals, physicians, and other providers/workers for a designated population (Resnick et al., 1994). Managed health care providers attempt to offer services at lower costs by limiting traditional services, using stringent review procedures, and using lower-cost brief treatment options (Glazer & Gray, 1996). These systems operate by marketing health care plans to employers or individuals. For a fixed prepaid fee, employers and individuals subscribe to a health service company or an **Health Maintenance Organization (HMO),** which entitles them to the services provided by that health plan (Resnick et al., 1994). These programs establish a treatment staff through a system of professionals, referred to as "panels," who are considered to have efficacy and efficiency in providing a wide range of services (Cummings, 1995). Some HMOs—referred to as open-panel systems—allow patients some choice of health providers

and allow any qualified professional in the community to participate. However, most are closed-panel systems, which limit the selection of available providers. The benefits vary from plan to plan and usually include limits on the problems covered or the maximum amount of care provided or services available. To keep costs low, some HMOs operate according to a system of "capitation," a method of payment in which a health provider contracts to deliver all the health care services required by a population for a fixed cost or flat fee per enrolled member or employee (Richardson & Austad, 1994). The HMOs assume some risk but capitation allows for great profit if the subscriber's fees can be set higher than the cost of health services.

Mental Health Treatment—Who Decides What Kind and How Long?

In one common approach to reducing health care costs, the managed care agency negotiates a reduced price directly with the health service provider. The provider then bills the health service organization for the time spent, and the HMO can obtain "low bid" services from the health professional (Richardson & Austad, 1994). This approach poses little financial risk to the provider. As might be apparent to the casual observer of managed care systems, the procedures for determining the amount of money paid to providers have frequently been a problem for mental health professionals—psychologists and psychiatrists (Resnick et al., 1994). The HMO representative or "gatekeeper" to reimbursement, often a medical generalist who is untrained in psychiatric disorders or psychosocial interventions, controls access to therapy and sometimes the type of treatment to be provided (Resnick et al., 1994). In some systems of managed care, the gatekeeper might be a business professional who is viewed by the health service provider as blocking adequate treatment by demanding that the clinician periodically justify treatment decisions to someone who has little or no background in mental health. In such situations conflicts frequently develop, and patients may be deprived of appropriate and necessary care (Resnick et al., 1994).

Managed care programs differ widely in the modes and quality of mental health services provided. Although their stated intention is to provide the most effective treatments available, decisions about what treatments to provide are often based more on business factors than on treatment considerations. HMOs that are overly cost conscious have come to be viewed by many in the field as simply tending to business to the neglect of the patient's needs (Karon, 1995; Hoyt & Austad, 1992; Schreter, Sharfstein, & Schreter, 1994).

Time-Limited Therapy

The mental health services typically covered by HMOs tend to favor less expensive and less labor-intensive approaches. As might be expected, pharmacotherapy is the most frequent mental health treatment provided by HMOs. About 10 percent of the population in the United States receives some prescribed psychoactive medication each year (Klerman et al., 1994). Interestingly, more psychotropic medication is now prescribed by primary care physicians than by psychiatrists (Brody, 1996). Some managed health care systems have advocated the expanded use of somatic therapies in an attempt to contain costs. Psychosocial interventions such as individual psychotherapy are discouraged or limited to relatively few sessions. Long-term psychotherapy has been virtually eliminated for all but a small number of wealthy private clients (Lazarus, 1996). On the other hand, group psychotherapy is often promoted and encouraged because it is often thought of as being cost effective.

Most managed care corporations have adopted the model of providing focused, brief, intermittent mental health treatment (Cummings, 1995; Hoyt & Austad, 1992) for most problems. Patients who require longer treatments or need inpatient hospitalization are typically not well served in managed care organizations (Gabbard, 1994). In fact, long-term mental health treatment is typically discouraged by managed health care organizations. For example, most managed care groups approve only short inpatient stays (less than ten days) and four to six sessions of outpatient mental health treatment at a time. Few if any of the decisions regarding the amount and type of services provided are directly guided by empirical criteria. Decisions as to whether to cover eight versus 20 sessions of psychotherapy, for example, are arbitrary and often seem capricious both to the practitioner and to the patient (Harwood et al., 1997).

A clear divide has developed between health service providers and managers. Available services are often governed more by financial concerns than by a mental health professional's judgment. Practitioners, as a result, are expressing outrage over the situation. One psychologist (Sank, 1997) recently suggested that ethics charges be filed against mental health professionals who violate patient-therapist confidentiality agreements by disclosing the process of therapy to HMOs. Lawsuits have been directed at health maintenance organizations for failing to provide appropriate and needed service. Managed care organizations are likely to face claims of negligence as a result of their legal exposure and obligation to provide services (Benda & Rozovsky, 1997). Sleek (1997) recently described a lawsuit in which seven psychologists were suing a managed care corporation for circumventing the psychologist's judgment, reducing necessary treatment sessions, and dropping them from the managed care panel. The extent to which such tactics will adversely affect the provision of mental health services is uncertain. It appears likely, however, that conflict will be prominent over the next few years as managed care systems assume more control over the mental health system. Some independent psychologists and psychiatrists have left the field because of the lack of a livable income from conducting psychotherapy.

Critics of managed care argue that there is no convincing evidence that current efforts are actually controlling costs (Gabbard, 1994; Harwood et al., 1997) and that there is no scientific support for the limited benefit options being exercised (England, 1994). Some have pointed out that the administrative costs for managed care centers (including high salaries for HMO executives) are exorbitant. Gabbard (1994), for example, estimated that about one-fourth of the health care expenditures in the United States goes for managed care administration.

The revolution in health care has clearly created controversy in the field of psychotherapy. The mental health field is being drastically altered by economic considerations. These growing pains are likely to continue as our society attempts to come to terms with the cost of health care and the need to provide care for citizens who desperately need help. One thing appears to be certain: the nature of the mental health professions is changing. Whether these changes are for better or worse is yet to be determined.

SUMMARY

Increasingly today, professionals are trying not only to cure mental health problems but also to prevent them, or at least reduce their effects. Prevention can be viewed as focusing on three levels: (1) universal interventions, which attempt to reduce the long-term consequences of having had a disorder; (2) selective interventions, which are aimed at reducing the possibility of disorder and fostering positive mental health efforts in subpopulations that are considered at special risk; and (3) indicated interventions, which attempt to reduce the impact or duration of a problem that has already occurred.

In recent years, several legal issues concerning the treatment of mental patients have surfaced. The commitment process and procedures for committing individuals for inpatient care have been reconsidered. Being "mentally ill" is not considered sufficient grounds for commitment. There must be, in addition, evidence that the individual is either dangerous to himself or herself or represents a danger to society. It is not an easy matter, even for trained professionals, to determine in advance if a person is "dangerous" and likely to cause harm to others. Nevertheless, professionals must, at times, make such judgments. Recent court rulings have found professionals liable when patients they were treating caused harm to others. The Tarasoff decision held that a therapist has a duty to protect potential victims if his or her patient has threatened to kill them.

Another important issue of forensic psychology involves the insanity plea for capital crimes. Many mental health and legal professionals, journalists, and laypersons have questioned the present use of the "not guilty by reason of insanity" (NGRI) defense. The original legal precedent, the M'Naughten Rule, held that, at the time of committing the act, the accused must have been laboring under such a defect of reason as to not know the nature and quality of the act or to not know that what he or she was doing was wrong. More recent broadenings of the insanity plea, as in the American Law Institute standard, leave open the possibility of valid NGRI pleas by persons who are not diagnosed to be psychotic. This broadening of the insanity plea led to its use in more and more cases, and decisions have often involved conflicting psychiatric testimony. The successful use of the NGRI defense by John Hinckley, attempted assassin of President Reagan, set off a storm of protest, resulting ultimately in widespread tightening of insanity defense laws. One effective and widely adopted reform was to shift the burden of proof to the defense in such cases.

There has been a great deal of legal controversy recently over deinstitutionalization—the release of patients from public mental hospitals—and the failure to provide adequate follow-up of these patients in the community. In their zeal to close large psychiatric institutions, many administrators underestimated the amount of care that would be needed after discharge, and overestimated communities' abilities to deal with patients with chronic problems. The result was that some chronic patients were placed in circumstances that required more adaptive abilities than they possessed. Recent work in the area of aftercare for former mental patients has provided clearer guidelines for discharge and therapeutic follow-up. Meanwhile, there has been a burgeoning use of private hospitalization in psychiatric care, an expensive alternative not normally available to the less than affluent.

A large number of organizations are concerned and involved with establishing organized efforts for mental health. Several government agencies have mental health as their primary mission. For example, federal agencies such as the National Institute of Mental Health (NIMH), the National Institute on Drug Abuse (NIDA), and the National Institute on Alcohol Abuse and Alcoholism (NIAAA) are devoted to promoting varied research, training, and service. State and county government agencies may focus their efforts on the delivery of mental health services to residents on an inpatient or outpatient basis.

Mental health programming in the United States is also the concern of several professional and mental health organizations, many corporations, and a number of voluntary mental health organizations. In addition, international organizations, such as the World Health Organization (WHO) and the World Federation for Mental Health, have contributed to mental health programs worldwide.

Changes in the health care industry have created multiple unresolved issues regarding who should determine the amount and type of treatment for mental problems and who should be responsible for deciding when treatment should be prolonged.

KEY TERMS

GLOSSARY

Many of the key terms listed in the glossary appear in boldface when first introduced in the text discussion. A number of other terms commonly encountered in this or other psychology texts are also included; you are encouraged to make use of this glossary both as a general reference tool and as a study aid for the course in abnormal psychology.

Abnormal behavior. Maladaptive behavior detrimental to an individual and/or a group.

Abnormal psychology. Field of psychology concerned with the study, assessment, treatment, and prevention of abnormal behavior.

Abstinence. Refraining altogether from the use of a particular addictive substance or from a particular behavior.

Accommodation. Cognitive process of changing existing cognitive frameworks to make possible the incorporation of discrepant information.

Acting out. Ego-defense mechanism of engaging in antisocial or excessive behavior without regard to negative consequences as a way of dealing with emotional stress.

Activation (arousal). Energy mobilization required for an organism to pursue its goals and meet its needs.

Actuarial approach. Application of probability statistics to human behavior.

Actuarial procedures. Methods whereby data about many subjects' behavior is stored in and analyzed by a computer.

Acute (disorder). Term used to describe a disorder of sudden onset, usually with intense symptoms.

Acute stress disorder. Disorder following a traumatic event that occurs within four weeks of the event and lasts for a minimum of two days and a maximum of four weeks.

Addictive behavior. Behavior based on the pathological need for a substance or activity; it may involve the abuse of substances, such as nicotine, alcohol, or cocaine, the excessive ingestion of high-caloric food, or gambling.

Adjustment. Outcome of a person's efforts to deal with stress and meet his or her needs.

Adjustment disorder. A disorder in which a person's response to a common stressor is maladaptive and occurs within three months of the stressor.

Adjustment disorder with depressed mood. Moderately severe mood disorder similar to dysthymic disorder but having an identifiable, though not severe, psychosocial stressor occurring within three months before the onset of depression, and not exceeding six months in duration.

Adoption method. Comparison of biological and adoptive relatives with and without a given disorder in order to assess genetic versus environmental influences.

Adrenal cortex. Outer layer of the adrenal glands; secretes the adrenal steroids and other hormones.

Adrenal glands. Endocrine glands located at the upper end of the kidneys; consist of inner adrenal medulla and outer adrenal cortex.

Adrenaline. Hormone secreted by the adrenal medulla during strong emotion; causes such bodily changes as an increase in blood sugar and a rise in blood pressure. Also called *epinephrine*.

Advocacy. Approach to meeting mental health needs in which advocates, often an interested group of volunteers, attempt to help children or others receive services that they need but often are unable to obtain for themselves.

Advocacy programs. Programs aimed at helping people in underserved populations to obtain aid with which to improve their situations.

Affect. Emotion or feeling.

Aftercare. Follow-up therapy after release from a hospital.

Aggression. Behavior aimed at hurting or destroying someone or something.

Agitation. Marked restlessness and psychomotor excitement.

Agoraphobia. Fear of being in places or situations from which escape would be physically difficult or psychologically embarrassing, or in which immediate help would be unavailable in the event that something bad happened.

AIDS-dementia complex (ADC). Generalized loss of cognitive functioning affecting a substantial proportion of AIDS patients.

AIDS-related complex (ARC). Pre-AIDS manifestation of HIV infection involving minor infections, various nonspecific symptoms (such as unexplained fever), blood cell count abnormalities, and sometimes cognitive difficulties.

Alarm and mobilization. First stage of responding to trauma, alerting and mobilizing a person's resources for coping with the trauma.

Alcoholic. Person with a serious drinking problem, whose drinking impairs his or her life adjustment in terms of health, personal relationships, and occupational functioning.

Alcoholism. Dependence on alcohol that seriously interferes with life adjustment.

Alexithymia. Term used to denote a personality pattern in which a person is unable to communicate distress in other than somatic language.

Alienation. Lack or loss of relationships to others.

Alter identities. In a person with dissociative identity disorder, personalities other than the host personality.

Alzheimer's disease. See **Dementia of the Alzheimer's type.**

Amnesia. Total or partial loss of memory.

Amnestic syndrome. Striking deficit in the ability to recall ongoing events more than a few minutes after they have taken place, or the inability to recall the recent past.

Amniocentesis. Technique that involves drawing fluid from the amniotic sac of a pregnant woman so that the sloughed-off fetal cells can be examined for chromosomal irregularities, including that of Down syndrome.

Amphetamine. Drug that produces a psychologically stimulating and energizing effect.

Analogue studies. Studies in which a researcher attempts to emulate the conditions hypothesized as leading to abnormality.

Anal stage. In psychoanalytic theory, stage of psychosexual development in which behavior is presumably focused on anal pleasure and activities.

Androgen. Hormone associated with the development and maintenance of male characteristics.

Anesthesia. Loss or impairment of sensitivity (usually to touch but often applied to sensitivity to pain and other senses as well).

Anhedonia. Inability to experience pleasure or joy.

Anorexia nervosa. Intense fear of gaining weight or becoming "fat" coupled with refusal to maintain adequate nutrition and severe loss of body weight.

Anoxia. Lack of sufficient oxygen.

Antabuse. Drug used in the treatment of alcoholism.

Anterograde amnesia. Loss of memory for events that occur *following* trauma or shock.

Antianxiety drugs. Drugs that are used primarily for alleviating anxiety.

Antibody. Circulating blood substance coded for detection of and binding to a particular antigen.

Antidepressant drugs. Drugs that are used primarily to elevate mood and relieve depression.

Antigen. Substance detected as "foreign" by the body's immune defenses, giving rise to the immune reaction.

Antipsychotic drugs. Group of drugs, that produce a calming effect on many patients as well as alleviate or reduce the intensity of psychotic symptoms, such as delusions and hallucinations.

Antisocial personality disorder. (ASPD). Continual violation of and disregard for the rights of others through deceitful, aggressive or antisocial behavior, typically without remorse or loyalty to anyone.

Anxiety. A general feeling of apprehension about possible danger.

Anxiety disorder. An unrealistic, irrational fear or anxiety of disabling intensity. DSM-IV recognizes seven types of anxiety disorder: phobic disorders (specific or social), panic disorder (with or without agoraphobia), generalized anxiety disorder, obsessive-compulsive disorder, and post-traumatic stress disorder.

Aphasia. Loss or impairment of ability to communicate and understand language symbols—involving loss of power of expression by speech, writing, or signs, or loss of ability to comprehend written or spoken language—resulting from brain injury or disease.

Apraxia. Loss of ability to perform purposeful movements.

Arousal. See **Activation.**

Arteriosclerosis. Degenerative thickening and hardening of the walls of the arteries, occurring usually in old age.

Asberger's disorder. Severe and sustained childhood impairment in social relationships and peculiar behaviors, but without language delays seen in autism.

Assertive community treatment (ACT). Persistent and vigorous followup with and aid to patients in managing life problems.

Assertiveness therapy. Behavior therapy technique for helping people become more self-assertive in interpersonal relationships.

Assimilation. Cognitive process whereby new expereinces tend to be worked into existing cognitive frameworks even if the new information has to be reinterpreted or distorted to make it fit.

Asylums. Institutions meant solely for the care of the mentally ill.

At risk. Condition of being considered vulnerable to the development of certain abnormal behaviors.

Atrophy. Wasting away or shrinking of a bodily organ, particularly muscle tissue.

Attention-deficit hyperactivity disorder (ADHD). Disorder of childhood characterized by difficulties that interfere with task-oriented behavior, such as impulsivity, excessive motor activity, and difficulties in sustaining attention. Also known as hyperactivity.

Attributions. Process of assigning causes to things that happen.

Autism. Pervasive developmental disorder beginning in infancy involving a wide range of problematic behaviors, including deficits in language, perceptual, and motor development; defective reality testing; and social withdrawal.

Autogynephilia. Paraphilia characterized by sexual arousal in men at the thought or fantasy of being a woman.

Autonomic nervous system. Section of the nervous system that regulates the internal organs; consists primarily of ganglia connected with the brain stem and spinal cord; may be subdivided into the sympathetic and parasympathetic systems.

Autonomic reactivity. Individual's characteristic degree of emotional reactivity to stress.

Autonomy. Self-reliance; the sense of being an independent person.

Autosome. Any chromosome other than those determining sex.

Aversion therapy. Form of behavior therapy in which punishment or aversive stimulation is used to eliminate undesired responses.

Aversive stimulus. Stimulus that elicits psychic or physical pain.

Avoidance conditioning. Form of conditioning in which a subject learns to behave in a certain way in order to avoid an unpleasant stimulus.

Avoidant personality disorder. Extreme social inhibition and introversion, hypersensitivity to criticism and rejection, limited social relationships, and low self-esteem.

Axes (of DSM). Evaluation of an individual according to five foci, the first three assessing the person's present clinical status or condition and the other two assesing broader aspects of the person's situation.

Barbiturates. Synthetic drugs that act as depressants to calm induce sleep.

Baseline. The initial level of responses emitted by an organism.

Behavioral contracting. Positive reinforcement technique using a contract, often between family members, to identify the behaviors to be changed and to specify privileges and responsibilities.

Behavioral medicine. Broad interdisciplinary approach to the treatment of physical disorders thought to have psychological factors as major aspects in their causation and/or maintenance.

Behavioral perspective. A theoretical viewpoint organized around the theme that learning is central in determining human behavior.

Behavioral sciences. Various interrelated disciplines, including psychology, sociology, and anthropology, that focus on human behavior.

Behavior disorder. Synonym for psychological problem.

Behaviorism. School of psychology that formerly restricted itself primarily to study of overt behavior.

Behavior modification. Change of specific behaviors by learning techniques.

Behavior therapy. Use of therapeutic procedures based primarily on principles of classical and operant conditioning.

Benign. Of a mild, self-limiting nature; not malignant.

Binge-eating disorder (BED). Distinct from nonpurging bulimia nervosa, whereby binging is not accompanied by inappropriate compensatory behavior to limit weight gain.

Biofeedback. Treatment technique in which a person is taught to influence his or her own physiological processes formerly thought to be involuntary.

Biogenic amines. Chemicals that serve as neurotransmitters or modulators.

Biological clocks. Regular biological cycles of sleep, activity, and metabolism characteristic of each species.

Biological viewpoint. Approach to mental disorders emphasizing biological causation.

Bipolar disorders. Mood disorders in which a person experiences both manic and depressive episodes.

Bipolar disorder with a seasonal pattern. Bipolar disorder with recurrences in particular seasons of the year.

Bisexuality. Sexual attraction to both females and males.

Blocking. Involuntary inhibition of recall, ideation, or communication (including sudden stoppage of speech).

Blood-injury-injection-phobia. Persistent and disproportionate fear of the sight of blood or injury, or the possibility of having an injection. Afflicted persons are likely to experience a drop in blood pressure and faint.

Body dysmorphic disorder (BDD). Obsession with some perceived flaw or flaws in a person's appearance.

Borderline personality disorder (BPD). Impulsivity and instability in interpersonal relationships, self-image, and moods.

Brain pathology. Diseased or disordered condition of the brain.

Brain waves. Minute oscillations of electrical potential given off by neurons in the cerebral cortex and measured by the electroencephalograph (EEG).

Brief Psychiatric Rating Scale (BPRS). Objective method of rating clinical symptoms that provides scores on 18 variables (e.g., somatic concern, anxiety, withdrawal, hostility, and bizarre thinking).

Brief psychotherapy. Short-term therapy, usually 8 to 10 sessions, focused on restoring an individual's functioning and offering emotional support.

Brief psychotic disorder. Brief episodes (lasting a month or less) of otherwise uncomplicated delusional thinking.

Bulimia nervosa. Frequent occurrence of binge-eating episodes, accompanied by a sense of loss of control of overeating and recurrent inappropriate behavior to prevent weight gain.

Caffeine. A drug of dependence found in many commonly available drinks and foods.

Cardiovascular. Pertaining to the heart and blood vessels.

Case study. An in-depth examination of an individual or family that draws from a number of data sources, including interviews and psychological testing.

Castrating. Refers to any source of injury to or deprivation of the genitals, or more broadly, to a threat to the masculinity or femininity of an individual.

Castration anxiety. As postulated by Freud, the anxiety a young boy experiences when he desires his mother while at the same time fearing that his father may harm him by cutting off his penis; this anxiety forces the boy to repress his sexual desire for his mother and his hostility toward his father.

Catalepsy. Condition seen in some schizophrenic psychoses, and some psychotic mood disorders, in which body postures are waxy and semirigid, with the limbs maintaining any position in which they are placed for prolonged periods.

Catecholamines. Class of monoamine compounds sharing a similar chemical structure. Known to be neurotransmitters—norepinephrine and dopamine.

Categorical approach. Approach to classifying abnormal behavior that assumes that (a) all human behavior can be sharply divided into the categories normal and abnormal, and (b) there exist discrete, nonoverlapping classes or types of abnormal behavior, often referred to as mental illnesses or diseases.

Catharsis. Discharge of emotional tension associated with something, such as by talking about past traumas.

CAT scan. See **Computerized axial tomography.**

Causal pattern. In a cause-and-effect relationship, a situation in which more than one causal factor is involved.

Causation. Relationship in which the preceding variable causes the other(s).

Central nervous system (CNS). The brain and spinal cord.

Cerebral arteriosclerosis. Hardening of the arteries in the brain.

Cerebral cortex. Surface layers of the cerebrum.

Cerebral hemorrhage. Bleeding into brain tissue from a ruptured blood vessel.

Cerebral laceration. Tearing of brain tissue associated with severe head injury.

Cerebral syphilis. Syphilitic infection of the brain.

Cerebral thrombosis. Formation of a clot or thrombus in the vascular system of the brain.

Cerebrovascular accident (CVA). Blockage or rupture of large blood vessel in brain leading to both focal and generalized impairment of brain function. Also called *stroke.*

Cerebrum. Main part of brain; divided into left and right hemispheres.

Chemotherapy. Use of drugs to treat mental disorders.

Child abuse. Infliction of physical or psychological damage on a child by parents or other adults.

Child advocacy. Movement concerned with protecting rights and ensuring well-being of children.

Chorea. Pathological condition characterized by jerky, irregular, involuntary movements. See also **Huntington's disease.**

Chromosomal anomalies. Inherited defects or vulnerabilities caused by irregularities in chromosomes.

Chromosomes. Chainlike structures within cell nucleus that contain genes.

Chronic. Term used to describe long-standing or frequently recurring disorder, often with progressing seriousnes.

Chronic schizophrenia. A schizophrenic patient whose condition has deteriorated and/or remained stable over a long period of time (years).

Circadian rhythms. The 24-hour rhythmic fluctuations in sleep activity, and metabolic processes of plants and animals. See also **Biological clocks.**

Civil commitment. Procedure whereby a person certified as mentally disordered can be hospitalized, either voluntarily or against his or her will.

Classical conditioning. A basic form of learning in which a neutral stimulus is paired repeatedly with an unconditioned stimulus (US) that naturally elicits an unconditioned response (UR). After repeated pairings the neutral stimulus becomes a conditioned stimulus (CS) that elicits a conditioned response (CR).

Claustrophobia. Irrational fear of small enclosed places.

Client-centered (person-centered) therapy. Nondirective approach to psychotherapy, developed chiefly by Carl Rogers, that focuses on the natural power of the organism to heal itself—to help clients accept and be themselves.

Clinical picture. Diagnostic picture formed by observation of patient's behavior or by all available assessment data.

Clinical problem checklist. Computer-administered psychological assessment procedure for surveying the range of psychological problems a patient is experiencing.

Clinical psychologist. Mental health professional with Ph.D. degree or Psy.D. degree in clinical psychology and clinical experience in assessment and psychotherapy.

Clinical psychology. Field of psychology concerned with the understanding, assessment, treatment, and prevention of maladaptive behavior.

Cocaine. Stimulating and pain-reducing psychoactive drug.

Cognition. Act, process, or product of knowing or perceiving.

Cognitive–behavioral perspective. A theory of abnormal behavior that focuses on how thoughts and information processing can become distorted and lead to maladaptive emotions and behavior.

Cognitive/cognitive-behavior therapy. Therapy based on altering dysfunctional thoughts and cognitive distortions.

Cognitive dissonance. Condition of tension existing when several of one's beliefs and attitudes are inconsistent with one another.

Cognitive map. Network of assumptions that form a person's "frame of reference" for interpreting and coping with his or her world.

Cognitive processes (cognition). Mental processes, including perception, memory, and reasoning, by which one acquires knowledge, solves problems, and makes plans.

Cognitive restructuring. Cognitive-behavior therapy that aims to change a person's false or maladaptive frame of reference.

Collective unconscious. Term used by Carl Jung to refer to that portion of the unconscious that he considered common to all humanity, based on wisdom acquired by our predecessors.

Coma. Profound stupor with unconsciousness.

Community mental health. Application of psychosocial and sociocultural principles to the improvement of given environments.

Community psychology. Use of community resources in dealing with maladaptive behavior; tends to be more concerned with community intervention rather than with personal or individual change.

Comorbidity. Occurrence of two or more identified disorders in the same psychologically disordered individual.

Compulsions. Overt repetitive behaviors (such as hand washing, checking (such as counting, praying, or saying certain words silently or ordering) or more covert mental acts that a person feels driven to perform in response to an obsession.

Compulsive gambling. See **Pathological gambling.**

Computer assessment. Use of computers to obtain or interpret assessment data.

Computerized axial tomography (CAT scan). Radiological technique used to locate and assess the extent of organic damage to the brain without surgery.

Concordance rates. The percentage of twins sharing a disorder or trait.

Conduct disorder. Childhood disorders that can appear by age 9 and are marked by persistent acts of aggressive or antisocial behavior that may or may not be against the law.

Confabulation. Filling in of memory gaps with false and often irrelevant details.

Confidentiality. Commitment on part of a professional person to keep information he or she obtains from a client confidential.

Conflict. Simultaneous arousal of opposing impulses, desires, or motives.

Congenital. Existing at birth or before birth but not necessarily hereditary.

Congenital defect. Genetic defect or environmental condition occurring before birth and causing a child to develop a physical or psychological anomaly.

Conjoint family therapy. Direct involvement of the family in improving communication, interaction, and relationships among family members and fostering a family system that better meets the needs of each member.

Consciousness. Awareness of inner and/or outer environment.

Constitution. Relatively constant biological makeup of an individual, resulting from the interaction of heredity and environment.

Constitutional liability. Any detrimental characteristic that is either innate or acquired so early and in such strength that it is functionally similar to a genetic characteristic.

Consultation. Community intervention approach that aims at helping individuals at risk for disorder by working indirectly through caretaker institutions (e.g., police and teachers).

Contingency. Relationship, usually causal, between two events in which one is usually followed by the other.

Continuous reinforcement. Reward or reinforcement given regularly after each correct response.

Contributary cause. A condition that increases the probability of developing a disorder but that is neither necessary nor sufficient for it to occur.

Control group. Group of subjects who do not exhibit the disorder being studied but who are comparable in all other respects to the criterion group. Also, a comparison group of subjects who do not receive a condition or treatment whose effects are being studied.

Conversion disorder. Pattern in which symptoms of some physical malfunction or loss of control appear without any underlying organic pathology; originally called *hysteria*.

Convulsion. Pathological, involuntary muscular contractions.

Coping strategies. Efforts to deal with stress.

Coprolalia. Verbal tic in which an individual utters obscenities aloud.

Coronary heart disease (CHD). Potentially lethal blockage of the arteries supplying blood to the heart muscle, or myocardium.

Corpus callosum. Nerve fibers that connect the two hemispheres of the brain.

Correlation. The tendency of two variables to covary. With positive correlation, as one variable goes up, so does the other; with negative correlation as one variable goes up the other goes down.

Corticovisceral control mechanisms. Brain mechanisms that regulate autonomic and other bodily functions.

Counseling psychology. Field of psychology that focuses on helping people with problems pertaining to education, marriage, or occupation.

Countertransference. Psychodynamic concept that the therapist brings personal issues based on his or her own vulnerabilities and conflicts to the therapeutic relationship.

Couples counseling. Treatment for disordered interpersonal relationships involving sessions with both members of the relationship present and emphasizing mutual need gratification, social role expectations, communication patterns, and similar interpersonal factors.

Coverants. Internal, private events, such as thoughts and assumptions, to which conditioning principles are applied in cognitive-behavior therapy.

Covert. Concealed, disguised, not directly observable.

Covert sensitization. Behavioral treatment method for extinguishing undesirable behavior by associating noxious mental images with that behavior.

Criminal responsibility. Legal question of whether a person should be permitted to use insanity as a defense after having committed a crime.

Crisis. Stressful situation that approaches or exceeds the adaptive capacities of an individual or group.

Crisis intervention. Provision of psychological help to an individual or group in times of severe and special stress.

Criterion group. Group of subjects who exhibit the disorder under study.

Cross-gender identification. The desire to be, or the insistence that one is, of the opposite sex.

Cultural-familial retardation. Mental retardation as a result of an inferior quality of interaction with the cultural environment and with other people, with no evidence of brain pathology.

Cultural relativism. Position that one cannot apply universal standards of normality or abnormality to all societies.

Cyclothymia. Mild mood disorder characterized by cyclical periods of manic and depressive symptoms.

Day hospital. Community-based mental hospital where patients are treated during the day, returning to their homes at night.

Defense mechanism. See **Ego-defense mechanism.**

Defense-oriented response. Behavior directed primarily at protecting the self from hurt and disorganization rather than at resolving the situation.

Deinstitutionalization. Movement to close mental hospitals and treat people with severe mental disorder in the community.

Delinquency. Antisocial or illegal behavior by a minor.

Delirium. State of mental confusion characterized by relatively rapid onset of widespread disorganization of the higher mental processes, caused by a generalized disturbance in brain metabolism. May include impaired perception, memory, and thinking and abnormal psychomotor activity.

Delirium tremens. Acute delirium associated with withdrawal from alcohol after prolonged heavy consumption; characterized by intense anxiety, tremors, fever and sweating, and hallucinations.

Delusions. False beliefs about reality but maintained in spite of strong evidence to the contrary.

Delusional disorder. Nuturing, giving voice to, and sometimes taking action on beliefs that are considered completely false and absurd by others, formerly called *paranoia*.

Delusional system. Internally coherent, systematized pattern of delusions.

Delusion of grandeur. False belief that one is a noted or famous person, such as Napoleon or the Virgin Mary.

Delusion of persecution. False belief that one is being mistreated or interfered with by one's enemies.

Dementia. Progressive deterioration of brain functioning occurring after the completion of brain maturation in adolescence. Characterized by deficits in memory, abstract thinking, acquisition of new knowledge or skills, visuospatial comprehension, motor control, problem solving, and judgment.

Dementia of the Alzheimer's type (DAT). Disorder associated with a progressive dementia syndrome ultimately terminating in death. Onset may be in middle or old age, and symptoms include memory loss, withdrawal, confusion, and impaired judgment.

Dementia praecox. Older term for schizophrenia.

Demonology. Viewpoint emphasizing supernatural causation of mental disorder, especially "possession" by evil spirits or forces.

Denial of reality. Ego-defense mechanism that protects the self from an unpleasant reality by refusing to perceive or face it.

Dependency. Tendency to rely overly on others.

Dependent personality disorder. Extreme dependence on others, particularly the need to be taken care of, leading to clinging and submissive behavior.

Dependent variable. In an experiment, the factor that is observed to change with changes in the manipulated (independent) variables.

Depersonalization. Loss of sense of personal identity, often with a feeling of being something or someone else.

Depersonalization disorder. Dissociative disorder in which there is a loss of the sense of self.

Depression. Emotional state characterized by extraordinary sadness and dejection.

Depressive personality disorder. Provisional category of personality disorder in DSM-IV that involves a pattern of depressive cognitions and behaviors that begins by early adulthood and is pervasive in nature.

Depressogenic schemas. Dysfunctional beliefs that are rigid, extreme, and counterproductive, and that are thought to leave one susceptible to depression when experiencing stress.

Derealization. Experience in which the external world is perceived as distorted and lacking a stable and palpable existence.

Desensitization. Therapeutic process by means of which reactions to traumatic experiences are reduced in intensity by repeatedly exposing a person to them in mild form, either in reality or in fantasy.

Desire phase. First phase of the human sexual response, consisting of fantasies about sexual activity or a sense of desire to have sexual activity.

Deterrence. Premise that punishment for criminal offenses will deter that criminal and others from future criminal acts.

Detox center. Center or facility for receiving and detoxifying alcohol- or drug-intoxicated individuals.

Detoxification. Treatment directed toward ridding the body of alcohol or other drugs.

Developmental disorder. Problem that is rooted in deviations in the development process itself, thus disrupting the acquisition of skills and adaptive behavior and often interfering with the transition to well-functioning adulthood.

Developmental psychopathology. Field of psychology that focuses on determining what is abnormal at any point in the developmental process by comparing and contrasting it with normal and expected changes that occur.

Developmental systems approach. Acknowledgment that genetic activity influences neural activity, which in turn influences behavior, which in turn influences the environment and that these influences are bidirectional.

Deviant behavior. Behavior that deviates markedly from the average or norm.

Diagnosis. Determination of the nature and extent of a specific disorder.

Diathesis. Predisposition or vulnerability toward developing a given disorder.

Diathesis stress models. View of abnormal behavior as the result of stress operating on an individual with a biological, psychosocial, or sociocultural predisposition toward developing a specific disorder.

Dimensional approach. Approach to classifying abnormal behavior that assumes that a person's typical behavior is the product of differing strengths or intensities of behavior along several definable dimensions, such as mood, emotional stability, aggressiveness, gender, identity, anxiousness, interpersonal trust, clarity of thinking and communication, social introversion, and so on.

Directive therapy. Type of therapeutic approach in which a therapist supplies direct answers to problems and takes much of the responsibility for the progress of therapy.

Disaster syndrome. Reactions of many victims of major catastrophes during the traumatic experience and the initial and long-lasting reactions after it.

Discordant marriage. Family in which one or both of the parents is not gaining satisfaction from the relationship and one spouse may express frustration and disillusionment in hostile ways, such as nagging, belittling, and purposely doing things to annoy the other person.

Discrimination. Learning to interpret and respond differently to two or more similar stimuli.

Disintegration. Loss of organization or integration in any organized system.

Disorganization. Severely impaired integration.

Disorientation. Mental confusion with respect to time, place, or person.

Displacement. Ego-defense mechanism that discharges pent-up feelings, often of hostility, on objects less dangerous than those arousing the feelings.

Disrupted family. Family that is incomplete as a result of death, divorce, separation, or some other circumstance.

Dissociation. The human mind's capacity to mediate complex mental activity in channels split off from or independent of conscious awareness.

Dissociative amnesia. Psychogenically caused memory failure.

Dissociative disorders. Conditions involving a disruption in a person's sense of personal identity.

Dissociative identity disorder. Condition in which a person manifests at least two more or less complete systems of identity. Formerly called *multiple personality disorder.*

Distress. Negative stress, associated with pain, anxiety or sorrow.

Disturbed family. Family in which one or both parents behave in grossly eccentric or abnormal ways and may keep the home in constant emotional turmoil.

Dizygotic (fraternal) twins. Twins that develop from two separate eggs.

DNA. Deoxyribonucleic acid, principal component of genes.

Dominant gene. A gene whose hereditary characteristics prevail in the offspring.

Dopamine. Catecholamine neurotransmitter substance.

Dopamine hypothesis. Hypothesis that schizophrenia is the result of an excess of dopamine activity at certain synaptic sites.

Double-bind. Situation in which a person will be disapproved for performing a given act and equally disapproved if he or she does not perform it.

Double-bind communication. Type of faulty communication in which the one person (e.g., a parent) presents to another (e.g., a child) ideas, feelings, and demands that are mutually incompatible.

Down syndrome. Form of moderate to severe mental retardation associated with chromosomal abnormality and typically accompanied by characteristic physical features.

Dream analysis. Method involving the recording, description, and interpretation of a patient's dreams.

Drive. Internal conditions directing an organism toward a specific goal, usually involving biological rather than psychological motives.

Drug abuse. Use of a drug to the extent that it interferes with health and/or occupational or social adjustment.

Drug addiction (dependence). Physiological and/or psychological dependence on a drug.

Drug therapy. See **Chemotherapy** and **Pharmacotherapy.**

DSM-IV. Current diagnostic manual of the American Psychiatric Association.

Dwarfism. Condition of arrested growth and very short stature.

Dyad. Two-person group.

Dynamic formulation. Integrated evaluation of an individual's personality traits, behavior patterns, environmental demands, and the like to describe the person's current situation and to hypothesize about what is driving the person to behave in maladaptive ways.

Dysfunction. Impairment or disturbance in the functioning of an organ or in behavior.

Dysfunctional beliefs. Negative beliefs that are rigid, extreme, and counterproductive.

Dyslexia. Impairment of the ability to read.

Dyspareunia. Painful coitus in a male or a female.

Dysrhythmia. Abnormal brain-wave pattern.

Dysthymia. Moderately severe mood disorder characterized by a persistently depressed mood extending for at least two years with brief periods of normal moods. Additional symptoms may include poor appetite, sleep disturbance, lack of energy, low self-esteem, difficulty concentrating, and feelings of hopelessness.

Eating disorders. Disorders of food ingestion, regurgitation, or attitude that affect health and well-being, such as anorexia, bulimia, or binge-eating.

Echolalia. Parrotlike repetition of a few words.

Edema. Swelling of tissues.

EEG. See **Electroencephalogram.**

Ego. In psychoanalytic theory, the rational part of the personality that mediates between the demands of the id constraints of the superego, and the realities of the external world.

Egocentric. Preoccupied with one's own concerns and relatively insensitive to the concerns of others.

Ego-defense mechanisms. Psychic mechanisms that discharge or soothe anxiety rather than coping directly with an anxiety-provoking situation; usually unconscious and reality-distorting. Also called *defense mechanism.*

Electra complex. Excessive emotional attachment (love) of a daughter for her father; the female counterpart of the Oedipus complex.

Electroconvulsive therapy (ECT). Use of electricity to produce convulsions and unconsciousness; a treatment used primarily to alleviate depressive and manic episodes. Also known as *electroshock therapy.*

Electroencephalogram (EEG). Graphic record of the brain's electrical activity, obtained by placing electrodes on the scalp and measuring the brain-wave impulses from various brain areas.

Embolism. Lodgment of a blood clot in a blood vessel too small to permit its passage.

Emotion. Strong feeling accompanied by physiological changes.

Emotional disturbance. Psychological disorder.

Emotional insulation. Ego-defense mechanism in which a person reduces anxiety by withdrawing into a shell of passivity.

Empathy. Ability to understand and to some extent share the state of mind of another person.

Encephalitis. Inflammation of the brain.

Encopresis. Disorder in children who have not learned appropriate toileting for bowel movements after age four.

Encounter group. Small group designed to provide an intensive interpersonal experience focusing on feelings and group interactions; used in therapy or to promote personal growth.

Endocrine glands. Ductless glands that secrete hormones directly into the lymph or bloodstream.

Endogenous factors. Factors originating within an organism that affect behavior.

Endorphins. Opiates produced in the brain and throughout the body which function like neurotransmitters to dampen pain sensations. They also play a role in the body building up tolerance to certain drugs.

Enuresis. Bed wetting; involuntary discharge of urine after the age of expected continence (age five).

Environmental psychology. Field of psychology focusing on the effects of an environmental setting on an individual's feelings and behavior.

Epidemiological studies. Attempts to establish the pattern of occurrence of certain (mental) disorders in different times, places, and groups of people.

Epidemiology. Study of the distribution of diseases, disorders, or health-related behaviors in a given population. Mental health epidemiology is the study of the distribution of mental disorders.

Epilepsy. Group of disorders varying from momentary lapses of consciousness to generalized convulsions.

Epinephrine. Hormone secreted by the adrenal medulla; also called *adrenaline.*

Episodic (disorder). Term used to describe a disorder that tends to abate and to recur.

Equilibrium. Steady state; balance.

Erotic. Pertaining to sexual stimulation and gratification.

Escape learning. Instrumental response in which a subject learns to terminate or escape an aversive stimulus.

Essential hypertension. High blood pressure with no specific physical cause known.

Estrogens. Female hormones produced by the ovaries.

Ethnic group. Group of people who are treated as distinctive in terms of culture and group patterns.

Etiology. Causal pattern of abnormal behavior.

Euphoria. Exaggerated feeling of well-being and contentment.

Eustress. Positive stress.

Exacerbate. Intensify.

Excitement phase. Second phase of the human sexual response in which there is generally a subjective sense of sexual pleasure and physiological changes, including penile erection in the male and vaginal lubrication and enlargement in the female.

Exhaustion. Third and final stage of responding to continued excessive trauma in which a person's adaptive resources are depleted and the coping patterns developed during the resistance stage fail.

Exhibitionism. Intentional exposure of genitals to others in inappropriate circumstances and without their consent.

Existential anxiety. Anxiety concerning one's ability to find a satisfying and fulfilling way of life.

Existentialism. View of human beings that emphasizes an individual's responsibility for becoming the kind of person he or she should be.

Existential neurosis. Disorder characterized by feelings of alienation, meaninglessness, and apathy.

Existential psychotherapy. Type of therapy that is based on existential thought and focuses on individual uniqueness and authenticity on the part of both client and therapist.

Exogenous. Originating from or due to external causes.

Exorcism. Religiously inspired treatment procedure designed to drive out evil spirits or forces from a "possessed" person.

Experimental group. Group of subjects used to assess the effects of independent variables.

Experimental method. Rigorous scientific procedure by which hypotheses are tested.

Expressed emotion (EE). Type of negative communication involving excessive criticism and emotional overinvolvement directed at a patient by family members.

Extinction. Gradual disappearance of a conditioned response when it is no longer reinforced.

Extraversion. Personality type oriented toward the outer world of people and things rather than concepts and intellectual concerns.

Factitious disorder. Feigning of symptoms to maintain the personal benefits that a sick role may provide, including the attention and concern of medical personnel and/or family members.

Factor analysis. Statistical technique used for reducing a large array of intercorrelated measures to the minimum number of factors necessary to account for the observed overlap or associations among them.

Fading. Technique whereby a stimulus causing some reaction is gradually replaced by a previously neutral stimulus, such that the latter acquires the property of producing the reaction in question.

False memories. "Memories" of events that did not actually happen, often produced by highly leading and suggestive techniques.

Familial. Pertaining to characteristics that tend to run in families and have a higher incidence in certain families than in the general population.

Family systems approach. Form of interpersonal therapy focusing on the within-family behavior of a particular family member and the assumption that it is largely influenced by the behaviors and communication patterns of other family members.

Fantasy. Daydream; also, an ego-defense mechanism by means of which a person escapes from the world of reality and gratifies his or her desires in fantasy achievements.

Fear. A basic emotion that involves the activation of the "fight-or-flight" response of the sympathetic nervous system.

Feedback. Explicit information pertaining to internal physiological processes or to the social consequences of one's overt behavior.

Female orgasmic disorder. Persistent or recurrent delay in or absence of orgasm following a normal sexual excitement phase.

Female sexual arousal disorder. Sexual dysfunction involving an absence of sexual arousal feelings and unresponsiveness to most or all forms of erotic stimulation.

Fetal alcohol syndrome. Observed pattern in infants of alcoholic mothers in which there is a characteristic facial or limb irregularity, low body weight, and behavioral abnormality.

Fetishism. Sexual variant in which sexual interest centers on some inanimate object or nonsexual part of the body.

Fetus. Embryo after the sixth week following conception.

Fixation. Ego-defense mechanism involving an unreasonable or exaggerated attachment to some person or arresting of emotional development on a childhood or adolescent level.

Fixed-interval schedule. Schedule of reinforcement based on fixed period of time after previously reinforced response.

Fixed-ratio schedule. Schedule of reinforcement based on reinforcement after fixed number of nonreinforced responses.

Flashback. Involuntary recurrence of perceptual distortions or hallucinations weeks or months after taking a drug, in post-traumatic stress disorder, a dissociative state in which the person briefly relives the traumatic experience.

Flooding. Anxiety-eliciting therapeutic technique involving having a client repeatedly experience the actual internal or external stimuli that had been identifed as producing anxiety reactions.

Folie á deux. See **Shared psychotic disorder.**

Follow-up study. Research procedure in which people are studied over a period of time or are recontacted at a later time after initial study.

Forensic psychology and psychiatry. Branches of psychology and psychiatry dealing with legal problems relating to mental disorders and the legal rights and protection of mental patients and members of society at large.

Fraternal twins. Dizygotic twins; fertilized by separate germ cells, thus not having same genetic inheritance. May be of the same or opposite sex.

Free association. Method for probing the unconscious by having patients talk freely about themselves, their feelings and their motives.

Free-floating anxiety. Anxiety not referable to any specific situation or cause.

Frontal lobe. Portion of the brain active in reasoning and other higher thought processes.

Frustration. Thwarting of a need or desire.

Frustration tolerance. Ability to withstand frustration without becoming impaired psychologically.

Fugue. Dissociative disorder that entails loss of memory accompanied by actual physical flight from one's present life situation to a new environment or less threatening former one.

Functional MRI (fMRI). Internal scanning technique that measures changes in local oxygenation (blood flow) to specific areas of brain tissue that in turn depend on neuronal activity in those specific regions, allowing the mapping of psychological activity such as sensations, images, and throughts.

Functional psychoses. Severe mental disorders for which a specific organic pathology has not been demonstrated.

Gambling. Wagering on games or events in which chance largely determines the outcome.

Gender dysphoria. Persistent discomfort about one's biological sex or the sense that the gender role of that sex is inappropriate.

Gender identity. Individual's identification as being male or female.

Gender identity disorder. Identification with members of the opposite sex, persistent discomfort with one's biological sexual identity, and strong desire to change to the opposite sex.

General adaptation syndrome. A model that helps explain the course of a person's biological decomposition under excessive stress; consists of three stages (alarm reaction, the stage of resistance, and exhaustion).

Generalization. Tendency of a response that has been conditioned to one stimulus to be elicited by other, similar stimuli.

Generalized anxiety disorder (GAD). Chronic excessive worry about a number of events or activities, with no specific threat present, accompanied by at least three of the symptoms of restlessness, fatigue, difficulty concentrating, irritability, muscle tension, or sleep disturbance.

Generalized reinforcer. Reinforcer, such as money, that may influence a wide range of stimuli and behaviors.

General paresis. Mental disorder associated with syphilis of the brain.

Genes. Ultramicroscopic areas of DNA that are responsible for the transmission of hereditary traits.

Genetic code. Means by which DNA controls the sequence and structure of proteins manufactured within each cell and also makes exact duplicates of itself.

Genetic counseling. Counseling prospective parents concerning the probability of their having defective offspring as a result of genetic defects.

Genetic inheritance. Potential for development and behavior determined at conception by egg and sperm cells.

Genetics. Science of the inheritance of traits and the mechanisms of this inheritance.

Genitalia. Organs of reproduction, especially the external organs.

Genital stage. In psychoanalytic theory, the final stage of psychosexual development involving shift from autoeroticism to heterosexual interest.

Genotype. A person's total genetic endowment.

Genotype–environment correlation. Genotypic vulnerability that can shape a child's environmental experiences.

Genotype–environment interaction. Differential sensitivity or susceptibility to their environments by people having different genotypes.

Geriatrics. Science of the diseases and treatment of the aged.

Germ cells. Reproductive cells (female ovum and male sperm) that unite to produce a new individual.

Gerontology. Science dealing with the study of old age.

Gestalt psychology. School of psychology that emphasizes patterns rather than elements or connections, taking the view that the whole is more than the sum of its parts.

Gestalt therapy. Type of psychotherapy emphasizing wholeness of the person and integration of thought, feeling, and action.

Glucocorticoids. Adrenocortical hormones involved in sugar metabolism but also having widespread effects on injury-repair mechanisms and resistance to disease; they include hydrocortisone, corticosterone, and cortisone.

Gonads. Sex glands.

Good premorbid schizophrenia. See **Reactive schizophrenia.**

Group therapy. Psychotherapy with several people at the same time.

Guilt. Feelings of culpability arising from behavior or desires contrary to one's ethical principles. Involves both self-devaluation and apprehension growing out of fears of punishment.

Guilty but mentally ill (GBMI). Plea and possible verdict that provides an option to plead not guilty by reason of insanity (NGRI) that allows placing a defendant in a treatment facility rather than in a prison.

Habituation. Process whereby a person's response to the same stimulus lessens with repeated presentations.

Halfway house. Facility that provides aftercare following institutionalization, seeking to ease a person's adjustment to the community.

Hallucinations. False perceptions such as things seen or heard that are not real or present.

Hallucinogens. Drugs thought to induce hallucinations; often referred to as psychedelics.

Hallucinosis. Persistent hallucinations in the presence of known or suspected organic brain pathology.

Hashish. Strongest drug derived from the hemp plant; a relative of marijuana that is usually smoked.

Health maintenance organization (HMO). Health plan that provides services to employers and individuals for a fixed prepaid fee.

Health psychology. Subspecialty within behavioral medicine that deals with psychology's contributions to diagnosis, treatment, and prevention of psychological components of physical dysfunction.

Hebephrenic schizophrenia. See **Schizophrenia, disorganized type.**

Hemiplegia. Paralysis of one lateral half of the body.

Heredity. Genetic transmission of characteristics from parents to their children.

Hermaphroditism. Anatomical sexual abnormality in which a person has some sex organs of both sexes.

Heroin. Powerful psychoactive drug, chemically derived from morphine, that relieves pain but is even more intense and addictive than morphine.

Heterosexuality. Sexual interest in a member of the opposite sex.

Hierarchy of needs. Concept that needs arrange themselves in a hierarchy in terms of importance, from the most basic biological needs to those psychological needs concerned with self-actualization.

High-risk. Term applied to persons showing great vulnerability to physical or mental disorders.

Histrionic personality disorder. Excessive attention-seeking and emotional instability, and self-dramatization.

Homeostasis. Tendency of organisms to maintain conditions making possible a constant level of physiological functioning.

Homosexuality. Sexual preference for a member of one's own sex.

Hormones. Chemical messengers secreted by endocrine glands that regulate development of and activity in various parts of the body.

Hostility. Emotional reaction or drive toward the destruction or damage of an object interpreted as a source of frustration or threat.

Host personality. The original personality in a person with dissociative identity disorder.

Humanistic-experiential therapies. Psychotherapies emphasizing personal growth and self-direction.

Humanistic perspective. Approach to understanding abnormal behavior that views basic human nature as "good" and emphasizes people's inherent capacity for growth and self-actualization.

Huntington's disease. Incurable disease of hereditary origin, which is manifested in jerking, twitching movements and mental deterioration. Formerly called *Huntington's chorea.*

Hydrocephalus. Relatively rare condition in which the accumulation of an abnormal amount of cerebrospinal fluid within the cranium causes damage to the brain tissues and enlargement of the skull.

Hydrotherapy. Use of hot or cold baths, ice packs, etc., in treatment.

Hyper-. Prefix meaning increased or excessive.

Hyperactivity. See **Attention-deficit hyperactivity disorder.**

Hyperobesity. Extreme overweight; 100 pounds or more above ideal body weight.

Hypertension. High blood pressure.

Hyperthymic temperament. Personality type involving life-long hypomanic adjustment.

Hyperventilation. Rapid breathing associated with intense anxiety.

Hypesthesia. Partial loss of sensitivity.

Hypnosis. Trancelike mental state induced in a cooperative subject by suggestion.

Hypnotherapy. Use of hypnosis in psychotherapy.

Hypo-. Prefix meaning decreased or insufficient.

Hypoactive sexual desire disorder. Sexual dysfunction in which either a man or a woman shows little or no sexual drive or interest.

Hypochondriacal delusions. Delusions concerning various horrible disease conditions, such as the belief that one's brain is turning to dust.

Hypochondriasis. Person's preoccupation with the fear that he or she has a serious disease, based on misinterpretations of bodily symptoms.

Hypomania. Mild form of mania.

Hypothalamus. Key structure at the base of the brain; important in emotion and motivation.

Hypothesis. Statement or proposition, usually based on observation, which is tested in an experiment; may be denied or supported by experimental results but never conclusively proved.

Hypoxia. Insufficient delivery of oxygen to an organ, especially the brain.

Hysteria. Older term used for conversion disorders; involves the appearance of symptoms of organic illness in the absence of any related organic pathology.

Id. In psychoanalytic theory, the of instinctual drives and the first structure to appear in infancy.

Identical twins. Monozygotic twins; developed from a single fertilized egg.

Identification. Ego-defense mechanism in which a person identifies himself or herself with some person or institution, usually of an illustrious nature.

Ideology. System of beliefs.

Illusion. Misinterpretation of sensory data; false perception.

Immaturity. Pattern of childhood maladaptive behaviors suggesting lack of adaptive skills.

Immune reaction. Complex defensive reaction initiated on detection of an antigen invading the body.

Immune system. The body's principal means of defending itself against the intrusion of foreign substances.

Implicit memory. Memory that occurs below the conscious level.

Implicit perception. Perception that occurs below the conscious level.

Incentive. External inducement to behave in a certain way.

Incest. Culturally prohibited sexual relations between family members, such as a brother and sister or a parent and child.

Incidence. Occurrence (onset) rate of a given disorder in a given population.

Independent variable. Factor whose effects are being examined and which is manipulated in some way while other variables are held constant.

Index case. In a genetic study, an individual who evidences the trait in which the investigator is interested. Same as **proband.**

Indicated prevention. Early detection and prompt treatment of maladaptive behavior in a person's family and community setting.

Infantile autism. See **Autism.**

Inhibition. Restraint of impulse or desire.

Innate. Inborn.

Inpatient. Hospitalized patient.

Insanity. Legal term for mental disorder, implying lack of responsibility for one's acts and inability to manage one's affairs.

Insanity defense (NGRI plea). "Not guilty by reason of insanity" plea used as a legal defense in criminal trials.

Insight. Clinically, a person's understanding of his or her illness or of the motivations underlying a behavior pattern; in general psychology, the sudden grasp or understanding of meaningful relationships in a situation.

Insight therapy. Type of psychotherapy focusing on helping a client achieve greater self-understanding with respect to his or her motives, values, coping patterns, and so on.

Insomnia. Difficulty in sleeping.

Instinct. Inborn tendency to particular behavior patterns under certain conditions in the absence of learning.

Instrumental (operant) conditioning. Reinforcement of a subject for making a correct response that either leads to receipt of something that is rewarding or escape from something that is unpleasant.

Insulin coma therapy. Physiological treatment for schizophrenia rarely used today that involved administration of increasing amounts of insulin until a patient went into shock.

Intellectualization. Ego-defense mechanism by which a person achieves some measure of insulation from emotional hurt by cutting off or distorting the emotional charge that normally accompanies hurtful situations.

Intelligence. The ability to learn, reason, and adapt.

Intelligence quotient (IQ). Measurement of "intelligence" expressed as a number or position on a scale.

Intelligence test. Test used in establishing a subject's level of intellectual capability.

Intensive care management (ICM). Use of multidisciplinary teams having limited caseloads to ensure that discharged patients don't get overlooked and "lost" in the system.

Interdisciplinary (multidisciplinary) approach. Integration of various scientific disciplines in understanding, assessing, treating, and preventing mental disorders.

Intermittent reinforcement. Reinforcement given intermittently rather than after every response.

International Classification of Diseases (ICD-10). System of classification of disorders published by the World Health Organization.

Interoceptive fears. Fear of various internal bodily sensations.

Interpersonal accommodation. Process through which two people develop patterns of communication and interaction that enable them to attain common goals, meet mutual needs, and build a satisfying relationship.

Interpersonal perspective. Approach to understanding abnormal behavior that views much of psychopathology as rooted in the unfortunate tendencies developed while dealing with our interpersonal environments; it thus focuses on our relationships, past and present, with other people.

Intrapsychic conflict. Inner mental struggles resulting from the interplay of the id, ego, and superego when the three subsystems are striving for different goals.

Introjection. Internal process by which a child incorporates symbolically, through images and memories, important people in his or her life.

Intromission. Insertion of the penis into the vagina or anus.

Introspection. Observing (and often reporting on) one's inner experiences.

Introversion. Direction of interest toward one's inner world of experience and toward concepts rather than external events and objects.

In vitro exposure. Taking place in the therapeutic or laboratory setting.

In vivo exposure. Taking place in a real-life situation as opposed to the therapeutic or laboratory setting.

Ionizing radiation. Form of radiation; major cause of gene mutations.

Isolation. Ego-defense mechanism by means of which contradictory attitudes or feelings that normally accompany particular attitudes are kept apart, thus preventing conflict or hurt.

Juvenile delinquency. Legal term used to refer to illegal acts committed by minors.

Juvenile paresis. General paresis in children, usually of congenital origin.

Klinefelter's syndrome. Type of mental retardation associated with sex chromosome anomaly.

La belle indifférence. Unconcern about serious illness or disability that is characteristic of conversion disorder.

Labeling. Assigning a person to a particular diagnostic category, such as schizophrenia.

Lability. Instability, particularly with regard to affect.

Latency stage. In psychoanalytic theory, a stage of psychosexual development during which sexual motivations recede in importance and a child is preoccupied with developing skills and other activities.

Latent. Inactive or dormant.

Latent content. In psychoanalytic theory, repressed actual motives of a dream that are seeking expression but are so painful or unacceptable that they are disguised by the manifest content of the dream.

Law of effect. Principle that responses that have rewarding consequences are strengthened and those that have aversive consequences are weakened or eliminated.

Learned helplessness theory of depression. A cognitive theory of depression that suggests that an organism that learns that it has no control over aversive events will show motivational, cognitive, and emotional deficits that are similar to those shown by depressed persons.

Learning. Modification of behavior as a consequence of experience.

Learning disabled (LD). Term used to describe children who exhibit deficits in academic skills.

Lesbian. Female homosexual person.

Lesion. Anatomically localized area of tissue pathology in an organ or part of the brain.

Lethality scale. Criteria used to assess the likelihood of a person's committing suicide.

Libido. In psychoanalytic theory, a term used to describe the instinctual drives of the id; the basic constructive energy of life, primarily sexual in nature.

Life crisis. Stress situation that approaches or exceeds a person's adjustive capacity.

Life history method. Technique of psychological observation in which the development of particular forms of behavior is traced by means of records of a subject's past or present behavior.

Lifestyle. General pattern of assumptions, motives, cognitive styles, and coping techniques that characterize a person's behavior and give it consistency.

Lifetime prevalence. The proportion of living persons in a population who have ever had a disorder up to the time of the epidemiological assessment.

Lobotomy. See **Prefrontal lobotomy.**

Locomotor ataxia. Muscular incoordination usually resulting from syphilitic damage to the spinal-cord pathways.

LSD (lysergic acid diethylamide). The most potent of the hallucinogens. It is odorless, colorless, and tasteless and can produce intoxication with an amount smaller than a grain of salt.

Lunacy. Old term roughly synonymous with insanity.

Lycanthropy. Delusion of being a wolf.

Lymphocyte. Generalized term for white blood cells involved in immune protection.

Macrocephaly. Rare type of mental retardation characterized by an increase in the size and weight of the brain, enlargement of the skull, visual impairment, convulsions and other neurological symptoms resulting from abnormal growth of glial cells that form the supporting structure for brain tissue.

Macrophage. Literally, "big eater." A white blood cell that destroys antigens by engulfment.

Madness. Nontechnical synonym for severe mental disorder.

Magnetic resonance imaging (MRI). Internal scanning technique involving measurement of variations in magnetic fields that allows visualization of the anatomical features of internal organs, including the central nervous system and particularly the brain.

Mainstreaming. Placement of mentally retarded children in regular school classrooms for all or part of the day.

Major depressive disorder. Severe mood disorder in which only depressive episodes occur most of every day for at least two weeks. Besides depression, the disorder involves other symptoms such as fatigue, sleep disturbance, loss of appetite and weight, psychomotor slowing, difficulty concentrating, self-denunciation, guilt, and recurrent thoughts of death or suicide.

Major tranquilizers. Antipsychotic drugs, such as the phenothiazines.

Maladaptive (abnormal) behavior. Behavior that is detrimental to the well-being of an individual and/or group.

Maladjustment. More or less enduring failure of adjustment; lack of harmony with self or environment.

Male erectile disorder. Sexual dysfunction in which a male is unable to achieve or maintain an erection sufficient for successful sexual intercourse; formerly known as impotence.

Male orgasmic disorder. Retarded ejaculation or the inability to ejaculate during intercourse.

Malingering. Consciously faking illness or disability symptoms to achieve some specific nonmedical objective.

Managed health care. System of corporations that secure services from hospitals, physicians, and other providers for treating a designated population, with the goal of holding down health care cost.

Mania. Emotional state characterized by intense and unrealistic feelings of excitement and euphoria.

Manic-depressive psychoses. Older term denoting a group of psychotic disorders characterized by prolonged periods of excitement and overactivity (mania) or by periods of depression and underactivity (depression) or by alternation of the two. Now known as *bipolar disorders*.

Manualized therapy. Standardization of psychosocial treatments (as in development of a manual) to fit the randomized clinical paradigm.

Manifest content. In psychoanalytic theory, the apparent meaning of a dream; masks the latent content.

Marijuana. Mild hallucinogenic drug derived from the hemp plant, often smoked in cigarettes called reefers or joints.

Marital schism. Marriage characterized by severe chronic discord that threatens continuation of the marital relationship.

Marital skew. Marriage maintained at the expense of a distorted relationship.

Marital therapy. See **Couples counseling.**

Masked disorder. "Masking" of underlying depression or other emotional disturbance by delinquent behavior or other patterns seemingly unrelated to the basic disturbance.

Masochism. Sexual stimulation and gratification from experiencing pain or degradation in relating to a lover.

Mass madness. Widespread occurrence of group behavior disorders that were apparently cases of hysteria.

Masturbation. Self-stimulation of genitals for sexual gratification.

Maternal deprivation. Lack of adequate care and stimulation by the mother or mother surrogate.

Maturation. Process of development and body change resulting from heredity rather than learning.

Medical model. View of disordered behavior as a symptom of a disease process, rather than a pattern representing faulty learning or cognition.

Melancholic type. Subtype of major depression that involves loss of interest or pleasure in almost all activities, and other symptoms, including early morning awakenings, worse depression in the morning, psychomotor agitation or retardation, loss of appetite or weight, excessive guilt, and qualitatively different sadness than usually experienced after a loss.

Meninges. Membranes that envelop the brain and spinal cord.

Mental age (MA). Scale unit indicating level of intelligence in relation to chronological age.

Mental disorder. Entire range of abnormal behavior patterns.

Mental hygiene movement. Movement that advocated a method of treatment that focused almost exclusively on the physical well-being of hospitalized mental patients.

Mental illness. Serious mental disorder.

Mental retardation. Significantly subaverage general intellectual functioning accompanied by significant limitations in adaptive functioning that is obvious during the developmental period.

Mescaline. Hallucinogenic drug derived from the peyote cactus.

Mesmerism. Theories of "animal magnetism" (hypnosis) formulated by Anton Mesmer.

Mesocorticolimbic dopamine pathway (MCLP). Center of psychoactive drug activation in the brain. This area is involved on the release of dopamine and in mediating the rewarding properties of drugs.

Methadone. Synthetic narcotic related to heroin; used in treatment of heroin addiction because it satisfies the craving for heroin without producing serious psychological impairment.

Microcephaly. Type of mental retardation resulting from impaired development of the brain and a consequent failure of the cranium to attain normal size.

Migraine. Intensely painful, recurrent headache that typically involves only one side of the head and may be accompanied by nausea and other disturbances.

Mild (disorder). Disorder of a low order of severity.

Milieu. Immediate environment, physical or social or both.

Milieu therapy. General approach to treatment for hospitalized patients that focuses on making the hospital environment itself a therapeutic community.

Minnesota Multiphasic Personality Inventory (MMPI/MMPI-2). Widely used and empirically validated personality scales.

Minor tranquilizers. Antianxiety drugs, such as the benzodiazepines.

Model. Analogy that helps a scientist order findings and see important relationships among them.

Modeling. Learning of skills by imitating another person who performs the behavior to be acquired.

Moderate (disorder). Disorder of an intermediate order of severity.

Monozygotic twins. Identical twins, developed from one fertilized egg.

Mood-congruent. Delusions or hallucinations that are consistent with a person's mood.

Mood disorders. Disturbances of mood that are intense and persistent enough to be clearly maladaptive.

Mood-incongruent. Delusional thinking that is inconsistent with a person's predominant mood.

Moral management. Wide-ranging method of treatment that focuses on a patient's social, individual, and occupational needs.

Moral therapy. Therapy based on provision of kindness, understanding, and favorable environment; prevalent during early part of the nineteenth century.

Morbid. Unhealthy, pathological.

Morphine. Addictive drug derived from opium that can serve as a powerful sedative and pain reliver.

Motivation. Often used as a synonym for drive or activation; implies that an organism's actions are partly determined in direction and strength by its own inner nature.

Motive. Internal condition that directs action toward some goal; term usually used to include both the drive and the goal to which it is directed.

Multi-infarct dementia. See **Vascular dementia.**

Multiple personality disorder. See **Dissociative identity disorder.**

Mutant gene. Gene that has undergone some change in structure.

Mutation. Change in the composition of a gene, usually causing harmful or abnormal characteristics to appear in the offspring.

Mutism. Refusal or inability to speak.

Nancy School, The. Group of physicians in nineteenth-century Europe who accepted the view that hysteria was a sort of self-hypnosis.

Narcissism. Self-love.

Narcissistic personality disorder. Exaggerated sense of self-importance, preoccupation with being admired, and lack of empathy for the feelings of others.

Narcolepsy. Disorder characterized by transient, compulsive states of sleepiness.

Narcotic drugs. Drugs, such as morphine, that lead to physiological dependence and increased tolerance.

Natural killer cell. White blood cell that destroys antigens by chemical dissolution.

Necessary cause. A condition that must exist for a disorder to occur.

Need. Biological or psychological condition whose gratification is necessary for the maintenance of homeostasis or for self-actualization.

Negative automatic thoughts. Thoughts that are just below the surface of awareness and that involve unpleasant pessimistic predictions.

Negative cognitive triad. Negative thoughts about the self, the world, and the future.

Negative-symptom schizophrenia. Schizophrenia characterized by an absence or deficit of normal behaviors, such as emotional expressiveness, communicative speech and reactivity to environmental events.

Negativism. Form of aggressive withdrawal that involves refusing to cooperate or obey commands, or doing the exact opposite of what has been requested.

Neologism. New word; feature of language disturbance in schizophrenia.

Neonate. Newborn infant.

Neoplasm. Tumor.

Nervous breakdown. General term used to refer broadly to lowered integration and inability to deal adequately with one's life situation.

Neurological examination. Examination to determine the presence and extent of organic damage to the nervous system.

Neurology. Field concerned with the study of the brain and nervous system and disorders thereof.

Neuron. Individual nerve cell.

Neurophysiology. Branch of biology concerned with the functioning of nervous tissue and the nervous system.

Neuropsychological assessment. Use of psychological tests that measure a person's cognitive, perceptual, and motor performance to obtain clues to the extent and locus of brain damage.

Neuropsychological disorders. Disorders that occur when there has been significant organic impairment or damage to a normal adolescent or adult brain.

Neuropsychological mood syndromes. Serious mood disturbances apparently caused by disruptions in the normal physiology of cerebral function.

Neuropsychological personality syndromes. Change in a person's general personality style or traits following brain injury of one or another type.

Neurosis. Term historically used to characterize maladaptive behavior resulting from intrapsychic conflict and marked by prominent use of defense mechanisms.

Neurosurgery. Surgery of the nervous system, especially the brain.

Neurosyphilis. Syphilis affecting the central nervous system.

Neurotic behavior. Anxiety-driven, exaggerated use of avoidance behaviors and defense mechanisms.

Neuroticism. Personality pattern including the tendency to experience anxiety, angry hostility, depression, self-consciousness, impulsiveness, and vulnerability.

Neurotransmitters. Chemical substances released into a synapse by the presynaptic neuron that transmit nerve impulses from one neuron to another.

Nicotine. Addictive akaloid that is the chief active ingredient in tobacco and a drug of dependence.

Night hospital. Mental hospital in which an individual may receive treatment during all or part of the night while carrying on his or her usual occupation in the daytime.

Nihilistic delusion. Fixed belief that everything is unreal.

Nondirective therapy. Approach to psychotherapy in which a therapist refrains from advice or direction of the therapy. See also **Client-centered psychotherapy.**

Norepinephrine. Catecholamine neurotransmitter substance.

Norm. Standard based on the measurement of a large group of people; used for comparing the scores of an individual with those of others in a defined group.

Normal. Conforming to the usual or norm; healthy.

Normal distribution. Tendency for most members of a population to cluster around a central point or average with respect to a given trait, with the rest spreading out to the two extremes in decreasing frequency.

NREM sleep. Stages of sleep not characterized by the rapid eye movements that accompany dreaming.

Objective tests. Structured tests, such as questionnaires, self-inventories, or rating scales, used in psychological assessment.

Object-relations. In psychoanalytic theory, this viewpoint focuses on an infant or young child's interactions with "objects" (that is, real or imagined people), as well as how they make symbolic representations of important people in their lives.

Observational method. Systematic technique by which observers are trained to watch and record behavior without bias.

Obsessions. Persistent and recurrent intrusive thoughts, images, or impulses that a person experiences as disturbing and inappropriate but has difficulty suppressing.

Obsessive-compulsive disorder (OCD). Anxiety disorder characterized by the persistent intrusion of unwanted and intrusive thoughts or distressing images; these are usually accompanied by compulsive behaviors designed to neutralize the obsessive thoughts or images or to prevent some dreaded event or situation.

Obsessive-compulsive personality disorder (OCPD). Perfectionism and excessive concern with maintaining order, control, and adherence to rules.

Occipital lobe. Portion of cerebrum concerned chiefly with visual function.

Oedipus complex. Desire for sexual relations with parent of opposite sex, specifically that of a boy for his mother with his father a hated rival.

Olfactory hallucinations. Hallucinations involving the sense of smell.

Operant (or instrumental) conditioning. Form of learning in which a particular response is reinforced and becomes more likely to be repeated on similar occasions.

Operational definition. Defining a concept on the basis of a set of operations that can be observed and measured.

Opium. Narcotic drug that leads to physiological dependence and the development of tolerance; derivatives are morphine, heroin, and codeine.

Oppositional defiant disorder. Childhood disorders that appear by age 6 and are characterized by persistent acts of aggressive or antisocial behavior that may or may not be against the law.

Oral stage. First stage of psychosexual development in Freudian theory, in which mouth or oral activities are the primary source of pleasure.

Organic mental disorders. Mental disorders associated with organic brain pathology. Called *brain disorders* in DSM-IV.

Organic viewpoint. Concept that all mental disorders have an organic basis. See also **Biological viewpoint.**

Orgasm. Third phase of the human sexual response during which there is a release of sexual tension and a peaking of sexual pleasure.

Outcome research. Studies of effectiveness of treatment.

Outpatient. Ambulatory client who visits a hospital or clinic for examination and treatment, as distinct from a hospitalized client.

Ovaries. Female gonads.

Overanxious disorder. Disorder of childhood characterized by excessive worry and persistent fears unrelated to any specific event; often includes somatic and sleeping problems.

Overcompensation. Type of ego-defense mechanism in which an undesirable trait is covered up by exaggerating a desirable trait.

Overloading. Subjecting an organism to excessive stress, e.g., forcing the organism to handle or "process" an excessive amount of information.

Overprotection. Shielding a child to the extent that he or she becomes too dependent on the parent.

Overt behavior. Activities that can be observed by an outsider.

Ovum. Female gamete or germ cell.

Pain disorder. Report of pain of sufficient duration and severity to cause significant life disruption in the absence of medical pathology that would explain it.

Panic. A basic emotion that involves the activation of the "fight-or-flight" response of the sympathetic nervous system.

Panic disorder. Occurrence of repeated unexpected panic attacks, often accompanied by intense anxiety about having another one.

Paradigm. Model or pattern; in research, a basic design specifying concepts considered legitimate and procedures to be used in the collection and interpretation of data.

Paranoia. Symptoms of delusions and impaired contact with reality but without the bizarreness, fragmentation, and severe personality disorganization characteristic of schizophrenia.

Paranoid personality disorder. Pervasive suspiciousness and distrust of others.

Paraphilias. Persistent sexual behavior patterns in which unusual objects, rituals, or situations are required for full sexual satisfaction.

Paraprofessional. Person who has been trained in mental health services, but not at the professional level.

Parasympathetic nervous system. Division of the autonomic nervous system that controls most of the basic metabolic functions essential for life.

Paresis. See **General paresis.**

Paresthesia. Exceptional sensations, such as tingling.

Parkinson's disease. Progressive disease characterized by a masklike, expressionless face and various neurological symptoms, such as tremors.

Passive-aggressive personality disorder. Provisional category of personality disorder in DSM-IV characterized by a pattern of passive resistance to demands in social or work situations, which may take such forms as simple resistance to fulfilling routine tasks, being sullen or argumentative, or alternating between defiance and submission.

Pathogenic. Pertaining to conditions that lead to pathology.

Pathological gambling. Progressive disorder characterized by loss of control over gambling, preoccupation with gambling and obtaining money for gambling, and irrational gambling behavior in spite of adverse consequences.

Pathology. Abnormal physical or mental condition.

PCP. Phencyclidine; developed as a tranquilizer but not marketed because of its unpredictability. Known on the street as "angel dust," this drug produces stuporous conditions and, at times, prolonged comas or psychoses.

Pedigree (family history) method. Observation of samples of relatives of each subject, or carrier of the trait or disorder in question.

Pedophilia. Paraphilia in which an adult's preferred or exclusive sexual partner is a prepubertal child.

Perception. Interpretation of sensory input.

Perceptual filtering. Processes involved in selective attention to aspects of the great mass of incoming stimuli that continually impinge on an organism.

Performance test. Test in which perceptual-motor rather than verbal content is emphasized.

Peripheral nervous system. Nerve fibers passing between the central nervous system and the sense organs, muscles, and glands.

Perseveration. Persistent continuation of a line of thought or activity once it is under way. Clinically inappropriate repetition.

Personality. Unique pattern of traits that characterizes an individual.

Personality disorders. Gradual development of inflexible and distorted personality and behavioral patterns that result in persistently maladaptive ways of perceiving, thinking, about, and relating to the world.

Personality of psychological decompensation. Inability to adapt to sustained or severe stressors.

Personality profile. Graphic summary from several tests or subtests of the same test battery or scale that shows the personality configuration of an individual or group of individuals.

Person-centered therapy. See **Client-centered therapy.**

Pervasive developmental disorders (PDD). Severely disabling conditions marked by deficits in language, perceptual, and motor development; defective reality testing; and inability to function in social situations.

Pessimistic attributional style. Cognitive style involving a tendency to make internal, stable, and global attributions for negative life events.

PET scan. See **Positron emission tomography.**

Phagocyte. Circulating white blood cell that binds to antigens and partially destroys them by engulfment.

Phallic stage. In psychoanalytic theory, the stage of psychosexual development during which genital exploration and manipulation occur.

Pharmacology. The science of drugs.

Pharmacotherapy. Treatment by means of drugs.

Phenomenological. Referring to the immediate perceiving and experiencing of an individual.

Phenotype. The observed structural and functional characteristics of a person that result from an interaction of the genotype and the environment.

Phenylketonuria (PKU). Type of mental retardation resulting from a baby's lack of a liver enzyme needed to break down phenylalanine, an amino acid found in many foods.

Phobia. Persistent and disproportionate fear of some specific object or situation that presents little or no actual danger to a person.

Physiological dependence. Type of drug dependence involving withdrawal symptoms when drug is discontinued.

Pick's disease. Form of presenile dementia.

Pineal gland. Small gland at the base of the brain that helps regulate the body's biological clock and may also pace sexual development.

Pituitary gland. Endocrine gland associated with many regulatory functions.

Placebo effect. Positive effect experienced after an inactive treatment is administered in such a way that a person thinks he or she is receiving an active treatment.

Play therapy. Use of play activities in psychotherapy with children.

Pleasure principle. Demand that an instinctual need be immediately gratified, regardless of reality or moral considerations.

Polygenic. Caused by the action of many genes together in an additive or interactive fashion.

Poor premorbid schizophrenia. See **Process schizophrenia.**

Positive reinforcer. Reinforcer that increases the probability of recurrence of a given response.

Positive-symptom schizophrenia. Schizophrenia symptoms characterized by something added to normal behavior and experience, such as marked emotional turmoil, motor agitation, delusions and hallucinations.

Positron emission tomography (PET scan). Scanning technique that measures metabolic processes to appraise how well an organ is functioning.

Posthypnotic amnesia. Subject's lack of memory for the period during which he or she was hypnotized.

Posthypnotic suggestion. Suggestion given during hypnosis to be carried out by a subject after he or she is brought out of hypnosis.

Postpartum depression. Depression occurring after childbirth.

Posttraumatic stress disorder (PTSD). Disorder that occurs following an extreme traumatic stress or in which a person shows symptoms of reexperiencing the event of avoiding reminders of the trauma, and of persistent symptoms of increased arousal.

Predisposition. Likelihood that a person will develop certain symptoms under given stress conditions.

Prefrontal lobotomy. Surgical procedure used before the advent of antipsychotic drugs in which the frontal lobes of the brain were severed from the deeper centers underlying them, resulting in permanent structural changes in the brain.

Prejudice. Emotionally toned conception favorable or unfavorable to some person, group, or idea—typically in the absence of sound evidence.

Premature ejaculation. Persistent and recurrent onset of orgasm and ejaculation with minimal sexual stimulation.

Prematurity. Birth of an infant before the end of a normal period of pregnancy.

Premorbid. Existing before the onset of mental disorder.

Prenatal. Before birth.

Presenile dementia. Mental disorders resulting from brain degeneration before old age.

Prevalence. Term that refers to the proportion of active cases in a population (in this case, a disorder) that can be identified at a given point in, or during a given period of, time.

Primary prevention. Older terminology for preventive efforts aimed at reducing the possibility of disease or disorder and fostering positive health. (See **Universal prevention.**)

Primary process thinking. Gratification of id demand by means of imagery or fantasy without the ability to undertake the realistic actions needed to meet those instinctual demands.

Primary reaction tendencies. Constitutional tendencies apparent in infancy, such as sensitivity and activity level.

Proband. In a genetic study, the original individual who evidences the trait in which the investigator is interested. Same as **index case.**

Problem checklist. Inventory used in behavioral assessment to determine an individual's fears, moods, and other problems.

Problem drinker. Behavioral term referring to one who has serious problems associated with drinking.

Process schizophrenia. Schizophrenic pattern—marked by seclusiveness, gradual lack of interest in the surrounding world, diminished emotional responsivity, and mildly inappropriate responses—that develops gradually and tends to be long-lasting; alternatively known as *poor premorbid schizophrenia* and *chronic schizophrenia.*

Prognosis. Prediction as to the probable course and outcome of a disorder.

Projection. Ego-defense mechanism that attributes a person's unacceptable motives or characteristics to others.

Projective tests. Techniques that use various ambiguous stimuli that a subject is encouraged to interpret and from which the subject's personality characteristics can be analyzed.

Prospective strategy. Method that focuses on individuals who have a higher-than-average likelihood of becoming psychologically disordered before abnormal behavior is observed.

Protective factors. Influences that modify a person's response to an environmental stressor, making it less likely that the person will experience the adverse effects of the stressor.

Prototypal approach. Approach to classifying abnormal behavior that assumes the existence of prototypes of behavior disorders that, rather than being mutually exclusive, may blend into others with which they share many characteristics.

Psilocybin. Hallucinogenic drug derived from a variety of mushrooms.

Psychedelic drugs. Drugs such as LSD that often produce hallucinations.

Psychiatric nursing. Field of nursing primarily concerned with mental disorders.

Psychiatric social worker. Professional having graduate training in social work with psychiatric specialization, typically involving a master's degree.

Psychiatrist. Medical doctor who specializes in the diagnosis and treatment of mental disorders.

Psychiatry. Field of medicine concerned with understanding, assessing, treating, and preventing mental disorders.

Psychic trauma. Any aversive experience that inflicts serious psychological damage on a person.

Psychoactive drugs. Drugs that affect mental functioning.

Psychoactive substance abuse. Pathological use of a substance resulting in potentially hazardous behavior or in continued use despite a persistent social, psychological, occupational, or health problem.

Psychoactive substance dependence. Use of a psychoactive substance to the point of a marked physiological need for increasing amounts of the substance to achieve the desired affects.

Psychoanalysis. Methods Freud used to study and treat patients.

Psychoanalytic perspective. Theory of psychopathology, initially developed by Freud, that emphasized the inner dynamics of unconscious motives.

Psychodrama. Psychotherapeutic technique in which the acting of various roles is a cardinal part.

Psychodynamic perspectives. Theories of psychopathology based on Freud's theories but modified and revised.

Psychodynamic therapy. Psychological treatment that focuses on individual personality dynamics, usually from a psychodynamic or some psychodynamically derived perspective.

Psychogenic. Of psychological origin: originating in the psychological functioning of an individual.

Psychogenic amnesia. Amnesia of psychological origin, common in initial reactions to traumatic experiences.

Psychogenic illness. Psychologically induced or maintained disease.

Psychohistory. A field of study analyzing history according to psychoanalytic principles.

Psychological autopsy. Analytical procedure used to determine whether or not death was self-inflicted and if so, why.

Psychological need. Need emerging out of environmental interactions, e.g., the need for social approval.

Psychological screening. Use of psychological procedures or tests to detect psychological problems among applicants in pre-employment evaluations.

Psychological test. Standardized procedure designed to measure a subject's performance on a specified task.

Psychomotor. Involving both psychological and physical activity.

Psychomotor retardation. Slowing down of psychological and motor functions.

Psychoneuroimmunology. Field whose focus is on the effects of stressors on the immune system.

Psychopathology. Abnormal behavior.

Psychopathy. A condition involving the features of antisocial personality disorder and such traits as lack of empathy, inflated and arrogant self-appraisal, and glib and superficial charm.

Psychopharmacology. Science of determining which drugs alleviate which disorders and why they do so.

Psychophysiologic (psychosomatic) disorders. Physical disorders in which psychological factors are believed to play a major causative role.

Psychosexual development. Freudian view of development as involving a succession of stages, each characterized by a dominant mode of achieving libidinal pleasure.

Psychosexual stages of development. According to Freudian theory, there are five stages of psychosexual development, each characterized by a dominant mode of achieving sexual pleasure: the oral stage, the anal stage, the phallic stage, the latency stage, and the genital stage.

Psychosis. Serious mental disorder involving a loss of contact with reality, as when hallucinations or delusions are present.

Psychosocial deprivation. Lack of needed stimulation and interaction during early life.

Psychosocial viewpoints. Approaches to understanding mental disorders that emphasize the importance of early experience and an awareness of social influences and psychological processes within an individual.

Psychosurgery. Brain surgery used in the past with excessive frequency in the treatment of functional mental disorders.

Psychotherapy. Treatment of mental disorders by psychological methods.

Psychotropic drugs. Drugs whose main effects are mental or behavioral in nature.

Q-sort. Personality inventory in which a subject, or a clinician, sorts a number of statements into piles according to their applicability to the subject.

Racism. Prejudice and discrimination directed toward individuals or groups because of their racial background.

Random sample. Sample drawn in such a way that each member of a population has an equal chance of being selected; hopefully representative of the population from which it is drawn.

Rape. Sexual activity that occurs under actual or threatened forcible coercion of one person by another.

Rapid cycling. A pattern of biploar disorder involving at least four manic or depressive episodes per year.

Rapport. Interpersonal relationship characterized by a spirit of cooperation, confidence, and harmony.

Rating scales. Formal structure for organizing information obtained from clinical observation and self-reports to encourage reliability and objectivity.

Rational-emotive therapy (REBT). Form of psychotherapy focusing on changing a client's maladaptive thought processes, on which maladaptive emotional responses and thus behavior are presumed to depend.

Rationalization. Ego-defense mechanism that involves the use of contrived "explanations" to conceal or disguise unworthy motives for a person's behavior.

Reaction formation. Ego-defense mechanism that prevents the awareness of or expression of unacceptable desires by an exaggerated adoption of seemingly opposite behavior.

Reactive schizophrenia. Schizophrenia pattern—marked by confusion and intense emotional turmoil—that normally develops suddenly and has identifiable precipitating stressors; alternatively known as *good premorbid schizophrenia (Type I schizophrenia),* and *acute schizophrenia.*

Reality principle. Awareness of the demands of the environment and adjustment of behavior to meet these demands.

Reality testing. Behavior aimed at testing or exploring the nature of a person's social and physical environment; often used more specifically to refer to the testing of the limits of permissiveness of the social environment.

Recessive gene. Gene that is effective only when paired with an identical gene.

Recidivism. Shift back to one's original behavior (often delinquent or criminal) after a period of treatment or rehabilitation.

Recompensation. Increase in integration or inner organization. Opposite of *decompensation.*

Recurrence. A new occurrence of a disorder after a remission period of at least two months.

Recurrent. Term used to describe a disorder pattern that tends to come and go.

Referral. Sending or recommending an individual and/or family for psychological assessment and/or treatment.

Regression. Ego-defense mechanism of retreat to an earlier developmental level involving less mature behavior and responsibility.

Rehabilitation. Use of reeducation rather than punishment to overcome behavioral deficits.

Reinforcement. The process of rewarding desired responses.

Relapse. Return of the symptoms of a disorder after a fairly short period of time.

Reliability. Degree to which a measuring device produces the same result each time it is used to measure the same thing, or when two or more different raters use it.

Remission. Marked improvement or recovery appearing in the course of a mental illness; may or may not be permanent.

REM sleep. Stage of sleep involving rapid eye movements (REM), associated with dreaming.

Representative sample. Small group selected in such a way as to be representative of the larger group from which it is drawn.

Repression. Ego-defense mechanism that prevents painful or dangerous thoughts from entering consciousness.

Resilience. The ability to adapt successfully to even very difficult circumstances.

Resistance. Second stage of responding to continuing trauma, involving finding some means to deal with the trauma and adjust to it. In psychodynamic treatment, the person's unwillingness or inability to talk about certain thoughts, motives, of experiences.

Resistance to extinction. Tendency of a conditioned response to persist despite lack of reinforcement.

Resolution. Final phase of the human sexual response, during which a person has a sense of relaxation and well-being.

Response shaping. Positive reinforcement technique used in therapy to establish by gradual approximation a response not initially in a person's behavioral repertoire.

Reticular activating system (RAS). Fibers going from the reticular formation to higher brain centers and presumably functioning as a general arousal system.

Reticular formation. Neural nuclei and fibers in the brain stem that apparently play an important role in arousing and alerting an organism and in controlling attention.

Retrograde amnesia. Loss of memory for events during a circumscribed period prior to brain injury or damage.

Retrospective research. Method of trying to uncover the probable causes of abnormal behavior by looking backward from the present.

Retrospective study. Research approach that attempts to retrace earlier events in the life of a subject.

Rigidity. Tendency to follow established coping patterns, with failure to see alternatives or extreme difficulty in changing one's established patterns.

Ritalin. Central nervous system stimulant often used to treat ADHD.

Role playing. Form of assessment in which a person is instructed to play a part, enabling a clinician to observe directly a client's behavior.

Rorschach test. Use of ten inkblot pictures to which a subject responds with associations that come to mind. Analysis of these responses enables a clinician to infer personality characteristics.

Sadism. Achievement of sexual gratification by inflicting physical or psychic pain or humiliation on a sexual partner.

Saint Vitus's dance. Name given to dancing mania (and mass hysteria) that spread from Italy to Germany and the rest of Europe in the Middle Ages.

Sample. Group on which measurements are taken; should normally be representative of the population about which an inference is to be made.

Sampling. The process of selecting a representative subgroup from a defined population of interest.

Scapegoating. Displacement of aggression onto some object, person, or group other than the source of frustration.

Schedule of reinforcement. Program of rewards for requisite behavior.

Schema. An underlying representation of knowledge that guides current processing of information and often leads to distortions in attention, memory, and comprehension.

Schizoaffective disorder. Major mood disorder in which a person also has at least two major symptoms of schizophrenia, such as hallucinations and delusions.

Schizoid personality disorder. Inability to form social relationships or express feelings and lack of interest in doing so.

Schizophrenia. Psychoses characterized by the breakdown of integrated personality functioning, withdrawal from reality, emotional blunting and distortion, and disturbances in thought and behavior.

Schizophrenia, catatonic type. Type of schizophrenia in which the central feature has pronounced motor symptoms, either of an excited or stuporous type, which sometimes make for difficulty in differentiating this condition from a psychotic mood disorder.

Schizophrenia, disorganized type. Type of schizophrenia that usually begins at an earlier age and represents a more severe disintegration of the personality than in the other types of schizophrenia.

Schizophrenia, paranoid type. Type of schizophrenia in which a person is increasingly suspicious, has severe difficulties in interpersonal relationships, and experiences absurd, illogical, and often changing delusions.

Schizophrenia, residual type. Diagnostic category used for people who have experienced a schizophrenic episode from which they have recovered sufficiently so as to not show prominent symptoms, but still manifesting some mild signs of their past disorder.

Schizophrenia, undifferentiated type. Type of schizophrenia in which a person meets the usual criteria for being schizophrenic—including (in varying combinations) delusions, hallucinations, thought disorder, and bizarre behavior—but does not clearly fit into one of the other types because of a mixed symptom picture.

Schizophreniform disorder. Category of schizophrenic-like psychoses of less than six months duration.

Schizophrenogenic. Schizophrenia-causing.

Schizotypal personality disorder. Excessive introversion, pervasive and social interpersonal deficits, cognitive and perceptual distortions, and eccentricities in communication and behavior.

Seasonal affective disorder. Mood disorder involving at least two episodes of depression in the past two years occuring at the same time of year (most commonly fall or winter), with remission also occurring at the same time of year (most commonly spring).

Secondary gain. External circumstances that tend to reinforce the maintenance of disability.

Secondary prevention. Older term for prevention techniques that typically involve emergency or crisis intervention, with efforts focused on reducing the impact, duration, or spread of a problem. (See Selective intervention.)

Secondary process thinking. Reality-oriented rational processes of the ego in dealing with the external world and the exercise of control over id demands.

Secondary reinforcer. Reinforcement provided by a stimulus that has gained reward value by being associated with a primary reinforcing stimulus.

Sedative. Drug used to reduce tension and induce relaxation and sleep.

Selective intervention. Mobilization of prevention resources to eliminate or reduce a particular type of problem (such as teenage pregnancy or alcohol or drug abuse).

Selective mutism. Condition that involves the persistent failure to speak in specific social situations and interferes with educational or social adjustment.

Self (ego). Integrating core of a personality that mediates between needs and reality.

Self-acceptance. Being satisfied with one's attributes and qualities while remaining aware of one's limitations.

Self-actualizing. Achieving one's full potentialities as a human being.

Self-concept. A person's sense of his or her own identity, worth, capabilities, and limitations.

Self-esteem. Feeling of personal worth.

Self-evaluation. Way in which an individual views the self, in terms of worth, adequacy, etc.

Self-ideal (ego-ideal). Person or "self" a person thinks he or she could and should be.

Self-identity. Individual's delineation and awareness of his or her continuing identity as a person.

Self-instructional training. Cognitive-behavioral method aimed at teaching a person to alter his or her covert behavior.

Self-monitoring. Observing and recording one's own behavior, thoughts, and feelings as they occur in various natural settings.

Self-reinforcement. Reward of self for desired or appropriate behavior.

Self-report inventory. Procedure in which a subject is asked to respond to statements in terms of their applicability to him or her.

Self-schemas. Our views of what we are, what we might become, and what is important to us.

Self-statements. A person's implicit verbalizations of what he or she is experiencing.

Senile. Pertaining to old age.

Senile dementia. Mental disorders that sometimes accompany brain degeneration in old age.

Sensate focus learning. Training to derive pleasure from touching one's partner and being touched by him or her; used in sexual therapy to enhance sexual feelings and help overcome sexual dysfunction.

Sensory deprivation. Restriction of sensory stimulation below the level required for normal functioning of the central nervous system.

Sentence-completion test. Projective technique utilizing incomplete sentences that a person is to complete, analysis of which enables a clinician to infer personality dynamics.

Separation anxiety disorder. Childhood disorder characterized by unrealistic fears, oversensitivity, self-consciousness, nightmares, and chronic anxiety.

Separation-individuation. According to Mahler, a developmental phase in which a child gains an internal representation of self as distinct from representations of other objects.

Sequelae. Symptoms remaining as the aftermath of a disorder.

Severe (disorder). Disorder of a high degree of seriousness.

Severe major depressive episode with psychotic features. Major depression involving loss of contact with reality, often in the form of delusions or hallucinations.

Sex chromosomes. Pair of chromosomes inherited by an individual that determine sex and certain other characteristics.

Sexual abuse. Sexual contact that involves physical or psychological coercion or when at least one individual cannot reasonably consent to the contact.

Sexual aversion disorder. Sexual dysfunction in which a person shows extreme aversion to, and avoidance of, all genital sexual contact with a partner.

Sexual dysfunction. Impairment either in the desire for sexual gratification or in the ability to achieve it.

Shaping. Form of instrumental conditioning; at first, all responses resembling the desired one are reinforced, then only the closest approximations, until finally the desired response is attained.

Shared psychotic disorder. Psychosis in which two or more people develop persistent, interlocking delusional ideas. Also known as *folie á deux.*

Sheltered workshops. Workshops where mentally retarded or otherwise handicapped persons can engage in constructive work in the community.

Short-term crisis therapy. Brief treatment that focuses on the immediate problem with which an individual or family is having difficulty.

Siblings. Offspring of the same parents.

Sick role. Protected role provided by society via the medical model for a person suffering from severe physical or mental disorder.

Signs. Objective observations of a patient's physical or mental disorder by a diagnostician.

Significant others. In interpersonal theory, parents or others on whom an infant is dependent for meeting all physical and psychological needs.

Simple phobia. See **Specific phobia.**

Simple tension headaches. Common headaches in which stress leads to contraction of the muscles surrounding the skull; these contractions, in turn, result in vascular constrictions that cause headache pain.

Situational test. Test that measures performance in a simulated life situation.

Sleepwalking disorder. Disorder of childhood that involves repeated episodes at leaving the bed and walking around without being conscious of the experience or remembering it later. Also known as *somnambulism.*

Social exchange view. Model of interpersonal relationships based on the premise that such relationships are formed for mutual need gratification.

Social introversion. Trait characterized by shy, withdrawn, and inhibited behavior.

Socialization. Process by which a child acquires the values and impulse controls deemed appropriate by his or her culture.

Social-learning programs. Behavioral programs using learning techniques, especially token economies, to help patients assume more responsibility for their own behavior.

Social norms. Group standards concerning behaviors viewed as acceptable or unacceptable.

Social pathology. Abnormal patterns of social organization, attitudes, or behavior; undesirable social conditions that tend to produce individual pathology.

Social phobias. Fear of situations in which a person might be exposed to the scrutiny of others and fear of acting in a humiliating or embarrassing way.

Social recovery. Ability to manage independently as an economically effective and interpersonally connected member of society.

Social role. Behavior expected of a person occupying a given position in a group.

"Social" self. Facade a person displays to others as contrasted with the private self.

Social work. Applied offshoot of sociology concerned with the analysis of social environments and providing services that assist the adjustment of a client in both family and community settings.

Social worker. Person in a mental health field with a master's degree in social work (MSW) plus supervised training in clinical or social service agencies.

Sociocultural viewpoint. Pertaining to broad social conditions that influence the development and/or behavior of individuals and groups.

Socioeconomic status. Position on social and economic scale in community; determined largely by income and occupational level.

Sociogenic. Having its roots in sociocultural conditions.

Sociopathic personality. See **Antisocial personality disorder.**

Sodium pentothal. Barbiturate drug sometimes used in psychotherapy to produce a state of relaxation and suggestibility.

Somatic. Pertaining to the body.

Somatic weakness. Special vulnerability of given organ systems to stress.

Somatization disorder. Multiple complaints of physical ailments over a long period, beginning before age 30, that are inadequately explained by independent findings of physical illness or injury and that lead to medical treatment or to significant life impairment.

Somatoform disorders. Conditions involving physical complaints or disabilities that occur without any evidence of physical pathology to account for them.

Somnambulism. See **Sleepwalking disorder.**

Spasm. Intense, involuntary, usually painful contraction of a muscle or group of muscles.

Spasticity. Marked hypertonicity or continual overcontraction of muscles, causing stiffness, awkwardness, and motor incoordination.

Specific learning disorders. Developmental disorders involving deficits in language, speech, mathematical, or motor skills.

Specific phobia. Persistent or disproportionate fears of various objects, places, or situations, such as fears of other species (snakes, spiders) or aspects of the environment (high places, water) or situations (airplanes or elevators).

Sperm. Male gamete or germ cell.

Split-brain research. Research associated with split-brain surgery, which cuts off the transmission of information from one cerebral hemisphere to the other, through severing the corpus callosum.

Spontaneous recovery. The return of a learned response at some time after extinction has occurred.

Stage of exhaustion. Third and final stage in the general adaptation syndrome, in which an organism is no longer able to resist continuing stress; may result in death.

Stage of resistance. Second stage of the general adaptation syndrome.

Standardization. Procedure for establishing the expected performance range on a test.

Stanford-Binet. Standardized intelligence test for children.

Startle reaction. Sudden involuntary motor reaction to intense unexpected stimuli; may result from mild stimuli if a person is hypersensitive.

Statutory rape. Sexual intercourse with a minor.

Steady states (homeostasis). Tendency of an organism to maintain conditions making possible a constant level or physiological functioning.

Stereotype. Generalized notion of how people of a given race, religion, or other group will appear, think, feel, or act.

Stereotypy. Persistent and inappropriate repetition of phrases, gestures, or acts.

Stimulants. Drugs that tend to increase feelings of alertness, reduce feelings of fatigue, and enable a person to stay awake over sustained periods of time.

Stimulus generalization. Spread of a conditioned response to some stimulus similar to, but not identical with, the conditioned stimulus.

Stress. Effects created within an organism by the application of a stressor.

Stress-inoculation therapy. Type of self-instructional training focused on altering self-statements that a person routinely makes in stress-producing situations.

Stress-inoculation training. Preventive strategy that prepares people to tolerate an anticipated threat by changing the things they say to themselves before the crisis.

Stressors. Adjustive demands that require coping behavior on the part of an individual or group.

Stress tolerance. A person's ability to withstand stress without becoming seriously impaired.

Stroke. See **Cerebrovascular accident.**

Structural family therapy. Treatment of an entire family by analysis of interaction among family members.

Stupor. Condition of lethargy and unresponsiveness, with partial or complete unconsciousness.

Sublimation. Ego-defense mechanism that channels frustrated sexual energy into substitutive activities.

Substance abuse. Maladaptive pattern of substance use manifested by recurrent and significant adverse consequences related to the use of the substance.

Substance dependence. Severe form of substance use disorder involving physiological dependence on the substance, tolerance, withdrawal, and compulsive drug taking.

Substance-related disorders. Patterns of maladaptive behavior centered on the regular use of a substance, such as drugs or alcohol.

Substitution. Acceptance of substitute goals or satisfactions in place of those originally sought after or desired.

Successive approximation. See **Shaping.**

Sufficent cause. A condition that guarantees the occurrence of a disorder.

Suicide. Taking one's own life.

Suicidology. Study of the causes and prevention of suicide.

Superego. Conscience; ethical or moral dimensions (attitudes) of personality.

Suppression. Conscious forcing of desires or thoughts out of consciousness; conscious inhibition of desires or impulses.

Surrogate. Substitute for another person, as parent or mate.

Symbol. Image, word, object, or activity that is used to represent something else.

Symbolism. Representation of one idea or object by another.

Sympathetic division. Division of the autonomic nervous system that is active in emergency conditions of extreme cold, violent effort, and emotions.

Symptoms. Patient's subjective description of a physical or mental disorder.

Synapse. Site of communication from the axon of one neuron to the dendrites or cell body of another neuron—a tiny filled space between neurons.

Syndrome. Group or pattern of symptoms that occur together in a disorder and represent the typical picture of the disorder.

System. Assemblage of interdependent parts, living or nonliving.

Systematic desensitization. Behavior therapy technique for extinguishing negatively reinforced behavior by teaching a person to relax or behave in some other way that is inconsistent with anxiety while in the presence of the anxiety-producing stimulus.

Tachycardia. Rapid heartbeat.

Tactual hallucinations. Hallucinations involving the sense of touch.

Tarantism. Dancing mania that occurred in Italy in the thirteenth century.

Tarasoff decision. Ruling by a California court (1974) that a therapist has a duty to warn a prospective victim of an explicit threat by a client in therapy.

Tardive dyskinesia. Neurological disorder resulting from excessive use of antipsychotic drugs. Side effects can occur months to years after treatment has been initiated or has stopped. The symptoms involve involuntary movements of the tongue, lips, jaw, and extremities.

Task-oriented response. Making changes in one's self, one's surroundings, or both, depending on the situation.

Tay-Sachs disease. Genetic disorder of lipoid metabolism usually resulting in death by age three.

T-cell. Generic type of lymphocyte crucial in immune functioning and having several subtypes that support and regulate the entire immune reaction.

Telepathy. Communication from one person to another without use of any known sense organs.

Temperament. Pattern of emotional and arousal responses and characteristic ways of self-regulation that are considered to be primarily hereditary or constitutional.

Temporal lobe. Portion of cerebrum located in front of the occipital lobe and separated from frontal and parietal lobes by the fissure of Sylvius.

Tension. Condition arising from the mobilization of psychobiological resources to meet a threat; physically, involves an increase in muscle tone and other emergency changes; psychologically, is characterized by feelings of strain, uneasiness, and anxiety.

Tertiary prevention. Older term for preventive techniques focusing on reducing long-term consequences of disorders or serious problems. (See Indicated prevention).

Testes. Male reproductive glands or gonads.

Testosterone. Male sex hormone.

Test reliability. Consistency with which a test measures a given trait on repeated administrations of the test to given subjects.

Test validity. Degree to which a test actually measures what it was designed to measure.

Thematic Apperception Test (TAT). Use of a series of simple pictures about which a subject is instructed to make up stories. Analysis of the stories gives a clinician clues about the person's conflicts, traits, personality dynamics, and the like.

Therapeutic. Pertaining to treatment or healing.

Therapeutic community. Hospital environment used for therapeutic purposes.

Therapy. Treatment; application of various treatment techniques.

Thyroid. Endocrine gland located in the neck that influences body metabolism, rate of physical growth, and development of intelligence.

Thyroxin. Hormone secreted by the thyroid glands.

Tic. Persistent, intermittent muscle twitch or spasm, usually limited to a localized muscle group, often of the facial muscles.

Token economies. Reinforcement techniques often used in hospital or institutional settings in which patients are rewarded for socially constructive behaviors with tokens that can then be exchanged for desired objects or activities.

Tolerance. Need for increased amounts of a substance to achieve the desired effects.

Tourette's syndrome. Extreme tic disorder involving uncontrollable multiple motor and vocal patterns.

Toxic. Poisonous.

Toxicity. Poisonous nature of a substance.

Trait. Characteristic of a person that can be observed or measured.

Trance. Sleeplike state in which the range of consciousness is limited and voluntary activities are suspended; a deep hypnotic state.

Tranquilizers. Drugs used for reduction of psychotic symptoms and/or reduction of anxiety and tension. See also **Major tranquilizers** and **Minor tranquilizers.**

Transference. In psychodynamic therapy, process whereby clients project attitudes and feelings that they have had for a parent or others close to them onto the therapist.

Transsexualism. Individuals who identify with members of the opposite sex (as opposed to acceptance of their own biological sex), and who strongly desire to (and often do) change their sex. In most cases this is gender identity disorder in adults.

Transvestic fetishism. Achievement of sexual arousal and satisfaction by dressing as a member of the opposite sex.

Trauma. Severe psychological or physiological stressor.

Traumatic. Pertaining to a wound or injury, or to psychic shock.

Traumatic brain injuries (TBI). Brain damage resulting from motor vehicle crashes, bullets or other objects entering the brain, and other severe impacts to the head.

Traumatic childhood abuse. Mistreatment in childhood severe enough to cause psychological damage.

Treatment contract. Explicit arrangement between a therapist and a client designed to bring about specific behavioral changes.

Tremor. Repeated fine spastic movement.

Twin method. The use of identical and nonidentical twins to study genetic influences on abnormal behavior.

Type A behavior pattern. Excessive competitive drive even when it is unnecessary, impatience or time urgency, and hostility.

Type I schizophrenia. Psychotic behavior of the positive syndrome variety thought to involve chiefly temporolimbic brain structures.

Type II schizophrenia. Psychotic behavior of the negative syndrome variety thought to involve chiefly frontal brain structures.

Unconscious, The. In psychoanalytic theory, a major portion of the mind is a hidden mass of instincts, impulses, memories that is not easily available to conscious awareness and yet plays an important role in behavior.

Underarousal. Inadequate physiological response to a given stimulus.

Undoing. Ego-defense mechanism of atoning for or magically trying to dispel unacceptable desires or acts.

Unipolar disorders. Mood disorders in which a person expereinces only depressive episodes, as opposed to bipolar disorder, in which both manic and depressive episodes occur.

Universal prevention. The tasks of altering conditions that cause or contribute to mental disorders (risk factors) and establishing conditions that foster positive mental health (protective factors).

Vaginismus. Involuntary spasm of the muscles at the entrance to the vagina that prevents penetration and sexual intercourse.

Validity. Extent to which a measuring instrument actually measures what it purports to measure.

Variable. Characteristic or property that may assume any one of a set of different qualities or quantities.

Vascular dementia (VAD). A brain disorder in which a series of circumscribed cerebral infarcts (small strokes) destroy neurons, leading to brain atrophy and behavioral impairments that ultimately mimic those of DAT.

Vasomotor. Pertaining to the walls of the blood vessels.

Vegetative. Withdrawn or deteriorated to the point of leading a passive, vegetable-like existence.

Verbal test. Test in which a subject's ability to understand and use words and concepts is important in making the required responses.

Vertigo. Dizziness.

Virilism. Accentuation of masculine secondary sex characteristsics, especially in a woman or young boy, caused by hormonal imbalance.

Viscera. Internal organs.

Voyeurism. Achievement of sexual pleasure through clandestine "peeping," usually watching other people disrobe and/or engage in sexual activities.

Vulnerabilities. Factors rendering a person susceptible to behaving abnormally.

Wechsler Intelligence Scale for Children (WISC). Standardized intelligence test for children.

Withdrawal. Intellectual, emotional, or physical retreat.

Withdrawal symptoms. Physical symptoms such as sweating, tremors, and tension that accompany abstinence from a drug.

Word salad. Jumbled or incoherent use of words by psychotic or disoriented individuals.

X chromosome. Sex-determining chromosome: all female gametes contain X chromosomes, and if the fertilized ovum has also received an X chromosome from its father it will be female.

XYY syndrome. Chromosomal anomaly in males (presence of an extra Y chromosome) possibly related to impulsive behavior.

Y chromosome. Sex-determining chromosome found in half of the total number of male gametes; uniting with X chromosome provided by a female produces a male offspring.

Zygote. Fertilized egg cell formed by the union of male and female gametes.

REFERENCES

JOURNAL ABBREVIATIONS

Acta Neurol. Scandin.—*Acta Neurologica Scandinavica*
Acta Psychiatr. Scandin.—*Acta Psychiatrica Scandinavica*
Aggr. Behav.—*Aggressive Behavior*
Alcoholism: Clin. Exper. Res.—*Alcoholism: Clinical and Experimental Research*
Am. J. Community Psychol.—*American Journal of Community Psychology*
Amer. J. Clin. Nutri.—*American Journal of Clinical Nutrition*
Amer. J. Drug Alcoh. Abuse—*American Journal of Drug and Alcohol Abuse*
Amer. J. Epidemiol.—*American Journal of Epidemiology*
Amer. J. Geriatr. Psychiat.—*American Journal of Geriatric Psychiatry*
Amer. J. Med. Genet.—*American Journal of Medical Genetics*
Amer. J. Med. Sci.—*American Journal of the Medical Sciences*
Amer. J. Ment. Def.—*American Journal of Mental Deficiency*
Amer. J. Ment. Retard.—*American Journal of Mental Retardation*
Amer. J. Nurs.—*American Journal of Nursing*
Amer. J. Occup. Ther.—*American Journal of Occupational Therapy*
Amer. J. Orthopsychiat.—*American Journal of Orthopsychiatry*
Amer. J. Psychiat.—*American Journal of Psychiatry*
Amer. J. Psychoanal.—*American Journal of Psychoanalysis*
Amer. J. Psychother.—*American Journal of Psychotherapy*
Amer. J. Pub. Hlth.—*American Journal of Public Health*
Amer. Psychol.—*American Psychologist*
Ann. Behav. Med.—*Annals of Behavioral Medicine*
Ann. Int. Med.—*Annals of Internal Medicine*
Ann. Neurol.—*Annals of Neurology*
Ann. NY Acad. Sci.—*Annals of the New York Academy of Science*
Ann. Sex Res.—*Annals of Sex Research*
Annu. Rev. Med.—*Annual Review of Medicine*
Annu. Rev. Psychol.—*Annual Review of Psychology*
Annu. Rev. Sex Res.—*Annual Review of Sex Research*
App. Prev. Psychol.—*Applied and Preventive Psychology*
Arch. Clin. Neuropsychol.—*Archives of Clinical Neuropsychology*
Arch. Gen. Psychiat.—*Archives of General Psychology*
Arch. Gerontol. Geriatr.—*Archives of Gerontology and Geriatrics*
Arch. Int. Med.—*Archives of Internal Medicine*
Arch. Neurol.—*Archives of Neurology*
Arch. Sex. Behav.—*Archives of Sexual Behavior*
Austral. N.Z. P. Psychiatr.—*Australian and New Zealand Journal of Psychiatry*
Behav. Gen.—*Behavior Genetics*
Behav. Mod.—*Behavior Modification*
Behav. Res. Ther.—*Behavior Research and Therapy*
Behav. Ther.—*Behavior Therapy*
Behav. Today—*Behavior Today*
Biol. Psychiat.—*Biological Psychiatry*
Brit. J. Addict.—*ritish Journal of Addiction*
Brit. J. Clin. Psychol.—*British Journal of Clinical Psychology*
Brit. J. Dev. Psychol.—*British Journal of Developmental Psychology*
Brit. J. Learn. Dis.—*British Journal of Learning Disabilities*
Brit. J. Psychiat.—*British Journal of Psychiatry*
Brit. Med. J.—*MDBRBritish Medical Journal*
Bull. Amer. Acad. Psychiatr. Law—*Bulletin of the American Academy of Psychiatry and Law*

Canad. J. Behav. Sci.—*Canadian Journal of Behavioral Science*
Canad. J. Psychiat.—*Canadian Journal of Psychiatry*
Child Ab. Negl.—*Child Abuse and Neglect*
Child Adoles. Psychiat.—*Child and Adolescent Psychiatry*
Child Adoles. Psychiatr. Clin. N. Amer.—*Child and Adolescent Psychiatric Clinics of North America*
Child Develop.—*Child Development*
Child Psychiat. Human Devel.—*Child Psychiatry and Human Development*
Clin. Neuropharmac.—*Clinical Neuropharmacology*
Clin. Pediat.—*Clinical Pediatrics*
Clin. Pharm.—*Clinical Pharmacy*
Clin. Psychol. Rev.—*Clinical Psychology Review*
Clin. Psychol. Sci. Prac.—*Clinical Psychology: Science and Practice*
Clin. Psychol.—*The Clinical Psychologist*
Clin. Res. Dig. Suppl. Bull.—
Cog. Ther. Res.—*Cognitive Therapy and Research*
Coll. Stud. J.—*College Student Journal*
Comm. Ment. Hlth. J.—*Community Mental Health Journal*
Compr. Psychiat.—*Comprehensive Psychiatry*
Contemp. Psychol.—*Contemorary Psychology*
Counsel. Psychol.—*Counseling Psychologist*
Crim. Just. Behav.—*Criminal Justice and Behavior*
Cult. Med. Psychiatr.—*Culture, Medicine, and Psychiatry*
Cultur. Psychiatr.—*Cultural Psychiatry*
Curr. Dis. Psychol. Sci.—*Current Directions in Psychological Science*
Develop. Med. Child Neurol.—*Developmental Medicine & Child Neurology*
Develop. Psychol.—*Developmental Psychology*
Develop. Psychopath.—*Development and Psychopathology*
Deviant Behav.—*Deviant Behavior*
Dis. Nerv. Sys.—*Diseases of the Nervous System*
Eat. Dis.—*Eating Disorders*
Eur. Arch. Psychiat. Clin. Neurosci.—*European Archives of Psychiatry and Clinical Neuroscience*
Except.—*Exceptionality*
Exper. Neurol.—*Experimental Neurology*
Fam. Hlth.—*Family Health*
Fam. Plann. Perspect.—*Family Planning Perspectives*
Fam. Process—*Family Process*
Fed. Proc.—*Federal proceedings*
Neurobiol. Aging—*neurobiology of Aging*
Neurosci. Lett.—*Neuroscience Letters*
New Engl. J. Med.—*New England Journal of Medicine*
Hlth. Psychol.—*Health Psychology*
Hosp. Comm. Psychiat.—*Hospital and Community Psychiatry*
Human Behav.—*Human Behavior*
Human Develop.—*Human Development*
Human Genet.—*Human Genetics*
Inf. Behav. Develop.—*Infant Behavior and Development*
Int. J. Clin. Exp. Hypn.—*International Journal of Clinical and Experimental Hypnosis*
Int. J. Eat. Dis.—*International Journal of Eating Disorders*
Int. J. Epidemiol.—*International Journal of Epidemiology*
Int. Rev. Psychiat.—*International Review of Psychiatry*
Integr. Psychiat.—*Integrative psychiatry*
Inter. J. Addict.—*International Journal of Addictions*
Inter. J. Ment. Hlth.—*International Journal of Mental Health*
Inter. J. Psychiat.—*International Journal of Psychiatry*
Inter. J. Psychoanal.—*International Journal of Psychoanalysis*

Inter. J. Soc. Psychiat.—*International Journal of Social Psychiatry*
J. Abn. Psychol.—*Journal of Abnormal Psychology*
J. Abnorm. Child Psychol.—*Journal of Abnormal Child Psychology*
J. Abnorm. Soc. Psychol.—*Journal of Abnormal and Social Psychology*
J. Affect. Dis.—*Journal of Affective Disorders*
JAMA—*Journal of the American Medical Association*
J. Amer. Acad. Adoles. Psychiat.—*Journal of the American Academy of Adolescent Psychiatry*
J. Amer. Acad. Child Adoles. Psychiat.—*Journal of the American Academy of Child and Adolescent Psychiatry*
J. Amer. Acad. Child Psychiat.—*Journal of the American Academy of Child Psychiatry*
J. Amer. Coll. Hlth.—*Journal of American College Health*
J. Amer. Geriat. Soc.—*Journal of the American Geriatrics Society*
J. Anxiety Dis.—*Journal of Anxiety Disorders*
J. Appl. Beh. Anal.—*Journal of Applied Behavior Analysis*
J. Autism Devel. Dis.—*Journal of Autism and Developmental Disorders*
J. Behav. Assess.—*Journal of Behavioral Assessment*
J. Behav. Med.—*Journal of Behavioral Medicine*
J. Behav. Ther. Exper. Psychiat.—*Journal of Behavior Therapy and Experimental Psychiatry*
J. Chem. Depen. Treat.—*Journal of Chemical Dependency Treatment*
J. Child Fam. Stud.—*Journal of Child and Family Studies*
J. Child Psychol. Psychiat.—*Journal of Child Psychology and Psychiatry*
J. Child Clin. Psychol.—*Journal of Child Clinical Psychology*
J. Clin. Geropsychol.—*Journal of Clinical Geropsychology*
J. Clin. Psychiat.—*Journal of Clinical Psychiatry*
J. Clin. Psychol. in Med. Set.—*Journal of Clinical Psychology in Medical Settings*
J. Clin. Psychol.—*Journal of Clinical Psychology*
J. Clin. Psychopharm.—*Journal of Clinical Psychopharmacology*
J. Cog. Neurosci.—*Journal of Cognitive Neuroscience*
J. Cog. Rehab.—*Journal of Cognitive Rehabilitation*
J. Coll. Stud. Psychother.—*Journal of College Student Psychotherapy*
J. Comm. Psychol.—*Journal of Community Psychology*
J. Cons. Clin. Psychol.—*Journal of Consulting and Clinical Psychology*
J. Couns. Psychol.—*Journal of Counseling Psychology*
J. Edu. Psychol.—*Journal of Educational Psychology*
J. Exper. Psychol.—*Journal of Experimental Psychology*
J. Fam. Pract.—*Journal of Family Practice*
J. Gen. Psychol.—*Journal of General Psychology*
J. Gerontol.—*Journal of Gerontology*
J. Head Trauma Rehab.—*Journal of Head Trauma Rehabilitation*
J. His. Behav. Sci.—*Journal of the History of the Behavioral Sciences*
J. Int. Neuropsycholog. Soc.—*Journal of the International Neuropsychological Society*
J. Intell. Develop. Dis.—*Journal of Intellectual Developmental Disability*
J. Intell. Dis. Res.—*Journal of Intellectual Disability Research*
J. Interpers. Violen.—*Journal of Interpersonal Violence*
J. Learn. Dis.—*Journal of Learning Disabilities*
J. Marit. Fam. Ther.—*Journal of Marital and Family Therapy*
J. Marr. Fam.—*Journal of Marriage and the Family*

J. Ment. Deficien. Res.—*Journal of Mental Deficiency Research*

J. Ment. Hlth. Couns.—*Journal of Mental Health Counseling*

J. Ment. Sci.—*Journal of Mental Science*

J. Nerv. Ment. Dis.—*Journal of Nervous and Mental Diseases*

J. Neurol. Neurosurg. Psychiat.—*Journal of Neurology, Neurosurgery, & Psychiatry*

J. Neuropsychiat. Clin. Neurosci.—*Journal of Neuropsychiatry and Clinical Neurosciences*

J. Off. Rehab.—*Journal of Offender Rehabilitation*

J. Pediat. Psychol.—*Journal of Pediatric Psychology*

J. Pers. Assess.—*Journal of Personality Assesment*

J. Pers. Soc. Psychol.—*Journal of Personality and Social Psychology*

J. Personal. Dis.—*Journal of Personality Disorders*

J. Personal.—*Journal of Primary Prevention*

J. Psychiat. Res.—*Journal of Psychiatric Research*

J. Psychiat.—*Journal of Psychiatry*

J. Psychoact. Drugs—*Journal of Psychoactive Drugs*

J. Psychohist.—*Journal of Psychohistory*

J. Psychol.—*Journal of Psychology*

J. Psychopath. Behav. Assess.—*Journal of Psychopathology and Behavioral Assessment*

J. Psychopharm.—*Journal of Psychopharmacology*

J. Psychosom. Res.—*Journal of Psychosomatic Research*

J. Sex Marit. Ther.—*Journal of Sex and Marital Therapy*

J. Sex. Res.—*Journal of Sex Research*

J. Speech Hear. Dis.—*Journal of Speech and Hearing Disorders*

J. Stud. Alcoh.—*Journal of Studies on Alcohol*

J. Subst. Abuse—*Journal of Substance Abuvs*

J. Trauma. Stress.—*Journal of Traumatic Stress*

Monogr. Soc. Res. Child. Develop.—*Monographs of the society for Research in Child Development*

N. Engl. J. Med.—*New England Journal of Medicine*

Personal. Indiv. Diff.—*Personality and Individual Differences*

Personal. Soc. Psychol. Bull.—*Personality and Social Psychology Bulletin*

Personal. Soc. Psychol. Rev.—*Personality and Social psychology Review*

Profess. Psychol.—*Professional Psychology*

Prog. Neuropsychopharmacol. Biol. Psychiatry—*Progress in Neuropsychopharmacology & Biological Psychiatry*

Psych. Today—*Psychology Today*

Psychiat. Ann.—*Psychiatric Annals*

Psychiat. Clin. N. Amer.—*Psychiatric Clinics of North America*

Psychiat. News—*Psychiatric News*

Psychiat. Res.—*Psychiatric Research*

Psychiatr. Q.—*Psychiatric Quarterly*

Psychiatr. Serv.—*Psychiatric Services*

Psychol. Aging—*Psychology and Aging*

Psychol. Assess.—*Psychological Assessment*

Psychol. Bull.—*Psychological Bulletin*

Psychol. Inq.—*Psychological Inquiry*

Psychol. Med.—*Psychological Medicine*

Psychol. Meth.—*Psychological Methods*

Psychol. Rep.—*Psychological Reports*

Psychol. Rev.—*Psychological Review*

Psychol. Sci.—*Psychological Science*

Psychopharm. Bull.—*Psychopharmacology Bulletin*

Psychosom. Med.—*Psychosomatic Medicine*

Psychother. Psychosom.—*Psychotherapy and Psychosomatics*

Q. J. Exp. Psych. [A]—*Quarterly Journal of Experimental Psychology: [A] Human Experimental Psychology*

Schizo. Bull.—*Schizophrenia Bulletin*

School Psychol. Rev.—*School Psychology Review*

Sci. News—*Science News*

Scientif. Amer.—*Scientific American*

Soc. Psychiat. Psychiatr. Epidemiol.—*Social Psychiatry and Psychiatric Epidemiology*

Soc. Psychiat.—*Social Psychiatry*

Soc. Sci. Med.—*Social Science and Medicine*

Transcult. Psychiat.—*Transcultural Psychiatry*

Abel, E. L. (1988). Fetal alcohol syndrome in families. *Neurotoxicology and Teratology, 10,* 1–2.

Abel, E. L. (1990). *Fetal alcohol syndrome.* New York: Plenum.

Abel, E. L. (1998). Fetal alcohol syndrome: The "American Paradox." *Alcohol & Alcoholism, 33*(3), 195–201.

Abel, E. L., Martier, Kruger, M., Ager, J., & Sokol, R. J. (1993). Ratings of fetal alcohol syndrome facial features by medical providers and biomedical scientists. *Alcoholism: Clin. Exper. Res., 17*(3), 717–721.

Abel, G. G., Barlow, D. H., Blanchard, E. B., & Guild, D. (1977). The components of rapists' sexual arousal. *Arch. Gen. Psychiat., 34,* 895–903.

Abel, G. G., Blanchard, E. B., Becker, J. V., & Djenderejian, A. (1978). Differentiating sexual aggressives with penile measures. *Crim. Just. Behav., 5,* 315–32.

Abel, G. G., & Rouleau, J. L. (1990). The nature and extent of sexual assault. In W. L. Marshall, D. R. Laws, & H. E. Barbaree (Eds.), *Handbook of sexual assault: Issues, theories, and treatment of the offender.* (pp. 9–22). New York: Plenum.

Abou-Saleh, M. T. (1992). Lithium. In E. S. Paykel (Ed.), *Handbook of affective disorders* (2nd ed.). New York: Guilford.

Abraham, H. D., & Wolf, E. (1988). Visual function in past users of LSD: Psychophysical findings. *J. Abn. Psychol., 97,* 443–47.

Abraham, K. (1960a). Notes on the psychoanalytic treatment of manic depressive insanity and allied conditions. In *Selected papers on psychoanalysis.* New York: Basic Books. (Original work published 1911.)

Abraham, K. (1960b). The first pregenital stage of libido. In *Selected papers on psychoanalysis.* New York: Basic Books. (Original work published 1916.)

Abrahamson, D. J., Barlow, D. H., & Abrahamson, L. S. (1989). Differential effects of performance demand and distraction on sexually functional and dysfunctional males. *J. Abn. Psychol., 98,* 241–47.

Abrahamson, D. J., Barlow, D. H., Sakheim, D. K., Beck, J. G., & Athanasiou, R. (1985). Effects of distraction on sexual responding in functional and dysfunctional men. *Behav. Ther., 16,* 503–15.

Abramowitz, A. J., Eckstrand, D., O'Leary, S. G., & Dulcan, M. K. (1992). Children's responses to stimulant medication and two intensities of a behavioral intervention. Special issue: Treatment of children with attention deficit hyperactivity disorder (ADHD). *Behav. Mod., 16,* 193–202.

Abrams, R. (1988). *Electroconvulsive treatment: It apparently works, but how and at what risks are not yet clear.* New York: Oxford University Press.

Abrams, R. (1992). *Electroconvulsive therapy.* Oxford: Oxford University Press.

Abrams, R. (1994). The treatment that will not die. *Psychiat. Clin. N. Amer., 17,* 525–30.

Abrams, R. (1997) On convulsive therapies.

Abrams, R. C., & Horowitz, S. V. (1996). Personality disorders after age 50: A meta-analysis. *J. Personal. Dis., 10*(3), 271–81.

Abramson, L., Alloy, L., & Metalsky, G. (1995). Hopelessness depression. In G. Buchanan & M. Seligman (Eds.), *Explanatory style.* (pp. 113–134). Hillsdale, NJ: Erlbaum.

Abramson, L. Y., Metalsky, G. I., & Alloy, L. B. (1989). Hopelessness depression: A theory-based subtype of depression. *Psychol. Rev., 96,* 358–372.

Abramson, L. Y., & Seligman, M. E. P. (1977). Modeling psychopathology in the laboratory: History and rationale. In M. Maser & M. E. P. Seligman (Eds.), *Psychopathology: Experimental models.* San Francisco: Freeman.

Abramson, L. Y., Seligman, M. E. P., & Teasdale, J. D. (1978). Learned helplessness in humans: Critique and reformulation. *J. Abn. Psychol., 87,* 49–74.

Abramson, R. K., Wright, H. H., Cuccaro, M. L., & Lawrence, L. G. (1992). Biological liability in families with autism. *J. Amer. Acad. Child Adoles. Psychiat., 31,* 370–71.

Abstract. (1997). *Means v. Baltimore County* [Abstract], Court of Appeals of Maryland, 344 Md 661 2d 1238.

Achenbach, T. M. (1985). *Assessment and taxonomy of child and adolescent psychopathology.* Beverly Hills, CA: Sage.

Achenbach, T. M., & Edelbrock, C. S. (1983). *Manual for the child behavior checklist and revised child behavior profile.* Burlington, VT: University of Vermont.

Achenbach, T. M., & Howell, C. T. (1993). Are American children getting worse? A 13-year comparison. *J. Amer. Acad. Child Adoles. Psychiat., 32,* 1145–54.

Achenbach, T. M., Howell, C. T., & McConaughy, S. H. (1995). Six-year predictors of problems in a national sample of children and youth: II. Signs of disturbance. *J. Amer. Acad. Child Adoles. Psychiat., 34*(4), 488–98.

Achenbach, T. M., Howell, C. T., McConaughy, S. H., Stanger, C., et al. (1995). Six-year predictors of problems in a national sample of children and youth: I. Cross-informant syndromes. *J. Amer. Acad. Child Adoles. Psychiat. 34*(3), 336–47.

Achenbach, T. M., & McConaughy, S. H. (1985). *Child interview checklist self-report form; Child interview checklist-observation form.* Burlington, VT: University of Vermont.

Achenbach, T. M., & Weisz, J. R. (1975). Impulsivity-reflectivity and cognitive development in preschoolers: A longitudinal analysis of developmental and trait variance. *Develop. Psychol., 11,* 413–14.

Acierno, R., et al. (1994). Review of the validation and dissemination of eye-movement desensitization and reprocessing: A scientific and ethical dilemma. *Clin. Psychol. Rev., 14,* 287–99.

Ackerson, J., Scogin, F., McKendree–Smith, N., & Lyman, R. (1998). Cognitive bibliotherapy for mild and moderate adolescent depressive symptomatology. *J. Cons. Clin. Psychol., 66*(4), 685–90.

ACSF Investigators. (1992). AIDS and sexual behaviour in France. *Nature, 360,* 407–9.

Adam, B. S., Everett, B. L., & O'Neal, E. (1992). PTSD in physically and sexually abused psychiatrically hospitalized children. *Child Psychiat. Human Develop., 23,* 3–8.

Adams, D. M., & Overholser, J. C. (1992). Suicidal behavior and history of substance abuse. *Amer. J. Drug Alcoh. Abuse, 18,* 343–54.

Adams, H. E., & McAnulty, R. D. (1993). Sexual disorders: The paraphilias. In P. Sutker & H. Adams (Eds.), *Comprehensive handbook of psychopathology.* (pp. 563–79). New York: Plenum.

Adams, M. A., & Ferraro, F. R. (1997). Acquired immunodeficiency syndrome dementia complex. *J. Clin. Psychol., 53*(7), 767–78.

Adams, M. S., & Neel, J. V. (1967). Children of incest. *Pediatrics, 40,* 55–62.

Adelman, S. A., & Weiss, R. D. (1989). What is therapeutic about inpatient alcoholism treatment? *Hosp. Comm. Psychiat., 40*(5), 515–19.

Ader, R., & Cohen, N. (1984). Behavior and the immune system. In W. D. Gentry (Ed.), *Handbook of behavioral medicine.* (pp. 117–73). New York: Guilford.

Adler, A. (1943). Neuropsychiatric complications in victims of Boston's Coconut Grove disaster. *JAMA, 123,* 1098–1101.

Adler, T. (1994). Alzheimer's causes unique cell death. *Sci. News, 146*(13), 198.

Adrien, J. L., Perrot, A., Sauvage, D., & Leddet, I. (1992). Early symptoms in autism from family home movies: Evaluation and comparison between 1st and 2nd year of life using I.B.S.E. scale. *Acta Paedopsychiatrica International Journal of Child and Adolescent Psychiatry, 55,* 71–75.

Affleck, G., Tennen, H., Urrows, S., & Higgins, P. (1994). Person and contextual features of daily stress reactivity: Individual differences in relations of undesirable daily events with mood disturbance and chronic pain intensity. *J. of Pers. Soc. Psychol., 66*(2), 329–40.

Agnew, J. (1985). Man's purgative passion. *Amer. J. Psychother., 39*(2), 236–46.

Agras, S. W., Telch, C. F., Arnow, B., Eldredge, K., et al. (1997). One-year follow–up of cognitive-behavioral therapy for obese individuals with binge eating disorder. *J. Cons. Clin. Psychol., 65*(2), 343–47.

Agras, W. S. (1982). Behavioral medicine in the 1980's: Nonrandom connections. *J. Cons. Clin. Psychol.*, *50*(6), 820–40.

Agras, W. S. (1993). Short term psychological treatments for binge eating. In C. Farirburn & G. T. Wilson (Eds.), *Binge eating: Nature, assessment, and treatment.* New York: Guilford.

Agras, W. S., Schneider, J. A., Arnow, B., Raeburn, S. D., & Telch, C. F. (1989). Cognitive-behavioral and response-prevention treatments for bulimia nervosa. *J. Cons. Clin. Psychol., 57*, 215–21.

Aiken, L. R. (1994). *Dying, death, and bereavement* (3rd ed.). Boston: Allyn & Bacon.

Aiken, L. R. (1996). *Rating scales and checklists.* New York: Wiley.

Ajdukovic, D. (1998). *Trauma recovery training.* Zagreb: Society for Psychological Assistance.

Akhtar, S. (1996). Further exploration of gender differences in personality disorders. *Amer. J. Psychiat., 153*(6), 846–47.

Akhtar, S., Wig, N. N., Varma, V. K., Pershad, D., & Verma, S. K. (1975). Phenomenological analysis of symptoms in obsessive-compulsive neurosis. *Brit. J. Psychiat., 127,* 342–98.

Akiskal, H. S. (1979). A biobehavioral approach to depression. In R. A. Depue (Ed.), *The psychobiology of depressive disorders: Implications for the effects of stress.* New York: Academic Press.

Akiskal, H. S. (1989). Validating affective personality types. In L. N. Robins & J. E. Barrett (Eds.), *The validity of psychiatric diagnosis.* New York: Raven Press.

Akiskal, H. S. (1997). Overview of chronic depressions and their clinical management. In H. S Akiskal, & G. B. Cassano (Eds.), *Dysthymia and the spectrum of chronic depressions.* (pp. 1–34). New York: The Guilford.

Akiskal, H. S., Chen, S., Davis, G., Puzantian, V., Kashgarian, M., & Bolinger, J. (1985). Borderline: An adjective in search of a noun. *Clinical psychiatry, 46,* 41–48.

Akiskal, H. S., Khani, M. K., & Scott-Strauss, A. (1979). Cyclothymic temperamental disorders. *Psychiat. Clin. N. Amer., 2,* 527–54.

Akiskal, H. S., Maser, J. D., Zeller, P. J., Endicott, J., Coryell, W., Keller, M., Warshaw, M., Clayton, P., & Goodwin, F. (1995). Switching from 'unipolar' to bipolar II. *Arch. Gen. Psychiat., 52,* 114–123.

Akiskal, H. S., & Simmons, R. C. (1985). Chronic and refractory depressions: Evaluation and management. In E. E. Becham & W. R. Leber (Eds.), *Handbook of depression: Treatment, assessment, and research.* (pp. 587–605). Homewood, IL: Dorsey Press.

Alander, R., & Campbell, T. (1975, Spring). An evaluation of an alcohol and drug recovery program: A case study of the Oldsmobile experience. *Human Resource Management,* 14–18.

Alarcon, M., et al. (1997). A twin study of mathematics disability. *J. Learn. Dis., 30*(6), 617–23.

Albee, G. W. (1996). Revolutions and counterrevolutions in prevention. *Amer. Psychol., 51*(11), 1130–33.

Albertson's Inc. v. Worker's Compensation Board of the State of California, 131, Cal App 3d, 182 Cal Reptr 304, 1982.

Albright v. Abington Memorial Hospital, 696 A.2d 1159 (Pa 1997).

Alcoholics Anonymous (1989). *Comments on AA's triennial surveys.* New York: AA World Service.

Alcoholics Anonymous Staff. Butcher, J. N. (1997). *Distribution of Chapters of Alcoholics Anonymous.*

Alden, L., & Capp, R. (1988). Characteristics predicting social functioning and treatment response in clients impaired by extreme shyness: Age of onset and the public/private shyness distinction. *Canad. J. Behav. Sci., 20,* 40–49.

Alexander, A. B. (1977). Chronic asthma. In R. B. Williams, Jr., & W. D. Gentry (Eds.), *Behavioral approaches to medical treatment.* (pp. 7–24). Cambridge, MA: Ballinger.

Alexander, A. B. (1981). Behavioral approaches to the treatment of bronchial asthma. In C. K. Prokop &

L. A. Bradley (Eds.), *Medical psychology: Contributions to behavioral medicine.* New York: Academic Press.

Alexander, F. (1946). Individual psychotherapy. *Psychosom. Med., 8,* 110–15.

Alexander, F. (1948). *Fundamentals of psychoanalysis.* New York: Norton.

Alexander, F. (1950). *Psychosomatic medicine.* New York: Norton.

Alexander, G. M., & Sherwin, B. B. (1993). Sex steroids, sexual behavior, and selective attention for erotic stimuli in women using oral contraceptives. *Psychoneuroendocrinology, 18,* 91–102.

Alexander, J. F., Holtzworth-Munroe, A., & Jameson, P. B. (1994). The process and outcome of marital and family therapy: Research review and evaluation. In A. E. Bergin & S. L. Garfield (Eds.), *Handbook of psychotherapy and behavior change* (4th ed., pp. 595–630). New York: Wiley.

Alexander, K., Huganir, L. S., & Zigler, E. (1985). Effects of different living settings on the performance of mentally retarded individuals. *Amer. J. Ment. Def., 90,* 9–17.

Alison, N. G. (1994). Fetal alcohol syndrome: Implications for psychologists. *Clin. Psychol. Rev., 14,* 91–111.

Al-Issa, I. (1982). Does culture make a difference in psychopathology? In I. Al-Issa (Ed.), *Culture and psychopathology.* Baltimore: University Park Press.

Allden, K., Poole, C., Chantavanich, S., Ohmar, K., Aung, N., & Mollica, R. (1996). Burmese political dissidents in Thailand: Trauma and survival among young adults in exile. *Amer. J. Pub. Hlth., 86*(11), 1561–169.

Allen, A. J., Leonarn, H., & Swedo, S. E. (1995). Current knowledge of medications for the treatment of childhood anxiety disorders. *J. Amer. Acad. Child & Adolescent Psychiatry, 34*(8), 976–86.

Allen, B., & Skinner, H. (1987). Lifestyle assessment using microcomputers. In J. N. Butcher (Ed.), *Computerized psychological assessment: A practitioner's guide.* New York: Basic Books.

Allen, J. S. (1997). At issue: Are traditional societies schizophrenogenic? *Schizo. Bull., 23*(3), 357–64.

Allerton, W. S. (1970). Psychiatric casualties in Vietnam. *Roche Medical Image and Commentary, 12*(8), 27.

Allodi, F. A. (1994). Posttraumatic stress disorder in hostages and victims of torture. *Psychiat. Clin. of N. Amer., 17,* 279–88.

Alloy, L. B., & Abramson, L. Y. (1997, May). *The Temple-Wisconsin cognitive vulnerability to depression project: Lifetime prevalence and prospective incidence of Axis I psychopathology.* Paper presented at Midwestern Psychological Association, Chicago.

Alloy, L. B., Kelly, K. A., Mineka, S., & Clements, C. M. (1990). Comorbidity in anxiety and depressive disorders: A helplessness/hopelessness perspective. In J. D. Maser & C. R. Cloninger (Eds.), *Comorbidity in anxiety and mood disorders,* (pp. 499–543). Washington, DC: American Psychiatric Press.

Alloy, L., Reilly-Harrington, N. A., & Fresco, D. M. (1997). *Cognitive styles and life events as predictors of bipolar and unipolar episodes.* Paper presented at the meeting of the Association for the Advancement of Behavior Therapy.

Alloy, L. B., & Tabachnick, N. (1984). Assessment of Covariation by humans and animals: The joint influence of prior expectations and current situational information. *Psychol. Rev., 91,* 112–149.

Alpert, J. E., Maddocks, A., Nierenberg, A. A., O'Sullivan, R., Pava, J. A., Worthington, J. J., Biederman, J., Rosenbaum, J. F., & Fava, M. (1996). Attention-deficit hyperactivity disorder in childhood among adults with major depression. *Psychiat. Res., 62,* 213–19.

Alpert, J. E., & Spillman, M. K. (1997). Psychotherapeutic approaches to aggressive and violent patients. *Psychiat. Clin. N. Amer., 20,* 453–472.

Alpert, J. E., Uebelacker, L. A., McLean, N. E., Nierenberg, A. A., Pava, J. A., Worthington III, J. J., Tedlow, J. R., Rosenbaum, J. F., & Fava, M. (1997). Social phobia, avoidant personality disorder and

atypical depression: Co-occurrence and clinical implications. *Psychol. Med., 27,* 627–633.

Alterman, A. I. (1988). Patterns of familial alcoholism, alcoholism severity, and psychopathology. *J. Nerv. Ment. Dis., 176,* 167–75.

Alterman, A. I., McDermott, P. A., Cacciola, J. S., Rutherford, M. J., Boardman, C. R., McKay, J. R., & Cook, T. G. (1998). A typology of antisociality in methadone patients. *J. Abn. Psychol., 107*(2), 412–22.

Alterman, A. I., Searles, J. S., & Hall, J. G. (1989). Failure to find differences in drinking behavior as a function of familial risk for alcoholism: A replication. *J. Cons. Clin. Psychol., 98,* 50–53.

Amato, P. R. (1988). Long-term implications of parental divorce for adult self concept. *Journal of Family Issues, 9,* 201–213.

Amato, P. R., & Keith, B. (1991a). Parental divorce and the well-being of children: A meta-analysis. *Psychol. Bull., 110,* 26–46.

Amato, P. R., & Keith, B. (1991b). Parental divorce and adult well-being: A meta-analysis. *Journal of Marriage and the Family, 53,* 43–58.

Ambrosini, P. J., Bianchi, M. D., Rabinovich, H., & Elia, J. (1993). Antidepressant treatments in children and adolescents: II Anxiety, physical, and behavioral disorders. *J. Amer. Acad. Child Adoles. Psychiat., 32,* 483–93.

Amcoff, S. (1980). The impact of malnutrition on the learning situation. In H. M. Sinclair & G. R. Howat (Eds.), *World nutrition and nutrition education.* New York: Oxford University Press.

American Medical Association Committee on Human Sexuality. (1972). *Human Sexuality.* (p. 40). Chicago: American Medical Association.

American Medical Association, Department of Mental Health. (1968). The crutch that cripples: Drug dependence, Part 1. *Today's Health, 46*(9), 11–12, 70–72.

American Psychiatric Association. (1968). *Diagnostic and statistical manual of mental disorders* (2nd ed.). Washington, DC: Author.

American Psychiatric Association. (1972). Classification of mental retardation. *Supplement to the Amer. J. Psychiat., 128*(11), 1–45.

American Psychiatric Association. (1980). *Diagnostic and statistical manual of mental disorders* (3rd ed.). Washington, DC: Author.

American Psychiatric Association. (1987). *Diagnostic and statistical manual of mental disorders* (3rd ed.—rev.). Washington, DC: Author.

American Psychiatric Association. (1990). *The Practice of ECT: Recommendations for treatment, training, priviliging.* Washington, DC: Author.

American Psychiatric Association. (1994). *Diagnostic and statistical manual of mental disorders (DSM-IV)* (4th ed.). Washington, DC: Author.

American Psychiatric Association. (1997). Practice guideline for the treatment of patients with Alzheimer's disease and other dementias of late life. *Amer. J. Psychiat., Supplement, 154*(5), 1–39.

American Psychiatric Association. (1997). Practice guideline for the treatment of patients with schizophrenia. *Amer. J. Psychiat.* (Supplement), *154*(4), 1–63.

American Psychological Association. (1970). Psychology and mental retardation. *Amer. Psychol., 25,* 267–68.

American Psychological Association. (1986). *Guidelines for computer-based tests and interpretations.* Washington, DC: Author.

American Psychological Association. (1992). Ethical principles of psychologists and code of conduct. *Amer. Psychol., 47*(12), 1597–611.

Ammerman, R. T., & Galvin, M. R. (1998). Child maltreatment. In R. T. Ammerman, J. V. Campo, et al. (Eds.), *Handbook of pediatric psychology and psychiatry: Vol 2. Disease, injury, and illness.* (pp. 31–69). Boston: Allyn & Bacon.

Ammerman, R. T., & Hersen, M. (1997). *Handbook of prevention and treatment with children and adolescents.* New York: Wiley.

Ammerman, R. T., Kane, V. R., Slomka, G. T., Reigel, D. H., Franzen, M. D., & Gadow, K. D. (1998). Psychiatric symptomatology and family functioning in children and adolescents with spina bifida. *J. Clin. Psychol. Med. Set., 5*(4), 449–65.

Anand, K. J. S., & Arnold, J. H. (1994). Opioid tolerance and dependence in infants and children. *Critical Care Medicine, 22,* 334–42.

Andersen, B. L. (1983). Primary orgasmic dysfunction: Diagnostic considerations and review of treatment. *Psychol. Bull., 93,* 105–36.

Andersen, B. L., & Cyranowski, J. M. (1995). Women's sexuality: Behaviors, responses, and individual differences. *J. Cons. Clin. Psychol., 63, 891–906.*

Anderson, B. L., Kiecolt-Glaser, J. K., & Glaser, R. (1994). A biobehavioral model of cancer stress and disease course. *Amer. Psychol., 49*(5), 389–404.

Anderson, C., Krull, D., & Weiner, B. (1996) Explanations: Processes and consequences. In E.T. Higgins, & A. Kruglanski (Eds.), *Social Psychology: Handbook of Basic Principles.* (pp. 271–296). New York: Guilford.

Anderson, E. M., & Lambert, M. J. (1995). Short-term dynamically oriented psychotherapy: A review and meta-analysis. *Clin. Psychol. Rev., 15*(6), 503–14.

Anderson, G., Yasenik, L., & Ross, C. A. (1993). Dissociative experiences and disorders among women who identify themselves as sexual abuse survivors. *Child Ab. Negl., 17,* 677–86.

Anderson, J. C., Williams, S., McGee, R., & Silva, P. A. (1987). DSM III disorders in preadolescent children. *Arch. Gen. Psychiat., 44,* 69–80.

Anderson, K., & Lehto, J. (1995). *Young people and alcohol, drugs and tobacco: European action plan.* Geneva: World Health Organization.

Anderson, N. B., & Jackson, J. S. (1987). Race, ethnicity, and health psychology: The example of essential hypertension. In G. C. Stone (Ed.), *Health psychology: A discipline and a profession.* (pp. 265–84). Chicago: University of Chicago Press.

Anderson, V. A., et al. (1997). Predicting recovery from head injury in young children: A prospective analysis. *J. Int. Neuropsychologic. Soc., 3*(6), 568–80.

Andrasik, F., Blanchard, E. B., Arena, J. G., Teders, S. J., Teevan, R. C., & Rodichok, L. D. (1982). Psychological functioning in headache sufferers. *Psychosom. Med., 44,* 171–82.

Andrasik, F., Holroyd, K. A., & Abell, T. (1979). Prevalence of headache within a college student population: A preliminary analysis. *Headache, 20,* 384–87.

Andreasen, N. C. (1982). Concepts, diagnosis and classification. In E. S. Paykel (Ed.), *Handbook of affective disorders.* New York: Guilford.

Andreasen, N. C. (1984). *The broken brain: The biological revolution in psychiatry.* New York: Harper & Row.

Andreasen, N. C. (1985). Positive vs. negative schizophrenia: A critical evaluation. *Schizo. Bull., 11,* 380–89.

Andreasen, N. C., & Carpenter, W. T., Jr. (1993). Diagnosis and classification of schizophrenia. *Schizo. Bull., 19*(2), 199–214.

Andreasen, N. C., et al., (1995). Symptoms of schizophrenia: Methods, meanings, and mechanisms. *Arch. Gen. Psychiat., 52*(5), 341–51.

Andreasen, N. C., Flaum, M., Swayze, V. W., Tyrrell, G., & Arndt, S. (1990). Positive and negative symptoms in schizophrenia: A critical reappraisal. *Arch. Gen. Psychiat., 47,* 615–21.

Andreasen, N. C., Nasrallah, H. A., Dunn, V., Olson, S. C., & Grove, W. M. (1986). Structural abnormalities in the frontal system in schizophrenia: A magnetic resonance imaging study. *Arch. Gen. Psychiat. 43,* 136–44.

Andreasen, N. C., Olsen, S. A., Dennert, J. W., & Smith, M. R. (1982a). Ventricular enlargement in schizophrenia: Definition and prevalence. *Amer. J. Psychiat., 139,* 292–96.

Andreasen, N. C., Olsen, S. A., Dennert, J. W., & Smith, M. R. (1982b). Ventricular enlargement in schizophrenia: Relationship to positive and negative symptoms. *Amer. J. Psychiat., 139,* 297–302.

Andreasen, N. C., Paradiso, S., & O'Leary, D. S. (1998). "Cognitive dysmetria" as an integrative theory of schizophrenia: A dysfunction in cortical-subcortical-cerebellar circuitry? *Schizo. Bull., 24*(2), 203–67.

Andreasen, N. C., Rezai, K., Alliger, R., Swayze, V. W., Flaum, M., Kirchner, P., Cohen, G., & O'Leary, D. S. (1992). Hypofrontality in neuroleptic-naive patients and in patients with chronic schizophrenia. *Arch. Gen. Psychiat., 49*(12), 959–65.

Andreasson, S., & Brandt, L. (1997). Mortality and morbidity related to alcohol. *Alcohol and Alcoholism, 32*(2), 173–78.

Andrews, G., & Harvey, R. (1981). Does psychotherapy benefit neurotic patients? A reanalysis of the Smith, Glass, and Miller data. *Arch. Gen. Psychiat., 38,* 1203–8.

Andrews, J. D. W. (1989a). Integrating visions of reality: Interpersonal diagnosis and the existential vision. *Amer. Psychol., 44,* 803–17.

Andrews, J. D. W. (1989b). Psychotherapy of depression: A self-confirmation model. *Psychol. Rev., 96,* 576–607.

Anthony, J. C., & Petronis, K. R. (1991). Panic attacks and suicide attempts. *Arch. Gen. Psychiat., 48,* 1114.

Anton, R. F. (1996). New methodologies for pharmacological treatment trials for alcohol dependence. *Alcoholism: Clin. Exper. Res., 20*(7), 3A–9A.

Antoni, M. H., Schneiderman, N., Fletcher, M. A., & Goldstein, D. A. (1990). Psychoneuroimmunology and HIV-1. *J. Cons. Clin. Psychol., 58,* 38–49.

Antonuccio, D. O., Thomas, M., & Danton, W. G. (1997). A cost-effectiveness analysis of cognitive-behavior therapy and fluoxetine (Prozac) in the treatment of depression. *Behav. Ther., 28*(2), 187–210.

Antony, M. M., & Barlow, D. H. (1996). Emotion theory as a framework for explaining panic attacks and panic disorder. In R. M. Rapee (Ed.), *Current controversies in the anxiety disorders.* (pp. 55–76). New York: Guilford.

Antony. M., Downie, F. , & Swinson R. (1998). Diagnostic issues and epidemiology in obsessive-compulsive disorder. In R. Swinson, M. Antony, S. Rachman, & M. Richter (Eds.), *Obsessive-compulsive disorder: Theory, research, and treatment.* (pp. 3-32). New York: Guilford.

Apfelbaum, B. (1989). Retarded ejaculation: A much-misunderstood syndrome. In S. R. Leiblum & R. C. Rosen (Eds.), *Principles and practice of sex therapy* (2nd ed.). (pp. 168–206). New York: Guilford.

Aponte, H., & Hoffman, L. (1973). The open door. A structural approach to a family with an anorectic child. *Fam. Process, 12,* 144.

Appelbaum, P. S. (1988). Who's on trial? Multiple personalities and the insanity defense. *Hosp. Comm. Psychiat., 45*(10), 965–66.

Appelbaum, P. S., Jick, R. Z., Grisso, T., Givelber, D., Silver, E., & Steadman, H. J. (1993). Use of posttraumatic stress disorder to support an insanity defense. *Amer. J. Psychiat., 150,* 229–34.

Apt, C. & Farley Hurlbert, D. (1994). The sexual attitudes, behavior, and relationships of women with histrionic personality disorder. *J. Sex. Marit. Ther., 20*(2), 125–33.

Arana, G. W., Baldessarini, R. J., & Ornsteen, M. (1985). The dexamethasone suppression test for diagnosis and prognosis in psychiatry: Commentary and review. *Arch. Gen. Psychiat, 42,* 1193–1204.

Arango, V., & Underwood, M. D. (1997). Serotonin chemistry in the brain of suicide victims. In R. W. Maris, M. M. Silverman, & S. S. Canetton (Eds.), *Review of Suicidology, 1997.* (pp. 237–50). New York: Guilford.

Arbitman-Smith, R., Haywood, H. C., & Bransford, J. D. (1984). Assessing cognitive change. In P. Brooks, C. M. Sperber, & R. McCauley (Eds.), *Learning and cognition in the mentally retarded.* (pp. 433–72). Hillsdale, NJ: Erlbaum.

Archer, J. (1994). Testosterone and aggression. *J. Off. Rehab., 21*(3-4), 3–39.

Archer, J. (1995). What can ethology offer the psychological study of human aggression? *Aggr. Behav., 21*(4), 243–55.

Archer, R., Griffin, R., & Aiduk, R. (1995). MMPI-2: Clinical correlates for ten common code types. *J. Pers. Assess., 65,* 391–408.

Aring, C. D. (1974). The Gheel experience: Eternal spirit of the chainless mind! *JAMA, 230*(7), 998–1001.

Aring, C. D. (1975a). Gheel: The town that cares. *Fam. Hlth., 7*(4), 54–55, 58, 60.

Aring, C. D. (1975b). Science and the citizen. *Scientif. Amer., 232*(1), 48–49; 52–53.

Arkowitz, H., & Messer, S. B. (Eds.). (1984). *Psychoanalytic and behavior therapy. Is integration possible?* New York: Plenum.

Arndt, I. O, McLellan, A. T., Dorozynsky, L., Woody, G. E., & O'Brien, C. P. (1994). Desipramine treatment for cocaine dependence: Role of antisocial personality disorder. *J. Ner. Ment. Dis., 182,* 151–56.

Arnett, P. A., Fischer, M., & Newby, R. F. (1996). The effects of Ritalin on response to reward and punishment in children with ADHD. *Child Study Journal, 26*(1), 51–70.

Arnkoff, D. B., & Glass, C. R. (1982). Clinical cognitive constructs: Examination, evaluation, and elaboration. In P. C. Kendall (Ed.), *Advances in cognitive-behavioral research and therapy* (Vol. 1, pp. 2–30). New York: Academic Press.

Arnold, M. B. (1962). *Story sequence analysis: A new method of measuring motivation and predicting achievement.* New York: Columbia University Press.

Arnold, S. E., et al. (1998). Absence of neurodegeneration and neural injury in the cerebral cortex in a sample of elderly patients with schizophrenia. *Arch. Gen. Psychiat., 55,* 225–32.

Aronoff, B. (1987). *Needs assessments: What have we learned? Experiences from Refugee Assistance Programs in Hawaii.* Paper given at the Refugee Assistance Program: Mental Health Workgroup Meeting, UCLA, February 12–13.

Asarnow, J. R. (1992). Suicidal ideation and attempts during middle childhood: Associations with perceived family stress and depression among child psychiatric inpatients. *J. Child Clinical Psychol., 21,* 35–40.

Ashton, A. K., Hamer, R., & Rosen, R. C. (1997). Serotonin reuptake inhibitor-induced sexual dysfunction and its treatment: A large-scale retrospective study of 596 psychiatric outpatients. *J. Sex and Marit. Ther., 23,* 165–175.

Aspis, S. (1997). Self-advocacy for people with learning difficulties: Does it have a future? *Disability & Society, 12*(4), 647–54.

Associated Press (1997, December 3). Crack-using woman admits guilt in the death of her fetus.

Athey, J. L., O'Malley, P., Henderson, D. P., & Ball, J. W. (1997). Emergency medical services for children: Beyond lights and sirens. *Profess. Psychol., 28*(5), 464–70.

Atkeson, B. M., Calhoun, K. S., Resick, P. A., & Ellis, E. M. (1982). Victims of rape: Repeated assessment of depressive symptoms. *J. Cons. Clin. Psychol., 50,* 96–102.

Atkeson, B. M., & Forehand, R. (1978). Parent behavior training for problem children: An examination of studies using multiple outcome measures. *J. Abnorm. Child Psychol., 6,* 449–60.

Atkinson, D. R. (1983). Ethnic similarity in counseling psychology: A review of research. *Counsel. Psychol, 11,* 79–92.

Atkinson, D. R., Furlong, M. J., & Poston, W. C. (1986). Afro-American preferences for counselor characteristics. *J. Couns. Psychol., 33,* 326–30.

Atkinson, J. W. (1992). Motivational determinants of thematic apperception. In C. P. Smith, J. W. Atkinson, & J. Veroff (Eds.). *Motivation and personality: Handbook of thematic content analysis.* (pp. 21–48). New York: Cambridge University Press.

Attie, I. & Brooks-Gunn, J. (1995). The development of eating regulation across the life span. In D. Cicchetti, & D. J. Cohen (Eds.), *Developmental Psychopathology: Vol. 2. Risk, disorder, and adaptation.* (pp. 332–368). New York: Wiley.

Auerbach, S. M., & Stolberg, A. L. (1986). *Crisis intervention with children and families.* New York: Hemisphere Press.

Averill, J. R. (1973). Personal control over aversive stimuli and its relationship to stress. *Psychol. Bull., 80*(4), 286–303.

Ayllon, T., & Azrin, N. H. (1968). *The token economy: A motivational system for therapy and rehabilitation.* New York: Appleton-Century-Crofts.

Azar, B. (1997). Researchers debunk myth of crack baby. *Monitor, 29*(12), 14–15.

Azari, N. P., Horwitz, B., Pettigrew, K. D., & Grady, C. L. (1994). Abnormal pattern of glucose metabolic rates involving language areas in young adults with Down syndrome. *Brain & Language, 46*(1), 1–20.

Babiak, P. (1995) When psychopaths go to work. *International Journal of Applied Psychology, 44,* 171–188.

Babor, T. F. (1996). The classification of alcoholics: Typology theories from the nineteenth century to the present. *Alcohol, Health, & Research World, 20*(1), 6–14.

Bachrach, L. L. (1976). *Deinstitutionalization: An analytic review and sociological perspective.* U.S. Department of Health, Education, and Welfare. National Institute of Mental Health, Washington, DC: U.S. Government Printing Office.

Badian, N. A. (1997). Dyslexia and the double deficit hypothesis. *Annals of Dyslexia, 47,* 69–87.

Baer, L., & Jenike, M. (1992). Personality disorders in obsessive compulsive disorder. *Psychiat. Clin. N. Amer., 15,* 803–12.

Baer, L., Jenike, M. A., Black, D. W., Treece, C., et al. (1992). Effect of Axis II diagnosis on treatment outcome with clomipramine in 55 patients with obsessive-compulsive disorder. *Arch. Gen. Psychiat., 49* (11), 862–6.

Baer, L., Jenike, M. A., Ricciardi, J. N., Holland, A. D., et al. (1990). Standardized assessment of personality disorders in obsessive-compulsive disorder. *Arch. Gen. Psychiat., 47*(9), 826–30.

Bailey, A., Le Couteur, A., & Gottesman, I. (1995). Autism as a strongly genetic disorder: Evidence from a British twin study. *Psychol. Med., 25*(1), 63–77.

Bailey, J. M., Gaulin, S., Agyei, Y., & Gladue, B. A. (1994). Effects of gender and sexual orientation on evolutionarily relevant aspects of human mating psychology. *J. Pers. Soc. Psychol. 66,* 1081–93.

Bailey, J. M. & Pillard, R. C. (1991). A genetic study of male sexual orientation. *Arch. Gen. Psychiat., 48,* 1089–96.

Bailey, J. M., Pillard, R. C., Neale, M. C., & Agyei, Y. (1993). Heritable factors influence female sexual orientation. *Arch. Gen. Psychiat., 50,* 217–23.

Bailey, J. M. & Shriver, A. (1999). Does childhood sexual abuse cause borderline personality disorder? *J. Sex Marit. Ther., 25,* 45–57.

Bailey, J. M., & Zucker, K. J. (1995). Childhood sextyped behavior and sexual orientation: A conceptual analysis and quantitative review. *Develop. Psychol., 31,* 43–55.

Baker, L. A., & Daniels, D. (1990). Nonshared environmental influences and personality differences in adult twins. *J. Pers. Soc. Psychol., 58,* 103–10.

Baldwin, A. L., Baldwin, C., Cole, R. E. (1990). Stress-resistant families and stress-resistant children. In J. Rolf, A. S. Masten, D. Cicchetti, K. H. Nuechterlein, & S. Weintraub (Eds.), *Risk and protective factors in the development of psychopathology.* New York: Cambridge University Press.

Bales, R. F. (1946). Cultural differences in rates of alcoholism. *Quarterly Journal of Studies in Alcoholism, 6,* 480–99.

Ballenger, J. C. (1988). The clinical use of carbamazepine in affective disorders. *J. Clin. Psychiat., 49,* 13–19.

Ballenger, J. C. (1996). An update on pharmacological treatment of panic disorder. In H. G. Westenberg, J. A. Den Boer, & D. L. Murphy (Eds.), *Advances in the neurobiology of anxiety disorders.* (pp. 229–246). Chichester, England: Wiley.

Balshem, M., Oxman, G., Van Rooyen, D., & Girod, K. (1992). Syphilis, sex and crack cocaine: Images of risk and morality. *Soc. Sci. and Med., 35,* 147–60.

Bandura, A. (1964). *Principles of behavior modification.* New York: Holt, Rinehart & Winston.

Bandura, A. (1969). *Principles of behavior modification.* New York: Holt, Rinehart & Winston.

Bandura, A. (1973). *Aggression: A social learning analysis.* Englewood Cliffs, NJ: Prentice-Hall.

Bandura, A. (1974). Behavior theory and the models of man. *Amer. Psychol., 29*(12), 859–69.

Bandura, A. (1977a). Self-efficacy: Toward a unifying theory of behavioral change. *Psychol. Rev., 84*(2), 191–215.

Bandura, A. (1977b). *Social learning theory.* Englewood Cliffs, NJ: Prentice-Hall.

Bandura, A. (1986). *Social foundations of thought and action: A social cognitive theory.* Englewood Cliffs, NJ: Prentice-Hall.

Bandura, A., & Walters, R. H. (1963). *Social learning and personality development.* New York: Holt, Rinehart & Winston.

Bannister, G., Jr. (1975). Cognitive and behavior therapy in a case of compulsive gambling. *Cog. Ther. Res., 1,* 223–27.

Barbach, L. G., & Levine, L. (1980). *Shared intimacies.* Garden City, NY: Anchor Press/Doubleday.

Barbaree, H. E. (1990). Stimulus control of sexual arousal: Its role in sexual assault. In W. L. Marshall, D. R. Laws, & H. E. Barbaree (Eds.), *Handbook of sexual assault.* (pp. 115–42). New York: Plenum.

Barbaree, H. E., Seto, M., Serin, R., Amos, N., & Preston, D. (1994). Comparisons between sexual and nonsexual rapist subtypes: Sexual arousal to rape, offense precursors, and offense characteristics. *Crim. Just. Behav., 21,* 95–114.

Barber, J. P., & Muenz, L. R. (1996). The role of avoidance and obsessiveness in matching patients to cognitive and interpersonal psychotherapy: Empirical findings from the Treatment of Depression Collaborative Research Program. *J. Cons. Clin. Psychol., 64*(5), 951–58.

Barber, T. X. (1969). *Hypnosis: A scientific approach.* New York: Van Nostrand Reinhold.

Barchas, J., Akil, H., Elliott, G., Holman, R., & Watson, S. (1978, May 26). Behavioral neurochemistry: Neuroregulators and behavioral states. *Science, 200,* 964–73.

Bard, D., Verger, P., & Hubert, P. (1997). Chernobyl, Ten years after: Health consequences. *Epidemiologic Reviews, 19*(2), 187–204.

Barlow, D. H. (1974). The treatment of sexual deviation: Toward a comprehensive behavioral approach. In K. S. Calhoun, H. E. Adams, & K. M. Mitchell (Eds.), *Innovative treatment methods in psychopathology.* New York: Wiley Interscience.

Barlow, D. H. (1986). Causes of sexual dysfunction: The role of anxiety and cognitive interference. *J. Cons. Clin. Psychol., 54,* 140–48.

Barlow, D. H. (1988). *Anxiety and its disorders: The nature and treatment of anxiety and panic.* New York: Guilford.

Barlow, D. H. (1991a). Disorders of emotion. *Psychological Inquiry, 2,* 58–71.

Barlow, D. H. (1991b). The nature of anxiety: Anxiety, depression, and emotional disorders. In R. M. Rapee & D. H. Barlow (Eds.), *Chronic Anxiety: Generalized anxiety disorder and mixed anxiety-depression.* (pp. 1–28). New York: Guilford.

Barlow, D. H. (Ed.). (1993). *Clinical handbook of psychological disorders* (2nd ed.). New York: Guilford.

Barlow, D. H., Brown, T. A., & Craske, M. G. (1994). Definitions of panic attacks and panic disorder in the DSM-IV: Implications for research. *J. Abn. Psychol., 103*(3), 553–64.

Barlow, D. H., & Cerny, J. A. (1988). *Psychological treatment of panic.* New York: Guilford.

Barlow, D. H., Chorpita, B., & Turovsky, J. (1996). Fear, panic, anxiety, and disorders of emotion. In D. Hope (Ed.), *Perspectives on anxiety, panic, and fear.* 43rd Annual Nebraska Symposium on Motivation. (pp. 251–328). Lincoln: University of Nebraska Press.

Barlow, D. H., Craske, M. G., Cerny, J. A., & Klosko, J. S. (1989). Behavioral treatment of panic disorder. *Behav. Ther., 20,* 261–82.

Barlow, D. H., Sakheim, D. K., & Beck, J. G. (1983). Anxiety increases sexual arousal. *J. Abn. Psychol., 92,* 49–54.

Barnard, K., Morisset, C., & Spieker, S. (1993). Preventative interventions: Enhancing parent-infant relationships. In C. H. Zeanah, Jr. (Ed.), *Handbook of infant development.* New York: Guilford.

Barnes, G. E., & Prosen, H. (1985). Parental death and depression. *J. Abn. Psychol., 94,* 64–69.

Barnett, P. A., & Gotlib, I. H. (1988a). Dysfunctional attitudes and psychosocial stress: The differential prediction of subsequent depression and general psychological distress. *Motivation and Emotion, 12,* 251–70.

Barnett, P. A., & Gotlib, I. H. (1988b). Psychosocial functioning and depression: Distinguishing among antecedents, concomitants, and consequences. *Psychol. Bull., 104,* 97–126.

Baroff, G. S. (1986). *Mental retardation: Nature, cause, and management.* Washington: Hemisphere.

Baron, I. S., & Goldberger, E. (1993). Neuropsychological disturbances of hydrocephalic children with implications for special education and rehabilitation. *Neuropsychological Rehabilitation, 3*(4), 389–410.

Barrett, D. H., Resnick, H., Foy, D. W., & Dansky, B. S. (1996). Combat exposure and adult psychosocial adjustment among U.S. Army veterans serving in Vietnam, 1965–1971. *J. Abn. Psychol. 105*(4), 575–81.

Barrett, P. M., Dadds, M. R., & Rapee, R. M. (1996). Family treatment of childhood anxiety disorder: A controlled trial. *J. Cons. Clin. Psychol., 64*(2), 333–42.

Barry, H., III. (1982). Cultural variations in alcohol abuse. In I. Al-Issa (Ed.), *Culture and psychopathology.* Baltimore: University Park Press.

Barsky, A. J., et al. (1998). A prospective 4- to 5-year study of DSM-III-R Hypochondriasis. *Arch. Gen. Psychiat., 5 5*(8), 737–44.

Barsky, A. J., Wool, C., Barnett, M. C., & Cleary, P. D. (1994). Histories of childhood trauma in adult hypochondriacal patients. *Amer. J. Psychiat., 151*(3), 397–401.

Barsky, A. J., Wyshak, G., & Klerman, G. L. (1992). Psychiatric comorbidity in DSM-III-R hypochondriasis. *Arch. Gen. Psychiat., 49*(2), 101–8.

Bartak, L. (1978). Educational approaches. In M. Rutter & E. Schopler (Eds.), *Autism: A reappraisal of concepts and treatment.* New York: Plenum.

Bartak, L., & Rutter, M. (1973). Special education treatment of autistic children: A comparative study, I. *J. Child Psychol. Psychiat., 14,* 161–79.

Bartak, L., & Rutter, M. (1976). Differences between mentally retarded and normally intelligent autistic children. *Journal of Autism and Childhood Schizophrenia, 6,* 109–20.

Bartholomew, R. (1997) The medicalization of the exotic: Latah as a colonialism-bound "syndrome." *Dev. Behav., 18,* 47-75.

Başoğlu, M., & Mineka, S. (1992). The role of uncontrollable and unpredictable stress in post-traumatic stress responses in torture survivors. In M. Başoğlu (Ed.), *Torture and its consequences: Current treatment approaches.* (pp. 182–225). Cambridge: Cambridge University Press.

Başoğlu, M., Mineka, S., Paker, M., Aker, T., Livanou, M., & Gok, S. (1997). Psychological preparedness for trauma as a protective factor in survivors of torture. *Psychol. Med., 27,* 1421–33.

Başoğlu, M., Paker, M., Paker, O., Ozmen, E., Marks, I., Sahin, D., & Sarimurat, N. (1994). Psychological effects of torture: A comparison of tortured and nontortured political activists in Turkey. *Amer. J. Psychiat., 151,* 76–81.

Bass, E., & Davis, L. (1988). *The courage to heal.* New York: Harper & Row.

Bassuk, E. L., & Gerson, S. (1978). Deinstitutionalization and mental health services. *Scientif. Amer., 238*(2), 46–53.

Bassuk, E. L., Schoonover, S. C., & Gelenberg, A. J. (1983). *The practitioner's guide to psychiatric drugs* (2nd ed.). New York: Plenum.

Bates, C. M., & Brodsky, A. M. (1989). *Sex in the therapy hour: A case of professional incest.* New York: Guilford.

Bateson, G. (1959). Cultural problems posed by a study of schizophrenic process. In A. Auerback (Ed.), *Schizophrenia: An integrated approach.* New York: Ronald Press.

Bateson, G. (1960). Minimal requirements for a theory of schizophrenia. *Arch. Gen. Psychiat., 2,* 477–91.

Bath, R., Morton, R., Uing, A., & Williams, C. (1996). Nocturnal enuresis and the use of desmopressin: Is it helpful? *Child: Care, Health & Development, 22*(22), 73–84.

Bathurst, K., Gottfried, A. W., & Gottfried, A. E. (1997). Normative data for the MMPI-2 in child litigation. *Psychol. Assess., 9,* 205–11.

Baucom, D. H. (1983). Sex role identity and the decision to regain control among women: A learned helplessness investigation. *J. Pers. Soc. Psychol., 44,* 334–43.

Bauer, A. M., & Shea, T. M. (1986). Alzheimer's disease and Down syndrome: A review and implications for adult services. *Education and Training of the Mentally Retarded, 21,* 144–50.

Baum, A., Gatchel, R. J., & Schaeffer, M. A. (1983). Emotional, behavioral, and physiological effects of chronic stress at Three Mile Island. *J. Cons. Clin. Psychol., 51,* 565–72.

Baumeister, R. F. (1990). Suicide as escape from self. *Psychol. Rev., 97,* 90–113.

Baumeister, R. F. & Butler, J. L. (1997). Sexual masochism: Deviance without pathology. In D. R. Laws & W. O'Donohue (Eds.), *Sexual deviance: Theory, assessment, and treatment.* New York: Guilford.

Baumrind, D. (1967). Child care practices anteceding three patterns of preschool behavior. *Genetic psychology Monographs, 75,* 43–88.

Baumrind, D. (1971). Current patterns of parental authority. *Develop. Psychol., 4*(1), 1–103.

Baumrind, D. (1975). *Early socialization and the discipline controversy.* Morristown, NJ: General Learning Press.

Baumrind, D. (1982). An explanatory study of socialization effects on black children: Some black-white comparisons. *Child Develop. 43,* 261–67.

Baumrind, D. (1991). Effective parenting during the early adolescent transition. In P. A. Cowan & E. M. Hetherington (Eds.), *Family transitions.* (pp. 111–164). Hillsdale, NJ: Erlbaum.

Baumrind, D. (1993). The average expectable environment is not good enough: A response to Scarr. *Child Develop., 64,* 1299–1317.

Baxter, L. R., Jr., Phelps, M. E., Mazziotta, J. C., Schwartz, J. M., & Gerner, R. H. (1985). Cerebral metabolic rates for glucose in mood disorders: Studies with positron emission tomography and fluorodeoxyglucose F18. *Arch. Gen. Psychiat., 42,* 441–47.

Baxter, L. R. Jr., Schwartz, J. M., Bergman, K. S., Szuba, M. P., Guze, B. H., Mazziota, J. C., Alazraki, A., Selin, C., Ferng, H. K., Munford, P. & Phelps, M. (1992). Caudate glucose metabolic rate changes with both drug and behavior therapy for obsessive-compulsive disorder. *Arch. Gen. Psychiat., 49,* 681–9.

Baxter, L. R., Jr., Schwartz, J. M., & Guze, B. H. (1991). Brain imaging: Toward a neuroanatomy of OCD. In J. Zohar, T. Insel, & S. Rasmussen (Eds.), *The psychobiology of obsessive-compulsive disorder.* New York: Springer.

Bayer, R. (1981). *Homosexuality and American psychiatry.* New York: Basic Books.

Beach, S. R. H., & O'Leary, K. D. (1992). Treating depression in the context of marital discord: Outcome and predictors of response of marital therapy versus cognitive therapy. *Behav. Ther., 23,* 507–28.

Beal, A. L. (1995). Post-traumatic stress disorder in prisoners of war and combat veterans of the Dieppe raid: A 50 year follow-up. *Canad. J. Psychiat., 40*(4), 177–84.

Beardslee, W. R., Bemporad, J., Keller, M. B., & Klerman, G. L. (1983). Children of parents with major affective disorder: A review. *Amer. J. Psychiat., 140,* 825–32.

Bearn, A., & Smith, C. (1998). How learning support is perceived by mainstream colleagues. *Support for Learning, 13*(1), 14–20.

Beason-Hazen, S., Nasrallah, H. A., & Bornstein, R. A. (1994). Self-report of symptoms and neuropsychological performance in asymptomatic HIV-positive individuals. *J. Neuropsychiat. Clin. Neurosci., 6*(1), 43–49.

Beaton, A. A. (1997). The relation of planum temporale asymmetry and morphology of the corpus callosum to handedness, gender, and dyslexia: A review of the evidence. *Brain and Language, 60*(2), 255–322.

Beauford, J. E., McNiel, D. E., & Binder, R. L. (1997). Utility of the initial therapeutic alliance in evaluating psychiatric patients' risk of violence. *Amer. J. Psychiat., 154*(9), 1272–76.

Bebbington, P., Brugha, T., McCarthy, B., Potter, J., Sturt, E., Wykes, T., Katz, R., & McGuffin, P. (1988). The Camberwell collaborative depression study I. Depressed probands: Adversity and the form of depression. *Brit. J. Psychiat., 152,* 754–65.

Beck, A. T. (1967). *Depression: Causes and treatment.* Philadelphia: University of Pennsylvania Press.

Beck, A. T. (1976). *Cognitive therapy and the emotional disorders.* New York: International University Press.

Beck, A. T. (1983). Cognitive therapy of depression: New perspectives. In P. J. Clayton & J. E. Barrett (Eds.), *Treatment of depression: Old controversies and new approaches.* (pp. 265–90). New York: Raven Press.

Beck, A. T. (1985). Theoretical perspectives on clinical anxiety. In A. H. Tuma & J. D. Maser (Eds.), *Anxiety and the anxiety disorders.* (pp. 183–98). Hillsdale, NJ: Erlbaum.

Beck, A. T., Beck, R., & Kovacs, M. (1975). Classification of suicidal behaviors: I. Qualifying intent and medical lethality. *Amer. J. Psychiat., 132*(3), 285–87.

Beck, A. T., Brown, G., & Steer, R. A. (1989). Prediction of eventual suicide in psychiatric inpatients by clinical ratings of hopelessness. *J. Cons. Clin. Psychol., 57,* 309–10.

Beck, A. T., & Emery, G., (with) Greenberg, R. L. (1985). *Anxiety disorders and phobias: A cognitive perspective.* New York: Basic Books.

Beck, A. T., Hollon, S. D., Young, J. E., Bedrosian, R. C., & Budenz, D. (1985). Treatment of depression with cognitive therapy and amitriptyline. *Arch. Gen. Psychiat., 42,* 142–48.

Beck, A. T., & Ward, C. H. (1961). Dreams of depressed patients: Characteristic themes in manifest content. *Arch. Gen. Psychiat. (Chicago), 5,* 462–67.

Beck, A. T., & Weishaar, M. (1989). Cognitive therapy. In A. Freeman, K. M. Simon, L. E. Beutler, & H. Arkowitz (Eds.), *Comprehensive handbook of cognitive therapy.* (pp. 21–36). New York: Plenum.

Beck, A. T., Freeman, A., and Associates (1990). *Cognitive therapy of personality disorders.* New York: Guilford.

Beck, A. T., Rush, A. J., Shaw, B., & Emery, G. (1979). *Cognitive therapy of depression: A treatment manual.* New York: Guilford.

Beck, A. T., Steer, R. A., Kovacs, M., & Garrison, B. (1985) Hopelessness and eventual suicide: A 10-year prospective study of patients hospitalized with suicidal ideation. *Amer. J. Psychiatr., 142,* 559–63.

Beck, A. T., Steer, R. A., Sanderson, W. C., & Skeie, T. M. (1991). Panic disorder and suicidal ideation and behavior: Discrepant findings in psychiatric outpatients. *Amer. J. Psychiat., 148,* 1195–9.

Beck, A. T., Wright, F., Newman, C., & Liese, B. (1993). *Cognitive therapy of substance abuse.* New York: Guilford.

Beck, J. G. (1992) Behavioral approaches to sexual dysfunction. In S. Turner, K. Calhoun, & H. Adams (Eds.), *Handbook of clinical behavior therapy* (2nd ed.). New York: Wiley.

Beck, J. G. (1995). Hypoactive sexual desire disorder: An overview. *J. Cons. Clin. Psychol., 63,* 919–27.

Becker, E., Rinck, M., & Margraf, J. (1994). Memory bias in panic disorder. *J. Abn. Psychol., 103,* 396–9.

Becker, J. V., Alpert, J. L., BigFoot, D. S., Bonner, B. L., et al. (1995). Empirical research on child abuse treatment: Report by the Child Abuse and Neglect Treatment Working Group: American Psychological Association. *J. Child Clin. Psychol., 24,* 23–46.

Becker, J. V., & Kaplan, M. S. (1991). Rape victims: Issues, theories, and treatment. *Ann. Rev. Sex Res., 2,* 267–92.

Beckham, E. E., & Leber, W. R. (1985a). The comparative efficacy of psychotherapy and pharmacotherapy for depression. In E. E. Beckham & W. R. Leber (Eds.), *Handbook of depression: Treatment, assessment, and research.* (pp. 316–42). Homewood, IL: Dorsey Press.

Beckham, E. E., & Leber, W. R. (Eds.). (1985b). *Handbook of depression: Treatment, assessment, and research.* Homewood, IL: Dorsey Press.

Bednar, R. L., & Kaul, T. (1994). Experiential group research. In A. E. Bergin & S. L. Garfield (Eds.), *Handbook of psychotherapy and behavior change.* (4th ed., pp. 631–63). New York: Wiley.

Beech, H. R., Burns, L. E., & Sheffield, B. F. (1982). *A behavioral approach to the management of stress.* New York: Wiley.

Beers, C. (1970). *A mind that found itself* (rev. ed.). New York: Doubleday.

Beitman, B. D., Klerman, G. L. (Eds.), (1991). *Integrating pharmacotherapy and psychotherapy.* Washington, DC: American Psychiatric Press.

Bekker, M. H. (1996). Agoraphobia and gender: A review. *Clin. Psychol. Rev., 16*(2), 129–46.

Bell, A. P., & Weinberg, M. S. (1978). *Homosexualities: A study of diversity among men and women.* New York: Simon & Schuster.

Bell, A. P., Weinberg, M. S., & Hammersmith, S. K. (1981). *Sexual preference: Its development in men and women.* Bloomington, IN: Indiana University Press.

Bell, E., Jr. (1958). The basis of effective military psychiatry. *Dis. Nerv. Sys., 19,* 283–88.

Bellack, A. S., Mueser, K. T., Gingerich, S., & Agresta, J. (1997). *Social skills training for schizophrenia.* New York: Guilford.

Bellak, L. (1993). *The Thematic Apperception Test, the Children's Apperception Test, and the Senior Apperception Test in clinical use* (5th ed.). Boston: Allyn & Bacon.

Bellak, L. & Abrams, D. M. (1993). *The Thematic Apperception Test, the Children's Apperception Test, and the Senior Apperception Technique in clinical use.* Boston: Allyn & Bacon.

Bellerson, K. J. (1997). *The complete and updated fat book.* New York: Avery Publishing.

Bellman, M. (1966). Studies on encopresis. *Acta Paediatr. Suppl., 170,* 121.

Belsher, G. & Costello, C. G. (1988). Relapse after recovery from unipolar depression: A critical review. *Psychol. Bull., 104,* 84–96.

Belsky, J. (1993). Etiology of child maltreatment: A developmental-ecological analysis. *Psychol. Bull., 114,* 413–34.

Belter, R. W., & Shannon, M. P. (1993). Impact of natural disasters on children and families. In C. F. Saylor (Ed.), *Children and disasters.* (pp. 85–104). New York: Plenum.

Bem, D. J. (1972). Self-perception theory. In L. Berkowitz (Ed.), *Advances in experimental social psychology* (Vol. 6). New York: Academic Press.

Bemis, K. M. (1978). Current approaches to the etiology and treatment of anorexia nervosa. *Psychol. Bull., 85,* 593–617.

Bemporad, J. R. (1995). Long-term analytic treatment of depression. In E. E. Beckham & W. R. Leber (Eds.), *Handbook of depression* (2nd ed.). (pp. 404–24). New York: Guilford.

Benda, C. G., & Rozovsky, F. A. (1997). *Managed care and the law: Liability and risk management, a practical guide.* Boston,: Little, Brown.

Benedict, R. (1934). Anthropology and the abnormal. *J. Gen. Psychol., 10,* 59–82.

Bengelsdorf, I. S. (1970, Mar. 5). Alcohol, morphine addictions believed chemically similar. *Los Angeles Times,* II, 7.

Benjamin, L. S. (1974). Structural analysis of social behavior. *Psychol. Rev., 81,* 392–425.

Benjamin, L. S. (1982). Use of structural analysis of social behavior (SASB) to guide intervention in psychotherapy. In J. C. Anchin & D. L. Kiesler (Eds.), *Handbook of interpersonal psychotherapy.* New York: Pergamon.

Benjamin, L. S. (1993). *Interpersonal diagnosis and treatment of personality disorders.* New York: Guilford.

Benjamin, L. S. (1994). SASB: A bridge between personality theory and clinical psychology. *Psychol. Inq., 5,* 273–316.

Benjamin, L. S. (1996). An interpersonal theory of personality disorders In J. F. Clarkin & M. F. Lenzenweger (Eds.), *Major Theories of Personality Disorder.* (pp. 141–220). New York: .

Benjamin, L. S. (1996). Interpersonal diagnosis and treatment of personality disorders (2nd ed.). New York: Guilford.

Benjamin, L. S., & Wonderlich, S. A. (1994). Social perceptions and borderline personality disorder: The relation to mood disorders. *J. Abn. Psychol., 103*(4), 610–624.

Ben Hamida, S., Mineka, S., & Bailey, J. M. (1998). Sex differences in perceived controllabilty of mate value: An evolutionary perspective. *J. Pers. Soc. Psychol., 75*, 953–66.

Bennett, A. E. (1947). Mad doctors. *J. Nerv. Ment. Dis., 106*, 11–18.

Bennett, J. B., & Lehman, W. E. K. (1996). Alcohol, antagonism, and witnessing violence in the workplace: Drinking climates and social alienation-integration. In G. R. Vandenbos & E. Q. Bulatao (Eds.), *Violence in the workplace.* (pp. 105–52). Washington: American Psychological Association.

Bennett, T. L., Dittmar, C., & Ho, M. R. (1997). The neuropsychology of traumatic brain injury. In A. M. Horton, D. Wedding, & J. Webster (Eds.), *The neuropsychology handbook* (Vol. 2). (pp. 123–72). New York: Springer.

Bennetto, L., Pennington, B. F., & Rogers, S. J. (1996). Intact and impaired memory functions in autism. *Child Develop., 67*(4), 1816–35.

Benotti, P. N., & Forse, R. A. (1995). The role of gastric surgery in the multidisciplinary management of severe obesity. *American Journal of Surgery, 169,* 361–67.

Ben-Porath, Y. S. (1997). Use of personality assessment instruments in empirically guided treatment planning. *Psychol. Assess., 9*(4), 361–68.

Ben-Porath, Y. S., & Butcher, J. N. (1989). The comparability of MMPI and MMPI-2 scales and profiles. *Psychol. Assess., 1,* 345–47.

Ben-Porath, Y. S., Shondrick, D., & Stafford, K. (1994). MMPI-2 and race in a forensic diagnostic sample. *Crim. Just. Behav., 22,* 19–32.

Bentler, P. M., & Prince, C. (1969). Personality characteristics of male transvestites. III. *J. Abn. Psychol., 74*(2), 140–43.

Bentler, P. M., & Prince, C. (1970). Psychiatric symptomology in transvestites. *J. Clin. Psychol., 264*), 434–35.

Bentler, P. M., Shearman, R. W., & Prince, C. (1970). Personality characteristics of male transvestites. *J. Clin. Psychol., 126*(3), 287–91.

Bentovim, A., Boston, P., & Van Elburg, A. (1987). Child sexual abuse—children and families referred to a treatment project and the effects of intervention. *Brit. Med. J., 295,* 1453–57.

Berenbaum, H., & Connelly, J. (1993). The effects of stress on hedonic capacity. *J. Abn. Psychol., 102*(3), 474–81.

Berenbaum, H., & Fujita, F. (1994). Schizophrenia and personality: Exploring the boundaries and connections between vulnerability and outcome. *J. Abn. Psychol., 103*(1), 148–58.

Berenbaum, H., & Oltmanns, T. F. (1992). Emotional experience and expression in schizophrenia and depression. *J. Abn. Psychol., 101*(1), 37–44.

Berenbaum, M. J., & Garske, J. P. (1993). The effect of stress on hedonic capacity. *J. Abn. Psychol., 102,* 474–81.

Berenbaum, S. A., & Hines, M. (1992). Early androgens are related to childhood sex-typed toy preferences. *Psychol. Sci., 3,* 203–6.

Berg, A. (1954). *The sadist* (O. Illner & G. Godwin, Trans.). New York: Medical Press of New York.

Bergem, A. L. M., Engedal, K., & Kringlen, E. (1997). The role of heredity in late-onset Alzheimer disease and vascular dementia. *Arch. Gen. Psychiat., 54*(3), 264–70.

Bergen, J. A., Eyland, E. A., Campbell, J. A., Jenkins, P., Kellehear, K., Richards, A., & Beumont, P. J. V. (1989). The course of tardive dyskinesia in patients on long-term neuroleptics. *Brit. J. Psychiat., 154,* 523–28.

Berger, P. A. (1978). Medical treatment of mental illness. *Science, 200,* 974–81.

Bergin, A. E., & Garfield, S. L. (Eds.). (1994). *Handbook of psychotherapy and behavior change* (4th ed.). New York: Wiley.

Bergin, A. E., & Lambert, M. J. (1978). The evaluation of therapeutic outcomes. In S. L. Garfield & A. E. Bergin (Eds.), *Handbook of psychotherapy and behavior change* (2nd ed.). New York: Wiley.

Bergin, R. M. (1997). What is psychopathology? And so what? *Clin. Psychol. Sci. Pract., 4*(3), 235–48.

Berlin, F. S. (1994, May). The case for castration, part 2. *Washington Monthly, 26,* 28–29.

Berlin, F. S., & Malin, H. M. (1991). Media distortion of the public's perception of recidivism and psychiatric rehabilitation. *Amer. J. Psychiat., 148,* 1572–76.

Berman, A. L., & Jobes, D. A. (1991). *Adolescent suicide.* Washington, DC: American Psychological Association.

Berman, A. L., & Jobes, D. A. (1992). Suicidal behavior of adolescents. In B. Bongar (Ed.), *Suicide: Guidelines for assessment, management and treatment.* New York: Oxford University Press.

Berman, K. F., Torrey, E. F., Daniel, D. G., & Weinberger, D. R. (1992). Regional cerebral blood flow in monozygotic twins discordant and concordant for schizophrenia. *Arch. Gen. Psychiat., 49*(12), 927–34.

Berman, S. L., Kurtines, W. M., Silverman, W. K., & Serafini, L. T. (1996). The impact of exposure to crime and violence on urban youth. *Amer. J. Orthopsychiat., 66*(3), 329–36.

Bernhardt, B., Meertz, E., & Schonfeldt-Bausch, P. (1985). Basal ganglia and limbic system pathology in schizophrenia: A morphometric study of brain volume and shrinkage. *Arch. Gen. Psychiat., 42,* 784–91.

Bernstein, D. P., Useda, D., & Siever, L. J. (1993). Paranoid personality disorder: Review of the literature and recommendations for DSM-IV. *J. Person. Dis., 7*(1), 53–62.

Bernstein, D. P., Useda, D., Siever, L. J. (1995). Paranoid personality disorder. In W. J Livesley (Ed), *The DSM-IV personality disorders. Diagnosis and treatment of mental disorders.* (pp. 45–57). New York: Guilford.

Bernstein, E. M., & Putnam, F. W. (1986). Development, reliability, and validity of a dissociation scale. *J. Nerv. Men. Dis., 174,* 727–35.

Bernstein, G. A., & Borchardt, C. M. (1991). Anxiety disorders of childhood and adolescence: A critical review. *J. Amer. Acad. Adoles. Psychiat., 30,* 519–32.

Berrios, G. (1990). A British contribution to the history of functional brain surgery. Special Issue: History of psychopharmacology. *J. Psychopharm., 4,* 140–44.

Berry, D. T. (1995). Detecting distortion in forensic evaluations with the MMPI-2. In Y. S. Ben-Porath, J. R. Graham, G. C. N. Hall, R. D. Hirschman, & M. S. Zaragoza (Eds.), *Forensic applications of the M-MPI-2.* (pp. 82–103). Thousand Oaks, CA: Sage.

Bertelsen, A., Harvald, B., & Hauge, M. (1977). A Danish twin study of manic depressive disorders. *Brit. J. Psychiat., 130,* 330–51.

Besharov, D. J. (1992, July). Yes: Consider chemical treatment. *ABA Journal, 78,* 42.

Beutler, L. E. (1992). Systematic treatment selection. In J. C. Norcross & M. R. Goldfried (Eds.), *Psychotherapy integration.* New York: Basic Books.

Beutler, L. E. (1995). Integrating and communicating findings. In L. Beutler and M. R. Berron (Eds.), *Integrative assessment of adult personality.* (pp. 25–624). New York: Guilford.

Beutler, L. E., Machado, P. P., & Neufeldt, S. A. (1994). Therapist variables. In A. E. Bergin & S. L. Garfield (Eds.), *Handbook of psychotherapy and behavior change* (4th ed.). (pp. 229–69). New York: Wiley.

Beveridge, A. W., & Renvoize, E. B. (1988). Electricity: A history of its use in the treatment of mental illness in Britain during the second half of the 19th century. *Brit. J. Psychiat., 153,* 157–62.

Bhandary, A. N. (1997). The chronic attention deficit syndrome. *Psychiat. Ann., 27*(8), 543–44.

Bibring, E. (1953). The mechanism of depression. In P. Greenacre (Ed.), *Affective disorders.* (pp. 13–48). New York: International University Press.

Bickel, W. K., Amass, L., Higgins, S. T., Badger, G. J., & Esch, R. A. (1997). Effects of adding behavioral treatment in opioid detoxification with Buprenorphine. *J. Cons. Clin. Psychol., 65*(5), 803–10.

Bickman, L. (1996). A continuum of care: More is not always better. *Amer. Psychol., 51,* 689–701.

Bieber, I., Dain, H. J., Dince, P. R., Drellich, M. G., Grand, H. G., Gundlach, R. H., Kremer, M. W., Rifkin, A. H., Wilbur, C. B. & Bieber, T. B. (1962). *Homosexuality: A psychoanalytic study of male homosexuals.* New York: Basic Books.

Biederman, J., Farone, S. V., Milberger, S., Jetton, J. G., Chen, L., Mick, E., Greene, R. W., & Russell, R. L. (1996). Is childhood oppositional defiant disorder a precursor to adolescent conduct disorder? Finding from a four-year follow-up of children with ADHD. *Child Adoles. Psychiat. 35*(9), 1193–1204.

Biederman, J., Rosenbaum, J. F., Hirschfeld, D. R., Faraone, S., Bolduc, E., Gersten, M., Meminger, S., Kagan, J., Snidman, N. & Reznick, J. S. (1990). Psychiatric correlates of behavioral inhibition in young children of parents with and without psychiatric disorders. *Arch. Gen. Psychiat., 47,* 21–26.

Biederman, J., Wilens, T., Mick, E., Milberger, S., Spencer, T. J., & Faraone, S. V. (1995). Psychoactive substance use disorders in adults with attention deficit hyperactivity disorder (ADHD): Effects of ADHD and psychiatric comorbidity. *Amer. J. Psychiat., 152*(11), 1652–58.

Bifulco, A. T., Brown, G. W., & Harris, T. O. (1987). Childhood loss of parent, lack of adequate parental care and adult depression: A replication. *J. Affect. Dis., 12,* 115–28.

Bigler, E. D. (1996). *Neuroimaging.* New York: Plenum.

Billet, E., Richter, J., & Kennedy, J. (1998). Genetics of obsessive-compulsive disorder. In R. Swinson, M. Antony, S. Rachman, & M. Richter (Eds.), *Obsessive-compulsive disorder: Theory, research, and treatment.* (pp.181–206). New York: Guilford.

Billings, A. G., Cronkite, R. C., & Moos, R. H. (1983). Social-environmental factors in unipolar depression: Comparisons of depressed patients and nondepressed controls. *J. Abn. Psychol., 92,* 119–33.

Billy, J. O. G., Tanfer, K., Grady, W. R., & Klepinger, D. H. (1993). The sexual behavior of men in the United States. *Fam. Plann. Perspect., 25,* 52–60.

Binder, J. L., & Strupp, H. H. (1997). "Negative process": A recurrently discovered and underestimated facet of therapeutic process and outcome in the individual psychotherapy of adults. *Clin. Psychol. Sci. Prac., 4*(2), 121–39.

Binder, R. L., & McNiel, D. E. (1988). Effects of diagnosis and context of dangerousness. *Amer. J. Psychiat., 145,* 788–92.

Birkhimer, L. J., Curtis, J. L., & Jann, M. W. (1985). Use of carbamazepine in psychiatric disorders. *Clin. Pharm., 4,* 425–34.

Birmaher, B., Ryan, S. W., Williamson, D., Brent, D., Kaufman, J., Dahl, R., Perel, J., & Nelson, B. (1996). Childhood and adolescent depression: A review of the past 10 years. Part I. *J. Amer. Acad. Child Adoles. Psychiat. 35,* 1427–39.

Birns, B., & Bridger, W. (1977). Cognitive development and social class. In J. Wortis (Ed.), *Mental retardation and developmental disabilities* (Vol. 9). (pp. 203–33). New York: Brunner/Mazel.

Bishop, E. R., Mobley, M. C., & Farr, W. F., Jr. (1978). Lateralization of conversion symptoms. *Compr. Psychiat., 19,* 393–96.

Bisnaire, L. M., Firestone, P., & Rynard, D. (1990). Factors associated with academic achievement in children following parental separation. *Amer. J. Orthopsychiat., 60,* 67–76.

Black, A. (1974). The natural history of obsessional neurosis. In H. R. Beech (Ed.), *Obsessional states.* London: Methuen.

Black, B., & Uhde, T. W. (1995). Psychiatric characteristics of children with selective mutism: A pilot study. *J. Amer. Acad. Child Adoles. Psychiat., 34*(7), 847–56.

Black, D. W., Noyes, R., Goldstein, R. B., & Blum, N. (1992). A family study of obsessive-compulsive disorder. *Arch. Gen. Psychiat., 49,* 362–368.

Black, D. W., Winoker, G., Bell, S., Nasrallah, A., & Hulbert, J. (1988). Complicated mania: Comorbidity and immediate outcome in the treatment of mania. *Arch. Gen. Psychiat., 45,* 232–36.

Black, D. W., Yates, W., Petty, F., Noyes, R., & Brown, K. (1986). Suicidal behavior in alcoholic males. *Compr. Psychiat., 273*(3), 227–33.

Blackburn, I. M., Bishop, S., Glen, A. I. M., Whalley, L. J., & Christie, J. E. (1981). The efficacy of cognitive therapy in depression: A treatment trial using cognitive therapy and pharmacotherapy, each alone and in combination. *Brit. J. Psychiat., 139,* 181–89.

Blackburn, R. (1993). *Psychology of criminal conduct.* New York: Wiley.

Blaine, J. D. (1992). Introduction. In J.D. Blaine (Ed.), *Buprenorphine: An alternative treatment for opioid dependence.* (pp. 1–4). Washington, DC: U.S. Department of Health and Human Services.

Blair, R. J. R., Jones, L., Clark, F., & Smith, M. (1997). The psychopathic individual: A lack of responsiveness to distress cues? *Psychophysiology, 34,* 192–198.

Blais, M. A., Hilsenroth, M. J., & Castlebury, F. D. (1997). Content validity of the DSM - IV borderline and narcissistic personality disorder criteria sets. *Compr. Psychiat., 38*(1), 31–37.

Blanchard, E. B. (1992). Psychological treatment of benign headache disorders. *J. Cons. Clin. Psychol., 60*(4), 537–51.

Blanchard, E. B. (1994). Behavioral medicine and health psycholgy. In A. E. Bergin & S. L. Garfield (Eds.), *Handbook of psychotherapy and behavior change.* (pp. 701–33). New York: Wiley.

Blanchard, E. B., & Andrasik, F. (1982). Psychological assessment and treatment of headache: Recent developments and emerging issues. *J. Cons. Clin. Psychol., 50*(6), 859–79.

Blanchard, E. B., Andrasik, F., Ahles, T. A., Teders, S. J., & O'Keefe, D. (1980). Migraine and tension headache: A meta-analytic review. *Behav. Ther., 11,* 613–31.

Blanchard, E. B., Andrasik, F., Neff, D. F., Saunders, N. L., Arena, J. G., Pallmeyer, T. P., Teders, S. J., & Jurish, S. G. (1983). Four process studies in the behavioral treatment of chronic headache. *Behav. Res. Ther., 21,* 209–20.

Blanchard, E. B., Appelbaum, K. A., Radnitz, C. L., Morrill, B., Michultka, D., Kirsch, C., Gaurinieri, P., Hillhouse, J., Evans, D. D., Jaccard, J., & Barron, K. D. (1990b). A controlled evaluation of thermal biofeedback and thermal biofeedback combined with cognitive therapy in the treatment of vascular headache. *J. Cons. Clin. Psychol., 58,* 216–24.

Blanchard, E. B., Appelbaum, K. A., Radnitz, C. L., Michultka, D., Morrill, B., Kirsch, C., Hillhouse, J., Evans, D. D., Guarnieri, P., Attanasio, V., Andrasik, F., Jaccard J., & Dentinger, M. P. (1990a). Placebo-controlled evaluation of abbreviated progressive muscle relaxation and of relaxation combined with cognitive therapy in the treatment of tension headache. *J. Cons. Clin. Psychol., 58,* 210–15.

Blanchard, E. B., & Epstein, L. H. (1978). *A biofeedback primer.* Reading, MA: Addison-Wesley.

Blanchard, E. B., Hickling, E. J., Barton, K., & Taylor, A. E. (1996). One-year prospective follow-up of motor vehicle accident victims. *Behav. Res. Ther., 34*(10), 775–86.

Blanchard, E. B., Hickling, E. J., Taylor, A. E., & Loos, W. (1995). Psychiatric morbidity associated with motor vehicle accidents. *J. Nerv. Ment. Dis., 183*(8), 495–504.

Blanchard, E. B., Miller, S. T., Abel G. G., Haynes, M. R., & Wicker, R. (1979). Evaluation of biofeedback in treatment of borderline essential hypertension. *J. Appl. Beh. Anal., 12,* 99–109.

Blanchard, E. B., & Young, L. D. (1973). Self-control of cardiac functioning: A promise as yet unfulfilled. *Psychol. Bull., 79,* 145–63.

Blanchard, E. B., & Young, L. D. (1974). Clinical applications of biofeedback training: A review of evidence. *Arch. Gen. Psychiat., 30,* 573–89.

Blanchard, J. J., & Neale, J. M. (1994). The neuropsychological signature of schizophrenia: Generalized or differential deficit. *Amer. J. Psychiat., 151*(1), 40–48.

Blanchard, R., (1985). Typology of maletofemale transsexualism. *Arch. Sex. Behav., 14,* 247–61.

Blanchard, R. (1989). The classification and labeling of nonhomosexual gender dysphorias. *Arch. Sex. Behav., 18.,* 315–34.

Blanchard, R. (1991). Clinical observations and systematic study of autogynephilia. *J. Sex Marit. Ther., 17,* 235–51.

Blanchard, R. (1992). Nonmonotonic relation of autogynephilia and heterosexual attraction. *J. Abnorm. Psych., 101,* 271–76.

Blanchard, R. (1993). Varieties of autogynephilia and their relationship to gender dysphoria. *Arch. Sex. Behav., 22,* 241–51.

Blanchard, R. (1994). A structural equation model for age at clinical presentation in nonhomosexual male gender dysphorics. *Arch. Sex. Behav., 23,* 311–32.

Blanchard, R., & Hucker S. J. (1991). Age, transvestitism, bondage, and concurrent paraphilic activities in 117 fatal cases of autoerotic asphyxia. *Brit. J. Psychiat., 159,* 371–77.

Bland, R., Orn, H., & Newman, S. (1988). Lifetime prevalence of psychiatric disorders in Edmonton. *Acta Psychiatr. Scandin., 77,* (Suppl. 338), 24–32.

Blashfield, R. K., & Breen, M. J. (1989). Face validity of the DSM-III-R personality disorders. *Amer. J. Psychiat., 146,* 1575–79.

Blaszczynski, A., McConaghy, N., & Frankova, A. (1989). Crime, antisocial personality and pathological gambling. *Journal of Gambling Behavior, 5,* 137–52.

Blatt, S. J. (1974). Levels of object representation in anaclitic and introjective depression. *The Psychoanalytic Study of the Child, 24,* 107–57.

Blatt, S. J., D'Afflitti, J. P., & Quinlan, D. M. (1976). Experiences of depression in normal young adults. *J. Abn. Psychol., 85,* 383–89.

Blatt, S. J., Sanislow, C. A., Zuroff, D. C., & Pilkonis, P. A. (1996a). Characteristics of effective therapists: Further analyses of the NIMH Treatment of Depression Collaborative Research Program. *J. Cons. Clin. Psychol., 64*(6), 1276–84.

Blatt, S., & Zuroff, D. C. (1992). Interpersonal relatedness and self definition: Two prototypes for depression. *Clin. Psychol. Rev., 12,* 527–62.

Blatt, S. J., Zuroff, D. C., Quinlan, D. M., & Pilkonis, P. A. (1996a). Interpersonal factors in brief treatment of depression: Further analyses of the NIMH Treatment of Depression Collaborative Research Program. *J. Cons. Clin. Psychol., 64*(1), 162–71.

Blazer, D. G. (1997). Depression in the elderly: Myths and misconceptions. *Psychiat. Clin. N. Amer., 20*(1), 111–20.

Blazer, D., George, L. K., Landerman, R., Pennybacker, M., & Melville, M. L. (1985). Psychiatric disorders: A rural/urban comparison. *Arch. Gen. Psychiat., 42,* 651–56.

Bleeker, E. (1968). Many asthma attacks psychological. *Sci. News, 93*(17), 406.

Blehar, M. C., & Rosenthal, N. E. (1989). Seasonal affective disorders and phototherapy: Report of a National Institute of Mental Health-sponsored workshop. *Arch. Gen. Psychiat., 46,* 469–74.

Bleuler, E. (1950). *Dementia praecox or the group of schizophrenias.* New York: International Universities Press. (Originally published in 1911.)

Bleuler, M. (1978). The long-term course of schizophrenic psychoses. In L. C. Wynne, R. L. Cromwell, & S. Matthysse (Eds.), *The nature of schizophrenia: New approaches to research and treatment.* (pp. 631–36). New York: Wiley.

Bloch, H. S. (1969). Army clinical psychiatry in the combat zone—1967–1968. *Amer. J. Psychiat., 126,* 289.

Block, J. H., Block, J., & Gjerde, P. F. (1986). The personality of children prior to divorce: A prospective study. *Child Develop., 57,* 827–840.

Block, J., & Gjerde, P. F. (1990). Depressive symptoms in late adolescence: A longitudinal perspective on personality antecedents. In J. Rolf, A. S. Masten, D. Cicchetti, K. H. Nuechterlein, & S. Weintraub (Eds.), *Risk and protective factors in the development of psychopathology.* New York: Cambridge University Press.

Block, J. H., Gjerde, P. F., & Bloack, J. H. (1991). Personality antecedents of depressive tendencies in 18-year-olds: A prospective study. *J. Pers. Soc. Psychol., 60,* 726–38.

Bloom, B. L. (1992). Computer-assisted psychological intervention: A review and commentary. *Clin. Psychol. Rev., 12,* 169–197.

Bloom, B. L., Asher, S. J., & White, S. W. (1978). Marital disruption as a stressor: A review and analysis. *Psychol. Bull., 85,* 867–94.

Blount, R. L., Dahlquist, L. M., Baer, R. A., & Wuori, D. (1984). A brief, effective method for teaching children to swallow pills. *Behav. Ther., 15,* 381–87.

Blum, R. (1969). *Society and drugs* (Vol. 1). San Francisco: Jossey-Bass.

Blume, E. S. (1990). *Secret survivors: Uncovering incest and its aftereffects.* New York: Ballantine.

Blumenthal, S. J. (1990). Youth suicide: Risk factors, assessment, and treatment of adolescent and young adult suicidal patients. *Psychiat. Clin. N. Amer., 13,* 511–56.

Bobashev, G. V., & Anthony, J. C. (1998). Clusters of marijuana use in the United States. *Amer. J. Publ. Hlth., 148*(12), 1168–73.

Bockhoven, J. S. (1972). *Moral treatment in community mental health.* New York: Springer.

Boehm, G. (1968). At last—a nonaddicting substitute for morphine? *Today's Health, 46*(4), 69–72.

Bogerts, B. (1993). Recent advances in the neuropathology of schizophrenia. *Schizo. Bull., 19*(2), 431–45.

Bogerts, B. (1997). The temporolimbic system theory of positive schizophrenic symptoms. *Schizo. Bull., 23*(3), 423–36.

Bohn, M. J. (1993). Alcoholism. *Psychiat. Clin. N. Amer., 16,* 679–92.

Bolen, D. W., & Boyd, W. H. (1968). Gambling and the gambler. *Arch. Gen. Psychiatr., 18*(5), 617–30.

Bolen, D. W., Caldwell, A. B., & Boyd, W. H. (1975, June). *Personality traits of pathological gamblers.* Paper presented at the Second Annual Conference on Gambling, Lake Tahoe, NV.

Bolger, N. (1990). Coping as a personality process: A prospective study. *J. Pers. Soc. Psychol., 59,* 525–37.

Boll, T. J. (1980). The Halstead-Reitan neuropsychological battery. In S. B. Filskov & T. J. Boll (Eds.), *Handbook of neurophysiology.* New York: Wiley Interscience.

Bolles, R. C., & Fanselow, M. S. (1982). Endorphins and behavior. *Annu. Rev. Psychol., 33,* 87–101.

Bonta, J., Law, M., & Hanson, K. (1998). The prediction of criminal and violent recidivism among mentally disordered offenders: A meta-analysis. *Psychol. Bull., 123*(2), 123–42.

Booth, B. M., Cook, C. L., & Blow, F. C. (1992a). Comorbid mental disorders in patients with AMA discharges from alcoholism treatment. *Hosp. Comm. Psychiat., 43,* 730–31.

Booth, B. M., Russell, D. W., Soucek, S., & Laughlin, P. R. (1992b). Social support and outcome of alcoholism treatment: An exploratory analysis. *Amer. J. Drug Alcoh. Abuse, 18,* 87–101.

Booth, B. M., Russell, D. W., Yates, W. R., & Laughlin, P. R. (1992). Social support and depression in men during alcoholism treatment. *J. Subst. Abuse, 4,* 57–67.

Booth-Kewley, S., & Friedman, H. S. (1987). Psychological predictors of heart disease: A quantitative review. *Psychol. Bull., 101,* 343–62.

Borg, W. R., & Ascione, F. R. (1982). Classroom management in elementary mainstreaming classrooms. *J. Educ. Psychol., 74,* 84–95.

Borkman, T. J., Kaskutas, L. A., Room, J., et al. (1998). An historical and developmental analysis of social model programs. *J. Subst. Abuse, 15*(1), 7–17.

Borkovec, T. D. (1970). Autonomic reactivity to sensory stimulation in psychopathic, neurotic, and normal juvenile delinquents. *J. Cons. Clin. Psychol., 35,* 217–22.

Borkovec, T. D. (1985). The role of cognitive and somatic cues in anxiety and anxiety disorders: Worry and relation-induced anxiety. In A. H. Tuma & J. D. Maser (Eds.), *Anxiety and the anxiety disorders.* (pp. 463–78). Hillsdale, NJ: Erlbaum.

Borkovec, T. D. (1988). Worry: Physiological and cognitive processes. In P. Eelen (Ed.), *Anxiety and the anxiety disorders.* Hillsdale, NJ: Erlbaum.

Borkovec, T. D. (1994). The nature, functions, and origins of worry. In G. L. C. Davey, & F. Tallis (Eds.), *Worrying, perspectives on theory, assessment, and treatment.* (pp. 5–34). Sussex, England: Wiley.

Borkovec, T. D. (1997). On the need for a basic science approach to psychotherapy research. *Psychol. Sci., 8*(3), 145–47.

Borkovec, T. D., Abel, J. L., & Newman, H. (1995). Effects of psychotherapy on comorbid conditions in generalized anxiety disorder. *J. Cons. Clin. Psychol., 63*(3), 479–83.

Borkovec, T. D., & Roemer, L. (1995). Perceived functions of worry among generalized anxiety disorder subjects: Distractions from more emotionally distressing topics. *J. Behav. Ther. Psychiat., 26*(1), 25–30.

Borkovec, T. D., Shadick, R. N., & Hopkins, M. (1991). The nature of normal and pathological worry. In R. M. Rapee & D. H. Barlow (Eds.), *Chronic Anxiety.* New York: Guilford.

Bornstein, R. F. (1992) The dependent personality: Developmental, social, and clinical perspectives. *Psychol. Bull., 112,* 3–23.

Bornstein, R. F. (1995). Comorbidity for dependent personality disorder and other psychological disorders: An integrative review. *J. Person. Dis., 9*(4), 286–303.

Bornstein, R.F. (1997) Dependent personality in the DSM-IV and beyond. *Clin. Psychol.: Sci. Prac., 4,* 175–187.

Borod, J. C. (1992). Interhemispheric and intrahemispheric control of emotion: A focus on unilateral brain damage. *J. Cons. Clin. Psychol., 60*(3), 339–48.

Boronow, J., Pickar, D., Ninan, P. T., Roy, A., & Hommer, D. (1985). Atrophy limited to the third ventricle in chronic schizophrenic patients: Report of a controlled series. *Arch. Gen. Psychiat., 42,* 266–71.

Borthwick-Duffy, S. A. (1994). Epidemiology and prevalence of psychopathology in people with mental retardation. *J. Cons. Clin. Psychol., 62*(1), 17–27.

Borum, R. (1996). Improving the clinical practice of violence risk assessment. *Amer. Psychol., 51,* 945–56.

Borus, J. F. (1974). Incidence maladjustment in Vietnam returnees. *Arch. Gen. Psychiat., 30*(4), 554–57.

Boscarino, J. A. (1996). Posttraumatic stress disorder, exposure to combat, and lower plasma cortisol among Vietnam veterans: Findings and clinical implications. *J. Cons. Clin. Psychol., 64*(1), 191–201.

Bose, K.C. (1932). *Pharmacopoeia Indica.* Calcutta, India: The Book Company.

Boskind-White, M., & White, W. C. (1983). *Bulimarexia: The binge-purge cycle.* New York: Norton.

Boskind-White, M., & White, W. C. (1986). Bulimarexia: A historical-sociocultural perspective. In K. D. Brownell & J. P. Foreyt (Eds.), *Handbook of eating disorders.* (pp. 353–66). New York: Basic Books.

Botvin, G. J. (1983). Prevention of adolescent substance abuse through the development of personal and social competence. *National Institute on Drug Abuse Research Monograph Series, 47,* 115–40.

Botvin, G. J., Baker, E., Dusenbury, L., Tortu, S., & Botvin, E. M. (1990). Preventing adolescent drug abuse through a multimodal cognitive-behavioral approach: Results of a 3 year study. *J. Cons. Clin. Psychol., 58,* 437–57.

Botvin, G. J., & Tortu, S. (1988). Preventing substance abuse through life skills training. In R. H. Price, E. L. Cowen, R. P. Lorion, & J. Ramos-McKay (Eds.), *14 ounces of prevention.* Washington, DC: American Psychological Association.

Boucher, J. (1981). Memory for recent events in autistic children. *J. Autism Devel. Dis., 11*(3), 293–301.

Bourdon, K. H., Boyd, J. H., Rae, D. S., Burns, B. J., Thompson, J. W., & Locke, B. Z. (1988). Gender differences in phobias: Results of the ECA community survey. *Journal of Anxiety Disorders, 2,* 227–41.

Bourne, P. G. (1970). Military psychiatry and the Vietnam experience. *Amer. J. Psychiat., 127*(4), 481–88.

Bouton, M. E. (1994). Conditioning, remembering, and forgetting. *J. Exper. Psychol.: Animal Behavior Processes, 20,* 219–231.

Bouton, M. E., & Nelson, J. B. (1997). The role of context in classical conditioning: Some implications for cognitive behavior therapy. In W. T. O'Donohue (Ed.), *Learning theory and behavior therapy.* (pp. 59-84). Boston, MA: Allyn & Bacon, Inc.

Bowen, R. C., Offord, D. R., & Boyle, M. H. (1990). The prevalence of overanxious disorder and separation anxiety disorder: Results from the Ontario Child

Health Study. *J. Amer. Acad. Child Adoles. Psychiat., 29,* 753–58.

Bowlby, J. (1960). Separation anxiety. *Inter. J. Psychoanal., 41,* 89–93.

Bowlby, J. (1969). *Attachment and loss* (Vol. 1). New York: Basic Books.

Bowlby, J. (1973). *Separation: Anxiety and anger. Psychology of attachment and loss series* (Vol. 3). New York: Basic Books.

Bowlby, J. (1980). *Attachment and loss, III: Loss, sadness, and depression.* New York: Basic Books.

Bowler, J. V., et al. (1997). Comparative evolution of Alzheimer disease, vascular dementia, and mixed dementia. *Arch. Neurol., 54*(6), 697–703.

Boyd, J. H., Burke, J. D., Gruenberg, E., Holzer, C. E., Rae, D. S., George, L. K., Karno, M., Stoltzman, R., McEvoy, L., & Nestadt, G. (1984). Exclusion criteria of DSM-III: A study of co-occurrence of hierarchy-free syndromes. *Arch. of Gen. Psychiat., 41,* 983–89.

Boyd, J. H., & Weissman, M. M. (1985). Epidemiology of major affective disorders. In R. Michels, J. O. Cavenar, H. K. H. Brodie, A. M. Cooper, S. B. Guze, L. L. Judd, G. L. Klerman, & A. J. Solnit (Eds.), *Psychiatry* (Vol. 3). Philadelphia: Lippincott.

Boyd, W. H., & Bolen, D. W. (1970). The compulsive gambler and spouse in group psychotherapy. *International Journal of Group Psychotherapy, 20,* 77–90.

Br. J. Ophthalmol.—*British Journal of Ophthalmology*

Bradbury, T. N., & Miller, G. A. (1985). Season of birth in schizophrenia: A review of evidence, methodology, and etiology. *Psychol. Bull., 98,* 569–94.

Bradford, J. M. (1990). The antiandrogen and hormonal treatment of sex offenders. In W. L. Marshall, D. R. Laws, & H. E. Barbaree (Eds.), *Handbook of sexual assault: Issues, theories, and treatment of the offender.* (pp. 363–85). New York: Plenum.

Bradley, L. A., & Prokop, C. K. (1981). The relationship between medical psychology and behavioral medicine. In C. K. Prokop & L. A. Bradley (Eds.), *Medical psychology: Contributions to behavioral medicine.* New York: Academic Press.

Bradley, L. A., & Prokop, C. K. (1982). Research methods in contemporary medical psychology. In P. C. Kendall & J. N. Butcher (Eds.), *Handbook of research methods in clinical psychology.* New York: Wiley Interscience.

Bradley, S. J., & Zucker, K. J. (1997). Gender identity disorder: A review of the past 10 years. *J. Amer. Acad. Child Adoles. Psychiat., 36,* 872–880.

Brady, K. T., Sonne, S. C., Anton, R., & Ballenger, J. C. (1995). Valproate in the treatment of acute affective episodes complicated by substance abuse: A pilot study. *J. Clin. Psychiat., 56,* 118–21.

Braff, D. L. (1993). Information processing and attention dysfunctions in schizophrenia. *Schizo. Bull., 19*(2), 233–59.

Braginsky, B. M., & Braginsky, D. D. (1974). The mentally retarded: Society's Hansels and Gretels. *Psych. Today, 7*(10), 18, 20–21, 24, 26, 28–30.

Braginsky, B. M., Braginsky, D. D., & Ring, K. (1969). *Methods of madness: The mental hospital as a last resort.* New York: Holt, Rinehart & Winston.

Brancaccio v. State of Florida. (1997). 69850.2d 597 (Fla. App. 4 Dist).

Brandsma, J. M., Maultsby, M. C., & Welsh, R. J. (1980). *Outpatient treatment of alcoholism: A review and comparative study.* Baltimore: University Park Press.

Brane, G. (1986). Normal aging and dementia disorders: Coping and crisis in the family. *Prog. in Neuropsychopharmacol. Biol. Psychiatry, 10,* 287–95.

Braun, B. G., & Sachs, R. G. (1985). The development of multiple personality disorder: Predisposing, precipitating, and perpetuating factors. In R. P. Kluft (Eds.), *Childhood antecedents of multiple personality disorder.* (pp. 37–64). Washington, DC: American Psychiatric Press.

Braun, P., Kochansky, G., Shapiro, R., Greenberg, S., Gudeman, J. E., Johnson, S., & Shore, M. (1981). Overview: Deinstitutionalization of psychiatric patients, a critical review of outcome studies. *Amer. J. Psychiat., 138*(6), 736–49.

Braun, S. (1996). *Buzz.* (1) New York: Oxford University Press.

Brayfield, A. H., et al. (1965). Special Issue: Testing and public policy. *Amer. Psychol., 20,* 857–1005.

Brebner, A., Hallworth, H. J., & Brown, R. I. (1977). Computer-assisted instruction programs and terminals for the mentally retarded. In P. Mittler (Ed.), *Research to practice in mental retardation* (Vol. 2). (pp. 421–26). Baltimore: University Park Press.

Brecksville V. A. Medical Center. (1981). *Annual report for 1981: Gambling treatment program.* Cleveland, OH.

Breggin, P. R. (1979). *Electroshock: Its brain-disabling effects.* New York: Springer.

Breggin, P. R. (1990). Brain damage, dementia, and persistent cognitive dysfunction associated with neuroleptic drugs: Evidence, etiology, implications. *Journal of Mind and Behavior, 11*(3–4), 425–63.

Breggin, P. R. (1991). *Toxic psychiatry.* New York: St. Martin's Press.

Breggin, P. R., & Breggin, G. R. (1995). The hazards of treating "attention deficit/hyperactivity disorder" with methylphenidate (Ritalin). *J. Coll. Stud. Psychother., 10*(2), 55–72.

Breier, A., Buchanan, R. W., Kirkpatrick, B., Davis, O. R., Irish, D., Summerfelt, A., & Carpenter, W. T. (1994). Effects of clozapine on positive and negative symptoms in outpatients with schizophrenia. *Amer. J. Psychiat., 151*(1), 20–26.

Breier, A., Charney, D. S., & Heninger, G. R. (1984). Major depression in patients with agoraphobia and panic disorder. *Arch. Gen. Psychiat., 41,* 1129–35.

Breiter, H. C., Rauch, S. L. et al. (1996). Functional magnetic resonance imagery of symptom provocation in obsessive-compulsive disorder. *Arch. Gen. Psychiat. 53*(7), 595–606.

Breitner, J. C. S., (1986). On methodology and appropriate inference regarding possible genetic factors in typical, late-onset AD. *Neurobiol. Aging, 7,* 476–77.

Breitner, J. C. S., Gatz, M., Bergem, A. L. M., Christian, J. C., Mortimer, J. A., McClearn, G. E., Heston, L. L., Welsh, K. A., Anthony, J. C., Folstein, M. F., & Radebaugh, T. S. (1993). Use of twin cohorts for research in Alzheimer's disease. *Neurology, 43,* 261–67.

Brekke, J. S., & Barrio, C. (1997). Cross-ethnic symptom differences in schizophrenia: The influence of culture and minority status. *Schizo. Bull., 23*(2), 305–16.

Brekke, J. S., Long, J. D., Nesbitt, N., & Sobel, E. (1997). The impact of service characteristics on functional outcomes from community support programs for persons with schizophrenia: A growth curve analysis. *J. Cons. Clin. Psychol., 65*(3), 464–75.

Bremner, J. D., Southwick, S. M., & Charney, D. S. (1995). Etiological factors in the development of posttraumatic stress disorder. In C. M. Mazure (Ed.), *Does stress cause psychiatric illness?* Washington, DC: American Psychiatric Association.

Brems, C. (1995). Women and depression: A comprehensive analysis. In E. E. Beckham & W. R. Leber (Eds.), *Handbook of depression* (2nd ed.). (pp. 539–66). New York: Guilford.

Brems, C., & Johnson, M. E. (1997). Clinical implications of the co-occurence of substance use and other psychiatric conditions. *Prof. Psychol., 28*(5), 437–47.

Brems, C., & Lloyd, P. (1995). Validation of the MMPI-2 low self-esteem scale. *J. Pers. Assess., 65*(3), 550–56.

Brent, D. A., Holder, D., Kolko, D., Birmaher, B., Baugher, M., Roth, C., Iyengar, S., & Johnson, B. A. (1997). A clinical psychotherapy trial for adolescent depression comparing cognitive, family, and supportive. *Arch. Gen. Psychia., 54,* 877–85.

Brent, D. A., Moritz, G., & Liotus, L. (1996). A test of the diathesis-stress model of adolescent depression in friends and acquaintances of suicide victims. In C. Pfeffer (Ed.), *Severe stress and mental disturbance in children.* (pp. 347–60). Washington: American Psychiatric Press.

Breslau, N. (1990). Does brain dysfunction increase children's vulnerability to environmental stress? *Arch. Gen. Psychiat., 47,* 15–20.

Breslau, N., Davis, G.C., Andreski, P., & Peterson, E. (1991). Traumatic events and posttraumatic stress disorder in an urban population of young adults. *Arch. Gen. Psychiat., 48*, 218–22.

Breslau, N., Davis, G. C., Andreski, P., Peterson, E. L., & Schultz, L. R. (1997). Sex differences in posttraumatic stress disorder. *Arch. Gen. Psychiat., 54*, 1044–48.

Breslau, N., Kessler, R. C., Chilcoat, H. D., Schultz, L. R., Davis, G. C., & Andreski, P. (1998). Trauma and posttraumatic stress disorder in the community. *Arch. Gen. Psychiat., 55*, 626–32.

Breton, J. J., Valla, J. P., & Lambert, J. (1993). Industrial disaster and mental health of children and their parents. *J. Amer. Acad. Child Adoles. Psychiat., 32*, 438–45.

Bretschneider, J. G., & McCoy, N. L. (1988). Sexual interest and behavior in healthy 80- to 102-year-olds. *Arch. Sex. Behav., 17*, 109–29.

Brewer, R. D., Morris, P. D., Cole, T. B., Watkins, S., Patetta, M. J., & Popkin, C. (1994). The risk of dying in alcohol-related automobile crashes among habitual drunk drivers. *New Engl. J. Med., 331*(8), 523–17.

Brewerton, T. D., Dansky, B. S., Kilpatrick, D. G., & O'Neil, P. M. (1997). The National Women's Study: Relationship of victimization and post-traumatic stress disorder in bulimia nervosa. *Int. J. Eat. Dis., 21*, 213–228.

Brewin, C. R., Andrews, B., & Gotlib, I. H. (1993). Psychopathology and early experience: A reappraisal of retrospective reports. *Psychol. Bull., 113*, 82–98.

Bridges, F. A., & Cicchetti, D. (1982). Mothers' ratings of the temperament characteristics of Down's Syndrome infants. *Develop. Psychol., 18*, 238–44.

Brinckerhoff, L. C. (1993). Self-advocacy: A critical skill for college students with learning disabilities. *Family & Community Health, 16*(3), 23–33.

Bringman, W. G., Luck, H., Miller, R., & Early, C. E. (Eds.). (1997). *A pictorial history of psychology.* Chicago: Quintessence Books.

Brodie, J. (1996, Jaunary 3). Personal health: Controlling your cholesterol. *New York Times.*

Brodsky, B. S., Cloitre, M., & Dulit, R. A. (1995). Relationship of Dissociation to self-mutilation and childhood abuse in borderline personality disorder. *Amer. J. Psychiat., 152*(12), 1788–92.

Brody, A. L., & Baxter L. (1996). Neuroimaging in obsessive compulsive disorder: Advances in understanding the mediating neuroanatomy. In H. G. Westenberg, J. A. Den Boer, & D. L. Murphy (Eds.), *Advances in the neurobiology of anxiety disorders.* (pp. 313–31). Chichester, England: Wiley.

Brom, D., Kleber, R. J., & Defares, P. B. (1989). Brief psychotherapy for posttraumatic stress disorders. *J. Cons. Clin. Psychol., 57*, 607–12.

Brom, D., Kleber, R. J., & Hofman, M. C. (1993). Victims of traffic accidents: Incidence and prevention of posttraumatic stress disorder. *J. Clin. Psychol., 49*, 131–40.

Brookoff, D., Cook, C. S., Williams, C., & Mann, C. S. (1994). Testing reckless drivers for cocaine and marijuana. *New Engl. J. Med., 331*, 518–22.

Brooks, D. N. (1974). Recognition, memory, and head injury. *J. Neurol. Neurosug. Psychiatry, 37*(7), 794–801.

Broun, H. & Leech, M. (1927). *Anthony Comstock: Roundsman of the Lord.* (pp. 55–56, 80–81). New York: Literary Guild of America.

Brown, G. D. A. (1997). Connectionism, phonology, reading, and regularity in developmental dyslexia. *Brain and Language, 59*, 207–35.

Brown, G. W. (1972). Life-events and psychiatric illness: Some thoughts on methodology and causality. *J. Psychosom. Res., 16*, 311–20.

Brown, G. W., & Harris, T. O. (1978). *Social origins of depression.* London: Tavistock.

Brown, G. W., & Harris, T. O. (1989). *Life events and illness.* New York: Guilford.

Brown, G. W., Harris, T. O., & Bifulco, P. M. (1985). Long-term effects of early loss of parent. In M. Rutter, C. E. Izard, & P. B. Read (Eds.), *Depression in young people: Clinical and developmental perspectives.* (pp. 251–96). New York: Guilford.

Brown, G. W., & Moran, P. M. (1997). Single mothers, poverty and depression. *Pychol. Med. 27*(1), 21–33.

Brown, J. D., & McGill, K. L. (1989). The cost of good fortune: When positive life events produce negative

health consequences. *J. Pers. Soc. Psychol., 57*, 1103–10.

Brown, J. F., & Menninger, K. A. (1940). *Psychodynamics of abnormal behavior.* New York: McGraw-Hill.

Brown, P. (1994). Toward a psychobiological model of dissociation and posttraumatic stress disorder. In S. J. Lynn & J. W. Rhue (Eds.), *Dissociation: Clinical and theoretical perspectives.* (pp. 94–122). New York: Guilford.

Brown, R. A., Evans, D. M., Miller, I. W., Burgess, E. S., & Mueller, T. L. (1997). Cognitive-behavioral treatment for depression in alcoholism. *J. Cons. Clin. Psychol., 65*(5), 715–36.

Brown, R. I. (1977). An integrated program for the mentally handicapped. In P. Mittler (Ed.), *Research to practice in mental retardation* (Vol. 2). (pp. 387–88). Baltimore: University Park Press.

Brown, R., Colter, N., Corsellis, J. A. N., Crow, T. J., & Frith, C. D. (1986). Postmortem evidence of structural brain changes in schizophrenia: Differences in brain weight, temporal horn area, and parahippocampal gyrus compared with average data. *Arch. Gen. Psychiat., 43*, 36–42.

Brown, S. J., Fann, J. R., & Grant, I. (1994). Postconcussional disorder: Time to acknowledge a common source of neurobehavioral morbidity. *J. Neuropsychiat. & Clin. Neurosci., 6*(1), 15–22.

Brown, T. A. (1996). Validity of the DSM-III-R and DSM-IV classification systems for anxiety disorders. In R. M. Rapee (Ed.), *Current controversies in the anxiety disorders.* (pp. 21–45). New York: Guilford.

Brown, T. A., Chorpita, B. F., & Barlow, D. H. (1998). Structural relationships among dimensions of the DSM-IV anxiety and mood disorders and dimensions of negative affect, positive affect, and autonomic arousal. *J . Abn. Psychol., 107*(2), 179–92.

Brown, T. A., O'Leary, T. A., & Barlow, D. H. (1993). Generalized anxiety disorder. In D. H. Barlow (Ed.), *Clinical handbook of psychological disorders.* New York: Guilford.

Brown, W. T., Jenkins, E. C., Cohen, I. L., Fisch, G. S., WolfSchein, E. G., Gross, A., Fein, D., Mason-Brothers, A., Ritvo, E., Ruttenberg, B. A., Bentley, W., & Castell, S. (1986). Fragile x and autism: A multicenter survey. *Amer. J. Med. Genet., 23*, 341–52.

Browne, A., & Finkelhor, D. (1986). Impact of child sexual abuse: A review of the research. *Psychol. Bull. 99*, 66–77.

Browne, E. G. (1921). *Arabian Medicine.* New York: Macmillan.

Brownell, K. D., & Rodin, J. (1994). The dieting maelstrom: Is it possible and advisable to lose weight? *Amer. Psychol., 39*, 781–91.

Brownell, K. D., & Wadden, T. A. (1992). Etiology and treatment of obesity: Understanding a serious, prevalent, and refractory disorder. *J. Cons. Clin. Psychol., 60*, 505–17.

Brownmiller, S. (1975). *Against our will: Men, women, and rape.* New York: Simon & Schuster.

Brozek, J., & Schurch, B. (1984). *Malnutrition and behavior: Critical assessment of key issues.* Lausanne, Switzerland: Nestle Foundation.

Bruch, H. (1973). *Eating disorders: Obesity, anorexia nervosa and the person within.* New York: Basic Books.

Bruch, H. (1986). Anorexia nervosa: The therapeutic task. In K. D. Brownell & J. P. Foreyt (Eds.), *Handbook of eating disorders.* (pp. 328–32). New York: Basic Books.

Bruch, H. (1988). *Conversations with anorexics.* New York: Basic Books.

Bruch, M. A. (1989). Familial and developmental antecedents of social phobia: Issues and findings. Special Issue: Social phobia. *Clin. Psychol. Rev., 9*(1), 37–47.

Bruck, M. (1987). Social and emotional adjustments of learning-disabled children. In S. J. Ceci (Ed.), *Handbook of cognitive, social, and neuropsychological aspects of learning disabilities* (Vol. 1). (pp. 361–80). Hillsdale, NJ: Erlbaum.

Bruck, M., Ceci., S.J., Francouer, E., & Renick, A. (1995). Anatomically detailed dolls do not facilitate

preschoolers' reports of a pediatric examination involving genital touch. *J. Exper. Psychol. Applied, 1*, 95–109.

Bry, B. H., McKeon, P., & Pandina, R. J. (1982). The extent of drug use as a function of number of risk factors. *J. Abn. Psychol., 91*(4), 273–79.

Buchanan, G. & Seligman, M. E. P. (Eds.) (1995) *Explanatory Style.* Hillsdale NJ: Erlbaum.

Buchanan, G. M., & Seligman, M. E. P. (1995). Afterword: The future of the field. In G. M. Buchanan & M. E. P. Seligman (Eds.), *Explanatory Style.* (pp. 247–52). Hillsdale, NJ: Erlbaum.

Buchanan, R. W., & Carpenter, W. T., Jr. (1997). The neuroanatomies of schizophrenia. *Schizo. Bull., 23*(3), 367–72.

Buchanan, R. W., Stevens, J. R., & Carpenter, W. T., Jr. (1997). The neuroanatomy of schizophrenia: Editors' introduction. *Schizo. Bull., 23*(23), 365–66.

Bucher, B., & Lovaas, O. I. (1967). Use of aversive stimulation in behavior modification. In M. R. Jones (Ed.), *Miami symposium on the prediction of behavior 1967: Aversive stimulation* (pp. 77–145). Coral Gables, FL: University of Miami Press.

Buchsbaum, M. S., Haier, R. J., Potkin, S. G., Nuechterlein, K., Bracha, H. S., Katz, M., Lohr, J., Wu, J., Lottenberg, S., Jerabek, P. A., Trenary, M., Tafalla, R., Reynolds, C., & Bunney, W. E., Jr. (1992). Frontostriatal disorder of cerebral metabolism in never-medicated schizophrenics. *Arch. Gen. Psychiat., 49*(12), 935–41.

Buchsbaum, M. S., Murphy, D. L., Coursey, R. D., Lake, C. R., & Zeigler, M. G. (1978). Platelet monoamine oxidase, plasma dopamine betahydroxylase and attention in a "biochemical high-risk" sample. In L. C. Wynne, R. L. Cromwell, & S. Matthysse (Eds.), *The nature of schizophrenia: New approaches to research and treatment.* (pp. 387–96). New York: Wiley.

Buckley, P. (1982). Identifying schizophrenic patients who should not receive medication. *Schizo. Bull., 8*, 429–32.

Buckley, P., Thompson, P., Way, L., & Meltzer, H. Y. (1994). Substance abuse among patients with treatment-resistant schizophrenia: Characteristics and implications for clozapine therapy. *Amer. J. Psychiat., 151*, 385–89.

Buckner, H. T. (1970). The transvestic career path. *Psychiatry, 3*(3), 381–89.

Budoff, M. (1977). The mentally retarded child in the mainstream of the public school: His relation to the school administration, his teachers, and his agemates. In P. Mittler (Ed.), *Research to practice in mental retardation* (Vol. 2). (pp. 307–13). Baltimore: University Park Press.

Bullard, D. M., Glaser, H. H., Heagarty, M. C., & Pivcheck, E. C. (1967). Failure to thrive in the neglected child. *Amer. J. Orthopsychiat., 37*, 680–90.

Bullman, T. A., & Kang, H. K. (1997). Posttraumatic stress disorder and the risk of traumatic deaths among Vietnam veterans. In C. S. Fullerton & R. J. Ursano (Eds.), *Posttraumatic stress disorders.* (pp. 175–89). Washington: American Psychiatric Press.

Bumbalo, J. H., & Young, D. E. (1973). The self-help phenomenon. *Amer. J. Nurs., 73*, 1588–91.

Bumpass, L. (1984). Some characteristics of children's second families. *American Journal of Sociology, 90*, 608–23.

Bunn, J. V., Booth, B. M., Cook, C. A. L., Blow, F. C., & Fortney, J. C. (1994). The relationship between mortality and intensity of inpatient alcoholism treatment. *Amer. J. Pub. Hlth., 84*, 211–14.

Burchard, J. D., & Schafer, M. (1992). Improving accountability in a service delivery system in children's mental health. *Clin. Psychol. Rev., 12*, 867–82.

Burgess, A. W., & Holmstrom, L. (1974). Rape trauma syndrome. *Amer. J. Psychiat., 131*, 981–86.

Burgess, A. W., & Holmstrom, L. (1976). Coping behavior of the rape victim. *Amer. J. Psychiat., 133*, 413–18.

Burke, K. C., Burke, J. D., Regier, D. A., & Rae, D. S. (1990). Age at onset of selected mental disorders in five community populations. *Arch. Gen. Psychiat., 47*, 511–18.

Burks, V. S., Dodge, K. A., & Price, J. M. (1995) Models of internalizing outcomes of early rejection. *Develop. Psychopath., 7*, 683–95.

Burns, D. (1980). *Feeling good.* New York: Signet.

Burns, G. W. (1972). *The science of genetics.* New York: Macmillan.

Burros, W. M. (1974). The growing burden of impotence. *Fam. Hlth., 6*(5), 18–21.

Burstein, A. (1985). How common is delayed posttraumatic stress disorder? *Amer. J. Psychiat., 142*(7), 887.

Bush, D. F., & O'Shea, P. G. (1996). Workplace violence: Comparative use of prevention practices and policies. In G. R. Vandenbos & E. Q. Bulatao (Eds.), *Violence in the workplace.* (pp. 283–98). Washington: American Psychological Association.

Bushnell, J. A., Wells, J. E., & Oakley-Browne, M. A. (1992). Long-term effects of intrafamilial sexual abuse in childhood. *Acta Psychiatr. Scandin., 85,* 136–42.

Busink, R. (1997). Reading and phonological awareness: What we have learned and how we can use it. *Reading Research and Instruction, 36*(3), 199–215.

Buss, D. M. (1989). Sex differences in human mate preferences: Evolutionary hypotheses tested in 37 cultures. *Behavioral and Brain Sciences, 12,* 1–49.

Buss, D. M. (1994). *The evolution of desire.* (pp. 144–48). New York: Basic Books.

Butcher, J. N. 1979. Use of the MMPI in industry. In J. N. Butcher (Ed.), *New developments in the use of the MMPI.* Minneapolis: University of Minnesota Press.

Butcher, J. N. (1980, Nov.). The role of crisis intervention in an airport disaster plan. *Aviation, Space and Environmental Medicine,* 1260–62.

Butcher, J. N. (1984). Current developments in MMPI use: An international perspective. In J. N. Butcher & C. D. Spielberger (Eds.), *Advances in personality assessment* (Vol. 4). Hillsdale, NJ: Erlbaum.

Butcher, J. N. (1993). *User's guide for the MMPI-2 Minnesota Report: Adult Clinical System.* Minneapolis: National Computer Systems.

Butcher, J. N. (1995). How to use computer-base reports. In J.N. Butcher (Ed.), *Clinical personality assessment: Practical considerations.* (pp. 78–94). New York: Oxford University Press.

Butcher, J. N. (1996) Understanding abnormal behavior across cultures: The use of objective personality assessment methods. In J. N. Butcher (Ed.), *International adaptations of the MMPI-2.* (pp. 3–25). Minneapolis: University of Minnesota Press.

Butcher, J. N. (Ed.). (1996). *International applications of the MMPI-2: A handbook of research and clinical applications.* Minneapolis, MN: University of Minnesota Press.

Butcher, J. N., Dahlstrom, W. G., Graham, J. R., Tellegen, A., & Kaemmer, B. (1989). *Minnesota Multiphasic Personality Inventory: MMPI-2: Manual for administration and scoring.* Minneapolis: University of Minnesota Press.

Butcher, J. N., & Dunn, L. (1989). Human responses and treatment needs in airline disasters. In R. Gist and B. Lubin (Eds.), *Psychosocial aspects of disaster.* New York: Wiley.

Butcher, J. N., & Graham, J. R. (1994). The MMPI-2: A new standard for personality assessment and research in counseling settings. *Measurement and Evaluation in Counseling and Development, 27,* 131–50.

Butcher, J. N., & Hatcher, C. (1988). The neglected entity in air disaster planning: Psychological services. *Amer. Psychol., 43,* 724–29.

Butcher, J. N., & Miller, K. (1998). Personality assessment in personal injury litigation. In A. Hess & I. I. Weiner (Eds.), *Handbook of forensic psychology* (2nd ed.). New York: Wiley.

Butcher, J. N., Narikiyo, T., & Vitousek, K. B. (1993). Understanding abnormal behavior in cultural context. In P. B. Sutker & H. E. Adams (Eds.), *Comprehensive handbook of psychopathology.* (pp. 83–105). New York: Plenum.

Butcher, J. N., & Pancheri, P. (1976). *Handbook of international MMPI research.* Minneapolis: University of Minnesota Press.

Butcher, J. N., & Rouse, S. (1996). Clinical personality assessment. *Ann. Rev. Psychol., 47,* 87–111.

Butcher, J. N., & Rouse, S. (in press). Personality assessment. *Ann. Rev. Psychol.*

Butcher, J. N., Rouse, S., & Perry, J. (1998). Empirical description of psychopathology in therapy clients: Correlates of MMPI-2 scales. In J. N. Butcher (Ed.), *Foundation sources for the MMPI-2.* Minneapolis: University of Minnesota Press.

Butcher, J. N., Stelmachers, Z. T., & Maudal, G. R. (1983). Crisis intervention and emergency psychotherapy. In I. Weiner (Ed.), *Handbook of clinical methods* (2nd ed.). New York: Wiley.

Butcher, J. N., Williams, C. L., Graham, J. R., Archer, R., Tellegen, A., Ben-Porath, Y. S., & Kaemmer, B. (1992). *MMPI-A: Manual for administration, scoring, and interpretation.* Minneapolis: University of Minnesota Press.

Butler, G. (1989). Issues in the application of cognitive and behavioral strategies to the treatment of social phobia. *Clin. Psychol. Rev., 9,* 91–186.

Butterfield, F. (1998,). Prisons replace hospitals for the nation's mentally ill. *New York Times,* pp. 1–17.

Button, E. (1993). *Eating disorders: Personal construct theory and change.* New York: Wiley.

Butzlaff, R. L., & Hooley, J. M. (1998). Expressed emotion and psychiatric relapse: A meta-analysis. *Arch. Gen. Psychol., 55*(6), 547–52.

Byassee, J. E. (1977). Essential hypertension. In R. B. Williams, Jr. & W. D. Gentry (Eds.), *Behavioral approaches to Medical treatment.* (pp. 113–37). Cambridge, MA: Ballinger.

Bychowski, G. (1950). On neurotic obesity. *Psychoanal. Rev., 37,* 301–19.

Cacioppo, J. T. (1994). Social neuroscience: Autonomic, neuroendocrine, and immune response to stress. *Psychophysiology, 31,* 113–28.

Cacioppo, J. T., et al. (1998). Cellular immune responses to acute stress in female caregivers of dementia patients and matched controls. *Hlth. Psychol., 17,* 182–89.

Cade, J. F. J. (1949). Lithium salts in the treatment of psychotic excitement. *Medical Journal of Australia, 36* (part II): 349–52.

Cadoret, R. J., Leve, L. D., & Devor, E. (1997). Genetics and aggressive behavior. *Psychiat. Clin. N. Amer., 20,* 301–22.

Cadoret, R. J., O'Gorman, T. W., Troughton, E., & Heywood, E. (1985). Alcoholism and antisocial personality: Interrelationships and environmental factors. *Arch. Gen. Psychiat., 42,* 161–67.

Cadoret, R. J., Troughton, E., & O'Gorman, T. W. (1987). Genetic and environmental factors in alcohol abuse and antisocial personality. *J. Stud. Alcoh., 48,* 1–8.

Caetano, R. , Clark, C. L., Tam, T. (1998). Alcohol consumption among racial/ethnic minorities, *Alcohol World: Health and Research, 22* (4), 233–42.

Calhoun, K. S., & Resick, P. A. (1993). Posttraumatic stress disorder. In D. H. Barlow (Eds.), *Clinical handbook of psychological disorders.* (pp. 48–98). New York: Guilford.

Callahan, L. A., & Silver, E. (1998). Factors associated with the conditional release of persons acquitted by reason of insanity: A decision tree approach. *Law and Human Behavior, 22*(2), 147–63.

Callahan, L. A., Robbins, P. C., Steadman, H., & Morrissey, J. P. (1995). The hidden effects of Montana's "abolition" of the insanity defense. *Psychiat. Q., 66*(2), 103–17.

Cameron, N. (1959). Paranoid conditions and paranoia. In S. Arieti (Ed.), *American handbook of psychiatry.* New York: Basic Books.

Camp, B. W., et al. (1998). Maternal and neonatal risk factors for retardation: Defining the "at risk" child. *Early Human Development, 50*(2), 159–73.

Campbell, D. (1926). *Arabian medicine and its influence on the Middle Ages.* New York: Dutton.

Campbell, M. (1987). Drug treatment of infantile autism: The past decade. In H. Meltzer (Ed.), *Psychopharmacology: The third generation of progress.* (pp. 1225–31). New York: Raven Press.

Campbell, M., & Cueva, J. E. (1995). Psychopharmacology in child and adolescent psychiatry: A review of

the past seven years. Part 1. *J. Amer. Acad. Child Adoles. Psychiat. 34*(9), 1124–32.

Campbell, S. B., Cohn, J. F., Ross, S., Elmore, M., & Popper, S. (1990, April). *Postpartum adaptation and postpartum depression in primiparous women.* International Conference of Infant Studies, Montreal.

Canetto, S. S. (1997). Gender and suicidal behavior: Theories and evidence. In R. W. Maris, M. M. Silverman, & S. S. Canetton (Eds.), *Review of Suicidology, 1997.* (pp. 138–67). New York: Guilford.

Cannon, M., et al., (1997). Premorbid social functioning in schizophrenia and bipolar disorder: Similarities and differences. *Amer. J. Psychiat., 154*(11), 1544–1550.

Cannon, T. D. (1998a). Genetic and perinatal influences in the etiology of schizophrenia: A neurodevelopmental model. In M. F. Lenzenweger & R. H. Dworkin (Eds.), *Origins and development of schizophrenia.* (pp. 67–92). Washington: American Psychological Association.

Cannon, T. D. (1998b). Neurodevelopmental influences in the genesis and epigenesis of schizophrenia: An overview. *App Prev. Psychol., 7*(1), 47–62.

Cannon, T. D., et al. (1998). The genetic epidemiology of schizophrenia in a Finnish twin cohort. *Arch. Gen Psychiat., 55*(1), 67–74,

Cannon, T. D., & Marco, E. (1994). Structural brain abnormalities as indicators of vulnerability to schizophrenia. *Schizo. Bull., 20*(1), 89–102.

Cannon, T. D., Mednick, S. A., Parnas, J., Schulsinger, F., Praestholm, J., & Vestergaard, A. (1993). Developmental brain abnormalities in the offspring of schizophrenic mothers: I. Contributions of genetic and perinatal factors. *Arch. Gen. Psychiat., 50*(7), 551–64.

Cannon, T. D., Mednick, S. A., Parnas, J., Schulsinger, F., Praestholm, J., & Vestergaard, A. (1994). Developmental brain abnormalities in the offspring of schizophrenic mothers: II. Structural brain characteristics of schizophrenia and schizotypal personality disorder. *Arch. Gen. Psychiat., 51*(12), 955–62.

Cannon, W. B. (1915). *Bodily changes in pain, hunger, and rage* (1st ed.). New York: D. Appleton.

Cannon, W. B. (1929). *Bodily changes in pain, hunger, fear and rage.* New York: Appleton.

Cantor, N., Smith, E., French, R. D. S., & Mezzich, J. (1980). Psychiatric diagnosis as prototype categorization. *J. Abn. Psychol., 89,* 181–93.

Cantwell, D. P., & Baker, L. (1989). Stability and natural history of DSM III childhood diagnoses. *J. Amer. Acad. Child Adoles. Psychiat. 28,* 691–700.

Capaldi, D. M., & Patterson, G. R. (1994). Interrelated influences of contextual factors on antisocial behavior in childhood and adolescence for males. In D. C. Fowles, P. Sutker, & S. H. Goodman (Eds.), *Progress in experimental personality and psychopathology research.* New York: Springer.

Capps, L., Kasari, C., Yirmiya, N., & Sigman, M. (1993). Parental perception of emotional expressiveness in children with autism. *J. Cons. Clin. Psychol., 61,* 475–84.

Capron, C. & Duyme, M. (1989). Assessment of effects of socio-economic status on IQ in a full cross-fostering study. *Nature, 340,* 552–554.

Cardenas, D. D. (1993). Cognition-enhancing drugs. *J. Head Trauma Rehab., 8*(4), 112–14.

Cardona, F., Camillo, E., Casini, M. P., Luchetti, A., & Muscetta, A. (1997). Tic disorders in childhood: A retrospective study. *Giornale di Neuropsichiatria dell'Eta Evolutiva, 17*(2), 120–26.

Cardoso, F., & Jankovic, J. (1997). Dystonia and dyskinesia. *Psychiatr. Clin. N. Amer., 20*(4), 821–38.

Carey, G. (1992). Twin imitation for antisocial behavior: Implications for genetic and family environment research. *J. Abn. Psychol., 101*(1), 18–25.

Carey, G. (1993). Genetics and violence. In A. J. Reiss & J. A. Roth (Eds.), *Understanding and preventing violence.* Washington, DC: National Academy Press.

Carey, G., & DiLalla, D. L. (1994). Personality and psychopathology: Genetic perspectives. *J. Abn. Psychol., 103,* 32–43.

Carey, G., & Goldman, D. (1997). The genetics of antisocial behavior. In D. M. Stoff, J. Breiling, & J. D. Maser (Eds.), *Handbook of antisocial behavior.* (pp. 243–254). New York: Wiley.

Carey, G., & Gottesman, I. I. (1981). Twin and family studies of anxiety, phobia and obsessive disorders. In D. F. Klien & J. Rabkin (Eds.), *Anxiety: New research and changing concepts.* (pp. 117–36). New York: Raven Press.

Carlier, I. V., & Gersons, B. P. (1997). Stress reactions in disaster victims following the Bijlmermeer plane crash. *J. Trauma. Stress, 10*(2), 329–35.

Carliner, I. V., Lamberts, R. D., Gersons, B. (1997). Risk factors for post-traumatic stress symptomatology in police officers: A prospective analysis. *J. Nerv. Ment. Dis. 185*(8), 498–506.

Carlson R. (1997, April). *Sildenafil: An effective oral drug for impotence. Inpharma, 1085: 11-12.* Annual Meeting of the American Urological Association, New Orleans.

Carlson, C. L., & Bunner, M. R. (1993). Effects of methylphenidate on the academic performance of children with Attention Deficit Hyperactivity Disorder and learning disabilities. *School Psychol. Rev., 22,* 184–98.

Carlson, C. R., & Hoyle, R. H. (1993). Efficacy of abbreviated progressive muscle relaxation training: A quantitative review of behavioral medicine research. *J. Cons. Clin. Psychol., 61*(6), 1059–67.

Carlson, E. A., & Sroufe, L. A. (1995). Contribution of attachment theory to developmental psychopathology. In D. Cicchetti, & D. J. Cohen (Eds.), *Developmental Psychopathology: Vol. 1 Theory and Methods.* (pp. 581–617). New York: Wiley.

Carlson, E. B., & Armstrong, J. (1994). The diagnosis and assessment of dissociative disorders. In S. J. Lynn & J. W. Rhue (Eds.), *Dissociation: Clinical and theoretical perspectives.* (pp. 159–74). New York: Guilford.

Carlson, E. B., & Rosser-Hogan, R. (1993). Mental health status of Cambodian refugees ten years after leaving their homes. *Amer. J. Orthopsychiat., 63,* 223–31.

Carlson, M. (1990, Jan. 29). Six years of torture. *Time, 135,* 26–27.

Carlsson, A. (1986). Searching for antemortem markers premature. *Neurobiol. Aging, 7,* 400–1.

Carlsson, A. (1988). The current status of the dopamine hypothesis of schizophrenia. *Neuropsychopharmacology, 1,* 179–86.

Carothers, J. C. (1947). A study of mental derangement in Africans, and an attempt to explain its peculiarities more especially in relation to the African attitude of life. *J. Ment. Sci., 93,* 548–97.

Carothers, J. C. (1951). Frontal lobe function and the African. *J. Ment. Sci., 97,* 12–48.

Carothers, J. C. (1959). Culture, psychiatry, and the written word. *Psychiatry, 22,* 307–20.

Carpenter, W. T., Jr. (1997). The risk of medication-free research. *Schizo. Bull., 23*(1), 11–18.

Carpenter, W. T., Buchanan, R. W., Kirkpatrick, B., Tamminga, C., & Wood, F. (1993). Strong inference, theory testing, and the neuroanatomy of schizophrenia. *Arch. of Gen. Psychiat., 50*(10), 825–31.

Carpenter, W. T., & Keith, S. J. (1986). Integrative treatments in schizophrenia. *Psychiat. Clin. N. Amer., 9,* 153–64.

Carpenter, W. T., & Strauss, J. S. (1979). Diagnostic issues in schizophrenia. In L. Bellak (Ed.), *Disorders of the schizophrenic syndrome.* New York: Basic Books.

Carpentieri, S., & Morgan, S. B. (1996). Adaptive and intellectual functioning in autistic and nonautistic retarded children. *J. Autism and Devel. Diso., 26*(6), 611–20.

Carr, A. (1997). Positive practice in family therapy. *J. Marit. Fam. Ther., 23*(3), 271–93.

Carr, A. T. (1971). Compulsive neurosis: Two psychophysiological studies. *Bull. Brit. Psychol. Soc., 24,* 256–57.

Carroll, B. J. (1982). The dexamethasone suppression test for melancholia. *Brit. J. Psychiat., 140,* 292–304.

Carroll, K. M. (1993). A comparison of alternate systems for diagnosing antisocial personality disorder in cocaine abusers. *Compr. Psychiat., 181,* 436–43.

Carroll, K. M. (1997). Manual-guided psychosocial treatment: A new virtual requirement for pharma-cotherapy trials? *Arch. Gen. Psychiat., 54*(10), 923–28.

Carroll, K. M., Ball, S. A., & Rounsaville, B. J. (1993). A comparison of alternate systems for diagnosing antisocial personality disorder in cocaine abusers. *J. Nerv. Ment. Dis., 181,* 436–43.

Carroll, K. M., Power, M. E., Bryant, K. J., & Rounsaville, B. J. (1992). One-year follow-up status of treatment-seeking cocaine abusers: Psychopathology and dependence severity as predictors of outcome. *J. Nerv. Ment. Dis., 181,* 71–79.

Carroll, K. M., & Rounsaville, B. J. (1993). History and significance and childhood attention deficit disorder in treatment-seeking cocaine abusers. *Compr. Psychiat., 34,* 75–82.

Carroll, K. M., Rounsaville, B. J., Gordon, L. T., Nich, C., Jatlow, P., Bisighini, R. M., & Gawin, F. H. (1994). Psychotherapy and pharmacotherapy for ambulatory cocaine abusers. *Arch. Gen. Psychiat., 51,* 177–87.

Carruthers, M., (1980). Hazardous occupations and the heart. In C. L. Cooper & R. Payne (Eds.), *Current concerns in occupational stress.* New York: Wiley.

Carskadon, M. A. (1990). Patterns of sleep and sleepiness in adolescents. *Pediatrician, 17,* 5–12.

Carson, R. C. (1979). Personality and exchange in developing relationships. In R. L. Burgess & T. L. Huston (Eds.), *Social exchange in developing relationships.* New York: Academic Press.

Carson, R. C. (1982). Self-fulfilling prophecy, maladaptive behavior, and psychotherapy. In J. C. Anchin & D. J. Kiesler (Eds.), *Handbook of interpersonal psychotherapy.* (pp. 64–77). New York: Pergamon.

Carson, R. C. (1989). Personality. *Ann. Rev. Psychol.* (Vol. 40). (pp. 227–48). Palo Alto, CA: Annual Reviews.

Carson, R. C. (1990a). Needed: A new beginning. *Contemp. Psychol., 35,* 11–12.

Carson, R. C. (1990b). Assessment: What role the assessor? *J. Pers. Assess., 54,* 435–45.

Carson, R. C. (1991). Tunnel vision and schizophrenia. In W. F. Flack, D. R. Miller, & M. Wiener (Eds.), *What is schizophrenia?* (pp. 245–49). New York: Springer-Verlag.

Carson, R. C. (1993). Can the Big Five help salvage the DSM? *Psychol. Inq., 4,* 98–100.

Carson, R. C. (1994a). Reflections on SASB and the assessment enterprise. *Psychol. Inq., 5,* 317–19.

Carson, R. C. (1996). Aristotle, Galileo, and the DSM Taxonomy: The case of schizophrenia. *J. Cons. Clin. Psychol., 64*(6), 1133–39.

Carson, R. C. (1996). Seamlessness in personality and its derangements. *J. Personal. Assess., 66*(2), 240–247.

Carson, R. C. (1997). Costly compromises: A critique of the diagnostic and statistical manual of mental disorders. In S. Fisher & R. P. Greenberg (Eds.), *From placebo to panacea: Putting psychiatric drugs to the test.* (pp. 98–112). New York: Wiley.

Carson, R. C., & Sanislow, C. A. (1993). The schizophrenias. In P. B. Sutker & H. E. Adams (Eds.), *Comprehensive handbook of psychopathology.* (pp. 295–333). New York: Plenum.

Carson, T. P., & Carson, R. C. (1984). The affective disorders. In H. E. Adams & P. B. Sutker (Eds.), *Comprehensive handbook of psychopathology.* New York: Plenum.

Carstairs, G. M., & Kapur, R. L. (1976). *The great universe of Kota: Stress, change and mental disorder in an Indian village.* Berkeley, CA: University of California Press.

Carter, C. S., Mintun, M., Nichols, T., & Cohen, J. D. (1997). Anterior cingulate gyrus dysfunction and selective attention deficits in schizophrenia: H2O PET study during single-trial Stroop task performance. *Amer. J. Psychiat., 154*(12), 1670–75.

Carter, C. S., Servan-Schreiber, D., & Perlstein, W. M. (1997). Anxiety disorders and the syndrome of chest pain with normal coronary arteries: Prevalence and pathophysiology. *J. Clin. Psychiat., 58*(3), 70–73.

Carter, J. C., & Fairburn, C. G. (1998). Cognitive behavioral self help for binge eating disorder: A controlled effectiveness study. *J. Cons. Clin. Psychol., 66*(4), 616–23.

Casey, R. J., & Berman, J. S. (1985). The outcome of psychotherapy with children. *Psychol. Bull., 98,* 388–400.

Cashdan, S. (1988). *Object relations therapy: Using the relationship.* New York: Norton.

Caspi, A., Elder, G. H., & Herbener, E. S. (1990). Childhood personality and the prediction of life-course patterns. In L. N. Robins & M. Rutter (Eds.), *Straight and devious pathways from childhood to adulthood.* Cambridge, UK: Cambridge University Press.

Caspi, A., & Moffitt, T. E. (1995). The continuity of maladaptive behavior: From description to understanding in the study of antisocial behavior. In D. Cicchetti & C. Cohen (Eds.), *Developmental psychopathology.* Vol 2: Risk, disorder and adaptation (pp. 472–511). New York: Wiley.

Cassano, G. B., Akiskal, H. S., Savino, M., Musetti, L., & Perugi, G. (1992). Proposed subtypes of bipolar II and related disorders: With hypomanic episodes (or cyclothymia) and with hyperthymic temperament. *J. Affect. Dis., 26,* 127–40.

Cassano, G. B., Musetti, L., Perugi, G., Mignani, V., Soriani, A., McNair, D.M., & Akiskal, H. S. (1987). *Major depression subcategories: Their potentiality for clinical research. In: Diagnosis and treatment of depression. "Quo Vadis?"* Symposium, Sanofi Group, May 11–12, Montpellier, France.

Cassidy, F., Forest, K., Murry, E., & Carroll, B. J. (1998). A factor analysis of the signs and symptoms of mania. *Arch. Gen. Psychiat., 55*(1), 27–32.

Castiglioni, A. (1946). *Adventures of the mind.* New York: Knopf.

Castro, J. (1993, May 31). What price mental health? *Time,* pp. 59–60.

Cate, R. M., & Lloyd, S. A. (1992). *Courtship.* Newbury Park, CA: Sage.

Cato, C., & Rice, B. D. (1982). *Report from the study group on rehabilitation of clients with specific learning disabilities.* St. Louis: National Institute of Handicapped Research.

Caton, C. L. M., Wyatt, R. J., Felix, A., Grunberg, J., & Dominguez, B. (1993). Follow-up of chronically homeless mentally ill men. *Ameri. J. Psychiat., 150*(11), 1639–42.

Cattell, R., Eber, H., & Tatsuoko, M. (1988). *Handbook for the Sixteen Personality Factor Questionnaire (16PF).* Champaign, IL: Institute for Personality and Ability Testing.

Caudill, B. D., Hoffman, J. A., Hubbard, R. L., Flynn, P. M., & Luckey, J. W. (1994). Parental history of substance abuse as a risk factor in predicting crack smokers' substance use, illegal activities, and psychiatric status. *Amer. J. Drug Alcoh. Abuse, 20,* 341–54.

Ceci, S. J. (1995). False beliefs: Some developmental and clinical considerations. In D. Schacter, (Ed.), *Memory distortions: How minds, brains and societies reconstruct the past.* (pp. 91–125). New York: Harvard University Press.

Ceci, S. J., & Baker, J. C. (1987). How shall we conceptualize the language problems of learning-disabled children? In S. J. Ceci (Ed.), *Handbook of cognitive, social, and neuropsychological aspects of learning disabilities* (Vol. 2). (pp. 103–14). Hillsdale, NJ: Erlbaum.

Center for Disease Control (1994). *Statistics on violent crimes in the United States.* Atlanta, GA: Author.

Center for Disease Control. (1997). Fire-arm related years of potential life lost before age 65 years—United States, 1980–1991. *MMWR—Morb-Mort Weekly Report, 43,* 609.

Centerwall, W. R., & Centerwall, S. A. (1961). Phenylketonuria (Folling's disease): The story of its discovery. *Journal of the History of Medicine, 16,* 292–96.

Chafel, J. A. (1992). Funding Head Start: What are the issues? *Amer. J. Orthopsychiat., 62*(1), 9–21.

Chambers, R. E. (1952). Discussion of "Survival factors. . ." *Amer. J. Psychiat., 109,* 247–48.

Chambless, D., et al. (1996). An update on empirically validated therapies. *Clin. Psychol., 49,* 5–18.

Chambless, D. L., et al. (1998). Update on empirically validated therapies, II. *Clin. Psychol., 51*(1), 3–16.

Chambless, D. L., & Mason, J. (1986). Sex, sex role stereotyping, and agoraphobia. *Behav. Res. Ther., 24,* 231–5.

Chance, P. (1986, Oct.). Life after head injury. *Psych. Today, 20,* 62–69.

Chandler, H. N. (1985). The kids-in-between: Some solutions. *J. Learn. Dis. 18,* 368.

Chappel, J. N. (1993). Long-term recovery from alcoholism. *Psychiat. Clin. N. Amer., 16,* 177–87.

Charlop-Christie, M. H., Schreibman, L., Pierce, K., & Kurtz, P. F. (1998). Childhood autism. In R. J. Morris, T. R. Kratochwill, et al. (Eds.), *The practice of child therapy.* (pp. 271–302). Boston: Allyn & Bacon.

Charman, T., Swettenham, J., Baron–Cohen, S., Cox, A., Baird, G., & Drew, A. (1997). Infants with autism: An investigation of empathy, pretend play, joint attention, and imitation. *Develop. Psychol., 33*(5), 781–89.

Charney, D., Grillon, C., & Bremner J. D. (1998). The neurobiological basis of anxiety and fear: circuits, mechanisms, and neurochemical interactions (Part I). *The Neuroscientist, 4,* 35–44.

Charney, D. S., Woods, S. W., Goodman, W. K., & Heninger, G. R. (1987). Neurobiological mechanisms of panic anxiety: Biochemical and behavioral correlates of yohombine-induced panic attacks. *Amer. J. psychiatr., 144,* 1030–1036.

Charney, F. L. (1979). Inpatient treatment programs. In W. H. Reid (Ed.), *The psychopath: A comprehensive study of antisocial disorders and behaviors.* New York: Brunner/Mazel.

Chase, T., The Troops for. (1990). *When rabbit howls.* New York: Jove.

Chase-Lansdale, P. L., Cherlin, A. J., & Kieran, K. E. (1995). The long-term effects of parental divorce on the mental health of young adults: A developmental perspective. *Child Develop., 66,* 1614–34.

Chassin, L., Curran, P. J., Hussong, A. M., & Colder, C. R. (1996). The relation of parent alcoholism to adolescent substance use: A longitudinal follow-up. *J. Abn. Psychol., 105*(1), 70–80.

Chassin, L., Pillow, D. R., Curran, P. J., Molina, B. S., & Barrera, M. (1993). Relation of parental alcoholism in early adolescent substance use: A test of three mediating mechanisms. *J. Abn. Psychol., 102,* 3–19.

Chassin, L., Rogosch, F., & Barrera, M. (1991). Substance use and symptomatology among adolescent children of alcoholics. *J. Abn. Psychol., 100,* 449–463.

Checkley, S. (1992). Neuroendocrinology. In E.S. Paykel (Ed.), *Handbook of affective disorders* (2nd ed.). New York: Guilford.

Chemtob, C. M., Hamada, R. S., Roitblat, H. L., & Muraoka, M. Y. (1994). Anger, impulsivity, and anger control in combat-related post-traumatic stress disorder. *J. Cons. Clin. Psychol., 62,* 827–32.

Chemtob, C. M., Novaco, R. W., Hamada, R. S., & Gross, D. M. (1997). Cognitive–behavioral treatment for severe anger in posttraumatic stress disorder. *J. Cons. Clin. Psychol., 65*(1), 184–89.

Chemtob, C. M., Tomas, S., Law, W., & Cremniter, D. (1997). Postdisaster psychosocial intervention: A field study of the impact of debriefing on psychological distress. *Amer. J. Psychiat., 154*(3), 415–17.

Chen, C. C., & Yeh, E. K. (1997). Population differences in ALDH levels and flushing response. In G. Y. San (Ed.), *Molecular mechanisms of alcohol.* New York: Humana.

Chess, S., & Thomas, A. (1984). *Origins and evolution of behavior disorders: From infancy to early adult life.* New York: Brunner/Mazel.

Chesser, E. (1971). *Strange loves: The human aspects of sexual deviation.* New York: William Morrow.

Cheung, F. M., & Song, W. Z. (1989). A review on the clinical applications of the Chinese MMPI. *Psychol. Assess., 1,* 230–38.

Chic, J., Gough, K., Falkowski, W., & Kershaw, P. (1992). Disulfiram treatment of alcoholism. *Brit. J. Psychiat., 161,* 84–89.

Chorpita, B. F., Albano, A. M., & Barlow, D. H. (1996). Cognitive processing in children: Relation to anxiety and family influences. *J. Clin. Child Psychol., 25*(2), 170–76.

Chorpita, B. F., Albano, A. M., & Barlow, D. H. (1998). The structure of negative emotions in a clinical sample of children and adolescents. *J. Abn. Psychol., 107,* 74–85.

Chorpita, B. F., & Barlow, D. H. (1998). The development of anxiety: The role of control in the early environment. *Psychol. Bull., 124*(1), 3–21.

Chowdhury, A. (1996) The definition and classification of Koro. *Cult., Med. Psychiat., 20,*41–65.

Christensen, A. & Heavy, C. L. (1999). Interventions for couples. In J. T. Spence, J. M. Darley, & D. J. Foss (Eds.). *Annual Review of Psychology.* (pp. 165–190). Palo Alt., CA: Annual Review.

Christensen, A., & Jacobson, N. S. (1994). Who (or what) can do psychotherapy: The status and challenge of nonprofessional therapies. *Psychol. Sci., 5*(1), 8–14.

Christiansen, B. A., Smith, G. T., Roehling, P. V., & Goldman, M. S. (1989). Using alcohol expectancies to predict adolescent drinking behavior after one year. *J. Cons. Clin. Psychol., 57,* 93–99.

Christie, B. L. (1981). Childhood enuresis: Current thoughts on causes and cures. *Social Work Health Care, 6*(3), 77–90.

Chrousos, G. B. & Gold, P. W. (1992). The concepts of stress and stress system disorders: Overview of physical and behavioral homeostasis. *JAMA, 267,* 1244–52.

Chu, J. A., & Dill, D. L. (1990). Dissociative symptoms in relation to childhood physical and sexual abuse. *Amer. J. Psychiat., 147,* 887–92.

Cicchetti, D. (1990). A historical perspective on the discipline of developmental psychopathology. In J. Rolf, A. S. Masten, D. Cicchetti, K. H. Nuechterlein, & S. Weintraub (Eds.), *Risk and protective factors in the development of psychopathology.* New York: Cambridge University Press.

Cicchetti, D., & Lynch, M. (1995). Failures in the expectable environment and their impact on individual development: The case of child maltreatment. In D. Cicchetti & D. J. Cohen (Eds.), *Developmental Psychopathology: Vol. 2. Risk, disorder, and adaptation.* (pp. 32–72). New York: Wiley.

Cicchetti, D., & Rogosch, F. (1999). Conceptual and methodological issues in developmental psychopathological research. In P.C. Kendall, J. N. Butcher, & G. Holmbeck (Eds.), *Research methods in clinical psychology* (2nd ed.). (pp. 433–65). New York: Wiley.

Cicchetti, D., & Toth, S. L. (1995a). A developmental psychopathology perspective on child abuse and neglect. *J. Amer. Acad. Child Adoles. Psychiat., 34*(5), 541–565.

Cicchetti, D., & Toth, S. L. (1995b). Developmental psychopathology and disorders of affect. In D. Cicchetti, & D. J. Cohen (Eds.), *Developmental Psychopathology Vol. 2: Risk, disorder, and adaptation.* (pp. 369–420). New York: Wiley.

Cicchetti, D., & Toth, S. L. (1998). The development of depression in children and adolescents. *Amer. Psychol., 53*(2), 221–41.

Cigrang, J. A., Pace, J. V., & Yasuhara, T. T. (1995). Critical incident stress intervention following fatal aircraft mishaps. *Aviation, Space, and Environmental Medicine, 66*(9), 880–82.

Cirinclone, C., Steadman, H., & McGreevy, M. A. (1995). Rates of insanity acquittals and the factors associated with successful insanity pleas. *Bull. Amer. Acad. Psychiat. Law, 23*(3), 399–409.

Clark, C. R. (1987). Specific intent and diminished capacity. In A. Hess and I. Weiner (Eds.), *Handbook of forensic psychology.* New York: Wiley.

Clark, D. A. (1997). Twenty years of cognitive assessment: Current status and future directions. *J. Cons. Clin. Psychol., 65*(6), 996–1000.

Clark, D. A., Beck, A. T., & Beck, J. S. (1994a). Symptom difference in major depression, dysthymia, panic disorder, and generalized anxiety disorder. *Amer. J. Psychiat., 151,* 205–9.

Clark, D. A., Beck, A. T., & Stewart, B. (1990). Cognitive specificity and positive-negative affectivity: Complementary or contradictory views on anxiety and depression. *J. Abn. Psychol., 99,* 148–55.

Clark, D. A., & Steer, R. A. (1996). Empirical status of the cognitive model of anxiety and depression. In P. M. Salkovskis (Ed.), *Frontiers of cognitive therapy.* (pp. 75–96). New York: Guilford.

Clark, D. A., Steer, R. A., & Beck, A. T. (1994b). Common and specific dimensions of self-reported anxiety and depression: Implications for the cognitive and tripartite models. *Amer. J. Psychiat., 103,* 645–54.

Clark, D. C. (1995). Epidemiology, assessment, and management of suicide in depressed patients. In E. E. Beckham & W. R. Leber (Eds.), *Handbook of depression* (2nd ed.). (pp. 526–38). New York: Guilford.

Clark, D. C., & Fawcett, J. (1992). Review of empirical risk factors for evaluation of the suicidal patient. In B. Bongar (Ed.), *Suicide: Guidelines for assessment, management and treatment.* New York: Oxford University Press.

Clark, D. M. & Wells, A. (1995). A cognitive model of social phobia. In R. G. Heimberg, M. R. Liebowitz, D. A. Hope, & Schneier, F. R. (Eds.), *Social phobia: Diagnosis, assessment, and treatment.* (pp. 69–93). New York: Guilford.

Clark, D. M. (1986). A cognitive approach to panic. *Behav. Res. Ther., 24,* 461–70.

Clark, D. M. (1988). A cognitive model of panic attacks. In S. Rachman, & J. D. Maser (Eds.), *Panic: Psychological perspectives.* Hillsdale, NJ: Erlbaum.

Clark, D. M. (1996). Panic disorder: From theory to therapy. In R. M. Rapee (Ed.), *Current controversies in the anxiety disorders.* (pp. 318–44). New York: Guilford.

Clark, D. M. (1997). Panic Disorder and Social Phobia. In D. M. Clark, & C. G. Fairburn (Eds.), *Science and practice of cognitive behaviour therapy.* (pp. 119–54). Oxford University press

Clark, D. M., Salkovskis, P. M., & Anastasiades, P. (1990). Cognitive mediation of lactate induced panic. In R. M. Rapee (Chair) Experimental investigations of panic disorder. Symposium conducted at the meeting of the Association for Advancement of Behavior Therapy, San Francisco.

Clark, D. M., Salkovskis, P. M., Hackmann, A., Middleton, H., Anastasiades, P., & Gelder, M. (1994). A comparison of cognitive therapy, applied relaxation, and imipramine in the treatment of panic disorder. *Brit. J. Psychiat., 164,* 759–69.

Clark, D. M., & Wells, A. (in press). A cognitive model of social phobia. To appear in R. G. Heimberg, M. Liebowitz, D. Hope, & F. Schneier (Eds.), *Social phobia: Diagnosis, assessment, and treatment.* New York: Guilford.

Clark, D. E., Salkovskis, P. M., Ost, L. G., Breitholtz, E., Koehler, K. A., Westling, B. E., Jeavons, A., & Gelder, M. (1997). Misinterpretations of body sensations in panic disorder. *J. Cons. Clin. Psychol., 65*(2), 203–13.

Clark, L. A. (1992). Resolving taxonomic issues in personality disorders: The value of large-scale analyses of symptom data. *J. Pers. Dis., 6,* 360–76.

Clark, L. A., & Livesley, W. J. (1994). Two approaches to identifying dimensions of personality disorder. Convergence on the five-factor model. In P. T. Costa, Jr., & T. A. Widiger (Eds.), *Personality disorders and the five-factor model of personality.* Washington, DC: American Psychological Association.

Clark, L. A., & Watson, D. (1991a). "Theoretical and Empirical issues in differentiating depression from anxiety." In J. Becker & A. Kleinman (Eds.), *Psychosocial aspects of depression.* Hillsdale, NJ: Erlbaum.

Clark, L. A., & Watson, D. (1991b). Tripartite model of anxiety and depression: Psychometric evidence and taxonomic implications. *J. Abnor. Psychol., 100,* 316–36.

Clark, L. A., Watson, D., & Mineka, S. (1994). Temperament, personality, and the mood and anxiety disorders. *J. Abn. Psychol., 103,* 103–16.

Clark, L. A., Watson, D., & Reynolds, S. (1995). Diagnosis and classification of psychopathology: Challenges to the current system and future directions. *Annu. Rev. Psychol., 46,* 121–53.

Clark, M. E. (1996). MMPI-2 negative treatment indicators content and content component scales: Clinical correlates and outcome prediction for men with chronic pain. *Psychol. Assess., 8,* 32–47.

Clark, R. F., & Goate, A. M. (1993). *Molecular genetics of Alzheimer's disease. Arch. Neurol., 50*(11), 1164–72.

Clarke, A. M., Clarke, A. D. B., & Berg, J. M. (Eds.). (1985). *Mental deficiency: The changing outlook* (4th ed.). London: Methuen.

Clarke, D. J., Littlejohns, C. S., Corbett, J. A., & Joseph, S. (1989). Pervasive developmental disorders and psychoses in adult life. *Brit. J. Psychiat., 155,* 692–99.

Clarke, G. N., Sack, W. H., & Goff, B. (1993). Three forms of stress in Cambodian adolescent refugees. *J. Abnor. Child Psychol., 21,* 65–77.

Clayton, P. J. (1982). Bereavement. In E. S. Paykel (Ed.), *Handbook of affective disorders.* New York: Guilford.

Cleckley, H. M. (1941). *The mask of sanity* (1st ed.). St. Louis, MO: Mosby.

Cleckley, H.M. (1982). *The mask of sanity* (rev. ed.). New York: Plume.

Clement, P. (1970). Elimination of sleepwalking in a seven-year-old boy. *J. Cons. Clin. Psychol., 34*(1), 22–26.

Clementz, B. A., Grove, W. M., Iacono, W. G., & Sweeney, J. A. (1992). Smooth-pursuit eye movement dysfunction and liability for schizophrenia: Implications for genetic modeling. *J. Abn. Psychol., 101*(1), 117–29.

Cloitre, M., Heimberg, R. G., Liebowitz, M. R., & Gitow, A. (1992). Perceptions of control in panic disorder and social phobia. *Cog. Ther. Res., 16* (5), 569–77.

Cloninger, C. R. (1986). Somatoform and dissociative disorders. In G. Winokur & P. Clayton (Eds.), *The medical basis of psychiatry.* (pp. 123–51). Philadelphia: Saunders.

Cloninger, C. R. (1987). A systematic method for clinical description and classification of personality invariants. *Arch. Gen. Psychiat., 44,* 161–67.

Cloninger, C. R., Bayon, C., & Pszybeck, T. R. (1997). Epidemiology and Axis I comorbidity of antisocial personality. In D. M. Stoff, J. Breiling, & J. D. Maser (Eds.), *Handbook of antisocial behavior.* (pp. 12–21). New York: Wiley.

Cloninger, C. R., Christiansen, K. O., Reich, T., & Gottesman, I. I. (1978). Implications of sex differences in the prevalences of antisocial personality, alcoholism, and criminality for familial transmission. *Arch. Gen. Psychiat., 35,* 941–51.

Cloninger, C. R., & Guze, S. B (1970). Psychiatric illness and female criminality: The role of sociopathy and hysteria in the antisocial woman. *Amer. J. Psychiat., 127*(3), 303–11.

Cloninger, C. R., Reich, T., Sigvardsson, S., von Knorring, A. L., & Bohman, M. (1986). The effects of changes in alcohol use between generations on the inheritance of alcohol abuse. In *Alcoholism: A medical disorder.* Proceedings of the 76th Annual Meeting of the American Psychopathological Association.

Cloninger, R., Sigvardsson, S., Von Knorring, A. L., & Bohman, M. (1984). An adoption study of somatoform disorders: II. Identification of two discrete somatoform disorders. *Arch. Gen. Psychiat., 41,* 863–71.

Clum, G. A., Clum, G. A., & Surls, R. (1993). A meta-analysis of treatments for panic disorder. *J. Con. Clin. Psychol., 61*(2), 317–26.

Coates, T. J., Perry, C., Killen, J., & Slinkard, L. A. (1981). Primary prevention of cardiovascular disease in children and adolescents. In C. K. Prokop & L. A. Bradley (Eds.), *Medical psychology: Contributions to behavioral medicine.* New York: Academic Press.

Cockayne, T. O. (1864–1866). Leechdoms, wort cunning, and star craft of early England. London: Longman, Green, Longman, Roberts & Green.

Cockerham, W. (1981). *Sociology of mental disorder.* Englewood Cliffs, NJ: PrenticeHall.

Coffey, C. E., Weiner, R. D., Djang, W. T., Figiel, G. S., Soady, S. A. R., Patterson, L. J., Holt, P. D., Spritzer, C. E., & Wilkinson, W. E. (1991). Brain anatomic effects of electroconvulsive therapy. *Arch. Gen. Psychiat., 48,* 1013–21.

Coffey, P., Leitenberg, H., Henning, K., Turner, T., & Bennett, R. T. (1996). The relation between methods of coping during adulthood with a history of childhood sexual abuse and current psychological adjustment. *J. Cons. Clin. Psychol., 64*(5), 1090–93.

Cohen, B. J., Nestadt, G., Samuels, J. F., Romanoski, A. J., McHugh, P. R., & Rabins, P. V. (1994). Personality disorder in later life: A community study. *Brit. J. Psychiat., 165,* 493–499.

Cohen, C. A., Gold, D. P., Shulman, K. I., & Wortley, J. T. (1993). Factors determining the decision to institutionalize dementing individuals: A prospective study. *Gerontologist, 33*(6), 714–20.

Cohen, C. I., et al. (1997). "Mixed dementia": Adequate or antiquated? A critical review. *Amer. J. Geriatr Psychiat., 5*(4), 279–83.

Cohen, D. (1997). A critique of the use of neuroleptic drugs in psychiatry. In S. Fisher & R. P. Greenberg (Eds.), *From placebo to panacea: Putting psychiatric drugs to the test.* (pp. 173–228). New York: Wiley.

Cohen, D., & Eisdorfer, C. (1988). Depression in family members caring for a relative with Alzheimer's disease. *J. Amer. Geriat. Soc., 36,* 885–89.

Cohen, J., & Hansel, M. (1956). *Risk and gambling: A study of subjective probability.* New York: Philosophical Library.

Cohen, M. L., Seghorn, T., & Calmas, W. (1969). Sociometric study of the sex offender. *J. Abn. Psychol., 74,* 249–55.

Cohen, P., Pine, D. S., Must, A., Kasen, S., & Brook, J. (1998). Prospective associations between somatic illness and mental illness from childhood to adulthood. *Amer. J. Epidemiol., 147*(3), 232–39.

Cohen, R., Singh, N. N., Hosick, J., & Tremaine, L. (1992). Implementing a responsive system of mental health services for children. *Clin. Psychol. Rev., 12,* 819–28.

Cohen, S., Tyrrell, D. A. J., & Smith, A. P. (1993). Negative life events, perceived stress, negative affect, and susceptibility to the common cold. *J. Pers. Soc. Psychol., 64*(1), 131–40.

Cohen, S. L., & Fiedler, J. E. (1974). Content analysis of multiple messages in suicide notes. *Life-Threatening Behavior, 4*(2), 75–95.

Cohler, B. J., Stott, F. M., & Musick, J. S. (1995). Adversity, vulnerability, and resilience: Cultural and developmental perspectives. In D. Cicchetti, & D. J. Cohen (Eds.), *Developmental Psychopathology: Vol. 2. Risk, disorder, and adaptation.* (pp. 753–800). New York: Wiley.

Cohn, J. F., & Tronick, E. Z. (1983). Three months infant's reaction to simulated maternal depression. *Child Develop. 54,* 185–93.

Coie, J. D. (1990). Toward a theory of peer rejection. In S. R. Asher & J. D. Coie (Eds.), *Peer rejection in childhood.* (pp. 365–402). New York: Cambridge University Press.

Coie, J. D. (1996). Effectiveness trials: An initial evaluation of the FAST track program. Paper presented at the Fifth National Institute of Mental Health Conference on Prevention Research, Washington.

Coie, J. D., & Cillessen, A. H. N. (1993). Peer rejection: Origins and effects on children's development. *Curr. Dir. Psychol. Sic., 2,* 89–92.

Coie, J. D., & Dodge, K. A. (1983). Continuity and changes in children's sociometric status: A five-year longitudinal study. *Merrill-Palmer Quarterly, 29,* 261–82.

Coie, J. D., & Dodge, K. A. (1988). Multiple sources of data on social behavior and social status in school: A cross-age comparison. *Child Develop., 57,* 815–829.

Coie, J. D., Dodge, K. A., & Kupersmidt, J. B. (1990). Peer group behavior and social status. In S. R. Asher & J. D. Coie (Eds.), *Peer rejection in childhood.* New York: Cambridge University Press.

Coie, J. D., Dodge, K. A., Terry, R., & Wright, V. (1991). The role of aggression in peer relations: An analysis of aggression episodes in boys' play groups. *Child Develop., 62,* 812–826.

Coie, J. D., & Kupersmidt, J. B. (1983). A behavioral analysis of emerging social status in boys' groups. *Child Develop., 54,* 1400–16.

Coie, J. D., & Lenox, K. F. (1994). The development of antisocial individuals. In D. C. Fowles, P. Sutker, & S. H. Goodman (Eds.), *Progress in experimental personality and psychopathology research.* New York: Springer.

Coie, J. D., Lochman, J. E., Terry, R., & Hyman, C. (1992). Predicting adolescent disorder from childhood aggression and peer rejection. *J. Cons. Clin. Psychol., 60*(5), 783–792.

Coie, J. D., Watt, N. F., West, S. G., Hawkins, J. D., Asarnow, J. R., Markman, H. J., Ramey, S. L., Shure, M. B., & Long, B. (1993). The science of prevention: A conceptual framework and some directions for a national research program. *Amer. Psychol., 48*(10), 1013–22.

Cole, D. A. (1989). Psychopathology of adolescent suicide: Hopelessness, coping beliefs, and depression. *J. Abn. Psychol., 98,* 248–55.

Cole, D. A., Martin, J. M., Peeke, L. G., Seroczynski, A., & Hoffman, K. (1998). Are cognitive errors of underestimation predictive or reflective of depressive symptoms in children: A longitudinal study. *J. Abn. Psychol. 107*(3), 481–96.

Cole, G., Neal, J. W., Fraser, W. I., & Cowie, V. A. (1994). Autopsy findings in patients with mental handicap. *J. Intell. Dis. Res., 38*(1), 9–26.

Cole, J. O., & Bodkin, J. A. (1990). Antidepressant drug side effects. *J. Clin. Psychiat., 51,* 21–26.

Collacott, R. A., & Cooper, S.-A. (1997). The five-year follow-up study of adaptive behavior in adults with Down syndrome. *J. Intell. Develop. Dis., 22*(3), 187–97.

Collacott, R. A., et al. (1998). Behavior phenotype for Down's syndrome. *Brit. J. Psychiat., 172,* 85–89.

Collins, G. B. (1993). Contemporary issues in the treatment of alcohol dependency. *Psychiat. Clin. N. Amer., 16,* 33–48.

Columbus, M., Allen, J. P., & Fertig, J. B. (1995). Assessment in alcoholism treatment: An overview. In NIAAA (Ed.), *Assessing alcohol problems: A guide for clinicians and researchers* (pp. 1–11). Washington: Department of Health and Human Services.

Comfort, A. (1984). Alzheimer's disease or Alzheimerism? *Psychiat. Ann., 14,* 130–32.

Compas, B. E., & Epping, J. E. (1993). Stress and coping in children and families: Implications for children coping with disaster. In C. F. Saylor (Ed.), *Children and disasters.* (pp. 11–28). New York: Plenum.

Comstock, B. S. (1992). Decision to hospitalize and alternatives to hospitalization. In B. Bongar (Ed.), *Suicide: Guidelines for assessment, management and treatment.* New York: Oxford University Press.

Cone, J. D. (1999). Observational assessment: Measure development and research issues. In P. C. Kendall, J. N. Butcher, & G. Holmbeck (Eds.), *Research methods in clinical psychology* (2nd ed.). (pp. 183–223). New York: Wiley.

Connors, G. J., Carroll, K. M., DiClemente, C. C., Longabaugh, R., & Donovan, D. M. (1997). The therapeutic alliance and its relationship to alcoholism treatment participation and outcome. *J. Cons. Clin. Psychol., 65,* 588–98.

Connors, G. J., Maisto, S. A., & Derman, K. H. (1994). Alcohol-related expectancies and their applications to treatment. In R. R. Watson (Ed.), *Drug and alcohol abuse reviews: Vol. 3. Alcohol abuse treatment.* (pp. 203–31). Totowa, NJ: Humana Press.

Conquest, R. (1986). *The harvest of sorrow: Soviet collectivization and the terror-famine.* New York: Oxford University Press.

Conrod, P. J., Pihl, R. O., & Vassileva, J. (1998). Differential sensitivity to alcohol reinforcement in groups of men at risk for distinct alcoholism subtypes. *Alcoholism: Clin. Exper. Res., 22*(3), 585–97.

Conte, H. R., & Karasu, T. B. (1992). A review of treatment studies of minor depression: 1980–1991. *Amer. J. Psychother., 46,* 58–74.

Conte, J., Berliner, L., & Schuerman, J. (1986). *The impact of sexual abuse on children* (Final Report No. MH 37133). Rockville, MD: National Institute of Mental Health.

Conwell, Y., & Caine, E. D. (1991). Suicide in the elderly chronic patient populations. In E. Light & B. D.

Lebowitz (Eds.), *The elderly with chronic mental illness.* (pp. 31–52). New York: Springer.

Cook, M., & Mineka, S. (1987). Second-order conditioning and overshadowing in the observational conditioning of snake fear in monkeys. *Behav. Res. Ther., 25,* 349–64.

Cook, M., & Mineka, S. (1989). Observational conditioning of fear to fear-relevant versus fear-irrelevant stimuli in rhesus monkeys. *J. Abn. Psychol., 98,* 448–59.

Cook, M., & Mineka, S. (1990). Selective associations in the observational conditioning of fear in monkeys. *J. Exper. Psychol.: Animal Behavior Processes, 16,* 372–89.

Cook, M., & Mineka, S. (1991). Selective associations in the origins of phobic fears and their implications for behavior therapy. In P. Martin (Ed.), *Handbook of behavior therapy and psychological science: An integrative approach.* (pp. 413–34). New York: Pergamon.

Cooke, D. J. (1996). Psychopathic personality in different cultures: What do we know? What do we need to find out? *J. Person. Dis., 10*(1), 23–40.

Cookerly, J. R. (1980). Does marital therapy do any lasting good? *Journal of Marital and Family Therapy, 6*(4), 393–97.

Coombe, P. (1996). The Cassel Hospital, London. *Austral. N. Z. J. Psychiat., 30*(5), 672–80.

Coombs, R. H., Paulson, M. J., & Palley, R. (1988). The institutionalization of drug use in America: Hazardous adolescence, challenging parenthood. *J. Chem. Depen. Treat., 1*(2), 9–37.

Coons, P. (1986). Child abuse and multiple personality disorder: Review of the literature and suggestions for treatment. *Child Abuse and Neglect, 10,* 455–62.

Coons, P. M. (1986). Treatment progress in 20 patients with multiple personality disorder. *J. Nerv. Men. Dis., 174,* 715–21.

Coons, P. M., Bowman, E. S., & Milstein, V. (1988). Multiple personality disorder: A clinical investigation of 50 cases. *J. Nerv. Ment. Dis., 176,* 519–27.

Cooper, A. J. (1969). A clinical study of "coital anxiety" in male potency disorders. *J. Psychosom. Res., 13*(2), 143–47.

Cooper, J. E., Kendell, R. E., Gurland, B. J., Sharpe, L., Copeland, J. R. M., & Simon, R. (1972). *Psychiatric diagnosis in New York and London.* London: Oxford University Press.

Cooper, M. L. (1994). Motivations for alcohol use among adolescents: Development and validation of a four-factor model. *Psychol. Assess., 6,* 117–28.

Cooper, S.-A. (1997). Deficient health and social services for elderly people with learning disabilities. *J. Intell. Dis. Res., 41*(4), 331–38.

Coovert, D. L., Kinder, B. N., & Thompson, J. K. (1989). The psychosexual aspects of anorexia nervosa and bulimia: A review of the literature. *Clin. Psychol. Rev., 9,* 169–80.

Copeland, J. (1968). Aspects of mental illness in West African students. *Soc. Psychiat., 3*(1), 7–13.

Coplan, J. A., & Klein, D. F. (1996). Pharmacological probes in panic disorder. In H. G. Westenberg, J. A. Den Boer, & D. L. Murphy (Eds.), *Advances in the neurobiology of anxiety disorders.* (pp. 173–196). Chichester, England: Wiley.

Cordova, J. V., & Jacobson, N. S. (1993). Couple distress. In D. H. Barlow (Ed.), *Clinical handbook of psychological disorders* (2nd ed.). (p. 481–512). New York: Guilford.

Cornblatt, B. A., & Keilp, J. G. (1994). Impaired attention, genetics, and the pathophysiology of schizophrenia. *Schizo. Bull., 20*(1), 31–46.

Cornblatt, B. A., Lenzenweger, M. F., Dworkin, R. H., & Erlenmeyer-Kimling, L. (1992). Childhood attentional dysfunctions predict social deficits in unaffected adults at risk for schizophrenia. *Brit. J. Psychiat., 16* (suppl. 18), 59–64.

Cornell, D. G., Warren, J., Hawk, G., Stafford, E., Oram, G., & Pine, D. (1996). Psychopathy in instrumental and reactive violent offenders. *J. Cons. Clin. Psychol., 64*(4), 783–790.

Corrao, G., Ferrari, P., Zambon, A., Torchio, P., Arico, S., & Decarli, A. (1997). Trends of liver cirrhosis mortality in Europe, 1970–1989: Age-period-cohort analysis and changing alcohol consumption. *Int. J. Epidemiol., 26*(1), 100–109.

Corrigan, P. W. (1995). Use of token economy with seriously mentally ill patients: Criticisms and misconceptions. *Psychiat. Serv., 46*(12), 1258–63.

Corrigan, P. W. (1997). Behavior therapy empowers persons with severe mental illness. *Behav. Mod., 21*(1), 45–61.

Coryell, W. (1997). Do psychotic, minor, and intermittent depressive disorders exist on a continuum? *J. Affect. Dis., 45,* 75–83.

Coryell, W., Endicott, J., & Keller, M. (1987). The importance of psychotic features to major depression: Course and outcome during a 2-year follow-up. *Acta Psychiatr. Scandin., 75,* 78–85.

Coryell, W., Endicott, J., Keller, M., Andreasen, N., Grove, W., Hirschfeld, R. M. A., & Scheftner, W. (1989). Bipolar affective disorder and high achievement: A familial association. *Amer. J. Psychiat., 146,* 983–88.

Coryell, W., Endicott, J., Maser, J. D., Mueller, T., Lavori, P., & Keller, M. (1995) The likelihood of recurrence in bipolar affective disorder: The importance of episode recency. *J. Affect. Dis., 33,* 201–206.

Coryell, W., Keller, M., Lavori, P., & Endicott, J. (1990a). Affective syndromes, psychotic features, and prognosis: I. Depression. *Arch. Gen. Psychiat., 47,* 651–57.

Coryell, W., Keller, M., Lavori, P., & Endicott, J. (1990b). Affective syndromes, psychotic features, and prognosis: II. Mania. *Arch. Gen. Psychiat., 47,* 658–62.

Coryell, W., & Winokur, G. (1982). Course and outcome. In E. S. Paykel (Ed.), *Handbook of affective disorders.* New York: Guilford.

Coryell, W., & Winokur, G. (1992). Course and outcome. In E. S. Paykel (Ed.), *Handbook of affective disorders* (2nd ed.). New York: Guilford.

Coryell, W., Winoker, G., Keller, M. B., & Scheftner, W. (1992). Alcoholism and primary major depression: A family study approach to co-existing disorders. *J. Affect. Dis., 24,* 93–99.

Costa, P. T., Jr., & McCrae, R. R. (1987). Neuroticism, somatic complaints, and disease: Is the bark worse than the bite? *J. Personal., 55,* 299–316.

Costa, P. T., Jr., & Widiger, T. A. (Ed.). (1994). *Personality disorders and the five-factor model of personality.* Washington, DC: American Psychological Association.

Costa, P. T., Jr., Whitfield, J. R., & Stewart, D. (Eds.). (1989). *Alzheimer's disease: Abstracts of the psychological and behavioral literature.* Washington, DC: American Psychological Association.

Costello, E. J. (1989). Developments in child psychiatric epidemiology. *J. Amer. Acad. Child Adoles. Psychiat., 28,* 836–41.

Costello, E. J., Messer, S. C., Bird, H. R., Cohen P., & Reinherz, H. Z. (1998). The prevalence of serious emotional disturbance: A re-analysis of community studies. *J. Child Fam. Stud., 7*(4), 411–32.

Cotler, S. B. (1971). The use of different behavioral techniques in treating a case of compulsive gambling. *Behav. Ther., 2,* 579–81.

Cotton, N. S. (1979). The familial incidence of alcoholism. *J. Stud. Alcoh., 40,* 89–116.

Cottraux, J., & Gerard, D. (1998). Neuroimaging and neuroanatomical issues in obsessive-compulsive disorder: Toward an integrative model-perceived impulsivity. In R. Swinson, M. Antony, S. Rachman, & M. Richter (Eds.), *Obsessive-compulsive disorder: Theory, research, and treatment.* (pp. 154–180). New York: Guilford.

Cox, Brian J. (1996). The nature and assessment of catastrophic thoughts in panic disorder. *Behav. Res. Ther., 34*(4), 363–74.

Cox, D. J. (1988). Incidence and nature of male genital exposure behavior as reported by college women. *J. Sex Res., 24,* 227–34.

Cox, D. J., Freundlich, A., & Meyer, R. G. (1975). Differential effectiveness of electromyographic feedback, verbal relaxation instructions, and medication placebo with tension headaches. *J. Cons. Clin. Psychol., 43,* 892–98.

Cox, W. M., & Klinger, E. (1988). A motivational model of alcohol use. *J. Abn. Psychol., 97,* 168–80.

Coyne, J. C. (1976). Depression and the response of others. *J. Abn. Psychol., 55*(2), 186–93.

Coyne, J. C. (1994). Self-reported distress: Analog or ersatz depression? *Psychol. Bull., 116*(1), 29–45.

Coyne, J. C., Kessler, R. C., Tal, M., Turnbull, J., Wortman, C., & Greden, J. (1987). Living with a depressed person: Burden and psychological distress. *J. Cons. Clin. Psychol., 55,* 347–52.

Coyne, J. C., & Whiffen, V. E. (1995). Issues in personality as diathesis for depression: The case of sociotropy-dependency and autonomy-self-criticism. *Psychol. Bull., 118*(3), 358–78.

Craighead, W. E., Craighead, L. W., & Ilardi, S. S. (1998). Psychosocial treatments for major depressive disorder. In P. E. Nathan, & J. M. Gorman *A guide to treatments that work.* (pp. 226–39). New York: Oxford University Press.

Craighead, W. E., Miklowitz, D. J., Vajk, F. C., & Frank, E. (1998). Psychosocial treatments for bipolar disorder. In P. E. Nathan, & J. M. Gorman *A guide to treatments that work.* (pp. 240–48). New York: Oxford University Press.

Craske, M. G., & Barlow, D. H. (1993). Panic disorder and agoraphobia. In D. H. Barlow (Eds.), *Clinical handbook of psychological disorders.* (pp. 1–47). New York: Guilford.

Craske, M. G., & Rowe, M. K. (1997). A comparison of behavioral and cognitive treatments of phobias. In G. C. L. Davey, (Ed.), *Phobias: A handbook of theory, research and treatment.* (pp. 247–80). Chichester, England: Wiley.

Crepeau, F., & Scherzer, P. (1993). Predictors and indicators of work status after traumatic brain injury: A meta-analysis. *Neuropsychological Rehabilitation, 3*(1), 5–35.

Crews, F. (1995). *The memory wars: Freud's legacy in dispute.* New York: Granta.

Crick, N. R., & Dodge, K. A. (1994). A review and reformulation of social information-processing mechanisms in children's social adjustment. *Psychol. Bull., 115*(1), 74–101.

Crino, R. D. (1991). Obsessive compulsive disorder. *Inter. Rev. Psychiat., 3,* 189–201.

Crisp, A. H., Douglas, J. W. B., Ross, J. M., & Stonehill, E. (1970). Some developmental aspects of disorders of weight. *J. Psychosom. Res., 14,* 313–20.

Crits-Christoph, P. (1992). The efficacy of brief dynamic psychotherapy: A meta-analysis. *Amer. J. Psychiat., 149*(2), 151–58.

Crits-Christoff, P., & Connolly, M. B. (in press). Empirical bases of supportive-expressive psychodynamic psychotherapy. In R. F. Bornstein & J. M. Masling (Eds.), *Empirical research on the psychoanalytic process.* Washington: American Psychological Association.

Crits-Christoph, P. (1998). Psychosocial treatments for personality disorders. In P. E. Nathan, & J. M. Gorman *A guide to treatments that work.* (pp. 544–53). New York: Oxford University Press.

Crittenden, P. M. (1985). Maltreated infants: Vulnerability and resilience. *J. Child Psychol. Psychiat., 26,* 85–96.

Crittenden, P. M., & Ainsworth, M. D. S. (1989). Child maltreatment and attachment theory. In D. Cicchetti & V. Carlson (Eds.), *Child maltreatment: Theory and research on the causes and consequences of child abuse and neglect.* (pp. 432–63). Cambridge: Cambridge University Press.

Crook, T., & Eliot, J. (1980). Parental death during childhood and adult depression: A critical review of the literature. *Psychol. Bull., 87,* 252–59.

Crouch, J. L., & Milner, J. S. (1993). Effective intervention with neglected families. *Crim. Just. Behav., 20,* 49–65.

Crow, T. J. (1985). The two syndrome concept: Origins and current status. *Schizo. Bull., 11,* 471–86.

Crow, T. J. (1997). Temporolimbic or transcallosal connections: Where is the primary lesion in schizophrenia and what is its nature? *Schizo. Bull., 23*(3), 521–24.

Crowe, R. R., Noyes, R., Pauls, D. L., & Slymen, D. (1983). A family study of panic disorder. *Arch. Gen. Psychiat., 40,* 1065–9.

Csernansky, J. G., & Bardgett, M. E. (1998). Limbic-cortical neuronal damage and the pathophysiology of schizophrenia. *Schizo. Bull., 24*(2), 231–48.

Csernansky, J. G., & Grace, A. A. (1998). New models of the pathophysiology of schizophrenia: Editors' introduction. *Schizo Bull., 24*(2), 185–87.

Culliton, B. J. (1970, Jan. 24). Pot facing stringent scientific examination. *Sci. News, 97*(4), 102–5.

Culliton, B. J. (1976). Psychosurgery: National Commission issues surprisingly favorable report. *Science, 194,* 299–301.

Cummings, E. M. (1987). Coping with background anger in early childhood. *Child Develop., 58,* 976–84.

Curry, S. J. (1993). Self-help interventions for smoking cessation. *J. Cons. Clin. Psychol., 61,* 790–803.

Custer, R. L. (1982). An overview of compulsive gambling. In P. A. Carone, S. F. Yolies, S. N. Kieffer, & L. W. Krinsky (Eds.), *Addictive disorders update.* New York: Human Sciences.

Dadds, M. R., Heard, P. M., & Rapee, R. M. (1991). Anxiety disorders in children. *Int. Rev. Psychiat., 3,* 231–41.

Dadds, M. R., Spence, S. H., Holland, D. E., Barren, P. M., & Laurens, K. R. (1997). Prevention and early intervention for anxiety disorders: A controlled study. *J. Cons. Clin. Psychol., 65*(4), 627–35.

Dahl, R. E. (1992). The pharmacologic treatment of sleep disorders. *Psychiat. Clin. N. Amer., 15,* 161–78.

Dahl, R. E., Pelham, W. E., Wierson, M. (1991). The role of sleep disturbances in attention deficit disorder symptoms: A case study. *J. Pediat. Psychol., 16,* 229–39.

Dahlstrom, W. G., Lachar, D., & Dahlstrom, L. E. (1986). *MMPI patterns of American minorities.* Minneapolis: University of Minnesota Press.

Dain, N. (1964). *Concepts of insanity in the United States: 1789–1865.* New Brunswick, NJ: Rutgers University Press.

Dalgleish, T., Rosen, K., Marks, M. (1996). Rhythm and blues: The theory and treatment of seasonal affective disorder. *Brit. J. Clini. Psychol., 35,* 163–82.

Daly, M., & Wilson, M. (1988). *Homicide.* New York: Aldine de Gruyter.

Daly, M., & Wilson, M. I. (1996). Violence against stepchildren. *Curr. Dir. Psychol. Sci., 5*(3), 77–81.

Daniel W. F., & Crovitz, H. F. (1983a). Acute memory impairment following electroconvulsive therapy: 1. Effects of electrical stimulus and number of treatments. *Acta Psychiatr. Scandin., 67,* 1–7.

Daniel, W. F., & Crovitz, H. F. (1983b). Acute memory impairment following electroconvulsive therapy: 2. Effects of electrode placement. *Acta Psychiatr. Scandin., 67,* 57–68.

Dansky, B. S., Kilpatrick, D. G., Brewerton, T. D. & O'Neil, P. M. (1997). *Int. J. Cat. Dis. 21,* 213–28.

Darbonne, A. R. (1969). Suicide and age: A suicide note analysis. *J. Cons. Clin. Psychol., 33,* 46–50.

Dare, C., & Eisler, I. (1997). Family therapy for anorexia nervosa. In D. M. Garner & P. E. Garfinkel (Eds.), *Handbook of treatment for eating disorders.* (pp. 307–24). New York: Guilford.

Darke, J. L. (1990). Sexual aggression: Achieving power through humiliation. In W. L. Marshall, D. R. Laws, & H. E. Barbaree (Eds.), *Handbook of sexual assault.* (pp. 55–72). New York: Plenum.

Davey, G. C. L. (1997). A conditioning model of phobias. In G. C. L. Davey, (Ed.), *Phobias: A handbook of theory, research and treatment.* (pp. 301–22). Chichester, England: Wiley.

Davidson, A. D. (1979a, Spring). Coping with stress reactions in rescue workers: A program that worked. *Police Stress.*

Davidson. A. D. (1979b). Personal communication.

Davidson, J. R., Hughes, D. I., Blazer, D. C., et al., (1991). Posttraumatic stress disorder in the community: An epidemiological study. *Psychol. Med., 21,* 713–21.

Davidson, K. M., & Tyrer, P. (1996). Cognitive therapy for antisocial and borderline personality disorders: Single case study series. *Brit. J. Clin. Psychol., 35,* 412–429.

Davidson, L. M., & Baum, A. (1986). Chronic stress and posttraumatic stress disorders. *J. Cons. Clin. Psychol., 54,* 303–8.

Davies, P. (1986). The genetics of Alzheimer's disease: A review and discussion of the implications. *Neurobiol. Aging, 7,* 459–66.

Davies, P. T., & Windle, M. (1997). Gender-specific pathways between maternal depressive symptoms, family discord, and adolescent adjustment. *Develop. Psychol., 33*(4), 657–68.

Davila, J., Hammen, C., Burge, D., Paley, B., & Daley, S. E. (1995). Poor interpersonal problem solving as a mechanism of stress generation in depression among adolescent women. *J. Abn. Psychol., 104*(4), 592–600.

Davis, J. M. (1978). Dopamine theory of schizophrenia: A two-factor theory. In L. C. Wynne, R. L. Cromwell, & S. Matthysse (Eds.), *The nature of schizophrenia: New approaches to research and treatment.* (pp. 105–15). New York: Wiley.

Dawe, S., & Richmond, R. (1997). Controlled drinking as a treatment goal in Australian alcohol treatment agencies. *J. Subst. Abuse, 14*(1), 81–6.

Dawkins, M. P. (1997). Drug use and violent crime among adolescents. *Adolescence, 32,* 395–405.

DAWN Project (1996). Heroin: Abuse and addiction. NIDA Research Report. Washington: National Household Survey on Drug Abuse.

DAWN Survey. (1996). *Annual trends in drug-related episodes. Monitoring the Future Study,*

Dawson, D. A., Harford, T. C., & Grant, B. F. (1992). Family history as a predictor of alcohol dependence. *Alcoholism: Clin. Exper. Res., 16,* 572–75.

Dawson, G., Panagiotides, H., Klinger, L. G., & Spieker, S. (1997). Infants of depressed and nondepressed mothers exhibit differences in frontal brain electrical activity during the expression of negative emotions. *Develop. Psychol., 33*(5), 650–56.

Dawson, P. M., Griffith, K., & Boeke, K. M. (1990). Combined medical and psychological treatment of hospitalized children with encopresis. *Child Psychiat. Human Devel., 20,* 181–290.

Deale, A., Chalder, T., Marks, I., & Wessely, S. (1997). Cognitive behavior therapy for chronic fatigue syndrome. *Amer. J. Psychiat., 154*(3), 408–14.

Deas-Nesmith, D., Brady, K. T., & Campbell, S. (1998). Comorbid substance use and anxiety disorders in adolescents. *J. Psychopath. Behav. Assess., 20*(2), 139–48.

Debettignles, B. H., Swihart, A. A., Green, L. A., & Pirozzolo, F. J. (1997). The neuropsychology of normal aging and dementia: An introduction. In J. A. M. Horton, D. Wedding, & J. Webster (Eds.), *The neuropsychology handbook* (Vol. 2). (pp. 173–210). New York: Springer.

Debuono, B. A., Zinner, S. H., Daamen, M., & McCormack, W. M. (1990). Sexual behavior of college women in 1975, 1986 and 1989. *New Eng. J. Med., 322,* 821–5.

DeCourville, N. H., & Sadova, S. W. (1997). The structure of problem drinking in adulthood: A confirmatory approach. *J. Stud. Alcoh., 58,* 146–54.

DeFazio, V. J., Rustin, S., & Diamond, A. (1975). Symptom development in Vietnam era veterans. *Amer. J. Orthopsychiat., 45*(1), 158–63.

DeGowin, R. L. (1994). *DeGowin & DeGowin's diagnostic examination* (6th ed.). New York: McGraw-Hill.

De Jongh, A., Muris, P., Ter Horst, T., & Duyx, M. P. M. A. (1995). Acquisition and maintenance of dental anxiety: The role of conditioning experiences and cognitive factors. *Behav. Res. Ther., 33*(2), 205–10.

DeKay, W. T., & Buss, D. M. (1992). Human nature, individual differences, and the importance of context: Perspectives from evolutionary psychology. *Curr. Dir. Psychol. Sci., 1*(6), 184–189.

DeLisi, L. E., Crow, T. J., & Hirsch, S. R. (1986a). The third biannual winter workshops on schizophrenia. *Arch. Gen. Psychiat., 43,* 706–11.

DeLisi, L. E., Goldin, L. R., Hamovit, J. R., Maxwell, E., & Kuritz, D. (1986b). A family study of the association of increased ventricular size with schizophrenia. *Arch. Gen. Psychiat., 43,* 148–53.

DeLisi, L. E., Mirsky, A. F., Buchsbaum, M. S., van Kammen, D. P., Berman, K. F., Phelps, B. H., Karoum, F., Ko, G. N., Korpi, E. R., et al. (1984). The Genain quadruplets 25 years later: A diagnostic and biochemical followup. *Psychiat. Res., 13,* 59–76.

Delk, E. W., & Meilman, P. W. (1996). Alcohol use among college students in Scotland compared with norms from the United States. *J. Amer. Coll. Hlth, 44,* 274–81.

Deltito, J. A., & Stam, M. (1989). Psychopharmacological treatment of avoidant personality disorder. *Compr. Psychiat., 30,* 498–504.

DeMarsh, J., & Kumpfer, K. L. (1985). Family-oriented interventions for the prevention of chemical dependency in children and adolescents. Special Issue: Childhood and Chemical Abuse: Prevention and Intervention. *J. Child. Contem. Soc., 18*(1–2), 117–51.

DeMause, L. (1981). What is psychohistory? *J. Psychohist., 9*(2), 179–84.

DeMause, L. (1990). The history of child assault. *J. Psychohist., 18,* 1–29.

Deming, M. P., Chase, N. D., & Karesh, D. (1996). Parental alcoholism and perceived levels of family health among college freshmen. *Alcoholism Treatment Quarterly, 14*(1), 47–56.

Den Boer, J. A., Vilet, I. M., & Westenberg, H. G. M. (1996). Advances in the psychopharmacology of social phobia. In H. G. Westenberg, J. A. Den Boer, & D. L. Murphy (Eds.), *Advances in the neurobiology of anxiety disorders.* (pp. 401–418). Chichester, England: Wiley.

Denicola, J., & Sandler, J. (1980). Training abusive parents in child management and self-control skills. *Behav. Ther., 11,* 263–70.

Dennes, B. (1974). Returning madness to an accepting community. *Comm. Ment. Hlth. J., 10*(2), 163–72.

Department of Labor. (1991, Feb.). *Employment and earnings.* Bureau of Labor Statistics. Washington, DC: U.S. Government Printing Office.

de Pauw, K. W., & Szulecka, T. K. (1988). Dangerous delusions: Violence and misidentification syndromes. *Brit. J. Psychiat., 152,* 91–96.

Depue, R. A. (1996). A neurobiological framework for the structure of personality and emotion: Implications for personality disorders. In J. F. Clarkin & M. F. Lenzenweger (Eds.), *Major theories of personality disorder.* (pp. 347–390). New York: Guilford.

Depue, R. A., & Iacono, W. G. (1989). Neurobehavioral aspects of affective disorders. *Ann. Rev. Psychol., 40,* 457–92.

Depue, R. A., & Monroe, S. M. (1986). Conceptualization and measurement of human disorder in life stress research: The problem of chronic disturbance. *Psychol. Bull., 99*(1), 36–51.

Depue, R. A., & Spoont, M. R. (1986). Conceptualizing a serotonin trait: A behavioral dimension of constraint. *Ann. NY Acad. Sci., 487,* 47–62.

Depue, R. A., Slater, J. F., Wolfstetter-Kausch, H., Klein, D., Goplerud, E., & Farr, D. (1981). A behavioral paradigm for identifying persons at risk for bipolar disorder: A conceptual framework. *J. Abn. Psychol., 90,* 381–437.

Derr, R. F., & Gutmann, H. R. (1994). Alcoholic liver disease may be prevented with adequate nutrients. *Medical Hypotheses, 42,* 1–4.

DeRubeis, R. (1997, May). *Cognitive therapy IS as effective as medication for severe depression: A mega-analysis.* Paper presented at the meeting of the Amercian Psychological Society, Washington.

De Silva, P., Rachman, S. J., & Seligman, M. E. P. (1977). Prepared phobias and obsessions: Therapeutic outcomes. *Behav. Res. Ther., 15,* 65–78.

Detera-Wadleigh, S. D., Berrettini, W. H., Goldin, L. R., Boorman, D., Anderson, S., & Gershon, E. S. (1987). Close linkage of c-harvey-ras-1 and the insulin gene to affective disorders is ruled out in three North American pedigrees. *Nature, 325,* 806–8.

Deutsch, A. (1948). *The shame of the states.* New York: Harcourt, Brace.

Devanand, D. P., et al. (1997). The course of psychopathologic features in mild to moderate Alzheimer disease. *Arch. Gen. Psychiat., 54*(3), 257–63.

Devanand, D. P. et al. (1994). Does ECT alter brain structure? *Amer. J. Psychiat., 151,* 957–70.

DeVane, C. L., & Sallee, F. R. (1996). Serotonin selective reuptake inhibitors in child and adolescent psychopharmacology: A review of published experience. *J. Clin. Psychiat., 57*(2), 55–66.

DeVeaugh-Geiss, J. (1991). Pharmacologic treatment of obsessive-compulsive disorder. In J. Zohar, T. Insel, & S. Rasmussen (Eds.), *The psychobiology of obsessive-compulsive disorder.* New York: Springer.

de Vries, L. B. A., Halley, D. J. J., Oostra, B. A., & Niermeijer, M. F. (1994). The fragile-X syndrome: A growing gene causing familial intellectual disability. *J. Intellect. Dis. Res., 38*(1), 1–8.

Dew, M. A., Bromet, E. J., & Schulberg, H. C. (1987). A comparative analysis of two community stressors' long-term mental health effects. *Am. J. Community Psychol., 15,* 167–184.

Dew, M. A., Penkower, L., & Bromet, E. J. (1991). Effects of unemployment on mental health in the contemporary family. *Behav. Mod., 15,* 501–544.

De Young, M. (1982) Innocent seducer and innocently seduced? The role of the child incest victim. *J. Clin. Child. Psychol, 11,* 56–60.

Diaferia, G., Bianchi, I., Bianchi, M. L., Cavedini, P., Eregovesi, S., & Bellodi, L. (1997). Relationship between obsessive-compulsive personality disorder and obsessive-compulsive disorder. *Compr. Psychiat., 38*(1), 38–42.

Diamond, M. C. (1988). *Enriching heredity: The impact of the environment on the anatomy of the brain.* New York: Free Press.

Diamond, M. J. (1974). Modification of hypnotizability: A review. *Psychol. Bull., 81*(3), 180–98.

DiClemente, C. C. (1993). Changing addictive behaviors: A process perspective. *Curr. Dir. Psychol. Sci., 2,* 101–6.

Dikmen, S. S., & Levin, H. S. (1993). Methodological issues in the study of mild head injury. *J. Head Trauma Rehab., 8*(3), 30–37.

Dikmen, S. S., Temkin, N. R., Machamer, J. E., & Holubkov, A. L. (1994). Employment following traumatic head injuries. *Arch. Neurol., 51*(2), 177–86.

Dilk, M. N., & Bond, G. R. (1996). Meta-analytic evaluation of skills training research for individuals with severe mental illness. *J. Cons. Clin. Psychol., 64*(6), 1337–46.

Diller, L., & Gordon, W. A. (1981). Interventions for cognitive deficits in brain-injured adults. *J. Cons. Clin. Psychol., 49,* 822–34.

Dimberg, U., & Öhman, A. (1983). The effect of directional facial cues on electrodermal conditioning to facial stimuli. *Psychophysiology, 20,* 160–7.

Dinwiddie, S. H. (1992). Patterns of alcoholism inheritance. *J. Subst. Abuse, 4,* 155–63.

Diokno, A. C., Brown, M. B., & Herzog, A. R. (1990). Sexual function in the elderly. *Arch. Int. Med., 150,* 197–200.

DiPietro, L., Mossberg, H.-O., & Stunkard, A. J. (1994). A 40-year history of overweight children in Stockholm: Lifetime overweight, morbidity, and mortality. *International Journal of Obesity, 18,* 585–90.

Dishion, T. (1994). The peer context of troublesome child and adolescent behavior. In P. E. Leone (Ed.), *Understanding troubled and troubling youth: Multidisciplinary perspectives.* Newbury Park, CA: Sage.

Dishion, T. P., & Patterson, G. R. (1997). The timing and severity of antisocial behavior: Three hypotheses within an ecological framework. In D. M. Stoff, J. Breiling, & J. D. Maser (Eds.), *Handbook of antisocial behavior.* (pp. 205–217). New York: Wiley.

Dixon, L., Weiden, P. J., Haas, G., & Sweeney, J. (1992). Increased tardive dyskinesia in alcohol-abusing schizophrenic patients. *Compr. Psychiat., 33,* 121–22.

Doane, J. A., Falloon, I. R. H., Goldstein, M. J., & Mintz, J. (1985). Parental affective style and the treatment of schizophrenia: Predicting course of illness and social functioning. *Arch. Gen. Psychiat., 42,* 34–42.

Doane, J. A., West, K., Goldstein, M. J., Rodnick, E., & Jones, J. (1981). Parental communication deviance and affective style as predictors of subsequent schizophrenia spectrum disorders in vulnerable adolescents. *Arch. Gen. Psychiat., 38,* 679–85.

Dobson, K. S. (1989). A meta-analysis of the efficacy of cognitive therapy for depression. *J. Cons. Clin. Psychol., 57,* 414–19.

Dodd, B., & Leahy, J. (1989). Facial prejudice. *Amer. J. Ment. Retard., 94,* 111.

Dodge, K. A. (1980). Social cognition and children's aggressive behavior. *Child Develop., 51,* 162–70.

Dodge, K. A. (1993). Social cognitive mechanisms in the development of conduct disorder and depression. *Ann. Rev. Psychol., 44,* 559–84.

Dodge, K. A., Bates, J. E., & Pettit, G. S. (1990). Mechanisms in the cycle of violence. *Science, 250,* 1678–83.

Dodge, K. A., Coie, J. D., & Brakke, N. P. (1982). Behavioral patterns of socially rejected and neglected preadolescents: The roles of social approach and aggression. *J. Abnorm. Child. Psychol. 10,* 389–410.

Dodge, K. A., & Frame, C. L. (1982). Social cognition biases and deficits in aggressive boys. *Child Develop., 53,* 620–35.

Dodge, K. A., Lochman, J. E., Harnish, J. D., Bates, J. E., & Pettit, G. S. (1997). Reactive and proactive aggression in school children and psychiatrically impaired chronically assaultive youth. *J. Abn. Psychol., 106*(1), 37–51.

Dodge, K. A., Murphy, R. R., & Buchsbaum, K. (1984). The assessment of intention-cue detection skills in children: Implications for developmental psychopathology. *Child Develop., 55,* 163–73.

Dodge, K. A., & Newman, J. P. (1981). Biased decision-making processes in aggressive boys. *J. Abn. Psychol., 90,* 375–79.

Dodge, K. A., Pettit, G. S., & Bates, J. E. (1994). Socialization mediators of the relation between socioeconomic status and child conduct problems. *Child Develop., 65,* 649–65.

Dodge, K. A., Pettit, G. S., Bates, J. E., & Valente, E. (1995). Social information-processing patterns partially mediate the effect of early physical abuse on later conduct problems. *J. Abn. Psychol., 104*(4), 632–43.

Dohrenwend, B. P. (1998). A psychosocial perspective on the past and future of psychiatric epidemiology. *Amer. J. Epidemiol., 147*(3), 222–29.

Dohrenwend, B. P., & Dohrenwend, B. S. (1982). Perspectives on the past and future of psychiatric epidemiology: The 1981 Rena Lapouse Lecture. *Amer. J. Pub. Hlth., 72*(1), 1271–79.

Dohrenwend, B. P., Dohrenwend, B. S., Gould, M. S., Link, B., Neugebauer, R., & Wunsch-Hitzig, R. (1980). *Mental illness in the United States: Epidemiological estimates.* New York: Praeger.

Dohrenwend, B. P., Shrout, P. E., Link, B. G., Skodol, A. E., & Martin, J. L. (1986). Overview and initial results from a risk factor study of depression and schizophrenia. In J.E. Barrett (Ed.), *Mental disorders in the community: Progress and challenge.* New York: Guilford Press.

Dohrenwend, B. P., Shrout, P. E., Link, B. G., Skodol, A. E., & Stueve, A. (1995). A case-control study of life events and other possible psychosocial risk factors for episodes of schizophrenia and major depression. In C. M. Mazure (Ed.), *Does stress cause psychiatric illness?* Washington, DC: American Psychiatric Press.

Dolberg, O. T., Iancu, I., Sasson, Y., & Zohar, J. (1996). The pathogenesis and treatment of obsessive-compulsive disorder. *Clin. Neuropharmac., 19*(2), 129–147.

Dolberg, O. T., Sasson, Y., Marazziti, D., Kotler, M., Kindler, S., & Zohar, J. (1996). New compounds for the treatment of obsessive-compulsive disorder. In H. G. Westenberg, J. A. Den Boer, & D. L. Murphy (Eds.), *Advances in the neurobiology of anxiety disorders.* (pp. 299–311). Chichester, England: Wiley.

Dole, V. P., & Nyswander, M. (1967). The miracle of methadone in the narcotics jungle. *Roche Report, 4*(11), 1–2, 8, 11.

Dollard, J., & Miller, N. E. (1950). *Personality and psychotherapy.* New York: McGraw-Hill.

Dolphus, S., et al., (1996). Identifying subtypes of schizophrenia by cluster analysis. *Schizo Bull., 22*(3), 545–55.

Donaldson, M. A., & Gardner, R., Jr. (1985). Diagnosis and treatment of traumatic stress among women after childhood incest. In C. R. Filley (Ed.), *Trauma and its wake: The study and treatment of posttraumatic stress disorder.* (pp. 356–77). Newbury Park, CA: Sage.

Donne, J. (1624). Meditation XVII. *Devotions upon emergent occasions.* London.

Dooley, D., & Catalano, R. (1980). Economic change as a cause of behavioral disorder. *Psychol. Bull., 87,* 450–68.

Dorwart, R. A., Schlesinger, M., Horgan, C., & Davidson, H. (1989). The privatization of mental health care and directions for mental health services research. In C. A. Taube, D. Mechanic, & A. A. Hohmann (Eds.), *The future of mental health services research.* (pp. 139–54). Washington, DC: U.S. Department of Health and Human Services.

Downey, G., & Coyne, J. C. (1990). Children of depressed parents: An integrative review. *Psychol. Bull., 108,* 50–76.

Downey, G., & Feldman, S. I. (1996). Implications of rejection sensitivity for intimate relationships. *J. Pers. Soc. Psychol., 70,*, 1327–43.

Draguns, J. G. (1979). Culture and personality. In A. J. Marsella, R. Tharp, & T. Cibowrowski (Eds.), *Perspectives in cross-cultural psychology.* New York: Academic Press.

Drewnowski, A. (1996). The behavioral phenotype in human obesity. In E. Capaldi et al. (Eds.), *Why we eat what we eat: The psychology of eating.* (pp. 291–308). Washington: American Psychological Association.

Drotar, D. (Ed.). (1985). *New directions in failure to thrive: Implications for research and practice.* New York: Plenum Press.

Drtikova, I., Balastikova, B., Lemanova, H., & Zak, J. (1996). Clonazepam, clonidine and tiapride in children with tic disorder. *Homeostasis in Health & Disease, 37*(5), 216.

Drug Enforcement Administration, Department of Justice. (1979). *Controlled Substance Inventory List.* Washington, DC.

Dryfoos, J. G. (1990). *Adolescents at risk: Prevalence and prevention.* New York: Oxford University Press.

Du Four, M. C., Stinson, F. S., & Cases, M. F. (1993). Trends in cirrhosis morbidity and mortality. *Seminars in Liver Disease, 13*(2), 109–25.

Dumas, J. E., Gibson, J. A., & Albin, J. B. (1989). Behavioral correlates of maternal depressive symptomatology in conduct-disorder children. *J. Cons. Clin. Psychol., 57,* 516–21.

Dunbar, F., (1943). *Psychosomatic diagnosis.* New York: Harper & Row.

Dunbar, P. (1954). *Emotions and bodily changes* (4th ed.). New York: Columbia University Press.

Duncan, G. J., Brooks-Gunn, J., & Klebanov, P. K. (1994). Economic deprivation and early childhood development. *Child Develop., 65,* 296–318.

Dunne, E. J. (1992). Following a suicide: Postvention. In B. Bongar (Ed.), *Suicide: Guidelines for assessment, management and treatment.* New York: Oxford University Press.

Dunner, D. L. (1993). *Psychiatric clinics of North America.* Philadelphia: Saunders.

DuPaul, G. I., & Barkley, R. A. (1990). Medication therapy. In R. A. Barkley (Ed.), *Attention deficit hyperactivity disorder: A handbook for diagnosis and treatment.* (pp. 573–612). New York: Guilford.

Dura, J. R., & Bornstein, R. A. (1989). Differences between IQ and school achievement in anorexia nervosa. *J. Clin. Psychol., 45,* 433–35.

Durkheim, E. (1951). *Suicide: A study in sociology* (J. A. Spaulding & G. Simpson, Trans., G. Simpson, Ed.). New York: Free Press. (Originally published 1897.)

Durrant, J. E. (1994). A decade of research on learning disabilities: A report card on the state of the literature. *J. Learn. Dis., 27*(1), 25–33.

Dwork, A. J. (1997). Postmortem studies on the hippocampal formation in schizophrenia. *Schizo. Bull., 23*(3), 385–402.

Dworkin, R. H., et al. (1998). Affective expression and affective experience in schizophrenia. In M. F. Lenzenweger & R. H. Dworkin (Eds.) *Origins and development of schizophrenia.* (pp. 385–426). Washington: American Psychological Association.

Dworkin, R. H., Cornblatt, B. A., Friedman, R., Kaplansky, L. M., Lewis, J. A., Rinaldi, A., Shilliday, C., & Erlenmeyer–Kimling, L. (1993). Childhood precursors of affective vs. social deficits in adolescents at risk for schizophrenia. *Schizo. Bull., 19*(3), 563–77.

Dyck, G. (1997). Management of geriatric behavior problems. *Psychiat. Clin. N. Amer., 20*(1), 165–80.

Eagly, A. H., & Steffen, V. J. (1986). Gender and aggressive behavior: A meta-analytic review of the social psychological literature. *Psychol. Bull., 100,* 309–30.

Earl, H. G. (1965). 10,000 children battered and starved: Hundreds die. *Today's Health, 43*(9), 24–31.

Earl, H. G. (1966). Head injury: The big killer. *Today's Health, 44*(12), 19–21.

Earlywine, M., & Finn, P. R. (1990, March). *Personality, drinking habits, and responses to cues for alcohol.* Paper presented at the 5th Congress of the International Society for Biomedical Research on Alcoholism and the Research Society on Alcoholism, Toronto, Canada.

East, W. N. (1946). Sexual offenders. *J. Nerv. Ment. Dis., 103,* 626–66.

Eaton, W. W. (1985). Epidemiology of schizophrenia. *Epidemiological Reviews,* 7, 105–26.

Eaton, W. W., Dryman, A., & Weissman, M. M. (1991). Panic and phobia. In L. N. Robins & D. A. Regier (Eds.), *Psychiatric disorders in America.* (pp. 155–79). New York: Free Press.

Eaton, W. W., Kessler, R. C., Wittchen, H. U., & Magee, W. J. (1994). Panic and panic disorder in the United States. *Amer. J. Psychiat., 151*(3), 413–20.

Eaton, W. W., & Keyl, P. M. (1990). Risk factors for the onset of Diagnostic Interview Schedule /DSM-III agoraphobia in a prospective, population based study. *Arch. Gen. Psychiat., 47,* 819–24.

Ebigo, P. O. (1982). Development of a culture specific (Nigeria) screening scale of somatic complaints indicating psychiatric disturbance. *Culture, Medicine and Psychiatry,* 6, 29–43.

Edwards, C. C. (1973). What you can do to combat high blood pressure. *Fam. Hlth., 5*(11), 24–26.

Egbert, L., Battit, G., Welch, C., & Bartlett, M. (1964). Reduction of postoperative pain by encouragement and instruction of patients. *New Engl. J. Med., 270,* 825–27.

Egeland v. City of Minneapolis, 344 N.W.2nd 597. (1984).

Egeland, B. & Sroufe, L. A. (1981). Attachment and early maltreatment. *Child Develop., 52,* 44–52.

Egeland, B., Cicchetti, D., & Taraldson, B. (1976, Apr. 26). Child abuse: A family affair. *Proceedings of the N. P. Masse Research Seminar on Child Abuse,* 28–52. Paper presented Paris, France.

Egeland, B., & Erickson, M. F. (1990). Rising above the past: Strategies for helping new mothers to break the cycle of abuse and neglect. *Zero to Three, 11,* 29–35.

Egeland, B., & Farber, E. A. (1984). Infant-mother attachment: Factors related to its development and change over time. *Child Develop., 55,* 753–71.

Egeland, J. A., Gerhard, D. S., Pauls, D. L., Sussex, J. N., Kidd, K. K., Allen, C. R., Hostetter, A. M., & Housman, D. E. (1987). Bipolar affective disorders linked to DNA markers on chromosome 11. *Nature, 325,* 783–87.

Egendorf, A. (1986). *Healing from the war.* Boston: Houghton Mifflin.

Ehlers, A. (1993). Somatic symptoms and panic attacks: A retrospective study of learning experiences. *Behav. Res. Ther., 31*(3), 269–278.

Ehlers, A. (1995). A 1-year prospective study of panic attacks: Clinical course and factors associated with maintenance. *J. Abn. Psychol.,* 104.

Ehlers, A., & Breuer, P. (1996). How good are patients with panic disorder at perceiving their heartbeats. *Biol. Psychol., 42,* 165–82.

Ehlers, A., Breuer, P., Dohn, D., & Fiegenbaum, W. (1995). Heartbeat perception and panic disorder: Possible explanations for discrepant findings. *Behav. Res. Ther., 33*(1), 69–76.

Ehlers, A., Mayou, R. A., & Bryant, B. (1998). Psychological predictors of chronic posttraumatic stress disorder after motor vehicle accidents. *J. Abnorm. Behav., 107*(3), 508–19.

Ehlers, A., Taylor, J., Margraf, J., Roth, W., & Birbaumer, R. (1988). Anxiety induced by false heart rate feedback in patients with panic disorder. *Behav. Res. Ther., 26,* 2–11.

Ehrhardt, A. A., & Meyer-Bahlburg, H. F. L. (1981). Effects of prenatal sex hormones on gender-related behavior. *Science, 211,* 1312–18.

Eisenberg, H. M. (1990). Behavioral changes after closed head injury in children. *J. Cons. Clin. Psychol., 58,* 93–98.

Eisenberg, P. & Lazarsfeld, P. F. (1938). The psychological effects of unemployment. *Psychol. Bull., 35,* 358–90.

El Guebaly, N., Staley, D., Leckie, A., & Koensgen, S. (1992). Adult children of alcoholics in treatment programs for anxiety disorders and substance abuse. *Canad. J. Psychiat., 37,* 544–48.

Elder, G. H., Shanahan, M. J., & Clipp, E. C. (1994). When war comes to men's lives: Life course patterns in family, work, and health. *Psychol. Aging, 9,* 3–17.

Eley, T. C. (1997). General genes: A new theme in developmental psychopathology. *Curr. Dir. Psychol. Sci., 6*(4), 90–95.

Elkin, I., Shea, M. T., Watkins, J. T., Imber, S. D., Sotsky, S. M., Collins, J. F., Glass, D. R., Pilkonis, P. A., Leber, W. R., Docherty, J. P., Fiester, S. J., & Parloff, M. B. (1989). National Institute of Mental Health Treatment of Depression Collaborative Research Program: General effectiveness of treatments. *Arch. Gen. Psychiat., 46,* 971–82.

Elkind, D. (1967). Middle-class delinquency. *Mental Hygiene, 51,* 80–84.

Ellicott, A., Hammen, C., Gitlin, M., Brown, G., & Jamison, K. (1990). Life events and the course of bipolar disorder. *Amer. J. Psychiat., 147,* 1194–98.

Elliott, D. M. (1997). Traumatic events: Prevalence and delayed recall in the general population. *J. Cons. Clin. Psychol., 65*(5), 811–20.

Elliott, D. S., Dunford, F. W., & Huizinga, D. (1987). The identification and prediction of career offenders utilizing self-reported and official data. In J. D. Burchard & S. N. Burchard (Eds.), *Prevention of delinquent behavior.* (pp. 90–121). Newbury Park, CA: Sage.

Elliott, G. (1989). Stress and illness. In S. Cheren (Ed.), *Psychosomatic medicine: Theory, physiology, and practice* (Vol. 1). (pp. 45–90). Madison, CT: International Universities Press.

Ellis, A. (1958). Rational psychotherapy. *J. Gen. Psychol., 59,* 35–49.

Ellis, A. (1970). *Reason and emotion in psychotherapy.* New York: Lyle Stuart.

Ellis, A. (1973). Rational-emotive therapy. In R. J. Corsini (Ed.), *Current psychotherapies.* Itasca, IL: Peacock Publishers.

Ellis, A. (1975). Creative job and happiness: The humanistic way. *The Humanist, 35*(1), 11–13.

Ellis, A. (1989). The history of cognition in psychotherapy. In A. Freeman, K. M. Simon, L. E. Beutler, & H. Arkowitz (Eds.), *Comprehensive handbook of cognitive therapy.* (pp. 5–19). New York: Plenum.

Ellis, A., & Dryden, W. (1997). *The practice of rational emotive behavior therapy* (2nd ed.). New York: Springer.

Ellis, E. M., Atkeson, B. M., & Calhoun, K. S. (1982). An examination of differences between multiple- and single-incident victims of sexual assault. *J. Abn. Psychol., 91,* 221–24.

Ellis, E. S. (1993). Integrative strategy instruction: A potential model for teaching content area subjects to adolescents with learning disabilities. *J. Learn. Dis., 26*(6), 358–83.

Ellis, L. (1989). *Theories of rape: Inquiries into the causes of sexual aggression.* New York: Hemisphere Publishing.

Ellison, K. (1977). Personal communication.

EMDR Institute (1997). Advertisement. *APA Monitor, 28*(9), 65.

Emery, R. E. (1982). Interparental conflict and the children of discord and divorce. *Psychol. Bull., 92,* 310–330.

Emery, R. E. (1989). Family violence. Special issue: Children and their development: Knowledge base, research agenda, and social policy application. *Amer. Psychol., 44,* 321–28.

Emery, R. E., & Kitzmann, K. M. (1995). The child in the family: Disruptions in family functions. In D. Cicchetti, & D. J. Cohen (Eds.), *Developmental Psychopathology: Vol. 2. Risk, disorder, and adaptation.* (pp. 3–31). New York: Wiley.

Emery, R. E., & Laumann–Billings, L. (1998). An overview of the nature, causes, and consequences

of abusive relationships: Toward differentiating maltreatment and violence. *Amer. Psychol., 53*(2), 121–35.

Emmelkamp, P. M. G. (1994). Behavior therapy with adults. In A. E. Bergin & S. L. Garfield (Eds.), *Handbook of psychotherapy and behavior change* (4th ed.). (pp. 379–427). New York: Wiley.

Emmelkamp, P. M. G., & Wessels, H. (1975). Flooding in imagination vs. flooding in vivo: A comparison with agoraphobics. *Behav. Res. Ther., 13*(1), 7–15.

Emslie, G. J., Rush, A. J., Weinberg, W. A., Kowatch, R. A., Hughes, C. W., Carmody, T., & Rintelmann, J. (1997). A double-blind, randomized, placebo–controlled trial of fluoxetine in children and adolescents with depression. *Arch. Gen. Psychiat., 54,* 1031–37.

Endicott, J., et al. (1986). Diagnosis of schizophrenia: Predictions of short-term outcome. *Arch. Gen. Psychiat., 43,* 13–19.

Endicott, N. A. (1989). Psychosocial and behavioral factors in myocardial infarction and sudden cardiac death. In S. Cheren (Ed.), *Psychosomatic Medicine: Theory, physiology, and practice* (Vol. 2). (pp. 611–60). Madison, CT: International Universities Press.

Endler, N. (1990). *Holiday of darkness: A psychologist's journey out of his depression* (rev. ed.). Toronto: Wall & Thompson.

Engdahl, B. E., Harkness, A. R., Eberly, R. E., & Bielinski, J. (1993). Structural models of captivity trauma, resilence, and trauma response among former prisoners of war 20 and 40 years after release. *Soc. Psychiat. Psychiat. Epidemiol., 28,* 109–15.

Engel, G. L. (1977). The need for a new medical model: A challenge for biomedicine. *Science, 196,* 129–36.

Engels, G. I., Garnefski, N., & Diekstra, R. F. W. (1993). Efficacy of rational-emotive therapy: A quantitative analysis. *J. Cons. Clin. Psychol., 61*(6), 1083–90.

Englander-Golden, P., Elconin, J., Miller, K. J., & Schwarzkopf, A. B., (1986). Brief SAY IT STRAIGHT training and follow-up in adolescent substance abuse prevention. *J. Prim. Preven., 6*(4), 219–30.

English, C. J. (1973). Leaving home: A typology of runaways. *Society, 10*(5), 22–24.

Enns, M. W. & Reiss, J. P. (1992). Position paper: Electroconvulsive therapy. *Canad. J. Psychiat., 37,* 671–78.

Epstein, H. (1979). *Children of the holocaust: Conversations with sons and daughters of survivors.* New York: Putnam.

Epstein, L. H. (1992). Role of behavior theory in behavioral medicine. *J. Cons. Clin. Psychol., 60*(4), 493–98.

Epstein, R. S., Fullerton, C. S., & Ursano, R. J. (1998). Posttraumatic stress disorder following an air disaster: A prospective study. *Amer. J. Psychiat., 155*(7), 934–38.

Epstein, S. (1994). Integration of the cognitive and the psychodynamic unconscious. *Amer. Psychol., 49*(8), 709–24.

Epstein, S., & Fenz, W. D. (1962). Theory and experiment on the measurement of approach-avoidance conflict. *J. Abnorm. Soc. Psychol., 64*(1), 97–112.

Epstein, S., & Fenz, W. D. (1965). Steepness of approach and avoidance gradients in humans as a function of experience: Theory and experiment. *J. Exper. Psychol., 70*(1), 1–12.

Equal Employment Opportunity Commission. (1991). *Americans with disability Act: A technical assistance manual on the employment provisions (Title 1).* Washington: Author.

Erdman, H. P., Klein, M., & Greist, J. H. (1985). Direct patient computer interviewing. *J. Cons. Clin. Psychol., 53*(6), 760–73.

Erickson, S. J., Feldman, S., Shirley, S., & Steiner, H. (1996). Defense mechanisms and adjustment in normal adolescents. *Amer. J. Psychiat., 153*(6), 826–28.

Erlenmeyer-Kimling, L., & Cornblatt, B. A. (1978). Attentional measures in a study of children at high risk for schizophrenia. In L. C. Wynne, R. L. Cromwell, & S. Matthysse (Eds.), *The nature of schizophrenia: New approaches to research and treatment.* (pp. 359–65). New York: Wiley.

Erlenmeyer-Kimling, L., & Cornblatt, B. A. (1992). A summary of attentional findings in the New York high-risk project. *J. Psychiat. Res., 26,* 405–26.

Erlenmeyer-Kimling, L., et al. (1997). The New York high risk project: Prevalence and comorbidity of Axis I disorders in offspring of schizophrenic parents at 25-year follow-up. *Arch. Gen Psychiat.,* 54(12), 1096–102.

Ernst, N. D., & Harlan, W. R. (1991). Obesity and cardiovascular disease in minority populations: Executive summary. Conference highlights, conclusions, and recommendations. *Amer. J. Clin. Nutri.,* 53, 1507S–11S.

Ernst, R. L., et al. (1997). Cognitive function and the costs of Alzheimer disease: An exploratory study. *Arch. Neurol.,* 54(6), 687–93.

Eron, L. D., Huesmann, L. R., Lefkowitz, M. M., & Walder, L. O. (1974). How learning conditions in early childhood—including mass media—relate to aggression in late adolescence. *Amer. J. Orthopsychiat.,* 44(3), 412–23.

Eron, L. D., & Peterson, R. A. (1982). Abnormal behavior: Social approaches. In M. R. Rosenzweig & L. W. Porter (Eds.), *Annu. Rev. Psychol.,* 33, 231–65.

Eronen, M., Hakola, P., & Tiihonen, J. (1996). Mental disorders and homicidal behavior in Finland. *Arch. Gen. Psychiat.,* 53(6), 497–501.

Errico, A. L., Parsons, O. A., & King, A. C. (1991). Assessment of verbosequential and visuospatial cognitive abilities in chronic alcoholics. *Psychol. Assess.,* 3, 693–96.

Esler, M., Julius, S., Zweifler, A., Randall, O., Harburgh, E., Gardiner, H., & DeQuattro, V. (1977). Mild high-renin essential hypertension: Neurogenic human hypertension? *New Engl. J. Med.,* 296, 405–11.

Esquirol, E. (1845). *Mental maladies: Treatise on insanity.* Philadelphia: Lea & Blanchard.

Eur. Child Adoles. Psychiatr.—*European Child and Adolescent Psychiatry*

Evans, D. A., Funkerstein, H., Albert, M. S., Scherr, P. A., Cook, N. R., Chown, M. J., Hebert, L. E., Hennekens, C. H., & Taylor, J. O. (1989). Prevalence of Alzheimer's disease in a community population of older persons. *JAMA,* 262, 2551–56.

Evans, D. W., King, R. A., & Leckman, J. F. (1996). Tic disorders. In E. J. Mash & R. A. Barkley (Eds.), *Child psychopathology.* (pp. 436–56). New York: Guilford.

Evans, J. A., & Hamerton, J. L. (1985). Chromosomal anomalies. In A. M. Clarke, A. D. B. Clarke, & J. M. Berg (Eds.). *Mental deficiency: The changing outlook* (4th ed.). (pp. 213–66). London: Methuen.

Evans, M. D., Hollon, S. D., DeRubeis, R. J., Piasecki, J. M., Grove, W. M., Garvey, M. J., & Tuason, V. B. (1992). Differential relapse following cognitive therapy and pharmacotherapy for depression. *Arch. Gen. Psychiat.,* 49(10), 802–8.

Evans-Ruth, K. (1996). Attachment relationships among children with aggressive problems: The role of disorganized early attachment patterns. *J. Cons. Clin. Psychol.,* 64(1), 64–73.

Everly, G. S. (1995). The role of the Critical Incident Stress Debriefing (CISD) process in disaster counseling. Special Issue: Disasters and crises: A mental health counseling perspective. *J. Ment. Hlth. Couns.,* 17(3), 278–90.

Ewing, C. P. (1994, July). Plaintiff awarded $500,000 in landmark "recovered memories" lawsuit. *APA Monitor,* p. 22.

Exner, J. E. (1987). Computer assistance in Rorschach interpretation. In J. N. Butcher (Ed.), *Computerized psychological assessment: A practitioner's guide.* New York: Basic Books.

Exner, J. E. (1991). *The Rorschach: A comprehensive system. Vol. 2: Interpretation.* New York: Wiley.

Exner, J. E. (1993). *The Rorschach: A comprehensive system. Vol. 1: Basic Foundations.* New York: Wiley.

Exner, J. E. (1995). Why use personality tests? A brief historical view. In J. N. Butcher (Ed.), *Clinical personality assessment: Practical considerations* (10th ed.). (pp. 10–18). New York: Oxford University Press.

Exner, J. E., & Weiner, I. B. (1994). *The Rorschach: A comprehensive system. Vol. 3: Assessment of children and adolescents.* New York: Wiley.

Eyman, J. R., & Eyman, S. K. (1992). Psychological testing for potentially suicidal individuals. In B. Bongar (Ed.), *Suicide: Guidelines for assessment, management and treatment.* New York: Oxford University Press.

Eysenck, H. J. (1952). The effects of psychotherapy: An evaluation. *J. Cons. Psychol., 16,* 319–24.

Eysenck, H. J. (1960). *Behaviour therapy and the neuroses.* London: Pergamon.

Eysenck, H. J. (1965). Extroversion and the acquisition of eyeblink and GSR conditioned responses. *Psychol. Bull., 63,* 258–70.

Eysenck, M. W., Mogg, K., May, J., Richards, A., & Mathews, A. (1991). Bias in interpretation of ambiguous sentences related to threat in anxiety. *J. Abn. Psychol.,* 100, 144–50.

Fabrega, H. (1981). Cultural programming of brain-behavior relationships. In J. R. Merikangas (Ed.), *Brain-behavior relationships.* Lexington, MA: Heath.

Faigel, H., & Heiligenstein, E. (1996). Medication for attention deficit hyperactivity disorder: Commentary and response. *J. Amer. Coll. Hlth, 45,* 40–42.

Fairbank, J. A., Schlenger, W. E., Caddell, J. M., & Woods, M. G. (1993). Posttraumatic stress disorder. In P. Sutker & H. E. Adams (Eds.), *Comprehensive handbook of psychopathology* (2nd ed.). (pp. 145–65). New York: Plenum.

Fairburn, C. G., Doll, H. A., Welch, S. L., Hay, P. J., Davies, B. A., & O'Conner, M. E. (1998). Risk factors for binge eating disorder: A community–based case control study. *Arch. Gen. Psychiat.,* 55(5), 425–32.

Fairburn, C. G., Jones, R., Peveler, R. C., Hope, R. A., & O'Connor, M. (1993). Psychotherapy and bulimia nervosa: Long-term effects of interpersonal psychotherapy, behavior therapy, and cognitive behavior therapy. *Arch. Gen. Psychiat.,* 50(6), 419–28.

Fairburn, C. G., Marcus, M. D., & Wilson, G. T. (1993). Cognitive-behavioral treatment for binge eating and bulimia nervosa. In C. G. Fairburn & G. T. Wilson (Eds.), *Binge eating: Nature, assessment, and treatment.* (pp. 361–404). New York: Guilford.

Fairburn, C. G., Peveler, R. C., Jones, R., Hope, R. A., & Doll, H., A. (in press). Predictors of 12-month outcome in bulimia nervosa and the influence of attitudes to shape and weight. *J. Cons. Clin. Psychol.*

Fairweather, G. W. (1994). *Keeping the balance: A psychologist's story.* Austin, TX: Fairweather Publishing.

Fairweather, G. W. (Ed.). (1980). *The Fairweather Lodge: A twenty-five year retrospective.* San Francisco: Jossey Bass.

Fairweather, G. W., & Fergus, E. O. (1993). *Empowering the mentally ill.* Austin, TX: Fairweather Publishing.

Fairweather, G. W., Sanders, D. H., Maynard, H., & Cressler, D. L. (1969). *Community life for the mentally ill: An alternative to institutional care.* Chicago: Aldine.

Fall, M. (1997). Self–efficacy: An additional dimension in play therapy. *International Journal of Play Therapy, 3*(2), 21–32.

Fallon, A. E., & Rozin, P. (1985). Sex differences in perceptions of desirable body shape. *J. Abn. Psychol., 94,* 102–5.

Falloon, I. R. H., Boyd, J. L., McGill, C. W., Williamson, M., & Razani, J. (1985). Family management in the prevention of morbidity of schizophrenia: Clinical outcome of a two-year longitudinal study. *Arch. Gen. Psychiat., 42,* 887–96.

Falsetti, S. A., Kilpatrick, D. G., Dansky, B. S., Lydiard, R. B., & Resnick, H. S. (1995). Relationship of stress to panic disorder: Cause or effect? In C.M. Mazure (Ed.), *Does stress cause psychiatric illness?* (pp. 111–47). Washington, DC: American Psychiatric Association.

Fals-Stewart, W., O'Farrell, T. J., & Birchler, G. R. (1997). Behavioral couples therapy for male substance-abusing patients: A cost outcomes analysis. *J. Cons. Clin. Psychol., 65*(5), 789–802.

Famularo, R., Kinscherff, R., Fenton, T., & Bolduc, S. M. (1990). Child maltreatment histories among runaway and delinquent children. *Clin. Pediat., 29,* 713–18.

Famy, C., Streissguth, A. P., & Unis, A. S. (1998). Mental illness in adults with fetal alcohol syndrome or fetal alcohol effects. *Amer. J. Psychiat., 155*(4), 552–34.

Fankhauser, M. P., Karumanchi, V. C., German, M. L., & Yates, A. (1992). A double-blind, placebo-controlled study of the efficacy of transdermal clonidine in autism. *J. Clin. Psychiat., 53,* 77–82.

Fantuzzo, J. W., Jurecic, L., Stovall, A., Hightower, A. D., Goins, C., & Schachtel, D. (1988). Effects of adult and peer social initiations on the social behavior of withdrawn, maltreated, preschool children. *J. Cons. Clin. Psychol., 56,* 40–47.

Faraone, S. V., Biederman, J., Lehman, B. F., Spencer, T., Norman, T., Seidman, L. J., Kraus, I., Perrin, J., Chen, W. J., & Tsuang, M. T. (1993b). Intellectual performance and school failure in children with Attention Deficit Hyperactivity Disorder and in their siblings. *J. Abn. Psychol., 102,* 616–91.

Faraone, S. V., Biederman, J., Lehman, B. K., & Keenan, K. (1993a). Evidence for the independent familial transmission of attention deficit hyperactivity disorder and learning disabilities: Results from a family genetic study. *Amer. J. Psychiat. 150*(6), 891–95.

Faraone, S. V., Biederman, J., & Milberger, S. (1994). An exploratory study of ADHD among second-degree relatives of ADHD children. *Biol. Psychiat., 35,* 398–402.

Faraone, S. V., Kremen, W. S., & Tsuang, M. T. (1990). Genetic transmission of major affective disorders: Quantitative models and linkage analysis. *Psychol. Bull., 108,* 109–27.

Farber, E. A., & Egeland, B. (1987). Invulnerability among abused and neglected children. In E. J. Anthony & B. Cohler (Eds.), *The invulnerable child.* (pp. 253–88). New York: Guilford.

Farberow, N. L. (1974). *Suicide.* Morristown, NJ: General Learning Press.

Farberow, N. L., & Litman, R. E. (1970). *A comprehensive suicide prevention program.* Suicide Prevention Center of Los Angeles, 1958–1969. Unpublished final report DHEW NIMH Grants No. MH 14946 & MH 00128. Los Angeles.

Farberow, N. L., Shneidman, E. S., & Leonard, C. (1963). Suicide among general medical and surgical hospital patients with malignant neoplasms. Veterans Administration, Dept. of Medicine and Surgery. *Medical Bulletin* MB9, Feb. 25, 1963, 1–11.

Faretra, G. (1981). A profile of aggression from adolescence to adulthood: An 18-year follow-up of psychiatrically disturbed and violent adolescents. *Amer. J. Orthopsychiat., 51,* 439–53.

Farley, F. H., & Farley, S. V. (1972). Stimulus seeking motivation and delinquent motivation among institutionalized delinquent girls. *J. Cons. Clin. Psychol., 39,* 94–97.

Faust, D. (1994). Comment on Putnam, Adams, and Schneider, "One-day test-retest reliability of neuropsychological tests in a personal injury case." *Psychol. Assess., 6,* 3–4.

Faust, M., Dimitrovsky, L., & Davidi, S. (1997). Naming difficulties in language-disabled children: Preliminary findings with the application of the tip-of-the-tongue paradigm. *Journal of Speech, Language, and Hearing Research, 40*(5), 1026–36.

Fava, M. & Rosenbaum, J. F. (1995). Pharmacotherapy and somatic therapies. In E. E. Beckham & W. R. Leber (Eds.), *Handbook of depression* (2nd ed.). (pp. 280–301). New York: Guilford.

Fava, M. (1997). Psychopharmacologic treatment of pathologic anger. *Psychiat. Clin. N. Amer., 20,* 427–52.

Fawcett, J., Scheftner, W., Clark, D., Hedeker, D., Gibbons, R., & Coryell, W. (1987). Clinical predictors of suicide in patients with major affective disorders: A controlled prospective study. *Amer. J. Psychiat., 144,* 35–40.

Fawzy, F. I., Fawzy, N. W., Hyun, C. S., Elashoff, R., Guthrie, D., Fahey, J. L., & Morton, D. L. (1993). Malignant melanoma: Effects of an early structured psychiatric intervention, coping, and affective state on recurrence and survival 6 years later. *Arch. Gen. Psychiat., 50*(9), 681–89.

Federal Bureau of Investigation. (1991). *Sourcebook of criminal justice statistics.* Washington, DC: U.S. Government Printing Office.

Federal Bureau of Investigation. (1995). *Crime in the United States.* Washington: U. S. Government Printing Office.

Feingold, B. F. (1977). Behavioral disturbances linked to the ingestion of food additives. *Delaware Medical Journal, 49,* 89–94.

Feitel, B., Margetson, N., Chamas, J., & Lipman, C. (1992). Psychosocial background and behavioral and emotional disorders of homeless and runaway youth. *Hosp. Comm. Psychiat., 43,* 155–59.

Feldman, L. (1992). *Integrating individual and family therapy.* New York: Brunner/Mazel.

Feldman, L. B., & Feldman, S. L. (1997). Conclusion: Principles for integrating psychotherapy and pharmocotherapy. *In Session: Psychotherapy in Practice, 3*(2), 99–102.

Feldman, R., & Weisfeld, G. (1973). An interdisciplinary study of crime. *Crime and Delinquency, 19*(2), 150–62.

Feldman, W., Feldman, E., Goodman, J. T., McGrath, P. J., Pless, R. P., Corsini, L., & Bennett, S. (1991). Is childhood sexual abuse really increasing in prevalence? An analysis of the evidence. *Pediatrics, 88,* 29–33.

Felsman, J. K., & Valliant, G. E. (1987). Resilient children as adults: A 40-year study. In E. J. Anthony & B. J. Cohler (Eds.), *The invulnerable child.* (pp. 289–314). New York: Guilford.

Fenna, D., et. al. (1971). Ethanol metabolism in various racial groups. *Canadian Medical Association Journal, 105,* 472–75.

Fennell, M. J. V. (1989). Depression. In K. Hawton, P. M. Salkovskis, J. Kirk, & D. M. Clark (Eds.), *Cognitive behaviour therapy for psychiatric problems: A practical guide.* Oxford, UK: Oxford University Press.

Fenton, W. S., & McGlashan, T. H. (1994). Antecedents, symptom progression, and long-term outcome of the deficit syndrome in schizophrenia. *Amer. J. Psychiat., 151*(3), 351–56.

Fenton, W. S., & McGlashan, T. H. (1997). We can talk: Individual psychotherapy for schizophrenia. *Amer. J. Psychiat., 154*(11), 1493–95.

Fenton, W. S., McGlashan, T. H., Victor, B. J., & Blyler, C. R. (1997). Symptoms, subtype, and suicidality in patients with schizophrenia spectrum disorders. *Amer. J. Psychiat., 154*(2), 199–204.

Fentress, et al. v. Shea Communications et al. (1990). Jefferson Circuit Court, No 90-CI-06033.

Fenz, W. D. (1971). Heart rate responses to a stressor: A comparison between primary and secondary psychopaths and normal controls. *Journal of Experimental Research in Personality, 5*(1), 7–13.

Ferholt, J. B., Rotnem, D. L., Genel, M., Leonard, M., Carey, M., & Hunter, D. E. K. (1985). A psychodynamic study of psychosomatic dwarfism. *J. Amer. Acad. Child Adol. Psychiat., 24,* 49–57.

Ferri, B. A., Gregg, N., & Heggoy, S. J. (1997). Profiles of college students demonstrating learning disabilities with and without giftedness. *J. Learn. Dis., 30*(5), 552–59.

Fersch, E. A., Jr. (1980). *Psychology and psychiatry in courts and corrections.* New York: Wiley.

Ferster, C. B. (1973). A functional analysis of depression. *Amer. Psychol., 28*(10), 857–70.

Ferster, C. B. (1974). Behavioral approaches to depression. In R. J. Friedman & M. M. Katz (Eds.), *The psychology of depression: Contemporary theory and research.* Washington DC: Hemisphere.

Feske, U. & Chambless, D. L. (1995). Cognitive behavioral versus exposure only treatment for social phobia: A meta-analysis. *Behav. Ther., 26*(4), 695–720.

Feske, U., & Goldstein, A. J. (1997). Eye movement desensitization and reprocessing treatment for panic disorder: A controlled outcome and partial dismantling study. *J. Cons. Clin. Psychol., 65*(6), 1026–35.

Feuerstein, R. (1977). Mediated learning experience: A theoretical basis for cognitive modifiability during adolescence. In P. Mittler (Ed.), *Research to practice in mental retardation* (Vol. 2). (pp. 105–16). Baltimore: University Park Press.

Field, T., Healy, B. T., Goldstein, S., Guthertz, M. (1990). Behavior-state matching and synchrony in mother-infant interactions of nondepressed versus depressed dyads. *Devel. Psychol., 26,* 7–14.

Fields, J. Z., Turk, A., Durkin, M., Ravi, N. V., & Keshavarzian, A. (1994). Increased gastrointestinal symptoms in chronic alcoholics. *American Journal of Gastroenterology, 89,* 382–86.

Fierman, E. J., Hung, M. F., Pratt, L. A., Warshaw, M. G., Yonkers, K. A., Peterson, L. G., Epstein-Kaye, T. M., & Norton, H. S. (1993). Trauma and posttraumatic stress disorder in subjects with anxiety disorders. *Amer. J. Psychiat., 150,* 1872–74.

Figueroa, E., & Silk, K. (1997). Biological implications of childhood sexual abuse in borderline personality disorder. *J. Person. Dis., 11* (1), 71–92.

Fillmore, K. M., Golding, J. M., Leino, E. V., Ager, C. R., & Ferrer, H. P. (1994). Societal-level predictors of groups' drinking patterns: A research synthesis from the Collaborative Alcohol-Related Longitudinal Project. *Amer. J. Pub. Hlth., 84,* 247–53.

Filskov, S. B., & Boll, T. J. (1986). *Handbook of clinical neuropsychology* (2nd ed.). New York: Wiley.

Filskov, S. B., & Goldstein, S. G. (1974). Diagnostic validity of the Halstead-Reitan Neuropsychology battery., *J. Cons. Clin. Psychol., 42,* 383–88.

Filskov, S. B., & Locklear, E. (1982). A multidimensional perspective on clinical neuropsychology research. In P. C. Kendall & J. M. Butcher (Eds.), *Handbook of research methods in clinical psychology.* New York: Wiley.

Fincham, F. D., Beach, S. R. H., Moore, T., & Diener, C. (1994). The professional response to child sexual abuse: Whose interests are served? *Family Relations, 43,* 244–54.

Fine, M. A., & Sansone, R. A. (1990). Dilemmas in the management of suicidal behavior in individuals with borderline disorder. *Amer. J. Psychother., 44,* 160–71.

Fine, R. (1979). *A history of psychoanalysis.* New York: Columbia University Press.

Fink, M. (1979). *Convulsive therapy: Theory and practice.* New York: Raven Press.

Fink, M. (1992). Electroconvulsive therapy. In E. S. Paykel (Ed.), *Handbook of affective disorders* (2nd ed.). New York: Guilford.

Finkelhor, D. (1979). *Sexually victimized children.* New York: Free Press.

Finkelhor, D. (1984). *Child sexual abuse.* New York: Free Press.

Finkelhor, D. (1990). Early and long term effects of child sexual abuse: An update. *Profess. Psychol.: Research and Practice, 21,* 325–30.

Finkelhor, D., & Dziumba-Leatherman, J. (1997). Children as victims of violence: A national survey. *Pediatrics, 94,* 413–20.

Finkelhor, D., Hotaling, G., Lewis, I. A., & Smith, C. (1990). Sexual abuse in a national survey of adult men and women: Prevalence, characteristics, and risk factors. *Child Ab. Neg., 14,* 19–28.

Finkelstein, J. R. J., Cannon, T. D., Gur, R. E., Gur, R. C., & Moberg, P. (1997). Attentional dysfunctions in neuroleptic-naive and neuroleptic-withdrawn schizophrenic patients and their siblings. *J. Abn. Psychol., 106*(2), 203–12.

Finkelstein, N. (1993). Treatment programming for alcohol and drug-dependent pregnant women. *Inter. J. Addictions, 28,* 1275–1309.

Finlay-Jones, R. A., & Brown, G. W. (1981). Types of stressful life events and the onset of anxiety and depressive disorders. *Psychol. Med., 11,* 803–15.

Finn, P. R. (1990, Mar.). *Dysfunction in stimulus-response modulation in men at high risk for alcoholism.* Paper presented at a symposium on the Genetics of Alcoholism: Recent Advances. Satellite Symposium of the Annual Meeting of the Research Society on Alcoholism, Montreal, Canada.

Finn, P. R., Earleywine, M., & Pihl, R. O. (1992). Sensation seeking, stress reactivity, and alcohol dampening discriminate the density of a family history of alcoholism. *Alcoholism: Clin. Exper. Res., 16,* 585–90.

Finn, P. R., & Pihl, R. O. (1987). Men at high risk for alcoholism: The effect of alcohol on cardiovascular response to unavoidable shock. *J. Abn. Psychol., 96,* 230–36.

Finn, P. R., Sharkansky, E. J., Viken, R., West, T. L., Sandy, J., & Bufferd, S. (1997). Heterogeneity in the families of sons of alcoholics: The impact of familial vulnerability type on offspring characteristics. *J. Abn. Psychol., 106*(1), 26–36.

Finn, P. R., Zeitouni, N., & Pihl, R. (1990). Effects of alcohol on psychophysiological hyperactivity to nonaversive and aversive stimuli in men at high risk for alcoholism. *J. Abn. Psychol., 99,* 79–85.

Finn, S. E. & Tonsager, M. E. (1992). Therapeutic effects of providing MMPI-2 test feedback to college students awaiting therapy. *Psychol. Assess., 4,* 278–87.

Finn, S. E., & Tonsager, M. E. (1997). Information-gathering and therapeutic models of assessment: Complementary paradigms. *Psychol. Assess., 9*(4), 374–85.

Finucci, J. M., Guthrie, T., Childs, A. L., Abbey, H., & Childs, B. (1976). The genetics of specific reading disability. *Ann. Human Genet., 40,* 1–23.

First, M. B., Williams, J. B. W., & Spitzer, R. L. (1997). *DTREE: The DSM-IV Expert.* Toronto: Multi-Health Systems.

Fischer, J. M. (1993). People with learning disabilities: Moral and ethical rights to equal opportunities. *Journal of Applied Rehabilitation Counseling, 24*(1), 3–7.

Fischer, M. (1971). Psychoses in the offspring of schizophrenic monozygotic twins and their normal co-twins. *Brit. J. Psychiat., 118,* 43–52.

Fischer, M. (1973). Genetic and environmental factors in schizophrenia: A study of schizophrenic twins and their families. *Acta Psychiatr. Scandin.,* Suppl. No. 238.

Fischer, P. J., Shapiro, S., Breakey, W. R., Anthony, J. C., & Kramer, M. (1986). Mental health and social characteristics of the homeless: A survey of mission users. *Amer. J. Pub. Hlth., 76*(5), 519–24.

Fischman, J. (1987, Feb.). Type A on trial. *Psych. Today, 21,* 42–50.

Fischman, M. W., & Schuster, C. R. (1982). Cocaine self-administration in humans. *Federal Proc., 41,* 241–46.

Fish, B., Marcus, J., Hans, S. L., Auerbach, J. G., & Perdue, S. (1992). Infants at risk for schizophrenia: Sequelae of a genetic neurointegrative defect: A review and replication analysis of pandysmaturation in the Jerusalem Infant Development Study. *Arch. Gen. Psychiat., 49*(3), 221–35.

Fisher, J. D., & Fisher, W. A. (1992). Changing AIDS-risk behavior. *Psychol. Bull., 111*(3), 455–74.

Fisher, J. E., & Carstensen, L. L. (1990). Behavior management for the dementias. *Clin. Psychol. Rev., 10,* 611–30.

Fisher, S., & Greenberg, R. P. (1997a). The curse of the placebo: Fanciful pursuit of a pure biological therapy. In S. Fisher & R. P. Greenberg (Eds.), *From placebo to panacea: Putting psychiatric drugs to the test.* (pp. 3–56). New York: Wiley.

Fisher, S., & Greenberg, R. P. (Eds.). (1997b). *From placebo to panacea: Putting psychiatric drugs to the test.* New York: Wiley.

Fiske, S., & Taylor, S. (1991). *Social cognition,* 2nd ed. New York: McGraw Hill.

Fitiello, B., & Jensen, P. S. (1997). Medication development and testing in children and adolescents. *Arch. Gen. Psychiat., 54,* 871–76.

Flaum, M., & Andreasen, N. C. (1991). Diagnostic criteria for schizophrenia and related disorders: Options for DSM-IV. *Schizo. Bull., 17*(1), 133–56.

Fleming, J. E., Offord, D. R., & Boyle, M. H. (1989). Prevalence of childhood and adolescent depression in the community: Ontario Health Study. *Brit. J. Psychiat., 155,* 647–54.

Flier, J. S., Underhill, L. H., & Lieber, C. S. (1995). Medical disorders of alcoholism. *New Engl. J. Med., 333*(6), 1058–65.

Flor, H., & Birbaumer, N. (1993). Comparison of the efficacy of electromyographic biofeedback, cognitive-behavior therapy, and conservative medical interventions in the treatment of chronic musculoskeletal pain. *J. Cons. Clin. Psychol., 61*(4), 653–58.

Fluoxetine Bulimia Nervosa Collaborative Study Group. (1992). Fluoxetine in the treatment of bulimia nervosa. *Arch. Gen. Psychiat., 49*(2), 139–47.

Flynn, C. F., Sturges, M. S., Swarsen, R. J., & Kohn, G. M. (1993, Apr.). Alcoholism and treatment in airline aviators: One company's results. *Aviation, Space, and Environmental Medicine,* 314–18.

Foa, E., Franklin, M., & Kozak, M. (1998). Psychosocial treatments for obsessive-compulsive disorder: Literature review. In R. Swinson, M. Antony, S. Rachman, & M. Richter (Eds.), *Obsessive-compulsive disorder: Theory, research, and treatment.* (pp. 258–76). New York: Guilford.

Foa, E., & Kozak, M. J. (1986). Emotional processing of fear: Exposure to corrective information. *Psychol. Bull., 99,* 20–35.

Foa, E. B., & Kozak, M. J. (1985). Treatment of anxiety disorders: Implications for psychopathology. In A. H. Tuma & J. D. Maser (Eds.), *Anxiety and the anxiety disorders.* (pp. 421–52). Hillsdale, NJ: Erlbaum.

Foa, E. B., & Meadows, E. A. (1997). Psychosocial treatments for posttraumatic stress disorder: A critical review. *Ann. Rev. Psychol., 48,* 449–80.

Foa, E. B., Steketee, G., & Young, M. C. (1984). Agoraphobia: Phenomenological aspects, associated characteristics, and theoretical considerations. *Clin. Psychol. Rev., 4,* 431–57.

Foelsch, P. A. & Kernberg, O. F. (1998). Transference-focused psychotherapy for borderline personality disorders. *In Session: Psychotherapy in Practice, 4*(2), 67–90.

Fogel, B. S. (1991). Beyond neuroleptics: The treatment of agitation. In E. Light & B. D. Lebowitz (Eds.), *The elderly with chronic mental illness.* (pp. 167–92). New York: Springer.

Foley, M. A. Santini, C., & Sopasakis, M. (1989) Discriminating between memories: Evidence for children's spontaneous elaboration. *Journal of Experimental Child Psychology.* 48, 146–69.

Foltin, R. W., & Fischman, M. W. (1997). A laboratory model of cocaine withdrawal in humans: Intravenous cocaine. *Experimental and Clinical Pharmacology, 5*(4), 404–11.

Fombonne, E., & du Mazaubrun, C. (1992). Prevalence of infantile autism in four French regions. *Soc. Psychiat. Psychiat. Epidemiol., 27,* 203–10.

Fontana, A., & Rosenheck, R. (1994). Traumatic war stressors and psychiatric symptoms among World War II, Korean, and Vietnam War veterans. *Psychol. Aging, 9,* 27–33.

Ford, M. R., & Widiger, T. A. (1989) Sex bias in the diagnosis of histrionic and antisocial personalty disorders. *J. Cons. Clin. Psychol., 57,* 301–305.

Forehand, R. (1993). Twenty years of research on parenting: Does it have practical implications for clinicians working with parents and children? *Clin. Psychol., 46,* 169–76.

Forehand, R., Wierson, M., Frame, C. L., & Kempton, T. (1991). Juvenile firesetting: A unique syndrome or an advanced level of antisocial behavior? *Behav. Res. Ther., 29,* 125–28.

Foreyt, J. P. (1986). Treating the diseases of the 1980s: Eating disorders. *Contemp. Psychol., 31,* 658–60.

Forgac, G. E., & Michaels, E. J. (1982). Personality characteristics of two types of male exhibitionists. *J. Abn. Psychol., 91,* 287–93.

Forman, S. G., & Linney, J. A. (1988). School-based prevention of adolescent substance abuse: Programs, implementation and future directions. *School Psychol. Rev., 17*(4), 550–58.

Forness, S. R., & Kavale, K. A. (1993). Strategies to improve basic learning and memory deficits in mental retardation: A meta-analysis of experimental studies. *Education and Training in Mental Retardation, 28*(2), 99–110.

Fowler, R. C., Rich, C. L., & Young, D. (1986). San Diego suicide study: Substance abuse in young cases. *Archiv. Gen. Psychiat., 43,* 962–65.

Fowler, R. D. (1987). Developing a computer based test interpretation system. In J. N. Butcher (Ed.), *Computerized psychological assessment: A practitioner's guide.* New York: Basic Books.

Fowler, R. D., & Butcher, J. N. (1986). Critique of Matarazzo's view of computerized testing: All sigma and no meaning. *Amer. Psychol., 41,* 94–96.

Fowler, R. D., Finkelstein, A., Penk, W., Bell, W., & Itzig, B. (1987). An automated problem-rating interview: The DPRI. In J. N. Butcher (Ed.), *Computerized psychological assessment: A practitioner's guide.* New York: Basic Books.

Fowles, D. C. (1980). The three arousal model: Implications of Gray's two-factor learning theory for heart rate, electrodermal activity, and psychopathy. *Psychophysiology, 17,* 87–104.

Fowles, D. C. (1993). Electrodermal activity and antisocial behavior: Empirical findings and theoretical issues. In J.-C. Roy, W. Boucsein, D. Fowles, & J. Gruzelier (Eds.), *Progress in electrodermal research.* London: Plenum.

Fowles, D. C., & Missel, K. A. (1994). Electrodermal hyporeactivity, motivation, and psychopathy: Theoretical issues. In D. C. Fowles, P. Sutker, & S. H. Goodman (Eds.), *Progress in experimental personality and psychopathology research.* New York: Springer.

Fowles, D. C., Sutker, P., & Goodman, S. H. (1994). *Progress in experimental personality and psychopathology research.* New York: Springer.

Frances, A. (1993). Dimensional diagnosis of personality: Not whether, but when and which. *Psychol. Inq., 4,* 110–11.

Frances, A., Widiger, T., & Fyer, M. R. (1990). The influence of classification methods on comorbidity. In J. D. Maser & C. R. Cloninger (Eds.), *Comorbidity of mood and anxiety disorders.* (pp. 42–59). Washington, DC: American Psychiatric Press.

Frances, A. J., et al. (1991). An A-to-Z guide to DSM-IV communications *J. Abn. Psychol., 100,* 907–12.

Frank, E., Anderson, C., & Rubenstein, D. (1978). Frequency of sexual dysfunction in normal couples. *New Engl. J. Med., 299,* 111–15.

Frank, E., Kupfer, D. J., Perel, J. M., Cornes, C., Jarrett, D. B., Mallinger, A. G., Thase, M. E., McEachran, A. B., & Grochocinski, V. J. (1990). Three-year outcomes for maintenance therapies in recurrent depression. *Arch. Gen. Psychiat., 47,* 1093–99.

Frank, E., Prien, R. F., Jarrett, R. B., Keller, M. B., Kupfer, D. J., Lavori, P. W., Rush, A. J., & Weissman, M. M. (1991). Conceptualization and rationale for consensus definitions of terms in major depressive disorder: Remission, recovery, relapse, and recurrence. *Arch. Gen. Psychiat., 48,* 851–55.

Frank, E., & Spanier, C. (1995). Interpersonal psychotherapy for depression: Overview, clinical efficacy, and future directions. *Clin. Psychol. Sci. Pract., 2,* 349–69.

Frank, J. D. (1978). *Persuasion and Healing* (2nd ed.). Baltimore: Johns Hopkins University Press.

Frankel, F. H. (1994). Dissociation in hysteria and hypnosis: A concept aggrandized. In S. J. Lynn & J. W. Rhue (Eds.), *Dissociation: Clinical and theoretical perspectives.* (pp. 80–93). New York: Guilford.

Frankenhauser, F. R. (1994). History of the development of antipsychotic medications. *Psychiat. Clin. N. Amer., 17*(3), 531–41.

Franklin, M. E., & Foa, E. B. (1998). Cognitive-behavioral treatments for obsessive-compulsive disorder. In P. E. Nathan & J. M. Gorman (Eds.), *A guide to treatments that work.* (pp. 339–57). New York: Oxford University Press.

Franzek, E., & Beckmann, H. (1998). Different genetic background of schizophrenia spectrum psychoses: A twin study. *Amer. J. Psychiat., 155*(1), 76–83.

Frasure-Smith, N., Lesperance, F., & Talajic, M. (1993). Depression following myocardial infarction: Impact on 6-month survival. *JAMA, 270,* 1819–25.

Frasure-Smith, N., Lesperance, F., & Talajic, M. (1995). Depression and 18-month prognosis following myocardial infarction. *Circulation, 91,* 999.

Frayser, S. G. (1985). *Varieties of sexual experience: an anthropological perspective on human sexuality.* New Haven, CT: HRAF Press.

Frazier, M., & Merrell, K. W. (1998). Issues in behavioral treatment of attention-deficit/hyperactivity disorder. *Education & Treatment of Children, 20*(4), 441–61.

Frazier, P., & Burnett, J. (1994). Immediate coping strategies among rape victims. *J. Couns. Devel. 72,* 633–39.

Frazier, P., & Schauben, L. (1994). Causal attributions and recovery from rape and other stressful life events. *J. Soc. Clin. Psychol., 14,* 1–14.

Frederick, C. J. (1985). An introduction and overview of youth suicide. In M. L. Peck, N. L. Farberow, & R. E. Litman (Eds.), *Youth Suicide.* (pp. 1– 6). New York: Springer.

Frederick, C. J. (1986). Post-traumatic stress disorder and child-molestation. In A. Burgess & C. Hartman (Eds.), *Sexual exploitation of parents by health professionals.* (pp. 133–42). New York: Praeger.

Freedheim, D. (Ed.). (1992). *The history of psychotherapy: A century of change.* Washington: American Psychological Association.

Freedman, B., & Chapman, L. J. (1973). Early subjective experience in schizophrenic episodes. *J. Abn. Psychol., 82*(1), 46–54.

Freeman, R. D., Malkin, S. F., & Hastings, J. O. (1975). Psychosocial problems of deaf children and their families: A comparative study. *Amer. Ann. Deaf, 120,* 391–405.

Freeman, T. (1960). On the psychopathology of schizophrenia. *J. Ment. Sci., 106,* 925–37.

Freeman, W. (1959). Psychosurgery. In S. Arieti (Ed.), *American handbook of psychiatry* (Vol. 2). (pp. 1521–40). New York: Basic Books.

Fremouw, W. J., de Perczel, M., & Ellis, T. E. (1990). *Suicide risk: Assessment and response guidelines.* Elmsford, NY: Pergamon.

French, S. A., & Jeffery, R. W. (1994). Consequences of dieting to lose weight: Effects on physical and mental health. *Hlth. Psychol., 13,* 195–212.

Freud, A. (1946). *Ego and the mechanisms of defense.* New York: International Universities Press.

Freud, S. (1909). Analysis of a phobia in a five-year-old boy. In *Standard edition, vol 10.* London: Hogarth Press (1955). First German edition 1909.

Freud, S. (1917). Mourning and Melancholia. In W. Gaylin (Ed.), *The meaning of despair: Psychoanalytic contributions to the understanding of depression.* New York: Science House.

Freud, S. (1935). Letter to an American mother. Reprinted in Paul Friedman (1959), Sexual deviations, in S. Arieti (Ed.), *American Handbook of Psychiatry* (Vol. 1). pp. 606–7. New York: Basic Books.

Freund, K., & Blanchard, R. (1993). Erotic target location errors in male gender dysphorics, paedophiles, and fetishists. *Brit. J. Psychiat., 162,* 558–63.

Freund, K., & Kuban, M. (1993). Deficient erotic gender differentiation in pedophilia: A followup. *Arch. Sex. Behav., 22,* 619–28.

Freund, K., Langevin, R., Zajac, Y., Steiner, B., & Zajac, A. (1974). The transsexual syndrome in homosexual males. *J. Nerv. Ment. Dis., 158,* 145–53.

Freund, K., Watson, R. J., & Rienzo, D. (1989). Heterosexuality, homosexuality, and erotic age preference. *J. Sex Res., 26,* 107–17.

Frick, P. J. (1998). Callous-unemotional traits and conduct problems: Applying the two-factor model of psychopathy to children. In D. J. Cooke, A. E. Forth, & R. D. Hare (Eds.), *Psychopathy: Theory, Research, and Implications for Society.* (pp. 161–187). Dordrecht, Netherlands: Kluwer Academic Publishers.

Frick, P. J. (1998). *Conduct disorders and severe antisocial behavior.* New York: Plenum.

Frick, P. J., Lahey, B. B., Loeber, R., & Stouthamer-Loeber, M. (1992). Familial risk factors to opposition defiant disorder and conduct disorder: Parental psychopathology and maternal parenting. *J. Cons. Clin. Psychol., 60,* 49–55.

Friedman, D., & Squires-Wheeler, E. (1994). Event-related potentials (ERPs) as indicators of risk for schizophrenia. *Schizo. Bull., 20*(1), 63–74.

Friedman, H. S., & Booth-Kewley, S. (1987a). Personality, Type A behavior, and coronary heart disease: The role of emotional expression. *J. Pers. Soc. Psychol., 53,* 783–92.

Friedman, H. S., & Booth-Kewley, S. (1987b). The "disease-prone" personality: A meta-analytic view of the construct. *Amer. Psychol., 42,* 539–55.

Friedman, H. S., Hawley, P. H., & Tucker, J. S. (1994). Personality, health, and longevity. *Curr. Dir. Psychol. Sci., 3*(2), 37–41.

Friedman, H. S., Tucker, J. S., Tomlinson-Keasey, C., Schwartz, J. E., Wingard, D. L., & Criqui, M. H. (1993). Does childhood personality predict longevity? *J. Pers. Soc. Psychol., 65*(1), 176–85.

Friedman, J. H. (1974). Woman's role in male impotence. *Med. Asp. Human Sex., 8*(6), 8–23.

Friedman, M., Manwaring, J. H., Rosenman, R. H., Donlon, G., & Ortega, P. (1973). Instantaneous and sudden death: Clinical and pathological differentiation in coronary artery disease. *JAMA, 225,* 1319–28.

Friedman, M., & Rosenman, R. H. (1959). Association of specific overt behavior pattern with blood and cardiovascular findings. *JAMA, 169,* 1286.

Friedman, M., & Ulmer, D. (1984). *Treating Type A behavior and your heart.* New York: Knopf.

Friedman, M. J., & Yehuda, R. (1995). Post-traumatic stress disorder and comorbidity: Psychobiological approaches to differential diagnosis. In M. J. Friedman, D. S. Charney, et al., *Neurobiological and clinical consequences of stress: From normal adaptation to post-traumatic stress disorder.* (pp. 429–45). Philadelphia: Lippincott-Raven.

Friedman, R., & Iwai, J. (1976). Genetic predisposition and stress-induced hypertension. *Science, 193,* 161–92.

Friedrich, W., Einbender, A. J., & Luecke, W. J. (1983). Cognitive and behavioral characteristics of physically abused children. *J. Cons. Clin. Psychol., 51*(2), 313–14.

Friman, P. C., & Warzak, W. J. (1990). Nocturnal enuresis: A prevalent, persistent, yet curable parasomnia. *Pediatrician, 17,* 38–45.

Fromm, E., & Shor, R. E. (1972). *Hypnosis: Research developments and perspectives.* Chicago: Aldine.

Fromm-Reichmann, F. (1948). Notes on the development of treatment of schizophrenics by psychoanalytic psychotherapy. *Psychiatry, 11,* 263–73.

Fruzzetti, A. E. (1996). Causes and consequences: Individual distress in the context of couple interactions. *J. Consult. Clin. Psychol., 64,* 1192–201.

Fullerton, C. S., & Ursano, R. J. (1997). The other side of chaos: Understanding the patterns of posttraumatic stress disorder. In C. S. Fullerton & R. J. Ursano (Eds.), *Posttraumatic stress disorder.* (pp. 3–20). Washington: American Psychiatric Association Press.

Fulmer, R. H., & Lapidus, L. B. (1980). A study of professed reasons for beginning and continuing heroin use. *Inter. J. Addictions, 15,* 631–45.

Furby, L., Weinrott, M. R., & Blackshaw, L. (1989). Sex offender recidivism: A review. *Psychol. Bull., 105,* 3–30.

Furlong, W. B. (1971). How "speed" kills athletic careers. *Today's Health, 49*(2), 30–33, 62, 64, 66.

Furst, M. (1995). The D-Tree. *Multi-Health Systems,* Toronto, Canada.

Futterman, A., Thompson, L., Gallagher-Thompson, D., & Ferris, R. (1995). Depression in later life: Epidemiology, assessment, etiology, and treatment. In E. E. Beckham & W. R. Leber (Eds.), *Handbook of depression* (2nd ed.). (pp. 494–525). New York: Guilford.

Fyer, A. J., Chapman, S., T. F., Martin, L. Y., & Klein, D. F. (1995). Specificity in familial aggregation of phobic disorders. *Arch. Gen. Psychiat., 52,* 564–73.

Fyer, A. J., Mannuzza, S., Chapman, T. F., Liebowitz, M. R., & Klein, D. F. (1993). A direct interview family study of social phobia. *Arch. Gen. Psychiat., 50,* 286–3.

Gabbard, G. O., Lazar, S. G., Hornberger, J., & Spiegel, D. (1997). The economic impact of psychotherapy: A review. *Amer. J. Psychiat., 154*(2), 147–55.

Gabuzda, D. H., & Hirsch, M. S. (1987). Neurologic manifestations of infection with human immunodeficiency virus: Clinical features and pathogenesis. *Ann. Int. Med., 107,* 383–91.

Gager, N., & Schurr, C. (1976). *Sexual assault: Confronting rape in America.* New York: Grosset & Dunlap.

Gagnon, J., & Simon, W. (1973). *Sexual conduct: The social origins of human sexuality.* Chicago: Aldine.

Gajdusek, D. C. (1986). On the uniform source of amyloid in plaques, tangles, and vascular deposits. *Neurobiol. Aging, 7,* 453–54.

Gajzago, C., & Prior, M. (1974). Two cases of "recovery" in Kanner syndrome. *Arch. Gen. Psychiat., 31*(2), 264–68.

Galin, D., Diamond, R., & Braff, D. (1977). Lateralization of conversion symptoms: More frequent on the left. *Amer. J. Psychiat., 134,* 578–80.

Galler, J. R. (Ed.) (1984). *Human nutrition: A comprehensive treatise: Vol. 5. Nutrition and Behavior.* New York: Plenum Press.

Gamble, T. J., & Zigler, E. (1989). The head start synthesis project: A critique. *J. App. Devel. Psychol., 10,* 267–74.

Ganju, V., & Quan, H. (1987). *Mental health service needs of refugees in Texas.* Paper given at the Refugee Assistance Program: Mental Health Workgroup Meeting, UCLA, February 12–13.

Garb, H. (1995). Using computers to make judgments: Correlation among predictors and the comparison of configural rules. *Computers in Human Behavior, 11*(2), 313–24.

Garb, H. N. (1989). Clinical judgment, clinical training, and professional experience. *Psychol. Bull., 105,* 387–96.

Garber, H. L. (1988). *The Milwaukee Project: Preventing mental retardation in children at risk.* Washington, DC: American Association on Mental Retardation.

Garber, J., Quiggle, N. L., Panak, W., & Dodge, K. A. (1994). Aggression and depression in children: Comorbidity, specificity, and cognitive processing. In D. Cicchetti & S. Toth (Eds.), *Rochester symposium on Developmental Psychopathology: Internalizing and externalizing expressions of dysfunctions.* (pp. 225–64). Hillsdale, NJ: Erlbaum.

Gardner, E. L. (1997). Brain reward mechanisms. In J. H. Lowinson, P. Ruiz, R. B. Millman, & J. G. Langrod (Eds.), *Substance abuse: A comprehensive textbook.* Baltimore: Williams & Wilkins.

Gardner, M. (1993, Summer). The false memory syndrome. *Skeptical Inquirer, 17,* 370–75.

Garfield, S. L. (1986). Research on client variables in psychotherapy. In S. L. Garfield & A. E. Bergin (Eds.), *Handbook of psychotherapy and behavior change* (3rd ed.). (pp. 213–56). New York: Wiley.

Garfield, S. L. (1994). Research on client variables in psychotherapy. In A. E. Bergin & S. L. Garfield (Eds.), *Handbook of psychotherapy and behavior change* (4th ed.). (pp. 190–228). New York: Wiley.

Garfield, S. L. (1998). Some comments on empirically supported treatments. *J. Cons. Clin. Psychol., 66*(1), 121–25.

Garmezy, N. (1978a). Current status of other high-risk research programs. In L. C. Wynne, R. L. Cromwell, & S. Matthysse (Eds.), *The nature of schizophrenia: New approaches to research and treatment.* New York: Wiley.

Garmezy, N. (1978b). Observations of high-risk research and premorbid development in schizophrenia. In L. C. Wynne, R. L. Cromwell, & S. Matthysse (Eds.), *The nature of schizophrenia: New approaches to research and treatment.* New York: Wiley.

Garner, D. M. (1986a). Cognitive-behavioral therapy for eating disorders. *Clin. Psychol., 39*(2), 36–39.

Garner, D. M. (1986b). Cognitive therapy for anorexia nervosa. In K. D. Brownell & J. P. Foreyt (Eds.), *Handbook of eating disorders.* (pp. 301–27). New York: Basic Books.

Garner, D. M., et al. (1980). Cultural expectations of thinness in women. *Psychol. Rep., 47,* 483–91.

Garner, D. M., & Garfinkel, P. E. (Eds.). (1997) *Handbook of treatment for eating disorders.* (2nd ed.). New York: Guilford.

Garner, D.M., & Wooley, S.C. (1991). Confronting the failure of behavioral and dietary treatments for obesity. *Clin. Psychol. Rev., 11,* 729–80.

Garrison, C. Z., Weinrich, M. W., Hardin, S. B., Weinrich, S., & Wang, L. (1993). Post-traumatic stress disorder in adolescents after a hurricane. *Amer. J. Epidemiol., 138,* 522–30.

Gatz, M., Kasl-Godley, J. E., & Karel, M. J. (1996). Aging and mental disorders. In J. E. Birren & K. W. Schaie (Eds.), *Handbook of the psychology of aging.* (pp. 365–83). New York: Academic Press.

Gatz, M., Lowe, B., Berg, S., Mortimer, J., & Pedersen, N. (1994). Dementia: Not just a search for the gene. *The Gerontologist, 34,* 251–55.

Gaudin, J.M., Jr. (1993). Effective intervention with neglectful families. *Crim. Just. Behav., 20,* 66–89.

Gaw, K. F., & Beutler, L. E. (1995). Integrating treatment recommendations. In L. Beutler and M. R. Berron (Eds.), *Integrative assessment of adult personality.* (pp. 280–319). New York: Guilford.

Gawin, F. H., & Kleber, H. D. (1986). Abstinence symptomatology and psychiatric diagnosis in cocaine abusers. *Arch. Gen. Psychiat., 43,* 107–13.

Gaynor, S. T., Baird, S. C., Nelson-Gray, R. (1999). Application of time-serious (single subject) designs in clinical psychology. In p. C. Kendall, J. N. Butcher, & G. Holmbeck (Eds.), *Research methods in clinical psychology* (2nd ed.). (pp. 297–329). New York: Wiley.

Gebhard, P. H., Gagnon, J. H., Pomeroy, W. B., & Christenson, C. V. (1965). *Sex offenders: An analysis of types.* New York: Harper & Row.

Geis, G. (1977). Forcible rape: An introduction. In D. Chappell, R. Geis, & G. Geis (Eds.), *Forcible rape, the crime, the victim, and the offender.* (pp. 1–37). New York: Columbia University Press.

Geiser, D. S. (1989). Psychosocial influences on human immunity. *Clin. Psychol. Rev., 9,* 689–715.

Geisz, D., & Steinhausen, H. (1974). On the "psychological development of children with hydrocephalus." (German) *Praxis der Kinderpsychologie und Kinderpsychiatrie, 23*(4), 113–18.

Gelehrter, T. D., Collins, F. S., & Ginsburg, D. (1998). *Principles of Medical Genetics.* Baltimore: Williams and Wilkins.

Gelfand, D. M., Jenson, W. R., & Drew, C. J. (1988). *Understanding child behavior disorders* (2nd ed.). New York: Holt, Rinehart & Winston.

Gelfand, D. M., & Teti, D. M. (1990). The effects of maternal depression on children. *Clin. Psychol. Rev., 10,* 329–53.

Gelles, R. J. (1978). Violence toward children in the United States. *Amer. J. Orthopsychiat., 48,* 580–90.

Gelles, R. J., & Cornell, C. P. (1990). *Intimate violence in families.* Newbury Park, CA: Sage.

Gentil, V., Lotufo-Neto, P., Andrade, L., Cordas, T., Bernik, M., Ramos, R., Maciel, L., Miyakawa, E., & Gorenstein, C. (1993). Clomipramine, a better reference drug for panic/agoraphobia. *J. Psychopharm., 7,* 316–24.

Gentry, J., & Eron, L. D. (1993). American Psychological Association Commission on violence and youth. *Amer. Psychol., 48,* 89.

Gentry, W. D. (1984). Behavioral medicine: A new research paradigm. In W. D. Gentry (Ed.), *Handbook of behavioral medicine.* (pp. 1–12). New York: Guilford.

Gentry, W. D., Chesney, A. P., Gary, H. G., Hall, R. P., & Harburg, E. (1982). Habitual anger-coping styles: I. Effect of mean blood pressure and risk for essential hypertension. *Psychosom. Med., 44,* 195–202.

George, L. K. (1984). *The burden of caregiving.* Center Reports of Advances in Research. Durham, NC: Duke University Center for the Study of Aging and Human Development.

George, L., & Neufeld, R. W. J. (1985). Cognition and symptomatology in schizophrenia. *Schizo. Bull., 11,* 264–85.

Gerner, R. H. (1993). Treatment of acute mania. *Psychiat. Clin. N. Amer., 16,* 443–60.

Gershon, E. S. (1990). In F. K. Goodwin & K. R. Jamison (Eds.), *Genetics in manic-depressive illness.* (pp. 373–401). New York: Oxford University Press.

Geschwind, N. (1975). The borderland of neurology and psychiatry: Some common misconceptions. In D. F. Benson & D. Blumer (Eds.), *Psychiatric aspects of neurological disease.* (pp. 1–9). New York: Grune & Stratton.

Gest, S. D. (1997). Behavioral inhibition: Stability and associations with adaptation from childhood to early adulthood. *J. Pers. Soc. Psychol., 72*(2), 467–75.

Giannetti, R. A. (1987). The GOLPH Psychosocial History: Response contingent data acquisition and reporting. In J. N. Butcher (Ed.), *Computerized psychological assessment: A practitioners guide.* New York: Basic Books.

Gibbons, H. L. (1988). Alcohol, aviation, and safety revisited: a historical review and a suggestion. *Aviation, Space, and Environmental Medicine, 59,* 657–60.

Gibbs, N. A. (1996). Nonclinical populations in research on obsessive-compulsive disorder: A critical review. *Clin. Psychol. Rev., 16*(8), 729–73.

Gilbert, C. (1991). Outcome in autistic-like conditions. *J. Amer. Acad. Child Adoles. Psychiat. 30,* 375–82.

Gilbert, J. G., & Lombardi, D. N. (1967). Personality characteristics of young male narcotic addicts. *J. Couns. Psychol., 31,* 536–38.

Gilbert, N. (1991, Spring). The phantom epidemic of sexual assault. Public Interest, 54–65 (12 pages).

Gilbert, N. (1992, May). Realities and mythologies of rape. *Society,* 4–11.

Giles, G. M. (1994). The status of brain injury rehabilitation. *Amer. J. Occup. Ther., 48*(3), 199–205.

Gilhooly, M. L. M., Sweeting, H. N., Whittick, J. E., & McKee, K. (1994). Family care of the dementing elderly. *Inter. Rev. Psychiat., 6*(1), 29–40.

Gill, D. (1996). Preventing violence in a structurally violent society: Mission impossible. *Amer. J. Orthopsychiat., 66*(1), 77–84.

Gillberg, C. (1989). *Diagnosis and treatment of autism.* New York: Plenum.

Gillberg, C. (1995). The prevalence of autism and autism spectrum disorders. In F. C. Verhulst & H. M. Koot (Eds.), *The epidemiology of child and adolescent psychopathology.* (pp. 227–57). New York: Oxford University Press.

Gillberg, C. U. (1998). Asperger syndrome and high–functioning autism. *Brit. J. Psychiat., 172,* 200–209.

Gillberg, C., Melander, H., von Knorring, A. L., Janols, L. O., Thernlund, G., Haggloff, B., Eidevall-Wallin, L., Gustafsson, P., & Kopp, S. (1997). Long-term stimulant treatment of children with attention-deficit hyperactivity disorder symptoms: A randomized double-blind, placebo controlled trial. *Arch. Gen. Psychiat., 54,* 857–864.

Gillberg, C. U. (1990). Autism and pervasive developmental disorders. *J. Child Psychol. Psychiatry, 31,* 99–119.

Gillberg, C., & Schaumann, H. (1981). Infantile autism and puberty. *J. Autism Develop. Dis., 11*(4), 365–71.

Gilley, D. W., et al. (1997). Psychotic symptoms and physically aggressive behavior in Alzheimer's disease. *J. Amer. Geriat. Soc., 45*(9), 1074–79.

Gillis, H. M. (1993). Individual and small-group psychotherapy for children involved in trauma and disaster. In C.F. Saylor (Ed.), *Children and disasters.* (pp. 165-186). New York: Plenum

Gingell, K., Parmar, R., & Sungum-Paliwal, S. (1996). Autism and multiple pituitary deficiency. *Develop. Med. Child Neuro., 38,* 545–53.

Ginsberg, S. D., Hof, P. R., McKinney, W. T., & Morrison, J. H. (1993a) Quantitative analyses of tuberoinfundibular tyrosine hydroxylase- activity and corticotropin-releasing factor-immunoreactive neurons in monkeys raised with differential rearing conditions. *Exper. Neur., 120,* 95–105.

Ginsberg, S. D., Hof, P. R., McKinney, W. T., & Morrison, J. H. (1993b) The noradrenergic innervation density of the monkey paraventricular nucleus is not altered by early social deprivation. *Neurosc. Lett., 158,* 130–134.

Gisele, G. M., Otto, M. W., McArdle, E. T., Worthington, J. J., Rosenbaum, J. F., & Pollack, M. H. (1996). Relationship of antecedent stressful life events to childhood and family history of anxiety and the course of panic disorder. *J. Affect. Dis., 41,* 135–39.

Gist, R., & Lubin, B. (Eds.). (1989). *Psychosocial aspects of disaster.* New York: Wiley.

Gitlin, M. J. (1993). Pharmacotherapy of personality disorders: Conceptual framework and clinical strategies. *J. Clin. Psychopharm., 13,* 343–53.

Gitlin, M. J. (1996). *The psychotherapist's guide to psychopharmacology* (2nd ed.). New York: Free Press.

Gittelman, R. (1983). Treatment of reading disorders. In M. Rutter (Ed.), *Developmental neuropsychiatry.* (pp. 520–39). New York: Guilford.

Gittelman, R. (Ed). (1986). *Anxiety disorders in childhood.* New York: Guilford.

Gittelman, R., Mannuzza, S., Shenker, R., & Bonagura, N. (1985). Hyperactive boys almost grown up. *Arch. Gen. Psychiat., 42,* 937–47.

Gittelman-Klein, R. (1980). Diagnosis and drug treatment of childhood disorders: Attention deficit disorder with hyperactivity. In D. F. Klein, R. Gittelman-Klein, F. Quitkin, & A. Rifkin (Eds.), *Diagnosis*

and drug treatment of psychiatric disorders: Adults and children (2nd ed.). (pp. 590–695). Baltimore, MD: Williams & Wilkins.

Glaser, R., Kiecolt-Glaser, J. K., Speicher, C. E., & Holliday, J. E. (1985). Stress, loneliness, and changes in herpes virus latency. *J. Behav. Med., 8,* 249–60.

Glaser, R., Rice, J., Sheridan, J., Fertel, R., Stout, J., Speicher, C., Pinsky, R., Kotur, M., Post, A., Beck, M., & Kiecolt-Glaser, J. (1987). Stress-related immune suppression: Health implications. *Brain, Behavior, and Immunity, 1,* 7–20.

Glasscote, R. (1978). What programs work and what programs do not work for chronic mental patients? In J. A. Talbott (Ed.), *The chronic mental patient: Problems, solutions and recommendations for a public policy.* Washington, DC: American Psychiatric Association.

Glatt, M. M. (1995). Controlled drinking after a third of a century. *Addiction, 90*(9), 1157–60.

Gleaves, D. L., & Eberenz, K. (1993). The psychopathology of anorexia nervosa: A factor analytic investigation. *J. Psychopath. Behav. Assess., 15*(2), 141–52.

Glenner, G. C. (1986). Marching backwards into the future. *Neurobiol. of Aging, 7,* 439–41.

Gleser, G., & Sacks, M. (1973). Ego defenses and reaction to stress: A validation study of the Defense Mechanisms Inventory. *J. Cons. Clin. Psychol., 40*(2), 181–87.

Glitz, D. A., & Balon, R. (1996). Serotonin-selective drugs in generalizes anxiety disorder: Achievements and prospects. In H. G. Westenberg, J. A. Den Boer, & D. L. Murphy (Eds.), *Advances in the neurobiology of anxiety disorders.* (pp. 335–58). Chichester, England: Wiley.

Glod, C. A. (1993). Long-term consequences of childhood physical and sexual abuse. *Archives of Psychiatric Nursing, 7,* 163–73.

Glosser, G., & Wexler, D. (1985). Participants' evaluation of education/support groups for families of patients with Alzheimer's disease and other dementias. *Gerontologist, 25,* 232–36.

Gochman, S. I., Allgood, B. A., & Geer, C. R. (1982). A look at today's behavior therapists. *Profess. Psychol., 13*(5), 605–9.

Goddard, A. W., Woods, S. W., & Charney, D. S. (1996). A critical review of the role of norepinephrine in panic disorder: Focus on its interaction with serotonin. In H. G. Westenberg, J. A. Den Boer & D. L. Murphy (Eds.), *Advances in the neurobiology of anxiety disorders.* (pp. 107–137). Chichester, England: Wiley.

Goetz, K. L., & Van Kammen, D. P. (1986). Computerized axial tomography scans and subtypes of schizophrenia: A review of the literature. *J. Nerv. Ment. Dis., 174,* 31–41.

Goffman, E. (1961). *Asylums.* New York: Doubleday.

Gold, E. R. (1986). Long-term effects of sexual victimization in childhood: An attributional approach. *J. Cons. Clin. Psychol., 54,* 471–75.

Gold, J., & Stricker, G. (Ed.). (1993). *Comprehensive handbook of psychotherapy integration.* New York: Plenum.

Gold, J. M., Carpenter, C., Randolph, C., Goldberg, T. E., & Weinberger, D. R. (1997). Auditory working memory and Wisconsin Card Sorting Test performance in schizophrenia. *Arch. Gen. Psychiat., 54*(2), 159–65.

Gold, M. S., & Rea, W. S. (1983). The role of endorphins in opiate addiction, withdrawal, and recovery. *Psychiat. Clin. N. Amer., 6,* 489–520.

Goldberg, C. (1997, October 1). A drinking death rattles elite M.I.T. *New York Times,* p. A10

Goldberg, D. P., & Bridges, K. (1988). Somatic presentations of psychiatric illness in primary care settings. *J. Psychoso. Res., 32,* 137–44.

Goldberg, J., True, W. R., Eisen, S. A., & Henderson, W. G. (1990). A twin study of the effects of the Vietnam War on posttraumatic stress disorder. *JAMA, 263,* 1227–32.

Goldberg, S., Schultz, C., Schultz, P., et al. (1986). Borderline and schizotypal personality disorders treated with low-dose thiothixene vs. placebo. *Arch. Gen. Psychiat., 43,* 680–86.

Golden, C. J. (1978). *Diagnosis and rehabilitation in clinical neuropsychology.* Springfield, IL: Charles C. Thomas.

Golden, D. A., & Davis, J. G. (1974). Counseling parents after the birth of an infant with Down's syndrome. *Children Today, 3*(2), 7–11.

Goldfeld, A. E., Mollica, R. R., Pesavento, B. H., & Faraone, S. V. (1988). The physical and psychological sequelae of torture—symptomatology and diagnosis. *JAMA, 259,* 2725–29.

Goldfinger, S. M., Schutt, R. K., Seidman, L. J., Turner, W. M., et al. (1996). Self report and observer measures of substance abuse among homeless mentally ill persons in the cross-section and over time. *J. Nerv. Ment. Dis., 184*(11), 667–72.

Goldfried, M. R. (1980). Toward the delineation of therapeutic change principles. *Amer. Psychol., 35,* (11) 991–99.

Goldfried, M. R., & Merbaum, M. (Eds.). (1973). *Behavior change through self control.* New York: Holt, Rinehart & Winston.

Goldfried, M. R., & Safran, J. D. (1986). Future directions in psychotherapy integration. In J. C. Norcross (Ed.), *Handbook of eclectic psychotherapy.* (pp. 463–83). New York: Brunner/Mazel.

Goldfried, M. R., Greenberg, L. S., & Marmar, C. (1990). Individual psychotherapy: Process and outcome. *Annu. Rev. Psychol.* (Vol. 41). (pp. 659–88). Palo Alto, CA: Annual Reviews.

Goldfried, M. R., Linehan, M. M., & Smith, J. L. (1978). Reduction of test anxiety through cognitive restructuring. *J. Cons. Clin. Psychol., 46*(1), 32–39.

Goldfried, M. R., & Wolfe, B. E. (1998). Toward a more clinically valid approach to therapy research. *J. Cons. Clin. Psychol., 66*(1), 143–50.

Golding, J. M. (1994). Sexual assault history and physical health in randomly selected Los Angeles women. *Hlth. Psychol., 13*(2), 130–38.

Golding, J. M., Cooper, M. L., & George, L. K. (1997). Sexual assault history and health perceptions: Seven general population studies. *Hlth. Psychol., 16*(5), 417–25.

Goldman, D. (1996). High anxiety. *Science, 274,* 1483–84.

Goldman, H. H., Feder, J., & Scanlon, W. (1986). Chronic mental patients in nursing homes: Reexamining data from the national nursing home survey. *Hosp. Comm. Psychiat., 37,* 269–72.

Goldman, L. S., Genel, M., Bezman, R. J., & Slanetz, P. J. (1998). Diagnosis and treatment of attention-deficit/hyperactivity disorder in children and adolescents. *JAMA, 279*(14), 1100–07.

Goldman-Rakic, P. S., & Selemon, L. D. (1997). Functional and anatomical aspects of prefrontal pathology in schizophrenia. *Schizo. Bull., 23,* 437–58.

Goldsmith, D. F., & Rogoff, B. (1997). Mother's and toddler's coordinated joint focus of attention: Variations with maternal dysphoric symptoms. *Develop. Psychol., 33,* 113–19.

Goldsmith, H. H., & Gottesman, I. I. (1996). Heritable variability and variable heritability in developmental psychopathology. In M. F. Lenzenweger & J. L. Haugaard (Eds.), *Frontiers of developmental psychopathology.* (pp. 5–43). New York: Oxford University Press.

Goldsmith, S. J., Anger, Friedfeld, K., Beren, S., & Rudolph, D. (1992). Psychiatric illness in patients presenting for obesity treatment. *International Journal of Eating Disorders, 12,* 63–71.

Goldsmith, W., & Cretekos, C. (1969). Unhappy odysseys: Psychiatric hospitalization among Vietnam returnees. *Amer. J. Psychiat., 20,* 78–83.

Goldstein, A., et al. (1974, Mar. 4). Researchers isolate opiate receptor. *Behav. Today, 5*(9), 1.

Goldstein, A. J., & Chambless, D. (1978). A reanalysis of agoraphobia. *Behav. Ther., 9,* 47–59.

Goldstein, M. J. (1985). Family factors that antedate the onset of schizophrenia and related disorders: The results of a fifteen year prospective longitudinal study. *Acta Psychiatr. Scandin.* (Suppl. No. 319), *71,* 7–18.

Goldstein, M. J. (1991). Schizophrenia and family therapy. In B. D. Beitman & G. L. Klerman (Eds.), *Integrating pharmacotherapy and psychotherapy.* (pp.

291–310). Washington, DC: American Psychiatric Press.

Goldstein, M. J., Rodnick, E. H., Jones, J. E., McPherson, S. R., & West, K. L. (1978). Family precursors of schizophrenia spectrum disorders. In L. C. Wynne, R. L. Cromwell, & S. Matthysse (Eds.), *The nature of schizophrenia: New approaches to research and treatment.* New York: Wiley.

Goldstein, M. J., & Strachan, A. M. (1987). The family and schizophrenia. In T. Jacob (Ed.), *Family interaction and psychopathology: Theories, methods, and findings.* (pp. 481–508). New York: Plenum.

Goldstein, S., & Goldstein, M. (1998). *Managing attention-deficit hyperactivity disorder in children: A guide for practitioners (2nd ed.).* New York: Wiley.

Golomb, M., Fava, M., Abraham, M., Rosenbaum, J. F. (1995). Gender differences in personality disorders. *Amer. J. Psychiat., 152*(4), 579–82.

Golub, A., & Johnson, B. D. (1994). A recent decline in cocaine use among youthful arrestees in Manhattan, 1987 through 1993. *Amer. J. Pub. Hlth., 84,* 1250–54.

Gomberg, E. S. (1989). Suicide rates among women with alcohol problems. *Amer. J. Pub. Hlth., 79,* 1363–65.

Gomes-Schwartz, B., Horowitz, J., & Cardarelli, A. (1990). *Child sexual abuse: The initial effects.* Newbury Park, CA: Sage.

Gonsiorek, J. C. (1982). The use of diagnostic concepts in working with gay and lesbian populations. In J. C. Gonsiorek, (Ed.), *Homosexuality and psychotherapy.* New York: Hayworth Press.

Good, B. J., & Kleinman, A. M. (1985). Culture and anxiety: Cross-cultural evidence for the patterning of anxiety disorders. In A. H. Tuma & J.D. Master (Eds.), *Anxiety and the anxiety disorders.* Hillsdale, NJ: Erlbaum.

Goode, E. (1994, Sept. 19). Battling deviant behavior. *U.S. News and World Report,* 74–75.

Goodman, G., & Aman, C. (1990). Children's use of anatomically detailed dolls to recount an event. *Child Develop., 61,* 1859–71.

Goodman, R. (1989). Infantile autism: A syndrome of multiple primary deficits? *J. Autism Devel. Dis., 19,* 409–24.

Goodman, W. K., Price, L. H., Woods, S. W., & Charney, D. S. (1991). Pharmacological challenges in obsessive-compulsive disorder. In J. Zohar, T. Insel, & S. Rasmussen (Eds.), *The psychobiology of obsessive-compulsive disorder.* New York: Springer.

Goodwin, D. K. (1988). *The Fitzgeralds and the Kennedys: An American saga.* New York: St. Martin's Press.

Goodwin, D. W., Schulsinger, F., Hermansen, L., Guze, S. B., & Winokur, G. (1973). Alcohol problems in adoptees raised apart from alcoholic biological parents. *Arch. Gen. Psychiat., 28*(2), 238–43.

Goodwin, D. W., Schulsinger, F., Moller, N., Hermansen, L., Winokur, G., & Guze, S. B. (1974). Drinking problems in adopted and nonadopted sons of alcoholics. *Arch. Gen. Psychiat., 31*(2), 164–69.

Goodwin, F. K., & Ghaemi, S. N. (1998). Understanding manic-depressive illness. *Arch. Gen. Psychiat., 55*(1), 23–25.

Goodwin, F. K., & Jamison, K. R. (1990). *Manic-depressive illness.* New York: Oxford University Press.

Goodwin, G. M. (1992). Tricyclic and newer antidepressants. In E. S. Paykel (Ed.), *Handbook of affective disorders* (2nd ed.). New York: Guilford.

Goodwin, L. (1992). Alcohol and drug use in fraternities and sororities. *Journal of Alcohol and Drug Education, 37*(2), 52–63.

Goplerud, E., & Depue, R. A. (1985). Behavioral response to naturally occurring stress in cyclothymia and dysthymia. *J. Abn. Psychol., 94,* 128–39.

Goran, D. A., Fabiano, R. J., & Crewe, N. (1997). Employment following severe traumatic brain injury: The utility of the Individual Ability Profile System (IAP). *Arch. Clin. Neuopsychol., 12*(7), 691–98.

Gordis, E. (1997). Patient-treatment matching. *Alcohol Alert, 36,* 1–4.

Gordis, E., Dufour, M. C., Warren, K. R., Jackson, R. J., Floyd, R. L., & Hungerford, D. W. (1995). Should physicians counsel patients to drink alcohol? *JAMA, 273,* 1–12.

Gordon, C. T., State, R. C., Nelson, J. E., et al. (1993). A double-blind comparison of clomipramine, desipramine, and placebo in the treatment of autistic disorder. *Arch. Gen. Psychiat., 50,* 441–47.

Gordon, M. (1992). The female fear. *Media Studies Journal, 6,* 130–136.

Gorenstein, E. E. (1982). Frontal lobe functions in psychopaths. *J. Abn. Psychol., 91,* 368–79.

Gorenstein, E. E. (1992). *The science of mental illness.* San Diego: Academic Press.

Gorin, N. (1980). Looking out for Mrs. Berwid. *Sixty Minutes.* (Narrated by Morley Safer.) New York: CBS Television News.

Gorin, N. (1982). It didn't have to happen. *Sixty Minutes.* (Narrated by Morley Safer.) New York: CBS Television News.

Gorlick, D. A. (1993). Overview of pharmacologic treatment approaches for alcohol and other drug addiction. *Psychiat. Clin. N. Amer., 16,* 141–56.

Gorman, J. M., Battista, D., Goetz, R. R., Dillon, D. J., Liebowitz, M. R., Fyer, A. J., Kahn, J. P., Sandberg, D., & Klein, D. F. (1989). A comparison of sodium bicarbonate and sodium lactate infusion in the induction of panic attacks. *Arch. Gen. Psychiat., 46,* 145–50.

Gorman, J. M., & Coplan, J. D. (1996). Comorbidity of depression and panic disorder. *J. Clin. Psychiat., 57*(10), 34–41.

Gortner, E. T., Gollan, J. K., & Jacobson, N. S. (1997). Psychological aspects of perpetrators of domestic violence and their relationships with the victims. *Psychiat. Clin. N. Amer., 20*(2), 327–52.

Gorton, G., & Akhtar, S. (1990). The literature on personality disorders, 1985–1988: Trends, issues, and controversies. *Hosp. Comm. Psychiat., 41,* 39–51.

Gospodinoff, M. L. (1989). Premature ejaculation: Clinical subgroups and etiology. *J. Sex Marit. Ther., 15,* 130–34.

Gosslin, C. C., & Eysenck, S. B. G. (1980). The transvestite "double image": A preliminary report. *Personal. Indiv. Diff., 1,* 172–73.

Gotlib, I. H., & Avison, W. (1993). Children at risk for psychopathology. In C. Costello (Ed.), *Basic issues in psychopathology.* (pp. 271–319). New York: Guilford.

Gotlib, I. H., & Colby, C. A. (1987). *Treatment of depression: An interpersonal systems approach.* New York: Pergamon.

Gotlib, I. H., & Hammen, C. L. (1992). *Psychological aspects of depression: Toward a cognitive-interpersonal integration.* Chichester, UK: Wiley.

Gotlib, I. H., Whiffen, V., Mount, J., Milne, K., & Cordy, N. (1989). Prevalence rates and demographic characteristics associated with depression in pregnancy and the postpartum. *J. Cons. Clin. Psychol., 57,* 269–74.

Gotlib, I. H., Whiffen, V., Wallace, P., & Mount, J. (1991). A prospective investigation of postpartum depression: Factors involved in onset and recovery. *J. Abn. Psychol., 100,* 122–32.

Gottesman, I. I. (1991). *Schizophrenia genesis: The origins of madness.* New York: Freeman.

Gottesman, I. I., & Bertelson, A. (1989). Confirming unexpected genotypes for schizophrenia: Risks in the offspring of Fischer's Danish identical and fraternal discordant twins. *Arch. Gen. Psychiat., 46,* 867–72.

Gottesman, I. I., & Goldsmith, H. H. (1994). Developmental psychopathology of antisocial behavior: Inserting genes into its ontogenesis and epigenesis. In C. Nelson (Ed.), *Threats to optimal development: Integrating biological, social, and psychological risk factors* (Vol. 27). Hillsdale, NJ: Erlbaum.

Gottesman, I. I., & Moldin, S. O. (1998). Genotype, genes, genesis, and pathogenesis in schizophrenia. In M. F. Lenzenweger & R. H. Dworkin (Eds.), *Origins and development of schizophrenia.* (pp. 5–26). Washington: American Psychological Association.

Gottesman, I. I., & Shields, J. (1982). *Schizophrenia: The epigenetic puzzle.* Cambridge, UK: Cambridge University Press.

Gottheil, E., Thornton, C. C., Skoloda, T. E., & Alterman, A. I. (1982). Follow-up of abstinent and nonabstinent alcoholics. *Amer. J. Psychiat., 139*(5), 560–65.

Gottlieb, G. (1992) *Individual development and evolution: The genesis of novel behavior.* New York: Oxford University Press.

Gottlieb, G., Wahlsten, D., & Lickliter, R. (1998) The significance of biology for human development: A developmental psychbiological systems view. In W. Damon & R. Lerner (Eds.), *Handbook of child psychology (5th ed.): Vol. 1: Theoretical models of human development.* (pp. 233–73). New York: Wiley.

Gottlieb, J. (1981). Mainstreaming: Fulfilling the promise? *Amer. J. Ment. Def., 86,* 115–26.

Gottman, J. M. (1998). Psychology and the Study of marital processes. In J. T. Spence, J. M. Darley, & D. J. Foss (Eds.), *Annual Review of Psychology.* (pp. 169–97). Palo Alto, CA: Annual Reviews.

Gottschalk, L. A., Haer, J. L., & Bates, D. E. (1972). Effect of sensory overload on psychological state: Changes in social alienation—personal disorganization and cognitive-intellectual impairment. *Arch. Gen. Psychiat., 27*(4), 451–56.

Gouvier, W. D., et al. (1997). Cognitive retraining with brain-damaged patients. In A. M. Horton, W. D, & J. Webster (Eds.), *The neuropsychology handbook* (Vol. 2). (pp. 3–46). New York: Springer.

Goy, R. W., & McEwen, B. S. (1980). *Sexual differentiation of the brain.* Cambridge: MIT Press.

Grace, A. A., & Moore, H. (1998). Regulation of information flow in the nucleus accumbens: A model for the pathophysiology of schizophrenia. In M. F. Lenzenweger & R. H. Dworkin (Eds.), *Origins and development of schizophrenia.* (pp. 123–60). Washington: American Psychological Association.

Grady, K., Gersick, K. E., & Boratynski, M. (1985). Preparing parents for teenagers: A step in the prevention of adolescent substance abuse. *Family Relations Journal of Applied Family and Child Studies, 34*(4), 541–49.

Graham, J. R. (1978a). *MMPI characteristics of alcoholics, drug abusers and pathological gamblers.* Paper presented at the 13th Annual Symposium on Recent Developments in the Use of the MMPI. Puebla, Mexico, March, 1978.

Graham, J. R. (1978b). The Minnesota Multiphasic Personality Inventory. In B. B. Wolman (Ed.), *Clinical diagnosis of mental disorders: A handbook.* New York: Plenum.

Gralnick, A. (1942). Folie a deux—The psychosis of association: A review of 103 cases and the entire English literature, with case presentations. *Psychiatric Quarterly, 14,* 230–63.

Grant, B. F. (1997). Prevalence and correlates of alcohol use and DSM–IV alcohol dependence in the United States: Results of the National Longitudinal Alcohol Epidemiologic Survey. *J. Stud. Alcoh., 58*(5), 464–73.

Grant, B. F., & Dawson, D. A. (1997). Age at onset of alcohol use and its association with DSM–IV alcohol abuse and dependency: Results from the National Longitudinal Alcohol Epidemiologic Survey. *J. Subst. Abuse, 9,* 103–10.

Grant, I., & Adams, K. M. (1996). *Neuropsychological assessment of neuropsychiatric disorders.* New York: Oxford University Press.

Grant, I., Atkinson, J. H., Hesselink, J. R., Kennedy, C. J., Richman, D. D., Spector, S. A., & McCutchan, J. A. (1987). Evidence for early central nervous system involvement in the acquired immunodeficiency syndrome (AIDS) and other human immunodeficiency virus (HIV) infections. *Ann. Int. Med., 107,* 828–36.

Grant, I., & Heaton, R. K. (1990). Human immunodeficiency virus-Type 1 (HIV-1) and the brain. *J. Cons. Clin. Psychol., 58,* 22–30.

Grant, S. J., & Sonti, G. (1994). Buprenorphine and morphine produce equivalent increases in extracellular single unit activity of dopamine neurons in the ventral tegmental area in vivo. *Synapse, 16,* 181–87.

Grant, V. W. (1953). A case study of fetishism. *J. Abnorm. Soc. Psychol., 48,* 142–49.

Gray, F., Gherardi, R., & Scaravilli, F. (1988). The neuropathology of the acquired immune deficiency syndrome (AIDS). *Brain, 111,* 245–66.

Gray, J. A. (1975). *Elements of a two-process theory of learning.* New York: Academic Press.

Gray, J. A. (1982). *The neuropsychology of anxiety.* New York: Oxford University Press.

Gray, J. A. (1987). *The psychology of fear and stress* (2nd edition). New York: Cambridge University Press.

Gray, J. A. (1991). Fear, panic, and anxiety: What's in a name? *Psycho. Inq., 2,* 77–78.

Gray, J. A., & McNaughton, N. (1996). The neuropsychology of anxiety: Reprise. In D. A. Hope (Ed.), *Perspectives on anxiety, panic, and fear Vol. 43 of the Nebraska Symposium on Motivation.* (pp. 61–134). Lincoln: University of Nebraska Press.

Gray, W. W., & Ramsey, B. K. (1982). The early training project: A lifespan view. *Human Develop., 25,* 48–57.

Gray-Little, B. (1995). The assessment of psychopathology in racial and ethnic minorities. In J. N. Butcher (Ed.), *Clinical personality assessment: Practical considerations.* (pp. 141–157). New York: Oxford University Press.

Grechanaia, T., Romanova, O., Williams, C. L., Perry, C. L., & Murray, P. (1997, Oct.). *Russian-American research project partners for prevention: Implementation of slick Tracey Home Team Program in Russia.* National Institute of Alcohol And Alcoholism. Washington: U.S. Government Printing Office.

Greeley, A. M. (1993, Mar. 20). How serious is the problem of sexual abuse by clergy? *America, 168,* 6–10.

Green, A. (1978). Self-destructive behavior in battered children. *Amer. J. Psychiat., 135,* 579–82.

Green, B. L., Korol, M., Grace, M. C., Vary, M. G., Leonard, A. C., Gleser, G. C., & Smitson Cohen, S. (1991). Children and disaster: Age, gender, and parental effects on PTSD symptoms. *J. Amer. Acad. Child Adoles. Psychiat., 30,* 945–51.

Green, B. L., & Lindy, J. D. (1994). Post traumatic stress disorder in victims of disasters. *Psychiat. Clin. N. Amer., 17,* 301–10.

Green, B. L., Lindy, J. D., Grace, M. C., & Leonard, A. C. (1992). Chronic posttraumatic stress disorder and diagnostic comorbidity in a disaster sample. *J. Nerv. Ment. Dis., 180,* 760–66.

Green, L., & Warshauer, D. (1981). Note on the "paradoxical" effect of stimulant drugs on hyperactivity with reference to the rate-dependency effect. *J. Nerv. Ment. Dis., 169*(3), 196–98.

Green, M. F., Nuechterlein, K. H., & Breitmeyer, B. (1997). Backward masking performance in unaffected siblings of schizophrenic patients: Evidence for a vulnerability indicator. *Arch. Gen. Psychiat., 54*(5), 465–72.

Green, R. (1987). *The "sissy boy syndrome" and the development of homosexuality.* New Haven: Yale University Press.

Green, R. (1992). *Sexual science and the law.* Cambridge: Harvard University Press.

Green, R. M. (1951). *Galen's hygiene.* Springfield, IL: Charles C. Thomas.

Green, R., & Fleming, D. (1990). Transsexual surgery followup: Status in the 1990's. In J. Bancroft, C. Davis, & H. Ruppel (Eds.) *Annual review of sex research.* Mt. Vernon, IA: Society for the Scientific Study of Sex.

Greenberg, L. S., Elliott, R. K., & Lietaer, G. (1994). Research on experiential psychotherapies. In A. E. Bergin & S. L. Garfield (Eds.), *Handbook of psychotherapy and behavior change.* (pp. 509–52). New York: Wiley.

Greenberg, M. D. (1997). Treatment implications of psychiatric comorbidity. In S. Fisher & R. P. Greenberg (Eds.), *From placebo to panacea: Putting psychiatric drugs to the test.* (pp. 57–97). New York: Wiley.

Greenberg, R. P., Bornstein, R. F., Greenberg, M. D., & Fisher, S. (1992). A meta-analysis of antidepressant outcome under "blinder" conditions. *J. Cons. Clin. Psychol., 60*(5), 664–69.

Greene, R. W., Biederman, J., Faraone, S. V., Sienna, M., & Garcia-Jetton, J. (1997). Adolescent outcome of boys with attention-deficit disorder and social dis-

ability: Results from a 4-year longitudinal study. *J. Cons. Clin. Psychol., 65*(5), 758–67.

Greene, S. M. (1989). The relationship between depression and hopelessness: Implications for current theories of depression. *Brit. J. Psychiat., 154,* 650–59.

Greenfield, B., Hechtman, L., & Tremblay, C. (1995). Short-term efficacy of interventions by a youth crisis team. *Canad. J. Psychiat., 40,* 320–24.

Greenfield, J. C., & Wolfson, J. M. (1935). Microcephalia vera. *Archives of Neurology and Psychiatry, 33,* 1296–1316.

Greenhill, L. L. (1992). Pharmacologic treatment of attention deficit hyperactivity disorder. *Psychiat. Clin. N. Amer., 15,* 1–28.

Greenhill, L. L. (1998). Childhood attention deficit hyperactivity disorer: Pharmacological treatments. In P. E. Nathan & J. M. Gorman (Eds.), *A guide to treatments that work.* (pp. 52–64). Oxford, England: Oxford University Press.

Greenhill, L. L., & Waslick, B. (1997). Management of suicidal behavior in children and adolescents. *Psychiat. Clin. N. Amer., 20*(3), 641–66.

Greenough, W. T., & Black, J. E. (1992) Induction of brain structure by experience: Substrates for cognitive development. In M. R. Gunnar & C. A. Nelson (Eds), *Minnesota Symposia on Child psychology: Developmental Neuroscience* (Vol. 24). (pp. 155–200). Hillsdale, NJ: Erlbaum.

Greenspan, S. (1997). Dead manual walking? Why the AAMR definition needs redoing. *Education & Training in Mental Retardation & Developmental Disabilities, 32*(3), 179–90.

Greer, S. (1964). Study of parental loss in neurotics and sociopaths. *Arch. Gen. Psychiat., 11*(2), 177–80.

Gregg, C., & Hoy, C. (1989). Coherence: The comprehension and production abilities of college writers who are normally achieving, learning disabled, and underprepared. *J. Learn. Dis., 22,* 370–72.

Gregoire, A. (1992). New treatments for erectile impotence. *Brit. J. Psychiat., 160,* 315–26.

Griest, D. L., & Wells, K. C. (1983). Behavioral family therapy with conduct disorders in children. *Behav. Ther., 14,* 37–53.

Greist, J. H. (1990). Treatment of obsessive-compulsive disorder: Psychotherapies, drugs, and other somatic treatments. *J. Clin. Psychiat., 51,* 44–50.

Gresham, F. M. (1982). Misguided mainstreaming: The case for social skills training with handicapped children. *Exceptional Children, 48,* 422–33.

Griffin, D., & Bartholomew, K. (1994). Models of the self and other: Fundamental dimensions underlying measures of adult attachment. *J. Pers. Soc. Psychol., 67,* 430–45.

Grilo, C. M., Becker, D. F., Fehon, D. C., Edell, W. S., & McGlashan, T. H. (1996). Conduct disorder, substance use disorders, and coexisting conduct and substance use disorders in adolescent inpatients. *Amer. J. Psychiat., 153*(7), 914–20.

Grimes, K., & Walker, E. F. (1994). Childhood emotional expressions, educational attainment, and age at onset of illness in schizophrenia. *J. Abn. Psychol., 103*(4), 784–90.

Grinfeld, M. J., & Wellner, M. (1998). Pill poisoned: The seasoning of medication defenses. *Forensic Echo, 2*(3), 4–10.

Grinker, R. R. (1969). An essay on schizophrenia and science. *Arch. Gen. Psychiat., 20,* 1–24.

Grinspoon, L., Ewalt, J. R., & Shader, R. I. (1972). *Schizophrenia: Pharmacotherapy and psychotherapy.* Baltimore: Williams & Wilkins.

Grisso, T., & Appelbaum, P. S. (1998). *Assessing competence to consent to treatment.* New York: Oxford University Press.

Grisso, T., & Tomkins, A. J. (1996). Communicating violence risk assessments. *Amer. Psychol., 51*(9), 928–30.

Grob, G. N. (1994). Mad, homeless, and unwanted: A history of the care of the chronically mentally ill in America. *Psychiat. Clin. N. Amer., 17*(3), 541–58.

Gross, B. H., Southard, M. J., Lamb, H. R., & Weinberger, L. (1987). Assessing dangerousness and responding appropriately: Hedland expands the clinician's liability established by Tarasoff. *J. Clin. Psychiat., 48,* 9–12.

Gross, R., Sasson, Y., Chopra, J., & Zohar, J. (1998). Biological models of obsessive-compulsive disorder: The serotonin hypothesis. In R. Swinson, M. Antony, S. Rachman, & M. Richter (Eds.), *Obsessive-compulsive disorder: Theory, research, and treatment.* (pp. 141–53). New York: Guilford.

Groth, A. N., Hobson, W. F., & Gary, T. (1982). Heterosexuality, homosexuality, and pedophilia: Sexual offenses against children. In A. Scacco (Ed.), *Male rape: A casebook of sexual aggression.* New York: AMS Press.

Groth, N. A. (1979). *Men who rape.* New York: Plenum.

Group for the Advancement of Psychiatry (1966). *Psychopathological disorders in childhood. Theoretical considerations and a proposed classification system.* Washington, DC: GAP Report # 2.

Grove, W. M., & Meehl, P. E. (1996). Comparative efficiency of informal (subjective impressionistic) and formal (mechanical, algorithmic) prediction procedures: The clinical statistical controversy. *Psychology, Public Policy, and the Law, 2*(2), 293–323.

Gruder, C. L., Mermelstein, R. J., Kirkendol, S., Hedeker, D., Wong, S. C., Schreckengost, J., Warnecke, R. B., Burzette, R., & Miller, T. Q. (1993). Effects of social support and relapse prevention training as adjuncts to a televised smoking cessation intervention. *J. Cons. Clin. Psychol., 61,* 113–20.

Grunebaum, H., & Perlman, M. S. (1973). Paranoia and naivete. *Arch. Gen. Psychiat., 28*(1), 30–32.

Guelfi, G. P., Faustman, W. O., & Csernansky, J. G. (1989). Independence of positive and negative symptoms in a population of schizophrenic patients. *J. Nerv. Ment. Dis., 177,* 285–90.

Guerra, F. (1971). *The pre-Columbian mind.* New York: Seminar Press.

Gugliemi, R. S. (1979). *A double-blind study of the effectiveness of skin temperature biofeedback as a treatment for Raynaud's disease.* Unpublished doctoral dissertation, University of Minnesota.

Gunderson, J. G. (1980). A reevaluation of milieu therapy for nonchronic schizophrenic patients. *Schizo. Bull., 6*(1), 64–69.

Gunderson, J. G., & Philips, K. A. (1991). A current view of the interface between borderline personality disorder and depression. *Amer. J. Psychiat., 148,* 967–75.

Gunderson, J. G., Phillips, K. A., Triebwasser, J., & Hirschfeld, R. M. A. (1994). The diagnostic interview for depressive personality. *Amer J. Psychiat., 151*(9), 1300–304.

Gunderson, J. G., Ronningstam, E., & Smith, L. E. (1995). Narcissistic personality disorder. In W. J. Livesley (Ed.), *The DSM-IV personality disorders.* (pp. 201–212). New York: Guilford.

Gunderson, J. G., & Singer, M. T. (1986). Defining borderline patients: An overview. In M. H. Stone (Ed.), *Essential papers on borderline disorders.* (pp. 453–74). New York: New York University Press.

Gunderson, J. G., Zanarini, M. C., Kisiel, C. L. (1995). Borderline personality disorder. In W. J. Livesley (Ed.), *The DSM-IV personality disorders.* (pp. 141–157). New York: Guilford.

Gunn, J. (1993). Castration is not the answer. *Brit. Med. J., 307,* 790–91.

Gupta, J. C., Deb, A. K., Kahali, B. S. (1943). Preliminary observations on the use of Rauwolfia perpentina berth in the treatment of mental disorder. *Indian Medical Gazette, 78,* 547–49.

Gur, R. E., et al. (1998). A follow-up magnetic resonance imaging study of schizophrenia: Relationship of neuroanatomical changes to clinical and neurobehavioral measures. *Arch. Gen. Psychiat., 55*(2), 145–52.

Gur, R. E., Mozley, P. D., Shtasel, D. L., Cannon, T. D., Gallacher, F., Turetsky, B., Grossman, R., & Gur, R. C. (1994). Clinical subtypes of schizophrenia: Differences in brain and CFS volume. *Amer. J. Psychiat., 151*(3), 343–50.

Gur, R. E., & Pearlson, G. D. (1993). Neuroimaging in schizophrenia research. *Schizo. Bull., 19*(2), 337–53.

Gureje, O., Bamidele, R., & Raji, O. (1994). Early brain trauma and schizophrenia in Nigerian patients. *Amer. J. Psychiat., 151*(3), 368–71.

Gureje, O., Vazquez–Barquero, J. L., & Janca, A. (1996). Comparisons of alcohol and other drugs: Experience from the WHO collaborative cross-cultural applicability research (CAR) study. *Addiction, 91*(10), 1529–38.

Gurland, B. J., & Cross, P. S. (1982). Epidemiology of psychopathology in old age. In L. F. Jarvik & G. W. Small (Eds.), *Psychiatric clinics of North America.* Philadelphia: Saunders.

Gurman, A. S., & Kniskern, D. P. (1978). Research on marital and family therapy: Progress, perspective and prospect. In S. L. Garfield & A. E. Bergin (Eds.), *Handbook of psychotherapy and behavior change.* New York: Wiley.

Gurman, A. S., Kniskern, D. P., & Pinsof, W. M. (1986). Research on marital and family therapies. In S. L. Garfield & A. E. Bergin (Eds.), *Handbook of psychotherapy and behavior change* (3rd ed.) (pp. 565–626). New York: Wiley.

Gurtman, M. B. (1986). Depression and the response of others: Reevaluating the reevaluation. *J. Abn. Psychol., 95,* 99–101.

Guze, S. B., (1995). Review of DSM-IV (no title). Amer. J. Psychiat., 152, 1228.

Guze, S. B., Cloninger, C. R., Martin, R. L., & Clayton, P. J. (1986). A follow-up and family study of Briquet's Syndrome. *Brit. J. Psychiat., 149,* 17–23.

Haaga, D. A., & Davison, G. C. (1989). Outcome studies of rational-emotive therapy. In M. Bernard & R. DeGiuseppe (Eds.), *Inside rationale-motive therapy.* New York: Academic Press.

Haaga, D. A., & Davison, G. C. (1992). Disappearing differences do not always reflect healthy integration: An analysis of cognitive therapy and rational-emotive therapy. *Journal of Psychotherapy Integration, 1,* 287–303.

Haaga, D. A. F., Dyck, M. J., & Ernst, D. (1991). Empirical status of cognitive theory of depression. *Psychol. Bull., 110* (2), 215–36.

Haas, G. (1997). Suicidal behavior in schizophrenia. In R. W. Maris, M. M. Silverman, & S. S. Canetton (Eds.), *Review of Suicidology, 1997.* (pp. 202–35). New York: Guilford.

Haber, S. N., & Fudge, J. L. (1997). The interface between dopamine neurons and the amygdala: Implications for schizophrenia. *Schizo. Bull., 23*(3), 471–82.

Haffner, H., et al. (1998). Causes and consequences of the gender difference in age at onset of schizophrenia. *Schizo. Bull., 24*(1), 99–114.

Haizlip, T. M., & Corder, B. E. (1996). Coping with natural disasters. In C. Pfeffer (Ed.), *Severe stress and mental disturbance in children* (pp. 131–52). Washington: American Psychiatric Association Press.

Halberstam, M. (1972). Can you make yourself sick? A doctor's report on psychosomatic illness. *Today's Health, 50*(12), 24–29.

Haley, J. (1962). Whither family therapy. *Family Process, 1,* 69–100.

Haley, S. A. (1978). Treatment implications of post-combat stress response syndromes for mental health professionals. In C. R. Figley (Ed.), *Stress disorders among Vietnam veterans.* New York: Brunner/Mazel.

Halford, W. K., & Haynes, R. (1991) Psychosocial rehabilitation of chronic schizophrenic patients: Recent findings on social skills training and family psychoeducation. *Clin. Psychol. Rev., 11,* 23–44.

Hall, G. (1994). Pavlovian conditioning: Laws of association. In N. J. Mackintosh (Ed.), *Animal learning and cognition.* (pp. 15–43). San Diego, CA: Academic Press.

Hallett, J. D., Zasler, N. D., Maurer, P., & Cash, S. (1994). Role change after traumatic brain injury in adults. *Amer. J. Occup. Ther., 48*(3), 241–46.

Hallgren, B. (1950). Specific dyslexia ("congenital word-blindness"). *Acta Neurol. Scandin.,* Suppl., 65, 1–287.

Hallworth, H. J. (1977). Computer-assisted instruction for the mentally retarded. In P. Milder (Ed.), *Research to practice in mental retardation* (Vol. 2). (pp. 419–20). Baltimore: University Park Press.

Halmi, K. A., Falk, J. R., & Schwartz, E. (1981). Binge-eating and vomiting: A survey of a college population. *Psychol. Med., 11,* 697–706.

Hamer, D. H., Hu, S., Magnuson, V. L., Hu, N., & Pattatucci, A. M. L. (1993). A linkage between DNA markers on the X chromosome and male sexual orientation. *Science, 261,* 321–27.

Hammen, C. L. (1991). Generation of stress in the course of unipolar depression. *J. Abnorm. Psychol., 100,* 555–61.

Hammen, C. L. (1995). Stress and the course of unipolar disorders. In C.M. Mazure (Ed.), *Does stress cause psychiatric illness?* Washington, DC: American Psychiatric Press.

Hammen, C., Adrian, C. L., Gordon, D., Burge, D., Jaenicke, C., & Hiroto, D. (1987). Children of depressed mothers: Maternal strain and symptom predictors of dysfunction. *J. Abn. Psychol., 96,* 190–98.

Hammen, C. L., & Peters, S. D. (1977). Differential responses to male and female depressive reactions. *J. Cons. Clin. Psychol., 45,* 994–1001.

Hammen, C. L., & Peters, S. D. (1978). Interpersonal consequences of depression: Responses to men and women enacting a depressed role. *J. Abn. Psychol., 87*(3), 322–32.

Hammen, C., & Gitlin, M. (1997). Stress reactivity in bipolar patients and its relation to prior history of disorder. *Amer. J. Psychiat., 154*(6), 856–857.

Hammen, C., & Rudolph, K. D. (1996). Childhood depression. In E. J. Mash & R. A. Barkley (Eds.), *Childhood psychopathology.* (pp. 153–94). New York: Guilford.

Handleman, J. S., Gill, M. J., & Alessandri, M. (1988). Generalization by severely developmentally disabled children: Issues, advances, and future directions. *The Behavior Therapist, 11,* 221–23.

Haney, B., & Gold, M. (1973). The juvenile delinquent nobody knows. *Psych. Today, 7*(4), 48–52, 55.

Hankin, B. L., Abramson, L. Y., Moffitt, T. E., Silva, P. A., McGee, R., & Angell, K. E. (1998). Development of depression from preadolescence to young adulthood: Emerging gender differences in a 10-year longitudinal study. *J. Abn. Psychol., 107*(1), 128–40.

Hannigan, J. H. (1996). What research with animals is telling us about alcohol-related neurodevelopmental disorder. *Pharmacology, Biochemistry & Behavior, 55*(4), 489–500.

Hanrahan, J., Goodman, W., & Rapagna, S. (1990). Preparing mentally retarded students for mainstreaming: Priorities of regular class and special school teachers. *Amer. J. Ment. Retard., 94,* 470–74.

Happe, F., & Frith, U. (1996). Theory of mind and social impairment in children with conduct disorder. *Brit. J. Develop. Psychol., 14,* 385–98.

Harburgh, E., Erfurt, J. C., Hauenstein, L. S., Chape, C., Schull, W. J., & Schork, M. A. (1973). Socioecological stress, suppressed hostility, skin color, and black-white male blood pressure: Detroit. *Psychosom. Med., 35,* 276–96.

Harder, D. W., Strauss, J. S., Greenwald, D. F., Kokes, R. F., et al. (1989). Life events and psychopathology severity: Comparisons between psychiatric inpatients and outpatients. *J. Clin. Psychol., 45,* 202–9.

Harding, C. M., Brooks, G. W., Ashikaga, T., Strauss, J. S., & Breier, A. (1987a). The Vermont longitudinal study of persons with severe mental illness, I: Methodology, study sample, and overall status 32 years later. *Amer. J. Psychiat., 144,* 718–26.

Harding, C. M., Brooks, G. W., Ashikaga, T., Strauss, J. S., & Breier, A. (1987b). The Vermont longitudinal study of persons with severe mental illness, II: Long-term outcome of subjects who retrospectively met DSM-III criteria for schizophrenia. *Amer. J. Psychiat., 144,* 727–35.

Hardy, J. A., Mann, D. M., Wester, P., & Winblad, B. (1986). An integrative hypothesis concerning the pathogenesis and progression of Alzheimer's disease. *Neurobiol. of Aging, 7,* 489–502.

Hardy, K. V., & Laszloffy, T. A. (1995). Therapy with African Americans and the phenomenon of rage. *In Session, 1*(4), 57–70.

Hare, E. H. (1962). Masturbatory insanity: The history of an idea. *J. Ment. Sci., 108,* 1–25.

Hare, R. D. (1968). Psychopathy, autonomic functioning and the orienting response. *J. Abnorm. Psychol., 73* (Monograph Suppl. 3, part 2), 1–24.

Hare, R. D. (1970). *Psychopathy: Theory and research.* New York: Wiley.

Hare, R. D. (1978a). Electrodermal and cardiovascular correlates of psychopathy. In R. D. Hare & D. Schalling (Eds.), *Psychopathic behavior: Approaches to research.* (pp. 107–43). Chichester, UK: Wiley.

Hare, R. D. (1978b). Psychopathy and electrodermal responses to nonsignal stimulation. *Biol. Psych., 6,* 237–46.

Hare, R. D. (1980). A research scale for the assessment of psychopathy in criminal populations. *Personal. Indiv. Diff., 1,* 111–19.

Hare, R. D. (1984). Performance of psychopaths on cognitive tasks related to frontal lobe function. *J. Abn. Psychol., 93*(2), 133–40.

Hare, R. D. (1985a). Comparison of the procedures for the assessment of psychopathy. *J. Cons. Clin. Psychol., 53,* 7–16.

Hare, R. D. (1985b). *The psychopathy checklist.* Unpublished manuscript, University of British Columbia, Vancouver, Canada.

Hare, R. D. (1991). *The Hare psychopathy checklist—Revised.* Toronto: Multi-Health systems.

Hare, R. D. (1998a). The Alvor Advanced Study Institute. In D. J. Cooke, A. E. Forth, & R. D. Hare (Eds.), *Psychopathy: Theory, research, and implications for society.* (pp. 1–11). Dordrecht, Netherlands: Kluwer Academic Publishers.

Hare, R. D. (1998b). Psychopathy, affect and behavior. In D. J. Cooke, A. E. Forth, & R. D. Hare (Eds.), *Psychopathy: Theory, research, and implications for society.* (pp. 105–37). Dordrecht, Netherlands: Kluwer Academic Publishers.

Hare, R. D., & Hart, S. D. (1993). Psychopathy, mental disorder, and crime. In S. Hodgins (Ed.), *Mental disorder and crime.* Newbury Park, CA: Sage.

Hare, R. D., Hart, S. D., & Harpur, T. J.(1991). Psychopathy and DSM-IV criteria for antisocial personality disorder. *J. Abn. Psychol., 100,* 391–98.

Hare, R. D., McPherson, L. M., & Forth, A. E. (1988). Male psychopaths and their criminal careers. *J. Cons. Clin. Psychology, 56,* 710–14.

Harford, T. C., & Parker, D. A. (1994). Antisocial behavior, family history, and alcohol dependence symptoms. *Alcoholism (NY), 18,* 265–68.

Hargrave, G. E., Hiatt, D., Ogard, E. M., & Karr, C. (1994). Comparison of MMPI and MMPI-2 for a sample of Peace Officers. *Psychol. Assess., 6,* 27–32.

Harkness, A. R., & Lilienfeld, S. O. (1997). Individual differences science for treatment planning: Personality traits. *Psychol. Assess., 9*(4), 349–60.

Harlow, J. M. (1868). Recovery from the passage of an iron bar through the head. *Publication of the Massachusetts Medical Society, 2,* 327.

Harlow, J. M. (1993). Recovery from the passage of an iron bar through the head. *History of Psychiatry, 4,* 271–81.

Harpur, T. J., & Hare, R. D. (1994). Assessment of psychopathy as a function of age. *J. Abn. Psychol., 103,* 604–9.

Harpur, T. J., Hare, R. D., & Hakstian, A. R. (1989). Two-factor conceptualization of psychopathy: Construct validity and assessment implications. *Psychol. Assess., 1* (1), 6–17.

Harpur, T. J., Hart, S. D., & Hare, R. D. (1993). The personality of the psychopath.

Harrington, P. J., Telch, M. J., Abplanalp, B., & Hamilton, A. C. (November 1995). *Lowering anxiety sensitivity in nonclinical subjects: Preliminary evidence for a panic prevention program.* Poster session presented at the meeting of the Association for the Advancement of Behavior Therapy, Washington.

Harrington, R., & Clark, A. (1998). Prevention and early intervention for depression in adolescence and early adult life. *Eur. Arch. Psychiat. Clin. Neurosci., 248*(1), 32–45.

Harrington, R., Rutter, M., & Fombonne, E. (1996). Developmental pathways in depression: Multiple meanings, antecedents, and end points. *Develop. Psychopath., 8,* 601–16.

Harris, G. T., Rice, M. E., & Cormier, C. A. (1991). Psychopathy and violent recidivism. *Law and Human Behavior, 15,* 625–37.

Harris, S. L., & Ersner-Hershfield, R. (1978). Behavioral suppression of seriously disruptive behavior in psychotic and retarded patients: A review of punishment and its alternatives. *Psychol. Bull., 85*, 1352–75.

Harris, T., Brown, G. W., & Bifulco, A. (1986). Loss of parent in childhood and adult psychiatric disorder: The role of lack of adequate parental care. *Psychol. Med., 16*, 641–59.

Harrow, M., Goldberg, J. F., Grossman, L. S., & Meltzer, H. Y. (1990). Outcome in manic disorders: A naturalistic follow-up study. *Arch. Gen. Psychiat., 47*, 665–71.

Hart, S. D. (1998). Psychopathy and risk for violence. In D. J. Cooke, A. E. Forth, & R. D. Hare (Eds.), *Psychopathy: Theory, research, and implications for society.* (pp. 355–373). Dordrecht, Netherlands: Kluwer Academic Publishers.

Hart, S. D., & Hare, R. D. (1997). Psychopathy: Assessment and association with criminal conduct. In D. M. Stoff, J. Breiling, & J. D. Maser (Eds.), *Handbook of antisocial behavior.* (pp. 22–35). New York: Wiley.

Hartford, J. T. (1986). A review of antemortem markers of Alzheimer's disease. *Neurobiol. of Aging, 7*, 401–2.

Hartlage, L., Asken, M., & Hornsby, J. (1987). *Essentials of neuropsychological assessment.* New York: Springer.

Hartmann, E., Milofsky, E., Vaillant, G., Oldfield, M., & Falke, R. (1984). Vulnerability to schizophrenia: Predormation. *Arch. Gen. Psychiat., 41*, 1050–56.

Hartup, W. W. (1983). Peer relations. In P. H. Mussen (Ed.), *Handbook of child psychology* (Vol. 4). (pp. 274–385). New York: Wiley.

Hasegawa, S., et al. (1997). Physical aging in persons with Down syndrome: Bases on external appearance and diseases. *Japanese Journal of Special Education, 35*(2), 43–49.

Hathaway, S. R., & McKinley, J. C. (1951). *The Minnesota multiphasic personality inventory* (rev. ed.). New York: Psychological Corporation.

Hatta, S.M. (1996) A Malay cross cultural worldview and forensic review of amok. *Austral. NZ J. Psychiat., 30*, 505–10.

Hauff, E., & Vaglum, P. (1994). Chronic posttraumatic stress disorder in Vietnamese refugees. *J. Nerv. Ment.Dis., 182*, 85–90.

Haug Schnabel, G. (1992). Daytime and nighttime enuresis: A functional disorder and its ethological decoding. *Behaviour, 120*, 232–61.

Haugland, G., Sigel, G., Hopper, K., & Alexander, M. J. (1997). Mental illness among homeless individuals in a suburban county. *Psychiat. Serv., 48*(4), 504–09.

Havens, L. L. (1974). The existential use of the self. *Amer. J. Psychiat., 131*(1), 1–10.

Hawkins, J. D., Arthur, M. W., & Olson, J. J. (1997). Community interventions to reduce risks and enhance protection against antisocial behavior. In D. M. Stoff, J. Breiling, & J. D. Maser (Eds.), *Handbook of antisocial behavior.* (pp. 365–374). New York: Wiley.

Hawton, K. (1992). Suicide and attempted suicide. In E. S. Paykel (Ed.), *Handbook of affective disorders* (2nd ed.). New York: Guilford.

Hawton, K., Catalan, J., & Fagg, J. (1992). Sex therapy for erectile dysfunction: Characteristics of couples, treatment outcome, and prognostic factors. *Arch. Sex. Behav., 21*, 161–75.

Hayden, M. F. (1998). Civil rights litigation for institutionalized persons with mental retardation: A summary. *Mental Retardation, 36*(1), 75–83.

Hayes, S. C. (1998). Resisting biologism. *Behavior Therapist, 21*(5), 95–97.

Haynes, S. G., Feinleib, M., & Kannel, W. B. (1980). The relationship of psychosocial factors to coronary heart disease in the Framingham study: III. Eight-year incidence of coronary heart disease. *Amer. J. Epidemiol., 111*, 37–58.

Haynes, S. N., Leisen, M. B., & Blaine, D. D. (1997). Design of individualized behavioral treatment programs using function analytic clinical case methods. *Psychol. Assess., 9*(4), 334–48.

Hayward, P. & Wardle, J. (1997). The use of medication in the treatment of phobias. In G. C. L. Davey,

(Ed.), Phobias. *A handbook of theory, research and treatment.* (pp. 281–98). Chichester, England: Wiley.

Haywood, H. C., Meyers, C. E., & Switsky, H. N. (1982). *Ann. Rev. Psychol., 33.*

Hazelrigg, M., Cooper, H., & Borduin, C. (1987). Evaluating the effectiveness of family therapies: An integrative review and analysis. *Psychol. Bull., 101*, 428–42.

Healy, D., & Williams, J. M. G. (1988). Dysrhythmia, dysphoria, and depression: The interaction of learned helplessness and circadian dysrhythmia in the pathogenesis of depression. *Psychol. Bull., 103*, 163–78.

Hearn, M. D., Murray, D. M., & Luepker, R. V. (1989). Hostility, coronary heart disease, and total mortality: A 33-year follow-up study of university students. *J. Behav. Med., 12*, 105–21.

Heather, J. (1995). The great controlled drinking consensus. Is it premature? *Addiction, 90*(9), 1160–63.

Heaton, R. K., Grant, I., & Matthews, C. G. (1991). *Comprehensive norms for an expanded Halstead–Reitan Battery.* Odessa, FL: Psychological Assessment Resources.

Heaton, R., Paulsen, J. S., McAdams, L. A., Kuck, J., Zisook, S., Braff, D., Harris, M. J., & Jesta, D. V. (1994). Neuropsychological deficits in schizophrenics: Relationship to age, chronicity, and dementia. *Arch. Gen. Psychiat., 51*(6), 469–76.

Hebert, R., Leclerc, G., Bravo, G., & Girouard, D. (1994). Efficacy of a support group programme for caregivers of demented patients in the community: A randomized control trial. *Arch. Gerontol. Gerialr., 18*, 1–14.

Hechtman, L. (1996a). Attention-deficit hyperactivity disorder. In L. Hechtman (Ed.), *Do they grow out of it?* (pp. 17–38). Washington: American Psychiatric Press.

Hechtman, L. (1996b). Families of children with attention deficit hyperactivity disorder: A review. *Canad. J. Psychiat., 41*, 350–60.

Hechtman, L., Weiss, G., & Perlman, T. (1980). Hyperactives as young adults: Self-esteem and social skills. *Canad. J. Psychiat., 25*(6), 478–83.

Hefez, A. (1985). The role of the press and the medical community in the epidemic of "mysterious gas poisoning" in the Jordan West Bank. *Amer. J. Psychiat., 142*, 833–37.

Hegarty, J. D., Baldessarini, R. J., Tohen, M., Waternaux, C., & Oepen, G. (1994). One hundred years of schizophrenia: A meta-analysis of the outcome literature. *Amer. J. Psychiat., 151*(10), 1409–16.

Heider, F. (1958). *The psychology of interpersonal relations.* New York: Wiley.

Heilbrun, K. (1992). The role of psychological testing in forensic assessment. *Law and Human Behavior, 16*, 257–72.

Heilbrun, K. (1997). Prediction versus management models relevant to risk assessment: The importance of legal decision-making context. *Law and Human Behavior, 21*(4), 347–59.

Heiligenstein, E., & Anders, J. (1997). Pemoline in adult attention deficit hyperactivity disorder: Predictors of nonresponse. *J. Amer. Coll. Hlth., 45*(5), 225–29.

Heiman, J. R. (1980). Female sexual response patterns. Interactions of physiological, affective, and contextual cues. *Arch. Gen. Psychiat., 37*, 1311–16.

Heiman, J. R., & Grafton-Becker, V. (1989). Orgasmic disorders in women. In S. R. Leiblum & R. C. Rosen (Eds.), *Principles and practice of sex therapy* (2nd ed.) (pp. 51–88). New York: Guilford.

Heimberg, R. G., & Juster, H. R. (1995) Cognitive-behavioral treatments: Literature review. In R. Heimberg, & M. Liebowitz, et al. (Eds.), *Social phobia: Diagnosis, assessment, and treatment.* (pp. 261–309). New York: Guilford.

Heller, K. (1996). Coming of age of prevention science: Comments on the 1994 National Institute of Mental Health–Institute of Medicine Prevention Reports. *Amer. Psychol., 51*(11), 1123–27.

Heller, K., Sher, K. J., & Benson, C. S. (1982). Problems associated with risk of overprediction in studies of offspring of alcoholics: Implications for prevention. *Clin. Psychol. Rev., 2*, 183–200.

Heller, T., Miller, A. B., & Factor, A. (1997). Adults with mental retardation as supports to their parents: Effects on parental caregiving appraisal. *Mental Retardation, 35*(5), 338–46.

Hellman, R., Green, R., Gray, J., & Williams, K. (1981). Childhood sexual identity, childhood religiosity, and homophobia as influences in the development of transsexualism, homosexuality and heterosexuality. *Arch. Gen. Psychiat., 38*, 910–15.

Helzer, J. E., Canino, G. J., Yeh, E. K., Bland, R., et al. (1990). Alcoholism—North America and Asia: A comparison of population surveys with the Diagnostic Interview Schedule. *Arch. Gen. Psychiat., 47*(4), 313–19.

Helzer, J. E., Robins, L. N., & McEvoy, L. (1987). Posttraumatic stress disorder in the general population: Findings from the Epidemiological Catchment Area Survey. *New Engl. J. Med., 317*, 1630–34.

Hemphill, J. F., Hart, S. D., & Hare, R. D. (1994). Psychopathy and substance use. *J. Person. Dis., 8*, 139–70.

Hemphill, J. F., Templeman, T., Wong, S., & Hare, R. D. (1998). Psychopathy and crime: Recidivism and criminal careers. In D. J. Cooke, A. E. Forth, & R. D. Hare (Eds.), *Psychopathy: Theory, research, and implications for society.* (pp. 375–399). Dordrecht, Netherlands: Kluwer Academic Publishers.

Henderson, V. W. (1986). Non-genetic factors in Alzheimer's disease pathogenesis. *Neurobiol. of Aging, 7*, 585–87.

Hendin, H. (1975). Student suicide: Death as a lifestyle. *J. Nerv. Ment. Dis., 160*(3), 204–19.

Henggeler, S. W. (1989). *Delinquency in adolescence.* Newberg Park, CA: Sage.

Hennessy, K. D., Rabideau, G. J., Cicchetti, D., & Cummings, M. E. (1994). Responses of physically abused and nonabused children to different forms of interadult anger. *Child Deveop., 65*, 815–28.

Henriques, J. B., & Davidson, R. J. (1990). Regional brain electrical asymmetries discriminate between previously depressed and healthy control subjects. *J. Abn. Psychol., 99*, 22–31.

Henriques, J. B., & Davidson, R. J. (1991). Left frontal hypoactivation in depression. *J. Abn. Psychol., 100*, 535–45.

Henry, W. P., & Strupp, H. H. (1994). The therapeutic alliance as interpersonal process. In A. O. Horvath & L. S. Greenberg (Eds.), *The working alliance: Theory, research, and practice.* (pp. 51–84). New York: Wiley.

Henry, W. P., Strupp, H. H., Schacht, T. E., & Gaston, L. (1994). Psychodynamic approaches. In A. E. Bergin & S. L. Garfield (Eds.), *Handbook of psychotherapy and behavior change* (4th ed.) (pp. 467–508). New York: Wiley.

Herbert, J. D., Hope, D. A., & Bellack, A. S. (1992). Validity of the distinction between generalized social phobia and avoidant personality disorder. *J. Abn. Psychol., 101*, 332–39.

Herbert, T. B., & Cohen, S. (1993). Depression and immunity: A meta-analytic review. *Psychol. Bull., 113*(3), 472–86.

Herd, J. A. (1984). Cardiovascular disease and hypertension. In W. D. Gentry (Ed.), *Handbook of behavioral medicine.* (pp. 222–81). New York: Guilford.

Herdt, G., & Stoller, R. G. (1990). *Intimate communications: erotics and the study of a culture.* New York: Columbia University Press.

Herek, G. (1989, Aug. 1). The tyranny of 10%. *The Advocate*, 46–49.

Hermalin, J., & Morell, J. A. (Eds.). (1986). *Prevention planning in mental health.* Beverly Hills, CA: Sage.

Herman, J. L. (1990). Sex offenders: A feminist perspective. In W. L. Marshall, D. R. Laws, & H. E. Barbaree (Eds.), *Handbook of sexual assault.* (pp. 177–94). New York: Plenum.

Herman, J. L. (1993, March/April). The abuses of memory. *Mother Jones, 18*, 3–4.

Herman, J. L. (1994, Spring). Presuming to know the truth. *Nieman Reports, 48*, 43–46.

Herman, J. L., Perry, J. C., & van der Kolk, B. A. (1989). Childhood trauma in borderline personality disorder. *Amer. J. Psychiat., 146*, 490–95.

Hermann, D. H. J. (1990). Autonomy, self determination, the right of involuntarily committed persons to refuse treatment, and the use of substituted judgment in medication decisions involving incompetent persons. *International Journal of Law and Psychiatry, 13*, 361–85.

Hernandez, J. T. (1992). Substance abuse among sexually abused adolescents. *Journal of Adolescent Health, 13,* 658–62.

Herrenkohl, R. C., Herrenkohl, E. C., & Egolf, B. P. (1983). Circumstances surrounding the occurrence of child maltreatment. *J. Cons. Clin. Psychol., 51*(3), 424–31.

Herrnstein, R., & Murray, C. (1994). *The bell curve.* New York: Free Press.

Herzog, D. B., & Rathbun, J. M. (1982). Childhood depression: Developmental considerations. *American Journal of Disorders in Children, 136*(2), 15–20.

Hester, R. K., & Delaney, H. D. (1997). Behavioral self-control program for Windows: Results of a controlled clinical trial. *J. Cons. Clin. Psychol., 65*(4), 686–93.

Heston, L. (1966). Psychiatric disorders in foster home reared children of schizophrenic mothers. *Brit. J. Psychiat., 112,* 819–25.

Hetherington, E. M. & Parke, R. D. (1993). *Child psychology: A contemporary viewpoint,* (4th ed.). New York: McGraw Hill.

Hetherington, E. M. (1991). The role of individual differences and family relationships in children's coping with divorce and remarriage. In P.S. Cowan & E. M. Hetherington (Eds.), *Family transitions.* (pp. 165–194). Hillsdale, NJ: Erlbaum.

Hetherington, E. M. (1998). Relevant issues in developmental science: Introduction to the special series. *Amer. Psychol., 53*(2), 93–5.

Hetherington, E. M., Bridges, M., & Insabella, G. (1998) What matters? What does not? Five perspectives on the association between marital transitions and children's adjustment. *Amer. Psychol., 53,* 167–84.

Hetherington, E. M., Stanley-Hagan, M., & Anderson, E. R. (1989). Marital transitions: A child's perspective. *Amer. Psychol., 44,* 303–312.

Hettema, J. M., Neale, M. C., & Kendler, K. S. (1995). Physical similarity and the equal-environment assumption in twin studies of psychiatric disorders. *Behav. Gen., 25*(4), 327–35.

Heyman, A., Wilkinson, W. E., Hurwitz, B. J., Helms, M. J., et al. (1987). Early-onset Alzheimer's disease: Clinical predictors of institutionalization and death. *Neurology, 37,* 980–84.

Heymsfield, S. B., Allison, D. B., Heshka, S., & Pierson, R. N. (1995). Assessment of human body composition. In D. B. Allison et al. (Eds.), *Handbook of assessment methods for eating behaviors and weight-related problems: Measures, theory, research.* (pp. 515–60). Thousand Oaks, CA: Sage.

Hibbert, G. A. (1984). Ideational components of anxiety: Their origin and content. *Brit. J. Psychiat., 144,* 618–24.

Higuchi, S., et al. (1997). Apolipoprotein E e4 allele and pupillary response to tropicamide. *Amer. J. Psychiat., 154*(5), 694–96.

Higuci, S. S., Matsushita, H., Imazeki, T., Kinoshita, T., Takagi, S., & Kono, H. (1994). Aldehyde de hydrogenase genotypes in Japanese alcoholics. *Lancet, 343,* 741–42.

Hijii, T., et al. (1997). Life expectancy and social adaptation in individuals with Down syndrome with and without surgery for congenital heart disease. *Clin. Pediat., 36*(6), 327–32.

Hilgard, E. R. (1973). The domain of hypnosis: With some comments on alternative paradigms. *Amer. Psychol., 28*(11), 972–82.

Hilgard, E. R. (1974). Weapon against pain: Hypnosis is no mirage. *Psych. Today, 8*(6), 120–22, 126, 128.

Hilgard, E. R. (1977). *Divided consciousness: Multiple controls in human thought and action.* New York: Wiley.

Hilgard, E. R. (1994). Neodissociation theory. In S. J. Lynn & J. W. Rhue (Eds.), *Dissociation: Clinical and theoretical perspectives.* (pp. 32–51). New York: Guilford.

Hill, A. L. (1975). Investigation of calendar calculating by an idiot savant. *Amer. J. Psychiat., 132*(5), 557–59.

Hillson, J. M., & Kuiper, N. A. (1994). A stress and coping model of child treatment. *Clin. Psychol. Rev., 14,* 261–85.

Himle, J. A., & Hill, E. M. (1991). Alcohol abuse and anxiety disorders: Evidence from the Epidemiologic Catchment Area Survey. *J. Anxiety Dis., 5,* 237–45.

Hinckley v. U.S. (1998). 140 F.3d 277 (D.C. Cir., 1998).

Hinrichsen, G. A., & Niederehe, G. (1994). Dementia management strategies and adjustment of family members of older patients. *Gerontologist, 34*(1), 95–102.

Hinshaw, S. F., & Anderson, C. A. (1996). Conduct and oppositional disorders. In E. J. Mash & R. A. Barkley (Eds.), *Child psychopathology.* (pp. 113–49). New York: Guilford.

Hinshaw, S. F., Zupan, B. A., Simmel, C., & Nigg, J. T. (1997). Peer status in boys with and without attention-deficit hyperactivity disorder: Predictions from overt and covert antisocial behavior, social isolation, and authoritative parents. *Child Develop., 68*(5), 880–96.

Hinshaw, S. P. (1992). Externalizing behavior problems and academic underachievement in childhood and adolescence: Causal relationships and underlying mechanisms. *Psychol. Bull., 111,* 127–55.

Hinshaw, S. P. (1994). Conduct disorder in childhood: Conceptualization, diagnosis, comorbidity, and risk status for antisocial functioning in adulthood. In D. C. Fowles, P. Sutker & S. H. Goodman (Eds.), *Progress in experimental personality and psychopathology research.* New York: Springer.

Hinton, W. L., Tiet, Q., Giaouyen, C., & Chesney, M. (1997). Predictors of depression among refugees from Vietnam: A longitudinal study of new arrivals. *J. Nerv. Ment. Dis., 185*(1), 39–45.

Hiroto, D. S., & Seligman, M. E. P. (1975). Generality of learned helplessness in man. *J. Pers. Soc. Psychol., 31*(2), 311–27.

Hirsch, S. R., & Leff, J. P. (1975). *Abnormalities in parents of schizophrenics.* London: Oxford University Press.

Hirschfeld, M. (1948). *Sexual anomalies.* (p. 167). New York: Emerson.

Hirschfeld, R. A. (1994). Major depression, dysthymia, and depressive personality disorder. *Brit. J. Psychiat., 165*(26), 23–30.

Hirschfeld, R. M. A. (1996). Panic disorder: Diagnosis, epidemiology, and clinical course. *J. Clin. Psychiat., 57*(10), 3–8.

Hirschfeld, R. M. A., & Cross, C. K. (1982). Epidemiology of affective categories. *Arch. Gen. Psychiat., 39,* 35–46.

Hirschfeld, R. M. A., Klerman, G. L., Andreasen, N. C., Clayton, P. J., & Keller, M. B. (1985). Situational major depressive disorder. Arch. Gen. Psychiat., 42, 1109–14.

Hirschfeld, R. M. A., Klerman, G. L., Clayton, P. J., Keller, M. B., McDonald-Scott, P., & Larkin, B. H. (1983). Assessing personality: Effects of the depressive state on trait measurement. *Amer. J. Psychiat., 140,* 695–99.

Hirschfeld, R. M. A., Klerman, G. L., Lavori, P., Keller, M. B., Griffith, P., & Coryell, W. (1989). Premorbid personality assessments of first onset of major depression. *Arch. Gen. Psychiat., 46,* 345–50.

Hirschfeld, R. M. A., Shea, M. T., & Weise, R. (1995). Dependent personality disorder. In W. J. Livesley (Ed.), *The DSM-IV personality disorders.* (pp. 239–256). New York: Guilford.

Hirshfeld, D. R., Rosenbaum, J. F., Biederman, J., Bolduc, F. A., Faraone, S. V., Snidman, N., Reznick, J. S., Kagan, J. (1992). Stable behavioral inhibition and its association with anxiety disorder. *J. Amer. Acad. Child Adoles. Psychiat., 31,* 103–111.

Hirst, W. (1982). The amnesic syndrome: Descriptions and explanations. *Psychol. Bull., 91,* 435–60.

Hobfoll, S. E., Johnson, R., Eyle, N., & Tzemach, M. (1994). A nation's response to attack: Israeli's depressive reactions to the Gulf War. *J. Trauma. Stress, 7,* 59–73.

Hobfoll, S., Ritter, C., Lavin, J., & Hulsizer, M. et al. (1995). Depression prevalence and incidence among inner-city pregnant and postpartum women. *J. Cons. Clin. Psychol., 3,* 445–453.

Hodkinson, S., Sherrington, R., Gurling, H., Marchbanks, R., Reeders, S., Mallet, J., McInnis, M., Petursson, H., & Brynjolfsson, J. (1987). Molecular evidence for heterogeneity in manic depression. *Nature, 325,* 805–6.

Hoffman, A. (1971). LSD discoverer disputes "chance" factor in finding. *Psychiat. News, 6*(8), 23–26.

Hoffman, J. L. (1943). Psychotic visitors to government offices in the national capital. *Amer. J. Psychiat., 99,* 571–75.

Hoffman, P. L., & Tabakoff, B. (1996). Alcohol dependence: A commentary on mechanisms. *Alcohol & Alcoholism, 31*(4), 333–40.

Hogarty, G. E., et al. (1997a). Three-year trials of personal therapy among schizophrenic patients living with or independent of family: I. Description of study and effects on relapse rate. *Amer. J. Psychiat., 154*(11), 1504–13.

Hogarty, G. E., et al. (1997b). Three-year trials of personal therapy among schizophrenic patients living with or independent of family, II: Effects on adjustment of patients. *Amer. J. Psychiat., 154*(11), 1514–24.

Hogarty, G. E., Anderson, C. M., Reiss, D. J., Kornblith, S. J., & Greenwald, D. P. (1986). Family psychoeducation, social skills training, and maintenance chemotherapy in the aftercare treatment of schizophrenia: 1. One-year effects of a controlled study. *Arch. Gen. Psychiat., 43,* 633–42.

Hogarty, G. E., McEvoy, J. P., Munetz, M., DiBarry, L., Bartone, P., Cather, R., Cooley, S. J., Ulrich, R. F., Carter, M., & Madonia, M. J. (1988). Dose of Fluphanazine, familial expressed emotion, and outcome in schizophrenia. *Arch. Gen. Psychiat., 45,* 797–805.

Hokanson, J. E., & Burgess, M. (1962). The effects of three types of aggression on vascular process. *J. Abnorm. Soc. Psychol., 64,* 446–49.

Hokanson, J. E., Hummer, J. T., & Butler, A. C. (1991). Interpersonal perceptions by depressed college students. *Cog. Ther. Res., 15,* 443–57.

Hokanson, J. E., Lowenstein, D. A., Hedeen, C., Howes, M. J. (1986). Dysphoric college students and roommates: A study of social behaviors over a three-month period. *Personality and Social Psychology Bulletin, 12,* 311–24.

Hokanson, J. E., Rubert, M. P., Welker, R. A., Hollander, G. R., & Hedeen, C. (1989). Interpersonal concomitants and antecedents of depression among college students. *J. Abn. Psychol., 98,* 209–17.

Holcomb, W. (1979). *Coping with severe stress: A clinical application of stress-inoculation therapy.* Unpublished doctoral dissertation, University of Missouri-Columbia.

Holden, R. R., Medonca, J. D., & Serin, R. C. (1989). Suicide, hopelessness, and social desirability: A test of an interactive model. *J. Cons. Clin. Psychol., 57,* 500–4.

Holder, H. D., Longabaugh, R., Miller, W. R., & Rubonis, A. V. (1991). The cost effectiveness of treatment for alcohol problems: A first approximation. *J. Stud. Alcohol., 52,* 517–40.

Holland, H. C. (1974). Displacement activity as a form of abnormal behavior in animals. In H. R. Beech (Ed.), *Obsessional states.* (pp. 161–73). London: Methuen.

Hollander, E., DeCaria, C. M., Nitescu, A., Gully, R., Suckow, R. F., et al. (1992). Serotonergic function in obsessive-compulsive disorder: Behavioral and neuroendocrine responses to oral m-chlorophenylpiperazine and fenfluramine in patients and healthy volunteers. *Arch. Gen. Psychiat., 49,* 21–28.

Hollander, E., Liebowitz, M. R., Gorman, J. M., Cohen, B., Fyer, A., & Klein, D. F. (1989). Cortisol and sodium lactate-induced panic. *Arch. Gen. Psychiat., 46,* 135–40.

Hollander, E., Stein, D. J., Decaria, C. M., Cohen, L., Saoud, J. B., Skodol, A., Kellman, D., Rosnick, L., & Oldham, J. M. (1994). Serotonergic sensitivity in borderline personality disorder: Preliminary Findings. *Amer. J. Psychiat., 151*(2), 277–280.

Hollon, S. D., & Beck, A. T. (1994). Cognitive and cognitive-behavioral therapies. In A. E. Bergin & S. L.

Garfield (Eds.), *Handbook of psychotherapy and behavior change* (4th ed.). (pp. 428–66). New York: Wiley.

Hollon, S. D., DeRubeis, R. J., & Evans, M. D. (1987). Causal mediation of change in treatment for depression: Discriminating between nonspecificity and noncausality. *Psychol. Bull., 102,* 139–49.

Hollon, S. D., DeRubeis, R. J., & Evans, M. D. (1996). Cognitive therapy in the treatment and prevention of depression. In P. M. Salkovskis (Ed.), *Frontiers of cognitive therapy.* (pp. 293–317). New York: Guilford.

Hollon, S. D., DeRubeis, R. J., Evans, M. D., Wiemer, M. J., Garvey, M. J., Grove, W. M., & Tuason, V. B. (1992). Cognitive therapy and pharmacotherapy for depression: Singly and in combination. *Arch. Gen. Psychiat., 49*(10), 774–81.

Hollon, S. D., Shelton, R. C., & Davis, D. D. (1993). Cognitive therapy for depression: Conceptual issues and clinical efficacy. *J. Cons. Clin. Psychol., 61*(2), 270–75.

Hollon, S. D., Evans, M., & DeRubeis, R. (1990). Cognitive mediation of relapse prevention following treatment for depression: Implications of differential risk. In R. Ingram (Ed.), *Psychological aspects of depression.* New York: Plenum.

Hollon, S. D., Shelton, R. C., & Loosen, P. T. (1991). Cognitive therapy and pharmacotherapy for depression. *J. Cons. Clin. Psychol., 59,* 88–99.

Hollon, S., & Beck, A. T. (1978). Psychotherapy and drug therapy: Comparisons and combinations. In S. L. Garfield & A. E. Bergin (Eds.), *Handbook of psychotherapy and behavior change.* (pp. 437–90). New York: Wiley.

Hollon, S., & Beck, A. T. (1986). Research on cognitive therapies. In S. L. Garfield & A. E. Bergin (Eds.), *Handbook of psychotherapy and behavior change* (3rd ed.). (pp. 443–82). New York: Wiley.

Holmes, D. L. (1998). *Autism through the lifespan: The Eden Model.* Bethesda, MD: Woodbine House.

Holmes, T. H., & Rahe, R. H. (1967). The social readjustment rating scale. *J. Psychosom. Res., 11*(2), 213–18.

Holohan, C. J., & Moos, R. H. (1991). Life stressors, personal and social resources, and depression: A 4-year structural model. *J. Abn. Psychol. 100,* 31–38.

Holroyd, K. A., & Andrasik, F. (1978). Coping and the self-control of chronic tension headache. *J. Cons. Clin. Psychol., 46,* 1036–45.

Holroyd, K. A., Andrasik, F., & Westbrook, T. (1977). Cognitive control of tension headache. *Cog. Ther. Res., 1,* 121–33.

Holsboer, F. (1992). The hypothalmic-pituitary-adrenocortical system. In E. S. Paykel (Ed.), *Handbook of affective disorders* (2nd ed.). New York: Guilford.

Holt, C. S., Heimberg, R. G., & Hope, D. A. (1992). Avoidant personality disorder and the generalized subtype of social phobia. *J. Abn. Psychol., 101,* 318–25.

Holvey, D. N., & Talbott, J. H. (Eds.). (1972). *The Merck manual of diagnosis and therapy* (12th ed.). Rahway, NJ: Merck, Sharp, & Dohme Research Laboratories.

Holzbeck, E. (1996). Thiamine absorption in alcoholic delirium patients. *J. Stud. Alcoh., 57*(6), 581–84.

Holzman, P. S., et al. (1998). How are deficits in motion perception related to eye-tracking dysfunction in schizophrenia. In M. F. Lenzenweger & R. H. Dworkin (Eds.), *Origins and development of schizophrenia.* (pp. 161–84). Washington: American Psychological Association.

Holzman, P. S., Kringlen, E., Matthysse, S., Flanagan, S. D., Lipton, R. B., Cramer, G., Levin, S., Lange, K., & Levy, D. L. (1988). A single dominant gene can account for eye tracking dysfunctions and schizophrenia in offspring of discordant twins. *Arch. Gen. Psychiat., 45,* 641–47.

Homans, G. C. (1961). *Social behavior: Its elementary forms.* New York: Harcourt Brace Jovanovich.

Homer, L. E. (1974). The anatomy of a runaway. *Human Behav., 3*(4), 37.

Homme, L. E. (1965). Perspectives in psychology: Control of coverants, the operants of the mind (Vol. 24). *Psychol. Rec., 15,* 501–11.

Hook, E. B. (1980). Genetic counseling dilemmas: Down's syndrome, paternal age, and recurrence risk after remarriage. *Amer. J. Med. Genet., 5,* 145–51.

Hooker, E. (1957). The adjustment of the male overt homosexual. *Journal of Projective Techniques, 21,* 18–30.

Hooley, J. M. (1985). Expressed emotion: A review of the critical literature. *Clin. Psychol. Rev., 5,* 119–39.

Hooley, J. M. (1986). Expressed emotion and depression: Interactions between patients and high-versus low-expressed-emotion spouses. *J. Abn. Psychol., 95,* 237–46.

Hooley, J. M. (1998). Expressed emotion and locus of control. *J. Nerv. Ment. Dis. 186,* 374–78.

Hooley, J. M., & Hiller, J. B. (1998). Expressed emotion and the pathogenesis of relapse in schizophrenia. In M. F. Lenzenweger & R. H. Dworkin (Eds.), *Origins and development of schizophrenia.* (pp. 447–68). Washington: American Psychological Association.

Hooley, J. M., Orley, J., & Teasdale, J. D. (1986). Levels of expressed emotion and relapse in depressed patients. *Brit. J. Psychiat., 148,* 642–47.

Hooley, J. M., & Teasdale, J. D. (1989). Predictors of relapse in unipolar depressives: Expressed emotion, marital distress, and perceived criticism. *J. Abn. Psychol., 98,* 229–35.

Hoon, P. W., Wincze, J. P., & Hoon, E. F. (1977). A test of reciprocal inhibition: Are anxiety and sexual arousal in women mutually inhibitory? *J. Abn. Psychol. 86,* 65–74.

Hope, D. A., & Heimberg, R. G. (1993). Social phobia and social anxiety. In D. H. Barlow (Eds.), *Clinical handbook of psychological disorders.* (pp. 99–136). New York: Guilford.

Hope, D. A., Rapee, R. M., Heimberg, R. G., & Dombeck, M. J. (1990). Representations of the self in social phobia: Vulnerability to social threat. *Cog. Ther. Res., 14,* 177–89.

Hops, H., Duncan, T. E., Duncan, S. C., & Stoolmiller, M. (1996). Parent substance use as a predictor of adolescent use: A six-year lagged analysis. *Ann. Behav. Med., 18*(3), 157–64.

Horevitz, R. (1994). Dissociation and multiple personality: Conflicts and controversies. In S. J. Lynn & J. W. Rhue (Eds.), *Dissociation: Clinical and theoretical perspectives.* (pp. 434–62). New York: Guilford.

Horevitz, R., & Loewenstein, R. J. (1994). The rational treatment of multiple personality disorder. In S. J. Lynn & J. W. Rhue (Eds.), *Dissociation: Clinical and theoretical perspectives.* (pp. 289–316). New York: Guilford.

Horn, W. F., Islongo, N. S., Pascoe, J. M., & et al. (1991). Additive effects of psychostimulants, parent training, and self-control therapy with ADHD children. *J. Amer. Acad. Child Adoles. Psychiat., 30,* 233–40.

Hornig, C. D., & McNally, R. J. (1995). Panic disorder and suicide attempt: A reanalysis of data from the Epidemiologic Catchment Area study. *Brit. J. Psychiat. 67,* 76–77.

Horowitz, L. M. (1996). The study of interpersonal problems: A Leary legacy. *J. Pers. Assess., 66*(2), 283–300.

Horowitz, L. M., Rosenberg, S. E., & Bartholomew, K. (1993). Interpersonal problems, attachment styles, and outcome in brief dynamic psychotherapy. *J. Cons. Clin. Psychol., 61*(4), 549–60.

Horowitz, M. J., Merluzzi, R. V., Ewert, M., Ghannam, J. H., Harley, D., & Stinson, C. H. (1991) Role-relationship models of configuration (RRMC) In M. Horowitz (Ed.), *Person schemas and maladaptive interpersonal patterns.* (pp. 115–54). Chicago: University of Chicago Press.

Horowitz, M. J., & Solomon, G. F. (1978). Delayed stress response syndromes in Vietnam veterans. In C. R. Figley (Ed.), *Stress disorders among Vietnam veterans: Theory, research, and treatment.* New York: Brunner/Mazel.

Horowitz, M. J., Wilner, N., & Alvarez, W. (1979). Impact of Events Scale: A measure of subjective stress. *Psychosom. Med., 41,* 209–18.

Horton, P. C., Louy, J. W., & Coppolillo, H. P. (1974). Personality disorder and transitional relatedness. *Arch. Gen. Psychiat., 30*(5), 618–22.

Horvath, A. O., & Greenberg, L. S. (Eds.). (1994). *The working alliance: Theory, research, and practice.* New York: Wiley.

Hoshino, Y., et al. (1980). Early symptoms of autism in children and their diagnostic significance, *Japanese Journal of Child and Adolescent Psychiatry, 21*(5), 284–99.

Houck, C. K. (1993). Ellis's "potential" Integrative Strategy Instruction model: An appealing extension of previous efforts. *J. Learn. Dis., 26*(6), 399–403.

House of Representatives. (1990). *No place to call home: Discarded children in America.* A report of the Select Committee on Children, Youth, and Families. Washington, DC: U.S. Government Printing Office.

Houts, A. C. (1991). Nocturnal enuresis as a biobehavioral problem. *Behav. Ther., 22,* 133–51.

Houts, A. C., Berman, J. S., & Abramson, H. (1994). Effectiveness of psychological and pharmacological treatments for nocturnal eneurisis. *J. Cons. Clin. Psychol., 62,* 737–45.

Howard, K. I., Davidson, C. V., O'Mahoney, M. T., & Orlinsky, D. E. (1989). Patterns of psychotherapy utilization. *Amer. J. Psychiat., 146,* 775–78.

Howard, K. I., Kopta, S. M., Krause, M. S., & Orlinsky, D. E. (1986). The dose-effect relationship in psychotherapy. *Amer. Psychol., 41,* 159–64.

Howes, M. J., Hokanson, J. E., & Loewenstein, D. A. (1985). Induction of depressive affect after prolonged exposure to a mildly depressed individual. *J. Pers. Soc. Psychol., 49,* 1110–13.

Howlin, P. (1998). Psychological and educational treatments for autism. *Journal of Child Psychology & Psychiatry & Allied Disciplines, 39*(3), 307–22.

Hser, Y. I., Anglin, M. D., & Powers, K. (1993). A 24 year follow-up of California narcotics addicts. *Arch. Gen. Psychiat., 50,* 577–84.

Hshieh, S. Y., & Srebalus, D. J. (1997). Alcohol treatment issues: Professional differences. *Alcoholism Treatment Quarterly, 15*(4), 63–73.

Hsu, L. K. G. (1989). The gender gap in eating disorders: Why are the eating disorders more common among women? *Clin. Psychol. Rev., 9,* 393–407.

Hsu, L. K., Benotti, P. N., Dwyer, J., Roberts, S. B., Saltzman, E., Shikora, S., Rolls, B. J., & Rand, W. (1998). Nonsurgical factors that influence the outcome of bariatric surgery: A review. *Psychosom. Med., 60,* 338–46.

Hu, T. W., Huang, L.-F., & Cartwright, W. (1986). Evaluation of the costs of caring for the senile demented elderly: A pilot study. *Gerontologist, 26,* 158–63.

Huber, L., & Edelberg, R. (1993). A community integration model of head injury rehabilitation. *J. Cogn. Rehab., 11*(2), 22–26.

Hudspeth, W. J., & Pribram, K. H. (1992). Psychophysiological indices of cerebral maturation. *International Journal of Psychophysiology, 12,* 19–29.

Hudziak, J. J; Boffeli, T. J., Kreisman, J. J., & Battaglia, M. M. (1996) Clinical study of the relation of borderline personality disorder to Briquet's syndrome (hysteria), somatization disorder, antisocial personality disorder, and substance abuse disorders. *Amer. J. Psychiat., 153,* 159–160.

Huff, F. W. (1969). A learning theory approach to family therapy. *The Family Coordinator, 18*(1), 22–26.

Hughes, A. L. (1992). The prevalence of illicit drug use in six metropolitan areas in the United States: Results from the 1991 National Household Survey on Drug Abuse. *Brit. J. Addict., 87,* 1481–1485.

Hughes, J. R., Higgins, S. T., & Hatsukami, D. K. (1990). Effects of abstinence from tobacco: A critical review. In L. T. Kozlowski, H. Annis, & H. D. Cappell, et al. (Eds.), *Recent advances in alcohol and drug problems* (Vol. 10). (pp. 317–97).

Hughes, J. R., & Pierattini, R. A. (1992). An introduction to pharmacotherapy for mental disorders. In J. Grabowski & G. R. VandenBos (Eds.), *Psychopharmabiology: Basic mechanisms and applied interventions* Washington, D. C.: American Psychological Association.

Hughes, P. L., Wells, L. A., Cunningham, C. J., & Ilstrup, D. M. (1986). Treating bulimia with desipramine: A double-blind, placebo-controlled study. *Arch. Gen. Psychiat., 43,* 182–86.

Humphrey, L. L. (1989). Observed family interactions among subtypes of eating disorders using Structural Analysis of Social Behavior. *J. Cons. Clin. Psychol., 57,* 206–14.

Humphreys, K., & Rappaport, J. (1993). From community mental health movement to the war on drugs: A study of the definition of social problems. *Amer. Psychol., 48*(8), 892–901.

Humphry, D., & Wickett, A. (1986). *The right to die: Understanding euthanasia.* New York: Harper & Row.

Hunt, M. (1975). *Sexual behavior in the 1970's.* New York: Dell.

Hunt, W. A. (1993). Are binge drinkers more at risk of developing brain damage? *Alcohol, 10,* 559–61.

Hunter, E. J. (1976). The prisoner of war: Coping with the stress of isolation. In R. H. Moos (Ed.), *Human adaptation: Coping with life crises.* Lexington, MA: Heath.

Hunter, E. J. (1978). The Vietnam POW veteran: Immediate and long-term effects. In C. R. Figley (Ed.), *Stress disorders among Vietnam veterans.* New York: Brunner/Mazel.

Hunter, E. J. (1981). Wartime stress: Family adjustment to loss (USIU Report No. TR-USIU-8-107). San Diego, CA: United States International University.

Husain, M. M., Meyer, D. E., Muttakin, M. H., & Weiner, M. F. (1993). Maintenance ECT for treatment of recurrent mania. *Amer. J. Psychiat., 150,* 985.

Hutchinson, N. L. (1993). Integrative Strategy Instruction: An elusive ideal for teaching adolescents with learning disabilities. *J. Learn. Dis., 26*(7), 428–32.

Huxley, A. (1965). Human potentialities. In R. E. Farson (Ed.), *Science and human affairs.* Palo Alto, CA: Science and Behavior Books.

Huynen, K. B., Lutzker, J. R., Bigelow, K. B., Touchette, R. E., & Campbell, R. V. (1996). Planned activities for mothers of children with developmental disorders. *Behav. Mod., 20*(4), 406–27.

Hyde, J. (1984). How large are gender differences in aggression? A developmental meta-analysis. *Develop. Psychol., 20,* 722–736.

Hyman, S. E. (1994). Why does the brain prefer opium to broccoli? *Harvard Review of Psychiatry, 2,* 43–6.

Hymel, S., & Rubin, K. H. (1985). Children with peer relationships and social skills problems: Conceptual, methodological, and developmental issues. *Annals of child development* (Vol. 2). Greenwich, CT: JAI Press.

Hynd, G. W., & Semrud-Clikeman, M. (1989). Dyslexia and brain morphology. *Psychol. Bull., 106,* 447–82.

Iacono, W. G., & Beiser, M. (1992). Where are the women in first-episode studies of schzophrenia? *Schizo. Bull., 18*(3), 471–80.

Iacono, W. G., Moreau, M., Beiser, M., Fleming, J. A. E., & Tsung-Yi, L. (1992). Smooth-pursuit eye tracking in first-episode psychotic patients and their relatives. *J. Abn. Psychol., 101*(1), 104–16.

Iezzi, A., & Adams, H. E. (1993). Somatoform and factitious disorders. In P. B. Sutker & H. E. Adams (Eds.), *Comprehensive handbook of psychopathology.* (pp. 167–202). New York: Plenum.

Ikemi, Y., Ago, Y., Nakagawa, S., Mori S., Takahashi, N., Suematsu, H., Sugita, M., & Matsubara, H. (1974). Psychosomatic mechanism under social changes in Japan. *J. Psychosom. Res., 18*(1), 15–24.

Imber, S. D., Glanz, L. M., Elkin, I., Sotsky, S. M., & Boyer, J. L. (1986). Ethical issues in psychotherapy research: Problems in a collaborative clinical trials study. *Amer. Psychol., 41,* 137–46.

Inch, R., Crossley, M., Keegan, D., & Thorarinson, D. (1997). Use of the Brief Psychiatric Rating Scale to measure success in a psychosocial day program. *Psychiat. Serv., 48*(9), 1135–37.

Innala, S. M., & Ernulf, K. E. (1989). Asphyxiophilia in Scandinavia. *Arch. Sex. Behav., 18,* 181–90.

Insel, T. R. (1992). Toward a neuroanatomy of obsessivecompulsive disorder. *Arch. Gen. Psychiat., 49,* 739–44.

Institute of Medicine. (1989). *Research on children and adolescents with mental, behavioral, and developmental disorders.* Washington, DC: National Academy Press.

Intrieri, R. C., & Rapp, S. R. (1994). Self-control skillfulness and caregiver burden among help-seeking elders. *J. Gerontol., 49*(1), P19–P23.

Ironside, R., & Batchelor, I. R. C. (1945). The ocular manifestations of hysteria in relation to flying. *Br. J. Ophthalmol., 29,* 88–98.

Irwin, M., Daniels, M., Smith, T. L., Bloom, E., & Weiner, H. (1987). Impaired natural killer cell activity during bereavement. *Brain, Behavior, and Immunity, 1,* 98–104.

Isaacson, R. L. (1970). When brains are damaged. *Psych. Today, 3*(4), 38–42.

Isacsson, G., & Rich, C. L. (1997). Depression, antidepressants, and suicide: Pharmacoepidemiological evidence for suicide prevention. In R. W. Maris, M. M. Silverman, & S. S. Canetton (Eds.), *Review of Suicidology, 1997.* (pp. 168–201). New York: Guilford.

Iscoe, I., Bloom, B. L., & Spielberger, C. D. (Eds.). (1977). *Community psychology in transition.* Washington, DC: Hemisphere.

Ismail, B., Cantor-Graae, E., & McNeil, T. F. (1998). Neurological abnormalities in schizophrenic patients and their siblings. *Amer. J. Psychiat., 155*(1), 84–89.

Isometsä, E., Henriksson, M., Aro, A., Heikkinen, M., Kuoppasalmi, K., & Lonnqvist, J. (1994). Suicide in psychotic major depression. *J. Affect. Dis., 31,* 187–91.

Isometsä, E. T., Henriksson, M. M., Aro, H. M., Heikkinen, M. E., Kuoppasalmi, K. I., Lonnqvist, J. K. (1994). Suicide in major depression. *Amer. J. Psychiat., 151,* 530–36.

Isralowitz, R. E., & Borowski, A. (1992). Australian university student alcohol behavior in perspective: A cross-cultural study. *Journal of Alcohol & Drug Education, 38*(1), 39–42.

Ivarsson, T., Larsson, B., & Gillberg, C. (1998). A 2–4 year follow up of depressive symptoms, suicidal ideation, and suicide attempts among adolescent psychiatric inpatients. *Eur. Child Adoles. Psychiat., 7*(2), 96–104.

Jablensky, A., et al. (1992). Schizophrenia: Manifestations, incidence, and course in different cultures. A World Health Organization ten-country study. *Psychological Medicine Monograph Supplement, 20,* 1–97.

Jackson, G. G., & Kirschner, S. A. (1973). Racial self-designation and preference for counselor race. *J. Couns. Psychol., 20,* 560–64.

Jackson, J. L., Calhoun, K., Amick, A. E., Maddever, H. M., & Habif, V. (1990). Young adult women who experienced childhood intrafamilial sexual abuse: Subsequent adjustment. *Arch. Sex. Behav., 19,* 211–21.

Jacobs, S. (1993) Pathologic grief: Maladaptation to loss. Washington, DC: American Psychiatric Press.

Jacobson, E. (1971). *Depression: Comparative studies of normal, neurotic, and psychotic conditions.* New York: International Universities Press.

Jacobson, J. W. (1990). Do some mental disorders occur less frequently among persons with mental retardation? *Amer. J. Ment. Retard., 94,* 596–602.

Jacobson, N. S., & Hollon, S. D. (1996). Prospects for future comparisons between drugs and psychotherapy: Lessons from the CBT-versus-pharmacotherapy exchange. *J. Cons. Clin. Psychol., 64*(1), 104–108.

Jacobson, N. S., Dobson, K., Fruzzetti, A. E., Schmaling, K. B., Salusky, S. (1991). Marital therapy as a treatment for depression. *J. Cons. Clin. Psychol., 59,* 547–57.

Jacobson, N. S., Gottman, J. M., Waltz, J., Rushe, R., Babcock, J., & Holtzworth-Munroe, A. (1994). Affect, verbal content, and psychophysiology in the arguments of couples with a violent husband. *J. Consult. Clin. Psychol., 62,* 982–88.

Jacobson, N. S., Holtzworth-Monroe, A., & Schmaling, K. B. (1989). Marital therapy and spouse involvement in the treatment of depression, agoraphobia, and alcoholism. *J. Cons. Clin. Psychol., 57,* 5–10.

Jaffe, A. (1992). Cognitive factors associated with cocaine abuse and its treatment. In T. R. Kosten & H.

D. Kleber (Eds.), *Cocaine: A clinician's guide.* New York: Guilford.

James, A. L., & Barry, R. J. (1981). General maturational lag as an essential correlate of early onset psychosis. *J. Autism Devel. Dis., 11*(3), 271–83.

James, W. (1890). *Principles of psychology.* New York: Holt.

Jamison, K. (1995). *An Unquiet Mind.* New York: Vintage Books.

Jamison, K. R. (1993). *Touched with fire.* New York: Free Press.

Jancar, J., & Jancar, P. J. (1996). Longevity in Down syndrome: A twelve year survey (1984–1995). *Italian Journal of Intellective Impairment, 9*(1), 27–30.

Jancar, J., & Johnston, S. J. (1990). Incest and mental handicap. *J. Men. Deficien. Res., 34,* 483–490.

Janicki, M. P., & Dalton, A. J. (1993). Alzheimer disease in a select population of older adults with mental retardation. *Irish Journal of Psychology: Special Issue, Psychological aspects of aging 14*(1), 38–47.

Janis, I. L. (1958). *Psychological stress: Psychoanalytic and behavioral studies of surgical patients.* New York: Wiley.

Janis, I. L., & Leventhal H. (1965). Psychological aspects of physical illness and hospital care. In B. B. Wolman (Ed.), *Handbook of Clinical psychology.* (pp. 1360–77). New York: McGraw-Hill.

Janis, I. L., Mahl, G. F., Kagan, J., & Holt, R. R. (1969). *From personality: Dynamics, development, and assessment.* New York: Harcourt Brace Jovanovich.

Janofsky, J. S., Dunn, M. H., Roskes, E. J., Briskin, J. K., & Rudolph, M. S. (1996). Insanity defense pleas in Baltimore city: An analysis of outcome. *Amer. J. Psychiat., 153*(11), 1464–68.

Jaranson, J. M., & Popkin, M. K. (1998). *Caring for victims of torture.* Washington: American Psychiatric Press.

Jarvik, M. E. (1967). The psychopharmacological revolution. *Psych. Today, 1*(1), 51–58.

Jeffrey, R. W., & French, S. A. (1996). Socioeconomic status and weight control practices among 20–45-year-old women. *Amer. J. Pub. Hlth., 86*(7), 1005–10.

Jeffrey, R. W., Wing, R. R., & Stunkard, A. J. (1978). Behavioral treatment of obesity: The state of the art, 1976. *Behav. Ther., 9,* 189–99.

Jemmott, J. B., III, & Locke, S. E. (1984). Psychosocial factors, immunologic mediation, and human susceptibility to infectious diseases: How much do we know? *Psychol. Bull., 95,* 78–108.

Jenike, M. A., Baer, L., Ballantine, H. T., Martuza, R. L., Giriunas, I. Tuttolph, M. L., & Cassem, N. H. (1991). Cingulotomy for refractory obsessive-compulsive disorder: A long-term follow-up of 33 patients. *Arch. Gen. Psychiat. 48,* 548–55.

Jenike, M., Baer, L., Minichiello, W., Schwarts, C., & Carey, R. (1986). Concomitant obsessive-compulsive disorder and schizotypal personality disorder. *Amer. J. Psychiat., 143,* 530–2.

Jenkins, C. D., Zyzansky, S. J., & Rosenman, R. H. (1971). Progress toward validation of a computer-scored test for the Type A coronary-prone behavior pattern. *Psychosom. Med., 33,* 193–202.

Jenkins, C. D., Zyzansky, S. J., & Rosenman, R. H. (1976). Risk of new myocardial infarction in middle-age men with manifest coronary heart disease. *Circulation, 53,* 342–47.

Jenkins, R. L. (1969). Classification of behavior problems of children. *Amer. J. Psychiat., 125*(8), 68–75.

Jennet, B., et al. (1976). Predicting outcome in individual patients after severe head injury. *Lancet, 1,* 1031.

Jenni, M. A., & Wollersheim, J. P. (1979). Cognitive therapy, stress-management training and the type A behavior pattern. *Cog. Ther. Res., 3*(1), 61–73.

Jensen, P. S., Watanabe, H. K., Richters, T. E., Cortes, R., et al. (1995.) Prevalence of mental disorder in military children and adolescents: Findings from a two-stage community survey. *J. Amer. Acad. Child Adoles. Psychiat., 34*(11), 1514–24.

Jernigan, T. L., Schafer, K., Butters, N., & Cermak, L. S. (1991). Magnetic resonance imaging of alcoholic Korsakoff patients. *Neuropsychopharmacology, 4,* 175–86.

Jeste, D., & Heaton, S. (1994). How does late-onset schizophrenia compare with early-onset schizophrenia. *Harvard Mental Health Letter, 10*(8).

Joffe, R. T., & Offord, D. R. (1990). Epidemiology. In G. MacLean (Ed.), *Suicide in children and adolescents.* Toronto: Hogrefe & Huber.

Johnson, A. M., Wadsworth, J., Wellings, K., Bradshaw, S., & Field, J. (1992). Sexual lifestyles and HIV risk. *Nature, 360,* 410–12.

Johnson, D. W. (1987). The behavioral control of high blood pressure. *Current Psychological Research Review, 6,* 99–114.

Johnson, J. (1969). The EEG in the traumatic encephalography of boxers. *Psychiatrica Clinica, 2*(4), 204–11.

Johnson, J. L., & McCown, W. G. (1993). Addictive behaviors and substance abuse. In P. B. Sutker & H. E. Adams (Eds.), *Comprehensive handbook of psychopathology* (2nd ed.). (pp. 437–49). New York: Plenum.

Johnson, J., Weissman, M. M., & Klerman, G. L. (1990). Panic Disorder, comorbidity, and suicide attempts. *Arch. Gen. Psychiat., 47,* 805–8.

Johnson, S. L., & Miller, I. (1997). Negative life events and time to recovery from episodes of bipolar disorder. *J. Abn. Psychol., 106*(3), 449–57.

Johnson, S. L., & Roberts, J. E. (1995). Life events and bipolar disorder: Implications from biological theories. *Psychol. Bull., 117,* 434–449.

Johnson, S., Fingerhut, R., Miller, I., Keitner, G., Ryan, C., Solomon, D. (1997, October). *Do minor life events predict course in bipolar disorder?* Paper presented at the Society for Research in Psychopathology. Palm Springs, CA.

Johnston, M. (1997). *Spectral Evidence.* Boston: Houghton Mifflin.

Joiner, T. E. (1995). The price of soliciting and receiving negative feedback: Self-verification theory as a vulnerability to depression theory. *J. Abn. Psychol., 104*(2), 364–72.

Joiner, T. E., & Metalsky, G. I. (1995). A prospective test of an integrative interpersonal theory of depression: A naturalistic study of college roommates. *J. Pers. Soc. Psychol., 69*(4), 778–88.

Joint Commission on the Mental Health of Children. (1970). *Crisis in child mental health: Challenge for the 1970's.* New York: Harper & Row.

Jones, E. E., Farina, A., Hastorf, A. H., Markus, H., & Miller, D. T. (1984). *Social stigma: The psychology of marked relationships.* New York: Freeman.

Jones, K. L., & Smith, B. W. (1975). The fetal alcohol syndrome. *Teratology, 12,* 1–10.

Jones, K. L., Smith, B. W., & Hansen, J. W. (1976). Fetal alcohol syndrome: A clinical delineation. *Ann. NY Acad. Sci., 273,* 130–37.

Jones, L. (1992). Specifying the temporal relationship between job loss and consequences: Implication for service delivery. *The Journal of Applied Social Sciences, 16,* 37–62.

Jones, M. (1953). *The therapeutic community.* New York: Basic Books.

Jones, M. C. (1924). A laboratory study of fear: The case of Peter. *Pedagogical Seminary, 31,* 308–15.

Jones, P. B., et al. (1998). Schizophrenia as a long-term outcome of pregnancy, delivery, and perinatal complications: A 28-year follow-up of the 1996 North Finland General Population Birth Cohort. *Amer. J. Psychiat., 155*(3), 355–64.

Jones, R. (1984). The pharmacology of cocaine. *National Institute on Drug Abuse Research Monograph Series 50.* Washington, DC: National Institute on Drug Abuse.

Jones, R. A. (1977). *Self-fulfilling prophecies: Social, psychological, and physiological effects of expectancies.* Hillsdale, NJ: Erlbaum.

Jones, R. E. (1983). Street people and psychiatry: An introduction. *Hosp. Comm. Psychiat., 34,* 807–11.

Jones, R. R., Reid, J. B., & Patterson, G. R. (1975). Naturalistic observation in clinical assessment. In P. M. Reynolds (Ed.), *Advances in psychological assessment* (Vol. 3). San Francisco: Jossey-Bass.

Joseph, S., Williams, R., & Yule, W. (1995). Psychosocial perspectives on post-traumatic stress disorder. *Clin. Psychol. Rev., 15*(6), 515–44.

Joyce, E. M., & Robbins, T. W. (1991). Frontal lobe function in Korsakoff and non-Korsakoff alcoholics: Planning and spatial working memory. *Neuropsychologia, 29,* 709–23.

Joyner, C. D., & Swenson, C. C. (1993). Community-level intervention after a disaster. In C. F. Saylor (Ed.)., *Children and disaster.* (pp. 211–32). New York: Plenum.

Kaada, B., & Retvedt, A. (1981). Enuresis and hyperventilation response in the EEG. *Develop. Med. Child Neurol., 23*(5), 591–99.

Kachur, S. P., Stennis, G. M., Powell, K. E., et al. (1996). School-associated violent deaths in the United States, 1992–1994. *JAMA, 275,* 1729

Kaelber, C. T., Moul, D. E., & Farmer, M. E. (1995). Epidemiology of depression. In E. E. Beckham & W. R. Leber (Eds.), *Handbook of depression* (2nd ed.). (pp. 3–35). New York: Guilford.

Kagan J. (1994). *Galen's Prophecy.* New York: Westview.

Kagan, J. (1997). Temperament and the reactions to unfamiliarity. *Child Develop., 68*(1), 139–43.

Kagan, J., Gibbons, J. L., Johnson, M. O., Reznick, J. S., & Snidman, N. (1990). A temperamental disposition to the state of uncertainty. In J. Rolf, A. S. Masten, D. Cicchetti, K. H. Nuechterlein, & S. Weintraub (Eds.), *Risk and protective factors in the development of psychopathology.* New York: Cambridge University Press.

Kagan, J., Reznick, J. S., & Snidman, N. (1988). Biological bases of childhood shyness. *Science, 240,* 167–71.

Kagan, J., Reznick, R. J., Clarke, C., Snidman, N., & Garcia-Coll, C. (1984). Behavioral inhibition and the unfamiliar. *Child Develop., 55,* 2212–25.

Kahan, J., Kemp, B., Staples, F. R., & Brummell-Smith, K. (1985). Decreasing the burden in families caring for a relative with a dementing illness: A controlled study. *J. Amer. Geriat. Soc., 33,* 664–70.

Kahana, B., Harel, Z., & Kahana, E. (1988). Predictors of psychological well-being among survivors of the Holocaust. In J. P. Wilson, Z. Harel, & B. Kahana (Eds.), *Human adaptation to extreme stress: From the Holocaust to Vietnam.* (pp. 171–92). New York: Plenum.

Kahler, C. W. (1995). Current challenges and an old debate. *Addiction, 90*(9), 1169–71.

Kahn, J. S., Kehle, T. J., Jenson, W. R., & Clark, E. (1990). Comparison of cognitive-behavioral, relaxation, and self-modeling interventions for depression among middle-school students. *School Psychol. Rev. 19,* 196–211.

Kahn, M. W., & Raifman, L. (1981). Hospitalization versus imprisonment and the insanity plea. *Crim. Just. Behav., 8*(4), 483–90.

Kalarchian, M. A., Wilson, G. T., Brolin, R. E., & Bradley, L. (1998). Binge eating in bariatric surgery patients. *Int. J. Eat. Dis., 23*(1), 89–92.

Kales, A., Paulson, M. J., Jacobson, A., & Kales, J. (1966). Somnambulism: Psychophysiological correlates. *Arch. Gen. Psychiat., 14*(6), 595–604.

Kalichman, S. C., Hunter, T. L., & Kelly, J. A. (1993). Perceptions of AIDS susceptibility among minority and nonminority women at risk for HIV infection. *J. Cons. Clin. Psychol., 60*(5), 725–32.

Kalin, N. H., Risch, S. C., Janowsky, D. S., & Murphy, D. L. (1981). Use of the dexamethasone suppression test in clinical psychiatry. *J. Clin. Psychopharm., 1,* 64–69.

Kalinowski, L. B., & Hippius, H. (1969). *Pharmacological, convulsive and other somatic treatments in psychiatry.* New York: Grune & Stratton.

Kalint, H. (1987). The nature of addiction: An analysis of the problem. In A. Goldstein (Ed.)., *Molecular and cellular aspects of the drug addictions.* (pp. 1–28). New York: Springer-Verlag.

Kallmann, F. J. (1958). The use of genetics in psychiatry. *J. Ment. Sci., 104,* 542–49.

Kalus, O., Bernstein, D. P., & Siever, L. J. (1995). Schizoid personality disorder. In W. J. Livesley (Ed.), *The DSM-IV personality disorders.* (pp.58–70). New York: Guilford.

Kamps, D. M., Leonard, B. R., Vernon, S., & Dugan, E. P. (1992). Teaching social skills to students with autism to increase peer interactions in an integrated first-grade classroom. *J. Appl. Beh. Anal., 25,* 281–88.

Kandel, D. B., & Davies, M. (1996). High school students who use crack and other drugs. *Arch. Gen. Psychiat., 53*(1), 71–80.

Kandel, D. B., Davies, M., Karus, D., & Yamaguchi, K. (1986). The consequences in young adulthood of adolescent drug involvement. *Arch. Gen. Psychiat., 43,* 746–54.

Kandel, E., & Fried, D. (1989) Frontal-lobe dysfunction and antisocial behavior: A review. *J. Clin. Psychol., 45,* 404–13.

Kandel, E., Mednick, S. A., Kirkegaard-Sorensen, L., Hutchings, B., Knop, J., Rosenberg, R., & Schulsinger, F. (1988). IQ as a protective factor for subjects at high risk for antisocial behavior. *J. Cons. Clin. Psychol., 56,* 224–26.

Kane, J. M., & Smith, J. M. (1982). Tardive dyskinesia: Prevalence and risk factors, 1959–79. *Arch. Gen. Psychiat., 39,* 473–81.

Kane, J., Honigfeld, G., Singer, J., Meltzer, H., & Clozapine Collaborative Study Group. (1988). Clozapine for the treatment-resistant schizophrenic: A double-blind comparison with chlorpromazine. *Arch. Gen. Psychiat., 45,* 789–96.

Kang, J., Lemaire, H.-G., Unterbeck, A., Salbaum, J. M., et al. (1987). The precursor of Alzheimer's disease amyloid A4 protein resembles a cell surface receptor. *Nature, 325,* 733–36.

Kanin, E. J. (1985). Date rapists: Differential sexual socialization and relative deprivation. *Arch. Sex. Behav., 14,* 219–31.

Kanner, L., (1943). Autistic disturbances of effective content. *Nervous Child, 2,* 217–40.

Kantorovich, F. (1930). An attempt at associative reflex therapy in alcoholism. *Psychological Abstracts,* 4282.

Kaplan, H. S. (1974). *The new sex therapy.* New York: Brunner/Mazel.

Kaplan, H. S. (1987). *The illustrated manual of sex therapy* (2nd ed.). New York: Brunner/Mazel.

Kaplan, M. S., & Krueger, R. B. (1997) Voyeurism: Psychopathology and theory. In D. R. Laws & W. O'Donohue (Eds.) *Sexual deviance: Theory, assessment, and treatment.* (pp. 297–310). New York: Guilford.

Karnesh, L. J. (with collaboration of Zucker, E. M.). (1945). *Handbook of psychiatry.* St. Louis: Mosby.

Karno, M., Golding, J. M., Sorenson, S. B., & Burnam, M. A. (1988). The epidemiology of obsessive-compulsive disorder in five U.S. communities. *Arch. Gen. Psychiat., 45,* 1094–99.

Karon, B. P., & Vandenbos, G. R. (1981) *Psychotherapy of schizophrenia: Treatment of choice.* New York: Jason Aronson.

Kasari, C., & Sigman, M. (1997). Linking parental perceptions to interactions in young children with autism. *J. Autism Develop. Dis., 27*(1), 39–57.

Kashani, J. H., Hodges, K. K., Simonds, J. F., & Hilderbrand, E. (1981a). Life events and hospitalization in children: A comparison with a general population. *Brit. J. Psychiat., 139,* 221–25.

Kashani, J. H., Husain, A., Shekim, W. O., Hodges, K. K., Cytryn, L., & McKnew, D. H. (1981b). Current perspectives on childhood depression: An overview. *Amer. J. Psychiat., 138*(2), 143–53.

Kashani, J. H., & Orvaschel, H. (1988). Anxiety disorders in mid-adolescence: A community sample. *Amer. J. Psychiat., 145,* 960–64.

Kaslow, N. J., Deering, C. G., & Racusin, G. R. (1994). Depressed children and their families. *Clin. Psychol. Rev., 14,* 39–59.

Katerndahl, D. A., & Realini, J. P. (1993). Lifetime prevalence of panic states. *Amer. J. Psychiat., 150,* 246–9.

Katon, W. (1994). Primary care-psychiatry panic disorder management. In B. E. Wolfe, & J. D. Maser (Eds.), *Treatment of panic disorder : A consensus development conference.* (pp. 41–56). Washington: American Psychiatric Press.

Katon, W., Egan, K., & Miller, D. (1985). Chronic pain: Lifetime psychiatric diagnoses and family history. *Amer. J. Psychiat., 142,* 1156–60.

Katon, W., Kleinman, A., & Rosen, G. (1982). Depression and somatization: A review. Part I. *Amer. J. Med., 72,* 127–35.

Katz, L. F., & Gottman, J. M. (1997). Buffering children from marital conflict and dissolution. *J. Clin. Child Psychol., 26*(2), 157–71.

Katz, M. M., Sanborn, K. O., Lowery, H. A., & Ching, J. (1978). Ethnic studies in Hawaii: On psychopathology and social deviance. In L. C. Wynne, R. L. Cromwell, & S. Matthysse (Eds.), *The nature of schizophrenia: New approaches to research and treatment.* (pp. 572–85). New York: Wiley.

Katz, R., Frazer, N., & Wilson, L. (1993). Sexual fears are increasing. *Psychol. Rep., 73,* 476–78.

Katz, R., & McGuffin, P. (1993). The genetics of affective disorders. In L. J. Chapman, J. P. Chapman, & D. C. Fowles (Eds.), *Progress in experimental personality and psychopathology research* (Vol. 16). New York: Springer.

Katz, S., & Kravetz, S. (1989). Facial plastic surgery for persons with Down syndrome: Research findings and their professional and social implications. *Amer. J. Ment. Retard., 94,* 101–10.

Katz, S., Kravetz, S., & Marks, Y. (1997). Parents' and doctors' attitudes toward plastic facial surgery for persons with Down syndrome. *J. Intell. Develop. Dis., 22*(4), 265–73.

Katzman, R., et al. (1997). Effects of apolipoprotein E on dementia and aging in the Shanghai Survey of Dementia. *Neurology, 49*(3), 779–85.

Kaufman, I., Frank, T., Heims, L., Herrick, J., Reiser, D., & Willer, L. (1960). Treatment implications of a new classification of parents of schizophrenic children. *Amer. J. Psychiat., 116,* 920–24.

Kaufman, J. & Zigler, E. (1989). The intergerational transmission of child abuse. In D. Cicchetti & V. Carlson (Eds.), *Child maltreatment: Theory and research on the causes and consequences of child abuse and neglect.* (pp. 129–150). Cambridge: Cambridge University Press.

Kay, S. R., & Singh, M. M. (1989). The positive-negative distinction in drug-free schizophrenic patients. *Arch. Gen. Psychiat., 46,* 711–18.

Kazdin, A. E. (1980). *Behavior modification in applied settings* (2nd ed.). Homewood, IL: Dorsey Press.

Kazdin, A. E. (1992). Child and adolescent dysfunction and paths toward maladjustment: Targets for intervention. *Clin. Psychol. Rev., 12,* 795–818.

Kazdin, A. E. (1994). *Conduct disorders in childhood and adolescence.* Newbury Park, CA: Sage.

Kazdin, A. E. (1994). Methodology, design, and evaluation in psychotherapy research. In A. E. Bergin & S. L. Garfield (Eds.), *Handbook of psychotherpay and behavior change.* (pp. 19–71). New York: Wiley.

Kazdin, A. E. (1995). Conduct disorder. In F. C. Verhulst & H. M. Koot (Eds.), *The epidemiology of child and adolescent psychopathology.* (pp. 258–90). New York: Oxford University Press.

Kazdin, A. E. (1998). Conduct disorder. In R. J. Morris, T. R. Kratochwill, et al. (Eds.), *The practice of child therapy* (3rd ed.). (pp. 199–230). Boston: Allyn & Bacon.

Kazdin, A. E., Bass, D., Ayers, W.A., & Rodgers, A. (1990). Empirical and clinical focus of child and adolescent psychotherapy research. *J. Cons. Clin. Psychol., 58,* 729–40.

Kazdin, A. E., Bass, D., Siegel, T., & Thomas, C. (1989). Cognitive behavioral therapy and relationship therapy in the treatment of children referred for antisocial behavior. *J. Cons. Clin. Psychol., 57,* 522–35.

Kazdin, A. E., Holland, L., & Crowley, M. (1997). Family experience of barriers to treatment and premature termination from child therapy. *J. Cons. Clin. Psychol., 65*(3), 453–63.

Kazdin, A. E., & Wilson, G. T. (1978). *Evaluation of behavior therapy: Issues, evidence and research strategies.* Cambridge, MA: Ballinger.

Keating, J. P. (1987, Aug.). *An overview of research on human response during disasters: Major fires, earthquakes, tornadoes, and airplane accidents since 1980.* Paper presented at the American Psychological Association, New York.

Keck, P. E., & McElroy, S. L. (1998). Pharmacological treatment of biopolar disorder. In P. E. Nathan & J. M. Gorman (Eds.), *A guide to treatments that work.* (pp. 249–69). Oxford, England: Oxford University Press.

Keefe, F. J., Dunsmore, J., & Burnett, R. (1992). Behavioral and cognitive-behavioral approaches to chronic pain: Recent advances and future directions. *J. Cons. Clin. Psychol., 60*(4), 528–36.

Keefe, F. J., & Williams, D. A. (1989). New directions in pain assessment and treatment. *Clin. Psychol. Rev., 9,* 549–68.

Keefe, K., Sue, S., Enomoto, K., Durvasula, R. S., & Chao, R. (1996). Asian-American and white college students performance on the MMPI-2. In J. N. Butcher (Ed.), *International adaptations of the MMPI-2.* (pp. 206–21). Minneapolis: University of Minnesota Press.

Keefe, R. S. E., et al. (1997). Eye tracking, attention, and schizotypal symptoms in nonpsychotic relatives of patients with schizophrenia. *Arch. Gen. Psychiat., 54*(2), 169–76.

Keita, G. P., & Jones, J. M. (1990). Reducing adverse reactions to stress in the workplace: Psychology's expanding role. *Amer. Psychol., 45*(10), 1137–41.

Keith, S. J. (1993). Understanding the experience of schizophrenia (Editorial). *Amer. J. Psychiat., 150*(11), 1616–17.

Keller, M. B. (1985). Chronic and recurrent affective disorders: Incidence, course, and influencing factors. *Advances in Biochemical Psychopharmacology, 40,* 11–120.

Keller, M. B., & Shapiro, R. W. (1982). "Double Depression": Superimposition of acute depressive episodes on chronic depressive disorders. *Amer. J. Psychiat., 139,* 438–42.

Keller, M. B., Lavori, P.W., Endicott, J., Coryell, W., & Flerman, G. (1983). "Double Depression": Two-year follow-up. *Amer. J. Psychiat., 140,* 689–94.

Keller, M. B., Lavori, P. W., Rice, J., Coryell, W., & Hirschfeld, R.M.A (1986). The persistant risk of chronicity in recurrent episodes of nonbipolar major depressive disorder: A prospective follow-up. *Amer. J. Psychiat., 143,* 24–28.

Keller, M. B., Hirschfeld, R. M. A., & Hanks, D. (1997). Double depression: A distinctive subtype of unipolar depression. *J. Affect. Dis., 45,* 65–73.

Keller, M. B., Shapiro, R. W., Lavori, P. W., & Wolfe, N. (1982). Recovery in major depressive disorder: Analysis with the life table and regression models. *Arch. Gen. Psychiatr., 39,* 905–910.

Kellner, R. (1982). Disorders of impulse control (not elsewhere classified). In J. H. Griest, J. W. Jefferson, & R. L. Spitzer (Eds.), *Treatment of mental disorders.* New York: Oxford University Press.

Kellner, R. (1985). Functional somatic symptoms and hypochondriasis: A survey of empirical studies. *Arch. Gen. Psychiat., 42,* 821–33.

Kellner, R. (1990). Somatization: Theories and research. *J. Nerv. Ment. Dis., 178,* 150–60.

Kelly, J. A., & Murphy, D. A. (1992). Psychological interventions with AIDS and HIV: Prevention and treatment. *J. Cons. Clin. Psychol., 60*(4), 576–85.

Kelsoe, J. R., Ginns, E. I., Egeland, J. A., Goldstein, A. M., Bale, S. J., Pauls, D. L., Long, R. T., Conte, G., Gerhard, D. S., Housman, D. E., & Paul, S. M. (1989). Re-evaluation of the linkage relationship between chromosome 11q loci and the gene for bipolar affective disorder in the Old Order Amish. *Nature, 325,* 238–43.

Kemeny, M. E., Weiner, H., Taylor, S. E., Schneider, S., Visscher, B., & Fahey, J. L. (1994). Repeated bereavement, depressed mood, and immune parameters in HIV seropositive and seronegative gay men. *Hlth. Psychol., 13*(1), 14–24.

Kempe, R., & Kempe, H. (1979). *Child Abuse.* London: Fontana/Open Books.

Kenardy, J., Arnow, B., & Agras, S. W. (1996). The aversiveness of specific emotional states associated with binge eating in obese patients. *Austral. N.Z. J. Psychiat., 30*(6), 839–44.

Kendall, P. C. (1982a). Cognitive processes and procedures in behavior therapy. In C. M. Franks, G. T. Wilson, P. C. Kendall, & K. D. Brownell, (Eds.), *Annual Review of Behavior Therapy* (Vol. 8). New York: Guilford.

Kendall, P. C. (1982b). Integration: Behavior therapy and other schools of thought. *Behav. Ther., 13,* 559–71.

Kendall, P. C. (1990). Cognitive processes and procedures in behavior therapy. In C. M. Franks, G. T. Wilson, P. C. Kendall, & J. P. Foreyt (Eds.), *Review of behavior therapy: Theory and Practice.* (pp. 103–37). New York: Guilford.

Kendall, P. C. (1994). Treating anxiety disorders in children: Results of a randomized clinical trial. *J. Cons. Clin. Psychol., 62*(1), 100–10.

Kendall, P. C. (1998). Empirically supported psychological therapies. *J. Cons. Clin. Psychol., 66*(1), 3–7.

Kendall, P. C., & Braswell, L. (1985). *Cognitive-behavioral therapy for impulsive children.* New York: Guilford.

Kendall, P. C., Flannery-Schroeder, E., Panichelli-Mindel, S. M., Southam-Gerow, M., Henin, A., & Warman, M. (1997). Therapy for youths with anxiety disorders: A second randomized clinical trial. *J. Cons. Clin. Psychol., 65*(3), 366–80.

Kendall, P. C., & Norton-Ford, J. D. (1982). Therapy outcome research methods. In P. C. Kendall & J. N. Butcher (Eds.), *Handbook of research methods in clinical psychology.* New York: Wiley.

Kendall-Tackett, K. A., Williams, L. M., & Finkelhor, D. (1993). Impact of sexual abuse on children: a review and synthesis of recent empirical studies. *Psychol. Bull., 113,* 164–80.

Kendler, K. S. (1993). Twin studies of psychiatric illness: Current status and future directions. *Arch. Gen. Psychiat., 50,* 905–915.

Kendler, K. S. (1996). Major depression and generalised anxiety disorder: same genes, (partly) different environments — revisited. *Brit. J. Psychiat., 168*(30), 68–75.

Kendler, K. S. (1997). The diagnostic validity of melancholic major depression in a population-based sample of female twins. *Arch. Gen. Psychiat., 54,* 299–304.

Kendler, K. S., & Davis, K. L. (1981). The genetics and biochemistry of paranoid schizophrenia and other paranoid psychoses. *Schizo. Bull., 7,* 689–709.

Kendler, K. S., & Diehl, S. R. (1993). The genetics of schizophrenia: A current, genetic-epidemiologic perspective. *Schizo. Bull.,19*(2), 261–85.

Kendler, K. S., & Gardner, C. O. (1997). The risk for psychiatric disorders in relatives of schizophrenic and control probands: A comparison of three independent studies. *Psychol. Med., 27,* 411–419.

Kendler, K. S., & Gruenberg, A. M. (1982). Genetic relationship between paranoid personality disorder and the "schizophrenic" spectrum disorders. *Amer. J. Psychiat., 139*(9), 1185–86.

Kendler, K. S., & Gruenberg, A. M. (1984). An independent analysis of the Danish adoption study of schizophrenia: VI. The relationship between psychiatric disorders as defined by DSM-III in the relatives and adoptees. *Arch. Gen. Psychiat., 41,* 555–64.

Kendler, K. S., Gruenberg, A. M., & Kinney, D. K. (1994a). Independent diagnoses of adoptees and relatives as defined by DSM-III in the provincial and national samples of the Danish adoption study of schizophrenia. *Arch. Gen. Psychiat., 51*(6), 456–68.

Kendler, K. S., & Karkowski-Shuman, L. (1997). Stressful life events and genetic liability to major depression: Genetic control of exposure to the environment? *Psychol. Med., 27,* 539–47.

Kendler, K. S., Kessler, R. D., Walters, E. E., MacLean, C., et al. (1995). Stressful life events, genetic liability, and onset of an episode of major depression in women. *Amer. J. Psychiat., 152*(2), 833–42.

Kendler, K. S., McGuire, M., Gruenberg, A. M., & Walsh, D. (1994b). Outcome and family study of the subtypes of schizophrenia in the west of Ireland. *Amer. J. Psychiat., 151*(6), 849–56.

Kendler, K. S., McGuire, M., Gruenberg, A. M., & Walsh, D. (1995). Examining the validity of DSM-III-R schizoaffective disorder and its putative subtypes in the Roscommon Family Study. *Amer. J. Psychiat., 152*(5) 755–64.

Kendler, K. S., Neale, M. C., Kessler, R. C., Heath, A. C., & Eaves, L. J. (1992a). Generalized anxiety disorder in women: A population-based twin study. *Arch. Gen. Psychiat., 49,* 267–72.

Kendler, K. S., Neale, M. C., Kessler, R. C., Heath, A. C., & Eaves, L. J. (1992b). The genetic epidemiology of phobias in women: The interrelationship of agoraphobia, social phobia, situational phobia, and simple phobia. *Arch. Gen. Psychiat., 49,* 273–81.

Kendler, K. S., Neale, M. C., Kessler, R. C., Heath, A. C., & Eaves, L. J. (1992d). Major depression and generalized anxiety disorder. Same genes, (partly) different environments? *Arch. Gen. Psychiat., 49,* 716–22.

Kendler, K. S., Neale, M. C., Kessler, R. C., Heath, A. C., & Eaves, L. J. (1993a). Panic disorder in women: A population-based twin study. *Psychological Medicine, 23,* 397–406.

Kendler, K. S., Neale, M. C., Kessler, R. C., Heath, A. C., & Eaves, L. J. (1992c). A population-based twin study of major depression in women: The impact of varying definitions of illness. *Arch. Gen. Psychiat., 49,* 257–66.

Kendler, K. S., Neale, M., Kessler, R., Heath, A., & Eaves, L. (1993b). A twin study of recent life events and difficulties. *Arch. Gen. Psychiat., 50*(10), 789–96.

Kendler, K. S., Ochs, A. L., Gorman, A. M., Hewitt, J. K., Ross D.E., & Mirsky, A. F. (1991). The structure of schizotypy: A pilot multitrait twin study. *Psychiat. Res., 36,* 19–36.

Kendler, K. S., & Tsuang, M. T. (1981). Nosology of paranoid schizophrenia and other paranoid psychoses. *Schizo. Bull., 7,* 594–610.

Kendler, K. S., & Walsh, D. (1995). Schizotypal personality disorder in parents and the risk for schizophrenia in siblings. *Schizo. Bull., 21*(1), 47–52.

Kendler, K. S., Walters, E. E., Neale, M. C., Kessler, R. C., Heath, A., & Eaves, L. J. (1995). The structure of the genetic and environmental risk factors for six major psychiatric disorders in women: Phobia, generalized anxiety disorder, panic disorder, bulimia, major depression, and alcoholism. *Arch. Gen. Psychiat., 52,* 374–83.

Kendler. K. S., Walters, E. E., & Kessler, R. C. (1997). The prediction of length of major depressive episodes: Results from an epidemiological sample of female twins. *Psychol. Med., 27,* 107–17.

Kennedy, J. F. (1963). Message from the President of the United States relative to mental illness and mental retardation. *Amer. Psychol., 18,* 280–89.

Kennedy, T. D., & Kimura, H. K. (1974). Transfer, behavioral improvement, and anxiety reduction in systematic desensitization. *J. Cons. Clin. Psychol., 42*(5), 720–28.

Kenny, J. T., et al. (1997). Cognitive impairment in adolescents with schizophrenia. *Amer. J. Psychiat., 154*(11), 1613–15.

Kent, G. (1997). Dental phobias. In G. C. L. Davey, (Ed.), *Phobias. A handbook of theory, research and treatment.* (pp. 107–27). Chichester, England: Wiley.

Keppel-Benson, J. M.. & Ollendick, T. H. (1993). Posttraumatic stress disorder in children and adolescents. In C.F. Saylor (Ed.), *Children and disasters.* (pp. 29–44). New York: Plenum.

Kern, P. A., Trozzolino, L., Wolfe, G., & Purdy, L. (1994). Combined use of behavior modification and very low-calorie diet in weight loss and weight maintenance. *Amer. J. Med. Sci., 307,* 325–28.

Kernberg, O. F. (1984). *Severe personality disorders.* New Haven, CT: Yale University Press.

Kernberg, O. F. (1985). *Borderline conditions and pathological narcissism.* Northvale, NJ: Jason Aronson.

Kernberg, O. F. (1996). A psychoanalytic theory of personality disorders. In J. F. Clarkin & M. F. Lenzenweger (Eds.), *Major theories of personality disorder.* (pp. 106–140). New York: Guilford.

Kershner, J. G., Cohen, N. J., & Coyne, J. C. (1998). Expressed emotion in families of clinically referred and nonreferred children: Toward a further understanding of the expressed emotion index. *Journal of Family Psychology, 10*(1), 97–106.

Kesey, K. (1962). *One flew over the cuckoo's nest.* New York: Signet.

Kessler, J. W. (1988). *Psychopathology of childhood* (2nd ed.). Englewood Cliffs, NJ: PrenticeHall.

Kessler, M., & Albee, G. W. (1975). Primary prevention. *Annu. Rev. Psychol., 26,* 557–91.

Kessler, R. C. (1997a). The effects of stressful life events on depression. *Annu. Rev. Psychol., 48,* 191–214.

Kessler, R. C. (1997b). The prevalence of psychiatric comorbidity. In S. Wetzler, & W. C. Sanderson (Eds.), *Treatment strategies for patients with psychiatric comorbidity.* (pp. 23–48). New York: Wiley.

Kessler, R. C., McGonagle, K. A., Zhao, S., Nelson, C. B., Hughes, M., Eshleman, S., Wittchen, H.-U., & Kendler, K. S. (1994). Lifetime and 12-month prevalence of DSM-III-R psychiatric disorders in the United States: Results from the national comorbidity survey. *Arch. Gen. Psychiat., 51,* 8–19.

Kessler, R. C., Sonnega, A., Bromet, E., Hughes, M., & Nelson, C. B. (1995). Posttraumatic stress disorder in the national comorbidity survey. *Arch. Gen. Psychiat., 52,* 1048–60.

Ketterer, M. W. (1993). Secondary prevention of ischemic heart disease. *Psychosimatics, 34,* 478–84.

Kety, S. S. (1974). From rationalization to reason. *Amer. J. Psychiat., 131,* 957–963.

Kety, S. S. (1987). The significance of genetic factors in the etiology of schizophrenia. *J. Psychiat. Res., 21,* 423–29.

Kety, S. S., Rosenthal, D., Wender, P. H., & Schulsinger, F. (1968). The types and prevalence of mental illness in the biological and adoptive families of adopted schizophrenics. In D. Rosenthal & S. S. Kety (Eds.), *The transmission of schizophrenia.* Elmsford, NY: Pergamon.

Kety, S. S., Rosenthal, D., Wender, P. H., Schulsinger, F., & Jacobsen, B. (1975). Mental illness in the biological and adoptive families of adopted individuals who have become schizophrenics: A preliminary report based on psychiatric interviews. In R. Fieve, P. Rosenthal, & H. Brill (Eds.), *Genetic research in psychiatry.* Baltimore: Johns Hopkins University Press.

Kety, S. S., Rosenthal, D., Wender, P. H., Schulsinger, F., & Jacobsen, B. (1978). The biologic and adoptive families of adopted individuals who became schizophrenic: Prevalence of mental illness and other characteristics. In L. C. Wynne, R. L. Cromwell, & S. Matthyse (Eds.), *The nature of schizophrenia: New approaches to research and treatment.* (pp. 25–37). New York: Wiley.

Kety, S. S., Wender, P. H., Jacobsen, B., Ingraham, L. J., Jansson, L., Faber, B., & Kinney, D. K. (1994). Mental illness in the biological and adoptive relatives of schizophrenic adoptees: Replication of the Copenhagen study in the rest of Denmark. *Arch. Gen. Psychiat., 51*(6), 442–55.

Kewman, D., & Roberts, A. H. (1979). *Skin temperature biofeedback and migraine headaches.* Paper presented at the Annual Conference of the Biofeedback Society of America, San Diego.

Keys, A., Brozek, J., Henschel, A., Mickelson, O., & Taylor, H. L. (1950). *The biology of human starvation.* Minneapolis: University of Minnesota Press.

Khan, A. E., Mirolo, H., Hughes, D., & Bierut, L. (1993). Electroconvulsive therapy. *Psychiat. Clin. N. Amer., 16,* 497–514.

Khan, A., Cowan, C., & Roy, A. (1997). Personality disorders in people with learning disabilities: A community survey. *J. Intell. Dis. Res., 41*(4), 324–30.

Kidd, K. K., & Morton, L. A. (1989). The genetics of psychosomatic disorders. In S. Cheren (Ed.), *Psychosomatic medicine: Theory, physiology, and practice* (Vol. 1). (pp. 385–424). Madison, CT: International Universities Press.

Kidson, M. A. (1973). Personality and hypertension. *J. Psychosom. Res., 17*(1), 35–41.

Kidson, M., & Jones, I. (1968). Psychiatric disorders among aborigines of the Australian Western Desert. *Arch. Gen. Psychiat., 19,* 413–22.

Kiecolt-Glaser, J., & Glaser, R. (1988). Psychological influences in immunity: Implications for AIDS. *Amer. Psychol., 43,* 892–98.

Kiecolt-Glaser, J. K., & Glaser, R. (1992). Psychoneuroimmunology: Can psychological interventions modulate immunity? *J. Cons. Clin. Psychol., 60*(4), 569–75.

Kiecolt-Glaser, J. K., Kennedy, S., Malkoff, S., Fisher, L., Speicher, D. E., & Glaser, R. (1988). Marital discord and immunity in males. *Psychosom. Med., 50,* 213–29.

Kiernan, C. (1985). Behaviour modification. In A. M. Clarke, A. D. B. Clarke, & J. M. Berg (Eds.), *Mental deficiency: The changing outlook* (4th ed.). (pp. 465–511). London: Methuen.

Kiersch, T. A. (1962). Amnesia: A clinical study of ninety-eight cases. *Amer. J. Psychiat., 119,* 57–60.

Kiesler, C. A. (1983). Social psychologic issues in studying consumer satisfaction with behavior therapy. *Behav. Ther., 14,* 226–36.

Kiesler, C. A. (1993b). Mental Health Policy and Mental Hospitalization. *Curr. Dir. Psychol. Sci., 2*(3), 93–95.

Kiesler, C. A., & Simpkins, C. G. (1993). *The unnoticed majority in inpatient psychiatric care.* New York: Plenum.

Kiesler, D. J. (1996). Contemporary interpersonal theory and research. New York: Wiley.

Kiev, A. (1972). *Transcultural psychiatry.* New York: Free Press.

Kihlstrom, J. F. (1990). The psychological unconscious. In L. Pervin (Eds.), *Handbook of personality: Theory and research.* (pp. 445–64). New York: Guilford.

Kihlstrom, J. F. (1994). One hundred years of hysteria. In S. J. Lynn & J. W. Rhue (Eds.), *Dissociation: Clinical and theoretical perspectives.* (pp. 365–94). New York: Guilford.

Kihlstrom, J. F., Glisky, M. L., & Angiulo, M. J. (1994). Dissociative tendencies and dissociative disorders. *J. Abn. Psychol., 103*(1), 117–24.

Kihlstrom, J. F., Tataryn, D. J., & Hoyt, I. P. (1993). Dissociative disorders. In P. B. Sutker & H. E. Adams (Eds.), *Comprehensive handbook of psychopathology.* (pp. 203–34). New York: Plenum.

Killen, J. D., Fortmann, S. P., Davis, L., & Varady, A. (1997). Nicotine patch and self-}help video for cigarette smoking cessation. *J. Cons. Clin. Psychol., 65*(4), 663–72.

Kilpatrick, D. G., Sutker, P. B., Roitch, J. C., & Miller, W. C. (1976). Personality correlates of polydrug users. *Psychol. Rep., 38,* 311–17.

Kim, A., Galanter, M., Castaneda, R., & Lifshutz, H. (1992). Crack cocaine use and sexual behavior among psychiatric inpatients. *Amer. J. Drug Alcoh. Abuse, 18,* 235–46.

Kim, K., & Jacobs, S. (1995). Stress bereavement and consequent psychiatric illness. In C. M. Mazure (Ed.), *Does stress cause psychiatric illness?* Washington, DC: American Psychiatric Association.

Kimerling, R., & Calhoun, K. S. (1994). Somatic symptoms, social support, and treatment seeking among sexual assault victims. *J. Cons. Clin. Psychol., 62,* 333–40.

Kimmel, H. D. (1974). Instrumental conditioning of autonomically mediated responses. *Amer. Psychol., 29,* 325–35.

Kinderman, P., & Bentall, R. P. (1997). Causal attributions in paranoia and depression: Internal, personal, and situational attributions for negative events. *J. Abn. Psychol., 106*(2), 341–45.

King, C. A. (1997). Suicidal behavior in adolescence. In R. W. Maris, M. M. Silverman, & S. S. Canetton (Eds.), *Review of Suicidology, 1997.* (pp. 61–95). New York: Guilford.

King, H. F., Carroll, J. L., & Fuller, G. B. (1977). Comparison of nonpsychiatric blacks and whites on the MMPI. *J. Clin. Psychol., 33,* 725–28.

Kinney, D. K., Holzman, P. S., Jacobsen, B., Jansson, L., Faber, B., Hildebrand, K., Kasell, E., & Zimbalist, M. E. (1997). Thought disorder in schizophrenic and control adoptees and their relatives. *Arch. Gen. Psychiat., 54*(5), 475–79.

Kinney, D. K., Woods, B. T., & Yurgelun-Todd, D. (1986). Neurologic abnormalities in schizophrenic patients and their families: II. Neurologic and psychiatric findings in relatives. *Arch. Gen. Psychiat., 43,* 665–68.

Kinon, B. J., & Lieberman, J. A. (1996). Mechanisms of action of atypical antipsychotic drugs: A critical analysis. *Psychophar. 124,* 2–34.

Kinsey, A. C., Pomeroy, W. B., & Martin, C. E. (1948). *Sexual behavior in the human male.* Philadelphia: Sanders.

Kinsey, A. C., Pomeroy, W. B., Martin, C. E., & Gebhard, P. H. (1953). *Sexual behavior in the human female.* Philadelphia: Saunders.

Kinzie, J. D., & Bolton, J. M. (1973). Psychiatry with the aborigines of West Malaysia. *Amer. J. Psychiat.,* 130(7), 769–73.

Kinzl, J., & Biebl, W. (1992). Long-term effects of incest: Life events triggering mental disorders in female patients with sexual abuse in childhood. *Child Ab. Negl., 16,* 567–73.

Kirch, D. G. (1993). Infection and autoimmunity as etiologic factors in schizophrenia: A review and reappraisal. *Schizo. Bull., 19*(2), 355–70.

Kirmayer, L. J. (1984). Culture, affect, and somatization: Part I. *Transcultural Psychiatric Research Review, 21,* 159–88.

Kirmayer, L. J. (1991). The place of culture in psychiatric nosology: Taijin Kyofusho and DSM III-R. *J. Nerv. Ment. Dis., 179,* 19–28.

Kirmayer, L. J., Robbins, J. M., & Paris, J. (1994). Somatoform disorders: Personality and the social matrix of somatic distress. *J. Abn. Psychol., 103*(1), 125–36.

Kirmayer, L. J., Young, A., Hayton, B. C. (1995). The cultural context of anxiety disorders. *Cultural Psychiat., 18*(3), 503–21.

Kirsch, I., Lynn, S. J., & Rhue, J. W. (1993). Introduction to clinical hypnosis. In J. W. Rhue, S. J. Lynn, & I. Kirsch (Eds.), *Handbook of clinical hypnosis.* (pp. 3–22). Washington, DC: American Psychological Association.

Kirstein, L., Prusoff, B., Weissman, M., & Dressler, D. M. (1975). Utilization review of treatment for suicide attempters. *Amer. J. Psychiat., 132*(1), 22–27.

Klackenberg, G. (1987). Incidence of parasomnias in children in a general population. In C. Guilleminault (Ed.), *Sleep and its disorders in children.* (pp. 99–113). New York: Raven Press.

Klassen, D., & O'Connor, W. A. (1988). A prospective study of predictors of violence in adult male mental health admissions. *Law and Human Behavior, 12,* 143–58.

Klee, H. (1998). The love of speed: An analysis of the enduring attraction of amphetamine sulphate for British youth. *Journal of Drug Issues, 28*(1), 33–56.

Klein, D. F. (1981). Anxiety reconceptualized. In D. F. Klein & J. Rabkin (Eds.), *Anxiety: New research and changing concepts.* New York: Raven Press.

Klein, D. F. (1993). False suffocation alarms, spontaneous panics, and related conditions. *Arch. Gen. Psychiat., 50,* 306–17.

Klein, D. N. (1990). Depressive personality: Reliability, validity, and relation to dysthymia. *J. Abn. Psychol., 99,* 412–21.

Klein, D. N., & Depue, R. A. (1984). Continued impairment in persons at risk for bipolar affective disorder: Results of a 19-month follow-up study. *J. Abn. Psychol., 93,* 345–47.

Klein, D. N., & Depue, R. A. (1985). Obsessional personality traits and risk for bipolar affective disorder: An offspring study. *J. Abn. Psychol., 94,* 291–397.

Klein, D. N., & Shih, J. H. (1998). Depressive personality: Association with DSM-III-R mood and personality disorders and negative and positive affectivity, 30-month stability, and prediciton of course of axis I depressive disorders. *J. Abn. Psychol., 107*(2), 319–327.

Klein, D. N., Depue, R. A., & Slater, J. F. (1985). Cyclothymia in the adolescent offspring of parents with bipolar affective disorder. *J. Abn. Psychol., 94,* 115–27.

Klein, D. N., Depue, R. A., & Slater, J. F. (1986). Inventory identification of cyclothymia: IX. Validations in offspring of bipolar I patients. *Arch. Gen. Psychiat., 43,* 441–45.

Klein, D. N., Riso, L. P., & Anderson, R. L. (1993). DSM-III-R dysthymia: Antecedents and underlying assumptions. In L.J. Chapman, J.P. Chapman, & D.C. Fowles (Eds.), *Experimental personality and psychopathology research* (Vol. 16). New York: Springer.

Klein, M. (1934). A contribution to the psychogenesis of manic-depressive states. In *Contributions to psychoanalysis, 1921–1945.* (pp. 282–310). London: Hogarth Press.

Klein, R. G. (1995). The role of methylphenidate in psychiatry. *Arch. Gen. Psychiat., 52,* 429–32.

Klein, R. G., Koplewicz, H. S., & Kanner, A. (1992). Imipramine treatment of children with separation anxiety disorder. *J. Amer. Acad. Child Adoles. Psychiat., 31,* 21–28.

Kleinknecht, R. A., Dinnel, D. L., & Kleinknecht, E. E. (1997). Cultural factors in social anxiety: A comparison of social phobia symptoms and Taijin Kyofusho. *J. Anxiety Dis., 11*(2), 157–77.

Kleinman, A. (1988). *Rethinking psychiatry: From cultural category to personal experience.* New York: Free Press.

Kleinman, A. M. (1986). *Social origins of distress and disease: Depression, neurasthenia and pain in modern China.* New Haven, CT: Yale University Press.

Kleinman, A. M., & Good, B. J. (1985). *Culture and depression.* Berkeley, CA: University of California Press.

Kleinman, P. H., Kang, S., Lipton, D. S., & Woody, G. E. (1992). Retention of cocaine abusers in outpatient psychotherapy. *Amer. J. Drug Alcoh. Abuse, 18,* 29–43.

Kleinmuntz, B. (1990). Why we still use our heads instead of formulas: Toward an integrative approach. *Psychol. Bull., 107,* 296–310.

Klem, M. L., Wing, R. R., McGuire, M. T., Seagle, H. M., & Hill, J. O. (1997). A descriptive study of individuals successful at long-term maintenance of substantial weight loss. *Amer. J. Clin. Nutri., 66,* 239–46.

Klepac, R. K., Hauge, G., Dowling, J., & McDonald, M. (1981). Direct and generalized effects of three components of stress-inoculation for increased pain tolerance. *Behav. Ther., 12,* 417–24.

Klerman, G. L. (1982). Practical issues in the treatment of depression and mania. In E. S. Paykel (Ed.), *Handbook of affective disorders.* New York: Guilford.

Klerman, G. L. (1990). The psychiatric patient's right to effective treatment: Implications of *Osheroff v. Chestnut Lodge. Amer. J. Psychiat., 147,* 409–18.

Klerman, G. L. (1991). Ideological conflicts in integrating pharmacotherapy and psychotherapy. In B. D. Beitman & G. L. Klerman (Eds.), *Integrating pharmocotherapy and psychotherapy.* (pp. 3–20). Washington, DC: American Psychiatric Press.

Klerman, G. L. (1994). Drugs and psychotherapy. In A. Bergin & S. Garfield (Eds.), *Handbook of psychotherapy and behavior change* (4th ed.). New York: Wiley.

Klerman, G. L., Weissman, M. M., Markowitz, J. C., Glick, I., Wilner, P. J., Mason, B., & Shear, M. K. (1994). Medication and psychotherapy. In A. E. Bergin & S. L. Garfield (Eds.), *Handbook of psychotherapy and behavior change* (4th ed.). (pp. 734–82). New York: Wiley.

Klerman, G. L., Weissman, M. M., Rounsaville, B. J., & Chevron, E. S. (1984). *Interpersonal psychotherapy of depression.* New York: Basic Books.

Klerman, G. L., & Weissman, M. M. (Ed.). (1993). *New applications of interpersonal psychotherapy.* Washington: American Psychiatric Press.

Kliewer, W., Lepore, S. J., Oskin, D., & Johnson, P. D. (1998). The role of social and cognitive processes in children's adjustment to community violence. *J. Cons. Clin. Psychol., 66*(1), 199–209.

Klinger, E. (1979). Modes of normal conscious flow. In K. S. Pope & J. L. Singer (Eds.), *The stream of consciousness: Scientific investigations into the flow of human experience.* New York: Plenum.

Klinger, E., & Kroll-Mensing, D. (1995). Idiothetic assessment. In J. N. Butcher (Ed.), *Clinical personality assessment: Practical considerations.* (pp. 267–77). New York: Oxford Unicersity Press.

Klingman, A. (1993). School-based intervention following a disaster. In C. F. Saylor (Ed.), *Children and disasters.* (pp. 187–210). New York: Plenum.

Klorman, R., Brumaghim, J. T., Fitzpatrick, P. A., Borgstedt, A. D., & Strauss, J. (1994). Clinical and cognitive effects of Methylphenidate on children with attention deficit disorders as a function of aggression, opporitionality and age. *J. Abn. Psychol., 103,* 206–21.

Klosko, J. S., Barlow, D. H., Tassinari, R., & Cerny, J. A. (1990). A comparison of alprazolam and behavior therapy in the treatment of panic disorder. *J. Cons. Clin. Psychol., 58,* 77–84.

Kluft, R. P. (1993). Basic principles in conducting the treatment of multiple personality disorder. In R. P. Kluft & C. G. Fine (Eds.), *Clinical perspectives on multiple personality disorder.* (pp. 53–73). Washington: American Psychiatric Press.

Knapp, P. H. (1989). Psychosomatic aspects of bronchial asthma: A review. In S. Cheren (Ed.), *Psychosomatic medicine: Theory, physiology, and practice* (Vol. 2). (pp. 503–64). Madison, CT: International Universities Press.

Knapp, S. (1980). A primer on malpractice for psychologists. *Profess. Psychol., 11*(4), 606–12.

Knight, R. A. (1997). *A unified model of sexual aggression: Consistencies and differences across noncriminal and criminal samples.* Paper presented at meeting of the Association for the Treatment of Sexual Abusers, Arlington, VA.

Knight, R., & Prentky, R. (1990). Classifying sexual offenders: The development and corroboration of taxonomic models. In W. L. Marshall, D. R. Laws, & H. E. Barbaree (Eds.), *Handbook of sexual assault: Issues, theories, and treatment of the offender.* (pp. 23–52). New York: Plenum.

Knight, R., Prentky, R., & Cerce, D. (1994). The development, reliability, and validity of an inventory for the multidimensional assessment of sex and aggression. *Crim. Just. Behav., 21,* 72–94.

Knowles, J. H. (1977). Editorial. *Science, 198,* 1103–4.

Kobak, K. A., Taylor, L., Dottl, S. L., Greist, J. H., et al. (1997). Computerized screening for psychiatric disorders in an outpatient community mental health clinic. *Psychiat. Serv., 48*(8), 1048–57.

Kobasa, S. C. O. (1979). Stressful life events, personality, and health: An inquiry into hardiness. *J. Pers. Soc. Psychol., 37*(1), 1–11.

Kobasa, S. C. O. (1985). Personality and health: Specifying and strengthening the conceptual fit. In P. Shaver (Ed.), *Self situations and social behavior.* (pp. 291–311). Beverly Hills, CA: Sage.

Koch, R. (1967). The multidisciplinary approach to mental retardation. In A. A. Baumeister (Ed.), *Mental retardation: Appraisal, education, and rehabilitation.* Chicago: Aldine.

Kocsis, J. H. (1997). Chronic depression: The efficacy of pharmacotherapy. In H. S Akiskal, & G. B. Cassano (Eds.), *Dysthymia and the spectrum of chronic depressions* (pp. 66–74). New York: Guliford.

Kocsis, J. H., Zisook, S., Davidson, J., Shelton, R., Yonkers, K., Hellerstein, D. J., Rosenbaum, J., Halbreich, U. (1997). Double-Blind comparisons of sertraline, imipramine, and placebo in the treatment of dysthymia: Psychosocial outcomes. *Amer. J. Psychiat., 154*(3), 390–95.

Koegel, L. K., Koegel, R. L., Hurley, C., & Frea, W. D. (1992). Improving social skills and disruptive behavior in children with autism through self-management. *J. Appl. Behav. Anal., 25,* 341–53.

Koegel, R. L., & Mentis, M. (1985). Motivation in childhood autism: Can they or won't they? *J. Child Psychol. Psychiat., 26*(2), 185–91.

Kog, E., & Vandereycken, W. (1985). Family characteristics of anorexia nervosa and bulimia: A review of the research literature. *Clin. Psychol. Rev., 5,* 159–80.

Kohn, M. L. (1973). Social class and schizophrenia: A critical review and a reformulation. *Schizo. Bull., 7,* 60–79.

Kohut, H. (1977). *The restoration of the self.* New York: International Universities Press.

Kohut, H., & Wolff, E. (1978). The disorders of the self and their treatment: An outline. *Inter. J. Psychoanal., 59,* 413–26.

Kolata, G. (1998, April 4). New drug for impotence raises hope for its use by women, too. *New York Times.*

Kolata, G. B. (1981a). Clues to the cause of senile dementia: Patients with Alzheimer's disease seem to be deficient in a brain neurotransmitter. *Science, 211,* 1032–33.

Kolata, G. B. (1981b). Fetal alcohol advisory debated. *Science, 214,* 642–46.

Kolko, D. J., & Kazdin, A. E. (1991). Aggression and psychopathology in match-playing and firesetting children. *J. Clin. Child Psychol., 20,* 191–201.

Koltek, M., Wilkes, T. C. R., & Atkinson, M. (1998). The prevalence of posttraumatic stress disorder in an adolescent inpatient unit. *Canad. J. Psychiat., 43*(1), 64–8.

Koob, G. F., & Nestler, E. J. (1997). Neurobiology of drug addiction. *J. Neuropsychiat. Clin. Neurosci., 9*(3), 482–97.

Koopman, C., Classen, C., & Spiegel, D. (1997). Multiple stressors following a disaster and dissociative symptoms. In C. S. Fullerton & R. J. Ursano (Eds.), *Posttraumatic stress disorder.* (pp. 21–35). Washington: American Psychiatric Press.

Kopelman, M. D. (1986). The cholinergic neurotransmitter system in human memory and dementia: A review. *Q. J. Exp. Psychol. [A], 38,* 535–73.

Kopelman, M. D. (1991). Non-verbal, short-term forgetting in the alcoholic Korsakoff syndrome and Alzheimer-type dementia. *Neuropsychologia, 29,* 737–47.

Kopelowicz, A. (1997). Integrating psychotherapy and pharmacotherapy for schizophrenia. *In Session: Psychotherapy in Practice, 3*(2), 79–98.

Kopelowicz, A., & Liberman, R. P. (1998). Psychosocial treatments for schizophrnia. In P. E. Nathan & J. M. Gorman (Eds.), *A guide to treatments that work.* (pp. 190–211). New York: Oxford University Press.

Kopp C. B., & Kaler, S. R. (1989). Risk in infancy: Origins and implications. Special issue: Children and their development: Knowledge base, research agenda, and social policy application. *Amer. Psychol., 44,* 224–230.

Koran, L. M., McElroy, S. L., Davidson, J. R. T., Rasmussen, S. A., Hollander, E., & Jenike, M. A. (1996). Fluvoxamine versus clomipramine for obsessive -compulsive disorder: A double-blind comparison. *J. Clin. Psychopharm., 16*(2), 121–29.

Koranyi, E. K. (1989). Physiology of stress reviewed. In S. Cheren (Ed.), *Psychosomatic medicine: Theory, physiology, and practice* (Vol. 1). (pp. 241–78). Madison, CT: International Universities Press.

Koreen, A. R., Lieberman, J., Alvir, J., Mayerhoff, D., Loebel, A., Chakos, M., Farooq, A., & Cooper, T. (1994). Plasma homovanillic acid levels in first-episode schizophrenia: Psychopathology and treatment response. *Arch. Gen. Psychiat., 51*(2), 132–38.

Kornberg, M. S., & Caplan, G. (1980). Risk factors and preventive intervention in child psychopathology: A review. *Journal of Prevention, 1,* 71–133.

Koscheyev, V. S. (1990, Oct.). *Psychological functioning of Chernobyl workers in the period after the nuclear accident.* Invited address. University of Minnesota.

Koscheyev, V. S., Martens, V. K., Kosenkov, A. A., Lartzev, M. A., & Leon, G. R. (1993). Psychological status of Chernobyl Nuclear Power Plant operators after the nuclear disaster. *J. Trauma. Stress, 6,* 561–68.

Koslow, S. H., Maas, J. W., Bowden, C. L., Davis, J. M., Hanin, I., & Javaid, J. (1983). CSF and urinary biogenic amines and metabolites in depression and mania: A controlled, univariate analysis. *Arch. Gen. Psychiat., 40,* 999–1010.

Koss, M. P. (1983). The scope of rape: Implications for the clinical treatment of victims. *Clin. Psychol., 36,* 88–91.

Koss, M. P. (1993). Detecting the scope of rape: A review of prevalence research methods. *J. Interpers. Violen., 8,* 198–222.

Koss, M. P., & Dinero, T. E. (1989). Discriminant analysis of risk factors for sexual victimization among a national sample of college women. *J. Cons. Clin. Psychol., 57,* 242–50.

Koss, M. P., Dinero, T. E., Seibel, C. A., & Cox, S. L. (1988). Stranger and acquaintance rape: Are there differences in the victim's experience? *Psychology of Women Quarterly, 12,* 1–23.

Koss, M. P., Gidycz, C. A., & Wisniewski, N. (1987). The scope of rape: Incidence and prevalence of sexual aggression and victimization in a national sample of higher education students. *J. Cons. Clin. Psychol., 55,* 162–70.

Koss, M. P., & Oros, C. J. (1982). Sexual experiences survey: A research instrument investigating sexual aggression and victimization. *J. Cons. Clin. Psychol., 50,* 455–57.

Koss, M., & Shiang, J. (1994). Research on brief psychotherapy. In A. E. Bergin & S. L. Garfield (Eds.), *Handbook of psychotherapy and behavior change* (4th ed.). (pp. 664–700). New York: Wiley.

Kosslyn, S. M., Alpert, N. M., Thompson, W. L., et al. (1993). Visual memory imagery activates topographically organized visual cortex: PET investigations. *J. Cog. Neurosci. 5*(3), 263–87.

Kosten, T. R. (1989). Pharmacotherapeutic interventions for cocaine abuse. Matching patients to treatments. *J. Nerv. Ment. Dis., 177,* 379–89.

Kosten, T. R. (1997). Substance abuse and schizophrenia. *Schizo. Bull., 23,* 181–86.

Kosten, T. R., & Rounsaville, B. J. (1986). Psychopathology in opioid addicts. *Psychiat. Clin. N. Amer., 9,* 515–32.

Kosten, T. R., Rounsaville, B. J., & Kleber, H. D. (1988). Antecedents and consequences of cocaine abuse among opioid addicts. A 2.5 year follow-up. *J. Nerv. Ment. Dis., 176,* 176–81.

Kosten, T. R., Silverman, D. G., Fleming, J., & Kosten, T. A. (1992). Intravenous cocaine challenges during naltrexone maintenance: A preliminary study. *Biol. Psychiat., 32,* 543–48.

Kosten, T. R., & Ziedonis, D. M. (1997). Substance abuse and schizophrenia: Editors' introduction. *Schizo. Bull., 23*(2), 181–86.

Kovacs, M. (1996). The course of childhood onset depressive disorders. *Psychiat. Ann., 26*(6), 326–30.

Kovacs, M., Devlin, B., Pollack, M., Richards, C., & Mukerji, P. (1997). A controlled family history study of childhood-onset depressive disorder. *Arch. Gen. Psychiat., (54),* 613–23.

Kozleski, E. B., & Jackson, L. (1993). Taylor's story: Full inclusion in her neighborhood elementary school. *Except., 4*(3), 153–75.

Kraemer, H. C. (1997). What is the 'right' statistical measure of twin concordance (or diagnostic reliability and validity)? *Arch. Gen. Psychiat., 54*(12), 1121–24.

Kraepelin, E. (1883). *Compendium der psychiatrie.* Leipzig: Abel.

Kraepelin, E. (1899). *Psychiatrie. Ein lehrbuch fur studierende und aerzte* (6th ed.). Leipzig: Barth.

Kraepelin, E. (1922). *Manic depressive insanity of paranoia* (trans. R. M. Barclay). Edinburgh: E. & S. Livingstone.

Krafft-Ebing, R. V. (1950). *Psychopathica sexualis.* New York: Pioneer Publications.

Kraines, S. H. (1948). *The therapy of the neuroses and psychoses* (3rd ed.). Philadelphia: Lea & Febiger.

Kramer, P. D. (1993). *Listening to Prozac: A psychiatrist explores antidepressant drugs and the remaking of the self.* New York: Viking Penguin.

Kramer, P. D. (1998, May 6). The mentally ill deserve job protection. *New York Times,* p. A19

Kramer, R. A., Warner, V., Olfson, M., Ebanks, C. M., Chaput, F., & Weissman, M. M. (1998). General medical problems among the offspring of depressed parents: A 10-year follow-up. *J. Amer. Acad. Child & Adoles. Psychiat., 37*(6), 602–11.

Kramer, R. M. (1998). Paranoid cognition in social systems: Thinking and acting in the shadow of doubt. *Personal. Soc. Psychol. Rev., 2*(4), 251–75.

Krantz, D. S., & Glass, D. C. (1984). Personality, behavior patterns, and physical illness: Conceptual and methodological issues. In W. D. Gentry (Ed.), *Handbook of behavioral medicine.* (pp. 38–86). New York: Guilford.

Kranzler, H. R., Del Boca, F. K., & Rounsaville, B. (1997). Comorbid psychiatric diagnosis predicts three-year outcomes in alcoholics: A posttreatment natural history study. *J. Stud. Alcoh., 57*(6), 619–26.

Kreitman, N., Sainsbury, P., Pearce, K., & Costain, W. R. (1965). Hypochondriasis and depression in outpatients at a general hospital. *Brit. J. Psychiat., 3,* 607–15.

Kremen, W. S., Seidman, L. J., Pepple, J. R., Lyons, M. J., Tsuang, M. T., & Faraone, S. V. (1994). Neuropsychological risk indicators for schizophrenia: A review of family studies. *Schizo. Bull., 20*(1), 103–19.

Kress, H. W. (1984). Role of family and networks in emergency psychotherapy. In E. L. Bassuk & A. Birk (Eds.), *Emergency Psychiatry.* New York: Plenum.

Kriechman, A. M. (1987). Siblings with somatoform disorders in childhood and adolescence. *J. Amer. Acad. Child Adoles. Psychiat., 26,* 226–31.

Kring, A. M. (1998, May 22). Emotion disturbance in schizophrenia. In Ann M. Kring (Chair), American Psychological Society, (p. 41). Washington.

Kring, A. M., Kerr, S. L., Smith, D. A., & Neale, J. M. (1993). Flat affect in schizophrenia does not reflect diminished subjective experience of emotion. *J. Abn. Psychol., 102*(4), 507–17.

Krippner, S. (1994). Cross-cultural treatment perspectives on dissociative disorders. In S. J. Lynn & J. W. Rhue (Eds.), *Dissociation: Clinical and theoretical perspectives.* (pp. 338–64). New York: Guilford.

Kroll, J., & Bachrach, B. (1984). Sin and mental illness in the Middle Ages. *Psychol. Med., 14,* 507–14.

Krupnick, J. L., et al. (1996). The role of therapeutic alliance in psychotherapy and pharmacotherapy outcome: Findings in the NIMH TDCRP. *J. Cons. Clin. Psychol., 64*(3), 532–39.

Krystal, H. (1968). *Massive psychic trauma.* New York: International Universities Press.

Krystal, J. H., Niehoff, D., & Charney, D. S. (1996). The biological basis of panic disorder. *J. Clin. Psychiat., 57*(10), 23–31.

Kuch, K. (1997). Accident phobia. In G. C. L. Davey, (Ed.), *Phobias. A handbook of theory, research and treatment.* (pp. 153–62). Chichester, England: Wiley.

Kuczmarski, R. J. (1992). Prevalence of overweight and weight gain in the United States. *Amer. J. Clin. Nutri., 55* (Suppl), 495S–502S.

Kuczmarski, R. J., Flegul, K. M., & Johnson, C. L. (1994). Increasing prevalence of overweight among U.S. adults. *JAMA, 272,* 205–11.

Kuechenmeister, C. A., Linton, P. H., Mueller, T. V., & White, H. B. (1977). Eye tracking in relation to age, sex, and illness. *Arch. Gen. Psychiat., 34,* 578–79.

Kuhn, T. S. (1962). *The structure of scientific revolutions.* Chicago: University of Chicago Press.

Kulka, R. A., Schlenger, W. E., Fairbank, J. A., Hough, R. L., Jordan, B. K., Marmar, C. R., & Weiss, D. S. (1990).*Trauma and the Vietnam War generation: Report of findings from the National Vietnam Veterans Readjustment Study.* NY: Brunner/Mazel.

Kumra, S., et al. (1996). Childhood-onset schizophrenia: A double-blind clozapine-haloperidol comparison. *Arch. Gen. Psychiat., 53*(12), 1090–97.

Kuperman, S., Black, D. W., & Burns, T.L. (1988). Excess mortality among formerly hospitalized child psychiatric patients. *Arch. Gen. Psychiat., 45,* 277–82.

Kupersmidt, J. B., Burchinal, M., & Patterson, C. J. (1995) Developmental patterns of childhood peer relations as predictors of externalizing behavior problems. *Develop. Psychopath., 7,* 825–43.

Kupersmidt, J. B., & Coie, J. D. (1990). Preadolescent peer status, aggression, and school adjustment as predictors of externalizing problems in adolescence. *Child Develop., 61,* 1350–62.

Kupersmidt, J. B., Coie, J. D., & Dodge, K. A. (1990). The role of poor peer relationships in the development of disorder. In S. R. Asher & J. D. Coie (Eds.), *Peer rejection in childhood.* (pp. 274–308). New York: Cambridge University Press.

Kushner, M. (1968). The operant control of intractable sneezing. In C. D. Spielberger (Ed.), *Contributions to general psychology: Selected readings for introductory psychology.* New York: Ronald Press.

Kutcher, S. & Mackenzie, S. (1988). Successful clonazepam treatment of adolescents with panic disorder. *J. Clin. Psychopharm., 8,* 299–301.

Kutcher, S. P., Reiter, S., Gardner, D. M., & Klein, R. G. (1992). The pharmacologic treatment of anxiety disorders in children and adolescents. *Psychiat. Clin. N. Amer., 15,* 41–68.

Kwapil, T. R. (1996). A longitudinal study of drug and alcohol use by psychosis-prone and impulsive-nonconforming individuals. *J. Abn. Psychol., 105*(1), 114–23.

Kwapil, T. R., Miller, M. B., Zinser, M. C., Chapman, J., & Chapman, L. J. (1997). Magical ideation and social anhedonia as predictors of psychosis proneness: A partial replication. *J. Abn. Psychol., 106*(3), 491–95.

Kwon, S. M., & Oei, T. P. (1994). The roles of two levels of cognitions in the development, maintenance, and treatment of depression. *Clin. Psychol. Rev., 14*(5), 331–58.

La Rue, A., & Swanda, R. (1997). Neuropsychological assessment. In P. D. Nussbaum (Ed.), *Handbook of neuropsychology and aging.* (pp. 360–84). New York: Plenum.

Laan, E., & Everaerd, W. (1995). Determinants of female sexual arousal: Psychophysiological theory and data. *Annu. Rev. Sex Res., 6,* 32–76.

Ladd, G. W. (1983). Social networks of popular, average, and rejected children in school settings. *Merrill-Palmer Quarterly, 29,* 283–308.

LaGreca, A. M., Silverman, W. K., Vernberg, E. M., & Prinstein, M. J. (1997). Symptoms of posttraumatic stress disorder in children after Hurricane Andrew: A prospective study. *J. Cons. Clin. Psychol., 64*(4), 712–23.

Lahey, B. B., Hartdagen, S. E., Frick, P. J., McBurnett, K., Connor, R., & Hynd, G. W. (1988). Conduct disorder: Parsing the confounded relation to parental divorce and antisocial personality. *J. Abn. Psychol., 97,* 334–37.

Lahey, B. B., Loeber, R., Quay, H. C., Frick, P. J., & Grimm, S. (1992). Oppositional defiant and conduct disorders: Issues to be resolved for DSM-IV. *J. Amer. Acad. Child Adoles. Psychiat., 29,* 620–26.

Lake, C. R., Pickar, D., Ziegler, M. G., Lipper, S., Slater, S., & Murphy, D. L. (1982). High plasma norepinephrine levels in patients with major affective disorder. *Amer. J. Psychiat., 139,* 1315–18.

Lakin, M. (1991). *Coping with ethical dilemmas in psychotherapy.* Elmsford, NY: Pergamon.

Lamb, H. R. (1984). Deinstitutionalization and the homeless mentally ill. *Hosp. Comm. Psychiat., 35,* 899–907.

Lamberg, L. (1998). Mental illness and violent acts: protecting the patient and the public. *JAMA, 280,* 407–08.

Lambert, M. C., Weisz, J. R., & Knight, F. (1989). Over and undercontrolled clinic referral problems of Jamaican and American children and adolescents: The culture general and culture specific. *J. Cons. Clin. Psychol., 57,* 467–72.

Lambert, M. C., Weisz, J. R., Knight, F., Desrosiers, M. F., Overly, K., & Thesiger, C. (1992). Jamaican and American perspectives on child psychopathology: Further exploration of the Threshold Model. *J. Cons. Clin. Psychol., 60*(1), 146–49.

Lambert, M. J. (1989). The individual therapist's contribution to psychotherapy process and outcome. *Clin. Psychol. Rev., 9,* 469–85.

Lambert, M. J., & Bergin, A. E. (1994). The effectiveness of psychotherapy. In A. E. Bergin & S. L. Garfield (Eds.), *Handbook of psychotherapy and behavior change* (4th ed.). (pp. 143–89). New York: Wiley.

Lambert, M. J., Shapiro, D. A., & Bergin, A. E. (1986). The effectiveness of psychotherapy. In S. L. Garfield & A. E. Bergin (Eds.), *Handbook of psychotherapy and behavior change.* New York: Wiley.

Landesman-Dwyer, S. (1981). Living in the community. *Amer. J. Ment. Def., 86,* 223–34.

Lang, A. R., & Kidorf, M. (1990). Problem drinking: Cognitive behavioral strategies for self control. In M. E. Thase, B. A. Edelstein, & M. Hersen (Eds.), *Handbook of outpatient treatment of adults.* (pp. 413–42). New York: Plenum.

Lang, A. R., & Marlatt, G. A. (1983). Problem drinking: A social learning perspective. In R. J. Gatchel, A. Baum, & J. E. Singer (Eds.), *Handbook of psychology and health* (Vol. 1). (pp. 121–69). Hillsdale, NJ: Erlbaum.

Lang, P. (1970). Autonomic control. *Psych. Today, 4*(5), 37–41.

Lang, P. J. (1968). Fear reduction and fear behavior: Problems in treating a construct. In J.M. Shlien (Ed.), *Research in psychotherapy* (Vol. 3). Washington DC: American Psychological Association.

Lang, P. J. (1971). Application of psychophysiological methods to the study of psychotherapy and behavior modification. In A. E. Bergin & S. L. Garfield (Eds.), *Handbook of psychotherapy and behavior change.* New York: Wiley

Lang, P. J. (1985). The cognitive psychophysiology of emotion: Fear and anxiety. In A. H. Tuma & J. D. Maser (Eds.), *Anxiety and the anxiety disorders.* Hillsdale, NJ: Erlbaum.

Lange, W. R., Cabanilla, B. R., Moler, G., Bernacki, E. J., & Frankenfield, D. (1994). Preemployment drug screening at the Johns Hopkins Hospital, 1989 and 1991. *Amer. J. Drug Alcoh. Abuse, 20,* 35–46.

Langevin, R., Handy, L., Day, D., & Russon, A. (1985). Are incestuous fathers pedophilic, aggressive, and alcoholic? In R. Langevin (Ed.), *Erotic preference, gender identity, and aggression.* (pp. 161–80). Hillsdale, NJ: Erlbaum.

Lansky, M. R., & Selzer, J. (1984). Priapism associated with trazodone therapy: Case report. *J. Clin. Psychiat., 45,* 232–33.

Lanyon, R. (1984). Personality assessment. *Annu. Rev. Psychol. 35,* 689–701.

Lanyon, R. I., Barrington, C. C., & Newman, A. C. (1976). Modification of stuttering through EMG biofeedback: A preliminary study. *Behav. Ther., 7,* 96–103.

Laporte, L., & Guttman, H. (1996). Traumatic childhood experiences as risk factors for borderline and other personality disorders. *J. Personal. Dis., 10*(3), 247–259.

Last, C. G., & Perrin, S. (1993). Anxiety disorders in African-American and white children. *J. Abnorm. Child Psychol., 21,* 153–64.

Lauer, C. J., Schreiber, W., Holsboer, F., & Krieg, J.-C. (1995). In quest of identifying vulnerability markers for psychiatric disorders by all-night polysomnography. *Arch. Gen. Psychiat., 52,* 145–53.

Lauer, J., Black D. W., & Keen, P. (1993) Multiple personality disorder and borderline personality disorder: Distinct entities or variations on a common theme? *Annals of Clinical Psychiatry, 5,* 129–134.

Laufer, R. S., Brett, E., & Gallops, M. S. (1985). Dimensions of posttraumatic stress disorder among Vietnam veterans. *J. Nerv. Ment. Dis., 173*(9), 538–45.

Lauriello, J., et al. (1997). Similar extent of brain dysmorphology in severely ill women and men with schizophrenia. *Amer. J. Psychiat., 154*(6), 819–25.

Law, W. A., & Mapou, R. L. (1997). Neuropsychological findings in HIV-1 disease and AIDS. In A. M. Horton, D. Wedding, & J. Webster (Eds.), *The neuropsychology handbook* (Vol. 2). (pp. 267–308). New York: Springer.

Lawton, H. (1990). The field of psychohistory. *J. Psychohist., 17,* 353–64.

Lazarus, A. A. (1981). *The practice of multimodal therapy.* New York: McGraw-Hill.

Lazarus, A. A. (Ed.). (1985). *Casebook of multimodal therapy.* New York: Guilford.

Lazarus, A. A. (1989). Dyspareunia: A multimodal psychotherapeutic perspective. In S. R. Leiblum & R. C. Rosen (Eds.), *Principles and practice of sex therapy* (2nd ed.). (pp. 89–112). New York: Guilford.

Lazarus, A. A. (1997a). Through a different lens: Commentary on "Behavior Therapy: Distinct but Acculturated." *Behav. Ther., 28*(4), 573–75.

Lazarus, A. A. (1997b). *Brief but comprehensive psychotherapy: The multimodal way.* New York: Springer.

Lazarus, R. S., & Folkman, S. (1984). *Stress appraisal and coping.* New York: Springer.

Le Couteur, A., Bailey, A., Goode, S., Pickles, A., Robertson, S., Gottesman, I., & Rutter, M. (1996). A broader phenotype of autism: The clinical spectrum in twins. *J. Child Clin. Psychiat., 37*(7), 785–801.

Leal, J., Ziedonis, D., & Kosten, T. (1994). Antisocial personality disorder as a prognostic factor for pharmacotherapy of cocaine dependence. *Drug and Alcohol Dependence, 35,* 31–35.

Leary, T. (1957). *Interpersonal diagnosis.* New York: Ronald.

Lease, C. A., & Ollendick, T. H. (1993). Development and psychopathology. In A. S. Bellack, & M. Hersen (Eds.), *Psychopathology in adulthood.* Needham, MA: Allyn and Bacon.

Lebedev, B. A. (1967). Corticovisceral psychosomatics. *Inter. J. Psychiat., 4*(3), 241–46.

Lebergott, S. (1964). *Manpower in economic growth: The American record since 1800.* New York: McGraw-Hill.

Lebra, W. (Ed.). (1976). Culture-bound syndromes, ethnopsychiatry and alternate therapies. In *Mental health research in Asia and the Pacific* (Vol. 4). Honolulu: University Press of Hawaii.

Lee, J. R., & Goodwin, M. E. (1987). Deinstitutionalization: A new scenario. *Journal of Mental Health Administration, 14,* 40–45.

Lees-Haley, P. R., Smith, H. H., Williams, C. W., & Dunn, J. T. (1996). Forensic neuropsychological test usage: An empirical survey. *Arch. Clin. Neuropsychol., 11,* 45–51.

Lees-Roitman, S. E., Cornblatt, B. A., Bergman, A., Obuchowski, M., Mitropoulou, V., Keefe, R. S. E., Silverman, J. M., & Siever, L. J. (1997). Attentional functioning in schizotypal personality disorder. *Amer. J. Psychiat., 154*(5), 655–660.

Leff, J., Kuipers, L., Berkowitz, R., & Sturgeon, D. A. (1982). A controlled trial of social intervention in the families of schizophrenic patients. *Brit. J. Psychiat., 141,* 121–34.

Lefkowitz, M. M., Eron, L. D., Walder, L. O., & Huesmann, L. R. (1977). *Growing up to be violent: A longitudinal study of the development of aggression.* New York: Pergamon.

Lefkowitz, M. M., & Tesiny, E. P. (1985). Depression in children: Prevalence and correlates. *J. Cons. Clin. Psychol., 53,* 647–56.

Lehman, A. F., et al. (1998). Patterns of usual care for schizophrenia: Initial results from the schizophrenia patient outcomes research team (PORT) client survey. *Schizo. Bull., 24*(1), 11–19.

Lehmann, H. E. (1967). Psychiatric disorders not in standard nomenclature. In A. M. Freedman, H. I. Kaplan, & H. S. Kaplan (Eds.), *Comprehensive textbook of psychiatry.* Baltimore: Williams & Wilkins.

Lehmann, L. (1985). The relationship of depression to other DSM-III Axis I disorders. In E. E. Beckham & W. R. Leber (Eds.), *Handbook of depression: Treatment, assessment, and research.* (pp. 669–99). Homewood, IL: Dorsey Press.

Lehrer, P. M., & Murphy, A. I. (1991). Stress reactivity and perception of pain among tension headache sufferers. *Behav. Res. Ther., 29,* 61–69.

Lehrer, P. M., Sargunaraj, D., & Hochron, S. (1992). Psychological approaches to the treatment of asthma. *J. Cons. Clin. Psychol., 60*(4), 639–643.

Lehto, J. (1995). *Approaches to alcohol control policy: European alcohol action plan.* Geneva: World Health Organization.

Leibenluft, E. (1996). Women with bipolar illness: Clinical and research issues. *Amer. J. Psychiat., 153*(2), 163–173.

Leiblum, S. R., & Pervin, L. A. (1980). *Principles and practice of sex therapy.* New York: Guilford.

Leiblum, S. R., & Rosen, R. C. (Eds.). (1989a). *Principles and practice of sex therapy* (2nd ed.). New York: Guilford.

Leiblum, S. R., & Rosen, R. C. (1989b). Introduction: Sex therapy in the age of AIDS. In S. R. Leiblum & R. C. Rosen (Eds.), *Principles and practice of sex therapy,* (2nd ed.). (pp. 1–18). New York: Guilford.

Leiblum, S. R., Pervin, L. A., & Campbell, E. H. (1989). The treatment of vaginismus: Success and failure. In S. R. Leiblum & R. C. Rosen (Eds.), *Principles and practice of sex therapy* (2nd ed.). (pp. 113–40). New York: Guilford.

Leichtman, M. (1995). Behavioral observations. In J. N. Butcher (Ed.). *Clinical personality assessment: Practical considerations.* (pp. 251–66). New York: Oxford University Press.

Leichtman, M. D. & Ceci, S. J. (1995). *The effects of stereotypes and suggestions on preschoolers' reports. Develop. Psychol., 31,* 568–78.

Lelliott, P., Marks, I., McNamee, G., & Tobena, A. (1989). Onset of panic disorder with agoraphobia. *Arch. Gen. Psychiat., 46,* 1000–4.

Lemert, E. M. (1962). Paranoia and the dynamics of exclusion. *Sociometry, 25,* 2–25.

Lencz, T., Raine, A., Scerbo, A., Redmon, M., Brodish, S., Holt, L., & Bird, L. (1993). Impaired eye tracking in undergraduates with schizotypal personality disorder. *Amer. J. Psychiat., 150,* 152–54.

Lenzenweger, M. F. (1994). Psychometric high-risk paradigm, perceptual aberrations, and schizotypy: An update. *Schizo. Bull., 20*(1), 121–35.

Lenzenweger, M. F. (1998). Schizotypy and schizotypic psychopathology: Mapping an alternative expression of schizophrenia liability. In M. F. Lenzenweger & R. H. Dworkin (Eds.), *Origins and development of schizophrenia.* (pp. 93–122). Washington: American Psychological Association.

Lenzenweger, M. F., & Dworkin, R. H. (Ed.). (1998). *Origins and development of schizophrenia: Advances in experimental psychopathology.* Washington: American Psychological Association.

Lenzenweger, M. F., & Korfine, L. (1994). Perceptual aberrations, schizotypy, and the Wisconsin Card Sorting Test. *Schizo. Bull., 20*(2), 345–56.

Leon, G. L., Butcher, J. N., Kleinman, M., Goldberg, A., & Almagor, M. (1981). Survivors of the holocaust and their children: Current status and adjustment. *J. Pers. Soc. Psychol., 41*(3), 503–16.

Leon, G. R., & Chamberlain, K. (1973). Emotional arousal, eating patterns, and body image as differential factors associated with varying success in maintaining a weight loss. *J. Cons. Clin. Psychol., 40,* 474–80.

Leon, G. R., Eckert, E. D., Teed, D., & Buckwald, H. (1978). Changes in body image and other psychological factors after intestinal bypass surgery for massive obesity. *J. Behav. Med., 2,* 39–59.

Leon, G. R., Fulkerson, J. A., Perry, C. L., & Cudeck, R. (1993). Personality and behavioral vulnerabilities associated with risk status for eating disorders in adolescent girls. *J. Abn. Psychol., 102*(3), 438–44.

Leonard, B. E. (1990). *Fundamentals of psychopharmacology.* New York: Wiley.

Leonard, K. E., & Senchak, M. (1996). Prospective prediction of husband marital aggression within newlywed couples. *J. Abn. Psychol., 105,* 369–80.

Leong, G. B., & Eth, S. (1991). Legal and ethical issues in electroconvulsive therapy. *Psychiat. Clin. N. Amer., 14,* 1007–16.

Lepine, J. P., Chignon, J. M., & Teherani, M. (1993). Suicide attempts in patients with panic disorder. *Arch. Gen. Psychiat., 50* (2), 144–9.

Lerman, P. (1981). *Deinstitutionalization: A cross-problem analysis.* Rockville, MD: U.S. Department of Health and Human Services.

Lerner, P. M. (1995). Assessing adaptive capacities by means of the Rorschach. In J. N. Butcher (Ed.), *Clinical personality assessment: Practical considerations.* (pp. 317–25). New York: Oxford University Press.

Lesch, K.-P., Bengel, D., Heils, A., Sabol, S., Greenburg, B., Petri, S., Benjamin, J., Muller, C., Hamer, D., & Murphy, D. (1996). Association of anxiety-related traits with a polymorphism in the serotonin transporter gene regulatory region. *Science, 274,* 1527–31.

Lester, D. (1988). Youth suicide: A cross-cultural perspective. *Adolescence, 23,* 955–58.

Leukefeld, C. G., Logan, P. R., Clayton, C., Martin, R., Zimmerman, A., Milch, R., & Lynam, D. (1998). Adolescent drug use, delinquency, and other behaviors. In T. P. Gullotta, G. R. Adams, & R. Montemayor (Eds.), *Advances in adolescent development: An annual book series. (Vol. 9).* (pp. 98–128). Thousand Oaks, CA: Sage.

Leung, P. W., & Connolly, K. (1996). Distractibility in hyperactive and conduct disordered children. *J. Child Psychol. Psychiat., 37*(3), 305–12.

Leung, P. W., Luk, S. L., Ho, T. P., Taylor, E., Mak, F. L., & Bacon-Shone, J. (1996). The diagnosis and prevalence of hyperactivity in Chinese boys. *Brit. J. Psychiat., 168,* 486–496.

LeVay, S. (1991). A difference in hypothalamic structure between heterosexual and homosexual men. *Science, 253,* 1034–37.

LeVay, S. (1993). *The sexual brain.* Cambridge, MA: MIT Press.

Levenson, A. J. (1981). Basic psychopharmacology. New York: Springer.

Leventhal, B. L., Cook, E. H., & Lord, C. (1998). The irony of autism. *Arch. Gen. Psychiat., 55,* 643–44.

Leventhal, H., Patrick–Muller, L., & Leventhal, E. A. (1998). It's long-term stressors that take a toll: Comment on Cohen et al. (1988). *Hlth. Psychol., 17*(3), 211–13.

Levin, S., & Yurgelun-Todd, D. (1989). Contributions of clinical neuropsychology to the study of schizophrenia. *J. Abn. Psychol., 98,* 341–56.

Levine, M. D. (1976). Children with encopresis: A descriptive analysis. *Pediatrics, 56,* 412.

Levine, M. D., & Bakow, H. (1975). Children with encopresis: A study of treatment outcomes. *Pediatrics, 58,* 845.

Levine, M., & Perkins, D. V. (1987). *Principles of community psychology: Perspectives and applications.* New York: Oxford University Press.

Levinson, D. F., et al., (1998). Genome scan of schizophrenia. *Amer. J. Psychiat., 155*(6), 741–50.

Levitan, H. (1989). Onset situation in three psychosomatic illnesses. In S. Cheren (Ed.), *Psychosomatic medicine: Theory, physiology, and practice* (Vol 1.). (pp. 119–34). Madison, CT: International Universities Press.

Levor, R. M., Cohen, M. J., Naliboff, B. D., & McArthur, D. (1986). Psychosocial precursors and correlates of migraine headache. *J. Cons. Clin. Psychol., 54,* 347–53.

Levy, D. L., Holzman, P. S., Matthysse, S., & Mendell, N. R. (1993). Eye tracking dysfunction and schizophrenia: A critical perspective. *Schizo. Bull., 19*(3), 461–536.

Levy, D. L., Holzman, P. S., Matthysse, S., & Mendell, N. R. (1994). Eye tracking and schizophrenia: A selective review. *Schizo. Bull., 20*(1), 47–62.

Levy, D. L., Yasillo, N. J., Dorcus, E., Shaughnessy, R. Gibbons, R. D., Peterson, J., Janicak, P.G., Gaviria, M., & Davis, J. M. (1983). Relatives of unipolar and bipolar patients have normal pursuit. *Psychiat. Res., 10,* 285–93.

Levy, F., Barr, C., & Sunohara, G. (1998). Directions of aetiologic research on attention deficit hyperactivity disorder. *Austral. N.Z. J. Psychiatr., 32*(1), 97–103.

Lewinsohn, P. M. (1974). A behavioral approach to depression. In R. J. Friedman & M. M. Katz (Eds.), *The psychology of depression: Contemporary theory and research.* New York: Halstead Press.

Lewinsohn, P. M., Clarke, G. N., Hops, H., & Andrews, J. (1990). Cognitive-behavioral treatment for depressed adolescents. *Behav. Ther., 21,* 385–401.

Lewinsohn, P. M., & Gotlib, I. H. (1995). Behavioral theory and treatment of depression. In E. E. Beckham & W. R. Leber (Eds.), *Handbook of depression* (2nd ed.). (pp. 352–75). New York: Guilford.

Lewinsohn, P. M., Gotlib, I. H., Lewinson, M., Seeley, J. R., & Allen, N. B. (1998). Gender differences in anxiety disorders and anxiety symptoms in adolescents. *J. Abn. Psychol. 107*(1), 109–17.

Lewinsohn, P. M., Hoberman, H. M., & Rosenbaum, M. (1988). A prospective study of risk factors for unipolar depression. *J. Abn. Psychol., 97,* 251–64.

Lewinsohn, P. M., Hoberman, H. M., Teri, L., & Hautzinger, M. (1985). An integrative theory of depression. In S. Reiss & R. Bootzin (Eds.), *Theoretical issues in behavior therapy.* (pp. 331–59). San Diego: Academic Press.

Lewinsohn, P. M., Hops, H., Roberts, R. E., Seeley, J. R., & Andrews, J. A. (1993). Adolescent psychopathology: I. Prevalence and incidence of depression and other DSM-III-R disorders in high school students. *J. Abn. Psychol., 102,* 133–44.

Lewinsohn, P. M., & Rohde, P. (1993). The cognitive behavioral treatment of depression in adolescents: Research and suggestions. *Clin. Psychol., 46,* 177–83.

Lewinsohn, P. M., Rohde, P., & Seeley, J. R. (1994). Psychosocial risk factors for future adolescent suicide attempts. *J. Cons. Clin. Psychol., 62,* 297–305.

Lewinsohn, P. M., Rohde, P., & Seeley, J. R. (1996). Epidemiology of adolescent suicide. *Clin. Psychol. Sci. Prac., 3,* 25–46.

Lewinsohn, P. M., Zeiss, A. M., & Duncan, E. M. (1989). Probability of relapse after recovery from an episode of depression. *J. Abn. Psychol., 98,* 107–16.

Lewis, C. E., Cloninger, C. R., & Pais, J. (1983). Alcoholism, anti-social personality, and drug use in a criminal population. *Alcohol and Alcoholism, 18,* 53–60.

Lewis, C. E., Robins, L., & Rice, J. (1985). Association of alcoholism with antisocial personality in urban men. *J. Nerv. Ment. Dis., 173*(3), 166–74.

Lewis, C. F., & Ednie, K. (1997) Koro and homicidal behavior. *Amer. J. Psychiat., 154,* 1169.

Lewis, J. M., Rodnick, E. H., & Goldstein, M. J. (1981). Intrafamilial interactive behavior, communication deviance, and risk for schizophrenia. *J. Abn. Psychol., 90,* 448–57.

Lewis, J. W., & Walter, D. (1992). Buprenorphine: Background to its development as a treatment for opiate dependence. In J. D. Blaine (Ed.), *Buprenorphine: An alternative treatment for opioid dependence.* (pp. 5–11). Washington, DC: U.S. Department of Health and Human Services.

Lewis, M. S. (1989a). Age incidence and schizophrenia: Part I. The season of birth controversy. *Schizo. Bull., 15,* 59–73.

Lewis, M. S. (1989b). Age incidence and schizophrenia: Part II. Beyond age incidence. *Schizo. Bull., 15,* 75–80.

Lewis, M. S. (1990). *Res ipsa loquitur:* The author replies. *Schizo. Bull., 16,* 17–28.

Lewis, M. S., & Griffin, P. A. (1981). An explanation for the season of birth effect in schizophrenia and certain other diseases. *Psychol. Bull., 89,* 589–96.

Lewis, N. D. C. (1941). *A short history of psychiatric achievement.* New York: Norton.

Lewis, O. (1997). Integrated psychodynamic psychotherapy with children. *Child Adoles. Psychiat. Clin. N. Amer., 6*(1), 53–68.

Lewis, R. J., Dlugokinski, E. L., Caputo, L. M., & Griffin, R. B. (1988). Children at risk for emotional disorders: Risk and resource dimensions. *Clin. Psychol. Rev., 8,* 417–40.

Lewis, W. C. (1974). Hysteria: The consultant's dilemma. *Arch. Gen. Psychiat., 30*(2), 145–51.

Lewis-Fernandez, R., & Kleinman, A. (1994). Culture, personality, and psychopathology. *J. Abn. Psychol., 103*(1), 67–71.

Lexow, G. A., & Aronson, S. S. (1975). Health advocacy: A need, a concept, a model. *Children Today, 4*(1), 2–6, 36.

Lezak, M. D. (1995). *Neuropsychological Assessment* (3rd ed.). New York: Oxford University Press.

Liberman, R. P., Mueser, K. T., & DeRisi, W. J. (1989). *Social skills training for psychiatric patients.* Elmsford, NY: Pergamon.

Liberman, R. P., & Raskin, D. E. (1971). Depression: A behavioral formulation. *Arch. Gen. Psychiat., 24*(6), 515–23.

Liddle, P. F., Barnes, T. R. E., Speller, J., & Kibel, D. (1993). Negative symptoms as a risk factor for tardive dyskinesia in schizophrenia. *Brit. J. Psychiat., 163,* 776–80.

Lidz, T. (1978). Egocentric cognitive regression and the family setting of schizophrenic disorders. In L. C. Wynne, R. L. Cromwell, & S. Matthysse (Eds.), *The nature of schizophrenia: New approaches to research and treatment.* (pp. 526–33). New York: Wiley.

Lidz, T. (1994). To the Editor. *Amer. J. Psychiat., 151,* 458–59.

Lidz, T., Fleck, S., & Cornelison, A. R. (1965). *Schizophrenia and the family.* New York: International Universities Press.

Lie, N. (1992). Follow-ups of children with attention deficit hyperactivity disorder (ADHD): Review of literature. *Acta Psychiatr. Scandin., 85,* 40–80.

Lieberman, J. A., Jody, D., Alvir, J. M. J., Ashtari, M., Levy, D. L., Bogerts, B., Degreef, G., Mayerhoff, D. I., & Cooper, T. (1993a). Brain morphology, dopamine, and eyetracking abnormalities in first-episode schizophrenia: Prevalence and clinical correlates. *Arch. Gen. Psychiat., 50*(5), 357–68.

Lieberman, J., Jody, D., Geisler, S., Alvir, J., Loebel, A., Szymanski, S., Woerner, M., & Borenstein, M. (1993b). Time course and biologic correlates of treatment response in first-episode schizophrenia. *Arch. Gen. Psychiat., 50*(5), 369–76.

Lieberman, J. A., & Koreen, A. R. (1993). Neurochemistry and neuroendocrinology of schizophrenia: A selective review. *Schizo. Bull., 19*(2), 371–429.

Lieberman, J. A., Safferman, A. Z., Pollack, S., Szymanski, S., Johns, C., Howard, A., Kronig, M., Bookstein, P., & Kane, J. M. (1994). Clinical effects of clozapine in chronic schizophrenia: Response to treatment and predictors of outcome. *Amer. J. Psychiat., 151*(12), 1744–52.

Lieberman, L. M. (1982). The nightmare of scheduling. *J. Learn. Dis., 15*, 57–58.

Liebman, J. M., & Cooper, S. J. (1989). *The neuropharmacological basis of reward.* New York: Clarendon Press.

Liebowitz, M. R., & Fyer, A. J. (1994). Diagnosis and clinical course of panic disorder with and without agoraphobia. In B. E. Wolfe. & J. D. Maser (Eds.), *Treatment of panic disorder.* Washington: Amercian Psychiatric Press.

Liebowitz, M. R., Fyer, A. J., Gorman, J. M., Dillon, D., Appleby, I. L., Levy, G., Anderson, S., Palij, M., Davies, S. O., & Klein, D. F. (1984). Lactate provocation of panic. *Arch. Gen. Psychiat., 41*, 764–70.

Liebowitz, M. R., Gorman, J. M., Fyer, A. J., Levitt, M., Dillon, D., Levy, P., Appleby, I. L., Anderson, S., Palij, M., Davis, S. O., & Klein, D. F. (1985). Lactate provocation of panic attacks: II. Biochemical and physiological findings. *Arch. Gen. Psychiat., 42*, 709–19.

Liebowitz, M. R., & Hollander, E. (1991). Obsessive-compulsive disorder: Psychobiological integration. In J. Zohar, T. Insel, & S. Rasmussen (Eds.), *The psychobiology of obsessive-compulsive disorder.* New York: Springer.

Liebowitz, M. R., Schneier, F. R., Campeas, R., Hollander, E., Hatterer, J., Fyer, A., Gorman, J., Papp, L., Davies, S., Gully, R., & Klein, D. R. (1992). Phenelzine vs. atenolol in social phobia: A placebo controlled comparison. *Arch. Gen. Psychiat., 49*, 290–300.

Liem, J. H. (1974). Effects of verbal communications of parents and children: A comparison of normal and schizophrenic families. *J. Cons. Clin. Psychol., 42*, 438–50.

Lifton, R. J. (1972). The "Gook syndrome" and "numbed warfare," *Saturday Review, 55*(47), 66–72.

Lilienfeld, S. O., & Andrews, B. P. (1996). Development and preliminary validation of a self-report measure of psychopathic personality traits in noncriminal populations. *J. Person. Assess., 66*(3), 488–524.

Lilienfeld, S. O., Waldman, I. D., & Israel, A. C. (1994). A critical examination of the use of the term and concept of comorbidity in psychopathology research. *Clin. Psychol. Sci. Prac., 1*, 71–83.

Liljefors, I., & Rahe, R. H. (1970). An identical twin study of psychosocial factors in coronary heart disease in Sweden. *Psychosom. Med., 32*(5), 523–42.

Lima, B. R., & Pai, S. (1993). Response to the psychological consequences of disasters in Latin America. *Inter. J. Ment. Hlth., 21*, 59–71.

Lincoln, J., Batty, J., Townsend, R., & Collins, M. (1992). Working for greater inclusion of children with severe learning difficulties in mainstream secondary schools. *Educational & Child Psychology, 9*(4), 46–51.

Lindman, R. E., & Lang, A. R. (1994). The alcohol-aggression stereotype: A cross-cultural comparison of beliefs. *Inter. J. Addict., 29*, 1–13.

Lindsay D. S., Johnson, M. K., & Kwon, P. (1991) Developmental changes in memory source monitoring. *Develop. Psychol., 52*, 297–318.

Lindsey, K. P., & Paul, G. L. (1989). Involuntary commitments to public mental institutions: Issues involving the overrepresentation of blacks and the assessment of relevant functioning. *Psychol. Bull., 106*, 171–83.

Linehan, M. M. (1987). Dialectical behavioral therapy: A cognitive behavioral approach to parasuicide. *J. Personal. Dis., 1*, 328–33.

Linehan, M. M. (1993). *Cognitive-behavioral treatment of borderline personality disorder: The dialectics of effective treatment.* New York: Guilford.

Linehan, M. M., Armstrong, H. E., Suarez, A., Allmon, D., & Heard, H. L. (1991). Cognitive-behavioral treatment of chronically parasuicidal borderline patients. *Arch. Gen. Psychiat., 48*, 1060–64.

Linehan, M. M., Heard, H. L., & Armstrong, H. E. (1993) Naturalistic follow-up of a behavioral treatment for chronically parasuicidal borderline patients. *Arch. Gen. Psychiat., 50*, 971–74.

Linehan, M. M., Tutek, D. A., Heard, H. L., & Armstrong, H. E. (1994). Interpersonal outcome of cognitive behavioral treatment for chronically suicidal borderline patients. *Amer. J. Psychiat., 151*(12), 1771–76.

Link, B. G., Cullen, F. T., Frank, J., & Wozniak, J.F. (1987). The social rejection of former mental patients: Understanding why labels matter. *American Journal of Sociology, 92*, 1461–1500.

Linszen, D. H., Dingemans, P. M., & Lenior, M. E. (1994). Cannabis abuse and the course of recent-onset schizophrenic disorders. *Arch. Gen. Psychiat., 51*(4), 273–79.

Linszen, D. H., et al. (1997). Patient attributes and expressed emotion as risk factors for psychotic relapse. *Schizo. Bull., 23*(1), 119–30.

Lintzeris, N., Holgate, F., & Dunlop, A. (1996). Addressing dependent amphetamine use: A place for prescription. *Drug and Alcohol Review, 15*(2), 189–95.

Lion, J.R. (1978). Outpatient treatment of psychopaths. In W. H. Reid (Ed.), *The psychopath: A comprehensive study of anti-social disorders and behaviors.* New York: Brunner/Mazel.

Lipowski, Z. J. (1988). Somatization: The concept and its clinical application. *Amer. J. Psychiat., 145*, 1358–68.

Lipton, D. N., McDonel, E. C., & McFall, R. M. (1987) Hetrosocial perception in rapists. *J. Cons. Clin. Psychol., 55*, 17–21.

Lipton, E. L., Steinschneider, A., & Richmond, J. B. (1966). Psychophysiologic disorders in children. In L. W. Hoffman & M. L. Hoffman (Eds.), *Review of child development research.* (pp. 169–220). Russell Sage Foundation.

Lisak, D., & Roth, S. (1988). Motivational factors in nonincarcerated sexually aggressive men. *J. Pers. Soc. Psychol., 55*, 795–802.

Lishman, W. A. (1990). Alcohol and the brain. *Brit. J. Psychiat., 156*, 635–44.

Lishman, W. A., Jacobson, R. R., & Acker, C. (1987). Brain damage in alcoholism: Current concepts. *Acta Medica Scandinavica* (Suppl. 717), 5–17.

Lissau, I., & Sorensen, T. I. A. (1994). Parental neglect during childhood and increased risk of obesity in young adulthood. *Lancet, 343*, 324–27.

Litman, R. E., et al. (1997). A quantitative analysis of smooth pursuit eye tracking in monozygotic twins discordant for schizophrenia. *Arch. Gen. Psychiat., 54*(5), 417–26.

Litwack, T. R., & Schlesinger, L. B. (1987). Assessing and predicting violence: Research, law, and applications. In A. Hess & I. Weiner (Eds.), *Handbook of forensic psychology.* New York: Wiley.

Litz, B. T., Orsillo, S. M., Friedman, M., Ehlich, P., et al. (1997). Post-traumatic stress disorder associated with peacekeeping duty in Somalia for U. S. military personnel. *Amer. J. Psychiat., 154*(2), 178–84.

Livesley, W. J. (1991). Classifying personality disorders: Ideal types, prototypes, or dimensions? *J. Personal. Dis., 5*, 52–59.

Livesley, W. J. (1995). Past achievements and future directions. In W. J. Livesley (Ed.), *The DSM-IV personality disorders.* (pp. 497–506). New York: Guilford.

Livesley, W. J., & Jackson, D. N. (1991). Construct validity and classification of personality disorders. In J. M. Oldham (Ed.), *Personality disorders: New perspectives on diagnostic validity.* Washington, DC: American Psychiatric Press.

Livesley, W. J., Jackson, D. N., & Schroeder, M. L. (1992). Factorial structure of traits delineating personality disorders in clinical and general population samples. *J. Abn. Psychol., 101*, 432–40.

Livesley, W. J., Jang, K. L., Jackson, D. N., & Vernon, P. A. (1993). Genetic and environmental contributions to dimensions of personality disorder. *Amer. J. Psychiat., 150*, 1826–31.

Livesley, W. J., Schroeder, M. L., Jackson, D. N., & Jang, K. L. (1994). Categorical distinctions in the study of personality disorder: Implications for classification. *J. Abn. Psychol., 103*, 6–17.

Livesley, W. J., West, M., & Tanney, A. (1985). Historical comment on the DSM-III schizoid and avoidant personality disorders. *Amer. J. Psychiat., 142*, 1344–47.

Livingston, J. (1974, Mar.). Compulsive gamblers: A culture of losers. *Psych. Today*, 51–55.

Lizardi, H., Klein, D. N., Ouimette, P. C., Riso, L. P., Anderson, R. L., & Donaldson, S. K. (1995). Reports of the childhood home environment in early-onset dysthymia and episodic major depression. *J. Abn. Psychol. 104*, 132–39.

Lobitz, W. C., & Lobitz, G. K. (1978). Clinical assessment in the treatment of sexual dysfunctions. In J. LoPiccolo & L. LoPiccolo (Eds.), *Handbook of sex therapy.* (pp. 85–102). New York: Plenum.

Lobovits, D. A., & Handel, P. (1985). Childhood depression: Prevalence using DSM-III criteria and validity of parent and child depression scales. *J. Pediat. Psychol., 10*(1), 45–54.

Loeber, R., Green, S. M., Lahey, B. B., Crist, M. A., & Frick, P. J. (1992). Developmental sequences in the age of onset of disruptive child behaviors. *Journal of Child and Family Studies, 1*, 21–41.

Loeber, R., & Farrington, D. P. (1998). *Serious and violent juvenile offenders: Risk factors and successful interventions.* Thousand Oaks, CA: Sage.

Loeber, R., & Stouthamer–Loeber, M. (1998). Development of juvenile aggression and violence: Some common misconceptions and controversies. *Amer. Psychol., 53*(2), 242–59.

Loftus, E. F. (1993). The reality of repressed memories. *Amer. Psychol., 48*(5), 518–537.

Loftus, E. F., Feldman, J., & Dashiell, R. (in press) The reality of illusory memories. In D. Schacter, J. Coyle, L. Sullivan, M. Mesulam, & G. Fischbach (Eds.), *Memory distortions: Interdisciplinary perspectives.* Cambridge: Harvard University Press.

Loftus, E. F., Feldman, J., & Garry, M. (1994). Forgetting sexual trauma: What does it mean when 38% forget? *J. Cons. Clin. Psychol., 62*, 1177–81.

Loftus, E. F., & Ketchum, K. (1994). *The myth of repressed memory : False memories and allegations of sexual abuse.* New York: St Martin's.

Lohr, B. A., Adams, H. E., & Davis, J. M. (1997). Sexual arousal to erotic and aggressive stimuli in sexually coercive and noncoercive men. *J. Abn. Psychol., 106*, 230–42.

Lohr, J. M., et al. (1995). The empirical status of the clinical application of eye movement desensitization and reprocessing. *J. Behav. Ther. Exper. Psychiat., 26*, 285–302.

Lohr, J. M., Tolin, D. F., & Lilienfeld, S. O. (1998). Efficacy of eye movement desensitization and reprocessing: Implications for behavior therapy. *Behav. Ther., 29*(1), 123–56.

Lombardo, V. S., & Lombardo, E. F. (1991). The link between learning disabilities and juvenile delinquency: Fact or fiction? *The Correctional Psychologist, 23*, 1–3.

Lomranz, J., Hobfoll, S., Johnson, R., Eyla, N., & Tzemach, M. (1994). A nation's response to attack: Israeli's depressive reactions to the Gulf War. *J. Traum. Stress, 7*, 59–73.

Long, J. V. F., & Valliant, G. E. (1984). Natural history of male psychological health, XI: Escape from the underclass. *Amer. J. Psychiat., 141*, 341–346.

Loosen, P. T. (1986). Hormones of the hypothalmic-pituitary thyroid axis: A psychoneuroendocrine perspective. *Pharmacopsychiatry, 19*, 401–15.

Lopez, O. L., et al. (1997). The apolioprotein E e4 allele is not associated with psychiatric symptoms or extra-pyramidal signs in probable Alzheimer's disease. *Neurology, 49*(3), 794–97.

Lopez, S. R., Lopez, A. A., & Fong, K. T. (1991). Mexican Americans' initial preferences for counselors: The role of ethnic factors. *J. Couns. Psychol., 38*, 487–96.

LoPiccolo, J. (1978). Direct treatment of sexual dysfunction. In J. LoPiccolo & L. LoPiccolo (Eds.), *Handbook of sex therapy.* (pp. 1–17). New York: Plenum.

LoPiccolo, J., & LoPiccolo, L. (Eds.). (1978). *Handbook of sex therapy.* New York: Plenum.

LoPiccolo, J., & Stock, W. E. (1986). Treatment of sexual dysfunction. *J. Cons. Clin. Psychol., 54*, 158–67.

Loranger, A. W., Oldham, J. M., & Tulis, E. H. (1982). Familial transmission of DSM-III borderline personality disorder. *Arch. Gen. Psychiat., 39*(7), 795–99.

Lord, C., & Magill-Evans, J. (1995). Peer interactions of autistic children and adolescents. *Develop. Psychopath., 7,* 611–26.

Lorenz, V. C., & Shuttlesworth, D. E. (1983). The impact of pathological gambling on the spouse of the gambler. *J. Comm. Psychol., 11,* 67–76.

Lorion, R. P. (1990). *Protecting the children: Strategies for optimizing emotional and behavioral development.* New York: Haworth.

Lorr, M., & Klett, C. J. (1968). Crosscultural comparison of psychotic syndromes. *J. Abn. Psychol., 74*(4), 531–43.

Los Angeles Times. (1973, Sept. 30). A transvestite's plea for understanding and tolerance. IV, 7.

Losel, F. (1998). Treatment and management of psychopaths. In D. J. Cooke, A. E. Forth, & R. D. Hare (Eds.), *Psychopathy: Theory, research, and implications for society.* (pp. 303-354). Dordrecht, Netherland: Kluwer Academic Publishers.

Lovaas, O. I. (1977). *The autistic child: Language development through behavior modification.* New York: Holsted Press.

Lovaas, O. I. (1987). Behavioral treatment of normal educational and intellectual functioning in young autistic children. *J. Cons. Clin. Psychol., 44,* 3–9.

Lovett, S. (1985). Microelectronic and computer-based technology. In A. M. Clarke, A. D. B. Clarke, & J. M. Berg (Eds.), *Mental deficiency: The changing outlook* (4th ed.). (pp. 549–83). London: Methuen.

Lovibond, S. H., & Caddy, G. R. (1970). Discriminated aversive control in the moderation of alcoholics' drinking behavior. *Behav. Ther. 1,* 437–44.

Lowenfels, A. B., & Winn, P. S. (1992). One less for the road: International trends in alcohol consumption and vehicular fatalities. *Annals of Epidemiology, 2*(3), 249–56.

Lozoff, B. (1989). Nutrition and behavior. Special issue: Children and their development: Knowledge base, research agenda, and social policy application. *Amer. Psychol., 44,* 231–236.

Lubin, B. (1976). Group therapy. In I. Weiner (Ed.), *Clinical methods in psychology.* New York: Wiley.

Lubin, B., Larsen, R. M., & Matarazzo, J. (1984). Patterns of psychological test usage in the United States, 1935–1982. *Amer. Psychol., 39,* 451–54.

Lubin, B., Larsen, R. M., Matarazzo, J. D., & Seever, M. F. (1985). Psychological test usage patterns in five professional settings. *Amer. Psychol., 40,* 857–61.

Luborsky, L., & Crits-Christoph. (1990). *Understanding transference.* New York: Basic Books.

Luborsky, L., et al. (1988). *Who will benefit from psychotherapy: Predicting therapeutic outcome.* New York: Basic Books.

Lucas, A. R., Duncan J. W., & Piens, V. (1976). The treatment for anorexia nervosa. *Amer. J. Psychiat., 133,* 1034–38.

Luchins, A. S. (1991). Moral treatment in Asylums and general hospitals in 19th Century America. *J. Psychol., 123,* 585–607.

Luckasson, R., Coulter, D. L., Polloway, E. A., Reiss, S., Schalock, R. L., Snell, M. E., Spitalnik, D. M., & Stark, J. A. (1992). *Mental retardation: Definition, classification, and systems of supports* (9th ed.). Washington, DC: American Association on Mental Retardation.

Lukas, C., & Seiden, H. M. (1990). *Silent grief: Living in the wake of suicide.* New York: Bantam Books.

Lund, S. N. (1975). *Personality and personal history factors of child abusing parents.* Unpublished doctoral dissertation, University of Minnesota.

Lung, C. T., & Daro, D. (1996). *Current trends in child abuse reporting and fatalities: The results of the 1995 annual 50-state survey.* Chicago: National Committee to Prevent Child Abuse.

Lunsing, R. J., Hadders Algra, M., Touwen, B. C., & Huisjes, H. J. (1991). Nocturnal enuresis and minor neurological dysfunction at 12 years: A follow-up study. *Develop. Med. Child Neurol., 33,* 439–45.

Luntz, B. K., & Spatz, W. (1994). Antisocial personality disorder in abused and neglected children grown up. *Amer. J. Psychiat., 151* (5), 670–674

Luntz, B. K., & Widom, C. S. (1994). Antisocial personality disorder in abused and neglected children grown-up. *Amer. J. Psychiat., 151,* 670–74.

Lusznat, R. M., Murphy, D. P., & Nunn, C. M. H. (1988). Carbamazepine vs. lithium in the treatment and prophylaxis of mania. *Brit. J. Psychiat., 153,* 198–204.

Luten, A., Ralph, I., & Mineka, S. (1995). *Pessimistic attributional style: Is it specific to depression versus anxiety versus negative affect?* Submitted for publication.

Luten, A., Ralph, J., & Mineka, S. (1997). Depressive attributional style: Is it specific to depression vs. anxiety vs. negative affect? *Behav. Res. Ther., 35,* 703–719.

Luthar, S. S., Doernberger, C. H., & Zigler, E. (1993). Resilience is not a unidimensional construct: Insights from a prospective study of inner-city adolescents. *Develop. Psychopath., 5,* 703–17.

Lutz, D. J., & Snow, P. A. (1985). Understanding the role of depression in the alcoholic. *Clin. Psychol. Rev., 5,* 535–51.

Lykken, D. T. (1957). A study of anxiety in the sociopathic personality. *J. Abn. Soc. Psychol., 55*(1), 6–10.

Lykken, D. T. (1995). *The Antisocial Personalities.* Hillsdale, NJ: Erlbaum.

Lynam, D. R. (1996). Early identification of chronic offenders: Who is the fledgling psychopath? *Psychol. Bull., 120*(2), 209–234.

Lynam, D. R. (1997). Pursuing the psychopath: Capturing the fledgling psychopath in a nomological net. *J. Abn. Psychol., 106*(3), 425–438.

Lynam, D., Moffitt, T. E., & Stouthamer-Loeber, M. (1993). Explaining the relation between IQ and delinquency: Class, race, test motivation, school failure, or self-control. *J. Abn. Psychol., 102,* 187–96.

Lynch, J. J. (1977). *The broken heart.* New York: Basic Books.

Lynch, J. P. (1996). Clarifying divergent estimates of rape from two national surveys. *Public Opinion Quarterly, 60,* 410–30.

Lynch, P. S., Kellow, J. T., & Willson, V. L. (1997). The impact of deinstitutionalization on the adaptive behavior of adults with mental retardation. *Education & Training in Mental Retardation & Developmental Disabilities, 32*(3), 255–61.

Lynd-Stevenson, R. M. (1996). A test of the hopelessness theory of depression in unemployed young adults. *Brit. J. of Clin. Psych., 35,* 117–32.

Lyness, S. A. (1993). Predictors of differences between Type A and B individuals in heart rate and blood pressure reactivity. *Psychol. Bull., 114*(2), 266–95.

Lyon, G. R., & Moats, L. C. (1997). Critical conceptual and methodological considerations in reading intervention research. *J. Learn. Dis., 30*(6), 578–88.

Lyon, M., Barr, C. E., Cannon, T. D., Mednick, S. A., & Shore, D. (1989). Fetal neural development and schzophrenia. *Schizo. Bull., 15,* 149–61.

Lyons-Ruth, K. (1996). Attachment relationships among children with aggressive behavior problems: The role of disorganized early attachment patterns. *J. Cons. Clin. Psychol., 64*(1), 64–73.

Lytton, H. (1980). *Parent-child interaction: The socialization process observed in twin and singleton families.* New York: Plenum.

Lyubomirsky, S., & Nolen-Hoeksema, S. (1995). Effects of self-focused rumination on negative thinking and interpersonal problem solving. *J. Pers. Soc. Psychol., 69*(1), 176–190.

Lyubomirsky, S., Caldwell, N. D., & Nolen-Hoeksema S. (1998). Effects of ruminative and distracting responses to depressed mood on retrieval of autobiographical memories. *J. Pers. Soc. Psychol., 75* 166–77.

McAlister, A., Puska, P., Koskela, K., Pallonen, U., & Maccoby, N. (1980). Mass communication and community organization for public health education. *Amer. Psychol., 35,* 375–79.

McBride, W. J., Murphy, J. M., Gatto, G. J., et al. (1992). CNS mechanisms of alcohol drinking in genetically selected lines of rats. *Alcohol and Alcoholism, 27* (supplement 2).

McBurnett, K. & Pfiffner, L. (1998). Comorbidities and biological correlates of conduct disorder. In D. J. Cooke, A. E. Forth, & R. D. Hare (Eds.), *Psychopathy: Theory, research, and implications for society.*

(pp. 189–204). Dordrecht, Netherlands: Kluwer Academic Publishers.

McCall, L. (1961). Between us and the dark (originally published in 1947). Summary in W. C. Alvarez, *Minds that came back.*

McCann, I. L., Sakheim, D. K., & Abrahamson, D. J. (1988). Trauma and victimization: A model of psychological adaptation. *Counsel. Psychol., 16,* 531–94.

McCarroll, J. E., Ursano, R. J., & Fullerton, C. S. (1995). Symptoms of PTSD following recovery of war dead: 13–15-month follow-up. *Amer. J. Psychiat., 152*(6), 939–41.

McCarthy, B. W. (1989). Cognitive-behavioral strategies and techniques in the treatment of early ejaculation. In S. R. Leiblum & R. C. Rosen (Eds.), *Principles and practice of sex therapy* (2nd ed.). (pp. 141–67). New York: Guilford.

McCarthy, P., & Foa, E. B. (1990). Treatment interventions for obsessive-compulsive disorder. In M. Thase, B. Edelstein, & M. Hersen (Eds.), *Handbook of outpatient treatment of adults.* New York: Plenum.

McCarton, C. M., Brooks-Gunn, J., Wallace, I. F., Bauer, C. R., Bennett, F. C., Bernbaum, J. C., Broyles, R. S., Casey, P. H., McCormick, M. C., Scott, D. T., Tyson, J., Tonascia J., & Meinert, C. L. (1997). Results at age 8 years of early intervention for low-birth-weight premature infants: The Infant Health and Development Program. *JAMA, 277*(2), 126–32.

McClellan, J. M., & Wherry, J. S. (1992). Schizophrenia. *Psychiat. Clin. N. Amer., 15,* 131–48.

McClelland, D. C. (1979). Inhibited power motivation and high blood pressure in men. *J. Abn. Psychol., 88*(2), 182–90.

McCloskey, L. A., Figueredo, A. J., & Koss, M. P. (1995) The effects of systemic family violence on children's mental health. *Child Develop., 66,* 1239–61.

Maccoby, E. E., & Martin, J. A. (1983). Socialization in the context of the family: Parent-child interaction. In E. M. Hetherington (Ed.), *Socialization, personality, and social development: Vol. 4. Handbook of child psychology.* New York: Wiley.

McCombie, S. L. (1976). Characteristics of rape victims seen in crisis intervention. *Smith College Studies in Social Work, 46,* 137–58.

McCord, J., & Tremblay, R. E. (1992). *Preventing antisocial behavior interventions from birth through adolescence.* New York: Guilford.

McCord, W., & McCord, J. (1964). *The psychopath: An essay on the criminal mind.* New York: Van Nostrand Reinhold.

McCracken, L. (1997). "Attention" to pain in persons with chronic pain: A behavioral approach. *Behav. Ther., 28*(2), 271–84.

McCutchan, J. A. (1990). Virology, immunology, and clinical course of HIV infection. *J. Cons. Clin. Psychol., 58,* 5–12.

McDonald, L., Billingham, S., Conrad, T., Morgan, A., et al. (1997). Families and schools together (FAST): Integrating community development with clinical strategies. *Families in Society, 78*(2), 140–55.

MacDonald, M. R., & Kuiper, N. A. (1983). Cognitive-behavioral preparations for surgery: Some theoretical and methodological concerns. *Clin. Psychol. Rev., 3,* 27–39.

McDonnell, J., Hardman, M. L., Hightower, J., & Keifer-O'Donnel, R. (1993). Impact of communitybased instruction on the development of adaptive behavior of secondary-level students with mental retardation. *Amer. J. Ment. Retard., 97*(5), 575–84.

McEwen, B. S., & Stellar, E. (1993). Stress and the individual. *Arch. Int. Med., 153,* 2093–101.

McFadden, K. L. (1997). Policy improvements for prevention of alcohol misuse by airline pilots. *Human Factors, 39*(1), 1–8.

McFall, M. E., Murburg, M. M., Grant, N., Veith, R. C. (1990). Autonomic responses to stress in Vietnam combat veterans with posttraumatic stress disorder. *Biol. Psychia., 27*(1), 1165–75.

McFall, R. M. (1990). The enhancement of social skills: An information-processing analysis. In W. L. Marshall, D. R. Laws, & H. E. Barbaree (Eds.), *Handbook of sexual assault: Issues, theories, and treatment of the offender* (pp. 311–30). New York: Plenum.

McFarlane, A. C. (1988). The longitudinal course of posttraumatic morbidity: The range of outcomes and their predictors. *J. Nerv. Ment. Dis., 176,* 30–39.

McFarlane, A. C., Clayer, J. R., & Bookless, C. L. (1997). Psychiatric morbidity following a natural disaster: An Australian bushfire. *Soc. Psychiat. Psychiatr. Epidemiol., 32*(5), 261–68.

McFarlane, W. R., et al. (1995). The multiple family group and psychoeducation in the treatment of schizophrenia. *Arch. Gen. Psychiat., 54,*679–87.

McGee, R., Feehan, M., & Williams, S. (1995). Long–term follow–up of a birth cohort. In F. C. Verhulst & H. M. Koot (Eds.), *The epidemiology of child and adolescent psychopathology.* (pp. 366–84). New York: Oxford Medical.

McGlashan, T. H. (1996). Early detection and intervention in schizophrenia: Research. *Schizo. Bull., 22*(2), 327–45.

McGlashan, T. H., & Fenton, W. S. (1992). The positive-negative distinction in schizophrenia: Review of natural history validators. *Arch. Gen. Psychiat., 49*(1), 63–72.

McGlashan, T. H., & Fenton, W. S. (1993). Subtype progression and pathophysiologic deterioration in early schizophrenia. *Schizo. Bull., 19*(1), 71–84.

McGue, M. (in press). Behavioral genetic models of alcoholism and drinking. In K. E. Leonard & H. T. Blane (Eds.), *Psychological theories of drinking and alcoholism.* New York: Guilford.

McGue, M., & Lykken, D. T. (1992). Genetic influence on risk of divorce. *Psychological Science, 3*(6), 368–73.

McGue, M., Pickens, R. W., & Svikis, D. S. (1992). Sex and age effects on the inheritance of alcohol problems: A twin study. *J. Abn. Psychol., 101*(1), 3–17.

McGuffin, P., & Gottesman, I. I. (1985). Genetic influences on normal and abnormal development. In M. Rutter & L. Hersov (Eds.), *Child and adolescent psychiatry: Modern approaches* (2nd ed.). Oxford: Blackwell Scientific.

McGuffin, P., Katz, R., & Rutherford, J. (1991). Nature, nurture and depression: A twin study. *Psychol. Med., 21,* 329–35.

McHugh, P. R. (1992). Psychiatric misadventures. *American-Scholar, 61,* 497–510.

McIntosh, J. L. (1992). Suicide of the elderly. In B. Bongar (Ed.), *Suicide: Guidelines for assessment, management and treatment.* New York: Oxford University Press.

McIvor, R. J., & Turner, S. W. (1995). Assessment and treatment approaches for survivors of torture. *Brit. J. Psychiat., 166,* 705–11.

McKay, J. R., Alterman, A. I., McLellan, A. T., & Snider, E. C. (1994). Treatment goals, continuity of care, and outcome in a day hospital substance abuse rehabilitation program. *Amer. J. Psychiat., 151,* 254–59.

Mackay, L. E. (1994). Benefits of a formalized traumatic brain injury program within a trauma center. *J. Head Trauma Rehab., 9*(1), 11–19.

Mackinnon, A., & Foley, D. (1996). The genetics of anxiety disorders. In H. G. Westenberg, J. A. Den Boer, & D. L. Murphy (Eds.), *Advances in the neurobiology of anxiety disorders.* (pp. 39–59). Chichester, England: Wiley.

Mackintosh, N. J. (1983). *Conditioning and associative learning.* Oxford: Clarendon.

McLaughlin, A. M., & Peters, S. (1993). Evaluation of an innovative cost-effective programme for brain injury patients: Response to a need for flexible treatment planning. *Brain Injury, 7*(1), 71–75.

Maclean, W. E., Jr. (Ed.). (1997). *Ellis' handbook of mental deficiency: Psychological theory and research.* Mahwah, NJ: Erlbaum.

McLellan, A. T., Arndt, I. O., Metzger, D. S., Woody, G. E., & O'Brien, C. P. (1993). The effects of psychosocial services in substance abuse treatment. *JAMA, 269,* 1953–59.

McLellan, A. T., Luborsky, L., Woody, G. E., O'Brien, C. P., & Druley, K. A. (1993). Predicting response to alcohol and drug abuse treatments. *Arch. Gen. Psychiat., 40,* 620–25.

MacLeod, C., & Cohen, I. L. (1993). Anxiety and the interpretation of ambiguity: A text comprehension study. *J. Abn. Psychol., 102* (2), 238–47.

MacLeod, C., & Mathews, A.M. (1991). Cognitive-experimental approaches to the emotional disorders. In P. Martin (Ed.), *Handbook of behavior therapy and psychological science: An integrative approach.* (pp. 116–50). New York: Pergamon.

McLoyd, V. C. (1998) Socioeconomic disadvantage and child development. *Amer. Psychol., 53,* 185–204.

McLoyd, V. C., Jayaratne, T. E., Rosario, C., & Borquez, J. (1994). Unemployment and work interruption among African-American single mothers: Effects on parenting and adolescent socioemotional functioning. *Child Develop., 65,* 562–89.

MacMillan, D. L., Gresham, F. M., & Siperstein, G. N. (1993). Conceptual and psychometric concerns about the 1992 AAMR definition of mental retardation. *Amer. J. Ment. Retard., 98*(3), 325–35.

McMillan, J. C., Smith, E. M., & Fisher, R. ,H. (1997). Perceived benefit and mental health after three types of disaster. *J. Cons. Clin. Psychol., 65*(5), 733–39.

McMinn, M. R., Buchanan, T., Ellens, B. M., Ryan, M. K. (1999). Technology, professional practice, and ethics: Survey findings and implications. *Professional Psychology: Research and Practice, 30*(2), 165–172.

McMurran, M., & Hollin, C. R. (1993). *Young offenders and alcohol related crime.* New York: Wiley.

McNally, R. (1987). Preparedness and phobias: A review. *Psychol. Bull., 101,* 283–303.

McNally, R. J. (1990). Psychological approaches to panic disorder: A review. *Psychol. Bull., 108*(3), 403–419.

McNally, R. J. (1994). *Panic disorder: A critical analysis.* New York: Guilford.

McNally, R. J., & Eke, M. (1996). Anxiety sensitivity, suffocation fear, and breath-holding duration as predictors of response to carbon dioxide challenge. *J. Abn. Psychol., 105*(1), 146–49.

McNally. R. J. (1996). Cognitive bias in anxiety disorders. In D. Hope (Ed.), *Perspectives on anxiety, panic and fear,* (pp. 211–50). Lincoln: University of Nebraska Press.

McNeal, E. T., & Cimbolic, P. (1986). Antidepressants and biochemical theories of depression. *Psychol. Bull., 99*(3), 361–74.

McNeil, D. E., & Binder, R. L. (1986). Violence, civil commitment, and hospitalization. *J. Nerv. Ment. Dis., 174*(2), 107–11.

McReynolds, P. (1996). Lightner Witmer: Little–known founder of clinical psychology. *Amer. Psychol., 51,* 237–240.

McReynolds, P. (1997). Lightner Witmer: The first clinical psychologist. In W. G. Bringmann, H. E. Luck, R. Miller, & C. E. Early (Eds.), *A pictorial history of psychology.* (pp. 465–470). Chicago: Quintessence Books.

McWhirter, D. P., & Mattison, A. M. (1978). The treatment of sexual dysfunction in gay male couples. *J. Sex Marit. Ther., 4,* 213–18.

Maddi, S. R., Bartone, P. T., & Puccetti, M. C. (1987). Stressful events are indeed a factor in physical illness: Reply to Schroeder and Costa. *J. Pers. Soc. Psychol., 52,* 833–43.

Maddux, J. F., Vogtsberger, K. N., Prihoda, T. J., Desmond, D. F., Watson, D. D., & Williams, M. L. (1994). Illicit drug injectors in three Texas cities. *Intern. J. Addict., 29,* 179–94.

Magee, W. J., Eaton, W. W., Wittchen, H., McGonagle, K. A., & Kessler, R. C. (1996). Agoraphobia, simple phobia, and social phobia in the National Comorbidity Survey. *Arch. Gen. Psychiat., 53,* 159–68.

Magnus, K., Diener, E., Fujita, F., & Pavot, W. (1993). Extraversion and neuroticism as predictors of objective life events: A longitudinal analysis. *J. Pers. Soc. Psychol., 65*(5), 1046–53.

Maher, J. J. (1997). Exploring effects on liver function. *Alcohol Health & Research, 2*(1), 5–12.

Mahler, M. (1976). *On Human symbiosis and the vicissitudes of individuation.* New York: Library of Human Behavior.

Mahoney, G., Glover, A., & Finger, I. (1981). Relationship between language and sensorimotor development of Down's syndrome and nonretarded children. *Amer. J. Ment. Def., 86,* 21–27.

Mahoney, M., & Arnkoff, D. (1978). Cognitive and self-control therapies. In S. Garfield & A. Bergin (Eds.), *Handbook of psychotherapy and behavior change: An empirical analysis.* New York: Wiley.

Maida, C. A., Gordon, N. S., & Farberow, N. L. (1989). *The crisis of competence.* New York: Bruner/Mazel.

Maier, S. F., Watkins, L. R., & Fleshner, M. (1994). Psychoneuroimmunology: The interface between behavior, brain, and immunity. *Amer. Psychol., 49*(12), 1004–17.

Maier, S., Seligman, M., & Solomon, R. (1969). Pavlovian fear conditioning and learned helplessness. In B. A. Campbell & R. M. Church (Eds.), *Punishment and aversive behavior.* New York: Appleton-Century-Crofts.

Main, M. B., & Weston, D. R. (1981). Security of attachment to mother and father: Related to conflict behavior and the readiness to establish new relationships. *Child Develop., 52,* 932–940.

Maisch, H. (1972). *Incest.* New York: Stein & Day.

Maisto, S. A., & McKay, J. R. (1995). Diagnosis. In National Institute of Alcohol And Alcoholism, *Assessing alcohol problems: A guide for clinicians and researchers.* (pp. 41–54). Washington: U.S. Department of Health and Human Services.

Maiuro, R. D., Cahn, T. S. Vitaliano, P. P., Wagner, B. C. & Zegree, J. B. (1988). Anger, hostility, and depression in domestically violent versus generally assaultive men and nonviolent control subjects. *J. Consult. Clin. Psychol., 56,* 17–23.

Maj, M., Satz, P., Janssen, R., Zaudig, M., Starace, F., D'Elia, L., Sughondhabirom, B., Mussa, M., Naber, D., Ndetei, D., Schulte, G., & Sartorius, N. (1994). WHO neuropsychiatric AIDS study, cross sectional Phase II: Neuropsychological and neurological findings. *Arch. Gen. Psychiat., 51*(1), 51–61.

Majcher, D., & Pollack, M. (1996). Childhood anxiety disorders. In L. Hechtman (Ed.), *Do they grow out of it?* (pp. 139–70). Washington: American Psychiatric Press.

Major, B., Richards, C., & Cooper, M. L. (1998). Personal resilience, cognitive appraisals, and coping: An integrative model of adjustment to abortion. *J. Pers. Soc. Psychol., 74,* 735–52.

Major, B., Zubek, J. M., Cooper, M. L., Cozzarelli, C., et al. (1997). Mixed messages: Implications of social conflict and social support within close relationships for adjustment to a stressful life event. *J. Pers. Soc. Psychol. 72*(6), 1349–63.

Makita, K. (1973). The rarity of "depression" in childhood. *Acta Psychiatr. Scandin. 40,* 37–44.

Malamud, N. (1975). Organic brain disease mistaken for psychiatric disorder: A clinicopathologic study. In D. F. Benson & D. Blumer (Eds.), *Psychiatric aspects of neurological disease.* (pp. 287–307). New York: Grune & Stratton.

Malamuth, N. M., Linz, D., Heavey, C. L., & Barnes, G. (1995). Using the confluence model of sexual aggression to predict men's conflict with women: A 10-year follow-up study. *J. Pers. Soc. Psychol., 69,* 353–369.

Malatesta, V. J., & Adams, H. (1993) The sexual dysfunctions. In P. Sutker & H. Adams (Eds.), *Comprehensive textbook of psychopathology.* New York: Plenum.

Malatesta, V. J., Sutker, P. B., & Treiber, F. A. (1981). Sensation seeking and chronic public drunkenness. *J. Cons. Clin. Psychol., 49,* 292–94.

Maldonado, J. R., Butler, L. D., & Spiegel, D. (1998). Treatments for dissociative disorders. In P. E. Nathan & J. M. Gorman (Eds.), *A guide to treatments that work.* (pp. 423–46). New York: Oxford University Press.

Male, D., & May, D. S. (1997). Burnout and workload in teachers of children with severe learning difficulties. *Brit. J. Learn. Dis., 25*(3), 117–21.

Malec, J. F., Smigielski, J. S., DePompolo, R. W., & Thompson, J. M. (1993). Outcome evaluation and prediction in a comprehensive-integrated post-acute outpatient brain injury rehabilitation programme. *Brain Injury, 7*(1), 15–29.

Maletsky, B. M. (1998). The paraphilias: Research and treatment. In P. E. Nathan & J. M. Gorman (Eds.), *A guide to treatments that work.* (pp. 472–500). New York: Oxford University Press.

Malinosky-Rummell, R., & Hansen, D.J. (1993). Long-term consequences of childhood physical abuse. *Psychol. Bull., 114,* 68–79.

Malinowski, B. (1927). *Sex and repression in savage society*. New York: Humanities.

Mandler, G. (1964). The interruption of behavior. In D. Levine (Ed.), *Nebraska symposium on motivation: 1964*. Lincoln, Nebraska: University of Nebraska Press.

Mandler, G. (1972). Helplessness: Theory and research in anxiety. In C. Spielberger (Ed.), *Anxiety: Current trends in theory and research*. (pp. 359–74). New York: Academic Press.

Manfro, G. G., Otto, M. W., McArdle, E. T., & Worthington, J. J. (1996). Relationships of antecedent stressful life events to childhood and family history of anxiety and the course of panic. *J. Affect. Dis.*, 41(2), 135–39.

Manglesdorff, D. (1985). Lessons learned and forgotten: The need for prevention and mental health interventions in disaster preparedness. *J. Comm. Psychol.*, 13, 239–57.

Mann, J. (1973). *Time-dated psychotherapy*. Cambridge, MA: Harvard University Press.

Mann, L. M., Chassin, L., & Sher, K. J. (1987). Alcohol expectancies and risk for alcoholics. *J. Cons. Clin. Psychol.*, 55, 411–17.

Mann, P. A. (1978). *Community psychology: Concepts and applications*. New York: Free Press.

Mannuzza, S., Gittelman, R., Bonagura, N., Konig, P. H., & Shenker, R. (1988). Hyperactive boys almost grown up. *Arch. Gen. Psychiat.*, 45, 13–18.

Mannuzza, S., Klein, R., Bessler, A., Malloy, P., & LaPadula, M. (1993). Adult outcome of hyperactive boys: Educational achievement, occupational rank, and psychiatric status. *Arch. Gen. Psychiat.*, 50, 565–76.

Marangell, L. B., Ketter, T. A., George, M. S., Pazzaglia, P. J., Callahan, A. M., Parekh, P., Andreason., P. J., Horwitz, B., Herscovitch, P., & Post, R. (1997). Inverse relationship of peripheral thyrotropin-stimulating hormone levels to brain activity in mood disorder. *Amer. J. Psychiat.*, 145(2), 224–30.

Marans, S., & Cohen, D. (1993). Children and inner–city violence: Strategies for intervention. In L. Leavitt & N. Fox (Eds.), *Psychological effects of war and violence on children*. (pp. 281–302). Hillsdale, NJ: Erlbaum.

March, J., & Leonard, H. (1998). Obsessive-compulsive disorder in children and adolescents. In R. Swinson, M. Antony, S. Rachman, & M. Richter (Eds.), *Obsessive-compulsive disorder: Theory, research, and treatment*. (pp. 367–94). New York: Guilford.

Marcos, T., Salamero, M., Gutierrez, F., Catalan, R., Gasto, C., & Lazaro, L. (1994). Cognitive dysfunctions in recovered melancholic patients. *J. Affect. Dis.*, 32, 133–37.

Marcourakis, T., Gorenstein, C., & Gentil, V. (1993). Clomipramine, a better reference drug for panic/agoraphobia: II Psychomotor and cognitive effects. *J. Psychopharm.*, 7, 325–30.

Marcus, E. R., & Bradley, S. S. (1990). Combination psychotherapy and psychopharmacotherapy with treatment-resistant inpatients with dual disorder. *Psychiat. Clin. N. Amer.*, 13, 209–14.

Marcus, J., Hans, S. L., Auerbach, J. G., & Auerbach, A. G. (1993). Children at risk for schizophrenia: The Jerusalem infant development study: II. Neurobehavioral deficits at school age. *Arch. Gen. Psychiat.*, 50(10), 797–809.

Marcus, J., Hans, S. L., Mednick, S. A., Schulsinger, F., & Michelson, N. (1985). Neurological dysfunctioning in offspring of schizophrenics in Israel and Denmark: A replication analysis. *Arch. Gen. Psychiat.*, 42, 753–61.

Marcus, M. D., Wing, R. R., & Hopkins, J. (1988). Obese binge eaters: Affect, cognitions, and response to behavioral weight control. *J. Cons. Clin. Psychol.*, 56, 433–39.

Marder, S. R., Ames, D., Wirshing, W. C., & Van Putten, T. (1993). Schizophrenia. *Psychiat. Clin. N. Amer.*, 16, 567–88.

Margolin, G., & Wampold, B. E. (1981). Sequential analysis of conflict and accord in distressed and non-distressed marital partners. *J. Cons. Clin. Psychol.*, 49(4), 554–67.

Margolis, R. D., & Zweben, J. E. (1998). *Treating patients with alcohol and other drug problems: An integrated approach*. Washington: American Psychological Association.

Margraf, J., Ehlers, A., & Roth, W. T. (1986a). Sodium lactate infusions and panic attacks: A review and critique. *Psychosom. Med.*, 48, 23–51.

Margraf, J., Ehlers, A., & Roth, W. (1986b). Biological models of panic disorder and agoraphobia—A review. *Behav. Res. Ther.*, 24, 553–67.

Margraf, J., & Schneider, S. (1995, July). *Psychological treatment of panic: What works in the long run?* Paper presented at the World Congress of Behavioural and Cognitive Therapies, Copenhagen, Denmark.

Mariotto, M., Paul, G. L. & Licht, M. H. (1995). Assessing the chronically mentally ill patient. In J. N. Butcher (Ed.), *Clinical personality assessment: Practical considerations* New York: Oxford University Press.

Maris, R. W. (1997). Social forces in suicide: A life review, 1965-1995. In R. W. Maris, M. M. Silverman, & S. S. Canetton (Eds.), *Review of Suicidology, 1997*, (pp. 42–60). New York: Guilford.

Markovitz, P. J., & Schulz, S.C. (1993). Drug treatment of personality disorders. *Brit. J. Psychiat.*, 162, 122.

Marks, I. M. (1969). *Fears and phobias*. New York: Academic Press.

Marks, I. M. (1982). Toward an empirical clinical science: Behavioral psychotherapy in the 1980's. *Behav. Ther.*, 13, 63–81.

Marks, I. M. (1987). *Fear, phobias, and rituals: Panic, anxiety, and their disorders*. New York: Oxford University Press.

Marks, I., & Nesse, R. M. (1991). Fear and fitness: An evolutionary analysis of anxiety disorders. Paper presented at the Eleventh National Conference on Anxiety Disorders. Chicago, IL.

Marks, I., Swinson, R. P., Başoğlu, M., Kunch, K. (1993). Alprazolam and exposure alone and combined in panic disorder with agoraphobia: A controlled study in London and Toronto. *Brit. J. Psychiat.*, 162, 776–787.

Marlatt, G. A. (1985). Cognitive assessment and intervention procedures for relapse prevention. In G. A. Marlatt & J. R. Gordon (Eds.), *Relapse prevention*. New York: Guilford.

Marlatt, G. A. (1992). Substance abuse: Implications of a biopsychosocial model for prevention, treatment, and relapse prevention. In J. Grabowsik & G. R. VandenBos (Eds.), *Psychopharmacology: Basic mechanisms and applied interventions*. (pp. 127–162). Washington, DC: American Psychological Association.

Marlatt, G. A., & Gordon, J. R. (1980). Determinants of relapse: Implications for the maintenance of behavior change. In P. Davidson & S. Davidson (Eds.), *Behavioral medicine: Changing health lifestyles*. New York: Brunner/Mazel.

Marlatt, G. A., Baer, J. S., Kivahan, D. R., Dimeoff, L. A., Larimer, M. E., Quigley, L. A., Somers, J. M., & Williams, E. (1998). Screening and brief intervention for high-risk college student drinkers: Results from a 2-year follow up assessment. *J. Cons. Clin. Psychol.*, 66(4), 604–15.

Marmor, J., & Woods, S. M. (Eds.). (1980). *The interface between psychodynamic and behavior therapies*. New York: Plenum.

Marsella, A. J. (1980). Depressive experience and disorder across cultures. In H. C. Triandis & J. Draguns (Eds.), *Handbook of cross-cultural psychology* (Vol. 6). Boston: Allyn & Bacon.

Marsella, A. J., Sartorius, N., Jablensky, A., & Fenton, F. R. (1985). Cross-cultural studies of depressive disorders: An overview. In A. Kleinman & B. Good (Eds.), *Culture and depression*. Berkeley, CA: University of California Press.

Marsh, L., et al. (1997). Structural magnetic resonance imaging abnormalities in men with severe chronic schizophrenia and an early age at clinical onset. *Arch. Gen. Psychiat.*, 54(12), 1104–12.

Marshall, W. L. (1974). A combined treatment approach to the reduction of multiple fetish-related behaviors. *J. Cons. Clin. Psychol.*, 42(4), 613–16.

Marshall, W. L. (1993). The treatment of sex offenders: What does the outcome data tell us? A reply to Quinsey, Harris, Rice, and Lalumiere. *J. Interpers. Viol.*, 8, 524–30.

Marshall, W. L. (1997). Pedophilia: Psychopathology and theory. In D. R. Laws & W. O'Donohue (Eds.), *Sexual deviance: Theory, assessment, and treatment*. (pp. 152–74). New York: Guilford.

Marshall, W. L., & Barbaree, H. E. (1990a). An integrated theory of the etiology of sexual offending. In W. L. Marshall, D. R. Laws, & H. E. Barbaree (Eds.), *Handbook of sexual assault*. (pp. 257–69). New York: Plenum.

Marshall, W. L., & Barbaree, H. E. (1990b). Outcome of comprehensive cognitive-behavioral treatment programs. In W. L. Marshall, D. R. Laws, & H. E. Barbaree (Eds.), *Handbook of sexual assault: Issues, theories, and treatment of the offender*. (pp. 363–85). New York: Plenum.

Marshall, W. L., Barbaree, H. E., & Christophe, D. (1986). Sexual offenders against female children: Sexual preferences for age of victim and type of behavior. *Canad. J. Behav. Sci.*, 18, 424–39.

Marshall, W. L., Jones, R., Ward, T., Johnston, P., & Barbaree, H. E. (1991). Treatment outcome with sex offenders. *Clin. Psychol. Rev.*, 11, 465–85.

Marshall, W. L., & Pithers, W. D. (1994). A reconsideration of treatment outcome with sex offenders. *Crim. Just. Behav.*, 21, 10–27.

Marshalll, R. D., & Klein, D. F. (1995). Pharmacotherapy in the treatment of posttraumatic stress disorder. *Psychiat. Ann.*, 23(10), 588–89.

Martell, D. A., & Dietz, P. E. (1992). Mentally disordered offenders who push or attempt to push victims onto subway tracks in New York City. *Arch. Gen. Psychiat.*, 49(6), 472–75.

Martin, C. L. (1990). Attitudes and expectations about children with nontraditional and traditional gender roles. *Sex Roles*, 22, 151–65.

Martin, E. S., et al. (1997). Studies in a large family with late-onset Alzheimer disease (LOAD). *Alzheimer Disease and Associated Disorders*, 11(3), 163–70.

Martin, R. L., Cloninger, R., Guze, S. B., & Clayton, P. J. (1985). Mortality in a follow-up of 500 psychiatric outpatients: I. Total mortality. *Arch. Gen. Psychiat.*, 42, 47–54.

Martin, S. E. (1992). The epidemiology of alcohol-related interpersonal violence. *Alcohol Health & Research World*, 16(2), 230–37.

Martinez, A., Malphurs, J., Field, T., Pickens, J., et al. (1996). Depressed mothers and their infants' interactions with nondepressed partners. *Infant Mental Health Journal*, 17(1), 74–80.

Marvit, R. C. (1981). Guilty but mentally ill—an old approach to an old problem. *Clin. Psychol.*, 34(4), 22–23.

Marx, J. (1991). Mutation identified as possible cause of Alzheimer's disease. *Science*, 251, 876–77.

Mash, E. J., & Dozois, D. J. A. (1996). Child psychopathology: A developmental perspective. In E. J. Mash & R. A. Barkley (Eds.), *Child psychopathology*. (pp. 3–60). New York: Guilford.

Mash, E. J., Handy, L. C., & Hamerlynck, L. A. (1976). *Behavior modification approaches to parenting*. New York: Brunner/Mazel.

Maslow, A. H. (1962). *Toward a psychology of being*. New York: Van Nostrand.

Maslow, A. H. (1969). Toward a humanistic biology. *Amer. Psychol.*, 24(8), 734–35.

Mason, B. J., & Ownby, R. L. (1998). Alcohol. In P. J. Goodnick et al. (Eds.), *Mania: Clinical and research perspectives*. (pp. 63–80). Washington: American Psychiatric Press.

Mason, F. L. (1997). Fetishism: Psychopathology and theory. In D. R. Laws & W. O'Donohue (Eds.) *Sexual deviance: Theory, assessment, and treatment*. (pp. 75–91). New York: Guilford.

Masten, A. S., Best, K., & Garmezy, N. (1990). Resilience and development: Contributions from the study of children who come adversity. *Develop. Psychopath.*, 2, 425–44.

Masten, A. S., & Coatsworth, J. D. (1995). Competence, resilience, and psychopathology. In D. Cicchetti, & D. J. Cohen (Eds.), *Psychopathology: Vol. 2. Risk, disorder, and adaptation*. (pp. 715–52). New York: Wiley.

Masten, A. S, & Coatsworth, J. D. (1998) The development of competence in favorable and unfavorable environments: Lessons from research on successful children. *Amer. Psychol., 53*, 205–20.

Masten, A. S., & O'Connor, M. J. (1989). Vulnerability, stress, and resilience in early development of a high risk child. *J. Amer. Acad. Child Adoles. Psychiat., 28*, 274–78.

Masters, J., Burish, T. Hollon, S., & Rimm, D. (1987). *Behavior therapy: Techniques and empirical findings* (3rd ed.). San Diego: Harcourt Brace Jovanovich.

Masters, W. H., & Johnson, V. E. (1966). *Human sexual response.* Boston: Little, Brown.

Masters, W. H., & Johnson, V. E. (1970). *Human sexual inadequacy.* Boston: Little, Brown.

Masters, W. H., & Johnson, V. E. (1975). *The pleasure bond: A new look at sexuality and commitment.* Boston: Little, Brown.

Masters, W. H., Johnson, V. E., & Kolodny, R. C. (1992). *Human sexuality.* New York: HarperCollins.

Masterson, J. (1987). Borderline and narcissistic disorders: An integrated developmental object-relations approach. In J. Grotstein, M. Solomon, & J. Lang (Eds.), *The borderline patient* (Vol. 1). (pp. 205–17). Hillsdale, NJ: Analytic Press.

Matarazzo, J. D. (1986). Computerized clinical psychological test interpretations: Unvalidated plus all mean and no sigma. *Amer. Psychol., 41*, 14–24.

Matheny, A. P. Jr. (1989). Children's behavioral inhibition over age and across situations: Genetic similarity for a trait during change. *J. Personal., 57*, 215–35.

Mathew, R. J., Wilson, W. H., & Melges, F. T. (1992). Temporal disintegration and its psychological and physiological correlates: Changes in the experience of time after marijuana smoking. *Annals of Clinical Psychiatry, 4*, 235–45.

Mathews, A. M. (1993). Anxiety and the processing of emotional information. In L. Chapman, J. Chapman, & D. Fowles (Eds.), *Models and methods of psychopathology: Progress in experimental personality and psychopathology research.* New York: Springer.

Mathews, A. M., & MacLeod, C. (1994). Cognitive approaches to emotion and emotional disorders. *Ann. Rev. Psychol., 45*, 25–50.

Mathis, H. I. (1970). *Emotional responsivity in the antisocial personality.* (Doctoral dissertation, George Washington University), Ann Arbor, MI: University Microfilms, 1970, No. 71–12, 299. Cited in Hare (1978b).

Matier, K., Halperin, J. M., Sharma, V., & Newcorn, J. H. (1992). Methylphenidate response in aggressive and non-aggressive ADHD children: Distinctions on laboratory measures of symptoms. *J. Amer. Acad. Child Adoles. Psychiat., 31*, 219–25.

Matson, J. L. (1981). Use of independence training to teach shopping skills to mildly mentally retarded adults. *Amer. J. Ment. Def., 86*, 178–83.

Matsunaga, E., Tonomura, A., Hidetsune, O., & Yasumoto, K. (1978). Reexamination of paternal age effect in Down's syndrome. *Human Genet., 40*, 259–68.

Matt, G., Vazquez, C., & Campbell, W. (1992). Mood-congruent recall of affectively toned stimuli: A meta-analytic review. *Clin. Psychol. Rev., 12*, 227–255.

Mattes, J. A., & Gittelman, R., (1981). Effects of artificial food colorings in children with hyperactive symptoms: A critical review and results of a controlled study. *Arch. Gen. Psychiat., 38*(6), 714–18.

Mattia, J. I., Heimberg, R. G., & Hope, D. A. (1993). The revised Stroop color-naming task in social phobics: Diagnostic and treatment outcome implications. *Behav. Res. Ther., 31*, 305–13.

Mattson, M. E., Allen, J. P., Longabaugh, R., Nickless, C. J., et al. (1994). A chronological review of empirical studies matching alcoholic clients to treatment. *J. Stud. Alcoh. 12*, 16–29.

Mattson, S. N., Jernigan, T. L., & Riley, E. P. (1994). MRI and prenatal alcohol exposure. *Alcohol Health & Research World, 18*(1), 49–52.

Mattson, S. N., Riley, E. P., Gramling, L., Delis, D. C., & Jones, K. L. (1998). Neuropsychological comparison of alcohol–exposed children with or without physical features of fetal alcohol syndrome. *Neuropsychology, 12*(1), 146–53.

Mattson, M. E., & Riley, E. P. (1998). A review of the neurobehavioral deficits in children with fetal alcohol syndrome or prenatal exposure to alcohol. *Alcoholism: Clin. Exper. Res., 22*(2), 279–94.

Maughan, B., & Rutter, M. (1997). Retrospective reporting of childhood adversity: Issues in assessing long-term recall. *J. Personal. Dis., 11*, 19–33.

Mavissakalian, M. R., & Perel, J. M. (1989). Imipramine dose-response relationship in panic disorder with agoraphobia. *Arch. Gen. Psychiat., 46*, 127–31.

Max, W. (1993). The economic impact of Alzheimer's disease. *Neurology, 43*(8, Suppl. 4), S6–S10.

Maxfield, M. G., & Widom, C. S. (1996). The cycle of violence: Revisited Six years later. *Archives of Pediatric and Adolescent Medicine, 150*, 390–95.

May, E. T. (1995). *Barren in the promised land.* Cambridge, MA: Harvard University Press.

May, R. (1969). *Love and will.* New York: Norton.

Mays, D. T., & Franks, C. M. (Eds.). (1985). *Negative outcome in psychotherapy and what to do about it.* New York: Springer.

Mays, J. A. (1974, Jan. 16). High blood pressure, soul food. *Los Angeles Times,* II, 7.

Mazure, C. M., & Druss, B. G. (1995). An historical perspective on stress and psychiatric illness. In C. M. Mazure (Ed.), *Does stress cause psychiatric illness?* Washington, DC: American Psychiatric Association.

Mazziotta, J. (1996). Mapping mental illness: A new era. *Arch. Gen. Psychiat. 53*(7), 574–6.

Mead, M. (1949). *Male and female.* New York: Morrow.

Mealiea, W. L., Jr. (1967). *The comparative effectiveness of systematic desensitization and implosive therapy in the elimination of snake phobia.* Unpublished doctoral dissertation, University of Missouri.

Mearns, J., & Lees-Haley, P. R. (1993). Discriminating of neuropsychological sequelae of head injury from alcohol-abuse-induced deficits: A review and analysis. *J. Clin. Psychol., 49*(5), 714–20.

Medea, A., & Thompson, K. (1974). *Against rape.* New York: Farrar, Straus & Giroux.

Medical Council on Alcoholism (1997). *Alcohol-related liver disease.* London: Author.

The Medical Letter. (1990). Sudden death in children treated with a tricyclic antidepressant. *Medical Letter Drug Therapy, 32*, 53.

Mednick, S. A. (1978). Berkson's fallacy and high-risk research. In L. C. Wynne, R. L. Cromwell, & S. Matthysse (Eds.), *The nature of schizophrenia: New approaches to research and treatment.* (pp. 442–52). New York: Wiley.

Mednick, S. A., et al. (1998). A two-hit working model of the etiology of schizophrenia. In M. F. Lenzenweger & R. H. Dworkin (Eds.), *Origins and development of schizophrenia.* (pp. 27–66). Washington: American Psychological Association.

Mednick, S. A., & Schulsinger, F. (1968). Some premorbid characteristics related to breakdown in children with schizophrenic mothers. In D. Rosenthal & S. S. Kety (Eds.), *The transmission of schizophrenia.* (pp. 267–91). Oxford: Pergamon.

Meehl, P. E. (1962). Schizotaxia, schizotypy, schizophrenia. *Amer. Psychol., 17*, 827–38.

Meehl, P. E. (1978). Theoretical risks and tabular asterisks: Sir Karl, Sir Ronald, and the slow progress of soft psychology. *J. Cons. Clin. Psychol., 46*, 806–34.

Meehl, P. E. (1989). Schizotaxia revisited. *Arch. Gen. Psychiat., 46*, 935–44.

Meehl, P. E. (1990a). Toward an integrated theory of schizotaxia, schizotypy, and schizophrenia. *J. Personal. Dis., 4*, 1–99.

Meehl, P. E. (1990b). Why summaries of research on psychological theories are often uninterpretable. *Psychol. Rep., 66*, 195–244.

Megargee, E. I. (1970). The prediction of violence with psychological tests. In C. D. Spielberger (Ed.), *Current topics in clinical and community psychology* (Vol. 2). New York: Academic Press.

Megargee, E. I. (1993). Aggression and violence. In P. B. Sutker & H. E. Adams (Eds.), *Comprehensive handbook of psychopathology* (2nd ed.). (pp. 617–44). New York: Plenum.

Megargee, E. I. (1995). Assessing and understanding aggressive and violent patients. In J. N. Butcher (Ed.), *Clinical personality assessment: Practical considerations.* (pp. 395–409). New York: Oxford University Press.

Megargee, E. I. (1995). Use of the MMPI-2 in correctional settings. In Y. S. Ben-Porath, J. R. Graham, G. N. Hall, R. D. Hirschman, & M. S. Zaragoza (Eds.), *Forensic applications of the MMPI-2.* (pp. 127–59) Thousand Oaks, CA: Sage.

Megargee, E. I. (1997). Using the Megargee MMPI–based classification system with the MMPI-2s of female prison inmates. *Psychol. Assess., 9*, 75–82.

Mehlum, L., Friis, S., Irion, T., Johns, S., Karterud, S., Vaglum, P., & Vaglum, S. (1991). Personality disorders 2–5 years after treatment: A prospective follow-up study. *Acta Psychiatr. Scandin., 84*, 72–77.

Meichenbaum, D. (1974). *Cognitive behavior modification.* General Learning Corporation, 16.

Meichenbaum, D. (1975). A self-instructional approach to stress management: A proposal for stress-inoculation training. In C. Spielberger & I. Sarason (Eds.), *Stress and anxiety* (Vol. 2). New York: Wiley.

Meichenbaum, D. (1985). *Stress inoculation training.* New York: Pergamon.

Meichenbaum, D. (1993). Changing conceptions of cognitive behavior modification: Retrospect and prospect. *J. Cons. Clin. Psychol., 61*, 202–204.

Meichenbaum, D., & Cameron, R. (1982). Cognitive behavior therapy. In G. T. Wilson & C. M. Franks (Eds.), *Contemporary behavior therapy: Conceptual and empirical foundations.* New York: Guilford.

Meichenbaum, D., & Cameron, R. (1983). Stress inoculation training: Toward a general paradigm for training coping skills. In D. Meichenbaum & M. E. Jaremko (Eds.), *Stress reduction and prevention.* (pp. 115–54). New York: Plenum.

Meichenbaum, D., & Jaremko, M. E. (1983). *Stress reduction and prevention.* New York: Plenum.

Meissner, W. W. (1978). *The paranoid process.* New York: Jason Aronson.

Meltzer, H. Y. (1992). Treatment of the neuroleptic-nonresponsive schizophrenic patient. *Schizo. Bull., 18*(3), 515–42.

Meltzer, H. Y. (1993). New drugs for the treatment of schizophrenia. *Psychiat. Clin. N. Amer., 16*, 365–86.

Meltzer, H. Y., Cola, P., Way, L. Thompson, S. et al. (1993) Cost-effectiveness of clozapine in neuroleptic-resistant schizophrenia. *Amer. J. Psychiat., 150*, 1630–38.

Meltzer, H. Y., & Stahl, S. M. (1976). The dopamine hypothesis of schizophrenia: A review. *Schizo. Bull., 2*(1), 19–76.

Mendels, J., & Frazer, A. (1974). Brain biogenic amine depletion and mood. *Arch. Gen. Psychiat., 30*, 447–51.

Mendelson, J. H., & Mello, N. (1992). Human laboratory studies of buprenorphine. In J. D. Blaine (Ed.), *Buprenorphine: An alternative treatment for opiate dependence.* (pp. 38–60). Washington, DC: U.S. Department of Health and Human Services.

Mendlewicz, J. (1985). Genetic research in depressive disorders. In E. E. Beckham & W. R. Leber (Eds.), *Handbook of depression: Treatment, assessment and research.* (pp. 795–815). Homewood, IL: Dorsey Press.

Mendlewicz, J., & Rainer, J. D. (1977). Adoption study supporting genetic transmission in manic-depressive illness. *Nature, 268*, 326–29.

Menninger, K. A. (1945). *The human mind* (3rd ed.). New York: Knopf.

Mental Health Law Project. (1987, October). Court decisions concerning mentally disabled people confined in institutions. *MHLP Newsletter.* Washington, DC.

Mental health: Does therapy help? (1995, November). *Consumer Reports,* pp. 734–39.

Merbaum, M. (1977). Some personality characteristics of soldiers exposed to extreme war stress: A follow-up study of post-hospital adjustment. *J. Clin. Psychol., 33*, 558–62.

Merbaum, M., & Hefez, A. (1976). Some personality characteristics of soldiers exposed to extreme war stress. *J. Cons. Clin. Psychol., 44*(1), 1–6.

Merikangas, K. R. (1990). Comorbidity for anxiety and depression: Review of family and genetic studies. In J. D. Maser & C. R. Cloninger (Eds.), *Comorbidity of mood and anxiety disorders.* Washington, DC: American Psychiatric Press.

Merikangas, K. R., Spence, M. A., & Kupfer, D. J. (1989). Linkage studies of bipolar disorder: Methodologic and analytic issues. *Arch. Gen. Psychiat., 46,* 1137–41.

Merikangas, K. R., & Swendsen, J. D. (1997). Genetic epidemiology of psychiatric disorders. *Epidemiological Reviews, 19*(1), 144–55.

Merikangas, K. R., Wicki, W., & Angst, J. (1994). Heterogeneity of depression: Classification of depressive subtypes by longitudinal course. *Brit. J. Psychiat., 164,* 342–48

Merson, S., & Tryer, P. (1991). Physical treatments for depression. In R. Horton & C. Katona (Eds.), *Biological aspects of affective disorders.* New York: Academic Press.

Mesibov, G. B., Adams, L. W., & Klinger, L. G. (1997). *Autism: Understanding the disorder.* New York: Plenum.

Messer, S. B., & Warren, C. S. (1995). *Models of brief psychodynamic therapy: A comparative approach.* New York: Guilford.

Meston, C. M. & Gorzalka, B. B. (1996) Differential effects of sympathetic activation on sexual arousal in sexually dysfunctional and functional women. *J. Abn. Psychol., 105,* 582–91.

Meston, C. M. & Palace, E. M. (1995). Differential effects of sympathetic activation on sexual arousal in sexually dysfunctional and functional women. *J. Abn. Psychol., 105,* 582–591.

Metalsky, G. I., Abrason, L. Y., Seligman, M. E. P., Semmel, A., & Peterson, C. R. (1982). Attributional styles and life events in the classroom: Vulnerability and invulnerability to depressive mood reactions. *J. Pers. Soc. Psychol., 43,* 612–17.

Metalsky, G. I., & Joiner, T. E. (1997). The hopelessness depression questionnaire. *Cog. Ther. Res., 21*(3), 359–84.

Metalsky, G. I., Joiner, T. E., Hardin, T. S., & Abramson, L. Y. (1993). Depressive reactions to failure in a naturalistic setting: A test of the hopelessness and self-esteem theories of depression. *J. Abn. Psychol., 102,* 101–9.

Metz, J. T., Johnson, M. D., Pliskin, N. H., & Luchins, D. J. (1994). Maintenance of training effects on the Wisconsin Card Sorting Test by patients with schizophrenia or affective disorders. *Amer. J. Psychiat., 151*(1), 120–22.

Metz, M. E., Pryor, J. L., Nesvacil, L. J., Abuzzahab, F., & Koznar, J. (1997). Premature ejaculation: A psychophysiological review. *J. Sex Marit. Ther., 23,* 3–23.

Meyer, C. B., & Taylor, S. E. (1986). Adjustment to rape. *J. Pers. Soc. Psychol., 50,* 1226–34.

Meyer, J. K. (1995) Paraphilias. In H. I. Kaplan & J. B. Sadock (Eds.), *Comprehensive textbook of psychiatry. (6th ed.).* (pp. 1334–47). Baltimore: Williams and Wilkins.

Meyer, R. E., & Mirin, S. M. (1979). *The heroin stimulus: Implications for a theory of addiction.* New York: Plenum.

Meyer, R. G., & Osborne, Y. H. (1996). *Case studies in abnormal behavior* (3rd ed.). Boston: Allyn & Bacon.

Meyers, J., & Parsons, R. D. (1987). Prevention planning in the school system. In J. Hermalin & J. A. Morell (Eds.), *Prevention planning in mental health.* Beverly Hills, CA: Sage.

Meyerson, B. A., & Mindus, P. (1988). Capsulotomy as treatment of anxiety disorders. In L. D. Lunsford (Ed.), *Modern stereotactic neurosurgery.* (pp. 353). Boston: Nijhoff.

Mezzione, J. C. (1996). Mapping mental illness: A new era. *Arch. Gen. Psychiat., 53*(7), 574–76.

Michael, R. T., Gagnon, J. H., Laumann, E. O., & Kolata, G. (1994). *Sex in America: A definitive survey.* Boston: Little, Brown.

Michaels, C. A., Lazar, J. W., & Risucci, D. A. (1997). A neuropsychological approach to the assessment of adults with learning disabilities in vocational rehabilitation. *J. Learn. Dis., 30*(5), 544–51.

Middleton, W., Burnett, P., Raphael, B., & Martinek, P. (1996). The bereavement response: A cluster analysis. *Brit. J. Psychiat., 169,* 167–71.

Miklowitz, D. J. (1996). Psychotherapy in combination with drug treatment for bipolar disorder. *J. Clin. Psychopharm., 16* (Suppl 1), 56S–66S.

Miklowitz, D. J., Goldstein, M. J., & Falloon, I. R. (1983). Premorbid and symptomatic characteristics of schizophrenics from families with high and low levels of expressed emotion. *J. Abn. Psychol. 92,* 359–67.

Miklowitz, D. J., Goldstein, M. J., Nuechterlein, K. H., Snyder, K. S., & Mintz, J. (1988). Family factors and the course of bipolar affective disorder. *Arch. Gen. Psychiat., 45,* 225–31.

Miklowitz, D. J., Strachan, A. M., Goldstein, M. J., Doane, J. A., & Snyder, K. S. (1986). Expressed emotion and communication deviance in families of schizophrenics. *J. Abn. Psychol., 95,* 60–66.

Milby, J. B. (1988). Methadone maintenance to abstinency: How many make it? *J. Nerv. Ment. Dis., 176,* 409–22.

Miles, C. (1977). Conditions predisposing to suicide: A review. *J. Nerv. Ment. Dis., 164,* 232–46.

Millar, J. D. (1990). Mental health and the workplace: An interchangeable partnership. *Amer. Psychol., 45*(10), 1165–66.

Miller v. City of Springfield (1998). 146 F.3d 612 (8th Cir.).

Miller, E. (1992). Some basic principles of neuropsychological assessment. In J. R. Crawford, D. M. Parker, & W. W. McKinlay (Eds.), *A handbook of neuropsychological assessment.* Hillsdale, NJ: Erlbaum.

Miller, F. T., Abrams, T., Dulit, R., & Fyer, M. (1993a). Psychotic symptoms in patients with borderline personality disorder and concurrent axis I disorder. *Hosp. Comm. Psychiat., 44,* 59–61.

Miller, F. T., Abrams, T., Dulit, R., & Fyer, M. (1993b). Substance abuse in borderline personality disorder. *Amer. J. Drug Alcoh. Abuse, 19,* 491–97.

Miller, H. L., Coombs, D. W ., Leeper, J. D., & Barton, S. N. (1984). An analysis of the effects of suicide prevention facilities on suicide rates in the United States. *Amer. J. Pub. Hlth., 74,* 340–43.

Miller, J. P. (1975, Spring). Suicide and adolescence. *Adolescence, 10*(37), 11–24.

Miller, K. A. (1989). Enhancing early childhood mainstreaming through cooperative learning: A brief literature review. *Child Study Journal, 19,* 285–92.

Miller, M. A., & Westermeyer, J. (1996). Gambling in Minnesota. *Amer. J. Psychiat., 153*(6), 845

Miller, N. S., & Gold, M. S. (1994). Criminal activity and crack addiction. *Inter. J. Addict., 29,* 1069–78.

Miller, R. (1970). Does Down's syndrome predispose children to leukemia? *Roche Report, 7*(16), 5.

Miller, R. C., & Berman, J. S. (1983). The efficacy of cognitive behavior therapies: A quantitative review of the research evidence. *Psychol. Bull., 94,* 39–53.

Miller, R. R., & Springer, A. D. (1974). Implications of recovery from experimental amnesia. *Psychol. Rev., 81*(5), 470–73.

Miller, W. R. (1978). Behavioral treatment of problem drinkers: A comparative outcome study of three controlled drinking therapies. *J. Cons. Clin. Psychol., 46,* 74–86.

Miller, W. R., Benefield, R. G., Tonigan, J. S. (1993). Enhancing motivation for change in problem drinking: A controlled comparison of two therapist styles. *J. Cons. Clin. Psychol. 61*(3), 455–61.

Miller, W. R., Brown, J. M., Simpson, T. L., Handmaker, N. S., Bien, T. H., Luckie, L. F., Montgomery, H. A., Hester, R. K., & Tonigan, J. S. (1995). What works? A methodological analysis of the alcohol treatment outcome literature. In R. K. Hester & W. R. Miller (Eds.), *Handbook of alcoholism treatment approaches:Effective alternatives.* (pp. 12–44). Needham, MA: Allyn & Bacon.

Miller, W. R., & Caddy, G. R. (1977). Abstinence and controlled drinking in the treatment of problem drinking. *J. Stud. Alcoh., 38,* 986–1003.

Miller, W. R., & Hester, R. K. (1986). Inpatient alcoholism treatment: Who benefits? *Amer. Psychol., 41,* 794–805.

Miller, W. R., Leckman, A. L., Tinkcom, M., & Rubenstein, J. (1986). *Longterm follow-up of controlled drinking therapies.* Paper given at the Ninety-fourth Annual Meeting of the American Psychological Association, Washington, DC.

Miller, W. R., & Munoz, R. F. (1976). *How to control your drinking.* Englewood Cliffs, NJ: Prentice-Hall.

Miller, W. R., & Rollnick, S. (1991). Using assessment results. In W. R. Miller & S. Rollnick (Eds.), *Motivational interviewing.* (pp. 89–99). New York: Guilford.

Millon, T. & Davis, R. D. (1996). An evolutionary theory of personality disorders. In J. F. Clarkin & M. F. Lenzenweger (Eds.), *Major theories of personality disorder.* (pp. 221–346). New York: Guilford.

Millon, T. & Martinez, A. (1995). Avoidant personality disorder. In W. J. Livesley (Ed.), *The DSM-IV personality disorders.* (pp. 218–233). New York: Guilford.

Millon, T. (1981). *Disorders of personality: DSM-III, Axis II.* New York: Wiley.

Millon, T. (1991). Classification in psychopathology: Rationale, alternatives, standards. *J. Abn. Psychol., 100*(3), 245–61.

Millon, T., & Davis, R. D. (1995). The development of personality disorders. In D. Cicchetti, & D. J. Cohen (Eds.), *Developmental psychopathology: Vol. 2. Risk, disorder, and adaptation.* (pp. 633–76). New York: Wiley.

Millon, T., & Radovanov, J. (1995). Passive-aggressive (negativistic) personality disorder. In W. J. Livesley (Ed.), *The DSM-IV personality disorders.* (pp. 312–325). New York: Guilford.

Mills, M. J. (1984). The so-called duty to warn: The psychotherapeutic duty to protect third parties from patients' violent acts. *Behavioral Sciences and the Law, 2,* 237–57.

Mills, M. J., Sullivan, G., & Eth, S. (1987). Protecting third parties: A decade after Tarasoff. *Amer. J. Psychiat., 144*(1), 68–74.

Milner, K. O. (1949). The environment as a factor in the aetiology of criminal paranoia. *J. Ment. Sci., 95,* 124–32.

Milns, R. D. (1986). Squibb academic lecture: Attitudes towards mental illness in antiquity. *Australian and New Zealand J. of Psychiat., 20,* 454–62.

Mindus, P., & Jenike, M. A. (1992). Neurosurgical treatment of malignant obsessive-compulsive disorder. *Psychiat. Clin. N. Amer., 15,* 921.

Mindus, P., Nyman, H., Lindquist, C., & Meyerson, B. A. (1993). *Neurosurgery for intractable obsessive-compulsive disorder, an update.* Paper presented at the International Workshop on Obsessive Disorder, Vail, Co.

Mindus, P., Rasmussen, S. A., & Lindquist, C. (1994). Neurosurgical treatment for refractory obsessive-compulsive disorder: Implications for understanding frontal lobe function. *J. Neuropsychiat. Clin. Neurosci., 6,* 467–77.

Mindus, P., Rauch, S. L., Nyman, H., Baer, L., Edman, G., & Jenike, M. A. (1994). Capsulotomy and cigulotomy as treatments for malignant obsessive-compulsive disorder: An update. In E. Hollander, J. Zohar, D. Marazziti, & B. Olivier (Eds.), *Current insights in obsessive compulsive disorder.* (pp. 245–76). Chichester, England: Wiley.

Mineka, S. & Nugent, K. (1995). Mood-congruent memory biases in anxiety and depression. In D. Schacter (Ed.), *Memory distortion: How minds, brains, and societies reconstruct the past.* (pp. 173–93). Cambridge, MA: Harvard University Press.

Mineka, S. & Thomas, C. (1999). Mechanisms of change during exposure treatments for anxiety disorders. In T. Dagleish, M. Power (Eds.), *Handbook of cognition and emotion.* (pp. 747–64). Chichester, England: Wiley.

Mineka, S. (1985a). Animal models of anxiety-based disorders: Their usefulness and limitations. In A. H. Tuma & J. D. Maser (Eds.), *Anxiety and the anxiety disorders.* Hillsdale, NJ: Erlbaum.

Mineka, S. (1985b). The frightful complexities of the origins of fears. In F. R. Brush & J. B. Overmier (Eds.), *Affect, conditioning, and cognition: Essays on the determinants of behavior.* Hillsdale, NJ: Erlbaum.

Mineka, S. (1992). Evolutionary memories, emotional processing and the emotional disorders. In D. Medin (Ed.), *The psychology of learning and motivation,* (Vol. 28). (pp. 161–206). New York: Academic Press.

Mineka, S. (1993). Animal models of obsessive-compulsive disorder. In J. Greist & J. Jefferson (Eds.), *Proceedings of the Third International Workshop on Obsessive-Compulsive Disorder,* Vail, CO.

Mineka, S., & Cook, M. (1986). Immunization against the observational conditioning of snake fear in monkeys. *J. Abnorm. Psycho., 95,* 307–18.

Mineka, S., & Cook, M. (1993). Mechanisms underlying observational conditioning of fear in monkeys. *J. Exper. Psychol.: General, 122,* 23–38.

Mineka, S., Cook, M., & Miller, S. (1984). Fear conditioned with escapable and inescapable shock: Effects of a feedback stimulus. *J. Exper. Psychol., 10,* 307–23.

Mineka, S., Davidson, M., Cook, M., & Keir, R. (1984). Observational conditioning of snake fear in Rhesus monkeys. *J. Abn. Psychol. 93*(4), 355–72.

Mineka, S., Gunnar, M., & Champoux, J. (1986). Control and early socioemotional development: Infant rhesus monkeys reared in controllable versus uncontrollable environments. *Child Develop. 57,* 1241–56.

Mineka, S., & Kelly, K. A. (1989). The relationship between anxiety, lack of control and loss of control. In A. Steptoe & A. Appels (Eds.), *Stress, personal control and health.* Brussels-Luxembourg: J. Wiley.

Mineka, S., & Nugent, K. (1995). Mood-congruent memory biases in anxiety and depression. In D. Schacter (Ed.), *Memory distortions: How minds, brains and societies reconstruct the past.* (pp. 173–93).Cambridge: Harvard University Press.

Mineka, S., Watson, D., & Clark, L. A. (1998). Comorbidity of anxiety and unipolar mood disorders. In J. T. Spence, J. M. Darley, & D. J. Foss (Eds.), Annual review of psychology. (pp. 377–412). Palo Alto. (A: Annual Reviews. *Annu. Rev. Psychol., 49,* 377–412.

Mineka, S., & Zinbarg, R. (1991). Animal models of psychopathology. In C.E. Walker (Ed.), *Clinical psychology: Historical and research foundations* (pp. 51–86. New York: Plenum.

Mineka, S., & Zinbarg, R. (1995). Conditioning and ethological models of social phobia. In R. Heimberg, M. Liebowitz, D. Hope, & F. Schneier (Eds.), *Social phobia: Diagnosis, assessment, and treatment.* New York: Guilford.

Mineka, S., & Zinbarg, R. (1996). Conditioning and ethological models of anxiety disorders: Stress-in-Dynamic Context Anxiety Models. In D. Hope (Ed.), *Perspectives on Anxiety, Panic, and Fear: Nebraska Symposium on Motivation.* Lincoln: University of Nebraska Press.

Mineka, S., & Zinbarg, R. (1998). Experimental approaches to the anxiety and mood disorders. In J. Adair, & D. Blanger (Eds.), *Advances in psychological science: (Vol. 1): Social, personal and cultural aspects.* (pp. 429–454). Hove, England UK: Psychology Press/Erlbaum.

Mintzer, J. E., et al. (1997). Effectiveness of a continuum of care using brief and partial hospitalization for agitated dementia patients. *Psychiatr. Serv., 48*(11), 1435–39.

Mintzer, M. Z., Guarino, J., Kirk, T., Roache, J. D., & Griffiths, R. R. (1997). Ethanol and Pentobarbital: Comparison of behavioral and subjective effects in sedative drug abusers. *Experimental and Clinical Psychopharmacology, 5*(3), 203–15.

Minuchin, S. (1974). *Families and family therapy.* Cambridge, MA: Harvard University Press.

Minuchin, S., Baker, L., Rosman, B., Liebman, R., Milman, L., & Todd, T. (1975). A conceptual model of

psychosomatic illness in children. *Arch. Gen. Psychiat., 32,* 1031–38.

Miranda, J., & Persons, J. B. (1988). Dysfunctional attitudes are mood state dependent. *J. Abn. Psychol., 97,* 76–79.

Miranda, J., Persons, J. B., & Byers, C. N. (1990). Endorsement of dysfunctional beliefs depends on current mood state. *J. Abn. Psychol., 99,* 237–41.

Mirsky, A. F., DeLisi, L. E., Buchsbaum, M. S., Quinn, O. W., Schwerdt, P., Siever, L. J., Mann, L., Weingartner, H., Zec, R., et al. (1984). The Genain quadruplets: Psychological studies. *Psychiat. Res., 13,* 77–93.

Mirsky, A. F., Silberman, E. K., Latz, A., & Nagler, S. (1985). Adult outcomes of high-risk children. *Schizo. Bull., 11,* 150–54.

Mischel, W. (1973). Toward a cognitive social learning reconceptualization of personality. *Psychol. Rev., 80*(4), 252–83.

Mischel, W. (1990). Personality dispositions revisited and revised: A view after three decades. In L. A. Pervin (Ed.). *Handbook of personality: Theory and research.* (pp. 111–135). New York: Guilford.

Mischel, W. (1993). *Introduction to personality,* 5th ed. Fort Worth, Texas: Harcourt, Brace & Jovanovich.

Mishler, E. G., & Waxler, N. E. (1968). *Interaction in families: An experimental study of family processes and schizophrenia.* New York: Wiley.

Mitchell, J. (1985). Healing the helper. In National Institute of Mental Health (Ed.), *Role stressors and supports for emergency workers.* (pp. 105–18). DHHS Publication No. ADM 85–1408), Washington, DC: U.S. Government Printing Office.

Mitchell, J. E., Pyle, R. L., Eckert, E. D., Hatsukami, D., Pomeroy, C., & Zimmerman, R. (1990). A comparison study of antidepressants and structured intensive group psychotherapy in the treatment of bulimia nervosa. *Arch. Gen. Psychiat., 47,* 149–57.

Mitchell, J. T., & Resnik, H. L. P. (1981). *Emergency response to crisis.* Bowie, MD: Robert J. Brady.

Miyakawa, T., Yagi, T., Kitazawa, H., Yasuda, M., Kawai, N., Tsuboi, K., & Niki, H. (1997). Fyn-Kinase as a determinant of ethanol sensitivity: Relation to NMDA receptor function. *Science, 278,* 698.

Moats, L. C., & Lyon, G. R. (1993). Learning disabilities in the United States: Advocacy, science, and the future of the field. *J. Learn. Dis., 26*(5), 282–94.

Moffatt, M. E. (1997). Nocturnal enuresis: A review of the efficacy of treatments and practical advice for clinicians. *Developmental and Behavioral Pediatrics, 18*(1), 49–56.

Moffitt, T. (1993a) Adolescence-limited and life-course-persistent antisocial behavior: A developmental taxonomy. *Psychological Review, 100,* 674–701.

Moffitt, T. E. (1993b). The neuropsychology of conduct disorder. *Development and Psychopathology, 5,* 135–51.

Moffitt, T. E. (1994). *Juvenile delinquency: Seed of a career in violent crime, just sowing wild oats or both?* Science and public policy seminars. Federation of behavioral, psychological and cognitive sciences.

Moffitt, T. E., & Lyman, D. (1994). The neuropsychology of conduct disorder and delinquency: Implications for understanding antisocial behavior. In D. C. Fowles, P. Sutker, & S. H. Goodman (Eds.), *Progress in experimental personality and psychopathology research.* New York: Springer.

Mohr, D. C., & Beutler, L. E. (1990). Erectile dysfunction: A review of diagnostic and treatment procedures. *Clin. Psychol. Rev., 10,* 123–50.

Mohr, J. W., Turner, R. E., & Jerry, M. B. (1964). *Pedophilia and exhibitionism: A handbook.* Toronto: University of Toronto Press.

Mohs, R. C., Breitner, J. C., Silverman, J. M., & Davis, K. L. (1987). Alzheimer's disease: Morbid risk among first-degree relatives approximates 50% by 90 years of age. *Arch. Gen. Psychiat., 44,* 405–8.

Moldin, S. O., & Gottesman, I. I. (1997). Genes, experience, and chance in schizophrenia—Positioning for the 21st century. *Schizo. Bull., 23*(4), 547–61.

Mollica, R. F., Wyshak, G., Lavelle, J., Truong, T., Tor, S., & Yang, T. (1990). Assessing symptom change in Southeast Asian refugees. *Amer. J. Psychiat., 147,* 83–88.

Monahan, J. (1981). *Predicting violent behavior: An assessment of clinical techniques.* Beverly Hills, CA: Sage.

Monahan, J. (1992). Mental disorder and violent behavior: Perceptions and evidence. *Amer. Psychol., 47*(4), 511–21.

Monahan, J., & Steadman, H. J. (1997). Violent storms and violent people: How meteorology can inform risk communication in mental health law. *Amer. Psychol., 51*(9), 931–38.

Money, J. (1985). *The destroying angel.* (pp. 17–31, 51–52, 61–68, 83–90, 107–20, 137–48) Buffalo, NY: Prometheus Books.

Money, J. (1986). Lovemaps: Clinical concepts of sexual/erotic health and pathology, paraphilia, and gender transposition. New York: Irvington.

Money, J. (1988). *Gay, straight, and in-between.* (p. 77). New York: Oxford University Press.

Money, J., & Ehrhardt, A. A. (1972). *Man & woman, boy & girl: Differentiation and dimorphism of gender identity from conception to maturity.* Baltimore: Johns Hopkins University Press.

Monroe, S. M., Roberts, J. E., Kupfer, D. J., & Frank, E. (1996). Life stress and treatment course of recurrent depression: II. Postrecovery associations with attrition, symptom course, and recurrence over 3 years. *J. Abn. Psychol., 105*(3), 313–28.

Monroe, S. M., & Simons, A. D. (1991). Diathesis-stress theories in the context of life stress research: Implications for the depressive disorders. *Psychol. Bull., 110,* 406–25.

Monroe, S. M., & Steiner, S. C. (1986). Social support and psychopathology: Interrelations with preexisting disorder, stress, and personality. *J. Abn. Psychol., 95,* 29–39.

Montgomery, S. A. (1994). Antidepressants in long-term treatment. *Ann. Rev. Med., 45,* 447–57.

Moolchan, E. T., & Hoffman, J. A. (1994). Phases of treatment: A practical approach to methadone maintenance treatment. *Inter. J. Addict., 151,* 165–68.

Mora, G. (1967). Paracelsus' psychiatry. *Amer. J. Psychiat., 124,* 803–14.

Moreno, J. L. (1959). Psychodrama. In S. Arieti, et al. (Eds.), *American handbook of psychiatry* (Vol. 2). New York: Basic Books.

Morey, L. C. (1988a). Personality disorders in DSM-III and DSM-III-R: Convergence, coverage, and internal consistency. *Amer. J. Psychiat., 145,* 573–77.

Morey, L. C. (1988b). The categorical representation of personality disorder: A cluster analysis of DSM-III-R personality features. *J. Abn. Psychol., 97,* 314–21.

Morey, L. C., Skinner, H. A., & Blashfield, R. K. (1984). A typology of alcohol abusers: Correlates and implications. *J. Abn. Psychol., 93,* 408–17.

Morgan, J. (1995). American Red Cross disaster mental health services: Implementation and recent developments. Special Issue: Disasters and stress: A mental health counseling perspective. *J. Ment. Hlth. Couns., 17*(3), 291–300.

Morganstern, J., Labouvie, E., McCrady, B. S., Kahler, C. W., & Frey, R. M. (1997). Affiliation with Alcoholics Anonomyous after treatment: A study of its therapeutic effects and mechanisms of action. *J. Cons. Clin. Psychol., 65*(5), 768–77.

Morganstern, J., Langenbucher, J., Labouvie, E., & Miller, K. J. (1997). The comorbidity of alcoholism and personality disorders in a clinical population. *J. Abn. Psychol., 106*(1), 74–84.

Mori, E., et al. (1997a). Medial temporal structures relate to memory impairment in Alzheimer's disease: An MRI volumetric study. *J. Neurol. Neurosurg. Psychiat., 63*(2), 214–21.

Mori, E., et al. (1997b). Premorbid brain size as a determinant of reserve capacity against intellectual decline in Alzheimer's Disease. *Amer. J. Psychiat., 154*(1), 18–24.

Moriarty, K. M., Alagna, S. W., & Lake, C. R. (1984). Psychopharmacology: An historical perspective. *Psychiat. Clin. N. Amer., 7*(3), 411–33.

Morlock, L. L. (1989). Recognition and treatment of mental health problems in the general health care sector. In C. A. Taube, D. Mechanic, & A. A.

Hohmann (Eds.), *The future of mental health services research.* (pp. 39–62). Washington, DC: U.S. Department of Health and Human Services.

Morrison, J. (1980). Adult psychiatric disorders in parents of hyperactive children. *Amer. J. Psychiat., 137*(7), 825–27.

Morrison, J. (1989). Childhood sexual histories of women with somatization disorder. *Amer. J. Psychiat., 146,* 239–41.

Morrison, T. L., Edwards, D. W., & Weissman, H. N. (1994). The MMPI and MMPI-2 as predictors of psychiatric diagnosis. *J. Pers. Assess., 62,* 17–30.

Morton, R. B., Uing, A., & Williams, C. (1996). Nocturnal enuresis and the use of desmopressin: Is it helpful? *Child Care Health and Development, 22*(2), 73–84.

Morton, T. L., & Ewald, L. S. (1987). Family-based interventions for crime and delinquency. In E. K. Morris & C. J. Braukmann (Eds.), *Behavioral approaches to crime and delinquency: A handbook of application, research, and concepts.* (pp. 271–94). New York: Plenum.

Mosbascher, D. (1988). Lesbian alcohol and substance abuse. *Psychiat. Ann., 18,* 47–50.

Moscato, B. S., Russell, M., Zielezny, M., Bromet, E., Egri, G., Mudar, P., & Marshall, J. R. (1997). Gender differences in the relation between depressive symptoms and alcohol problems: A longitudinal perspective. *Amer. J. Epidemiol., 146*(11), 966–74.

Motavalli, N. (1995). Fluoxetine for (s)elective mutism. *J. Amer. Acad. Child Adoles. Psychiat., 34*(6), 701–02.

Mott, F. W. (1919). *War neuroses and shell shock.* Oxford: Oxford Medical Publications.

Mowbray, R. M. (1959). Historical aspects of electric convulsant therapy. *Scott Medical Journal, 4,* 373–78.

Mowrer, O. H. (1947). On the dual nature of learning: A reinterpretation of "conditioning" and "problem solving." *Harvard Educational Review, 17,* 102–148.

Mowrer, O. H., & Mowrer, W. M. (1938). Enuresis—a method for its study and treatment. *Amer. J. Orthopsychiat., 8,* 436–59.

Mrazek, P. J., & Haggerty, R. J. (1994). *Reducing risks for mental disorders: Frontiers for prevention intervention research.* Washington: National Academy Press.

Mucha, T. F., & Reinhardt, R. F. (1970). Conversion reactions in student aviators. *Amer. J. Psychiat., 127,* 493–97.

Mueser, K. T., Bellack, A. S., & Blanchard, J. B. (1992). Comorbidity of schizophrenia and substance abuse: Implications for treatment. *J. Cons. Clin. Psychol., 60,* 845–56.

Mueser, K. T., Drake, R. E., Ackerson, T. H., Alterman, A. I., Miles, K. M., & Noordsy, D. L. (1997). Antisocial personality disorder, conduct disorder, and substance abuse in schizophrenia. *J. Abn. Psychol., 106*(3), 473–77.

Mueser, K. T., et al. (1998). Models of community care for severe mental illness: A review of research on case management. *Schizo. Bull., 24*(1), 37–74.

Mueser, K. T., Yarold, P. R., & Bellack, A. S. (1992). Diagnostic and demographic correlates of substance abuse in schizophrenia and major affective disorders. *Acta Psychiatr. Scandin., 85,* 48–55.

Mufson, L., Weissman, M. M., & Warner, V. (1992). Depression and anxiety in parents and children: A direct interview study. *J. Anxiety Dis., 6,* 1–13.

Mukherjee, S., Sackeim, H. A., & Schnur, D. B. (1994). Electroconvulsive therapy of acute manic episodes: A review of 50 years' experience. *Amer. J. Psychiat., 151,* 169–76.

Munoz, R. F., Mrazek, P. J., & Haggerty, R. J. (1996). Institute of Medicine report on prevention of mental disorders: Summary and commentary. *Amer. Psychol., 51*(11), 1116–22.

Munro, J. F., & Duncan, L. J. P. (1972). Fasting in the treatment of obesity. *The Practitioner, 208,* 493–98.

Murphy, C. M., Meyer, S-L, & O'Leary, K. D. (1994). Dependency characteristics of partner asssaultive men. *J. Abn. Psychol., 103,* 729–35.

Murphy, D. L., Greenburg, B., Altemus, M., Benjamin, J., Grady, T., & Pigott, T. (1996). The neuropharmacology and neurobiology of obsessive-compulsive disorder: An update on the serotonin Hypothesis. In H. G. Westenberg, J. A. Den Boer, & D. L. Mur-

phy(Eds.), *Advances in the neurobiology of anxiety disorders.* (pp. 279–97). Chichester, England: Wiley.

Murphy, G. E. (1988). Suicide and substance abuse. *Arch. Gen. Psychiat., 45,* 593–94.

Murphy, G. E., Simons, A. D., Wetzel, R. D., & Lustman, P. J. (1984). Cognitive therapy and pharmacotherapy: Singly and together in the treatment of depression. *Arch. Gen. Psychiat., 41,* 33–41.

Murphy, G. E., & Wetzel, R. D. (1982). Family history of suicidal behavior among suicide attempters. *J. Nerv. Ment. Dis., 170,* 86–90.

Murphy, G. E., & Wetzel, R. D. (1990). The lifetime risk of suicide in alcoholism. *Arch. Gen. Psychiat., 47,* 383–92.

Murphy, G. M., Taylor, J., Kraemer, H. C., Yesavage, J., & Tinklenberg, J. R. (1997). No association between apolipoprotein E e4 allele and rate of decline in Alzheimer's disease. *Amer. J. Psychiat., 154*(5), 603–608.

Murphy, H. B. (1968). Cultural factors in the genesis of schizophrenia. In D. Rosenthal & S. S. Kety (Eds.), *The transmission of schizophrenia.* (pp. 137–52). Elmsford, NY: Pergamon.

Murphy, J. M. (1976). Psychiatric labeling in cross-cultural perspective. *Science, 191* (4231), 1019–28.

Murphy, S., & Irwin, J. (1992). "Living with the dirty secret": Problems of disclosure for methadone maintenance clients. *J. Psychoact. Drugs, 24,* 257–64.

Murphy, W., D. (1990). Assessment and modification of cognitive distortions in sex offenders. In W. L. Marshall, D. R. Laws, & H. E. Barbaree (Eds.), *Handbook of sexual assault: Issues, theories, and treatment of the offender.* (pp. 331–42). New York: Plenum.

Murphy, W. D. (1997). Exhibitionism: Psychopathology and theory. In D. R. Laws & W. O'Donohue (Eds.) *Sexual deviance: Theory, assessment, and treatment* (pp. 22–39). New York: Guilford.

Murray, C. J. L., & Lopez, A. D. (1996). *The global burden of disease.* Cambridge, MA: Harvard University Press.

Murray, D. C. (1973). Suicidal and depressive feelings among college students. *Psychol. Rep., 33*(1), 175–81.

Murray, L. & Cooper, P. (1997). Postpartum depression and child development. *Psychol. Med., 27,* 253–60.

Murray, L., Fiori–Cowley, A., Hooper, R., & Cooper, P. (1996). The impact of postnatal depression and associated adversity on early mother-infant interactions and later infant outcomes. *Child Develop., 67*(5), 2512–26.

Musante, G. J., Costanzo, P. R., & Friedman, K. E. (1998). The comorbidity of depression and eating dysregulation processes in a diet-seeking obese population: A matter of gender specificity. *Int. J. Eat. Dis., 23*(1), 65–75.

Myers, J. K., Weissman, M. M., Tischler, G. L., Holzer, C. E., Leaf, P. J., & Stoltzman, R. (1984). Six-month prevalence of psychiatric disorders in three communities: 1980 to 1982. *Arch. Gen. Psychiat., 41,* 959–67.

Myers, M. B., Templer, D. I., & Brown, R. (1985). Reply to Wieder on rape victims. Vulnerability does not imply responsibility. *J. Cons. Clin. Psychol., 53,* 431.

Myers, R., Cunningham, V., & Bailey, D. (1996). *Quantification of brain functions using PET.* London: Academic Press.

Nace, E. P., Orne, M. T., & Hammer, A. G. (1974). Posthypnotic amnesia as an active psychic process. *Arch. Gen. Psychiat., 31*(2), 257–60.

Nada-Raja, S., Langley, J. D., McGee, R., Williams, S. M., Begg, D. J., & Reeder, A. I. (1997). Inattentive and hyperactive behaviors and driving offenses in adolescence. *J. Amer. Acad. Child Adoles. Psychiat. 36*(4), 515–22.

Nadder, T. S., Silberg, J. L., Eaves, L. J., Maes, H. H., & Meyer, J. M. (1998). Genetic effects on ADHD symptomatology in 7- to 13-year-old twins: Results from a telephone survey. *Behav. Gen., 28*(2), 83–99.

Nagaraja, J. (1974). Somnambulism in children: Clinical communication. *Child Psychiatry Quarterly, 7*(1), 18–19.

Nanson, J. L., & Hiscock, M. (1990). Attention deficits in children exposed to alcohol prenatally. *Alcoholism: Clin. Exper. Res., 14,* 656–661.

Narby, J. (1982). The evolution of attitudes towards mental illness in preindustrial England. *Orthomolecular Psychiatry, 11,* 103–10.

Narrow, W. E., Regier, D. A., Rae, D. S., Manderscheid, R. W., & Locke, B. Z. (1993). Use of services by persons with mental and addictive disorders: Findings from the National Institute of Mental Health Epidemiologic Catchment Area Program. *Arch. Gen. Psychiat., 50,* 95–107.

Nash, M. R., Hulsey, T. L., Sexton, M. C., Harralson, T. L., & Lambert, W. (1993). Long-term sequelae of childhood sexual abuse: Perceived family environment, psychopathology, and dissociation. *J. Cons. Clin. Psychol., 61*(2), 276–83.

Nathan, P. E., & Gorman, J. M. (Eds.). (1998). *A guide to treatments that work.* New York: Oxford University Press.

National Advisory Mental Health Council. (1990). *National plan for research on child and adolescent mental disorders.* Washington, DC: National Institute of Mental Health.

National Association for Mental Health. (1979, Mar. 23). *Bulletin* No. 103.

National Center for Health Statistics. (1982). Washington, DC: U.S. Government Printing Office.

National Committee to Prevent Child Abuse. (1996). *Study of the national incidence and prevalence of child abuse and neglect.* Washington D.C.: Author.

National Institute for Drug Abuse (1998). *Director's report: 1997.* Washington: Author.

National Institute of Drug Abuse. (1981). *Trend report: January 1978–September 1980.* Data from Client Oriented Data Acquisition Program (CODAP) (Series E, No. 24). Washington, DC: U.S. Department of Health and Human Services.

National Institute of Drug Abuse. (1990). Washington, DC: U.S. Department of Health and Human Services.

National Institute of Mental Health. (1971). Amphetamines approved for children. *Sci. News, 99*(4), 240.

National Institute of Mental Health. (1976, Apr. 20). Rising suicide rate linked to economy. Los Angeles Times, VIII, 2, 5.

National Institute of Mental Health. (1978a, Oct.). *Third report on alcohol and health.* Washington, DC: U.S. Government Printing Office.

National Institute of Mental Health. (1978b). *Indirect services* (Statistical Note No. 147). Washington, DC: U.S. Government Printing Office.

National Institute of Mental Health. (1985a). *Electroconvulsive therapy Consensus Development Conference statement.* Bethesda, MD: U.S. Department of Health and Human Services.

National Institute of Mental Health. (1985b). *Mental Health, United States, 1985.* Washington, DC: U.S. Government Printing Office.

National Mental Health Association. (1997). *Working for America's mental health.* Alexandria, VA: Author.

National Transportation Safety Board. (1977). *Human Factors specialist's factual report of investigation. Accident to Capitol Airways DC8.* Washington, DC: NTSB (NTSB-DCA-77-A-A008).

Navia, B. A., Jordan, B. D., & Price, R. W. (1986). The AIDS dementia complex: I. Clinical features. *Ann. Neurol., 19,* 517–24.

Neale, J. M., & Oltmanns, T. F. (1980). *Schizophrenia.* New York: Wiley.

Neale, M. C., Walters, E. E., Eaves, L. J., & Hermine, M. H. (1994). Mutivariate genetic analysis of twin-family data on fears: Mx models. *Behavior Genetics, 24*(2), 119–39.

Nee, L. F., Eldridge, R., Sunderland, T., Thomas, C. B., et al. (1987). Dementia of the Alzheimer type: Clinical and family study of 22 twin pairs. *Neurology, 37,* 359–63.

Neisser, U. (1967). *Cognitive psychology.* New York: Appleton Century Crofts.

Neisser, U. (Ed.) (1982). *Memory observed: Remembering in natural contexts.* San Francisco: Freeman.

Nelson, C. A., & Bloom, F. E. (1997) Child development and neuroscience. *Child Develop., 68,* 970–87.

Nelson, F. L. (1984). Suicide: Issues of prevention, intervention, and facilitation. *J. Clin. Psychol., 40,* 1328–33.

Nelson, H. (1971, Jan. 26). County suicide rate up sharply among young. *Los Angeles Times*, II, 1.

Nelson, H. (1973, Mar. 27). High blood pressure found in third of adults in survey. *Los Angeles Times*, II, 1, 3.

Nelson, L. D., & Adams, K. M. (1997). Challenges for neuropsychology in the treatment rehabilitation of brain-injured patients. *Psychol. Assess., 9*(4), 368–73.

Nelson, Z. P., & Mowry, D. D. (1976). Contracting in crisis intervention. *Comm. Ment. Hlth. J., 12*, 37–43.

Nemeroff, C. B., & Schatzberg, A. F. (1998). Pharmacological treatment of unipolar depression. In P. E. Nathan & J. M. Gorman (Eds.), *A guide to treatments that work.* (pp. 212–25). Oxford, England: Oxford University Press.

Nemiah, J. C. (1961). *Foundations of psychopathology.* Cambridge: Oxford University Press.

Nemiah, J. C. (1975). Obsessive-compulsive neurosis. In A.M. Freedman, H.I. Kaplan, & B.J. Sadock (Eds.), *Comprehensive textbook of psychiatry* (2nd ed., Vol 1.). Baltimore: Williams & Wilkins.

Nesdale, D., Rooney, R., & Smith, L. (1997). Migrant ethnic identity and psychological distress. *Journal of Cross-Cultural Psychology, 28*(5), 569–88.

Nestor, P. G., Shenton, M. E., McCarley, R. W., Haimson, J., Smith, S., O'Donnell, B., Kimble, M., Kikinis, R., & Jolesz, F. A. (1993). Neuropsychological correlates of MRI temporal lobe abnormalities in schizophrenia. *Amer. J. Psychiat., 150*(12), 1849–55.

Neufeld, R. W. (1990). Coping with stress, coping without stress, and stress with coping: In interconstruct redundencies. *Stress Medicine, 6*, 117–25.

Neugarten, B. L. (1977). Personality and aging. In J. E. Birren & K. W. Schaie (Eds.), *Handbook of the psychology of aging.* New York: Van Nostrand.

Newman, B., Selby, J. V., Quesenberry, C. P., King, M., Friedman, G. D., & Fabsitz, R. P. (1990). Nongenetic influences of obesity on other cardiovascular disease risk factors: An analysis of identical twins. *Amer. J. Pub. Hlth., 80*, 675–78.

Newman, J. P. (1997). Conceptual models of the nervous system: Implications for antisocial behavior. In D. M. Stoff, J. Breiling, & J. D. Maser (Eds.), *Handbook of antisocial behavior.* (pp. 324–335). New York: Wiley.

Newman, J. P., & Kosson, D. S. (1986). Passive avoidance learning in psychopathic and nonpsychopathic offenders. *J. Abn. Psychol., 95*, 252–56.

Newman, J. P., Kosson, D. S., & Patterson, C. M. (1992). Delay of gratification in psychopathic and nonpsychopathic offenders. *J. Abn. Psychol., 101*, 630–36.

Newman, L., Henry, P. B., DiRenzo, P., & Stecher, T. (1988–89). Intervention and student assistance: The Pennsylvania model. Special Issue: Practical approaches in treating adolescent chemical dependency: A guide to clinical assessment and intervention. *J. Chem. Depen. Treat., 2*(1), 145–62.

Newman, L. S., Duffe, K. J., & Baumeister, R. F. (1997). A new look at defensive projection: Thought suppression, accessibility, and biased person perception. *J. Pers Soc. Psychol., 72*(5), 980–1001.

Newman, M. G., & Cates, M. S. (1977). *Methadone treatment in narcotic addiction.* New York: Academic Press.

Newman, M. L., & Greenway, P. (1997). Therapeutic effects of providing MMPI-2 test feedback to clients in a university counseling service. *Psychol. Assess., 9,* 122–31.

New York Times (1994, May 9). Multiple personality cases perplex legal system. pp. 143.

NIAAA Eighth Special Report to the U.S. Congress. (1994). *Comorbidity of alcohol use disorders with other psychopathology.* Washington, DC: U.S. Government Printing Office.

Niccols, G. A. (1994). Fetal alcohol syndrome: Implications for psychologists. *Clin. Psychol. Rev., 14,* 91–112.

Nicholson, R. A., & Berman, J. S. (1983). Is follow-up necessary in evaluating psychotherapy? *Psychol. Bull., 93,* 261–78.

Niederehe, G. & Schneider. (1998). Treatments for depression and anxiety in the aged. In P. E. Nathan & J. M. Gorman, *A guide to treatments that work.* (pp. 270–87). New York: Oxford University Press.

Niederland, W. G. (1968). Clinical observations of the survivor syndrome. *Inter. J. Psychoanal., 49,* 313–16.

Nietzel, M. T., & Harris, M. J. (1990). Relationship of dependency and achievement/autonomy to depression. *Clin. Psychol. Rev., 10,* 279–97.

Nigg, J. T., & Goldsmith, H. H. (1994). Genetics of personality disorders: perspectives from personality and psychopathology research. *Psychol. Bull., 115,* 346–80.

NIH Consensus Statement on Treatment of Panic Disorder. (1991). In B. E. Wolfe & J. D. Maser (Eds.), (1994). *Treatment of panic disorder. A consensus development conference.* Washington, DC: American Psychiatric Press.

NIMH Psychopharmacology Service Center Collaborative Study Group. (1964). Phenothiazine treatment in acute schizophrenia: Effectiveness. *Arch. Gen. Psychiat., 10,* 246–61.

Nisbett, R. E., & Wilson, T. D. (1977). Telling more than we can know: Verbal reports on mental processes. *Psychol. Rev., 84,* 231–59.

Noble, E. P. (Ed.). (1979). *Alcohol and health: Technical support document.* Third special report to the U.S. Congress (DHEW Publication No. ADM79–832). Washington, DC: U.S. Government Printing Office.

Noble, P., & Rodger, S. (1989). Violence by psychiatric inpatients. *Brit. J. Psychiat., 155,* 384–90.

Noia, G., De Santis, M., Fundaro, C., Mastromarino, C., Trivellini, C., Rosati, P., Caruso, A., Segni, G., & Mancuso, S. (1994). Drug addiction in pregnancy: 13 years of experience. *Fetal Diagnosis and Therapy, 9,* 116–24.

Nolan, E. E., & Gadow, K. D. (1997). Children with ADHD and tic disorder and their classmates: Behavioral normalization with methylphenidate. *J. Amer. Acad. Child Adoles. Psychiat. 36*(5), 597–604.

Nolan, S., Mineka, S., & Gotlib, I. (submitted). Verbal, nonverbal, and gender-related factors in negative interpersonal reactions toward depressed and anxious individuals.

Nolen-Hoeksma, S. (1987). Sex differences in unipolar depression: Evidence and theory. *Psychol. Bull., 101,* 259–82.

Nolen-Hoeksma, S. (1990). *Sex differences in depression.* Stanford, CA: Stanford University Press.

Nolen-Hoeksma, S., & Girgus, J. S. (1994). The emergence of gender differences in depression during adolescence. *Psychol. Bull., 115*(3), 424–43.

Nolen-Hoeksma, S., Morrow, J., & Fredrickson, B. L. (1993). Response styles and the duration of episodes of depressed mood. *J. Abn. Psychol., 102*(1), 20–28.

Nolen-Hoeksma, S., Parker, L. E., & Larson, J. (1994). Ruminative coping with depressed mood following loss. *J. Pers. Soc. Psychol., 67*(1), 92–104.

Noll, K. M., Davis, J. M., & DeLeon-Jones, F. (1985). Medication and somatic therapies in the treatment of depression. In E. E. Beckham & W. R. Leber (Eds.), *Handbook of depression: Treatment, assessment, and research.* (pp. 220–315). Homewood, IL: Dorsey Press.

Nopoulos, P., Flaum, M., & Andreasen, N. C. (1997). Sex differences in brain morphology in schizophrenia. *Amer. J. Psychiat., 154*(12), 1648–54.

Norcross, J. C., & Goldfried, M. R. (Ed.). (1992). *Handbook of psychotherapy integration.* New York: Basic Books.

Norden, K. A., Klein, D. N., Donaldson, S. K., Pepper, C. M., & Klein, L. M. (1995). Reports of the early home environment in DSM-III-R personality disorders. *J. Person. Dis., 9*(3), 213–223.

Norris, F. H., & Kaniasty, K. (1994). Psychological distress following criminal victimization in the general population: Cross-sectional, longitudinal, and prospective analyses. *J. Cons. Clin. Psychol., 62,* 111–23.

North, C. S., Smith, E. M., & Spitznagel, E. L. (1994). Post-traumatic stress disorders in survivors of a mass shooting. *Amer. J. Psychiat., 151,* 82–88.

Norton, K., & Hinshelwood, R. D. (1996). Severe personality disorder. Treatment issues and selection for in-patient psychotherapy. *Brit. J. Psychiat., 168,* 723–731.

Novaco, R. W. (1977). A stress inoculation approach to anger management in the training of law enforcement officers. *Am. J. Community Psychol., 5,* 327–46.

Novaco, R. W. (1979). The cognitive regulation of anger and stress. In P. Kendall & S. Hollon (Eds.), *Cognitive-behavioral intervention: Theory, research, and procedures.* New York: Academic Press.

Novaco, R. W. (1977). Stress inoculation: A cognitive therapy for anger and its application to a case of depression. *J. Cons. Clin. Psychol., 45,* 600–8.

Novy, D. M., Blumentritt, T. L., Nelson, D. V., & Gaa, A. (1997). The Washington University Sentence Completion Test: Are the two halves alternate forms? Are the female and male forms comparable? *J. Pers. Assess., 68*(3), 616–27.

Noyes, R., Jr., Clarkson, C., Crowe, R. R., Yates, W. R., & McChesney, C. M. (1987). A family study of generalized anxiety disorder. *Amer. J. Psychiat., 144,* 1019–24.

Noyes, R., Jr., Crowe, R. R., Harris, E. L., Hamra, B. J., & McChesney, C. M. (1986). Relationship between panic disorder and agoraphobia: A family study. *Arch. Gen. Psychiat., 43,* 227–32.

Noyes, R., Kathol, R. G., Fisher, M. M., Phillips, B. M., Suelzer, M. T., & Holt, C. S. (1993). The validity of DSM-III-R hypochondriasis. *Arch. Gen. Psychiat., 50*(12), 961–70.

Noyes, R., Jr., Woodman, C., Holt, C. S., Reich, J. H., Zimmerman, M. B. (1995). Avoidant personality traits distinguish social phobic and panic disorder subjects. *J. Nerv. Ment. Dis., 183*(3), 145–153.

Neuchterlein, K. H., Snyder, K. S., & Mintz, J. (1992). Paths to relapse: Possible transactional processes connecting patient illness onset, expressed emotion, and psychotic relapse. *Brit. J. Psychiat., 161* (Suppl. 18), 88–96.

Nurnberger Jr., J. I., & Gershon, E. S. (1992). Genetics. In E. S. Paykel (Ed.), *Handbook of affective disorders* (2nd ed.). New York: Guilford.

Nurnberger, J., Roose, S. P., Dunner, D. S., & Fieve, R. R. (1979). Unipolar mania: A distinct clinical entity? *Amer. J. Psychiat., 136,* 1420–23.

O'Brien, D. (1979, Mar.). Mental anguish: An occupational hazard. *Emergency,* 61–64.

Obrzut, J. E., Paquette, A., & Flores, M. M. (1997). On the neurobiological and neuropsychological basis of learning disabilities. In J. A. M. Horton, D. Wedding, & J. Webster (Eds.), *The neuropsychology handbook* (Vol. 2). (pp. 237–66). New York: Springer.

O'Connell, M., Cooper, S., Perry, J. C., & Hoke, L. (1989). The relationship between thought disorder and psychotic symptoms in borderline personality disorder. *J. Nerv. Ment. Dis., 177,* 273–78.

O'Connell, P. (1976, Nov.). Trends in psychological adjustment: Observations made during successive psychiatric follow-up interviews of returned Navy–Marine Corps POWs. In R. Spaulding (Ed.), *Proceedings of the 3rd annual joint meeting concerning POW/MIA matters.* (pp. 16–22). San Diego.

O'Connor, B. P., McGuire, S., Reiss, D., Hetherington, E. M., & Plomin, R. (1998). Co-occurence of depressive symptoms and antisocial behavior in adolescence: A common genetic liability. *J. Abn. Psychol., 107*(1), 27–37.

Odell, J. D., Warren, R. P., Warren, W., Burger, R. A., & Maciulis, A. (1997). Association of genes within the major histocompatibility complex with attention-deficit hyperactivity disorder. *Neuropsychobiology, 35*(4), 181–86.

O'Dell, S. (1974). Training parents in behavior modification: A review. *Psychol. Bull., 81*(7), 418–33.

O'Donnell, C. R. (1995). Firearm deaths among children and youth. *Amer. Psychol., 50*(9), 771–76.

O'Donnell, I., & Farmer, R. (1995). The limitations of official suicide statistics. *Brit. J. Psychiat., 166,* 458–61.

O'Donnell, I., Farmer, R., & Catalan, J. (1996). Explaining suicide: The views of survivors of serious suicide attempts. *Brit. J Psychiat., 168,* 780–86.

O'Donnell, P., & Grace, A. A. (1998). Dysfunctions in multiple interrelated systems as the neurobiological bases of schizophrenic symptom clusters. *Schizo. Bull.*, 24(2), 267–84.

O'Hara, M., Schlecte, J., Lewis, D., & Varner, M. (1991). Controlled prospective study of postpartum mood disorders: Psychological, environmental, and hormonal variables. *J. Abn. Psychol.*, 100, 63–73.

O'Hara, M., Zekoski, E., Philipps, L., & Wright, E. (1990). Controlled prospective study of postpartum mood disorders: Comparison of childbearing and nonchildbearing women. *J. Abn. Psychol.*, 99, 3–15.

O'Leary, A. (1985). Self-efficacy and health. *Behav. Res. Ther.*, 23, 437–51.

O'Leary, D., & Wilson, G. T. (1987). *Behavior therapy* (2nd ed.). Englewood Cliffs, NJ: Prentice-Hall.

O'Leary, K. D. (1995). Assessment and treatment of partner abuse. *Clin. Res. Dig. Suppl. Bull, 12, 13,* 1–2.

O'Leary, K. D., & Beach, S. R. H. (1990). Marital therapy: A viable treatment for depression and marital discord. *Amer. J. Psychiat.*, 147, 183–86.

O'Leary, K. D., Christian, J. L., & Mendell, N. R. (1994). A closer look at the link between marital discord and depressive symptomatology. *J. Soc. Clin. Psychol.*, 13, 33–41.

O'Malley, S., Adamse, M., Heaton, R. K., & Gawin, F. H. (1992). Neuropsychological impairment in chronic cocaine abusers. *Amer. J. Drug Alcoh. Abuse*, 18, 131–44.

O'Malley, S. S., Foley, S. H., Rounsaville, B. J., Watkins, J. T., Sotsky, S. M., Imber, S. D., & Elkin, I. (1988). Therapist competence and patient outcome in interpersonal psychotherapy of depression. *J. Cons. Clin. Psychol.*, 56, 496–501.

O'Malley, S. S., Jaffe, A. J., Rode, S., & Rounsaville, B. (1996). Experience of a "slip" among alcoholics treated with naltrexone or placebo. *Amer. J. Psychiat.*, 153(2), 281–83.

Oetting, E. R., & Beauvais, F. (1990). Adolescent drug use: Findings of national and local surveys. *J. Cons. Clin. Psychol.*, 58, 385–94.

Office of Juvenile Justice and Delinquency Prevention. *1995 Youth Gang survey.* (1995). Washington: U.S. Government Printing Office.

Office of Technology Assessment, U.S. Congress. (1986, Dec.)*Children's mental health: Problems and services.* (OTA Publication No. OTABP-H-33). Washington, DC: U.S. Government Printing Office.

Office of Technology Assessment. (1993). *Biological components of substance abuse and addiction.* Washington, DC: United States Congress, Office of Technology Assessment.

Offord, D. R., & Bennett, K. J. (1996). Conduct disorder. In L. Hechtman (Ed.), *Do they grow out of it?* (pp. 77–100). Washington: American Psychiatric Press.

Ogata, S. N., Silk, K. R., Goodrich, S., Lohr, N. E., & Hill, E. M. (1990). Childhood sexual and physical abuse in adult patients with borderline personality. *Amer. J. Psychiat.*, 147, 1008–13.

Ogloff, J. R. P. (1995). The legal basis of forensic applications of the MMPI-2. In Y. S. Ben-Porath, J. R Graham, G. C. Hall, R. D. Hirschman, & M. S. Zargoza (Eds.), *Forensic applications of the MMPI-2.* Newbury Park, CA: Sage.

Öhman, A. (1986). Face the beast and fear the face: Animal and social fears as prototypes for evolutionary analyses of emotion. *Psychophysiology*, 23, 123–45.

Öhman, A. (1996). Preferential preattentive processing of threat in anxiety: Preparedness and attentional biases. In R. M. Rapee (Ed.), *Current controversies in the anxiety disorders (pp. 253–90).* New York: Guilford.

Öhman, A., Dimberg, U., & Esteves, F. (1989). Preattentive activation of aversive emotions. In T. Archer & L. G. Nilsson (Eds.), *Aversion, avoidance, and anxiety: Perspectives on aversively motivated behavior.* (pp. 169–99). Hillsdale, NJ: Erlbaum.

Öhman, A., Dimberg, U., & Öst, L. G. (1985). Animal and social phobias: Biological constraints on learned fear responses. In S. Reiss & R. Bootzin (Eds.), *Theoretical issues in behavior therapy.* (pp. 123–75). New York: Academic Press.

Öhman, A., & Mineka, S. (submitted). *Revisiting Preparedness: Toward an evolved module of fear learning.*

Öhman, A., & Soares, J. (1993). On the automatic nature of phobic fear: Conditioned electrodermal responses to masked fearrelevant stimuli. *J. Abn. Psychol.*, 102, 121–32.

Ohtsuka, K., Bruton, E., DeLuca, L., & Borg, V. (1997). Sex differences in pathological gambling using gaming machines. *Psychol. Rep.*, 80(3), 1051–57.

Okura, K. P. (1975). Mobilizing in response to a major disaster. *Community Health Journal*, 2(2), 136–44.

Oldenburg, B., Perkins, R. J., & Andrews, G. (1985). Controlled trial of psychological intervention in myocardial infarction. *J. Cons. Clin. Psychol.*, 53, 852–59.

Oldham, J. M. (1991). *Personality disorders: New perspectives on diagnostic validity.* Washington, DC: American Psychiatric Press.

Oldham, J. M., Skodol, A. E., Kellman, H. D., Hyler, S. E., Rosnick, L., & Davies, M. (1992). Diagnosis of DSM-III-R personality disorders by two structured interviews: Patterns of comorbidity. *Amer. J. Psychiat.*, 149, 213–20.

Olds, D. L., Henderson, C., & Tatelbaum, R. (1994). Prevention of intellectual impairment in children of women who smoke cigarettes during pregnancy. *Pediatrics*, 93, 228–233.

Olds, D. L., Henderson, C., Tatelbaum, R., & Chamberlin, R. (1986). Improving the delivery of prenatal care and outcomes of pregnancy: A randomized trial of nurse home visitation. *Pediatrics*, 77, 16–28.

Olds, S. (1970). Say it with a stomach ache. *Today's Health*, 48(11), 41–43, 88.

Oles, B. (1994). *Psychosocially-imposed homosexuality: Institutionalized mate-guarding in Melanesia.* Paper presented at the sixth annual meeting of the Human Behavior and Evolution Society, June 15–19, Ann Arbor, Michigan.

Olfson, M. (1993). Trends in the prescription of antidepressants by office-based psychiatrists. *Amer. J. Psychiat.*, 150, 571–77.

Olivera, A. A., Kiefer, M. W., & Manley, M. K. (1990). Tardive dyskinesia in psychiatric patients with substance use disorders. *Amer. J. Drug Alcoh. Abuse*, 16, 57–66.

Ollendick, T. H. (1981). Self-monitoring and self-administered overcorrection: The modification of nervous tics in children. *Behav. Mod.*, 5(1), 75–84.

Ollendick, T. H. (1997). Violence in youth: where do we go from here? Behavior therapy's response. *Behav. Ther.*, 27(4), 485–514.

Ollendick, T. H., Yang, B., King, N. J., Dong, Q., et al. (1996). Fears in American, Australian, Chinese, and Nigerian children and adolescents: A cross-cultural study. *Journal of Child Psychology & Psychiatry & Allied Sciences*, 37(2), 213–20.

Oltmanns, T. F., & Maher, B. A. (Eds.). (1988). *Delusional beliefs.* New York: Wiley.

Opler, M. K., & Singer, J. L. (1959). Ethnic differences in behavior and psychopathology. *Inter. J. Soc. Psychiat.*, 2, 11–23.

Oppenheim, J. (1991). *Shattered nerves.* New York: Oxford University Press.

Oren, D. A., & Rosenthal, N. E. (1992). Seasonal affective disorders. In E. S. Paykel (Ed.), *Handbook of affective disorders* (2nd ed.). (pp. 551–67). New York: Guilford.

Orford, J. (1985). *Excessive appetites: A psychological view of addiction.* New York: Wiley.

Orleans, C. T., Kristeller, J. L., & Gritz, E. R. (1993). Helping hospitalized smokers quit: New directions for treatment and research. *J. Cons. Clin. Psychol.*, 61, 778–89.

Orne, M. T., Dinges, D. F., & Orne, E. C. (1984). On the differential diagnosis of multiple personality in the forensic context. *Int. J. Clin. Exp. Hypn.*, 32, 118–69.

Oros, C. J., & Koss, M. P. (1978, Aug.). *Women as rape victims.* Paper presented at the American Psychological Association Annual Meeting, Toronto.

Osborn, A. F. (1992). Social influences on conduct disorder in mid-childhood. *Studia Psychologica*, 34, 29–43.

Oscar-Berman, M., Shagrin, B., Evert, D. L., & Epstein, C. (1997). Impairments of brain and behavior. *Alcohol Health and Research World*, 21(1), 65–75.

Osler, W. (1892). *Lectures on Angina Pectoris and allied states.* New York: Appleton-Century-Crofts.

Osofsky, J. (1995). The effects of exposure to violence on young children. *Amer. Psychol.*, 50(9), 782–88.

Öst, L. G. (1987). Age of onset of different phobias. *J. Abn. Psychol.*, 96, 223–9.

Öst, L-G. (1997). Rapid treatment of specific phobias. In G. C. L. Davey, (Ed.), Phobias. A handbook of theory, research and treatment (2nd ed.). (pp. 227–46). Chichester, England: Wiley.

Öst, L-G., & Hellstrom, K. (1997). Blood-injury-injection phobia. In G. C. L. Davey, (Ed.), *Phobias. A handbook of theory, research and treatment.* (pp.63–80). Chichester, England: Wiley.

Öst, L. G., & Hugdahl, K. (1985). Acquisition of blood and dental phobia and anxiety response patterns in clinical patients. *Behav. Res. Ther.*, 23(1), 27–34.

Öst, L.G., & Hugdahl, K.(1981). Acquisition of phobias and anxiety response patterns in clinical patients. *Behav. Res. Ther.*, 19, 439–47.

Otto, M. W., Fava, M., Penava, S. J., Bless, E., et al. (1997). Life event, mood, and cognitive predictors of perceived stress before and after treatment for major depression. *Cog. Ther. Res.*, 21(4), 403–20.

Otto, R. M., Poythress, N., Starr, C. B., & Darkes, J. (1993). An empirical study of the Reports of APAs Peer Review Panel in the Congressional Review of the *U.S.S. Iowa* incident. *J. Pers. Assess.*, 61, 425–42.

Ouimette, P. C., & Klein, D. N. (1993). Convergence of psychoanalytic and cognitive-behavioral theories of depression: An empirical review and new data on Blatt's and Beck's models. In *Psychoanalytic perspectives on psychopathology.* (pp. 191–223). Washington: American Psychological Association.

Overall, J. E., & Hollister, L. E. (1982). Decision rules for phenomenological classification of psychiatric patients. *J. Cons. Clin. Psychol.*, 50(4), 535–45.

Overmier, J. B., & Seligman, M. E. P. (1967). Effects of inescapable shock upon subsequent escape and avoidance learning. *Journal of Comparative and Physiological Psychology*, 63, 23–33.

Owen, C., Rutherford, M. J., Jones, M., Tennant, C., & Smallman, A. (1997). Noncompliance in psychiatric aftercare. *Comm. Ment. Hlth. J.*, 33, 25–34.

Owen, F. W. (1978). Dyslexia—genetic aspects. In A. L. Benton & D. Pearl (Eds.), *Dyslexia: In appraisal of current knowledge.* (pp. 267–84). New York: Oxford University Press.

Ozdemir, V., Bremner, K. E., & Naranjo, C. A. (1994). Treatment of alcohol withdrawal syndrome. *Annals of Medicine*, 26, 101–6.

Pachter, H. M. (1951). *Magic into science: The story of Paracelsus.* New York: Schumen.

Page, A. C. (1994). Blood-injury phobia. *Clin. Psychol. Rev.*, 14(5), 443–61.

Page, A. C., & Martin, N. G. (1998). Testing a genetic structure of blood-injury-injection fears. *Am. J. Med. Genet.*, 81 377–84.

Page, W. F., Engdahl, B. E., & Eberly, R. E. (1997). Persistence of PTSD in former prisoners of war. In C. S. Fullerton & R. J. Ursano (Eds.), *Posttraumatic stress disorder.* (pp. 147–58). Washington: American Psychiatric Press.

Palace, E. M. (1995). Modification of dysfunctional patterns of sexual response through autonomic arousal and false feedback. *J. Cons. Clin. Psychol.*, 63, 604–15.

Palace, E. M., & Gorzalka, B. B. (1990). The enhancing effects of anxiety on arousal in sexually dysfunctional and functional women. *J. Abn. Psychol.*, 99, 403–11.

Palmer, C. T. (1988). Twelve reasons why rape is not sexually motivated: A skeptical examination. *J. Sex Res.*, 25, 512–30.

Palosaari, U., & Laippala, P. (1996). Parental divorce and depression in young adulthood: Adolescents' closeness to parents and self-esteem as mediating factor. *Acta Psychiat. Scandin.*, 93(1), 20–36.

Pan, H. S., Neidig, P. H., & O'Leary, K. D. (1994). Predicting mild and severe husband-to-wife physical aggression. *J. Consult. Clin. Psychol.*, 62, 975–81.

Papp, L., & Gorman, J. M. (1990). Suicidal preoccupation during fluoxetine treatment. *Amer. J. Psychiat., 147,* 1380.

Paris, J., Zweig-Frank, H., & Guzder, J. (1994). Psychological risk factors for borderline personality disorder in female patients. *Compr. Psychiat., 35*(4), 301–305.

Paris, J., Zweig-Frank, H., & Guzder, J. (1994). Risk factors for borderline personality disorders in male outpatients. *J. Nerv. Ment. Dis., 182,* 375–80.

Parker, G., Hadzi-Pavlovic, D., Roussos, J.; Wilhelm, K.; Mitchell, P.; Austin, M.-P.; Hickie, I.; Gladstone, G.; Eyers, K. (1998) Non-melancholic depression: The contribution of personality, anxiety and life events to subclassification. *Psychological Medicine, 28,* 1209–19.

Parker, G., Johnston, P., & Hayward, L. (1988). Parental "expressed emotion" as a predictor of schizophrenic relapse. *Arch. Gen. Psychiat., 45,* 806–13.

Parker, J. G., Rubin, K. H., Price, J. M., & DeRossier, M. E. (1995). Peer relationships, child development, and adjustment: A developmental psychopathology perspective. In D. Cicchetti & D. J. Cohen (Eds.), *Developmental psychopathology: Vol. 2. Risk, disorder, and adaptation.* (pp. 96–161). New York: Wiley.

Parker, R. I. (1993). Comments on Ellis's Integrative Strategy Instruction model. *J. Learn. Dis., 26*(7), 443–47.

Parkes, C. M., Benjamin, B., & Fitzgerald, R. G. (1969). Broken heart: A statistical study of increased mortality among widowers. *Brit. Med. J., 1,* 740–43.

Parkin, M. (1974). Suicide and culture in Fairbanks: A comparison of three cultural groups in a small city of interior Alaska. *Psychiatry, 37*(1), 60–67.

Parsons, Oscar A. (1998). Neurocognitive deficits in alcoholics and social drinkers: A continuum? *Alcoholism: Clin. Exper. Res. 22*(4), 954–61.

Pasewark, R. A., Pantle, M. L., & Steadman, H. J. (1982). Detention and rearrest rates of persons found not guilty by reason of insanity and convicted felons. *Amer. J. Psychiat., 139*(7), 892–97.

Paternite, C. E., & Loney, J. (1980). Childhood hyperkinesis: Relationships between symptomatology and home environment. In C. K. Whelan & B. Henker (Eds.), *Hyperactive children: The social ecology of identification and treatment.* New York: Academic Press.

Paterson, R. J., & Neufeld, R. W. (1987). Clear danger: Situational determinants of the appraisal of threat. *Psychol. Bull., 101,* 404–16.

Patrick, C. J., Bradley, M. M., & Lang, P. J. (1993). Emotion in the criminal psychopath: Startle reflex modulation. *J. Abn. Psychol., 102*(1), 82–92.

Patrick, C. J., Cuthbert, B. N., & Lang, P. J. (1994). Emotion in the criminal psychopath: Fear image processing. *J Abnorm. Psychol., 103,* 523–34.

Patterson, C. H. (1989). Eclecticism in psychotherapy: Is integration possible? *Psychotherapy, 26,* 157–61.

Patterson, C. M., & Newman, J. P. (1993) Reflectivity and learning from aversive events: Toward a psychological mechanism for the syndromes of disinhibition. *Psychol. Rev., 100,* 716–36.

Patterson, G. R. (1979). Treatment for children with conduct problems: A review of outcome studies. In S. Feshbach & A. Fraczek (Eds.), *Aggression and behavior change: Biological and social processes.* New York: Praeger.

Patterson, G. R. (1996). Characteristics of developmental theory for early onset delinquency. In M. F. Lenzenweger & J. L. Haugaard (Eds.), *Frontiers of developmental psychopathology* (pp. 81–124). New York: Oxford University Press.

Patterson, G. R., Capaldi, D., & Bank, L. (1991). An early starter model for predicting delinquency. In D. Pepler & K. H. Rubin (Eds.), *The development and treatment of childhood aggression.* (pp. 139–168). Hillsdale, NJ: Erlbaum.

Patterson, G. R., DeBarsyshe, B. D., & Ramsey, E. (1989). A developmental perspective on antisocial behavior. *Amer. Psychol., 44,* 329–35.

Patterson, G. R., Reid, J. B., & Dishion, T. J. (1991). *Antisocial boys.* Eugene, OR: Castalia.

Patterson, W. M. (1993). Fluoxetine-induced sexual dysfunction. *J. Clin. Psychiat., 54,* 71.

Paul, G. L. (1979). New assessment systems for residential treatment, management, research and evaluation: A symposium. *J. Behav. Assess., 1*(3), 181–84.

Paul, G. L. (1982). *The development of a "transportable" system of behavioral assessment for chronic patients.* Invited address. University of Minnesota, Minneapolis.

Paul, G. L., & Lentz, R. J. (1977). *Psychosocial treatment of chronic mental patients: Milieu versus social-learning programs.* Cambridge, MA: Harvard University Press.

Paul, G. L., & Menditto, A. A. (1992). Effectiveness of inpatient treatment programs for mentally ill adults in public psychiatric facilities. *Applied and Preventive Psychology: Current Scientific Perspectives, 1,* 41–63.

Paul, G. L., Stuve, P., & Cross, J. V. (1997). Real-world inpatient programs: Shedding some light—A critique. *App. Prev. Psychol., 6*(4), 193–204.

Paul, N. (1971, May 31). The family as patient. *Time,* 60.

Pauls, D. L., Alsobrooke, J. P., Goodman, W., Rasmussen, S., & Leckman, J. F. (1995). A family study of obsessive-compulsive disorder. *Amer. J. Psychiat., 152*(1), 76–84.

Pauls, D. L., Raymond, C. L., & Robertson, M. (1991). The genetics of obsessive-compulsive disorder: A review. In J. Zohar, T. Insel, & S. Rasmussen (Eds.), *The psychobiology of obsessive-compulsive disorder.* New York: Springer.

Pauls, D. L., Towbin, K. E., Leckman, J. F., Zahner, G. E., & Cohen, D. J. (1986). Gilles de la Tourette's Syndrome and obsessive-compulsive disorder. *Arch. Gen. Psychiat., 43,* 1180–2.

Pausnau, R. O., & Russell, A. T. (1975). Psychiatric resident suicide. An analysis of five cases. *Amer. J. Psychiat., 132*(4), 402–6.

Pavlov, I. P. (1927). *Conditioned reflexes.* London: Oxford University Press.

Pavone, L., Meli, C., Nigro, F., & Lisi, R. (1993). Late diagnosed phenylketonuria patients: Clinical presentation and results of treatment. *Developmental Brain Dysfunction, 6*(1–3), 184–87.

Paykel, E. S. (Ed.). (1982a). *Handbook of affective disorders.* New York: Guilford.

Paykel, E. S. (1982b). Life events and early environment. In E. S. Paykel (Ed.), *Handbook of affective disorders.* New York: Guilford.

Paykel, E. S., Brayne, C., Huppert, F. A., Gill, C., Barkley, C., Gehlhaar, E., Beardsall, L., Girling, D. M., Pollitt, P., & O'Connor, D. (1994). Incidence of dementia in a population older than 75 years in the United Kingdom. *Arch. Gen. Psychiat., 51*(4), 325–32.

Paykel, E. S., Hallowell, C., Dressler, D. M., Shapiro, D. L., & Weissman, M. M. (1974). Treatment of suicide attempters. *Arch. Gen. Psychiat., 31*(4), 487–91.

Payne, R. L. (1975). Recent life changes and the reporting of psychological states. *J. Psychosom. Res., 19*(1), 99–103.

Pearlson, G. D., Kim, W. S., Kubos, K. L., Moberg, P. J., Jayaram, G., Bascom, M. J., Chase, G. A., Goldfinger, A. G., & Tune, L. E. (1989). Ventricle-brain ratio, computed tomographic density, and brain area in 50 schizophrenics. *Arch. Gen. Psychiat., 46,* 690–97.

Peck, M. A., & Schrut, A. (1971). Suicidal behavior among college students. *HSMHA Health Reports, 86*(2), 149–56.

Peeke, P. M., & Chrousos, G. P. (1995). Hypercortisolism and obesity. In G. P. Chrousos, R. McCarty, et al. (Eds.), *Stress: Basic mechanisms and clinical implications.* (pp. 515–60). New York: New York Academy of Sciences.

Pelham, W. E., Carlson, C., Sams, S. E., Vallano, G., Dixon, M. J., & Hoza, B. (1993). Separate and combined effects of methylphenidate and behavior modification on boys with attention-deficit hyperactivity disorder in the classroom. *J. Cons. Clin. Psychol., 61,* 506–15.

Pelham, W. E., Murphy, D. A., Vannatta, K., Milich, R., Licht, B. G., Gnagy, E. M., Greenslade, K. E., Greiner, A. R., & Vodde-Hamilton, M. (1992). Methylphenidate and attributions in boys with at-tention-deficit hyperactivity disorder. *J. Cons. Clin. Psychol., 60,* 282–92.

Pelham, W. E., Schnedler, R. W., Bologna, N. C., & Contreras, J. A. (1980). Behavioral and stimulant treatment of hyperactive children. A therapy study with methylphenidate probes in a within subject design. *J. Appl. Beh. Anal., 13*(2), 221–36.

Pelham, W. E., Swanson, J. M., Furman, M., & Schwindt, H. (1996). Pemoline effects on children with ADHD: A time response by dose-response analysis on classroom measures. *Annual Progress in child Psychiatry & Child Development, 1996,* 473–93.

Penk, W. E., Charles, H. L., & Van Hoose, T. A. (1978). Comparative effectiveness of day hospital and inpatient psychiatric treatment. *J. Cons. Clin. Psychol., 46,* 94–101.

Penn, D. L., Corrigan, P. W., Bentall, R. P., Racenstein, J. M., & Newman, L. (1997). Social cognition in schizophrenia. *Psychol. Bull., 121*(1), 114–32.

Penna, M. W. (1986). Classification of personality disorders. In J. R. Lion (Ed.), *Personality disorders: Diagnosis and management.* (pp. 10–31). Malabar, FL: Robert F. Kreiger.

Pennebaker, J. W. (1997). *Opening up: The healing power of expressing emotions.* New York: Guilford.

Pennisi, E. (1994). One team, two clues in Alzheimer's puzzle. *Sci. News, 146*(20), 308–9.

Penrose, L. S. (1963). *Biology of mental defect* (3rd ed.). New York: Grune & Stratton.

Pentz, M. A. (1983). Prevention of adolescent substance abuse through social skill development. *National Institute on Drug Abuse Research Monograph Series, 47,* 195–232.

Perez, C. M., & Widom, C. S. (1994). Childhood victimization and long-term intellectual and academic outcomes. *Child Ab. Negl., 18*(8), 617–33.

Perlberg, M. (1979, Apr.). Adapted from Trauma at Tenerife: The psychic aftershocks of a jet disaster. *Human Behav.,* 49–50.

Perlin, M. L. (1996). Myths, realities, and the political world*; the anthropology of insanity defense attitudes. *Bull. Amer. Acad. Psychiat. Law, 24*(1), 5–25.

Perls, F. S. (1967). Group vs. individual therapy. *ETC: A Review of General Semantics, 34,* 306–12.

Perls, F. S. (1969). *Gestalt therapy verbatim.* Lafayette, CA: Real People Press.

Perris, C. (1979). Recent perspectives in the genetics of affective disorders. In J. Mendlewicz & B. Shopsin (Eds.), *Genetic aspects of affective illness.* New York: SP Medical & Scientific Books.

Perris, C. (1982). The distinction between bipolar and unipolar affective disorders. In E. S. Paykel (Ed.), *Handbook of affective disorders.* New York: Guilford.

Perris, C. (1992). Bipolar-unipolar distinction. In E. S. Paykel (Ed.), *Handbook of affective disorders* (2nd ed.). New York: Guilford.

Perry, C. L., & Murray, D. M. (1985). The prevention of adolescent drug abuse: Implications from etiological, developmental, behavioral, and environmental models. *J. Prim. Prevent., 6*(1), 31–52.

Perry, C. L., Williams, C. L., Forster, J. L., Wolfson, M., Wagenaar, A. C., Finnegan, J. R., McGovern, P. G., Veblen-Mortensen, S., Komro, K. A., & Anstine, P. S. (1993). Background, conceptualization, and design of a community-wide research program on adolescent alcohol use: Project Northland. *Health Education Research: Theory and Practice, 8*(1), 125–36.

Perry, T. (1970). The enigma of PKU. *The Sciences, 10*(8), 12–16.

Persons, J., Thase, M., & Crits-Christoph, P. (1996). The role of psychotherapy in the treatment of depression. *Arch. Gen. Psychiatr., 53,* 283–90.

Pert, C. B., & Snyder, S. H. (1973, Mar. 9). Opiate receptor: Demonstration in nervous tissue. *Science, 179*(4077), 1011–14.

Peters, R. H., & Kearns, W. D. (1992). Drug abuse history and treatment needs of jail inmates. *Amer. J. Drug Alcoh. Abuse, 18,* 355–66.

Petersen, A. C., Compas, B. E., Brooks-Gunn, J., Stemmler, M., Ey, S., & Grant, K. E. (1993). Depression in adolescence. *Amer. Psychol., 48,* 155–68.

Peterson, C., Maier, S. F., & Seligman, M. E .P. (1993). *Learned Helplessness: A theory for the age of personal control.* New York: Oxford University Press.

Peterson, C., & Seligman, M. E. P. (1987). Explanatory style and illness. *J. Personal., 55,* 237–65.

Peterson, C., Seligman, M. E. P., & Vaillant, G. E. (1988). Pessimistic explanatory style is a risk factor for physical illness: A thirty-five-year longitudinal study. *J. Pers. Soc. Psychol., 55,* 23–27.

Peterson, R. A., & Reiss, S. (1987). *Test maual for the anxiety sensitivity index.* Orland Park, IL: International Diagnostic Systems.

Petito, C. K. (1988). Review of central nervous system pathology in human immunodeficiency virus infection. *Ann. Neurol.,* Suppl., *23,* 54–57.

Petraitis, J., Flay, B. R., Miller, T. Q. et al. (1998). Illicit substance use among adolescents: A matrix of prospective predictors. *Substance Use & Misuse, 33*(13) 2661–604.

Petronko, M. R., Harris, S. L., & Kormann, R. J. (1994). Community-based behavioral training approaches for people with mental retardation and mental illness. *J. Cons. Clin. Psychol., 62*(1), 49–54.

Pfeffer, C. R. (1981). The family system of suicidal children. *Amer. J. Psychother., 35,* 330–41.

Pfeffer, C. R. (1996a). Suicidal behavior in response to stress. In C. R. Pfeffer (Ed.), *Severe stress and mental disturbance in children.* (pp. 327–46). Washington: American Psychiatric Association.

Pfeffer, C. R. (1996b). Suicidal behavior. In L. Hechtman (Ed.), *Do they grow out of it?* (pp. 121–38). Washington: American Psychiatric Press.

Pfeffer, C. R., Hurt, S. W., Kakuma, T., Peskin, J., Siefker, C. A., & Nagbhairava, S. (1994). Suicidal children grow up: Suicidal episodes and effects of treatment during followup. *J. Amer. Acad. Child Adoles. Psychiat., 33,* 225–30.

Pfohl, B. (1995). Histrionic personality disorder. In W. J. Livesley (Ed.), *The DSM-IV personality disorders.* (pp. 173–192). New York: Guilford.

Pfohl, B., & Blum, N. (1995). Obsessive-compulsive personality disorder. In W. J. Livesley (Ed.), *The DSM-IV personality disorders.* (pp. 261–276). New York: Guilford.

Phares, V., & Compas, B. E. (1992). The role of fathers in child and adolescent psychopathology: Make room for daddy. *Psychol. Bull., 111,* 387–412.

Phelps, J. A., Davis, J. O., & Schartz, K. M. (1997). Nature, nurture, and twin research strategies. *Curr. Dir. Psychol. Sci., 6*(5), 117–20.

Phifer, J. F., & Murrell, S. A. (1986). Etiologic factors in the onset of depressive symptoms in older adults. *J. Abn. Psychol., 95,* 282–91.

Phillips, K. (1996). *The broken mirror: Understanding and treating body dysmorphic disorder.* New York: Oxford University Press.

Phillips, K. A., Hirschfeld, R. M. A., Shea, M. T., & Gunderson, J. G. (1995). In W. J. Livesley (Ed.), *The DSM-IV personality disorders.* (pp. 287–302). New York: Guilford.

Piccinelli, M., & Wilkinson, G. (1994). Outcome of depression in psychiatric settings. *Brit. J. Psychiat., 164,* 297–304.

Pickworth, W. B., Rohrer, M. S., & Fant, R. V. (1997). Effects of abused drugs on psychomotor performance. *Experimental and Clinical Psychopharmacology, 5*(3), 235–41.

Pigott, T., & Seay, S. (1998). In R. Swinson, M. Antony, S. Rachman, & M. Richter (Eds.), *Obsessive-compulsive disorder: Theory, research, and treatment.* (pp. 298–326). New York: Guilford.

Pigott, T. M., Myers, K. R., & Williams, D. A. (1996). Obsessive-compulsive disorder: A neuropsychiatric perspective. In R. M. Rapee (Ed.), *Current controversies in the anxiety disorders.* (pp. 134–60). New York: Guilford.

Pillard, R. C. (1988). Sexual orientation and mental disorder. *Psychiatr. Ann., 18,* 52–56.

Pine, D. S., Cohen, P., Brook, J., & Coplan, J. D. (1997). Psychiatric symptoms in adolescence as predictors of obesity in early adulthood: A longitudinal study. *Amer. J. Pub. Hlth., 87,* 1303–10.

Pinsof, W. M. (1995). *Integrative problem-centered therapy: A synthesis of family, individual, and biological therapies.* New York: Basic Books.

Piotrowski, C., & Keller, J. W. (1992). Psychological testing in applied settings: A literature review from 1982–1992. *Journal of Training and Practice in Professional Psychology, 6,* 74–82.

Piotrowski, C., & Zalewski, C. (1993). Training in psychodiagnostic testing in APA aproved PsyD and PhD clinical psychology programs. *J. Pers. Assess., 61,* 394–405.

Pitman, R. (1993). Biological findings in posttraumatic stress disorder. In J.R. Davidson & E. B. Foa (Eds.), *Post-Traumatic Stress Disorder: DSM IV and Beyond.* (pp. 173–189). Washington, DC: American Psychiatric Press.

Pitman, R. K., van der Kolk, B. A., Orr, S. P., Bessel, A., Manchester, N. H., & Greenberg, M. S. (1990). Naloxone-reversible analgesic response to combat related stimuli in post traumatic stress disorder. *Arch. Gen. Psychiat., 47,* 541–44.

Pitt, B. (1982). Depression and childbirth. In E. S. Paykel (Ed.), *Handbook of affective disorders.* New York: Guilford.

Plassman, B. L., & Breitner, J. C. (1997). The genetics of dementia in late life. *Psychiat. Clin. N. Amer., 20*(1), 59–76.

Plato. (n.d.). *The laws* (Vol. 5). (G. Burges, Trans.). London: George Bell & Sons.

Platt, S. D. (1984). Unemployment and suicidal behaviour: A review of the literature. *Social Science and Medicine, 19,* 93–115.

Pliner, P. L., & Cappell, H. D. (1974). Modification of affective consequences of alcohol: A comparison of social and solitary drinking. *J. Abn. Psychol., 83*(4), 418–25.

Pliszka, S. R. (1989). Effect of anxiety on cognition, behavior, and stimulant response in ADHD. *J. Amer. Acad. Child Adoles. Psychiat., 28*(6), 882–87.

Pliszka, S. R. (1991). Antidepressants in the treatment of child and adolescent psychopathology. Special issue: Child psychopharmacology. *J. Clin. Child Psychol., 20,* 313–20.

Plomin, R. (1986). *Development, genetics and psychology.* Hillsdale, NJ: Erlbaum.

Plomin, R. (1989). Environment and genes: Determinants of behavior. *Amer. Psychol., 44,* 105–111.

Plomin, R. (1990). The role of inheritance in behavior. *Science, 248,* 183–188.

Plomin, R. (1991). Genetic risk and psychosocial disorders: Links between the normal and abnormal. In M. Rutter & P. Casaer (Eds.), *Biological risk factors for psychosocial disorders.* Cambridge: Cambridge University Press.

Plomin, R., & Daniels, D. (1987). Why are children in the same family so different from one another? *Behavioral and Brain Sciences, 10,* 1–15.

Plomin, R., De Fries, J. C., McClearn, G. E., & Rutter, M. (1997). *Behavior genetics* (3rd ed.). New York: W. H. Freeman.

Plomin, R., & McClearn, G. E. (Eds.). (1993). *Nature, nurture, and psychology.* Washington: American Psychological Association.

Plotkin, R. (1981). When rights collide: Parents, children and consent to treatment. *J. Pediat. Psychol., 6*(2), 121–30.

Polich, J. M., Armor, D. J., & Braiker, H. B. (1981). *The course of alcoholism: Four years after treatment.* New York: Wiley Interscience.

Politzer, R. M., Yesalis, C. E., & Hudak, C. J. (1992). The epidemiologic model and the risks of legalized gambling: Where are we headed? *Health Values, 16,* 20–27.

Polivy, J., Zeitlin, S., Herman, P., & Beal, L. (1994). Food restriction and binge eating: A study of former prisoners of war. *J. Abn. Psychol., 103,* 409–411.

Pollack, J. M. (1979). Obsessive-compulsive personality: A review. *Psychol. Bull. 86*(2), 225–41.

Pollak, J. M. (1995). Commentary on obsessive-compulsive personality disorder. In W. J. Livesley (Ed.), *The DSM-IV personality disorders.* (pp. 277–283). New York: Guilford.

Pollard, C. A., Pollard, H. J., & Corn, K. J. (1989). Panic onset and major events in the lives of agoraphobics: A test of contiguity. *J. Abn. Psychol., 98,* 318–21.

Polvan, N. (1969). Historical aspects of mental ills in Middle East discussed. *Roche Reports, 6*(12), 3.

Ponce, F. Q., & Atkinson, D. R. (1989). Mexican-American acculturation, counselor ethnicity, counseling style, and perceived counselor credibility. *J. Couns. Psychol., 36,* 203–208.

Pope, H. G., Jr., Mangweth, B., Negrao, A. B., Hudson, J. I., & Cordas, T. A. (1994). Childhood sexual abuse and bulimia nervosa: A comparison of American, Austrian, and Brazilian women. *Amer. J. Psychiat., 151*(5), 732–37.

Pope, K. S. (1996). Memory, abuse, and science: Questioning claims about the false memory syndrome epidemic. *Amer. Psychol., 51,* 957–74.

Pope, K. S., Butcher, J. N., & Seelen, J. (1993). *MMPI/MMPI-2/MMPI-A in court: A practical guide for expert witnesses and attorneys.* Washington, DC: American Psychological Association.

Pope, K. S., Sonne, J. L., & Holroyd, J. (1993). *Sexual feelings in psychotherapy: Explorations for therapists and therapists-in-training.* Washington, DC: American Psychological Association.

Pope, K. S., & Vetter, V. A. (1991). Prior therapist-patient sexual involvement among patients seen by psychologists. *Psychotherapy, 28,* 429–38.

Popkin, J. (1994, Sept. 19). Sexual predators. *U.S. News and World Report,* 65–73.

Porter, B., & O'Leary, D. (1980). Marital discord and child behavior problems. *J. Abnorm. Child Psychol., 8,* 287–295.

Posener, J. A., Le Haye, A., & Cheifetz, P. N. (1989). Suicide notes in adolescence. *Canad. J. Psychiat., 34,* 171–76.

Post, R., Rubinow, D. R., & Ballenger, J. C. (1986). Conditioning and sensitization in the longitudinal course of affective illness. *Brit. J. Psychiat., 149,* 191–201.

Post, R. M. (1975). Cocaine psychoses: A continuum model. *Amer. J. Psychiat., 132*(3), 225–31.

Post, R. M. (1992). Anticonvulsants and novel drugs. In E. S. Paykel (Ed.), *Handbook of affective disorders* (2nd ed.). New York: Guilford.

Post, R. M. (1992). Transduction of psychosocial stress into the neurobiology of recurrent affective disorder. *Amer. J. Psychiat., 149*(8), 999–1010.

Post, R. M., Weiss, S. R. B., & Smith, M. A. (1995). Sensitization and kindling: Implications for the evolving neural substrates of post-traumatic stress disorder. In M. J. Friedman, D. S. Charney, et al. *Neurobiological and clinical consequences of stress: From normal adaptation to post-traumatic stress disorder.* (pp. 203–24). Philadelphia: Lippincott-Raven.

Potts, N. L., & Davidson., J. R. T. (1995). Pharmacological treatments: Literature review. In R. G. Heimberg, M. R. Liebowitz, D. A. Hope, & Schneier, F. R. (Eds.), *Social phobia: Diagnosis, assessment, and treatment* (pp. 334–65). New York: Guilford.

Powell, G. E., & Wilson, S. L. (1994). Recovery curves for patients who have suffered very severe brain injury. *Clinical Rehabilitation, 8*(1), 54–69.

Powell, T. A., Holt, J. C., & Fondacaro, K. M. (1997). The prevalence of mental illness among inmates in a rural state. *Law & Human Behavior, 21*(4), 427–38.

Powers, M. (1992). Early intervention for children with autism. In D.E. Berkell (Ed.), *Autism.* (pp. 225–72). Hillsdale, NJ: Erlbaum.

Prasher, V. P., et al. (1997). ApoE genotype and Alzheimer's disease in adults with Down syndrome: Meta-analysis. *Amer. J. Ment. Retard., 102*(2), 103–10.

Prasher, V. P., & Kirshnan, V. H. (1993). Age of onset and duration of dementia in people with Down syndrome: Integration of 98 reported cases in the literature. *International Journal of Geriatric Psychiatry, 8*(11), 915–22.

President's Commission on Mental Health. (1978). *Report to the President.* Washington, DC: U.S. Government Printing Office.

Pretzer, J. L., & Beck, A. T. (1996). A cognitive theory of personality disorders. In J. F. Clarkin & M. F. Lenzenweger (Eds.), *Major theories of personality disorder.* (pp. 36–105). New York: Guilford.

Pribor, E. F., Yutzy, S. H., Dean, J. T., & Wetzel, R. D. (1993). Briquet's syndrome, dissociation, and abuse. *Amer. J. Psychiat., 150*(10), 1507–11.

Price, R. W., Brew, B., Sidtis, J., Rosenblum, M., Scheck, A. C., & Cleary, P. (1988a). The brain in AIDS: Central nervous system HIV-1 infection and the AIDS dementia complex. *Science, 239,* 586–92.

Price, R. W., Sidtis, J., & Rosenblum, M. (1988b). The AIDS dementia complex: Some current questions. *Ann. Neurol.,* Suppl., *23,* 27–33.

Prichard, J. C. (1835). *A treatise on insanity.* London: Sherwood, Gilbert, & Piper.

Prien, R. F. (1992). Maintenance treatment. In E.S. Paykel (Ed.), *Handbook of affective disorders* (2nd ed.). New York: Guilford.

Prien, R. F., Kupfer, D. J., Mannsky, P. Q., Small, J. G., Tuason, V. B., Voss, C. B., Johnson, W. E. (1984). Drug therapy in the prevention of recurrences in unipolar and bipolar affective disorders. *Arch. Gen. Psychiat., 41,* 1096–104.

Prien, R. F., & Potter, W. Z. (1990). Report on the treatment of bipolar disorder. *Psychopharm. Bull., 26,* 409–27.

Prigatano, G. P. (1992). Personality disturbances associated with traumatic brain injury. *J. Cons. Clin. Psychol., 60*(3), 360–68.

Prigerson, H., Bierhals, A. J., Kasl, S. V., Reynolds, C. F., et al. (1997). Traumatic grief as a risk factor for mental and physical morbidity. *Amer. J. Psychiat., 154*(5), 616–23.

Prior, M., & Wherry, J. S. (1986). Autism, schizophrenia, and allied disorders. In H. C. Quay & J. S. Wherry (Eds.), *Psychopathological disorders of childhood* (3rd ed.). (pp. 156–210). New York: Wiley.

Pritchard, W. S. (1986). Cognitive event-related potential correlates of schizophrenia. *Psychol. Bull., 100*(1), 43–66.

Prizant, B. M. (1983). Language acquisition and communicative behavior in autism: Toward an understanding of the "whole" of it. *J. Speech Hear. Dis., 46,* 241–49.

Prizant, B. M., & Duchan, J. F. (1981). The functions of immediate echolalia in autistic children. *J. Speech Hear. Dis., 465*(3), 241–49.

Project DAWN Drug Enforcement Agency. (1988). Drug Abuse Warning Newtwork: Project DAWN.

Project Match Group. (1997). Project MATCH: Rationale and methods for a multisite clinical trial matching patients to alcoholism treatment. *Alcoholism: Clin. Exper. Res., 17*(6), 1130–45.

Provence, S., & Lipton, R. C. (1962). *Infants in institutions.* New York: International Universities Press.

Pryor, J. C., & Sulser, F. (1991). Evolution of the monoamine hypothesis of depression. In R. Horton & C. Katona (Eds.), *Biological aspects of affective disorders.* San Diego, CA: Academic Press.

Psychological Corporation. (1997). *WAIS-III manual.* San Antonio, TX: Author.

Psychological Corporation. (1997). *Wechsler Memory Scale III manual.* San Antonio, TX: Author.

Psychological Medicine, *28,* 1209–1219.

Puig-Antich, J., Goetz, D., Davies, M., Kaplan, T., Davies, S., Ostrow, L., Asnis, L., Twomey, J., Iyengar, S., & Ryan, N. D. (1989). A controlled family history study of prepubertal major depressive disorder. *Arch. Gen. Psychiat., 46,* 406–18.

Puig-Antich, J., Lukens, D., Davies, M., Goetz, D., & Brennan-Quattrock, J. (1985). Psychosocial functioning in prepubertal major depressive disorders: I. Interpersonal relationships during the depressive episode. *Arch. Gen. Psychiat., 42,* 500–57.

Puri, B. K., Baxter, R., & Cordess, C. C. (1995). Characteristics of fire–setters: A study and proposed multiaxial psychiatric classification. *Brit. J. Psychiat., 166,* 393–96.

Purisch, A. D., & Sbordone, R. J. (1997). Forensic neuropsychology: Clinical issues and practice. In A. M. Horton, D. Wedding, & J. Webster (Eds.), *The neuropsychology handbook* (Vol. 2). (pp. 309–56). New York: Springer.

Puska, P. (1983, Feb./Mar.). Television can save lives. *World Health.* Geneva, Switzerland: Magazine of the World Health Organization, 8–11.

Puska, P., Tuomqwehto, J., Salonen, J., Neittaanmaki, L., Maki, J., Virtamo, J., Nissinen, A., Koskela, K., & Takalo, T. (1979). Changes in coronary risk factors during a comprehensive five-year community

programme to control cardiovascular diseases (North Karelia Project). *Brit. Med. J., 2,* 1173–78.

Putallaz, M., & Gottman, J. M. (1983). Social relationship problems in children: An approach to intervention. In B. B. Lahey & A. E. Kazdin (Eds.), *Advances in clinical child psychology* (Vol. 6). New York: Plenum.

Putnam, F. W. (1989). *Diagnosis and treatment of multiple personality disorder.* New York: Plenum.

Putnam, F. W., Guroff, J. J., Silberman, E. K., Barban, L., & Post, R. M. (1986). The clinical phenomenology of multiple personality disorder: Review of 100 recent cases. *J. Clin. Psychiat., 47,* 285–93.

Pynoos, R. S., Frederick, C., Nader, K., Arroyo, W., Steinberg, A., Eth, S., Nunez, F., & Fairbanks, L. (1987). Life threat and posttraumatic stress in school-age children. *Arch. Gen. Psychiat., 44,* 1057–63.

Quay, H. C. (1965). Psychopathic personality as pathological stimulation seeking. *Amer. J. Psychiat., 122*(2), 180–83.

Quinsey, V. L., & Earls, C. M. (1990). The modification of sexual preferences. In W. L. Marshall, D. R. Laws, & H. E. Barbaree (Eds.), *Handbook of sexual assault: Issues, theories, and treatment of the offender.* (pp. 279–95). New York: Plenum.

Quinsey, V. L., Harris, G. T., Rice, M. E., & Lalumiere, M. L. (1993). Assessing treatment efficacy in outcome studies of sex offenders. *J. Interpers. Viol., 8,* 512–23.

Quinton, D., & Rutter, M. (1988). *Parenting breakdown: The making and breaking of intergenerational links.* Aldershot, Hants: Avebury.

Quinton, D., Rutter, M., & Liddle, C. (1984). Institutional rearing, parenting difficulties, and marital support. *Psychol. Med., 14,* 102–124.

Rabin, A. I., Doneson, S. L., & Jentons, R. L. (1979). Studies of psychological functions in schizophrenia. In L. Bellak (Ed.), *The schizophrenic syndrome.* New York: Basic Books.

Rabiner, D., & Coie, J. (1989). Effect of expectancy induction on rejected children's acceptance by unfamiliar peers. *Develop. Psychol., 25,* 450–457.

Rabinowitz, D. (1990, May). From the mouths of babes to a jail cell. *Harper's Magazine,* pp. 52–63.

Rabkin, J. (1972). Public attitudes about mental illness: A review of the literature. *Schizo. Bull., 10,* 9–33.

Rabow, J., & Duncan-Schill, M. (1995). Drinking among college students. *Journal of Alcohol & Drug Education, 40*(3), 52–64.

Rachman, J. G., & Hodgson, R. (1980). *Obsessions and compulsions.* Englewood Cliffs, NJ: Prentice-Hall.

Rachman, S. J. (1990). *Fear and courage.* New York: Freeman.

Rachman, S. J. (1997). Claustrophobia. In G. C. L. Davey, (Ed.), *Phobias: A handbook of theory, research and treatment.* (pp. 163–181). Chichester, England: Wiley.

Rachman, S., & DeSilva, P. (1978). Abnormal and normal obsessions. *Behav. Res. Ther., 16,* 233–48.

Rachman, S., & Shafran, R. (1998). Cognitive and behavioral features of obsessive-compulsive disorder. In R. Swinson, M. Antony, S. Rachman, & M. Richter (Eds.), *Obsessive-compulsive disorder: Theory, research, and treatment.* (pp. 51–78). New York: Guilford.

Rado, S. (1956). *Psychoanalysis and behavior.* New York: Grune & Stratton.

Rado, S. (1962). *Psychoanalysis of behavior II,* (p. 96). New York: Grune & Stratton.

Ragland, D. R., & Brand, R. J. (1988). Type A behavior and mortality from coronary heart disease. *New Engl. J. Med., 318,* 65–69.

Rahe, R. H. (1974). Life changes and subsequent illness reports. In K. E. Gunderson & R. H. Rahe (Eds.), *Life stress and illness.* Springfield, IL: Thomas.

Rahe, R. H., & Arthur, R. J. (1978). Life changes and illness studies: Past history and future directions. *Journal of Human Stress, 4,* 3–15.

Raine, A., Brennan, P., & Mednick, S. A. (1994). Birth complications combined with early maternal rejection at age 1 year predispose to violent crime at age 18 years. *Arch. Gen. Psychiat., 51,* 984–988.

Rainer, M. (1997). Galanthamine in Alzheimer's disease: A new alternative to tacrine? *CNS Drugs,* 7(2), 89–97.

Ramey, C. T., & Haskins, R. (1981). The causes and treatment of school failure: Insights from the Carolina Abecedarian Project. In M. J. Begab, H. C. Haywood, & H. L. Garber (Eds.), *Psychosocial influences in retarded performance* (Vol. II). Baltimore: University Park Press.

Ramey, C. T., & Ramey, S. L. (1998). Early intervention and early experience. *Amer. Psychol., 53*(2), 109–20.

Ramirez, L. F., McCormick, R. A., & Russo, A. M. (1984). Patterns of substance abuse in pathological gamblers undergoing treatment. *Addictive Behavior, 8,* 201–03.

Rao, U., Weissman, M. M., Martin, J. A., & Hammond, R. W. (1993). Childhood depression and risk of suicide: A preliminary report of a longitudinal study. Special section: Longitudinal studies of depressive disorders in children. *J. Amer. Acad. Child Adoles. Psychiat., 32,* 21–27.

Rapaport, J. (1989). *The boy who couldn't stop washing: The experience and treatment of obsessive-compulsive disorder.* New York: Penguin.

Rapaport, K., & Burkhart, B. R. (1984). Personality and attitudinal characteristics of sexually coercive college males. *J. Abn. Psychol., 93,* 216–21.

Rapee, R. M. (1996). Information-processing views of panic disorder. In R. M. Rapee (Ed.), *Current controversies in the anxiety disorders.* (pp. 77–93). New York: Guilford.

Rapee, R. M., & Barlow, D. H. (1993). Generalized anxiety disorder, panic disorder, and the phobias. In P. B. Sutker, & H. E. Adams (Eds.), *Comprehensive handbook of psychopathology* (2nd ed.). New York: Plenum.

Rapoport, J., et al. (1997). Childhood-onset schizophrenia: Progressive ventricular change during adolescence. *Arch. Gen. Psychiat., 54*(10), 897–903.

Rapoport, J. L., & Wise, S. P. (1988). Obsessive-compulsive disorder: Evidence for basil ganglia dysfunction. *Psychopharm. Bull., 24,* 380–4.

Raskin, A., Pelchat, R., Sood, R., Alphs, L. D., & Levine, J. (1993). Negative symptom assessment of chronic schizophrenia patients. *Schizo. Bull., 19*(3), 627–35.

Raskin, V. D. (1993). Psychiatric aspects of substance use disorders in childbearing populations. *Psychiatr. Clin. N. Amer., 16,* 157–65.

Rasmussen, S., & Eisen, J. L. (1991). Phenomenology of OCD: Clinical subtypes, heterogeneity and coexistence. In J. Zohar, T. Insel & S. Rasmussen (Eds.), *The psychobiology of obsessive-compulsive disorder.* New York: Springer.

Rasmussen, S. A., & Tsuang, M. T. (1986). Clinical characteristics and family history in DSM-III obsessivecompulsive. *Amer. J. Psychiat., 143,* 317–22

Ratakonda, S., et al. (1998). Characterization of psychotic conditions: Use of the domains of psychopathology model. *Arch. Gen. Psychiat., 55*(1), 75–81.

Rauch, S. L., & Jenike, M. A. (1998) Pharmacological treatment of obsessive-compulsive disorder. In P. E. Nathan & J. M. Gorman (Eds.), *A guide to treatmentst that work* (pp. 358–76). Oxford, England: Oxford University Press.

Rauh, V. A., Achenbach, T. M., Nurcombe, B., Howell, C. T., Teti, D. M. (1988). Minimizing adverse effects of low birth-weight: Four-year results of an early intervention program. *Child Develop., 59,* 544–553.

Rawson, H. E., & Tabb, C. L. (1993). Effects of therapeutic intervention on childhood depression. *Child and Adolescent Social Work Journal, 10,* 39–52.

Ray, O. & Ksir, C. (1995). *Drugs, society and human behavior.* New York: McGraw-Hill.

Raz, S. (1993). Structural cerebral pathology in schizophrenia: Regional or diffuse? *J. Abn. Psychol., 102*(3), 445–52.

Razran, G. (1961). The observable unconscious and the inferable conscious in current Soviet psychophysiology: Interoceptive conditioning, semantic conditioning, and the orienting reflex. *Psychol. Rev., 68,* 81–147.

Read, J. (1997). Child abuse and psychosis: A literature review and implications for professional psychology. *Profess. Psychol., 28*(5), 448–56.

Real, T. (1997). *I don't want to talk about it: Overcoming the secret legacy of male depression.* New York: Scribner.

Realmuto, G. M., Jensen, J. B., & Wescoe, S. (1990). Specificity and sensitivity of sexually anatomically correct dolls in substantiating abuse: a pilot study. *J. Amer. Acad. Child Adoles. Psychiat., 29,* 743–46.

Realmuto, G., M., & Wescoe, S. (1992),. Agreements among professionals about a child's sexual abuse status: Interviews with sexually anatomically correct dolls as indicators of abuse. *Child Ab. Negl., 16,* 719–25.

Redmond, D. E., Jr. (1985). Neurochemical basis for anxiety and anxiety disorders: Evidence from drugs which decrease human fear of anxiety. In A. H. Tuma & J. D. Maser (Eds.), *Anxiety and the anxiety disorders.* Hillsdale, NJ: Erlbaum.

Reed, S. D., Katkin, E. S., & Goldband, S. (1986). Biofeedback and behavioral medicine. In F. H. Kanfer & A. P. Goldstein (Eds.), *Helping people change: A textbook of methods* (3rd ed.). Elmsford, NY: Pergamon.

Rees, T. P. (1957). Back to moral treatment and community care. *J. Ment. Sci., 103,* 303–13. In H. B. Adams "Mental illness" or interpersonal behavior? *Amer. Psychologist, 1964, 19,* 191–97.

Regier, D. A., Boyd, J. H., Burke, J. D., Rae, D. S., Myers, J. K., Kramer, M., Robins, L. N., George, L. K., Karno, M., & Locke, B. Z. (1988). One-month prevalence of mental disorders in the United States. *Arch. Gen. Psychiat., 45,* 877–986.

Regier, D. A., Narrow, W. E., Rae, D. S., Manderscheid, R. W., Locke, B. Z., & Goodwin, F. K. (1993). The de facto US mental and addictive disorders service system: Epidemiologic Catchment Area prospective 1-year prevalence rates of disorders and services. *Arch. Gen. Psychiat., 50,* 85–94.

Rehm, L. P., & Tyndall, C. I. (1993). Mood disorders: Unipolar and bipolar. In P. B. Sutker & H. E. Adams (Eds.), *Comprehensive handbook of psychopathology* (2nd ed.). New York: Plenum.

Reich, J., Noyes, R., & Troughton, E. (1987). Dependent personality disorder associated with phobic avoidance in patients with panic disorder. *Amer. J. Psychiat., 144,* 323–6.

Reich, J. H., & Green, A. I. (1991). Effects of personality disorders on outcome of treatment. *J. Nerv. Ment. Dis., 179,* 74–82.

Reid, A. H. (1985). Psychiatric disorders. In A. M. Clarke, A. B. D. Clarke, & J. M. Berg (Eds.), *Mental deficiency: The changing outlook.* (4th ed.). (pp. 291–325). London: Methuen.

Reid, J. B., & Eddy, J. M. (1997). The prevention of antisocial behavior: Some considerations in the search for effective interventions. In D. M. Stoff, J. Breiling, & J. D. Maser (Eds.), *Handbook of antisocial behavior.* (pp. 343–356). New York: Wiley.

Reilley, P., Clark, H., & Shopshire, M. (1994). Anger management and temper control: Critical components of post–traumatic stress disorder and substance abuse treatment. *Psychoactive Drugs, 26,* 401–07.

Reisman, J. M. (1991). *A history of clinical psychology.* New York: Hemisphere Press.

Reiss, S., & McNally, R. J. (1985). Expectancy model of fear. In S. Reiss & R. R. Bootzin (Eds.), *Theoretical issues in behavior therapy.* (pp. 107–121). San Diego, CA: Academic Press.

Reitan, R. M., & Wolfson, D. (1985). *The Halstead-Reitan Neuropsychological Test Battery: Theory and clinical interpretation.* Tuscon, AZ: Neuropsychology Press.

Renvoize, E. B., Mindham, R. H., Stewart, M., McDonald, R., et al. (1986). Identical twins discordant for presenile dementia of the Alzheimer type. *Brit. J. Psychiat., 149,* 509–12.

Rescorla, R. A. (1974). Effect of inflation of the unconditioned stimulus value following conditioning. *Journal of Comparative and Physiological Psychology, 86,* 101–6.

Rescorla, R. A., (1988). Pavlovian Conditioning: It's not what you think it is. *Amer. Psychol., 43,* 151–160.

Resnick, H. S., Kilpatrick, D. G., Dansky, B. S., Saunders, B., & Best, C. L. (1993). Prevalence of civilian trauma and posttraumatic stress disorder in a rep-

resentative national sample of women. *J Cons. Clin. Psychol., 61,* 984–991.

Reynaud, M., Leleu, X., Bernoux, A., Meyer, L., Lery, J. F., & Ruch, C. (1997). Alcohol use disorders in French hospital patients. *Alcohol and Alcoholism, 32*(6), 749–55.

Rhoades, L. J. (1981). *Treating and assessing the chronically mentally ill: The pioneering research of Gordon L. Paul.* U.S. Department of Health and Human Services. Public Health Service. (Library of Congress Catalog #81-600097). Washington, DC: U.S. Government Printing Office.

Rhue, J. W., & Lynn, S. J., & Kirsch, I. (Eds.). (1993). *Handbook of clinical hypnosis.* Washington: American Psychological Association.

Ricciuti, H. N. (1993). Nutrition and mental development. *Curr. Dir. Psychol. Sci., 2*(2), 43–46.

Rice, M. E., & Harris, G. T. (1997). The treatment for adult offenders. In D. M. Stoff, J. Breiling, & J. D. Maser (Eds.), *Handbook of antisocial behavior.* (pp. 425–435). New York: Wiley.

Rice, M. E., Quinsey, V. L., & Harris, G. T. (1991). Sexual recidivism among child molesters released from a maximum security psychiatric institution. *J. Cons. Clin. Psychol., 59,* 381–86.

Rich, B. E., Paul, G. L., & Mariotto, M. J. (1988). Judgmental relativism as a validity threat to standardized psychiatric relating scales. *J. Psychopath. Behav. Assess., 10,* 241–57.

Rich, C. L., Fowler, R. C., Fogarty, L. A., & Young, D. (1988). San Diego suicide study: III. Relationships between diagnoses and stressors. *Arch. Gen. Psychiat., 45,* 589–92.

Rich, C. L., Young, D., & Fowler, R. C. (1986). San Diego suicide study: I. Young vs. old subjects. *Arch. Gen. Psychiat., 43,* 577–82.

Richards, J., Smith, D. J., Harvey, C. A., & Pantelis, C. (1997). Characteristics of the new long-stay population in an inner Melbourne acute psychiatric hospital. *Austral. N.Z. J. Psychiat., 31*(4), 488–95.

Richardson, S. A., Koller, H., & Katz, M. (1985). Relationship of upbringing to later behavior disturbance of mildly mentally retarded young people. *Amer. J. Ment. Def., 90,* 18.

Richelson, E. (1993). Treatment of acute depression. *Psychiat. Clin. N. Amer., 16,* 461–78.

Richters, J. E., & Martinez, P. E. (1993). Violent communities, family choices, and children's chances: An algorithm for improving the odds. *Develop. Psychopath., 5,* 609–27.

Rickels, K., Schweizer, E., Weiss, S., & Zavodnick, S. (1993). Maintenance drug treatment for panic disorder: II. Short and long-term outcome after drug taper. *Arch. Gen. Psychiat., 50 (1),* 61–68.

Rieder, R. O. (1979). Children at risk. In L. Bellak (Ed.), *The schizophrenic syndrome.* New York: Basic Books.

Rifkin, L., & Gurling, H. (1991). Genetic aspects of affective disorders. In R. Horton & C. Katona (Eds.), *Biological aspects of affective disorders.* San Diego: Academic Press.

Riggs, D. S., & Foa, E. B. (1993). Obsessive compulsive disorder. In D. H. Barlow (Eds.), *Clinical handbook of psychological disorders.* (pp. 189–239). New York: Guilford.

Rimm, D. C., & Lefebvre, R. C. (1981). Phobic disorders. In S. M. Turner, K. S. Calhoun, & H. E. Adams (Eds.), *Handbook of clinical behavior therapy.* New York: Wiley.

Ringwalt, C. L., Greene, J. M., Robertson, M., & McPheeters, M. (1998). The prevalence of homelessness among adolescents in the United States. *Amer. J. Pub. Hlth., 88*(9), 1325–29.

Rittson, B. (1995). *Community and municipal action on alcohol: European alcohol action plan.* Geneva: World Health Organization.

Ritvo, E. R., & Freeman, B. J. (1978). Current research on the syndrome of autism. *J. Amer. Acad. Child Psychiat., 17,* 565–75.

Ritvo, E. R., Freeman, B. J., Pingree, C., Mason-Brothers, A., Jorde, L., Jenson, W. R., McMahon, W. M., Peterson, P. B., Mo, A., & Ritvo, A. (1989). The UCLA-University of Utah epidemiologic survey of autism: Prevalence. *Amer. J. Psychiat., 146,* 194–99.

Ritvo, E., Brothers, A. M., Freeman, B. J., & Pingree, J. C. (1988). Eleven possibly autistic parents. *J. Autism Devel. Dis., 18,* 139–43.

Ritvo, E., & Ornitz, E. (1970). A new look at childhood autism points to CNS disease. *Roche Report, 7*(18), 6–8.

Ritzler, B. A. (1981). Paranoia—prognosis and treatment: A review. *Schizo. Bull., 7,* 710–28.

Rivera, F. P., Muellar, B. A., Somes, G., Mendoza, C. T., Rushforth, N. B., & Kellerman, A. L. (1997). Alcohol and illicit drug abuse and the risk of violent death in the home. *JAMA, 278*(7), 569–75.

Roberts, J. E., Gotlib, I. H. & Kassel, J. D. (1996). Adult attachment security and symptom of depression. The mediating told of dysfunctional attitudes and low self-esteem. *J. Pers. Soc. Psychol., 70,* 301–20.

Roberts, M. C., & Peterson, L. (1984). *Prevention of problems in childhood.* New York: Wiley Interscience.

Robins, C. J., Bagby, M., Rector. N. A., Lynch, T. R., & Kennedy, S. H. (1997). Sociotropy, autonomy, and patterns of symptoms in patients with major depression: A comparison of dimensional and categorical approaches. *Cog. Ther. Res., 21*(3), 285–300.

Robins, C. J., & Hayes, A. M. (1993). An appraisal of cognitive therapy. *J. Cons. Clin. Psychol., 61*(2), 205–14.

Robins, L. N. (1978). Aetiological implications in studies of childhood histories relating to antisocial personality. In R.D. Hare & D. Schalling (Eds.), *Psychopathic behavior: Approaches to research.* (pp. 255–71). Chichester, UK: Wiley.

Robins, L. N. (1991). Conduct disorder. *J. Child Psychol. Psychiat., 32,* 193–212.

Robins, L. N., Helzer, J. E., Weissman, M. M., Orvaschel, H., Gruenberg, E., Burke, J. D., & Regier, D. (1984). Lifetime prevalence of specific psychiatric disorders in three sites. *Arch. Gen. Psych., 41,* 949–58.

Robins, L. N., & Price, R. (1991). Adult disorders predicted by childhood conduct problems: Results from the NIMH Epidemiologic Catchment Area Project. *Psychiatry, 54,* 116–32.

Robins, L. N., & Regier, D. A. (Eds.). (1991). *Psychiatric disorders in America.* New York: Free Press.

Robinson R. G., & Downhill, J. E. (1995). Lateralization of psychopathology in response to focal brain injury. In R. J. Davidson & K. Hugdahl (Eds.), *Brain asymmetry.* (pp. 693–711). Cambridge, MA: MIT Press.

Robinson, N. M., & Robinson, H. B. (1976). *The mentally retarded child* (2nd ed.). New York: McGraw-Hill.

Robinson, R. G., Kubos, K. L., Starr, L. B., Rao, K., & Price, T. R. (1984). Mood disorders in stroke patients: Importance of location of lesion. *Brain, 107,* 81–93.

Robinson-Whelen, S., & Kiecolt-Glaser, J. (1997). Spousal caregiving: Does it matter if you have a choice? *J. Clin. Geropsychol., 3*(4), 283–99.

Rodriguez de Fonesca, F., et al. (1997). Activation of corticotropin-release factor in the limbic system during cannabinoid withdrawal. *Science, 276,* 2050–54.

Rodriguez, N., Ryan, S. W., Kemp, H. V., & Foy, D. W. (1997). Posttraumatic stress disorder in adult female survivors of childhood sexual abuse: A comparison study. *J. Cons. Clin. Psychol., 65*(1), 53–9.

Roeleveld, N., Zielhuis, G. A., & Gabreels, F. (1997). The prevalence of mental retardation: A critical review of recent literature. *Develop. Med. Child Neurol., 39*(2), 125–32.

Roemer, L., Molina, S., & Borkovec, T. D. (1997). An investigation of worry content among generally anxious individuals. *J. Nerv. Ment. Dis., 185*(5), 314–19.

Rogers, C. R. (1951). *Client-centered therapy.* Boston: Houghton Mifflin.

Rogers, C. R. (1959). A theory of therapy, personality, and interpersonal relationships as developed in the client-centered framework. In S. Koch (Ed.), *Psychology: A study of a science* (Vol. 3). (pp. 184–256). New York: McGraw-Hill.

Rogers, C. R. (1961). *On becoming a person: A client's view of psychotherapy.* Boston: Houghton Mifflin.

Rogers, C. R. (1966). Client-centered therapy. In S. Arieti et al. (Eds.), *American handbook of psychiatry* (Vol. 3). New York: Basic Books.

Rogers, C. R., & Dymond, R. F. (Ed.). (1954). *Psychotherapy and behavior change.* Chicago: University of Chicago Press.

Rogers, C. R., Gendlin, G. T., Kiesler, D. J., & Truax, C. B. (1967). *The therapeutic relationship and its impact: A study of psychotherapy with schizophrenics.* Madison: University of Wisconsin Press.

Rogers, S. J., Bennetto, L., McEvoy, R., & Pennington, B. F. (1996). Imitation and pantomine in high-functioning adolescents with autism spectrum disorders. *Child Develop., 67*(5), 2060–73.

Rogosch, F. A., Cicchetti, D., & Aber, J. L. (1995). The role of child maltreatment in early deviations in cognitive and affective processing abilities and later peer relationship problems. *Develop. Psychopath., 7,* 591–609.

Rohde, P., Lewinsohn, P. M., Seeley, J. R. (1990). Are people changed by the experience of having an episode of depression? A further test of the scar hypothesis. *J. Abn. Psychol., 99,* 264–71.

Roiphe, K. (1993). *The morning after: Sex, fear, and feminism on campus.* Boston: Little, Brown.

Roitman, S. E. L., et al. (1997). Attentional functioning in schizotypal personality disorder. *Amer. J. Psychiat., 154*(5), 655–60.

Rolf, J., Masten, A. S., Cicchetti, D., Nuechterlein, K., & Weintraub, S. (Eds.) (1990). *Risk and protective factors in the development of psychopathology.* New York: Cambridge University Press.

Rolfs, R. T., Goldberg, M., & Sharrar, R. G. (1990). Risk factors for syphillis: Cocaine use and prostitution. *Amer. J. Pub. Hlth., 80,* 853–57.

Romach, M. K., & Sellers, E. M. (1998). Alcohol dependency: Women, biology, and pharmacotherapy. In E. F. McCance-Katz & T. R. Kosten (Eds.), *New treatments for chemical addictions.* Washington, American Psychiatric Press.

Ronningstam, E., & Gunderson, J. G. (1989). Descriptive studies on narcissistic personality disorder. *Psychiat. Clin. N. Amer., 12,* 585–601.

Ronningstam, E., Gunderson, J., & Lyons, M. (1995). Changes in pathological narcissism. *Amer. J. Psychiat., 152*(2), 253–257.

Roose, S. P., Galssman, A. H., Attia, E., & Woodring, R. N. (1994). Comparative efficacy of selective serotonin reupatke inhibitors and tricyclics in the treatment of melancholia. *Amer. J. Psychiat., 151*(12), 1735–39.

Rooth, G. (1974). Exhibitionists around the world. *Human Behav., 3*(5), 61.

Rorvik, D. M. (1970, Apr. 7). Do drugs lead to violence? *Look,* 58–61.

Rosen, A. J. (1986). Schizophrenic and affective disorders: Rationale for a biopsychosocial treatment model. *Integr. Psychiat., 4,* 173–85.

Rosen, D. H. (1970). The serious suicide attempt: Epidemiological and follow-up study of 886 patients. *Amer. J. Psychiat., 127*(6), 64–70.

Rosen, R. C. (1996). Erectile dysfunction: The medicalization of male sexuality. *Clin. Psychol. Rev., 16,* 497–519.

Rosen, R. C., & Leiblum, S. J. (1995). Treatment of sexual disorders in the 1990s: An integrated approach. *J. Cons. Clin. Psychol., 63,* 877–90.

Rosen, R. C., & Leiblum., S. J. (1987). Current approaches to the evaluation of sexual desire disorders. *J. Sex Res., 23,* 141–62.

Rosen, R. C., & Leiblum, S. R. (1989). Assessment and treatment of desire disorders. In S. R. Leiblum & R. C. Rosen (Eds.), *Principles and practice of sex therapy,* (2nd ed.). (pp. 19–50). New York: Guilford.

Rosenbaum, G., Shore, D. L., & Chapin, K. (1988). Attention deficit and schizotypy: Marker versus symptom variables. *J. Abn. Psychol., 97,* 41–47.

Rosenbaum, J. F., Biederman, J., Pollock, R. A., & Hirshfeld, D. R. (1994). The etiology of social phobia. *J. Clin. Psychiat., 55*(6), 10–16.

Rosenbaum, M., Leibel, R. L., & Hirsch, J. (1997). Medical progress: Obesity. *N. Engl. J. Med., 337*(6), 396–407.

Rosenberg, L. A., Brown, J., & Singer, H. S. (1995). Behavioral problems and severity of tics. *J. Clin. Psychol., 51*(6), 760–67.

Rosenblatt, A. (1984). Concepts of the asylum in the care of the mentally ill. *Hosp. Comm. Psychiat., 35,* 244–50.

Rosenman, R. H. (1978). The interview method of assessment of the coronary-prone behavior pattern. In T. P. Dembroski, S. M. Weiss, J. L. Shields, S. G. Haynes, & M. Feinleib (Eds.), *Coronary-prone behavior.* New York: Springer-Verlag.

Rosenman, R. H., Brand, R. J., Jenkins, C. D., Friedman, M., & Straus, R. (1975). Coronary heart disease in the Western Collaborative Group Study: Final follow-up experience of 8 1/2 years. *JAMA, 233,* 872–77.

Rosenthal, D. (Ed.). (1963). *The Genain quadruplets.* New York: Basic Books.

Rosenthal, D., Wender, P. H., Kety, S. S., Schulsinger, F., Welner, J., & Ostergaard, L. (1968). Schizophrenics' offspring reared in adoptive homes. In D. Rosenthal & S. S. Kety (Eds.), *The transmission of schizophrenia.* (pp. 377–92). New York: Pergamon.

Rosenthal, N. E., Sack, D. A., Gillin, J. C., Lewry, A. J., Goodwin, F. K., Davenport, Y., Mueller, P. S., Newsome, D. A., & Wehr, T. A. (1984). Seasonal affective disorder: A description of the syndrome and preliminary findings with light therapy. *Arch. Gen. Psychiat., 41,* 72–80.

Rosenthal, R. J. (1992). Pathological gambling. *Psychiat. Ann., 22,* 72–78.

Rosler, A., & Witztum, E. (1998). Treatment of men with paraphilia with a long-acting analogue of gonadotropin-releasing hormone. *New Engl. J. Med., 338,* 416–22.

Ross, C. A. (1989). *Multiple personality disorder: Diagnosis, clinical features, and treatment.* New York: Wiley.

Ross, C. A., et al. (1990). Structured interview data on 102 cases of multiple personality disorder from four centers. *Amer. J. Psychiat., 147,* 596–601.

Ross, C. A., Norton, G. R., & Wozney, K. (1989). Multiple personality disorder: An analysis of 236 cases. *Canad. J. Psychiat., 34,* 413–18.

Ross, M. (1974). This doctor will self-destruct. . . . *Human Behav., 3*(2), 54.

Ross, M. J., & Berger, R. S. (1996). Effects of stress inoculation training on athletes' postsurgical pain and rehabilitation after orthopedic injury. *J. Cons. Clin. Psychol., 64*(2), 406–10.

Rossi, P. H. (1990). The old homeless and the new homelessness in historical perspective. *Amer. Psychol., 45,* 954–59.

Rossini, E. D., & Moretti, R. J. (1997). Thematic Apperception Test (TAT) interpretation: Practice recommendations from a survey of clinical psychology doctoral programs accredited by the American Psychological Association. *Professional Psychology, 28*(4), 393–98.

Rossow, I. (1996). Alcohol–related violence: The impact of drinking pattern and drinking context. *Addiction, 91*(11), 1651–61.

Rosten, R. A. (1961). *Some personality characteristics of compulsive gamblers.* Unpublished dissertation, UCLA.

Roth, A., & Fonagy, P. (1996). *What works for whom? A critical view of psychotherapy research.* New York: Guilford.

Roth, M. E. (1993). Advances in Alzheimer's disease: A review for the family physician. *J. Fam. Pract., 37*(6), 593–607.

Roth, M., & Mountjoy, C. Q. (1997). The need for the concept of neurotic depression. In H. S Akiskal, & G. B. Cassano (Eds.), *Dysthymia and the spectrum of chronic depressions.* (pp. 96–129). New York: Guilford.

Roth, S., & Lebowitz, L. (1988). The experience of sexual trauma. *J. Trauma. Stress, 1,* 79–107.

Rothbart, M. K., & Ahadi, S. A. (1994). Temperament and the development of personality. *J. Abn. Psychol., 103,* 55–66.

Rothbart, M .K., Posner, M. I., & Hershey, K. L. (1995). Temperament, attention, and developmental psychopathology In D. Cicchetti, & D. J. Cohen (Eds.), *Developmental psychopathology: Vol. 1. Theory and Methods.* (pp. 315–42). New York: Wiley.

Rothbaum, B. O., et al. (1995a). The efficacy of virtual reality graded exposure in the treatment of acrophobia. *Amer. J. Psychiat., 152,* 626–28.

Rothbaum, B. O., et al. (1995b). Virtual reality graded exposure in the treatment of acrophobia: A case report. *Behav. Ther., 26,* 547–54.

Rothbaum, B. O., et al. (1996). Virtual reality exposure therapy in the treatment of fear of flying: A case report. *Behav. Res. Ther., 34,* 477–81.

Rounsaville, B. J., Dolinsky, Z. S., Babor, T. F., & Meyer, R. E. (1987). Psychopathology as a predictor of treatment outcome in alcoholics. *Arch. Gen. Psychiat., 44,* 505–13.

Rounsaville, B., Kranzler, H. R., Ball, S., Tennen, H., Poling, J., & Triffleman, E. (1998). Personality disorders in substance abuse: Relation to substance use. *J. Nerv. Ment. Dis., 186*(2), 87–95.

Rounsaville, B. J., Weissman, M. M., & Prusoff, B. A. (1981). Psychotherapy with depressed outpatients: Patient and process variables as predictors of outcome. *Amer. J. Psychiat., 138,* 67–74.

Rouse, S. V., Sullivan, J., & Taylor, J. (1997). Treatment-oriented MMPI/MMPI-2 studies. In J. N. Butcher (Ed.), *Personality assessment in managed care: Using the MMPI-2 in treatment planning.* (pp. 173–200). New York: Oxford University Press.

Rousseau, C., Drapeau, A., & Corin, E. (1996). School performance and emotional problems in refugee children. *Amer. J. Orthopsychiat., 66*(2), 239–51.

Rovner, S. (1990, Nov.). Dramatic overlap of addiction, mental illness. *Washington Post Health,* 14–15.

Rowland, D. L., & Slob, A. K. (1997). Premature ejaculation: Psychophysiological considerations in theory, research, and treatment. *Annu. Rev. Sex Res., 8,* 224–53.

Rowland, D. L., Slob, A. K., & Kallan, K. (1997). Yohimbine, erectile capacity, and sexual response in men. *Arch. Sex. Behav., 26,* 49–62.

Roy, A. (1985). Early parental separation and adult depression. *Arch. Gen. Psychiat., 42,* 987–91.

Roy-Byrne, P. P., & Katon, W. (1997). Generalized anxiety disorder in primary care: The precurser /modifier pathway to increased health care utilization. *J. Clin. Psychiat., 58*(3), 34–38.

Roy-Byrne, P. P., Cowley, D. S. (1998). Pharmacological treatment of panic, generalized anxiety, and phobic disorders. In P. E. Nathan & J. M. Gorman (Eds.), *A guide to treatments that work.* (pp. 319–38). Oxford, England: Oxford University Press.

Rozensky, R. H., Sweet, J. J., & Tovian, S. M. (1997). *Psychological assessment in medical settings.* New York: Plenum.

Rubber, M. (1987a). Psychosocial resilience and protective mechanisms. *Amer. J. Orthopsychiat., 51,* 316–331.

Rubenstein, J. L., Heeren, T., Houseman, D., Rubin, C., & Stechler, G. (1989). Suicidal behavior in "normal" adolescents: Risk and protective factors. *Amer. J. Orthopsychiat., 59,* 59–71.

Rubin, R. T., Reinisch, J. M., & Haskett, R. F. (1981). Postnatal gonadal steroid effects on human behavior. *Science, 211,* 1318–24.

Rubonis, A. V., & Bickman, L. (1991). Psychological impairment in the wake of disaster: The disaster's psychopathology relationship. *Psychol. Bull. 109*(3), 384–99.

Ruegg, R., & Frances, A. (1995). New research in personality disorders. *J. Personal. Dis., 9*(1), 1–48.

Runnheim, V. A., Frankenberger, W. R., & Hazelkorn, M. N. (1996). Medicating students with emotional and behavioral disorders and ADHD: A state survey. *Behavioral Disorders, 21*(4), 306–14.

Rush, A. J., Beck, A. T., Kovacs, M., & Hollon, S. (1977). The comparative efficacy of cognitive therapy and imipramine in the treatment of depressed outpatients. *Cog. Ther. Res., 1*(1), 17–37.

Rush, A. J., Beck, A. T., Kovacs, M., Weissenburger, J., & Hollon, S. D. (1982). Comparison of the effects of cognitive therapy and pharmacotherapy on hopelessness and self-concept. *Amer. J. Psychiat., 139,* 862–66.

Rush, A. J., & Hollon, S. D. (1991). Depression. In B. D. Beitman & G. L. Klerman (Eds.). *Integrating phar-*

macotherapy and psychotherapy. (pp. 121–142). Washington, DC: American Psychiatric Press.

Rush, A. J., Khatami, M., & Beck, A. T. (1975). Cognitive and behavior therapy in chronic depression. *Behav. Ther., 6,* 398–404.

Rush, A. J., Kovacs, M., Beck, A. T., Weissenburger, J., & Hollon, S. D. (1981). Differential effects of cognitive therapy and pharmacotherapy on depressive symptoms. *J. Affect. Dis., 3,* 221–29.

Rush, B. (1812). *Medical inquiries and observations upon diseases of the mind.* Philadelphia: Grigg and Elliot.

Rush, J., Giles, D. E., Schlesser, M. A., Orsulak, P. J., Weissenburger, J. E., Fulton, C., Fairchild, C. J., & Roffwarg, H. P. (1997). Dexamethasone response, Thyrotropin-releasing hormone stimulation, rapid eye movement latency, and subtypes of depression. *Biol. Psychiat., 41,* 915–28.

Russ, M. J., Roth, S. D., Kakuma, T., Harrison, K., & Hull, J. (1994). Pain perception in self-injurious borderline patients: Naloxone effects. *Biol. Psychiat., 35,* 207–09.

Russ, M. J., Roth, S. D., Lerman, A., Kakuma, T., et al. (1992). Pain perception in self injurious patients with borderline personality disorder. *Biol. Psychiat., 32,* 501–11.

Russell, A. J., Munro, J. C., Jones, P. B., Hemsley, D. R., & Murray, R. M. (1997). Schizophrenia and the myth of intellectual decline. *Amer. J. Psychiat., 154*(5), 635–39.

Russell, D. E. H. (1983). The incidence and prevalence of intrafamilial and extrafamilial sexual abuse of female children. *Child Ab. Negl., 7,* 133–46.

Russell, D. E. H. (1984). *Sexual exploitation: Rape, child sexual abuse, and workplace harassment.* Beverly Hills, CA: Sage.

Russell, D. E. H. (1986). *The secret trauma: Incest in the lives of girls and women.* New York: Basic Books.

Russell, S. (1975). *The development and training of autistic children in separate training centres and in centres for retarded children.* Special Publication No. 6. Victoria: Mental Health Authority.

Russo, D. C., Carr, E. G., & Lovaas, O. I. (1980). Self-injury in pediatric populations. In J. Ferguson & C. R. Taylor (Eds.), *Comprehensive handbook of behavioral medicine, Vol. 3: Extended applications and issues.* Holliswood, NY: Spectrum.

Russo, J., Vitaliano, P. P., Brewer, D. D., Katon, W., & Becker, J. (1995). Psychiatric disorders in spouse caregivers of care recipients with Alzheimer's disease and matched controls: A diathesis-stress model of psychopathology. *J. Abn. Psychol., 104,* 197–204.

Rutter, M. (1971). Parent-child separation: Psychological effects on the children. *J. Child Psychol. Psychiat., 12,* 233–60.

Rutter, M. (1979). Maternal deprivations. 1972–1978: New findings, new concepts, new approachs. *Child Develop., 50,* 283–305.

Rutter, M. (1981). Stress, coping and development: Some issues and some questions. *J. Child Psychol. Psychiatr., 22,* 323–356.

Rutter, M. (1982). Epidemiological-longitudinal approaches to the study of development. In W. A. Collins (Ed.), *The concept of development. Minnesota Symposia on Child Psychology* vol. 15. Hillsdale, NJ: Erlbaum.

Rutter, M. (1985). The treatment of autistic children. *Journal of Child Psychiatry, 26*(2), 193–214.

Rutter, M. (1987a). Psychosocial resilience and protective mechanisms. *Amer. J. Orthopsychiat., 51,* 316–31.

Rutter, M. (1987b). Continuities and discontinuities from infancy. In J. D. Osofsky (Ed.), *Handbook of infant development* (2nd ed.). (pp. 1256–1296). New York: Wiley.

Rutter, M. (1988). Epidemiological approaches to developmental psychopathology. *Arch. Gen. Psychiat., 45,* 486–500.

Rutter, M. (1990). Psychosocial resilience and protective mechanisms. In J. Rolf, A. S. Masten, D. Cicchetti, K. H. Nuechterlein, & S. Weintraub (Eds.), *Risk and protective factors in the development of psychopathology.* New York: Cambridge University Press.

Rutter, M. (1991a). Nature, nurture, and psychopathology: A new look at an old topic. *Develop. Psychopath., 3,* 125–136.

Rutter, M. (1991b). Autism as a genetic disorder. In P. McGuffin & R. Murray (Eds.), *The new genetics of mental illness.* (pp. 225–244). Oxford: Heinmann Medical.

Rutter, M. (1996). Introduction: Concepts of antisocial behavior, of cause, and of genetic influences. In G. R. Bock & J. A. Goode (Eds.), *Genetics of criminal and anti-social behavior CIBA Foundation, Vol. 194.* (pp. 1–20). Chichester, England and New York: Wiley.

Rutter, M. (1997). Child psychiatric disorder. *Arch. Gen. Psychiat., 54,* 785–88.

Rutter, M. L. (1997). Nature-nurture integration: The example of antisocial behavior. *Amer. Psychol., 52*(4), 390–98.

Rutter, M., & Maughan, B. (1997). Psychosocial adversities in childhood and adult psychopathology. *J. Personal. Dis., 11,* 4–18.

Rutter, M., & Quinton, D. (1984a). Long term follow-up of women institutionalized in childhood: Factors promoting good functioning in adult life. *British Journal of Developmental Psychology, 18,* 255–234.

Rutter, M., & Quinton, D. (1984b). Parental psychiatric disorder: Effects on children. *Psychol. Med., 14,* 853–80.

Rutter, M., Silberg, J., & Simonoff, E. (1993) Whither behavioral genetics?—A developmental psychopathological perspective. In R. Plomin & G. McClearn (Eds.), *Nature, nuture, and psychology.* (pp. 433–56). Washington: American Psychological Association.

Rutter, M., Tizard, J., & Whitmore, K. (1970). *Education, health and behavior: Psychological and medical study of childhood development.* New York: Wiley.

Ryan, N. D. (1992). The pharmacologic treatment of child and adolescent depression. *Psychiat. Clin. N. Amer., 15,* 29–40.

Ryan, N. D., Puig-Antich, J., Ambrosini, P., Rabinovich, H., Robinson, D., Nelson, B., Iyengar, S., & Twomey, J. (1987). The clinical picture of major depression in children and adolescents. *Arch. Gen. Psychiat., 44,* 854–61.

Sacco, W. P., & Beck, A. T. (1995). Cognitive theory and therapy. In E. E. Beckham & W. R. Leber (Eds.), *Handbook of depression* (2nd ed.). (pp. 329–51). New York: Guilford.

Sachar, E. J., Gruen, P. H., Altman, N., Langer, G., & Halpern, F. S. (1978). Neuroendocrine studies of brain dopamine blockade in humans. In L. C. Wynne, R. L. Cromwell, & S. Matthysse (Eds.), *The nature of schizophrenia: New approaches to research and treatment.* (pp. 95–104). New York: Wiley.

Sack, A., Sperling, M. B., Fagen, G., & Foelsch, P. (1996). Attachment style, history, and behavioral contrasts for a borderline and normal sample. *J. Person. Dis., 10*(1), 88–102.

Sack, D. A., Rosenthal, N. E., Perry, B. L., & Wehr, T. A. (1987). Biological rhythms in psychiatry. In H.Y. Meltzer (Ed.), *Psychopharmacology: The third generation of progress.* New York: Raven Press.

Sack, R. L., Lewry, A. J., White, D. M., Singer, C. M., Fireman, M. J., & Vandiver, R. (1990). Morning vs. evening light treatment for winter depression: Evidence that the therapeutic effects of light are mediated by circadian phase shifts. *Arch. Gen. Psychiat., 47,* 343–51.

Sack, R. L., & Miller, W. (1975). Masochism: A clinical and theoretical overview. *Psychiatry, 38*(3), 244–57.

Sackeim, H., Prudic, J., Devanand, D. P., Kiersky, J. E., et al. (1993). Effects of stimulus intensity and electrode placement on the efficacy and cognitive effects of electroconvulsive therapy. *New Engl. J. Med., 328,* 839–846.

Safer, D. J. (1997). Central stimulant treatment of childhood attention-deficit hyperactivity disorder: Issues and recommendations from a U.S. perspective. *CNS Drugs, 7*(4), 264–72.

Safer, D. J. (1997). Self-reported suicide attempts by adolescents. *Annals of Clinical Psychiatry, 9*(4), 263–69.

Safer, D. J., & Krager, J. M. (1988). A survey of medication treatment for hyperactive/inattentive students. *JAMA, 260,* 2256–58.

Safran, J. D. (1990a). Towards a refinement of cognitive therapy in light of interpersonal theory: I. Theory. *Clin. Psychol. Rev., 10,* 87–105.

Safran, J. D. (1990b). Towards a refinement of cognitive therapy in light of interpersonal theory: II. Practice. *Clin. Psychol. Rev., 10,* 107–21.

Safran, J. D., & Messer, S. B. (1997). Psychotherapy integration: A postmodern critique. *Clin. Psychol. Sci. Prac., 4,* 140–52.

Saghir, M. T., & Robins, E. (1973). *Male and female homosexuality: A comprehensive investigation.* Baltimore: William & Wilkins.

Salekin, R., Rogers, R., & Sewell, K. (1996). A review and meta-analysis of the Psychopathy Checklist and Psychopathy Checklist-Revised: Predictive validity of dangerousness. *Clin. Psychol.: Sci. Pract., 3,* 203–215.

Salkovskis, P. M., Clark, D. M., & Gelder, M. G. (1996). Cognition-Behavior links in the persistence of panic. *Behav. Res. Ther., 34*(5/6), 453–58.

Salkovskis, P. M., & Harrison, J. (1984). Abnormal and normal obsessions: A replication. *Behav. Res. Ther., 22,* 549–52.

Salkovskis, P. M., & Kirk, J. (1997). Obsessive-compulsive disorder. In D. M. Clark, & C. G. Fairburn (Eds.), *Science and practice of cognitive behaviour therapy.* (pp. 179–208). New York: Oxford University Press.

Salter, A. (1949). *Conditioned reflex therapy.* New York: Creative Age Press.

Salter, A. C. (1991). Epidemiology of child sexual abuse. In W. O'Donohue & J. H. Geer (Eds.), *The sexual abuse of children: Theory and research* (Vol. 1). Hillsdale, NJ: Erlbaum.

Samborn, R. (1994, Jul. 4). Priests playing hardball to battle abuse charges. *National Law Journal, 16,* A1.

Sameroff, A. J. (1995). General systems theories and developmental psychopathology. In D. Cicchetti, & D. J. Cohen (Eds.), *Developmental psychopathology: Vol. 1. Theory and methods.* (pp. 659–95). New York: Wiley.

Sameroff, A., Seifer, R., & Zax, M. (1982). Early development of children at risk for emotional disorders. *Monogr. Soc. Res. Child Develop., 47,* (7 No. 199).

Sameroff, A., Seifer, R., Zax, M., & Barocas, R. (1987). Early indicators of developmental risk: Rochester longitudinal study. *Schizo. Bull., 13,* 383–94.

Samson, H. H., & Harris, R. A. (1992). Neurobiology of alcohol abuse. *Trends in Pharmacological Science, 13,* 206–11.

Sandbak, T., Murison, R., Sarviharju, M., & Hyytiae, P. (1998). Defensive burying and stress gastric erosions in alcohol-preferring AA and alcohol-avoiding ANA rats. *Alcoholism: Clin. Exper. Res., 22*(9), 2050–54.

Sandberg, J. G., Johnson, L. N., Dermer, S. B., Gfeller–Strouts, L. L., et al. (1997). Demonstrated efficacy of models of marriage and family therapy: An update of Gurman, Kniskern, and Pinsof's chart. *American Journal of Family Therapy, 25*(1), 121–37.

Sanders, B., & Giolas, M. H. (1991). Dissociation and childhood trauma in psychologically disturbed adolescents. *Amer. J. Psychiat., 148,* 50–54.

Sanders, M. J., Kapphahn, C. J., & Steiner, H. (1998). Eating disorders. In R. T. Ammerman & J. V. Campo (Eds.), *Handbook of pediatric psychology and psychiatry: Vol. 1. Psychological and psychiatric issues in the pediatric setting.* (pp. 287–312). Boston: Allyn & Bacon.

Sanders, M. R., Shepherd, R. W., Cleghorn, G., & Woolford, H. (1994). The treatment of recurrent abdominal pain in children: A controlled comparison of cognitive-behavioral family intervention and standard pediatric care. *J. Cons. Clin. Psychol., 62*(2), 306–14.

Sanderson, W. C., & Barlow, D. H. (1990). A description of patients diagnosed with DSM-III-Revised generalized anxiety disorder. *J. Nerv. Ment. Dis., 178,* 588–91.

Sanderson, W. C., Rapee, R. M., & Barlow, D. H. (1989). The influence of an illusion of control on panic attacks induced via inhalation of 5.5%-carbon dioxide-enriched air. *Arch. Gen. Psychiat., 46,* 157–62.

Sanderson, W. C., & Wetzler, S. (1991). Chronic anxiety and generalized anxiety disorder: Issues in comorbidity. In R. M. Rapee & D. H. Barlow (Eds.), *Chronic anxiety: Generalized anxiety disorder and mixed anxiety-depression.* (pp. 119–35). New York: Guilford.

Sanderson, W. C., & Woody, S. (1995). Manuals for empirically validated treatments. *Clin. Psychol., 48*(4), 7–11.

Sandford, J. L. (1966). Electric and convulsive treatments in psychiatry. *Dis. Nerv. Sys., 27,* 333–38.

Sandhu, H. S., & Cohen, L. M. (1989). Endocrine disorders. In S. Cheren (Ed.), *Psychosomatic medicine: Theory, physiology, and practice,* (Vol. 2). (pp. 661–706). Madison, CT: International Universities Press.

Sands, J., & Harrow, M. (1995). Vulnerability to psychosis in unipolar major depression: Is premorbid functioning involved? *Amer. J. Psychiat., 152*(7), 1009–15.

Sank, L. I. (1997). Taking on managed care: One reviewer at a time. *Profess. Psychol., 28,* 548–54.

Santiago, J. M., McCall-Perez, F., Gorcey, M., & Beigel, A. (1985). Long-term psychological effects of rape in 35 rape victims. *Amer. J. Psychiat., 142,* 1338–40.

Santich, M., & Kavanagh, D. J. (1997). Social adaptation of children with mild intellectual disability: Effects of partial integration within primary school classes. *Australian Psychologist, 32*(2), 126–30.

Sanua, V. D. (1969). Sociocultural aspects. In L. Bellak & L. Loeb (Eds.), *The schizophrenic syndrome.* New York: Grune & Stratton.

Sapolsky, R. M. (1994). *Why zebras don't get ulcers.* New York: W. H. Freeman.

Sapolsky, R. M. (1996). Why stress is bad for your brain. *Science, 273*(5276), 749–50.

Saracoglu, B., Minden, H., & Wilchesky, M. (1989). The adjustment of students with learning disabilities to university and its relationship to self-esteem and self-efficacy. *J. Learn. Dis., 22,* 590–92.

Sarbin, T. R., & Juhasz, J. B. (1967). The historical background of the concept of hallucination. *J. Hist. Behav. Sci., 3,* 339–58.

Sargent, M. (1982a, Jul. 16). Schizophrenic quads not identically ill, studies show. *ADAMHA News, 8*(13), 4–5.

Sargent, M. (1982b, Dec. 3), Researcher traces Alzheimer's disease eight generations back in one family. *ADAMHA News, 8*(23), 3.

Sartorius, N., Kaelber, C. T., Cooper, J. E., Roper, M. T., Rae, D. S., Gulbinat, W., Ustun, T. B., & Regier, D. A. (1993). Progress toward achieving a common language in psychiatry: Results from the field trial of the clinical guidelines accompanying the WHO classification of mental and behavioral disorders in ICD-10. *Arch. Gen. Psychiat., 50,* 115–24.

Sarvis, M. A. (1962). Paranoid reactions: Perceptual distortion as an etiological agent. *Arch. Gen. Psychiat., 6,* 157–62.

Sarwer, D. B., Wadden, T. A., & Foster, G. D. (1998). Assessment of body image dissatisfaction in obese women: Specificity, severity, and clinical significance. *J. Cons. Clin. Psychol., 66*(4), 651–54.

Sasaki, M., & Hara, Y. (1973). Paternal origin of the extra chromosome in Down's syndrome. *Lancet, 2*(7840), 1257–58.

Satir, V. (1967). *Conjoint family therapy* (rev. ed.). Palo Alto, CA: Science and Behavior Books.

Satterfield, J. H., Satterfield, B. T., & Cantwell, D. P. (1981). Three year multimodal treatment study of 100 hyperactive boys. *Journal of Pediatrics, 98,*(4), 650–55.

Satz, P., et al., (1997). Mild head injury in children and adolescents: A review of studies (1970–1995). *Psychol. Bull., 122*(2), 107–31.

Saudino, K. J. (1997). Moving beyond the heritability question: New directions in behavioral genetic studies of personality. *Curr. Dir. Psychol. Sci., 4,* 86–90.

Sauter, S. L., Murphy, L. R., & Hurrell, J. J., Jr. (1990). Prevention of work-related psychological disorders: A national strategy proposed by the National Institute for Occupational Safety and Health (NIOSH). *Amer. Psychol., 45*(10), 1146–58.

Savacir, I., & Erol, N. (1990). The Turkish MMPI: Translation, standardization, and validation. In J. N. Butcher & C. D. Spielberger (Eds.), *Advances in personality assessment* (Vol. 8). Hillsdale, NJ: Erlbaum.

Sawyer, J. B., Sudak, H. S., & Hall, S. R. (1972, Winter). A follow-up study of 53 suicides known to a suicide prevention center. *Life-Threatening Behavior, 2*(4), 227–38.

Saxe, G. N., Chinman, G., Berkowitz, R., Hall, K., Lieberg, G., Schwartz, J., & van der Kolk, B. A. (1994). Somatization in patients with dissociative disorders. *Amer. J. Psychiat., 151*(9), 1329–34.

Sayette, M. A. (1994). Effects of alcohol on self-appraisal. *Inter. J. Addictions, 29,* 127–33.

Saykin, A. J., Shtasel, D. L., Gur, R. E., Kester, D. B., Mozley, L. H., Stafiniak, P., & Gur, R. C. (1994). Neuropsychological deficits in neuroleptic naive patients with first-episode schizophrenia. *Arch. Gen. Psychiat., 51*(2), 124–31.

Sbrocco, T., Barlow, D. H. (1996) Conceptualizing the cognitive component of sexual arousal: Implications for sexuality research and treatment. Salkovskis, P. M. (Ed), *Frontiers of cognitive therapy.* (pp. 419–449). New York: Guilford

Scalf-McIver, L., & Thompson, K. J. (1989). Family correlates of bulimic characteristics in college females. *J. Clin. Psychol., 45,* 467–72.

Scarr, S. (1992). Developmental theories for the 1990s: Development and individual differences. *Child Develop., 63,* 1–19.

Schaar, K. (1974). Suicide rate high among women psychologists. *APA Monitor, 5*(7), 1, 10.

Schacter, D. L., Norman, K. A., & Koustaal, W. (1998). The cognitive neuroscience of constructive memory. In J. T. Spence, J. M. Darley, & D. J. Foss (Eds.), *Annual review of psychology.* (pp. 289–318). Palo Alto, CA: Annual Reviews.

Schaefer, J. M. (1977, Aug. 30). *Firewater myths revisited: Towards a second generation of ethanol metabolism studies.* Paper presented at Cross-cultural Approaches to Alcoholism. Physiological variation: Invited Symposium. NATO Conference, Bergen, Norway.

Schaefer, J. M. (1978). Alcohol metabolism reactions among the Reddis of South India. *Alcoholism: Clin. Exper. Res., 2*(1), 61–69.

Schalling, D. (1978). Psychopathy-related personality variables and the psychophysiology of socialization. In R. D. Hare & D. Schalling (Eds.), *Psychopathic behavior: Approaches to research.* (pp. 85–106). Chichester, UK: Wiley.

Schalock, R. L., Harper, R. S., & Carver, G. (1981). Independent living placement: Five years later. *Amer. J. Ment. Def., 86,* 170–77.

Schapiro, M. B., Haxby, J. V., & Grady, C. L. (1992). Nature of mental retardation and dementia in Down syndrome: Study with PET, CT, and neuropsychology. *Neurobiol. of Aging, 13*(6), 723–734.

Schapiro, M. B., & Rapoport, S. I. (1987). "Pathological similarities between Alzheimer's disease and Down's syndrome: Is there a genetic link?": Commentary. *Integr. Psychiat., 5,* 167–69.

Scharfman, M., & Clark, R. W. (1967). Delinquent adolescent girls: Residential treatment in a municipal hospital setting. *Arch. Gen. Psychiat., 17*(4), 441–47.

Scheff, T. J. (1984). *Being mentally ill: A sociological theory* (2nd ed.). New York: Aldine.

Scheibel, A. (1996). Structural and functional changes of the aging brain. In J. E. Birren & K. W. Schaie (Eds.), *Handbook of the psychology of aging.* (pp. 105–28). New York: Academic Press.

Scheier, M. F., & Carver, C. S. (1987). Dispositional optimism and physical well-being: The influence of generalized outcome expectancies on health. *J. Personal., 55,* 169–210.

Scheier, M. F., & Carver, C. S. (1992). Effects of optimism on psychological and physical well-being: Theoretical overview and empirical update. *Cog. Ther. Res., 16*(2), 201–28.

Scheiffelin, E. (1984). *The cultural analysis of depressive affect: An example from New Guinea.* Unpublished manuscript. University of Pennsylvania.

Schenk, J. W. (1998, March 9). Do "Megan's Laws" make a difference? Pariah status may not deter sex offenders. *U.S. News and World Report,* p. 27.

Schildkraut, J. J. (1965). The catecholamine hypothesis of affective disorders: A review of supporting evidence. *Amer. J. Psychiat., 122,* 509–22.

Schilling, R. F., & McAlister, A. L. (1990). Preventing drug use in adolescents through media interventions. *J. Cons. Clin. Psychol., 58,* 416–24.

Schleifer, S. J., Keller, S. E., Bond, R. M., Cohen, J., & Stein, M. (1989). Major depressive disorder and immunity: Role of age, sex, severity, and hospitalization. *Arch. Gen. Psychiat., 46,* 81–87.

Schleifer, S. J., Keller, S. E., & Stein, M. (1985). Central nervous system mechanisms and immunity: Implications for tumor responses. In S. M. Levy, *Behavior and cancer.* (pp. 120–33). San Francisco: Jossey-Bass.

Schmalz, J. (1993, Mar. 5). Poll finds an even split on homosexuality's cause. *New York Times,* p. 11.

Schmand, B., et al. (1997a). The effects of intelligence and education on the development of dementia: A test of the brain reserve hypothesis. *Psychol. Med., 27*(6), 1337–44.

Schmand, B., et al. (1997b). Subjective memory complaints in the elderly: Depressive symptoms and future dementia. *Brit. J. Psychiat., 171,* 373–76.

Schmidt, N. B., Lerew, D. R., & Jackson, R. J. (1997). The role of anxiety sensitivity in the pathogenesis of panic: Prospective evaluation of spontaneous panic attacks during acute stress. *J. Abn. Psychol., 106,* 355–65.

Schmidt, N. B., & Telch, M. J. (1997). Nonpsychiatric medical comorbidity, healthy perceptions, and treatment outcome in patients with panic disorder. *Hlth. Psychol., 16*(2), 114–22.

Schneider, J. A. (1995). Eating disorders, addictions, and unconscious fantasy. *Bulletin of the Menninger Clinic, 59*(2), 177–90.

Schneider, M. L. (1992) The effects of mild stress during pregnancy on birthweight and neuromotor maturation in Rhesus monkey infants (*Macaca mulatta*). *Inf. Behav. Develop., 15,* 389–403.

Schneider, S. (1978). Attitudes toward death in adolescent offspring of holocaust survivors. *Amer. J. Orthopsychiat., 13,* 575–83.

Schneider-Rosen, K., & Cicchetti, D. (1984). The relationships between affect and cognition in maltreated infants: Quality of attachment and the development of self-recognition. *Child Develop., 55,* 648–658.

Schoeneman, T. J. (1984). The mentally ill witch in textbooks of abnormal psychology: Current status and implications of a fallacy. *Profess. Psychol., 15*(3), 299–314.

Schofield, W. (1964). *Psychotherapy: The purchase of friendship.* Englewood Cliffs, NJ: Prentice-Hall.

Schopler, E. (1978). Changing parental involvement in behavioral treatment. In M. Rutter & E. Schopler (Eds.), *Autism: A reappraisal of concepts and treatment.* New York: Plenum.

Schopler, E. (1983). New developments in the definition and diagnosis of autism. In B. B. Lahey & A. E. Kazdin (Eds.), *Advances in clinical child psychology* (Vol. 6). (pp. 93–127). New York: Plenum.

Schopler, E., Mesibov, G., & Baker, A. (1982). Evaluation of treatment for autistic children and their parents. *J. Amer. Acad. Child Psychiat., 21,* 262–67.

Schowalter, J. E. (1980). Tics. *Pediatrics in Review, 2,* 55–57.

Schreiber, F. R. (1973). *Sybil.* New York: Warner Paperback.

Schreibman, L., & Charlop-Christie, M. H. (1998). Autistic disorder. In T. H. Ollendick, M. Hersen, et al. (Eds.), *Handbook of child psychopathology* (3rd ed.). (pp. 157–79). New York: Plenum.

Schreibman, L., & Koegel, R. L. (1975). Autism: A defeatable horror. *Psych. Today, 8*(10), 61–67.

Schreibman, L., & Pierce, K. (1993). Achieving greater generalization of treatment effects in children with autism: Pivotal response training and self-management. *Clin. Psychol., 46,* 184–91.

Schreiner-Engel., P., Schiavi, R., White, D., & Ghizzani, A. (1989). Low sexual desire in women: The role of reproductive hormones. *Hormones and Behavior, 23*, 221–34.

Schuckit, M. A. (1996). Recent developments in the pharmacotherapy of alcohol dependence. *J. Cons. Clin. Psychol., 64*(4), 669–76.

Schuckit, M. A., & Gould, R. O. (1988). A simultaneous evaluation of multiple markers of ethanol/placebo challenges in sons of alcoholics and controls. *Arch. Gen. Psychiat., 45*, 211–16.

Schuckit, M. A., Tipp, J. E., Smith, T. L., & Bucholtz, K. K. (1997). Periods of abstinence following the onset of alcohol dependence in 1853 men and women. *J. Stud. Alcoh., 58*, 581–89.

Schudson, M. (1995). Collective memory and modes of distortion. In D. Schachter, J. Coyle, L. Sullivan, M. Mesulam, & G. Fishbach (Eds.), *Memory distortion: Interdisciplinary perspectives.* Cambridge: Harvard University Press.

Schulsinger, F. (1972). Psychopathy: Heredity and environment. *Inter. J. Ment. Hlth., 1*, 190–206.

Schulsinger, F. (1980). Biological psychopathology. *Annu. Rev. Psychol., 31*, 583–606.

Schulsinger, F., Knop, J., Goodwin, D. W., Teasdale, T. W., & Mikkelsen, U. (1986). A prospective study of young men at high risk for alcoholism. *Arch. Gen. Psychiat., 43*, 755–60.

Schultz, R. K., Braun, B. G., & Kluft, R. P. (1989). Multiple personality disorder: Phenomenology of selected variables in comparison to major depression. *Dissociation, 2*, 45–51.

Schumm, J. S., & Vaughn, S. (1992). Planning for mainstreamed special education students: Perceptions of general classroom teachers. *Except., 3*(2), 81–98.

Schwalberg, M. D., Barlow, D. H., Alger, S. A., & Howard, L. J. (1992). Comparison of bulimics, obese binge eaters, social phobics, and individuals with panic disorder on comobidity across DSM-III-R anxiety disorders. *J. Abn. Psychol., 101*, 675–81.

Schwartz, C. C., & Myers, J. K. (1977). Life events and schizophrenia: I. Comparison of schizophrenics with a community sample. *Arch. Gen. Psychiat., 34*, 1238–41.

Schwartz, C. E., Snidman, N., & Kagan, J. (1996). Early childhood temperament as a determinant of externalizing behavior in adolescence. *Develop. Psychopath., 8*(3), 527–37.

Schwartz, D. A. (1963). A review of the "paranoid" concept. *Arch. Gen. Psychiat., 8*, 349–61.

Schwartz, D., Dodge, K.A., & Coie, J. D. (1993). The emergence of chronic peer victimization in boys' play groups. *Child Develop., 64*, 1755–72.

Schwartz, E. D., & Perry, B. D. (1994). The posttraumatic response in children and adolescents. *Psychiat. Clin. N. Amer., 17*, 311–26.

Schwartz, G. E. (1978). Psychobiological foundations of psychotherapy and behavior change. In S. L. Garfield & A. E. Bergin (Eds.), *Handbook of psychotherapy and behavior change* (2nd ed.). (pp. 63–99). New York: Wiley.

Schwartz, G. E. (1989). Disregulation theory and disease: Toward a general model for psychosomatic medicine. In S. Cheren (Ed.), *Psychosomatic medicine: Theory, physiology, and practice* (Vol. 1). (pp. 91–118). Madison, CT: International Universities Press.

Schwartz, G. E., & Weiss, S. M. (1978). Behavioral medicine revisited: An amended definition. *J. Behav. Med., 1*, 249–51.

Schwartz, L., Slater, M. A., & Birchler, G. R. (1994). Interpersonal stress and pain behaviors in patients with chronic pain. *J. Cons. Clin. Psychol., 62*(4), 861–64.

Schwartz, R. C., Barrett, M. J., & Saba, G. (1983, Oct.). *Family therapy for bulimia.* Paper presented at American Association for Marriage and Family Therapy, Washington, DC.

Schwartz, S., & Johnson, J. H. (1985). *Psychopathology of childhood: A clinical-experimental approach,* (2nd ed.). New York: Pergamon.

Schwarzwald, J., Weisenberg, M., Waysman, M., Soloman, Z., & Klingman, A. (1993). Stress reaction of school-age children to bombardment by SCUD missles. *J. Abn. Psychol., 102*, 404–10.

Schweizer, E., & Rickels, K. (1996). The long-term management of generalized anxiety disorder: Issues and dilemmas. *J. Clin. Psychiat., 57*(7), 9–12.

Schweizer, E., & Rickels, K. (1997). Strategies for treatment of generalized anxiety in the primary care setting. *J. Clin. Psychiat., 58*(3), 27–31.

Schwitzgebel, R. L., & Schwitzgebel, R. K. (1980). *Law and psychological practice.* New York: Wiley.

Scott, F. J., & Baron-Cohen, S. (1996). Logical, analogical, and psychological reasoning in autism: A test of the Cosmides theory. *Develop. Psychopath., 8*, 235–45.

Scovern, A. W., & Kilmann, P. R. (1980). Status of electron-convulsive therapy: A review of the outcome literature. *Psychol. Bull., 87*, 260–303.

Seaman, B., Roberts, P., Gilewski, M., & Nagai, J. (1993). Clinic to the real world: Community reintegration of head injured patients. *J. Cogn. Rehab., 11*(2), 6–11.

Searles, J. S. (1991). The genetics of alcoholism: Impact on family and sociological models of addiction. *Family Dynamics of Addiction Quarterly, 1*, 8–21.

Sears, R. R. (1961). Relation of early socialization experiences to aggression in middle childhood. *J. Abnorm. Soc. Psychol., 63*, 466–92.

Sedvall, G., Farde, L., Persson, A., & Wiesel, F. A. (1986). Imaging of neurotransmitter receptors in the living human brain. *Arch. Gen. Psychiat., 43*, 995–1005.

Seeley, M. F. (1997). The role of hotlines in the prevention of suicide. In R. W. Maris, M. M. Silverman, & S. S. Canetton (Eds.), *Review of Suicidology, 1997.* (pp. 251–70). New York: Guilford.

Segal, D. S., Yager, J., & Sullivan, J. L. (1976). *Foundations of biochemical psychiatry.* Boston: Butterworth.

Segal, S. (1978). Attitudes toward the mentally ill: A review. *Social Work, 23*, 211–17.

Segal, Z. V., & Stermac, L. E. (1990). The role of cognition in sexual assault. In W. L. Marshall, D. R. Laws, & H. E. Barbaree (Eds.), *Handbook of sexual assault.* (pp. 161–75). New York: Plenum.

Segraves, R.T., Althof, S. (1998) Psychotherapy and pharmacotherapy of sexual dysfunctions. In P. Nathan & J. Gorman (Eds.), *A Guide to Treatments that Work.* (pp. 447–71). New York: Oxford University Press.

Segraves, R. T., & Segraves, K. B. (1991). Diagnosis of female arousal disorder. *Sex. Marit. Ther., 6*, 9–13.

Seidl, F. W. (1974). Community oriented residential care: The state of the art. *Child Care Quarterly, 3*(3), 150–63.

Seligman, M. E. P. (1971). Phobias and preparedness. *Behav. Ther., 2*, 307–20.

Seligman, M. E. P. (1974). Depression and learned helplessness. In R.J. Friedman & M. M. Katz (Eds.), *The psychology of depression: Contemporary theory and research.* Washington, DC: Hemisphere.

Seligman, M. E. P. (1975). *Helplessness: On depression, development, and death.* San Francisco: Freeman.

Seligman, M. E. P. (1990). Why is there so much depression today? The waxing of the individual and the waning of the commons. In R. E. Ingram (Ed.), *Contemporary psychological approaches to depression.* New York: Plenum.

Seligman, M. E. P. (1995). The effectiveness of psychotherapy: The Consumer Reports study. *Amer. Psychol., 50*, 965–74.

Seligman, M. E. P. (1998). Afterword—A plea. In P. E. Nathan & J. M. Gorman (Eds.). *A guide to treatments that work* (pp. 568–71). New York: Oxford University Press.

Seligman, M. E. P., & Binik, Y. (1977). The safety signal hypothesis. In H. Davis & H. M. B. Hurwitz (Eds.), *Operant-Pavlovian interactions.* (pp. 165–88). Hillsdale, NJ: Erlbaum.

Selkin, J. (1975). Rape. *Psych. Today, 8*(8), 70–72.

Selkoe, D. J. (1986). Altered structural protein in plaques and tangles: What do they tell us about the biology of Alzheimer's disease? *Neurobiol. of Aging, 7*, 425–32.

Sell, R. L., Wypij, D., & Wells, J. A. (1995). The prevalence of homosexual behavior and attraction in the United States, the United Kingdom, and France:

Results of national population-based samples. *Arch. Sex. Behav., 24*, 235–48.

Selling, L. S. (1943). *Men against madness.* New York: Garden City Books.

Selye, H. (1956). *The stress of life.* New York: McGraw-Hill.

Selye, H. (1976a). *Stress in health and disease.* Woburn, MA: Butterworth.

Selye, H. (1976b). *The stress of life* (2nd ed.). New York: McGraw-Hill.

Senft, R. A., Polen, M. R., Freeborn, D. K., & Hollis, J. F. (1997). Brief intervention in a primary care setting for hazardous drinkers. *American Journal of Preventive Medicine, 13*(6), 464–70.

Seppa, N. (1998). Amyloid can trigger brain damage. *Sci. News, 154*(July 4), 4.

Serrano, A. C., Zuelzer, M. B., Howe, D. D., & Reposa, R. E. (1979). Ecology of abusive and nonabusive families, *J. Amer. Acad. Child Psychiat., 18*, 167–75.

Seto, M. C., & Barbaree, H. E. (1995). The role of alcohol in sexual aggression. *Clin. Pscyhol. Rev., 15*(6), 545–66.

Sewell, D. W., Jeste, D. V., Atkinson, J. H., Heaton, R. K., Hesselink, J. R., Wiley, C., Thal, L., Chandler, J. L., & Grant, I. (1994). HIV-associated psychosis: A study of 20 cases. *Amer. J. Psychiat., 151*(2), 237–42.

Shadish, W. R., et al. (1997). Evidence that therapy works in clinically representative conditions. *J. Cons. Clin. Psychol., 65*(3), 355–65.

Shadish, W. R., Montgomery, L. M., Wilson, P., Wilson, M. R., Bright, I., & Okwumabua, T. (1993). Effects of family and marital psychotherapies: A meta-analysis. *J. Cons. Clin. Psychol., 61*(6), 992–1002.

Shaffer, H. J. & LaSalvia, T. A. (1992). Patterns of substance use among methadone maintenance patients: Indicators of outcome. *Journal of Substance Abuse Treatment, 9*, 143–47.

Shakow, D. (1969). On doing research in schizophrenia. *Arch. Gen. Psychiat., 20*(6), 618–42.

Shaley, A. Y., Bonne, O., & Eth, S. (1996). Treatment of posttraumatic stress disorder: A review. *Psychosom. Med., 58*, 165–82.

Shapiro, A. K., & Morris, L. A. (1978). The placebo effect in medical and psychological therapies. In S. L. Garfield & A. E. Bergin (Eds.), *Handbook of psychotherapy and behavior change* (2nd ed.). (pp. 369–410). New York: Wiley.

Shapiro, F. (1989). Efficacy of the eye movement desensitization procedure in the treatment of traumatic memories. *J. Trauma. Stress, 2*, 199–223.

Shapiro, F. (1995). *Eye movement desensitization and reprocessing: Basic principles, protocols, and procedures.* New York: Guilford.

Shapiro, F. (1996). Eye movement desensitization and reprocessing (EMDR): Evaluation of controlled PTSD research. *J. Behav. Ther. Exper. Psychiat., 27*, 209–18.

Shapiro, F., & Forest, M. S. (1997). *EMDR: The breakthrough therapy for overcoming anxiety, stress and trauma.* New York: Basic Books.

Sharkey, J. (1997, Sept. 28). You're not bad, you're sick. It's in the book. *New York Times,* pp. 1, 5.

Shaw, E. D., Stokes, P. E., Mann, J. J., & Manevitz, A. Z. A. (1987). Effects of lithium carbonate on the memory and motor speed of bipolar outpatients. *J. Abn. Psychol., 96*, 64–69.

Shaw, J. A. (1990). Stress engendered by military action on military and civilian populations. In J. D. Noshpitz & R. D. Coddington (Eds.), *Stressors and the adjustment disorders.* New York: Wiley Intersciences.

Shaw, W. S., et al. (1997). Longitudinal analysis of multiple indicators of health decline among spousal caregivers. *Ann. Behav. Med., 19*(2), 101–109.

Shay, J. J. (1996). "Okay, I'm here, but I'm not talking!" Psychotherapy with the reluctant male. *Psychotherapy, 33*(3), 503–13.

Shea, M. T. (1995). Interrelationships among categories of personality disorders. In W. J. Livesley (Ed.), *The DSM-IV personality disorders.* (pp. 397–406). New York: Guilford.

Shea, M. T., Elkin, I., Imber, S. D., Sotsky, S. M., Watkins, J. T., Collins, J. F., Pilkonis, P. A., Beckham, E., Glass, D. R., Dolan, R. T., & Parloff, M. B. (1992). Course of depressive symptoms over follow-up: Findings from the National Institute of Mental Health Treatment of Depression Collaborative Research Program. *Arch. Gen. Psychiat., 49*(10), 782–87.

Shedler, J., & Block, J. (1990). Adolescent drug use and psychological health: A longitudinal inquiry. *Amer. Psychol., 45,* 612–30.

Shedler, J., Mayman, M., & Manis, M. (1993). The *illusion* of mental health. *Amer. Psychol., 48*(11), 1117–31.

Sheehan, D. Z. (1982). Panic attacks and phobias. *New Engl. J. Med., 307,* 156–8.

Sheehan, D. Z. (1983). *The anxiety disease.* New York: Bantum Books.

Sheitman, B. B., Kinon, B. J., Ridgway, B. A., Lieberman, J. A. (1998). Pharmacological treatments of schizophrenia. In P. E. Nathan & J. M. Gorman (Eds.), *A guide to treatments that work.* (pp. 167–89). Oxford, England: Oxford University Press.

Shelby, J. S., & Tredinnick, M. G. (1995). Crisis intervention with survivors of natural disaster: Lessons from Hurricane Andrew. *Journal of Counseling and Development, 73*(5), 491

Shelton, R. C., Hollon, S. D., Purdon, S. E., Loosen, P. T. (1991). Biological and psychological aspects of depression. *Behav. Ther., 22,* 201–28.

Shephard, M. (1974). The psycho-historians: A psychiatrist's scepticism. *Encounter,* March, 36.

Shepher, J. (1971). Mate selection among second generation kibbutz adolescents and adults. *Arch. Sex. Behav., 1,* 293–307.

Shepherd, J., & Brickley, M. (1996). The relationship between alcohol intoxication, stressors, and injury in urban violence. *British Journal of Criminology, 36*(4), 546–66.

Sher, K. J., Frost, R. O., & Otis, R. (1983). Cognitive deficits in compulsive checkers: An exploratory study. *Behav. Res. Ther., 21,* 357–64.

Sher, K. J., Frost, R. O., Kushner, M., Crews, T. M., & Alexander, J. E. (1989). Memory deficits in compulsive checkers: A replication and extension in a clinical example. *Behav. Res. Ther., 27,* 65–69.

Sher, K. J., & Trull, T. J. (1994) Personality and disinhibitory psychopathology: Alcoholism and antisocial personality disorder. *J. Abn. Psychol., 103,* 92–102.

Sher, K. J., Wood, M. D., Wood, P. D., & Raskin, G. (1996). Alcohol outcome expectancies and alcohol use: A latent variable cross–lagged panel study. *J. Abn. Psychol., 105*(4), 561–74.

Sherrod, B. (1968). *Dallas Times Herald* (n.d.). Quoted in D. Bolen & W. H. Boyd, Gambling and the gambler. *Arch. Gen. Psychiat., 18*(5), 617–30.

Sherwin, B. B. (1988). A comparative analysis of the role of androgen in human male and female sexual behavior: Behavioral specificity, critical thresholds, and sensitivity. Special Issue: Sexual differentiation and gender-related behaviors. *Psychobiology, 16,* 416–25.

Sherwin, B. B. (1991). The psychoendocrinology of aging and female sexuality. *Annu. Rev. Sex Res., 2,* 181–98.

Sherwin, I., & Geschwind, N. (1978). Neural substrates of behavior. In A. M. Nicholi (Ed.), *The Harvard guide to modern psychiatry.* (pp. 59–80). Cambridge, MA: Harvard University Press.

Sheung-Tak, C. (1996) A critical review of Chinese koro. *Cult., Med. Psychiat., 20,* 67–82.

Shneidman, E. S. (1997). The suicidal mind. In R. W. Maris, M. M. Silverman, & S. S. Canetton (Eds.), *Review of Suicidology, 1997.* (pp. 22–41). New York: Guilford.

Shore, J. H., Vollmer, W. M., & Tatum, E. L. (1989). Community patterns of posttraumatic stress disorders. *J. Nerv. Ment. Dis., 177,* 681–85.

Short, C. (1997). The myth of community care: A historical review for people with mental handicap. *Italian Journal of Intellective Impairment, 9*(2), 219–29.

Short, K. H., & Johnston, C. (1997). Stress, maternal distress, and children's adjustment following immigration: The buffering role of social support. *J. Cons. Clin. Pscyhol., 65*(3), 494–503.

Short, R. H., & Hess, G. C. (1995). Fetal alcohol syndrome: Characteristics and remedial implications. *Developmental Disabilities Bulletin, 23*(1), 12–29.

Shrout, P. E., Link, B. G., Dohrenwend, B. P., Skodol, A. E., Stueve, A., & Mirotznik, J. (1989). Characterizing life events as risk factors for depression: The role of fateful loss events. *J. Abn. Psychol., 89,* 460–67.

Sidtis, J. J., Gatsonis, C., & Price, R. W. (1993). Zidovudine treatment of the AIDS dementia complex: Results of a placebo-controlled trial. *Ann. Neurol., 33,* 343–49.

Siegel, B. (1996). *The world of the autistic child.* New York: Oxford University Press.

Siegel, J. M., & Kuykendall, D. H. (1990). Loss, widowhood, and psychological distress among the elderly. *J. Cons. Clin. Psychol. 58,* 519–24.

Siegel, R. K. (1984). Hostage hallucinations: Visual imagery induced by isolation and life-threatening stress. *J. Nerv. Ment. Dis., 172*(5), 264–72.

Siegelman, M. (1979). Adjustment of homosexual and heterosexual women: A cross-national replication. *Arch. Sex. Behav., 8,* 121–26.

Siever, L. J. (1985). Biological markers in schizotypal personality disorder. *Schizo. Bull., 11,* 564–75.

Siever, L. J. (1986). Schizoid and schizotypal personality disorders. In J. R. Lion (Ed.), *Personality disorders: Diagnosis and management.* (pp. 32–64). Malabar, FL: Robert F. Kreiger.

Siever, L. J., Bernstein, D. P., & Silverman, J. M. (1995). Schizotypal personality disorder. In W. J. Livesley (Ed.), *The DSM-IV personality disorders.* (pp. 71–90). New York: Guilford.

Siever, L. J., & Davis, K. L. (1985). Overview: Toward a dysregulation hypothesis of depression. *Amer. J. Psychiat., 142,* 1017–31.

Siever, L. J., & Davis, K. L. (1991). A psychobiological perspective on the personality disorders. *Amer. J. Psychiat., 148,* 1647–58.

Siever, L. J., Silverman, J. M., Horvath, T. B., Klar, H., Coccaro, E., Keefe, R. S. E., Pinkham, L., Rinaldi, P., Mohs, R. C., & Davis, K. L. (1990). Increased morbidity risk for schizophrenia-related disorders in relatives of schizotypal personality disordered patients. *Arch. Gen. Psychiat., 47,* 634–40.

Sifneos, P. E. (1973). The prevalence of "alexithymic" characteristics in psychosomatic patients. *Psychotherapy and Psychosomatics, 22,* 255–62.

Sigal J. J., Silver, D., Rakoff, V., & Ellin, B. (1973, Apr.). Some second-generation effects of survival of the Nazi persecution. *Amer. J. Orthopsychiat., 43*(3), 320–27.

Sigel, G. S., & Kane, R. J. (1997). Violence prediction reconsidered. *The Forensic Examiner, 6*(11–12), 21–4.

Sigerist, H. E. (1943). *Civilization and disease.* Ithaca, NY: Cornell University Press.

Sigman, M. (1996). Behavioral research in childhood autism. In M. F. Lenzenweger & J. L. Haugaard (Eds.), *Frontiers of developmental psychopathology.* (pp. 190–208). New York: Oxford University Press.

Sigman, M., Kasari, C., Kwon, J., & Yirmiya, N. (1992). Responses to the negative emotions of others by autistic, mentally retarded, and normal children. *Child Develop., 63,* 796–807.

Sigvardsson, S., Von Knorring, A. L., Bohman, M., & Cloninger, C. R. (1984). An adoption study of somatoform disorders: I. The relationship of somatization to psychiatric disability. *Arch. Gen. Psych., 41,* 853–59.

Silberman, E. K., & Tassone, E. P. (1985). The Israeli high-risk study: Statistical overview and discussion. *Schizo. Bull., 11,* 138–45.

Silk, K. R., Eisner, W., Allport, C., DeMars, C., Miller, C., Justice, R. W., & Lewis, M. (1994). Focused time-limited inpatient treatment of borderline personality disorder. *J. Person. Dis., 8*(4), 268–278.

Silk, K., & Lohr, N. E. (1996). Drs. Silk and Lohr Reply. *Amer. J. Psychiat., 153*(6), 848–49.

Silver, E. (1995). Punishment or treatment? Comparing the lengths of confinement of successful and unsuccessful insanity defendants. *Law and Human Behavior, 19*(4), 375–88.

Silverman, K., Higgins, S. T., Brooner, R. K., & Montoya, I. D. (1996). Sustained cocaine abstinence in methadone maintenance patients through voucher-based reinforcement therapy. *Arch. Gen. Psychiat., 53*(3), 409–15.

Silverman, M. M. (1997). Current controversies in suicidology. In R. W. Maris, M. M. Silverman, & S. S. Canetton (Eds.), *Review of Suicidology, 1997.* (pp. 1–21). New York: Guilford.

Silverman, P. R., & Klass, D. (1996). Introduction: What's the problem? In D. Klass, P. R. Silverman, & S. L. Nickman (Eds.), *Continuing bonds: New understandings of grief.* (pp. 3–27). Washington: Taylor & Francis.

Silverman, W. H., & Wallander, J. L. (1993). Bridging research and practice in interventions with children: Introduction to the special issue. *Clin. Psychol., 46,* 165–168.

Silverman, W. H., & Silverman, M. M. (1987). Comparison of key informants, parents, and teenagers for planning adolescent substance abuse prevention programs. *Psychology of Addictive Behaviors, 1*(1), 30–37.

Silverstein, A. B., Legutki, G., Friedman, S. L., & Takayama, D. L. (1982). Performance of Down's syndrome individuals on the Stanford-Binet Intelligence Scale. *Amer. J. Ment. Def., 86,* 548–5.

Silverton, L., Finello, K. M., Schulsinger, F., & Mednick, S. A. (1985). Low birth weight and ventricular enlargement in a high-risk sample. *J. Abn. Psychol., 94,* 405–9

Simmons, D., Goode, S., & Fombonne, E. (1997). Elective mutism and chromosome 18 abnormality. *Eur. Child Adoles. Psychiat., 6*(2), 112–14.

Simon, G. E. (1998). Management of somatoform and factitious disorders. In P. E. Nathan & J. M. Gorman (Eds.), *A guide to treatments that work.* (pp. 408–22). New York: Oxford University Press.

Simon, R. J., & Aaronson, D. E. (1988). *The insanity defense.* New York: Praeger.

Simon, W. (1975). Male sexuality: The secret of satisfaction. *Today's Health, 53*(4), 32–34, 50–52.

Simons, A. D., Angell, K. L., Monroe, S. M., & Thase, M. E. (1993). Cognition and life stress in depression: Cognitive factors and the definition, rating, and generation of negative life events. *J. Abn. Psychol., 102,* 584–91.

Simons, A. D., Murphy, G. E., Levine, J. L., & Wetzel, R. D. (1986). Cognitive therapy and pharmacotherapy for depression: Sustained improvement over one year. *Arch. Gen. Psychiat., 43,* 43–48.

Simons, R. C. (1987). Applicability of the DSM-III to psychiatric education. In G. L. Tischler (Ed.), *Diagnosis and classification in psychiatry: A critical appraisal of DSM-III.* (pp. 510–29). New York: Cambridge University Press.

Simons, R. C., & Hughes, C. C. (Eds.). (1985). *The culture bound syndromes.* Boston: Reidel.

Simpson, J. A., Rholes, W. S. & Phillips, D. (1996). Conflict in close relationships: An attachment perspective. *J. Pers. Soc. Psychol., 71,* 899–914.

Singer, J. E. (1980). Traditions of stress research: Integrative comments. In I. G. Sarason & C. D. Spielberger (Eds.), *Stress and anxiety* (Vol. 7). (pp. 3–10). Washington, DC: Hemisphere.

Singer, J., & Singer, I. (1978). Types of female orgasm. In J. LoPiccolo & L. LoPiccolo (Eds.), *Handbook of sex therapy.* (pp. 175–86). New York: Plenum.

Singer, M., & Wynne, L. C. (1963). Differentiating characteristics of the parents of childhood schizophrenics, childhood neurotics and young adult schizophrenics. *Amer. J. Psychiat., 120,* 234–43.

Singer, M., & Wynne, L. C. (1965a). Thought disorder and family relations of schizophrenics. III. Methodology using projective techniques. *Arch. Gen. Psychiat., 12,* 182–200.

Singer, M., & Wynne, L. C. (1965b). Thought disorder and family relations of schizophrenics. IV. Results and implications. *Arch. Gen. Psychiat., 12,* 201–12.

Singer, M. T., Wynne, L. C., & Toohey, M. L. (1978). Communication disorders and the families of schizophrenics. In L. C. Wynne, R. L. Cromwell, & S. Matthysse (Eds.), *The nature of schizophrenia: New approaches to research and treatment.* (pp. 499–511). New York: Wiley.

Skinner, B. F. (1990). Can psychology be a science of mind? *Amer. Psychol. 45,* 1206–10.

Skodol, A. E., Oldham, J. M., Hyler, S. E., Stein, D. J. (1995). Patterns of anxiety and personality disorder comorbidity. *J. Psychiat. Res., 29*(5), 361–74.

Skodol, A. E., Rosnick, L., Kellman, H. D., Oldham, J. M., & Hyler, S. E. (1991). Development of a procedure for validating structured assessments of Axis II. In J. Oldham (Ed.), *Personality disorders: New perspectives on diagnostic validity.* Washington DC: American Psychiatric Press.

Slap, G. B., Vorters, D. F., Chaudhuri, S., & Centor, R. (1989). Risk factors for attempted suicide during adolescence. *Pediatrics, 84,* 762–72.

Slater, E., with the assistance of J. Shields. (1953). *Psychotic and neurotic illness in twins.* Special Report Series No. 278. Medical Research Council (Great Britain).

Slater, J., & Depue, R. A. (1981). The contribution of environmental events and social support to serious suicide attempts in primary depressive disorder. *J. Abn. Psychol., 90,* 275–85.

Sloan, S. J., & Cooper, C. L. (1984). Health-related lifestyle habits in commercial airline pilots. *British Journal of Aviation Medicine, 2,* 32–41.

Sloane, R. B., Staples, F. R., Cristol, A. H., Yorkston, N. J., & Whipple, K. (1975). *Psychotherapy versus behavior therapy.* Cambridge, MA: Harvard University Press.

Sloman, L. (1991). Use of medication in pervasive developmental disorders. *Psychiat. Clin. N. Amer. 14,* 165–82.

Sloper, P., Turner, S., Knussen, C., & Cunningham, C. C. (1990). Social life of school children with Down's syndrome. *Child: Care, Health, and Development, 16,* 235–51.

Slovenko, R. (1994). Legal aspects of post-traumatic disorder. *Psychiat. Clin. N. Amer., 17,* 439–46.

Slutsky, W. S., Heath, A. C., Dinwiddie, S. H., Madden, P. A., & Bucholz, K. K. (1998). Common genetic risk factors for conduct disorder and alcohol dependence. *J. Abn. Psychol., 107*(3), 363–74.

Slutsky, W. S., Heath, A. C., Dunne, M. P., Statham, D. J., Dinwiddie, S. H., Madden, P. A. F., Martin, N. G., & Bucholz, K. K. (1997). Modeling genetic and environmental influences in the etiology of conduct disorder: A study of 2,682 adult twin pairs. *J. Abn. Psychol., 100*(2), 266–79.

Smalley, S. L. (1991). Genetic influences in autism. *Psychiat. Clin. N. Amer., 14,* 125–39.

Smith G., & Smith, D. (1985). A mainstreaming program that really works. *Learn. Dis., 18,* 369–72.

Smith, D. (1982). Trends in counseling and psychotherapy. *Amer. Psychol., 37*(7), 802–9.

Smith, G. F., & Berg, J. M. (1976). *Down's anomaly.* New York: Churchill Livingstone (Distributed by Longman).

Smith, G. T., Goldman, M. S., Greenbaum, P. E., & Christiansen, B. A. (1995). Expectancy for social facilitation from drinking: The diveregent paths of high-expectancy and low-expectancy adolescents. *J. Abn. Psychol., 104,* 32–40.

Smith, I. M. & Bryson, S. (1994). Imitation and action in autism: A critical review. *Psychol. Bull., 116*(2), 259–73.

Smith, M. L., Glass, G. V., & Miller, T. I. (1980). *The benefits of psychotherapy.* Baltimore: Johns Hopkins University Press.

Smith, R. J. (1978). *The psychopath in society.* New York: Academic Press.

Smith, R. J. (1979). Study finds sleeping pills overprescribed. *Science, 204,* 287–88.

Smith, R. S. (1976). Voyeurism: A review of the literature. *Arch. Sex. Behav., 5,* 585–608.

Smith, S. S., & Newman, J. P. (1990). Alcohol and drug abuse dependence disorders in psychopathic and nonpsychopathic criminal offenders. *J. Abn. Psychol., 99,* 430–39.

Smith, W. (1989). *A profile of health and disease in America.* New York: Facts on File.

Smithyan, S. D. (1978). *The undetected rapist.* Ph.D. Dissertation, Claremont Graduate School. University Microfilms International: Ann Arbor, MI.

Smyth, J. M. (1998). Written emotional expression: Effect sizes, outcome types, and moderating variables. *J. Cons. Clin. Psychol., 66*(1), 174–84.

Snow, D. L., & Kline, M. L. (1995). Preventive interventions in the work site to reduce negative psychiatric consequences of work and family stress. In C.M. Mazure (Ed.), *Does stress cause psychiatric illness?* Washington, DC: American Psychiatric Association.

Snowden, K. R., & Cheung, F. K. (1990). Use of inpatient mental health services by members of ethnic minority groups. *Amer. Psychol., 45,* 347–55.

Snyder, D. K., & Wills, R. M. (1989). Behavioral versus insight-oriented marital therapy: Effects on individual and interspousal functioning. *J. Cons. Clin. Psychol. 57,* 39–46.

Snyder, P. J., & Nussbaum, P. D. (1998). *Clinical neuropsychology: A pocket handbook for assessment.* Washington: American Psychological Association.

Snyder, S. H. (1978). Dopamine and schizophrenia. In L. C. Wynne, R. L. Cromwell & S. Matthysse (Eds.), *The nature of schizophrenia: New approaches to research and treatment.* (pp. 87–94). New York: Wiley.

Sobell, M. B., & Sobell, L. C. (1995). Controlled drinking after 25 years: How important was the great debate? *Addiction, 90*(9), 1149–53.

Sokol, M. S., & Pfeffer, C. R. (1992). Suicidal Behavior of children. In B. Bongar (Ed.), *Suicide: Guidelines for assessment, management and treatment.* New York: Oxford University Press.

Soloff, P. H., Cornelius, J., George, A. (1991). The depressed borderline: One disorder or two? *Psychopharma. Bull., 27,* 23–30.

Soloff, P. H., Lis, J. A., Kelly, T., Cornelius, J., & Ulrich, R. (1994). Risk factors for suicidal behavior in borderline personality disorder. *Amer. J. Psychiat., 151*(9), 1316–23.

Solomon, Z., & Kleinhauz, M. (1996). War-induced psychic trauma: An 18-year follow-up of Israeli veterans. *Amer. J. Orthopsychiat., 66*(1), 152–60.

Sommers-Flanagan, J., & Sommers-Flanagan, R. (1996). Efficacy of antidepressant medication with depressed youth: What psychologists should know. *Profess. Psychol., 27*(2), 145–53.

Soni, S. D., & Rockley, G. J. (1974). Socio-cultural substrates of folie à deux. *Brit. J. Psychiat., 125*(9), 230–35.

Sonnenberg, S. M. (1988). Victims of violence and post-traumatic stress disorder. *Psychiat. Clin. N. Amer., 11,* 581–90.

Sorenson, S. B., Rutter, C. M., & Aneshensel, C. S. (1991). Depression in the community: An investigation into age of onset. *J. Cons. Clin. Psychol., 59,* 541–46.

Soroka v. Dayton-Hudson, Corp., 753 Cal.App.3d 654,1 Cal Rptr.2d 77 (Cal.App.1. Dist.1991) (1991).

Southam-Gerow, M. A., & Kendall, P. C. (1997). Parent-focused and cognitive-behavioral treatments of antisocial youth. In D. M. Stoff, J. Breiling, & J. D. Maser (Eds.), *Handbook of antisocial behavior.* (pp. 384–394). New York: Wiley.

Southwick, S. M., Yehuda, R., & Charney, D. S. (1997). Neurobiological alterations in PTSD: Review of the clinical literature. In *Posttraumatic stress disorder.* (pp. 241–66). Washington: American Psychiatric Press.

Southwick, S. M., Yehuda, R., & Morgan, C. A. (1995). Clinical studies of neurotransmitter alterations in post-traumatic stress disorder. In M. Friedman & D. S. Charney, et al. (Eds.), *Neurobiological and clinical consequences of stress: From normal adaptation to post-traumatic stress disorder.* (pp. 335–49). Philadelphia: Lippincott-Raven.

Spanos, N. P. (1986). Hypnosis, nonvolitional responding, and multiple personality. In B. Maher & W. Maher (Eds.), *Progress in experimental personality research.* (pp. 1–62). New York: Academic Press.

Spanos, N. P. (1994). Multiple identity enactments and multiple personality disorder: a sociocognitive perspective. *Psychol. Bull., 116,* 143–65.

Spanos, N. P. (1996). *Multiple identies and false memories: A sociocognitive perspective.* Washington, DC: American Psychological Association.

Spanos, N., & Burgess, C. (1994). Hypnosis and multiple personality disorder: A sociocognitive perspective. In S. J. Lynn & J. W. Rhue (Eds.), *Dissociation: Clinical and theoretical perspectives.* (pp. 136–58). New York: Guilford.

Spanos, N. P., Weekes, J. R., & Bertrand, L. D. (1985). Multiple personality: A social psychological perspective. *J. Abn. Psychol., 94,* 362–76.

Speed, N., Engdahl, B., Schwartz, J., & Eberly, R. (1989). Posttraumatic stress disorder as a consequence of the POW experience. *J. Nerv. Ment. Dis. 177,* 147–53.

Speer, D. C. (1992). Clinically significant change: Jacobson and Truax (1991) revisited. *J. Cons. Clin. Psychol., 60*(3), 402–08.

Speier, P. L., Sherak, D. L., Hirsch, S., & Cantwell, D. P. (1995). Depression in children and adolescents. In E. E. Beckham & W. R. Leber (Eds.), *Handbook of depression* (2nd ed.). (pp. 467–493). New York: Guilford.

Spencer, G. (1989). *Projections of the population of the United States, by age, sex, and race: 1988–2080.* U.S. Department of Commerce, Bureau of Census. Washington, DC: U. S. Government Printing Office.

Sperling, E. (1997). The collateral treatment of parents with children and adolescents in psychotherapy. *Child Adoles. Psychiatr. Clin. N. Amer., 6*(1), 81–95.

Sperling, E. (1997). The role of play in child psychotherapy. *Child Adoles. Psychiat. Clin. N. Amer., 6*(1), 68–79.

Spiegel, D. A., & Bruce, T. J. (1997). Benzodiazepines and exposure-based cognitive-behavior therapies for panic disorder: Conclusions from combined treatment trials. *Amer. J. Psychiat., 154*(6), 773–81.

Spielberger, C. D., Johnson, E. H., Russell, S. F., Crane, R. J., & Worden, T. J. (1985). The experience and expression of anger. In M. A. Chesney & R. H. Rosenman (Eds.), *Anger and hostility in cardiovascular and behavioral disorders.* New York: Hemisphere.

Spiess, W. F. J., Geer, J. H., & O'Donohue, W. T. (1984). Premature ejaculation: Investigation of factors in ejaculatory latency. *J. Abn. Psychol., 93,* 242–45.

Spitz, R. A. (1945). Hospitalization: An inquiry into the genesis of psychiatric conditions of early childhood. In R. S. Eissler, A. Freud, H. Hartman, & E. Kris (Eds.), *The psychoanalytic study of the child* (Vol. 1). New York: International Universities Press.

Spitz, R. A. (1946). Anaclitic depression. In *Psychoanalytic study of the child* (Vol. 2). New York: International Universities Press.

Spitzer, R. L., Gibbon, M., Skodol, A. E., Williams, J. B. W., & First, M. B. (1989). *DSM-III-R casebook.* Washington, DC: American Psychiatric Press.

Spitzer, R. L., Gibbon, M., Skodol, A. E., Williams, J. B. W., & First, M. B. (Ed.). (1994). *DSM-IV casebook* (4th ed.). Washington: American Psychiatric Press.

Spitzer, R. L., Skodol, A. E., Gibbon, M., & Williams, J. B. W. (1981). *DSM-III casebook.* Washington, DC: American Psychiatric Association.

Spitzer, R. L., Skodol, A. E., Gibbon, M., & Williams, J. B. W. (1983). *Psychopathology: A casebook.* New York: McGraw-Hill.

Sponheim, B. (1996). Changing criteria for autistic disorders: A comparison of the ICD-10 research criteria and DSM-IV with DSM-IIIR, CARS, and ABC. *J. Autism Devel. Dis., 26*(5), 513–25.

Spoont, M. R. (1992). Modulatory role of serotonin in neural information processing: Implications for human psychopathology. *Psychol. Bull., 112*(2), 330–50.

Spreen, O., & Strauss, E. (1998). *A compendium of neuropsychological tests.* New York: Oxford University Press.

Spring, B. J., & Zubin, J. (1978). Attention and information-processing as indicators of vulnerability to schizophrenic episodes. In L. C. Wynne, R. L. Cromwell, & S. Matthysse (Eds.), *The nature of schizophrenia: New approaches to research and treatment.* (pp. 366–175). New York: Wiley.

Spunt, B., Goldstein, P., Brownstein, H., & Fendrich, M. (1994). The role of marijuana in homicide. *Inter. J. Addict., 29,* 195–213.

Squire, L. R. (1977). ECT and memory loss. *Amer. J. Psychiat., 134,* 997–1001.

Squire, L. R., & Slater, P. C. (1978). Bilateral and unilateral ECT: Effects on verbal and nonverbal memory. *Amer. J. Psychiat., 135,* 1316–20.

Squire, L. R., Slater, P. C., & Chase, P. M. (1975). Retrograde amnesia: Temporal gradient in very long-term memory following electroconvulsive therapy. *Science, 187,* 77–79.

Squires-Wheeler, E., Friedman, D., Amminger, G. P., Skodol, A., Looser-Ott, S., Roberts, S., Pape, S., & Erlenmeyer-Kimling, L. (1997). Negative and positive dimensions of schizotypal personality disorder. *J. Personal. Dis., 11*(3), 285–300.

Stabenau, J. R. (1984). Implications of family history of alcoholism, antisocial personality, and sex differences in alcohol dependence. *Amer. J. Psychiat., 141*(10), 1178–82.

Stabenau, J., & Pollin, W. (1968). Comparative life history differences of families of schizophrenics, delinquents and "normals." *Amer. J. Psychiat., 124*, 1526–34.

Stabenau, J. R., Tupin, J., Werner, M., & Pollin, W. (1965). A comparative study of families of schizophrenics, delinquents, and normals. *Psychiatry, 28*, 45–59.

Stacy, A. W., Widaman, K. F., & Marlatt, G. A. (1990). Expectancy models of alcohol use. *J. Pers. Soc. Psychol., 58*, 918–28.

Stafford, K. P., & Ben-Porath, Y. S. (1995). Assessment of criminal responsibility. In J. N. Butcher (Ed.), *Foundations of clinical personality assessment: Practical considerations.* New York: Oxford University Press.

Stafford, S. H., & Green, V. P. (1993). Facilitating preschool mainstreaming: Classroom strategies and teacher attitude. *Early Child Development & Care, 91*, 93–98.

Staley, D., Wand, R., & Shady, G. (1997). Tourette Disorder: A cross-cultural review. *Compr. Psychiat., 38*(1), 6–16.

Stampfl, T. G., (1975). Implosive therapy: Staring down your nightmares. *Psych. Today, 8*(9), 66–68, 72–73.

Stanley, E. J., & Barter, J. T. (1970). Adolescent suicidal behavior. *Amer. J. Orthopsychiat., 40*(1), 87–96.

Stanton, B., Baldwin, R. M., & Rachuba, L. (1997). A quarter century of violence in the United States. *Psychiat. Clin. N. Amer., 20*, 269–82.

Stanton, M. D., & Todd, T. C. (1976, June). *Structural family therapy with heroin addicts: Some outcome data.* Paper presented at the Society for Psychotherapy Research. San Diego.

Starck, L. C., Branna, S. K., & Tallen, B. J. (1994). Mesoridazine use and priapism. *Amer. J. Psychiat., 151*, 946.

Stare, F. J., Whelan, E. M., & Sheridan, M. (1980). Diet and hyperactivity: Is there a relationship? *Pediatrics, 6*(4), 521–25.

Stark, L. J., Spirito, A., Lewis, A. V., & Hart, K. J. (1990). Encopresis: Behavioral paramaters associated with children who fail medical management. *Child Psychiat. Human Develop., 20*, 169–79.

Stattin, H., & Klackenberg-Larsson, I. (1993). Early language and intelligence development and their relationship to future criminal behavior. *J. Abn. Psychol., 102*(3), 369–78.

Steadman, H. J., McGreevy, M. A., Morrissey, J. P., Callahan, L. A., Robbins, P. C., & Cirincione, C. (1993). *Before and after Hinckley: Evaluating insanity defense reform.* New York: Guilford.

Steadman, H. J., Mulvey, E. P., Monahan, J., Robbins, P. C., Appelbaum, P. S., Grisso, T., Roth, L. H., & Silver, E. (1998). Violence by people discharged from acute psychiatric inpatient facilities and by others in the same neighborhoods. *Arch. Gen. Psychiat., 55*, 393–401.

Steele, R. G., & Forehand, R. (1997). The role of family processes and coping strategies in the relationship between parental chronic illness and childhood internalizing problems. *J. Abnorm. Child Psychol., 25*, 83–94.

Steer, R. A., Clark, D., Beck, A. T., & Ranieri, W. F. (1995). Common and specific dimensions of self-reported anxiety and depression: A replication. *J. Abn. Psychol., 104*(3), 542–45.

Steffenberg, S., & Gillberg, C. (1986). Autism and autistic-like conditions in Swedish rural and urban areas: A population study. *Brit. J. Psychiat.* 149, 81–87.

Stein, J. (1970). *Neurosis in contemporary society: Process and treatment.* Belmont, CA: Brooks/Cole.

Stein, J., & Walsh, V. (1997). To see but not to read: The magnocellular theory of dyslexia. *Trends in Neurosciences, 20*(4), 147–52.

Stein, M. I. (1998). *The Thematic Apperception Test.* Washington: American Psychological Association.

Stein, S. (1987). Computer-assisted diagnosis for children and adolescents. In J. N. Butcher (Ed.), *Computerized psychological assessment: A practitioner's guide.* New York: Basic Books.

Steinhausen, H. C., & Adamek, R. (1997). The family history of children with elective mutism: A research report. *Eur. Child Adoles. Psychiat., 6*(2), 107–11.

Steinhausen, H. C., & Juzi, C. (1996). Elective mutism: An analysis of 100 cases. *J. Amer. Acad. Child Adoles. Psychiat., 35*(5), 606–14.

Steinhausen, H. C., Williams, J., & Spohr, H.-L. (1993). Long-term psychopathological and cognitive outcome of children with fetal alcohol syndrome. *J. Amer. Acad. Child Adoles. psychiatr., 32*, 990–994.

Steinmann, A., & Fox, D. J. (1974). *The male dilemma: How to survive the sexual revolution.* New York: Jason Aronson.

Steketee, G. S. (1993). *Treatment of obsessive-compulsive disorder.* New York: Guilford.

Steketee, G., & Foa, E. B. (1985). Obsessive-compulsive disorder. In D. H. Barlow (Ed.), *Clinical handbook of psychological disorders.* (pp. 69–144) New York: Guilford.

Stelmachers, Z. T. (1995). Assessing suicidal patients. In J. N. Butcher (Ed.), *Clinical personality assessment: Practical considerations* New York: Oxford University Press.

Stelmack, R. M., Houlihan, M., & McGarry-Roberts, P. A. (1993). Personality, reaction time, and event-related potentials. *J. Pers. Soc. Psychol., 65*(2), 399–409.

Stene, J., Stene, E., Stengel-Rutkowski, S., & Murken, J. D. (1981). Paternal age and Down's syndrome, data from prenatal diagnoses (DFG). *Human Genet., 59*, 119–74.

Stephens, R. S., Roffman, R. A., & Simpson, E. E. (1994). Treating adult marijuana dependence: A test of the relapse prevention model. *J. Cons. Clin. Psychol., 62*, 92–99.

Stephens, R., & Cottrell, E. (1972). A follow-up study of 200 narcotic addicts committed for treatment under the narcotic addiction rehabilitation act. *Brit. J. Addict., 67*, 45–53.

Stermac, L., Hall, K., & Henskens, M. (1989). Violence among child molesters. *J. Sex Res., 26*, 450–59.

Stermac, L. E., Segal, Z. V., & Gillis, R. (1990). Social and cultural factors in sexual assault. In W. L. Marshall, D. R. Laws, & H. E. Barbaree (Eds.), *Handbook of sexual assault.* (pp. 143–60). New York: Plenum.

Stern, D. B. (1977). Handedness and the lateral distribution of conversion reactions. *J. Nerv. Ment. Dis., 164*, 122–28.

Stern, E. & Silbersweig, D. A. (1998). Neural mechanisms underlying hallucinations in schizophrenia: Theole of abnormal fronto-temporal interactions. In M. F. Lenzenweger & R. H. Dworkin (Eds.), *Origins and development of schizophrenia: Advances in experimental psychopathology.* (pp. 235–46). Washington, DC: American Psychological Association.

Sternberg, K. J., Lamb, M. B., Greenbaum, C., & Cicchetti, D. (1992). Effects of domestic violence on children's behavior problems and depression. *Develop. Psychol., 29*, 44–52.

Stevens, J. R. (1997). Anatomy of schizophrenia revisited. *Schizo. Bull., 23*(3), 373–373.

Stevens, J. R., & Hallick, L. M. (1992). Viruses and schizophrenia. In S. Specter, M. Bendinelli, & H. Friedman (Eds.), *Viruses and immunity.* (pp. 303–16). New York: Plenum.

Stewart, J. B., Hardin, S. B., Weinrich, S., & McGeorge, S. (1992). Group protocol to mitigate disaster stress and enhance social support in adolescents exposed to Hurricane Hugo. *Issues in Mental Health Nursing, 13*, 105–19.

Stewart, S. H., Finn, P. R., & Pihl, R. O. (1990, Mar.). *The effects of alcohol on the cardiovascular stress response in men at high risk for alcoholism: A dose response study.* Paper presented at the annual meeting of the Canadian Psychological Association, Ottawa.

Stiles, W. B., & Shapiro, D. A., (1989). Abuse of the drug metaphor in psychotherapy process-outcome research. *Clin. Psychol. Rev., 9*, 521–43.

Stiles, W. B., Shapiro, D. A., & Elliott, R. (1986). "Are all psychotherapies equivalent?" *Amer. Psychol., 41*, 165–80.

Stokes, P. E., & Sikes, C. R. (1987). Hypothalamic-pituitary-adrenal axis in affective disorders. In H. Y. Meltzer (Ed.), *Psychopharmacology: A third generation of progress.* (pp. 589–607). New York: Raven Press.

Stoller, R. U. (1977). Sexual deviations. In F. Beach (Ed.), *Human sexuality in four perspectives.* Baltimore, MD: Johns Hopkins University Press.

Stone, G. C., Weiss, S. M., Matarazzo, J. D., Miller, N. E., Rodin, J., Belar, C. D., Follick, M. J., & Singer, J. E. (Eds.), (1987). *Health psychology: A discipline and a profession.* Chicago: University of Chicago Press.

Stone, L. J., & Hokanson, J. E. (1969). Arousal reduction via self-punitive behavior. *J. Pers. Soc. Psychol., 12*, 72–79.

Stone, S. (1937). Psychiatry through the ages. *J. Abnorm. Soc. Psychol., 32*, 131–60.

Storandt, M., & Vanden Bos, G. (1994). *Neuropsychological assessment of dementia and depression in older adults.* Washington: American Psychological Association.

Strack, S., & Coyne, J. C. (1983). Social confirmation of dysphoria: Shared and private reactions to depression. *J. Pers. Soc. Psychol., 44*, 798–806.

Strakowski, S. M. (1994). Diagnostic validity of schizophreniform disorder. *Amer. J. Psychiat., 151*(6), 815–24.

Strang, J. P. (1989). Gastrointestinal disorders. In S. Cheren (Ed.), *Psychosomatic medicine: Theory, physiology, and practice* (Vol. 2). (pp. 427–502). Madison, CT: International Universities Press.

Strange, R. E., & Brown, D. E., Jr. (1970). Home from the wars. *Amer. J. Psychiat., 127*(4), 488–92.

Strauman, T. J., Lemieux, A. M., & Coe, C. L. (1993). Self-discrepancy and natural killer cell activity: Immunological consequences of negative self-evaluation. *J. Pers. Soc. Psychol., 64*(6), 1042–52.

Strauss, T. S. (1979). Social and cultural influences on psychopathology. *Annu. Rev. Psychol., 30*(4), 397–415.

Strayer, R., & Ellenhorn, L. (1975). Vietnam veterans: A study exploring adjustment patterns and attitudes. *Journal of Social Issues, 31*, 81–93.

Strean, H. S. (1985). *Resolving resistances in psychotherapy.* New York: Wiley Interscience.

Street, W. (1994). *A chronology of noteworthy events in American psychology.* Washington: American Psychological Association.

Streiner, D. L., & Norman, G. R. (1995). *Health measurement scales.* New York: Oxford University Press.

Streissguth, A. P. (1976). Maternal alcoholism and the outcome of pregnancy: A review of the fetal alcohol syndrome. In M. Greenblatt & M. A. Schuckit (Eds.), *Alcoholism: Problems in women and children.* New York: Grune & Stratton.

Strine, G. (1971, Mar. 30). Compulsive gamblers pursue elusive dollar forever. *Los Angeles Times,* III, 1–6.

Strober, M. (1986). Anorexia nervosa: history and psychological concepts. In K. D. Brownell & J. P. Foreyt (Eds.), *Handbook of eating disorders.* (pp. 231–46). New York: Basic.

Stroebe, M. S., & Stroebe, W. (1983). Who suffers more? Sex differences in health risks of the widowed. *Psychol. Bull., 93*(2), 279–301.

Strupp, H. H. (1981). Toward a refinement of time-limited dynamic psychotherapy. In S. H. Budman (Ed.), *Forms of brief therapy.* New York: Guilford.

Strupp, H. H. (1993). The Vanderbilt psychotherapy studies: Synopsis. *J. Cons. Clin. Psychol., 61*(3), 431–33.

Strupp, H. H., & Binder, J. L. (1984). *Psychotherapy in a new key: A guide to time-limited dynamic psychotherapy.* New York: Basic Books.

Strupp, H. H., Hadley, S. W., & Gomes-Schwartz, B. (1977). *Psychotherapy for better or worse: An analysis of the problem of negative effects.* New York: Jason Aronson.

Stuart, R. B. (1967). Behavioral control of overeating. *Behav. Res. Ther., 5*, 357–65.

Stuart, R. B. (1971). A three-dimensional program for the treatment of obesity. *Behav. Res. Ther., 9,* 177–86.

Stunkard, A. J., Harris, J. R., Pedersen, N. L., & Mc-Clearn, G. E. (1990). A separated twin study of the body mass index. *New Engl. J. Med., 322,* 1483–87.

Sturgis, E. T. (1993). Obsessive-compulsive disorders. In P. B. Sutker & H. E. Adams (Eds.), *Comprehensive handbook of psychopathology* (2nd ed.). New York: Plenum.

Sturmey, P., & Sevin, J. (1993). Dual diagnosis: An annotated bibliography of recent research. *J. Intell. Dis. Res., 37*(5), 437–48.

Sturt, E. (1986). Application of survival analysis to the inception of dementia. *Psychol. Med., 16,* 583–93.

Stuss, D. T., Gow, C. A., & Hetherington, C. R. (1992). "No longer Gage": Frontal lobe dysfunction and emotional changes. *J. Cons. Clin. Psychol., 60*(3), 349–59.

Suddath, R. L., Christison, G. W., Torrey, E. F., Casanova, M. F., & Weinberger, D. R. (1990). Anatomical abnormalities in the brains of monozygotic twins discordant for schizophrenia. *New Engl. J. Med., 322,* 789–94.

Sue, D., & Sue, S. (1987). Cultural factors in the clinical assessment of Asian Americans. *J. Cons. Clin. Psychol., 55,* 479–87.

Sue, S., Fujino, D. C., Hu, L., Takeuchi, D. T., & Zane, N. W. S. (1991) Community mental health services for ethnic minority groups: A test of the cultural responsiveness hypothesis. *J. Cons. Clin. Psychol., 59,* 533–40.

Sue, S., Zane, N., & Young, K. (1994). Research on psychotherapy with culturally diverse populations. In A. E. Bergin & S. L. Garfield (Eds.), *Handbook of psychotherapy and behavior change.* (pp. 783–820) New York: Wiley.

Suedfeld, P., & Landon, P. B. (1978). Approaches to treatment. In R. D. Hare & D. Schalling (Eds.), *Psychopathic behavior: Approaches to research.* (pp. 347–76). New York: Wiley.

Sulkunen, P. (1976). Drinking patterns and the level of alcohol consumption: An international overview. In R. I. Gibbons et al. (Eds.), *Research advances in alcohol and drug problems* (Vol. 3). New York: Wiley.

Sullivan, H. S. (1953). In H. S. Perry & M. L. Gawel (Eds.), *The interpersonal theory of psychiatry.* New York: Norton.

Sultzer, D. L., Levin, H. S., Mahler, M. E., High, W. M., & Cummings, J. L. (1993). A comparison of psychiatric symptoms in vascular dementia and Alzheimer's disease. *Amer. J. Psychiat., 150*(12), 1806–12.

Summerfelt, L., Huta, V., & Swinson, R. (1998). In R. Swinson, M. Antony, S. Rachman, & M. Richter (Eds.), *Obsessive-compulsive disorder: Theory, research, and treatment.* (pp. 79–119). New York: Guilford.

Summers, F. (1979). Characteristics of new patient admissions to aftercare. *Hosp. Comm. Psychiat., 30*(3), 199–202.

Sundberg, N. D., & Tyler, L. E. (1962). *Clinical psychology.* New York: Appleton-Century-Crofts.

Surwit, R. S., Shapiro, D., & Good, M. L. (1978). Comparison of cardiovascular biofeedback, neuromuscular biofeedback, and meditation in the treatment of borderline essential hypertension. *J. Cons. Clin. Psychol., 46,* 252–53.

Susser, E., Moore, R., & Link, B. (1993). Risk factors for homelessness. *Amer. J. Epidemiol., 15,* 546–66.

Suter, B. (1976). Suicide and women. In B. B. Wolman & H. H. Krauss (Eds.), *Between survival and suicide.* (pp. 129–61). New York: Gardner.

Sutker, P. B. & Allain, A. N. (1995). Psychological assessment of aviators captured in World War II. *Psychol. Assess., 7,* 66–68.

Sutker, P. B., Allain, A. N., Johnson, J. J., & Butters, N. M. (1992). Memory and learning performances in POW survivors with history of malnutrition and combat veteran controls. *Archives of Clinical Neuropsychology, 7,* 431–44.

Sutker, P. B., Archer, R. P., & Kilpatrick, D. G. (1979). Sociopathy and antisocial behavior: Theory and treatment. In S. M. Turner, K. S. Calhoun, & H. E.

Adams (Eds.), *Handbook of clinical behavior therapy.* New York: Wiley.

Sutker, P. B., Bugg, F., & West, J. A. (1993). Antisocial personality disorder. In P. B. Sutker & H. E. Adams (Eds.), *Comprehensive handbook of psychopathology* (2nd ed.). New York: Plenum.

Sutker, P. B., Galina, H., & West, J. A. (1990). Trauma-induced weight loss and cognitive deficits among former prisoners of war. *J. Cons. Clin. Psychol., 58,* 323–28.

Sutker, P. B., Uddo, M., Brailey, K., Vasterling, J. J., & Errera, P. (1994). Psychopathology in warzone deployed and non-deployed Operation Desert Storm troops assigned to graves registration duties. *J. Abn. Psychol., 103,* 383–90.

Sutker, P. B., Vasterling, J. J., Brailey, K., Allain, A. N., et al. (1995). Memory, attention, and executive deficits of POW survivors: Contributing biological and psychological factors. *Neuropsychology, 9,* 118–25.

Svanum, S., & Schladenhauffen, J. (1986). Lifetime and recent alcohol consumption among male alcoholics. *J. Nerv. Ment. Dis., 174*(4), 214–20.

Sverd, J., Sheth, R., Fuss, J., & Levine, J. (1995). Prevalence of pervasive developmental disorder in a sample of psychiatrically hospitalized children and adolescents. *Child Psychiat. Human Devel., 25*(4), 221–40.

Swadi, H., & Zeitlin, H. (1988). Peer influence and adolescent substance abuse: A promising side? *Brit. J. Addiction, 83*(2), 153–57.

Swain, R. A., Armstrong, K. E., Comery, T. A., Humphreys, A. G., Jones, T. A., Klein, J. A., & Greenough, W. T. (1995). Speculations on the fidelity of memories stored in synaptic connections. In D. Schactern (Ed.), *Memory distortions: How minds, brains, and societies reconstruct the past.* (pp. 274–297). Cambridge: Harvard University Press.

Swann, W. B., Jr. (1996). *Self-Traps.* New York: W. H. Freeman.

Swann, W. B., Jr. (1997). The trouble with change: Self-verification and allegiance to the self. *Psychol. Sci. 8*(3), 177–80.

Swanson, D. W., Bohnert, P. J., & Smith, J. A. (1970). *The paranoid.* Boston: Little, Brown.

Swedo, S. E., Pietrini, P., Leonard, H. L., Schapiro, M. B., Rettew, D. C., Goldberger, E., Rapoport, S., Rapoport, J., & Grady, C. (1992). Cerebral glucose metabolism in childhood-onset obsessive-compulsive disorder. *Arch. Gen. Psychiat., 49,* 690–4.

Swedo, S. E., Rapoport, J. L., Leonard, H., Lenane, M., & Cheslow, D. (1989). Obsessive-compulsive disorder in children and adolescents: Clinical phenomenology of 70 consecutive cases. *Arch. Gen. Psychiat., 46,* 335–41.

Sweeney, J. A., Clementz, B. A., Haas, G. L., Escobar, M. D., Drake, K., & Frances, A. J. (1994). Eye tracking dysfunction in schizophrenia: Characterization of component eye movement abnormalities, diagnostic specificity, and the role of attention. *J. Abn. Psychol., 103*(2), 222–30.

Sweeney, P. D., Anderson, K., & Bailey, S. (1986). Attributional style in depression: A meta-analytic review. *J. Pers. Soc. Psychol., 50,* 974–91.

Sweet, W. H. & Meyerson, B. A. (1990). Neurosurgical aspects of primary affective disorders. In J. R. Youmans (Ed.), *Neurological surgery.* (pp. 335). Philadelphia: Saunders.

Swendsen, J., Hammen, C., Heller, T., Gitlin, M. (1995). Correlates of stress reactivity in patients with bipolar disorder. *Amer. J. Psychiat., 152*(5), 795–97.

Swenson, C. C., Powell, P., Foster, K. Y. & Saylor, C. E. (1991). *The long-term reactions of young children to natural disaster.* Paper presented at the annual convention of the American Psychological Association, San Francisco.

Swenson, C. R., & Wood, M. J. (1990). Issues involved in combining drugs with psychotherapy for the borderline patient. *Psychiat. Clin. N. Amer. 13,* 297–306.

Switzky, H. N. (1997). Mental retardation and the neglected construct of motivation. *Education & Training in Mental Retardation & Developmental Disabilities, 32*(3), 194–200.

Sylvain, C., Ladouceur, R., & Boisvert, J. M. (1997). Cognitive and behavioral treatment of pathological gambling: A controlled study. *J. Cons. Clin. Psychol., 65*(5), 727–32.

Symonds, M. (1976). The rape victim. Psychological patterns of response. *Amer. J. Psychoanal., 36*(1), 27–34.

Symons, D. (1979). *The evolution of human sexuality.* New York: Oxford University Press.

Szapocznik, J., Perez-Vidal, A., Brickman, A. L., Foote, F. H., Santisteban, D., Hervis, O., & Kurtines, W. M. (1988). Engaging adolescent drug abusers and their families in treatment: A strategic structural systems approach. *J. Cons. Clin. Psychol., 56,* 552–57.

Szasz, T. (1974). *The myth of mental illness* (rev. ed.). (pp. 17–80). New York: Harper & Row.

Szmukler, G. I., & Russell, G. F. M. (1986). Outcome and prognosis of anorexia nervosa. In K. D. Brownell & J. P. Foreyt (Eds.), *Handbook of eating disorders* (pp. 283–300). New York: Basic Books.

Tacke, U. (1990). Fluoxetine: An alternative to the tricyclics in the treatment of major depression. *Amer. J. Med. Sci., 298,* 126–29.

Takei, N., et al. (1997). Prenatal exposure to influenza and increased cerebrospinal fluid spaces in schizophrenia. *Schizo. Bull., 22*(3), 521–34.

Takei, N., Sham, P., O'Callaghan, E., Murray, G. K., Glover, G., & Murray, R. M. (1994). Prenatal exposure to influenza and the development of schizophrenia: Is the effect confined to females? *Amer. J. Psychiat., 151*(1), 117–19.

Takeshita, T. K., Morimoto, X., Mao, Q., Hashimoto, T., & Furyuama, J. (1993). Phenotypic differences in low Km Aldehyde de hydrogenase in Japanese workers. *Lancet, 341,* 837–38.

Talamini, J. T. (1982). *Boys will be girls: The hidden world of the heterosexual male transvestite.* Washington, DC: University Press of America.

Talbott, J. A. (1985). Community care for the chronically mentally ill. *Psychiat. Clin. N. Amer., 8,* 437–48.

Talley, P. F., Strupp, H. H., & Morey, L. C. (1990). Matchmaking in psychotherapy: Patient-therapist dimensions and their impact on outcome. *J. Cons. Clin. Psychol., 58,* 182–88.

Tallis, F. (1997). The neuropsychology of obsessive-compulsive disorder: A review and consideration of clinical implications. *Brit. J. Clin. Psychol., 36,* 3–20.

Tardiff, K. (1998). Unusual diagnoses among violent patients. *Psychiat. Clin. N. Amer., 21*(3), 567–76.

Tardiff, K., Marzuk, P. M., Leon, A. C., Hirsch, C. S., Stajic, M., Portera, L., & Hartwell, N. (1994). Homicide in New York City: Cocaine use and firearms. *JAMA, 272,* 43–46.

Tarjan, G., & Eisenberg, L. (1972). Some thought on the classification of mental retardation in the United States of America. *Amer. J. Psychiat., Suppl., 128*(11), 14–18.

Tarler-Beniolo, L. (1978). The role of relaxation in biofeedback training: A critical review of the literature. *Psychol. Bull., 85*(4), 727–55.

Tarrier, M., & Barrowclough, C. (1990) Family interventions for schizophrenia. *Behav. Mod., 14,* 408–40.

Tarter, R. E. (1988). Are there inherited behavioral traits that predispose to substance abuse? *J. Cons. Clin. Psychol., 56,* 189–196.

Tasto, D. L., & Hinkle, J. E. (1973). Muscle relaxation treatment for tension headaches. *Behav. Res. Ther., 11,* 347–50.

Tate, D. C., Reppucci, N. D., & Mulvey, E. P. (1995). Violent juvenile delinquents: Treatment effectiveness and implications for future action. *Amer. Psychol., 50,* 777–81.

Tatem, D. W., & DelCampo, R. L. (1995). Selective mutism in children: A structural family therapy approach to treatment. *Contemporary Family Therapy: An International Journal, 17*(2), 177–94.

Tavel, M. E. (1962). A new look at an old syndrome: Delirium tremens. *Arch. Int. Med., 109,* 129–34.

Taves, I. (1969). Is there a sleepwalker in the house? *Today's Health, 47*(5), 41, 76.

Taylor, A. J. W. (1989). *Disasters and disaster stress.* New York: AMS Press.

Taylor, C., & Meux, C. (1997). Individual cases: The risk, the challenge. *Int. Rev. Psychiat., 9*(2), 285–302.

Taylor, H. G., & Alden, J. (1997). Age-related differences in outcomes following childhood brain insults: An introduction and overview. *J. Int. Neuropsychologic. Soc., 3*(6), 555–67.

Taylor, S. (1995). Anxiety Sensitivity: Theoretical perspectives and recent findings. *Behav. Res. Ther., 33*(3), 243–58.

Taylor, S. (1996). Meta-analysis of cognitive-behavioral treatments for social phobia. *J. Behav. Ther. Exp. Psychiat., 27*(1), 1–9.

Taylor, S. E., & Brown, J. (1988). Illusion and well-being: A social psychological perspective on mental health. *Psychol. Bull., 103,* 193–210.

Teasdale, J. (1988). Cognitive vulnerability to persistent depression. *Cognition and Emotion, 2,* 247–74.

Teasdale, J. D. (1996). Clinically relevant therapy: Integrating clinical insight with cognitive science. In P. M. Salkovskis (Ed.), *Frontiers of cognitive therapy.* (pp. 26–47). New York: Guilford.

Teicher, M. H., Glod, C. A., Magnus, E., Harper, D., Benson, G., Krueger, K., & McGreenery, C. E. (1997). Circadian rest-activity disturbances in seasonal affective disorder. *Arch. Gen. Psychiat., 54,* 124–30.

Telch, M. (1995, July). *Singular and combined efficacy of in vivo exposure and CBT in the treatment of panic disorder with agoraphobia.* Paper presented at the World Congress of Behavioural and Cognitive Therapies, Copenhagen, Denmark.

Telch, M. J. (1981). The present status of outcome studies: A reply to Frank. *J. Cons. Clin. Psychol., 49*(3), 472–75.

Telch, M. J., Alpbanalp, B., Harrington, P., Owen, C., & Hattiengadi, N. (1997). *Can reduction in anxiety sensitivity reduce vulnerability to panic attacks?* Unpublished manuscript.

Telch, M. J., Lucas, J. A., Schmidt, N. B., Hanna, H. H., Jaimez, T. L., & Lucas, R. (1993). Group cognitive-behavioral treatment of panic disorder. *Behav. Res. Ther., 31,* 279–87.

Telch, M. J., Schmidt, N. B., LaNae Jaimez, T., Jacquin, K. M., & Harrington, P. J. (1995). Impact of cognitive-behavioral treatment on quality of life in panic disorder patients. *J. Cons. Clin. Psychol., 63*(5), 823–30.

Tellegen, A. (1985). Structures of mood and personality and their relevance to assessing anxiety, with an emphasis on self-report. In A. H. Tuma & J. Maser (Eds.), *Anxiety and the anxiety disorders.* Hillsdale, NJ: Erlbaum.

Tennen, H., & Affleck, G. (1987). The costs and benefits of optimistic explanations and dispositional optimism. *J. Pers., 55,* 377–93.

Teri, L., et al. (1997). Behavioral treatment of depression in dementia patients: A controlled clinical trial. *J. Gerontol.,* Series B, 52B, P159–P166.

Teri, L., & Wagner, A. (1992). Alzheimer's disease and depression. *J. Cons. Clin. Psychol., 60*(3), 379–91.

Thacher, M. (1978, Apr.). First steps for the retarded. *Human Behav.*

Thackwray, D. E., Smith, M. C., Bodfish, J. W., & Meyers, A. W. (1993). A comparison of behavioral and cognitive-behavioral interventions for bulimia nervosa. *J. Cons. Clin. Psych., 61*(4), 639–45.

Thapar, A., & McGuffin, P. (1996). The genetic etiology of childhood depressive symptoms: A developmental perspective. *Develop. Psychopath., 8*(4), 751–60.

Tharp, R. G. (1991) Cultural diversity and treatment of children. *J Cons. Clin. Psychol., 59,* 799–812.

Thase, M. E., Frank, E., & Kupfer, D. J. (1985). Biological processes in major depression. In E. E. Beckham & W. R. Leber (Eds.), *Handbook of depression: Treatment, assessment, and research.* (pp. 816–913). Homewood, IL: Dorsey Press.

Thase, M. E., & Howland, R. H. (1995). Biological Processes in depression: An updated review and integration. In E. E. Beckham & W. R. Leber (Eds.), *Handbook of depression* (2nd ed.). (pp. 213–279). New York: Guilford.

Thase, M. E., Simons, A. D., Cahalane, J. F., & McGeary, J. (1991). Cognitive behavior therapy of endoge-nous depression: Part 1: An outpatient clinical replication series. *Behav. Ther., 22,* 457–68.

Theodor, L. H., & Mandelcorn, M. S. (1973). Hysterical blindness: A case report and study using a modern psychophysical technique. *J. Abn. Psychol., 82*(3), 552–53.

Thibaut, J. W., & Kelley, H. H. (1959). *The social psychology of groups.* New York: Wiley.

Thomas, J. D. & Riley, E. P. (1998). Fetal alcohol syndrome: Does alcohol withdrawal play a role?, *Alcohol World: Health and Research, 22* (1), 47–53.

Thompson-Pope, S. K., & Turkat, I. D. (1993). Schizotypal, schizoid, paranoid, and avoidant personality disorders. In P. B. Sutker & H. E. Adams (Eds.), *Comprehensive handbook of psychopathology* (2nd ed.). New York: Plenum.

Thomsen, P. H. (1998). Obsessive-compulsive disorder in children and adolescents: Clinical guidelines. *Eur. Chid Adoles. Psychiat., 7*(1), 1–11.

Thoreson, C. E., & Powell, L. H. (1992). Type A behavior pattern: New perspectives on theory, assessment, and intervention. *J. Cons. Clin. Psychol., 60*(4), 595–604.

Tiefer, L., & Melman, A. (1989). Comprehensive evaluation of erectile dysfunction and medical treatments. In S. R. Leiblum & R. C. Rosen (Eds.), *Principles and practice of sex therapy* (2nd ed.). (pp. 207–36). New York: Guilford.

Tien, A. Y., & Anthony, J. C. (1990). Epidemiological analysis of alcohol and drug use as risk factors for psychotic experiences. *J. Nerv. Ment. Dis., 178,* 473–80.

Tien, A. Y., & Eaton, W. W. (1992). Psychopathologic precursors and sociodemographic risk factors for the schizophrenia syndrome. *Archi. Gen. Psychiat., 49*(1), 37–46.

Tienari, P. (1991). Interaction between genetic vulnerability and family environment: The Finnish adoptive family study of schizophrenia. *Acta Psychiatr. Scandin., 84,* 460–65.

Tienari, P. (1994). The Finnish adoption study of schizophrenia. Implications for family research. *Brit. J. Psychiat., 164,* 20–26.

Tienari, P., Lahti, I., Sorri, A., Naarala, M., Moring, J., Wahlberg, K.-E., & Wynne, L. C. (1987). The Finnish adoptive family study of schizophrenia. *J. Psychiat. Res., 21,* 437–45.

Tienari, P., Sorri, A., Lahti, I., Naarala, M., Wahlberg, K.-E., Pohjola, J., & Moring, J. (1985). Interaction of genetic and psychosocial factors in schizophrenia. *Acta Psychiatr. Scandin.* (Suppl. No. 319), *71,* 19–30.

Tillman, J. G., Nash, M. R., & Lerner, P. M. (1994). Does trauma cause dissociative pathology? In S. J. Lynn & J. W. Rhue (Eds.), *Dissociation: Clinical and theoretical perspectives.* (pp. 395–414). New York: Guilford.

Timbrook, R. E, & Graham, J. R. (1994). Ethnic differences on the MMPI-2? *Psychol. Assess., 6,* 212–17.

Time. (1966, June 17). From shocks to stop sneezes, p. 72.

Time. (1974, Apr. 22). Alcoholism: New victims, new treatment, pp. 75–81.

Time. (1983, Apr. 18). Ailing schoolgirls. p. 52.

Tinius, T., & Ben-Porath, Y. S. *A comparative study of Native American and Caucasian Americans undergoing substance abuse treatment.* Paper presented at the annual meeting on Recent Developments in the Use of the MMPI-2, St. Petersburg, FL.

Tinker, J. E., & Tucker, J. A. (1997). Motivations for weight loss and behavior change strategies associated with natural recovery from obesity. *Psychology of Addictive Behaviors, 11,* 98–106.

Tizard, B. & Hodges, J. (1978). The effect of early institutional rearing on the development of eight-year-old children. *J. Child Psychol. Psychiat., 19,* 99–118.

Tizard, J. (1975). Race and IQ: The limits of probability. *New Behaviour, 1,* 6–9.

Tobler, N. S. (1986). Meta-analysis of 143 adolescent drug prevention programs: Quantitative outcome results of program participation compared to a control or comparison group. *Journal of Drug Issues, 16,* 537–68.

Tollefson, G. D., et al. (1997). Olanzapine versus haloperidol in the treatment of schizophrenia and schizoaffective and schizophreniform disorders: Results of an international collaborative trial. *Amer. J. Psychiat., 154*(4), 457–65.

Tollison, C. D., & Adams, H. E. (1979). *Sexual disorders.* New York: Gardner Press.

Tomarken, A., Sutton, S., & Mineka, S. (1995). Dear-relevant illusory correlations: What types of associative linkages promote judgmental bias? *J. Abn. Psychol., 104,* 312–26.

Tomarken, A. J., Mineka, S., & Cook, M. (1989). Fear-relevant selective associations and covariation bias. *J. Abn. Psychol., 98,* 381–94.

Tomarken, A. J., Simien, C., & Garber, J. (1994). Resting frontal brain asymmetry discriminates adolescent children of depressed mothers from low-risk controls. *Psychophysiology, 31,* 97–98.

Tomes, N. (1994). Feminist histories of psychiatry. In M. Micale & R. Porter (Eds.), *Discovering the history of psychiatry.* (pp. 348–383). New York: Oxford University Press.

Tonigan, J. S., Toscova, R., & Miller, W. R. (1995). Meta-analysis of the literature on Alcoholics Anonymous. *J. Stud. Alcoh., 57*(1), 65–72.

Took, K. J., & Buck, B. L. (1996). Enuresis with combined risperidone and SSRI use. *J. Acad. of Child Adoles. Psychiat. 35*(7), 840–41.

Toomey, R., et al. (1997). Revisiting the factor structure for positive and negative symptoms: Evidence from a large heterogeneous group of psychiatric patients. *Amer. J. Psychiat., 154*(3), 371–77.

Torgersen, S. (1983). Genetic factors in anxiety disorders. *Arch. Gen. Psychiat., 40,* 1085–89.

Torgersen, S. (1993). Genetics. In A. S. Bellack & M. Hersen (Eds.), *Psychopathology in adulthood.* Needham Heights, MA: Allyn and Bacon.

Torgerson, S. (1984). Genetic and nosological aspects of schizotypal and borderline personality disorders. *Arch. Gen. Psychiat., 41,* 546–54.

Torrey, E. F. (1973). Is schizophrenia universal? An open question. *Schizo. Bull, 7,* 53–59.

Torrey, E. F. (1979). Epidemiology. In L. Bellak (Ed.), *Disorders of the schizophrenic syndrome.* New York: Basic Books.

Torrey, E. F. (1987). Prevalence studies in schizophrenia. *Brit. J. Psychiat., 150,* 598–608.

Torrey, E. F. (1997). *Out of the shadows: Confronting America's mental illness crisis.* New York: Wiley.

Torrey, E. F., Bower, A. E., Taylor, E. H., & Gottesman, I. I. (1994). *Schizophrenia and manic-depressive disorder: The biological roots of mental illness as revealed by the landmark study of identical twins.* New York: Basic Books.

Torrey, E. F., Bowler, A. E., Rawlings, R., & Terrazas, A. (1993). Seasonality of schizophrenia and stillbirths. *Schizo. Bull., 19*(3), 557–62.

Toth, S. L. & Cicchetti, D. (1996). Patterns of relatedness, depressive symptomatology, and perceived competence in maltreated children. *J. Cons. Clin. Psychol., 64*(1), 32–41.

Toth, S. L., Manly, J. T., & Cicchetti, D. (1992). Child maltreatment and vulnerability to depression. *Develop. Psychopath., 4,* 97–112.

Tower, R. B., Kasl, S. V., & Moritz, D. J. (1997). The influence of spouse cognitive impairment on respondents' depressive symptoms: The moderating role of marital closeness. *J. Gerontol.,* Series B, 52B(5), S270–S278.

Townsend, J., Harris, N. S., & Courchesne, E. (1996). Visual attention abnormalities in autism: Delayed orienting to location. *J. Int. Neuropsycholog. Assoc., 2,* 541–50.

Townsley, R., Turner, S., Beidel, D., & Calhoun, K. (1995). Social phobia: An analysis of possible developmental factors. *J. Abn. Psychol., 104,* 526–31.

Townsley, R. M. (1992). Social phobia: Identification of possible etiological factors. University of Georgia, unpublished doctoral dissertation.

Trasler, G. (1978). Relations between psychopathy and persistent criminality-methodological and theoretical issues. In R. D. Hare & D. Schalling (Eds.), *Psychopathic behavior: Approaches to research.* New York: Wiley.

Travis, J. (1996). Visualizing vision in dyslexic brains. *Sci. News, 149,* 105.

Tremble, J., Padillo, A., & Bell, C. (1994). *Drug abuse among ethnic minorities, 1987:* Washington, DC: U.S. Department of Health and Human Services.

Trickett, P. K., & Putnam, F. W. (1993). Impact of child sexual abuse on females: Toward a developmental, psychobiological integration. *Psychological Science, 4*(2), 81–87.

Trinder, H., & Salkovskis (1994). Personally relevant intrusions outside the laboratory: Long-term suppression increases intrusion. *Behav. Res. Ther., 32*(8), 833–42.

Triplett, F. (1986, July 21). The madman on the ferry; released from a hospital, a mental patient kills two people. *Time,* p. 28.

Tripp, C. A. (1975). *The homosexual matrix.* New York: McGraw-Hill.

Trivedi, M. H. (1996). Functional neuroanatomy of obsessive-compulsive disorder. *J. Clin. Psychiat., 57*(8), 26–36.

Tronick, E. Z., & Cohn, J. F. (1989). Infant-mother face-to-face interaction: Age and gender differences in coordination and miscoordination. *Child Develop., 59,* 85–92.

Trull, T. J., Widiger, T. A., & Frances, A. (1987). Covariation of criteria sets for avoidant, schizoid, and dependent personality disorders. *Amer. J. Psychiat., 144,* 767–71.

Tryer, P. (1995). Are personality disorders well classified in DSM-IV. In W. J. Livesley (Ed.), *The DSM-IV personality disorders.* (pp. 29–42). New York: Guilford.

Tsai, L. Y., & Ghaziuddin, M. (1992). Biomedical research in autism. In D. M. Berkell (Ed.), *Autism.* (pp. 53–76). Hillsdale: Erlbaum.

Tseng, W. S. (1973). The development of psychiatric concepts in traditional Chinese medicine. *Arch. Gen. Psychiat., 29*(4), 569–75.

Tseng, W., Asai, M., Kitanishi, K., McLaughlin, D. G., & Kyomen, H. (1992). Diagnostic patterns of social phobia: Comparison in Tokyo and Hawaii. *J. Nerv. Ment. Dis., 180,* 380–5.

Tucker, J. S., Friedman, H. S., Schwartz, J. E., Criqui, M. H., Tomlinson-Keasey, C., & Wingard, D. L. (1997). Parental divorce: Effects on individual behavior and longevity. *J. Pers. Soc. Psychol., 73*(2), 381–91.

Tuckman, J., Kleiner, R., & Lavell, M. (1959). Emotional content of suicide notes. *Amer. J. Psychiat.* 116, 59–63.

Tulving, E. (1993). What is episodic memory? *Curr. Dir. Psychol. Sci., 2*(3), 67–70.

Turk, D., Meichenbaum, D., & Genest, M. (1983). *Pain and behavioral medicine: A cognitive-behavioral perspective.* New York: Plenum.

Turkheimer, E. (1991). Individual and group differences in adoption studies of IQ. *Psychol. Bull., 110*(3), 392–405.

Turner, S. M., Beidel, D. C., & Costello, A. (1987). Psychopathology in the offspring of anxiety disorder patients. *J. Cons. Clin. Psychol., 55,* 229–35.

Turner, S. M., Beidel, D. C., & Townsley, R. M. (1992). Social phobia: A comparison of specific and generalized subtypes and avoidant personality disorder, *J. Abn. Psychol., 101,* 326–31.

Tyor, P. L., & Bell, L. V. (1984). *Caring for the retarded in America: A history.* Westport, CT: Greenwood Press.

Tyrer, P. (1988). What's wrong with DSM III personality disorders? *J. Personal. Dis., 2,* 281–91.

Tyrka, A. R., Cannon, T. D., Haslam, N., Mednick, S. A., Schulsinger, F., Schulsinger, H., & Parnas, J. (1995). The latent structure of schizotypy: I. Premorbid indicators of a taxon of individuals at risk for schizophrenia-spectrum disorders. *J. Abn. Psychol., 104*(1), 173–183.

U.S. Bureau of the Census (1989). *Statistical abstract of the United States* (109th ed.), Washington DC: Author.

U.S. Bureau of the Census (1992) *Marital status and living arrangements: March 1992* (No. 468, Tables G & 5, Current population reports, Series P-20). Washington: Government Printing Office.

U.S. Bureau of the Census. (1995). *Statistical abstract of the United States 1995.* Washington: Author.

U.S. Department of Health and Human Services. (1988). *The Health Consequences of Smoking: Nicotine addiction.* Public Health Service, Office on Smoking and Health, Maryland.

U.S. Department of Health and Human Services. (1989). *Reducing the Consequences of Smoking: 25 years of Progress.* Public Health Service, Office on Smoking and Health, Maryland.

U.S. Department of Labor. (1999). *Current statistics on unemployment* Washington: Government Printing Office.

Uchida, I. A. (1973). Paternal origin of the extra chromosome in Down's syndrome. *Lancet, 2*(7840), 1258.

Udry, J. R. (1993). The politics of sex research. *J. Sex Res., 30,* 103–10.

Uecker, A., Mangan, P. A., Obrzut, J. E., & Nadel, L. (1993). Down syndrome in neurobiological perspective: An emphasis on spatial cognition. *J. Clin. Child Psychol., 22*(2), 266–76.

Uhde, T. W. (1990). Caffeine provocation of panic: A focus on biological mechanisms. In J. C. Ballenger (Ed.), *Neurobiology of panic disorder.* (pp. 219–242). New York: Wiley-Liss.

Ullmann, L. P., & Krasner, L. (1975). *Psychological approach to abnormal behavior* (2nd ed.). Englewood Cliffs, NJ: PrenticeHall.

Umana, R. F., Gross, S. J., & McConville, M. T. (1980). *Crisis in the family.* New York: Gardner Press.

Umbricht, D., & Kane, J. M. (1997). Medical complications of new antipsychotic drugs. *Schizo. Bull., 22*(3), 475–83.

Uniform Crime Reports, (1989). *Federal Bureau of Investigation.* Washington, DC: U.S. Government Printing Office.

Uniform Crime Reports. (1992). *Federal Bureau of Investigation.* Washington, DC: U.S. Government Printing Office.

United Press International. (1982, Oct. 24). "Tylenol hysteria" hits 200 at football game. *Chicago Tribune,* Sec. 1, p. 1, p. 4.

Ursano, R. J., Boydstun, J. A., & Wheatley, R. D. (1981). Psychiatric illness in U.S. Air Force Vietnam prisoners of war: A five-year follow-up. *Amer. J. Psychiat., 138*(3), 310–14.

USDHHS. (1981). Surgeon General's Advisory on alcohol and pregnancy. *FDA Drug Bulletin,* 11, 9–10.

USDHHS. (1994). Preventing tobacco use among young people: A report of the Surgeon General. *U.S. Department of Health and Human Services.*

Uva, J. L. (1995). Autoerotic asphyxiation in the United States. *Journal of Forensic Sciences, 40,* 574–81.

Vaillant, G. E. (1975). Sociopathy as a human process: A viewpoint. *Arch. Gen. Psychiat., 32*(2), 178–83.

Vaillant, G. E. (1978). The distinction between prognosis and diagn osis in schizophrenia: A discussion of Manfred Bleuler's paper. In L. C. Wynne, R. L. Cromwell, & S. Matthysse (Eds.), *The nature of schizophrenia: New approaches to research and treatment.* (pp. 637–40). New York: Wiley.

Vailliant, G. E. (1983). Natural history of male alcoholism V: Is alcoholism the cart or the horse to sociopathy? *Brit. J. Addict., 711,* 317–26.

Vailliant, G. E. (1987). A developmental view of old and new perspectives of personality disorders. *J. Personal. Dis., 1,* 146–56.

Vaillant, G. E., & Milofsky, E. S. (1991). The etiology of alcoholism: A prospective viewpoint. In D. J. Pittman, H. R. White, et al. (Eds.), *Society, culture, and drinking patterns reexamined.* (pp. 492–512). New Brunswick, NJ: Rutgers Center of Alcohol Studies.

Vaillant, G. E., & Schnurr, P. (1988). What is a case? *Arch. Gen. Psychiat., 45,* 313–19.

Valenstein, E. S. (1986). *Great and desperate cures.* New York: Basic Books.

Valenstein, E. S. (Ed.).(1980). *The psychosurgery debate: Scientific, legal, and ethical perspectives.* San Francisco: Freeman.

Valentiner, D. B., Foa, E. B., Riggs, D. S., & Gershuny, B. S. (1996). Coping strategies and posttraumatic stress disorder in female victims of sexual and nonsexual assault. *J. Abn. Psychol., 105*(3), 455–58.

Vallacher, R. R., Wegner, D. M., & Hoine, H. (1980). A postscript on application. In D. Megner & R. R. Val-

lacher (Eds.), *The self in social psychology.* New York: Oxford University Press.

Valleni-Basile, L. A., Garrison, C. Z., Jackson, K. I., Waller, J. L., McKeown, R. E., Addy, C. I., & Cuffe, S. P. (1994). Frequency of obsessive-compulsive disorder in a community sample of young adolescents. *J. Amer. Acad. Child Adoles. Psychiat., 33,* 782–91.

Van Broeckhoven, C., Genthe, A. M., Vandenberghe, A., Horsthemke, B., et al. (1987). Failure of familial Alzheimer's disease to segregate with the A4-amyloid gene in several European families. *Nature, 329,* 153–55.

van den Boom, D. C. (1989) Neonatal irritability and the development of attachment. In G. A. Kohnstamm, J. E. Bates, and M. K. Rothbart (Eds.) *Temperament in childhood.* (pp.229–318). Chichester, England: Wiley.

VandenBos, G. R. (1986). Psychotherapy research: A special issue. *Amer. Psychol., 41,* 111–12.

VandenBos, G. R. (1993). U. S. Mental Health Policy: Proactive evolution in the midst of health care reform. *Amer. Psychol., 48*(3), 283–90.

van den Hout, M. A. (1988). The explanation of experimental panic. In S. Rachman, & J. D. Maser (Eds.), *Panic: Psychological perspectives.* Hillsdale, NJ: Erlbaum.

Vandereycken, W.(1982). Paradoxical strategies in a blocked sex therapy. *Amer. J. Psychother., 36,* 103–8.

van der Kolk, B. A. (1987). *Psychological trauma.* Washington, DC: American Psychological Association Press.

Van der Kolk, B. A., & Saporta, J. (1993). Biological responses to psychic trauma. In J. P. Wilson, B. Raphael et al., *International handbook of traumatic stress syndromes.* (pp. 25–33). New York: Plenum.

Van Der Sande, R., Van Rooijen, L., Buskens, E., Allart, E., Hawton, K., VanDer Graaf, Y., & Van Engeland, H. V. (1997). Intensive in-patient and community intervention versus routine care after attempted suicide. *Brit. J. Psychiat., 171,* 35–41.

Van Ree, J. M. (1996). Endorphins and experimental addiction. *Alcohol, 13*(1), 25–30.

Van Velzen, C. J. M., & Emmelkamp, P. M. G. (1996). The assessment of personality disorders: Implications for cognitive and behavior therapy. *Behav. Res. Ther., 34*(8), 655–668.

Vargas, M. A., & Davidson, J. (1993). Posttraumatic stress disorder. *Psychiat. Clin. N. Amer., 16,* 737–48.

Vasiljeva, O. A., Kornetov, N. A., Zhankov, A. I., & Reshetnikov, V. I. (1989). Immune function in psychogenic depression. *Amer. J. Psychiat., 146,* 284–85.

Vasterling, J. J., Seltzer, B., & Watrous, W. (1997). Longitudinal assessment of deficit unawareness in Alzheimer's disease. *Neuropsychiatry, Neuropsychology, & Behavioral Neurology, 10*(3), 197–202.

Vaughn, C. E., & Leff, J. P. (1976). The influence of family and social factors on the course of psychiatric illness: A comparison of schizophrenic and depressed neurotic patients. *Brit. J. Psychiat., 129,* 125–37.

Vaughn, C. E., Snyder, K. S., Jones, S., Freeman, W. B., & Falloon, I. R. H. (1984). Family factors in schizophrenic relapse: Replication in California of British research on expressed emotion. *Arch. Gen. Psychiat., 41,* 1169–77.

Veale, D., Gournay, K., Dryden, W., Boocock, A. et al. (1996) Body dysmorphic disorder: A cognitive behavioral model and pilot randomized control trial. *Behav. Res. & Ther., 34,* 717–29.

Vega, W. A., & Rumbaut, R. G. (1991). Reasons of the heart: Ethnic minorities and mental health. *Annual Review of Sociology, 17.*

Vega, W. A., Zimmerman, R. S., Warheit, G. J., Apospori, E., & Gil, A. G. (1993). Risk factors for early adolescent drug use in four ethnic and racial groups. *Amer. J. Pub. Hlth., 83,* 185–89.

Veith, I. (1977). Four thousand years of hysteria. In M. J. Horowitz (Ed.), *Hysterical personality.* (pp. 7–93). New York: Jason Aronson.

Velasquez, R. J., Gonzales, M., Butcher, J. N., Castillo-Canez, I., Apodace, J. X., & Chavira, D. (1997). Use of the MMPI-2 with Chicanos: Strategies for counselors. *Journal of Multicultural Counseling and Development, 25,* 107–20.

Velez, C. N., & Cohen, P. (1987). Suicidal behavior and ideation in a community sample of children: Maternal and youth reports. *J. Amer. Acad. Child Adoles. Psychiat., 27,* 349–56.

Vellutino, F. R. (1987). Linguistic and cognitive correlates of learning disability: Review of three reviews. In S. J. Ceci (Ed.), *Handbook of cognitive, social and neuropsychological aspects of learning disabilities* (Vol. 1). (pp. 317–35). Hillsdale, NJ: Erlbaum.

Velting, D. M., & Gould, M. S. (1997). Suicide contagion. In R. W. Maris, M. M. Silverman, & S. S. Canetton (Eds.), *Review of Suicidology, 1997.* (pp. 96–137). New York: Guilford.

Verdoux, H., et al. (1997). Obstetric complications and age at onset in schizophrenia: An international collaborative meta-analysis of individual patient data. *Amer. J. Psychiat., 154*(9), 1220–27.

Verhulst, F. C., & Achenbach, T. M. (1995) Empirically based assessment and taxonomy of psychopathology: Cross cultural applications. A review. *Eur. Child Adoles. Psychiat., 4,* 61–76.

Verhulst, F. C., & Koot, H. M. (1992). *Child psychiatric epidemiology: Concepts, methods, and findings.* Beverly Hills, CA: Sage.

Verhulst, J. H., Van Der Lee, J. H., Akkerhuis, G. W., Sanders-Woudstra, J. A. R., Timmer, F. C., & Donkhorst, I. D. (1985). The prevalence of nocturnal enuresis: Do DSM-III criteria need to be changed: A brief research report. *J. Child Psychol. Psychiat., 26*(6), 983–93.

Viets, V. C. L., & Miller, W. R. (1998). Treatment approaches for pathological gamblers. *Clin. Psychol. Rev., 17*(7), 689–702.

Viney, W. (1996). Dorthea Dix: An intellectual conscience for psychology. In G. A. Kimble, C. A. Boneau, & M. Wertheimer (Eds.), *Portraits of pioneers in psychology.* (pp. 15–33). Washington: American Psychological Association.

Viney, W., & Bartsch, K. (1984). Dorthea Lynde Dix: Positive or negative influence on the development of treatment for the mentally ill. *Social Science Journal, 21,* 71–82.

Vinokur, A. D., Price, R. H. & Caplan, R. D. (1996). Hard times and hurtful partners: How financial strain affects depression and relationship satisfaction of unemployed persons and their spouses. *J. Pers. Soc. Psychol., 71,* 166–79.

Vitiello, B. & Jensen, P. S. (1997). Medication development and testing in children and adolescents: Current problems, future directions. *Arch. Gen. Psychiat., 54*(9), 871–76.

Vitousek, K., & Manke, F. (1994). Personality variables and disorders in anorexia and bulimia nervosa. *J. Abn. Psychol., 103*(1), 137–47.

Vogel, E. M., & Vogel, J. M. (1993). Interventions with children after disasters. *J. Clin. Child Psychol., 22,* 485–98.

Vogel, J. M., & Vernberg, E. M. (1993). Children's psychological responses to disaster. *J. Clin. Child Psychol., 22,* 485–98.

Volberg, R. A. (1990). *Estimating the prevalence of pathological gambling in the United States.* Paper presented at the Eighth International Conference on Risk and Gambling. (August).

Volberg, R. A. (1994). The prevalence and demographics of pathological gamblers: Implications for public health. *Amer. J. Pub. Hlth., 84,* 237–41.

Volberg, R. A., & Steadman, H. J. (1989). Prevalence estimates of pathological gambling in New Jersey and Maryland. *Amer. J. Psychiat., 146,* 1618–19.

Volkmar, F. R., Hoder, E. L., & Cohen, D. J. (1985). Compliance, "negativism," and the effects of treatment structure in autism: A naturalistic behavioral study. *J. Child Psychol. Psychiat., 26*(6), 865–77.

Volkow, N. D., Ding, Y. S., Fowler, J. S., Ashby, C., Liebermann, J., Hitzemann, R., & Wolf, A. P. (1995). Is methylphenidate like cocaine? Studies on their pharmacokinetics and distribution in the human brain. *Arch. Gen. Psychiat., 52,* 456–63.

Von Korff, M., Ormel, J., Katon, W., & Lin, E. H. B. (1992). Disability and depression among high utilizers of health care: A longitudinal analysis. *Archi. Gen. Psychiat., 49*(2), 91–100.

Vredenbrug, K., Flett, G. L., & Krames, L. (1993). Analogue versus clinical depression: A critical reappraisal. *Psychol. Bull., 113* (2), 327–44.

Wachtel, E. F. (1994). *Treating troubles children and their families.* New York: Guilford.

Wachtel, P. L. (1977). *Psychoanalysis and behavior therapy: Toward an integration.* New York: Basic Books.

Wachtel, P. L. (1982). What can dynamic therapies contribute to behavior therapy? *Behav. Ther., 13,* 594–609.

Wachtel, P. L. (1987). *Action and insight.* New York: Guilford.

Wachtel, P. L. (1993). *Therapeutic communication: Principles and effective practice.* New York: Guilford.

Wachtel, P. L. (1997). *Psychoanalysis, behavior therapy, and the relational world.* Washington: American Psychological Association.

Wachtel, P. L., & Messer, S. B. (Eds.). (1997). *Theories of psychotherapy: Origins and evolution.* Washington: American Psychological Association.

Wadden, T. A., Foster, G. D., & Letizia, K. A. (1994). One-year behavioral treatment of obesity: Comparison of the moderate and severe caloric restriction and the effects of weight maintenance procedures. *J. Cons. Clin. Psychol., 62,* 165–71.

Wadden, T. A., Luborsky, L., Greer, S., & Crits-Christopher, P. (1985). The behavioral treatment of essential hypertension: An update and comparison with pharamacological treatment. *Clin. Psychol. Rev., 4,* 403–29.

Wagenaar, A. C., & Perry, C. L. (1995). Community strategies for the reduction of youth drinking: Theory and application. In G. M. Boyd, J. Howard, & R. A. Zucker (Eds.), *Alcohol problems among adolescents.* (pp. 197–223). Hillsdale, NJ: Erlbaum.

Wagner, B. M. (1997). Family risk factors for child and adolescent suicidal behavior. *Psychol. Bull., 121*(2), 246–98.

Wagner, G. (1981). Methods for differential diagnosis of psychogenic and organic erectile failure. In G. Wagner & R. Green (Eds.), *Impotence: Physiological, psychological, surgical diagnosis and treatment.* New York: Plenum.

Wagner, G., & Green, R. (Eds.). (1981). *Impotence: Physiological, psychological, surgical diagnosis and treatment.* New York: Plenum.

Wagner, M. T., et al. (1997). Unawareness of cognitive deficit in Alzheimer disease and related dementias. *Alzheimer Disease & Associated Disorders, 11*(3) 125–31.

Wahlberg, K.-E., et al. (1997). Gene-environment interaction in vulnerability to schizophrenia: Findings from the Finnish adoptive family study of schizophrenia. *Amer. J. Psychiat., 154*(3), 355–62.

Wahler, R. G. (1980). The insular mother: Her problems in parent-child treatment. *J. Appl. Beh. Anal., 13,* 207–19.

Wahler, R. G., Hughey, J. B., & Gordon, J. S. (1981). Chronic patterns of mother-child coercion: Some differences between insular and noninsular families. *Analysis and Intervention in Developmental Disorders, 1,* 145–56.

Wakefield, J. C. (1992a). Disorder as harmful dysfunction: a conceptual critique of DSM-III-R's definition of mental disorder. *Psychol. Rev., 99*(2), 232–247.

Wakefield, J. C. (1992b). The concept of mental disorder: On the boundary between biological facts and social values. *Amer. Psychol., 47*(3), 373–388.

Walker, E., Katon, W., Harrop-Griffiths, J., Holm, L., Russo, J., & Hickok, L. R. (1988). Relationship of chronic pelvic pain to psychiatric diagnoses and childhood sexual abuse. *Amer. J. Psychiat., 145,* 75–80.

Walker, E. F., Baum, K. M., & Diforio, D. (1998). Developmental changes in the behavioral expression of vulnerability for schizophrenia. In M. F. Lenzenweger & R. H. Dworkin (Eds.), *Origins and development of schizophrenia.* (pp. 469–92). Washington: American Psychological Association.

Walker, E. F., & Diforio, D. (1997). Schizophrenia: A neural diathesis-stress model. *Psychol. Rev., 104*(4), 667–85.

Walker, E. F., Grimes, K. E., Davis, D. M., & Smith, A. J. (1993). Childhood precursors of schizophrenia: Facial expressions of emotion. *Amer. J. Psychiat., 150*(11), 1654–60.

Walker, E. F., Savoie, T., & Davis, D. (1994). Neuromotor precursors of schizophrenia. *Schizo. Bull., 20*(3), 441–51.

Wallace, J. (1996). Theory of 12 step-oriented treatment. In F. Rotgers, D. S. Keller, et al. (Eds.), *Treating substance abuse: Theory and technique.* (pp. 13–26). New York: Guilford.

Wallace, R. A. (1987). *Biology: The world of life.* Glenview, IL: Scott, Foresman.

Waller, G. (1994). Childhood sexual abuse and borderline personality disorder in the eating disorders. *Child Ab. Negl., 18,* 97–101.

Wallerstein, J. S. (1991). The long-term effects of divorce on children: A review. *J. Amer. Acad. Child Adoles. Psychiat., 30,* 349–60.

Wallerstein, J. S., & Kelly, J. B. (1980). Surviving the breakup: How children and parents cope with divorce. New York: Basic Books.

Wallerstein, R. S. (1989). The psychotherapy research project of the Menninger Foundation: An overview. *J. Cons. Clin. Psychol., 57,* 195–205.

Wallin, A., & Blennow, K. (1993). Heterogeneity of vascular dementia: Mechanisms and subgroups. *Journal of Geriatric Psychiatry and Neurology, 6*(3), 177–88.

Walsh, D. (1969). Mental illness in Dublin: First admissions. *Brit. J. Psychiat., 115,* 449–56.

Walsh, D., O'Hare, A., Blake, B., Halpenny, J. V., & O'Brien, P. F. (1980). The treated prevalence of mental illness in the Republic of Ireland: The three county case register study. *Psychol. Med., 10,* 465–70.

Walsh, J. (1993). The promise and pitfalls of Integrated Strategy Instruction. *J. Learn. Dis., 26*(7), 438–42.

Walsh, T. B. (1980). The endocrinology of anorexia nervosa. *Psychiat. Clin. N. Amer., 3*(2), 299–312.

Walter, A. A., & Carter, A. S. (1997). Gilles de la Tourette's syndrome in childhood: A guide for school professionals. *School Psychol. Rev., 26*(1), 28–46.

Walters, J. A., & Croen, L. G. (1993). An approach to meeting the needs of medical students with learning disabilities. *Teaching and Learning in Medicine, 5*(1), 29–35.

Wampold, B. E., Mondlin, G. W. Moody, M., & Hyunnie, A. (1997). The flat earth as metaphor for evidence of uniform efficacy of bona fide psychotherapies: Reply to Crits-Christoff (1997) and Howard et al. (1997). *Psychol Bull., 122*(3), 226–30.

Ward, N. G. (1991). Psychosocial approaches to pharmacotherapy. In B.D. Beitman & G. Klerman (Eds.). *Integrating pharmacotherapy and psychotherapy.* (pp. 69–104). Washington, DC: American Psychiatric Press.

Warner, R. (1994). Recovery from schizophrenia: Psychiatry and political economy (2nd ed.). New York: Routledge-Kegan Paul.

Warnes, H. (1973). The traumatic syndrome. *Ment. Hlth. Dig., 5*(3), 33–34.

Warren, J. I., Dietz, P. E., & Hazelwood, R. R. (1996). The sexually sadistic serial killer. *Journal of Forensic Sciences, 41,* 970–74.

Warrington, E. K., & Weiskrantz, L. (1973). An analysis of short-term and long-term memory defects in man. In J. A. Deutsch (Ed.), *The psychological basis of memory.* New York: Academic Press.

Warshaw, M. G., Massion, A. O., Peterson, L. G., Pratt, L. A., & Keller, M. B. (1995). Suicidal behavior in patients with panic disorder: Retrospective and prospective data. *J. Affect. Dis., 34,* 235–47.

Wasserman, D. R., & Leventhal, J. M. (1993). Maltreatment of children born to cocaine-dependent mothers. *Archives of Pediatrics and Adolescent Medicine, 147,* 1324–28.

Wasserstein, S. B., & La Greca, A. M. (1996) Can peer support buffer against behavioral consequences of parental discord. *J. Clin. Child. Psychol., 25*(2), 177–82.

Watanabe, H., Kawauchi, A., Kitamori, T., & Azuma, Y. (1994). Treatment system for nocturnal enuresis according to an original classification system. *European Urology, 25,* 43–50.

Waterhouse, L., & Fein, D. (1997). Genes tPA, Fyn, and FAK in autism? *J. Autism Devel. Dis., 27*(3), 220–23.

Watkins, B., & Bentovim, A. (1992). The sexual abuse of male children and adolescents: A review of current research. *J. Child Psychol. Psychiat., 33,* 197–248.

Watson, D., Clark, L. A., Harkness, A. R. (1994). Structures of personality and their relevance to psychopathology. *J. Abn. Psychol., 103,* 18–31.

Watson, D., Clark, L. A., Weber, K., Assenheimer, J. S., Strauss, M. E., & McCormick, R. A. (1995a). Testing a tripartite model: I. Evaluating the convergent and discriminant validity of anxiety and depression symptom scales. *J. Abn. Psychol., 104,* 3–14.

Watson, D., Clark, L. A., Weber, K., Assenheimer, J. S., Strauss, M. E., & McCormick, R. A. (1995b). Testing a tripartite model: II. Exploring the symptom structure of anxiety and depression in student, adult, and patient samples. *J. Abn. Psychol., 104,* 15–25.

Watson, D., & Pennebaker, J. W. (1989). Health complaints, stress, and distress: Exploring the central role of negative affectivity. *Psychol. Rev., 96*(2), 234–54.

Watson, J. (1924). *Behaviorism.* The People's Institute Publishing Co., Inc.

Watt, N. F., Anthony, E. J., Wynne, L. C., & Rolf, J. E. (Eds.). (1984). *Children at risk for schizophrenia: A longitudinal perspective.* Cambridge: Cambridge University Press.

Watten, R. G. (1995). Negative affectivity and consumption of alcohol: A general population study. *Journal of Community & Applied Social Psychology, 5*(3), 173–81.

Weary, G., & Mirels, H. L. (1982). *Integrations of clinical and social psychology.* New York: Oxford University Press.

Weatherby, N. L., Shultz, J. M., Chitwood, D. D., & McCoy, H. V. (1992). Crack cocaine use and sexual activity in Miami, Florida. *J. Psychoact. Drugs, 24,* 373–80.

Webster-Stratton, C. (1991). Annotation: Strategies for helping families with conduct disordered children. *J. Child Psychol. Psychiat., 32,* 1047–62.

Wechsler, D. (1981). *Manual for the Wechsler Adult Intelligence Scale.* New York: Psychological Corporation.

Wechsler, H., Davenport, A., Dowdall, G., Moeykens, M. S., & Castillo, S. (1994). Health and behavioral consequences of binge drinking in college. *JAMA, December,* 1672–77.

Wechsler, H., Dowdall, G. W., Maenner, G., Gledhill-Hoyt, J., Lee, H. (1998). Changes in binge drinking and related problems among American college students between 1993 and 1997. *J. Amer. Coll. Hlth., 47*(2), 57–68.

Weddington, W. W. (1993). Cocaine: Diagnosis and treatment. *Psychiat. Clin. N. Amer., 16,* 87–95.

Weekes, J. R., Lynn, S. J., Green, J. P., & Brentar, J. T. (1992). Pseudomemory in hypnotized and task-motivated subjects. *J. Abn. Psychol., 101*(2), 356–60.

Wegner, D. M. (1989). *White bears and other unwanted thoughts.* New York: Viking.

Wegner, D. M. (1994). Ironic processes of mental control. *Psychol. Rev., 101*(1), 34–52.

Wegner, D. M., Schneider, D. J., Carter, S. R., & White, T. L. (1987). Paradoxical effects of thought suppression. *J. Pers. Soc. Psychol., 53* (1), 5–13.

Wehr, T. A., & Goodwin, F. K. (1987). Can antidepressants cause mania and worsen the course of affective illness? *Amer. J. Psychiat., 144,* 1403–11.

Wehr, T. A., Jacobsen, F. M., Sack, D. A., Arendt, J., Tamarkin, L., & Rosenthal, N. E. (1986). Phototherapy of seasonal affective disorder. *Arch. Gen. Psychiat., 43,* 870–75.

Weickert, C. S., & Weinberger, D. R. (1998). A candidate molecule approach to defining developmental pathology in schizophrenia. *Schizo. Bull., 24*(2), 303–316.

Weinberg, J., & Elieli, R. (1995). *The Holocaust Museum in Washington.* New York: Rizzoli International Publications.

Weinberg, M. S., Williams, C. J., & Pryor, D. W. (1994). *Dual Attraction.* New York: Oxford University Press.

Weinberger, D. R. (1984). Brain disease and psychiatric illness: When should a psychiatrist order a CAT scan? *Amer. J. Psychiat., 141,* 1521–27.

Weinberger, D. R. (1997). On localizing schizophrenic neuropathology. *Schizo. Bull., 23*(3), 537–40.

Weinberger, D. R., DeLisi, L. E., Perman, G. P., Targum, S., & Wyatt, R. J. (1982). Computed tomography in schizophreniform disorder and other acute psychiatric disorders. *Arch. Gen. Psychiat., 39,* 778–83.

Weiner, H. (1977). *Psychobiology and human disease.* New York: Elsevier.

Weiner, H., & Fawzy, F. I. (1989). An integrative model of health, disease, and illness. In S. Cheren (Ed.), *Psychosomatic medicine: Theory, physiology, and practice* (Vol. 1). (pp. 9–44). Madison, CT: International Universities Press.

Weiner, I. (1998). *Principles of Rorschach interpretation.* Hillsdale, NJ: Erlbaum.

Weiner, R. D., & Krystal, A. D. (1994). The present use of electroconvulsive therapy. *Annu. Rev. Med., 45,* 273–81.

Weiner, S. (1998). The addiction of overeating; self-help groups as treatment models. *J. Clin. Psychol., 54*(2), 163–67.

Weinrot, M. R., & Riggan, M. (1996). *Vicarious sensitization: A new method to reduce deviant arousal in adolescent offenders.* Manuscript submitted for publication.

Weinstein, A. S. (1983). The mythical readmissions explosion. *Amer. J. Psychiat., 140*(3), 332–35.

Weisenberg, M. (1977). Pain and pain control. *Psychol. Bull., 84,* 1008–44.

Weisman, A., Lopez, S. R., Karno, M., & Jenkins, J. (1993). An attributional analysis of expressed emotion in Mexican-American families with schizophrenia. *J. Abn. Psychol., 102*(4), 601–6.

Weiss, B., Weisz, J. R., & Bromfield, R. (1986). Performance of retarded and nonretarded persons on information-processing tasks: Further tests of the similar structure hypothesis. *Psychol. Bull., 100,* 157–75.

Weiss, G., & Hechtman, L. (1979). The hyperactive child syndrome. *Science, 205,* 1348–54.

Weiss, G., Hechtman, L., Perlman, T., Hopkins, J., & Wener, A. (1979). Hyperactives as young adults: A controlled prospective ten-year follow-up of 75 children. *Arch. Gen. Psychiat., 36,* 675–81.

Weiss, J. & Sampson, H. (1986). The research: A broad view. In J. Weiss, & H. Sampson (Eds.), *The psychoanalytic process.* (pp. 337–348). New York: Guilford.

Weiss, J. M. (1984). Behavioral and psychological influences on gastrointestinal pathology: Experimental techniques and findings. In W. D. Gentry (Ed.), *Handbook of behavioral medicine.* (pp. 174–221). New York: Guilford.

Weiss, S. M., Herd, J. A., & Fox. B. H. (1981). *Perspectives on behavioral medicine.* New York: Academic Press.

Weiss, T., & Engel, B. T. (1971). Operant conditioning of heart rate in patients with premature ventricular contractions. *Psychosom. Med., 33,* 301–21.

Weisse, C. S. (1992). Depression and immunocompetence: A review of the literature. *Psychol. Bull., 111*(3), 475–89.

Weissman, M. M. (1990). Evidence for comorbidity of anxiety and depression: Family and genetic studies of children. In J. D. Maser & C. R. Cloninger (Eds.), *Comorbidity of mood and anxiety disorders.* Washington, DC: American Psychiatric Press.

Weissman, M. M. (1993). The epidemiology of personality disorders: A 1990 update. *J. Personal. Dis., Supplement,* 44–62.

Weissman, M. M., Bland, R. C., Canino, G. J., Greenwald, S., Hwu, H. G., Lee, C. K., Newman, S. C., Oakley-Browns, M. A., Rubio-Stipec, M., Wickramaratne, P. J., Wittchen, H. U., & Yeh, E. K. (1994). The cross-national epidemiology of obsessive-compulsive disorder. *J. Clin. Psychiat., 55,* 5–10.

Weissman, M. M., Fendrich, M., Warner, V., & Wickramaratne, P. (1992). Incidence of psychiatric disorder in offspring at high and low risk for depression. *J. Amer. Acad. Child Adoles. Psychiat., 31,* 640–48.

Weissman, M. M., Gammon, D., John, K., Merikangas, K. R., Warner, V., Prusoff, B. A., & Sholomskas, D. (1987). Children of depressed parents. *Arch. Gen. Psychiat., 44,* 847–53.

Weissman, M. M., Klerman, G. L., Markowitz, J. S., & Ouellette, R. (1989). Suicidal ideation and suicide attempts in panic disorder and attacks. *New Eng. J. Med., 321 (18),* 1209–14.

Weissman, M. M., Leaf, P. J., Blazer, D. G., Boyd, J. H., & Florio, L. (1986). The relationship between panic disorder and agoraphobia: An epidemiologic perspective. *Psychopharm. Bull., 43,* 787–91.

Weissman, M. M., Pottenger, M., Kleber, H., Ruben, H. L., Williams, D., & Thompson, D. (1977). Symptom pattern in primary and secondary depression. *Arch. Gen. Psychiat., 34,* 854–62.

Weisz, J. R., McCarty, C. A., Eastman, K. L., Chaiyasit, W., & Suwanlert, S. (1997) Developmental psychopathology and culture: Ten lessons from Thailand. In S. Luthar, J. Burack, D. Cicchetti, & J. Weisz (Eds.), *Developmental psychopathology: Perspectives an adjustment, risk, and disorder* (pp. 568–92) Cambridge, England: Cambridge University Press.

Weisz, J. R., Suevanlert, S., Chaiyasit, W., Weiss, B., Achenbach, T. M., & Eastman, K. L. (1993). Behavior and emotional problems among Thai and American adolescents: Parent reports for ages 12–16. *J. Abn. Psychol., 102,* 395–403.

Weisz, J. R., Suwanlert, S., Chaiyasit, W., & Walter, B. R. (1987). Over and undercontrolled clinic-referral problems among Thai and American children and adolescents: The wat and wai of cultural differences. *J. Cons. Clin. Psychol., 55,* 719–726.

Weisz, J. R., & Weiss, B. (1991) Studying the referability of child clinical problems. *J. Cons. Clin. Psychol., 59,* 266–73.

Weisz, J. R., Weiss, B., & Donenberg, G. R. (1992). The lab versus the clinic: Effects of child and adolescent psychotherapy. *Amer. Psychol., 47,* 1578–85.

Weisz, J. R., Weiss, B., Alicke, M. D., & Klotz, M. L. (1987). Effectiveness of psychotherapy with children and adolescents: A meta-analysis for clinicians. *J. Cons. Clin. Psychol., 55,* 542–49.

Weizman, A., Zohar, J., & Insel, T. (1991). Biological markers in obsessive-compulsive disorder. In J. Zohar, T. Insel, & S. Rasmussen (Eds.), *The psychobiology of obsessive-compulsive disorder.* New York: Springer.

Weizman, R., Laor, N., Barber, Y., Selman, A., Schujovizky, A., Wolmer, L., Laron, Z., & Gil-Ad, I. (1994). Impact of the Gulf war on the anxiety, cortisol, and growth hormone levels of Israeli civilians. *Amer. J. Psychiat., 151,* 71–75.

Wekstein, L. (1979). *Handbook of suicidology: Principles, problems, and practice.* New York: Brunner/Mazel.

Welch, S. L., & Fairburn, C. G. (1994). Sexual abuse and bulimia nervosa: Three integrated case control comparisons. *Amer. J. Psychiat., 151*(3), 402–7.

Wells, A., & Butler, G. (1997). Generalized anxiety disorder. In D. M. Clark & C. G. Fairburn (Eds.), *Science and practice of cognitive behaviour therapy.* (pp. 155–178). Oxford University Press.

Wells, A., & Clark, D. M. (1997). Social phobia: A cognitive perspective. In G. C. L. Davey (Ed.), *Phobias: A handbook of description, treatment, and theory.* Chicherster, England: Wiley.

Wells, A., & Papageorgiou, C. (1995). Worry and the incubation of intrusive images following stress. *Behav. Res. Ther., 33,* 579-583.

Wells, K. B., & Sturm, R. (1996). Informing the policy process: From efficacy to effectiveness data on pharmocotherapy. *J. Cons. Clin. Psychol., 64*(4), 638–45.

Wenar, C. (1990). *Developmental psychopathology: From infancy through adolescence* (2nd ed.). New York: McGraw-Hill.

Wender, P. H., Kety, S. S., Rosenthal, D., Schulsinger, F., Ortmann, J. & Lunde, I. (1986). Psychiatric disorders in the biological and adoptive families of adopted individuals with affective disorders. *Arch. Gen. Psychiat., 43,* 923–29.

Wender, P. H., Kety, S. S., Rosenthal, D., Schulsinger, F., Ortmann, J., & Lunde, I. (1986). Psychiatric disorders in the biological and adoptive families of adopted individuals with affective disorders. *Arch. Gen. Psychiat., 43,* 923–29.

Wender, P. H., Reimherr, F. W., & Wood, D. R. (1981). Attention deficit disorder (minimal brain dysfunction) in adults. *Arch. Gen. Psychiat., 38,* 449–56.

Wender, P. H., Rosenthal, D., Kety, S. S., Schulsinger, F., & Weiner, J. (1974). Cross-fostering: A research strategy for clarifying the role of genetic and experimental factors in the etiology of schizophrenia. *Arch. Gen. Psychiat., 30*(1), 121–28.

Wennerholm, M., & Lopez-Roig, L. (1983). *Use of the MMPI with executives in Puerto Rico.* Paper given at the Eighth Annual Conference on Personality Assessment, Copenhagen, Denmark.

Wenzlaff, R. M., Wegner, D. M., & Klein, S. B. (1991). The role of thought suppression in the bonding of thought and mood. *J. Pers. Soc. Psychol., 60 (4),* 500–8.

Werner, E. E., & Smith, R. S. (1982). *Vulnerable but invincible: A study of resilient children.* New York: McGraw-Hill.

Werry, J. S. (1979). The childhood psychosis. In H. C. Quay & J. S. Werry (Eds.), *Psychopathological disorders of childhood.* New York: Wiley.

Westen, D., & Shedler, J. (1999a). Revising and assessing Axis II, Part I: Developing a clinically and empirically valid assessment method. *Amer. J. Psychiat., 156,* 258–72.

Westen, D. & Shedler, J. (1999b). Revising and assessing Axis II, Part II: Toward an empirically based and clinically useful classification of personality disorder. *Amer. J. Psychiat., 156,* 273–85.

Wester, P., Eriksson, S., Forsell, A., Puu, G., & Adolfsson, R. (1988). Monoamine metabolite concentrations and cholinesterase activities in cerebrospinal fluid of progressive dementia patients: Relation to clinical parameters. *Acta Neurol. Scandin., 77,* 12–21.

Westermeyer, J. (1982a). Bag ladies in isolated cultures, too. *Behav. Today, 13*(21), 1–2.

Westermeyer, J. (1982b). *Poppies, pipes and people: Opium and its use in Laos.* Berkeley, CA: University of California Press.

Westermeyer, J., (1987). Public health and chronic mental illness. *Amer. J. Pub. Hlth., 77*(6), 667–68.

Westermeyer, J. (1989). Paranoid symptoms and disorders among 100 Hmong refgugees: A longitudinal study. *Acta psychiatr. Scandin. 80,*(1), 47–59.

Westermeyer, J., & Janca, A. (1997) Language, culture and psychopathology: Conceptual and methodological issues. *Transcult. Psychiatry, 34,* 291–311.

Westermeyer, J., Neider, J., & Callies, A. (1989). Psychosocial adjustment of Hmong refugees during their first decade in the United States. A longitudinal study. *J. Nerv. Ment. Dis., 177,* 132–39.

Westermeyer, J., Williams, C. L., & Nguyen, N. (Eds.). (1991). *Mental health and social adjustment: A guide to clinical and prevention services.* Washington, DC: U.S. Government Printing Office.

Wetherby, A. M., & Prizant, B. M. (1992). Facilitating language and communication development in autism: Assessment and intervention guidelines. In D. E. Berkell (Ed.), *Autism.* (pp. 107–34). Hillsdale, NJ: Erlbaum.

Wethington, E., Brown, G. W., & Kessler, R. C. (1994). Interview measurement of stressful life events. In S. Cohen, R. Kessler & L. Underwood-Gordon (Eds.), *Measuring stress.* New York: Oxford University Press.

Whalen, C. K., Henker, B., Buhrmester, D., Hinshaw, S. P., Huber, A., & Laski, K. (1989). Does stimulant medication improve the peer status of hyperactive children? *J. Cons. Clin. Psychol., 57,* 545–49.

Wherry, J. S. (1996). Pervasive developmental, psychotic, and allied disorders. In L. Hechtman (Ed.), *Do they grow out of it?* (pp. 195–223). Washington: American Psychiatric Press.

Whiffen, V. E. (1992). Is postpartum depression a distinct diagnosis? *Clin. Psychol. Rev., 12,* 485–508.

Whiffen, V. L., & Clark, S. E. (1997). Does victimization account for sex differences in depressive symptoms? *Brit. J. Clin. Psychol., 36,* 185–93.

Whiffen, V. E., & Gotlib, I. H. (1989). Infants of postpartum depressed mothers: Temperament and cognitive status. *J. Abn. Psychol., 98,* 274–79.

Whitaker, L. C. (1992). *Schizophrenic disorders: Sense and nonsense in conceptualization, assessment, and treatment.* New York: Plenum.

White, A. D. (1896). *A history of the warfare of science with theology in Christendom.* New York: Appleton.

White, J., Moffitt, T. E., & Silva, P. A. (1989). A prospective replication of the protective effects of IQ in subjects at high risk for juvenile delinquency. *J. Clin. Cons. Psychol., 57,* 719–24.

White, K., & Davey, G. (1989) Sensory preconditioning and UCS inflation in human "fear" conditioning. *Behav. Res. & Ther., 2,* 161–66.

Whitehouse, P. J. (1993). Cholinergic therapy in dementia. *Acta Neurol. Scandin., 88* (Suppl. 149), 42–45.

Whitehouse, P. J., et al. (1982). Alzheimer's disease and senile dementia: Loss of neurons in the basal forebrain. *Science, 215,* 1237–39.

Whiteley, J. S. (1991). Developments in the therapeutic community. *Psychiatriki, 2*(1), 34–41.

Whitman, B. Y., & Munkel, W. Multiple personality disorder: a risk indicator, diagnostic marker and psychiatric outcome for severe child abuse. *Clin. Pediat., 30,* 422–28.

Whybrow, P. C. (1997). *A mood apart.* New York: Basic Books.

Wickizer, T., Maynard, C., Atherly, A., Frederick, M., Koepsell, T., Krupski, A., & Stark, K. (1994). Completion rates of clients discharged from drug and alcohol treatment programs in Washington State. *Amer. J. Pub. Hlth., 84,* 215–21.

Widiger, T. A. (1992). Categorical versus dimensional classification: Implications from and for research. *J. Personal. Dis., 6,* 287–300.

Widiger, T. A. (1993). The DSM-III-R categorical personality disorder diagnoses: A critique and alternative. *Psychol. Inq., 4,* 75–90.

Widiger, T. A. (1998). Sex biases in the diagnosis of personality disorders. *J. Personal. Dis. , 12,* 95–118.

Widiger, T. A., & Chat, L. (1994). The DSM-IV personality disorders: Changes from DSM-III-R. In P. Wilner (Ed.), *Psychiatry.* (Chap. 14.2, pp. 1–13). B. Lippincott: Philadelphia.

Widiger, T. A., & Corbitt, E.M. (1993). Antisocial personality disorder: Proposals for DSM-IV. *J. Personal. Dis., 7,* 63–77.

Widiger, T. A. & Corbitt, E. M. (1995). Antisocial personality disorder. In W. J. Livesley (Ed.), *The DSM-IV personality disorders.* (pp. 103–126). New York: Guilford.

Widiger, T. A., & Costa, P. T. (1994). Personality and personality disorders. *J. Abn. Psychol., 103,* 78–91.

Widiger, T. A., & Frances, A. (1985). Axis II personality disorders: Diagnostic and treatment issues. *Hosp. Comm. Psychiat., 36,* 619–27.

Widiger, T. A., & Frances, A. J. (1994). Toward a dimensional model for the personality disorders. In P. T. Costa, Jr., & Widiger (Eds.), *Personality Disorders and the Five-Factor Model of Personality.* (pp. 19-39). Washington: American Psychological Association.

Widiger, T., & Rogers, J. (1989). Prevalence and comorbidity of personality disorders. *Psychiat. Ann., 19,* 132–36.

Widiger, T. A., Frances, A. J., Pincus, H. A., Davis, W. W., & First, M. B. (1991). Toward an empirical classification for the DSM-IV. *J. Abn. Psychol., 100* (3), 280–88.

Widiger, T. A., Frances, A., & Trull, T. J. (1987). A psychometric analysis of social-interpersonal and cognitive-perceptual items for the schizotypal personality disorder. *Arch. Gen. Psychiat., 44,* 741–45.

Widiger, T. A., Frances, A., Warner, L., & Bloom, C. (1986). Diagnostic criteria for the Borderline and Schizotypal Personality Disorders. *J. Abn. Psychol., 95*(1), 43–51.

Widiger, T. A., & Sanderson, C. J. (1995). Toward a dimensional model of personality disorders. In W. J. Livesley (Ed.), *The DSM-IV personality disorders.* (pp. 433–458). New York: Guilford.

Widiger, T., & Trull, T. J. (1993) Borderline and narcissistic personality disorders. In P. B. Sutker & H. E. Adams (Eds.), *Comprehensive handbook of psychopathology* (2nd ed.). New York: Plenum.

Widom, C. S. (1977). A methodology for studying noninstitutionalized psychopaths. *J. Cons. Clin. Psychol., 45,* 674–83.

Widom, C. S. (1989). Does violence beget violence? A critical examination of the literature. *Psychol. Bull., 106,* 3–28.

Weins, A. N. (1991). Diagnostic interviewing. In M. Hersen, A. E. kazdin, & A. S. Bellack (Eds.), *The clinical psychology handbook.* (2nd ed.). (pp. 345–61). New York: Pergamon.

Wiesbeck, G. A., Schuckit, M. A., Kalmijin, J. A., Tipp, J. E., et al. (1996). An evaluation of the history of a marijuana withdrawal syndrome in a large population. *Addiction, 91*(10), 1469–78.

Wiese, D., & Daro, D. (1995). *Current trends in child abuse reporting and fatalities: The results of the 1994 Annual 50-State Survey.* Chicago: NCPCA.

Wiggins, J. S. (1982). Circumplex models of interpersonal behavior in clinical psychology. In P. C. Kendall & J. N. Butcher (Eds.), *Handbook of research methods in clinical psychology.* New York: Wiley Interscience.

Wilbur, R. S. (1973, June 2). In S. Auerbach (Ed.), POWs found to be much sicker than they looked upon release. *Los Angeles Times,* Part I, p. 4.

Wilcox, B. L. & Naimark, H. (1991). The rights of the child: Progress toward human dignity. *Amer. Psychol., 46,* 49–52.

Wilczenski, F. L. (1993). Comparison of academic performances, graduation rates, and timing of drop out for LD and nonLD college students. *Coll. Stud. J., 27*(2), 184–94.

Wilder, D. A., et al. (1997). A simplified method of toilet training adults in residential settings. *J. Behav. Ther Exper. Psychiat., 28*(3), 241–46.

Wilfley, D. E., Agras, W. S., Telch, C. F., Rossiter, E. M., Schneider, J. A., Cole, A. G., Sifford, L., & Raeburn, S. D. (1993). Group cognitive-behavioral and group interpersonal psychotherapy for the nonpurging bulimic individual: A controlled comparison. *J. Cons. Clin. Psychol., 61*(2), 296–305.

Wilhelm, K., Parker, G., & Hadzi-Pavlovic. (1997). Fifteen years on: Evolving ideas in researching sex differences in depression. *Psychol. Med., 27,* 875–83.

Wille, R. & Beier, K. M. (1989). Castration in Germany. *Ann. Sex Res., 2,* 103–133.

Williams, C. L. & Perry, C. L. (1998). Lessons from Project Northland: Preventing alcohol problems during adolescence. *Alcohol World: Health and Research, 22* (2), 95–106.

Williams, C. L., Perry, C. L., Dudovitz, B., Veblen-Mortenson, S., Anstine, P. S., Komro, K. A., & Toomey, T. L. (1995). A home-based prevention program for sixth grade alcohol use: Results from Project northlands. *J. Prim. Preven, 16,* 125–147.

Williams, C. L., Solomon, S. D., & Bartone, P. (1988). Primary prevention in aircraft disasters: Integrating research and practice. *Amer. Psychol., 43,* 724–39.

Williams, J. A., Koegel, R. L., & Egel, A. L. (1981). Response-reinforcer relationships and improved learning in autistic children. *J. Appl. Beh. Anal., 14*(1), 53–60.

Williams, J. M., Watts, F. N., MacLeod, C., & Mathews, A. (1997). *Cognitive psychology and emotional disorders.* Chichester, Engalnd: Wiley.

Williams, K. E., Chambless, D. L., & Ahrens, A. (1997). Are emotions frightening? An extension of the fear of fear construct. *Behav. Res. Ther., 35*(3), 239–48.

Williams, L. M. (1994). Recall of childhood trauma: A prospective study of women's memories child sexual abuse, *J. Cons. Clin. Psychol., 62,* 1167–76.

Williams, L. M., & Finkelhor, D., (1990). The characteristics of incestuous fathers: A review of recent studies. In W. L. Marshall, D. R. Laws, & H. E. Barbaree (Eds.), *Handbook of sexual assault.* (pp. 231–56). New York: Plenum.

Williams, R. B., Barefoot, J. C., Blumenthal, J. A., Helms, M. J., et al. (1997). Psychosocial correlates of job strain in a sample of working women. *Arch. Gen. Psychiat. 54*(6), 543–48.

Williams, R. B., Jr. (1977). Headache. In R. B. Williams, Jr., & W. D. Gentry (Eds.), *Behavioral approaches to medical treatment.* (pp. 41–53). Cambridge, MA: Ballinger.

Williams, R. B., Jr., Barefoot, J. C., & Shekelle, R. B. (1985). The health consequences of hostility. In M.

A., Chesney, S. E., Goldston, & R. H. Rosenman, (Eds.), *Anger, hostility, and behavioral medicine.* (pp. 173–85). New York: Hemisphere/McGraw-Hill.

Williams, R. B., Jr., & Gentry, W. D. (Eds.). (1977). *Behavioral approaches to medical treatment.* Cambridge, MA: Ballinger.

Williams, R. B., Jr., Haney, T. L., Lee, K. L., Kong, V., & Blumenthal, J. A. (1980). Type A behavior, hostility, and coronary atherosclerosis. *Psychosom. Med., 42*, 529–38.

Williams, S. L., Turner, S. M., & Peer, D. F. (1985). Guided mastery and performance desensitization treatments for severe acrophobia. *J. Cons. Clin. Psychol., 53*, 237–47.

Williams, S. L., & Zane, G. (1989). Guided mastery and stimulus exposure treatments for severe performance anxiety in agoraphobics. *Behav. Res. Ther., 27*, 237–45.

Williams, W. M., & Ceci, S. J. (1997). Are Americans becoming more or less alike: Trends in race, class, and ability differences in intelligence. *Amer. Psychol., 52*(11), 1226–35.

Wilson, G. T. (1998). Manual-based treatment and clinical practice. *Clin. Psychol. Sci. Prac., 5*, 363–75.

Wilson, G. T., & Fairburn, C. G. (1993). Cognitive treatments for eating disorders. *J. Cons. Clin. Psychol., 61*(2), 261–69.

Wilson, G. T., & Fairburn, C. G. (1998). Treatments for eating disorders. In P. E. Nathan & J. M. Gorman (Eds.), *A guide to treatments that work.* (pp. 501–30). New York: Oxford University Press.

Wilson, G. T., Fairburn, C. G., & Agrus, W. S. (1997). Cognitive-behavioral therapy for bulimia nervosa. In D. M. Garner & P. E. Garfinkel (Eds.), *Handbook of treatment for eating disorders.* (pp. 67–93). New York: Guilford.

Wilson, M. (1993). DSM-III and the transformation of American psychiatry: A history. *Amer. J. Psychiat., 150*, 399–410.

Wilson, M. I., & Daly, M. (1996). Male sexual proprietariness and violence against wives. *Curr. Dir. Psychol. Sci., 5*, 2–7.

Wilson, S. A., Becker, L. A., & Tinker, R. H. (1997). Fifteen-month follow-up of eye movement desensitization and reprocessing (EMDR) treatment for posttraumatic stress disorder and psychological trauma. *J. Cons. Clin. Psychol., 65*(6), 1047–56.

Wincze, J. P., & Carey, M. P. (1991). *Sexual dysfunction: A guide for assessment and treatment.* New York: Guilford.

Wing, L. (1980). Childhood autism and social class: A question of selection. *Brit. J. Psychiat., 137*, 410–17.

Wing, L. K. (1976). Diagnosis, clinical description and prognosis. In L. Wing (Ed.), *Early childhood autism.* London: Pergamon.

Wing, S., & Manton, K. G. (1983). The contribution of hypertension to mortality in the U.S.: 1968, 1977. *Amer. J. Pub. Hlth., 73*(2), 140–44.

Winick, B. J. (1997). *The right to refuse mental health treatment.* Washington: American Psychological Association.

Winick, M. (Ed.). (1976). *Malnutrition and brain development.* New York: Oxford University Press.

Winokur, G. (1985). The validity of neurotic-reactive depression: New data and reappraisal. *Arch. Gen. Psychiat., 42*, 1116–22.

Winokur, G, Corywell, W., Akisal, H. S., Endicott, J., Keller, M., & Mueller, T. (1994). Manic-depressive (bipolar) disorder: The course in light of a prospective ten-year follow-up of 131 patients. *Acta Psychiatr. Scandin., 89*, 102–10.

Winokur, G., & Tsuang, M. T. (1996). *The natural history of mania, depression, and schizophrenia.* Washington: American Psychiatric Press.

Winslow, J. T., & Insel, T. R. (1991). Neuroethological models of obsessive-compulsive disorder. In J. Zohar, T. Insel, & S. Rasmussen (Eds.), *The psychobiology of obsessive-compulsive disorder.* New York: Springer.

Winston, A., Laikin, M., Pollack, J., Samstag, L.W., McCullough, L., & Muran, C. (1994). Short-term psychotherapy of personality disorders. *Amer. J. Psychiat., 151*, 190–94.

Winters, K. C., & Neale, J. M. (1985). Mania and low self-esteem. *J. Abn. Psychol., 94*, 282–90.

Wise, R. A. (1996). Addictive drugs and brain stimulation reward. *Annual Review of Neuroscience, 19*, 319–40.

Wise, R. A., & Munn, E. (1995). Withdrawl from chronic amphetamine elevates baseline intracranial self-stimulation thresholds. *Psychopharmacology, 117*(2), 130–36.

Witkin, M. J., Atay, J., & Manderscheid, R. W. (1998). Trends in state and county mental hospitals in the U.S. from 1970 to 1992. *Psychiat. Serv., 47*(10), 1079–81.

Wittchen, H., Zhao, S., Kessler, R. C., Eaton, W. W. (1994). DSM-III-R generalized anxiety disorder in the National Comorbidity Survey. *Arch. Gen. Psychiat., 51*, 355–64.

Woike, B. A., Osier, T. J. & Candela, K. (1996). Attachment styles and violent imagery in thematic stories about relationships. *Pers. Soc. Psychol. Bull., 22*, 1030–34.

Wolf, A. P. (1970). Childhood association and sexual attraction: a further test of the Westermarck hypothesis. *American Anthropologist, 72*, 503–15.

Wolf, M., Risley, T., & Mees, H. (1964). Application of operant conditioning procedures to the behavior problems of an autistic child. *Behav. Res. Ther., 1*, 305–12.

Wolf, S. L., Nacht, M., & Kelly, J. L. (1982). EMG feedback training during dynamic movement for low back pain patients. *Behav. Ther., 13*, 395–406.

Wolfe, B. E., & Maser, J. D. (1994). Treatment of panic disorder: Consensus statement. In B. E. Wolfe & J. D. Maser (Eds.), *Treatment of panic disorder. A consensus development conference.* (pp. 237–255). Washington, DC: American Psychiatric Press.

Wolfe, D. A., Edwards, B., Manion, I., & Koverola, C. (1988). Early intervention for parents at risk of child abuse and neglect: A preliminary investigation. *J. Cons. Clin. Psychol., 56*, 34–39.

Wolfe, D. A., & Wekerle, C. (1993). Treatment strategies for child physical abuse and neglect: A critical progress report. *Clin. Psychol. Rev., 13*, 473–500.

Wolfe, V. V., Gentile, C., & Wolfe, D. A. (1989). The impact of sexual abuse on children: A PTSD formulation. *Behav. Ther., 20*, 215–28.

Wolff, H. G. (1950). Life stress and cardiovascular disorders. *Circulation, 1*, 187–203.

Wolff, H. G. (1960). Stressors as a cause of disease in man. In J. M. Tanner (Ed.), *Stress and psychiatric disorder.* London: Oxford University Press.

Wolff, P. H. (1972). Ethnic differences in alcohol sensitivity. *Science, 175*, 449–50.

Wolff, W. M., & Morris, L. A. (1971). Intellectual personality characteristics of parents of autistic children. *J. Abn. Psychol., 77*(2), 155–61.

Wolkin, A., Sanfilipo, M., Wolf, A. P., Angrist, B., Brodie, J. D., & Rotrosen, J. (1992). Negative symptoms and hypofrontality in chronic schizophrenia. *Arch. Gen. Psychiat., 49*(12), 959–65.

Wolpe, J. (1958). *Psychotherapy by reciprocal inhibition.* Stanford, CA: Stanford University Press.

Wolpe, J. (1969a). For phobia: A hair of the hound. *Psych. Today, 3*(1), 34–37.

Wolpe, J. (1969b). *The practice of behavior therapy.* New York: Pergamon.

Wolpe, J. (1988). *Life with out fear. Anxiety and its cure.* Oakland, CA: New Harbinger Publications, Inc.

Wolpe, J. (1993). Commentary: The cognitivist oversell and comments on symposium contributions. *J. Behav. Ther. Exper. Psychiat., 24*(2), 141–47.

Wolpe, J. & Rachman, S. J. (1960). Psychoanalytic evidence: A critique based on Freud's case of Little Hans. *J. Nerv. Ment. Dis., 131*, 135–45.

Wolrich, M. L., Hannah, J. N., Baumgaertel, A., & Feurer, I. D. (1998). Examination of DSM-IV criteria for attention deficit disorder in a county–wide sample. *Journal of Developmental & Behavioral Pediatrics, 19*(3), 162–68.

Wolrich, M. L., Hannah, J. N., Pinnock, T. Y., Baumgaertel, A., & Brown, J. (1996). Comparison of diagnostic criteria for attention-deficit hyperactivity disorder in a county-wide sample. *J. Amer. Acad. Child Adoles. Psychiat. 35*(3), 319–24.

Wood, C. (1986). The hostile heart. *Psych. Today, 20*, 10–12.

Wood, J. M., Bootzin, R. R., Rosenhan, D., Nolen-Hocksema, S., & Jourden, F. (1992). Effects of the 1989 San Francisco earthquake on frequency and content of nightmares. *J. Abn. Psychol., 101*, 219–24.

Woodruff, P. W. R., et al. (1997). Auditory hallucinations and the temporal cortical response to speech in schizophrenia: A functional magnetic resonance imaging study. *Amer. J. Psychiat., 154*(12), 1676–82.

Woods, B. T., Kinney, D. K., & Yurgelun-Todd, D. (1986). Neurologic abnormalities in schizophrenic patients and their families: I. Comparison of schizophrenic, bipolar, and substance abuse patients and normal controls. *Arch. Gen. Psychiat., 43*, 657–63.

Woods, S. W., Charney, D. S., Goodman, W. K., & Heninger, G. R. (1987). Carbon dioxide-induced anxiety: Behavioral, physiologic, and biochemical effects of 5% CO_2 in panic disorder patients and 5 and 7.5% CO_2 in healthy subjects. *Arch. Gen. Psychiat., 44*, 365–75.

Woodworth, R. S. (1920). *The personal data sheet.* Chicago: Stoelting Press.

Woody, G. E., Luborsky, L., McLellan, L., O'Brien, C. P., Beck, A. T., Blaine, J., Herman, I., & Hole, A. (1983). Psychotherapy for opiate addicts: Does it help? *Arch. Gen. Psychiat., 40*, 639–45.

Woody, G. E., McLellan, A. T., Luborsky, L., & O'Brien, C. P. (1985). Sociopathy and psychotherapy outcome. *Arch. Gen. Psychiat., 42*, 1081–86.

Woody, G. E., McLellan, A. T., Luborsky, L., & O'Brien, C. P. (1987). Twelve month follow-up of psychotherapy for opiate dependence. *Amer. J. Psychiat., 144*, 590–96.

Woo-Ming, A. & Siever, L. (1998). Psychopharmacological treatment of personal disorders. In P. Nathan & J. Gorman (Eds.), *A Guide to treatments that work.* (pp. 554–567). New York: Oxford University Press.

Worden, P. E. (1986). Prose comprehension and recall in disabled learners. In S. J. Ceci (Ed.), *Handbook of cognitive, social and neuropsychological aspects of learning disabilities* (Vol. 1). (pp. 241-62). Hillsdale, NJ: Erlbaum.

Workman, E. A., & La Via, M. F. (1987). T-lymphocyte polyclonal proliferation: Effects of stress and stress response style on medical students taking national board examinations. *Clinical Immunology and Immunopathology, 43*, 308–13.

World Health Organization (1997). *Executive summary.* Geneva: Author.

World Health Organization. (1978a, Apr.). *Report of the director-general.* Geneva: Author.

World Health Organization. (1978b). *Mental disorders: Glossary and guide to their classification in accordance with the ninth revision of the International Classification of Diseases.* Geneva: Author.

World Health Organization. (1989). *Lexicon of psychiatric and mental health terms.* Geneva: Author.

World Health Organization. (1992). *ICD-10 classification of mental and behavioral disorders: Clinical descriptions and diagnostic guidelines.* Geneva: Author.

World Health Organization. (1993). *A lexicon of alcohol and drug terms.* Geneva: Author.

World Health Organization. (1997). *World Health Organization Report, 1997: Conquering suffering, furthering humanity.* Geneva: Author.

Worthington, E. R. (1978). Demographic and pre-service variables as predictors of post-military adjustment. In C. R. Figley (Ed.), *Stress disorders among Vietnam veterans.* New York: Brunner/Mazel.

Wortman, C. B., & Silver, R. C. (1989). The myths of coping with loss. *J. Cons. Clin. Psychol., 57*, 349–57.

Wright, L. (1994). *Remembering Satan.* New York: Knopf.

Wright, P., Takei, N., Rifkin, L., & Murray, R. M. (1995). Maternal influenza, obstetric complications, and schizophrenia. *Amer. J. Psychiat., 152*(12), 1714–20.

Wyatt, R. J., et al. (1995). An economic evaluation of schizophrenia—1991. *Soc. Psychiat. Psychiatr. Epidemiol, 30*, 196–205.

Wynne, L. C., Toohey, M. L., & Doane, J. (1979). Family studies. In L. Bellak (Ed.), *The schizophrenic syndrome.* New York: Basic Books.

Yablonsky, L. (1975). Psychodrama lives. *Human Behav., 4,* 24–29.

Yager, J., Grant, I., & Bolus, R. (1984). Interaction of life events and symptoms in psychiatric patient and nonpatient married couples. *J. Nerv. Ment. Dis., 171*(1), 21–25.

Yang, B., & Clum, G. A. (1996). Effects of early negative life experience on cognitive functioning and risk for suicide: A review. *Clin. Psychol. Rev., 16*(3), 177–95.

Yanok, J. (1993). College students with learning disabilities enrolled in developmental education programs. *Coll. Stud. J., 27*(2), 166–74.

Yap, P. M. (1951). Mental diseases peculiar to certain cultures: A survey of comparative psychiatry. *J. Ment. Sci., 97*(3), 313.

Yapko, M. D. (1994). *Suggestions of abuse: True and false memories of childhood sexual trauma.* New York: Simon & Schuster.

Yeates, K. O., et al. (1997). Preinjury family environment as a determinant of recovery from traumatic brain injuries in school-age children. *J. Int. Neuropsychologic Soc., 3*(6), 617–30.

Yeh, M., Takeuchi, D. T., Sue, S. (1994) Asian-American children treated in the mental health system: A comparison of parallel and mainstream outpatient service centers. *J. Clin. Child Psychol., 23,* 5–12.

Yehuda, R. (1998). *Psychological trauma.* Washington: American Psychiatric Press.

Yehuda, R., Marshall, R., & Giller, E. L. (1998). Psychopharmacological treatment of post-traumatic stress disorder. In P. E. Nathan & J. M. Gorman (Eds.), *A guide to treatments that work.* (pp. 377–97). Oxford, England: Oxford University Press.

Yehuda, R., Resnick, H., Schmeidler, J., Yang, R. K., & Pitman, R. K. (1998). Predictors of cortisol and 3-Methoxy-4-hydroxy-penylglycol responses in the acute aftermath of rape. *Biol. Psychiat., 43*(11), 855–59.

Yehuda, R., Southwick, S. M., Giller, E. L., et al. (1992). Urinary catecholamine excretion and severity of PTSD symptoms in Vietnam combat veterans. *J. Nerv. Ment. Dis., 180,* 321–25.

Yehuda, R., Teicher, M. H., Trestman, R. L., Levengood, R. A., & Siever, L. J. (1996). Cortisol regulation in posttraumatic stress disorder and major depression: A chronobiological analysis. *Biological Psychiatry, 40,* 79–88.

Young, M. A., Fogg, L. F., Scheftner, W. A., Keller, M. B., & Fawcett, J. A. (1990). Sex differences in the lifetime prevalence of depression: Does varying the diagnostic criteria reduce the female/male ratio? *J. Affect. Dis., 18,* 187–92.

Youth Suicide in the United States, 1970–1980. (1986). Atlanta, GA: Centers for Disease Control.

Yule, W., & Rutter, M. (1985). Reading and other learning difficulties. In M. Rutter & L. Hersov (Eds.), *Child and adolescent psychiatry: Modern approaches* (2nd ed.). (pp. 444–64). Oxford, UK: Blackwell.

Zahn, T. P., et al. (1997). Autonomic nervous system markers of psychopathology in childhood-onset schizophrenia. *Arch. Gen. Psychiat., 54*(10), 904–12.

Zakowski, S., Hall, M. H., & Baum, A. (1992). Stress, stress management, and the immune system. *Applied & Preventive Psychology, 1,* 1–13.

Zalewski, C., et al. (1998). A review of neuropsychological differences between paranoid and nonparanoid schizophrenia patients. *Schizo. Bull., 24*(1), 127–46.

Zametkin, A., & Liotta, W. (1997). The future of brain imaging in child psychiatry. *Child Adoles. Psychiat. Clin. N. Amer. , 6*(2), 447–60.

Zanarini, M. C., Gunderson, J. G., Marino, M. F., Schwartz, E. O., & Frankenburg, F. R. (1989). Childhood experiences of borderline patients. *Comp. Psychiat., 30,* 18–25.

Zanarini, M. C., Williams, A. A., Lewis, R. E., Reich, R. B., Vera, S. C., Marino, M. F., Levin, A., Yong, L., & Frankenburg, F. R. (1997). Reported pathological childhood experiences associated with the development of borderline personality disorder. *Amer. J. Psychiat., 154*(8), 1101–06.

Zasler, N. D. (1993). Mild traumatic brain injury: Medical assessment and intervention. *J. Head Trauma Rehab., 8*(3), 13-29.

Zborowski, M. J., & Garske, J. P. (1993). Interpersonal deviance and consequent social impact in hypothetically schizophrenia-prone men. *J. Abn. Psychol., 102*(3), 482–89.

Zeidner, M. (1993). Coping with disaster: The case of Israeli adolescents under threat of missile attack. *Journal of Youth and Adolescence, 22,* 89–108.

Zeitlin, H. (1986). *The natural history of psychiatric disorder in childhood.* New York: Oxford University Press.

Zelikovsky, N., & Lynn, S. J. (1994). The aftereffects and assessment of physical and psychological abuse. In S. J. Lynn & J. W. Rhue (Eds.), *Dissociation: Clinical and theoretical perspectives.* (pp. 190–214). New York: Guilford.

Zetlin, A., & Murtaugh, M. (1990). Whatever happened to those with borderline IQs? *Amer. J. Ment. Retard., 94,* 463–69.

Zetzer, H. A., & Beutler, L. E. (1995). The assessment of cognitive functioning and the WAIS-R. In L. E. Beutler and M. R. Berren (Eds.), *Integrative assessment of adult personality.* (pp. 121–186). New York: Guilford.

Zheng, Y. P., & Lin, K. M. (1994). A nationwide study of stressful life events in Mainland China. *Psychosom. Med., 56,* 296–305.

Zigler, E., Abelson, W. D., Trickett, P. K., & Seitz, V. (1982). Is an intervention program necessary in order to improve economically disadvantaged children's IQ scores? *Child Develop., 53,* 340–48.

Zigler, E., & Muenchow, S. (1992). *Head Start: The inside story of America's most successful educational experiment.* New York: Basic Books.

Zigler, E., & Styfco, S. J. (1994). Head Start: Criticisms in a constructive context. *Amer. Psychol., 49*(2), 127–32.

Zilbergeld, B., & Evans, M. (1980, Jan.). The inadequacy of Masters and Johnson. *Psych. Today,* 29–43.

Zilbergeld, B., & Kilmann, P. R. (1984). The scope and effectiveness of sex therapy. *Psychotherapy, 21,* 319–26.

Zilboorg, G., & Henry, G. W. (1941). *A history of medical psychology.* New York: Norton.

Zill, N., & Schoenborn, G. A. (1990). Developmental, learning, and emotional problems: Health of our nation's children. *Advance data: National Center for Health Statistics* (Number 190).

Zimmerman, M. (1983). Methodological issues in the assessment of life events: A review of issues and research. *Clin. Psychol. Rev, 3,* 339–70.

Zimmerman, M., & Coryell, W. (1989). DSM-III personality disorder diagnoses in a nonpatient sample: Demographic correlates and comorbidity. *Arch. Gen. Psychiat., 46,* 682–89.

Zimmerman, M., & Coryell, W. (1990). Diagnosing personality disorders in the community. A comparison of self report and interview measures. *Arch. Gen. Psychiat., 47,* 527–31.

Zimring, F. (1979). *American youth violence.* Chicago: University of Chicago Press.

Zinbarg, R. E., & Barlow, D. H. (1996). Structure of anxiety and the anxiety disorders: a hierarchical model. *J. Abn. Psychol., 105,* 181–93.

Zinbarg, R. E., Barlow, D. H., Brown, T. A., & Hertz, R. M. (1992). Cognitive-behavioral approaches to the nature and treatment of anxiety disorders. *Annu. Rev. Psychol., 43,* 235–67.

Zipursky, R. B., Lambe, E. K., Kapur, S., & Mikulis, D. J. (1998). Cerebral gray matter volume deficits in first episode psychosis. *Arch. Gen. Psychiat., 55*(6), 540–46.

Zoccolillo, M., Meyers, J., & Assiter, S. (1997). Conduct disorder, substance dependence, and adolescent motherhood. *Amer. J. Orthopsychiat., 67*(1), 152–57.

Zoccolillo, M., Pickles, A., Quinton, D., & Rutter, M. (1992). The outcome of conduct disorder: Implications for defining adult personality disorder and conduct disorder. *Psychol. Med., 22,* 971–86.

Zohar, A. H., Ratzoni, G., Pauls, D. L., Apter, A., Bleich, A., Kron, S., Rappaport, M., Weizman, A., & Cohen, D. J. (1992). An epidemiological study of obsessive compulsive disorder and related disorders in Israeli adolescents. *J. Amer. Acad. Child Adoles. Psychiat., 31,* 1057–61.

Zohar, J., Mueller, E. A., Insel, T. R., Zohar-Kadouch, R., & Murphy, D. L. (1987). Serotonergic responsivity in obsessive-compulsive disorder: Comparison of patients and healthy controls. *Arch. Gen. Psychiat., 44,* 946–51.

Zola, I. K. (1966). Culture and symptoms—An analysis of patients' presenting complaints. *American Sociological Review, 31,* 615–30.

Zubin, J., & Spring, B. J. (1977). Vulnerability: A new view of schizophrenia. *J. Abn. Psychol., 86,* 103–26.

Zucker, K. J. & Blanchard, R. (1997). Transvesticfetishism: Psychopathology and theory. In D. R. Laws & W. O'Donohue (Eds.), *Sexual deviance: Theory, assessment, and treatment.* (pp. 253–79). New York: Guilford.

Zucker, K. J., & Bradley, S. J. (1995). *Gender identity disorder and psychosexual problems in children and adolescents.* New York: Guilford.

Zucker, K. J., Sanikhani, M., & Bradley, S. J. (1997). Sex differences in referral rates of children with gender identity disorder: Some hypotheses. *J. Abnorm. Child Psychol., 25,* 217–27.

Zuckerman, M. (1972). *Manual and research report for the Sensation Seeking Scale (SSS).* Newark, DE: University of Delaware.

Zuckerman, M. (1978). Sensation seeking and psychopathy. In R. D. Hare and D. Schalling (Eds.), *Psychopathic behavior: Approaches to research.* New York: Wiley.

Zuckerman, M. (1990). The psychophysiology of sensation seeking. *J. Personal., 58,* 313–45.

Zuger, B. (1984). Early effeminate behavior in boys: Outcome and significance for homosexuality. *J. Nerv. Ment. Dis., 172,* 90–97.

Zung, W. W. K. (1969). A cross-cultural survey of symptoms in depression. *Amer. J. Psychiat., 126*(1), 116–21.

Zweben, J. E., & O'Connell, K. (1992). Strategies for breaking marijuana dependence. *J. Psychoact. Drugs, 24,* 165–71.

Zwelling, S. S. (1985). *Quest for a cure.* Williamsburg, VA: The Colonial Williamsburg Foundation.

Acknowledgments

TEXT CREDITS

Page 9: Table 1.1: DSM-IV Diagnostic Criteria for Somatization Disorder. From American Psychiatric Association, 1994, page 449–450; page 11: Table 1.2: Global Assessment of Functioning (GAF) Scale. From American Psychiatric Association, 1994, page 32; page 15: Highlight 1.1: Sample Items from the Somatization Disorder Section of the Structured Clinical Interview for DSM. From R.L. Spitzer, J.B.W.Williams, M. Gibbon, and M.B. First. Structured Clinical Interview for DSM-III-R-Patient Version (SCID-P, 4/1/88). Biometrics Research Department, New York State Psychiatric Institute, New York, NY; page 73: Figure 3.2: Human Chromosome Pairs. From T.D. Gelehrter, F.S. Collins, and D. Ginsburg, *Principles of Medical Genetics*. Copyright © 1998. Reprinted by permission of Lippincott/Williams & Wilkins; page 79: Figure 3.3: Bidirectional Influences. From Gilbert Gottlieb, *Individual Development and Evolution: The Genesis of Novel Behavior*. New York: Oxford University Press. Copyright © 1992 Oxford University Press, Inc; page 85: Table 3.1: Ego-Defense Mechanisms. Based on A. Freud (1946): American Psychiatric Association, 1994, pages 751–753; page 173: Case 5.5: Mindy Markowitz, American Psychiatric Association, 1994; page 174: Case 5.6: A mother with panic disorder. American Psychiatric Association, 1994; page 177: Figure 5.1: The Brain. From Gorman, et al. A comparison of sodium bicarbonate and sodium lactate infusion in the indiction of panic attacks. *Archives of General Psychiatry*, 46:145–150. Copyright © 1989. Reprinted by permission of the American Medical Association; page 179: Figure 5.2: The Panic Circle. Reprinted from A. Clark, Cognitive approach to panic. *Behavior Research Theory*, 24:461–470. Copyright © 1986. Reprinted with permission from Elsevier Science, Ltd; page 186: Table 5.2: Frequency of Symptoms in 100 Cases of Generalized Anxiety Disorder. From Beck and Emery, *Anxiety Disorders & Phobias: A Cognitive Approach*. Copyright © 1985 Basic Books, page 87–88; page 215: Case 6.2: A Dysthymic Junior Executive. American Psychiatric Association, 1994; page 220: Case 6.5: A Cyclothymic Car Salesman. American Psychiatric Association, 1994; page 222: Figure 6.1: The Manic-Depressive Spectrum. From Frederick K. Goodwin and Kay J. Jaimson, *Manic-Depressive Illness*. Copyright © 1990 Oxford University Press, Inc. Used by permission of Oxford University Press, Inc.; page 235: Figure 6.2: Depression. From K. Hawton, et al., *Cognitive Behaviour Therapy for Psychiatric Problems: A Practical Guide*. Copyright © 1989. Reprinted by permission of Oxford University Press; page 251: Figure 6.4: Robert Schuman's Work. Adapted from E. Slater and A. Meyer. Contributions to a pathology of the musicians: Robert Schumann. C*onfinia Psychiatrics*, 2(1959):65–94. Reprinted by permission of Karger, Basel, Switzerland; page 257: Figure 6.5: Rates of Suicide in the Elderly. From *Suicide: Guidelines for Assessment, Management and Treatment*, edited by Brice Bongar. Copyright © 1992 Oxford University Press. Used by permission of Oxford University Press, Inc; page 269: Case 7.1: A Woman and Her Yet Undiscovered Illness. American Psychiatric Association, 1994; page 270: Case 7.2: A Radiologist's Abdominal Mass. American Psychiatric Association, 1994; page 274: Case 7.5: A Desperate Wife's Vertigo. American Psychiatric Association, 1994; page 282: Case 7.6: A Middle Manager's Dissociative Fugue. American Psychiatric Association, 1994; page 282: Case 7.7: Mary, Marian and other alters. American Psychiatric Association, 1994; page 288: Figure 7.2: Documented Childhood Abuse in 12 Cases of DID Among Convicted Murderers. American Psychiatric Association, 1997; page 300: Highlight 8.1: A Bulimic's Morning. From Marlene Boskind White and William C. White, Jr., *Bulimarexia: The Binge/Purge Cycle*. Copyright © 1983 by Marlene Boskind-White and William White, Jr. Reprinted by permission of W.W. Norton & Company, Inc.; page 317: Highlight 8.2: Heart Attack. From *Discover* magazine, 1988; page 334: DSM-IV's Five Criteria. American Psychiatric Association, 1994; page 336: Case Study: A Paranoid Construction Worker. American Psychiatric Association, 1994; page 339: Case Study: The Disconnectedness of a Schizotypal Woman. American Psychiatric Association, 1994; page 341: Case Study: A Narcissistic Graduate Student. American Psychiatric Association, 1994; page 343: Case Study: Self-Mutilation in a Woman with Borderline Personality Disorder. American Psychiatric Association, 1994; page 348: Case Study: A Passive-Aggressive Psychiatrist. American Psychiatric Association, 1994; page 350: Table 9.2: Typical Overdeveloped and Underde-veloped Strategies. From Beck and Freeman, Cognitive Therapy of Personality Disorders. Copyright © 1990 Guilford Publishing; page 360: Case Study: A Psychopath in Action. From R.D. Hare, *Psychotherapy: Theory and Research*. Copyright © 1970. Reprinted by permission of John Wiley & Sons, Inc; page 367: Case Study: Cognitive Therapy with a Psychopath. From Beck and Freeman, *Cognitive Therapy of Personality Disorders*. Copyright © 1990 Guilford Publishing; page 366: Figure 9.1: Model for the Association of Family Context and Antisocial. From Capaldi and Patterson, Interelated influences of contextual factors on antisocial behavior in childhood and adolescence in males. In D.C. Fowles, et al., *Progress in Experimental Personality and Psychopathology Research*. Copyright © 1994. Reprinted by permission of Springer Publishing Company; page 375: Highlight 10.1: DSM-IV criteria for Substance Abuse. Adapted from American Psychiatric Association, 1994; page 379: Table 10.2: Alcohol Levels in the Blood After Drinks. From "Alcohol Levels in the Blood" *Time*, April 22, 1974. Copyright © 1974 Time, Inc; page 429: Case Study: A Transvestite's Dilemma. American Psychiatric Association, 1994; page 432: Case Study: Autoerotic Asphyxia. American Psychiatric Association, 1994; page 426: Table 11.1: Sex Typical and Sex Atypical Behavior in Childhood in Homosexual and Heterosexual Women and Men. From a study by the Kinsey Institute (Bell, Weinberg, & Hammersmith, 1981); page 465: Figure 12.1: Age Distribution of Onset of Schizophrenia for Men and Women. From Haffner, et al. (1998) Causes and consequences of the gender difference in age onset of schizophrenia. *Schizophrenia Bulletin*, 24(1):99–114; page 468: Table 12.2: DSM-IV Criteria for the Diagnosis of Schizophrenia. American Psychiatric Association, 1994: pages 285–286; page 470: Case Study: He Thought He Could Move Mountains. American Psychiatric Association, 1994; page 472: Case Study: Catatonia in a 16-year-old. American Psychiatric Association, 1994; page 477: Figure 12.2: Schizophrenia Genesis: The Origins of Madness. From Irving I. Gottesman, *Schizophrenia Genesis*. Copyright © 1991 by Irving I. Gottesman. Used by permission of W.H. Freeman and Company; page 480: Figure 12.3: Pairwise Twin Concordance Rates for Schizophrenia. From Torrey, *Schizophrenia & Manic-Depressive Disorder: The Biological Roots of Mental Illness as Revealed by the Landmark Study of Identical Twins*. Copyright © 1994 Basic Books, Inc.; page 488: Figure 12.4: Severity of Psychopathology and Responsivity to Treatment. From J.G. Csernansky, and M.E. Bardgett (1998) Limbic-cortical neuronal damage and the patholophysiology of schizophrenia. *Schizophrenia Bulletin*, 24(2):231–248; page 499: Figure 12.6: Paranoid Social Cognition. From R.M. Kramer; paranoid cognition in social systems: Thinking and acting in the shadow of doubt; *Personality and Social Psychology Review*, 4(2):251–275; page 532: Table 13.4: Average IQs of 586 Milwaukee Children. From Garber, *The Milwaukee Project; Preventing Mental Retardation in Children at Risk*. Copyright © 1988. Reprinted by permission of the Association on Mental Retardation; page 637: Highlight 16-3: Excerpts from *An Unquiet Mind*. From Kay Redfield *An Unquiet Mind*. Copyright © 1995 by Kay Redfield Jamison. Reprinted by permission of Alfred A. Knopf, Inc; page 652: Highlight 17.1: An Example of Psychodynamic Interpersonal Psychotherapy. From PAGEA. Foelsch and O.F. Kernberg (1998) Transference-focused psycotherapy for borderline personality disorders. *Session: Psychotherapy in Practice*, 4(2):67–90: John Wiley & Sons, Inc; page 686: Figure 18.1: The Mental Health Intervention Spectrum for Mental Disorders. From Mrazek and R.J. Haggerty (eds.) *Reducing Risks for Mental Disorders: Frontiers for Preventive Research*. Washington, DC: National Academy Press, page 23. Copyright © 1994 by National Academy Press. Reprinted by permission.

PHOTO CREDITS

Page 1: Case no. 18, inventory no. 184/Zentsch/Prinzhorn-Sammlung der Psychiatrischen Universitätsklinik Heidelberg; page 2: Lee Snider/The Image Works; page 4: Corbis/Bettmann; page 5: Rick Smolen/Against All Odds; page 7: Tony Freeman/PhotoEdit; page 10: Larry Mulvehill/Photo Researchers, Inc.; page 13: AP / Wide World Photos, Inc.; page 17: Christopher Morrow/Stock, Boston; page 20: Corbis/Reuters; page 22: Robert Brenner/PhotoEdit; page 24: Hank Morgan/Rainbow; page 28: James Prince/Photo Researchers, Inc.; page 31: Case no. 244, inventory no. 2939/Zentsch/Prinzhorn-Sammlung der Psychiatrischen Universitätsklinik

Heidelberg; page 33: Granger Collection; page 36: Granger Collection; page 37: Granger Collection; page 39: Sven Nackstrand/Liaison Agency, Inc.; page 40: Granger Collection; page 43 (top): Bulloz; page 43 (bottom): Mary Evans Picture Library; page 44: Granger Collection; page 47: Historical Pictures/Stock Montage; page 49: Brown Brothers; page 54: Wellcome Institute Library, London; page 55 (top): Corbis; page 55 (bottom): Corbis; page 57: Corbis; page 58 (top left): Granger Collection; page 58 (top right): Granger Collection; Page 58 (bottom left): Granger Collection; page 58 (bottom right): Mary Evans Picture Library; page 59 (top left): Granger Collection; page 59 (top right): Granger Collection; page 59 (bottom left): Historical Pictures/Stock Montage; page 59 (bottom right): Corbis; page 62: Case no. 160, inventory no. 1891n/Zentsch/Prinzhorn-Sammlung der Psychiatrischen Universitatsklinik Heidelberg; page 66: Mike Mazzaschi/Stock, Boston; page 69: Mark Richards/PhotoEdit; page 75 (left and right): D. Gorton/*Time* magazine; page 80: Corbis/Reuters; page 86: Laura Dwight/Peter Arnold, Inc; page 87 (left): Corbis; page 87 (center): Margaret Mahler; page 87 (Right): Barbara Young/Photo Researchers, Inc.; page 88: M. Gratton/Vision/Photo Researchers, Inc.; page 89 (left): William Alanson White Psychiatric Institute; page 89 (center): Association for the Advancement of Psychoanalysis of the Karen Horney Psychoanalytic Institute and Center, New York; page 89 (right): Courtesy of New York University; page 90: Jon Erickson; page 94: Rockefeller University; page 96 (left): Dr. Albert Bandura; page 96 (right): Aaron T. Beck M.D./Center for Cognitive Therapy; page 97: Christopher Bissell/Tony Stone Images; page 98: Chuck Savage/Uniphoto; page 101: Mark Elias/AP/Wide World Photos; page 102: Charles Gupton/Stock, Boston; page 104: Lawrence Migdale/Stock, Boston; page 107: J. Greenberg/The Image Works; page 110: Mimi Forsyth / Monkmeyer / Forsyth; page 114: Michael O'Brien; page 119: Case no. 61, inventory no. 881/Zentsch/Prinzhorn-Sammlung der Psychiatrischen Universitatsklinik Heidelberg; page 121: Thomas Friedman/Photo Researchers, Inc., Inc.; page 124: F. Hoffmann/The Image Works; page 126: Valery Zufarov/Sovfoto; page 128: R. Maiman/Sygma; page 131: Bob Daemmrich/Stock, Boston; page 132: Camera M.D. Studios; page 134: Corbis/Reuters; page 135: Corbis/Reuters; page 140: Okoniewski/The Image Works; page 144: K. Bernstein/Spooner/Liaison Agency, Inc.; page 145: United States Coast Guard; page 148: Larry Burrows/*Life* magazine; page 151: Sipa Press; page 154: Justin Sutcliffe/Sipa Press; page 158: Case no. 516, inventory no. 6053/Zentsch/Prinzhorn-Sammlung der Psychiatrischen Universitatsklinik Heidelberg; page 160: Peter Weimann/Animals Animals; page 162: J. Griffin/The Image Works; page 164: David Wells/The Image Works; page 165: Susan Mineka; page 166: Michael Newman/PhotoEdit; page 167: Billy Horsman/Stock, Boston; page 174: David Gifford/Science Photo Library/Photo Researchers, Inc.; page 179: Hattie Young/Science Photo Library/Photo Researchers, Inc.; page 186: Kevin Horan/Stock, Boston; page 189: Christopher Bissell/Tony Stone Images; page 193: Scott Foresman Library; page 197: Andy Schwartz/Photofest; page 209: Case no. 244, inventory no. 2942/Zentsch/Prinzhorn-Sammlung der Psychiatrischen Universitatsklinik Heidelberg; page 213: Bob Daemmrich/Stock, Boston; page 217: Sheila Terry/Science Photo Library/Photo Researchers, Inc.; page 219: Beringer-Dratch/The Image Works; page 223 (left): Corbis; page 223 (right): Harcourt Brace Jovanovich, Inc.; page 227 (top): Dr. Richard Davidson; page 227 (bottom): Dr. Richard Davidson; page 230: Corbis/Peter Turnley; page 234: Corbis/John Bellissimo; page 242: Snider/The Image Works; page 243: Richard Hutchings/Photo Researchers, Inc.; page 247: Drs. Michael E; p helps and John C. Mazziotta; page 249: Penny Tweedie/Woodfin Camp & Associates; page 263: Mary Kate Denney/PhotoEdit; page 267: Case no. 402, inventory no. 4494/Zentsch/Prinzhorn-Sammlung der Psychiatrischen Universitatsklinik Heidelberg; page 270: Martin/Custom Medical Stock Photo; page 273: Bob Daemmrich/Stock, Boston; page 276: Kerbs/Monkmeyer Press Photo; page 279: Grantpix/Photo Researchers, Inc.; page 281: Susan Greenwood/Liaison Agency, Inc.; page 286: Dennis Budd/Stock, Boston; page 288: L. S. Stepanowicz/Index Stock; page 293: Case no. 160, inventory no. 4267/Zentsch/Prinzhorn-Sammlung der Psychiatrischen Universitatsklinik Heidelberg; page 294: Najlah Feanny/Stock, Boston; page 297: William Thompson/Index Stock; page 298: Sipa Press; page 304: Lawrence Schwartswald/Liaison Agency, Inc.; page 306: Dorothy Greco/The Image Works; page 309: Leinwand/Monkmeyer Press Photo; page 310: Frank Siteman/Stock, Boston; page 312: The Incredible Machine/Boehringer Ingelheim Zentrale GmbH; page 314: David Young-Wolff/PhotoEdit; page 320: Robert Frerk/Odyssey Productions; page 325: Jeff Greenberg/Stock, Boston; page 328: David Lissy/Index Stock; page 332: Case no. 355, inventory no. 3927/Zentsch/Prinzhorn-Sammlung der Psychiatrischen Universitatsklinik Heidelberg; page 335: Frank Siteman/Stock, Boston; page 338: M. Antman/The Image Works; page 341: Joel Gordon Photography; page 345: M. Bridwell/PhotoEdit; page 348: Frank Siteman/PhotoEdit; page 352 (left): Otto Kernberg; page 352 (right): Norton Professional Books; page 360: Corbis/UPI; page 364: Louis Fernandez/Black Star; page 373: Case no. 18, inventory no. 176/Zentsch/Prinzhorn-Sammlung der Psychiatrischen Universitatsklinik Heidelberg; page 377: Paul Conklin/PhotoEdit; page 382: George Steinmetz; page 386: A. Farnsworth/The Image Works; page 390: Serge Attal/The Image Bank; page 394: J. B. Boykin/PhotoEdit; page 396: R. Lord/The Image Works; page 401: D & I MacDonald/Index Stock; page 404: Sharon Guynup/The Image Works; page 409: Larry Mulvehill/Photo Researchers, Inc.; page 411: Dennis MacDonald/PhotoEdit; page 414: Zigy Kaluzny/Tony Stone Images; page 419: Ricco/Maresca Gallery, NY; page 421: Will & Deni McIntyre/Photo Researchers, Inc.; page 425: A. Ramey/PhotoEdit; page 429: Peter Yates/Mercury; page 433: Barry Yee/Liaison Agency, Inc.; page 436 (left): AP/Wide World Photos; page 436 (right): Corbis /UPI; page 439: Mary Ellen Mark; page 444 (left): Courtesy the survivors living and deceased of convicted pedophile, former priest James Porter; page 444 (right): Corbis/Reuters; page 447: Maynard/Sipa Press; page 453: Bill Bachmann/Stock, Boston; page 456: Scott Camazine/Photo Researchers, Inc.; page 462: Ricco/Maresca Gallery, NY; page 463: Barbara J. Feigles/Stock, Boston; page 467: Alfred Gescheidt/The Image Bank; page 471: Al Vercoutere, Malibu, CA; page 473: Monkmeyer Press Photo; page 475: Al Vercoutere, Malibu, CA; page 478: NIMH; page 485: NIMH; page 486: Max Aguilera/Hellweg; page 488: Larry Mulvehill/Photo Researchers, Inc.; page 491: Billy E. Barnes/PhotoEdit; page 492: David Alan Harvey/Woodfin Camp & Associates; page 499: Spencer Grant/Index Stock; page 503: Case no. 27, inventory no. 238/Zentsch/Prinzhorn-Sammlung der Psychiatrischen Universitatsklinik Heidelberg; page 506: Leonard Lessin/Peter Arnold, Inc.; page 510: Lynn Johnson/ Black Star; page 513: Dan McCoy/Rainbow; page 516: Custom Medical Stock Photo; page 517: Dr. Dennis J. Selkoe/Brigham and Women's Hospital, Harvard Medical School; page 519: R. Sidney/The Image Works; page 521: Harvard Medical School/Warren Anatomical Museum; page 523: Hank Morgan/Photo Researchers, Inc.; page 525: Lawrence Migdale/Stock, Boston; page 527: Stock, Boston; page 529 (top): Custom Medical Stock Photo; page 529 (bottom): Elaine Rebman/Photo Researchers, Inc.; page 532: Guy Gillette/Photo Researchers, Inc.; page 542: Phyllis Kind Gallery, NY; page 544: Ursula Markus/Photo Researchers, Inc., Inc.; page 548: Aurora; page 554: Frank Siteman/Stock, Boston; page 556: Stewart Cohen/Tony Stone Images, Inc.; page 561: Laura Dwight/PhotoEdit; page 566: Abraham Menashe; page 569: Will & Deni Mcintyre/Photo Researchers, Inc., Inc.; page 573: Heron/Monkmeyer Press Photo; page 577: Alex Tehrani/Liaison Agency, Inc.; page 580: Douglas Burrows/Liaison Agency, Inc.; page 583: Phyllis Kind Gallery, NY; page 586 (left): Network Productions/The Image Works; page 586 (right): Dean Abramson/Stock, Boston; page 588: J. Pickerell/The Image Works; page 589: Hank Morgan/ Rainbow; page 592: Will & Deni McIntyre/Photo Researchers, Inc., Inc.; page 597: Bob Daemmrich/Stock, Boston; page 599: Peter Vandermark/Stock, Boston; page 601: Merrim/Monkmeyer Press Photo; page 607: Drew Crawford/The Image Works; page 609: Jay Freis/The Image Bank; page 615: Frank Siteman/Rainbow; page 618: Case no. 90, inventory no. 1490/Zentsch/Prinzhorn-Sammlung der Psychiatrischen Universitatsklinik Heidelberg; page 621: Will McIntyre/Photo Researchers, Inc.; page 623: Corbis /UPI; page 631: Peter Simon/Stock, Boston; page 638: Tony Freeman/PhotoEdit; page 643: Case no. 61, inventory no. 880/Zentsch/Prinzhorn-Sammlung der Psychiatrischen Universitatsklinik Heidelberg; page 645: Lerner/Woodfin Camp & Associates; page 647: S. Agricola/The Image Works; page 649: Richard Hutchings/Photo Researchers, Inc., Inc.; page 655: Courtesy of Dr. Joseph Wolpe; page 657: Jacques Chenet/Woodfin Camp & Associates; page 658: Alan Carey/The Image Works; page 661: Erika Stone/Peter Arnold, Inc.; page 663: David K. Crow/PhotoEdit; page 667: Smith/Monkmeyer Press Photo; page 674: Joseph Nettis/Photo Researchers, Inc.; page 676: Stephen Frisch/Stock, Boston; page 684: Phyllis Kind Gallery, NY; page 687: A. Ramey/Woodfin Camp & Associates; page 689: Bob Daemmrich/Stock, Boston; page 692: AP/Wide World Photos; page 697: Christopher Morris/Black Star; page 701: Robert Brenner/PhotoEdit; page 706: Bruce Ely/Liaison Agency, Inc.; page 709: Joseph Schuyler/Stock, Boston; page 710: Eric Roth/Index Stock.

Name Index

Buckley, P., 386
Buckner, H. T., 428
Bucknill, J. C., 620
Budoff, M., 534
Bugg, F., 359
Bullard, D. M., 101
Bullman, T. A., 146
Bundy, T., 360, 432
Bunner, M. R., 549
Burchard, J. D., 578
Burchinal, M., 108
Burgess, A. W., 142, 446
Burgess, C., 283
Burks, V. S., 108
Burman, B., 326
Burnett, J., 141, 142
Burnett, R., 326
Burns, L. E., 153
Burns, T. L., 544
Burr, G., 13
Burstein, A., 148
Burton, R., 39, 59
Bush, D. F., 395
Bushnell, J. A., 575
Busink, R., 537
Buss, D. M., 421, 446
Butcher, J. N., 109, 320, 600, 602, 603, 604, 606, 607, 608, 609, 691, 694
Butler, G., 184, 186, 187, 190, 192
Butler, L. D., 289
Butow, P., 305
Butterfield, F., 710
Butzlaff, R., 242, 255, 491
Bychowski, G., 410

Cacioppo, J. T., 131, 314
Cade, J. F. J., 636
Cadoret, R. J., 386, 552
Caldwell, N. D., 239
Calhoun, K. S., 447, 657
Callahan, L. A., 706, 707
Callies, A., 149
Camargo, C. A., Jr., 296
Cambyses, King of Persia, 376
Cameron, N., 500
Cameron, R., 153
Camp, B. W., 532
Campbell, D., 36
Campbell, M., 550, 562, 565, 569
Campbell, S., 386, 561
Campbell, T., 395
Candela, K., 245
Canetto, S. S., 261
Canino, G. J., 376
Cannon, T. D., 339, 464, 485, 486, 487
Cannon, W. B., 129, 311, 327
Cantor-Graae, E., 484
Cantwell, D. P., 558
Capaldi, D. M., 108, 365, 555
Caplan, R. D., 244
Capp, R., 345
Capps, L., 566
Capron, C., 76
Cardarelli, A., 576

Cardona, F., 565
Carey, G., 72, 233, 350, 351, 359, 362
Carey, M. P., 316
Carlat, D. J., 296
Carliner, I. V., 694
Carlson, R., 455
Carlson, C. L., 549
Carlson, C. R., 323, 328, 329, 661
Carlson, E. A., 90, 91, 103
Carlson, E. B., 148, 284, 289
Carlson, M., 439
Carlsson, A., 483
Carothers, J. C., 249
Carpenter, K., 295, 307
Carpenter, W. T., Jr., 469, 486
Carpentieri, S., 567
Carr, A., 572
Carroll, K. M., 386, 404, 549
Carruthers, M., 130
Carskadon, M. A., 79
Carson, R. C., 8, 12, 27, 28, 89, 113, 234, 320, 335, 469, 489, 598, 608, 651
Carstairs, G. M., 204
Carstensen, L. L., 516, 518
Carter, A. S., 565
Carter, C. S., 173
Carter, J. C., 309, 412
Cartwright, W., 519
Carver, C. S., 309
Carver, G., 525
Cases, M. F., 380
Casey, R. J., 573
Cashdan, S., 651
Caspi, A., 365
Cassano, G. B., 221
Cassidy, F., 220, 221
Castiglioni, A., 40
Castillo, S., 388–89
Castlebury, F. D., 340
Castro, J., 716
Catalan, J., 261
Catalano, R., 114
Cates, M. S., 403
Cato, C., 539
Cato, M., 376
Cattell, J. M., 56, 59
Cattell, R., 610
Caudill, B. D., 571
Ceci, S. J., 439, 440–41, 441, 538
Centerwall, S. A., 530
Centerwall, W. R., 530
Cerce, J., 446
Cerletti, U., 620
Cerny, J. A., 184
Chafel, J. A., 532
Chambers, R. E., 146
Chambless, D. L., 172, 175, 178, 662, 681
Champoux, M., 189
Chandler, H. N., 535
Chaney, J. M., 307
Chapin, K., 484
Chappel, J. N., 394
Charcot, J., 52–54

Charles, Prince of Wales, 295
Charlop-Christie, M. H., 567, 569
Charman, T., 566
Charney, D., 143, 177, 178, 192
Chase, N. D., 385
Chase-Lansdale, P. L., 106
Chassin, L., 103, 376, 385, 386
Chat, L., 348, 349
Checkley, S., 226
Cheit, R., 442
Chemtob, C. M., 145, 146, 154, 695
Chen, C. C., 384
Cherlin, A. J., 106
Chess, S., 555
Cheung, F. K., 493
Chic, J., 391
Chilcoat, H. D., 135
Chopra, J., 202
Chorpita, B. F., 160,189,557, 559
Christensen, A., 673, 678
Christian, J. L., 244
Christiansen, B. A., 387
Christophe, D., 444
Chrousos, G. B., 129
Chrousos, G. P., 410
Chu, J. A., 438
Chung Ching, 38
Cicchetti, D., 100, 101, 102, 103, 105, 115, 529, 543, 574, 575, 576
Cigrang, J. A., 154
Cillessen, A. H. N., 107, 108
Cirinclone, C., 707
Clark, A., 571
Clark, C. R., 112
Clark, D. A., 236, 241, 665
Clark, D. C., 256, 257, 258, 261, 262
Clark, D. E., 124
Clark, D. M., 169, 171, 172, 178, 179, 182, 183, 232, 233, 236, 240, 335, 667
Clark, H. W., 155
Clark, L. A., 10, 28, 77, 95, 141, 161, 191, 216, 231, 240, 335, 336, 370, 371, 386
Clark, M. E., 607
Clark, R. F., 517
Clark, S. E., 238
Clarke, G. N., 148
Classen, C., 140
Clayer, J. R., 694
Clayton, P. J., 213
Cleckley, H. M., 356, 358
Clement, P., 564
Clementz, B. A., 484
Cloitre, M., 171, 344
Cloninger, C. R., 278, 359, 361, 383
Clum, G. A., 259, 662
Coatsworth, J. D., 65, 66, 104, 107, 114, 127, 544
Cockayne, T. O., 39
Coe, C. L., 314
Coffey, P., 575
Cohen, B. J., 333

Cohen, C. A., 519
Cohen, C. I., 519
Cohen, D., 464, 486, 518, 552
Cohen, D. J., 568
Cohen, I. L., 190
Cohen, N., 315
Cohen, N. J., 126
Cohen, P., 554, 560
Cohen, S., 312, 314
Cohler, B. J., 109, 112, 115
Cohn, J. F., 561
Coie, J. D., 107, 108, 369, 555
Cole, D. A., 561
Cole, G., 530
Cole, J. O., 632
Cole, R. E., 105
Collacott, R. A., 528, 529
Collaer, M., 71
Collins, G. B., 396
Columbus, M., 391
Compas, B. E., 103, 544
Comstock, A., 422
Comstock, B. S., 262
Cone, J. D., 593
Connolly, J., 43, 120
Connolly, K., 547
Connolly, M. B., 651
Connors, G. J., 387, 395
Conrod, P. J., 416
Conte, J., 576
Cook, C. L., 390
Cook, E. H., 569
Cook, M., 93, 165–66, 168
Cook, S., 439
Cooke, D. J., 365, 366
Cookerly, J. R., 673
Coombe, P., 695
Coombs, R. H., 690
Coons, P. M., 281, 289, 438
Cooper, H., 572
Cooper, M. L., 127, 142, 315, 387
Cooper, P., 243
Cooper, S. A., 528, 537
Cooper, S. J., 383, 385
Coplan, J. A., 176
Coplan, J. D., 175
Corbitt, E. M., 357, 370
Corder, B. E., 545
Cordess, C. C., 554
Cordova, J. V., 660, 672
Corin, E., 149
Corn, K. J., 181
Cornblatt, B. A., 482, 484
Cornelison, A. R., 490
Cornelius, J., 344
Cornell, D. G., 357
Corrigan, P. W., 695
Coryell, W., 218, 219, 221, 223, 224, 250, 255, 350, 370, 387
Costa, P. T., Jr., 278, 304, 310, 336, 518
Costanzo, P. R., 410
Costello, E. J., 543
Cotton, N. S., 383
Cottraux, J., 202
Council, J. R., 307

Subject Index